MASSACHUSETTS
RULES OF COURT

VOLUME I – STATE

2020

THOMSON REUTERS™

Mat #42622758

ISBN 978-1-539-21239-3

PREFACE

Designed for use in the office or courtroom, this pamphlet contains the Massachusetts State rules.

WHAT'S NEW

Massachusetts Rules of Court, Volume I – State, 2020, includes rules and associated material governing practice before the Massachusetts state courts. It replaces the 2019 edition, and any accompanying supplements. It is current with amendments received through January 15, 2020.

CONTACT US

For additional information or research assistance, call the reference attorneys at 1-800-REF-ATTY (1-800-733-2889). Contact our U.S. legal editorial department directly with your questions and suggestions by e-mail at editors.us-legal@tr.com.

Thank you for subscribing to this product. Should you have any questions regarding this product please contact Customer Service at 1-800-328-4880 or by fax at 1-800-340-9378. If you would like to inquire about related publications, or to place an order, please contact us at 1-888-728-7677 or visit us at legal.thomsonreuters.com.

THE PUBLISHER

February 2020

TABLE OF CONTENTS

CIVIL, CRIMINAL, AND APPELLATE RULES

SUPREME JUDICIAL COURT

APPEALS COURT

TRIAL COURT

TABLE OF CONTENTS

DISTRICT COURTS AND BOSTON MUNICIPAL COURT

HOUSING COURT

JUVENILE COURT

LAND COURT

PROBATE AND FAMILY COURT

SUPERIOR COURT

TABLE OF CONTENTS

JUDICIAL CONDUCT

BOARD OF BAR OVERSEERS AND CLIENTS' SECURITY BOARD

APPELLATE TAX BOARD

GUIDE TO EVIDENCE

INDEX

MASSACHUSETTS RULES OF CIVIL PROCEDURE

Effective July 1, 1974

Research Note

See Massachusetts General Laws Annotated, vols. 46 and 46A, for case annotations, historical notes, cross references, and research references relating to the Massachusetts Rules of Civil Procedure.

See Smith and Zobel, Massachusetts Practice—Rules Practice, vols. 6 and 7 (2nd Edition), for a discussion of the Massachusetts Rules of Civil Procedure. Perlin and Blum, Massachusetts Practice—Procedural Forms Annotated, vols. 10, 10A, 10B and 10C (6th Edition), sets forth and discusses many forms used in civil practice in Massachusetts.

Table of Rules

I. SCOPE OF RULES—ONE FORM OF ACTION

Rule 1. Scope of Rules

These rules govern the procedure before a single justice of the Supreme Judicial Court or of the Appeals Court, and in the following departments of the Trial Court: the Superior Court, the Housing Court, the Probate and Family Court in proceedings seeking equitable relief, the Juvenile Court in proceedings seeking equitable relief, in the Land Court, in the District Court and in the Boston Municipal Court, in all suits of a civil nature whether cognizable as cases at law or in equity, with the exceptions stated in Rule 81. They should be construed, administered, and employed by the court and the parties to secure the just, speedy, and inexpensive determination of every action and proceeding.

As used in these rules the following terms shall be deemed to have the following meanings:

"Superior Court" shall mean the Superior Court Department of the Trial Court, or a session thereof for holding court.

"Housing Court" shall mean a division of the Housing Court Department of the Trial Court, or a session thereof for holding court.

"Probate Court" shall mean a division of the Probate and Family Court Department of the Trial Court, or a session thereof for holding court.

"Land Court" shall mean the Land Court Department of the Trial Court, or a session thereof for holding court.

"District Court" or "Municipal Court" shall mean a division of the District Court Department of the Trial Court, or a session thereof for holding court; except when the context means something to the contrary, said words shall include the Boston Municipal Court Department.

"Municipal Court of the City of Boston" or "Boston Municipal Court" shall mean a division of the Boston Municipal Court Department of the Trial Court, or a session thereof for holding court.

"Juvenile Court" shall mean the Juvenile Court Department of the Trial Court, or a session thereof for holding court.

Amended June 27, 1974, effective July 1, 1974; November 9, 1979, effective January 1, 1980; December 13, 1981, effective January 1, 1982; amended effective June 8, 1989; July 1, 1996; April 5, 2007, effective June 1, 2007; November 28, 2007, effective March 1, 2008; June 29, 2016, effective August 1, 2016.

Reporter's Notes—1973

This rule is substantially the same as Federal Rule 1, substituting Massachusetts references for those of the United States. The rules apply to cases at law or in equity. (See Rule 2 for merger of law and equity.) The reference in Rule 1 to cases at law or in equity in no way attempts to enlarge the jurisdiction of any court.

In cases of concurrent jurisdiction, the litigation is controlled by the rules applicable in the court where the action rests. Thus an action for divorce which is triable in either the Probate Court or the Superior Court, is, when commenced in the Superior Court, controlled by these rules, even though if, had it been commenced in the Probate Court, it would be controlled by the extant Probate Court rules. Cases involving switches between the Superior Court and a district court or the Boston Municipal Court are governed by Rule 81(f) and 81(g). See also Rule 13(j).

Reporter's Notes—1996

With the merger of the District/Municipal Courts Rules of Civil Procedure into the Massachusetts Rules of Civil Procedure in 1996, minor changes have been made to Rule 1 with the addition of references to the District Court and to the Boston Municipal Court.

Reporter's Notes—2007

The 2007 amendments to Rule 1 make the Massachusetts Rules of Civil Procedure applicable to proceedings in the Juvenile Court where equitable relief is sought. For example, a civil action brought in the Juvenile Court seeking specific performance of a post-adoption contract (G.L. c. 210, § 6D) will be governed by the Massachusetts Rules of Civil Procedure.

Reporter's Notes—2008

The definition of "Municipal Court of the City of Boston" has been amended in light of legislation in 2003 transferring various Divisions of the District Court Department located in Suffolk County to the Boston Municipal Court. See G.L. c. 218, § 1 and G.L. c. 218, § 50.

Whenever the term "District Court" is used in the Massachusetts Rules of Civil Procedure, the reference is to be construed as including the Boston Municipal Court, unless "the context means something to the contrary." Mass. R. Civ. P. 1, sixth definition.

Reporter's Notes—2016

The amendment to Rule 1, adopted from the Federal Rules of Civil Procedure, changed the second sentence of the first paragraph so that it reads: "They [the Massachusetts Rules of Civil Procedure] should be construed, administered, and employed by the court and the parties to secure the just, speedy, and inexpensive determination of every action and proceeding."

The purpose of the change was to acknowledge that both the court and the parties have the obligation to employ the rules for the purposes set forth.

Rule 1A. Transitional Rule for District Court Litigation in Progress on July 1, 1996 [Repealed]

Repealed November 28, 2007, effective March 1, 2008.

Reporter's Notes—2008

Rule 1A, entitled Transitional Rule for District Court Litigation in Progress on July 1, 1996, was repealed in 2008.

Rule 1B. Transitional Rule for Probate Accounts in Litigation on July 1, 1977 [Deleted]

Rule 2. One Form of Action

There shall be one form of action to be known as "civil action".

Reporter's Notes—1973

"Merger" of Law and Equity, refers only to the *procedure* involved, i.e., the manner of framing and trying the issues, and the type of relief. "Merger" does not alter the traditional substantive distinctions between legal and equitable *remedies*. Although the once separate procedures have been merged, the right to equitable remedies still exists; now, however, a party may seek legal and equitable relief simultaneously. All issues in a dispute, legal or equitable, may now be tried in the same form and in the same action. Grauman v. City Company of New York, 31 F.Supp. 172 (S.D.N.Y.1939). Unified procedure takes away no rights in either law or equity; rather, it merely affords a more simple and effective way of enforcing such rights.

Rule 2 also abolishes distinctive "forms of action". Henceforth all litigation, whatever the claimed basis for relief, will be known as "civil action". A plaintiff need only plead those facts necessary to show that he is entitled to a relief which the law recognizes; he need not frame his action into one of several possible forms of action. In Nester v. Western Union Telegraph Co., 25 F.Supp. 478, 481 (S.D.Cal.1938) the court discussed the effect of Federal Rule 2:

> Under the liberal rules of reformed procedure, a plaintiff is entitled to recover not on the basis of allegations of damages or of his theory of damages but rather on the basis of the facts as to damages shown in the record. Differences in the forms of claims being abolished, the plaintiff should be denied relief only when under the facts proved, he is entitled to none.

Rule 2 relates to several other rules. Rule 8(a) allows a party to demand "relief in the alternative or of several different types"; Rule 8(e) allows a party to "state as many separate claims or defenses as he has regardless of consistency and whether based on legal or equitable grounds;" Rule 18(a) allows a party to join "as many claims, legal or equitable as he has against an opposing party"; Rule 13(a) demands that a pleader with certain exceptions, assert as a counterclaim "any claim" which the pleader has against the opposing party if it arises out of the same transaction or occurrence that is the subject matter of the opposing party's claim; Rule 13(b) permits a pleader to assert as a counterclaim "any claim" regardless of its connection with the opposing party's claim.

Because Massachusetts previously maintained a separate procedural system for actions at law and suits in equity, the merger of the two systems brings about a substantial change in existing practice.

Rule 2, together with Rule 13(a), makes the assertion of a legal or equitable counterclaim compulsory if it arises out of the same transaction or occurrence (subject to the specific exceptions of Rule 13(a)), regardless of the nature of the counterclaim.

Rule 2 abolishes the previously existing tripartite division of personal action: (1) Contracts, including assumpsit, covenant, debt; (2) Tort, including trespass, trespass on the case, trover; and (3) Replevin.

The kind of relief previously afforded by either legal or equitable replevin is available under Rule 2. However the right of the plaintiff in a replevin action to obtain immediate possession of the property by the delivery of a bond is abolished.

For a complete discussion of the effect of the law-equity merger on the right to a jury trial see the Reporters' Notes to Rule 38.

II. COMMENCEMENT OF ACTION; SERVICE OF PROCESS, PLEADINGS, MOTIONS AND ORDERS

Rule 3. Commencement of Action

A civil action is commenced by (1) mailing to the clerk of the proper court by certified or registered mail a complaint and an entry fee prescribed by law, or (2) filing such complaint and an entry fee with such clerk. Actions brought pursuant to G.L. c. 185 for registration or confirmation shall be commenced by filing a surveyor's plan and complaint on a form furnished by the Land Court.

Amended December 13, 1981, effective January 1, 1982.

Reporter's Notes—1973

Rule 3, substantially enlarges Federal Rule 3, and drastically alters prior Massachusetts practice, by eliminating the trifurcation of delivery to an officer, service, and "entry". Henceforth, an action is considered commenced, for all purposes, including the applicable statute of limitations, when either the plaintiff mails to the clerk the complaint and any required entry fee, *or* the clerk *receives* the complaint and the fee. The requirement of certified or registered mail is calculated to minimize problems of proof. The phrase "proper court" means the court in which requirements of venue and jurisdiction (personal and subject matter) are met.

Rule 4. Process

(a) **Summons: Issuance.** Upon commencing the action the plaintiff or his attorney shall deliver a copy of the complaint and a summons for service to the sheriff, deputy sheriff, or special sheriff; any other person duly authorized by law; a person specifically appointed to serve them; or as otherwise provided in subdivision (c) of this rule. Upon request of the plaintiff separate or additional summons shall issue against any defendant. The summons may be procured in blank from the clerk, and shall be filled in by the plaintiff or the plaintiff's attorney in accordance with Rule 4(b).

(b) Same: Form. The summons shall bear the signature or facsimile signature of the clerk; be under the seal of the court; be in the name of the Commonwealth of Massachusetts; bear teste of the first justice of the court to which it shall be returnable who is not a party; contain the name of the court and the names of the parties; be directed to the defendant; state the name and address of the plaintiff's attorney, if any, otherwise the plaintiff's address, and the time within which these rules require the defendant to appear and defend; and shall notify him that in case of his failure to do so judgment by default may be rendered against him for the relief demanded in the complaint.

(c) By Whom Served. Except as otherwise permitted by paragraph (h) of this rule, service of all process shall be made by a sheriff, by his deputy, or by a special sheriff; by any other person duly authorized by law; by some person specially appointed by the court for that purpose; or in the case of service of process outside the Commonwealth, by an individual permitted to make service of process under the law of this Commonwealth or under the law of the place in which the service is to be made, or who is designated by a court of this Commonwealth. A subpoena may be served as provided in Rule 45. Notwithstanding the provisions of this paragraph (c), wherever in these rules service is permitted to be made by certified or registered mail, the mailing may be accomplished by the party or his attorney.

(d) Summons: Personal Service Within the Commonwealth. The summons and a copy of the complaint shall be served together. The plaintiff shall furnish the person making service with such copies as are necessary. Service shall be made as follows:

(1) Upon an individual by delivering a copy of the summons and of the complaint to him personally; or by leaving copies thereof at his last and usual place of abode; or by delivering a copy of the summons and of the complaint to an agent authorized by appointment or by statute to receive service of process, provided that any further notice required by such statute be given. If the person authorized to serve process makes return that after diligent search he can find neither the defendant, nor defendant's last and usual abode, nor any agent upon whom service may be made in compliance with this subsection, the court may on application of the plaintiff issue an order of notice in the manner and form prescribed by law.

(2) Upon a domestic corporation (public or private), a foreign corporation subject to suit within the Commonwealth, or an unincorporated association subject to suit within the Commonwealth under a common name: by delivering a copy of the summons and of the complaint to an officer, to a managing or general agent, or to the person in charge of the business at the principal place of business thereof within the Commonwealth, if any; or by delivering such copies to any other agent authorized by appointment or by law to receive service of

process, provided that any further notice required by law be given. If the person authorized to serve process makes return that after diligent search he can find no person upon whom service can be made, the court may on application of the plaintiff issue an order of notice in the manner and form prescribed by law.

(3) Upon the Commonwealth or any agency thereof by delivering a copy of the summons and of the complaint to the Boston office of the Attorney General of the Commonwealth, and, in the case of any agency, to its office or to its chairman or one of its members or its secretary or clerk. Service hereunder may be effected by mailing such copies to the Attorney General and to the agency by certified or registered mail.

(4) Upon a county, city, town or other political subdivision of the Commonwealth subject to suit, by delivering a copy of the summons and of the complaint to the treasurer or the clerk thereof; or by leaving such copies at the office of the treasurer or the clerk thereof with the person then in charge thereof; or by mailing such copies to the treasurer or the clerk thereof by registered or certified mail.

(5) Upon an authority, board, committee, or similar entity, subject to suit under a common name, by delivering a copy of the summons and of the complaint to the chairman or other chief executive officer; or by leaving such copies at the office of the said entity with the person then in charge thereof; or by mailing such copies to such officer by registered or certified mail.

(6) In any action in which the validity of an order of an officer or agency of the Commonwealth is in any way brought into question, the party questioning the validity shall forthwith forward to the Attorney General of the Commonwealth by hand or by registered or certified mail a brief statement indicating the order questioned.

(e) Same: Personal Service Outside the Commonwealth. When any statute or law of the Commonwealth authorizes service of process outside the Commonwealth, the service shall be made by delivering a copy of the summons and of the complaint: (1) in any appropriate manner prescribed in subdivision (d) of this Rule; or (2) in the manner prescribed by the law of the place in which the service is made for service in that place in an action in any of its courts of general jurisdiction; or (3) by any form of mail addressed to the person to be served and requiring a signed receipt; or (4) as directed by the appropriate foreign authority in response to a letter rogatory; or (5) as directed by order of the court.

(f) Return. The person serving the process shall make proof of service thereof in writing to the court promptly and in any event within the time during which the person served must respond to the process. If service is made by a person other than a sheriff, deputy sheriff, or special sheriff, he shall make affidavit thereof. Proof of service outside the Commonwealth may be made by affidavit of the individual who made the service or in the manner prescribed by the law of the Commonwealth, or the law of the place in which the service is made for proof of service in an action in any of its courts of general jurisdiction. When service is made by mail, proof of service shall include a receipt signed by the addressee or such other evidence of personal delivery to the addressee as may be satisfactory to the court. Failure to make proof of service does not affect the validity of the service.

(g) Amendment. At any time in its discretion and upon such terms as it deems just, the court may allow any process or proof of service thereof to be amended, unless it clearly appears that material prejudice would result to the substantial rights of the party against whom the process is issued.

(h) Certain Actions in Probate Courts: Service. Notwithstanding any other provision of these rules, in actions in the Probate Courts in the nature of petitions for instructions or for the allowance of accounts, service may be made in accordance with G.L. c. 215, § 46, in such manner and form as the court may order.

(i) Land Court. In actions brought in the Land Court, service shall be made by the court where so provided by statute.

(j) Summons: Time Limit for Service. If a service of the summons and complaint is not made upon a defendant within 90 days after the filing of the complaint and the party on whose behalf such service was required cannot show good cause why such service was not made within that period, the action shall be dismissed as to that defendant without prejudice upon the court's own initiative with notice to such party or upon motion.

Amended February 24, 1975, effective July 1, 1974; December 17, 1975, effective January 1, 1976; June 2, 1976, effective July 1, 1976; December 13, 1982, effective January 1, 1982; March 29, 1988, effective July 1, 1988.

Reporter's Notes—1973

Rule 4 deals with process and service. It extensively changes Federal Rule 4 to meet state conditions and to adopt such existing state law as the "long-arm" statute, G.L. c. 223A, §§ 1–8.

Rule 4(a), unlike Federal Rule 4(a), puts the onus of delivering process to the server upon the plaintiff or his attorney, rather than upon the clerk. It explicitly allows the plaintiff or the attorney to obtain the blank summons form in advance.

Rule 4(c) permits special court appointment of process servers.

Rule 4(d) somewhat changes the Massachusetts rule that in actions of tort or contract, not involving an attachment, the summons need not contain a copy of the declaration. Under Rule 4(d), the summons does not *contain* the complaint, but the two must be served together.

Rule 4(d)(1) allows process to be "left at [defendant's] last and usual place of abode," G.L. c. 223, § 31. The Rule makes clear that service on a statutorily authorized agent may also require the giving of additional notice, and that the plaintiff must consult the statute and fulfill its requirements. If service in any of the modes prescribed by Rule 4(d)(1) is impossible, the plaintiff may obtain an order of notice. See G.L. c. 223, § 34; c. 227, § 7. Divorce proceedings brought in the Superior Court, c. 208, § 6, although governed by these rules, are, in matters of notice and service, controlled by G.L. c. 208, § 8.

Rule 4(d)(1) incorporates prior law covering service upon infants and incompetents. No statute treats the situation precisely, of G.L. c. 206, § 24. At common law, an infant or an incompetent must be served like any other defendant, and service must precede the appointment of a guardian ad litem, Taylor v. Lovering, 171 Mass. 303, 306, 50 N.E. 612, 613 (1898); Reynolds v. Remick, 327 Mass. 465, 469, 470–471, 99 N.E.2d 279, 281–282 (1951).

Rule 4(d)(2) governs service upon a business entity. Basically, it allows the entity to be served via its officers, manager, or service-receiver designated by appointment or statute. A domestic entity may, alternatively, be served by leaving the papers at the principal office with the person in charge of the business. This somewhat widens prior Massachusetts practice. For an example of the kind of statutory notice covered by the proviso clause of Rule 4(d)(2), see G.L. c. 181, § 4. The "order-of-notice" provision follows Rule 4(d)(1).

Rule 4(d)(2), unlike the cognate Federal Rule, does not refer to "partnerships". Because Massachusetts law so clearly treats partners as individuals for purposes of suit, Shapira v. Budish, 275 Mass. 120, 126, 175 N.E. 159, 161 (1931), use of the federal language would work an undesirable change in substantive law.

Rule 4(d)(3), like Federal Rule 4(d)(4), covers service upon the sovereign or one of its agencies. Service is complete upon delivery to the Attorney General's office *or* upon the mailing of the papers to him by registered or certified mail.

Rule 4(d)(4) governs service upon political subdivisions of the Commonwealth subject to suit. It simplifies the procedure set out in G.L. c. 223, § 37, and applies the principles of the rest of Rule 4 to service of political subdivisions. Rule 4(d)(4) requires the plaintiff to bring the fact of suit to the attention of the person who is most likely to sound the litigational alarm; but it does not require him to do more.

Rule 4(d)(5) applies the principles of Rule 4(d) to service of public entities subject to suit under a common name.

Rule 4(d)(6) is designed to ensure that the Attorney General receives prompt notification of any possible court test (however collateral) of an order of an officer or agency of the Commonwealth. The Rule seeks to minimize the inconvenience to the public which results when such test does not come to the Attorney General's attention until late in the litigation. Rule 4(d)(6) is therefore a mandate of convenience. Failure to observe it will not vitiate otherwise valid service; courts should, however, be alert to compel observance of its requirements.

Rule 4(e) controls out-of-state service. It embodies the procedure set out in the long-arm statute (G.L. c. 223A, §§ 6–7), which in turn relied heavily upon Federal Rule 4(i) (a section omitted, therefore, from these rules). Rule 4(e) is largely self-explanatory and is flexible enough, when read with Rule 4(d)(1) and (2) and G.L. c. 223, § 37; c. 223A, §§ 1–3, to cover most order-of-notice situations. See also c. 227, § 7.

Rule 4(f) requires direct filing by the server. It should be emphasized that any delay by the process server does not bar the plaintiff. See Peeples v. Ramspacher, 29 F.Supp. 632, 633 (E.D.S.C.1939).

Rule 4(g) tracks Federal Rule 4(h) verbatim. It follows the spirit of the Federal Rules, refusing to allow "technicalities" to obstruct justice. See Rule 15 (covering amendments to pleadings) and Rule 60 (covering relief from judgments). It will work no substantial change in Massachusetts practice. See G.L. c. 231, § 51.

Reporter's Notes—February 1975

Rule 4(c) has been amended to make clear that process in the types of actions covered by Rule 4(h) need not be served by any of the individuals enumerated in Rule 4(c).

Rule 4(h) has been inserted to correct a serious inconvenience resulting from the apparent applicability to such Probate Court matters as petitions for instructions and accounts of Rule 4's general service requirements. If Rule 4, as originally promulgated, applied to this type of case, the cost of service might frequently assume excessive proportions. A petition for instructions involving a trust with numerous beneficiaries could require substantial service charges; an account in a common trust fund with over a thousand participants would impose massive expenses.

Prior to July 1, 1974, it was unquestioned that notice of the pendency of a petition for instructions, or the presentation for allowance of an account could be—and invariably was—effected by citation, served in hand or by publication. Moreover, a statute, G.L. c. 215, § 46, authorized the court to direct service to be made by registered mail, thus permitting appreciable saving in service costs. (Another statute, G.L. c. 4, § 7, equating certified mail with registered mail for this purpose, permitted an even less expensive procedure.)

As the amendatory legislation accompanying the Rules, Acts, 1974, c. 1114, repealed neither G.L. c. 215, § 46, nor G.L. c. 4, § 7, many probate courts continued to issue citations in the old form even after July 1, 1974. Others required service in accordance with Rule 4.

To eliminate the confusion, and to maximize flexibility in the particular class of actions affected, Rule 4(h) now explicitly approves both methods of procedure: In any Probate Court action seeking instructions or the allowance of an account, service may—but need not—be made by citation. In those rare cases whose strategy dictates service by an officer, the usual Rule 4 procedure is available.

Although the change in Rule 4(c) and the language of Rule 4(h) are both declaratory of existing practice as to accounts, the Supreme Judicial Court, in the order of February 24, 1975 promulgating the amendments, specifically made the new material retroactive to July 1, 1974. Thus service between July 1, 1974 and February 24, 1975 was valid, so long as it was made either: (1) In accordance with a citation; or (2) In accordance with Rule 4.

Reporter's Notes—December 1975

The last sentence of Rule 4(c) makes clear that whenever a statute, like the so-called long-arm statute, G.L. Chapters 223A, Sections 1-3, authorizes service by certified or registered mail, it is not necessary to enlist the aid of a process server to do the mailing.

Reporter's Notes—1976

Rule 4(d)(3) governs service upon the Commonwealth or one of its agencies (but not upon a political subdivision, see Rule 4(d)(4), or an authority or board (Rule 4(d)(5)). As originally promulgated, the rule made no provision for service upon the agency directly. Moreover, certain sections of the Administrative Procedure Act, G.L. Chapter 30A, Sections 14(1), (2), seemed to conflict with Rule 4(d)(3). In order to rationalize the procedure for appealing from an administrative decision, legislation has been prepared to amend G.L. Chapter 30A, Sections 14(1) and (2). Essentially, the amendments ensure that in all appeals of this sort, the appellant will serve the agency – and every party to the agency proceedings – pursuant to the Massachusetts Rules of Civil Procedure governing service of process. Thus service upon the agency itself follows Rule 4(d)(3), and service upon the other parties looks to Rule 4(d)(1) (which remains unamended).

The original Rule 4(d)(3) required service only upon the Attorney General, not upon the agency. Such service, however, could be effected by certified or registered mail. As amended, Rule 4(d)(3) requires service upon the agency (through either its chairman, any one of its members, or its secretary or clerk). The rule also retains the old requirement of service upon the Attorney General, explicitly directed to the Boston office, to expedite handling. But each service, whether on the agency or the Attorney General, may be made by certified or registered mail. Moreover, as the amendment to Rule 4(c) makes explicit, the actual mailing may be accomplished by the party or his attorney, rather than any of the usual process servers.

It is worth realizing that, although the amendment to Rule 4(d)(3) resulted primarily from a desire to integrate the Massachusetts Rules of Civil Procedure and the Administrative Procedure Act, the new, simplified service procedure which the amendment establishes applies to any action against the Commonwealth or any agency, not merely to administrative appeals. It does not, of course, alter any substantive principles concerning administrative review or the Commonwealth's liability to suit.

Finally, the amendment to Rule 4(d)(3) does not affect the requirement of Rule 4(d)(6) that, when in any action to which the Commonwealth is not a party, the validity of an agency (or other official) order comes into question, the party raising the question must notify the Attorney General.

Reporter's Notes—1988

This amendment sets a 90 day limit after filing for the service of the summons and complaint upon defendants, unless "good cause" is shown. On April 7, 1986 the Supreme Judicial Court ordered, inter alia, that: "The time standards set forth below for the trial, settlement or other disposition of civil cases are hereby adopted applicable to cases entered in any department of the Trial Court on or after July 1, 1988: CIVIL CASES OTHER THAN FAMILY LAW CASES, Superior Court, District Court, and Boston Municipal Court, all jury and non-jury cases within 24 months after filing." The amendment should aid parties and the courts in meeting the time standards promulgated by the Supreme Judicial Court. The amendment is patterned after Fed. R. Civ. P. 4(j), but the Massachusetts amendment prescribes a 90 day limit, rather than the 120 days in the Federal Rules, in order to further aid in the timely disposition of cases.

If a party does not think it will be able to obtain service within the 90 day period, a timely motion can be made for "cause shown" for an enlargement of time pursuant to Mass. R. Civ. P. 6(b)(1). Moreover, Mass. R. Civ. P. 4(j) also permits a party to "show good cause why such service was not made within" the 90 day period.

Reporter's Notes—1996

With the merger of the District/Municipal Courts Rules of Civil Procedure into the Massachusetts Rules of Civil Procedure in 1996, two differences that had existed between the two sets of rules have been eliminated. Prior to the merger, the District Court version of Rule 4(f) required proof of service to be made to the court and to the party; in addition, the District Court version included constables among those who are not required to make an affidavit of service. The merged set of rules adopts the version of Rule 4(f) contained in the Massachusetts Rules of Civil Procedure. Under the merged set of rules, proof of service in the District Court is required to be made only to the court and constables are required to make affidavit of service.

It should be noted that there may be additional requirements in connection with service of process imposed by statute. See, for example, G.L. c. 223, § 31, which provides that where service is made at the defendant's last and usual place of abode in District Court actions, "the officer making service shall forthwith mail first class a copy of the summons to such last and usual place of abode. The date of mailing and the address to which the summons was sent shall be set forth ... in the officer's return."

Rule 4.1. Attachment

(a) Availability of Attachment. Subsequent to the commencement of any action under these rules, real estate, goods and chattels and other property may, in the manner and to the extent provided by law, but subject to the requirements of this rule, be attached and held to satisfy the judgment for damages and costs which the plaintiff may recover.

(b) Writ of Attachment: Form. The writ of attachment shall bear the signature or facsimile signature of the clerk, be under the seal of the court, be in the name of the Commonwealth, contain the name of the court, the names and residences (if known) of the parties and the date of the complaint, bear teste of the first justice of the court to which it is returnable who is not a party; state the name and address of the plaintiff's attorney (if any), be directed to the sheriffs of the several counties or their deputies, or any other person duly authorized by law, and command them to attach the real estate or personal property of the defendant to the value of an amount approved by the court, and to make due return of the writ with their doings thereon. The writ of attachment shall also state the name of the justice who entered the order approving attachment of property and the date thereof.

(c) Same: Service. The writ of attachment may be procured in blank from the clerk and shall be filled out by the plaintiff or plaintiff's attorney as provided in subdivision (b) of this rule, either of whom shall deliver to the officer making the attachment the original writ of attachment upon which to make his return and a copy thereof.

No property may be attached unless such attachment for a specified amount is approved by order of the court. Except as provided in subdivision (f) of this rule, the order of approval may be entered only after notice to the defendant and hearing and upon a finding by the court that there is a reasonable likelihood that the plaintiff will recover judgment, including interest and costs, in an amount equal to or greater than the amount of the attachment over and above any liability insurance shown by the defendant to be available to satisfy the judgment.

An action in which attachment of property is sought may be commenced only by filing the complaint with the court, together with a motion for approval of the attachment. The motion shall be supported by affidavit or affidavits meeting the requirements set forth in subdivision (h) of this rule. Except as provided in subdivision (f) of this rule, the motion and affidavit or affidavits with the notice of hearing thereon shall be served upon the defendant in the manner provided by Rule 4, at the same time the summons and complaint are served upon him.

Inclusion of a copy of the complaint in the notice of hearing shall not constitute personal service of the complaint upon the defendant. The notice shall inform the defendant that by appearing to be heard on the motion for approval of an attachment he will not thereby submit himself to the jurisdiction of the court nor waive service of the complaint and summons upon him in the manner provided by law.

Except as provided in subdivision (e) of this rule, any attachment of property shall be made within 30 days after the order approving the writ of attachment. When attachments of any kind of property are made subsequent to service of the summons and complaint upon the defendant, a copy of the writ of attachment with the officer's endorsement thereon of the date or dates of the attachments shall be promptly served upon the defendant in the manner provided by Rule 5.

(d) Attachment on Counterclaim, Cross-Claim or Third-Party Complaint. An attachment may be made by a party bringing a counterclaim, a cross-claim, or a third-party complaint in the same manner as upon an original claim.

(e) Subsequent Attachment. Either before or after expiration of the applicable period prescribed in subdivision (c) of this rule for making attachments, the court may, subject to the provisions of subdivision (f) of this rule, order another or an additional attachment of real estate, goods, and chattels or other property.

(f) Ex Parte Hearings on Property Attachments. An order approving attachment of property for a specific amount may be entered ex parte upon findings by the court that there is a reasonable likelihood that the plaintiff will recover judgment in an amount equal to or greater than the amount of the attachment over and above any liability insurance known or reasonably believed to be available, and that either (i) the person of the defendant is not subject to the jurisdiction of the court in the action, or (ii) there is a clear danger that the defendant if notified in advance of attachment of the property will convey it, remove it from the state or will conceal it, or (iii) there is immediate danger that the defendant will damage or destroy the property to be attached. The motion for such ex parte order shall be accompanied by a certificate by the plaintiff or his attorney of the amount of any liability insurance which he knows or has reason to believe will be available to satisfy any judgment against the defendant in the action. The motion, in the filing of which the plaintiff's attorney shall be subject to the obligations of Rule 11, shall be supported by affidavit or affidavits meeting the requirements set forth in subdivision (h) of this rule.

(g) Dissolution or Modification of Ex Parte Attachments. On two days' notice to the plaintiff or on such shorter notice as the court may prescribe, a defendant whose real or personal property has been attached pursuant to an ex parte order entered under subdivision (f) of this rule may appear without thereby submitting his person to the jurisdiction of the court, and move the dissolution or modification of the attachment, and in that event the court shall proceed to hear and determine such motion as expeditiously as the ends of justice require. At such hearing the plaintiff shall have the burden of justifying any finding in the ex parte order which the defendant has challenged by affidavit. Nothing herein shall be construed to abolish or limit any means for obtaining dissolution, modification or discharge of an attachment that is otherwise available by law.

(h) Requirements for Affidavits. Affidavits required by this rule shall set forth specific facts sufficient to warrant the required findings and shall be upon the affiant's own knowledge, information or belief; and, so far as upon information and belief, shall state that he believes this information to be true.

(i) Form of Hearing. At any hearing held under this rule, either party may adduce testimony and may call witnesses (including any opposing party). The court, for cause shown on the evidence so adduced, may make such interlocutory orders concerning disposition of the property sought to be attached as justice may require.

Amended June 27, 1974, effective July 1, 1974.

Reporter's Notes—1973

Rule 4.1, like Rules 4.2 and 4.3, does not appear in the Federal Rules, which look to "the law of the state in which the district court is held." Federal Rule 64. The practitioner should realize that attachment under Rule 4.1 does not discharge the plaintiff's obligation to effectuate service of the summons and complaint as specified in Rule 4.

The rule, conforming to recent decisional abrogations of the right to attach, does not otherwise substantially change Massachusetts practice: it limits the use of the attachment process to what the law now permits. G.L. c. 223, §§ 42–83A contain detailed regulations pertaining to attachment. These are obviously too minute and lengthy for insertion in a set of procedural rules, but the practitioner contemplating any sort of attachment of any type of property, real or personal, is strongly urged to consult the statute.

Rule 4.1(b) does not significantly alter Massachusetts law, under which the clerk must sign the writ. See Moriarty v. King, 317 Mass. 210, 213–214, 57 N.E.2d 633, 635–636 (1944). See also G.L. c. 223, §§ 16, 21. The Massachusetts writ must be under seal, see G.L. c. 223, §§ 16, 21; see also Const.Pt. 2, c. 6, art. 5, and must bear the teste of the first justice of the court to which it is returnable; see G.L.

c. 223, §§ 16, 21; see also Const.Pt. 2, c. 6, art. 5, and must identify the parties; Tyler v. Boot & Shoe Workers Union, 285 Mass. 54, 55, 188 N.E. 509, 510 (1933); see also G.L. c. 214, § 12. An attachment of land or of an interest therein must contain the name and last known residence of the defendant. G.L. c. 223, § 62. An attachment of goods also must describe the defendant. See Eaton v. Walker, 244 Mass. 23, 30, 138 N.E. 798, 800 (1923). A Massachusetts writ, under present practice, contains the date of its issuance, which is prima facie evidence of the time of the bringing of the action. Moriarty v. King, 317 Mass. 210, 214, 57 N.E.2d 633, 636 (1944); see also Lapp Insulator Co., Inc. v. Boston and Maine Railroad, 330 Mass. 205, 213, 112 N.E.2d 359, 364 (1953). Massachusetts writs run throughout the Commonwealth, G.L. c. 223, § 20; this will be true under Rule 4.1(b). Like Rule 4.1(b), present statutory practice limits the attachment to the amount of the claim, plus interest and costs. G.L. c. 223, § 42A; see also G.L. c. 223, § 114. If attachment is made subsequent to service of the original complaint and summons, Rule 4.1(c) requires service upon the defendant of a copy of the writ of attachment which must contain a copy of any endorsement by the officer on the original writ. Such service, although it must be made "promptly" (that is, as soon as may be), may be made by mailing the copy to the defendant's attorney, or to the defendant, if he is unrepresented. See Rule 5(b).

Rule 4.1(c) changes Massachusetts practice as to service of the summons. After the attachment of a resident defendant's property, Massachusetts formerly required that a separate summons be served on the defendant stating the value of the goods attached. The service of that summons constituted sufficient service of the original summons. See G.L. c. 223, § 17; Callaghan v. Whitmarsh, 145 Mass. 340, 341, 14 N.E. 149, 151 (1887); Wilbur v. Ripley, 124 Mass. 468, 469 (1878). Service upon a non-resident was accomplished in the same manner, if the court could acquire sufficient personal jurisdiction. Peabody v. Hamilton, 106 Mass. 217, 220 (1870).

In an equity suit, the court generally issued a subpoena, served in the same manner as an original writ of summons. See G.L. c. 214, § 7 and Squire v. Lincoln, 137 Mass. 399, 403 (1884). A defendant was given a copy of an original summons or subpoena. G.L. c. 223, § 41.

Rule 4.1(c)'s limitation of thirty days changes Massachusetts practice. G.L. c. 223, § 30 allows the summons to be served at any time after the attachment has been made, if it is served the required number of days before the return day for the service of the original writ. The equity practice is the same as the practice at law, former G.L. c. 223, § 41.

Rule 4.1(c), establishes a basic procedure to ensure that attachment of defendant's property (real or personal) hews to constitutional lines. Fuentes v. Shevin, 407 U.S. 67, 80 (1972); Schneider v. Margossian, 349 F.Supp. 741, 745 (D.Mass.1972); Bay State Harness Horse Racing & Breeding Association v. PPG Industries, 365 F.Supp. 1299 (D.Mass. 1973). Rule 4.1(f) affords a remedy against plaintiff's unfairly being deprived of security for his judgment.

The basic principle—no attachment without a prior court order after notice and hearing—is thus subject to limited exception if fair security is imperilled. And even this exception requires a court hearing (albeit ex parte) on a motion supported by affidavits. See Rule 4.1(h) and 4.1(i). Moreover the procedure for dissolution of an attachment obtained ex parte is summary and weighted in defendant's favor.

Rule 4.1(d)'s allowing of attachment in the case of a counterclaim, a cross-claim, or a third party complaint did not formerly exist in Massachusetts practice.

Rule 4.1(e) is similar to existing practice, G.L. c. 223, § 85, and covers two situations: (1) cases in which attachment is made for the first time, after service of process; (2) cases in which attachment was made when process was served, and an additional attachment is sought thereafter.

Rule 4.2. Trustee Process

(a) **Availability of Trustee Process.** Subsequent to the commencement of any personal action under these rules, except actions only for specific recovery of goods and chattels, for malicious prosecution, for slander or libel, or for assault and battery, trustee process may be used, in the manner and to the extent provided by law, but subject to the requirements of this rule, to secure satisfaction of the judgment for damages and costs which the plaintiff may recover, provided, however, that no person shall be adjudged trustee for any amount due from him to the defendant for wages or salary for personal labor or services of the defendant except on a claim that has first been reduced to judgment or otherwise authorized by law; and in no event shall the attachment exceed the limitations prescribed by law.

(b) **Summons to Trustee: Form.** The summons to a trustee shall bear the signature or facsimile signature of the clerk, be under the seal of the court, be in the name of the Commonwealth, contain the name of the court, the names and residences (if known) of the parties and the date of the filing of the complaint, bear teste of the first justice of the court to which it is returnable who is neither a party nor a trustee; state the name and address of the plaintiff's attorney (if any), be directed to the trustee, shall notify him that the goods, effects or credits of the defendant in the hands of the trustee have been attached to the value of the amount authorized by the court, shall state the time within which these rules require the trustee to answer, shall notify him that in case of his failure to do so he will be defaulted and adjudged trustee as alleged, and, if wages, a pension, or a bank account is sought to be attached, shall notify him of such amount of wages, pension, or bank account as are by law exempt from attachment and shall direct him to pay over to the defendant the exempted amount. The summons to the trustee shall also state the name of the justice who entered the order approving the trustee attachment and the date thereof.

(c) **Same: Service.** The trustee summons may be procured in blank from the clerk and shall be filled out by the plaintiff or the plaintiff's attorney as provided in subdivision (b) of this rule, either of whom shall deliver to the person who is to make service the original trustee summons upon which to make his return and a copy thereof.

No trustee summons may be served unless attachment on trustee process for a specified amount has been approved by order of the court. Except as provided in subdivision (g) of this rule, the order of approval may be entered only after notice to the defendant and hearing and upon a finding by the court that there is a reasonable likelihood that the plaintiff will recover judgment, including interest and costs, in an amount equal to or greater than the amount of the trustee process over and above any liability insurance shown by the defendant to be available to satisfy the judgment.

An action in which trustee process is sought may be commenced only by filing the complaint with the court, together with a motion for approval of attachment on trustee process. The motion shall be supported by affidavit or affidavits meeting the requirements set forth in Rule 4.1(h). Except as provided in subdivision (g) of this rule, the motion and affidavit or affidavits with the notice of hearing thereon shall be served upon the defendant in the manner provided by Rule 4, at the same time the summons and complaint are served upon him; and the defendant shall also be served with a copy of the trustee summons in cases where attachment has been approved ex parte as provided in subdivision (g) of this rule. Inclusion of a copy of the complaint in the notice of hearing shall not constitute personal service of the complaint upon the defendant. The notice shall inform the defendant that by appearing to be heard on the motion for approval of an attachment on trustee process he will not thereby submit himself to the jurisdiction of the court nor waive service of the complaint and summons upon him in the manner provided by law.

Except as provided in subdivision (f) of this rule, any trustee process shall be served within 30 days after the date of the order approving the attachment. Promptly after the service of the trustee summons upon the trustee or trustees, a copy of the trustee summons with the officer's endorsement thereon of the date or dates of services shall be served upon the defendant in the manner provided by Rule 5.

(d) Answer by Trustee; Subsequent Proceedings. A trustee shall file, but need not serve, his answer, under oath, or signed under the penalties of perjury, within 20 days after the service of the trustee summons upon him, unless the court otherwise directs. The answer shall disclose plainly, fully, and particularly what goods, effects or credits, if any, of the defendant were in the hands or possession of the trustee when the trustee summons was served upon him. The proceedings after filing of the trustee's answer shall be as provided by law.

(e) Trustee Process on Counterclaim, Cross-Claim or Third-Party Complaint. Trustee process may be used by a party bringing a counterclaim, a cross-claim, or a third-party complaint in the same manner as upon an original claim. Such party may use trustee process, even though the trustee does not reside or maintain a usual place of business in the county where the action is pending.

(f) Subsequent Trustee Process. Either before or after expiration of the applicable period prescribed in subdivision (c) of this rule for serving trustee process, the court may, subject to the provisions of subdivision (g) of this rule, order another or an additional service of the trustee summons upon the original trustee.

(g) Ex Parte Hearings on Trustee Process. An order approving trustee process for a specific amount may be entered ex parte upon findings by the court that there is a reasonable likelihood that the plaintiff will recover judgment in an amount equal to or greater than the amount of the trustee process over and above any liability insurance known or reasonably believed to be available, and that either (i) the person of the defendant is not subject to the jurisdiction of the court in the action, or (ii) there is a clear danger that the defendant if notified in advance of the attachment on trustee process will withdraw the goods or credits from the hands and possession of the trustee and remove them from the state or will conceal them, or (iii) there is immediate danger that the defendant will dissipate the credits, or damage or destroy the goods to be attached on trustee process. The motion for an ex parte order shall be accompanied by a certificate by the plaintiff or his attorney of the amount of any liability insurance which he knows or has reason to believe will be available to satisfy any judgment against the defendant in the action. The

motion, in the filing of which the plaintiff's attorney shall be subject to the obligations of Rule 11, shall be supported by affidavit or affidavits meeting the requirements set forth in Rule 4.1(h).

(h) Dissolution or Modification of Ex Parte Trustee Process. On two days' notice to the plaintiff or on such shorter notice as the court may prescribe, a defendant whose goods or credits have been attached on trustee process pursuant to an ex parte order entered under subdivision (g) of this rule may appear, without thereby submitting his person to the jurisdiction of the court, and move the dissolution or modification of the trustee process, and in that event the court shall proceed to hear and determine such motion as expeditiously as the ends of justice require. At such hearing the plaintiff shall have the burden of justifying any finding in the ex parte order which the defendant has challenged by affidavit. Nothing herein shall be construed to abolish or limit any means for obtaining dissolution, modification or discharge of an attachment that is otherwise available by law.

(i) Form of Hearing. At any hearing held under this rule, either party may adduce testimony and may call witnesses (including any opposing party). The court, for cause shown on the evidence so adduced, may make such interlocutory orders concerning disposition of the goods or credits sought to be subject to trustee process as justice may require.

Amended June 27, 1974, effective July 1, 1974.

Reporter's Notes

Rule 4.2 indicates the availability of trustee process as a means of commencing a lawsuit and of securing any potential judgment. It does not appear in the Federal Rules, which refer to state procedure. The rule, based on Maine and Rhode Island variants, does not attempt to cover the subject completely; it specifically refers to "law" as a supplement to the rule's provisions. G.L. c. 246 is entirely devoted to trustee process; the attorney contemplating use of such process ought certainly to consult the statute before proceeding.

Rule 4.2, like Rule 4.1 has been drafted to meet constitutional requirements. Its provisions as to notice and hearing (Rule 4.2(c)); ex parte hearings (Rule 4.2(g)); affidavits (Rule 4.2(g)), incorporating (Rule 4.1(h)); and dissolution of attachment (Rule 4.2(h)) parallel Rule 4.1, which together with its Reporters' Notes, should be consulted. See also Sniadach v. Family Finance Corp., 395 U.S. 337 (1969); 15 U.S.C. §§ 1671–1677 (the Federal Consumer Protection Act).

Rule 4.2(a) and Form 2–A in the Appendix of Forms capsulize the most important basic existing rules pertaining to trustee process: (1) The types of action in which it is unavailable (G.L. c. 246, §§ 1, 32); (2) The preferred position of wages, pensions, and salaries generally (G.L. c. 246, §§ 28, 32); and (3) The ceiling on trustee attachment of wages, pensions and bank accounts (G.L. c. 246, §§ 28, 28A).

Certain actions cannot be commenced by trustee process at all, others not unless a bond is filed. See G.L. c. 246, § 1.

Under Massachusetts practice, the statutory requirements are strictly enforced. If the complaint includes a count for a cause of action in which trustee process is not available (e.g., slander), the entire attachment will be void, even though the complaint also contains a "trusteeable" cause of action *and* plaintiff waives the slander count. Buono v. Nardella, 344 Mass. 257, 259, 182 N.E.2d 142, 143–144 (1962). This is not regarded as discretionary; it may not be cured by amendment because the court "never had jurisdiction to entertain the action or to amend the [complaint]." A. Sandler Co. v. Portland Shoe Manufacturing Co., 291 Mass. 326, 327, 197 N.E. 1 (1935).

Similarly, if the action is one in which the bond requirement is statutorily waived, the statutory terms must be complied with exactly.

Thus the statute exempts from the bond requirement "a writ which contains a statement that the action is . . . for money due under a contract in writing," G.L. c. 246, § 1. A statement that the action is "an action of contract (in writing)" was held not to comply with the statute. Farber v. Lubin, 327 Mass. 128, 130, 97 N.E.2d 419, 420 (1951). The defect is jurisdictional, and cannot be cured by amendment. Tennessee Plastics, Inc. v. New England Elec. Heating Co., Inc., 345 Mass. 575, 577, 188 N.E.2d 569, 570–571 (1963). The court may allow an amendment only if the complaint states, however irrelevantly, one of the statutory exemptions. So long as the action is in fact based on *any* of the exceptions, the court may permit the necessary amendment. Tennessee Plastics, Inc. v. New England Electric Heating Co., Inc., *supra* at 577. 188 N.E.2d at 570–571.

Rules 15 (allowing liberal amendment) and 18 (allowing free joinder of claims) alter prior practice, and abrogate the strict rules heretofore laid down in interpreting G.L. c. 246, § 1.

Rule 4.2(b) prescribes the form of trustee process. It closely follows Rule 4(b), relying on Massachusetts Const.Pt. 2, c. 6, Art. V; G.L. c. 223, § 16.

Rule 4.2(c), covering service procedure, relates explicitly to the service of other process under Rule 4. Rule 4.2(c) requires service of the trustee process within 30 days after filing the complaint, i.e. within 30 days after commencement of the action. The problem did not arise under prior practice, because seizure had to precede entry; that is, in Massachusetts formerly an action (although commenced for statute of limitations purposes when the writ was filled out with the intention to serve, Rosenblatt v. Foley, 252 Mass. 188, 190, 147 N.E. 558, 559 (1925)), was not "in court" until the writ was entered and the declaration filed.

. The principles of Rule 4.1(c), as discussed in the Reporters' Notes to that rule, apply to Rule 4.2(c).

Rule 4.2(d), by reference to "law," includes such statutory provisions as G.L. c. 246, §§ 10–19. The requirement of a signature under the penalties of perjury comes from G.L. c. 246, § 11. The 20–day requirement conforms to the general time-to-answer provision of the rules (Rule 12(a)); it enlarges the time formerly allowed by ten days (Supreme Judicial Court), G.L. c. 246, § 10.

Rule 4.2(e) makes trustee process available on claims against the plaintiff (counterclaims), or between parties on the same side of the *versus* (cross-claims), or against parties newly brought into the litigation by the defendant (third-party claims). Rule 4.2(e) eliminates venue requirements, G.L. c. 246, § 2, in any counterclaim situations, whether the counterclaim is compulsory or permissive, see Rule 13. If the counterclaim is *compulsory*, the defendant must raise it, or else abandon it forever, Rule 13(a). It would be unfair to allow venue rules to deprive such a defendant of the valuable right to trustee process. If the counterclaim is merely *permissive*, the unfairness argument does not apply. But the whole idea behind encouraging permissive counterclaims is the minimizing and compressing of litigation. That purpose seems clearly superior to the rationale behind the trustee venue statute, viz., the convenience of the trustee. This is particularly true under Rule 4.1(c), which contemplates that in the great majority of cases, the trustee will participate in the litigation entirely on paper. Even in those rare instances requiring "live" participation, no particular unfairness will result. In such a geographically compact state as Massachusetts, it does not seem unreasonable to require, say, a Boston bank to send a representative to testify in a Pittsfield lawsuit.

Rule 4.2(f) incorporates existing statutory law concerning plural service on the same trustee, G.L. c. 246, § 8. Such service, like fresh service on additional trustees, G.L. c. 246, § 8, requires appropriate court approval.

Reporter's Notes—1994

The ninth paragraph of the Reporters' Notes to Rule 4.2 states in part that Rule 4.2(c) requires service of the trustee summons within 30 days after commencement of the action. In fact, Rule 4.2(c) requires

service of the trustee process within 30 days after the order of approval of the trustee attachment.

Rule 4.3. Arrest: Supplementary Process: Ne Exeat

(a) Arrest; Availability of Remedy. Except in cases of civil contempt or as specifically authorized by law, no civil arrest shall be permitted in connection with any action under these rules, except as provided in section (c) of this rule.

(b) Supplementary Process. Supplementary process shall be available in the form, manner, and to the extent provided by law.

(c) Ne Exeat. An order of arrest may be entered upon motion with or without notice when the plaintiff has obtained a judgment or order requiring the performance of an act, the neglect or refusal to perform which would be punishable by the court as a contempt, and where the defendant is not a resident of the Commonwealth or is about to depart therefrom, by reason of which nonresidence or departure there is danger that such judgment or order will be rendered ineffectual. The motion shall be accompanied by an affidavit showing that the plaintiff is entitled to the relief requested. The court may fix such terms as are just, and shall in any event afford the defendant an opportunity to obtain his release by the giving of an appropriate bond. In this rule the words "plaintiff" and "defendant" mean respectively the party who has obtained the judgment or order and the person whose arrest is sought.

Reporter's Notes—1973

Rule 4.3 has no Federal counterpart. Massachusetts arrest procedure, to the extent that it is still viable, is governed by G.L. c. 224, §§ 1–30; the related subject of bail is covered by G.L. c. 226, §§ 1–25. There is serious question whether civil arrest, notwithstanding its ancient lineage, could survive a constitutional attack; cf. Sniadach v. Family Finance Corp., 395 U.S. 337, 89 S.Ct. 1820, 23 L.Ed.2d 349 (1969).

Rule 4.3(a) thus eliminates arrest as a vehicle for the commencement of an action; arrest is still available, however, to enforce a judgment of contempt or to effectuate orders of court in the unusual circumstances covered by Rule 4.3(c).

Rule 4.3(b) refers to existing law, covering supplementary process. See G.L. c. 224, §§ 14–30. The subject is not appropriate for detailed treatment in the rules.

Rule 4.3(c) treats the writ of ne exeat regno, or ne exeat, ("let him not leave the realm") which is entirely the creature of "the common law and general equity jurisprudence." Cohen v. Cohen, 319 Mass. 31, 36, 64 N.E.2d 689, 692 (1946). It is designed to keep a defendant within the jurisdiction (by physical arrest, if necessary) so that the court's orders can continue to have effect. The writ " 'is regarded as little more than an order to hold to equitable bail. The party may generally get rid of it by giving security to abide the event of the cause in litigation.' . . . [It] operates in restraint of personal liberty. It is to be granted with caution. It is to be continued in force with caution." Cohen v. Cohen, supra at 37, 64 N.E.2d at 692–693. An order of arrest is available to assure compliance with any court order, *even an order obtained ex parte,* provided: (1) the original order or judgment was lawfully obtained; and (2) the court considering the application for the order of arrest is satisfied that justice demands issuance of that order. The requirements of proviso (2) will rarely be met; orders of arrest, therefore will ordinarily not be issued.

The last two sentences of Rule 4.3(c) are designed to prevent indiscriminate application for orders of arrest. Among the terms which a court might properly fix would be "a requirement that the plaintiff give bond to secure the defendant's damages and costs if the arrest proves unlawful or the defendant prevails on the merits." 1 Field, McKusick & Wroth, Maine Civil Practice 163 (1970).

Rule 5. Service and Filing of Pleadings and Other Papers

(a) Service: When Required. Except as otherwise provided in these Rules, or unless the court on motion with or without notice or of its own initiative otherwise orders, every order required by its terms to be served, every pleading subsequent to the original complaint, every paper relating to discovery required to be served upon a party, every written motion other than one which may be heard ex parte, and every written notice, notice of change of attorney, appearance, demand, brief or memorandum of law, offer of judgment, designation of record on appeal, and similar paper shall be served upon each of the parties. No service need be made on any party in default for failure to appear except that any pleading asserting new or additional claims for relief against him shall be served upon him in the manner provided for service of summons in Rule 4 and except as otherwise provided in Rule 55(b)(2) with regard to notice of a hearing on the amount of damages.

(b) Same: How Made. Whenever under these rules service is required or permitted to be made upon a party represented by an attorney the service shall be made upon the attorney unless service upon the party himself is ordered by the court. Service upon the attorney or upon a party shall be made by delivering a copy to him or by mailing it to him at his last known address or, if no address is known, by leaving it with the clerk of the court. Delivery of a copy within this rule means: handing it to the attorney or to the party; or leaving it at his office with his clerk or other person in charge thereof; or, if there is no one in charge, leaving it in a conspicuous place therein; or if the office is closed or the person to be served has no office, leaving it at his dwelling house or usual place of abode with some person of suitable age and discretion then residing therein. Service by mail is complete upon mailing.

(c) Same: Multiple Defendants. The court, on motion with or without notice or of its own initiative, may order that service of the pleadings of the defendants and replies thereto need not be made as between the defendants and that any cross-claim, counterclaim, or matter constituting an avoidance or affirmative defense contained therein shall be deemed to be denied or avoided by all other parties and that the filing of any such pleading and service thereof upon the plaintiff constitutes due notice of it to the parties. A copy of every such order shall be served upon the parties in such manner and form as the court directs.

(d) Filing Generally, and Nonfiling of Discovery Materials.

(1) Except as otherwise provided in Rule 5(d)(2), all papers after the complaint required to be served upon a party shall be filed with the court either before service or within a reasonable time thereafter. Such filing by a party's attorney shall constitute a representation by him, subject to the obligations of Rule 11, that a copy of the paper has been or will be served upon each of the other parties as required by Rule 5(a). No

further proof of service is required unless an adverse party raises a question of notice. In such event, prima facie proof of service shall be made out by a statement signed by the person making service, or by a written acknowledgment signed by the party or attorney served; and such statement or acknowledgment shall be filed within a reasonable time after notice has been questioned. Failure to make proof of service does not affect the validity of service.

(2) Unless the court, generally or in a specific case, on motion ex parte by any party or concerned citizen, or on its own motion shall otherwise order, the following shall not be presented or accepted for filing: notices of taking depositions, transcripts of depositions, interrogatories under Rule 33, answers and objections to interrogatories under Rule 33, requests under Rule 34, and responses to requests under Rule 34. The party taking a deposition or obtaining material through discovery is responsible for its preservation and delivery to court if needed or so ordered. Notwithstanding anything in this Rule 5(d)(2), any party pressing or opposing any motion or other application for relief may file any document pertinent thereto.

(e) Filing With the Court Defined. The filing of pleadings and other papers with the court as required by these rules shall be made by filing them with the clerk of the court, except that a judge may permit the papers to be filed with him, in which event he shall note thereon the filing date and forthwith transmit them to the office of the clerk.

(f) Effect of Failure to File. If any party fails within five days after service to file any paper required by this rule to be filed, the court on its own motion or the motion of any party may order the paper to be filed forthwith; if the order be not obeyed, it may order the paper to be regarded as stricken and its service to be of no effect.

(g) Information Required. On any pleading or other paper required or permitted by these rules to be filed with the court, there shall appear the name of the court and the county, the title of the action, the docket number, the designation of the nature of the pleading or paper, and the name and address of the person or attorney filing it. In any case where an endorsement for costs is required, the name of any attorney of this Commonwealth appearing on the complaint filed with the court shall constitute such an endorsement in absence of any words used in connection therewith showing a different purpose.

(h) Protection of Personal Identifying Information. Publicly accessible documents filed with the court shall conform to Supreme Judicial Court Rule 1:24, Protection of Personal Identifying Information in Publicly Accessible Court Documents.

Amended effective September 16, 1975; amended August 3, 1982, effective January 1, 1983; January 30, 1989, effective March 1, 1989; March 5, 2002, effective May 1, 2002; October 24, 2012, effective January 1, 2013; January 25, 2017, effective February 1, 2017.

Reporter's Notes—1973

Rule 5 regulates the service and filing of virtually every court document connected with a pending matter. Essentially, it requires that every party affected by a document receive appropriate notice at every step of the action after the original service of process. Obviously, the opposing party or his attorney is entitled to receive a copy of the answer, and of any motion or other paper required to be served; the reference in Rule 5(a) to "similar paper" indicates that the list of other documents is not to be taken as exhaustive.

The phrase "except as otherwise provided" in Rule 5(a) refers to motions which may be made ex parte: (Rule 6(b)—request for enlargement of time made prior to expiration of the applicable period); (Rule 6(d)—application to hear a motion within 7 days); (Rule 65—application for a temporary restraining order); and (Rule 77(d)—requiring the clerk to give notice of the entry of all orders).

Parties in default for failure to appear need not be served, unless the paper in question contains a new or additional claim for relief; in such case, Rule 4 applies. Another exception to the blanket service requirement is any case involving numerous defendants in which the court has ordered a partial abrogation of such service (see Rule 5(c)).

Formerly in Massachusetts, although notice that a motion had been marked up for hearing had to be furnished to "all parties interested" a copy of the motion itself did not have to be supplied unless the opposing party demanded it. Of course, almost all attorneys routinely send copies of all papers to opposing counsel. Rule 5(a) will merely codify that salutary practice.

Rule 5(b) permits service to be made by delivering a copy to the attorney or party (if the party appears pro se), or by mailing one to him at his last known address; or if no such address is known, to the clerk of court. If a party has more than one attorney of record, service upon one of them suffices. Except for permitting service on the clerk in the rare case in which the address is unknown, this portion of Rule 5(b) works no substantial change in Massachusetts practice.

The concept of "delivery" is clearly set out in Rule 5(b). Prior Massachusetts practice did not precisely define this concept. The few cases which have considered the question suggest that the Massachusetts rule concerning delivery was more constrictive than Rule 5(b). For example, effective delivery under former Super.Ct. Rule 3 seemed to require personal receipt by the party or his attorney. Although the manner in which the paper reached the attorney or party was not essential, actual delivery was crucial. "The words 'delivering the same personally' as used in former Super.Ct. Rule 3 did not require the service in hand which is familiar in connection with a writ or process of the court. They were satisfied if the notice was caused to reach the party or his counsel in person." Checkoway v. Cashman Bros. Co., 305 Mass. 470, 472, 26 N.E.2d 374, 375 (1940). The individual giving the notice may use the post office for delivery, "if he is willing to take the chance that it will actually reach the opposing party or his counsel in person." Ibid.

Unlike Rule 5(b), which allows delivery by leaving the copy with a clerk or other person in charge of the recipient's office (or if the office is empty, by leaving the copy in a conspicuous place therein), Massachusetts strictly required personal delivery. In Foley v. Talbot, 162 Mass. 462, 463, 39 N.E. 40 (1894), the attorney had left notice of filing a bill of exceptions in the office of opposing counsel. The Court held that a notice thus left was not duly served unless it actually reached its addressee.

Under Rule 5(b), service may be made by mailing the paper to the party or attorney at his last known address; if no address is known, the paper may be left with the clerk of court. Prior Massachusetts practice made no provision in cases where the address was unknown.

Notice must be written. In the absence of a waiver of written notice, an oral notice is void. Chertok v. Dix, 222 Mass. 226, 227, 110 N.E. 272 (1915). On the other hand, under Rule 5(b), notice by mailing is complete upon depositing the correctly-addressed, postage-prepaid notice in the mailbox. This conforms to previous practice. Checkoway v. Cashman Bros. Co., 305 Mass. 470, 471, 26 N.E.2d 374, 375 (1940); Blair v. Laflin, 127 Mass. 518, 521 (1879).

Rule 5(c) is a kind of "housekeeping" measure designed to enable the court to relieve parties of unnecessary paperwork and postage. This provision, which has no counterpart in prior Massachusetts law,

will doubtless be construed by the courts in such a way as to alleviate the problem of excessive service, and not to create the worse difficulty of insufficient service.

The Supreme Judicial Court has held that under prior rules and statutes, filing must *precede* notice. In Arlington Trust Co. v. Le Vine, 289 Mass. 585, 586, 194 N.E. 725, 726 (1935), one attorney had prepared a bill of exceptions and sent them to his opponent with the following letter: "I am enclosing herewith copy of the Defendant's Bill of Exceptions in the above entitled matter, original of which I am this day filing with the Clerk of the Superior Court at Boston." The applicable statute, G.L. c. 231, § 113, and rule, Super.Ct. Rule 3, required that exceptions be reduced to writing and "notice thereof in writing shall be given to the adverse party." The Court held that the notice did not fulfill these requirements. (But see Curran v. Burkhardt, 310 Mass. 466, 468, 38 N.E.2d 622, 624 (1941); and note that S.J.C. Rule 2:28 requires only that copies be given "not later than the day of filing"). Rule 5(d) will relax the heretofore strict Massachusetts practice and will give the attorney the option of serving his opponent after filing, or a reasonable time before filing.

Federal Rule 5 makes no provision for proof of service of pleading and papers subsequent to the complaint (cf. Rule 4(d)); the matter is controlled by local rule in many Districts. Rule 5(d) has been expanded to eliminate all formalities as to proof of service of papers upon other parties. If an adverse party challenges the adequacy of notice, the serving party will of course have to prove service. In order to minimize frivolous challenges, Rule 5(d) provides that a simple statement signed under the penalties of perjury will suffice to establish prima facie proof of service: "I certify that on October 9, 1974, I served the within Answer on plaintiff by mailing a copy thereof, postage-prepaid, directed to his attorney, John Adams, Esq., at his office, 78 Court Street, Boston, Massachusetts. Signed under the penalties of perjury."

The last sentence of Rule 5(d) is designed to make explicit that the attorney's failure to supply proper proof of service does not invalidate the service if in fact it has been properly completed.

Rule 5(e) has no specific Massachusetts analogue, although various statutes and rules indicate strongly that filing must take place at the clerk's office. See, e.g., G.L. c. 231, §§ 13, 113; Super.Ct. Rule 73. The portion of Rule 5(e) permitting service with the judge is new to Massachusetts. It is designed to cover that rare circumstance in which a party's ability to obtain immediately necessary relief might be unjustly impeded were he required first to file his paper with the clerk.

Rule 5(f) makes clear that the court, either of its own motion, or on application from the adverse party, has power to compel filing of papers; such power necessarily requires an appropriate sanction, in this case, nullifying the service and the papers themselves.

The "backing" requirement of Rule 5(g) codifies familiar Massachusetts practice. The reference to endorsement for costs deals with the requirement of G.L. c. 231, §§ 42 and 43 that initial papers must, if the plaintiff is not an inhabitant of the Commonwealth, be endorsed before entry by a "responsible" inhabitant, who then becomes liable for costs if the plaintiff is unable or unwilling to pay them. This requirement does not affect the large majority of cases, in which the plaintiff is a resident. Shute v. Bills, 198 Mass. 544, 545, 84 N.E. 862, 863 (1908). An endorsement from the office of an attorney is a sufficient compliance with the statute; the attorney thus becomes liable for the costs. Johnson v. Sprague, 183 Mass. 102, 104, 66 N.E. 422, 423 (1903). Rule 5(g) merely clarifies existing law and clearly implies that if the attorney does not wish to be liable for costs, he may so indicate on the backer of the complaint. In that case, the plaintiff must find someone else to endorse the backer.

Reporter's Notes—1983

Rule 5(a) has been amended by adding discovery documents to those which must be served upon each of the parties. Absent this provision, one must repeatedly consult the docket to keep abreast of the case and to ascertain whether further discovery is necessary. The Standing Advisory Committee considered the potential for large reproduction and mailing costs in multiple-party litigation; this can be controlled, however, by the court's authority to "otherwise order" which is already present in Rule 5(a). This amendment draws the Massachusetts Rule closer to Federal Rule 5(a).

Reporter's Notes—1989

As a result of this amendment, which adds a subparagraph (2) to Rule 5(d), specified discovery documents shall ordinarily no longer "be presented or accepted for filing." The discovery documents that shall not be filed, except by leave of court, are: notices of taking and transcripts of depositions, and requests and responses to requests under Rule 34. However, in order to give the court access to relevant documents when a ruling is required, a party "pressing or opposing any motion or other application for relief may file any document pertinent thereto."

Interrogatories and answers thereto are not covered by this amendment, and must be filed in accordance with Rule 5(d)(1).*

The reasons for this amendment are that some courthouses have insufficient storage space, and the filing of discovery documents requires valuable clerical time. This amendment is largely patterned after Superior Court Department Standing Order No. 3–87 (Applicable to the Middlesex Division) entitled "SUBJECT: PAPERS IN CIVIL ACTIONS WHICH WILL NOT BE ACCEPTED FOR FILING." The United States District Court for the District of Massachusetts has a similar local rule entitled "Nonfiling of Discovery Materials." Local Rule 16(g).

There may not be a need for the new non-filing requirement in some counties or specific courthouses. The amendment permits a court to require filing "generally," thus authorizing a court to order the filing of all discovery, or categories of discovery, in all cases or in categories of cases. There may be occasions when a party, the press, or other concerned citizen has a good reason to have more discovery filed than is normally permitted under the amendment. Consequently, the amendment permits the court, "on motion ex parte by any party or concerned citizen, or on its own motion," to make a different order as to the filing of discovery either "generally or in a specific case."

* **Publisher's Note:** Superior Court Administrative Directive 90–2, effective December 3, 1990, provides "on a temporary basis and until further notice" for the non-filing of interrogatories and answers in offices of Superior Court Clerks.

Reporter's Notes—1996

With the merger of the District Court Rules into the Massachusetts Rules of Civil Procedure, differences that had existed in the District Court rules have been eliminated in merged Rule 5. District Court Rule 5(d) had required that papers after the complaint that are required to be served upon a party must be filed with the court either before service or within five days thereafter (as opposed to a reasonable period of time thereafter as set forth in the Rule 5 of the Mass.R.Civ.P.). Also, by merging the two sets of rules, the 1989 amendment to Mass.R.Civ.P. 5(d) regarding the non-filing of specified discovery materials is now clearly applicable in the District Court and Boston Municipal Court.

Reporter's Notes to Amendment to Rule 5(d)—2002

The 2002 amendment to Rule 5(d) added interrogatories under Rule 33 and answers and objections to interrogatories under Rule 33 to the listing of discovery materials that are not to be filed in court (unless leave of court is obtained). This amendment is intended to relieve the parties and court personnel of the burden of filing interrogatories and answers in court. Limitations on the filing of discovery documents were first added to Rule 5(d) in 1989, at which time the following documents were no longer to be filed: notices of taking and transcripts of depositions and requests and responses to requests under Rule 34.

In recent years, some courts have provided, by Standing Order or Administrative Directive, that interrogatories and answers to interrogatories not be filed, notwithstanding the express language of Rule 5(d). See Superior Court Administrative Directive No. 90–2, Housing Court Standing Order No. 1–96, District Court Standing Order No. 1–98 (applicable in Berkshire, Essex, Middlesex and Norfolk Counties). The 2002 amendment to Rule 5(d) has eliminated the conflict between the Massachusetts Rules of Civil Procedure and any such Standing Orders or Directives.

It should be noted that this amendment to the Massachusetts Rules of Civil Procedure does *not* change the requirement of Rule 7(a) of the Uniform Summary Process Rules (Trial Court Rule I) that discovery demands be served *and* filed in court (which results in an automatic postponement of the trial date pursuant to Uniform Summary Process Rule 7(b)). The Massachusetts Rules of Civil Procedure are applicable in summary process actions only if they are not inconsistent with the Uniform Summary Process Rules (see Uniform Summary Process Rule 1), and the provisions of the latter set of rules regarding filing of discovery are now inconsistent with Mass. R. Civ. P. 5(d).

Reporter's Notes—2013

The amendment to Rule 5(a) in 2013 was part of a group of amendments to Rules 5(a), 54(c), and 55(b)(2) that responded to the Supreme Judicial Court's decision in Hermanson v. Szafarowicz, 457 Mass. 39 (2010). The *Hermanson* case dealt with the conflict between G.L. c. 231, § 13B, which limits a plaintiff's ability to demand a specific monetary amount in a complaint, and Rule 54(c), which provides that a default judgment may not exceed the amount requested in the demand for judgment.

Detailed analysis of the amendments to these three rules is set forth in the Reporter's Notes to the 2013 amendments to Rule 55(b)(2).

Reporter's Notes—2017

The 2017 amendment, adding Rule 5(h), serves to alert attorneys, parties, and interested members of the public to the requirements of Supreme Judicial Court Rule 1:24, Protection of Personal Identifying Information in Publicly Accessible Court Documents (effective November 1, 2016). Under Supreme Judicial Court Rule 1:24, unless there is an exception, personal identifying information, such as social security numbers, parent's birth surnames, driver's license numbers, and financial account numbers, may not be included in documents filed in court unless redacted as set forth in the rule.

Rule 6. Time

(a) Computation. In computing any period of time prescribed or allowed by these rules, by order of court, or by any applicable statute or rule, the day of the act, event, or default after which the designated period of time begins to run shall not be included. The last day of the period so computed shall be included, unless it is a Saturday, a Sunday, or a legal holiday, in which event the period runs until the end of the next day which is not a Saturday, a Sunday, or a legal holiday. When the period of time prescribed or allowed is less than 7 days, intermediate Saturdays, Sundays, and legal holidays shall be excluded in the computation. As used in this rule and in Rule 77(c), "legal holiday" includes those days specified in Mass.G.L. c. 4, § 7 and any other day appointed as a holiday by the President or the Congress of the United States or designated by the laws of the Commonwealth.

(b) Enlargement. When by these rules or by a notice given thereunder or by order or rule of court an act is required or allowed to be done at or within a specified time, the court for cause shown may at any time in its discretion (1) with or without motion or notice order the period enlarged if request therefor is made before the expiration of the period originally prescribed or as extended by a previous order; or (2) upon motion made after the expiration of the specified period permit the act to be done where the failure to act was the result of excusable neglect; or (3) permit the act to be done by stipulation of the parties; but it may not extend the time for taking any action under Rules 50(b), 52(b), 59(b), (d), and (e), and 60(b), except to the extent and under the conditions stated in them.

(c) For Motions-Affidavits. A written motion, other than one which may be heard ex parte, and notice of the hearing thereof shall be served not later than 7 days before the time specified for the hearing, unless a different period is fixed by these rules or by order of the court. Such an order may for cause shown be made on ex parte application. When a motion is supported by affidavit, the affidavit shall be served with the motion; and, except as otherwise provided in Rule 59(c), opposing affidavits may be served not later than 1 day before the hearing, unless the court permits them to be served at some other time.

(d) Additional Time After Service by Mail. Whenever a party has the right or is required to do some act or take some proceedings within a prescribed period after the service of a notice or other papers upon him and the notice or paper is served upon him by mail, 3 days shall be added to the prescribed period.

Reporter's Notes—1973

Rule 6(a) does not significantly alter Massachusetts law. G.L. c. 4, § 9 provides:

"Except as otherwise provided, when the day or the last day of the performance of any act, including the making of any payment or tender of payment, authorized or required by statute or by contract, falls on Sunday or a legal holiday, the act may, unless it is specifically authorized or required to be performed on Sunday or on a legal holiday, be performed on the next succeeding business day."

At the common law, if the limited time was less than a week, Sundays were excluded in calculating the time. Cunningham v. Mahan, 112 Mass. 58 (1873); Stevenson v. Donnelly, 221 Mass. 161, 108 N.E. 926 (1915). If however, the time limit exceeded one week, Sundays were included in the calculation of the time, even where the

last day for doing the act fell on a Sunday. Haley v. Young, 134 Mass. 364 (1883).

Rule 6(a) liberalizes the common law, excluding not only Sundays but Saturdays and legal holidays as well, and slightly liberalizes G.L. c. 4, § 9 by excluding all Saturdays.

G.L. c. 4, § 9 extends the expiration date of a statute of limitations from a Sunday to the following Monday. See Smith v. Pasqualetto, 246 F.2d 765 (1st Cir.1957). Federal Rule 6(a) has been held to extend a federal statute of limitations where the last day fell on a Sunday. See Rutledge v. Sinclair Refining Co., 13 F.R.D. 477 (S.D.N.Y.1953).

With certain exceptions, Rule 6(b) permits the court to extend the time for doing acts required under the Rules. The exceptions are governed by the language of the specific applicable rules:

50(b)—a motion for judgment notwithstanding the verdict;

52(b)—motion to amend findings;

59(b)—motion for a new trial;

59(d)—new trial on court's initiative;

59(e)—motion to alter or amend a judgment;

60(b)—a motion for relief from a judgment.

Rule 6(b) applies: (a) where the time period has already expired, as well as (b) where the time period has not expired, although in the *former* situation the failure to act within the time period must have been the result of excusable neglect.

Rule 6(b) does not change Massachusetts practice. The power of the courts in Massachusetts to allow extension of time applies also to permission for late filing. See Whitney v. Hunt–Spiller Mfg. Corp., 218 Mass. 318, 105 N.E. 1054 (1914); Prunier v. Schulman, 261 Mass. 417, 158 N.E. 785 (1927); Hill v. Trustees of Glenwood Cemetery, 323 Mass. 388, 82 N.E.2d 238 (1948).

Federal Rule 6(c) was rescinded in 1966 and is not included in Rule 6. Rules 6(c) and 6(d) are the same as Federal Rules 6(d) and 6(e). They do not substantially affect prior law.

Reporter's Notes—1996

Prior to the merger of the District Court Rules into the Massachusetts Rules of Civil Procedure, the District Court version of Rule 6(b) contained no reference to Rule 50(b) regarding motions for judgment notwithstanding the verdict. This difference has been eliminated in the merged set of rules.

III. PLEADINGS AND MOTIONS

Rule 7. Pleadings Allowed: Form of Motions

(a) Pleadings. There shall be a complaint and (except as provided by law) an answer, and a trustee's answer under oath if trustee process is used; a reply to a counterclaim denominated as such; an answer to a cross-claim, if the answer contains a cross-claim; a third-party complaint, if a person who was not an original party is summoned under the provisions of Rule 14; and a third-party answer, if a third-party complaint is served. No other pleading shall be allowed, except that the court may order a reply to an answer or a third-party answer. In the Land Court, answers in actions for registration, confirmation, or tax foreclosure shall conform to G.L. c. 185, § 41, and G.L. c. 60, § 68, where applicable.

(b) Motions and Other Papers.

(1) An application to the court for an order shall be by motion which, unless made during a hearing or trial, shall be

made in writing, shall state with particularity the grounds therefor, and shall set forth the relief or order sought.

(2) The rules applicable to captions, signing, and other matters of form of pleadings apply to all motions and other papers provided for by these rules.

(c) Demurrers, Pleas, etc., Abolished. Demurrers, pleas, and exceptions for insufficiency of a pleading shall not be used.

Amended December 13, 1981, effective January 1, 1982.

Reporter's Notes—1973

Rule 7 is virtually identical to Federal Rule 7, although Rule 7(a) includes as a permissible pleading, a trustee's answer under oath if trustee process is used. Rule 7 reflects the belief that extensive and complex pleadings are not desirable as a vehicle for the narrowing of issues in a case and that this function can be better performed by discovery and the use of the pretrial conference.

Except where there is a counterclaim, cross-claim or third-party complaint, the only pleadings allowed are the complaint and answer, although the court may order a reply to an answer. In federal practice such orders are rare, because of the availability of other devices, such as discovery, for narrowing the issues. See Keller-Dorian Colorfilm Corp. v. Eastman Kodak Co., 10 F.R.D. 39, 41 (S.D.N.Y.1950). Absent an order, a reply is not permissible. Where no reply to an answer is required, allegations in the answer are deemed denied or avoided. See Rule 8(d). Thus in the usual case, the only pleadings will be the complaint and the answer. Any deficiencies in the pleadings which presently are attacked by such devices as demurrers, pleas, answers in abatement, and the like will be raised by motion or answer.

The limitation of pleadings subsequent to the answer does not substantially alter Massachusetts practice.

Rule 7(a) provides also for an answer to a cross-claim; a third-party answer, if a thirty-party complaint is served; and a reply to a counterclaim *denominated as such.*

The italicized language relieves the plaintiff from deciding at his peril whether the defendant's pleading constitutes a counterclaim, since failure to reply to a properly denominated counterclaim has the effect of admitting its allegations. (See, however, Rule 6(b), which permits the Court in its discretion upon a showing of excusable neglect to provide relief from the consequences of failure to file a reply within the twenty-day period specified by Rule 12(a)(1).)

If an answer contains a counterclaim which is not so labeled the plaintiff is not required to reply. In fact, theoretically, he is not entitled to reply. However, under Rule 8(c), the Court on terms, if justice so requires, shall treat the pleading as having been so denominated and thus allow a reply. Where the defendant denominates as a counterclaim what is actually a defense the cautious lawyer will no doubt reply.

The plaintiff's reply to a properly designated counterclaim should only relate to matters in the counterclaim and should not traverse allegations of the answer which are not part of the counterclaim.

Under Rule 7(c), demurrers, pleas, and exceptions for insufficiency of a pleading are abolished. The functions of these various devices are served under the rules by either motion or answer. See Rule 12(b).

Rule 8.   General Rules of Pleading

(a) Claims for Relief. A pleading which sets forth a claim for relief, whether an original claim, counterclaim, cross-claim, or third-party claim shall contain (1) a short and plain statement of the claim showing that the pleader is entitled to relief, and (2) a demand for judgment for the relief to which he deems himself entitled. Relief in the alternative or of several different types may be demanded.

(b) Defenses: Form of Denials. A party shall state in short and plain terms his defenses to such claim asserted and shall admit or deny the averments upon which the adverse party relies. If he is without knowledge or information sufficient to form a belief as to the truth of an averment, he shall so state and this has the effect of a denial. Denials shall fairly meet the substance of the averments denied. When a pleader intends in good faith to deny only a part or a qualification of an averment, he shall specify so much of it as is true and material and shall deny only the remainder. Unless the pleader intends in good faith to controvert all the averments of the preceding pleading, he may make his denials as specific denials of designated averments or paragraphs, or he may generally deny all the averments except such designated averments or paragraphs as he expressly admits; but, when he does so intend to controvert all its averments, he may do so by

general denial subject to the obligations set forth in Rule 11. The signature to an instrument set forth in any pleading shall be taken as admitted unless a party specifically denies its genuineness. An allegation in any pleading that a place is a public way shall be taken as admitted unless a party specifically denies such allegation.

(c) Affirmative Defenses. In pleading to a preceding pleading, a party shall set forth affirmatively accord and satisfaction, arbitration and award, assumption of risk, contributory negligence, discharge in bankruptcy, duress, estoppel, failure of consideration, fraud, illegality, injury by fellow servant, laches, license, payment, release, res judicata, statute of frauds, statute of limitations, waiver, and any other matter constituting an avoidance or affirmative defense. When a party has mistakenly designated a defense as a counterclaim or a counterclaim as a defense, the court on terms, if justice so requires, shall treat the pleading as if there had been a proper designation.

(d) Effect of Failure to Deny. Averments in a pleading to which a responsive pleading is required, other than those as to the amount of damage, are admitted when not denied in the responsive pleading. Averments in a pleading to which no responsive pleading is required or permitted shall be taken as denied or avoided.

(e) Pleading to Be Concise and Direct; Consistency.

(1) Each averment of a pleading shall be simple, concise, and direct. No technical forms of pleading or motions are required.

(2) A party may set forth two or more statements of a claim or defense alternatively or hypothetically, either in one count or defense or in separate counts or defenses. When two or more statements are made in the alternative and one of them if made independently would be sufficient, the pleading is not made insufficient by the insufficiency of one or more of the alternative statements. A party may also state as many separate claims or defenses as he has regardless of consistency and whether based on legal or equitable grounds. All statements shall be made subject to the obligations set forth in Rule 11.

(f) Construction of Pleadings. All pleadings shall be so construed as to do substantial justice.

Reporter's Notes—1973

Rule 8(a), unlike Federal Rule 8(a)(1), does not contain requirement that the claim set forth "a short and plain statement of the grounds upon which the court's jurisdiction depends." Such a statement, although essential in the federal courts, is of minimal value in the state courts.

Rule 8(b) provides that the signature to an instrument set forth in any pleading shall be taken as admitted unless a party specifically denies its genuineness. The only Massachusetts statutes dealing with this point, G.L. c. 231, § 29 and G.L. c. 106, § 3–307, reach the same result. To comport with prior law, Rule 8(b) also includes a provision that an allegation in any pleading that a place is a public way shall be taken as admitted unless a party specifically denies such allegation.

That part of former G.L. c. 231, § 30 concerning an allegation that a party is an executor, administrator, guardian, trustee, assignee, conservator, receiver or corporation, was not included in Rule 8(b) because this matter is adequately covered in Rule 9(a). While Rule 9(a) deals only with the matter of capacity of a party to sue or be sued, whereas the language of G.L. c. 231, § 30 could reasonably be interpreted to deal with the matter of capacity of a party for other purposes, these latter instances are so rare that they do not warrant specific mention in Rule 8(b).

G.L. c. 231, § 85A imposes upon the defendant-registered owner of an automobile involved in a collision the responsibility for setting up as an affirmative defense in his answer a denial that the automobile was being operated by a person for whose conduct the defendant was legally responsible. This requirement was omitted from Rule 8(b) for several reasons:

(1) Unlike the questions of the genuineness of a signature or the public ownership of a place, which are susceptible of definite answers and will not often be denied, the legal relationship between the registered owner of a motor vehicle and its operator will often call for a conclusion upon which reasonable minds may differ. When there is any good faith doubt on the matter, the allegation will be denied by the defendant, and properly so.

(2) G.L. c. 231, §§ 85B and 85C are intertwined with the provisions of § 85A. Any subsequent statutory amendments to G.L. c. 231, §§ 85A, 85B, and 85C would likely entail a revision of the rule.

(3) Since one of the major purposes of Rule 8(b) is elimination of the general denial except in those rare cases where the pleader intends in good faith to controvert all the averments of the preceding pleading, particularization of specific situations requiring a specific denial tends to weaken the emphasis on this goal.

Rule 8 reflects the view that the primary function of pleadings is not to formulate the precise issues for trial but rather to give fair notice of the claims and defenses of the parties. Particularized pleadings do occasionally expose the plaintiff's lack of a viable case or the defendant's lack of a valid defense. More often, however, particularized pleadings merely result in wasted time and effort, because the claimed defects are matters of form which are subsequently corrected by amendment. In the occasional case where the plaintiff does not have a valid claim, a trial can still be avoided by the use of discovery and either a motion to dismiss for failure to state a claim upon which relief can be granted (Rule 12(b)(6)), or a motion for summary judgment. (Rule 56).

Rule 8(a)(1) provides that a pleading shall contain "a short and plain statement of the claim showing that the pleader is entitled to relief alters prior practice."

G.L. c. 231, § 7 provides in part:

"Second, the declaration shall state concisely and with substantial certainty the substantive facts necessary to constitute the cause of action."

The change is epitomized by the statutory terms "substantive facts" and "cause of action". Under prior law, a pleading had to state precise facts rather than general conclusions, Becker v. Calnan, 313 Mass. 625, 630, 48 N.E.2d 668, 671 (1943), and the substantive allegations had to set forth the essential elements of a recognized cause of action. Brighams Cafe Inc. v. Price Bros. Co., 334 Mass. 708, 137 N.E.2d 923 (1957).

Rule 8(a)(1) makes no reference to facts or causes of action. Under this rule, if a plaintiff fairly notifies the defendant of the nature of the plaintiff's claim and the grounds on which he relies, the action should not be dismissed because it does so through what might be termed "conclusions of law." See Conley v. Gibson, 355 U.S. 41, 45, 78 S.Ct. 99, 101, 2 L.Ed.2d 80 (1957). Certain statutes pertaining to real estate may, however, require unique particularity. See G.L. c. 185, §§ 28, 29; c. 237, § 3; c. 240, § 1.

While Rule 8(a)(1) allows the pleading of conclusions, Rule 12(e) (motion for more definite statement) and Rule 12(f) (motion to strike) cure the only real impropriety of the pleading of conclusions, namely, that the pleading is too vague to form a responsive pleading. It should be emphasized that Rule 8(a)(1) does not alter the statutory requirements regarding the omission of names in Superior Court divorce proceedings, G.L. c. 208, § 10.

Rule 8(a)(2) provides that the claim contain a demand for judgment for the relief to which the pleader deems himself entitled. This will control in the event of a default judgment, see Rule 54(c). It is also important in shaping the judgment, see Rule 54(c) and in determining whether a jury trial is warranted.

Unlike prior procedure, Rule 8(a)(2) permits the pleader to seek in his claim both legal and equitable relief, either together or in the alternative.

Behind Rule 8(b) lies the simple principle that a defendant's answer should unmistakably indicate to both Court and plaintiff precisely which aspects of the complaint are admitted, and which are controverted. Accordingly, the answer must serially respond to each paragraph of the complaint (with an exception to be discussed shortly). Only three responses are proper: (1) an admission of the allegations of the paragraph; (2) a denial of those allegations; or (3) a disclaimer of knowledge or information sufficient to form a belief as to the truth of those allegations. The provisions of Rule 15 are available to relieve the defendant of the consequences of any admission subsequently discovered to be incorrect. The strictures of Rule 11 apply to encourage admission of those allegations which defendant knows to be true, even if without such admission, plaintiff would be put to expense or difficulty in proving them, or might even be unable to prove them at all. See Arena v. Luckenbach Steamship Company, 279 F.2d 186, 188–189 (1st Cir.1960), cert. denied, 364 U.S. 895, 81 S.Ct. 222, 5 L.Ed.2d 189 (1960): "It is difficult to believe that counsel who signed this answer had good grounds to assert, among other things, that his client did not either own, operate, or manage the vessel, that the plaintiff was not employed by the stevedore, and that he was not injured, or even aboard the vessel. It is a breach of counsel's obligation to the court to file an answer creating issues that counsel does not affirmatively believe have a basis."

Rule 8(b) thus proscribes promiscuous use of the general denial except in those rare cases where defendant (and, more important, his attorney) in good faith denies each and every allegation in the complaint. In this respect, it differs from G.L. c. 231, § 22, which permitted "the general issue" in real and mixed actions. However, G.L. c. 231, § 25, required a separate denial "in clear and precise terms" of each "substantive fact intended to be denied", or a declaration of ignorance (cognate under Rule 8(b) to a disclaimer of knowledge or information).

If instead of denying the plaintiff's assertions (or in addition to denying them, see Rule 8(e)(2)), the defendant wishes only to controvert their effect, he may do so by the modern equivalent of the old "confession and avoidance." Under Rule 8(c) such disputation is called an affirmative defense; the Rule requires the defendant to set forth any and all affirmative defenses, including, as under prior law, "any facts which would entitle him in equity to be absolutely and unconditionally relieved against the plaintiff's claim or cause of action or against a judgment recovered by the plaintiff in such action," G.L. c. 231, § 31.

It does not, however, seek to regulate the substantive question of distribution of the burden of producing evidence or of persuading the trier of fact. The rule merely establishes the burden of pleading, i.e., of raising the issue. On the other hand, by raising for the first time an issue on which he does not have the burden of production or persuasion, a defendant may conceivably run afoul of the doctrine of "invited error." This principle, which so far as the Reporters can determine has not yet been enunciated by the Massachusetts Court, holds that if a defendant alleges a fact, he cannot be heard to complain if the trial court charges the jury that the defendant has assumed the burden of proving that fact. The Reporters agree with Professor Moore, 2A Moore, Federal Practice, § 8.27[2], that the mere raising of the defense should not shift any burden to the defendant; they recommend this position unequivocally.

A somewhat related point concerns the possible working of an estoppel on the defendant who pleads, first, a denial of all operative allegations, then an affirmative defense. Under prior Massachusetts practice, Payson v. Macomber, 85 Mass. 69, 73 (1861), as well as under the Federal Rules, such estoppel is of doubtful validity; nonetheless cautious counsel for defendants will probably wish to preface affirmative defenses with some such language as: "If plaintiff suffered injury, as in his complaint is alleged, which is denied. . . ."

In raising an affirmative defense, whoever may be obliged to assume the burden of production and persuasion, the defendant need only give the plaintiff "fair notice," 2A Moore, Federal Practice § 8.27[3]. This is of course the natural corollary of the notice-pleading theory behind the Rules generally and Rule 8(a) in particular.

Rule 8(d) sets up a straightforward way of dealing with failure to deny averments:

(1) If the averments are contained in a pleading to which a responsive pleading is authorized, the pleader must either utilize the opportunity or be taken to have waived it. Rule 8(d) makes the admission automatic.

(2) If the averments are contained in a pleading to which responsive pleading is not authorized, all averments are automatically taken to have been denied. The chief subject of this Rule will be the answer, see Rule 7(a), unless the court orders a reply.

Rule 8(e)(1) merely emphasizes the fact that under Rule 8 no technical forms of pleading are required.

Rule 8(e)(2) permits a party to state as many separate claims or defenses as he has, regardless of consistency and whether based on legal or equitable grounds. This changes prior Massachusetts practice.

Under previous Massachusetts law, besides being unable to join legal and equitable claims in one pleading, a plaintiff could not join causes of action unless they arose out of the same matter (G.L. c. 231, § 1A) or unless they belonged to the same division of actions. (G.L. c. 231, § 7 Fifth and Sixth); Twombly v. Monroe, 136 Mass. 464 (1884); Vigoda v. Barton, 338 Mass. 302, 155 N.E.2d 409 (1959). In equity practice, a bill would be objectionable as multifarious if separate and distinct wrongs, each dependent upon its own facts, were joined in a bill. Coughlin v. Coughlin, 312 Mass. 452, 456, 45 N.E.2d 388, 391 (1942).

Rule 8(e)(2) also permits a party to set forth two or more statements of a claim or defense alternately or hypothetically, either in one count or defense or in separate counts or defenses. To some extent this rule changes Massachusetts practice, which permitted different causes of action to be joined (with the exceptions mentioned previously), so long as the causes of action were stated in different counts. See G.L. c. 231, § 7 Fifth, Sixth. See also Davis v. H.S. & M.W. Snyder, Inc., 252 Mass. 29, 143 N.E. 319 (1925); McNulty v. Whitney, 273 Mass. 494, 174 N.E. 121 (1931). Because Rule 8(e)(2) permits the plaintiff to set forth two or more statements of a claim in one count, the rule that allegations in one count will not be read into the allegations of another count, Kenney v. Boston & Maine R. R., 301 Mass. 271, 274, 17 N.E.2d 103, 104 (1938) is eliminated.

A party's right under Rule 8(e)(2) to state claims based upon inconsistent remedies does not alter Massachusetts practice, see G.L. c. 231, § 7 (Sixth) (providing that a plaintiff shall not be required to elect between causes of action where the remedies are inconsistent). Obviously, separate judgments, based upon inconsistent theories, against the same person for the same acts, cannot be outstanding simultaneously. See Rock–Ola Mfg. Corp. v. Music & Television Corp., 339 Mass. 416, 425, 426, 159 N.E.2d 417, 419 (1959).

Rule 8(e)(2) changes practice with respect to defenses. Heretofore, at law different *consistent* defenses could be separately stated in the same answer or plea. See Payson v. Macomber, 85 Mass. 69, 73 (1861). In equity, however, an answer could state as many defenses, in the alternative, regardless of consistency, as the defendant deemed essential to his defense. See S.J.C. Rule 2:12. Rule 8(e)(2) makes the equity principle applicable to all cases.

Rule 8(f) alters the prior Massachusetts rule that pleadings must be construed most strictly against the party drafting them. Hawes v. Ryder, 100 Mass. 216, 218 (1868).

The difference between the philosophy of Rule 8 and that of former Massachusetts pleading practice emerges vividly from a comparison of the "substantial justice" construction requirement of Rule 8(f) with G.L. c. 231, § 38: "The allegations and denials of each party shall be so construed by the court as to secure as far as possible substantial precision and certainty."

Rule 8.1. Special Requirements for Certain Consumer Debts

(a) Definitions. As used in this rule, the following definitions shall apply:

(1) "Action" means a proceeding where the plaintiff seeks to collect a debt incurred pursuant to a revolving credit agreement.

(2) "Charge–off" means the treatment of a receivable balance as a loss or expense because payment is unlikely.

(3) "Debt" means any obligation or alleged obligation to pay money arising out of a transaction in which the money, personal property, insurance, or services which are the subject of the transaction are primarily for personal, family, or household purposes. Debt shall not include obligations to pay money arising out of a loan secured by real property.

(4) "Original creditor" means the person or entity first owed the debt.

(5) "Revolving credit agreement" means an agreement pursuant to which the consumer may purchase, at retail, goods or services or merchandise certificates on credit from time to time and under the terms of which a finance charge is to be computed in relation to the consumer's balance from time to time.

(b) Special requirements. In any action as defined in subdivision (a)(1) of this rule involving a debt as defined in (a)(3), the plaintiff shall file simultaneously with the complaint the affidavits, documentation, and certification provided for in subdivisions (c)–(f) of this rule. The affidavits, documentation, and certification shall be served on the defendant with the complaint.

(c) Affidavit regarding debt. An affidavit disclosing the following information with particularity:

(1) The name, position, and employer of the affiant;

(2) The name of the current owner of the debt;

(3) The name of the original creditor, including the name under which the original creditor did business with the defendant, if different;

(4) For debt arising from a credit card sponsored or co-sponsored by a retailer, the name of the sponsoring or co-sponsoring retailer;

(5) The last four digits of the account number(s) assigned by the original creditor;

(6) The amount and date of the defendant's last payment, if any, or a representation by the affiant that no payment has been made;

(7) The date of charge-off;

(8) The amount of the debt on the date of charge-off;

(9) For the portion of the debt incurred after the date of charge-off, an itemization of the debt (broken down by principal, interest, fees, or other charges) and the method of calculating such principal, interest, fees, or other charges;

(10) A chronological listing of the names of all prior owners of the debt and the date of each transfer of ownership of the debt, beginning with the original creditor; and

(11) An attestation that the affiant personally reviewed records sufficient to establish the information requested in this subdivision (c).

(d) Affidavit providing documentation of debt. An affidavit with legible copies of the following documents:

(1) Documents establishing the existence, amount, and terms and conditions applicable to the debt, including:

(A) A document provided to the defendant before the date of charge-off demonstrating the defendant incurred the debt and the amount owed;

(B) Documents establishing the terms and conditions applicable to the debt;

(C) The written document, if any, signed by the defendant evidencing the defendant's agreement to the terms and conditions described in the documents in (d)(1)(B) or, if a signed copy of such document is not within the possession, custody, or control of the plaintiff, documents evidencing the defendant's acceptance of such terms and conditions (which may include the most recent monthly statement reflecting a purchase, payment, or balance transfer authorized by the defendant before the date of charge–off); and

(2) Each bill of sale, assignment, or other document evidencing the transfer of ownership of the debt, beginning with the original creditor. Such documentation must include a specific reference to the defendant or the defendant's account number.

(e) Affidavit regarding address verification. An affidavit stating that the defendant's residential address has been verified within three months prior to the commencement of the action by at least one of the following methods:

(1) Receipt of correspondence from the defendant with that return address or other verification from the defendant within the three-month period that such address is current;

(2) Certified mail receipt signed by the defendant with that address within the three-month period; or

(3) Sending a letter by first-class mail to that address for the defendant that has not been returned to sender by the postal service, and verifying the same address as current using a paid subscriber-based commercial online database and, if available, either a municipal record, such as a street list or tax records, or a state motor vehicle registry.

The affidavit shall describe the verification method(s) used and the date(s) of the verification. If any database or municipal or state record(s) used shows more than one address for the defendant during the last 12 months, the plaintiff shall state the basis for selecting the address(es) to be used for service. Documents reflecting such verification shall be attached.

(f) Statute of limitations certification. A certification from the plaintiff or counsel for the plaintiff stating:

(1) Whether the terms and conditions applicable to the debt included a choice of law or limitations provision, and, if so, what such provision(s) stated;

(2) The statute or other law establishing the limitations period, if any; and

(3) That, based on reasonable inquiry, the applicable limitations period has not expired.

Adopted May 22, 2018, effective January 1, 2019.

Reporter's Notes—2019

Rule 8.1 and Rule 55.1, effective in 2019, apply to collection actions against consumers involving debts arising out of revolving credit agreements. Rule 8.1 requires the plaintiff to (1) file with the complaint documentation regarding the debt, (2) verify the defendant's address prior to commencement of the action, and (3) certify that the statute of limitations has not expired. Rule 55.1 (1) prohibits entry of default against a defendant where the documentation required by Rule 8.1 has not been provided; (2) requires a determination that the plaintiff is entitled to judgment in the amount claimed prior to entry of a default judgment; and (3) requires reverification of the defendant's address under specified circumstances prior to entry of a default judgment.

Collection actions involving credit cards make up a significant portion of the civil actions commenced in the Massachusetts courts, with many of them filed in the District Court and Boston Municipal Court. Many of these cases proceed to judgment by default, sometimes raising questions whether the plaintiff has used a current address for service of process.

Requiring additional documentation with the complaint is a recognition that consumers in the past often lacked critical information needed when sued for credit card debts. When an assignee of the debt is named as plaintiff in the action and a complaint is served on the defendant, the defendant may have difficulty in ascertaining the identity of the original creditor. The documentation will help consumers to identify the original creditor in instances where an assignee is seeking to collect an assigned debt and the documentation will help to confirm the amount owed. The requirement of address verification mandates extra steps to help to ensure that an address used by a plaintiff to serve a defendant is as accurate as can reasonably be expected.

The addition of special requirements in litigation involving certain types of debts is not a new phenomenon in Massachusetts. Additional documentation and address verification requirements for certain types of debts have been applicable in small claims cases since 2009 (Rules 2(b), Uniform Small Claims Rules) and in civil actions on the regular civil docket in the District Court and Boston Municipal Court since 2015 (Boston Municipal Court and District Court Joint Standing Order No. 2–15).

Rule 8.1(a). The rule applies to a "debt incurred pursuant to a revolving credit agreement" (Rule 8.1(a)(1)). This would encompass, but is not limited to, a collection action arising out of credit card debt. The definition of debt is limited to consumer debt but excludes a revolving credit agreement involving real estate (Rule 8.1(a)(3)). Thus, Rule 8.1 is not applicable to a suit on a debt arising out of a home equity line of credit where the collateral is real estate.

Rule 8.1(b). The required items must be served on the defendant with the complaint. Accordingly, copies of all such items should be sent to the process server to be served together with the summons and complaint.

Rule 8.1(c). In connection with preparing an affidavit regarding debt, care should be taken not to include personal identifying data. Rule 5(h). Credit card numbers and other personal identifying information must be redacted consistent with Supreme Judicial Court Rule 1:24, Protection of Personal Identifying Information in Publicly Accessible Court Documents. See SJC Rule 1:24, §§ 3 and 4.

Rule 8.1(d). These documents are intended to provide a defendant with details about the nature of the claim, the amount allegedly owed, and the identity of the original creditor.

Rule 8.1(e). The address verification requirements provide various methods for the plaintiff to determine and confirm the defendant's address. The verification must have occurred within three months prior to plaintiff having commenced the action.

Rule 8.1(f). The plaintiff must certify, based on a reasonable inquiry, that the statute of limitations has not expired on the claim and must provide the statutory or caselaw basis for the period of limitations applicable to the debt. Even though the statute of limitations is a listed affirmative defense under Rule 8(c), this requirement places the burden on the plaintiff to determine, and certify, that the action is not stale. A regulation of the Massachusetts Attorney General provides that it is an unfair or deceptive act or practice for a debt collector to attempt to collect a consumer debt that "the creditor knows, or has reason to know based on a good faith determination, is a time-barred debt" unless the creditor makes certain disclosures, including that the debt may be unenforceable because it is time-barred. 940 CMR § 7.07(24).

Rule 9. Pleading Special Matters

(a) Capacity. It is not necessary to aver the capacity of a party to sue or be sued or the authority of a party to sue or be sued in a representative capacity or the legal existence of an organized association of persons that is made a party. When a party desires to raise an issue as to the legal existence of any party or the capacity of any party to sue or be sued or the authority of a party to sue or be sued in a representative capacity, he shall do so by specific negative averment, which shall include such supporting particulars as are peculiarly within the pleader's knowledge.

(b) Fraud, Mistake, Duress, Undue Influence, Condition of the Mind. In all averments of fraud, mistake, duress or undue influence, the circumstances constituting fraud, mistake, duress or undue influence shall be stated with particularity. Malice, intent, knowledge, and other condition of mind of a person may be averred generally.

(c) Conditions Precedent. In pleading the performance or occurrence of conditions precedent, it is sufficient to aver generally that all conditions precedent have been performed or have occurred. A denial of performance or occurrence shall be made specifically and with particularity.

(d) Official Document or Act. In pleading an official document or official act it is sufficient to aver that the document was issued or the act done in compliance with law.

(e) Judgment. In pleading a judgment or decision of a domestic or foreign court, judicial or quasi-judicial tribunal, or of a board or officer, it is sufficient to aver the judgment or decision without setting forth matter showing jurisdiction to render it.

(f) Time and Place. For the purpose of testing the sufficiency of a pleading, averments of time and place are material and shall be considered like all other averments of material matter.

(g) Special Damage. When items of special damage are claimed, they shall be specifically stated.

Reporter's Notes—1973

Rule 9 is substantially the same as Federal Rule 9 and does not substantially alter Massachusetts practice.

Rule 9(a), which abolishes any requirement that the pleadings aver the legal existence of a party or the capacity or authority of a party to sue or be sued, is based upon the assumption that in most cases the capacity, authority or legal existence of a party is not in issue; thus the pleadings should not be cluttered with unnecessary verbiage. Of course, the caption of the complaint would contain the capacity of the parties in the action. Thus, for example, the name of the plaintiff appearing in the complaint, "Alpha Corporation," would indicate that the plaintiff is a corporation. Under Rule 9(a), however, the complaint would not have to recite the fact of incorporation or indicate the state of incorporation. Likewise, while the caption of the complaint would name the plaintiff as "John Jones, Executor under the will of Mary Smith," it would not be necessary to recite in the complaint the fact of the appointment.

Most of the Massachusetts cases dealing with the capacity of a party to sue or be sued have involved the application of G.L. c. 231, § 30 which provides in part:

"If it is alleged in any civil action or proceeding that a party is an executor, administrator, guardian, trustee, assignee, conservator or receiver or is a corporation ... such allegation shall be taken as admitted unless the party controverting it files in court, within the time allowed for the answer thereto, or within ten days after the filing of the paper containing such allegation, or within such further time as the court may allow on motion and notice, a special demand for its proof."

For cases applying this statute see Boudreau v. New England Transportation Co., 315 Mass. 423, 53 N.E.2d 92 (1944) (administrator); Salvato v. Di Silva Transportation Co., 329 Mass. 305, 108 N.E.2d 51 (1953) (corporation); Schwartz v. Abbot Motors, Inc., 344 Mass. 28, 181 N.E.2d 334 (1962) (trustees under a declaration of trust and assignees).

Like prior law, Rule 9(a) places on the party disputing capacity, authority or legal existence the initial burden of controverting it.

Massachusetts cases hold that, unless the lack of capacity appears on the face of the pleadings, the question of alleging lack of capacity to sue or be sued is a matter in abatement. See Friedenwald Co. v. Warren, 195 Mass. 432, 434, 81 N.E. 207 (1907). If the lack of capacity to sue or be sued appears on the face of the pleading, a motion to dismiss is the proper procedure. Tyler v. Boot and Shoe Workers' Union, 285 Mass. 54, 188 N.E. 509 (1933).

The federal cases have held that where lack of capacity appears on the face of the pleadings it may be raised by a motion to dismiss. Klebanow v. New York Produce Exchange, 344 F.2d 294, 296, fn. 1 (2d Cir.1965); Hershel California Fruit Products Co., Inc. v. Hunt Foods Inc., 119 F.Supp. 603, 607 (D.C.Cal.1954); Coburn v. Coleman, 75 F.Supp. 107, 109 (D.C.S.C.1947).

Rule 9(b) does not alter Massachusetts law, which has long held that averments of fraud must be stated with particularity, Nichols v. Rogers, 139 Mass. 146, 29 N.E. 377 (1885); Cohen v. Santoianni, 330 Mass. 187, 112 N.E.2d 267 (1953), and that allegations of duress must be similarly stated, Fleming v. Dane, 298 Mass. 216, 10 N.E.2d 85 (1937).

That part of Rule 9(b) permitting a general averment with respect to malice, intent and knowledge and other conditions of a person's mind also comports with prior law. See Gabriel v. Borowy, 326 Mass. 667, 672, 96 N.E.2d 243, 245 (1951).

Because under former practice, allegations of duress had to be stated with particularity (see Fleming v. Dane, supra) the reasons for the requirement that fraud and mistake be stated with particularity also apply to duress and undue influence, which Rule 9(b) specifically includes.

Rule 9(c) does constitute a change in prior Massachusetts law. G.L. c. 231, § 7 provided in part:

"Twelfth, The condition of a bond or other conditional obligation, contract or grant declared on shall be set forth. The breaches relied on shall be assigned, and the performance of conditions precedent to the right of the plaintiff to maintain his action shall be averred or his reason for the nonperformance thereof stated."

The failure of the plaintiff to allege the performance of conditions precedent to the right of the plaintiff to maintain his action was held sufficient grounds to sustain the defendant's demurrer. Mirachnick v. Kaplan, 294 Mass. 208, 1 N.E.2d 40 (1936); Muchnick v. Bay State Harness Horse Racing & Breeding Association, Inc., 341 Mass. 578, 171 N.E.2d 163 (1961). An allegation that "the plaintiff has done and performed all things on its part in said agreement contained to be done and performed, and that it has kept all of the conditions of said agreement" has been held insufficient to avoid a demurrer. In Newton Rubber Works v. Graham, 171 Mass. 352, 353, 50 N.E. 547, 548–549 (1898), the Court held that the conditions should also be set out.

Rule 9(d) and (e) require little comment. While some common law authority holds that the jurisdiction of the court rendering a foreign judgment must be pleaded, no Massachusetts decision directly so states. In Upham v. Damon, 94 Mass. (12 Allen) 98 (1866), an action on a judgment rendered by a magistrate of another state, the Court held that an objection by the defendant that the declaration did not show that the magistrate had jurisdiction can only be taken by demurrer. "We have not therefore considered whether, if so taken [it] would have availed the defendant" Id. at 99. The presumption in favor of the regularity and validity of a judgment rendered by a court of general and superior jurisdiction of another state, Tuells v. Flint, 283 Mass. 106, 186 N.E. 222 (1933), while concerned with the matter of proof, may have some bearing on the pleading issue.

It should be noted that Rule 9(e) makes no distinction between domestic and foreign judgments.

Rule 9(f) makes averments of time and place material for purposes of testing the sufficiency of the complaint. This alters the common law rule that time and place in most instances are not material. Shipman, Common Law Pleading, 458–460 (1923). See Pierce v. Pickens, 16 Mass. 470 (1820); Folger v. Fields, 66 Mass. 93 (1853).

It should be noted that Rule 9(f) does not require specificity in pleading time and place. See Supreme Wine Co. v. Distributors of New England, Inc., 198 F.Supp. 318 (D.Mass.1961). Rule 9(f) provides only that when specific allegations of time and place are made, they are material, that is they must be able to withstand a motion under Rule 12. Any defect can be cured by amendment under Rule 15.

The chief importance of Rule 9(f) lies in connection with the statute of limitations. Under prior law the defense of the statute of limitations, even though apparent from the face of the declaration, had to be set up as an affirmative defense not by demurrer. Aisenberg v. Royal Insurance Co. Ltd., 266 Mass. 543, 165 N.E. 682 (1929). Because time is material under Rule 9(f), a motion to dismiss under Rule 12(b)(6) may be utilized whenever the time alleged in the complaint shows that the cause of action has not been brought within the statutory period.

Rule 9(g) states prior law, Antokol v. Barber, 248 Mass. 393, 143 N.E. 350 (1924), and does not purport to determine what precisely are special damages. Prior law will govern this.

The justification for Rule 9(g) and prior law is that the defendant ought to be guarded against surprise at the trial by evidence tending to prove damages of which he had no previous notice and which would not normally be implied from the facts set forth in the complaint.

The words "special damage" in Rule 9(g) have three appropriate meanings:

1. Special damages are sometimes considered "damages not necessarily flowing from the acts set out in the declaration, and of which the defendant could not be supposed to have notice unless they were properly averred." Baldwin v. Western Railroad Corp., 4 Gray 333, 336 (1855). Special damages "are not implied by law" from allegation of general damages "because they do not necessarily arise from the act complained of." Id. Thus, in an action for injury to real estate, damages for the loss of rent may not be recovered unless they are specially pleaded. Parker v. City of Lowell, 11 Gray 353, 358 (1858). These are to be contrasted with general damages; "all damages which are the natural or necessary consequences of the cause of action." "Damages such as the law will imply from the facts set forth in the declaration." Antokol v. Barber, 248 Mass. 393, 395, 143 N.E. 350, 351 (1924). Thus, in a case involving an automobile accident, both the expense of repairing the vehicle and the fair value of its use while being repaired were considered elements of general damages, Id., because they were "such damages as any other person as well as the plaintiff, might under the circumstances have sustained from the acts set out in the declaration." Baldwin v. Western Railroad Corp., 4 Gray 333 (1855).

2. In an action for slander, unless the words alleged are "slanderous per se", the plaintiff, in order to withstand a motion under Rule 12(b)(6) (failure to state a claim upon which relief can be granted) must allege special damage, i.e. particular allegations of the way the plaintiff has suffered money damages from the defendant's words. Lynch v. Lyons, 303 Mass. 116, 119, 20 N.E.2d 953, 955 (1939).

3. In personal-injury litigation the words "special damages" (or more colloquially, "specials") refer to such specific, allocable items of damage as the plaintiff's loss of earning capacity, his hospital and medical bills, and any other out-of-pocket losses, although arguably, some of these items might be considered general damages under the principles discussed earlier. For example, Millmore v. Boston Elevated Railroad, 198 Mass. 370, 84 N.E. 468 (1908) held that a housewife's claim for impairment of earning capacity caused by personal injury constituted general damages and not special damages.

Under prior Massachusetts practice (Super.Ct.Rule 33A) the plaintiff was required to file "a statement setting forth the facts in full and itemized detail upon which the plaintiff then relies as constituting the damages." Rule 9(g) makes no more stringent requirement.

Under Federal Practice, Rule 9(g) has been interpreted to require a plaintiff "to inform defending parties as to the nature of the damages claimed in order to avoid surprise; and to inform the court of the substance of the complaint." Great American Indemnity Co. v. Brown, 307 F.2d 306, 308 (5th Cir.1962). Thus, for example, Form 9, which is by definition sufficient under the rules (Rule 84), contains no other reference to damages, general or special, than the following: "As a result plaintiff was thrown down and had his leg broken and was otherwise injured, was prevented from transacting his business, suffered great pain of body and mind, and incurred expenses for medical attention and hospitalization in the sum of one thousand dollars."

Rule 9(g) has been interpreted to place upon the *defendant* the onus of requiring strict compliance. Faced with a complaint which he believes to contain inadequate notice of special damages, a defendant "should file a motion for a more definite statement" under Rule 12(e), Great American Indemnity Co. v. Brown, 307 F.2d 306, 308 (5th Cir.1962). Defendant's failure to raise this point in the pleadings stage constitutes a waiver of the requirements. Niedland v. United States, 338 F.2d 254, 259 (3rd Cir.1964).

Rule 10. Form of Pleadings

(a) Caption; Names of Parties. Every pleading shall contain a caption setting forth the name of the court, the county, the title of the action, the docket number, and a designation as in Rule 7(a). In the complaint the title of the action shall include the names of all the parties, but in other pleadings it is sufficient to state the name of the first party on each side with an appropriate indication of other parties.

(b) Paragraphs; Separate Statements. All averments of claim or defense shall be made in numbered paragraphs, the contents of each of which shall be limited as far as practicable to a statement of a single set of circumstances; and a paragraph may be referred to by number in all succeeding pleadings. Each claim founded upon a separate transaction or occurrence and each defense other than denials shall be stated in a separate count or defense whenever a separation facilitates the clear presentation of the matters set forth.

(c) Adoption by Reference; Exhibits. Statements in a pleading may be adopted by reference in a different part of the same pleading or in another pleading or in any motion. A copy of any written instrument which is an exhibit to a pleading is a part thereof for all purposes.

(d) Parties' Residence or Place of Business. The complaint, and any subsequent pleading stating a claim against a person not originally a party to the action, shall state the respective residences or usual places of business of the party stating a claim and of each person against whom a claim is stated, if known to the pleader; if unknown, the complaint or pleading shall so state.

(e) Two–Sided Documents. The text of any document may appear on both sides of the page.

Amended December 14, 1976, effective January 1, 1977; amended March 5, 2010, effective May 1, 2010.

Reporter's Notes—1973

Rule 10(a) works no substantial change in Massachusetts practice except for requiring that the county be stated in the caption, and that "file" be changed to "docket."

Prior law required that actions be divided into "divisions of personal actions", viz. contract, tort, and replevin. G.L. c. 231, § 1. Causes of action for tort and contract could be joined in a single declaration, provided they derived from the same subject matter, G.L. c. 231, § 7. By statute, a declaration could "contain any number of counts for different causes of action in the same division of action." G.L. c. 231, § 7. The word "count" in Massachusetts thus signified a statement of a complete and independent cause of action.

Rule 10(b) changes prior law. The word "count" no longer carries any talismanic significance. Under Rule 10 the pleader must utilize an additional count only when such use will facilitate clear exposition of the contents of the pleadings. Further, the concept of division of actions is no longer relevant. By Rule 8(e)(2), the pleader is entitled to state "as many separate claims ... as he has regardless of consistency and whether based on legal or equitable grounds."

Rule 10(c) aims to reduce the size of pleadings. Incorporating other parts of the pleading by reference will eliminate the need for repetition. Making a copy of a written instrument annexed to a pleading a part of the pleading for all purposes will likewise simplify proceedings. It should be noted that Rule 10(c) does not purport to require that any document be made part of any particular pleading. The option remains with the pleader, as it did under earlier law, G.L. c. 231, § 7, G.L. c. 231, § 147(10), whether (1) to annex a copy of the document to the pleading; or (2) merely to rely on appropriate stating language in the body of the pleading.

Rule 10(c) abrogates that portion of G.L. c. 231, § 7 which permitted the court, upon motion of the defendant, to require the plaintiff to set out a copy of the original of the contract sued on. The net effect, however, will be the same. A defendant may, under appropriate discovery provisions, compel production by the plaintiff of the contract (or a copy); by deposition or interrogatories, he may, if the instrument is lost or destroyed, discover the particulars of the loss or destruction.

Actions on promissory notes or accounts will continue in substantially the present form. The approved forms for such actions generally follow prior Massachusetts practice. The note or account is either set out in the complaint or annexed thereto as an exhibit (and incorporated by reference), see Forms 3 and 4.

Reporter's Notes—2010

Rule 10(e) was added in 2010 to recognize the existing practice by which some attorneys include text on both the front and back of a page. The language of Rule 10(e) is similar to a 1999 amendment to Appellate Rule 20(a)(4) regarding briefs and other documents filed in the appellate courts.

Although the two-sided document language has been added to Rule 10, which governs the form of pleadings, the provisions of Rule 10, including the two-sided document language, are also applicable to motions and other papers filed under the Massachusetts Rules of Civil Procedure. See Rule 7(b)(2).

Rule 11.   Appearances and Pleadings

(a) Signing. Every pleading of a party represented by an attorney shall be signed in his individual name by at least one attorney who is admitted to practice in this Commonwealth. The address of each attorney, telephone number, and e-mail address if any shall be stated. A party who is not represented by an attorney shall sign his pleadings and state his address, telephone number, and e-mail address if any. Except when otherwise specifically provided by rule or statute, pleadings need not be verified or accompanied by affidavit. The signature of an attorney to a pleading constitutes a certificate by him that he has read the pleading; that to the best of his knowledge, information, and belief there is a good ground to support it; and that it is not interposed for delay. If a pleading is not signed, or is signed with intent to defeat the purpose of this Rule, it may be stricken and the action may proceed as though the pleading had not been filed. For a wilful violation of this rule an attorney may be subjected to appropriate disciplinary action. Similar action may be taken if scandalous or indecent matter is inserted.

(b) Appearances.

(1) The filing of any pleading, motion, or other paper shall constitute an appearance by the attorney who signs it, unless the paper states otherwise.

(2) An appearance in a case may be made by filing a notice of appearance, containing the name, address, and telephone number of the attorney or person filing the notice.

(3) No appearance shall, of itself, constitute a general appearance.

(c) Withdrawals. An attorney may, without leave of court, withdraw from a case by filing written notice of withdrawal, together with proof of service on his client and all other parties, provided that (1) such notice is accompanied by the appearance of successor counsel; (2) no motions are then pending before the court; and (3) no trial date has been set. Under all other circumstances, leave of court, on motion and notice, must be obtained.

(d) Change of Appearance. In the event an attorney who has heretofore appeared, ceases to act, or a substitute attorney or additional attorney appears, or a party heretofore represented by attorney appears without attorney, or an attorney appears representing a heretofore unrepresented party, or a heretofore stated address or telephone number is changed, the party or attorney concerned shall notify the court and every other party (or his attorney, if the party is represented) in writing, and the clerk shall enter such cessation, appearance, or change on the docket forthwith. Until such notification the court, parties, and attorneys may rely on action by, and notice to, any attorney previously appearing (or party heretofore unrepresented), and on notice, at an address previously entered.

(e) Verification Generally. When a pleading is required to be verified, or when an affidavit is required or permitted to be filed, the pleading may be verified or the affidavit made by the party, or by a person having knowledge of the facts for and on behalf of such party.

Amended March 5, 2010, effective May 1, 2010.

Reporter's Notes—1973

Rule 11(a) requires that papers be signed by an attorney admitted to practice in Massachusetts; this ensures that all litigation in courts of the Commonwealth will be the nominal responsibility of a member of the Bar here, even if the litigation is in fact being conducted by out-of-state counsel admitted pro hac vice. Far from multiplying costs to litigants, this requirement guarantees to other parties and the court that service and notice can be made on a local attorney, and that the court need not delay the progress of its docket to accommodate distant counsel.

The requirement of the telephone number is designed to accommodate the court and clerk's office.

The two-witness rule in Federal Rule 11(a) does not apply in Massachusetts, and hence is deleted. The words "sham and false" appearing in the Federal Rule do not seem to add to the force of the Rule. If a pleading is signed mala fide, the court's power to strike does not require an additional supporting reason.

Like Federal Rule 11, Rule 11(a) prescribes no specific sanctions against the offending attorney. Violation of the Rule would probably constitute a breach of DR 7–102(A) and (B), American Bar Association, Code of Professional Responsibility. It would also transgress the Massachusetts attorney's oath, G.L. c. 221, § 38: "I ... solemnly swear that I will do no falsehood, nor consent to the doing of any in court; I will not wittingly or willingly promote or sue any false, groundless, or unlawful suit, nor give aid or consent to the same...." The United States Court of Appeals for the First Circuit has indicated unmistakably that a defendant's attorney violates the Rule when counsel files "an answer creating issues that counsel does not affirmatively believe have a basis," **Arena v. Luckenbach Steamship Co., 279 F.2d 186, 188–189 (1st Cir.1960)**. Yet, so far as the Reporters have been able to discover, no attorney has ever been formally disciplined for violation of Federal Rule 11. The punitory limit seems to have been the Court's action in **American Automobile Association, Inc. v. Rothman, 104 F.Supp. 655, 656 (S.D.N.Y.1952)**: "This opinion should be filed separately in the office of the Clerk of this Court, and indexed against the name of the defendant's attorney, so that, in the event that his professional conduct in any other connection shall become a subject of inquiry, this case and this record can be referred to for such instruction as it may yield."

Rule 11(b), (c) and (d) express concisely and clearly how an attorney (or a party pro se) appears in or withdraws from a case. They reflect Massachusetts court policy.

Rule 11(b)(2) permits the entry of formal appearance prior to answer. Pre-answer appearance "will not prevent an entry of default by the clerk if the answer is not timely filed, but it will entitle the party to notice of an application for a judgment by default," 1 Field, McKusick & Wroth, Maine Civil Practice 242 (1970). See Rule 55(b).

Although under the Federal Rules, "the age-old distinction between general and special appearances" has been "abolished", **Orange Theatre Corp. v. Rayherstz Amusement Corp., 139 F.2d 871, 874 (3d Cir.1944)**, no Federal Rule explicitly so states. Massachusetts has up to now retained the distinction. To ensure complete understanding, therefore, it seemed essential to include in the Rules a clear indication that the mere filing of an appearance no longer constitutes a general appearance. The Rules encourage the parties to raise as many simultaneous dispositive objections as possible. A defendant may therefore, prior to answer, move to dismiss for failure to state a claim upon which relief can be granted (the Rules' rough equivalent of a demurrer) and in the same paper move to dismiss for improper venue. The cases construing Federal Rule 12 have unanimously agreed that such a double-barrelled motion does not entail a general appearance (2A Moore, Federal Practice ¶ 12.07). Rule 11(b) makes this learning explicit. Finally, under the Rules, a defendant may, during the 20–day grace period before the answer is due, pursue some of the discovery devices (e.g., depositions); it therefore seemed necessary to indicate that such pursuit does not constitute a general appearance. Admittedly, a defendant objecting on the grounds of, say, improper venue, will have little need for discovery. Cases, however, can be imagined where discovery would be necessary. A defendant in those circumstances does not appear generally simply because he seeks to bolster his defenses through discovery.

Rule 11(d) is based on prior Massachusetts practice. Its principle is simple: for the convenience of court, clerk, and other parties, any party undergoing change in representation bears the onus of bringing word of that change to all concerned; until such notification, anyone is entitled to rely on the previous record.

Reporter's Notes—2010

Rule 11(a) has been amended to require attorneys and unrepresented parties to include their e-mail addresses, if any, on pleadings. The requirement of e-mail addresses already exists in the Federal Rules of Civil Procedure (Rule 11(a), as amended in 2007) and in the Rules of the Superior Court (Rule 9A(6)), effective March 2, 2009).

The Advisory Committee Notes to the 2007 amendment to the Federal Rules of Civil Procedure state that "[p]roviding an e-mail address is useful, but does not of itself signify consent to filing or service by e-mail." Likewise, the 2010 amendment to Rule 11(a) "does not of itself signify consent to filing or service by e-mail" in civil actions in Massachusetts.

Rule 12. Defenses and Objections—When and How Presented—by Pleading or Motion— Motion for Judgment On Pleadings

(a) When Presented.

(1) After service upon him of any pleading requiring a responsive pleading, a party shall serve such responsive pleading within 20 days unless otherwise directed by order of the court.

(2) The service of a motion permitted under this rule alters this period of time as follows, unless a different time is fixed by order of the court: (i) if the court denies the motion or postpones its disposition until the trial on the merits, the responsive pleading shall be served within 10 days after notice of the court's action; (ii) if the court grants a motion for a more definite statement, the responsive pleading shall be served within 10 days after the service of the more definite statement.

(b) How Presented. Every defense, in law or fact, to a claim for relief in any pleading, whether a claim, counterclaim, cross-claim, or third-party claim, shall be asserted in the responsive pleading thereto if one is required, except that the following defenses may at the option of the pleader be made by motion:

(1) Lack of jurisdiction over the subject matter;

(2) Lack of jurisdiction over the person;

(3) Improper venue;

(4) Insufficiency of process;

(5) Insufficiency of service of process;

(6) Failure to state a claim upon which relief can be granted.

(7) Failure to join a party under Rule 19;

(8) Misnomer of a party;

(9) Pendency of a prior action in a court of the Commonwealth;

(10) Improper amount of damages in the Superior Court as set forth in G.L. c. 212, § 3 or in the District Court as set forth in G.L. c. 218, § 19.

A motion making any of these defenses shall be made before pleading if a further pleading is permitted. No defense or objection is waived by being joined with one or more other defenses or objections in a responsive pleading or motion. If a pleading sets forth a claim for relief to which the adverse party is not required to serve a responsive pleading, he may assert at the trial any defense in law or fact to that claim for relief. If, on any motion asserting the defense numbered (6), to dismiss for failure of the pleading to state a claim upon which relief can be granted, matters outside the pleading are presented to and not excluded by the court, the motion shall be treated as one for summary judgment and disposed of as provided in Rule 56, and all parties shall be given reasonable opportunity to present all material made pertinent to such a motion by Rule 56. A motion, answer, or reply presenting the defense numbered (6) shall include a short, concise statement of the grounds on which such defense is based.

(c) Motion for Judgment on the Pleadings. After the pleadings are closed but within such time as not to delay the trial, any party may move for judgment on the pleadings. If, on a motion for judgment on the pleadings, matters outside the pleadings are presented to and not excluded by the court, the motion shall be treated as one for summary judgment and disposed of as provided in Rule 56, and all parties shall be given reasonable opportunity to present all material made pertinent to such a motion by Rule 56.

(d) Preliminary Hearings. The defenses specifically enumerated (1)–(10) in subdivision (b) of this rule, whether made in a pleading or by motion, and the motion for judgment mentioned in subdivision (c) of this rule shall be heard and determined before trial on application of any party, unless the court orders that the hearing and determination thereof be deferred until the trial.

(e) Motion for More Definite Statement. If a pleading to which a responsive pleading is permitted is so vague or ambiguous that a party cannot reasonably be required to frame a responsive pleading, he may move for a more definite statement before interposing his responsive pleading. The motion shall point out the defects complained of and the details desired. If the motion is granted and the order of the court is not obeyed within 10 days after notice of the order or within such time as the court may fix, the court may strike the pleading to which the motion was directed or make such order as it deems just.

(f) Motion to Strike. Upon motion made by a party before responding to a pleading or, if no responsive pleading is permitted by these rules, upon motion made by a party within 20 days after the service of the pleading upon him or upon the court's own initiative at any time, the court may after hearing order stricken from any pleading any insufficient defense, or any redundant, immaterial, impertinent, or scandalous matter.

(g) Consolidation of Defenses in Motion. A party who makes a motion under this rule may join with it any other motions herein provided for and then available to him. If a party makes a motion under this rule but omits therefrom any defense or objection then available to him which this rule permits to be raised by motion, he shall not thereafter make a motion based on the defense or objection so omitted, except a motion as provided in subdivision (h)(2) hereof on any of the grounds there stated.

(h) Waiver or Preservation of Certain Defenses.

(1) A defense of lack of jurisdiction over the person, improper venue, insufficiency of process, insufficiency of service of process, misnomer of a party, pendency of a prior action, or improper amount of damages is waived (A) if omitted from a motion in the circumstances described in subdivision (g), or (B) if it is neither made by motion under this rule nor included in a responsive pleading or an amendment thereof permitted by Rule 15(a) to be made as a matter of course.

(2) A defense of failure to state a claim upon which relief can be granted, a defense of failure to join a party indispensable under Rule 19, and an objection of failure to state a legal defense to a claim may be made in any pleading permitted or ordered under Rule 7(a), or by motion for judgment on the pleadings, or at the trial on the merits.

(3) Whenever it appears by suggestion of a party or otherwise that the court lacks jurisdiction of the subject matter, the court shall dismiss the action.

Amended November 28, 2007, effective March 1, 2008; May 6, 2008, effective July 1, 2008.

Reporter's Notes—1973

Rule 12 prescribes the basic timetable for responsive pleading and the basic mechanism for raising defenses based solely on the pleadings. Rule 56 (Summary Judgments) interrelates with the remedies afforded by Rule 12, especially Rule 12(b)(6) and Rule 12(c). But Rule 56 encompasses matters (as, for example, supporting affidavits) not confined strictly to the pleadings. A court in deciding any motion brought under any part of Rule 12 initially looks only at the pleadings.

Under Rule 12(a)(1) the deadline for filing responsive pleadings is 20 from receipt of the pleading calling for a response. In actions involving the United States, Federal Rule 12(a) extends this period to 60 days principally to allow the necessary correspondence with the Department of Justice and any other department or agency involved in the litigation. No such extension is necessary in Massachusetts, so Rule 12 makes no special provision for suits against the Commonwealth, its subdivisions, officers, agencies, and the like.

Filing any motion under Rule 12 "stops the clock" on the 20–day responding period. The clock resumes when the court either denies the motion or indicates a postponement of its decision until the trial. From the date of notice of the denial or indication, the moving party (the party obligated to respond to the pleading) has 10 days to serve his response unless the court orders otherwise. If the court grants the motion, the pleading is stricken (that is, the complaint is dismissed or the answer is stricken). In Federal practice, the dismissal or the striking is usually conditional; by amending within a period set by the court, or by otherwise eliminating the defect, the pleader can reinstate the pleading. From that point, the party originally required to respond must do so within whatever time may remain of the original period of response, or 10 days, whichever is longer, unless the court orders otherwise, Rule 15(a).

It will be convenient here to consider, out-of-order, motions for more definite statement under Rule 12(e). Because the type of "notice pleading" authorized by the Rules encourages indefinite and generalized complaints, motions for more definite statements are rarely justified. They will generally be granted only if after an indulgent reading the court concludes that the party required to respond to the pleading will not be able fairly to meet the pleading's allegations. If such motion is granted, the court will order that a more definite statement be served within any time the court may order. From receipt of the amended pleading, the opposing party has 10 days to serve his response.

Rule 12(b), taken, with the exception of Rule 12(b)(8) and (9), directly from Federal Rule 12(b), is the heart of the defensive pleading rules. It covers all the defensive maneuvers previously available in Massachusetts practice: motion to dismiss, special answer, pleas or answer in abatement, plea in bar, and demurrer. The pleader may if he chooses raise any of the nine numbered defenses in his responsive pleading. If, as will much more likely be the case, he elects to raise them by motion, he is bound by three restrictions:

(a) He must make the motion before serving any responsive pleading (Rule 12(b));

(b) He must include in his motion any defense or objection *then* available (Rule 12(g) and 12(h)(1)); and

(c) If his motion fails to object to personal jurisdiction, venue, process, service of process, or misnomer of a party, he permanently waives any such omitted objection (Rule 12(h)(1)–(2)). The idea here is to conserve judicial time by preventing a defendant from serially raising objections which the plaintiff might well be able to meet. Each of the defects covered by Rule 12(b)(2)–(5) and (8) is curable. Were a defendant permitted to raise such objections one at a time, the court might have to hear and determine as many as five separate motions. By contrast, lack of subject-matter jurisdiction (Rule 12(b)(1)) is generally not curable, and certainly not waivable. Because such a defect is central to the court's basic power to hear the action at all, the issue should remain open throughout, as under prior law. Jones v. Jones, 297 Mass. 198, 202, 7 N.E.2d 1015, 1018 (1937). Failure of a pleading to state a claim upon which relief can be granted, failure to state a legal defense, and failure to join an indispensable party are, true enough, curable defects, in the sense that a pleading may be amended or (frequently though not invariably) a hitherto absent party may be brought into the lawsuit. But such matters are so central to the justiciability of the dispute that failure to raise them by motion should not preclude raising them at an appropriate later stage in the litigation.

It should be emphasized here that although the three "favored" objections must be included in any pre-response motion, failure so to include them merely precludes their being raised by any subsequent or additional pre-pleading motion. They may, however, be raised (Rule 12(h)(2)):

(a) In the responsive pleading itself;

(b) In a motion for judgment on the pleadings under Rule 12(c); or

(c) At the trial on the merits, presumably by motion.

The lack of subject-matter jurisdiction may be raised at any time up to final judgment on appeal, in any way, by any party, or by the court sua sponte.

Under prior Massachusetts practice, the courts resolve the problem of successive proceedings based upon the same facts in different ways, depending upon the classification of the dispute, see Stahler v. Sevinor, 324 Mass. 18, 23, 84 N.E.2d 447, 449 (1949), and cases there cited: (1) if the two actions were both at law, the court ordinarily ordered abatement of the second action; (2) if the two suits were in equity, the plaintiff had to elect dismissal of one; and (3) if one proceeding was at law and the other in equity, the plaintiff likewise had to elect. Rule 12(b)(9) alters these principles. It assumes that the court, rather than the parties should determine the location of the ultimate litigation; conceivably, for example, the presence in the subsequent action of additional parties might dictate that judicial time and energy would best be conserved by concentrating the litigation in the second court. Whatever the decision, the rule sets up the mechanism to effectuate the court's determination: (a) The court may dismiss the later action; or (b) it may require the parties to stipulate a voluntary dismissal of the prior action. Such stipulation is necessary in order to meet the requirements of Rule 41(a)(1)(ii).

A motion under Rule 12(b)(6), like the traditional demurrer, tests the legal sufficiency of the complaint, counterclaim, or cross-claim. It should be allowed if and only if "*it appears to a certainty that [the claiming pleader] is entitled to no relief under any state of facts which could be proved in support of the claim.*" 2A Moore, Federal Practice 2245 (original emphasis).

A demurrer looked only to the pleading which it treated. A Rule 12(b)(6) motion may be similarly limited. If, however, in treating the motion, either at the preliminary hearing prescribed in Rule 12(d) or otherwise, the court considers matters outside the pleadings, including uncontroverted allegations by counsel, the motion will be treated as a motion for summary judgment under Rule 56, and all parties, including parties who may not be joining in the original motion, will be afforded an opportunity to present material pertinent to a Rule 56 motion. Under prior practice, a "speaking" demurrer would be dismissed. Davenport v. Town of Danvers, 332 Mass. 580, 582, 126 N.E.2d 530, 531 (1955).

One other distinction between Rule 12(b)(6) and demurrer practice should be noted. In Massachusetts, a demurrer had to stand alone and could not be presented along with other motions or with an answer to the declaration or bill. The Rules encourage, indeed require, concentration of defensive pleadings and motions. Therefore the defense raised by Rule 12(b)(6), whether in motion, answer, or otherwise, may be presented either alone or in combination. A motion under Rule 12(b)(6) must contain a statement of grounds. This closely resembles prior practice, G.L. c. 231, § 16.

Rule 12(c) is designed to cover the rare case where the answer admits all the material allegations of the complaint (or the reply admits all the allegations of the counterclaim) so that no material issue of fact remains for adjudication. Because under Rule 8(d) all allegations in the usual answer (that is, one to which no reply is required or permitted) are taken as denied, a defendant will normally not even be eligible to move for judgment on the pleadings. If, in any event, the court considers matters outside the pleadings, the motion will be treated as one for summary judgment under Rule 56.

The Rules abolish the bill of particulars, see e.g., G.L. c. 231, § 14 (a bill of particulars must be filed in an action on the common counts). Under the principles of notice-pleading espoused by the Rules, a responding party is supposed to obtain clarification of his opponent's vague pleading through use of the various discovery procedures, particularly interrogatories (Rule 33) and depositions (Rule 30). Occasionally, however, a pleading may be so murky that it defies any intelligent response. In that rare case, Rule 12(e) permits the responding party to bring his specific inability to the court's attention and permits the court to order an appropriate amendment.

Rule 12(f) indicates explicitly that although the court may, sua sponte, clean up the pleadings (literally and figuratively) at any time, it may strike an insufficient defense only if the plaintiff takes the initiative. A motion to strike a defense as insufficient is the counterpart of a motion under Rule 12(b)(6), see Lehmann Trading Corp. v. J & H Stolow, Inc., 184 F.Supp. 21, 22 (S.D.N.Y.1960). Although Federal Rule 12(f) makes no provision for the court's consideration of matters outside the pleadings, the federal courts have done so, Wilkinson v. Field, 108 F.Supp. 541, 545 (W.D.Ark.1952), 2A Moore, Federal Practice 2320. Accordingly, the Reporters felt that such provision ought to be made explicit. Under Rule 12(f), as under existing federal practice, a motion to strike an insufficient defense searches the pleadings; in hearing such a motion, the court may properly dismiss the *complaint* for failure to state a claim upon which relief can be granted, just as though the defendant had been the moving party under Rule 12(b)(6), Gunder v. New York Times Co., 37 F.Supp. 911, 912 (S.D.N.Y.1941).

Reporter's Notes—2008

Rule 12(b) has been amended to add a new numbered defense, 12(b)(10). This defense permits a defendant to raise by motion to dismiss the issue whether the amount of damages that the plaintiff is reasonably likely to recover meets the requirements of G.L. c. 212, § 3 (Superior Court) or G.L. c. 218, § 19 (District Court and Boston Municipal Court). Under G.L. c. 212, § 3, an action may proceed in the Superior Court "only if there is no reasonable likelihood that recovery by the plaintiff will be less than or equal to $25,000 ..." Under G.L. c. 218, § 19, an action may proceed in the District Court or Boston Municipal Court "only if there is no reasonable likelihood that recovery by the plaintiff will exceed $25,000 ..."

Before the addition of new Rule 12(b)(10), the issue whether the plaintiff met the statutory requirements regarding the $25,000 amount was not included among the defenses enumerated in Rule 12(b), and presumably could be raised only in the answer. With this amendment, the issue may now also be raised by a motion to dismiss. In addition, Rule 12(h) has been amended to provide that failure to raise improper amount of damages in a motion to dismiss or answer constitutes a waiver.

Violation of the statutory requirements regarding the $25,000 amount is procedural, not jurisdictional. G.L. c. 212, § 3A(b); G.L. c. 218, § 19A(b). See Sperounes v. Farese, 449 Mass. 800 (2007).

In *Sperounes*, the Court held that under the statewide one-trial system, a District Court judge *must* dismiss an action where an objection has been made and where there is a reasonable likelihood the plaintiff will recover more than $25,000. However, where the defendant does not object, a District Court judge has the discretion to dismiss the action *sua sponte* or to permit it to proceed. Sperounes v. Farese, *supra* at 806–807.

A 2008 amendment to Rule 12 added a new numbered defense, 12(b)(10), improper amount of damages in the Superior Court, District Court, and Boston Municipal court. This prior amendment was part of a group of amendments to the Massachusetts Rules of Civil Procedure in light of the adoption of the statewide one-trial system for civil cases.

This second 2008 amendment to Rule 12 corrects an oversight in the prior group of amendments. The correction changes the language in Rule 12(d) from "defenses specifically enumerated (1)–(9) in subdivision (b)" to "defenses specifically enumerated (1)–(10) in subdivision (b)." The amendment to 12(d) is technical in nature and merely reflects the additional numbered defense provided by Rule 12(b)(1)–(10).

Rule 13. Counterclaim and Cross–Claim

(a) Compulsory Counterclaims. A pleading shall state as a counterclaim any claim for relief the court has power to give which at the time of serving the pleading the pleader has against any opposing party, if it arises out of the transaction or occurrence that is the subject matter of the opposing party's claim and does not either require for its adjudication the presence of third parties over whom the court cannot acquire jurisdiction or constitute an action required by law to be brought in a county or judicial district, as the case may be, other than the county or judicial district in which the court is sitting. But the pleader need not state the claim if (1) at the time the action was commenced the claim was the subject of another pending action, or (2) the opposing party brought suit upon his claim by attachment or other process by which the court did not acquire jurisdiction to render a personal judgment on that claim, and the pleader is not stating any counterclaim under this Rule 13, or (3) if part or all of the pleader's claim is based upon property damage arising out of a collision, personal injury, including actions for consequential damages, or death. In actions in the Land Court for registration and confirmation pursuant to G.L. c. 185, and tax title foreclosures, brought pursuant to G.L. c. 60, no party may assert a counterclaim under this subdivision or subdivision (b), except by leave of court.

(b) Permissive Counterclaims. A pleading may state as a counterclaim any claim against an opposing party.

(c) Counterclaim Exceeding Opposing Claim. A counterclaim may or may not diminish or defeat the recovery sought by the opposing party. It may claim relief exceeding in amount or different in kind from that sought in the pleading of the opposing party.

(d) Counterclaim Against the Commonwealth. These rules shall not be construed to enlarge beyond the limits now fixed by law the right to assert counterclaims or to claim credits against the Commonwealth of Massachusetts or a political subdivision thereof, or any of their officers and agencies.

(e) Counterclaim Maturing or Acquired After Pleading. A claim which either matured or was acquired by the pleader after serving his pleading may, with the permission of the court, be presented as a counterclaim by supplemental pleading.

(f) Omitted Counterclaim. When a pleader fails to set up a counterclaim through oversight, inadvertence, or excusable neglect, or when justice requires, he may by leave of court set up the counterclaim by amendment.

(g) Cross-Claim Against Co-party. A pleading may state as a cross-claim any claim by one party against a co-party arising out of the transaction or occurrence that is the subject matter either of the original action or of a counterclaim therein or relating to any property that is the subject matter of the original action. Such cross-claim may include a claim that the party against whom it is asserted is or may be liable to the cross-claimant for all or part of a claim asserted in the action against the cross-claimant.

(h) Joinder of Additional Parties. Persons other than those made parties to the original action may be made parties to a counterclaim or cross-claim in accordance with the provisions of Rules 19 and 20.

(i) Separate Trials; Separate Judgments. If the court orders separate trials as provided in Rule 42(b), judgment on a counterclaim or cross-claim may be rendered in accordance with the terms of Rule 54(b) when the court has jurisdiction so to do, even if the claims of the opposing party have been dismissed or otherwise disposed of.

Amended December 13, 1981, effective January 1, 1982; amended effective July 1, 1996; November 28, 2007, effective March 1, 2008.

Reporter's Notes—1973

Rule 13 regulates claims of relief by defendants against plaintiffs (counterclaims) and as between parties on the same side of the versus (cross-claims). Rule 13 changes prior practice.

Under prior practice, by statute, G.L. c. 232, §§ 1–11, if a defendant had a liquidated or readily calculable claim in *contract*, he could seek *set off*. The respective claims of the plaintiff and the defendant need not have arisen out of the same transaction; but they must have been mutual. Thus if a plaintiff sued two defendants on, say, a note, the claim sought to be set off must have been due from the plaintiff to *both* defendants, G.L. c. 232, § 3. Set off would not lie for a tort claim, Lane v. Volunteer Cooperative Bank, 307 Mass. 508, 511, 30 N.E.2d 821, 823 (1940); Pitts v. Holmes, 10 Cush. 92, 94 (1852). Affirmative relief was available.

At common-law, a defendant could seek *recoupment*, provided: (1) his claim arose out of the same contract or transaction as that sued on; and (2) he was content merely to cancel out plaintiff's claim, without obtaining any affirmative relief, Wright v. Graustein, 248 Mass. 205, 210, 142 N.E. 797, 799 (1924).

In equity, a defendant could plead a *counterclaim*. If the defendant's claim arose out of the subject matter of the suit, and could itself support an independent suit in equity, the counterclaim was compulsory. The counterclaim was, however, only permissive if the defendant's claim: (1) arose out of the same transaction, but was legal in nature; or (2) arose out of a different transaction, but was equitable in nature. A counterclaim had the same effect as a cross-bill in equity; it enabled the court in appropriate circumstances to grant affirmative relief.

Cross-claims, that is, claims against one or more co-parties, could be brought either: (a) in a separate action, consolidated for trial; or (b) (if the case was in equity) by way of so-called counterclaim under S.J.C.Rule 2:13 or Super.Ct.Rule 32, whose strictures have just been discussed.

Rule 13(a) greatly simplifies pre-existing procedure. Basically, with exceptions discussed below, it requires a defendant or third-party defendant (hereinafter jointly referred to as "defendant") to assert against the plaintiff or third-party plaintiff (hereinafter "plaintiff") any claim which the defendant may have against the plaintiff provided the claim arises out of the factual nexus of the plaintiff's claim. The requirement is mandatory if the counterclaim arises out of the transaction or occurrence which is the subject of the plaintiff's claim; the defendant must assert it, or forever lose it. Such a counterclaim is denominated "compulsory" precisely because failure seasonably to raise it permanently forfeits it. This feature sharply differs from prior Massachusetts practice, at least with regard to set-off. Prior law permitted the defendant to withhold pleading a set-off without risk of waiver, see Hunt v. Brown, 146 Mass. 253, 255, 15 N.E. 587, 590 (1888). With respect, however, to a compulsory counterclaim under Super.Ct.Rule 32 (and presumably also under S.J.C.Rule 2:13), it appears that a failure to plead invites loss of right, see Buckley v. John, 314 Mass. 719, 721, 51 N.E.2d 317, 319 (1943).

Classification of a counterclaim as compulsory or permissive depends in turn upon a definition of "transaction or occurrence." The word "transaction", in the present context, has been defined thus: " '[A] transaction is where both causes of action proceed from the same wrong.' " Potier v. A.W. Perry, Inc., 286 Mass. 602, 608, 190 N.E. 822, 824–825 (1934). As the court there suggested, the governing rule "should be construed in a sense to effectuate the settlement in one proceeding of controversies so closely connected as appropriately to be combined in one trial in order to prevent duplication of testimony, to avoid unnecessary expense to the parties and to the public, and

to expedite the adjudication of suits." Interpreting the old Federal Equity Rule 30, the United States Supreme Court expressed a similar view: " 'Transaction' is a word of flexible meaning. It may comprehend a series of many occurrences, depending not so much upon the immediateness of their connection as upon their logical relationship." Moore v. New York Cotton Exchange, 270 U.S. 593, 610, 46 S.Ct. 367, 371, 70 L.Ed. 750 (1926). Approximately the same meaning should be assigned to the phrase "transaction or occurrence", as it appears in Rule 13(a). "The use of the word 'occurrence' in the rule in connection with the word 'transaction' can serve no other purpose than to make clear the meaning of the word 'transaction.' ... The word 'transaction' commonly indicates an act of transacting or conducting business but in the rule under consideration it is not restricted to such sense. It is broad enough to include an occurrence. ... The words 'transaction' and 'occurrence' probably mean, whatever may be done by one person which affects another's rights and out of which a cause of action may arise. ... A familiar test may be applied by inquiring whether the same evidence will support or refute the opposing claims." Williams v. Robinson, 1 F.R.D. 211, 213 (D.D.C.1940).

Even though a given counterclaim arises out of the transaction or occurrence that underlies the plaintiff's claim, it may still avoid being labelled compulsory, provided one of the following conditions obtains:

(a) The court lacks power to confer the relief sought.

(b) The defendant does not have the claim at the time he serves his answer. Any later-blooming claims may be asserted by way of appropriate amendment, either under Rule 13(e) or Rule 15(a).

(c) To award relief upon the counterclaim, the court would require the presence of parties over whom it cannot acquire jurisdiction.

(d) The counterclaim is already the subject of an action by the present defendant against the present plaintiff. Rule 12(b)(9) and Rule 42(a) (consolidation) will permit the court to take any appropriate steps to prevent improper duplication of effort.

(e) The plaintiff commenced his action by process which did not subject the defendant to an unlimited judgment. Assume, for example, that the action was begun by trustee process against a non-resident's bank account. If the defendant appears merely to defend the dollar amount trusteed, without raising any counterclaim, it does not seem fair to require him—on pain of permanent preclusion—to assert a counterclaim which he might otherwise have chosen to commence in a different forum. Of course, if the defendant voluntarily chooses to raise *any* counterclaim, there seems no reason why he should not be required, as a matter of sensible judicial economy, to raise all counterclaims, which would normally be labelled "compulsory."

(f) If part or all of the pleader's claim is based upon property damage arising out of a collision, personal injury, including actions for consequential damages, or death. This exception is *primarily* directed at actions arising out of automobile accidents.

The application of the compulsory counterclaim rule to automobile accidents, where the defendant is usually represented by an attorney for the insurance company, presents several difficulties. These difficulties are set out in the following excerpt from 1 Field, McKusick & Wroth, Maine Civil Practice, pp. 263–264 (1970):

"The objective of Rule 13(a) as originally promulgated was to avoid the possibility of two trials on the same facts and the further possibility of the defendant's inadvertent loss of his own claim by reason of the adverse determination in the first trial of facts essential to that claim. Desirable though that objective may be conceded to be, the rule did not work satisfactorily in motor vehicle actions in which, as is usually the case, the defendant carried liability insurance.

"Under the terms of its policy, the insurer controls the defense of such actions. Counsel for the insurer properly felt obligated to notify the assured of the compulsory counterclaim rule; with the likely result that the assured would request him to handle the counterclaim. If counsel acceded to the request, it caused resentment on the part of the 'plaintiff bar' that a member of the 'defendant bar' had pre-empted law business which he would not have had under the prior practice where an independent action was required. This resentment was particularly serious in the mind of the attorney who by reason of former representation of the assured in other matters looked upon him as a regular client. Moreover, when the same lawyer was charged with protecting both the interests of the insurance company in defending a claim and the interests of the assured in asserting a claim, problems of conflict of interest would naturally arise. On the other hand, if the insurer's counsel told the assured that he must retain his own lawyer for the prosecution of the counterclaim, the assured found it hard to understand why two lawyers were necessary to do the work of one. The layman's reaction was likely to be adverse both to the insurer's attorney and the legal profession generally.

"Criticism of the rule was statewide and came both from lawyers who habitually represented plaintiffs and those who habitually represented insurance companies. After several months of experience with the rule, the Supreme Judicial Court concluded that there was sufficient merit to this criticism to warrant the elimination of the compulsory counterclaim requirement in these cases. Since the complaints evoked by the rule involved motor vehicle cases, the Court limited the amendment to this type of case."

Massachusetts Rule 13(a) does not limit the application of the exception to the compulsory counterclaim to motor vehicle accidents for two reasons:

1. In actions for property damage the same reasons which warrant the exception in cases of motor vehicle accidents are present in cases involving other types of collisions (e.g., a collision of motor boats). Thus the language "property damage arising out of a collision" appears appropriate.

2. Most personal injury cases involve actions against owners or possessors of property for injury resulting from a defective condition of the premises, or actions arising out of collisions. Representation by an attorney for an insurance company is just as likely in the former type of case as in the latter. While it is obvious that the former type of case would rarely lend itself to the use of the counterclaim, if a counterclaim does exist, it should not, for the same reasons present in the collision cases, be compulsory.

Rule 13(b) tracks Federal Rule 13(b), but omits the final clause, thus making clear that the defendant may at his option assert as a counterclaim any claim whatsoever, even though some other portion of Rule 13 might give the defendant the option of omitting it.

Rule 13(c) changes prior Massachusetts practice which, as previously indicated, permitted affirmative recovery only in set-off, not in recoupment. It will also allow the defendant who raises a legal counterclaim against an equitable claim by the plaintiff to retain his jury right on the counterclaim. This too will change prior law, Gulesian v. Newton Trust Co., 302 Mass. 369, 371, 19 N.E.2d 312, 313–314 (1939).

Rule 13(d) reemphasizes that the Rules do not purport to change substantive rights, in this case against the Commonwealth, its political subdivisions, or any of their officers and agencies.

Rule 13(e) echoes the general assumption of the Rules that issues between the parties should be resolved in as few lawsuits as possible. In Massachusetts, a claim acquired after commencement of the action was not available in set-off. Jump v. Leon, 192 Mass. 511, 513, 78 N.E. 532 (1906). Rule 13(e) changes this practice. A late-arising counterclaim may be added at any time by leave of court. Presumably, if at the time the counterclaim is acquired, a reply has not yet been served to the original counterclaim, the defendant may add the new counterclaim by way of amendment under Rule 15(a).

If the defendant owned the counterclaim at the time of serving his original answer, but omitted it excusably, Rule 13 allows the court to permit an amendment; this is similar to prior Massachusetts practice,

Scullin v. Cities Service Oil Co., 304 Mass. 75, 22 N.E.2d 666 (1939); Hall v. Rosenfield, 177 Mass. 397, 59 N.E. 68 (1901). Under appropriate circumstances, a Rule 15(a) amendment may also be allowed.

For applicable periods of limitation, see G.L. c. 260, § 36 (as amended).

Up to this point, Rule 13 has dealt with claims back against the plaintiff by the defendant. Rule 13(g) regulates claims between co-parties, that is, parties on the same side of the *versus*. Previously, defendants in equity suits could cross-claim (the Massachusetts Rules used the word "counterclaim") under the same conditions regulating a counterclaim against the plaintiff. Rule 13(g) somewhat narrows this practice. It permits a cross-claim under only two sets of circumstances: (1) the cross-claim arises out of the transaction or occurrence underlying the original action or a counterclaim; or (2) the cross-claim relates to property which is the subject matter of the original action.

This Rule does not purport to prescribe machinery for resolving in one litigation all the disputes between all the parties. To begin with, it is entirely permissive. Failure to assert a cross-claim will never forfeit the right to commence an independent action. Further, the rule allows only those cross-claims fairly closely associated with the principal dispute.

Rule 13(g) permits assertion against a co-party of what is in effect a third-party complaint under Rule 14. The chief difference is that under Rule 13(g), both co-parties are, by definition, potentially liable to the opposing party; under Rule 14, the third-party defendant will not even be potentially liable to the plaintiff unless the plaintiff chooses specially to assert such a claim directly against the third-party defendant.

Rule 13(h) makes effective as to counterclaims and cross-claims the provisions of Rules 19 and 20. These deal respectively with the joinder of necessary parties, and the joinder of additional parties. The practice is reasonably familiar in Massachusetts. For the manner of serving such parties, see Rule 4(f).

Rule 13(i) authorizes the court to order separate trials (Rule 42) and to enter separate judgment on a cross-claim or a counterclaim (Rule 54(b)). Rule 13(i), like earlier Massachusetts practice, Bordonaro v. Vandenkerckhaven, 322 Mass. 278, 281, 76 N.E.2d 755, 757 (1948), permits the court to give judgment on a counterclaim or cross-claim even though the plaintiff's claim may have been dismissed.

Since the rules are not applicable to the district courts, Rule 13(j) provides for cases transferred, appealed or removed to the Superior Court. Rule 13(j) provides for a twenty-day period from the transfer, removal or appeal during which the defendant must (if Rule 13(a) is applicable) or may (if Rule 13(b) is applicable) amend the answer so as to assert any counterclaims. This twenty-day period applies only to asserting a counterclaim; the time for reply to a counterclaim would be governed by Rule 12(a). Rule 13(j) also sets a similar 20–day time limit for assertion of cross-claims (i.e., claims between parties on the same side of the *versus*). The requirements of Rule 13(j) do not apply to any case which was *tried* in a district court before removal or appeal.

Reporter's Notes—1996

Rule 13(a) has been amended to add references to "judicial district" to take into account the applicability of the Rules to the District Court and Boston Municipal Court. It should be noted that Rule 13(j), which did not appear in the District Court version of the Rules, appears in the merged set of Rules.

Reporter's Notes—2008

Rule 13(j) ("Transferred, Appealed and Removed Actions") has been deleted. It had been included in the original version of the Mass. R. Civ. P. because the Massachusetts Rules of Civil Procedure, when first promulgated, did not apply in the District Court.

Rule 14. Third–Party Practice

(a) When Defendant May Bring in Third Party. At any time after commencement of the action a defending party, as a third-party plaintiff, may (except in cases of registration and confirmation in the Land Court brought pursuant to G.L. c. 185) cause a summons and complaint to be served upon a person who is or may be liable to him for all or part of the plaintiff's claim against him. The third-party plaintiff need not obtain leave to make the service if he files the third-party complaint not later than 20 days after he serves his original answer. Otherwise he must obtain leave on motion upon notice to all parties to the action. The person served with the summons and third-party complaint, hereinafter called the third-party defendant, shall make his defenses to the third-party plaintiff's claim as provided in Rule 12 and his counterclaims against the third-party plaintiff and cross-claims against other third-party defendants as provided in Rule 13. The third-party defendant may assert against the plaintiff any defenses which the third-party plaintiff has to the plaintiff's claim. The third-party defendant may also assert any claim against the plaintiff arising out of the transaction or occurrence that is the subject matter of the plaintiff's claim against the third-party plaintiff, and the plaintiff thereupon shall assert his defenses as provided in Rule 12 and his counterclaims as provided in Rule 13. The plaintiff may assert any claim against the third-party defendant arising out of the transaction or occurrence that is the subject matter of the plaintiff's claim against the third-party plaintiff, and the third-party defendant thereupon shall assert his defenses as provided in Rule 12 and his counterclaims and cross-claims as provided in Rule 13. Any party may move to strike the third-party claim, or for its severance or separate trial. A third-party defendant may proceed under this rule against any person who is or may be liable to him for all or part of the claim made in the action against the third-party defendant.

(b) When Plaintiff May Bring in Third Party. When a counterclaim is asserted against a plaintiff, he may cause a third party to be brought in under circumstances which under this rule would entitle a defendant to do so.

Amended December 13, 1981, effective January 1, 1982.

Reporter's Notes—1973

Rule 14 largely tracks Federal Rule 14; it also closely approximates G.L. c. 231, § 4B as amended, which was deliberately patterned upon that version of Federal Rule 14 extant at the time the statute was passed (1964).

Rule 14 allows a defendant to implead a third party defendant without leave of court if the third party complaint is served within 20 days after service of the original answer; thereafter leave of court is required. This changes prior law which allowed 90 days after service of the answer for impleader without leave of court. See Mass.G.L. c. 231 § 4B as amended in 1973.

In most cases, the defendant/third-party plaintiff will be fully aware of potential third-party defendants well before the deadline. He will therefore file his third-party pleadings promptly. Admittedly, sometimes even diligent preparation will not disclose to the original defendant's attorney the possibility of a third-party action until the deadline has passed. In such cases, the court will grant leave almost as of course. The purpose behind the restriction is the belief that unbridled third-party practice offers an unscrupulous attorney an opportunity to delay trial; by commencing a third-party suit, he can hold up the proceedings for the length of time necessary to permit the new third-

party defendant to answer and otherwise defend. Under the Rule, however, the court will have an opportunity to examine any late-blooming third-party claims. It can (and should) deny leave when it is convinced that the third-party claim is not bona fide, or is interposed for the purpose of delay.

The amendment to G.L. c. 231 § 4B struck from the statute the words "not a party to the action", which therefore do not appear in Rule 14(a). This eliminates a doubt which existed prior to the amendment, viz., whether a third-party complaint could be served only on a non-party. The deletion emphasizes that the purpose of Rule 14 is to encourage the joinder in a law suit of all parties who may reasonably be said to have an interest (in the legal sense) in the final disposition of the litigation. The combined effect of Rule 14 and Rule 13 (which is explicitly referred to in the body of Rule 14(a)) will be to ensure a single piece of litigation where previously two or more had been necessary.

Rule 14 frankly aims at telescoping litigation. It will therefore find appropriate use in situations of indemnity, and in situations testing the possibility of contribution among joint tortfeasors (G.L. c. 231B §§ 1–4), although these latter will more generally be resolved by cross-claims under Rule 13. Because Rule 14 expressly allows what is in effect anticipatory litigation, a third-party defendant may not and should not object on the grounds that the defendant's liability has not yet been established.

It should be noted that Rule 14, like Federal Rule 14 and G.L. c. 231 § 4B as amended, does not permit the defendant to "tender" an additional defendant to the plaintiff. If the plaintiff has not chosen to sue the prospective third-party defendant, the original defendant may bring in the third-party defendant only if the third-party defendant "is or may be liable to" the original defendant. If the prospective third-party defendant is also potentially directly liable to the plaintiff, then the plaintiff, as the rule explicitly states, "may assert any claim against the third-party defendant;" but he need not do so. The rule already requires responses from the third-party defendant; language has been inserted to extend this requirement to the plaintiff in the event that the third-party defendant asserts any claim against him. It is not clear why such language does not appear in the Federal Rule (although the requirement has been assumed, 3 Moore, Federal Practice 614). The insertion will remove all doubt.

Rule 15.   Amended and Supplemental Pleadings

(a) Amendments. A party may amend his pleading once as a matter of course at any time before a responsive pleading is served and prior to entry of an order of dismissal or, if the pleading is one to which no responsive pleading is permitted and the action has not been placed upon the trial calendar, he may so amend it at any time within 20 days after it is served. Otherwise a party may amend his pleading only by leave of court or by written consent of the adverse party; and leave shall be freely given when justice so requires. A party shall plead in response to an amended pleading within the time remaining for response to the original pleading or within 10 days after service of the amended pleading, whichever period may be the longer, unless the court otherwise orders.

(b) Amendments to Conform to the Evidence. When issues not raised by the pleadings are tried by express or implied consent of the parties, they shall be treated in all respects as if they had been raised in the pleadings. Such amendment of the pleadings as may be necessary to cause them to conform to the evidence and to raise these issues may be made upon motion of any party at any time, even after judgment; but failure so to amend does not affect the result of the trial of these issues. If evidence is objected to at the trial on the ground that it is not within the issues made by the pleadings, the court may allow the pleadings to be amended and shall do so freely when the presentation of the merits of the action will be subserved thereby and the objecting party fails to satisfy the court that the admission of such evidence would prejudice him in maintaining his action or defense upon the merits. The court may grant a continuance to enable the objecting party to meet such evidence.

(c) Relation Back of Amendments. Whenever the claim or defense asserted in the amended pleading arose out of the conduct, transaction, or occurrence set forth or attempted to be set forth in the original pleading, the amendment (including an amendment changing a party) relates back to the original pleading.

(d) Supplemental Pleadings. Upon motion of a party the court may, upon reasonable notice and upon such terms as are just, permit him to serve a supplemental pleading setting forth transactions or occurrences or events which have happened since the date of the pleading sought to be supplemented. Permission may be granted even though the original pleading is defective in its statement of a claim for relief or defense. If the court deems it advisable that the adverse party plead to the supplemental pleading it shall so order, specifying the time therefor.

Reporter's Notes—1973

The first part of Rule 15(a) allows a party to amend his pleading prior to entry of an order of dismissal, under certain circumstances, once, as a matter of course. The circumstances are: (1) the pleading is one with respect to which a responsive pleading is permitted (see Rule 7(a)) and no responsive pleading has yet been served; or (2) the pleading is one to which no responsive pleading is permitted (see Rule 7(a)) and the action has not yet been placed on the trial calendar. In the first case, no time limit is imposed; in the second, amendment must take place within 20 days after service of the original pleading.

Rule 15(a) is the same as Federal Rule 15(a) except that it also specifically limits the right of amendment *as a matter of course* to the situation where there has not been an order of dismissal.

Because a motion is not considered a pleading within the meaning of Rule 15 (see Rule 7(a)), Federal Rule 15(a) if read literally, would permit a plaintiff to amend his pleading, without leave of court, even after the Court had granted a motion to dismiss or a motion for summary judgment.

Most of the federal courts which have considered the matter have held that a motion is not a pleading within the meaning of Rule 15(a). Thus a mere *filing* of a motion to dismiss does not prevent the plaintiff from amending his complaint as a matter of right. See Keene Lumber Co. v. Leventhal, 165 F.2d 815 (1st Cir.1948). It is however unclear whether the plaintiff should be entitled to amend his complaint as a matter of right after a motion to dismiss or a motion for summary judgment has been *granted.* The Court in *Keene Lumber Co.* held that the plaintiff's right to amend as a matter of course ended with the granting of the motion to dismiss; so have most courts which have considered the matter. There are however enough contrary decisions to cause the matter to be handled by a specific provision in Rule 15(a). See Breier v. Northern California Bowling Prop. Ass'n, 316 F.2d 787, 789 (9th Cir.1963); Peckham v. Scanlon, 241 F.2d 761 (7th Cir.1957).

The right to amend as a matter of course should not extend beyond the granting of a motion to dismiss or a motion for summary judgment. Because the plaintiff, who has already had an opportunity to amend prior to the disposition of the motion, nonetheless chose to stand (unsuccessfully) on his original pleading, the defendant who successfully moved against such pleading should at the least be allowed to oppose the amendment. This does not burden the plaintiff unduly, since even if leave of court is made a requirement, such leave

will be liberally granted. See Moore, Federal Practice § 15.07[2], (2d ed. 1968). And even if leave to amend is not granted, the plaintiff may still move for relief under Rules 59(e) or 60(b). These rules contain time limits, while present post-dismissal practice under Rule 15(a) does not.

The second part of Rule 15(a) deals with amendments by leave of court or by written consent of the adverse party. Rule 15(a) specifically provides that "leave shall be freely given when justice so requires."

In Foman v. Davis, 371 U.S. 178, 83 S.Ct. 227, 9 L.Ed.2d 222 (1962), the Court strongly reaffirmed this mandate.

Rule 15(a) clearly alters prior Massachusetts practice. Amendment as a matter of right did not exist in Massachusetts. See G.L. c. 231, §§ 51–56. Motions to amend were addressed to the discretion of the trial judge. Reilly v. Revere Racing Ass'n Inc., 349 Mass. 763, 208 N.E.2d 232 (1965). Thus an exception to the denial of a motion to amend merely raises the question of abuse of discretion by the trial judge. Magaletta v. Millard, 346 Mass. 591, 195 N.E.2d 324 (1964).

Under the interpretation of Federal Rule 15(a) in *Keene Lumber,* supra, the plaintiff has the *right* to one amendment, without leave of court, even though the defendant has filed a motion to dismiss the complaint.

Rule 15(a) changes Massachusetts law in another material respect. Under prior practice an amendment setting out new causes of action could not be allowed. Boston Trust Funds Inc. v. Henderson, 341 Mass. 730, 170 N.E.2d 318 (1960); Beckwith v. Massachusetts Turnpike Authority, 354 Mass. 766, 238 N.E.2d 364 (1968). No such limitation exists under Rule 15. Indeed, Rule 15(d) permits the court, on terms, to allow a party to serve a supplemental pleading setting out further transactions or occurrences or events which have happened since the date of the pleading sought to be supplemented. Previously, Massachusetts law did not allow an amendment to a declaration attempting to introduce a cause of action that did not exist when the action was brought. Sharpe v. Metropolitan Transit Authority, 327 Mass. 171, 97 N.E.2d 399 (1951).

Rule 15(b), which tracks Federal Rule 15(b), does not significantly change Massachusetts procedure. Issues, to whose trial the parties expressly or impliedly consent, will, even if not raised by the pleadings, be treated in all respects as if they had been so raised. Although such amendment of the pleadings to conform to the evidence may be made at any time, failure to amend does not affect the result of the trial.

If a party objects at the trial to evidence on the ground that it is not within the issues made by the pleadings, Rule 15(b) enjoins the court freely to allow amendment unless the objecting party satisfies the court that admission of such evidence would prejudice his case on the merits. A continuance may be granted to the objecting party to meet the evidence.

This rule differs slightly from previous Massachusetts practice. Although language of Mass.G.L. c. 231, § 51 ("at any time before judgment") appears sufficiently broad to permit the trial judge to allow amendment during trial where an objection is made to the admission of certain evidence, the Court in Lewis v. Russell, 304 Mass. 41, 45, 22 N.E.2d 606, 608–609 (1939) held that defective pleading cannot be cured merely by reference to the plaintiff's evidence. But even in *Lewis,* supra, the Court concluded: "This decision does not affect the power of the Superior Court in its discretion to allow the defendant to amend her answer on motion filed before judgment if, under all of the circumstances, justice appears to require such amendment."

Rule 15(c) provides for the relation back of amendments whenever the claim or defense asserted arose out of the conduct, transaction or occurrence attempted to be set forth in the original pleading. This provision ties directly to the statute of limitations.

Under Federal Rule 15(c) an amendment changing the party against whom a claim is asserted may relate back (and thus preclude a statute of limitations defense) if the claim in the amended pleading arose out of the conduct, transaction or occurrence set forth or attempted to be set forth in the original pleading and, within the period provided by law for commencing the action against him, the party to be brought in by amendment (1) has received such notice of the institution of the action that he will not be prejudiced in maintaining his defense on the merits and (2) knew or should have known that, but for a mistake concerning the identity of the proper party, the action would have been brought against him.

Massachusetts practice is more liberal than Federal Rule 15(c) in allowing amendments adding or substituting party defendants after expiration of the period of limitations. The Massachusetts rule is set out in detail in Wadsworth v. Boston Gas Company, 352 Mass. 86, 88–89, 223 N.E.2d 807, 809–810 (1967) in the following language:

"... It has often been said that the running of the statute of limitations is not a reason for denying an amendment and may furnish a reason for allowing it. Johnson v. Carroll, 272 Mass. 134, 138, 172 N.E. 85; Peterson v. Cadogan, 313 Mass. 133, 134, 46 N.E.2d 517, and cases cited. In general, the law in this Commonwealth with respect to amendments is more liberal than elsewhere, and cases from other jurisdictions are not in point. Neszery v. Beard, 226 Mass. 332, 334, 115 N.E. 420. See Ideal Financing Ass'n Inc. v. McPhail, 320 Mass. 521, 523, 70 N.E.2d 311.

"There is ample authority for the proposition that where an action has been commenced before the statute of limitations has run, a plaintiff may be allowed to substitute one defendant for another after the statute of limitations has run against the proposed substitute defendant. McLaughlin v. West End St. Ry., 186 Mass. 150, 151, 71 N.E. 317. Genga v. Director Gen. of Railroads, 243 Mass. 101, 104, 137 N.E. 637, and cases cited. After the amendment has been allowed and the defendant brought into court by due process, the substitution relates back to the date of the writ and makes the substituted defendant a party from that date. Johnson v. Carroll, 272 Mass. 134, 137, 172 N.E. 85. We discern no difference in principle between permitting a plaintiff to substitute a defendant and permitting a plaintiff to add a defendant. See Cohen v. Levy, 221 Mass. 336, 337, 108 N.E. 1074; McPherson v. Boston Edison Co., 336 Mass. 94, 97, 142 N.E.2d 758. The effect in both cases is that a different defendant is called upon to defend the action. We hold, therefore, that the propriety of allowing the amendment in both cases is governed by the same rules."

For statutory requirements governing amendment of names in Superior Court divorce proceedings, see G.L. c. 208 § 10.

Rule 15(d) provides that the court, upon motion of a party, may allow the party to serve a supplemental pleading setting forth transactions, occurrences, or events postdating the pleading sought to be supplemented. This liberalizes Massachusetts law, which did not allow an amendment to sustain a new cause of action not intended when the writ was drawn. See Church v. Boylston and Woodbury Cafe Co., 218 Mass. 231, 105 N.E. 883 (1914).

Rule 16.   Pre–Trial Procedure: Formulating Issues

In any action, the court may in its discretion direct the attorneys for the parties and any unrepresented parties to appear before it for a conference to consider:

(1) The simplification of the issues;

(2) The necessity or desirability of amendments to the pleadings;

(3) The possibility of obtaining admissions of fact and of documents which will avoid unnecessary proof;

(4) The limitation of the number of expert witnesses;

(5) The timing and extent of discovery;

(6) The preservation and discovery of electronically stored information;

(7) Agreements or proceedings for asserting claims of privilege or of protection as trial preparation material after information is produced;

(8) The advisability of a preliminary reference of issues to a master;

(9) The possibility of settlement;

(10) Agreement as to damages; and

(11) Such other matters as may aid in the disposition of the action.

The court shall make an order which recites the action taken at the conference, the amendments allowed to the pleadings, and the agreements made by the parties as to any of the matters considered, and which limits the issues for trial to those not disposed of by admissions or agreements of counsel; and such order when entered controls the subsequent course of the action, unless modified at the trial to prevent manifest injustice.

Amended September 24, 2013, effective January 1, 2014.

Reporter's Notes—1973

Although in recent years, the Superior Court has been unable to make consistent systematized use of pre-trial conferences, the device is well-worth preserving, regulating, and encouraging. Coupled with the liberal discovery provisions in the Rules, pre-trial procedure can simplify and expedite every type of litigation. The basic principle of Rule 16, including the trial judge's power to modify the pre-trial order "to prevent manifest injustice," are quite familiar. Gurman v. Stowe-Woodward, Inc., 302 Mass. 442, 444–445, 19 N.E.2d 717, 718 (1939) and cases cited; Mitchell v. Walton Lunch Co., 305 Mass. 76, 80, 25 N.E.2d 151, 154 (1940).

The word "master" as used in Rule 16(5) includes an auditor. See Rule 53(a). The changes in Rule 16(5) from Federal Rule 16(5) are designed to reflect Massachusetts practice. Because an auditor's findings are by their very nature evidence utilizable before a jury (see, e.g., Roth v. Rubin Bros., 344 Mass. 604, 607, 183 N.E.2d 856, 858–859 (1962)), it has not been considered necessary to say so. Rule 16(6) and Rule 16(7), taken from Superior Court Rule 58, are designed to emphasize that agreements about money, in either partial or full resolution of the dispute, are the most valuable by-products of a pre-trial system.

Reporter's Notes—2014

The 2014 amendments are the first amendments to Rule 16 since the adoption of the Massachusetts Rules of Civil Procedure in 1973. They were part of a series of amendments concerning discovery of electronically stored information. For background, see the 2014 Reporter's Notes to Rule 26.

Rule 16 has been amended to add three discovery provisions to the listing of considerations at a pre-trial conference: (5) "The timing and extent of discovery;" (6) "The preservation and discovery of electronically stored information;" and (7) "Agreements or proceedings for asserting claims of privilege or of protection as trial preparation material after information is produced." The items previously designated as (5) through (8) have been renumbered as (8) through (11). The new items are consistent with topics added to Rule 16 of the Federal Rules of Civil Procedure in 2006, and are appropriate items for a judge to consider in making a pre-trial order regarding discovery.

Rule 16 conferences that deal with discovery of electronically stored information may be of significant value to the parties and to the court. New item (6) makes specific reference to consideration at the pre-trial conference of matters relating to electronically stored information. Conferences with the court in cases involving discovery of electronically stored information may be particularly appropriate given the complexity and costs involved in electronic discovery.

Various court departments currently require a case management conference and a scheduling order by virtue of Standing Orders or internal rules. The amendments to Rule 16 do not alter the language of Rule 16 that "a court may in its discretion" order a conference. Courts that require case management conferences by virtue of Standing Orders or internal rules should consider adding specific references to the three items that are now part of Rule 16.

The 2014 amendments also added language to the first sentence of the rule to make clear that a court may order unrepresented parties to appear at a conference. The addition of the reference to unrepresented parties conforms this portion of the first sentence of Rule 16 to a similar amendment to Rule 16 of the Federal Rules of Civil Procedure in 1983.

IV. PARTIES

Rule 17. Parties Plaintiff and Defendant: Capacity

(a) **Real Party in Interest.** Except for any action brought under General Laws, chapter 152, section 15, every action shall be prosecuted in the name of the real party in interest. A personal representative, guardian, conservator, bailee, trustee of an express trust, a party with whom or in whose name a contract has been made for the benefit of another, or a party authorized by statute may sue in his own name without joining with him the party for whose benefit the action is brought; and when a statute so provides, an action for the use or benefit of another shall be brought in the name of the Commonwealth. An insurer who has paid all or part of a loss may sue in the name of the assured to whose rights it is subrogated. No action shall be dismissed on the ground that it is not prosecuted in the name of the real party in interest until a reasonable time has been allowed after objection for ratification of commencement of the action by, or joinder or substitution of, the real party in interest; and such ratification, joinder, or substitution shall have the same effect as if the action had been commenced in the name of the real party in interest.

(b) **Infants or Incompetent Persons or Incapacitated Persons.** Whenever an infant or incompetent person, or an incapacitated person as defined in G.L. c.190B has a representative, such as a guardian, conservator, or other like fiduciary, the representative may sue or defend on behalf of the infant or incompetent person, or incapacitated person as defined in G.L. c.190B. If an infant or incompetent person, or an incapacitated person as defined in G.L. c.190B does not have a duly appointed representative, he may sue by his next friend or by a guardian ad litem. The court shall appoint a guardian ad litem for an infant or incompetent person, or an incapacitated person as defined in G.L. c.190B not otherwise represented in an action or shall make such other order as it deems proper for the protection of the infant or incompetent person, or an incapacitated person as defined in G.L. c.190B.

Amended June 24, 2009, effective July 1, 2009; December 14, 2011, effective January 2, 2012.

Reporter's Notes—1973

Rule 17 is a modified version of Federal Rule 17; the requirement that actions be prosecuted in the name of the real party in interest is new to Massachusetts law. At common law in Massachusetts, the subrogee had no right to sue the tortfeasor in his own name. His rights were considered equitable in nature, entitling him to bring the action only in the insured's name. See Gray v. United States, 77 F.Supp. 869 (D.Mass.1948), reversed on other grounds, 172 F.2d 737 (1st Cir.1949). By statute (G.L. c. 231 § 5), the assignee of a non-negotiable legal chose in action which has been assigned in writing *may* maintain an action thereon in his own name. With several exceptions, Rule 17(a) makes compulsory a suit in the name of the real party in interest. One of the exceptions is not contained in Federal Rule 17: "An insurer who has paid all or part of a loss may sue in the name of the assured to whose right it is subrogated."

The second sentence in Rule 17(a) does not really qualify the first sentence. Individuals such as executors, bailees, trustees, etc. have a "real interest" in the litigation.

The last sentence of Rule 17(a) permits a reasonable time for ratification by, or joinder or substitution of, the real party in interest. It tracks a 1966 amendment to Federal Rule 17(a). This provision is consistent with Massachusetts practice, which allows amendments as to parties (G.L. c. 231 § 51).

Rule 17(b), which copies Federal Rule 17(c) without change, accords with prior Massachusetts law. See G.L. c. 201. Federal Rule 17(b) is omitted from Rule 17 as inapplicable to state practice.

Reporter's Notes—2009

The 2009 amendments reflect changes resulting from the adoption of the Massachusetts Uniform Probate Code.

Reporter's Notes—2012

The rule is updated to reflect terminology changes introduced by the Massachusetts Uniform Probate Code, G.L. c. 190B.

Rule 18. Joinder of Claims and Remedies

(a) **Joinder of Claims.** A party asserting a claim to relief as an original claim, counterclaim, cross-claim, or third party claim, may join, either as independent or as alternate claims, as many claims, legal or equitable, or both, as he has against an opposing party.

(b) **Joinder of Remedies: Fraudulent Conveyances.** Whenever a claim is one heretofore cognizable only after another claim has been prosecuted to a conclusion, the two claims may be joined in a single action; but the court shall grant relief in that action only in accordance with the relative substantive rights of the parties. In particular, a plaintiff may state a claim for money and a claim to have set aside a conveyance fraudulent as to him, without first having obtained a judgment establishing the claim for money.

Reporter's Notes—1973

Rule 18(a) works a major change in Massachusetts practice. Under prior law, causes of action could be joined only "when they arise out of the same matter" (Mass.G.L. c. 231 §§ 1A, 7 (part sixth)) or if they belong to the same division of actions (G.L. c. 231 § 1; Mass.G.L. c. 231 § 7 (part fifth)). Legal and equitable claims could not be joined in a single action. Although equity rules were more liberal as to joinder, "multifarious" admixture of claims was forbidden. Coughlin v. Coughlin, 312 Mass. 452, 456, 45 N.E.2d 388, 391–392 (1942); Strasnick v. American Wood Products Corp., 319 Mass. 723, 65 N.E.2d 310 (1946). Now all disputed issues between the parties may be resolved in one lawsuit.

Rule 18(b) accords with case law. In litigation under G.L. c. 214 § 3(8), a single bill in equity "to reach and apply property fraudulently conveyed combine[d] in one proceeding matters both of law and equity. The first [was] the establishment of indebtedness by the defendant to the plaintiff. The second [was] the equitable process for collecting the debt out of property fraudulently conveyed." Salvucci v. Sheehan, 349 Mass. 659, 662, 212 N.E.2d 243, 244–245 (1965).

The adoption of 18(b) does not, however, permit the plaintiff to bring a single action (1) to establish liability for a tort and (2) to reach and apply the obligation of an insurance company in satisfaction of the judgment. See G.L. c. 214 § 3(9). A specific prohibition against such telescoping is unnecessary, because G.L. c. 214 § 3(9) prohibits a suit being maintained unless the judgment against the tortfeasor has remained unsatisfied for 30 days; see also Rogan v. Liberty Mutual Insurance Co., 305 Mass. 186, 188, 25 N.E.2d 188, 189 (1940).

Reporter's Notes—1996

Prior to the merger of the District Court Rules into the Massachusetts Rules of Civil Procedure, the District Court version of Rule 18(b) contained no reference to fraudulent conveyances. Under the merged set of rules, the reference to fraudulent conveyances is maintained, but the merger itself does not serve to confer jurisdiction on the District Court which otherwise does not exist. See Rule 83.

Rule 19.   Joinder of Persons Needed for Just Adjudication

(a) Persons to Be Joined if Feasible. A person who is subject to service of process shall be joined as a party in the action if (1) in his absence complete relief cannot be accorded among those already parties, or (2) he claims an interest relating to the subject of the action and is so situated that the disposition of the action in his absence may (i) as a practical matter impair or impede his ability to protect that interest or (ii) leave any of the persons already parties subject to a substantial risk of incurring double, multiple, or otherwise inconsistent obligations by reason of his claimed interest. If he has not been so joined, the court shall order that he be made a party. If he should join as a plaintiff but refuses to do so, he may be made a defendant.

(b) Determination by Court Whenever Joinder Not Feasible. If a person as described in subdivision (a)(1)–(2) hereof cannot be made a party, the court shall determine whether in equity and good conscience the action should proceed among the parties before it, or should be dismissed, the absent person being thus regarded as indispensable. The factors to be considered by the court include: first, to what extent a judgment rendered in the person's absence might be prejudicial to him or those already parties; second, the extent to which, by protective provisions in the judgment, by the shaping of relief, or other measures, the prejudice can be lessened or avoided; third, whether a judgment rendered in the person's absence will be adequate; fourth, whether the plaintiff will have an adequate remedy if the action is dismissed for nonjoinder.

(c) Pleading Reasons for Nonjoinder. A pleading asserting a claim for relief shall state the names, if known to the pleader, of any persons as described in subdivision (a)(1)–(2) hereof who are not joined, and the reasons why they are not joined.

(d) Exception of Class Actions. This rule is subject to the provisions of Rule 23.

Reporter's Notes—1973

Rule 19 deals with compulsory joinder of parties. With the exception of the language in Rule 19(a) pertaining to jurisdiction, involuntary plaintiffs and venue, it follows Federal Rule 19.

Rule 19(a) sets out the general rule as to those persons with respect to whom joinder is compulsory. (See Rule 20 as to permissive joinder.) Rule 19 covers, generally, those individuals who under prior Massachusetts practice would be classified as necessary parties or indispensable parties.

Rule 19(b) deals with persons who fall within Rule 19(a) but cannot be made parties. If under the tests set out in Rule 19(b) such an absent person is regarded as indispensable, the action will be dismissed; otherwise the court may proceed with the parties before it, with judgment obviously binding those parties only.

Rules 19(a) and 19(b) are quite similar to prior equity practice. Eustis Manufacturing Co. v. Saco Brick Co., 198 Mass. 212, 219–220, 84 N.E. 449, 452–453 (1908); Franks v. Markson, 337 Mass. 278, 284, 149 N.E.2d 619, 623 (1958).

Under that practice a court could of its own motion order a cause to stand over in order that an indispensable party might be joined. Sutcliffe v. Cawley, 240 Mass. 231, 239, 132 N.E. 406, 409 (1921). "Whenever the lack of indispensable parties has become manifest the court may dismiss the bill of its own motion." Turner v. United Mineral Lands Corp., 308 Mass. 531, 539, 33 N.E.2d 282, 286–287 (1941). As in federal practice under Rule 19, under Massachusetts equity practice if a person who should join as a plaintiff refused to do so, he would be made a party-defendant. Billings v. Mann, 156 Mass. 203, 205, 30 N.E. 1136, 1137 (1892).

In a few actions at law, prior practice made joinder compulsory. In contract actions, joint obligees were indispensable parties. Thomas v. Benson, 264 Mass. 555, 556, 163 N.E. 181, 182 (1928). However joint obligors were only conditionally necessary parties; failure to join a joint obligor was merely a defect in form, and could be pressed only by a plea in abatement. *Id.* at 556–557, 163 N.E. at 182. The reason for this rule was that each of such persons was liable for the whole amount claimed by the plaintiff.

In personal actions of tort, even though the wrongdoers were joint tortfeasors, the plaintiff could elect between joining them and suing them separately. Thus it was not a ground of abatement that others potentially liable were not served. Donnelly v. Larkin, 327 Mass. 287, 296, 98 N.E.2d 280, 285–286 (1951).

The language of Rule 19(a) will not effect these common law doctrines.

Rule 19(c) is the same as Federal Rule 19(c). It requires a pleading asserting a claim for relief to state the names, if known to the pleader, of any persons described in Rule 19(a) who were not joined and the reasons why they were not joined. The usual reason for non-joinder will be that such person was not subject to the jurisdiction of the court. Before making such allegation the plaintiff should assure himself that the "long-arm" statute (G.L. c. 223A) does not make the absent defendant amenable to process.

Rule 19(d) merely makes Rule 19 subject to the provisions of Rule 23 (Class Actions).

Rule 20.   Permissive Joinder of Parties

(a) Permissive Joinder. All persons may join in one action as plaintiffs if they assert any right to relief jointly, severally, or in the alternative, in respect of or arising out of the same transaction, occurrence, or series of transactions or occurrences and if any question of law or fact common to all these persons will arise in the action.

All persons may be joined in one action as defendants if there is asserted against them jointly, severally, or in the alternative, any right to relief in respect of or arising out of the same transaction, occurrence, or series of transactions or occurrences and if any question of law or fact common to all defendants will arise in the action. A plaintiff or defendant need not be interested in obtaining or defending against all the relief demanded. Judgment may be given for one or more of the plaintiffs according to their respective rights to relief, and against one or more of the defendants according to their respective liabilities, and the court may issue one or more executions and make such order relative to costs as may be necessary and proper. In any action in which persons not asserting any right to recover jointly join as plaintiffs, and in which the relief sought is not wholly equitable, the entry fee shall be an amount equal to the aggregate of the entry fees which would have been required had separate actions been brought.

(b) Separate Trials. The court may make such orders as will prevent a party from being embarrassed, delayed, or put to expense by the inclusion of a party against whom he asserts no claim and who asserts no claim against him, and may order separate trials or make other orders to prevent delay or prejudice.

Amended June 27, 1974, effective July 1, 1974.

Reporter's Notes—1973

Rule 20(a) is the same as Federal Rule 20(a) except for: (1) the deletion of a reference to admiralty law, and (2) the addition of a reference to executions and costs taken from G.L. c. 231, § 4A.

Rule 20(a) changes prior law slightly. G.L. c. 231, § 4A allowed joinder where the rights or liabilities arose out of the same transaction, occurrence, or series of transactions or occurrences. Rule 20(a) adds the requirement, taken from Federal Rule 20(a), that there be a common question of law or fact.

The principal difference between Rule 20(a) and the prior statute is that the latter applied solely to actions at law whereas the former applies to all claims for relief.

Joinder of parties under Rule 20(a) obviously does not affect the substantive rights of the parties involved. For example, Rule 20(a) permits the joinder of a master and his servant. This follows prior law, see Kabatchnick v. Hanover–Elm Building Corp., 331 Mass. 366, 369, 119 N.E.2d 169, 172–173 (1954), but does not however convert the several liability of the master into a joint tort liability with his servant. Id.

Just as the prejudicial operation of Rule 18 (Joinder of Claims and Remedies) can be avoided by the court (Rule 42(b)), so also can embarrassment, delay and expense to a party be avoided by the court, acting under Rule 20(b).

Rule 21.   Misjoinder and Non–Joinder of Parties

Misjoinder of parties is not ground for dismissal of an action. Parties may be dropped or added by order of the court on motion of any party or of its own initiative, after hearing, at any stage of the action and on such terms as are just. Any claim against a party may be severed and proceeded with separately.

Reporter's Notes—1973

Rule 21 embodies prior law: G.L. c. 231, § 4A; §§ 51–54, and adds to Federal Rule 21 the requirement of a hearing before parties may be dropped or added.

Rule 22.   Interpleader

Persons having claims against the plaintiff may be joined as defendants and required to interplead when their claims are such that the plaintiff is or may be exposed to double or multiple liability. It is not ground for objection to the joinder that the claims of the several claimants or the titles on which their claims depend do not have a common origin or are not identical but are adverse to and independent of one another, or that the plaintiff avers that he is not liable in whole or in part to any or all of the claimants. A defendant exposed to similar liability may obtain such interpleader by way of cross-claim or counterclaim. The provisions of this rule supplement and do not in any way limit the joinder of parties permitted in Rule 20.

Reporter's Notes—1973

Rule 20 allows joinder of defendants where it is uncertain which of them is liable. Rule 22 acts as a useful corollary to Rule 20 by making the same free joinder available to the person against whom a claim might otherwise be pressed by several different persons. See 7 Wright & Miller, Federal Practice and Procedure, § 1702.

Rule 22 is identical with Federal Rule 22(1). Federal Rule 22(2) is inappropriate to Massachusetts practice.

Rule 22 removes a number of technical statutory and case-law restrictions under prior law. It avoids the confusion between the so-called strict interpleader (see Gonia v. O'Brion, 223 Mass. 177, 179, 111 N.E. 787, 788 (1916)) and bills in the nature of interpleader (see Savage v. McCauley, 301 Mass. 162, 164, 16 N.E.2d 639, 640 (1938)). It eliminates any requirement that the claims be identical or based upon a common origin or title. Further, it allows the person asking relief to aver that he is not liable in whole or in part to any or all of the claimants. In other words he may plead that he owes no claimant anything; but that if he does, he does not know which. As under prior law (see Perkins v. Darker, 345 Mass. 763, 764, 186 N.E.2d 607 (1962)), Rule 22 makes the impleader remedy completely available to the plaintiff as well as the defendant, and allows interpleader by way of cross-claim or counterclaim.

Rule 22 does not specifically cover the following case: P sues D; D denies his liability but maintains that if he is liable at all, he may instead be liable to T. Rule 22 does not mention "impleader" in the catalogue of defendant's remedies. The Reporters believe, however, that Rule 20 (Permissive Joinder of Parties) would allow T to be joined as a plaintiff; D could then assert an appropriate claim for interpleader.

Under pre-Rules Massachusetts caselaw, if the party seeking to compel interpleader has incurred a personal liability to either of the other parties, independent of the question between the claimants themselves, interpleader will not lie. Gonia v. O'Brion, supra; National Security Bank of Boston v. Batt, 215 Mass. 489, 102 N.E. 691 (1913). Rule 22 is silent on this point. There is however one federal decision Olivier v. Humble Oil and Refining Co., 225 F.Supp. 536, 539 (D.La. 1963), holding that under Federal Rule 22 it is immaterial that the party counterclaiming for interpleader has a so-called independent liability to the plaintiff or that the claims of the parties sought to be interpleaded are independent of the claims of the plaintiff. This same result was reached by a state court construing identical language. See Jersey Insurance Company of New York v. Altieri, 5 N.J.Super. 577, 68 A.2d 852 (1949).

Rule 23.   Class Actions

(a) Prerequisites to Class Action. One or more members of a class may sue or be sued as representative parties on behalf of all only if (1) the class is so numerous that joinder of all members is impracticable, (2) there are questions of law or fact common to the class, (3) the claims or defenses of the representative parties are typical of the claims or defenses of the class, and (4) the representative parties will fairly and adequately protect the interests of the class.

(b) Class Actions Maintainable. An action may be maintained as a class action if the prerequisites of subdivision (a) are satisfied, and the court finds that the questions of law or fact common to the members of the class predominate over any questions affecting only individual members, and that a class action is superior to other available methods for the fair and efficient adjudication of the controversy.

(c) Dismissal or Compromise. A class action shall not be dismissed or compromised without the approval of the court. The court may require notice of such proposed dismissal or compromise to be given in such manner as the court directs. The court shall require notice to the Massachusetts IOLTA Committee for the purpose set forth in subdivision (e)(3) of this rule.

(d) Orders to Insure Adequate Representation. The court at any stage of an action under this rule may require such security and impose such terms as shall fairly and adequately protect the interests of the class in whose behalf the action is brought or defended. It may order that notice be given, in such manner as it may direct, of the pendency of the action, of a proposed settlement, of entry of judgment, or of any other proceedings in the action, including notice to the absent persons that they may come in and present claims and defenses if they so desire. Whenever the representation appears to the court inadequate fairly to protect the interests of absent parties who may be bound by the judgment, the court may at any time prior to judgment order an amendment of the pleadings, eliminating therefrom all reference to representation of absent persons, and the court shall order entry of judgment in such form as to affect only the parties to the action and those adequately represented.

(e) Disposition of Residual Funds.

(1) "Residual Funds" are funds that remain after the payment of all approved class member claims expenses, litigation costs, attorneys' fees, and other court-approved disbursements to implement the relief granted. Nothing in this rule is intended to limit the parties to a class action from suggesting, or the trial court from approving, a settlement that does not create residual funds.

(2) Any order, judgment or approved compromise in a class action certified under this rule that establishes a process for identifying and compensating members of the class may provide for the disbursement of residual funds. In matters where the claims process has been exhausted and residual funds remain, the residual funds shall be disbursed to one or more nonprofit organizations or foundations (which may include nonprofit organizations that provide legal services to low income persons) which support projects that will benefit the class or similarly situated persons consistent with the objectives and purposes of the underlying causes of action on which relief was based, or to the Massachusetts IOLTA Committee to support activities and programs that promote access to the civil justice system for low income residents of the Commonwealth of Massachusetts.

(3) Where residual funds may remain, no judgment may enter or compromise be approved unless the plaintiff has given notice to the Massachusetts IOLTA Committee for the limited purpose of allowing the committee to be heard on whether it ought to be a recipient of any or all residual funds.

Amended November 25, 2008, effective January 1, 2009; April 24, 2015, effective July 1, 2015.

Reporter's Notes—1973

Prior Massachusetts practice in the area of class suits was governed entirely by case law. The requirements for maintaining a class suit in Massachusetts were set out as follows:

"Class bills may be maintained where a few individuals are fairly representative of the legal and equitable rights of a *large number* who cannot readily be joined as parties. The persons suing as representatives of a class must show by the allegations of their bill that all the persons whom they profess to represent have a common interest in the subject matter of the suit *and a right and interest to ask for the same relief against the defendants.* It is not essential that the interest of each member of the class be identical in all aspects with that of the plaintiffs. The interest must arise out of a common relationship to a definite wrong. There must be a joint prejudice to all the class whom the plaintiff seeks to represent. The wrong suffered must be subject to redress by some common relief beneficial to all. The plaintiffs must be fairly representative in all essential particulars of the class for which they seek to act.... Mere community of interest in the questions of law or of fact at issue in a controversy or in the kind of relief to be afforded does not go far enough to warrant a class suit. Avoidance of multiplicity of suits is not enough." Spear v. H.V. Greene Co., 246 Mass. 259, 266–267, 140 N.E. 795, 797–798 (1923). (emphasis supplied)

This rule likewise applies where the action was brought *against* a class. Thus in Thorn v. Foy, 328 Mass. 337, 338, 103 N.E.2d 416, 417 (1952) a suit was held properly brought against the officers of a labor union, individually and as representatives of the members of the union, because it was found that the members were too numerous to be sued individually and the named defendants adequately represented the entire membership.

Rule 23(a) sets out four prerequisites to a class action. These prerequisites, which are also contained in Federal Rule 23(a) as amended in 1966, closely parallel prior Massachusetts practice as stated in Spear v. H.V. Greene Co., supra.

"(1) the class is so numerous that joinder of all members is impracticable."

Federal courts have drawn very few lines with respect to how large a class must be in order to allow the class action. Most courts would agree that mere numbers should not be the sole test of practicability of joinder.

"But courts should not be so rigid as to depend upon mere numbers as a guideline on the practicability of joinder; a determination of practicability should depend upon all the circumstances surrounding a case." Demarco v. Edens, 390 F.2d 836, 845 (2d Cir.1968).

The Supreme Judicial Court has never attempted to set any minimum number which would be necessary for a class suit. The opinions use such language as "large number who cannot readily be joined as parties," Spear v. H.V. Greene Co., 246 Mass. at 266, 140 N.E. at 797; "When the parties interested are very numerous, so that it would be difficult and expensive to bring them all before the court ... the court will not require a strict adherence to the [general] rule [that all interested persons be made parties]." Stevenson v. Austin, 44 Mass. (3 Metc.) 474, 480 (1842).

Rule 23(a)(1) will have little effect on prior Massachusetts practice.

"(2) there are questions of law or fact common to all."

The requirement of common questions of law or fact is the same as that established for joinder under Rule 20 and intervention under Rule 24. It should, however, be noted that Rule 23(a)(2), unlike Rules 20 and 24, does not also require a single transaction or series of transactions or a single occurrence or series of occurrences. However, the language of Rule 23(b) concerning the predominance of the questions of law or fact over questions affecting individual members would imply the need for a single transaction or occurrence or a series of transactions or occurrences.

Rule 23(a)(2) should have little effect on prior Massachusetts law. "The persons suing as representatives of a class must show by the allegations of their bill that all the persons whom they profess to represent have a common interest in the subject matter of the suit and a right and interest to ask for the same relief against the defendants." Spear v. H.V. Greene Co., 246 Mass. at 266, 140 N.E. at 797.

"(3) the claims or defenses of the representative parties are typical of the claims or defenses of the class, and (4) the representative parties will adequately protect the interests of the class."

Prerequisite (3) was written into Federal Rule 23 when it was amended in 1966. It should be read with prerequisite (4). Both requirements state the need for the ability of the representatives of the class to protect its interests. The word "typical" does not require that all members of the class be identically situated. Siegel v. Chicken Delight, Inc., 271 F.Supp. 722, 726–727 (N.D.Cal.1967). This is similar to the language of the Supreme Judicial Court in the *Spear* case: "It is not essential that the interest of each member of the class be identical in all respects with that of the plaintiffs. The interest must arise out of a common relationship to a definite wrong." Spear v. H.V. Greene Co., 246 Mass. at 266, 140 N.E. at 797.

Rule 23(a)(3) and (4) should have little effect on prior Massachusetts law.

Rule 23(b) deletes substantial portions of Federal Rule 23(b) which are unnecessary to state practice. Beyond the four requirements set out in Rule 23(a) for maintaining a class action the only further requirements set out in Rule 23(b) are findings by the Court: (1) that the questions of law or fact common to the members of the class predominate over any questions affecting only individual members; and (2) that a class action is superior to other available methods for the fair and efficient adjudication of the controversy.

Rule 23(c) and (d) are designed to afford protection to absent members of the class.

Unlike Federal Rule 23, the Massachusetts class action rule does not *require* the giving of notice to members of the class; nor does it provide to members of the class the opportunity to exclude themselves. Instead Rule 23(d) provides that the court may order that notice be given, in such manner as it may direct, of the pendency of the action, of a proposed settlement, of entry of judgment, or of any other proceedings in the action, including notice to the absent persons that they may come in and present claims and defenses if they so desire. No doubt the trial judge will order the giving of appropriate notice to members of the class, of the commencement of the action where fairness and justice so require, particularly where the failure to give notice may raise subsequent problems of res judicata.

Reporter's Notes—1996

With the merger of the District Court civil rules into the Mass. R.Civ.P., Rule 23 of the Mass.R.Civ.P. governing class actions is made applicable to District Court proceedings.

Reporter's Notes—2008

The 2008 amendment, effective January 1, 2009, added Rule 23(e) concerning residual funds in class action proceedings. This amendment was recommended to the Supreme Judicial Court by the Massachusetts IOLTA Committee.

Rule 23.1. Derivative Actions by Shareholders

In a derivative action brought by one or more shareholders or members to enforce a right of a corporation or of an unincorporated association, the corporation or association having failed to enforce a right which may properly be asserted by it, the complaint shall be verified by oath and shall allege that the plaintiff was a shareholder or member at the time of the transaction of which he complains or that his share or membership thereafter devolved on him by operation of law from one who was a stockholder or member at such time. The complaint shall also allege with particularity the efforts, if any, made by the plaintiff to obtain the action he desires from the directors or comparable authority and, if necessary, from the shareholders or members, and the reasons for his failure to obtain the action or for not making the effort. The derivative action may not be maintained if it appears that the plaintiff does not fairly and adequately represent the interests of the shareholders or members similarly situated in enforcing the right of the corporation or association. The action shall not be dismissed or compromised without the approval of the court, and notice of the proposed dismissal or compromise shall be given to shareholders or members in such manner as the court directs.

Reporter's Notes—1973

Rule 23.1 with some minor changes is the same as Federal Rule 23.1. Prior to the 1966 amendments to the federal rules, Federal Rule 23.1 was part of Federal Rule 23, "Class Actions" (Rule 23(b)). The 1966 change was effected because derivative suits are not class actions and have distinctive aspects which warrant treatment in a separate rule. A derivative suit is brought on behalf of a corporation or other association for a wrong done to the corporation or association. The corporation is an indispensable party in a derivative suit. Turner v. United Mineral Lands Corp., 308 Mass. 531, 538–539, 33 N.E.2d 282, 286–287 (1941). It is joined as a party defendant. While the shareholder controls the action, any recovery is for the corporation. Shaw v. Harding, 306 Mass. 441, 448, 28 N.E.2d 469, 473 (1940). The plaintiff has no direct or personal interest in the suit, except as the value of his stock might be enhanced by recovery by the corporation. The bill cannot be maintained to enforce any personal right of the plaintiff. Id.

A class action, on the other hand, is brought to redress a wrong committed directly against the members of the class. It may be maintained where a few individuals are fairly representative of the legal and equitable rights of a large number of individuals who cannot readily be joined as parties. Spear v. H.V. Greene Co., 246 Mass. 259, 266, 140 N.E. 795, 797 (1923). Thus if an action is brought by shareholders against the directors of the corporation for mismanagement, the action is derivative because the harm is directly to the corporation and only indirectly to the shareholders. If, however, an action is brought by the shareholders against the directors to compel the payment of dividends arbitrarily withheld, the action would be in the nature of a class suit because the harm is directly to the shareholders. cf. Fernald v. Frank Ridlon Co., 246 Mass. 64, 140 N.E. 421 (1923).

Rule 23.1 makes a few minor changes in Federal Rule 23.1. The language of Federal Rule 23.1 pertaining to the conferring of jurisdiction is deleted as inapplicable to state practice. Also, Rule 23.1 adds the words "by oath" to the verification requirement. It is hoped that this language will tend to discourage "strike suits" which suits are brought primarily for the purpose of coercing "corporate managers to settle worthless claims in order to get rid of them." Surowitz v. Hilton Hotels Corporation, 383 U.S. 363, 86 S.Ct. 845, 15 L.Ed.2d 807 (1966).

Rule 23.1 includes the contemporaneous-ownership-of-stock requirement of Federal Rule 23.1. The purpose of this requirement is to prevent an individual from purchasing stock solely for the purpose of maintaining a derivative suit with the hope of coercing the corporate managers to make a personal settlement. Massachusetts, by statute, requires contemporaneous-ownership-of-stock with respect to derivative actions against the corporation's stockholders, directors or officers. G.L. c. 156B, § 46. Rule 23.1 broadens the requirement of G.L. c. 156B, § 46, making it applicable in all derivative actions rather than merely those actions against the corporation's stockholders, directors or officers. The language *"from one who was a stockholder at such time"* was added to Rule 23.1 to bring it in harmony with G.L. c. 156B, § 46, and to make clear that a person receiving stock under a will or by intestacy cannot maintain a particular derivative suit unless the decedent could have done so prior to death.

Before a shareholder can maintain a derivative suit in Massachusetts he must first make a demand upon the corporation's board of directors for action, unless such a demand would be futile because a majority of the directors are not disinterested. S. Solomont & Sons Trust, Inc. v. New England Theatres Operating Corporation, 326 Mass. 99, 113, 93 N.E.2d 241, 248 (1950). If the board is thus disqualified, or if, after such a demand, the directors refuse to act, the shareholder must make demand upon the corporate shareholders, unless such demand would be futile because a majority of them are not disinterested. Most of the cases decided subsequent to *Solomont,* applying this principle, arose in the federal courts. Pomerantz v. Clark, 101 F.Supp. 341, 344, 346 (D.Mass.1951), held, applying Massachusetts law that the *Solomont* requirements must usually be satisfied no matter how many and how scattered were the corporation's shareholders. This view was, by dicta, subsequently repudiated in Levitt v. Johnson, 334 F.2d 815, 818–819 (1st Cir.1964). See also In re Kauffman Mutual Fund Actions, 479 F.2d 257, 263–264 (1st Cir.1973).

While quite similar, the requirements of *Solomont* go further than those imposed by Rule 23.1. *Solomont* held that a vote of a majority of the shareholders of a corporation, undominated and uncontrolled, acting reasonably and in good faith, can bar the bringing of a derivative suit by a minority shareholder or shareholders, regardless of the nature of the cause of action. 326 Mass. at 114–115, 93 N.E.2d at 248–249. The rationale is that from a business viewpoint it is not always best to insist upon all of one's legal rights; and since honest and intelligent men differ as to business policy, the will of the majority, acting fairly, should control. Halprin v. Babbit, 303 F.2d 138 (1st Cir.1962), applying Massachusetts law, held that if, after a demand upon the shareholders, the shareholders fail to act, the minority shareholder may proceed with the action. In other words, under the *Solomont* rule, the minority shareholder does not need the express approval of the majority of the shareholders in order to bring the action. Inaction on their part is sufficient.

The Advisory Committee believes that the holding of *Solomont* is *not* repealed by implication by Rule 23.1 and that a majority of the shareholders, undominated and uncontrolled, acting reasonably and in good faith, can bar the bringing of a derivative suit.

Reporter's Notes—1996

With the merger of the District Court civil rules into the Mass. R.Civ.P., Rule 23.1 of the Mass.R.Civ.P. governing shareholder derivative actions is made applicable to District Court proceedings.

Rule 23.2. Actions Relating to Unincorporated Associations

An action brought by or against the members of an unincorporated association as a class by naming certain members as representative parties may be maintained only if it appears that the representative parties will fairly and adequately protect the interests of the association and its members. In the conduct of the action the court may make appropriate orders corresponding with those described in Rule 23(d). Further, the provisions of Rule 23(c), concerning dismissal or compromise of the action are applicable to this Rule.

Reporter's Notes—1973

Rule 23.2 is substantially the same as Federal Rule 23.2, the only difference being the references to Rule 23. Federal Rule 23.2 was added in 1966 in conjunction with the 1966 amendment completely rewriting and revising Federal Rule 23 and also adding Federal Rule 23.1 (derivative actions).

The Advisory Committee's notes to Federal Rule 23.2 read as follows:

"Although an action by or against representatives of the membership of an unincorporated association has often been viewed as a class action, the real or main purpose of this characterization has been to give 'entity treatment' to the association when for formal reasons it cannot sue or be sued as a jural person under Rule 17(b).... Rule 23.2 deals separately with these actions, referring where appropriate to Rule 23."

Massachusetts practice permits individuals to sue or be sued in a representative capacity on behalf of an association, such as a labor union, when it is made to appear that the individuals represent the group. Leonard v. Eastern Mass. St. Ry. Co., 335 Mass. 308, 140 N.E.2d 187 (1957) (representative suit by labor union); Thorn v. Foy, 328 Mass. 337, 103 N.E.2d 416 (1952) (representative suit against officers of labor union). Where such an action is brought, the unincorporated association should not be described as a party to the suit. Donahue v. Kenney, 327 Mass. 409, 99 N.E.2d 155 (1951).

Rule 23.2 does not change the rule in Massachusetts that with some statutory exceptions (i.e., suits against certain voluntary associations and business trusts—G.L. c. 182, § 6) unincorporated associations do not have the capacity to sue or be sued.

In view of Rule 23, it may appear that Rule 23.2 is redundant. It is not entirely clear, however, that an action by or against representatives of an unincorporated association is technically a class action. Rule 23.2 emphasizes that whether or not such representative suits are class actions, they are maintainable. The protective provisions of Rule 23, namely sections (c) and (d) are incorporated into Rule 23.2.

Reporter's Notes—1996

With the merger of the District Court civil rules into the Mass. R.Civ.P., Rule 23.2 of the Mass.R.Civ.P. governing actions relating to unincorporated associations is made applicable to District Court proceedings.

Rule 24. Intervention

(a) Intervention of Right. Upon timely application anyone shall be permitted to intervene in an action: (1) when a statute of the Commonwealth confers an unconditional right to intervene or (2) when the applicant claims an interest relating to the property or transaction which is the subject of the action and he is so situated that the disposition of the action may as a practical matter impair or impede his ability to protect that interest, unless the applicant's interest is adequately represented by existing parties.

(b) Permissive Intervention. Upon timely application anyone may be permitted to intervene in an action: (1) when a statute of the Commonwealth confers a conditional right to intervene; or (2) when an applicant's claim or defense and the main action have a question of law or fact in common. When a party to an action relies for ground of claim or defense upon any statute or executive order administered by a federal or state governmental officer or agency or upon any regulation, order, requirement, or agreement issued or made pursuant to the statute or executive order, the officer or agency upon timely application may be permitted to intervene in the action. In exercising its discretion the court shall consider whether the intervention will unduly delay or prejudice the adjudication of the rights of the original parties.

(c) Procedure. A person desiring to intervene shall serve a motion to intervene upon the parties as provided in Rule 5. The motion shall state the grounds therefor and shall be accompanied by a pleading setting forth the claim or defense for which intervention is sought.

(d) Intervention by the Attorney General. When the constitutionality of an act of the legislature or the constitutionality or validity of an ordinance of any city or the by-law of any town is drawn in question in any action to which the Commonwealth or an officer, agency, or employee thereof is not a party, the party asserting the unconstitutionality of the act or the unconstitutionality or invalidity of the ordinance or by-law shall notify the attorney general within sufficient time to afford him an opportunity to intervene.

Reporter's Notes—1973

Rule 24(a), with the exception of the substitution of "Commonwealth" for the "United States" is identical to Federal Rule 24(a). It permits the intervention of a party as a matter of right in two instances: (1) where permitted by statute and (2) where the disposition of the action may as a practical matter impair or impede the applicant's ability to protect his claimed interest, unless such interest is adequately represented by existing parties.

Prior to a 1966 amendment to Federal Rule 24, apart from statutory authorization, intervention was allowed as a matter of right only upon a showing (1) that the applicant might be bound by a judgment in the action, and that existing parties would inadequately represent his interests; or (2) that the applicant would be adversely affected by a distribution or other disposition of property in the custody or subject to the control or disposition of the court.

The Advisory Committee on the Federal Rules felt that the "res judicata" or "fund" requirements of the former Federal Rule 24(a) were unnecessarily restrictive. If the interests of an absentee who would be substantially affected in a practical sense by the determination are not adequately represented by existing parties, he should, as a matter of right, be allowed to intervene.

The amended version of Federal Rule 24(a) coordinates more closely intervention with joinder (Rule 19) and class actions (Rule 23). The amendment provides that an applicant is entitled to intervene in an action when his position is comparable to that of a person under Rule 19(a)(2)(i) unless his interest is already adequately represented by existing parties.

Adequacy of representation under Rule 24(a) is not confined to formal representation like that provided by a trustee for his beneficiary or a representative party in a class action for a member of the class. Ford Motor Co. v. Bisanz Bros. Inc., 249 F.2d 22 (8th Cir.1957) presents a good illustration of practical representation and of the wisdom of eliminating the res judicata requirement of the former version of Federal Rule 24(a). *Ford* involved an action by property owners against a railroad company to enjoin the operation of freight cars on certain trackage. Ford, which owned an assembly plant which was serviced by this particular trackage, sought to intervene under Federal Rule 24(a). The United States Court of Appeals vacated an order of the District Court and allowed Ford to intervene. On the argument of plaintiff that Ford should not be allowed to intervene because it would not be bound by any judgment against the railroad, the Court held that a judgment against the railroad would have the practical effect of denying Ford a service essential to its operation. As amended, Rule 24(a) codifies this reasoning.

Apart from a few isolated situations covered by statute (see G.L. c. 12, § 8; G.L. c. 149, § 29; G.L. c. 151D, § 3; G.L. c. 241, § 6), intervention as a matter of right did not exist under prior Massachusetts practice.

A person could intervene in Massachusetts only upon a showing that he had a substantial interest in the subject matter of the litigation (Check v. Kaplan, 280 Mass. 170, 178, 182 N.E. 305, 308 (1932)). In all cases a motion to intervene was addressed to the sound judicial discretion of the presiding judge; his decision would not be reversed unless it clearly appeared that there has been an abuse of such discretion. Haverhill v. Di Burro, 337 Mass. 230, 235, 236, 148 N.E.2d 642, 645, 646 (1958).

Rule 24(b) provides for permissive intervention when allowed by statute or where an applicant's claim or defense and the main action have a question of law or fact in common. The purpose of Rule 24(b) is to facilitate the disposal in one action of claims involving common questions of law or fact, thus avoiding both court congestion and undue delay and expense to all parties. On the other hand, one could argue that intervention may unduly delay or prejudice the adjudication of the right of the original parties.

Rule 24(b) clearly alters Massachusetts practice which required as a condition for the allowance of intervention a showing by the applicant of a substantial interest in the subject matter of the litigation. See Check v. Kaplan, supra.

Rule 24(c) regulates the form of the prospective intervenor's notice to the parties.

Under Rule 24(d), the obligation to notify the attorney general that the constitutionality of an act of the legislature or of a municipality is being questioned in the action is placed upon the party asserting the unconstitutionality of the act (or the unconstitutionality or invalidity of an ordinance or by-law) rather than, as in Federal Rule 24(c), on the court.

Rule 25. Substitution of Parties

(a) Death.

(1) If a party dies and the claim is not thereby extinguished, the court may order substitution of the proper parties. The motion for substitution may be made by any party or by the representative of the deceased party and, together with the notice of hearing, shall be served on the parties as provided in Rule 5 and upon persons not parties in the manner provided in Rule 4 for the service of a summons. Unless the motion for substitution is made within one year after the date of approval of the bond of the representative of the deceased party, the action shall, upon notice and hearing, be dismissed unless the failure of the surviving party to move for substitution was the result of excusable neglect. If the court finds that the representative of the deceased party has failed within a reasonable period of time after the date of the approval of his bond to notify in writing the surviving party of the decedent's death and to file a suggestion of death upon the record it shall find excusable neglect for purposes of this rule and Rule 6(b).

(2) In the event of the death of one or more of the plaintiffs or of one or more of the defendants in an action in which the right sought to be enforced survives only to the surviving plaintiffs or only against the surviving defendants, the action does not abate. The death shall be suggested upon the record and the action shall proceed in favor of or against the surviving parties.

(b) Incompetency or Incapacity. If a party becomes incompetent or incapacitated as defined in G.L. c.190B, the court upon motion served as provided in subdivision (a) of this rule may allow the action to be continued by or against his representative.

(c) Transfer of Interest. In case of any transfer of interest, the action may be continued by or against the original party, unless the court upon motion directs the person to whom the interest is transferred to be substituted in the action or joined with the original party. Service of the motion shall be made as provided in subdivision (a) of this rule.

(d) Public Officers; Death or Separation From Office.

(1) When a public officer is a party to an action in his official capacity and during its pendency dies, resigns, or otherwise ceases to hold office, the action does not abate and his successor is automatically substituted as a party. Proceedings following the substitution shall be in the name of the substituted party, but any misnomer not affecting the substantial rights of the parties shall be disregarded. An order of substitution may be entered at any time, but the omission to enter such an order shall not affect the substitution.

(2) When a public officer sues or is sued in his official capacity, he may be described as a party by his official title rather than by name; but the court may require his name to be added.

Amended June 24, 2009, effective July 1, 2009.

Reporter's Notes—1973

Rule 25(a) deals with the substitution of the proper parties in the event of the death of any party. Rule 25(a)(1) treats the situation where the claim for or against the deceased party survives the death. Rule 25(a) is not limited to the situation involving the death of a *sole* plaintiff whose claim survives or a *sole* defendant against whom the claim survives. Thus if P sues D(1) and D(2) on a claim which survives a defendant's death then upon the death of D(1), his representative may be substituted under Rule 25(a)(1).

In the case of death of one of several defendants, where the claim does *not* survive against the deceased defendant, Rule 25(a)(2) allows the action to continue against the remaining defendants. Thus if P sued D(1) and D(2) on a claim which does not survive a defendant's

death, then upon the death of D(1), the action will continue against D(2).

Under prior law, substitution of the representative of a deceased party could occur in one of two ways: (1) the representative could voluntarily appear; or (2) the surviving party could obtain a court citation requiring the representative to appear and assume the prosecution or defense of the action. Rule 25(a)(1) supplants the citation procedure with the motion for substitution. If it is the representative of the deceased party who seeks substitution, he must give notice to the other parties as provided in Rule 5. If a surviving party seeks the substitution, service must be made upon the representative in the manner prescribed by Rule 4, because the representative is not yet a party.

Rule 25(a)(1) differs in several respects from Federal Rule 25(a)(2). The federal rule requires that the motion for substitution take place within ninety days after the death is suggested upon the record; the Massachusetts rule allows the motion to be made within one year after the date of approval of the bond of the representative of the deceased party. This period is more consistent with prior Massachusetts law for issuance of a citation. Prior law provided for one year from the time the representative had given bond whereas Rule 25(a)(1) provides for one year from the approval of the bond.

Rule 25(a)(1) allows a dismissal of the action upon notice and hearing if the motion for substitution is not timely made, unless the failure of the surviving party to make the motion was the result of excusable neglect. Failure on the part of the decedent's representative to notify the surviving party within a reasonable time from the approval of the bond and to file a suggestion of death upon the record requires a finding of excusable neglect.

Rule 25(b) does not alter prior practice. Neither does Rule 25(c). See Henri Peladeau Lte. v. Fred Gillespie Lumber Co., 285 Mass. 10, 13–14, 188 N.E. 380, 381–382 (1933); Shapiro v. McCarthy, 279 Mass. 425, 428, 181 N.E. 842, 843 (1932).

Rule 25(d) changes prior practice slightly by allowing substitution of a successor officer in place of the officer against whom the action was originally brought. See Knights v. Treasurer & Receiver General, 236 Mass. 336, 341, 342, 128 N.E. 637, 639 (1920).

Reporter's Notes—2009

The 2009 amendments reflect changes resulting from the adoption of the Massachusetts Uniform Probate Code.

V. DEPOSITIONS AND DISCOVERY

Rule 26. General Provisions Governing Discovery

(a) Discovery Methods. Parties may obtain discovery by one or more of the following methods except as otherwise provided in Rule 30(a) and Rule 30A(a), (b): depositions upon oral examination or written questions; written interrogatories; production of documents or things or permission to enter upon land or other property, for inspection and other purposes; physical and mental examinations; and requests for admission. Unless the court orders otherwise, or unless otherwise provided in these rules, the frequency of use of these methods is not limited.

(b) Scope of Discovery. Unless otherwise limited by order of the court in accordance with these rules, the scope of discovery is as follows:

(1) *In General.* Parties may obtain discovery regarding any matter, not privileged, which is relevant to the subject matter involved in the pending action, whether it relates to the claim or defense of the party seeking discovery or to the claim

or defense of any other party, including the existence, description, nature, custody, condition and location of any books, documents, or other tangible things and the identity and location of persons having knowledge of any discoverable matter. It is not ground for objection that the information sought will be inadmissible at the trial if the information sought appears reasonably calculated to lead to the discovery of admissible evidence.

(2) *Insurance Agreements.* A party may obtain discovery of the existence and contents of any insurance agreement under which any person carrying on an insurance business may be liable to satisfy part or all of a judgment which may be entered in the action or to indemnify or reimburse for payments made to satisfy the judgment. Information concerning the insurance agreement is not by reason of disclosure admissible in evidence at trial. For purposes of this paragraph, an application for insurance shall not be treated as part of an insurance agreement.

(3) *Trial Preparation: Materials.* Subject to the provisions of subdivision (b)(4) of this rule, a party may obtain discovery of documents and tangible things otherwise discoverable under subdivision (b)(1) of this rule and prepared in anticipation of litigation or for trial by or for another party or by or for that other party's representative (including his attorney, consultant, surety, indemnitor, insurer, or agent) only upon a showing that the party seeking discovery has substantial need of the materials in the preparation of his case and that he is unable without undue hardship to obtain the substantial equivalent of the materials by other means. In ordering discovery of such materials when the required showing has been made, the court shall protect against disclosure of the mental impressions, conclusions, opinions, or legal theories of an attorney or other representative of a party concerning the litigation.

A party may obtain without the required showing a statement concerning the action or its subject matter previously made by that party. Upon request, a person not a party may obtain without the required showing a statement concerning the action or its subject matter previously made by that person. If the request is refused, the person may move for a court order. The provisions of Rule 37(a)(4) apply to the award of expenses incurred in relation to the motion. For purposes of this paragraph, a statement previously made is (A) a written statement signed or otherwise adopted or approved by the person making it, or (B) a stenographic, mechanical, electrical, or other recording, or a transcription thereof, which is a substantially verbatim recital of an oral statement by the person making it and contemporaneously recorded.

(4) *Trial Preparation: Experts.* Discovery of facts known and opinions held by experts, otherwise discoverable under the provisions of subdivision (b)(1) of this rule and acquired or developed in anticipation of litigation or for trial, may be obtained only as follows:

(A) (i) A party may through interrogatories require any other party to identify each person whom the other party expects to call as an expert witness at trial, to state the subject matter on which the expert is expected to testify, and to state the substance of the facts and opinions to which the expert is expected to testify and a summary of the grounds for each opinion. (ii) Upon motion, the court may order further discovery by other means, subject to such restrictions as to scope and such provisions, pursuant to subdivision (b)(4)(C) of this rule, concerning fees and expenses as the court may deem appropriate.

(B) A party may discover facts known or opinions held by an expert who has been retained or specially employed by another party in anticipation of litigation or preparation for trial and who is not expected to be called as a witness at trial, only as provided in Rule 35(b) or upon a showing of exceptional circumstances under which it is impracticable for the party seeking discovery to obtain facts or opinions on the same subject by other means.

(C) Unless manifest injustice would result, (i) the court shall require that the party seeking discovery pay the expert a reasonable fee for time spent in responding to discovery under subdivisions (b)(4)(A)(ii) and (b)(4)(B) of this rule; and (ii) with respect to discovery obtained under subdivision (b)(4)(A)(ii) of this rule the court may require,

and with respect to discovery obtained under subdivision (b)(4)(B) of this rule the court shall require, the party seeking discovery to pay the other party a fair portion of the fees and expenses reasonably incurred by the latter party in obtaining facts and opinions from the expert.

(5) *Claims of Privilege or Protection of Trial Preparation Materials.*

(A) *Information Withheld.* When a party withholds information otherwise discoverable by claiming that the information is privileged or subject to protection as trial-preparation material, the party must:

(i) expressly make the claim; and

(ii) describe the nature of the documents, communications, or tangible things not produced or disclosed—and do so in a manner that, without revealing information itself privileged or protected, will enable other parties to assess the claim.

The court, upon motion, may order the withholding party to provide such additional information as is necessary to assess the claim of privilege.

(B) *Information mistakenly produced; claim of privilege.* If information produced in discovery is subject to a claim of privilege or of protection as trial-preparation material, the party making the claim may notify any party that received the information of the claim and the basis for it. After being notified, a party shall promptly return, sequester, or destroy the specified information and any copies it has; shall not use or disclose the information until the claim is resolved; shall take reasonable steps to retrieve the information if the party disclosed it before being notified; and may promptly present the information to the court under Trial Court Rule VIII, Uniform Rules on Impoundment Procedure, for a determination of the claim. The producing party shall preserve the information until the claim is resolved.

In resolving any such claim, the court should determine whether:

(i) the disclosure was inadvertent;

(ii) the holder of the privilege or protection took reasonable steps to prevent disclosure; and

(iii) the holder promptly took reasonable steps to rectify the error

(C) *Effect of a ruling.* If the court, following such procedure, or pursuant to an order under Rule 26(f)(3), upholds the privilege or protection in a written order, the disclosure shall not be deemed a waiver in the matter before the court or in any other proceeding.

(c) **Protective Orders.** Upon motion by a party or by the person from whom discovery is sought, and for good cause shown, the court in which the action is pending or alternatively, on matters relating to a deposition, the court in the county or judicial district, as the case may be, where the deposition is to be taken may make any order which justice requires to protect a party or person from annoyance, embarrassment, oppression, or undue burden or expense, including one or more of the following: (1) that the discovery not be had; (2) that the discovery may be had only on specified terms and conditions, including a designation of the time, place, or manner; or the sharing of costs; (3) that the discovery may be had only by a method of discovery other than that selected by the party seeking discovery; (4) that certain matters not be inquired into, or that the scope of the discovery be limited to certain matters; (5) that discovery be conducted with no one present except persons designated by the court; (6) that a deposition after being sealed be opened only by order of the court; (7) that a trade secret or other confidential research, development, or commercial information not be disclosed or be disclosed only in a designated way; (8) that the parties simultaneously file specified documents or information enclosed in sealed envelopes to be opened as directed by the court.

Factors bearing on the decision whether discovery imposes an undue burden or expense may include the following:

(1) whether it is possible to obtain the information from some other source that is more convenient or less burdensome or expensive;

(2) whether the discovery sought is unreasonably cumulative or duplicative; and

(3) whether the likely burden or expense of the proposed discovery outweighs the likely benefit of its receipt, taking into account the parties' relative access to the information, the amount in controversy, the resources of the parties, the importance of the issues, and the importance of the requested discovery in resolving the issues.

If the motion for a protective order is denied in whole or in part, the court may, on such terms and conditions as are just, order that any party or person provide or permit discovery. The provisions of Rule 37(a)(4) apply to the award of expenses incurred in relation to the motion.

(d) Sequence and Timing of Discovery. Unless the court upon motion, for the convenience of parties and witnesses and in the interests of justice, orders otherwise, methods of discovery may be used in any sequence and the fact that a party is conducting discovery, whether by deposition or otherwise, shall not operate to delay any other party's discovery.

(e) Supplementation of Responses. A party who has responded to a request for discovery with a response that was complete when made is under no duty to supplement his response to include information thereafter acquired, except as follows:

(1) A party is under a duty seasonably to supplement his response with respect to any question directly addressed to (A) the identity and location of persons having knowledge of discoverable matters, and (B) the identity of each person expected to be called as an expert witness at trial, the subject matter on which he is expected to testify, and the substance of his testimony.

(2) A party is under a duty seasonably to amend a prior response if he obtains information upon the basis of which (A) he knows that the response was incorrect when made, or (B) he knows that the response though correct when made is no longer true and the circumstances are such that a failure to amend the response is in substance a knowing concealment.

(3) A duty to supplement responses may be imposed by order of the court, agreement of the parties, or at any time

prior to trial through new requests for supplementation of prior responses.

(f) Electronically Stored Information.

(1) *Definition.*

"Inaccessible electronically stored information" means electronically stored information from sources that the party identifies as not reasonably accessible because of undue burden or cost.

(2) *Electronically Stored Information Conferences.*

(A) *Conference as of right.* Upon the written request of any party made no later than 90 days after the service of the first responsive pleading by any defendant, the parties shall confer regarding electronically stored information. Such request shall be served on each party that has appeared, but it shall not be filed with the court. The conference shall be held as soon as practicable but no later than 30 days from the date of service of the request.

(B) *Conference by agreement of the parties.* At any time more than 90 days after the service of the first responsive pleading, any party may serve on each party that has appeared a request that all parties confer regarding electronically stored information. Such request shall not be filed with the court. If within 30 days after the request all parties do not agree to confer, any party may move that the court conduct a conference pursuant to Rule 16 regarding electronically stored information.

(C) *Purpose of electronically stored information conference among the parties.* The purpose of an electronically stored information conference is for the parties to develop a plan relating to the discovery of electronically stored information. Within 14 days after such conference the parties shall file with the court the plan and a statement concerning any issues upon which the parties cannot agree. At any electronically stored information conference the parties shall discuss:

(i) any issues relating to preservation of discoverable information;

(ii) the form in which each type of the information will be produced;

(iii) what metadata, if any, shall be produced;

(iv) the time within which the information will be produced;

(v) the method for asserting or preserving claims of privilege or of protection of trial preparation materials, including whether such claims may be asserted after production;

(vi) the method for asserting or preserving confidential and proprietary status of information either of a party or a person not a party to the proceeding;

(vii) whether allocation among the parties of the expense of production is appropriate, and,

(viii) any other issue related to the discovery of electronically stored information.

(3) *Electronically Stored Information Orders.* The court may enter an order governing the discovery of electronically stored information pursuant to any plan referred to in subparagraph (2)(C), or following a Rule 16 conference, or upon

motion of a party or stipulation of the parties, or *sua sponte*, after notice to the parties. Any such order may address:

(A) whether discovery of the information is reasonably likely to be sought in the proceeding;

(B) preservation of the information;

(C) the form in which each type of the information is to be produced;

(D) what metadata, if any, shall be produced;

(E) the time within which the information is to be produced;

(F) the permissible scope of discovery of the information;

(G) the method for asserting or preserving claims of privilege or of protection of the information as trial-preparation material after production;

(H) the method for asserting or preserving confidentiality and the proprietary status of information relating to a party or a person not a party to the proceeding;

(I) allocation of the expense of production; and

(J) any other issue relating to the discovery of the information.

(4) *Limitations on Electronically Stored Information Discovery.*

(A) A party may object to the discovery of inaccessible electronically stored information, and any such objection shall specify the reason that such discovery is inaccessible.

(B) On motion to compel or for a protective order relating to the discovery of electronically stored information, a party claiming inaccessibility bears the burden of showing inaccessibility.

(C) The court may order discovery of inaccessible electronically stored information if the party requesting discovery shows that the likely benefit of its receipt outweighs the likely burden of its production, taking into account the amount in controversy, the resources of the parties, the importance of the issues, and the importance of the requested discovery in resolving the issues.

(D) The court may set conditions for the discovery of inaccessible electronically stored information, including allocation of the expense of discovery.

(E) The court may limit the frequency or extent of electronically stored information discovery, even from an accessible source, in the interests of justice. Factors bearing on this decision include the following:

(i) whether it is possible to obtain the information from some other source that is more convenient or less burdensome or expensive;

(ii) whether the discovery sought is unreasonably cumulative or duplicative;

(iii) whether the party seeking discovery has had ample opportunity by discovery in the proceeding to obtain the information sought; or

(iv) whether the likely burden or expense of the proposed discovery outweighs the likely benefit.

Amended December 16, 1980, effective January 1, 1981; amended effective July 1, 1996; February 27, 2008, effective April 1, 2008; September 24, 2013, effective January 1, 2014; May 31, 2016, effective July 1, 2016; July 11, 2017, effective September 1, 2017.

Reporter's Notes—1973

As a result of S.J.C. Rule 3:15, Massachusetts practitioners are reasonably familiar with a broadened philosophy of discovery. The discovery rules (Rules 26–37) are in many respects similar to S.J.C. Rule 3:15. This is understandable, as Rule 3:15 and the new discovery rules were patterned in large measure upon Federal Rules of Civil Procedure, 26–37. On March 30, 1970, however, the Supreme Court promulgated an amended version of the federal discovery rules, containing several significant departures from existing patterns (and hence from Rule 3:15). Rules 26–37, although patterned closely upon the revised federal discovery rules, depart from them in several significant particulars. In each instance, the Advisory Committee felt the departure to be warranted either by Massachusetts needs or by ingrained Massachusetts practice.

Rule 26 expresses the overall philosophy of the discovery rules. It lists the types of available discovery; it emphasizes that, unless the Rules otherwise provides, the methods may be used as frequently as necessary; it specifies the scope of discovery in terms not of admissibility at the trial, but rather in terms of the possibility of discovering admissible evidence; and it spells out the procedure for relief from harassment-by-discovery.

Unlike S.J.C. Rule 3:15, Rule 26 explicitly permits the discovery of the existence and contents of an insurance agreement where such insurance may be the basis for satisfaction of the judgment, either directly or by way of indemnity. The insurance application, however, is not similarly discoverable. Of course, in an action in which the insurance policy or the application therefor is an essential element of the case, as, for example, in an action for the proceeds of a life insurance policy, the contents of both the policy and the application would be discoverable; Rule 26(b)(2) does not apply.

The first paragraph of Rule 26(b)(3) regulates the discovery of materials prepared in anticipation of litigation. First, such materials are not discoverable at all, unless they meet the requirements of Rule 26(b)(1); that is, they must be relevant to the subject matter of the pending action and/or reasonably calculated to lead to the discovery of admissible evidence. Second, the party seeking discovery must show (a) that he has substantial need of the materials to prepare his case; and (b) that he would sustain severe hardship were he to be forced to obtain the equivalent of such materials by means other than discovery. It will be noted that the "good cause" requirement of former Federal Rule 34 (and S.J.C. Rule 3:15) has been eliminated, to be replaced by a specified special showing. The language, which is taken verbatim from Federal Rule 26(b)(3), as amended, is designed to "conform to the holdings of the cases" construing the former Federal Rules, 48 F.R.D. 497, 500 (1970).

Third, in keeping with the rule of Hickman v. Taylor, 329 U.S. 495 (1947), discovery, except in extremely unusual circumstances, may not be had of an attorney's mental impressions and similar intellectual work-product. This protection applies also to "other representative(s) of a party", provided their work relates to litigation. This pertains to "mental impressions and subjective evaluations of investigators and claim-agents," 48 F.R.D. 500, 502 (1970).

The second paragraph of Rule 26(b)(3) is taken verbatim from its federal counterpart. "Many, but not all, of the considerations supporting a party's right to obtain a statement applies also to the non-party witness. Insurance companies are increasingly recognizing that a witness is entitled to a copy of a statement and are modifying their regular practice accordingly," 48 F.R.D. 497, 503 (1970).

Rule 26(b)(4) contains the full text of the cognate federal rule. It permits the following means of discovering certain information pertaining to experts:

1. Through interrogatories:

a. The identity of each prospective expert witness;

b. The subject matter on which he is expected to testify; and

c. The facts, opinions (and grounds therefor) as to which the expert is expected to testify.

2. Upon obtaining a court order, discovery may continue "by other means", which presumably includes discovery of documents, and depositions. (The question of fees and expenses will be considered hereafter.) An expert retained for litigation purposes need divulge his opinion only upon a showing of circumstances which preclude the discovering party's obtaining the information by other means.

The exceptional circumstances of this rule do not apply to the report of a non-witness examining physician, which is specially regulated by Rule 35(b).

In the usual situation, the party seeking discovery must pay the expert's fee for time spent in, for example, attending a discovery deposition and for time spent by a non-witness expert in responding to any kind of "exceptional circumstances" discovery. Moreover, in the former case, the court *may* require the discovering party to pay his opponent a portion of the expense incurred in initially obtaining the fact and opinion from the expert; in the case of "exceptional circumstances" discovery of expert opinion, the court *must* order payment.

Rule 26(c), which substantially copies Federal Rule 26(c), provides the mechanism by which a person (whether party or not) from whom discovery is sought may obtain court relief in the event he believes he is being unfairly oppressed. Generally, the order will be sought in the court in which the action is pending. However, in the case of a deposition being taken in another county, the order may be sought from the court in the county where the deposition is to be taken. It is assumed that the latter court will be co-equal to the former court. Thus, in an action pending in the Barnstable Superior Court, in which a deposition is being taken at Boston, the application for relief will be made to the Suffolk Superior Court.

Rule 26(d) copies Federal Rule 26(d) and makes clear that the so-called "rule of due diligence" no longer obtains. The parties, that is, may conduct discovery simultaneously; no longer will the party who first files notice of his opponent's deposition win, for that reason alone, priority in the conducting of depositions. The rule does contemplate that in certain situations, convenience and justice may require a court-imposed order of discovery. In the ordinary case, however, discovery will proceed in whatever order the parties select.

Rule 26(e) follows Federal Rule 26(e). Rule 26(e)(1) requires supplementation of previously complete responses to discovery (either in a deposition or by interrogatories, or otherwise) in only certain limited respects: (a) the identity and location of persons having any knowledge of discoverable matters, provided the identity and location of such persons was previously *directly* sought by discovery; and (b) the identity of each prospective expert witness and the subject on which he is expected to testify, again provided that such information was *directly* sought by previous discovery. Rule 26(e)(1)(B) also requires disclosure of the substance of the expert's testimony. Otherwise, a party who desires to force his opponent to supplement prior discovery may do so only (a) if he obtains an order of court; (b) if he obtains his opponent's agreement; or (c) if he strictly requests supplementation of prior answers to make this clear.

Reporter's Notes—1996

Rule 26(c) has been amended to add a reference to "judicial district" to take into account the applicability of the Rules to the District Court and Boston Municipal Court.

Reporter's Notes—2008

The addition of subparagraph (5) to Rule 26(b) adds to the Massachusetts discovery rules the requirement of a "privilege log."

The first sentence of subparagraph (5) is taken in part from the 1993 amendment to Rule 26(b) of the Federal Rules of Civil Procedure that sets out a procedure in connection with a claim of privilege or

protection in response to a discovery request. This 1993 amendment has not been previously adopted in Massachusetts. Unlike the cognate Federal rule, the Massachusetts rule specifically uses the term "privilege log."

Language has been added to the first sentence of the Massachusetts version in order to facilitate judicial review of the appropriateness of a claim that a matter is privileged or otherwise subject to protection. The second sentence of the rule allows the party seeking discovery and the party withholding the information, by written agreement, or the court to waive the requirement of a privilege log or to limit the log to "certain documents, written communications, or things." The rule also makes clear that a party need not include information in the privilege log that is itself privileged.

As is the case with the federal rule, there is no specific requirement in the Massachusetts rule that the privilege log be produced simultaneously with the claim of privilege or protection.

In an attempt to resolve discovery disputes without the need for court intervention, the parties are encouraged to confer and resolve areas of disagreement regarding privilege or protection, including agreeing on the timing of the production of the privilege log. See Superior Court Rule 9C ("Settlement of Discovery Disputes") and Boston Municipal Court and District Court Joint Standing Order No. 1–04 ("Civil Case Management"), III, D, 4 ("Contested Discovery").

The requirement of a privilege log applies to a claim of privilege or right to protection asserted by a *party* only. This rule imposes no obligation to provide a privilege log on the part of a non-party who withholds privileged information after service of a subpoena for the production of documentary evidence under Rule 45(b), although a court would appear to have authority to order preparation of a log.

Reporter's Notes—2014

Background to 2014 Amendments

The 2014 amendments to Rule 26 were part of a series of amendments concerning discovery of electronically stored information. Amendments have been made to Rules 16, 26, 34, 37, and 45.

For a number of years, the Standing Advisory Committee on the Rules of Civil Procedure of the Supreme Judicial Court (Standing Advisory Committee) had been considering the amendments to Federal Rules of Civil Procedure that dealt with discovery of electronically stored information in litigation.

The driving force behind the decision to consider rules for electronic discovery in Massachusetts is the staggering growth of information in electronic form today. In preparing draft electronic discovery rules, a subcommittee of the Standing Advisory Committee drew on two primary sources: the 2006 amendments to the Federal Rules of Civil Procedure that addressed electronically stored information and the 2007 Uniform Rules Relating to the Discovery of Electronically Stored Information (National Conference of Commissioners on Uniform State Laws). Helpful comments on the background that fueled the decision to amend the Federal Rules and to adopt Uniform Rules can be found in the Advisory Committee Notes to the 2006 Federal Rules amendments and the Comments to the Uniform Rules.

The following excerpts from the Prefatory Note that accompanied the Uniform Rules illustrate the scope of the problems created by electronically stored information and the litigation process. Footnotes from the following excerpts have been deleted.

"With very few exceptions, when the state rules and statutes concerning discovery in civil cases were promulgated and adopted, information was contained in documents in paper form. Those documents were kept in file folders, filing cabinets, and in boxes placed in warehouses. When a person, business or governmental entity decided that a document was no longer needed and could be destroyed, the document was burned or shredded and that was the end of the matter. There was rarely an argument about sifting through the ashes or shredded material to reconstruct a memo that had been sent.

"In today's business and governmental world, paper is a thing long past. By some estimates, 93 percent or more of corporate information is being stored in some sort of digital or electronic format. This difference in storage medium for information creates enormous problems for a discovery process created when there was only paper. Principal among these differences is the sheer volume of information in electronic form, the virtually unlimited places where the information may appear, and the dynamic nature of the information. These differences are well documented in the report of the Advisory Committee on the Federal Rules of Civil Procedure (Civil Rules Advisory Committee). The Civil Rules Advisory Committee recommended adoption of new Federal Rules to accommodate the differences:

The *Manual for Complex Litigation (4*th) illustrates the problems that can arise with electronically stored information.

The sheer volume of such data, when compared with conventional paper documentation, can be staggering. A floppy disk, with 1.44 megabytes is the equivalent of 720 typewritten pages of plain text. A CD-ROM with 650 megabytes, can hold up to 325,000 typewritten pages. One gigabyte is the equivalent of 500,000 typewritten pages. Large corporate computer networks create backup data measured in terabytes, or 1,000,000 megabytes; each terabyte represents the equivalent of 500 billion typewritten pages of plain text.

Electronically stored information may exist in dynamic databases that do not correspond to hard copy materials. Electronic information, unlike words on paper, is dynamic. The ordinary operation of computers—including the simple act of turning a computer on and off or accessing a particular file—can alter or destroy electronically stored information, and computer systems automatically discard or overwrite as part of their routine operation. Computers often automatically create information without the operator's direction or awareness, a feature with no direct counterpart in hard copy materials. Electronically stored information may be "deleted" yet continue to exist, but in forms difficult to locate, retrieve or search. Electronic data, unlike paper, may be incomprehensible when separated from the system that created it. The distinctive features of electronic discovery often increase the expense and burden of discovery."

After making a preliminary decision to move forward with a recommendation to adopt rules on electronic discovery, the Standing Advisory Committee also decided that it would be preferable to integrate any changes dealing with electronic discovery directly into the relevant existing rules of the Massachusetts Rules of Civil Procedure and rejected the alternative of promulgating a separate set of rules that would govern electronic discovery.

The Committee also discussed whether electronic discovery rules should be applicable to all Trial Court Departments or should be limited to those courts that regularly heard "larger" civil cases where the costs, time associated with, and burdens of, electronic discovery were perceived to be significant. The Committee ultimately decided that electronic discovery was a matter of concern in all courts of the Commonwealth, and concluded that the electronic discovery rules should be applicable to all trial courts in Massachusetts, and not be limited to courts such as the Superior Court.

The Standing Advisory Committee believes that the proposed amendments to the Massachusetts Rules of Civil Procedure reflect the goals that were identified in the Prefatory Note to the Uniform Rules describing the 2006 amendments to the Federal Rules of Civil Procedure: "to (1) provide early attention to electronic discovery issues, (2) provide better management of discovery into electronically stored information, (3) set out a procedure for assertions of privilege after production, (4) clarify the application of the rules relating to interrogatories and requests for production of documents to electronically

stored information, and (5) clarify the application of the sanctions rules to electronically stored information."

There is a danger in attempting to describe "key" or "major" provisions of rules changes, since any significant change in a rule has the potential to change the dynamic of litigation. But it is fair to say that a major focus of the Committee charged with recommending the 2014 amendments was crafting a process: (1) by which the parties, and the court if necessary, deal with electronic discovery early in the litigation, including the format for production of electronically stored information; (2) that addresses how to handle electronically stored information that is "inaccessible;" (3) that recognizes that privileged information may be inadvertently disclosed in the context of electronic discovery and sets forth a remedy for such disclosure; and (4) that provides protection where electronically stored information is lost by virtue of the "good-faith operation of an electronic information system." These matters are all addressed in the Reporter's Notes that accompany the 2014 amendments.

The rules governing electronic discovery apply in all courts and in all proceedings governed by the Massachusetts Rules of Civil Procedure. However, a particular department of the Trial Court may consider whether supplemental rules or standing orders that address special needs of the department, including considerations common to self-represented litigants, would be appropriate. Of course, any departmental rule or standing order regarding electronic discovery may not be "inconsistent with" the provisions of the Massachusetts Rules of Civil Procedure. Mass. R. Civ. P. 83. See Sullivan v. Iantosca, 409 Mass. 796 (1991).

The 2014 Amendments

The 2014 amendments relating to electronically stored information have resulted in changes to Rule 26(b) and (f).

Rule 26(b).

The existing paragraph that had constituted Rule 26(b)(5) ("Claims of Privilege or Protection of Trial Preparation Materials: Privilege Log") was designated as 26(b)(5)(A), with no changes made to the text. Simultaneously, new provisions were added that have been designated as 26(b)(5)(B) and (C) to deal with information that was mistakenly produced in discovery and subject to a claim of privilege or protection.

The provisions of the first paragraph of Rule 26(b)(5)(B) were adapted from Rule 26(b)(5)(B) of the Federal Rules of Civil Procedure. The provisions of the second paragraph of Rule 26(b)(5)(B) and Rule 26(b)(5)(C) were adapted from Rule 502 of the Federal Rules of Evidence. The language addresses concerns that have been raised about inadvertent waiver of a privilege or claim of protection for trial-preparation material that may result from production of materials in connection with discovery. The problem has become particularly acute in light of the increased likelihood that privileged and protected material can easily be inadvertently produced in discovery where the materials are embedded in voluminous material in electronic format that has been turned over in discovery. But the language of the rule is not restricted to privilege or protection in connection with electronically stored information.

The Standing Advisory Committee decided that an appropriate place to add "clawback" provisions to the Massachusetts Rules was in Rule 26(b)(5), which prior to the 2014 amendment, dealt with privilege and privilege logs. A simultaneous amendment to Mass. R. Civ. P. 16 in 2014 also added this topic to the list of items to be discussed at a pretrial conference.

The Comment to Rule 9 of the Uniform Rules Relating to the Discovery of Electronically Stored Information aptly summarizes the scope of the problem as follows: "The risk of privilege waiver and the work necessary to avoid it add to the costs and delay of discovery. When the review is of electronically stored information, the risk of waiver and the time and effort to avoid it can increase substantially because of the volume of electronically stored information and the difficulty of ensuring that all information to be produced has in fact been reviewed. This rule provides a procedure for a party to assert a claim of privilege or trial-preparation material protection after information is produced in discovery and, if the claim is contested, permits any party that received the information to present the matter to the court for resolution ..."

The Massachusetts version of the "clawback" rule provides that a party may present the information to the court for resolution pursuant to the provisions of the Uniform Rules on Impoundment Procedure, Trial Court Rule VIII. The cognate language in the federal rules uses "under seal" terminology that the Standing Advisory Committee thought to be less appropriate under Massachusetts practice.

Although Rule 26(b)(5)(B) sets forth a "clawback" provision, there is nothing in the rule that precludes the parties from modifying the procedures set forth in the rule to deal with information within the scope of a privilege or protection.

The language of Rule 26(b)(5)(C) provides that if the procedure is used and a court enters a written order upholding the privilege or protection, "the disclosure shall not be deemed a waiver in the matter before the court or in any other proceeding." Such an order is necessary to avoid a waiver of privilege or protection as to non-parties.

Rule 26(c).

Rule 26(c) includes a listing of types of protective orders that a court may enter. Item (2) in the list provides for an order that discovery "be had only on specified terms and conditions, including a designation of the time, place, or manner; or the sharing of costs." The reference to "manner" would, for example, permit an order that discovery be provided on a compact disc. The reference to "sharing of costs" makes clear that the court may order sharing of costs in light of the expenses associated with electronic discovery.

Rule 26(f).

Rule 26(f) is new and deals with conferences regarding electronically stored information.

The definition set forth in Rule 26(f)((*l*) that the term "inaccessible electronically stored information" is "electronically stored information from sources that the party identifies as not reasonably accessible because of undue burden or cost" is taken from Federal Rule 26(b)(2)(B).

Unlike the Federal Rules of Civil Procedure and the Uniform Rules Relating to the Discovery of Electronically Stored Information, the Massachusetts version of Rule 26(f) does not require a conference between the parties as a matter of course (sometimes referred to as a "meet and confer" conference, although a telephonic conference may be permissible). The Massachusetts version, on the contrary, is a recognition that courts in Massachusetts may not necessarily be set up to provide in all instances a right to a conference with the judge as a matter of course in all litigation at the early stages of litigation.

The approach taken by Rule 26(f), however, recognizes that a conference between the parties at the early stages of litigation will often be helpful where there may be discovery of electronically stored information. Thus, the Massachusetts rule has been drafted to encourage a meaningful conference between the parties to deal with electronically stored information.

The Massachusetts version is an attempt to foster communication between counsel on issues of electronic discovery in a court environment that is not set up, as is the case in the federal courts, to provide individual conferences or individual court management of litigation in all instances. A similar approach that did not adopt the federal model in full can be seen in the "Guidelines For State Trial Courts Regarding Discovery of Electronically–Stored Information," approved by the Conference of Chief Justices, August 2006 (available on the Internet at: http://www.ncsconline.org/images/EDiscCCJGuidelinesFinal.pdf. See generally, Guideline 3 and the Comments that accompany Guideline 3.

Conference as of right. Under Rule 26(f)(2)(A), a party has a right to demand a conference with the other party by serving a written request for a conference "no later than 90 days after the service of the

first responsive pleading" of a defendant. The term "pleading" as used in this rule is intended to reflect the definition of "pleading" as set forth in Rule 7(a). Thus, an answer of a defendant would be a pleading that would trigger the right to serve a request for a conference, whereas a motion to dismiss would not. The rule specifically provides that the request for a conference not be *filed* with the clerk's office, in an attempt not to overburden an already-beleaguered court system with additional filings. The conference must be held no later than thirty days from the date a party served the request.

Although the rule itself does not define the term "conference," the parties should not feel that they are required to meet in person. A conference by telephone or through electronic communication is satisfactory.

Conference by agreement. If there has been no request for a conference as of right within the 90–day period, Rule 26(f)(2)(B) allows a party to request a conference at a later point. Such a request should not be filed with the clerk's office. If the other parties to the case do not agree to such a conference, a party desiring a conference may move that the court conduct a conference under the provisions of Rule 16 to deal with matters relating to electronically stored information.

Purpose of conference; plan. Rule 26(f)(2)(C) sets forth the purpose of the conference, whether occurring as of right or by agreement of the parties— to develop a plan that relates to discovery of electronically stored information. The rule sets forth a variety of topics that must be discussed at the conference, adapted in part from Rule 3 of the Uniform Rules Relating to the Discovery of Electronically Stored Information.

The parties must discuss at the conference the preservation of electronically stored information (see item (i), "any issues relating to preservation of discoverable information"). Given the practice that exists in many organizations of deleting or disposing of electronic files after a set period of time, discussion of preservation may serve to avoid later disputes about the availability and expense of retrieving electronic information.

The language of the rule makes specific reference to the production of metadata as a subject to be discussed at the conference (see item (iii), "what metadata, if any, shall be produced"). Specific reference to metadata has also been added to the rule regarding a court order governing electronically stored information (Rule 26(f)(3)).

The parties may also want to address at the conference details regarding how the responding party accesses electronically stored information. This may aid the requesting party in formulating or refining discovery requests involving electronically stored information.

Within fourteen days after the conference, the parties must file with the court a plan that deals with electronically stored information. If the parties are not able to agree on certain issues, they shall file a statement so indicating. The parties must submit a plan to the court whether there was a conference as of right or by agreement, or by order of the court.

Electronically stored information orders. The language of Rule 26(f)(3) provides a court with discretion to enter an order relating to electronically stored information and sets forth the matters that may be addressed in such an order. These matters are drawn in part from Rule 4 of the Uniform Rules Relating to the Discovery of Electronically Stored Information.

A court may enter an order after the parties have filed a plan, or upon motion or stipulation of the parties, or *sua sponte.* A court order may be entered whether or not the parties have conferred. If the parties have agreed about the method to assert or preserve a claim of privilege or protection (Rule 26(f)(3)(F)), the court order may so state.

Limitations on electronically stored information discovery. Rule 26(f)(4) is drawn from Rule 8 of the Uniform Rules Relating to the Discovery of Electronically Stored Information. It provides considerations for a judge to limit discovery of electronically stored information and to allocate the costs involved. Rule 26(f)(4) applies regardless of whether the parties have had a conference or not.

The philosophy behind Rule 26(f)(4) is similar to that of Federal Rule 26(b)(2)(B), reflecting a two-tiered approach to electronic discovery. Upon request, electronic discovery shall be produced, unless limited under Rule 26(f)(4)(E). However, a party believing that electronically stored information is "inaccessible" (as defined in Rule 26(f)(1)) may object to the discovery. In the event that there is a motion to compel the discovery, or a motion for protective order, the court will then determine whether to order the discovery. See Rule 26(f)(4)(C).

Reporter's Notes—2016

At the request of the Rules Committee of the Supreme Judicial Court, the Standing Advisory Committee on the Massachusetts Rules of Civil and Appellate Procedure ("Standing Advisory Committee") considered possible changes to the Massachusetts discovery rules that were based on amendments to the federal discovery rules. The proposed amendments to the Massachusetts discovery rules were intended to address the burdens of discovery that have been the subject of significant debate across the country over the past few years.

There were three proposed changes involving the Massachusetts discovery rules, all taken from amendments to the federal discovery rules.

The first proposed change to Rule 26(b) would have involved the scope of discovery by deleting the language that discovery must be "relevant to the subject matter involved" in the action. The proposal would have added in place of the deleted language that discovery must be relevant to a party's claim or defense. This language was drawn from a 2000 amendment to Rule 26 of the Federal Rules of Civil Procedure refining the scope of discovery.

The second proposed change to Rule 26(b) would have adopted the principle of proportionality for discovery requests—i.e., discovery should be "proportional to the needs of the case." This proposed amendment would have adopted the principle of proportionality as set forth in amendments to the Federal Rules of Civil Procedure that were effective in 2015. The proposed rule listed the factors that were to be taken into account in determining whether a discovery request was proportional to the needs of a case: "the importance of the issues at stake in the action, the amount in controversy, the parties' relative access to relevant information, the parties' resources, the importance of the discovery in resolving the issues, and whether the burden or expense of the proposed discovery outweighs its likely benefit."

The third proposed change would have deleted the language in Rule 26(b)(1) that "[i]t is not ground for objection that the information sought will be inadmissible at the trial if the information sought appears reasonably calculated to lead to the discovery of admissible evidence." In its place, the proposal would have added language that information "need not be admissible in evidence to be discoverable."

The Standing Advisory Committee reviewed the many comments submitted by both lawyers and judges after the proposal was published for public comment and voted not to recommend to the Supreme Judicial Court adoption of the three changes to the discovery rules. The comments reflected significant opposition to the proposed changes and described them as unnecessary and inadvisable at the present time. The principal objection to the amendments by the Standing Advisory Committee was based on the perception by many Committee members of drawbacks and unintended consequences of imposing the federal changes on the Massachusetts trial courts, as well as the newness of the federal changes. Most Committee members were in favor of a "wait and see" approach that would allow review of how the federal amendments affect litigants and civil litigation prior to considering whether similar amendments should be adopted in Massachusetts.

The Standing Advisory Committee also prepared draft language for consideration by the Supreme Judicial Court that alluded to proportionality in discovery, not in the context of the scope of discovery, but in the context of a court's decision to grant a protective order involving discovery under Rule 26(c). The Standing Advisory Committee referred to this as "compromise" language in the event that the Supreme Judicial Court did not accept the Standing Advisory Committee's recommendation not to change the Massachusetts discovery rules, at least until there is sufficient experience under the federal amendments. It is this compromise language that the Supreme Judicial Court adopted in 2016.

The amendment to the protective order language of Rule 26(c) lists factors similar to those that are relevant to a court's decision to limit the discovery of electronically stored information under Rule 26(f)(4)(E). These factors are:

(1) whether it is possible to obtain the information from some other source that is more convenient or less burdensome or expensive;

(2) whether the discovery sought is unreasonably cumulative or duplicative; and

(3) whether the likely burden or expense of the proposed discovery outweighs the likely benefit of its receipt, taking into account the parties' relative access to the information, the amount in controversy, the resources of the parties, the importance of the issues, and the importance of the requested discovery in resolving the issues.

Under Rule 26(f)(4)(E)(iii), a relevant factor in limiting electronic discovery is "whether the party seeking discovery has had ample opportunity by discovery in the proceeding to obtain the information sought." This factor has been omitted from the listing of factors in the 2016 amendment to Rule 26(c).

The addition of these factors to Rule 26(c) should not result in any significant change to Massachusetts practice. The amendment confirms the existing authority of a trial judge in determining whether to grant a protective order.

Reporter's Notes—2017

The 2017 amendment to Rule 26(b)(5)(A) changed the procedure involving assertions of a claim of privilege or protection of trial preparation materials in connection with discovery requests. It deleted the language that a privilege log must contain specified information—author, recipient, date and type of document, etc.—where a party responding to discovery claimed privilege or protection from discovery.

In 2008, an amendment to Rule 26(b)(5) added the requirement of a privilege log to the Massachusetts discovery rules. The procedure adopted required a designation of each item withheld, document-by-document. Where information was withheld from discovery on the basis that it was privileged or otherwise subject to protection, the withholding party was required to produce a privilege log, unless the parties agreed otherwise in writing. The privilege log was required to list the author and sender (if different) of the document, the recipient, the date and type of document, and the subject matter of the withheld information. In many instances, the requirement of a privilege log listing each document with the required information has proven to be burdensome and in some instances, impractical, given the large number of matters that may exist in an electronic format. This may be especially true where discovery seeks production of electronic mail, text messages, or other forms of electronic communication. Hence, a decision was made to revisit the process.

The 2017 amendment to Rule 26(b)(5)(A) eliminated the requirement of producing a document-by-document log in the first instance containing the specified information. In its place, it adopted an approach used under the Federal Rules of Civil Procedure since 1993. It requires a party seeking to claim privilege or protection to "expressly make the claim" and to "describe the nature of the documents, communications, or tangible things not produced or disclosed...in a manner that, without revealing information itself privileged or protected, will enable other parties to assess the claim."

To comply with the revised rule, a party may respond with a privilege log or index in any appropriate way that allows other parties to evaluate the claim. The 1993 Notes of the Advisory Committee on the Federal Rules of Civil Procedure regarding Rule 26(b)(5)(A) of the Federal Rules state:

> The rule does not attempt to define for each case what information must be provided when a party asserts a claim of privilege or work product protection. Details concerning time, persons, general subject matter, etc., may be appropriate if only a few items are withheld, but may be unduly burdensome when voluminous documents are claimed to be privileged or protected, particularly if the items can be described by categories.

By virtue of the 2017 change in the Massachusetts rule, there is no longer a requirement that each item withheld be listed together with the name of the sender, etc. For example, a categorical privilege log may be appropriate where a request for documents encompasses a large number of communications between a lawyer and a client such that a document-by-document listing would be unduly burdensome. See Games2U, Inc. v. Game Trucking Licensing, LLC, 2013 WL 4046655 (U.S.D.C. D. Ariz. 2013); Companion Property and Casualty Ins. Co. v. U.S. Bank National Assoc., 2016 WL 6539344 (U.S.D.C. D. S.C. 2016). If the requesting party is of the view that such a categorical response is not adequate to allow it to make an intelligent decision as to whether all such documents are privileged, the party may seek appropriate relief in court. See Automobile Club of New York, Inc. v. Port Authority of New York and New Jersey, 297 F.R.D. 55 (U.S.D.C. S.D. N.Y. 2013) (motion for an order requiring defendant to amend the privilege log; court ordered categorical privilege log to be supplemented).

The rule as amended is not intended to prohibit a document-by-document privilege log containing detailed information if a party chooses to respond with one.

The final paragraph of Rule 26(b)(5)(A) provides that upon motion, a court may order the withholding party to provide additional information to enable the requesting party to assess a claim of privilege. This sentence is intended to address the point made in the 1993 notes of the Advisory Committee on the Federal Rules of Civil Procedure that when withholding information, a "party must also provide sufficient information to enable other parties to evaluate the applicability of the claimed privilege or protection."

Rule 27.   Depositions Before Action or Pending Appeal

(a) Before Action.

(1) *Petition*. A person who desires to perpetuate his own testimony or that of another person regarding any matter that may be cognizable in any court where these rules apply may file a verified petition in the Superior Court in the county or District Court in the judicial district, as the case may be, of the residence of any expected adverse party. The petition shall be entitled in the name of the petitioner and shall show: 1, that the petitioner expects to be a party to an action cognizable in a court where these rules apply but is presently unable to bring it or cause it to be brought, 2, the subject matter of the expected action and his interest therein, 3, the facts which he desires to establish by the proposed testimony and his reasons for desiring to perpetuate it, 4, the names or a description of the persons he expects will be adverse parties and their addresses so far as known, and 5, the names and addresses of the persons to be examined and the substance of the testimony which he expects to elicit from each, and shall ask for an order authorizing the petitioner to take the depositions of the persons to be examined named in the petition, for the purpose of perpetuating their testimony.

(2) *Notice and Service*. The petitioner shall thereafter serve a notice upon each person named in the petition as an expected adverse party, together with a copy of the petition, stating that the petitioner will apply to the court, at a time and place named therein, for the order described in the petition. At least 20 days before the date of hearing the notice shall be served either within or without the Commonwealth in the manner provided in Rule 4 for service of summons; but if such service cannot with due diligence be made upon any expected adverse party named in the petition, the court may make such order as is just for service by publication or otherwise, and shall appoint, for persons not served in the manner provided in Rule 4, an attorney who shall represent them, and, in case they are not otherwise represented, shall cross-examine the deponent. If any expected adverse party is a minor or incompetent, or an incapacitated person as defined in G.L. c. 190B the provisions of Rule 17(b) apply.

(3) *Order and Examination*. If the court is satisfied that the perpetuation of the testimony may prevent a failure or delay of justice, it shall make an order designating or describing the persons whose depositions may be taken and specifying the subject matter of the examination and whether the depositions shall be taken upon oral examination or written interrogatories. The depositions may then be taken in accordance with these rules; and the court may make orders of the character provided for by Rules 34 and 35. For the purpose of applying these rules to depositions for perpetuating testimony, each reference therein to the court in which the action is pending shall be deemed to refer to the court in which the petition for such deposition was filed.

(4) *Use of Deposition*. If a deposition to perpetuate testimony is taken under these rules or if, although not so taken, it would be admissible in evidence in the courts of the Commonwealth, it may be used in any action involving the same subject matter subsequently brought in such a court, in accordance with the provisions of Rule 32(a).

(b) **Pending Appeal.** If an appeal has been taken from a judgment of a court of this Commonwealth or before the taking of an appeal if the time therefor has not expired, the court in which the judgment was rendered may allow the taking of the depositions of witnesses to perpetuate their testimony for use in the event of further proceedings in that court. In such case the party who desires to perpetuate the testimony may make a motion in that court for leave to take the depositions, upon the same notice and service thereof as if the action was pending in that court. The motion shall show (1) the names and addresses of persons to be examined and the substance of the testimony which he expects to elicit from each; (2) the reasons for perpetuating their testimony. If the court finds that the perpetuation of the testimony is proper to avoid a failure or delay of justice, it may make an order allowing the depositions to be taken and may make orders of the character provided for by Rules 34 and 35, and thereupon the depositions may be taken and used in the same manner and under the same conditions as are prescribed in these rules for depositions taken in pending actions.

(c) Perpetuation by Action. This rule does not limit the power of a court to entertain an action to perpetuate testimony.

Amended effective July 1, 1996; amended June 24, 2009, effective July 1, 2009.

Reporter's Notes—1973

Rule 27, substantially tracking Federal Rule 27, regulates the taking of depositions for a purpose other than discovery, i.e., for preservation of testimony before an action is commenced, or for a similar purpose after trial, but during the pendency of an appeal. Rule 27 supersedes G.L. c. 233, §§ 46–63. Rule 27 contains no provision for recording the deposition in the Registry of Deeds (or anywhere else); compare practice under G.L. c. 233, § 50. The major substantive difference between Rule 27 and prior practice is that under Rule 27(a)(3), a deposition may not be taken unless a court determines that the perpetuation of testimony "may prevent a failure or delay of justice". Under G.L. c. 233, § 46, no similar determination had to be made; the person desiring to perpetuate testimony merely applied in writing to a justice of the peace and a notary public (or any two justices or notaries) requesting them to take the deposition.

Reporter's Notes—1996

Rule 27(a)(1) has been amended to add a reference to the District Court in the relevant judicial district to take into account the applicability of the Rules to the District Court and Boston Municipal Court.

Reporter's Notes—2009

The 2009 amendments reflect changes resulting from the adoption of the Massachusetts Uniform Probate Code.

Rule 28. Persons Before Whom Depositions May Be Taken

(a) Within the United States. Within the United States or within a territory or insular possession subject to the jurisdiction of the United States, depositions shall be taken before an officer authorized to administer oaths by the laws of the United States or of the place where the examination is held, or before a person appointed by the court in which the action is pending. A person so appointed has power to administer oaths and take testimony. The term officer as used in Rules 30, 31 and 32 includes a person appointed by the court or designated by the parties under Rule 29.

(b) In Foreign Countries. In a foreign country, depositions may be taken (1) on notice before a person authorized to administer oaths in the place in which the examination is held, either by the law thereof or by the laws of the United States, or (2) before a person commissioned by the court, and a person so commissioned shall have the power by virtue of his commission to administer any necessary oath and take testimony, or (3) pursuant to a letter rogatory. A commission or a letter rogatory shall be issued on application and notice and on terms that are just and appropriate. It is not requisite to the issuance of a commission or a letter rogatory that the taking of the deposition in any other manner is impracticable or inconvenient; and both a commission and a letter rogatory may be issued in proper cases. A notice or commission may designate the person before whom the deposition is to be taken either by name or descriptive title. A letter rogatory may be addressed "To the Appropriate Authority in [here name the country]." Evidence obtained in response to a letter rogatory need not be excluded merely for the reason that it is not a verbatim transcript or that the testimony was not taken under oath or

for any similar departure from the requirements for depositions taken within the United States under these rules.

(c) Disqualification for Interest. No deposition shall be taken before a person who is a relative or employee or attorney or counsel of any of the parties, or is a relative or employee of such attorney or counsel, or is financially interested in the action.

Amended October 27, 1981, effective January 1, 1982.

Reporter's Notes—1973

Rule 28 copies Federal Rule 28. It describes the persons before whom depositions may be taken, either within the United States or abroad. Within the United States, any person authorized to give oaths may preside at the taking of a deposition. As a practical matter, virtually every court reporter holds a commission as a notary public; accordingly, in almost every instance, the court reporter administers the oath and then takes the testimony.

Rule 29. Stipulations Regarding Discovery Procedure

Unless the court orders otherwise, the parties may by written stipulation (1) provide that depositions may be taken before any person, at any time or place, upon any notice, and in any manner and when so taken may be used like other depositions; and (2) modify the procedures provided by these rules for other methods of discovery.

Reporter's Notes—1973

Rule 29 changes Federal Rule 29. The Federal Rule requires court approval for any extension of time: (a) to answer interrogatories; (b) to produce documents, etc.; or (c) to respond to a request for admission. This requirement clashes squarely with Massachusetts practice. Under G.L. c. 231 § 72, "[p]arties may make agreements relative to amendments and the time of filing papers, which shall be equivalent to an order of the court to the same effect." Because existing practice seems to have worked so well, and because the requirement of prior court approval seems so likely to produce unnecessary anguish to bench and bar, Rule 29 follows Massachusetts procedure. It should be noted that even Arizona, which has otherwise adopted a firm policy of tracking the Federal Rules without change (see Frank, "Arizona and the Federal Rules," 41 F.R.D. 79, 86–87 (1966)), has rejected the court-approval requirement of Federal Rule 29.

Rule 30. Depositions Upon Oral Examination

(a) When Depositions May Be Taken. After commencement of the action, any party may take the testimony of any person, including a party, by deposition upon oral examination. Leave of court, granted with or without notice, must be obtained only if: (i) the plaintiff seeks to take a deposition prior to the expiration of 30 days after service of the summons and complaint upon any defendant or service made under Rule 4(e) (except that leave is not required (1) if a defendant has served a notice of taking deposition or otherwise sought discovery, or (2) if special notice is given as provided in subdivision (b)(2) of this rule); (ii) there is no reasonable likelihood that recovery will exceed $5,000 if the plaintiff prevails; (iii) the action is pending in the Superior Court and there has been a trial in a District Court before a transfer; (iv) there has been a hearing before a master; or (v) the relief sought is the custody of minor children, divorce, affirmance or annulment of marriage, separate support, or any like relief.

The attendance of witnesses may be compelled by subpoena as provided in Rule 45. The deposition of a person confined in prison may be taken only by leave of court on such terms as the court prescribes.

(b) Notice of Examination: General Requirements; Special Notice; Non-Stenographic Recording; Production of Documents and Things; Deposition of Organization.

(1) A party desiring to take the deposition of any person upon oral examination shall give at least seven days' notice in writing to every other party to the action. The notice shall state the time and place for taking the deposition and the name and address of each person to be examined, if known, and, if the name is not known, a general description sufficient to identify him or the particular class or group to which he belongs. If a subpoena duces tecum is to be served on the person to be examined, the designation of the materials to be produced as set forth in the subpoena shall be attached to or included in the notice.

(2) Leave of court is not required for the taking of a deposition by plaintiff if the notice (A) states that the person to be examined is about to go out of the county where the action is pending and more than 100 miles from the place of trial, or is about to go out of the United States, or is bound on a voyage abroad, and will be unavailable for examination unless his deposition is taken before expiration of the 30-day period, and (B) sets forth facts to support the statement. The plaintiff's attorney shall sign the notice, and his signature constitutes a certification by him that to the best of his knowledge, information, and belief the statement and supporting facts are true. The sanctions provided by Rule 11 are applicable to the certification.

If a party shows that when he was served with notice under this subdivision (b)(2) he was unable through the exercise of diligence to obtain counsel to represent him at the taking of the deposition, the deposition may not be used against him.

(3) The court may for cause shown enlarge or shorten the time for taking the deposition.

(4) Any oral deposition may be recorded by (i) stenographic or (ii) stenographic and audio-visual means. If the deposition is recorded by stenographic and audio-visual means, the parties shall comply with the provisions of Mass.R.Civ.P. 30 and 30A. With prior notice to the deponent and other parties, any party may designate another method for recording the testimony in addition to that specified in the original notice. Except as otherwise provided by this rule, the rules governing the practice and procedure in depositions and discovery shall apply. The party choosing to have the testimony recorded by stenographic and audio-visual means shall bear the entire cost of the audio-visual recording, except that each party shall bear the cost for a copy of the audio-visual recording and the stenographic record. By leave of court upon motion with notice and an opportunity to be heard in opposition, or by stipulation in writing of all parties, a party taking an oral deposition may have the testimony recorded by other than stenographic or stenographic and audio-visual means. The stipulation or order shall designate the person before whom the deposition shall be taken, the manner of recording, preserving and filing the deposition, and may include other provisions to assure that the recorded testimony will be accurate and trustworthy. A party may arrange to have a stenographic

transcription made at his own expense. Any objections under subdivision (c), any changes made by the witness, his signature identifying the deposition as his own or the statement of the officer that is required if the witness does not sign, as provided in subdivision (e), and the certification of the officer required by subdivision (f) shall be set forth in a writing to accompany a deposition recorded by non-stenographic means. In any event, however, where testimony is to be recorded by audio-visual means, the provisions of Rule 30A shall apply.

(5) The notice to a party deponent may be accompanied by a request made in compliance with Rule 34 for the production of documents and tangible things at the taking of the deposition. The procedure of Rule 34 shall apply to the request and, notwithstanding the provisions of subdivision (b)(1) of this Rule, the party making the request shall give at least 30 days' notice in writing to every other party to the action. The court may on motion with or without notice allow a shorter or longer time.

(6) A party may in his notice and in a subpoena name as the deponent a public or private corporation or a partnership or association or governmental agency and describe with reasonable particularity the matters on which examination is requested. The organization so named shall designate one or more officers, directors, or managing agents, or other persons who consent to testify on its behalf, and may set forth, for each person designated, the matters on which he will testify. A subpoena shall advise a non-party organization of its duty to make such a designation. The persons so designated shall testify as to matters known or reasonably available to the organization. This subdivision (b)(6) does not preclude taking a deposition by any other procedure authorized in these rules.

(7) By leave of court upon motion with notice and an opportunity to be heard in opposition, or by stipulation in writing of all parties, a deposition may be taken by telephone. For the purpose of this rule and Rules 28(a), 37(a)(1), 37(b)(1) and 45(d), a deposition taken by telephone is taken in the county and at the place where the deponent is to answer questions propounded to him.

(c) Examination and Cross-Examination; Record of Examination; Oath; Objections. Examination and cross-examination of witnesses may proceed as permitted at the trial under the provisions of Rule 43(b). The officer before whom the deposition is to be taken shall put the witness on oath and shall personally, or by someone acting under the officer's direction and in the officer's presence, record the testimony of the witness. The testimony shall be taken stenographically or by voice writing or recorded by any other means ordered in accordance with subdivision (b)(4) of this rule. If requested by one of the parties, the testimony shall be transcribed. In lieu of participating in the oral examination, parties may serve written questions in a sealed envelope on the party taking the deposition and such party shall transmit them to the officer, who shall propound them to the witness and record the answers verbatim.

All objections made at the time of the examination to the qualifications of the officer taking the deposition, or to the manner of taking it, or to the evidence presented, or to the conduct of any party, and any other objection to the proceedings, shall be noted by the officer upon the deposition; but the examination shall proceed. Any objection to testimony during a deposition shall be stated concisely and in a non-argumentative and non-suggestive manner. Testimony to which objection is made shall be taken subject to the objections. Counsel for a witness or a party may not instruct a deponent not to answer except where necessary to assert or preserve a privilege or protection against disclosure, to enforce a limitation on evidence directed by the court or stipulated in writing by the parties, or to terminate the deposition and present a motion to the court pursuant to Rules 30(d) or 37(d).

(d) Motion to Terminate or Limit Examination. At any time during the taking of the deposition, on motion of any party or of the deponent and upon a showing that the examination is being conducted in bad faith or in such manner as unreasonably to annoy, embarrass, or oppress the deponent or party, the court in which the action is pending or the court in the county or judicial district, as the case may be, where the deposition is being taken may order the officer conducting the examination to cease forthwith from taking the deposition, or may limit the scope and manner of the taking of the deposition as provided in Rule 26(c). If the order made terminates the examination, it shall be resumed thereafter only upon the order of the court in which the action is pending. Upon demand of the objecting party or deponent, the taking of the deposition shall be suspended for the time necessary to make a motion for an order. The provisions of Rule 37(a)(4) apply to the award of expenses incurred in relation to the motion.

(e) Submission to Witness; Changes; Signing. When the testimony is fully transcribed the deposition transcript and any audio-visual recording thereof shall be submitted to the witness for examination and the deposition transcript shall be read to or by the witness, unless such examination and reading are waived by the witness and by the parties. Any changes in form or substance which the witness desires to make shall be entered upon the deposition transcript by the officer with a statement of the reasons given by the witness for making them. The deposition transcript shall then be signed by the witness, unless the parties by stipulation waive the signing or the witness is ill or cannot be found or refuses to sign. If the deposition transcript is not signed by the witness within 30 days of its submission to him, the officer shall sign it and state on the record the fact of the waiver or of the illness or absence of the witness or the fact of the refusal to sign together with the reason, if any, given therefor; and the deposition transcript may then be used as fully as though signed, unless on a motion to suppress under Rule 32(d)(4) the court holds that the reasons given for the refusal to sign require rejection of the deposition in whole or in part.

(f) Certification and Delivery by Officer; Exhibits; Copies; Notice of Receipt.

(1) The officer shall certify on the deposition transcript that the witness was duly sworn by him and that the deposition transcript is a true record of the testimony given by the witness. Unless otherwise ordered by the court generally or in a specific case or stipulated by the parties, he shall then securely seal the deposition transcript in an envelope endorsed with the title of the action and marked "Deposition of [here insert name of witness]" and shall promptly deliver or send it to the party taking the deposition.

Documents and things produced for inspection during the examination of the witness, shall, upon the request of a party, be marked for identification and annexed to the deposition transcript and may be inspected and copied by any party, except that if the person producing the material desires to retain them he may (A) offer copies to be marked for identification and annexed to the deposition and to serve thereafter as originals if he affords to all parties fair opportunity to verify the copies by comparison with the originals, or (B) offer the originals to be marked for identification, after giving to each party an opportunity to inspect and copy them, in which event the materials may then be used in the same manner as if annexed to the deposition. Any party may move for an order that the original be annexed to and returned with the deposition transcript to the court, pending final disposition of the case.

(2) Upon payment of reasonable charges therefor, the officer shall furnish a copy of the deposition transcript to any party or to the deponent.

(3) The party taking the deposition shall give prompt notice of its receipt to all other parties.

(g) Failure to Attend or to Serve Subpoena; Expenses.

(1) If the party giving the notice of the taking of a deposition fails to attend and proceed therewith and another party attends in person or by attorney pursuant to the notice, the court may order the party giving the notice to pay to such other party the amount of the reasonable expenses incurred by him and his attorney in so attending, including reasonable attorney's fees.

(2) If the party giving the notice of the taking of a deposition of a witness fails to serve a subpoena upon him and the witness because of such failure does not attend, and if another party attends in person or by attorney because he expects the deposition of that witness to be taken, the court may order the party giving the notice to pay to such other party the amount of the reasonable expenses incurred by him and his attorney in so attending, including reasonable attorney's fees.

Amended December 16, 1980, effective January 1, 1981; October 27, 1981, effective January 1, 1982; May 25, 1982, effective July 1, 1982; January 30, 1989, effective March 1, 1989; amended effective July 1, 1996; amended October 1, 1998, effective November 2, 1998; July 11, 2017, effective September 1, 2017.

Reporter's Notes—1973

Although patterned on Federal Rule 30, Rule 30 has been altered to encompass existing practice under S.J.C. Rule 3:15. The situations in which leave of court must first be obtained closely follow the strictures of S.J.C. Rule 3:15. The rest of the procedural scheme is thoroughly familiar. In order to fill what appeared to be a hiatus in Federal Rule 30, the Advisory Committee inserted in Rule 30(b)(5) language to ensure that a party seeking documentary discovery at an oral deposition provide his opponent with at least 30 days' notice.

Reporter's Notes—1989

Because of the simultaneous amendment to Mass.R.Civ.P. 5(d) which states that transcripts of depositions shall no longer ordinarily be presented or accepted for filing, the obligation of the officer at the deposition to file the deposition has been changed. "Unless otherwise ordered," the officer must now "deliver or send" the deposition "to the party taking the deposition" (Rule 30(f)(1)), and the party taking the deposition "shall give prompt notice of its receipt to all other parties" (Rule 30(f)(3)). See, also, Reporter's Notes to the Amendment to Rule 5(d).

Reporter's Notes—1996

Rule 30(d) has been amended to add a reference to "judicial district" to take into account the applicability of the Rules to the District Court and Boston Municipal Court. Certain provisions from Mass.R.Civ.P. 30 which did not appear in the District Court version of Rule 30 (regarding leave of court where the action is pending in the Superior Court after District Court trial and where the action relates to domestic relations matters) now apply in the merged set of Rules.

Reporter's Notes—1998

The purpose of the 1998 amendments to Rule 30, modeled after 1993 amendments to Federal Rule 30, is to address the problem created by objections during a deposition and by directions to a deponent by counsel not to answer a question.

Under the revised rule, objections must "be stated concisely and in a non-argumentative and non-suggestive manner." The Notes of the Advisory Committee on the 1993 federal change aptly described the problem concerning objections as follows: "Depositions frequently have been unduly prolonged, if not unfairly frustrated, by lengthy objections and colloquy, often suggesting how the deponent should respond."

A related problem concerns instructions by counsel to a deponent not to answer. This issue is addressed by the 1998 amendments by adding language to Rule 30(c), taken in part from 1993 amendments to Federal Rule 30, that such instructions are permissible only in the case of a privilege (such as attorney-client privilege) or protection against disclosure (such as the "work product" protection set forth in Mass.R.Civ.P. 26(b)(3)); where a court has imposed limitations on the deposition testimony; where the parties have entered into a written stipulation setting forth limitations; or to terminate the deposition in order to move in court for an appropriate order regarding the deposition (for example, a motion under Mass.R.Civ.P. 30(d) to terminate or limit the deposition on the basis that "the examination is being conducted in bad faith or in such manner as unreasonably to annoy, embarrass, or oppress the deponent or party").

It should be noted that Mass.R.Civ.P. 30(c) makes clear that if there is objection to certain aspects of the deposition, the deposition shall proceed and the objection preserved. Objecting counsel does have the option, of course, under Mass.R.Civ.P. 30(d), to suspend the deposition for purposes of seeking a court order to terminate or limit the deposition. Counsel considering such a move, however, may want to consider the technique of recommending that the objectionable questions be set aside until later in the deposition in order to allow the rest of the deposition to move forward without interruption. After the rest of the questioning is complete, counsel may then consider whether it is necessary to bring the objections to the attention of the court.

The 1998 amendments have also moved the last sentence of the second paragraph of Rule 30(c) to the first paragraph for clarity purposes, thus leaving the focus of the second paragraph on objections and evidence at depositions.

Finally, minor changes have been made to the first paragraph of Rule 30(c) in order to make the language gender-neutral.

Reporter's Notes to Rule 30(c)—2001

In 1998, the Supreme Judicial Court amended Rule 30 in an attempt to deal with "deposition abuse." Rule 30(c) now provides that objections during a deposition "shall be stated concisely and in a non-argumentative and non-suggestive manner." Further, the amended rule prohibits an instruction to a deponent not to answer except where a privilege may exist or where some other legal protection against disclosure may apply. The language of the Massachusetts rule was drawn from Federal Rule 30.

Despite the 1998 amendment which requires that objections be made in a non-argumentative and non-suggestive manner, suggestive objections or comments continue to be made at depositions. Further commentary is therefore in order. The intent of the 1998 amendment

was to prevent the indirect coaching of witnesses by objections or comments from counsel. Thus, the attorney who, after a question, interjects the suggestive objection or comment "if you remember," "if you understand," or "if you have personal knowledge," acts contrary to the language and spirit of the new rule by indirectly suggesting how the witness should respond. The questioning attorney may consider taking appropriate action in response to such coaching suggestions, including suspending the deposition for purposes of obtaining an appropriate court order (Rule 30(d)).

It has been suggested that some attorneys, cognizant of the prohibition against suggestive comments or hints during the deposition, may accomplish the same result by seeking to confer with the client in private prior to the client answering the question. It appears that the rule does not permit such conferences except where appropriate to preserve a privilege or protection against disclosure. A deponent, for example, may not realize that the privilege against self-incrimination provides a legal basis to decline to answer a question; intervention of counsel and a conference with counsel may be necessary to determine whether the deponent will invoke the privilege. In other circumstances, however, the use of private conferences between lawyer and deponent would serve to provide an end-run around the 1998 rule against suggestive objections and the general rule that examination of witnesses at depositions "may proceed as permitted at the trial..." (Rule 30(c)). Just as a lawyer may not interrupt the questioning of a witness in order to confer in private and develop strategy with the witness, nor should the lawyer be allowed to interrupt the flow of questions at a deposition. Nor may the deponent stop the deposition in order to seek the advice of counsel (except in the case of a privilege or protection against disclosure).

Reporter's Notes—2017

Since the 1980s, the Massachusetts Rules of Civil Procedure have provided for two types of audio-visual depositions. The first is an audio-visual deposition by leave of court or by stipulation of the parties under Rule 30A(a)–(k). The second is an "audio-visual expert witness deposition for trial" under Rule 30A(m). Rule 30A(m) allows a party to depose a treating physician or expert witness whom the party intends to call at trial as his or her own witness without the need to obtain leave of court or a stipulation and to use that deposition at trial in lieu of live testimony. Rule 30A(m) does not apply to another party's treating physician or expert.

The 2017 amendments to Rule 30 and Rule 30A deal with the first type of audio-visual deposition and make no change to the Rule 30A(m) deposition. The changes allow audio-visual depositions as a matter of right, making Massachusetts practice consistent with the approach in other jurisdictions and consistent with the Federal Rules of Civil Procedure. The amendments recognize the advantages of audio-visual depositions in addition to written transcripts of depositions.

Rule 30(b). Rule 30(b)(4) allows a party as a matter of right to record a deposition by stenographic and audio-visual means. Where a deposition is recorded by stenographic and audio-visual means, the parties must comply with both Rule 30 and Rule 30A. The party who chooses to have testimony recorded by stenographic and audio-visual means is required to bear the cost of the audio-visual recording. A party who requests a copy of the audio-visual recording is required to bear the cost of a copy of the recording.

Rule 30(e). The recording of an audio-visual deposition must be submitted to the witness for examination together with the transcript of the deposition, unless waived by the witness and the parties. This provides the deponent with the opportunity to view the video before signing the written transcript of the deposition. The rule does not set forth details regarding the manner of submission or location for the viewing of an audio-visual deposition, leaving these matters to be worked out by the parties.

Rule 30A. Audiovisual Depositions and Audiovisual Evidence

(a) Authorization of Audio–Visual Depositions. Any oral deposition may be recorded by stenographic and audio-visual means by complying with the provisions of this rule. Except as otherwise provided by this rule, the rules governing the practice and procedure in depositions and discovery shall apply. At the taking of any such deposition, unless the parties otherwise stipulate, or the court for good cause otherwise orders, there shall also be prepared a simultaneous stenographic record of the deposition. The party choosing to have the testimony recorded by audio-visual means shall bear the entire cost of the audio-visual recording, except that each party shall bear the cost for a copy of the audio-visual recording and the stenographic record.

(b) Notice. Every notice for the taking of an audio-visual deposition and the subpoena for attendance at that deposition shall state that it is to be recorded by audio-visual means and the name and address of the person whose deposition is to be taken. If the operator is an employee of the attorney choosing the audio-visual recording, the notice shall so indicate.

(c) Procedure. The party taking the audio-visual deposition shall be responsible for assuring that the necessary equipment for making an audio-visual recording of the deposition is present at the time the deposition is taken.

The following procedure shall be observed in recording an audio-visual deposition:

(1) *Opening of Deposition.* The deposition shall begin with an oral or written statement on camera which includes:

(i) the operator's name and business address;

(ii) the name and address of the operator's employer;

(iii) the date, time and place of the deposition;

(iv) the caption of the case;

(v) the name of the witness-deponent;

(vi) the name of the party on whose behalf the deposition is being taken; and

(vii) any stipulation by the parties.

The opening statement, if oral, shall be made by the operator, unless counsel agree that one of counsel will make the statement.

(2) *Counsel.* Counsel shall identify themselves on camera by stating their names, their addresses, and the names of the parties or persons for whom they appear at the deposition, and nothing more.

(3) *Oath.* The officer before whom the deposition is taken shall then identify himself and swear or affirm the witness on camera.

(4) *Multiple Units.* When the length of the deposition requires the use of more than one recording unit, the end of each recording unit and the beginning of each succeeding recording unit shall be announced on camera by the operator.

(5) *Closing of Deposition.* At the conclusion of the deposition, a statement shall be made on camera that the deposition is concluded. A statement may be made on camera setting forth any stipulation made by counsel con-

cerning the custody of the audio-visual recording and exhibits and other pertinent matters.

(6) *Index.* The deposition shall be timed by a digital clock on camera which shall show continually each hour, minute and second of each recording unit of the deposition, or otherwise suitably indexed by a time generator. The date(s) on which the deposition is taken shall be shown.

(7) *Objections.* An objection shall be made as in the case of depositions taken solely by stenographic means.

(8) *Interruption of Recording.* No party shall be entitled to cause the operator to interrupt or halt the recording of the audio-visual deposition without the assent of all other parties present.

(9) *Submission to Witness; Changes; Signing.* Unless the parties have stipulated that a simultaneous stenographic record of the deposition not be prepared, the provisions of Rule 30(e) shall apply to the stenographic record of the deposition.

(10) *Certification.* The operator before whom the audio-visual deposition is taken shall attach to the original audio-visual recording a certificate stating that the audio-visual recording is a true record of the testimony given by the witness.

(d) Recording Officer; Use of Camera; Copies. The operator before whom an audio-visual deposition is taken shall be subject to the provisions enumerated in Rule 28(a)–(c).

During the taking of the audio-visual deposition, the operator shall assure that the audio-visual recording records the witness in a standard fashion at all times during the deposition, unless all counsel agree otherwise, or unless on motion before the court, the court directs otherwise. In no event shall the operator use, or permit the use of, audio-visual recording techniques to vary the view which is being recorded for presentation in the courtroom unless agreed upon or ordered by the court as recited above. As an exception to the foregoing, the operator shall, at the request of the attorney questioning the witness, cause a close-up view of a deposition exhibit or visual aid to be taken while the witness is being questioned concerning the exhibit.

Upon the request of any of the parties, the officer shall provide, at the cost of the party making the request, a copy of the deposition transcript in the form of an audio-visual recording or a written transcription.

(e) Custody; Filing; Notice of Filing. Unless the parties have otherwise stipulated, the officer shall take custody of each recording unit upon its completion and shall retain custody of all completed units throughout the deposition. When a deposition is to be completed on another day, the officer shall also take custody of any uncompleted recording unit during the interval.

(f) Inspection and Release of Audio–Visual Recordings. Except upon order of the court and upon such terms as may be provided, the audio-visual recordings on file with the clerk of the court in which the action is pending shall not be available for inspection or viewing after their filing and prior to their use at the trial of the case or their disposition in accordance with this rule. The clerk may release the audio-visual recording to the operator taking the deposition, without an order of court, for the purpose of preparing a copy at the request of a party as provided in subdivisions (a) and (d) of this rule.

(g) Rulings on Objections; Editing of Recording. If any party has any objections to the audio-visual deposition which would otherwise be made at trial, pursuant to Rule 32(b), such objections shall if practicable, be submitted to the trial judge prior to commencement of the trial or hearing for the purpose of obtaining rulings on such objections. An audio copy of the sound track or the transcript may be submitted in lieu of the audio-visual recording for this purpose. For the purpose of ruling on the objections, the trial judge may view the entire audio-visual recording, or view only those parts of the audio-visual recording pertinent to the objections made, or he may listen to an audio recording submitted in lieu of the audio-visual recording, or he may read the transcript. The trial judge shall, if practicable, rule on the objections prior to the commencement of the trial or hearing and shall return the recording to the party who took the audio-visual deposition, with notice to all parties of his rulings and of his instructions as to editing. The editing shall reflect the rulings of the trial judge and shall then remove all references to the objections. After making a copy of the audio-visual recording, the officer shall cause said copy to be edited in accordance with the court's instructions. He shall then cause both the original audio-visual recording and the edited version thereof, each clearly identified, to be returned to the trial judge for use during the trial or hearing. The original audio-visual recording shall be preserved intact and unaltered.

(h) Transcribing of Audio Portion; Marking for Identification. At a trial or hearing, that part of the audio portion of an audio-visual deposition which is offered in evidence and admitted, or which is excluded on objection, shall be transcribed in the same manner as the testimony of other witnesses. Both the original unedited audio-visual recording and the edited version shall be marked for identification.

(i) Use of Audio–Visual Deposition and Responsibility for Assuring Necessary Equipment at Time of Use. An audio-visual deposition may be used for any purpose and under any circumstances in which a stenographic deposition may be used.

The party desiring to use the audio-visual deposition for any purpose shall be responsible for assuring that the necessary equipment for playing the audio-visual recording back is available when the audio-visual deposition is to be used. When an audio-visual deposition is used during a hearing, a trial, or any other court proceeding, the party first using such audio-visual deposition in whole or in part shall assure the availability of the same or comparable audio-video playback equipment to any other party for such other party's use in further showing such audio-visual deposition during the hearing, the trial, or other court proceeding or at any rehearing, recess, or continuation thereof.

(j) Discrepancy Between Audio–Visual Recording and Stenographic Transcript. Upon the claim of a party that a discrepancy exists between the audio-visual recording and the stenographic transcript, the trial judge shall determine: (i) whether such discrepancy reasonably appears; and (ii) whether the relevant part of the audio-visual recording is intelligible. If the relevant part of the audio-visual recording is not intelli-

gible, the stenographic transcript controls. If the relevant part of the audio-visual recording is intelligible and the trial judge rules that a discrepancy reasonably appears, the jury, in a jury action, shall determine from the audio-visual recording the deponent's testimony. The trial judge, in his discretion, may permit the jury to be aided in its determination by the stenographic transcript.

(k) Evidence by Audio–Visual Recording.

(1) *Authorization of Audio–Visual Testimony or Other Evidence.* Upon motion with notice and an opportunity to be heard, or by stipulation of all parties approved by the court, or upon the court's motion, the court may order, in the interest of justice and with due regard to the importance of presenting the testimony of witnesses orally in open court, that all or part of the testimony, and such other evidence as may be appropriate, may be presented at trial by audio-visual means. The provisions of Rule 30A shall govern such audio-visual recordings.

(2) *Introduction as Evidence.* Notwithstanding Rule 30A(i) or Rule 32(a)(3), but subject to rulings on objections pursuant to Rule 30A(k)(3), any party may introduce any such audio-visual recording, that has been authorized under Rule 30A(k)(1), at trial if the court finds its introduction to be in the interest of justice.

(3) *Objections.* Before such audio-visual recording is admitted at trial, the trial judge shall rule upon any objection to any portion thereof and the recording shall be edited to reflect the rulings. The objections shall be presented to the trial judge and the editing to reflect the rulings shall be accomplished, each in accordance with the provisions of Rule 30A(g).

(4) *Part of the Record; Not an Exhibit.* Any portion of the audio-visual recording so introduced shall be part of the record, and subject to the provisions of Rule 30A(h), but not an exhibit.

(*l*) Costs. The reasonable expense of recording, editing, and using an audio-visual deposition may be taxed as costs, pursuant to the provisions of Rule 54(e).

(m) Audio–Visual Depositions of Treating Physicians and Expert Witnesses for Use at Trial.

(1) *Authorization and Definitions.* Unless the court upon motion orders otherwise, any party intending to call a treating physician or expert witness at trial as that party's own witness may take the oral deposition of any such treating physician or expert witness by audio-visual means for the purpose of its being used as evidence at trial in lieu of oral testimony. Such depositions shall be known as "audio-visual expert witness depositions for trial." This rule 30A(m) does not apply to another party's treating physician or expert, discovery from whom is subject to the provisions of Rule 26(b)(4)(A) or 26(b)(4)(B). A "treating physician" is a physician who has provided medical treatment to a party or other person involved in the lawsuit, and who will be questioned about such treatment and matters related thereto. An "expert witness" is a person qualified as an expert by knowledge, skill, experience, training, or education to testify in the form of an opinion or otherwise.

(2) *Timing, Curriculum Vitae, and Report.* Except by leave of court, a notice for the taking of an audio-visual

expert witness deposition for trial shall not be served (i) sooner than six (6) months after the action has been commenced, and (ii) until thirty (30) days after a written report of that witness has been furnished to all parties. Such report shall contain a curriculum vitae of that witness, shall cover the subjects described in, Rule 26(b)(4)(A)(i) and, in the case of a treating physician, a description of the treatment and its costs. Any party may move for further discovery of that witness, to take place prior to the audio-visual expert witness deposition for trial, in accordance with Rule 26(b)(4)(A)(ii).

(3) *Notice; Opposition.* In addition to the requirements of rule 30A(b), every notice for the taking of an audio-visual expert witness deposition for trial shall state that it is to be recorded by audio-visual means with the purpose of its being used as evidence at trial in lieu of oral testimony. Any motion in opposition to the taking of an audio-visual expert witness deposition for trial must be filed within fourteen (14) days of receipt of the notice or on or before the specified time for taking of the audio-visual expert witness deposition for trial, if such time is less than fourteen (14) days from receipt of the notice. The audio-visual expert witness deposition shall not occur until the court rules on the motion opposing the deposition.

(4) *Ruling on Objections; Editing of Recording.* When an audio-visual expert witness deposition for trial is taken, all evidential objections shall, to the extent practicable, be made during the course of the deposition. If any party has made objections during the course of the audio-visual expert witness deposition for trial, or has any objections to such deposition which would otherwise be made at trial, pursuant to Rule 32(b), such objections shall be filed with the trial judge or a motion judge, if the trial judge has not yet been designated, no later than twenty-one (21) days before the commencement of the trial. Objections not so submitted shall be deemed waived, except to the extent that events at the trial, which could not have reasonably been foreseen by the objecting party, necessitate an objection at trial. The nonobjecting party shall file a response to the submissions by the objecting party within fourteen (14) days of the receipt of the objecting party's submissions. Failure to respond to an objection shall constitute a waiver with respect thereto. The party making the objection shall be responsible for providing the judge with a stenographic record of the deposition, unless it is already on file at the court, and, if the judge requests, with the audio-visual recording or an audio copy of the sound track. For the purpose of ruling on the objections, the judge may utilize the entire stenographic record, audio-visual recording, or audio recording, or those portions that are pertinent to the objections made. The judge shall rule on the objections prior to the commencement of trial or hearing and give notice to all parties of the rulings and instructions as to editing. The editing shall reflect the rulings of the judge and shall remove all references to the objections. The operator shall cause a copy of the audio-visual recording to be edited in accordance with the court's instructions. The operator shall then cause copies of the edited version thereof to be delivered to the parties who ordered them, and to the court, if so instructed by the court. The stenographic record, and the original audio-visual recording and the edited version thereof, if any, shall be preserved intact and unaltered.

(5) *Use at Trial.* Unless the court upon motion orders otherwise, an audio-visual expert witness deposition for trial may be used by any party for any purpose and under any circumstances in which a stenographic deposition may be used and, in addition, may be used at trial in lieu of oral testimony whether or not such witness is available to testify.

(6) *Applicability of Rule 30A(a)–(l).* Except as altered by Rule 30(A)(m), the provisions of rule 30A(a)–(*l*) shall apply to audio-visual expert witness depositions for trial.

Adopted December 16, 1980, effective January 1, 1981. Amended July 20, 1984, effective January 1, 1985; October 23, 1989, effective January 1, 1990; July 11, 2017, effective September 1, 2017.

Reporter's Notes—1984

This amendment permits a court to authorize in advance of trial, or at the trial, the use of an audio-visual recording as testimony or other evidence "in the interest of justice and with due regard to the importance of presenting the testimony of witnesses orally in open court." The major purpose of this rule is to permit judges to prevent the delay of trials which often occurs in order to accommodate the schedule of witnesses, particularly experts. Rule 30A(k)(3) makes the obtaining of rulings on objections and the editing of the audio-visual recordings subject to the provisions of 30A(g). Rule 30A(k)(4) provides that any portion of the audio-visual recording that is introduced "shall be part of the record, but not an exhibit." This is so testimony by audio-visual recording is not accorded more weight than live testimony. Rule 30A(k)(4) makes any portion of the audio-visual recording that is introduced subject to the transcription and marking provisions of Rule 30A(h).

Even without a Rule 30A(k)(1) order, one may still be able to use an audio-visual deposition at trial pursuant to the provisions of Rule 32(a). (See Rule 30A(i).)

Reporter's Notes—1989

These amendments accompany the simultaneous amendment adding Mass.R.Civ.P. 30A(m), which creates a new category of videotape depositions called "audio-visual expert depositions for trial." See Reporter's Notes to Proposed Amendment Adding Mass.R.Civ.P. 30A(m). That amendment will make audio-visual depositions a more frequent occurrence. In considering the addition of Rule 30A(m), it made sense to make some clarifications for all audio-visual depositions. The provisions of Rule 30A(a)–(*l*) apply to audio-visual expert depositions for trial except when altered by Rule 30A(m). Mass.R.Civ.P. 30A(m)(6).

The amendment to Mass.R.Civ.P. 30A(c) gives the party taking any audio-visual deposition the responsibility for assuring that the necessary equipment is available at the time the deposition is taken. The amendment to Mass.R.Civ.P. 30A(i) requires the party first using an audio-visual deposition in whole or in part to be responsible for providing the necessary play-back equipment for the use of all parties at such hearing, trial, or any other court proceeding or "at any rehearing, recess, or continuation thereof."

The amendment to Mass.R.Civ.P. 30A(d) adds to the recording officer's duties the obligation to assure "that the audio-visual tape records the witness in a standard fashion at all times during the deposition, unless all counsel agree otherwise, or unless on motion before the court, the court directs otherwise." The purpose is to make the audio-visual deposition as close as possible to what the fact-finder would see and hear if the witness were present in the courtroom.

Mass.R.Civ.P. 30A(c), (d), and (i) are otherwise left intact, except for appropriate changes to the titles in Rules 30(d) and (i) which reflect the additions.

The amendments borrow in part from a similar rule in South Carolina (S.C.Cir.Ct.Prac.R. 99C.(4) and 99K.).

Rule 30A deals generally with "Audio-visual Depositions and Audio-visual Evidence." This amendment adds a new set of provisions dealing specifically with "Audio–Visual Depositions of Treating Physicians and Expert Witnesses for Use at Trial."

Delays in court have been a substantial problem in the Commonwealth. Many lawyers and judges believe that a major reason for the seeking and granting of continuances in the past has been the unavailability of expert witnesses and treating physicians on the day set for trial. Unlike Rule 30A(k)(1), which requires prior court approval for the use of audio-visual testimony at the trial, the amendment authorizes such use with respect to a party's own treating physicians and expert witnesses or neutral treating physicians and expert witnesses whom that party intends to call at trial as that party's own witness, regardless of whether the witness is available to testify in person, unless the court orders otherwise. Rule 30A(m)(5). The goals are to eliminate a major reason for continuances; to facilitate intelligent settlement, since the lawyers will know in advance that the testimony of such expert or treating physician will be available for the trial; and to aid physicians and other experts in more predictably scheduling and efficiently utilizing their time.

The amendment does not apply to "another party's treating physician or expert, discovery from whom is subject to the provisions of Rule 26(b)(4)(A) or 26(b)(4)(B)." Rule 30(m)(1).

The amendment covers both treating physicians and experts, because there may be occasions when a treating physician's testimony relates only to observable facts and not expert opinion. The amendment's inclusion of the treating physician, whether or not the physician's testimony is technically that of an expert, should both help to eliminate disputes over the boundary between fact and opinion and to meet the other goals of the amendment, such as eliminating a major reason for continuances.

Because such audio-visual testimony is in lieu of live testimony, the amendment contains a number of protections for the opposing party, e.g., notice in advance that the audio-visual deposition is for the "purpose of its being used as evidence at trial in lieu of oral testimony" (Rule 30A(m)(3)); the requirement that a curriculum vitae and a report covering "the substance of the facts and opinions to which the expert is expected to testify and a summary of the grounds for each opinion," and, in the case of a treating physician, providing a description of the treatment and its costs, be furnished to all parties at least thirty days before such audio-visual deposition (Rule 30A(m)(2)); the ability to move for a discovery deposition prior to the audio-visual expert witness deposition (Rule 30A(m)(2)); the ability to move to oppose the deposition before it is taken, with the deposition stayed until the court rules on the motion (Rule 30A(m)(3)); and detailed provisions for the ruling on objections and the editing of the audio-visual recording (Rule 30A(m)(4)).

Rule 30A(m)(5) permits a party either to use live testimony of the treating physician or expert, or the audio-visual expert witness deposition for trial, but not both. However, if a party chooses to use the live testimony of the witness, the opponent may still cross-examine and use portions of the audio-visual expert witness deposition for trial for appropriate purposes.

Except where this amendment changes the audio-visual deposition rules for this specific type of deposition for use at trial, the remaining provisions of Rule 30A apply. Rule 30A(m)(6). Consequently, all of Rule 30A applies to audio-visual expert witness depositions for trial, except the first sentence of Rule 30A(a) (requiring prior leave of court or stipulation of all parties to authorize the deposition), the provisions of Rule 30A(g) (Rulings on Objections, Editing of Recording), and Rule 30A(k)(1)(2)(3) (Evidence by Audio–Visual Recording). Rule 30A(k)(4), making any portion of an audio-visual recording introduced at the trial part of the record, but not an exhibit, is applicable to audio-visual expert witness depositions for trial. Although Rule 30A(b)

(Notice) is applicable to Rule 30A(m) depositions, Rule 30A(m)(2) adds an additional requirement related to the timing of such deposition (requirement of written report) and Rule 30A(m)(3) requires additional information in the notice for the taking of such deposition.

There may be occasions when a party becomes aware of the need for an audio-visual deposition of a treating physician or expert witness at a time too close to trial to permit compliance with all of the provisions of Rule 30A(m). The discretionary motions under Rule 30A(a) and 30A(k)(1), and the court's authorization under Rule 30A(k)(2), remain available to meet such emergency situations.

The amendment borrows in part from a similar rule in New Jersey (N.J.Civ.Prac.R. 4:14–9) and from a paragraph of the South Carolina videotaped deposition rule (S.C.Cir.Ct.Prac.R. 99 I.). The definition of "expert witness" (30A(m)(1)) is derived from a portion of Fed.R.Evid. 702 and Proposed Mass.R.Evid. 702.

Reporter's Notes—1996

With the merger of the District Court civil rules into the Mass. R.Civ.P., Rule 30A of the Mass.R.Civ.P. governing audio-visual depositions is made applicable to District Court proceedings.

Reporter's Notes—2017

Since the 1980s, the Massachusetts Rules of Civil Procedure have provided for two types of audio-visual depositions. The first is an audio-visual deposition by leave of court or by stipulation of the parties under Rule 30A(a)–(k). The second is an "audio-visual expert witness deposition for trial" under Rule 30A(m). Rule 30A(m) allows a party to depose a treating physician or expert witness whom the party intends to call at trial as his or her own witness without the need to obtain leave of court or a stipulation and to use that deposition at trial in lieu of live testimony. Rule 30A(m) does not apply to another party's treating physician or expert.

The 2017 amendments to Rule 30 and Rule 30A deal with the first type of audio-visual deposition and make no change to the Rule 30A(m) deposition. The changes allow audio-visual depositions as a matter of right, making Massachusetts practice consistent with the approach in other jurisdictions and consistent with the Federal Rules of Civil Procedure. The amendments recognize the advantages of audio-visual depositions in addition to written transcripts of depositions.

Rule 30A(a). Rule 30A(a) allows a party as a matter of right to record a deposition by stenographic and audio-visual means. The party who chooses to have testimony recorded by stenographic and audio-visual means is required to bear the cost of the audio-visual recording. A party who requests a copy of the audio-visual recording is required to bear the cost of a copy of the recording.

Rule 30A(b). Prior to amendment, Rule 30A(b) precluded service of a notice of taking of an audio-visual deposition prior to six months after commencement of the action. The six-month provision has been deleted by virtue of the 2017 amendments.

Rule 31.   Depositions of Witnesses Upon Written Questions

(a) Serving Questions; Notice. After commencement of the action, any party may take the testimony of any person, including a party, by deposition upon written questions. The attendance of witnesses may be compelled by the use of subpoena as provided in Rule 45. The deposition of a person confined in prison may be taken only by leave of court on such terms as the court prescribes.

A party desiring to take a deposition upon written questions shall serve them upon every other party with a notice stating (1) the name and address of the person who is to answer them, if known, and if the name is not known, a general description sufficient to identify him or the particular class or group to which he belongs, and (2) the name or descriptive title and address of the officer before whom the deposition is to be taken. A deposition upon written questions may be taken of a public or private corporation or a partnership or association or governmental agency in accordance with the provisions of Rule 30(b)(6).

Within 30 days after the notice and written questions are served, a party may serve cross questions upon all other parties. Within 10 days after being served with cross questions, a party may serve redirect questions upon all other parties. Within 10 days after being served with redirect questions, a party may serve recross questions upon all other parties. The court may for cause shown enlarge or shorten the time.

(b) Officer to Take Responses and Prepare Record. A copy of the notice and copies of all questions served shall be delivered by the party taking the deposition to the officer designated in the notice, who shall proceed promptly, in the manner provided by Rule 30(c), (e), and (f), to take the testimony of the witness in response to the questions and to prepare, certify, and deliver or send the deposition to the party taking the deposition, attaching thereto the copy of the notice and questions received by him.

(c) Notice of Receipt. When the deposition is received the party taking it shall promptly give notice thereof to all other parties.

Amended January 30, 1989, effective March 1, 1989.

Reporter's Notes—1973

Rule 31, a copy of Federal Rule 31, governs the little-used practice of conducting a deposition on written interrogatories, a process which has been aptly described as washing one's hands without removing one's gloves.

Reporter's Notes—1989

This amendment is necessitated by the amendment to Mass.R.Civ.P. 5(d). Since depositions will no longer be filed in court, except as otherwise ordered by the court, this amendment requires the officer who takes responses at depositions upon written questions to "deliver or send the deposition to the party taking the deposition." Rule 31(b). The party who took the deposition is required promptly to notify all other parties of receipt of the deposition from the officer. Rule 31(c). See, also, Reporter's Notes to the Amendment to Rule 5(d).

Rule 32. Use of Depositions in Court Proceedings

(a) Use of Depositions. At the trial or upon the hearing of a motion or an interlocutory proceeding, any part or all of a deposition, so far as admissible under the rules of evidence applied as though the witness were then present and testifying, may be used against any party who was present or represented at the taking of the deposition or who had due notice thereof, in accordance with any one of the following provisions:

(1) Any deposition may be used by any party for the purpose of contradicting or impeaching the testimony of deponent as a witness.

(2) The deposition of a party or of any one who at the time of taking the deposition was an officer, director, or managing agent, or a person designated under Rule 30(b)(6) or 31(a) to testify on behalf of a public or private corporation, partnership or association or governmental agency which is a party may be used by an adverse party for any purpose.

(3) The deposition of a witness, whether or not a party, may be used by any party for any purpose if the court finds: (A) that the witness is dead; or (B) that the witness is out of the Commonwealth, unless it appears that the absence of the witness was procured by the party offering the deposition; or (C) that the witness is unable to attend or testify because of age, sickness, infirmity, or imprisonment; or (D) that the party offering the deposition has been unable to procure the attendance of the witness by subpoena; or (E) upon application and notice, that such exceptional circumstances exist as to make it desirable, in the interest of justice and with due regard to the importance of presenting the testimony of witnesses orally in open court, to allow the deposition to be used.

(4) If only part of a deposition is offered in evidence by a party, an adverse party may require him to introduce any other part which ought in fairness to be considered with the part introduced, and any party may introduce any other parts.

Substitution of parties pursuant to Rule 25 does not affect the right to use depositions previously taken; and when an action has been brought in any court of the United States or of any state and another action involving the same subject matter is afterward brought between the same parties or their representatives or successors in interest, all depositions lawfully taken and duly filed in the former action may be used in the latter as if originally taken therefor.

(b) Objections to Admissibility. Subject to the provisions of Rules 28(b) and subdivision (d)(3) of this rule, objection may be made at the trial or hearing to receiving in evidence any deposition or part thereof for any reason which would require the exclusion of the evidence if the witness were then present and testifying.

(c) Effect of Taking or Using Depositions. A party does not make a person his own witness for any purpose by taking his deposition. The introduction in evidence of the deposition or any part thereof for any purpose other than that of contradicting or impeaching the deponent makes the deponent the witness of the party introducing the deposition, but this shall not apply to the use by an adverse party of a deposition under subdivision (a)(2) of this rule. At the trial or hearing any party may rebut any relevant evidence contained in a deposition whether introduced by him or by any other party.

(d) Effect of Errors and Irregularities in Depositions.

(1) *As to Notice.* All errors and irregularities in the notice for taking a deposition are waived unless written objection is promptly served upon the party giving the notice.

(2) *As to Disqualification of Officer.* Objection to taking a deposition because of disqualification of the officer before whom it is to be taken is waived unless made before the taking of the deposition begins or as soon thereafter as the disqualification becomes known or could be discovered with reasonable diligence.

(3) *As to Taking of Deposition.*

(A) Objections to the competency of a witness or to the competency, relevancy, or materiality of testimony are not waived by failure to make them before or during the taking of the deposition, unless the ground of the objection is one which might have been obviated or removed if presented at that time.

(B) Errors and irregularities occurring at the oral examination in the manner of taking the deposition, in the form of the questions or answers, in the oath or affirmation, or in the conduct of parties, and errors of any kind which might be obviated, removed, or cured if promptly presented, are waived unless seasonable objection thereto is made at the taking of the deposition.

(C) Objections to the form of written questions submitted under Rule 31 are waived unless served in writing upon the party propounding them within the time allowed for serving the succeeding cross or other questions and within 5 days after service of the last questions authorized.

(4) *As to Completion and Return of Deposition.* Errors and irregularities in the manner in which the testimony is transcribed or the deposition is prepared, signed, certified, sealed, indorsed, transmitted, filed, or otherwise dealt with by the officer under Rules 30 and 31 are waived unless a motion to suppress the deposition or some part thereof is made with reasonable promptness after such defect is, or with due diligence might have been, ascertained.

Amended October 27, 1981, effective January 1, 1982; April 25, 1984, effective July 1, 1984.

Reporter's Notes—1973

Rule 32 tracks Federal Rule 32, as amended, and substantially embodies S.J.C. Rule 3:15, which was in turn based upon the un-amended Federal Rule 32. It sets out the procedure for use of depositions in court. In general, and subject to substantive evidentiary objections, a deposition can be used without limit for purposes of impeaching the deponent if he testifies in court; the deposition of a party can be used without limit (including the proof of the adverse party's case) by an adverse party; the deposition of a justifiably absent witness may be used for any purpose. Rule 32(a)(4) protects against unfair piecemeal use of a deposition. The rest of Rule 32 sets out in detail the preservation of objections.

Reporter's Notes—1984

Before this amendment, Mass.R.Civ.P. 32(a)(3)(B) permitted a deposition to be "used by any party for any purpose if the court finds: . . . (B) that the witness is at a greater distance than 100 miles from the place of trial or hearing, or is out of the United States, unless it appears that the absence of the witness was procured by the party offering the deposition . . ." This prior language was taken from the Fed.R.Civ.P. The amendment changes the text to "out of the Commonwealth" because the "out of the United States" language is inappropriate for a state system. Moreover, the state boundaries, which also delimit the subpoena power, provide a more logical and easier test to apply than "100 miles."

Rule 33. Interrogatories to Parties

(a) Availability: Procedures for Use.

(1) *In General.* Any party may serve upon any other party written interrogatories to be answered by the party served or, if the party served is a public or private corporation or a partnership or association or governmental agency, by any officer or agent, who shall furnish such information as is available to the party. Interrogatories may, without leave of court, be served upon the plaintiff after commencement of the action and upon any other party with or after service of the summons and complaint upon that party.

(2) *Number.* No party shall serve upon any other party as of right more than thirty interrogatories, including interrogatories subsidiary or incidental to, or dependent upon, other interrogatories, and however the same may be grouped or combined; but the interrogatories may be served in two or more sets, as long as the total number of interrogatories served does not exceed thirty. The court on motion for good cause shown may allow service of additional interrogatories; or the party interrogated, subject to Rule 29, may agree to such service. All interrogatories shall be numbered consecutively.

(3) *Answers; Final Request for Answers.* Each interrogatory shall be answered separately and fully in writing under the penalties of perjury, unless it is objected to, in which event the reasons for objection shall be stated in lieu of the answer; each answer or objection shall be preceded by the interrogatory to which it responds. The answers are to be signed by the person making them, the objections by the person or attorney making them. The party upon whom the interrogatories have been served shall serve answers and objections, if any, within 45 days after the service of the interrogatories. The court may, on motion with or without notice, specify a shorter or longer time. Unless otherwise specified, further answers to interrogatories shall be served within 30 days of the entry of the order to answer further. The interrogating party may move for an order under Rule 37(a) with respect to any objection to or other failure to answer an interrogatory. Alternatively, for failure to serve timely answers or objections to interrogatories (or further answers, as the case may be), the interrogating party may serve a final request for answers, specifying the failure. The final request for answers shall state that the interrogating party may apply for final judgment for relief or dismissal pursuant to paragraph 4 in the event that answers or objections are not timely received. The party upon whom the interrogatories have been served shall serve the answers or objections either within 30 days from the date of service of the final request or prior to the filing of an application for a final judgment for relief or dismissal, whichever is later.

(4) *Application for Final Judgment; Affidavit.* In the event that answers or objections have not been received and after the expiration of 40 days from the date of service of the final request for answers, or such further time as the parties may agree upon in writing or the court may allow, the interrogating party may file a written application for entry of final judgment for relief or dismissal. The period of time set forth in the previous sentence shall be deemed to include the three-day period allowed pursuant to Rule 6(d). The application must be accompanied by a copy of the final request for answers and an affidavit containing the following information:

a. the date and manner in which interrogatories were served on the party against whom relief is sought;

b. the fact that the 45–day time period for service of answers or objections has expired, and no answers have been received;

c. the date and manner in which the final request for answers was served;

d. the fact that the 40–day time period for answers or objections after a final request for answers has expired, and that no answers or objections have been received; and

e. that the party now applies for final judgment for relief or dismissal.

(5) Motion to Extend. The pendency of a motion to extend any time hereunder, unless the motion be assented to, or heard within 30 days of filing, shall not stay the entry of any judgment.

(6) Entry of Judgment. Upon receipt of the application for final judgment and only if accompanied by a copy of the final request for answers and by the required affidavit as set forth above, the clerk shall enter an appropriate judgment, subject to the provisions of Rules 54(b), 54(c), 55(b)(1), 55(b)(2) (final sentence), 55(b)(4) and 55(c).

(b) Scope: Use at Trial. Interrogatories may relate to any matters which can be inquired into under Rule 26(b), and the answers may be used to the extent permitted by the rules of evidence.

An interrogatory otherwise proper is not necessarily objectionable merely because an answer to the interrogatory involves an opinion or contention that relates to fact or the application of law to fact, but the court may order that such an interrogatory need not be answered until after designated discovery has been completed, or until a pretrial conference, or other later time.

(c) Option to Produce Business Records. Where the answer to an interrogatory may be derived or ascertained from the business records of the party upon whom the interrogatory has been served or from an examination, audit or inspection of such business records, including a compilation, abstract or summary thereof, and the burden of deriving or ascertaining the answer is substantially the same for the party serving the interrogatory as for the party served, it is a sufficient answer to such interrogatory to specify the records from which the answer may be derived or ascertained and to afford to the party serving the interrogatory reasonable opportunity to examine, audit or inspect such records and to make copies, compilations, abstracts or summaries. A specification shall be in sufficient detail to permit the interrogating party to locate and to identify, as readily as can the party served, the records from which the answer may be ascertained.

Amended June 27, 1974, effective July 1, 1974; September 16, 1975, effective January 1, 1976; October 27, 1981, effective January 1, 1982; March 5, 2002, effective May 1, 2002; June 24, 2009, effective August 1, 2009.

Reporter's Notes—1973

Rule 33 governs interrogatory practice. It changes Massachusetts practice slightly.

Interrogatories may be served, as of right, by the *defendant* at any time after commencement of the action (i.e., after filing of the complaint; see Rule 3); by the *plaintiff* simultaneously with, or after, service of summons and complaint upon the defendant to whom the interrogatories are addressed.

The Massachusetts thirty-interrogatory limit, G.L. c. 231, § 61, has been adopted, with one important modification: the permitted thirty interrogatories may be divided into "sets", provided that the total number of interrogatories served may never exceed thirty. This modification changes the rule that a "party shall not interrogate an

adverse party more than once unless the court otherwise orders." G.L. c. 231, § 63. The following examples illustrate what is permitted and what is forbidden:

Case # 1:   Three sets, each with 10 interrogatories. *Permissible.*

Case # 2:   Four sets, three of six interrogatories, one of 12. *Permissible.*

Case # 3:   Two sets, one of 16 interrogatories, one of 15. *Impermissible* without court order. In the absence of such order, the clerk will, upon the application of the party being interrogated, strike the second set; the interrogating party may then prepare, serve, and file a set of 14 interrogatories or less (i.e., so that his total is reduced to thirty or less).

Rule 33 also liberalizes the Massachusetts practice concerning failure to answer interrogatories. Super.Ct. Rule 36; see also Super.Ct. Rule 27. Under Rule 33, a party has thirty days as of right to answer interrogatories. Upon his failure to answer, the interrogating party may file a verified application, which in turn causes the clerk to notify all parties that unless answers are filed within an additional 30 days, a dismissal or judgment shall be entered. If the answers are not on file by the end of thirty days, the dismissal or judgment shall be entered, subject to vacation as of course by the clerk if answers are filed within 20 additional days. (The parties, by agreement, or the court, on motion with notice, may enlarge or shorten any of these times, or may vacate the dismissal or judgment.)

It should be observed that under Rule 33 the guillotine for refusal to answer interrogatories does not fall until:

	30 days originally to answer,
plus	30 days after first notice,
plus	20 days after notice of conditional dismissal or judgment
total	80 days.

Further, entry of judgment is governed by Rule 55, which requires a hearing on the issue of damages, of which hearing the defendant is entitled to an additional 7 days' notice.

Dismissal, which is the equivalent under these rules of the old nonsuit, does not entail the same consequences as judgment (the equivalent of the old default), hence no additional hearing need be held.

One final aspect of Rule 33 is notable. Under Rule 33(c) a party whose answer depends on an examination of business records may, in lieu of answering, offer the interrogating party the right to inspect the records and derive his own answer. This privilege is conditioned upon an equality of bother. Only if the bother of deriving the information would be substantially the same for both parties may the party interrogated shift the burden to his opponent; otherwise, he may not. This procedure is taken verbatim from amended Federal Rule 33(c).

Reporter's Notes—1975

In order to simplify the policing of interrogatory practice, Rule 33(a) has been amended to establish a more rational procedure. The basic period for answering original interrogatories will now be 45 days after service, although the court may order a longer or shorter time. If the court has ordered further answers to interrogatories, they must be filed within 30 days of the entry of the order, unless the court specifies otherwise. (The original Rule 33(a) provided no deadline for filing further answers to interrogatories after court order.) If at the expiration of allowed time the original answers or further answers have not been filed, the interrogating party may, at his option, move for an order under Rule 37. In most cases, however, the party will take advantage of the simplified procedure established by Rule 33(a). He will file a written application with the clerk asking (if he is plaintiff) for the relief sought in the complaint, or (if he is defendant) for dismissal of the action. The clerk, upon receipt, notifies all parties; within 30 days from the date of the notice, the interrogating party may again apply in writing, and the appropriate final judgment will be entered. The judgment will be treated as a default judgment; if the plaintiff is the prevailing party, judgment will be entered in the amount prayed for, provided it can be ascertained by inspection of the complaint or by a ready computation. In other cases, the court will hold a hearing to establish the amount of damages.

Rule 33(a) thus gives a party, in the case of original interrogatories, 75 days, and in the case of further answers, 60 days, to file answers before the guillotine can fall. And even then, the dilatory party may file a motion to extend his time to answer. So long as that motion is heard within 30 days of filing, it too can stave off the judgment. On the other hand, the mere filing of a motion to extend time does not, as in the past, of itself stay the entry of any judgment. However, even after a judgment has been entered, Rule 33(a), by specific reference to Rule 55(c), allows a party to seek to have the judgment vacated, provided he can fit through one of the limited openings afforded by Rule 60(b).

In originally answering interrogatories, the responding party has 45 days, and in which to *serve* a copy of the answers and objections; because service is complete upon mailing, Mass.R.Civ.P.5(b), this means that he need only place the answers in the mail before the deadline. In furnishing further answers to interrogatories, however, he is obligated not merely to serve them within 30 days after the entry of the order for further answers, but actually to file them in the clerk's office by that time. This means that he must ensure that the further answers are in the clerk's hands on or before the deadline date. This same requirement applies to the 30—day grace period after the original 45—day (or in the case of further answers to interrogatories 30—day) period has expired. To avoid the entry of the appropriate final judgment, the delinquent party must cause his answers to be *filed* * the clerk's office; mere mailing by that time does not suffice. Indeed, in each of these situations, even early mailing may not be enough if, through any inadvertence (including an error by the postal service), see Pierce v. Board of Appeals of Carver, 3 Mass.App.Ct. 352, 329 N.E.2d 774, 777 (1975), the paper is not at the clerk's office, indeed actually filed there, Hackney v. Butler, 339 Mass. 605, 609, 162 N.E.2d 68, 71 (1959).

The revision changes Rule 33(a) in three other minor ways:

(1) As before, a party must answer each interrogatory or precisely state his reasons for objecting to it. Now, however, when preparing the response, the responding party must place each respective interrogatory on the paper, so that it immediately precedes the answer or objection to which it responds.

(2) The revision makes explicit that after serving a copy of the answers (or objections) on the interrogating party within the appropriate period, the responding party must file the original (i.e. ribbon copy) with the court.

(3) Unlike original Rule 33(a), the revision establishes a definite initial period (30 days) for furnishing court-ordered further answers. In all other respects, the obligation to supply further answers must conform to the same procedural requirements which govern original answers.

Reporter's Notes to Amendment to Rule 33(a)—2002

In 2002, Rule 5(d) was amended to provide that interrogatories under Rule 33 and answers and objections to interrogatories no longer were to be filed in court, unless otherwise ordered by the court. The non-filing requirement of amended Rule 5(d) necessitated changes in the Rule 33 procedure by which a party who has served interrogatories seeks to have judgment entered against another party for failure to respond to the interrogatories.

Prior to the 2002 amendment, Rule 33(a) provided that a party upon whom interrogatories had been served must serve answers (and any

objections) within 45 days of service and must file the original answers in court. If answers were not served within the 45–day period, the interrogating party had the option of filing with the court an application requesting final judgment for relief or dismissal. The filing of the application then triggered a 30–day period for filing of the answers. If answers were not filed within the 30–day period, the interrogating party could then file a reapplication for final judgment for relief or dismissal. After a reapplication had been filed and upon determination by the clerk that the answers had not been filed, the clerk would then enter a final judgment.

The 2002 amendment adopts a procedure, taken in part from Superior Court Administrative Directive No. 91–1, for obtaining judgment for failure to answer interrogatories that takes into account that the clerk of court will now be unable to determine whether the interrogatories have been answered (because answers are no longer to be filed with the court).

The 2002 amendment also added subdivisions and headings to Rule 33(a).

Rule 33(a)(1), entitled "In General." There has been no change to the first paragraph of former Rule 33(a), other than the addition of the number (1) and the title.

Rule 33(a)(2), entitled "Number." Likewise, there has been no change to the second paragraph of former Rule 33(a), other than the addition of the number (2) and the title.

The third and fourth paragraphs of Rule 33(a) are rewritten as follows.

Rule 33(a)(3), entitled "Answers; Final Request for Answers." The revised rule provides that if answers or objections are not served within 45 days, the interrogating party may *serve* (but not file) a *final request for answers*. (The former language requiring a written application for final judgment has been changed to take into account that under the revised procedure, there is no filing made in the clerk's office at this point.) The final request must also contain a notice that the interrogating party intends to apply for final judgment, thereby putting the latter on notice of the serious consequences of a failure to answer the interrogatories. The act of serving the request on the interrogated party will trigger an additional 30–day period for the interrogated party to answer or object.

Rule 33(a)(4), entitled "Application for Final Judgment; Affidavit." Rule 33(a)(4) provides that if answers or objections to the interrogatories still have not been received and 40 days have expired from the date of service of the final request for answers, the interrogating party may *file* a written application (under the former procedure, referred to as a reapplication) for final judgment for relief or dismissal. A copy of the application must also be served on each party to the case (see Rule 5(a)). In calculating the 40–day period set forth in Rule 33(a)(4), the additional three days that otherwise would be granted under Rule 6(d) after service by mail are not to be included. The application must be accompanied by a copy of the final request that had been earlier served on the interrogated party and an affidavit containing specified information setting forth the chronology leading up to the application. As long as a copy of the final request for answers and the requisite affidavit have been filed, the clerk shall then enter judgment for relief or dismissal (see Rule 33(a)(6)).

The 2002 amendments also eliminated the provision that an agreement to extend the time for answering be filed in court. Given the non-filing requirements for interrogatories and answers, this provision is now unnecessary.

Rule 33(a)(5), entitled "Motion to Extend." There has been no change to the text of this paragraph (formerly the last paragraph of Rule 33(a)), other than the addition of the number (5) and the title.

Rule 33(a)(6), entitled "Entry of Judgment." Rule 33(a)(6) is drawn from the final sentence of the former fourth paragraph of Rule 33(a), with some housekeeping changes designed to correct an omission made in 1996 when the District Court rules were merged into the

Massachusetts Rules of Civil Procedure. In connection with the merger in 1996, certain paragraph numbers in Rule 55(b) were changed, but corresponding changes were not made to the references to Rule 55(b) that were contained in Rule 33(a).

* Probably should read "in the clerk's office".

Reporter's Notes—2009

Amendments to Rule 55(b) effective March 1, 2008 eliminated differing default provisions for the Superior Court and the District Court and resulted in changes to the numbering of some of the subparagraphs of Rule 55(b). The March 2008 amendments were part of a group of amendments to the Massachusetts Rules of Civil Procedure in light of the adoption of the statewide one-trial system for civil cases.

The 2009 amendment to Rule 33(a)(6) corrects an oversight in the March 2008 amendments by correcting the cross-references to Rule 55(b) that are found in Rule 33(a)(6).

Rule 34. Producing Documents, Electronically Stored Information, and Tangible Things, or Entering Onto Land, for Inspection and Other Purposes

(a) In General. A party may serve on any other party a request within the scope of Rule 26(b):

(1) to produce and permit the requesting party or its representative to inspect, copy, test, or sample the following items in the responding party's possession, custody, or control:

(A) any designated documents or electronically stored information — including writings, drawings, graphs, charts, photographs, sound recordings, images and other data or data compilations—stored in any medium from which information can be obtained either directly or, if necessary, after translation by the responding party into a reasonably usable form; or

(B) any designated tangible things; or

(2) to permit entry onto designated land or other property possessed or controlled by the responding party, so that the requesting party may inspect, measure, survey, photograph, test, or sample the property or any designated object or operation on it.

(b) Procedure.

(1) *Contents of the Request.* The request may, without leave of court, be served upon the plaintiff after commencement of the action and upon any other party with or after service of the summons and complaint upon that party. The request shall set forth the items to be inspected either by individual item or by category, and describe each item and category with reasonable particularity. The request shall specify a reasonable time, place, and manner of making the inspection and performing the related acts, and it may specify the form in which electronically stored information is to be produced.

(2) *Responses and Objections.*

(A) *In General.* The party upon whom the request is served shall serve a written response within 30 days after the service of the request, except that a defendant may serve a response within 45 days after service of the summons and complaint upon that defendant. The court may allow a shorter or longer time. The response shall state, with respect to each item or category, that inspection and related activities will be permitted as requested, unless the request is objected to, in which event the reasons for objection shall be stated. If objection is made to part of an item or category, the part shall be specified. The party submitting the request may move for an order under Rule 37(a) with respect to any objection to or other failure to respond to the request or any part thereof, or any failure to permit inspection as requested.

(B) *Responding to a request for production of electronically stored information.* The response may state an objection to a requested form for producing electronically stored information. If the responding party objects to a requested form — or if no form was specified in the request — the party shall state the form or forms it intends to use.

(C) *Producing the documents or electronically stored information.* Unless otherwise stipulated or ordered by the court, these procedures apply to producing documents or electronically stored information:

(i) A party shall produce documents as they are kept in the usual course of business or shall organize and label them to correspond to the categories in the request;

(ii) The producing party may produce copies of the documents, including by electronic means, provided that, if requested, the producing party affords all parties a fair opportunity to verify the copies by comparison with the originals.

(iii) If a request does not specify a form for producing electronically stored information, a party shall produce it in a form or forms in which it is ordinarily maintained or in a reasonably usable form or forms; and

(iv) A party need not produce the same electronically stored information in more than one form.

(c) Persons Not Parties.

(1) This rule does not preclude an independent action against a person not a party for production of documents and things and permission to enter upon land.

(2) As provided in Rule 45, a nonparty may be compelled to produce documents and tangible things or to permit an inspection.

Amended October 27, 1981, effective January 1, 1982; September 24, 2013, effective January 1, 2014; June 29, 2016, effective August 1, 2016.

Reporter's Notes—1973

Rule 34 copies Federal Rule 34, which in turn changed earlier Federal Rule 34 and S.J.C. Rule 3:15. Previously, a party seeking discovery of documents or objects was required to move for a court order compelling such discovery. Under Rule 34, the party seeking discovery need merely serve a request upon his opponent. Only if the opponent objects to the request must the discovering party obtain a court order.

Reporter's Notes—2014

The 2014 amendments to Rule 34 were part of a series of amendments concerning discovery of electronically stored information. For background, see the 2014 Reporter's Notes to Rule 26.

The title to Rule 34 has been changed to add a reference to "electronically stored information". The title to Rule 34 is now consistent with the title to Rule 34 of the Federal Rules of Civil Procedure.

The 2014 amendments made some stylistic changes in Rule 34(a) so as to conform the rule to the format set forth in Rule 34(a) of the Federal Rules of Civil Procedure. In addition, the phrase "or electronically stored information" has been added to Rule 34(a)(1)(A), also in conformity with the cognate federal rule.

Formatting and stylistic changes have been made in Rule 34(b), again modeled after Rule 34(b) of the Federal Rules of Civil Procedure, but no substantive changes were intended. Language has been added to Rule 34(b)(1) to the effect that a request for production "may specify the form in which electronically stored information is to be produced."

Rule 34(b)(2)(B) and (C), modeled after Federal Rule 34(b)(2)(D) and (E), have been added to deal with responding to a request for production of electronically stored information and the important aspect of the form for producing such information.

Issues surrounding the production of electronically stored information, including the format for production, should be discussed by the parties in their conference regarding electronically stored information, if there is one. See Rule 26(f)(2).

Reporter's Notes—2016

Rule 34 was amended in 2016 to recognize the common practice of producing copies of documents rather than permitting inspection of the originals (Rule 34(b)(2)(C)(ii)). This amendment reflects a similar amendment to the Federal Rules of Civil Procedure effective in 2015.

The 2016 amendment further states that upon request, the producing party shall provide "all parties a fair opportunity to verify the copies by comparison with the originals." This language, which is not part of the Federal Rules, reinforces the requesting party's right to inspect the original documents under the existing language of Rule 34(a). To the extent that producing the original is deemed unduly burdensome or expensive, the producing party may seek a protective order under Rule 26(c). Such an order may restrict access to the original document, or may allow access upon payment of costs associated with production of the original.

Rule 34(c) was also amended to add a cross-reference to Rule 45 (Rule 34(c)(2)). Rule 45 had been amended in 2015 to allow a "documents only" subpoena against a nonparty (Rule 45(d)).

Rule 35. Physical and Mental Examination of Persons

(a) Order for Examination. When the mental or physical condition (including the blood group) of a party, or of a person in the custody or under the legal control of a party, is in controversy, the court in which the action is pending may order the party to submit to a physical or mental examination by a physician or to produce for examination the person in his custody or legal control. The order may be made only on motion for good cause shown and upon notice to the person to be examined and to all parties and shall specify the time, place, manner, conditions, and scope of the examination and the person or persons by whom it is to be made.

(b) Report of Examining Physician.

(1) If requested by the party against whom an order is made under Rule 35(a) or the person examined, the party causing the examination to be made shall deliver to him a copy of a detailed written report of the examining physician setting out his findings, including results of all tests made, diagnoses and conclusions, together with like reports of all earlier examinations of the same condition. After delivery the party caus-

ing the examination shall be entitled upon request to receive from the party against whom the order is made a like report of any examination, previously or thereafter made, of the same condition, unless, in the case of a report of examination of a person not a party, the party shows that he is unable to obtain it. The court on motion may make an order against a party requiring delivery of a report on such terms as are just, and if a physician fails or refuses to make a report the court may exclude his testimony if offered at the trial.

(2) By requesting and obtaining a report of the examination so ordered or by taking the deposition of the examiner, the party examined waives any privilege he may have in that action or any other involving the same controversy, regarding the testimony of every other person who has examined or may thereafter examine him in respect of the same mental or physical condition; but he does not otherwise waive his right to object at the trial to the introduction into evidence of the report or any part thereof.

(3) This subdivision applies to examinations made by agreement of the parties, unless the agreement expressly provides otherwise. This subdivision does not preclude discovery of a report of an examining physician or the taking of a deposition of the physician in accordance with the provisions of any other rule.

Reporter's Notes—1973

Rule 35 tracks Federal Rule 35 (as amended). The general procedural framework remains identical to that under S.J.C. 3:15. No one need submit to a physical examination except upon a court order granted only "for good cause shown". If the person examined obtains from the discovering party a copy of the report of the examination (which he is entitled to do, as of right), the discovering party is entitled to any reports of any other examination (prior or subsequent) pertaining to the same condition which the person examined may have.

Rule 36. Requests for Admission

(a) Request for Admission. A party may serve upon any other party a written request for admission, for purposes of the pending action, only, of the truth of any matters within the scope of Rule 26(b) set forth in the request that relate to statements or opinions of fact or of the application of law to fact, including the genuineness of any documents described in the request. Copies of documents shall be served with the request unless they have been or are otherwise furnished or made available for inspection and copying. The request may, without leave of court, be served upon the plaintiff after commencement of the action and upon any other party with or after service of the summons and complaint upon that party.

Each matter of which an admission is requested shall be separately set forth. The matter is admitted unless, within 30 days after service of the request, or within such shorter or longer time as the court may allow, the party to whom the request is directed serves upon the party requesting the admission either (1) a written statement signed by the party under the penalties of perjury specifically (i) denying the matter or (ii) setting forth in detail why the answering party cannot truthfully admit or deny the matter; or (2) a written objection addressed to the matter, signed by the party or his attorney, but, unless the court shortens the time, a defendant shall not be required to serve answers or objections before the expiration of 45 days after service of the summons and complaint upon him. If objection is made, the reasons therefor shall be stated. A denial shall fairly meet the substance of the requested admission, and when good faith requires that a party qualify his answer or deny only a part of the matter of which an admission is requested, he shall specify so much of it as is true and qualify or deny the remainder. An answering party may not give lack of information or knowledge as a reason for failure to admit or deny unless he states that he has made reasonable inquiry and that the information known or readily obtainable by him is insufficient to enable him to admit or deny. A party who considers that a matter of which an admission has been requested presents a genuine issue for trial may not, on that ground alone, object to the request; he may, subject to the provisions of Rule 37(c), deny the matter or set forth reasons why he cannot admit or deny it. Each admission, denial, objection, or statement shall be preceded by the request to which it responds.

The party who has requested the admissions may move to determine the sufficiency of the answers or objections. Unless the court determines that an objection is justified, it shall order that an answer be served. If the court determines that an answer does not comply with the requirements of this rule, it may order either that the matter is admitted or that an amended answer be served. The court may, in lieu of these orders, determine that final disposition of the request be made at a pre-trial conference or at a designated time prior to trial. The provisions of Rule 37(a)(4) apply to the award of expenses incurred in relation to the motion.

(b) Effect of Admission. Any matter admitted under this rule is conclusively established unless the court on motion permits withdrawal or amendment of the admission. Subject to the provisions of Rule 16 governing amendment of a pre-trial order, the court may permit withdrawal or amendment when the presentation of the merits of the action will be subserved thereby and the party who obtained the admission fails to satisfy the court that withdrawal or amendment will prejudice him in maintaining his action or defense on the merits. Any admission made by a party under this rule is for the purpose of the pending action only and is not an admission by him for any other purpose nor may it be used against him in any other proceeding.

Reporter's Notes—1973

Rule 36, tracking amended Federal Rule 36, governs Requests for Admission, a procedure long familiar to Massachusetts practitioners as "Notices to Admit", G.L. c. 231, § 69. Although the matters subject to such request under Rule 36 are somewhat broader than those under the statute, Rule 36 should cause no difficulty; the expanded response period (30 days, as opposed to 10 under G.L. c. 231, § 69) should in fact permit more flexible use of this discovery device.

Rule 37. Failure to Make Discovery: Sanctions

(a) Motion for Order Compelling Discovery. Upon reasonable notice to other parties and all persons affected thereby, a party may apply for an order compelling discovery as follows:

(1) *Appropriate Court.* An application for an order to a party may be made to the court in which the action is pending, or on matters relating to a deposition, to the court in the county or judicial district, as the case may be, where the deposition is being taken. An application for an order to a deponent who is not a party shall be made to the court in the county or judicial district, as the case may be, where the deposition is being taken.

(2) *Motion.* If a deponent fails to answer a question propounded or submitted under Rules 30 or 31, or a corporation or other entity fails to make a designation under Rule 30(b)(6) or 31(a), or a party fails to answer an interrogatory submitted under Rule 33, or if a party, in response to a request for inspection submitted under Rule 34, fails to respond that inspection will be permitted as requested or fails to permit inspection as requested, the discovering party may move for an order compelling an answer or a designation or an order compelling inspection in accordance with the request. When taking a deposition on oral examination, the proponent of the question may complete or adjourn the examination before he applies for an order. If the court denies the motion in whole or in part, it may make such protective order as it would have been empowered to make on a motion made pursuant to Rule 26(c).

(3) *Evasive or Incomplete Answer.* For purposes of this subdivision an evasive or incomplete answer is to be treated as a failure to answer.

(4) *Award of Expenses of Motion.* If the motion is granted, the court may, after opportunity for hearing, require the party or deponent whose conduct necessitated the motion or the party or attorney advising such conduct or both of them to pay to the moving party the reasonable expenses incurred in obtaining the order, including attorney's fees, unless the court finds that the opposition to the motion was substantially justified or that other circumstances make an award of expenses unjust.

If the motion is denied, the court may, after opportunity for hearing, require the moving party or the attorney advising the motion or both of them to pay to the party or deponent who opposed the motion the reasonable expenses incurred in opposing the motion, including attorney's fees, unless the court finds that the making of the motion was substantially justified or that other circumstances make an award of expenses unjust.

If the motion is granted in part and denied in part, the court may apportion the reasonable expenses incurred in relation to the motion among the parties and persons in a just manner.

(b) Failure to Comply With Order.

(1) *Sanctions by Court in County or District Where Deposition is Taken.* If a deponent fails to be sworn or to answer a question after being directed to do so by the court in the county or judicial district, as the case may be, in which the deposition is being taken, the failure may be considered a contempt of that court.

(2) *Sanctions by Court in Which Action Is Pending.* If a party or an officer, director, or managing agent of a party or a person designated under Rule 30(b)(6) or 31(a) to testify on behalf of a party fails to obey an order to provide or permit discovery, including an order made under subdivision (a) of this rule or Rule 35, the court in which the action is pending may make such orders in regard to the failure as are just, and among others the following:

(A) An order that the matters regarding which the order was made or any other designated facts shall be taken to be established for the purposes of the action in accordance with the claim of the party obtaining the order;

(B) An order refusing to allow the disobedient party to support or oppose designated claims or defenses, or prohibiting him from introducing designated matters in evidence;

(C) An order striking out pleadings or parts thereof, or staying further proceedings until the order is obeyed, or dismissing the action or proceeding or any part thereof, or rendering a judgment by default against the disobedient party;

(D) In lieu of any of the foregoing orders or in addition thereto, an order treating as a contempt of court the failure to obey any orders except an order to submit to a physical or mental examination;

(E) Where a party has failed to comply with an order under Rule 35(a) requiring him to produce another for examination, such orders as are listed in paragraphs (A), (B), and (C) of this subdivision, unless the party failing to comply shows that he is unable to produce such person for examination.

In lieu of any of the foregoing orders or in addition thereto, the court may require the party failing to obey the order or the attorney advising him or both to pay the reasonable expenses, including attorney's fees, caused by the failure.

(c) Expenses on Failure to Admit. If a party fails to admit the genuineness of any documents or the truth of any matters as requested under Rule 36, and if the party requesting the admissions thereafter proves the genuineness of the document or the truth of the matter, he may apply to the court for an order requiring the other party to pay him the reasonable expenses incurred in making that proof, including reasonable attorney's fees. The court shall make the order unless it finds that (1) the request was held objectionable pursuant to Rule 36(a), or (2) the admission sought was of no substantial importance, or (3) the party failing to admit had reasonable grounds to believe that he might prevail on the matter, or (4) there was other good reason for the failure to admit.

(d) Failure of Party to Attend at Own Deposition or Serve Answers to Interrogatories or Respond to Request for Inspection. If a party or an officer, director, or a managing agent of a party or a person designated under Rule 30(b)(6) or 31(a) to testify on behalf of a party wilfully fails (1) to appear before the officer who is to take his deposition, after being served with a proper notice, or (2) to serve answers or objections to interrogatories submitted under Rule 33, after proper service of the interrogatories, or (3) to serve a written response to a request for inspection submitted under Rule 34, after proper service of the request, the court in which the action is pending on motion may make such orders in regard to the failure as are just, and among others it may take any action authorized under paragraphs (A), (B), and (C) of subdivision (b)(2) of this rule. In lieu of any order or in addition thereto, the court may require the party failing to act or the attorney advising him or both to pay the reasonable expenses, including attorney's fees, caused by the failure.

The failure to act described in this subdivision may not be excused on the ground that the discovery sought is objectiona-ble unless the party failing to act has applied for a protective order as provided by Rule 26(c).

(e) Expenses Against Commonwealth. Except to the extent permitted by statute, expenses and fees may not be awarded against the Commonwealth under this rule.

(f) Failure to Provide Electronically Stored Information. Absent exceptional circumstances, a court may not impose sanctions on a party for failing to produce electronically stored information lost as a result of the routine, good-faith operation of an electronic information system.

Amended June 27, 1974, effective July 1, 1974; December 2, 1983, effective January 1, 1984; amended effective May 1, 1994; July 1, 1996; September 24, 2013, effective January 1, 2014.

Reporter's Notes—1973

Rule 37 substantially follows Federal Rule 37. The sanctions imposed are those listed in S.J.C. Rule 3:15, with the addition of penalties for willful disobedience of a physical-examination order under Rule 35. Rule 37, like Rule 3:15, but unlike Federal Rule 37, makes clear that an order of contempt may issue only if the refusal to obey a discovery order is willful; similarly, only a willful failure to produce another person for a physical examination justifies the imposition of any sanctions at all.

Reporter's Notes—1983

This amendment permits the court to apply sanctions against those who fail to comply with a discovery order, without the necessity of finding that the noncompliance was wilful. The amendment makes the rule consistent with Fed.R.Civ.P. 37(b), upon which it was patterned. The amendment's purpose is to increase compliance with discovery orders, by making it easier for parties to achieve, and judges to award, sanctions for the failure to comply with a discovery order.

Reporter's Notes to Amendment to Mass.R.Civ.P. 37(a)(4)—1994

Prior to this amendment, there was an anomaly in Mass.R.Civ.P. 37(a)(4). The first paragraph, relating to motions for orders to compel discovery which are granted, says "the court may, after opportunity for hearing, require" the payment of reasonable expenses, including attorney's fees, "incurred in obtaining the order." The second paragraph, concerning such motions that are denied, used the verb "shall" instead of "may". Although the companion Federal Rule uses "shall" in both paragraphs, the Standing Advisory Committee believes that "may" makes more sense. First, as was pointed out in Smith and Zobel, Massachusetts Practice, Rules Practice, Vol. 7 (1975), at Sec. 37.3, "[e]ach paragraph contains explicit language allowing the court not to order the payment if it finds either that the opposition or pressing of the motion, as the case may be, were substantially justified, or that 'other circumstances make an award of expenses unjust.'" Therefore both paragraphs should "be taken in the permissive rather than the mandatory sense." Second, hearings are time-consuming, and it does not make sense to require hearings in all cases when the net result will usually be either the imposition of no sanction or a modest sanction. After the amendment, whether the motion to compel discovery has been won or lost, the judge may (but does not have to) order the payment of reasonable expenses, but such an order for payment cannot be made without first providing the opportunity for a hearing.

Reporter's Notes—1996

The 1996 amendments to paragraphs (a)(1) and (b)(1) merely add appropriate references to "judicial district" to take into account the applicability of the Rules to the District Court and Boston Municipal Court as result of the merger.

Reporter's Notes—2014

The 2014 amendments to Rule 37 were part of a series of amendments concerning discovery of electronically stored information. For background, see the 2014 Reporter's Notes to Rule 26.

These amendments added section (f) to Rule 37. This section establishes a "safe harbor" provision that will preclude imposition of sanctions where electronically stored information "is lost as a result of the routine, good-faith operation of an electronic information system." It is taken from Rule 37(e) of the Federal Rules of Civil Procedure and Rule 5 of the Uniform Rules Relating to the Discovery of Electronically Stored Information.

The 2014 amendment to Rule 37, as well as the other amendments to the discovery rules regarding electronically stored information, was not intended to change any existing law in Massachusetts on the obligation to preserve evidence when litigation is reasonably anticipated or has commenced. A duty to preserve may exist as a matter of common law, statutory law, or by reason of a court order.

The following comment from the 2006 Advisory Committee Notes to Federal Rule 37 is equally applicable in Massachusetts:

> The good faith requirement of Rule 37(f) means that a party is not permitted to exploit the routine operation of an information system to thwart discovery obligations by allowing that operation to continue in order to destroy specific stored information that it is required to preserve. When a party is under a duty to preserve information because of pending or reasonably anticipated litigation, intervention in the routine operation of an information system is one aspect of what is often called a "litigation hold."

VI. TRIALS

Rule 38. Jury Trial of Right

(a) Right Preserved. The right of trial by jury as declared by Part 1, Article 15 of the Constitution of this Commonwealth or as given by a statute shall be preserved to the parties inviolate.

(b) Demand. Any party may demand a trial by jury of any issue triable of right by a jury by serving upon the other parties a demand therefor in writing at any time after the commencement of the action and not later than 10 days after the service of the last pleading directed to such issue. Such a demand may be endorsed upon a pleading of the demanding party. In an action transferred, retransferred, removed or appealed from a District Court or the Municipal Court of the City of Boston, a demand for a trial by jury by a party entitled of right thereto shall be made in accordance with the statute governing such transfer, retransfer, removal, or appeal; but if the statute makes no provision for such demand, he shall be deemed to have waived such right unless within 10 days after the entry of the action in the Superior Court he files such demand therein.

(c) Same: Specification of Issues. In his demand a party may specify the issues which he wishes so tried; otherwise he shall be deemed to have demanded trial by jury for all the issues so triable. If he has demanded trial by jury for only some of the issues, any other party within 10 days after service of the demand or such lesser time as the court may order, may serve a demand for trial by jury of any other or all of the issues of fact in the action.

(d) Waiver. The failure of a party to serve a demand as required by this rule and to file it as required by Rule 5(d) constitutes a waiver by him of trial by jury. A demand for trial by jury made as herein provided may not be withdrawn without the consent of the parties.

Amended June 27, 1974, effective July 1, 1974; amended effective July 1, 1996; November 28, 2007, effective March 1, 2008.

Reporter's Notes—1973

Rule 38 is substantially the same as Federal Rule 38. Rule 38(a) substitutes Part 1, Article 15 of the Massachusetts Constitution for the "Seventh Amendment to the [United States] Constitution" and deletes the words "of the United States" after the word "statute".

Rule 38(b) includes language taken substantially from Super.Ct.Rule 44 covering cases transferred, removed or appealed from a District Court.

While Rule 2 merges law and equity into one form of action, Rule 38(b), by using the language "of any issue triable of right by jury," retains the principle that in an action seeking purely equitable relief, neither party has a constitutional right to a jury trial. See Parker v. Simpson, 180 Mass. 334, 346, 62 N.E. 401, 405–406 (1902). Thus, for purposes of determining such a right, differences between legal and equitable remedies are preserved. U.S. v. Malakie, 188 F.Supp. 592, 593 (E.D.N.Y.1960).

The merger of law and equity under Rule 2 together with Rule 38(b) does alter prior Massachusetts practice in one respect. Formerly once a plaintiff commenced a proceeding in equity he was held to have waived any right which he might have to a jury trial despite the fact that his action involved primarily legal issues. See McAdams v. Milk, 332 Mass. 364, 367, 125 N.E.2d 122, 123–124 (1955) [plaintiff, in a bill to reach and apply, is not entitled, as a matter of right, to the framing of jury issues]. Gulesian v. Newton Trust Co., 302 Mass. 369, 371, 19 N.E.2d 312, 314 (1939) held that when a plaintiff "voluntarily went into equity he submitted himself to all the incidents of equity practice, including the hearing without jury of a counterclaim, even one based upon a purely legal cause of action." With the merger of law and equity, the distinction adumbrated in these decisions will no longer be viable. The United States Supreme Court has held that if a demand for a jury trial has been made in accordance with Federal Rule 38(b), and both legal and equitable issues are presented in a single case, any legal issues must be submitted to a jury (if one is demanded) *before* related equitable issues are decided by the judge. Beacon Theatres, Inc. v. Westover, 359 U.S. 500, 79 S.Ct. 948, 3 L.Ed.2d 988 (1959); Dairy Queen, Inc. v. Wood, 369 U.S. 469, 82 S.Ct. 894, 8 L.Ed.2d 44 (1962).

The demand requirement of Rule 38(b) is not substantially different from prior Massachusetts practice. The relevant portion of former G.L. c. 231, § 60 allows a jury trial if "... a party before issue joined, or within ten days after the time allowed for filing the answer or plea, or within ten days after answer or plea has by consent of the plaintiff or permission of the court been filed, *or within such time after the parties are at issue as the court by general or special order directs,* files a notice that he desires a jury trial...." (Emphasis supplied).

The italicized language made clear that the court might in its discretion extend the period for demanding a jury trial. See Gechijian v. Richmond Ins. Co., 305 Mass. 132, 143, 25 N.E.2d 191, 198 (1940). While no such language appears in Rule 38(b), the same result may be reached under Rule 39(b), which grants the court discretion, in cases where a jury could have been demanded under Rule 38, upon motion to order a jury trial of any or all issues.

No previous rule or statute in Massachusetts allowed a party in the Superior Court to specify issues which he wished jury-tried. cf. G.L. c. 185, § 15. Rule 38(c) does permit such limited jury demand. This in no way prejudices the opposing party, because he is entitled, within 10 days after service of the demand or such lesser time as the court may order, to serve a counter-demand for jury trial of any or all the remaining issues of fact in the action.

The first sentence of Rule 38(d) reaches the same result as prior Massachusetts practice. See Alpert v. Mercury Publishing Co., 272 Mass. 39, 42, 172 N.E. 221, 222–223 (1930).

The second sentence of Rule 38(d) alters prior practice. Under Rule 38(d) a demand for a trial by jury may not be withdrawn without the consent of the parties. Under former G.L. c. 231, § 60A, any party to the proceeding could waive a jury trial which had been claimed. This presented a possible trap. Suppose P demanded a jury trial within the time permitted by G.L. c. 231, § 60. Relying on P's demand, D did not make a similar demand. Subsequently, after the period set out in § 60, if P waived his jury trial claim, D could subsequently be granted a jury trial only at the court's discretion, not as a matter of right. See Gouzoulas v. F.W. Stock & Sons, 223 Mass. 537, 538, 112 N.E. 221, 222 (1916). The approach of Rule 38(d) eliminates this pitfall.

Reporter's Notes—1996

The 1996 amendment to Rule 38 adds a new section (e), making the rule inapplicable to District Court proceedings. This is consistent with the approach taken by the now-repealed District/Municipal Courts Rules of Civil Procedure. However, Rule 38 will apply in the District Court in those limited circumstances where trial by jury in civil cases is provided by statute. See, for example, G.L. c. 218, §§ 19A and 19B (civil jury trials in Worcester and Haverhill).

Reporter's Notes—2008

Rule 38(e), entitled "District Court," has been deleted, now that jury trials are available in the District Court under the statewide one-trial system, applicable to civil actions commenced on or after August 31, 2004 (St. 2004, c. 252). Thus, the provisions of Rule 38 governing the right to jury trial, demand, specification, and waiver, are applicable in the District Court.

Rule 39.   Trial by Jury or by the Court

(a) By Jury. When trial by jury has been demanded as provided in Rule 38, the action shall be designated upon the docket as a jury action. In the District Court, the action shall be designated upon the docket as a jury action in accordance with the statutory provisions governing trials by jury in the District Court. The trial of all issues so demanded shall be by jury, unless (1) the parties or their attorneys of record, by written stipulation filed with the court or by an oral stipulation made in open court and entered in the record, consent to trial by the court sitting without a jury as to some or all of the issues or (2) the court upon motion or of its own initiative finds that a right of trial by jury of some or all of those issues does not exist under the constitution or statutes of this commonwealth.

(b) By the Court. Issues not demanded for trial by jury as provided in Rule 38 shall be tried by the court; but notwithstanding the failure of a party to demand a jury in an action in which such a demand might have been made of right, the court in its discretion upon motion may order a trial by jury of any or all issues.

(c) Framing Jury Issues. In all actions not triable of right by a jury, the court, except where otherwise provided by law, may upon motion frame issues of fact to be tried by a jury.

Amended effective July 1, 1996; November 28, 2007, effective March 1, 2008.

Reporter's Notes—1973

Rule 39 is substantially the same as Federal Rule 39.

Rule 39(a) in essence states that even though a demand for a jury trial has been made, the parties or their attorneys may subsequently, by stipulation, consent to trial without a jury. While Rule 39(a) does not literally so indicate, such stipulation may be made with respect to fewer than all of the issues. Further, the trial judge may determine that a right to trial by jury of some or all of the issues does not exist under the constitution or statutes of the Commonwealth.

Rule 39(b) authorizes the trial judge, in his discretion, upon motion, to order a jury trial on any or all of the issues despite the fact that a timely demand for a jury trial was not made under Rule 38(b). Some courts have taken the position that before relieving a party from waiver of a jury trial under Rule 38(d) the court should require a showing of highly exceptional circumstances, and that mere inadvertence of counsel in failing to make a timely demand for a jury trial does not justify the judge's exercise of discretion. Lemelson v. Gerber Products Co., 39 F.R.D. 336, 337 (E.D.N.Y.1966); see also Transocean Air Lines v. Pan American World Airways, Inc., 36 F.R.D. 43, 45 (S.D.N.Y.1964). Other courts have held the trial judge's discretion to order a jury trial largely unlimited. Britt v. Knight Publishing Co., 42 F.R.D. 593, 595 (D.S.C.1967). This latter position more closely resembles prior Massachusetts practice and is the proper interpretation of Rule 39(b). See former G.L. c. 231, § 60; Gechijian v. Richmond Ins. Co., 305 Mass. 132, 25 N.E.2d 191 (1940).

Rule 39(c) differs substantially from Federal Rule 39(c), which authorizes the court, in all actions not triable of right by a jury, upon motion or of its own initiative to try any issue with an advisory jury. Findings of such a jury are only advisory in nature unless both parties have consented that the verdict be binding.

Rule 39(c) does not adopt the advisory jury, but retains the prior practice of framing issues of fact to be tried by a jury. See former G.L. c. 214, §§ 34, 36. Because Rule 39(c) by definition refers only to actions "not triable of right by a jury," it will apply principally in actions where the plaintiff seeks only equitable relief. Therefore the reference to framing issues of fact should be taken to incorporate prior "equity" practice with respect to such issues. Under prior law, the framing of issues of fact was not a matter of right. See Marcoux v. Charroux, 329 Mass. 687, 688, 110 N.E.2d 362, 363 (1953). If, however, issues were framed for a jury the jury was not merely advisory. Whether the original proceeding was in equity, Westfield Savings Bank v. Leahey, 291 Mass. 473, 475, 197 N.E. 160, 161 (1935), or in probate, Lambert v. Cheney, 221 Mass. 378, 380, 108 N.E. 1078, 1079 (1915), the jury's verdict bound both parties, subject to the court's common law supervisory powers, Crocker v. Crocker, 188 Mass. 16, 20, 73 N.E. 1068, 1070 (1905).

Reporter's Notes—1996

The 1996 amendment to Rule 39 adds a new section (d), making the rule inapplicable to District Court proceedings. This is consistent with the approach taken by the now-repealed District/Municipal Courts Rules of Civil Procedure. However, Rule 39 will apply in the District Court in those limited circumstances where trial by jury in civil cases is provided by statute. See, for example, G.L. c. 218, §§ 19A and 19B (civil jury trials in Worcester and Haverhill).

Reporter's Notes—2008

A new second sentence has been added to Rule 39(a) to deal with statutory requirements in the District Court regarding designating an action on the docket as a jury action. The statewide one-trial statute provides in G.L. c. 218, § 19B(a) as follows:

In any case in which a party has filed a timely demand for a jury trial, the action shall not be designated upon the docket as a jury action until after the completion of a pretrial conference, a hearing on the results of the conference and until the disposition of any pretrial discovery motion and compliance with any order of the court pursuant to the motions.

Rule 39(d), entitled "District Court," has been deleted, since jury trials are available under the statewide one-trial system in District Court civil actions. Thus, Rule 39, as amended by the addition of the above sentence to Rule 39(a), will be applicable in the District Court.

Rule 40. Assignment of Cases for Trial: Continuances

(a) Assignment of Cases for Trial. Cases may be assigned to the appropriate calendar or list for trial or other disposition by order of the court including general rules and orders adopted for the purpose of assignment. Precedence shall be given to actions entitled thereto by statute.

(b) Continuances. Continuances shall be granted only for good cause, in accordance with general rules and orders which the court may from time to time adopt.

(c) Affidavit or Certificate in Support of Motion. The court need not entertain any motion for a continuance based on the absence of a material witness unless such motion be supported by an affidavit which shall state the name of the witness and, if known, his address, the facts to which he is expected to testify and the basis for such expectation, the efforts which have been made to procure his attendance or deposition, and the expectation which the party has of procuring his testimony or deposition at a future time. Such motion may, in the discretion of the court, be denied if the adverse party will admit that the absent witness would, if present, testify as stated in the affidavit. The same rule shall apply, with the necessary changes in points of detail, when the motion is grounded on the want of any material document, thing, or other evidence.

Reporter's Notes—1973

Rule 40 governs in a general way the final progress of cases toward trial. Federal Rule 40, on the other hand, deals only with the *assignment* of cases for trial. It says nothing of continuances.

It should be emphasized that Rule 40 states general principles pertaining to assignment and continuances. It does not attempt to lay down detailed regulations. Thus the matters covered by Super.Ct.R. 57, 57a, and 59–70 will still require the promulgation of standing court orders, and Rule 40(a) anticipates this.

Rule 40(a) does not alter practice. In Massachusetts, courts have the inherent power to place cases on the trial list even without request of the parties, Sweeny v. Home Owners' Loan Corporation, 307 Mass. 165, 166, 29 N.E.2d 712 (1940).

Rule 40(a) makes no explicit provision for advancing an action for speedy trial. G.L. c. 231, § 59A allows the Court upon motion for cause shown to advance an action for speedy trial. The final sentence of Rule 40(a) embodies this practice. See also, G.L. c. 231, §§ 59B–E, for other examples of statutory special preferences. (Even without statute, the Court seems to have power to advance cases for speedy trial. See Merchants' National Bank of Bangor v. Glendon Company, 120 Mass. 97, 99 (1876).)

Rule 40(b) and Rule 40(c) state general principles pertaining to continuances. By and large, they codify existing practice. The grant-

ing or denial of a continuance is discretionary with the court; the court's exercise of discretion will not be disturbed on appeal, absent a showing of abuse. Mowat v. Deluca, 330 Mass. 711, 712, 116 N.E.2d 322, 323 (1953). The Court may grant a discretionary continuance at any time prior to trial, indeed at any time prior to judgment. American Woodworking Machinery Co. v. Forbush, 193 Mass. 455, 457, 79 N.E. 770, 771 (1907).

Rule 41. Dismissal of Actions

(a) Voluntary Dismissal: Effect Thereof.

(1) *By Plaintiff; By Stipulation.* Subject to the provisions of these rules and of any statute of this Commonwealth, an action may be dismissed by the plaintiff without order of court (i) by filing a notice of dismissal at any time before service by the adverse party of an answer or of a motion for summary judgment, whichever first occurs, or (ii) by filing a stipulation of dismissal signed by all parties who have appeared in the action. Unless otherwise stated in the notice of dismissal or stipulation, the dismissal is without prejudice, except that a notice of dismissal operates as an adjudication upon the merits when filed by a plaintiff who has once dismissed in any court of the United States or of this or any other state an action based on or including the same claim.

(2) *By Order of Court.* Except as provided in paragraph (1) of this subdivision (a), an action shall not be dismissed at the plaintiff's instance save upon order of the court and upon such terms and conditions as the court deems proper. If a counterclaim has been pleaded by a defendant prior to the service upon him of the plaintiff's motion to dismiss, the action shall not be dismissed against the defendant's objection unless the counterclaim can remain pending for independent adjudication by the court. Unless otherwise specified in the order, a dismissal under this paragraph is without prejudice.

(b) Involuntary Dismissal: Effect Thereof.

(1) *On Court's Own Motion.* The court may on notice as hereinafter provided at any time, in its discretion, dismiss for lack of prosecution any action which has remained upon the docket for three years preceding said notice without activity shown other than placing upon the trial list, marking for trial, being set down for trial, the filing or withdrawal of an appearance, or the filing of any paper pertaining to discovery. The notice shall state that the action will be dismissed on a day certain, (not less than one year from the date of the notice) unless before that day the case has been tried, heard on the merits, otherwise disposed of, or unless the court on motion with or without notice shall otherwise order. The notice shall be mailed to the plaintiff's attorney of record, or, if there be none, to the plaintiff if his address be known. Otherwise such notice shall be published as directed by the court. Dismissal under this paragraph shall be without prejudice.

(2) *On Motion of the Defendant.* On motion of the defendant, with notice, the court may, in its discretion, dismiss any action for failure of the plaintiff to prosecute or to comply with these rules or any order of court. After the plaintiff, in an action tried by the court without a jury, has completed the presentation of his evidence, the defendant, without waiving his right to offer evidence in the event the motion is not granted, may move for a dismissal on the ground that upon the facts and the law the plaintiff has shown no right to relief. The court as trier of the facts may then determine them and

render judgment against the plaintiff or may decline to render any judgment until the close of all the evidence. If the court renders judgment on the merits against the plaintiff the court shall make findings as provided in Rule 52(a).

(3) *Effect.* Unless the dismissal is pursuant to paragraph (1) of this subdivision (b), or unless the court in its order for dismissal otherwise specifies, a dismissal under this subdivision (b) and any dismissal not provided for in this rule, other than a dismissal for lack of jurisdiction, for improper venue, or for failure to join a party under Rule 19, or for improper amount of damages in the Superior Court as set forth in G. L. c. 212, § 3 or in the District Court as set forth in G. L. c. 218, § 19, operates as an adjudication upon the merits.

(c) Dismissal of Counterclaim, Cross-Claim, or Third-Party Claim. The provisions of this rule apply to the dismissal of any counterclaim, cross-claim, or third-party claim. A voluntary dismissal by the claimant alone pursuant to paragraph (1) of subdivision (a) of this rule shall be made before a responsive pleading or a motion for summary judgment is served, whichever first occurs, or, if there is none, before the introduction of evidence at the trial or hearing.

(d) Costs of Previously-Dismissed Action. If a plaintiff who has once dismissed an action in any court commences an action based upon or including the same claim against the same defendant, the court may make such order for the payment of costs of the action previously dismissed as it may deem proper and may stay the proceedings in the action until the plaintiff has complied with the order.

Amended June 24, 2009, effective August 1, 2009.

Reporter's Notes—1973

Rule 41(a) provides for voluntary dismissal. Under Rule 41(a)(1), the plaintiff may dismiss without order of court merely by filing a notice of dismissal prior to an answer or a motion for summary judgment. Thereafter dismissal by the plaintiff, without court order, requires the filing of a stipulation signed by all parties. Unless otherwise provided in the notice or stipulation, such dismissal is without prejudice. If, however, the plaintiff has previously dismissed the same claim in any state or federal court, a notice of dismissal operates as an adjudication on the merits. The two-dismissal rule applies automatically only to a notice of dismissal. It does not so apply if the second dismissal is (a) by stipulation (Cornell v. Chase Brass & Copper Co., 49 F.Supp. 979, 981 (S.D.N.Y.1943)); or (b) by order of court under Rule 41(a)(2).

Rule 41(a) alters prior Massachusetts practice, which allowed a plaintiff to dismiss (discontinue) an action at law *as of right* at any time before trial. Marsch v. Southern New England R. Corp., 235 Mass. 304, 307, 126 N.E. 519, 520 (1920); Alpert v. Mercury Publishing Co., 272 Mass. 39, 40–41, 172 N.E. 221, 222 (1930); Burnham v. MacWhinnie, 350 Mass. 17, 18–19, 213 N.E.2d 385, 386 (1965). Leave to dismiss a suit in equity without prejudice had to be obtained from the court once the defendant's situation materially changed. Keown v. Keown, 231 Mass. 404, 406–407, 121 N.E. 153, 154–155 (1918); Nicolai v. Nicolai, 283 Mass. 241, 246, 186 N.E. 240, 241–242 (1933).

The two-dismissal rule will effect only a slight change in Massachusetts practice. While a discontinuance would not operate as res judicata unless a judgment had been rendered on the merits, Pontiff v. Alexander, 320 Mass. 514, 516, 70 N.E.2d 5, 6 (1946), the statute of limitations eventually terminated the right of action. Cf. Farnum v. Brady, 269 Mass. 53, 54, 168 N.E. 165 (1929).

Rule 41(a)(2) requires that an order of court precede any dismissal not covered by Rule 41(a)(1). Dismissals under Rule 41(a)(2) are without prejudice unless otherwise stated. If the defendant has counterclaimed prior to service of the motion to dismiss, the action may not be dismissed over defendant's objection unless the counterclaim can remain pending for independent adjudication. This latter point changes prior practice. Verdone v. Verdone, 345 Mass. 773, 774, 187 N.E.2d 853, 854 (1963).

Rule 41(b)(1) does not appear in Federal Rule 41(b). It has been adopted to follow salutory Massachusetts practice.

Rule 41(b)(2) provides for involuntary dismissal upon motion of the defendant on one of two grounds: (1) failure to comply with the rules or any order of the court; or (2) in an action tried without a jury, if, upon the facts and the law, the plaintiff has shown no right to relief.

No pre-rule procedure existed in Massachusetts for dismissal of a jury-waived or equity case, after the plaintiff has rested, on the ground that upon the facts and the law the plaintiff had shown no right to relief. Under Rule 41(b)(2) this procedure applies to all non-jury cases, whether the relief sought is legal or equitable.

Rule 41(b)(3) provides that involuntary dismissal under Rule 41(b)(2) operates as an adjudication on the merits unless the court otherwise orders.

Rule 41(c) makes the provisions of Rule 41 applicable to counterclaims, cross-claims and third-party claims.

Rule 41(d), pertaining to allowing first-action costs as precondition for a second action, does not alter existing Massachusetts law. G.L. c. 261, § 10.

Boyajian v. Hart, 312 Mass. 264, 267, 44 N.E.2d 964, 966 (1942), held that even apart from statute:

"... whenever the prevention of vexatious litigation and the interests of justice require, a court has power, both in actions at law and in suits in equity, to stay a new proceeding for substantially the same cause as a former one until costs for which the plaintiff has become liable in the former proceeding have been paid ... and ... the court has the power in appropriate cases to dismiss the second proceeding altogether."

Reporter's Notes—1996

Prior to the merger of the District Court Rules into the Mass.R.Civ. P., the District Court version of Rule 41(b)(1) provided for dismissal for lack of prosecution after two years. As result of the merger, the three-year provision of the Mass.R.Civ.P. now applies in the District Court.

Reporter's Notes—2009

An amendment to Rule 12(b), effective March 1, 2008 added a new numbered defense, 12(b)(10), dismissal for improper amount of damages in the Superior Court as set forth in G.L. c. 212, § 3 or in the District Court as set forth in G.L. c. 218, § 19.

The 2009 amendment to Rule 41(b)(3) makes clear that such a dismissal does not operate as an adjudication upon the merits unless the court orders otherwise.

Rule 42. Consolidation: Separate Trials

(a) Courts Other Than District Court: Consolidation. When actions involving a common question of law or fact are pending before the court, in the same county or different counties, it may order a joint hearing or trial of any or all the matters in issue in the actions; it may order all the actions consolidated; and it may make such orders concerning proceedings therein as may tend to avoid unnecessary costs or delay.

(b) Courts Other Than District Court: Separate Trials. The court, in furtherance of convenience or to avoid prejudice, or when separate trials will be conducive to expedition and economy, may order a separate trial in the county where the action is pending or in a different county of any claim, cross-claim, counterclaim, or third-party claim, or of any separate issue or of any number of claims, cross-claims, counterclaims, third-party claims, or issues, always preserving inviolate the right of trial by jury as declared by the constitution of this Commonwealth or as set forth in a statute.

(c) District Court: Joinder for Trial; Consolidation. When actions involving a common question of law or fact are pending before a single District Court, it may order a joint hearing or trial of any or all the matters in issue in the actions; it may order all the actions consolidated; and it may make such orders concerning proceedings therein as may tend to avoid unnecessary cost or delay.

A party who moves for the consolidation and trial together of cross actions between the same parties or two or more actions, including other court proceedings, arising out of or connected with the same accident, event or transaction, pending in more than one District Court, shall file the original copy of the motion in any such court. The party making such motion shall send notices thereof forthwith, together with a copy of the motion, to interested parties and to the clerk(s) of the other court(s) involved in the requested consolidation. The party making such motion shall annex thereto a certificate stating the time and place of filing such motion, the names and addresses of all interested parties, and showing that the party has given such notices and the time and manner of giving the same. The said motion and certificate shall then be forwarded forthwith by the clerk to the presiding justice of the Appellate Division District of the said court and it shall be marked for hearing and all parties so notified. The clerk shall note upon the motion and docket the day and hour of the filing of same. All notices received by a clerk of the filing of a motion for consolidation in another court shall be docketed by the clerk in the proper case.

Upon allowance of any such motion, the presiding justice or some justice designated by the presiding justice shall make an order providing for the consolidated trial of the actions involved, and copies of such order shall be forwarded to the clerks of the courts involved in the requested consolidation. The clerk of the court in which the consolidated actions will be heard shall notify all interested parties of the order to consolidate. All papers filed in the case, all bonds, and a certified copy of the docket entries shall be forwarded by the clerk(s) of the court(s) of origin to the court where such actions or proceedings are consolidated, and such actions or proceedings shall thereafter proceed in the court to which they are thus transferred as though originally entered there.

If all the parties to any such actions agree upon consolidation and trial together, the order therefor shall be signed by the presiding justice or some justice designated by the presiding justice.

Whenever in this rule any reference is made to the presiding justice, in the Municipal Court of the City of Boston it shall be deemed to refer to the Chief Justice of that court.

(d) District Court: Separate Trials. The court, in furtherance of convenience or to avoid prejudice, or when separate trials will be conducive to expedition and economy, may order a separate trial of any claim, cross-claim, counterclaim, or third-party claim, or of any separate issue or of any number of claims, cross-claims, counterclaims, third-party claims, or

issues, always preserving inviolate the right of trial by jury as declared by the constitution of this Commonwealth or as set forth in a statute.

Amended effective July 1, 1996; November 28, 2007, effective March 1, 2008.

Reporter's Notes—1973

Except for the language pertaining to counties, Rule 42(a) tracks Federal Rule 42(a). By authorizing the court to order a joint trial of any or all the matters in issue in the actions or to order all the actions consolidated, it complements the liberal provisions for permissive joinder of claims (Rule 18) and of parties (Rule 20).

Under Rule 42(a) the court's order may apply to separate issues and not necessarily to entire cases. For example, if several plaintiffs are suing the same defendant for injuries arising from the same accident, the court may order a joint trial on the issue of liability, leaving the issue of damages to be determined separately in each case, should the liability issue be determined against the defendant. See Hassett v. Modern Maid Packers, Inc., 23 F.R.D. 661 (D.Md.1959). Where however the issues of liability and damages are significantly related, it has been held error to order a separate trial of the liability issue. United States Air Lines, Inc. v. Wiener, 286 F.2d 302 (9th Cir.1961).

Rule 42(a) does permit the consolidation of separate actions seeking legal and equitable relief as concomitant of the merger of law and equity effected by Rule 2. It also changes past practice, Stoneman v. Coakley, 266 Mass. 64, 65–66, 164 N.E. 802, 803 (1929), by permitting, in any appropriate situation, consolidation for trial of two cases pending in different counties.

Rule 42(b) is necessary primarily because of the liberal joinder provisions of Rules 18 and 20. The authority in the court to order separate trials is necessary in some cases to avoid unwieldy litigation.

Reporter's Notes—1996

The amendments to Rule 42 effective in 1996 add new sections (c) and (d), applicable in the District Court, and retitle the headings to Rule 42(a) and (b). New sections (c) and (d) of Rule 42 correspond respectively to now-repealed Rule 42(a) and (b) of the Dist./Mun.Cts.R.Civ.P.

The "Comments" to now-repealed Rule 42(a) of the Dist./Mun.Cts.R.Civ.P. describe the District Court provisions by noting that under District Court Rule 42(a) (now Mass.R.Civ.P. 42(c)), the first paragraph governs only consolidation of cases pending in a single District Court, while the second paragraph governs consolidation of actions pending in two or more District Courts.

The "Comments" to now-repealed Rule 42(b) of the Dist./Mun.Cts.R.Civ.P. describe the District Court provisions by noting that District Court Rule 42(b) (now Mass.R.Civ.P. 42(d)) does not contain the power of one District Court to separate claims or issues in a case before it and order that any such claims or issues be heard in a different District Court. Such power does exist for other courts governed by the Mass.R.Civ.P. pursuant to section (b) as retitled. The "Comments" finally point out that District Court Rule 42(b) (now Mass.R.Civ.P. 42(d)) does not contain language dealing with trial by jury.

Reporter's Notes—2008

Rule 42(d) has been amended to add language that appears in Rule 42(b) regarding the constitutional right to trial by jury.

In light of the 2003 legislation transferring various divisions of the District Court Department located in Suffolk County to the Boston Municipal Court Department and with the creation of divisions in the Boston Municipal Court Department (G.L. c. 218, § 1 and G.L. c. 218, § 50), Rule 42(c) and Rule 42(d) are also applicable in the Boston Municipal Court Department.

Rule 43. Evidence

(a) Form and Admissibility. In all trials the testimony of witnesses shall be taken orally in open court, unless otherwise provided by these rules. All evidence shall be admitted which is admissible under the statutes of this Commonwealth or under the rules of evidence applied in this Commonwealth. The competency of a witness to testify shall be determined in like manner.

(b) Scope of Examination and Cross-Examination. A party may interrogate any unwilling or hostile witness by leading questions. A party may call an adverse party or an officer, director, or managing agent of a public or private corporation or of a partnership or association which is an adverse party, and interrogate him by leading questions and contradict and impeach him in all respects as if he had been called by the adverse party, except by evidence of bad character, and the witness thus called may be contradicted and impeached by or on behalf of the adverse party also, and may be cross-examined by the adverse party only upon the subject matter of his examination in chief. Any other witness may be cross-examined without regard to the scope of his testimony on direct, subject only to the trial judge's sound discretion.

(c) Record of Excluded Evidence. In an action tried by a jury, if an objection to a question propounded to a witness is sustained by the court, the examining attorney may make a specific offer of what he expects to prove by the answer of the witness. The court may require the offer to be made out of the hearing of the jury. The court may add such other or further statement as clearly shows the character of the evidence, the form in which it was offered, the objection made, and the ruling thereon. In actions tried without a jury the same procedure may be followed, except that the court upon request shall take and report the evidence in full, unless it clearly appears that the evidence is not admissible on any ground or that the witness is privileged.

(d) Affirmation in Lieu of Oath. Whenever under these rules an oath is required to be taken, a solemn affirmation under the penalties of perjury may be accepted in lieu thereof.

(e) Evidence on Motions. When a motion is based on facts not appearing of record the court may hear the matter on affidavits presented by the respective parties, but the court may direct that the matter be heard wholly or partly on oral testimony or depositions.

(f) Interpreters. The court may appoint an interpreter of its own selection and may fix his reasonable compensation. The compensation shall be paid out of funds provided by law or by one or more of the parties as the court may direct, and may be taxed ultimately as costs, in the discretion of the court.

(g) Examination of Witnesses. Unless otherwise permitted by the court, the examination and cross-examination of any witness shall be conducted by one attorney only for each party. The attorney shall stand while so examining or cross-examining unless the court otherwise permits.

Reporter's Notes—1973

Except for the deletion of material which is inapplicable to state practice, Rule 43(a) tracks its federal counterpart. Rule 43(a) does not affect Massachusetts law since it incorporates existing law on the admissibility of evidence and the competency of witnesses.

Rule 43(b) follows Federal Rule 43(b). It does not alter Massachusetts practice, which (1) allows interrogation of a hostile witness by leading questions, Commonwealth v. Monahan, 349 Mass. 139, 207 N.E.2d 29 (1965); Commonwealth v. Coshnear, 289 Mass. 516, 194 N.E. 900 (1935); (2) allows an adverse party to be called and cross-examined, G.L. c. 233, § 22; (3) allows a corporate officer or agent to be examined as an adverse party, G.L. c. 233, § 22; (4) permits the adverse party's impeachment, except as to character, G.L. c. 233, § 23; Labrie v. Midwood, 273 Mass. 578, 581–582, 174 N.E. 214, 216 (1931); and (5) normally permits the adverse party-witness to be "cross-examined" by his own attorney only upon the subject matter of the direct examination. Phillips v. Vorenberg, 259 Mass. 46, 73, 156 N.E. 61, 65 (1927). The final sentence of Rule 43(b) makes it clear that any other witness may be cross-examined without regard to the scope of his testimony on direct, Moody v. Rowell, 34 Mass. (17 Pick.) 490, 498 (1835), subject only to the trial judge's sound discretion, Commonwealth v. Granito, 326 Mass. 494, 95 N.E.2d 539 (1950).

Rule 43(c) is similar to prior Massachusetts practice. If an objection to the admission of evidence is sustained, the proponent of the evidence should make an offer of proof, to preserve the record. See Petition of Mackintosh, 268 Mass. 138, 139, 167 N.E. 273, 274 (1929); cases collected in Hughes, Massachusetts Evidence, 240–242 (1961). Note that if the evidence is excluded on *cross*-examination, the offer of proof need not be made. Stevens v. William S. Howe Co., 275 Mass. 398, 402, 176 N.E. 208, 210 (1931).

Rule 43(d), dealing with oaths, is basically the same as G.L. c. 233, §§ 15 to 19.

Rule 43(e) is supported by Super.Ct. Rule 46, although the latter does not specifically allow the introduction of oral testimony or depositions.

Rule 43(f), dealing with interpreters, follows Federal Rule 43(f). Massachusetts appears not to have had any settled practice on this question.

Rule 43(g) which does not appear in the Federal Rules, is taken virtually verbatim from Super.Ct. Rule 51, and embodies long-settled Massachusetts courtroom etiquette.

Reporter's Notes—1996

As result of the merger of the District Court rules into the Mass.R.Civ.P., Rule 43(c) has been made applicable to District Court proceedings.

Rule 44. Proof of Official Records

(a) Authentication.

(1) *Domestic.* An official record kept within the Commonwealth, or an entry therein, when admissible for any purpose, may be evidenced by an official publication thereof or by a copy attested by the officer having legal custody of the record, or by his deputy. If the record is kept in any other state, district, commonwealth, territory or insular possession of the United States, or within the Panama Canal Zone, the Trust Territory of the Pacific Islands, or the Ryukyu Islands, any such copy shall be accompanied by a certificate that such custodial officer has the custody. This certificate may be made by a judge of a court of record of the district or political subdivision in which the record is kept, authenticated by the seal of the court, or may be made by any public officer having a seal of office and having official duties in the district or political subdivision in which the record is kept, authenticated by the seal of his office.

(2) *Foreign.* A foreign official record, or an entry therein, when admissible for any purpose, may be evidenced by an official publication thereof; or a copy thereof, attested by a

person authorized to make the attestation, and accompanied by a final certification as to the genuineness of the signature and official position (i) of the attesting person, or (ii) of any foreign official whose certificate of genuineness of signature and official position relates to the attestation or is in a chain of certificates of genuineness of signature and official position relating to the attestation. A final certification may be made by a secretary of embassy or legation, consul general, consul, vice consul, or consular agent of the United States, or a diplomatic or consular official of the foreign country assigned or accredited to the United States. If reasonable opportunity has been given to all parties to investigate the authenticity and accuracy of the documents, the court may, for good cause shown, (i) admit an attested copy without final certification, or (ii) permit the foreign official record to be evidenced by an attested summary with or without a final certification.

(b) Lack of Record. A written statement that after diligent search no record or entry of a specified tenor is found to exist in the records designated by the statement, authenticated as provided in subdivision (a)(1) of this rule in the case of a domestic record, or complying with the requirements of subdivision (a)(2) of this rule for a summary in the case of a foreign record, is admissible as evidence that the records contain no such record or entry.

(c) Other Proof. This rule does not prevent the proof, by any other method authorized by law, of the existence of, or the lack of, an official record, or of entry, or lack of entry therein.

Reporter's Notes—1973

Rule 44, like Federal Rule 44, deals only with the problems of (1) authenticating an official record, and (2) establishing the lack of such record. Rule 44 does not cover the authentication of non-official records (as, e.g., hospital records under G.L. c. 233, § 79). Neither does it regulate the extent to which the contents of the record, once authenticated, may be admissible (as, e.g., the question of "liability" evidence in hospital records, G.L. c. 233, § 79, or death records, G.L. c. 46, § 19).

Rule 44 largely follows Federal Rule 44, with one significant exception. Federal Rule 44(a)(1) requires that any official record be doubly-certified: (1) The officer having custody of the record must certify its validity; (2) The judge or officer must certify the status of the custodial officer. Rule 44(a)(1) eliminates this double certification with respect to records kept within the Commonwealth. In other respects, Rule 44 accords with prior Massachusetts practice. See G.L. c. 233, §§ 75–79G.

Rule 44(a)(2) deals with foreign records. It does not alter prior Massachusetts practice. G.L. c. 233, § 69, G.L. c. 223A, § 13. Rule 44(b) allows a lack of record to be proved in the same manner as proof of the existence of an official record.

Rule 44(c) modifies Federal Rule 44(c) slightly to make clear that proof of either the existence of a record, or lack of such record, or entries therein may be proved by methods other than those set out in sections (a) and (b). Thus the case law in Massachusetts permitting proof of the absence of a record or entry therein by parol evidence remains unaffected. See Bristol County Savings Bank v. Keary, 128 Mass. 298, 303 (1880); Blair's Foodland, Inc. v. Shuman's Foodland, Inc., 311 Mass. 172, 175–176, 40 N.E.2d 303, 305–306 (1942).

Rule 44.1.   Determination of Foreign Law

A party who intends to raise an issue concerning the law of the United States or of any state, territory or dependency thereof or of a foreign country shall give notice in his pleadings or other reasonable written notice. The court, in deter-

mining such law, may consider any relevant material or source, including testimony, whether or not submitted by a party or admissible under Rule 43. The court's determination shall be treated as a ruling on a question of law.

Reporter's Notes—1973

Rule 44.1 is similar to Federal Rule 44.1, which was added to the Federal Rules in 1966. The Reporters have extended the provisions of Federal Rule 44.1 to encompass the law of the United States or any other state, territory or dependency of the United States.

Rule 44.1 does not significantly alter pre-rule practice. G.L. c. 233, § 70 provides: "The courts shall take judicial notice of the law of the United States or of any state, territory or dependency thereof or of a foreign country whenever the same shall be material." While the word "shall" is used in G.L. c. 233, § 70, the court need not take judicial notice of the law of a foreign jurisdiction unless it is brought to the court's attention. Tsacoyeanes v. Canadian Pacific Railway Co., 339 Mass. 726, 728, 162 N.E.2d 23, 24 (1959). This judicial requirement is not satisfied simply by mentioning the appropriate reference to foreign law. "Merely to direct attention to the law of a foreign country written in a foreign tongue does not make it a matter for judicial notice." Rodrigues v. Rodrigues, 286 Mass. 77, 83, 190 N.E. 20, 22 (1934).

In New England Trust Co. v. Wood, 326 Mass. 239, 243, 93 N.E.2d 547, 549 (1950) the court, while holding that it could take judicial notice of the Turkish law of descent and distribution, although not brought to its attention by the parties, refused to do so because it was not equipped to make its own investigation of Turkish law. It is unlikely that Rule 44.1 affects the philosophy of these holdings.

Rule 44.1 permits the court to consider "any relevant material or source"; this follows Massachusetts practice. The trial judge's attention may be directed to the law of another jurisdiction by oral testimony of a qualified witness as well as by citation of statutes and decisions. Eastern Offices, Inc. v. P.F. O'Keefe Advertising Agency, Inc., 289 Mass. 23, 26, 193 N.E. 837, 838 (1935). See also Petition of Mazurowski, Petitioner, 331 Mass. 33, 38–39, 116 N.E.2d 854, 857–858 (1954), which approved the Probate Court's (and the Supreme Judicial Court's) obtaining information from various United States government departments; Lenn v. Riche, 331 Mass. 104, 109, 117 N.E.2d 129, 132 (1954) (French Code and commentaries).

The last sentence of Rule 44.1 is designed to make clear that the trial court's determination of foreign law is a matter of law (and therefore reversible if the appellate court disagrees) not a finding of fact, which may be reversed only if the appellate court decides that the trial court was "clearly erroneous." See Rule 52.

Rule 45.   Subpoena

(a) For Attendance of Witnesses; Form; Issuance. Every subpoena shall be issued by the clerk of court, by a notary public, or by a justice of the peace, shall state the name of the court and the title of the action, and shall command each person to whom it is directed to do the following at a specified time and place: to attend and give testimony; to produce designated documents, electronically stored information, or tangible things in that person's possession, custody, or control; or to permit inspection of premises. The clerk, notary public, or justice of the peace shall issue a subpoena signed but otherwise in blank, to a party requesting it, who shall fill it in before service.

(b) Combining or Separating a Command to Produce or to Permit Inspection; Specifying the Form for Electronically Stored Information. A command to produce documents, electronically stored information, or tangible things or to permit the inspection of premises may be included in a subpoena commanding attendance at a deposition, hearing, or trial, or may be set out in a separate subpoena. A subpoena may specify the form or forms in which electronically stored information is to be produced. A party or attorney responsible for issuing and serving a subpoena must take reasonable steps to avoid imposing undue burden or expense on a person subject to the subpoena. The court upon motion made promptly and in any event at or before the time specified in the subpoena for compliance therewith, may (1) quash or modify the subpoena if it is unreasonable and oppressive or (2) condition denial of the motion upon the advancement by the person in whose behalf the subpoena is issued of the reasonable cost of producing the documents, electronically stored information, or tangible things. A command in a subpoena to produce documents, electronically stored information, or tangible things requires the responding person to permit inspection, copying, testing, or sampling of the materials. A person commanded to produce documents, electronically stored information, or tangible things, or to permit inspection of premises, need not appear in person at the place of production or inspection unless also commanded to appear for a deposition, hearing, or trial.

(c) Service. A subpoena may be served by any person who is not a party and is not less than 18 years of age. Service of a subpoena upon a person named therein shall be made by delivering a copy thereof to such person, or by exhibiting it and reading it to him, or by leaving a copy at his place of abode; and, if the person's attendance is required, by tendering to him the fees for one day's attendance and the mileage allowed by law. When the subpoena is issued on behalf of the United States or the Commonwealth or a political subdivision thereof, or an officer, or agency of either, fees and mileage need not be tendered.

(d) Subpoenas for Taking Deposition and for Command to Produce; Place of Examination.

(1) No subpoena for the taking of a deposition shall be issued prior to the service of a notice to take the deposition. If a subpoena commands only the production of documents, electronically stored information, or tangible things or the inspection of premises before trial, then before it is served on the person to whom it is directed, a copy of the subpoena shall be served on each party. The party serving a subpoena requiring production or inspection before trial shall also serve on each party a copy of any objection to the commanded production or inspection and a notice of any production made or, alternatively, provide a copy of the production to each party.

The subpoena commanding the person to whom it is directed to produce documents, electronically stored information, or tangible things, which constitute or contain evidence relating to any of the matters within the scope of the examination permitted by these rules, is subject to the provisions of Rule 26(c) and subdivision (b) of this rule.

A subpoena upon a party which commands the production of documents, electronically stored information, or things must give the party at least 30 days for compliance after service thereof. Such subpoena shall not require compliance of a defendant within 45 days after service of the summons and complaint on that defendant. The court may allow a shorter or longer time.

A person commanded to produce documents or tangible things or to permit inspection may within 10 days after the service thereof or on or before the time specified in the subpoena for compliance if such time is less than 10 days after service, serve upon the party or attorney designated in the subpoena written objection to inspecting, copying, testing, or sampling any of the materials; to inspecting the premises; or to producing electronically stored information in the form or forms requested. If objection is made, the party serving the subpoena shall not be entitled to inspect, copy, test, or sample the materials or inspect the premises except pursuant to an order of the court from which the subpoena was issued. The party serving the subpoena may, if objection is made, move at any time upon notice to the commanded person for an order compelling production or inspection. Such an order to compel production or inspection shall protect a person who is neither a party nor a party's officer from undue burden or expense resulting from compliance.

(2) Unless the court orders otherwise, other than for a hearing or trial, a resident of this Commonwealth shall not be required to attend an examination or produce documents, electronically stored information, or tangible things at a place more than 50 airline miles distant from either his residence, place of employment, or place of business, whichever is nearest to the place to which he is subpoenaed. Other than for a hearing or trial, a nonresident of the Commonwealth when served with a subpoena within the Commonwealth may be required to attend or produce documents, electronically stored information, or tangible things only in that county wherein he is served, or within 50 airline miles of the place of service, or at such other convenient place as is fixed by an order of court.

(e) Subpoena for a Hearing or Trial. At the request of any party subpoenas for attendance or to produce documents, electronically stored information, or tangible things at a hearing or trial shall be issued by any of the persons directed in subdivision (a) of this rule. A subpoena requiring the attendance of a witness or production of documents, electronically stored information, or tangible things at a hearing or trial may be served at any place within the Commonwealth.

(f) Duties in Responding to a Subpoena.

(1) *Producing Documents or Electronically Stored Information.* These procedures apply to producing documents or electronically stored information:

(A) *Documents.* A person responding to a subpoena that requires production of documents shall produce them as they are kept in the ordinary course of business or shall organize and label them to correspond to the categories in the demand. Other than for a deposition, hearing, or trial, unless the production of original documents is requested, the producing party may produce copies of the documents, including by electronic means, provided that, if requested, the producing party affords all parties a fair opportunity to verify the copies by comparison with the originals.

(B) *Form for producing electronically stored information not specified.* If a subpoena does not specify a form for producing electronically stored information, the person responding shall produce it in a form or forms in which it is ordinarily maintained or in a reasonably usable form or forms.

(C) *Electronically stored information produced in only one form.* The person responding need not produce the same electronically stored information in more than one form.

(D) *Inaccessible electronically stored information.* The person responding may object to the discovery of inaccessible electronically stored information, and any such objection shall specify the reason that such discovery is inaccessible. On motion to compel or for a protective order, the person claiming inaccessibility bears the burden of showing inaccessibility. If that showing is made, the court may nonetheless order discovery from such sources if the requesting party shows good cause, considering the limitations of Rule 26(f)(4)(C) and (D). The court may specify conditions for the discovery.

(2) *Claiming Privilege or Protection.*

(A) *Information withheld.* A person withholding subpoenaed information under a claim that it is privileged or subject to protection as trial-preparation material shall make the claim expressly and provide information that will enable the parties to assess the claim. A privilege log need not be prepared, except by agreement or order of the court.

(B) *Information mistakenly produced.* If information produced in response to a subpoena is subject to a claim of privilege or of protection as trial-preparation material, the person making the claim may notify any party that received the information of the claim and the basis for it. The provisions of Rule 26(b)(5)(B) and (C) are applicable.

(3) *Further Protection.* Any person subject to a subpoena under this rule may move the court:

(A) for a protective order under rule 26(c) or

(B) to be deemed entitled to any protection set forth in any discovery or procedural order previously entered in the case.

(g) **Contempt.** Failure by any person without adequate excuse to obey a subpoena served upon him may be deemed a contempt of the court in which the action is pending.

Amended August 3, 1982, effective January 1, 1983; November 17, 1986, effective January 1, 1987; September 24, 2013, effective January 1, 2014; January 29, 2015, effective April 1, 2015.

Reporter's Notes—1973

Rule 45 closely follows Federal Rule 45 with changes to coincide with prior Massachusetts practice. In these Rules, the word "subpoena" is the equivalent of "witness summons" in prior Massachusetts practice. The word "summons" in these Rules always means "summons of complaint." The first sentence of Rule 45(a) embodies the provisions of G.L. c. 233, § 1:

A clerk of a court of record, or notary public or a justice of the peace may issue summonses for witnesses in all cases pending before courts. . . .

Rule 45(b) incorporates the familiar Massachusetts practice of issuing subpoenas duces tecum. The rule specifically allows the subpoena to be used to command the production of books, papers, documents or tangible things. The section incorporates a protective device on behalf of the person to whom the subpoena is addressed. By motion made promptly, the producent can have the court modify or quash the

subpoena if it is unreasonable and oppressive, or require the party seeking the production to pay the costs thereof. Quashing or modifying a subpoena which is unreasonable is well established in Massachusetts practice. See Finance Commission of the City of Boston v. McGrath, 343 Mass. 754, 765, 180 N.E.2d 808, 815–816 (1962); Bull v. Loveland, 27 Mass. 9 (1830). Observe the relation between Rule 45(b) and Rule 26(c), which gives the person served with a notice for the taking of a deposition the right to move the court for appropriate relief, including an order that the deposition may not be taken or that it may be taken only at some designated place, or that the scope of inquiry be limited. Rule 45(b)(1) gives a non-party under a subpoena duces tecum the right to seek a protective order. Without the language of Rule 45(b)(1), a non-party subpoenaed merely to force the production of documents (as, for example, the custodian of records of a hospital) would not be explicitly empowered to seek appropriate court relief; indeed, the silence of the rules on the point might be interpreted to mean that he has no such right. The language of Rule 45(b)(1) is designed to eliminate all such confusion.

Rule 45(c) allows service of a subpoena to be made by any non-party who is over 18 years of age. This accords with G.L. c. 233, § 2 which allows service of a summons to be made "by an officer qualified to serve civil process or by a disinterested person." Both statute and rule thus permit service by a party's attorney. Although permissible, this practice may be unwise *cf.* ABA, Canons of Professional Ethics, Canon 19; ABA Code of Professional Responsibility DR 5–102; EC 5–9, 5–10.

Rule 45(c) permits service to be made in accordance with pre-rule Massachusetts practice. See G.L. c. 233, § 2. The requirement that the fees be tendered to the witness accords with G.L. c. 233, § 3:

No person shall be required to attend as a witness in a civil case . . . unless the legal fees for one day's attendance and for travel to and from the place where he is required to attend are paid or tendered to him.

Rule 45(d) provides the mechanism for using a subpoena to compel the attendance of a witness at a deposition. It also permits the subpoena to be used to compel the deponent to produce at the deposition designated papers, documents, books or tangible things. Such use of a subpoena is not intended to circumvent whatever good-cause-for-production requirements may remain in the discovery rules, at least as to parties. Rule 45(d)(1) indeed gives a non-party deponent substantially all the objection-rights of a party. A subpoena for the attendance of a witness at a deposition may not be issued without a showing that service of notice to take a deposition as provided for in the discovery rules has been made.

Rule 45(d)(1) regulates the place-of-taking-of in Massachusetts depositions only. It does not attempt to regulate the problem of enforcement of subpoenas out-of-state. Whether the state will honor a Massachusetts subpoena is a question that depends on reciprocal arrangements between Massachusetts and the state in question, and must be resolved ad hoc. Presumably, the state enforcing the Massachusetts subpoena will in its order of enforcement make explicit the place where the deposition is to be taken. An in-state deponent may not be summoned to a deposition more than 50 miles from where he lives or works. The mileage is specified in airline (i.e., straight-line) terms in order to obviate disputes over road distances.

Rule 45(e) provides that a subpoena shall issue as a matter of course upon the request of any party. This section is applicable to hearings as well as trials and follows pre-rule Massachusetts practice. See G.L. c. 233, §§ 1, 7, 8.

Rule 45(f) likewise works no change in Massachusetts practice; it preserves the existing law as to penalties for failure to comply with the requirements of a subpoena. Failure of a party to submit to discovery is also punishable by an appropriate order under Rule 37.

Reporter's Notes—1983

This amendment makes clear that one cannot circumvent the time periods in Rule 30(b)(5) and Rule 34(b) by serving a deposition subpoena duces tecum on another party.

A subpoena is unnecessary to compel a party to appear or to produce documents at a party's deposition. See Rules 37(d) and 30(b)(5).

Reporter's Notes—1986

This amendment makes clear that a deposition subpoena can require, in addition to production, permission to inspect and copy designated books, papers, documents, or tangible things. The amendment brings the Massachusetts Rule closer to the wording of Fed. R.Civ.P. 45(d).

Reporter's Notes—2008

In 2008, Rule 26(b)(5) was amended to require the production of a privilege log by a party who makes a claim of privilege or protection in response to a discovery request. The requirement of a privilege log applies to a claim of privilege or right to protection asserted by a *party* only. Rule 26(b)(5) imposes no obligation to produce a privilege log on the part of a non-party who withholds information after service of a subpoena for the production of documentary evidence under Rule 45(b), although a court would appear to have authority to order preparation of a log.

Reporter's Notes—2014

The 2014 amendments to Rule 45 were part of a series of amendments concerning discovery of electronically stored information. For background, see the 2014 Reporter's Notes to Rule 26.

The 2014 amendments relating to electronically stored information have resulted in a number of changes to Rule 45.

Language has been added to Rule 45(b) recognizing a duty on the party issuing a subpoena to "take reasonable steps to avoid imposing undue burden or expense on a person subject to the subpoena." This language makes the Massachusetts rule similar to its federal counterpart. It is a recognition of the burden involving time and expense that a subpoena imposes upon a third person, often with no stake in the outcome and often without counsel. Although this provision has been added in connection with amendments that relate to electronic discovery, the requirement of taking steps to avoid undue burden and expense is not limited to subpoenas involving electronically stored information.

References to "electronically stored information" have been added to Rule 45(b) and (d).

Existing Rule 45(f) (contempt) has been redesignated as Rule 45(g).

Rule 45(f), taken from Rule 45(d) of the Federal Rules of Civil Procedure, has been added. Rule 45(f) sets forth procedures applicable to producing documents, including electronically stored information.

Rule 45(f)(2) is modeled after Rule 45(d)(2)(A) of the Federal Rules of Civil Procedure, but with the added proviso that a person subpoenaed need not prepare a privilege log, a recognition of the burden that otherwise would be imposed on a non-party claiming a privilege.

Rule 45(f)(2)(B), dealing with information mistakenly produced that is subject to a claim of privilege or protection, incorporates the "clawback" provisions and procedures set forth in Rule 26(b)(5)(B) and (C).

Reporter's Notes–2015

Background to 2015 Amendments

In 2013, the Standing Advisory Committee on the Rules of Civil Procedure of the Supreme Judicial Court (Standing Advisory Committee) undertook a review of Rule 45 governing subpoenas. Two matters that prompted the Committee to undertake this review were changes to Rule 45 of the Federal Rules of Civil Procedure effective December 1, 2013 and changes to Rule 45 of the Massachusetts Rules of Civil Procedure resulting from a series of rules amendments that dealt with discovery of electronically stored information effective January 1, 2014.

The most significant change in Rule 45 as result of this review was the adoption for Massachusetts practice of a "documents only" subpoena directed to a non-party, a practice that has existed under the Federal Rules of Civil Procedure since 1991.

Without the formal rules-based ability to subpoena documents from a non-party, Massachusetts lawyers have accomplished a result similar to that allowed under the Federal Rules by resorting to a practice of noticing the deposition of a keeper of records together with a deposition subpoena that required the production of documents at the deposition. See Rules 30(b)(1) and 45(d) (prior to the instant amendment). As long as there was no need to depose the keeper of records and only a desire to obtain the requested documents, the party seeking the discovery would agree to "waive" the appearance at the deposition if the documents themselves were produced. With the adoption of a documents only subpoena in 2015, there is no longer a need in Massachusetts to use deposition practice in regard to a non-party for the sole purpose of document production.

Other changes were made to Rule 45 to bring the rule up-to-date and to make the rule consistent with current subpoena practice.

The 2015 Amendments

A number of changes have been made to Rule 45 to deal with the dual nature of the subpoena— to command the appearance of a non-party witness and to command production of documents, etc. from the non-party witness. The following is a section-by-section analysis describing the significant changes.

Rule 45(a).

As amended, Rule 45(a) states that a subpoena may command a person, in addition to giving testimony, "to produce designated documents, electronically stored information, or tangible things in that person's possession, custody or control; or to permit inspection of premises" and to do so "at a specified time and place." The addition of the quoted language formally adopts the concept of a documents only subpoena for Massachusetts civil practice.

A specific reference to electronically stored information has been added, consistent with other changes made to the discovery rules in 2014 regarding discovery of electronically stored information.

The language added to Rule 45(a) has been adapted from Rule 45(a)(1)(A)(iii) of the Federal Rules of Civil Procedure.

Rule 45(b).

As revised, this rule implements the documents only provisions of the new rule. The new title to Rule 45(b) and language that a command to produce documents, etc. may be included in a subpoena to attend a deposition or in a separate subpoena are taken from Rule 45(a)(1)(C) of the Federal Rules of Civil Procedure.

The last sentence of the revised rule makes clear that a command to produce documents, etc. does not require the person upon whom it is served to "appear in person at the place of production or inspection unless also commanded to appear for a deposition, hearing, or trial." See Rule 45(d)(2)(A) of the Federal Rules of Civil Procedure.

Rule 45(c).

Rule 45(c), dealing with service of the subpoena, makes clear that the requirement of tendering of fees to the person served with the subpoena applies only if the person's attendance is commanded and does not apply if the subpoena commands production only.

Rule 45(d).

A provision has been added to Rule 45(d)(1) that prior to service of a documents only subpoena before trial, a copy of the subpoena must be served on each party. This language differs from Rule 45(a)(4) of the

Federal Rules of Civil Procedure, which requires that both a notice and a copy of the subpoena to be served on each party. The Massachusetts version reflects the belief that the requirement of a notice in addition to a copy of the subpoena is not needed. Service of a copy of the subpoena will provide sufficient notice to allow other parties to monitor discovery and to raise any objection to the subpoena.

The party serving the subpoena must also serve on all parties to the case a copy of any objection received to the subpoena as well as a notice of any production made or alternatively, a copy of the production. Similar requirements do not appear in the Federal Rules. The Massachusetts addition was provided so that parties to the case, other than the party who served the subpoena, are aware of the scope of production and are aware of any objection to production made by the non-party who has been served with the subpoena. The language also gives the option to the party who receives the documents to provide copies of the documents to the other parties, as often was the prior practice.

The last paragraph of Rule 45(d)(1) states that if there is an objection to production by the person served with the subpoena, the party seeking production may move to compel production. "Such an order to compel production or inspection shall protect a person who is neither a party nor a party's officer from undue burden or expense resulting from compliance." This quoted language in the Massachusetts rule differs from the cognate provision in Rule 45(d)(2)(B)(ii) of the Federal Rules of Civil Procedure. The federal rule provides that an order of production must protect the person "from significant expense resulting from compliance."

This is an intentional variation from the federal rules. The Massachusetts version adopts the same language that was added to Rule 45(b) in connection with the 2014 amendments regarding electronically stored information. A party issuing a subpoena is required to "take reasonable steps to avoid imposing undue burden or expense on a person subject to the subpoena." Rule 45(b), as amended effective January 1, 2014. The 2014 Reporter's Notes to the Massachusetts amendments described the philosophy behind the language "undue burden or expense" as follows:

It is a recognition of the burden involving time and expense that a subpoena imposes upon a third person, often with no stake in the outcome and often without counsel. Although this provision has been added in connection with amendments that relate to electronic discovery, the requirement of taking steps to avoid undue burden and expense is not limited to subpoenas involving electronically stored information.

The Massachusetts language is intended to provide judges with broad discretion on a case-by-case basis to deal with the burden on a non-party to a case, and the possible expense, involved in responding to a subpoena. Its language is sufficiently broad to allow a court to require cost-sharing in its discretion as part of an order to produce.

The title of Rule 45(d) has also been revised to reflect the new procedure for a documents only subpoena.

Rule 45(e).

The pre–2015 version of Rule 45(e) dealt with a subpoena requiring attendance at a hearing or trial. The 2015 amendments added language making this provision applicable as well to a subpoena requiring production of documents, etc.

Rule 45(f).

A sentence has been added to Rule 45(f)(1)(A) to address the question whether copies of documents or originals of documents must be produced in response to a subpoena. The sentence states that in the case of a documents only subpoena, the producing person may produce copies of the documents, unless originals were requested in the command. However, if requested, the producing party must provide "all parties a fair opportunity to verify the copies by comparison with the originals."

This sentence is not in the federal rules. It is intended to recognize the general practice in Massachusetts of producing copies of documents, and not the originals, other than at a deposition, hearing, or trial. This is consistent with the procedure applicable where documents are produced in connection with a deposition and the producing party desires to retain the originals. Rule 30(f)(1), second paragraph, provides that under such circumstances, the producing party may (A) offer copies to be marked for identification and annexed to the deposition and to serve thereafter as originals if he affords to all parties fair opportunity to verify the copies by comparison with the originals, or (B) offer the originals to be marked for identification, after giving to each party an opportunity to inspect and copy them, in which event the materials may then be used in the same manner as if annexed to the deposition.

The sentence provides that copies may be produced "by electronic means." This language recognizes the benefits of producing copies by such methods as electronic transfer of files by e-mail, CD–ROM, or Internet connection.

The last sentence of Rule 45(f)(1)(2)(A) has been amended to provide that even though a privilege log is not required in the case of a subpoena to a third person where there is an objection on the basis of privilege, the parties may agree to the preparation of a privilege log or the court may so order.

Rule 45(g).

There are no changes to Rule 45(g) dealing with contempt for failure to obey a subpoena.

Rule 46. Exceptions Unnecessary

Formal exceptions to rulings or orders of the court are unnecessary; but for all purposes for which an exception has heretofore been necessary it is sufficient that a party, at the time the ruling or order of the court is made or sought, makes known to the court the action which he desires the court to take or his objection to the action of the court and his grounds therefor; and, if a party has no opportunity to object to a ruling or order at the time it is made, the absence of an objection does not thereafter prejudice him.

Reporter's Notes—1973

Under Rule 46, which is identical to Federal Rule 46, a party need no longer mouth the magic word "exception" to save his right to review a questionable ruling by the trial judge. The party must merely clearly indicate to the court what he wants the court to do or object to the action of the court stating his grounds therefor.

Although Rule 46 presumes the requirement of objection, it does eliminate exceptions and bills of exceptions. This severely changes Massachusetts practice, where an objection was considered a mere preliminary gesture indicating to the judge that alleged error was about to occur. Thus the opposing party was warned of the possibility of error so that he might correct the defect, if he could and would, and the trial judge was given an opportunity to exercise his judgment on the contention. An objection in Massachusetts formerly preserved *no* rights. That could be done only by claiming an exception following an adverse ruling on an objection. Consequently, an exception, properly taken and preserved, was necessary and sufficient to obtain appellate review of a question; an objection, although a necessary basis of an exception, Mouradian v. Giblin, 254 Mass. 478, 479, 150 N.E. 215 (1926), did not suffice to obtain review, Leyland v. Pingree, 134 Mass. 367, 370 (1883).

Under Rule 46, these purposes are served entirely by an objection. The same specificity formerly required in taking an exception, Graunstein v. Boston & Me. R.R., 317 Mass. 164, 167, 57 N.E.2d 570, 572 (1944) would under Rule 46 be required in making an objection. See Maulding v. Louisville & Nashville R. Co., 168 F.2d 880 (7th Cir.1948). General objections are regarded with the same disfavor as general exceptions used to be and will be found adequate only if the grounds can not possibly be misunderstood. See Johnston v. Reily, 160 F.2d 249 (D.C.1947). Without a *specific* objection and a ruling on it, the appellate court under Rule 46 will generally not review the question, any more than it would review an overruled objection to which under prior practice a specific exception was not taken. In the federal system, if the trial court has committed "fundamental error" (sometimes called "plain error"), the Court of Appeals may review the point, even though no objection was raised below. See Sibbach v. Wilson, 312 U.S. 1, 16, 61 S.Ct. 422, 427, 85 L.Ed. 479 (1941). Massachusetts does not follow the "fundamental error" doctrine. The Reporters know no case in which the Supreme Judicial Court has allowed late-claimed error to affect the outcome. The closest the Court has come to considering such error was Newell v. West, 149 Mass. 520, 531–532, 21 N.E. 954, 958–959 (1889), where a "purely clerical" error in an account was corrected on appeal, even though not questioned below.

Reporter's Notes—1996

Rule 46 has been applicable in the District Court since the adoption of the District/Municipal Courts Rules for Appellate Division Appeal in 1994. Note that under the terms of this rule, no objection is necessary in the District Court to preserve for appeal rulings made by the court in response to written requests for rulings. See Rule 64A of these rules.

Rule 47.   Jurors

(a) **Examination of Jurors.** The trial judge shall examine on oath all persons called as jurors, in each case, and shall ask: (1) whether any juror or any member of his family is related to any party or attorney therein; (2) whether any has any interest therein; (3) whether any has expressed any opinion on the case; (4) whether any has formed any opinion thereon; (5) whether any is sensible of any bias or prejudice therein; and (6) whether any knows of any reason why he cannot or does not stand indifferent in the case. The jurors shall respond to each question separately before the next is propounded. The trial judge may submit, of his own motion or on that of any party, such additional questions as he deems proper. The trial judge may also, on motion of any party, permit the parties or their attorneys to make such further inquiry of the jurors on oath as he deems proper.

(b) **Courts Other Than District Courts: Additional Jurors.** The court may order impanelled a jury of not more than sixteen members and the court shall have jurisdiction to try the case with such jury as provided by law. Each side is entitled to 1 peremptory challenge in addition to those otherwise allowed by law if 1 or 2 additional jurors are to be impanelled, and 2 peremptory challenges if 3 or 4 additional jurors are to be impanelled.

(c) **District Court: Additional Jurors.** The court may order impanelled a jury of not more than eight members and the court shall have jurisdiction to try the case with such jury as provided by law. Each side is entitled to 1 peremptory challenge in addition to those otherwise allowed by law if 1 or 2 additional jurors are to be impanelled.

Amended November 28, 2007, effective March 1, 2008.

Reporter's Notes—1973

Rule 47(a) changes Federal Rule 47 and clarifies ambiguities in the controlling statute, G.L. c. 234, § 28. The statute reads in part:

"Upon motion of either party, the court shall, or the parties or their attorneys may under the direction of the court, examine on oath a person who is called as a juror therein, to learn whether he is related to either party or has any interest in the case, or has expressed or formed an opinion, or is sensible of any bias or prejudice, therein; and the objecting party may introduce other competent evidence in support of the objection. If the court finds that the juror does not stand indifferent in the case, another shall be called in his stead."

Rule 47(a) makes clear that the court, rather than the clerk, is *required* to ask certain questions. Prior practice, which permitted the clerk to ask the questions, did not convey to the jurors with necessary clarity the significance of the questions. Rule 47(a) has been divided into numbered classes. The court is to ask each question separately; the jurors are to respond to each question before the judge propounds the next question.

The questions themselves are taken from G.L. c. 234, § 28. Rule 47(a)(1) emphasizes not merely relation to a party, but to a participating attorney; this last relationship may be as productive of prejudice as relation to a party. Rules 47(a)(2), (3), (4) and (5) are taken almost verbatim from the statute. Rule 47(a)(6) is a catchall designed to ensure that each juror has an opportunity, under judicial interrogation, to reveal any reason for his disqualification not covered by the rest of the rule.

The final sentence of Rule 47(a) allows the court to permit the parties or attorneys to make whatever direct inquiry the court may deem proper.

Rule 47(a) further permits the court to submit to the jurors any question in addition to the six specified questions.

An addition to G.L. c. 234, § 28, enacted in 1973 (see Chapter 919 of the Acts of 1973), provides that

"if it appears that, as a result of the impact of considerations which may cause a decision or decisions to be made in whole or in part upon issues extraneous to the case, including, but not limited to, community attitudes, possible exposure to potentially prejudicial material or possible preconceived opinions toward the credibility of certain classes of persons, the juror may not stand indifferent, the court may, or the parties or their attorneys may, with the permission and under the direction of the court, examine the juror specifically with respect to such considerations, attitudes, exposure, opinions or any other matters which may, as aforesaid, cause a decision or decisions to be made in whole or in part upon issues extraneous to the issues in the case. Such examination may include a brief statement of the facts of the case, to the extent the facts are appropriate and relevant to the issues of such examination, and shall be conducted individually and outside the presence of other persons about to be called as jurors or already called."

Such additional questions would be likewise authorized by the last two sentences of Rule 47(a).

The procedure under Rule 47(a) applies to any juror called to replace any juror challenged or otherwise excused, as well as to any alternate jurors.

The net effect of Rule 47(a) will be:

(1) Initial questions will be asked by the judge;

(2) The judge on his own motion or on motion of the parties may ask any further questions; and

(3) On motion of a party the judge may (but need not) permit limited voir dire.

Under Federal Rule 47(b) the court may direct that not more than six additional jurors may be called and impanelled. Rule 47(b) adopts the existing Massachusetts practice of four additional jurors, G.L. c. 234, § 26B. Federal Rule 47(b) requires all the additional jurors to be impanelled as designated alternate jurors; under Massachusetts practice those jurors who are designated as alternate jurors, with the exception of the foreman, are not determined until the case is ready for submission to the jury. Rule 47(b) follows the Massachusetts approach; a juror is likely to be more attentive if it is probable that he will be called upon to participate in reaching a verdict.

Also, under Federal Rule 47(b), an alternate juror who does not replace a regular juror must be discharged after the jury retires to consider its verdict. Under Massachusetts practice, as incorporated in Rule 47(b), even after the case has been submitted to the jury, if a juror is unable to perform his duty, an alternate juror will be selected and the jury will renew its deliberations with the alternate juror.

Reporter's Notes—1996

With the merger of the District Court rules into the Mass.R.Civ.P., Rule 47 has been made applicable to the District Court, to the extent that Massachusetts law permits trial by jury in District Court civil actions.

Reporter's Notes—2008

Rule 47 has been amended to add an additional section (c) dealing with six-person juries in the District Court. Rule 47(b) applies to all courts other than the District Court.

New Rule 47(c) provides for impanelling up to eight jurors. The statewide one-trial statute provides that the number of peremptory challenges is two for each party. G.L. c. 218, § 19(B)(c).

Rule 48.   Number of Jurors—Majority Verdict

The parties may stipulate that the jury shall consist of any number less than twelve, or less than six in the District Court, or that a verdict or a finding of a stated majority of the jurors shall be taken as the verdict or finding of the jury.

Amended November 28, 2007, effective March 1, 2008.

Reporter's Notes—1973

Rule 48 is the same as Federal Rule 48. Its provisions should be read in connection with Mass.G.L. c. 234, §§ 34A and 34B. Under section 34A, an agreement of five-sixths of the jury suffices to render a verdict. Under section 34B, if during trial a juror is unable to perform his duty for good cause (e.g.—death, illness) the trial may proceed with the remaining jurors, except that no trial may proceed with less than ten jurors unless the parties agree to the lesser number.

Reporter's Notes—1996

With the merger of the District Court rules into the Mass.R.Civ.P., Rule 48 has been made applicable to the District Court, to the extent that Massachusetts law permits trial by jury in District Court civil actions.

Reporter's Notes—2008

The title of Rule 48 has been changed to "Number of Jurors— Majority Verdict" in light of the fact that there are six-person juries in the District Court. The language of Rule 48 has likewise been amended.

Rule 49.   Special Verdicts and Interrogatories

(a) **Special Verdicts.** The court may require a jury to return only a special verdict in the form of a special written finding upon each issue of fact. In that event the court may submit to the jury written questions susceptible of categorical or other brief answer or may submit written forms of the several special findings which might properly be made under the pleadings and evidence; or it may use such other method of submitting the issues and requiring the written findings thereon as it deems most appropriate. The court shall give to the jury such explanation and instruction concerning the matter thus submitted as may be necessary to enable the jury to make its findings upon each issue. If in so doing the court omits any issue of fact raised by the pleadings or by the evidence, each party waives his right to a trial by jury of the issue so omitted unless before the jury retires he demands its submission to the jury. As to an issue omitted without such demand the court may make a finding; or, if it fails to do so, it shall be deemed to have made a finding in accord with the judgment on the special verdict.

(b) **General Verdict Accompanied by Answer to Interrogatories.** The court may submit to the jury, together with appropriate forms for a general verdict, written interrogatories upon one or more issues of fact the decision of which is necessary to a verdict. The court shall give such explanation or instruction as may be necessary to enable the jury both to make answers to the interrogatories and to render a general verdict, and the court shall direct the jury both to make written answers and to render a general verdict. When the general verdict and the answers are harmonious, the appropriate judgment upon the verdict and answers shall be entered pursuant to Rule 58. When the answers are consistent with each other but one or more is inconsistent with the general verdict, judgment may be entered pursuant to Rule 58 in accordance with the answers, notwithstanding the general verdict, or the court may return the jury for further consideration of its answers and verdict or may order a new trial. When the answers are inconsistent with each other and one or more is likewise inconsistent with the general verdict, judgment shall not be entered, but the court shall return the jury for further consideration of its answers and verdict or shall order a new trial.

Reporter's Notes—1973

Rule 49, identical to Federal Rule 49, prescribes two special methods by which the court may submit issues of fact to a jury: the special verdict, and the general verdict accompanied by answers to interrogatories. Under Rule 49(a) the court may require a jury to return only a special verdict. The issue may be put to the jury under this rule in one of three ways: (1) It may submit written questions; (2) it may submit written alternative special findings (so long as they are within the pleading and evidence), or (3) it may use such other method as it deems "appropriate."

If the court omits any issue of fact, each party waives his right to trial by jury as to that issue unless he objects before the jury retires. The court may make a finding as to that issue; if it fails to make any finding, the issues will be deemed to have been decided in accordance with the judgment on the special verdict. Palmiero v. Spada Distributing Co., 217 F.2d 561 (9th Cir.1954).

The special verdict, well known in Massachusetts practice, originated in common law. See Frati v. Jannini, 226 Mass. 430, 431, 115 N.E. 746, 747 (1917). It is recognized by G.L. c. 231, § 124, G.L. c. 231A, § 1 (declaratory judgment) and G.L. c. 231, § 85 (comparative negligence). Except for cases falling under Mass.G.L. c. 231, § 85 (comparative negligence), under prior practice the trial judge had full discretion to determine whether or not the jury should return a general or a special verdict, Stone v. Orth Chevrolet Co., Inc., 284 Mass. 525, 528, 187 N.E. 810, 812 (1933). The Reporters have found no limitation on the court's discretion as to the form or nature of the questions to be presented to the jury other than Mass.G.L. c. 231, § 85, supra, requiring the jury to find: (1) the amount of damages which would have been recoverable had there been no contributory negligence; and (2) the degree of negligence of each party expressed as a percentage.

The provision of Rule 49(a) that a party waives his jury right pro tanto if any issue is not submitted by the court to the jury is new to

Massachusetts, as is the provision permitting the judge to find the facts of any such non-submitted issue. In Fitzgerald v. Young, 225 Mass. 116, 121, 113 N.E. 777, 778–779 (1916) the judge failed to submit an issue of material fact to the jury. The jury returned with findings tending to show that the defendant was not liable. Over the plaintiff's objection, the judge thereupon directed a verdict for the defendant. The Supreme Judicial Court held that the plaintiff had a right to a jury trial on the omitted issue of fact. See also Stone v. Orth Chevrolet Co., Inc., 284 Mass. 525, 528, 187 N.E. 910, 912 (1933).

Note that in *Fitzgerald* the plaintiff's objection was held to be timely, even though it was made *after* the judge directed a verdict for the defendant. This directly conflicts with Rule 49(a). Further, the *Fitzgerald* jury in fact returned a "special verdict," as the term is used in Rule 49(a). It answered the special questions submitted to it; the judge then directed a defendant's verdict. Under Rule 49(a), the judge would merely have entered judgment for the defendant; the net effect is identical. Rule 49(a), in other words, allows the jury to find the basic facts, with the judge then applying the law to those facts and entering judgment for the appropriate party.

Rule 49(b) allows the court to require the jury to return, not merely a general verdict, but also specific answers to one or more special interrogatories. In federal practice, the court has full discretion as to whether or not special questions should be submitted to the jury, Moyer v. Aetna Life Insurance Co., 126 F.2d 141, 145 (1941). If the general verdict and the answers to the interrogatories are consistent the court will enter the appropriate judgment. If the answers to the interrogatories are consistent with each other but inconsistent with the general verdict the court has three options: (1) enter judgment in accordance with the answers to interrogatories notwithstanding the general verdict; (2) return the jury for further consideration; or (3) order a new trial.

Under Federal Rule 49(b), "every reasonable intendment in favor of the general verdict should be indulged in an effort to harmonize the two. The answers override the general verdict and warrant the entry of judgment in disregard of the latter only where the conflict on a material question is beyond reconciliation on any reasonable theory consistent with the evidence and its fair inferences." Mayer v. Petzelt, 311 F.2d 601, 603n. (7th Cir.1962), quoting Theurer v. Holland Furnace Co., 124 F.2d 494, 498 (10th Cir.1941).

If the answers to interrogatories are inconsistent with each other and one or more is also inconsistent with the general verdict, the court may only (1) order the jury out for further consideration; or (2) order a new trial.

In Massachusetts, the practice of submitting special questions to the jury along with a request for a general verdict is recognized by statute, G.L. c. 231, § 124 and G.L. c. 231A, § 1. But the court's power to utilize the procedure is not statutory, Burgess v. Giovannucci, 314 Mass. 252, 256, 49 N.E.2d 907, 909 (1943), and the court has full discretion as to whether or not special questions should be submitted, Viaux v. John T. Scully Foundation, 247 Mass. 296, 301, 142 N.E. 81, 83 (1924).

The Reporters know no Massachusetts case dealing specifically with the problem of a general verdict which is inconsistent with one or more special questions. In Dorr v. Fenno, 29 Mass. 520, 525–526 (1832), a case involving jury misconduct (quotient verdict), the court indicated by way of dictum that a judge could either send the jury back for further deliberations or set the verdict aside in the event that the general verdict was inconsistent with the answers to special questions.

Rule 49(b) is inconsistent with Massachusetts practice in two respects. Rule 49(b) requires that special questions be in writing; under prior Massachusetts practice the judge could put the questions to the jury orally, Newell v. Rosenberg, 275 Mass. 455, 458, 176 N.E. 616, 617 (1931). Rule 49(b) also requires that the special questions be submitted "*together with* appropriate forms for a general verdict" (emphasis added); prior Massachusetts practice permitted the judge

to submit questions after the jury had returned with a general verdict, Id.

Reporter's Notes—1996
With the merger of the District Court rules into the Mass.R.Civ.P., Rule 49 has been made applicable to the District Court, to the extent that Massachusetts law permits trial by jury in District Court civil actions.

Rule 50. Motion for a Directed Verdict and for Judgment Notwithstanding the Verdict

(a) Motion for Directed Verdict: When Made; Effect. A party may move for a directed verdict at the close of the evidence offered by an opponent, and may offer evidence in the event that the motion is not granted, without having reserved the right so to do and to the same extent as if the motion had not been made. A party may also move for a directed verdict at the close of all the evidence. A motion for a directed verdict which is not granted is not a waiver of trial by jury even though all parties to the action have moved for directed verdicts. A motion for a directed verdict shall state the specific grounds therefor. The order of the court granting a motion for a directed verdict is effective without any assent of the jury.

(b) Motion for Judgment Notwithstanding the Verdict. Whenever a motion for a directed verdict made at the close of all the evidence is denied or for any reason is not granted, the court is deemed to have submitted the action to the jury subject to a later determination of the legal questions raised by the motion. Not later than 10 days after entry of judgment, a party who has moved for a directed verdict may serve a motion to have the verdict and any judgment entered thereon set aside and to have judgment entered in accordance with the motion for a directed verdict; or if a verdict was not returned such party, within 10 days after the jury has been discharged, may serve a motion for judgment in accordance with the motion for a directed verdict. A motion for a new trial may be joined with this motion, or a new trial may be prayed for in the alternative. If a verdict was returned the court may allow the judgment to stand or may reopen the judgment and either order a new trial or direct the entry of judgment as if the requested verdict had been directed. If no verdict was returned the court may direct the entry of judgment as if the requested verdict had been directed or may order a new trial.

(c) Same: Conditional Rulings on Grant of Motion.

(1) If the motion for judgment notwithstanding the verdict, provided for in subdivision (b) of this rule is granted, the court shall also rule on the motion for a new trial, if any, by determining whether it should be granted if the judgment is thereafter vacated or reversed, and shall specify the grounds for granting or denying the motion for the new trial. If the motion for a new trial is thus conditionally granted, the order thereon does not affect the finality of the judgment. In case the motion for a new trial has been conditionally granted and the judgment is reversed on appeal, the new trial shall proceed unless the appellate court has otherwise ordered. In case the motion for a new trial has been conditionally denied, the appellee on appeal may assert error in that denial; and if the judgment is reversed on appeal, subsequent proceedings shall be in accordance with the order of the appellate court.

(2) The party whose verdict has been set aside on motion for judgment notwithstanding the verdict may serve a motion for a new trial pursuant to Rule 59 not later than 10 days after entry of the judgment notwithstanding the verdict.

(d) Same: Denial of Motion. If the motion for judgment notwithstanding the verdict is denied, the party who prevailed on that motion may, as appellee, assert grounds entitling him to a new trial in the event the appellate court concludes that the trial court erred in denying the motion for judgment notwithstanding the verdict. If the appellate court reverses the judgment, nothing in this rule precludes it from determining that the appellee is entitled to a new trial, or from directing the trial court to determine whether a new trial shall be granted.

Amended October 1, 1998, effective November 2, 1998.

Reporter's Notes—1973

Rule 50(a) is patterned upon Federal Rule 50(a), with the first sentence revised for clarity. It liberalizes the Massachusetts practice governing defendant's motion for a directed verdict at the close of the plaintiff's evidence. Formerly, the judge could refuse to rule upon the defendant's motion unless the defendant rested his case upon his opponent's evidence, thereby surrendering his right to put in his own case. See Hurley v. O'Sullivan, 137 Mass. 86, 87 (1884). "The defendant was not entitled to a ruling upon plaintiff's case, reserving to himself the right to put in his own case afterwards." McMahon v. Tyng, 96 Mass. 167, 169 (1867). Under Rule 50(a), the defendant retains just that right. The judge may still refuse to decide such motion when made, but must rule on it at a later stage of the trial.

"Plaintiff says that 50(a) itself provides no right of reservation or later determination of the motion by the court. The answer to this contention is that nowhere in 50(a) is there evidence of any intention to take from the court its power to reserve a motion at the end of plaintiff's case and later dispose of that motion. . . . [W]here the court has taken a motion under advisement under 50(a) it not only can but *must* decide the issue." Sattler v. Great Atlantic & Pacific Tea Co., 18 F.R.D. 271, 274 (W.D.La.1955); see also, Stevens v. G.L. Rugo & Sons Inc., 115 F.Supp. 61, 62 (D.Mass.1952), reversed on other grounds, 209 F.2d 135 (1st Cir.1953).

Until now, the only formal requirements for a motion for directed verdict were that it be in writing, (Super.Ct.R. 71), and that if the declaration contained more than one count the motion specify the particular count upon which a verdict is sought. The provision of Rule 50(a) that a motion for a directed verdict "state the specific grounds therefor," although often strongly advocated by the Supreme Judicial Court, is new to Massachusetts practice. "When a judge is not prepared to grant such a motion, a prudent practice for him to adopt is to require the moving party to state all the grounds upon which he relies in support of the motion as otherwise an exception to the denial of the motion leaves open every ground in support of the motion even though not mentioned or even thought of at the time of the trial", Trites v. City of Melrose, 318 Mass. 378, 380, 61 N.E.2d 656, 657 (1945).

The motion for judgment notwithstanding the verdict is new to Massachusetts practice. Unlike practice under former G.L. c. 231, § 120 (entry of verdict or finding in accordance with leave reserved), a motion for judgment n.o.v. does not depend upon the judge's discretionary reservation of leave to review the sufficiency of either party's case. Rule 50(b) presumes such a reservation in every case in which an unsuccessful motion for directed verdict has been made at the close of all the evidence.

The provisions of Rule 50(b) make a party's motion for directed verdict a prerequisite to his motion for judgment notwithstanding the verdict. In Massachusetts, no preliminary motion was required before a party could move that a verdict be entered in his favor under leave

reserved. Interstate Busses Corp. v. McKenna, 329 Mass. 1, 2, 105 N.E.2d 852, 853 (1952).

There is no Massachusetts practice similar to the provisions of Rule 50(c) and (d). They aim at expediting judicial administration by requiring the trial judge to make "if-it-should-be-determined-I-have-erred" rulings with respect to a motion for new trial made concurrently with the motion for judgment n.o.v.

Reporter's Notes—1996

With the merger of the District Court rules into the Mass.R.Civ.P., Rule 50 has been made applicable to the District Court, to the extent that Massachusetts law permits trial by jury in District Court civil actions.

Reporter's Notes—1998

Prior to amendment in 1998, the language of Rule 50(b) provided that a party may "move" for judgment notwithstanding the verdict within ten days of entry of judgment. The Appeals Court has construed this language to require *service* of the motion within the ten-day period, rather than filing. Russell v. Pride Convenience, Inc., 37 Mass. App. Ct. 502 (1994). Filing in court should be made within a reasonable time after service. Mass.R.Civ.P. 5(d). The Supreme Judicial Court has endorsed this interpretation. F.W. Webb Co. v. Averett, 422 Mass. 625, 629, n.5 (1996).

The 1998 amendment to Rule 50(b) adopts this interpretation by deleting the term "move" and substituting language requiring *service* of the motion within ten days. The change is not intended to alter existing practice. Rather, it serves to harmonize the language of Rule 50(b) with that of Rule 59, the latter requiring a motion for new trial to be "served" not later than ten days after judgment.

Rule 51. Argument: Instructions to Jury

(a) Time for Argument. Counsel for each party shall be allowed thirty minutes for argument; but before the argument commences, the court, on motion or sua sponte, may reasonably reduce or extend the time. When two or more attorneys are to be heard on behalf of the same party, they may divide their time as they elect.

(b) Instructions to Jury: Objection. At the close of the evidence or at such earlier time during the trial as the court reasonably directs, any party may file written requests that the court instruct the jury on the law as set forth in the requests. The court shall inform counsel of its proposed action upon the requests prior to their arguments to the jury, but the court shall instruct the jury after the arguments are completed. No party may assign as error the giving or the failure to give an instruction unless he objects thereto before the jury retires to consider its verdict, stating distinctly the matter to which he objects and the grounds of his objection. Opportunity shall be given to make the objection out of the hearing of the jury.

Reporter's Notes—1973

Rule 51(a) will work no change in Massachusetts practice.

Rule 51(b) copies Federal Rule 51, and tracks prior Massachusetts practice.

Because the adoption of Rule 46 will eliminate the present formal Massachusetts requirement for exceptions, Rule 51(b) will only work a formal change in Massachusetts practice. Instead of taking an exception, an attorney under 51(b) must object to the giving or the failure to give a requested instruction before the jury retires to consider its verdict. He must also state his grounds therefor. Under former practice, failure properly to except resulted in waiver of objection, Herrick v. Waitt, 224 Mass. 415, 417, 113 N.E. 205 (1916); failure to object seasonably will have a similar effect under the new rules. Nimrod v. Sylvester, 369 F.2d 870, 872–873 (1st Cir.1966).

Reporter's Notes—1996

With the merger of the District Court rules into the Mass.R.Civ.P., Rule 51 in its entirety has been made applicable to the District Court, to the extent that Massachusetts law permits trial by jury in District Court civil actions.

Rule 52. Findings by the Court

(a) Courts Other Than District Court: Effect. In all actions tried upon the facts without a jury, the court shall find the facts specially and state separately its conclusions of law thereon, and judgment shall be entered pursuant to Rule 58. Requests for findings are not necessary for purposes of review. Findings of fact shall not be set aside unless clearly erroneous, and due regard shall be given to the opportunity of the trial court to judge of the credibility of the witnesses. The findings of a master, to the extent that the court adopts them, shall be considered as the findings of the court. If an opinion or memorandum of decision is filed, it will be sufficient if the findings of fact and conclusions of law appear therein. Findings of fact and conclusions of law are unnecessary on decisions of motions under Rules 12 or 56 or any other motion except as provided in Rule 41(b)(2).

(b) Courts Other Than District Court: Amendment. Upon motion of a party made not later than 10 days after entry of judgment the court may amend its findings or make additional findings and may amend the judgment accordingly. The motion may be made with a motion for a new trial pursuant to Rule 59. When findings of fact are made in actions tried by the court without a jury, the question of the sufficiency of the evidence to support the findings may thereafter be raised whether or not the party raising the question has made in the trial court an objection to such findings or has made a motion to amend them or a motion for judgment.

(c) District Court: Effect. In all actions tried upon the facts without a jury, except as otherwise provided in Rule 65.3, the court shall find the facts specially and state separately its conclusions of law thereon, provided that any party submits before the beginning of any closing arguments proposed findings of fact and rulings of law. Upon request made before the beginning of any closing arguments, such party shall have the right to submit supplemental proposed findings of fact and rulings of law within three days. Each proposed finding of fact and ruling of law should be set forth concisely in a separately numbered paragraph covering one subject. Judgment shall be entered pursuant to Rule 58. Findings of fact shall not be set aside unless clearly erroneous, and due regard shall be given to the opportunity of the trial court to judge the credibility of the witnesses. If an opinion or memorandum of decision is filed, it will be sufficient if the findings of fact and conclusions of law appear therein. Findings of fact and conclusions of law are unnecessary on decisions of motions under Rules 12 or 56 or any other motion except as provided in Rule 41(b)(2).

(d) District Court: Amendment. Upon motion of a party made not later than 10 days after entry of judgment, or upon its own initiative not later than 10 days after entry of judgment, the court may amend its findings, if any, or make additional findings and may amend the judgment accordingly.

The motion may be made with a motion for a new trial pursuant to Rule 59.

Amended effective July 1, 1996; November 28, 2007, effective March 1, 2008.

Reporter's Notes—1973

Rule 52 is almost identical to Federal Rule 52. It omits the phrase "or with an advisory jury" in the first sentence, because such juries are unknown to Massachusetts practice, and have not been included in Rule 39. Rule 52 does constitute a departure from the Massachusetts practice articulated by the court in Matter of Loeb, 315 Mass. 191, 196, 52 N.E.2d 37, 40–41 (1943): "On the law side of the court a judge cannot be required to make any express findings of fact." See also Maglio v. Lane, 268 Mass. 135, 137, 167 N.E. 228, 229 (1929). Even though the trial judge is not *required* to itemize his findings of fact, he may do so voluntarily. In actions tried without a jury, although the judge was required to pass on rulings of law requested by the parties. Ashapa v. Reed, 280 Mass. 514, 182 N.E. 859 (1932), he need not, unless he wished, make findings of fact. "Findings of fact not infrequently are made in more or less detail by a trial judge and the reasons stated for the information of parties and counsel, but that is a practice of convenience." Id. at 516, 182 N.E. at 859.

In Massachusetts equity practice, on the other hand, the trial judge was obligated, if the losing party requested, to "report the material facts" upon which his decision was based. If no request was made, a report was discretionary. See also Matter of Loeb, 315 Mass. 191, 196 note, 52 N.E.2d 37, 40–41 (1943).

Under Rule 52(a), the trial court's findings of fact cannot be set aside unless the appellate court determines them to be "clearly erroneous". "A finding is 'clearly erroneous' when although there is evidence to support it, the reviewing court on the entire evidence is left with the definite and firm conviction that a mistake has been committed." United States v. United States Gypsum Co., 333 U.S. 364, 395, 68 S.Ct. 525, 542, 92 L.Ed. 746 (1948).

The rule emphasizes the "opportunity of the trial court to judge the credibility of the witnesses." This is similar to prior Massachusetts equity practice.

In equity cases (where the judge made findings of fact), the full Supreme Judicial Court had to make its own evaluation of the testimony, giving due weight to the trial judge's findings. Those findings would not be reversed unless "plainly wrong." McMahon v. Monarch Life Ins. Co., 345 Mass. 261, 262, 263, 186 N.E.2d 827, 828–829 (1962); Sulmonetti v. Hayes, 347 Mass. 390, 391, 198 N.E.2d 297, 298–299 (1964). Like Rule 52(a), Massachusetts decisions emphasize that the trial judge is "in the best position to determine the weight and credibility of the evidence," Oberg v. Burke, 345 Mass. 596, 598, 188 N.E.2d 566, 568 (1963); Murphy v. Hanlon, 322 Mass. 683, 685, 79 N.E.2d 292, 293 (1948).

In Massachusetts, the findings in a confirmed master's report were binding upon the court unless they were "mutually inconsistent or plainly wrong." Rose v. Homsey, 347 Mass. 259, 260, 197 N.E.2d 603, 605 (1964); Lukas v. Leventhal, 344 Mass. 762, 183 N.E.2d 879 (1962).

Under Rule 52(b) the court, upon motion of a party within 10 days after entry of judgment, "may amend its findings or make additional findings and may amend the judgment accordingly." Under former practice, the trial judge had discretion to allow a rehearing and to amend his findings prior to the entry of the final decree. See, e.g., Stern v. Stern, 330 Mass. 312, 316, 113 N.E.2d 55, 58 (1953); Souza v. Souza, 325 Mass. 761, 762, 90 N.E.2d 572, 573 (1950). However, "after the entry of a final decree in equity, as after the entry of a final judgment in a suit at law, the case is finally disposed of by the court, subject to such rights of appeal, if any, as the statute gives, and the court has no further power to deal with the case except upon a bill of review." White v. Gove, 183 Mass. 333, 340, 67 N.E. 359, 362 (1903).

The change engendered by Rule 52(b) stems largely from the difference between "judgment" under the Rules and the Massachusetts concept of "judgment". See Reporters' Notes to Rule 58.

Reporter's Notes—1996

The amendments to Rule 52 effective in 1996 add new sections (c) and (d), applicable in the District Court, and retitle the headings to Rule 52(a) and (b). New sections (c) and (d) of Rule 52 are identical to the now-repealed provisions of Dist./Mun.Cts.R.Civ.P. 52(a) and (b), respectively. The "Comments" to now-repealed Dist./Mun.Cts.R.Civ.P. 52 provided as follows:

The revision of paragraph (a) [now Mass.R.Civ.P. 52(c)] evidences the decision not to follow the MRCP procedure of requiring an automatic set of judicial findings of fact and conclusions of law in every case tried without a jury. Rather, this rule provides that the court may make detailed findings of fact and rulings of law, and is required, as has been true in the past, to make rulings of law in response to requests for rulings submitted by any of the parties to the litigation. This procedure, and the whole mechanism of appeal to the Appellate Division of which it is the foundation, is set forth in Rule 64 of these rules. [Since July 1, 1994, appeal to the Appellate Division is governed by the District/Municipal Courts Rules for Appellate Division Appeal.]

The decision to favor the present appeal mechanism over the MRCP approach in cases tried without a jury is based on several factors. Important among these is the fact that in many of the District Courts, and particularly the Boston Municipal Court, a judge will frequently hear a large number of civil cases in the course of a single day, and on successive days, and the fact that most of these cases turn on questions of fact, which in turn relate to questions of credibility. If there were a mandatory requirement that written findings and rulings be made in each case under such circumstances, this would impose a tremendous burden in those courts. Even if adequate stenographic assistance were available to these courts for this purpose (which is not the case), this would require a large expenditure of judicial time in preparing such findings where the element of credibility would be decisive, and would merely bring into play the provisions of MRCP, Rule 52, that "[f]indings of fact shall not be set aside unless clearly erroneous, and due regard shall be given to the opportunity of the trial court to judge of the credibility of the witnesses." In short, the present appellate mechanism is well suited to current District Court jurisdiction, and is well understood by those members of the bar familiar with District Court practice.

A clause has been added in the first sentence of paragraph (b) [now Mass.R.Civ.P. 52(d)] which allows the court *on its own initiative* to amend its findings and judgment, so long as it acts within ten days of the entry of judgment.

Lastly, the words "if any" have been added after the word "findings" in the first sentence of paragraph (b) [now Mass.R.Civ.P. 52(d)]. This is consistent with the fact that this rule leaves it discretionary with the trial court whether findings of fact will be made.

It should be noted that although findings of fact and conclusions of law are not generally required in the District Court, section (c), by its reference to Rule 65.3 dealing with civil contempt, *will* require such findings and conclusions in District Court civil contempt actions.

Reporter's Notes—2008

Rule 52 has been amended to require findings of fact and rulings of law in jury-waived cases in the District Court and Boston Municipal Court, but only if a party has submitted, before the beginning of any closing arguments, proposed findings and rulings. This differs from practice in the Superior Court under Rule 52(a), which requires Superior Court judges to make findings and rulings as a matter of course in jury-waived actions, whether or not a party has submitted proposed findings and rulings.

Requiring a party to submit proposed findings and rulings as a condition to the court's making findings and rulings is justified by the volume and nature of the civil caseload in the District Court and Boston Municipal Court. The rule also provides a party with the absolute right to a three-day period in which to submit supplemental proposed findings and rulings, as long as that party, before the beginning of any closing arguments, has filed proposed findings and rulings *and* has made a request to file supplemental proposed findings and rulings. The proposed findings and rulings and the request to file supplemental proposed findings and rulings may be contained in the same document.

The amendments to Rule 52(c) include a general description of the format and content of proposed findings and rulings by a provision that they be set forth concisely and in separately numbered paragraphs covering one subject for each request. In doing so, the rule intends to state a preferred, but not mandatory, format and content for proposed findings and rulings.

A judge in the District Court or Boston Municipal Court may make findings and rulings, *sua sponte*, even where doing so is not required by this rule.

Simultaneously with the amendments to Rule 52(c), Rule 64A, Requests for Rulings of Law in District Court, was repealed. The repeal of Rule 64A eliminates the "requests for rulings" procedure that had been in place in the District Court and Boston Municipal Court. Under that procedure, a party could obtain rulings of law from the court by filing requests for rulings of law prior to the beginning of any closing arguments. This prior procedure merely required the court to allow or deny a requested ruling of law, and did not require the court to make its own rulings of law. Under the prior procedure, there was no mechanism for a party to require findings of fact in District Court and Boston Municipal Court jury-waived actions. Under the amended language of Rule 52(c), a party now has the opportunity to require both findings of fact and rulings of law from the trial judge.

The repeal of Rule 64A also eliminates the provisions regarding "warrants" requests. These were requests that the evidence warrants a finding for the requesting party or does not warrant a finding for the opposing party.

The requirement of findings and rulings under Rule 52(c) applies to all District Court and Boston Municipal Court cases governed by the Massachusetts Rules of Civil Procedure, that is, "cases traditionally considered tort, contract, replevin, or equity actions, except small claims actions." Rule 81(a)(2). No attempt has been made in the rule or in the Reporter's Notes to list all of the types of District Court and Boston Municipal Court actions in which findings and rulings are not required. Supplementary process is one example where findings and rulings should not be required, since supplementary process is a statutory proceeding not falling within the ambit of cases that would be "traditionally considered tort, contract, replevin, or equity."

Summary process, however, presents a different example and a different result. Although under the Massachusetts Rules of Civil Procedure, findings and rulings are not required in District Court and Boston Municipal Court summary process actions (because of the language in Rule 81(a)(2)), the application of Rule 1 of the Uniform Summary Process Rules would result in a requirement of findings and rulings in District Court and Boston Municipal Court summary process cases pursuant to the procedure set forth in Rule 52(c). Rule 1 of the Uniform Summary Process Rules adopts the Massachusetts Rules of Civil Procedure, "insofar as the latter are not inconsistent with" the Uniform Summary Process Rules. Thus, Uniform Summary Process Rule 1 would make amended Rule 52(c), with its requirement of findings and rulings in the District Court and Boston Municipal Court upon the filing of proposed findings and rulings, applicable to summary process cases in those courts. It should be noted that in summary process cases in the Superior Court and Housing Court, findings and rulings are required as a matter of course pursuant to

Rule 52(a) (made applicable to summary process cases in those courts by virtue of Uniform Summary Process Rule 1).

Rule 53.   Masters

(a) Definition.   The following words, as used in this rule, shall mean:

(i) "master" shall mean any person, however designated, who is appointed by the court to hear evidence in connection with any action and report facts.

(ii) "stenographer" shall mean a stenographer appointed by the master before commencement of the hearing.

(b) Appointment.

(1) *Member of Bar.*   The court in which an action is pending may appoint a master therein subject, however, to a standing order, if any, of the Administrative Justice designating classes of cases not to be tried to a master, and provided further that in the District Court, no master may be appointed without the assent of all parties.   No master shall be appointed who is not a member in good standing of the bar of one of the United States or of the District of Columbia.

(2) *Selection by Agreement.*   Prior to appointment of a master, the court shall inquire whether the parties can agree upon a master.   The court shall appoint the person agreed upon unless the court is of the opinion that the proposed master is unqualified, or for other good reason should not be appointed.

(3) *Selection Without Agreement.*   If the parties cannot agree upon a master, the court whenever practicable shall select a master from such official standing list of masters, if any, as may have been approved by the department in which the action is pending.   The court may select from such list a non-resident of the county in which the action is pending or a person whose office is not in said county.   If the court finds that special circumstances make it advisable to select and appoint a master whose name is not on an official standing list, in making such appointment it shall forthwith file with the clerk a statement containing its specific reasons for selecting and appointing a master not on such list.

(4) *Objection to Master Selected.*   If an objection is made by any party to the appointment of a master selected by the court, whether from the official standing list, if any, or otherwise, the objecting party shall file with the court within five (5) days of notice of such appointment a written objection to such appointment, and notice of such filing shall be forwarded forthwith by the clerk of court to the referring justice.   The grounds for such objection shall not be included within such written objection but shall be furnished to the referring justice upon his request and in the form that the referring justice shall order.

(5) *Inability to Serve.*   Upon receipt of an order of reference as herein provided, a person appointed a master shall notify the referring justice immediately if he is unable or unwilling to serve as master in the case.   No person shall accept appointment as master in any case in which he cannot be impartial.   If there are circumstances known to the master, which may give the appearance of partiality, including the existence of any pending matter between the master and any party to the litigation or any party's counsel, the master must make full written disclosure to the referring justice and all parties immediately after receipt of the order of reference.

(c) Compensation.   The compensation allowed to a master may be charged in whole or in part upon the parties, or out of any fund or subject matter of the action which is in the custody or control of the court, or, when authorized by law, upon the Commonwealth, as the court may direct.   The rate of compensation to be paid by the parties or out of any fund or subject matter of the action shall be fixed by the court; the rate of compensation to be paid by the Commonwealth shall be fixed from time to time by rule of each department.   Where compensation is to be paid by the Commonwealth, no additional compensation shall be accepted from the parties, unless approved by the court and stated in the order of reference.   When a party ordered to pay the compensation allowed by the court does not pay it after notice and within the time prescribed by the court, the master is entitled to a writ of execution against the delinquent party.

(d) Order of Reference.   A master shall be appointed by a written order of reference.   Said order: (i) shall either fix definite times for the hearings or fix the time when or before which hearings shall be begun and the time within which they shall be ended; (ii) shall fix the time for the filing of the master's report; (iii) may specify or limit the master's powers and may direct him to report only upon particular issues or to do or perform particular acts.

(e) Powers.   Subject to the specifications and limitations stated in the order of reference, the master has and shall exercise the power to regulate all proceedings in every hearing before him and to do all acts and take all measures necessary or proper for the efficient performance of his duties under the order.   He may require the production before him of evidence upon all matters embraced in the reference, including the production of all books, papers, vouchers, documents, and writings applicable thereto.   He may rule upon the admissibility of evidence unless otherwise directed by the order of reference and he shall have the authority to put witnesses on oath and may himself examine them and may call the parties to the action and examine them upon oath.

(f) Proceedings.

(1) *Hearings.*   When a reference is made, the clerk shall forthwith furnish the master with a copy of the order of reference.   Upon receipt thereof the master shall forthwith notify the parties or their attorneys of the time, date and place of the first hearing.   The order of reference may require that the hearings proceed from day to day, Saturdays, Sundays and holidays excepted, until completed.   If the court does not order the master to proceed from day to day, nevertheless he shall proceed as nearly as possible on consecutive days, and shall grant no adjournment for a longer period than seven (7) days except by order of the court.   Either party, on notice to the parties and master, may apply to the court for an order requiring the master to speed the proceedings and to make his report.   The court may change or extend the time for hearings.   Hearings shall be held at a court house, unless the parties and the master agree otherwise or, upon application by the master, the court expressly orders that hearings be held elsewhere.

(2) *Evidence.*   Rules 43(a), (b), (d) and (g) will govern hearings before masters.   If an objection to a question pro-

pounded to a witness is sustained by the master, and there is a stenographer present, upon request the master shall take the proffered evidence as an offer of proof unless the master finds that the proffered evidence is privileged.

(3) *Interpreters.* The master may appoint an interpreter whose compensation shall be fixed by the court. The compensation shall be paid out of funds provided by law or by one or more of the parties as the court may direct, and may be taxed ultimately as costs in the discretion of the court.

(4) *Stenographers.* No master shall, without prior approval of the court, appoint a stenographer to be paid by the Commonwealth.

(5) *Statement of Accounts.* When matters of accounting are in issue before the master, he may prescribe the form in which the accounts shall be submitted and in any proper case may require or receive in evidence a statement by a certified public accountant who is called as a witness. Upon objection of a party to any of the items thus submitted or upon showing that the form of statement is insufficient, the master may require a different form of statement to be furnished, or the accounts or specific items thereof to be proved by oral examination of the accounting parties or upon written interrogatories or in such other manner as he directs.

(6) *Failure to Appear.* If all parties fail to appear at a hearing without showing good cause, the master shall report forthwith to the clerk of the court in which the action is pending, and the clerk shall bring such report forthwith to the attention of the referring justice, if practicable, otherwise to any justice of the court. If a party fails to appear at the time and place appointed, the master may proceed ex parte or, in his discretion, adjourn the proceedings to a future day, giving notice to the absent party of the adjournment, or apply to the court, with notice to the parties, for the imposition of sanctions.

(7) *Witnesses.* The parties may procure the attendance of witnesses before the master by the issuance and service of subpoenas as provided in Rule 45. If without adequate excuse a witness fails to appear or give evidence, he may be punished by the court as for a contempt.

(g) Master's Report.

(1) *Contents.* The master shall prepare a report upon the matters submitted to him by the order of reference, and, if required by the order of reference to make findings of fact and conclusions of law, he shall set them forth in the report. The master's report will contain the master's general finding upon each issue that is within the order of reference and will include and clearly identify the subsidiary findings upon which each general finding is based. No general findings will be presumed by the court to be supported by subsidiary findings which are not stated in the report as the basis therefor. In a jury case, the master's report shall contain findings on damages, separately stated, irrespective of his determination of liability. In a non-jury case the master need not make findings on damages if he determines that there is no liability. Any party, at the conclusion of the evidence may file with the master requests for findings of fact and conclusions of law.

(2) *Filing.* At least 20 days before filing his report, the master shall submit a draft thereof to counsel for all parties. Counsel for any party may submit to the master suggested amendments in writing, copies of which must be contemporaneously submitted to counsel for all of the parties. The master may, in his discretion, allow a hearing on any suggested amendments. If any suggested amendment is adopted by the master, he shall furnish counsel for all parties with copies of said amendment contemporaneously with the filing of his report. Within 60 days after the close of the evidence, unless the court, on motion or otherwise, for good cause shown, shall alter the time, the master shall file his report and the original exhibits with the clerk of the court. The clerk shall forthwith mail to all parties notice of the filing.

(h) Master's Report in Non-jury Cases.

(1) *Status of Report.* In an action to be tried without a jury, the court shall accept the master's subsidiary findings of fact unless they are clearly erroneous, mutually inconsistent, unwarranted by the evidence before the master as a matter of law or are otherwise tainted by error of law. Any party who contends that the master's subsidiary findings are clearly erroneous, mutually inconsistent, unwarranted by the evidence before the master or are otherwise tainted by error of law must make such contentions by objection as hereinafter provided. The court may draw its own inferences from the master's subsidiary findings. The court may make findings in accordance with Rule 52, which are in addition to the master's findings and not inconsistent therewith, based either on evidence presented to the court or evidence before the master which was recorded by means approved by the master before commencement of the hearing.

(2) *Objections to Report.* Within 30 days after service of notice of the filing of the report or such other time as the court may allow, any party may serve written objections thereto upon every other party making any of the contentions referred to in paragraph (1) of this section, clearly stating the grounds for each objection and the relief sought. At any time after the filing of objections or the expiration of the time therefor, any party may move the court, with notice to all other parties, to act upon the report and upon any objections thereto, provided, however, the court may so act upon its own motion after notice to all parties.

(3) *Limitations on Review.* The court will not review a question of law dependent upon evidence before the master unless the evidence was recorded by a stenographer and a transcript of so much of the proceedings before the master as is necessary to dispose of the objections adequately is served, together with the objections, upon every other party. Any party may designate additional portions of the transcript for submission to the court by the service of notice within 10 days after service of the objections. The objecting party shall serve such additional portions upon every other party; but if the objecting party shall refuse to do so, the party designating such additional portions shall either serve them upon every other party or shall move the court to require the objecting party to do so. At the time of ordering a transcript from the stenographer, a party shall make satisfactory arrangements with the reporter for payment of the cost of any transcript ordered. The parties are encouraged to agree as to the portions of the transcript that will accompany the objections.

(4) *Action on Report.* The court may adopt the report, strike it in whole or in part, modify it, recommit it to the master with instructions or take any other action that justice

requires. Any motion to adopt a report shall be deemed to include a motion to enter judgment and shall be accompanied by a proposed form of judgment.

(i) Master's Report in Jury Cases.

(1) *Status of Report.* In an action to be tried by a jury the master's findings upon all the issues submitted to him are admissible as prima facie evidence of the matters found and may be read to the jury and, in the discretion of the court, may be submitted to the jury as an exhibit, subject, however, to the rulings of the court upon any objections properly preserved as hereinafter provided.

(2) *Objections to Report.* Within 30 days after service of notice of the filing of the report or within such further time as the court may allow any party may serve written objections thereto upon every other party objecting to the findings as mutually inconsistent, unwarranted by the evidence before the master as matter of law or otherwise tainted by error of law, clearly stating the grounds for each objection and the relief sought. Within 45 days after service of objections or such further time as the court may allow, the objecting party shall move the court to act upon the objections and within said 45 days or such further time as the court may allow said motion must be heard by the court.

(3) *Limitations on Review.* The court will not review a question of law dependent upon evidence before the master unless the evidence was recorded by a stenographer and a transcript of so much of the proceedings before the master as is necessary to dispose of the objections adequately is served together with the objections upon every other party. Any party may designate additional portions of the transcript for submission to the court by the service of notice within 10 days after service of the objections. The objecting party shall serve such additional portions upon every other party; but if the objecting party shall refuse to do so, the party designating such additional parts shall either serve them upon every other objecting party or shall move the court to require the objecting party to do so. At the time of ordering the transcript from the stenographer, a party shall make satisfactory arrangements with the reporter for payment of the cost of any transcript ordered. The parties are encouraged to agree as to the portions of the transcript that will accompany the objections.

(4) *Action on Report.* The court may strike the report in whole or in part, modify it, recommit it to the master with instructions or take any other action that justice requires.

Amended effective February 24, 1975; amended May 25, 1982, effective July 1, 1982; amended effective July 1, 1996.

Reporter's Notes—1973

Rule 53, taken largely from Federal Rule 53, covers all quasi-judicial court-appointed fact-finders, including masters, referees, auditors, examiners, commissioners, and assessors.

Under prior Massachusetts practice a master could sit only in equity; an auditor could sit only in actions at law. Under the Rules, the distinction between an auditor and a master disappear. See Rule 2. The change in nomenclature should make little difference.

Under Rule 53(a) the amount and source of a master's compensation will continue to be court-regulated, either ad hoc, or by a standing order.

If a party fails to pay the master, after the court directs him to, the master has only those rights of an ordinary judgment creditor. He may not withhold his report; the rule does not recognize a master's lien.

Reference may be made when the parties agree to it. Rule 53(b). This provision, which is not a part of Federal Rule 53, honors existing Massachusetts practice.

Under Rule 53(c), as under prior practice, Spiegel v. Beacon Participations, 297 Mass. 398, 406, 8 N.E.2d 895, 902 (1937), the order of reference may impose binding limitations upon the master. Subject to these restrictions, he can regulate all proceedings in hearings before him, including requiring the production before him of evidence, ruling on the admissibility of evidence, putting witnesses and/or parties on oath and examining them. Rule 53(c) requires the master, upon request, to make a record of the evidence offered and excluded. This follows prior law. Whenever an auditor made a ruling as to the admissibility of evidence, and objection was taken thereto, the auditor if requested so to do, had to make a statement of such ruling in his report. G.L. c. 221, § 56.

Rule 53(d) requires the master, unless otherwise instructed by the order of reference, to set a time and place for the first meeting of the parties or their attorneys; this first meeting must be held within 20 days after the date of the order of reference. Rule 53(d), like prior Massachusetts practice, stresses the importance of the master's diligence. Rule 53(d)(1) permits either party, after notice to the parties and master, to apply to the court for an order to speed the proceedings. If a party fails to appear at the hearing, the master may proceed ex parte or, in his discretion, adjourn the proceedings to a future day giving notice to the absent party of the adjournment. Under prior law judgment could be entered for the adverse party upon the recommendation of the auditor, G.L. c. 221, § 58; or he could proceed ex parte, Super.Ct. Rule 87. A master, faced with a similar situation, could proceed ex parte, Id. Under S.J.C. Rule 2:32, Super.Ct. Rule 87 and Prob.Ct. Rule 21, not only *could* the officer proceed ex parte in the absence of a party, but he *had* to do so "on motion of the party appearing." Rule 53 thus ameliorates the rigor of prior Massachusetts practice. It gives the master a discretionary choice. He may proceed ex parte or adjourn the proceedings to a future day.

Under Rule 53(d)(2), the parties may procure the attendance of witnesses before the master by the issuance and service of subpoenas. An unexcused failure to appear is punishable as contempt of court, thus subjecting the absent witness to the penalties and remedies in Rules 37 and 45. This does not significantly alter prior practice. Note that the court, not the master, finds the contempt and imposes appropriate sanctions.

Under Rule 53(d)(3) the form of accounts is a matter for the master's discretion. This appears consistent with prior Massachusetts practice, which set no form for the auditor's or master's report. See Zuckernik v. Jordan Marsh Co., 290 Mass. 151, 194 N.E. 892 (1935).

Rule 53(e) requires that the master report upon the matters submitted to him by the order of reference and also report any findings of fact and conclusions of law he was required to make.

Massachusetts courts have permitted an auditor at his discretion to set forth the subsidiary facts which he found, as well as the inferences and conclusions which he drew, Fair v. Manhattan Ins. Co., 112 Mass. 320, 329 (1893). Masters had to make and report all findings of facts material to issues raised by the pleadings including not only the master's conclusions but enough subsidiary findings to enable the court to follow the steps taken by the master. Smith v. Lloyd, 224 Mass. 173, 174, 112 N.E. 615, 616 (1961). Rule 53(e)(1) preserves this practice.

Under Rule 53, as before, the master files his report with the clerk of court, who notifies the parties forthwith. Super.Ct.Rule 87 required that the master's report be filed within 30 days after the hearing had been closed. This provision has been incorporated into Rule 53(e)(1).

Rule 53(e)(2) has been amended to retain the Superior Court requirement, Super.Ct.Rule 90, that objections to a master's report clearly state the grounds. It applies the "clearly erroneous" standard to a master's findings in a nonjury case. This follows prior Massachusetts practice, where the master's findings of basic fact would stand "unless plainly wrong, mutually inconsistent or contradictory or vitiated in view of controlling principles of law." Sturtevant v. Ford, 280 Mass. 303, 308, 182 N.E. 560, 562 (1932).

Under Rule 53(e)(2), parties have a 10–day period in which to object to any findings of the master in an action seeking equitable relief or any action in which the master's findings are to be final. The court, as in existing Massachusetts practice, may accept, reject or recommit a master's report. C.A. Briggs Co. v. National Wafer Co., 215 Mass. 100, 108, 102 N.E. 87, 90 (1913).

Rule 53(e)(3) closely follows Federal Rule 53(e)(3). The language has been modified to make clear that a master's report will have "prima facie" effect if introduced at the trial. G.L. c. 221, § 56; Cook v. Farm Service Stores, Inc., 301 Mass. 564, 17 N.E.2d 890 (1938).

Rule 53(e)(4) precludes further litigation of facts in cases where the parties have stipulated that the master's findings of fact will be final.

Under Rule 53(e)(5), a master must submit a draft of his report to counsel for all parties for the purpose of receiving their suggestions. This embodies existing Massachusetts practice, Super.Ct.Rules 87, 88, 89, 90.

Reporter's Notes—1975

As originally promulgated, Rule 53(e)(1) required the master to file his report and the original exhibits within 30 days after the hearing had been "closed". This presented an ambiguity, because a hearing in which the evidence has been completed, but the parties had not yet filed briefs, could fairly be said not yet to have been "closed." Accordingly, the rule has been amended to indicate that the master's filing deadline dates from the close of the evidence, i.e., the final resting of the parties. To allow for the filing of briefs, if desired, the master's time to report has been enlarged from 30 days to 45 days.

Reporter's Notes—1982

Rule 53 ("Masters") consolidates into one rule many of the provisions of the former Rule 53 and former Superior Court Rule 49. There are several new provisions, however, which appeared in neither of the former Rules. For example, Rule 53(b)(1) now explicitly provides that a master must be a "member in good standing of the bar." Rule 53(b)(5) requires the master to "make full written disclosure" of "circumstances known to the master, which may give the appearance of partiality."

The most significant new features of Rule 53 are found in Rule 53(g) ("Master's Report"), Rule 53(h) ("Master's Report in Non–Jury Cases"), and Rule 53(i) ("Master's Report in Jury Cases"). These new provisions describe what a Master's Report must contain, the timing of each step, the role of objections, and the limitations on review by the trial court. Under new Rule 53(g)(1), the master in a jury case must make findings on damages, even if the master has determined that there is no liability; these damage findings are admissible as prima facie evidence at the jury trial (Rule 53(i)(1)). Rule 53(g)(1) now expressly authorizes, but does not require, requests for findings of fact. New Rule 53(i)(1) abolishes "facts final" references in jury cases which were previously countenanced in the form for orders of reference to a master in jury actions, which was a part of Superior Court Rule 49. Such "facts final" references were eliminated as probably inconsistent with a jury trial. The new Rule substitutes "objections to report" (Rule 53(h)(2) and (i)(2)) for the multiple steps of filing objections in the nature of exceptions and then filing separate motions, such as those to strike or recommit. In jury cases, a party objecting to any aspect of the report must within 45 days after service of the objections "move the court to act upon" them, unless the court allows further time (Rule 53(i)(2)).

New Rules 53(h)(3) and 53(i)(3) now condition review of "a question of law dependent upon evidence before the master" on the existence of "a transcript of so much of the proceedings before the master as is necessary to dispose of the objections adequately." A master is no longer required to prepare a summary of the evidence, as under previous Superior Court Rules 49(7) and (8). The new process is comparable to Massachusetts Rule of Appellate Procedure 8(b)(1). In new Rules 53(h)(4) and 53(i)(4) the reviewing court is given the power, along with specifically enumerated powers, to "take any other action that justice requires" with respect to the report. The reviewing court can, when appropriate, reverse a master's ultimate finding, and enter a finding for the opposing party (compare old Rule 53(e)(2) and old Superior Court Rule 49(8)).

Turning now to each new rule consecutively, Rule 53(a) defines "master" and "stenographer." "Master" means "any person . . . who is appointed by the court to hear evidence in connection with any action and report facts." As in previous Rule 53, the distinction between "auditor" and "master" is eliminated.

Rule 53(b) deals with "Appointment." Rule 53(b)(1) requires that masters be members in good standing of the bar, since masters deal with legal issues and render legal conclusions. A court, under this Rule, may appoint a master in any case except those classes of cases, "if any," designated by the Administrative Justice "not to be tried to a master." The Supreme Judicial Court has frequently commented on the potential delay and confusion resulting from references to masters, and cautioned that the judicial discretion to refer cases "should be exercised most discriminately and reasonably sparingly." O'Brien v. Dwight, 363 Mass. 256, 280, 294 N.E.2d 363, 378 (1973). Also see, for examples, Peter v. Wallach, 366 Mass. 622, 626, 321 N.E.2d 806, 808 (1975), and Jet Spray Cooler, Inc. v. Crampton, 377 Mass. 159, 163, 385 N.E.2d 1349, 1352, 1353 (1979). It is important, therefore, that the Administrative Justice has the power to designate entire classes of cases "not to be tried to a master."

Rule 53(b)(2), "Selection by Agreement," requires the court to "inquire whether the parties can agree upon a master," prior to appointment. Unless the court "is of the opinion that the proposed master is unqualified, or for other good reason should not be appointed," the court "shall appoint the person agreed upon." This is similar to previous Superior Court Rule 49(1)(b).

Rules 53(b)(2) through 53(b)(5) dictate how a master is to be appointed when the parties cannot agree; how and when a party may object to "the appointment of a master selected by the Court;" and the responsibility of a newly appointed master to give notice "if he is unable or unwilling to serve." Rule 53(b)(5) also requires a person to decline appointment as master "in any case in which he cannot be impartial," and to make full written disclosure "if there are circumstances known to the master, which may give the appearance of partiality."

Rule 53(c) contains "Compensation" provisions, and tracks much of the previous Rule 53(a) compensation language, except, in keeping with the results of Court Reorganization, references to the "county" and "rule of the justices of the court" have been replaced by "the Commonwealth" and "rule of each department."

Rules 53(d) ("Order of Reference") and 53(e) ("Powers") contain much of what was previously found in Rule 53(c). Provisions with respect to evidence and objections, which were previously covered in Rule 53(c), are now governed by a new Rule 53(f)(2).

Rule 53(f), entitled "Proceedings," has seven sections. Rule 53(f)(1), "Hearings," provides for the timing and location of hearings. Rule 53(f)(2), "Evidence," provides that Rules 43(a), (b), (d) and (g), which also deal with evidence issues, "will govern hearings before masters." Rule 53(f)(3) covers "Interpreters," and Rule 53(f)(4), "Stenographers." Rule 53(f)(5), "Statement of Accounts," is identical to previous Rule 53(d)(3). Rule 53(f)(6), "Failure to Appear," provides more specific options than previous Rule 53(d)(1) about the consequences of a party's failure to appear. Under the new rule, if a party fails to appear, the master may proceed ex parte, or adjourn the proceedings, or apply to the court for the imposition of sanctions. Rule 53(f)(7), "Witnesses," permits "subpoenas as provided in Rule 45," and also provides for the possible imposition of a punishment by the court "as for a contempt" in the event a witness fails to appear "without adequate excuse." This "Witnesses" section, unlike previous Rule 53(d)(2), no longer includes "consequences, penalties, and remedies provided in Rules 37 and 45" for failure to honor a subpoena.

Rule 53(g), Rule 53(h), and Rule 53(i) contain the provisions relating to Master's Reports. Rule 53(g) is a general rule, with separate sections on "Contents" and "Filing." Rule 53(h) provides specific rules with respect to a "Master's Report in Non–Jury Cases," and Rule 53(i) does the same for a "Master's Report in Jury Cases." Rule 53(g), (h), and (i), taken together, cover questions previously dealt with in Rule 53(e) and Superior Court Rule 49(7) and (8).

Rule 53(g)(1) requires the master's report to "contain the master's general finding upon each issue that is within the order of reference" and to "include and clearly identify the subsidiary findings upon which each general finding is based." In jury cases the master must make "findings on damages, separately stated," but "in a non-jury case the master need not make findings on damages if he determines that there is no liability." Parties may file requests for findings "at the conclusion of the evidence."

Rule 53(g)(2) obligates the master to submit a draft report "at least 20 days before filing his report." Previous Rule 53(e)(5), on draft reports, did not have this specific time period. The master's report must be filed "within 60 days after the close of the evidence," unless the court alters the time. This changes the 45 day period under previous Rule 53(e)(1). Counsel may submit suggested amendments in writing to the draft report, and the "master may, in his discretion, allow a hearing on any suggested amendments."

Rule 53(h), "Master's Report in Non–Jury Cases," and Rule 53(i), "Master's Report in Jury Cases," are each divided up into four sections: "(1) Status of Report," "(2) Objections to Report," "(3) Limitations of Review," and "(4) Action on Report." Rule 53(i) abolishes "facts final" references.

In a non-jury case, "the court shall accept the master's subsidiary findings of fact unless they are clearly erroneous, mutually inconsistent, unwarranted by the evidence before the master as a matter of law or are otherwise tainted by error of law" (Rule 53(h)(1)). In a

jury case, "the master's findings upon all the issues submitted to him are admissible as prima facie evidence of the matters found . . . , subject, however, to the rulings of the court upon any objections properly preserved . . ." (Rule 53(i)(1)).

Challenges to the master's report in a non-jury or jury action are made by the filing of objections "clearly stating the grounds for each objection and the relief sought," (Rule 53(h)(2) and Rule 53(i)(2)). Thereafter, in a non-jury case, either party may at any time move the court to act upon the report and the objections (Rule 53(h)(2)). In a jury case, within forty-five days after service of the objections, unless the court allows further time, the objecting party "shall move the court to act upon the objections" (Rule 53(i)(2)). Unlike previous practice, counsel no longer file objections in the nature of exceptions, nor file separate motions to strike and to recommit.

In a non-jury or jury case the court will review a question of law dependent upon evidence before the master if the evidence was recorded by a stenographer and if "a transcript of so much of the proceedings before the master as is necessary to dispose of the objections adequately is served, together with the objections, upon every other party" (Rule 53(h)(3) and Rule 53(i)(3)). The procedure for designating portions of the transcript for submission to the court is similar to that contained in Massachusetts Rule of Appellate Procedure 8(b). Under new Rule 53, counsel no longer request the master to summarize relevant evidence, as was the case under Superior Court Rule 49(7) and (8). The court will have transcripts to review rather than masters' summaries.

Rule 53(h)(4) and Rule 53(i)(4) describe the action which a court may take on the master's report in non-jury and jury cases respectively. In both jury and non-jury cases, the court may strike all or part of the report, modify it, recommit it with instructions, or take other action that justice requires. In non-jury cases the court may also "adopt the report."

Reporter's Notes—1996

With the merger of the District Court rules into the Mass.R.Civ.P., the version of Mass.R.Civ.P. 53 as amended in 1982 is made applicable to the District Court. The specific language that had been included in now-repealed Rule 53(a) of the Dist./Mun.Cts.R.Civ.P. providing that a master may not be appointed in District Court proceedings without the assent of all parties has been retained in the merged rule for District Court civil proceedings.

VII. JUDGMENT

Rule 54. Judgments: Costs

(a) Definition; Form. The terms "judgment" and "final judgment" include a decree and mean the act of the trial court finally adjudicating the rights of the parties affected by the judgment, including:

(1) judgments entered under Rule 50(b) and Rule 52(a) and (b);

(2) judgments entered under Rule 58 upon a general verdict of a jury, or upon a decision by the court that a party shall recover only a sum certain or costs or that all relief shall be denied, or upon a special verdict under Rule 49(a) or a general verdict accompanied by answers to interrogatories under Rule 49(b).

A judgment shall not contain a recital of pleadings, the report of a master or the record of prior proceedings.

(b) Judgment Upon Multiple Claims or Involving Multiple Parties. When more than one claim for relief is presented

in an action, whether as a claim, counterclaim, cross-claim, or third-party claim, or when multiple parties are involved, the court may direct the entry of a final judgment as to one or more but fewer than all of the claims or parties only upon an express determination that there is no just reason for delay and upon an express direction for the entry of judgment. In the absence of such determination and direction, any order or other form of decision, however designated, which adjudicates fewer than all the claims or the rights and liabilities of fewer than all the parties shall not terminate the action as to any of the claims or parties, and the order or other form of decision is subject to revision at any time before the entry of judgment adjudicating all the claims and the rights and liabilities of all the parties.

(c) Demand for Judgment. A judgment by default shall not be different in kind from that prayed for in the demand for judgment. If only damages that are a sum certain or a sum which can by computation be made certain are demanded, a judgment by default shall not exceed the amount demanded.

Except as to a party against whom a judgment is entered by default, every final judgment shall grant the relief to which the party in whose favor it is rendered is entitled, even if the party has not demanded such relief in his pleadings.

(d) Costs. Except when express provision therefor is made either in a statute of the Commonwealth or in these rules, costs shall be allowed as of course to the prevailing party unless the court otherwise directs; but costs against the Commonwealth, its officers, and agencies shall be imposed only to the extent permitted by law. Except for those costs which are subject to the discretion of the court, costs shall be taxed by the clerk according to law.

Costs which are subject to the discretion of the court may be taxed by the court upon 5 days' notice. Costs which are taxable by the clerk may be taxed without notice unless a party notifies the clerk at any time after judgment and before execution that he desires to be present at the taxation of costs. Such notification shall be in writing and entered on the docket. If such notification is given, the clerk shall set a time for the taxation of costs, and shall give notice to all interested parties. The clerk shall include in the costs taxed only such items as are shown by the record and files at the time of taxation. On motion served within 5 days after receipt of notice of taxation of costs by the clerk, the action of the clerk may be reviewed by the court.

A party claiming costs shall file such certificates, affidavits and vouchers pertaining to items of costs, as he desires to have considered in taxing costs. Copies of such certificates, affidavits and vouchers shall be served by said party upon all other parties at least 5 days prior to the taxation of costs.

Whenever costs are awarded to two adverse parties in the same case, the court may order one sum to be set off against the other. If such set-off is not ordered, each party may have execution for the costs due him.

(e) Costs on Depositions. The taxation of costs in the taking of depositions, including audio-visual depositions, shall be subject to the discretion of the court, but in no event shall costs be allowed unless the court finds that the taking of the deposition was reasonably necessary, whether or not the deposition was actually used at the trial. Taxable costs may include the cost of service of subpoena upon the deponent, the reasonable fees of the officer before whom the deposition is taken, the fees and mileage allowances of the witnesses, the stenographer's reasonable fee for attendance, and the cost of the transcript of the testimony or such part thereof as the court may fix. When an audio-visual deposition is taken, taxable costs may include a reasonable fee for the use of the audio-visual equipment and for the services of the operator both in recording the deposition and editing it.

(f) Interest. Every judgment for the payment of money shall bear interest up to the date of payment of said judgment. Interest accrued up to the date of entry of a judgment shall be computed by the clerk according to law. Unless otherwise ordered by the court, interest from the date of entry of a judgment to the date of execution or order directing the payment of said judgment shall also be computed by the clerk,

and the amount of such interest shall be stated on the execution or order.

Amended April 18, 1980, effective July 1, 1980; December 16, 1980, effective January 1, 1981; October 24, 2012, effective January 1, 2013.

Reporter's Notes—1973

Rule 54(a) crystallizes the meaning of "judgment" (and "final judgment"), and emphasizes the difference between these terms and the concept of "judgment" under pre-existing Massachusetts practice. Heretofore, "judgment" has meant the last step in the case, which cuts off all appellate review (unless the losing party can successfully press a petition to vacate the judgment). Under the Rules, "judgment" is merely the final adjudicating act of the trial court, and starts the timetable for appellate review. Briefly stated, a case which "went to judgment" under the old practice was, except in the rarest circumstances, forensically dead; henceforth, a case in which judgment is "entered" is ready for appeal. See Rule 58 and Appellate Rules 3 and 4. For a definition of "appeal" see Appellate Rule 1.

Because the Rules merge "law" and "equity," see Rule 2, the word "judgment" also incorporates what used to be called a "decree".

Practice under Federal Rule 54(b) (identical to Rule 54(b)) is to wait until all claims are ripe for judgment before entering judgment on any of them. However, the court may "direct entry of a final judgment as to one or more but fewer than all of the claims or parties," although "only upon an express determination that there is no just reason for delay." This exception is necessary to avoid the injustice that may result from reserving judgment until final adjudication of all of several remotely-related claims.

Rule 54(c) requires that a judgment by default extend only to what is prayed for in the demand for judgment; otherwise, a judgment should grant the relief to which the prevailing party is entitled.

Rule 54(c) also provides that every final judgment (except a default judgment) shall grant the relief to which the party is entitled, regardless of whether he requested it or not. Thus a party may be granted equitable relief when he asked for damages, or damages when he requested equitable relief. A party may be awarded greater damages than the ad damnum.

Rule 54(d) accords with G.L. c. 261, § 1: "In civil actions the prevailing party shall recover his costs, except as otherwise provided." Costs fixed by statute are of course taxed in accordance therewith. Costs in actions whose costs are not thus regulated may not be taxed more broadly than in regulated actions. See G.L. c. 261, § 13. In the latter event, however, both rules and statute vest the court with discretion as to whether costs shall be taxed at all.

Massachusetts practice with respect to taxation of costs can be found in G.L. c. 261, § 19. The clerk may tax the costs without notifying any party, unless the adverse party has given "seasonable notice in writing to the clerk of his desire to be present at the taxation or causes such notice to be entered on the docket." This procedure will continue under Rule 54(d).

Rule 54(e) deals with the taxation of costs incident to depositions. These costs are entirely subject to the court's discretion. But costs may never be allowed unless the court finds the taking of the deposition to have been reasonably necessary. Items includible as "taxable costs" are also listed in Rule 54(e). Rule 54(e) is for all practical purposes identical to S.J.C.Rule 3:15, Section 9. The only difference is that Rule 54(e) permits taxation of witnesses' fees and mileage allowances.

Reporter's Notes—1986

Under Rule 54(f), the initial entry of judgment by the trial court should be the sum of the verdict and interest on that verdict to the time of said entry. Post-judgment interest should be computed on that total. See, e.g., *Boston Edison v. Tritsch*, 370 Mass. 260, 266 (1976); *Charles D. Bonanno Linen Service, Inc. v. McCarthy*, 550 F.Supp. 231, 248 (D.Mass.1982).

With the merger of the District Court rules into the Mass.R.Civ.P., minor differences which had existed between Mass.R.Civ.P. 54 and Dist./Mun.Cts.R.Civ.P. 54 have been eliminated. These differences were based on the lack of civil jury trials in the District Court. Although there are still no civil jury trials in the District Court (with some exceptions), the differences are not significant enough to merit any changes in the merged set of civil rules.

The amendment to Rule 54(c) in 2013 was part of a group of amendments to Rules 5(a), 54(c), and 55(b)(2) that responded to the Supreme Judicial Court's decision in Hermanson v. Szafarowicz, 457 Mass. 39 (2010). The *Hermanson* case dealt with the conflict between G.L. c. 231, § 13B, which limits a plaintiff's ability to demand a specific monetary amount in a complaint, and Rule 54(c), which provides that a default judgment may not exceed the amount requested in the demand for judgment.

Detailed analysis of the amendments to these three rules is set forth in the Reporter's Notes to the 2013 amendments to Rule 55(b)(2).

Rule 55. Default

(a) Entry. When a party against whom a judgment for affirmative relief is sought has failed to plead or otherwise defend as provided by these rules and that fact is made to appear by affidavit or otherwise, the clerk shall enter his default.

(b) Judgment. Judgment by default may be entered as follows:

(1) *By the Clerk.* When the plaintiff's claim against a defendant is for a sum certain or for a sum which can by computation be made certain, the clerk upon request of the plaintiff and upon affidavit of the amount due and affidavit that the defendant is not an infant or incompetent person, or an incapacitated person as defined in G. L. c. 190B shall enter judgment for that amount and costs against the defendant, if he has been defaulted for failure to appear.

(2) *By the Court.* In all other cases the party entitled to a judgment by default shall apply to the court therefor; but no judgment by default shall be entered against an infant or incompetent person or an incapacitated person as defined in G. L. c. 190B unless represented in the action by a guardian, conservator, or other such representative who has appeared therein. The court shall not conduct a hearing unless the party entitled to a judgment by default has provided notice to all other parties, including the party against whom a judgment by default is sought, of the date, time, and location of the hearing. Such notice must include a statement setting forth the nature and type of all damages requested and the amount of any damages that are a sum certain or a sum which can by computation be made certain. The notice shall be sent at least fourteen days prior to the date of hearing by first-class mail to the last known address or by other means approved by the court. If, in order to enable the court to enter judgment or to carry it into effect, it is necessary to take an account or to determine the amount of damages or to establish the truth of any averment by evidence or to make an investigation of any other matter, the court may conduct such hearings or order such references as it deems necessary and proper and shall accord a right of trial by jury to the parties when and as required by statute.

(3) The provisions of subparagraph (b)(2) supplement, but do not supersede, any other requirements of notice established by law.

[Text of subd. (b)(4) effective until March 15, 2020. See, also, text effective March 15, 2020.]

(4) *Affidavit Required.* Notwithstanding the foregoing, no judgment by default shall be entered until the filing of an affidavit made by any competent person, on the affiant's own knowledge, setting forth facts showing that the defendant is not a person in military service as defined in the "Servicemembers Civil Relief Act," as set forth in 50 U.S.C. §§ 3901 et seq., except upon order of the court in accordance with the Act.

[Text of subd. (b)(4) effective March 15, 2020. See, also, text effective until March 15, 2020.]

(4) *Affidavit Required.* Notwithstanding the foregoing, no judgment by default shall be entered until the filing of an affidavit made by any competent person, on the affiant's own knowledge, setting forth facts showing whether or not the defendant is in military service or, if the plaintiff is unable to determine whether or not the defendant is in military service, stating that the plaintiff is unable to determine whether or not the defendant is in military service, as set forth in the "Servicemembers Civil Relief Act," 50 U.S.C. §§ 3901 et seq., except upon order of the court in accordance with the Act.

(c) Setting Aside Default. For good cause shown the court may set aside an entry of default and, if a judgment has been entered, may likewise set it aside in accordance with Rule 60(b).

(d) Plaintiffs, Counterclaimants, Cross-Claimants. The provisions of this rule apply whether the party entitled to the judgment by default is a plaintiff, a third-party plaintiff, or a party who has pleaded a cross-claim or counterclaim. In all cases a judgment by default is subject to the limitations of Rule 54(c).

Amended effective July 1, 1996; amended November 28, 2007, effective March 1, 2008; June 24, 2009, effective July 1, 2009; October 24, 2012, effective January 1, 2013; April 26, 2017, effective May 1, 2017; November 26, 2019, effective March 15, 2020.

Rule 55 embraces two separate and distinct procedures:

(1) The entry of default, and (2) the entry of judgment by default. Rule 55(a) deals solely with entry of default, a formal, ministerial act of the clerk which does not constitute a judgment. Rule 55(b) provides the procedure for entering judgment by default which, in most cases, binds the defendant to the same degree as if he had appeared in the action and contested the allegations of the complaint. Riehle v. Margolies, 279 U.S. 218, 225, 49 S.Ct. 310, 313, 73 L.Ed. 669 (1928).

The entry of default by the clerk under Rule 55(a) is specifically limited to situations (1) where affirmative relief is sought; and (2) where there has been a failure to plead or otherwise to defend on the part of the opposing party. The clerk is authorized to make the entry when the above factors are brought to his attention by affidavit or otherwise.

Rule 55(a) authorizes the entry of default when the opposing party has "failed to plead or otherwise defend". The language includes a defendant's complete failure to file any papers at all, as well as his failure, after filing an appearance, to file an answer.

Rule 55(b)(1) changes slightly the language of Federal Rule 55(b)(1) by requiring the party seeking the default judgment to file an affidavit that the defendant is not an infant or incompetent. This amendment relieves the clerk of responsibility for determining the status of the defendant.

The filing of an appearance does not prevent the entry of default for failure to plead or otherwise defend, but it does, under Rule 55(b)(2), entitle a party to at least 7 days written notice of the application to the court for judgment on the default.

Rule 55(a) will produce no substantial change in Massachusetts practice. Generally, the Massachusetts rules of court and G.L. c. 231, § 57 authorized the clerk to enter a default for failure of a defendant to appear and answer. The plaintiff, however, was not required specially to request a default; if the return of service was in order, the clerk would automatically enter one.

In the federal system, a party who without answering attacks service or moves to dismiss is not liable to default for failure to appear. Bass v. Hoagland, 172 F.2d 205, 210 (5th Cir.1949). However, he is not usually held to have submitted himself to jurisdiction. This interpretation of Rule 55(a) may well change Massachusetts practice. See Dist.Ct.Rule 13.

Rule 55(b)(1) authorizes the clerk to enter a default judgment in certain limited circumstances. He shall do so upon plaintiff's request if:

(1) the claim against the defendant is for a sum certain or for a sum which by computation can be made certain; and

(2) the default has been entered for failure to appear; and

(3) the defendant is not an infant or incompetent.

The absence of any one of the above factors precludes the clerk from entering the judgment and presents a Rule 55(b)(2) situation.

Under Rule 55(b)(1) the plaintiff must request the clerk to enter the judgment by default and submit affidavits establishing the amount due and stating that the defendant is not an infant or an adjudged incompetent person. The section is also affected by the Soldiers' and Sailors' Civil Relief Act, 50 U.S.C.App. § 520, which is discussed below.

Rule 55(b)(2) empowers the court to enter judgment by default in cases not covered by Rule 55(b)(1). Judgment by default entered by the court must be preceded by an application from the party entitled to judgment. Denial of the motion for default judgment is interlocutory and is not an appealable order. McNutt, Jr. v. Cordox Corporation, 329 F.2d 107 (6th Cir.1964). Relief from such an order lies under Rule 55(c) or Rule 60(b).

Where the party in default is an infant or incompetent the court may enter judgment only if the infant or incompetent is represented, as provided in Rule 55(b)(2), and the representative has appeared in the action. If the party has no representative or if the representative has not appeared, a default judgment may not be entered. The power to enter judgment by default under Rule 55(b)(1) or (2) is limited by the Soldiers' and Sailors' Civil Relief Act, 50 U.S.C. § 520, which applies to state litigation as well as federal. Before a judgment based on a default of appearance is entered the plaintiff is required to file an affidavit satisfying the provisions of Rule 55(b)(4).

If the defaulting party has not appeared in the action, he is not entitled to notice of the plaintiff's pending application for judgment. Bowles v. Branick, 66 F.Supp. 557 (W.D.Mo.1946). If the defaulting party has filed an appearance, the defaulted party must be served with written notice of the application for judgment at least 7 days prior to the hearing on such application. Federal Rule 55(b)(2) specifies a three-day notice period; the time has been extended to conform with the notice period for motions prescribed in Rule 6. Failure to serve the required notice is considered a serious procedural irregularity warranting reversal by an appellate court, Hoffman v. New Jersey Federation of Young Men's and Young Women's Hebrew Assn's, 196

F.2d 204 (3d Cir.1939), or setting aside the trial court's judgment, Meeker v. Rizley, 324 F.2d 269 (10th Cir.1963). It has been held, however, that failure to give written notice may not prevent the entry of judgment if the defendant has actual notice of the pending application. I.C.C. v. Smith, 82 F.Supp. 39 (E.D.Pa.1949).

The purpose of Rule 55(b)(3) is to make it clear that the notice provisions of subparagraph (b)(2) supplement rather than supersede other notice requirements established by law. Thus, for example, Rule 55(b)(2) will have no effect upon G.L. c. 231, § 58A which provides that if a defendant is defaulted for failure to appear in a tort action wherein payment of the judgment is secured by a motor vehicle liability policy or bond, damages shall not be assessed until the expiration of four days after the plaintiff has given notice of such default to the issuing company and has filed an affidavit to that effect.

No hearing is provided if judgment is entered by the clerk. Where the court is required to enter the judgment, Rule 55 provides for a hearing. The hearing is not a trial; if the court determines that the defendant is in default, his liability is established and may not be contested. The defaulted party is, however, provided an opportunity to contest the amount of damages; the court may hold such hearings as it deems necessary including an accounting or reference to a master. In addition, a jury trial may be proper where provided by statute. Rule 55 is subject to the provisions of Rule 54(c) that a judgment by default may not be different in kind or exceed in amount that prayed for in the complaint. Neither Rule 54(c) nor Rule 55 should be interpreted to *require* the court to grant any relief at all. Thus if a complaint on its face seeks improper relief, e.g. an injunction against speech which is clearly constitutionally protected, the court need grant no relief at all, even though the defendant has been defaulted.

Rule 55(b) does not substantially change Massachusetts practice. It merely distinguishes those situations where the clerk may enter judgment by default from those where court action is required.

Rule 55(c) allows the court to set aside the entry of default for "good cause"; and may, for any of the grounds set forth in Rule 60(b), set aside a judgment by default. Because the entry of default is an interlocutory order, a motion under 55(c) is addressed to the sound judicial discretion of the trial judge and will not be reversed except for abuse of that discretion. Although an adequate basis for the motion must be shown, any doubt should be resolved in favor of setting aside defaults so that cases may be decided on their merits. Alopari v. O'Leary, 154 F.Supp. 78 (E.D.Pa.1957).

Rule 55(c) is similar to prior Massachusetts practice. G.L. c. 231, § 57 specifically provides that at any time before judgment a default may be set aside for good cause shown. The grounds for relief from a judgment in Massachusetts are substantially similar to those recognized in the federal system.

Rule 55(d) makes clear that the party entitled to a judgment by default may be a third-party plaintiff, or a party who has pleaded a cross-claim or counterclaim.

Reporter's Notes—1996

The 1996 amendments to Rule 55 changes the numbering of prior subparagraphs (b)(3) and (b)(4) to (b)(5) and (b)(6), respectively, in order to accommodate new subparagraphs (b)(3) and (b)(4). New subparagraphs (b)(3) and (b)(4) are drawn verbatim from now-repealed Rule 55 of the Dist./Mun.Cts.R.Civ.P., thus retaining the original District Court version of Rule 55. Changes in the title to subparagraphs (b)(1) and (b)(2) have been added to make clear that these two subparagraphs do not apply in the District Court. New subparagraph (b)(5) corresponds to what had been (b)(3), with minor changes, while new subparagraph (b)(6) is identical to what had been subparagraph (b)(4).

The following "Comments" to Rule 55, as originally adopted in the District Court in 1975 (and as later amended), explain the differences between default procedure in the District Court and in courts governed by the Mass.R.Civ.P.:

> This rule represents a significant departure from the MRCP version. Changes were made primarily because of the high default rate in District Courts in contract actions where the claim is "for a sum certain or for a sum which can by computation be made certain."

> Under this rule, the question of whether the clerk or the court enters the default judgment no longer depends on whether the defendant has appeared. Rather, if the claim is for a sum certain, the clerk enters judgment according to (b)(1), and if it is not for a sum certain, the court enters judgment according to (b)(2).

In summary, the merger of the District Court rules into the Mass.R.Civ.P. has effected no change in the procedures by which default judgments are entered in the respective courts involved.

Reporter's Notes—2008

Prior to the 2008 amendments, there were different provisions regarding default for the Superior Court and District Court. In the Superior Court, the pre–2008 version of this rule authorized the clerk to enter a judgment by default in "sum certain" cases if the defendant had been defaulted for failure to appear; otherwise, the matter had to be presented to the court (Rule 55(b)(1) and (2)). In the District Court, the pre–2008 version of this rule authorized the clerk to enter a judgment by default in "sum certain" cases, regardless of whether the default had been based on defendant's failure to appear (Rule 55(b)(3) and (4)). See Reporter's Notes to the 1996 amendments to the Mass. R. Civ. P. (merging the District Court Rules into the Mass. R. Civ. P.).

The 2008 amendments to Rule 55 serve to eliminate the differing default provisions for the Superior Court and the District Court. The amended language adopts for the District Court the Superior Court version of Rule 55. Accordingly, Rule 55(b)(3) and (4), which had contained the District Court version, have been deleted. Also, Rule 55(b)(5) and (6) have been renumbered as Rule 55(b)(3) and (4).

In light of the above, the titles to subparagraphs (1) and (2) of Rule 55(b) have been changed to read "(1) By the Clerk" and "(2) By the Court." In addition, the text of the pre–2008 version of subparagraph (5)—now renumbered as subparagraph (3)—has been amended to delete the reference to (b)(4).

Unrelated to the statewide one-trial system, the reference in renumbered Rule 55(b)(4) to the "Soldiers' and Sailors' Civil Relief Act" of 1940 has been deleted and replaced with the "Servicemembers Civil Relief Act." Congress renamed the Act and updated the Act in 2003.

Reporter's Notes—2009

The 2009 amendments reflect changes resulting from the adoption of the Massachusetts Uniform Probate Code.

Reporter's Notes—2013

Amendments to Rules 5(a), 54(c), and 55(b)(2) in 2013 responded to the Supreme Judicial Court's decision in Hermanson v. Szafarowicz, 457 Mass. 39 (2010).

The Hermanson Problem. The *Hermanson* case dealt with G.L. c. 231, § 13B, which prohibits a demand for a specific monetary amount in a complaint (unless the damages "are liquidated or ascertainable by calculation and a statement under oath" accompanies the complaint) and the first sentence of Mass. R. Civ. P. 54(c), which provides that a default judgment may not exceed the amount requested in the demand for judgment.

The Court ruled that there was an "irreconcilable conflict" between the statute and the court rule, and accordingly, the statute prevailed over the rule. As a result, the language of Rule 54(c) that provided for a ceiling on the amount of a default judgment that may enter against a defendant was rendered ineffective. The Court noted, however, that the ineffective first sentence of Rule 54(c) served the "sound" policy of allowing a defendant, served with a complaint, to

make a reasoned decision whether it might be financially worth a default rather than defending the case.

The Court referred to the Standing Advisory Committee on the Rules of Civil and Appellate Procedure the question whether the policy underlying the sentence "might continue to be served by an amendment to the rule that would eliminate reference to the 'demand for judgment' in the complaint but add a reference to the amount of damages set out in the civil action cover sheet" that accompanies the complaint.

The Standing Advisory Committee considered the matter at a number of meetings. The committee agreed that a mechanism should be found to provide a defendant with fair notice of the amount in controversy so that a defendant could make a reasoned decision whether it made sense to defend the case or to default. However, the committee did not recommend amending the civil action cover sheet to require a specific amount of damages. The committee noted that cover sheets are not universally used in all of the departments of the Trial Court with jurisdiction over damage claims. Further, the committee believed that such an approach—with a requirement that the cover sheet include a specific amount of damages—would undermine the legislative determination in G.L. c. 231, § 13B against inclusion of unliquidated amounts in civil complaints.

Rather than proposing that the amount of damages be contained in the cover sheet, the Standing Advisory Committee recommended to the Court, and the Court adopted, an approach that requires the party seeking a default judgment to provide advance notice to the defendant of the nature and type of damages sought that are not a sum certain. This approach required amendments to three rules: Rules 5(a), 54(c), and 55(b)(2).

Rule 55(b)(2) Statement of Damages. The 2013 amendments struck the second sentence of Mass. R. Civ. P. 55(b)(2) which provided for a seven-day notice to a defendant who had appeared in the action prior to a hearing on an application for default judgment.

Added to Rule 55(b)(2) were the following two sentences: "The court shall not conduct a hearing unless the party entitled to a judgment by default has provided notice to all other parties, including the party against whom a judgment by default is sought, of the date, time, and location of the hearing. Such notice must include a statement setting forth the nature and type of all damages requested and the amount of any damages that are a sum certain or a sum which can by computation be made certain." The "all damage" language in the revised rule requires the party seeking a default judgment to set forth the nature and type of so-called "unliquidated" damages (for example, tort action for pain and suffering damages or loss of consortium damages) and the amount of any "sum certain" damages.

The notice must be sent by first-class mail to the last known address at least fourteen days prior to the hearing or by some other method that the court approves. Thus, a defendant who has been defaulted will have notice of the extent of his or her financial exposure prior to the hearing. The longer period of fourteen days for the notice (rather than the seven-day period in the prior version of the rule) recognizes the difficulties that may occur in providing notice to a defendant who has not appeared in the action.

The fourteen-day notice with its statement setting forth damages should also be filed with the clerk's office. Mass. R. Civ. P. 5(d)(1).

Rule 54(c) Limitation Remains for Sum Certain Claims. The conflict between G.L. c. 231, § 13B and the first sentence of Mass. R. Civ. P. 54(c) that was addressed in the *Hermanson* case dealt with so-called unliquidated claims. The statute does not prohibit, and in fact recognizes, monetary demands in complaints where the damages are "liquidated or ascertainable by calculation" (if accompanied by a statement under oath). Accordingly, the 2013 amendments replaced the first sentence of Rule 54(c) with language that provides for a ceiling on damages that may be awarded after default in cases where damages that are set forth in the complaint are a "sum certain or a sum which can by computation be made certain" (language taken from Rule 55(b)(1)).

Only a party seeking a default judgment including any damages that are not a sum certain must serve the fourteen-day notice on the defendant prior to assessment of damages by virtue of the language added to Rule 55(b)(2) in 2013. Rule 55(b)(1) will continue to control entry of judgment by default where the demand for judgment is for only sum certain damages.

Rule 5(a) Service Requirements. The new requirement of a fourteen-day notice to a defaulted defendant prior to a hearing on damages (Rule 55(b)(2)) necessitated an amendment to Mass. R. Civ. P. 5(a). Rule 5(a) had provided that service of a document need not be made on a defendant in default (with an exception of a pleading asserting "new or additional claims for relief." As amended in 2013, Rule 5(a) adds another exception to the "no service" provision. The exception requires service on a defaulted defendant of the new fourteen-day notice describing the damages.

Reporter's Notes—2017

Rule 55(b)(4) has been amended to reflect that the federal Servicemembers Civil Relief Act was relocated in the United States Code from 50 U.S.C. App. §§ 501 et seq. to 50 U.S.C. §§ 3901 et seq. in 2015.

Reporter's Notes—2020

An amendment to Rule 55(b)(4) deals with the requirement of a military affidavit which is a prerequisite to a default judgment. The amendment is intended to make the Massachusetts rule consistent with the language of the federal Servicemembers Civil Relief Act, 50 U.S.C. §§ 3901 et seq., so as to provide more information about whether or not a defendant is in military service.

The previous language of Rule 55(b)(4) required an affidavit "setting forth facts showing that the defendant is not a person in military service. ..." The federal statute, however, provides that the plaintiff must file an affidavit "stating whether or not the defendant is in military service and showing necessary facts to support the affidavit" or "if the plaintiff is unable to determine whether or not the defendant is in military service, stating that the plaintiff is unable to determine whether or not the defendant is in military service." 50 U.S.C. § 3931(b)(1)(A) and (B). The revised language of Rule 55(b)(4) more closely tracks the federal language.

In recommending this amendment, the Standing Advisory Committee on the Rules of Civil Procedure of the Supreme Judicial Court also suggested that the Trial Court update the military affidavit form commonly in use in the Massachusetts trial courts to comply with the amendment and that a revised form indicate whether the plaintiff conducted a search of the Servicemembers Civil Relief Act Website in making a determination regarding the defendant's military status; to attach the results of any such search to the form; and if such a search was not conducted, to state facts in the form that would support the plaintiff's statement that the defendant is not in military service.

Rule 55.1. Special Requirements for Defaults and Default Judgments for Certain Consumer Debts

(a) Applicability. In addition to the requirements of Rule 55, the provisions of this rule shall apply to the entry of default for failure to appear or otherwise defend and to the entry of judgment after default in all actions subject to the requirements of Rule 8.1.

(b) Default.

(1) *Affidavit required.* When requesting a default, or upon request of the clerk for the purpose of entering a default, counsel for the plaintiff shall sign, serve, and file an affidavit stating that (i) counsel has personally reviewed the documentation filed and served pursuant to Rule 8.1; (ii) the documentation meets all requirements of Rule 8.1(c)–(f) (with any exceptions specifically stated); and (iii) the documentation establishes the plaintiff's entitlement to judgment in the amount claimed by the plaintiff. A self-represented plaintiff shall sign, serve, and file an affidavit with the same content. In entering a default, the clerk may rely upon the affidavit.

(2) *Non-entry of default.* If the plaintiff has not complied with the requirements of Rule 8.1 and subdivision (b)(1) of this rule, the clerk shall not enter a default against the defendant and shall so notify the parties. The court shall dismiss the complaint without prejudice on or after the 30th day after the date of notice by the clerk unless the plaintiff shows cause, with notice to the defendant, why the complaint should not be dismissed.

(c) Judgment. No default judgment against the defendant shall enter unless the clerk (if under Rule 55(b)(1)) or court (if under Rule 55(b)(2)) determines that the documentation filed and served by the plaintiff pursuant to Rule 8.1 and the affidavit pursuant to subdivision (b)(1) of this rule establish the plaintiff's entitlement to judgment in the amount claimed by the plaintiff. In entering a default judgment, the clerk or court may rely upon the affidavit pursuant to subdivision (b)(1) of this rule.

(d) Service. The plaintiff's request for entry of default judgment must be served on the defendant in accordance with Rule 5(b). The plaintiff must file proof of service of the request with the clerk or court. If service is to be made by mailing the request to the defendant's residential address, the plaintiff shall, within three months prior to the request, reverify the defendant's current residential address and shall file a new address verification affidavit pursuant to Rule 8.1(e).

Adopted May 22, 2018, effective January 1, 2019.

Reporter's Notes—2019

Rule 8.1 and Rule 55.1, effective in 2019, apply to collection actions against consumers involving debts arising out of revolving credit agreements. Rule 8.1 requires the plaintiff to (1) file with the complaint documentation regarding the debt, (2) verify the defendant's address prior to commencement of the action, and (3) certify that the statute of limitations has not expired. Rule 55.1 (1) prohibits entry of default against a defendant where the documentation required by Rule 8.1 has not been provided; (2) requires a determination that the plaintiff is entitled to judgment in the amount claimed prior to entry of a default judgment; and (3) requires reverification of the defendant's address under specified circumstances prior to entry of a default judgment.

Collection actions involving credit cards make up a significant portion of the civil actions commenced in the Massachusetts courts, with many of them filed in the District Court and Boston Municipal Court. Many of these cases proceed to judgment by default, sometimes raising questions whether the plaintiff has used a current address for service of process.

Requiring additional documentation with the complaint is a recognition that consumers in the past often lacked critical information needed when sued for credit card debts. When an assignee of the debt is named as plaintiff in the action and a complaint is served on the defendant, the defendant may have difficulty in ascertaining the identity of the original creditor. The documentation will help consumers to identify the original creditor in instances where an assignee is seeking to collect an assigned debt and the documentation will help to confirm the amount owed. The requirement of address verification mandates extra steps to help to ensure that an address used by a plaintiff to serve a defendant is as accurate as can reasonably be expected.

The addition of special requirements in litigation involving certain types of debts is not a new phenomenon in Massachusetts. Additional documentation and address verification requirements for certain types of debts have been applicable in small claims cases since 2009 (Rules 2(b), Uniform Small Claims Rules) and in civil actions on the regular civil docket in the District Court and Boston Municipal Court since 2015 (Boston Municipal Court and District Court Joint Standing Order No. 2–15).

Rule 55.1(a). Rule 55.1 applies where the plaintiff seeks to default the defendant for failure to answer or otherwise defend or where the clerk sua sponte enters a default for failure to answer or otherwise defend. The rule is inapplicable to default for other reasons, such as failure of the defendant to attend a pretrial conference or as a discovery sanction.

In order to obtain a default and judgment by default in a collection action against a consumer involving a debt arising out of a revolving credit agreement, the plaintiff must comply with both Rule 55 and Rule 55.1. All of the provisions of Rule 55 are applicable to such an action. Thus, a plaintiff must request entry of default under Rule 55(a), and a judgment after default may be entered by the clerk (if the action is one for a sum certain, Rule 55(b)(1)) or by the court (if the action is one other than for a sum certain, Rule 55(b)(2)). The requirement of a military affidavit pursuant to the federal Service-members Civil Relief Act (Rule 55(b)(4)) is applicable to collection actions covered by Rule 8.1.

Rule 55.1(b)(1). In addition to satisfying the requirements of Rule 55(a), counsel for the plaintiff or a self-represented party seeking a default must serve and file an affidavit setting forth various matters regarding the documentation required under Rule 8.1. Even where the plaintiff has not sought a default, the clerk may request that an affidavit be filed. This might occur, for example, in courts in which clerks have a practice of reviewing the docket for the purpose of entering a default sua sponte where the defendant has not answered or moved to dismiss within the time provided by Rule 12(a).

Rule 55.1(b)(2).

Even though a plaintiff has satisfied the provisions of Rule 55(a) for entry of default, Rule 55.1(b)(2) prevents the clerk from entering a default if the clerk determines that the plaintiff has not provided the information required by Rule 8.1 with the complaint or has not filed an affidavit under Rule 55.1(b)(1). In making this determination, the clerk is not required to review the various items that must be filed with the complaint under Rule 8.1, but may rely upon the Rule 55.1(b)(1) affidavit.

The clerk is required to notify the parties of the non-entry of default. The rule requires a judge (and not the clerk) to order dismissal of the complaint on or after the 30th day after the date the clerk sends notice of non-entry of default, but provides the plaintiff with an opportunity to avoid dismissal by showing cause why the complaint should not be dismissed. This period of time allows the plaintiff to remedy the defect by supplying the required missing information to the clerk or to persuade a judge that there is cause justifying non-compliance with the requirements of Rule 8.1, provided that cause for non-compliance is consistent with the purposes of the rule.

A party who disagrees with a clerk's determination whether to enter a default should bring the matter to a judge for resolution. The plaintiff must provide notice to the defendant of any attempt to show cause to avoid dismissal and provide the defendant with copies of any filings.

Rule 55.1(c).

Even though a plaintiff has satisfied the provisions of Rule 55(b)(1) for entry of default judgment by the clerk or Rule 55(b)(2) for entry of default judgment by the court, the clerk (if under Rule 55(b)(1)) or the court (if under Rule 55(b)(2)) must make a determination that the plaintiff is entitled to a judgment in the amount sought by the plaintiff. This will require a determination that the plaintiff has complied with Rule 8.1 and that the submitted documentation demonstrates the plaintiff is entitled to the damages sought. The clerk or court must also determine that the plaintiff has filed the affidavit required under Rule 55.1(b)(1). The rule provides the option to the clerk or court to rely upon the plaintiff's Rule 55.1(b)(1) affidavit in the determination whether there has been compliance with Rule 8.1. Reliance on the Rule 55.1(b)(1) affidavit relieves the clerk or court from independently having to review the filings required by Rule 8.1(c)–(f).

Rule 55.1(d). This provision requires the plaintiff to serve the request for default judgment on the defendant in accordance with Rule 5(b) by delivery or by mail to the defendant's last known address. A plaintiff who uses the mail option must reverify the defendant's address as set forth in Rule 8.1.

Rule 56. Summary Judgment

(a) For Claimant. A party seeking to recover upon a claim, counterclaim, or cross-claim or to obtain a declaratory judgment may, at any time after the expiration of 20 days from the commencement of the action or after service of a motion for summary judgment by the adverse party, move with or without supporting affidavits for a summary judgment in his favor upon all or any part thereof.

(b) For Defending Party. A party against whom a claim, counterclaim, or cross-claim is asserted or a declaratory judgment is sought may, at any time, move with or without supporting affidavits for a summary judgment in his favor as to all or any part thereof.

(c) Motion and Proceedings Thereon. The motion shall be served at least 10 days before the time fixed for the hearing. The adverse party prior to the day of hearing may serve opposing affidavits. The judgment sought shall be rendered forthwith if the pleadings, depositions, answers to interrogatories, and responses to requests for admission under Rule 36, together with the affidavits, if any, show that there is no genuine issue as to any material fact and that the moving party is entitled to a judgment as a matter of law. A summary judgment, interlocutory in character, may be rendered on the issue of liability alone although there is a genuine issue as to the amount of damages. Summary judgment, when appropriate, may be rendered against the moving party.

(d) Case Not Fully Adjudicated on Motion. If on motion under this rule judgment is not rendered upon the whole case or for all the relief asked and a trial is necessary, the court at the hearing of the motion, by examining the pleadings and the evidence before it and by interrogating counsel, shall if practicable ascertain what material facts exist without substantial controversy and what material facts are actually and in good faith controverted. It shall thereupon make an order specifying the facts that appear without substantial controversy, including the extent to which the amount of damages or other relief is not in controversy, and directing such further proceedings in the action as are just. Upon the trial of the action the facts so specified shall be deemed established, and the trial shall be conducted accordingly.

(e) Form of Affidavits; Further Testimony; Defense Required. Supporting and opposing affidavits shall be made on personal knowledge, shall set forth such facts as would be admissible in evidence, and shall show affirmatively that the affiant is competent to testify to the matters stated therein. Sworn or certified copies of all papers or parts thereof referred to in an affidavit shall be attached thereto or served therewith. The court may permit affidavits to be supplemented or opposed by depositions, answers to interrogatories, or further affidavits. When a motion for summary judgment is made and supported as provided in this rule, an adverse party may not rest upon the mere allegations or denials of his pleading, but his response, by affidavits or as otherwise provided in this rule, must set forth specific facts showing that there is a genuine issue for trial. If he does not so respond, summary judgment, if appropriate, shall be entered against him.

(f) When Affidavits Are Unavailable. Should it appear from the affidavits of a party opposing the motion that he cannot for reasons stated present by affidavit facts essential to justify his opposition, the court may refuse the application for judgment or may order a continuance to permit affidavits to be obtained or depositions to be taken or discovery to be had or may make such other order as is just.

(g) Affidavits Made in Bad Faith. Should it appear to the satisfaction of the court at any time that any of the affidavits presented pursuant to this rule are presented in bad faith or solely for the purpose of delay, the court shall forthwith order the party employing them to pay to the other party the amount of the reasonable expenses which the filing of the affidavits caused him to incur, including reasonable attorney's fees, and any offending party or attorney may be adjudged guilty of contempt.

Amended March 7, 2002, effective May 1, 2002.

Reporter's Notes—1973

Except in a narrow class of cases, Massachusetts has up to now lacked any procedural device for terminating litigation in the interim between close of pleadings and trial. Under G.L. c. 231, §§ 59 and 59B, only certain contract actions could be disposed of prior to trial. In all other types of litigation, no matter how little factual dispute involved, resolution had to await trial.

Rule 56, which, with a small addition, tracks Federal Rule 56 exactly, responds to the need which the statutes left unanswered. It proceeds on the principle that trials are necessary only to resolve issues of fact; if at any time the court is made aware of the total absence of such issues, it should on motion promptly adjudicate the legal questions which remain, and thus terminate the case.

The statutes, so far as they went, embodied this philosophy. They aimed "to avoid delay and expense of trials in cases where there is no genuine issue of fact." Albre Marble & Tile Co., Inc. v. John Bowen Co., Inc., 338 Mass. 394, 397, 155 N.E.2d 437, 439 (1959). Rule 56 will extend this principle beyond contract cases. Thus in tort actions where the facts are not disputed, summary judgment for one party will be appropriate. Should the facts concerning liability be undisputed, but damages controverted, Rule 56(c) authorizes partial summary judgment: the court may determine the liability issue, leaving for trial only the question of damages.

The important thing to realize about summary judgment under Rule 56 is that it can be granted if and only if there is "no genuine issue as to any material fact." If any such issue appears, summary judgment *must* be denied. So-called "trial by affidavits" has no place under Rule 56. Affidavits (or pleadings, depositions, answers to interrogatories, or admissions) are merely devices for demonstrating the absence of any genuine issue of material fact. Introduction of material controverting the moving party's assertions of fact raises such an issue and precludes summary judgment.

On the other hand, because Rule 56 recognizes only "genuine" material issues of fact, Rule 56(e) requires the opponent of any summary judgment motion to do something more than simply deny the proponent's allegations. Faced with a summary judgment motion supported by affidavits or the like, an opponent may not rely solely upon the allegations of his pleadings. He bears the burden of introducing enough countervailing data to demonstrate the existence of a genuine material factual issue.

If, however, the opponent is convinced that even on the movant's undisputed affidavits, the court should not grant summary judgment, he may decline to introduce his own materials and may instead fight the motion on entirely legal (as opposed to factual) grounds. Indeed, the final sentence of Rule 56(c) makes clear that in appropriate cases, summary judgment may be entered *against* the moving party. This is eminently logical. Because by definition the moving party is *always* asserting that the case contains no factual issues, the court should have the power, no matter who initiates the motion, to award judgment to the party legally entitled to prevail on the undisputed facts.

Reporter's Notes to Rule 56(c)—2002

The 2002 amendment to Rule 56(c) deletes the phrase "on file" from the third sentence, in recognition of the fact that discovery documents are generally no longer separately filed with the court. See Rule 5(d)(2) and Superior Court Administrative Directive No. 90–2. The previous reference to admissions has also been replaced by a reference to "responses to requests for admission under Rule 36." The amendment is merely of the housekeeping variety and no change in practice is intended.

Rule 57. Declaratory Judgment

The procedure for obtaining a declaratory judgment pursuant to General Laws c. 231A shall be in accordance with these rules, and the right to trial by jury may be demanded under the circumstances and in the manner provided in Rules 38 and 39. The existence of another adequate remedy does not preclude a judgment for declaratory relief in cases where it is appropriate. The court may order a speedy hearing of an action for a declaratory judgment and may advance it on the calendar.

Reporter's Notes—1973

G.L. c. 231A is the Uniform Declaratory Judgment Act with minor changes and additions. Rule 57, specifically referring to the statute, does not effect any essential change in Massachusetts practice. The main thrust of Rule 57 is that actions for declaratory judgment are to be brought in accordance with the Rules. Although the statute is quite detailed procedurally (see, e.g., G.L. c. 231A, §§ 7 and 8 dealing respectively with costs and necessary parties), the specificity of the Act should cause no conflict with the Rules.

The abolition, by Rule 2, of the distinction between law and equity requires only verbal adjustment of prior practice. The rule (S.J.C. Rule 2:23) prohibiting the plaintiff's attorney in a declaratory judgment proceeding from representing the defendant remains unchanged.

The last sentence of Rule 57 specifically authorizes priority trial treatment for declaratory judgment actions. It does not materially alter the assignment judge's power (see Super.Ct. Rules 59 and 63); and it makes clear to bench and bar that declaratory judgment proceedings, which by their nature frequently require summary disposition, may receive whatever special treatment they need.

Reporter's Notes—1996

With the merger of the District Court rules into the Mass.R.Civ.P., minor differences which had existed between Mass.R.Civ.P. 57 and Dist./Mun.Cts.R.Civ.P. 57 have been eliminated.

Rule 58.   Entry of Judgment

(a) After Trial or Hearing or by Agreement. Subject to the provisions of Rules 54(b) and 23(c): (1) upon a general verdict of a jury, or upon a decision by the court that a party shall recover only a sum certain or costs or that all relief shall be denied, or upon a written agreement for judgment for a sum certain or denying relief, the clerk, unless the court otherwise orders, shall forthwith prepare, sign and enter judgment without awaiting any direction by the court; (2) upon a decision by the court granting other relief, or upon a special verdict under Rule 49(a) or a general verdict accompanied by answers to interrogatories under Rule 49(b), the court shall promptly approve the form of the judgment, and the clerk shall thereupon enter it.   Every judgment shall be set forth on a separate document; but when any party files an agreement for judgment, or a notice or stipulation of dismissal pursuant to Rule 41(a)(1), the agreement, notice, or stipulation, as the case may be, shall, upon being filed, constitute the judgment, for all purposes, and no separate document need be prepared.   A judgment is effective only when so set forth or filed and when entered as provided in Rule 79(a).   Entry of the judgment shall not be delayed for the taxing of costs. Attorneys shall submit forms of judgment upon direction of the court.   The court, on motion, may allow a hearing on the form of the judgment.

(b) Upon Order of Supreme Judicial Court. The clerk shall enter any judgment specifically directed by the Supreme Judicial Court.

Amended December 14, 1976, effective January 1, 1977.

Reporter's Notes—1973

Rule 58 tracks Federal Rule 58 and works a substantial change in Massachusetts practice.

The rule deals with the ministerial act of "entry" of judgment as opposed to the judicial act of "rendition" of judgment.   Its aim is to ascertain the exact date when a judgment becomes effective.   That date is important because it begins the allowable period for making most of the post-verdict motions included in the Rules, and (in some cases) for taking an appeal.

The provisions of the rule are subject to Rule 54(b) and Rule 23(c). Rule 54 operates as to the entry of final judgment on any issue or as to any party in a suit which involves multiple claims or multiple parties.   Under Rule 54(b) the court may direct the entry of final judgment as to one or more but fewer than all of the claims, provided the court makes "an express determination that there is no just reason for delay" and "makes an express direction for the entry of judgment." Rule 23(c) prohibits dismissal or compromise of a class action without court approval.

Rule 58 contemplates two basic situations.   In one, the clerk enters final judgment according to Rule 79(a) without any direction from the court; in the other, the clerk awaits the court's approval of the judgment before effectuating it by entry in the civil docket.

In case of (1) a general verdict of a jury, or (2) a determination by the court that a party shall recover only a sum certain or costs or that all relief shall be denied, or (3) a written agreement for judgment for a sum certain or denying relief, Rule 58(1) requires the clerk immediately to enter judgment on the civil docket in accordance with Rule 79(a).

In these situations the clerk does not await the court's direction before entering judgment.   The court, however, retains power to order otherwise where, for example, the court has before it a motion for judgment n.o.v. (Rule 50(b)) and directs that the clerk not enter judgment on a general verdict immediately.   Voelkier v. Delaware, Lackawanna & Western R. Co., 31 F.Supp. 515, 516 (W.D.N.Y.1939). The language of Rule 58 and the policy underlying the prompt entry of judgment suggest that only in the most exceptional circumstances will a court not direct entry of judgment on a jury's general verdict.

Rule 58(a)(2) deals with the more complex situations where (1) a jury returns a general verdict accompanied by answers to interrogatories under Rule 49(b); (2) there is a special verdict; or (3) the court grants "other relief."   Since these areas require specific judicial resolution, the rule requires the clerk to defer entry of judgment until the court approves its form.

Even in these situations, however, Rule 58(a)(2) emphasizes speed and simplicity by requiring the court to approve the form of judgment "promptly."   An example of a situation within the ambit of Rule 58(a)(2) would be a special verdict returned pursuant to Rule 49. Such a verdict merely recites the facts found.   It then becomes necessary for the court to apply the law to those facts and render a judgment.   Until the court has done so, the clerk is not in a position to enter it on the docket.

The requirement that every judgment "be set forth on a separate document" makes clear that a judicial opinion alone cannot serve as a directive to a clerk to enter judgment pursuant to Rule 79(a).   The judgment to be effective must satisfy *two* conditions:

(1) It must be set out on a separate document distinct from any opinion or memorandum (unless the opinion or memorandum includes a specific order for entry of judgment); and

(2) It must be entered according to Rule 79(a).

In the absence of either of these preconditions, the judgment is not effective; any appellate procedure is premature.   Thus a concluding sentence in an opinion which merely states "the complaint is dismissed" is not an effective entry of judgment by itself.   The requirement that the judgment be explicitly set forth on a separate document is not limited to situations where the court writes an opinion.   It extends to *all* judgments, whether based on jury verdict or court decision.

For purposes of the other rules the date of effective entry is crucial. For example, a motion to amend findings or make additional findings under Rule 52(b) may be made not later than 10 days after entry of judgment.   A motion for a new trial under Rule 59(b), a motion to alter or amend the judgment under Rule 59(e), and the awarding of a new trial on the court's own motion are subject to the same time limitation.   The specific date of the notation of the judgment by the clerk pursuant to Rule 79(a) constitutes the date of effective judgment for purposes of the above rules.

In accord with the policy of prompt entry of judgment, Rule 58 provides that the entry of judgment shall not be delayed for the taxing of costs.   Thus, judgment can be entered with the notation "with costs," leaving the exact amount for later determination.   "The postponement of judgment until after the amount of costs can be determined is contrary to the letter and purpose of Rule 58."   Danzig v. Virgin Isle Hotel, Inc., 278 F.2d 580, 582 (3rd Cir.1960).

Rule 58 effects a major change in Massachusetts practice.   Under the previous separate procedural systems for actions at law and suits in equity, a "judgment" was a final decision at law while a "decree" was the terminal document in a suit in equity.   With the adoption of Rule 2, both situations are covered by the one term: Judgment.

The practice heretofore in "equity" cases required the party in whose favor a decree was entered to submit to the court the form of the decree.   S.J.C. Rule 2:44; Super.Ct. Rule 82.   The last sentence of Federal Rule 58 discourages such submissions, but Massachusetts Rule 58 has been drafted to accord specifically with familiar practice.

Reporter's Notes—1996

With the merger of the District Court rules into the Mass.R.Civ.P., minor differences which had existed between Mass.R.Civ.P. 58 and Dist./Mun.Cts.R.Civ.P. 58 have been eliminated.

Rule 59. New Trials: Amendment of Judgments

(a) Grounds. A new trial may be granted to all or any of the parties and on all or part of the issues (1) in an action in which there has been a trial by jury, for any of the reasons for which new trials have heretofore been granted in actions at law in the courts of the Commonwealth; and (2) in an action tried without a jury, for any of the reasons for which rehearings have heretofore been granted in suits in equity in the courts of the Commonwealth. A new trial shall not be granted solely on the ground that the damages are excessive until the prevailing party has first been given an opportunity to remit so much thereof as the court adjudges is excessive. A new trial shall not be granted solely on the ground that the damages are inadequate until the defendant has first been given an opportunity to accept an addition to the verdict of such amount as the court adjudges reasonable. On a motion for a new trial in an action tried without a jury, the court may open the judgment if one has been entered, take additional testimony, amend findings of fact and conclusions of law or make new findings and conclusions, and direct the entry of a new judgment.

(b) Time for Motion. A motion for a new trial shall be served not later than 10 days after the entry of judgment.

(c) Time for Serving Affidavits. When a motion for new trial is based upon affidavits they shall be served with the motion. The opposing party has 10 days after such service within which to serve opposing affidavits, which period may be extended for an additional period not exceeding 20 days either by the court for good cause shown or by the parties by written stipulation. The court may permit reply affidavits.

(d) On Initiative of Court. Not later than 10 days after entry of judgment the court of its own initiative may order a new trial for any reason for which it might have granted a new trial on motion of a party. After giving the parties notice and an opportunity to be heard on the matter, the court may grant a motion for a new trial, timely served, for a reason not stated in the motion. In either case, the court shall specify in the order the grounds therefor.

(e) Motion to Alter or Amend a Judgment. A motion to alter or amend the judgment shall be served not later than 10 days after entry of the judgment.

Reporter's Notes—1973

Rule 59(a) allows the court to grant a new trial as to any or all of the parties or as to any or all of the issues. This power applies to both jury and non-jury cases and is entirely discretionary. Yates v. Dann, 11 F.R.D. 386 (D.Del.1951). This provision seeks to limit the issue on retrial to those which the court considers were not properly adjudicated in the first trial. Thus a partial new trial may be granted as to liability alone, if the court considers that the damages have been properly ascertained. Calaf v. Fernandez, 239 F. 795 (1st Cir.1917). Conversely, as in *Yates,* supra, the new trial is often limited to the issue of damages, if liability has been properly determined.

The partial new trial device may only be used if the issues as to which the new trial is ordered are so distinct and independent from the remainder of the case that they may be separately tried without

injustice. If the issues or parties to which the motion is addressed are not severable or are interwoven with the remaining issues, the court may not order a partial retrial. Gasoline Products Co. v. Champlin Refining Co., 283 U.S. 494, 51 S.Ct. 513, 75 L.Ed. 1188 (1931).

In conformity with the spirit of the entire Federal Rules, Rule 59(a) also provides that in non-jury cases "the court may open the judgment if one has been entered, take additional testimony, amend findings of fact and conclusions of law and direct the entry of a new judgment."

The provisions of Rule 59(a), in most instances, substantially follow former Massachusetts practice. The grounds for a new trial are unchanged.

Rule 59(a) treats two types of cases: (1) actions tried by a jury and (2) actions tried without a jury. In the first classification new trials may be granted for any of the reasons for which new trials have heretofore been granted in actions at law. In the second, new trials may be granted "for any of the reasons for which rehearings have heretofore been granted in suits in equity." This latter standard applies both to jury-waived actions and actions in which equitable relief is sought.

Rule 59(a) incorporates the remittitur and additur provisions of G.L. c. 231, § 127. While Federal Rule 59(a) does not specifically refer to the remittitur, established federal practice allows it, within the discretion of the trial judge. Neese v. Southern Ry., 350 U.S. 77, 76 S.Ct. 131, 100 L.Ed. 60 (1955). The additur, however, is not allowed in the federal system. Dimick v. Schiedt, 293 U.S. 474, 55 S.Ct. 296, 79 L.Ed. 603 (1934). This distinction is not attributable to any language of Federal Rule 59(a); it is based upon the Supreme Court's interpretation of the Seventh Amendment. The decision in *Dimick* does not bind the state courts because the states are not bound by the provisions of the Seventh Amendment, either directly, Pearson v. Yewdall, 95 U.S. 294, 24 L.Ed. 436 (1877), or by reason of its being incorporated into the due process clause of the Fourteenth Amendment. Walker v. Sauvinet, 92 U.S. 90, 23 L.Ed. 678 (1875).

The possibility remains that the additur could be held unconstitutional under Article 15 of the Massachusetts Declaration of Rights. The California Supreme Court held the additur unconstitutional under similar language of the California Constitution. See Dorsey v. Barba, 38 Cal.2d 350, 357, 240 P.2d 604, 608 (1952).

The promulgation of Rule 59(a) by the Supreme Judicial Court does not constitute a binding decision that the Massachusetts additur provision is constitutional under Article 15. The promulgation is analogous to an advisory opinion. Advisory opinions are not adjudications by the court and do not fall within the doctrine of stare decisis; thus if the same question arises later in the course of other litigation, the Court is obliged to consider it anew, unaffected by the advisory opinion. Dodge v. Prudential Insurance Company of America, 343 Mass. 375, 379–380, 179 N.E.2d 234, 239–240 (1961).

The time limit for making a motion under Rule 59(b) is computed from the date of effective entry of judgment under Rule 58. The wording of 59(b), however, allows a motion to be made both before or after the entry of judgment. Patridge v. Presley, 189 F.2d 645 (D.C.Cir.1951); McCulloch Motors Corp. v. Oregon Saw Chain Corp., 245 F.Supp. 851 (S.D.Cal.1965).

Some courts have held, however, that a motion for a new trial made prior to the entry of judgment is to be taken as denied by a subsequent entry of judgment. Mosier v. Federal Reserve Bank of New York, 132 F.2d 710 (2nd Cir.1942); Agostino v. Ellamer Packing Co., 191 F.2d 576 (9th Cir.1951).

Generally, present federal practice allows the motion to be made either before or after entry of judgment. This is evidenced by the fact that the Supreme Court adopted the words "not later than" (rather than the proposed "within") 10 days after entry of judgment. Furthermore, Rule 59(a) allows the court to open judgment *"if one has been entered"* (emphasis supplied) in response to a motion by a party.

Except for motions made during the trial or hearing, Rule 7(b) requires that the motion be in writing and state specifically the grounds and the relief or order sought. A motion under Rule 59 which does not meet the requirements of Rule 7(b) will be insufficient and considered a nullity. National Farmers Union Auto & Casualty v. Wood, 207 F.2d 659 (10th Cir.1953); Collins v. Risner, 22 F.R.D. 14 (E.D.Pa.1958). The exception in Rule 7(b) refers to the situation where a motion is made "during the trial or hearing" as, for example, during the actual trial or immediately after pronouncement of the verdict. In such a case, the motion need not be in writing. See Douglas v. Union Carbide Corp., 311 F.2d 182, 185 (4th Cir.1962).

Because a motion under Rule 59(b) affects the finality of judgment and tolls the time for taking an appeal, the 10–day limit may not be enlarged by the court. Rule 6(b). Some authority indicates that the parties themselves can extend the time, Whayne v. Glenn, 114 F.Supp. 784 (W.D.Ky.1953); however, the safer view is that Rule 6(b) bars any such extension. John E. Smith's Sons Co. v. Lattimer Foundry & Machine Co., 239 F.2d 815 (3rd Cir.1956).

The 10–day period, it should be emphasized, begins to run from the date of effective entry of judgment under Rule 58. This provision applies even though a party has not received notice of the judgment under Rule 77(d) from the clerk or adverse party; or even if the clerk fails to record a correct copy of the judgment as required by Rule 79(b).

A motion under Rule 59 suspends the finality of the judgment and tolls the time for appeal. It is established in federal practice that an amendment may be made to a motion for a new trial. For example, the court can allow a subsequent amendment of the motion to state additional or different grounds. Alcavo v. Jean Jordeau, Inc., 3 F.R.D. 61 (D.N.J.1942). The weight of judicial authority, however, supports the view that such an amendment may not be made after the 10–day period has elapsed. McCloskey v. Kane, 285 F.2d 297 (D.C.Cir.1960); Marks v. Philadelphia Wholesale Drug Co., 125 F.Supp. 369 (E.D.Pa.1954). The court has the power to grant a new trial on its own initiative for any reason not stated in the motion, provided the court acts within the 10–day period.

Rule 59(b) substantially changes former Massachusetts practice. The rule allows a motion for new trial after judgment has been entered, while the practice in Massachusetts was that a new trial may be ordered at any time before judgment. The difference springs from the differing meaning of "judgment". See Reporters' Notes to Rule 54.

The 10–day deadline under Rule 59(b) enlarges the former three day period for jury cases. Like Rule 59(b), former Massachusetts practice required that the motion be in writing. By statute and court rule, hearings supported by affidavits on motions for a new trial were allowed in Massachusetts, G.L. c. 231, § 127; Super.Ct.Rules 46 and 55. The state rules also provided that unless an application for hearing was made within 10 days of filing of the motion, the trial judge could act upon the motion without a hearing.

Under Rule 59(c), when a motion is supported by affidavits, the latter must be filed *with the motion*. Former practice allowed the affidavits to be filed at the hearing.

Rule 59(d), taken unchanged from Federal Rule 59(d), substantially departs from former Massachusetts practice. It allows the court, on its own initiative, to order a new trial "for any reason for which it might have granted a new trial on motion of a party." The second part of Rule 59(d) allows the trial judge to grant a motion for a new trial for a reason not stated in the motion. Under prior law, in jury cases, a new trial could be ordered only on motion and only for the reasons set forth in the motion.

Rule 59(d) continues the former Massachusetts practice of allowing the parties a hearing in any action proposed to be taken sua sponte by the trial judge, and continues to require that the court specify the grounds for whatever action it takes.

A motion under Rule 59(e) (taken with only slight changes from Federal Rule 59(e)), authorizes the court to alter or amend a judgment provided the motion is filed within 10 days of entry of judgment. Since such a motion affects the finality of the judgment, it tolls the time for taking an appeal from the judgment; the time does not begin to run again until after disposition of the motion.

Rule 59(e) encompasses many motions seeking relief of a type which technically might not be considered a motion for a new trial: for example, a motion for rehearing, reconsideration or vacation; a motion to amend a judgment of dismissal "without prejudice"; or one to vacate a dismissal for want of jurisdiction. Market v. Swift & Co., 173 F.2d 517 (2nd Cir.1949).

The significance of a motion under Rule 59(e) is that such a motion stops the appeal clock. If the relief sought does not fit under Rule 59(e) or is made later than 10 days after judgment, it is considered to fall within Rule 60(b), which does not toll the appeal time.

Reporter's Notes to Rule 59(e)—as amended, 1994 (third paragraph from end)

A motion under Rule 59(e) (taken with only slight changes from Federal Rule 59(e)), authorizes the court to alter or amend a judgment provided the motion is served within 10 days of entry of judgment. Since such a motion affects the finality of the judgment, it tolls the time for taking an appeal from the judgment; the time does not begin to run again until after disposition of the motion. It should be noted that, as in the case of a motion for new trial under Rule 59(b), the motion to alter or amend judgment under Rule 59(e) must be served not later than 10 days after entry of judgment. See Arthur D. Little, Inc. v. East Cambridge Savings Bank, 35 Mass.App.Ct. 734, 743, note 7, 625 N.E.2d 1383 (1994), commenting on a prior misstatement in these Reporters' Notes that a motion under Rule 59(e) must be "filed" within 10 days of entry of judgment. The difference between service and filing should be emphasized. Service is accomplished pursuant to Rule 5(b) by delivery or mail to all parties or their attorneys; the papers "shall be filed with the court either before service or within a reasonable time thereafter." Rule 5(d). See Albano v. Bonanza International Development Co., 5 Mass.App.Ct. 692, 369 N.E.2d 473 (1977).

Reporter's Notes—1996

With the merger of the District Court rules into the Mass.R.Civ.P., minor differences which had existed between Mass.R.Civ.P. 59 and Dist./Mun.Cts.R.Civ.P. 59 have been eliminated (most of which concerned references to jury trial).

Reporter's Notes—2013

The 1973 Reporter's Notes to Rule 59, last paragraph, state: "The significance of a motion under Rule 59(e) is that such a motion stops the appeal clock. If the relief sought does not fit under Rule 59(e) or is made later than 10 days after judgment, it is considered to fall within Rule 60(b), which does not toll the appeal time." In 2013, however, an amendment to Rule 4(a) of the Massachusetts Rules of Appellate Procedure provided that a Rule 60 motion, if served within ten days after entry of judgment, tolls the time period to claim an appeal. See 2013 Reporter's Notes to Mass. R. A. P. 4(a).

Rule 60.   Relief From Judgment or Order

(a) Clerical Mistakes. Clerical mistakes in judgments, orders or other parts of the record and errors therein arising from oversight or omission may be corrected by the court at any time of its own initiative or on the motion of any party and after such notice, if any, as the court orders. During the pendency of an appeal, such mistakes may be so corrected before the appeal is docketed in the appellate court, and thereafter while the appeal is pending may be so corrected with leave of the appellate court.

(b) Mistake; Inadvertence; Excusable Neglect; Newly Discovered Evidence; Fraud, etc. On motion and upon such terms as are just, the court may relieve a party or his legal representative from a final judgment, order, or proceeding for the following reasons: (1) mistake, inadvertence, surprise, or excusable neglect; (2) newly discovered evidence which by due diligence could not have been discovered in time to move for a new trial under Rule 59(b); (3) fraud (whether heretofore denominated intrinsic or extrinsic), misrepresentation, or other misconduct of an adverse party; (4) the judgment is void; (5) the judgment has been satisfied, released, or discharged, or a prior judgment upon which it is based has been reversed or otherwise vacated, or it is no longer equitable that the judgment should have prospective application; or (6) any other reason justifying relief from the operation of the judgment. The motion shall be made within a reasonable time, and for reasons (1), (2), and (3) not more than one year after the judgment, order or proceeding was entered or taken. A motion under this subdivision (b) does not affect the finality of a judgment or suspend its operation. This rule does not limit the power of a court to entertain an independent action to relieve a party from a judgment, order, or proceeding, or to set aside a judgment for fraud upon the court. Writs of review, of error, of audita querela, and petitions to vacate judgment are abolished, and the procedure for obtaining any relief from a judgment shall be by motion as prescribed in these rules or by an independent action.

Reporter's Notes—1973

Rule 60 encompasses two basic situations: (a) the correction of mere clerical mistakes in the judgment or other part of the record, and (b) substantive relief from a final judgment. Included in Rule 60(b) are all possible grounds for relief from a final judgment. A motion under Rule 60(b) performs the same function as the former Massachusetts procedures of writ of review, writ of error, writ of audita querela and petition to vacate judgment. As will be noted below, Rule 60 preserves the substance of these remedies. But with the adoption of Rule 60, the relief is available through simple "motion" under Rule 60(b). In addition, Rule 60 does not prohibit the court from entertaining an independent action to relieve a party from a judgment.

A motion under Rule 60 is addressed to the trial judge's judicial discretion, and is generally not reviewable except for a clear abuse of discretion. Farmers Co-operative Elevator Association v. Strand, 382 F.2d 224 (8th Cir.1967). Further, because a Rule 60(b) motion does not affect the finality of the judgment, it does not toll the time for taking an appeal. Compare Rule 62(e).

Rule 60(a) is limited to the correction of purely clerical errors. Errors within the purview of Rule 60(a) include "misprisions, oversights, omissions, unintended acts or failures to act." First National Bank v. National Airlines, 167 F.Supp. 167 (S.D.N.Y.1958). In effect, Rule 60(a) merely seeks to ensure that the record of judgment reflects what actually took place. Substantive errors or mistakes are outside the scope of Rule 60(a). See Stowers v. United States, 191 F.Supp. 795 (N.D.Ga.1961) holding that failure to consider interest as an element of a judgment is a substantive matter beyond Rule 60(a).

Further, Rule 60(a) does not apply unless the mistake springs from some oversight or omission; it does not cover mistakes which result from deliberate action. Ferraro v. Arthur M. Rosenberg Co., Inc., 156 F.2d 212 (2d Cir.1946). The word "record" in Rule 60(a) refers not only to process, pleadings, and verdict but also to evidentiary documents, testimony taken, instructions to the jury, and all other matters pertaining to the case of which there is a written record. Rule 60(a) covers mistakes or errors of the clerk, the court, the jury, or a party. The taking of an appeal does not divest the trial court of power to correct errors. However, once the case is docketed in the appellate

court, the trial court can only grant relief after first obtaining the appellate court's leave.

Rule 60(b) affords a "party or his legal representative" a means of obtaining substantial relief from a "final judgment, order or proceeding." Interlocutory judgments thus do not fall within Rule 60(b). They remain subject to the complete power of the court rendering them to afford such relief from them as justice requires. This has long been the federal rule. John Simmons Co. v. Grier Brothers Co., 258 U.S. 82, 12 S.Ct. 196, 66 L.Ed. 475 (1922). Rule 60(b) leaves this unchanged. Rule 60(b) incorporates all possible grounds for relief from judgment; such relief must be sought by "motion as prescribed in these rules or by an independent action." The phrase "independent action" has been interpreted to mean, not that a party could still utilize the older common law and equitable remedies for relief from judgment, but rather "that courts no longer are to be hemmed in by the uncertain boundaries of these and other common law remedial tools." Klapprott v. United States, 335 U.S. 601, 69 S.Ct. 384, 93 L.Ed. 266 (1949). The court now has power "to vacate judgments whenever such action is appropriate to accomplish justice." Id. Thus, as presently interpreted, Rule 60(b) contains the substance of the older remedies while simplifying the procedure for obtaining such relief.

Rule 60(b)(1) allows relief for "mistake, inadvertence, surprise or excusable neglect." It applies to acts of the court, parties or third persons. Thus Rule 60(b)(1) has been held to permit granting of relief where the court overlooked one small item of damages concerned with the major issues of the case. Southern Fireproofing Co. v. R.F. Ball Construction Co., 334 F.2d 122 (8th Cir.1964). Similarly, the oversight of an attorney's law clerk in failing to serve a more definite statement of claim may be ground for vacating a judgment dismissing the complaint under the mistake or inadvertence clause of Rule 60(b)(1). Weller v. Socony Vacuum Oil Co. of New York, 2 F.R.D. 158 (S.D.N.Y. 1941). Where a default judgment was based on a misunderstanding as to appearance and representation by counsel, relief was granted under Rule 60(b)(1). Standard Grate Bar Co. v. Defense Plant Corp., 3 F.R.D. 371 (M.D.Pa.1944).

The "excusable neglect" clause of the section has been frequently interpreted. It seems clear that relief will be granted only if the party seeking relief demonstrates that the mistake, misunderstanding, or neglect was excusable and was not due to his own carelessness. See Petition of Pui Lan Yee, 20 F.R.D. 399 (N.D.Cal.1957); Kahle v. Amtorg Trading Corp., 13 F.R.D. 107 (D.N.J.1952). The party seeking the relief bears the burden of justifying failure to avoid the mistake or inadvertence. The reasons must be substantial. For example, the misplacing of papers in the excitement of moving an attorney's office was held not to constitute excusable neglect sufficient to relieve the party from a default judgment entered for failure to file an answer. Standard Newspaper Inc. v. King, 375 F.2d 115 (2nd Cir.1967). Likewise, ignorance of the rules of civil procedure has been held not to be "excusable neglect." Ohliger v. U.S., 308 F.2d 667 (2nd Cir.1962).

Rule 60(b)(2) affords a party relief from a final judgment, order or proceeding on the ground of newly discovered evidence.

The movant bears the burden of showing that the evidence could not have been discovered by due diligence in time to move for a new trial under Rule 59(b). See Flett v. W.A. Alexander & Co., 302 F.2d 321, 324 (7th Cir.), cert. denied, 371 U.S. 841, 83 S.Ct. 71, 9 L.Ed.2d 77 (1962):

"Rule 60(b) provides for extraordinary relief and may be invoked only upon a showing of exceptional circumstances."

It is also settled practice that the phrase "newly discovered evidence" refers to evidence in existence at the time of trial but of which the moving party was excusably ignorant. Brown v. Penn. R.R., 282 F.2d 522 (3rd Cir.1960), cert. denied 365 U.S. 818, 81 S.Ct. 690, 5 L.Ed.2d 696 (1961). The results of a new physical examination are not "newly discovered evidence" within the meaning of the Rules, Ryan v. U.S. Lines Co., 303 F.2d 430 (2nd Cir.1962).

Finally, the evidence must be of a material nature and so controlling as probably to induce a different result. Giordano v. McCartney, 385 F.2d 154 (3rd Cir.1967).

Rule 60(b)(3) allows relief from a final judgment, order or proceeding on the basis of "fraud (whether heretofore denominated intrinsic or extrinsic), misrepresentation or other misconduct of an adverse party".

The section does not limit the power of the court to:

1) entertain an independent action to enjoin enforcement of a judgment on the basis of fraud; or

2) set aside a judgment on its own initiative for fraud upon the court.

Since neither the fraud nor misrepresentation is presumed the moving party has the burden of proving by clear and convincing evidence that the alleged fraud or misrepresentation exists and that he is entitled to relief.

Prior to the adoption of Federal Rule 60(b), relief was afforded for extrinsic fraud, that is, fraud collateral to the subject matter, but denied for intrinsic fraud relating to the subject matter of the action. Because of difficulty in differentiation, Rule 60(b) explicitly abolishes the distinction, at least with respect to a timely motion under Rule 60(b)(3). These distinctions may, however continue to exist with respect to the independent action and the action of the court on its own initiative.

Rule 60(b)(3) includes any wrongful act by which a party obtains a judgment under circumstances which would make it inequitable for him to retain its benefit. Fraud covered by Rule 60(b)(3) must be of such a nature as to have prevented the moving party from presenting the merits of his case. Assmann v. Fleming, 159 F.2d 332 (8th Cir.1947). See also U.S. v. Rexach, 41 F.R.D. 180 (D.P.R.1966).

Rule 60(b)(3) refers to "misconduct of an adverse party," and thus does not literally apply to the conduct of third persons. However, it is safe to assume that if the fraud is derivatively attributable to one of the parties (as for example, fraud by his attorney), it is within Rule 60(b)(3). Even if the fraud is not attributable to one of the parties, relief may still be available through an "independent action" or the residual clause, Rule 60(b)(6).

Rule 60(b)(4) allows relief from a void judgment; it gives no scope to the court's discretion. A judgment is either void or valid. Having resolved that question, the court must act accordingly.

An erroneous judgment is not a void judgment. A judgment is void only if the court rendering it lacked jurisdiction of the subject matter or of the parties, or where it acted in a manner inconsistent with due process of law.

Although Rule 60(b)(4) is ostensibly subject to the "reasonable" time limit of Rule 60(b), at least one court has held that no time limit applies to a motion under the Rule 60(b)(4) because a void judgment can never acquire validity through laches. See Crosby v. Bradstreet Co., 312 F.2d 483 (2nd Cir.) cert. denied, 373 U.S. 911, 83 S.Ct. 1300, 10 L.Ed.2d 412 (1963) where the court vacated a judgment as void 30 years after entry. See also Marquette Corp. v. Priester, 234 F.Supp. 799 (E.D.S.C.1964) where the court expressly held that clause Rule 60(b)(4) carries no real time limit.

Finally, a party may obtain relief from a void judgment through an independent action to enjoin its enforcement.

Rule 60(b)(5) affords relief if "the judgment has been satisfied, released or discharged, or a prior judgment upon which it is based has been reversed or otherwise vacated, or it is no longer equitable that the judgment should have prospective application." The time for moving under Rule 60(b)(5) is stated to be a "reasonable time", to be determined in light of all the circumstances of the case.

It is important to note that relief under this clause is available only where the judgment is *based* on a prior judgment which has been reversed or otherwise vacated. Rule 60(b)(5) may not be used as a substitute for appeal. It does not authorize relief from a judgment on the ground that the law applied by the court in making its adjudication has been subsequently overruled or declared erroneous in another and unrelated proceeding. Berryhill v. United States, 199 F.2d 217 (6th Cir.1952).

Rule 60(b)(5) significantly affects appellate procedure where, for example, a judgment is based upon a prior judgment and the two judgments are appealed simultaneously. In this situation it would be proper for the appellate court to consolidate the two appeals and make a final adjudication based on both judgments. See Butler v. Eaton, 141 U.S. 240, 11 S.Ct. 985, 35 L.Ed. 713 (1891).

The third clause of Rule 60(b)(5) only applies to judgments having a prospective effect, as, for example, an injunction, or a declaratory judgment. It does not apply in the usual money damages situation because such a judgment lacks prospective effect. Ryan v. U.S. Lines Co., 303 F.2d 430 (2d Cir.1962). Specifically, the clause allows relief from a judgment which was valid and equitable when rendered but whose prospective application has, because of changed conditions, become inequitable. This power to grant relief from the prospective features of a judgment has always been clearly recognized in equity. See State of Pennsylvania v. Wheeling & Belmont Bridge Co., 18 How. 421 (1855).

Rule 60(b)(6) contains the residual clause, giving the court ample power to vacate a judgment whenever such action is appropriate to accomplish justice. Pierre v. Bemuth, Lembeke Co., 20 F.R.D. 116 (S.D.N.Y.1956). Rule 60(b)(6) is, however, subject to two important internal qualifications. First, the motion must be based upon some other reason than those stated in Rule 60(b)(1)–(5); second, the other reason urged must be substantial enough to warrant relief.

A motion under Rule 60(b)(5) or (6) must be made within a "reasonable time." A motion under Rule 60(b)(4) probably has, as noted above, no effective time limit.

Motions under Rule 60(b)(1)–(3) are also subject to a "reasonable time" limitation which may never exceed one year after the judgment, order or proceeding in question. Further, Rule 60(b) explicitly prohibits the enlargement of Rule 60(b) time limits.

The saving clause in Rule 60(b) which allows the court to set aside a judgment for fraud upon the court contains no time limit. Likewise, the time limitations of Rule 60(b) do not apply to the independent action preserved by the rule. Presumably, concepts of reasonableness and laches would control.

When equitable principles warrant relief a party may obtain relief even though time for a Rule 60(b) motion has expired, through an independent action on the basis of accident, fraud, mistake, or newly discovered evidence. West Virginia Oil & Gas Co. v. George E. Breece Lumber Co., 213 F.2d 702 (5th Cir.1954). See also the Federal Advisory Committee Note of 1946:

> "If the right to make a motion is lost by the expiration of the time limits fixed in these rules, the only other procedural remedy is by a new or independent action to set aside a judgment upon those principles which have heretofore been applied in such an action. Where the independent action is resorted to, the limitations of time are those of laches or statutes of limitations."

It is not clear, however, just what statute of limitations applies.

In an independent action, the same requirements outlined above with respect to motions under Rule 60(b) must be met.

There should logically be no distinction between intrinsic or extrinsic fraud, if the independent action is based on Rule 60(b)(3), discussed above. However, it has been held that the troublesome distinction between intrinsic and extrinsic fraud is still effective with respect to independent actions and that only extrinsic fraud will support such an action. Dowdy v. Hawfield, 189 F.2d 637 (D.C.Cir.) cert. denied 342 U.S. 830, 72 S.Ct. 54, 96 L.Ed. 628 (1951).

Although nothing in Rule 60(b) so specifies, the concepts of sound judicial administration suggest that the independent action should ordinarily be brought in the court (subject to statutory venue requirements) which heard the original action.

Generally, Rule 60(b) affords the same relief formerly available. The former procedures for such relief included:

(1) *By general consent* of all parties and the court. Brooks v. Twitchell, 182 Mass. 443, 447, 65 N.E. 843, 845 (1903). (2) *By motion of the prevailing party within three months,* G.L. c. 250, § 14. Marsch v. Southern New England Railroad, 235 Mass. 304, 305, 126 N.E. 519, 520 (1920). (3) *Where* the execution has been in no part satisfied, *by petition to vacate judgment, brought within one year.* G.L. c. 250, §§ 15–20. Gould v. Converse, 246 Mass. 185, 140 N.E. 785 (1923). Maker v. Bouthier, 242 Mass. 20, 136 N.E. 255 (1922). Shour v. Henin, 240 Mass. 240, 133 N.E. 561 (1922). (4) *By writ of review,* in some cases without petition, and generally but not always within one year. G.L. c. 250, § 21 et seq. Lynn Gas & Electric Co. v. Creditors National Clearing House, 235 Mass. 114, 126 N.E. 364 (1920). Carrique v. Bristol Print Works, 8 Met. 444, 446 (1844). Silverstein v. Daniel Russell Boiler Works, Inc., 268 Mass. 424, 167 N.E. 676 (1929). (5) *By writ of error, usually within six years.* Former G.L. c. 250, § 3 et seq. Lee v. Fowler, 263 Mass. 440, 443, 161 N.E. 910, 911 (1928). (6) *By bill in equity to compel the vacation of the judgment and to restrain its enforcement.* Brooks v. Twitchell, supra at 447, 65 N.E. at 845. Joyce v. Thompson, 229 Mass. 106, 118 N.E. 184 (1918). Nesson v. Gilson, 224 Mass. 212, 112 N.E. 870 (1916). Farquhar v. New England Trust Co., 261 Mass. 209, 158 N.E. 836 (1927).

In addition to the above, the remedy of audita querela also existed in Massachusetts, G.L. c. 214, § 1, but was rarely used.

Reporter's Notes—2013

The 1973 Reporter's Notes to Rule 60, second paragraph state in part: "...[B]ecause a Rule 60(b) motion does not affect the finality of the judgment, it does not toll the time for taking an appeal." In 2013, however, an amendment to Rule 4(a) of the Massachusetts Rules of Appellate Procedure provided that a Rule 60 motion, if served within ten days after entry of judgment, tolls the time period to claim an appeal.

The 2013 amendment to Mass. R. A. P. 4(a) was intended to address the confusion that sometimes arose when a post-judgment motion, denominated a motion for "reconsideration," was served within ten days after entry of judgment. Since the text of the Massachusetts Rules of Civil Procedure does not refer to motions for reconsideration, a motion for reconsideration, if served within ten days of judgment, could have been treated as a motion under Rule 59 (for new trial or to alter or amend judgment) or as a motion under Rule 60(b) (for relief from judgment). If treated as a Rule 59 motion, the motion for reconsideration would have operated to toll the time period to claim an appeal. If treated as a Rule 60(b) motion, the motion for reconsideration would *not* have served to toll the time period to claim an appeal. Mass. R. A. P. 4(a), as it existed prior to the 2013 amendment. The 2013 amendment to Mass. R. A. P. 4(a) eliminates this potential for confusion by tolling the time period to claim an appeal where a post-judgment motion for reconsideration is served within ten days after entry of judgment.

See 2013 Reporter's Notes to Mass. R. A. P. 4(a).

Rule 61. Harmless Error

No error in either the admission or the exclusion of evidence and no error or defect in any ruling or order or in anything done or omitted by the court or by any of the parties is ground for granting a new trial or for setting aside a verdict or for vacating, modifying or otherwise disturbing a judgment or order, unless refusal to take such action appears to the court inconsistent with substantial justice. The court at every stage of the proceeding must disregard any error or defect in the proceeding which does not affect the substantial rights of the parties.

Reporter's Notes—1973

Federal Rule 61 is adopted without change. It is declarative of existing Massachusetts law as expressed in former G.L. c. 231, §§ 132 and 144 and in the decided cases. See, e.g., Runshaw v. Bernstein, 347 Mass. 405, 407–408, 198 N.E.2d 293, 295–296 (1964).

Reporter's Notes—1996

With the merger of the District Court rules into the Mass.R.Civ.P., minor differences which had existed between Mass.R.Civ.P. 61 and Dist./Mun.Cts.R.Civ.P. 61 have been eliminated.

Rule 62. Stay of Proceedings to Enforce a Judgment

(a) Automatic Stay; Exceptions—Injunctions and Receiverships. Except as stated herein, no execution shall issue upon a judgment nor shall proceedings be taken for its enforcement until the time for appeal from the judgment has expired. In the District Court, in the case of a default judgment, no execution shall issue until 10 days after entry of such judgment. Unless otherwise ordered by the court, an interlocutory or final judgment in an action for an injunction or in a receivership action shall not be stayed during the period after its entry and until an appeal is taken or during the pendency of an appeal. The provisions of subdivision (c) of this rule govern the suspending, modifying, restoring, or granting of an injunction during the pendency of an appeal.

(b) Stay on Motion to Vacate Judgment. In its discretion and on such conditions for the security of the adverse party as are proper, the court may stay the execution of or any proceedings to enforce a judgment pending the disposition of a motion for relief from a judgment or order made pursuant to Rule 60.

(c) Injunction Pending Appeal. When an appeal is taken from an interlocutory or final judgment granting, dissolving, or denying an injunction, the court in its discretion may suspend, modify, restore, or grant an injunction during the pendency of the appeal upon such terms as to bond or otherwise as it considers proper for the security of the rights of the adverse party.

(d) Stay Upon Appeal. Except as otherwise provided in these rules, the taking of an appeal from a judgment shall stay execution upon the judgment during the pendency of the appeal.

(e) Power of Appellate Court Not Limited. The provisions in this rule do not limit any power of the appellate court or of a single justice thereof to stay proceedings during the pendency of an appeal or to suspend, modify, restore, or grant an injunction during the pendency of an appeal or to make any order appropriate to preserve the status quo or the effectiveness of the judgment subsequently to be entered.

(f) Stay of Judgment as to Multiple Claims or Multiple Parties. When a court has ordered a final judgment under the conditions stated in Rule 54(b), the court may stay enforcement of that judgment until the entering of a subsequent judgment or judgments and may prescribe such conditions as are necessary to secure the benefit thereof to the party in whose favor the judgment is entered.

Amended April 18, 1980, effective July 1, 1980; amended effective July 1, 1996.

Reporter's Notes—1973

Federal Rule 62, which permits execution to issue immediately after judgment, has been modified to reflect existing Massachusetts law as to the period during which execution is automatically stayed. Federal Rules 62(e) and 62(f) are inapplicable to state practice and have been omitted.

Under Rule 62(a) execution is automatically stayed "until the time for appeal from the judgment has expired." Heretofore, in actions at law in the Superior Court, entry of judgment was delayed until the expiration of the 20–day period for claiming an appeal (former G.L. c. 231, § 96). This obviates provision for stay of execution. However, Rule 58 requires judgment to be entered immediately upon the determination of the rights of the parties. Rule 62(a) will automatically stay execution for 30 days (60 days if the Commonwealth or one of its officers or agencies is a party) following entry of judgment. See Appellate Rule 4. No bond will be required during the waiting period.

Formerly, in equity matters, under G.L. c. 214, § 29, no execution could issue upon a final decree of the Superior Court or the Supreme Judicial Court until the expiration of 20 days from entry of the decree. This was the period allowed by former G.L. c. 214, § 19 for appeal from the decree.

The automatic stay provision of Rule 62(a) does not apply to a judgment ordering an injunction or a judgment in a receivership action. In those cases, the judgment is immediately enforceable, unless a stay is ordered by the court. This provision of Rule 62(a) must be read with Rule 62(c), which provides that when an appeal is taken from an interlocutory or final judgment granting, dissolving, or denying an injunction, the court in its discretion may suspend, modify, restore, or grant an injunction during the pendency of the appeal upon such terms as to bond or otherwise as it considers proper for the security of the rights of the adverse party.

Rules 62(a) and (c) do not substantially alter prior Massachusetts practice with respect to the stay of enforcement of a judgment in an action for an injunction or in a receivership action. "Proceedings under a final decree are stayed under G.L. (Ter.Ed.) c. 214, § 19, but only after an appeal has been seasonably claimed and the appeal is entered.... During the time which must necessarily elapse before appeal can be perfected, there is a statutory power in the court that entered the decree.... to grant any needed injunction and to make any other proper interlocutory order, pending appeal. G.L. (Ter.Ed.) c. 214, §§ 21, 22." Carlson v. Lawrence H. Oppenheim Co., 334 Mass. 462, 465, 136 N.E.2d 205, 207 (1956).

Rule 62(b) is an abbreviated version of Federal Rule 62(b). References to Rules 50, 52 and 59 are omitted. The language of section (a) encompasses these situations since the time for claiming an appeal, as computed under Appellate Rule 4, is suspended during the pendency of such motions. A motion for relief from judgment under Rule 60 replaces those provisions of G.L. c. 250, dealing with writs of error, vacating judgment, and writs of review. Rule 62(b) states familiar Massachusetts practice requiring a bond before an application for such relief can stay proceedings to enforce a judgment.

Rule 62(d) declares prior practice. But because Rule 58 reverses the appeal/entry-of-judgment sequence, Rule 62(d) makes clear that the taking of an appeal stays execution upon the judgment during the pendency of the appeal.

Rule 62(e) also follows prior practice.

Rule 62(f) is a corollary of Rule 54(b), which deals with multiple claims or multiple parties, and allows judgments to be entered as to one or more, but fewer than all, claims or parties upon an express determination that there exists no reason for delay. Rule 62(f) allows the court to stay enforcement of such judgments until the entering of a subsequent judgment or judgments. The stay may relate to a period beyond the time for appeal of such judgments. Rule 62(f) also permits the court to prescribe whatever conditions may be necessary to protect the party in whose favor the judgment has been entered.

Reporter's Notes—1996

The 1996 amendment to Rule 62(a) retains in a new second sentence the procedure that had been applicable in the District Court prior to the merger dealing with default judgments. The "Comments" to Rule 62, as originally adopted in the District Court in 1975, explain the rationale for the District Court approach as follows:

This sentence insures a stay of executions on default judgments for a period of time similar to the stay of executions allowed for other judgments during the period in which they may be appealed. Unless extended, the period for appeal of judgments other than default judgments is ten days....

Rule 63.   Disability of a Judge

If by reason of death, sickness, resignation, removal, or other disability, a judge before whom an action has been tried is unable to perform the duties to be performed by the court under these rules after a verdict is returned or findings of fact and conclusions of law are filed, then any other judge regularly sitting in or assigned to the court in which the action was tried may, on assignment by the Chief Justice of such court, or in case of disability of such Chief Justice, by the senior justice present and qualified to act, perform those duties; but if such other judge is satisfied that he cannot perform those duties because he did not preside at the trial or for any other reason, he may in his discretion grant a new trial.

Reporter's Notes—1973

Rule 63 closely follows Federal Rule 63 with the following additions: (1) The enumerated disabilities have been expanded specifically to include resignation and removal; (2) An assignment mechanism has been added.

Rule 63 permits any other judge regularly sitting in or assigned to the court in which the action was tried to perform the duties of the judge who by reason of some disability is unable to perform his own duties after a verdict has been returned or after he has filed findings of fact and conclusions of law. The rule provides, however, that only by assignment may the successor judge perform the duties of the disabled judge.

If the successor judge cannot perform his substituted duties satisfactorily either because he did not preside at the trial or "for any other reason", he may in his discretion grant a new trial. See St. Louis Southwestern Ry. Co. v. Henwood, 157 F.2d 337 (8th Cir.1946); Brennan v. Grisson, 198 F.2d 532 (D.C.Cir.1952).

Reporter's Notes—1996

With the merger of the District Court rules into the Mass.R.Civ.P., minor differences which had existed between Mass.R.Civ.P. 63 and Dist./Mun.Cts.R.Civ.P. 63 have been eliminated.

VIII. PROVISIONAL AND FINAL REMEDIES AND SPECIAL PROCEDURES

Rule 64. Report of Case

(a) **Courts Other Than District Court.** The court, after verdict or after a finding of facts under Rule 52, may report the case for determination by the appeals court. If the trial court is of opinion that an interlocutory finding or order made by it so affects the merits of the controversy that the matter ought to be determined by the appeals court before any further proceedings in the trial court, it may report such matter, and may stay all further proceedings except such as are necessary to preserve the rights of the parties. The court, upon request of the parties, in any case where the parties agree in writing as to all the material facts, may report the case to the appeals court for determination without making any decision thereon. In an action commenced before a single justice of the supreme judicial court, the court may report the case in the circumstances above described to either the appeals court or the full supreme judicial court; provided further that a single justice of the supreme judicial court may at any time reserve any question of law for consideration by the full court, and shall report so much of the case as is necessary for understanding the question reserved.

(b) **District Court.** Report of a case or a ruling by the court to the Appellate Division shall be governed by District/Municipal Courts Rules for Appellate Division Appeal 5.

Amended effective July 1, 1996.

Reporter's Notes—1973

Rule 64 preserves the former report procedure which gives a trial judge discretionary power to obtain appellate court determination of controlling questions of law without the necessity of a prior judgment in the trial court. Amended Mass.G.L. c. 231, §§ 111, 112 provide the statutory foundation for this procedure. Cases must be reported to the appeals court, except that a case pending before a single justice may be reported to either appellate court. This accords with former Mass.G.L. c. 214, §§ 31, 31A.

An important aspect of the rule is its provision for the report of an interlocutory order. This provision is drawn from former Mass.G.L. c. 214, §§ 30, 30A; Mass.G.L. c. 231, § 111. Since there is no procedure for appeal of an interlocutory order, compare the federal practice, 28 U.S.C. § 1292(b), a judge's authority to report a decisive order is the only effective way to obtain appellate review at an early stage of litigation, regulating and perhaps even obviating further proceedings in the trial court.

Rule 64 must be read in conjunction with Appellate Rule 5 which provides that a report is the equivalent of a notice of appeal for purposes of the Massachusetts Rules of Appellate Procedure.

Reporter's Notes—1996

The 1996 amendments to Rule 64 create new sections (a) and (b). Rule 64(a) contains the pre-existing language of Rule 64 of the Mass.R.Civ.P., while Rule 64(b) contains the language of Rule 64 of the now-repealed Dist./Mun.Cts.R.Civ.P. as it existed effective July 1, 1994. Rule 64(b), applicable to the District Court and Boston Municipal Court, merely refers to Rule 5 of the District/Municipal Courts Rules for Appellate Division Appeal, which sets forth the procedures for a report to the Appellate Division.

Prior to July 1, 1994, Rule 64 of the Dist./Mun.Cts.R.Civ.P. dealt with "Preservation of Issues and Appeal to the Appellate Division." Effective July 1, 1994, these matters can be found in the District/Municipal Courts Rules for Appellate Division Appeal. It should be noted, however, that the pre-July 1994 version of Dist./Mun.Cts.R.Civ.P. 64 may still have application to appeals of matters occurring before July 1, 1994. See Rule 1A of the District/Municipal Courts Rules for Appellate Division Appeal.

Rule 64A. Requests for Rulings of Law in District Court [Repealed]

Repealed November 28, 2007, effective March 1, 2008.

Reporter's Notes—2008

Rule 64A, entitled Requests for Rulings of Law in District Court, was repealed in 2008. For procedure to obtain findings of fact and rulings of law in jury-waived cases in the District Court and Boston Municipal Court, see Rule 52(c), as amended in 2008.

Rule 65. Injunctions

(a) **Temporary Restraining Order; Notice; Hearing; Duration.** A temporary restraining order may be granted without written or oral notice to the adverse party or his attorney only if it clearly appears from specific facts shown by affidavit or by the verified complaint that immediate and irreparable injury, loss, or damage will result to the applicant before the adverse party or his attorney can be heard in opposition. Every temporary restraining order granted without notice shall be indorsed with the date and hour of issuance; shall be filed forthwith in the clerk's office and entered of record; and shall expire by its terms within such time after entry, not to exceed 10 days, as the court fixes, unless within the time so fixed the order, for good cause shown, is extended for a like period or unless the party against whom the order is directed consents that it may be extended for a longer period. In case a temporary restraining order is granted without notice, the application for a preliminary injunction shall be set down for hearing at the earliest possible time, and in any event within 10 days, and takes precedence of all matters except older matters of the same character; and when the matter comes on for hearing the party who obtained the temporary restraining order shall proceed with the application for a preliminary injunction and, if he does not do so, the court shall dissolve the temporary restraining order. On 2 days' notice to the party who obtained the temporary restraining order without notice or on such shorter notice to that party as the court may prescribe, the adverse party may appear and move its dissolution or modification and in that event the court shall proceed to hear and determine such motion as expeditiously as the ends of justice require.

(b) **Preliminary Injunction.**

(1) *Notice.* No preliminary injunction shall be issued without notice to the adverse party.

(2) *Consolidation of Hearing With Trial on Merits.* Before or after the commencement of the hearing of an application for a preliminary injunction, the court may order the trial of the action on the merits to be advanced and consolidated with the hearing of the application. This subdivision (b)(2) shall be so construed and applied as to save to the parties any rights they may have to trial by jury.

(c) Security. Unless the court, for good cause shown, shall otherwise order, no restraining order or preliminary injunction shall issue except upon the giving of security by the applicant, in such sum as the court deems proper, for the payment of such costs and damages as may be incurred or suffered by any party who is found to have been wrongfully enjoined or restrained. No such security shall be required of the United States or of the Commonwealth or of a political subdivision of the Commonwealth or of any officer or agency of any of them.

The provisions of Rule 65.1 apply to a surety upon a bond or undertaking under this rule.

(d) Form and Scope of Injunction or Restraining Order. Unless the court, for good cause shown, otherwise orders, an injunction or restraining order shall be specific in terms; shall describe in reasonable detail, and not by reference to the complaint or other document, the act or acts sought to be restrained; and is binding only upon the parties to the action, their officers, agents, servants, employees, and attorneys, and upon those persons in active concert or participation with them who receive actual notice of the order by personal service or otherwise.

(e) Labor Disputes. These rules are subject to any statutory provisions relating to restraining orders and injunctions in actions involving or growing out of labor disputes.

Reporter's Notes—1973

Rule 65 is taken with little change from Federal Rule 65. The order of the first two sections has been reversed, to conform with the usual sequence of litigation. The requirement of Rule 65(a) of an affidavit or verified complaint showing immediate and irreparable harm before a court will issue a temporary restraining order does not alter former Massachusetts law. Rule 65(a) contains a provision for the extension of a temporary restraining order, which is familiar to Massachusetts practice. See Stathopoulos v. Reeksting, 252 Mass. 542, 544, 147 N.E. 853, 854 (1925).

Rule 65(a), like former Massachusetts practice, gives a motion for a preliminary injunction precedence over all matters and allows an adverse party an opportunity to move to dissolve or modify a temporary restraining order.

Rule 65(b)(1) provides that no court shall issue an injunction unless proper notice is given to the adverse party; former Massachusetts practice also required notice, although the usual procedure had been an order to show cause. Under federal practice, although an order to show cause may itself constitute sufficient notice, a motion is the preferable procedure. Walling v. Moore Milling Co., 62 F.Supp. 378, 382 (W.D.Va.1945).

Rule 65(b)(2) provides for the consolidation of a hearing on an application for a preliminary injunction with a trial on the merits. This was not part of former Massachusetts practice. Under Rule 65(b)(2), the consolidation may be ordered before or after the commencement of the hearing of an application for a preliminary injunction. See Brotherhood of Railroad Carmen v. Chicago and N.W.Ry. Co., 354 F.2d 786, 787 (8th Cir.1965).

Former Massachusetts law contained no requirement that the plaintiff file a bond as a condition precedent to the issuance of either a temporary restraining order or preliminary injunction. See American Circular Loom v. Wilson, 198 Mass. 182, 211, 84 N.E. 133, 139 (1908); Weinberg v. Goldstein, 241 Mass. 259, 261, 135 N.E. 126, 127 (1922). The requirement of a bond was left to the court's discretion. Under Rule 65(c), a court also need not require a bond. Under the Federal Rules, courts have at times not required a bond. Continental Oil Co. v. Frontier Refining Co., 338 F.2d 780, 782–783 (10th Cir.1964); Ferguson v. Tabah, 288 F.2d 665, 675 (2d Cir.1961).

The language of Rule 65(d), emphasizing precision in the framing of injunctions and restraining orders, expresses former Massachusetts practice (see e.g., forms of decree set out in Reed, Equity §§ 981–1014 (1952)), although the Reporters have found no case saying so explicitly. "Specificity has long been a hallmark of the well-drafted injunctive decree. An injunction circumscribes the defendant's conduct with the threat of punishments similar to those of the criminal law, and the defendant is entitled to fair notice [of the bounds] · · · Some defendants may take advantage of a vague decree intentionally." *Developments in the Law–Injunctions,* 78 Harv.L.Rev. 994, 1065 (1965).

Rule 65(e), which is new, is designed to show unmistakably that such anti-injunction statutes as G.L. c. 214, § 9A are not affected by the rule.

Reporter's Notes—1996

With the merger of the District Court Rules into the Mass.R.Civ.P., minor differences which had existed between Mass.R.Civ.P. 65 and Dist./Mun.Cts.R.Civ.P. 65 have been eliminated. These differences were found in Rule 65(b)(2) (reference to jury trial) and Rule 65(e) (labor disputes). The merger of the two sets of rules, of course, does not serve to enlarge District Court jurisdiction. See Rule 82.

Rule 65.1   Security: Proceedings Against Security Provider

Whenever these rules require or permit the giving of security by a party, and security is given with one or more security providers, each provider submits to the jurisdiction of the court and irrevocably appoints the clerk of the court as agent upon whom any papers affecting the liability on the security may be served. The security provider's liability may be enforced on motion without the necessity of an independent action. The motion and such notice of the motion as the court prescribes may be served on the clerk of the court, who shall forthwith send copies to each security provider whose address is known.

Amended October 1, 2019, effective November 1, 2019.

Reporter's Notes—1973

Rule 65.1 effects a substantial change in former Massachusetts practice. Formerly, a party who took a bond as security had to institute a separate action in contract to enforce the obligation of the sureties to the bond. Castaline v. Swardlick, 264 Mass. 481, 482, 163 N.E. 62 (1928). Rule 65.1, providing for enforcement on motion makes unnecessary the costly and lengthy process of a second civil suit. The rule provides for notice to those whose obligations are sought to be enforced. G.L. c. 214, § 9A clauses 2 and 3, requires that an undertaking be filed with the court when a preliminary injunction is issued in a labor dispute. A decree may be rendered upon such undertaking in the suit for the injunction; no second suit is necessary. The statute further states that the complainant and surety submit themselves to the jurisdiction of the court for the purpose of such undertaking. Both provisions accord with Rule 65.1.

That portion of Rule 65.1 providing that "each surety submits himself to the jurisdiction of the court and irrevocably appoints the clerk of the court as his agent upon whom papers affecting his liability on the bond or undertaking may be served" does not substantially change former law. Apart from specific statutory provisions, one who undertakes to be a surety on a bond is subject to process (to enforce the obligation) by virtue of his being an inhabitant of the Commonwealth or by virtue of his minimal contact with the state under Massachusetts G.L. c. 223A, § 3(f), the "long-arm" statute.

G.L. c. 175, § 151 provides that foreign fidelity and corporate insurance companies must file a power of attorney appointing the commissioner of insurance lawful attorney upon whom legal process may be served. This statute will not affect Rule 65.1; the rule merely permits the party proceeding against the surety to "serve" the surety by filing the necessary papers with the clerk.

The Reporters take the position that the notice which must be mailed by the clerk of court to the surety under Rule 65.1 need not comply with the requirements of seal and teste prescribed by Part II, c. 6, art. 5 of the Massachusetts Constitution. The enforcement of liability against the surety is not a new action. While notice may be the means for bringing a defendant into court for all purposes connected with an already commenced action, an order of notice is not a writ within the meaning of Part II, c. 6, art. 5 of the Massachusetts Constitution. Taplin v. Atwater, 297 Mass. 302, 306, 8 N.E.2d 786, 788 (1937).

Reporter's Notes—2019

Prior to amendment in 2019, the title of Rule 65.1 was "Security: Proceedings Against Sureties." The 2019 amendments changed the title and the text of the rule to provide for enforcement proceedings against any security provider, rather than against only a surety.

Rule 62(b) allows a court to stay proceedings to enforce a judgment in connection with a Rule 60 motion "on such conditions for the security of the adverse party as are proper ..." Rule 62(c) allows a court to suspend or modify an injunction during the pendency of an appeal "upon such terms as to bond or otherwise as it considers proper." Under these rules, a surety bond, cash, or other property may be used, yet the enforcement proceeding under Rule 65.1 had been limited to sureties. The amendment to Rule 65.1 allows enforcement proceedings to be brought against any security provider, whether a surety bond has been posted or not.

The last sentence of the rule was also amended to provide that the clerk shall "send" a copy of the motion for enforcement to the security provider rather than "mail" it. For example, this would allow notice to be sent by electronic means or by private delivery service.

These changes were modeled after similar changes to Rule 65.1 of the Federal Rules of Civil Procedure, effective in 2018.

Rule 65.2 Redelivery of Goods or Chattels

In an action for the redelivery of goods or chattels brought pursuant to General Laws c. 214, § 3, an order that a party redeliver goods or chattels may be made ex parte, pursuant to the provisions of Rule 65(a) and existing law governing the issuing of restraining orders, or with notice and hearing, pursuant to Rule 65(b) and existing law governing the issuing of preliminary injunctions. No restraining order or preliminary injunction for the redelivery of goods or chattels shall issue except upon the applicant's giving security, in such sum as the court deems proper, for the payment of such costs and damages as may be incurred or suffered by any party who is found to have been wrongfully enjoined or restrained.

Adopted December 22, 1978, effective January 15, 1979.

Reporter's Notes—1979

Two Massachusetts statutes govern actions to recover goods or chattels: G.L. c. 247 (Replevin) permits plaintiff to obtain the disputed property prior to trial, without hearing, and without justification such as imminent destruction, transfer, or concealment of the property. This statute is probably unconstitutional (see Fuentes v. Shevin, 407 U.S. 67, 92 S.Ct. 1983, 32 L.Ed.2d 556 (1972)). The other statute, G.L. c. 214, § 3 gives the Supreme Judicial Court and Superior Court equitable jurisdiction to order redelivery of goods or chattels taken or detained from the owner, without requiring the owner first to establish inadequacy of the legal remedy. "The supreme judicial and superior courts shall have original and concurrent jurisdiction of the following

cases: (1) Actions to compel the redelivery of goods or chattels taken or detained from the owner . . ." G.L. c. 214, § 3.

As G.L. c. 214, § 3 provides a legal vehicle for recovery of property, its marriage with Rule 65 (Injunctions) provides a simple and flexible procedure, affording the same constitutional safeguards as a detailed statute. Although "injunction" and "restraining order", as used in Rule 65, literally imply restraint or inaction, the rule clearly also covers any order requiring affirmative conduct, the so-called "mandatory injunction", International Longshoremen's Ass'n, Local No. 1291 v. Philadelphia Marine Trade Ass'n, 389 U.S. 64, 75–76, 88 S.Ct. 201, 207–208, 19 L.Ed.2d 236 (1967).

Rule 65(a) allows the ex parte recovery of property only "if it clearly appears from specific facts shown by affidavit or by the verified complaint that immediate and irreparable injury, loss or damage will result to the applicant before the adverse party or his attorney can be heard in opposition." Even then, the time provisions of Rule 65(a) provide a wronged defendant the opportunity to obtain an immediate hearing. Likewise, plaintiff seeking a preliminary injunction must establish (1) an irremediable deprivation of his rights during pendency of the action; and (2) the likelihood that he will ultimately succeed on the merits. Under Rule 65.2, these provisions control the pre-trial recovery of property.

Unlike Rule 65(c), Rule 65.2 requires security in all cases, although it leaves the amount to the determination of the court. Because the pre-trial recovery of property is so constitutionally sensitive, security should be mandatory. On the other hand, the rule does not impose an arbitrary dollar requirement (as, for example, twice the value of the property). Sometimes defendant has wrongfully taken or withheld plaintiff's property as security for a disputed debt less than the value of the property. Certainly, a bond in the amount of the debt is adequate.

Reporter's Notes—1996

With the merger of the District Court Rules into the Mass.R.Civ.P., Rule 65.2 has now been made applicable to the District Court. However, the applicability of this rule to the District Court does not serve to grant jurisdiction to the District Court over actions to compel redelivery of goods pursuant to G.L. c. 214, § 3. This statute grants jurisdiction only to the Supreme Judicial Court and the Superior Court. See Rule 82.

Rule 65.3 Proceedings for Civil Contempt

(a) Applicability. Enforcement of compliance with the following court orders shall be sought by means of a separate civil proceeding denominated as a "civil contempt proceeding":

(1) temporary restraining orders, preliminary or permanent injunctions pursuant to Rule 65, or stipulations in lieu thereof;

(2) orders issued pursuant to Rule 70; and

(3) any other orders or judgments entered pursuant to these rules, for the violation of which civil contempt is an appropriate remedy, except for matters cognizable under Rules 26(c), 36(a) and 37.

(b) Commencement. A civil contempt proceeding shall be commenced by the filing of a complaint for contempt with the clerk of the court whose injunction, stipulation, order or judgment is claimed to have been violated.

No entry fee shall be required in connection with the filing of the complaint for civil contempt. The proceeding shall be considered part of the civil action out of which the contempt arose.

(c) Contents of the Complaint. The complaint for civil contempt shall:

(1) contain a complete verbatim statement of the injunction, stipulation, order or judgment involved, or a copy thereof if available, and the name of the issuing judge where appropriate;

(2) identify the court that issued the injunction, order or judgment, or in which the stipulation was filed:

(3) contain the case caption and the docket number of the case in which the injunction, order or judgment was issued, or the stipulation was filed;

(4) include a short, concise statement of the facts on which the asserted contempt is based;

(5) include a prayer for the issuance of a summons as specified in subsection (d) below;

(6) be verified or supported by affidavits complying with the provisions of Rule 11(e); and

(7) otherwise comply with the provisions of Rules 8, 9, 10 and 11.

(d) Summons. The summons shall issue only on a judge's order and shall direct the parties to appear before the court not later than ten days thereafter for the purpose or purposes specifically stated therein of: scheduling a trial, considering whether the filing of an answer is necessary, holding a hearing on the merits of the complaint, or considering such other matters or performing such other acts as the court may deem appropriate.

(e) Service of the Summons and Complaint. A copy of the summons, the complaint for contempt, and any accompanying affidavits shall be served, in hand, upon the defendant in accordance with the provisions of Rule 4, unless the court orders some other method of service or notice.

(f) Answer. Unless the court otherwise orders, the defendant shall serve an answer within twenty days after service of the summons and complaint for contempt. The answer shall comply with the provisions of Rules 8, 9, 10 and 11.

(g) Discovery. A party, by motion, may seek an order permitting discovery. Such motion shall set forth the particular need for discovery, the type of discovery sought and the time required for obtaining the discovery. A motion for discovery in a civil contempt proceeding may be heard on three days' notice.

(h) Trial. The complaint for contempt shall be tried upon the facts in accordance with Rule 52. The court shall find the facts specially and state separately its conclusions of law thereon, and judgment shall be entered pursuant to Rule 58.

Adopted May 25, 1982, effective July 1, 1982.

Reporter's Notes—1982

Prior to the adoption of this rule, no provisions existed in the Rules of Civil Procedure to specifically govern civil contempt proceedings. See Nolan, Equitable Remedies, 31 Massachusetts Practice, § 193. There is no analogous federal rule.

Under Rule 65.3(a) the rule is made applicable to all proceedings to enforce compliance with temporary, preliminary or permanent injunctions; stipulations in lieu thereof; Rule 70 orders; and other similar orders "for the violation of which civil contempt is an appropriate remedy." It is not applicable to discovery sanctions, under Rules 26(b), 36(a) and 37, nor to small claims cases (Rule 81(a)(7)). This rule excludes discovery sanctions because when a discovery order is violat-

ed, the parties are usually already before the court and there are a wide range of available sanctions, other than contempt. A distinct civil contempt proceeding, with its own summons, pleadings, and potential evidentiary hearing, seems unnecessary in the context of most disputes over the violations of a discovery order.

Section (b) tells how to commence a civil contempt proceeding, and clarifies that such proceeding shall have the same docket number and be otherwise treated as part of "the civil action out of which the contempt arose." Consequently, no entry fee is required.

Rule 65.3(c)(1)–(7) prescribes what must be included in a civil contempt complaint, and, because of the serious nature of an allegation of civil contempt, requires verification or accompanying appropriate affidavits.

Rule 65.3(d) endows the summons with unusual significance. Because of the expedited and grave nature of a civil contempt proceeding, the summons (i) "issues only on a judge's order," (ii) must "direct the parties to appear before the court not later than ten days" after issuance of the order; and (iii) must specifically state what will happen when the parties appear. The rule places the responsibility on the party filing a complaint for contempt to obtain the summons.

Rule 65.3(d) is constructed to meet two different goals. The first is to permit flexibility with respect to what occurs when the parties first appear in answer to the summons. Depending on the nature of the alleged contempt, a case may or may not benefit from the filing of an answer, expedited discovery, or an immediate hearing. Consequently, the rule gives wide discretion to the judge to determine what should happen when the parties appear: a "hearing on the merits," if it makes sense to have that quickly; scheduling a trial; considering dispensing with an answer; expediting discovery, if discovery is necessary; requiring initial compliance by the defendant pending a hearing; considering other appropriate matters; or requiring other appropriate acts to be performed.

The second goal is to eliminate, to the extent reasonably possible, surprising the parties. The parties should know, for example, whether a trial will take place when they appear in response to the summons. The word "specifically" in "for the purpose or purposes specifically stated therein" is to emphasize the importance of informing the parties what to expect. To merely place in each summons a laundry list of everything which might happen or "whatever the court may deem appropriate" will not comply with either the language or spirit of this rule.

Rule 65.3(e) provides that service of the summons and complaint and "any accompanying affidavits" will normally be "in hand."

Rule 65.3(f) provides for an answer within 20 days, unless "the court otherwise orders" in the summons or when the parties appear. The judge may, for instance, decide an answer is unnecessary, or that it should be served in fewer than 20 days.

Under Rule 65.3(g) a party must seek an "order permitting discovery," unlike the normal discovery provisions which permit parties, on their own, to initiate discovery. The rule requires the parties seeking discovery to particularize the need for, type, and timing of the discovery sought. The purpose is to constrict the more wide-open discovery which can occur in other proceedings. It is important to note that in an unusual case, the court can order discovery in the initial summons under Rule 65.3(d) or at the hearing which occurs when the parties respond to the summons.

Rule 65.3(h) makes Rules 52 (Findings by the Court) and 58 (Entry of Judgment) applicable to civil contempt proceedings.

Reporter's Notes—1996

With the merger of the District Court Rules into the Mass.R.Civ.P., Rule 65.3 is now applicable in the District Court. It had previously been held by the Supreme Judicial Court that Rule 65.3 was not applicable in the District Court, although the provisions thereof might have been applied by analogy in District Court civil contempt proceedings. Mahoney v. Commonwealth, 415 Mass. 278, 612 N.E.2d 1175 (1993).

Rule 66. Receivers

(a) An action wherein a receiver has been appointed shall not be dismissed except by order of the court. The practice in the administration of estates by receivers or by other similar officers appointed by the court shall be in accordance with the practice heretofore followed in the courts of this Commonwealth and with the laws thereof. In all other respects the action in which the appointment of a receiver is sought or which is brought by or against a receiver is governed by these rules.

(b) Every receiver, within thirty days after his appointment, shall file a detailed inventory of the property of which he has possession or the right to possession, with the estimated values thereof, together with a list of the encumbrances thereon; and also a list of the creditors of the receivership and of the party whose property is in the hands of the receiver, so far as known to him.

(c) Every receiver shall file, not later than the fifteenth day of February of each year, a detailed account under oath of his receivership to and including the last day of the preceding year, substantially in the form required for an account by a conservator in the probate courts, together with a report of the condition of the receivership. He shall also file such further accounts and reports as the court may order.

(d) When an attorney at law has been appointed a receiver, no attorney shall be employed by the receiver or receivers except upon order of court, which shall be made only upon the petition of a receiver, stating the name of the attorney whom he desires to employ and showing the necessity of such employment.

(e) No order discharging a receiver from further responsibility will be entered until he has settled his final account.

(f) The court, in its discretion, may relieve any receiver from any requirement imposed by sections (b)–(e) of this rule.

Amended June 24, 2009, effective July 1, 2009.

Reporter's Notes—1973

Rule 66 presents no conflict with prior Massachusetts practice; Rule 66(a) indeed explicitly incorporates existing law. See G.L. c. 200, 205, and 206. Succeeding subsections of the rule incorporate Super.Ct. Rule 91 in its entirety. Rule 66(e) dealing with discharge of a receiver accords with S.J.C. Rule 2:47. Rule 66(f) imparts flexibility to permit abrogation of requirements in appropriate cases, as for example a rent receivership.

Reporter's Notes—1996

With the merger of the District Court Rules into the Mass.R.Civ.P., minor differences which had existed between Mass.R.Civ.P. 66 and Dist./Mun.Cts.R.Civ.P. 66 have been eliminated.

Reporter's Notes—2009

The 2009 amendments reflect changes resulting from the adoption of the Massachusetts Uniform Probate Code.

Rule 67. Deposit in Court

In an action in which any part of the relief sought is a judgment for a sum of money or the disposition of a sum of money or the disposition of any other thing capable of delivery, a party, upon notice to every other party, and by leave of court, may deposit with the court all or any part of such sum or thing. Money paid into court under this rule shall be deposited and withdrawn in accordance with the provisions of any applicable statute or rule.

Reporter's Notes—1973

While no prior statute or rule of court in Massachusetts authorized deposits in court, some prior statutes and rules of court did deal with the mechanics of comparable procedures. Among these is the familiar "payment into court under the common rule." See Super.Ct. Rule 42. Another is G.L. c. 231, § 40, which authorizes the payment of money into court in an interpleader action. See also G.L. c. 35, § 23; S.J.C. Rule 2:29; Super.Ct. Rule 41. None of these statutes or rules however, has provided for the deposit of a non-monetary object into court as Rule 67 does.

Rule 68. Offer of Judgment

At any time more than 10 days before the trial begins, a party defending against a claim may serve upon the adverse party an offer to allow judgment to be taken against him for the money or property or to the effect specified in his offer, with costs then accrued. If within 10 days after the service of the offer the adverse party serves written notice that the offer is accepted, either party may then file the offer and notice of acceptance together with proof of service thereof and thereupon the clerk shall enter judgment. An offer not accepted shall be deemed withdrawn and evidence thereof is not admissible except in a proceeding to determine costs. If the judgment exclusive of interest from the date of offer finally obtained by the offeree is not more favorable than the offer, the offeree must pay the costs incurred after the making of the offer. The fact that an offer is made but not accepted does not preclude a subsequent offer. When the liability of one party to another has been determined by verdict or order or judgment, but the amount or extent of the liability remains to be determined by further proceedings, the party adjudged liable may make an offer of judgment, which shall have the same effect as an offer made before trial if it is served within a reasonable time not less than 10 days prior to the commencement of hearings to determine the amount or extent of liability.

Reporter's Notes—1973

With one slight exception Rule 68 is the same as Federal Rule 68. The addition incorporates the provision of G.L. c. 231, § 75 excluding interest from a judgment in determining whether it is more favorable than the offer. It does not, however, prevent the plaintiff's obtaining interest on the judgment from the date of the offer if the judgment obtained is not more favorable than the offer. Merely because interest is excluded in determining whether the judgment is more favorable than the offer, it does not logically follow that the plaintiff should be deprived of interest when the judgment is not more favorable than the offer. G.L. c. 231, § 75 did not deprive the plaintiff of interest from the date of the offer. Because the defendant has the use of the money even from the date of the offer there is no reason why he should not pay interest to the plaintiff for the use of that money; to provide otherwise, would be tantamount to assessing a penalty against the plaintiff for not accepting an offer.

Rule 68 slightly changes preexisting Massachusetts practice. The offer of judgment is no longer limited to those suits "wherein damages only are sought to be recovered." G.L. c. 231, § 74. The requirement that the offer be made at least 10 days before the trial begins is new to Massachusetts practice, which did not specify a time for the offer; the time for acceptance of an offer was limited to 10 days. G.L. c. 231, § 74 permitted such further time as the court allowed.

Rule 68 clearly identifies the party entitled to make an offer of judgment. The federal rule permits any "party defending against a claim" to make such offer. This phrase has been interpreted as covering by its express terms either an original defendant or a plaintiff defending against a counterclaim. The term defending party "does not confine itself to a defendant in the technical sense." Moore, Federal Practice, § 68.02, p. 2303. Rules 8(a) and 13(a) make clear that the word "claim" would refer also to a counterclaim. The Massachusetts statute (G.L. c. 231, § 74), permitted any "defendant in an action . . ." to make an offer of judgment. No reported case has defined the term "defendant". Presumably the word as used in G.L. c. 231, § 74 included plaintiffs defending against a counterclaim. Rule 68 clarifies this matter.

Rule 68 requires the defending party to serve upon the adverse party his offer of judgment. The court enters the picture only after acceptance. At that time either party may file "the offer and notice of acceptance together with proof of service thereof and thereupon the clerk shall enter judgment."

Rule 68 specifies that the mere fact of an offer's nonacceptance does not preclude a subsequent offer. Massachusetts law had previously been silent on this point.

Rule 69.   Execution

Process to enforce a judgment for the payment of money shall be a writ of execution, unless the court directs otherwise. The procedure on execution, in proceedings on and in aid of execution shall be in accordance with applicable statutes. In aid of the judgment or execution, the judgment creditor or his successor in interest when that interest appears of record, may obtain discovery from any person, including the judgment debtor, in the manner provided in these rules.

Reporter's Notes—1973

Rule 69 is a shortened version of Federal Rule 69. It provides that the procedure on execution shall accord with existing statutes. See G.L. c. 235 and G.L. c. 236. In aid of judgment or execution, depositions may be taken in accordance with these rules.

Rule 70.   Judgment for Specific Acts: Vesting Title

If a judgment directs a party to execute a conveyance of land or to deliver deeds or other documents or to perform any other specific act and the party fails to comply within the time specified, the court may direct the act to be done at the cost of the disobedient party by some other person appointed by the court and the act when so done has like effect as if done by the party. On application of the party entitled to performance, the clerk shall issue a writ of attachment against the property of the disobedient party to compel obedience to the judgment. The court may also in proper cases adjudge the party in contempt. If real or personal property is within the Commonwealth, the court in lieu of directing a conveyance thereof may enter a judgment divesting the title of any party and vesting it in others and such judgment has the effect of a conveyance executed in due form of law. When any order or judgment is for the delivery of possession, the party in whose favor it is entered is entitled to a writ of execution upon application to the clerk.

Reporter's Notes—1973

Rule 70, with a few minor changes, is the same as Federal Rule 70. Former Massachusetts practice with respect to enforcement of judgments for specific acts was generally less permissive, making no provision for alternative performance by a person appointed by the court.

G.L. c. 183, §§ 43, 44 operates identically to that portion of Rule 70 concerning the vesting of title to real property "in the party entitled thereto by the decree". Rule 70 however applies also to personal property.

Rule 70 allows the application of what are essentially legal remedies to the enforcement of equitable decrees. The effect is to ensure swift performance of obligations established by the court.

Reporter's Notes—1996

With the merger of the District Court Rules into the Mass.R.Civ.P., minor differences which had existed between Mass.R.Civ.P. 70 and Dist./Mun.Cts.R.Civ.P. 70 have been eliminated. These differences related to judgments for specified types of equitable relief not within District Court jurisdiction. The elimination of these differences does not broaden District Court jurisdiction. See Rule 82.

Rule 71.   Process in Behalf of and Against Persons Not Parties

When an order is made in favor of a person who is not a party to the action, he may enforce obedience to the order by the same process as if he were a party; and, when obedience to an order may be lawfully enforced against a person who is not a party, he is liable to the same process for enforcing obedience to the order as if he were a party.

Reporter's Notes—1973

Rule 71 is the same as Federal Rule 71. It permits a person, not a party to the action, in whose favor an order has been made, to enforce obedience to the order by the same process as if he were a party. See Woods v. O'Brien, 78 F.Supp. 221 (D.Mass.1948). An example of the operation of this rule would be a foreclosure in which the court orders the property delivered to the purchaser. The purchaser is entitled to any process to enforce the order to which a party might be entitled. See 12 Wright & Miller, Federal Practice & Procedure 80 (1973). Rule 71 requires that the order sought to be enforced be made in favor of that person. It is not enough that the person seeking to enforce obedience be indirectly benefited by the decree. See United States v. American Society of Composers, Authors and Publishers, 341 F.2d 1003, 1007–1008 (2d Cir.1965), cert. denied, 382 U.S. 877, 86 S.Ct. 160, 15 L.Ed.2d 119 (1965). The court there held that a radio broadcaster not a party to the government's antitrust action against a music licensor lacked standing to move to punish the licensor for contempt for alleged failure to comply with the decree.

The final clause of Rule 71 does not purport to affect the general rule that ordinarily a judgment may be enforced only against a party. It merely provides that in those rare cases where such a right exists, the person in question is liable to the same process for enforcing obedience to the order as if he were a party. Suppose, for example, the person knowingly aids or abets the disobeying of the injunction. See Robert Findlay Mfg. Co. v. Hygrade Lighting Fixture Corp., 288 Fed. 80 (D.C.N.Y.1923). The latter portion of Rule 71 will also apply to those situations, as under the discovery rules, where a person not a party may be held liable for expenses and attorney's fees. An order against such a person may be enforced by the same methods as if the person were a party. See 12 Wright & Miller, Federal Practice & Procedure 82 (1973).

Rule 72.   Probate Accounts [Repealed]

Repealed December 14, 2011, effective January 2, 2012.

Reporter's Notes—2012
Rule 72 titled Probate Accounts was repealed in 2012. For the procedure regarding the allowance of accounts filed in the Probate and Family Court, see Rule 72 of the Supplemental Rules of the Probate and Family Court as adopted in 2012.

Rules 73 to 76.   [Reserved]

IX.   COURTS AND CLERKS

Rule 77.   Courts and Clerks

(a) **Courts Always Open.** Unless otherwise provided by law, the courts shall be deemed always open for the purpose of filing any pleading or other proper paper, of issuing and returning process, and of making and directing all interlocutory motions, orders, and rules.

(b) **Clerk's Office and Orders by Clerk.** The clerk's office with a clerk or assistant clerk in attendance shall be open during business hours on all days except Saturdays, Sundays, and legal holidays. All motions and applications in the clerk's office for issuing mesne process, for issuing final process to enforce and execute judgments, for entering defaults or judgments by default, and for other proceedings which do not require allowance or order of the court are grantable of course by the clerk; but his action may be suspended or altered or rescinded by the court upon cause shown.

(c) **Filing Date of All Papers Received by Clerk.** The clerk shall date-stamp all papers whatsoever received by him, whether by hand or by mail. Any paper so received, whether stamped or not, shall be deemed to have been filed as of the date of receipt. If at any subsequent time, any party disputes the fact of such filing, the court shall determine the question, taking whatever evidence it deems appropriate. Proof of mailing shall constitute prima facie proof of receipt.

(d) **Notice of Entry of Orders or Judgments.** Unless an order or judgment is entered in open court in the presence of the parties or their counsel, the clerk shall immediately upon the entry of an order or judgment serve upon each party who is not in default for failure to appear a notice of the entry by at least one of the following means, at the option of the clerk:

(1) *By Mail.* By mail in the manner provided for in Rule 5 and shall make a note in the docket of the mailing. Such mailing is sufficient notice for all purposes for which notice of the entry of an order or judgment is required by these rules; but any party may in addition serve a notice of such entry in the manner provided in Rule 5 for the service of papers.

(2) *By Electronic Means.* By electronic means in the manner selected by the clerk, which may include: (a) e-mail to an attorney's e-mail address on file with the Massachusetts Board of Bar Overseers; (b) e-mail to an e-mail address provided by an attorney or party pursuant to a court rule or order; or (c) electronic transmission to an address and in a form provided by the attorney or party and specifically accepted by the clerk for such purpose. Transmission of such electronic notice is sufficient notice for all purposes for which notice of the entry of an order or judgment is required by these rules, without need for mailing; provided that the clerk shall notify by mail, pursuant to

subsection (d)(1), any self-represented litigant who does not provide an e-mail address voluntarily to the clerk for purposes of notice and any attorney who has not provided such an e-mail address and is not required to maintain an e-mail address with the Board of Bar Overseers. The clerk shall make a note in the docket of electronic notice. Where a self-represented litigant wishes to withdraw his or her voluntary agreement to electronic service under this rule, the litigant shall notify the court in writing of his or her withdrawal of voluntary agreement to receive electronic notices and shall confirm the mailing address to which subsequent notices may be mailed.

Lack of notice of the entry by the clerk does not affect the time to appeal or relieve or authorize the court to relieve a party for failure to appeal within the time allowed, except as permitted in Rule 4 of the Massachusetts Rules of Appellate Procedure or Rule 4 of the District/Municipal Courts Rules for Appellate Division Appeal, and except as relevant to a motion for relief from judgment under Rule 60(b)(6) of these rules.

(e) **Transmittal of Papers.** In courts other than the District Court, at the direction of any judge of the court, the clerks for the several counties shall transmit the papers in any action from one county to another when a matter has been duly set down for hearing in a county other than that in which the action is pending. Pleadings, motions, and papers to be filed in such case shall be filed in the office of the clerk for the county in which the case is pending. The clerk for the county in which the case is heard shall certify the proceedings had in his county to the clerk for the county in which the case is pending and, at the direction of any judge of the court, shall return to such clerk all the papers, to be kept there on file.

When the court orders a change of venue, such order shall include a direction to the clerk to transmit all papers to the clerk for the county to which the action is transferred and thereafter all the papers shall be filed and all proceedings taken as if the action had been commenced in the county to which it is transferred.

Amended December 2, 1983, effective January 1, 1984; amended effective July 1, 1996; amended June 24, 2009, effective August 1, 2009; January 25, 2017, effective March 1, 2017.

Reporter's Notes—1973
Rule 77(a) is taken substantially from Federal Rule 77(a). It does not require the clerk's office to be physically open at all times for the filing of pleadings or other papers. (G.L. c. 220, § 6 provides that "Courts shall not be open on Sunday or a legal holiday, and courts, other than district courts, shall not be open on Saturday. . . .") Nor does this rule mean that "filing" may be accomplished by slipping the paper under the door of the clerk's office. It permits the filing of papers with the clerk, or with the judge if he so permits (see Rule 5(e)) at other than business hours and outside the courthouse.

Rule 77(b) requires the clerk's office to be open during business hours except Saturdays, Sundays and legal holidays. Business hours refers to normal business hours as observed by the community. Rule 77(b) also authorizes the clerk to issue process and make entries which do not require allowance or order of the court. This confirms the authority conferred upon the clerk by Rule 55 (default), Rule 58 (entry of judgment) and Rule 68 (offer of judgment).

Rule 77(c) remedies the difficulties occasionally arising where a clerk returns for correction without endorsement of receipt, a paper received by him for filing.

Rule 77(d) requires the clerk, immediately upon entry of an order or judgment to serve a notice of entry by mail upon each party not·in default, except where the order or judgment is entered in open court in the presence of the parties or their counsel. Such notice by mail is sufficient for all purposes under the rules. A party may, however, to ensure notice, serve notice of entry of a judgment or order in the manner provided in Rule 5.

Although under Rule 77(d) lack of notice does not authorize the court to relieve a party for failure to appeal within the time allowed, Appellate Rule 4 provides that upon a showing of excusable neglect the court may extend the time for appeal. A failure to learn of the entry of judgment could, in appropriate circumstances, so qualify. Denial of a motion to extend the time for appeal, where failure to appeal in a timely manner was due to a clerk's failure to give notice, has been held to constitute an abuse of discretion. See Commercial Credit Corp. v. United States, 175 F.2d 905 (8th Cir.1949).

Rule 77(e) does not appear in the federal rules. If a case is to be heard in a county other than the county where the case was properly commenced (e.g., because of consolidation) the case remains on the docket of the original county and all papers are filed there. After the hearing, the papers in the case are returned to the county where the action was commenced. However if a case is transferred in response to a court order for change of venue, all the papers in the case are transferred to the transferee county and all further papers are filed there.

Reporter's Notes—Mass.R.Civ.P.

The purpose of this amendment is to remind lawyers that although Mass.R.Civ.P. 77(d) provides that "[l]ack of notice of the entry [of a judgment] by the clerk does not affect the time to appeal or relieve or authorize the court to relieve a party for failure to appeal within the time allowed . . .", the lack of notice may be relevant to a motion for relief from judgment under Mass.R.Civ.P. 60(b)(6). See, for example, Chavoor v. Lewis, Mass.Adv.Sh. (1981) 1467, 422 N.E.2d 1353 (1981), in which a plaintiff, whose counsel averred that he had never received notification of a call of the list nor of entry of judgment, had the judgment vacated almost two years after judgment pursuant to Mass.R.Civ.P. 60(b)(6). See also 8A Smith and Zobel, Massachusetts Practice—Rules Practice, § 77.5, and citations therein.

Reporter's Notes—1996

The merger of the District/Municipal Courts Rules of Civil Procedure into the Massachusetts Rules of Civil Procedure necessitated minor changes to Rule 77. The language "for each county" previously appearing in the first sentence of Rule 77(b) has been deleted to take into account the fact that a county may contain a number of District Court divisions. A new second sentence has been added to Rule 77(d), drawn from now-repealed Rule 77(d) of the Dist./Mun.Cts.R.Civ.P., requiring that notice of entry of judgment in District Court civil actions must indicate "the court's ruling on any requests for ruling which may have been made." The last sentence of Rule 77(d) has also been amended to refer to the relevant rule governing appeal from the District Court to the Appellate Division of the District Court, namely Rule 4 of the District/Municipal Courts Rules for Appellate Division Appeal.

Some changes to now-repealed Rule 77 of the Dist./Mun.Cts.R.Civ.P. as result of the merger should also be noted. Previously, Rule 77(b) of the Dist./Mun.Cts.R.Civ.P. provided that the clerk's office was to be open on all days "except Sundays and legal holidays." This has been eliminated in favor of the Mass.R.Civ.P. version, excepting Saturdays, Sundays, and legal holidays. This should effect no change in existing District Court practice. The occasion of the merger of the two sets of rules also provided the opportunity to eliminate now-outdated references appearing in Rule 77(d) of the Dist./Mun.Cts.R.Civ.P. to a request for report and to a draft report, both of which were eliminated in 1994 with the adoption of the District/Municipal Courts Rules for Appellate Division Appeal.

Reporter's Notes—2009

Amendments to Rule 52(c) effective March 1, 2008 require findings of fact and rulings of law in jury-waived cases in the District Court if a party timely submits proposed findings and rulings. The March 2008 amendments were part of a group of amendments to the Massachusetts Rules of Civil Procedure in light of the adoption of the statewide one-trial system for civil cases. These amendments also deleted Rule 64A, which provided that a party seeking rulings of law in jury-waived cases in the District Court must submit to the court Requests for Rulings of Law.

In light of the elimination of the procedure involving Requests for Rulings of Law, the 2009 amendment deleted the following sentence from Rule 77(d): "In the District Court, such notice shall indicate the court's ruling on any requests for rulings which may have been made." The deletion of this sentence is not intended to change the existing practice by which the clerk sends to the parties or counsel a copy of the court's findings and rulings.

Reporter's Notes—2017

The 2017 amendment to Rule 77(d) adds electronic means as an option in addition to mail for the clerk to provide notice of an order or judgment to a party. The clerk may send notice to an attorney's e-mail address on file with the Board of Bar Overseers; to an e-mail address that the attorney or party has provided pursuant to a court order or court rule; or to an e-mail address that an attorney or party has provided to the clerk for that purpose. As in the case of mail notice, the clerk must make a note on the docket of the electronic notice. Where electronic notice is given, the clerk need not provide notice by mail.

The rule contains provisions to address the situation where a self-represented litigant has not provided an e-mail address or no longer desires to receive electronic notice or where an attorney is not required to provide an e-mail address with the Board of Bar Overseers.

Rule 78.   Motion Day

The court shall establish regular times and places, at intervals sufficiently frequent for the prompt dispatch of business, at which motions requiring notice and hearing may be heard and disposed of; but a judge at any time or place and on such notice, if any, as he considers reasonable may make orders for the advancement, conduct, and hearing of such motions.

To expedite its business, the court may provide by order for the submission and determination of motions without oral hearing upon brief written statements of reasons in support and opposition.

The court may require the filing of briefs, in such form and within such time as it may direct.

Reporter's Notes—1973

The first paragraph of Rule 78 generalizes what are essentially housekeeping details in Super.Ct.Rules 62, 64 and 66 and includes a provision for flexibility governed by judicial discretion in allowing deviation from the established hearing procedure. This reservation of judicial discretion is similar to Super.Ct.Rule 47. See also, Worster v. Yeaton, 198 Mass. 335, 337, 84 N.E. 461, 462 (1908).

The provision of Rule 78 calling for "brief written statements of reasons in support and opposition" is similar to the requirement of Super.Ct.Rule 46 and S.J.C.Rule 2:30 that matters of fact pertinent to decision on a motion be placed before the court by affidavit or other signed statement.

Rule 79. Books and Records Kept by the Clerk and Entries Therein

(a) Civil Docket. The clerk shall keep the civil docket and shall enter therein each civil action to which these rules are made applicable. Actions shall be assigned consecutive file numbers. The file number of each action shall be noted on the folio of the docket whereon the first entry of the action is made. All papers filed with the clerk, all process issued and returns made thereon, all appearances, orders, verdicts, and judgments shall be entered chronologically in the civil docket on the folio assigned to the action and shall be marked with its file number. These entries shall be brief but shall show the nature of each paper filed or writ issued and the substance of each order or judgment of the court and of the returns showing execution of process. The entry of an order or judgment shall show the date the entry is made. When in an action trial by jury has been properly demanded or ordered the clerk shall enter the word "jury" on the folio assigned to that action.

(b) Indices; Calendars. Suitable indices of the civil docket shall be kept by the clerk according to law under the direction of the court.

(c) Other Books and Records of the Clerk. The clerk shall also keep such other books and records as may be required by law or by direction of the court.

(d) Land Court. In the Land Court, the clerk may assign to actions for registration and confirmation, actions for tax liens, and miscellaneous other actions, separate dockets, each having consecutive file numbers, designated respectively, "Registration and Confirmation," "Tax Lien," and "Miscellaneous."

Amended December 13, 1981, effective January 1, 1982.

Reporter's Notes—1973

Rule 79 is substantially the same as the cognate Federal Rule. It follows prior Massachusetts practice.

Reporter's Notes—1996

With the merger of the District Court rules into the Mass.R.Civ.P., a minor difference which had existed between Mass.R.Civ.P. 79 and Dist./Mun.Cts.R.Civ.P. 79 (last sentence of Rule 79(a) dealing with jury trial) has been eliminated.

Rule 80. Stenographic Report or Transcript

(a) Courts Other Than District Court: Evidence in Subsequent Trial. Whenever the testimony of a witness at a trial or hearing which was officially stenographically reported is admissible in evidence at a later trial, it may be proved by the transcript thereof duly certified by the person who reported the testimony.

(b) Courts Other Than District Court: Part of Record on Appeal. A transcript, duly certified by the person officially reporting the testimony, shall be considered part of the record on appeal. The trial court need not appoint said person a commissioner to report the evidence.

(c) District Court: Stenographers. The appointment of stenographers in District Court proceedings shall be in accordance with the applicable statute. Whenever the testimony of a witness at a trial or hearing which was officially stenographically reported is admissible in evidence at a later trial, it may be proved by the transcript thereof duly certified by the person who reported the testimony. Subject to the discretion of the court, parties may be permitted to record stenographically the proceedings in civil actions at their own expense.

(d) District Court: Sound Recording Devices. The use of sound recording devices to record civil proceedings shall be governed by Rule 114 of the District/Municipal Courts Supplemental Rules of Civil Procedure.

Amended effective July 1, 1996; November 28, 2007, effective March 1, 2008.

Reporter's Notes—1973

Rule 80(a) is similar both in wording and import to G.L. c. 233, § 80 and G.L. c. 221, § 91C. It aims to abolish the requirement set forth in G.L. c. 214, § 24 and Super.Ct.Rule 76 (applicable to equity cases) that in order to make the report of the evidence available on appeal to the full bench, the court must formally appoint the stenographer a commissioner to report the evidence. See Thayer Company v. Binnall, 326 Mass. 467, 482–483, 95 N.E.2d 193, 202–203 (1950); Price v. Price, 348 Mass. 663, 665, 204 N.E.2d 902, 904 (1965).

Reporter's Notes—1996

New sections (c) and (d) have been added to Rule 80 as result of the merger of the District Court rules into the Mass.R.Civ.P. and sections (a) and (b) have been retitled. As amended, Rule 80(a) and (b) now are applicable in all courts other than the District Court. Rule 80(c) adopts for District Court proceedings the provisions contained in now-repealed Rule 80(a) of the Dist./Mun.Cts.R.Civ.P., while Rule 80(d) adopts for District Court proceedings the provisions of Rule 80(b) of the Dist./Mun.Cts.R.Civ.P. The "Comments" to now-repealed Rule 80 of the Dist./Mun.Cts.R.Civ.P. explain the significance of the different provisions for District Court proceedings:

This rule totally rewrites Rule 80 of the MRCP. Since no "official" stenographers are used in the District Courts, paragraph (a) [now (c)] has been revised merely to allow the use of stenographers. The use to which the resulting record may be put is not dealt with by this rule. The swearing of the stenographer may be added merely to formalize the procedure.

Paragraph (b) [now (d)] has dropped the MRCP discussion of how the record may be proved. Instead, paragraph (b) [now (d)] of this rule deals with the use of mechanical sound recording devices, and does so merely by referring to Rule 114 of the District/Municipal Courts Supplemental Rules of Civil Procedure which covers the topic.

Reporter's Notes—2008

Rule 80(c), dealing with stenographic reports in the District Court, has been amended in light of the following language in the statewide one-trial law (see G.L. c. 218, § 19B(d)):

(d) The justice presiding at the jury of 6 session may, upon the request of a party, appoint a stenographer; provided, however, that where the party claims indigency, the appointment is determined to be reasonably necessary in accordance with chapter 261; and provided, further, that the court electronic recording system is not available or not properly functioning ... The request for the appointment of a stenographer to preserve the testimony at a trial shall be given to the clerk of the court by a party, in writing, no later than 48 hours before the proceeding for which the stenogra-

pher has been requested ... The original recording of proceedings in a district court or in the Boston municipal court made with a recording device under the exclusive control of the court shall be the official record of the proceedings ...

X. GENERAL PROVISIONS

Rule 81. Applicability of Rules

(a) Applicability in General.

(1) *Courts Other Than District Court.* These rules apply to all civil proceedings in courts whose proceedings they govern except:

1. proceedings pertaining to the writ of habeas corpus;

2. proceedings pertaining to naturalization;

3. proceedings pertaining to the disciplining of an attorney;

4. proceedings pertaining to juvenile delinquency;

5. proceedings pertaining to contested elections;

6. proceedings pertaining to dissolution of corporations and distribution of their assets;

7. proceedings pertaining to summary process, small claims, and supplementary process;

8. proceedings pertaining to the adjudication, commitment and release of sexually dangerous persons;

9. proceedings for divorce or for the annulment or affirmation of marriage; and

10. proceedings to foreclose any mortgage on real estate brought in compliance with the "Servicemembers Civil Relief Act," as set forth in 50 U.S.C. §§ 3901 et seq.

(2) *District Court.* These rules apply to all civil proceedings involved in cases traditionally considered tort, contract, replevin, or equity actions, except small claims actions.

(3) In respects not governed by statute, or in the case of the District Court not governed by other District Court rules, the practice in civil proceedings to which these rules do not apply shall follow the course of the common law, as near to these rules as may be, except that depositions shall not be taken, nor interrogatories served, save by order of the court on motion, with notice, for good cause shown.

(b) Writs Abolished. The following writs are abolished: audita querela; certiorari; entry; error; mandamus; prohibition; quo warranto; review; and scire facias. In any action seeking relief formerly obtainable under any such writ, procedure shall follow these rules.

(c) Superior Court: Trial of Framed Jury Issues. These rules govern the trial of any issues framed in another court for trial in the Superior Court; but nothing herein contained shall authorize the use of discovery procedures contained in these rules, except as a justice of the Superior Court, on motion with notice, may allow for good cause shown.

(d) Terminology in Statutes. In applying these rules to any proceedings to which they apply, the terminology of any statute which also applies shall, if inconsistent with these rules, be taken to mean the analogous device or procedure proper under these rules.

(e) Procedure Not Specifically Prescribed. When no procedure is specifically prescribed, the court shall proceed in any lawful manner not inconsistent with the Constitution of this Commonwealth, these rules, or any applicable statute.

(f) Superior Court: Actions Removed, Transferred or Appealed From Another Court. Except as otherwise provided in subdivision (a) of this rule, these rules apply to civil actions removed, transferred or appealed to the Superior Court from any other court. Repleading is not necessary unless a justice of the Superior Court so orders. If the defendant has not answered prior to removal or transfer, he shall answer or present the other defenses or objections available to him under these rules within 20 days after the receipt through service or otherwise of a copy of the initial pleading setting forth the claim for relief upon which the action or proceeding is based, or within 20 days after the service of summons upon such initial pleadings, then filed, or within 5 days after the filing of the removal or transfer papers, whichever period is longest.

(g) Actions Transferred or Remanded to District Court. In any action commenced in the Superior Court and transferred to a district court or the Boston Municipal Court, or in any action remanded to either such court after removal to the Superior Court, the rules for the time being in force in the district court or the Boston Municipal Court shall control all proceedings subsequent to the filing of the order for transfer or remand; but all proceedings in the Superior Court shall be governed by these rules.

Amended June 27, 1974, effective July 1, 1974; amended effective February 24, 1975; February 1, 1995; July 1, 1996; November 28, 2007, effective March 1, 2008; December 19, 2018, effective January 1, 2019.

Reporter's Notes—1973

Rule 81, based partly on the analogous Federal Rule, treats various questions of applicability.

Rule 81(a) exempts seven types of proceedings, none of which would be appropriately governed by the general civil rules. By proviso, however, Rule 81(a) commands adherence to these rules, unless statutorily contradicted. Even so, no depositions may be had nor interrogatories served unless the court approves.

Rule 81(b) abolishes a series of venerable, and in many instances, arcane, writs. Burial of these antiques, however, does not mean elimination of the relief they afforded. It does mean that an application for such relief will henceforth be commenced like any other civil action under these rules, viz., by complaint and summons, with the former containing a prayer for the appropriate relief.

Rule 81(c) makes clear that if the Probate Court, for example, frames jury issues for trial in the Superior Court, G.L. c. 215, § 16, *trial* in the Superior Court will accord with these rules; but unlimited discovery will not automatically ensue, unless, of course, these rules controlled the initial Probate Court proceedings (see Rule 1).

Rule 81(d) covers cases in which an applicable statute uses terminology which, although analogous to appropriate language of these rules, departs from it somewhat. The rule makes clear that the intent of the statutory wording should be effectuated through the comparable language of the rules.

Rule 81(e) provides a safety valve for those rare instances in which no procedure seems authorized by statute, common law, or these rules. It is not calculated to permit wholesale judicial procedural innovation; rather, it is designed to guide bench and bar through unforeseeable future thickets.

Rule 81(f), based on Federal Rule 81(c), deals with cases which have been brought from a district court to the Superior Court for trial (removed cases), or re-trial (appealed cases). It makes clear that any pleadings previously filed in the court below need not be redrafted to accord with these rules. In removed cases, G.L. c. 231, § 104, the papers, including bond, must be filed in such a short time after commencement of the action that the defendant may not have previously filed his answer. If he has not, then he must do so in accordance with a fairly liberal timetable set out in Rule 81(f). The rule also requires the defendant promptly to exercise his right to demand a jury trial; because that right is usually the reason for the removal anyway, this requirement should not cause much difficulty. It should be noted that in a removed case, the plaintiff, too, has the right to demand a jury trial, G.L. c. 231, § 103; Rule 81(f) also governs his exercise of the right.

Rule 81(g) deals with the converse of the Rule 81(f) situation. Here, the case has either been commenced in the Superior Court or removed there, but has, for lack of sufficient amount in controversy, been transferred to the appropriate district court (if it was commenced in the Superior Court) or remanded there (if it had originally been commenced in the district court and then removed to the Superior Court), G.L. c. 231, § 102c. In either event, Rule 81(g) makes clear that when the case goes to the district court, that court's rules apply; but while it is in the Superior Court, the instant rules control the proceedings.

Reporter's Notes—1975

Real estate mortgage foreclosures brought in compliance with the Soldiers and Sailors Civil Relief Act, Acts 1943, c. 57, §§ 1–3, as amended by Acts, c. 120, § 1 (not a part of the codified General Laws, but printed following M.G.L.A., c. 244, § 14) have presented a problem. The Act prescribes a distinct procedure, well-suited for the purpose, governing foreclosures. Attempts to fit this integrated arrangement into the Rules format since July 1, 1974, caused considerable difficulty to bench, bar, and clerks. Rather than press the Procrustean effort, the entire matter of real estate mortgage foreclosures complaint to the Act has been removed from the Rules, by addition of Rule 81(a)(10). Because the difficulty proceeds from the language of the Act, no other mortgage foreclosures have been similarly treated. Thus whenever a real estate mortgage foreclosure does not fall within the Act, the Rules will continue to govern.

Reporter's Notes—1988

Rule 81(a)(7) excepts, inter alia, "proceedings pertaining to summary process" from the application of the Massachusetts Rules of Civil Procedure. However, the bar should be aware that Uniform Summary Process Rule 1 states, in part, that "[p]rocedures in such actions that are not prescribed by these rules shall be governed by the Massachusetts Rules of Civil Procedure insofar as the latter are not inconsistent with . . ." the Uniform Summary Process Rules. Stated another way, the Uniform Summary Process Rules have incorporated by reference the Massachusetts Rules of Civil Procedure to be used in a residuary capacity when they are not "inconsistent" with the Uniform Summary Process Rules or "with applicable statutory law or with the jurisdiction of the particular court in which they would be applied." Uniform Summary Process Rule 1 should be applied as written. It is not unusual in law for one set of rules (in this instance, the Massachusetts Rules of Civil Procedure) that do not by their own provisions apply in a situation to be incorporated by reference by another set of rules (in this instance, the Uniform Summary Process Rules). For example, federal law often incorporates aspects of state law, and contracts often incorporate a body of law from elsewhere.

Reporter's Notes—1995

The amendment to Rule 81(f) makes clear that the Rules of Civil Procedure are not intended to apply to actions removed, transferred or appealed to the Superior Court and involving the types of proceedings listed in Rule 81(a). For example, where a petition for dissolution of a corporation is filed directly in the Supreme Judicial Court (see G.L. c. 156B, § 99) and thereafter transferred by the Court to the Superior Court (pursuant to G.L. c. 211, § 4A), proceedings in the Superior Court would not be governed by the Massachusetts Rules of Civil Procedure.

Reporter's Notes—1996

A number of technical changes to Rule 81 have been made as result of the merger of the Dist./Mun.Cts.R.Civ.P. into the Mass.R.Civ.P. in 1996. These changes essentially retain the respective versions of Rule 81 that had existed in the two sets of rules prior to the merger.

Rule 81(a) has been subdivided into new subsections (1), (2), and (3).

Subsection (1) of Rule 81(a) is applicable to all courts other than the District Court, and is identical to the pre–1996 version of Rule 81(a) of the Mass.R.Civ.P., with the exception of the last paragraph of Mass. R.Civ.P. 81(a) as it existed prior to the merger. Thus, in all courts governed by the rules other than the District Court, the Mass.R.Civ.P. apply in all civil proceedings except for the ten types of proceedings specifically listed.

Subsection (2) of Rule 81(a) is applicable to the District Court and the Boston Municipal Court, and is identical to the premerger language that had been contained in the first paragraph of Rule 81(a) of the Dist./Mun.Cts.R.Civ.P. Thus, the "merged" set of rules "apply to all civil proceedings involved in [District Court] cases traditionally considered tort, contract, replevin, or equity actions, except small claims actions." Small claims actions are specifically mentioned because they otherwise could be deemed to come within the language of "cases traditionally considered" as tort or contract. The number of District Court proceedings to which the rules are inapplicable is sufficiently large such that a comprehensive listing of such exceptions (as occurs in Rule 81(a)(1) for courts other than the District Court) would be difficult, and in all likelihood, incomplete. The difference in approach between Rule 81(a)(1) and (2), therefore, should not be taken to signify that there has been any change in applicability of the civil rules in District Court proceedings as result of the merger of the two sets of rules in 1996. The following rationale for the different approach to setting forth the applicability of the rules in District Court proceedings, as explained in the "Comments" to now-repealed Rule 81 of the Dist./Mun.Cts.R.Civ.P., is still apt:

> Several significant changes from Rule 81 of the MRCP have been made in this rule. First, it is stated that these rules apply to proceedings in cases traditionally considered tort, contract, replevin, or equity actions. Small claims actions, expressly excluded from coverage under these rules, are governed by Rules 170–185 of the District/Municipal Courts Supplemental Rules of Civil Procedure. The reference to "tradition" is in deference to the fact that under these rules there are no longer any separate "causes of action." (See Rule 2 and accompanying comments.) No attempt is made to list the many other District Court civil proceedings to which these rules do not apply, such as those involving compensation to victims of violent crime, repossession hearings, summary process, supplementary procedure, hearings on denials of gun permits, civil commitments, etc. It should be noted that this rule does not enlarge District Court jurisdiction; the only equity actions covered by these rules are the few which the District Courts have the statutory power to hear and decide.

Some of the proceedings mentioned in the "Comments" quoted above are now governed by other rules. Some examples follow. Summary process actions are governed by the Uniform Summary

Process Rules (Trial Court Rule I). Small claims actions are no longer governed by the District/Municipal Courts Supplemental Rules of Civil Procedure, but rather by the Uniform Small Claims Rules, Trial Court Rule III. Proceedings regarding compensation to victims of violent crime are governed by Rules 150 and 151 of the District/Municipal Courts Supplemental Rules of Civil Procedure.

Subsection (3) of Rule 81(a) contains the guidelines concerning procedure in cases where the rules are inapplicable and combines into one paragraph the essential aspects of what had been contained in the last paragraph of Mass.R.Civ.P. 81(a) and Dist./Mun.Cts.R.Civ.P. 81(a).

The only change to Rule 81(c) is contained in the title to the section. The addition of the reference to the Superior Court in the title is intended to make clear that Rule 81(c) is applicable only in the Superior Court.

Likewise, the title to Rule 81(f) has been changed to make clear that Rule 81(f) is applicable only in the Superior Court.

Reporter's Notes—2008

Unrelated to the statewide one-trial system, the reference in item 10 of Rule 81(a)(1) is amended to delete the reference to the "Soldiers' and Sailors' Civil Relief Act," which was renamed as the "Servicemembers Civil Relief Act" and updated by Congress in 2003.

Reporter's Notes—2019

Rule 81(a)(1) has been amended to reflect that the federal Servicemembers Civil Relief Act was relocated in the United States Code from 50 U.S.C. App. §§ 501 et seq. to 50 U.S.C. §§ 3901 et seq. in 2015. A similar amendment was made to Rule 55(b)(4) in 2017.

Rule 82. Jurisdiction and Venue Unaffected

These rules shall not be construed to extend or limit the jurisdiction of the courts or the venue of actions therein.

Reporter's Notes—1973

Rule 82, taken with minor changes from Federal Rule 82, makes clear that the new Rules are entirely procedural, and that they have left unchanged the various statutes setting out jurisdiction of the courts and venue of actions.

Rule 83. Supplemental Rules

Any court whose procedure is regulated in whole or in part by these rules may from time to time make and amend supplemental rules, or continue in force existing rules, governing its procedure not inconsistent with these rules. In instances not provided for by rule, each said court may regulate its practice in a manner not inconsistent with these rules and the said supplemental rules.

Adopted June 27, 1974, effective July 1, 1974.

Reporter's Notes—1994

This rule permits the promulgation of supplemental rules by courts whose procedure is governed by these rules. However, the provisions of the Massachusetts Rules of Civil Procedure will prevail whenever there is inconsistency between them and supplemental rules or standing orders. See Sullivan v. Iantosca, 409 Mass. 796, 801 (1991).

It should be noted, however, that a supplemental rule containing a time period shorter than that set out in the rules of civil procedure is not necessarily inconsistent with the rules of civil procedure. For example, where a Superior Court rule required that affidavits in opposition to a motion for summary judgment be filed within ten days after service of the summary judgment motion, the Appeals Court noted that "[t]rial court rules 'more demanding than the requirements of Rule 56 . . . are not necessarily inconsistent with the general provisions' in the rule [allowing the filing of counter-affidavits prior to the hearing day]." Ruggiero v. Costa, 28 Mass.App.Ct. 967, 968 (1990), citing 10A Wright & Miller, Federal Practice and Procedure § 2719, at 13 (1983). See also 12 Wright & Miller, Federal Practice and Procedure § 3153 (1973) (citing federal cases interpreting similar language in Federal Rule 83).

Reporter's Notes—1996

Rule 83, which had been "reserved" in the Dist./Mun.Cts.R.Civ.P., is now applicable in the District Court as result of the merger of the District Court civil rules into the Mass.R.Civ.P. in 1996.

Rule 84. Forms [Repealed]

Repealed November 30, 2016, effective January 1, 2017.

Reporter's Notes—2017

Rule 84 was repealed and the related Appendix of Forms was deleted from the Massachusetts Rules of Civil Procedure effective January 1, 2017. Prior to repeal, Rule 84 provided in part: "The forms contained in the Appendix of Forms are sufficient under the rules and are intended to indicate the simplicity and brevity of statement which the rules contemplate."

Many of the forms in the Appendix of Forms are out of date, and the Appendix is not widely used in its current form. In addition, the value of the Appendix of Forms has been diminished with the availability of a multiplicity of forms that are accessible on the website of the Massachusetts court system and from a variety of sources on-line.

For similar reasons, Rule 84 of the Federal Rules of Civil Procedure and the federal Appendix of Forms were likewise repealed in 2015.

Rule 85. Title

These rules may be known and cited as the Massachusetts Rules of Civil Procedure (Mass.R.Civ.P.).

Reporter's Notes—1973

This tracks Federal Rule 85.

Reporter's Notes—1996

With the merger of the District/Municipal Courts Rules of Civil Procedure into the Massachusetts Rules of Civil Procedure in 1996, the former title has been eliminated. The Mass.R.Civ.P. now also apply in the District Court and in the Boston Municipal Court.

MASSACHUSETTS RULES OF CRIMINAL PROCEDURE

Effective July 1, 1979

Research Note

See Massachusetts General Laws Annotated, vol. 47, for case annotations, cross references, and research references relating to the Massachusetts Rules of Criminal Procedure.

The Massachusetts Rules of Criminal Procedure are discussed in Cypher, Massachusetts Practice—Criminal Practice and Procedure, vols. 30, 30A and 30B (4th Edition).

Table of Rules

Rule 1. Title; Scope

[Text of rule applicable to cases initiated (by indictment or complaint) on or after September 7, 2004.]

(a) Title. These rules may be known and cited as the Massachusetts Rules of Criminal Procedure. (Mass.R.Crim. P.)

(b) Scope. These rules govern the procedure in all criminal proceedings in the District Court, in all criminal proceedings in the Superior Court, in all delinquency and youthful offender proceedings in the Juvenile Court, District Court and Superior Court consistent with the General Laws, and in proceedings for post-conviction relief.

Amended March 8, 2004, effective September 7, 2004.

Reporter's Notes—Revised, 2004

Rule 1 is drawn from and combines Fed. R. Crim. P. 60 and 1. The substance of the rule defines the scope and applicability of the remainder of the rules.

These rules are applicable to the criminal process in those courts having general criminal jurisdiction. This code represents an attempt to consolidate into a single document rules of procedure to apply with the fewest possible exceptions to the appropriate departments of the Trial Court of the Commonwealth. Those exceptions are delineated in each rule where different procedures must prevail. There is, of course, a limitation inherent in any comprehensive set of procedural rules. That is, a variety of special procedures or factual situations exist where the mechanical application of the rules would work an unnecessary hardship or an injustice. In those limited circumstances, sound judicial discretion will require a construction of the rules so as to secure simplicity in procedure, fairness in the administration of the criminal justice system, and the elimination of unnecessary expense and delay as required by Rule 2(a).

In order to be of broad application to criminal practice, it was necessary for the rules to prescribe general procedures suitable for all courts within their scope. It is necessary that the rules be general and flexible, prescribing only basic essentials, rather than rigid and detailed. It is also necessary that the Rules be reviewed periodically to assess their operation and to take account of changes in both law and society over time. Such a comprehensive review was undertaken beginning in 1995, resulting in subsequent amendments to several of the rules, including a set of major revisions promulgated in 2004.

While these rules are intended to constitute a comprehensive code of criminal procedure for cases in the enumerated courts, nevertheless there are areas of criminal practice which were left unregulated. Among these matters are pretrial diversion, search- and arrest-warrant procedures, wire-tapping procedures, and other similar matters. As to some of these practices, it was determined that the state of the law, especially regarding constitutional issues, was so fluid as to defy codification. These matters were necessarily left to an *ad hoc* determination on specific facts by the courts. In other areas it was recognized that local practice in individual courts — whether by accepted usage or court rules — could give the criminal justice system some flexibility as required by special conditions not susceptible to general regulation.

These rules are not intended to pre-empt the adoption of rules by the several departments of the Trial Court to address specific problems which are inevitably encountered in those courts and which are not dealt with by these rules.

Nor are these rules intended to be a comprehensive guide or statement with respect to the procedures used by the clerks of court. It is expected that those offices will continue to develop efficient methods to assist in the expeditious disposal of criminal matters consistent with the letter and spirit of these rules.

By a 2004 amendment, Rule 1 was revised to explicitly state that the Rules of Criminal Procedure govern "all delinquency and youthful offender proceedings in the Juvenile Court." Thus the same rules apply to juvenile court proceedings that apply to delinquency and criminal proceedings in the other trial courts. This accords with M.G.L. c. 218, sec. 59, which provides that "Except as otherwise provided by law, the divisions of the juvenile court department shall have and exercise, within their respective jurisdictions, the same powers, duties, and procedure as the divisions of the district court department; and all laws relating to district courts or municipal courts in their respective counties or officials thereof or proceedings therein, shall, so far as applicable, apply to said divisions of the juvenile court department . . ." The application of the Rules of Criminal Procedure to juvenile proceedings does not, however, imply that they are identical to adult criminal cases in all other respects. Special procedures for the hearing of juvenile offenses have been established under G.L. c. 119 and are designed to treat juveniles as children in need of aid, encouragement and guidance, rather than as criminals. Metcalf v. Commonwealth, 338 Mass. 648, 156 N.E.2d 649 (1959). G.L. c. 119, § 53 directs that proceedings against juveniles under G.L. c. 119 shall not be deemed criminal proceedings, but such matters must still be governed by constitutional due process standards. In re Gault, 87 S.Ct. 1428, 387 U.S. 1, 18 L.Ed.2d 527 (1967). Therefore, these rules are intended to be construed liberally so as to comply with the goals and purposes of G.L. c. 119, while G.L. c. 119, § 53 is not to operate to deny the procedural safeguards contained within these rules.

Rule 2. Purpose; Construction; Definition of Terms

(Applicable to District Court and Superior Court)

(a) Purpose; Construction. These rules are intended to provide for the just determination of every criminal proceeding. They shall be construed to secure simplicity in procedure, fairness in administration, and the elimination of expense and delay.

(1) Words or phrases importing the singular number may extend and be applied to several persons or things, words importing the plural number may include the singular, and words importing the masculine gender may include the feminine and neuter.

(2) When in these rules reference is made to a subdivision of a rule, that reference is to that subdivision and to any subdivisions thereof.

(b) Definition of Terms. In construing these rules the following words and phrases shall have the following meanings unless a contrary intent clearly appears from the context in which they are used:

(1) "Indigent" means any defendant who is unable to procure counsel with his funds as defined in Supreme Judicial Court Rule 3:10.

(2) "Indigent but able to contribute" means any defendant who is unable to procure counsel with his funds but is able to contribute funds for the cost of counsel as defined in Supreme Judicial Court Rule 3:10.

(3) "Capital Crime" means a charge of murder in the first degree.

(4) "Commonwealth" includes the prosecuting office or agency and all officers or agents responsible thereto.

(5) "Court" includes a judge, special magistrate, or clerk.

(6) "District Attorney" or "Attorney General" include assistant district attorneys or assistant attorneys general and other attorneys specially appointed to aid in the prosecution of a case.

(7) "District Court" includes all divisions of the District Court Department of the Trial Court, the Boston Municipal Court Department of the Trial Court, and the Juvenile Court Department of the Trial Court, or sessions thereof for holding court.

(8) "Interested Person" includes the adverse party, a co-defendant, and a witness who is to be deposed.

(9) "Judge" includes a judge of a court or one properly assigned to a court or a special magistrate when in the performance of those duties imposed and authorized by these rules.

(10) "Juvenile Court" means a division of the Juvenile Court Department of the Trial Court, or a session thereof for holding court.

(11) "Mailing" means the use of regular mail and shall not require registered or certified mail.

(12) "Prosecuting Attorney" means the attorney general or assistant attorneys general, district attorney, assistant district attorneys, special assistant district attorneys, or legal assis-

tants to the district attorney, or other attorneys specially appointed to aid in the prosecution of a case.

(13) "Prosecutor" means any prosecuting attorney or prosecuting officer, and shall include a city solicitor, a police prosecutor, or a law student approved for practice pursuant to and acting as authorized by the rules of the Supreme Judicial Court.

(14) "Related Offense" means one of two or more offenses which are based on the same criminal conduct or episode or arise out of a course of criminal conduct or series of criminal episodes connected together or constituting parts of a single scheme or plan.

(15) "Return Day" means the day upon which a defendant is ordered by summons to first appear or, if under arrest, does first appear before a court to answer to the charges against him, whichever is earlier.

(16) "Special Magistrate" means any person who is appointed pursuant to, and empowered to administer those functions authorized by, rule forty-seven of these rules.

(17) "Summons" means

(A) criminal process issued to a person requiring him to appear at a stated time and place to answer to criminal charges; or

(B) process issued to a person requiring him to appear at a stated time and place to give testimony in a criminal proceeding; or

(C) process issued to a person requiring him to appear and produce at a stated time and place books, designated papers, documents, or other objects for use in a criminal proceeding.

(18) "Superior Court" means the Superior Court Department of the Trial Court, or a session thereof for holding court.

Amended May 29, 1986, effective July 1, 1986.

Reporter's Notes

Rule 2 is perhaps the most significant of the rules in advancing the trend toward a high degree of procedural fairness in the administration of criminal justice. This is so because the rule not only permits but requires the rules to be construed and applied in a manner which provides for fairness in their administration to the end that a just determination in every criminal proceeding shall be achieved. The rules must be approached with sympathy for this purpose; they must be interpreted with common sense.

The rules were not intended to be administered inflexibly without regard for the circumstances of the particular case. Where a literal interpretation of a rule and its application in a specific situation would lead to unnecessary expense or delay, would unduly complicate the proceedings, or would operate unfairly or produce an unjust result, that interpretation is to yield to the principle enunciated in Rule 2(a).

This is not to imply that the rules were conceived as merely guidelines or suggested procedures to which the courts and counsel need adhere only as will further their particular interests. They have the force and effect of law.

The appellate courts have made it increasingly clear that abuse of power by the prosecution or by trial judges is not to be tolerated. *See e.g.*, S.J.C. Rule 3:22A, *Disciplinary Rules Applicable to Practice as a Prosecutor or as a Defense Lawyer*, PF 1–14 (Feb. 14, 1979); Commonwealth v. St. Pierre, Mass.Adv.Sh. (1979) 834, 387 N.E.2d 1135; Commonwealth v. Soares, Mass.Adv.Sh. (1979) 593, 387 N.E.2d 499; Commonwealth v. Ellison, Mass.Adv.Sh. (1978) 2072, 379 N.E.2d 560;

Commonwealth v. Earltop, Mass.Adv.Sh. (1977) 532, 539, 361 N.E.2d 220 (Hennessey, C.J., concurring); Commonwealth v. Redmond, 370 Mass. 591, 351 N.E.2d 501 (1976); Commonwealth v. Sneed, Mass.Adv. Sh. (1978) 3156, 383 N.E.2d 843. It is equally apparent that a high standard of conduct is demanded of defense counsel. *See* S.J.C. Rule 3:22A, supra, DF 1–15. A disregard for these rules of court or a failure to adhere to their provisions are abuses of the system which can be expected to produce problems in the administration of justice and unfairness to the Commonwealth, defendants, and the public, and which, therefore, should not be tolerated by either the trial or appellate courts.

Subdivision (a). The language of the first paragraph is drawn virtually without change from Fed.R.Crim.P. 2. These rules are intended to minimize complicated proceedings and needless expense and delay and are to be construed so as to achieve that goal.

The principle of construction stated in subdivision (a)(1) is taken from G.L. c. 4, § 6, cl. fourth, which relates to the construction of the General Laws.

Subdivision (a)(2) is designed to avoid any confusion in reading references to subdivisions. Included in a reference to a subdivision are all paragraphs, subparagraphs, and clauses of that subdivision.

Subdivision (b). These definitions are to be used in construing these rules unless a contrary interpretation is clearly demanded by the context within which the term is used. See G.L. c. 4, § 7; c. 3, § 63.

(1) *Appointed Counsel.* This definition is suggested by Superior Court Rule 53(3) (1974); it is to be distinguished from "Assigned Counsel," infra.

(2) *Assigned Counsel.* The terms "appointed counsel" and "assigned counsel" have been used interchangeably in the case law. *See* e.g., Costarelli v. Municipal Court of the City of Boston, 367 Mass. 35, 323 N.E.2d 859 (1975). However, for the purposes of these rules, each term has been given a separate and distinct definition. In these rules, "assigned counsel" means a member of a publicly funded or charitable organization, such as the Massachusetts Defenders Committee (G.L. c. 221, § 34D. See Rule 8[b]), or a county defender. "Appointed counsel" denotes a private attorney who is designated by a judge or magistrate to represent a defendant who cannot afford counsel. Both assigned and appointed counsel may include senior law students appearing without compensation on behalf of indigent defendants as permitted by S.J.C. Rule 3:11 (1974: 366 Mass. 867, as amended, 1975: 367 Mass. 914).

(3) *Capital Crime.* This definition is drawn from existing case law, e.g., Commonwealth v. Capalbo, 308 Mass. 376, 32 N.E.2d 225 (1941); Commonwealth v. Ibrahim, 184 Mass. 255, 68 N.E. 231 (1903); Green v. Commonwealth, 94 Mass. (12 Allen) 155 (1866). *Compare* G.L. c. 278, § 33E (capital crime defined "for the purposes of . . . [appellate] review" only). General Laws c. 274, § 2 provides that, "Whoever aids in the commission of a felony, or is accessory thereto before the fact by counselling, hiring or otherwise procuring such felony to be committed, shall be punished in the manner provided for the punishment of the principal felon." Therefore, an indictment of a defendant as an accessory before the fact of first degree murder sets out a capital crime. Grady v. Treasurer of the County of Worcester, 352 Mass. 702, 704, 227 N.E.2d 490 (1967).

(4) *Commonwealth.* The definition of this term reflects the meaning of the word as commonly used in the case law and statutes.

(5) *Court.* This term is used in the rules to include those officials most intimately involved in the process of adjudicating cases. When so generically used, the word is not to be construed so as to expand or limit those duties traditionally or by law within the prerogative of certain officials.

(6) *District Attorney or Attorney General.* As with "Commonwealth," supra, these terms are used both in the sense of the office and the personnel thereof in their official capacity.

(7) *District Court.* General Laws c. 211B, § 1 (inserted by St.1978, c. 478, § 110) established the Trial Court of the Commonwealth which consists in part of the Superior Court Department, the District Court Department, the Boston Municipal Court Department, and the Juvenile Court Departments. For ease of reference throughout these rules, the latter three Departments are included within the term "District Court."

It is in keeping with the policy of these rules to secure simplicity and uniformity in procedure to make the Juvenile Court Department subject to these rules, insofar as they are consistent with juvenile practice. See District Court Special Rule 2 (1974), which applies the rules of the District Court to juvenile proceedings insofar as they are "pertinent."

(8) *Interested Person.* This term specifies those persons who are entitled to notice of, for example, the filing of motions, Mass.R.Crim.P. 13, 32, or the taking of a deposition, Mass.R.Crim.P. 36.

(9) *Judge.* In addition to its accepted meaning, for purposes of these rules this term is to include a magistrate when used in reference to a function which that official is authorized to perform by Mass. R.Crim.P. 48.

(10) *Juvenile Court.* See G.L. c. 211B, § 1 (inserted by St.1978, c. 478, § 110), c. 218, §§ 57–60 (St.1978, c. 478, §§ 212–16).

The divisions of the Juvenile Court Department, within their respective jurisdictions, have and exercise the same powers, duties and procedures as the District Court or Municipal Court Departments and are subject to the laws relating thereto, so far as applicable. G.L. c. 218, § 59 (as amended, St.1978, c. 478, § 215).

(11) *Mailing.* It is intended that unless specifically provided for elsewhere in these rules, neither registered nor certified mailing is required.

(12) *Prosecuting Attorney.* This term includes those attorneys who prosecute the majority of criminal cases in the Commonwealth.

(13) *Prosecutor.* This definition is broader than that of "prosecuting attorney," and reflects the fact that many cases in the District Courts are prosecuted by a police prosecutor. Under these rules, some prosecutorial functions can be carried on only by a district attorney or attorney general. *See* e.g., Mass.R.Crim.P. 15(d)(1)(B). A prosecutor may include senior law students appearing on behalf of the Commonwealth pursuant to S.J.C. Rule 3:11 (1974: 366 Mass. 867, as amended, 1975: 367 Mass. 914).

(14) *Related Offense.* For further explanation of this definition, see Mass.R.Crim.P. 9 and Reporter's Notes.

(15) *Return Day.* The "return day" is the date upon which a defendant under arrest first appears in court or the date upon which a defendant not under arrest is scheduled to appear pursuant to summons. It is the date upon which speedy trial rights attach (Mass. R.Crim.P. 36[b][1]) and from which other time limits are measured.

(16) *Special Magistrate.* The office of "Special Magistrate" is defined in terms of its powers and duties. See Mass.R.Crim.P. 47. Special Magistrates are to be distinguished from "Magistrates in the Trial Court" under G.L. c. 221, §§ 62B–62C (inserted by St.1978, c. 478, § 250).

(17) *Summons.* This definition includes process issued pursuant to Mass.R.Crim.P. 6 and 17. The definitions contained in subdivisions (b)(17)(B) and (C) of this rule replace the older term "subpoena."

(18) *Superior Court.* See G.L. c. 211B, § 1 (inserted by St.1978, c. 478, § 110), c. 212 (as amended, St.1978, c. 478, §§ 115–25).

Rule 3.   Complaint and Indictment; Waiver of Indictment; Probable Cause Hearing

[Text of rule applicable to cases initiated (by indictment or complaint) on or after September 7, 2004.]

(a) Commencement of Criminal Proceeding. A criminal proceeding shall be commenced in the District Court by a complaint and in the Superior Court by an indictment, except that if a defendant is charged in the District Court with a crime as to which the defendant has the right to be proceeded against by indictment and the defendant has waived the right to an indictment pursuant to subdivision (c), the Commonwealth may proceed in the Superior Court upon the complaint.

(b) Right to Indictment. A defendant charged with an offense punishable by imprisonment in state prison shall have the right to be proceeded against by indictment except when the offense charged is within the concurrent jurisdiction of the District and Superior Courts and the District Court retains jurisdiction.

(c) Waiver of Indictment.

(1) *Right to Waive Indictment.* A defendant charged in a District Court with an offense as to which the defendant has the right to be proceeded against by indictment shall have the right, except when the offense charged is a capital crime, to waive indictment, unless the Commonwealth proceeds by indictment pursuant to subdivision (e) of this rule.

(2) *Procedure for Waiving Indictment.* The defendant may waive the right to be proceeded against by indictment by filing a written waiver of that right in the District Court prior to the determination to bind the case over to the Superior Court for trial. The District Court may for cause shown grant relief from that waiver. After the determination by the District Court to bind the case over to the Superior Court for trial, the defendant may waive the right to be proceeded against by indictment by filing a written waiver of that right, with the consent of the prosecutor, in the Superior Court.

(d) Transmission of Papers. If the defendant is bound over to the Superior Court for trial after a finding of probable cause or after the defendant waives a probable cause hearing, the clerk of the District Court shall transmit to the clerk of the Superior Court a copy of the complaint and of the record; the original recognizances; a list of the witnesses; a statement of the expenses and the appearance of the attorney for the defendant, if any is entered; the waiver of the right to be proceeded against by indictment, if any is executed; the pretrial conference report, if any has been filed; and the report of the department of mental health as to the mental condition of the defendant, if such report has been filed under the provisions of the General Laws.

(e) Indictment after Waiver. Notwithstanding the defendant's waiver of the right to be proceeded against by indictment, the prosecuting attorney may proceed by indictment.

(f) Probable Cause Hearing. Defendants charged in a District Court with an offense as to which they have the right to be proceeded against by indictment and defendants charged in a District Court with an offense within the concurrent jurisdiction of the District and Superior Courts for which the District Court will not retain jurisdiction, have the right to a probable cause hearing, unless an indictment has been returned for the same offense. If the District Court finds that there is probable cause to believe that the defendant committed the crime or crimes alleged in the complaint, the court shall bind the defendant over to the Superior Court. If the

District Court finds that there is no probable cause to believe that the defendant committed the crime or crimes alleged in the complaint, the court shall dismiss the complaint.

(g) The Complaint Process.

(1) *Procedure for Obtaining a Complaint.* Any person having knowledge, whether first hand or not, of the facts constituting the offense for which the complaint is sought may be a complainant. The complainant shall convey to the court the facts constituting the basis for the complaint. The complainant's account shall be either reduced to writing or recorded. The complainant shall sign the complaint under oath, before an appropriate judicial officer.

(2) *Probable Cause Requirement.* The appropriate judicial officer shall not authorize a complaint unless the information presented by the complainant establishes probable cause to believe that the person against whom the complaint is sought committed an offense.

Amended March 8, 2004, effective September 7, 2004.

Reporter's Notes—Revised, 2004

WHILE DRAWN IN PART FROM THE GENERAL LAWS AND INCORPORATING MANY PROCEDURES DICTATED BY THE CASE LAW OF THE COMMONWEALTH, RULE 3 ALTERS PRESENT PRACTICE IN SOME RESPECTS. AS ORIGINALLY PROMULGATED IN 1979, RULE 3 WAS DESIGNED TO FORCE ALL NONCAPITAL DEFENDANTS IN THE DISTRICT COURT WHO HAD A RIGHT TO AN INDICTMENT TO MAKE AN ELECTION BETWEEN HAVING THEIR CASES CONSIDERED BY A GRAND JURY OR OBTAINING A PROBABLE CAUSE HEARING. THIS "FORCED WAIVER" PROVISION WAS RARELY USED IN PRACTICE BECAUSE OF CONCERNS THAT IT WOULD INFRINGE ON A DEFENDANT'S CONSTITUTIONAL RIGHT TO INDICTMENT AND STATUTORY RIGHT TO A PROBABLE CAUSE HEARING. A 2004 AMENDMENT TO THE RULE ELIMINATED THE "FORCED WAIVER" PROVISION. THE RATIONALE FOR THE "FORCED WAIVER" PROVISION WAS BASED ON A CONCERN FOR EFFICIENCY. HOWEVER, EVEN WITHOUT FORCING A DEFENDANT TO CHOOSE BETWEEN A PROBABLE CAUSE HEARING AND AN INDICTMENT, THE PROSECUTOR CAN PREVENT UNNECESSARY DUPLICATION OF PROCEDURE SIMPLY BY INDICTING THE DEFENDANT PRIOR TO THE PROBABLE CAUSE HEARING. IF IT IS INEFFICIENT TO HAVE A PROBABLE CAUSE HEARING, THE PROSECUTOR IS IN THE BEST POSITION TO RECOGNIZE THAT FACT AND TO TAKE THE STEPS NECESSARY TO AVOID IT. THE 2004 AMENDMENT ALSO ELIMINATED A REFERENCE TO JUVENILE PROCEDURE MADE IRRELEVANT BY STATUTE AND ADDED PROVISIONS DESCRIBING THE COMPLAINT PROCESS.

Subdivision (a). This subdivision in part restates G.L. c. 263, § 4. Approximate parallels may be found in Rules of Criminal Procedure (ULA) Rule 23(a) (1974); ALI Model Code of Pre–Arraignment Procedure §§ 330.1(3), 340.1(2) (POD 1975).

General Laws c. 263, § 4 provides that "[n]o person shall be held to answer in any court for an alleged crime, except upon an indictment by a grand jury or upon a complaint before a district court ..." It is only the issuance of a complaint or an indictment that begins the criminal process, initiates a defendant's right to counsel under the Sixth Amendment to the United States Constitution, and tolls the statute of limitations. See Commonwealth v. Valchuis, 40 Mass. App. Ct. 556, 560 (1996) (statute of limitations not tolled by application for complaint or citation, but by complaint itself).

The District Courts are empowered by G.L. c. 218, § 32, to "receive complaints and issue warrants and other processes for the apprehen-

sion of persons charged with crime ..." and pursuant to G.L. c. 218, § 30, shall bind over for trial in the Superior Court defendants who appear to be guilty of crimes not within their final jurisdiction, and may bind over defendants appearing guilty of crimes within their final jurisdiction. Where the charge is by complaint and the accused is under arrest not having been indicted by grand jury, he is entitled "as soon as may be" to a probable cause hearing to determine whether he should be held for trial. G.L. c. 276, § 38.

Subdivision (b). This subdivision in large part restates the essentials of prior practice. The right to indictment is not mentioned in the Constitution of the Commonwealth. It was not until 1857 that the Supreme Judicial Court defined that right, holding that "punishment in the state prison is an infamous punishment, and cannot be imposed without ... indictment ..." Jones v Robbins, 74 Mass. (8 Gray) 329, 349 (1857). Therefore, subdivision (b) affords the right to be proceeded against by indictment to "a defendant charged with an offense punishable by imprisonment in state prison ...," that is, Massachusetts Correctional Institution, Cedar Junction. G.L. c. 125, § 1(o). The right to indictment is not extended to defendants charged with a crime within the concurrent jurisdiction of the District and Superior Courts if the District Court retains jurisdiction. Section 27 of chapter 218 of the General Laws provides in part:

> [District Courts] may impose the same penalties as the superior court for all crimes of which they have jurisdiction, except that they may not impose a sentence to state prison.

General Laws c. 279, § 23 states that "[n]o sentence of a male convict to imprisonment or confinement for more than two and one half years shall be executed in any jail or house of correction." General Laws c. 218, §§ 26—27 and c. 279, § 23, when construed together, have led to the settled practice of the District Court, although having jurisdiction of felonies punishable by less than five years at Cedar Junction, sentencing to a jail or house of correction for not more than two and one half years.

Because a defendant tried in District Court is not subject to a sentence to state prison, there is no right to be proceeded against by indictment.

Subdivision (c) (1) While intended to secure a benefit to the accused, a grand jury indictment is but the formal accusation or presentation of charges against the accused, see Commonwealth v. Woodward, 157 Mass. 516, 518 (1893), and may be waived. See DeGolyer v. Commonwealth, 314 Mass. 626, 632–33 (1943); e.g. Commonwealth v. Thurston, 419 Mass. 101 (1994). Statutory authorization for such waiver in instances of defendants committed or bound over to the Superior Court for trial was found in former G.L. c. 263, § 4A (St 1934, c 358).

A defendant who is bound over to the Superior Court after a finding of probable cause has the right to indictment and the right to waive indictment. However, a defendant charged with a capital crime cannot waive indictment. G.L. c. 263, § 4A (as amended).

If after a waiver of indictment, probable cause is found to bind the defendant over for trial, G.L. c. 218, § 30, the Superior Court shall have as full jurisdiction over the case on the complaint as if an indictment has been found. See DeGolyer v. Commonwealth, 314 Mass. 626, 632 (1943).

(c) (2) Under the original version of the provision now contained in Rule 3 (c), the judge was required to advise a defendant who had a right to an indictment that he or she might waive indictment and proceed upon the complaint. In the 2004 revision of the rule, the elimination of the "forced waiver" provision made it unnecessary to require that a defendant receive such a warning. The right to waive indictment remains, however, except in a capital case where the General Laws prohibit it. See G.L. c. 263, § 4A. The defendant may exercise the option to waive indictment in the District Court, before being bound over, or afterward, in Superior Court. In either event, the approval of the judge is not necessary, although the court must ensure that the waiver is valid. This means that it must be intelligent and voluntary, *see* DeGolyer v. Commonwealth, 314 Mass. 626, 632 (1943), and that the defendant either has counsel or has waived the right to the assistance of counsel. The waiver must be in writing.

A juvenile who would otherwise be entitled to an indictment by virtue of G.L. c. 263 § 4 may also waive indictment under the procedure established in this subdivision.

Subdivision (d) This subdivision was formerly Rule 3(c)(2) prior to the revision of the Rule in 2004. It generally governs the transmission of the papers in the case after a defendant is bound over to the Superior Court. It is implicit in the rule that the defendant may waive the probable cause hearing to which he or she is entitled thereby proceeding immediately to the Superior Court upon the complaint. *E.g.* Commonwealth v. Tanso, 411 Mass. 640 (1992). Subdivision (d) provides for that contingency.

Subdivision (e). If the defendant waives indictment and probable cause is found the case moves immediately to the Superior Court for trial or other disposition unless the Commonwealth chooses to seek an indictment. The prosecution may wish to so proceed because of defects in the complaint, because there are other chargeable crimes— e.g., related offenses arising out of the same criminal episode—or to avail itself of the investigative power of the grand jury.

The prosecutor also has the option of obtaining an indictment in cases where the defendant does not have the right to one and the District Court would otherwise exercise final jurisdiction over the offense. So long as the District Court has not already placed the defendant in jeopardy, *cf.* Commonwealth v. Aldrich, 21 Mass. App. Ct. 221 (1985) (indictment barred by jeopardy where defendant pled guilty to complaint in District Court), the return of an indictment for the same offense as alleged in a complaint is ordinarily sufficient reason for the court to dismiss the complaint. *Compare* Commonwealth v. Burt, 393 Mass. 703 (1985) (judge acted properly in dismissing complaint upon return of indictment) *with* Commonwealth v. Raposa, 386 Mass. 666 (1982) (where judge refused to dismiss complaint upon return of indictment, it was proper for prosecutor to nolle prosequi). The prosecutor should not abuse this power however, such as by waiting until the day of trial to obtain an indictment, *see Raposa*, 386 Mass. at 669 n. 8 ("We would not look with favor, however, on a prosecutor's deliberate obstruction of the criminal process and waste of judicial resources by waiting until the day of trial in the District Court to seek indictments."), or by removing a case to Superior Court to avoid having to comply with a District Court order denying a continuance, *see* Commonwealth v. Thomas, 353 Mass. 429 (1967).

Subdivision (f). This subdivision was added by amendment in 2004.

Defendants whose cases are going to be ultimately disposed of in Superior Court, either because the District Court lacks or declines jurisdiction, are entitled to a probable cause hearing unless the prosecutor obtains an indictment for the same offense charged in the complaint. The return of an indictment constitutes a finding of probable cause and ordinarily renders unnecessary a probable cause hearing. *See* Lataille v District Court of Eastern Hampden, 366 Mass. 525, 531 (1974). There may be circumstances, however, where the prosecutor's bad faith in obtaining an indictment entitles the defendant to a probable cause hearing in any event. *Cf.* Hadfield v. Commonwealth, 387 Mass. 252, 257 (1982) (*dicta*) (circumventing probable cause hearing may be invalid where "effrontery to district court," "obstruction of criminal process," or "waste of judicial resources."); Commonwealth v. Spann, 383 Mass. 142, 145 (1981) (if prosecutor promised that defendant would not be indicted before a probable cause hearing and if defendant relied on promise to his detriment, promise would be enforced); Lataille v. District Court of Eastern Hampden, 366 Mass. 525, 531 n. 6 (1974) (agreement between counsel might entitle defendant to further pursuit of probable cause hearing which was in progress at time of indictment). Absent these unusual circumstances, however, the ordinary course of events after an indictment has been returned is for the District Court to dismiss the complaint, or for the prosecutor to enter a nolle prosequi, once the defendant has been arraigned in the Superior Court.

If an indictment has not already been returned, a defendant charged with a crime not within the jurisdiction of the District Court must be given a probable cause hearing "as soon as may be." See G.L. c. 276, § 38. The policy underlying this subdivision looks to liberal granting of continuances to the prosecution in order that indictments may be sought in cases that are scheduled for a probable cause hearing.

Even if the complaint charges a defendant with a crime within the jurisdiction of the District Court (which includes misdemeanors for which there would otherwise be no right to an indictment) the court may hold a probable cause hearing, *see* G.L. c. 218 § 30, if the judge in the exercise of discretion determines that the interest of justice would be served by having the Superior Court dispose of the defendant's case. This would typically be the case either to allow the consolidation of cases or in recognition of the exclusive power of the Superior Court to sentence defendants charged with a concurrent jurisdiction felony to state prison. *Cf.* Commonwealth v. Zannino, 17 Mass. App. Ct. 73, 79 (1983) (the power to exercise jurisdiction or to bind the defendant over for trial in the Superior Court "is not to be used arbitrarily, but in view of the circumstances of each particular case"). While it is ordinarily the prosecutor who institutes a request that a matter within the District Court's jurisdiction be treated as a probable cause matter rather than a trial on the merits, the ultimate decision is the judge's. *See* Commonwealth v. Zannino, 17 Mass. App. Ct. 73, 78–79 (1983) ("if the crime charged is within the final jurisdiction of the District Court, the threshold decision whether to conduct a full trial on the merits or only a probable cause hearing is, at least ordinarily, a question for the judge and not the prosecutor").

If a case is within the final jurisdiction of the District Court, the judge must announce that the court is going to decline jurisdiction prior to hearing sworn testimony from any witnesses, which is when jeopardy would otherwise attach in a non-jury trial. *See* Commonwealth v. DeFuria, 400 Mass. 485, 487 (1987); Crist v. Bretz, 437 U.S. 28, 37 n.15 (1978). If the court does not make a clear announcement that it is declining jurisdiction, any hearing that follows at which sworn testimony is received will be considered as a trial on the merits at which jeopardy has attached. *See* Commonwealth v. Clemmons, 370 Mass. 288, 291 n.2 (1976); Corey v. Commonwealth, 364 Mass. 137, 142 n. 7 (1973). *Compare* Commonwealth v. Crosby, 6 Mass. App. Ct. 679 (1978) (since judge failed to announce that he was declining jurisdiction prior to hearing sworn testimony offered in the course of an admission to sufficient facts, the proceedings constituted a trial on the merits and jeopardy barred the defendant's indictment) *with* Commonwealth v. DeFuria, 400 Mass. 485 (1987) (judge's failure to announce declination of jurisdiction prior to prosecutor's recitation of facts at an admission to sufficient findings did not bar further prosecution since no sworn testimony taken). *Cf.* Commonwealth v. Mesrobian, 10 Mass. App. Ct. 355, 356 n. 2 (1980) ("fundamental fairness dictates that the Commonwealth ought to be required to state unequivocally at the outset of the hearing its intention [to proceed on the basis of probable cause rather than a trial on the merits]"). Since defense strategy at a probable cause hearing differs significantly from that at a trial, the judge should provide notice to the defendant of the decision to decline jurisdiction as far in advance of the hearing as possible. The District Court rules promulgated on January 1, 1996 contemplate that the pretrial hearing is the appropriate stage at which to make the decision. District/Municipal Courts Rules of Criminal Procedure, Rule 4(f).

Whether a probable cause hearing concerns an offense outside the jurisdiction of the District Court or results from a decision of the court to decline jurisdiction over an offense for which it could have held a trial, the standard that the court should apply at the probable cause hearing to determine whether to bind the case over to the Superior Court is the same. It is the test a trial judge uses to determine a motion for a required finding of not guilty. *See* Myers v. Commonwealth, 363 Mass. 843, 850 (1973) ("The examining magistrate should view the case as if it were a trial and he were required to rule on whether there is enough credible evidence to send the case to the jury. Thus, the magistrate should dismiss the complaint when, on the evidence presented, a trial court would be bound to acquit as a matter of law.") This standard is more stringent than the one that governs the grand jury's determination. *See* Commonwealth v. McCarthy, 385 Mass. 160, 163 (1982) (an indictment cannot stand unless, at a minimum, it is supported by evidence sufficient to establish probable cause to arrest); Commonwealth v. O'Dell, 392 Mass. 445, 451–52 (1984) (grand jury requirement of sufficient evidence to establish the identity of the accused and probable cause to arrest him is considerably less exacting than a requirement of sufficient evidence to warrant a guilty finding).

At a probable cause hearing, the defendant must be given a meaningful opportunity to cross-examine witnesses and present evidence on his or her own behalf to assure an accurate appraisal of probable cause. *See* Myers v Commonwealth, 363 Mass. 843 (1973); Corey v Commonwealth, 364 Mass. 137 (1973). Following the lead of the United States Supreme Court in Coleman v Alabama, 399 U.S. 1 (1970), the Supreme Judicial Court held that a probable cause hearing is such a critical stage in criminal proceedings as to require the assistance of counsel. *See* Commonwealth v Britt, 362 Mass. 325 (1972). The rules of evidence at a probable cause hearing should in general be the same as are applicable at a trial, that is, a finding of probable cause to hold the defendant for trial "must be based on competent testimony which would be admissible at trial." Myers v Commonwealth, *supra* at 849 n 6. Further, the defendant may have the proceedings taken by a stenographer at his or her own expense, *see* G.L. c. 221, § 91B; Commonwealth v. Shea, 356 Mass. 358, 360—61 (1969); Commonwealth v. Britt, 362 Mass. 325, 328—29 (1972) and the transcript is admissible in subsequent proceedings when otherwise competent. *See* G L c 221, § 91B, c 233, § 80; Commonwealth v. DiDietro, 373 Mass. 369 (1977).

If the evidence meets the appropriate standard and the case is bound over to Superior Court, the District Court retains jurisdiction to rule on ancillary matters until an indictment is returned. *See* Commonwealth v. Tanso, 411 Mass. 640, 644 (1992). If the evidence presented at the probable cause hearing does not meet the appropriate standard, the complaint should be dismissed. *See* Commonwealth v. Ortiz, 393 Mass. 523, 524 (1984). Since jeopardy does not attach at a probable cause hearing, *see* Commonwealth v. Scala, 380 Mass. 500, 505 n. 3 (1980), nor is a finding of no probable cause subject to appeal, a District Court's dismissal based on a failure of the evidence to meet the standard does not bar a further proceedings, either by way of a subsequent indictment for the same offense, *see* Commonwealth v. Juvenile, 409 Mass. 49, 52 (1991); Burke v Commonwealth, 373 Mass. 157, 160 (1977), or holding another probable cause hearing based on a new complaint, *see* Juvenile v. Commonwealth, 375 Mass. 104, 106 (1978) ("Additional probable cause hearings may be held, especially if additional evidence is to be offered at the subsequent hearing."). However, if the institution of further proceedings constitutes harassment, the defendant is entitled to relief. *See* Juvenile v. Commonwealth, 375 Mass. 104, 106 n. 1 (1978); Maldonado, petitioner, 364 Mass. 359, 364–365 (1973).

Subdivision (g) (1). This subdivision and the one following were added to Rule 3 by a 2004 amendment.

The General Laws identify the appropriate judicial officers who play a role in the process of authorizing the issuance of a criminal complaint and administering the oath. *See e.g.,* General Laws c. 218 § 7 (justices and special justices may administer oaths); c. 218 § 10A (deputy assistant clerks may administer oath); c. 218 § 33 (clerks, assistant clerks, temporary clerks, and temporary assistant clerks may receive complaints and administer the oath); c. 218 § 35 (justice or special justice may receive complaints); c. 218 § 37 (justices, special justices, clerks, assistant clerks, temporary clerks and temporary assistant clerks may issue process resulting from a hearing upon an application for a complaint).

General Laws c. 276, § 22 provides that a complainant is to be examined "on oath" and that the complaint is to be "subscribed by the complainant." The preferred procedure is to administer the oath to the complainant before he or she makes the statements which will serve as the basis for the complaint, but a complaint is still valid if the complainant swears to the truth of statements tendered to the appropriate judicial official after they have been made. *See* Commonwealth v. Cote, 15 Mass. App. Ct. 229, 236 (1983). There is no requirement that the statements offered in support of the issuance of a complaint be based on personal knowledge or observation. A complainant may properly present statements of which he or she has no first-hand knowledge. *See* Commonwealth v. Dillane, 77 Mass. (11 Gray) 67 (1858); Commonwealth v. Cote, 15 Mass. App. Ct. 229 (1983). Nor does a complainant have to have a personal stake in the matter. *See* Commonwealth v. Haddad, 364 Mass. 795, 797 (1974) ("anyone may make a criminal complaint in a District Court who is competent to make oath to it.") The practice in many courts where a single officer applies for complaints for offenses of which the officer has no first-hand knowledge is not only appropriate, but a sound administrative procedure. *Cf.* District Court Standards of Judicial Practice, THE COMPLAINT PROCEDURE, standard 3:23, commentary at 41–42 (1975). Rule 3(g) (1) authorizes the signing of the complaint by persons other than the arresting officer in order to avoid requiring the officer's presence at any time prior to the probable cause hearing or trial. The subdivision is grounded in the desire to avoid removing an officer from a regular work shift to execute the mere formality of personally signing the complaint.

The person against whom a complaint is sought does not have a right to be present at the procedure described in this subdivision. *See* Commonwealth v. Smallwood, 379 Mass. 878 (1980). However, in cases where no arrest has been made and all of the offenses the complainant seeks are misdemeanors, *see* Commonwealth v. Cote, *supra*, 15 Mass. App. Ct. at 235, as well as in certain felony cases, G.L. c. 218 § 35A provides for notice and a hearing before a complaint is authorized, subject to exceptions where there is a risk of bodily injury, commission of a crime, or flight from the jurisdiction.

"The implicit purpose of the § 35A hearings is to enable the court clerk to screen a variety of minor criminal or potentially criminal matters out of the criminal justice system through a combination of counseling, discussion, or threat of prosecution ..." Snyder, Crime and Community Mediation — The Boston Experience: A Preliminary Report on the Dorchester Urban Court Program, 1978 Wis. L. Rev. 737, 746 *quoted with approval* in Gordon v. Fay, 382 Mass. 64, 69–70 (1980).

This subdivision changes existing practice by requiring that in all cases, the facts on which a complaint is based either be submitted in writing or, in the discretion of the appropriate judicial official, conveyed orally so long as the oral statement is transcribed or otherwise recorded. The facts on which the complaint is based may be memorialized in any of the following three ways. First is a written statement submitted by the complainant. The written account of the facts can come from a police report, from a motor vehicle citation, *see* G.L. c. 90C § 3(B)(2), from a statement memorialized on the form for an application for a complaint promulgated by the District Courts, *see* District/Municipal Courts Rules of Criminal Procedure, Rule 2 (effective Jan. 1, 1996), or from any other written source. Second is a written statement made by the appropriate judicial official based on information conveyed by the complainant. And third is to record an oral statement by the complainant. Nothing in this subsection is intended to require the recording of hearings under G.L. c. 218 § 35A.

A number of other jurisdictions follow the practice of requiring the basis for a criminal complaint to be memorialized. *See* Fed. Rules Crim. Pro., Rules 3 & 4; Colo. Rules Crim. Pro., Rule 4(a); Minn. Rules Crim. Pro., Rule 2.01; R.I. Rules Crim. Pro., Rule 3. The purpose of this requirement is twofold. First, requiring a record of the facts presented to the court will protect the integrity of the complaint process. And second, in those cases where a defendant has the right to litigate the basis on which a complaint was issued, *see e.g.,* Commonwealth v. DiBennadetto, 436 Mass. 310 (2002), the existence of a record will facilitate judicial review.

(g) (2). This subdivision changes the existing practice concerning the authorization of criminal complaints in some cases. Under prior practice, where a complaint was sought against an individual who had been arrested, the appropriate judicial officer did not evaluate the justification for initiating criminal proceedings. It was only if the complainant applied for process to issue, either a summons or warrant, that a determination of probable cause was necessary. STANDARDS OF JUDICIAL PRACTICE: THE COMPLAINT PROCEDURE, 2:03, Administrative Office of the District Courts (1975). Under this subdivision, a finding of probable cause must be made for all cases, whether the defendant has been arrested or not. In requiring a probable cause determination in every case, this subdivision follows the federal model, see Fed. Rules Crim. Pro., 4(a) & 5(a), and that of a number of other states, e.g., Conn. Practice Book, § 617; Minn. Rules Crim. Pro., Rule 2.01; N.J. Rules Crim. Pro., Rule 3:4–1(a).

The consequence, if any, of the failure of the record in a particular case to demonstrate probable cause is a matter that the rule does not address. The Supreme Judicial Court, in Commonwealth v. DiBennadetto, supra at 313, has held, however, that where a complaint was authorized after a § 35A hearing, "the issuance of [the] complaint … is not to be revisited by a further show cause hearing; the defendant's remedy is a motion to dismiss."

The purpose of a probable cause determination prior to the authorization of a complaint is to screen out cases that do not belong in the criminal justice system at the earliest possible stage. The standard of probable cause to authorize a complaint is the same as the standard that governs the grand jury's decision to issue an indictment. "[A]t the very least the grand jury must hear sufficient evidence to establish the identity of the accused … and probable cause to arrest him." Commonwealth v. O'Dell, 392 Mass. 445, 450 (1984), quoting Commonwealth v. McCarthy, 385 Mass. 160, 163 (1982). As in the grand jury or arrest context, the probable cause determination at this stage of the process may be based on hearsay. All that is required is "reasonably trustworthy information … sufficient to warrant a prudent man in believing that the defendant had committed … an offense," O'Dell, 385 Mass. at 450 *. This standard is considerably less exacting than the one that a judge must apply at a probable cause hearing under subdivision (f). Id. at 451. If a case cannot even meet the standard necessary under subdivision (g), it would be a waste of judicial resources and an unnecessary burden on the individual for the case to move any further in the process.

This subsection does not alter existing case law that gives courts in circumstances where a private citizen is a complainant, the power to refuse to issue a complaint even though there is probable cause to do so. See Victory Distributors v. Ayer Division of the District Court Dept., 435 Mass. 136 (2001). Where the Commonwealth seeks a complaint, however, the court must issue it so long as it is legally valid. Id. Although there is no explicit provision in the Rules of Criminal Procedure for the process that follows from an initial denial of an application for a complaint, the Supreme Judicial Court has held that judges have inherent authority to rehear such applications. See Bradford v. Knights, 427 Mass. 748 (1998).

* Probably should be 392 Mass. at 450.

Rule 3.1. Determination of Probable Cause for Detention

[Text of rule applicable to cases initiated (by indictment or complaint) on or after September 7, 2004.]

(a) No person shall be held in custody more than twenty-four hours following an arrest, absent exigent circumstances, unless:

(i) a warrant or other judicial process authorizes the person's detention,

(ii) a complaint has been authorized under Rule 3 (g), or

(iii) a determination of probable cause for detention has been made pursuant to subsection (b).

(b) A determination of probable cause for detention shall be made by an appropriate judicial officer. The appropriate officer shall consider any information presented by the police, whether or not known at the time of arrest. The police shall present the information under oath or affirmation, or under the pains and penalties of perjury. The police may present the information orally, in person or by any other means, or in writing. If presented in writing, the information may be transmitted to the appropriate judicial officer by facsimile transmission or by electronic mail or by such other electronic means as may be found acceptable by the court. The determination of probable cause for detention shall be an ex parte proceeding. The person arrested has no right to appear, either in person or by counsel.

(c) Where subsection (a) requires a determination of probable cause for detention, the police shall present the information necessary to obtain such determination to the appropriate judicial officer as soon as reasonably possible after the arrest, but no later than twenty-four hours after arrest, absent exigent circumstances.

(d) The judicial officer shall promptly reduce to writing his or her determination as to probable cause and notify the police. A copy of the written determination shall be transmitted to the police, by facsimile transmission or other means, as soon as possible.

(e) The judicial officer shall apply the same standard in making the determination of probable cause for detention as in deciding whether an arrest warrant should issue. If the judicial officer determines that there is probable cause to believe the person arrested committed an offense, the judicial officer shall make a written determination of his or her decision which shall be filed with the record of the case together with all the written information submitted by the police.

(f) If there is no probable cause to believe that the person arrested committed an offense, the judicial officer shall order the person's prompt release from custody. The order and a written determination of the judicial officer shall be filed in the District Court having jurisdiction over the location of the arrest, together with all the written information submitted by the police. These documents shall be filed separately from the records of criminal and delinquency cases, but shall be public records.

Added March 8, 2004, effective September 7, 2004.

Reporter's Notes—Revised, 2004

Rule 3.1 was added in 2004 to implement the requirements described by the Supreme Judicial Court in Jenkins v. Chief Justice of the District Court Department, 415 Mass. 221 (1993), dealing with the topic of obtaining a judicial determination of probable cause for persons held in custody after a warrantless arrest. It is based on the procedure promulgated in 1994 by Trial Court Rule XI. The only major substantive change that Rule 3.1 makes in the procedure dictated by Trial Court Rule XI is in the standard to use in determining if the custody of the individual is lawful. Trial Court Rule XI directed the "judicial officer [to determine whether] … there is probable cause to believe that such arrestee committed one or more of the offenses for which he or she was arrested." Rule 3.1 directs the judicial officer to determine if "there is probable cause to believe the person arrested committed an offense." The language of Rule 3.1 more accurately focuses on the appropriate issue that is crucial to the question of the legality of an individual's detention prior to being brought to court.

Subdivision (a) In *Jenkins*, the Court held that Article 14 of the Declaration of Rights requires the police to obtain a judicial determination of probable cause as soon as reasonably possible after they have made a warrantless arrest, which in the usual circumstances means no more than twenty-four hours. This subdivision identifies the only four exceptions to the police following the procedure that the balance of Rule 3.1 establishes. One is when the arrestee will not be held more than twenty-four hours. For example, if the police have arrested someone who is going to be bailed at the police station within twenty-hours, Rule 3.1 is not applicable. Another is when the arrest was based on process issued by a judicial officer, such as an arrest warrant, or when process exists which authorizes the detention of an arrestee on another charge. In the former circumstance, the police are merely executing a judicial order rather than making an independent judgment to deprive someone of their liberty. In the latter circumstance, where for example the police arrest someone without a warrant and then discover that there is a pre-existing outstanding warrant for the arrestee, there is already judicial authorization to deprive the arrestee of his or her liberty. The third is when a complaint charging the arrestee with a crime has already been authorized under Rule 3(g), which independently requires a judicial officer to make the same sort of probable cause determination as Rule 3.1 contemplates. Last is when exigent circumstances exist which make it not possible to obtain judicial approval for an extended deprivation of the arrestee's liberty.

Subdivision (b) This subsection describes the procedure for a determination of probable cause for detention after a warrantless arrest. It requires the police to present the information that supports a deprivation of an arrestee's liberty to an appropriate judicial officer. These officials include judges and those individuals in the clerk-magistrate's office who are empowered to authorize complaints. *See* Reporters' Notes to Rule 3(g); G.L. c. 218 § 33. The Court held in *Jenkins*, 416 Mass. at 337–38 that:

> like the issuance of a warrant, the postarrest determination need not necessarily be made by a judge. *See* Commonwealth v. Smallwood, 379 Mass. 878, 885, 401 N.E.2d 802 (1980) ("While District Court judges are authorized to receive complaints and issue warrants, G. L. c. 218, § 32, a clerk or assistant clerk may also receive complaints, administer the required oath, and issue warrants in the name of the court. G. L. c. 218, § 33. Commonwealth v. Penta, 352 Mass. 271, 273, 225 N.E.2d 58 [1967]").

The police may present the appropriate judicial officer with the information providing probable cause for the arrestee's detention in writing or orally. This subdivision contemplates that the medium of providing the information be as flexible as possible. Physical submission of a written report, faxed copies or e-mail are all appropriate, as are telephone conversations. No matter how the police submit the information, however, it should be sworn to under oath or affirmation. The arrestee has no right to appear or participate at this proceeding, either in person or through counsel. *See Jenkins*, 416 Mass. at 244–45.

Subdivision (c) This subsection directs the police to present the information justifying the detention of an arrestee's liberty within twenty-four hours of the arrest, unless there are exigent circumstances. The exception for exigent circumstances addresses situations such as communication failures and natural disasters and not exigencies that relate solely to the investigative needs of the police.

Subdivision (d) This subsection incorporates essentially the same requirement for reducing the results of a determination of probable cause for detention to writing and transmitting it to the police as contained in Trial Court Rule XI(e).

Subdivision (e) This subdivision deals with the standard that governs the determination of probable cause for detention and the consequence of an affirmative finding. As to the first of these issues, the subdivision addresses two questions: what the standard should be and the issues to which the standard should be applied. The Court in *Jenkins* held that the Declaration of Rights requires a postarrest determination of probable cause to be "governed by the same legal standards as apply to the issuance of a warrant." *Jenkins*, 416 Mass. at 239. Rule 3.1 follows Trial Court Rule XI (b), in adopting this same familiar standard as the measure of whether further detention of an arrestee is warranted. However, the subdivision differs from Trial Court Rule XI (b) in the question of what issues must meet this standard. The Trial Court Rule focused on whether the individual committed one or more of the offenses for which he or she was arrested. This subdivision focuses on whether there is probable cause to believe individual committed any offense.

The procedure that Rule 3.1 addresses is directed to the question of probable cause for the arrestee's detention, not whether probable cause existed to justify the person's arrest. Given the nature of the determination, the legality of the arrestee's detention should not depend on the ability of the police accurately to identify the precise offense for which the person should be held. For example, it is sometimes the case that police with probable cause to arrest someone for a particular crime put down the wrong offense on the documents they fill out afterwards. Under the language of Trial Court Rule XI (d), such a person would have to be released despite clear probable cause to charge him or her with the correct crime. Under Rule 3.1, the police could detain such an individual and charge him or her with the appropriate offense. The approach that Rule 3.1 takes to this issue is similar to the rules of other jurisdictions. *See* Fla. R. Crim. Pro., Rule 3.133(a)(3); Me. R. Crim. Pro., Rule 5(d); Minn. R. Crim. Pro., Rule 4.03.

The subdivision also addresses the issue of the consequence of a determination that there exists probable cause for detention. If probable cause exits, a written finding together with the supporting documents are to be filed with the record of the case. A defendant does not have the right to have the probable cause determination reviewed at arraignment. By the time a defendant subject to the process described in Rule 3.1 is arraigned, a judicial officer not only will have made a determination of probable cause for detention, but also a determination pursuant to Rule 3(g) that probable cause exists for each of the offenses with which the defendant has been charged. There is no need for a judge at arraignment routinely to reconsider the matter of probable cause.

Subdivision (f) This subdivision deals with the issue of the consequence of a determination that there does not exist probable cause for detention. It is essentially the same in this regard as Trial Court Rule XI (e)(3).

Rule 4.   Form and Contents of Complaint or Indictment; Amendment

(Applicable to District Court and Superior Court)

(a) Contents of Indictment or Complaint. An indictment and a complaint shall contain a caption as provided by law, together with a plain, concise description of the act which constitutes the crime or an appropriate legal term descriptive thereof.

(b) Subscription of Application for Issuance of Process. An application for issuance of process may be subscribed by the arresting officer, the police chief, or any police officer within the jurisdiction of a crime, a prosecutor, or a private person.

(c) Indictment Based Upon Secondary Evidence. An indictment shall not be dismissed on the grounds that the evidence presented before the grand jury consisted in whole or in part of the record from the defendant's probable cause hearing or that other hearsay evidence was presented before the grand jury.

(d) Amendment. Upon his own motion or the written motion of either party, a judge may allow amendment of the form of a complaint or indictment if such amendment would not prejudice the defendant or the Commonwealth.

Reporter's Notes

Subdivision (a). Rule 4(a) is a restatement of Massachusetts statutory law. A caption is required for indictments and complaints by G.L. c. 277, §§ 17, 79. See 30 MASS.PRACTICE SERIES (Smith) § 342 (1970). Although the indictment or complaint may contain more than one count (see Mass.R.Crim.P. 9[a][2], [b]), a single caption is sufficient. G.L. c. 277, §§ 17, 79.

The statement of the charges can be in the form of a description of the criminal act or in the form of a legal term descriptive of the act. "The words used in a statute to define a crime, or other words conveying the same meaning, may be used." G.L. c. 277, § 17. An indictment or complaint must, however, set forth all the elements of the crime charged and if a statute does not contain all those elements, an indictment or complaint drawn in terms of that statute is insufficient. G.L. c. 277, § 17; Commonwealth v. Palladino, 358 Mass. 28, 260 N.E.2d 653 (1970). The forms established by G.L. c. 277, § 79 contain sufficient descriptions of the crimes listed therein.

To survive a motion to dismiss, an indictment (together with a bill of particulars, if any. See Rule [13][b]) must describe the offense charged "'fully, plainly, substantially and formally,' with as much certainty as the known circumstances of the case . . . [will] permit." Commonwealth v. Soule, 6 Mass.App. 973, 384 N.E.2d 235 (1979) 69 (Rescript). *Accord* Commonwealth v. Burke, 339 Mass. 521, 523, 159 N.E.2d 856, 77 A.L.R.2d 451 (1959); Commonwealth v. Gill, 5 Mass. App. 337, 363 N.E.2d 267 (1977).

Subdivision (b). General Laws c. 276, § 22 provides that a complainant is to be examined "on oath" and that the complaint is to be "subscribed by the complainant." While this requirement has been strictly construed, Commonwealth v. Barhight, 75 Mass. (9 Gray) 113 (1857), there is no requirement that the statements offered in support of the issuance of process be based on personal knowledge or observation. A complainant may properly present statements of which he has no first-hand knowledge. Commonwealth v. Dillane, 77 Mass. (11 Gray) 67 (1858). The practice in many courts where a single officer presents applications for issuance of process for offenses of which he has no first-hand knowledge is not only appropriate, but a sound administrative procedure. District Court Standards of Judicial Practice, THE COMPLAINT PROCEDURE, standard 3:23, commentary at 41–42 (1975). Rule 4(b) authorizes the signing of the complaint by persons other than the arresting officer in order to avoid requiring the officer's presence at any time prior to the probable cause hearing or trial. The subdivision is grounded in the desire to avoid removing an officer from his regular work shift to execute the mere formality of personally signing the complaint.

Subdivision (c). This subdivision of the rule refers to hearsay and other types of evidence which may be inadmissible at trial, but may properly be considered by a grand jury. Commonwealth v. Gibson, 368 Mass. 518, 333 N.E.2d 400 (1975), reaffirmed the long-recognized rule in the Commonwealth that evidence which is not legally competent at trial is sufficient upon which to base an indictment, and that an indictment which is in fact based exclusively upon hearsay will not be invalidated at trial for that reason. Commonwealth v. Woodward, 157 Mass. 516 (1893); Commonwealth v. Walsh, 255 Mass. 317, 151 N.E. 300 (1926); Commonwealth v. Ventura, 294 Mass. 113, 1 N.E.2d 30 (1936); Commonwealth v. Lammi, 310 Mass. 159, 37 N.E.2d 250 (1941); Commonwealth v. Geagan, 339 Mass. 487, 159 N.E.2d 870 (1959), cert. denied, 80 S.Ct. 200, 361 U.S. 895, 4 L.Ed.2d 152;

Commonwealth v. Monahan, 349 Mass. 139, 207 N.E.2d 29 (1965); Commonwealth v. Beneficial Finance Co., 360 Mass. 188, 275 N.E.2d 33, 52 A.L.R.3d 1143 (1971).

The United States Supreme Court, in Costello v. United States, 76 S.Ct. 406, 350 U.S. 359, 100 L.Ed. 397 (1956), disposed of constitutional arguments against the practice, holding "[a]n indictment returned by a legally constituted and unbiased grand jury . . . is enough to call for a trial of the charge on the merits. The Fifth Amendment requires nothing more." Id. at 363. The Court affirmed and expanded upon this holding in United States v. Dionisio, 93 S.Ct. 764, 410 U.S. 1, 35 L.Ed.2d 67 (1973), in which it stated that:

A grand jury has broad investigative powers to determine whether a crime has been committed and who has committed it. The jurors may act on tips, rumors, evidence offered by the prosecutor, or their own personal knowledge.

Id. at 15. More recently, that Court has said, "[t]he grand jury's sources of information are widely drawn, and the validity of an indictment is not affected by the character of the evidence considered." United States v. Calandra, 94 S.Ct. 613, 414 U.S. 338, 344–45, 38 L.Ed.2d 561 (1974).

Subdivision (d). This subdivision for the most part restates prior Massachusetts practice. The substance of this subdivision was taken from G.L. c. 277, § 35A, but a significant modification of the statute has been effected. The change involves the expansion of the right to seek amendments. Under the statute, only the prosecutor could move for amendment of a complaint or indictment; under the rule either party can seek amendments, and the court can allow amendments on its own motion.

It is preferable that a party seeking an amendment of the charges file a written motion to that effect in order that a sufficient record be preserved on that issue should there be an appeal. However, a court may allow an amendment upon oral motion. In such event, or in the event that the court amends the charges on its own motion, the court should make certain that the amendment, as well as the charges as originally framed, are made a part of the record.

The most common prejudice resulting from an amendment of the charges is that the amendment materially alters the substantive offense charged. *See* Commonwealth v. Gallo, 2 Mass.App. 636, 318 N.E.2d 187 (1974). Such an amendment would be one of substance and not of form and would thus be impermissible. Commonwealth v. Snow, 269 Mass. 598, 603, 169 N.E. 542, 68 A.L.R. 920 (1930). An unessential element of a crime charged in an indictment or complaint, such as the time of stealing in larceny, may be amended without prejudice to the defendant. Commonwealth v. Jervis, 368 Mass. 638, 643–44, 335 N.E.2d 532 (1975). See Commonwealth v. Grasso, 375 Mass. 138, 375 N.E.2d 708 (1978); Commonwealth v. Sitko, 372 Mass. 305, 361 N.E.2d 1258 (1977).

One test for determining whether an amendment is one of substance or of form is whether an acquittal on the original charge would act as a bar on double jeopardy grounds to a prosecution of the defendant on the amended charges. If not, then the amendment would be deemed one of substance rather than of form. *Commonwealth v. Snow*, supra.

Although the power of the court to amend indictments under this rule and under existing statutory law is the same as its power to amend complaints, it should be noted that the restrictions on its power to allow amendment of indictments reaches constitutional dimensions. Since defendants charged with felonies have the constitutional right to indictment (Jones v. Robbins, 74 Mass. [8 Gray] 329 [1857]; see Reporters' Notes to Rule, supra), an amendment which goes to the substance of the offense charged in an indictment so as to "materially change the work of the grand jury" interferes with the defendant's right to have a grand jury frame those charges upon which he is to be tried. Commonwealth v. Benjamin, 358 Mass. 672, 679, 266 N.E.2d 662 (1971); Commonwealth v. Ohanian, 6 Mass.App. 965, 384 N.E.2d 218 (1979).

As to complaints, the power of the court is not so restricted. Therefore, the District Court judge should review each complaint carefully to assure that it fulfills the statutory requirements. If it does not, the judge should order it amended. This course of action will prevent defective complaints from entering the Superior Court system after a waiver of indictment. Further, if during a probable cause hearing it appears to the judge that the evidence would warrant charges of other or related offenses, he should order a new complaint to be prepared.

Rule 5.   The Grand Jury

[Text of rule applicable to cases initiated (by indictment or complaint) on or after September 7, 2004.]

(a) Summoning Grand Juries. As prescribed by law, the appropriate number of jurors shall be summoned in the manner and at the time required, from among whom the court shall select not more than twenty-three grand jurors to serve in said court as long as and at those specific times required by law, or as required by the court.

The regular grand jury shall be called upon and directed to sit by the Chief Justice of the Superior Court Department whenever within his or her discretion the conduct of regular criminal business and timely prosecution within a particular county so dictate. Notwithstanding the foregoing, special grand juries shall be summoned in the manner prescribed by the General Laws.

(b) Foreperson, Foreperson Pro Tem, Clerk, Clerk Pro Tem. After the grand jurors have been impanelled they shall retire and elect one of their number as foreperson. The foreperson and the prosecuting attorney shall have the power to administer oaths and affirmations to witnesses who appear to testify before the grand jury, and the foreperson shall, under his or her hand, return to the court a list of all witnesses sworn before the grand jury during the sitting. If the foreperson is unable to serve for any part of the period the grand jurors are required to serve, a foreperson pro tem shall be elected in the same manner as provided herein for election of the foreperson. The foreperson pro tem shall serve until the foreperson returns or for the remainder of the term if the foreperson is unable to return. The grand jury may also appoint one of their number as clerk to be charged with keeping a record of their proceedings, and, if the grand jury so directs, to deliver such record to the attorney general or district attorney. If the clerk is unable to serve for any part of the period the grand jurors are required to serve, a clerk pro tem may be appointed.

(c) Who May be Present. Attorneys for the Commonwealth who are necessary or convenient to the presentation of the evidence, the witness under examination, the attorney for the witness, and such other persons who are necessary or convenient to the presentation of the evidence may be present while the grand jury is in session. The attorney for the witness shall make no objections or arguments or otherwise address the grand jury or the prosecuting attorney. No witness may refuse to appear because of unavailability of counsel for that witness.

(d) Secrecy of Proceedings and Disclosures. The judge may direct that an indictment be kept secret until after arrest. In such an instance, the clerk shall seal the indictment and no person may disclose the finding of the indictment except as is necessary for the issuance and execution of a warrant. A person performing an official function in relation to the grand jury may not disclose matters occurring before the grand jury except in the performance of his or her official duties or when specifically directed to do so by the court. No obligation of secrecy may be imposed upon any person except in accordance with law.

(e) Finding and Return of Indictment. An indictment may be found only upon the concurrence of twelve or more jurors. The indictment shall be returned by the grand jury to a judge in open court.

(f) No Bill; Discharge of Defendant. The grand jury shall during its session make a daily return to the court of all cases as to which it has determined not to present an indictment against an accused. Each such complaint shall be endorsed "no bill" and shall be filed with the court.

If upon the filing of a no bill the accused is held on process, he or she shall be discharged unless held on other process.

(g) Deliberation. The prosecuting attorney shall not be present during deliberation and voting except at the request of the grand jury.

(h) Discharge. A grand jury shall serve until the first sitting of the next authorized grand jury unless it is discharged sooner by the court or unless its service is extended to complete an investigation then in progress.

Amended March 8, 2004, effective September 7, 2004.

Reporter's Notes—Revised, 2004

Rule 5 is modeled in large part upon Fed. R Crim. P. 6 and substantially conforms to the General Laws.

Subdivision (a). This subdivision is drawn from Fed. R. Crim. P. 7(a) and G.L. c. 277, §§ 1, 2, 2A—2H. General Laws c. 277, § 3 provides that grand jurors are to drawn, G.L. c. 234, §§ 17—24C, summoned, GL c 234, §§ 10—14, 16, 24, and returned in the same manner as traverse jurors from a list compiled in compliance with G.L. c. 234, §§ 4—9. By a 2004 amendment, this subdivision was amended to eliminate a reference to a specific number of veniremen who must be summonsed, since the number differs from county to county. The statutes require that twenty-three jurors be selected to make up the grand jury, G.L. c. 277, §§ 1, 2, 2A—2H, and authorize the issuance of writs of venire facias to fill any deficiency in that number. G.L. c. 277, § 4. A number less than twenty-three is competent to return an indictment, however, so long as at least thirteen are present and twelve concur in the return. *See* Commonwealth v. Wood, 56 Mass (2 Cush) 149 (1848). *Accord,* Crimm v Commonwealth, 119 Mass. 326 (1876).

Subdivision (a) generally governs the time of issuance of writs of venire facias and provides that such writs for special grand juries shall be issued pursuant to G.L. c. 277, § 2A. In addition to the statutory regular and special grand jury sitting, the Administrative Justice of the Superior Court is empowered to call a "regular" grand jury session whenever the amount of criminal business and the need for timely prosecution within a particular county requires. This provision is intended to provide the Superior Court with much needed flexibility in responding to the fluctuating demand for grand jury action among counties.

Subdivision (b). Although similar to Fed. R. Crim. P. 6(c), this subdivision is wholly adopted from former GL c 277, §§ 7—10. The federal rule provides for the simultaneous court appointment of a foreperson and deputy foreperson; under Rule 5 the foreperson is elected by the other jurors and a replacement, the foreperson pro tem, is chosen only if the first cannot serve Provision for a clerk pro tem is new with this rule.

Those parts of subdivision (b) dealing with the administration of oaths and listing of witnesses and with the appointment and duties of the clerk are restatements, respectively, of former G.L. c. 277, §§ 9 and 10.

Subdivision (c). This subdivision was patterned on Fed. R. Crim. P. 6(d), although it omitted the provision of the federal rule that excluded all persons other than jurors from deliberations or voting.

Grand jury proceedings are ordinarily secret and the presence of an unauthorized person will void an indictment. *See* Commonwealth v. Pezzano, 387 Mass. 69, 72–73 (1982). The importance of keeping the grand jury process from becoming public rests on several policy considerations: preventing individuals from facing the notoriety associated with a grand jury investigation unless probable cause is found against them and an indictment is returned; shielding the grand jury from any outside influences having the potential to distort their investigatory or accusatory functions; protecting witnesses from improper influence; encouraging the full disclosure of information to the grand jury; and facilitating the freedom of the grand jury's deliberations. *See* WBZ–TV4 v. District Attorney for Suffolk Dist., 408 Mass. 595, 600 (1990).

However, prior to the adoption of Rule 5, the Supreme Judicial Court recognized that grand jury secrecy would not be compromised by the presence of persons who were necessary to the work of the grand jury. For example, Commonwealth v. Favulli, 352 Mass 95 (1967), held that a prosecutor has discretion as to the use of assistants and may have present such reasonable number as he or she deems appropriate to the efficient presentation of the evidence. *Id.* at 106. *Accord*, Commonwealth v. Beneficial Finance Co., 360 Mass. 188, 207—09 (1971) (no greater number than is "necessary"). Besides the jury, the prosecutors and the witness under examination, other persons "necessary or convenient to the presentation of the evidence" may include counsel for a witness (G.L. c. 277, § 14A), an interpreter, an officer to guard a dangerous prisoner-witness, an attendant for a sick witness (*see* 30 MASS PRACTICE SERIES [Smith] § 812 [1970]), a stenographer (G.L. c. 221, § 86), or the operator of a recording device. It should be noted that G.L. c. 221, § 86, which permits the appointment of a stenographer to take notes of testimony given before a grand jury does not authorize the recording of any statement or testimony of a grand juror.

The provision in Rule 5(c) allowing the prosecutor to be present at request of grand jurors does not deny defendant due process. *See* Commonwealth v. Smith, Mass. 437 (1993).

Under this subdivision, it may be proper for a federal prosecutor who was involved in the investigation of the case, *see* Commonwealth v. Angiulo, 415 Mass. 502, 513 (1993) or a victim-witness advocate accompanying a child witness, *see* Commonwealth v. Conefrey, 410 Mass. 1, 7 (1991) to be present during testimony before the grand jury. However, it is ordinarily not proper for a police officer to be present, except as a witness. *See Pezzano supra.*

Subdivision (d). Adopted from Fed. R. Crim. P. 6(e), this subdivision incorporates the substance of former G.L. c. 277, §§ 12—13. Nothing in this rule nor in the General Laws prevents a witness before a grand jury from disclosing his or her testimony. *See* Commonwealth v. Schnackenburg, 356 Mass. 65 (1969); Silverio v. Mun. Court of Boston, 355 Mass. 623, *cert. denied*, 396 US 878 (1969). The last phrase, "except in accordance with law" is intended to comprehend statute, court rule, rule or order of an administrative agency, and case law.

Subdivision (e) In order to return an indictment, the grand jury "must hear sufficient evidence to establish the identity of the accused ... and probable cause to arrest him" (citations omitted). Commonwealth v. McCarthy, 385 Mass. 160, 163 (1982).

Although an indictment may be based solely on hearsay, Commonwealth v. O'Dell, 392 Mass. 445, 450–51 (1984), the Supreme Judicial

Court has expressed a "preference for the use of direct testimony," Commonwealth v. St. Pierre, 377 Mass. 650, 656 (1979). A prosecutor need not present the grand jury all the evidence available to the Commonwealth, even if some of it is exculpatory. *See* O'Dell, 392 Mass. at 447. However, if there is exculpatory evidence that would greatly undermine either the credibility of an important witness or likely affect the grand jury's decision, the prosecutor should inform the grand jury. *Id.*

Although there is no statute which mandates the concurrence of at least twelve jurors in the return of an indictment, the requirement expressed in this subdivision is long-established in Massachusetts practice. *See* Commonwealth v. Smith, 9 Mass. 107 (1812). Grand jurors voting to return an indictment need not hear all of the evidence presented against a defendant. *See* Commonwealth v. Wilcox, 437 Mass. 33 (2002).

Subdivision (f). General Laws c. 277, § 15, requiring daily reports of cases where no indictment is returned, is the basis of this subdivision.

Subdivision (g). Prior Massachusetts procedure permitted the prosecutor to be present, *See* Commonwealth v. Favulli, *supra* at 107. A major change is worked by this subdivision, pursuant to which the prosecuting officer may be present during deliberations and voting only if his or her presence is requested by the grand jurors. It is believed that this will operate to enhance the independence of the grand jury, thus alloying fears that it is merely "a tool of the prosecutor".

Subdivision (h). This subdivision essentially restates those provisions of G.L. c 277, §§ 1, 2, and 2A–2H relative to the duration of sittings of grand juries and of § 1A relative to extensions. Grand juries in Suffolk (§ 2), Middlesex (§ 2B), Worcester (§ 2E), Norfolk (§ 2F) and Bristol (§ 2H) counties are to serve for six months and in Hampden (§ 2C), Essex (§ 2G) and Plymouth counties (§ 2D) for four months "and until another grand jury has been impanelled in their stead." Notwithstanding these express statutory provisions, the summoning of the grand jury and the duration of its term is subject to the discretion of the Administrative Justice of the Superior Court pursuant to subdivision (a).

Rule 6. Summons to Appear; Arrest Warrant

(Applicable to District Court and Superior Court)

(a) Issuance of Process.

(1) *Summons.* A defendant not under arrest or otherwise in custody shall, except as provided in subdivision (a)(2) of this rule, be notified of the criminal proceedings against him and of the date of the return day by means of a summons. A copy of the complaint or indictment shall accompany the summons. If the accused is a juvenile, a summons and copy of the complaint or indictment shall also be served upon the parent or legal guardian of the juvenile or upon the person with whom the juvenile resides. Such notice shall also advise the defendant to report in person to the probation department before the return day.

(2) *Warrant.* The District Court may authorize the issuance of a warrant in any case except where the accused is a juvenile less than twelve years of age. Upon the return of an indictment against a defendant, the Superior Court may authorize the issuance of a warrant. The decision to issue a warrant may be based upon the representation of a prosecutor made to the court that the defendant may not appear unless arrested. If a defendant fails to appear in response to a summons or for any reason is not amenable to service, the prosecutor may request that a warrant issue or may resummon the defendant.

(b) Form.

(1) *Warrant.* An arrest warrant issued pursuant to this rule shall be signed by the official issuing it and shall contain the name of the defendant or, if his name is unknown, any name or description by which he can be identified with reasonable certainty. The warrant shall recite the substance of the offense charged in the complaint or indictment. It shall command that the defendant be arrested and brought before the court.

(2) *Summons.* A summons shall be in the same form as a warrant except that it shall summon the defendant to appear before the court at a stated time and place.

(c) Service or Execution; Return.

(1) *By Whom.* A summons may be served in the manner provided by subdivision (c)(3) of this rule by any person authorized by the General Laws to serve criminal process. A warrant shall be directed to and executed by an officer authorized by the General Laws to serve criminal process.

(2) *Territorial Limits.* A summons may be served or a warrant executed at any place within the Commonwealth.

(3) *Manner.* A summons shall be served upon a defendant by delivering a copy to him personally, or by leaving it at his dwelling house or usual place of abode with some person of suitable age and discretion then residing therein, or by mailing it to the defendant's last known address. A warrant shall be executed by the arrest of the defendant. The officer need not have the warrant in his possession at the time of the arrest, but upon request he shall show the warrant to the defendant as soon as possible. If the officer does not have the warrant in his possession at the time of the arrest, he shall then inform the defendant that a warrant has issued and of the offense charged, but if the officer does not then know of the offense charged, he shall inform the defendant thereof within a reasonable time after arrest.

(4) *Return.* On or before the return day, the person to whom a summons was delivered for service shall make return thereof to the issuing court. The clerk shall maintain a list of those summonses returned unserved which shall include a statement of the efforts made by the person to whom the summonses were delivered for service to serve them. If a summons is mailed pursuant to subdivision (c)(3) of this rule and returned, the clerk shall record that fact upon the list. The officer executing a warrant shall make return thereof to the issuing court. At the request of the prosecutor any unexecuted warrant shall be returned to the issuing court and may be cancelled by that court upon its own motion or upon the motion of the prosecutor. At the request of the prosecutor made at any time while a complaint or an indictment is pending, a summons returned unserved or a warrant returned unexecuted and not cancelled may be delivered to an authorized person for service or execution.

(d) Default.

(1) *Costs.* A judge may order that expenses incurred as a result of the entry of a default against a defendant are to be assessed as costs against the defendant.

(2) *Preservation of Testimony.* If counsel for a defendant is present upon the entry of a default against the defendant and if the judge finds that to require the attendance at a later time of a witness then present in court would constitute a hardship upon the witness because of age, infirmity, illness, profession or other sufficient reason, the judge may order that the testimony of the witness be taken and preserved for subsequent use at trial or any other proceeding. The witness shall be examined in open court by the party on whose behalf he is present and the adverse party shall have the right of cross-examination. The expense of taking and preserving the testimony may be assessed as costs against the defendant.

Reporter's Notes

Rule 6 was drafted with the aim of dispensing with unnecessary appearances by defendants, their counsel, and witnesses and insuring that defendants who are unlikely to flee pending their initial appearance may be at liberty without restriction.

Subdivision (a). Under prior practice, after a finding of probable cause—whether upon an application for issuance of process or upon presentment to a grand jury—arrest warrants were to be issued in the majority of cases. G.L. c. 276, § 22. The issuance of a summons in lieu of a warrant was the exception under the law, if not in practice.

Under G.L. c. 276, § 24, a summons was to be issued only in those instances where the District Court had final jurisdiction over the offense charged and the court believed a summons would sufficiently guarantee the defendant's appearance in court.

Under this rule the permissible use of a summons is greatly expanded. Whenever it is determined that process shall issue upon an application, the District Court shall authorize the issuance of a warrant, except in cases where the accused is a juvenile less than twelve years of age. G.L. c. 119, § 54. Whenever a direct indictment is returned against a defendant, the Superior Court shall authorize the issuance of a warrant. In both instances, however, the warrant will not be immediately issued for execution unless the court determines that the defendant will not likely appear upon a summons alone.

This rule reflects the policy underlying current efforts to secure the release prior to trial of all defendants who have sufficient roots in the community to guarantee their presence at trial. Federal Rule of Criminal Procedure 4 requires a magistrate to issue a summons rather than an arrest warrant only "upon the request of the attorney for the government" after probable cause is found. Section 3.3 of the ABA *Standards Relating to Pretrial Release* (Approved Draft, 1968) provides for the use of a summons instead of a warrant except where specific grounds exist for the use of an arrest warrant. *Accord* Rules of Criminal Procedure (U.L.A.) Rule 221(c) (1974); National Advisory Commission on Criminal Justice Standards & Goals, *Courts,* Standard 4.2 (1973). See Vermont R.Crim.P. 4 (1974).

The preference for the issuance of summonses operates to conserve law enforcement resources by releasing the police for other duties, and conserves the resources of the court and parties.

The preference for the issuance of a summons instead of a warrant is based on the same policy mandating the release of arrested defendants on personal recognizance rather than on bail. That policy is bottomed on the belief that defendants should be burdened with the fewest restrictions on their pretrial liberty that will adequately assure their presence at trial.

There is, however, one significant difference between the decision made concerning the issuance of a summons and that concerning the appropriate conditions of release after arrest. When a decision on bail is made, the court or magistrate has more information concerning the defendant than when a summons or warrant is to be issued. In the former instance, the defendant is present before the court and can be questioned in order to establish a sufficient basis for a determination of the appropriate conditions of his release. In addition, under Mass.R.Crim.P. 28, the judge is authorized to review the probation report concerning the defendant prior to the bail determination.

In light of these considerations, it is intended that the court not be prohibited from issuing an arrest warrant where there is an absence of sufficient information to make an intelligent choice concerning the appropriate process to be issued. Where there is a dearth of information concerning the defendant, it is expected that the court will place much reliance upon the nature of the offense charged and will order the arrest of defendants charged with serious crimes. An arrest in such situations will not unduly prejudice a defendant, because, if he is suitable for pretrial release on his own recognizance, the court can so order when the defendant is initially brought before it after arrest.

Subdivision (a)(1) provides that, except when the issuance of a warrant is necessitated, the defendant is to be notified of the criminal proceedings against him and the date of his scheduled appearance by means of a summons coupled with a copy of the complaint or indictment. See Rules of Criminal Procedure (U.L.A.) Rule 222(d) (1974). This notice shall also advise the defendant to personally report to the probation department before his scheduled appearance for the purpose of an interview to determine whether counsel need be assigned. If the defendant has retained counsel, and counsel has filed his appearance, the defendant need not attend until his next scheduled appearance.

Subdivision (a)(1) also deals with the requirement of G.L. c. 119, § 55 that notice to the parent or guardian of the defendant is necessary when the accused is a juvenile. Although notice to and appearance by a parent or guardian is thus required, nothing in this rule is to be construed as making the parent or guardian of the juvenile a party defendant. Robinson v. Commonwealth, 242 Mass. 401, 403, 136 N.E. 241 (1922).

Subdivision (a)(2) provides that upon the prosecuting officer's recital to the court that the defendant will not appear unless arrested, a warrant may be issued. This is less restrictive than the guidelines provided by the ABA *Standards Relating to Pretrial Release*, § 3.3 (Approved Draft, 1968), which require an application for an arrest warrant to reveal the defendant's residence, employment, family ties, criminal record, and whether he had previously responded to a citation or summons. If a magistrate fails to issue a summons instead of an arrest warrant, he is required to state the reason therefor. *Compare* Rule 221(c) of the *Uniform Rules of Criminal Procedure* (U.L.A.) (1974).

The factors to be considered by the court in its decision upon the conditions necessary to assure the defendant's presence are reflected in the *Rules of the Superior Court Governing Persons Authorized to Take Bail* 2 (1972):

> The purpose of setting terms for any pretrial release is to assure the presence at court of the person released. Any person charged with an offense, other than an offense punishable by death [sic], is required by law to be released on his personal recognizance pending trial unless the person setting the terms of release determines, in the exercise of his discretion, that such a release will not reasonably assure the appearance of the person as required. In making a determination as to what form of release to set, the following factors shall be considered: (1) the nature and circumstances of the offense charged, (2) the accused's family ties, (3) his financial resources, (4) his length of residence in the community, (5) his character and mental condition, (6) his record of convictions and appearances at court proceedings or of any previous flight to avoid prosecution or (7) any failure to appear at any court proceedings.

Accord G.L. c. 276, § 58 (as amended, St.1978, c. 478, § 286).

Moreover, this subdivision provides that if a defendant fails to respond to summons, then the court may order that a warrant issue, or may permit the defendant to be served with a new summons. This accords with practice under G.L. c. 276, § 26, which makes the willful failure to appear in response to criminal process a separate offense. See ABA *Standards Relating to Pretrial Release* § 1.3 (Approved Draft, 1968); Rules of Criminal Procedure (U.L.A.) rule 221(e)(2) (1974).

Subdivision (b). General Laws c. 276, § 21, c. 218, § 33 (as amended, St.1978, c. 478, § 191), and c. 218, § 35 (as amended, St.1978, c. 478, § 192) enumerate those officials who are empowered to issue arrest warrants.

Subdivision (b)(1) restates the Massachusetts practice, dating from Commonwealth v. Crathy, 92 Mass. (10 Allen) 403 (1865), which requires that if the warrant does not contain a name by which the accused is known, it must contain a sufficient description by which the arresting officer will be able to identify the accused with reasonable certainty. This subdivision follows the practice in Massachusetts which mandates that the warrant shall recite the substance of the accusation, G.L. c. 276, § 22, a requirement fulfilled at common law by attaching the complaint or a copy thereof to the warrant. Commonwealth v. Dean, 75 Mass. (9 Gray) 283 (1857). General Laws c. 276, § 22 details the procedure to be followed by the arresting officer when the accused is located.

Support for the rule that the warrant must be directed to an officer authorized to serve criminal process is found in In re Graves, 236 Mass. 493 (1920). In *Graves,* the court held that a warrant which by express direction would have permitted unqualified persons to execute it was invalid on its face.

Subdivision (c)(3) is also borrowed from ALI *Model Code of Pre-Arraignment Procedure* § 120.3(2) (P.O.D.1975), and is similar to Rules of Criminal Procedure (U.L.A.) rule 223(c) (1974). The ALI *Model Code,* supra, § 120.4, permits service of the summons by mail.

It is well established in Massachusetts that an officer need not have the warrant authorizing the arrest in his possession when the accused is placed under arrest. This principle is grounded on the judicial determination that an arrest is valid if based on probable cause even if the warrant upon which the arrest was made is void. Commonwealth v. Bowlen, 351 Mass. 655, 223 N.E.2d 391 (1967). However, if the arrest is based upon a warrant, the accused should be afforded an opportunity to examine it within a reasonable time.

Subdivision (c)(4) complies substantially with Rule 225 of the Rules of Criminal Procedure (U.L.A.) (P.O.D.1975) and with Fed.R.Crim.P. 4(c)(4).

General Laws c. 218, § 32 states that warrants are returnable before a court in the county where trial of the case is to be held. The only restrictions on the time in which a warrant must be executed is that a delay in its execution must not be unreasonable. *See generally* Commonwealth v. Sullivan, 354 Mass. 598, 239 N.E.2d 5 (1968). However, if execution of the warrant is wilfully delayed by the person to whom it was committed for service, that person is subject to the penalties provided by G.L. c. 268, §§ 22–23 irrespective of whether the warrant is valid.

Subdivision (d). This subdivision introduces two new practices. The first, in subdivision (d)(1), allows the court to assess as costs against the defendant those expenses which result from the defendant's failure to appear. While the assessment is discretionary, it is intended to be exercised only upon the willful default of a defendant and as to those costs which directly result therefrom. As under Mass.R.Crim.P. 10(b), relating to assessment of costs upon a continuance, expenses which may be assessed under this rule include fees of witnesses then present, extra compensation of police officers, travel costs, and stenographer's attendance fees if one is appointed.

Subdivision (d)(2) provides that if a witness is present in court and the trial cannot proceed because the defendant is absent, the testimony of that witness may be ordered taken and recorded by deposition. This is an extraordinary practice, and is to be utilized only when to require the later appearance of the witness would constitute a hardship due to his age, infirmity, profession or other sufficient reason. "Profession" in this context does not signify solely the recognized professions, but refers to the manner of earning a livelihood of one who will lose income or wages if required to attend further proceedings.

There is no issue as to confrontation in this situation. A defendant has the right to be present at the taking of a deposition, see Mass. R.Crim.P. 18(a), but "his failure to appear after notice and without cause shall constitute a waiver of the right to be present." Mass. R.Crim.P. 35(c). This subdivision is but a logical extension of that provision. The defendant has had notice to appear for trial and has chosen to absent himself. It is assumed for purposes of this rule that defendant's counsel is present to examine or cross-examine the deponent and to preserve objections to his testimony. Thus the essential need of the defendant to be present is fulfilled.

The defendant is protected from a "default" by the Commonwealth by Mass.R.Crim.P. 10(c), pursuant to which the court may order that the taking of depositions of Commonwealth witnesses be made a condition upon the grant of a continuance.

FORM DC–CR–7. SUMMONS FOR DEFENDANT/SUMMONS FOR WITNESS

☐ SUMMONS FOR DEFENDANT ☐ SUMMONS FOR WITNESS DOCKET NUMBER	Trial Court of Massachusetts District Court Department

SESSION: ☐ CRIMINAL ☐ JUVENILE ☐ JURY ☐ MAGISTRATE HEARING

NAME, ADDRESS AND ZIP CODE OF DEFENDANT

NAME AND ADDRESS OF COURT DIVISION

←— YOU MUST APPEAR AT THIS COURT ADDRESS ON THE DATE AND TIME SPECIFIED HEREIN ←—

DATE AND TIME OF APPEARANCE

_____ AT _____ M.
DATE   TIME

NAME, ADDRESS AND ZIP CODE OF WITNESS

OFFENSE(S)

TO ANY PERSON AUTHORIZED TO SERVE CRIMINAL PROCESS IN THE COMMONWEALTH:

You are hereby commanded to forthwith serve the annexed summons upon the defendant or witness named within by delivering it to the defendant or witness personally, or by leaving it at the dwelling house or usual place of abode of the defendant or witness with some person of suitable age and discretion then residing therein, or by mailing it to the last known address of the defendant or witness.

NOTE: A summons for a witness may also be served by any person authorized to serve a summons in a civil action. See Rule 17(d)(1) of the Massachusetts Rules of Criminal Procedure.

To the above named   ☐ Defendant   ☐ Witness:

You are hereby ordered to appear in this Court on the appearance date noted above

☐ To answer to a criminal complaint charging you with the offense(s) listed above.

☐ To give evidence and testify on behalf of the ☐ Commonwealth ☐ Defendant in the matter described above, and to appear from time to time and day to day thereafter as ordered. You are further required to bring with you:

_____
_____
_____

WITNESS:	FIRST JUSTICE	DATE OF ISSUE	CLERK-MAGISTRATE

RETURN OF SERVICE

I hereby certify that I served the within summons upon the above named ☐ Defendant ☐ Witness by

☐ Delivering a copy of it personally to the defendant or witness.

☐ Leaving a copy of it at the dwelling house or usual place of abode of the defendant or witness with a person of suitable age and discretion residing therein.

☐ Mailing a copy of it to the last known address of the defendant or witness

☐ I received the summons on _____ but I was unable to make service because: _____

DATE RECEIVED

DATE OF SERVICE	SIGNATURE OF PERSON MAKING SERVICE X	TITLE OF PERSON MAKING SERVICE

DC–CR–7 (1/84)

```
┌─────────────────────────────────┬──────────────┬────────────────────────────────┐
│ ☐  SUMMONS FOR DEFENDANT         │ DOCKET NUMBER│ Trial Court of Massachusetts   │
│ ☐  SUMMONS FOR WITNESS           │              │ District Court Department      │
├─────────────────────────────────┴──────────────┼────────────────────────────────┤
│                                                 │ NAME AND ADDRESS OF COURT      │
│ SESSION: ☐ CRIMINAL ☐ JUVENILE ☐ JURY ☐         │ DIVISION                       │
│ MAGISTRATE HEARING                              │                         ←—     │
│ NAME, ADDRESS AND ZIP CODE OF DEFENDANT         │             YOU MUST           │
│                                                 │             APPEAR AT          │
│   ┌                          ┐                  │             THIS COURT         │
│                                                 │             ADDRESS ON         │
│                                                 │             THE DATE           │
│                                                 │             AND TIME           │
│                                                 │             SPECIFIED          │
│   └                          ┘                  │             HEREIN             │
│ NAME, ADDRESS AND ZIP CODE OF WITNESS           │ DATE AND TIME OF APPEARANCE ←— │
│                                                 │                                │
│   ┌                          ┐                  │ _____ AT _____ M.          │
│                                                 │    DATE      TIME              │
│                                                 │ OFFENSE(S)                     │
│   └                          ┘                  │                                │
├─────────────────────────────────────────────────┴───────────────────────────────┤
│                                                                                   │
│                                                                                   │
│ To the above named   ☐ Defendant   ☐ Witness:                                     │
│                                                                                   │
│ You are hereby ordered to appear in this Court on the appearance date noted above │
│                                                                                   │
│ ☐  To answer to a criminal complaint charging you with the offense(s) listed above.│
│                                                                                   │
│ ☐  To give evidence and testify on behalf of the ☐ Commonwealth ☐ Defendant in the matter │
│    described above, and to appear from time to time and day to day thereafter as ordered.  You are │
│    further required to bring with you:                                            │
│    _____           │
│    _____           │
│    _____           │
├──────────────────────┬──────────────────┬───────────────────────────────────────┤
│         FIRST JUSTICE │  DATE OF ISSUE   │      CLERK-MAGISTRATE                  │
│ WITNESS:              │                  │                                       │
├──────────────────────┴──────────────────┴───────────────────────────────────────┤
│               WARNING TO DEFENDANT OR WITNESS:                                    │
│                                                                                   │
│   Failure to appear in accordance with this summons may result in the issuance of a │
│   warrant for your arrest.  Please bring this document with you to court.          │
│                                                                                   │
│                         ATENCIÓN:                                                 │
│                                                                                   │
│              Esta es una notificación oficial de la corte.                        │
│              Si usted no sabe leer inglés, obtenga traducción!                    │
└───────────────────────────────────────────────────────────────────────────────────┘
DC-CR-7(1/84)
```

Rule 7. Arraignment

(a) Time of Arraignment; Probation Interview; Indigency and Bail Reports

(1) *Upon Arrest or Summons.* A defendant who has been arrested and is not released shall be brought for arraignment before a court if then in session, and if not, at its next session. A defendant who receives a summons or who has been arrested but is thereupon released shall be ordered to appear before the court for arraignment on a date certain.

(2) *Arrest of a Juvenile.* Upon the arrest of a juvenile, the arresting officer shall notify the parent or guardian of the juvenile and the probation office.

(3) *Probation Interview.* On the day of the arraignment, the probation department shall interview the defendant; the probation department shall report to the court the pertinent information reasonably necessary to determine the issues of bail and indigency.

(b) Arraignment Procedure.

(1) *Notice; Plea; and Bail.* The court shall:

(A) read the charges to the defendant in open court, except that the reading of the charges in open court may be waived by the defendant if he or she is represented by counsel;

(B) enter the defendant's plea to the charges;

(C) inform the defendant of all warnings and advisories required by law; and,

(D) determine the conditions of the defendant's release, if any.

(2) *Appointment of Counsel.* If the court finds that the defendant is indigent or indigent but able to contribute and has not knowingly waived the right to counsel under the procedures established in Supreme Judicial Court Rule 3:10, the Committee for Public Counsel Services shall be assigned to provide representation for the defendant.

(3) *Provision of Criminal Record; Preservation of Evidence.* The court shall ensure that at or before arraignment, (i) a copy of the defendant's criminal record, if any, as compiled by the Commissioner of Probation is provided to the defense and to the prosecution, and (ii) the parties are afforded an opportunity to move for the preservation of evidence pursuant to Rule 14(a)(1)(E).

(4) *Order Scheduling Pretrial Proceedings.* At a District Court arraignment on a complaint which is outside of the District Court's final jurisdiction or on which jurisdiction is declined, the court shall schedule the case for a probable cause hearing. In all other District and Superior Court cases the court shall issue an order at arraignment requiring the prosecuting attorney and defense counsel to (1) engage in a pretrial conference on a date certain, and (2) appear at a pretrial hearing on a specified subsequent date.

(c) Appearance of Counsel.

(1) *Filing.* An appearance shall be entered by the attorney for the defendant and the prosecuting attorney on or before the arraignment. The appearance may be entered either by personally appearing before the clerk or by submitting an appearance slip, which shall include the name, Board of Bar Overseers number, address, and telephone number of the attorney. An attorney appearing on behalf of an organization shall also file with the court proof of the attorney's authorization to represent the organization.

(2) *Effect; Withdrawal.* An appearance shall be in the name of the attorney who files the appearance and shall constitute a representation that the attorney shall represent the defendant for trial or plea or shall prosecute the case, except that, if at the arraignment such a representation cannot be made and no contrary legal restriction applies, (1) the court may permit an appearance to be entered by an attorney to represent the defendant or prosecute the case for such time as the court may order, and (2) the court shall permit an appear-ance in the name of the prosecuting agency, which shall constitute representations that the agency will prosecute the case, will ensure that throughout the duration of the appearance a prosecutor is assigned to the case, and upon request of the court or a party will identify the prosecutor assigned to the case. If the attorney who files an appearance for the defendant on or before the arraignment wishes to withdraw the appearance, he or she may do so within fourteen days of the arraignment, provided that the attorney who shall represent the defendant at trial files an appearance simultaneously with such withdrawal; thereafter no appearance shall be withdrawn without permission of the court. The appearance of the prosecuting officer shall be withdrawn only with permission of the court.

(3) *Notice.* A copy of all appearances and withdrawals of appearance shall be filed and shall be served upon the adverse party pursuant to Rule 32.

Amended May 29, 1986, effective July 1, 1986; March 8, 2004, effective September 7, 2004; February 27, 2012, effective June 1, 2012.

Reporter's Notes—Revised, 2004

Rule 7 governs the initial appearance and arraignment. It is based in part upon Fed. R. Crim. P. 5, 5.1, and 10. See ALI Model Code of Pre–Arraignment Procedure § 310.1, .3, .5 (POD 1975); Rules of Criminal Procedure (ULA) rules 311—13, 321 (1974). In 2004, Rule 7 was amended in four respects. The revisions mandate: that in some circumstances counsel be permitted to enter a limited appearance; that the defendant receive a copy of his or her criminal record at arraignment; that the parties have an opportunity to move to preserve evidence at arraignment; and that pretrial conference and hearing dates, or alternatively a probable cause hearing date, be assigned at the initial appearance. These revisions are addressed in detail infra.

Subdivision (a)(1). Subdivision (a) provides that when a defendant has been arrested, he or she is to be brought immediately to appear before a court if then in session, and if not, then at its next session.

Pursuant to G.L. c 119, § 67, notice of the arrest of a juvenile is required to be given to the parent of the juvenile and to the probation officer for the district in which the accused is arrested, unless the juvenile was arrested as a child in need of service pursuant to G.L. 119, § 39H, which contains alternative notification requirements. The purpose of this notice is to permit the prompt release of a juvenile, consistent with G.L. c 119, § 66, which discourages the detention of juvenile offenders, unless, in the opinion of the arresting officer or the probation department, cause exists to hold him or her.

Massachusetts case law requires that an arrested defendant be brought before a court for arraignment as soon after arrest as is reasonably possible. Commonwealth v. Dubois, 353 Mass. 223 (1967); Keefe v. Hart, 213 Mass. 476 (1913). Whether or not delay has been unreasonable is to be determined on a case-by-case basis, Commonwealth v. Banuchi, 335 Mass. 649 (1957), and in light of all the circumstances. Commonwealth v. Perito, 417 Mass. 674, 680 (1994); Commonwealth v. Hodgkins, 401 Mass. 871, 876–77 (1988). Generally, arraignment the next morning following arrest is not unreasonable when a defendant is arrested late in the day. United States v. Connell, 213 F. Supp. 741 (D. Mass. 1963); Commonwealth v. Daniels, 366 Mass. 601 (1975); Commonwealth v. Dubois, *supra.* Rule 7(a) codifies this case law by mandating that the defendant be brought before the court immediately if the court is in session, and if not, then at its next session. This requirement is primarily intended to prevent both unlawful detentions and unlawfully obtained statements. Commonwealth v. Cote, 386 Mass. 354, 361 n. 11 (1982). However, in Commonwealth v. Rosario, 422 Mass. 48 (1996), the S.J.C. established a bright line rule that an otherwise admissible statement taken within a six-hour period following arrest should not be excluded, even if the court was in session at the time.

This initial appearance before the court serves several functions. First, at this time, the defendant will be interviewed by the probation department. The results of this interview, together with an investigative report by the probation department as to prior criminal prosecutions and juvenile complaints, will be communicated to the court. See Mass. R. Crim. P. 28(d)(1)—(2). This information will form the basis of decisions as to pretrial release. Moreover, this information will be used to determine whether a defendant is indigent or indigent but able to contribute. If the court so determines, then it will assign the Committee for Public Counsel Services to represent him according to the requirements of G.L. c. 211D and Supreme Judicial Court Rule 3:10. If the defendant was arrested without a warrant, there must also be a judicial determination of probable cause within twenty-four hours, as provided in Rule 3.1. See Jenkins v. Chief Justice of the District Court Dep't, 416 Mass. 221 (1993). Finally, at this time the court shall establish a time for arraignment or other proceeding.

The initial appearance and arraignment, although distinguishable by their respective functions, need not be separate events. The preferred practice, however, is to postpone arraignment until such time as the defendant has had a meaningful opportunity to consult with counsel. See District Court Initial Rule of Criminal Procedure 2, comment (1971).

The vital importance of the component parts of arraignment must not be lost in the tedium of repetition so as to foreclose inadvertently the rights of the uninformed defendant. Among the decisions to be made is whether to plead guilty or nolo contendere, or to admit to sufficient facts. Mass. R. Crim. P. 12. Representation by counsel is necessary to ensure that the defendant understands that by selecting among these alternatives he or she is exercising or waiving substantial rights. Counsel should also be available to advise the defendant whether to exercise "drug rights," G.L. c. 111E, § 10; whether to undergo examination for competence, G.L. c 123, § 15; whether he or she may qualify for diversion as a selected offender, G.L. c. 276A; whether arrangements should be made for a stenographer, G.L. c. 221, § 91B; whether to consider mediation in cases where it is offered; and whether the charges may be subject to dismissal. In addition, at arraignment the defendant may waive reading of the charges, subdivision (c), infra; and the case will be ordered to conference, Mass. R. Crim. P. 11. These considerations are all important to the ultimate rights of the defendant and decisions should not be casual or perfunctory. Therefore, if counsel is to be provided, there should be a prompt assignment or appointment, and time should be allowed for consultation. The initial appearance and arraignment can be held on the same day if assigned or appointed counsel is then present in court or is available without delay, and if there is an opportunity for adequate consultation.

The fact that a defendant is to be afforded time to discuss the case with counsel is not to be relied upon by the prosecution to justify undue delay in bringing the defendant before the court for arraignment.

Subdivision (a)(2). If a defendant is issued a summons instead of being arrested, a procedure different from that under subdivision (a)(1) prevails. In such an instance a defendant who has retained counsel need not be present at the scheduled initial appearance if his or her counsel enters an appearance prior thereto. This is required in order that the prosecution and any witnesses of the parties may be notified not to attend. When counsel enters an appearance, the clerk will set the time for the next scheduled event which will require the defendant's presence—usually the pretrial conference or pretrial hearing — and counsel will notify the defendant thereof.

Subdivision (a)(2) does not require the defendant's presence on the date specified on the summons (unless that is the date established by the clerk when counsel enters his or her appearance) because the purposes for the initial appearance outlined in subdivision (a)(1) have

been fulfilled. See Rules of Criminal Procedure (ULA), *supra*, rule 312.

The purpose of this subdivision is to conserve judicial resources and those of the defendant by dispensing with unnecessary appearances. Further, the pretrial liberty of defendants who are likely to appear for arraignment is not compromised.

The defendant who cannot afford or who does not have retained counsel must attend at the initial appearance at the time set in the summons. Prior to that time, the defendant must have appeared at the probation department so that information relative to the issues of bail and indigency may be gathered.

If a defendant intends to waive counsel, the waiver should be executed at the initial appearance.

Subdivision (b). This subdivision governs the entry and withdrawal of appearances by counsel. It combines and revises former subdivisions (b) and (c), which had treated District Court and Superior Court appearances differently. Following the abolition of the district court *de novo* system, a 2004 amendment to this Rule instituted a uniform procedure for both trial courts. It also revised the rule to permit limited appearances in some circumstances — a more efficient option when fully competent counsel is present but unable to submit an appearance guaranteeing representation throughout the case. Assistant district attorneys often do not represent the Commonwealth in a case from beginning to end, and sometimes a public defender or bar advocate is on duty for bail and arraignment sessions only. The original formulation of this subdivision deflected progress in the case by generally barring the appearance of counsel for such limited purposes.

As amended, subdivision (b) provides that the entry of an appearance by *defense counsel* presumes that he or she will represent the defendant at the tender of a plea or at trial, but permits the court to order an appearance for a shorter period when no contrary constitutional, legislative or judicial restriction applies. For example, District Court Dept. Supplemental Rule of Criminal Procedure 8(8) authorizes the appointment of an attorney "for arraignment only," but prohibits any other kind of limited appointment. Rule 7(b) as amended is not intended to preempt such court rules, but to provide the flexibility necessary for courts to formulate and revise such rules over time. An appearance entered by defense counsel may only be withdrawn as of right within fourteen days after arraignment and provided substitute counsel has simultaneously entered an appearance.

A second revision introduces a responsible degree of flexibility with regard to appearances by the *prosecution*. An appearance entered by a prosecutor constitutes a representation that he or she will prosecute a case at trial and may only be withdrawn with permission of the court. However, if such a representation cannot be made, subdivision (b)(2) allows an appearance to be entered in the name of the prosecuting agency, but this requires the office (a) to ensure that throughout the duration of the appearance a prosecutor is assigned to the case, and (b) upon request of the court or other counsel, to identify the prosecutor then assigned to the case. These requirements were added to the rule in 2004 to ameliorate a difficulty in then-existing district court practice: defense counsel was too often unable to speak with a district attorney about the case between arraignment and the next scheduled date because no assistant district attorney had yet been assigned to it. This revised procedure will facilitate early discussions between the parties, and also insure that notices delivered to the offices of the Attorney General or a District Attorney will be brought to the immediate attention of the assistant handling the case.

Subdivision (c). The major functions of the arraignment are to inform the defendant of the charge and to receive his or her plea thereto. Subdivision (c)(1) permits the defendant to waive the reading of the charges if represented by counsel. This is a restatement of District Court Initial Rule of Criminal Procedure 1 (1971); accord, Rules of the Municipal Court of the City of Boston Sitting for Criminal Business 1 (1971).

If the defendant's attendance at the initial appearance is excused, subdivision (c)(2) provides for the automatic entry of a plea of not guilty. Implicit in (c)(2) is a waiver of the reading of the charge. There is then no arraignment as defined in this Rule and the next event is usually the pretrial conference.

Subdivision (d). This subdivision mandates two additional procedures at arraignment. First it requires that the defendant be provided with his or her criminal record at arraignment. This was customarily the case long before the promulgation of this subdivision in 2004, and in district court was already mandated by Dist./Mun. Cts. R. Crim. P. 3. (That Rule goes beyond this subdivision, however, by also requiring the prosecution to provide certain police statements to the defendant at a district court arraignment.) Second, subdivision (d) provides an opportunity at arraignment for the parties to seek an order to preserve evidence that is not subject to a Rule 14 discovery order. Rule 14 discovery reaches only items in the possession, custody or control of the prosecution, its team, or those working with it on the case. But private parties or government agencies not working on the case may have relevant evidence that could be destroyed absent court action. Such evidence should not be subject to an individual's unfettered decision to destroy it in cases where counsel for a party considers preservation important. Therefore, under Rule 14(a)(1)(E), the parties may move for an order preserving this evidence. Subdivision (d) of Rule 7 simply guarantees the parties an opportunity to be heard on this motion at the initial appearance, since expedition may be crucial in such cases.

When a preservation order is requested at arraignment, the non-party custodian of the evidence is not likely to be present to assert its interests. However, the non-party may subsequently contest the order, or request the court to use its authority under subdivision 14(a)(1)(E)(ii) to "modify or vacate such an order upon a showing that preservation of particular evidence will create significant hardship, on condition that the probative value of said evidence is preserved by a specified alternative means."

Subdivision (e). This subdivision, promulgated in 2004, requires the District Court to issue an order at the initial appearance scheduling subsequent pretrial proceedings. For this purpose the subdivision distinguishes between a "probable cause track" and a "pretrial conference/pretrial hearing" track. The latter requires the court to schedule both a pretrial conference (between the attorneys) and a pretrial hearing, each further addressed in Rule 11. As to the former, some District Court arraignments are continued for probable cause hearings rather than pretrial conferences. Under the statutory mandate that probable cause hearings be held "as soon as may be", G.L. c 276 § 38, the Court should not assign any intervening pretrial conferences or hearings when it intends to, or by statute must, bind over the case. The subdivision's recognition of a separate "probable cause track" is necessary to effectuate this statutory requirement. However, nothing in Rule 7(e) prevents the court from subsequently continuing the probable cause hearing to another date, or (in concurrent jurisdiction cases) from ordering a short continuance of the initial hearing to permit counsel to prepare arguments on whether district court jurisdiction should be declined.

Reporter's Notes—2012

In 2012, Rule 7 was amended in several respects. These revisions are discussed below.

Subdivision (a)(1). Defendants who are released on bail prior to the issuance of a complaint or those who receive a summons must be ordered to appear in court for their arraignment on a date certain. Courts may establish their own policy on whether that date falls on the same day of every week or within a particular time frame. The 2012 amendments eliminated the separate event of an initial appearance prior to arraignment. The widespread availability of counsel to represent defendants at arraignment made this separate event unnecessary. The 2012 amendments also eliminated the procedure that

allowed a summonsed defendant who had retained counsel to be excused from appearing until the pretrial conference or trial.

Subdivision (b)(1). By referring to "the court" as the responsible agency for conducting all of the activities surrounding the arraignment, this subdivision is meant to include judges, special magistrates, and any Superior Court clerk-magistrates authorized to conduct arraignments.

Subdivision (b)(1)(A). This provision requires that the arraignment take place in open court. It restates accepted practice, reflected in the mandate of *Foley v. Commonwealth*, 429 Mass. 496, 498 (1999). The concept of an open court means that the public must be allowed access absent "an overriding interest based on findings that closure is essential to preserve higher values and is narrowly tailored to serve that interest." *Boston Herald v. Superior Court*, 421 Mass. 502, 505 (1995), quoting *Press-Enter. Co. v. Superior Court*, 464 U.S. 501, 510 (1984). Arraignments may take place outside of a courtroom, in settings such as correctional facilities, *see Foley, supra,* or hospitals, *see Boston Herald, supra,* so long as the public's right of access to the proceedings is as free as in a courthouse, subject to the same considerations that might lead a judge to close a courtroom to the public.

Subdivision (b)(1)(C). This provision is intended to alert all the participants at the arraignment of the provisions for notice that appear outside the Rules of Criminal Procedure, such as the bail warning mandated by G. L. c. 276, § 58, and the requirement of G. L. c. 111E, § 10, that defendants charged with drug offenses have a right to request an examination concerning drug dependency.

Subdivision (c)(1). When an attorney in a criminal case appears for an organization, whether incorporated or not, he or she must present the court with proof of authority to act on behalf of the defendant. The proof of authority that this subdivision requires can come in the form of a resolution by a board of directors in the case of a corporate defendant or a similar statement from the person or group authorized to make litigation decisions on behalf of an unincorporated organization. SJC Rule 1:21 already requires corporate defendants in criminal cases to file a disclosure form revealing the identity of any parent corporation or any publicly listed company that owns 10% or more of its shares.

Rule 8.   Assignment of Counsel

(Applicable to District Court and Superior Court)

If a defendant charged with a crime for which a sentence of imprisonment or commitment to the custody of the Department of Youth Services may be imposed initially appears in any court without counsel, the judge shall follow the procedures established in G.L. c. 211D and in Supreme Judicial Court Rule 3:10.

Amended May 29, 1986, effective July 1, 1986.

Reporter's Notes

This rule is in large part derived from former Supreme Judicial Court Rule 3:10 (1967: 351 Mass. 791, as amended, 1969: 355 Mass. 803), and District Court Initial Rules of Criminal Procedure 2, 10 (1971). See Fed.R.Crim.P. 44.

Subdivision (a).

The present state of the law is that counsel is required in all cases where the defendant faces possible imprisonment unless the defendant properly waives his right to the assistance of counsel. Argersinger v. Hamlin, 92 S.Ct. 2006, 407 U.S. 25, 32 L.Ed.2d 530 (1972).

The Supreme Court has held the right to assistance of counsel fundamental in certain juvenile proceedings as well:

A proceeding where the issue is whether the child will be found to be delinquent and subjected to the loss of his liberty is comparable in seriousness to a felony prosecution. The juvenile needs the assistance of counsel to cope with problems of law, to make skilled inquiry into the facts, to insist upon regularity of the proceedings, and to ascertain whether he has a defense and to prepare and submit it.

In re Gault, 87 S.Ct. 1428, 387 U.S. 1, 36, 18 L.Ed.2d 527 (1967). There the Court concluded that in delinquency proceedings where the juvenile faces a risk of commitment, the juvenile *and* his parent must be notified of the juvenile's right to counsel and that counsel will be assigned by the court if the juvenile is indigent. *In re Gault,* supra, at 41; Marsden v. Commonwealth, 352 Mass. 564, 567, 227 N.E.2d 1 (1967); District Court Special Rule 207 (1974).

The stages of criminal proceedings at which the right to counsel has been held to apply include arraignment (Hamilton v. Alabama, 82 S.Ct. 157, 368 U.S. 52, 7 L.Ed.2d 114 [1961]; *see* Commonwealth v. White, 362 Mass. 193, 285 N.E.2d 110 [1972]), probable cause hearing (White v. Maryland, 83 S.Ct. 1050, 373 U.S. 59, 10 L.Ed.2d 193 [1963]; *see* Arsenault v. Massachusetts, 89 S.Ct. 35, 393 U.S. 5, 21 L.Ed.2d 5 [1968]), when the plea is tendered (Moore v. Michigan, 77 S.Ct. 150, 352 U.S. 907 [1956]), trial (Gideon v. Wainwright, 83 S.Ct. 792, 372 U.S. 335, 9 L.Ed.2d 799 [1963]), sentencing (Townsend v. Burke, 71 S.Ct. 286, 334 U.S. 736, 95 L.Ed. 661 [1948]), appellate proceedings (Douglas v. California, 83 S.Ct. 814, 372 U.S. 353, 9 L.Ed.2d 811 [1963]; *see* Arsenault v. Massachusetts, supra; *compare* Ross v. Moffitt, 94 S.Ct. 2437, 417 U.S. 600, 41 L.Ed.2d 341 [1975]), probation revocation proceedings (Williams v. Commonwealth, 350 Mass. 732, 216 N.E.2d 779 [1966]), lineups after the defendant has been formally charged (Kirby v. Illinois, 92 S.Ct. 1877, 406 U.S. 682, 32 L.Ed.2d 411 [1972]; Commonwealth v. Mendes, 361 Mass. 507, 281 N.E.2d 243 [1972] and cases cited), and transfer hearings to determine whether a juvenile is to be tried as an adult offender (Kent v. United States, 86 S.Ct. 1045, 383 U.S. 541, 561, 16 L.Ed.2d 84 [1966]; *see* Marsden v. Commonwealth, 352 Mass. 564, 567 n. 5, 227 N.E.2d 1 [1967]).

Counsel is also to be available to a defendant at the taking of a deposition pursuant to Mass.R.Crim.P. 32 (*see* 18 U.S.C. § 3503[c] [1970] from which Rule 32 derived) and during plea discussions under Mass.R.Crim.P. 12(b)(1).

In requiring that a defendant be advised of his right to, and provided with, counsel upon any appearance in court, Rule 8 is in accord with ABA *Standards Relating to Providing Defense Services* § 5.1 (Approved Draft, 1968), which directs that counsel should be provided "as soon as feasible."

General Laws c. 221, § 34D states in part that the Massachusetts Defenders Committee

shall provide counsel at any stage of a criminal proceeding, other than capital, . . . provided . . . that [the] defendant is unable to obtain counsel by reason of his inability to pay.

Consistent with § 34D, for purposes of this rule, inability to obtain counsel is intended to include only financial inability. There are, however, no criteria supplied by statute or court rule to govern the judicial determination of who qualifies for assigned counsel, despite the fact that G.L. c. 261, § 27C(2), applicable to criminal cases, requires the clerk to "conspicuously post in that part of his office open to the public a notice specifying the indigency limits currently in force. . . ."

In answering the question of whether, under G.L. c. 221, § 34D, the defendant is "unable to obtain counsel by reason of his inability to pay," the judge may choose to rely on the opinion of the probation department, which is required to be prepared by G.L. c. 221, § 34D. However, since the final decision on indigency is the responsibility of the judge, neither the probation department's opinion nor its report of relevant information can be considered conclusive. The judge or special magistrate must "interrogate the defendant to satisfy himself that the defendant is unable to procure counsel." District Court Initial Rule of Criminal Procedure 2 (1971) requires that the interro-

gation be conducted in open court, but its dimensions are left to the judge's discretion.

General Laws c. 119, § 29A states that the parent of an unemancipated minor is liable for the minor's legal expenses, not to exceed three hundred dollars. While the resources of the parents may be included in the determination of the juvenile's indigency, if the parents refuse to retain counsel, the juvenile is entitled to court-provided counsel. It is the practice in some courts of the Commonwealth to impose costs for legal expenses of a juvenile upon the parents, notwithstanding the three-hundred-dollar limit of § 29A, supra, on the grounds that services of counsel are a necessity for which the parents are liable.

The assignment of counsel for, or the election to proceed without counsel by, a juvenile is governed by these rules.

Subdivision (b). This subdivision is drawn from and restates the substance of former S.J.C. Rule 3:10, paragraph 2 (1967: 351 Mass. 791, as amended, 1969: 355 Mass. 803). It is thus intended that counsel shall be assigned from the Massachusetts Defenders Committee, G.L. c. 221, § 34D, or from "a voluntary charitable group, corporation, or association," unless exceptional circumstances such as a conflict of interests or a need for foreign language speaking counsel justify appointing private counsel. *See* Superior Court Rule 53(3) (1974). Commonwealth v. Sheeran, 370 Mass. 82, 345 N.E.2d 362 (1976).

While the court in its discretion may appoint counsel other than from the Massachusetts Defenders Committee or similar organization, that discretion is to be exercised "sparingly" and not "unnecessarily." Abodeely v. County of Worcester, 352 Mass. 719, 227 N.E.2d 486 (1967).

The statutes provide compensation for appointed counsel only in capital cases (G.L. c. 276, § 37A: "reasonable compensation") and more particularly in murder cases (G.L. c. 277, § 55: "reasonable compensation" and § 56: "reasonable expenses"). Sections 55–56 provide that compensation is to be paid by the county where the indictment is found. The court in Abodeely v. County of Worcester, 352 Mass. 719, 227 N.E.2d 486 (1967), held that G.L. c. 213, § 8, which had been construed to compel the counties (now the Commonwealth: see G.L. c. 213, § 8, as amended, St.1978, c. 478, § 127) to pay the expense of prosecuting non-capital criminal cases, should be extended to cover also the costs of appointed defense counsel in such cases.

If we are to provide proper prosecution we must also provide appropriate defence under the Constitution. . . . [W]hen the court assigns counsel for the defence in cases of needy criminal defendants then counsel should be paid from the county treasury. . . .

352 Mass. at 723–24. General Laws c. 276, § 37A and c. 277, §§ 55–56, provide for "reasonable" compensation and expenses. Superior Court Rule 53 imposes a maximum limit on what will be allowed unless an excess is authorized in advance, Rule 53(2), (3)(c), or is deemed necessary in extraordinary circumstances, Rule 53(3)(d).

Subdivision (c). Provision for an assignment docket to be maintained by the clerk is drawn from former S.J.C. Rule 3:10, paragraph 3 (1967: 351 Mass. 791, as amended, 1969: 355 Mass. 803) and is consistent with prior law.

Subdivision (d). If a defendant is found to be financially able to retain counsel at his own expense it is, of course, incumbent upon him to do so. If a defendant is dilatory in engaging counsel, the court is empowered to take reasonable steps to keep the proceedings moving, even if the defendant's failure to arrange representation leaves him without counsel. Commonwealth v. Jackson, 376 Mass. 790, 383 N.E.2d 835 (1978). *See* Ungar v. Sarafite, 84 S.Ct. 841, 376 U.S. 575, 588–91, 11 L.Ed.2d 921 (1964); United States v. White, 529 F.2d 1390, 1394 (8th Cir.1976); United States v. Sperling, 506 F.2d 1323, 1337 n. 19 (2d Cir.1974), cert. denied, 95 S.Ct. 1351, 420 U.S. 962 (1975); Glenn v. United States, 303 F.2d 536, 542–43 (5th Cir.1962), cert. denied sub nom., Belvin v. United States, 83 S.Ct. 737, 372 U.S. 922, 9

L.Ed.2d 726 (1963). *Compare* Commonwealth v. Cavanaugh, 371 Mass. 46, 51, 353 N.E.2d 732 (1976) (myopic insistence upon expeditiousness in the face of a justifiable request for delay can render right to counsel an empty formality).

Subdivision (e). If the defendant wishes to waive counsel and proceed pro se, that right is guaranteed by the sixth and fourteenth amendments to the United States Constitution. Faretta v. California, 95 S.Ct. 2525, 422 U.S. 806, 45 L.Ed.2d 562 (1975). The right to self-representation is recognized in Massachusetts in Article 12 of the Declaration of Rights: "every subject shall have a right . . . to be fully heard in his defense by himself or his counsel, at his election." Commonwealth v. Mott, 2 Mass.App. 47, 51, 308 N.E.2d 557 (1974).

However, the "waiver of counsel will not be presumed from a silent record." Williams v. Commonwealth, 350 Mass. 732, 734, 216 N.E.2d 779 (1966). Since the right to counsel is a constitutional right, the court should insure that a defendant's waiver of that right is both voluntary and intelligent. *See* Johnson v. Zerbst, 58 S.Ct. 1019, 304 U.S. 458, 464, 82 L.Ed. 1461 (1938). Section 7.2 of the ABA *Standards Relating to Providing Defense Services* (Approved Draft, 1968) is instructive on this issue:

> The accused's failure to request counsel or his announced intention to plead guilty should not of itself be construed to constitute a waiver. An accused should not be deemed to have waived the assistance of counsel until the entire process of offering counsel has been completed and a thorough inquiry into the accused's comprehension of that offer and his capacity to make the choice intelligently and understandingly has been made. No waiver should be found to have been made where it appears that the accused is unable to make an intelligent and understanding choice because of his mental condition, age, education, experience, the nature or the complexity of the case, or other factors.

The requirement of this rule that the waiver be in writing and signed by the defendant and certified by the judge or special magistrate is supportive of the notion that any waiver to be constitutional must be both voluntary and intelligent.

Both the United States Supreme Court and the Supreme Judicial Court of Massachusetts have made it clear that the right to proceed pro se is not unqualified. Under the *Faretta* decision, supra, although it is recognized that the right to proceed pro se is personal to the defendant and constitutionally guaranteed, nonetheless the trial judge must make an inquiry into whether the accused is choosing to proceed pro se in an intelligent and competent manner.

> Although a defendant need not himself have the skill and experience of a lawyer in order competently and intelligently to choose self-representation, he should be made aware of the dangers and disadvantages of self-representation.

Faretta, supra, at 835.

Massachusetts case law is in accord with this rule, and qualifies the waiver of counsel further. First, the request to proceed pro se must be unequivocal. Second, it should be asserted before trial. Finally, an inquiry as to the defendant's competence and intelligence in making the decision must be conducted and the motivation of the defendant examined. The defendant must also be told of the possible disadvantages of representing himself. Commonwealth v. Cavanaugh, 371 Mass. 46, 353 N.E.2d 732 (1976); *Commonwealth v. Mott*, supra. *See* Commonwealth v. Jackson, 376 Mass. 790, 383 N.E.2d 835 (1978).

The qualification that the waiver be unequivocal results in leaving a later request due to change of mind to the discretion of the trial judge—the defendant is no longer entitled to counsel as of right. Commonwealth v. Jackson, 376 Mass. 790, 383 N.E.2d 835 (1978). *See* Commonwealth v. Drolet, 337 Mass. 396, 149 N.E.2d 616 (1958).

Moreover, the assertion of the right to proceed pro se should be made before trial. "Once the trial has begun with the defendant represented by counsel, . . . his right thereafter to discharge his lawyer and to represent himself is sharply curtailed." Commonwealth

v. Mott, 2 Mass.App. 47, 308 N.E.2d 557. The courts on both the federal and state levels have construed the language "sharply curtailed" very strictly. In United States ex rel. Maldonado v. Denno, 348 F.2d 12 (2d Cir.1965), it was held that after commencement of trial

> there must be a showing that the prejudice to the legitimate interests of the defendant overbalances the potential disruption of proceedings already in progress, with considerable weight being given to the trial judge's assessment of this balance.

Id. at 15.

If a defendant is to proceed pro se, he must have waived counsel "knowingly and intelligently." *Faretta*, supra, held that technical, legal knowledge is not the test, but rather whether the defendant is literate, competent, and understanding, and is voluntarily exercising his free will. *Accord* Commonwealth v. Jackson, 376 Mass. 790, 383 N.E.2d 835 (1978). Impliedly, if the court finds that the defendant fails this test after an inquiry, it may appoint counsel notwithstanding the defendant's motion to proceed pro se. *See* subdivision (f), infra.

In Von Moltke v. Gillies, 68 S.Ct. 316, 332 U.S. 708, 92 L.Ed. 309 (1948) the Supreme Court laid down a searching formula to be used by trial judges in making certain that a defendant understandingly waives his right to counsel. Massachusetts, however, has not strictly interpreted *Von Moltke*. A judge is not required

> literally to fulfill all elements of a formula describing his responsibilities for acceptance of waiver of counsel. Substance rather than form is the guiding criterion for reviewing courts.

Commonwealth v. Fillippini, 2 Mass.App. 179, 182, 310 N.E.2d 147 (1974). Moreover, the *Faretta* decision, which recognizes emphatically the right to proceed pro se, would seem to erode the need for use of any rigid formula as long as the waiver was knowing and intelligent.

In *Mott*, supra, the court stated:

> We think that even in cases where the accused is harming himself by insisting on conducting his own defense, respect for individual autonomy requires that he be allowed to go to jail under his own banner if he so desires and if he makes the choice with eyes open.

Mott, supra, at 52, *quoting* United States ex rel. Maldonado v. Denno, 348 F.2d 12, 15 (2d Cir.1965).

However, under Massachusetts law, which is more liberal than *Von Moltke*, it is necessary for the trial judge to inquire into the defendant's motivation. "The motivation of the accused in making the request should be examined, and the accused should be apprised of the pitfalls in proceeding pro se." *Mott*, supra, at 52.

Subdivision (f). This subdivision is drawn from Rules of Criminal Procedure (U.L.A.) rule 711 (1974). See ABA *Standards Relating to the Function of the Trial Judge* § 6.7 (Approved Draft, 1972).

As long as the standby counsel assists only when called upon by the defendant and calls the attention of the court to matters favorable to the defendant upon which the court should rule upon its own motion, there is no interference with the defendant's representing himself. See Illinois v. Allen, 90 S.Ct. 1057, 397 U.S. 337, 25 L.Ed.2d 353 (1970); Commonwealth v. Maynard, 2 Mass.App. 894, 319 N.E.2d 453 (1974) (Rescript).

> A judge has broad discretion to appoint and order payment of . . . counsel to represent or advise . . . [an indigent defendant], to whatever extent he will accept representation, advice, and assistance, in an effort to ensure a fair, orderly and expeditious trial.

Jackson v. Commonwealth, 370 Mass. 855, 856, 346 N.E.2d 714 (1976) (Rescript).

Rule 9.　Joinder of Offenses or Defendants

(Applicable to District Court and Superior Court)

(a) Joinder of Offenses.

(1) *Related Offenses.* Two or more offenses are related offenses if they are based on the same criminal conduct or episode or arise out of a course of criminal conduct or series of criminal episodes connected together or constituting parts of a single scheme or plan.

(2) *Joinder of Related Offenses in Complaint or Indictment.* If two or more related offenses are of the same or similar character, they may be charged in the same indictment or complaint, with each offense stated in a separate count.

(3) *Joinder of Related Offenses for Trial.* If a defendant is charged with two or more related offenses, either party may move for joinder of such charges. The trial judge shall join the charges for trial unless he determines that joinder is not in the best interests of justice.

(4) *Joinder of Unrelated Offenses.* Upon the written motion of a defendant, or with his written consent, the trial judge may join for trial two or more charges of unrelated offenses upon a showing that failure to try the charges together would constitute harassment or unduly consume the time or resources of the parties. The trial judge shall join the charges for trial unless he determines that joinder is not in the best interests of justice.

(b) Joinder of Defendants. Two or more defendants may be joined in the same indictment or complaint if the charges against them arise out of the same criminal conduct or episode or out of a course of criminal conduct or series of criminal episodes so connected as to constitute parts of a single scheme, plan, conspiracy or joint enterprise. The defendants may be charged separately or together in one or more counts; all of the defendants need not be charged in each count.

(c) Consolidation of Offenses or Defendants on Motion of Court. The trial judge may order two or more indictments or complaints to be tried together if the offenses and the defendants, if more than one, could have been joined in a single indictment or complaint. The procedure shall be the same as if the prosecution were under a single indictment or complaint.

(d) Relief From Prejudicial Joinder.

(1) *In General.* If it appears that a joinder of offenses or of defendants is not in the best interests of justice, the judge may upon his own motion or the motion of either party order an election of separate trials of counts, grant a severance of defendants, or provide whatever other relief justice may require.

(2) *Motion by the Defendant.* A motion of the defendant for relief from prejudicial joinder shall be in writing and made before trial and shall be supported by an affidavit setting forth the grounds upon which any alleged prejudice rests, except that a motion for severance may be made before or at the close of all the evidence if based upon a ground not previously known.

(e) Conspiracy. An indictment or complaint for conspiracy to commit a substantive offense shall not be tried simultaneously with an indictment or complaint for the commission of the substantive offense, unless the defendant moves for joinder of such charges pursuant to subdivision (a) of this rule.

Reporter's Notes

The substance of Rule 9 is taken from several sources. These are Fed.R.Crim.P. 8 and 13, the ABA *Standards Relating to Joinder and Severance* (Approved Draft, 1968), Uniform Rules of Criminal Procedure (U.L.A.) Rules 471–73 (1974), and ALI Model Penal Code §§ 1.07–1.09 (1962). *See* Commonwealth v. Gallarelli, 372 Mass. 573, 362 N.E.2d 923 (1977) (Kaplan, J., concurring). The language is drawn largely from the Uniform Rules.

Subdivision (a). Although subdivisions (a) and (b) of the rule are consistent with their statutory precedent, former G.L. c. 277, § 46 (St.1861, c. 181), the rule is more explicit in defining what charges may be joined in a single indictment.

Related offenses are defined in (a)(1) as those which 1) are based on the same criminal conduct or episode, or 2) arise out of a course of criminal conduct or a series of criminal episodes connected together or constituting parts of a single scheme or plan. "Conduct" means an act or omission to act; "episode" means an occurrence or connected series of occurrences and developments which may be viewed as distinctive and apart although part of a larger or more comprehensive series. ABA *Standards Relating to Joinder and Severance* § 1.3(a), comment at 20–21 (Approved Draft, 1968).

Under Federal Rule 8, offenses may be joined if they 1) are based on the same transaction, 2) are parts of a common scheme or plan, or 3) are of the same or similar character. Offenses that are based on the same underlying facts or are each part of a larger plan are related in such a way as to insure an overlap in the evidence to be presented upon each offense.

Rule 9 takes the position that the goal of judicial economy will rarely be paramount to affording the defendant a trial as free from prejudice as possible; therefore, joinder of unrelated offenses is prohibited except at the instance of the defendant or with his written consent.

Rule 9 permits joint trial of offenses committed in furtherance of a common scheme or plan, but factually independent, and thus conforms to case law under former G.L. c. 277, § 46.

General Laws c. 277, § 46, which governed joinder of offenses, stated:

Two or more counts describing different crimes depending upon the same facts or transactions may be set forth in the same indictment if it contains an averment that the different counts therein are different descriptions of the same acts.

If read narrowly the statute would prohibit joint trial of offenses which were part of a joint scheme or plan, but not dependent upon the same underlying facts. The statute has, however, been interpreted more broadly, allowing joint trial of offenses related in ways other than as literally permitted by § 46. *See* e.g., Harding v. Commonwealth, 283 Mass. 369, 186 N.E. 556 (1933).

Subdivision (a)(3) allows the parties to request that the charges pending against the defendant be joined for trial. By granting the court discretionary power to deny the defendant's motion to join the charges, the rule protects the prosecution from being effectively "forced" to try charges on which it has not yet organized a sufficient case to warrant proceeding. See Mass.R.Crim.P. 37(a), (b)(2), which require the approval of the prosecutor for charges to be transferred for plea, sentence, or trial.

Subdivision (b). This subdivision is in form virtually identical to the corresponding federal rule provision, but substitutes "conduct" and "criminal episode" for the terms used in the federal rule, "act" and "transaction."

Although there is no statute in the Commonwealth analogous to the joinder of defendants provision contained in subdivision (b), it seems to be in harmony with former Massachusetts practice. Prior to the promulgation of these rules, such joinder was permitted in two instances: when the defendants were charged with joint participation in a single series of events based on identical facts, Commonwealth v. Nicholson, 4 Mass.App. 87, 341 N.E.2d 688 (1976); Englehart v. Commonwealth, 353 Mass. 561, 233 N.E.2d 737 (1968), and when there existed sufficient evidence to indicate that the defendant and co-defendant were engaged in a common enterprise, and the issue of fact to be tried against each defendant was similar, as in Commonwealth v. Smith, 353 Mass. 442, 232 N.E.2d 917 (1968).

Subdivision (c). This subdivision allows otherwise permissive joinder of offenses or defendants to be accomplished by the trial court on its own motion. This provision is included in order to achieve the principle goal of the rule, judicial economy, while protecting the defendant's right to a reasonably prejudice-free trial. Although it is contemplated that joinder will be effected by the prosecution at the indictment or complaint stage in all possible cases, should the prosecution elect to proceed in a manner contrary to the goal of judicial economy this subsection empowers the court to rectify the situation on its own motion without having to depend on a motion by the defendant. *Compare* Commonwealth v. Benjamin, 358 Mass. 672, 678, 266 N.E.2d 662 (1971) (order for amendment of indictments).

Subdivision (d). Subdivision (d)(1) is essentially drawn from Fed. R.Crim.P. 14 and is consonant with prior Massachusetts practice. Subdivision (d)(2) is taken from ABA *Standards Relating to Joinder & Severance* § 2.1(a) (Approved Draft, 1968).

> As a general proposition, the decision whether to allow a motion to sever two or more indictments which have been joined for purposes of trial rests in the sound discretion of the trial judge.

Commonwealth v. Jervis, 368 Mass. 638, 645, 335 N.E.2d 356 (1975). *Accord,* United States v. Luna, 585 F.2d 1, 4–5 (1st Cir.1978); Commonwealth v. Cruz, 373 Mass. 676, 369 N.E.2d 996 (1977); Commonwealth v. Drew, 4 Mass.App. 30, 340 N.E.2d 524 (1976).

Where "substantially the same evidence, or evidence connected with a single line of conduct," Commonwealth v. Rosenthal, 211 Mass. 50, 54, 97 N.E. 609 (1912), substantiates two or more indictments for "offenses [which] are kindred and liable to punishment of the same general character," Commonwealth v. Veal, 362 Mass. 877, 289 N.E.2d 844 (1972) (Rescript), there is no abuse of discretion in denying the defendant's motion for severance. *Commonwealth v. Drew, supra,* at 53. The legal standards which must guide the exercise of the court's discretion in determining a motion to sever have been articulated as follows:

> No sound reason can be given why several indictments charging different crimes arising out of a single chain of circumstances should not be tried together. Where several offenses might have been joined in one indictment, and would be proved by substantially the same evidence, or evidence connected with a single line of conduct, and grow out of what is essentially one transaction, and where it does not appear that any real right of the defendant has been jeopardized, it would be a refinement not demanded by the law or by justice to require in all instances a separate trial, simply because separate indictments have been found for each offense.

Commonwealth v. Cruz, 373 Mass. 676, 369 N.E.2d 996 (1977). *Accord* Commonwealth v. Blow, 362 Mass. 196, 200, 285 N.E.2d 400 (1972); *Commonwealth v. Rosenthal, supra.*

The assertion of prejudicial joinder does not challenge the propriety of the initial order for consolidation. Rather, the prejudice is found in facts peculiar to a defendant's case. Defendants may move for severance of their cases, or of counts therein, on the grounds of misjoinder and prejudicial joinder.

Misjoinder. It is important to know what the minimal grounds for joinder of defendants or offenses are when considering a claim of misjoinder because such a claim is an assertion that the minimal requirements have not been satisfied. Thus, when a motion for severance of defendants or for separate trials of more than one count is based on the ground that the consolidated offenses should not have been joined, i.e., that there has been a misjoinder, the standards upon which the motion is to be judged are stated in subdivisions (a)(1)–(2) of this rule.

A misjoinder can result in two ways. First, the offenses joined might have been improperly joined in one indictment and, secondly, two indictments may have been improperly consolidated for trial. In both cases, however, the same standard is to be used to determine the propriety of the joinder.

Two other aspects of this subdivision deserve mention. First, subdivision (d)(1) permits a court to grant a severance upon its own motion. Although this authorizes a court to review its initial order of consolidation of the charges for trial to see if the minimum grounds are satisfied, its primary significance is that it permits the court to exercise its discretion in deciding initially whether to proceed by joint or separate trials even though one of the minimum grounds for joinder is satisfied. In effect, this provision permits the trial judge to consider the prejudice to the defendant in his initial decision as well as at later stages of the trial.

Secondly, it is recommended in the ABA *Standards Relating to Joinder and Severance* § 2.1(c)–(d), comment at 28 (Approved Draft, 1968), that a motion by the prosecution for severance, unless consented to by the defendant, be required to be made prior to trial to avoid giving the defendant upon retrial the defense of double jeopardy. As is stated therein, however, this proposition does not derive from any judicial holdings to that effect. While this subdivision contemplates that prosecution motions for severance shall be limited to a pretrial posture, it is likely that if a severance upon the prosecution's motion after the commencement of trial is a "manifest necessity" such that the "ends of public justice would otherwise be defeated," United States v. Perez, 22 U.S. (9 Wheat.) 579, 580 (1824), courts of this Commonwealth would hold that the severance was not a bar to future prosecution on the severed charges, even if the defendant did not consent. *Compare* Price v. Slayton, 347 F.Supp. 1269 (W.D.Va.1972).

Prejudicial Joinder. Satisfying the minimum joinder standards is only one consideration affecting a court's decision on consolidation. The court is lodged with the discretion to determine in each case whether justice would be served better by joint or separate trials. The countervailing considerations affecting this decision are the defendant's interests and the interests of the court and prosecution in having the adjudication as short and as inexpensive as possible. The merits of each side's claims will differ from case to case. Only the trial judge is in a position to balance effectively the competing interests, and, in most cases, his discretion is very broad.

In its initial decision upon the issue of consolidating charges for a single trial, in addition to determining whether minimum grounds for joinder exist, the court should consider whether the defendant would be adversely affected by joinder. If he would and if this prejudice overrides the interests of the prosecutor, the public, and the courts in an expeditious trial, joinder should not be ordered.

At any stage after joinder has been ordered, the court on motion of the defendant or on its own motion may wish to reconsider whether the interests of justice are better served by separate trials. At such time, the court should again weigh the competing interests as well as considering how far the prosecution of the charges has proceeded and whether a severance would involve an undue relitigation of issues already presented to the court. In both its initial decision and at any later reconsideration of prejudice to the defendant, the court is determining whether there exists a prejudicial joinder of charges.

The Supreme Judicial Court summarized the duty of the trial court in protecting a defendant's rights as follows:

> It is the heavy obligation of the trial court sedulously to take care that the defendant is not confounded in his defense, that the attention of the jury is not distracted and that in no aspect are the substantial rights of the defendant adversely affected by requiring him to proceed to trial on separate complaints for different offenses or on separate counts for different offenses in one complaint.

Commonwealth v. Slavski, 245 Mass. 405, 412–13, 140 N.E. 465 (1923). It is made clear by the court that the trial court's discretion is circumscribed by its duty to guarantee a fair trial.

A court may find prejudice on its own motion or the motion of either party. However, where a defendant initiates the motion for relief from prejudice, he has a strong burden of persuasion. Sagansky v. United States, 358 F.2d 195 (1st Cir.1966), cert. denied, 87 S.Ct. 36, 385 U.S. 816, 17 L.Ed.2d 55. This heavy burden is placed upon the defendant because the trial judge has already determined once that the defendant was not likely to be prejudiced by consolidated trials.

A defendant first must make his motion at the appropriate time. If a motion is filed before the prejudicial grounds have materialized, the motion should be dismissed. The grounds of prejudice may become known to a defendant at any stage of the pretrial of trial proceedings. He has the duty to inform the court of these grounds whenever he first learns of them. If a motion is made at trial based upon grounds known prior to the commencement of the trial, the defendant has waived his opportunity to object. Subdivision (d)(2).

Secondly, a defendant has the related burden of showing a specific ground of prejudice. It is not enough for a defendant merely to claim that his chances of acquittal are reduced in a joint trial, or that a joint trial presents him with a number of *potential* dangers. The defendant must point to definite prejudice that presently exists.

One other class of cases deserves mention. In these, a separate trial must be granted because of an established principle of law; the decision is non-discretionary. In cases not of this class, the decision regarding a joint trial rests upon the peculiar arrangement of the facts, whereas here the facts are less significant. This class is composed mostly of claims that a defendant's constitutional rights will be infringed by a consolidated trial. Bruton v. United States, 88 S.Ct. 1620, 391 U.S. 123, 20 L.Ed.2d 476 (1968), establishes the most significant principle in this area. Basing its decision on a defendant's sixth amendment right to confront adverse witnesses, the Supreme Court held that a severance was required where a co-defendant's confession implicating the defendant is to be offered at trial. It had always been true that such a confession was inadmissible against the non-confessor, but prior to this decision a limiting instruction to the jury was deemed sufficient to protect the rights of the non-confessing defendant. The distinction between this decision and others where continued reliance on jury instructions is found is that a defendant's constitutional right is in issue here and less flexibility in balancing competing interests is tolerated.

The scope of the *Bruton* decision has been delimited since the time of its issuance, and a severance is not always required where one defendant's confession mentions other participants in the criminal acts. The following are examples where a severance is not required:

1. Commonwealth v. Scott, 355 Mass. 471, 245 N.E.2d 415 (1969), holds that a confession implicating the defendant may be admitted in a joint trial when the defendant does not contest his participation in the crime. This occurs when a defendant asserts a special defense, e.g., insanity.

2. When the statement refers to other participants without identifying them or when the statement can be cured of any constitutional defect by excision, it may be admitted at a joint trial. *See* Commonwealth v. French, 357 Mass. 356, 259 N.E.2d 195, 46 A.L.R.3d 1106 (1970); ABA *Standards*, supra, § 2.3(a). But sufficient identification may be found even when names are not used. Commonwealth v. Sarro, 356 Mass. 100, 248 N.E.2d 286 (1969).

3. The confessing co-defendant can testify at trial, thereby giving the implicated defendant the opportunity to cross-examine the witness on any statements made by him that were admitted at trial. Santoro v. United States, 402 F.2d 920 (9th Cir.1968). *See* Commonwealth v. Hicks, Mass.Adv.Sh. (1979) 1, 384 N.E.2d 1206; Commonwealth v. Murphy, Mass.App.Adv.Sh. (1978) 533.

Another example of a severance being required because of the threat of impairing a defendant's constitutional rights is offered by DeLuna v. United States, 308 F.2d 140, 1 A.L.R.3d 969 (5th Cir.1962). Only one defendant took the stand, and his counsel commented upon the failure of his client's co-defendant to testify in an attempt to show that only an innocent defendant has the courage to deny his guilt at trial. The Court of Appeals held it error to permit one defendant to comment adversely upon his co-defendant's exercise of his fifth amendment privilege not to testify.

In sum, prejudice to a defendant is to be found in the facts of his case. Most claims of prejudice are to be decided by the trial court in the exercise of its discretion, and the majority of these claims are rejected. A severance is required in some cases because certain facts relating to either trial strategy or the nature of the offenses establish as a matter of law the existence of prejudice. In other cases, a severance is mandated by constitutional considerations.

Subdivision (e). This subdivision prohibits trial on an indictment or complaint for conspiracy to commit a substantive offense simultaneously with the trial on the substantive offense, except upon motion of the defendant. This provision is retained from former G.L. c. 278, § 2A (St.1968, c. 721, § 2) pursuant to which the prohibition against joint trials of the conspiracy and substantive charges was absolute. *See* Commonwealth v. Gallarelli, Mass.Adv.Sh. (1977) 1013, 1017, 362 N.E.2d 923. Under this rule, however, the defendant may move for joinder of such charges.

The Supreme Judicial Court has noted that "[t]he legislative history affords no indication of why § 2A, which may add new complications to enforcement of the criminal law, was adopted at all...." Commonwealth v. French, 357 Mass. 356, 375 n. 20, 259 N.E.2d 195, 46 A.L.R.3d 1106 (1970). *Accord* Commonwealth v. Gallarelli, Mass.Adv. Sh. (1977) 1013, 1024, 362 N.E.2d 923 (Kaplan, J., concurring). The intent of the rule is to guard against the possibility that a jury, if permitted to hear evidence on both the conspiracy and the substantive offense, might convict on the charge of the substantive offenses of a matter of course after convicting on the conspiracy charge, in spite of the court's instruction as to the distinct evidence required to establish a conspiracy. This is because of the much broader scope of admissibility of evidence permitted to prove the conspiracy charge.

The defendant should be allowed to proceed by a joint trial, however, so long as it is determined by the judge to be in the best interests of justice. This practice accords with that under Fed.R.Crim.P. 8(b), pursuant to which conspiracy and substantive charges may be joined. E.g., United States v. Graham, 548 F.2d 1302, 1310 (8th Cir.1977); United States v. Beasley, 519 F.2d 233, 238 (5th Cir.1975); United States v. Banks, 465 F.2d 1235, 1242–43 (5th Cir.), cert. denied, 401 U.S. 924 (1972); Gordon v. United States, 438 F.2d 858, 878 (5th Cir.), cert. denied sub nom., Crandall v. United States, 92 S.Ct. 63, 404 U.S. 828, 30 L.Ed.2d 56 (1971). See ABA *Standards Relating to Joinder and Severance* § 1.2(b), comment at 15 (Approved Draft, 1968).

Rule 10.   Continuances

(Applicable to District Court and Superior Court)

(a) Continuances.

(1) After a case has been entered upon the trial calendar, a continuance shall be granted only when based upon cause and only when necessary to insure that the interests of justice are served.

(2) The factors, among others, which a judge shall consider in determining whether to grant a continuance in any case are:

(A) Whether the failure to grant a continuance in the proceeding would be likely to make a continuation of the proceeding impossible, or result in a miscarriage of justice.

(B) Whether the case taken as a whole is so unusual or so complex, because of the number of defendants or the nature of the prosecution or otherwise, that it is unreasonable to expect adequate preparation of the case at the time it is scheduled for trial.

(C) Whether the overall caseload of defense counsel routinely prohibits his making scheduled appearances, whether there has been a failure of diligent preparation by a party, and whether there has been a failure by a party to use due diligence to obtain available witnesses.

(3) An attorney who is to be otherwise engaged in a trial, evidentiary hearing, or appellate argument so as to require a continuance shall notify the court and the adverse party or the attorney for the adverse party of such conflicting engagement not less than twenty-four hours before the scheduled appearance, or within such other time as is reasonable under the circumstances.

(4) A motion for a continuance may include a request that the court rule on the motion without a hearing. If such a motion is filed at least three court days prior to the scheduled appearance or trial date and indicates that all parties have agreed to the continuance, the court shall, prior to the scheduled date, rule on the motion without a hearing unless it deems a hearing to be necessary. In any other case, the court may in its discretion rule on a continuance motion without a hearing, provided that all parties have had an adequate opportunity to file an opposition to the motion. If the court continues the case without a hearing, defendant's counsel shall inform the defendant of the revised date. Any motion filed pursuant to this subdivision shall provide one or more proposed continuance dates and state all supporting grounds, and any factual allegations shall be supported by affidavit.

(b) Assessment of Costs. When a continuance is granted upon the motion of either the Commonwealth or the defendant without adequate notice to the adverse party, causing the adverse party to incur unnecessary expenses, a judge may in his discretion assess those expenses as costs against the party or counsel requesting the continuance.

(c) Preservation of Testimony. A judge may order as a condition upon the granting of a continuance that the testimony of a witness then present in court be taken and preserved for subsequent use at trial or any other proceeding. The witness shall be examined in open court by the party on whose behalf he is present and the adverse party shall have the right of cross-examination. The expense of taking and preserving the testimony shall be assessed as costs against the party requesting the continuance.

Amended October 14, 1997, effective December 1, 1997.

Reporter's Notes

This rule is modeled in part after 18 U.S.C. § 3161(h)(8)(B)–(C) (Supp. 1, 1975). Subdivisions (b) and (c), while novel to Massachusetts criminal practice, are not without precedent, *see* Superior Court Rule 21 (1974); District Court Supplemental Rule of Civil Procedure 103 (1975); G.L. c. 276, § 50.

Subdivision (a). This subdivision is modeled after 18 U.S.C. § 3161(h)(8)(B)–(C) (Supp. 1, 1975). The controlling principle underlying this subdivision is that a continuance should be granted only when justice requires. See ABA *Standards Relating to Speedy Trial* § 1.3 (Approved Draft, 1968); *the Defense Function* § 1.2(b), (c) (Approved Draft, 1971); *the Prosecution Function* § 2.9(a), (c) (Approved Draft, 1971); Rules of Criminal Procedure (U.L.A.) Rule 721(d) (1974). Consensual continuances and continuances which are helpful, but which fall short of being necessary, are not to be granted, because in

such cases justice is generally promoted by proceeding to trial without delay and because the need for the prompt disposition of criminal cases transcends the desires of the immediate participants in the proceedings. *Compare* Commonwealth v. Silva, Mass.App.Adv.Sh. (1978) 374 (Rescript), 374 N.E.2d 353.

Whether a motion for a continuance should be granted traditionally lies within the discretion of the trial judge, whose action will not be disturbed unless there is a clear abuse of discretion. Commonwealth v. Jackson, Mass.Adv.Sh. (1978) 3062, 3064, 383 N.E.2d 835; Commonwealth v. Watkins, Mass.Adv.Sh. (1978) 1646, 1671, 379 N.E.2d 1040; Commonwealth v. Funderberg, Mass.Adv.Sh. (1978) 601, 604, 373 N.E.2d 963; Commonwealth v. Grieco, Mass.App.Adv.Sh. (1977) 598, 604, 362 N.E.2d 1204. In ruling on a motion for a continuance, the judge should balance the moving party's need for additional time against the possible inconvenience, increased costs, and prejudice which may be incurred by the opposing party, as well as giving due weight to the interest of the judicial system in avoiding delays which would not measurably contribute to the resolution of a particular controversy. Commonwealth v. Gilchrest, 364 Mass. 272, 276–77, 303 N.E.2d 331 (1973). *Accord Commonwealth v. Grieco,* supra, at 605, Mass.App.Adv.Sh. (1977) 598, 362 N.E.2d 1204.

Common grounds asserted by counsel as a basis for a requested continuance are:

Illness of the defendant or important witnesses or defense counsel, conflicting engagements of counsel, lack of time for preparation by counsel or prejudicial publicity or a combination of several of the factors....

30 MASS. PRACTICE SERIES (Smith) § 1013 (1970, Supp.1978).

A determination of a motion for a continuance to secure the attendance of witnesses will depend upon a showing that the desired testimony is of more than "marginal significance" and not "merely cumulative" to or corroborative of other available testimony to the same effect. Commonwealth v. Watkins, Mass.Adv.Sh. (1978) 1646, 1670–71, 379 N.E.2d 1040; Commonwealth v. Funderberg, 374 Mass. 577, 373 N.E.2d 963 (1978); Commonwealth v. Hanger, Mass.App.Adv. Sh. (1978) 633, 648, aff'd, Mass.Adv.Sh. (1979) 647; Commonwealth v. Darden, 5 Mass.App. 522, 364 N.E.2d 1092 (1977), where the adverse party would not be prejudiced by a continuance and the testimony is significant, a denial of the continuance constitutes an abuse of discretion, Commonwealth v. Silva, Mass.App.Adv.Sh. (1978) 374 (Rescript), 374 N.E.2d 353, assuming that the desired witness may be expected to become available within a reasonable time. *Compare* Commonwealth v. Ambers, 4 Mass.App. 647, 357 N.E.2d 323 (1976), (witness missed ride) with Commonwealth v. Swenor, 3 Mass.App. 65, 66–67, 323 N.E.2d 742 (1975) (witness in federal custody; authorities would not honor writ of habeas corpus ad testificandum). *See* Commonwealth v. Hanger, Mass.App.Adv.Sh. (1978) 633, 647, 376 N.E.2d 877. Subdivision (a)(2)(C) adds as a consideration that the moving party must have exercised due diligence to obtain the presence of available witnesses.

As for conflicting engagements of counsel, subdivision (a)(2)(C) indicates that delays attributable to the heavy case load of desired defense counsel which would prevent the commencement of trial for an unreasonable time period do not establish good cause for a continuance. The right of a defendant to retain counsel of his choice does not include the right to choose an attorney who is unable to comply with the demands of the trial calendar. United States v. DiStefano, 464 F.2d 845, 846 n. 1 (2d Cir.1972). *See* United States v. Poulack, 556 F.2d 83, 86 (1st Cir.1977); United States v. Tortora, 464 F.2d 1202, 1210 (2d Cir.1972); Commonwealth v. Perry, Mass.App.Adv.Sh. (1978) 840, 850, 378 N.E.2d 1384.

Other conflicting engagements of counsel afford no right to the continuance of any particular case.... [T]his is the only way in which the trial of causes can proceed in an orderly and expeditious way under present conditions.... No attorney can accept ... a larger number of cases than he can try as and when they are reached and expect courts to continue any case for his convenience or that of his clients. Commonwealth v. Festo, 251 Mass. 275, 277, 146 N.E. 700 (1925). *See* Commonwealth v. Dabrieo, 370 Mass. 728, 736–37, 352 N.E.2d 186 (1976) (counsel was engaged in court appearances in several counties and "unavailable for trial of this case" for seven months). There are those instances, however, where a conflicting engagement is unavoidable and justice would best be served by the granting of a continuance. In such an instance, subdivision (a)(3) requires counsel to notify the court and the adverse party of the conflict in order to minimize their inconvenience.

The sixth and fourteenth amendments to the United States Constitution, which afford a defendant the right to counsel in a prosecution which may result in a loss of liberty, Argersinger v. Hamlin, 92 S.Ct. 887, 407 U.S. 25, 27 L.Ed.2d 805 (1972), are not satisfied by the mere presence of a competent attorney if that attorney is not prepared. Commonwealth v. Cavanaugh, 371 Mass. 46, 57, 353 N.E.2d 732 (1976). In addition to the factors listed in subdivision (a)(2)(B) relative to the reasonableness of expecting adequate preparation, the court may consider the length of time the attorney has been assigned or appointed to the case. In ruling on a motion for a continuance on this ground, the judge's discretion cannot be exercised so as to impair the constitutional right to prepared counsel; a "myopic insistence upon expeditiousness in the face of a justifiable request for delay can render the right ... an empty formality." *Commonwealth v. Cavanaugh,* supra, 371 Mass. at 51. On the other hand, where there is ample justification for the conclusion that a last-minute claim of lack of preparation is merely a dilatory tactic, is unsupported by the facts, or is the result of a failure of diligent preparation, a denial of a continuance is no abuse of discretion. Commonwealth v. Jackson, Mass.Adv.Sh. (1978) 3062, 3064, 3070, 383 N.E.2d 835; Commonwealth v. Perry, Mass.App.Adv. Sh. (1978) 840, 848–50, 378 N.E.2d 1384; subdivision (a)(2)(C). *See also* Commonwealth v. Coward, Mass.App.Adv.Sh. (1979) 273 (Rescript) 386 N.E.2d 256.

Pursuant to Mass.R.Crim.P. 11(a)(2)(B) and (b)(2)(B), if the required pretrial conference report is not filed and a party does not appear at the scheduled time to explain the failure, "no request of that party for a continuance of the trial date ... shall be granted...."

Subdivision (b). This subdivision deviates from previous Massachusetts criminal procedure. Former practice dictated that if a continuance was granted, each party was to bear his own costs, unless the defendant was assessed the costs of prosecution. *See* generally G.L. c. 280, § 6. However, the courts have long applied a similar assessment rule to the costs of continuances in civil proceedings. Superior Court Rule 21 (1974) provides, and District Court Civil Rule 16 (1965) provided, that when a case is postponed on the motion of a party, that party may be responsible for the costs and expenses of the adverse party in addition to his own.

The decision to assess the costs rests solely within the discretion of the judge, and payment is to be made directly to the adverse party for the benefit of whomever incurred the expenses and not to the court. The purposes of this rule are to discourage parties or their attorneys from requesting continuances on short notice and to reimburse parties for expenses they incur as a result of the tardiness of the adverse side in requesting a continuance. As stated in the District Court and Superior Court rules, supra, the court should not assess costs against a party in cases where his opponent has incurred expenses because of a requested continuance when: 1) the continuance is granted because of improper conduct of the adverse party; or 2) adequate notice was in fact given the adverse party (*see* [a][3], infra); or 3) grounds for the continuance were not discovered in time to give sufficient notice to prevent the expense to the adverse party.

Assessable costs under this rule are those costs directly caused by the insufficient notice. Assessable costs generally include witness fees, extra compensation paid to police witnesses, travel costs, costs of depositions pursuant to subdivision (c), infra, and perhaps stenographers' attendance fees in District Court. *See* Mass.R.Crim.P. 6(d)(1).

Subdivision (c). A new practice is instituted by this subdivision: if a witness is present in court and a party has requested a continuance, the judge may condition the grant of the continuance upon the taking and preservation of that witness' testimony for use at trial or other proceeding. While similar in many respects to a court-ordered deposition after a finding that a witness was unlikely to appear at the continued proceeding (former G.L. c. 276, § 50 [St.1851, c. 71]), the procedure permitted under this rule is not termed a deposition. This is to avoid conflict with the formal summons and notice requirements of Mass.R.Crim.P. 35(b)(c)(h). In all other respects the procedure is compatible with Rule 35 deposition practice.

While utilization of the procedure established by this subdivision should be undertaken only in "exceptional circumstances" when "deemed to be in the interests of justice," Mass.R.Crim.P. 35(a), it is not intended to be so restricted as that under Mass.R.Crim.P. 6(d)(2), pursuant to which testimony may be taken upon the default of a defendant only if "to require the attendance at a later time of a witness ... would constitute a hardship because of age, infirmity, illness, profession or other sufficient reason." Once taken and preserved, the witness' testimony may be used as substantive evidence in any subsequent proceeding as if the witness were "unavailable" under Mass.R.Crim.P. 35(g).

This procedure does not deny the defendant's right to confrontation of witnesses, since it is presumed that the defendant will be present when the continuance is requested and the witness will, of course, be in attendance. The witness is to be examined in open court by the party calling him and the adverse party is permitted to cross-examine. In these circumstances, the constitutional requirement is satisfied. Commonwealth v. DiPietro, 373 Mass. 369, 367 N.E.2d 811 (1977); aff'g Commonwealth v. DiPietro, 4 Mass.App. 845, 356 N.E.2d 269 (1976).

Reporter's Notes—1997

(a)(4). In 1997, Rule 10 was amended by adding new subsection (a)4. This amendment allows the judge to rule on a continuance motion without a hearing, provided all other parties have had a chance to file an opposition to the motion. Previously a continuance motion was often argued in court, even if it was agreed to by all parties, because no other formal procedure was available. Either the case was advanced for hearing on the motion, compounding client expense and court congestion; or the continuance motion was argued on the trial day, leaving parties uncertain whether it would be granted and requiring the defendant and witnesses to be present in case the motion was denied. Subsection (a)(4) is designed to rectify these problems and provide a more efficient procedure, while continuing to maintain ultimate authority in the court over whether to grant a continuance even when the parties are in agreement.

Criminal Rule 10 continues to provide for a ruling by the judge on a continuance motion in every case, consistent with Uniform Magistrate's Rule 2. Although this rule generally permits actions on uncontested, nonevidentiary motions by the magistrate, subdivision (c) prohibits the magistrate from acting on continuances.

As with Rule 7, when a case is continued in the absence of the defendant, defense counsel is charged with the responsibility of so notifying his or her client.

Rule 11. Pretrial Conference and Pretrial Hearing

[Text of rule applicable to cases initiated (by indictment or complaint) on or after September 7, 2004.]

(a) The Pretrial Conference.

At arraignment, except on a complaint regarding which the court will not exercise final jurisdiction, the court shall order the prosecuting attorney and defense counsel to attend a pretrial conference on a date certain to consider such matters as will promote a fair and expeditious disposition of the case.

The defendant shall be available for attendance at the pretrial conference. The court may require the conference to be held at court under the supervision of a judge or clerk-magistrate.

(1) *Conference Agenda.* Among those issues to be discussed at the pretrial conference are:

(A) Discovery and all other matters which, absent agreement of the parties, must be raised by pretrial motion. All motions which cannot be agreed upon shall be filed pursuant to Rule 13(d).

(B) Whether the case can be disposed of without a trial.

(C) If the case is to be tried, (i) the setting of a proposed trial date which shall be subject to the approval of the court and which when fixed by the court shall not be changed without express permission of the court; (ii) the probable length of trial; (iii) the availability of necessary witnesses; and (iv) whether issues of fact can be resolved by stipulation.

(2) *Conference Report.*

(A) Filing. A conference report, subscribed by the prosecuting attorney and counsel for the defendant, and when necessary to waive constitutional rights or when the report contains stipulations as to material facts, by the defendant, shall be filed with the clerk of the court pursuant to subdivision (b)(2)(i). The conference report shall contain a statement of those matters upon which the parties have reached agreement, including any stipulations of fact, and a statement of those matters upon which the parties could not agree which are to be the subject of pretrial motions. Agreements reduced to writing in the conference report shall be binding on the parties and shall control the subsequent course of the proceeding.

(B) Failure to File. If a party fails to participate in a pretrial conference or to cooperate in the filing of a conference report, the adverse party shall notify the clerk of such failure. If a conference report is not filed and a party does not appear at the pretrial hearing, no request of that party for a continuance of the trial date as scheduled shall be granted and no pretrial motion of that party shall be permitted to be filed, except by leave of court for cause shown. If the parties fail to file a conference report or do not appear at the pretrial hearing, the case shall be presumed to be ready for trial and shall be scheduled for trial at the earliest possible time. The parties shall be subject to such other sanctions as the judge may impose.

(b) The Pretrial Hearing.

At arraignment, except on a complaint regarding which the court will not exercise final jurisdiction, the court shall order the prosecuting attorney and defense counsel to appear before the court on a date certain for a pretrial hearing. The defendant shall be available for attendance at the hearing. The pretrial hearing may include the following events:

(1) *Tender of Plea.* The defendant may tender a plea, admission or other requested disposition, with or without the agreement of the prosecutor.

(2) *Pretrial Matters.* Unless the Court declines jurisdiction over the case or disposes of the case at the pretrial hearing, the pretrial hearing shall include the following events:

(i) Filing of Pretrial Conference Report. The prosecuting attorney and defense counsel shall file the pretrial conference report with the clerk of court.

(ii) Discovery and Pretrial Motions. The court shall hear all discovery motions pending at the time of the pretrial hearing. Other pending pretrial motions may be heard at the pretrial hearing, continued to a specified date for a hearing, or transmitted for hearing and resolution by the trial session.

(iii) Compliance and Trial Assignment. The court shall determine whether the pretrial conference report is complete, all discovery matters have been resolved, and compliance with all discovery orders has been accomplished. If so, the court shall obtain the defendant's decision on waiver of the right to a jury trial, and assign a trial date or trial assignment date. If completion of either the pretrial conference report or discovery is still pending, the court shall schedule and order the parties to appear for a compliance hearing pursuant to Rule 11(c) unless the aggrieved party waives the right to a compliance hearing.

(iv) The court may issue such additional orders as will promote the fair, speedy and orderly disposition of the case.

(c) Compliance Hearing.

A compliance hearing ordered pursuant to Rule 11(b)(2)(iii) shall be limited to the following court actions:

(1) determining whether the pretrial conference report and discovery are complete and, if necessary, hearing and deciding discovery motions and ordering appropriate sanctions for non-compliance;

(2) receiving and acting on a tender of plea or admission; and

(3) if the pretrial conference report and discovery are complete, obtaining the defendant's decision on waiver of the right to a jury trial, and scheduling the trial date or trial assignment date.

Amended March 8, 2004, effective September 7, 2004.

Reporter's Notes—Revised, 2004

Rule 11 is designed to promote the speedy and orderly disposition of cases at a time certain which is most convenient to all parties, and to that end it calls upon defendants' counsel to aid the court in the disposition of all preliminary motions and other matters relative to pending cases. *See* Commonwealth v. Durning, 406 Mass. 485, 495 (1990). Although the title of the rule would appear to limit its application to those cases which are destined to be tried, it is intended that in some cases the conference will result in the resolution of issues so as to make trial unnecessary. At the least the pretrial conference should assist the parties in channeling their attention and resources to matters genuinely in issue and aid the court in focusing the elaborate mechanism of a full trial upon the material issues in dispute.

The 2004 Amendments. In 2004, the Rule was substantially rewritten to mandate a uniform pretrial process in all criminal courts. Under the rule, at arraignment (except on a complaint regarding which the court will not exercise final jurisdiction, in which case a probable cause hearing will be scheduled as required by Rule 7), the court will schedule the case for both a pretrial conference and a pretrial hearing, to be held on separate dates. Following the pretrial conference, the parties will prepare a pretrial conference report, memorializing their agreements and disagreements. This report controls the scope of subsequent motions practice. Rule 11 also mandates a pretrial hearing on a subsequent date, at which a plea may be taken or pretrial matters may be raised and/or resolved. Rule 11 as revised reflects this three step process, setting out the functions of the pretrial conference, the report, and the pretrial hearing. Additionally, if discovery remains incomplete at the time of the pretrial hearing, a compliance hearing will be scheduled to insure that discovery is complete before the case proceeds.

Subdivision (a). The Pretrial Conference and Conference Report. Rule 11 originally required pretrial conferences in both Superior and District Court jury sessions, leaving the District Court primary session with the option of scheduling a conference or not. By a 2004 amendment, pretrial conferences are now mandatory in all cases, regardless of whether the case is docketed in a superior, juvenile, district, or municipal court. Under Rules 7 and 11, at arraignment the court will schedule the case for *both* a pretrial conference and a pretrial hearing. Regarding the pretrial conference, the rule allows but does not require the court to order that this conference take place before a judge or magistrate. The Boston Municipal Court practice of holding a conference before a magistrate has proven quite efficient, but because some district courts may not have adequate personnel and courtrooms for this purpose the subdivision leaves this issue to be determined by each court.

Subdivisions (a)(1)(A)—(C) outline suggested issues which may be discussed and resolved prior to the trial. The catalog is not to be considered exhaustive.

Subdivision (a)(1)(A), in conjunction with Mass. R. Crim. P. 13, seeks to reduce the number of "boiler plate" pretrial motions which are routinely filed. *See* Commonwealth v. Hall, 369 Mass. 715, 723 (1976). If the substance of a motion is agreed upon, that fact and the agreement are set out in the conference report [(a)(2)(A)], *infra*; only pretrial motions which are not agreed upon are permitted to be filed. Mass. R. Crim. P. 13(d).

While it is unlikely that a plea arrangement will immediately result from the conference, the defendant, following disclosure of the Commonwealth's case, may decide that a plea is the best alternative. Therefore, the subject is properly discussed at that time [(a)(1)(B)]. If an arrangement is in fact concluded, it should be stated in the conference report. *See* Mass. R. Crim. P. 12(b)(2), which requires counsel to notify the court of the existence of any agreement contingent upon the defendant's plea.

Among the matters to be discussed under subdivision (a)(1)(C)(i) is the setting of the trial date. It must be emphasized that one consequence of a failure to comply with this rule is that the case will be presumed to be ready for trial and a trial date will be set for the earliest available time, [a] [2] [B], *infra*. Agreements as to subdivision (C)(ii) will assist the court in the management of its docket, see Mass. R. Crim. P. 36(a)(2), and understandings as to the availability of necessary witnesses will reduce the need for continuances to secure their attendance, Mass. R. Crim. P. 10. If stipulations of fact are agreed upon after discussion under (C)(iv) they are to be recorded in the conference report, [a] [2] [A], *infra*.

The defendant may also request information concerning the Commonwealth's intended use of prior acts or convictions for proof of knowledge, intent, or modus operandi, and use of prior convictions to impeach the testimony of the defendant. This information, while not specifically mentioned in Rule 11, is a proper subject of discussion at the pretrial conference. It is contemplated that compliance with this subdivision will obviate the necessity for resorting to the more time-consuming procedures of Mass. R. Crim. P. 14 and 23, expedite the taking of testimony at the trial, and allow counsel to better prepare for trial.

Pursuant to Mass. R. Crim. P. 9(a)(3), either party may move for consolidation of pending charges. This matter, if resolved at confer-

ence, will avoid the time delay required for the court to conduct a hearing and act upon a motion for joinder. This is true also as to motions to transfer other pending charges for plea, sentence or trial. Mass. R. Crim. P. 37(b)(1)—(2).

It should be noted that a motion to take a deposition, not contemplated within subdivision (a)(1) of this rule, if considered at conference and agreed upon, need not be filed with the court, since the parties are permitted to depose witnesses by agreement pursuant to Mass. R. Crim. P. 35(i).

The parties may also wish to stipulate as to the application and effect of the excludable time provisions of Mass. R. Crim. P. 36(b), e.g., whether time should be excluded from the speedy trial limits due to the absence of an essential witness and, if so, how much. Mass. R. Crim. P. 36(b)(2)(B).

The 2004 revision eliminated a provision then numbered (a)(1)(C), which required the defendant to reveal "the nature of the defense" at the pretrial conference, and whether he or she intends to defend by alibi, insanity or privilege. Such discovery to the prosecution is now mandatory discovery under Rule 14, at a more realistic and constitutionally appropriate phase of the pretrial proceedings. The pretrial conference is generally held too early to expect the defendant to know and convey the defense, especially since full discovery may not yet have been provided by the prosecution. Indeed, because under the Fifth and Fourteenth Amendments to the United States Constitution the defense can only be compelled to disclose information it has decided to use at trial, Williams v. Florida, 399 U.S. 78 (1970), prosecutorial discovery should not be required before the defendant is in a position to make an informed decision.

Subdivision (a)(2)(A) outlines the contents of the pretrial conference report and establishes the requirement that it be signed by the defendant when it contains agreements which amount to waivers of constitutional right or stipulations to material facts. The defendant's signature should not be pro forma, but should be subscribed only after his counsel has explained the consequences of this act to him. To expedite this procedure, subdivisions (a) and (b) mandate that the defendant "shall be available for attendance" at both the pretrial conference and the pretrial hearing. This requirement assures also that the defendant's assent to other agreements may readily be obtained.

The pretrial conference report must set out all agreements of the parties. Such agreements have the force of a court order, and are enforceable by the same sanctions. Commonwealth v. Viriyahiranpaiboon, 412 Mass. 224, 228 (1992); Commonwealth v. Durning, *supra* at 495; Commonwealth v. Gallarelli, 399 Mass. 17, 20 (1987); Commonwealth v. Chapee, 397 Mass. 508, 517 (1986), *habeas denied sub nom.* Chappee v. Vose, 843 F.2d 25 (1st Cir. 1988); Commonwealth v. Delaney, 11 Mass. App. Ct. 398 (1981). Only pretrial motions whose subject matter could not be agreed on at the conference may be filed. The conference report is filed with the clerk, whose responsibility it is to monitor filing and advancement of cases for trial.

Subdivision (a)(2)(B) sets out the sanctions to be imposed upon a failure to file a report and to appear to explain that failure. If counsel refuse to cooperate in the conference procedure, the court may also invoke its authority under subdivision (a)(1) to require a conference be held at court under the supervision of a judge or clerk-magistrate.

Subdivision (b). The pretrial hearing. This subdivision originally concerned conference procedures in the District Court jury-waived sessions. By a 2004 amendment, Rule 11(a)'s pretrial conference requirements were made uniform for all sessions, and subdivision (b) is instead devoted to the pretrial hearing. New subdivision 11(b) allows a District Court judge to decline jurisdiction and schedule a probable cause hearing expeditiously (and in such case the judge may entertain discovery motions prior to the probable cause hearing, Commonwealth v. Silva, 10 Mass. App. Ct. 784, 791 (1980)). Otherwise a pretrial hearing is to be held in order to accomplish the pretrial matters enumerated in the subdivision. Subparagraph (b)(1) authorizes the court to receive a plea, admission, or other requested disposition. If there is no plea or disposition, subparagraph (b)(2)(i) requires the parties to file the pretrial conference report; (b)(2)(ii) requires the pretrial hearing judge to hear all pending discovery motions, and permits him or her to hear other pretrial motions as well; and (b)(2)(iii) requires the court to schedule the next court date. If the pretrial report or discovery is not complete, the court will schedule a compliance hearing unless waived by the aggrieved party (see subdivision (c)). If they are complete, the court will ask the defendant to elect or waive a jury trial, and then assign "the trial date or trial assignment date." Ideally, the rule would have simply required the assignment of a trial date, rather than offering the option of scheduling a "trial assignment date," which allows for yet another intermediate hearing date; but practical constraints require this option, as many courts are presently unable to guarantee a particular trial date as early as the pretrial hearing. Although the jury decision should be fully considered and resolved at this time, nothing in the rule prevents a defendant who elects a jury trial from waiving the right at a later date.

Subdivision (c). Compliance Hearing. This subdivision makes a compliance hearing mandatory if a party failed to complete a pretrial conference report or provide discovery, unless the aggrieved party waives such a hearing. Such a hearing was optional before this subdivision was promulgated in 2004, leading to routine inefficiencies this subdivision is designed to eliminate. In courts that did not have compliance hearings, the aggrieved party had confronted an unfair choice between the sometimes burdensome task of obtaining an expedited hearing simply to obtain overdue discovery, or waiting until the trial date to receive discovery (which itself presented the prospect of either a continuance or an immediate trial with unprepared counsel). Moreover, municipal and district courts without compliance hearings had to defer jury waivers until the trial date pursuant to G.L. c. 218 sec. 28, which prohibits a waiver decision until discovery has been delivered. It promoted delays and inconvenience to witnesses for the court to remain ignorant up to the trial date as to whether a jury session would be required.

Therefore, this subdivision requires a compliance hearing when required discovery has not been forthcoming, and limits the hearing to certain enumerated matters mostly derived from Dist./Mun. Cts. R. Crim. P. 5. The court must determine whether the pretrial report and discovery are complete; must hear and decide pending discovery motions; and may order sanctions for non-compliance. If discovery is completed, it may receive a plea or admission; obtain the defendant's decision on whether to elect or waive a jury trial; and schedule the trial date or trial assignment date.

Rule 12.   Pleas and Withdrawals of Pleas

[Text of rule applicable to cases initiated (by indictment or complaint) on or after September 7, 2004.]

(a) Pleas In General.

(1) *Pleas That May Be Entered and by Whom.* A defendant may plead not guilty, or guilty, or with the consent of the judge, nolo contendere, to any crime with which the defendant has been charged and over which the court has jurisdiction. A plea of guilty or nolo contendere shall be received only from the defendant personally except pursuant to the provisions of Rule 18(b). Pleas shall be received in open court and the proceedings shall be recorded. If a defendant refuses to plead or if the judge refuses to accept a plea of guilty or nolo contendere, a plea of not guilty shall be entered.

(2) *Admission to Sufficient Facts.* In a District Court, a defendant may, after a plea of not guilty, admit to sufficient facts to warrant a finding of guilty.

(3) *Acceptance of Plea of Guilty, a Plea of Nolo Contendere, or an Admission to Sufficient Facts.* A judge may accept a plea of guilty or a plea of nolo contendere or an admission to sufficient facts only after first determining that it is made voluntarily with an understanding of the nature of the charge and the consequences of the plea or admission. A judge may refuse to accept a plea of guilty or a plea of nolo contendere or an admission to sufficient facts.

(b) Plea Discussions; Pleas Without Plea Agreement and With Plea Agreement.

(1) *In General.* The defendant may tender a guilty plea, a plea of nolo contendere, or an admission to sufficient facts to warrant a finding of guilty without entering into a plea agreement with the prosecutor. Alternatively, if the defendant intends to tender a plea of guilty or an admission to sufficient facts, the prosecutor and the defendant may enter into a plea agreement pursuant to Rule 12(b)(5).

(2) *Plea Discussions.* The judge may participate in plea discussions at the request of one or both of the parties if the discussions are recorded and made part of the record.

(3) *Inquiry as to the Existence of a Plea Agreement.* After being informed that a defendant intends to plead guilty or to admit to sufficient facts, the judge shall inquire as to the existence of a plea agreement.

(4) *Pleas Without an Agreement.* If the defendant intends to plead guilty or nolo contendere or to admit to sufficient facts and there is no agreement under Rule 12(b)(5), the judge shall follow the procedures set forth in Rule 12(c).

(5) *Pleas Conditioned Upon an Agreement.* The defendant may enter into a plea agreement with the prosecutor if the defendant intends to plead guilty or admit to sufficient facts but not if the defendant intends to plead nolo contendere.

(A) A plea agreement may specify both that the parties agree on a specific sentence, including the length of any term of probation, and that the prosecutor will make one or more of the following charge concessions: amend an indictment or complaint; dismiss, reduce, or partially dismiss charges; not seek an indictment; or not bring other charges. The judge shall follow the procedures set forth in Rule 12(d) when the parties enter into a plea agreement that includes both an agreement to a specific sentence and a charge concession. If the judge accepts the plea agreement and the defendant's plea, Rule 12(d) requires the judge to sentence the defendant according to the terms of the plea agreement.

(B) When the plea is conditioned on a plea agreement other than one described in Rule 12(b)(5)(A), the judge shall follow the procedures set forth in Rule 12(c).

(6) *Pleas Reserving Appellate Review.* With the written agreement of the prosecutor, the defendant may tender a plea of guilty or an admission to sufficient facts while reserving the right to appeal any ruling or rulings that would, if reversed, render the Commonwealth's case not viable on one or more charges. The written agreement must specify the ruling or rulings that may be appealed, and must state that reversal of the ruling or rulings would render the Commonwealth's case not viable on one or more

specified charges. The judge, in an exercise of discretion, may refuse to accept a plea of guilty or an admission to sufficient facts reserving the right to appeal. If the defendant prevails in whole or in part on appeal, the defendant may withdraw the guilty plea or the admission to sufficient facts on any of the specified charges. If the defendant withdraws the guilty plea or the admission to sufficient facts, the judge shall dismiss the complaint or indictment on those charges, unless the prosecutor shows good cause to do otherwise. The appeal shall be governed by the Massachusetts Rules of Appellate Procedure, provided that a notice of appeal is filed within thirty days of the acceptance of the plea.

(c) Procedure If No Plea Agreement or If Plea Agreement Does Not Include Both a Specific Sentence and a Charge Concession.

(1) *Disclosure of the Terms of Any Plea Agreement.* If the parties have entered into a plea described in Rule 12(b)(5)(B), the parties shall disclose the terms of that agreement on the record in open court unless the judge for good cause allows the parties to disclose the terms of the plea agreement in camera on the record.

(2) *Tender of Plea.* The defendant's plea or admission shall be tendered to the judge.

(3) *Colloquy.* The judge shall:

(A) Provide notice to the defendant of the consequences of a plea. The judge shall inform the defendant:

(i) that by a plea of guilty or nolo contendere, or an admission to sufficient facts, the defendant waives the right to trial with or without a jury, the right to confrontation of witnesses, the right to be presumed innocent until proved guilty beyond a reasonable doubt, and the privilege against self-incrimination;

(ii) of the maximum possible sentence on the charge, and, if applicable,

(a) any different or additional punishment based upon subsequent offense provisions of the General Laws;

(b) that the defendant may be subject to adjudication as a sexually dangerous person and required to register as a sex offender;

(c) the mandatory minimum sentence on the charge; and

(d) that a conviction or plea of guilty for an offense listed in G.L. c. 279, § 25(b) implicates the habitual offender statute, and that upon conviction or plea of guilty for the third or subsequent of said offenses: (1) the defendant may be imprisoned in the state prison for the maximum term provided by law for such third or subsequent offense; (2) no sentence may be reduced or suspended; and (3) the defendant may be ineligible for probation, parole, work release or furlough, or to receive any deduction in sentence for good conduct;

(iii) of the following potential immigration consequences of the plea:

(a) that, if the defendant is not a citizen of the United States, the guilty plea, plea of nolo contendere, or

admission may have the consequence of deportation, exclusion of admission, or denial of naturalization; and

(b) that, if the offense to which the defendant is pleading guilty, nolo contendere, or admitting to sufficient facts is under federal law one that presumptively mandates removal from the United States and federal officials decide to seek removal, it is practically inevitable that this conviction would result in deportation, exclusion from admission, or denial of naturalization under the laws of the United States.

(B) Factual basis for the charge. The prosecutor shall present the factual basis of the charge.

(C) Rights of Victims and Witnesses of Crimes. If applicable, the judge shall inquire of the prosecutor as to compliance with the requirements of G.L. c. 258B, Rights of Victims and Witnesses of Crimes. At any time prior to imposing sentence, the judge shall give any person entitled under G.L. c. 258B to make an oral and/or written victim impact statement the opportunity to do so.

(4) *Disposition Requests.*

(A) When there is no agreed-upon recommendation as to sentence. The judge shall give both parties the opportunity to recommend a sentence to the judge. In the District Court, the judge shall inform the defendant that the disposition imposed will not exceed the terms of the defendant's request without first giving the defendant the right to withdraw the plea. In the Superior Court, the judge shall inform the defendant that the disposition imposed will not exceed the terms of the prosecutor's recommendation without first giving the defendant the right to withdraw the plea. At any time prior to accepting the plea or admission, the judge may continue the hearing on the judge's own motion to ensure that the judge has been provided with, and has had an opportunity to consider, all of the facts pertinent to a determination of a just disposition in the case.

(B) Where there is an agreed-upon recommendation as to disposition. The judge shall inform the defendant that the sentence imposed will not exceed the terms of the agreement without first giving the defendant the right to withdraw the plea. At any time prior to accepting the plea or admission, the judge may continue the hearing on the judge's own motion to ensure that the judge has been provided with, and has had an opportunity to consider, all of the facts pertinent to a determination of a just disposition in the case.

(5) *Findings of Judge; Acceptance of Plea.* The judge shall inquire whether the defendant still wishes to plead guilty or nolo contendere or admit to sufficient facts. If so, the judge will then make findings as to whether the plea or admission is knowing and voluntary, and whether there is an adequate factual basis for the charge. The defendant's failure to acknowledge all aspects of the factual basis shall not preclude a judge from accepting a guilty plea or admission. At the conclusion of the hearing, the judge shall accept or reject the tendered plea or admission.

(6) *Sentencing.* After acceptance of a plea of guilty or nolo contendere or an admission, the judge shall sentence the defendant.

(A) Conditions of Probation. If the judge's disposition includes a term of probation, the judge, with the assistance of probation where appropriate and after considering the recommendations of the parties, shall impose appropriate conditions of probation.

(B) Intent to Impose Sentence Exceeding Requested Disposition. In District Court, if the judge decides to impose a sentence that will exceed the defendant's request for disposition under Rule 12(c)(4)(A) or the parties' request for disposition under Rule 12(c)(4)(B), the judge shall, on the record, advise the defendant of that intent and shall afford the defendant the opportunity to withdraw the plea or admission. In Superior Court, if the judge decides to impose a sentence that will exceed the prosecutor's request for disposition under Rule 12(c)(4)(A) or the parties' request for disposition under Rule 12(c)(4)(B), the judge shall, on the record, advise the defendant of that intent and shall afford the defendant the opportunity to withdraw the plea or admission. In both District and Superior Court, the judge may indicate to the parties what sentence the judge would impose.

(d) Procedure If Plea Agreement Includes Both a Specific Sentence and a Charge Concession.

(1) *Disclosure of the Terms of the Plea Agreement.* The parties shall disclose the terms of the plea agreement on the record in open court unless the judge for good cause allows the parties to disclose the terms of the plea agreement in camera on the record.

(2) *Tender of Plea.* The defendant's plea or admission shall be tendered to the judge.

(3) *Colloquy.* The judge shall:

(A) Provide notice to the defendant of the consequences of a plea. The judge shall inform the defendant:

(i) that by a plea of guilty or an admission to sufficient facts, the defendant waives the right to trial with or without a jury, the right to confrontation of witnesses, the right to be presumed innocent until proved guilty beyond a reasonable doubt, and the privilege against self-incrimination;

(ii) of the maximum possible sentence on the charge, and, if applicable,

(a) any different or additional punishment based upon subsequent offense provisions of the General Laws;

(b) that the defendant may be subject to adjudication as a sexually dangerous person and required to register as a sex offender;

(c) the mandatory minimum sentence on the charge; and

(d) that a conviction or plea of guilty for an offense listed in G.L. c. 279, § 25(b) implicates the habitual offender statute, and that upon conviction or plea of guilty for the third or subsequent of said offenses: (1) the defendant may be imprisoned in the state prison for the maximum term provided by law for such third or subsequent offense; (2) no sentence may be reduced or suspended; and (3) the defendant may be ineligible for

probation, parole, work release or furlough, or to receive any deduction in sentence for good conduct;

(iii) of the following potential immigration consequences of the plea:

(a) that, if the defendant is not a citizen of the United States, the guilty plea or admission may have the consequence of deportation, exclusion from admission, or denial of naturalization; and

(b) that, if the offense to which the defendant is pleading guilty or admitting to sufficient facts is under federal law one that presumptively mandates removal from the United States and federal officials decide to seek removal, it is practically inevitable that this conviction would result in deportation, exclusion from admission, or denial of naturalization under the laws of the United States.

(B) Factual basis for the charge. The prosecutor shall present the factual basis of the charge.

(C) Rights of Victims and Witnesses of Crimes. If applicable, the judge shall inquire of the prosecutor as to compliance with the requirements of G.L. c. 258B, Rights of Victims and Witnesses of Crimes. The judge shall give any person entitled under G.L. c. 258B to make an oral and/or written victim impact statement the opportunity to do so.

(4) *Review; Acceptance or Rejection of Plea Agreement.* The judge must accept or reject the plea agreement before the judge accepts a guilty plea or admission. The judge should not accept a plea agreement without considering whether the proposed disposition is just. At any time prior to the acceptance or rejection of the plea agreement, the judge may continue the plea hearing on the judge's own motion to ensure that the judge has been provided with, and has had an opportunity to consider, all of the facts pertinent to a determination whether the plea agreement provides for a just disposition in the case.

(A) Accepted Plea Agreement. If the judge accepts the plea agreement, the judge shall inform the defendant that the judge will impose the sentence, including the length of any term of probation, provided in the plea agreement.

(B) Rejected Plea Agreement. If the judge rejects the plea agreement, the judge shall, on the record and in open court (or, for good cause, in camera on the record):

(i) inform the parties that the judge rejects the plea agreement, but the judge may indicate to the parties what sentence the judge would impose or what additional information the judge will require before the judge may make this determination;

(ii) allow either party to withdraw from the plea agreement; and

(iii) allow the defendant to withdraw his or her plea or admission.

(5) *Findings of Judge as to Plea Agreement and Plea; Acceptance of Plea.* If the judge has accepted the plea agreement, the judge shall inquire whether the defendant still wishes to plead guilty or admit to sufficient facts. If so, the judge will then make findings as to whether the plea

agreement and plea or admission are knowing, voluntary, and supported by an adequate factual basis. The defendant's failure to acknowledge all aspects of the factual basis shall not preclude a judge from accepting a guilty plea or admission. At the conclusion of the hearing, the judge shall accept or reject the tendered plea or admission.

(6) *Sentencing.* After accepting the plea agreement and the plea or admission, the judge shall impose sentence according to the terms of the plea agreement. If the plea agreement includes a term of probation, the judge, with the assistance of probation where appropriate and after considering the recommendations of the parties, shall impose appropriate conditions of probation.

(e) Availability of Criminal Record and Presentence Report. Prior to sentencing under Rule 12(c)(6) or to the judge's decision to accept or reject a plea agreement under Rule 12(d)(4), the judge, prosecutor, and counsel for the defendant shall have an opportunity to review the defendant's criminal record and any report of the presentence investigation as described in Rule 28(d)(2). In extraordinary cases, the judge may except from disclosure to the parties parts of the report which are not relevant to a proper sentence, diagnostic opinion which might seriously disrupt a program of rehabilitation, sources of information obtained upon a promise of confidentiality, or any other information which, if disclosed, might result in harm, physical or otherwise, to the defendant or other persons. If the report is not made fully available, the portions thereof which are not disclosed shall not be relied upon in determining sentence. No party may make any copy of the presentence report.

(f) Inadmissibility of Pleas, Offers of Pleas, and Related Statements. Except as otherwise provided in this subdivision, evidence of a plea of guilty, or a plea of nolo contendere, or an admission, or of an offer to plead guilty or nolo contendere or an admission to the crime charged or any other crime, later withdrawn, or statements made in connection with, and relevant to, any of the foregoing pleas or offers, is not admissible in any civil or criminal proceedings against the person who made the plea or offer. However, evidence of a statement made in connection with, and relevant to, a plea of guilty, later withdrawn, or a plea of nolo contendere, or an admission or an offer to plead guilty or nolo contendere or an admission to the crime charged or any other crime, is admissible in a criminal proceeding for perjury if the statement was made by the defendant under oath, on the record, and in the presence of counsel, if any.

Amended June 12, 1986, effective January 1, 1987; March 8, 2004, effective September 7, 2004; January 29, 2015, effective May 11, 2015; July 17, 2019, effective September 1, 2019.

Reporter's Notes—Revised, 2004

Although analogous to Fed. R. Crim. P. 11, in its original form in 1979 this rule was drawn from a number of sources. *See, e.g.,* A.B.A. Standards Relating to Pleas of Guilty (Approved Draft, 1968); A.L.I. Model Code of Pre–Arraignment Procedure §§ 350.1—.9 (POD 1975); National Advisory Commission on Criminal Justice Standards & Goals, Courts, Standards 3.1 *et seq.* (1973); President's Commission on Law Enforcement & Administration of Justice, Task Force Report: The Courts 4—13 (1967). The rule was amended in 1987 to remove the option, contained in original subdivision (c)(2)(B), which allowed a judge to sentence a defendant more harshly than the terms of a prosecutor's sentence recommendation without giving the defendant

an opportunity to withdraw the plea. In 2004, the rule was further amended, retaining its basic structure but bringing the details of the process up to date, in light of the abolition of trial de novo and other developments in the law.

As the United States Supreme Court has observed:

Whatever may be the situation in an ideal world, the fact is that the guilty plea and the often concomitant plea bargain are important components of this country's criminal justice system. Properly administered, they can benefit all concerned.

Blackledge v. Allison, 431 U.S. 63, 71 (1977). *Accord,* Bordenkircher v. Hayes, 434 U.S. 357, 361—62 (1978). Rule 12 is intended to guarantee the proper administration of the guilty plea and plea bargaining process.

The proffer by a defendant of a guilty plea is a significant step in the criminal process. It represents a decision by the defendant not to put the Commonwealth to the test of proving his or her guilt beyond a reasonable doubt. Plea bargaining, of course, flows from the "mutuality of advantage" to defendants and prosecutors, each with their own reasons for wanting to avoid trial, Bordenkircher v. Hayes, 434 U.S. 357, 363 (1978), but the Commonwealth and the public have an interest in promoting fairness by insuring that each plea is an accurate reflection of guilt and a fair termination of criminal proceedings against a defendant. Rule 12 is intended to promote attainment of those goals.

Subdivision (a).

(a)(1). This subdivision is adopted from A.B.A. Standards Relating to Pleas of Guilty § 1.1 (Approved Draft, 1968), which substantially accords with Fed. R. Crim. P. 11(a)—(b).

Under criminal practice prior to the adoption of rule 12, former G.L. c 227, § 47A (St 1978, c 478, § 298) provided that the defendant could plead not guilty, guilty, or nolo contendere. Rule 12 preserves these options.

The Rule does not establish the precise words a defendant must use in order to plead guilty. While the absence of the actual phrase "I plead guilty" or the word "guilty" is not sufficient by itself to invalidate a purported guilty plea, *see* Commonwealth v. Cavanaugh, 12 Mass. App. Ct. 543 (1981), in order to avoid confusion, a judge should clarify the intent of any defendant who does not use clear language to identify a desire to enter a guilty plea. Stipulations by the defendant to the truth of facts that are conclusive of guilt are the functional equivalent of a guilty plea and fall within the confines of Rule 12. *See* Commonwealth v. Hill, 20 Mass. App. Ct. 130 (1985). On the other hand, if all the defendant stipulates to is that the Commonwealth's witnesses would testify in the manner described by the prosecutor, then the defendant's act would not be the complete waiver that a guilty plea entails, *see* Commonwealth v. Garcia, 23 Mass App 259, 265 (1986).

The requirements of this subdivision are to insure that the fact that the plea was the informed and voluntary act of the defendant appears upon a contemporaneous record of the proceeding, thus reducing the likelihood of a post-conviction attack on the validity of a plea of guilty or nolo contendere. *See, e.g.,* Commonwealth v Foster, 368 Mass 100 (1975).

Therefore, except where a corporation is the defendant, or where the defendant is permitted by the General Laws to pay a fine by mail or by appearing before a clerk personally or by authorized agent, the defendant personally must plead if the plea is to be guilty or nolo contendere. The defendant must also personally plead not guilty except where his or her appearance is excused pursuant to Mass. R. Crim. P. 7(a)(2) and the court enters the plea on the defendant's behalf. Mass. R. Crim. P. 7(d)(2).

The requirement that the plea be accepted in open court is based upon G.L. c. 263 § 6, and furthers the goal that it be free from the suspicion of coercion and that it is a knowing and intelligent waiver of the defendant's right to a trial. Thus, all pleas should be entered under the scrutiny of the judge in formal proceedings and be recorded, whether by stenographic or electronic means.

(a)(2). An admission to sufficient facts to warrant a finding of guilty is a procedural device that had its genesis in the trial de novo system. Rather than entering a guilty plea, which would have had the consequence of limiting the de novo trial to the issue of the sentence, a defendant in the first tier of the de novo system could admit to sufficient facts and preserve his option of a full trial de novo. Admissions to sufficient facts have proved useful for another reason however. They offer a way to allow the defendant's case to be continued without a guilty finding, something that a traditional guilty plea is ill suited to accomplish. As the Supreme Judicial Court has recognized, a continuance without a finding (cwof) is a procedure that often serves the best interests of both the Commonwealth and the defendant. *See* Commonwealth v. Duquette, 386 Mass. 834, 840 (1982). Admissions to sufficient facts and cwofs were common at both levels of the trial de novo system in the District Courts. After the abolition of trial de novo, they continue to be prevalent in the District Court and Juvenile systems. *See* G.L. c 278 § 18 (allowing a District Court defendant to request that a case be continued without a finding and requiring that an admission to sufficient facts be treated as the equivalent of a guilty plea for purposes of the "defense capped plea" procedure discussed *infra* in subsection (c)(2)(B)).

If a defendant desires to admit to sufficient facts, the judge should interrogate the defendant personally to insure that the defendant understands the nature and consequences of such an admission. In the years since Rule 12 was originally promulgated, the Supreme Judicial Court has held that an offer to admit to sufficient facts triggers essentially the same safeguards required when a defendant offers to plead guilty. *See* Commonwealth v. Lewis, 399 Mass. 761, 763 (1987); Commonwealth v. Duquette, 386 Mass. 834, 838 (1982).

(a)(3). Requiring the permission of the court to enter a guilty plea or plea of nolo contendere accords with the practice that prevailed prior to the adoption of Rule 12. By court rule, no defendant was permitted to plead guilty or nolo contendere to a complaint for which a sentence of imprisonment may be imposed unless the judge was fully satisfied that certain conditions had been met. *See* District Court Initial Rules of Criminal Procedure 4 (1971); Rules of the Mun. Ct. for the City of Boston Sitting for Criminal Business 4 (1971).

A defendant does not have a constitutional right to have a guilty plea accepted by the court, *see* North Carolina v. Alford, 400 U.S. 25, 38 n. 11 (1970); Commonwealth v. Dilone, 385 Mass. 281 (1982); Commonwealth v. Kelliher, 28 Mass. App. Ct. 915 (1989). An admission to sufficient facts is very much like an *Alford* plea or a plea of nolo contendere, in that the defendant does not explicitly admit guilt. The same considerations that may inform a judge's decision to refuse to accept that latter two pleas apply equally in the case of the former.

A judge may refuse to accept a guilty plea, admission to sufficient facts, or plea of nolo contendere for a variety of reasons. So long as the judge's decision is not arbitrary or based on an impermissible factor, the sound exercise of discretion supports a decision to refuse to accept a plea. *See* Rossman, Guilty Pleas, 2 Criminal Law Advocacy, ¶ 8.04(3)(a). Among the common reasons to refuse to accept plea are: the plea is involuntary; the defendant does not understand the nature of the charge [c] [5] [A], *infra* or the consequences of the plea [c] [3], *infra*; there is no factual basis for the plea [c] [5] [a], *infra*; or there is a factual dispute that should be litigated at trial.

Subdivision (b). Section (e)(1)—(5) of Federal Rule of Criminal Procedure 11 is the prototype for this subdivision.

(b)(1). This subdivision outlines the scope of agreements as to concessions or other actions which the defendant and the prosecution may arrive at prior to plea proceedings before a judge. It must be emphasized that these negotiations are to be between defense counsel, or the defendant in an appropriate case, and the prosecution. Judges should not "participate as active negotiators in plea bargaining discussions," Commonwealth v. Gordon, 410 Mass. 498, 501 n. 3 (1991).

When a judge takes part in plea negotiations, it raises several troubling possibilities:

[it] (1) can create the impression in the mind of the defendant that he would not receive a fair trial were he to go to the trial before this judge; (2) ... makes it difficult for the judge objectively to determine the voluntariness of the plea when it is offered; (3) ... is inconsistent with the theory behind the use of the presentence investigation report; and (4) the risk of not going along with the disposition apparently desired by the judge may seem so great to the defendant that he will be induced to plead guilty even if innocent.

Commonwealth v. Damiano, 14 Mass. App. Ct. 615, 618 n.7 (1982) (quoting § 3.3(a) of the A.B.A. Standards *supra*). For the type of participation that a judge should avoid, *see* Commonwealth v. Carter 50 Mass App 902 (2000) (judge's statement at side bar that if defendant proceeded with trial and was found guilty, he would impose sentence of 18–20 years, but that if defendant pleaded guilty, sentence would be six years to six years and one day was coercive, making defendant's guilty plea involuntary).

The list of actions set out in this subsection that a prosecutor may include in a plea agreement is not exhaustive and allows for considerable flexibility. For example, the parties may agree to a joint sentence recommendation or to present disparate positions, and may propose that the agreement either does not bind the judge or to one that allows the defendant to withdraw the plea if the judge does not agree. Some of the concessions a prosecutor may make in plea negotiations relate to action over which the judge has control, such as the imposition of a particular sentence. Other concessions, as in an agreement not to bring additional charges, are totally within the purview of the prosecutor. Since the doctrine of separation of powers gives the prosecutor the authority to decide what criminal charge the Commonwealth should bring against a defendant, a judge may not accept a guilty plea to a lesser included offense over the prosecutor's objection. *See* Commonwealth v. Gordon, 410 Mass. 498, 503 (1991).

(b)(2). Early and full disclosure of a plea arrangement reduces the risk of an unfair agreement—unfair to the public because of an unwarranted concession by an overburdened prosecutor anxious to avoid trial, or unfair to the defendant because the concession is either illusory, or so irresistible in light of the inevitable risks of trial as to induce an innocent defendant to plead guilty. *E.g.*, Jones v. United States, 423 F.2d 252, 255 (9th Cir 1970). Disclosure of the terms of a plea agreement also will allow the court to monitor the prosecutor's performance. In addition, placing the agreement on the record will avoid disputes that may arise in an attack on the validity of the guilty plea. For these reasons and to expedite the proceedings, this subdivision requires that the court be informed at the outset of the existence of any agreement. If upon inquiry under subdivision (c)(1), *infra*, the defendant denies any such agreement, it is incumbent upon the prosecutor to notify the court if an agreement in fact has been made. For an example of the difficulties that can arise when the parties do not disclose the terms of a plea agreement, *see* Commonwealth v. Johnson, 11 Mass. App. Ct. 835 (1981).

A judge does not improperly participate in plea negotiations simply by having the parties disclose the substance of a plea arrangement pursuant to this subdivision.

Subdivision (c).

Subdivision (c)(1) is a product of Santobello v. New York, 404 U.S. 257 (1971), where it was held that:

when a plea rests in any significant degree on a promise or agreement of the prosecutor, so that it can be said to be part of the inducement or consideration, such promise must be fulfilled.

Id. at 262. The Court stated further that the adjudicative element inherent in accepting a plea of guilty must be attended by safeguards to insure the defendant what is reasonably due in the circumstances and if a plea is induced by promises, their essence must in some way be known. 404 U.S. 261, 262.

If upon inquiry the defendant replies that no promises have been made, the judge should instruct the defendant that any promises relating to the imposition of sentence are in no way binding on the court. *See* Subdivisions (b)(1)—(2), *supra*. This is because defendants are often loathe to disclose such promises, although it is believed that the increased acceptability of the plea arrangement procedure of this rule will obviate such difficulties.

The effect of such an instruction will depend on the facts of each case, but in no case can it cure the prejudice resulting from a broken promise.

The words of the Supreme Court as to the binding character of defense-prosecution agreements deserve repetition:

> when a plea rests in any significant degree on a promise or agreement of the prosecutor, so that it can be said to be a part of the inducement or consideration, such promise must be fulfilled.

Santobello v. New York, 404 U.S. 257, 262 (1971). This accords with established doctrine in the Commonwealth long before the adoption of Rule 12. The Supreme Judicial Court, in 1899, stated that:

> When ... promises are made by the public prosecutor or with his authority, the court will see that due regard is paid to them, and that the public faith which has been pledged by him is duly kept.

Commonwealth v. St. John, 173 Mass. 566, 569 (1899). *See also*, Commonwealth v. Benton, 356 Mass. 477 (1969); Commonwealth v. Harris, 364 Mass. 236, 238 (1973); Commonwealth v. Santiago, 394 Mass. 25 (1985); Commonwealth v. Parzyck, 41 Mass. App. Ct. 195 (1996).

Whether a plea bargain actually exists that obligates the prosecutor to perform a promise upon which the plea is contingent depends on an objective evaluation of the underlying circumstances that led to the plea. *See* Blaikie v. District Attorney for Suffolk County, 375 Mass. 613, 616 n. 2 (1978) (the prosecutor's subjective understanding of the bargain is irrelevant); Commonwealth v. Santiago, 394 Mass. 25, 28 (1985) ("The touchstone for determining whether a defendant has been improperly denied the advantages he expected from a plea bargain is whether that defendant has reasonable grounds for reliance on his interpretation of the prosecutor's promise."); Rossman, Guilty Pleas, 2 Criminal Law Advocacy, ¶7.05(1) (subjective impressions alone never entitle the defendant to the benefit of an illusory agreement).

If the court determines that a plea agreement existed, and that the defendant has fulfilled his or her part of the bargain, the defendant is entitled to the benefit of the prosecutor's performance of the countervailing promise. If the Commonwealth seeks to avoid performance on the ground that the defendant has not lived up to the terms of the agreement, then the prosecutor bears the burden of proof on this issue. *See* Doe v. District Attorney for Plymouth Dist., 29 Mass. App. Ct. 671, 677 n.6 (1991). In the usual course of events, all the defendant need do to fulfill his or her obligation under a plea agreement is to offer a guilty plea. However, the right to enforce a plea agreement may arise beforehand, if the defendant has relied to his or her detriment on a prosecutor's promise. *See id.* at 674 ("concerns about fairness which underlie the requirement that the government abide by its agreements are solidly engaged once an accused person has relied to his detriment upon a plea agreement, even if that occurs before entry of a guilty plea.") *Compare* Blaikie v. District Attorney for Suffolk County, 375 Mass. 613, 618 (1978) (Specific performance is in no sense mandated where no guilty plea has been entered, and the defendant's position has not been adversely affected).

The purposes of subdivision (c)(1) are fourfold. First, airing plea agreements in open court enhances public confidence in the administration of justice. *E.g.*, Jones v. United States, 423 F.2d 252, 255 (9th Cir 1970). Secondly, disclosure of prosecutorial promises is the best way to test the voluntariness of the plea. By testing the strength of the inducement, the court obtains the best available evidence of its

effect upon the defendant. Thirdly, this helps to implement the "factual basis" requirement of subdivision (c)(5)(A), for promises that offer unusual leniency to a defendant are suspect. Finally, this requirement will help to uncover promises that are by their nature improper and thus help to eliminate whatever incentive the prosecution might have to offer improper inducements.

Pursuant to this subdivision and subdivision (b)(2), *supra*, the prosecutor and defense counsel have the duty to come forward and disclose the existence and terms of a plea arrangement if the defendant balks at his opportunity to do so (even if the court does not specifically question the prosecutor or defense counsel on this issue). *See* Commonwealth v. Santon, 2 Mass. App. Ct. 614 (1974). This is important practically because often the defendant will not fully disclose the terms of the arrangement. It is important legally because the prosecutor and defense counsel should inform the court whenever they are aware that testimony offered in court is not in full accord with the truth as they know it. *See* Supreme Judicial Court Rule 3:07, MA Rules of Pro. Conduct, R. 3.3

(c)(2). Under subdivision (c)(2)(A) the judge may inform the defendant that the court is disposed to accept the prosecutor's sentence recommendation, pending the outcome of the hearing required by subdivision (c)(5), and that the judge will not exceed that recommendation without giving the defendant an opportunity to withdraw the plea. As originally promulgated, subdivision (c)(2)(b) allowed the judge an alternative course of action, indicating that the court did not intend to entertain or consider any recommendation, in which event the judge's sentencing discretion would be unrestricted. In 1987, this provision was eliminated from the Rule. The effect of the amendment was to provide defendants pleading guilty pursuant to a sentencing bargain more certainty about their fate.

Prior to the 1987 amendment, a judge could force a defendant who chose to plead guilty on the strength of a plea agreement specifying that he or she should receive a particular sentence to "plead in the dark." If the judge took advantage of option (B) of the original subsection, he or she could categorically refuse to tell a defendant who entered a negotiated plea whether the court would abide by the recommendation or not. Such a judge forced the defendant to bear the risk of waiving the right to trial and receiving nothing in return. After 1987, defendants entering plea agreements based on a joint sentence recommendation knew where they stood prior to irrevocably waiving their right to a trial.

In 2004, this subsection was amended to add new subdivision (c)(2)(B), to reflect the "defense capped plea" procedure provided for by statute in the District and Juvenile Courts. Part of the legislation that abolished the trial de novo system, G.L. c. 278 § 18, gave defendants in District Court who did not reach an agreement with the prosecutor the right to offer a guilty plea or admission to sufficient facts contingent upon the judge's accepting any disposition of the case within the court's jurisdiction. The new subdivision (c)(2)(B) reflects this practice. The defense capped plea procedure applies in all District, Municipal and Juvenile courts. *See* G.L. ch. 119, § 55B. Neither Rule 12 nor G.L. c. 278 § 18 establish how many times a defendant may tender a defense capped plea. Individual judges are free to formulate their own policy on this issue as the needs of their particular courts dictate. A District or Juvenile Court judge has the power to accept a proposed disposition under this procedure even if it entails continuing the case without a finding over the objection of the prosecutor. Although ordinarily the separation of powers doctrine prevents a judge from foreclosing the prosecution's effort to conclude a case with either a conviction or acquittal on the original charge, the legislature's specific sanction of the cwof option in the defense capped plea procedure legitimates it. *Compare* Commonwealth v. Pyles, 423 Mass. 717 (1996) (grant of authority by G.L. c. 278 § 18 specifically gives District Court judges authority to continue a case without a finding over the objection of the prosecutor) *with* Commonwealth v. Cheney, 440 Mass. 568 (2003) (Superior Court judge lacks power to dismiss case in the interest of justice over the objection of the prosecutor as this procedure is only available under G.L. c. 278 § 18 which applies only to District and Juvenile Courts); Commonwealth v. Tim T., 437 Mass 592 (2002) (without statutory authority akin to G.L. c. 278 § 18, Juvenile Court judge lacks power to place defendant on pretrial probation over the objection of the prosecutor). However, if a judge does accept the defendant's proposal to continue a case without a finding over the prosecutor's objection, the record should reflect the reasons for the conclusion that this action is in the best interests of justice. *See Pyles, supra,* at 723.

If the defendant has offered a plea or admission under either subdivision (c)(2)(A) or (c)(2)(B), the judge may not impose a sentence harsher than the one upon which the defendant's action is predicated. Judges should pay careful attention to dispositions involving probationary terms or a suspended sentence to ensure that they conform to the legitimate sentence expectation of the defendant. *See e.g.*, Commonwealth v. Glines, 40 Mass. App. Ct. 95 (1996) (where District Court judge imposed a sentence of probation with a suspended term of five years, it was more severe than the defendant's request for probation with 2 1/2 years suspended); Commonwealth v. Barber, 37 Mass. App. Ct. 599 (1994) (where pursuant to a plea agreement, prosecutor recommended the defendant receive a 12–15 year sentence concurrent with other sentences the defendant received, and the judge imposed a suspended sentence of 12–15 years, consecutive to the other sentences the defendant received, and placed the defendant on probation for two years, the judge exceeded the terms of the prosecutor's recommendation).

(c)(3). This subdivision was originally patterned after Fed. R. Crim. P. 11(c)—(d). In addition, it drew upon District Court Initial R. Crim. P. 4 (1971); Sections 1.4 and 1.5 of the ABA Standards Relating to Pleas of Guilty (Approved Draft, 1968); A.B.A. Standards Relating to the Function of the Trial Judge § 4.2 (Approved Draft, 1972); Rules of Criminal Procedure (U.L.A.) rule 444(b) (1974); A.L.I. Model Code of Pre–Arraignment Procedure § 350.4 (POD 1975); and the National Advisory Commission on Criminal Justice Standards &. Goals, Courts, standard 3.7 (1973).

In 2004, this subdivision was amended to eliminate a provision allowing defense counsel to conduct the colloquy with the defendant. The Supreme Judicial Court has disapproved of defense counsel conducting guilty plea colloquies, as far back as Commonwealth v. Morrow, 363 Mass. 601 (1973) ("the spontaneity and flexibility of the dialogue, which supports a conclusion of voluntariness, can best be achieved where the judge asks the questions. This also avoids even the appearance that the colloquy is but a prearranged script. Therefore, we think it would be better practice for the judge to ask the questions.") By statute, defense counsel cannot conduct the part of the colloquy dealing with warnings of immigration consequences, *see* Commonwealth v. Villalobos, 437 Mass. 797 (2002).

The responsibility for conducting a meaningful colloquy with the defendant properly rests on the judge's shoulders. This requires "a continuing effort on the part of trial judges, with the help of counsel, so to direct their questions *as to make them a real probe of the defendant's mind* ... It is not to become a 'litany' but is to attempt a live evaluation of whether the plea has been sufficiently meditated by the defendant with guidance of counsel, and whether it is not being extracted from the defendant under undue pressure." Commonwealth v. Fernandes, 390 Mass. 714, 716 (1984) *quoting* Commonwealth v. Foster, 368 Mass. 100, 107 (1975) (emphasis added). The colloquy should include an inquiry into any mental illness from which the defendant may be suffering, and whether the defendant is under the influence of alcohol or drugs. *See* Commonwealth v. Correa, 43 Mass. App. Ct. 714, 717–718 (1997).

The Supreme Judicial Court has suggested the utility of using a checklist to ensure that a plea colloquy is both comprehensive in scope and meaningful in substance. *See* Commonwealth v Colon (2003) 439 Mass 519, 530 *quoting* Commonwealth v. Nolan, 19 Mass. App. Ct. 491, 501–502, (1985):

[Post conviction attacks on the validity of a plea can] be minimized if not wholly avoided, and justice better and more humanely administered in the first instance, if judges permitted themselves to be assisted by the carefully drafted and fully inclusive model questionnaires that have long been available ... We do not suggest that any model should be followed mechanically; indeed such a practice would be unwise because it could interfere with a probing exchange. Nevertheless a model can serve as a guide and checklist. We would suggest, as well, that a duty is cast on the lawyers on both sides to be alert and helpful if it appears that the judge through inadvertence may not be carrying out the full requirements of the rule. (Footnote omitted)

The information about the consequences of a conviction should be part of the oral dialogue between the judge and the defendant. It is not sufficient for a judge to rely on the defendant's acknowledgment of this information on a written form. *See* Commonwealth v. Rodriguez, 52 Mass. App. Ct. 572 (2001); Commonwealth v. Hilaire, 51 Mass. App. Ct. 818, 823 (2001) ("During a colloquy, the judge has the opportunity to observe and interact with the defendant and can communicate the warnings to the ... defendant with greater assurance than can be supplied by the preprinted ... form.")

While the judge is the one who conducts the colloquy, all the parties share the responsibility to make certain that defendants are informed of the consequences of a plea or admission. As the United States Supreme Court said, with respect to the obligation of defense attorneys in federal criminal cases:

Apart from the small class of rights that require specific advice from the court under Rule 11(c), it is the responsibility of defense counsel to inform a defendant of the advantages and disadvantages of a plea agreement and the attendant statutory and constitutional rights that a guilty plea would forgo.

Libretti v. United States, 516 U.S. 29, 50–51 (1995). The prosecutor also has a role to play in ensuring that the court is aware of any information that might bear on the legitimacy of the plea and that the colloquy covers all of the necessary topics. *See* State v. Rodriguez, 112 Ariz. 193, 540 P.2d 665 (1975).

Subdivision (c)(3)(A) enumerates the plea's immediate consequences of which a defendant must be specifically informed. It imposes a responsibility on the judge not only in cases where the defendant has tendered a traditional guilty plea or a nolo contendere plea, but also where a defendant has offered to admit to sufficient facts to warrant a finding of guilty. The Rule was amended in 2004 to cover this last category in recognition of the fact that in the years since Rule 12 was originally promulgated, the Supreme Judicial Court held that an offer to admit to sufficient facts triggers the essentially the same safeguards required when a defendant offers to plead guilty. *See* Commonwealth v. Duquette, 386 Mass. 834, 838 (1982) (an admission to sufficient facts is the functional equivalent of a guilty plea and the record must reflect the defendant waived the right to trial knowingly and voluntarily); Commonwealth v. Lewis, 399 Mass. 761, 763 (1987).

The United States Supreme Court held in Boykin v. Alabama, 395 U.S. 238, 243 (1969) not only that a defendant must understand that he or she waives the privilege against self incrimination, the right to trial by jury, and the right to confront one's accusers by entering a guilty, but also that a court could not presume a waiver of these rights from a silent record. Prior to the adoption of Rule 12 in 1979, the Supreme Judicial Court held in Commonwealth v. Morrow, 363 Mass 601, 604—05 (1973), that "it would be better practice to include specific inquiry as to the defendant's understanding waiver of the three constitutional rights."

In 2004, this subdivision was amended to require an additional warning of rights be given to the defendant, concerning the right to be presumed innocent until proved guilty beyond a reasonable doubt. Although not constitutionally required, it is sound practice to include it. The Supreme Judicial Court has recommended its use in cases where the defendant is willing to plead guilty but does not acknowledge all of the elements of the factual basis. *See* Commonwealth v.

Earl, 393 Mass. 738, 742 (1985) ("when a judge concludes that he is satisfied that there is a factual basis for a charge to which a defendant is willing to plead guilty, but the defendant does not acknowledge all the elements of the factual basis, it would be better practice for the plea judge to advise the defendant that his guilty plea waives his right to be presumed innocent until proved guilty beyond a reasonable doubt.")

It has been recommended that the proper formulation for advising a defendant as to his waiver of a jury trial is that "by pleading guilty he [gives] up his right to a 'trial with or without a jury,'" Commonwealth v. Hamilton, 3 Mass. App. Ct. 554, 557 n. 4 (1975). This instruction will serve to emphasize that, upon acceptance of a guilty plea, no trial will be held and all that remains is the imposition of sentence. However, the judge does not have to include information about the difference between a jury trial and a bench trial. *See* Commonwealth v. Gonsalves 57 Mass App 925 (2003). Nor does the colloquy have to include information about the loss of the opportunity to appeal issues, such as the court's action in denying a suppression motion. *See* Commonwealth v. Quinones, 414 Mass. 423, 435 (1993); Commonwealth v. Hamilton, 3 Mass App Ct 554, 558 n. 6 (1975) (if such information is given, it will "require careful formulation to avoid creating confusion as to the right to appeal to the Appellate Division of the Superior Court and the right to post-conviction remedies under special circumstances.")

Pursuant to subdivision (c)(3)(B), the defendant is to be informed of the sentencing consequences of a conviction based upon the tender of a plea or admission. The judge should inform the defendant of the maximum sentence of each offense to which the defendant is offering a plea or admission. In some circumstances, the maximum sentence will depend on whether the defendant has previously been convicted. The judge must take this possibility into account. General Laws c. 279, § 25, which mandates the maximum sentence for a felony defendant who has been previously convicted of two felonies and sentenced to more than three years on each, is an example of that type of provision contemplated by the "second offense" language of (c)(3)(B).

If probation is not a sentencing option, the judge must inform the defendant of any applicable mandatory minimum sentence as well. If the judge imposes a sentence of straight probation (one without a concomitant suspended term), the judge must inform the defendant of the maximum term, and any mandatory minimum term, that could be imposed if probation is revoked. *See* Commonwealth v. Rodriguez, 52 Mass. App. Ct. 572 (2001). In 2004, this subsection was amended to eliminate the requirement that the judge inform the defendant of the maximum sentence possible if the defendant received consecutive sentences. *See* United States v. Kikuyama, 109 F.3d 536 (9th Cir. 1997) (where it is not mandatory to impose consecutive sentences, defendant need not be informed of that possibility in order to enter a knowing and intelligent guilty plea); United States v. Hamilton, 568 F.2d 1302, (9th Cir.) *cert. denied* 436 U.S. 934 (1978) (the possibility of consecutive sentences was implicit in the separate explanation of the possible sentence on each charge).

Conviction of certain sex crimes carries with it three consequences that also must be included in the plea colloquy in a relevant case. First, if the defendant is subject to commitment as a sexually dangerous person, *see* G.L. c. 123A, the judge must include notice of that possibility prior to accepting the plea or admission. This provision has been part of Rule 12 since its adoption, changing the practice that prevailed prior to 1979. *See* Commonwealth v Morrow, 363 Mass 601, 606 (1973) (being subject to the "sexually dangerous person" provision "is but one of many contingent consequences of being confined" after conviction, and therefore need not be explained to a defendant). Since a 2004 amendment to G.L. c. 123A § 12 makes a defendant subject to commitment as a sexually dangerous person despite the nature of the offense to which the defendant is pleading guilty, so long as the defendant has been convicted any time in the past of a designated sex offense, a warning of the possibility of commitment under c. 123A

should be included as a matter of routine unless it is clear from the defendant's prior record that it is not relevant.

Second, if the defendant is tendering a plea or admission to an offense which might subject him or her to the possibility of community parole supervision for life, a 2004 amendment to this subsection requires the judge to notify the defendant of this possibility. Because the prospect of life time parole is an additional form of punishment, it should be part of the information the defendant receives about the maximum sentence he faces. GL c. 265 § 45 specifically refers to community parole supervision for life as punishment.

Third, a 2004 amendment incorporated into this subsection the requirement of G.L. c. 6, § 178E(d), that a court accepting a plea for a sex offense inform the defendant that the plea may result in the defendant's being subject to the provisions of the sex offender registration statute. The statute states that failure to provide this information shall not be grounds to vacate or invalidate the plea, and the inclusion of this requirement in Rule 12(c)(3)(B) does not enlarge the grounds on which a defendant can invalidate a plea after the fact.

The failure to inform the defendant of the sentencing consequences of a plea may result in the conviction being set aside because the plea was not a knowing and intelligent waiver. *E.g.*, Commonwealth v. Rodriguez, 52 Mass. App. Ct. 572 (2001) (failure to inform the defendant of the maximum sentence and mandatory minimum sentence upon revocation of probation). However, "not every omission of a particular from the protocol of the rule ... entitles a defendant at some later stage to negate his plea and claim a trial." Commonwealth v. Nolan, 19 Mass. App. Ct. 491, 494 (1984). *E.g.*, Commonwealth v. Cavanaugh, 12 Mass. App. Ct. 543, 545–546 (1981) (where defendant received the sentence recommended by the prosecutor, the judge's failure to inform him of the maximum possible sentence was harmless beyond a reasonable doubt).

While there are consequences beyond those enumerated in this subdivision that might influence a defendant's decision to plead guilty, if they are collateral, in the sense of being contingent upon some future event or subject to discretion or under the control of the federal government or that of another state, they need not be incorporated into the plea colloquy. For example, ordinary parole consequences need not be part of the judge's warnings, *see* Commonwealth v. Santiago, 394 Mass. 25, 30 (1985), nor is ineligibility to receive good time deductions from a sentence being served after conviction of certain crimes, *see* Commonwealth v. Brown, 6 Mass. App. Ct. 844 (1978) (rescript).

Subdivision (c)(3)(c) was added in 2004, and is based on the requirement in G.L. c. 278, § 29D, that a defendant who pleads guilty or nolo contendere must be advised that if he or she is not a United States citizen, a conviction may have the consequences of deportation, exclusion of admission, or denial of naturalization. This subdivision, however, is broader than the statute. The Supreme Judicial Court has held that this warning is also required when the defendant offers an admission to sufficient facts, *see* Commonwealth v. Mahadeo, 397 Mass. 314 (1986), and so the Rule requires an "alien" warning in those cases as well. In addition, the Rule requires the defendant to be warned of the potential adverse impact of the plea or admission, rather than of a conviction, as the statute requires. Under current immigration law, the statute's warning may be misleading since adverse consequences can flow from an admission to sufficient facts not followed by a conviction. *See* Commonwealth v. Villalobos, 437 Mass. 797 (2002). By warning the defendant that a plea or admission can have adverse immigration consequences, the court necessarily conveys not only the message about the effect of an ensuring conviction but also alerts the defendant to the possibility of adverse consequences from the plea or admission itself.

(c)(4). To this point the court has been informed of the existence of and substance of a plea arrangement, has indicated a willingness to entertain that arrangement, and has informed, or caused, the defendant to be informed of the consequences of acceptance of the plea. The defendant now formally tenders a plea or admission to the court,

which then conducts a hearing to determine whether it is a knowing, intelligent, and voluntary waiver.

(c)(5). By requiring an inquiry into the "voluntariness" of the plea or admission, this subdivision requires the judge to ensure two basic foundations for a valid waiver. First is that the defendant understands the consequences of his or her act. Courts often refer to this standard as requiring the plea to be a knowing and intelligent act. In addition, the defendant's decision must be free from improper influence. As the Supreme Court, in Johnson v. Zerbst, 304 U.S. 458 (1938), declared, a waiver is "an *intentional* relinquishment or abandonment of a *known* right or privilege." *Id.* at 464 (emphasis supplied).

In order to enter a valid guilty plea, the defendant must be competent. Under both the federal and state constitutions, the test of competence to plead is the same as that for standing trial. *See* Godinez v. Moran, 509 U.S. 389 (1993); Commonwealth v. Blackstone, 19 Mass. App. Ct. 209 (1985). The standard for determining competency to stand trial is "whether [the defendant] has sufficient present ability to consult with his lawyer with a reasonable degree of rational understanding — and whether he has a rational as well as factual understanding of the proceedings against him." Commonwealth v. Russin, 420 Mass. 309, 317 (1995) *quoting* Dusky v. United States, 362 U.S. 402, 402 (1960). The substituted judgment doctrine, by which the court appoints a guardian to act, is not an appropriate vehicle for an incompetent defendant who offers to plead guilty. *See* Commonwealth v. Del Verde, 398 Mass. 288 (1986).

In Huot v. Commonwealth, 363 Mass. 91, 99—101 (1973), the court recognized that Boykin v. Alabama, 397 U.S. 238 (1969) placed the burden of establishing on review that a guilty plea is made voluntarily and intelligently is on the prosecution. The Commonwealth must meet that burden and the hearing that this subsection establishes is designed to meet that end.

The Supreme Judicial Court, in Commonwealth v. Lopez, 426 Mass. 657, 660, (1998), stated the appropriate standard:

As a general proposition of constitutional law, a guilty plea may be withdrawn or nullified if it does not appear affirmatively that the defendant entered the plea freely and voluntarily. Boykin v. Alabama, 395 U.S. 238, 242–243 (1969). *See* Brady v. United States, 397 U.S. 742, 748 (1970); Commonwealth v. Foster, 368 Mass. 100, 106 (1975). Rule 12 (c) (3) of the Massachusetts Rules of Criminal Procedure, requires that a defendant be informed on the record of the three constitutional rights which are waived by a guilty plea: the right to trial, the right to confront one's accusers, and the privilege against self-incrimination. *See* Boykin v. Alabama, *supra* at 243; Commonwealth v. Lewis, 399 Mass. 761, 764 (1987). Moreover, the plea record must demonstrate either that the defendant was advised of the elements of the offense or that he admitted facts constituting the unexplained elements. *See* Henderson v. Morgan, 426 U.S. 637, 646, (1976); Commonwealth v. Colantoni, 396 Mass. 672, 678–679 (1986). Finally, the plea record must demonstrate that the defendant pleaded guilty voluntarily and not in response to threats or undue pressure. *See* Commonwealth v. Foster, *supra* at 107.

The first distinct requirement is that the defendant understand the nature of the charge. A plea may be involuntary because the defendant has such an incomplete understanding of the charge that the plea is an unintelligent admission of guilt. Without adequate notice of the nature of the charge against him, or an indication that the defendant in fact comprehends the charge, the plea cannot stand as voluntary. *See* Smith v. O'Grady, 312 U.S. 329 (1941). In Henderson v. Morgan, 426 U.S. 637 (1976), the Supreme Court held that a guilty plea to a charge of second-degree murder was involuntary because the defendant was not informed that intent to cause death was an element of that crime. The Court assumed, without deciding, that notice of the true nature, or substance, of a charge does not always require a description of every element of the offense, however. *Id.* at 647 n. 18. The Court agreed with the government that in the usual case, the

reviewing court should examine the totality of the circumstances and determine whether the substance of the charge, as opposed to its technical elements, was conveyed to the defendant, rather than testing the voluntariness of his plea according to whether a ritualistic litany of the formal legal elements of the offenses was read to him.

There are three ways that the record of a plea or admission can serve as satisfactory evidence that the defendant had the requisite knowledge of the elements of the charge: 1) the judge can explain the elements of the crime; 2) counsel may represent that he or she has explained them to the defendant; or, 3) the defendant may admit or stipulate to facts constituting the elements. *See* Commonwealth v. Colantoni, 396 Mass. 672, 679 (1986). The defendant's signature on a form that he or she is aware of the elements of the charge is not sufficient. *See* Commonwealth v. Jones, 60 Mass. App. Ct. 88 (2003).

While in a post-conviction context it may suffice for the record to reflect that counsel stated that the defendant was advised of the elements, or for the defendant to have admitted an act constituting the elements, the judge should not rely on these means as the primary method of establishing the requisite knowledge. *See* Colantoni, *supra*, 396 Mass. at 679 n. 5. The best way to ensure that the defendant knows the elements of the crime is for the judge to explain them as part of the colloquy. This can be fairly easily done in most cases by reading to the defendant the indictment or complaint. However, in some cases, it may require more than a simple statement of the crime itself. *E.g.* Commonwealth v. Jones, 60 Mass. App. Ct. 88 (2003) (simply telling the defendant that he is charged with assault and battery does not sufficiently apprise him of the elements of the crime); Commonwealth v. Pixley, 48 Mass. App. Ct. 917 (2000) (telling the defendant only that he was charged with possession of cocaine with intent to distribute did not satisfy requirement of explaining the elements as mandated by this subsection).

For an example of the scope of the examination conducted to satisfy the *Boykin* requirement of an affirmative showing of understanding and voluntariness, *see* Commonwealth v Taylor, 370 Mass 141, 144–45 n. 5 (1976). In conducting the examination, the judge is to rely on his or her own observations and discernment in concluding that the defendant understands the questions. *See* Commonwealth v Leate, 367 Mass 689, 696 (1975)

In order for the plea or admission to be voluntary, the defendant's decision to waive a trial must be free from the influence of factors that have no legitimate role to play in the process. *See* Rossman, Guilty Pleas, 2 Criminal Law Advocacy, ¶ 2.03 (listing improper threats, such as physical abuse). Therefore, the judge should inquire whether the defendant's decision to waive a trial is a result of any threats or inducements apart from those identified in the plea agreement. *See* Commonwealth v. Fernandes 390 Mass. 714, 719 (1984). While no particular form of words need be used to make this inquiry, *see* Commonwealth v. Lewis, 399 Mass. 761, 764 (1987), a brief colloquy that does not probe the defendant's mind will not do. *See* Commonwealth v. Quinones, 414 Mass. 423, 434 (1992); *Fernandes, supra*, 390 Mass. at 717–719. It is useful, however, for the judge to include in the colloquy a question about whether the defendant has consulted with counsel about the decision to waive a trial and is satisfied with counsel's assistance. *Cf. Fernandes, supra*, 390 Mass. at 718.

The pressure of a plea bargain that holds out no more than the possibility of a harsher sentence if the defendant goes to trial and is convicted is not by itself an improper influence that would render a guilty plea not voluntary. *See* Commonwealth v Tirrell 382 Mass 502, 510 (1981):

neither this court nor the Supreme Court has required total absence of psychological or emotional pressure. In any plea bargaining situation the defendant is necessarily put to a difficult choice — the risk of a more serious sentence after trial and conviction against the probabilities of the trial judge's accepting the prosecutor's recommended leniency. The defendant's fond hopes for acquittal must be tempered by his understanding of the strength of the case against him, his prior record, and the completely unknowable reaction of the trier of fact. *See* Commonwealth v. Leate, 367 Mass. 689, 694 (1975). Without some showing of peculiar susceptibility, which rendered the defendant so gripped by fear of the . . . penalty or hope of leniency that he . . . could not . . . rationally weigh the advantages of going to trial against the advantages of pleading guilty," Brady v. United States, 397 U.S. 742, 750 (1970). We cannot say that the pressure of the decision per se destroys voluntariness. *Contrast* Pate v. Robinson, 383 U.S. 375, 385–386 (1966) (record of irrational conduct required hearing on defendant's incompetency to stand trial).

(c)(5)(A). This subdivision is based upon A.B.A. Standards Relating to Pleas of Guilty § 1.6 (Approved Draft, 1968) and accords with District Court Initial R. Crim. P. 5 (1971). *See* Fed. R. Crim. P. 11(f).

The "factual basis" standard can be met by having the prosecutor state for the record the evidence that the Commonwealth would have presented had the case gone to trial. In addition, the court may require sworn testimony from a prosecution witness or of the defendant. *See* 8 J. Moore, Federal Practice ¶ 11.03 [3] at 11–75 (1978); A.B.A. Standards Relating to Pleas of Guilty § 1.6, comment at 32 (Approved Draft, 1968).

North Carolina v. Alford, 400 U.S. 25 (1970), establishes that the United States Constitution does not prohibit the court from accepting a guilty plea from a defendant who nevertheless asserts his or her innocence. An *Alford* plea is a permissible way to establish a defendant's guilt without a trial. *See* Commonwealth v. Nikas, 431 Mass. 453 (2000); Hout v. Commonwealth, 363 Mass. 91 (1973). "Under *Alford*, a defendant who professes innocence may nevertheless plead guilty and 'voluntarily, knowingly and understandingly consent to the imposition of a prison sentence,' if the State can demonstrate a 'strong factual basis' for the plea." Commonwealth v. DelVerde, 398 Mass. 288, 297(1986), *quoting* North Carolina v. Alford, 400 U.S. 25, 38 (1970). If a factual basis for such a plea exists, it is only fair to allow a defendant who is aware of the law, the facts, and the consequences of his plea, to attempt to reduce the severity of his or her punishment by pleading guilty. *See* Commonwealth v Hubbard, 371 Mass. 160 (1976). The defendant is free to weigh the strength of the Commonwealth's evidence and on this basis to waive the right to trial. If the waiver is voluntary and intelligent it should be upheld.

Subdivision (c)(5)(A) is not made applicable to nolo pleas. The purpose of permitting a nolo plea is to relieve the defendant of the adverse repercussions that can result from the introduction of evidence from the present criminal proceedings. This purpose would be undermined to the extent that disclosures led to subsequent civil proceedings or evidence to be used at such proceedings, notwithstanding the fact that the disclosures themselves could not be used in evidence. The Federal Rules Advisory Committee stated in its note to Fed. R. Crim. P. 11: "it is desirable in some cases to permit entry of judgment upon a plea of nolo contendere without inquiry into the factual basis for the plea."

(c)(5)(B). At the conclusion of the hearing, if the judge finds that the plea "is the defendant's own, guided by reasonable advice of his counsel, his own knowledge of what he has done, and a fair understanding of the alternatives," it will be considered voluntary. Commonwealth v Manning, 367 Mass 699, 706 (1975). The judge may then accept the plea or, notwithstanding the fact that it is voluntary, reject it. *See* subdivision (c)(6), *infra*.

(c)(5)(C). If the plea or admission is accepted, the judge shall proceed with sentencing as after a verdict or finding of guilty under Mass. R. Crim. P. 28(b).

(c)(6). This subdivision is drawn in part from Fed. R. Crim. P. 11(e)(3)–(4) and from A.B.A. Standards Relating to Pleas of Guilty § 2.1 (Approved Draft, 1968). *See* Rules of Criminal Procedure (U.L.A.) rule 444(e) (1974). *Compare* Fed. R. Crim. P. 32(d) (plea may be withdrawn after sentence only "to correct manifest injustice") *with* A.L.I. Model Code of Pre-Arraignment Procedure § 350.6 (POD

1975) (defendant may withdraw plea if sentence to be imposed is more severe than that provided in plea agreement).

Previously existing statutes relative to the withdrawal of pleas after imposition of sentence are intended to be unaffected by this rule. General Laws c. 278 §§ 29A (St 1962, c 310, § 2) and 29C (St 1959, c 167, § 1) permitted the retraction of any sentence and the withdrawal of any plea upon which the sentence was imposed within sixty days of sentencing if justice has not been done. Now *see* Mass. R. Crim. P. 29. In a case where the defendant has the right to counsel and is neither represented nor validly waived counsel, General Laws c. 278, § 29B grants the defendant an absolute right to withdraw a plea prior to sentencing.

This subdivision addresses two classes of cases. One is where the defendant's plea or admission is contingent upon a prosecutor's sentence recommendation. The other, referred to in language added in 2004, occurs where the defendant has tendered a defense capped plea. In either case, the judge has many available options. After reviewing the arrangement and, if desired, the probation report, the judge may concur in the disposition; concur in the disposition, but condition the concurrence upon facts being found consistent with representations made by the parties; refuse to accept the disposition; or propose an alternative disposition, giving the defendant a reasonable opportunity to consider the alternative before deciding whether to persist in the plea or admission or proceed to trial. If the judge intends to vary from the recommended or tendered disposition in a manner which is detrimental or prejudicial to the interests of the defendant, the defendant has an absolute right to withdraw the plea or admission.

It should be noted that where a plea or admission is predicated on a promise by the prosecutor to take unilateral action over which the judge has no control, such as entering a nolle prosequi to certain charges, this subsection is not applicable. The "[p]ower to enter a nolle prosequi is absolute in the prosecuting officer . . . except possibly in instances of scandalous abuse of the authority." Commonwealth v. Dascalakis, 246 Mass. 12, 18 (1923). *See* Mass. R. Crim. P. 16. In a case such as this, disclosure to the court prior to the tender of the plea serves no purpose other than determining whether the plea is knowingly and voluntarily made.

While this subdivision is the only provision in Rule 12 that explicitly addresses the issue of a defendant's withdrawing a plea, a judge has authority to entertain such a motion on other grounds. Prior to its amendment in 1987, Rule (c)(2)(B) contained an explicit statement that if the defendant persisted in pleading guilty despite notice of the judge's intention to exceed the prosecutor's recommended sentence, the defendant could not thereafter withdraw the plea except "in the discretion of the judge." This provision was eliminated in 1987. The former subsection (c)(2)(B) gave the judge "broad discretion to allow a defendant to withdraw [a] plea before . . . sentence [has been] imposed." Commonwealth v. DeMarco, 387 Mass. 481, 484 (1982); *see also* Commonwealth v. Clerico, 35 Mass. App. Ct. 407, 413 n. 7(1991). The removal from Rule 12 of the reference to a judge's discretion to allow the defendant to withdraw a plea does not alter the law that otherwise controls in this situation. If the defendant can show that the plea was not voluntary or tendered knowingly, then a motion for withdrawal should be granted, for these requirements are constitutional prerequisites to the validity of the plea. If, on the other hand, the defendant seeks to withdraw a plea prior to sentencing despite its being knowing and voluntary, the judge should balance the reason put forward by the defendant against any prejudice to the Commonwealth. *Cf.* Commonwealth v. Nolan, 19 Mass. App. Ct. 491, 494 (1984). After sentencing, however, the proper vehicle to seek to withdraw a guilty plea is a motion under Rule 30 (b).

The 2004 revision of Rule 12 deleted subdivision (d), which was designed to discourage the practice of "judge shopping" by tendering, withdrawing, and retendering a guilty plea until a judge is found who will agree to the disposition favored by the defendant. A uniform policy on whether a defendant may ask more than one judge to accept a sentence recommendation or defense capped plea is unnecessary.

Individual judges still retain the discretion to refuse to entertain such requests.

(e). The conditions governing the availability to the defendant of the probation report are the same as those which control under Mass. R. Crim. P. 28(d)(3). It is important for the defendant to have access to this information so that he or she can more effectively bargain with the prosecutor and more accurately predict how the court will react to proposed dispositions. The judge need not always view the probation report to properly decide whether it should be released to the defendant. The judge can rely on representations made by the probation department or by the prosecutor in reaching this decision. The judge may examine the defendant's criminal record before accepting a plea or admission. *See* Commonwealth v. Whitford, 16 Mass. App. Ct. 448, 453 (1983).

Subdivision (f). In its original form, this subdivision changed the prior rule in Massachusetts that a plea that has been withdrawn may be introduced in subsequent proceedings as an admission by the defendant. *See* Morrisey v. Powell, 304 Mass. 268 (1939). The current position reflected in this subdivision is consistent with the modern trend and with the rule in federal courts. *See* A.B.A. Standards Relating to Pleas of Guilty, §§ 2.2, 3.4 (Approved Draft, 1968); Rules of Criminal Procedure (U.L.A.) rule 444(f) (1974); A.L.I. Model Code of Pre–Arraignment Procedure § 350.7 (POD 1975). It is drawn from Fed. Cr. Crim. P. 11(e)(6), although it is broader in scope, since unlike the federal rule, its application to statements made in the course of plea negotiations is not limited only to circumstances where the defendant is negotiating with a government attorney. *See* Commonwealth v. Wilson, 430 Mass. 440, 443 (1999). However, simply expressing a desire to plead guilty to a police officer who does not have any authority to bind the Commonwealth does not bring a defendant's statement within the scope of this subdivision. *Id.*

In 2004, the subdivision was amended to include admissions to sufficient facts among the category of actions by the defendant that are not admissible if later withdrawn.

Permitting a prosecutor to offer evidence that a defendant unsuccessfully tendered a plea or admission undermines the rationale behind the decision allowing the plea or admission to be withdrawn in the first place. *See* Kercheval v. United States, 274 U.S. 220 (1927). Additionally, juries tend to give undue weight to the introduction of prior pleas. Of course, if the reason why the plea or admission was withdrawn was that it was not knowing and voluntary, then the federal Constitution prohibits its use in a subsequent proceeding. *Cf.* White v. Maryland, 373 U.S. 59 (1963) (barring use of evidence that the defendant had entered a guilty plea without the assistance of counsel, where the defendant did not validly waive the right to counsel).

While an offer to plead guilty is inadmissible pursuant to this subdivision, the fact that a defendant refused to enter a guilty plea or rejected a plea agreement is not, conversely, admissible by implication. *See* Commonwealth v. DoVale, 57 Mass. App. Ct. 657 (2003).

Reporter's Notes—January 2015

Rule 12 Pleas and Plea Agreements

As the title of Rule 12 suggests, the 2015 revision of the rule resulted in a more carefully delineated and somewhat expanded role for plea agreements in the process of a judge's consideration and acceptance of a proffered guilty plea. The rule's amendment was in response to the Supreme Judicial Court's interpretation of Rule 12 in *Commonwealth v. Rodriguez*, 461 Mass. 256 (2012), and *Commonwealth v. Dean–Ganek*, 461 Mass. 305 (2012), holding that former Rule 12 permitted a judge to impose a sentence more lenient than the sentence agreed to in a plea agreement accepted by the judge. The Court further held that jeopardy attaches when the judge accepts a plea, *see Dean–Ganek*, 461 Mass. at 312–313, thus preventing the prosecution's withdrawal in such a case, even when the plea agreement included negotiated charge concessions.

As amended, Rule 12 provides that, if (1) the parties enter a plea agreement which includes both a specific, agreed sentence and a prosecutorial charge concession and (2) the judge accepts that agreement, then the judge is bound to impose the agreed sentence. If, on the other hand, the judge rejects such an agreement, either party may withdraw. In all other pleas or admissions, whether conditioned on a plea agreement or not, the amended rule provides that the judge is not bound by the sentencing recommendations of the parties. However, in such cases, the amended rule permits the defendant to withdraw the plea if the judge indicates an intent to impose a sentence more severe than (1) an agreed recommendation (but without charge concessions), (2) the prosecutor's recommendation if there is no agreed sentencing recommendation, or (3) in District Court, the disposition requested by the defendant. Finally, in order to promote fair and efficient plea bargaining and to establish rules to govern the previously unregulated and widely varying practice of lobby conferences, amended Rule 12 provides for judicial participation in plea negotiations at the request of a party and requires that plea discussions with judicial participation be recorded.

Rule 12(a) Pleas in General

The 2015 amendments made no substantive changes to Rule 12(a). The only changes were stylistic, designed to make the rule more specific and clear.

Rule 12(b) Plea Discussions; Pleas Without Plea Agreement and With Plea Agreement

Rule 12(b)(1) In General

Rule 12(b)(1) makes it clear that the defendant may tender a guilty plea, a nolo contendere plea, or, in District Court, an admission to sufficient facts, without entering into a plea agreement. *See* Rule 2(b)(7) (defining "District Court" to include all divisions of the District Court, Boston Municipal Court, and Juvenile Court). However, the rule also provides that the parties may condition a guilty plea (or, in District Court, an admission to sufficient facts) on a plea agreement under Rule 12(b)(5), discussed below. Rule 12(b)(1) omits nolo contendere pleas from those that can be conditioned on a plea agreement, an omission that Rule 12(b)(5) makes explicit, thus limiting the benefits of a plea agreement to those defendants who take responsibility for the crimes to which they are pleading.

Rule 12(b)(2) Plea Discussions

Rule 12(b)(2) provides that the judge may participate in plea discussions at the request of either party provided that any such discussions are recorded and made part of the record. Such limited judicial participation in plea negotiations facilitates fair and efficient case management, particularly in courts with crowded dockets, and it has been a longstanding though largely unregulated practice in many courts. The rule maintains the recognized benefits of this practice while providing important safeguards to curb its potential for abuse.

Recognizing that judicial participation in plea negotiations can be coercive and leave the impression of unfairness, this provision addresses these concerns by conditioning such participation on the request of one or both parties and further requiring that these discussions be recorded and made a part of the record. *See Murphy v. Boston Herald, Inc.*, 449 Mass. 42, 57 n. 15 (2007) (stressing the importance of recording lobby conferences). The rule does not, however, preclude a judge's uninvited announcement that he or she is willing to participate in plea discussions if invited to do so by either party. The rule's requirement that the discussions be recorded and made part of the record is not meant to require that they invariably be conducted in open court. As with other potentially sensitive matters, judges have discretion under the appropriate circumstances to conduct plea discussions in a manner that restricts immediate public access, most likely at sidebar, provided they are recorded. Judges are experienced in determining when sidebars or other such restrictions are appropriate, and the rule anticipates that they will continue to apply that experience injudiciously exercising this discretion.

Rule 12(b)(3) Inquiry as to the Existence of a Plea Agreement

Rule 12(b)(3) provides that, when a defendant indicates an intent to plead guilty or to admit to sufficient facts, the judge shall inquire if there is a plea agreement. Because plea procedures vary depending on whether there is an agreement that will bind the judge if accepted, such an inquiry is necessary in order to determine which procedure is applicable. Because Rule 12 does not permit a nolo contendere plea to be conditioned on a plea agreement, the rule does not require the judge to ask if there is a plea agreement in such a case. However, it may make sense for the judge nevertheless to make this preliminary inquiry in the case of a nolo plea, if only to ensure that the parties understand that any such plea agreement is outside the rule, constituting at best a joint recommendation that the judge is free to disregard.

Rule 12(b)(4) Pleas Without an Agreement

If there is no plea agreement under Rule 12(b)(5), Rule 12(b)(4) provides that the procedure for taking a plea or admission set forth in Rule 12(c) applies. In such a case, the parties are each free to make any dispositional request permitted by law.

Rule 12(b)(5) Pleas Conditioned Upon an Agreement

Rule 12(b)(5) provides that a defendant may condition an intended guilty plea or admission on a plea agreement with the prosecutor. As noted, the rule explicitly precludes a plea agreement if the intended plea is nolo contendere. The rule divides plea agreements into two categories. Rule 12(b)(5)(A) provides for a type of plea agreement that, if accepted by the judge, binds the judge to sentence in accordance with the agreement, and Rule 12(b)(5)(B) provides, in effect, that no other plea agreement binds the judge to impose a particular sentence.

Under Rule 12(b)(5)(A), an accepted plea agreement will bind the judge if the parties have agreed both to a particular charge concession(s) by the prosecutor and to a specific sentence, including the length of any probationary term. Rule 12(b)(5)(A)'s reach is intentionally narrow. The rule carves out an exception to judicial sentencing discretion, an exception applicable only to a plea bargain that expressly includes both a prosecutorial charge concession and an agreed sentence to a specific term of incarceration, to a specific period of probation, or to a specific term of incarceration coupled with a specific period of probation (e.g., a term of probation to be served in lieu of a suspended sentence of incarceration, or a term of probation to be served on and after a term of incarceration). If the parties enter into such an agreement, the rule requires the judge to follow the plea procedures set forth in Rule 12(d), noting that those procedures mandate imposition of the agreed sentence if the judge accepts the plea agreement and the plea. *See* Rule 12(d)(4)(A) and (6), discussed below. As discussed below, Rule 12(d) further provides that, if the judge rejects such a plea agreement, either party may withdraw from the agreement and thus from the plea. *See* Rule 12(d)(4)(B).

Even though Rule 12(b)(5)(A) permits the parties to include a specific period of probation within a binding plea agreement, the rule does not permit the parties to bind the judge to impose specific conditions of probation. Any agreement by the parties concerning conditions of probation is treated as a non-binding recommendation for the judge to consider, with the assistance of probation, in deciding what probationary conditions are appropriate in the case. *See* Rule 12(d)(6), discussed below. Finally, nothing in Rule 12 is intended to limit a judge's lawful discretion to modify probationary conditions during the course of probation or to adjust the probationary term upon a finding of a probation violation. In short, a plea agreement containing a charge concession and an agreed-upon period of probation will bind a judge who accepts that agreement to impose the agreed term of probation, but the parties may not by agreement trench upon the longstanding prerogative of the judge to determine and subsequently to modify any conditions of probation during that probationary term. *See Commonwealth v. Goodwin,* 458 Mass. 11,17–19(2010).

Under Rule 12(b)(5)(B), pleas conditioned on plea agreements other than those described in Rule 12(b)(5)(A) are governed by the procedures set forth in Rule 12(c), the procedures that also govern pleas in which there is no plea agreement. As discussed below, Rule 12(c) treats any agreement contained in a Rule 12(b)(5)(B) plea agreement as a non-binding, joint recommendation. For example, if the parties agree to a specific sentence unaccompanied by a charge concession, to a charge concession unaccompanied by an agreement to a specific sentence, or to some other dispositional alternative such as incarceration in a particular facility, that agreement would not bind the judge in imposing sentence. As was true under former Rule 12(b), the parties are free to enter into an agreement to recommend any disposition, or kind of disposition, permitted by law in the case in question. However, unless the agreement provides for both a charge concession and a specific sentence, the judge cannot be bound to follow that recommendation.

Rule 12(c) Procedure If No Plea Agreement or If Plea Agreement Does Not Include Both a Specific Sentence and a Charge Concession

Rule 12(c) provides for the plea procedure in cases in which the parties have not entered a binding plea agreement under Rule 12(b)(5)(A). Rule 12(c)'s procedure is parallel to that set forth in Rule 12(d), which is applicable to pleas and admissions when there is a Rule 12(b)(5)(A) binding plea agreement. The two sections diverge in their respective timing of receipt of victim impact statements, *compare* Rule 12(c)(3)(C) *with* Rule 12(d)(3)(C), treatment of the parties' sentencing recommendations, *compare* Rule 12(c)(4) *with* Rule 12(d)(4), and sentencing, *compare* Rule 12(c)(6) *with* Rule 12(d)(6). Otherwise, the two plea procedures are substantively identical.

Rule 12(c)(1) Disclosure of Terms of Plea Agreement

As discussed above, if the plea is conditioned on a plea agreement, the applicability of Rule 12(c)'s procedures depends on the provisions of that agreement. If the agreement provides for both a prosecutorial charge concession and an agreed specific sentence, the procedures under Rule 12(d) apply; if not, Rule 12(c) applies. It is thus important for the parties and the judge to be clear about the terms of any agreement before the plea procedure begins.

Rule 12(c)(2) Tender of Plea

Because Rule 12(c) applies to pleas in which there is no agreement as well as to pleas conditioned on an agreement, Rule 12(c)(2) moves the tender of plea or admission to the beginning of the plea procedure so that from the outset the terms of the plea or admission are clear even if there is no agreement. Although the plea tender precedes Rule 12(c)(3)'s colloquy, which includes the notice of the consequences of the plea, Rule 12(c)(5) permits the defendant to withdraw the tendered plea or admission subsequent to the colloquy but prior to the judge's acceptance of the plea or admission. In a District–Court plea in which there will be a recommendation of probation, whether unagreed or agreed, the party(ies) must consult with the probation department before tendering the plea so that probation will be in a position to provide any assistance that the judge may require in sentencing. *See* Dist./Mun. Ct. R. Crim. P. 4(c).

Rule 12(c)(3) Colloquy

Rule 12(c)(3)(A) requires the judge to begin the plea colloquy by notifying the defendant of the consequences of the tendered plea or admission. The notice of consequences is substantively identical to former Rule 12(c)(3)'s required notice of consequences with two exceptions. First, unlike its predecessor, Rule 12(c)(3)(A)(ii)(d) requires the notice mandated by the 2012 amendments to the habitual-offender statute. *See* G.L. c. 279, § 25(d) (requiring notice of potential habitual-offender consequences "prior to accepting a guilty plea for any qualifying offense listed in subsection (b) [of the statute]" but further providing that the failure to give such notice is not a basis to vacate an otherwise valid plea or conviction).

Second, Rule 12(c)(3)(A)(iii) expands former Rule 12(c)(3)(C)'s required noncitizen warning. As did former Rule 12(c)(3)(C), Rule 12(c)(3)(A)(iii)(a) requires the warning mandated by G.L. c. 278,

§ 29D, advising a defendant that, if he or she is a noncitizen, his or her plea or admission may result in deportation, exclusion from admission, or denial of naturalization. Rule 12(c)(3)(A)(iii)(b) advises further that, if (1) the offense to which the defendant is pleading is under federal law one that "presumptively mandates removal from the United States" (a so-called "removable offense," see Padilla v. Kentucky, 559 U.S. 356, 363–364 (2010)) and (2) federal officials seek removal, it is "practically inevitable that [defendant's] conviction would result in deportation, exclusion from admission, or denial of naturalization."

This additional warning recognizes that under federal immigration law there are a substantial number of crimes—including "all controlled substances convictions except for the most trivial of marijuana possession offenses," see Padilla, 559 U.S. at 368; 8 U.S.C. § 1227(a)(2)(B)(i) (2008)—the conviction for which make "deportation practically inevitable" if federal officials seek the defendant's removal. See Commonwealth v. DeJesus, 468 Mass. 174, 181 & n. 5 (2014). See also Moncrieffe v. Holder, 133 S. Ct. 1678, 1682 (2013) (cited in DeJesus, noting that the federal Immigration and Nationality Act prohibits discretionary relief for deportations based on convictions for a wide range of crimes no matter how compelling the circumstances). Further, as the warning states, once deported due to such a conviction, a defendant would almost certainly be denied both re-admission to the United States and naturalization. See, e.g., L. Rosenberg, D. Kanstroom & J. Smith, Immigration Consequences of Criminal Proceedings, Massachusetts Criminal Practice § 42.2 (E. Blumenson & A. Leavens eds., 4th ed. 2012). It is important to appreciate that Rule 12(c)(3)(A)(iii)(b)'s warning is limited to the consequences of a conviction for a "removable offense." The narrow focus of this enhanced warning is purposeful and should not be read to suggest that convictions for other crimes would have no serious immigration consequences. Under federal law, conviction for—or even an admission to conduct constituting—a broader range of crimes than those presumptively mandating removal can also result in denial of re-admission and of naturalization. Id. §§ 42.2–42.3.

Finally, as Rule 12(c)(3)(A)(iii)'s warning provides, under federal immigration law, "convictions" include admissions to sufficient facts even when the result is a continuance without a finding (CWOF), if the continuance is conditioned on "some form of punishment, penalty or restraint" such as payment of costs or restitution. See DeVaga v. Gonzalez, 503 F.3d 45, 49 (1st Cir. 2007) (holding that a CWOF conditioned on payment of restitution satisfies 8 U.S.C. § 1101(a)(48)(A)(ii)'s provision that an admission to sufficient facts constitutes a "conviction" if the admission results in "some form of punishment, penalty or restraint"); Matter of Cabrera, 24 I. & N. Dec. 459, 462 (BIA 2008) (holding that imposition of costs and surcharges following a plea is a "penalty" or "punishment" for purposes of § 1101(a)(48)(A)(ii)).

This noncitizen warning is not meant to displace the critical role of counsel in providing more particular advice concerning the immigration consequences of a particular plea. Quite the contrary, the warning is meant to trigger that advice if, under circumstances best known by counsel, a defendant is risking serious immigration consequences by pleading guilty or admitting to sufficient facts. See Padilla v. Kentucky, 559 U.S. 356, 368–369 (2010); Commonwealth v. Clarke, 460 Mass. 30, 45–46, 48–49 & n. 20 (2011) (noting that then-Rule 12's requirement of "[immigration] warnings is not an adequate substitute for defense counsel's professional obligation to advise her client of the likelihood of specific and dire immigration consequences that might arise from such a plea"), partially abrogated on other grounds, Chaidez v. United States, 133 S. Ct. 1103 (2013); DeJesus, 468 Mass. at 182 (holding that counsel's advice to a noncitizen defendant that he would be "eligible for deportation" and would "face deportation" if he pled guilty to possession of cocaine with intent to distribute (a removable offense under the immigration statute) was constitutionally inadequate).

Rule 12(c)(3)(B) requires the prosecutor to present the factual basis of the charge. Unlike former Rule 12(c)(5)(A), Rule 12(c)(3)(B) does not exclude nolo contendere pleas from the requirement that the prosecutor present a factual basis for the tendered plea or admission. The factual basis of a nolo plea provides information essential to crafting an appropriate sentence, but, because the defendant is not called upon to acknowledge or admit those facts, they will not be admissible in any subsequent proceeding against the defendant. See, e.g., Mass. Guide to Evidence § 803(22) (2014) (explicitly excluding judgments based on nolo contendere pleas from the hearsay exception generally applicable to judgments of conviction).

The prosecutor can present the factual basis in the traditional manner, stating the facts that he or she expects to prove if the case goes to trial, but the rule also permits presenting sworn testimony, at the request of the judge or otherwise, as a way to satisfy this requirement. If the plea is an Alford plea, i.e., one in which the defendant declines to admit one or more elements of the offense to which he or she is nevertheless pleading guilty, the Supreme Court requires "strong evidence of [the defendant's] guilt." See North Carolina v. Alford, 400 U.S. 25, 37–38 (1970). In such a case, the prosecutor should give particular attention to this testimonial option. See E. Cypher, Procedure if Defendant pleads Guilty or Nolo Contendere but does not admit Participation in Crime, 30A Mass. Prac., Criminal Practice & Procedure, § 24:78 n. 4 (2014) ("[I]f an Alford plea is offered, the Commonwealth should . . . [offer] sworn testimony to show the case is strong against the defendant, his defense is non-existent, and the defendant has presented reasons why the plea should be accepted").

As the final part of the colloquy, Rule 12(c)(3)(C) requires the judge to inquire of the prosecutor as to compliance with G.L. c. 258B. However, the judge is granted discretion concerning when to hear any victim-impact statements. The judge does not need this input until deciding whether to accept or reject the plea and then to impose sentence. However, hearing victim-impact statements at this stage of the proceeding—just before hearing the parties' respective sentencing recommendations and arguments—may provide the judge with the proper perspective for considering those recommendations and deciding what is a just disposition in the case.

Rule 12(c)(4) Disposition Requests

Rule 12(c)(4) gives the parties the opportunity to make their respective sentencing recommendations. This section has two subdivisions: Rule 12(c)(4)(A) applies to cases in which there is no agreed-upon sentence recommendation, and Rule 12(c)(4)(B) applies to cases in which there is. Rule 12(c)(4)(A) requires a District Court judge to inform a defendant of the statutory right to withdraw the plea if the judge imposes a sentence that exceeds the defendant's request, see G.L. c. 278, § 18, and a Superior Court judge to inform a defendant of the right to withdraw the plea if the disposition imposed exceeds the prosecutor's recommendation. If the parties have agreed on a sentence recommendation, Rule 12(c)(4)(B) requires the judge to inform the defendant that the plea may be withdrawn if the sentence imposed exceeds the agreed-upon recommendation. However, unlike Rule 12(d)(4)(B)(ii), which applies to binding plea agreements, Rule 12(c)(4)(B) does not give the prosecution the right to withdraw from the plea agreement and the plea if the judge announces an intent to impose a sentence more lenient than the sentence jointly recommended.

If in considering the parties' joint or respective recommendations the judge decides that he or she needs more information or time to determine a just disposition in the case, both subsections of Rule 12(c)(4) allow the judge to continue the plea hearing for that purpose. Among the factors pertinent to the judge's sentencing decision are the nature of the offense committed, the manner in which it was committed, the impact that the offense had on any victims, the defendant's criminal history, and the defendant's circumstances (e.g., his or her mental health, substance abuse, and/or psychological issues). The judge, in consultation with probation where appropriate, should take the time and consider the facts necessary to craft a sentence, including any term and conditions of probation, that is fair, appropriate to the crime, and designed to diminish the risk of recidivism.

Rule 12(c)(5) Findings of Judge; Acceptance of Plea

Rule 12(c)(5) requires the judge to inquire if the defendant still wishes to plead guilty or admit to sufficient facts. At this point, the defendant has received the notice of consequences of the plea or admission, has heard the factual basis for the charged offense(s), and is aware of the respective sentencing recommendations of the parties. The defendant may have also heard the victim-impact statement(s), if any. The defendant must now elect to go forward with his or her tendered plea or admission, or choose to withdraw it and go to trial. If the defendant elects to go forward, the judge then makes the necessary inquiries to ensure that the plea or admission is knowing and voluntary. The amended rule is intended to make no change to former Rule 12(c)(5)'s provision for this voluntariness hearing, either in its form or substance.

The rule also requires the judge to find that there is an adequate factual basis for the plea or admission. As did its predecessor, Rule 12(c)(5) provides that the defendant's failure to acknowledge all aspects of the factual basis shall not preclude a judge from accepting a guilty plea. The rule is not intended to work any change to former Rule 12(c)(5)(A) in this regard.

If the judge is satisfied that the plea or admission is knowing, voluntary, and supported by an adequate factual basis, the judge is then in a position to accept the tendered plea or admission. Of course, if the judge is not satisfied in this regard, or, if for some other reason the judge determines that the plea or admission would not result in a just disposition of the case, the judge is permitted to reject the plea or admission. Nothing in the rule is meant to deprive the judge of this longstanding discretion. *See Commonwealth v. Dilone*, 385 Mass. 281, 285 (1982) (acceptance of a guilty plea is "wholly discretionary with the judge"), citing *Santobello v. New York*, 404 U.S. 257 (1971); E. Cypher, 30A Mass. Prac., Criminal Practice & Procedure, Judge may refuse to accept guilty plea, plea of nolo contendere or admission to sufficient facts, § 24:60 (4th ed. 2014).

Rule 12(c)(6) Sentencing

If the judge accepts the plea or admission, the judge then imposes sentence under Rule 12(c)(6). As required by G.L. c. 278, § 18, Rule 12(c)(6)(B) explicitly permits a District Court defendant to withdraw his or her tendered plea or admission if the intended sentence exceeds the defendant's requested disposition. Similarly, in Superior Court a defendant may withdraw his or her plea if the intended sentence exceeds the parties' agreed-upon recommendation or, if there is no agreed-upon recommendation, the recommendation of the prosecutor. In either event, the judge may indicate to the parties what sentence the judge would impose if the plea were to go forward.

Rule 12(d) Procedure If Plea Agreement Includes Both a Specific Sentence and a Charge Concession

The procedure set out in Rule 12(d) applies to pleas and admissions conditioned on a plea agreement that includes both an agreed charge concession by the prosecutor and an agreement to a specific sentence. *See* Rule 12(b)(5)(A), discussed above. Under Rule 12(d)(6), discussed below, if the judge accepts such a plea agreement, the judge is bound to impose the agreed sentence. If, however, the judge rejects the plea agreement, either party may withdraw from the agreement. *See* Rule 12(d)(4)(B), discussed below. Because jeopardy attaches when the judge accepts a tendered plea or admission, at that point foreclosing the prosecutor's withdrawal from any plea agreement, *see Commonwealth v. Dean–Ganek*, 461 Mass. 305, 312–313 (2012), the rule requires that the judge accept or reject a Rule 12(b)(5)(A) plea agreement prior to accepting the plea or admission. And, because such a plea agreement binds the judge if accepted, Rule 12(d) is structured to ensure that, at the time the judge must accept or reject the agree-

ment, the judge has the necessary information to determine if the agreed disposition would be just and appropriate for the case.

Rule 12(d)(1) Disclosure of the Terms of the Plea Agreement

Rule 12(d)(1) requires disclosure of the plea agreement at the beginning of the plea hearing. Because acceptance of the agreement binds the judge to sentence according to its terms, it is essential that this disclosure include a clear explanation on the record of those terms.

Rule 12(d)(2) Tender of Plea

Rule 12(d)(2) moves the tender of plea to the beginning of the plea procedure so that the terms of the plea or admission are clear at the outset. In District Court, if the plea agreement includes any probationary terms or conditions, the parties must consult with the probation department before tendering the plea so that probation will be in a position to provide any assistance that the judge may require in considering the plea or the plea agreement. *See* Dist./Mun. Ct. R. Crim. P. 4(c). The plea tender precedes Rule 12(d)(3)'s colloquy, which includes the notice of the consequences of the plea or admission, but Rule 12(d)(5) permits the defendant to withdraw the tendered plea or admission subsequent to being informed of its consequences and prior to the judge's acceptance of it.

Rule 12(d)(3) Colloquy

Rule 12(d)(3)(A) provides for the notice of consequences in terms substantively identical to those of 12(c)(3)(A). The above discussion of Rule 12(c)(3)(A) thus applies here with equal force.

Rule 12(d)(3)(B) and (C) respectively require the prosecutor's presentation of the factual basis for the charge and any victim-impact statements mandated by G.L. c. 258B. As with Rule 12(c)(3)(B), the prosecutor can satisfy this obligation to inform the judge of the factual basis of the charge in the traditional manner, stating the facts that he or she expects to prove if the case goes to trial, but the rule also permits presenting sworn testimony, at the request of the judge or otherwise. Rule 12(d)(3)(C) provides for the receipt of any victim-impact statements at this time. While in some instances it may not be necessary for the judge to hear the victim-impact statements before deciding whether to accept the plea agreement, the judge should not defer hearing from the victims absent the most unusual circumstances. Victim–impact statements delivered after the judge accepts the plea agreement can have no effect on the sentence.

Rule 12(d)'s placement of the facts describing the offense and its impact on the victims at this point in the procedure is necessary because, as noted, the rule requires that the judge accept or reject the plea agreement prior to accepting the plea itself, and that, if accepted, the plea agreement binds the judge to sentence according to the agreement. It is thus essential that a judge have access to all of the facts pertinent to a just and appropriate disposition in the case prior to deciding whether to accept or reject the plea agreement under Rule 12(d)(4).

Rule 12(d)(4) Review; Acceptance or Rejection of Plea Agreement

As noted, to avoid the double-jeopardy bar to the prosecutor's withdrawal from a rejected plea agreement, the judge must accept or reject the plea agreement before accepting the plea or admission. *See Dean–Ganek*, 461 Mass. at 312–313. Rule 12(d)(4) imposes that timing requirement. At this point in the procedure, the judge has heard the facts of the charged offense and its impact on any victims. Moreover, in reviewing the plea agreement, the judge will hear from the parties concerning the agreed disposition and will have access to the probation department concerning the defendant, including any criminal history. *See* Rule 12(e), discussed below. However, if the judge believes that there might be other information pertinent to a just disposition in the case, the rule permits the judge *sua sponte* to continue the plea hearing in order to obtain and consider that information. Once the judge accepts the agreement, he or she is bound by its terms, and it is therefore essential that at this point the judge be fully satisfied that the agreed-upon sentence is fair, appropriate to the crime, and designed to diminish the risk of recidivism. The only timing requirement imposed by Rule 12(d)(4) is that the judge accept or reject such a plea agreement prior to accepting the guilty plea.

If the judge accepts the plea agreement, Rule 12(d)(4)(A) requires the judge to inform the defendant that the judge will impose the sentence provided in the agreement. If the judge rejects the agreement, Rule 12(d)(4)(B) requires that the judge so inform the parties and permit either party to withdraw from the plea agreement and further permit the defendant to withdraw the tendered plea. Rule 12(d)(4)(B)(i) here gives the judge discretion to inform the parties what sentence he or she would impose if the plea were to go forward. The judge's doing so gives the parties the opportunity to proceed on that basis without agreement under Rule 12(c), to refashion their plea agreement to conform to the judge's suggestion (thus binding the judge if the judge accepts that amended agreement), or to forego the plea and try the case. If the judge has doubts concerning the wisdom or fairness of the agreed disposition and believes that additional information might help to resolve those doubts, Rule 12(d)(4)(B)(i) permits the judge so to inform the parties. This gives the parties the opportunity, if one or the other has the requested information and is in a position to divulge it, to do so before the judge decides whether to accept or reject the agreement.

Rule 12(d)(5) Findings of Judge as to Plea Agreement and Plea; Acceptance of Plea

If the judge accepts the plea agreement, Rule 12(d)(5) provides that the judge ask the defendant if the defendant wishes to go forward with the tendered plea or admission. At this point, the judge has informed the defendant of the consequences of the plea, including what the sentence will be, and the defendant has heard the factual basis of the charged offense and any victim statements as to its impact. If the defendant elects to go forward with the plea, the judge must then make the necessary inquiries to satisfy the judge that the plea agreement and the plea or admission are knowing and voluntary. Rule 12(d)(5) is intended to make no change to former Rule 12(c)(5)'s provision for a voluntariness hearing except that the hearing also applies to the plea agreement on which the plea or admission is conditioned.

Rule 12(d)(5) requires the judge to find that there is an adequate factual basis for the plea or admission. Rule 12(d)(5) preserves the former Rule 12(c)(5)(A)'s provision that the defendant's failure to acknowledge all aspects of the factual basis shall not preclude a judge from accepting a guilty plea, and the rule is not intended to work any change on its predecessor in this regard.

Once satisfied that the plea agreement and the plea or admission are knowing and voluntary, and that the plea or admission is supported by an adequate factual basis, the judge is in a position to accept the tendered plea or admission. Of course, if the judge is not satisfied in this regard, or, if for some other reason the judge determines that the plea or admission is not just, the judge is permitted to reject the plea or admission. Rule 12(d)(5) is not intended to deprive the judge of this longstanding discretion, even if the judge has accepted the plea agreement on which the plea or admission is conditioned. *See Commonwealth v. Dilone*, 385 Mass. 281, 285 (1982) (acceptance of a guilty plea is "wholly discretionary with the judge"), citing *Santobello v. New York*, 404 U.S. 257 (1971); E. Cypher, 30A Mass. Prac., Criminal Practice & Procedure, Judge may refuse to accept guilty plea, plea of nolo contendere or admission to sufficient facts, § 24:60 (4th ed. 2014).

Rule 12(d)(6) Sentencing

If the judge accepts the plea or admission, the judge must impose a sentence according to the terms of the plea agreement, including any agreed-upon probationary term. It lies with the judge, however, in consultation with probation where appropriate, to decide what conditions of probation are appropriate. To the extent that the plea agreement contains agreed-upon recommended conditions of probation, they are not binding on the judge; rather, they are to be considered as joint recommendations for the judge to consider, and

neither party has the right to withdraw the plea or from the agreement if the judge declines to follow such recommendations. Unlike Rule 12(c)(6), Rule 12(d)(6) does not provide for the defendant's right to withdraw his or her plea in District Court. That right, afforded by G.L. c. 278, § 18, does not here apply. Under Rule 12(b)(5), the defendant agreed to and thus requested the sentence set forth in the plea agreement. A sentence that comports with that agreement therefore cannot exceed the defendant's requested disposition.

Rule 12(e) Availability of Criminal Record and Presentence Report

Rule 12(e) is amended to recognize an admission to sufficient facts in District Court as the equivalent of a guilty plea, *see, e.g.,* Rule 12(a)(2), and to omit the requirement that the parties must file a written motion to obtain a presentence report. The former amendment conforms Rule 12(e) to Rule 12(a)(2) as it was amended in 2004, and the latter amendment achieves consistency between Rule 12(e) and Rule 28(d)(2). Further, the rule is amended to ensure that a judge considering whether to accept a binding plea agreement under Rule 12(d)(4) has both an updated record of the defendant's criminal record and any presentence report prepared by probation under Rule 28(d)(2).

Rule 12(f) Inadmissibility of Pleas, Offers of Pleas, and Related Statements

The 2015 amendments made no changes to Rule 12(f).

Reporter's Notes—2019

Subdivision (b)(6) is added in response to a referral in *Commonwealth v. Gomez*, 480 Mass. 240 (2018), requesting that the Committee propose a rule providing for conditional guilty pleas in Massachusetts. Like the federal rules and the rules of many states, it enables a defendant to enter a plea reserving a right to appeal (commonly called a "conditional plea"). Under this rule, a defendant may, with the prosecutor's agreement, plead guilty (or in District or Juvenile Courts admit to sufficient facts), appeal a ruling the defendant believes is erroneous and, if successful on appeal, withdraw the plea (or the admission to sufficient facts) and presumptively obtain dismissal of the charge. A guilty plea or admission to sufficient facts reserving appellate review of a specified ruling or rulings may be tendered under either Mass. R. Crim. P. 12(c) or 12(d). In all respects other than reserving the right to appeal, this subdivision works no change in existing rules governing pleas, sentencing, or appeal.

A guilty plea, voluntarily and intelligently made, ordinarily "waives all nonjurisdictional defects." *Commonwealth v. Cabrera*, 449 Mass. 825, 830 (2007) (*citing Garvin v. Commonwealth*, 351 Mass. 661, 663–664 (1967)). Adverse rulings thus cannot be appealed, even by a defendant who might otherwise plead guilty, without the time and expense of a trial. As the Supreme Judicial Court recognized in *Commonwealth v. Gomez*, 480 Mass. 240 (2018), the Federal Rules of Criminal Procedure and the law of most states permit defendants to enter a guilty plea conditioned on the right to appeal a specified ruling of the court. *See, e.g.,* Fed. R. Crim. P. 11(a)(2). In *Gomez*, the Court exercised its superintendence authority under G.L. c. 211, § 3 to authorize conditional guilty pleas provided the Commonwealth and the court agreed, and the defendant specified the ruling on which appellate review was sought. *Gomez, supra* at 252. This subdivision implements *Gomez* by permitting guilty pleas or admissions to sufficient facts in which the defendant reserves for appellate review one or more rulings.

This procedure facilitates plea bargaining and conserves judicial resources. These savings are greatest when the rulings reserved for appeal effectively dispose of the case; thus, the procedure requires that the Commonwealth agree that reversal of the ruling subject to appeal would render its case on the specified charge or charges not viable. While most conditional pleas involve legally dispositive rulings, even certain non-dispositive rulings can be subject to conditional pleas. See *Gomez*, 480 Mass. at 252. The rule thus extends to situations in which, should the reserved ruling be reversed, the Commonwealth would choose not to proceed because the case would no longer be viable for prosecution. The viability standard also appears in S.J.C. Order regarding Applications to a Single Justice Pursuant to Mass. R. Crim. P. 15(a)(2) (June 8, 2016) (applications for interlocutory appeal by the Commonwealth must include a "statement whether the Commonwealth has a viable case without the suppressed evidence, and the strength of that case, if viable").

This rule requires the parties to specify, by written agreement, the ruling or rulings reserved for appeal, and the charge or charges that would presumptively be dismissed if the defendant prevails on appeal and chooses to withdraw the guilty plea or admission to sufficient facts. The ruling or rulings should be identified by stating the name of the motion or pleading ruled upon, the date of the ruling or rulings, and the judge who issued the ruling. The charge or charges should be identified by reference to the complaint and offense or count of the indictment. The written agreement should be filed with the court and become part of the record for appeal. A guilty plea or admission to sufficient facts reserving appellate review of a specified ruling or rulings may be tendered under either Mass. R. Crim. P. 12(c) or 12(d). As with any guilty plea, the judge has discretion to refuse to accept a plea reserving appellate review. *See* Mass. R. Crim. P. 12(a)(3). While a plea that does not result in a conviction would ordinarily not merit appeal, in special circumstances the collateral consequences of even a continuance without a finding may warrant a defendant pursuing an appeal. *See, e.g., Commonwealth v. Henry,* 88 Mass. App. Ct. 446 (2015) (admission to sufficient facts and continuance without a finding equivalent to a guilty plea in evaluating immigration consequences, *citing Commonwealth v. Grannum,* 457 Mass. 128, 130 n. 4 (2010)); *Burke v. Bd. of Appeal on Motor Vehicle Liability Policies and Bonds,* 90 Mass. App. Ct. 203, rev. denied 476 Mass. 1101 (2016) (admission to sufficient facts in connection with continuance without a finding on first offense operating under the influence could qualify as a conviction for purposes of lifetime revocation of driver's license pursuant to G.L. c. 90 § 24(1)(d)). The process for taking appellate review of the specified ruling or rulings is governed by the Massachusetts Rules of Appellate Procedure, provided that the notice of appeal is filed within thirty days of the acceptance of the plea.

If the defendant prevails in whole or in part on appeal, the defendant has the choice whether to withdraw the guilty plea, or the admission to sufficient facts, on the specified charge or charges. If the defendant elects to withdraw the plea or admission, dismissal of the specified charge or charges, which the Commonwealth previously agreed would not be viable should the defendant prevail on appeal, is presumptively appropriate. In cases in which, for example, the defendant prevails on appeal in part (e.g., the appellate court suppresses some but not all the evidence which the defendant sought to exclude), the Commonwealth has an opportunity to show good cause that the court should not dismiss the charge or charges. If the judge does not intend to dismiss the specified charge or charges, the judge should indicate that intention to the defendant before the defendant withdraws the guilty plea or admission to sufficient facts.

Appellate relief for the defendant may necessitate re-sentencing. As when a conviction or sentencing provision is vacated, in the normal course the trial judge has an opportunity to reassess the sentence given the remaining convictions and sentencing options. *Commonwealth v. Sallop,* 472 Mass. 568, 570 (2015); *Commonwealth v. Kruah,* 47 Mass. App. Ct. 341, 348 (1999); *Commonwealth v. Clermy,* 37 Mass. App. Ct. 774, 779, aff'd, 421 Mass. 325 (1995).

Rule 13. Pretrial Motions

[Text of rule applicable to cases initiated (by indictment or complaint) on or after September 7, 2004.]

(a) In General.

(1) *Requirement of Writing and Signature; Waiver.* A pretrial motion shall be in writing and signed by the party making the motion or the attorney for that party. Pretrial motions shall be filed within the time allowed by subdivision (d) of this rule.

(2) *Grounds and Affidavit.* A pretrial motion shall state the grounds on which it is based and shall include in separately numbered paragraphs all reasons, defenses, or objections then available, which shall be set forth with particularity. If there are multiple charges, a motion filed pursuant to this rule shall specify the particular charge to which it applies. Grounds not stated which reasonably could have been known at the time a motion is filed shall be deemed to have been waived, but a judge for cause shown may grant relief from such waiver. In addition, an affidavit detailing all facts relied upon in support of the motion and signed by a person with personal knowledge of the factual basis of the motion shall be attached.

(3) *Service and Notice.* A copy of any pretrial motion and supporting affidavits shall be served on all parties or their attorneys pursuant to Rule 32 at the time the originals are filed. Opposing affidavits shall be served not later than one day before the hearing. For cause shown the requirements of this subdivision (3) may be waived by the court.

(4) *Memoranda of Law.* The judge or special magistrate may require the filing of a memorandum of law, in such form and within such time as he or she may direct, as a condition precedent to a hearing on a motion or interlocutory matter. No motion to suppress evidence, other than evidence seized during a warrantless search, and no motion to dismiss may be filed unless accompanied by a memorandum of law, except when otherwise ordered by the judge or special magistrate.

(5) *Renewal.* Upon a showing that substantial justice requires, the judge or special magistrate may permit a pretrial motion which has been heard and denied to be renewed.

(b) Bill of Particulars.

(1) *Motion.* Within the time provided for the filing of pretrial motions by this rule or within such other time as the judge may allow, a defendant may request or the court upon its own motion may order that the prosecution file a statement of such particulars as may be necessary to give both the defendant and the court reasonable notice of the crime charged, including time, place, manner, or means.

(2) *Amendment.* If at trial there exists a material variance between the evidence and bill of particulars, the judge may order the bill of particulars amended or may grant such other relief as justice requires.

(c) Motion to Dismiss or to Grant Appropriate Relief.

(1) All defenses available to a defendant by plea, other than not guilty, shall only be raised by a motion to dismiss or by a motion to grant appropriate relief.

(2) A defense or objection which is capable of determination without trial of the general issue shall be raised before trial by motion.

(d) Filing. Only pretrial motions the subject matter of which could not be agreed upon at the pretrial conference shall be filed with the court.

(1) *Discovery Motions.* Any discovery motions shall be filed prior to the conclusion of the pretrial hearing, or thereafter for good cause shown. A discovery motion filed after the conclusion of the pretrial hearing shall be heard and considered only if (A) the discovery sought could not reasonably have been requested or obtained prior to the conclusion of the pretrial hearing, (B) the discovery is sought by the Commonwealth, and the Commonwealth could not reasonably provide all discovery due to the defense prior to the conclusion of the pretrial hearing, or (C) other good cause exists to warrant consideration of the motion.

(2) *Non–discovery Pretrial Motions.* A pretrial motion which does not seek discovery shall be filed before the assignment of a trial date pursuant to Rule 11(b) or (c) or within 21 days thereafter, unless the court permits later filing for good cause shown.

(e) Hearing on Motions. The parties shall have a right to a hearing on a pretrial motion. The opposing party shall be afforded an adequate opportunity to prepare and submit a memorandum of law prior to the hearing.

(1) *Discovery Motions.* All pending discovery motions shall be heard and decided prior to the defendant's election of a jury or jury-waived trial. Any discovery matters pending at the time of the pretrial hearing or the compliance hearing shall be heard at that hearing. Discovery motions filed pursuant to subdivision (d)(1) after the defendant's election shall be heard and decided expeditiously.

(2) *Non–Discovery Pretrial Motions.* A non-discovery motion filed prior to the pretrial hearing may be heard at the pretrial hearing, at a hearing scheduled to address the motion, or at the trial session. A non-discovery motion filed at or after the pretrial hearing shall be heard at the next scheduled court date unless otherwise ordered.

(3) Within seven days after the filing of a motion, or if the motion is transmitted to the trial session within seven days after the transmittal, the clerk or the judge shall assign a date for hearing the motion, but the judge or special magistrate for cause shown may entertain such motion at any time before trial. If the parties have agreed to a mutually convenient time for the hearing of a pretrial motion, and the moving party so notifies the clerk in writing at the time of the filing of the motion, the clerk shall mark up the motion for hearing at that time subject to the approval of the court. The clerk shall notify the parties of the time set for hearing the motion.

Amended March 8, 2004, effective September 7, 2004.

Reporter's Notes—Revised, 2004

This rule establishes the form of, and manner for the presentation of, pretrial motions. Not every motion that is made in a pretrial posture is governed exclusively by this rule. For example, a continuance motion is subject to the provisions of Rule 10(a)(3) and (4), and the requirements of a motion for relief from prejudicial joinder are contained in Rule 9(d). Where, however, no other rules or statutes provide otherwise, pretrial motions should be made in conformity with the provisions of this rule.

The primary sources of this rule as originally formulated are Rule 3.190 of the Florida Rules of Criminal Procedure (1974) and the existing statutory law of the Commonwealth. The rule has an abbreviated counterpart in Rule 47 of the Federal Rules of Criminal Procedure. In 2004 the rule was revised with regard to its provisions governing filing, filing deadlines, and hearings. The formal requirements concerning motions, affidavits, supporting memoranda, service and notice were unchanged in all respects. So too were the specific provisions in 13(b) and 13(c) concerning bills of particulars and motions to dismiss respectively.

Subdivision (a). Motions in general. This subdivision is derived in large part from the Florida Rule, but essentially restates existing practice and is supported in large part by Rule 9 of the Superior Court Rules (1974). The references to pretrial motions are to include pleadings in response to a motion where such exist.

Subdivision (a)(1) requires a pretrial motion to be in writing. Although an oral motion may be considered, **Commonwealth v. Geoghegan, 12 Mass. App. Ct. 575, 575–76 (1981)**, it need not be because it violates this requirement. **Commonwealth v. Pope, 392 Mass. 493, 498 n. 8 (1984).**

Subdivision (a)(2) is taken from Rules 9 and 61 of the Superior Court Rules (1974). The requirement of an affidavit in support of factual assertions is supported additionally by former G.L. c. 277, § 74. (RS [1836] c 136, § 31). The affidavit need not be signed by the defendant but must be signed by someone with personal knowledge of the facts therein, *see* **Commonwealth v. Santosuosso, 23 Mass. App. Ct. 310 (1986)**(affidavit by counsel), except for those affidavits accompanying a motion requesting a summons for the production of documentary evidence and objects, *see* **Commonwealth v. Lampron, 441 Mass. 265, 270–71 (2004)** (an affidavit accompanying a motion requesting a summons for production of documentary evidence or objects may be based on hearsay from a reliable source, which the affidavit must identify).

The reference in subdivision (a)(3) to opposing affidavits is to apply only if there are opposing affidavits. It is not intended to require them.

Subdivision (a)(4) is taken from Rule 9 of the Superior Court Rules (1974).

Subdivision (a)(5) provides that although a motion has been once heard and denied, it may be renewed if "substantial justice requires" that action. This is appropriate where new or additional grounds are alleged which could not reasonably have been known when the motion was originally filed. See (a)(2), *supra.* Moreover, at times it may be necessary to renew a motion in order to preserve it for appeal. For example, the Supreme Judicial Court has held that a suppression motion was waived when counsel failed to renew it at the time the evidence was offered at trial. **Commonwealth v. Acosta, 416 Mass. 279 (1993).**

Subdivision (b). Bill of Particulars. Former G.L. c. 277, § 40 (St 1887, c 436, § 2) permitted the court to require the prosecution to file particulars in order to more fully apprise the defendant or the court of the nature of the charges. This subdivision incorporates that practice into this rule.

The distinction which was drawn in the statute between particulars ordered by a court with jurisdiction over the offense charged and those ordered by a court without jurisdiction of the offense charged has not been retained in this rule. However, the judge may in his discretion order whatever particulars he deems necessary under the circumstances, and this would permit him to order a more complete statement of particulars where it is required in the interests of justice. Indeed, particulars may be constitutionally required in some cases under article 12 of the Massachusetts Declaration of Rights, which protects a defendant from having to answer charges "until the same is fully and plainly, substantially and formally, described to him." *See also* **Commonwealth v. Baker, 368 Mass. 58, 77 (1975)**(suggesting a liberal standard for granting particulars).

If the specifications supplied in conformity with the court's order are irrelevant or prejudicial, defense counsel must file a motion to strike those deemed improper. 30 MASS. PRACTICE SERIES (Smith) § 1296 (1983).

Although the rule requires motions for bills of particulars to be made before trial, it is not intended to be construed so as to limit the inherent power of the court in an appropriate situation to order a bill at any time.

Subdivision (c). Motions to Dismiss or Grant Appropriate Relief.

This is a restatement of former G.L. c. 277, § 77A (St 1965, c 617, § 1). It should be noted that G.L. c. 277, § 47A abolished at least in name all the other pleas, demurrers, challenges, and motions to quash; it effectively consolidated all of them under the general heading of a motion to dismiss or grant appropriate relief, in effect retaining the statutory and common law of the Commonwealth governing such pleas. Section 47A (as amended) now provides for relief from the waiver of defenses not timely raised, upon a showing of cause.

In a criminal case, any defense or objection based upon defects in the institution of the prosecution or in the complaint or indictment, other than a failure to show jurisdiction in the court or to charge an offense, shall only be raised prior to trial and only by a motion in conformity with the requirements of the Massachusetts Rules of Criminal Procedure. The failure to raise any such defense or objection by motion prior to trial shall constitute a waiver thereof, but a judge or special magistrate may, for cause shown, grant relief from such waiver. A defense or objection based upon a failure to show jurisdiction in the court or the failure to charge an offense may be raised by motion to dismiss prior to trial, but shall be noticed by the court at any time.

Id. See also **Commonwealth v. Chou, 433 Mass. 229 (2001).** "Cause" should be read to include grounds of which the moving party was not previously aware. See Mass. R. Crim. P. 46(b); **Commonwealth v. Bongarzone, 390 Mass. 326, 337–38 (1983).** Additionally, case law and statutory law establish that certain motions and objections must be heard even if raised for the first time at trial, such as claims that the complaint or indictment fails to state a charge, or is outside the court's jurisdiction, G.L. c. 277, s. 47A and **Commonwealth v. Cantres, 405 Mass. 238, 239–40 (1989);** that wiretap evidence should be suppressed, **Commonwealth v. Picardi, 401 Mass. 1008 (1988);** that a statement was taken in violation of the *Miranda* rule, **Commonwealth v. Adams, 389 Mass. 265, 269–70 & n. 1 (1983);** or that the defendant was not criminally responsible by reason of insanity, Mass. R. Crim. P. 14(b)(2).

Subdivision (d). Filing motions.

This subdivision sets out the filing deadlines for pretrial motions. It was amended in 2004 to eliminate provisions relating to filing motions in the now-abolished *de novo* district court system, and to remove a conflict between this rule and the statutory filing deadlines subsequently established for district courts by the single-trial legislation, G.L. c. 278 sec. 18.

Under subdivision (d)(1), discovery motions are to be filed prior to the conclusion of the pretrial hearing, or after for good cause shown. The subdivision also specifies two specific, *non-exhaustive* circumstances which shall be deemed to constitute good cause. One self-evident basis is that the discovery sought could not reasonably have been requested or obtained prior to the pretrial hearing [(d)(1)(A)]. The other, specified in (d)(1)(B), allows later filing by the Commonwealth if it "could not reasonably provide all discovery due to the defense prior to the conclusion of the pretrial hearing." This asymmetrical provision is necessary because under the rules, the Commonwealth must fulfill its discovery obligations in order to receive discovery. If the Commonwealth has been unable to provide discovery prior to the pretrial hearing for good reason, it should not be prejudiced by having its reciprocal discovery rights foreclosed. Provision 13(d)(1)(ii) is necessary to preserve the Commonwealth's discovery rights in such a situation. In any event, with the institution in 2004 of automatic and comprehensive discovery without motion under Rule 14, motions for discovery should be unnecessary in many cases.

Under subdivision (d)(2), non-discovery pretrial motions are to be filed no later than 21 days after the court's assignment of a trial date or trial assignment date, unless the court permits later filing for good cause shown. (Additionally, the defendant must also provide notice of intent to defend by reason of insanity, or by reason of license or privilege, within this time period. Rule 14(b)(2) and (3), respectively). In effect, this provides 21 days after the pretrial hearing or compliance hearing, whichever is later, since under Rule 11 it is there that the trial date or trial assignment date must be set (and, in district court, a jury election or waiver must be taken, the event that commences the 21–day deadline for motions mandated by the district court single trial legislation). The time limits provided in this rule for the filing of pretrial motions are intended to set the norm. Ample opportunity is left for the court to exercise its discretion in the interest of justice, however, by the inclusion of the "for cause shown" provision in subdivisions (d)(1) and (d)(2). *See also* Commonwealth v. Bongarzone, *supra.*

A clerk is not generally empowered to refuse to accept and docket a motion without the court's express approval, but if this occurs counsel may move to have the motion docketed. **Bolton v. Commonwealth, 407 Mass. 1003, 1003–4 (1990).**

Subdivision (d) also makes explicit what is already implicit in Mass. R. Crim. P. 11, namely, that the only pretrial motions which may be filed are those as to the substance of which counsel were unable to agree. Counsel should ascertain whether the opposing party or parties will agree to all potential motions before or during the pretrial conference (or, if the motion could not have been anticipated until after the pretrial conference, promptly when the need for the motion becomes apparent). By requiring that the substance of any pretrial motions a party intends to file be discussed with the adverse party, this subdivision institutes a rule of judicial economy. It is contemplated that having parties compare all the motions they intend to file before trial at the pretrial conference will make the conference more productive by eliminating many "boiler plate" motions. If a conflict between this subdivision and the general filing and service of papers provisions of Rule 32 should arise, this subdivision is controlling as to motions to which it is applicable.

Subdivision (e). This subdivision provides the parties with a right to a hearing on a pretrial motion, and governs the scheduling of the hearing. Subdivision (e)(3) provides that within seven days of filing (or if the motion is transmitted to the trial session within seven days after the transmittal), the clerk should schedule the motion for hearing. However, the clerk will be guided by other provisions in subdivision (e). First, the court must afford the opposing party an adequate opportunity to prepare and submit a memorandum prior to the hearing. Second, *discovery motions* must be heard and decided prior to the defendant's election of a jury or jury waived trial; if any discovery motions are pending at the time of the pretrial hearing or the compliance hearing, they should be heard at that time [(e)(1)]. *See* Rule 11(b)(2)(iii) and (c)(3); Dist./Mun. Ct. Rule of Criminal Procedure 4(e). Third, *non–discovery motions* may be scheduled to be heard at the pretrial hearing, at a hearing scheduled to address the motion, or at the trial session, although the default date for motions filed at the pretrial hearing is the next scheduled court date [(e)(2)]. The clerk must notify the parties of the date assigned. This provision allows individual courts to decide how to schedule non-discovery motions. Finally, subdivision (e)(3) provides a method for the parties to agree to a mutually convenient time for hearing when the motion is filed.

Although not enumerated in the rule, precedent establishes that some motions may be heard *ex parte*, especially when they do not affect an interest of the opposing party or would reveal privileged or other information to which the opposing party is not entitled. For example, motions to fund indigent expenses need not be heard in the presence of the prosecution. **Commonwealth v. Dotson, 402 Mass.**

185, 187 (1988); Commonwealth v. Haggerty, 400 Mass. 437, 441 (1987).

Rule 14. Pretrial Discovery

[Text of rule applicable to cases initiated (by indictment or complaint) on or after September 7, 2004.]

(a) Procedures for Discovery.

(1) *Automatic Discovery.*

(A) Mandatory Discovery for the Defendant. The prosecution shall disclose to the defense, and permit the defense to discover, inspect and copy, each of the following items and information at or prior to the pretrial conference, provided it is relevant to the case and is in the possession, custody or control of the prosecutor, persons under the prosecutor's direction and control, or persons who have participated in investigating or evaluating the case and either regularly report to the prosecutor's office or have done so in the case:

(i) Any written or recorded statements, and the substance of any oral statements, made by the defendant or a co-defendant.

(ii) The grand jury minutes, and the written or recorded statements of a person who has testified before a grand jury.

(iii) Any facts of an exculpatory nature.

(iv) The names, addresses, and dates of birth of the Commonwealth's prospective witnesses other than law enforcement witnesses. The Commonwealth shall also provide this information to the Probation Department.

(v) The names and business addresses of prospective law enforcement witnesses.

(vi) Intended expert opinion evidence, other than evidence that pertains to the defendant's criminal responsibility and is subject to subdivision (b)(2). Such discovery shall include the identity, current curriculum vitae, and list of publications of each intended expert witness, and all reports prepared by the expert that pertain to the case.

(vii) Material and relevant police reports, photographs, tangible objects, all intended exhibits, reports of physical examinations of any person or of scientific tests or experiments, and statements of persons the party intends to call as witnesses.

(viii) A summary of identification procedures, and all statements made in the presence of or by an identifying witness that are relevant to the issue of identity or to the fairness or accuracy of the identification procedures.

(ix) Disclosure of all promises, rewards or inducements made to witnesses the party intends to present at trial.

(B) Reciprocal Discovery for the Prosecution. Following the Commonwealth's delivery of all discovery required pursuant to subdivision (a)(1)(A) or court order, and on or before a date agreed to between the parties, or in the absence of such agreement a date ordered by the court, the defendant shall disclose to the prosecution and permit the Commonwealth to discover, inspect, and copy any material and relevant evidence discoverable under subdivision (a)(1)(A) (vi), (vii) and (ix) which the defendant intends to offer at trial, including the names, addresses, dates of birth, and statements of those persons whom the defendant intends to call as witnesses at trial.

(C) Stay of Automatic Discovery; Sanctions. Subdivisions (a)(1)(A) and (a)(1)(B) shall have the force and effect of a court order, and failure to provide discovery pursuant to them may result in application of any sanctions permitted for non-compliance with a court order under subdivision 14(c). However, if in the judgment of either party good cause exists for declining to make any of the disclosures set forth above, it may move for a protective order pursuant to subdivision (a)(6) and production of the item shall be stayed pending a ruling by the court.

(D) Record of Convictions of the Defendant, Codefendants, and Prosecution Witnesses. At arraignment the court shall order the Probation Department to deliver to the parties the record of prior complaints, indictments and dispositions of all defendants and of all witnesses identified pursuant to subdivisions (a)(1)(A)(iv) within 5 days of the Commonwealth's notification to the Department of the names and addresses of its witnesses.

(E) Notice and Preservation of Evidence. (i) Upon receipt of information that any item described in subparagraph (a)(1)(A)(i)–(viii) exists, except that it is not within the possession, custody or control of the prosecution, persons under its direction and control, or persons who have participated in investigating or evaluating the case and either regularly report to the prosecutor's office or have done so in the case, the prosecution shall notify the defendant of the existence of the item and all information known to the prosecutor concerning the item's location and the identity of any persons possessing it. (ii) At any time, a party may move for an order to any individual, agency or other entity in possession, custody or control of items pertaining to the case, requiring that such items be preserved for a specified period of time. The court shall hear and rule upon the motion expeditiously. The court may modify or vacate such an order upon a showing that preservation of particular evidence will create significant hardship, on condition that the probative value of said evidence is preserved by a specified alternative means.

(2) *Motions for Discovery.* The defendant may move, and following its filing of the Certificate of Compliance the Commonwealth may move, for discovery of other material and relevant evidence not required by subdivision (a)(1) within the time allowed by Rule 13(d)(1).

(3) *Certificate of Compliance.* When a party has provided all discovery required by this rule or by court order, it shall file with the court a Certificate of Compliance. The certificate shall state that, to the best of its knowledge and after reasonable inquiry, the party has disclosed and made available all items subject to discovery other than reports of experts, and shall identify each item provided. If further discovery is subsequently provided, a supplemental certificate shall be filed with the court identifying the additional items provided.

(4) *Continuing Duty.* If either the defense or the prosecution subsequently learns of additional material which it would have been under a duty to disclose or produce pursuant to any provisions of this rule at the time of a previous

discovery order, it shall promptly notify the other party of its acquisition of such additional material and shall disclose the material in the same manner as required for initial discovery under this rule.

(5) *Work Product.* This rule does not authorize discovery by a party of those portions of records, reports, correspondence, memoranda, or internal documents of the adverse party which are only the legal research, opinions, theories, or conclusions of the adverse party or its attorney and legal staff, or of statements of a defendant, signed or unsigned, made to the attorney for the defendant or the attorney's legal staff.

(6) *Protective Orders.* Upon a sufficient showing, the judge may at any time order that the discovery or inspection be denied, restricted, or deferred, or make such other order as is appropriate. The judge may alter the time requirements of this rule. The judge may, for cause shown, grant discovery to a defendant on the condition that the material to be discovered be available only to counsel for the defendant. This provision does not alter the allocation of the burden of proof with regard to the matter at issue, including privilege.

(7) *Amendment of Discovery Orders.* Upon motion of either party made subsequent to an order of the judge pursuant to this rule, the judge may alter or amend the previous order or orders as the interests of justice may require. The judge may, for cause shown, affirm a prior order granting discovery to a defendant upon the additional condition that the material to be discovered is to be available only to counsel for the defendant.

(8) A party may waive the right to discovery of an item, or to discovery of the item within the time provided in this Rule. The parties may agree to reduce or enlarge the items subject to discovery pursuant to subsections (a)(1)(A) and (a)(1)(B). Any such waiver or agreement shall be in writing and signed by the waiving party or the parties to the agreement, shall identify the specific items included, and shall be served upon all the parties.

(b) Special Procedures.

(1) *Notice of Alibi.*

(A) Notice by Defendant. The judge may, upon written motion of the Commonwealth filed pursuant to subdivision (a)(2) of this rule, stating the time, date, and place at which the alleged offense was committed, order that the defendant serve upon the prosecutor a written notice, signed by the defendant, of his or her intention to offer a defense of alibi. The notice by the defendant shall state the specific place or places at which the defendant claims to have been at the time of the alleged offense and the names and addresses of the witnesses upon whom the defense intends to rely to establish the alibi.

(B) Disclosure of Information and Witness. Within seven days of service of the defendant's notice of alibi, the Commonwealth shall serve upon the defendant a written notice stating the names and addresses of witnesses upon whom the prosecutor intends to rely to establish the defendant's presence at the scene of the alleged offense and any other witnesses to be relied on to rebut testimony of any of the defendant's alibi witnesses.

(C) Continuing Duty to Disclose. If prior to or during trial a party learns of an additional witness whose identity, if known, should have been included in the information furnished under subdivision (b)(1)(A) or (B), that party shall promptly notify the adverse party or its attorney of the existence and identity of the additional witness.

(D) Failure to Comply. Upon the failure of either party to comply with the requirements of this rule, the judge may exclude the testimony of any undisclosed witness offered by such party as to the defendant's absence from or presence at the scene of the alleged offense. This rule shall not limit the right of the defendant to testify.

(E) Exceptions. For cause shown, the judge may grant an exception to any of the requirements of subdivisions (b)(1)(A) through (D) of this rule.

(F) Inadmissibility of Withdrawn Alibi. Evidence of an intention to rely upon an alibi defense, later withdrawn, or of statements made in connection with that intention, is not admissible in any civil or criminal proceeding against the person who gave notice of that intention.

(2) *Mental Health Issues.*

(A) Notice. If a defendant intends at trial to raise as an issue his or her mental condition at the time of the alleged crime, or if the defendant intends to introduce expert testimony on the defendant's mental condition at any stage of the proceeding, the defendant shall, within the time provided for the filing of pretrial motions by Rule 13(d)(2) or at such later time as the judge may allow, notify the prosecutor in writing of such intention. The notice shall state:

(i) whether the defendant intends to offer testimony of expert witnesses on the issue of the defendant's mental condition at the time of the alleged crime or at another specified time;

(ii) the names and addresses of expert witnesses whom the defendant expects to call; and

(iii) whether those expert witnesses intend to rely in whole or in part on statements of the defendant as to his or her mental condition.

The defendant shall file a copy of the notice with the clerk. The judge may for cause shown allow late filing of the notice, grant additional time to the parties to prepare for trial, or make such other order as may be appropriate.

(B) Examination. If the notice of the defendant or subsequent inquiry by the judge or developments in the case indicate that statements of the defendant as to his or her mental condition will be relied upon by a defendant's expert witness, the court, on its own motion or on motion of the prosecutor, may order the defendant to submit to an examination consistent with the provisions of the General Laws and subject to the following terms and conditions:

(i) The examination shall include such physical, psychiatric, and psychological tests as the court-appointed examiner (examiner) deems necessary to form an opinion as to the mental condition of the defendant at the relevant time. No examination based on statements of the defendant may be conducted unless the judge has found that (a) the defendant then intends to offer into evidence expert testimony based on his or her own statements or (b) there is a reasonable likelihood that the defendant will offer that evidence.

(ii) No statement, confession, or admission, or other evidence of or obtained from the defendant during the course of the examination, except evidence derived solely from physical examinations or tests, may be revealed to the prosecution or anyone acting on its behalf unless so ordered by the judge.

(iii) The examiner shall file with the court a written report as to the mental condition of the defendant at the relevant time.

Unless the parties mutually agree to an earlier time of disclosure, the examiner's report shall be sealed and shall not be made available to the parties unless (a) the judge determines that the report contains no matter, information, or evidence which is based upon statements of the defendant as to his or her mental condition at the relevant time or which is otherwise within the scope of the privilege against self-incrimination; or (b) the defendant files a motion requesting that the report be made available to the parties; or (c) after the defendant expresses the clear intent to raise as an issue his or her mental condition, the judge is satisfied that (1) the defendant intends to testify, or (2) the defendant intends to offer expert testimony based in whole or in part on statements made by the defendant as to his or her mental condition at the relevant time.

At the time the report of the examiner is disclosed to the parties, the defendant shall provide the Commonwealth with a report of the defense psychiatric or psychological expert(s) as to the mental condition of the defendant at the relevant time.

The reports of both parties' experts must include a written summary of the expert's expected testimony that fully describes: the defendant's history and present symptoms; any physical, psychiatric, and psychological tests relevant to the expert's opinion regarding the issue of mental condition and their results; any oral or written statements made by the defendant relevant to the issue of the mental condition for which the defendant was evaluated; the expert's opinions as to the defendant's mental condition, including the bases and reasons for these opinions; and the witness's qualifications.

If these reports contain both privileged and nonprivileged matter, the court may, if feasible, at such time as it deems appropriate prior to full disclosure of the reports to the parties, make available to the parties the nonprivileged portions.

(iv) If a defendant refuses to submit to an examination ordered pursuant to and subject to the terms and conditions of this rule, the court may prescribe such remedies as it deems warranted by the circumstances, which may include exclusion of the testimony of any expert witness offered by the defense on the issue of the defendant's mental condition or the admission of evidence of the refusal of the defendant to submit to examination.

(C) Discovery for the purpose of a court-ordered examination under Rule 14(b)(2)(B).

(i) If the judge orders the defendant to submit to an examination under Rule 14(b)(2)(B), the defendant shall, within fourteen days of the court's designation of the examiner, make available to the examiner the following:

(a) All mental health records concerning the defendant, whether psychological, psychiatric, or counseling, in defense counsel's possession;

(b) All medical records concerning the defendant in defense counsel's possession; and

(c) All raw data from any tests or assessments administered to the defendant by the defendant's expert or at the request of the defendant's expert.

(ii) The defendant's duty of production set forth in Rule 14(b)(2)(C)(i) shall continue beyond the defendant's initial production during the fourteen-day period and shall apply to any such mental health or medical record(s) thereafter obtained by defense counsel and to any raw data thereafter obtained from any tests or assessments administered to the defendant by the defendant's expert or at the request of the defendant's expert.

(iii) In addition to the records provided under Rule 14(b)(2) (C)(i) and (ii), the examiner may request records from any person or entity by filing with the court under seal, in such form as the Court may prescribe, a writing that identifies the requested records and states the reason(s) for the request. The examiner shall not disclose the request to the prosecutor without either leave of court or agreement of the defendant.

Upon receipt of the examiner's request, the court shall issue a copy of the request to the defendant and shall notify the prosecutor that the examiner has filed a sealed request for records pursuant to Rule 14(b)(2)(C)(iii). Within thirty days of the court's issuance to the defendant of the examiner's request, or within such other time as the judge may allow, the defendant shall file in writing any objection that the defendant may have to the production of any of the material that the examiner has requested. The judge may hold an ex parte hearing on the defendant's objections and may, in the judge's discretion, hear from the examiner. Records of such hearing shall be sealed until the report of the examiner is disclosed to the parties under Rule 14(b)(2)(B)(iii), at which point the records related to the examiner's request, including the records of any hearing, shall be released to the parties unless the court, in its discretion, determines that it would be unfairly prejudicial to the defendant to do so.

If the judge grants any part of the examiner's request, the judge shall indicate on the form prescribed by the Court the particular records to which the examiner may have access, and the clerk shall subpoena the indicated record(s). The clerk shall notify the examiner and the defendant when the requested record(s) are delivered to the clerk's office and shall make the record(s) available to the examiner and the defendant for examination and copying, subject to a protective order under the same terms as govern disclosure of reports under Rule 14(b)(2)(B)(iii). The clerk's office shall maintain these records under seal except as provided herein. If the judge denies the examiner's request, the judge shall notify the examiner, the defendant, and the prosecutor of the denial.

(iv) Upon completion of the court-ordered examination, the examiner shall make available to the defendant all raw data from any tests or assessments administered to the defendant by the Commonwealth's examiner or at the request of the Commonwealth's examiner.

(D) Additional discovery. Upon a showing of necessity, the Commonwealth and the defendant may move for other material and relevant evidence relating to the defendant's mental condition.

(3) *Notice of Other Defenses.* If a defendant intends to rely upon a defense based upon a license, claim of authority or ownership, or exemption, the defendant shall, within the time provided for the filing of pretrial motions by Rule 13(d)(2) or at such later time as the judge may direct, notify the prosecutor in writing of such intention and file a copy of such notice with the clerk. If there is a failure to comply with the requirements of this subdivision, a license, claim of authority or ownership, or exemption may not be relied upon as a defense. The judge may for cause shown allow a late filing of the notice or grant additional time to the parties to prepare for trial or make such other order as may be appropriate.

(4) *Self Defense and First Aggressor.*

(A) Notice by Defendant. If a defendant intends to raise a claim of self defense and to introduce evidence of the alleged victim's specific acts of violence to support an allegation that he or she was the first aggressor, the defendant shall no later than 21 days after the pretrial hearing or at such other time as the judge may direct for good cause, notify the prosecutor in writing of such intention. The notice shall include a brief description of each such act, together with the location and date to the extent practicable, and the names, addresses and dates of birth of the witnesses the defendant intends to call to provide evidence of each such act. The defendant shall file a copy of such notice with the clerk.

(B) Reciprocal Disclosure by the Commonwealth. No later than 30 days after receipt of the defendant's notice, or at such other time as the judge may direct for good cause, the Commonwealth shall serve upon the defendant a written notice of any rebuttal evidence the Commonwealth intends to introduce, including a brief description of such evidence together with the names of the witnesses the Commonwealth intends to call, the addresses and dates of birth of other than law enforcement witnesses and the business address of law enforcement witnesses.

(C) Continuing Duty to Disclose. If prior to or during trial a party learns of additional evidence that, if known, should have been included in the information furnished under subdivision (b)(4)(A) or (B), that party shall promptly notify the adverse party or its attorney of such evidence.

(D) Failure to Comply. Upon the failure of either party to comply with the requirements of this rule, the judge may exclude the evidence offered by such party on the issue of the identity of the first aggressor.

(c) Sanctions for Noncompliance.

(1) *Relief for Nondisclosure.* For failure to comply with any discovery order issued or imposed pursuant to this rule, the court may make a further order for discovery, grant a continuance, or enter such other order as it deems just under the circumstances.

(2) *Exclusion of Evidence.* The court may in its discretion exclude evidence for noncompliance with a discovery order issued or imposed pursuant to this rule. Testimony of the defendant and evidence concerning the defense of lack of criminal responsibility which is otherwise admissible cannot be excluded except as provided by subdivision (b)(2) of this rule.

(d) Definition. The term "statement", as used in this rule, means:

(1) a writing made, signed, or otherwise adopted by a person having percipient knowledge of relevant facts and which contains such facts, other than drafts or notes that have been incorporated into a subsequent draft or final report; or

(2) a written, stenographic, mechanical, electrical, or other recording, or transcription thereof, which is a substantially verbatim recital of an oral declaration, except that a computer assisted real time translation, or its functional equivalent, made to assist a deaf or hearing impaired person, that is not transcribed or permanently saved in electronic form, shall not be considered a statement.

Amended March 8, 2004, effective September 7, 2004; April 4, 2005, effective May 1, 2005; December 17, 2008, effective April 1, 2009; June 26, 2012, effective September 17, 2012; November 5, 2015, effective January 1, 2016.

Reporter's Notes—Revised, 2004

This rule is based on the concept of reciprocity and has as its aim full pretrial disclosure of items normally within the range of discovery. It is emphasized, however, that this rule establishes a formal discovery procedure and is not intended to discourage those disclosures which may take place at a pretrial conference under Mass. R. Crim. P. 11 or whatever other informal discovery may be agreed upon by the parties. *See* Commonwealth v. Delaney, 11 Mass. App. Ct. 398 (1981).

The 2004 amendments. The substance of the original version promulgated in 1979 was drawn from Fed. R. Crim. P. 12.1, 12.2 and 16, N.J.R. Crim. P. 3:13–3 (1972), Fla. R. Crim P. 3.220 (1975), and the ABA *Standards Relating to Discovery and Procedure Before Trial* (Approved Draft, 1979). As more fully discussed *infra*, in 2004 the Rule was substantially revised to eliminate the requirement of pretrial motions in many routine areas of discovery, instead mandating that such discovery be (1) mandatory, and (2) provided automatically to both prosecution and defense. These automatic discovery obligations stem directly from the rule itself, but pursuant to subdivision (a)(1)(C) have all the force and effect of a court order. Discovery of items not included in the automatic discovery regime remains subject to the court's discretion, and may be requested by pretrial motion.

The decision to broaden the ambit of mandatory discovery reflects a conviction that full, automatic, and even-handed discovery to both sides will improve both the administration and delivery of justice. Comprehensive discovery affords counsel a full opportunity to prepare the case, rather than be hijacked by surprise evidence, as the Supreme Court has noted. See Wardius v. Oregon, 412 U.S. 470, 473-74 (1973)("the end of justice will best be served by a system of liberal discovery which gives both parties the maximum possible amount of information with which to prepare their cases and thereby reduce surprise at trial.") It also brings Rule 14 in line with the broad discovery requirements that have existed in district court since the abolition of trial·de novo in 1994 under G.L. c. 218, s. 26A and District Court/BMC Rule 3(c). Finally, the decision to afford mandatory discovery to the prosecution as well as the defense assures that one party will not be disadvantaged by a comparative inability to prepare.

A second major innovation – mandating discovery without the need for motions or argument – is designed to manage court events more efficiently. In areas where discovery is routinely afforded in practice, requiring motions and hearings simply delayed the case and absorbed court and counsel time and expense. The revision recognizes that it is far more efficient to provide automatic discovery of such items to both sides, so long as all parties have a full opportunity to argue against discovery of any of these items where special circumstances in the case warrant divergence from these presumptive procedures. Moreover, automatic discovery early in the case provides the defense with notice of the Commonwealth's case prior to plea negotiations or the filing of other pretrial motions. The grounds for such motions, and the advisability of a plea, may only be revealed through discovery.

The 2004 amendments made some additional, more minor changes to Rule 14. A revision to Rule 14(d) modified the definition of "statements" for purposes of this rule, as described below. Rule 14(e), which formerly specified the timing requirements for discovery motions, was deleted because revised Rule 13(d) now governs all pretrial motion deadlines, including discovery motions. The 2004 amendments did not make substantive changes to section (b), concerning notice of certain defenses to the prosecution, or section (c), concerning sanctions for non-disclosure.

Subdivision (a). Initially Rule 14(a) classified the items now included in sections (a)(1)(iv) through (ix) as "discretionary discovery," to be ordered within the sound discretion of the trial judge. In 2004, however, subdivision (a) was substantially revised to require these items to be produced to the opposing party automatically. However, if a party believes good cause exists for non-discovery of an item listed as automatic discovery, it may resist disclosure pursuant to Rule 14(a)(1)(C), providing for a mandatory stay of discovery of any item that the obligated party believes should not be disclosed, pending resolution by the court.

Subdivision (a)(1) of this rule details the parties' automatic discovery rights. 14(a)(1)(a) sets out the defendant's rights to certain mandatory discovery without motion, and (a)(1)(b) provides reciprocal automatic discovery rights to the prosecution. To a very large extent, the scope of disclosure called for by this subdivision is a codification of prior Massachusetts practice.

Subdivision (a)(1)(A). Mandatory Discovery for the Defendant. This provision lists the items that the prosecution must produce for discovery, with the qualification that the prosecutor's automatic discovery obligation is confined to ascertaining and delivering relevant material it and/or its agents already possess or control. The first paragraph of this subsection limits the Commonwealth's discovery obligation to material "in the possession, custody or control of the prosecutor, persons under its direction and control, or persons who have participated in investigating or evaluating the case and either regularly report to the prosecutor's office or have done so in the case ..." This language, inserted in 2004, is not intended to change existing case law but to reflect it. The language is specifically drawn from *Commonwealth v. Daye*, 411 Mass. 719, 734 (1992)(also stating that a prosecutor "cannot be said to suppress that which is not in his possession or subject to his control"). *Daye* and many cases since describe the prosecution's duty of disclosure as extending to all discoverable material existing in its own files and in the files of others who have participated with them in the prosecution. The latter officials are usually police, but may include others assisting in the prosecution. Thus in Commonwealth v. Martin, 427 Mass. 816, 823–24 (1998), the S.J.C. reversed a conviction because the prosecutor failed to turn over evidence he did not know existed, but which was known to the Commonwealth's crime lab, because "the prosecution had a duty to inquire" concerning the existence of such tests. *Id.* at 823. *See also* Commonwealth v. Bing Sial Liang, 434 Mass. 131, 135 (2001)(victim

witness advocates are part of prosecution team and are subject to the same discovery rules); Commonwealth v. Gallarelli, 399 Mass. 17, 20 n. 4 (1987). It is also clear, however, that the scope of the prosecutor's duty of disclosure does not extend to complainants and independent witnesses who are not agents of the prosecution with regard to some aspect of the case. *Commonwealth v. Lampron*, 441 Mass. 265, 269 n. 4 (2004)(records of medical and social service providers, including D.S.S.); *Commonwealth v. Beal*, 429 Mass. 530 (1999)(complainant); *Commonwealth v. Wanis*, 426 Mass. 629 (1998)(Rule 14 does not reach Internal Affairs Division records because the IAD is not part of the prosecution team).

Under (a)(1)(A), each of the following items must be produced for the defense at or before the pretrial conference, provided it exists and is (1) relevant to the case, (2) within the possession or control of the prosecution or its agents as just defined, and (3) not the subject of a motion for a protective order, which stays its production under subdivision (a)(1)(C)). Even before the 2004 revision, the prosecution was required to turn over most of these items in District Court and the Boston Municipal Court pursuant to Dist./Mun. Ct. Rule 3 and M.G.L. c. 218, sec. 26A, which eliminated trial de novo and mandated broad discovery to the defense.

(a)(1)(A)(i). Statements of the defendant(s). Rule 14 previously included the written or recorded statements of the defendant and any co-defendants in its category of mandatory discovery which must be disclosed. The 2004 revision includes these items as automatic discovery, and adds "the substance of any oral statements" of the defendant or co-defendants. This addition reflects the broader discovery requirement established by case law. The substance of the defendant's oral statements must be provided "as a matter of course to counsel for the defendant" according to Commonwealth v. Lewinski, 367 Mass. 889, 903 (1975). See also Commonwealth v. Gilbert, 377 Mass. 887, 892–94 (1979); Commonwealth v. Lopes, 25 Mass. App. Ct. 988 (1988); Commonwealth v. Lapka, 13 Mass. App. Ct. 24, 31 (1982); Commonwealth v. Janard, 16 Mass. App. Ct. 931, 933 (1983).

Subdivision (a)(1)(A)(ii). Grand jury minutes and statements of grand jury witnesses. The rule had developed in both the Massachusetts and federal courts that pretrial discovery of grand jury minutes was to be allowed when the defendant showed a "particularized need" that the release of a part or all of the minutes would serve. Dennis v. United States, 384 U.S. 855 (1966); Commonwealth v. Cook, 351 Mass. 231 (1966), cert denied, 385 U.S. 981. The Supreme Judicial Court in Commonwealth v. Stewart, 365 Mass. 99 (1974), announced a new rule mandating that the court routinely order discovery of "the grand jury testimony of any person called as a Commonwealth witness which is related to the subject matter of his testimony at trial. The defense will not be required to show 'particularized need.'" *Id.* at 105–06.

Superior Court Rule 63 (1974) mandates that stenographic notes of all testimony given before a grand jury shall be taken, but that transcripts thereof need be furnished only as required by the prosecuting officer unless the court orders otherwise. It is within the judge's discretion under this subdivision to order the transcription of a stenographic record. *Compare* Commonwealth v. Pimental, 5 Mass. App. Ct. 463 (1977)(no error in ordering trial to proceed despite Commonwealth's failure to comply with order to supply defendant with copy of grand jury minutes where minutes not transcribed).

Commonwealth v. Stewart, supra, required production of the grand jury testimony of "any person called as a Commonwealth witness." 365 Mass. 106. However, since 1979 Rule 14 has required the pretrial production of the relevant "written or recorded statements of a person who has testified before a grand jury," whether or not the Commonwealth intends to call that person at trial. There is no requirement that the grand jury testimony have been given before the grand jury which returned the indictment against the defendant, Commonwealth v. Cavanaugh, 371 Mass. 46, 57–58 (1976), as long as that testimony is relevant to an issue at trial. *See* Commonwealth v. Barnett, 371 Mass. 87, 94 (1976). However, a 2004 amendment requires the prosecution to also provide automatic discovery of the minutes of the grand jury that brought the indictment in the case.

Although the relevant grand jury testimony must be routinely supplied by the Commonwealth, if the judge rules that the requested testimony is either not relevant or is to be the subject of a protective order, a motion for production under Mass. R. Crim. P. 23 must be made at the time the witness testifies on direct examination.

(a)(1)(A)(iii). Exculpatory evidence. This provision requires the prosecution to provide automatic discovery of "any facts of an exculpatory nature." It derives from the constitutional requirement established in Brady v. Maryland, 373 U.S. 83 (1963), that "the suppression by the prosecution of evidence favorable to an accused upon request violates due process where the evidence is material either to guilt or punishment, irrespective of the good faith or bad faith of the prosecution." *Id.* at 87. *Accord,* United States v. Agurs, 427 U.S. 97 (1976); Moore v. Illinois, 408 U.S. 786, 794 (1972); Commonwealth v. Adrey, 376 Mass. 747, 753 (1978); Commonwealth v. Ellison, 376 Mass. 1, 21 (1978). This duty is also an ethical one, imposed on the prosecution by S.J.C.Rule 3:07, R. P.C. 3.8(d).

The term "exculpatory" is not intended to be technically construed as encompassing alibi or other complete proof of innocence. Rather, case law *at present* defines exculpatory evidence to include (but not necessarily be limited to) all information that is material and favorable to the accused because it tends to cast doubt on defendant's guilt as to any essential element of the crime charged, including the degree of the crime; or tends to cast doubt on the credibility of a Commonwealth witness, or on the accuracy of scientific evidence, that the government anticipates offering in its case-in-chief. In Commonwealth v. Ellison, 376 Mass. 1, 22 n. 9 (1978), the S.J.C. interpreted the Brady obligation as encompassing "evidence which provides some significant aid to the defendant's case, whether it furnishes corroboration of the defendant's version of facts, calls into question a material, although not indispensable, element of the prosecution's version of the events, or challenges the credibility of a key Commonwealth witness." *See also* United States v. Bagley, 473 U.S. 667, 676–77 (1985) (impeachment material); Commonwealth v. Hill, 432 Mass. 704 (2000); Commonwealth v. Tucceri, 412 Mass. 401, 414 (1992); Blumenson, Fisher and Kanstroom, *Massachusetts Criminal Practice,* Sec. 16.6 (1998) (defining exculpatory evidence and the legal consequences of non–disclosure). The S.J.C. has advised that even minor prior inconsistent statements are exculpatory in the case of an important witness, and urged prosecuting attorneys to "become accustomed to disclosing all material which is even possibly exculpatory, as a prophylactic against reversible error and in order to save court time arguing about it." Commonwealth v. St. Germain, 381 Mass. 256, 262 n. 10 (1980).

To establish a violation of the rule of Brady v. Maryland, *supra,* as incorporated herein, the defendant must demonstrate upon review that evidence actually existed, Commonwealth v. Adams, 374 Mass. 722, 732–33 (1978); that evidence would have tended to exculpate him, Commonwealth v. Pisa, 372 Mass. 590, 595 (1977), cert denied, 434 U.S. 869 (1977); and that the Commonwealth failed to disclose it upon proper request, Commonwealth v. Gilday, 367 Mass. 474, 487 (1975). *Accord,* Commonwealth v. Adrey, 376 Mass. 747. (1978). Evidence in possession of the police is Brady material even if the prosecutor is unaware of it, so the prosecutor has a constitutional duty of inquiry. Commonwealth v. Martin, 427 Mass. 816, 823–24 (1998); Commonwealth v. Baldwin, 385 Mass. 165, 177 n. 12 (1982); Kyles v. Whitley, 514 U.S. 419 (1995); However, there is no duty to search for exculpatory evidence outside the Commonwealth's possession. Commonwealth v. Martinez, 437 Mass. 84 (2002); Arizona v. Youngblood, 488 U.S. 51 (1988) (police do not have a constitutional duty to perform any particular tests). Evidence in government hands but not within the possession, custody or control of the prosecution team presents a special problem. In Commonwealth v. Wanis, 426 Mass. 639 (1998), the Supreme Judicial Court found that particular evidence in the files of the Internal Affairs Division of the police could be exculpatory evidence to which the defendant was constitutionally entitled, but

because the I.A.D. was not a part of the prosecution team it could not be reached by the discovery mechanisms of Rule 14. The proper mechanism in such cases is a subpoena. *Id.* at 644; *Commonwealth v. Lampron,* 441 Mass. 265, 269 n. 4 (2004) (records of medical and social service providers, including D.S.S.);

Although exculpatory evidence is included within automatic discovery, if the defense is aware of items that may be exculpatory that have not been delivered by the pretrial conference, it should file a discovery motion specifying that evidence under subdivision (a)(2), as the magnitude of the error in non-disclosure is in part a function of the specificity of the motion. Commonwealth v. Tucceri, 412 Mass. 401 (1992); Commonwealth v. Gallarelli, 399 Mass. 17, 21 n.5 (1987). In addition to preserving the issue for appeal, specificity can operate to avoid appeals by directing the attention of the prosecutor to those particular materials which the defendant believes would be helpful. A prosecutor cannot be expected to appreciate the significance of every item of evidence in his possession to any possible defense which the defendant may assert. Commonwealth v. Pisa, 372 Mass. 590, 595 (1977), cert denied, 434 U.S. 869 (1977). Assembly and disclosure of those materials — and thus the entire pretrial phase of the proceedings — is expedited by specific motions in such cases.

(a)(1)(A)(iv). Names, addresses, and dates of birth of the Commonwealth's prospective non-law enforcement witnesses. Names, addresses, and the criminal records of prospective witnesses were originally denominated discretionary discovery in Rule 14(a). However, some case law emerging around the time of the Rule's promulgation mandated such discovery. Commonwealth v. Adams, 374 Mass. 722, 732 (1978); Commonwealth v. Clark, 363 Mass. 467, 474 (1973); Commonwealth v. Ferrara, 368 Mass. 182 (1975) (confrontation right to juvenile records which indicate bias despite confidentiality of juvenile records). *But see* Halner v. Commonwealth, 378 Mass. 388, 390 (1979). Legislation since makes defense discovery of names and addresses of Commonwealth witnesses a matter of right in district courts, and also requires the court to order the Probation Department to produce the prior criminal record of these witnesses. G.L. c. 218 s. 26A.

Therefore, in 2004 Rule 14 was amended to include this provision, which requires automatic discovery of the names, addresses, and birthdates (which are necessary to locate a witness' criminal record) of prospective witnesses *other than* law enforcement witnesses, which are covered by subdivision (a)(1)(v)). It also requires the Commonwealth to provide this information to the Probation Department. A separate provision in this Rule, (a)(1)(D), requires the court to order the Probation Department to furnish the parties with the criminal record of all defendants and Commonwealth witnesses within five days of the Commonwealth's notification to the department of its prospective witnesses.

In some cases, there may be special circumstances warranting non-disclosure of a witness' address. For example, if a witness may be threatened or endangered by a defendant, disclosure should not be compelled. See e.g., Commonwealth v. Rivera, 424 Mass. 266, 269–72 (1997); Commonwealth v. French, 357 Mass. 356, 399 (1970). The identity of informants may be privileged against disclosure in some cases. Commonwealth v. Abdelnour, 11 Mass. App. Ct. 531. 538 (1981); Roviaro v. United States, 353 U.S. 53 (1957). There are several options available in such cases. Ordinarily the Commonwealth will move for a protective order under subdivision (a)(6), which stays automatic discovery of the contested item until the issue can be resolved by the court. If after a witness' identity and address have been disclosed, the court is advised that his safety is endangered, there is provision in Mass. R. Crim. P. 35 for the perpetuation of testimony. Once a witness' testimony is recorded, little reason remains for the defendant to attempt to intimidate him. Finally, subdivisions (a)(6) and (a)(7) provide specifically that the court can order information (including witnesses' names) to be disclosed only to defendant's counsel and not to the defendant himself. *See also* G.L. 258B s. 3(h), which allows a person to request non-disclosure of his or her address, telephone number, or place of employment or education, and if granted then prohibits disclosure of that information in open court.

If, after the initial phase of discovery, it is determined that additional witnesses will be called, the defendant may, in the discretion of the court, be granted time within which to investigate and interview that witness. *See generally* Commonwealth v. Lopez, 433 Mass. 406, 413–414 (2001); Commonwealth v. Baldwin, 385 Mass. 165, 176–77 (1982); Commonwealth v. Mains, 374 Mass. 733 (1978).

The Commonwealth's Probation Department records reveal with assurance only Massachusetts convictions; where known facts suggest that a witness has a record elsewhere, an inquiry as to out-of-state convictions may be a reasonable practice. Commonwealth v. Corradino, 368 Mass. 411, 422 (1975). *See also* Commonwealth v. Donahue, 396 Mass. 590, 599 (1986)(normally the state must produce the federal "rap sheet" of witnesses to the defendant).

(a)(1)(A)(v). Names and business addresses of prospective law enforcement witnesses. In the first two decades of practice under Rule 14, it had become routine for the Commonwealth to provide the business address of a police witness when ordered to provide all prospective witness addresses. The 2004 amendment recognized this, and the fact that felons are statutorily barred from serving as police officers, by creating this subdivision that modifies the Commonwealth's obligation with regard to prospective witnesses who are law enforcement officers. In such cases the Commonwealth must provide automatic discovery of the name and business address of the witness. Further discovery concerning the witness, including home address and birthdate, may be pursued by motion under subdivision (a)(2). However, in the rare case where a prospective police witness has a criminal record which could be used for impeachment, the Commonwealth should provide automatic discovery of this fact under subdivision (a)(1)(A)(iii)(exculpatory evidence).

(a)(1)(A)(vi). Intended expert opinion evidence. The Commonwealth's intended expert opinion evidence was made part of automatic, mandatory discovery to the defense under this 2004 provision. The subdivision specifies that expert opinion evidence includes "the identity, current curriculum vitae, and list of publications of each intended expert witness, and all reports prepared by the expert that pertain to the case." Discovery of the prosecution's expert opinion is also a matter of statutory right in district court. G.L. c. 218, s. 26A.

Subdivision (vi) does *not* apply to experts who may have been interviewed or retained but whose testimony or reports are not intended for use at trial. It also does not apply to expert evidence relevant to a defendant's criminal responsibility or to a mental impairment relevant to mens rea, which are governed by Rule 14(b)(2) as described *infra*.

Under the general automatic discovery provisions of subdivision (a)(1)(A), only evidence in the possession, custody or control of the prosecution at the time of the pretrial conference is due at that time. A party may discover or retain an expert later in the course of trial preparation, at which point it must provide discovery of its intended expert opinion evidence under the continuing duty requirement of subdivision (a)(4).

(a)(1)(A)(vii). Material and relevant police reports, photographs, tangible objects, intended exhibits, reports of physical examinations of any person or of scientific tests or experiments, and statements of persons the Commonwealth intends to call as witnesses. Most of these items were treated as "discretionary discovery" in the original provisions of Rule 14. The 2004 amendments to Rule 14 make discovery of these items mandatory and automatic. However, in district court defense discovery of these items had been mandated since 1994 under M.G.L. c. 218, s. 26A par. 2, which requires the prosecution to provide discovery of certain specified items and also "any material and relevant evidence [and] documents." Because subdivision (vii) does not include the latter term but only specified items, the Commonwealth's mandatory discovery obligation remains broader in district courts than in courts where sec. 26A does not apply.

Nevertheless, the items included in this subdivision are likely to exhaust the Commonwealth's evidence in many cases and therefore obviate the need for filing motions to obtain further discovery in those cases.

This provision encompasses "statements of persons," but with regard to this item limits the scope of discovery to statements of only those persons whom the Commonwealth intends to call as witnesses at trial. Rule 14(d), described *infra*, defines the term "statement." Mass. R. Crim. P. 23(b) affords an overlapping right to a testifying witness' statements prior to cross examination. Similarly, subdivision (iii) requires that a witness' prior inconsistent statement be provided to opposing counsel as exculpatory evidence, insofar as it would diminish the credibility of the witness. Commonwealth v. St. Germain, 381 Mass. 256, 262 (1980). Some statements of persons who may *not* be prospective witnesses must be produced for defense discovery pursuant to other provisions, such as police reports included in this subdivision, co-defendants' statements pursuant to subdivision (i), grand jury minutes and relevant testimony pursuant to subdivision (ii), exculpatory statements pursuant to subdivision (iii), and statements made by or in the presence of an identifying witness relevant to the issue of identity pursuant to subdivision (viii).

This subdivision also mandates automatic discovery of any relevant reports of physical examinations or scientific tests or experiments. Often but not always, these will be in conjunction with expert opinion evidence, which must be produced pursuant to subdivision (vi). Under this provision such reports must be produced if relevant, whether or not intended for use at trial and whether or not prepared by an expert. When tests of physical evidence have been conducted by the Commonwealth, the defense also has a right of access to that evidence to conduct its own independent tests, at least unless the testing of another available item would be as probative on the issue. Commonwealth v. Neal, 392 Mass. 1, 10 (1984); Commonwealth v. Nicholson, 20 Mass. App. Ct. 9, 16 n.4 (1985). Regarding access to the government's evidence for investigation generally, *see* California v. Trombetta, 467 U.S. 479, 485 (1984) (Sixth Amendment right); Commonwealth v. Balliro, 349 Mass. 505 (1965) (art. 12 right).

(a)(1)(A)(viii). Identification procedures and statements. Under this subdivision promulgated in 2004, the Commonwealth must provide automatic discovery of any statements made by, or in the presence of, an identifying witness if relevant to the issue of identity or to the fairness or accuracy of the identification procedures. It must also provide a summary of identification procedures to the defense.

Many cases are not "wrong man" cases. In such cases, if there have been no identification procedures the prosecution is not required to do anything under this subdivision. But where identification is at issue and procedures have been used they should be disclosed. Commonwealth v. Dougan, 377 Mass. 303, 316 (1979)(the due process right to fair identification procedures "would mean little if it did not carry with it the right to be informed of the details of any out-of-court identification, even if it were not used at trial"). Prior Massachusetts case law (as well as the constitutional obligation to disclose exculpatory evidence) affords the defendant a right to discover whether the witness previously failed to identify him. Commonwealth v. Clark, 378 Mass. 392, 403 (1979).

(a)(1)(A)(ix). Promises, rewards or inducements made to prospective witnesses. Such inducements offered by the prosecution affect the credibility of the witness, and the defense is constitutionally entitled to discover it. See Commonwealth v. Hill, 432 Mass. 704, 715 (2000); Gigilo v. United States, 405 U.S. 150, 154–55 (1972); Commonwealth v. Luna, 410 Mass. 131, 139–40 (1991). An implicit quid pro quo may exist, and must be disclosed, even in the absence of any explicit promise. Even if there are no explicit promises, any implicit quid pro quo must be revealed. Commonwealth v. Johnson, 21 Mass. App. Ct. 28, 40–41 (1985). Moreover, even if there is *no* quid pro quo by which consideration is given in return for testimony, any material understanding or agreement between the government and a key witness or his attorney must be revealed. Commonwealth v. Collins,

386 Mass. 1, 11–12 (1982); Commonwealth v. Gilday, 382 Mass. 166, 175–76 (1980)(promise to witness' attorney not known to witness must be disclosed); California v. Trombetta, 467 U.S. 479, 485 (1984).

This subdivision requires the Commonwealth to disclose promises, rewards or inducements to only those witnesses it *intends to present at trial.* However, this obligation does not exhaust the Commonwealth's constitutional obligation to disclose all exculpatory evidence, or its parallel obligation under subdivision (iii) of this Rule. Such exculpatory evidence could, for example, include a promise or inducement made to a hearsay declarant whom the Commonwealth does not intend to present at trial.

(a)(1)(B). Reciprocal discovery to the prosecution. Originally, Rule 14(a)(3) (as then numbered) provided that a court could order reciprocal discovery to the prosecution in its discretion. This provision derived from then-recent holdings of the Supreme Court relative to the rights of the prosecution to discover the defendant's case.

The very integrity of the judicial system and public confidence in the system depend on full disclosure of all the facts, within the framework of the rules of evidence. To ensure that justice is done, it is imperative to the function of courts that compulsory process be available for the production of evidence needed either *by the prosecution* or by the defense.

United States v. Nixon, 418 U.S. 683, 709 (1973)(emphasis supplied). Under these cases, the prosecution was empowered to call upon the power of the court to compel production of evidence which will facilitate full disclosure of all the relevant facts. United States v. Nobles, 422 U.S. 225 (1975). *See* Commonwealth v. Hanger, 377 Mass. 503 (1979); Blaisdell v. Commonwealth, 372 Mass. 753 (1977); Commonwealth v. Edgerly, 372 Mass. 337 (1977); Commonwealth v. Lewinski, 367 Mass. 889, 903 n. 10 (1975).

Revisions to Rule 14 in 2004 expanded the defense obligation by making reciprocal discovery mandatory, not discretionary. Under Rule 14(a)(1)(B), when the prosecution certifies that it has disclosed and made available the discoverable items it has, it is entitled to automatic reciprocal discovery of specified categories of defense evidence. Any differences between the obligations on the defense and prosecution result from asymmetrical constitutional requirements. There are two, deriving from the defendant's right to due process and privilege against self-incrimination. First, the defense obligation is limited to evidence it intends to introduce at trial, whereas the prosecution must turn over some evidence it may intend not to use (and in the case of exculpatory evidence, is constitutionally required to do so). Since its promulgation in 1979, Rule 14 has limited reciprocal discovery to "intended" defense evidence because the U.S. Supreme Court case of Williams v. Florida, 399 U.S. 78 (1970), upheld the constitutionality of prosecutorial discovery only on the basis of this limitation. According to *Williams*, the Fifth Amendment privilege limits prosecutorial discovery to evidence the defendant intends to introduce. Intention in this context is, of course, fluid as investigation and discovery progress and the defendant is subject to the continuing duty imposed by subdivision (a)(4), *infra.* The second difference between the prosecution and defense obligations is in the order of disclosure: the prosecution gets its discovery only after it has produced discovery for the defense. In Wardius v. Oregon, 412 U.S. 470 (1973), the Supreme Court found reversible error, in violation of due process, for the prosecution to receive categories of discovery without discovery of those same categories to the defense. To assure against such reversible error, and to allow defendants to assess what evidence they should introduce as required by the *Williams* "intended evidence" constitutional limitation, the Rule provides for defense discovery to take place first.

Under subdivision (a)(1)(B), automatic reciprocal discovery to the prosecution commences only after the Commonwealth has delivered all defense discovery required pursuant to the automatic discovery provisions of (a)(1)(A) and any other extant discovery orders. After that point, and by a date agreed to by the parties or ordered by the court,

the defense is obligated to provide the Commonwealth with discovery of the names, addresses, dates of birth, and statements of its intended witnesses; and of every relevant item described in subdivisions (a)(1)(A) (vi), (vii), and (ix) that it intends to use at trial. In Commonwealth v. Reynolds, 429 Mass. 388 (1999), a pretrial agreement signed by the parties obligated defense counsel to provide not only statements of witnesses it intended to introduce, but also statements of *Commonwealth* witnesses that it intended to use in cross examination. The specified obligations under this subdivision do not go so far. Just as subdivision (a)(1)(A)(vii) requires the Commonwealth to disclose the statements of *its own* intended witnesses, subdivision (a)(1)(B) requires the defense to provide discovery of the statements of its own witnesses, not all witnesses. Discovery of other statements must be pursued by motion.

A separate provision in this Rule affords the prosecution notice of certain defenses if the defendant intends to assert one of them at trial. As discussed *infra*, under subdivision (b), the defense must provide notice and/or discovery if it intends to defend on the basis of alibi, lack of criminal responsibility, or the existence of a license, claim of authority or ownership, or exemption.

(a)(1)(C). Stay of automatic discovery; sanctions. According to this subdivision, the automatic discovery provisions of subdivision (a)(1) which stem directly from the Rule "shall have the force and effect of a court order." If a party violates one of its automatic discovery obligations, the court may impose any of the sanctions permitted for noncompliance with a court order under subdivision 14(c). *Id.*

This provision also allows a party to seek a judicial determination of whether an item should not be subject to discovery, notwithstanding its inclusion in the automatic discovery regime. If a party has good cause for declining to provide such discovery, it should move for a protective order. This subdivision provides that the filing of such a motion stays production of the item pending a ruling by the court.

(a)(1)(D). Record of convictions of the defendant, codefendants and prosecution witnesses. Under this provision, at arraignment the court must issue an order to the Probation Department, directing it to deliver to all parties its record of all prior complaints, indictments, and dispositions of the defendants and all witnesses identified pursuant to subdivision (a)(1)(A)(iv). Under the latter provision, the Commonwealth must notify the Probation Department of its intended witnesses. The court's order must also require the Probation Department to provide this information no later than 5 days after it has been notified by the Commonwealth of its witnesses. *See also* Reporter's Notes to (a)(1)(A)(iv).

(a)(1)(E). Notice and preservation of evidence. Under this provision promulgated in 2004, *if* the prosecutor becomes aware of the existence of an item that would be subject to mandatory discovery but for the fact that it is not within the prosecutor's possession, custody or control, the prosecutor must notify the defendant of the existence (and if known, the location) of the item. The defendant may then move for an order requiring the individual or entity in possession of the item to preserve it for a specified period of time. If either party successfully moves for such a preservation order under subsection (E)(ii), that party should insure that the order is served on the individual or entity in possession of the item.

This subdivision does not require the prosecution to search for new evidence. It applies only to evidence *already* known to exist without inquiry; and only to evidence held by independent third parties who are *not* part of the prosecution team and thus not subject to rule 14 discovery. In addition to insuring that the defense is aware of potentially significant evidence known to the prosecution, this provision is intended to place the defendant in a position to move the court for an order preventing destruction of the evidence so that a subsequent defense subpoena may be effective. To provide a party or independent witness with recourse when a preservation order is inappropriate or unnecessary, the rule provides for motions to vacate or modify the preservation order, or to protect the probative value of the evidence by alternative means.

(a)(2). Motions for discovery. Although most discovery is made automatic under the rule, there may be additional items not encompassed by Rule (a)(1)(A) that are properly discoverable. Rule 14(a)(2) provides for motions to discover such material. Such a motion may only be made for discovery of material and relevant evidence that is not encompassed by the automatic discovery provisions; if items in the latter category are not produced, the proper response is to file a motion to compel discovery or, in an appropriate case, a motion for sanctions under (a)(1)(C).

The timing and deadlines for discovery motions are set out in Rule 13(d)(1). Additionally, because the Commonwealth must provide discovery before it can obtain reciprocal discovery, subdivision (a)(2) provides that the Commonwealth may file a motion for discovery only after it has filed a Certificate of Compliance under subdivision (a)(3).

Nothing in this Rule is intended to prohibit the court from ex parte consideration of discovery motions in appropriate circumstances, consistent with law.

(a)(3). Certificates of compliance. Under this subdivision, each party must file a certificate of compliance when it has met its automatic or court-ordered discovery obligations (other than disclosure of expert reports, which may be written late in the case). The certificate must identify each item provided.

The certificate is properly filed when, to the best of its knowledge and after reasonable inquiry, the party has provided discovery of all covered items it *then* has. The provision recognizes that additional discovery will likely occur as new information and witnesses are obtained, and mandates a supplemental certificate for that purpose.

(a)(4). Continuing duty. This is taken from Rule 3.220(f) of the Florida Rules of Criminal Procedure and has a counterpart in the Federal Rule, the New Jersey Rule and the ABA Standards Relating to Discovery and Procedure Before Trial (Approved Draft, 1970). This subdivision imposes a continuing duty to promptly provide court-ordered discovery as additional information is acquired. The duty continues throughout the trial, Commonwealth v. Costello, 392 Mass. 393 (1984), and includes an obligation to correct previous disclosures that have turned out to be inaccurate. Commonwealth v. Borans, 379 Mass. 117, 153 (1979); Commonwealth v. Gilbert, 377 Mass. 887, 893 (1979).

(a)(5). Work product. Work product is protected under the federal rule and the ABA Standards, *supra.* The sanctity of a party's "work product" is a well recognized principle that was specifically approved by the Supreme Court relating to its application to discovery under the Federal Rules of Civil Procedure, Hickman v. Taylor, 329 U.S. 495 (1947). The principle has equal applicability to criminal discovery.

The definition of "work product" is drawn in part from Rules of Criminal Procedure (ULA) rule 421(b)(1)(1974). The subdivision defines "work product" as limited to portions of documents containing the "legal research, opinions, theories or conclusions of the adverse party or its attorney and legal staff" or statements of the defendant made to counsel or counsel's legal staff. Although witness statements obtained by counsel are not deemed work product under this definition, *see* Commonwealth v. Paszko, 391 Mass. 164, 186–88 & n.27 (1984) and Commonwealth v. Bing Sial Liang, 434 Mass. 131, 140 (2001), in some cases "witness statements may be so commingled with counsel's theories, or so revealing of counsel's mental processes by virtue of the areas covered, as to be unsegregable and constitute work product." Blumenson, Fisher and Kanstroom, Massachusetts Criminal Practice (1998), Sec. 16.2C, citing Commonwealth v. Lewinski, 367 Mass. 889, 902 (1975) and Upjohn v. United States, 449 U.S. 383, 400–01 (1981).

(a)(6)(Protective orders) and (a)(7)(Amendment of discovery orders). Although Rule 14(a) provides for automatic, mandatory discovery, if danger or abuse can be shown, or a privilege preventing disclosure

applies, discovery need not be granted. The power of the court to restrict the scope of otherwise permissible discovery is recognized in the Federal Rule, the New Jersey Rule, the Florida Rule, and the ABA Standards, *supra.*

Protective orders are designed for the unusual case in which the granting of discovery will work to the injury of the person whose material is to be discovered or to the injury of some third person. Although a party must move for such an order, this does not imply that the moving party always has the burden of proof. Ordinarily the party or person opposing discovery has the burden of showing why the discovery of requested materials must be denied or granted subject to restriction, but in certain cases including some privileges, statutory or case law may provide that the party seeking disclosure has the burden of proof. Therefore the 2004 revision added to this subdivision an explicit recognition that "nothing in this provision shall be deemed to alter the allocation of the burden of proof with regard to the matter at issue, including privilege."

With respect to automatic discovery mandated under subdivision (a)(1), a motion for a protective order stays the discovery obligation pending a ruling by the court. Subdivision (a)(1)(C). With respect to discretionary discovery sought by motion under subdivision (a)(2), a protective order may be sought only to restrict (and not prevent completely) the scope of discovery, because if reasons exist to wholly deny discovery *ab initio*, it is within the discretion of the court to deny the discovery motion, without requiring the opponent to the motion to seek a protective order. If what is sought is the modification of an existing discovery order the following subdivision, (a)(7), provides the appropriate remedy.

The provisions of these subdivisions that the court may, in certain situations, grant discovery to a defendant on condition that the material to be discovered be available only to counsel for the defendant, is merely a corollary to that sentence of subdivision (a)(6) which gives the court the power, upon a sufficient showing, to deny, restrict, or defer discovery or inspection. Fed. R. Crim. P. 16(d) and ABA Standards § 4.4 give the judge this same power. The commentary accompanying the ABA Standard indicates that this restriction on disclosure means "such adjustment of the time, place, recipient, and use of disclosures as may commend themselves in the particular case." ABA Standards, supra, comment at 102. Since it is constitutionally permissible to limit pretrial discovery in criminal cases, United States v. Randolph, 456 F2d 132 (3d Cir 1972), there should be no objection to the Commonwealth's giving material only to defendant's counsel in certain situations, which is preferable to denying discovery altogether. It is contemplated that this provision of Rule 14 will sometimes be used to prevent a defendant from seeing his own psychiatric report. In some instances, the mental well-being of the defendant could be adversely affected if he or she has access to such a report. United States v. Moody, 490 F2d 866 (5th Cir 1974). Although the defendant in Moody had been convicted, the same rationale is applicable to the defendant awaiting trial.

Nothing in this Rule is intended to prohibit the court from *ex parte* consideration of a motion for a protective order in appropriate circumstances, consistent with law.

(a)(8). Waivers and agreements to alter discovery rights. Rule (a)(8) allows the parties to change discovery requirements by waiver or agreement, including both the scope and timing of discovery. The waiver or agreement must be in writing, signed by the waiving party or the parties to the agreement, identify the specific items included, and be served upon all parties.

Subdivision (b). Special procedures. Rule 14(b), governing notice to the prosecution of certain intended defenses, was left essentially unchanged by the 2004 revision, except for the substitution of gender neutral language. Under this provision, the prosecution is entitled to notice, and in some cases discovery, when the defendant intends to defend on the basis of alibi, lack of criminal responsibility, or the existence of a license, claim of authority or ownership, or exemption.

The philosophy and provisions of this subdivision are drawn from Commonwealth v. Edgerly, 372 Mass. 337 (1977); Blaisdell v. Commonwealth, 372 Mass. 753 (1977); and a number of other sources. *See* Commonwealth v. Hanger, 377 Mass. 503 (1979); Commonwealth v. Lewinsky, 367 Mass. 889, 902–03 and n. 10 (1975); Fed. R. Crim. P. 12.1, 12.2; Fla. R. Crim. P. 3.200; Rules of Criminal Procedure (ULA) rule 423(a)(1) (2) (1974); National Advisory Commission on Criminal Justice Standards and Goals, *Courts*, standard 4.9 (1973).

The Supreme Court in Williams v. Florida, 399 U.S. 78 (1970), held that a prosecutor could obtain discovery from a defendant by requesting information pertaining to evidence which the defendant intended to offer at trial without violating the fifth amendment privilege against self-incrimination. Although the defense is compelled to make an accelerated determination of the evidence it is to introduce at trial, the nature of this compulsion is such that it is not unconstitutional. While the holding of the Supreme Court related only to the discovery of a defendant's prospective alibi defense, the decision indicates that the rule announced is applicable to other forms or prosecutorial discovery as well. *See* Commonwealth v. Lewinsky, 367 Mass. 889, 903 n 10 (1975). The types of disclosures mandated by subdivision (b)(1)–(3) occur in those situations where in fairness the Commonwealth is entitled at least to notification.

(b)(1).   Notice of alibi. Notice–of–alibi rules have been in existence at least since 1927 and as of 1978 at least half the statutes had such rules. *See* Williams v. Florida, 399 U.S. 78, 81–82 (1970). The substance of this subdivision is taken from Commonwealth v. Edgerly, 372 Mass. 337, 344–45(1977).

In Gilday v. Commonwealth, 360 Mass. 170 (1971), the Supreme Judicial Court, mindful of the implications of the Supreme Court's decision in Williams v. Florida, 399 U.S. 78 (1970), held that discovery by the prosecution of the defendant's intent to interpose an alibi defense and of the names of any prospective witnesses in support of the alibi violated due process because in Massachusetts a defendant did not have an equal right to discovery from the prosecution. Nearly all a defendant's rights to discovery had been subject to judicial discretion under Massachusetts law. The Supreme Court in Wardius v. Oregon, 412 U.S. 470 (1973), specifically held that reciprocity in discovery rights was a constitutional prerequisite to the validity of prosecutorial discovery. That requirement is supplied by subdivisions (b)(1)(B)–(C).

The purpose of such a rule is two-fold. First, alibi defenses are the most frequently and easily fabricated defenses. *See*, for example, Commonwealth v. Harris, 364 Mass. 236, 238 (1973). By requiring the defendant to give the Commonwealth pretrial notice of his intent to interpose such a defense and a list of witnesses to be used in support of the alibi, the defendant is prevented from using an eleventh hour defense, and the Commonwealth is given the tools necessary to uncover fabrication. Fairness to the defendant is insured by granting him discovery of the identities of rebuttal witnesses. Second, the need to grant continuances on the basis of surprise at trial will no longer exist.

As the *Edgerly* court observes, if, in the court's discretion, no other order is appropriate to serve the purposes of this rule, it may exclude the testimony of any undisclosed witness offered by either party as to the defendant's absence from, or presence at, the scene of the alleged offense. 372 Mass. at 345. Exclusion of such alibi testimony, other than the defendant's, is authorized in subdivision (b)(1)(D). *See* Commonwealth v. Cutty, 47 Mass. App. Ct. 671, 673 (1999). If a defendant against whom a sanction is imposed is convicted, he or she may, of course, preserve for argument on appeal the issue of whether imposition of that sanction amounted to an abuse of discretion or the denial of any constitutional right. *Commonwealth v. Edgerly, supra* at 339 and 343. *See generally* Commonwealth v. Reynolds, 429 Mass. 388, 398–399 (1999); Commonwealth v. Durning, 406 Mass. 485, 496 (1990); Commonwealth v. Chappee, 397 Mass. 508, 518 (1986); Taylor v. Illinois, 484 U.S. 400 (1988). In Commonwealth v. Hanger, 377 Mass. 503 (1979), the procedure authorized by this subdivision was substantially approved in the absence of any rule, even though the Commonwealth's motion was not presented until the second day of trial.

(b)(2).   Notice of intent to defend by lack of criminal responsibility or mental incapacity. The subject matter of this subdivision was treated by the Supreme Judicial Court in Blaisdell v. Commonwealth, 372 Mass. 753 (1977), and the procedures contained herein substantially restate those dictated by the court in that opinion. At its inception, this subdivision governed only a prospective insanity defense, but since then the Supreme Judicial Court has extended its scope to govern other defense claims based on mental impairment or incapacity, including mental incapacity to entertain mens rea, Commonwealth v. Diaz, 431 Mass. 822 (2000), or to voluntarily waive Miranda rights, Commonwealth v. Ostrander, 441 Mass. 344 (2004).

Provisions requiring notice of an intent to rely upon a defense of lack of criminal responsibility or diminished mental capacity have a different purpose than notice-of-alibi provisions. The latter, as noted above, are directed at preventing "eleventh-hour" or fabricated alibis. On the other hand, because rebuttal of an insanity defense requires a degree of expertise on the part of a cross-examiner that can only be gained through pretrial research, this subdivision is intended to meet the need of a prosecutor to become familiar with the complex nature of this type of defense.

The Supreme Judicial Court in Gilday v. Commonwealth, 360 Mass. 170 (1971), upheld an order to the defendant to disclose his intent with regard to the interposition of a defense of not guilty by reason of insanity despite the fact that the system of discovery then in effect was non-reciprocal. Implicit in the court's opinion is the fact that due process did not require reciprocation by the Commonwealth because only notice of intent to interpose the defense, and not the identity of the defendant's witnesses nor the evidence intended to support of that defense, was required. In short, the only response by the Commonwealth would be that opposition to that defense would be presented, which does not reasonably require notice.

As the court recognized in *Blaisdell v. Commonwealth*, the privilege against self-incrimination is not implicated by a mere notice requirement. 372 Mass. at 767. Nor is there anything in that privilege which precludes

> an order requiring a defendant to reveal on motion of the prosecution the information of (a) whether a defendant pursuant to such defense intends to offer expert testimony thereon; (b) the names and addresses of such expert witnesses as the defense intends to call; (c) whether a defendant's experts intend to rely in whole or in part on statements of the defendant pertaining to his mental state at or about the time of the commission of the alleged crime or as it may be otherwise relevant to the issue of his mental responsibility therefor.

Id. That information is required by subdivisions (b)(2)(A)(ii)–(iii) of this rule. If the defendant files the notice of intent, the Commonwealth is subject to the reciprocity requirements of this rule and as imposed by Commonwealth v. Edgerly, 372 Mass. 337, 342 (1977); Blaisdell v. Commonwealth, 372 Mass. 753 (1977).

If in answer to subdivision (b)(2)(A)(iii) the defendant responds that his expert witnesses intend to rely upon statements of the defendant as a foundation for their testimony, or if that fact becomes apparent from inquiry by the judge or developments in the case, the judge may order that the defendant submit to a psychiatric examination. (b)(2)(B).

If . . . a defendant voluntarily submits to psychiatric interrogation as to his inner thoughts, the alleged crime and other relevant factors bearing on his mental responsibility and, on advice of counsel, voluntarily proffers such evidence to the jury, we feel that the offer of such expert testimony based in whole or in part on a defendant's testimonial statements constitutes a waiver of the privilege [against self–incrimination] for such purposes . . . In short, by adopting this approach, a defendant who seeks to put in issue his statements as the basis of psychiatric expert opinion in his behalf opens to the State the opportunity to rebut such testimonial evidence in essentially the same way as if he himself has testified ... Under such a view there would be no violation of his privilege should the court then order him under c 123, § 15, to submit to psychiatric examination so that the jury may have the benefit of countervailing expert views, based on similar testimonial statements of a defendant in discharging its responsibility of making a true and valid determination of the issues thus opened by a defendant.

Blaisdell v. Commonwealth, 372 Mass. 753, 765–766 (1977)(citation omitted). The privilege against self-incrimination does not bar the Commonwealth's use of evidence which incriminates the defendant, but rather the compelled production of such evidence by the defendant; yet it is clear that an examination pursuant to this subdivision constitutes compelled production. Blaisdell v. Commonwealth, supra, 372 Mass. at 758. *See also* Commonwealth v. Baldwin, 426 Mass. 105 (1997); Commonwealth v. Wayne W., 414 Mass. 218, 228–30 (1993). Therefore, if the psychiatric report contains evidence of a testimonial character, it is not to be made available to either party unless the defendant is to testify on his own behalf or is to offer expert testimony based on his statements ([b][2][B][iii][c]) or unless the defendant, by motion, requests that it be made available. ([b][2][B][iii][b]). Ordering the examination to be conducted prior to a defendant's formal waiver of the privilege against self-incrimination is justified on the basis that:

To require the Commonwealth to wait may ... well cause it to be disadvantaged in meeting the issues raised by a defendant's evidence by virtue of the fact that its expert witnesses will lack adequate time to examine properly a defendant and his evidence in order to prepare for trial. Alternatively, a continuance of the trial may cause needless expense to the Commonwealth, unnecessary inconvenience to the court and to the jurors, and disruption of the progress of the trial which may cause harm to either the prosecution or the defense. To require the Commonwealth to wait until such a waiver occurs at trial seems not only inexpedient and unwise but also unnecessary.

Blaisdell v. Commonwealth, supra, 372 Mass. at 767.

(b)(3). Notice of defenses based on license, authority, ownership or exemption. This subdivision, promulgated in 1979, requires the defendant to furnish the prosecution with notice of his intent to rely upon a defense based upon a license, claim of authority or ownership, or exemption.

A "license" is defined as a right granted by the Commonwealth or other competent authority to do a particular act or carry on a particular business which, without such license, would be unlawful. A "claim of authority" is an assertion that the claimant has received an express or implied right to do an act from one lawfully empowered to grant such right. A "claim of ownership" is an assertion that the claimant has a right of possession enforceable in a court. An "exemption" is a release from a duty or obligation to which others are subject.

The requirement of disclosure in this subdivision is reasonable when considered in light of "the proposition that the end of justice will best be served by a system of liberal discovery which gives both parties the maximum possible amount of information with which to prepare their cases and thereby reduce surprise at trial." Wardius v. Oregon, 412 U.S. 470, 473 (1973).

The concept of mandating notice of criminal defenses other than alibi and insanity, subdivisions (b)(1)–(2) supra, was advocated by the American Bar Association in the ABA *Standards Relating to Discovery and Procedure Before Trial* (Approved Draft, 1970):

Subject to constitutional limitations, the trial court may require that the prosecuting attorney be informed of the nature of *any* defense which defense counsel intends to use at trial ...

Id., § 3.3 (emphasis supplied).

Considerations of reciprocity, dealt with by the United States Supreme Court in connection with notice-of-alibi statutes in Wardius v.

Oregon, 412 U.S. 470 (1973) and Williams v. Florida, 399 U.S. 78 (1970), and by the Supreme Judicial Court in Gilday v. Commonwealth, 360 Mass. 170 (1971), are inapposite to subdivision (b)(3). The Williams–Wardius cases hold that state statutes requiring notice to be given the prosecution that an alibi defense is to be raised at trial, with the names of witnesses to be called in support of the alibi, are constitutionally valid only if the defendant is allowed reciprocal rights to receive the names of governmental rebuttal witnesses. The statutes in those decisions, unlike Rule 14(b)(3), involved the furnishing of prosecutors with both notice of, and information pertaining to, the intended defense. See subdivisions (b)(1) and (b)(2), *supra*. It was to this information gathering aspect of the Oregon and Florida statutes that the Supreme Court addressed itself:

It is fundamentally unfair to require the defendant to divulge *the details* of his own case while at the same time subjecting him to the hazard of surprise concerning refutation of the very pieces of evidence which he disclosed to the State.

Wardius, supra at 476 (emphasis added).

Subdivision (b)(3) involves the giving only of notice. The defendant is not required to divulge the details of his intended defense. Mere notification of intent to raise a defense without more does not trigger considerations of reciprocity. *See* Commonwealth v. Gilday, 360 Mass. 170 (1971); Blaisdell v. Commonwealth, 372 Mass. 764, 767 (1977).

The sanction for failure to comply with the requirement of subsection (b)(3) is drawn from Fed. R. Crim. P. 12.1 and 12.2. *See also* ABA *Standards, supra*, § 4.7. The court may "for cause shown" ease or lift the requirements of this subdivision.

Subdivision (c). Sanctions for noncompliance. Sanctions may be issued under this subdivision for violations of discovery obligations established either by the court's order or by the automatic discovery provisions of the rule. The automatic discovery obligations of subsections (a)(1)(A)(discovery to the defense) and (a)(1)(B)(discovery to the prosecution) stem from the rule itself rather than an order issued by the court, but subdivision (a)(1)(C) provides that they "have the force and effect of a court order, and failure to provide discovery pursuant to them may result in application of any sanctions permitted for noncompliance with a court order under subdivision 14(c)."

The general sanction provision of subdivision (c)(1) is paralleled by Fed. R. Crim. P. 16(d)(2) and New Jersey R. Crim. P. 3:13–3(f). The power to exclude alibi evidence other than the defendant's testimony is recognized in Commonwealth v. Edgerly, 372 Mass. 337, 342 (1977), and is express in subdivision (b)(1)(D), *supra*. See Federal Rule 12.1; ABA Standards Relating to Discovery and Procedure Before Trial § 4.7(a) (Approved Draft, 1970). Subdivision (b)(2)(B), *supra*, provides the sanction for failure of the defendant to comply with a court-ordered psychiatric examination.

"Rights and duties are ephemeral indeed without remedies." ABA Standards, supra, comment at 107. Subdivision (c)(1) is intended to provide the general rule and is based on that assumption that the trial court is in the best situation to consider the opposing arguments concerning a failure to comply with a discovery order and to fashion an appropriate remedy. Remedies for non-compliance with discovery requirements could include a further order for discovery, a continuance, exclusion of certain testimony, or "such other order as [the Court] deems just under the circumstances." (c)(1). A continuance or in some cases a mistrial may be the proper remedy when delayed disclosure leaves the defendant unable to "make effective use of the evidence in preparing and presenting his case." *See* Commonwealth v. Baldwin, 385 Mass. 165, 175 & n.10 (1982); Commonwealth v. St. Germain, 381 Mass. 256, 262–63 (1980). (There is, it should be noted, a statutory limitation on the court's power to grant a continuance without the defendant's consent. When the defendant is in custody, General Laws c 276, § 35 provides a thirty day limit in such instances.) A dismissal barring retrial may be required when a discovery violation has resulted in irremediable harm to the defendant's opportunity to obtain a fair trial.

Although the court may exercise its general sanction power under subdivision (c)(2) to exclude evidence, it is generally better to grant each party the freedom to present all relevant evidence at trial. However, in regard to alibi evidence, there is sufficient likelihood of abuse to require specifically empowering the court to exclude extrinsic alibi evidence other than the defendant's testimony, and this is specifically authorized by section (b)(1)(D). A court should only employ this sanction, however, when convinced that a failure to comply with an order was deliberate and prejudicial to the Commonwealth. Subdivision (c)(2) also provides that evidence concerning the defense of lack of criminal responsibility cannot be excluded except as provided by subdivision (b)(2).

Subdivision (d). Definition of "statement." The definition of the term "statement" was initially drawn from 18 USC § 3500(e)(1)–(2) (1969, Supp. 1976) and Commonwealth v. Lewinski, 367 Mass. 889 (1975). Definition (d)(1) defines "statements" which have been written by the percipient witness himself or herself. Definition (d)(2) defines "statements" which have been contemporaneously recorded by someone other than the speaker or writer.

The definition in (d)(1) was amended in 2004 to delete the requirement that writings by witnesses be signed or otherwise adopted by the author. In Commonwealth v. Lewinski, 367 Mass. 889, 901–903 (1975), the Court stated that without any showing of particularized need, a defendant was entitled to all "prior written statements of prosecution witnesses which are available to the prosecution and are related to the subject," and subdivided this into three categories of mandatorily discoverable statements: "any statement made by the witness and in some definite way approved by him, a transcript of a contemporaneous verbatim or substantially verbatim stenographic or other recording of an oral statement by the witness, and a written report consisting of a statement by the witness." The 2004 revision reflects a decision that the definition of written statements made by a witness should encompass *written* statements of a percipient witness which have not been formally adopted by the witness, and the third category in Lewinsky, although not without ambiguity, implies as much. Under 14(d)(1), these will have been written by the percipient witness himself, and under 14(d)(2), such statements must still be "a *substantially verbatim* recital of an oral declaration and which is *recorded contemporaneously* with the making of the oral declaration" (emphasis added). In both cases, such evidence is generally relevant at trial; for example, one need not show a prior statement was adopted as accurate and complete by the writer in order to admit and demonstrate its inconsistencies. Prior informal statements, not intended for court, are not only often admissible at trial but often more probative than formal signed statements in anticipation of litigation. On this view, if the police have taken a statement of a witness who will testify, it should be discoverable to the defense.

However, the revised definition does not extend to "drafts or notes that have been incorporated into a subsequent draft or final report." It would be unnecessary and burdensome to require that every rough draft of a police report or other statement to be turned over in addition to the final one.

Subdivision (e), which formerly specified the time limits for discovery, was deleted as part of the 2004 revisions. In the amended rules, the deadlines for automatic, non-motion discovery are detailed in Rule 14(a)(1)(a) and (b), and the deadlines for discovery (and other) motions are found in Rule 13(d).

Reporter's Notes—2008

The definition of a statement was revised in 2008 to exempt the means by which hearing impaired attorneys gain access to an electronic display of the words a witness utters. Whether through a computer assisted real time translation or other means, so long as the witness' words are not transcribed or saved in electronic form, as in a computer file, the fact that a contemporaneous transcript of the witness' words appears on a screen to assist a hearing impaired attorney does not fit the definition of a statement under the terms of Rule 14. This amendment does not affect any other aspect of an attorney's discovery obligations, such as the requirement that a prosecutor reveal exculpatory evidence.

Reporter's Notes—2012

In 2012, Rule 14 was amended in several respects. These revisions are discussed below.

Subdivision (b)(2). Mental health issues

This amendment responds to the Supreme Judicial Court's expansion of the *Blaisdell* procedure to analogous situations such as defenses based on an inability to form the requisite intent for an element of the crime, see Commonwealth v. Dias, 431 Mass. 822, 829 (2000), on an inability to premeditate, see Commonwealth v. Contos, 435 Mass. 19, 24 n.7 (2001), and where the defendant places at issue his or her mental ability voluntarily to waive *Miranda* rights, see Commonwealth v. Ostrander, 441 Mass. 344, 352 (2004). In addition, the Court has indicated in *dicta* that the same would hold true in the case of a defense based on battered woman syndrome, see Ostrander, 441 Mass. at 355 (2004).

There are two different dimensions to the problem that this subsection addresses. One concerns giving notice to the Commonwealth of a complex issue that the prosecutor otherwise would have no reason to expect to litigate. The other deals with redressing the unfairness of allowing a defense expert to testify based on statements obtained from the defendant without giving the prosecution an opportunity to obtain equivalent access for its expert.

The proposed amendment addresses the first concern by expanding the scope of the notice provision beyond the context of *Blaisdell* to include all mental health defenses. A mental health defense is one that places in issue the defendant's mental condition at the time of the alleged crime, based on a claim that some mental disease or defect or psychological impairment, such as battered woman syndrome, affected the defendant's cognitive ability. These are complex issues for which the prosecutor should have time to prepare, whether an expert testifies for the defense or not. As used in this subsection, the term "mental health defense" does not include a claim that the defendant's cognitive ability was affected by intoxication, an issue that arises more frequently and does not present the same level of complexity as do the former examples.

The proposed amendment addresses the second concern by requiring notice whenever the defendant intends to rely on expert testimony concerning the defendant's mental condition at any stage of the process on any issue, whether it related to culpability, competency or because it concerns the admission of evidence. Thus, for example, if the defendant intends to introduce expert testimony in support of a claim that a confession was not voluntary, as in *Ostrander*, the notice would specify that the witness would testify as to the defendant's mental condition at the time of the confession. If it appears that the expert will rely on statements of the defendant as to his or her mental condition, then the judge may order the defendant to submit to an examination pursuant to subsection 14(b)(2)(B).

Subdivision (b)(2)(B)(i)

The proposed amendment deletes "physiological tests" from those that may be included in a court-ordered examination. This deletion is not intended to work any substantive change to the rule but rather to eliminate a superfluous term. Under the rule, "physical tests" is meant to include "physiological tests," including but not limited to neurological tests and examinations such as magnetic resonance imaging (MRI) and positron emission tomography (PET) scans.

Subdivision (b)(2)(B)(iii)

The Rule applies not only to experts who are psychiatrists, but to psychologists as well.

The regime for disclosure of expert reports has been amended in light of Commonwealth v. Sliech–Brodeur, 457 Mass. 300 (2010). The timing of the release of the Commonwealth's expert's report was altered only to make clear that the parties can agree on its disclosure at a time earlier than previously set out in the Rule. *See Sliech–Brodeur*, 457 Mass. at 325 n.34 (2010). As required by *Sliech–Brodeur*, defense experts as well as the prosecution's must prepare and disclose reports. In order to avoid infringing on the defendant's privilege against self incrimination, the defense expert's report is released to the prosecution at the same time that the defendant receives the report of the Commonwealth's expert. The Rule also has been amended to address the timing of the exchange of reports. The latest date of exchange would be when the defendant expresses a "clear intent" to rely on mental impairment as an issue in the case, relying in part on the defendant's statements or testimony. This will often occur at the final pretrial conference or comparable event. The Rule attempts to avoid the delay and inconvenience of disclosing the reports only after the defendant's expert offers testimony on direct examination. Finally, the rule as amended makes clear the judge's discretion to review any expert report filed with and sealed by the court, and, if feasible and appropriate, to release to the parties any unprivileged material contained in the report prior to the report's full disclosure to the parties.

Once the reports have been released to the parties, they may be shared with the respective experts for each side.

The Rule has been amended to require more detail in the content of the report that both prosecution and defense experts must file. This portion of the Rule is patterned after 18 U.S.C.S. § 4247(c). In one major respect, however, the Rule goes beyond the federal model by requiring the report to contain a complete account of the statements of the defendant that are relevant to the issue of his or her mental condition. This includes both statements relating to the underlying incident as well as any statements prior to or following it that are relevant to the defendant's mental condition. If the examiner considered written statements of the defendant, the report should contain the relevant portions. If the examiner considered oral statements of the defendant, the report should include the substance of what the defendant said that bears on the question of his or her mental condition. In reporting on the defendant's statements, examiners should not withhold relevant evidence contrary to their own position.

The protection of the work product doctrine and the principle that notes or preliminary drafts are not discoverable if they are incorporated into a final report, applicable elsewhere in the discovery regime that Rule 14 establishes, apply as well in this context.

Subdivision (b)(2)(C)

This provision gives trial judges the flexibility to require the parties to provide additional discovery beyond the information contained in the notice that the defendant must give and the reports that the experts must file. It is a very limited grant of discretion and should be reserved for cases presenting discovery issues that are out of the ordinary. In this respect, it is more restrictive than the analogous discovery provision in Rule 14(a)(2).

Subdivision (b)(4). Self Defense and First Aggressor.

This amendment implements the discovery obligation created by *Commonwealth v. Adjutant*, 4.43 Mass. 649 (2005). The procedure it mandates applies only to situations such as those in *Adjutant*, where the defendant intends to rely on self defense claiming that the victim was the first aggressor. The notice procedure established in this amendment does not apply to other instances where prior violent conduct by the victim may be admissible, such as where the defendant intends to introduce evidence of a violent act by the victim of which he or she was aware at the time of the incident that is the subject of the criminal case before the court. *See Commonwealth v. Fontes*, 396 Mass. 733, 735–36 (1986). However, in a case where the defendant wishes to introduce evidence of an act of prior violence by the victim to support a claim based on both *Adjutant* and *Fontes*, the notice provision of this subsection would apply.

Beyond notice of an intent to raise the issue of prior violent acts by the alleged victim as it bears on the identity of the first aggressor, the amendment also requires the defendant to provide specific information about each incident. Where the defendant lacks specific details as to the time and place of a prior incident, the notice should contain as much information as is available, subject to a continuing duty to supplement the notice as counsel becomes aware of further facts.

The reciprocal obligation on the Commonwealth extends to all evidence that it intends to introduce to rebut the defendant's claim that the victim was the first aggressor. This may concern the victim's role in the incidents of prior violence upon which the defendant may rely, or any other evidence the Commonwealth may introduce in rebuttal.

Nothing in this amendment is intended to derogate from the discovery obligations of Rule 14(a)(1)(A)–(B) concerning physical evidence or documents that either party may rely on with respect to prior acts of violence by the victim.

This subsection does not affect the ultimate decision the judge must make on the admissibility of the evidence contained in the defendant's notice, or of any rebuttal evidence the prosecution might offer. The rule does contemplate, however, that failure to provide notice in advance may bar a party from offering evidence that might otherwise be admissible.

Subdivision (d). Definition.

In 2012, Rule 23 was eliminated because the 2004 revision of Rule 14 largely made it irrelevant. Almost all of the statements that Rule 23 required a party to produce after a witness testified were made part of the automatic pretrial discovery mechanism of Rule 14. Because a small class of statements covered by Rule 23 was not included in the definition of a statement in the 2004 revision of Rule 14(d), an amendment to this subsection was made. The amendment brings within the confines of Rule 14 the remaining class of statements that were subject to the discovery provision of the former Rule 23.

Section 14(d)(1) was amended to include not only writings made by a witness, but also writings made by another and signed or otherwise adopted by the witness. A person otherwise adopts a statement when he or she approves it or accepts it as accurate. *See, e.g., Smith v. United States*, 31 F.3d 1294, 1301 (4th Cir. 1994) ("[n]otes taken by prosecutors and other government agents during a pretrial interview of a witness may qualify as a 'statement' . . . if the witness has reviewed them in their entirety—either by reading them himself or by having them read back to him—and formally and unambiguously approved them—either orally or in writing—as an accurate record of what he said during the interview.")

Section 14(d)(2) was amended to remove the requirement that a witness's statement has been recorded contemporaneously. This is an issue that will only be relevant with respect to written accounts of what the witness said, since by their nature stenographic, mechanical, electrical or other means of recordings must be made contemporaneously. With respect to written accounts, Rule 14(d) includes substantially verbatim statements of a witness that are contained in a document written by someone else, whether the document consists solely of the witness's statement or the witness's statements appear only in part of the document. In the latter case, only that portion of the document that consists of the substantially verbatim account of the witness's statement must be produced. This provision is intended only to require the production of statements that can "fairly be deemed to reflect fully and without distortion" what the witness said. *See Palermo v. United States*, 360 U.S. 343, 352–53 (1959); *United States v. Hodges*, 556 F.2d 366 (5th Cir. 1977) *cert. den.* 434 US 1016 (1978) (that investigators' notes contained occasional verbatim recitation of phrases used by the person interviewed did not make such notes discoverable).

Reporter's Notes—2015 Rule 14(b)(2)(C)

Rule 14(b)(2)(C) Discovery for the purpose of a court-ordered examination under Rule 14(b)(2)(B)

In *Commonwealth v. Hanright*, 465 Mass. 639, 648 (2013), the Supreme Judicial Court held that, when a judge orders a defendant under Rule 14(b)(2)(B) to submit to a forensic mental evaluation, the judge may also require the defendant to disclose to the court-appointed examiner ("Commonwealth's examiner" or "examiner") treatment records necessary to conduct that forensic evaluation. Rule 14(b)(2)(C) sets out the scope and sequence of that disclosure and the procedure by which it is implemented. Under the rule, both experts—the Commonwealth's examiner and the defendant's expert—must be given equal access to the information they collectively deem necessary to conduct an effective forensic examination and produce a competent report. The rule achieves this result, without involving the prosecutor, through a reciprocal discovery process that makes available to each expert (1) the defendant's pertinent medical and mental-health records and (2) the raw data from tests or assessments of the defendant administered during the course of the experts' respective examinations of the defendant. By ensuring that the experts are working from a common, comprehensive set of records and objective, test-generated data, the rule advances the reliability and fairness of the examinations and the ensuing reports, and it promotes efficiency in the examination process.

Rule 14(b)(2)(C)(i)

Rule 14(b)(2)(C)(i) outlines the defendant's disclosure obligation. The rule requires that the defendant make available to the Commonwealth's examiner, within 14 days of the examiner's appointment, three categories of information: (a) the defendant's mental-health records, broadly defined, that are possessed by defense counsel, (b) the defendant's medical records that are possessed by defense counsel, and (c) the raw data from any tests or assessments administered to the defendant in the course of the defense expert's examination of the defendant. This discovery obligation is intended to provide equal and full access for both parties to the defendant's pertinent mental-health and medical history at the time each expert is conducting his or her examination of the defendant. Full discovery of pertinent source material at this point, when the examiners are forming their respective opinions concerning the defendant's mental health without yet having access to the opinions of the other, promotes the truth-seeking function of the trial, see *Hanright*, 465 Mass. at 644–645, while making the examination process more efficient.

In defining the scope of the mental-health and medical records to be produced as those possessed by defense counsel, the rule intends as wide a reach as is reasonably possible, covering every such record that the defense collected in the course of considering whether to assert this defense. At this point in the process, the defendant has waived any privilege that might preclude producing his statements and records to the Commonwealth's examiner, see *Hanright*, 465 Mass. at 645–648, and the rule means to give both experts access to every record reasonably available, relying on the experts independently to decide which records are relevant to the inquiry. If, in examining the defendant and the records that the defendant produced, the Commonwealth's examiner identifies a mental-health or medical record that the defense overlooked, or chose not to collect, and thus did not produce, Rule 14(b)(2)(C)(iii), discussed below, provides for a process by which the examiner can seek that record. Any such records would, under the rule, be available to both experts.

The raw testing data that Rule 14(b)(2)(C)(i) requires the defendant to produce consists of objective, uninterpreted test results, for example, multiple-choice, bubble outputs from a psychological test with quantification on various scales. As discussed below, Rule 14(b)(2)(C)(iv) requires the same disclosure from the Commonwealth's examiner. The intent is to provide both experts with all of the relevant, objective testing data available at the time each writes his or her report, thus avoiding the need for supplemental reports or evaluations that consider pertinent testing data first revealed in the other expert's report. Not only would the necessity of such supplemental reports or evaluations extend the examination process, but these reports would necessarily be written after reviewing the opposing

expert's report, thus putting in question the independence of this supplemental evaluation of these testing data. The rule's discovery obligation reaches only raw testing data; it does not apply to the defense expert's work product, such as notes interpreting this raw testing data or notes relating to a clinical interview of the defendant. This mandatory disclosure of raw testing data generated by the experts during the course of their respective examinations works no unfair advantage to either side. The discovery obligation is mutual. As with defendant's mental-health and medical records, the raw data resulting from tests administered to the defendant are essential to determining the defendant's mental-health at the time in question, and all of these data must be considered by both examiners if their respective reports are to serve their truth-seeking function. Finally, the test results will ultimately be released with the final reports under Rule 14(b)(2)(B)(iii); the only question Rule 14(b)(2)(C)(i) & (iv) address is the timing of that release.

Rule 14(b)(2)(C)(ii)

As noted, Rule 14(b)(2)(C)(i) requires the defendant to produce the mental-health and medical records and raw testing data within 14 days after the judge appoints the Commonwealth examiner. Under Rule 14(b)(2)(C)(ii), the defendant's duty to disclose records and raw testing data continues throughout the examination period provided under Rule 14(b)(2)(B). If the defendant discovers records or raw testing data that was subject to production under Rule 14(b)(2)(C)(i) but was not produced, those records or data must be produced as soon as they are discovered. Moreover, if subsequent to the initial production under Rule 14(b)(2)(C)(i) defense counsel obtains records covered by the rule or the defense expert generates test data covered by the rule, Rule 14(b)(2)(C)(ii) requires that these materials be promptly produced to the Commonwealth's examiner.

Rule 14(b)(2)(C)(iii)

As noted, this subsection anticipates the possibility that the Commonwealth's examiner will learn of additional medical or mental-health records that he or she believes necessary to conducting a professionally competent examination. For example, a record provided by the defendant, or a comment by the defendant during the court-ordered examination, might refer to an earlier hospitalization of the defendant for which the defendant did not produce records. If the examiner concludes that there is a reasonable possibility that such records exist and should be reviewed, Rule 14(b)(2)(C)(iii) provides for a procedure by which the examiner can file with the court a prescribed form under seal identifying the requested records (with as much specificity as circumstances reasonably permit) and stating the reason(s) for the request. Because at this point the court has yet to find sufficient evidence of privilege waiver by the defendant to permit the prosecutor's involvement in the examination process, see Rule 14(b)(2)(B)(iii), under Rule 14(b)(2)(C)(iii), the examiner may not inform the prosecutor of the document request or its contents, absent permission from either the defense or the court.

Upon receiving the sealed request, the court must issue a copy to the defendant, notifying the Commonwealth only that a sealed request for additional records has been filed. The defendant has 30 days to file ex parte a written objection to the requested production. If the defendant timely files such an objection, the judge has the discretion to hold an ex parte hearing on it, including, again in the judge's discretion, permitting the Commonwealth's examiner to participate. If the judge grants any part of the examiner's request, the judge must inform the clerk to which records the examiner may have access, and the clerk must then subpoena those records. When the records arrive at the clerk's office, the clerk must notify the examiner and the defendant of the records' availability for examination and copying, subject to a protective order forbidding their disclosure to the prosecutor unless the judge determines that the conditions set forth in Rule 14(b)(2)(B)(iii) for permitting prosecutorial access to the examiners' reports are met. The clerk's office must maintain the records under seal.

When the report of the Commonwealth's examiner is disclosed to the parties under Rule 14(b)(2)(B)(iii), the records related to the examiner's Rule 14(b)(2)(C)(iii) request for additional records shall also be released to the parties, subject to the judge's narrow discretion to forbid such release. At this point in the process, the defendant has effectively waived any claim of privilege concerning evidence relating to the mental-health defense. See *Hanright*, 465 Mass. at 645–647. The only reason for withholding from the prosecutor information concerning the examiner's request for additional records would presumably be a concern that information there set forth would have little or no relevance to the mental-health defense and would cause unfair prejudice to the defendant in conducting the mental-health defense, a balancing of interests with which judges are quite familiar. As is so with the release of the examiners' reports and supporting records, the release of records relating to a request for additional records would be confined to the parties; these records would remain sealed to the public. Granting the prosecutor access to the records relating to a denial of an examiner's request for records would not only permit full communication between the prosecutor and the examiner in preparing for trial, but it would also allow the Commonwealth to weigh the possibility, however remote, of seeking appellate review of the denial.

Rule 14(b)(2)(C)(iv)

As noted above, once the Commonwealth's examiner completes his or her examination of the defendant, the examiner must disclose to the defendant all raw data from any tests or assessments that the examiner conducted or requested. This ensures full reciprocity between the parties. Presumably, the only mental-health or medical records available to the examiner would be those provided by the defendant or produced in response to a court order under Rule 14(b)(2)(C)(iii), making any reciprocal discovery of such records unnecessary. The production of raw testing data by the court-ordered examiner would result in both experts having full access to the same records and raw testing data before they complete and file their respective reports.

Rule 15.   Interlocutory Appeal

(Applicable to District Court and Superior Court)

(a) Right of Interlocutory Appeal.

(1) *Right of Appeal Where Pretrial Motion to Dismiss or for Appropriate Relief Granted.* The Commonwealth shall have the right to appeal to the Appeals Court a decision by a judge granting a motion to dismiss a complaint or indictment or a motion for appropriate relief made pursuant to the provisions of Rule 13(c).

(2) *Right of Appeal Where Motion to Suppress Evidence Determined.* A defendant or the Commonwealth shall have the right and opportunity to apply to a single justice of the Supreme Judicial Court, in the form and manner prescribed by a standing order of that court, for leave to appeal an order determining a motion to suppress evidence prior to trial. If the single justice determines that the administration of justice would be facilitated, the justice may grant that leave and may hear the appeal or may order it to the full Supreme Judicial Court or to the Appeals Court for determination.

(3) *Right of Appeal Where Delinquency Defendant Discharged.* The Commonwealth shall have the right to appeal to the Appeals Court a decision by a judge discharging a person pursuant to G. L. c. 119, § 72A.

(4) *Probable Cause Hearings.* No interlocutory appeal or report may be taken of matters arising out of a probable cause hearing.

(b) Procedural Requirements.

(1) *Time for Filing Appeal.* An appeal under Rule 15(a)(1) shall be taken by filing a notice of appeal in the trial court within thirty days of the date of entry of the order being appealed. An application for leave to appeal under Rule 15(a)(2) shall be made by filing within thirty days of the date of entry of the order being appealed, or such additional time as either the trial judge or the single justice of the Supreme Judicial Court shall order, (a) a notice of appeal in the trial court, and (b) an application to the single justice of the Supreme Judicial Court for leave to appeal.

(2) *Record.* The record for an interlocutory appeal shall be defined and assembled pursuant to Massachusetts Rule of Appellate Procedure 8.

(3) *Findings.* The judge shall make all findings of fact relevant to the appeal or the application for leave to appeal within the period specified in Rule 15(b)(1) for filing the notice of appeal.

(c) Determination of Motions.
Any motion the determination of which may be appealed pursuant to this rule shall be decided by the judge before the defendant is placed in jeopardy under established rules of law.

(d) Costs upon Appeal.
If an appeal or application therefor is taken by the Commonwealth, the appellate court, upon the written motion of the defendant supported by affidavit, shall determine and approve the payment to the defendant of his or her costs of appeal together with reasonable attorney's fees to be paid on the order of the trial court upon the entry of the rescript or the denial of the application.

(e) Stay of the Proceedings.
If the trial court issues an order which is subject to the interlocutory procedures herein, the trial of the case shall be stayed and the defendant shall not be placed in jeopardy until interlocutory review has been waived or the period specified in Rule 15(b)(1) for instituting interlocutory procedures has expired. If an appeal is taken or an application for leave to appeal is granted, the trial shall be stayed pending the entry of a rescript from or an order of the appellate court. If an appeal or application therefor is taken by the Commonwealth, the defendant may be released on personal recognizance during the pendency of the appeal.

Amended April 29, 1986, effective July 1, 1986; amended effective April 14, 1995; March 1, 1996; June 8, 2016, effective August 1, 2016; January 25, 2017, effective March 1, 2017.

Reporter's Notes

The 2016 amendments to Rule 15 respond to the Supreme Judicial Court's decision in *Commonwealth v. Jordan*, 469 Mass. 134 (2014), a case in which the Commonwealth sought interlocutory review of a suppression order through a late-filed notice of appeal and application for leave to appeal. In agreeing to consider the appeal in spite of the late filings, the Court acknowledged that the procedures governing the timeliness of such appeals lacked clarity, *id.* at 145, a problem that the Court addressed by announcing specific procedures prospectively applicable to Rule 15 filings seeking leave to appeal suppression orders. *Id.* at 147–148. In addition to this clarification of Rule 15 filing procedures, the Court expressed concern that then–Rule 15(b)(1)'s ten-day filing period for such appeals might be insufficient. *Id.* at 149–150. As discussed below, amended Rule 15 implements the procedural framework mandated in *Jordan* and expands to thirty days the time for filing a notice of appeal and an application for leave to appeal from an order determining a motion to suppress evidence.

Amended Rule 15 also includes non-substantive changes that clarify its mandate and update it to reflect current law.

Rule 15(a)(1) Right of Appeal Where Pretrial Motion to Dismiss or for Appropriate Relief Granted. Amended Rule 15(a)(1) reflects longstanding case law, making it clear that the Appeals Court is the court to which the Commonwealth may appeal the allowance of a motion to dismiss or of a motion for appropriate relief other than to suppress evidence. See *Commonwealth v. Friend*, 393 Mass. 310, 314 (1984) (Commonwealth's appeal from allowance of a motion to dismiss must be to the Appeals Court).

Rule 15(a)(2) Right of Appeal Where Motion to Suppress Evidence Determined. Amended Rule 15(a)(2) implements the late-filing procedures mandated by the Supreme Judicial Court in *Commonwealth v. Jordan*, 469 Mass. 134 (2014) for interlocutory appeals of an order determining a motion to suppress. Former Rule 15(a)(2) did not specify what showing an applicant for such relief must make concerning the timeliness of the necessary filings, hampering the efforts of single justices to be consistent in addressing the threshold issue of whether the notice of appeal and application for leave to appeal were timely filed and, if not, whether they should nevertheless be considered. See *Jordan*, 469 Mass. at 145 (acknowledging a "lack of clarity" in the single justices' application of procedural rules governing timeliness of Rule 15(a)(2) filings).

Amended Rule 15(a)(2) cures this deficiency, incorporating by reference the Supreme Judicial Court's standing order prescribing with specificity the form and manner for making an application to a single justice for leave to appeal a suppression order. This standing order, Supreme Judicial Court Order Regarding Applications to A Single Justice Pursuant to Mass. R. Crim. P. 15(a)(2) (2016), in effect codifies *Jordan*'s procedural framework for addressing timeliness issues, including a requirement that an application for leave to appeal a suppression order contain an affirmative representation that the application and notice to appeal are, or are not, timely under Rule 15(b)(1). If the appeal or application is untimely, the standing order requires that the application be accompanied by a motion to enlarge time for filing, supported by an affidavit providing "in meaningful detail the reasons for the delay." See Supreme Judicial Court Order Regarding Applications to A Single Justice Pursuant to Mass. R. Crim. P. 15(a)(2), § (a)(7) (2016). See also *Commonwealth v. Jordan*, 469 Mass. 134, 147–148 (2014) (setting out "Rule 15 procedure in future cases").

The purpose of this provision is to permit the single justice to whom the application is made to decide (1) whether the application satisfies Rule 15's timing requirements, and, if it does not, (2) whether the application should nevertheless be considered, before proceeding to the merits of the application and, if appropriate, the appeal. This threshold determination by the single justice is intended to be final, foreclosing further consideration of this procedural issue by the full court or the Appeals Court if the single justice refers the appeal to either for determination. See *Jordan*, 469 Mass. at 148 (2014).

Rule 15(a)(3) Right of Appeal Where Transfer of Delinquency Proceeding is Denied. Rule 15(a)(3), permitting the Commonwealth to appeal a judge's denial of a requested transfer of a delinquency proceeding to Superior or District Court for criminal prosecution, is deleted. G. L. c. 119, § 61, which provided for such transfers, was repealed, making Rule 15(a)(3) obsolete. This section is reserved for possible amendment to reflect current law.

Rule 15(b)(1) Time for Filing Appeal. Rule 15(b)(1), as amended, increases the time to file a notice of appeal and an application for leave to appeal a suppression order to thirty days, clarifying that the starting point for that time period is the date that the order being appealed is entered by the lower court. This filing period is meant to balance the need for adequate time to consider and prepare an application for interlocutory review of a suppression order against the potential for unnecessary, widespread delays in resolving the many criminal cases which involve suppression orders. Thirty days, the filing period applicable to other interlocutory appeals under Rule 15

and presumptively applicable to all appeals in criminal cases, see Rule 4(b), Mass. R. A. P., as amended, 431 Mass. 1601 (2000), should ordinarily suffice. However, if in a particular case a party can demonstrate with specificity that thirty days is insufficient, the rule provides for leave to seek additional time from either the trial judge or single justice. If there is a timely motion to reconsider the suppression order in question, the thirty-day time period for filing an application for interlocutory review does not commence until the trial court enters its order deciding the motion to reconsider. See *Jordan*, 469 Mass. at 147 n. 24.

The SJC's standing order incorporated in amended Rule 15(a)(2) provides that the party opposing interlocutory appeal of the suppression order may file a memorandum in opposition to that application within fourteen days after the application for leave to appeal is entered. Supreme Judicial Court Order Regarding Applications to A Single Justice Pursuant to Mass. R. Crim. P. 15(a)(2), § (c) (2016). The order further permits the single justice to extend or shorten the time to file such opposition and provides that a party deciding not to file an opposition must serve notice of that intention within the time allowed for filing the opposition. *Id.*

Rule 15(b)(2) Record; Rule 15(b)(3) Findings. Rule 15(b)(2) and Rule 15(b)(3) contain the provisions of former Rule 15(b)(2), renumbered to separate former Rule 15(b)(2) into two parts, Rule 15(b)(2) providing for definition and assembly of the record and Rule 15(b)(3) requiring timely findings by the trial judge.

Rule 16. Dismissal by the Prosecution

(Applicable to District Court and Superior Court)

(a) Entry of a Nolle Prosequi. A prosecuting attorney may enter a nolle prosequi of pending charges at any time prior to the pronouncement of sentence. A nolle prosequi shall be accompanied by a written statement, signed by the prosecuting attorney, setting forth the reasons for that disposition.

(b) Entry of Nolle Prosequi During Trial. After jeopardy attaches, a nolle prosequi entered without the consent of the defendant shall have the effect of an acquittal of the charges contained in the nolle prosequi.

Reporter's Notes

While similar to Fed.R.Crim.P. 48, this rule is a formalization of prior Massachusetts practice.

Subdivision (a). The decision to enter a nolle prosequi as to all or any distinct part of pending charges is discretionary with the prosecuting attorney.

Power to enter a nolle prosequi is absolute in the prosecuting officer from the return of the indictment up to the beginning of trial, except possibly in instances of scandalous abuse of the authority.

Commonwealth v. Dascalakis, 246 Mass. 12, 18, 140 N.E. 470 (1923). *See* Manning v. Municipal Court of Roxbury, Mass.Adv.Sh. (1977) 679, 682–83, 361 N.E.2d 1274; Commonwealth v. Massod, 350 Mass. 745, 217 N.E.2d 191 (1966). This rule is consistent with the common law. See 30 MASS. PRACTICE SERIES (Smith) §§ 854, 858 (1970, Supp. 1978).

Rule 48(a) of the Federal Rules of Criminal Procedure permits dismissal by the prosecution only with leave of court. It did not seem advisable to engraft this additional requirement onto the Massachusetts rule, however, since it is doubted that the court has the power to compel the Commonwealth to proceed with a case which it does not believe warrants prosecution. See 3 C. WRIGHT, FEDERAL PRACTICE & PROCEDURE: CRIMINAL § 812 at 304 (1969).

The term "prosecuting attorney" in this rule is intended to include municipal attorneys, e.g., city solicitors, prosecuting a case. See G.L. c. 278, § 15.

General Laws c. 277, § 70A is the basis for the second sentence of this subdivision which requires the prosecuting attorney to file a statement of his reasons for entering a nolle prosequi. 30 MASS. PRACTICE SERIES (Smith) § 857 (1970, Supp.1978); see ABA *Standards Relating to the Prosecution Function* § 4.4 (Approved Draft, 1971).

Subdivision (b). Once a case has reached trial, the defendant has been placed in jeopardy and has the right to have the issue of his guilt adjudicated. Commonwealth v. Massod, 350 Mass. 745, 217 N.E.2d 154 (1966). If after commencement of trial, but before return of the verdict, the prosecuting attorney enters a nolle prosequi without the consent of the defendant, the defendant is effectually acquitted of those charges which are the subject of the nolle prosequi. Commonwealth v. Hart, 149 Mass. 7, 20 N.E. 310 (1889); Commonwealth v. Dascalakis, 246 Mass. 12, 140 N.E. 470 (1923); Commonwealth v. Sitko, Mass.Adv.Sh. (1977) 668, 361 N.E.2d 1258; 30 MASS. PRACTICE SERIES (Smith) § 855 (1970). This comports substantially with Fed.R.Crim.P. 46(a), which prohibits the filing of a dismissal during trial without the consent of the defendant.

Rule 17. Summonses for Witnesses

(Applicable to District Court and Superior Court)

(a) Summons.

(1) *For Attendance of Witness; Form; Issuance.* A summons shall be issued by the clerk or any person so authorized by the General Laws. It shall state the name of the court and the title, if any, of the proceeding and shall command each person to whom it is directed to attend and give testimony at the time and place specified therein.

(2) *For Production of Documentary Evidence and of Objects.* A summons may also command the person to whom it is directed to produce the books, papers, documents, or other objects designated therein. The court on motion may quash or modify the summons if compliance would be unreasonable or oppressive or if the summons is being used to subvert the provisions of Rule 14. The court may direct that books, papers, documents, or objects designated in the summons be produced before the court within a reasonable time prior to the trial or prior to the time when they are to be offered in evidence and may upon their production permit the books, papers, documents, objects, or portions thereof to be inspected and copied by the parties and their attorneys if authorized by law.

(b) Defendants Unable to Pay. At any time upon the written ex parte application of a defendant which shows that the presence of a named witness is necessary to an adequate defense and that the defendant is unable to pay the fees of that witness, the court shall order the issuance of an indigent's summons. The witness so summoned shall be paid in accordance with the provisions of subdivision (c) of this rule. If the court so orders, the costs incurred shall be assessed to the defendant in accordance with the General Laws or the provisions of these rules.

(c) Payment of Witnesses. Expenses incurred by a witness summoned on behalf of a defendant determined to be indigent under this rule as well as expenses incurred by a witness summoned on behalf of the Commonwealth, as such expenses are determined in accordance with the General

Laws, shall be paid after the witness certifies in a writing filed with the court the amount of his travel and attendance.

(d) Service.

(1) *By Whom; Manner.* A summons may be served by any person authorized to serve a summons in a civil action or to serve criminal process. A summons shall be served upon a witness by delivering a copy to him personally, by leaving it at his dwelling house or usual place of abode with some person of suitable age and discretion then residing therein, or by mailing to the witness' last known address.

(2) *Place of Service.*

(A) Within the Commonwealth. A summons requiring the attendance of a witness at a hearing or a trial may be served at any place within the Commonwealth.

(B) Outside the Commonwealth or Abroad. A summons directed to a witness outside the Commonwealth or abroad shall issue and be served in a manner consistent with the General Laws.

(3) *Return.* The person serving a summons pursuant to this rule shall make a return of service to the court.

(e) Failure to Appear. If a person served with a summons pursuant to this rule fails to appear at the time and place specified therein and the court determines that such person did receive actual notice to appear, a warrant may issue to bring that person before the court.

Publisher's Note

The Summons for Witness form follows Rule 6, supra.

Reporter's Notes

The prototype for this rule is found in Fed.R.Crim.P. 17. See Massachusetts and Federal Rule of Civil Procedure 45; Rules of Criminal Procedure (U.L.A.) Rule 731 (1974). Rule 17 is for the most part in accord with prior Massachusetts law. Statutes which are consistent with this rule—e.g., G.L. c. 233, §§ 5–6, which authorize sanctions for a witness' failure to comply with a summons—are to remain in effect.

"Summons" as used in this rule (and Mass.R.Crim.P. 35[b]) is intended to refer to what has traditionally been expressed by the terms "summons" and "subpoena."

The right of a defendant to have process issued for the attendance of necessary witnesses is founded in the Constitution:

[I]t is the Sixth Amendment itself that in terms guarantees 'compulsory process for obtaining witnesses in [the accused's] favor,' and this is paralleled in substance by article 12 of our Declaration of Rights.

Blazo v. Superior Court, 366 Mass. 141, 145, 315 N.E.2d 857 (1974). A defendant's right to have summonses issued on his behalf may also be grounded in the sixth amendment right of confrontation.

Subdivision (a). This subdivision is drawn with little change from Fed.R.Crim.P. 17(a), (c); *accord* Rules of Criminal Procedure (U.L.A.) rule 731(a), (c) (1974).

Subdivision (a)(1). General Laws c. 233, § 1 provides that persons in addition to the clerk of court, i.e., notaries public and justices of the peace, may issue summonses for witnesses in criminal cases but only "upon request of the attorney general, district attorney or other person who acts in the case in behalf of the Commonwealth or of the defendant."

The proceedings contemplated by this subdivision include depositions to perpetuate testimony pursuant to Mass.R.Crim.P. 35.

Subdivision (a)(2). The provision of this subdivision authorizing the court to order the production of evidence prior to its use at trial or in other judicial proceedings is not intended to permit the use of summonses to subvert the discovery rule, Mass.R.Crim.P. 14. Rather, it is to permit the court to avoid delay where the production of many books, papers, documents, or other objects would delay the proceedings if not ordered until their commencement.

Subdivision (b). The subdivision, loosely modeled upon Fed. R.Crim.P. 17(b), is drafted in response to the Supreme Judicial Court's decision in Blazo v. Superior Court, 366 Mass. 141, 315 N.E.2d 857 (1974). There the court held that when indigency and the necessity for witnesses are shown, a defendant is to have the witnesses summoned at the expense of the Commonwealth, suggesting the following procedure:

> [A] defendant believing himself entitled will apply to the competent judge—ex parte if the defendant should so desire—supporting his application by affidavit showing his inability to pay the fees involved, setting out the names and addresses (if known) of the persons to be summoned, and stating why their attendance is necessary to an adequate defence. The judge may require the submission of further data.

Id. at 145–46 (footnote omitted). The court further explained that the reason for permitting ex parte application

> is that, just as a defendant able to foot the costs need not explain to anyone his reasons for summoning a given witness, so an impecunious defendant should be able to summons his witnesses without explanation that will reach the adversary.

Id. at 145 n. 8.

There is a significant difference between this subdivision and its counterpart under the federal rule. The summons that is to be issued under this rule is a prosecutor's summons, G.L. c. 277, § 68, and not a court summons, G.L. c. 233, § 1. This is because G.L. c. 233, § 3 provides that witnesses summoned on behalf of the defendant are entitled to prepayment of some of their expenses. If this requirement were applicable to witnesses for indigent defendants, an added burden would be imposed on the court clerks. Therefore, witnesses for indigent defendants are to be summoned by the Commonwealth pursuant to G.L. c. 277, §§ 68–69, and will not require prepayment. This procedure parallels that of Rules of Criminal Procedure (U.L.A.) Rule 731(b) (1974). Compare Fed.R.Crim.P. 17(b), (d).

Subdivision (c). The expenses involved in securing the attendance of a witness on behalf of a defendant or the Commonwealth in a criminal proceeding consist of the fees of the officer serving the process and fees to the witness for travel and attendance. G.L. c. 233, §§ 2–3; c. 262, §§ 8(B)(3), 29.

General Laws c. 262, § 29 requires that a witness certify in writing the amount of his travel and attendance costs and serves as a basis for this subdivision. The statute additionally provides that where the witness has been summoned by the Commonwealth, the certificate must be accompanied by a voucher signed by the attorney general or the district attorney stating that such fees are due the witness for his attendance. This rule adds witnesses summoned by indigent defendants to this category and provides for the payment of their expenses in the same manner as the expenses of Commonwealth witnesses are paid. Where the district attorney is prosecuting the case, G.L. c. 12, § 24 (as amended, St.1978, c. 478, § 10) authorizes the payment of expenses of government-summoned witnesses from Commonwealth funds. See G.L. c. 213, § 8, which the Supreme Judicial Court in Blazo stated would authorize county payment (now the Commonwealth, § 8 as amended, St.1978, c. 478, § 127) of witnesses ordered to attend on behalf of an indigent defendant. Blazo v. Superior Court, supra, at 146.

Under this rule, all witnesses are to be paid established witness fees. This is a departure from prior law, G.L. c. 277, § 69, which required prosecution witnesses to attend without pay unless the court directed the payment of their fees and expenses.

Subsection (d). The first sentence of subdivision (d)(1) embodies the substance of Mass.R.Civ.P. 45(c), which permits service "by any person who is not a party and is not less than 18 years of age." Compare Fed.R.Civ.P. 45(c) with Fed.R.Crim.P. 17(d). This procedure accords with that under G.L. c. 233, § 2, which provides that a summons for a witness may be served by an officer qualified to serve civil process or by some other disinterested person. Added is provision for service of summonses by persons authorized to serve criminal process. The rule would appear to allow service by counsel for the defendant or Commonwealth, although this practice has been criticized as perhaps "unwise." 8 MASS. PRACTICE SERIES (Smith & Zobel) Reporter's Notes at 136 (1977); compare Supreme Judicial Court Rule 3:22, incorporating ABA Canons of Professional Ethics, Canon 19 (1972); ABA Code of Professional Responsibility DR 5–102, EC 5–9, 5–10 (1970).

The manner of service under this rule is for the most part consistent with procedure under prior law and the civil rules, G.L. c. 233, § 2; Mass.R.Civ.P. 45(c), but adds that a summons may be served by mail. This last means of service is not available in cases of witnesses summoned by non-indigent defendants, since tender or payment of fees to the witness is a prerequisite to compelling his attendance. G.L. c. 233, § 3.

Subdivision (d)(2)(A) is taken from the second sentence of Mass. R.Civ.P. 45(e).

General Laws c. 233, §§ 13A–13C; otherwise known as the Uniform Law to Secure the Attendance of Witnesses from Without the State in Criminal Proceedings, provides a simple solution to the problem of obtaining out-of-state witnesses to appear in criminal proceedings. As long as the subject jurisdiction has adopted the Act the court will be able to secure attendance. Notwithstanding the provisions of G.L. c. 233, §§ 13A–13C and c. 277, § 66, it has been stated that the right of a defendant to compulsory process for witnesses who are necessary to his defense does not by statute automatically extend beyond the territory of the Commonwealth. Commonwealth v. Dirring, 354 Mass. 523, 238 N.E.2d 508 (1968). Accord Commonwealth v. Edgerly, Mass.App.Adv.Sh. (1978) 400, 375 N.E.2d 1.

Even though a defendant may not have the statutory right to compulsory process for necessary witnesses, the Constitution requires that the state make a good faith effort to obtain the presence of certain witnesses. In addition to the Uniform Act, state courts should avail themselves of two other avenues to secure the attendance of witnesses. The court in Barber v. Page, 88 S.Ct. 1318, 390 U.S. 719, 20 L.Ed.2d 255 (1968), determined that where the defendant has a constitutional right to confront a witness, a state must seek his attendance via: (1) 28 U.S.C. § 2241(c)(5) (1971), which gives federal courts the power to issue writs of habeas corpus ad testificandum at the request of state prosecutors in the case of the prospective witnesses currently in federal custody; and (2) the issuance of a writ of habeas corpus ad testificandum by state courts. The existing policy of the United States Bureau of Prisons is to permit federal prisoners to testify in state court criminal proceedings pursuant to the issuance of such writs.

With respect to witnesses who are citizens or residents of the United States, but currently beyond its jurisdiction, the Court in Mancusi v. Stubbs, 92 S.Ct. 2308, 408 U.S. 204, 33 L.Ed.2d 293 (1972), enunciated the limitations of the applicability of 28 U.S.C. § 1783 (1966), which provides in pertinent part:

> (a) A court of the United States may order the issuance of a subpoena requiring the appearance as a witness before it, or before a person or body designated by it, of a national or resident of the United States who is in a foreign country, or requiring the production of a specified document or other thing by him, if the court finds that particular testimony or the production of the document or other thing by him is necessary in the interest of justice * * *

With respect to § 1783, the court stated:

> We have been cited to no authority applying this section to permit subpoena by a federal court for testimony in the state felony trial, and certainly the statute on its face does not appear to be designated for that purpose.

Id. at 212. (Footnote omitted.)

The *Mancusi* court concluded that Tennessee was powerless to compel the attendance of the absent witness, then a resident of Sweden, and that, therefore, the state had not denied the respondent the right of confrontation as guaranteed by the sixth and fourteenth amendments.

NOTICE OF A HEARING REGARDING THE RELEASE OF RECORDS	DOCKET NO.	Trial Court of Massachusetts

CASE NAME

Commonwealth v.

NOTICE IS ISSUED TO:	COURT NAME & ADDRESS
third-party subject	
keeper of records	

NOTICE OF A HEARING REGARDING THE RELEASE OF RECORDS [1]

To:

name of third-party subject	name of keeper of records
address 1	address 1
address 2	address 2
city, state, zip code	city, state, zip code

The defendant in this case has filed a motion with the Court to be allowed to inspect the records of

_____ for the dates from _____ to _____
(third-party subject)   (date range)

made by _____
        (name and professional title of caregiver or other person/entity that created the records, if known)

that are being held by _____
                      (name and address of keeper of records)

---

1 For use in criminal, youthful offender, or delinquency cases whenever a defendant seeks pretrial inspection of a third party's records that are likely to be covered by a statutory privilege. Use a separate form for each keeper of records and each third-party subject.

AOTC 12/2007

THE COURT HAS ORDERED THE PROSECUTING ATTORNEY'S OFFICE TO NOTIFY YOU THAT A HEARING ON THE ATTACHED MOTION HAS BEEN SCHEDULED FOR

_____ in Courtroom _____ of the _____ Courthouse,
(date and time)

which is located at: _____.

    At the hearing, the judge will decide if the records are privileged and if they are relevant to the case against the defendant. Under the law, certain records (e.g., psychiatric or other counseling records) may be confidential, or "privileged." The purpose of the hearing is to determine whether the judge will order the records to be sent to Court for the defendant's lawyer to inspect. If the judge allows the defendant's motion, the Court will make privileged records available only to defense counsel, pending further order of the Court, except for limited disclosures to support staff and to other attorneys for purposes of consultation as described in the Protective Order that counsel will be required to sign before reviewing the records.

    If the records are privileged under the law, the Court will assume that you do not wish to give up (waive) any privilege at this time, unless you provide (or have provided) a written waiver before or at the hearing. Your absence from the hearing will not constitute a waiver of any privilege you may have under the law.

    You have the right to attend the hearing. You can take part in the hearing yourself or you may (but need not) obtain a lawyer to represent you. Victims have the right to talk to the prosecuting attorney before the hearing.

THIS HEARING WILL BE YOUR ONLY OPPORTUNITY TO ADDRESS THE COURT REGARDING THE RELEASE OF THESE RECORDS.

_____   _____
date   signature of Assistant District Attorney/Assistant Attorney General

If you have any questions about this notice, you may contact _____
                                                             (name of prosecutor or advocate)

at _____ at telephone number _____.
   (name of prosecuting office)

AOTC 12/2007

NOTICE ACCOMPANYING COURT-ORDERED SUMMONS FOR NON-PRIVILEGED RECORDS	DOCKET NO.	Trial Court of Massachusetts

CASE NAME

Commonwealth v.

KEEPER OF RECORDS TO WHOM THIS NOTICE IS ISSUED AND ADDRESS	COURT NAME & ADDRESS

Pursuant to Rule 17(a)(2) of the Massachusetts Rules of Criminal Procedure, 378 Mass. 885 (1979), the Court has issued the enclosed summons to produce records in the above-captioned matter. A judge has determined that the records ordered produced are not likely to be protected by a statutory privilege, or the third-party subject has waived any applicable statutory privilege.

The records ordered by the Court must be delivered to: _____

_____

(address of Clerk of Court)

on or before the return date on the summons in a sealed envelope or box clearly marked as follows:

COMMONWEALTH v. _____ **(defendant)**

DOCKET NUMBER: _____

From: _____ **(name of keeper of records)**

Date: _____

NON-PRIVILEGED RECORDS: NOT FOR PUBLIC INSPECTION

	Clerk of Court
Entered: _____	By: _____

AOTC: 12/2007

NOTICE ACCOMPANYING COURT-ORDERED SUMMONS FOR PRESUMPTIVELY PRIVILEGED RECORDS	DOCKET NO.	Trial Court of Massachusetts

CASE NAME

Commonwealth v.

KEEPER OF RECORDS TO WHOM THIS NOTICE IS ISSUED AND ADDRESS	COURT NAME & ADDRESS

Pursuant to Rule 17(a)(2) of the Massachusetts Rules of Criminal Procedure, 378 Mass. 885 (1979), the Court has issued the enclosed summons to produce records in the above-captioned matter. A judge has determined that the records ordered produced are "presumptively privileged," which means that they are likely to be protected by a statutory privilege.

The records ordered by the Court must be delivered to: _____

_____

(address of Clerk of Court)

on or before the return date on the summons in a sealed envelope or box clearly marked as follows:

COMMONWEALTH v. _____ (defendant)

DOCKET NUMBER: _____

From: _____ (name of keeper of records)

Date: _____

PRIVILEGED RECORDS: IMPOUNDED

Entered: _____	Clerk of Court By: _____

AOTC 12/2007

PROTECTIVE ORDER FOR DEFENSE COUNSEL	DOCKET NO.	Trial Court of Massachusetts

CASE NAME

Commonwealth v.

On consideration of the defendant's motion pursuant to Rule 17(a)(2) of the Massachusetts Rules of Criminal Procedure, 378 Mass. 885 (1979), it is hereby ORDERED that defense counsel ("counsel") who has signed this protective order and filed it with the Clerk of Court in the above-captioned case be provided access to presumptively privileged records subject to the following terms and conditions:

1. Counsel shall have access to presumptively privileged records solely in his or her capacity as an officer of the Court. Counsel shall review any presumptively privileged records in the Clerk's office, or a space within the courthouse designated by the Clerk, during regular business hours under arrangements to be made with the Clerk.

2. Counsel shall not copy, and shall not directly or indirectly disclose, disseminate, or otherwise make available to any person, including the defendant, any of the presumptively privileged records, any portion thereof, or any of their contents without prior application to and an order of the Court.

3. Counsel may read and make notes concerning the presumptively privileged records. Any such notes shall be governed by this Protective Order.

4. Presumptively privileged records reviewed pursuant to this Protective Order shall not be used for any purpose other than the defense of the above-captioned case.

5. If counsel believes that copying or disclosure of any presumptively privileged records, or portions thereof, is necessary to prepare this case for trial, he or she may file a motion to modify this Protective Order to permit copying of records or disclosure to specifically identified individuals. The motion shall be accompanied by an affidavit, and notice shall be provided to all parties. If the Court enters an order vacating or modifying any term of this Protective Order, counsel shall then be bound by the terms of that Court order.

6. At the conclusion of the trial, direct appeal, or other disposition of the above-captioned case, the signatory shall deliver to the Clerk of Court, under seal, any and all copies of any records produced pursuant to any modified protective order or any other order of the Court. Notwithstanding the entry of any order terminating the case, this Protective Order shall remain in effect unless terminated by entry of a Court order.

7. The prohibitions against disclosure shall not apply to communications made under the following circumstances:

    (a) where counsel is engaged in the private practice of law, communications with other attorneys in counsel's law firm, provided that such communications are for the purpose of consultation in this matter;

    (b) where counsel is a staff attorney employed by the Committee for Public Counsel Services ("CPCS"), communications with other staff attorneys employed by CPCS, provided that such communications are for the purpose of consultation in this matter;

AOTC. 12/2007

(c) where counsel is private counsel assigned by CPCS, communications with attorneys employed or assigned by CPCS, provided that such communications are for the purpose of consultation in this matter; or

(d) communications with counsel's support staff, operating under counsel's direction, for the purpose of preparing pleadings and other documents in this matter.

In making any of the above communications, counsel shall, insofar as possible, use a pseudonym in place of the true name of the person protected by the privilege. Counsel will instruct any person receiving a communication pursuant to paragraph 7 of the court-ordered confidentiality of the material disclosed.

The Court and any counsel shall report any violation of this order to the Board of Bar Overseers. Violations may also be reported to the Court and/or Board of Bar Overseers by the privilege holder, the keeper of records, and any other person who believes, in good faith, that the terms of this Order have been violated.

Entered:	By the Court, (, J.) x _____ Signature of Justice
CERTIFICATION BY COUNSEL	
I agree to be bound by the terms of this Protective Order. SIGNED UNDER THE PAINS AND PENALTIES OF PERJURY.	
Date:	Signature of Counsel: x
BBO. No.:	Printed Name and Address of Counsel:

ORDER ALLOWING ACCESS TO PRIVILEGED RECORDS BY PERSONS OTHER THAN COUNSEL	DOCKET NO.	Trial Court of Massachusetts

CASE NAME

Commonwealth v.

On consideration of the _____ 's motion to disclose records, it is hereby
                        (defense or prosecuting attorney)

ORDERED that _____
                        (name, address, title of person permitted access)

is permitted access to the records of _____ held by
                                    (name of third-party subject)
_____ for the period from _____ to _____ ,
     (keeper of records)   (date range)

subject to the following terms and conditions:

1. Any person granted access to records by this Court ("authorized person") must sign and file a copy of this Order with the Clerk of Court in the above-captioned case before receiving access to the records.

2. An authorized person shall have access to records solely for use in the defense or prosecution of the above-captioned case. An authorized person shall not copy or directly or indirectly disclose, disseminate, or otherwise make available to any person, including the defendant, any portion of the records or their contents without a written Court order authorizing such copying or disclosure.

3. An authorized person may take notes regarding the records. Any such notes shall be governed by the terms of paragraph 2, above.

4. At the conclusion of trial or other disposition of the above-captioned case, an authorized person shall deliver to the defense or prosecuting attorney any copies of the records and any notes made pursuant to paragraph 3, above. Notwithstanding the entry of any order terminating the case, this Order shall remain in effect unless terminated by the the Court.

Entered:	By the Court, (, J.)
	X _____
	Signature of Justice

I agree to be bound by the terms of this Court Order. **I UNDERSTAND THAT VIOLATION OF THIS COURT ORDER IS PUNISHABLE AS CRIMINAL CONTEMPT AND MAY SUBJECT THE VIOLATOR TO A FINE AND/OR TERM OF IMPRISONMENT.**

SIGNED UNDER THE PAINS AND PENALTIES OF PERJURY.

Signature
x

Printed Name:	Address:

AOTC 12/2007

PROTECTIVE ORDER FOR PROSECUTING ATTORNEY	DOCKET NO.	Trial Court of Massachusetts

CASE NAME

Commonwealth v.

It is hereby ORDERED that the prosecutor who has signed this protective order and filed it with the Clerk of Court in the above-captioned case be provided access to presumptively privileged records subject to the following terms and conditions:

1. The prosecutor shall have access to presumptively privileged records solely in his or her capacity as an officer of the Court. The prosecutor shall review any presumptively privileged records in the Clerk's office, or a space within the courthouse designated by the Clerk, during regular business hours under arrangements to be made with the Clerk.

2. The prosecutor shall not copy, and shall not directly or indirectly disclose, disseminate, or otherwise make available to any person, any of the presumptively privileged records, any portion thereof, or any of their contents without prior application to and an order of the Court.

3. The prosecutor may read and make notes concerning the presumptively privileged records. Any such notes shall be governed by this Protective Order.

4. Presumptively privileged records reviewed pursuant to this Protective Order shall not be used for any purpose other than the prosecution of the above-captioned case.

5. If the prosecutor believes that copying or disclosure of any presumptively privileged records, or portions thereof, is necessary to prepare this case for trial, he or she may file a motion to modify this Protective Order to permit copying of records or disclosure to specifically identified individuals. The motion shall be accompanied by an affidavit, and notice shall be provided to all parties. If the Court enters an order vacating or modifying any term of this Protective Order, counsel shall then be bound by the terms of that Court order.

6. At the conclusion of the trial, direct appeal, or other disposition of the above-captioned case, the signatory shall deliver to the Clerk of Court, under seal, any and all copies of any records produced pursuant to any modified protective order or any other order of the Court. Notwithstanding the entry of any order terminating the case, this Protective Order shall remain in effect unless terminated by entry of a Court order.

7. The prohibitions against disclosure shall not apply to communications made under the following circumstances:

    (a) communications with any victim-witness advocate working with the prosecuting attorney in this matter;

    (b) communications with other prosecuting attorneys, provided that such communications are for the purpose of consultation in this matter; or

    (c) communications with counsel's support staff, operating under counsel's direction, for the purpose of preparing pleadings and other documents in this matter.

AOTC. 12/2007

In making any of the above communications authorized by subparagraph (b) and (c), counsel shall, insofar as possible, use a pseudonym in place of the true name of the person protected by the privilege. Counsel will instruct any person receiving a communication pursuant to paragraph 7 of the court-ordered confidentiality of the material disclosed.

The Court and any counsel shall report any violation of this order to the Board of Bar Overseers. Violations may also be reported to the Court and/or Board of Bar Overseers by the privilege holder, the keeper of records, and any other person who believes, in good faith, that the terms of this Order have been violated.

Entered:	By the Court, (, J.)
	X _____
	Signature of Justice

CERTIFICATION BY COUNSEL

I agree to be bound by the terms of this Protective Order.

SIGNED UNDER THE PAINS AND PENALTIES OF PERJURY.

Date:	Signature of Counsel:
	x
BBO. No.:	Printed Name and Address of Counsel:

AOTC 12/2007

Rule 18. Presence of Defendant

(Applicable to District Court and Superior Court)

(a) Presence of Defendant. In any prosecution for crime the defendant shall be entitled to be present at all critical stages of the proceedings.

(1) *Defendant Absenting Himself.* If a defendant is present at the beginning of a trial and thereafter absents himself without cause or without leave of court, the trial may proceed to a conclusion in all respects except the imposition of sentence as though the defendant were still present.

(2) *Waiver of Presence in Misdemeanor Cases.* A person prosecuted for a misdemeanor may at his own request, with leave of court, be excused from attendance if represented by counsel or an agent authorized by law and may be excused from attendance without leave of court if so authorized by the General Laws.

(3) *Presence Not Required.* A defendant need not be present at a revision or revocation of sentence pursuant to Rule 29 or at any proceeding where evidence is not to be taken.

(b) Presence of Corporation. A corporation may appear by a duly authorized agent for the purposes of this rule.

Reporter's Notes

This rule is patterned primarily upon Rule 3.180 of the Florida Rules of Criminal Procedure and is a codification of accepted Massachusetts practice.

Under the Florida rule a defendant's presence is commanded at certain specifically enumerated "critical stages" of a criminal proceeding: arraignment, entry of plea, pretrial conference, all trial proceedings before the court, jury view, rendition of verdict, pronouncement of judgment and imposition of sentence. See Uniform Rule 713, which would grant the defendant the right to be present "at *every stage* of the trial ... and at the disposition hearing" (emphasis supplied), and which would *require* his presence unless he is represented by counsel and has waived the right to be present, has voluntarily failed to be present, or has been justifiably excluded. Rules of Criminal Procedure (U.L.A.) Rule 713 (1974). Rule 18 neither presumes to define those stages of a proceeding when the defendant's presence is constitutionally mandated, nor to compel his presence at every stage, rather it instructs that he is to be present at "all critical stages." The term "critical" is unrelated to its use for other purposes, e.g., assignment of counsel, and is to be interpreted in light of relevant judicial decisions.

The defendant's presence is constitutionally required during all critical stages because fairness demands that the defendant be present when his substantial rights are at stake, and those instances are not limited to the specific proceedings listed in the Florida rule. Conversely, there are matters which the court and defendant's counsel can determine in the defendant's absence; to require the defendant's presence at all times could in some instances unduly prolong the disposition of the case. Thus, under this rule, the detailing of what stages are deemed critical is left to judicial determination.

The sixth amendment to the United States Constitution guarantees a defendant the right to confront witnesses at trial, which right is also guaranteed by article 12 of the Massachusetts Declaration of Rights and by statute, G.L. c. 278, § 6. However, the primary constitutional protection is afforded by the due process clause of the fourteenth amendment. "[T]he presence of the defendant is a condition of due process to the extent that a fair and just hearing would be thwarted by his absence...." Snyder v. Massachusetts, 54 S.Ct. 330, 291 U.S. 97, 107–08, 78 L.Ed. 674, 90 A.L.R. 575 (1934). Thus, the Constitution requires the presence of the defendant at proceedings other than trial if his presence would be essential to preserve substantial rights.

Subdivision (a). Where a stage of the proceedings is deemed critical, the defendant's presence is required and the court is not to proceed in his absence without determining that he has effectively waived or forfeited the right to be present. Taylor v. United States, 94 S.Ct. 194, 414 U.S. 17, 38 L.Ed.2d 174 (1973). Most hearings either before or after trial do not require the defendant's presence. *See* Mass.R.Crim.P. 30. For example, his presence is not required at pretrial motions, including motions for a change of venue, Mass.R.Crim.P. 37, and motions for a continuance, Mass.R.Crim.P. 10, Commonwealth v. Robichaud, 358 Mass. 300, 264 N.E.2d 374 (1970). And his presence is not generally required at post-trial proceedings. Commonwealth v. Dupont, 2 Mass.App. 566, 317 N.E.2d 83 (1974); Mass.R.Crim.P. 30. But the defendant's presence is required at all trial proceedings (See *Commonwealth v. Robichaud*, supra), at arraignment (Mass.R.Crim.P. 6), when a plea is made (Mass.R.Crim.P. 12), and at sentencing (Thompson v. United States, 495 F.2d 1304 [1st Cir.1974]; Mass.R.Crim.P. 28).

(a)(1). Although a defendant is entitled to be present at critical stages, he may waive or forfeit that right. Commonwealth v. McCarthy, 163 Mass. 458, 40 N.E. 766 (1895). He may waive his right to be present at the trial of a felony in either of two ways. First, he may voluntarily absent himself from trial, in which case the trial may continue in his absence. Commonwealth v. Flemmi, 360 Mass. 693, 277 N.E.2d 523 (1971). Secondly, the defendant may become so obstreperous as to require his removal from court in order to preserve the orderliness of judicial proceedings. Illinois v. Allen, 90 S.Ct. 1057, 397 U.S. 337, 25 L.Ed.2d 353 (1970); Commonwealth v. Senati, 3 Mass.App. 304, 327 N.E.2d 906 (1975); Mass.R.Crim.P. 45; See ABA *Standards Relating to the Function of the Trial Judge* § 6.8 (Approved Draft, 1972). However, trial cannot begin in the defendant's absence, Diaz v. United States, 32 S.Ct. 250, 223 U.S. 442, 455, 56 L.Ed. 500 (1912), thereby eliminating the possibility that a defendant, by voluntarily absenting himself can be deemed to have waived his right to be present at the inception of trial.

The defendant is not prohibited by this rule from waiving his right to be present at the trial of capital cases. The traditional rule enunciated in *Diaz v. United States*, supra, is that in capital crimes the defendant is not permitted to be tried in absentia because of the severity of the potential punishment. The rule was recently reaffirmed in *Taylor v. United States*, supra. However, the prohibition against waiver of the right to be present in capital cases does not exist in Rule 43 of the Federal Rules of Criminal Procedure, nor is it suggested by Rule 713 of the Uniform Rules of Criminal Procedure (U.L.A.) (1974). As the Advisory Committee Note to Federal Rule 43 recognizes, the present state of the law on this issue is not clear. As with the federal rule, this rule does not attempt to resolve this disputed issue, but leaves the matter to future judicial decisions.

(a)(2). This is a restatement of G.L. c. 278, § 6. General Laws c. 274, § 1 defines felonies and misdemeanors.

(a)(3). See generally the discussion of when a defendant's presence *is* required, supra.

Subdivision (b). Federal Rule of Criminal Procedure 43(c)(1) provides that "a corporation may appear by counsel for all purposes." It is, therefore, unnecessary for an officer of the corporation to be present at arraignment plea, trial, or sentencing (unless individually charged) in any case, whether misdemeanor or felony. 8B J. MOORE, FEDERAL PRACTICE para. 43.02[3] (Rev. ed. 1978). Under Mass.R.Crim.P. 18, the corporation may appear for all purposes by "duly authorized agent" which does not require counsel.

Rule 19. Trial by Jury or by the Court

(Applicable to Superior Court and jury
sessions in District Court)

(a) General. A case in which the defendant has the right to be tried by a jury shall be so tried unless the defendant waives a jury trial in writing with the approval of the court and files the waiver with the clerk, in which instance he shall be tried by the court instead of by a jury. If there is more than one defendant, all must waive the right to trial by jury, and if they do not so waive, there must be a jury trial unless the court in its discretion severs the cases. The court may refuse to approve such a waiver for any good and sufficient reason provided that such refusal is given in open court and on the record.

(b) Less Than a Full Jury. If after jeopardy attaches there is at any time during the progress of a trial less than a full jury remaining, a defendant may waive his right to be tried by a full jury and request trial by the remaining jurors by signing a written waiver which shall be filed with the court. If there is more than one defendant, all must sign and file a waiver unless the court in its discretion severs the cases.

Reporter's Notes

The right to trial by jury, which is guaranteed by art. 3, § 2, cl. 3 of the United States Constitution and the sixth amendment, is applicable to the states through the fourteenth amendment. Duncan v. Louisiana, 88 S.Ct. 1444, 391 U.S. 145, 20 L.Ed.2d 491, 522 (1968). The Massachusetts Constitution, part 1, art. 12, also guarantees defendants the right to trial by jury. Further, G.L. c. 278, § 2, applicable to the Superior Court, provides that "[i]ssues of fact ... shall ... be tried by a jury ... unless the person indicted or complained against elects to be tried by the court...." General Laws c. 218, § 26A, inserted by St.1978, c. 478, § 188, provides that trials in the District Court and the Boston Municipal Court "shall be by a jury of six, unless the defendant files a written waiver and consents to be tried by the court...." Under prior law a juvenile defendant had no right to a trial by jury during the adjudicative phase of a delinquency proceeding. McKeiver v. Pennsylvania, 91 S.Ct. 1976, 403 U.S. 528, 29 L.Ed.2d 647 (1971); Commonwealth v. Page, 339 Mass. 313, 316, 159 N.E.2d 82 (1959). However, by G.L. c. 119, § 55A, inserted by St.1978, c. 478, § 56, delinquency proceedings shall be by jury unless waived. If a juvenile appeals from an adjudication of delinquency in a jury waived session, his appeal to the jury session will be tried and determined in like manner as an appeal by an adult criminal defendant. G.L. c. 119, § 56 (as amended, St.1978, c. 478, § 57). *See* Sylvester v. Commonwealth, 253 Mass. 244, 148 N.E. 449 (1925).

Subdivision (a). This subdivision is drawn from Fed.R.Crim.P. 23(a) and G.L. c. 119, § 55A; c. 218, § 26A; c. 263, § 6. The requirement that the waiver be in writing is not universal. See ABA *Standards Relating to Trial by Jury*, § 1.2(b) (Approved Draft, 1968); Rules of Criminal Procedure (U.L.A.) rule 511 (1974). In Boykin v. Alabama, 89 S.Ct. 1709, 395 U.S. 238, 23 L.Ed.2d 274 (1969), the Court held that a waiver of a jury trial cannot be presumed from a silent record. While *Boykin* would be satisfied by an oral waiver when the proceedings are recorded, the requirement in Massachusetts is that the waiver be written and filed with the clerk. Commonwealth v. Hesser, 1 Mass.App. 850, 302 N.E.2d 927 (1973) (Rescript); Gallo v. Commonwealth, 343 Mass. 397, 402, 179 N.E.2d 231, 93 A.L.R.2d 406 (1961); G.L. c. 263, § 6. The federal rule imposes this stricter requirement "to ensure a greater probability of a defendant understanding what he is doing...." Pool v. United States, 344 F.2d 943, 945 (9th Cir.1966). Likewise, the Massachusetts rule seeks to "avoid unnecessary controversy and to provide a procedural safeguard...." *Gallo v. Commonwealth*, supra.

"A waiver is ... an intentional relinquishment or abandonment of a known right...." Johnson v. Zerbst, 58 S.Ct. 1019, 304 U.S. 458, 464, 82 L.Ed. 1461 (1938). Waiver of a constitutional right must be "intelligent and competent." Id. at 465. The waiver of the right to a jury trial must be "express and intelligent." Patton v. United States, 50 S.Ct. 253, 281 U.S. 276, 312, 74 L.Ed. 854, 70 A.L.R. 263 (1930).

Subdivision (a) incorporates that portion of the federal rule which provides that a waiver of trial by jury must be approved by the court. Although a defendant is free to waive his jury trial, *Patton*, supra, there is no constitutional impediment to conditioning that waiver upon the consent of the trial judge. Singer v. United States, 85 S.Ct. 783, 380 U.S. 24, 36, 13 L.Ed.2d 630 (1965) (construing Fed.R.Crim.P. 23[a]). See ABA *Standards Relating to Trial by Jury* § 1.2(a), comment at 32–34 (Approved Draft, 1968). The defendant in a capital case may not waive a jury trial in any event. G.L. c. 263, § 6 (as amended); Commonwealth v. O'Brien, 371 Mass. 605, 358 N.E.2d 786 (1976). *Accord* Commonwealth v. Marshall, Mass.Adv.Sh. (1977) 1530, 1532–33, 364 N.E.2d 1237.

The decision whether to waive trial by jury is properly that of the defendant after full consultation with counsel. ABA *Standards Relating to the Defense Function* § 5.2 (Approved Draft, 1971).

If there are multiple defendants and one desires to waive the right to trial by jury, then all must waive. United States v. Farries, 459 F.2d 1057, 1061 (3d Cir.), cert. denied, 93 S.Ct. 143, 409 U.S. 888 (1972), 34 L.Ed.2d 145, 410 U.S. 912, 35 L.Ed.2d 275 (1973). In a rare case, severance may be the best course if not all defendants choose waiver. In *Farries*, however, the enormous expense and serious security problems involved in a trial where the defendants and many witnesses were inmates of various federal penitentiaries was held to outweigh the interests of a defendant in severance.

Subdivision (b). This subdivision is in accord with current Massachusetts practice as stated in G.L. c. 234, § 26A. The provision authorizing the court to disallow a waiver of the right to be tried by a full jury is not inconsistent with prior law even though a similar provision does not appear in G.L. c. 234, § 26A. See Commonwealth v. Roby, 29 Mass. 496, 502 (1832). *Compare* United States v. Jorn, 91 S.Ct. 547, 400 U.S. 470, 27 L.Ed.2d 543 (1971).

Rule 20. Trial Jurors

(Applicable to Superior Court and jury
sessions in District Court)

(a) Motion for Appropriate Relief. Either party may challenge the array by a motion for appropriate relief pursuant to Rule 13(c). A challenge to the array shall be made only on the ground that the prospective jurors were not selected or drawn according to law. Challenges to the array shall be made and decided before any individual juror is examined unless otherwise ordered by the court. A challenge to the array shall be in writing supported by affidavit and shall specify the facts constituting the ground of the challenge. Challenges to the array shall be tried by the court and may in the discretion of the court be decided on the basis of the affidavit filed with the challenge. Upon the hearing of a challenge to the array, a witness may be examined on oath by the court and may be so examined by either party. If the challenge to the array is sustained, the court shall discharge the panel.

(b) Challenge for Cause.

(1) *Examination of Juror.* The court shall, or upon motion, the parties or their attorneys may under the direction of the court, examine on oath a person who is called as a juror in a case to learn whether he is related to either party, has any interest in the case, has expressed or formed an opinion, or is sensible of any bias or prejudice. The objecting party may, with the approval of the court, introduce other competent evidence in support of the objection.

(2) *Examination Upon Extraneous Issues.* The court shall examine or cause a juror to be examined upon issues extrane-

ous to the case if it appears that the juror's impartiality may have been affected by the extraneous issues. The examination may include a brief statement of the facts of the case, to the extent the facts are appropriate and relevant to the issues of such examination, and shall be conducted individually and outside the presence of other persons about to be called or already called as jurors.

(3) *Challenge of Juror.* Either party may challenge an individual prospective juror before the juror is sworn to try the case. The court may for cause shown permit a challenge to be made after the juror is sworn but before any evidence is presented. When a juror is challenged for cause, the ground of the challenge shall be stated. A challenge of a prospective juror and the statement of the grounds thereof may be made at the bench. The court shall determine the validity of each such challenge.

(c) Peremptory Challenges.

(1) *Number of Challenges.* Upon the trial of an indictment for a crime punishable by imprisonment for life, each defendant shall be entitled to twelve peremptory challenges of the jurors called to try the case; in any other criminal case tried before a jury of twelve, each defendant shall be entitled to four peremptory challenges; and in a case tried before a jury of six, each defendant shall be entitled to two peremptory challenges. Each defendant in a trial of an indictment for a crime punishable by imprisonment for life in which additional jurors are impaneled under subdivision (d) of this rule shall be entitled to one additional peremptory challenge for each additional juror. Each defendant in a case in which several indictments or complaints are consolidated for trial shall be entitled to no more peremptory challenges than the greatest number to which he would have been entitled upon trial of any one of the indictments or complaints alone. In every criminal case the Commonwealth shall be entitled to as many peremptory challenges as equal the whole number to which all the defendants in the case are entitled.

(2) *Time of Challenge.* Peremptory challenges shall be made before the jurors are sworn and may be made after the determination that a person called to serve as a juror stands indifferent in the case.

(d) Alternate Jurors.

(1) *Impanelling Jury With Alternate Jurors.* If a jury trial is likely to be protracted, the judge may impanel a jury of not more than sixteen members and the court shall have jurisdiction to try the case with that jury.

(2) *Selection of Twelve Jurors.* If at the time of the final submission of the case to the jury more than twelve members of the jury who have heard the whole case are alive and not incapacitated or disqualified, the judge shall direct the clerk to place the names of all the remaining jurors except the foreman in a box and draw the names of a sufficient number to reduce the jury to twelve members. Those jurors whose names are drawn shall not be discharged, but shall be known as alternate jurors and shall be kept separate and apart from the other jurors in some convenient place, subject to the same rules and regulations as the other jurors, until the jury has agreed upon a verdict or has been otherwise discharged.

(3) *Disabled Juror: Selection of Alternate.* If, at any time after the final submission of the case by the court to the jury

but before the jury has agreed on a verdict, a juror dies, becomes ill, or is unable to perform his duty for any other cause, the judge may order him to be discharged and shall direct the clerk to place the names of all the remaining alternate jurors in a box and draw the name of an alternate who shall take the place of the discharged juror on the jury, which shall renew its deliberations with the alternate juror.

(e) Regulation and Separation of Jurors.

(1) *Sequestration.* After the jurors have been sworn they shall hear the case as a body and, within the discretion of the trial judge, may be sequestered.

(2) *After Submission of the Cause.* Unless the jurors have been sequestered for the duration of the trial, the judge after the final submission of the case, may order that the jurors be permitted to separate for a definite time to be fixed by the judge and then reconvene in the courtroom before retiring for consideration of their verdict.

(3) *After Commencement of Deliberations.* After final submission of the case to the jury and after deliberations have commenced, the judge may allow the jurors, under proper instructions, to separate for a definite time to be fixed by the judge and to reconvene in the courtroom before retiring for further deliberation of their verdict.

Reporter's Notes

This rule is primarily a distillation of Massachusetts statutory law. G.L. c. 234, §§ 26B, 28–29; former G.L. c. 277, § 47A (St.1978, c. 478, § 298). *See e.g.,* Fed.R.Crim.P. 24; Fla.R.Crim.P. 3.370; ABA *Standards Relating to Trial by Jury* §§ 2.3–2.7 (Approved Draft, 1968); Rules of Criminal Procedure (U.L.A.) Rules 511–513, 532 (1974); National Advisory Commission on Criminal Justice Standards and Goals, *Courts* §§ 4.13–4.14 (1973).

Subdivision (a). Although G.L. c. 277, § 47A, inserted by St.1965, c. 617, § 1, abolished in terms "challenges to the array and to the manner of selection of grand or traverse jurors," the relief formerly available thereunder remains available by a "motion to grant appropriate relief." Despite the statutory change in nomenclature, the courts continue to refer to such motions as challenges to the array. *See e.g.,* Commonwealth v. Underwood, 3 Mass.App. 522, 535, 335 N.E.2d 915 (1975).

A motion for appropriate relief from trial by a jury allegedly not selected in accordance with law—that is, a motion for discharge of the panel—is properly made only before trial. G.L. c. 277, § 47A. Brunson v. Commonwealth, 369 Mass. 106, 337 N.E.2d 895 (1975); Commonwealth v. Rodriquez, 364 Mass. 87, 91, 300 N.E.2d 192 (1973); Commonwealth v. Underwood, 3 Mass.App. 522, 536, 335 N.E.2d 915 (1975). Mass.R.Crim.P. 13(c).

See ABA *Standards Relating to Trial by Jury* § 2.3 (Approved Draft, 1968), Rules of Criminal Procedure (U.L.A.) rule 511(d) (1974) (incorporating by reference Uniform Jury Selection and Service Act [U.L.A.] § 12 [1970]); Fed.R.Crim.P. 6(b)(1).

Subdivision (b).

(b)(1). This subdivision is based upon the first paragraph of G.L. c. 234, § 28. *See* Fed.R.Crim.P. 24(a); ABA *Standards Relating to Trial by Jury* § 2.4 (Approved Draft, 1968); ABA *Standards Relating to the Prosecution Function* § 5.3(c) (Approved Draft, 1971); ABA *Standards Relating to the Defense Function* § 7.2(c) (Approved Draft, 1971); Rules of Criminal Procedure (U.L.A.) Rule 512(b) (1974).

The purpose of G.L. c. 234, § 28 and of this rule is manifestly to determine whether prospective jurors are free from interest, bias, and prejudice in the case in which they are drawn to sit. Commonwealth v. Beneficial Finance Co., 360 Mass. 188, 295, 275 N.E.2d 33, 52 A.L.R.3d 1143 (1971), cert. denied, 92 S.Ct. 2433, 407 U.S. 910, 914, 32

L.Ed.2d 689 (1972); *accord* Commonwealth v. Montecalvo, 367 Mass. 46, 50, 323 N.E.2d 888 (1975).

It has been consistently held that Federal Rule 24(a) permits the trial judge a large range of discretion in the latitude and manner of voir dire examination, subject to the essential demands of fairness. E.g., Eastern Renovating Corp. v. Roman Catholic Bishop of Springfield, 554 F.2d 4 (1st Cir.1977); United States v. Desmarais, 531 F.2d 632, 633 (1st Cir.1976). This comports with Massachusetts practice which has been uniformly stated to give the trial judge broad discretion "whether to refine or improve on the subjects of . . . § 28, by going into more detail." Commonwealth v. Lacy, 371 Mass. 363, 373, 358 N.E.2d 419 (1976); Commonwealth v. Harrison, 368 Mass. 366, 371, 331 N.E.2d 873 (1975). E.g., Commonwealth v. Kudish, 362 Mass. 627, 631–32, 289 N.E.2d 856 (1972). Because the trial judge has "a fair leeway in deciding how deep the probe should go, having in view the nature of the case as . . . [he] apprehends it at the start," *Harrison,* supra, there is no requirement that any particular form or number of questions be asked. *See* e.g., Commonwealth v. Hicks, Mass.Adv.Sh. (1979) 1, 384 N.E.2d 1206; Commonwealth v. Horton, Mass.Adv.Sh. (1978) 2548, 380 N.E.2d 687; Commonwealth v. McCants, 3 Mass.App. 596, 598, 337 N.E.2d 918 (1975).

The provision of this subdivision which requires the approval of the court for the introduction of extrinsic evidence is consistent with prior practice although not statutorily mandated. Commonwealth v. DiStasio, 294 Mass. 273, 1 N.E.2d 189 (1936).

Prior practice was to pose the so-called "statutory questions" to the jurors as a group in non-capital cases and individually, out of the presence of other prospective jurors, in capital cases. Commonwealth v. Ventura, 294 Mass. 113, 1 N.E.2d 30 (1936). Because the need to interrogate each juror regarding the death penalty no longer exists, there is likewise no reason in the usual case why the statutory questions may not be asked of the jurors as a group. Commonwealth v. Montecalvo, 367 Mass. 46, 48–49, 323 N.E.2d 888 (1975). *See* Commonwealth v. Harrison, 368 Mass. 366, 369 n. 5, 331 N.E.2d 873 (1975). Individual questioning may be commanded, however, by the facts and circumstances of the particular case. *Commonwealth v. Montecalvo,* supra at 50 n. 2. *Compare* subdivision (b)(2), infra.

Whether the questions upon voir dire are to be posed by the judge or by the parties or their attorneys is another matter fully within the discretion of the trial judge. The sole purpose of the voir dire is to provide the parties with a means of discovering grounds for challenges for cause and to enable them to intelligently exercise peremptory challenges. The procedure is subject to abuse by counsel who utilize voir dire to influence jurors, however, ABA *Standards Relating to Trial by Jury,* § 2.4, comment at 64 (Approved Draft, 1968), and unless carefully regulated, can consume an inordinate amount of court time. For these reasons, it is suggested that the better practice when voir dire is confined to the subjects of G.L. c. 234, § 28 is for the judge to conduct the interrogation. If further questioning is desirable, it should be by the judge upon suggestion of counsel. *Compare* ABA *Standards,* supra (judge is to submit such additional questions as he deems proper), and Rules of Criminal Procedure (U.L.A.) Rule 512(b) (1974) (judge *shall* permit questioning by the parties).

(b)(2). The basis of this subdivision is found in the second paragraph of G.L. c. 234, § 28, as amended, St.1975, c. 335. The amendment of § 28 conformed the statute to the Supreme Court's decision in Ham v. South Carolina, 93 S.Ct. 848, 409 U.S. 524, 35 L.Ed.2d 46 (1973), which recognized that some cases present circumstances in which an impermissible threat to the fair trial guaranteed by the due process clause of the fourteenth amendment is posed when a judge refuses to question prospective jurors specifically as to racial prejudice. *Ham* did not announce a universally applicable rule, however, but a standard requiring assessment of the facts of each case. Ristaino v. Ross, 96 S.Ct. 1017, 424 U.S. 589, 47 L.Ed.2d 258 (1976).

General Laws c. 234, § 28 is not limited by its terms to racial prejudice, but is directed at any bias which may result from

the impact of considerations which may cause a decision or decisions to be made in whole or in part upon issues extraneous to the case, including, but not limited to, community attitudes, possible exposure to potentially prejudicial material or possible preconceived opinions toward the credibility of certain classes of persons. . . .

It should perhaps be noted that "community attitudes" or "exposure to potentially prejudicial material" may be so pervasive as to suggest a motion to transfer for prejudice if recognized prior to trial. Mass. R.Crim.P. 38(b)(1).

The procedure under § 28 is in two steps. It must first appear to the satisfaction of the court that a prospective juror or jurors may not be indifferent as a result of matters extraneous to the case. It is preferable that the court be apprised of the possibility of bias by a motion that prospective jurors be interrogated as to possible prejudice, *see* Commonwealth v. Lumley, 367 Mass. 213, 216, 327 N.E.2d 683 (1975); Commonwealth v. Rodriques, 364 Mass. 87, 92–93, 300 N.E.2d 192 (1973), and that the motion be accompanied by an affidavit specifying the facts which defendant alleges make him subject to bias. *See* Commonwealth v. Pinckney, 365 Mass. 70, 309 N.E.2d 495 (1974). In Commonwealth v. Harrison, 2 Mass.App. 775, 321 N.E.2d 672 (1975), affirmed, 368 Mass. 366 (1975), the court found inadequate an affidavit which

amounted to no more than an argument of law intended to persuade the court to adopt the defendant's position on the utility of the requested questions and in no way informed the judge as to the possible injection into the case of prejudice stemming from possibly disparate political views or cultural values.

Id. at 779. *Accord Commonwealth v. Pinckney,* supra. *See* Commonwealth v. Peters, Mass.Adv.Sh. (1977) 684, 689, 361 N.E.2d 1277 ("absence of even minimal substantiation").

If the court finds that there is a basis to the allegations, "the court *shall,* or the parties or their attorneys may . . . examine the juror specifically" as to the extraneous issues. G.L. c. 234, § 28 (emphasis added). Under prior case law, and pursuant to § 28 previous to its 1975 amendment, this specific examination was discretionary even if impaired indifference were shown.

Both under this subdivision and G.L. c. 234, § 28 the questioning of each venireman as to extraneous issues is to be conducted out of the presence of those not yet or already called.

(b)(3). The time for challenge of prospective juror is generally considered to end once the jury is impanelled. Commonwealth v. Galvin, 323 Mass. 205, 80 N.E.2d 825 (1948). It has been held, however, that the right of a judge to dismiss a juror for cause and to provide for the selection of another juror in his place continues even after the jury is impanelled but before the trial actually starts. Commonwealth v. Monahan, 349 Mass. 139, 207 N.E.2d 29 (1965); 30 MASS.PRACTICE SERIES (Smith) § 1047 (1970, Supp.1978). *See* ABA *Standards Relating to Trial by Jury* § 2.5 (Approved Draft, 1968); Rules of Criminal Procedure (U.L.A.) Rule 512(c) (1974).

Subdivision (c). The substance of subdivision (c)(1) is taken from G.L. c. 234, § 29. See Superior Court Rule 6 (1974); ABA *Standards Relating to Trial by Jury* § 2.6 (Approved Draft, 1968); Rules of Criminal Procedure (U.L.A.) Rule 512(d) (1974).

"The essential nature of the peremptory challenge is that it is one exercised without a reason stated, without inquiry and without being subject to the court's control." Swain v. Alabama, 85 S.Ct. 824, 380 U.S. 202, 220, 13 L.Ed.2d 759 (1965). Therefore, it had been held that a claim of denial of trial by an impartial jury based on the fact that the Commonwealth utilizes its peremptory challenges to exclude a particular sex or race from the panel must fail. Commonwealth v. Mitchell, 367 Mass. 419, 420, 326 N.E.2d 6 (1975). However, in Commonwealth v. Soares, Mass.Adv.Sh. (1979) 593, 387 N.E.2d 499, decided under article 12 of the Declaration of Rights rather than the equal protection clause of the fourteenth amendment, the Supreme Judicial Court held that the use of peremptory challenges to exclude prospective jurors solely by virtue of their membership in, or affiliation with, particular, defined groupings in the community is proscribed. Id. at 624–25.

[The] exercise of peremptory challenges to exclude members of discrete groups, solely on the basis of bias presumed to derive from that individual's membership in the group, contravenes the requirement [of the jury drawn from a representative cross-section of the community] inherent in art. 12 of the Declaration of Rights. In so holding, we recognize that no defendant is entitled to a petit jury proportionally representing every group in the community; nor are members of particular groups insulated from the proper use of peremptory challenges to exclude any individual on any other ground. What both parties are constitutionally entitled to expect is "a petit jury that is as near an approximation of the ideal cross-section of the community as the process of random draw permits."

Id. at 627, *quoting, People v. Wheeler,* 22 Cal.3d 258, 277, 148 Cal.Rptr. 890, 583 P.2d 748 (1978). While the proper use of peremptory challenges may be presumed, that presumption is rebuttable by either party on a showing that: 1) a pattern of conduct has developed whereby several prospective jurors who have been challenged peremptorily are members of a discrete group, and 2) there is a likelihood that they are being excluded from the jury solely by reason of their group membership. Id. at 628–29.

If the court finds that the burden of justification is not sustained as to any of the questioned peremptory challenges, the presumption of their validity is rebutted. Accordingly, the court must then conclude that the jury as constituted fails to comply with the representative cross-section requirement, and it must dismiss the jurors thus far selected. So too it must quash any remaining venire, since the complaining party is entitled to a random draw from an entire venire—not one that has been partially or totally stripped of members of a cognizable group by the improper use of peremptory challenges. Upon such dismissal a different venire shall be drawn and the jury selection process may begin anew.

Id. at 631–32, *quoting People v. Wheeler,* supra, at 282.

Subdivision (c)(2) is borrowed almost entirely from G.L. c. 234, § 29.

It should be noted that no irregularity in a writ of venire facias or in the drawing, summoning, returning, or *impanelling* of jurors is sufficient to set aside a verdict unless the objecting party has been "injured" by the irregularity and unless the objection is made before verdict. G.L. c. 234, § 32. Commonwealth v. Montecalvo, 367 Mass. 46, 51, 323 N.E.2d 888 (1975); Commonwealth v. McKay, 363 Mass. 220, 223–24, 294 N.E.2d 213 (1973).

Subdivision (d). This subdivision parallels G.L. c. 234, § 26B (as amended). *Compare Rules of Criminal Procedure* (U.L.A.) Rule 511(c) (1974), which provides for "additional" jurors, *with ABA Standards Relating to Trial by Jury* § 2.7. (Approved Draft, 1968), which has provisions for both "alternate" and "additional" jurors. Under an alternate juror system, one or more persons specifically identified as alternates are chosen in advance of trial and will be designated to take the place of a juror who is discharged prior to the time the jury retires, or in some jurisdictions, prior to verdict. ABA *Standards,* supra, comment at 79. *See* Fed.R.Crim.P. 24(c). Massachusetts employs the additional juror system, G.L. c. 234, § 26B, approved in Uniform Rule 511(c), *supra,* and preferred by the ABA *Standards,* supra, comment at 80.

Subdivision (d)(3) adopts a procedure contained in Cal.Penal Code § 1089 (Deering, 1971). This practice has been rejected, however, by the ABA *Standards,* supra, comment at 82, and in the 1975 amendments to the Federal Rules of Criminal Procedure.

Subdivision (e).

(e)(1). This subdivision reiterates prior Massachusetts practice in leaving the decision whether to sequester the jury in the discretion of the trial judge. 30 MASS.PRACTICE SERIES (Smith) § 1042 (1970); Commonwealth v. Marshall, Mass.Adv.Sh. (1977) 1530, 364 N.E.2d 1237.

(e)(2)–(3). Drawn in part from Fla.R.Crim.P. 3.370 (1975), these subdivisions represent a significant departure from prior Massachusetts practice. In cases where sequestration is unnecessary, forcing the jury to remain in a body after submission of the case or the beginning of deliberations may cause hardship to jurors or their families which is not, in balance, necessary for protection of the defendant's interests, nor justified by the interests of justice. *See* Commonwealth v. Watkins, Mass.Adv.Sh. (1978) 1646, 1673–74, 379 N.E.2d 1040 (defendant's motion to excuse jury from further deliberation for the evening within the discretion of judge).

Rule 21. Sequestration of Witnesses

(Applicable to District Court and Superior Court)

Upon his own motion or the motion of either party, the judge may, prior to or during the examination of a witness, order any witness or witnesses other than the defendant to be excluded from the courtroom.

Reporter's Notes

This rule is based upon former G.L. c. 276, § 39 (Rev.St. [1836] c. 135, § 14) which was applicable to the District Court.

The power of a judge to control the progress and, within the limits of the adversary system, the shape of a trial, is universally held to include the broad discretionary power to sequester witnesses before, during, and after their testimony. Geders v. United States, 96 S.Ct. 1330, 425 U.S. 80, 47 L.Ed.2d 592 (1976); Holder v. United States, 150 U.S. 91, 92 (1893); United States v. Robinson, 502 F.2d 894 (7th Cir.1974); United States v. Eastwood, 489 F.2d 818, 821 (5th Cir. 1973); Commonwealth v. Dougan, Mass.Adv.Sh. (1979) 380, 400; Commonwealth v. Watkins, 373 Mass. 849, 370 N.E.2d 701 (1977); Commonwealth v. Vanderpool, 367 Mass. 743 (1975); Commonwealth v. Blackburn, 354 Mass. 200, 237 N.E.2d 35 (1968); Commonwealth v. Follansbee, 155 Mass. 274, 29 N.E.2d 471 (1892); Commonwealth v. Parry, 1 Mass.App. 730, 736, 306 N.E.2d 855 (1974).

Although sequestration may be well used to prevent the occurrence of perjury, it serves an equally important function in preventing one witness' testimony from being inadvertently molded by the testimony of other witnesses. "The process of sequestration consists merely in preventing one prospective witness from being taught by hearing another's testimony...." 6 J. WIGMORE EVIDENCE § 1838 at 461 (Chadbourne rev. 1976). It additionally aids in detecting testimony which is less than candid, see WIGMORE, supra, and prevents improper attempts during recess to influence the witness' testimony in light of that already given. *Geders v. United States,* supra, at 87.

Since the sequestration of witnesses is within the discretion of the judge, the judge may order that only some of the witnesses be removed from the courtroom or kept separated. In Commonwealth v. Therrien, 359 Mass. 500, 269 N.E.2d 687 (1971), it was held proper for the trial judge to except from a general order of sequestration one witness deemed "essential to the management of the case." Id. at 508.

In conformity with prior practice, the court is to have discretionary power to exclude the testimony of a witness who remains in court in violation of a court order. In Commonwealth v. Crowley, 168 Mass. 121, 46 N.E. 415 (1897), a witness called by the defendant to impeach the testimony of a prosecution witness was not allowed to testify because he had remained in court in violation of a court order. Although at the time of the court order the defense had not intended to use that witness at trial, the exclusion of his testimony was upheld because during the progress of the trial it became apparent that he might be called for impeachment purposes. Conversely, the court may receive the testimony of a witness who is present at trial in violation of a sequestration order. Commonwealth v. Shagoury, Mass. App.Adv.Sh. (1978) 927, 380 N.E.2d 708; Commonwealth v. Hall, 86 Mass. (4 Allen) 305, 306 (1862). In addition, a trial judge may revoke or modify a previous sequestration order. Commonwealth v. Parry, 1 Mass.App. 730, 736, 306 N.E.2d 855 (1974).

The rule by its terms is inapplicable to a defendant. A sequestration order would affect a defendant quite differently from the way it affects a non-party witness, because of the defendant's need to consult with counsel. *Geders v. United States*, supra, at 88.

In addition, the defendant as a matter of right can be and usually is present for all testimony. E.g., Mass.R.Crim.P. 18, unless removed for disruptive behavior, Mass.R.Crim.P. 45.

Rule 22. Objections

(Applicable to Superior Court and jury sessions in District Court)

Exceptions to rulings or orders of the court are unnecessary and for all purposes for which an exception has heretofore been necessary, it is sufficient that a party, at the time the ruling or order of the court is made or sought, makes known to the court the action which he desires the court to take or his objection to the action of the court, but if a party has no opportunity to object to a ruling or order, the absence of an objection does not thereafter prejudice him.

If a party objects to a ruling or order of the court, he may state the precise legal grounds of his objection, but he shall not argue or further discuss such grounds unless the court calls upon him for such argument or discussion.

Reporter's Notes

Rule 22 restates Rule 51 of the Federal Rules of Criminal Procedure and is substantially similar to Rule 46 of both the Massachusetts and Federal Rules of Civil Procedure. *See* Superior Court Rule 8 (1974).

For generations of Massachusetts practitioners the relationship between the saving of an exception and the right of review was so firmly established in the appellate procedure of the Commonwealth and so universally understood and applied that discussion of the validity of the requirement was foreclosed. *See* e.g., Commonwealth v. Underwood, 358 Mass. 506, 509, 265 N.E.2d 577 (1970); SUPERIOR COURT RULES, 1974, ANNOTATED, 281–82 (Mass.Bar ed. 1975). The proper saving of an exception was the first and fundamental step to secure a review by bill of exceptions or by appeal, *Commonwealth v. Underwood*, supra; Commonwealth v. Dinnall, 366 Mass. 165, 314 N.E.2d 903 (1974), and the failure to seasonably except vitiated the right to review of the issue to which exception was not taken, Commonwealth v. Boudreau, 362 Mass. 378, 285 N.E.2d 915 (1972), save for the rare instance when an appellate court would review such questions because of a "substantial risk of a miscarriage of justice." Commonwealth v. Freeman, 352 Mass. 556, 564, 227 N.E.2d 3 (1967); Commonwealth v. Williams, Mass.App.Adv.Sh. (1979) 253, 386 N.E.2d 744 (Rescript); Commonwealth v. Harris, 371 Mass. 462, 471, 358 N.E.2d 982 (1976); Commonwealth v. Fields, 371 Mass. 274, 277, 356 N.E.2d 1211 (1976).

It is felt that the requirement of exceptions exalts form over substance in an unnecessarily ritualistic and time-consuming procedure. The draftsmen of Mass.R.Civ.P. 46 followed the lead of both the federal civil and criminal rules in abolishing the exception. This rule eliminates the requirement from criminal trials. That decision is premised upon the practical observation that an objection by counsel or counsel's request for specific action is sufficient to indicate to the court counsel's position on any issue and that to additionally require an exception is superfluous. *See* Rules of Criminal Procedure (U.L.A.) rule 755 (1974).

It has been argued that the requirement of an exception should be retained to provide the trial judge with an opportunity to reconsider his ruling on an objection and to eliminate specious arguments by

counsel, Commonwealth v. Foley, 358 Mass. 233, 263 N.E.2d 451 (1970). Realistically, however, the taking of an exception apprises the judge of nothing which is apt to affect his initial ruling, nor does the requirement of an exception in any way compel counsel to take exception only to rulings on substantial matters.

The practice of requiring exceptions had led appellate courts to scrutinize records so as to determine whether holding that a defendant had waived objections by his failure to save exceptions could result in a miscarriage of justice. The scope of such review equates with that if no exceptions were required. *See* e.g., Commonwealth v. Williams, Mass.App.Adv.Sh. (1979) 253, 386 N.E.2d 744 (Rescript). Further, rigidly requiring that exceptions be saved led to "anomalous" results. In Commonwealth v. Nelson, 3 Mass.App. 90, 101, 323 N.E.2d 752 (1975), the court reviewed the denial of a motion for a new trial to which denial no exception was taken because the appellant's co-defendant had properly saved an exception to a similarly-grounded motion.

Superior Court rule 8 (1974) provides that in criminal cases, objections to evidence shall be decided without argument unless the presiding justice calls upon the parties to state the grounds on which the evidence is offered or objected to.

Having once stated the grounds, if so requested, counsel is not to further comment thereon unless the court requires elucidation. *See* Fed.R.Evid. 103(a). It is the intent of this rule that if a statement of grounds is requested, the court may allow such statement to be made in open court or at the bench and out of hearing of the jury. *See* Fed.R.Evid. 103(c).

Rule 23. Stipulations

(a) Essential Elements. Any stipulation to an essential element of a charged offense entered by the parties before or during trial shall be in writing and signed by the prosecutor, the defendant, and defense counsel. Any such stipulation shall be read to the jury before the close of the Commonwealth's case and may be introduced into evidence.

(b) Other Stipulations. Any other stipulation shall be placed on the record before the close of evidence and may be read or otherwise communicated to the jury or introduced into evidence in the discretion of the court.

Adopted April 29, 2015, effective July 1, 2015.

Reporter's Notes

Rule 23 is intended to fill a gap in the Rules of Criminal Procedure identified by the Supreme Judicial Court in *Commonwealth v. Ortiz*, 466 Mass. 475 (2013). The rule provides for the manner in which stipulations of fact agreed to by the parties before or during trial are to be memorialized and used at trial. Rule 11 governs stipulations of fact agreed to at the pretrial conference, but prior to Rule 23 there were no rules that applied to such stipulations reached after the filing of the pretrial conference report at the pretrial hearing. Rule 23 remedies that deficiency, supplementing Rule 11's provisions concerning stipulations of fact.

Rule 23(a) Essential Elements

Rule 23(a) is modeled on Rule 11 in its treatment of stipulations of fact, but its coverage is narrower. Rule 11(a)(2)(A) requires that the pretrial conference report include "any stipulations of fact" agreed to by the parties at the pretrial conference and further provides that the report be "subscribed by the prosecuting attorney and counsel for the defendant, and . . . when the report contains stipulations as to material facts, by the defendant." Rule 11(a)(2)(A) requires the parties to file the pretrial conference report with the clerk of court and provides that agreements contained in the report, including stipulations, "shall be binding on the parties and shall control the subsequent course of the proceeding." These requirements for binding stipulations of fact are consistent with such rules of other states. See, e.g., Ark. R. Cr. P. 20.4, Pretrial Conference; Vt. R. Cr. P. 17.1, Pretrial Conference; Ia. R. Cr. P. 2.16, Pretrial Conference; Haw. R. Cr. P. 17.1, Pretrial Conference.

Unlike Rule 11, Rule 23(a) is limited to stipulations to "an essential element of a charged offense," that is, a fact that the Commonwealth must prove beyond a reasonable doubt in order to secure a conviction. To take a common example, in a trial for operating a motor vehicle while under influence of intoxicating liquor, G.L. c. 90, § 24(1)(a)(1), the Commonwealth must prove three elements, one of which is "that the defendant operated a motor vehicle." *Commonwealth v. Cabral*, 77 Mass. App. Ct. 909, 909, rev. denied, 458 Mass. 1107 (2010). See Criminal Model Jury Instruction for Use in the District Court 5.310, *Operating Under the Influence of Intoxicating Liquor* (2013). If the parties stipulate to such operation, the Commonwealth's burden of production for that element is satisfied, foreclosing the need for further proof in that regard. See *Commonwealth v. Ortiz*, 466 Mass. 475, 481 (2013). Rule 23(a) thus requires that a stipulation subject to its coverage be memorialized, that the defendant formally express his or her agreement to the stipulation, and that it be made a matter of record. Moreover, because the stipulated fact constitutes sufficient evidence, maybe the only evidence, of the element in question, the rule requires that the stipulation be read to the jury before the prosecution rests, affording the judge the discretion to decide whether it should further be entered into evidence and given to the jury as an exhibit. The model jury instructions for the charged crime set out its constituent elements, providing a ready reference for the facts subject to Rule 23(a).

Although a stipulated element under Rule 23(a) relieves the Commonwealth of its burden of producing evidence to prove that element, *Ortiz*, 466 Mass. at 481, it is distinct from a so-called stipulated trial, in which a defendant stipulates to all of the facts conclusive of guilt in order to preserve his or her right to appeal the judge's rulings on one or more pretrial issues. See, e.g., *Commonwealth v. Brown*, 55 Mass. App. Ct. 440 (2002). Because a stipulated trial is tantamount to a guilty plea, the defendant is entitled to the safeguards applicable in a guilty plea or admission to sufficient facts, informing him or her of the consequences of the stipulation and providing a hearing to ensure that the stipulation was entered into knowingly and voluntarily. *Id.* at 448–449. See Rule 12. In contrast, a stipulated element under Rule 23(a) occurs in the context of a contested trial, and it represents a considered, tactical decision by the defendant and defense counsel which is a part of the defendant's litigation strategy. In the ordinary case, Rule 23(a)'s requirement, following that of Rule 11(a)(2)(A), that the stipulation be written and signed by the defendant should adequately demonstrate that the defendant understands and agrees with the decision to stipulate. Requiring in addition a colloquy such as that required for a guilty plea or an admission to sufficient facts seems unnecessary. Cf. *Commonwealth v. Ramsey*, 466 Mass. 489, 496 n. 8 (2013) (observing that plea colloquies required for stipulated trials had no application to a defendant's trial concession, as part of a litigation strategy, that he possessed crack and powder cocaine). Of course, if the judge thinks it appropriate in the circumstances of a particular case to inquire, on the record out of the presence of the jury, in order to make the record clear that the defendant understands the evidentiary consequences of the stipulation and/or that the defendant's agreement to the stipulation is voluntary, the judge has the discretion to do so. See, e.g., *Commonwealth v. Walorz*, 79 Mass. App. Ct. 132, 135–36, rev. denied, 460 Mass. 1103 (2011) (noting trial judge's detailed explanation to defendant of the effect of a stipulation to two elements of the charged offense in holding that a colloquy was not required).

A stipulated element subject to Rule 23(a) is also distinct from a defendant's concession that an essential element will be proved or that he or she is guilty of a lesser included offense. Unlike a stipulation of fact agreed to by the parties, the Commonwealth is not a participant in a defendant's strategic decision to concede that the evidence is sufficient to satisfy a portion of the charged offense. Nor does such a concession relieve the Commonwealth of its burden to prove every element of the charged offense beyond a reasonable doubt. See *Commonwealth v. Charles*, 456 Mass. 378, 383 (2010) (in a narcotics case, defense counsel's concession in opening and closing that defendant possessed "drugs" neither amounted to a tacit stipulation of that fact nor relieved the Commonwealth of its burden to prove each element beyond a reasonable doubt). Rather, a defendant's concession that some part of the Commonwealth's case is beyond dispute is a recognized trial tactic that, like other defense tactics, ordinarily requires no confirmation that the defendant understands its risks and agrees with its employment. The Supreme Judicial Court accordingly has declined to exercise its supervisory authority to require a colloquy to confirm that a defendant understands, and agrees with, a trial concession that he is guilty of a lesser included offense, deferring instead to the sound discretion of the trial judge concerning the need for any such inquiry. See *Commonwealth v. Evelyn*, 470 Mass. 765, 770 (2015). Similarly, Rule 23, including Rule 23(a)'s requirement of a signed writing, does not apply to a defendant's concession of some fact, element, or guilt of a lesser included offense.

Rule 23(b) Other Stipulations

The purpose of limiting Rule 23(a) to facts constituting an essential element of a charged offense is to avoid requiring a formal writing, subscribed by counsel and the defendant, to the variety of other factual stipulations that have long been a non-problematic part of criminal trials. Those stipulations are treated by the less formal provisions of Rule 23(b), which applies to stipulations during trial to evidentiary facts, such as those necessary to authenticate a document or to qualify a witness as an expert, and to facts that, while material, are not sufficient to prove an essential element of a charged offense. For example, in the above-hypothesized trial for operating under the influence, the fact that the defendant had told the police that he was driving a car at the time in question would certainly be material in determining whether he had operated a motor vehicle. However, standing alone, that confession would not be sufficient to prove the element of operation, see *Commonwealth v. Leonard*, 401 Mass. 470, 473 (1988), and the parties' stipulation that the defendant had so confessed would not be subject to Rule 23(a)'s requirements. Such stipulations of evidentiary and material facts have long been utilized to expedite trials where—in the judgment of the parties—nothing would be gained by insisting on a formal mode of proof. Requiring a subscribed, written stipulation in such circumstances would undercut its utility without any apparent gain.

Rule 23(b) does not require that stipulations subject to its coverage be written, mandating only that they be placed on the record before the close of evidence. The rule leaves it to the judge to decide how that is done and, for stipulations of a material fact, how the stipulation should be communicated to the jury. Nothing in the rule prohibits a judge, as a matter of discretion, from requiring that a particular stipulation of fact be reduced to writing, whether because of its complexity or for any other good cause.

Rule 24. Opening Statements; Arguments; Instructions to Jury

(Applicable to Superior Court and jury sessions in District Court)

(a) Opening and Closing Statements; Arguments.

(1) *Order of Presentation*. The Commonwealth shall present its opening statement first. The defendant may present an opening statement of his defense after the opening statement of the Commonwealth or after the close of the Commonwealth's evidence. The defendant shall present his closing argument first.

(2) *Time Limitation.* Counsel for each party shall be allowed fifteen minutes for an opening statement and thirty minutes for argument; but before the opening or the argument commences, the judge on motion or sua sponte, may reasonably reduce or extend the time.

(b) Instructions to Jury; Objection. At the close of the evidence or at such earlier time during the trial as the judge reasonably directs, any party may file written requests that the judge instruct the jury on the law as set forth in the requests. The judge shall inform counsel of his proposed action upon requests prior to their arguments to the jury. No party may assign as error the giving or the failure to give an instruction unless he objects thereto before the jury retires to consider its verdict, specifying the matter to which he objects and the grounds of his objection. Upon request, reasonable time shall be given to each party to object to the charge before the jury retires. Where either party wishes to object to the charge or to request additional instructions, the objection or the request shall be made out of the hearing of the jury, or where appropriate, out of the presence of the jury.

Reporter's Notes

The language of this rule substantially parallels that of Mass. R.Civ.P. 51. *See* National Advisory Commission on Criminal Justice Standards and Goals, *Courts*, Standard 4.15 (1973).

Subdivision (a). Drawn from Rules of Criminal Procedure (U.L.A.) Rule 521 (1974), this subdivision (a)(1) establishes the order of presentation of opening statements and closing arguments.

The fifteen-minute limitation on opening statements and thirty-minute limitation on arguments of subdivision (a)(2) are carried over from earlier rules of court. Superior Court Rules 7, 68 (1974); Supreme Judicial Court Rule 2:48 (1967: 351 Mass. 768). It is intended that under this rule only one attorney for each side is to participate, contrary to the provisions of Mass.R.Civ.P. 51 and Supreme Judicial Court Rule 2:48.

While placing time limits upon opening statements and arguments, and limiting arguments to a single counsel, Rule 24 does not otherwise affect their respective functions.

The proper function of an opening is to outline in a general way the nature of the case which counsel expects to be able to prove or support by evidence. He should not be allowed to state facts which are irrelevant or for any reason plainly incompetent.

Posell v. Herscovitz, 237 Mass. 513, 514, 130 N.E. 69 (1921); *see* **Commonwealth v. Clark, 292 Mass. 409, 410, 198 N.E. 641 (1935); Commonwealth v. LePage, 352 Mass. 403, 409, 226 N.E.2d 200 (1967).** The refusal by counsel to confine his opening statement within the established boundaries constitutes unprofessional conduct, S.J.C. Rule 3:22A, *Disciplinary Rules Applicable to Practice as a Prosecutor or as a Defense Lawyer*, PF 11, DF 12 (February 14, 1979), and may amount to such misconduct as to warrant his expulsion from the courtroom and subjection to disciplinary proceedings. **United States v. Dinitz, 96 S.Ct. 1075, 424 U.S. 600, 47 L.Ed.2d 267 (1976).**

An opening statement has a narrow purpose and scope. It is to state what evidence will be presented, to make it easier for the jurors to understand what is to follow, and to relate parts of the evidence and testimony to the whole; it is not an occasion for argument. To make statements which will not or cannot be supported by proof is, if it relates to significant elements of the case, professional misconduct. Moreover, it is fundamentally unfair to an opposing party to allow an attorney, with the standing and prestige inherent in being an officer of the court, to present to the jury statements not susceptible of proof but intended to influence the jury in reaching a verdict.

A trial judge is under a duty, in order to protect the integrity of the trial, to take prompt and affirmative action to stop such professional misconduct.

United States v. Dinitz, supra, Burger, C.J., *concurring* at 612. *See* **Commonwealth v. Fazio, Mass.Adv.Sh. (1978) 1617, 378 N.E.2d 648;** ABA *Standards Relating to the Prosecution Function* § 5.5 (Approved Draft, 1971); ABA *Standards Relating to the Defense Function* § 7.4 (Approved Draft, 1971).

Although Massachusetts practice permits counsel "great latitude" in closing argument, **Commonwealth v. Pettie, 363 Mass. 836, 840, 298 N.E.2d 836 (1973),**

[i]t is the duty of a judge sitting with a jury to guard against improper arguments.... Whether he shall do this by stopping counsel in the course of such an argument, by instructing the jury to disregard such an argument, or by combining both methods, rests largely in the discretion of the judge.

Commonwealth v. Witschi, 301 Mass. 459, 462, 17 N.E.2d 549 (1938). *Accord* **Commonwealth v. Montecalvo, 367 Mass. 46, 56, 323 N.E.2d 888 (1975).** *See* **Commonwealth v. Earltop, Mass.Adv.Sh. (1977) 532, 539, 361 N.E.2d 220** (Hennessey, C.J., concurring) and cases cited: ABA *Standards Relating to the Function of the Trial Judge* § 5.10 (Approved Draft, 1972).

Where counsel "repeatedly and deliberately sail[s] unnecessarily close to the wind . . . beyond permissible limits," **Commonwealth v. Redmond, 370 Mass. 591, 597, 351 N.E.2d 501 (1976),** thus bringing unsworn testimony to the attention of the jury, the cumulative prejudice may be such that curative instructions are insufficient. The remedy in such instance is an order for a new trial. *Commonwealth v. Redmond*, supra. Further, where counsel misstates the law, a request for a curative instruction is denied, and the judge's general instruction that arguments are not evidence to be weighed by the jury is insufficient to allay the resulting prejudice, a new trial is required. **Commonwealth v. Killelea, 370 Mass. 638, 351 N.E.2d 509 (1976).** Because of these serious consequences, it is obvious that overreaching in argument—as in openings—may constitute unprofessional conduct. S.J.C. Rule 3:22A, *Disciplinary Rules Applicable to Practice as a Prosecutor or as a Defense Lawyer*, PF 13, PF 14 (February 14, 1979).

Subdivision (b). The incorporation of the civil practice form of requests for and objection to instructions into criminal practice is felt to be appropriate because the same basic principles apply to both types of proceedings. *Compare* Fed.R.Crim.P. 30 *with* Fed.R.Civ.P. 51. Subdivision (b) adopts what had been a long-standing practice before its formalization as a rule of the Superior Court. SUPERIOR COURT RULES, 1974, ANNOTATED 290–91 (Mass.Bar.Ed.1975); *see* e.g., **Commonwealth v. Boutwell, 162 Mass. 230, 38 N.E. 441 (1894); Commonwealth v. Hassan, 235 Mass. 26, 31, 126 N.E. 287 (1920).**

The rule differs from Mass.R.Civ.P. 51 in requiring that objections to the charge or requests for additional instructions be made out of the hearing or presence of the jury in all cases. This comports with Rules of Criminal Procedure (U.L.A.) Rule 523(b) (1974) and ABA *Standards Relating to Trial by Jury* § 4.6(c) (Approved Draft, 1968). *See* Fed.R.Crim.P. 30.

Rule 25. Motion for Required Finding of Not Guilty

(Applicable to District Court and Superior Court)

(a) Entry by Court. The judge on motion of a defendant or on his own motion shall enter a finding of not guilty of the offense charged in an indictment or complaint or any part thereof after the evidence on either side is closed if the evidence is insufficient as a matter of law to sustain a conviction on the charge. If a defendant's motion for a required finding of not guilty is made at the close of the Commonwealth's evidence, it shall be ruled upon at that time. If the motion is denied or allowed only in part by the judge, the defendant may offer evidence in his defense without having reserved that right.

(b) Jury Trials.

(1) *Reservation of Decision on Motion.* If a motion for a required finding of not guilty is made at the close of all the evidence, the judge may reserve decision on the motion, submit the case to the jury, and decide the motion before the jury returns a verdict, after the jury returns a verdict of guilty, or after the jury is discharged without having returned a verdict.

(2) *Motion After Discharge of Jury.* If the motion is denied and the case is submitted to the jury, the motion may be renewed within five days after the jury is discharged and may include in the alternative a motion for a new trial. If a verdict of guilty is returned, the judge may on motion set aside the verdict and order a new trial, or order the entry of a finding of not guilty, or order the entry of a finding of guilty of any offense included in the offense charged in the indictment or complaint.

(c) Appeal.

(1) *Right of Appeal Where Motion for Relief Under Subdivision (b) Is Allowed After a Jury Verdict of Guilty.* The Commonwealth shall have the right to appeal to the appropriate appellate court a decision of a judge granting relief under the provisions of subdivisions (b)(1) and (2) of this rule on a motion for required finding of not guilty after the jury has returned a verdict of guilty or on an order for the entry of a finding of guilt of any offense included in the offense charged in the indictment or complaint.

(2) *Costs Upon Appeal.* If an appeal or application therefor is taken by the Commonwealth, the appellate court, upon the written motion of the defendant supported by affidavit, may determine and approve the payment to the defendant of his costs of appeal together with reasonable attorney's fees, if any, to be paid on the order of the trial court upon the entry of the rescript or the denial of the application.

Amended April 6, 1983, effective July 1, 1983; amended effective April 14, 1995.

Reporter's Notes

Rule 25 is derived with a minimum of change from former G.L. c. 278, § 11 (St.1964, c. 108, §§ 1, 2) and conforms in substance to Fed.R.Crim.P. 29. *See* ABA *Standards Relating to Trial by Jury* § 4.5 (Approved Draft, 1968); Rules of Criminal Procedure (U.L.A.) rule 522 (1974); Vt.R.Crim.P. 29; Me.R.Crim.P. 29.

The practical effect of this rule is to abolish the common law motion for a directed verdict and to substitute therefor a motion for a required finding of not guilty. This is essentially a change in terminology and does not presume to alter practice as it has developed relative to the directed verdict. The new term is not unknown in Massachusetts practice. *See* e.g., Commonwealth v. Coyne, 372 Mass. 599, 363 N.E.2d 256 (1977).

Motion for findings of not guilty are a part of Massachusetts practice in the context of nonjury cases, *see* e.g., Commonwealth v. Pursley, 2 Mass.App. 910, 321 N.E.2d 830 (1975) (Rescript), and are extended by this rule to include jury trials in recognition of the fact that juries have no proper function in this area. *See* ABA *Standards*

Relating to Trial by Jury § 4.5(a), comment at 106–08 (Approved Draft, 1968).

Subdivision (a). The requirement that the court rule on a defendant's motion made at the close of the Commonwealth's case at the time such motion is made has recently been added to Massachusetts procedure. *See* Commonwealth v. Kelley, 370 Mass. 147, 149–50, 346 N.E.2d 368 (1976). This rule adopts this approach because of the difference between such a motion and a motion made at the close of all the evidence: in either case a defendant is requesting a judgment on the basis of evidence then before the court, but that evidence is very different at each of the two stages of trial. *See* ABA *Standards Relating to Trial by Jury* § 4.5(b), comment at 108 (Approved Draft, 1968).

On a defendant's motion for a directed verdict at the close of the Commonwealth's case, the defendant's rights become "fixed." If this motion is improperly denied on the basis of the condition of the case when the motion was made, the defendant is entitled to a reversal of the judgment, notwithstanding the introduction of further evidence. Of course, the Commonwealth's proof might deteriorate between the time the Commonwealth rests and the close of all the evidence. In such a case, on renewal of his motion, the defendant's rights would be reappraised in consideration of all the evidence. *Commonwealth v. Kelley,* supra, at n. 1; Commonwealth v. Blow, 370 Mass. 401, 407 n. 4, 348 N.E.2d 794 (1976); Commonwealth v. Aguiar, 370 Mass. 490, 498, 350 N.E.2d 436 (1976).

Under this rule the defendant may offer evidence in his defense without having reserved that right. Fairness requires this result. As the court stated in Jackson v. United States, 250 F.2d 897 (5th Cir.1958), the motion "would be a futile thing if the court could reserve its ruling and force the defendant to an election between resting and being deprived of the benefit of his motion," Id. at 901, because the defendant would be compelled to forfeit either his right to move for acquittal or his right to present evidence in his defense.

Subdivision (b)(1). This subdivision permits the court to reserve a decision on a motion made at the close of all the evidence. The objection stated in the *Jackson* case, supra, is not present in this situation, and G.L. c. 278, § 11 in fact expressly condoned the propriety of what often is referred to in as a judgment notwithstanding the verdict.

Subdivision (b)(2). By giving the court the power to enter a finding of guilty of any lesser included offense or, in the language of G.L. c. 278, § 33E, a lesser degree of guilt, after a verdict of guilty, this rule deviates sharply from prior criminal practice under G.L. c. 278, § 11. Commonwealth v. Jones, 366 Mass. 805, 323 N.E.2d 726 (1975). This has the practical effect of extending to the trial courts, post-verdict, a power in all cases much like that which had previously been reserved to the Supreme Judicial Court in capital cases under G.L. c. 278, § 33E (as amended). This increases the options available to the trial judge after verdict. It is anticipated that through this extension greater judicial economy will result where the evidence will not support the charge, but where the weight of the evidence clearly requires the conviction of a lesser included offense. *See Jones,* supra.

It should be noted that the motion for a new trial which may be made under this subdivision is in addition to those rights which a defendant has under Rule 30(b). Obviously the court should order a new trial pursuant to this rule only upon motion of a defendant since otherwise the subsequent proceeding would be subject to constitutional attack on double jeopardy grounds.

Rule 26.   Requests for Rulings

(Applicable to jury-waived trials in District Court and Superior Court)

Requests for rulings in the trial of a case shall be in writing and shall be presented to the court before the beginning of closing arguments, unless consent of the court is given to present requests later.

Reporter's Notes

Provisions comparable to Rule 26 are found in Fed.R.Crim.P. 23(c) and Rules of Criminal Procedure (U.L.A.) Rule 511(e) (1974). In addition, this rule reflects existing practice under District Court Rule 27 (1972) and Superior Court Rule 70 (1974), which deal with requests for rulings of law in non-jury trials. This rule is intended to secure for the purpose of review a separation of law from fact in cases where the trial judge acts both as factfinder and applier of law. *See* Caleb Pierce, Inc. v. Commonwealth, 354 Mass. 306, 237 N.E.2d 63 (1968).

Although much of the case law concerning requests for rulings has arisen out of the litigation of civil actions, *see* SUPERIOR COURT RULES, 1974, ANNOTATED 290–96 (Mass.Bar Ed.1975), a rule which provides the court with adequate opportunity to pass upon the soundness of requested rulings is equally appropriate in criminal practice. Commonwealth v. Hassan, 235 Mass. 26, 31, 126 N.E. 287 (1920).

Requiring the requests to be made before the beginning of closing arguments serves the function of apprising opposing counsel of the law under which the case will be decided. In Wilson v. United States, 250 F.2d 312, 324 (9th Cir.1957), the court recognized that the failure to honor requests for rulings on the law could hinder the administration of justice, since there is no real difference between the giving of improper instructions in a jury trial and the judge in a nonjury trial effectually instructing himself improperly on the law.

The failure to present written requests seasonably, however, which results in a trial judge's refusal to allow such requests, vitiates any claim of error in the refusal. Commonwealth v. Lammi, 310 Mass. 159, 164, 37 N.E.2d 250 (1941). It is a matter within the sound discretion of the trial judge whether to grant special leave for requests. *See* Finkelman v. Kaufman, 337 Mass. 770, 150 N.E.2d 285 (1958) (Rescript).

It should be noted that under this rule requests are to be made for rulings of law only, and not for findings of fact. Neither this rule nor the prior practice in the Commonwealth requires a judge to honor requests for findings of fact. Stella v. Curtis, 348 Mass. 458, 461, 204 N.E.2d 457 (1965).

Rule 27.   Verdict

(Applicable to jury trials in District Court and Superior Court)

(a) Return. The verdict shall be unanimous. It shall be a general verdict returned by the jury to the judge in open court. The jury shall file a verdict slip with the clerk upon the return of the verdict.

(b) Several Offenses or Defendants. If there are two or more offenses or defendants tried together, the jury may, with the consent of the judge at any time during its deliberations return or be required by the judge to return a verdict or verdicts with respect to the defendants or charges as to which a verdict has been reached; and thereafter the jury may in the discretion of the judge resume deliberation. The judge may declare a mistrial as to any charges upon which the jury cannot agree upon a verdict; provided, however, that the judge may first require the jury to return verdicts on those charges upon which the jury can agree and direct that such verdicts be received and recorded.

(c) Special Questions. The trial judge may submit special questions to the jury.

(d) Poll of Jury. When a verdict is returned and before the verdict is recorded, the jury may be polled in the discretion of the judge. If after the poll there is not a unanimous concurrence, the jury may be directed to retire for further deliberations or may be discharged.

Reporter's Notes

This rule is patterned after Rule 31 of the Federal Rules of Criminal Procedure. Substantially, it reflects current Massachusetts practice as embodied in the common law and in statute. *See* former G.L. c. 278, § 11 (St.1964, c. 108, §§ 1–2).

Subdivision (a). This subdivision requires that the verdict be unanimous. This is consistent with Fed.R.Crim.P. 31(a).

Accord, Me.R.Crim.P. 31(a); Rules of Criminal Procedure (U.L.A.) Rule 535(b) (1974). *But see* ABA *Standards Relating to Trial by Jury* § 1.1(b) (Approved Draft, 1968), which allows for less than a unanimous verdict.

The requirement that the jury return a verdict slip with the verdict is a change from existing practice. The verdict slip is a written recital of the verdict. This practice conforms to Rule 535(a) of the Uniform Rules of Criminal Procedure (U.L.A.) (1974). The use of a verdict slip will help reduce errors in the rendering and announcing of verdicts. *See* Commonwealth v. Brown, 367 Mass. 24, 27–29, 323 N.E.2d 902 (1975) (verdicts of not guilty returned, affirmed, and recorded and jury discharged; no error in permitting corrected verdicts to be entered since jury had remained undispersed, in custody, and had not been influenced), pet. for habeas corpus denied sub nom. Brown v. Gunter, 428 F.Supp. 889 (D.Mass.1977), aff'd, 562 F.2d 122 (1st Cir.1977).

Subdivision (b). This subdivision permits a jury in multiple-defendant or multiple-offense cases, with the consent of the court, to return a verdict at any time during their deliberations with respect to charges or defendants as to which a verdict has been reached. This rule also permits the court to require the return of such verdicts before the jury has reached a verdict as to all the defendants or charges. In either case, if the court directs, the jury is to continue its deliberations after rendering the verdicts under this subdivision. To the extent that this rule permits the jury to return such verdicts without having reached a decision on all the charges or defendants, it is consistent with Fed. R.Crim.P. 31(b)–(c). *Accord* Rules of Criminal Procedure (U.L.A.) Rule 535(c)–(d) (1974).

This rule also provides that the court may declare a mistrial in cases where the jury is unable to reach a verdict. However, it must first receive and record the verdicts which the jury can agree upon. *See* ABA *Standards Relating to Trial by Jury* §§ 5.4–.5 (Approved Draft, 1968); Rules of Criminal Procedure (U.L.A.), supra, Rule 541.

Subdivision (b) does not prohibit retrial of those defendants as to whom the jury is unable to reach a verdict. This is consistent with Fed.R.Crim.P. 31(b), which provides that, in cases of multiple defendants, disagreement as to one or more defendants has no effect upon the verdict as to any other defendant, and such defendant may be retried without violating the protection of the double jeopardy clause. 8A J. MOORE, FEDERAL PRACTICE para. 31.02[2] (1978 rev.). It has long been settled that jeopardy does not attach where the jury is discharged after inability to reach a verdict. United States v. Perez, 22 U.S. 579, 9 Wheat. 579, 6 L.Ed. 165 (1824); Thames v. Commonwealth, 365 Mass. 477, 312 N.E.2d 687 (1974). It is within the discretion of the court to declare a mistrial where there is a "manifest necessity." *United States v. Perez*, supra at 580. Unless such "manifest necessity" exists, a second prosecution will be barred by the double jeopardy clause. Since *Perez*, it has been held that where the jury has been unable to agree upon a verdict, the declaration of a mistrial is a "classic example" of manifest necessity. United States v. Castellanos, 478 F.2d 749, 751 (2d Cir.1973). Thus the defendant may be retried without twice being placed in jeopardy.

Subdivision (c). One change in Massachusetts law is the elimination of the special verdict. General Laws c. 278, § 11 had authorized the jury to return a special verdict, although this procedure was seldom used. This subdivision does, however, recognize the practice of submitting special questions to the jury. *See Commonwealth v. Beneficial Finance Co.*, 360 Mass. 188, 299–300, 275 N.E.2d 33, 62 A.L.R.3d 1143 (1971), cert. denied, 92 S.Ct. 2433, 407 U.S. 910, 32 L.Ed.2d 689 (1972). Special questions should, however, be used sparingly as they can "'catechize' a reluctant juror away from an acquittal and towards a seemingly more 'logical' conviction." *Heald v. Mullaney*, 505 F.2d 1241, 1245 (1st Cir.1974), cert. denied, 95 S.Ct. 1339, 420 U.S. 955, 43 L.Ed.2d 432 (1975).

Subdivision (d). This subdivision is based upon Fed.R.Crim.P. 31(d), but differs in that the polling of the jury is to be discretionary with the court rather than a right of the defendant so as to conform to existing Massachusetts practice. That this discretion is well-settled in the Commonwealth was recently reaffirmed in *Commonwealth v. Stewart*, Mass.Adv.Sh. (1978) 1521, 1533–34, 377 N.E.2d 693. *See also Commonwealth v. Valliere*, 366 Mass. 479, 497, 321 N.E.2d 625 (1974); *Commonwealth v. Caine*, 366 Mass. 366, 375, 318 N.E.2d 901 (1974); *Commonwealth v. Fleming*, 360 Mass. 404, 408, 274 N.E.2d 809 (1971) (jurors polled); *Commonwealth v. Beneficial Finance Co.*, supra, at 300–301. Under Rule 31 of the Federal Rules of Criminal Procedure and under the ABA *Standards Relating to Trial by Jury* § 5.5 (Approved Draft, 1968), a jury is to be polled only at the request of a party or upon the court's own motion.

In any case, where a jury has been polled and there is not a unanimous concurrence, *compare Commonwealth v. Fleming*, supra, or it appears that the verdict was a compromise or other serious doubts are raised as to its integrity, *see Commonwealth v. Stewart*, supra, the court may declare a mistrial, or alternatively, order further deliberations. *Accord*, Rules of Criminal Procedure (U.L.A.) Rule 535(e) (1974).

Rule 28.   Judgment

(Applicable to District Court and Superior Court)

(a) Judgment. If the defendant has been determined to be guilty, a verdict or finding of guilty shall be rendered, or if he has been determined to be not guilty, a verdict or finding of not guilty shall be rendered, in open court, and shall be entered on the court's docket.

(b) Imposition of Sentence. After a verdict, finding, or plea of guilty, or a plea of nolo contendere, or an admission to sufficient facts, the defendant shall have the right to be sentenced without unreasonable delay. Pending sentence the court may commit the defendant or continue or alter the bail as provided by law. Before imposing sentence the court shall afford the defendant or his counsel an opportunity to speak on behalf of the defendant and to present any information in mitigation of punishment.

(c) Notification of Right to Appeal. After a judgment of guilty is entered, the court shall advise the defendant of his right to appeal. In the District Court, upon the request of the defendant, the clerk of the court shall prepare and file forthwith a notice of appeal.

(d) Presentence Investigation.

(1) *Criminal Record.* The probation officer shall inquire into the nature of every criminal case or juvenile complaint brought before the court and report to the court information concerning all prior criminal prosecutions or juvenile complaints, if any, and the disposition of each such prosecution, except where the defendant was found not guilty. Such information is to be presented before a defendant is admitted to bail in court, and also before disposition of the case against him.

(2) *Report.* The report of the presentence investigation shall contain any prior criminal or juvenile prosecution record of the defendant, but shall not contain any information relating to criminal or juvenile prosecutions in which the defendant was found not guilty. In addition, the report shall include such other available information as may be helpful to the court in the disposition of the case.

(3) *Availability to Parties.* Prior to the disposition the presentence report shall be made available to the prosecutor and counsel for the defendant for inspection. In extraordinary cases, the judge may except from disclosure parts of the report which are not relevant to a proper sentence, diagnostic opinion which might seriously disrupt a program of rehabilitation, sources of information obtained upon a promise of confidentiality, or any other information which, if disclosed, might result in harm, physical or otherwise, to the defendant or other persons. If the report is not made fully available, the portions thereof which are not disclosed shall not be relied upon in determining sentence. No party may make any copy of the presentence report.

(e) Filing. The court may file a case after a guilty verdict or finding without imposing a sentence if the defendant and the Commonwealth both consent. With the consent of both parties, the judge may specify a time limit beyond which the case may not be removed from the file, and may specify any events that may cause the case to be removed from the file. The defendant shall file a written consent with the court as to both the filing of the case and any time limit or events regarding removal from the file. Prior to accepting the defendant's consent, the court shall inform the defendant on the record in open court:

(i) that the defendant has a right to request sentencing on any or all filed case(s) at any time;

(ii) that subject to any time limit imposed by the court, the prosecutor may request that the case be removed from the file and sentence imposed if a related conviction or sentence is reversed or vacated or upon the prosecutor's establishing by a preponderance of the evidence either that the defendant committed a new criminal offense or that an event occurred on which the continued filing of the case was expressly made contingent by the court; and

(iii) that if the case is removed from the file the defendant may be sentenced on the case.

In sentencing the defendant after the removal of a case from the file, the court shall consider the over-all scheme of punishment employed by the original sentencing judge.

December 17, 2008, effective April 1, 2009.

Reporter's Notes

The format and much of the language of this rule is derived from Rule 32 of the Federal Rules of Criminal Procedure. Subdivision (c) is taken from Rule 3.670 of the Florida Rules of Criminal Procedure (1975). The Federal Rule has been significantly modified so as to conform to existing Massachusetts practice.

Subdivision (a). This subdivision is a restatement of Rule 3.670 of the Florida Rules of Criminal Procedure (1975). It requires the verdict or finding, whether it is guilty or not guilty, to be rendered in open court and entered on the court's docket. *See* Fed.R.Crim.P. 32(b)(1); Rules of Criminal Procedure (U.L.A.) Rule 621 (1974).

Subdivision (b). The defendant has the right to prompt sentencing. *See* G.L. c. 279, § 4; Commonwealth v. Kossowan, 265 Mass. 436, 165 N.E. 22 (1929); In re Lebowitch, 235 Mass. 357 (1920). *See* ABA *Standards Relating to Sentencing Alternatives & Procedures* § 5.4(a) (Approved Draft, 1968). However, the defendant can waive that right. When the defendant consents to a continuance of the case or a probationary term, he has by implication waived his right to prompt sentencing. *Compare* Fla.R.Crim.P. 3.670 (1975).

Pending the pronouncement of sentence, the court may commit the defendant, place him on probation, or release him on bail in a manner consistent with existing law. *See* G.L. c. 276, §§ 58, 65, 87. The terms of his release may subsequently be altered by the court. *See* ABA *Standards Relating to Post Conviction Remedies* § 5.2(b) (Approved Draft, 1968); Rules of Criminal Procedure (U.L.A.) Rule 611 (1974); 18 U.S.C. § 3148.

Finally, this subdivision grants to the defendant or his counsel the opportunity to speak on behalf of the defendant and to offer any information which may serve to mitigate the sentence to be imposed. While there is no constitutional or other right to allocution, Commonwealth v. Curry, Mass.App.Adv.Sh. (1978) 977, 380 N.E.2d 1325 (Rescript); Jeffries v. Commonwealth, 94 Mass. (12 Allen) 145, 153 (1866), this opportunity has traditionally been afforded the defendant at common law and may have therapeutic value for the defendant as well as potential for mitigation. 8A J. MOORE, FEDERAL PRACTICE para. 32.05 (1978 rev.). In Green v. United States, 81 S.Ct. 653, 365 U.S. 301, 5 L.Ed.2d 670 (1961), the Supreme Court indicated that the right to allocution was a personal one and could not be satisfied by only affording the opportunity to the defendant's counsel. "The most persuasive counsel may not be able to speak for a defendant as the defendant might, with halting eloquence, speak for himself." Id. at 304. For the procedure to be followed if a denial of the right to allocution is found, see Hill v. United States, 82 S.Ct. 468, 368 U.S. 424, 7 L.Ed.2d 417 (1962). *See* ABA *Standards Relating to Sentencing Alternatives & Procedures* § 5.4(a)(iii) (Approved Draft, 1968); Rules of Criminal Procedure (U.L.A.) rule 613(2) (1974).

Subdivision (c). This subdivision is meant to assure that the defendant is informed of his right to appeal following a finding of guilty, a finding of sufficient facts to warrant a finding of guilty, or imposition of sentence in a District Court jury-waived session or after a verdict or finding of guilt in a District Court jury session or the Superior Court. *See* Superior Court Rule 65 (1974, as amended, 1977).

General Laws c. 278, § 18 (as amended, St.1978, c. 478, § 302) permits a defendant convicted in District Court jury-waived session to appeal either from a sentence or from a finding of guilty where no sentence is imposed. Rule 9 of the District Court Initial Rules of Criminal Procedure (1971) provides that either the judge or the sessions clerk may inform the defendant of his right to his de novo appeal to a jury session. That practice is in conformity with this rule. *Compare* Fed.R.Crim.P. 32(a)(2) *with* Rules of Criminal Procedure (U.L.A.) 613(4) (1974), both of which provide that the judge is to inform the defendant of his right to appeal.

This rule is much more limited in its operation than the federal rule, which requires notice of the defendant's right to appellate review to correct errors. This rule does, however, direct the District Court clerk to file the notice of appeal on behalf of the defendant upon his request, which is consistent with the federal rule.

Subdivision (d). This rule preserves the distinction between the defendant's criminal record and the full probation report which was emphasized in Commonwealth v. Martin, 355 Mass. 296, 244 N.E.2d 303 (1969).

Subdivision (d)(1) is essentially a restatement of existing law. See G.L. c. 276, § 85; G.L. c. 279, § 4A, pursuant to which the defendant is given the right to see his criminal record. This rule affords the

court the important right to inspect probation records regarding a defendant's prior criminal convictions or other dispositions, exclusive of not guilty findings, prior to his release on bail. *But see* District Court Initial Rules of Criminal Procedure 8 (1971), which would prohibit the use of probation records for bail determinations.

Support can be found for the position taken in this subdivision in G.L. c. 119, §§ 60, 60A (as amended, St.1978, c. 478, § 64). Section 60 authorizes the consideration of juvenile delinquency records before imposition of sentence in criminal proceedings. Section 60A provides the same basic standard for the availability of juvenile records for inspection in appeals to a juvenile appeals session from adjudications of delinquency as does subdivision (d)(3), infra, for the availability of the records of criminal and juvenile prosecutions prior to sentencing in criminal proceedings.

Although G.L. c. 279, § 4A mandates that the criminal record is not to include information concerning prior charges of which the defendant was acquitted, it does not require exclusion of information as to other *pending* charges. Commonwealth v. Franks, 372 Mass. 866, 362 N.E.2d 362 (1977) (Rescript); Commonwealth v. LeBlanc, 370 Mass. 217, 222, 346 N.E.2d 874 (1976); Commonwealth v. Settipane, 5 Mass.App. 648, 368 N.E.2d 1213 (1977). The consideration of other charges is appropriate as long as the judge makes clear that he is not passing on guilt or innocence on the untried charges, the resulting sentence is within statutory limits and there is no basis in the record for apprehension of vindictiveness or retaliatory motivation. *Settipane,* supra. *Accord Franks,* supra.

There is no constitutional objection to a judge knowing of other pending charges, although due process would require resentencing if inaccurate, unreliable or misleading information had been considered at sentencing, or if the judge had undertaken to punish the defendant for conduct other than that of which he is immediately convicted. *Commonwealth v. LeBlanc,* supra at 221, and cases cited. For a similar example of factors beyond the scope of consideration for sentencing, *see* Commonwealth v. Murray, 4 Mass.App.Ct. 493, 351 N.E.2d 555 (1976).

Subdivision (d)(2) contemplates a probation report concerning the defendant which will include the criminal record of subdivision (d)(1) and also other information about the defendant which may assist the court in disposing of the case. The authorization for such reports is found in G.L. c. 276, § 100, as noted in *Commonwealth v. Martin,* supra. The probation report of this subdivision may be used by the court for purposes of sentencing as well as for other purposes, such as the setting of bail. To the extent that this report is multiple-purpose, it is somewhat different than the pre-sentence investigation report of Fed.R.Crim.P. 32(c)(1)–(2), which is used primarily for the purpose of sentencing following a determination of guilt. *See* Rules of Criminal Procedure (U.L.A.) Rule 612 (1974). Other sources also recommend the use of pre-sentence investigative reports following a guilty finding. *See* ABA *Standards Relating to Sentencing Alternatives & Procedures* §§ 4.1(b), 4.2(a), 4.3, 4.4(a)–(b) (Approved Draft, 1968); ALI *Model Code of Pre-Arraignment Procedure* § 320.4 (P.O.D.1975); National Advisory Commission on Criminal Justice Standards & Goals, *Corrections,* Standards 5.14(1), (3); 5.15(1); 5.16; 16.10 (1973).

Subdivision (d)(3) states that generally the report compiled by the probation department shall be made available to the defendant and his counsel and to the prosecutor. The court in *Commonwealth v. Martin,* supra, held that the defendant did not have a right to see the report, but stated that "the administration of justice would be improved by a liberal and generous use of the power to disclose." Id. at 303, *quoting* United States v. Fischer, 381 F.2d 509, 512–13 (2d Cir.), cert. denied, 88 S.Ct. 1064, 390 U.S. 973, 19 L.Ed.2d 1185 (1967). The court stated that the main consideration against full disclosure is the prospect that the revelation of certain material given the probation officer in confidence, would result in the destruction of the sources of such material and its availability. *Commonwealth v. Martin,* supra, at 303.

This subdivision further conditions availability upon the judge's determination that disclosure would not "result in harm, physical or otherwise, to the defendant or other persons." This qualification accords with Fed.R.Crim.P. 32(c)(3)(A). ABA *Standards Relating to Sentencing Alternatives and Procedures* § 4.4 (Approved Draft, 1968), also recommends disclosure of presentence reports with certain exceptions, as does ALI, *Model Code of Pre–Arraignment Procedure* § 320.4 (P.O.D.1975).

The next to last sentence of this subdivision provides that if any portion of the report is not made available, then the judge is not to rely upon any information contained in that portion in determining sentence. *See* Gardner v. Florida, 97 S.Ct. 1197, 430 U.S. 349, 51 L.Ed.2d 393 (1977) (denial of due process to impose death sentence on basis of information contained in undisclosed presentence report which defendant could not deny or explain).

Reporter's Notes—2008

This section was added to meet the concerns the Supreme Judicial Court expressed in its opinion in Commonwealth v. Simmons, 448 Mass. 68 (2007). It addresses the procedure for placing a case on file without a sentence after a guilty verdict, a guilty finding or a plea of guilty. Before a court can place a complaint or indictment on file, both the defendant and the Commonwealth must consent. The defendant's consent is necessary because the suspension of the case deprives the defendant of the right to be sentenced in a timely fashion and the right to appeal. *See Simmons*, 448 Mass. at 698; Commonwealth v. Delgado, 367 Mass. 432, 438 (1975); Marks v. Wentworth, 199 Mass. 44, 45 (1908). The defendant's consent must be in writing and made part of the record in the case.

The Commonwealth's consent is necessary both because it accords with the historical practice, *see* Commonwealth v. Dowdican's Bail, 115 Mass. 133, 136 (1874) ("It has long been a common practice in this Commonwealth . . . to order, with the consent of the defendant *and of the attorney for the Commonwealth,* and upon such terms as the court in its discretion may impose, that the indictment be laid on file . . .") (emphasis added), and because of the general public interest in seeing the timely imposition of a sentence.

If the judge does not otherwise specify, a filed case remains inactive indefinitely. The judge may, however, provide for the time frame within which the case may be brought forward as well as the occurrence of any events that would serve as the predicate for removing the case from the file. *See, e.g.,* Commonwealth v. Marinucci Bros. & Co., 354 Mass. 743, 745 (1968) (defendant paying restitution); Commonwealth v. Pelletier, 62 Mass. App. Ct. 145, 146–147 (2004) (defendant serving a specified term in prison before being paroled). Since both the Commonwealth and the defendant have a right to have the judge impose a sentence, by implication if the judge sets a time limit or establishes a contingency that would bring the case forward, both parties must agree.

The notice the defendant must receive about the implications of filing a case without imposing sentence is similar to a guilty plea colloquy in that it must occur in open court on the record. It is, however, not as detailed as a guilty plea colloquy nor must the judge specifically address the question of voluntariness, as would be the case with a guilty plea. *Cf.* Rule 12(a)(5). The defendant must, however, file with the court a signed statement agreeing to the filing of the case without a sentence and acknowledging the time frame within which the case can be removed from the file as well as the occurrence of any events that would serve as the predicate for its removal.

Subsection (i) requires the court to inform the defendant that he or she has the right to request that a case be removed from the file at any time. This reflects the historical practice surrounding the filing procedure, *see* Commonwealth v. Chase, Thacher's Crim. Cas. 267, 268–269 (Boston Mun. Ct. 1831) *quoted in* Commonwealth v. Simmons, 448 Mass. 687, 696 (2007) ("the [defendant] might at any time [appear] in court, and [demand] the judgment of law."); Commonwealth v. Dowdican's Bail, 115 Mass. 133, 136 (1874) ("[the practice of filing]

leaves it within the power of the court at any time, upon the motion of either party, to bring the case forward"). Since a defendant ordinarily cannot obtain appellate review of a filed case, *see* Commonwealth v. Delgado, 367 Mass. 432, 438 (1975), allowing the defendant to remove a case from the file is the only way to effectuate the right to appeal.

Subsection (ii) requires the defendant to receive notice of the reasons why the case can be removed from the file. One contingency that must be part of the notice in every case is the possibility that a related conviction was reversed or a related sentence vacated or modified. In the usual instance, a related conviction will be one that was joined for trial with the complaint or indictment that is being filed. *See, e.g.,* Commonwealth v. Owens, 414 Mass. 595, 596 (1993). In some circumstances, however, a conviction that results from a separate proceeding may be based on the same course of criminal conduct as the filed case. In that situation, if the conviction or sentence in the separate case were reversed or vacated, the filed case could be brought forward.

Another element of the notice the defendant must receive under subsection (ii) is that the case may be removed from the file if the defendant commits a new criminal offense. The Supreme Judicial Court has recognized that historically, an implicit condition of a case remaining on file was the defendant's good behavior. *See* Commonwealth v. Simmons, 448 Mass. 687, 697 (2007). In *Simmons* itself, the Court approved the removal of an indictment from the file because the defendant was charged with a new offense. "Future criminal conduct" rather than "good behavior" is a more appropriate standard to incorporate into contemporary procedure given the existence of probation and the need to provide fair notice to the defendant of the reasons why a case might be brought forward for sentencing. If a defendant's future behavior has to be monitored on a long-term basis beyond the specific criterion of avoiding future criminal conduct, probation is a more appropriate vehicle than placing a case on file. The notice also informs the defendant that the issue of future criminal behavior is one that the prosecutor must establish by a preponderance of the evidence in order to justify removing a case from the file and having the court impose a sentence. The preponderance standard is the one that governs a probation revocation hearing, which is the closest analogy to removing a case from the file. *See* Commonwealth v. Holmgren, 421 Mass. 224, 226 (1995). It is also the standard that a judge must apply in sentencing. *See* Nichols v. United States, 511 U.S. 738, 748 (1994); Commonwealth v. Nawn, Jr., 394 Mass. 1, 7 (1985).

Subsection (ii) also recognizes that in an individual case a judge may make bringing the case forward contingent upon a specific event, such as the defendant paying restitution, *see e.g.* Commonwealth v. Marinucci Bros. & Co., 354 Mass. 743, 745 (1968), or serving a specified term in prison before being paroled, *see e.g.* Commonwealth v. Pelletier, 62 Mass. App. Ct. 145, 146–147 (2004). The defendant must receive explicit notice of any such contingency.

Subsection (iii) requires the court to inform the defendant that if the case is removed from the file, the defendant can receive a sentence that entails additional punishment. *Cf. Simmons*, 448 Mass. at 695 n.9. This provision does not require the type of colloquy concerning the details of a maximum sentence that must accompany a guilty plea. *Cf.* Rule 12(c)(3)(B). The defendant must, however, be made aware of the possibility of additional punishment and the judge should tailor the amount of information on this topic to the needs of each specific case.

The last provision in this section addresses the power of a judge to impose a sentence after a case is removed from the file. The Supreme Judicial Court has made clear that when a case is brought forward from the file, the judge, in deciding on what sentence to impose, must conform the new sentence to "the over-all scheme of punishment employed by the trial judge." *Simmons*, 448 Mass. at 699. This requirement means the sentencing judge has to take into account two limitations. One is the length of the original sentencing scheme. In *Simmons*, for example, the Court determined that the disparity between the two sentences was too great where a defendant was originally sentenced to concurrent terms of eight to twelve years on six armed robbery indictments and five years later received a sentence of eighteen to twenty years on a single count of armed assault with intent to rob that had been removed from the file. *See id.* at 699. It may be appropriate in some cases for the judge who orders a case placed on file to indicate what type of sentence is contemplated if the case is ever removed from the file. The other limitation stems from the requirement of due process that a defendant not be punished for conduct other than that for which he or she was convicted. *See* Commonwealth v. Bianco, 390 Mass. 254, 259 (1983). Since an allegation of new criminal conduct will often be the occasion for bringing a case out of the file, the judge should take care not to impose a harsher sentence on the filed case because the defendant "has not demonstrated his innocence of [the] unrelated, pending charge." Commonwealth v. LeBlanc, 370 Mass. 217 (1976).

Rule 29. Revision or Revocation of Sentence

(Applicable to District Court and Superior Court)

(a) Revision or Revocation.

(1) *Illegal Sentences.* The trial judge, upon the judge's own motion, or the written motion of the prosecutor, filed within sixty days after imposition of a sentence, may revise or revoke such sentence if the judge determines that any part of the sentence was illegal.

(2) *Unjust Sentences.* The trial judge, upon the judge's own motion, or the written motion of a defendant, filed within sixty days after the imposition of a sentence or within sixty days after issuance of a rescript by an appellate court on direct review, may, upon such terms and conditions as the judge shall order, revise or revoke such sentence if it appears that justice may not have been done.

(b) Affidavits. If a party files a motion pursuant to this rule, the party shall file and serve, and the other party may file and serve, affidavits in support of their respective positions. The judge may deny a motion filed pursuant to this rule on the basis of facts alleged in the affidavits without further hearing.

(c) Notice. The moving party shall serve the other party with a copy of any motion and affidavit filed pursuant to this rule. If the judge orders that a hearing be held on the motion, the court shall give the parties reasonable notice of the time set for the hearing.

(d) Place of Hearing. A motion filed pursuant to this rule may be heard by the trial judge wherever the judge is then sitting.

(e) Appeal. An appeal from a final order under this rule may be taken to the Appeals Court, or the Supreme Judicial Court in an appropriate case, by either party.

Amended June 8, 2016, effective September 1, 2016.

Reporter's Notes

This amendment to Rule 29 is intended to fill a gap in the Rules of Criminal Procedure identified by the Supreme Judicial Court in *Commonwealth v. Selavka*, 469 Mass. 502 (2014), in which the Court upheld the Commonwealth's authority to move to correct an illegal sentence. After noting that neither former Rule 29(a) nor Rule 30(a) permitted a Commonwealth motion to revise or revoke an illegal sentence, the Court concluded that "rule 29(a), with its sixty-day time frame, is the proper vehicle by which the Commonwealth may challenge illegal sentences." *Selavka*, 469 Mass. at 508. This amendment to Rule 29 permits the Commonwealth to seek such relief.

Rule 29(a) Revision or Revocation.

Rule 29(a)(1), Illegal Sentences, provides that, within 60 days after a trial judge imposes a sentence, either the Commonwealth or the judge may move to revise or revoke that sentence if any part of the sentence is illegal. While Rule 29(a) has long authorized a trial judge to increase a sentence under Rule 29(a), either because the sentence imposed is illegal or, on reflection, unjust, see *Commonwealth v. Aldoupolis*, 386 Mass. 260, 268–270 (1982), former Rule 29 did not authorize the Commonwealth to seek revision or revocation of a sentence for any purpose. See *Selavka*, 469 Mass. at 506. Rule 29(a)(1) makes it clear that the judge's authority to correct an illegal sentence remains unchanged, but the rule further permits the Commonwealth to seek such relief. This narrow provision for a Commonwealth motion to revise or revoke a sentence is intentionally limited to correcting an illegal sentence; it does not permit a motion to increase a legal sentence that the prosecutor considers to be legal but unduly lenient.

Rule 29(a)(1)'s authority to challenge an illegal sentence within 60 days of sentencing is limited to the Commonwealth and the trial judge for two reasons. First, the defendant is already authorized to file such a motion. Rule 29(a)(2), Unjust Sentences, leaves unchanged the defendant's right to challenge a sentence "if it appears that justice may not have been done," which includes a sentence imposing punishment not permitted by law. See *Selavka*, 469 Mass. 508 n. 7. Quite apart from Rule 29(a), Rule 30(a) gives the defendant the right to challenge an illegal sentence at any time.

Second, a successful prosecution or judicial motion to revise or revoke an illegal sentence that is too lenient would result in additional punishment, which, if unduly belated, would implicate the defendant's double-jeopardy interest in sentence finality even though the original sentence was illegal. See *Selavka*, 469 Mass. at 509. The Court in *Selavka* concluded that limiting the potential for such upward adjustment of an illegal sentence to Rule 29(a)'s 60–day timeframe marks a reasonable balance between a defendant's interest in sentence finality and society's interest in enforcement of the sentencing laws. *Selavka*, 469 Mass. at 508. Rule 29(a)(1) thus provides for a 60–day time limit for the Commonwealth to file a motion seeking, or for the judge to initiate consideration of, the revision or revocation of an illegal sentence. After that, any motion to revise or revoke an illegal sentence must come from the defendant under Rule 30(a), which would raise no double-jeopardy problems.

Rule 29(a)(1) includes revocation as a potential remedy for an illegal sentence that is too lenient, in part because that sentence might have been the result of a guilty plea from which the defendant could have withdrawn had the sentence been more harsh than it was. See Rule 12(c)(4) (permitting defendant to withdraw (1) from a District–Court plea if the judge intends to impose a sentence in excess of defendant's request and (2) from a Superior–Court plea if the judge intends to sentence in excess of either the agreed recommendation or the prosecutor's recommendation); Rule 12(d)(4) (requiring a judge who accepts a plea agreement providing for both a charge concession and a specific sentence to impose the agreed sentence and permitting the defendant to withdraw if the judge rejects the plea agreement); former Rule 12(c)(2) (permitting defendant to withdraw (1) from a District–Court plea if the judge intends to impose a sentence in excess of defendant's request and (2) from a Superior–Court plea if the judge intends to sentence in excess of an agreed recommendation on which the plea was contingent). At the very least, such a case would require re-sentencing, with the defendant presumably having the right to withdraw the plea if Rule 12 would have afforded that right at the plea hearing and initial sentencing. See *Selavka*, 469 Mass. at 514–515.

Rule 29(a)(2), Unjust Sentences, clarifies former Rule 29(a)'s provision for filing a motion to revise or revoke an unjust sentence following appellate review.

First, the rule makes clear that, other than the imposition of sentence, the only event that triggers the sixty-day period to file a Rule 29(a)(2) motion is the appellate court's issuance of the rescript in a case on direct review. If the conviction is affirmed, the issuance of the rescript marks the point at which the conviction becomes final, see *Foxworth v. St. Amand*, 457 Mass. 200, 206 (2010), making it an appropriate time for filing a motion to revise or revoke the sentence based on that conviction. Although on its face the rule does not limit such motions to cases in which the conviction is affirmed, as a practical matter, a conviction's reversal would result in vacation of the sentence, leaving nothing to revise or revoke.

Pegging the beginning of the sixty-day filing period to the rescript's issuance permits a defendant whose conviction is affirmed by the Appeals Court to seek either rehearing or further appellate review without impinging on the time period for filing a motion to revise and revoke. Rule of Appellate Procedure 23 requires the Appeals Court, after deciding an appeal and mailing the decision to the parties, to wait twenty-eight days before issuing the rescript, see Mass. R.A.P. 23, thereby affording the parties time to file for rehearing or further review. See Mass. R.A.P. 27 (petition for rehearing to be filed within fourteen days of decision); Mass. R.A.P. 27.1 (application for further review to be filed within twenty days of decision). If either is granted, the rescript's issuance is stayed pending disposition of that proceeding. See Mass. R.A.P. 23. Finally, the appellate court's issuance of the rescript, finalizing a conviction which is affirmed, is a procedural event of which the defendant would surely be aware and thus a fair time for the sixty-day filing period to begin. The amendment eliminates the uncertainty caused by basing the time period on the trial court's receipt of the rescript, which was subject to the vagaries of mail delivery and clerical document processing.

Second, by confining the extension of the sixty-day filing period to cases on direct review, Rule 29(a)(2) clarifies the reach of its predecessor. Former Rule 29(a) did not specify whether a rescript on appellate review of a collateral attack on a sentence would allow a Rule 29 motion, though the Appeals Court found in an unpublished opinion that it would not. *Commonwealth v. White*, No. 08–P–766, 74 Mass. App. Ct. 1115, 2009 Mass. App. Unpub. LEXIS 788, at *3–*6 (Mass. App. Ct. June 4, 2009). The rule's purpose is to permit the trial judge to revise or revoke a sentence that, based on the facts existing at the time of sentencing, appears in retrospect to have been unjust. See *Commonwealth v. Rodriguez*, 461 Mass. 256, 260 (2012); *Commonwealth v. DeJesus*, 440 Mass. 147, 152 (2003). This purpose is best served if the sentence review prompted by the motion occurs reasonably soon after the sentence's imposition. See *Commonwealth v. Barclay*, 424 Mass. 377, 380 (1997) (holding Rule 29 motion must be decided within reasonable time of its filing); *Commonwealth v. Layne*, 386 Mass. 291, 295–296 (1982) (noting that, with "the passage of time from the date of sentencing, it becomes increasingly difficult for a trial judge to make the determination called for by [then Rule 29(a)] without improperly considering postsentencing events"). Rule 29(a)(2) accordingly limits the filing time to sixty days from the imposition of sentence or from the issuance of the rescript in any direct appeal, the latter filing period commencing as soon as the conviction becomes final. The former rule's provision permitting filing within sixty days of any appellate court order or judgment "denying review of, or having the effect of upholding, a judgment of conviction" has been deleted as being either redundant (if the order or judgment in question is part of the rescript concluding a direct appeal), or not sufficiently clear.

Finally, Rule 29(a)(2) achieves gender neutrality.

Rule 29(b) Affidavits

Rule 29(b), Affidavits, is amended to accommodate the Commonwealth's narrow authority to file a motion to revise or revoke an illegal sentence under the rule, authorizing both parties to file appropriate affidavits in that event. Consistent with Rule 18(a)(3), the amended rule further provides that the judge may deny a motion filed under Rule 29(a) without a hearing, based solely on the affidavits. Mass. R. Cr. P. 18(a)(3), Presence [of Defendant] Not Required, 378 Mass. 887 (1979) ("A defendant need not be present at a revision or revocation of sentence pursuant to Rule 29 or at any proceeding where evidence is not to be taken."). However, any revision or revocation of a sentence

under Rule 29, whether because the sentence imposed is illegal or unjust, must be predicated on a hearing. See E. B. Cypher, Revise or Revoke of Sentence Hearings, 30A Criminal Practice and Procedure, § 30:27 (4th ed. Mar. 2015). See also *Thompson v. United States*, 495 F.2d 1304, 1307 (1st Cir. 1974) (vacating post-trial sentence imposed *in absentia* to correct an illegal sentence, holding defendant must be present for re-sentencing; cited by Reporter's Notes to Mass. R. Cr. P. 18(a), Presence of Defendant, as example of sentencing requiring defendant's presence). Although the defendant does not have the right to present evidence at this hearing, see *Commonwealth v. Coggins*, 324 Mass. 552, 556–557, cert. denied, 338 U.S. 881 (1949), he or she has the right to be present and to be heard. See *Aldoupolis v. Commonwealth*, 386 Mass. 260, 275–276 (1982); E. B. Cypher, Presence of the Defendant at the [Rule 29] Hearing, 30B Criminal Practice and Procedure, § 41:12 (4th ed. Mar. 2015). Further, any victim(s) covered by G.L. c. 258B, Rights of Victims and Witnesses of Crime, may present a victim-impact statement at such a hearing. See *Commonwealth v. Doucette*, 81 Mass. App. Ct. 740, 742, rev. denied, 463 Mass. 1103 (2012) (upholding judge's discretion under G.L. c. 258B, § 3(p) to permit victims to be heard on Rule 30(a) motion for a new trial, adding that "[t]he victim's family was also entitled [under the statute] to make a victim impact statement at sentencing or disposition").

Rule 29(c) Notice—(d) Place of Hearing

Rule 29(c), Notice, and Rule 29(d), Place of Hearing, are amended (1) to recognize the Commonwealth's narrow authority to file a motion to revise or revoke an illegal sentence, and (2) to achieve gender neutrality.

Rule 29(e) Appeal

Rule 29(e) provides that either party may appeal from a final order under the rule. This provision clarifies that the Commonwealth may appeal a denial of its motion to revise or revoke an illegal sentence. Prior to Rule 29(e), a defendant's right to appeal the denial of a motion to revise or revoke a sentence was well established, see *Commonwealth v. Richards*, 44 Mass. App. Ct. 478, 481 (1998), as was the Commonwealth's right to appeal the allowance of such a motion. See *Commonwealth v. Cowan*, 422 Mass. 546, 547 (1996) (recognizing Commonwealth's right under G.L. c. 211, § 3 to appeal District Court allowance of Rule 29 motion); *Commonwealth v. Amirault*, 415 Mass. 112, 115 (1993) (same under G.L. c. 278, § 28E for Superior Court motion). In contrast, while the Commonwealth had the right to move to correct an illegal sentence and presumably the attendant right to appeal the denial of such a motion, see *Commonwealth v. Selavka*, 469 Mass. 502, 507 & n. 6 (2014), its avenue for pursuing that appeal was not clear. *Id.* Rule 29(e) cures that deficiency.

Rule 30. Post Conviction Relief

(a) Unlawful Restraint. Any person who is imprisoned or whose liberty is restrained pursuant to a criminal conviction may at any time, as of right, file a written motion requesting the trial judge to release him or her or to correct the sentence then being served upon the ground that the confinement or restraint was imposed in violation of the Constitution or laws of the United States or of the Commonwealth of Massachusetts.

(b) New Trial. The trial judge upon motion in writing may grant a new trial at any time if it appears that justice may not have been done. Upon the motion the trial judge shall make such findings of fact as are necessary to resolve the defendant's allegations of error of law.

(c) Post Conviction Procedure.

(1) *Service and Notice.* The moving party shall serve the office of the prosecutor who represented the Commonwealth in the trial court with a copy of any motion filed under this rule.

(2) *Waiver.* All grounds for relief claimed by a defendant under subdivisions (a) and (b) of this rule shall be raised by the defendant in the original or amended motion. Any grounds not so raised are waived unless the judge in the exercise of discretion permits them to be raised in a subsequent motion, or unless such grounds could not reasonably have been raised in the original or amended motion.

(3) *Affidavits.* Moving parties shall file and serve and parties opposing a motion may file and serve affidavits where appropriate in support of their respective positions. The judge may rule on the issue or issues presented by such motion on the basis of the facts alleged in the affidavits without further hearing if no substantial issue is raised by the motion or affidavits.

(4) *Discovery.* Where affidavits filed by the moving party under subdivision (c)(3) establish a prima facie case for relief, the judge on motion of any party, after notice to the opposing party and an opportunity to be heard, may authorize such discovery as is deemed appropriate, subject to appropriate protective order.

(5) *Counsel.* The judge in the exercise of discretion may assign or appoint counsel in accordance with the provisions of these rules to represent a defendant in the preparation and presentation of motions filed under subdivisions (a) and (b) of this rule. The court, after notice to the Commonwealth and an opportunity to be heard, may also exercise discretion to allow the defendant costs associated with the preparation and presentation of a motion under this rule.

(6) *Presence of Moving Party.* A judge may entertain and determine a motion under subdivisions (a) and (b) of this rule without requiring the presence of the moving party at the hearing.

(7) *Place and Time of Hearing.* All motions under subdivisions (a) and (b) of this rule may be heard by the trial judge wherever the judge is then sitting. The parties shall have at least 30 days notice of any hearing unless the judge determines that good cause exists to order the hearing held sooner.

(8) *Appeal.* An appeal from a final order under this rule may be taken to the Appeals Court, or to the Supreme Judicial Court in an appropriate case, by either party.

(A) If an appeal is taken, the defendant shall not be discharged from custody pending final decision upon the appeal; provided, however, that the defendant may, in the discretion of the judge, be admitted to bail pending decision of the appeal.

(B) If an appeal or application therefor is taken by the Commonwealth, upon written motion supported by affidavit, the Appeals Court or the Supreme Judicial Court may determine and approve payment to the defendant of the costs of appeal together with reasonable attorney's fees, if any, to be paid on the order of the trial court after entry of the rescript or the denial of the application. If the final order grants relief other than a discharge from custody, the trial court or the court in which the appeal is pending may, upon application by the Commonwealth, in its discretion,

and upon such conditions as it deems just, stay the execution of the order pending final determination of the matter.

(9) *Appeal under G.L. c. 278, § 33E.* If an appeal or application for leave to appeal is taken by the Commonwealth under the provisions of Chapter 278, Section 33E, upon written notice supported by affidavit, the Supreme Judicial Court may determine and approve payment to the defendant of the costs of appeal together with reasonable attorney's fees to be paid on order of the trial court after entry of the rescript or the denial of the application.

Amended effective April 14, 1995; amended September 6, 2001, effective October 1, 2001.

Reporter's Notes

This rule, which marks a significant departure from prior Massachusetts practice, is derived from a number of sources. *See* Fed.R.Crim. P., Rules 33, 35; ABA *Standards Relating to Post-Conviction Remedies* (Approved Draft, 1968); *Rules of Criminal Procedure* (U.L.A.) Rule 632 (1974).

The moving party is to seek post conviction relief from the trial judge presiding at the initial trial. *See* Commonwealth v. Sullivan, 385 Mass. 497, 498 n. 1 (1981) (the judge who presided at a defendant's trial normally should hear that defendant's motion for a new trial). The trial judge is familiar with the case which "may make for more efficient handling." ABA *Standards, supra,* § 1.4, comment at 30. *See* McCastle, Petitioner, 401 Mass. 105, 107 (1987) (Rule 30 "assigns the motion to the trial judge who heard the case, on the theory that [the judge's] familiarity with the case can assist in its effective handling.") However, for this same reason the trial judge may bring to the hearing a prejudice that another judge would not have. Recusal of the trial judge should thus be liberally exercised, particularly where it is requested by the moving party. See ABA *Standards, supra,* § 1.4(c). A second advantage to be gained from giving the trial court original jurisdiction to hear post conviction motions is that the necessary witnesses, if any, are likely to be convenient to the court.

Subdivision (a). When originally adopted in 1979, this subdivision consolidated the previously distinct procedures of habeas corpus and writ of error. The purpose of the revision was to simplify post conviction procedure, while maintaining the full scope of relief previously available. *See* ABA *Standards Relating to Post-Conviction Remedies* § 1.1 (Approved Draft, 1968). However, the writ of habeas corpus still has limited application in cases contending that the term of a lawfully imposed sentence has expired and basing a claim for relief on grounds distinct from issues arising at the indictment, trial, conviction or sentencing stages. *See e.g.,* Averett, Petitioner, 404 Mass. 28, 30 (1988) (forfeiture of good time credits). A petition for a writ of habeas corpus is appropriate only where the petition alleges that the petitioner is entitled to immediate release. *See* Stewart, Petitioner, 411 Mass. 566, 568 (1991). On the other hand, a rule 30(a) motion is not available to contest the legality of a sentence that the defendant has already completed. *Cf.* Commonwealth v. Lupo, 394 Mass. 644, 646 (1985) ("Rule 30 [a] is intended primarily to provide relief for defendants incarcerated in violation of Federal law or of the laws of the Commonwealth.")

In addition to permitting convicted defendants to seek release from illegal confinement or other restraint on their liberty, this subdivision permits them to seek the correction of an illegal sentence. A distinction is drawn between an illegal sentence and a sentence imposed in an illegal manner. *See* Fed.R.Crim.P., Rule 35.

The concepts of an illegal sentence and an illegally-imposed sentence are narrow and permit the trial judge no discretion in the decision to modify a sentence. Both concepts presume that a defendant's conviction is in all ways valid and that only the sentence is in some manner defective. The difference between the two is that an illegal sentence is one that is not permitted by law for the offense committed by the defendant, *e.g.*, a sentence that exceeds the permissible maximum. *See e.g.*, Commonwealth v. Ambers, 397 Mass. 705 (1986) (challenge to legality of consecutive sentences); Commonwealth v. Harris, 23 Mass.App.Ct. 687, 691–92 (1987) (court sentenced defendant for an offense other than that for which the jury convicted). Illegality has been held to include not only facially illegal sentences, but sentences premised upon a major misunderstanding by the sentencing judge as to the legal bounds of the judge's authority. *E.g.*, United States v. Lewis, 392 F.2d 440 (4th Cir. 1968) (sentencing judge believed parole permissible upon imposition of maximum sentence); Thomas v. United States, 368 F.2d 941 (5th Cir. 1966) (sentence constituted penalty upon exercise of defendant fifth amendment rights); Robinson v. United States, 313 F.2d 817 (7th Cir. 1963) (sentencing judge recommended parole when defendant ineligible). An illegally-imposed sentence is one where the irregularity lies with the procedure employed in imposing the sentence. *See e.g.*, Hill v. United States, 368 U.S. 424 (1962), where the trial court denied the defendant his right of allocution, which was held to be a procedural irregularity. In the context of a probation revocation order, a motion under Rule 30(a) would be appropriate only as a vehicle for challenging the legality of the sentence the defendant received and not the legality of the order revoking probation. Irregularities in the probation revocation process should be challenged through a direct appeal. *See* Commonwealth v. Christian, 429 Mass. 1022 (1999).

An illegal sentence must be corrected by the court at any time upon proper motion by the defendant. An illegally-imposed sentence can only be corrected upon a motion filed within the time permitted by Mass.R.Crim.P., Rule 29(a), that is, within 60 days after imposition. *See Rules of Criminal Procedure* (ULA) Rule 632 (1974). The only restriction upon the correction of an illegal sentence is that it cannot be increased if it has been partially executed. *See* United States v. Benz, 282 U.S. 304 (1931).

Subdivision (b). This subdivision was taken primarily from Fed. R.Crim.P., Rule 33. The standard established in the first sentence is, however, taken directly from former G.L. c. 278, § 29 (St.1966, c. 301).

Prior to 1964 a motion for a new trial under G.L. c. 278, § 29 could only be granted within one year after the end of the trial. *See* Fine v. Commonwealth, 312 Mass. 252 (1942); Commonwealth v. Sacco, 261 Mass. 12 (1927). However, a 1964 amendment rewrote the statute so that the court could consider such a motion filed at any time after judgment. St.1964, c. 82.

In the absence of constitutional error, whether to grant a motion for a new trial on an issue that has been properly presented to the court is within the sound discretion of the trial judge. *See* Commonwealth v. Smith, 318 Mass. 141, 142 (1980). The basis for a new trial can either relate to the conduct of the trial, *see e.g.*, Commonwealth v. Vaidulas, 433 Mass. 247, 250 (2001) ("The only means of revisiting after trial a matter raised in a motion in limine is through a motion for postconviction relief under rule 30."); Commonwealth v. Francis, 411 Mass. 579, 585–86 (1992) (improper jury instruction); Commonwealth v. Westmoreland, 388 Mass. 269, 271 (1983) (ineffective assistance of counsel); Commonwealth v. Schand, 420 Mass. 783, 787–88 (1995) (prosecutor's failure to disclose exculpatory evidence); Commonwealth v. Nickerson, 388 Mass. 246, 249–250 (1983) (defendant's mental incompetence); Commonwealth v. Ciminera, 11 Mass.App.Ct. 101, 107–110, *aff'd* 384 Mass. 807 (1981) (jury misconduct), or to the discovery of new facts that bear on the question of guilt, *see e.g.*, Commonwealth v. Pires, 389 Mass. 657, 664–666 (1983) (newly–discovered evidence); Commonwealth v. Watson, 377 Mass. 814, 815 (1979) (recanted testimony).

A defendant seeking a new trial on the basis of newly discovered evidence must establish both that the evidence is newly discovered and that it casts real doubt on the justice of the conviction. *See* Commonwealth v. Pike, 431 Mass. 212, 218 (2000). The allegedly new evidence must be material and credible, and "carry a measure of strength in support of the defendant's position." Commonwealth v. Grace, 397 Mass. 303, 305–06 (1986). A defendant must also show that the evidence was unknown to the defendant or the defendant's counsel, and not discoverable through "reasonable pretrial diligence" at the time of trial or at the time of the presentation of any earlier motion for a new trial. *See Pike*, 431 Mass. at 218. "The motion judge decides not whether the verdict would have been different, but rather whether the new evidence would probably have been a real factor in the jury's deliberations. This process of judicial analysis requires a thorough knowledge of the trial proceedings and can, of course, be aided by a trial judge's observation of events at trial." Commonwealth v. Moore, 408 Mass. 117, 126–27 (1990) *quoting* Commonwealth v. Grace, 397 Mass. 303, 305–06 (1986).

A new trial motion under Rule 30(b) is the appropriate vehicle to attack the validity of a guilty plea or an admission to sufficient facts. *See* Commonwealth v. Fanelli, 412 Mass. 497 (1992) (treating the defendant's postsentence motion to withdraw guilty pleas as a motion for a new trial pursuant to Mass.R.Crim.P. 30); Dunbrack v. Commonwealth, 398 Mass. 502 (1986) (the appropriate method for attacking the lawfulness of the admission to sufficient facts and the sentence imposed is a postconviction motion for new trial pursuant to rule 30(b) and not a petition under c. 211 § 3). A Rule 30(b) motion is also appropriate where the defendant has been deprived of a constitutionally protected right by counsel's failure to appeal. *See* Commonwealth v. Cowie, 404 Mass. 119, 121 (1989). However, granting a new trial because the verdict is against the weight of the evidence should be done according to Rule 25(b)(2), not Rule 30. *See* Commonwealth v. Preston, 393 Mass. 318, 324 (1984).

The requirement that the trial judge make findings upon a motion for a new trial is contrary to the traditional rule in the Commonwealth, *see* Commonwealth v. Morgan, 280 Mass. 392 (1932), but is based upon the following language of the court in Earl v. Commonwealth, 356 Mass. 181 (1969):

> We recognize that the single justice has power to entertain writs of error in such cases but it is preferable that these questions be resolved in the first instance by the trial judge upon a motion for new trial. The effect of this practice will be to place in the hands of the trial judge, rather than in the hands of the single justice, the task of resolving factual disputes underlying alleged constitutional errors.

Id. at 183. *Accord*, Commonwealth v. Penrose, 363 Mass. 677 (1973). *Cf.* Commonwealth v. Preston, 393 Mass. 318, 323 n. 4 (1984) (declining to address the issue whether findings are required in response to all rule 30(b) motions regardless of outcome). The absence of a finding of fact hampers appellate review of the judge's decision on a new trial motion. *See e.g.*, Commonwealth v. Caban, 48 Mass.App.Ct. 179, 184 (1999) (remanding case for finding of fact).

General Laws c. 279, § 41 provides that judgment should be entered against a corporation that fails to appear in court to answer charges against it. If the corporation can later show cause to excuse its prior neglect, it should be permitted to have the prior judgment vacated upon a motion for a new trial.

The original Reporter's Notes to Rule 30 intended that the remedy available under this subdivision be truly post-conviction, that is, not open to a defendant until the validity of the finding or verdict of guilt was conclusively established by an appellate court if an appeal was taken. This policy was designed to avoid complex and duplicitous proceedings and to protect the interests of the defendant, who is ordinarily limited to a single motion for a new trial. In the years since this subdivision was first promulgated, however, it has not been unusual for defendants to file a rule 30(b) motion after a notice of appeal has been filed. If the motion is pending at the time the appeal is entered, counsel then request a stay of the appeal until the motion is disposed of so that any appeal from the ruling can be consolidated with that from the judgment. *See* Commonwealth v. Powers, 21 Mass.App.Ct. 570, 572 n. 2 (1986). The Supreme Judicial Court has recognized that a judge may rule on a new trial motion prior to the determination of an appeal from the conviction. *See* Commonwealth v. Hallet, 427 Mass. 552, 555 (1998) (describing considerations a judge should take into account in deciding whether to rule on the merits of a new trial motion presented prior to the determination of an appeal); Commonwealth v. Smith, 384 Mass. 519, 524 (1981) ("defendant's appeal from his conviction should, when possible, be combined for review with his appeal from the denial of any motion for a new trial").

This rule does not limit access of a criminal defendant to review pursuant to G.L. c. 211, § 3, which grants the Supreme Judicial Court "general superintendence of all courts of inferior jurisdiction to correct and prevent errors and abuses therein if no other remedy is expressly provided . . . ." That power, however, should be and has been exercised only in exceptional circumstances, when necessary to protect substantive rights. *See* McGuinness v. Commonwealth, 420 Mass. 495, 497 (1995); Forte v. Commonwealth, 418 Mass. 98, 99 (1994); Commonwealth v. McCarthy, 375 Mass. 409, 414 (1978) and cases cited.

Subdivision (c).

(c)(1). In 2001, this subsection was amended to eliminate the requirement that the Attorney General be served in every case where a motion is filed under Rule 30(a). The subsection now requires service of a motion for a new trial, under either subsection (a) or subsection (b), upon the office of the prosecutor who represented the Commonwealth in the trial court, whether a District Attorney's Office or the Attorney General's Office. The prosecutor's office which maintains the original trial file is in the best position, and is responsible for, responding to motions for a new trial.

(c)(2). Subdivision (c)(2) was modeled after ME REV STAT ANN, tit. 14 § 5507 (1964), and was intended to establish finality of convictions and to eliminate "piecemeal litigation . . . whose only purpose is to vex, harass, or delay." Sanders v. United States, 373 U.S. 1, 18 (1963). *See* Commonwealth v. Donahue, 6 Mass.App.Ct. 971 (1979) (defendant's fourth motion for new trial). This rule is not intended to foreclose from future consideration grounds which were not known and could not have been found out with the exercise of due diligence. The constitutionality of the Maine statute from which this subdivision is taken was upheld by the Supreme Court in Murch v. Mottram, 409 U.S. 41 (1972). *See ABA Standards Relating To Post-Conviction Remedies* § 6.2(b)(i) (Approved Draft, 1968).

The rule of waiver established in the subdivision applies, as a result of case law, to claims that were not preserved at trial or not raised in an appeal, as well as to claims that were not put forward in a prior new trial motion. *See* Rodwell v. Commonwealth, 432 Mass. 1016, 1017 (2000) ("If a defendant fails to raise a claim that is generally known and available at the time of trial or direct appeal or in the first motion for postconviction relief, the claim is waived."); Commonwealth v. McLaughlin, 364 Mass. 211, 229 (1973), *quoting* from Commonwealth v. Dascalakis, 246 Mass. 12, 24 (1923) ("It has been the unbroken practice both under the statute [former G.L. c. 278 § 29 on which Rule 30 was based] and at common law respecting motions for new trial not to examine anew the original trial for the detection of errors which might have been raised by exceptions taken at the trial.") Waiver applies equally to constitutional and non-constitutional claims. *See* Commonwealth v. Deeran, 397 Mass. 136, 139 (1986).

Where a new trial motion presents a claim that could have been raised at trial but was not, the discretion a judge has to entertain the issue, as well as the scope of appellate review of the judge's decision, differs depending on the timing of the motion. Where the motion is presented to the court prior to the determination of an appeal, the motion judge, especially if the judge presided over the original trial, has wide discretion to consider an issue that was not raised at trial. *See* Commonwealth v. Hallet, 427 Mass. 552, 554–55 (1998). If the judge does consider the issue on its merits, it opens the issue up to full appellate review. *Id.* If the judge does not consider the issue on the merits, however, and denies relief based on the waiver doctrine, the standard on appellate review is confined to whether there was a substantial risk of a miscarriage of justice. *Id.* at 554. A judge should take into account in deciding to deny a new trial motion on the merits rather than on the basis of waiver, the advantage and disadvantage of making full appellate review available. *Id.*

Since it affects the scope of appellate review, if the judge is going to deny the motion, the judge should make clear whether the decision is based on a consideration of the merits, or on the basis that the error did not raise a substantial risk of a miscarriage of justice – which is the standard for considering issues that have been waived because they were not preserved at trial. *See id.* at 555. ("The judge should recognize that, unless the asserted error concerns a manifest injustice or created a substantial risk of a miscarriage of justice, she has wide discretion whether to consider any new trial issue fully on its merits.") *Cf.* Commonwealth v. Depace, 433 Mass. 379, 382 n. 2 (2001) (where the judge considered the matter only on the threshold question whether the defendant raised a substantial issue necessitating an evidentiary hearing, the issue was not preserved for full appellate review); Commonwealth v. Oliveira, 431 Mass. 609, 612 (2000) (where the judge considered the matter only to determine if the issue raised an asserted error that created a substantial risk of a miscarriage of justice, the issue was not preserved for full appellate review).

If a new trial motion is presented after an appeal has been decided, the discretion the judge has to consider an issue that could have been raised earlier, is much more limited. In this posture, the Supreme Judicial Court has recommended restricting consideration of such ordinarily waived issues to "those extraordinary cases where, upon sober reflection, it appears that a miscarriage of justice might otherwise result." Commonwealth v. Watson, 409 Mass. 110, 112 (1991). In determining if a substantial risk of a miscarriage of justice warrants the judge in considering a claim that would otherwise be precluded because it was not raised earlier, the judge should take into account three factors, taken from Commonwealth v. Miranda, 22 Mass.App.Ct. 10, 21 n. 22 (1986); whether there is a genuine question of guilt or innocence; whether the error was significant enough in the context of the trial to make it plausible to infer that the result might have been different but for the error; and, whether counsel's failure to object at trial was simply a reasonable tactical decision. *See* Commonwealth v. Amirault, 424 Mass. 618, 647 (1997). However, where a new trial motion raises an issue for the first time whose constitutional significance was not established until after the trial and appeal, so that the defendant did not have a genuine opportunity to preserve the issue in the normal course of events, the judge may consider it. *See* Commonwealth v. Burkett, 396 Mass. 509, 511 (1986). The standard of review from the denial of a new trial motion filed after an appeal has been decided is the same whether the motion judge considered the issue or not, whether there was a substantial risk of a miscarriage of justice. *See* Commonwealth v. Curtis, 417 Mass. 619, 624 n. 4 (1994).

(c)(3). The primary purpose of subdivision (c)(3) is to encourage the disposition of post conviction motions upon affidavit. In accordance with prior practice, *see* Commonwealth v. Hubbard, 371 Mass. 160, 174 (1976) *quoting* Commonwealth v. Coggins, 324 Mass. 552, 556–57, *cert. denied*, 338 U.S. 881 (1949), such motions should ordinarily be heard on the facts as presented by affidavit, although in particular circumstances, the judge may in the exercise of discretion receive oral testimony. *See* Commonwealth v. Figueroa, 422 Mass. 72, 77 (1996) (the decision whether to hold an evidentiary hearing on a new trial motion under Rule 30 is within the sound discretion of the judge). Where a substantial issue is raised, however, the better practice is to conduct an evidentiary hearing. *See* Blackledge v. Allison, 431 U.S. 63, 75–76 (1977). *Compare* Commonwealth v. Licata, 412 Mass. 654, 660 (1992) (error to refuse a hearing on new trial motion which raised a substantial issue of ineffective assistance of counsel) *with* Commonwealth v. Stewart, 383 Mass. 253, 257 (1981) (not error to refuse a hearing on new trial motion which failed to raise substantial issue concerning perjury by prosecution witness). In determining whether the motion raises a substantial issue which merits an evidentiary hearing, the judge should look not only at the seriousness of the issue asserted, but also to the adequacy of the defendant's showing. *See id.* at 257–58. Whether or not a substantial issue is presented must, of course, be determined on the face of the motion and affidavit. The motion should specify the grounds for relief, *see* Commonwealth v. Saarela, 15 Mass.App.Ct. 403, 407 (1983), and the affidavit should provide the factual support necessary to determine the issue. The court is fully warranted in dismissing a motion unaccompanied by affidavit, *see* Commonwealth v. Colantonio, 31 Mass.App.Ct. 299, 302 (1991); or one whose the factual allegations are "obscure," *cf.* Sayles v. Commonwealth, 373 Mass. 856 (1977), "impressionistic and conclusory," *cf.* Commonwealth v. Coyne, 372 Mass. 599, 600 (1977), or untrustworthy, *see* Commonwealth v. Lopez, 426 Mass. 657, 662 (1998).

The only change contemplated by this subdivision is that the use of this established procedure is to be extended to all cases where it is deemed appropriate by the trial judge.

(c)(4). Discovery in the context of a new trial motion is not a matter of right. The motion must first establish a prima facie case for relief before discovery is available. However, where that hurdle is met and discovery would be appropriate to develop facts necessary to support the claim, it is within the judge's discretion to allow discovery. Discovery is appropriate where specific allegations before the court show reason to believe that the petitioner may, if the facts are fully developed, be able to demonstrate that he or she is entitled to relief. *Cf.* Harris v. United States, 394 U.S. 286, 300 (1969). This subsection provides that the Commonwealth, as well as the defendant, may obtain discovery. *Cf. Rules Governing § 2254 Cases in the United States District Courts*, Rule 6(c) (recognizing the right of the respondent in a habeas corpus case to take the deposition of the petitioner). If, upon completion of discovery, the defendant is totally unable to make a reasonable proffer of evidence on a crucial element of the case, no hearing need be held and the motion may be dismissed.

In 2001, this subsection was amended to eliminate confusion arising from the reference to discovery in civil cases. The judge has wide discretion to allow the appropriate form of discovery, *see* Commonwealth v. Stewart, 383 Mass. 253, 261 (1981), which may include orders to produce evidence or statements, as provided in the Rules of Criminal Procedure, and in an unusual case may include depositions or other modes of discovery provided in the Rules of Civil Procedure. Where necessary, a party subject to discovery may seek an appropriate protective order.

In 2001, this subsection was also amended to require the opposing party to receive notice and an opportunity to be heard before the judge grants a discovery request. This provision is particularly important in the context of a request that evidence in the possession of the Commonwealth be made available to the defendant for scientific testing, such as DNA analysis. Before ordering such discovery, the judge must take into account a number of issues whose resolution requires the Commonwealth's participation, including the potential relevance of the results to the ground the motion advances for a new trial, the feasibility of successful testing, and the details of access to and testing of the evidence. *See generally* National Commission on the Future of DNA Evidence, *Postconviction DNA Testing: Recommendations For Handling Requests* (Nat'l. Inst. Justice 1999) at 52–53.

(c)(5). As a matter of constitutional obligation, the state need only ensure that indigent defendants have meaningful access to whatever post conviction proceedings are generally available. *See* Commonwealth v. Conceicao, 388 Mass. 255 (1983). Counsel is not necessary in every case to ensure that end. *Id.* at 261. The decision whether to appoint counsel on a motion for a new trial is within the discretion of the trial judge. However, where the motion raises a meritorious, or even colorable claim, "it is much the better practice to assign counsel." *Id.* at 262. G.L. c. 211D § 14 provides for the Committee for Public Counsel Services to represent indigent defendants in post conviction proceedings, and judges may refer requests for counsel to the Committee for initial screening.

If the motion is frivolous, repetitive, or the issues are so simple and easy that an attorney is not necessary to elucidate them, the judge

may deny a motion for the appointment of counsel. *See* Conceicao, *supra*, 388 Mass. at 261–62. Where the motion is presented to the trial judge, the judge may take into account the fact of familiarity with the original record, or with that in prior new trial motions, in declining to appoint counsel. *Id.* at 261.

By amendment in 2001, this subsection gave judges discretion to allow for the payment of costs associated with the preparation and presentation of a new trial motion. Such costs may include the preparation of a transcript, obtaining the services of an investigator, retaining the services of an expert, or paying for scientific testing. As with the decision to appoint counsel, there is no constitutional right to have the state pay for these types of costs associated with a new trial motion. *See* Commonwealth v. Davis, 410 Mass. 680, 684 n. 7 (1991). But where the defendant seeks costs that are reasonably necessary to develop support for a well founded basis for granting a new trial, it is appropriate for the judge to exercise discretion and allow the request. In making the decision to allow costs associated with a new trial motion, the judge should take into account the likelihood that the expenditure will result in the defendant's being able to present a meritorious ground for a new trial. Where the request concerns scientific testing of evidence in the Commonwealth's possession, as with DNA analysis, the court should consider a request for funds in conjunction with the appropriate discovery motion under subsection (c)(4) seeking access to the evidence in question.

By amendment in 2001, this subsection required that the Commonwealth be given notice and an opportunity to be heard with respect to a request for costs in connection with a new trial motion. Unlike a request for costs prior to trial, in the context of a new trial motion there is no reason to deny the Commonwealth an opportunity to participate in a hearing on this type of request in order to avoid the prejudice that can result from the defendant's being forced to reveal trial strategy prematurely. *Cf.* McKinney v. Paskett, 753 F.Supp. 861, 864 (D.C. Id. 1990). The sound exercise of a judge's discretion to allow the defendant costs will depend in part on an evaluation of the legal theory which the expenditure of funds would support. The Commonwealth's participation in this process will result in a better informed decision. This subsection, however, does not give the Commonwealth a right to participate in the determination of a request for the initial appointment of counsel.

(c)(6). Subdivision (c)(6) was originally taken from 28 U.S.C. § 2255 (1949) and authorizes the court to make a determination—with or without a hearing—without requiring the presence of the moving party.

The defendant's presence is not required at a hearing on a motion for a new trial. *See* Commonwealth v. Owens, 414 Mass. 595, 604 (1993) *citing* Commonwealth v. Costello, 121 Mass. 371, 372 (1876). Where the defendant's presence will be of little help to the court—e.g., at the determination of purely legal issues—a proper determination can be made in his absence. Sanders v. United States, 373 U.S. 1, 21 (1963); Howard v. United States, 274 F.2d 100, 104 (8th Cir. 1960). *See* Mass.R.Crim.P., Rule 18 and Reporters' Notes. It is therefore appropriate to screen post-conviction motions carefully, and to utilize other than summary disposition only where an evidentiary hearing to resolve factual issues requires the presence of the defendant. ABA *Standards Relating to Post-Conviction Remedies* § 4.5(a); § 4.6, commentary at 74–75 (Approved Draft, 1968).

(c)(7). This subdivision is designed to expedite the determination of motions filed pursuant to this rule. In 2001, it was amended to give the parties at least 30 days notice of a hearing on a new trial motion, unless the judge determines that good cause exists to order the hearing held sooner. In light of the fact that the Commonwealth need not respond to every new trial motion, since some may be denied on their face as without merit, the primary objective of this provision is to avoid the problem of having the Commonwealth placed in the position of having to respond to a new trial motion without adequate time to prepare.

(c)(8) & (c)(9). Subdivision (c)(8) was originally patterned after CAL PENAL CODE § 1506 (Deering Supp. 1976).

Appeals from new trial motions in cases subject to G.L. c. 278, § 33E go to the Supreme Judicial Court. In all other cases, the Appeals Court is the appropriate venue. Either party may appeal from an adverse determination on a new trial motion. A ruling in favor of a defendant on a motion for relief from unlawful restraint or for a new trial pursuant to this rule does not preclude a Commonwealth appeal, since a successful appeal would merely reinstate the verdict or finding of guilt and would not subject the defendant to reprosecution or multiple punishment. United States v. Wilson, 420 U.S. 332 (1975).

A defendant's request for release on bail pending appeal is a matter within the discretion of the trial judge. *See* Forte v. Commonwealth, 418 Mass. 98, 100 (1994). However, the provision giving the judge discretion to release a defendant on bail pending appeal applies only to appeals from an order for a new trial or an order determining that the defendant's sentence should be reduced to a term of imprisonment less than the time he already has served. *See* Stewart v. Commonwealth, 413 Mass. 664 (1992).

Under subdivisions (c)(8)(B) and (c)(9), the appellate court is to determine the defendant's costs of appeal which are then to be paid to the defendant by the Commonwealth on the order of the trial court. In 1995, the Standing Advisory Committee on Criminal Procedure reconsidered the several rules concerning the payment of reasonable attorney's fees to insure that they were consistent. In Latimore v. Commonwealth, 417 Mass. 805 (1994), the Commonwealth filed an application for leave to appeal the allowance of the defendant's motion for a new trial under the provisions of G.L. c. 278, § 33E. The application was denied by the single justice and the defendant moved for costs and attorney's fees. Because the application for appeal in a capital case was controlled by section 33E, rather than Rule 30(c)(8)(B), no specific provision for payment of fees and costs were available. The court observed that this situation, while rare, presented an anomaly in the rules.

The committee reconsidered the appropriate rules and added language to address the situation where the Commonwealth is making application for leave to appeal and adds directions for payment of fees and costs upon the denial of the application.

The Single Justice in the Memorandum of Decision in the County Court in Commonwealth v. Latimore, Supreme Judicial Court for Suffolk Co. 92–0469 said that in appropriate circumstances he would read the authority granted to the Appeals Court to include the Supreme Judicial Court. To confirm this authority to include both appellate courts, Rule 30(c)(8)(B) was amended to specifically include both courts.

The specific shortcoming of the rules addressed in *Latimore* was corrected by the addition of Rule 30(c)(9) which provides the Supreme Judicial Court with authority to award fees and costs in capital cases under the provision of G.L. c. 278, § 33E.

Rule 31. Stay of Execution; Relief Pending Review; Automatic Expiration of Stay

(a) Imprisonment. If a sentence of imprisonment is imposed upon conviction of a crime, the entry of an appeal shall not stay the execution of the sentence unless the judge imposing it or, pursuant to Mass. R. App. P. 6, a single justice of the court that will hear the appeal, determines in the exercise of discretion that execution of said sentence shall be stayed pending the determination of the appeal. If execution of a sentence of imprisonment is stayed, the judge or justice may at that time make an order relative to the custody of the defendant or for admitting the defendant to bail.

(b) If the application for a stay of execution of sentence is allowed, the order allowing the stay may state the grounds upon which the stay may be revoked and, in any event, shall state that upon release by the appellate court of the rescript affirming the conviction, stay of execution automatically expires unless extended by the appellate court. Any defendant so released shall provide prompt written notice to the clerk of the trial court regarding the defendant's current address and promptly notify the clerk in writing of any change thereof. The clerk shall notify the appellate court that will hear the appeal that a stay of execution of sentence has been allowed. At any time after the stay expires, the Commonwealth may move in the trial court to execute the sentence. The court shall schedule a prompt hearing and issue notice thereof to the defendant unless the prosecutor requests, for good cause shown, that a warrant shall issue.

(c) Fine. If a reservation, filing, or entry of an appeal is made following a sentence to pay a fine or fine and costs, the sentence shall be stayed by the judge imposing it or by a single justice of the court that will hear the appeal if there is a diligent perfection of appeal.

(d) Probation or Suspended Sentence. An order placing a defendant on probation or suspending a sentence may be stayed if an appeal is taken.

Amended June 24, 2009, effective October 1, 2009.

Reporter's Notes

Subdivision (a). The substance of this subdivision is drawn from G.L. c. 279, § 4 (as amended). The defendant convicted of a crime and sentenced to a term of imprisonment may petition the trial judge or a single justice of the Supreme Judicial or Appeals Court by motion that execution of his sentence be stayed pending appeal. The motion is directed to the discretion of the judge. DiPietro v. Commonwealth, 369 Mass. 964, 339 N.E.2d 924 (1976) (Rescript); Stranad v. Commonwealth, 366 Mass. 847, 318 N.E.2d 617 (1974) (Rescript); Commonwealth v. Allen, Mass.App.Adv.Sh. (1979) 147, 385 N.E.2d 532 (Rescript).

There are few cases construing G.L. c. 279, § 4 and while all are concerned with the element of discretion, in no one is an abuse of that discretion found. *Commonwealth v. Allen*, supra; Commonwealth v. Roberts, Mass.Adv.Sh. (1977) 927, 362 N.E.2d 904 (Rescript); *DiPietro v. Commonwealth*, supra; *Stranad v. Commonwealth*, supra; Fine v. Commonwealth, 312 Mass. 252, 261, 44 N.E.2d 659, 145 A.L.R. 392 (1942); Lebowitch, Petitioner, 235 Mass. 357, 363, 126 N.E. 831 (1920); Commonwealth v. Drohan, 210 Mass. 445, 448, 97 N.E. 89 (1912); Commonwealth v. Brown, 167 Mass. 144, 146, 45 N.E. 1 (1896).

The sine qua non for finding an abuse of discretion in the denial of a motion for a stay is that the movant must have established on the record "a reasonable likelihood of success on appeal." *DiPietro v. Commonwealth*, supra. *Accord Commonwealth v. Roberts*, supra. *But see Commonwealth v. Allen*, S.J.C. No. 79–100 Civ. (Mem., March 20, 1979) (single justice decision overturning *Commonwealth v. Allen*, supra: "[T]he standard is one of sound discretion and may be exercised if the circumstances warrant without a requirement that there be a finding made of a reasonable likelihood of success on appeal.").

The amendment of G.L. c. 276, § 87 by St.1974, c. 614, allows the judge to place the convicted defendant, with his consent, on probation for such term and upon such conditions as the judge deems proper. This provides the judge with a flexible alternative to traditional bail procedures pending appeal which may be used at his discretion for defendants convicted of all but those offenses enumerated in the statute.

Subdivision (b). This subdivision departs from the federal rule in that a stay of the payment of a fine is mandatory under this rule. This provision is adopted in recognition of the difficulty a defendant has, upon the successful appeal of his conviction, in recovering money he has paid in satisfaction of a fine.

Subdivision (c). This subdivision is based, in part, on Fed.R.Crim.P. 38(a)(4) and upon G.L. c. 279, § 4.

Reporter's Notes to Rule 31

This Rule was revised in 2009. As originally adopted in 1979, it codified existing practice under G.L. c. 279 § 4, which governed the procedure for a stay of execution pending appeal prior to the adoption of the Rules of Criminal Procedure.

Subdivision (a). Practice in the Commonwealth is that sentences are not routinely stayed pending appeal. *See Hagen v. Commonwealth*, 437 Mass. 374, 378 (2002). However, where a defendant meets the appropriate requirements, it has been a long standing tradition to grant a stay in the interest of justice, to avoid imprisoning one whose conviction may not survive appellate review. *See Commonwealth v. Levin*, 7 Mass. App. Ct. 501, 513 (1979).

A judge should order a stay only when the defendant has met the two concerns which guide the exercise of discretion in this area. The first and most important is the likelihood of the defendant establishing on appeal that the conviction will be overturned. *Cf. Commonwealth v. Stewart*, 413 Mass. 664 (1992) (bail pending appeal is not appropriate if the only consequence of the defendant's success would be reducing the term of his sentence and not immediate discharge). This requirement does not demand that the defendant establish that the appeal is more likely than not to be successful, only that it presents "an issue which is worthy of presentation to an appellate court, one which offers some reasonable possibility of a successful decision in the appeal." *See Commonwealth v. Hodge*, 380 Mass. 851, 855 (1980); *Commonwealth v. Allen*, 378 Mass. 489, 498 (1979). In this respect, the Massachusetts practice is more liberal than its federal counterpart. *Compare* 18 U.S.C. 3143(b)(1)(B) (the defendant must establish that the appeal "raises a substantial question of law or fact likely to result in" a favorable outcome).

The other factor that informs a judge's exercise of discretion in granting a stay is the question of security: whether the defendant will flee, commit another crime. or present a danger to the community. *See Hodge*, 380 Mass. at 855. The same facts that are relevant to the decision to grant a defendant bail prior to trial are pertinent in this context as well. *See Allen*, 378 Mass. at 498.

In granting a stay, a judge may impose appropriate conditions on the defendant's release. *Cf. Commonwealth v. Beauchemin*, 410 Mass. 181, 186 (1991) (defendant not leave his home and have no minor visitors). G.L. c. 276 § 87 can be used as a vehicle for having the probation department monitor the defendant's conduct during a stay.

The trial judge may entertain a motion for a stay either before or after the entry of an appeal. Whether the judge grants or denies the motion, no statement of reasons is necessary nor must the judge make any particular finding or certification. *See Allen*, 378 Mass. at 1034.

This Rule does not address stays of execution of a sentence when an appeal is not pending. *See Commonwealth v. McLaughlin*, 431 Mass. 506, 518 (2000) (raising but not deciding the question of a judge's inherent power to stay a sentence for other reasons).

Appellate Rule 6 establishes the procedure that is available after the trial judge acts on a motion for a stay. Either the defendant or the Commonwealth may seek relief from a single justice of the court that will hear the appeal concerning the trial judge's decision to deny, *e.g., Commonwealth v. Aviles*, 422 Mass. 1008 (1996), or grant, *e.g. Commonwealth v. Hodge*, 380 Mass. 851 (1980), a stay. In the ordinary course of events, for all but first degree murder cases a single justice of the Appeals Court is the appropriate forum.

Subdivision (b). Stay orders must inform the defendant of the conditions upon which they were issued. Mandatory conditions in-clude the defendant's continuing obligation to provide the court in writing with a current address and to prosecute the appeal in a diligent manner. *See* Mass. R. A.P. 6 (b)(4). The court should craft whatever additional conditions are appropriate to each case.

The stay automatically expires when the appellate court considering the appeal releases a rescript affirming the conviction, unless the appellate court states otherwise. A rescript is "released" when it is announced to the public and the appellate court notifies the parties that the court has decided the case. *Cf.* Mass. R. App. P. 23 (requiring the clerk of the appellate court to mail the parties a copy of the rescript and the opinion, if any). In the ordinary course of events, the rescript "issues" twenty-eight days following the release date or upon the denial of any petition for rehearing or application for further appellate review, whichever is later. *Id*

The court that decided the appeal may exercise its discretion to extend a stay of execution pending a petition for rehearing, application for further appellate review, or petition for certiorari. Unless otherwise specified, an extended stay expires when the rescript issues. The appellate court may act *sua sponte* or pursuant to the defendant's motion, which may be filed before the appeal is decided or after the rescript is released. If the appeal is lodged in the Appeals Court, the defendant should file the motion with the panel that has the responsibility for deciding the merits of the appeal.

In order to ensure that the clerk of the appellate court can notify the parties that a stay has automatically expired, *see* Mass. R. App. P. 6 (b)(6), the clerk of the trial court must notify the appellate court whenever a stay is granted.

Once a rescript affirming the conviction is released, the burden is on the Commonwealth, not the defendant, to initiate the process for the sentence to be executed. *See Commonwealth v. Ly*, 450 Mass. 16, 20 (2007). This requires the prosecutor to file a motion with the trial court and for the court to schedule a hearing and notify the defendant. The court should schedule the hearing promptly. *Id.* at 22. If possible, the prosecutor should agree on a date for the hearing with the defendant's current counsel (in most cases that will be the lawyer who represented the defendant on appeal). The procedure for ensuring the defendant's appearance at the hearing to execute the sentence is modeled after the one described in Rule 6 (a). Ordinarily, the court should simply issue a notice to the defendant of the time and date of the hearing. The prosecutor, however, may accompany the motion for a hearing with a request that the court issue a warrant for the arrest of the defendant. If the prosecutor's submission establishes good cause to believe that a warrant is necessary in order to ensure the defendant's appearance, the court may order the defendant's arrest. The defendant is not entitled to be heard on the question of whether a warrant should issue.

Subdivision (c). This subdivision departs from federal rule in that a stay of the payment of a fine is mandatory under this rule. This provision was adopted in recognition of the difficulty a defendant has, upon the successful appeal of his judgment, in recovering money he has paid in satisfaction of a fine.

Subdivision (d). This subdivision was originally based, in part, on Fed. R. Crim. P. 38(a)(4) and upon G.L. c. 279 § 4.

Rule 32. Filing and Service of Papers

(Applicable to District Court and Superior Court)

(a) Service: When Required. Written motions other than those which are heard ex parte, written notices, and similar papers shall be served upon each of the parties.

(b) Service: How Made. Whenever under these rules or by order of court service is required or permitted to be made upon a party represented by an attorney, service shall be made upon the attorney, unless service upon the party himself is ordered by the court. Service upon the attorney or upon a party shall be made in the manner provided for in civil actions.

(c) Notice of Orders and Judgments. If upon the entry of a judgment or order made on a written motion either or both of the parties are not present in court, the clerk shall immediately mail to the absent party or parties a notice of that entry and shall record the mailing in the docket.

(d) Filing. Papers required to be served shall be filed with the court. Papers shall be filed in the manner provided for in civil actions.

(e) Additional Time After Service by Mail. Whenever a party has the right or is required to do an act within a prescribed period after the service of a notice or other paper upon him and the notice or other paper is served upon him by mail, three days shall be added to the prescribed period.

(f) Protection of Personal Identifying Information. Publicly accessible documents filed with the court shall conform to Supreme Judicial Court Rule 1:24, Protection of Personal Identifying Information in Publicly Accessible Court Documents.

Amended January 25, 2017, effective February 1, 2017.

Reporter's Notes

This rule is closely patterned after Fed.R.Crim.P. 49. Subdivisions (a), (b) and (d) are identical to their federal counterparts and subdivision (c) has been adopted with slight revision. Subdivision (e) has been taken from Fed.R.Crim.P. 45(e) and Mass.R.Civ.P. 6(d).

Subdivision (a). This subdivision is similar to Fed.R.Civ.P. and Mass.R.Civ.P. 5(a). Service is required "upon each of the parties" to avoid the interpretive questions that arose under the "adverse party" language of the federal rule prior to its 1966 amendment, such as the problem of when is a co-defendant an adverse party. The rule is also designed to promote full exchange of information among all parties. However, no restriction is intended upon agreements among co-defendants or between the defendant and the prosecutor restricting mutual exchange of papers in the interest of eliminating unnecessary expense. Advisory Committee Note to Rule 49.

Service is required of motions, notices and similar papers. The latter category embraces opposing affidavits and the like. But this rule does not apply to service of a summons for a witness under Mass.R.Crim.P. 17, or the execution or service of a warrant or summons under Mass.R.Crim.P. 6. *See* 8B J. MOORE, FEDERAL PRACTICE para. 49.02 (1978 rev.).

Subdivision (b). The first sentence of this subdivision is the same as the first sentence of Mass.R.Civ.P. 5(b) and Fed.R.Civ.P. 5(b). When a party has appeared and is represented by an attorney, service is required to be made upon the attorney, unless the court orders service to be made upon the party himself in cases where the court deems such service necessary. An order, disobedience of which is punishable as a contempt, or an order to show cause why a party should not be punished for contempt, are papers which the court would, as a practical matter, generally order to be served upon the party himself. A civil contempt proceeding, however, is merely a continuance of the original action and a step in the enforcement of a previous order or judgment, so that service of papers to have a party adjudged in civil contempt may validly be made on his attorney of record, unless it is unreasonable to regard the attorney as a representative of the party at that time. 2 J. MOORE, FEDERAL PRACTICE para. 5.06 (2d ed. 1978).

The second sentence of Mass.R.Crim.P. 32(b) incorporates by reference Mass.R.Civ.P. 4.

Subdivision (c). This subdivision is similar to Fed.R.Crim.P. 49(d) as it appeared prior to its 1966 amendment. The federal rule is an adaptation for criminal proceedings of Fed.R.Civ.P. 77(d). No consequences are attached to the failure of the clerk to give the prescribed notice. However, it is intended that in a case where the losing party, in reliance upon the clerk's obligation to send a notice, fails to file a timely notice of appeal, the trial judge may, in the exercise of his discretion, vacate the judgment because of the clerk's failure to give notice and may enter a new judgment. The time period for appeal would then begin to run when the second judgment is entered. *See* Hill v. Hawes, 64 S.Ct. 334, 320 U.S. 520, 88 L.Ed. 283, 149 A.L.R. 736 (1944). Since oral motions are generally ruled on in the presence of the parties, there can be no reliance on the clerk's failure to send notice and the applicable time limits for appeal must be observed.

Subdivision (d). This subdivision incorporates by reference Mass. R.Civ.P. 5(d)–(e), which govern the procedure for filing papers. Under Mass.R.Civ.P. 5(e), papers must be filed with the clerk of the court "except that a judge may permit the papers to be filed with him, in which event he shall note thereon the filing date and forthwith transmit them to the office of the clerk."

Subdivision (e). This subdivision is identical to Mass.R.Civ.P. 6(a) and Fed.R.Civ.P. 6(e) and to Fed.R.Crim.P. 45(e). The reason for this rule is that under Mass.R.Civ.P. 5(b), service by mail is complete upon mailing, and various prescribed time periods begin to run after service of notice or other papers. This subdivision adds three days to these prescribed periods since a day or more may intervene between the mailing of a pleading or paper and the actual receipt thereof.

Rule 33. Counsel for Defendants Indigent and Indigent But Able to Contribute

(Applicable to District Court and Superior Court)

The assignment of counsel for defendants determined to be indigent or indigent but able to contribute shall be governed by the provisions of G.L. c. 211D and Supreme Judicial Court Rule 3:10.

Amended May 29, 1986, effective July 1, 1986.

Reporter's Notes

The Municipal Court for the City of Boston established in 1974 the Marginally Indigent Defendant's Attorneys Program (MIDA). This rule establishes a program of similar content for all District and Superior Courts.

A substantial number of defendants who appear in court to answer to criminal charges are found to be indigent and are provided with the services of counsel at public expense. Others with adequate resources retain private counsel. There is also a middle group composed of defendants who, because their incomes or assets are sufficient to prevent their being classed indigent, but are insufficient to enable them to comfortably retain counsel, are often denied representation.

Many of this latter group are willing to pay for legal services to the extent of their ability, but are frustrated in attempting to retain counsel by their limited means. It has become the practice of many judges, when advised of such defendants' unsuccessful attempts to obtain representation, to assign counsel, thus adding to the cost of administering the public defender programs and to the caseload of Massachusetts Defenders Committee.

It is the intent of this rule that an attorney be provided at a fee which is affordable by a defendant who does not qualify as an indigent, but who nonetheless cannot pay the total expense of a criminal defense without undue hardship. The rule applies only to reduced rates for attorney's fees; it does not apply to other defense services.

Under existing practice there is no system of partial eligibility. It is expected that this rule—which makes competent attorneys available at reduced fees—will serve the dual function of providing defense counsel to a large number of defendants while reducing an unnecessary drain on the public treasury. *See* ABA *Standards Relating to Providing Defense Services* § 6.2 (Approved Draft, 1968).

Subdivision (a). This rule is to be read in conjunction with Mass. R.Crim.P. 8, *Assignment of Counsel.*

For many years, indigents who have needed attorneys have received the services of volunteers. Many bar associations have assumed the responsibility of providing legal services without charge to those unable to pay for their criminal defense. However, as constitutional considerations have multiplied, an increased number of defendants and an increased number of appearances for each defendant have created a tremendous burden on public revenues. James v. Strange, 92 S.Ct. 2027, 407 U.S. 128, 141, 32 L.Ed.2d 600 (1972). It is not the purpose of this rule to deprive any defendant of the services of appointed counsel. Rather, it is recognized that many defendants who receive the services of court-appointed counsel are as able to pay part of their legal expenses as some defendants are to pay the entire expenses of retained counsel.

Subdivision (b). The referral process for the appointed attorney shall be monitored by either the local bar association or the clerk of the District Court. The list of attorneys should be comprised of those who volunteer and who are qualified to provide competent legal assistance. An established list will better ensure fairness in the distribution of appointments and will "avoid the appearance of patronage." ABA *Standards*, supra § 2.3.

Subdivision (c). In determining the eligibility of a defendant for the appointment of counsel under this rule, the court should consider the same relevant factors as mentioned in the Reporter's Notes to Mass. R.Crim.P. 8: employment status, income, obligations, dependents, etc. See G.L. c. 261, § 27C. The final determination as to the defendant's eligibility as marginally indigent is within the court's discretion.

Where special circumstances require, *see* Mass.R.Crim.P. 8(b), an appointment can be made of an attorney who is not on the list.

It should be clearly understood by both the defendant and the appointed attorney that the established fee is to be the only remuneration for the services rendered. Upon appointment of counsel, a form, which details the required information, is to be signed by the defendant.

Within seven days after entry of judgment or other disposition of the case, the attorney shall complete a report indicating the offense of which the defendant was charged and the fees charged and received.

Subdivision (d). The defendant is to make the initial contact and it is his responsibility to afford the attorney adequate time for investigation and preparation before trial. If appointed counsel chooses not to, or is unable to, represent the defendant, he is to notify the court and the defendant.

Subdivision (e). As provided in Mass.R.Crim.P. 8(d), the case may proceed to trial on the set date notwithstanding the fact that the attorney has not been contacted by the accused or has been given insufficient time for preparation.

All parties, unless the attorney has withdrawn his appearance pursuant to subdivision (d), must appear in court on the trial date. If the attorney has properly withdrawn and no continuance has been granted, the defendant must appear in court on the trial date. The case should proceed to trial unless for compelling reasons the court determines that justice requires a continuance. *See* Mass.R.Crim.P. 9.

Subdivision (f). Upon appointment of counsel, the defendant should be told that the expense of appointed counsel will be assessed against him as costs, and he should be informed of the possible effects of non-compliance with any court order regarding payment of these costs. To insure that the defendant understands the operation of this rule, the defendant will be required to sign a statement to that effect.

The court should then make an initial estimate of the costs of defense (keeping in mind the maximum established by the District Court and Superior Court Rules and other rules of court that deter-mine the rate of attorneys' compensation) and of the defendant's ability to satisfy all or part of those costs out of present assets and expected earnings. In determining the availability of present assets to meet these costs, the court should consider the defendant's liabilities and continuing obligations. In determining the amount of income available to meet those costs, the court should additionally consider how long (if at all) the defendant will be working prior to the commencement of trial (if there is to be a trial). See G.L. c. 261, § 27C, which does not attempt to establish standards for determining indigency, but requires that such standards be posted by the court. The court may also utilize G.L. c. 93, § 51 to obtain records from a consumer reporting agency in order to evaluate defendant's affidavit of indigency under G.L. c. 261, § 27B.

Where the court finds that there are assets or income available to be used for the benefit of counsel, the court may then enter an order that the defendant pay a reasonable amount to the court out of his present assets and that he pay a reasonable amount out of future income on an installment basis for a definite duration. This order, like all subsequent orders regarding the payment of costs, may be modified by the court upon a showing by either the defense or the prosecution of changed circumstances.

A defendant can be ordered to pay in installments to be satisfied out of future income, and to this extent the timing of the burden may be different. However, this can in no way be seen as coercive pressure to find employment, or to maintain present employment or one's present income level, because changed circumstances are grounds for modification of the court order. Thus, the only difference relates to the timing of the burden which does not impede the exercise of one's right to counsel.

The Supreme Court in Fuller v. Oregon, 94 S.Ct. 2116, 417 U.S. 40, 38 L.Ed.2d 737 (1974), affirmed the validity of such reasoning:

> The fact that an indigent who accepts state-appointed legal representation knows that he might someday be required to repay the costs of these services in no way affects his eligibility to obtain counsel. The Oregon statute is carefully designed to insure that only those who actually become capable of repaying the State will ever be obliged to do so....
>
> A defendant in a criminal case who is just above the line separating the indigent from the non-indigent must borrow money, sell off his meager assets, or call upon his family or friends in order to hire a lawyer. We cannot say that the Constitution requires that those only slightly poorer must remain forever immune from any obligation to shoulder the expenses of their legal defense, even when they are able to pay without hardship.

Id. at 53–54.

The provisions of subdivision (f)(3) for assignment to defense counsel of any cash bail deposited is new to Massachusetts procedure.

Rule 34. Report

[Text of rule applicable to cases initiated (by indictment or complaint) on or after September 7, 2004.]

If, prior to trial, or, with the consent of the defendant, after conviction of the defendant, a question of law arises which the trial judge determines is so important or doubtful as to require the decision of the Appeals Court, the judge may report the case so far as necessary to present the question of law arising therein. If the case is reported prior to trial, the case shall be continued for trial to await the decision of the Appeals Court.

Amended March 8, 2004, effective September 7, 2004.

Reporter's Notes—Revised, 2004

Under prior practice, the authority of a judge to report a question of law for the decision of the full court was wholly a creature of statute,

Commonwealth v. Cronin, 245 Mass. 163 (1923), and the procedure was expressly confined to instances where a person had been convicted, G.L. c. 278, § 30 (St. 1830, c. 113, § 4), or before trial had commenced. G.L. c. 278, § 30A (St.1954, c. 528). The language of this rule is comprised of the statutory provisions of those two sections.

Prior to 1954, a trial judge was authorized to report a question of law only after the conviction of a defendant; no provision granted the court the authority to report an interlocutory question before trial. Commonwealth v. Baldi, 250 Mass. 528 (1925). The addition of § 30A by chapter 528 of the Statutes of 1954 gave the court the power to report and have decided a question arising prior to trial, and this procedure has been used increasingly in recent years with the expanded application of fourth, fifth and sixth amendment rights. *See,* e.g., Commonwealth v. Baker, 343 Mass. 162 (1961) (admission to bail); Commonwealth v. Mekalian, 346 Mass. 496 (1963) (motion to suppress evidence); Commonwealth v. O'Leary, 347 Mass. 387 (1964) (assignment of counsel).

Once trial has commenced, the court may not report a question until after a conviction of the defendant. The definition of "conviction" for purposes of this rule is that provided by the Supreme Judicial Court in Commonwealth v. Baldi, 250 Mass. 528 (1925), which may include the judgment of the court following a verdict of guilty or confession of guilt, or may mean a verdict of guilty against the defendant or his confession in open court, without judgment or sentence. *Id.* at 536–37.

Although a report may be made after trial if the defendant consents, it does not preclude the defendant from taking an appeal. *See* Commonwealth v. Giles, 350 Mass. 102 (1966), in which the judge found the defendant guilty and suspended the execution of sentence pending answer to his report from the Supreme Judicial Court. The defendant later appealed the entire case. Conversely, the procedure has also been used to afford a defendant as full a review as he could have obtained had his counsel properly filed an assignment of errors after notice of the completion of the summary of the record. In Commonwealth v. Pratt, 360 Mass. 708 (1972), the Supreme Judicial Court treated such a case as if it had been properly brought on appeal. *See* Commonwealth v. Dorius, 346 Mass. 323, 324 (1963).

The decision to report rests within the discretion of the trial judge. Commonwealth v. Eagleton, 402 Mass. 199, 208 (1988). This discretion is to be guided in part by the standard set out by the Supreme Judicial Court in Commonwealth v. Cavanaugh, 366 Mass. 277 (1974). This standard, though stated in connection with interlocutory appeals, is, as the court clearly states, applicable to decisions to report:

An interlocutory appeal, *like a report,* may be appropriate when the alternatives are a prolonged, expensive, involved or unduly burdensome trial or a dismissal of the indictment.

Id. at 279. (Emphasis added). Accord Commonwealth v. Vaden, 373 Mass. 397 (1977).

A case may be reported if in the judge's opinion a question of law is so important or doubtful as to require a determination by a higher court, Commonwealth v. A Juvenile, 381 Mass. 727, 728 n.2 (1980). The judge must then refer facts sufficient to make intelligible the question of law reported. Commonwealth v. Yacobian, 393 Mass. 1005, 1005–06 (1984); Commonwealth v. O'Neil, 233 Mass. 535 (1919). In Commonwealth v. Ficksman, 340 Mass. 744 (1960), the Supreme Judicial Court decided that the record before it was insufficient to determine properly the question reported. The court therefore discharged the report and remanded the case to the lower court. The judge should refuse to report a case upon the defendant's motion if he finds there is no question of law so important as to require higher court resolution, Commonwealth v. McKnight, 289 Mass. 530 (1935), or because there is no issue of law. Commonwealth v. Chase, 348 Mass. 100 (1964).

The Supreme Judicial Court held in Commonwealth v. Henry's Drywall Co., Inc., 362 Mass. 552 (1972), that an interlocutory report was not appropriate under the circumstances of the case. Quoting

John Gilbert, Jr. Co. v. C.M. Fauci Co., 309 Mass. 271, 273 (1941), Justice Quirico stated that:

Interlocutory matters should be reported only where it appears that they present serious questions likely to be material in the ultimate decision, and that subsequent proceedings in the trial court will be substantially facilitated by so doing.

362 Mass. at 557. The report was discharged since a decision would have avoided what appeared to the court to be only a short trial which might effectively resolve the issues reported. See Commonwealth v. Henry's Drywall Co., Inc., 366 Mass. 539 (1974). Interlocutory reports are not to "be permitted to become additional causes of the delays . . . which are already too prevalent." Commonwealth v. Vaden, 373 Mass. 397 (1977). However, in Commonwealth v. Shields, 402 Mass. 162, 163 (1988), the S.J.C. found questions concerning the constitutionality of sobriety roadblocks were appropriately reported because the answers were likely to be dispositive, the questions were likely to recur, and an improper ruling by the trial court would have resulted in an unnecessary waste of judicial resources at trial.

To help the appellate court decide whether an interlocutory report is appropriate, the reporting court should explain its reasons for declining to wait until after the trial is completed. Commonwealth v. Wallace, 431 Mass. 705, 705 n.1 (2000). *See also* Commonwealth v. Vaden, 373 Mass. 397 (1977) ("the report itself, or . . . [an] accompanying stipulation or [the] record" should indicate why the issue is appropriate for interlocutory review).

After conviction of the defendant, the trial judge has the authority to make a report whether or not the trial was heard by a jury, so long as it is determined that the defendant is guilty. *See* Commonwealth v. Kemp, 254 Mass. 190 (1926), as to authority to report in a jury-waived trial.

The granting of jurisdiction to the Appeals Court concurrent with the Supreme Judicial Court conforms to existing statutory law. G. L. c. 211A, § 10 established the concurrent jurisdiction:

Subject to such further appellate review by the supreme judicial court as may be permitted pursuant to section eleven or otherwise, the appeals court shall have concurrent appellate jurisdiction with the supreme judicial court, to the extent review is otherwise allowable, with respect to a determination made in the appellate tax board and in the superior court department, the housing court department, the land court department, the probate and family court department, the Boston municipal court department in criminal session, the Boston municipal court department appellate division, the juvenile court department, the district court department in criminal session, and the district court department appellate divisions, except in review of convictions for first degree murder. A report from any such department of the trial court of any case, in whole or in part, or any question of law arising therein shall be deemed to be within the concurrent appellate jurisdiction of the supreme judicial court and the appeals court.

A trial judge is to report a case to the Appeals Court. Section 10 states further that appellate review, "if within the jurisdiction of the appeals court, shall be in the first instance by the appeals court . . ."

Previously a defendant in District Court, except in a jury session trial, was precluded from requesting the judge to report a question. By a 2004 amendment, however, the caption limiting application of this rule was removed. That amendment brings Rule 34 into conformity with legislation that abolished the de novo district court system and established that "review may be had directly by the appeals court, by appeal, report or otherwise in the same manner provided for trials of criminal cases in the superior court." G.L. c. 218, secs. 26A and 27A(g), applicable to judge and jury sessions respectively. Rule 34 now applies to all superior, juvenile, district and municipal courts.

The Supreme Judicial Court is also given general discretionary powers of superintendence under c. 211, §§ 3 and 4A, with which it can review significant interlocutory matters.

The supreme judicial court may . . . direct any cause or matter to be transferred from a lower court to it in whole or in part for further action or directions, and in case of partial transfer may issue such orders or direction in regard to the part of such cause or matter not so transferred as justice may require.

G.L. c. 211, § 4A. Under § 3, it may do so "to correct and prevent errors and abuses . . . if no other remedy is expressly provided," and in the interests of "the furtherance of justice and . . . the regular execution of the laws."

The broad statutory standard governing matters acceptable for review under §§ 3 and 4A has been narrowly interpreted by the Supreme Judicial Court. The Court has stated that "[o]nly in the most exceptional circumstances will we review interlocutory rulings in criminal cases under our general superintendence powers." Gilday v. Commonwealth, 360 Mass. 170, 171 (1971). To fulfill this requirement there must be a substantial claim of violation of a substantive right and irremediable error, such that the defendant cannot be placed in status quo in the regular course of appeal. Morrissette v. Commonwealth, 380 Mass. 197, 198 (1980). See also Gilday, supra, at 171; Mass. R. Crim. P. 30, Reporter's Notes, supra (collecting cases). Moreover, as in the case of a report, the fact that an appeal may be taken from a final judgment after the case has been tried does not prevent the court from acting within its powers of superintendence. Barber v. Commonwealth, 353 Mass. 236, 239 (1967).

In A Juvenile v. Commonwealth, 370 Mass. 272 (1976), the plaintiff filed a petition for relief in the nature of certiorari with the Supreme Judicial Court under c. 211, § 3. This procedure was sufficient to bring the matter to the court for review.

Rule 35. Depositions to Perpetuate Testimony

(Applicable to District Court and Superior Court)

(a) General Applicability. Whenever due to exceptional circumstances, and after a showing of materiality and relevance, it is deemed to be in the interest of justice that the testimony of a prospective witness of the defendant or the Commonwealth be taken and preserved, the judge may at any time after the filing of a complaint or return of an indictment, upon his own motion or the motion of either party with notice to all interested persons, order that the testimony of the witness be taken by deposition and that any designated book, paper, document, record, recording, or other material not privileged be produced at the same time and place. If a witness is committed for failure to give bail to appear to testify at a trial or hearing, the judge may direct that his deposition be taken. A copy of a deposition ordered upon the judge's own motion shall be transmitted to the court by the person administering the deposition. In determining a motion filed pursuant to this rule, the judge may order a hearing or may determine whether exceptional circumstances exist and the materiality and relevance of the testimony on the basis of the supporting affidavit.

(b) Summonses. An order to take a deposition shall authorize the issuance by the clerk of summonses pursuant to Rule 17 for the persons and objects named or described in such order. A witness whose deposition is to be taken may be required to attend at any place designated by the trial court, taking into account the convenience of the witness and the parties.

(c) Notice of Taking of Deposition. The party on whose motion a deposition is to be taken shall give all interested persons reasonable written notice of the time and place for the taking of the deposition. If a defendant is in custody, the officer having custody of the defendant shall be notified by the court of the time and place set for the taking of the deposition and shall produce the defendant at that time and place and keep him in the presence of the witness during the taking of the deposition. A defendant not in custody shall have the right to be present at the taking of a deposition, but his failure to appear after notice and without cause shall constitute a waiver of the right to be present and of all objections based upon that right.

(d) Payment of Expenses. Whenever a deposition is taken upon motion of the Commonwealth, the court shall direct that the reasonable expenses of travel and subsistence of the defendant and his counsel and the witness be paid for by the Commonwealth. Expenses for a deposition taken upon motion of a defendant may be assessed to the defendant to be paid forthwith or in such other manner as the judge may determine.

(e) Scope of Examination. Subject to such additional conditions as the judge may specify and except as otherwise provided in these rules, the taking of depositions in criminal cases shall be in the manner provided for in civil actions. The scope and manner of examination and cross-examination at the taking of the deposition shall be such as would be allowed in the trial itself.

(f) Objections to Deposition Testimony. Objections to deposition testimony or evidence or parts thereof and the grounds for the objections shall be stated at the time of the taking of the deposition.

(g) Admissibility. At a trial or upon any hearing, a part or all of a deposition, so far as it is otherwise admissible under the law of evidence, may be used as substantive evidence if the judge finds that the deponent is unavailable or if the deponent gives testimony at the trial or hearing which is inconsistent with his deposition. Any deposition may be used by any party for the purpose of contradicting or impeaching the testimony of the deponent as a witness. "Unavailable" as a witness includes situations in which the deponent:

(1) is exempt by a ruling of the judge on the ground of privilege from testifying concerning the subject matter of his deposition;

(2) persists in refusing to testify concerning the subject matter of his deposition despite an order of the judge to do so;

(3) lacks memory of the subject matter of his deposition;

(4) is unable to be present or to testify at the trial or hearing because of death or physical or mental illness or infirmity;

(5) is absent from the trial or hearing and the proponent of the deposition has been unable to procure the deponent's attendance by process or other reasonable means; or

(6) is absent from the trial or hearing and his testimony was ordered taken and preserved pursuant to Rule 6(d)(2).

A deponent is not unavailable as a witness if his exemption, refusal, claim of lack of memory, inability, or absence is due to the procurement or wrongdoing of the proponent of his deposition for the purpose of preventing the deponent from attending or testifying.

(h) Notice.

(1) *District Court.* All interested parties shall be given reasonable notice by the clerk of the time set for hearing motions filed under this rule.

(2) *Superior Court.* The moving party shall notify all interested parties of the time set for hearing motions filed under this rule at least seven days prior to the hearing.

(i) Deposition by Agreement Not Precluded. Nothing in this rule shall preclude the taking of a deposition, orally or upon written questions, by agreement of the parties with the consent of the judge.

Reporter's Notes

This rule was written in substantial conformity with 18 U.S.C. § 3503 (1970) and is to be governed by the provisions of Mass. R.Crim.P. 13 wherever the two rules are not inconsistent. *See* Rules of Criminal Procedure (U.L.A.) rules 431–32 (1974), Fed.R.Crim.P. 15.

Previous comparable statutory law in the Commonwealth concerning the taking of depositions in criminal proceedings was General Laws c. 277, § 76 (Rev.St. [1836] 136, § 32) which provided that:

[Where] an issue of fact is joined upon an indictment, the court may, upon application of the defendant, grant a commission to examine any material witnesses residing out of the commonwealth, in the same manner as in civil causes; and the prosecuting officer may join in such commission and may name any material witnesses to be examined on the part of the commonwealth.

Section 77 of that same chapter (Rev.St. [1836] c. 136, § 33) provided:

When such commission is issued ... and the depositions taken thereon ... [are] returned, [they] shall be read in the same manner and with the like effect ... subject to the same exceptions, as in civil cases; but if the defendant on his trial declines to use the deposition so taken, the prosecuting officer shall not, without the defendant's consent, make use of any deposition taken on behalf of the commonwealth.

Although these statutes provide a basis for this rule, they are superseded by it. The statement that depositions are to be conducted and used "as in civil causes" formerly operated to incorporate by reference G.L. c. 233, §§ 46–63 and Superior Court Rule 37 (1954). This rule is to govern the taking of depositions in criminal cases, but should reference to civil practice be necessary it shall be to Mass.R.Civ.P. 27 and to Superior Court Rules 71–72 (1974), insofar as they are consistent with this rule. *See* SUPERIOR COURT RULES, 1974, ANNOTATED 297–309 (Mass.Bar Ed.1975).

Subdivision (a). This rule has adopted the approach set out in the Federal Rules: A request to take a deposition in a criminal case will be granted only in exceptional situations. United States v. Whiting, 308 F.2d 537 (2d Cir.1962). This is because criminal depositions are not for the discovery of information; rather they are intended to preserve evidence. United States v. Steffes, 35 F.R.D. 24 (1964).

While it is true that it is far more desirable to secure the actual presence of a potential witness in criminal cases, there are situations in which the use of depositions is required in order to assure that the ends of justice are met, e.g., when a witness' attendance cannot be secured because of sickness or infirmity. (*See* subdivision [g][4], infra). Or, notwithstanding the provisions of G.L. c. 233, § 13A and c. 277, § 66, the right of a defendant to compulsory process for witnesses who are necessary to his defense does not automatically extend beyond the territory of the Commonwealth. Commonwealth v. Dirring, 354 Mass. 523, 238 N.E.2d 508 (1968). *Accord* Commonwealth v. Watkins, Mass.Adv.Sh. (1978) 1646, 1668–69, 379 N.E.2d 1040. *See* subdivision (g)(5), infra.

The Supreme Judicial Court in Smith v. Commonwealth, 331 Mass. 585, 121 N.E.2d 707 (1954), specifically mentioned the availability of depositions in criminal cases. In *Smith,* a convicted defendant petitioned for a writ of error alleging that his alibi defense which was

supported by affidavits and letters had not received sufficient recognition during the prosecution of his case. The court said that where the defendant's material allegations could have been supported by the testimony of known people residing out of state, the deposition procedure detailed in G.L. c. 277, §§ 76–77 could have been used advantageously. It is in such a case that the procedures detailed in this rule should be used.

Another set of exceptional circumstances warranting the taking of a deposition was established by statute. Former General Laws c. 276, § 50 (St.1851, c. 71) provided that the deposition of a witness unable to provide sufficient sureties guaranteeing his appearance in court could be taken upon order of the court with the consent of the defendant. This subdivision does not require the defendant's consent when the court finds that exceptional circumstances justify an order that a witness' deposition be taken.

Subdivision (b). This subdivision conforms to Fed.R.Crim.P. 17(f) in explicitly empowering the clerk of the court to issue compulsory process in order to effect the taking of a deposition. It should be noted that it authorizes orders to produce documents, objects, etc., at the taking of the deposition as well. Summonses are treated in full under Mass.R.Crim.P. 17.

Subdivision (c). Whenever a defendant is incarcerated, the moving party is responsible for insuring that the defendant has the opportunity to be present while the deponent is being examined. This can be accomplished in either of two ways: by designating the detention facility where the defendant is incarcerated as the place where the deposition is to be taken, or by authorizing the defendant's temporary release for the purpose of attending the examination. The second alternative would require the issuance of a writ of habeas corpus or other similar judicial order.

A defendant not in custody has the responsibility of attending the taking of a deposition unless he has cause for not attending. Insufficient notice and not having been tendered expenses are examples of sufficient cause for non-attendance. By implication, the failure to attend after sufficient notice and tendering of expenses constitutes a waiver of the right to be present unless other cause is shown. Where the defendant has established cause for non-attendance, the deposition should not be used over his objection.

Subdivision (d). The provision in this subdivision authorizing payment from public funds is supported by G.L. c. 12, § 24 (as amended, St.1978, c. 478, § 10), which authorizes district attorneys to expend state monies for the necessary costs of prosecuting a case.

Subdivision (e). This subdivision conforms substantially to Fed. R.Crim.P. 15(d), although the Massachusetts rule makes no provision for discovery, a subject which is covered in depth by Mass.R.Crim.P. 14. For deposition practice in civil actions, see Mass.R.Civ.P. 27.

Subdivision (f). It is intended that objections to testimony and the grounds therefor are to be stated at the taking of the deposition, consistent with civil practice under Superior Court Rule 71 (1974). *See* SUPERIOR COURT RULES, 1974, ANNOTATED 302–03 (Mass.Bar Ed.1975). The requirement that objections be stated at the taking of a deposition accords with Fed.R.Crim.P. 15(f).

Subdivision (g). For all or part of a deposition to be admissible as evidence, the deponent must be unavailable as that term is defined in this subdivision. Prior to the promulgation of this rule, there was no statute or rule which defined "unavailability" in the present context. Commonwealth v. DiPietro, 373 Mass. 397, 367 N.E.2d 621 (1977). Further, the deposition must be otherwise admissible within the law of evidence, i.e., the former testimony exception to the hearsay rule. *See* Fed.R.Evid. 804(b)(1); Commonwealth v. McLaughlin, 364 Mass. 211, 219–21, 303 N.E.2d 338 (1973); *Commonwealth v. DiPietro,* supra, at 1984–92 (collecting cases), Commonwealth v. Canon, 373 Mass. 494, 368 N.E.2d 1181 (1977).

As with other manifestations of the sixth amendment right to confrontation, the significant feature is whether the party against whom the deposition is offered had through counsel an adequate opportunity for cross-examination of the deponent. *Pointer v. Texas,* 85 S.Ct. 1065, 380 U.S. 400, 406–07, 13 L.Ed.2d 923 (1965). *Accord Commonwealth v. Canon,* supra; Commonwealth v. DiPietro, 4 Mass. App. 845, 356 N.E.2d 269 (1976), aff'd, 373 Mass. 369, 367 N.E.2d 811 (1977); Commonwealth v. Caine, 366 Mass. 366, 371–72, 318 N.E.2d 901 (1974); Commonwealth v. Clark, 363 Mass. 467, 295 N.E.2d 163 (1973); Commonwealth v. Mustone, 353 Mass. 490, 498, 233 N.E.2d 1 (1968). Actual cross-examination is not required, the constitutional requirement is satisfied if the party against whom the deposition is offered was afforded an adequate opportunity to cross-examine. *Pointer v. Texas,* supra; *Commonwealth v. Canon,* supra; *Commonwealth v. DiPietro,* supra; In re Andrews, 368 Mass. 468, 334 N.E.2d 15 (1975). That opportunity is to be afforded pursuant to subdivision (e), infra, under which the scope and manner of cross-examination is to be such as allowed in trials.

A deposition otherwise admissible may be introduced as substantive evidence of the matters contained therein if the deponent is unavailable. Any deposition may be used to impeach in accord with established rules of evidence.

Subdivisions (g)(1)–(g)(5) are essentially restatements of Fed. R.Evid. 804(a)(1)–(5). Subdivision (g)(6) is included to make this rule consistent with Mass.R.Crim.P. 6(d)(2).

Subdivision (g)(1) is consistent with Commonwealth v. Canon, 373 Mass. 494, 368 N.E.2d 1181 (1977) (witness invoked fifth amendment privilege against self-incrimination) and Commonwealth v. DiPietro, 373 Mass. 369, 367 N.E.2d 811 (1977) (witness invoked marital privilege). The *DiPietro* court properly distinguished between the unavailability of a witness and the unavailability of the testimony of that witness:

"[T]he important element is whether the testimony of the witness is sought and is available and not whether the witness's body is available." The physical presence without the testimony contributes nothing to the later trial.

Mass.Adv.Sh. (1977) at 1987, *quoting* Mason v. United States, 408 F.2d 903, 906 (10th Cir.1969), cert. denied 91 S.Ct. 462, 400 U.S. 993, 27 L.Ed.2d 441 (1971).

Subdivisions (g)(2) and (3) are also concerned with the situation where the witness is present, but unable or unwilling to testify.

As to a deceased or incapacitated witness, subdivision (g)(4), *see* e.g., Commonwealth v. Richards, 35 Mass. (18 Pick.) 434, 29 Am.Dec. 608 (1837); Temple v. Phelps, 193 Mass. 297, 79 N.E. 482 (1906).

For "unavailability" in terms of the witness who cannot be found or is not amenable to process, *see* e.g., Commonwealth v. Gallo, 275 Mass. 320, 324, 175 N.E. 718, 79 A.L.R. 1380 (1931).

Mass.R.Crim.P. 6(d)(2) authorizes the court to order that the testimony of a witness present in court upon the default of a defendant be taken and preserved, and Mass.R.Crim.P. 10(c) permits the court to condition a continuance upon the taking of and preservation of the testimony of witnesses then present. It is presumed under the former that if a deposition of a witness then present in court is ordered upon the default of a defendant, defendant's counsel is present in court so as to protect the right of the defendant to confront his accusers under the sixth amendment and *Pointer v. Texas,* supra. The voluntary absence of a defendant from trial operates as a waiver of his sixth amendment right to confrontation. Taylor v. United States, 94 S.Ct. 194, 414 U.S. 17, 3 L.Ed.2d 174 (1973); Commonwealth v. Flemmi, 360 Mass. 693, 277 N.E.2d 523 (1971). *See also* Illinois v. Allen, 90 S.Ct. 435, 397 U.S. 337, 342–43, 24 L.Ed.2d 420 (1970); Commonwealth v. Snyder, 282 Mass. 401, 185 N.E. 376 (1933), aff'd sub nom., Snyder v. Massachusetts, 54 S.Ct. 330, 291 U.S. 97, 105–06, 78 L.Ed. 674, 90 A.L.R. 575 (1934). There is evident a clear analogy between the situation where the defendant voluntarily absents himself from trial and that contemplated by Mass.R.Crim.P. 6(d)(2) where the defendant is found in default.

The summons which is issued pursuant to Mass.R.Crim.P. 6(b)(2) is formulated to give the defendant adequate notice that his willful default may result in the taking of depositions so as to avoid the sixth amendment confrontation issues raised in *Taylor v. United States,* supra.

Subdivision (h). This subdivision, generally governing notice, is supplemental to Mass.R.Crim.P. 32.

Subdivision (i). Drawn from Fed.R.Crim.P. 15(g), this subdivision recognizes that the parties may find it to their joint advantage to preserve testimony by deposition, or to utilize a deposition at trial, and permits them to do so without having to call upon the court for authorization. If depositions are contemplated, that fact is appropriate for discussion at the pretrial conference. Mass.R.Crim.P. 11(a), (b), Reporter's Notes, supra.

Rule 36.   Case Management

(Applicable to District Court and Superior Court)

(a) General Provisions.

(1) *Order of Priorities.* The trial of defendants in custody awaiting trial and defendants whose pretrial liberty is reasonably believed to present unusual risks to society shall be given preference over other criminal cases.

(2) *Function of the Court.*

(A) District Court. The court shall determine the sequence of the trial calendar.

(B) Superior Court. The court shall determine the sequence of the trial calendar after cases are selected for prosecution by the district attorney.

(b) Standards of a Speedy Trial. The time limitations in this subdivision shall apply to all defendants as to whom the return day is on or after the effective date of these rules. Defendants arraigned prior to the effective date of these rules shall be tried within twenty-four months after such effective date.

(1) *Time Limits.* A defendant, except as provided by subdivision (d)(3) of this rule, shall be brought to trial within the following time periods, as extended by subdivision (b)(2) of this rule:

(A) During the first twelve-month period following the effective date of this rule, a defendant shall be tried within twenty-four months after the return day in the court in which the case is awaiting trial.

(B) During the second such twelve-month period, a defendant shall be tried within eighteen months after the return day in the court in which the case is awaiting trial.

(C) During the third and all successive such twelve-month periods, a defendant shall be tried within twelve months after the return day in the court in which the case is awaiting trial.

(D) If a retrial of the defendant is ordered, the trial shall commence within one year after the date the action occasioning the retrial becomes final, as extended by subdivision (b)(2) of this rule. The order of an appellate court requiring a retrial is final upon the issuance by the appellate court of the rescript. In the event that the clerk of the appellate court fails to issue the rescript within the time provided for in Massachusetts Rule of Appellate Procedure 23, retrial shall commence within one year after the date when the rescript should have issued.

If a defendant is not brought to trial within the time limits of this subdivision, as extended by subdivision (b)(2), he shall be entitled upon motion to a dismissal of the charges.

(2) *Excluded Periods.* The following periods shall be excluded in computing the time within which the trial of any offense must commence:

(A) Any period of delay resulting from other proceedings concerning the defendant, including, but not limited to:

(i) delay resulting from an examination of the defendant, and hearing on, his mental competency, or physical incapacity;

(ii) delay resulting from a stay of the proceedings due to an examination or treatment of the defendant pursuant to section 47 of chapter 123 of the General Laws;

(iii) delay resulting from a trial with respect to other charges against the defendant, which period shall run from the commencement of such other trial until fourteen days after an acquittal or imposition of sentence;

(iv) delay resulting from interlocutory appeals;

(v) delay resulting from hearings on pretrial motions;

(vi) delay resulting from proceedings relating to transfer to or from other divisions or counties pursuant to Rule 37;

(vii) delay reasonably attributable to any period, not to exceed thirty days, during which any proceeding concerning the defendant is actually under advisement.

(B) Any period of delay resulting from the absence or unavailability of the defendant or an essential witness. A defendant or an essential witness shall be considered absent when his whereabouts are unknown and he is attempting to avoid apprehension or prosecution or his whereabouts cannot be determined by due diligence. A defendant or an essential witness shall be considered unavailable whenever his whereabouts are known but his presence for trial cannot be obtained by due diligence or he resists appearing at or being returned for trial.

(C) Any period of delay resulting from the fact that the defendant is mentally incompetent or physically unable to stand trial.

(D) If the complaint or indictment is dismissed by the prosecution and thereafter a charge is filed against the defendant for the same or a related offense, any period of delay from the date the charge was dismissed to the date the time limitation would commence to run as to the subsequent charge.

(E) A reasonable period of delay when the defendant is joined for trial with a codefendant as to whom the time for trial has not run and there is no cause for granting a severance.

(F) Any period of delay resulting from a continuance granted by a judge on his own motion or at the request of the defendant or his counsel or at the request of the prosecutor, if the judge granted the continuance on the basis of his findings that the ends of justice served by taking such action outweighed the best interests of the public and the defendant in a speedy trial. No period of delay resulting from a continuance granted by the court in accordance with this paragraph shall be excludable under this subdivision unless the judge sets forth in the record of the case, either orally or in writing, his reasons for finding that the ends of justice served by the granting of the continuance outweigh the best interests of the public and the defendant in a speedy trial.

(G) Any period of time between the day on which a defendant or his counsel and the prosecuting attorney agree in writing that the defendant will plead guilty or nolo contendere to the charges and such time as the judge accepts or rejects the plea arrangement.

(H) Any period of time between the day on which the defendant enters a plea of guilty and such time as an order of the judge permitting the withdrawal of the plea becomes final.

(3) *Computation of Time Limits.* In computing any time limit other than an excluded period, the day of the act or event which causes a designated period of time to begin to run shall not be included. Computation of an excluded period shall include both the first and the last day of the excludable act or event.

(c) **Dismissal for Prejudicial Delay.** Notwithstanding the fact that a defendant is not entitled to a dismissal under subdivision (b) of this rule, a defendant shall upon motion be entitled to a dismissal where the judge after an examination and consideration of all attendant circumstances determines that: (1) the conduct of the prosecuting attorney in bringing the defendant to trial has been unreasonably lacking in diligence and (2) this conduct on the part of the prosecuting attorney has resulted in prejudice to the defendant.

(d) **Special Procedures: Persons Serving Term of Imprisonment.**

(1) *General Provisions.* A person serving a term of imprisonment either within or without the prosecuting jurisdiction is entitled to all safeguards afforded him under subdivisions (a), (b), and (c) of this rule in the conduct of any criminal proceeding, subject to the limitations stated herein.

(2) *Persons Detained Within the Commonwealth.* Any person who is detained within the Commonwealth upon the unexecuted portion of a sentence imposed pursuant to a criminal proceeding is entitled to be tried upon any untried indictment or complaint pending against him in any court in this Commonwealth within the time prescribed by subdivision (b) of this rule.

(3) *Persons Detained Outside the Commonwealth.* Any person who is detained outside the Commonwealth upon the unexecuted portion of a sentence imposed pursuant to a criminal proceeding, and against whom an untried indictment or complaint is pending within the Commonwealth shall, subsequent to the filing of a detainer, be notified by the prosecutor by mail of such charges and of his right to demand a speedy trial. If the defendant pursuant to such notification does demand trial, the person having custody shall so certify to the prosecutor, who shall promptly seek to obtain the presence of the defendant for trial. If the prosecutor has unreasonably delayed (A) in causing a detainer to be filed with the official having custody of the defendant, or (B) in seeking to obtain

the defendant's presence for trial, and the defendant has been prejudiced thereby, the pending charges against the defendant shall be dismissed.

(e) Effect of a Dismissal. A dismissal of any charge ordered pursuant to any provision of this rule shall apply to all related offenses.

(f) Case Status Reports.

(1) *District Court.* The First Justice of each division of the District Court shall be advised periodically by the clerk of the status of all cases which have been pending in that court for six months or longer. The report shall be transmitted to the Administrative Justice for the District Court Department.

(2) *Superior Court.* The Administrative Justice for the Superior Court Department shall be notified by the clerk for each county of the status of all cases which have been pending in that court for six months or longer within the following time periods:

(A) for the first twelve-month period following the effective date of this rule, sixty days after the last day of a sitting;

(B) for the second such twelve-month period, forty-five days after the last day of a sitting;

(C) for the third and all successive such twelve-month periods, thirty days after the last day of a sitting.

Such notice shall include the number of the case, the name of the defendant, the offense charged, the name of defense counsel, if any, and the name of the prosecutor.

Amended effective March 1, 1996.

Reporter's Notes

This rule is taken in part from the ABA *Standards Relating to Speedy Trial* (Approved Draft, 1968) and to a lesser extent from the Federal Speedy Trial Act, 18 U.S.C. §§ 3161–74 (Supp. 1, 1975), and former G.L. c. 277, §§ 72 (St.1784, c. 72) and 72A (St.1965, c. 343). *See* Rules of Criminal Procedure (U.L.A.) rule 722 (1974); ABA *Standards Relating to Speedy Trial* (2d ed., Approved Draft, 1978).

The Supreme Court held in Barker v. Wingo, 92 S.Ct. 2182, 407 U.S. 514, 33 L.Ed.2d 101 (1972), that a defendant's constitutional right to a speedy trial cannot be established by any inflexible rule, but can be determined only on an ad hoc balancing basis in which the conduct of the defendant and the prosecution are weighed.

[A]ny inquiry into a speedy trial claim necessitates a functional analysis of the right in the particular context of the case. . . .

Barker v. Wingo, supra at 522. The Court refused to objectify a "fixed point in the criminal process when the State can put the defendant to the choice of either exercising or waiving the right to a speedy trial," 407 U.S. at 521, choosing not to engage in legislative or rulemaking activity.

We find no constitutional basis for holding that the speedy trial right can be quantified into a specified number of days or months. *The States, of course, are free to prescribe a reasonable period consistent with constitutional standards,* but our approach must be less precise.

407 U.S. at 523 (Emphasis supplied).

Since the Supreme Court's decision in Klopfer v. North Carolina, 87 S.Ct. 988, 386 U.S. 213, 18 L.Ed.2d 1 (1967), wherein the speedy trial guarantee secured by the sixth amendment was made applicable to and enforceable against the states by virtue of the due process requirements of the fourteenth amendment, three-quarters of the

states have enacted, either by court rule or statute, speedy trial provisions. This would seem to indicate that the majority of states have experienced difficulty in affording uniformly fair justice on a case-by-case basis and are seeking to objectify the right so as to ease its application. The Supreme Court in *Barker* does not deny the states this prerogative so long as its exercise is consistent with constitutional standards. 407 U.S. at 530 n. 29.

While Rule 36 does quantify the time limits beyond which a defendant's speedy trial rights shall be deemed to have been denied, it is, as its title makes clear, primarily a management tool, designed to assist the trial courts in administering their dockets.

Subdivision (a).

Subdivision (a)(1). This subdivision is taken from § 1.1 of the ABA *Standards Relating to Speedy Trial* (Approved Draft, 1968). *See* ABA *Standards Relating to the Function of the Trial Judge,* § 3.8(c) (Approved Draft, 1972); Rules of Criminal Procedure (U.L.A.) rule 721(b) (1974).

Incarcerated defendants under existing Massachusetts law are accorded certain rights. This subdivision is first a general restatement of the principles underlying prior law, rather than a substitute for former statutes, and secondly an aid in the continued implementation of the policy of former G.L. c. 277, § 72, which provided for the release of a defendant from pretrial detention if he had not been tried within the criminal session next following six months of incarceration.

Additionally, the preference given to the trial of criminal defendants held in jail for offenses not punishable by death or life imprisonment over the trial of civil cases by G.L. c. 212, § 29 is to retain its vitality though not expressly adopted by this rule. See G.L. c. 212, § 24. *See* ABA *Standards Relating to Speedy Trial, Standard* 12–1.1(a) (2d ed. Approved Draft, 1978), Fed.R.Crim.P. 50(a).

Subdivision (a)(2). This is modeled after *Standard* 12–1.2 of the ABA *Standards Relating to Speedy Trial,* supra, and is consonant with the policy of G.L. c. 278, § 1 in that the trial court is given ultimate control over the calendar. *See* Rules of Criminal Procedure (U.L.A.) rule 721(a) (1974). The guiding principle behind this section was enunciated by the Eighth Circuit:

The government and, for that matter, the trial court are not without responsibility for the expeditious trial of criminal cases. The burden of trial promptness is not solely upon the defense.

Hodges v. United States, 408 F.2d 543, 551 (8th Cir.1969). *Accord* United States v. Drummond, 511 F.2d 1046, 1053 (2d Cir.1975). *See* Barker v. Wingo, 92 S.Ct. 2182, 407 U.S. 514, 527, 33 L.Ed.2d 101 (1972).

(a)(2)(A). In District Court jury-waived sessions, the court is to prepare and control the trial lists consistently with prior practice.

(a)(2)(B). General Laws c. 278, § 1 requires the district attorney to submit a list to the court of defendants to be tried at each sitting of the Superior Court, and it states that the cases will be tried in the order of the list unless otherwise ordered by the court.

Practice remains unchanged by this rule—the district attorneys are to place cases on the list in the order of priority they believe appropriate; the court may re-order arrangement of the list once it is submitted—but this procedure is extended to District Court jury sessions. General Laws c. 218, § 26A (St.1978, c. 478, § 188) provides for a jury trial in the first instance of all charges over which the District Court has original jurisdiction. If a defendant elects not to waive jury trial, or, having waived that right, claims an appeal to a jury session after conviction, G.L. c. 218, § 27A(g) (St.1978, c. 478, § 189) mandates that a District Attorney shall appear and prosecute the case. Further, G.L. c. 278, § 27A(e) provides that District Court jury sessions shall proceed in accordance with jury trials in the Superior Court. Therefore, subdivision (a)(2)(B) is to be read to empower the District Attorney to select those cases which are to be placed on the District Court jury session trial list. General Laws c. 278, § 1 establishes burdens on the prosecutor who is to keep current the list of cases to be tried and on the court which is to have the ultimate responsibility for the timely trial of those cases. *See* ABA *Standards Relating to the Function of the Trial Judge,* § 3.8(a) (Approved Draft, 1972). Practice under this rule will aid in the effective implementation of the speedy trial guarantee for there is a periodic check by the court on the prosecutor. Subdivision (f), infra.

Subdivision (b). General Laws c. 277, § 72 formerly provided for trial within six months after demand by an incarcerated defendant. This subdivision is an expansion of that statutory right, ultimately securing to all defendants the right to trial within twelve months after the filing of charges. Subdivision (b) is intended to insure that a defendant is not denied that right by providing for the dismissal of the charges for undue delay in bringing the defendant to trial.

The effect of this subdivision is not only to establish a specific time limit for commencement of trial, but also to shift the burden of proof concerning a deprivation of the defendant's right to trial within twelve months. The constitutional protection puts the burden on the defendant to show that the delay was undue and to his prejudice, whereas under this rule, once a twelve-month lapse has been shown, the burden shifts to the prosecutor to explain the delay.

General Laws c. 277, § 72 provided that a defendant held in custody upon an indictment had the right to be released on his own recognizance if not brought to trial by the time of the court's sitting next after six months from his commitment. General Laws c. 277, § 72A gave an incarcerated defendant the right to be tried on pending charges within six months after his application for a speedy trial or the charges would be dismissed. Those statutes were designed to alleviate hardships imposed upon particular defendants by pretrial delay. This subdivision is founded upon the premise that all defendants are liable to suffer from undue delay and that a definite time limit should be made available to them on an equal basis.

Subdivision (b)(1). Unlike former G.L. c. 277, § 72A, this subdivision is phrased so that only a *trial* upon charges against the defendant will satisfy the requirements of this rule. General Laws c. 277, § 72A required either a prompt "trial or *other* disposition thereof" (emphasis supplied), thus permitting a defendant's demand to be satisfied by other than a trial upon the charges. Commonwealth v. Fields, 371 Mass. 274, 280 (1976); Commonwealth v. Stewart, 361 Mass. 857, 356 N.E.2d 1211 (1972) (Rescript); Commonwealth v. Royce, 358 Mass. 597, 599, 266 N.E.2d 308 (1971); Commonwealth v. Ambers, Mass.App. Adv.Sh. (1978) 1141, 1145–46, 378 N.E.2d 451; Commonwealth v. Anderson, Mass.App.Adv.Sh. (1978) 775, 779, 378 N.E.2d 451. This change is intended to offer a defendant relief from pending charges and their attendant burdens, thereby giving substance to the speedy trial concept. A dismissal of charges on other grounds, a disposition of the charges by plea, or a filing of the case, of course, vitiates any need for trial, and in such an instance the rule does not apply.

For purposes of this rule, a trial is deemed to have commenced when jeopardy attaches. "In the case of a jury trial, jeopardy attaches when a jury is empaneled and sworn.... In a nonjury trial, jeopardy attaches when the court begins to hear evidence." Serfass v. United States, 95 S.Ct. 1055, 420 U.S. 377, 388, 43 L.Ed.2d 265 (1975). *Accord* Commonwealth v. Ludwig, 370 Mass. 31, 33, 345 N.E.2d 386 (1976). *See* Commonwealth v. Brandano, 359 Mass. 332, 334–35, 269 N.E.2d 84 (1971); 30 MASS.PRACTICE SERIES (Smith) § 563 at 290 (1970). If neither of these stages of prosecution has been reached within twelve months after the return day in the court in which the case is pending, the charges must be dismissed upon motion of the defendant. The mandatory sanction for failure to comply with the twelve-month time limit is dismissal of the charges, such dismissal to be a bar to any subsequent prosecution for the same offense or any related offenses, whether by later complaint in the District Court or indictment in the Superior Court. Commonwealth v. Fields, 371 Mass. 274, 356 N.E.2d 1211 (1976); *Commonwealth v. Ludwig,* supra, at 35; subdivision (e), infra.

Under this rule, the right to a speedy trial attaches upon "the return day in the court in which the case is awaiting trial," that is, the date on which "a defendant is ordered by summons to first appear or, if under arrest, does first appear ... to answer to the charges...." Mass.R.Crim.P. 2(b)(15). Therefore, if a defendant is bound over to the Superior Court after a probable cause hearing (Mass.R.Crim.P. 3[c]) or the Commonwealth elects to proceed by direct indictment in a case commenced by complaint which is within the District Court's jurisdiction (Mass.R.Crim.P. 3[e]), the time limits of this rule begin anew upon the return day in the Superior Court. *See* ABA *Standards Relating to Speedy Trial,* Standard 12–2.2 (2d ed., Approved Draft, 1978); Rules of Criminal Procedure (U.L.A.) Rule 722(d) (1974).

As to re-trials, the right accrues when the certainty of that trial is established, *e.g.,* by a judicial order for a new trial. Subdivision (b)(1)(D). As originally drafted, the Rule left some ambiguity as to when this condition was satisfied in practice. *See* Commonwealth v. Levin, 390 Mass. 857, 860 n. 4, 460 N.E.2d 578 (1984) and Commonwealth v. Bodden, 391 Mass. 356, 357–58, 461 N.E.2d 803 (1984). A 1996 amendment settled this issue by declaring that a retrial order is final upon the issuance by the appellate court of the rescript or, if the clerk failed to issue the rescript as required, when it should have issued.

Subdivision (b)(2). This is patterned after 18 U.S.C. § 3161(h) (Supp. 1, 1975). See ABA Standards Relating to Speedy Trial §§ 2.1, 2.3 (Approved Draft, 1968); Rules of Criminal Procedure (ULA) Rule 722(f) (1974).

The Supreme Judicial Court has stated that "in addition to periods of time specifically excluded by the rule, periods during which a defendant acquiesced in, is responsible for, or benefitted from a delay are also not counted." Commonwealth v. Lauria, 411 Mass. 63, 68, 576 N.E.2d 1368 (1991). *See also* Commonwealth v. Conefrey, 410 Mass. 1, 4–5, 570 N.E.2d 1384 (1991); Commonwealth v. Farris, 390 Mass. 300, 455 N.E.2d 433 (1983); Commonwealth v. Look, 379 Mass. 893, 402 N.E.2d 470 (1980); Commonwealth v. Alexander, 371 Mass. 726, 359 N.E.2d 306 (1977); Commonwealth v. Boyd, 367 Mass. 169, 178, 326 N.E.2d 320 (1975); Commonwealth v. Loftis, 361 Mass. 545, 549–50, 281 N.E.2d 258 (1972); Commonwealth v. McCants, 25 Mass. App.Ct. 735, 522 N.E.2d 15 (1988); Commonwealth v. Jones, 6 Mass. App.Ct. 750, 752–53, 383 N.E.2d 527 (1978) (interpreting G.L. c. 277, § 72A). But because the Commonwealth has the primary obligation for setting a trial date, a thorough examination of the record is necessary to determine whether failure to object should be counted against the defendant. Commonwealth v. Spaulding, 411 Mass. 503, 507, 583 N.E.2d 1257 (1992). The specific periods listed in this subdivision are those where the delay is not to be attributed to the prosecution.

Under prior cases in which the *Barker v. Wingo* sixth amendment analysis was applied, absent a showing of culpability on the part of the Commonwealth in delaying trial, the burden was on the defendant to demonstrate that the Commonwealth unreasonably caused prejudicial delay. Commonwealth v. Gilbert, 366 Mass. 18, 22, 314 N.E.2d 111 (1974). *Accord* Commonwealth v. Campbell, 5 Mass.App. 571, 366 N.E.2d 44 (1977); Commonwealth v. Burhoe, 3 Mass.App. 590, 594, 337 N.E.2d 913 (1975); Commonwealth v. Jackson, 3 Mass.App. 511, 517, 335 N.E.2d 367 (1975). Under this rule, however, no demonstration of prejudice is necessary (except under subdivision [c], infra; once the defendant has established a *prima facie* case for dismissal— i.e., that twelve months have elapsed since the return day—the burden is on the Commonwealth to establish justification for the delay. The rule *requires* the court to dismiss the charges (rather than making the decision discretionary and dependent upon a balancing of all relevant considerations) unless an explanation is deemed sufficient to excuse the delay.

Under this subdivision, the court is given the discretion to consider and determine whether a proffered explanation for delay is a valid excluded period. But, once it is determined that a period of delay is within the contemplation of this subdivision, that period shall be excluded from computation of the twelve-month limit. The rationale underlying this subdivision is that the Commonwealth should not be penalized when the defendant elects to avail himself of those procedures which are certain to result in delay, or when the causes for delay are beyond its control.

(b)(2)(A)(i). This subdivision excludes delay due to a mental or physical examination of the defendant to determine his competency or physical capacity to stand trial and the resultant hearing on the matter. This delay is a common occurrence and often essential to a fair trial. *See* Commonwealth v. Boyd, 367 Mass. 169, 178–79, 321 N.E.2d 320 (1975); Commonwealth v. Rise, Mass.App.Ct.Adv.Sh. (1979) 254, 255–57, 386 N.E.2d 745. It is intended that the excluded period shall begin on the date the order for examination is given and shall extend until such date as the court finds the defendant mentally competent or physically able to stand trial. The court's finding should be made within 30 days after receipt by the court of the examiner's report ([b][2][A][vii], infra) and the excludable period shall continue until such finding is made. It should be noted that the actual time period under (b)(2)(A)(i) may be extended by (b)(2)(C) to exclude any delay resulting from the fact that the defendant is found mentally incompetent or physically unable to stand trial. Fairness requires that a balance be struck between the defendant's right to a speedy trial and those delays which of necessity accompany the examination process and which are beyond the control of the prosecution once the procedure has been ordered.

(b)(2)(A)(ii). It is intended by this subdivision that the excluded period shall begin when the defendant is advised by the court that he may request an examination to determine whether he is a drug dependent person pursuant to G.L. c. 123, § 47. The defendant is then given five days under § 47 in which to exercise his right to an examination. If an examination is not requested within the provided time limit, the excludable period shall terminate. However, if the defendant elects an examination, the period of time during which he is being examined shall be excluded. Once the defendant has requested examination, the court may, in its discretion, determine without an examination that the defendant would benefit from treatment and shall inform him that he may request treatment in a drug facility. The period of time during which the defendant is undergoing treatment for drug addiction will be excluded under (b)(2)(A)(ii). It is intended that the excluded period shall cover the entire period of delay generated by § 47 examination or treatment.

(b)(2)(A)(iii). This subdivision is intended to be inclusive of trials of the defendant on other charges in any state or federal court including the court where charges are then pending against the defendant. *See* Commonwealth v. Anderson, Mass.App.Adv.Sh. (1978) 775, 780–81, 378 N.E.2d 451; Commonwealth v. Fasano, Mass.App.Adv.Sh. (1978) 521, 375 N.E.2d 361. The period shall run from the date such other trial begins and it is intended that the period shall conclude 14 days after a verdict of acquittal or imposition of sentence in the case. For the purpose of this subdivision, trial shall include the impanelling of the jury, hearings on motions deferred to the trial date, and any periods during which trial is suspended. The 14–day period following acquittal or sentencing is included in order to provide defense counsel with adequate preparation time for the second trial.

(b)(2)(A)(iv). It is intended that the excluded period under this subdivision run from the date the notice of appeal is filed until the rescript is received by the clerk of the lower court. The period covers any time during which interlocutory appeals are pending. *See* Commonwealth v. Underwood, 3 Mass.App. 522, 528–29, 335 N.E.2d 915 (1975). Where delay is occasioned by the Commonwealth's successful interlocutory appeal under Mass.R.Crim.P. 15, such delay does not prejudice the defense nor deny the defendant his right to a speedy trial. *See* United States v. Rosenbloom, 167 U.S.App. 211, 511 F.2d 777 (D.C.Cir.1974).

(b)(2)(A)(v). Delay attributable to the securing of a judicial resolution of issues raised by a defendant's pretrial motions are excluded from the running of the time limits. *See* Commonwealth v. Morgan, Mass.App.Adv.Sh. (1978) 1047, 381 N.E.2d 1126 (Rescript); Commonwealth v. Fasano, Mass.App.Adv.Sh. (1978) 521, 531–532, 375 N.E.2d

361; Commonwealth v. Campbell, 5 Mass.App. 571, 366 N.E.2d 44 (1977); Commonwealth v. Burhoe, 3 Mass.App. 590, 593, 337 N.E.2d 913 (1975); Commonwealth v. Underwood, 3 Mass.App. 522, 528–29, 335 N.E.2d 915 (1975); Commonwealth v. Jackson, 3 Mass.App. 511, 516–517, 335 N.E.2d 367 (1975).

The excludable period under this subdivision is intended to run from the date on which the request for hearing on the pretrial motion is filed, or, if no such request is filed, from the date the hearing is ordered, until the conclusion of the hearing.

(b)(2)(A)(vi). This subdivision provides that delay due to proceedings related to transfer under Mass.R.Crim.P. 37 shall be an excluded period. In cases transferred pursuant to Rule 37(a)(1) and (2), it is intended that the time limit begin to run on the date the clerk of the court in the transferee district receives the papers from the clerk of the court in the transferor district. In cases where the defendant moves for transfer of the case to another district pursuant to Rule 37(b), an excludable period shall run from the date of the hearing on the motion for transfer. If the motion is denied the period terminates at that time. If the motion is allowed and the case is subsequently transferred, the conclusion of the period will be determined by the court in that district to which the case is transferred. Under this rule, periods that are excluded are not restricted to the proceedings, directly related to transfer pursuant to Rule 37, but are intended to provide as well for delays caused by the transfer of papers from one district to another in transfer proceedings. This is to account for reasonable administrative delays while the court awaits the transfer papers.

(b)(2)(A)(vii). This subdivision provides for those delays which are necessary for the court to pass on proceedings concerning the defendant, exclusive of those periods for consideration of pretrial motions under (2)(A)(v). It is intended by this rule that the excluded period run during the time that the matter is actually under advisement until an order or ruling is entered, but in no event shall the period exceed 30 days. *See* 18 U.S.C. § 3161(h)(1)(G). It is not the intent of (2)(A)(vii) to preclude a continuance under Mass.R.Crim.P. 10 after the 30–day time limit is expired, but it is believed that the 30–day limit is reasonable in most cases. Where the matter under advisement is complex, the court may continue the case upon its own motion under (b)(2)(F), infra.

(b)(2)(B). If a defendant has made himself unavailable for trial for the purpose of avoiding prosecution, the interests of justice require that he not be allowed to subsequently claim violation of his right to a speedy trial. Commonwealth v. Underwood, 3 Mass.App. 522, 527–28, 335 N.E.2d 915 (1975). *Accord* Commonwealth v. Jones, Mass.App. Adv.Sh. (1978) 1218, 1225, 383 N.E.2d 527. Similarly, delays granted to allow the defendant or the Commonwealth to locate a key witness are justified and not properly chargeable against the Commonwealth. *See e.g.*, Commonwealth v. Daggett, 369 Mass. 790, 793–94, 343 N.E.2d 409 (1976); Commonwealth v. Boyd, 367 Mass. 169, 178, 326 N.E.2d 320 (1975); Commonwealth v. Jones, Mass.App.Adv.Sh. (1978) 1218, 1225, 383 N.E.2d 527; Commonwealth v. Alves, Mass.App.Adv.Sh. (1978) 912, 917 n. 3, 380 N.E.2d 701; Commonwealth v. Campbell, 5 Mass.App. 571, 366 N.E.2d 44 (1977); Commonwealth v. Ambers, 4 Mass.App. 647, 357 N.E.2d 323 (1976). An exclusion under this subdivision will be established by a party on motion for a continuance. It is intended that the excludable period run from the date the motion for a continuance is filed until the date when the defendant or witness is found by the court to have become available for trial. Mass. R.Crim.P. 10 provides that a continuance shall not be granted if a party fails to exercise due diligence to obtain an available witness for trial. Therefore, a party moving for a continuance under this subdivision should set forth with particularity the reasons why a continuance will enable him to obtain the witness and should state those facts as to which the witness is expected to testify. This will enable the court to make the necessary determination, on the facts presented, whether the unavailable witness is so "essential" as to warrant a continuance.

It is intended by this subdivision that a motion for a continuance on the ground of the absence of the defendant explain the facts of the defendant's absence. Since such absence may occur at any time during the proceedings, it may become necessary for the court to determine how long the defendant has been absent and whether he is attempting to avoid prosecution or whether his whereabouts cannot be determined by due diligence. It is recommended practice under this rule that if a party learns or has reason to believe that a witness will be unavailable, and if the party does not wish to proceed to trial without that witness, that the party move for a continuance as far in advance of trial as is feasible. Counsel should inform the court and the adverse party promptly of the availability of the defendant or witness.

The definition of an absent defendant or witness has been adapted from the ABA *Standards Relating to Speedy Trial* § 2.3(e) (Approved Draft, 1968); *accord Standard* 12–2.3(e) (2d ed., Approved Draft, 1978).

(b)(2)(C). Subdivision (b)(2)(A)(i) provides for an excluded period during examination and hearing on the defendant's competency or ability to stand trial. It is intended that if the court should find the defendant unable to stand trial, a new period will begin under this subdivision, such excluded period to conclude upon a court finding that the defendant is competent and able to stand trial.

(b)(2)(D). This subdivision provides for an excluded period when the prosecution nol prosses the charges pending against the defendant pursuant to Mass.R.Crim.P. 16 and subsequently brings new charges for the same offense. Only the time period during which there are no charges pending against the defendant is to be excluded from the twelve-month limit under (b)(1). The excluded time period will run only from the time the prosecution dismisses the charges until the return day as to the subsequent charge. For example, if the return day as to certain charges is January 1 and those charges are dismissed by the prosecution six months later, followed by a new complaint or indictment for the same offenses, as to which the return day is August 1, the prosecution has until February 1 to bring the defendant to trial. The one-month period during which no charges were pending is excluded, but the previous six months during which charges were outstanding is counted against the Commonwealth. *See* Commonwealth v. Gove, 366 Mass. 351, 359, 320 N.E.2d 900 (1974).

(b)(2)(E). Under this subdivision, reasonable delay where no motion for severance has been granted and the time for trial has not run as to the joined defendant shall be an excluded period. *See* Commonwealth v. Beckett, Mass.Adv.Sh. (1977) 1922, 1925, 378 N.E.2d 69; Commonwealth v. Carr, 3 Mass.App. 654, 656–57, 338 N.E.2d 844 (1975). Situations may arise where the period of delay could prove unreasonable; for example, where the joined defendant is indefinitely unavailable for trial or cannot be brought into custody. In such a situation it is not intended that the trial of the defendant presently in custody pending trial be deferred.

(b)(2)(F). This subdivision excludes delay resulting from a continuance granted upon a finding that "the ends of justice . . . outweigh the best interests of the public and the defendant in a speedy trial." It is implicit that (b)(2)(F) does not countenance an after-the-fact appraisal of the causes of delay by a reviewing court; in order to be excluded, the delay must have been the subject of a formal continuance. This does not, of course, preclude the appellate court from considering whether the grant or denial of a continuance constituted an abuse of discretion. See Mass.R.Crim.P. 10. Since only a judge may grant a continuance under Rule 10, the Commonwealth's failure to bring a case to trial without such a continuance, or its unilateral rescheduling a case to a later trial list, see G.L. c. 278, § 1, will not toll the speedy trial clock under this subsection. Commonwealth v. Spaulding, 411 Mass. 503, 508–10, 583 N.E.2d 1257 (1992) (failure of defendant to object to delay in scheduling did not toll period); Barry v. Commonwealth, 390 Mass. 285, 296 n. 13, 455 N.E.2d 437 (1983) (Commonwealth's setting of trial date does not toll period).

When a formal continuance is granted, this subdivision incorporates the procedure stated to be "advisable" under former G.L. c. 277, § 72A which requires the trial judge to state the reasons for any extension of time hereunder. Commonwealth v. Fields, 371 Mass. 274, 280 n. 8, 356 N.E.2d 1211 (1976); Commonwealth v. Boyd, 367 Mass. 169, 179, 326 N.E.2d 320 (1975); Commonwealth v. Loftis, 361 Mass. 545, 549, 281 N.E.2d 258 (1972); Commonwealth v. Ambers, 4 Mass. App.Ct. 647, 357 N.E.2d 323 (1976).

Delay which is justified under this subdivision may include that required for the Commonwealth to comply with a discovery order, Commonwealth v. Anderson, 6 Mass.App.Ct. 492, 378 N.E.2d 451 (1978); that required by newly-appointed counsel to prepare the case, e.g., Commonwealth v. Campbell, 5 Mass.App.Ct. 571, 366 N.E.2d 44 (1977); or that occasioned by the illness of the defendant, a co-defendant, counsel for the defendant or the Commonwealth, or the judge. Commonwealth v. Campbell, supra.

On the other hand, undue delay attributable to a defendant's desire to be represented by particular counsel is not justified. E.g., Commonwealth v. Dabrieo, 370 Mass. 728, 739, 352 N.E.2d 186 (1976). See Mass.R.Crim.P. 10(a)(2)(c) and Reporter's Notes, supra.

While the Supreme Judicial Court has indicated that court congestion will not be tolerated as an adequate ground for denying a "reasonably prompt trial," Commonwealth v. Beckett, 373 Mass. 329, 332, 335, 366 N.E.2d 1252 (1977), delay "inherent in the general problems of the administration of justice in a congested county," Commonwealth v. Rego, 360 Mass. 385, 392, 274 N.E.2d 795 (1971), is an often-cited excuse for an extension of time limits. Commonwealth v. Gove, 366 Mass. 351, 362–63, 320 N.E.2d 900 (1974); Commonwealth v. Fontaine, 8 Mass.App.Ct. 51, 391 N.E.2d 1234 (1979); Commonwealth v. Jones, 6 Mass.App.Ct. 750, 755–56, 383 N.E.2d 527 (1978) (interpreting G.L. c. 277, § 72A); Commonwealth v. Campbell, 5 Mass.App.Ct. 571, 366 N.E.2d 44 (1977); Commonwealth v. Ambers, 4 Mass.App.Ct. 647, 357 N.E.2d 323 (1976); Commonwealth v. Burhoe, 3 Mass.App.Ct. 590, 593, 337 N.E.2d 913 (1975). Although crowded dockets, lack of counsel, and other factors make some delays inevitable, Commonwealth v. Beckett, supra, a judge presented with a motion for a continuance on this ground is to carefully weigh the interests of the defendant and the public. *See also* Commonwealth v. Plantier, 22 Mass.App.Ct. 314, 493 N.E.2d 534 (1986) (dismissal within court's discretion where defendant prepared but case continued due to prosecutor's request or court congestion).

Although the Rule does not say so, caselaw since its promulgation has held that the defendant's failure to object to a continuance may render the continuance period excludable. Commonwealth v. Dias, 405 Mass. 131, 139, 539 N.E.2d 59 (1989); Commonwealth v. Farris, 390 Mass. 300, 455 N.E.2d 433 (1983); Commonwealth v. Fleenor, 39 Mass.App.Ct. 25, 27, 652 N.E.2d 899 (1995); Commonwealth v. Domingue, 18 Mass.App.Ct. 987, 470 N.E.2d 799 (1984), review denied 393 Mass. 1105, 474 N.E.2d 181 (1985). Moreover, as indicated in the Reporter's Notes, supra at (b)(2), caselaw has enunciated a broader rule which may exclude some delays which the defense acquiesced in, is responsible for, or benefitted from.

(b)(2)(G). This subdivision extends the rule that a valid plea of guilty constitutes a waiver of any claim to a denial of a speedy trial to the situation where, pursuant to Mass.R.Crim.P. 12(b), the defendant and the Commonwealth have concluded a plea arrangement. Becker v. Nebraska, 435 F.2d 157 (8th Cir.1970), cert. denied 91 S.Ct. 1684, 402 U.S. 981, 29 L.Ed.2d 145 (1971); Fowler v. United States, 391 F.2d 276, 277 (5th Cir.1968); United States v. Doyle, 348 F.2d 715, 718–19 (2d Cir.), cert. denied sub nom. Doyle v. United States, 86 S.Ct. 89, 382 U.S. 843, 46 L.Ed.2d 394 (1965). *See* Commonwealth v. L'Italien, 3 Mass.App. 763, 330 N.E.2d 214 (1975).

(b)(2)(H). The same principle which governs in subdivision (b)(2)(G) operates to exclude the time between which a plea is tendered and accepted by the court under Mass.R.Crim.P. 12(c)(5) and the time at which it is withdrawn by the defendant pursuant to Mass.R.Crim.P. 12(d).

It is intended that the excluded period run from the date the plea of guilty is first offered and accepted until the date the court permits withdrawal of the plea.

Subdivision (b)(3). The provision as to excluded periods is contrary to G.L. c. 4, § 7 and Mass.R.Crim.P. 46(a), which state that the day on which a limited period commences shall be excluded from the computation. This subdivision is in other respects consistent with prior law. *See* Commonwealth v. Daggett, 369 Mass. 790, 792 n. 1, 343 N.E.2d 409 (1976). *See* ABA *Standards Relating to Speedy Trial* § 3.2 (Approved Draft, 1968), *Standard* 12–3.2 (2d ed., Approved Draft, 1978).

Subdivision (c). It is possible, although unusual, that a delay of less than twelve months could be deemed prejudicial and therefore violative of a defendant's right to be tried with reasonable dispatch. Under this subdivision a dismissal of charges would be warranted in such a situation.

For those defendants who are not yet entitled to the mandatory dismissal upon motion under subdivision (b)(1), this subdivision states the standard by which an allegation of a denial of a speedy trial may nonetheless be judged: it is a statement of the fundamental constitutional guarantee. The twelve-month rule sets a standard which is quantitative and whose limits are easily determined, whereas the constitutional standard is a relative qualitative concept demanding that the severity of the denial of its protection to a defendant be dependent upon the facts of his case.

Barker v. Wingo, 92 S.Ct. 2182, 407 U.S. 514, 33 L.Ed.2d 101 (1972), and Commonwealth v. Horne, 362 Mass. 738, 291 N.E.2d 629 (1973), make it clear that a balancing approach must be used to determine whether a defendant's constitutional right to a speedy trial has been violated. E.g., Commonwealth v. Beckett, 373 Mass. 329, 366 N.E.2d 1252 (1977); Commonwealth v. Dabrieo, 370 Mass. 728, 352 N.E.2d 186 (1976); Commonwealth v. Daggett, 369 Mass. 790, 343 N.E.2d 409 (1976); Commonwealth v. Gove, 366 Mass. 351, 361–65, 320 N.E.2d 900 (1974). For purposes of this analysis, the right to a speedy trial under art. II of the Massachusetts Declaration of Rights and under the sixth amendment to the United States Constitution are considered to be coextensive. *Commonwealth v. Gove,* supra at 356 n. 6; Commonwealth v. Underwood, 3 Mass.App. 522, 526, 335 N.E.2d 915 (1975).

This subdivision puts the constitutional standard into manageable operational terms. Four factors were mentioned by the United States Supreme Court in *Barker* as among those to be considered: the length of delay, the reason for delay, the resulting prejudice to the defendant, and the assertion of the right by the defendant. This subdivision isolates two essential factors which are the substance of the constitutional protection. These are unreasonable prosecutorial delay and resulting prejudice to the defendant.

Subdivision (c)(1) states that only prosecutorial delay is within the scope of the relief afforded by this subdivision. This protection is compatible with the constitutional protection. Commonwealth v. Lauria, 359 Mass. 168, 268 N.E.2d 363 (1971); Commonwealth v. Thomas, 353 Mass. 429, 233 N.E.2d 25 (1967). This subdivision requires the defendant to establish first that the delay he has endured is unreasonable and secondly that it was caused by the prosecutor. If the delay is of that nature, the defendant has conclusively established one of the two requisites to a finding that his motion to dismiss the charges is to be granted.

There is no disagreement with the proposition that only an unreasonable delay is prohibited by the Constitution and that what is unreasonable depends upon the peculiar facts of each case. For example, the amount of time that a prosecutor needs to prepare a case in which several defendants have been joined for trial is normally greater than the time needed to prepare for the trial of a single defendant. *See* Commonwealth v. Dominico, 1 Mass.App. 693, 306 N.E.2d 835 (1974).

Subdivision (c)(2) establishes the second element which the defendant must show to support his motion: that he has been prejudiced by the delay. Prejudice in the context of this subdivision is not restricted to prejudice to the preparation or presentation of the defense. The Supreme Court in *Barker v. Wingo,* supra, listed three distinct functions served by the prohibition against unreasonable delay: "(i) to prevent oppressive pretrial incarceration; (ii) to minimize anxiety and concern of the accused; and (iii) to limit the possibility that the defense will be impaired." *Id.* at 532.

If the defendant is able to show that deliberate, unreasonable prosecutorial delay has operated to his prejudice, the appropriate sanction is dismissal of the charges with prejudice to the Commonwealth. Support for such a sanction is even stronger when imposed for constitutional reasons. The Supreme Court in Strunk v. United States, 93 S.Ct. 2260, 412 U.S. 434, 37 L.Ed.2d 56 (1973), declared that dismissal with prejudice was the only permissible remedy for violation of the constitutional speedy trial protection.

The judge is always given discretion in his determination of whether the defendant has been prejudiced to an extent that will require dismissal of the indictment due to prosecutorial delay.

Subdivision (d). This subdivision is based upon G.L. c. 277, §§ 72–72A. *See* ABA *Standards Relating to Speedy Trial,* § 3.1 (Approved Draft, 1968), *Standard* 12–3.1 (2d ed., Approved Draft, 1978).

The statement in subdivision (d)(1) that prisoners are entitled to all the safeguards of a defendant whose liberty is not similarly impaired recognizes that a prisoner does not by reason of his status alone lose the protection of the Constitution or of this rule. It is not intended to declare, however, that all substantive rights of an unimprisoned defendant are to be accorded a prisoner. The same rights can apply with equal force in different circumstances and impose differing duties on the Commonwealth. A separate subdivision is devoted to prisoners' speedy trial rights because the substance of those rights is different from that of other accused persons. Imprisonment necessarily affects both the duty which the Commonwealth has to deliver a defendant to trial and the nature of the prejudice that might result from a delayed trial.

Subdivision (d)(2) extends to defendants incarcerated within the Commonwealth for other crimes the same speedy trial rights guaranteed to other defendants by subdivisions (b)(1) and (c).

Subdivision (d)(3) is largely a restatement of G.L. c. 277, § 72A, which is applied to prisoners incarcerated "outside" the Commonwealth. This is to be read to include prisoners within federal custody, although physically present within Massachusetts.

The Constitution has been interpreted to require of the prosecutor only that which he is reasonably able to accomplish. Commonwealth v. McGrath, 348 Mass. 748, 205 N.E.2d 710 (1965). Where a defendant is imprisoned in a foreign jurisdiction and his extradition is impeded— whether by his own opposition or by that of the executive of the incarcerating jurisdiction—it would be unfair to attribute the delay in bringing the defendant to trial to the Commonwealth if it had made all reasonable efforts to secure the defendant's presence. It would be equally unfair to require the Commonwealth to guarantee trial within a specified time limit.

There is disagreement among jurisdictions as to what the speedy trial provision of the Constitution requires of a state seeking to obtain the presence of a prisoner incarcerated in another jurisdiction, although it is clear that where a defendant's presence *cannot* be obtained because the incarcerating state refuses to deliver him, there is no denial of the defendant's constitutional right to a speedy trial. *See* ABA *Standards Relating to Speedy Trial,* § 3.1, comment at 31 (Approved Draft, 1968). It is also clear that Massachusetts is one of the many states to require the prosecution to use all reasonable efforts to obtain the presence of a foreign prisoner for trial upon pending charges, although this position is not universally accepted. Commonwealth v. Green, 353 Mass. 687, 690, 234 N.E.2d 534 (1968).

Uniform acts dealing with extradition have been adopted by many states. The *Agreement On Detainers,* G.L. c. 276, App. §§ 1–1 et seq., gives prisoners the right to have a trial within one hundred eighty days of their delivery to the jurisdiction where charges are pending. This statute, which has been adopted by thirty-two jurisdictions, gives substance to the rights of prisoners and is to be read as a complement to this rule. The *Uniform Criminal Extradition Act,* G.L. c. 276, §§ 11–20R, which has been adopted by forty-seven jurisdictions, establishes procedures for orderly extradition; it sets out proper procedures for a request for delivery, the arrest of the alleged criminal, and his delivery to the requesting state. Section 20G of this statute, however, still affords governors the discretion to refuse delivery of prisoners.

Massachusetts courts have required the Commonwealth to use due diligence in seeking to bring a foreign prisoner to trial. In light of the legal limitations of rendition this is a fair standard. This rule attempts to put the diligence standard in operational terms. The speedy trial rights of a foreign prisoner are defined under this rule as follows: the Commonwealth must diligently notify a foreign prisoner of pending charges and must promptly seek to obtain his presence for trial; if the Commonwealth is dilatory in either filing a detainer or seeking to obtain the defendant's presence and the prisoner is prejudiced by the delay, the charges must be dismissed. The defendant is given the right to make a demand, although the demand under this rule does not affect the Commonwealth's duty to obtain the defendant's presence. The Commonwealth must use due diligence whether or not a demand has been made. However, the demand is relevant to a determination of the prejudice incurred by the defendant, and under the *Agreement on Detainers,* a demand entitles a defendant to a trial within one hundred eighty days of his delivery.

Subdivision (e). In Commonwealth v. Gove, 1 Mass.App. 614, 304 N.E.2d 589 (1973), aff'd, 366 Mass. 351, 320 N.E.2d 900 (1974), it was held that a defendant did not have the right to be simultaneously charged with all the offenses which might have been committed in the course of a single act or a closely related series of acts. One result is that a dismissal of the charge of one of a number of related offenses on denial of speedy trial grounds would not bar the Commonwealth from charging the defendant with another of the related offenses. A second result is that if a significant amount of time had elapsed between the filing of charges of two related offenses, and the earlier charge was dismissed because the twelve-month limit of this rule had passed, the Commonwealth could proceed to trial on the later charge. Subdivision (e) effectively vitiates the *Gove* decision.

Standard 12–4.1 of the ABA *Standards Relating to Speedy Trial* (2d ed., Approved Draft, 1978), states that if a charge is dismissed on speedy trial grounds "[s]uch discharge should forever bar prosecution for the offense charged and for any other offense required to be joined with that offense."

The Supreme Judicial Court, citing with approval ABA *Standards* § 4.1, (Approved Draft, 1968), has held that

the dismissal of a complaint in the District Court on the ground that the defendant has been denied his right to a speedy trial is a bar to any subsequent prosecution for the *same offense* whether by later complaint . . . or by an indictment. . . .

Commonwealth v. Ludwig, 370 Mass. 31, 35, 345 N.E.2d 386 (1976) (emphasis supplied). *Accord* Commonwealth v. Fields, 371 Mass. 274, 275, 356 N.E.2d 1211 (1976) (dismissal of complaint in District Court on speedy trial grounds bar to subsequent prosecution of same offense by indictment in Superior Court). While agreeing with the ABA *Standards* insofar as holding dismissal to constitute an absolute discharge of the prosecution of the offense charged, the *Ludwig* court did not reach the issue of whether such a discharge was to encompass other offenses.

Subdivision (e) states that a dismissal of any charge ordered pursuant to Rule 36 "shall apply to all related offenses." Offenses are related when they

are based on the same criminal conduct or episode or arise out of a course of criminal conduct or series of criminal episodes connected together or constituting parts of a single scheme or plan.

Mass.R.Crim.P. 2(b)(14); 9(a)(1). This subdivision expands the principle of ABA *Standard* 12–4.1 further, mandating that the dismissal shall be not only as to charges required to be joined with that dismissed, but also as to any charges which *could* have been joined under Mass.R.Crim.P. 9(a)(2).

This position is advanced in the interests of fairness to a defendant. Without such a provision, a defendant could be subjected to harassment by a prosecutor who might essentially relitigate the same issues he was barred from litigating for failure to accord the defendant his rights under this rule.

Subdivision (f). Under this rule, the respective clerks are to have the burden of periodically informing the first justice of each District Court division and the Administrative Justice of the Superior Court Department of cases which have been pending longer than six months.

Rule 37. Transfer of Cases

(Applicable to District Court and Superior Court)

(a) Transfer for Plea and Sentence.

(1) *District Court.* A defendant against whom a complaint is pending and who appears in District Court, whether under arrest or pursuant to a summons, and against whom a complaint is pending in a division other than that in which he appears, may state in writing that he wishes to plead guilty or nolo contendere, to waive trial in the division in which the other complaint is pending, and to consent to disposition of the case in the division in which he appears. The District Court in which the defendant appears may order that the other complaint be transferred for disposition, subject to the written approval of the prosecutor in each division.

(2) *Superior Court.* A defendant against whom a complaint or indictment is pending and who appears in Superior Court, whether under arrest or pursuant to a summons, and against whom a complaint or indictment is pending in a county other than that in which he appears, may state in writing that he wishes to plead guilty or nolo contendere, to waive trial in the county in which the other complaint or indictment is pending, and to consent to disposition of the case in the county in which he appears. The Superior Court in which the defendant appears may order that the other complaint or indictment be transferred for disposition, subject to the written approval of the prosecuting attorney in each county.

(3) *Effect of Not Guilty Plea.* If after a proceeding has been transferred pursuant to subdivision (a) of this rule the defendant pleads not guilty, the clerk shall return the papers transmitted pursuant to subdivision (c) of this rule to the court in which the prosecution was commenced, and the proceeding shall be restored to the docket of that court.

(b) Transfer for Trial.

(1) *Transfer for Prejudice.* A judge upon his own motion or the motion of a defendant or the Commonwealth made prior to trial may order the transfer of a case to another division or county for trial if the court is satisfied that there exists in the community where the prosecution is pending so great a prejudice against the defendant that he may not there obtain a fair and impartial trial.

(2) *Transfer of Other Cases*. A judge, upon motion of a defendant made pursuant to subdivision (3) or (4) of Rule 9(a), and after taking into account the convenience of the court, the parties, and their witnesses, may with the written approval of the prosecuting attorney in each division or county order the transfer and consolidation for trial of any or all charges pending against the defendant in the several divisions or counties of the Commonwealth.

(c) Proceedings on Transfer. Upon receipt of the defendant's statement and the written approval of the prosecutor required by this rule, the clerk of the court in which a complaint or indictment is pending shall transfer the papers in the case and any bail taken to the clerk of the court to which the case is transferred. The clerk of the transferee court shall make immediate entry of the case upon the docket of that court and shall so notify the clerk of the transferor court so that the case may be closed on the docket of that court. The prosecution shall continue in the transferee court.

Reporter's Notes

This rule is drawn from Fed.R.Crim.P. 20, 21 and 22 and substantially expands Massachusetts practice relative to the transfer of pending criminal proceedings.

Subdivision (a). Subdivisions (a)(1) and (2), applicable respectively to the District and Superior Court Departments, are modeled after Fed.R.Crim.P. 20(a) and 22. It is intended that the request to consolidate complaints or indictments for plea and sentence is to be made at the initial appearance. The arraignment date is to be set at a time sufficiently after the initial appearance to allow the transmittal of the necessary papers (*See* subdivision [c], infra). The rule is not to be read to permit the consolidation of an indictment with a complaint for trial or plea in the District Court. Nor may complaints pending in District Court be consolidated with Superior Court proceedings (except where the defendant waives indictment and is bound over so that the case is properly in Superior Court. Mass.R.Crim.P. 3). Where the defendant appears in Superior Court upon a complaint or indictment and there are complaints outstanding in divisions of the District Court within that same county, the District Attorney may proceed by direct indictment (Mass.R.Crim.P. 3[e]), may make an appropriate disposition of the lower court charges pursuant to a plea arrangement (Mass.R.Crim.P. 12[b]), or may nol prosse the charges (Mass. R.Crim.P. 16) if the interests of the parties and the court so dictate.

Subdivision (a)(3) is substantially identical to Fed.R.Crim.P. 20(c).

Subdivision (b). Subdivision (b)(1) parallels Fed.R.Crim.P. 21(a) and has a statutory precedent in G.L. c. 277, § 51.

Under most circumstances a trial is held where the indictment or complaint is pending. This in fact is a constitutional right of the defendant. Article 13 of the Massachusetts Declaration of Rights provides:

In criminal prosecutions, the verification of facts in the vicinity where they happen, is one of the greatest securities of the life, liberty, and property of the citizen.

However, the common law recognized the right of a defendant to have the case removed to another community for the purpose of achieving an impartial trial. Commonwealth v. Handren, 261 Mass. 294, 296–97, 158 N.E. 894 (1927); Crocker v. Justices of the Superior Court, 208 Mass. 162, 174–75, 94 N.E. 369, 21 Ann.Cas. 1061 (1911). And the right to a fair and impartial trial to the fourteenth amendment to the United States Constitution, which right includes the right "to show that a change of venue *is* required" in a particular case. Groppi v. Wisconsin, 91 S.Ct. 490, 400 U.S. 505, 511, 27 L.Ed.2d 571 (1971).

A defendant in a capital case has a statutory right to seek a transfer of the trial to any adjoining county. G.L. c. 277, § 51. This statutory

right is, in many cases, too limited to permit removal to a venue uninfected by the prejudice and the statute is not to maintain its vitality except as precedent for the broader rule. *See generally* Commonwealth v. Turner, 371 Mass. 803, 807, 359 N.E.2d 626 (1977). In some cases, the transfer need not be to another county if an impartial jury panel can be found in another court within the same county.

The motion must be made prior to trial. *See* Commonwealth v. Noxon, 319 Mass. 495, 550, 66 N.E.2d 814 (1946). If the jury has been impanelled, and the court is satisfied that the jurors are impartial, the defendant cannot later claim that the situs of trial was improper.

The trial court has discretion as to whether pretrial publicity has so infected the community where proper venue lies as to require a transfer to another community. E.g., Commonwealth v. Turner, 371 Mass. 803, 806–07, 359 N.E.2d 626 (1977). The transfer, however, should not be ordered without a substantial showing of prejudice. As the Supreme Judicial Court said in Crocker v. Justices of the Superior Court, 208 Mass. 162, 94 N.E. 369, 21 Ann.Cas. 1061 (1911):

Such a motion ought not to be granted upon mere suggestion, nor unless the reason for it is fully established. It is a jurisdiction which should be exercised with great caution and only after a solid foundation of fact has been first established. Manifestly, it should be resorted to only in aid of justice, and it should not be permitted to be employed as an instrument of obstruction or as a means of delay.

Id. at 180.

The mere fact that a juror has been exposed to pretrial publicity concerning the case does not mean that his impartiality has been affected. This normally can be adequately tested during the voir dire. Commonwealth v. Smith, 357 Mass. 168, 258 N.E.2d 13 (1970). In addition to questioning prospective jurors as to their bias, the court should consider the extent of the publicity concerning the case and the nature of the charges. Some crimes give rise to heightened community response more readily than others. *See* Commonwealth v. Blackburn, 354 Mass. 200, 203–04, 237 N.E.2d 35 (1968); Commonwealth v. Smith, 353 Mass. 487, 489–90, 232 N.E.2d 915 (1968). In some cases the extent of the publicity will be so great as to mandate a transfer of the trial. It is presumed in these cases that an impartial jury cannot be obtained from the mere fact of the exposure of the crime to the public. Rideau v. Louisiana, 83 S.Ct. 1417, 373 U.S. 723, 10 L.Ed.2d 663 (1963).

Subdivision (b)(2), drawn from Fed.R.Crim.P. 21(b), provides for the inter-division or inter-county transfer of charges of related offenses for trial. Such transfer is contingent upon the approval of the court and of the prosecutors involved. The rule is intended to conserve judicial resources by obviating the need for separate trials of related offenses which were committed in different divisions or counties.

Subdivision (c). This subdivision is in conformity with both Fed. R.Crim.P. 20(a) and 21(c) and with G.L. c. 277, § 52. The language was taken in part from each source.

Other statutes in Massachusetts are applicable to the transfer of cases in specific factual situations, and these are to maintain their vitality. General Laws c. 277, § 53 is applicable when the transfer is to a different county and the defendant is in custody. It should be noted that while this rule is concerned with the transfer of cases which are to be tried in Superior Court upon indictment, it is intended to be equally applicable to cases to be tried in District or Superior Court upon complaint. In this respect, the rule goes beyond the provisions of G.L. c. 277, §§ 51–54 which are, technically speaking, applicable only to trial upon indictment.

Rule 38. Disability of Judge

(Applicable to Superior Court and jury sessions in District Court)

(a) During Trial. If by reason of death, sickness, or other disability the judge before whom a jury trial has commenced is unable to proceed with the trial, any other judge of that court or properly assigned to that court, upon certifying in writing that he has familiarized himself with the record of the trial, may proceed with and finish the trial.

(b) Receipt of Verdict. Any judge of a court or any judge properly assigned to that court may receive a verdict of the jury.

(c) After Verdict or Finding of Guilt. If by reason of absence, unavailability, death, sickness, or other disability the judge before whom the defendant has been tried is unable to perform the duties to be performed by the judge after a verdict or finding of guilt, any other judge of that court or properly assigned to that court may perform those duties; but if the other judge is satisfied that he cannot perform those duties because he did not preside at the trial or for any other reason, he may, in his discretion or upon motion of the defendant, order a new trial.

Reporter's Notes

Rule 38 has no counterpart in the statutory or case law of the Commonwealth. The rule closely parallels Fed.R.Crim.P. 25, although there is some deviation. *See* Rules of Criminal Procedure (U.L.A.) Rule 741 (1974); ABA *Standards Relating to Trial by Jury* (2d ed., Approved Draft, 1978).

Subdivision (a). This subdivision is drawn nearly verbatim from ABA *Standards Relating to Trial by Jury* § 4.3 (Approved Draft, 1968), differing in that under the rule the substituted judge must be of the same court in which the proceeding is held, or properly assigned to that court. It has been intimated that the federal analogue to this subdivision, Fed.R.Crim.P. 25(a), is open to constitutional inquiry. 2 C. WRIGHT, FEDERAL PRACTICE & PROCEDURE: CRIMINAL § 392 (1969, Supp.1978). It is suggested further, however, that no substantial constitutional infirmity exists if a defendant consents to the substitution of judges during the trial. Id. *See* Rules of Criminal Procedure (U.L.A.) Rule 741(e) (1974), which would require the parties' consent to the substitution of a specified judge. Whether or not constitutionally mandated, it would be the better practice to obtain the defendant's consent to substitution in writing to be made a part of the record.

Subdivision (b). This subdivision constitutes the most significant departure from Federal Rule 25. It is felt that the receipt of a verdict is a court function ministerial in nature and need not be performed by the judge who presided at trial. Subdivision (b) is intended to implement the efficient use of judicial manpower by permitting a single judge to take verdicts in more than one trial and to circumvent the need for a judge to interrupt other business to receive a verdict.

Subdivision (c). The constitutionality of the federal equivalent of this subdivision, Fed.R.Crim.P. 25(b), was questioned as to the power of a substitute judge to act in the case. Its validity was sustained in Connelly v. United States, 249 F.2d 576 (8th Cir.1957), cert. denied 78 S.Ct. 700, 356 U.S. 921, 2 L.Ed.2d 716 (1958). *See* Rules of Criminal Procedure (U.L.A.) Rule 741(f) (1974).

The power granted to the succeeding judge to "perform the duties to be performed by the court after a verdict or finding of guilt" is intended to encompass the authority and duty to hear post-conviction proceedings under Mass.R.Crim.P. 30. *See* former G.L. c. 278, § 31A, which permitted a substitute justice to examine and allow or disallow a bill of exceptions.

The final clause of subdivision (c) gives rise to potential problems of constitutional dimension regarding the ordering of a new trial by a successor judge. Under this rule, the successor judge may order such a trial "in his discretion, or upon motion of the defendant...." A new trial in the latter situation raises no issue and is supported by precedent. *See* United States v. Tateo, 84 S.Ct. 1587, 377 U.S. 463, 12 L.Ed.2d 448 (1964).

Regarding the former situation, however, for a trial judge to grant a new trial sua sponte, and presumably, over defendant's objection, may raise fifth amendment problems of double jeopardy. 2 C. WRIGHT, FEDERAL PRACTICE AND PROCEDURE: CRIMINAL § 551 at 483 (1969, Supp.1978). *See* United States v. Smith, 67 S.Ct. 1330, 331 U.S. 469, 474–75, 91 L.Ed. 1610 (1947).

The current law with respect to the double jeopardy implications of a declaration of a mistrial over a defendant's objections involves a balancing of competing interests:

A defendant has a 'valued right to have his trial completed by a particular tribunal.' [citations omitted]. Because of this right, a court may not declare a mistrial without consent of the defendant unless there is a 'manifest necessity for the act, or the ends of public justice would otherwise be defeated.' [citations omitted].

United States v. Lansdown, 460 F.2d 164, 168 (4th Cir.1972). *See* Wade v. Hunter, 69 S.Ct. 834, 336 U.S. 684, 689, 93 L.Ed. 974 (1949). This doctrine of "manifest necessity," enunciated in the early case of United States v. Perez, 22 U.S. 579 (9 Wheat.) 579, 6 L.Ed. 165 (1824), remains consistently adhered to and approved by the Supreme Court. Illinois v. Somerville, 93 S.Ct. 1066, 410 U.S. 458, 35 L.Ed.2d 425 (1973); United States v. Jorn, 91 S.Ct. 547, 400 U.S. 470, 27 L.Ed.2d 543 (1971). *See also* United States v. Wilson, 95 S.Ct. 1013, 420 U.S. 332, 344, 43 L.Ed.2d 232 (1975).

At the same time, the *Perez* formulation, the Supreme Court has emphasized, is not so rigid as to be mechanically applied:

This formulation ... abjures the application of any mechanical formula by which to judge the propriety of declaring a mistrial *in the varying and often unique situations arising during the course of a criminal trial*. The broad discretion reserved to the trial judge in such circumstances has been consistently reiterated in decisions of this court.

Illinois v. Somerville, supra at 462 (Emphasis added).

The relatively rare, if not unique, issue posed by subdivision (c) presents several new considerations. The "broad discretion reserved," *Illinois v. Somerville*, supra, will be wielded in this context by a successor to the disabled trial judge. Furthermore, the Court's admonition that trial judges must not "foreclose the defendant's option" to proceed to the first jury until they have completed a "scrupulous exercise" of their discretion, *United States v. Jorn*, supra at 485, takes on heightened significance where, as here, the defendant has already gone to the first jury.

Nevertheless, it is submitted that the *Perez* doctrine as refined by the Court today applies to the post-verdict situation in this subdivision. *See Illinois v. Somerville, supra* at 467, where the Court intimates a distinction between mistrials declared prior to and those declared after verdict. Thus, in the careful exercise of his discretion, a trial judge, or successor judge, must weigh the defendant's "valued right to have his trial completed by a particular tribunal" against "the public's interest in fair trials designed to end in just judgments." *Wade v. Hunter*, supra at 689. If the judge, then, "is satisfied that he cannot perform ... [the post-verdict duties of the court], he may ... order a new trial" without unconstitutionally subjecting a defendant to double jeopardy.

Rule 39. Records of Foreign Proceedings and Notice of Foreign Law

(Applicable to District Court and Superior Court)

(a) Records of Courts of Other States or of the United States. The records and judicial proceedings of a court of another state or of the United States shall be competent evidence in this Commonwealth if authenticated by the attestation of the clerk or other officer who has charge of the records of such court under its seal.

(b) Notice of Foreign Law. The court shall upon request take judicial notice of the law of the United States or of any state, territory, or dependency thereof or of a foreign country whenever it shall be material.

Reporter's Notes

Rule 39 substantially conforms to G.L. c. 233, §§ 69–70. *See* Fed.R.Crim.P. 26.1.

Subdivision (a). General Laws c. 233, § 69, from which this subdivision is taken, does not require "that a record be fully extended in order to afford proof of judgment if the facts essential thereto are set forth," Commonwealth v. Rondoni, 333 Mass. 384, 386, 131 N.E.2d 187 (1955). *Rondoni* should be examined as illustrative of what serves as sufficient attestation by the officer in charge of judicial records. *Id.* at 385–86.

Subdivision (b). This is taken with little change from G.L. c. 233, § 70. Although nearly all of the cases which have construed that section are civil, it applies to criminal proceedings as well. *See* e.g., Commonwealth v. White, 358 Mass. 488, 491, 265 N.E.2d 473 (1970).

The rule states that a court shall notice foreign law upon request when that law is material. This is not intended to limit a court's authority under § 70 to notice foreign law in the absence of a request if the court so chooses. Dicker v. Klein, 360 Mass. 735, 736–37, 277 N.E.2d 514 (1972); De Gategno v. De Gategno, 336 Mass. 426, 431, 146 N.E.2d 497 (1957). Even upon request, however, a court is not required to notice foreign law unless it is brought to the attention of the court. Tsacoyeanes v. Canadian Pac. Ry. Co., 339 Mass. 726, 162 N.E.2d 23 (1959). Massachusetts practice is in accord with Fed. R.Evid. 201 which states that "(c) . . . A court may take judicial notice, whether requested or not [and] (d) . . . shall take judicial notice if requested by a party and supplied with the necessary information." *See* Me.R.Evid. 201 (c)–(d).

When a party does make a request for the court to take judicial notice of foreign law, that party carries the burden of proof as to what the law is. Finer v. Steuer, 255 Mass. 611, 152 N.E. 220 (1926). The attention of the court may be directed to the law of another jurisdiction by oral testimony of a qualified witness as well as by citation of statutes and decisions. Eastern Offices, Inc. v. P.F. O'Keefe Ad. Agency, Inc., 289 Mass. 23, 193 N.E. 837 (1935). The requirement of bringing the law to the attention of the court and proving it is not satisfied by simply mentioning the appropriate reference to foreign law. "Merely to direct attention to the law of a foreign country written in a foreign tongue does not make it a matter for judicial knowledge." Rodrigues v. Rodrigues, 286 Mass. 77, 83, 190 N.E. 20 (1934). However, where there is not sufficient information available to the litigants as to what is the pertinent foreign law, the court may use other channels available to it in order to determine the law. In Mazurowski, petitioner, 331 Mass. 33, 116 N.E.2d 854 (1954), the court drew upon the superior sources of foreign law and regulations available through the State Department, to which neither party to the litigation has access.

Rule 40. Proof of Official Records

(Applicable to District Court and Superior Court)

(a) Authentication.

(1) *Domestic.* An official record kept within the Commonwealth, or an entry therein, when admissible for any purpose, may be evidenced by an official publication thereof or by a copy attested by the officer having legal custody of the record, or by his deputy. If the record is kept in any other state, district, commonwealth, territory or insular possession of the United States, or within the Panama Canal Zone or the Trust Territory of the Pacific Islands, any such copy shall be accompanied by a certificate that such custodial officer has the

custody. This certificate may be made by a judge of a court of record of the district or political subdivision in which the record is kept, authenticated by the seal of the court, or may be made by any public officer having a seal of office and having official duties in the district or political subdivision in which the record is kept, authenticated by the seal of his office.

(2) *Foreign.* A foreign official record, or an entry therein, when admissible for any purpose, may be evidenced by an official publication thereof, or a copy thereof, attested by a person authorized to make the attestation, and accompanied by a final certification as to the genuineness of the signature and official position (i) of the attesting person, or (ii) of any foreign official whose certificate of genuineness of signature and official position relates to the attestation or is in a chain of certificates of genuineness of signature and official position relating to the attestation. A final certification may be made by a secretary of embassy or legation, consul general, consul, vice consul, or consular agent of the United States, or a diplomatic or consular official of the foreign country assigned or accredited to the United States. If reasonable opportunity has been given to all parties to investigate the authenticity and accuracy of the documents, the court may, for good cause shown, (i) admit an attested copy without final certification, or (ii) permit the foreign official record to be evidenced by an attested summary with or without a final certification.

(b) Lack of Record. A written statement that after diligent search no record or entry of a specified tenor is found to exist in the records designated by the statement, authenticated as provided in subdivision (a)(1) of this rule in the case of a domestic record, or complying with the requirements of subdivision (a)(2) of this rule for a summary in the case of a foreign record, is admissible as evidence that the records contain no such record or entry.

(c) Other Proof. This rule does not prevent the proof, by any other method authorized by law, of the existence of, or the lack of, an official record, or of entry, or lack of entry therein.

Reporter's Notes

This rule is identical to Mass.R.Civ.P. 44. *See* Fed.R.Crim.P. 27, which incorporates by reference the provisions of Fed.R.Civ.P. 44.

Prior to the promulgation of this rule, no statute or rule expressly provided for the proof of official records in criminal cases. The practice developed of utilizing the law applicable to the proof of such records in civil cases. Rule 40 formally recognizes that practice.

Like its civil counterpart, Rule 40 is addressed only to authenticating an official record or establishing the lack thereof. It does not govern the authentication of unofficial records, nor does it regulate the extent to which the contents of an authenticated official record are admissible.

The term "official record" has been defined generally as including records of any governmental entity, 8A J. MOORE, FEDERAL PRACTICE para. 27.02 at 27–6 (1978), and more particularly as "all documents prepared by public officials pursuant to a duty imposed by law or required by the nature of their offices. . . ." Olender v. United States, 210 F.2d 795, 801 (9th Cir.1954). *See* Fed.R.Evid. 901(b)(7), 902(1)–(3).

Subdivision (a). It should be noted that subdivision (a)(1), unlike its federal counterpart, does not require certification by a judge or other officer of the status of the custodial official if the records are kept within the Commonwealth. As for domestic records kept outside the Commonwealth (subdivision [a][1]) and foreign records (subdivision

[a][2]), the requirement of double certification is retained. Subdivision (a)(2) is in all other respects in accord with former Massachusetts practice.

Subdivision (b). This subdivision permits the written statement of a custodial officer that no particular record can be found, authenticated pursuant to subdivision (a), to suffice as proof that no such record exists.

Subdivision (c). Rule 40(c) incorporates all pre-existing statutory methods of proving the existence of, or lack of the existence of, official records. Those statutes are unaffected by the promulgation of this rule. *See*, e.g., G.L. c. 46, § 19 (records relative to birth, marriage, and death); G.L. c. 233, §§ 76, 76A, 76B (records of departments of government).

Rule 41. Interpreters and Experts

(Applicable to District Court and Superior Court)

The judge may appoint an interpreter or expert if justice so requires and may determine the reasonable compensation for such services and direct payment therefor.

Reporter's Notes

This rule is an abbreviated version of Fed.R.Crim.P. 28 as it appeared prior to amendment in 1975. Federal Rule 28 now deals only with interpreters; the provisions governing expert witnesses, formerly Federal Rule 28(a), are now contained in Fed.R.Evid. 706. *See* Main R.Crim.P. 28.

The right of a defendant to be present at trial, *see* e.g., Lewis v. United States, 146 U.S. 370, 372 (1892)—in the sense of being able to comprehend and participate meaningfully in the proceeding, United States ex rel. Negron v. New York, 434 F.2d 386 (2d Cir.1970)—the requirement that a defendant have "sufficient . . . ability to consult with his lawyer with a reasonable degree of rational understanding," Dusky v. United States, 80 S.Ct. 788, 362 U.S. 402, 4 L.Ed.2d 824 (1960), and the sixth amendment right to be confronted with adverse witnesses, applicable to the states through the fourteenth amendment, Pointer v. Texas, 85 S.Ct. 1065, 380 U.S. 400, 13 L.Ed.2d 923 (1965), mandate that an interpreter be available to the defendant or witness who cannot effectively communicate. "Otherwise, '[t]he adjudication loses its character as a reasoned interaction . . . and becomes an invective against an insensible object.'" *United States ex rel. Negron,* supra at 389, *quoting* Note, Incompetency to Stand Trial, (1969) 81 HARVARD L.REV. 454, 458.

Whenever an interpreter is placed between the witness and counsel, the judge, and the jury, problems of distortion and confusion may arise. For example, where some of the jurors understand the language of the witness and the judge or counsel does not, the jurors may hear testimony that should have been excluded. The Supreme Judicial Court has suggested the following:

1. Counsel should address his questions to the witness in the second person, and not to the interpreter.

2. The interpreter should translate the question exactly without any additional or supplementary remarks of his own.

3. The interpreter should then translate the answer of the witness in the first person, neither editing nor adding to the witness' words. Even if the answer is non-responsive, the interpreter should give it and allow the judge to pass on its admissibility, for the interpreter's sole function is to translate.

4. Extraneous conversations between the witness and the interpreter should not be permitted. If such conversations do occur for some reason, they should be translated into English for the judge and counsel to hear.

5. When there are sitting on the jury individuals who understand the language of the witness, they are to be instructed that it is the interpreted testimony in English that is evidence and not their own translations of the witness' answers.

6. Neither party has the right to have a juror excused solely because that juror understands the language of a witness. However, in certain circumstances the judge in his discretion may decide whether to excuse such a juror is appropriate. For example, this action may be desirable on motion of the defendant in a criminal matter in which the progress of the trial will not be interrupted by the removal of the juror, sufficient alternate jurors have been empaneled, and interpreted testimony constitutes a major part of the case.

Commonwealth v. Festa, 369 Mass. 419, 429–30, 341 N.E.2d 276 (1976) (footnote omitted).

While the Supreme Court has established that it is within the discretion of the court whether to appoint an interpreter, Perovich v. United States, 27 S.Ct. 456, 205 U.S. 86, 91, 51 L.Ed. 722 (1907), it has not found a right to state-provided interpreters to be a constitutional absolute since that issue has never been squarely presented. Lower federal courts have held, however, that if the court is put on notice that a defendant has a language difficulty, the court must make it unmistakably clear to him that he has the right to have a competent translator assist him, at state expense if he is indigent, throughout the proceeding. United States v. Carrion, 488 F.2d 12, 15 (1st Cir.1973), cert. denied, 94 S.Ct. 1613, 416 U.S. 907, 40 L.Ed.2d 112 (1974); United States ex rel. Negron v. New York, 434 F.2d 386, 390–91 (2d Cir.1970). Conversely, if the need for an interpreter's services is not apparent nor are such services requested, it is no abuse of discretion to fail to advise a defendant of their availability. United States v. Barrios, 457 F.2d 680, 682 (9th Cir.1972).

The justices of the Superior Court, G.L. c. 221, § 92, the Boston Municipal Court, G.L. c. 218, § 67, and the East Boston District Court, G.L. c. 218, § 68, may appoint official interpreters for the sessions of those courts. Other District Courts may employ interpreters as the need therefor arises. G.L. c. 262, § 32. Interpreters are to be compensated for their services by the Commonwealth. G.L. c. 221, §§ 92, 92A; c. 262, § 32. The appointment of interpreters in civil actions is governed by Mass.R.Civ.P. 43(f).

The federal rule does not indicate that it was intended to benefit only the indigent defendant.

The view that the Rule should be restricted overlooks the fact that the interpreter's services, though required by the defendant's own language problem, benefit the court and prosecution as well as the defense. The integrity of the judicial process—not to mention the desirability of avoiding collateral attacks—demands an accurate and impartial translation. Such a translation can only be guaranteed by court appointment of interpreters.

8A J. MOORE, FEDERAL PRACTICE Para. 28.02[2] at 28–3 (1978). *But see* United States v. Desist, 384 F.2d 889, 901–03 (2d Cir.1967), aff'd on other grounds 89 S.Ct. 1030, 394 U.S. 244, 22 L.Ed.2d 248 (1969). Former practice in Massachusetts appeared to be that interpreters, unless retained by non-indigent defendants, were paid by the court. Official interpreters are expressly barred from receiving gratuities, bonuses or fees beyond that compensation paid by the Commonwealth. G.L. c. 218, § 67; c. 221, § 92.

The use of interpreters is not limited to situations where the defendant or a witness is not English-speaking. General Laws c. 221, § 92A provides for the appointment of interpreters for the deaf. The court in United States v. Addonizio, 451 F.2d 49, 68 (3d Cir.), cert. denied 92 S.Ct. 949, 405 U.S. 936, 30 L.Ed.2d 812 (1972), held that the appointment as interpreter of the wife of a witness whose illness made his speech difficult to understand was not an abuse of discretion. *See* Fairbanks v. Cowan, 551 F.2d 97 (6th Cir.1977) (father of retarded adult). The appointment of such a person should only be after a finding that he is disinterested in the outcome of the case. *United States v. Addonizio,* supra; Price v. Beto, 426 F.2d 875 (5th Cir.1970) (appointment of husband of deaf-mute victim held violative of due process). *See* Maine R.Crim.P. 28, which provides for appointment of a "disinterested" interpreter of the court's own selection.

The courts' power to appoint expert witnesses to assist the indigent defendant or the court itself is nowhere express; rather, it is grounded upon the long-standing belief "that it is for the interest of the Commonwealth . . . that all proper investigations should be made, in order to guard against the danger of doing injustice to the prisoner. . . ." Attorney General, petitioner, 104 Mass. 537, 544 (1870). The Supreme Judicial Court has approved the practice of the trial judge's authorization, on a proper showing, of an indigent defendant to expend public funds for expert assistance. *See* Commonwealth v. Silva, 371 Mass. 819, 821, 359 N.E.2d 942 (1977) (psychiatric expert).

Under Superior Court Rule 54 (1974), the court is not to allow compensation for the services of an expert witness unless his employment by the defendant was authorized by the court. If the compensation of defense experts is approved by the court, it is paid by the Commonwealth. G.L. c. 280, §§ 4, 16; c. 261, §§ 27A–G.

Pursuant to G.L. c. 261, § 27B, applicable by its terms to criminal cases, a defendant may file an affidavit of indigency and request waiver, substitution or payment by the Commonwealth of costs and fees. Substitution means that if an alternative to a translator is available at lower or no cost, the judge may order that this alternative be used if it is "substantially equivalent . . . and does not materially impair the rights of any party." G.L. c. 261, § 27F. If, after hearing, the court finds that certain services are "reasonably necessary to assure the [defendant] as effective a . . . defense as he would have if he were financially able to pay," the court must grant the defendant's request for payment by the Commonwealth of "extra fees and costs," defined in G.L. c. 261, § 27A as including "expert assistance."

The indigent defendant cannot as of right nominate the expert whom he wishes to employ, Commonwealth v. Erickson, 356 Mass. 63, 248 N.E.2d 270 (1969); Commonwealth v. Medeiros, 354 Mass. 193, 199–200, 236 N.E.2d 642 (1968), cert. denied sub nom., Bernier v. Massachusetts, 89 S.Ct. 699, 393 U.S. 1058, 21 L.Ed.2d 699 (1969), but in practice most judges will permit the defendant to specify an expert, although a ceiling may be established on the amount which may be expended. 30 MASS.PRACTICE SERIES (Smith) § 492 (1970, Supp. 1978).

In addition to appointing experts to assist the defendant in the preparation or presentation of his defense, the court is empowered to call experts on its own motion to aid in its determination of issues of fact or law. *See* Commonwealth v. Lykus, 367 Mass. 191, 327 N.E.2d 671 (1975) (Separate opinion of Kaplan J., 206 at 213).

Rule 42.   Clerical Mistakes

(Applicable to District Court and Superior Court)

Clerical mistakes in judgments, orders, or other parts of the record and errors therein arising from oversight or omission may be corrected by the court at any time of its own initiative or on the motion of any party and after such notice, if any, as the court orders. During the pendency of an appeal, such mistakes may be corrected before the appeal is docketed in the appellate court, and thereafter while the appeal is pending may be corrected with leave of the appellate court.

Reporter's Notes

This rule is substantially identical to Mass.R.Civ.P. 60(a). *See* Fed.R.Crim.P. 36; Fed.R.Civ.P. 60(a).

Rule 42 is limited to the correction of "clerical mistakes" or errors "arising from oversight or omission" and does not apply to the correction of errors of substance, such as an illegal sentence or improperly obtained conviction. The federal criminal analogue is said to be typically invoked when the court has authority to impose

consecutive as well as concurrent sentences, but the record is ambiguous as to which was in fact given. 8A J. MOORE, FEDERAL PRACTICE Para. 36.02 at 36–1 n. 1 (1978). *See* e.g., Borum v. United States, 409 F.2d 433, 439–41, 133 U.S.App. 147 (D.C.Cir.1967), cert. denied 89 S.Ct. 1765, 395 U.S. 916, 23 L.Ed.2d 230 (1968).

Errors which may be corrected pursuant to this rule must arise out of "misprisions, oversights, omissions, unintended acts or failures to act," First Nat'l Bank v. National Airlines, 167 F.Supp. 167, 169 (S.D.N.Y.1958) (construing Fed.R.Civ.P. 60[a]), and not result from deliberate action, Ferrao v. Arthur M. Rosenblum Co., 156 F.2d 212 (2d Cir.1946). *See* 8 MASS.PRACTICE SERIES (Smith & Zobel) Reporters' Notes at (1977).

Clerical mistakes are due to a failure to accurately record statements made or action taken by the court or parties. E.g., Costello v. United States, 252 F.2d 750 (5th Cir.1958). 8A J. MOORE, FEDERAL PRACTICE Para. 36.02 at 36–2 (1978). Errors which are due to oversight or omission generally require correction so as to conform to the intent of the court or a party which may not be reflected in their recorded statements. E.g., Green v. Clerk of Mun. Ct., 321 Mass. 487, 74 N.E.2d 19 (1947); Lott v. United States, 309 F.2d 115 (5th Cir.1962), cert. denied 83 S.Ct. 504, 371 U.S. 950, 9 L.Ed.2d 498 (1963). *But* cf. United States v. Raftis, 427 F.2d 1145 (8th Cir.1970); 8A J. MOORE, supra at 36–2.

The term "record" is intended to be broadly read so as to encompass not only process, pleadings, and verdict, but also evidentiary documents, testimony, instructions and all other matters pertaining to the case of which there is a written record. 8 MASS.PRACTICE SERIES, supra at 461; 8A J. MOORE, supra at 36–2.

The entry of an appeal does not divest the trial court of its power to correct error. If the case has been docketed in the appellate court, the trial court is still empowered to correct error, but only with permission of the appellate court. *See* 8 MASS.PRACTICE SERIES, supra at 461; Fed.R.App.P. 10(a), (e).

Rule 43.   Summary Contempt Proceedings

(a) When Warranted. A criminal contempt may be punished summarily when

(1) summary punishment is necessary to maintain order in the courtroom;

(2) the contemptuous conduct occurred in the presence of, and was witnessed by, the presiding judge;

(3) the presiding judge enters a preliminary finding at the time of the contemptuous conduct that a criminal contempt occurred; and

(4) the punishment for each contempt does not exceed three months imprisonment and a fine of $2,000.

(b) Procedure.

(1) Upon making a preliminary finding that a criminal contempt occurred, the presiding judge shall give the alleged contemnor notice of the charges and shall hold a hearing to provide at least a summary opportunity for the alleged contemnor to produce evidence and argument relevant to guilt or punishment. For good cause shown, the presiding judge may continue the hearing to enable the contemnor to obtain counsel or evidence.

(2) The presiding judge may order the alleged contemnor held, subject to bail and/or conditions of release, pending the hearing provided for in subsection (b)(1) if the judge finds it necessary to maintain order in the courtroom or to assure the alleged contemnor's appearance.

(3) (i) If, after the hearing provided for in subsection (b)(1), the presiding judge determines that summary contempt is not appropriate because the appropriate punishment for the alleged contempt exceeds three months imprisonment and a fine of $2,000, the judge shall refer the alleged contemnor for prosecution under Rule 44. If necessary to maintain order in the courtroom or to assure the alleged contemnor's appearance, the judge may order the alleged contemnor held, subject to bail and/or conditions of release, for a reasonable period of time, not to exceed 15 days absent good cause shown, pending the issuance of a complaint or indictment under Rule 44(a).

(ii) If, after the hearing, the presiding judge determines that summary contempt is not appropriate because one or more of the requirements in subsection (a)(1), (a)(2), or (a)(3) is not satisfied, or for another reason, the judge shall discharge the alleged contemnor. The judge, in his or her discretion, may refer the matter to the government for investigation and possible prosecution, and nothing in this subsection shall preclude such investigation or prosecution, whether undertaken in response to the judge's referral or independently.

(iii) If, after the hearing, the presiding judge determines that summary contempt is appropriate, the judge shall make a finding on the record of summary contempt, setting forth the facts upon which that finding is based. The court shall further announce a judgment of summary contempt in open court, enter that judgment on the court's docket, and notify the contemnor of the right to appeal. The judge may defer sentencing, or the execution of any sentence, where the interests of orderly courtroom procedure and substantial justice require. If necessary to maintain order in the courtroom or to assure the contemnor's appearance, the judge may order the contemnor held, subject to bail and/or conditions of release, pending sentencing.

(c) Appeal. A contemnor may appeal a judgment of summary contempt to the Appeals Court.

Amended October 30, 2013, effective January 1, 2014.

Reporter's Notes

Rule 43 is based upon Fed.R.Crim.P. 42(a) as that rule was affected by the Supreme Court decision in Bloom v. Illinois, 88 S.Ct. 1477, 391 U.S. 194, 20 L.Ed.2d 522 (1968), and upon Fla.R.Crim.P. 3.830 (1975).

Bloom v. Illinois, supra, signaled a departure from the traditional approach to adjudicating criminal contempt. The Court's guidelines established in *Bloom*, which have been consistently followed and clarified since the issuance of the opinion, comprise the substance of this rule.

In *Bloom* the Court de-emphasized the long-standing distinction between so-called direct and indirect contempt, focusing instead on the issue of potential penalty. Beginning with the premise that criminal contempts are so similar to other criminal proceedings as to be in their practical—and constitutional—aspects indistinguishable, and following its decision in Duncan v. Louisiana, 88 S.Ct. 1444, 391 U.S. 145, 20 L.Ed.2d 491, 522 (1968), the Court held that while summary punishment of criminal contempt may be necessary to preserve the dignity and efficacy of the judicial process, those interests are outweighed by the need to provide the defendant with all the procedural safeguards deemed fundamental in our judicial system. The Court concluded that a defendant charged with a serious contempt, whether direct or indirect, is entitled to a full jury trial.

Subdivision (a). In Codispoti v. Pennsylvania, 94 S.Ct. 2687, 418 U.S. 506, 41 L.Ed.2d 912 (1974), the Court stated that "where the

necessity of circumstances warrants, a contemnor may be summarily tried...." Id. at 514. The Court recognized, however, that where "there is no overriding necessity for instant action to preserve order.... [there is] no justification for dispensing with the ordinary rudiments of due process." Id. at 515. The present rule incorporates that principle: summary proceedings are available *only* when they are necessary to preserve order. *Accord* Sussman v. Commonwealth, 374 Mass. 692, 374 N.E.2d 1195 (1978).

By limiting the use of summary disposition of contempts to those cases where the alleged contemptuous conduct was committed in the presence of the trial judge, subdivision (a)(1) conforms to the common law practice based on the direct-indirect contempt distinction and to practice under Fed.R.Crim.P. 42(a). One basis for the common law principle is that the judge cannot determine the facts surrounding an allegation of contempt without a hearing unless he personally viewed the contemptuous conduct.

Subdivision (a)(2) stems from the principle expressed in Taylor v. Hayes, 94 S.Ct. 2697, 418 U.S. 488, 41 L.Ed.2d 897 (1974), that when the adjudication of contempt is delayed until after the contemptuous conduct has occurred, summary disposition is improper. Although in most cases the same principle would apply when the punishment is delayed, the Supreme Court recognized that in some cases, particularly those involving lawyers, summary punishment is permissible when the punishment alone has been delayed.

Subdivision (a)(2) goes beyond the minimum constitutional requirements that must be afforded to contemnors. *Taylor v. Hayes*, supra, expressly allows the court to punish without a full scale trial, though it disallows summary disposition of contempts when the judgment of contempt is not entered contemporaneously with the commission of the contempt. Accordingly, under this rule, a trial is required in such situations. The rationale for such requirement is that where necessity does not demand immediate action, a contemnor is to have the same rights as other criminal defendants. *See* Commonwealth v. Sussman, 374 Mass. 692, 374 N.E.2d 1195 (1978).

Courts have generally defined serious contempt to mean one for which in excess of six months' imprisonment may be imposed, *Duncan*, supra, or for which a fine of more than $500 may be levied, United States v. Polk, 438 F.2d 377 (6th Cir.1971). The Supreme Court has not addressed the specific question whether and in what circumstances—if at all—"the imposition of a fine for criminal contempt, unaccompanied by imprisonment, may require a jury trial." Muniz v. Hoffman, 95 S.Ct. 2178, 422 U.S. 454, 476, 45 L.Ed. 319 (1975). Muniz has been read narrowly so as to preserve the traditional standard of $500 as constituting serious contempt. Douglas v. First National Realty Corp., 543 F.2d 894 (D.C.Cir.1976).

Subdivision (a)(3) reflects this demarcation between serious and petty offenses. Any contempt which the trial judge would punish by a sentence of at least three months cannot be tried summarily and must be tried before a jury if the contemnor so elects. *See* Mass.R.Crim.P. 45(a)–(b).

Codispoti v. Pennsylvania, supra, imposes a further restriction on the availability of summary proceedings that relates to the six-month rule. Where the adjudication of contempt is delayed until after trial and where there are at least two sentences imposed that are consecutive and cumulative more than six months, summary proceedings are not available. This is an interpretation of the six-month rule adopted by *Bloom* and subsequent cases as applied to consecutive sentences for contempt imposed at one trial. This limitation does not apply where the judgments of contempt are entered serially during the progress of the trial as the contemptuous conduct occurs. *Codispoti v. Pennsylvania*, supra at 513–15. Sentences will be aggregated for purposes of the six-month rule, however, where the citations for contempt occur during trial but imposition of sentences is delayed until the conclusion thereof. United States v. Prewitt, 553 F.2d 1082, 1087–90 (7th Cir.1977). The foregoing principles, while fully applicable under this rule, are to be read in terms of *three* months as dictated by subdivision (a)(3).

Subdivision (b). This subdivision outlines the procedures to be followed in a summary adjudication of contempt. While these procedures go beyond the minimum requirements of due process set out in *Taylor v. Hayes,* they do comport with suggestions by the Supreme Court as to the proper procedure to be followed.

"Summary punishment always, and rightly, is regarded with disfavor," Sacher v. United States, 72 S.Ct. 451, 343 U.S. 1, 8, 96 L.Ed. 717 (1952). *Accord Taylor v. Hayes,* supra, at 497–98; Groppi v. Leslie, 92 S.Ct. 582, 404 U.S. 496, 502–05, 30 L.Ed.2d 632 (1972). Unless the contempt occurs in the presence of the judge and immediate punishment is needed to prevent demoralization of the court's authority or to enforce lawful orders essential to prevent a breakdown of the proceedings, many of the due process safeguards available in criminal proceedings should apply to a contempt proceeding. Sussman v. Commonwealth, 374 Mass. 692, 374 N.E.2d 1195 (1978). Except in cases of flagrant contemptuous conduct, the trial judge should not exercise the power of summary contempt in the absence of a prior warning as to the conduct which will place the offender in contempt. *Sussman,* supra at 759. If an adjudication of, and punishment for, contempt is carried out summarily, the contemnor is denied an opportunity to present facts in mitigation of the charge. *See Groppi v. Leslie,* supra, 503, 505. It is for this reason that a contemnor should in all cases be given notice and granted at least a summary opportunity to present evidence on his own behalf. An adequate opportunity to defend or explain one's conduct is a minimum requirement before imposition of punishment. *Sussman,* supra, at 762. As stated in the ABA *Standards Relating to the Function of the Trial Judge,* § 7.4, comment at 95 (Approved Draft, 1972):

> Although there is authority that in-court contempts can be punished without notice of charges or an opportunity to be heard, Ex parte Terry, 9 S.Ct. 77, 128 U.S. 289, 32 L.Ed. 405 (1888), such a procedure has little to commend it, is inconsistent with the basic notions of fairness, and is likely to bring disrespect upon the court. Accordingly, notice and at least a brief opportunity to be heard should be afforded as a matter of course.

The last sentence of subdivision (b) is intended to cover those "circumstances, particularly where the offender is a lawyer representing a client on trial ... [where summary punishment] may be postponed until the conclusion of the proceedings." *Taylor v. Hayes,* supra at 498. *See Sussman v. Commonwealth,* supra at 762–63.

It should be recognized that the power to punish for contempt is to be used cautiously and is not an appropriate device to control every act of courtroom disrespect. This rule is intended to authorize summary punishment only for disruptive conduct that is willfully contemptuous and that has been preceded by a prior warning in all but the most flagrant violations. *See ABA Standards Relating to the Function of the Trial Judge* § 7.2, comment at 93 (Approved Draft, 1972); United States v. Wilson, 95 S.Ct. 1802, 421 U.S. 309, 44 L.Ed.2d 186 (1975).

Subdivision (c). The elimination of the writ of error by Rule 30 necessitated a change in the method of review provided for in criminal contempt cases. Formerly, under G.L. c. 250, § 9, a sentence to punish for criminal contempt was a judgment in a criminal case which could be reexamined upon a writ of error. Hansen v. Commonwealth, 344 Mass. 214, 216, 181 N.E.2d 843 (1962); Dolan v. Commonwealth, 304 Mass. 325, 328, 23 N.E.2d 904 (1939). Review was limited to errors of law and matters of fact not heard and decided at the trial under review. *Blankenburg v. Commonwealth,* 260 Mass. 369, 376–77, 157 N.E. 693 (1927).

Subdivision (c) establishes the taking of an appeal as the sole means of review for criminal contempts. Review by appeal has already gained a foothold in Massachusetts practice for contempt findings against witnesses who have been previously granted immunity and have refused to testify. G.L. c. 233, § 20H. Under subdivision (c) review will be by the Appeals Court.

Reporter's Notes—2014

Rule 43 Summary Contempt

This amendment to Rule 43 is intended to clarify the procedures by which a judge can impose summary punishment for criminal contempt or, alternatively, refer an alleged contemnor for prosecution by complaint or indictment under Rule 44. *See Vizcaino v. Commonwealth,* 462 Mass. 266, 279 n. 11 (2012) (suggesting a need for clarification in the operation of Rule 43). Amended Rule 43 resolves ambiguities concerning the prerequisites for summary punishment of contempt and the procedural steps in a summary-contempt proceeding. Further, amended Rule 43(b) explicitly recognizes discretionary authority that judges have presumably enjoyed in summary contempt proceedings, principally the common-law authority to hold an accused contemnor if necessary to maintain courtroom order or to assure his or her appearance at any subsequent proceeding. The amended rule also increases the maximum fine permitted from $500 to $2,000.

Rule 43(a) When Warranted

Subdivision (a). Amended Rule 43(a), like its predecessor, provides for the four conditions necessary to warrant summary punishment for contempt. Such punishment must be necessary to maintain courtroom order; the contemptuous conduct must occur in the presence of and be witnessed by the judge; the judge must enter a finding of contempt at the time it occurs; and the punishment cannot exceed three months' imprisonment and a fine of $2,000. As discussed below, amended Rule 43(a)(3) clarifies an ambiguity in former Rule 43(a), the amended rule expressly providing that this threshold, contemporaneous finding of contempt be preliminary. As such, it gives notice to the alleged contemnor of the charges, but it is subject to reconsideration after affording the alleged contemnor an opportunity to be heard as required under Rule 43(b)(1).

Former Rule 43(a)(2) referred to the threshold, contemporaneous finding as a "judgment of contempt," leading to possible confusion between it and the final "judgment of contempt" which, under former Rule 43(b), the judge could make only after "giv[ing] the contemnor notice of the charges and at least a summary opportunity to adduce evidence or argument relevant to guilt or punishment." Mass. R. Crim. P. 43, 378 Mass. 919 (1979). *See Vizcaino v. Commonwealth,* 462 Mass. 266, 276 (2012) (holding that an opportunity to be heard followed by entry of the judgment on docket are necessary predicates to a Rule 43 judgment of summary contempt); *Commonwealth v. Segal,* 401 Mass. 95, 99-100 (1987) (same). Amended Rule 43(a)(3) makes it clear that the judge's threshold, contemporaneous finding of contempt is preliminary. While the Supreme Judicial Court had read former Rule 43(a)(2) to provide that this preliminary "judgment of contempt" be written, *see Vizcaino v. Commonwealth,* 462 Mass. 266, 272 & n. 7 (2012) (interpreting Rule 43(a)'s contemporaneity requirement to permit reasonable, minor delays in preparing Rule 43(a)(2)'s written judgment of contempt), amended Rule 43(a)(2) neither provides nor contemplates that the preliminary finding of contempt be written. Such a requirement seems unnecessary given that the judge's finding is in open court and presumably subject to transcription if necessary. Moreover, requiring a written finding could delay both the alleged contemnor's opportunity to be heard and the trial in which the contemptuous conduct occurred. Finally, as noted, the amended rule increases the maximum fine for summary contempt from $500 to $2,000, an increase that partially accounts for the inflation that has occurred since the rule's adoption in 1979. This maximum fine is well within the punishment that may be imposed without implicating the Sixth Amendment right to a jury trial. *See Blanton v. City of N. Las Vegas,* Nev., 489 U.S. 538, 544-45 (1989) (holding no Sixth Amendment right to jury trial for offense the maximum punishment for which was six months imprisonment and $1,000 fine, noting the possible fine was "well below" the $5,000 federal benchmark utilized in identifying petty offenses that can be tried without a jury); *Furtado v. Furtado,* 380 Mass. 137, 142 n. 5 (1980) (noting Supreme Judicial Court has not interpreted article 12 to impose a stricter jury-trial requirement).

Rule 43(b) Procedure

As did former Rule 43(b), amended Rule 43(b)(1) provides that, following the preliminary finding of contempt under Rule 43(a)(3), the judge must conduct a hearing, affording the accused contemnor at least a summary opportunity to produce evidence and/or argument relevant to guilt or punishment. The amended rule further gives the judge discretion, for good cause shown, to continue the hearing so that the accused contemnor can obtain evidence or counsel.

Rule 43(b)(2) authorizes the judge to hold the accused contemnor, subject to bail and/or conditions of release, pending the summary-contempt hearing if necessary to maintain courtroom order or to assure the contemnor's appearance. Judges presumably had such common-law authority under former Rule 43, see In re Terry, 128 U.S. 289, 307-13 (1888) (recognizing longstanding judicial authority to apprehend, commit, and summarily punish one who engages in contemptuous conduct in the judge's presence); see also G.L. c. 276, § 57 (authorizing justices of the superior and district courts to admit a committed prisoner to bail upon finding that such release will reasonably assure the prisoner's future appearance before the court), but the amended rule makes it explicit.

Amended Rule 43(b)(3) sets out the respective procedures for the three possible results of the Rule 43(b)(1) hearing.

First, under Rule 43(b)(3)(i), if the judge determines that summary contempt is not appropriate because the accused contemnor deserves greater punishment than that permitted for summary contempt, the judge must refer the alleged contemnor for prosecution by complaint or indictment under Rule 44. In that event, if necessary to maintain courtroom order or the appearance of the accused, the rule recognizes the judge's common-law authority to hold the alleged contemnor subject to bail and/or conditions of release for up to 15 days, extendable for good cause shown, pending issuance of the contempt complaint or indictment under Rule 44(a). Although the judge has wide discretion in determining what constitutes good cause to extend the 15-day limitation, it would ordinarily include a superior court referral in which there is no grand jury in session during that 15-day period.

Second, Rule 43(b)(3)(ii) covers the case in which, after considering the facts and arguments presented in the summary-contempt hearing, the judge decides for whatever reason that summary contempt is not appropriate. This possibility, although inferable under former Rule 43(b), is here explicit. Under Rule 43(b)(3)(ii), such a decision to forgo further proceedings and to discharge the alleged contemnor does not bar the alleged contemnor's prosecution for the alleged contempt. The rule explicitly provides that, in spite of this termination of summary-contempt proceedings, the judge has discretion to refer the matter to the government for investigation and possible prosecution, and that, even in the absence of such a judicial referral, the government may investigate and prosecute the alleged contempt. Cf. Vizcaino, 462 Mass. at 274-75 (holding that, where judge had not entered summary contempt judgment on the court's docket as required by Rule 43(b), further prosecution for nonsummary contempt under Rule 44 not barred by double jeopardy).

Third, Rule 43(b)(3)(iii) sets out the procedure if, after the hearing, the judge decides that summary punishment for the contempt is appropriate. The judge must make a finding of summary contempt on the record, setting out the facts on which it is based. Unlike former Rule 43(b), this finding need not be written; a transcript of the factual finding provides an adequate record for purposes of appeal. The rule further provides that, as in any criminal conviction, the court must announce the summary-contempt judgment in open court, enter the judgment on the docket, and notify the contemnor of the right to appeal. See Mass. R. Crim. P. 28(a), 378 Mass. 898 (1979). As did former Rule 43(b), Rule 43(b)(3)(iii) allows the judge discretion to defer summary-contempt sentencing or its execution where orderly courtroom procedure and substantial justice require. Although the rule does not explicitly limit the purpose or length of such sentence deferral, as was so under former Rule 43(b), it ordinarily would be reserved for cases of summary contempt by one of the parties or lawyers in the trial, see Taylor v. Hayes, 418 U.S. 488, 497-98 (1974),

and imposition or execution of sentence would be deferred until after the trial is completed. The rule further permits the judge, if necessary, to order the contemnor held, subject to bail and/or conditions of release, pending sentencing.

Rule 43(c), providing for the right of appeal to the Appeals Court, remains in substance unchanged.

Rule 44.   Contempt

(Applicable to District Court and Superior Court)

(a) **Nature of the Proceedings.** All criminal contempts not adjudicated pursuant to Rule 43 shall be prosecuted by means of complaint, unless the prosecutor elects to proceed by indictment. Except as otherwise provided by these rules, the case shall proceed as a criminal case in the court in which the contempt is alleged to have been committed.

(b) **Special Provisions for District Court.** The District Court shall have jurisdiction to try all contempts committed therein except those prosecuted by indictment. Whenever a contemnor asserts his right to a jury trial in District Court, the trial shall be held before a jury in District Court. The contemnor's only right of appeal shall be to the Appeals Court.

(c) **Disqualification of the Judge.** The contempt charges shall be heard by a judge other than the trial judge whenever the nature of the alleged contemptuous conduct is such as is likely to affect the trial judge's impartiality.

Reporter's Notes

Contempts that are not or cannot be tried summarily in accordance with Rule 43 must be tried under the provisions of Rule 44. Rule 44 carries the recent developments in the law of contempt to a logical conclusion by requiring all contempts not summarily tried to be prosecuted under the procedures established for the trial of other criminal offenses.

In any alleged contempt to be adjudicated pursuant to this rule, the defendant has the right to a jury trial. Bloom v. Illinois, 88 S.Ct. 1477, 391 U.S. 194, 20 L.Ed.2d 522 (1968), adopted the standard established in Duncan v. Louisiana, 88 S.Ct. 1444, 391 U.S. 145, 20 L.Ed.2d 491, 522 (1968) for determining when the right to a jury trial accrues to a defendant and applied that standard to criminal contempt. Duncan accepted the established rule that maximum sentences of under six months denote petty offenses. It was established in Baldwin v. New York, 90 S.Ct. 1886, 399 U.S. 66, 69, 26 L.Ed.2d 437 (1970), that authorized maximum punishment of greater than six months indicated a serious offense. Since the maximum punishment for contempt is often not regulated by statute, the determination of whether a particular contempt charge is a serious or petty offense is to be made with reference to the penalty actually imposed. See Bloom v. Illinois, supra at 211; Codispoti v. Pennsylvania, 94 S.Ct. 2687, 418 U.S. 506, 512, 41 L.Ed.2d 912 (1974). Under Mass.R.Crim.P. 43(a)(3), that reference will be to whether the sentence exceeds three months' imprisonment or a fine of $500.

Initiation of prosecution by complaint is an historically recognized manner of bringing charges for indirect contempt in the Commonwealth. Dolan v. Commonwealth, 304 Mass. 325, 337, 23 N.E.2d 904 (1939). See generally, the cases cited by the Court in Dolan at 337 for further similarities existing between prosecutions for indirect contempt and other criminal prosecutions.

One exception to the claim of similarity between a contempt prosecution under this rule and other criminal prosecutions should be noted: the right to indictment by grand jury, to which contemnors are not entitled at present, is not to be extended to them by interpreting this rule broadly. In ordinary criminal prosecutions, a defendant has the right to indictment for those crimes punishable by a term in the state prison. Jones v. Robbins, 74 Mass. (8 Gray) 329, 350 (1857). General Laws c. 220, § 14, as interpreted by the Court in Hurley v. Commonwealth, 188 Mass. 443, 448, 74 N.E. 677, 3 Ann.Cas. 757 (1905), precludes contempt commitments other than to the "common jail." Since the maximum term of imprisonment in a jail or house of correction is set at two and one-half years by G.L. c. 279, § 23, and since no grand jury indictment is required to confine a defendant for that period of time (see Mass.R.Crim.P. 3, Complaint; Indictment), it is apparent that no right to prosecution by indictment exists in contempt cases. Federal case law is in accord on this point. Green v. United States, 78 S.Ct. 632, 356 U.S. 165, 183, 2 L.Ed.2d 672 (1958); United States v. Eichhorst, 554 F.2d 1383, 1386 (7th Cir.1976); Mitchell v. Fiore, 470 F.2d 1149, 1153 (3rd Cir.1972); United States v. Bukowski, 435 F.2d 1094, 1101 (7th Cir.1970).

Rule 45. Removal of the Disruptive Defendant

(Applicable to District Court and Superior Court)

(a) Removal of Defendant. Upon the direction of the trial judge, a defendant may be removed from the courtroom during his trial when his conduct has become so disruptive that the trial cannot proceed in an orderly manner. Gagging or shackling may be employed if the trial judge has found such restraint reasonably necessary to maintain order. If the trial judge orders such restraint, he shall enter into the record of the case the reasons therefor. Whenever physical restraint of a defendant or witness occurs in the presence of the jury trying the case, or whenever the defendant is removed, the judge, at the request of the defendant, shall instruct the jury that such restraint or removal is not to be considered in assessing the proof and determining guilt.

(b) Defendant's Rights After Removal. A defendant once removed shall be required to be present in the court building while the trial is in progress. At the time of his removal he shall be advised that he has the right to be returned to the courtroom upon his request and assurances of good behavior. Notwithstanding the failure of a defendant to request to be returned to the courtroom, he shall be returned to the courtroom, at appropriate intervals in the absence of the jury, and shall be advised in open court that he will be permitted to remain upon the giving of assurances of good behavior.

Reporter's Notes

Rule 45 is drawn from § 6.8 of the ABA *Standards Relating to the Function of the Trial Judge* (Approved Draft, 1972), but differs in that the rule requires that at the time of removal the defendant is to be informed of his right to return upon his request and assurance of good conduct. Section 4.1 of the ABA *Standards Relating to Trial by Jury* (Approved Draft, 1968) in part provides the basis of subdivision (a). See Fed.R.Crim.P. 43(b)(2); Rules of Criminal Procedure (U.L.A.) Rule 713(b)(3) (1974).

This rule, in conjunction with Rules 43–44, Summary Contempt and Contempt, provides a means of dealing with obstreperous defendants. In many cases the measures provided by this rule may be viewed as less drastic than invocation of the contempt power to control the unruly defendant.

While the sixth and fourteenth amendments guarantee the right of a defendant to confront the witnesses against him in a state criminal proceeding, that right has been held by the Supreme Court to be less than absolute. In Snyder v. Massachusetts, 51 S.Ct. 330, 291 U.S. 97, 78 L.Ed.2d 674, 90 A.L.R. 575 (1934), the Court indicated that there was "[n]o doubt the privilege [of personally confronting witnesses] may be lost by consent or at times even by misconduct." Id. at 106. In Illinois v. Allen, 90 S.Ct. 1057, 397 U.S. 337, 25 L.Ed.2d 353 (1970),

a unanimous Court affirmed the principle that the sixth amendment right to confront witnesses can be forfeited.

Subdivision (a). The *Allen* Court recognized three methods of dealing with an obstreperous defendant as constitutionally permissible: (1) binding and gagging the defendant while present in the courtroom; (2) citing the defendant for contempt; or (3) removing the defendant from the courtroom until he promises to conduct himself properly. Id. at 343–44.

While gagging, shackling and other unusual measures are obviously less offensive to the defendant's right to be present at trial than his removal, such measures are not without attendant difficulties:

> These displays tend to create prejudice in the minds of the jury by suggesting that a defendant is a bad and dangerous person whose guilt may be virtually assumed; they may interfere with a defendant's thought processes and ease of communication with counsel; intrinsically they give affront to the dignity of the trial process.

Commonwealth v. Brown, 364 Mass. 471, 475, 305 N.E.2d 830 (1973) (Footnote omitted). While *Brown* dealt specifically with defendants who presented unusual security risks, the potential for prejudice to the unruly defendant is no less real, albeit mitigated perhaps by the fact that the jury will have observed the disruptive behavior and not presume guilt of the offense charged. In either case, "[w]hen special restraints are imposed, the judge's charge to the jury should seek to quell prejudice by reasoning and warning against it." *Commonwealth v. Brown*, supra at 476. *Accord* Commonwealth v. Cavanaugh, 371 Mass. 46, 58, 383 N.E.2d 732 (1977). See ABA *Standards Relating to Trial by Jury* § 4.1(c) (Approved Draft, 1968); ABA *Standards Relating to the Function of the Trial Judge* § 5.3(b)(ii) (Approved Draft, 1972).

In Commonwealth v. Senati, 3 Mass.App.Ct. 304, 327 N.E.2d 906 (1975), on facts similar to *Illinois v. Allen*, supra, the Appeals Court approved the practice of removing a defendant who refuses to observe standards of courtroom decorum. Section 6.8 of the ABA *Standards Relating to the Function of the Trial Judge* (Approved Draft, 1972) endorses this practice as preferable to gagging or shackling the disruptive defendant.

Whether the obstreperous defendant is restrained or removed, the trial judge is to state his reasons for such action on the record. See *Commonwealth v. Brown*, supra at 479; ABA *Standards Relating to the Function of the Trial Judge* § 5.3(b)(i) (Approved Draft, 1972).

Subdivision (b). The defendant who has been removed from the courtroom is accorded certain rights by this subdivision. First, the defendant is to be kept present in the court building while his trial is in progress. This is not intended to be read literally, but rather only to require that the defendant be kept in custody within reasonable proximity to the court, i.e., in a jail or police station adjacent to the courthouse.

Further, the defendant is to be given the opportunity of learning of the progress of his trial through his counsel at reasonable intervals. ABA *Standards Relating to the Function of the Trial Judge* § 6.8 (Approved Draft, 1972). Where feasible, the defendant should be provided with means to monitor the proceedings. See concurring opinion of Justice Brennan in Illinois v. Allen, 90 S.Ct. 1057, 397 U.S. 337, 351, 25 L.Ed.2d 353 (1970).

Secondly, the defendant is to be advised at the time of his removal of his continuing right to return upon his request and assurance of good behavior. ABA *Standards*, supra.

Finally, and notwithstanding the defendant's failure to request return, he is to be returned to the courtroom periodically and advised that he will be permitted to remain upon the giving of assurances of good behavior. To the ABA *Standards*, supra, is added the provision that the defendant is to be returned with the jury not present.

Rule 46. Time

(Applicable to District Court and Superior Court)

(a) Computation. In computing any period of time prescribed or allowed by these rules, by order of court, or by any applicable statute or rule, the day of the act, event, or default after which the designated period of time begins to run shall not be included. The last day of the period so computed shall be included, unless it is a Saturday, a Sunday, or a legal holiday, in which event the period runs until the end of the next day which is not a Saturday, a Sunday, or a legal holiday. When the period of time prescribed or allowed is less than seven days, intermediate Saturdays, Sundays, and legal holidays shall be excluded in the computation. As used in this rule, "legal holiday" includes any day appointed as a holiday by the President or the Congress of the United States or so designated by the laws of the Commonwealth.

(b) Enlargement. When by these rules or by a notice given thereunder or by order or rule of court an act is required or allowed to be done at or within a specified time, the court for cause shown may at any time in its discretion (1) with or without motion or notice order the period enlarged if a request therefor is made before the expiration of the period originally prescribed or as extended by a previous order; or (2) upon motion made after the expiration of the specified period permit the act to be done where the failure to act was the result of excusable neglect; or (3) permit the act to be done by stipulation of the parties; but the court may not extend the time for taking any action under Rules 25 and 29 except to the extent and under the conditions stated therein.

(c) For Motions, Affidavits in Superior Court. A written motion, other than one which may be heard ex parte, and notice of the hearing thereof shall be served on all interested parties not later than seven days prior to the hearing unless a different period is fixed by these rules or by order of the court. For cause shown, such an order may issue upon an ex parte application. When a motion is supported by affidavit, the affidavit shall be served with the motion. Opposing affidavits shall be served not later than one day before the hearing, unless the court permits them to be served at a later time.

Reporter's Notes

Rule 46 is drawn from and closely parallels Mass.R.Civ.P. 6. It is substantially the same as Rule 6 of the Federal Rules of Civil Procedure and Rule 45 of the Federal Rules of Criminal Procedure. This rule does not substantially alter prior Massachusetts practice.

Subdivision (a). Under the common law, Sundays were excluded from the calculation of a limited time period of seven days or less; if the period exceeded seven days, Sundays were included, even if the final day for the performance of an act fell upon a Sunday. 6 MASS.PRACTICE SERIES (Smith & Zobel) Reporter's Notes at 155 (1974). Like Mass.R.Civ.P. 6(a), this rule excludes Saturdays and legal holidays as well as Sundays from prescribed periods of less than seven days. It provides that a limited period shall not end on a Saturday, Sunday or legal holiday, but shall end on the next succeeding business day. See G.L. c. 4, § 9, which does not exclude Saturdays. Those legal holidays which shall be excluded are catalogued in G.L. c. 4, § 7, cl. 18 (as amended, St.1978, c. 12).

An exception to the first sentence is found in the Case Management rule, which provides that in the computation of that rule's time limits, an excluded period shall include both the first and last days of the excludable act or event. Mass.R.Crim.P. 36(b)(3).

Uniform Rule 753 is also phrased in terms of a "designated period of time" and is intended to "not authorize automatic exclusion of the first day or of Saturdays, Sundays, or holidays in complying with provisions which require action 'promptly,' 'without unnecessary delay,' within a 'reasonable' time, or the like." Rules of Criminal Procedure (U.L.A.) Rule 753(a) Comment (1974). Similar requirements prescribed by these rules or by court order are likewise not extended by the excludable days of this rule.

Subdivision (b). This subdivision grants the court discretion to relieve the parties from strict compliance with time requirements in three situations: first, upon request made before the expiration of an original period or a previously-extended period; secondly, upon motion made after the expiration of a period; and thirdly, upon agreement of the parties. In all three instances the party is entitled to relief "for cause shown." In the second situation, the failure to act must have been due to "excusable neglect." Because a motion must state with particularity the grounds on which it is based, Mass.R.Crim.P. 13(b), a bare assertion of excusable neglect without more is insufficient. *See* 6 MASS.PRACTICE SERIES, supra, comments § 6.4.

Neither the federal civil nor criminal rules expressly authorize enlargement by stipulation. While it is stated that under prior Massachusetts practice a stipulation as to enlargement ordinarily did not need court approval, 6 MASS.PRACTICE SERIES, supra, § 6.5, Mass.R.Civ.P. 6(b)(3) appears to require such approval. It is intended that under this rule the approval of the court is to be obtained.

A motion for a required finding of not guilty must be made at the close of the Commonwealth's or the defendant's case, Mass.R.Crim.P. 25(a). Under subdivision (b)(2) of that rule, the motion, if denied, can be renewed within five days after the jury is discharged. In neither case can the court enlarge the time within which the motion is to be made.

A motion to reduce or revoke a sentence is to be filed within sixty days after the imposition of the sentence and such time is not to be enlarged. Mass.R.Crim.P. 29(a).

Subdivision (c). It should be noted that the provisions that an affidavit in support of a motion must be served with the motion and that opposing affidavits are to be served at least one day before the hearing are applicable to pretrial motions under Mass.R.Crim.P. 13.

Rule 47. Special Magistrates

(Applicable to Superior Court)

The Justices of the Superior Court may appoint special magistrates to preside over criminal proceedings in the Superior Court. Such special magistrates shall have the powers to preside at arraignments, to set bail, to assign counsel, to supervise pretrial conferences, to mark up pretrial motions for hearing, to make findings and report those findings and other issues to the presiding justice or Administrative Justice, and to perform such other duties as may be authorized by order of the Superior Court. The doings of special magistrates shall be endorsed upon the record of the case. Special magistrates shall be compensated in the same manner as is provided by the General Laws for the compensation of masters in civil cases.

Reporter's Notes

Under prior law, magistrates served primarily as bail commissioners. G.L. c. 262, §§ 23–24. Sections 62B and 62C of chapter 221 of the General Laws, inserted by St.1978, c. 478, § 250, established the office of Magistrate in all Departments of the Trial Court and gave to that official certain quasi-judicial powers. This rule is not intended to expand the powers which such statutory Trial Court Magistrates may exercise, but to create the new and separate position of Special Magistrate in the Superior Court Department.

Special Magistrates in criminal cases shall have the authority to assign counsel (Mass.R.Crim.P. 8), set bail, and preside at arraignment (Mass.R.Crim.P. 7), and their duties shall include the supervision of pretrial conferences (Mass.R.Crim.P. 11) and the marking up of pretrial motions for hearing (Mass.R.Crim.P. 13). The rule is broad enough to permit assignment of some fact finding functions to Special Magistrates, although the exact dimension of those functions is left to definition by appropriate order of the Administrative Justice of the Superior Court Department. In this respect the Special Magistrate will differ little from masters as appointed by the Supreme Judicial Court under longstanding practice, especially in habeas corpus proceedings.

It is intended that Special Magistrates under this rule, because of the nature of their quasi-judicial responsibilities, be at the least attorneys admitted to practice before the bar and preferably that they be retired judges. Special Magistrates are to be compensated as are masters in civil practice. G.L. c. 221, § 55 (as amended, St.1978, c. 478, § 247); Mass.R.Civ.P. 53(a), Superior Court Rule 49(3) (1974).

While similar to federal magistrates, the office of Special Magistrate under this rule does not carry with it such broad powers. The federal officer can conduct trials for minor offenses and sentence those who are found guilty. 18 U.S.C. §§ 3401–02. Before a federal magistrate can conduct a trial, however, the defendant must consent in writing and specifically waive both a trial before a District Court judge and the right to trial by jury, subject to enumerated qualifications. Under this rule the defendant is to have no objection to proceeding before a Special Magistrate since the functions to be performed by the office of Special Magistrate are administrative rather than adjudicatory.

Rule 48. Sanctions

(Applicable to District Court and Superior Court)

A willful violation by counsel of the provisions of these rules or of an order issued pursuant to these rules shall subject counsel to such sanctions as the court shall deem appropriate, including citation for contempt or the imposition of costs or a fine.

Reporter's Notes

This rule is intended to supplement rather than supplant the provisions of prior law relative to the power of the courts to regulate the conduct of attorneys who practice therein and to discipline those whose actions fall short of accepted standards. The rule applies equally to attorneys and to defendants who appear pro se.

In addition to the sanctions of citations for contempt and the imposition of costs or a fine, the rule contemplates referral to the Board of Bar Overseers where appropriate.

See e.g., Supreme Judicial Court Rule 3.22A, *Disciplinary Rules Applicable to Practice as a Prosecutor or as a Defense Lawyer* (Feb. 14, 1979); ABA *Standards Relating to the Prosecution Function* § 1.1 (Approved Draft, 1971); ABA *Standards Relating to the Defense Function* § 1.1 (Approved Draft, 1971).

MASSACHUSETTS RULES OF APPELLATE PROCEDURE

Effective July 1, 1974

Table of Rules

Rule 1. Scope of Rules: Definitions

(a) Scope and Construction of Rules. These rules govern procedure in appeals to an appellate court. They shall be construed, administered, and employed to secure the just, speedy, and inexpensive determination of appeals. They shall be construed in conjunction with the rules and standing orders of the appellate courts.

(b) Rules Not to Affect Jurisdiction. These rules shall not be construed to extend or limit the jurisdiction, as established by law, of the Supreme Judicial Court or the Appeals Court.

(c) Definitions. As used in these rules, unless the context clearly indicates otherwise:

"appeal" means an appeal to an appellate court and supersedes any procedure other than reservation and report by which matters have heretofore been brought before an appellate court for review.

"appellate court" means the full Supreme Judicial Court, the full Appeals Court, or a statutory quorum of either, as the case may be, whichever court is exercising jurisdiction over the case at bar.

"child welfare case" means any case that is before a court of competent jurisdiction pursuant to G.L. c. 119, §§ 21–39J; G.L. c. 190B regarding guardianship of minors; or G.L. c. 210, §§ 1–11.

"clerk" means "clerk," "register," "recorder," and their respective assistants or deputies; "clerk of the appellate division" means the clerk of the trial court from which the action was reported to the appellate division.

"decision" means, when referring to an appellate court, the court's written opinion, memorandum and order pursuant to Appeals Court Rule 1:28, or other final adjudicative order in the case.

"first class mail or its equivalent" means (1) use of the United States Postal Service through first class postage or other class of mail that is at least as expeditious, postage prepaid or (2) dispatch to a third-party commercial carrier for delivery within 3 days. Registration or certification shall not be required unless specifically stated to be necessary.

"indigent party" means a person who is a party to a legal proceeding and whom a court has determined meets the statutory criteria to obtain waiver, reduction, or payment of certain fees and costs incident to civil and criminal litigation, including appeals in that proceeding.

"lower court" means the single justice, court, appellate division, board, commission, or other body whose decision is the subject of a direct appeal to an appellate court; for the purpose of Rule 9, the term includes any member of the lower court.

"party" means a person or entity appearing in a case, including an appeal. In the context of performing any act under these rules, a party means counsel, where a party is represented by counsel, and, when a party is not represented by counsel, it means the self-represented litigant.

"rescript" means the appellate court's order, direction, or mandate to the lower court disposing of the appeal.

"single justice" means a single justice of whichever appellate court is exercising jurisdiction over the case at bar.

"transmission" or "transmit" means the sending or conveying of a document or court record through a medium authorized by the court or these rules, and may include, but is not limited to, first class mail or its equivalent, electronic filing, electronic mail, facsimile, or electronic file share.

(d) Construction. Words or phrases importing the singular number may extend and be applied to several persons or things, and words importing the plural number may include the singular.

Amended May 15, 1979, effective September 1, 1979; May 29, 1986, effective July 1, 1986; amended effective July 28, 1987; November 15, 1995; amended July 28, 1999, effective September 1, 1999; June 24, 2009, effective July 1, 2009; October 31, 2018, effective March 1, 2019.

Reporter's Notes—1973

The Appellate Rules, modelled almost entirely upon the Federal Rules of Appellate Procedure, drastically alter the procedure for judicial review in non-criminal cases as heretofore known in Massachusetts. Mass.R.Civ.P. 46 having eliminated the concept of the exception, all existing authority and learning pertaining to bills of exceptions are now obsolete. In addition, the Appellate Rules eradicate heretofore existing distinctions between bills of exceptions, appeals, claims of reports, and the like. The Appellate Rules are drafted to apply to any "procedure by which matters have heretofore been brought before an appellate court for review," except reservation and report (see Mass.R.Civ.P. 64; M.R.A.P. 5). The word "appeal" by definition includes all such preexisting procedures. The Appellate Rules apply to any review by the full Supreme Judicial Court or the Appeals Court of the decision of any "lower court," which latter term is defined to include any "single justice, court, appellate division, board, commission, or other party whose decision is the subject of an appeal."

Note that in the Appellate Rules "appellate court" refers to *either* the full Supreme Judicial Court *or* the full Appeals Court, whichever is then exercising jurisdiction, and that "single justice" similarly refers to a single justice of either court.

"Rescript", a term well-known to Massachusetts practice, covers the meaning of "mandate", the term used in the Federal Rules, F.R.A.P. 41.

Reporter's Notes—1979

Subdivision (a) of Rule 1 is amended by the deletion of the word "civil," thereby enlarging the scope of the Rules of Appellate Procedure to encompass both civil and criminal appeals. As thus amended, the rules govern interlocutory appeals in criminal cases (G.L. c. 278, § 28E, as amended; Mass.R.Crim.P. 15 [1979]), appeals from single justice proceedings and appeals from final convictions.

Bills of exceptions (former G.L. c. 278, § 31), writs of error (former G.L. c. 250, §§ 1–2, 9–13), and the limited "appeal" from a judgment of the Superior Court based on a "matter of law apparent upon the record" (former G.L. c. 278, § 28) are superseded by an appeal under these rules by virtue of subdivision (c). The appeal available pursuant to the rules is similar in many respects to the direct appeal on the transcript previously provided by G.L. c. 278, §§ 33A–33H, but the assignment of error as a vehicle for isolating and identifying issues

(G.L. c. 278, § 28D) is abolished. Reports in Criminal cases are governed by Mass.R.Crim.P. 34 and Mass.R.App.P. 5.

"Lower court" as defined in subdivision (c) may include a justice of the district court department sitting in a jury-waived session. While ordinarily the only avenue for review of a judgment or order in a jury-waived session will be by way of appeal to a jury session, the Commonwealth is granted an interlocutory appeal of orders granting motions to dismiss or to suppress evidence by G.L. c. 278, § 28E, as amended, and Mass.R.Crim.P. 15(a).

Reporter's Notes—1987

This amendment deletes the reference to appeals from "a decision of the Appellate Division of the District Courts". Pursuant to G.L. c. 211A, § 10, as amended, review of such decisions is in the first instance by the Appeals Court.

Reporter's Notes—1995

The 1995 amendment to Mass.R.A.P. 1(b), effective November 15, 1995, provides that the Rules of Appellate Procedure are not applicable to proceedings governed by Supreme Judicial Court Rule 2:21, also effective November 15, 1995. Supreme Judicial Court Rule 2:21 regulates the procedure for appeal to the full court of a single justice's denial of relief from an interlocutory ruling in the trial court.

Reporter's Notes—1999

The 1999 amendment to Appellate Rule 1(c) was part of a comprehensive set of amendments to the Appellate Rules (Rules 1, 3, 4, 8, and 10) that had been proposed by the Supreme Judicial Court Committee on Appeals of Child Welfare Cases. The Committee's recommendations were intended to: (1) provide a uniform appeal period for child welfare cases; (2) establish a procedure for filing a notice of appeal which would eliminate the taking of appeals on behalf of absent and disinterested clients; (3) establish a procedure for the appointment of appellate counsel which makes it clear that trial counsel continues to be responsible for all trial court proceedings; (4) expedite the assembly of the record; and (5) provide notice to the trial court, for jurisdictional purposes, when appeals are entered in the appellate courts.

The amendment to Appellate Rule 1(c) defines the term "child welfare case" as it is used in the Appellate Rules.

Reporter's Notes—2019

These Reporter's Notes describing the 2019 amendments were prepared by the subcommittee appointed by the Supreme Judicial Court Standing Advisory Committee on the Rules of Civil and Appellate Procedure, in conjunction with the Standing Advisory Committee on the Rules of Criminal Procedure.

I. Overview.

In 2015, the Supreme Judicial Court Standing Advisory Committee on the Rules of Civil and Appellate Procedure, in conjunction with the Standing Advisory Committee on the Rules of Criminal Procedure, appointed a subcommittee to review the Massachusetts Rules of Appellate Procedure (hereinafter "Rules"). The Rules were enacted in 1974 and, although many isolated amendments were adopted over the ensuing years, no full-scale review of the Rules had occurred in over four decades. Accordingly, the Standing Advisory Committee charged the subcommittee to review the Rules and identify proposals that would:

• make the Rules more easily understood and followed;

• facilitate the just and expeditious resolution of appeals;

• clarify and simplify filing and formatting requirements;

• eliminate arcane language and incorporate consistent style and terminology;

• incorporate existing practices and procedures; and

• facilitate the appellate and trial courts' development of paperless processes.

In 2017, the subcommittee posted many proposed amendments for a period of public comment and review. Numerous public comments were submitted. The subcommittee studied the comments and made many significant changes in response.

Where possible, the subcommittee sought to preserve the current Rules' language and related procedures so not to disrupt established practices that, for the most part, operate well. Consequently, many proposed amendments are merely stylistic or organizational, and require minimal change to current procedures. Other proposed amendments are substantive and intended to improve a rule or procedure consistent with the subcommittee's charge.

The subcommittee also compared the relevant Federal Rules of Appellate Procedure, aware of both the differences between the Massachusetts and Federal courts and case types, and of the recent Federal "restyling" amendments designed to make those rules more comprehensible. While the subcommittee followed the spirit of the Federal restyling amendments, the subcommittee concluded the preferable route in most instances would be to maintain the existing Massachusetts Rules' language, style, and procedures instead of proposing a wholesale adoption of the current Federal rules. However, in certain situations the subcommittee derived amendments from adopted Federal language. See, e.g., Rules 4(d) and 13(a)(2) (timeliness of filings by a self-represented party confined in an institution); Rules 20(a)(2) and (a)(3) (word count alternative to page limitation for briefs).

The subcommittee's proposals were endorsed by the Supreme Judicial Court Standing Advisory Committee on the Rules of Civil and Appellate Procedure, and by the Standing Advisory Committee on the Rules of Criminal Procedure. In 2018, the Supreme Judicial Court approved the amendments and identified their effective date.

II. Global Amendments.

The following global amendments were made, where appropriate, throughout the Rules:

(1) Gender Neutrality. Masculine gender pronouns were removed in favor of gender-neutral phrases.

(2) Provisions Rendered Obsolete by Technology. The amendments removed certain provisions that had become obsolete because of technological developments and work processes.

(3) Word Count. The Rules were amended to allow, as does Fed. R. App. P. 32(a)(7), the use of a word limit together with a proportionally spaced font, as an alternative to a page limit, in setting the permissible lengths of principal and reply briefs, amicus briefs, motions for reconsideration or modification of decision (previously called petitions for rehearing), and applications for and responses to direct and further appellate review. The word limits are not intended to allow for longer documents.

The word limits are: 11,000 for a principal brief in all cases except cross appeals (Rule 20(a)(2)(A)); 4,500 for a reply brief in all cases except cross appeals (Rule 20(a)(2)(B)); 11,000 for an appellant's principal brief in a cross appeal (Rule 20(a)(3)(A)); 13,000 for an appellee's principal/response brief in a cross appeal (Rule 20(a)(3)(B)); 11,000 for an appellant's response/reply brief in a cross appeal (Rule 20(a)(3)(C)); 4,500 for an appellee's reply brief in a cross appeal (Rule 20(a)(3)(D)); 7,500 for an amicus brief (Rules 20(a)(2)(C) and (a)(3)(E)); 2,000 for a motion for reconsideration or modification of decision (Rules 27(b) and (c)); 2,000 for argument in applications for direct appellate review and for further appellate review, as well as any response to those documents (Rules 11(b), 11(c), and 27.1); and 1,000 for a response to a transfer from the Supreme Judicial Court (Rule 11.1).

The amendments exclude items for inclusion in the length limits consistent with current Rule 16(h), and current Fed. R. App. P. 32(a)(7)(B)(ii), except that the signature block also is excluded. See Rules 20(a)(2)(D) and 20(a)(3)(E). The amendments to Rule 16(k) require a certification as to how compliance with the brief-length limit

was ascertained. See Rules 20(a)(2)(F), 20(a)(3)(G) and 16(k). The Federal rules likewise require a certificate of compliance for word count. See Fed. R. App. P. 32(a)(7)(C).

This amendment eliminates the considerable time parties sometimes spend using formatting devices solely to comply with the current page limits.

The amendments are consistent with the word limit/proportional font approach in the Federal rules.

Importantly, the amendments allow for no more than the amount of text that currently fits into a properly formatted 50–page principal brief or 20–page reply brief. The subcommittee reviewed the Federal rules for guidance as to comparative ratios among the different types of briefs (i.e., principal, reply, and amicus), but not for the absolute numbers of words, since it was determined that adopting the Federal word count applicable to the various briefs would lead to substantially longer briefs than the 50 pages currently authorized in the Massachusetts rules. For this reason, the word limits for briefs are less than their Federal counterparts and, as stated above, allow no more than the amount of text permitted under the prior rules.

Under the amended rule, a significant change is that for briefing in a cross appeal, the appellee's principal brief may include approximately the amount of text that fits into a properly formatted 60–page brief. This is consistent with the Federal approach by recognizing that in an appellee/cross-appellant's brief, the appellee must both respond to the arguments in the appellant's brief and present the appellee's arguments in the cross appeal. For a further discussion of the amendments regarding the briefing process in a cross appeal, see the Reporter's Note to Rule 20(a)(3).

(4) Freestanding Paragraphs: Separation into Smaller Segments and Numbering. Multiple prior rules had long, freestanding paragraphs either comprising the complete rule or contained within multiple paragraphs of a rule. This decreased readability of the rule and made reference to particular provisions of a rule more difficult. Accordingly, in 2019 many freestanding paragraphs were numbered and separated into distinct paragraphs, making it easier to locate and refer to different sections. Where appropriate, titles were also added.

(5) Consistent Numbering. Throughout the Rules, numbers were consistently changed to numeral format. Excluded from this change are internal rule cross-references and other citations, as well as numbers that begin a sentence.

(6) Changing "Paper" to "Document." The word "paper" is replaced with "document" throughout the Rules. The word "document" encompasses more media (e.g., PDFs) and is consistent with the courts' transition to electronic filing and storage of electronic documents.

(7) Changing Deadlines to Increments of 7 Days. Many filing deadlines in the Rules were revised to be in increments of 7. Most 10–day deadlines were converted to 14–day deadlines, and all 20–day deadlines to 21–day deadlines. Because a court's action is often the event that triggers a deadline, changing the deadlines to increments of 7 will guarantee that the final day falls on a weekday. For example, if the Appeals Court releases a decision on a Tuesday, the final day for filing an application for further appellate review is certain to fall 21 days later on the third following Tuesday. See Rules 23(a) and 27.1(a). This clarifies filing dates for parties and makes processing filings easier in the appellate courts. The change also significantly decreases the likelihood that a deadline will fall on a non-business day, which causes confusion to litigants who are not aware that such a deadline is extended to the next business day. See Rule 14(a). Deadlines in increments of 30 or 40 days are unchanged because those are well established and traditionally referenced time periods that are not as affected by weekends as the shorter time periods referenced above.

(8) Changing "Trial" Court to "Lower" Court. All references to the "trial court" are amended to lower court, consistent with the definition of "lower court" in Rule 1(c).

(9) Changing "Opposition" to "Response." All references to "opposition" are amended to "response" to reflect that, depending on the particular circumstances of a case or motion, the nonmoving party may want to respond to the moving party's request, but not necessarily oppose that request. Parties remain free to caption a response as an "opposition" if they so desire.

(10) Form of Cross–References. Internal rule cross-references to other Massachusetts Rules of Appellate Procedure are changed to be in the form "Rule 6(a)(2)" instead of "paragraph (a)(2) of this rule," to clarify the cross-reference.

III. Amendments to Rule 1.

Rule 1(a). The title of this subdivision was amended by adding "and Construction" to clarify the content of the rule. In addition, a new second sentence was added stating that the Rules should be construed in order to secure the just, speedy, and inexpensive determination of appeals. This sentence is consistent with Fed. R. Civ. P. 1 and Mass. R. Civ. P. 1. As stated in the 2015 Reporter's Notes to Mass. R. Civ. P. 1, "The purpose of the change was to acknowledge that both the court and the parties have the obligation to employ the rules for the purposes set forth." The appellate courts and the parties have the same obligation as the lower court, leading to this amendment.

A new sentence has been added to acknowledge and highlight that these Rules are not to be viewed in isolation. In addition to complying with these Rules, parties must also comply with the Rules of the Supreme Judicial Court, Appeals Court Rules, and standing orders of the appellate courts, including but not limited to: S.J.C. Rule 1:15 (impoundment procedure in the appellate courts), S.J.C. Rule 1:21 (corporate disclosure statement), and Appeals Court Rule 1:28 (summary disposition).

Including in Rule 1(a) a reference to the appellate courts' rules and standing orders also removes a so-called "trap for the unwary," as individuals who rely only on the Rules of Appellate Procedure may miss additional procedural requirements and potentially compromise their appellate rights. See Commonwealth v. Hartsgrove, 407 Mass. 441, 444–445 (1990) ("The Massachusetts Rules of Appellate Procedure were intended to simplify the procedure by which individuals take a case from the trial court to the appellate court, removing many of the traps for the unwary which previously prevented a litigant from having his appeal heard on the merits."). To the extent possible, the 2019 amendments have incorporated and cross-referenced other appellate court requirements, to eliminate such "traps."

Rule 1(b). The second sentence of this subdivision was deleted as unnecessary in light of the broad language of the first sentence. An appeal from a decision of a single justice of the Supreme Judicial Court must be to the Supreme Judicial Court, but other proceedings related to such an appeal may not be. See Pixley v. Commonwealth, 453 Mass. 827 (2009) (describing subsequent proceedings related to the appeal to take place in the Appeals Court); Commonwealth v. Pixley, 77 Mass. App. Ct. 624 (2010) (related proceedings in the Appeals Court).

Rule 1(c). The clause "unless the context clearly indicates otherwise" was added to the beginning of the rule to address instances when the words, as used in the Rules, are more broad or narrow than that included in the definitions. Rule 1(c) was also amended by adding new or revising existing definitions as follows:

"Appellate Court": The word "statutory" before "jurisdiction" was removed because appellate court jurisdiction is derived from additional sources than only a statute. For instance, the jurisdiction of the Supreme Judicial Court is derived primarily from the Massachusetts Constitution and the Appeals Court's statutory jurisdiction has been expanded by decisions of the Supreme Judicial Court.

"Child welfare case": The reference to G.L. c. 190B in the definition of "child welfare case" was revised to clarify that only the provisions of G.L. c. 190B regarding guardianship of minors is encompassed in the definition, so as to ensure the definition is neither over- nor under-inclusive.

"Decision": A definition of "decision" was added to distinguish between the appellate court's written opinion, memorandum and order pursuant to Rule 1:28, or other final adjudicative order in the case (the decision), and the "rescript," which is the appellate court's order, direction, or mandate disposing of the appeal. The prior rules' use of "rescript" caused some confusion for parties as to when to begin calculating the time to file a petition for rehearing and an application for further appellate review. In accordance with this definition, the word "rescript" was replaced with "decision" in Rules 27(a), 27.1(a) and 27.1(b), as well as in Rules 23(a), 23(b), and 31(c).

"First class mail or its equivalent": This definition has been expanded to include "or its equivalent" to first class mail and specify that a third-party commercial carrier is permissible. Including third-party carriers within the definition of "first class mail" conforms with the parallel Fed. R. App. P. 25(a)(2)(B). In addition, this definition better serves the parties by making it clear that these services may be used. Requiring "delivery within 3 days" ensures that use of a third-party carrier is comparable to the use of United States Postal Service first class mail.

"Indigent Party": A definition of "indigent party" was added. This new term replaces the prior term, "in forma pauperis," throughout the Rules. "In forma pauperis" was not commonly used in practice or in the relevant legal authorities. "Indigent party" is the term set forth in the relevant Massachusetts statutes, see G. L. c. 261, §§ 27A–27D and 29, and rules of court, see S.J.C. Rule 3:10.

"Lower court": The definition was amended by revising "whose decision is the subject of an appeal" to "whose decision is the subject of a direct appeal to an appellate court." This amendment is intended to clarify that where an appeal from an administrative agency decision is first reviewed by the lower court, such as the Superior Court pursuant to G.L. c. 30A, the other body is not the lower court.

"Party": A new definition of "party" is intended to recognize that, as used throughout the Rules, a "party" may mean a person or entity participating in a proceeding or appeal (such as an appellant, appellee, petitioner, respondent, etc.). When used to describe any act that is performed under the Rules (such as filing or serving documents), "party" may mean counsel, where a party is represented by counsel, or, when a party is not represented by counsel, it means the self-represented litigant. This recognizes the reality that if a person or entity is represented by counsel in an appeal, it will be counsel that is performing the acts necessary to carry out the appeal. This definition avoids the need to explicitly reference both counsel and any self-represented litigant in each of the numerous places "party" is used in the Rules in connection with performing an act. The definition is not intended to make any substantive change to the rights of a person or entity to participate in a legal proceeding or appeal.

"Rescript": A stylistic revision to "rescript" is made to clarify rescript "means the appellate court's order, direction, or mandate to the lower court disposing of the appeal." No substantive change is intended.

"Single justice": The word "statutory" was removed before "jurisdiction" because the single justice's authority is derived from other means than statute.

"Transmission" or "transmit": A new definition was added to clarify that these words allow for the sending or conveying of documents or court records using a method authorized by the court. The definition provides a non-exhaustive list of current methods of transmission used by the courts and is intended to allow for future methods as new technologies are adopted by the courts.

Rule 1(d). The last clause of prior Rule 1(d) which stated "words importing the masculine gender may include the feminine and neuter[,]" was removed. The sentence was no longer necessary as words that import the masculine gender were globally removed from the Rules and replaced with gender-neutral language.

Rule 2. Suspension of Rules

In the interest of expediting decision, or for other good cause shown, the appellate court or a single justice may, except as otherwise provided in Rule 14(b), suspend the requirements or provisions of any of these rules in a particular case, on such reasonable terms as the court or the single justice may order, on application of a party or on its own motion and may order proceedings in accordance with its direction.

Amended October 31, 2018, effective March 1, 2019.

Reporter's Notes—1973

Appellate Rule 2, substantially tracking F.R.A.P. 2, injects flexibility into the appellate structure. It permits relaxation of the rules in the interest of expedition, or for good cause, except enlarging appeal time beyond one year from the date the appeals period begins to run.

Reporter's Notes—2019

The last sentence of Rule 2, which stated that "[s]uch a suspension [of the Rules] may be on reasonable terms," was struck and its substance relocated and incorporated within the rule's principal sentence. The amended language continues to require that any suspension of the Rules must be on "reasonable terms" and that either "the court or the single justice may" enter an order suspending the requirements or provisions of any of these Rules in a particular case.

With regard to the preparation of the 2019 Reporter's Notes to this Rule, see the first paragraph of the 2019 Reporter's Notes to Rule 1. For an overview of the 2019 amendments to the Rules and a summary of the global amendments to the Rules, see 2019 Reporter's Notes to Rule 1, sections *I.* and *II.*

Rule 3. Appeal—How Taken

(a) Filing the Notice of Appeal.

(1) An appeal permitted by law from a lower court shall be taken by filing a notice of appeal with the clerk of the lower court within the time allowed by Rule 4, with service upon all parties. Failure of an appellant to take any step other than the timely filing of a notice of appeal shall not affect the validity of the appeal, but shall be ground only for such action as the appellate court deems appropriate, which may include dismissal of the appeal.

(2) A party need not claim an appeal from an interlocutory order to preserve the party's right to have such order reviewed upon appeal from the final judgment; but for all purposes for which an appeal from an interlocutory order has heretofore been necessary, it is sufficient that the party comply with the requirement of Massachusetts Rules of Civil Procedure 46 or Massachusetts Rules of Criminal Procedure 22, whichever was applicable to the trial of the case in the lower court.

(b) Appeals by Multiple Parties.
If 2 or more persons are entitled to appeal from a judgment, decree, adjudication, order, or part thereof of a lower court and their interests are such as to make joinder practicable, they may file a joint notice of appeal, or may join in appeal after filing separate timely notices of appeal.

(c) Content of the Notice of Appeal.

(1) *Content of the Notice of Appeal, Generally.* The notice of appeal shall specify the party or parties taking the appeal and shall, in civil cases, designate the judgment, decree, adjudication, order, or part thereof appealed from.

(2) *Content of the Notice of Appeal in Child Welfare Cases.* In child welfare cases, the notice of appeal and any request for a transcript, if required, shall be signed by the person or persons, or by counsel for the entity, taking the appeal; however, if the appellant is a minor, the notice and request shall be signed by the minor's counsel. A notice of appeal that is not so signed shall not be accepted for filing by the clerk.

(d) Service of the Notice of Appeal.
The clerk of the lower court shall serve notice of the filing of a notice of appeal by transmitting a copy thereof to counsel of record for each party other than the appellant, or, if a party is not represented by counsel, to the party. The clerk shall note on each copy served the date on which the notice of appeal was filed. Failure of the clerk to serve notice shall not affect the validity of the appeal. Service shall be sufficient notwithstanding the death of a party or counsel. The clerk shall note in the docket the names of the persons to whom copies are transmitted, and the date of transmission.

(e) Change of Counsel on Appeal in Criminal and Certain Non-criminal Cases.
If the defendant in a criminal case, or any party in any other proceeding, excluding child welfare cases, in which counsel is required to be made available to such party pursuant to Supreme Judicial Court Rule 3:10, was represented by counsel at trial, the trial court counsel shall continue to represent that party on appeal until an appearance is filed by substitute counsel, if such assignment of counsel is made by the Committee for Public Counsel Services. In such proceedings, assigned trial court counsel shall, no later than the day on which the notice of appeal is filed, notify the Committee for Public Counsel Services that appellate counsel should be assigned. Assigned appellate counsel shall promptly file a notice of appearance in the trial court, following which trial court counsel may file a notice of withdrawal.

(f) Appointment of Appellate Counsel in Child Welfare Cases.

(1) Subject to the provisions of Rule 10(d), any party to a child welfare case in which counsel was appointed pursuant to Supreme Judicial Court Rule 3:10 and who was represented by counsel at trial, shall continue to be represented by that counsel on appeal until either the lower court has appointed counsel for appellate purposes and an appearance has been filed by appellate counsel or the lower court has denied a motion to appoint counsel for appellate purposes.

(2) Lower court counsel shall, on the day upon which the signed notice of appeal is filed, file, and request a hearing on, a motion to allow reasonable costs associated with the appeal in the lower court. At the same time, if lower court counsel is not appellate certified by the Committee for Public Counsel Services, counsel shall also file, and request a hearing on, a motion to appoint counsel for appellate purposes in the lower court. Subject to the provisions of Supreme Judicial Court Rule 3:10, § 7, lower court counsel shall continue to represent the party at all lower court proceedings.

(3) If the motion to appoint counsel for appellate purposes is allowed, the Committee for Public Counsel Services shall be assigned to provide representation according to the procedures established in Supreme Judicial Court Rule 3:10.

(4) If counsel has not filed a motion to withdraw appearance in the lower court, or counsel has filed a motion to withdraw but the motion has not been allowed by the lower court prior to the date that the lower court transmits to the appellate court the notice of assembly of the record pursuant to Rule 9, lower court counsel will be designated as counsel in the appellate court. Any motion to withdraw filed thereafter shall comply with Rule 10(d).

Amended May 15, 1979, effective July 1, 1979; May 29, 1986, effective July 1, 1986; amended July 28, 1999, effective September 1, 1999; October 31, 2018, effective March 1, 2019.

Reporter's Notes—1973

An appeal is initiated by filing in *the lower court* a notice of appeal, within 30 days following the order or judgment appealed from. If the Commonwealth or any office or agency thereof is a party, however, the appeal time is extended to 60 days. After the notice of appeal has been filed, the clerk of the lower court notifies all other parties by mail of the notice's having been filed. It is the date of the filing, however, not the date of the notice, which controls the timeliness of the appeal.

Reporter's Notes—1979

The second paragraph of subdivision (a) is amended by the addition of a reference to Mass.R.Crim.P. 22, "Objections," to clarify that a party need not claim an exception to an interlocutory order adverse to his position to preserve his right to have that order subsequently reviewed on appeal.

Subdivision (b), regulating joint or consolidated appeals, is consistent with prior criminal appellate practice.

Subdivision (c) is amended to reflect the fact that in a civil case, the notice of appeal must designate the judgment, order, or part thereof which is appealed from. It would also be appropriate in an interlocutory appeal in a criminal case for the notice of appeal to designate the order from which an appeal is being taken (e.g., denial of motion to suppress, grant of motion to dismiss), but this is not required by the rule because there is seldom any question about the matter being appealed.

General Laws, c. 278, § 33B (St.1955, c. 352, § 2) formerly provided that the clerk was to notify the District Attorney of a claim of appeal "forthwith." Subdivision (d) is more explicit in setting out the manner of notice and will require notification of co-defendants, if any, when a notice of appeal is filed.

Subdivision (e), "Change of Counsel on Appeal in Criminal Cases," is new and addresses the continuing responsibility of the trial attorney to provide assistance to a client beyond entry of final judgment in the trial court. See ABA *Standards Relating to Criminal Appeals* 21–2.2(a) (2d ed., Approved Draft, 1978). This subdivision seeks to avoid a hiatus in legal representation during a critical period when the defendant has questions as to the meaning and effect of conviction and the option of whether to appeal. ABA *Standards,* supra, commentary at 10.

In Pires v. Commonwealth, Mass.Adv.Sh. [1977] 2601 the Supreme Judicial Court held that a lawyer has a professional obligation to his client which goes beyond the trial of the case. The court adopted the provisions of the American Bar Association Project on Standards for Criminal Justice as the appropriate measure of the responsibility of counsel. Standard 8.2 of the Defense Function (Approved Draft 1971), provides:

8.2 Appeal. (a) After conviction, the lawyer should explain to the defendant the meaning and consequences of the court's judgment and his right of appeal. The lawyer should give the defendant his professional judgment as to whether there are meritorious grounds for appeal and as to the probable results of an appeal. He should also explain to the defendant the advantages and disadvantages of an appeal. The decision whether to appeal must be the defendant's

own choice. (b) The lawyer should take whatever steps are necessary to protect the defendant's right of appeal.

Reporter's Notes—1999

The 1999 amendments to Appellate Rule 3 were part of a comprehensive set of amendments to the Appellate Rules (Rules 1, 3, 4, 8, and 10) that had been proposed by the Supreme Judicial Court Committee on Appeals of Child Welfare Cases. The purpose of the 1999 amendments is described in the 1999 Reporter's Notes to Appellate Rule 1(c).

Appellate Rule 3(c) has been amended to require that in child welfare cases, the notice of appeal must be signed by the party or parties taking the appeal unless the appellant is the minor who is the subject of the action. The clerk is directed not to accept an appeal that is not so signed. The purpose of this change is to eliminate the taking of an appeal on behalf of an absent and disinterested client.

The amendment to Appellate Rule 3(f) make it clear that until appellate counsel files an appearance, trial counsel is obligated to continue representation of the client. Even after appellate counsel has filed an appearance, trial counsel will continue to represent the party at all proceedings in the trial court.

Reporter's Notes—2019

Rule 3(a). The phrase "with service upon all parties" was added to the first sentence to clarify the appellant's duty to serve all other parties when filing a notice of appeal. Although the clerk of the lower court is still required to serve notice on the parties pursuant to Rule 3(d), this amendment is consistent with Mass. R. Civ. P. 5(a) and Mass. R. Crim. P. 32(a), which require documents (other than those allowed to be filed ex parte) filed in court to be served on all other parties.

Rule 3(b). The title of this subdivision was revised from "Joint or Consolidated Appeals" to "Appeals by Multiple Parties." The designation of parties proceeding on appeal as a single appellant is most often made by the appellate court when the appeal is docketed in the appellate court, and not by the lower court after the notice of appeal is filed there. Accordingly, language relating to consolidated appeals and authorizing parties to proceed on appeal as a single appellant was relocated to Rules 10(a)(5) and (6). The first sentence of Rule 3(b) was revised to clarify that in addition to a judgment or order, an appeal may be taken from a "decree, adjudication ... or part thereof." The addition of these terms makes this subdivision consistent with other parts of the Rules. See Rules 3(c), 4(a)(1), and 4(b)(1).

Rule 3(c) was reformatted to clarify the required content of a notice of appeal. Rule 3(c)(1) applies "generally" to civil and criminal cases and Rule 3(c)(2) applies to child welfare cases. Because the requirements related to a notice of appeal in a child welfare case are different, a separate paragraph addressing those particular requirements clarifies the rule. Regarding the signing of the notice of appeal in a child welfare case where the appellant is not a minor, the reference is amended from "party or parties taking the appeal," to "person or persons, or by counsel for the entity, taking the appeal," to be consistent with the new definition of "party" in Rule 1(c), and because the term "person" ordinarily does not apply to government entities, such as the Department of Children and Families, which may take appeals in child welfare cases and which can act only through counsel.

Rule 3(d) was updated to replace "mailing" with "transmitting," to accommodate the fact that the lower court may have procedures by which the clerk transmits electronic notice. See Mass. R. Civ. P. 77(d)(2).

Rule 3(e), governing the change of counsel on appeal in criminal and certain noncriminal cases, was amended to change the procedure for counsel to withdraw an appearance upon the filing of a notice of appeal in the common situation that the Committee for Public Counsel Services (CPCS) assigns substitute counsel to handle a party's appeal. The prior procedure required the defendant's counsel to file a motion to withdraw that required action by the trial court before notice was made to CPCS to provide appellate representation. The new procedure requires the defendant's counsel with an appearance in the trial court to notify CPCS no later than the day on which the notice of appeal is to be filed that appellate counsel should be assigned. CPCS will then assign appellate counsel, who is required to file a prompt notice of appearance in the trial court. After the appellate attorney has entered the appearance, the prior counsel of record in the trial court may file a notice of withdrawal.

Rule 3(f)(4) is an entirely new paragraph that explains the existing practices that occur when counsel who has been active in the lower court either has not filed a motion to withdraw appearance in the lower court or when such a motion has been filed and not acted upon prior to the lower court's issuance of the notice of assembly of the record on appeal. In such instances, the lower court counsel's appearance in the case will continue and that counsel will be designated as active counsel in the appellate court. Rule 3(f)(4) includes a reference to new Rule 10(d), which governs motions to withdraw appearance after the lower court's issuance of the notice of assembly and docketing of an appeal in the appellate court.

The addition of Rule 3(f)(4) is intended to clarify that counsel listed as active on the lower court docket at the time the lower court issues the notice of assembly per Rule 9 will be listed as active counsel on the docket of the appellate court, and encourage such counsel to file a prompt notice of withdrawal in the lower court. This is consistent with Mass. R. Civ. P. 11(d) and Mass. R. Prof. C. 1.16(c). Rule 3(f)(4) also clarifies that, after an appeal is docketed in an appellate court, a motion to withdraw must be filed in the appellate court, not the lower court. The inclusion of this longstanding practice into the Rules will reduce confusion on the part of attorneys as to why their appearance was entered on the appellate court docket in circumstances where the attorney was retained or assigned as lower court counsel only, and clarifies that a motion to withdraw appearance should be filed in the appellate court once that court has jurisdiction of a case. See Rule 10(d).

Further organizational and stylistic revisions were made to this rule in 2019 in accordance with a global review and revision of all of the Appellate Rules. These revisions are described in the 2019 Reporter's Notes to Rule 1.

With regard to the preparation of the 2019 Reporter's Notes to this Rule, see the first paragraph of the 2019 Reporter's Notes to Rule 1. For an overview of the 2019 amendments to the Rules and a summary of the global amendments to the Rules, see 2019 Reporter's Notes to Rule 1, sections *I.* and *II.*

Rule 4. Appeal—When Taken

(a) Appeals in Civil Cases.

(1) In a civil case, unless otherwise provided by statute, the notice of appeal required by Rule 3 shall be filed with the clerk of the lower court within 30 days of the date of the entry of the judgment, decree, appealable order, or adjudication appealed from; but if the Commonwealth or an officer or agency thereof is a party, the notice of appeal may be filed by any party within 60 days of such entry, except in child welfare cases, in which the notice of appeal shall be filed within 30 days from the date of the entry of the judgment, decree, appealable order, or adjudication. If a notice of appeal is mistakenly filed in an appellate court, the clerk of such appellate court shall note the date on which it was received and transmit it to the clerk of the lower court from which the appeal was taken and it shall be deemed filed in such lower court on the date so noted. If a timely notice of appeal is filed by a party, any other party may file a notice of appeal within 14 days of the date on which the first notice of appeal was

filed, or within the time otherwise prescribed by this rule, whichever period last expires.

(2) If a motion is made or served in a timely manner under the Massachusetts Rules of Civil Procedure and filed with the lower court by any party, the time to file an appeal runs for all parties from the entry of the order disposing of the last remaining motion:

(A) for judgment under Rule 50(b);

(B) under Rule 52(b) to amend or make additional findings of fact, whether or not an alteration of the judgment would be required if the motion is granted;

(C) to alter or amend a judgment under Rule 59 or for relief from judgment under Rule 60(b), however titled, but only if either motion is served within 10 days after entry of judgment; or

(D) under Rule 59 for a new trial.

(3) A notice of appeal filed before the disposition of any timely motion listed in Rule 4(a)(2) shall have no effect. A new notice of appeal must be filed within the prescribed time measured from the entry of the order disposing of the last such remaining motion.

(b) Appeals in Criminal Cases.

(1) In a criminal case, unless otherwise provided by statute or court rule, the notice of appeal required by Rule 3 shall be filed with the clerk of the lower court within 30 days after entry of the judgment, appealable order, or adjudication appealed from, or entry of a notice of appeal by the Commonwealth,; or the imposition of sentence, whichever comes last.

(2) The running of the time for filing a notice of appeal shall be terminated as to the moving party by a motion for a new trial pursuant to Massachusetts Rules of Criminal Procedure 25(b)(2) and 30 filed in the lower court within 30 days after the verdict or finding of guilt or within 30 days after imposition of sentence, and the full time fixed by this rule shall commence to run and shall be computed from the date of entry of an order denying such motion.

(c) Extension of Time for Filing Notice of Appeal. Upon a showing of excusable neglect, the lower court may extend the time for filing the notice of appeal or notice of cross appeal by any party for a period not to exceed 30 days from the expiration of the time otherwise prescribed by this rule. Such an extension may be granted before or after the time otherwise prescribed by this rule has expired; but if a request for an extension is made after such time has expired, it shall be made by motion with service upon all other parties.

(d) Appeal by a Self-Represented Party Confined in an Institution. If an institution has a system designed for legal mail, a self-represented party confined there must use that system to receive the benefit of this rule. If such party files a notice of appeal in either a civil or criminal case, the notice is timely if deposited in the institution's internal mail system on or before the last day for filing and is accompanied by a signed certificate in compliance with Rule 13(a)(1)(B) setting out the date of deposit. If the notice of appeal is not received by the last day for filing, the certificate shall give rise to a presumption of timely filing provided it shows compliance with this rule. Failure to attach the certificate shall not of itself render the notice of appeal invalid or untimely, and the lower court

may permit the later filing of a certificate. If such party files the first notice of appeal in a civil case under Rule 4(d), the 14–day period provided in Rule 4(a)(1) for another party to file a notice of appeal runs from the date when the lower court enters the first notice.

Amended May 15, 1979, effective July 1, 1979; July 20, 1984, effective January 1, 1985; June 7, 1985, effective July 1, 1985; July 28, 1999, effective September 1, 1999; March 6, 2000, effective April 3, 2000; March 22, 2013, effective May 1, 2013; October 31, 2018, effective March 1, 2019.

Reporter's Notes—1973

Certain motions toll the running of the appeal time. These motions, enumerated in Appellate Rule 4, pertain to the allowance or denial of a judgment, the opening of the record, the altering or amending of a judgment, and the seeking of a new trial. The new, *full* appeal period begins to run from the day the court finally decides a motion in any of the foregoing classes. The time for filing an appeal may be enlarged by order of an appellate court or an appellate justice, but such extension can never exceed one year from the date of the judgment or order appealed from, see Appellate Rule 14(b).

Reporter's Notes—1979

The first two paragraphs of former Rule 4 have been denominated subdivision (a) and are limited to civil cases.

Added to Rule 4 is the substance of subdivision (b), which enlarges the time for filing a claim of appeal in criminal cases from twenty days to thirty (see former G.L. c. 278, § 28 [St.1820, c. 79, § 4]; Superior Court Rule 65 [1974]; G.L. c. 278, § 33B [St.1955, c. 352, § 2]), and which provides that if a motion for a new trial (Mass.R.Crim.P. 30[b]) which is filed within thirty days after verdict or imposition of sentence is ultimately denied, a new thirty-day period for filing the claim of appeal from the conviction shall commence to run. While this latter provision may appear to foster delay, it actually formalizes prior practice.

This subdivision also recognizes the defendant's right to claim an appeal from a guilty verdict or finding as well as his right to appeal from the sentence. This was intended to avoid any ambiguity as to whether a claim of appeal prior to the final judgment was out of time and ineffective. See Commonwealth v. Dascalakis, 246 Mass. 12, 19 "Sentence is final judgment in a criminal case."

The third paragraph of former Rule 4 is now subdivision (c) and is applicable to both civil and criminal appeals. Under former G.L. c. 278, § 33B, the twenty-day limit was mandatory and could not be extended by consent of the parties or by the court; an untimely claim of appeal divested the appellate court of jurisdiction. Commonwealth v. Rodrigues, 333 Mass. 501 (1956); Commonwealth v. McKnight, 289 Mass. 530, 538, 540 (1935).

See also Commonwealth v. Dorius, 343 Mass. 533 (1962) where it was held that after the time for filing the claim of appeal had expired the trial court was without jurisdiction to extend the period by allowing a motion to make the case subject to then G.L. c. 278, § 33E as amended St.1979, c. 346, § 2 which would thereby trigger a new appeal period.

See Silvia v. Laurie, 594 F.2d 892 (1st Cir.1978) where the Court of Appeals also held the time limit for filing the claim of appeal under the Federal Rules of Appellate Procedure was jurisdictional.

[T]he time limits of [Fed.R.App.P.] 4 are not merely procedural requirements that can be waived at the discretion of the court, but rather are limits on . . . [the appellate] court's power to review decisions of the . . . [lower] courts. . . . While the application of this rule may lead to apparently harsh results in some cases, it serves important interests of finality.

594 F.2d at 893. Subdivision (c) permits the lower court to extend the time for filing a notice of appeal by an additional thirty days upon "a

showing of excusable neglect." Such an extension, whether granted before or after the expiration of the thirty days prescribed by subdivision (b), may not enlarge the time beyond sixty days after the verdict or finding of guilt or imposition of sentence. See Silvia v. Laurie, supra. Compare Mass.R.App.P. 14(b) (Appellate court or single justice may extend time for noticing appeal up to one year after verdict or sentence).

Reporter's Notes—1984

This amendment makes Mass.R.A.P. 4(a) conform, in part, to a 1979 federal amendment. See F.R.A.P. 4(a)(4). Its primary purpose is to clarify an ambiguity as to the effect of filing an appeal prior to a decision on specified timely motions under Mass.R.Civ.P. 50(b), 52(b) and 59.

Reporter's Notes—1985

The added sentence conforms the Massachusetts Rule to the last sentence of F.R.A.P. 4(a)(1). The purpose is to protect appellants who mistakenly, but in otherwise timely fashion, file a notice of appeal in an appellate court rather than in the lower court.

The change from ten days to fourteen days for the filing of a cross-appeal conforms the time period to that found in F.R.A.P. 4(a)(3). Such conformity of time periods may aid practitioners.

Reporter's Notes—1999

The 1999 amendments to Appellate Rule 4(a) were part of a comprehensive set of amendments to the Appellate Rules (Rules 1, 3, 4, 8, and 10) that had been proposed by the Supreme Judicial Court Committee on Appeals of Child Welfare Cases. The purpose of the 1999 amendments is described in the 1999 Reporter's Notes to Appellate Rule 1(c).

Appellate Rule 4(a) has been amended to provide for a uniform 30–day period for filing a notice of appeal in all child welfare cases. See G.L. c. 119, § 27, as amended by St. 1999, c. 3, § 11.

Reporter's Notes—2000

Appellate Rule 4(b) was amended in 2000 in light of the Supreme Judicial Court's opinion in Commonwealth v. White, 429 Mass. 258 (1999). In *White*, the Court ruled that in criminal cases, "a notice of appeal of any judgment or order appealed from must be filed within thirty days after the entry of the order," even though Appellate Rule 4 may not have been clear on the matter. Specific language has now been added to Rule 4(b) to eliminate any ambiguity.

Prior to the 2000 amendment, Appellate Rule 4(b) also provided that the notice of appeal was to be filed within thirty days, unless otherwise provided by statute. The rule now states that the notice of appeal is to be filed within thirty days unless otherwise provided by statute *or court rule*.

Reporter's Notes—2013

The 2013 amendment to Appellate Rule 4(a) changed item (3) to provide that, if served within ten days after entry of judgment, a motion under Mass. R. Civ. P. 59 to alter or amend a judgment or a motion under Mass. R. Civ. P. 60 for relief from judgment will toll the time period to claim an appeal from the underlying judgment.

The language "however titled" in the amended version is intended to make clear that the substance and not the title of the motion should control. See Pentucket Manor Chronic Hospital, Inc. v. Rate Setting Commission, 394 Mass. 233, 235–236 (1985). Thus a post-judgment motion under either Mass. R. Civ. P. 59 or 60, whether titled as a motion to alter, amend, or vacate, for relief from judgment, or for reconsideration, if served within ten days, will toll the time period to file a notice of appeal.

The 2013 amendment to Mass. R. A. P. 4(a) was intended to address the confusion that sometimes arose when a post-judgment motion, denominated a motion for "reconsideration," was served within ten days after entry of judgment. Since the text of the Massachusetts

Rules of Civil Procedure does not refer to motions for reconsideration, a motion for reconsideration, if served within ten days of judgment, could have been treated as a motion under Rule 59 (for new trial or to alter or amend judgment) or as a motion under Rule 60(b) (for relief from judgment). If treated as a Rule 59 motion, the motion for reconsideration would have operated to toll the time period to claim an appeal. If treated as a Rule 60(b) motion, the motion for reconsideration would *not* have served to toll the time period to claim an appeal. Mass. R. A. P. 4(a), as it existed prior to the 2013 amendment. The 2013 amendment to Mass. R. A. P. 4(a) eliminates this potential for confusion by tolling the time period to claim an appeal where a motion for reconsideration is served within ten days after entry of judgment.

This amendment is not intended to provide a litigant with multiple opportunities to extend the time period to claim an appeal. Assume that the defendant serves a motion for relief from judgment within ten days of entry of judgment, thereby staying the time period to claim an appeal from the judgment. Two months later, the judge enters an order denying the motion for relief. Entry of that order starts the clock running to file a notice of appeal. If the defendant moves for reconsideration of the order denying relief from judgment, the motion for reconsideration should have no effect on the time period to claim appeal from the original judgment.

A 2009 amendment to Rule 4(a)(4)(a) of the Federal Rules of Appellate Procedure similarly recognized that a motion for relief from judgment under Rule 60 tolls the time period to file a notice of appeal.

Reporter's Notes—2019

Rule 4 continues to set forth the time period when a notice of appeal must be filed. While Rules 4(a) and 4(b) continue to govern, respectively, civil cases and criminal cases, the 2019 amendments divided these subdivisions to improve their clarity by distinguishing among their separate topics. Rules 4(a)(1) and 4(b)(1) govern the time period to file a notice of appeal, and Rules 4(a)(2), 4(a)(3), and 4(b)(2) govern the tolling of the time period.

Rules 4(a)(1) and 4(b)(1) continue to specify the types of lower court dispositions that may be appealed, but were amended to add language consistent with Rule 3(c). Rule 3(c), which governs the contents of a notice of appeal, specifies that the notice of appeal shall "designate the judgment, decree, adjudication, order, or part thereof appealed from," while the prior Rule 4(a) referenced only "judgment." Accordingly, Rule 4(a)(1) (governing civil cases) was amended to include "judgment, decree, appealable order, or adjudication." Similarly, Rule 4(b)(1) (governing criminal cases) was amended to provide that a notice of appeal may be filed from a "judgment, appealable order, or adjudication" in addition to the other categories stated in Rule 4(b)(1). Importantly, in both Rules 4(a)(1) and 4(b)(1), the word "appealable" was added before the word "order" to clarify the lower court dispositions from which an appeal may be taken. Not every "order" may be appealed. An "appealable order" includes those orders authorized by statute, rule, or case law as immediately appealable. These 2019 amendments ensure consistency and completeness and were not intended to alter the types of lower court dispositions that are appealable.

As set forth in Rule 4(a)(2), certain motions toll the time period to claim an appeal. Prior to these amendments, the time period for filing a notice of appeal was tolled when a "timely motion under the Massachusetts Rules of Civil Procedure is filed in the lower court by any party." However, the pertinent Massachusetts Rules of Civil Procedure use different terms, including "filed," "served," and "made," to determine whether a post-judgment motion is timely. See Mass. R. Civ. P. 50(b) ("serve"), 52(b) ("made"), 59(b) ("served"), 59(e) ("served"), and 60(b)("made"). Therefore, in 2019, Rule 4(a)(2) was amended to include the phrase "made or served in a timely manner" to clarify that the time period to file a notice of appeal is tolled when a party timely complies with the requirements established for bringing a post-judgment motion under the applicable Massachusetts Rules of Civil Procedure, including that the motion "is filed."

The word "filed" is retained in Rule 4(a)(2) to clarify that, regardless of the language used in the applicable Massachusetts Rules of Civil Procedure, the post-judgment motion must actually be filed with the lower court to toll the time period to file a notice of appeal. This phrasing is intended to address the situation where a party serves a post-judgment motion in compliance with a lower court standing order or rule, such as Superior Court Rule 9A, but then never files the motion with the lower court. In that situation, the time period to file a notice of appeal is not tolled because the motion was only served and not filed. Finally, the last clause of the prior sentence was relocated and revised slightly to clarify that the time for filing a notice of appeal for all parties begins on the date when the lower court enters the order disposing of the last remaining motion enumerated in the rule.

Rule 4(a)(2)(C) was amended to clarify that only a motion "for relief from judgment under Rule 60(b)" tolls the time period to file a notice of appeal. The 2013 amendments' inclusion of "relief from judgment under Rule 60, however titled" was intended to encompass only Mass. R. Civ. P. 60(b) motions since Mass. R. Civ. P. 60(a) does not reference or provide for "relief from judgment." Instead, a Mass. R. Civ. P. 60(a) motion allows the court to correct certain clerical mistakes arising from oversight or omission. A Mass. R. Civ. P. 60(a) motion is intended to correct the record to reflect the original adjudication and may not be used to alter the substantive rights of the parties. See 1973 Reporter's Note to Mass. R. Civ. P. 60. Moreover, the phrase "however titled," added in 2013, was not intended to expand the scope of the rule to include Mass. R. Civ. P. 60(a) motions. See 2013 Reporter's Note to Rule 4. Unlike Fed. R. App. P. 4(a)(4)(A)(vi), which tolls the time period to file a notice of appeal upon a timely motion "for relief under Rule 60[,]" which includes both a Fed. R. Civ. P. 60(a) and a 60(b) motion, the prior Massachusetts rule, as amended in 2013, more narrowly tolled the time period only where there was a timely motion for "relief from judgment under Rule 60, however titled." However, the text of the rule after the 2013 amendment could inadvertently cause some litigants to believe, incorrectly, that a Mass. R. Civ. P. 60(a) motion would toll the time period to file a notice of appeal. Accordingly, in 2019, Rule 4(a)(2)(C) was amended to clarify that only a Mass. R. Civ. P. 60(b) motion, and not a Mass. R. Civ. P. 60(a) motion, will toll the time period to file a notice of appeal.

Rule 4(a)(3) includes the requirement of prior Rule 4(a) that a notice of appeal filed before the disposition of any post-judgment motion listed in Rule 4(a)(2) has no effect, and that a new notice of appeal must be filed. The provision is revised to clarify that the requirement applies to motions that are "timely." It further clarifies that entry in the lower court of the order disposing of the last remaining post-judgment motion begins the time period for filing a new notice of appeal.

The final revision to Rule 4(a) is the deletion of the reference to fees for filing a notice of appeal. The only existing fees required for the filing of a notice of appeal are in the Appellate Divisions of the District Court and Boston Municipal Court, which are not governed by these Rules. Deleting reference to such fees removes potential for confusion.

The phrase "whichever comes last" was added at the end of Rule 4(b)(1) to clarify that the time for filing a notice of appeal runs from the happening of the last occurrence enumerated in the rule.

Rule 4(b)(2) was amended to clarify that a motion filed pursuant to Mass. R. Crim. P. 25(b)(2) terminates the time for filing a notice of appeal for the moving party. Like a motion filed pursuant to Mass. R. Crim. P. 30, a motion filed pursuant to Mass. R. Crim. P. 25(b)(2) calls the judgment of conviction into question. If a motion filed pursuant to either rule is allowed, the conviction is vacated and an appeal by the moving party is unnecessary. If the motion is denied, the full time period fixed by Rule 4(b)(1) commences to run from the date of entry of the order denying the motion.

Rule 4(c) was amended to specifically state that service upon all other parties is required when a party seeks by motion an extension of time for filing a notice of appeal.

Rule 4(d) is a new subdivision that incorporates the so-called "inmate mailbox rule" concerning the filing of a notice of appeal by self-represented parties confined in an institution. Rule 4(d) is intended to address the concerns highlighted by the Supreme Judicial Court in Commonwealth v. Hartsgrove, 407 Mass. 441, 445 (1990), as to the limitations of a person confined in an institution to effectuate the "mailing" of a document on a certain day. The subdivision is modeled on Fed. R. App. P. 4(c), with slight changes.

In Commonwealth v. Hartsgrove, 407 Mass. 441, 445 (1990), the Supreme Judicial Court relied on the United States Supreme Court's interpretation of Fed. R. App. P. 4 in Houston v. Lack, 487 U.S. 266, 270–272 (1988), to hold that a self-represented party confined in an institution would be deemed to have filed a notice of appeal with the trial court, in accordance with Mass. R. App. P. 4(b), upon the inmate having deposited the notice of appeal in the prison's institutional mailbox. The Supreme Judicial Court observed that "[t]he Supreme Court's reasoning bears quoting at length":

> The situation of prisoners seeking to appeal without the aid of counsel is unique. Such prisoners cannot take the steps other litigants can take to monitor the processing of their notices of appeal and to ensure that the court clerk receives and stamps their notices of appeal before the 30–day deadline. Unlike other litigants, *pro se* prisoners cannot personally travel to the courthouse to see that the notice is stamped "filed" or to establish the date on which the court received the notice. Other litigants may choose to entrust their appeals to the vagaries of the mail and the clerk's process for stamping incoming papers, but only the *pro se* prisoner is forced to do so by his situation ... [T]he *pro se* prisoner has no choice but to entrust the forwarding of his notice of appeal to prison authorities whom he cannot control or supervise and who may have every incentive to delay. No matter how far in advance the *pro se* prisoner delivers his notice to the prison authorities, he can never be *sure* that it will ultimately get stamped "filed" on time. And if there is a delay the prisoner suspects is attributable to the prison authorities, he is unlikely to have any means of proving it, for his confinement prevents him from monitoring the process sufficiently to distinguish delay on the part of prison authorities from slow mail service or the court clerk's failure to stamp the notice on the date received. Unskilled in law, unaided by counsel, and unable to leave the prison, his control over the processing of his notice necessarily ceases as soon as he hands it over to the only public officials to whom he has access-the prison authorities-and the only information he will likely have is the date he delivered the notice to those prison authorities and the date ultimately stamped on his notice.

Id. at 445–446, quoting Houston v. Lack, 487 U.S. at 270–272. The Supreme Judicial Court held that the filing of the notice of appeal should be deemed to have occurred upon the inmate's relinquishment of control of the notice of appeal to the prison authorities, and not on the date the clerk received it. Id. at 444.

Because Hartsgrove concerned a notice of appeal in a criminal matter, the court did not reach the question of its applicability to civil matters. Although the Supreme Judicial Court in Hartsgrove did not construe the word "inmate," some Federal circuit courts of appeal have construed the word "inmate" to refer to civilly committed persons as well as prisoners. See Brown v. Taylor, 829 F.3d 365 (5th Cir. 2016); Parrish v. McCulloch, 481 Fed. Appx. 254, 254 (7th Cir. 2012); Jones v. Blanas, 393 F.3d 918, 926 (9th Cir. 2004). The committee agreed with this approach and concluded civilly committed persons were within the intended scope of the rule announced in Hartsgrove. Accordingly, the language of the 2019 amendment adding Rule 4(d) both incorporates the Supreme Judicial Court's decision in Hartsgrove and extends its application to the filing of notices of appeal by all self-represented persons confined in an institution, including civilly committed persons. See G.L. c. 123, §§ 1, 7, 35; G.L. c. 123A, § 12. This is consistent with Fed. R. App. P. 4(c). Whether the case involves a criminal or civil appeal, the concerns as to the limitations placed on

persons confined in an institution regarding access to mail are the same, and thus Rule 4(d) applies equally to both types of cases.

Rule 4(d) provides that the notice of appeal is to be deemed filed on the date the document is deposited for mailing in the institution's internal mailing system. The subdivision requires a party to show timely filing by including a certificate in compliance with Rule 13(a)(1)(B). This certificate creates a presumption of timely filing. However, not including this certificate will not itself render the notice of appeal invalid or untimely because Rule 4(d) permits the lower court to allow later filing of the certificate. Unlike Fed. R. App. P. 4(c)(1)(A), this subdivision requires only that the party's certificate set forth the date of deposit, and does not include the further requirement that the party also state that first-class postage has been prepaid because some Massachusetts institutions affix postage after the item leaves the inmate or civilly committed person's hands.

Rule 4(d), consistent with Fed. R. App. P. 4(c)(2), establishes that in a civil case, the 14–day time period for another party to file a notice of appeal begins when the filing of the first notice of appeal is docketed in the lower court.

Further organizational and stylistic revisions were made to this rule in 2019 in accordance with a global review and revision of all of the Appellate Rules. These revisions are described in the 2019 Reporter's Notes to Rule 1.

With regard to the preparation of the 2019 Reporter's Notes to this Rule, see the first paragraph of the 2019 Reporter's Notes to Rule 1. For an overview of the 2019 amendments to the Rules and a summary of the global amendments to the Rules, see 2019 Reporter's Notes to Rule 1, sections *I.* and *II.*

Rule 5.   Report of a Case for Determination

A report of a case for determination by an appellate court shall for all purposes under these rules be taken as the equivalent of a notice of appeal. Whenever a case or any part of it is reported after decision or verdict, the aggrieved party (as designated by the lower court) shall be treated as the appellant. Whenever a case or any part of it is reported without decision or verdict, the plaintiff in a civil action or the defendant in a criminal case shall be treated as the appellant. The clerk of the lower court shall serve notice of the filing of the report by transmitting a copy thereof to each party.
Amended May 15, 1979, effective July 1, 1979; October 31, 2018, effective March 1, 2019.

Reporter's Notes—1973

No federal analogue to Appellate Rule 5 exists. Read in conjunction with Mass.R.Civ.P. 64 (Report of Case), it prescribes the adversarial framework at the appellate level for cases reported, either after an interlocutory ruling, upon an agreed statement of facts, or on a question of law reserved by a single justice of the Supreme Judicial Court (see Mass.R.Civ.P. 64). Whatever the form of the report, no party need file a separate notice of appeal (compare Appellate Rule 3); the report itself serves that function.

Reporter's Notes—1979

This rule is amended to provide that if a case is reported by the trial court prior to a decision or verdict, the plaintiff in a civil action or the defendant in a criminal case is to be the appellant. If a whole case or any issue arising therein is reported after a decision or verdict, the aggrieved party, as determined by the trial court, shall be designated as the appellant. As to reports in criminal cases generally, see Mass.R.Crim.P. 34 (1979) and Reporter's Notes.

Reporter's Notes—2019

Rule 5 was revised to reflect notification methods include "transmitting" notice, which may include electronic or conventional mail. Minor changes were made to the final sentence of Rule 5 to remove terms rendered unnecessary by the new definition of "party" added to Rule 1(c) in 2019.

With regard to the preparation of the 2019 Reporter's Notes to this Rule, see the first paragraph of the 2019 Reporter's Notes to Rule 1. For an overview of the 2019 amendments to the Rules and a summary of the global amendments to the Rules, see 2019 Reporter's Notes to Rule 1, sections *I.* and *II.*

Rule 6. Stay or Injunction Pending Appeal

(a) Civil Cases.

(1) *Stay Must Ordinarily Be Sought in the First Instance in Lower Court; Motion for Stay in Appellate Court.* In civil cases, an application for a stay of the judgment or order of a lower court pending appeal, or for approval of a bond under Rule 6(a)(2), or for an order suspending, modifying, restoring, or granting an injunction during the pendency of an appeal must ordinarily be made in the first instance in the lower court. A motion for such relief may be made to the appellate court or to a single justice, but the motion shall show that application to the lower court for the relief sought is not practicable, or that the lower court has denied an application, or has failed to afford the relief which the applicant requested, with the reasons given by the lower court for its action. The motion shall also show the reasons for the relief requested and the facts relied upon, and if the facts are subject to dispute, the motion shall be supported by affidavits or other statements signed under the penalties of perjury or copies thereof. With the motion shall be filed such parts of the record as are relevant. Reasonable notice of the motion shall be given to all parties. The motion shall be filed with the clerk of the appellate court to which the appeal is being taken. If the court is the Supreme Judicial Court, the motion shall be filed with the clerk of the Supreme Judicial Court for Suffolk County.

(2) *Stay May Be Conditioned Upon Giving of Bond; Proceedings Against Sureties.* Relief available in the appellate court under this rule may be conditioned upon the filing of a bond or other appropriate security in the lower court. If security is given in the form of a bond or stipulation or other undertaking with 1 or more sureties, each surety thereby shall submit to the jurisdiction of the lower court and irrevocably appoint the clerk of the lower court as an authorized agent upon whom any documents affecting liability on the bond or undertaking may be served. A surety's liability may be entered against the surety on motion in the lower court without the necessity of an independent action. The motion and such notice of the motion as the lower court prescribes may be served on the clerk of the lower court, who shall forthwith mail copies to the sureties if their addresses are known.

(3) *Terms.* Relief available in the appellate court under this rule, or denial of such relief, may be conditioned on such reasonable terms as the appellate court or single justice may impose. For failure to observe such terms, the appellate court or single justice may make such further order as it or the single justice deems just and appropriate.

(b) Criminal Cases.
A motion for a stay of execution of a sentence shall be governed by Rule 6(b) and by Massachusetts Rules of Criminal Procedure 31.

(1) *Stay Must Ordinarily Be Sought in the First Instance in Lower Court; Motion for Stay in Appellate Court.* In criminal cases, an application for a stay of execution of a sentence pending appeal must ordinarily be made in the first instance in the lower court. A motion for such relief may be made to the single justice of the appellate court to which the appeal is being taken, but the motion shall show that application to the lower court for the relief sought is not practicable, or that the lower court has previously denied an application for a stay or has failed to afford the relief which the applicant requested with the reasons given by the lower court for its action. The motion shall also show the reasons for the relief requested and the facts relied upon, and if the facts are subject to dispute, the motion shall be supported by affidavits or other statements signed under the penalties of perjury or copies thereof. With the motion shall be filed such parts of the record as are relevant. The motion shall be filed with the clerk of the appellate court to which the appeal is being taken. If the court is the Supreme Judicial Court, the motion shall be filed with the clerk of the Supreme Judicial Court for Suffolk County).

(2) *Reasonable Notice.* Reasonable notice of the motion for a stay shall be given to the Commonwealth.

(A) If the motion is filed prior to the docketing of the appeal in an appellate court, the time for response shall be governed by Rule 15.

(B) After an appeal has been docketed pursuant to Rule 10(a)(2),

(i) if the motion is filed at least 30 days prior to the date the appellant's brief is due, the time for a response shall be governed by Rule 15; or

(ii) if the motion is filed at any other time, the Commonwealth shall have 30 days to respond.

(C) A single justice may shorten or extend the time for responding to any motion authorized by this rule.

(3) *Appealability of Single Justice Order; Finality.* An order by the single justice allowing or denying an application for a stay may be appealed to the appellate court in which the appeal is pending. An order by the appellate court in which the appeal is pending, allowing or denying an application for a stay, shall be final.

(4) *Revocation of Stay Pending Appeal.* If a defendant fails at any time to take any measure necessary for the hearing of an appeal or report, a stay of execution of a sentence may, on motion of the Commonwealth, be revoked.

(5) *Expiration of Stay.* Upon the release of the decision by the appellate court of a judgment affirming the conviction, the stay of execution of the sentence automatically expires, unless extended by the appellate court.

(6) *Notice of Expiration of Stay.* Upon release of a decision affirming the conviction, the clerk of the appellate court shall notify the clerk of the lower court and the parties that the conviction has been affirmed and that therefore, the stay of execution of the sentence has automatically expired.

Amended December 14, 1976, effective January 1, 1977; May 15, 1979, effective July 1, 1979; June 24, 2009, effective October 1, 2009.; October 31, 2018, effective March 1, 2019.

Reporter's Notes—1973

Appellate Rule 6, patterned on F.R.A.P. 8, allows the court (first the lower court, then the appellate court) to grant such relief as may be necessary to preserve the rights of the parties during the pendency of an appeal. Appellate Rule 6 does not substantially alter the powers of the court under existing practice. See G.L. c. 214, § 19. City of Boston v. Santosuosso, 308 Mass. 202, 210, 31 N.E.2d 572, 578 (1941); G.L. c. 231, § 116. Appellate Rule 6(c), which is new, codifies existing federal practice. See also Mass.R.Civ.P. 62(c). Prior Massachusetts practice will, however continue to control stays in criminal cases. G.L. c. 278, § 28B, c. 279, §§ 4, 49A.

Reporter's Notes—1979

Subdivision (a) of Rule 6, requiring applications or motions for stays to be ordinarily filed in the lower court in the first instance, is expanded to cover both civil and criminal cases.

Subdivisions (b) and (c) of former Rule 6 are made (b)(1) and (b)(2) of the amended rule, and are applicable only to civil cases.

A new subdivision (c), relative to motions for stays of execution of sentence in criminal cases, incorporates by reference Mass.R.Crim.P. 31 (1979).

The Appeals Court in Commonwealth v. Levin, Mass.App.Ct.Adv. Sh. (1979) 857 further app. rev. denied Mass.Adv.Sh. (1979) 1610 and the Supreme Judicial Court in Commonwealth v. Allen, Mass.Adv.Sh. (1979) 1819 established the criteria for determining whether a stay of sentence pending appellate review ought to be granted. These cases establish that the same judgment and discretion as used by the lower courts in bail applications can properly be considered on questions on motions for stay. These cases acknowledge that considerations such as whether the defendant was likely to be a danger to any other person or to the community and as to the likelihood of further criminal conduct during the pendency of the appeal were appropriate.

Under these decisions the lower court is also empowered to require that the appeal present "an issue which is worthy of presentation to an appellate court, one which offers some reasonable possibility of a successful decision in the appeal." Commonwealth v. Levin, Mass. App.Ct.Adv.Sh. (1979) 857, 860.

The Supreme Judicial Court in Allen further held that the application of this standard was open, de novo, to the full bench of the appellate court after a determination of the single justice of that court denying a stay.

Subdivision (c) also establishes that a stay of execution, once granted, is always subject to being vacated if the defendant is not diligent in prosecuting his appeal. See ABA Standards Relating to Criminal Appeals 21–2.5(a) & commentary at 15 (2d ed., Approved Draft, 1978).

The second paragraph of subdivision (c) was added to ensure that an appeal, where a stay of sentence had been allowed, is prosecuted with reasonable dispatch under all the circumstances. It is expected that this provision will be used to vacate a stay for serious delays caused by the appellant and not for mere technical lapses which do not disrupt the schedule of the appellate court.

Reporter's Notes—2009

[The notes to the 2009 amendments were drafted by the Reporter for the Massachusetts Rules of Criminal Procedure]

This Rule was revised in 2009 to describe more fully the procedure for obtaining a stay of execution of a criminal sentence in an appellate court. It complements Rule 31 of the Rules of Criminal Procedure.

The 2009 amendment clarified the appellate process for stays of execution of a criminal sentence pending an appeal. As in civil cases, requests for a stay must first be presented to the trial court, unless such an application is not practicable. Either the defendant or the Commonwealth may seek relief from a single justice of the court that will hear the appeal concerning the trial judge's decision to deny, e.g., Commonwealth v. Aviles, 422 Mass. 1008 (1996), or grant, e.g. Com-

monwealth v. Hodge, 380 Mass. 851 (1980), a stay. Only the parties may do so. See Hagen v. Commonwealth, 437 Mass. 374, 375 (2002) (crime victim lacks standing to request revocation of stay). In the ordinary course of events, for all but first-degree murder cases a single justice of the Appeals Court is the appropriate forum. The single justice does not review the decision of the trial judge, but considers the matter de novo. See Commonwealth v. Allen, 378 Mass. 489, 497 (1979).

Rule 6(b)(2) recognizes that it is important to give the Commonwealth adequate time to prepare a response to a motion for a stay, since that will often require substantial effort in addressing the merits of the underlying appeal.

After the single justice decides the issue, there is only one further step in the process: an appeal to the panel of the Appeals Court that will decide the merits, or the full bench of the Supreme Judicial Court if the case will be decided there. This changes prior practice, which allowed a party aggrieved by the decision of a single justice of the Appeals Court the option of seeking relief both by appealing the decision in that court and asking a single justice of the Supreme Judicial Court to entertain the matter. See e.g., Duong v. Commonwealth, 434 Mass. 1006 (2001). The appeal from the decision of the single justice may be accompanied by a motion for an expedited ruling. See e.g., Restucci v. Commonwealth, 442 Mass. 1045 (2004).

As also provided in Mass. R. Crim. P. 31, a stay of execution of sentence automatically expires when the appellate court considering the appeal releases a rescript affirming the conviction, unless the appellate court decides to extend it. A rescript is "released" when it is announced to the public and the appellate court notifies the parties that the court has decided the case. Cf. Mass. R. App. P. 23 (requiring the clerk of the appellate court to mail the parties a copy of the rescript and the opinion, if any). In the ordinary course of events, the rescript "issues" twenty-eight days following the release date or upon the denial of any petition for rehearing or application for further appellate review, whichever is later. Id.

When a rescript is released affirming a conviction, the clerk of the appellate court, in addition to the obligation that Mass. R. App. P. 23 imposes, shall notify the parties and the trial court clerk that the stay of execution of sentence has automatically expired. If the defendant wishes to apply for a new stay, in order to seek a rehearing or further appellate review, such a request should go to the appellate court that decided the case (either the panel of the Appeals Court or the full bench of the Supreme Judicial Court).

The court that decided the appeal may exercise its discretion to extend a stay of execution pending a petition for rehearing, application for further appellate review, or petition for certiorari. Unless otherwise specified, an extended stay expires when the rescript issues. The appellate court may act sua sponte or pursuant to the defendant's motion, which may be filed before the appeal is decided or after the rescript is released.

Reporter's Notes—2019

Rule 6(b)(2) was revised to clarify the standard time period for the Commonwealth to file a response to a motion for a stay of execution of a sentence. A motion to stay execution of a sentence may be filed in the appellate court either prior to completion of the record assembly process and the docketing of the appeal, or after the underlying appeal has been assembled and docketed pursuant to Rules 9 and 10. The timing of the motion affects the timing of the Commonwealth's response. Rules 6(b)(2)(A) and 6(b)(2)(B)(i) provide that if the motion to stay sentence is filed prior to the docketing of the appeal in the appellate court, or after docketing of the appeal and at least 30 days prior to the due date for the appellant's brief, the Commonwealth's response time is governed by Rule 15. Otherwise, the Commonwealth has 30 days to respond pursuant to Rule 6(b)(2)(B)(ii). This clarification will eliminate any misapprehension that the Commonwealth has 30 days to respond in all circumstances. In either situation, the time for response may be shortened or extended by a single justice.

Further organizational and stylistic revisions were made to this rule in 2019 in accordance with a global review and revision of all of the Appellate Rules. These revisions are described in the 2019 Reporter's Notes to Rule 1.

With regard to the preparation of the 2019 Reporter's Notes to this Rule, see the first paragraph of the 2019 Reporter's Notes to Rule 1. For an overview of the 2019 amendments to the Rules and a summary of the global amendments to the Rules, see 2019 Reporter's Notes to Rule 1, sections *I.* and *II.*

Rule 7. Disability of a Member of the Lower Court

If a judge whose decision has been appealed to the appellate court becomes unable to participate further, then any other judge of or assigned to the lower court may be substituted.

Amended October 31, 2018, effective March 1, 2019.

Reporter's Notes—1973

This rule, which does not appear in the Federal Rules of Appellate Procedure, reads into appellate procedure the provisions of Mass. R.Civ.P. 63, and ensures that whenever the Appellate Rules require action by the lower court judge, his disability will not of itself impede the appellate process.

Reporter's Notes—1979

Disability of the trial judge in criminal cases was formerly dealt with in Supreme Judicial Court Rule 1:10 (1975: 366 Mass. 859–60) and Appeals Court Rule 1:10 (1975: 3 Mass.App.Ct. 803), which are superseded by the application of this rule to criminal proceedings. As to disability of the judge under the trial rules, see Mass.R.Civ.P. 63 (1974) and Mass.R.Crim.P. 38 (1979).

Reporter's Notes—2019

Rule 7 was substantially revised to eliminate an enumerated list of the reasons a lower court judge may become unable to participate further in a case on appeal and to clarify that judicial substitutions may be made as needed. The revised language is consistent with Mass. R. Civ. P. 63 and Mass. R. Crim. P. 38.

With regard to the preparation of the 2019 Reporter's Notes to this Rule, see the first paragraph of the 2019 Reporter's Notes to Rule 1. For an overview of the 2019 amendments to the Rules and a summary of the global amendments to the Rules, see 2019 Reporter's Notes to Rule 1, sections *I.* and *II.*

Rule 8. The Record on Appeal

(a) Definition. The record on appeal shall consist of the documents and exhibits on file, the transcript of the proceedings, if any, and the docket entries.

(b) Producing the Transcript of Proceedings.

(1) *Cases Other than Child Welfare Cases.*

(A) Transcript Orders and Certifications. For those proceedings relevant to the appeal that were recorded by a court reporter, the appellant shall order a transcript of those proceedings within 14 days of filing the notice of appeal in accordance with procedures set by the Chief Justice of the Trial Court, unless the appellant certifies to the clerk (i) that no lower court proceedings are relevant to the appeal or (ii) that the transcript is on file with the court. For those proceedings relevant to the appeal that were electronically recorded, the appellant shall request the transmission of the audio recording of those proceedings and order the transcription of those proceedings within 14 days of filing the notice of appeal in accordance with procedures set by the Chief Justice of the Trial Court, unless the appellant certifies to the clerk (i) that no lower court proceedings are relevant to the appeal or (ii) that the transcript of all proceedings relevant to the appeal is on file with the court. The appellant shall at the same time file a copy of the transcript orders or certifications with the clerk and serve a copy on all other parties. Within 14 days of service of the appellant's transcript orders or certifications, any other party may order a transcript of additional proceedings in accordance with procedures set by the Chief Justice of the Trial Court. Such party shall at the same time file a copy of the transcript order with the clerk and serve a copy on all other parties.

(B) Stipulation that Transcript is Unnecessary. To the extent consistent with the appellant's duty to provide an adequate record to the appellate court, the parties may stipulate that the transcription of some or all of the proceedings relevant to the appeal is unnecessary to the adjudication of the appeal, in which case the appellant need order only the transcript of the proceedings, if any, that the parties agree are necessary to the adjudication of the appeal. The parties shall file the stipulation with the clerk within 14 days of the filing of the notice of appeal.

(C) Costs of Transcription. In any criminal case and in a civil case in which the appellant is entitled to have counsel made available pursuant to Supreme Judicial Court Rule 3:10, the Commonwealth shall pay for the cost of providing the transcript of all proceedings relevant to the appeal, including those designated by the appellee, to the lower court clerk. In all other cases, unless ordered otherwise by the lower court, the appellant shall pay for such costs. If the parties cannot agree on which proceedings are relevant to the appeal, the lower court shall settle the matter upon motion. Payment, if required, for copies of the transcript for the parties shall be governed by procedures set by the Chief Justice of the Trial Court.

(2) *Child Welfare Cases.* Upon the filing of a notice of appeal, unless the parties file a stipulation designating the parts of the proceedings which need not be transcribed or a statement of intent to proceed under Rule 8(d), the clerk of the lower court shall order, within 14 days and in accordance with procedures set by the Chief Justice of the Trial Court, a transcript of the proceedings relevant to the appeal and shall serve a copy of the transcript order on the parties.

(3) *Delivery of the Transcript.* Upon completion, the transcriber shall deliver the transcript to the clerk of the lower court in accordance with procedures set by the Chief Justice of the Trial Court. The delivery of transcripts to the parties shall be governed by procedures set by the Chief Justice of the Trial Court. Upon receipt of all of the transcripts ordered by the parties, the clerk shall notify all parties within 14 days that the transcripts have been received.

(c) Statement of the Proceedings When No Report or Transcript is Available. If no report of the evidence or proceedings at a hearing or trial was made and a transcript is unavailable, the appellant shall file a motion to reconstruct the record within 14 days of the filing of the notice of appeal. The parties shall confer and reconstruct the record. Within such time as the lower court shall allow, the appellant shall file a proposed statement of the proceedings Within 14 days of service of the proposed statement, any other party may file objections or proposed amendments or additions. The lower court shall promptly settle any disputes and approve a statement of the proceedings for inclusion in the record on appeal.

(d) Agreed Statement as the Record on Appeal. If the parties intend to submit an agreed statement as the record on appeal in lieu of the procedures set forth in Rule 8(a)–(c), the parties shall notify the clerk in writing within 14 days of the filing of the notice of appeal. Within 28 days of the filing of the notice to the clerk, the parties shall submit to the lower court an agreed statement of the record on appeal containing such information as is necessary for consideration of the appeal. If the statement conforms to the truth, the lower court shall approve the statement, along with any additions the lower court considers useful to the appellate court.

(e) Correction or Modification of the Record.

(1) *Omissions.* If anything material is omitted from the record, the parties may supply it by stipulation and submit the stipulation for the approval of the lower court. If the parties are unable to agree, the lower court on motion shall settle the dispute and add to the record on appeal. On motion of the parties or on its own motion, the appellate court or a single justice may direct that any omission be rectified.

(2) *Corrections.* If any part of the record on appeal fails to accord with what occurred in the lower court, the parties may correct the record by stipulation and submit the stipulation for the approval of the lower court. If the parties are unable to agree, the lower court on motion shall settle any disputes and conform the record to the truth. On motion of the parties or on its own motion, the appellate court or a single justice may direct that any part of the record be corrected.

(3) *Inaudible Recording.* If portions of the proceedings cannot be transcribed because they are unintelligible, the parties shall promptly use reasonable efforts to stipulate to their content, and shall submit any such stipulation for the approval of the lower court. If the parties are unable to agree, the lower court shall settle the dispute on motion.

Amended June 27, 1974, effective July 1, 1974; amended effective February 24, 1975; amended May 15, 1979, effective July 1, 1979; June 28, 1979, effective July 1, 1979; February 17, 1983, effective April 1, 1983; May 29, 1986, effective July 1, 1986; June 23, 1986, effective July 1, 1986; October 1, 1998, effective November 2, 1998; July 28, 1999, effective September 1, 1999; June 26, 2002, effective September 3, 2002; October 31, 2018, effective March 1, 2019.

Reporter's Notes—1973

Based on F.R.A.P. 10, Appellate Rule 8 describes the record on appeal, which should be carefully distinguished from the record appendix. The record consists of the original papers and exhibits, plus a transcript of the proceedings and a certified copy of the docket entries, as well as any certified copy of the lower court's final order. The record appendix (see Appellate Rule 18) is that distillation of the decision-essential portions of the record which is filed in connection with appellate brief.

The appellant is responsible for attending to the preparation of a transcript; this transcript must be sufficiently extensive to cover all points raised by the appeal. The phrase "description of the parts of the transcript," refers to such a description as "the plaintiff's entire

testimony," rather than a designation by page and line, unless a more precise description is necessary.

If no transcript was made, the appellant may prepare a statement of the evidence in the proceedings in the most expeditious manner possible; after inspection by the appellee, this statement will be submitted to the lower court for approval. The statement of issues need be only extensive enough to enable the appellee to determine the need for ordering a transcript of other parts of the testimony.

The parties may, alternatively, prepare and file an agreed statement of facts. This is similar to existing practice, see G.L. c. 231, § 111; cf. Paulino v. Concord, 259 Mass. 142, 144, 155 N.E. 870, 871 (1927).

Reporter's Notes—1975

As originally promulgated, Appellate Rule 8 required the inclusion, in the record on appeal, of a certified copy of the order appealed from and the opinion. Because the record includes all "original papers" anyway, this requirement was superfluous. Accordingly, it has been eliminated.

Reporter's Notes—1979

The second sentence of subdivision (a) of former Rule 8 is amended to clarify that it applies to appeals in civil cases from the Appellate Division of the District Court Department (G.L. c. 231, § 108, as amended, St.1978, c. 478, § 264) and not to the Appellate Division of the Superior Court Department for review of sentences in criminal cases (G.L. c. 278, §§ 28A–28D).

Subdivision (b) of the former rule has been divided into subdivisions (b)(1), applicable to civil cases, and (b)(2), applicable to criminal cases. Subdivision (b)(1) is identical to former 8(b). Subdivision (b)(2) is wholly new.

Consonant with practice under former G.L. c. 278, §§ 33A–33H, a defendant is entitled to a complete transcript on appeal. Charpentier v. Commonwealth, Mass.Adv.Sh. (1978) 2163, 2172. Pursuant to (b)(2), upon the filing of a notice of appeal in a criminal case, the clerk of the lower court automatically orders from the court reporter a transcript of the proceedings out of which the appeal arises. Since counsel is no longer obligated to take this mechanical step, one point of delay under prior practice is thus eliminated. The parties may—and are encouraged by the rule to—file a stipulation as to those parts of the proceedings which are unnecessary to the appeal and which therefore need not be transcribed. The provision for stipulations as to parts of the proceedings which need not be transcribed is not applicable to capital cases under G.L. c. 278, § 33E, as amended, because in such cases, the "entire case" is before the Supreme Judicial Court, "including a transcript of the entire proceedings." E.g., *Charpentier*, supra at 2173 n. 9. A "capital case" is a case in which the defendant was convicted of murder in the first degree. G.L. c. 278, § 33E, as amended. *See Commonwealth v. O'Brien*, Mass.Adv.Sh. (1976) 2926; Mass.R.Crim.P. 2(b)(3).

When the transcript is completed, the court reporter is to deliver it to the clerk of the lower court who prepares copies thereof for the appellate court, the appellant or appellants, and the appellee or appellees. The parties' copies are delivered to them, while the original and one copy are retained by the clerk for transmission to the appellate court as part of the record (Rule 9[d]).

In the district court jury sessions, the General Laws (G.L. c. 218, § 27A(h)) provide a procedure for appointment of a court reporter to transcribe the proceedings and in the alternative for an electronic recording of the proceedings. These rules as well as G.L. c. 218, § 27A(g) provide that appeals from the district court jury sessions are to proceed in the same manner as appeals from the superior court.

Because of the unavailability of a court reporter in some cases in the district court jury sessions or where the defendant has not taken advantage of section 27A(h) it may be necessary for the clerk, who has the responsibility under this rule for the completion of the record, including the transcript, to cause a transcript to be made from an electronic recording.

After this necessary preliminary step has been taken by the district court clerk copies of the transcript are to be made and distributed as provided by this rule and rule 9(d).

The cost of preparation of the original transcript and of the copies required by this rule is borne by the Commonwealth except where the defendant is not indigent. In that case the defendant is to pay the clerk for the cost of producing his copy. The provision requiring production of the whole transcript is intended to provide for more expeditious and just disposition of questions on appeal. In the first place, the Commonwealth could not in all cases determine whether a partial transcript was adequate to serve its needs until such time as the defendant's brief was filed. Secondly, without a full transcript, appellate courts cannot resolve issues of plain error, a miscarriage of justice, or harmless error.

Subdivision (c) has been amended to enlarge the time within which a statement of the evidence or proceedings may be filed from ten to thirty days. Procedure like that provided under this subdivision has been followed by the Supreme Judicial Court in a criminal case when a transcript was unavailable. Commonwealth v. Harris, Mass.Adv.Sh. (1978) 2155.

It should be noted that the appellant may prepare and submit a statement of the evidence or proceeding from the best available means. However, as stated in Ingersoll Grove Nursing Home, Inc. v. Springfield Gas Light Co., Mass.Adv.Sh. (1979) 203, 204 a substitution is available only "if no report of the evidence or proceedings at a hearing or trial was made, or if a transcript is unavailable." In a case in which the transcript is "made and available" the plaintiff is not entitled to substitute a statement of the evidence under subdivision (c).

Subdivision (d) however allows the parties to "prepare and sign a statement of the case" in lieu of the record. The term "statement of the evidence or proceeding" of subdivision (c) is not to be used interchangeably with "statement of the case" in subdivision (d) since the rules outline different procedures with respect to these terms.

The agreed statement permitted by subdivision (d) must now be filed within thirty days after the notice of appeal is filed; prior to this amendment no time limit was specified. The parties electing to proceed under the subdivision should notify the clerk that no transcript is to be ordered and, in addition, that the agreed statement shall be substituted for the record as defined in subdivision (a). Filing of the agreed statement as the appendix required by Rule 18 has been made mandatory.

Subdivision (e), relative to correction or modification of the record, as applied to criminal cases, is similar in operation to prior provisions for settling a bill of exceptions (G.L. c. 278, § 31 [St.1974, c. 540, § 1]) or for correcting errors in a transcript (G.L. c. 278, § 33A [St.1974, c. 540, § 2]), although much broader in the scope of relief available.

Reporter's Notes to Addition of Rule 8(b)(3)—1983

Rule 8(b)(3) has been added to deal with tape-recorded transcripts. It is quite detailed because judges, clerks, and lawyers have complained about a lack of specificity with respect to the utilization of cassettes on appeal.

Rule 8(b)(3)(i) indicates when Rule 8(b)(3) applies. The Rule does not apply to court reporters, including voice writers, or to cases where a complete transcript has already been produced for use by the trial court, and is available to the parties. Rule 8(b)(3)(ii) gives the duties of appellants and clerks, and provides for appointment of a transcriber. A major purpose is to facilitate a speedy appeal. Consequently, an appellant must order a cassette at the time of appeal and state the date of receipt to insure that the designation is timely. Another major purpose is to reduce the number of steps required of the clerk. This rule permits the parties, if they can agree, to choose the transcriber. The appellant must inform the clerk at the time of transcript designation whether the parties have so agreed. The parties must order their

copies directly from the transcriber and make their own payment arrangements; the transcriber delivers transcripts directly to them. Rule 8(b)(3)(ii), unlike 8(b)(1), does not specify when an appellant must transcribe all evidence relevant to a finding or conclusion. This is not meant to change the law, but rather leave it to the parties to determine what must be transcribed in order to protect their appeal. The Standing Advisory Committee wants to discourage unnecessary transcription.

Rule 8(b)(3)(iii) gives the duties of the appellee with respect to ordering a cassette or arranging to borrow the appellant's, counter-designation, and ordering copies. Rule 8(b)(3)(iv) describes the transcriber's duties, and the certificate which the transcriber must file. Rule 8(b)(3)(v) covers the situation where a portion of the cassette is unintelligible; it requires the parties first to attempt to stipulate the contents of such portion, and provides for the trial judge, if possible, to settle differences. Rule 8(b)(3)(vi) requires that when the Commonwealth must pay for an original transcript or copy, the designating parties must certify that they have designated only necessary portions. Again, the purpose is to reduce costs.

Rule 8(b)(3) does not have its own provision concerning enlargements of time, but is subject to the general computation and extension of time provisions contained in Appellate Rule 14.

Here is a chronology of the major steps and time periods under this rule:

1. Simultaneously with filing the notice of appeal, the appellant, if desirous of a transcript, orders the cassette. Rule 8(b)(3)(ii).

2. The clerk promptly provides the cassette (Rule 8(b)(3)(ii)), unless an entire transcript is already available; in such event, the clerk notifies the parties, and the normal designation rules in Rule 8(b)(1) or 8(b)(2) apply. Rule 8(b)(3)(i). In such event, the appellant's time for ordering a transcript is within ten days after the clerk's notification. Rule 8(b)(3)(i). The clerk also notifies the parties if there has been a previous transcription of a portion of the cassette, so that the parties may utilize the prior partial transcription if they wish. Rule 8(b)(3)(ii).

3. Within fifteen days after receipt of the cassette from the clerk, the appellant designates which portions are to be included in the transcript. Rule 8(b)(3)(ii). If the appellant wants the entire cassette transcribed, then appellant also delivers the cassette to the transcriber and places the order within said fifteen day period. Rule 8(b)(3)(ii).

4. When the appellant has not ordered the transcription of the entire transcript, the appellee has fifteen days from service of the appellant's designation to file and serve a counter-designation. Rule 8(b)(3)(iii).

5. When the appellant has not already designated the entire cassette for transcription, the appellant delivers the cassette to the transcriber and places the order promptly after twenty days have expired from service upon the appellee of the appellant's designation. Rule 8(b)(3)(ii). This, in effect, gives the appellant at least five days to deliver the cassette to the transcriber and place the order, for the appellee had to file and serve the counter-designation within fifteen days.

In summary, from the time the appellant receives the cassette from the clerk, the entire designation process takes fifteen days if appellant orders the entire cassette transcribed, and "promptly" after thirty-five days if appellant has designated less than the entire cassette.

Reporter's Notes—1998

The 1998 amendment to Appellate Rule 8(b)(3) deals with appeals in proceedings that were electronically-recorded on court-controlled recording equipment and not recorded by an official court reporter.

The existing rule allows the appellant to designate either the entire cassette or only specified portions of the cassette to be transcribed for purposes of preparing the appellate record. The existing rule further provides that where less than the entire cassette is to be designated, the appellant must inform the appellee of those portions of the cassette that are to be transcribed. This allows the appellee to counter-designate additional portions of the cassette for transcription. However, the current rule does not require the appellant to inform the appellee of the issues that the appellant intends to present on the appeal, thus making it difficult for the appellee to make such counter-designation intelligently.

The 1998 amendment resolves this dilemma by requiring the appellant to file and serve on the appellee a statement of the issues together with the appellant's designation of transcript.

Reporter's Notes—1999

The 1999 amendments to Appellate Rule 8(b) were part of a comprehensive set of amendments to the Appellate Rules (Rules 1, 3, 4, 8, and 10) that had been proposed by the Supreme Judicial Court Committee on Appeals of Child Welfare Cases. The purpose of the 1999 amendments is described in the 1999 Reporter's Notes to Appellate Rule 1(c).

Appellate Rule 8(b)(1) (concerning ordering the transcript) and Rule 8(b)(3) (concerning electronically-recorded proceedings) have been made inapplicable to child welfare cases. Instead, the ordering of the transcript of the proceeding is now controlled by Rule 8(b)(5). Rule 8(b)(5) shifts the duty of ordering the cassettes and transcripts from the appellant to the clerk of the lower court. Modeled in part after the procedures applicable in criminal cases, new Rule 8(b)(5) is intended to expedite preparation of the transcript in child welfare cases.

Reporter's Notes to Appellate Rule 8(b)(2)—2002

The 2002 amendment to Appellate Rule 8(b)(2) requires that upon the filing of a notice of appeal in a criminal case, the clerk of the lower court shall order a transcript from the court reporter within ten days. Prior to this amendment, there was no time period prescribed for ordering the transcript.

This amendment will make the practice in criminal cases consistent with that already in existence in civil cases in Massachusetts. Appellate Rule 8(b)(1) requires that in a civil case, the appellant shall order the transcript within ten days after filing of the notice of appeal. It should be noted that Rule 10(b)(1) of the Federal Rules of Appellate Procedure likewise requires that the transcript in civil and criminal cases in federal court be ordered within ten days of the filing of the notice of appeal.

Reporter's Notes—2019

The 2019 revisions to Rules 8 and 9(a) were recommended by the Trial Court Committee on Transcript Production, a committee convened by the Chief Justice of the Trial Court in 2016 to address widespread dissatisfaction with the complexity and lack of flexibility afforded by the prior rules. The revisions facilitate assembly of the record on appeal by streamlining the requirements for production of the transcript of the lower court proceedings.

Rule 8(a) was revised to simplify the description of the record on appeal. The requirement that the docket entries be certified was eliminated, consistent with revisions to Rule 9(e)(2)(D). The reference to inclusion in the record of "the report of the trial judge to the appellate division" was deleted because such a report would be part of the documents on file with the lower court.

Rule 8(b)(1) governs all appeals except appeals in child welfare cases. Under Rule 8(b)(1)(A), within 14 days of the filing of a notice of appeal, the appellant must either order transcripts of "all court proceedings relevant to the appeal," certify that no court proceedings are relevant to the appeal, or certify that the relevant transcripts have already been filed with the lower court. The orders or certifications are filed with the lower court clerk and the appellant is required to give notice to the other parties. If proceedings were electronically recorded, the appellant must order the recording and the transcript at the same time. Prior requirements regarding designation were deleted from this rule. If the appellee believes that other proceedings should be transcribed, the appellee may order the transcript of those

proceedings within 14 days of the appellant's order. The procedural mechanics of the parties' orders are to be determined by the Chief Justice of the Trial Court in an Administrative Order, to allow flexibility in the transcript request and production processes as technology advances.

Rule 8(b)(1)(B) retains the right of the parties to stipulate that transcription of some or all of the court proceedings is unnecessary to the appeal. The parties must file the stipulation with the lower court clerk with 14 days of the filing of a notice of appeal.

The requirement in prior Rule 8(1)(b)(2) that the clerk of the lower court in a criminal case order the transcript without the prompting of the appellant was deleted. The appellant's trial counsel is better able than the clerk to determine which dates and hearings are potentially relevant to an appeal.

Rule 8(b)(1)(C) governs the cost of producing the transcript. The Commonwealth is responsible for paying for the transcript for the lower court in all criminal cases and in civil cases in which the appellant was entitled to appointed counsel. In other cases, the appellant is required to pay for the transcript for the lower court for all proceedings relevant to the appeal, regardless of whether the appellant or the appellee ordered them. The lower court may settle any dispute over whether transcripts ordered by the appellee are relevant to the appeal and has the authority to shift costs in the interests of justice. Payment of costs for the copies of the transcripts to be provided to the parties is determined by the Chief Justice of the Trial Court in an Administrative Order because it concerns contracts between the Trial Court and transcribers and court reporters, and will be influenced by the expansion of electronic processes.

Rule 8(b)(2) governs child welfare cases, which continues prior Rule 8(b)(5)'s recognition of the urgency of child welfare appeals. Rule 8(b)(2) requires the lower court clerk to order the transcript of the court proceedings relevant to the appeal, unless the parties stipulate otherwise within 14 days of the filing of a notice of appeal.

Rule 8(b)(3) clarifies that, in all cases, the transcriber must deliver the transcript directly to the lower court clerk, rather than providing it to the ordering party for delivery to the clerk. This clarification is intended to avoid unnecessary delays. The mechanics of such delivery is governed by an Administrative Order published by the Chief Justice of the Trial Court, which is intended to allow the Trial Court to take immediate advantage of advances in technology regarding electronic delivery. The lower court clerk has the duty of informing all parties when all transcripts have been received. Of course, a clerk may also inform parties when transcripts of some, but not all, proceedings are received.

Rule 8(c) was revised to modify the procedure for reconstructing the record when a transcript is unavailable. Under the modified procedure, the appellant must file a motion to reconstruct the record within 14 days of the filing of the notice of appeal. Unlike prior Rule 8(c), the duty is on the parties to confer prior to the filing of a proposed reconstruction in the lower court. This process is more likely to achieve the objective of reconstructing a record adequate for the appellate court and better reflects the Supreme Judicial Court's admonition that "'[a]ll those with ... relevant evidence, but particularly the attorneys involved at the trial, are under an affirmative duty to use their best efforts to ensure that a sufficient reconstruction is made if at all possible.'" Drayton v. Commonwealth, 450 Mass. 1028, 1030 (2008), quoting Commonwealth v. Harris, 376 Mass. 74, 79 (1978). Once the parties have conferred, the appellant shall file a proposed reconstruction within such time as the lower court shall allow, and any other party may file objections, amendments, or additions, and the lower court shall settle the matter. The deadline for filing such objections, amendments, or additions is changed from 10 days to 14 days after the filing of a proposed reconstruction.

Rule 8(d) continues prior Rule 8(d)'s provisions authorizing the parties to file an agreed statement of the record on appeal. Unlike the prior rule, however, the parties must notify the lower court clerk of their intention to do so within 14 days of the filing of a notice of appeal. The agreed statement is to be filed within 28 days of the parties' notification to the clerk.

Rule 8(e) was revised to clarify the procedures for correction or modification of the record. The subdivision was separated into three paragraphs, each addressing a different method for modification of the record: omissions, corrections, or an inaudible recording. In each case, the parties may stipulate to a correction and submit the stipulation to the lower court for approval. If the parties cannot agree, they may submit the dispute to the lower court for resolution. The provision of prior Rule 8(e) that allowed parties to stipulate to an addition to the transcripts, but not a correction without lower court approval, was deleted. In both instances, the amended rule requires approval of the lower court. The appellate court may benefit from any guidance the lower court judge may be able to provide. The appellate court retains the ability to order a correction or addition to the transcripts, with or without lower court input.

Further organizational and stylistic revisions were made to this rule in 2019 in accordance with a global review and revision of all of the Appellate Rules. These revisions are described in the 2019 Reporter's Notes to Rule 1.

With regard to the preparation of the 2019 Reporter's Notes to this Rule, see the first paragraph of the 2019 Reporter's Notes to Rule 1. For an overview of the 2019 amendments to the Rules and a summary of the global amendments to the Rules, see 2019 Reporter's Notes to Rule 1, sections *I.* and *II.*

Rule 9. Assembly of the Record; Reproduction of Exhibits; Notice of Assembly; and Transmission of Documents from the Lower Court

(a) **Assembly.**

(1) Upon the filing of a notice of appeal, the clerk of the lower court shall promptly review the file and ensure the accuracy of the docket entries and that all documents are properly numbered in order of filing or identified with reasonable specificity. The clerk shall prepare a list of all exhibits filed in the lower court and ensure that all exhibits are properly numbered and labeled. The clerk shall maintain the file until the final disposition of the appeal, unless otherwise ordered by a judge.

(2) The lower court or the appellate court or a single justice thereof may order the record to be assembled, and the appellate court or a single justice thereof may order the appeal to be docketed, at any time.

(b) **Exhibits.** The lower court shall make such orders as it deems necessary for the preservation of exhibits, and shall not transmit any exhibit to the appellate court unless pursuant to an order of the appellate court or a justice thereof. The parties may reproduce exhibits for inclusion in the record appendix insofar as necessary to their appeal, pursuant to Rule 18.

(c) **Impounded materials.** When an appeal has been taken in a case in which material has been impounded, the clerk of the lower court shall provide written notification to the appellate court clerk that material was impounded by the lower court when notice of the assembled record is transmitted. Such notification shall specify the materials or portions thereof which were impounded below and shall include a copy of the order of impoundment, if any, or a reference to other authority for the impoundment. Unless otherwise ordered by the appellate court, or otherwise provided in the lower court order of impoundment, material impounded in the lower court shall remain impounded in the appellate courts.

(d) **Appellant's Obligation.**

(1) *In General.* In a civil or criminal case, upon request by the clerk of the lower court, a party shall forthwith perform any act reasonably necessary to enable the clerk to assemble the record.

(2) *Civil Cases.* Notwithstanding any other obligation which these rules may impose, but excepting electronically recorded proceedings governed by Rule 8(b)(1), each appellant in a civil case shall, within 14 days after filing a notice of appeal, deliver to the clerk of the lower court either

(A) a transcript or those portions of the transcript of the lower court proceedings which the appellant deems necessary for determination of the appeal,

(B) a signed statement certifying that the appellant has ordered such portions, or

(C) a signed statement certifying that the appellant has not ordered and does not intend to order the transcript or any portion thereof.

(3) *Denial of Motion for Post–Conviction Relief in a Criminal Case.* Excepting an appellant in a criminal case in which the defendant was convicted of murder in the first degree, and notwithstanding any other obligation these rules may impose, after the direct appeal, each appellant in a criminal case in which the appeal concerns the denial of a motion for post-conviction relief shall, within 14 days after filing a notice of appeal, deliver to the clerk of the lower court an electronically formatted transcript of the lower court proceedings related to the appellant's underlying conviction or a statement that such a transcript may not be obtained with due diligence, is not relevant, or has been ordered and not yet produced. In lieu of a copy of the transcript, the appellant may file with the clerk of the lower court a certification that a copy of the transcript is available in the appellate court. The certification shall include the appellate court docket number of the case in which the transcript is available. The clerk of the lower court shall transmit the transcript of the lower court proceedings or the certification to the appellate court when notice of the assembled record is transmitted.

(e) **Duty of Clerk; Transmission.**

(1) Unless otherwise ordered by the lower court or the appellate court or a single justice thereof pursuant to Rule 9(a)(2), the clerk of the lower court shall complete the assembly of the record and transmit notice of the assembled record to the parties and the clerk of the appellate court either:

(A) within 21 days from the later of

(i) the clerk's receipt of the transcript of proceedings, if any, in the lower court; or

(ii) the clerk's receipt of notice from the appellant that no transcript will be ordered; or

(iii) the expiration of the time for filing any other notice of appeal after the filing of a first notice of appeal pursuant to Rule 4(a); or

(B) if the parties notify the clerk of their intent to file an agreed statement as to the record on appeal pursuant to

Rule 8(d), within 21 days of the lower court's approval of the statement.

(2) The notice of assembly transmitted to the appellate court shall be accompanied by the following:

(A) a completed appellate court entry statement;

(B) a copy of the notice of assembly issued to the parties;

(C) a copy of the notice(s) of appeal;

(D) a copy of the docket entries;

(E) the written notification regarding impounded materials as required by Rule 9(c);

(F) a list of all the exhibits; and,

(G) in criminal cases, any electronically formatted transcript, if a transcript is necessary for the appeal.

(3) In case of an order to transmit, transmission shall be effected when the clerk of the lower court mails or otherwise forwards a copy of the notice of assembly and other information as required in this rule to the clerk of the appellate court.

(4) The clerk of the lower court shall indicate, by endorsement on the face of the notice of assembly, the date upon which it is transmitted to the appellate court.

Amended May 15, 1979, effective July 1, 1979; amended effective May 1, 1994; June 26, 2002, effective September 3, 2002; October 31, 2018, effective March 1, 2019.

Reporter's Notes—1973

Appellate Rule 9, changing federal practice (which requires transmission of the entire record in all cases, see F.R.A.P. 11) responds to the Massachusetts practice of not sending the actual original papers to the appellate court. The rule, however, recognizes that occasionally it may be essential for such papers to be transmitted, and thus requires the clerk to assemble all the original papers in a case, including a transcript if any, and hold them, subject to an order by the appellate court to transmit the record to that court. The appellant must take whatever action is necessary to assure assembly; failure to do so jeopardizes the appeal, see Appellate Rule 10(c).

Reporter's Notes—1979

Subdivision (a) of Rule 9, as made applicable to criminal cases, supersedes the provisions of former G.L. c. 278, § 33C (St.1974, c. 458, § 1) relative to the preparation of the record.

Subdivision (b), relative to exhibits, is amended by the addition of a sentence which restates the substance of the first sentence of former Appeals Court Rule 1:06(3) (1975: 3 Mass.App.Ct. 802) and Supreme Judicial Court Rule 1:06(3) (1975: 366 Mass. 858–59). Subdivision (b) was previously incorporated into criminal appellate procedure by Appeals Court and Supreme Judicial Court Rules 1:06(1) (1975: 3 Mass.App.Ct. 802; 366 Mass. 858), except that "record appendix" in the appellate rule was taken to mean "record" in the context of a criminal appeal. This provision, which states that certain risk-associated exhibits are not to be transmitted to the appellate court absent an order, is applicable in civil as well as criminal cases.

Subdivision (c) is amended by limiting the forty-day time for appellants' assistance in assembly of the record to civil cases, and by requiring the appellant in a criminal case to forthwith perform any act reasonably necessary to enable the clerk to assemble the record. The provision for delivery to the clerk of the necessary parts of the transcript for inclusion in the record in civil cases is inapplicable to criminal cases since the clerk orders the transcript, makes and distributes the required copies to the parties and transmits the original and a copy to the appellate court, (Rule 8[b][2]). The entire transcript is included unless the parties stipulate otherwise (Id.).

The requirement of subdivision (d) that the clerk of the lower court transmit two copies of the docket entries to the appellate court in a criminal case conforms to procedure under former Appeals Court and Supreme Judicial Court Rules 1:09 (1975: 3 Mass.App.Ct. 802; 366 Mass. 859). Subdivision (d) additionally provides that the original and one copy of the transcript (see Rule 8[b][2]) and a list of all the exhibits (see former Appeals Court and Supreme Judicial Court Rules 1:06[3], supra) shall be transmitted with the record.

Reporter's Notes—1986

This rule [subdivision (b) of Rule 9], inter alia, requires the clerk of the lower court to "transmit any exhibit to the appellate court at the request of any party made at any time after the filing of the record appendix." It is important to realize, however, that the transmittal of such exhibits does not automatically permit lawyers to refer to them. Rule 18(a) states that ". . . the court may decline to permit the parties to refer to portions of the record omitted from the appendix, unless leave be granted prior to argument." *See* Iverson v. Board of Appeals of Dedham, 14 Mass.App.Ct. 951 (1982).

Reporter's Notes—1994

At several places in this Rule, and in Rule 8, the word "record" or the words "record on appeal" are used. It is critical that litigants realize that there is a profound difference between the "record" and the "appendix". The record is what the lower clerk assembles and retains "until the final disposition of the appeal, except as the record or any part of it is ordered to be transmitted by the appellate court or a single justice." Mass.R.A.P. 9(a). The appendix is what the appellant must file in accordance with Mass.R.A.P. 18. A 1993 amendment to Mass.R.A.P. 18, which was made to reflect the language of Shawmut Community Bank, N.A. v. Zagami, 411 Mass. 807, 810–812 (1992), emphasizes "the responsibility of the parties to include materials necessary to their appeal, including exhibits, in the appendix."

It is important to realize that when Mass.R.A.P. 9(b) says that "[n]o exhibit need be reproduced for the record, except by order of an appellate court, a single justice, or the judge of the lower court," it is talking about "the record" and not "the appendix". The fact that the rule goes on to say that "[a]ny counsel may reproduce any exhibit in several copies for the convenience of the court," also does not relieve the parties of their obligation to put copies of exhibits they rely upon in the appendix in accordance with Mass.R.A.P. 18.

Reporter's Notes to Mass.R.A.P. 9(c)(2)—1994

There has been an ambiguity in Mass.R.A.P. 9(c)(2) in those cases in which there has been an electronically recorded proceeding in trial court. Rule 9(c)(2) calls for the appellant, within forty days after filing the notice of appeal, to deliver to the clerk of the trial court either portions of the transcript or a signed statement certifying that the appellant has ordered such portions from the court reporter. Rule 8(b)(3), covering electronically recorded proceedings, has distinct provisions for obtaining a transcript which do not mesh perfectly with Rule 9(c)(2). For instance, as the dissent of Justice O'Connor (with whom Wilkins and Greaney, JJ. joined) explained in Russell v. McOwen-Hanelt, 413 Mass. 106, 114 (1992), the appellant in that case had a minimum of fifty-six days to order transcription of the cassette, so that the forty day notice provision in Rule 9(c)(2) did not fit. Nonetheless, in that case, the majority, relying on Hawkins v. Hawkins, 397 Mass. 401, 406 (1986), read Rule 9(c) to require the appellant in appeals from electronically recorded proceedings " 'to deliver either a transcript or a signed statement certifying that the tapes [are] being transcribed, to the clerk or register's office, [no later than] forty days after [the] appeal was filed.' " Russell v. McOwen-Hanelt, at 109.

The Standing Advisory Committee believes that Rule 9(c)(2) should be clarified so that henceforth it does not apply to electronically recorded proceedings. There are special problems when a tape recorder rather than a stenographer has been used to record a trial. For instance, an appellant must order and receive the cassette from the lower court before the designation process can begin and a person or firm must be selected to prepare the transcript. Consequently, the requirements in Rule 8(b)(3) are different from those in Rule 9(c)(2). This amendment resolves the previous ambiguity by creating an exception from the requirements of Rule 9(c)(2) where there has been an electronically recorded proceeding covered by Rule 8(b)(3). This amendment renders inapplicable the contrary holding in Russell v. McOwen-Hanelt, 413 Mass. 106 (1992) and Hawkins v. Hawkins, 397 Mass. 401 (1986).

Reporter's Notes to Appellate Rule 9(c)(2)—2002

Rule 9(c)(2) was amended in 2002 to reduce the time period after the filing of a notice of appeal from 40 to ten days in which the appellant in a civil case must deliver to the clerk of the lower court either the transcript or a certification that the appellant has ordered the transcript from the court reporter.

This amendment serves to bring Rule 9(c)(2) in line with the requirement of Rule 8(b)(1) that the appellant must order the transcript within ten days of filing the notice of appeal.

A further change was made in the first sentence of Rule 9(c)(2). Prior to the 2002 amendment, that sentence required the appellant to provide to the clerk of the lower court either (1) a transcript of the proceedings which the appellant deems necessary or (2) a statement that the appellant has ordered such transcript. A third option, (iii), has been added for cases where the appellant is not ordering the transcript (or any portion thereof). The appellant, by certifying that no transcript has been ordered and that the appellant does not intend to order the transcript, will thereby put the appellee on notice that the appellee must, if a transcript is desired, take steps to order the transcript. See Rule 8(b)(1).

Reporter's Notes—2019

Rule 9. The title of Rule 9 was revised from "Assembly and Transmission of the Record: Exhibits" to "Assembly of the Record; Reproduction of Exhibits; Notice of Assembly; and Transmission of Documents from the Lower Court." The revised title more accurately describes the processes encompassed in the rule.

Rule 9(a) was divided into two paragraphs and the contents substantially revised. Rule 9(a)(1) is concerned with the lower court clerk's duty of reviewing the file and confirming the accuracy of the docket entries. Archaic language regarding spindling, binding, and tying papers in preparation for the appeal was deleted.

Rule 9(a)(2). The content of the second sentence of prior Rule 9(c)(1) was relocated to Rule 9(a)(2) because Rule 9(a) relates to the authority of the appellate court or a single justice to order a record assembled or appeal docketed. The remainder of prior Rule 9(c)(1) was designated Rule 9(d)(1) in the amended rules, and relates to the appellant's obligations.

Rule 9(b). The significant revisions to Rule 9(b) simplify the requirements regarding trial court exhibits and clarify the distinction between the record and the appendix. The amendments clarify that exhibits are not transmitted to the appellate court with the notice of assembly from the lower court, but remain in the lower court, and that parties can, and must, reproduce exhibits in their appendices when pertinent to the issues raised on appeal. See Rule 18(a)(1)(A), (D), and (F).

Rule 9(c) is a new subdivision requiring the clerk of the lower court to notify the clerk of the appellate court that information in the record was impounded by the lower court. The language of Rule 9(c) follows the requirements in S.J.C. Rule 1:15, §§ 2(a) and (b). This subdivision was added to ensure that the Rules are consistent with S.J.C. Rule 1:15 and current appellate court practices, and that impounded information is not inadvertently made available. It also clarifies for the lower court clerk that an affirmative notice to the appellate court clerk as to impounded information is required at the time of transmission of the notice of assembly of the record to the appellate court. See S.J.C. Rule 1:15, § 2(a).

Rule 9(d)(3) is a new paragraph. Except in an appeal from a conviction of murder in the first degree, the new paragraph requires the appellant in a criminal case concerning the denial of a motion for post-conviction relief to deliver to the clerk of the lower court a copy, in electronic form, of the transcript of the lower court proceedings related to the appellant's underlying conviction. Alternatively, in an appropriate case, the appellant may file a statement that the transcript may not be obtained by due diligence, is not relevant, has been ordered and not yet produced, or may file a certification that the transcript is already available in the appellate court, such as from the defendant's prior direct appeal. When transmitting the notice of assembly to the appellate court, the clerk of the lower court is required to transmit the transcript or certification. This paragraph was added to facilitate consideration of the appeal by the appellate court because the lower court's assembly of the record on appeal from a motion for post-conviction relief does not include the transcript of the underlying trial, which the appellate court needs to determine the subsequent appeal.

Rule 9(e), prior Rule 9(d), was divided into two paragraphs. Rule 9(e)(1) establishes a timeframe for the lower court clerk to assemble the record, and Rule 9(e)(2) denominates the items that the clerk is to include with the notice of assembly transmitted to the appellate court clerk. Rule 9(e)(1) includes a new provision requiring the clerk of the lower court to complete assembly of the record within 21 days of the last of the clerk's (1) receipt of the transcript, (2) receipt of notice from the appellant that no transcript will be ordered, (3) the expiration of the time for filing any other notice of appeal after the filing of the first notice of appeal, or (4) approval of an agreed statement of the record. In the common situation where multiple days of transcript have been ordered, the clerk will not assemble the record until all transcript volumes have been received. This amendment is intended to prevent delay in completion of the assembly of the record.

Rule 9(e)(2) identifies the documents that must be transmitted by the lower court clerk to the appellate court with the notice of assembly. The documents include a completed appellate court entry statement, a copy of the notice of assembly sent to the parties, a copy of the notice(s) of appeal, any notice of impounded information, and an exhibit list. The requirement that two "certified" copies of the docket entries be transmitted was reduced to one copy, which need not be certified. Removing the requirement that the lower court docket be certified recognizes that it can be presumed that the docket is authentic because it is transmitted directly from the lower court, facilitates transmission of the notice of assembly and accompanying documents to the appellate court, and is consistent with the requirements in Rule 18 (the copy of the docket included in the appendix need not be certified). Moreover, any incorrect docket entry transmitted to the appellate court can be corrected pursuant to the procedures in Rule 8(e). Removing this requirement eliminates the need for manual certification of the docket which consumes the time and effort of lower court personnel. In criminal cases, the prior requirement that an original and one copy of the transcript be transmitted was revised to a single electronically-formatted transcript. These amendments reflect current practice regarding the information required by the appellate courts from the lower court for entry of an appeal.

Prior Rule 9(e), titled "Record for Preliminary Hearing in the Appellate Court," was deleted because other rules currently provide processes for parties to obtain the relief that had been provided for in that rule. See Rules 2, 6, and 15.

Further organizational and stylistic revisions were made to this rule in 2019 in accordance with a global review and revision of all of the Appellate Rules. These revisions are described in the 2019 Reporter's Notes to Rule 1.

With regard to the preparation of the 2019 Reporter's Notes to this Rule, see the first paragraph of the 2019 Reporter's Notes to Rule 1. For an overview of the 2019 amendments to the Rules and a summary of the global amendments to the Rules, see 2019 Reporter's Notes to Rule 1, sections *I.* and *II.*

Rule 10. Docketing the Appeal

(a) Docketing the Appeal.

(1) *Civil Cases.*

(A) Within 14 days after receiving from the clerk of the lower court the notice of assembly of the record, each appellant, including each cross-appellant and each appellant in a joint appeal, shall pay to the clerk of the appellate court the docket fee required by law or request waiver of the fee, and the clerk shall thereupon enter the appeal of such appellant or cross-appellant upon the docket. If an appellant is authorized to prosecute the appeal without payment of fees, the clerk shall enter the appeal upon the docket at the written request of a party.

(B) When payment or request for waiver is made by first class mail or its equivalent, it shall be deemed timely if accompanied by a certificate attesting that the day of mailing was within 14 days of receipt of the notice of assembly.

(2) *Criminal Cases.* Upon receipt of the notice of assembly of the record, pursuant to Rule 9(e), the clerk of the appellate court shall enter the appeal upon the docket.

(3) *In General.* Upon docketing of the appeal, the clerk shall serve written notice thereof upon each party and the clerk of the lower court. Upon motion, the lower court or a single justice of the appellate court may, for cause shown, enlarge the time for docketing the appeal or permit the appeal to be docketed out of time. An appeal shall be docketed under the title given to the action in the lower court, with the appellant identified as such, but if such title does not contain the name of the appellant, then the party's name, unless permitted to proceed under a pseudonym, identified as appellant, shall be added to the title.

(4) *Certain Constitutional Claims.* Within 14 days after the docketing of any civil appeal that draws into question the constitutionality of an act of the legislature, if neither the Commonwealth nor an officer, agency, or employee thereof is a party to the appeal, the party asserting the unconstitutionality of the act shall notify the attorney general of such challenge. If such a question becomes apparent to a party after the 14-day period has expired, the party shall immediately notify the attorney general. Such notice shall be given either in writing or by use of any electronic method the attorney general may designate for this purpose.

(5) *Consolidated Appeals.* Appeals may be consolidated by order of the appellate court upon its own motion or upon motion of a party, on such terms as the court may order.

(6) *Joint Appeal.* Upon entry of an appeal pursuant to Rule 10(a)(1) or 10(a)(2), parties who have filed a joint notice of appeal shall proceed on appeal as a single appellant, unless upon motion the appellate court grants leave to proceed separately.

(7) *Cross Appeals.* If a cross appeal is filed, the party who files a notice of appeal first is the appellant for the purposes of these Rules. If notices are filed on the same day, the plaintiff in the proceeding below is the appellant. These designations may be modified by the parties' agreement, filed with the appellate court, or by court order.

(b) Filing.

The clerk of the appellate court shall file upon receipt any part of the record or any document authorized to be filed in lieu of the record under any provision of Rule 9, following timely docketing of the appeal. The clerk shall immediately give notice to all parties of the date of each such filing.

(c) Dismissal for Failure of Appellant in a Civil Case to Comply With Rule 9(d) or Rule 10(a).

If any appellant in a civil case shall fail to comply with Rule 9(d) or Rule 10(a)(1), the lower court may, on motion with notice by any appellee, dismiss the appeal, but only upon a finding of inexcusable neglect; otherwise, the court shall enlarge the appellant's time for taking the required action. If, prior to the lower court's hearing such motion for noncompliance with Rule 9(d), the appellant shall have cured the noncompliance, the appellant's compliance shall be deemed timely.

(d) Withdrawal of Counsel.

In all cases, any counsel who does not intend to continue representing a client on appeal, for any reason, should file a motion to withdraw his or her appearance in the lower court as soon as is practicable. After an appeal has been docketed in an appellate court, any motion to withdraw appearance of counsel shall be filed with the appellate court. The motion shall include a certificate of service in compliance with Rule 13, which shows service upon all parties to the appeal, including those represented by counsel filing the motion, at the party's or parties' last known address.

Amended June 27, 1974, effective July 1, 1974; amended effective February 24, 1975; amended May 15, 1979, effective July 1, 1979; amended effective May 1, 1994; amended July 28, 1999, effective September 1, 1999; amended September 6, effective October 1, 2001; October 31, 2018, effective March 1, 2019.

Reporter's Notes—1973

Appellate Rule 10 covers the mechanics of docketing the appeal in the appellate court.

Reporter's Notes—1975

The amendment requires the clerk to give written notice of the docketing to counsel for each party (or to each unrepresented party directly). This ensures that all parties receive notice of the docketing date, which is the starting point for various periods under the Rules; see, e.g. Appellate Rules 11, 11.1, and 19.

In Appellate Rule 10(c) substitution of "Rule 9(c)" for "Rule 9(b)" merely corrects a previous typographical error.

Reporter's Notes—1979

The substance of former subdivision (a) has been divided into subdivisions (a)(1), applicable to civil cases, and (a)(3), applicable to both civil and criminal cases.

Subdivision (a)(2), which provides for the automatic docketing of an appeal in a criminal case upon receipt by the clerk of the appellate court of notice of assembly of the record or approval of an agreed statement, is added.

The provision of a subdivision (a)(3) for notice to the parties of the docketing of a criminal appeal conforms to prior practice under former Appeals Court Rule 1:11 (1975: 3 Mass.App.Ct. 803) and Supreme Judicial Court Rule 1:11 (1975: 366 Mass. 860).

Since in a criminal appeal the appellant is responsible neither for initiating assembly of the record (see Rules 8[b][2], 9[c]) nor for taking any step to docket the appeal ([a][2], supra), subdivision (c) is limited in application to civil cases.

Reporter's Notes to Mass.R.A.P. 10(c)—1994

This amendment eliminates noncompliance with Mass.R.A.P. 10(a)(1) (the appellant's obligation to pay the docket fee within the ten day period described in Mass.R.A.P. 10(a)(1)) from the instances of noncompliance that can be cured prior to a hearing on a motion to dismiss for noncompliance. Noncompliance with Rule 9(c) (appellant's obligations re: assembly of the record and transmission of the transcript) can still be cured prior to a hearing for dismissal based on such noncompliance.

Many lawyers and pro se litigants relied on the previous version of the last sentence of Mass.R.A.P. 10(c) as their rationale for paying the filing fee only after there had been a motion to dismiss and before the lower court's hearing of such a motion, even though Mass.R.A.P. 10(a)(1) specifically required the payment "[w]ithin ten days after receiving from the clerk of the lower court notice of assembly of the record, or of approval by the lower court of an agreed statement ..." Although the last sentence of Rule 10(c) seemed to permit such late payment as a matter of right, the practice in the Appeals Court was to refuse to accept a docket fee sent by the appellant subsequent to the ten day period described in Rule 10(a)(1) even if it was paid before a hearing described in Rule 10(c). The appellant who attempted to file the fee late was told that he or she must be successful on a motion to docket late in order for the Appeals Court to accept the payment, and that this motion would not ordinarily be entertained by the single justice while a motion to dismiss was pending in the trial court.

The prior wording of the last sentence of Rule 10(c) was therefore misleading to appellants who thought they had a right to pay the fee after the ten day period but before the hearing on a motion to dismiss; moreover, the practice of the Appeals Court may have been in disregard of the clear language of the same sentence. It does not make sense to have a ten day period in which to pay a filing fee which is widely ignored. Consequently, this amendment removes the excuse and automatic permission to pay the fee late and also makes the Rule in accord with the practice of the Appeals Court. This amendment in no way eliminates or alters the right of an indigent pro se litigant to obtain a waiver of the obligation to pay the filing fee.

Reporter's Notes—1999

The 1999 amendments to Appellate Rule 10(a) were part of a comprehensive set of amendments to the Appellate Rules (Rules 1, 3, 4, 8, and 10) that had been proposed by the Supreme Judicial Court Committee on Appeals of Child Welfare Cases. The purpose of the 1999 amendments is described in the 1999 Reporter's Notes to Appellate Rule 1(c).

Prior to the 1999 amendment, Appellate Rule 10(a)(3) required that upon the docketing of the appeal in the appellate court, the clerk serve written notice of the docketing upon each party. The 1999 amendment requires that the clerk of the appellate court also serve written notice on the clerk of the lower court whose decision is subject to the appeal.

It is significant to note that although the 1999 amendments were part of a package of amendments that related to child welfare appeals, the amendment to Appellate Rule 10(a)(3) applies not only to child welfare appeals, but all other appeals as well.

Reporter's Notes to Appellate Rule 10(a)(1)—2001

Prior to amendment in 2001, the first sentence of Appellate Rule 10(a)(1) provided that "the appellant" was to pay the docket fee to the clerk of the appellate court within ten days after receipt of notice of the assembly of the record or approval of an agreed statement. Where there have been multiple appellants or cross-appeals, the appellate clerks have required each appellant or cross-appellant to pay a separate docket fee. The 2001 amendment makes clear that separate docket fees are required.

Reporter's Notes—2019

Rule 10(a)(1)(A) contains the entirety of prior Rule 10(a)(1) and was amended to expand the time period to docket the appeal from 10 to 14 days. The subparagraph was also amended to specify that when the lower court has authorized the appellant to proceed on appeal without payment of fees, the docketing of the appeal in the appellate court will proceed upon the "written request" of the appellant. This amendment clarifies that verbal requests to docket the appeal are not permitted.

Rule 10(a)(1)(B) is a new subparagraph which provides that the payment or request for waiver of the docket fee is timely if accompanied by a certificate attesting that the day of its mailing was within 14 days of the appealing party's receipt of the lower court's notice of assembly of the record.

Rule 10(a)(2), concerning the automatic docketing of criminal appeals in the appellate court, was revised to delete the clause in the prior rule authorizing docketing upon approval by the lower court of an agreed statement pursuant to Rule 8(d). This amendment is necessary because, even in Rule 8(d) situations, a notice of assembly should issue. Related revisions to Rule 9(e) also clarify that the notice of assembly should issue in this circumstance and provides a time-frame within which the notice should issue.

Rule 10(a)(3) contains new language to provide that an appellate court clerk should not add a party's name to the title of an appeal if that party has been permitted to proceed under a pseudonym.

Rule 10(a)(4) is a new paragraph added to provide notice to the Office of the Attorney General of constitutional challenges to acts of the legislature. The paragraph is modelled after existing Mass. R. Civ. P. 24(d) and Fed. R. Civ. P. 44(b), with minor changes to specify the timing and manner of notice.

Rule 10(a)(5) is a new paragraph that addresses consolidated appeals. The substance of this paragraph was moved from prior Rule 3(b). Rule 3 prescribes how an appeal is taken, and relates to actions the appealing party must take in the lower court to initiate an appeal. In contrast, Rule 10 is concerned with docketing an appeal and consolidation happens at the time of, or after, the docketing of the appeal in the appellate court. Relocating the paragraph from Rule 3(b) to Rule 10(a) presents it in a more appropriate context.

Rule 10(a)(6) is a new paragraph that addresses joint appeals. Pursuant to prior Rule 3(b), parties with similar interests could file a joint notice of appeal in the lower court or could join in an appeal after filing separate notices of appeal and then proceed on appeal as a single appellant, but still needed to enter their cases separately in the appellate court. This caused confusion for parties who sought to pay one docketing fee on behalf of all parties who have joined in an appeal. Rule 10(a)(6) clarifies that, when an appeal is docketed in the appellate court and the parties file a joint notice of appeal, they shall automatically proceed as a single appellant without leave of court. If the parties' interests are aligned, judicial economy and efficiency are advanced by having them proceed in the appellate court as a single appellant.

Rule 10(a)(7) is a new paragraph that encompasses the content of the first sentence in prior Rule 16(j), which concerned the designation of parties to a cross-appeal. Moving this provision to Rule 10(a)(7) clarifies for the parties at the outset of the appeal which party is the appellant and which is the appellee. In addition to relocating the provision, the designation of the parties was revised to deem the party filing the first notice of appeal as the appellant, absent agreement or court order otherwise, consistent with Fed. R. App. P. 28.1(b).

Rule 10(c) applies to an appellant's compliance with Rules 9(d) and 10(a). The reference to Rule 10(a)(3) was removed from the first sentence of this subdivision because Rule 10(a)(3) applies to clerks, not appellants.

Rule 10(d) is a new subdivision added to resolve confusion on the part of attorneys who have appeared in the lower court but seek to withdraw from representation for purposes of an appeal. Adding this subdivision clarifies that, after an appeal is docketed in the appellate court, a motion to withdraw must be filed in the appellate court, not the lower court. This will reduce confusion as to which court the motion should be filed in after an appellate court has jurisdiction of a case.

Further organizational and stylistic revisions were made to this rule in 2019 in accordance with a global review and revision of all of the Appellate Rules. These revisions are described in the 2019 Reporter's Notes to Rule 1.

With regard to the preparation of the 2019 Reporter's Notes to this Rule, see the first paragraph of the 2019 Reporter's Notes to Rule 1. For an overview of the 2019 amendments to the Rules and a summary of the global amendments to the Rules, see 2019 Reporter's Notes to Rule 1, sections *I.* and *II.*

Rule 11. Direct Appellate Review

(a) Application; When Filed; Grounds. An appeal within the concurrent appellate jurisdiction of the Appeals Court and Supreme Judicial Court shall be docketed in the Appeals Court before a party may apply to the Supreme Judicial Court for direct appellate review. Within 21 days after the docketing of an appeal in the Appeals Court, any party to the case (or 2 or more parties jointly) may apply in writing to the Supreme Judicial Court for direct appellate review, provided the questions presented by the appeal are (1) questions of first impression or novel questions of law which should be submitted for final determination to the Supreme Judicial Court; (2) questions of law concerning the Constitution of the Commonwealth or questions concerning the Constitution of the United States which have been raised in a court of the Commonwealth; or (3) questions of such public interest that justice requires a final determination by the full Supreme Judicial Court.

(b) Contents of Application; Form. The application for direct appellate review shall contain, in the following order: (1) a request for direct appellate review; (2) a statement of prior proceedings in the case; (3) a short statement of facts relevant to the appeal; (4) a statement of the issues of law raised by the appeal, together with a statement indicating whether the issues were raised and properly preserved in the lower court; (5) a brief argument thereon (consisting of not more than either 10 pages of text in monospaced font or 2,000 words in proportional font, as defined in Rule 20(a)(4)(B)) including appropriate authorities, in support of the applicant's position on such issues; and (6) a statement of reasons why direct appellate review is appropriate. A copy of the docket entries shall be appended to the application. The applicant shall also append a copy of any written decision, memorandum, findings, rulings, or report of the lower court relevant to the appeal. The application shall comply with the requirements of Rule 20(a), and shall contain a certification of such compliance, including a statement of how compliance with the foregoing length limit was ascertained, as specified in Rule 16(k).

(c) Response; Form. Within 14 days after the filing of the application, any other party to the case may, but need not, file and serve a response thereto (consisting of not more than either 10 pages of text in monospace font or 2,000 words in proportional font, as defined in Rule 20(a)(4)(B)) setting forth reasons why the application should or should not be granted. The response shall not restate matters described in Rule 11(b)(2) and (3) unless the party is dissatisfied with the statement thereof contained in the application. The response shall comply with the requirements of Rule 20(a), and shall contain a certification of such compliance, including a state-

ment of how compliance with the foregoing length limit was ascertained, as specified in Rule 16(k). A response may be filed in a different form as permitted by the court.

(d) Filing; Service. One copy of the application and of each response shall be filed in the office of the clerk of the full Supreme Judicial Court. Filing and service of the application and of any response shall comply with Rule 13.

(e) Effect of Application Upon Appeal. The filing of an application for direct appellate review shall not extend the time for filing briefs or doing any other act required to be done under these rules.

(f) Vote of Direct Appellate Review; Certification. If any 2 justices of the Supreme Judicial Court vote for direct appellate review, or if a majority of the justices of the Appeals Court shall certify that direct appellate review is in the public interest, an order allowing the application (or transferring the appeal sua sponte) or the certificate, as the case may be, shall be transmitted to the clerk of the Appeals Court with notice to the lower court. The clerk of the Appeals Court shall forthwith transmit to the clerk of the full Supreme Judicial Court all documents filed in the case.

(g) Cases Transferred for Direct Review; Time for Serving and Filing Briefs. In any appeal transferred to the full Supreme Judicial Court from the Appeals Court:

(1) If at the time of transfer all parties have served and filed briefs in the Appeals Court, no further briefs may be filed by the parties except that a reply brief may be served and filed on or before the last date allowable had the case not been transferred, or within 14 days after the date on which the appeal is docketed in the full Supreme Judicial Court, whichever is later.

(2) If at the time of transfer only the appellant's brief has been served and filed in the Appeals Court the appellant may, but need not, serve and file an amended brief within 21 days after the date on which the appeal is docketed in the full Supreme Judicial Court. The appellee shall serve and file a brief within 30 days after service of any amended brief of the appellant, or within 50 days after the date on which the appeal is docketed in the full Supreme Judicial Court, whichever is later.

(3) Service and filing of a reply brief shall comply with Rule 19.

(4) If at the time of transfer to the full Supreme Judicial Court no party to the appeal has served or filed a brief, the appellant shall serve and file a brief within 21 days after the date on which the appeal is docketed in the full Supreme Judicial Court or within 40 days after the date on which the appeal was docketed in the Appeals Court, whichever is later.

Amended May 15, 1979, effective July 1, 1979; amended effective July 1, 1991; April 14, 1995; January 29, 1996; amended October 30, 1997, effective January 1, 1998; June 26, 2002, effective September 3, 2002; October 31, 2018, effective March 1, 2019.

Reporter's Notes—1973

Appellate Rule 11 implements the statutorily-authorized direct review by the Supreme Judicial Court of cases which would otherwise first be heard and determined in the Appeals Court; G.L. c. 211A, § 10. (For procedure subsequent to an Appeals Court decision, see Appellate Rule 27.1). Direct review may result if: (1) The Supreme

Judicial Court (or two justices thereof) shall so order, either (a) sua sponte, or (b) on application of one or more parties; or (2) The Appeals Court (or a majority of the justices thereof) shall certify that direct review is in the public interest.

The rule deals with the mechanics of application for direct review, and also prescribes the procedure governing cases accorded direct review, no matter what the means which caused such review (order by the Supreme Judicial Court ex mero motu, order on application, or certification by the Appeals Court).

Of the routes to direct review, only one—Supreme Judicial Court order after application—ought appropriately to be governed by the Appellate Rules. The other two, self-initiated exercises of judicial discretion and administration, are intracourt matters not subject to procedural regulation.

What Appellate Rule 11(a)–(d) accomplishes, therefore, is to assure appellate parties the right to put the matter before the Supreme Judicial Court and to urge direct review; the rule leaves all other means by which review may be granted out of the parties' control entirely, and completely in the dispositive power of the respective courts.

The application for direct review proceeds parallel to the usual requirements, Appellate Rule 11(e). Application does not in any way "stop the clock" with respect to normal appellate procedure. Once review is granted, however, a special timetable controls, Appellate Rule 11(g). In general, any brief already filed in the Appeals Court need not be re-filed in the Supreme Judicial Court; if no party has yet filed, the briefing schedule, proceeding as though the appeal had commenced initially in the Supreme Judicial Court, is controlled by Appellate Rule 19.

Reporter's Notes—1979

Appellate Rule 11 was previously applicable to direct appellate review in criminal cases by virtue of Supreme Judicial Court Rule 3:24, § 4(1) (1975) 366 Mass. 870, (1975) except that the words "the appeal is docketed" were taken to mean "the case is entered." That distinction is no longer viable (see Rule 10([a][2]).

Only two changes are made in the former rule. A new first sentence is added to subdivision (a), which restates the first sentence of Supreme Judicial Court Rule 3:24 supra § 3. Section 3 also provided that:

All matters preliminary to the entry of . . . appeals [within the concurrent appellate jurisdiction of the Appeals and Supreme Judicial Court] which require action by an appellate court shall be presented to and disposed of by the Appeals Court.

That requirement is implicit in Rule 11.

Secondly, the time within which an application for direct appellate review may be filed is increased from ten to twenty days after the docketing of the appeal in the Appeals Court. The remainder of the rule is unchanged.

Reporter's Notes—1996

The 1996 amendment to Mass.R.A.P. 11(f), effective January 29, 1996, is a technical amendment to that portion of the first sentence relating to certification that direct appellate review by the Supreme Judicial Court is in the public interest. The amendment provides for certification by "a majority of the justices of the Appeals Court," replacing earlier language providing for certification by "all of the justices of the Appeals Court or any majority thereof."

Reporter's Notes—1997

The 1997 amendment to Appellate Rule 11(d) increased to seventeen the number of copies of an application for direct appellate review and of each opposition to be filed in the clerk's office of the Supreme Judicial Court. The amendment also clarified that an original is to be filed together with the seventeen copies.

Reporter's Notes—1999

The cover of applications for direct appellate review shall be white. See Appellate Rule 20(b), as amended in 1999.

Reporter's Notes to Appellate Rule 11(b)—2002

In 2002, the Supreme Judicial Court amended Appellate Rule 11(b) to require that an application for direct appellate review contain "a statement indicating whether the issues were raised and properly preserved in the lower court" and that "a copy of any written decision, memorandum, findings, rulings, or report of the lower court relevant to the issues on appeal" be appended to the application. Having a statement regarding whether issues were raised below and a copy of the lower court's decision will serve to benefit the court's determination in considering the application for direct appellate review.

Reporter's Notes—2019

Rule 11(a) was amended to remove the statement that no oral argument will be allowed in support of an application for direct appellate review. Oral argument is not ordinarily permitted under this rule and removing the reference to oral argument is consistent with Supreme Judicial Court practice.

Rule 11(d) was revised to reduce the number of copies of an application or response to an application for direct appellate review that must be filed from "an original and seventeen copies" to 1 copy. Due to advances in paperless practices, the Supreme Judicial Court now only requires 1 copy to properly process and review these documents. The requirement that a copy of the application be filed in the Appeals Court was deleted because the Appeals Court receives automatic notification from the Supreme Judicial Court when an application for direct appellate review is filed.

Rule 11(f) was revised to align the rule with court practices. According to the prior rule, although the Supreme Judicial Court entered and sent notice of an order granting direct appellate review, the order would not actually be "deemed granted" until the Appeals Court received it. The amendments to this rule delete the phrase "upon receipt, direct appellate review shall be deemed granted" to clarify that the order is effective upon its entry. Rule 11(f) was also amended to substitute the Supreme Judicial Court in place of the Appeals Court as the court sending notice to the lower court when direct appellate review is granted.

Rule 11(g)(1) was amended by inserting "by the parties" after "If at the time of transfer all parties have served and filed briefs in the Appeals Court, no further briefs may be filed" to clarify that in cases that are fully briefed prior to transfer, the prohibition against filing additional briefs does not apply to amicus briefs.

Further organizational and stylistic revisions were made to this rule in 2019 in accordance with a global review and revision of all of the Appellate Rules. These revisions are described in the 2019 Reporter's Notes to Rule 1.

With regard to the preparation of the 2019 Reporter's Notes to this Rule, see the first paragraph of the 2019 Reporter's Notes to Rule 1. For an overview of the 2019 amendments to the Rules and a summary of the global amendments to the Rules, see 2019 Reporter's Notes to Rule 1, sections *I.* and *II.*

Rule 11.1. Transfer from Supreme Judicial Court

In the case of a direct appeal to the Supreme Judicial Court, except as to any appeal concerning a conviction of murder in the first degree, within 14 days after the appeal has been docketed, or such further time as a single justice upon motion for cause shown may allow, any party may serve and file a motion to transfer the appeal to the Appeals Court. The motion (a) shall not exceed either 5 pages of text in mono-spaced font or 1,000 words in proportional font, as defined in Rule 20(a)(4)(B); (b) shall succinctly specify the grounds for transfer; and (c) shall conform to Rules 13, 14, 15, and 20(b). Within 7 days after filing of the motion, any other party may serve and file a response to the transfer. The response (a) shall not exceed either 5 pages of text in monospaced font or 1,000 words in proportional font, as defined in Rule 20(a)(4)(B); (b) shall succinctly specify the reasons why transfer should or should not be granted; and (c) shall conform to Rules 13, 14, 15, and 20(b).

Amended October 31, 2018, effective March 1, 2019.

Reporter's Notes—1973

Appeals which have proceeded direct to the Supreme Judicial Court without application of a party, that is, on judicial certification or order, see Appellate Rule 11(f), have by definition not afforded the parties an opportunity to oppose direct review. (Review after application, of course, has resulted from a procedure permitting the party not applying for direct review to oppose it, Appellate Rule 11(c).) Appellate Rule 11.1 permits either party to an appeal which has been brought up to the Supreme Judicial Court without application to indicate any reason why the case should be transferred back to the Appeals Court.

Reporter's Notes—2019

Rule 11.1 was revised to add the word count alternative to page limits, explained in the Reporter's Notes to Rule 1. The phrase "except as to any appeal concerning a conviction of murder in the first degree" was added to explicitly exclude those appeals from transfer to the Appeals Court because the Appeals Court does not have concurrent appellate jurisdiction over such appeals. See G. L. c. 278, § 33E and G. L. c. 211A, § 10. Since the Supreme Judicial Court's practice is that oral argument is not ordinarily permitted in connection with a motion to transfer the appeal to the Appeals Court or response to such a motion, reference to such oral argument was deleted.

Further organizational and stylistic revisions were made to this rule in 2019 in accordance with a global review and revision of all of the Appellate Rules. These revisions are described in the 2019 Reporter's Notes to Rule 1.

With regard to the preparation of the 2019 Reporter's Notes to this Rule, see the first paragraph of the 2019 Reporter's Notes to Rule 1. For an overview of the 2019 amendments to the Rules and a summary of the global amendments to the Rules, see 2019 Reporter's Notes to Rule 1, sections *I.* and *II.*

Rule 12.　Proceedings Involving an Indigent Party

(a) Leave to Proceed on Appeal as an Indigent Party from Lower Court to Appellate Court. Either a lower court or the appellate court or a single justice thereof, for cause shown and after reasonable notice, may authorize an appeal to be prosecuted by an indigent party, upon such reasonable terms as such court or justice may prescribe.

(b) Form of Briefs, Appendices, and Other Documents. Parties allowed to proceed as indigent may upon motion and with leave of the appellate court or a single justice thereof, file and serve a reduced number of copies of briefs, appendices, and other documents than otherwise required by these rules.

Amended October 31, 2018, effective March 1, 2019.

Reporter's Notes—1973

Appellate Rule 12 regulates proceedings in forma pauperis, and works no serious change in existing practice. Unlike the cognate F.R.A.P. 24, it allows the justice entertaining the application to proceed in forma pauperis large discretion to tailor the terms of the order to the needs of the case.

Reporter's Notes—2019

References to "in forma pauperis" throughout Rule 12 were changed to "indigent party" consistent with the new definition of "indigent party" in Rule 1(c). See 2019 Reporter's Note to Rule 1(c).

Rule 12(b) was amended to both highlight that a party allowed under Rule 12(a) to proceed as indigent may seek to file a reduced number of copies of briefs, appendices, or other documents, and clarify that leave of court to do so is required. In addition, Rule 12(b) was amended to eliminate the reference to proceeding on the original record without producing an appendix or copies of the record. Proceeding on the original record was similarly stricken from Rule 18(f) and the reasons for the deletion are described in the Reporter's Notes to Rule 18.

Further organizational and stylistic revisions were made to this rule in 2019 in accordance with a global review and revision of all of the Appellate Rules. These revisions are described in the 2019 Reporter's Notes to Rule 1.

With regard to the preparation of the 2019 Reporter's Notes to this Rule, see the first paragraph of the 2019 Reporter's Notes to Rule 1. For an overview of the 2019 amendments to the Rules and a summary of the global amendments to the Rules, see 2019 Reporter's Notes to Rule 1, sections *I.* and *II.*

Rule 13.　Filing and Service

(a) Filing. Documents required or permitted to be filed in the appellate court shall be filed with the clerk.

(1) *Filing Generally.* Except as provided in Rule 13(a)(2), filing may be accomplished in hand, through any electronic means provided by the clerk or by first class mail or its equivalent, addressed to the clerk, but filing shall not be timely unless the documents are received by the clerk within the time fixed for filing, except that briefs and appendices shall be docketed on the date of receipt and shall be deemed timely filed if

　(A) received within the time fixed for filing, or

　(B) when filed by first class mail or its equivalent, they are accompanied by a certificate attesting that the day of mailing was within the time fixed for filing.

If a motion requests relief which may be granted by a single justice, the justice may permit the motion to be filed, in which event the justice shall note thereon the date of filing and shall thereafter transmit it to the clerk.

(2) *Documents Filed by a Self–Represented Party Confined in an Institution.* If an institution has a system designed for legal mail, a self-represented party confined in an institution must use that system to receive the benefit of this rule. A document other than a notice of appeal filed by such party is timely if it is deposited in the institution's internal mail system on or before the last day for filing and is accompanied by a signed certificate in compliance with Rule 13(a)(1)(B) setting out the date of deposit. If the document is not received by the last day for filing, the certificate shall give rise to a presumption of timely filing provided it shows compliance with this rule. Failure to attach the certificate shall not of itself render the document invalid or untimely, and the appellate court may permit the later filing of a certificate. The time period for the opposing party to file any response to the document runs from the date when the appellate court dockets the document.

(b) Service of All Documents Required. Copies of all documents filed by any party shall, at or before the time of filing, be served by a party on all other parties to the appeal or review.

(c) Manner of Service. Service may be personal or by first class mail or its equivalent. Personal service includes delivery of the copy to the party's mailing address. Service by first class mail or its equivalent is complete on mailing. Service may also be completed electronically with the consent of the party being served.

(d) Certificate of Service of All Documents Other than Briefs and Appendices.

(1) *Requirement.* Documents presented for filing, other than a brief or appendix, shall contain a certificate of service. A certificate of service may appear on or be affixed to the document filed. The clerk may permit documents to be filed without a certificate of service but shall require such certificate to be filed promptly thereafter.

(2) *Contents.* A certificate of service shall be in the form of a statement certifying

(A) the date and manner of service;

(B) the name, mailing address, and, if known, electronic address of the person(s) served; and

(C) the printed and signed name, Board of Bar Overseers (BBO) number, if any, mailing and electronic addresses, and telephone number of the person who made service, and if that person is affiliated with a firm or office, the office name.

(e) Certificate of Service of Briefs and Appendices.

(1) *Requirement.* Briefs and appendices presented for filing shall be accompanied by a certificate of service. The certificate of service shall appear as a part of the brief being filed as required in Rule 16(a)(15).

(2) *Contents.* The certificate of service shall be in the form of a certification that includes

(A) the name of the court and the number of the case;

(B) the title of the case;

(C) the title of the brief;

(D) the party on whose behalf service was made;

(E) the printed and signed name, Board of Bar Overseers (BBO) number, if any, mailing and electronic addresses, and telephone number of the person who made service, and, if that person is affiliated with a firm or office, the office name;

(F) the name and mailing address and, if known, electronic address of the person(s) served; and

(G) the date and manner of service.

Amended October 23, 1989, effective January 1, 1990; October 31, 2018, effective March 1, 2019.

Reporter's Notes—1973

Appellate Rule 13 governs filing and service requirements. Papers may be filed by mail; they must be actually received by the clerk within the filing deadline, except that briefs and appendices are regarded as having been filed upon mailing so long as the most expeditious form of mailing is utilized; special delivery need not be used. Service as between parties is, if accomplished by first class mail, complete upon mailing. Personal service may be made to a responsible person in the office of counsel for the recipient.

Reporter's Notes—1989

Mass.R.A.P. 31(b) requires that "[a]ll papers filed with the clerk . . . shall be entered chronologically in the docket . . ." But prior to this amendment, Mass.R.A.P. 13(a) stated that "briefs and appendices shall be deemed filed on the day of mailing if the most expeditious form of delivery by mail, excepting special delivery, is used." This clash in language has caused some problems for clerks, including additional clerical time spent modifying computerized dockets. The amended rule requires briefs and appendices be docketed on the date of receipt, but by utilizing affidavits by counsel, continues to permit counsel to mail within the time fixed for filing, even if receipt at the clerk's office is subsequent thereto. Consequently, there will no longer be a need for asterisks or other special notations on the dockets.

Reporter's Notes—2019

Rule 13(a)(1), prior Rule 13(a), was amended to incorporate modern means of service. A party may file either in hand, through any electronic means provided by the clerk, or by first class mail or its equivalent. The phrase "any electronic means provided by the clerk" includes any electronic filing system offered by the clerk. The phrase "first class mail or its equivalent" is new and defined in Rule 1(c). Rule 13(a)(1) was also amended to simplify the provision allowing a party to mail a brief to the appellate court on the day it is due and have the clerk deem it timely filed even when received after the due date. Instead of the past requirement of an affidavit attesting that the day of mailing of a brief was within the time fixed for filing, the new provision permits a certificate attesting the date is within the time. This certificate will provide the appellate court clerk with sufficient information to determine the date of mailing.

Rule 13(a)(2) is a new paragraph that incorporates the so-called "inmate mailbox rule" into the appellate rules and governs an incarcerated or civilly committed person's filing of briefs, motions, and other documents, except a notice of appeal, which is governed by Rule 4(d). Rule 13(a)(2) is intended to address the concerns highlighted by the Supreme Judicial Court in Commonwealth v. Hartsgrove, 407 Mass. 441, 445 (1990), as to the limitations of a person confined in an institution to effectuate the "mailing" of a document on a certain day. This provision is consistent with Rule 4(d) and Fed. R. App. P. 25(a)(2)(C). However, unlike the Federal rule, a party's certificate need not state that first-class postage has been prepaid because some Massachusetts institutions affix postage after the item leaves the inmate or civilly committed person's hands. Importantly, the rule is written to encompass filings by any self-represented person confined in an institution. This includes persons confined on criminal or civil grounds, such as a sexually dangerous person commitment or a court-ordered involuntary civil commitment for mental illness or for alcohol and substance abuse disorders. See Reporter's Note to Rule 4(d).

Rule 13(b) was revised to remove reference to service by the clerk. This amendment clarifies that it is the party's obligation to serve documents on all parties to the appeal. The clerk will still serve notice of the filing of a notice of appeal pursuant to Rule 3(d), but the filer always has the obligation to serve a copy of a document upon the parties to an appeal unless specifically provided otherwise.

Rule 13(c) was revised to explicitly allow electronic service where a party consents to such service.

Rules 13(d) and 13(e) are substantially revised subdivisions that detail the requirement for, and contents of, a certificate of service. Rule 13(d) governs all documents other than briefs and appendices, which are governed by Rule 13(e). Under both subdivisions, a party must include in the certificate of service the electronic and mailing addresses of the person served. The inclusion of this information promotes consistency with the electronic-filing procedures implemented in the appellate courts. Prior Rule 13(d)'s provisions allowing acknowledgment by the person served as an alternative to proof of service and requiring a statement under the penalties of perjury were struck. The revised subdivisions are consistent with Mass. R. Civ. P.

5(d)(1) and Mass. R. Crim. P. 32(b), which do not require the certificate of service to be made under the penalties of perjury.

Rule 13(e)(1) is a new subdivision that requires the certificate of service of a brief and appendix be contained within the brief itself. This requirement is intended to simplify the process of filing a brief. This language departs from the Appeals Court's prior practice of requesting parties to file a separate certificate of service. Finally, Rule 13(e)(2) specifies the contents of a certificate of service of a brief and appendix, and contains additional requirements than a Rule 13(d) certificate of service for other documents.

Further organizational and stylistic revisions were made to this rule in 2019 in accordance with a global review and revision of all of the Appellate Rules. These revisions are described in the 2019 Reporter's Notes to Rule 1.

With regard to the preparation of the 2019 Reporter's Notes to this Rule, see the first paragraph of the 2019 Reporter's Notes to Rule 1. For an overview of the 2019 amendments to the Rules and a summary of the global amendments to the Rules, see 2019 Reporter's Notes to Rule 1, sections *I.* and *II.*

Rule 14.   Computation and Extension of Time

(a) Computation of Time. In computing any period of time prescribed by these rules, by order of court, or by any applicable statute, the day of the act, event, or default after which the designated period of time begins to run shall not be included. The last day of the period shall be included, unless it is a Saturday, Sunday, or a legal holiday, in which event the period shall extend until the end of the next day which is not a Saturday, Sunday, or legal holiday. When the period of time prescribed or allowed is less than 7 days, intermediate Saturdays, Sundays, and legal holidays shall be excluded in the computation. As used in this rule "legal holiday" means those days specified in G.L. c. 4, § 7 and any other day appointed as a holiday by the President or the Congress of the United States or so designated by the laws of the Commonwealth.

(b) Enlargement of Time. The appellate court or a single justice of the appellate court in which the appeal will be, or is, docketed for good cause shown may upon motion enlarge the time prescribed by these rules or by its order for doing any act, or may permit an act to be done after the expiration of such time; but neither the appellate court nor a single justice may enlarge the time for filing a notice of appeal beyond 1 year from the date of entry of the judgment or order sought to be reviewed, or, in a criminal case, from the date of the verdict or finding of guilt or the date of imposition of sentence, whichever date is later.

(c) Additional Time After Service by First Class Mail or Its Equivalent. Whenever a party is required or permitted to do an act within a prescribed period after service of a document upon the party and the document is served by first class mail or its equivalent, 3 days shall be added to the prescribed period.

Amended May 15, 1979, effective July 1, 1979; October 31, 2018, effective March 1, 2019.

Reporter's Notes—1973

Appellate Rule 14(a), dealing with computation of time, follows Mass.R.Civ.P. 6. By countenancing enlargement of appeal time up to one year after entry of the order or judgment appealed from, Appellate Rule 14(b) relaxes the cognate F.R.A.P. 26(b). Read together, Appellate Rules 4 and 14(b) mean that an "excusable neglect" exten-

sion may be granted only on such terms as to cause the extension to expire within the one-year period prescribed by Appellate Rule 14(b).

Reporter's Notes—1979

The only change in Rule 14 is the addition to subdivision (b) of language restricting the appellate court's power to enlarge the time within which a notice of appeal may be filed in a criminal case to no longer than one year after the date of the verdict or finding of guilt or the date of the imposition of sentence, whichever date is later. Compare Rule 4(c), which limits any extension granted by the lower court to no more than sixty days after verdict or sentence. The failure of a party to notice his appeal prior to the expiration of the thirty-day limit of Rule 4(b), or within sixty days if extended may be rectified by the appellate court, or a single justice as long as it does not extend beyond one year past verdict or sentence.

Reporter's Notes—2019

Rule 14(b) was revised by adding text to clarify that the single justice referred to is a single justice of the appellate court in which the appeal will be or is docketed.

Rule 14(c) was revised to be consistent with the new definition in Rule 1(c) of "first class mail or its equivalent."

Further organizational and stylistic revisions were made to this rule in 2019 in accordance with a global review and revision of all of the Appellate Rules. These revisions are described in the 2019 Reporter's Notes to Rule 1.

With regard to the preparation of the 2019 Reporter's Notes to this Rule, see the first paragraph of the 2019 Reporter's Notes to Rule 1. For an overview of the 2019 amendments to the Rules and a summary of the global amendments to the Rules, see 2019 Reporter's Notes to Rule 1, sections *I.* and *II.*

Rule 15.   Motions

(a) Content of Motions; Response; Reply. Unless another form is elsewhere prescribed by these rules, an application for an order or other relief shall be made by filing a motion for such order or relief with proof of service upon all other parties. The motion shall comply with Rule 20(b)(2) and shall contain or be accompanied by any matter required by a specific provision of these rules governing such a motion, shall state with particularity the grounds on which it is based, shall set forth the order or relief sought, and, if known, should state whether the motion is assented to, or that no other party is in opposition, or if any party intends to file an opposition or other response. If a motion is supported by briefs, affidavits, or other documents, they shall be served and filed with the motion. Any party may file a response to a motion other than for a procedural order (for which see Rule 15(b)) within 7 days after service of the motion, but motions authorized by Rule 6 may be acted upon after reasonable notice, and the appellate court or a single justice may shorten or extend the time for responding to any motion.

(b) Determination of Motions for Procedural Orders. Notwithstanding the provisions of the preceding paragraph as to motions generally, motions for procedural orders, including any motion under Rule 14(b), may be acted upon at any time, without awaiting a response thereto. Any party adversely affected by such action may request reconsideration, vacation, or modification of such action.

(c) Power of a Single Justice to Entertain Motions. In addition to the authority expressly conferred by these rules or by law, a single justice may entertain and may grant or deny any request for relief which under these rules may properly be sought by motion, except that a single justice may not dismiss or otherwise determine an appeal or other proceeding, and except that the appellate court may provide by order or rule that any motion or class of motions shall be acted upon by the appellate court. The action of a single justice may be reviewed by the appellate court.

(d) Motions for New Trial in Capital Cases. After the docketing of an appeal in a "capital case" as defined in G. L. c. 278, § 33E, and until the issuance of a rescript by the appellate court, any motion for a new trial pursuant to Massachusetts Rules of Criminal Procedure 30 shall be filed in the appellate court and may be remitted to the trial judge for hearing and determination at such time as the appellate court may direct.

Amended May 15, 1979, effective July 1, 1979; October 31, 2018, effective March 1, 2019.

Publisher's Note

On March 29, 1988, the Supreme Judicial Court adopted the following order:

ORDERED: Pursuant to Mass. R.A.P. 15(c), applications for stays pending the United States Supreme Court's consideration of applications for writs of certiorari shall be considered upon the filing of a motion with the Clerk of the Supreme Judicial Court for the Commonwealth. Reasonable notice of the motion shall be given to all parties. The motion may be decided with or without a hearing by the panel whose decision is sought to be reviewed. At its discretion, the court may order a hearing by a single justice who was a member of that panel either for the justice's recommendation or decision. Relief available under this order, or denial of such relief, may be conditioned on such reasonable terms as the panel or single justice may impose, including appropriate conditions for the security of the adverse party.

This order shall take effect on July 1, 1988.

Reporter's Notes—1973

Appellate Rule 15 governs motion practice. Appellate Rule 15(c) permits a single justice to dispose of any motion except a motion to dismiss an appeal (and, of course, except as otherwise provided by the Appellate Court). For the required number of copies see Appellate Rule 19(b); for the form of motions, see Appellate Rule 20(b).

Reporter's Notes—1979

Subdivision (d), drawn from G.L. c. 278, § 33E (as amended) merely recognizes that while after docketing, a motion for a new trial (Mass. R.Crim.P. 30) is required to be filed in the appellate court, it should ordinarily be heard and determined by the trial judge (unless disabled, see Mass.R.Crim.P. 38[c]), since he is in a better position to weigh its merits. *See, e.g., Commonwealth v. Grace*, 370 Mass. 746 (1976). The need for familiarity with the trial proceedings may vary, however, as a function of the grounds asserted (e.g., newly-discovered evidence as opposed to a verdict allegedly against the weight of evidence).

Reporter's Notes—2019

The second sentence of Rule 15(a) was revised to reference Rule 20(b) to clarify that the form of motions is governed by Rule 20(b).

Rule 15(b) continues to allow an appellate court or a single justice to act on motions for procedural orders at any time without awaiting a response thereto. Notwithstanding this authority, text was added to Rule 15(a) to express the appellate courts' preference for knowing, at the time a motion is filed, whether a motion is assented to or if it is known that any party opposes the motion, and, if so, whether the party intends to file an opposition or other response. The amendment is intended to encourage the parties to communicate about whether a response will be filed prior to the filing of a motion to avoid the unnecessary consumption of time, effort, and expense to both the parties and the appellate court. See Reporter's Note to Rule 1(a).

Rule 15(d) was revised to replace "murder in the first degree" with "'capital case' as defined in G. L. c. 278, § 33E" to encompass the statute's definition of a "capital case" as including certain habitual offender convictions in addition to convictions of murder in the first degree.

Further organizational and stylistic revisions were made to this rule in 2019 in accordance with a global review and revision of all of the Appellate Rules. These revisions are described in the 2019 Reporter's Notes to Rule 1.

With regard to the preparation of the 2019 Reporter's Notes to this Rule, see the first paragraph of the 2019 Reporter's Notes to Rule 1. For an overview of the 2019 amendments to the Rules and a summary of the global amendments to the Rules, see 2019 Reporter's Notes to Rule 1, sections *I.* and *II.*

Rule 16. Briefs

(a) Brief of the Appellant. The brief of the appellant shall be formatted and paginated as provided in Rule 20(a)(4), and contain under appropriate headings and in the order here indicated:

(1) *Cover.* The cover of the brief shall contain the information identified in Rule 20(a)(6)(B).

(2) *Corporate Disclosure Statement.* A corporate disclosure statement, if required pursuant to Supreme Judicial Court Rule 1:21, shall be contained within the brief.

(3) *Table of Contents.* The table of contents shall list each section of the brief, including the headings and subheadings of each section, and the page on which they begin.

(4) *Table of Authorities.* The table of authorities shall list each case, statute, rule, and other authority cited in the brief, with references to each page on which it is cited. The authorities shall be listed alphabetically or numerically, as applicable.

(5) *Statement of Issues.* The statement of issues shall concisely and particularly describe each issue presented for review.

(6) *Statement of Case.* The statement of the case shall briefly describe the nature of the appeal, the procedural history relevant to the issues presented for review, with page references to the record appendix or transcript in accordance with Rule 16(e), and the disposition of these issues by the lower court.

(7) *Statement of Facts.* The statement of the facts shall describe the facts relevant to the issues presented for review, but need not repeat items otherwise included in the statement of the case, and each statement of fact shall be supported by page references to the record appendix or transcript in accordance with Rule 16(e).

(8) *Summary of Argument.* In a brief with more than 20 pages of argument, or more than 4,500 words if produced in a proportionally spaced font, there shall be a summary of the argument, that contains a succinct, clear, and accurate statement of the arguments made in the body of the brief, which must not merely repeat the argument headings, and is to include page references to where in the body of the brief each argument is made.

(9) *Argument.* The argument shall contain:

(A) the contentions of the appellant with respect to the issues presented, and the reasons therefor, with citations to the authorities and parts of the record on which the appellant relies. The appellate court need not pass upon questions or issues not argued in the brief; and

(B) for each issue, a concise statement of the applicable standard of review (which may appear in the discussion of the issue or under a separate heading placed before the discussion of the issues).

(10) *Request for Attorney's Fees and Costs.* Any request for appellate attorney's fees and costs must be included in the brief, with a citation to the authority therefor.

(11) *Conclusion.* The brief shall contain a short conclusion stating the precise relief sought.

(12) *Signature Block.* The signature block shall contain

(A) the printed and signed name(s), Board of Bar Overseers (BBO) number(s), if any, mailing and electronic addresses, and telephone number(s) of the person(s) who prepared the brief, and, if any individual counsel is affiliated with a firm or office, the office name; and

(B) the date of signing.

(13) *Addendum.* An addendum, contained within the brief, shall consist of the following:

(A) a table of contents listing each item contained therein and the page on which it begins;

(B) any appealed judgment or order (including any written opinion, memorandum of decision, or findings of fact and conclusions thereon relating to an issue raised on appeal, including a typed version of any pertinent handwritten or oral endorsement, notation, findings, or order made by the lower court);

(C) copies of constitutional provisions, statutes, rules, regulations, or relevant parts thereof, as in effect at the relevant time, consideration of which is required for determination of the issues presented;

(D) a copy of any unpublished decision cited in the brief; and

(E) in a case where geographical facts are of importance, unless appropriate plans are reproduced in the printed record or record appendix, an outline plan (preferably based on exhibits in evidence). This outline plan should be suitable for reproduction on 1 page of the printed law reports.

(14) *Certificate of Compliance.* The certification required by Rule 16(k) shall be contained within the brief.

(15) *Certificate of Service.* The certificate of service required by Rule 13(e) shall be contained within the brief.

(b) Brief of the Appellee. The brief of the appellee shall conform to the requirements of Rule 16(a), except as follows:

(1) *Statements of the Issues, Case, Facts, and Standard(s) of Review.* Statements of the issues, of the case, of the facts, and of the applicable standard(s) of review need not be made unless the appellee is dissatisfied with the statements of the appellant.

(2) *Argument.* The argument shall contain the contentions of the appellee with respect to the issues presented, and the reasons therefor, with citations to the authorities and parts of the record on which the appellee relies.

(3) *Addendum.* The addendum shall include copies of items required by Rule 16(a)(13) insofar as pertinent to the issues argued by the appellee, even if included in the addendum of the appellant.

(c) Appellant's Reply Brief. The appellant may file a reply brief responding to the appellee's argument. No new issues shall be raised in the reply brief. No further briefs may be filed except with leave of the appellate court or a single justice. The reply briefs shall comply with the requirements of Rule 16 (a)(1), (3), (4), (9), and (11)–(15).

(d) References in Briefs to Parties. Parties will be expected in their briefs and oral argument to keep to a minimum references to parties by such designations as "appellant" and "appellee." It promotes clarity to use the designations used in the lower court, or the actual names of the parties, or descriptive terms such as "the employee," "the injured person," "the taxpayer," "the landlord," etc. If the name of a party has been impounded or has been made confidential by statute, rule, or court order, the party shall preserve confidentiality in briefs and oral arguments.

(e) References in Briefs to the Record. Any factual statement in a brief shall be supported by a citation to the volume number(s) and page number(s) at which it appears in an appendix, and if not contained in an appendix, to the volume number(s) and page number(s) at which it appears in the transcript(s) or exhibits volume(s). Only clear abbreviations may be used, for example, RAII/55 (meaning Record Appendix volume II at page 55) or TRIII/231–232 (meaning Transcript volume III at pages 231–232). Any record material cited in a brief must be reproduced in an appendix or transcript or exhibit volume. Any record material cited in a brief that is included in the addendum should also include a citation to the addendum. If reference is made to evidence the admissibility of which is in controversy, reference shall be made to the pages of the appendix or of the transcript at which the evidence was identified, offered, and received or rejected.

(f) Reserved.

(g) Massachusetts Citations. Citations to Massachusetts decisions, statutes, and regulations shall be made only to the official report of the decision or to the official publication containing the statute or regulation, if any. References to decisions should include, in addition to the page at which the decision begins, a page reference to the particular material therein upon which reliance is placed, and the year of the decision.

(h) Length of Briefs in Cases Other than Cross Appeals. In any case other than a cross appeal, the length of briefs shall comply with Rule 20(a)(2).

(i) Briefs in Cases Involving Cross Appeals. In a cross appeal,

(1) the length of briefs shall comply with Rule 20(a)(3);

(2) the appellee's principal and response brief shall contain the issues and argument involved in the appellee's appeal as well as the answer to the brief of the appellant;

(3) the appellee may file a reply brief responding to the appellant's argument as to the issues presented by the cross appeal; and

(4) except with leave of the appellate court or a single justice, an appellee that has cross-appealed may file only a single brief in reply to the responses of multiple appellants to the issues presented by the cross appeal.

(j) Briefs in Cases Involving Multiple Appellants or Appellees. In cases involving more than one appellant or appellee, including cases consolidated for purposes of the appeal per Rule 10(a)(5),

(1) any number of either may join in a single brief or reply brief, provided appropriate notice is given to the clerk and other parties;

(2) any appellant or appellee may adopt by reference any part of the brief of another; and

(3) except with leave of the appellate court or a single justice, an appellee may file only a single brief in response to multiple appellant briefs, and an appellant may file only a single brief in reply to multiple appellee briefs.

(k) Required Certification; Non-complying Briefs. The last page of each brief shall include a certification by the party, that the brief complies with the rules of court that pertain to the filing of briefs, including, but not limited to: Rule 16(a)(13) (addendum); Rule 16(e) (references to the record); Rule 18 (appendix to the briefs); Rule 20 (form and length of briefs, appendices, and other documents); and Rule 21 (redaction). The certification shall specify how compliance with the applicable length limit of Rule 20 was ascertained, by stating either (1) the name, size, and number of characters per inch of the monospaced font used and the number of non-excluded pages, or (2) the name and size of the proportionally spaced font used, the number of non-excluded words, and the name and version of the word-processing program used. A brief not complying with these rules (including a brief that does not contain a certification) may be struck from the files by the appellate court or a single justice.

(l) Citation of Supplemental Authorities. When pertinent and significant authorities come to the attention of a party after the party's brief has been filed, or after oral argument but before decision, a party may promptly advise the clerk of the court, by letter setting forth the citations. There shall be a reference either to the page of the brief or to a point argued orally to which the citations pertain, but the letter shall without argument state the reasons for the supplemental citations. Any response shall be made promptly and shall be similarly limited. Filing and service of any letter pursuant to this paragraph shall comply with Rule 13.

(m) References to Impounded Material. Upon the filing of any brief or other document containing references to matters that are impounded or have been made confidential by statute, rule, or order, the party shall file a written notice with the clerk, with a copy to all parties, so indicating. Wherever possible, the party shall not disclose impounded material. Where it is necessary to include impounded material in a brief, the cover of the brief shall clearly indicate that impounded information is included therein.

(n) Amendment of Brief. On motion for good cause, the court may grant leave for a party to file an amended brief. The motion shall describe the nature and reason for the amendment. The party shall file with the motion the amended brief marked as such on the front page or cover. Except as the court otherwise orders, the filing of an amended brief has no effect on any filing deadlines.

Amended effective February 24, 1975; amended May 15, 1979, effective July 1, 1979; May 25, 1982, effective July 1, 1982; November 17, 1986, effective January 1, 1987; November 24, 1987, effective January 1, 1988; amended effective May 5, 1989; February 1, 1991; January 1, 1992; January 1, 1997; amended June 11, 1997, effective July 1, 1997; December 1, 1998, effective January 1, 1999; February 5, 2003, effective March 3, 2003; April 27, 2005, effective October 1, 2005; October 31, 2018, effective March 1, 2019.

Reporter's Notes—1973

Appellate Rule 16 establishes the form of the briefs: table of contents; statement of the issues; statement of the case; arguments; and conclusion. Appellate Rule 16(f) also requires the reproduction of relevant statutes and the like. None of the requirements will substantially change existing practice. Appellate Rule 16(e), stating the requirements in briefs for references to the record, likewise follows existing practice. See S.J.C. Rule 1:15; Appeals Court Rule 1:15.

Reporter's Notes—1975

As originally promulgated, Appellate Rule 16(a)(4) made optional the use of a summary of argument. The new rule makes such a summary mandatory, if the brief contains more than 24 pages of argument (i.e. not including table of contents, table of cases, statutes, and authorities, statement of issues, and statement of the case). By explicit language, the summary must be something more than a mere recital of the argument headings.

Amended Appellate Rule 16(a)(4) makes explicit the long-standing principle that failure to discuss an issue in the brief may, at the discretion of the court, preclude reliance upon that point in oral argument. On the other hand, if the brief does include the question, failure to argue it orally does not waive the point.

Although earlier Massachusetts appellate citation form omitted the year of decision, the amendment to Appellate Rule 16(g) ensures that the year will be included in any citation.

Reporter's Notes—1979

Rule 16 was previously incorporated into criminal appellate procedure by Appeals Court Rule 1:15 (1975: 3 Mass.App.Ct. 803) and Supreme Judicial Court Rule 1:15 (1975: 366 Mass. 861). The rule is unchanged beyond amendment of subdivision (e) to reflect the fact that there may be more than one appendix in a criminal case. (Mass.R.App.P. 19[a]).

The last two sentences of subdivision (a)(4) which provide that questions or issues not argued in the brief need not be decided, but that a failure to orally argue an issue does not waive it if argued in the brief, supersede the last two sentences of former Appeals Court and Supreme Judicial Court Rules 1:13 (1972: 1 Mass.App.Ct. 889, amended 1975: 3 Mass.App.Ct. 801. 1967: 351 Mass. 738, amended, 1975: 366 Mass. 801).

Reporter's Notes—1982

Appellate Rule 16(l) is the same as F.R.A.P. 28(j), which became effective in 1979. Its purpose is to allow a concise letter to inform the court in a non-argumentative manner of a "pertinent and significant" authority discovered after the filing of a brief or oral argument. The amendment does not authorize reargument in the disguise of a supplementary citation.

Reporter's Notes—1986

This amendment is to clarify that reply briefs of more than twenty pages shall contain the tables and references required of other appellate briefs of that length. Such tables and references aid opposing parties and the court. This amendment corresponds, in part, to the 1986 amendment to Fed.R.A.P. 28(c).

Reporter's Notes—1991

Mass.R.A.P. 16(a)(7) and 20(a), final sentence, clause (5):

These amendments require individual counsel who are affiliated with a firm to include the firm name on filed briefs. Appellate judges need to know the firm names in order to determine correctly whether it is necessary to withdraw from a case.

Reporter's Notes—1997

The amendment to Appellate Rule 16(a)(1), effective January 1, 1997, eliminates the provision that a table of contents and a table of cases, statutes, and other authorities be included only in briefs of twenty pages or more. All briefs must include these items.

The 1997 amendments to Appellate Rule 16(d) and (m) serve as a reminder to counsel to maintain confidentiality in briefs and oral argument of any information that has been impounded or designated as confidential. For example, where the name of a person is not subject to disclosure, counsel may use a generic term such as "child" or "juvenile" or may use a pseudonym or initials.

Illustrative statutes requiring confidentiality include G.L. c. 112, § 12S (petitions by minors seeking judicial determination of maturity in connection with abortion; see also Superior Court Standing Order No. 5–81, as amended, requiring that papers "shall be designated anonymously" such as with the titles "Mary Moe" or "Mary Doe"); G.L. c. 119, § 38 (names in care and protection proceedings); G.L. c. 119, § 65 (juvenile proceedings); G.L. c. 209A, § 8 (in abuse prevention proceedings, plaintiff's address and case records involving a minor); G.L. c. 209C, § 13 (papers in paternity proceedings and a party's address); and G.L. c. 210, § 5C (adoption proceedings).

Illustrative rules providing for confidentiality include Mass.R.Civ.P. 26(c) (trade secrets and other matters in connection with discovery) and Probate Court Supplemental Rule 401 (financial statements in connection with requests for support or alimony). The Uniform Rules on Impoundment Procedure also provide a mechanism to preserve confidentiality of matters contained in case papers.

Illustrative cases using pseudonyms include *Care and Protection of Stephen*, 401 Mass. 144, 514 N.E.2d 1087 (1987); *C.C. v. A.B.*, 406 Mass. 679, 550 N.E.2d 365 (1990); *Oscar F. v. County of Worcester*, 412 Mass. 38, 587 N.E.2d 208 (1992); *Adoption of Carla*, 416 Mass. 510, 623 N.E.2d 1118 (1993); *Doe v. Superintendent of Schools of Worcester*, 421 Mass. 117, 653 N.E.2d 1088 (1995); *Doe v. Purity Supreme, Inc.*, 422 Mass. 563, 664 N.E.2d 815 (1996); and *Commonwealth v. Wotan*, 422 Mass. 740, 665 N.E.2d 976 (1996).

There may be instances, however, where counsel will find it necessary to include confidential information in a brief in order to allow for full appellate review of the issue. In such instances, Rule 16(m) provides that counsel must alert the clerk's office that confidential information is contained in a filing. In this way, the rule shifts the burden to counsel to alert the clerk's office to the presence of impounded material so that the latter can take appropriate steps to safeguard the material in accordance with Supreme Judicial Court Rule 1:15, Impoundment Procedure.

These amendments, together with amendments to Appellate Rule 18, serve to preserve confidentiality of material in briefs, appendices, and oral argument.

Reporter's Notes—1999

New paragraph (6), added to Appellate Rule 16(a) effective in 1999, requires that any findings (written or oral) or memorandum of decision by the trial court pertinent to an appellate issue be included in an addendum to the appellant's brief. Although findings or a memorandum of decision are already required to be included in the appendix to the brief (Mass.R.A.P. 18(a)), incorporating such matters in an addendum to the brief will enable a judge on appeal to locate quickly the trial court's rationale for its decision, especially where there is a multivolume appendix.

The reference to oral findings is intended to cover the situation where the trial judge has dictated findings into the record that have been transcribed or otherwise recorded. These findings must now also be included in an addendum to the brief.

This additional requirement will not serve to reduce the maximum number of pages for a principal brief. The page limitations contained in Mass.R.A.P. 16(h) are inapplicable to an addendum to a brief.

Reporter's Notes—1999

The 1999 amendments to Appellate Rule 16(h) were made together with the updating of Appellate Rule 20, the latter governing the form of briefs and appendices. The 1999 amendments to Appellate Rule 20 deleted references to standard typographic printing in recognition of the practice that briefs today are produced through computer word-processing and no longer through a typesetting and printing process. Accordingly, the page limitation for briefs produced by "standard typographic printing" of forty pages (and fifteen pages for reply briefs) has been deleted from the rule.

The existing page limitation on principal briefs produced by computer wordprocessing remains fifty pages, with reply briefs twenty pages.

Reporter's Notes—2003

By virtue of the 2003 amendment to Appellate Rule 16(h), a party seeking leave to file a brief with additional pages must specify the issues involved and why they require additional pages. The rule also sets forth a standard of "extraordinary reasons" for the allowance of such a motion.

Reporter's Notes—2005

In order to reduce the number of non-complying briefs, Appellate Rule 16(k) was amended in 2005 to require a certification that the brief complies with all of the rules of court that govern briefs. Counsel should be aware that a brief that does not contain the required certification may be struck by the court for non-compliance with the rule.

Reporter's Notes—2019

Rule 16(a) was revised and reorganized to detail in sequential order the contents of an appellant's brief. The revised rule is organized as a checklist intended to assist the parties in preparing a brief in compliance with the Rules, and to eliminate any heretofore unreferenced requirements raised by other court rules or decisions. The rule cross-references Rule 20(a)(4) for brief formatting and pagination requirements.

Rule 16(a)(1) is a new paragraph that begins the checklist format. It merely crossreferences Rule 20(a)(6), which sets forth color and contents of the cover of a brief.

Rule 16(a)(2) is a new paragraph that cross-references S.J.C. Rule 1:21, which requires the inclusion of a corporate disclosure statement in specified circumstances. The corporate disclosure statement is to be included immediately after the cover, and before the table of contents in a party's principal brief. See S.J.C. Rule 1:21.

Rules 16(a)(3) and 16(a)(4) are derived from prior Rule 16(a)(1) and provide the required format of the table of contents and table of authorities, respectively.

Rule 16(a)(5) continues the requirement from prior Rule 16(a)(2) for a statement of the issues presented. The rule was revised to highlight that the statement of issues is to describe each issue concisely and with particularity.

Rule 16(a)(6) continues the requirement from prior Rule 16(a)(3) that the brief include a statement of the case. The revised rule requires the statement of the case to include reference to the record appendix or transcript, a requirement that was required in prior Rule 16(e), although not expressly so stated. See also Fed. R. App. P. 28(a)(6).

Rule 16(a)(7) continues the requirement from prior Rule 16(a)(3) for a statement of facts relevant to the issues presented for review, with supporting references to the record. New language clarifies that the statement of facts need not repeat items included in the statement of the case. The rule also clarifies that each statement of fact must be supported by specific page references to the record appendix or transcript, similar to the requirements in prior Rules 16(a)(3) and 16(e).

Rule 16(a)(8) continues prior Rule 16(a)(4)'s requirement for a summary of the argument that does not merely repeat argument headings. Under prior Rule 16(a)(4), a summary of the argument was required only when the argument exceeded 24 pages. The page limit was reduced to arguments exceeding 20 pages, or equivalent length under the word count alternative if a proportionally spaced font is used. The paragraph continues to require page references to the pages in the body of the brief where each argument is presented. See also Fed. R. App. P. 28(a)(7).

Rule 16(a)(9) governs the argument portion of the brief and is derived from prior Rule 16(a)(4). The rule was divided into two subparagraphs, the first, Rule 16(a)(9)(A), concerning the argument section generally, and the second, Rule 16(a)(9)(B), concerning presentation of the individual issues. The final sentence of prior Rule 16(a)(4) was relocated to Rule 22, because it concerns oral argument ("Nothing argued in the brief shall be deemed waived by a failure to argue orally"). Rule 16(a)(9)(B) includes a new requirement, derived from Fed. R. App. P. 28(a)(8), that the party include the standard of review for each issue raised. The standard of review is a critical factor in every appeal, constituting the lens through which the court views the issues presented.

Rule 16(a)(10) is a new paragraph added to ensure litigants comply with the requirement derived from case law, that any request for attorney's fees and costs must be included in the brief. See Yorke Management v. Castro, 406 Mass. 17, 19 (1989). Such a request must be made even where the request is not based upon a fee-shifting statute. Beal Bank, SSB v. Eurich, 448 Mass. 9, 10 (2006). An appellate court may excuse or modify this requirement if the circumstances so warrant. Lowell v. Massachusetts Comm'n Against Discrimination, 65 Mass. App. Ct. 356, 358 (2006). This new rule also requires that a request for fees and costs identify the specific source (e.g., statute, court rule, or case law) which authorizes the request.

Rule 16(a)(11) continues the requirement of prior Rule 16(a)(5) for a conclusion to the brief that states the precise relief requested from the appellate court.

Rule 16(a)(12) delineates the requirements of the brief's signature block and expands upon prior Rule 16(a)(8). The signature block must include both the mailing and electronic addresses of the person who prepared the brief, whether by counsel or a self-represented party. This is consistent with amendments to Rules 13(e), 20(a)(6)(B), and 20(b)(2)(B).

Rule 16(a)(13) specifies the contents of the addendum to a principal brief. It contains substantially revised text relocated from prior Rules 16(a)(6) and 16(a)(7). The amendment was intended to consolidate into a single provision the various items required to be included in an addendum. Rule 16(a)(13)(A) requires the addendum to include a table of contents listing each item contained in the addendum and the page number on which the document begins. Rule 16(a)(13)(B) continues the requirement of prior Rule 16(a)(6) that a copy of any memorandum of decision or findings of the lower court be included in the addendum. The provision was expanded to require that when the addendum includes a document bearing a handwritten endorsement by

the lower court, the addendum also include a typed copy of that endorsement. A lower court judge will often endorse a motion or other paper with a handwritten notation that is difficult to decipher. Requiring both a copy of the original endorsement and a typed version facilitates review in the appellate court. If the lower court clerk provides a typed notice of docket entry containing the full text of the judge's order, a copy of the notice would suffice for purposes of this rule.

Rule 16(a)(13)(D) is a new subparagraph requiring that when a brief cites to an unpublished decision, a copy of the entire decision is to be included in the addendum. The Appeals Court already requires that any party citing to a Memorandum of Decision and Order pursuant to Appeals Court Rule 1:28 decision is to include the full text of that decision in the addendum to a brief. See Chace v. Curran, 71 Mass. App. Ct. 258 (2008); Appeals Court Rule 1:28, as amended in 2008. The amendment codifies this requirement in the Rules, and expands the requirement to apply to any unpublished decision cited in a brief to either appellate court.

Rule 16(a)(13)(E) is nearly identical to prior Rule 16(a)(7), omitting "or chalk" as superfluous.

Rules 16(a)(14) and 16(a)(15) are new paragraphs which specify that the brief is to conclude with the Rule 16(k) certificate of compliance and the Rule 13(e) certificate of service. Adding these paragraphs to the "checklist" portion of Rule 16(a) highlights that the certifications are necessary parts of a brief and identify the proper location of the certifications in the brief.

Rule 16(b) was revised and separated into three paragraphs. The rule specifies, in greater detail than prior Rule 16(b), the contents of the appellee's brief. The rule requires the appellee's brief to conform to the requirements of Rule 16(a) except as provided in paragraphs (1)–(3) of the rule, and including that the statements of the issues, case, facts, and applicable standard(s) of review need not be made unless the appellee is dissatisfied with the statements of the appellant. A new provision, Rule 16(b)(3), requires the appellee to include an addendum that contains the same materials required in the appellant's addendum in Rule 16(a)(13), insofar as the items are pertinent to the appellee's arguments, even if the items were included in the appellant's addendum.

Prior Rule 16(c) was revised to specify the format of a reply brief, and expressly state that the reply brief may not raise new issues different from those raised in the principal briefs. Accord Krapf v. Krapf, 439 Mass. 97, 110 (2003) (where Supreme Judicial Court, citing prior Rules 16(a)(4) and (c), declined to consider issues raised for the first time in a reply brief). The words "or a single justice" are added to the prior requirement that "leave of the appellate court" be obtained before an appellee may file a reply brief, otherwise known as a sur-reply brief. The sentence in prior Rule 16(c) authorizing an appellee who has cross-appealed to file a reply brief responding to the appellant's argument as to the issues presented in the cross appeal was relocated to Rule 16(i), the rule addressing brief requirements in a cross appeal.

Rule 16(e) continues to require that parties support factual statements in a brief with citation to the record. This subdivision was amended to specify that the citation references shall be to both the supporting volume number(s), if applicable, and page number(s) in the appendix, transcript, exhibits, or addendum. All citations must be clear and may follow the examples found in the text of the rule. References to Rules 18(c) and 18(f) were deleted consistent with revisions to those subdivisions as described in the Reporter's Note to Rule 18.

Prior Rule 16(f) (reproduction of statutes, rules, regulations, etc., in the addendum) was deleted entirely because its substance was relocated to Rule 16(a)(13). The subdivision was kept as "reserved" instead of renumbering the subdivisions that follow because subsequent subdivisions 16(k) and 16(l) are commonly referred to by their respective numbers and maintaining the lettering will avoid confusion for filers in the appellate courts.

Rule 16(g), regarding Massachusetts citations, was amended to remove language referencing old volumes of the Massachusetts Reports, since those are not as commonly cited today. The language was revised to state more simply that citations to Massachusetts authorities need to be to the official reporter of the decision or the official publication containing the statute or regulation, if an official report or publication exists. Language related to quotations of statutory material and citation examples were also relocated to these Reporter's Notes. Examples of citations to Massachusetts authorities are as follows:

Supreme Judicial Court:	Commonwealth v. Dorelas, 473 Mass. 496, 502–503 (2016);
Appeals Court:	Amaral v. Seekonk Grand Prix Corp., 89 Mass. App. Ct. 1, 3–5 (2016);
Unpublished decision:	Parks vs. Petraglia, Boston Hous. Ct., No. 93–CV–00155 (Jan. 20, 1995);
General Laws:	G. L. c. 261, § 27D.

Citations to these and other authorities should be made consistent with the Supreme Judicial Court Style Manual, available at http://www.mass.gov/courts/docs/sjc/docs/reporter–of–decisions–style–guide.pdf.

Rule 16(h) was renamed "Length of Briefs in Cases Other Than Cross Appeals," to be consistent with Rule 16(i), which governs the length of briefs in cross appeals. The current contents of the Rule are deleted entirely, and replaced with a cross-reference to Rule 20(a)(2), which establishes the brief length requirements.

Rule 16(i) continues to govern briefs in cases involving cross appeals. The rule was revised and separated into four paragraphs. The first sentence of this provision was deleted and relocated to Rule 10(a)(6), docketing of a joint appeal. Rule 10(a)(6) is a more appropriate location for a provision designating the parties for purposes of a cross appeal, rather than in the rule concerning the briefs. The parties' designation for purposes of the appeal applies to all aspects of the appeal, starting at the docketing stage, and is not simply for purposes of briefing. Rule 16(i)(1) cross-references Rule 20(a)(3) regarding requirements for the length of briefs in a cross appeal. In addition, Rule 16(i)(2) updates the rule to align it with Federal language concerning cross appeals (e.g., principal brief and response brief). See Fed. R. App. P. 28.1(c). The sentence in prior Rule 16(c) authorizing an appellee that has cross-appealed to file a reply brief responding to the appellant's argument as to the issues presented in the cross appeal was relocated to Rule 16(i)(3). Finally, Rule 16(i)(4) clarifies that, except with leave of the appellate court or a single justice, an appellee who has cross-appealed may file only a single reply brief in response to the issues presented by the cross appeal regardless if multiple appellants have filed responses to the issues presented by the cross appeal.

Rule 16(j) was amended to cross-reference Rule 10(a)(5) concerning consolidated appeals. The specific reference to Rule 10(a)(5) clarifies the phrase "cases consolidated for purposes of the appeal." The rule was revised and separated into three paragraphs. The rule continues to authorize parties to join in another party's brief in the same case. The rule was revised to clarify that reply briefs can be joined in the same manner as principal briefs. In addition, a clause requiring notice to the clerk and other parties was added. The notice informs the clerk to designate that party as having joined another party's brief and alerts the other parties that a separate brief will not be filed. Finally, a new provision, encompassed in Rule 16(j)(3), codifies existing practice that, except with leave of the appellate court or a single justice, in cases involving more than one appellant or appellee, an appellee may file only a single brief regardless of the number of appellant briefs that are filed, and an appellant may file only a single reply brief regardless of the number of appellee briefs that are filed.

Rule 16(k) continues to require a certification of compliance with the formatting requirements of these Rules. Rule 16(k) was amended to add language that the certification is to specify how compliance with the applicable length limit of Rule 20 was ascertained. This requirement will also assist the appellate court clerks' offices in verifying the brief's compliance with applicable rules. This requirement is similar to the certification required by Fed. R. App. P. 32(g)(1).

Rule 16(*l*) was amended to remove the phrase "with a copy to all counsel" and add the sentence, "Filing and service of any letter pursuant to this paragraph shall comply with Rule 13." Parties often neglect to adhere to the service requirements of Rule 13 when filing letters submitted pursuant to Rule 16(*l*). An express reference to that rule will increase compliance with these requirements and clarify that service requirements apply to such letters.

Rule 16(n) is a new subdivision that codifies existing appellate court practice regarding the filing of an amended brief. The amended document is to be submitted to the court contemporaneous with a motion seeking leave to file the amended document. An "amended" (which sometimes is titled "revised" or "corrected") brief typically contains typographical corrections or required redactions.

Further organizational and stylistic revisions were made to this rule in 2019 in accordance with a global review and revision of all of the Appellate Rules. These revisions are described in the 2019 Reporter's Notes to Rule 1.

With regard to the preparation of the 2019 Reporter's Notes to this Rule, see the first paragraph of the 2019 Reporter's Notes to Rule 1. For an overview of the 2019 amendments to the Rules and a summary of the global amendments to the Rules, see 2019 Reporter's Notes to Rule 1, sections *I.* and *II.*

Rule 17.   Brief of an Amicus Curiae

(a) General. A brief of an amicus curiae may be filed only (1) by leave of the appellate court or a single justice granted on motion or (2) when solicited by the appellate court, except that leave shall not be required when the brief is presented by the Commonwealth or its officer or agency. The brief may be conditionally filed with the motion for leave. A motion for leave shall identify the interest of the applicant and shall state the reasons why a brief of an amicus curiae is desirable.

(b) Timing. In all cases, an amicus curiae shall file its brief no later than 21 days before the date of oral argument for that case unless the appellate court or a single justice for cause shown shall grant leave for later filing. Any party may request leave from the appellate court or a single justice to file a response to a brief filed by an amicus curiae.

(c) Cover, Length, and Content. An amicus brief must comply with Rule 20. In addition to the requirements of Rule 20, the cover must identify the party or parties supported and indicate whether the brief supports affirmance or reversal or neither. An amicus brief need not comply with all the requirements of Rule 16, but must include the following:

(1) if the amicus curiae is a corporation, a disclosure statement like that required of parties by Supreme Judicial Court Rule 1:21;

(2) a table of contents with page references, in accord with Rule 16(a)(3);

(3) a table of authorities, in accord with Rule 16(a)(4);

(4) a concise statement of the identity of the amicus curiae and its interest in the case;

(5) unless the brief is presented by the Commonwealth or its officer or agency, a declaration that indicates whether

(A) a party or a party's counsel authored the brief in whole or in part;

(B) a party or a party's counsel contributed money that was intended to fund preparing or submitting the brief;

(C) a person or entity—other than the amicus curiae, its members, or its counsel—contributed money that was intended to fund preparing or submitting the brief and, if so, identifying each such person or entity; and

(D) the amicus curiae or its counsel represents or has represented one of the parties to the present appeal in another proceeding involving similar issues, or was a party or represented a party in a proceeding or legal transaction that is at issue in the present appeal, and, if so, identifying the proceeding or transaction, its relevance to the present appeal, and the parties involved;

(6) a summary of argument, in accord with Rule 16(a)(8), if the argument is more than 20 pages in length or more than 4,500 words if produced in a proportionally spaced font;

(7) an argument, which need not include a statement of the applicable standard of review;

(8) a signature block, in accord with Rule 16(a)(12);

(9) a certificate stating that the brief complies with the requirements of this rule and Rule 20 and specifying how compliance with the length limit of Rule 20(a)(3)(E) was ascertained, by stating either (A) the name, size, and number of characters per inch of the monospaced font used and the number of non-excluded pages, or (B) the name and size of the proportionally spaced font used, the number of non-excluded words, and the name and version of the word-processing program used; and

(10) a certificate of service, in accord with Rule 13(e).

A brief not complying with these rules (including a brief that does not contain a certification) may be struck from the files by the appellate court or a single justice.

(d) **Filing.** The same number of copies of the brief of an amicus curiae shall be filed with the clerk and served on each party as required by Rule 19(d).

(e) **Oral argument.** A motion of an amicus curiae to participate in the oral argument will be granted only for good cause.

Amended October 30, 1997, effective January 1, 1998; October 31, 2018, effective March 1, 2019.

Reporter's Notes—1973

No existing rule governs briefs of an amicus curiae. Appellate Rule 17, limiting the right to file such a brief to an amicus who has obtained leave of the full appellate court or a single justice on motion, follows existing practice. It should be noted that the Commonwealth need never obtain leave to file an amicus brief.

Reporter's Notes—1979

Rule 17 is unchanged, its provisions having been incorporated into criminal appellate procedure by former Appeals Court and Supreme Judicial Court Rules 1:15 (1975: 3 Mass.App.Ct. 803, 366 Mass. 861).

Reporter's Notes—1997

The 1997 amendment to Appellate Rule 17 added a new last sentence requiring that the number of copies of an amicus brief to be filed with the appellate court and served on counsel be the same as set forth in Appellate Rule 19(b).

Reporter's Notes—2019

Rule 17 was divided into separate subdivisions for clarity and substantively revised as described below.

Rule 17(a) contains the first three sentences of prior Rule 17. The words "or its officer or agency" were added at the end of the second sentence to make it clear that an officer or agency of the Commonwealth may also file an amicus brief as of right. This language was adopted from a similar provision in Fed. R. App. P. 29(a)(2). The phrase "at the request of the appellate court" was amended to "when solicited by the appellate court" to clarify when an amicus brief may be filed without leave of court. In accordance with Rule 17(a)(2), an amicus curiae need not move for leave to file a brief in a case where an appellate court has issued an announcement requesting submission of amicus briefs. The words "consent or" were struck because they were redundant of "leave" of court to file an amicus brief.

Rule 17(b) revises the fourth sentence of prior Rule 17 to allow an amicus curiae to file an amicus brief no later than 21 days before the date of oral argument for that case, unless leave is granted for later filing. This is intended to establish an ascertainable date for the filing of an amicus brief on behalf of any party, provide all parties with sufficient time to prepare a response to an amicus brief, and allow the appellate court sufficient time to review any amicus brief or response. Rule 17(b) was also amended to explicitly allow any party to seek leave from the appellate court or single justice to respond to any amicus brief.

Rule 17(c) is a new subdivision that governs the cover, length, and content of an amicus brief. An amicus brief must comply with the formatting and length requirements of Rule 20. However, an amicus brief does not need to comply with all of the content requirements applicable to a party's brief under Rule 16. Instead, Rule 17(c) explicitly references certain provisions of Rule 16 that are applicable to an amicus brief. Text was also added to clarify an amicus brief may be struck by an appellate court or single justice if it does not comply with Rule 17(c).

Rules 17(c)(4) and (c)(5) require the amicus curiae to identify its interest in the case in an amicus brief, so that it will be readily apparent to the appellate court when considering the brief. These paragraphs were modelled on Fed. R. App. P. 29(a)(4)(D)–(E), with a few changes. As with the analogous Federal rule, these paragraphs are not intended to require the amicus to disclose mere coordination of arguments or sharing of drafts with a party. The paragraphs are, however, intended to discourage the use of amicus briefs as an instrument to reiterate arguments made by a party to the appeal.

Rule 17(c)(5)(D) requires disclosure concerning whether "the amicus curiae or its counsel represents or has represented one of the parties to the present appeal in another proceeding involving similar issues, or was a party or represented a party in a proceeding or legal transaction that is at issue in the present appeal," in accord with Aspinall v. Philip Morris Co., Inc., 442 Mass. 381, 385 n.8 (2004), and Champa v. Weston Public Schools, 473 Mass. 86, 87 n.2 (2015). In determining whether another proceeding involves similar issues, the amicus and its counsel need only consider issues that have been explicitly raised in, and that are directly relevant to, the other proceeding and the present appeal. Likewise, in determining whether another proceeding or transaction is at issue in the present appeal, the amicus and its counsel need only consider whether that proceeding or transaction has been explicitly put at issue in the appeal. Similar to Fed. R. App. P. 29(a)(4)(E), the Commonwealth and its officer or agency are exempted from the requirements in Rule 17(c)(5).

Rule 17(d) contains the last sentence of prior Rule 17 as a stand-alone subdivision. The text "counsel for each party separately represented" was replaced with "each party," consistent with the with the new definition of "party" in Rule 1(c). The cross-reference to Rule 19(b) was changed to Rule 19(d) to conform to changes in Rule 19.

Rule 17(e) contains the fifth sentence of prior Rule 17 as a stand-alone subdivision. The standard for allowing a motion of an amicus curiae to participate in oral argument was changed from "extraordinary reasons" to "good cause" to reflect that an amicus curiae's participation at oral argument may be desirable for a variety of reasons, even if those reasons might not be fairly described as "extraordinary."

Further organizational and stylistic revisions were made to this rule in 2019 in accordance with a global review and revision of all of the Appellate Rules. These revisions are described in the 2019 Reporter's Notes to Rule 1.

With regard to the preparation of the 2019 Reporter's Notes to this Rule, see the first paragraph of the 2019 Reporter's Notes to Rule 1. For an overview of the 2019 amendments to the Rules and a summary of the global amendments to the Rules, see 2019 Reporter's Notes to Rule 1, sections *I.* and *II.*

Rule 18. Appendix to the Briefs: Contents, Cost, Filing, and Service

(a) Duty of Appellant to Prepare and File; Content of Appendix; Time for Filing; Number of Copies. The appellant shall prepare and file an appendix to the briefs which shall be separately bound. The parties are cautioned that, under Rule 9, the lower court does not ordinarily transmit the entire record to the appellate court. Therefore, the appendix or appendices must include the items specified in this rule.

(1) *Requirements in Civil and Criminal Cases.*

(A) The appendix shall contain, in the order hereinafter provided:

(i) a cover that conforms substantially to Rules 20(a)(5)(A) and (a)(6).

(ii) a table of contents, listing the parts of the record reproduced therein, and including a detailed listing of exhibits, affidavits, and other documents associated with those parts, with references to the pages of the appendix at which each begins;

(iii) the docket entries in the lower court proceedings;

(iv) any order of impoundment or confidentiality from the lower court; and

(v) in chronological order of filing in the lower court:

(a) any parts of the record relied upon in the brief, and in a criminal case, a copy of the complaint or indictment;

(b) any document, or portion thereof, filed in the case relating to an issue which is to be argued on appeal;

(c) any findings or memorandum of decision or order by the lower court pertinent to an issue on appeal, including a typed version of any pertinent handwritten or oral endorsement, notation, findings, or order made by the lower court;

(d) the judgment, decree, order, or adjudication in question; and

(e) the notice(s) of appeal.

(B) Except where they have independent relevance, memoranda of law in the lower court should not be included in the appendix.

(C) The first volume of a multi-volume appendix shall include a complete table of contents referencing all volumes of the appendix, and each individual volume shall include a table of contents for that volume.

(D) The court may decline to permit the parties to refer to portions of the record omitted from the appendix, but the fact that parts of the record are not included in the appendix shall not prevent the court from relying on such parts.

(E) When an appendix contains materials from more than 1 lower court case, the table of contents shall clearly indicate, by reference to the lower court docket number, the case in which each paper was filed and by whom it was filed.

(F) Any reproduction of an exhibit in an appendix shall be of high quality to ensure a legible and accurate representation of the exhibit, including color if color is relevant. A color photograph marked or admitted as an exhibit in the lower court and included in the appendix must be reproduced in color. Lower court color-coded forms need not be reproduced in color.

(2) *Additional Requirements in a Criminal Case.*

(A) The appellee in a criminal case must include any part of the record relied on by the appellee not otherwise included in the appellant's appendix or contained in the transcript.

(B) An appendix may contain relevant excerpts of the transcript, but should not duplicate the entire transcript transmitted from the lower court to the appellate court.

(b) Determination of Contents of Appendix in Civil Cases; Cost of Producing; Supplemental Appendix.

(1) The parties are encouraged to agree as to the contents of the appendix. In the absence of agreement, the appellant shall, not later than 14 days after receiving from the clerk of the lower court the notice of assembly of the record, serve on the appellee a designation of the parts of the record which the appellant intends to include in the appendix and a statement of the issues which the appellant intends to present for review. If the appellee deems it necessary to direct the particular attention of the court to parts of the record not designated by the appellant, the appellee shall, within 14 days after receipt of the designation, serve upon the appellant a designation of those parts. The parties shall not engage in unnecessary designation and may refer to parts of the record not included in the appendix if permitted by the appellate court or a single justice pursuant to the provisions of Rule 18(a)(1)(D). However, this does not affect the responsibility of the parties to include materials necessary to their appeal, including exhibits, in the appendix.

(2) Where a party designates as part of the record any matter that has been impounded or has been made confidential by statute, rule, or order, the designation shall so state.

(3) Unless the parties otherwise agree, the cost of producing the appendix shall initially be paid by the appellant, but if the appellant considers that parts of the record designated by the appellee for inclusion are unnecessary for the determination of the issues presented the appellant may so advise the appellee and the appellee shall advance the cost of including

such parts. In the event of a dispute as to the parts to be included or the cost advance required to include them, the matter shall be settled by the lower court on motion and notice. The cost of producing the appendix shall be taxed as costs in the case, but if either party shall cause matters to be included in the appendix unnecessarily the court may impose the cost of producing such parts on the party.

(4) Depending on the issues raised on appeal and the applicable standards of review, it may be necessary for the party filing the appendix to reproduce the entire transcript of the relevant lower court proceedings. Failure to reproduce the entire transcript may result in waiver of the issue. If the party does not reproduce a transcript of the entire proceedings, the party shall, preceding each portion of transcript reproduced, insert a concise statement identifying:

(A) the witness whose testimony is being reproduced;

(B) the party originally calling the witness;

(C) the party questioning the witness;

(D) the classification of the witness's examination (direct, cross, or other); and

(E) the transcript volume and page number from which the reproduced testimony is derived.

(5) *Supplemental Appendix in a Civil Case.* Except with leave of the appellate court or a single justice granted on motion, an appellee or cross-appellee in a civil case shall not file a supplemental appendix. Where such leave is granted, the appendix shall

(A) be filed and served with the brief pursuant to Rules 18(f) and 19, unless otherwise ordered;

(B) include only materials that are part of the record;

(C) not generally include materials already in the appellant's appendix, unless necessary for context; and

(D) be in the form prescribed by Rules 18(a)(1) and 20(a)(5) and (a)(6).

(c) **Reproduction of Transcripts in Civil Cases.** In a civil case, transcripts or portions thereof shall be reproduced for inclusion in the appendix consistent with Rule 18(b)(4).

(d) **Reproduction of Impounded Materials.** If the entire case has been impounded, the cover of the appendix shall clearly indicate that the appendix is impounded. If the entire case has not been impounded, a separate appendix volume shall be filed containing the impounded material and a copy of any lower court order(s) impounding the material, and the cover thereof shall clearly indicate that it contains impounded material.

(e) **Reproduction of electronic audio or audiovisual exhibit.** At the time of filing an appendix containing a reproduction of an electronic audio or audio-visual exhibit that was part of the lower court record, the filing party shall file a written notice with the clerk, with a copy of the notice sent to all parties, so indicating the inclusion of such reproduction, and specifying the form in which it is reproduced.

(f) **Filing and Service.** Any appendix, including exhibits and transcripts or portions thereof in a civil case, shall be filed and served with the brief in accordance with Rule 19.

(g) **Amendment of Appendix.** On motion for good cause, the court may grant leave for a party to file an amended appendix volume. The motion shall describe the nature and reason for the amendment. The party shall file with the motion the amended appendix volume marked as such on the front page or cover. Except as the court otherwise orders, the filing of an amended appendix volume has no effect on any filing deadlines.

Amended effective February 24, 1975; amended June 2, 1976, effective July 1, 1976; May 15, 1979, effective July 1, 1979; April 25, 1984, effective July 1, 1984; November 17, 1986, effective January 1, 1987; amended effective February 1, 1991; May 1, 1994; amended June 11, 1997, effective July 1, 1997; October 1, 1998, effective November 2, 1998; October 31, 2018, effective March 1, 2019.

Reporter's Notes—1973

Appellate Rule 18 indicates the required contents of the appendix, preparation of which is appellant's responsibility; the appendix must be filed with appellant's brief. Appellate Rule 18(b) encourages the parties to agree as to the contents of the joint appendix. Appellate Rule 18(c) permits the parties, at the election of the appellant, with leave of the appellate court or a single justice, to defer preparation of the appendix until after the briefs have been filed; it sets out detailed regulations for appropriate pagination of the deferred appendix and consequent references in the briefs. It should be emphasized that transcript pages included in the appendix may be reproduced by Xerography or a similar process; they need not be retyped. See Appellate Rule 20(a). The procedures set out in Appellate Rule 18, although necessarily somewhat different from existing practice, should not cause any serious practitional dislocation. See S.J.C. Rule 1:22.

Reporter's Notes—1975

The amendment to Appellate Rule 18(d) ensures that in a multiparty appeal, each paper appearing in the reproduced appendix bears sufficient identification to permit the reader easily to understand the document's particular genesis and significance.

Reporter's Notes—1979

A major change in criminal appellate procedure is worked by the application of Rule 18, as amended, to criminal cases. Under prior practice, after the record was assembled by the clerk, he would prepare a "summary of the record" which included a copy of the indictment or complaint and copies of pleadings and motions designated by the parties (former G.L. c. 278, § 33C [St.1974, c. 458, § 1]). This summary, in the required number of copies (former G.L. c. 278, § 33 [St.1978, c. 478, § 308]; Appeals Court and Supreme Judicial Court Rules 1:01 [1975: 3 Mass.App.Ct. 801–02. 366 Mass. 858, amended March 2, 1978]) was reproduced at the expense of the Commonwealth. The summary, together with two copies of the transcript and the assignment of errors (former G.L. c. 278, § 33D [St.1974, c. 458, § 2]), constituted the record on appeal (former G.L. c. 278, § 33E [St.1974, c. 457]). Under Rule 8(a), as amended, the record on appeal now consists of the original papers and exhibits on file, the transcript and a copy of the docket entries. The entire record is not transmitted to the appellate court except upon that court's order (Rule 9[a], [d]). The place of the summary of the record is taken by an appendix to the briefs, the contents of which are described in Rule 18(a). Responsibility for preparation of the appendix (properly "record appendix") rests with the appellant. If the appellee wishes to direct the particular attention of the court to parts of the record not contained in the appendix prepared by the appellant, he may prepare and file with his brief a supplemental appendix.

As in civil cases, the record appendix "is that distillation of the decision-essential portions of the record [on appeal]." Mass.R.App.P. 8, Reporter's Notes [1974]).

Subdivision (a) is changed by reducing from twenty-five to fifteen the number of copies of the appendix required to be filed, and, as amended, applies to both civil and criminal cases.

Subdivisions (b) and (c) are limited in application to civil cases.

Subdivision (d) restates in part the requirements of former Appeals Court and Supreme Judicial Court Rules 1:01, supra, relative to the contents of the record appendix and designation of the papers in a record.

Subdivisions (e) and (f) are unchanged.

Reporter's Notes—1984

Under previous Mass.R.A.P. 18(e) a party on appeal could put "exhibits designated for inclusion in the appendix" in "a separate volume, or volumes" and then file only "five copies," plus serve one copy "on counsel for each party separately represented." This reduced the number of copies of exhibits otherwise required under Mass.R.A.P. 18(a). The present amendment to Mass.R.A.P. 18(e) adds "transcripts or portions thereof in civil cases" to "exhibits," to further decrease the cost of appeals and reduce the number of documents which must be handled and stored by appellate courts.

The reference to Mass.R.A.P. 18(e), which has now been added to Rule 18(a), is to remind counsel to check Rule 18(e) in order to consider whether they wish to reduce the required copies of exhibits and "transcripts or portions thereof in civil cases" from fifteen, plus two for "counsel for each party separately represented," to five, plus one copy for such counsel. This change also makes clear that the "five copies" option in Rule 18(e) is instead of, and not in addition to, the "fifteen copies" otherwise required by the provisions of Rule 18(a).

These amendments do not alter the rules in criminal cases, which obligate the clerk of the lower court to transmit to the appellate court the "original and one copy of the transcript and a list of all the exhibits" and provide that ". . . the appendix need not contain relevant portions of the transcript . . ." (Mass.R.A.P. 9(d) and 18(a)).

Reporter's Notes—1986

This amendment corresponds to a 1986 amendment to F.R.A.P. 30(a). As the Committee Note to that amendment suggests, the inclusion of memoranda of law can make an appendix bulky and less useful to the appellate court, and also increase litigation costs. "There are occasions when such trial court memoranda have independent relevance in the appellate litigation. For instance, there may be a dispute as to whether a particular point was raised or whether a concession was made in the . . . [lower court]. In such circumstances, it is appropriate to include pertinent sections of such memoranda in the appendix."

Reporter's Notes—1991

This amendment reduces the number of copies of the appendix required to be filed in the Appeals Court from fifteen to the numbers of copies of the brief required under Mass.R.A.P. 19(b). For example, unless an exception applies, a party is required to file seven copies of both the briefs and the appendix in the Appeals Court and fifteen copies in the Supreme Judicial Court. The reasons for the reduction are explained in the Reporter's Notes to Amended Rule 19(b).

Reporter's Notes to Mass.R.A.P. 18(b)—1994

The prior language in Mass.R.A.P. 18(b) stated that "[i]n designating parts of the record for inclusion in the appendix, the parties shall have regard for the fact that the entire record is always available to the court for reference and examination and shall not engage in unnecessary designation." Since the parties have the obligation in Rule 18(a) and (b) to designate portions of the record upon which they will rely, and in civil cases must include relevant portions of the transcript, it was unclear what it meant "to have regard for the fact that the entire record is always available to the court." This phrase was particularly ambiguous because the parties in civil cases have no right to rely upon portions of the transcript that are not designated.

Rules 18(b) and 18(f), which under some circumstances permit the parties to rely on parts of the record that have not been included in the appendix, specifically refer to leave granted prior to argument or a motion in advance granted by the appellate court or a single justice. The new language is in keeping with the normal expectation of appellate judges that the parties will provide appellate courts with an appendix which includes the materials upon which they rely. See Shawmut Community Bank, N.A. v. Zagami, 411 Mass. 807, 810–812 (1992).

Reporter's Notes—1997

The 1997 amendment to Appellate Rule 18(a) requires that where any matter has been impounded or made confidential in the lower court, a copy of the lower court order of impoundment, if any, be included in the appendix. The amendment to Appellate Rule 18(b) requires that where such matter is to be included in the record, the fact that the matter has been impounded or made confidential be indicated in the designation of the record.

The amendment to Appellate Rule 18(g) places the burden on counsel to inform the appellate clerk's office that confidential information is contained in an appendix and to prepare a separate appendix volume in instances where less than the entire case has been impounded. The purpose of this amendment, as is the purpose of the simultaneous amendments to Appellate Rules 16(d) and (m), is to facilitate the work of the clerk's office in maintaining the confidentiality of information filed in the appellate court. See Reporter's Notes to Appellate Rules 16(d) and (m).

Reporter's Notes to Mass.R.A.P. 18(e)—1998

This amendment is intended to further decrease the cost of appeals and further reduce the quantity of documents which must be handled and stored by the appellate courts. In the Appeals Court, the number of transcript copies in civil cases (if separately bound) has been reduced to two, which is the same requirement as in criminal cases (see Mass.R.A.P. 9(d)). If a case is transferred to the Supreme Judicial Court after the filing of a reduced number of copies in the Appeals Court, three additional copies of the transcript must be filed in the Supreme Judicial Court.

Reporter's Notes—2019

Rule 18 was reorganized and substantially revised to clarify the required contents of the record appendix, as well as the procedures governing the cost, filing, and service of the record appendix. In accordance with these revisions, the title of this rule was amended to "Appendix to the Briefs: Contents, Cost, Filing, and Service."

Rule 18(a). The entire subdivision was reorganized and separated into numbered paragraphs to improve clarity and for easy reference. The rule was also amended to require all paper appendices to be bound and filed separately from the brief. This is intended to facilitate the appellate courts' paperless practices, which includes the scanning of paper briefs, and is consistent with the requirements for electronically filed briefs. A cautionary note was added to alert parties that the entire record ordinarily is not transmitted by the lower court to the appellate court, and therefore the appendix must include the items identified in the rule. Because the appendix is filed at the same time as a brief, the requirements related to filing and service of the appendix in prior Rule 18(a) were revised and relocated to Rule 19. See Reporter's Notes to Rule 19.

Rule 18(a)(1) was revised to present, in a checklist format, the common items that must be included in a record appendix filed in civil and criminal cases.

Rule 18(a)(1)(A) lists the items in the order in which they must appear in an appendix. Prior Rule 18(a) did not explicitly specify the arrangement of an appendix. As a result, the format of appendices was often inconsistent, making it difficult to locate necessary parts of the record below. This amendment is intended to streamline the rule as to the content and arrangement of an appendix, reduce confusion for litigants, help ensure appendices are complete, and facilitate review by the appellate court.

Language was added to require inclusion of the notice(s) of appeal and any written or oral findings or memorandum of decision issued by the lower court and relevant to the appeal. Notably, although Rule 16(a)(13) requires the judge's order or decision at issue to be included in a brief's addendum, it also must be included in the appendix. The duplication is required because of the different purposes served by the addendum and appendix: the addendum is for the convenient reference of the judges and parties, and the appendix is a compilation of all relevant lower court documents and is used for record reference purposes.

In Rule 18(a)(1)(A)(iii), the word "relevant" that qualified "docket entries" in prior Rule 18(a) was removed. The inclusion of the entire trial court docket provides a better context for review of the issues on appeal. A printout or copy of the lower court docket is acceptable.

Rule 18(a)(1)(A)(v)(d). The amendment requiring the inclusion of the "judgment, decree, order, or adjudication in question" does not necessarily mean verdict slips must be included in the appendix, but might if the verdict slips are relevant to an issue on appeal.

Rule 18(a)(1)(B) continues the requirement from prior Rule 18(a) that memoranda of law filed in the lower court should not be included in the appendix unless they have independent relevance. As stated in the 1986 Reporter's Notes to Rule 18:

> the inclusion of memoranda of law can make an appendix bulky and less useful to the appellate court, and also increase litigation costs. There are occasions when such trial court memoranda have independent relevance in the appellate litigation. For instance, there may be a dispute as to whether a particular point was raised or whether a concession was made in the ... [lower court]. In such circumstances, it is appropriate to include pertinent sections of such memoranda in the appendix.'

Rule 18(a)(1)(C) is a new subparagraph intended to facilitate the reading of appendices in electronic form, consistent with the appellate court's paperless practices, and particularly in cases in which multiple appendix volumes are filed. The first volume of the appendix is to include a complete table of contents referencing all volumes of the appendix, and each individual volume must include a table of contents for that volume. To facilitate review by the court, the table of contents should identify each separate document included in each respective volume and the page in the volume where the document begins. Further, when a principal document contains multiple documents attached as exhibits, such as a motion for summary judgment package or administrative agency record, the table of contents should list the motion and each individual document filed with the motion, and the page of the appendix where each document is located.

Rule 18(a)(1)(D) relocates and clarifies the provision included in prior Rule 18(a) regarding an appellant's obligation to include all relevant portions of the record in the appendix. However, although an appellant must provide the reviewing court with all relevant portions of the record, Shawmut Community Bank, N.A. v. Zagami, 411 Mass. 807, 811 (1992), an appellate court is entitled, in its discretion, to rely on parts of the record even if not included in the record appendix. Commonwealth v. Morse, 50 Mass. App. Ct. 582, 586 n.3 (2000). As stated in the 1994 Reporter's Notes to an amendment to Rule 18(b):

> Rules 18(b) and 18(f), which under some circumstances permit the parties to rely on parts of the record that have not been included in the appendix, specifically refer to leave granted prior to argument or a motion in advance granted by the appellate court or a single justice. The new language is in keeping with the normal expectation of appellate judges that the parties will provide appellate courts with an appendix which includes the materials upon which they rely. See Shawmut Community Bank, N.A. v. Zagami, 411 Mass. 807, 810–812 (1992).

Rule 18(a)(1)(E) relocates language from prior Rule 18(d) regarding an appendix that contains materials from more than one lower court case. Similar to the prior rule, the appendix must indicate the case to which each document belongs and by whom it was filed.

Rule 18(a)(1)(F) is a new subparagraph that requires any exhibit reproduced in the appendix to be of high quality to ensure it is a legible and accurate reproduction, including color, if the color is relevant. The rule requires that a color photograph marked or admitted as an exhibit in the lower court and included in the appendix be reproduced in color. The rule specifically excludes court forms which are color coded and which may be submitted in black and white instead of color, but must be legible. Frequently, parties file a record appendix containing exhibits that were copied, scanned, or reproduced in such poor quality that it is difficult or impossible for the appellate court to read or view the exhibit. With the advent of electronic filing in the appellate courts and the use of electronic devices to view appendices, this amendment is necessary to ensure that the highest possible quality images are provided.

Language in prior Rule 18(a) that referred to a process for deferral of a record appendix pursuant to prior Rule 18(c) was deleted because Rule 18(c) was deleted in the amended rules, as described below.

Rule 18(a)(2) is a new paragraph titled "Additional Requirements in a Criminal Case," which specifies items in addition to those required in Rule 18(a)(1) that must be included in the appendix in criminal cases only. Rule 18(a)(2)(A) is a new subparagraph which imposes an obligation on the appellee in a criminal case to include any part of the record on which the appellee relies that is not otherwise included in the appellant's appendix or contained in the transcript. This requirement addresses situations where necessary documents are omitted from both parties' appendices even though they are discussed in the appellee's brief. As in prior Rule 18(a), the appellee in a criminal case may file a supplemental appendix containing relevant portions of the lower court record without filing a motion, when the supplemental appendix is filed at the same time as the appellee's brief. Rule 18(a)(2)(B) provides for optional inclusion in the appendix of excerpts of the transcript in criminal cases. In criminal cases, either party may, but are not required to, reproduce relevant portions of the transcript in the appendix but should not duplicate the entire transcript as it is already available to the appellate court.

Prior Rule 18(b) was amended to create three numbered paragraphs. The timeframe regarding the parties' agreement as to the contents of an appendix in a civil case is included in Rule 18(b)(1). Rule 18(b)(1) was amended to be triggered by the appellant "receiving from the clerk of the lower court the notice of assembly of the record." This phrase replaces the prior phrase "the date on which the clerk notifies the parties that the record has been assembled" in the second sentence. The change is consistent with amendments to Rule 10(a). The reference to prior Rule 18(f) was struck, as that subdivision was deleted from the amended rule for the reasons stated below.

Rule 18(b)(4) outlines the requirements, relocated from prior Rule 18(d), applicable when a party in a civil case reproduces only portions of a transcript. A cautionary note is added to this paragraph to alert the parties that it may be necessary to reproduce the entire transcript of the relevant court proceedings; otherwise waiver of one or more issues may result. It is essential that parties provide the relevant portions of the transcripts of proceedings in the lower court. Parties often relied on the prior rule to submit incomplete transcripts to support their appellate arguments, and subsequently the appellate court reviewing the appeal determined that additional portions of the transcript, or even the entire transcript, were necessary for proper review of the issues on appeal. This language makes clear that a partial transcript may not be appropriate for every civil case.

Rule 18(b)(5) is a new paragraph which addresses the filing of a supplemental appendix in civil cases. The requirements for filing a supplemental appendix are included in separate subparagraphs for ease of reference. Appellees and cross-appellees in civil cases often submit supplemental appendices without realizing that leave of court is required. This rule clarifies the process for filing a supplemental appendix in a civil appeal and incorporates current practice requiring leave of court for such filing. This rule promotes judicial efficiency by reducing delays associated with the submission of a supplemental appendix without leave of court and ensures that the docket will note the filing of a supplemental appendix. In addition, requiring leave of court in a civil matter encourages parties to abide by the provisions of Rule 18(b) regarding designation and agreement as to the contents of the record appendix at the outset of the case.

Prior Rule 18(c) was deleted in its entirety. The subdivision permitted the appellant to elect, with the court's permission, to defer preparation of the appendix until after the briefs had been filed. In practice, requests to defer appendix preparation pursuant to Rule 18(c) were rarely filed, and, if filed, were rarely allowed. Deferral of preparation of the appendix resulted in delay in the appellate process and unnecessary duplication of the parties' efforts. In the future rare circumstance where deferral of appendix preparation may be appropriate, Rule 2, which allows for suspension of the rules by the appellate court or a single justice, and Rule 15(c), which governs motions generally, would suffice to afford the parties an opportunity to request leave to defer the appendix.

The filing and service requirements related to exhibits and transcripts in prior Rule 18(e), were relocated, with slight revisions, to Rule 19(d)(2). This amendment was made because exhibits and transcripts are filed and served contemporaneous with a brief. See Reporter's Notes to Rule 19(d)(2). The remainder of prior Rule 18(e) was designated in the amended rules as Rule 18(c), and is revised to clarify that in civil cases parties are authorized to reproduce exhibits and transcripts or portions thereof for inclusion in the appendix.

Prior Rule 18(f) was deleted in its entirety. Parties sometimes requested to proceed on the original record for purposes of expediency or instead of incurring the expense of preparation of an appendix. Such motions were rarely, if ever, allowed because the appendix materials and organization are essential to the appellate courts' review of the issues on appeal, and multiple copies of the pertinent record materials are required because multiple justices are involved in reviewing the record. In the rare circumstance where allowance of such a motion may be appropriate, Rule 2, which allows for suspension of the rules by the appellate court or a single justice, and Rule 15(c), which governs motions generally, would suffice to enable proceeding in this alternative manner.

Rule 18(d), which comprises prior Rule 18(g), adds a requirement to the prior rule that when a separate appendix of impounded material is filed, any lower court order impounding the material must be included in the impounded appendix volume(s). This amendment codifies current impoundment procedures and further ensures the protection of the impounded information.

Rule 18(e) is a new subdivision addressing the reproduction of electronic audio or audiovisual exhibits. This subdivision requires parties who include reproductions of these exhibits in their appendix to notify the clerk, with a copy of this notice sent to all parties, indicating the inclusion of such reproduction and specifying the form in which the material is reproduced. Parties sometimes file a reproduction of an electronic audio or audiovisual exhibit but do not alert the appellate court clerk that it has been included in the appendix. The requirement of filing a written notice with the clerk's office ensures that the appellate court is aware that the electronic audio or audiovisual exhibit has been included and can be properly processed and stored.

Rule 18(f) is a new subdivision addressing filing and service of the appendix, including exhibits and transcripts or portions thereof filed in a civil case. The subdivision incorporates the requirements of Rule 19 to the filing and service of the appendix.

Rule 18(g) is a new subdivision that codifies existing appellate court practice regarding the filing of an amended appendix volume. The amended document (which sometimes is titled "revised" or "correct-

ed") is to be submitted to the court contemporaneous with a motion seeking leave to file the amended document.

Further organizational and stylistic revisions were made to this rule in 2019 in accordance with a global review and revision of all of the Appellate Rules. These revisions are described in the 2019 Reporter's Notes to Rule 1.

With regard to the preparation of the 2019 Reporter's Notes to this Rule, see the first paragraph of the 2019 Reporter's Notes to Rule 1. For an overview of the 2019 amendments to the Rules and a summary of the global amendments to the Rules, see 2019 Reporter's Notes to Rule 1, sections *I.* and *II.*

Rule 19. Filing and Serving of Briefs, Appendices, and Certain Motions

(a) Time for Serving and Filing Briefs and Appendices in All Cases Except Cross Appeals. Except as provided in Rule 19(c) (first degree murder appeals), Rule 11(g)(4) (direct appellate review), and Rule 27.1(f) (further appellate review), the following briefs and appendices shall be due as stated below:

(1) *Appellant Brief and Appendix.* The appellant shall serve and file a brief and appendix within 40 days after the date on which the appeal is docketed in the appellate court.

(2) *Appellee Brief.* The appellee shall serve and file a brief within 30 days after service of the brief of the appellant (or, in the case of multiple appellants, service of the last appellant brief).

(3) *Reply Brief.* Except by leave of court, any reply brief must be served and filed by the earlier of

(A) 14 days after service of the brief of the appellee (or, in the case of multiple appellees, service of the last appellee brief), or

(B) 7 days before argument.

(b) Time for Serving and Filing Briefs and Appendices in Cases Involving Cross Appeals. Except as provided in Rule 19(c) (first degree murder appeals), Rule 11(g) (direct appellate review), and Rule 27.1(f) (further appellate review), the following briefs and appendices shall be due when stated:

(1) *Appellant's Principal Brief and Appendix.* The appellant/cross-appellee shall serve and file a brief and appendix within 40 days after the date on which the appeal is docketed in the appellate court.

(2) *Appellee's Principal and Response Brief and Appendix.* The appellee/cross-appellant shall serve and file a brief and appendix within 30 days after service of the brief and appendix of the appellant (or, in the case of multiple appellants, service of the last appellant brief).

(3) *Appellant's Response and Reply Brief.* The appellant/cross-appellee reply brief must be served and filed within 30 days after service of the brief of the appellee/cross-appellant.

(4) *Appellee's Reply Brief.* Except by leave of court, any reply brief must be served and filed by the appellee/cross-appellant by the earlier of (A) 14 days after service of the brief of the appellant/cross-appellee (or, in the case of multiple appellants/cross-appellees, service of the last appellant/cross-appellee brief), or (B) 7 days before argument.

(c) Time for Serving and Filing Briefs, Appendices, and Motions for New Trial in First Degree Murder Appeals.

(1) In the case of a direct appeal by an appellant who has been convicted of first degree murder, the appellant shall within 120 days after the date on which the appeal is docketed in the Supreme Judicial Court: (A) serve and file the appellant's brief and appendix; (B) serve and file a motion for a new trial; or (C) for good cause shown, seek a further enlargement of time for filing a brief and appendix or a motion for a new trial. The Commonwealth shall serve and file its brief within 90 days after service of the brief of the appellant. The appellant may serve and file a reply brief within the 30 days after service of the brief of the Commonwealth.

(2) If during the pendency of the direct appeal a motion for a new trial is remanded to the Superior Court, the direct appeal of the conviction will ordinarily be stayed until the motion is decided. The matter shall be heard and determined expeditiously in the Superior Court. The appellant shall file with the Clerk of the Supreme Judicial Court for the Commonwealth status reports as directed by the Court. An appeal by the defendant from the denial of a motion for a new trial shall be consolidated with the direct appeal. An appeal by the Commonwealth or by the defendant from the determination of a motion for a new trial shall have the same docket number as the direct appeal. The Clerk of the Supreme Judicial Court for the Commonwealth shall establish a briefing schedule.

(d) Number of Copies to Be Filed and Served.

(1) *Briefs and Appendices.*

(A) Appeals Court. Except as provided in the Appeals Court Standing Order Concerning Electronic Filing, on appeal to the Appeals Court, 4 copies of each brief and appendix shall be filed with the clerk, unless the court by order in a particular case shall direct a different number, and 2 copies shall be served on counsel for each party separately represented, 2 copies of each shall be served on counsel for all jointly represented parties, and 2 copies of each shall be served on each self-represented party to the appeal, unless the parties agree in writing or the court shall by rule or by order direct the filing or service of a different number.

(B) Supreme Judicial Court.

(i) On appeal to the Supreme Judicial Court, 7 copies of each brief and appendix shall be filed with the clerk, unless the court by order in a particular case shall direct a different number, and 2 copies shall be served on counsel for each party separately represented, 2 copies of each shall be served on counsel for all jointly represented parties, and 2 copies of each shall be served on each self-represented party to the appeal, unless the parties agree in writing or the court shall by rule or by order direct the filing or service of a different number.

(ii) Appeals Transferred to the Supreme Judicial Court from the Appeals Court. In any appeal transferred to the full Supreme Judicial Court, in which briefs and appendices have already been filed in the Appeals Court, 7 copies of each brief and appendix shall be promptly filed with the clerk of the Supreme Judicial Court, unless the court by order in a particular case shall direct a different number.

(2) *Exhibits and Transcripts in Civil Cases.* Exhibits and transcripts or portions thereof in civil cases, designated for inclusion in the appendix, may be contained in separate volumes, suitably indexed.

(A) Appeals Court. Except as provided in the Appeals Court Standing Order Concerning Electronic Filing, on appeal to the Appeals Court, 2 copies of the exhibit volume or volumes, and 1 copy of the transcript volume or volumes shall be filed with the brief and appendix and 1 copy of each shall be served on counsel for each party separately represented, 1 copy of each shall be served on counsel for all jointly represented parties, and 1 copy of each shall be served on each self-represented party to the appeal, unless the parties agree in writing or the court shall by rule or order direct the filing or service of a different number.

(B) Supreme Judicial Court.

(i) On appeal to the Supreme Judicial Court, and on further appellate review, 2 copies of the exhibit volume or volumes and 2 copies of the transcript volume or volumes shall be filed with the brief and appendix and 1 copy of each shall be served on counsel for each party separately represented, 1 copy of each shall be served on counsel for all jointly represented parties, and 1 copy of each shall be served on each self-represented party to the appeal, unless the parties agree in writing or the court shall by rule or by order direct the filing or service of a different number.

(ii) Appeals Transferred to the Supreme Judicial Court from the Appeals Court. In any appeal transferred to the full Supreme Judicial Court, in which copies of the exhibits and transcripts have already been filed in the Appeals Court pursuant to this rule, 2 copies of the transcript volume or volumes shall be promptly filed with the clerk of the Supreme Judicial Court, unless the court by order in a particular case shall direct a different number.

(e) Consequence of Failure to File Briefs and Appendices. If an appellant fails to file a brief and appendix, other than a reply brief, within the time provided by this rule, or within the time as extended, the appellate court may, upon motion or sua sponte, dismiss the appeal. Any appellee who elects not to file a principal brief shall timely notify the appellate court and all parties that no brief will be filed. If an appellee fails to file a brief within the time provided by this rule, or within the time as extended, the appellate court may, upon motion or sua sponte, deem the case ready for consideration by the appellate court. An appellee who fails to file a timely brief will not be heard at oral argument except by permission of the appellate court.

Amended May 15, 1979, effective July 1, 1979; amended effective February 1, 1991; July 1, 1991; amended October 30, 1997, effective January 1, 1998; July 28, 1999, effective October 1, 1999; February 25, 2004, effective April 1, 2004; October 31, 2018, effective March 1, 2019.

Reporter's Notes—1973

Appellate Rule 19 sets the time table for the filing of briefs. Appellant must file his brief within 40 days after the docketing of the appeal (which occurs ten days after the record is assembled, see Appellate Rule 10(a); assembly occurs "as soon as may be after the filing of the notice of appeal," Appellate Rule 9(a)). Thus appellant's brief ordinarily must be filed approximately 50 days after the filing of his notice of appeal, (plus however long the lower court clerk requires for assembling the record). Appellee must file his brief within 30 days after service of appellant's brief. The appellant may serve a reply brief within 14 days after service of the appellee's brief. Although Appellate Rule 19 somewhat enlarges previous appellate timetables, see S.J.C. Rule 1:16 and Appeals Court Rule 1:16, it should occasion no unusual difficulties.

Reporter's Notes—1979

There is no change in the substance of subdivision (a), but applying the rule to criminal appeals does enlarge the times for filing of the appellant's brief found in former Appeals Court and Supreme Judicial Court Rules 1:16 (1975: 3 Mass.App.Ct. 804. 366 Mass. 861–62) from twenty-eight to forty days after docketing (Mass.R.App.P. 10[b]). Further, under the former court rules, the appellee's brief was required to be filed within forty-nine days after entry of the case, while up to seventy days after docketing is allowed by this rule (within thirty days after service of appellant's brief). Thus, in the usual appeal, the defendant's brief is due forty days after docketing and the Commonwealth's brief thirty days thereafter. The abolishing of assignments of error (former G.L. c. 278, § 33D [St.1974, c. 458, § 2]) eliminate one step in prior appellate procedure which generated a great deal of delay. Section 33D of chapter 278 required that assignments were to be filed within thirty days after receipt of notice of the completion of the summary of the record (G.L. c. 278, § 33C [St.1974, c. 458, § 1]), but that time could be extended by a justice of an appellate or lower court. Much of the delay was attributable to the fact that assignments could not be prepared until the trial transcript had been received and reviewed for error.

Appeals Court and Supreme Judicial Court Rules 1:16 permitted either party to file a reply brief; under Rule 19, only the appellant may do so. Twenty-five copies of each were required to be filed by both the former court rules and by Appellate Rule 19(b). Subdivision (b) has been amended to reduce that number to fifteen, the reduction being applicable in civil and criminal cases alike. The requirement in subdivision (b) that two copies of briefs be served upon each party separately represented is consistent with former Appeals Court and Supreme Judicial Court Rules 1:16.

Reporter's Notes—1991

Experience has demonstrated that seven copies of briefs are needed by the Appeals Court and fifteen by the Supreme Judicial Court. This amendment, reducing the number of copies from fifteen in the Appeals Court, should save money for the parties and the Commonwealth, as well as storage space for the court. When a case is transferred from the Appeals Court to the Supreme Judicial Court, in which briefs have already been filed, the clerk of the Appeals Court must transmit the seven copies of the briefs already filed (Mass.R.A.P. 11(f)), and the parties must promptly deliver an additional eight copies to the clerk of the Supreme Judicial Court (Mass.R.A.P. 19(b)(3)).

Reporter's Notes—1997

The 1997 amendments to Appellate Rule 19(b) were prompted by the need for additional copies of filings to accommodate the practice in which all seven Justices of the Supreme Judicial Court sit on many cases.

Appellate Rule 19(b)(2), dealing with appeals to the Supreme Judicial Court, was amended to increase to seventeen the number of copies of each brief to be filed with the clerk of the Supreme Judicial Court, unless otherwise ordered. The amendment also clarified that an original is to be filed together with the seventeen copies.

Appellate Rule 19(b)(3), dealing with appeals transferred to the Supreme Judicial Court from the Appeals Court in cases where briefs had already been filed in the Appeals Court, was amended to increase to eleven the number of additional copies to be filed with the clerk of the Supreme Judicial Court, unless otherwise ordered.

Reporter's Notes—1999

The 1999 amendments added new Appellate Rule 19(d) to deal with direct appeals to the Supreme Judicial Court from first-degree murder convictions pursuant to G.L. c. 278, § 33E. The changes to Appellate Rule 19 were based on recommendations made by the Ad Hoc Supreme Judicial Court Committee on Appeals in Cases of Murder in the First Degree, a committee consisting of defense attorneys and prosecutors who handle first degree murder appeals. The major purpose of the amendments was to establish realistic time periods for the briefing of such appeals.

Paragraph (1) of Appellate Rule 19(d) substantially lengthens the time period for the service and filing of briefs that is provided for cases other than first-degree murder appeals in Appellate Rule 19(a). The time period for the appellant's brief has been increased from 40 days to 120 days; the time period for the Commonwealth's brief has been increased from 30 days to 90 days (and any reply brief by the appellant to be served and filed within 30 days). A defendant must serve and file a motion for new trial within 120 days of docketing the appeal in the Supreme Judicial Court.

Paragraph (2) of Appellate Rule 19(d) provides for a stay of the direct appeal in the event the Supreme Judicial Court remands to the Superior Court a motion for new trial. In such event, the appellant must file status reports with the Clerk of the Supreme Judicial Court for the Commonwealth every 30 days. An appeal by the defendant from the Superior Court judge's denial of a motion for new trial is to be consolidated with the direct appeal under the same docket number. In such a case, the Clerk of the Supreme Judicial Court will establish the schedule for briefing.

Reporter's Notes—2004

The first sentence of Appellate Rule 19(a) has been amended to be consistent with the simultaneous amendment to Appellate Rule 27.1(f). As amended in 2004, Appellate Rule 27.1(f) provides that upon further appellate review in the Supreme Judicial Court, a party may rely on the brief filed in the Appeals Court or may request permission to file a new brief in lieu of the Appeals Court brief.

Reporter's Notes—2019

The title of Rule 19 was amended to add "Certain" before "Motions" to clarify this rule only governs certain motions, unlike Rule 15 which governs motions generally. Reference to "Appendices" was also added to the title because the rule, as amended, governs the requirements for the filing and service of appendices. A provision in prior Rule 18(a) governed the filing and service of appendices. Since amended Rule 19 clarifies that briefs and appendices are filed contemporaneously, relocating these requirements to Rule 19 streamlined the filing and service requirements for these documents. This amendment is also consistent with the deletion of the provision contained in prior Rule 18(c) which allowed parties to defer the filing of an appendix in a civil case. See Reporter's Notes to Rule 18.

Rules 19(a) and (b). Prior Rule 19(a)'s provision for the timely filing and service of briefs was separated into two subdivisions: Rule 19(a) concerns cases where there is no cross appeal, and Rule 19(b) concerns cases involving cross appeals. Expressly excluded from both subdivisions are briefs filed pursuant to Rules 19(c) (first degree murder appeals), 11(g) (direct appellate review), and 27.1(f) (further appellate review).

Rule 19(a)(1) clarifies that the appellant's brief and appendix are both due at the same time.

Rule 19(a)(2), governing the due date for an appellee's brief, was revised to clarify that in an appeal involving multiple appellants, and in which more than one appellant brief is being filed, the appellee's brief is not due until 30 days after service of the last appellants' brief.

Rule 19(a)(3) amends the time period a party is allowed to file a reply brief. A reply brief must be filed by the earlier of either 14 days after service of the appellee's brief or 7 days prior to a scheduled argument before the appellate court.

Rule 19(b) is a new subdivision that concerns the time for filing and serving briefs and appendices in cases involving cross appeals, and is modelled on Fed. R. App. P. 28.1(f). It is intended to clarify the time frame for filing briefs, and the types of briefs that can be filed, in such cases.

Rule 19(c), encompassing prior Rule 19(d), was revised to reflect that G.L. c. 278, § 33E, was amended in 2012 to include certain habitual offender convictions. The revision clarifies that the extraordinary provisions of Rule 19(c) apply only to first degree murder appeals. No determination has been made that these provisions will apply to those habitual offender appeals that are now covered by G.L. c. 278, § 33E. References to Rule 19(c) were updated in the remainder of the rule to reflect the new title.

Rule 19(d), prior Rule 19(b), is a substantively revised subdivision that provides, in a single rule, the varying requirements for the filing and service of a brief and the brief-related documents that must be filed with the brief in each of the appellate courts. Under the prior rules, these requirements were located in several different rules (prior Rules 18(a), 18(e), and 19(b)) and often caused confusion for the parties.

Rules 19(d)(1)(A) and 19(d)(2)(A) reduce the number of copies of documents that must be filed in the Appeals Court. Rule 19(d)(1)(A) reduces the number of copies of each brief and appendix to be filed in the Appeals Court from 7 to 4. Rule 19(d)(2)(A), which applies to civil cases, was relocated to Rule 19 from prior Rule 18(e) to consolidate and streamline the filing and service requirements previously contained in Rules 18 and 19. See Reporter's Notes to Rule 18. The amendments reduce the number of copies of each exhibit and transcript volume that was required in prior Rule 18(e). The required number of copies of each exhibit volume was reduced from 5 to 2, and copies of each transcript volume from 2 to 1. Due to advances in the Appeals Court's paperless practices, fewer copies of each document are now required to properly process and review filings. In both Rules 19(d)(1)(A) and 19(d)(2)(A), reference was added to the Appeals Court Standing Order Concerning Electronic Filing, which supplements the Rules of Appellate Procedure to the extent that it requires certain documents to be electronically filed, and, if electronically filed, provides no paper copies are required.

Rules 19(d)(1)(B) and 19(d)(2)(B) similarly reduce the number of copies of documents that must be filed in the Supreme Judicial Court. The Supreme Judicial Court now requires 7 copies of each brief and appendix volume. In civil cases, 2 copies of each exhibit volume and transcript volume are required. Under the prior rules, fewer copies of these documents were required to be filed in the Supreme Judicial Court if a case was transferred from the Appeals Court after briefs, appendices, exhibits, or transcripts were filed in the Appeals Court. This distinction has been eliminated. Under the new rules the number of required copies is the same regardless of how or when an appeal enters in the Supreme Judicial Court. Rules 19(d)(1)(B)(ii) and 19(d)(2)(B)(ii) retain the prior requirement that where an appeal is transferred to the Supreme Judicial Court after briefs, appendices, exhibits, or transcripts were filed in the Appeals Court, the additional required copies must be "promptly filed" with the clerk of the Supreme Judicial Court.

Rules 19(d)(1)(A), 19(d)(1)(B)(i), 19(d)(2)(A), and 19(d)(2)(B)(i) add text to clarify the service requirements depending on the representation status of the parties. In cases involving jointly represented parties, 2 copies of the brief and appendix must be served and 1 copy of each exhibit volume and transcript volume must be served on counsel for all jointly represented parties. In cases involving self-represented parties, 2 copies of the brief and appendix and 1 copy of each exhibit volume and transcript volume must be served on each self-represented party. These amendments are intended to reduce confusion parties often have regarding service requirements in cases involving jointly represented parties or self-represented parties.

Rule 19(e), prior Rule 19(c), was revised to clarify that an appellate court may, upon motion or sua sponte, dismiss an appeal if an appellant fails to file a brief and appendix (other than a reply brief). In addition, a provision was added requiring any appellee who will not be filing a brief to timely notify the court. Timely notification is considered to be within the time period allotted for the filing of the brief. This notification is essential to the appellate court's processing of an appeal. Otherwise, the court awaits the filing of the brief, which can result in a significant delay in the timing of the court's consideration and disposition of the appeal. An additional provision was added to provide that, if an appellee fails to file a brief within the time provided by the rule, or any enlargement granted by the court, the appellate court may, upon motion or sua sponte, deem the case ready for consideration by the court. This provision is consistent with the appellate courts' practices.

Further organizational and stylistic revisions were made to this rule in 2019 in accordance with a global review and revision of all of the Appellate Rules. These revisions are described in the 2019 Reporter's Notes to Rule 1.

With regard to the preparation of the 2019 Reporter's Notes to this Rule, see the first paragraph of the 2019 Reporter's Notes to Rule 1. For an overview of the 2019 amendments to the Rules and a summary of the global amendments to the Rules, see 2019 Reporter's Notes to Rule 1, sections *I.* and *II.*

Rule 20. Form and Length of Briefs, Appendices, and Other Documents

(a) Form and Length of Briefs, Appendices, and Applications for and Responses to Direct and Further Appellate Review.

(1) *Form.* Except on order of the appellate court or a single justice, or if filed on behalf of a party allowed to proceed as an indigent party, all briefs, appendices, and applications for and responses to direct and further appellate review shall be produced by any duplicating or copying process which produces a clear black image on white paper. However produced, the page shall be 8.5 inches in width and 11 inches in height. Pages shall be firmly bound at the left, and a cover or front page shall be used.

(2) *Length of Briefs in All Cases Other than Cross Appeals.* The following rules shall govern the length of briefs in all cases other than cross appeals:

(A) A principal brief shall either be produced in a monospaced font and not contain more than 50 pages, or be produced in a proportionally spaced font and not contain more than 11,000 words.

(B) A reply brief shall either be produced in a monospaced font and not contain more than 20 pages, or be produced in a proportionally spaced font and not contain more than 4,500 words.

(C) An amicus curiae brief shall either be produced in a monospaced font and not contain more than 35 pages, or be produced in a proportionally spaced font and not contain more than 7,500 words.

(D) In all briefs, only those parts required by Rule 16(a)(5)–(11), including headings, footnotes, and quotations, count towards the length limits.

(E) A motion to exceed these length limits shall specify the relevant issue or issues and why such issues merit additional pages or words, and will not be granted except for extraordinary reasons.

(F) The certification required pursuant to Rule 16(k) shall specifically state how compliance with the length limits of this rule was ascertained, as specified therein.

(3) *Length of Briefs in Cases Involving Cross Appeals.* The following rules shall govern the length of briefs in cases involving cross appeals:

(A) An appellant's principal brief shall either be produced in a monospaced font and not contain more than 50 pages, or be produced in a proportionally spaced font and not contain more than 11,000 words.

(B) An appellee's principal and response brief shall either be produced in a monospaced font and not contain more than 60 pages, or be produced in a proportionally spaced font and not contain more than 13,000 words.

(C) An appellant's response and reply brief shall either be produced in a monospaced font and not contain more than 50 pages, or be produced in a proportionally spaced font and not contain more than 11,000 words.

(D) An appellee's reply brief shall either be produced in a monospaced font and not contain more than 20 pages, or be produced in a proportionally spaced font and not contain more than 4,500 words.

(E) An amicus curiae brief shall either be produced in a monospaced font and not contain more than 35 pages, or be produced in a proportionally spaced font and not contain more than 7,500 words.

(F) In all briefs, only those parts required by Rule 16(a)(5)–(11), including headings, footnotes, and quotations, count towards the length limits.

(G) A motion to exceed these length limits shall specify the relevant issue or issues and why such issues merit additional pages or words, and will not be granted except for extraordinary reasons.

(H) The certification required pursuant to Rule 16(k) shall specifically state how compliance with the length limits of this rule was ascertained, as specified therein.

(4) *Format and Pagination of Text.* The following rules shall govern the format of text on the pages of all briefs and applications for and responses to direct or further appellate review:

(A) If a monospaced font is used, the top and bottom margins shall be at least 1 inch. The left and right margins shall be at least 1.5 inches. If a proportionally spaced font is used, the top, bottom, left, and right margins shall be at least 1 inch. Page numbers shall appear in the margin with the cover paginated as page 1 pursuant to Rule 20(a)(6)(B)(vii) and pages thereafter numbered consecutively through the last page, including any addendum.

(B) The typeface of all text, including footnotes, shall be either (i) a monospaced font (such as Courier New) of 12 point or larger size and not exceeding 10.5 characters per inch; or (ii) a proportionally spaced font (such as Times New Roman) of 14 point or larger size.

(C) Text shall be double-spaced, except that argument headings, footnotes, and indented quotations may be single-spaced. For purposes of this rule, single spacing means not more than 6 lines of text per vertical inch; double spacing means not more than 3 lines of text per vertical inch and not more than 27 double-spaced lines on a page.

(D) The text may appear on both sides of the page.

(5) *Format, Pagination, and Length of Appendix.* The following rules shall govern the format of appendices:

(A) The cover of each volume of the appendix shall be designated by a Roman numeral and paginated as page 1, and pages thereafter numbered consecutively through the volume's last page. The cover shall also contain the information identified in Rule 20(a)(6)(B).

(B) Each volume of the appendix shall be separately paginated, beginning at page 1.

(C) No single volume of an appendix, transcript or exhibit shall be more than 1.5″ thick.

(D) The text of appendices filed on paper may appear on both sides of the page.

(6) *Color and Contents of Cover.* The following rules shall govern the color and contents of the cover of all briefs, appendices, and applications for or responses to direct or further appellate review:

(A) Color. The cover of the brief of the appellant shall be blue; that of the appellee, red; that of a party intervening in the appeal, yellow; that of an amicus curiae, green; that of any reply brief, gray. The cover of the appendix shall be white. The cover or front page of an application for or response to direct or further appellate review shall be white. A color cover is not required for any electronically-filed brief.

(B) Contents. The front covers of the briefs and appendices, in addition to the requirements for covers of appendices in Rule 20(a)(5), and of applications for or responses to direct or further appellate review shall contain:

(i) the name of the court and the number of the case;

(ii) the title of the case (see Rule 10(a));

(iii) the nature of the proceeding in the appellate court (e.g., Appeal; Application for Review) and the name of the lower court;

(iv) the title of the document (e.g., Brief for Appellant, Appendix);

(v) the name(s), Board of Bar Overseers (BBO) number(s), if any, mailing and electronic addresses, and telephone number(s) of the person(s) filing the document, and, if any individual counsel is affiliated with a firm or office, the office name; and

(vi) where it is necessary to include impounded material in a brief, the notification required by Rule 16(m).

(vii) The cover shall be paginated as page 1.

(7) *Substantial Compliance Required.* Briefs, appendices, or applications for or responses to direct or further appellate review not in substantial compliance with these rules shall not be docketed unless the appellate court or a single justice shall otherwise order.

(b) Form of Other Documents.

(1) *Motions for Reconsideration or Modification.* Motions for reconsideration or modification shall be produced in a manner prescribed by Rule 27(b).

(2) *Motions and Other Documents.*

(A) A motion or other document addressed to an appellate court shall contain a caption setting forth the name of the court, the title of the case, the docket number, and a brief descriptive title indicating the purpose of the document; the caption shall appear on the first page. Lines of text shall be double-spaced and shall be in 12 point or larger font, with side and top margins no less than 1 inch, and shall be no longer than reasonably necessary. Consecutive pages shall be stapled at the upper left margin.

(B) Such motion or document shall contain, at the end thereof

(i) the printed and signed name(s), Board of Bar Overseers (BBO) number(s), if any, mailing and electronic addresses, and telephone number(s) of the person(s) filing the document, and, if any individual counsel is affiliated with a firm or office, the office name, and

(ii) the date of signing.

Amended effective February 24, 1975; February 1, 1991; January 1, 1992; amended December 1, 1998, effective January 1, 1999; March 5, 2010, effective May 1, 2010; October 31, 2018, effective March 1, 2019.

Reporter's Notes—1973

Appellate Rule 20 permits briefs and appendices to be reproduced *either* by printing or by any duplicating process which produces a clear black image on white paper. Thus briefs may be xeroxed. However produced, briefs must be firmly bound or stapled, and must ordinarily bear color-coded covers: blue for the appellant; red for the appellee; gray for the reply brief; green for an amicus (if allowed, see Appellate Rule 17). The record appendix, if separately produced, should be covered in white.

Motions may be either typewritten or xeroxed.

Reporter's Notes—1975

The amendment to Appellate Rule 20(b) eliminates the requirement of "backing" the caption, so as to conform to the introduction of flat filing, see S.J.C. Rule 3:20.

Reporter's Notes—1979

Subdivision (a) of Rule 20 was made applicable to criminal cases by former Appeals Court and Supreme Judicial Court Rules 1:14 (1975: 3 Mass.App.Ct. 803. 366 Mass. 860) and is unchanged.

Reporter's Notes—1991

Experience has shown that volumes of appendices that are more than one and a half inches thick often fall apart and are clumsy to use. The limitation of each individual volume of the appendix to a thickness no greater than one and a half inches should solve the problem. If the appendix is larger in size, multiple volumes should be used.

Mass.R.A.P. 16(a)(7) and 20(a), final sentence, clause (5):

These amendments require individual counsel who are affiliated with a firm to include the firm name on filed briefs. Appellate judges need to know the firm names in order to determine correctly whether it is necessary to withdraw from a case.

Reporter's Notes to Mass.R.A.P. 20(a)—1999

I. Introduction.

Since the adoption of the Massachusetts Rules of Appellate Procedure in 1974, there have been only a few changes to Appellate Rule 20. With the advances in computer technology that have ensued since the 1970s, the Standing Advisory Committee on the Rules of Civil Procedure of the Supreme Judicial Court agreed with the recommendation of the clerks of the Supreme Judicial Court and of the Appeals Court that the time had come to re-examine Appellate Rule 20.

II. Briefs.

A number of changes to the existing rule were made in recognition of the fact that briefs today are typically computer-generated, whether an attorney produces a brief in-house or utilizes the services of a commercial firm. For example, outmoded references in the first paragraph of Rule 20(a) such as "standard typographic printing" and "printed matter" have been deleted. The reference to carbon copies has also been deleted.

The 1999 amendment also addresses a problem that has developed in recent years in the appellate courts of the Commonwealth. Judges have commented that in some instances briefs have been difficult to read because of the small size of letters. In addition, today's computer technology has provided opportunity for circumvention of the page limitations on briefs by compressing or condensing letters. If a brief is rejected by the clerk's office for such reasons, frustration and the additional expense of producing a replacement brief result. See "Strict Rule on Briefs Frustrates Litigators," 26 Massachusetts Lawyers Weekly 55 (September 15, 1997). A new second paragraph has been added to Rule 20(a) to address these and other matters of form.

It should be noted the existing page limitations on briefs produced by computer wordprocessing--as contained in Appellate Rule 16(h)--remain the same.

The following provisions numbered (1) through (4) are applicable to all briefs under the amended rule:

(1) *Margins.* Top and bottom margins on a page shall be at least one inch; left and right margins must be at least one and one-half inches. The rule specifically allows a page number to be placed within a margin. Uniformity in margins will also facilitate the placing of text on both sides of a page of a document, a practice permitted by Rule 20(a)(4).

(2) *Typeface.* Only a monospaced font is allowed. Therefore, attorneys may no longer use a proportional font such as Times New Roman. The typeface must be a 12 point or larger size and a limitation of 10.5 characters per inch is imposed. It should be noted that these limitations are applicable to footnotes as well as text. These requirements should eliminate the problem brief where page limitations have been circumvented by means of reducing, compressing, or condensing typeface.

Right margin justification (the process by which the lettering on a line is spaced so that the last letter on each line is flush to the right margin) is not prohibited by this rule, as long as the right margin is at least one and one-half inches and the limitation of 10.5 characters per inch is observed.

(3) *Line Spacing.* Documents are to be double-spaced. Argument headings, footnotes, and indented quotations, however, may be single-spaced. The revised rule defines the terms double-spaced and single-spaced--terms which may have been obvious in the context of a brief produced by a typewriter--so that there will be no more than three lines per vertical inch for double spacing and no more than six lines per vertical inch for single spacing (with an overall limit of 27 double-spaced lines on a page).

(4) *Text May Appear on Both Sides.* The prior version of Rule 20(a) did not speak to the issue of text appearing on both sides of a page. In recent years, some attorneys have begun to submit briefs where the text appears on the front and back of a page. The 1999 amendment specifically allows this practice. Although it is not required that text must appear on both sides of a page, attorneys are encouraged to produce briefs in this fashion. It is hoped that the practice of putting text on the front and back of a page will significantly reduce the storage problems in the clerks' offices of the appellate courts by reducing the overall size of briefs.

Where counsel is unable to comply with the technical requirements of Rule 20, it would be advisable to move in the appellate court in advance for leave to file a non-conforming brief rather than risk rejection of the filing at a point where time deadlines may be about to expire.

III. Appendices.

The 1999 changes regarding briefs do not apply to the appendix. An appendix may contain existing documents, transcripts, and other matters that were not originally prepared by counsel. However, in an effort to help reduce the storage problems in the clerk's offices of the appellate courts, a sentence has been added to Appellate Rule 20(a) allowing the text of the appendix to be reproduced on both sides of a page, a practice that is also allowed (and in fact, encouraged) for briefs.

Reporter's Notes to Mass.R.A.P. 20(b)—1999

Appellate Rule 20(b), governing the form of papers other than briefs and appendices, has been amended to require that the cover of applications for direct appellate review (Rule 11) and for further appellate review (Rule 27.1) be white. This will allow the clerk's office more easily to identify such documents.

Reporter's Notes—2010

Rule 20(a)(4) has been amended to require attorneys to include their e-mail addresses, if any, on the front cover of briefs and appendices. A similar amendment to Mass. R. Civ. P. 11(a) was adopted in 2010 requiring attorneys to include their e-mail addresses on pleadings.

Reporter's Notes—2019

The title of Rule 20 was amended to indicate that it encompasses the length of the referenced appellate documents, as well as the form. In addition, prior Rule 20's paragraphs were numbered, reordered, revised, and new paragraphs were added for clarity and ease of reference.

Rule 20(a). The title of this subdivision was amended to indicate that it applies both to the form and length of briefs, appendices, and applications for, and responses to, direct and further appellate review.

Rule 20(a)(1) addresses the form of briefs, appendices, and applications for, and responses to, direct and further appellate review. Reference to the format of appendices in the first paragraph of the prior rule was deleted and the content, with revisions, was relocated to Rule 20(a)(5).

Rules 20(a)(2) and 20(a)(3) are new paragraphs. Rule 20(a)(2) addresses the length of briefs in all cases other than cross appeals, and Rule 20(a)(3) establishes the length of briefs in cross appeals. These paragraphs allow the use of a word limit together with a proportionally spaced font, as an alternative to a page limit, in setting the permissible lengths of principal and reply briefs. The word limits are not intended to allow for longer documents. The limits allow no more than the amount of text permitted under the prior rules. For a comprehensive discussion of the word count amendment, see the 2019 Reporter's Notes to Rule 1.

Rule 20(a)(4). The content from the second paragraph of prior Rule 20(a) concerning the format of text on the pages of the documents encompassed in the rule was revised and relocated to Rule 20(a)(4). The revisions include the addition of applications for, and responses to, direct and further appellate review to clarify that the text requirements also apply to these documents. In addition, the rule was amended to include the word count alternative to the page limit.

Rule 20(a)(4)(A) provides that if a proportionally spaced font is used, all margins shall be at least one inch. This is intended to improve readability and is consistent with the analogous Federal rule. See Fed. R. App. P. 32(a)(4). The subparagraph retains the traditional 1.5 inch left and right margins from prior Rule 20(a)(1) only if a monospaced font is used.

Rule 20(a)(4)(A) also specifies the pagination requirements for briefs and applications for and responses to direct or further appellate review. The page numbers shall appear in the margin with the cover paginated as page one pursuant to Rule 20(a)(6)(B)(vii), and pages thereafter numbered consecutively through the last page. Any addendum is included in this requirement and should continue the pagination of the document itself without beginning again at page one. This provision is intended to facilitate reading documents in electronic form.

Rule 20(a)(5) is a new paragraph addressing the format and length of a record appendix. The rule requires that the cover of each volume of the appendix be designated by a Roman numeral, that each volume of the appendix be separately paginated with the cover designated as page 1, and that pages thereafter be numbered consecutively through the volume's final page. This paragraph is intended to facilitate reading appendices in electronic form.

Rule 20(a)(6). The content from the final paragraph of prior Rule 20(a) was revised, relocated to Rule 20(a)(6), and separated into new subparagraphs. Rule 20(a)(6)(A) addresses the color of the cover of briefs, appendices, and applications for or responses to direct or further appellate review. Rule 20(a)(6)(B) specifies the contents of the cover of briefs and appendices.

Rule 20(a)(6)(A). The content of the prior rule was revised to change the color of the cover of a brief filed by a party intervening in the appeal from green to yellow. This is intended to prevent confusion with the color of a brief of an amicus curiae, which is required to be green. Text was also added to clarify that the cover to applications for, or responses to, direct or further appellate review are white. Finally, the phrase "if separately bound" was removed from the existing requirement that appendix covers be white because under Rule 18(a), as amended, all appendices must now be bound separately from the brief. Color requirements do not apply to electronically-filed briefs.

Rule 20(a)(6)(B). The requirements regarding the contents of the cover of these documents were revised. The word "e-mail address" was revised to "electronic address," to clarify that both "mailing and electronic addresses" are required. Explicit reference to Rule 16(m) was added to ensure briefs referencing impounded material are clearly marked.

Rule 20(a)(7). The content from the first sentence of the third paragraph of prior Rule 20(a) was converted into new stand-alone Rule 20(a)(7). This amendment was made in order to separate the requirements for the form and length of briefs and appendices from the consequences should a brief or appendix not be in substantial compliance with Rule 20.

Prior Rule 20(b) was divided into two separate paragraphs. The first paragraph of prior Rule 20(b) is now Rule 20(b)(1). Reference to "[p]etitions for rehearing" was changed to "motion for reconsideration or modification," consistent with revisions to Rule 27. See 2019 Reporter's Notes to Rule 27. Language prescribing the form of a motion for reconsideration or modification was stricken and replaced with an explicit reference to Rule 27, which provides for the form of such a motion.

The remaining paragraphs of prior Rule 20(b) now encompass Rule 20(b)(2). Specifying in one paragraph the required structure for motions promotes clarity for parties submitting motions, and will promote a consistent format for review by the court. Rule 20(b)(2)(A) was added to specify basic formatting and length requirements of motions. There is no page limit for motions, but motions "shall be no longer than reasonably necessary." In some circumstances, the appellate courts have specified page limits of a motion. See Appeals Court Standing Order Governing Motions to Stay a Judgment or Execution of Sentence Filed Pursuant to Mass. R.A.P. 6 (setting 5 page limit for motion and 15 page limit for supporting memorandum of law). Rule 20(b)(2)(B) includes language added to the requirements for the end of a motion included in the prior rule to specify that "address" includes both the electronic and mailing address of the party, and to require the inclusion of the date of signing.

Further organizational and stylistic revisions were made to this rule in 2019 in accordance with a global review and revision of all of the Appellate Rules. These revisions are described in the 2019 Reporter's Notes to Rule 1.

With regard to the preparation of the 2019 Reporter's Notes to this Rule, see the first paragraph of the 2019 Reporter's Notes to Rule 1. For an overview of the 2019 amendments to the Rules and a summary of the global amendments to the Rules, see 2019 Reporter's Notes to Rule 1, sections *I.* and *II.*

Rule 21. Protection of Personal Identifying Information

Publicly accessible documents filed with the court shall conform to Supreme Judicial Court Rule 1:24, Protection of Personal Identifying Information in Publicly Accessible Court Documents.

Amended October 31, 2018, effective March 1, 2019.

Reporter's Notes—1973

Appellate Rule 21 allows the court to conduct a prehearing conference. Modelled on F.R.A.P. 33, it has no Massachusetts parallel at the appellate level.

Reporter's Notes—2019

Rule 21 was completely revised in 2019. Prior Rule 21 allowed the court to hold a prehearing conference "to consider the simplification of the issues and such other matters as may aid in the disposition of the proceeding by the court." This rule was stricken entirely as such conferences are not held. Even without such a rule, an appellate court or a single justice thereof still has the inherent authority to order such a conference.

Rule 21 was revised to encompass requirements related to the redaction of publicly available documents. The amendment serves to alert attorneys, parties, and interested members of the public to the requirements of S.J.C. Rule 1:24, Protection of Personal Identifying Information in Publicly Accessible Court Documents. Under S.J.C. Rule 1:24, unless there is an exception, personal identifying information, such as social security numbers, parent's birth surnames, driver's license numbers, and financial account numbers, may not be included in documents filed in court unless redacted as set forth in the rule. Identical cross-references to S.J.C. Rule 1:24 were added in 2017 to Mass. R. Civ. P. 5(h) and Mass. R. Crim. P. 32(f).

With regard to the preparation of the 2019 Reporter's Notes to this Rule, see the first paragraph of the 2019 Reporter's Notes to Rule 1. For an overview of the 2019 amendments to the Rules and a summary of the global amendments to the Rules, see 2019 Reporter's Notes to Rule 1, sections *I.* and *II.*

Rule 22. Oral Argument

(a) Notice of Argument; Postponement. The clerk shall advise all parties of the time and place at which oral argument will be heard. A request for postponement of the argument must be made by motion filed reasonably in advance of the date fixed for hearing.

(b) Time Allowed for Argument. Unless otherwise enlarged or limited by the appellate court, each side will be allowed 15 minutes for argument, except in a criminal case in which the defendant is appealing from a conviction of murder in the first degree, in which case each side will be allowed 20 minutes for argument. Reasonably in advance of the date fixed for oral argument, a party may move for additional time for good cause shown. The appellate court may terminate the argument whenever in its judgment further argument is unnecessary.

(c) Order and Content of Argument.

(1) *Oral Argument.* The appellant will argue first. Nothing argued in the brief shall be deemed to be waived by a failure to argue orally.

(2) *Post–Argument Filings.* After the oral argument of a case has been concluded or the case has been submitted on the documents without oral argument, no brief, memorandum, or letter relating to the case, except a citation of supplemental authorities letter filed pursuant to Rule 16(*l*), shall be submitted to the court, except to correct a factual misstatement during oral argument, or when such a writing was expressly allowed or requested by the court during the argument, or upon allowance of a motion to submit such a writing. Any such writing allowed during oral argument shall state that the court allowed the submission. A submission containing argument on the merits and not otherwise in compliance with this rule may be struck by the court.

(d) Cross and Separate Appeals. A cross or separate appeal shall be argued with the initial appeal at a single argument, unless the appellate court otherwise directs. If separate appellants support the same argument, care shall be taken to avoid duplication of argument.

(e) Non-appearance of Parties. Parties are expected to appear for oral argument unless prior arrangements have been made with the court. If the appellee fails to appear to present argument, the appellate court will hear argument on behalf of the appellant, if present. If the appellant fails to appear, the court may hear argument on behalf of the appellee, if present. If neither party appears, the case will be decided on the briefs unless the appellate court shall otherwise order.

(f) Submission on Briefs. By agreement of the parties, a case may at any time be submitted for decision on the briefs, but the appellate court may direct that the case be argued. At any time, any party may, by written notice filed and served, waive the party's right to oral argument. No criminal case in which the defendant was convicted of murder in the first degree may be submitted for decision on the briefs without oral argument unless the appellate court or a justice thereof shall have approved the submission prior to the week the case has been scheduled for argument.

(g) Use of Physical Exhibits at Argument; Removal. If physical exhibits other than documents are to be used at the argument, the party shall arrange to have them placed in the court room before the court convenes on the date of the argument. After the argument, the exhibits shall be left with the clerk unless the court otherwise directs. If exhibits are not reclaimed by the party within a reasonable time after notice is given by the clerk, they shall be destroyed or otherwise disposed of as the clerk shall think best.

Amended May 15, 1979, effective July 1, 1979; December 2, 1983, effective January 1, 1984; amended effective May 1, 1994; November 1, 1994; amended May 3, 2002, effective September 3, 2002; October 31, 2018, effective March 1, 2019.

Reporter's Notes—1973

Appellate Rule 22 governs the conduct of oral argument. A modification of F.R.A.P. 34, it codifies prior practice. Enlargements of argument time beyond thirty minutes will rarely be allowed; compare F.R.A.P. 34(b). Rebuttal argument, a matter of right, Appellate Rule 22(c), is strictly limited to new matter raised in appellee's argument. Although failure explicitly to reserve rebuttal does not waive the right, failure to preserve for rebuttal purposes a portion of the thirty-minute argument time will effect a de facto waiver in the absence of leave granted.

Reporter's Notes—1979

The only change in Rule 22 is that the substance of Supreme Judicial Court Rule 1:20 (1975: 366 Mass. 862), relative to submission of capital cases on briefs, is added to subdivision (g) of the former rule. The provisions of Rule 22 were previously applicable to criminal appeals by virtue of Supreme Judicial Court Rule 1:20, supra and Appeals Court Rule 1:20 (1975: 3 Mass.App.Ct. 804).

Reporter's Notes—1983

The purpose of this amendment is to conform Rule 22(b) to the actual practice in the appellate courts.

The purpose of this amendment is to conform Rule 22(c) to the actual practice in the appellate courts.

Reporter's Notes to Mass.R.A.P. 22(h)—1994

Mass.R.A.P. 22(h) does *not* give permission to counsel to refer to physical exhibits during oral argument. It only instructs counsel as to their obligation to arrange to have the physical exhibits in the court room before the court convenes if they are going to use them, and of the clerk's obligations afterwards.

Counsel should remember that it is their obligation to include in the appendix any portions of the record they are relying upon, including exhibits, in accordance with the provisions of Mass.R.A.P. 18(a) and 18(b). The third paragraph of Mass.R.A.P. 18(a) makes clear that ". . . the court may decline to permit the parties to refer to portions of the record omitted from the appendix, unless leave be granted prior to argument."

Physical exhibits cannot be actually placed in an appendix. Consequently, counsel on appeal who intend to refer to a physical exhibit, such as a revolver or a piece of clothing, should "prior to argument" seek leave of court to refer to such objects. Many appellate justices prefer to have pages in an appendix to refer to whenever possible. It is sound practice for counsel on appeal to have a photograph of physical exhibits appear on a page or pages of the appendix, even if prior permission has been given to use the actual physical exhibit at the oral argument.

Reporter's Notes to Appellate Rule 22(b)—2002

In 2002, the Supreme Judicial Court amended Appellate Rule 22(b) to reduce the time allowed for oral argument in first degree murder cases from thirty minutes to twenty minutes for each side. The time for oral argument in all other cases remains fifteen minutes for each side. As amended, Appellate Rule 22(b) further provides that if counsel desires additional time for oral argument, "counsel may request additional time for good cause shown." This latter provision replaces the former language that had provided that requests for additional time "will rarely be granted."

Reporter's Notes—2019

Rule 22(b) was amended to clarify that requests for additional argument time must be made reasonably in advance of the date fixed for oral argument.

Rule 22(c) was revised into two paragraphs. Rule 22(c)(1) addresses the rules for oral argument. The sentence providing that nothing argued in a brief is deemed waived by a failure to argue orally was relocated from prior Rule 16(a)(4) because Rule 22 is a more appropri-

ate location as it concerns procedures for oral argument. Rule 22(c)(2) is a new paragraph that clarifies the procedure and limits of a post-argument filing. Once oral argument is completed, a party may not submit any additional argument on the merits in the case other than a citation of supplemental authorities pursuant to Rule 16(*l*), a letter correcting a factual misstatement of any party during oral argument, or when otherwise allowed by leave of court. Although a letter containing citation of supplemental authorities pursuant to Rule 16(*l*) does not require leave of court, a submission containing argument on the merits does, and may be struck by the court if no leave has been granted. This amendment is not intended to modify existing practice where a justice requests or permits a party to file a letter at oral argument. A party who is given leave during oral argument should identify that leave has been given in the party's post-argument filing.

Rule 22(d) previously included a sentence relating to designation of the parties in a cross appeal. The substance of this sentence was moved to Rule 10(a)(7), which governs the docketing of an appeal. A party's designation, including in any cross appeal, is important at the outset of the case.

Rule 22(e). The first sentence was added to clarify that parties do not have the option not to attend oral argument without prior arrangements having been made with the court.

Rule 22(f), which previously prohibited an attorney who has been a witness in a case from appearing at oral argument without leave of court was stricken because there are several circumstances in which an attorney may testify under Mass. R. Prof. C. 3.7(a). The subsequent subdivisions were re-lettered.

Further organizational and stylistic revisions were made to this rule in 2019 in accordance with a global review and revision of all of the Appellate Rules. These revisions are described in the 2019 Reporter's Notes to Rule 1.

With regard to the preparation of the 2019 Reporter's Notes to this Rule, see the first paragraph of the 2019 Reporter's Notes to Rule 1. For an overview of the 2019 amendments to the Rules and a summary of the global amendments to the Rules, see 2019 Reporter's Notes to Rule 1, sections *I.* and *II.*

Rule 23. Notice of Decision; Issuance of Rescript; Stay of Rescript

(a) The clerk of the appellate court shall send to all parties copies of or a link to the rescript and the decision, if one was written, on the day the decision is released.

(b) The rescript and the decision of the appellate court shall issue to the lower court 28 days after the date of the decision unless the time is shortened or enlarged by order, except as provided by Rule 23(c).

(c) The issuance of the rescript will automatically be stayed, unless otherwise ordered by the appellate court, by the timely filing of: (1) a motion for reconsideration or modification pursuant to Rule 27; or (2) an application for further appellate review pursuant to Rule 27.1. The rescript shall issue forthwith after both the disposition of any motions for reconsideration or modification and the denial of any applications for further appellate review, unless the appellate court or a single justice orders otherwise. If an application for further appellate review is granted, the rescript of the Appeals Court shall not issue to the lower court.

Amended effective February 24, 1975. Amended October 31, 2018, effective March 1, 2019.

Reporter's Notes—1973

A rescript is the equivalent at the appellate level, of judgment in the trial court, Appellate Rule 1(c); Mass.R.Civ.P. 54(a). It is the appellate court's enunciation of its disposition of the appeal, the order directing the lower court's further conduct of the case. Usually, the rescript will issue to the lower court within fourteen days of its utterance by the appellate court. But a timely application for rehearing, Appellate Rule 27, or for further appellate review (if appropriate), Appellate Rule 27.1, will stay the issuance of the rescript.

Reporter's Notes—1975

The amendment enlarges the period for the issuance of rescript from 14 days to 28 days. This change was required by the amendment to Appellate Rule 27.1(a), extending the period within which the party could apply for further appellate review from 10 days to 20 days. Without the amendment to Appellate Rule 23, therefore, a party properly waiting until the twentieth day to file his application for further appellate review might find that the rescript had issued six days earlier, thus cutting off his additional appellate rights. The other amendment to Appellate Rule 23 merely substitutes "petition" for "request", to conform with the language of Appellate Rule 27.

Reporter's Notes—1979

The current text is unchanged but made applicable to criminal as well as civil cases.

Reporter's Notes—2019

The title and body of Rule 23 were revised for consistency with the new definition of "decision," and revised definition of "rescript" in Rule 1(c). These revisions clarify the distinction between the clerk's release of a decision to the parties and the clerk's issuance of the rescript to the lower court. Prior Rule 23's use of the word "rescript" often confused parties because it referred both to the appellate court's decision and to the order or direction to the lower court disposing of the appeal that is transmitted to the lower court 28 days after the release of the court's decision. This confusion resulted sometimes in parties not filing timely petitions for rehearing (the term used for Rule 27's motion for reconsideration or modification of decision prior to the 2019 amendments to the Rules) or applications for further appellate review since each filing was due within a specific time after the date of the rescript.

Rule 23(a) identifies the clerk's responsibilities to issue notice of the appellate court's release of a decision, and in Rule 23(b) to issue the rescript to the lower court. When read together, the amendments to Rules 23(a), 23(b), 27(a), and 27.1(a), establish the sequence of events that occur when an appellate court releases a decision: the clerk notifies the parties, the time period commences for filing a motion for reconsideration or modification (and, if the decision is released by the Appeals Court, an application for further appellate review), and the clerk issues the rescript and decision to the lower court 28 days later unless such issuance is stayed for one of the reasons delineated in Rule 23(c). Rule 23(a) was also revised to include that the appellate court clerk may electronically transmit a decision and rescript.

Rule 23(c). Consistent with amendments to Rule 27, the term "petition to rehearing" was changed to "motion for reconsideration or modification."

Further organizational and stylistic revisions were made to this rule in 2019 in accordance with a global review and revision of all of the Appellate Rules. These revisions are described in the 2019 Reporter's Notes to Rule 1.

With regard to the preparation of the 2019 Reporter's Notes to this Rule, see the first paragraph of the 2019 Reporter's Notes to Rule 1. For an overview of the 2019 amendments to the Rules and a summary of the global amendments to the Rules, see 2019 Reporter's Notes to Rule 1, sections *I.* and *II.*

Rule 24.   Justices' Participation

(a) Other Justices May Participate Without Reargument. Whenever the justices before whom a case has been heard so desire, others of the justices may be called in to take part in the decision, upon a review of the record and briefs, and the recording of any oral argument, without reargument.

(b) Replacement of Justices. If a justice who has participated in a case becomes unable to participate further, then the Chief Justice of the appellate court may substitute another justice.

(c) Justice May Review Own Ruling in Certain Cases. No justice shall sit on the hearing of any proceeding in the nature of a review of any judgment, decree, order, or ruling made by that justice; provided, however, that this shall not apply where it is necessary to secure a quorum or where the other justices of the court shall be equally divided in opinion.

Amended October 31, 2018, effective March 1, 2019.

Reporter's Notes—1973

Appellate Rule 24(a) permits the participation in a decision of a justice who has not heard argument. Appellate Rule 24(b) regulates a justice's participation in review of his own ruling. The rule codifies prior practice, S.J.C. Rule 1:18, 1:19; Appeals Court Rule 1:18.

Reporter's Notes—1979

Rule 24 is unchanged, but in criminal cases supersedes former Appeals Court and Supreme Judicial Court Rules 1:18 (1972: 1 Mass.App.Ct. 892, amended, 1975: 3 Mass.App.Ct. 801. 1967: 351 Mass. 731, amended, 1975: 366 Mass. 853) and 1:19 (1975: 3 Mass. App.Ct. 804. 1967: 351 Mass. 741–42, amended, 1975: 366 Mass. 853).

Reporter's Notes—2019

Rule 24(a) was revised to clarify that the recording of any oral argument is part of the record for review of a justice called in to take part in a decision after oral argument. The word "perusal" was replaced with "review." Although the terms have nearly identical meanings, "review" is more commonly used today.

Rule 24(b) is a new subdivision and, conformably with current practice, allows for the replacement of a justice should that justice become unable to participate in the case. The Chief Justice of the appellate court has the authority to make the substitutions as needed. Prior Rule 24(b) was re-lettered Rule 24(c).

Further organizational and stylistic revisions were made to this rule in 2019 in accordance with a global review and revision of all of the Appellate Rules. These revisions are described in the 2019 Reporter's Notes to Rule 1.

With regard to the preparation of the 2019 Reporter's Notes to this Rule, see the first paragraph of the 2019 Reporter's Notes to Rule 1. For an overview of the 2019 amendments to the Rules and a summary of the global amendments to the Rules, see 2019 Reporter's Notes to Rule 1, sections *I.* and *II.*

Rule 24.1.   [Rescinded]

Rule 24.1. Reporter's Notes—2019

Prior Rule 24.1 described the procedure for when there is a divided vote on further appellate review. The procedure governing applications for further appellate review is otherwise set forth in Rule 27.1. Instead of having separate but related parts of the same topic in nonconsecutive rules, the 2019 revision deleted Rule 24.1 and relocated its substance to Rule 27.1(g).

With regard to the preparation of the 2019 Reporter's Notes to this Rule, see the first paragraph of the 2019 Reporter's Notes to Rule 1.

For an overview of the 2019 amendments to the Rules and a summary of the global amendments to the Rules, see 2019 Reporter's Notes to Rule 1, sections *I.* and *II.*

Rule 25. Damages for Frivolous Appeal in Civil Cases

If an appellate court determines that an appeal in a civil case is frivolous, it may award just damages and single or double costs to the appellee, and such interest on the amount of the judgment as may be allowed by law. The appellate court shall calculate the amount of any award after a separately filed motion or notice from the court and reasonable opportunity to respond.

Amended December 22, 1978, effective January 15, 1979; May 15, 1979, effective July 1, 1979; October 31, 2018, effective March 1, 2019.

Reporter's Notes—1973

Appellate Rule 25, taken from F.R.A.P. 38, allows the court to award damages and appropriate costs if it determines that an appeal was taken frivolously. See Oscar Gruss & Son v. Lumberman's Mutual Casualty Co., 422 F.2d 1278, 1283–1284 (2d Cir.1970). This is new to Massachusetts practice.

Reporter's Notes—1979

Rule 25 is limited to civil cases.

Reporter's Notes—2019

The title of Rule 25 was revised by replacing the word "Delay" with "Frivolous" to more accurately describe the topic addressed by the rule. Additionally, the substance of the free-standing parenthetical subtitle "(Applicable to Civil Cases)" indicating the rule applies only in civil cases was moved to the title of the rule and expressly referenced in the body of the rule to improve clarity. The final sentence was added to reflect existing practice of the appellate courts, and is similar to Fed. R. App. P. 38.

With regard to the preparation of the 2019 Reporter's Notes to this Rule, see the first paragraph of the 2019 Reporter's Notes to Rule 1. For an overview of the 2019 amendments to the Rules and a summary of the global amendments to the Rules, see 2019 Reporter's Notes to Rule 1, sections *I.* and *II.*

Rule 26. Costs in Civil Cases

This rule applies only to civil cases.

(a) **To Whom Allowed.** Except as otherwise provided by law or ordered by the court, (1) if an appeal is dismissed, costs shall be taxed against the appellant unless otherwise agreed to by the parties; (2) if a judgment is affirmed, costs shall be taxed against the appellant; (3) if a judgment is reversed, costs shall be taxed against the appellee; (4) if a judgment is affirmed in part, reversed in part, modified, or vacated, costs are taxed only as ordered by the appellate court. Costs shall not be taxed against a party determined indigent in the same proceeding.

(b) **Costs For and Against the Commonwealth.** In cases involving the Commonwealth or an agency or officer thereof, if an award of costs against the Commonwealth is authorized by law, costs shall be awarded in accordance with the provisions of Rule 26(a); otherwise, costs shall not be awarded for or against the Commonwealth.

(c) **Costs of Briefs and Appendices.** The cost of printing or otherwise producing necessary copies of briefs and appendices shall be taxable in the lower court at rates not higher than those generally charged for such work in the Commonwealth. A party who desires such costs to be taxed shall state them in an itemized and verified bill of costs which shall be filed with the clerk of the lower court, with proof of service, within 14 days after the entry of judgment.

(d) **Clerk to Insert Costs in Lower Court Judgment; Costs Taxable.** The clerk of the lower court shall prepare and certify an itemized statement of costs on appeal for insertion in the lower court judgment. The following costs on appeal are taxable in the lower court for the benefit of the party entitled to costs under this rule:

(1) copies under Rule 26(c);

(2) costs incurred in the preparation and transmission of the record;

(3) the reporter's transcript, if necessary to determine the appeal;

(4) the premiums paid for any bond to preserve rights pending appeal;

(5) the fee for docketing the appeal under Rule 10(a)(1); and

(6) the cost of any convenience fees and other administrative fees levied for the privilege of paying fees or costs by credit card or other means, including, but not limited to, fees for electronic filing of documents or pleadings with the court.

Amended May 15, 1979, effective July 1, 1979; October 31, 2018, effective March 1, 2019.

Reporter's Notes—1973

Appellate Rule 26, based on F.R.A.P. 39, governs the allowance of costs, and follows prior practice. See G.L. c. 261, § 22. Costs are taxable against the Commonwealth as against an individual. G.L. c. 261, §§ 14, 16. Appellate Rule 26(c), dealing with costs of briefs, enlarges existing practice somewhat, see former G.L. c. 261, § 25; previously a prevailing party could recover only $50 of the cost of printing his brief, unless the court allowed a larger discretionary sum; under Appellate Rule 26(c) the prevailing party recovers the necessary costs of producing the briefs at a rate not higher than such costs generally charged in the Commonwealth.

Reporter's Notes—1979

Rule 26 is limited to civil cases.

Reporter's Notes—2019

The free-standing parenthetical subtitle "(Applicable to Civil Cases)" in prior Rule 26 was deleted and its substance moved to the title of Rule 26 and to the introductory sentence.

Rule 26(a) was revised to simplify the language of the sentence and add numbering to the various scenarios in which costs may be taxed. The list was also expanded to include judgments affirmed in part or modified in those situations where the costs are taxed only as ordered by the appellate court. New language was added to provide that costs are not to be taxed against a party determined indigent in the same proceeding.

Rule 26(c). Language including copies of records authorized by prior Rule 18(f) as taxable costs was deleted consistent with the deletion of that provision as described in the 2019 Reporter's Notes to Rule 18(f).

Rule 26(d). Language indicating that a fee for filing a notice of appeal will be taxed as a cost was deleted. Though the prior language of this Rule tracked the Federal rule, a fee for filing the notice of appeal does not exist for appeals that will be heard in the Appeals Court or the Supreme Judicial Court. Rather, a fee, if required, is paid upon docketing. The language was updated to reflect this practice. In addition, language was added indicating that certain administrative and convenience fees are recoverable costs, such as credit card convenience fees, fees incurred when electronically filing, and other such costs. This change updates the rule to reflect current costs that may be incurred by a party in prosecuting an appeal.

Further organizational and stylistic revisions were made to this rule in 2019 in accordance with a global review and revision of all of the Appellate Rules. These revisions are described in the 2019 Reporter's Notes to Rule 1.

With regard to the preparation of the 2019 Reporter's Notes to this Rule, see the first paragraph of the 2019 Reporter's Notes to Rule 1. For an overview of the 2019 amendments to the Rules and a summary of the global amendments to the Rules, see 2019 Reporter's Notes to Rule 1, sections *I.* and *II.*

Rule 27. Motion for Reconsideration or Modification of Decision

(a) Time for Filing; Content; Action by Court if Granted. Within 14 days after the date of the decision of the appellate court, any party to an appeal may file a motion for reconsideration or modification of decision unless the time is shortened or enlarged by order. It shall state with particularity the points of law or fact which it is contended the court has overlooked or misapprehended and shall contain such argument in support of the motion as the movant desires to present. Oral argument in support of the motion will not be permitted, except by order of the appellate court which decided the appeal. The motion shall be decided by the quorum or panel of the appellate court which decided the appeal.

(b) Form of Motion; Length. Except by permission of the appellate court, a motion shall not exceed either 10 pages of text in monospaced font or 2,000 words in proportional font, as defined in Rule 20(a)(4)(B), and shall contain a certification of such compliance, including a statement of how compliance with the foregoing length limit was ascertained, as specified in Rule 16(k).

(c) Response. No response to a motion for reconsideration or modification will be docketed unless requested by the appellate court, but reconsideration will ordinarily not be granted in the absence of such a request. Any response filed pursuant to this provision shall comply with the form and length requirements in Rule 27(b).

(d) Filing and Service. The motion, and any requested response, shall be filed in the office of the clerk of the appellate court that released the decision. In the Supreme Judicial Court, a paper original and 7 copies of the motion shall be filed. In the Appeals Court, the motion shall be filed in electronic form and no paper original or copies are required. Service of the motion, and any requested response, shall comply with Rule 13.

(e) Ruling on Motion. Upon consideration of a motion and any response, the appellate court may make a final disposition of the case without reargument or may restore it to the calendar for reargument or resubmission or may make such other orders as are deemed appropriate under the circumstances of the particular case. Action upon a motion is in the discretion of such appellate court, which may award costs, including a reasonable attorney's fee, to the prevailing party.

(f) Notice to Supreme Judicial Court. A party seeking further appellate review shall promptly notify the Supreme Judicial Court of any action taken on the motion.

Amended June 7, 1985, effective July 1, 1985; January 28, 1986, effective February 1, 1986; amended effective July 1, 1991; amended October 31, 2018, effective March 1, 2019.

Reporter's Notes—1973

Appellate Rule 27, taken from F.R.A.P. 40, governs petitions for rehearing. It will not change prior practice, under which a petition for rehearing was addressed to the discretion of the court, Merrill v. Beckwith, 168 Mass. 72, 75, 46 N.E. 400, 401 (1897), and ordinarily could not be supported by oral argument, Wall v. Old Colony Trust Company, 177 Mass. 275, 278, 58 N.E. 1015, 1016 (1901).

Reporter's Notes—1985

The change from ten days to fourteen days after the date of the rescript for a petition for rehearing conforms the time period to that found in Fed.R.A.P. 40(a). Such conformity of time periods may aid practitioners.

Reporter's Notes—1986

This amendment provides for review of petitions for rehearing by the quorum or panel which decided the appeal. The purpose of the amendment is to conform Rule 27 to the actual practice in the appellate courts.

Reporter's Notes—2019

The title of Rule 27 was changed from "petition for rehearing" to "motion for reconsideration or modification of decision." This revision more appropriately describes such filings which rarely, if ever, seek an oral argument and rehearing of a case before the justices and instead typically request a reconsideration or modification of the decision.

The term "rescript" in Rule 27(a) was changed to "decision of the appellate court," consistent with the new definitions in Rule 1(c). This change clarifies that a motion is due 14 days after the date of the decision, making it clear to the parties that it is the decision that triggers commencement of the time period, and not the clerk's issuance of the rescript to the lower court. Language relating to an "answer to a petition," now referred to as a "response," was moved to Rule 27(c) to promote clarity of the related procedures.

Consistent with the revisions to other rules, Rule 27(b) was amended to include the new option for a word count using proportionally spaced font and to clarify that the page limit option follows the monospaced font requirement in Rule 20(a). The first sentence of prior Rule 27(b), concerning the form of a "petition" as a letter addressed to the senior justice was deleted as inapplicable in light of the change to the title and form of these documents.

Rule 27(c) is a new subdivision titled "Response." The language for this subdivision comes from prior Rule 27(a). The word "answer" is no longer used to signify a response to a motion for reconsideration or modification of decision. Lastly, this new subdivision clarifies the formatting requirements applicable to a requested response.

Rule 27(d) is a new subdivision titled, "Filing and Service." Under prior Rule 27(b), litigants sometimes mailed the request directly to the senior justice and/or panel that decided the appeal instead of filing it in the appellate court clerk's office. Adding language about filing and service requirements clarifies the appropriate filing procedures.

Rule 27(e) is a new subdivision titled, "Ruling on Motion." The contents of the subdivision are taken from prior Rule 27(a). Placing this information in its own subdivision increases the readability of the Rules and makes it easier to refer to its requirements.

Rule 27(f), prior Rule 27(c), was revised by striking the first sentence of prior Rule 27(c), which is redundant considering Rule 27(e) now authorizes the appellate court to order review or revision of opinions when a motion is allowed. The language in the remaining sentence is updated for consistency with the revisions made in the preceding subdivisions, e.g., "petition" is changed to "motion." In addition, language regarding notification to the Supreme Judicial Court of any action on the motion is streamlined, and a requirement that this notification be made "promptly" is added.

Further organizational and stylistic revisions were made to this rule in 2019 in accordance with a global review and revision of all of the Appellate Rules. These revisions are described in the 2019 Reporter's Notes to Rule 1.

With regard to the preparation of the 2019 Reporter's Notes to this Rule, see the first paragraph of the 2019 Reporter's Notes to Rule 1. For an overview of the 2019 amendments to the Rules and a summary of the global amendments to the Rules, see 2019 Reporter's Notes to Rule 1, sections *I.* and *II.*

Rule 27.1.   Further Appellate Review

(a) Application; When Filed; Grounds. Within 21 days after the date of the decision of the Appeals Court, any party to the appeal may file an application for further appellate review of the case by the Supreme Judicial Court. Such application shall be founded upon substantial reasons affecting the public interest or the interests of justice. Oral argument in support of an application shall not be permitted except by order of the court.

(b) Contents of Application; Form. The application for further appellate review shall contain, in the following order: (1) a request for further appellate review; (2) a statement of prior proceedings in the case (including whether any party is seeking a reconsideration or modification in the Appeals Court); (3) a short statement of facts relevant to the appeal (but facts correctly stated in the decision of the Appeals Court shall not be restated); (4) a statement of the points with respect to which further appellate review of the decision of the Appeals Court is sought; and (5) a brief statement (consisting of not more than either 10 pages of text in monospaced font or 2,000 words in proportional font as defined in Rule 20(a)(4)(B)), including appropriate authorities, indicating why further appellate review is appropriate. A copy of the rescript and decision of the Appeals Court shall be appended to the application. In addition, if the Appeals Court entered a memorandum and order under Appeals Court Rule 1:28 which refers to another document, such as a brief or judge's findings and rulings, a copy of that document, or, if appropriate, the pertinent pages of that document, shall be appended to the application. The application shall comply with the requirements of Rule 20(a), and shall contain a certification of such compliance, including a statement of how compliance with the foregoing length limit was ascertained, as specified in Rule 16(k).

(c) Response; Form. Within 14 days after the filing of the application, any other party to the appeal may, but need not, file and serve a response thereto (consisting of not more than either 10 pages of text in monospaced font or 2,000 words of text in proportional font, as defined in Rule 20(a)(4)(B)) setting forth reasons why the application should or should not be granted. The response shall not restate matters described in Rule 27.1(b)(2) and (3) unless the opposing party is dissatisfied with the statement thereof contained in the application. A response shall comply with the requirements of Rule 20(a), and shall contain a certification of such compliance, including a statement of how compliance with the foregoing length limit was ascertained, as specified in Rule 16(k). A response may be filed in a different form as permitted by the court.

(d) Filing; Service. One copy of the application and of each response shall be filed in the office of the clerk of the full Supreme Judicial Court. No copy of the application or any response need be filed in the Appeals Court. Filing and service of the application and of any response shall comply with Rule 13.

(e) Vote for Further Appellate Review; Certification. If any 3 justices of the Supreme Judicial Court shall vote for further appellate review for substantial reasons affecting the public interest or the interests of justice, or if a majority of the justices of the Appeals Court or a majority of the justices of the Appeals Court deciding the case shall certify that the public interest or the interests of justice make desirable a further appellate review, an order allowing the application or the certificate, as the case may be, shall be transmitted to the clerk of the Appeals Court with notice to the lower court. The clerk of the Appeals Court shall forthwith transmit to the clerk of the full Supreme Judicial Court all documents filed in the case.

(f) Briefs. Any party may apply to the Supreme Judicial Court within 14 days after the date on which the appeal is docketed in the full Supreme Judicial Court for permission to file a new brief. If the application is granted, the new brief must be filed in accordance with the briefing schedule established by the clerk of the Supreme Judicial Court, and the court may impose terms as to the length and filing of such brief and any response thereto. If a new brief is filed, it will be considered in lieu of the Appeals Court brief. If permission to file a new brief is denied or not sought, cases in which further appellate review has been granted shall be argued on the briefs filed in the Appeals Court.

(g) Equally Divided Vote on Further Appellate Review. If, following allowance of an application for further appellate review, the justices of the Supreme Judicial Court are equally divided in opinion, unless a majority of the participating justices decides otherwise, the court shall issue an order noting such equal division, the effect of which shall be the same as if the court had denied the application for further appellate review.

Amended effective February 24, 1975; July 1, 1991; January 1, 1994; November 1, 1994; February 1, 1995; April 14, 1995; amended October 30, 1997, effective January 1, 1998; May 2, 2001, effective June 1, 2001; February 25, 2004, effective April 1, 2004; October 31, 2018, effective March 1, 2019.

Reporter's Notes—1973

G.L. c. 211A, § 11 permits the Supreme Judicial Court, for substantial reasons of justice or the public interest, to review cases determined in the Appeals Court, provided three justices of the Supreme Judicial Court so order, or a majority of the Appeals Court or a majority of the Appeals Court panel deciding the case certify the desirability of further review. Appellate Rule 27.1 regulates the application for such review.

Further review is analogous to the granting of certiorari by the Supreme Court of the United States. Applications for such review will not ordinarily entail oral argument; and if granted, review will usually be argued on the briefs and record appendix filed in the Appeals Court.

Reporter's Notes—1975

As originally promulgated, a party desiring further appellate review had 10 days from the date of rescript to file an appropriate application. Because, in practice, this period did not suffice, it has been enlarged to 20 days. In addition, an amendment to Appellate Rule 27.1(f) allows a party who so desires to apply to the Supreme Judicial Court for leave to file a brief different from or supplementary to his brief in the Appeals Court. As originally promulgated, Rule 27.1(f) did not make clear that the party had a right to lodge such a request. However, absent leave of court, whether because the court denies the application or because the party fails to file it initially, the case will be argued on the Appeals Court papers.

Reporter's Notes—1979

Appellate Rule 27.1 was previously applicable to further appellate review in criminal cases by virtue of Supreme Judicial Court Rule 3:24, § 7 (1975: 366 Mass. 874), except that the words "record appendix" (prepared by the appellant) were taken to mean "record" (assembled by the clerk, former G.L. c. 278, § 33C [St.1974, c. 458, § 1]). That distinction is no longer viable (see Rule 18[a]).

In criminal cases, § 7 of Supreme Judicial Court Rule 3:24 imposes two requirements additional to those of Appellate Rule 27.1. Subdivision 27.1(d) calls for copies of an application for further appellate review and any opposition to be filed with the clerks of the Appeals and Supreme Judicial Courts; Rule 3:24, § 7 further mandates that a copy of the application is to be served on the clerk of the trial court the action of which is on appeal. Subdivision 27.1(e) provides for notice to the clerk of the lower court by the clerk of the Appeals Court when an application for further appellate review is granted; Rule 3:24, § 7 further requires such notice in criminal cases if an application is denied.

Reporter's Notes—1994

In those cases in which the Appeals Court has reversed or vacated the judgment in the Trial Court and the Supreme Judicial Court has allowed further appellate review, Rule 27.1(g) places the applicant for further appellate review in the position of appellant for the purpose of order of argument. See Rule 22(c). The court by order or the parties by agreement may change the order of argument. In a case in which both parties apply for further appellate review, order of argument will be controlled by such agreement of the parties or order of the court.

Reporter's Notes—1995

The 1995 amendment to appellate Rule 27.1(e) makes the rule consistent with the practice of the Supreme Judicial Court which is to vote for further appellate review but not to sign an order concerning such vote.

Reporter's Notes—1997

The 1997 amendment to Appellate Rule 27.1(d) increased to seventeen the number of copies of an application for further appellate review and of each opposition to be filed in the clerk's office of the Supreme Judicial Court. The amendment also clarified that an original is to be filed together with the seventeen copies.

Reporter's Notes—1999

The cover of applications for further appellate review shall be white. See Appellate Rule 20(b), as amended in 1999.

Reporter's Notes—2001

Where further appellate review has been granted after consideration of a case by the Appeals Court, the case will be reviewed in the Supreme Judicial Court based on the brief that was earlier filed in the Appeals Court. Prior to the 2001 amendment, Appellate Rule 27.1(f) provided that a party may request permission to file a separate or supplemental brief in the Supreme Judicial Court within ten days of the order *granting further appellate review*. However, time periods regarding service and filing of briefs in the appellate courts are generally measured from the date the appeal is *docketed* in the appellate court. See, for example, Appellate Rule 11(g).

To maintain consistency, therefore, the clerk's office of the Supreme Judicial Court requested that Appellate Rule 27.1(f) be amended. The amended rule provides that the time period to request permission to file a separate or supplemental brief on further appellate review runs from the date the appeal is docketed in the Supreme Judicial Court.

Reporter's Notes—2004

The 2004 amendment to Appellate Rule 27.1(f) revises the practice of requesting permission to file a separate or supplemental brief in cases where further appellate review in the Supreme Judicial Court has been granted. The parties have the option to rely upon the Appeals Court brief or to request permission (within ten days after the appeal is docketed in the Supreme Judicial Court) to file a new brief in lieu of the Appeals Court brief. Thus, under the revised procedure, only one brief from each party will be considered by the Supreme Judicial Court. No party may file both the brief from the Appeals Court and a new brief.

Reporter's Notes—2019

Rule 27.1(a). The word "rescript" was replaced with "decision" consistent with the new definitions contained in Rule 1(c), and the related amendments made to Rule 23, to clarify the distinction between the clerk's release of a decision to the parties and the clerk's issuance of the rescript to the lower court, (see 2019 Reporter's Notes to Rules 1(c) and 23), and that is the appellate court's release of the decision that commences the timeframe for filing an application for further appellate review. A party has 21 days after the date of the decision of the Appeals Court to file an application for further appellate review in the Supreme Judicial Court. The time period does not commence on the date the Appeals Court issues the rescript to the lower court.

Rules 27.1(a) and (b). References to "an application for leave to obtain further appellate review" were revised to "an application for further appellate review" to simplify the phrase. No substantive change was intended. See G.L. c. 211A, § 11.

Rules 27.1(b) and (c), governing the length requirements of both the application and response, were revised to include the new word count alternative to the page limit, as explained in the 2019 Reporter's Notes to Rule 1.

Rule 27.1(c) was amended to change "opposition" to "response" to more generally describe an answer to an application since not all applications are opposed.

Rule 27.1(d) was revised to reduce the number of copies of an application or response to an application for further appellate review that must be filed from "an original and seventeen copies" to 1 copy and the requirement that a copy need be filed in the Appeals Court was deleted. Fewer copies are required in the Supreme Judicial Court due to advances in paperless practices and no copy is required in the Appeals Court because the Appeals Court receives automatic notification from the Supreme Judicial Court when an application for further appellate review, or a response to an application, is filed, and an electronic copy of the document is automatically shared with the Appeals Court.

Rule 27.1(e). The phrase "upon receipt, further appellate review shall be deemed granted" was removed. According to the prior rule, although the Supreme Judicial Court entered and sent notice of an order granting further appellate review, the application would not be "deemed granted" until the Appeals Court received the order. By deleting this phrase, consistent with all other orders issued by an appellate court, the order is effective upon entry. The rule was also amended to require the Supreme Judicial Court to send notice to the lower court when it grants further appellate review.

The content of prior Rule 27.1(g), governing order of oral argument in cases argued on further appellate review, was removed. The order of argument in a case where further appellate review is granted will be the same as in any other case, with the appellant arguing first. See Rule 22(c)(1). As prior Rule 24.1 (Divided Vote on Further Appellate Review) and Rule 27.1 are closely-related, prior Rule 24.1 was deleted and its content moved to Rule 27.1(g). See 2019 Reporter's Note to Rule 24.1.

Further organizational and stylistic revisions were made to this rule in 2019 in accordance with a global review and revision of all of the Appellate Rules. These revisions are described in the 2019 Reporter's Notes to Rule 1.

With regard to the preparation of the 2019 Reporter's Notes to this Rule, see the first paragraph of the 2019 Reporter's Notes to Rule 1. For an overview of the 2019 amendments to the Rules and a summary of the global amendments to the Rules, see 2019 Reporter's Notes to Rule 1, sections *I.* and *II.*

Rule 28.   Procedure in Lower Court Following Rescript

(a) Civil Cases. In a civil case, when the rescript from the appellate court sets forth the text of the judgment to be entered, the clerk of the lower court shall, upon receipt of the rescript, prepare, sign, and enter the judgment which has been ordered. If the rescript orders settlement of the form of the judgment in the lower court, the clerk of the lower court shall sign and enter the judgment after settlement. Notation of a judgment in the lower court docket constitutes entry of the judgment.

(b) Criminal Cases. If the rescript has the effect of entitling the defendant to immediate release from custody, counsel for the defendant, the Commonwealth, and the clerk of the lower court shall immediately take any action necessary to ensure that the defendant is released from custody forthwith. In all other criminal cases, unless the rescript affirms the lower court, the clerk of the lower court shall, upon receipt of the rescript, schedule a hearing forthwith to be held no later than 30 days from the clerk's entry of the rescript.

Amended May 15, 1979, effective July 1, 1979; October 31, 2018, effective March 1, 2019.

Reporter's Notes—1973

Appellate Rule 28 prescribes the duties of the lower court clerk upon receipt of the appellate court rescript. It should always be remembered that it is the judgment of the lower court, not the rescript (however much the terms of the rescript may shape the final judgment), which regulates the nature and quantum of any relief obtained. Until that judgment has been made to conform to the rescript, the litigation is not terminated. The rescript may dictate the text of the judgment or it may enjoin the parties to "settle," i.e., jointly work out a draft of a judgment to be approved by the appellate court before transmission to the lower court clerk for entry.

Reporter's Notes—1979

Rule 28 is limited in applicability to civil cases. The existing practice in criminal cases, to be continued under the Rules, is to enter the rescript on the docket rather than to prepare a separate "judgment" as is done in civil cases.

Reporter's Notes—2019

The title of Rule 28 was revised to "Procedure in Lower Court Following Rescript," to clarify the content and applicability of the rule. The parenthetical indicating that Rule 28 applies only to civil cases was deleted because the rule, as amended, also applies to criminal cases.

Rule 28 was separated into two subdivisions, one concerning civil cases and the other concerning criminal cases. The prior language, found in Rule 28(a), encompasses the procedure in civil cases. Rule 28(b) was added to govern the procedure in criminal cases. The language requires action when the rescript reverses or remands a case to the lower court, to ensure a timely hearing is scheduled for further proceedings.

With regard to the preparation of the 2019 Reporter's Notes to this Rule, see the first paragraph of the 2019 Reporter's Notes to Rule 1. For an overview of the 2019 amendments to the Rules and a summary of the global amendments to the Rules, see 2019 Reporter's Notes to Rule 1, sections *I.* and *II.*

Rule 29.   Voluntary Dismissal of Appeal or Other Proceeding

(a) Voluntary Dismissal in the Lower Court. Before an appeal has been docketed in the appellate court, the lower court may dismiss the appeal on the filing of a stipulation signed by all the parties or on the appellant's motion with notice to all parties.

(b) Voluntary Dismissal in the Appellate Court.

(1) *Civil Cases.* If the parties to a civil appeal or other civil proceeding shall sign and file with the clerk of the appellate court a stipulation or motion that the proceeding be dismissed with prejudice, specifying the terms as to payment of costs and attorney's fees, and shall pay whatever fees are due, the clerk shall enter the case as dismissed. An appeal may be dismissed on motion of the appellant upon such terms as may be agreed upon by the parties or fixed by the court.

(2) *Criminal Cases.* A criminal appeal or other criminal proceeding may be dismissed by the appellate court on motion of the appellant, and the clerk shall enter the case as dismissed. If the appellant is the defendant, the motion shall include an affidavit by the defendant, or an attestation by counsel, that the defendant assents to the court's dismissal of the appeal with prejudice. If the motion states that the appeal is moot, an affidavit by the defendant is not required.

(c) Settlement; Obligation of Appellant. In the event a case is settled or otherwise disposed of while an appeal is pending, it shall be the duty of the appellant to notify the clerk of the appellate court forthwith.

(d) Notice to Lower Court. The clerk of the appellate court shall promptly notify the clerk of the lower court whenever an appeal is dismissed pursuant to this rule.

Amended May 15, 1979, effective July 1, 1979; October 31, 2018, effective March 1, 2019.

Reporter's Notes—1973

Appellate Rule 29, based on F.R.A.P. 42, is a housekeeping measure regulating voluntary dismissal of appeals and the settlement of cases. Appellate Rule 29(c) is designed to ensure that the court is kept informed of any out-of-court disposition.

Reporter's Notes—1979

Rule 29 is changed only in that paragraph (b) of Rule 29, governing dismissal of an appeal in the appellate court, now provides for notification of the clerk of the lower court by the clerk of the appellate court whenever an appeal in a criminal case is dismissed in the appellate court.

Reporter's Notes—2019

Rule 29(a) was revised to improve clarity. No substantive change was intended.

Rule 29(b). The title of this subdivision was amended to include the word "voluntary" to more accurately reflect the substance of the subdivision. Rule 29(b) was divided into two separate paragraphs, one addressing voluntary dismissal in civil cases and another addressing voluntary dismissal in criminal cases, because the processes differ. Rule 29(b)(2) provides that although a criminal appeal or other proceeding may be voluntarily dismissed, if the appellant is the defendant, an affidavit by the defendant or an attestation by counsel is required stating that the defendant assents to the dismissal of the appeal with prejudice. This language is consistent with existing practice.

Rule 29(d) is a new subdivision that requires the appellate court clerk to notify promptly the lower court when an appeal is dismissed pursuant to Rule 29. Under prior Rule 29(b), such a requirement was only applicable in a criminal case.

Further organizational and stylistic revisions were made to this rule in 2019 in accordance with a global review and revision of all of the Appellate Rules. These revisions are described in the 2019 Reporter's Notes to Rule 1.

With regard to the preparation of the 2019 Reporter's Notes to this Rule, see the first paragraph of the 2019 Reporter's Notes to Rule 1. For an overview of the 2019 amendments to the Rules and a summary of the global amendments to the Rules, see 2019 Reporter's Notes to Rule 1, sections *I.* and *II.*

Rule 30. Substitution of Parties in Civil Cases

This rule applies only to civil cases.

(a) Death of a Party. If a party dies after a notice of appeal is filed in the lower court or while a proceeding is pending in the appellate court, the personal representative of the deceased party may be substituted as a party on motion filed by the representative or by any party with the clerk of the appropriate court. The motion of a party shall be served upon the representative in accordance with the provisions of Rule 13. If the deceased party has no representative, any party may suggest the death on the record and proceedings shall then be had as the appellate court or a single justice may direct. If a party against whom an appeal may be taken dies after entry of a judgment or order in the lower court but before a notice of appeal is filed, an appellant may proceed as if death had not occurred. After the appeal is docketed, substitution shall be effected in the appellate court in accordance with this subdivision. If a party entitled to appeal shall die before filing a notice of appeal, the notice of appeal may be filed by the party's personal representative, or, if the party has no personal representative, by the party's attorney of record within the time prescribed by these rules. After the appeal is docketed, substitution shall be effected in the appellate court in accordance with this subdivision.

(b) Substitution for Other Causes. If substitution of a party in the appellate court is necessary for any reason other than death, substitution shall be effected in accordance with the procedure prescribed in Rule 30(a).

(c) Public Officers; Death or Separation from Office.

(1) When a public officer is a party to an appeal or other proceeding in an appellate court in the public officer's official capacity and during its pendency dies, resigns, or otherwise ceases to hold office, the action does not abate and the public officer's successor is automatically substituted as a party.

Proceedings following the substitution shall be in the name of the substituted party, but any misnomer not affecting the substantial rights of the parties shall be disregarded. An order of substitution may be entered at any time, but the omission to enter such an order shall not affect the substitution.

(2) When a public officer is a party to an appeal or other proceeding in the public officer's official capacity, the public officer may be described as a party by official title rather than by name; but the court may require the public officer's name to be added.

Amended May 15, 1979, effective July 1, 1979; October 31, 2018, effective March 1, 2019.

Reporter's Notes—1973

Appellate Rule 30 governs the substitution of a party, whether because of death or for some other cause, and also regulates the substitution of public officers. It is based on F.R.A.P. 43; see also Mass.R.Civ.P. 25.

Reporter's Notes—2019

Rule 30 was amended by striking a free-standing parenthetical subtitle ("Applicable to Civil Cases"), and adding "in Civil Cases" to the title of the rule. The amendment was made to clarify the content and applicability of the rule and to eliminate a drafting technique unique to only a few prior rules that may have led to confusion.

Further organizational and stylistic revisions were made to this rule in 2019 in accordance with a global review and revision of all of the Appellate Rules. These revisions are described in the 2019 Reporter's Notes to Rule 1.

With regard to the preparation of the 2019 Reporter's Notes to this Rule, see the first paragraph of the 2019 Reporter's Notes to Rule 1. For an overview of the 2019 amendments to the Rules and a summary of the global amendments to the Rules, see 2019 Reporter's Notes to Rule 1, sections *I.* and *II.*

Rule 31. Duties of Clerks

(a) General Provisions. The Supreme Judicial Court and the Appeals Court shall be deemed always open for the purpose of filing any proper document, of issuing and returning process, and of making motions and orders. The office of the clerk with a clerk in attendance shall be open during regular court business hours on all weekdays except State and Federal holidays recognized by the Commonwealth

(b) The Docket; Calendar; Other Records Required.

(1) The clerk shall keep an electronic docket, in such form and style as may be prescribed by the appellate court, and shall enter therein each case. Cases shall be assigned consecutive docket numbers. All filings, orders, decisions, and rescripts shall be entered chronologically on the docket. Entries shall show the nature of each filing, order, decision, or rescript.

(2) The clerk shall prepare, under the direction of the appellate court, a calendar of cases awaiting argument. In placing cases on the calendar for argument, the clerk shall give preference to appeals in child welfare and criminal cases, and to appeals and other proceedings entitled to preference by law.

(3) The clerk shall keep such other records as may be required from time to time by law or by the appellate court.

(c) Notice of Orders, Decisions, or Rescripts. Upon the entry of an order, decision, or rescript, including an order on an application for direct or further appellate review, the clerk of the appellate court shall send a notice of entry to each party, and include a copy of or a link to any decision and rescript. The clerk shall send such notice to the electronic business address of an attorney that is registered with the Board of Bar Overseers, and may send paper notice by conventional mail. The clerk shall send such notice to the mailing or electronic address of a self-represented party, depending upon such party's address preference as registered with the clerk.

(d) Custody of Records and Documents. The clerk shall have custody of the records and documents of the appellate court. The clerk shall not permit any original record or document to be taken from the clerk's custody except as authorized by the orders or instructions of the court or a single justice. Original documents transmitted as the record on appeal or review shall be returned to the lower court.

Amended October 31, 2018, effective March 1, 2019.

Reporter's Notes—1973

Appellate Rule 31, based on F.R.A.P. 45, outlines the duties and responsibilities of the clerk and his assistants. Note that although the clerk's office is open only during normal business hours, the court is deemed open at all times for purposes of filing motions, papers, and the like. See also Mass.R.Civ.P. 77.

Reporter's Notes—1979

The duties of clerks set out in this Rule have been applicable to criminal appellate procedure since the effective dates of Appeals Court Rule 1:27 (February 27, 1975: 3 Mass.App.Ct. 805) and Supreme Judicial Court Rule 1:27 (January 1, 1975: 366 Mass. 862).

Reporter's Notes—1984

Under the provisions of Mass.R.A.P. 31(d), transcripts filed in the appellate court need not be returned to the lower court. For this purpose, transcripts are not part of the "original papers." See Mass.R.A.P. 8(a), which lists "original papers" as distinct from "the transcript of proceedings."

Reporter's Notes—2019

Rule 31(a). The first two sentences of the prior rule were deleted as unnecessary because the clerk's oath and bond requirements are established by statute (G.L. c. 221, § 12) and the prohibition on practicing law has been superseded by S.J.C. Rule 3:02 and S.J.C.

Rule 3:12, Canon 3. The provisions regarding specific business hours of court (weekdays and holidays) were removed because they are outside the scope of the Rules of Appellate Procedure.

Rule 31(b) was separated into three paragraphs for clarity, and the language updated for consistency, with current practices and the revisions to the definitions in Rule 1(c). Consistent with the appellate courts' longstanding practices, the revised rule includes child welfare cases as proceedings to be given preference by the clerk when scheduling cases for argument. Criminal cases and other proceedings are entitled to preference by law. See G.L. c. 211, § 7 and G.L. c. 211A, § 13.

Rule 31(c). The title of this rule was amended to include "decision" given its addition in 2019 to Rule 1(c). Language was added authorizing the clerk to send notices to an attorney's electronic business address registered with the Board of Bar Overseers, and providing that paper notice by conventional mail may be sent. In addition, the clerk is authorized to send electronic or paper notice to self-represented parties, depending upon such party's preference as registered with the clerk.

Rule 31(d). In the last sentence, the phrases "upon the disposition of the case" and "from which they were received" were deleted. The first phrase was deleted because it is current practice to return original documents transmitted to an appellate court back to the lower court when review of the case is completed; the clerk does not presently wait for disposition of the case before doing so. The second phrase was deleted as unnecessary; the clerk of the appellate court only returns original documents to the lower court which had transmitted the records.

Further organizational and stylistic revisions were made to this rule in 2019 in accordance with a global review and revision of all of the Appellate Rules. These revisions are described in the 2019 Reporter's Notes to Rule 1.

With regard to the preparation of the 2019 Reporter's Notes to this Rule, see the first paragraph of the 2019 Reporter's Notes to Rule 1. For an overview of the 2019 amendments to the Rules and a summary of the global amendments to the Rules, see 2019 Reporter's Notes to Rule 1, sections *I.* and *II.*

Rule 32.   Title

These rules may be known and cited as the Massachusetts Rules of Appellate Procedure.

Reporter's Notes—1973

The formal title of the Appellate Rules is "Massachusetts Rules of Appellate Procedure." They may be cited "Mass.R.A.P."

RULES OF THE SUPREME JUDICIAL COURT

Effective January 1, 1981

Table of Rules

CHAPTER ONE. GENERAL RULES

Rule 1:01. Definitions; Conflict With Other Rules

These rules shall be construed to secure the just, speedy and inexpensive determination of every case. Words or phrases importing the singular number may extend and be applied to several persons or things, words importing the plural number may include the singular, and words importing the masculine gender may include the feminine and neuter. As used in these rules the following terms shall be deemed to have the following meanings:

"Superior Court" shall mean the Superior Court Department of the Trial Court, or a session thereof for holding court.

"Housing Court" shall mean a division of the Housing Court Department of the Trial Court, or a session thereof for holding court.

"Probate Court" shall mean a division of the Probate and Family Court Department of the Trial Court, or a session thereof for holding court.

"Land Court" shall mean the Land Court Department of the Trial Court, or a session thereof for holding court.

"District Court" or "Municipal Court" shall mean a division of the District Court Department of the Trial Court, or a session thereof for holding court. Except when the context means something to the contrary, said words shall include the Boston Municipal Court Department.

"Municipal Court of the City of Boston" shall mean the Boston Municipal Court Department of the Trial Court, or a session thereof for holding court.

"Juvenile Court" shall mean the Boston Division, the Worcester Division, the Springfield Division, and the County of Bristol Division of the Juvenile Court Department of the Trial Court, or a session thereof for holding court.

"Chief Justice" of a Trial Court Department shall mean the "Administrative Justice" of that Department.

To the extent of any conflict between the Massachusetts Rules of Civil Procedure, the Massachusetts Rules of Criminal Procedure, the Massachusetts Rules of Appellate Procedure and the rules of the Supreme Judicial Court, the Appeals Court, and the various Departments of the Trial Court, the Massachusetts Rules of Civil, Criminal and Appellate Procedure shall control.

Amended May 29, 1986, effective July 1, 1986; June 16, 1987, effective July 1, 1987; amended effective June 8, 1989; amended June 9, 1997, effective January 1, 1998; March 30, 1999, effective April 5, 1999.

Rule 1:02. Sittings of the Supreme Judicial Court

Sittings of the full court for hearing questions of law pursuant to G. L. c. 211, § 12, as amended, shall be held at Boston on the first Monday of October, November, December, January, February, March, April and May, and at such other places or times as the court from time to time may order.

Rule 1:03. Uniform Certification of Questions of Law

Section 1. Authority to Answer Certain Questions of Law. This court may answer questions of law certified to it by the Supreme Court of the United States, a Court of Appeals of the United States, or of the District of Columbia, or a United States District Court, or the highest appellate court of any other state when requested by the certifying court if there are involved in any proceeding before it questions of law of this state which may be determinative of the cause then pending in the certifying court and as to which it appears to the certifying court there is no controlling precedent in the decisions of this court.

Section 2. Method of Invoking. This rule may be invoked by an order of any of the courts referred to in Section 1 upon that court's own motion or upon the motion of any party to the cause.

Section 3. Contents of Certification Order. A certification order shall set forth

(1) the question of law to be answered; and

(2) a statement of all facts relevant to the questions certified and showing fully the nature of the controversy in which the questions arose.

Section 4. Preparation of Certification Order. The certification order shall be prepared by the certifying court, signed by the judge presiding at the hearing, and forwarded to this court by the clerk of the certifying court under its official seal. This court may require the original or copies of all or of any portion of the record before the certifying court to be filed with the certification order, if, in the opinion of this court, the record or portion thereof may be necessary in answering the questions.

Section 5. Costs of Certification. Fees and costs shall be the same as in civil appeals docketed before this court and shall be equally divided between the parties unless otherwise ordered by the certifying court in its order of certification.

Section 6. Briefs and Arguments. Proceedings in this court shall be those provided in these rules, the Massachusetts Rules of Appellate Procedure or statutes governing briefs and arguments, so far as reasonably applicable.

Section 7. Opinion. The written opinion of this court stating the law governing the questions certified shall be sent by the clerk under the seal of this court to the certifying court and to the parties.

Section 8. Power to Certify. This court on its own motion or the motion of any party may order certification of questions of law to the highest court of any state when it appears to the certifying court that there are involved in any proceeding before the court questions of law of the receiving state which may be determinative of the cause then pending in the certifying court and it appears to the certifying court that there are no controlling precedents in the decisions of the highest court or intermediate appellate courts of the receiving state.

Section 9. Procedure on Certifying. The procedures for certification from this state to the receiving state shall be those provided in the laws of the receiving state.

Section 10. Uniformity of Interpretation. This rule shall be so construed as to effectuate its general purpose to make uniform the law of those states which adopt it; or enact a uniform certification statute.

Section 11. Short Title. This rule may be cited as the Uniform Certification of Questions of Law Rule.

Rule 1:04.   Judicial Conference

G.L. c. 211, § 3B, as amended *

* provides statutory authority for this rule.

(1) The Massachusetts Judicial Conference is hereby constituted to consist of the following: (a) the Chief Justice (who shall serve as chairman of the Conference) and the Associate Justices of this court; (b) the Chief Justice of the Appeals Court; (c) the Chief Administrative Justice of the Trial Court; (d) the Administrative Justice of the Superior Court Department; (e) the Administrative Justice of the Probate and Family Court Department; (f) the Administrative Justice of the Land Court Department; (g) the Administrative Justice of the Housing Court Department; (h) the Administrative Justice of the District Court Department; (i) the Administrative Justice of the Boston Municipal Court Department; (j) the Administrative Justice of the Juvenile Court Department; (k) the Chairman of the Judicial Council; (l) the Trial Court Administrator; and (m) the Administrative Assistant to the Supreme Judicial Court (G.L. c. 211, § 3A), who shall act as secretary and as the principal administrative officer of the Conference.

(2) The judges and officers mentioned in paragraph (1) shall serve as the members of the Conference until further order of this court. Any member may designate another member of the court or body which he represents to act for him at any meeting.

(3) The Conference may invite other judges and members of the bar (a) to participate in any one or more projects, studies, meetings, or other activities, or (b) to prepare and present studies, recommendations, and comments upon matters concerning which the Conference desires information.

(4) The Conference (a) may consider and make recommendations on matters relating to the conduct of judicial business, the improvement of the judicial system, and the administration of justice in such manner as the Conference from time to time may deem appropriate; (b) may initiate and conduct legal research; (c) shall assist this court in coordinating the activities of the several courts; (d) may conduct general conferences and educational meetings; (e) may appoint reporters, advisers, research assistants, and other employees, either for the general work of the Conference or for designated projects and, subject to the availability of necessary funds, may make expenditures, including the payment of the foregoing persons; (f) may employ such facilities of universities, law schools, colleges, bar associations, foundations, and other institutions, as may be made available to it; and (g) may appoint standing or special committees. The Chief Justice of this court may appoint a vice-chairman of the Conference and may delegate to him duties with respect to the Conference.

(5) The Conference shall meet at such times as may be designated by the Chief Justice or a majority of the Justices of this court.

Rule 1:05.   Certain Contracts by Judicial Officers

(1) Except as provided by paragraph (4), by statute, or by other rule or order of this court, no judge of a court shall enter into, order, or approve a contract on behalf of the Commonwealth or any of its political subdivisions requiring the expenditure of funds or the incurring of a liability in excess of any appropriation therefor, or for which no appropriation has been made, without the written approval of the appropriate judicial officer designated by this court. The following officers are so designated: for the Appeals Court, its Chief Justice; for each department of the Trial Court, its Administrative Justice. Every judge seeking such approval shall file a written request for approval with the appropriate judicial officer and a copy with the Chief Administrative Justice of the Trial Court. Every request shall be in the form of a memorandum and shall set forth the following: (a) the nature and cost of the facilities, goods or services sought; (b) an explanation of the circumstances causing the judge to consider it reasonably necessary to the proper execution of the court's responsibilities; (c) a chronological account of administrative action previously taken to secure it; and (d) a statement of the action contemplated by the judge.

(2) The appropriate judicial officer may approve in writing a request made under paragraph (1) only upon a finding that the facilities, goods or services sought are reasonably necessary to the proper execution of the court's responsibilities, and subject to such instructions as he deems appropriate. If such request is approved by the judicial officer, he shall forthwith submit a copy of his approval to the Chief Administrative Justice.

(3) Any judge whose request under paragraph (1) is denied may appeal in writing to the Chief Administrative Justice, who shall make a final determination thereon.

(4) The only exception to paragraph (1) shall be in instances where failure to obtain the required facilities, goods or services expeditiously and without delay will frustrate the execution of the court's responsibilities. In every such instance, the judge entering into, ordering or approving a contract on behalf of the Commonwealth or any of its political subdivisions shall forthwith submit a memorandum of the type required by paragraph (1) to the appropriate judicial officer, with a copy to the Chief Administrative Justice.

(5) Upon receipt of a copy of a memorandum filed under paragraph (1) or (4) the Chief Administrative Justice shall forthwith notify the Chief Justice of this court.

Rule 1:06. Records of the Supreme Judicial Court, of the Appeals Court, and of the Superior Court Department. Form, Style, and Size of Papers

G.L. c. 221, § 27, as amended *

* provides statutory authority for this rule.

(1) The records of the Supreme Judicial Court, of the Appeals Court, and of the Superior Court Department in the several counties shall consist of the docket, the files, any extended record, which shall have been made at the promulgation of these rules, and whatever other specific records may be required by special statutes, and no others.

(2) There shall be two dockets in the Supreme Judicial Court: a full court docket and a single justice docket. The single justice docket shall be kept by the clerk in each county.

(3) There shall be two dockets in the Superior Court Department: a civil action docket and a criminal docket.

(4) The dockets are records wherein the clerk shall register, by its title, every action, suit or proceeding, civil and criminal, commenced in, or transferred or appealed to, the court whereof he is clerk, according to the date of its actual entry. He shall note therein, according to the date thereof, the filing or return of any paper or process, the making of any order, rule, or other direction in or concerning such action, suit or proceeding, civil and criminal, the verdict or finding, the allowance of exceptions, and the entry of final judgment, final decree or order.

(5) The criminal docket shall be kept in the form heretofore in common usage, being substantially as provided in paragraph (4) hereof.

(6) The files are all papers and processes filed with or by the clerk of the court in any action, suit or proceeding therein, or before the justice thereof, including executions, with their returns. So far as reasonably practicable, they shall comply with S.J.C. Rule 1:08 in size and in other respects therein stated. All such papers and processes shall be numbered consecutively in each case as entered.

(7) Resort may be had to the docket, files, and any extended record, or full extended record, which has been made at the time of the promulgation of these rules, but the full extended record, where one has been made, shall control.

(8) The docket shall be kept either by the loose-leaf system or by a computer based record keeping system. Under the loose-leaf system the record shall be kept in typewriting, or partly in typewriting and partly in print, except as otherwise ordered by the court. Typewriter ribbons of permanent character shall be used. Those authorized for use on public records shall be regarded as sufficient under this rule, unless otherwise ordered by the court. The leaves of both docket and record when completed shall be strongly bound in volumes of appropriate size. Under the computer based record keeping system upon the completion of each case a printed paper copy of the docket shall be produced to provide a permanent record of the docket. The printed paper copy of the docket shall be strongly bound in volumes of appropriate size.

(9) Immediately after the final disposition of each action, suit or proceeding, complaint or indictment, papers constituting the files shall be assembled, collated, and arranged in order as theretofore numbered, and thereafter shall be kept in such order, except that executions may for greater safety be kept in a more secure place.

(10) The docket, files, and such extended and full extended records which shall have been made at the time of the promulgation of these rules, are to be kept in the clerk's office or in the custody of the clerk, and he is to be strictly responsible for them. They shall not be taken from his custody except in cases authorized by statute, by rule of court, for the preparation of the record for the full court, or for use by a justice of the court; but the parties may at all times have copies.

Amended effective September 3, 1991.

Rule 1:07. Fee Generating Appointments and the Maintenance of Appointment Dockets in All Courts

Preamble

The Justices understand the importance of allowing judges the flexibility of selecting appointees based on the particular expertise needed in a given case. In recognition of the necessity to safeguard judicial discretion, a waiver from the requirement of successive appointments has been included in Rule 1:07. In making an appointment, a judge may select a qualified person who is not on the list or who is not next in order on the list by making a brief notation of the reasons for the selection.

The goal of this rule is to assure that all fee-generating appointments made by the courts of the Commonwealth are made on a fair and impartial basis with equal opportunity and access for all qualified candidates for appointments. The Justices have concluded that the fairest way to accomplish this goal, and at the same time avoid favoritism or the appearance of favoritism, is by requiring each court to create lists of qualified candidates and then generally make appointments from those lists in rotation or sequential order.

(1) **Annual Publication.** At the beginning of each fiscal year, the chief justice of each Trial Court department and the chief justices of the appellate courts shall submit to the Chief Justice for Administration and Management (CJAM) a listing of the types of fee-generating appointments made in their department or court and the qualifications for those appoint-

ments. The CJAM shall compile the listings into a unified report which shall be published annually by the CJAM. The report shall include a description of the educational, professional, and other qualifications required for each type of appointment. The report shall state the method by which a person may apply to be considered for each particular type of appointment. It shall also include a statement that appointments of counsel for indigent defendants in criminal matters and for parties in certain non-criminal matters are governed by the Committee for Public Counsel Services (CPCS). An address and telephone number for interested persons to receive information on CPCS appointments shall be included in the report. This annual publication shall be accompanied by a statement from the Supreme Judicial Court that the appointments in the report are open to all qualified persons without regard to race, sex, religion, national origin, disability, age, sexual orientation or socioeconomic status.

(2) **Court Lists.** Every individual court making fee-generating appointments shall maintain a list of persons eligible for each type of appointment made by the court. The list shall be generated by the court or, where applicable, by CPCS. All court-generated lists shall be open to all qualified candidates and shall not be restricted to a fixed number of candidates. The method for removing individuals from a list shall be the responsibility of CPCS, in the case of CPCS-generated lists, and of the CJAM, in the case of court-generated lists. The lists shall be public.

(3) **Successive Appointments.** Each court appointment shall be made from the list maintained pursuant to section (2) of this rule, except as otherwise provided in section (4). Appointments from the list shall be made successively, except that, if an appointment is not made in successive order, the judge (or other person) making the appointment shall provide a brief written statement of reasons for not following the order of the list. For appointees compensated by CPCS, such written statement shall be kept by the Clerk, Register or Recorder in a separate file marked "CPCS appointments." A judge may direct that an appointment made successively from the list be entered administratively by the clerk, register, or recorder.

(4) **Persons Not On List.** If a judge appoints a person not on the list maintained pursuant to section (2), the judge (or other person) making the appointment shall provide a brief written statement of reasons for not appointing from the list.

(5) **Appointment Docket.** All clerks, registers, and recorders, for trial and appellate courts, shall establish and maintain, currently indexed, as part of the public records of the court open during regular business hours to public inspection, an appointment docket with respect to the appointment by the court of each fee-generating appointment, excluding appointees compensated by CPCS. The appointment dockets shall include the following:

(a) guardian ad litem,

(b) investigator appointed pursuant to G.L. c. 208, § 16,

(c) appraiser in any estate estimated to have gross assets in excess of $100,000,

(d) commissioner to sell real estate,

(e) appellate court conference counsel,

(f) master or special master,

(g) counsel in any civil matter,

(h) monitor for the administration of antipsychotic medications,

(i) investigator in care and protection proceedings,

(j) title examiner,

(k) administrator, trustee, guardian, conservator, or receiver, whose appointment was not prayed for by name in a petition, pleading, or written motion, and any guardian or conservator who is an attorney, social worker or other social service professional unrelated to the ward by blood or marriage,

(l) any other fee-generating appointment not compensated by CPCS and not otherwise excluded by this section. The appointment of a guardian ad litem to serve process under G.L. c. 215, § 56B, shall not be entered on the appointment docket. The appointment of an executor, administrator, trustee, guardian, conservator or receiver shall not be entered on the appointment docket except as required by section (5)(k). Appointments shall be entered on the appointment docket regardless of the anticipated source, if any, of payment to the appointee.

(6) **Data Collection.** Such docket shall contain at a minimum the following:

(a) the docket number and, if the case file is available for public inspection or if access to the information is not otherwise prohibited, the name of the case,

(b) the date of the appointment,

(c) the name of the appointee,

(d) the position to which appointed,

(e) by whom the appointment was made,

(f) a notation if the appointment was not made successively from the court's list or if the appointee was a person not on the list, and

(g) the amount of any payment received and the source thereof (party, estate, or Commonwealth) or whether payment was waived or declined.

(7) **Payments.** No payment shall be made or received on account of any appointment required to be recorded in the appointment docket until a statement under the penalties of perjury, certifying the services provided, amount of payment, and itemization of expenses, is filed with the clerk, register, or recorder, to be placed with the papers in the case. No person holding an appointment required to be recorded in the appointment docket under section (5) of this rule shall make any payment to himself or herself until such payment is approved by the court.

(8) **Compliance.** Each appointment made under this rule shall include language on the document of appointment itself that section (7) of this rule must be complied with. After July 1, 2000, no person whose appointment is subject to this rule shall accept reappointment unless he or she has filed a certification that all fee reports for payments received in the previous fiscal year have been filed.

(9) Implementation. The CJAM shall promulgate, subject to the approval of the Supreme Judicial Court, such uniform practices as are necessary to implement this rule.

(10) Alternative Dispute Resolution Exclusion. The provisions of this rule are not applicable to fee-generating appointments made pursuant to Rule 1:18, Uniform Rules on Dispute Resolution.

Amended December 6, 1988, effective January 1, 1989; January 7, 1999, effective July 1, 1999 and April 3, 2000; March 6, 2000, effective April 3, 2000.

Uniform Practice I. Removal From Fee Generating Appointment List

1.) All requests for the involuntary removal of an individual from a court generated list of persons eligible for fee generating appointments maintained under paragraph (2) of Rule 1:07, shall be in writing, shall specify the grounds upon which the request for removal is based, and shall be addressed to the Chief Justice of the Department, hereinafter Chief Justice.[1]

2.) If the request for involuntary removal raises serious concerns as to the individual's qualifications or suitability to perform the duties and/or functions of the type of appointment(s) for which he or she is eligible, the Chief Justice shall have the discretion to temporarily suspend the individual from one or more of the court generated lists of his or her Department. The Chief Justice may remove the temporary suspension at any time during the review of a request for involuntary removal.

3.) The Chief Justice shall send a copy of the request to the individual whose involuntary removal is sought along with a notice indicating that the individual may file a written response.

4.) After receipt and review of the individual's written response or upon the expiration of 30 days if no written response is received, the Chief Justice shall determine if an investigation should be conducted into the facts and circumstances that form the basis for the request. If an investigation is not needed because the facts are not in dispute, the Chief Justice shall make his or her determination. If the Chief Justice determines that no action is required on the request for involuntary removal, he or she shall inform in writing both the requesting party and the individual whose involuntary removal was sought that no action will be taken on the request. If the Chief Justice determines that the individual should be removed from one or more of the court's lists or that a lesser sanction should be imposed, he or she shall make such recommendation in writing to the Chief Justice for Administration and Management. Lesser sanctions which the Chief Justice may recommend shall include, but are not limited to, suspension from the list for a specific period of time, caseload limits, assignment of a mentor, a directive to obtain additional training or referral to Lawyer's Concerned for Lawyers. If the Chief Justice's decision is that an investigation is necessary, he or she shall appoint an individual to conduct an investigation.

5.) The investigator so selected under paragraph (4) shall conduct a complete and full investigation into the facts and circumstances that provide the basis for the request for involuntary removal and shall report the results of the investigation in writing.

6.) The investigator's report shall be submitted to the Chief Justice and a copy shall be forwarded to the individual whose involuntary removal is sought. The Chief Justice shall afford to the individual whose involuntary removal is sought an opportunity to submit a written response. The Chief Justice may, in his or her discretion, meet with the individual whose involuntary removal is sought and such others as the Chief Justice deems appropriate or he or she may conduct a hearing at which the individual whose involuntary removal is sought may be heard. Based upon the investigator's report and such other information as the Chief Justice has obtained, he or she shall make a determination. If the Chief Justice determines that no action is required on the request for involuntary removal, he or she shall inform in writing both the requesting party and the individual whose involuntary removal was sought that no action will be taken on the request. If the Chief Justice determines that the individual should be removed from one or more of the court's lists or that a lesser sanction should be imposed, he or she shall make such recommendation in writing to the Chief Justice for Administration and Management.

7.) If the Chief Justice decides to recommend the removal of the individual from one or more of the court's lists, or that a lesser sanction be imposed, the Chief Justice shall set forth in his or her written recommendation the basis for said recommendation and forward it along with a copy of the investigator's report and such other documentation as has been submitted, to the Chief Justice for Administration and Management. A copy of the recommendation shall also be sent to the individual whose involuntary removal is sought.

8.) The Chief Justice for Administration and Management shall consider the recommendation submitted by the Chief Justice and shall, within sixty days, either accept or reject the recommendation. That decision shall be final. A copy of the Chief Justice for Administration and Management's decision shall be sent to the Chief Justice, the requesting party and the individual whose involuntary removal is sought.

9.) The initial request for involuntary removal, any report prepared by an investigator appointed under paragraph 4, any written response submitted under paragraph 3, any written recommendation prepared pursuant to paragraph's[2] 4, 6 or 7, any written response submitted under paragraph 6, and any hearing conducted under paragraph 6 shall be considered to be confidential and shall not be open to the public.

10.) If, within 30 days after the Chief Justice sends the copy referred to in paragraph 3, the individual does not respond in writing objecting to the requested involuntary removal, the person's name may be removed from the list in question (or a lesser sanction imposed) by the Chief Justice without following the procedures set forth in paragraphs 4 through 9. The Chief Justice shall notify the Chief Justice for Administration and Management of the action by the Chief Justice under this paragraph and shall send a copy of that notification to the individual whose name has been removed.

11.) Notwithstanding the foregoing, and provided that a request for involuntary removal is not pending against him or her, any person may voluntarily remove his or her own name from a court list for fee generating appointments by sending a written request for such voluntary removal to the Chief Justice.

Adopted December 4, 2003, effective January 1, 2004.

[1] If the request for involuntary removal is initiated by a Chief Justice, then he or she shall designate another justice of his or her Department to perform the functions of the Chief Justice under this Uniform Practice.

[2] So in original.

Interim Uniform Practices for the Establishment and Maintenance of Appointment Dockets Pursuant to Supreme Judicial Court Rule 1:07, As Amended Effective January 1, 1989 [REPEALED]

Adopted January 30, 1989, effective March 1, 1989. Repealed December 4, 2003, effective December 4, 2003.

Rule 1:08. Form, Style, and Size of Papers Filed in All Courts

(Applicable to all cases and to all courts. See S.J.C. Rules 1:06[7], 2:02, Rule 5[g] of Mass.R.Civ.P., and Rule 20 of Mass.R.A.P., each as amended.)

(1) Except as provided in this rule, papers (except exhibits) and processes filed with or by the clerk of the court in any court in the Commonwealth, or before a justice thereof, in any action, suit, or proceeding therein, including executions, with their returns, shall be, so far as reasonably practicable, approximately (but not larger than) eight and one-half inches by eleven in size, of standard quality of paper with adequate margins, and, except writs and other processes, approved Probate and Family Court Department printed forms, and printed briefs, shall be printed or typewritten upon one side only. It is desirable that blanks be filled in in typewriting. All papers filed in appeals (civil or criminal) to the full Supreme Judicial Court, the full Appeals Court, or a statutory quorum of either shall comply with the informational requirements of Rule 20(b) of the Massachusetts Rules of Appellate Procedure. All papers filed in all other proceedings shall bear the name of the court and the county, the title of the action, the designation of the nature of the pleading or paper, and the name (written in capital letters or typed legibly, in addition to any signature required), address, and telephone number of the person or attorney filing the same, and, with respect to such papers filed by an attorney in the Supreme Judicial Court for the Commonwealth, the Supreme Judicial Court for Suffolk County and the Appeals Court, the attorney's Board of Bar Overseers (BBO) number. The court number of the case shall appear on each paper filed after the assignment of such a number.

(1A) With the exceptions appearing in paragraphs (1) an (2) of this rule and, with the exception of the Probate and Family Court Department, and applications for admission to the bar filed in the county court, all papers and processes in cases commenced after January 1, 1975, filed with or by the clerk of the court in any court in the Commonwealth shall not be folded. Backers are not required and should not be used.

(2) The District Court Department and the Boston Municipal Court Department by rule may exempt from the operation of this rule papers filed in small claims proceedings and in criminal cases. The District Court and the Juvenile Court Departments by rule may exempt from the operation of this rule papers filed in juvenile cases. However, when the clerks of these courts enter in the Superior Court Department papers exempted under this paragraph they shall adapt such papers to the requirements of this rule. In all courts there may be exempted by rule or order papers filed by parties appearing pro se.

(3) Any court by rule or order may provide for the effective enforcement of this rule.

Amended effective January 1, 1992.

Rule 1:09. Form of Original Executions for All Courts of the Commonwealth

G.L. c. 235, §§ 22, 23, as amended *

* provides statutory authority for this rule.

Original executions to be issued in all courts of the Commonwealth on judgments against executors, administrators, and other fiduciary officers in their representative capacity, including any such original execution running against two or more parties, any one or more of whom are fiduciary officers as aforesaid in their representative capacity, or against sheriffs under G.L. c. 37, § 10, or special judgments entered under G.L. c. 235, § 24, shall in the last sentence after the words "in sixty days from the date hereof" contain the clause "or within ten days after this writ has been satisfied or discharged."

All other original executions to be issued on judgments in all courts of the Commonwealth shall contain a last sentence reading as follows:

"Hereof fail not, and make return of this writ with your doings thereon into the clerk's office of our said Court, at   within our county of   , within twenty years after the date of said judgment, or within ten days after this writ has been satisfied or discharged."

No execution shall be invalid which conforms in substance to the provisions of this rule.

Rule 1:10. Form of Alias Executions for All Courts of the Commonwealth

G.L. c. 235, § 22, as amended *

* provides statutory authority for this rule.

Alias and successive executions to be used in all courts of the Commonwealth shall contain the following: Immediately after the words, "We command you, therefore," there shall be inserted "as we have commanded you."

The last sentence shall be:

"Hereof fail not, and make return of this writ with your doings thereon into the clerk's office of our said Court at   within our county of   within five years from the date hereof, or within ten days after this writ is satisfied in whole or discharged by law."

No execution shall be invalid which conforms in substance to the provisions of this rule.

Rule 1:11. Rule Relative to the Disposal of Court Papers and Records

G.L. c. 221, § 27A, as amended *

* provides statutory authority for this rule.

Section 1. Scope. This Rule shall govern the disposal of all court case records, regardless of the form in which they were created or are retained.

Section 2. Definitions. The following definitions apply in this Rule:

Clerk—the clerks of the Supreme Judicial Court, the clerk of the Appeals Court, the recorder of the Land Court, the registers of Probate, and the clerks of the Boston Municipal Court, District Court, Housing Court, Juvenile Court and Superior Court departments of the Trial Court.

Case records—case papers or records that have been filed or deposited in paper or electronic form in any court of the commonwealth or that are in the custody of any clerk.

Docket—the paper or electronic list of case information maintained by the clerk that contains the case caption, case number, and a chronological entry identifying the date and title of each paper, document, exhibit, order, or judgment filed in a case, and the scheduling and occurrence of events in the case.

Extended record—as described in G. L. c. 34, § 9E: an abbreviated chronicle of all matters entered upon the docket, under the same or a similar title or an abstract thereof, and under the same number, and shall contain a brief and concise narrative of the essential features of the matter. Any final judgment, decree or order affecting the title to land shall be copied therein at length.

Minor violation records—case records, other than dockets, filed in or relating to a proceeding involving civil motor vehicle infractions, parking, littering, bicycles, pedestrians, municipal dog control, the decriminalized disposition of violations of municipal ordinances or by-laws or other decriminalized regulatory offenses.

Sampling—the process of retaining designated case records in accordance with an Order re Sampling of Case Records issued from time to time by the Supreme Judicial Court.

Section 3. Required Permanent Retention of Case Records. The following types of case records shall be retained permanently and shall not be subject to the provisions of Section 7 regarding the destruction of case records:

A. *The Supreme Judicial Court and the Appeals Court.*

(1) all trial court transcripts in cases decided by the Supreme Judicial Court shall be retained.

(2) all case records under the custody of the clerks of the Supreme Judicial Court or the clerk of the Appeals Court shall be retained except:

    (a) papers unrelated to the appellate courts' deliberation and decision, after the rescript issues to the trial court;

    (b) record appendices upon final disposition of the case; and

    (c) original exhibits transmitted pursuant to an order or rule of court, which shall be returned to the trial court after review by the appellate court.

B. *All Departments of the Trial Court.* The following types of case records shall be retained permanently in all departments of the Trial Court:

(1) case records in all cases decided by the Supreme Judicial Court;

(2) old case records, defined as:

    (a) any records dated or known to have been filed earlier than 1800; and

    (b) all records from any predecessor court to the District Court or the Boston Municipal Court;

(3) dockets and extended records, except for dockets and extended records for minor violation records, which shall be subject to the sampling provisions set forth in an Order issued by the Supreme Judicial Court pursuant to Section 6;

(4) divorce judgments nisi and absolute and judgments in annulment actions; and

(5) naturalization records prior to 1906.

In addition, for time periods in which both dockets and extended records are missing from a trial court in a particular courthouse, all other case records from that time period in that trial court at that courthouse shall be retained.

C. *Individual Departments of the Trial Court.* In addition to the case records that shall be retained permanently in every department, the following case records shall be retained by individual departments:

(1) District Court, Boston Municipal Court, Juvenile Court and Probate and Family Court. The following shall be retained permanently:

    (a) all case records, acknowledgments and agreements filed to establish paternity pursuant to G. L. c. 209C; and

    (b) all case records filed in or relating to an adoption filed pursuant to G. L. c. 210, or a name change filed pursuant to G. L. c. 210, § 12.

(2) Land Court. The following shall be retained permanently:

    (a) all registration case records, abstracts, plans and proceedings subsequent to registration; and

    (b) all case records relating to the foreclosure of the right of redemption pursuant to G. L. c. 60, § 65.

(3) Probate and Family Court. The following shall be retained permanently:

    (a) all case records in conservatorship, trusts and estate administration; and

    (b) all orders and judgments in equity.

(4) Superior Court. The following shall be retained permanently:

    (a) all case records filed before 1860;

    (b) all case records filed in Barnstable, Dukes, Essex, and Nantucket counties before 2000; and

    (c) for time periods in which any case records in a particular courthouse are missing or substantially damaged, all other case records from that time period at that courthouse.

Section 4. Retention Periods for Certain Non–Permanent Case Records in the Probate and Family Court Department.

A. The following shall be retained for 20 years:

(1) all case records in divorce or annulment actions except for judgments, which must be retained permanently;

(2) all case records in complaints filed pursuant to G. L. c. 208 and G. L. c. 209C except for acknowledgements and agreements which must be retained permanently; and

(3) all case records in equity matters other than orders and judgments which must be retained permanently.

B. The following shall be retained for 10 years after final disposition or allowance of the accounts, whichever is later, and then may be destroyed without the need to sample under Section 6:

(1) guardian ad litem reports and reports of the office of the commissioner of probation pursuant to G.L. c. 276, § 85B;

(2) fiduciary account subsidiary schedules, but not cover pages; and

(3) financial statements under Supplemental Probate and Family Court Rule 401.

C. The following shall apply to records in guardianship proceedings:

(1) case records regarding the guardianship of a minor pursuant to G. L. c. 190B, § 5–204 shall be retained for at least 10 years or until the minor has reached the age of 20, whichever is the later date; and

(2) case records regarding the guardianship of an incapacitated person pursuant to G. L. c. 190B, § 5–303 shall be retained for at least 10 years or until 5 years after the incapacitated person's death, whichever is the later date.

Section 5. Retention Periods for Certain Non–Permanent Case Records in the Juvenile Court Department.
All case records filed in or relating to a care and protection case filed pursuant to G. L. c. 119, § 24, or to matters where the Department of Children and Families has responsibility pursuant to G. L. c. 119, § 23(f) shall be retained for at least 10 years, or until the youngest child or young adult named on the petition has reached the age of twenty-two, whichever is the later date.

Section 6. Sampling of Case Records.
Case records not required to be retained pursuant to Section 3 may be sampled in accordance with an Order issued by the Supreme Judicial Court. The Order shall set forth the sampling requirements for case records in all the departments of the Trial Court.

Section 7. Destruction of Case Records.

A. Case records not required to be retained pursuant to Section 3 may be destroyed ten years after final disposition of a case provided that:

(1) unless this rule states that sampling is not necessary, a sample pursuant to Section 6 has been retained;

(2) the clerk certifies to the appropriate Chief Justice that the dockets for any case records to be destroyed contain essential information including:

(a) entries indicating that a party was represented by counsel or waived counsel pursuant to S.J.C. Rule 3:10 in cases where counsel is required; and

(b) in civil cases, information sufficient to permit execution on a judgment within twenty years after the date of the judgment.

(3) in any criminal case in which a defendant has been sentenced to more than ten years' imprisonment, the case records shall be retained for the period of time that the defendant remains in the custody of the Commonwealth or under parole or probation supervision in connection with that case;

(4) transcripts in cases not decided by the Supreme Judicial Court may be destroyed ten years after final disposition of a case without the need to sample under Section 6; and

(5) sealed case records not otherwise required to be retained by this rule may be destroyed 100 years after final disposition of the case.

B. *Notice.* At least thirty days before destroying case records, the clerk shall give public notice that case records are proposed to be destroyed pursuant to this rule. The notice shall identify the types of cases and the beginning and ending dates of the cases to be destroyed (e.g. civil cases, 1900 through 1950). The Record Management Coordinator of the Trial Court (RMC) shall give such notice for any records under the RMC's custody.

(1) Before publication, the notice shall be approved by the appropriate clerk, the appropriate Chief Justice and the first justice of the division, if any, in which the case records are stored. The clerk or RMC shall send a copy of the notice to the Chief Justices of the Supreme Judicial Court and of the Trial Court.

(2) Notice shall be posted on the court's website or in a manner to be determined by the Chief Justice of the Trial Court, or, in the appellate courts, by the appropriate Chief Justice.

C. *Court Order.* No case records shall be destroyed in the Land Court, Probate and Family Court or Superior Court without an order of the Chief Justice of the appropriate court. No case records shall be destroyed in the Boston Municipal Court, District Court, Juvenile Court or Housing Court without an order, approved by the Chief Justice of the department and the first justice of the division where the records are stored. Before destroying any records, the clerk or RMC shall notify the appropriate Chief Justice of any responses received as a result of the publication of the notice.

D. *Exceptions.*

(1) Discretion to preserve case records. A Chief Justice or clerk may exercise discretion at any time to retain any case records under the clerk's custody even if such records could be destroyed under this rule.

(2) Excess papers. Regardless of other provisions of this rule, a clerk may destroy any excess case records, such as transmittal letters and duplicate copies.

Section 8. Digital Storage.

A. With the exception of the case records listed in Section 8B, all case records subject to retention under this rule may be destroyed once the case record has been converted to, and stored in, a PDF–A format or in another archival digital format which has been approved by the Supreme Judicial Court.

B. The following case records shall be retained in their original form even if electronic copies are available:

(1) any original paper dated or known to have been filed before the year 1800;

(2) all case records created prior to 1900;

(3) all wills, case records filed in or relating to an adoption filed pursuant to G. L. c. 210, a name change filed pursuant to G. L. c. 210 § 12, or the establishment of paternity pursuant to G. L. c. 209C;

(4) all dockets and extended records; and

(5) any other paper or record designated for retention by the Chief Justice of the Trial Court, or, in the appellate courts, by the appropriate chief justice.

C. Section 8A shall take effect in the Trial Court after the Court Administrator and Chief Justice of the Trial Court determine that the Trial Court has adopted adequate policies and procedures to permanently protect case records stored in PDF–A format or any other approved archival digital format. In the appellate courts, such determination shall be made by the appropriate chief justice. Redetermination shall occur at least every five years and before any new archival digital format is used.

Amended December 16, 1980, effective January 1, 1981; amended effective October 22, 1982; amended June 16, 1987, effective July 1, 1987; amended effective September 1, 1991; October 2, 1995; amended June 27, 2018, effective October 1, 2018.

Rule 1:12. Rule Relative to the Disposal of Stenographic Notes of Testimony Taken in the Courts of the Commonwealth

G.L. c. 221, § 27A, as amended *

* provides statutory authority for this rule.

Stenographic notes of testimony made in any court of the Commonwealth in accordance with any provisions of law may be destroyed by the lawful custodian thereof after the expiration of six years from the date when such notes were taken; provided, however, that this rule shall not apply to notes of which a transcript shall have been ordered and not completed, or to notes as to which the court in which they were taken shall otherwise order.

Rule 1:13. Time for Report of Material Facts in the Probate and Family Court Department for Cases Under G.L. c. 215, § 11

When, in accordance with G.L. c. 215, § 11, a judge of a division of the Probate and Family Court Department has been requested to report the material facts found by him, he shall report such facts within thirty days after the request is made.

Rule 1:14. Interest on Pecuniary Legacies and Trust Distributions Under G.L. c. 197, § 20 [Stricken]

Stricken June 18, 2015, eff. September 1, 2015.

Rule 1:15. Impoundment Procedure in the Supreme Judicial Court and Appeals Court

Section 1. Requests for Impoundment in the First Instance.

(a) Supreme Judicial Court.

(i) As used herein, "impoundment" shall mean the act of keeping some or all of the papers, documents, or exhibits, or portions thereof, in a case separate and unavailable for public inspection.

(ii) Requests for impoundment in proceedings in the Supreme Judicial Court shall be made by written motion describing with particularity the information sought to be impounded and the period of time for which impoundment is sought, and demonstrating good cause for the impoundment. The motion shall be accompanied by an affidavit in support thereof.

(iii) An order of impoundment may be entered by the court for good cause shown and in accordance with applicable law. In determining good cause, the court shall consider the nature of the parties and the controversy, the type of information and the privacy interests involved, the extent of community interest, the reason(s) for the request, and any other relevant factors.

(iv) Upon filing of the motion to impound and accompanying affidavit, the motion, affidavit, and the information sought to be impounded shall be treated by the court as temporarily impounded pending a ruling on the motion. Subsequent to the ruling on the motion, the motion, affidavit, and any impoundment order shall be part of the public docket and not impounded unless otherwise ordered by the court. If the motion is denied, the information sought to be impounded shall be part of the public docket.

(v) Hearings, if any, on requests under this rule shall be scheduled at the discretion of the court.

(vi) Upon entry of an order of impoundment, the Clerk of the Supreme Judicial Court or his or her assistants shall make a notation in the docket indicating what material has been impounded. All impounded material shall be kept separate from other papers in the case and shall not be available for public inspection. Such impounded material shall be available to the court, the attorneys of record, the parties to the case, and the clerk, unless otherwise ordered by the court.

(b) Appeals Court. Requests for impoundment in proceedings in the Appeals Court shall be governed by the provisions of Trial Court Rule VIII with the following exceptions: (i) the term "clerk" shall mean the Clerk of the Appeals Court and his or her assistants; and (ii) the Appeals Court or a single justice thereof has discretion to enter, either *sua sponte* or upon motion, any order relating to impoundment without holding a hearing.

Section 2. Maintaining Confidentiality of Previously Impounded Material in Cases on Appeal.

(a) Duties of Trial Court Clerks. When an appeal has been taken in a case in which material has been impounded, the clerk of the trial court shall notify the clerk of the appellate court, in writing, at the time of the transmission of the record that material was impounded by the trial court. Such notification shall specify those papers, documents or exhibits, or portions thereof, which were impounded below and shall include a copy of the order of impoundment, if any, or a reference to other authority for the impoundment.

(b) Duties of Appellate Court Clerk. Unless otherwise ordered by the appellate court, or otherwise provided in the trial court order of impoundment, material impounded in the trial court shall remain impounded in the appellate courts and material impounded in the Appeals Court shall remain impounded in the Supreme Judicial Court. The clerk shall keep all impounded material separate from other papers in the case and unavailable for public inspection. Such impounded material shall be available to the court, the attorneys of record, the parties to the case and the clerk, unless otherwise ordered by the court.

(c) Duties of the Parties. When an appeal has been taken in a case in which material has been impounded, the parties shall protect the confidentiality of the impounded material. Unless it is necessary to do so, the parties shall not include impounded information in briefs and appendices filed with the court. If material filed with the court contains impounded information, the parties shall so notify the clerk and shall identify the impounded material, which shall be unavailable for public inspection. The appellate court, a single justice, or the clerk thereof may require any party filing a document containing impounded information to file a redacted copy of the document that the appellate court may make available for public inspection.

During oral argument in public sessions the parties shall not disclose impounded material, provided that in cases where such disclosure is necessary the parties shall notify the clerk in advance and, in appropriate cases, shall make such disclosures in a manner that protects the confidentiality of the parties.

Adopted October 27, 1987, effective January 1, 1988. Amended September 24, 2015, effective October 1, 2015.

Rule 1:16. Judicial Performance Enhancement Programs

Section 1. Confidentiality. Except as provided in section 2 of this rule, any written, recorded, or oral data, information and materials received or developed under a judicial performance enhancement program shall be confidential and shall not be disclosed. The identity of individuals who furnish information concerning judges under a program shall be confidential and shall not be disclosed.

Section 2. Disclosure.

(a) Information concerning an individual judge may be disclosed to that judge, to that judge's chief justice or administrative justice, to the Chief Administrative Justice, and to the judges supervising the judicial performance enhancement program, provided that it is presented in a manner that will not disclose the identity of any person furnishing any information.

(b) From time to time, the Supreme Judicial Court, or the supervisory committee may issue public statements or reports describing the judicial performance enhancement programs and the procedures used in such programs, and summarizing information compiled under such programs, provided that such statements and reports shall not identify, directly or indirectly, any individual judge or any person who furnished information concerning a judge or judges under a program.

Adopted October 24, 1989, effective January 1, 1990.

Rule 1:17. Subpoenas to Officials of the Supreme Judicial Court and Appeals Court

(1) Subpoenas to compel the testimony of a justice or clerk or assistant clerk of the Supreme Judicial Court or Appeals Court shall be governed by the provisions of Rule 1 of Trial Court Rule IX.

(2) Subpoenas to compel the production of court records or administrative records of a clerk, assistant clerk or other official keeper of records in the Supreme Judicial Court or Appeals Court shall be governed by the provisions of Rule 2 of Trial Rule IX.

(3) For purposes of this rule, the term "justice," as used in Trial Court Rule IX, shall mean a judge of the Supreme Judicial Court or Appeals Court; the terms "magistrate" or "clerk-magistrate," as used in Trial Court Rule IX, shall mean the Clerk of the Supreme Judicial Court for the Commonwealth, the Clerk of the Supreme Judicial Court for Suffolk County, the Clerk of the Appeals Court, and their employees.

Adopted January 6, 1995, effective February 1, 1995.

RULE 1:18. UNIFORM RULES ON DISPUTE RESOLUTION

Adopted May 1, 1998

Table of Contents

[This Table of Contents is provided for convenience of reference only and is not part of the Uniform Rules on Dispute Resolution or the order adopting such rules.]

Rule 1. Court–Connected Dispute Resolution

(a) Scope, Applicability and Purpose of Rules. These rules govern court-connected dispute resolution services provided in civil and criminal cases in every department of the Trial Court. The Ethical Standards in Rule 9 also apply to neutrals who provide court-connected dispute resolution services in the Supreme Judicial Court and the Appeals Court. The purpose of the rules is to increase access to court-connected dispute resolution services, to ensure that these services meet standards of quality and procedural fairness, and to foster innovation in the delivery of these services. The rules shall be construed so as to secure those ends. To the extent that there is any conflict between these rules and the Massachusetts Rules of Civil Procedure, the Massachusetts Rules of Criminal Procedure, the Massachusetts Rules of Appellate Procedure, the Massachusetts Rules of Domestic Relations Procedure, the Juvenile Court Rules, the Standards and Forms For Probation Offices of the Probate and Family Court Department (hereinafter the "Probation Standards") promulgated by the Office of the Commissioner of Probation effective July 1, 1994, or the Rules of the Supreme Judicial Court and the Appeals Court, then the Massachusetts Rules of Civil, Criminal, Appellate, and Domestic Relations Procedure, the Juvenile Court Rules, the Probation Standards, or the Supreme Judicial Court and Appeals Court rules shall control. The Supreme Judicial Court, the Appeals Court, the Chief Justice for Administration and Management, and each Trial Court department may adopt additional rules or administrative procedures to supplement these rules, provided that they are consistent with these rules.

(b) Guiding Principles. The interpretation of these rules shall be guided by the following principles:

(i) *Quality.* The judiciary, collaborating with others experienced in dispute resolution, is responsible for assuring the high quality of the dispute resolution services to which it refers the public.

(ii) *Integrity.* Dispute resolution services should be provided in accordance with ethical standards and with the best interest of the disputants as the paramount criterion.

(iii) *Accessibility.* Dispute resolution services should be available to all members of the public regardless of their ability to pay.

(iv) *Informed choice of process and provider.* Wherever appropriate, people should be given a choice of dispute resolution processes and providers and information upon which to base the choice.

(v) *Self–determination.* Wherever appropriate, people should be allowed to decide upon the issues to be discussed during a dispute resolution process, and to decide the terms of their agreements.

(vi) *Timely services.* Dispute resolution services, to be most effective, should be available early in the course of a dispute.

(vii) *Diversity.* The policies, procedures and providers of dispute resolution services should reflect the diverse needs and background of the public.

(viii) *Qualification of neutrals.* Dispute resolution services should be performed only by qualified neutrals. There are many ways in which a neutral may become competent, and there are many ways to determine qualifications of neutrals, such as assessing performance and considering a neutral's education, training, experience and subject matter expertise.

Adopted May 1, 1998, effective June 1, 1998.

Rule 2. Definitions

As used in these rules, the following terms shall have the following meanings:

"Arbitration" means a process in which a neutral renders a binding or non-binding decision after hearing arguments and reviewing evidence.

"Case evaluation" means a process in which the parties or their attorneys present a summary of their cases to a neutral who renders a non-binding opinion of the settlement value of the case and/or a non-binding prediction of the likely outcome if the case is adjudicated.

"Clerk" means the clerk, clerk-magistrate, recorder, or register of a court, or a designated assistant clerk-magistrate, assistant recorder or assistant register of probate.

"Community mediation program" means a non-profit, charitable program whose goals are to promote the use of mediation and related conflict resolution services by volunteers to resolve disputes including those that come to, or might otherwise come to, the courts.

"Conciliation" means a process in which a neutral assists parties to settle a case by clarifying the issues and assessing the strengths and weaknesses of each side of the case, and, if the case is not settled, explores the steps which remain to prepare the case for trial.

"Court" means the Land Court, the Boston Municipal Court, or a division of the District Court, the Superior Court, the Probate and Family Court, the Housing Court or the Juvenile Court. The provisions of these rules addressed to courts shall apply to judges, clerks, probation officers and other employees of these courts. For the purposes of Rule 9, "court" also includes the appellate courts.

"Court-connected dispute resolution services" means dispute resolution services provided as the result of a referral by a court. "To refer," for purposes of this definition, means to provide a party to a case with the name of one or more dispute resolution services providers or to direct a party to a particular dispute resolution service provider.

"Dispute intervention" means a process used in the Probate and Family Court and in the Housing Court in which a neutral identifies the areas of dispute between the parties, and assists in the resolution of differences.

"Dispute resolution service" means any process in which an impartial third party is engaged to assist in the process of settling a case or otherwise disposing of a case without a trial, including arbitration, mediation, case evaluation, conciliation, dispute intervention, early neutral evaluation, mini-trial, summary jury trial, any combination of these processes, and any comparable process determined by the Chief Justice for Administration and Management of the Trial Court or the Supreme Judicial Court to be subject to these rules. The term "dispute resolution service" does not include a pretrial conference, an early intervention event, a screening, a trial, or an investigation.

"Early intervention" means a compulsory, judicially supervised event, early in the life of a case, with multiple objectives relating to both scheduling of litigation and selection of dispute resolution services.

"Early neutral evaluation" means case evaluation which occurs early in the life of a dispute.

"Immediate family" means the individual's spouse, domestic partner, guardian, ward, parents, children, and siblings.

"Mediation" means a voluntary, confidential process in which a neutral is invited or accepted by disputing parties to assist them in identifying and discussing issues of mutual concern, exploring various solutions, and developing a settlement mutually acceptable to the disputing parties.

"Mini-trial" means a two-step process to facilitate settlement in which (a) the parties' attorneys present a summary of the evidence and arguments they expect to offer at trial to a neutral in the presence of individuals with decision-making authority for each party, and (b) the individuals with decision-making authority meet with or without the neutral to discuss settlement of the case.

"Neutral" means an individual engaged as an impartial third party to provide dispute resolution services and includes but is not limited to a mediator, an arbitrator, a case evaluator, and a conciliator. "Neutral" also includes a master, clerk, clerk-magistrate, register, recorder, family service officer, housing specialist, probation officer, and any other court employee when that individual is engaged as an impartial third party to provide dispute resolution services. For purposes of Rule 9, "neutral" also means an administrator of a program providing court-connected dispute resolution services.

"Program" means an organization with which neutrals are affiliated, through membership on a roster or a similar relationship, which administers, provides and monitors dispute resolution services. A program may be operated by a court employee or by an organization independent of the court, including a corporation or a governmental agency. A program operated by a court employee may include one or more court employees or non-employees or a combination of court employees and non-employees on its roster.

"Provider" or "provider of dispute resolution services" means a program which provides dispute resolution services or a neutral who provides dispute resolution services.

"Screening" means an orientation session in which parties to a case and/or their attorneys receive information about dispute resolution services. The case is reviewed to determine whether referral to a dispute resolution service is appropriate, and, if so, to which one. In a screening, there may also be discussion to narrow the issues in the case, to set discovery parameters, or to address other case management issues.

"Summary jury trial" means a non-binding determination administered by the court in which (a) the parties' attorneys present a summary of the evidence and arguments they expect to offer at trial to a six-person jury chosen from the court's jury pool, (b) the jury deliberates and returns a non-binding decision on the issues in dispute, (c) the attorneys may discuss with the jurors their reaction to the evidence and reasons for the verdict, and (d) the presiding neutral may be available to conduct a mediation with the parties.

Adopted May 1, 1998, effective June 1, 1998.

Rule 3. Administrative Structure for Court–Connected Dispute Resolution Services

(a) **Appointment of Standing Committee on Dispute Resolution.** There shall be a Standing Committee on Dispute Resolution consisting of up to twenty persons appointed by the Chief Justice for Administration and Management in consultation with the Chief Justices of the Trial Court departments. Each department of the Trial Court shall be represented on the Standing Committee. Members shall be appointed for three year terms and may be reappointed for additional terms when their terms expire. The Standing Committee shall be composed of: judges; other court personnel; attorneys; members of the public; academics; and providers of dispute resolution services. In order to achieve diversity in the membership of the Standing Committee, the Trial Court shall attempt to make funds available for expenses associated with participation in the Committee.

(b) Duties of Standing Committee on Dispute Resolution. The Standing Committee shall advise the Chief Justice for Administration and Management of the Trial Court with respect to standards for court-connected dispute resolution services and the implementation and oversight of court-connected dispute resolution services throughout the Trial Court. The Standing Committee shall work to ensure access to court-connected dispute resolution services, to ensure the quality of the services, and to foster innovation in the delivery of the services.

(c) Trial Court Departments. The Chief Justice of each Trial Court department may appoint an advisory committee on that department's court-connected dispute resolution services composed of judges, other court personnel, attorneys, academics, members of the public, and providers of dispute resolution services, including representatives of community mediation programs where they provide services to that court department. In order to achieve diversity in the membership of an advisory committee, the court shall attempt to make funds available for expenses associated with participation in the committee. An advisory committee shall function so as to avoid conflict of interest or the appearance of conflict of interest. Each such Chief Justice may designate an employee as the department coordinator of court-connected dispute resolution services. Every Trial Court chief justice who approves dispute resolution programs pursuant to Rule 4(a) shall develop written policies and procedures governing program operations and record-keeping that will enable evaluation of the program.

(d) Local Dispute Resolution Services Coordinator. The First Justice or the justice with administrative supervision of each court or division within every Trial Court department shall designate one court staff member as the dispute resolution services coordinator for that court or division. By agreement of affected First Justices, one person may be designated as dispute resolution services coordinator for divisions or courts in more than one department which are located in the same or a nearby building. The dispute resolution services coordinator shall maintain information about court-connected dispute resolution services and assist the public in making informed choices about the use of those services. The coordinator, in collaboration with the program or programs to which the court division refers cases, shall develop a system to record and compile data as required by Rule 6(g).

(e) Technical Assistance for Implementation of Dispute Resolution Services. The Chief Justice for Administration and Management shall, subject to appropriation, provide advice and consultation to Trial Court departments, courts, advisory committees and designated dispute resolution staff to assist in developing and operating court-connected dispute resolution services in accordance with the rules.

Adopted May 1, 1998, effective June 1, 1998. Amended July 21, 2004, effective January 1, 2005.

Rule 4. Implementation of Court–Connected Dispute Resolution

(a) Development of List of Approved Programs. (i) The Chief Justice of each Trial Court department, subject to review for compliance by the Chief Justice for Administration and Management, shall approve programs to receive court referrals in accordance with these rules. In order to be approved, programs must: agree to meet the operations standards in Rule 7; agree to ensure that the neutrals on their roster who provide court-connected dispute resolution services meet the qualifications standards in Rule 8; and agree to ensure that the neutrals on their roster follow the ethical standards in Rule 9 when providing court-connected dispute resolution services. The list of approved programs shall be developed and maintained through an open process which includes at least the following: advertisement of the opportunity to apply to be on the list; fair assessment of programs; efforts to ensure diversity among neutrals as to race, gender, ethnicity, experience, and training; policies about the length and termination of participation on the list; and procedures for removing a program from the list for cause and/or as a result of a complaint filed pursuant to Rule 4(f).

(ii) The Chief Justice for Administration and Management shall distribute a combined list of the programs approved pursuant to subparagraph (i). The list shall include information as to each program regarding geographic region, fees, and dispute resolution processes; and information as to each program's expertise, including process and subject matter expertise;

(b) Trial Court Department Plans. Each Trial Court department shall develop plans each fiscal year for the use of court-connected dispute resolution services by the courts in the department. The Chief Justice shall develop the plan in consultation with the department advisory committee, the department coordinator of court-connected dispute resolution services, and the courts in the department. Services may be provided only by programs on the list developed pursuant to paragraph (a) of Rule 4. The plan shall set forth information about court-connected dispute resolution services in the department, including at least the following: current status, goals and objectives, plans for the coming year, any plans for collaborating with other departments, a budget request, case selection and screening criteria, plans for early intervention, and needs for education programs. Where appropriate, each portion of the plan shall address: plans with respect to access to dispute resolution services, the quality of the services, and efforts to foster innovation in the delivery of services. Plans shall ensure that court-connected dispute resolution services are available to those who lack the financial resources to pay for the services and those who would not otherwise have access to the services. The plans shall be submitted by September 1 of each year to the Chief Justice for Administration and Management for review and approval.

(c) Pilot Programs for Mandatory Participation in Dispute Resolution Services. Any Trial Court department may propose to the Chief Justice for Administration and Management for review and approval an experimental pilot program which requires parties in civil cases to participate in nonbinding forms of dispute resolution services. No Trial Court department shall administer such a pilot program without the approval of the Chief Justice for Administration and Management. Case types not suitable for dispute resolution services should be identified. The pilot program may provide for the mandatory participation of the parties and shall be assessed regularly to control quality. The minimal requirements for mandatory participation shall be as follows:

(i) each party shall be provided with an opportunity to terminate the dispute resolution services, upon motion to the court for good cause shown, but unwillingness to participate shall not be considered good cause;

(ii) the court shall give preference to a dispute resolution process upon which the parties agree;

(iii) the court shall explicitly inform parties that, although they are required to participate, they are not required to settle the case while participating in dispute resolution services; and

(iv) no fees may be charged for mandatory participation in dispute resolution services, but the court may charge fees for elective dispute resolution services.

(d) **Funding of Court-connected Dispute Resolution Services.** As part of the annual budget requests required by G.L. c. 211B, § 10(viii) and (x), the Chief Justice of each Trial Court department shall include a request for funding for court-connected dispute resolution services. The budget request shall provide for the funding of court-connected dispute resolution services for those parties who lack the financial resources to pay for the services or who would not otherwise have access to the services. Funds may be used for approved programs to provide screening and to provide and/or administer the services. Budget requests shall estimate funds needed to maintain previously funded services provided by approved programs. Additional amounts shall be used for the expansion or improvement of services or for innovative services. Expenditures shall be subject to the approval of the Chief Justice for Administration and Management after consultation with the Standing Committee.

(e) **Contracts for Court-connected Dispute Resolution Services.** (i) If public funds are appropriated or otherwise available and allocated by the Chief Justice for Administration and Management of the Trial Court for contracts with court connected dispute resolution programs, the Chief Justice for Administration and Management, in consultation with First Justices or other justices with administrative responsibility for courts and the Chief Justices of affected departments, shall issue one or more requests for proposals for dispute resolution services to be provided by contracts with approved programs, shall select programs through a competitive bidding process, and shall execute contracts for services on behalf of departments and courts which may extend for no more than three years. These contracts may provide for a program to receive payments approved under paragraph (d) and may provide that a court will refer all or most of its cases requiring dispute resolution services to one or more contracting programs.

(ii) If public funds are not involved, but courts seek an exclusive arrangement with a program or programs for court-connected dispute resolution services, the Chief Justice of the affected department or his or her designee shall, in consultation with the Chief Justice for Administration and Management, issue one or more requests for proposals to be provided by contracts with approved programs, shall select programs through a competitive process, and, with the approval of the Chief Justice for Administration and Management, shall execute contracts for services on behalf of departments and courts which may extend for no more than three years. These contracts may provide that a court will refer all or most of its cases requiring dispute resolution services to one or more contracting programs.

(iii) In selecting programs with which to contract, the Chief Justice for Administration and Management, or the Chief Justice of the department, as applicable, is encouraged to give preference to programs which demonstrate a record of and commitment to maintaining a diverse roster and operating in a manner which is accountable to the community.

(iv) The competitive bidding requirements in this subsection shall not apply to programs in which dispute resolution services are provided exclusively by court employees.

(f) **Complaint Mechanism.** The Chief Justice for Administration and Management, in consultation with the Chief Justices of the departments and with the advice of the Standing Committee, shall develop a uniform procedure for handling complaints regarding court-connected dispute resolution services.

Adopted May 1, 1998, effective June 1, 1998. Amended July 21, 2004, effective January 1, 2005.

Rule 5.   Early Notice of Court–Connected Dispute Resolution Services

Clerks shall make information about court-connected dispute resolution services available to attorneys and unrepresented parties. This information should state that selection of court-connected dispute resolution services can occur at the early intervention event or sooner, and that no court may compel parties to mediate any aspect of an abuse prevention proceeding under G.L. c. 209A, § 3. Insofar as possible, information should be available in the primary language of the parties. Attorneys shall: provide their clients with this information about court-connected dispute resolution services; discuss with their clients the advantages and disadvantages of the various methods of dispute resolution; and certify their compliance with this requirement on the civil cover sheet or its equivalent.

Adopted May 1, 1998, effective February 1, 1999.

Rule 6.   Duties of Courts with Respect to Court–Connected Dispute Resolution Services

(a) **Referral of Cases.** No court may refer cases to a provider of dispute resolution services unless the provider is an approved program included on the list developed pursuant to Rule 4(a). In all cases, courts shall inform parties that they are free to choose any approved program on the list, subject to such reasonable limitations as the court may impose, or any other provider of dispute resolution services. If the parties are unable or unwilling to choose a program from the list or another provider, a court may make a referral to a specific program on the list in which the court has confidence, whether or not the court has a contract for services with that program. The court shall make a reasonable effort to distribute such specific referrals fairly among programs on the list, taking into consideration geographic proximity, subject matter competence, special needs of the parties, and fee levels. In the alternative, a court may refer all or most of its cases requiring dispute resolution services to one or more approved programs in which the roster consists exclusively of one or more court employees or with which it has a contract for services pursuant to Rule 4(e). Notwithstanding the foregoing, a court may refer a case to a provider that is not on the list in exceptional circumstances, when special needs of the parties cannot be met by a program on the list. The judge shall report any such referral and the exceptional circumstances which required it to the Chief Justice of the department. In a criminal case, the court shall consult with the prosecuting attorney and obtain the approval of the defendant and, where applicable, the victim, before making a referral to a dispute resolution program.

(b) Screening. In civil cases, courts may require parties and/or their attorneys to attend a screening session or an early intervention event regarding court-connected dispute resolution services except for good cause shown.

(c) Time for Dispute Resolution. A court may establish a deadline for the completion of a court-connected dispute resolution process, which may be extended by the court upon a showing by the parties that continuation of the process is likely to assist in reaching resolution.

(d) Choice. No court shall require parties to participate in dispute resolution services without meeting the minimal requirements set forth in Rule 4(c), except that Probate and Family Courts may require parties to participate in dispute intervention. Except in a case affected by a pilot program under Rule 4(c) or a case involving such a referral to dispute intervention, the court shall inform litigants, both at the time of referral and at the beginning of the dispute resolution process, that the decision to participate in a dispute resolution process is voluntary.

(e) Space for Dispute Resolution Sessions. Courts may, subject to guidelines issued by the Chief Justice for Administration and Management of the Trial Court, provide available courthouse space or other resources for court-connected dispute resolution services provided by approved programs. The space provided shall be sufficiently private and readily accessible. Reasonable accommodation shall be made for disabled individuals.

(f) Communication with Program or Neutral. (i) The court shall give a program which is providing court-connected dispute resolution services sufficient information to process the case effectively.

(ii) The program shall give the court's administrative staff sufficient case-specific and aggregate information to permit monitoring and evaluation of the services.

(iii) Communication with the court during the dispute resolution process shall be conducted only by the parties or with their consent. The parties may agree, as part of the dispute resolution process, as to the scope of the information which

they, the program, or the neutral will provide to the court. Absent an agreement of the parties and subject to the provisions of Rule 9 regarding confidentiality and subparagraph (iv) below, the program or neutral may provide only the following information to the court: a request by the parties for additional time to complete dispute resolution, the neutral's assessment that the case is inappropriate for dispute resolution, and the fact that the dispute resolution process has concluded without parties' having reached agreement.

(iv) At the conclusion of conciliation or dispute intervention, the program or neutral may communicate to the court recommendations, a list of those issues which are and are not resolved, and the program's or neutral's assessment that the case will go to trial or settle, provided that the parties are informed at the initiation of the process that such communication may occur.

(g) Data Collection. The court, in collaboration with the approved program or programs to which it refers cases, shall develop a system to record accurately and compile regularly data sufficient to track cases, monitor services, and provide any information required or requested by the applicable Trial Court department chief justice or the Chief Justice for Administration and Management.

(h) Intake and Selection. Every court shall evaluate cases to ensure that they are appropriate for dispute resolution based on the case selection criteria of the applicable department developed pursuant to Rule 4(b).

(i) Inappropriate Pressure to Settle. Courts shall inform parties that, unless otherwise required by law, they are not required to make offers and concessions or to settle in a court-connected dispute resolution process. Courts shall not impose sanctions for nonsettlement by the parties. The court shall give particular attention to the issues presented by unrepresented parties, such as the need for the neutral to memorialize the agreement and the danger of coerced settlement in cases involving an imbalance of power between the parties. In dispute intervention, in cases in which one or more of the parties is not represented by counsel, a neutral has a responsibility, while maintaining impartiality, to raise questions for the parties to consider as to whether they have the information needed to reach a fair and fully informed settlement of the case.

(j) Sanctions for Failure to Attend Sessions. A court may impose sanctions for failure without good cause to attend a mandatory screening session, an early intervention event, or a scheduled dispute resolution session.

Adopted May 1, 1998, effective February 1, 1999.

Rule 7. Duties of Approved Programs with Respect to Court–Connected Dispute Resolution Services

(a) Program Administration. Programs shall be monitored and evaluated on a regular basis. Settlement rates shall not be the sole criterion for evaluation. Every program shall evaluate its neutrals on a regular basis. Every program shall develop and comply with written policies and procedures governing program administration and operations, including policies regarding evaluation, facilities, communication with the court, data collection, pressure to settle, and intake and selection, which are consistent with policies developed by Trial Court departments pursuant to Rule 3(c) and with Rules 4(a) and 6(a), (e), (f), (g), (h) and (i). A program may refuse to accept a referral from a court if the case does not meet the program's intake and selection criteria.

(b) Diversity. Programs shall be designed with knowledge of and sensitivity to the diversity of the communities served. The design shall take into consideration such factors as the languages, dispute resolution styles, and ethnic traditions of communities likely to use the services. Programs shall not discriminate against staff, neutrals, volunteers, or clients on the basis of race, color, sex, age, religion, national origin, disability, political beliefs or sexual orientation. Programs shall actively strive to achieve diversity among staff, neutrals, and volunteers.

(c) Rosters. Programs shall (i) assemble, maintain and administer rosters of qualified neutrals in conformity with these rules; (ii) except in the case of programs in which the roster consists exclusively of court employees, make a reasonable effort to distribute referrals fairly among individuals on the list, taking into consideration geographic proximity, subject matter competence, special needs of the parties, scheduling, and fee levels; (iii) adopt a fair and reasonable method by which qualified individuals may join the roster at its inception, when vacancies occur, or when the caseload requires additional neutrals; and (iv) adopt a fair and reasonable method by which individuals may be removed from the roster, including a provision for a periodic review of the roster. The methods used by the program for adding and removing neutrals shall be set forth in writing and made available to individuals applying for affiliation.

(d) Presence of Advisers. Parties, in consultation with their attorneys, if any, shall be permitted to decide whether their attorney, advocate or other adviser will be present at court-connected dispute resolution sessions.

(e) Fees. Programs may charge fees for service. Parties shall not be charged a fee for attendance at a mandatory screening session or an early intervention event, or for dispute resolution services provided by court employees. Fees charged by a provider of court-connected dispute resolution services shall be approved by the Chief Justice of the applicable court department. The fee schedule shall provide for fee waived or reduced fee services to be made available to indigent and low income litigants. Fees may not be contingent upon the result of the dispute resolution process or the amount of the settlement. Neutrals may assist parties to negotiate an equitable allocation of fees.

(f) Dispute Resolution Sessions. The program shall make reasonable efforts to schedule dispute resolution sessions at the convenience of the parties. The program shall allow adequate time in the dispute resolution session to discuss issues and reach settlement.

(g) Written Agreement. If a settlement is reached, the agreement shall be prepared in writing and signed by the parties, who shall forward for docketing a notice of the disposition of the case to the clerk of the court in which the case is pending. The neutral may participate in the preparation of the written agreement. At the parties' request, the court may allow an oral agreement instead of a written one.

(h) Orientation and Supervision of Neutrals. The program shall ensure that neutrals are familiar with the policies and operations of the court and the program. The program shall supervise its neutrals. During dispute resolution sessions, newly trained neutrals shall have immediate access to an experienced neutral.

(i) Enforcement of Qualifications Standards and Ethical Standards. Each approved program shall be responsible for enforcing the qualifications standards in Rule 8 and the ethical standards in Rule 9, and for taking appropriate action if a neutral on its roster fails or ceases to meet the qualifications standards or violates the ethical standards. Appropriate actions include referral for further training, suspension from the roster, or removal from the roster. If the Chief Justice of a Trial Court Department directs a program to take such action as a result of a complaint about the neutral and the program refuses to act, the Chief Justice may revoke the program's status as a program approved to receive referrals from that department.

Adopted May 1, 1998, effective February 1, 1999. Amended November 20, 2003, effective January 1, 2005.

Rule 8. Qualifications Standards for Neutrals

(a) Purpose and applicability. The purpose of setting qualifications standards for neutrals who receive court referrals is to foster high quality dispute resolution services. This rule shall apply to neutrals who provide mediation, arbitration, conciliation, case evaluation, dispute intervention, mini-trials or summary jury trials in court-connected programs.

(b) General Provisions.

(i) General Qualifications Requirements. To be qualified to provide dispute resolution services for cases referred by a court to an approved program, a neutral shall satisfy the requirements specified in this rule for the particular process which he or she provides unless exempted pursuant to Rule 8(k). A neutral may meet one or all of these requirements using the alternative method, if any, specified for the particular process, pursuant to Rule 8(j). To remain qualified, neutrals shall satisfy the continuing education and continuing evaluation requirements, if any, specified in this rule for the particular process.

(ii) Additional Qualifications. Trial Court Departments may establish additional qualifications for neutrals in approved programs in addition to those set forth in this rule provided they are consistent with these rules. In establishing such additional standards, court departments may provide for consideration of such factors as an individual's experience as a neutral, educational background, work experience, or subject matter expertise, and may also require such neutrals to complete specialized training or demonstrate subject matter expertise. Academic degrees and professional licensure may be among the factors considered but cannot be used as preclusive criteria by court departments in establishing additional qualifications for mediators or arbitrators participating in approved programs.

(iii) Competence. In qualifying mediators and arbitrators to handle court referrals, approved programs may consider such factors as an individual's experience as a mediator or arbitrator, educational background, work experience and sub-

ject matter expertise. Academic degrees and professional licensure may be among the factors considered but cannot be used as preclusive criteria by approved programs in qualifying mediators and arbitrators for inclusion in court panels. Academic degrees and professional licensure may be used as preclusive criteria for qualifying conciliators, case evaluators, mini-trial neutrals and summary jury trial neutrals.

(iv) Duties of the Chief Justice for Administration and Management. The Chief Justice for Administration and Management (CJAM) shall oversee and monitor the implementation of this rule, and suggest changes as needed. The CJAM shall, in consultation with the Standing Committee, develop guidelines for implementing the provisions of this rule. The CJAM shall collect, publish and distribute to approved programs any changes in the guidelines, and shall maintain the annual certifications submitted by approved programs as to the training, evaluation, mentoring and continuing education of neutrals.

(v) Duties of Approved Programs. Each approved program shall ensure that the neutrals on its roster meet the applicable training, mentoring, evaluation, continuing education, continuing evaluation, professional and experience requirements set forth in this rule and the guidelines adopted pursuant to Rule 8(b)(iv), and any additional qualification requirements adopted by a Trial Court Department. Each approved program shall ensure that the neutrals meet the standards set forth in the rule and guidelines, that any alternative method relied upon by a neutral to meet the standards is in compliance with Rule 8(j) and the guidelines, and that reliance upon the limited exemption is in compliance with Rule 8(k). To carry out these duties, each program shall take the following specific actions:

(a) Attest in its application for program approval that it will assign cases referred by a court only to neutrals who meet the qualifications standards;

(b) Maintain for the tenure of the neutral's association with the program, and for three years thereafter, documentation which demonstrates that the neutral meets the qualifications standards. Such documentation shall include, without limitation, the following:

(i) Name of the neutral;

(ii) Name of the training organization where the neutral satisfactorily completed any required training (or documentation of the neutral's compliance with the alternative method of meeting any training requirement pursuant to Rule 8(j));

(iii) Outcome of any required mentoring and evaluation for each neutral (or documentation of the neutral's compliance with the alternative method of meeting any evaluation requirement pursuant to Rule 8(j));

(iv) Documentation of the neutral's participation in any required continuing education and in any required continuing evaluation;

(v) Documentation demonstrating that the neutral meets any applicable requirements as to professional licensure, experience or subject matter expertise; and

(vi) Documentation demonstrating that the neutral qualifies for the limited exemption set forth in Rule 8(k).

(c) Certify annually to the AOTC that the neutrals on its roster meet the requirements for training, mentoring and evaluation, and continuing education set forth in this rule and the guidelines.

(d) Make the documentation demonstrating a neutral's qualification and the documentation demonstrating the program's compliance with the rules and the guidelines available to the AOTC and to the Chief Justices of the Trial Court Departments for inspection and copying upon request.

(c) Mediators.

(i) Training Requirement. A mediator shall successfully complete a basic mediation training course of at least thirty hours and a court orientation, both of which comply with the guidelines adopted pursuant to Rule 8(b)(iv). A mediator shall also complete any additional, specialized training required by a Trial Court Department.

(ii) Mentoring and Evaluation Requirement. A mediator shall complete the mentoring and evaluation requirements contained in the Guidelines adopted pursuant to Rule 8(b)(iv).

(iii) Continuing Education. A mediator shall participate in any continuing education required by the approved program with which he or she is affiliated or by the court department in which he or she is providing services.

(iv) Continuing Evaluation. A mediator shall participate in regular evaluation as required by Rule 7.

(d) Arbitrators.

(i) Training Requirement. An arbitrator shall successfully complete a basic arbitration training course of at least eight hours and a court orientation, both of which comply with the guidelines adopted pursuant to Rule 8 (b)(iv). An arbitrator shall also complete any additional, specialized training required by a Trial Court Department.

(ii) Mentoring and Evaluation Requirement. An arbitrator shall complete the mentoring and evaluation requirements contained in the guidelines adopted pursuant to Rule 8(b)(iv).

(iii) Continuing Education. An arbitrator shall participate in any continuing education required by the approved program with which he or she is affiliated or by the court department in which he or she is providing services.

(iv) Continuing Evaluation. An arbitrator shall participate in regular evaluation as required by Rule 7.

(e) Conciliators.

(i) Professional Qualifications. A conciliator must be admitted to the bar of the Commonwealth of Massachusetts, be in good standing with the Board of Bar Overseers, and have engaged in the practice of law within the Commonwealth of Massachusetts for at least three years.

(ii) Training Requirement. A conciliator shall successfully complete a conciliation training course of at least eight hours and a court orientation, both of which comply with the guidelines adopted pursuant to Rule 8(b)(iv). A conciliator shall also complete any additional, specialized training required by a trial court department.

(iii) Mentoring and Evaluation Requirement. A conciliator shall, if required to do so at the discretion of the approved program with which he or she is affiliated, complete the

mentoring and evaluation requirements of that program contained in the guidelines adopted pursuant to Rule 8(b)(iv).

(iv) Continuing Education. A conciliator shall participate in any continuing education required by the approved program with which he or she is affiliated or by the court department in which he or she is providing services.

(v) Continuing Evaluation. A conciliator shall participate in regular evaluation as required by Rule 7.

(f) Case Evaluators.

(i) Professional Qualifications. A case evaluator must be admitted to the bar of the Commonwealth of Massachusetts, be in good standing with the Board of Bar Overseers, and must have seven years of trial experience within the Commonwealth of Massachusetts as an attorney or judge.

(ii) Training Requirement. A case evaluator shall successfully complete a basic case evaluation training of at least eight hours and a court orientation, both of which comply with the guidelines adopted pursuant to Rule 8(b)(iv). A case evaluator shall also complete any additional, specialized training required by a Trial Court Department for case evaluators.

(iii) Mentoring and Evaluation Requirement. A case evaluator shall complete the mentoring and evaluation requirements contained in the guidelines adopted pursuant to Rule 8(b)(iv).

(iv) Continuing Education. A case evaluator shall participate in any continuing education required by the approved program with which he or she is affiliated or by the court department in which he or she is providing services.

(v) Continuing Evaluation. A case evaluator shall participate in regular evaluation as required by Rule 7.

(g) Mini–Trial Neutrals.

(i) Professional Qualifications. A mini-trial neutral shall have at least ten years experience evaluating legal disputes as a judge, arbitrator, attorney, or executive level decision-maker.

(ii) Training Requirements. A mini-trial neutral shall successfully complete the training required for mediators in Rule 8(c)(i), and the training required for case evaluators in Rule 8(f)(ii).

(iii) Mentoring and Evaluation Requirement. A mini-trial neutral shall complete the mentoring and evaluation requirements contained in the guidelines adopted pursuant to Rule 8(b)(iv).

(iv) Continuing Education. A mini-trial neutral shall participate in any continuing education required by the approved program with which he or she is affiliated or by the court department in which he or she is providing services.

(v) Continuing Evaluation. A mini-trial neutral shall participate in regular evaluation as required by Rule 7.

(h) Summary Jury Trial Neutrals.

(i) Professional Qualifications. A summary jury trial neutral shall be an arbitrator qualified under this rule, an attorney, or a former judge, with at least ten years of experience as an arbitrator, trial attorney, or judge. The summary jury trial neutral must be in good standing in any jurisdiction in which he or she is licensed to practice law.

(ii) Continuing Education. A summary jury trial neutral shall participate in any continuing education required by the approved program with which he or she is affiliated or by the court department in which he or she is providing services.

(iii) Continuing Evaluation. A summary jury trial neutral shall participate in regular evaluation as required by Rule 7.

(i) Dispute Intervention Neutrals.

(i) Training Requirement. A provider of dispute intervention services shall successfully complete a training course and a court orientation, both of which comply with the guidelines adopted pursuant to Rule 8(b)(iv). A provider of dispute resolution services shall also complete any additional specialized training required by the Trial Court Department in which he or she is providing dispute intervention services.

(ii) Mentoring and Evaluation Requirement. A provider of dispute intervention services shall complete the mentoring and evaluation requirements set forth in the guidelines adopted pursuant to Rule 8(b)(iv).

(iii) Continuing Education. A provider of dispute resolution services shall participate in any continuing education required by the approved program with which he or she is affiliated or by the court department in which he or she is providing services.

(iv) Continuing Evaluation. A provider of dispute resolution services shall participate in regular evaluation as may be required by the relevant Trial Court Department.

(j) Alternative Methods of Satisfying Requirements. A neutral may be qualified by a program to handle cases referred by a court by demonstrating that he or she meets the alternative methods set forth in the guidelines of satisfying the training, mentoring and evaluation requirements set forth in this rule and the guidelines. Programs that seek to qualify neutrals through the alternative methods provision are required to compile necessary documentation pursuant to Rule 8(b)(v) and applicable guidelines.

(k) Limited Exemption from Training, Mentoring and Evaluation Requirements. As a general rule, all neutrals in approved programs shall satisfy the training, mentoring and evaluation requirements set forth in Rule 8. However, the Chief Justice of any Trial Court Department may elect, as a one-time exception to this rule, to exempt mediators, arbitrators, case evaluators, and conciliators from those requirements, subject to the provisions set forth below. The Chief Justice for Administration and Management shall establish a process for notification and a deadline for submission by departmental Chief Justices of their decision to utilize the exemption, and for programs to apply for the exemption.

(i) One Time Exemption of Certain Neutrals. This exemption will be a one-time option available only to those mediators, arbitrators, case evaluators and conciliators who meet the requirements set forth in Rule 8(k). No other neutral shall be exempted from the training, mentoring or evaluation requirements of Rule 8.

(ii) Designation of Neutrals. Each program approved on or before July 1, 2002, by a Department in which this exemption is available pursuant to this Rule and which continues as an approved program on the date on which Rule 8 becomes effective shall submit to the Chief Justice of that Department

pursuant to the process established by the Chief Justice for Administration and Management, a list of any mediators, arbitrators, case evaluators and conciliators who qualify for the exemption. The program shall include a complete and detailed description of the qualifications of each such mediator, arbitrator, case evaluator or conciliator as evidence of his or her eligibility.

(iii) Requirements for Exemption. A program may consider a neutral eligible for this exemption only if he or she was serving as of July 1, 2002, on a panel of a program approved on or before that date which continues as an approved program on the date on which Rule 8 becomes effective. In addition, a program shall consider the neutral's overall experience and other factors under Rule 8 (e.g. prior training, mentoring, evaluation, the recency of his or her experience and the number and types of cases handled). An eligible individual must have served in the process for which he or she is seeking exemption for five years during the last six years prior to July 1, 2002, and meet the following additional requirement:

(a) Mediators. Must have provided at least 300 hours of mediation during that period.

(b) Arbitrators. Must have provided at least 150 hours of arbitration during that period.

(c) Case Evaluators. Must have provided at least 100 hours of case evaluation during that period.

(d) Conciliators. Must have provided at least 100 hours of conciliation during that period.

(iv) Transferability of Exemption. A mediator, arbitrator, case evaluator or conciliator who qualifies for this exemption in a Trial Court Department shall be qualified to provide services in the process in which he or she is exempted in another approved program within that Department subject to the approval of the other program. A mediator, arbitrator, case evaluator or conciliator who seeks exemption in another Department must meet the exemption through a program approved in that other Department.

(v) Limitations on Exemption. This provision does not exempt any mediator, arbitrator, case evaluator or conciliator from complying with the continuing education and continuing evaluation requirements of Rule 8.

(*l*) Effective Date. The effective date of this rule shall be January 1, 2005, except that to be qualified to provide dispute intervention, individuals employed by the courts on the effective date of this rule shall have until January 1, 2007 to demonstrate compliance with the requirements set forth in this rule. Employees hired to provide dispute intervention after the effective date of this rule must satisfy all the requirements of this rule within thirty-six (36) months of the date of hire.

Adopted November 20, 2003, effective January 5, 2005.

Rule 9. Ethical Standards

(a) Introduction. These Ethical Standards are designed to promote honesty, integrity and impartiality by all neutrals and other individuals involved in providing court-connected dispute resolution services. These standards seek to assure the courts and citizens of the Commonwealth that such services are of the highest quality, and to promote confidence in these dispute resolution services. In addition, these standards are intended as a foundation on which appellate courts and Trial Court departments can build their dispute resolution policies, programs and procedures to best serve the public. These Standards apply to all neutrals as defined in these Standards when they are providing court-connected dispute resolution services for the Trial Court and the appellate courts, including those who are state or other public employees. State and other public employees are subject to the Massachusetts Conflict of Interest Law, M.G.L. c. 268A, and therefore, to the extent that these standards are in any manner inconsistent with M.G.L. c. 268A, the statute shall govern. In addition, to the extent that these standards are in any manner inconsistent with the Standards and Forms For Probation Offices of the Probate and Family Court Department promulgated by the Office of the Commissioner of Probation effective July 1, 1994, the Probation Standards shall govern. All courts providing dispute resolution services and all court-connected dispute resolution programs shall provide the neutrals with a copy of these Ethical Standards. These Standards shall be made a part of all training and educational programs for approved programs, and shall be available to the public.

(b) Impartiality. A neutral shall provide dispute resolution services in an impartial manner. Impartiality means freedom from favoritism and bias in conduct as well as appearance.

(i) A neutral shall provide dispute resolution services only for those disputes where she or he can be impartial with respect to all of the parties and the subject matter of the dispute.

(ii) If at any time prior to or during the dispute resolution process the neutral is unable to conduct the process in an impartial manner, the neutral shall so inform the parties and shall withdraw from providing services, even if the parties express no objection to the neutral continuing to provide services.

(iii) No neutral or any member of the neutral's immediate family or his or her agent shall request, solicit, receive, or accept any in-kind gifts or any type of compensation other than the court-established fee in connection with any matter coming before the neutral.

(c) Informed Consent. The neutral shall make every reasonable effort to ensure that each party to the dispute resolution process (a) understands the nature and character of the process, and (b) in consensual processes, understands and voluntarily consents to any agreement reached in the process.

(i) A neutral shall make every reasonable effort to ensure at every stage of the proceedings that each party understands the dispute resolution process in which he or she is participating. The neutral shall explain (aa) the respective responsibilities of the neutral and the parties, and (bb) the policies, procedures and guidelines applicable to the process, including circumstances under which the neutral may engage in private communications with one or more of the parties.

(ii) If at any time the neutral believes that any party to the dispute resolution process is unable to understand the process or participate fully in it—whether because of mental impairment, emotional disturbance, intoxication, language barriers, or other reasons—the neutral shall (aa) limit the scope of the dispute resolution process in a manner consistent with the party's ability to participate, and/or recommend that the party obtain appropriate assistance in order to continue with the process, or (bb) terminate the dispute resolution process.

(iii) Where a party is unrepresented by counsel and where the neutral believes that independent legal counsel and/or independent expert information or advice is needed to reach an informed agreement or to protect the rights of one or more of the parties, the neutral shall so inform the party or parties.

(iv) A neutral may use his or her knowledge to inform the parties' deliberations, but shall not provide legal advice, counseling, or other professional services in connection with the dispute resolution process.

(v) The neutral shall inform the parties of their right to withdraw from the process at any time and for any reason, except as is provided by law or court rule.

(vi) In mediation, case evaluation, and other processes whose outcome depends upon the agreement of the parties, the neutral shall not coerce the parties in any manner to reach agreement.

(vii) In dispute intervention, in cases in which one or more of the parties is not represented by counsel, a neutral has a responsibility, while maintaining impartiality, to raise questions for the parties to consider as to whether they have the information needed to reach a fair and fully informed settlement of the case.

(d) **Fees.** A neutral shall disclose to the parties the fees that will be charged, if any, for the dispute resolution services being provided.

(i) A neutral shall inform each party in a court-connected dispute resolution process in writing, prior to the start of the process, of (aa) the fees, if any, that will be charged for the process, (bb) if there will be a fee, whether it will be paid to the neutral, court, and/or the program, and (cc) whether the parties may apply for a fee-waiver or other reduction of fees.

(ii) If a fee is charged for the dispute resolution process, the neutral shall enter into a written agreement with the parties, before the dispute resolution process begins, stating the fees and time and manner of payment.

(iii) Fee agreements may not be contingent upon the result of the dispute resolution process or amount of the settlement.

(iv) Neutrals shall not accept, provide, or promise a fee or other consideration for giving or receiving a referral of any matter.

(v) If the court has established fees for its dispute resolution services, no neutral shall request, solicit, receive, or accept any payment in any amount greater than the court-established fees when providing court-connected dispute resolution services.

(e) **Conflict of Interest.** A neutral shall disclose to all parties participating in the dispute resolution process all actual or potential conflicts of interest, including circumstances that could give rise to an appearance of conflict. A neutral shall not serve as a neutral in a dispute resolution process after he or she knows of such a conflict, unless the parties, after being informed of the actual or potential conflict, give their consent and the neutral has determined that the conflict is not so significant as to cast doubt on the integrity of the dispute resolution process and/or neutral.

(i) As early as possible and throughout the dispute resolution process, the neutral shall disclose to all parties participating in the process, all actual or potential conflicts of interest, including but not limited to the following:

(aa) any known current or past personal or professional relationship with any of the parties or their attorneys;

(bb) any financial interest, direct or indirect in the subject matter of the dispute or a financial relationship (such as a business association or other financial relationship) with the parties, their attorneys, or immediate family member of any party or their attorney, to the dispute resolution proceeding; and

(cc) any other circumstances that could create an appearance of conflict of interest.

(ii) Where the neutral determines that the conflict is so significant as to cast doubt on the integrity of the dispute resolution process and/or neutral, the neutral shall withdraw from the process, even if the parties express no objection to the neutral continuing to provide services.

(iii) Where the neutral determines that the conflict is not significant, the neutral shall ask the parties whether they wish the neutral to proceed. The neutral shall obtain consent from all parties before proceeding.

(iv) A neutral must avoid even the appearance of a conflict of interest both during and after the provision of services.

(aa) A neutral shall not use the dispute resolution process to solicit, encourage or otherwise procure future service arrangements with any party.

(bb) A neutral may not subsequently act on behalf of any party to the dispute resolution process, nor represent one such party against the other, in any matter related to the subject of the dispute resolution process.

(cc) A neutral may not subsequently act on behalf of any party to the dispute resolution process, nor represent one such party against the other, in any matter unrelated to the subject of the dispute resolution process for a period of one year, unless the parties to the process consent to such action or representation.

(v) A neutral shall avoid conflicts of interest in recommending the services of other professionals.

(f) **Responsibility to Non–Participating Parties.** A neutral should consider, and where appropriate, encourage the parties to consider, the interests of persons affected by actual or potential agreements and not participating or represented in the process.

(i) If a neutral believes that the interests of parties not participating or represented in the process will be affected by actual or potential agreements, the neutral should ask the parties to consider the effects of including or not including the absent parties and/or their representatives in the process. This obligation is particularly important when the interests of children or other individuals who are not able to protect their own interests are involved.

(g) **Advertising, Soliciting, or Other Communications by Neutrals.** Neutrals shall be truthful in advertising, soliciting, or other communications regarding the provision of dispute resolution services.

(i) A neutral shall not make untruthful or exaggerated claims about the dispute resolution process, its costs and benefits, its outcomes, or the neutral's qualifications and abilities.

(ii) A neutral shall not make claims of specific results, benefits, outcomes, or promises which imply favor of one side over another.

(h) Confidentiality. A neutral shall maintain the confidentiality of all information disclosed during the course of dispute resolution proceedings, subject only to the exceptions listed in this section.

(i) The information disclosed in dispute resolution proceedings that shall be kept confidential by the neutral includes, but is not limited to: the identity of the parties; the nature and substance of the dispute; the neutral's impressions, opinions, and recommendations; notes made by the neutral; statements, documents or other physical evidence disclosed by any participant in the dispute resolution process; and the terms of any settlement, award, or other resolution of the dispute, unless disclosure is required by law or court rule.

(ii) *Confidentiality vis-á-vis nonparties.* The neutral shall inform the participants in the dispute resolution process that he or she will not voluntarily disclose to any person not participating in the mediation any of the information obtained through the process, unless such disclosure is required by law.

(iii) *Confidentiality within mediation.* A neutral shall respect the confidentiality of information received in a private session or discussion with one or more of the parties in a dispute resolution process, and shall not reveal this information to any other party in the mediation without prior permission from the party from whom the information was received.

(iv) Neutrals who are part of a court-connected dispute resolution program may, for purposes of supervising the program, supervising neutrals and monitoring of agreements, discuss confidential information with other neutrals and administrative staff in the program. This permission to discuss confidential information does not extend to individuals outside their program.

(v) Neutrals may, with prior permission from the parties, use information disclosed by the parties in dispute resolution proceedings for research, training, or statistical purposes, provided the materials are adapted so as to remove any identifying information.

(i) Withdrawing from the Dispute Resolution Process. A neutral shall withdraw from the dispute resolution process if continuation of the process would violate any of the Ethical Standards, if the safety of any of the parties would be jeopardized, or if the neutral is unable to provide effective service.

(i) Withdrawal must be accomplished in a manner which, to the extent possible, does not prejudice the rights or jeopardize the safety of the parties.

(ii) A neutral may withdraw from the dispute resolution process if the neutral believes that (aa) one or more of the parties is not acting in good faith; (bb) the parties' agreement would be illegal or involve the commission of a crime; (cc) continuing the dispute resolution process would give rise to an

appearance of impropriety; (dd) in a process whose outcome depends upon the agreement of the parties, continuing with the process would cause severe harm to a non-participating party, or the public; and (ee) continuing discussions would not be in the best interest of the parties, their minor children, or the dispute resolution program.

Adopted May 1, 1998, effective February 1, 1999.

Rule 1:19.   Electronic Access to the Courts

1.   Covert photography, recording or transmission prohibited. No person shall take any photographs, or make any recording or transmission by electronic means, in any courtroom, hearing room, office, chambers or lobby of a judge or magistrate without prior authorization from the judge or magistrate then having immediate supervision over such place.

2.   Electronic access by the news media. A judge shall permit photographing or electronic recording or transmitting of courtroom proceedings open to the public by the news media for news gathering purposes and dissemination of information to the public, subject to the limitations of this rule. Subject to the provisions of paragraph (d), the news media shall be permitted to possess and to operate in the courtroom all devices and' equipment necessary to such activities. Such devices and equipment include, without limitation, still and video cameras, audio recording or transmitting devices, and portable computers or other electronic devices with communication capabilities.

The "news media" shall include any authorized representative of a news organization that has registered with the Public Information Officer of the Supreme Judicial Court or any individual who is so registered. Registration shall be afforded to organizations that regularly gather, prepare, photograph, record, write, edit, report or publish news or information about matters of public interest for dissemination to the public in any medium, whether print or electronic, and to individuals who regularly perform a similar function, upon certification by the organizations or individuals that they perform such a role and that they will familiarize themselves or their representatives, as the case may be, with the provisions of this rule and will comply with them.

In his or her discretion, a judge may entertain a request to permit electronic access as authorized by this rule to a particular matter over which the judge is presiding by news media that have not registered with the Public Information Officer.

(a) *Substantial likelihood of harm.* A judge may limit or temporarily suspend such access by the news media if it appears that such coverage will create a substantial likelihood of harm to any person or other serious harmful consequence.

(b) *Limitations.* A judge shall not permit:

(i) photography or electronic recording or transmission of voir dire hearings concerning jurors or prospective jurors.

(ii) electronic recording or transmission of bench and side-bar conferences, conferences between counsel, and conferences between counsel and client; or

(iii) frontal or close-up photography of jurors and prospective jurors.

A judge may impose other limitations necessary to protect the right of any party to a fair trial or the safety and well-being of any party, witness or juror, or to avoid unduly distracting participants or detracting from the dignity and decorum of the proceedings.

If the request is to record multiple cases in a session on the same day, a judge, in his or her discretion, may reasonably restrict the number of cases that are recorded to prevent undue administrative burdens on the court.

(c) Minors and sexual assault victims may not be photographed without the consent of the judge.

(d) *Positioning of equipment.* All equipment and devices shall be of a type and positioned and operated in a manner which does not detract from the dignity and decorum of the proceeding. Unless the judge permits otherwise for good reason, only one stationary, mechanically silent video camera shall be used in the courtroom for broadcast television, a second mechanically silent video camera shall be used for other media, and, in addition, one silent still camera shall be used in the courtroom at one time. Unless the judge otherwise permits, photographic equipment and its operator shall be in place in a fixed position within the area designated by the judge and remain there so long as the court is in session, and movement shall be kept to a minimum, particularly in jury trials. The operator shall not interrupt a court proceeding with a technical problem.

(e) *Advance notice.* A judge may require reasonable advance notice from the news media of their request to be present to photograph or electronically record or transmit at a particular session. In the absence of such notice, the judge may refuse to admit them. A judge may defer acting on such a request until the requester has seasonably notified the parties and, during regular business hours, the Bureau Chief or News Editor of the Associated Press, Boston, using the email address of apboston@ap.org A judge hearing any motion under this rule may reasonably limit the number of counsel arguing on behalf of the several interested media.

(f) *Non-exclusive access.* A judge shall not make an exclusive arrangement with any person or organization for news media coverage of proceedings in the courtroom. If there are multiple requests to photograph or electronically record the same proceeding, the persons making such requests must make arrangements among themselves for pooling or cooperative use and must do so outside of the courtroom and before the court session without judicial intervention.

(g) *Objection by a party.* Any party seeking to prevent any of the coverage which is the subject of this rule may move the court for an appropriate order, but shall first deliver electronic notice of the motion during regular business hours to the Bureau Chief or News Editor of the Associated Press, Boston, using the email address of apboston@ap.org as seasonably as the matter permits. The judge shall not hear the motion unless the movant has certified compliance with this paragraph, but compliance shall relieve the movant and the court of any need to postpone hearing the motion and acting on it, unless the judge, as a matter of discretion, continues the hearing.

3. Other recordings. A judge may permit the use of electronic or photographic means the presentation of evidence or the perpetuation of a record when authorized by law, for other purposes of judicial administration, or for the preparation of materials for educational or ceremonial purposes.

4. Definitions. For purposes of this rule, the term "judge" shall include a magistrate presiding over a proceeding open to the public. The term "minor" shall be defined as a person who has not attained the age of eighteen.

Adopted October 1, 1998, effective November 2, 1998. Amended December 15, 1999, effective January 3, 2000; February 28, 2012, effective September 17, 2012.

Rule 1:20. Address Confidentiality Program

The purpose of this rule is to allow persons certified by the Secretary of the Commonwealth as program participants under the Address Confidentiality Program, G.L. c. 9A, §§ 1 *et seq.* to use "substitute addresses" provided in that program in certain court proceedings. The words "address," "program participant" and "Secretary" as used in this rule shall have the same meaning as designated for said words in G.L. c. 9A, § 1.

This rule shall supersede any court rule, standing order or administrative directive to the contrary.

Any address confidentiality program participant and minor child(ren) residing with the program participant who are listed with the Secretary of the Commonwealth as included within the program, shall be entitled to use the address designated for him or her by the Secretary of the Commonwealth pursuant to Chapter 9A of the General Laws as his or her address. This address may be used in connection with any civil proceeding that is open to the public, except youthful offender cases, and except as may be ordered by the court, provided that the program participant first submits to the court in which the particular action is pending or is to be filed, an affidavit for use of substitute address on a form provided in this rule. The actual address of the program participant may be used by court personnel in the furtherance of their official duties, but such address shall not be used for purposes of mailing any documents, notices or orders.

Any person who submits such an affidavit in connection with a particular action shall have an affirmative duty to notify the court if his or her certification is canceled by the Secretary of the Commonwealth or expires during the pendency of the particular action. Such person shall also file a new affidavit whenever there is a change in the actual address as listed on the affidavit filed with the court. Said affidavit shall be impounded by operation of this rule without any further judicial action. The Clerk, Register, or Recorder shall segregate the impounded affidavit from the other papers and shall not make the information contained therein available to other parties.

AFFIDAVIT FOR USE OF "SUBSTITUTE ADDRESS"

RE: _____ v. _____

Docket Number: _____

  Name: _____

Address Designated by Secretary of the Commonwealth as my substitute address: _____

  I hereby swear or affirm that pursuant to Chapter 9A of the General Laws I was certified by the Secretary of the Commonwealth on _____ to participate in the Address Confidentiality Program and that the certification remains in full force and effect.

My actual residential address is _____.

The minor children residing with me at that address who are also participants in the Address Confidentiality Program are: _____

_____

Signed under the penalties of perjury this _____ day of _____ in the year ___.

Certified Program Participant

NOTICE

As a Program participant you may use the substitute address provided by the State Secretary of the Commonwealth and need not use your actual address in this court proceeding except as the court may otherwise order. However, you should be aware that other individuals who know your actual address might use that address in documents filed with the court or during the court proceedings related to this case. Furthermore, your actual address may appear in case files in other court proceedings not related to this case. You should consider seeking a protective order and/or an order of impoundment of all court documents containing your actual address to protect your safety further.

Adopted March 5, 2002, effective April 1, 2002.

Rule 1:21. Corporate Disclosure Statement on Possible Judicial Conflict of Interest

(a) **Who Must File.** In civil and criminal cases in the Trial Court and appellate courts, any nongovernmental corporate party to a proceeding must file a statement identifying all its parent corporations and listing any publicly held corporation that owns 10% or more of the party's stock or stating that there is no such corporation. In a criminal case, if an organization is a victim of the alleged criminal activity, the government must file a statement identifying the victim and if the victim is a corporation providing the information required by this paragraph.

(b) **Time for Filing.** The manner of filing the corporate disclosure statement shall be as follows:

(i) *Appellate Court.* In an appellate court, a party must file an original and nine copies of the statement required in paragraph (a) within thirty days of the entry of the appeal upon the docket. In the single justice session of the Supreme Judicial Court, a party must file in accordance with subparagraph (ii). Even if such statement has already been filed, the party's principal brief must include the statement before the table of contents.

(ii) *Trial Court; Civil Case.* In a civil case in the Trial Court, a party must file an original and one copy of the statement required in paragraph (a) with its first appearance, pleading, petition, motion, response or other request. A copy of the statement must also be filed with each contested motion.

(iii) *Trial Court; Criminal Case.* In a criminal case in the Trial Court, a party must file an original and one copy of the statement required in paragraph (a) upon the defendant's initial appearance pursuant to Mass.R.Crim.P.7. A copy of the statement must also be filed with each contested motion.

(c) **Supplemental Filing.** In any case, a party shall promptly file a supplemental statement upon any change in the information that the statement requires.

Adopted June 26, 2002, effective September 3, 2002.

Rule 1:22. Motions to Recuse

(a) Any motion seeking to recuse a Justice of this court from a full court case shall be in writing, and shall comply in all respects with Mass. R. A. P. 15 (a). The motion shall be filed at or before the time for filing the moving party's brief. The court may allow the filing of a motion to recuse after the filing of the brief if the motion is based on grounds not known, and that reasonably could not have been known, at the time the brief was filed, and provided that the motion is filed as soon as practicable after the alleged ground for recusal becomes known. Late filed motions are strongly discouraged.

(b) If the motion is denied by the Justice whose recusal is sought, the moving party may request review of that ruling by the other Justices, by filing with the clerk, within seven days of the ruling, a written request for review. To facilitate this review, a Justice who denies a motion to recuse is encouraged to provide a brief statement of his or her reasons for the ruling.

The review shall be on the papers, and limited to the information that was before the Justice whose recusal was sought, unless the court requests further information. A party requesting review shall therefore file, along with the request for review, eight copies of the motion to recuse and all material related to the motion that was before the Justice initially, including any supporting or opposing memoranda and affidavits. The Justices reviewing the ruling will act as soon as practicable, and, time permitting, before oral argument or submission of the case on briefs.

(c) This rule applies only to full court cases. Recusal rulings in single justice cases are, and will continue to be, reviewable in the regular course on appeal from any adverse final judgment in the single justice case.

(d) Nothing in this rule is intended to change the substantive law governing recusals.

Adopted September 20, 2010, effective November 1, 2010.

Rule 1:23. Attorney General Approved Modifications of Certain Gift Instruments Under G.L. c. 180A, Section 5(d)

1.0 Administrative Equitable Deviation.

If an institution determines that a restriction contained in a gift instrument on the management, investment or duration of an institutional fund has become impractical or wasteful, impairs the management or investment of the fund or if, because of circumstances not anticipated by the donor, a modification of a restriction will further the purposes of the fund, the institution, without application to the court, but with the consent of the Attorney General given in accordance with procedures adopted pursuant to Section 3.0, may modify the restriction. This Section 1.0 shall apply only if the fund subject to the restriction has a total value of seventy five thousand dollars ($75,000) or less, as determined as of the end of the institution's last fiscal year, and has been in existence for twenty (20) years or longer. To the extent practicable, the modification shall be made in accordance with the donor's probable intention.

2.0 Administrative *Cy Pres*.

If an institution determines that a particular charitable purpose or a restriction contained in a gift instrument on the use of an institutional fund has become unlawful, impracticable, impossible to achieve or wasteful, the institution, without application to the court, but with the consent of the Attorney General given in accordance with procedures adopted pursuant to Section 3.0, may modify the purpose of the fund or the restriction on the use of the fund in a manner consistent with the charitable purposes expressed in the gift instrument. This Section 2.0 shall apply only if the fund subject to the restriction has a total value of seventy five thousand dollars ($75,000) or less, as determined as of the end of the institution's last fiscal year, and has been in existence for twenty (20) years or longer.

3.0 Attorney General Procedures.

The Attorney General may adopt such requirements, definitions, forms and procedures for granting or withholding consent as are not inconsistent with the forgoing and applicable laws governing charitable funds.

4.0 De Novo Proceedings.

Any institution aggrieved by the decision of the Attorney General may proceed, de novo, under G.L. c. 180A, §§ 5(b) or 5(c).

Adopted November 22, 2010, effective January 1, 2011.

Rule 1:24. Protection of Personal Identifying Information in Publicly Accessible Court Documents

Section 1. Purpose and Scope. This rule is intended to prevent the unnecessary inclusion of certain personal identifying information in publicly accessible documents filed with or issued by the Courts, in order to reduce the possibility of using such documents for identity theft, the unwarranted invasion of privacy, or other improper purposes. The rule applies to publicly accessible documents filed in civil and criminal cases; documents offered in evidence at any trial or hearing; and any order, decision, or other document issued by a court that will be publicly accessible. The rule does not prevent a document's filer from requesting more or less protection of personal identifying information than this rule requires. The rule does not limit a court's authority to enter specific orders in particular cases, and it does not relieve a filer of any greater obligations imposed by the law or a court. Further, the rule does not prohibit any Department of the Trial Court, or any appellate court, from adopting a rule or standing order providing additional protections for personal identifying information covered by this rule, or protecting

additional categories of personal identifying information. The rule applies only to filings made after its effective date.

Section 2. Definitions. As used in this rule, the following terms shall have the following meanings:

"Clerk" shall mean a Clerk, Clerk–Magistrate, Register of Probate, the Recorder of the Land Court, and their assistants.

"Court" shall mean all Departments of the Trial Court; the Appeals Court; and the Supreme Judicial Court.

"Document" shall mean any material filed in a court, in paper or electronic form.

"Filer" shall mean any person or entity, including a corporation or government entity, that files documents in a court, and is not limited to parties.

"Personal identifying information" shall mean a social security number, taxpayer identification number, driver's license number, state-issued identification card number, or passport number, a parent's birth surname if identified as such, a financial account number, or a credit or debit card number.

"Redacted" shall mean a filing that either does not include complete personal identifying information or has portions of such information whited or blacked out so they are not readable.

Section 3. Personal Identifying Information: Requirement of Limited Disclosure. When filing a document in court that will be publicly accessible, a filer may not, unless otherwise allowed by this rule, include personal identifying information, except when the filer redacts it as follows:

(a) **Government–Issued Identification Numbers.** If a social security number, taxpayer identification number, driver's license number, state-issued identification card number, or passport number must be included, all but the last four digits of that number shall be redacted.

(b) **Parent's Birth Surname, if Identified as Such.** If the birth surname of a person's parent, identified as such, must be included, all but the first initial of the birth surname shall be redacted.

(c) **Financial Account Numbers and Credit Card Numbers.** If a financial account number or credit or debit card number must be included, all but the last four digits of the number shall be redacted.

Section 4. Methods of Redaction. Documents shall be redacted as set forth below.

(a) **Documents Drafted for Filing in Court.** In the case of a document drafted for filing in court, the omitted information shall be replaced by three "x" characters or, where appropriate, by the phrase "beginning with" or "ending in."

(b) **All Other Documents.** In all documents that were not drafted for filing in court, such as copies of pre-existing exhibits, the filer shall partially redact all personal identifying information as required by this rule. All redactions shall be made in a way that prevents the redacted information from being read or made visible. Any document redacted in this way shall be clearly marked to show the name of the filer making the redaction and the date on which it was made. The location of each redaction in the document must be visible. The filer shall keep an unredacted copy of the document while the case is pending, including during any related appeal, and furnish it (i) to the court promptly upon request, and (ii) to any party promptly upon that party's request, or if such a request is refused, the court may order production upon the requesting party's motion showing good cause and affirming that the information will be secured in a manner sufficient to avoid misuse or disclosure to third parties.

Section 5. General Exceptions. Unless the court orders otherwise, unredacted personal identifying information may be included in documents filed with the court if any of the following exceptions applies:

(a) A law, court rule, standing order, court-issued form, or an order issued in the proceeding specifically requires including the personal identifying information in the document.

(b) The document including the personal identifying information is a transcript of the court proceeding, filed directly by a court reporter or transcriber, or is the official record of another court proceeding, filed by that court.

(c) The document including the personal identifying information is a record of administrative adjudicatory or quasi-adjudicatory proceedings, filed by the administrative agency, and the applicable department of the Trial Court or other court has adopted its own rule or standing order governing redaction of personal identifying information in such records.

(d) The document including the personal identifying information is produced directly to or in the court by a nonparty in response to a subpoena, summons or other court order, and is not publicly accessible. Any party that intends to offer such a document in evidence shall make a copy of it, redact the copy as required by this rule, and offer the redacted copy.

(e) The document includes a financial account number that is necessary to identify an account that is the subject of a forfeiture proceeding, in which case the number need not be redacted.

Section 6. Exceptions in Criminal and Youthful Offender Cases. In criminal and youthful offender cases, unless the court orders otherwise, the following documents need not be redacted when filed originally, but shall be redacted when attached by an attorney as exhibits unless the original filing is in the same court file:

(a) a court filing that is related to a criminal matter or investigation and that is prepared before the filing of a criminal case or is not filed as part of any docketed criminal case;

(b) an arrest or search warrant; or

(c) a charging document, including an application for a criminal complaint, and supporting documents filed in support of any charging document.

Section 7. Responsibility for Redaction. The filer is responsible for redacting personal identifying information. The clerk will not review each filed document for compliance.

Section 8. Noncompliance.

(a) In the event of a filer's noncompliance with this rule, the court, on its own initiative or on motion of a party or the person whose personal identifying information is at issue, may require corrective action. Corrective action may include, but is not limited to: (i) striking and returning to the filer any noncompliant document, with or without an order that a properly-redacted copy be filed in its place; (ii) requiring the filer to file a redacted version of the document and move to impound the unredacted version; (iii) forfeiting any protection under this rule for the filer's own personal identifying information, if the information has become public or if other parties or persons would be unduly prejudiced by treating the information as protected, or if the filer's noncompliance is either willful or repeated; (iv) entering orders to ensure the filer's future compliance or to protect the interests under this rule of other parties and persons; and (v) imposing monetary sanctions, if the filer's noncompliance is either willful or repeated.

(b) The filer shall have the burden to prove any claim that the noncompliance was inadvertent. The filing of a document that contains the filer's personal identifying information does not by itself make this rule inapplicable to that information. If a filer files a document that includes another person's personal identifying information, that person or any other interested person may still move for an order impounding the document or requiring that it be returned to the filer and that a properly-redacted copy be filed in its place. A filer may waive the applicability of this rule to the filer's own personal identifying information, but only by an express statement of waiver filed in writing or made in open court.

Section 9. Applicability to Court Orders and Other Court-Issued Documents. In any order, decision, or other document issued by the court that will be publicly accessible, the court shall avoid including a complete version of any personal identifying information covered by this rule, unless including it (a) is specifically required by law, court rule, standing order, or court-issued form or (b) is necessary to serve the document's purpose.

Section 10. Appellate Court Filings. In addition to the other requirements of this rule, filers in the Supreme Judicial Court, the Appeals Court, or the Appellate Divisions of the District and Boston Municipal Courts shall comply with the following requirements:

(a) **Brief.** If a filer includes any complete personal identifying information in a publicly accessible brief, the filer shall at the same time file one additional, unbound copy of the brief, with that personal identifying information redacted according to this rule, clearly marked "Limited Personal Identifying Information" on the cover and without including any addendum or appendix.

(b) **Record Appendix.** If a document to be included in the record appendix was redacted when filed in or issued by the trial court, the same version of the document shall be included in the record appendix. If a document to be included in the record appendix was not redacted when filed in or issued by the trial court, even where complete personal identifying information was included under an exception in Section 5 or 6, the party that wants to include the document in the record appendix shall redact it as required by Section 3, unless the party obtains leave of the appellate court to include the document in unredacted form.

Adopted July 22, 2016, effective November 1, 2016.

Commentary of the Standing Advisory Committee on the Rules of Civil and Appellate Procedure on S.J.C. Rule 1:24

This Commentary was drafted by the Supreme Judicial Court's Standing Advisory Committee on the Rules of Civil and Appellate

Procedure, which recommended the adoption of this Rule. The Court's Standing Advisory Committee on the Rules of Criminal Procedure furnished helpful input on Section 6 and the Commentary thereto. The Commentary does not constitute part of the Rule and has not been formally adopted by the Court but is provided as an aid to understanding and applying the Rule.

Section 1

This rule applies to paper documents, as well as to electronic documents that are now or may in the future be filed with or issued by all Departments of the Trial Court; the Appeals Court; and the Supreme Judicial Court. The rule does not govern the separate question whether various court documents should be made publicly available on the Internet.

The reference in Section 1 to "greater obligations imposed by the law or court" is intended to include statutes and rules that require, or authorize a court to require, impoundment or confidentiality, however labeled. *See, e.g.*, G.L. c. 265, § 24C (requiring that court records containing rape victims' names be "withheld from the public"); G.L. c. 6, § 178M (on judicial review of Sex Offender Registry Board decisions, records to be kept "confidential and . . . impounded"); G.L. c. 209A, § 8 (requiring that certain personal information filed in connection with requests for abuse prevention orders be "withheld from public inspection except by order of the court"); Mass. R. App. P. 16(m) (governing "references to impounded material"). Litigants should also be aware that other court rules, such as the forthcoming Uniform Rules on Access to Court Records (Trial Court Rule XIV), may impose limits on whether or how certain personal information may be included in court filings.

Section 2

The term "filer" as used in Section 2 and throughout this rule includes any person or governmental or other entity making a filing (including, *e.g.*, persons applying for criminal complaints, police officers applying for search warrants, putative interveners, and amici curiae) regardless of their status as parties.

In the definition of "Personal identifying information," the term "financial account numbers" includes, but is not limited to, insurance policies, and account numbers and loan numbers assigned by financial service providers.

Section 3

Section 3 refers to "filing" documents in court. Exhibits offered at evidentiary hearings, although not "filed" as that term is used in Mass. R. Civ. P. 5 or Mass. R. Crim. P. 32, are subject to this rule. Prior to trial or other evidentiary hearing, the parties should discuss how to handle exhibits in compliance with this rule, as well as any issues of waiver of the rule's protection pursuant to Section 8.

Section 4

In the case of documents drafted for filing in court as described in Section 4(a) (*e.g.*, motions, memoranda, and affidavits, as opposed to pre-existing exhibits), this rule does not require the filer to prepare a second version with complete personal identifiers. Nothing in this rule limits the court's power to order that such complete information be supplied to other parties or non-parties.

The provision in Section 4(b) requiring the filer to mark redactions creates a record that helps protect against claims of improper alteration of documents. Particularly in documents with multiple redactions, the required notation of each redaction need be no more than an asterisk or similar mark, together with a single statement, on or accompanying the document, explaining that redactions so marked were made by the filer on a specified date.

Section 5

The exception in Section 5(a) does not permit inclusion of complete personal identifying information in a filing merely because such information may be useful to include in an order to be issued in the

proceeding as requested by the filing. Alternatives are often available.

Thus, a motion for an order to a third party to produce records, such as a person's hospital records under G.L. c. 233, § 79, or a person's criminal offender record information (CORI), shall not include the person's unredacted personal identifying information. The motion and any resulting order may instead include redacted information, and the moving party may then, at the time the order is served on the entity required to respond to it, provide any unredacted information the entity requires in order to respond.

Similarly, a filer shall not include bank or other asset account numbers in court filings in connection with court orders that serve to secure assets to satisfy a judgment. If complete account numbers are necessary, the filer (usually the plaintiff) may provide this information separately, along with any other unredacted personal identifying information necessary to identify an account holder, to those who may need it to carry out the order.

Likewise, a bank responding to a trustee summons shall not include the entire account number in the trustee's answer. Section 1 and Section 9 recognize that courts and filers retain flexibility to deal with such situations without unnecessarily making personal identifying information publicly accessible.

The exception in Section 5(b) for transcripts is included to avoid undue burden on the court reporter or transcriber. Section 5(b) also creates an exception for the official record of another court proceeding, filed by that court, *e.g.*, in a certiorari action under G.L. c. 249, § 4, for review of a District Court or Boston Municipal Court decision. Ordinarily the documents in that record will already have been redacted in accordance with this Rule, either by the parties at the time of filing or by the court at the time of issuance. This provision of Section 5(b) makes clear that the court need not independently review all of those documents to ensure that they were properly redacted.

The exception in Section 5(c) recognizes that departments of the Trial Court or the appellate courts may adopt their own rules or standing orders governing redaction of personal identifying information in the official record of an administrative adjudicatory proceeding filed by the administrative agency. This provision is included to afford flexibility to the courts in dealing with the particular redaction problems raised by the filing of these often voluminous records. The term "adjudicatory proceedings" refers to proceedings that are judicially reviewed primarily or exclusively on the agency record, under G.L. c. 30A or other law such as G.L. c. 249, § 4. The qualifier "adjudicatory" is used because the reasons for different treatment of the records of such proceedings are less likely to apply to documents concerning other, less formal administrative proceedings.

The exception in Section 5(d) is intended to cover documents produced by a non-party pursuant to Mass. R. Civ. P. 45(b), Mass. R. Crim. P. 17(a)(2), Superior Court Rule 13 and G.L. c. 233, § 79 (hospital records), and similar court rules or laws. It is intended to be consistent with the *Dwyer* protocol applicable to defendants' motions for Rule 17(a)(2) summonses. *See Commonwealth v. Dwyer*, 448 Mass. 122, 147–50 (2006). The exception recognizes that requiring the non-party to redact, particularly where some or all of the records may never become available to the public, would be unduly burdensome.

Section 6

This section is based, with some Massachusetts-specific alterations, on Fed. R. Crim. P. 49.1(b)(7)–(9). This section addresses special considerations related to charging documents and documents created by police or other investigative entities prior to the initiation of a criminal case. Requiring redaction of such documents would impose a substantial burden on these law enforcement agencies, which necessarily must document the personal identifying information relied upon for investigative purposes. Moreover, requiring redaction of these documents would deprive clerks initiating a new criminal case or issuing an arrest warrant of the information necessary to properly identify the defendant and enter the case or warrant into, and search for existing information about the defendant already contained in, databases such as MassCourts and the warrant management system. This is necessary to ensure, among other things, that information about prior cases or warrants involving that defendant is available to the court in the pending matter, and that information about the pending matter is available to the court in any future cases involving that defendant.

Unlike the federal rule, however, Section 6 does ordinarily require redaction when one of these documents is filed by an attorney as an exhibit in another case. Thus, an attorney might need to file a search warrant, District Court charging document, or police report attached to an application for a criminal complaint, as an attachment to a motion to dismiss or suppress, or an opposition thereto, in a related Superior Court case. In that circumstance, there would be no burden on the investigative agency or need for the Superior Court clerk to have access to that information. The attorney, therefore, would be required to redact the document of personal identifying information. If that document, however, already appeared in the same court file (for example, an application for complaint attached to a District Court motion to dismiss), there would be no point in redacting the document when filed as an exhibit, and an attorney would not need to do so.

In any event, the court may make other orders regarding the redaction of documents in a criminal case file, if a different practice is warranted in a particular case.

Section 7

This section makes clear that clerks are not responsible for reviewing every filed document for compliance, but it does not preclude clerks from reviewing selected documents for compliance—for example, at the time a member of the public asks to see a case file.

Section 8

In determining issues concerning corrective action, the court has the discretion to consider all relevant circumstances, including but not limited to whether the violation of this rule was willful or repeated, whether it has caused or is likely to cause harm to privacy interests or financial interests, and the nature and amount of information improperly filed in unredacted form.

Section 9

The exception in Section 9 for inclusion of complete personal identifying information where "necessary to serve the document's purpose" is included because some types of court documents, although directed to parties or non-parties that require specific identifying information, are included in the court file, where they are publicly accessible as a matter of law. Although the inclusion of personal identifying information should be minimized when drafting such documents, it must be recognized that sometimes, unredacted information will be necessary to serve the purpose of the document.

Section 10

Section 10(b)'s provision governing documents not redacted when filed in or issued by the trial court is included because the rationales underlying the exceptions in Sections 5 and 6 ordinarily would not apply, and would not serve any useful purpose if applied, to documents presented to the appellate court in the record appendix. If inclusion of an unredacted document is warranted, Section 10(b) allows the party to do so if leave of the appellate court is obtained.

RULE 1:25. MASSACHUSETTS RULES OF ELECTRONIC FILING

Table of Contents

Rule 1. Scope

(a) Scope. These Rules of Electronic Filing (E–Filing Rules) shall govern the general procedures of electronic filing and service of documents in the participating Massachusetts trial and appellate courts, as supplemented by any procedures specified by a court or a court department relating to its particular case types and requirements. To the extent that any Massachusetts Court Rules and Orders concerning conventional filing methods are inconsistent with these rules, the E–Filing Rules shall govern.

(b) Court Record. The official court record in a case shall include electronic records pertaining to that case, together with any documents and exhibits filed under the conventional method.

(c) Use of These Rules. All filers shall become familiar with these E–Filing Rules and all training and documentation materials provided for use by the Provider or the court(s).

Adopted June 7, 2018, effective September 1, 2018.

Rule 2. Definitions

"Clerk" shall refer to the clerk, clerk magistrate, recorder, or register of any court, as well as his/her respective assistants or deputies.

"Conventional method" shall refer to court rules and procedures that would apply in the absence of electronic filing. Parties or counsel who are ordered or opt to proceed "conventionally," as provided in these E–Filing Rules, must follow the appropriate Massachusetts Court Rules and Orders.

"Electronic record" shall refer to the electronic record maintained on a court's case management and document management systems.

"Electronic filing," "e-filing," or "electronically filed" shall refer to the submission of documents through the e-filing system for purposes of filing in a case. E-mailing or sending a document by facsimile does not constitute "e-filing" a document.

"Electronic filing system" or "e-filing system" shall refer to the Provider's system of electronic filing and electronic service of documents via the internet.

"Electronic service" or "e-service" shall refer to the electronic transmission of a notice of filing to the electronic mail (e-mail) address of a party who has consented to electronic service through the Provider. The notice will contain a hyperlink to access the document that was filed electronically for the purpose of accomplishing service. E-service according to these E–Filing Rules shall be deemed in compliance with the Massachusetts Court Rules and Orders that govern service and notice. Service of process or summons to gain jurisdiction over persons or property may not be made by e-service.

"Electronic signature" or "electronically signed" shall mean a signature from a User, judge, or clerk, that complies with the requirements set forth in Rule 13, below.

"Envelope" shall refer to a submission containing one or more filings to be filed in a single case by a filing User.

"Massachusetts Court Rules and Orders" shall mean the Rules of Civil, Criminal, and Appellate Procedure, the Rules of the Supreme Judicial Court, Appeals Court, and Trial Court, the Rules of the various Trial Court Departments, and the Rules Governing Time Standards and Case Management, together with all Standing Orders.

"Non–Registered Participant" shall mean a party to a case who has not registered with the Provider.

"PDF" shall mean "portable document format," the file format compatible with the latest version of Adobe Reader. Types of PDFs include electronically converted PDFs and scanned PDFs.

Electronically converted PDFs are created from an electronic source (MS Word, WordPerfect, etc.) using Adobe Acrobat or similar software. They are text searchable, accessible, and their file size is small. Electronically converted PDFs are preferred.

Scanned PDFs are created from documents run through an optical scanner. Scanned PDFs have a larger file size and lower quality image and should be avoided when possible. Pursuant to Rule 9(a), scanned PDFs must contain optical character recognition of text.

"Provider" shall refer to the Electronic Filing Service Provider designated by the courts.

"Provider Notification" shall mean a provider-generated notice acknowledging activity within the e-filing system.

"Public access terminal" shall mean a publicly accessible computer provided by a court for the purposes of allowing e-filing and viewing public electronic court records. The public access terminal shall be located at the courthouse and will be available during normal business hours.

"Service Contact" shall mean an individual to be served electronically by the electronic filing system.

"User" shall refer to a participant in a case who has properly registered with the e-filing system.

"User ID" shall refer to the e-mail address provided during registration that is used to login to the e-filing system.

"Waiver Account" shall refer to a method whereby court and provider fees may be waived. The acceptance of any document filed under a waiver account shall be subject to the court's determination that use of the account is appropriate, given the nature of the filing.

Adopted June 7, 2018, effective September 1, 2018.

Rule 3.   Eligibility and Conditions of Registration

(a) Eligibility. Participation in the Electronic Filing Program shall be determined by order of the particular department or court. In general, registration for the Electronic Filing Program may include:

(1) Attorneys who are members of the Massachusetts Bar.

(2) Attorneys who are admitted to practice in a Massachusetts court *pro hac vice*.

(3) Self-represented parties.

(4) Any non-party who is seeking or has obtained permission of the court to participate in the case (e.g., a witness seeking a protective order, an intervenor, amicus curiae, or court investigator).

(b) Registration. Registration is accomplished by completing the online e-filing system registration, a link to which is available on the Provider's website. An e-mail address will be required for registration.

(1) Attorneys who are members of the Massachusetts Bar shall register for a firm account and furnish their primary business e-mail address on file with the Board of Bar Overseers, and shall keep their account e-mail up to date.

(2) Non-attorneys who are representing themselves and attorneys who are not members of the Massachusetts Bar shall register for a self-represented account, unless otherwise ordered.

(3) An attorney representing him or herself shall register for a self-represented account with a unique e-mail address.

(c) Law Firm or Agency Registration. The Provider shall allow a firm or agency administrator to register a central account profile on behalf of a firm or agency's multiple Users.

Once an administrator has completed this central registration, the administrator can add additional Users to that account.

(d) Conditions of Registration. By registering, the User acknowledges that:

(1) Registration shall constitute consent to receipt of Provider notifications, electronic court notifications, and e-service in all cases.

(2) It is the User's responsibility to ensure that the court and the Provider have the User's correct e-mail address at all times. Users shall update the Provider within 7 days of any change in the information provided at registration.

(e) User ID. The e-mail address provided during registration will serve as a unique User ID.

(f) User Password. At registration the User must designate a unique password in accordance with the specifications given by the Provider. Users may reset their password for the e-filing system at any time.

(g) Confidentiality of User ID and Password. The combination of the User ID and password shall be used only by the User and any other person that the User authorizes. Use of the User ID and password shall be deemed authorized by the User. Users should contact the court if they believe a filing was submitted falsely under their User ID.

Adopted June 7, 2018, effective September 1, 2018.

Rule 4.   Electronic Filing Procedures

(a) E-filing Through the Provider. E-filing shall be performed only through the Provider's e-filing system. The Provider shall receive electronic filings 24 hours per day except when undergoing maintenance or repair.

(b) Receipt of Provider Notifications. Whenever a User submits a document to the court through the e-filing system, a Provider Notification will automatically generate and transmit to the User, acknowledging the submission. Provider notifications shall also be sent at the time the court accepts or rejects any submitted document.

(c) Determination of Date of Filing and Commencement of Civil Action.

(1) *Date of Filing.* Any document submitted through the e-filing system by 11:59 P.M. on a business day shall be deemed filed on that date, unless it is rejected by the court. See Rule 4(d). A document submitted on a Saturday, Sunday, or legal holiday shall be considered filed the next business day, unless it is subsequently rejected by the court.

(2) *Commencement of Civil Action.* The date of filing provided in Rule 4(c)(1) shall constitute the date of filing of any case initiating document or entry fee when determining the commencement of an action under Mass. R. Civ. P. 3.

(d) Clerk's Review of Electronically Filed Documents. Prior to entry upon the docket, the clerk shall review each document submitted through the e-filing system for compliance with these E-filing Rules, the court's Electronic Filing Program, and the Massachusetts Court Rules and Orders. Upon the clerk's acceptance, the document shall be considered "filed" with the court at the time the original submission to the e-filing system was complete, as stated on the Provider Notification transmitted pursuant to Rule 4(b), subject to Rule 4(c), and a Provider Notification of the acceptance will be transmitted. If a filing is rejected, the filing User will receive notice from the Provider, which shall note the rejection and the court's reason(s) therefore.

(e) Correction of Errors. Upon the discovery of any error made during the e-filing process, the User may cancel the transaction while the cancel option is available in the e-filing system. The cancel option is not available once the court begins the review process pursuant to Rule 4(d). After this period, the User should abide by the Massachusetts Court Rules and Orders for correcting filings containing errors.

(f) Exchange of Discovery and Other Materials. The e-filing system may be used for the electronic exchange of discovery materials and other communications between the parties that are not intended to be filed with the court. Use of the e-filing system for these purposes should be decided by the parties.

Adopted June 7, 2018, effective September 1, 2018.

Rule 5. Rejection of Electronic Documents for Technical Nonconformance with the Rules of Court

The clerk may reject any document filed electronically for any technical nonconformance with the Rules of Court and may identify the error to be corrected and may state a deadline for the party to resubmit the document in a conforming format. This rule shall not, however, extend the mandatory or statutory time, including any statute of limitations, for the filing of such document.

Adopted June 7, 2018, effective September 1, 2018.

Rule 6. Electronic Filing and Service of Civil Case Initiating Documents

(a) Filing of Case Initiating Documents. Where permitted by a court, case initiating documents, such as a complaint or petition, may be submitted for filing through the e-filing system, accompanied by electronic payment of the required filing fee. Motions to waive fees may be submitted through the e-filing system in accordance with Rule 8(d).

(b) Court Action Upon Acceptance of Case Initiating Document. Upon acceptance of a case initiating document for filing, a case number will be assigned and the document will be processed. If the case initiating document is rejected, the User will be informed as provided in Rule 4(d).

(c) Service of Case Initiating Documents Shall Be By Conventional Methods. Unless otherwise determined by the court, or unless the responding party has consented in writing to accept electronic service or service by some other method, case initiating documents shall be served by conventional methods, together with a notice to the responding party stating that the case has been electronically commenced.

Adopted June 7, 2018, effective September 1, 2018.

Rule 7. Service of Electronically Filed Documents

(a) All Documents E-filed Must Be Served. Except as otherwise provided in the Massachusetts Court Rules and Orders, or as otherwise ordered by the court, all electronically filed documents must be served on all other parties. Any document filed through the e-filing system must include a certificate of service. Subject to a court's specific requirement, the certificate of service may appear as a part of the document being filed or may be filed as a separate document.

(b) Electronic Service Accomplished Through the Electronic Filing Service Provider; Conventional Service Required for Non–Registered Participants. All Users in a case may be served electronically through the e-filing system, even when the parties to a case comprise both Users and Non–Registered Participants. When the parties to a case comprise both Users and Non–Registered Participants, the User submitting the document for filing through the e-filing system is responsible for serving a copy of the document to all parties who are Non–Registered Participants in accordance with other Massachusetts Court Rules and Orders.

(c) Conventional Service Required If Electronic Service Notification Is Undeliverable. If a filing User receives notice that electronic service on any party was undeliverable, the filing User shall then serve the document on that party by conventional methods.

(d) Electronic Notification Shall Signal Completion of Electronic Service. Electronic service shall be deemed complete at the time of transmission to the e-mail account of the Service Contact.

(e) Calculation of Time To Respond. For the purpose of computing time to respond to documents electronically filed, whenever a User has the right or is required to do some act within a prescribed period after the completion of electronic service of a notice or other documents upon him/her and the notice or document is either served upon him/her by electronic means, or the document was filed electronically and served by conventional methods, three days shall be added to the prescribed period.

Adopted June 7, 2018, effective September 1, 2018.

Rule 8. Payment of Fees

(a) Provider May Charge Fee for Civil Filings. The e-filing Provider may charge a fee per envelope for its services related to filings in civil cases, in an amount approved by the Supreme Judicial Court. The Provider will provide for one or more methods of electronic payment.

(b) Provider May Charge Fee for Non–Indigent Criminal Defendant Filings. The e-filing Provider may charge a fee for its services related to filings in criminal cases only when counsel is not appointed pursuant to S.J.C. Rule 3:10 and the defendant is not indigent.

(c) Payments Shall Be Made at Time of Filing. All applicable fees are due and payable at the time of e-filing unless waived by the court. Failure to timely pay a required fee may cause the document submitted to be refused by the clerk under Rule 4(d) or stricken by the court. The payment will be debited when the clerk accepts the document.

(d) Payments Shall Be Transmitted Through the E–Filing System. Users shall make any payment due to the clerk through the e-filing system unless otherwise ordered by the court.

(e) Request to Waive Court Fees. Where permitted by the court, Users may submit a motion for waiver of court fees accompanied by a separate affidavit of indigency through the e-filing system. If the court allows a waiver of a court fee, any related Provider fee shall also be waived.

(f) Request to Waive Provider Fees. Upon request, the court shall waive a Provider fee upon a showing the filing party is indigent or is represented by court-appointed counsel. Upon request, the court may waive a Provider fee for multiple envelopes simultaneously submitted in the same case.

(g) Recoverable Costs. The cost of any convenience fees and other administrative fees levied for the ability to pay fees or costs by credit card or other means, including, but not limited to, Provider fees for electronic filing of documents or pleadings with the court, may be recovered pursuant to any applicable Massachusetts Court Rules and Orders.

Adopted June 7, 2018, effective September 1, 2018.

Rule 9.   Format and Content of Documents

(a) Documents Shall Be Filed in Searchable PDF. Except where specifically provided, all documents submitted for e-filing must be in searchable Portable Document Format (PDF). Documents should be submitted as electronically converted PDFs rather than scanned PDFs whenever possible. Scanned PDFs shall be made searchable using optical-character-recognition software, such as Adobe Acrobat. Documents shall not be locked or otherwise password protected.

(b) Documents Shall Be Formatted in Compliance with Massachusetts Court Rules and Orders. Users shall format all documents in accordance with the Massachusetts Court Rules and Orders governing formatting of paper documents, including page limits and font style and size, unless a deviation has been allowed by court order.

(c) Internal Links Are Allowed. Each document submitted for e-filing may contain electronic links, but only to navigate within the same document.

(d) Paper Filing Required. Each court may identify documents that must be filed by conventional methods in paper form only.

Adopted June 7, 2018, effective September 1, 2018.

Rule 10.   File Size Limitations and Legibility

(a) File Size Limitations. The Provider has set a maximum megabyte size for each document, and a maximum envelope size for all documents contained in one envelope. A User must limit the size of each electronically filed document, and the total size of all the documents filed within one envelope, to comply with the maximum file size and envelope size permitted by the Provider. Documents exceeding those limits cannot be transmitted by the Provider.

(b) Submission of Oversized Documents. Documents or envelopes larger than the maximum allowed file size may be submitted for e-filing if they are broken up into separate segments, each of which complies with the Provider's size restrictions. The User shall indicate in the document "Description" field that a filing is part of multiple parts (for example, "Volume 1 of 2"). The additional envelopes necessary to submit multiple parts may be filed under a waiver account, subject to review by the court.

(c) Scan Settings for Text Documents. To minimize file size, Users must configure their scanners to scan text documents at 200 dpi and in black and white rather than in color.

(d) Color and High Resolution Images. For documents that consist of images beyond text, such documents shall be scanned at sufficient resolution to ensure a legible and accurate representation of the image. Black and white images should be scanned in grayscale. Images should only be scanned in color if color is relevant, such as color photographs used as an exhibit.

(e) Users Must Verify Document Legibility and Orientation. A PDF produced under these rules must be of high quality sufficient to ensure a legible and accurate reading of the entire document. A User must verify the legibility and orientation of scanned documents before submitting them for e-filing.

Adopted June 7, 2018, effective September 1, 2018.

Rule 11.   Filing of Impounded Information

(a) Filing of Impounded Documents. Except as otherwise provided, impounded documents should be filed in hard copy with the clerk's office. Such documents must be clearly labeled as impounded, with the appropriate accompanying notice of impoundment or motion to impound pursuant to the Uniform Rules of Impoundment Procedure, and any other applicable Massachusetts Court Rules and Orders.

(b) Electronic Filing of Impounded Documents. When permitted by a court, impounded documents may be e-filed through the e-filing system. The User shall identify the document as impounded at the time of filing.

(c) Identification of Impounded Documents By User. Where an impounded document is submitted through the e-filing system, the User shall mark the cover or first page of the document as impounded.

(d) Motions to Impound. A User may submit for e-filing a motion to file an impounded document. If the motion is granted, the User shall then submit by conventional methods the impounded document to the clerk's office for filing. A paper copy of the order granting the motion must be attached to documents so filed and delivered to the clerk.

(e) Confidentiality. The confidentiality of an electronic record or an electronic or paper copy thereof is equivalent to that of a paper record. Where an impounded document is scanned or otherwise placed in the e-filing system, access may be permitted only to the extent provided by law.

Adopted June 7, 2018, effective September 1, 2018.

Rule 12.   Protection of Personal Identifying Information

Publicly accessible documents filed with the court shall conform to Supreme Judicial Court Rule 1:24, Protection of

Personal Identifying Information in Publicly Accessible Court Documents. A User is responsible for redacting personal identifying information. The clerk will not review filed documents for compliance. See S.J.C. Rule 1:24, § 7.

Adopted June 7, 2018, effective September 1, 2018.

Rule 13.   Electronic Signature

(a) **Attorneys.** An attorney's use of the e-filing system to file documents shall serve as the attorney's signature for purposes of Mass. R. Civ. P. 11 and for all other purposes under the Massachusetts Court Rules and Orders. In addition, all documents submitted for e-filing must include either a scan of the individual's handwritten signature, an electronically inserted image intended to substitute for a signature, or a "/s/ name of signatory" block, which shall have the same validity and effect as a handwritten signature, and must set forth the attorney's name, Board of Bar Overseers number, address, telephone number, and e-mail address.

When using the "s" option, the name of the User must be preceded by an "/s/" and typed in the space where the signature would otherwise appear. For example:

/s/ John A. Smith

John A. Smith

BBO#123456

123 Main Street

Boston, MA 02210

617–123–4567

jasmith@internetprovider.com

(b) **Self–Represented Litigants.** All documents submitted for e-filing must include either a scan of the individual's handwritten signature, an electronically inserted image intended to substitute for a signature, or a "/s/ name of signatory" block, which shall have the same validity and effect as a handwritten signature, and must set forth the individual's name, address, telephone number and e-mail address. When using the "s" option, the "/s/" must be typed in the space where the signature would otherwise appear. For example:

/s/ John B. Doe

John B. Doe

123 Main Street

Boston, MA 02210

617–123–4567

johnbdoe@isp.com

(c) **Multiple Signatories.** A User who submits a document for e-filing that bears more than one signature (e.g., stipulations, joint motions, joint status reports, etc.) must ensure that all signatures comply with Rule 13(a) and (b).

(d) **Signature of Notary; Retention of Original.** Notarized documents containing a handwritten signature and physical seal may be submitted for e-filing. The User shall submit a scanned copy of the notarized document through the e-filing system, and the court shall maintain the scanned document as the official court record. The court may require the User to produce the original paper document. The User shall retain the original for future production, if necessary, until two years after the conclusion of the case, including any appeal.

(e) **Summons and Complaint.** A summons and complaint, petition, or other case initiating document that is signed in compliance with this Rule bears a sufficient signature under any applicable Massachusetts Court Rules and Orders.

Adopted June 7, 2018, effective September 1, 2018.

Rule 14.   Orders and Judgments

(a) **Orders and Judgments May Be Electronically Signed.** The assigned judge or clerk may electronically sign all orders, judgments, and notifications.

(b) **Electronic Signatures Shall Have the Force of Conventional Signatures.** Any order signed electronically has the same force and effect as if the judge or clerk had affixed his/her signature to a paper copy of the order and it had been entered on the docket in the conventional method.

(c) **Clerk May Enter Orders By Text–Only Entry.** A clerk may enter orders, issued by a judge or clerk as the case may be, by a text-only entry upon the docket. The text-only entry shall constitute the court's only order on the matter.

(d) **Notification.** All Users and Non–Registered Participants of record in the case will receive notification either electronically or by conventional methods.

Adopted June 7, 2018, effective September 1, 2018.

Rule 15.   Technological Failures and Timeliness of Filing

(a) **Technological Failure of the Provider May Excuse Untimely Filing.** A User whose filing is made untimely as a result of a technological failure of the Provider may seek appropriate relief from the court. The court may enter an order permitting the document to be deemed filed or served as of the date it was first attempted to be transmitted electronically. If appropriate, the court may adjust the schedule for responding to these documents or for the court's hearing, or provide other relief.

(b) **Scheduled Maintenance Will Not Excuse Untimely Filing.** Notice of known system outages or maintenance will be posted by the Provider in advance on the User login screen. The notice will be posted as soon as the scheduled date and time is confirmed. Users will also receive e-mail notification of the upcoming downtime. Scheduled maintenance will not constitute a technological failure under these E–Filing Rules nor excuse an untimely filing.

(c) **User Error Will Not Excuse Untimely Filing.** Problems on the User's end, e.g., problems with the User's Internet Service Provider (ISP), hardware, or software problems, will not constitute a technological failure under these E–Filing Rules nor excuse an untimely filing,

Adopted June 7, 2018, effective September 1, 2018.

Rule 16.   Title

These rules may be known and cited as the Massachusetts Rules of Electronic Filing (Mass. R. E. F.).

Adopted June 7, 2018, effective September 1, 2018.

CHAPTER ONE–A. GENERAL RULES PARTIALLY SUPERSEDED BY THE MASSACHUSETTS RULES OF CIVIL PROCEDURE OR THE MASSACHUSETTS RULES OF CRIMINAL PROCEDURE

Rule 1:01A. [Stricken]

Stricken May 29, 1986, effective July 1, 1986.

Rule 1:02A. Depositions and Discovery

(Applicable to certain civil cases.)

Section 1. Depositions Pending Action

(a) *When Depositions May Be Taken.* Any party to an original civil proceeding pending in the Supreme Judicial Court, other than such a proceeding governed by the Massachusetts Rules of Civil Procedure, or to a civil proceeding pending in the Land Court Department, other than such a proceeding governed by the Massachusetts Rules of Civil Procedure, may take the testimony of any person, including a party, by deposition upon oral examination for the purpose of discovery or for use as evidence or for both purposes. After service of process the deposition may be taken without leave of court except that leave, granted with or without notice, must be obtained if notice of the taking is served by the plaintiff prior to the time allowed the defendant for appearance; or where in an action at law there is no reasonable likelihood that recovery will exceed five thousand dollars if the plaintiff prevails; or in an action at law there has been a hearing before an auditor. The attendance of witnesses may be compelled by the use of summons or subpoena as provided by Section 4(a). The deposition of a person confined in prison may be taken only by leave of court on such terms as the court prescribes.

(b) *Scope of Examination.* Unless otherwise ordered by the court as provided by Section 4(b) or (d), the deponent may be examined regarding any matter, not privileged, which is relevant to the subject matter involved in the pending proceeding, whether it relates to the claim or defense of the examining party or to the claim or defense of any other party, including the existence, description, nature, custody, condition and location of any books, documents, or other tangible things and the identity and location of persons having knowledge of relevant facts. It is not ground for objection that the testimony will be inadmissible at the trial if the testimony sought appears reasonably calculated to lead to the discovery of admissible evidence. The party taking the deposition shall not require the production or submission for inspection of any writing, plan, recording, model, photograph, or other thing prepared by or for the adverse party, his attorney, surety, indemnitor, or agent in anticipation of litigation or in preparation for trial unless the court otherwise orders on the ground that a denial of production or inspection will result in an injustice or undue hardship; nor shall the deponent be required to produce or submit for inspection any part of a writing which reflects an attorney's mental impressions, conclusions, opinions, or legal theories, or, except as provided in Section 7(b) the conclusions

of an expert. The deponent may not be examined on or be required to produce for inspection any liability insurance policy or indemnity agreement unless such policy or agreement would be admissible in evidence at the trial of the action.

(c) *Examination and Cross-Examination.* Examination and cross-examination of deponents may proceed as permitted at trial in the court where the proceeding is pending.

(d) *Use of Depositions.* At the trial or upon the hearing of a motion or an interlocutory proceeding, any part or all of a deposition, so far as admissible under the rules of evidence, may be used against any party who was present or represented at the taking of the deposition or who had due notice thereof, in accordance with any one of the following provisions:

(1) Any deposition may be used by any party for the purpose of contradicting or impeaching the testimony of deponent as witness.

(2) The deposition of a party or of any one who at the time of taking the deposition was an officer, director or managing agent of a public or private corporation which is a party may be used by an adverse party for any purpose.

(3) The deposition of a witness, whether or not a party, may be used by any party for any purpose if the court finds: (i) that the witness is dead; or (ii) that the witness is out of state, unless it appears that the absence of the witness was procured by the party offering the deposition; or (iii) that the witness is unable to attend or testify because of age, sickness, infirmity, or imprisonment; or (iv) that the party offering the deposition has been unable to procure the attendance of the witness by subpoena; or (v) upon application and notice, that such exceptional circumstances exist as to make it desirable, in the interest of justice and with due regard to the importance of presenting the testimony of witnesses orally in open court, to allow the deposition to be used.

(4) If only part of a deposition is offered in evidence by a party, an adverse party may require him to introduce all of it which is relevant to the part introduced, and any party may introduce any other parts. Substitution of parties does not affect the right to use depositions previously taken; and, when a proceeding in any court of the United States or of any state has been dismissed and another proceeding involving the same subject matter is afterward brought between the same parties or their representatives or successors in interest, all depositions lawfully taken and duly filed in the former proceeding may be sued in the latter as if originally taken therefor.

(e) *Objections to Admissibility.* Subject to the provisions of Sections 2(b) and 5(c), objections may be made at the trial or hearing to receiving in evidence any deposition or part thereof for any reason which would require the exclusion of the evidence if the witness were then present and testifying.

(f) *Effect of Taking or Using Depositions.* A party shall not be deemed to make a person his own witness for any purpose by taking his deposition. The introduction in evidence of the deposition or any part thereof for any purpose other than that of contradicting or impeaching the deponent makes the deponent the witness of the party introducing the deposition, but this shall not apply to the use by an adverse party of a deposition as described in paragraph (2) of subsection (d) of this section. At the trial or hearing any party may rebut any relevant evidence contained in a deposition whether introduced by him or by any other party.

Section 2. Persons Before Whom Depositions May Be Taken.

(a) *Within the Commonwealth.* Within the Commonwealth depositions shall be taken before an officer authorized to administer oaths by the laws of the Commonwealth or the United States, or before a person appointed by the court, in which the proceeding is pending. A person so appointed has the power to administer oaths and take testimony.

(b) *Outside the Commonwealth.* Within another state, or within a territory or insular possession subject to the dominion of the United States, or in a foreign country, depositions may be taken (1) on notice before a person authorized to administer oaths in the place in which the examination is held, whether by the law thereof or by the law of the United States, or (2) before a person commissioned by the court, and a person so commissioned shall have the power by virtue of his commission to administer any necessary oath and take testimony, or (3) pursuant to a letter rogatory. A commission or a letter rogatory shall be issued on application and notice and on terms that are just and appropriate. It is not requisite to the issuance of a commission or a letter rogatory that the taking of the deposition in any other manner is impracticable or inconvenient; and both a commission and a letter rogatory may be issued in proper cases. A notice or commission may designate the person before whom the deposition is to be taken either by name or descriptive title. A letter rogatory may be addressed "To the Appropriate Authority in [here name the state, territory, or country]." Evidence obtained in a foreign country in response to a letter rogatory need not be excluded merely for the reason that it is not a verbatim transcript or that the testimony was not taken under oath or for any similar departure from the requirements for depositions taken within the United States under these rules.

(c) *Disqualification for Interest.* No deposition shall be taken before a person who is a relative or employee or attorney or counsel of any of the parties, or is a relative or employee or partner or associate of such attorney or counsel, or is financially interested in the proceeding.

Section 3. Stipulations Regarding the Taking of Depositions. If the parties so stipulate in writing, depositions may be taken before any person, at any time or place, upon any notice, and in any manner and when so taken may be used like any other depositions.

Section 4. Procedures for Depositions Upon Oral Examination.

(a) *Notice of Examination: Time and Place.* A party desiring to take the deposition of any person upon oral examination, at least seven days before the time of the taking of the deposition, shall give notice in writing to every other party to the proceeding and file a copy of the notice in court in the proceeding. The notice shall state the time and the place for taking the deposition and the name and address of each person to be examined, if known, and, if the name is not known, a general description sufficient to identify him or the particular class or group to which he belongs. On motion of any party to the proceeding, the court may for cause shown enlarge or shorten the time. A resident of the Commonwealth shall not be required by subpoena to travel a distance of more than fifty miles from his place of residence or from his place of business or employment, unless the court otherwise orders. A nonresident of the Commonwealth may be required by subpoena to attend only within fifty miles from the place within the Commonwealth wherein he is served with a subpoena, or at such other convenient place as is fixed by an order of court. The court may regulate at its discretion the time, place and order of taking depositions as shall best serve the convenience of the parties and witnesses and the interest of justice.

(b) *Orders for the Protection of Parties and Deponents.* After notice is served for taking a deposition by oral examination, upon motion seasonably made by any party or by the person to be examined and upon notice and for good cause shown, the court in which the proceeding is pending may make an order that the deposition shall not be taken, or that it may be taken only at some designated place other than that stated in the notice, or that it may be taken only on written interrogatories, or that certain matters shall not be inquired into, or that the scope of the examination shall be limited to certain matters, or that the examination shall be held with no one present except the parties to the proceeding and their officers or counsel, or that the deposition be sealed and opened only by order of the court, or that secret processes, developments, or research need not be disclosed, or that the parties shall simultaneously file specified documents or information enclosed in sealed envelopes to be opened as directed by the court; or the court may make any other order which justice requires to protect the party or witness from annoyance, undue expense, embarrassment, or oppression. The court may in its discretion where notice is given of the taking of depositions outside the state and at great distances from the place where the case is to be tried, require the party taking the deposition to pay the traveling expenses of the opposite party and of his attorney where their attendance is reasonably necessary at the taking of said deposition; and where it appears that the witness whose deposition is sought is under the control of the party taking the deposition, the court may require such witness to be brought within the state and his deposition taken there. The power of the court under this rule shall be exercised with liberality toward the accomplishment of its purpose to protect parties and witnesses.

(c) *Record of Examination; Oath; Objections.* The officer before whom the deposition is to be taken shall put the witness on oath and shall personally, or by someone acting under his direction and in his presence, record the testimony of the witness. The testimony shall be taken stenographically and transcribed unless the parties agree otherwise. The cost thereof shall be borne by the party taking the deposition, except that the court may for cause shown order the cost of stenographer or transcription equitably apportioned among the parties. All objections made at the time of the examination to the qualifications of the officer taking the deposition, or to the manner of taking it, or to the evidence presented, or to the conduct of any party, and any other objection to the proceedings, shall be noted by the officer upon the deposition. Evidence objected to shall be taken subject to the objections. In lieu of participating in the oral examination, parties may transmit written interrogatories to the officer, who shall propound them to the witness and record the answers verbatim.

(d) *Motion to Terminate or Limit Examination.* At any time during the taking of the deposition, on motion of any party or of the deponent and upon a showing that the examination is being conducted in bad faith or in such manner as unreasonably to annoy, embarrass, or oppress the deponent or party, any justice of the court in which the action is pending may order the officer conducting the examination to cease forthwith from taking the deposition, or may limit the scope and manner of the taking of the deposition as provided in subdivision (b). If the order made terminates the examination, it shall be resumed thereafter only upon the order of the court in which the proceeding is pending. Upon demand of the objecting party or deponent, the taking of the deposition shall be suspended for the time necessary to make a motion for an order. In granting or refusing such order the court may impose upon either party or upon the witness the requirement to pay such costs or expenses as the court may deem reasonable.

(e) *Submission to Witness; Changes; Signing.* When the testimony is fully transcribed the deposition shall be submitted to the witness for examination and shall be read to or by him, unless such examination and reading are waived by the witness and by the parties. Any changes in form or substance which the witness desires to make shall be entered upon the deposition by the officer with a statement of the reasons given by the witness for making them. The deposition shall then be signed by the witness, unless the parties by stipulation waive the signing or the witness is ill or cannot be found or refuses to sign. If the deposition is not signed by the witness, the officer shall sign it and state on the record the fact of the waiver or of the illness or absence of the witness or the fact of the refusal to sign together with the reason, if any, given therefor; and the deposition may then be used as fully as though signed, unless on a motion to suppress under Section 5(d) the court holds that the reasons given for the refusal to sign require rejection of the deposition in whole or in part.

(f) *Certification and Filing by Officer; Copies; Notice of Filing.*

(1) The officer shall certify on the deposition that the witness was duly sworn by him and that the deposition is a true record of the testimony given by the witness. He shall then securely seal the deposition in an envelope indorsed with the title of the proceeding and marked "Deposition of [here insert name of witness]" and shall promptly deliver or mail it to the clerk of the court in which the proceeding is pending. The parties by stipulation may waive transcription and filing of the deposition.

(2) Upon payment of reasonable charges therefor, the officer shall furnish a copy of the deposition to any party or to the deponent.

(3) The party taking the deposition shall give prompt notice of its filing to all other parties.

(4) Upon being filed, the deposition shall be open to inspection unless otherwise ordered by the court.

(g) *Failure to Attend or to Serve Summons or Subpoena; Expenses.*

(1) If the party giving the notice of the taking of a deposition fails to attend and proceed therewith and another party attends in person or by attorney pursuant to the notice, the court may order the party giving the notice to pay to such other party the amount of the reasonable expenses incurred by him and his attorney in so attending, including reasonable attorney's fees.

(2) If the party giving the notice of the taking of a deposition of a witness fails to serve a summons or subpoena upon him and the witness because of such failure does not attend, and if another party attends in person or by attorney because he expects the deposition of that witness to be taken, the court may order the party giving the notice to pay to such other party the amount of the reasonable expenses incurred by him and his attorney in so attending, including reasonable attorney's fees.

(h) *Engagements of Counsel.* The engagement of counsel at the taking of a deposition shall be recognized to the extent that the court in which the proceeding is pending shall order upon application in writing to the court not less than three days prior to the time for the taking of a deposition.

Section 5. Effect of Errors and Irregularities in Depositions.

(a) *As to Notice.* All errors and irregularities in the notice for taking a deposition are waived unless written objection is promptly served upon the party giving the notice.

(b) *As to Disqualification of Officer.* Objection to taking a deposition because of disqualification of the officer before whom it is to be taken is waived unless made before the taking of the deposition begins or as soon thereafter as the disqualification becomes known or could be discovered with reasonable diligence.

(c) *As to Taking of Deposition.*

(1) Objections to the competency of a witness or to the competency, relevancy, or materiality of testimony are not waived by failure to make them before or during the taking of the deposition, unless the ground of the objection is one which might have been obviated or removed if presented at that time.

(2) Errors and irregularities occurring at the oral examination in the manner of taking the deposition, in the form of the questions or answers, in the oath or affirmation, or in the conduct of parties and errors of any kind which might be obviated, removed, or cured if promptly presented, are waived unless seasonable objection thereto is made at the taking of the deposition.

(d) *As to Completion and Return of Deposition.* Errors and irregularities in the manner in which the testimony is transcribed or the deposition is prepared, signed, certified, sealed, indorsed, transmitted, filed, or otherwise dealt with by the officer under Section 4 are waived unless a motion to suppress the deposition or some part thereof is made with reasonable promptness after such defect is, or with due diligence might have been, ascertained.

Section 6. Discovery and Production of Documents and Things for Inspection, Copying, or Photographing.

Upon motion of any party showing good cause therefor and upon notice to all other parties, and subject to the provisions of Section 4(b), the court may (1) order any party to produce and permit the inspection and copying or photographing, by or on behalf of the moving party, of any designated documents, papers, books, accounts, letters, photographs, objects, or tangible things, not privileged, which constitute or contain evidence relating to any of the matters within the scope of examination permitted by Section 1(b) and which are in his possession, custody, or control; or (2) order any party to permit entry upon designated land or other property in his possession or control for the purpose of inspecting, measuring, surveying, testing, or photographing the property or any designated object or operation thereon within the scope of examination permitted by Section 1(b). The order shall specify the time, place, and manner of making the inspection and taking the copies and photographs and may prescribe such terms and conditions as are just.

Section 7. Physical and Mental Examination of Persons.

(a) *Order for Examination.* In a proceeding in which the mental or physical condition of a party is in controversy, or may affect the conduct of the proceedings, the court in which the proceeding is pending may order him to submit to a physical or mental examination by a physician. The order may be made only on motion for good cause shown and upon notice to the party to be examined and to all other parties and shall specify the time, place, manner, conditions, and scope of the examination and the person or persons by whom it is to be made.

(b) *Report of Findings.*

(1) If requested by the person examined, the party causing the examination to be made shall deliver to him a copy of a detailed written report of the examining physician setting out his findings and conclusions. After such request and delivery the party causing the examination to be made shall be entitled upon request to receive from the party examined a like report of any examination, previously or thereafter made, of the same mental or physical condition. If the party examined refuses to deliver such report the court on motion and notice may make an order requiring delivery on such terms as are just, and if a physician fails or refuses to make such a report the court may exclude his testimony if offered at the trial.

(2) By requesting and obtaining a report of the examination so ordered or by taking the deposition of the examiner, the party examined waives any privilege he may have in that proceeding or any other involving the same controversy, regarding the testimony of every other person who has examined or may thereafter examine him in respect of the same mental or physical condition.

Section 8. Refusal to Make Discovery; Consequences.

(a) *Refusal to Answer.* If a party or other deponent refuses to answer any questions propounded upon oral examination, the examination shall be completed on other matters or adjourned, as the proponent of the question may prefer. Thereafter, on reasonable notice to all persons affected thereby, he may apply to the court for an order compelling an answer. If the motion is granted and if the court finds that the refusal was without substantial justification the court shall require the refusing party or deponent and the party or attorney advising the refusal or either of them to pay to the examining party the amount of the reasonable expenses incurred in obtaining the order, including reasonable attorney's fees. If the motion is denied and if the court finds that the motion was made without substantial justification, the court shall require the examining party or the attorney advising the motion or both of them to pay to the refusing party or witness the amount of the reasonable expenses incurred in opposing the motion, including reasonable attorney's fees.

(b) *Failure to Comply With Order.*

(1) Contempt. If a party or other witness refuses to be sworn or refuses to answer any question after being directed to do so by the court, the refusal may be considered a contempt of court.

(2) Other Consequences. If any party or an officer or managing agent of a party refuses to obey an order made under subdivision (a) of this section requiring him to answer designated questions, or an order made under Section 6 to produce any document or other thing for inspection, copying, or photographing or to permit it to be done, or to permit entry upon land or other property, or an order under Section 7 requiring him to submit to a physical or mental examination, the court may make such orders in regard to the refusal as are just, and among others the following:

(i) An order that the matters regarding which the questions were asked, or the character or description of the thing or land, or the contents of the paper, or the physical or mental condition of the party, or any other designated facts shall be taken to be established for the purposes of the proceeding in accordance with the claim of the party obtaining the order;

(ii) An order refusing to allow the disobedient party to support or oppose designated claims or defenses, or prohibiting him from introducing in evidence designated documents or things or items of testimony, or from introducing evidence of physical or mental condition;

(iii) An order striking out pleadings or parts thereof, or staying further proceedings until the order is obeyed, or dismissing the proceeding or any part thereof, or rendering a judgment by default against the disobedient party;

(iv) In lieu of any of the foregoing orders or in addition thereto, an order directing the arrest of any party or agent of a party for disobeying any of such orders except an order to submit to a physical or mental examination.

(c) *Failure of a Party to Attend or Serve Answers.* If a party or an officer or managing agent of a party wilfully fails to appear before the officer who is to take his deposition, after being served with a proper notice, the court on motion and notice may strike out all or any part of any pleading of that party, or dismiss the proceeding or any part thereof, or enter a judgment by default against that party.

(d) *Expenses Against the Commonwealth.* Expenses and attorney's fees are not to be imposed upon the Commonwealth under this section.

Section 9. Costs on Depositions. The taxing of costs in the taking of depositions shall be subject to the discretion of the court. No costs shall be allowed unless the court finds that the taking of the deposition was reasonably necessary, whether or not the deposition was actually used at trial. Taxable costs may include the costs of service of summons or subpoena upon the deponent, the reasonable fee of the officer before whom the deposition is taken, the stenographer's reasonable fee for attendance, and the costs of transcription or such part thereof as the court may fix.

Amended October 27, 1999, effective January 1, 2000.

Rule 1:03A.   Trustee Process

(Applicable to certain civil cases.)

(1) Availability of Trustee Process. In connection with any personal action or proceeding not governed by the Massachusetts Rules of Civil Procedure, the Massachusetts Rules of Domestic Relations Procedure (adopted by the judges of the Probate and Family Court Department), or the District/Municipal Courts Rules of Civil Procedure, trustee process may be used in the manner and to the extent provided by law, but subject to the requirements of this rule, to secure satisfaction of a judgment which the plaintiff may recover, provided, however, that no person shall be adjudged trustee for any amount due from him to the defendant for wages or salary for personal labor or services of the defendant except on a claim that has first been reduced to judgment or otherwise authorized by law; and in no event shall the attachment exceed the limitations prescribed by law.

(2) Necessity of Prior Hearing. No trustee process may be served unless attachment on trustee process for a specified amount has been approved by order of the court. Except as provided in paragraph (8) of this rule, the order of approval may be entered only after notice to the defendant and hearing and upon a finding by the court that there is a reasonable likelihood that the plaintiff will recover judgment, including interest and costs, in an amount equal to or greater than the amount of the trustee process over and above any liability insurance shown by the defendant to be available to satisfy the judgment.

(3) Procedure. A plaintiff who desires to trustee goods, effects, or credits of the defendant shall file in the court to which the action is returnable the writ, properly completed, the declaration, and a motion for approval of attachment on trustee process. The motion shall be supported by affidavit or affidavits meeting the requirements set forth in paragraph (10) of this rule. Except as provided in paragraph (8) of this rule, a copy of the writ, declaration, motion and supporting affidavit or affidavits, together with notice of hearing thereon, shall be mailed to the defendant by certified mail, return receipt requested, at his last known place of residence, or delivered to him, seven days (or if the credits to be attached include wages, ten days) at least before the date set for the hearing.

Except as provided in paragraph (7) of this rule, any trustee process shall be served within thirty days after the date of the order approving the attachment. Promptly after the service of the trustee process upon the trustee or trustees, a copy of the trustee process with the officer's endorsement thereon of the date or dates of service shall be mailed to the defendant in the manner provided in paragraph (3).

(4) Appearance of Defendant. Inclusion of a copy of the writ in the notice of hearing shall not constitute personal service of the writ upon the defendant. The notice shall inform the defendant that by appearing to be heard on the motion for approval of an attachment he will not thereby submit himself to the jurisdiction of the court nor waive service of the writ and summons or citation upon him in the manner provided by law.

(5) Answer by Trustee; Subsequent Proceedings. A trustee shall file, but need not serve, his answer, under oath, or signed under the penalties of perjury, within the time prescribed in G.L. c. 246, § 10, unless the court otherwise directs. The answer shall disclose plainly, fully, and particularly what goods, effects or credits, if any, of the defendant were in the hands or possession of the trustee when the trustee process was served upon him. The proceedings after filing of the trustee's answer shall be as provided by law. A trustee's failure to file an answer within the time allowed by this rule shall subject him to default in accordance with law.

(6) Trustee Process in Third-Party Action. Trustee process may be used by a party bringing a third-party action in the same manner as upon an original action.

(7) Subsequent Trustee Process. Either before or after expiration of the applicable period prescribed in paragraph (3) of this rule for serving trustee process, the court may, subject to the provisions of paragraph (8) of this rule, order another or an additional service of the trustee process upon the original trustee. A trustee not named in the original writ may be served subject to the provisions of all paragraphs of this rule, except that if the defendant has previously been served with process the plaintiff need not mail him a copy of the writ; and if the plaintiff has previously filed any motion pursuant to paragraph (3) of this rule, or paragraph (3) of Rule 1:04A, he need not mail the defendant a copy of either the writ or the declaration.

(8) Ex Parte Hearings on Trustee Process. An order approving trustee process for a specific amount may be entered ex parte upon findings by the court that there is a reasonable likelihood that the plaintiff will recover judgment in an amount equal to or greater than the amount of the trustee process over and above any liability insurance known or reasonably believed to be available, and that either (a) the person of the defendant is not subject to the jurisdiction of the court in the action, or (b) there is a clear danger that the defendant if notified in advance of the attachment on trustee process will withdraw the goods, effects or credits from the hands and possession of the trustee and remove them from the Commonwealth or will conceal them, or (c) there is immediate danger that the defendant will dissipate the credits, or damage or destroy the goods or effects to be attached on trustee process. The motion for an ex parte order shall be accompanied by a certificate by the plaintiff or his attorney of the amount of any liability insurance which he knows or has reason to believe will be available to satisfy any judgment against the defendant in the action, and shall be supported by affidavit or affidavits meeting the requirements set forth in paragraph (10) of this rule.

(9) Dissolution or Modification of Ex Parte Trustee Process. On two days' notice to the plaintiff, or on such shorter notice as the court may prescribe, a defendant whose goods, effects or credits have been attached on trustee process pursuant to an ex parte order entered under paragraph (8) of this rule may appear, without thereby submitting his person to the jurisdiction of the court, file a motion, supported by affidavit, for the dissolution or modification of the trustee process, and in that event the court shall proceed to hear and determine such motion as expeditiously as the ends of justice require. One day at least before such hearing the plaintiff shall furnish the defendant with a copy of the writ, declaration, motion for the ex parte order, and supporting affidavits. At the hearing the plaintiff shall have the burden of justifying any finding in the ex parte order which the defendant has challenged by affidavit. Nothing herein shall be construed to abolish or limit any means for obtaining dissolution, modification or discharge of an attachment that is otherwise available by law.

(10) Requirements for Affidavits. Affidavits required by this rule shall set forth specific facts sufficient to warrant the required findings and shall be upon the affiant's own knowledge, information and belief, and, so far as upon information and belief, shall state that he believes this information to be true.

(11) Form of Hearing. At any hearing held under this rule, either party may adduce testimony and may call witnesses (including any opposing party).

(12) Definitions. The term "plaintiff" shall include a petitioner; "defendant" shall include a respondent; "writ" shall include a summons or an order of notice in the action or proceeding; "declaration" shall include any initial pleading; and "judgment" shall include an order or decree.

Rule 1:04A. Attachment

(Applicable to certain civil cases.)

(1) Availability of Attachment. Real estate, goods, chattels and other property may be attached in any personal action or proceeding, not governed by the Massachusetts Rules of Civil Procedure, the Massachusetts Rules of Domestic Relations Procedure (adopted by the judges of the Probate and Family Court Department), or the District/Municipal Courts Rules of Civil Procedure, in the manner and to the extent provided by law but subject to the requirements of this rule.

(2) Necessity of Prior Hearing. No attachment upon an original writ may be made unless such attachment for a specified amount has been approved by a justice of the court to which the writ is returnable. The approval of such justice shall be endorsed upon the writ. Except as provided in paragraph (5) of this rule, such approval may be endorsed only after notice to the defendant and hearing and upon a finding by the court that there is a reasonable likelihood that the plaintiff will recover judgment, including interest and costs, in an amount equal to or greater than the amount of the attachment over and above any liability insurance shown by the defendant to be available to satisfy the judgment.

(3) Procedure. A plaintiff who desires to attach real estate, goods, chattels or other property of the defendant shall file in the court to which the writ is returnable the writ in the action, properly completed, the declaration, and a motion for approval of the attachment. The motion shall be supported by affidavit or affidavits meeting the requirements of paragraph (7) of this rule. The motion shall be marked for hearing and, except as provided in paragraph (5) of this rule, a copy of the writ, declaration, motion, supporting affidavit or affidavits, and a notice of hearing shall be mailed to the defendant by certified mail, return receipt requested, at his last known place of residence, or delivered to him, seven days at least before the date set for hearing. Except as provided in paragraph (9) of this rule, any attachment shall be made within thirty days after the date of the order approving the attachment. Promptly after the attachment is made, a copy of the writ with the officer's endorsement thereon of the date of any attachment shall be mailed to the defendant in the manner provided in paragraph (3).

(4) Appearance of Defendant. Inclusion of a copy of the writ in the notice of hearing shall not constitute personal service of the writ upon the defendant. The notice shall inform the defendant that by appearing to be heard on the motion for approval of an attachment he will not thereby submit himself to the jurisdiction of the court nor waive service of the writ and summons or citation upon him in the manner provided by law.

(5) Ex Parte Approval. Approval of an attachment and endorsement thereof upon the writ may be granted ex parte upon findings by the court that there is a reasonable likelihood that the plaintiff will recover judgment in an amount equal to or greater than the amount of the attachment over and above any liability insurance known or reasonably believed to be available, and that either (a) the person of the defendant is not subject to the jurisdiction of the court in the action, or (b) there is a clear danger that the defendant if notified in advance of attachment of his property will remove it from the Commonwealth or conceal or convey it, or (c) there is immediate danger that the defendant will damage, destroy or waste the property to be attached. The motion for such ex parte approval of attachment shall be accompanied by a certificate by the plaintiff or his attorney of the amount of any liability insurance which he knows or has reason to believe will be available to satisfy any judgment, and shall be supported by affidavit or affidavits meeting the requirements of paragraph (7) of this rule.

(6) Dissolution or Modification of Ex Parte Attachments. On two days' notice to the plaintiff, or on such shorter notice as the court may prescribe, a defendant whose real estate, goods, chattels or other property has been attached upon a writ approved ex parte as provided in paragraph (5) of this rule may appear, without thereby submitting his person to the jurisdiction of the court, and move the dissolution or modification of the attachment. Such motion shall be heard and determined as expeditiously as the ends of justice require. At such hearing the plaintiff shall have the burden of justifying any finding made in the ex parte order which the defendant has challenged by affidavit. Nothing herein shall be construed to abolish or limit any means for obtaining dissolution, modification or discharge of an attachment that is otherwise available by law.

(7) Requirements for Affidavits. Affidavits required by this rule shall set forth specific facts sufficient to warrant the required findings, and shall be upon the affiant's own knowledge, information or belief and, so far as upon information and belief, shall state that he believes this information to be true.

(8) Form of Hearing. At any hearing held under this rule, either party may adduce testimony and may call witnesses (including any opposing party).

(9) Subsequent Attachment. Property subject to attachment may, during the pendency of the action or proceeding, be attached subject to the provisions of this rule, except that if the defendant has previously been served with process the plaintiff need not mail the defendant a copy of the writ; and if the plaintiff has previously filed any motion pursuant to paragraph (3) of this rule, or paragraph (3) of Rule 1:03A, he need not mail the defendant a copy of either the writ or the declaration or similar pleading.

(10) Definitions. The term "plaintiff" shall include a petitioner; "defendant" shall include a respondent; "writ" shall include a summons or an order of notice in the action or proceeding; "declaration" shall include any initial pleading; and "judgment" shall include an order or decree.

CHAPTER TWO. RULES FOR THE REGULATION OF PRACTICE BEFORE THE SINGLE JUSTICE OF THE SUPREME JUDICIAL COURT

Rule 2:01. Fixing Time for Pleadings and Proceedings

(Applicable to all cases.)

The court in its discretion may order or permit pleadings to be filed, or any act to be done, at other times than are provided in these rules.

Whenever in the progress of any case it becomes necessary that a pleading be filed or other step taken so that the case may proceed, and the matter is not covered by any provision of statute or rule, the court may fix the time for the filing of such pleading or make any other appropriate order.

Rule 2:02. Form and Indorsement of Papers

(Applicable to all cases. See S.J.C. Rule 1:08.)

All papers filed in the county court shall be legibly typed with double spacing. The page shall be eight and three-eighths or eight and one-half inches in width and ten and three-fourths or eleven inches in height. The left hand margin shall be not less than one and three-fourths inches. The right hand margin shall be not less than one inch. Documents shall be bound at the left side only. They shall be filed unfolded except applications for admission to the bar.

All information required by S.J.C. Rule 1:08 shall be indorsed on the paper before filing in the clerk's office.

In case of failure to comply with this rule, the court may entertain a motion to strike such paper from the files, and may allow such motion to strike or deny it upon terms against the party at fault.

Rule 2:03. Appearances

(Applicable to criminal cases.)

The name, address, and business telephone number of the attorney for every party, or of the party if no attorney appears for him, shall be entered upon the docket as they appear upon the paper or papers constituting the appearance, or some paper transmitted to the clerk therewith. Where no address of the attorney or party, as the case may be, appears upon the docket, notice to such party may be given by posting the same publicly in the clerk's office or in a room, hall or passage adjacent thereto. The clerk upon request shall post the same.

A substitution of attorneys or change of address or telephone number shall be entered by the clerk upon the docket on written request filed in the particular case. The court and the parties, until such substitution or change is entered, and thereafter until the parties have notice thereof, may rely on action by, and notice to, any attorney previously appearing, and on notice at an address previously entered.

Any appearance shall constitute a general appearance unless the purposes thereof are specified in writing.

Rule 2:04. Giving of Notice

(Applicable to criminal cases.)

A notice to a party required by or given in pursuance of these rules, or any statute relative to procedure not requiring a different notice, shall be in writing, and, except as otherwise permitted by Rule 2:03, shall be given to such party or his attorney or any of his attorneys by delivering the same personally to him or by mailing the same, postage prepaid, to him at his business address or the address entered under Rule 2:03.

An affidavit of the person giving the notice shall be evidence thereof.

This rule shall not apply to original process or notice to bring a party before the court.

The words "registered mail" in these rules shall include "certified mail."

Rule 2:05. Time for Pleadings and Proceedings When Last Day for Performance Falls On Saturday, Sunday, or A Legal Holiday

(Applicable to criminal cases.)

When the day or the last day for the performance of any act authorized or required by these rules or by any order of the court falls on Saturday, Sunday, or a legal holiday, the act may be performed on the next succeeding business day, unless a contrary intent appears.

Rule 2:06. Eliminating Requirement for Verification by Oath or Affirmation

(Applicable to criminal cases.)

No written statement in any proceeding in this court required to be verified by affidavit shall be required to be verified by oath or affirmation if it contains or is verified by a written declaration that it is made under the penalties of perjury.

Rule 2:07. Hearings Before Single Justice. Notice

(Applicable to civil cases.)

When any party desires a hearing before a single justice, except at a sitting of the court held in Suffolk County, he may apply to a justice to appoint a time and place for the hearing; and when such time and place have been appointed, notice shall be given in accordance with the Massachusetts Rules of Civil Procedure (see, e.g., Rule 5 of Mass.R.Civ.P.) or the Massachusetts Rules of Appellate Procedure, where applicable (see, e.g., Rule 1[b], 13, and 15[c] of Mass.R.A.P., and S.J.C. Rule 2:20). But this rule shall not prevent a party from obtaining a temporary restraining order, or a dissolution of the same or of an injunction, or other order, upon a shorter notice, or without notice, if the court shall think the same reasonable.

And cases may be heard by consent of parties, and the permission of the court, without such notice.

Rule 2:08. Jury Issues

(Applicable to criminal cases.)

Whenever it is necessary or proper to have any fact tried and determined by a jury, the court will direct an issue for that purpose, to be framed by the parties, containing a distinct affirmation and denial of the points in question, or in such form as the court shall order; and the issue thus framed and joined shall be submitted to a jury together with such part of the answers, depositions, and other proceedings in the cause as the court shall direct.

Rule 2:09. Copies to Adverse Parties

(Applicable to criminal cases.)

When any pleading or motion is filed after the bill, complaint, or petition, or when any bill of particulars or specifications or answers to interrogatories are filed, a copy thereof shall be given not later than the day of filing to each of the adverse parties in the manner provided for notices by Rule 2:04.

In case of failure to comply with this rule, the court may entertain a motion to strike such paper from the files, and may allow such motion to strike or deny it upon terms against the party at fault.

Rule 2:10. Money Paid Into Court

(Applicable to civil cases.)

Money paid into court shall be in the custody of the clerk, whose duty it shall be to receive it when paid under the authority of law or rule or order of the court. He shall pay it as directed by the court; but money paid into court upon tender, or otherwise for the present and unconditional use of a party, shall be paid, on request, without special order, with any interest which has accrued thereon, to such party, at whose risk it shall be from the time when it is paid into court. Money payable to a party may be paid to his attorney of record.

No interest shall be deemed to accrue on any sum less in amount than the minimum on which interest is payable in the depositary in which the money is deposited.

Rule 2:11. Hearings Upon Motions Grounded on Facts

(Applicable to criminal cases.)

The court need not hear any motion, or opposition thereto, grounded on facts, unless the facts are verified by affidavit, or apparent upon the record and files, or are agreed and stated in writing signed by the attorneys for the parties interested.

Rule 2:12. Postponement for Want of Evidence

(Applicable to criminal cases.)

The court need not entertain any motion for postponement, grounded on the want of material testimony, unless supported by an affidavit, which shall state (1) the name, and, if known, the residence, of the witness whose testimony is wanted, (2) the particular testimony which he is expected to give, with the grounds of such expectation, and (3) the endeavors and means that have been used to procure his attendance or deposition; to the end that the court may judge whether due diligence has been used for that purpose. The party objecting to the postponement shall not be allowed to contradict the statement of what the absent witness is expected to testify, but may disprove any other fact stated in such affidavit. Such motion will not ordinarily be granted if the adverse party will admit that the absent witness would, if present, testify as stated in the affidavit, and will agree that the same shall be received and considered as evidence at the trial or hearing, as though the witness were present and so testified; and such agreement shall be in writing, upon the affidavit, and signed by such adverse party or his attorney. The same rule shall apply, mutatis mutandis, when the motion is grounded on the want of any material document, thing, or other evidence. In all cases the granting or denial of a motion for postponement shall be discretionary, whether the foregoing provisions have been complied with or not.

Rule 2:13. Special Masters and Commissioners

(Applicable to all cases.)

The full court may designate special masters and commissioners to deal with specified cases or with such matters as may be referred to them by a written order of a single justice or of the full court. The acts of any such special master and commissioner, when confirmed or approved, by a single justice or by the full court, as the case may be, shall have all the force and effect of a decision by a single justice or by the full court.

Rule 2:14. Writ of Protection

(Applicable to all cases.)

A writ of protection shall issue only upon the application of the person for whom the writ of protection is to be issued, or some person in his behalf, and upon order of the court, and then only in case it is made to appear to the court, by affidavit and any other evidence that the court may require, (1) that the application is made in good faith and for the purpose of enabling such person to attend this court as a party or witness in some specified case pending, (2) if such person is a party, that such case has not been brought collusively to enable him to obtain a writ of protection, and (3) if such person is a witness, that he has not been required to attend as a witness by his own request or procurement to enable him to obtain a writ of protection.

Rule 2:15. Objections

(See Mass.R.Civ.P. 46.)

(1) Civil Cases. Objections to evidence in civil cases shall be decided without argument, unless the presiding judge calls upon the parties to state the grounds upon which the evidence is offered or objected to.

(2) Criminal Cases. Exceptions to rulings or orders of the court in criminal cases are unnecessary and for all purposes for which an exception has heretofore been necessary, it is sufficient that a party, at the time the ruling or order of the court is made or sought, makes known to the court the action which he desires the court to take or his objection to the action of the court, but if a party has no opportunity to object to a ruling or order, the absence of an objection does not thereafter prejudice him.

If a party objects to a ruling or order of the court, he may state the precise legal grounds of his objection, but he shall not argue or further discuss such grounds unless the court calls upon him for such argument or discussion.

Objections to any opinion, ruling, direction or judgment made in the absence of counsel shall be taken by a writing filed with the clerk within three days after receipt from the clerk of notice thereof.

Rule 2:16. Requests for Rulings

(Applicable to all cases.)

Requests for rulings, when appropriate, shall be made in writing before the closing arguments unless special leave is given to present further requests later.

Rule 2:17. Time for Arguments

(Applicable to criminal cases.)

All arguments shall be limited to one-half hour on each side unless, for good cause shown, the court shall allow further time; and, when more than one counsel are to be heard on the same side, the time may be divided between them as they may elect.

Rule 2:18. Order of Business. Single Justice Sittings

The justice designated to hear matters within the jurisdiction of a single justice at Boston will hear such matters once each week, except in the weeks in which his or her attendance with the full court is required during consultation or argument, and except as the number of cases to be heard does not require sitting. The sitting shall be on Wednesday, unless the single justice otherwise directs. A weekly list for hearing in Boston will be made up on which cases from any county may be set down, either by order of the court or by joint request of counsel, the hearing of which cases shall be subject to the discretion of the court. Matters to be heard before a single justice will be heard in Boston unless the full court or the single justice shall otherwise order. The single justice in his or her discretion may set any matter down for hearing in any place within the Commonwealth.

Amended effective October 2, 1995; January 1, 1997; amended May 7, 2002, effective July 1, 2002.

Rule 2:19. Reviews of Orders of Department of Public Utilities

(Applicable to proceedings to review orders, etc., of the department of public utilities.)

So far as the Massachusetts Rules of Civil Procedure are applicable, they shall govern proceedings brought under the provisions of G.L. c. 25, § 5, or acts in amendment thereof.

Unless the interests of justice plainly require, no stay of an order of the department of public utilities shall be ordered except after notice to the Attorney General or the commissioners of the department.

An order of the department fixing the rates, fares, charges, or prices for service furnished by a person or corporation under its jurisdiction shall not be stayed unless provision be made by the party applying for such stay by bond or other security for the repayment, in the event the order is finally sustained, of so much of rates, fares, charges, or prices collected, while such stay is in effect, as is in excess of those fixed in the order.

Rule 2:20. Appeals from Decisions of Appellate Tax Board

Interlocutory matters arising in appeals from the decisions of the Appellate Tax Board and questions of final disposition thereof when further proceedings appear unnecessary may be presented to a single justice, who may after notice hear and determine the same both as to questions of law and of fact or reserve and report the case.

Rule 2:21. Appeal from Single Justice Denial of Relief on Interlocutory Ruling

(Applicable to civil and criminal cases.)

(1) When a single justice denies relief from a challenged interlocutory ruling in the trial court and does not report the denial of relief to the full court, the party denied relief may appeal the single justice's ruling to the full court. Unless the court otherwise orders, the notice of appeal shall be filed with the Clerk of the Supreme Judicial Court for Suffolk County within seven days of the entry of the judgment appealed from. Unless the single justice or the full court orders otherwise, neither the trial nor the interlocutory ruling in the trial court shall be stayed.

(2) The appeal shall be presented to the full court on the papers filed in the single justice session, including any memorandum of decision. Nine copies of the record appendix must be filed in the Office of the Clerk for the Supreme Judicial Court for the Commonwealth within fourteen days after the date on which the appeal is docketed in the full Supreme Judicial Court. The record appendix shall be accompanied by eight copies of a memorandum of not more than ten pages, double-spaced, in which the appellant must set forth the reasons why review of the trial court decision cannot adequately be obtained on appeal from any final adverse judgment in the trial court or by other available means. No response from the prevailing party shall be filed, unless requested by the court.

(3) This rule shall not apply to interlocutory appeals governed by Rule 15 of the Massachusetts Rules of Criminal Procedure.

(4) The full court will consider the appeal on the papers submitted pursuant to this rule, unless it otherwise orders.

Adopted effective November 15, 1995; amended May 2, 2001, effective June 1, 2001.

Rule 2:22. Petitions Under G.L. c. 211, § 3

(Applicable to civil and criminal cases.)

Any petition seeking to invoke the general superintendency power of the court pursuant to G.L. c. 211, § 3, shall name as respondents and make service upon all parties to the proceeding before the lower court, including in criminal cases the Commonwealth through the District Attorney or Attorney General as appropriate. When the lower court is named as a respondent, service upon the lower court shall be made in accordance with Rule 4(d)(3) of the Rules of Civil Procedure by delivering a copy to the clerk of the lower court and to the Boston office of the Attorney General. Unless otherwise ordered by the single justice, the lower court shall thereafter be treated as a nominal party which may, but need not, appear and be heard.

Adopted effective May 13, 1996.

Rule 2:23. Appeals in Bar Discipline Cases

(Applicable to all bar discipline cases entered in
the Supreme Judicial Court for Suffolk
County after April 1, 2009.)

(a) A party aggrieved by a final order or judgment of the single justice in a bar discipline case may appeal to the full court for review of the order or judgment. A notice of appeal must be filed with the clerk of the Supreme Judicial Court for Suffolk County within ten days of entry of the final order or judgment for which review is sought. An appeal shall not stay any order or judgment of suspension or disbarment unless the single justice or this court so orders.

(b) The appeal shall initially be presented to the full court on the record that was before the single justice, together with a preliminary memorandum from the appellant and, if requested, from the appellee. The appellant shall be responsible for preparing and filing a record appendix containing copies of all the relevant papers from the single justice proceeding, including but not limited to the hearing committee report, appeal panel report, if any, board of bar overseers memorandum, the order or judgment of the single justice, and any memorandum of decision of the single justice. The appellant's preliminary memorandum, which shall not exceed twenty pages, double spaced, shall set forth the relevant background and summarize the appellant's arguments on appeal, with citations to applicable authority. It is incumbent on the appellant to demonstrate in this memorandum that there has been an error of law or abuse of discretion by the single justice; that the decision is not supported by substantial evidence; that the sanction is markedly disparate from the sanctions imposed in other cases involving similar circumstances; or that for other reasons the decision will result in a substantial injustice.

Nine copies of the record appendix and preliminary memorandum shall be filed with the clerk of the Supreme Judicial Court for the Commonwealth within thirty days after the appeal has been docketed in the full court; one copy of the record appendix and memorandum shall be served on each other party. In the case of multiple appellants or cross-appellants, each appellant shall be permitted to file a preliminary memorandum within this time frame, but in such a case, the appellants shall submit, and share the cost of, a single record appendix. If requested by the court, the appellee may file a responsive memorandum, not to exceed twenty pages, double spaced, within twenty days of the court's request. Extensions of time for filing memoranda will rarely be granted and should not be anticipated.

(c) Based on its review of the parties' memoranda and the record appendix, the full court may affirm, reverse, or modify the order or judgment of the single justice without oral argument; alternatively, the court may direct the appeal to proceed in the regular course, in which case the parties will be permitted to file full briefs conformably with the Rules of Appellate Procedure and the case will be scheduled for oral argument.

(d) The Rules of Appellate Procedure shall apply to appeals covered by this rule to the extent they are not inconsistent with this rule.

Adopted March 19, 2015, effective April 1, 2015.

CHAPTER THREE. ETHICAL REQUIREMENTS AND RULES CONCERNING THE PRACTICE OF LAW

RULE 3:01. ATTORNEYS

Preamble

Persons desiring admission to the Massachusetts bar may petition to: (1) sit for the Uniform Bar Examination as provided in Section 1.1; (2) transfer a Uniform Bar Examination score earned in another jurisdiction as provided in Section 1.2; or (3) be admitted by motion as provided by Section 6.1 or 6.2.

Adopted November 7, 2017, effective March 1, 2018.

Section 1. Filing Requirements for Admission

1.1 Admission by Written Uniform Bar Examination. Persons desiring admission to the bar of the Commonwealth by written examination in Massachusetts or a concurrent written exam in another Uniform Bar Examination jurisdiction shall petition by filing with the Clerk of the Supreme Judicial Court for the county of Suffolk:

1.1.1 Petition for Admission accompanied by the recommendation of a member of the bar of this Commonwealth or of any state, district or territory of the United States;

1.1.2 Petitioner's Statement;

1.1.3 Authorization Form;

1.1.4 Law School Certificate;

1.1.5 Multistate Professional Responsibility Examination Score Report that sets forth a passing scaled score that meets or exceeds the Massachusetts required score;

1.1.6 Two (2) Letters of Recommendation for Admission; and

1.1.7 Current Certificate(s) of Admission and Good Standing from the highest judicial court of each state, district, territory or foreign country to which the petitioner is admitted, if applicable.

1.2 Admission by Transfer of Uniform Bar Examination Score Previously Earned in Another Jurisdiction. Persons desiring admission to the bar of the Commonwealth by transfer of a Uniform Bar Examination score previously earned in another jurisdiction shall petition by filing with the Clerk of the Supreme Judicial Court for the County of Suffolk;

1.2.1 Petition for Admission accompanied by the recommendation of a member of the bar of this Commonwealth or of any other state, district, or territory of the United States;

1.2.2 Petitioner's Statement;

1.2.3 Authorization Form;

1.2.4 Law School Certificate;

1.2.5 Multistate Professional Responsibility Examination Score Report that meets or exceeds the Massachusetts required score;

1.2.6 Written confirmation, issued by the National Conference of Bar Examiners, that the petitioner has submitted a request to transfer a Uniform Bar Examination transcript that sets forth a passing scaled score for Massachusetts that was achieved by an administration of the Uniform Bar Examination not more than 36 months prior to the date of filing;

1.2.7 Two Letters of Recommendation for Admission; and

1.2.8 Current Certificate(s) of Admission and Good Standing from the highest judicial court of each state, district, territory or foreign country to which the petitioner is admitted, if applicable.

1.3 Admission by Motion. Persons desiring admission to the bar of the Commonwealth by motion, pursuant to Rule 3:01, Section 6.1 or 6.2, shall petition by filing with the Clerk of the Supreme Judicial Court for the county of Suffolk:

1.3.1 Petition for Admission accompanied by the recommendation of a member of the bar of this Commonwealth or of any state, district or territory of the United States;

1.3.2 Petitioner's Statement;

1.3.3 Multistate Professional Responsibility Examination Score Report that meets or exceeds the Massachusetts required score;

1.3.4 *(section deleted)*

1.3.5 For admission by motion pursuant to Section 6.1, three (3) letters of Recommendation for Admission from members of the bar of the Commonwealth or of the bar of the state, district or territory of the United States where the petitioner is admitted or last practiced. At least one letter must be from a member of the bar of the state, district or territory of the United States where the petitioner is admitted;

1.3.6 For admission by motion pursuant to Section 6.2, three (3) letters of Recommendation for Admission from members of the bar of the Commonwealth or of the bar of the province or territory of Canada where the petitioner is admitted or last practiced. At least one letter must be from a member of the bar of the province or territory of Canada where the petitioner is admitted;

1.3.7 Current Certificate(s) of Admission and Good Standing from the highest judicial court of each state, district, territory, province or foreign country to which the petitioner is admitted;

1.3.8 Letter from the grievance or disciplinary entity of each state, district, territory, province or foreign country to which the petitioner is admitted indicating that there are no charges pending against the petitioner;

1.3.9 For admission by motion pursuant to Section 6.1, proof of active practice or teaching of law in a state, district or territory of the United States for five out of the past seven years immediately preceding the filing of petition for admission by motion.

1.3.10 For admission by motion pursuant to Section 6.2, proof of active practice or teaching of law in a province or territory of Canada for five out of the past seven years immediately preceding the filing of petition for admission by motion.

1.4 Referral to Board of Bar Examiners. All petitions for admission shall be referred to the Board of Bar Examiners for a report as to the character, acquirements and qualifications of the petitioner. See Rules V and VI of the Rules of the Board of Bar Examiners.

Amended effective October 2, 1995; April 1, 2009, effective July 1, 2009; June 10, 2010, effective July 1, 2010; October 7, effective November 1, 2016; November 7, 2017, effective March 1, 2018.

Section 2. Bar Examination

2.1 Time and Place. Law examinations shall be held at least twice a year in Massachusetts. The Board of Bar Examiners shall fix the times and places of the examinations and shall give due notice thereof.

Amended April 1, 2009, effective July 1, 2009; November 7, 2017, effective March 1, 2018.

Section 3. Qualifications.

3.1 Graduates of law schools in a state, district or territory of the United States.

3.1.1 *(section deleted)*

3.1.2 *College.* Each petitioner shall have completed the work acceptable for a bachelor's degree in a college or university, or have received an equivalent education in the opinion of the Board of Bar Examiners.

3.1.3 *Law School.* Each petitioner shall have graduated with a degree of bachelor of laws or juris doctor from a law school which, at the time of graduation, is approved by the American Bar Association or is authorized by statute of the Commonwealth to grant the degree of bachelor of laws or juris doctor.

3.2 Graduates of Foreign Law Schools. Graduates of law schools in foreign countries must have a college and legal education that is, in the opinion of the Board of Bar Examiners, similar in nature and quality to that of graduates of law schools approved by the American Bar Association. Before permitting such a petitioner to petition for admission by sitting for the written law examination in Massachusetts or a concurrent written exam in another Uniform Bar Examination jurisdiction, or to petition for admission based on transfer of a Uniform Bar Examination score earned previously in another jurisdiction, the Board of Bar Examiners in its discretion may, as a condition to such permission, require such petitioners to take such further legal studies as the Board of Bar Examiners may designate at a law school approved by the American Bar Association.

3.3 Massachusetts Law Component Requirement. Each petitioner shall have successfully completed the Massachusetts Law Component Examination.

Amended September 17, 1981; December 21, 1982, effective January 1, 1983; amended effective March 18, 1987; amended December 20, 2000, effective March 1, 2001; amended effective May 7, 2002; amended February 9, 2006, effective March 1, 2006; April 1, 2009, effective July 1, 2009; June 10, 2010, effective July 1, 2010; November 7, 2017, effective March 1, 2018.

Section 4. Public Notice

4.1 Notice and Publication. Before the Board of Bar Examiners reports to the Court on the character, acquirements, and qualifications of a petitioner for admission, the Board of Bar Examiners shall publish the names of those petitioners who passed the written law examination in Massachusetts or a concurrent written exam in another Uniform Bar Examination jurisdiction, or transferred a qualifying Uniform Bar Examination score earned previously in another jurisdiction (under Rule 3:01, § 3) and who, if no objection is made, may be recommended to the Supreme Judicial Court for admission.

The Board of Bar Examiners shall publish the names on the websites of the Massachusetts Judicial Branch and the Board of Bar Examiners. The names shall remain published for no fewer than seven business days from a date fixed by the Board of Bar Examiners, in consultation with the Office of the Clerk of the Supreme Judicial Court for the County of Suffolk.

4.2 Report to the Court. Not sooner than ten days after the date fixed for publication by the Board of Bar Examiners, the Board of Bar Examiners may report to the Supreme Judicial Court the names of those petitioners then found qualified for admission under § 3.

Amended April 1, 1986, effective May 1, 1986; November 7, 2017, effective March 1, 2018.

Section 5. Disposition of Petitions for Admission

5.1 Qualified Petitioners. The petitions for admission of those who pass the written law examination in Massachusetts or a concurrent written exam in another Uniform Bar Examination jurisdiction, or transfer a passing Uniform Bar Examination score earned previously in another jurisdiction and who are found by the Board of Bar Examiners to be of good moral character and of sufficient acquirements and qualifications may be allowed and the petitioners may be admitted either (a) in open court upon subscription to the attorney's oaths, at such times and places as the Supreme Judicial Court shall appoint, or (b) by mail in accordance with procedures established by the Supreme Judicial Court and administered by the Clerk of the Supreme Judicial Court for the County of Suffolk.

5.2 Admissions of Qualified Petitioners within a Limited Time. Except as otherwise ordered by a Justice of the Supreme Judicial Court, a qualified petitioner for admission may be sworn and enrolled as an attorney within one year of the report to the Court (Rule 3:01, subsection 4.2) concerning the petitioner, and, if not so sworn and enrolled, the petitioner may thereafter be sworn and enrolled only if he or she satisfies the Board of Bar Examiners as to his or her current legal knowledge, qualifications, and good moral character.

5.3 Non–Qualified Petitioners. The petitions of those found not qualified shall be dismissed at the expiration of sixty days from the Board of Bar Examiners' report of non-qualification, unless within that period the Chief Justice of the Supreme Judicial Court, on application of the petitioner, shall order a hearing on the matter.

Amended effective February 11, 1992; November 7, 2017, effective March 1, 2018.

Section 6. Admission by Motion.

6.1 Persons admitted to practice in the United States. A person who has been admitted as an attorney of the highest judicial court of any state, district or territory of the United States may petition to the Supreme Judicial Court for admission by motion as an attorney in this Commonwealth. The Board of Bar Examiners may, in its discretion, excuse the petitioner from taking the written law examination or transferring a qualifying Uniform Bar Examination score earned previously in another jurisdiction on the petitioner's compliance with the following conditions:

6.1.1 The petitioner shall have been admitted in another state, district or territory of the United States for at least five years prior to petitioning for admission in the Commonwealth, and shall have engaged in the active practice or teaching of law in a state, district or territory of the United States for five out of the past seven years immediately preceding the filing of the petition for admission by motion.

6.1.2 The petitioner shall have so engaged in the practice or teaching of law since the prior admission as to satisfy the Board of Bar Examiners of his or her good moral character and professional qualifications.

6.1.3 *(section deleted)*

6.1.4 *Graduates of law schools in a state, district or territory of the United States.* The petitioner shall have completed work for a bachelor's degree at a college or university, or its equivalent, and graduated from a law school which at the time of graduation was approved by the American Bar Association or was authorized by a state statute to grant the degree of bachelor of laws or juris doctor.

Graduates of Foreign Law Schools. Graduates of law schools in foreign countries must have a college and legal education that is, in the opinion of the Board of Bar Examiners, similar in nature and quality to that of graduates of law schools approved by the American Bar Association.

6.1.5 The petitioner shall pass the Multistate Professional Responsibility Examination if he or she has not previously passed that examination in another jurisdiction.

6.1.6 *Massachusetts Law Component Requirement.* Each petitioner shall have successfully completed the Massachusetts Law Component Examination.

6.2 Graduates of Canadian law schools who are admitted to practice in Canada. A person who has graduated from a law school in Canada, and who has been admitted as an attorney in the Law Society of any Canadian province or territory, may petition to the Supreme Judicial Court to be admitted by motion as an attorney in this Commonwealth. The Board of Bar Examiners may, in its discretion, excuse the petitioner from taking the written law examination or transferring a qualifying Uniform Bar Examination score earned previously in another jurisdiction on the petitioner's compliance with the following conditions:

6.2.1 The petitioner shall have completed a college and legal education that is, in the opinion of the Board of Bar Examiners, similar in nature and quality to that of graduates of law schools approved by the American Bar Association.

6.2.2 The petitioner shall have been admitted in a Canadian province or territory for at least five years prior to petitioning for admission in the Commonwealth, and shall have engaged in the active practice or teaching of law in such province or territory for five out of the seven years immediately preceding the filing of the petition for admission by motion.

6.2.3 The petitioner shall have so engaged in the practice or teaching of law since the prior admission as to satisfy the Board of Bar Examiners of his or her good moral character and professional qualifications.

6.2.4 The petitioner shall pass the Multistate Professional Responsibility Examination if he or she has not previously passed the examination in another jurisdiction.

6.2.5 The petitioner shall have successfully completed the Massachusetts Law Component Examination.

6.3 Massachusetts Law Component Requirement. All persons desiring admission to the bar are required to certify their successful completion of the Massachusetts Law Component Examination to the Board of Bar Examiners.

6.4 Notice and Publication for Admission under Section 6. Before the Board of Bar Examiners reports to the Court on the character, acquirements, and qualifications of petitioners for admission, the Board of Bar Examiners shall publish the names of petitioners who, if no objection is made, may be recommended to the Supreme Judicial Court for admission.

The list of names shall be published on the web sites of the Massachusetts Judicial Branch and the Board of Bar Examiners and shall remain posted for at least seven business days from a date fixed by the Board of Bar Examiners.

6.5 Report to the Court. Not sooner than ten days after the date fixed for publication by the Board of Bar Examiners, the Board of Bar Examiners may report to the Supreme Judicial Court the names of those petitioners then found qualified for admission under § 6.

6.6 Time Limitation for Enrollment. Except as otherwise ordered by a Justice of the Supreme Judicial Court, a qualified petitioner may be sworn and enrolled as an attorney within one year of the report to the Court. Failure to be so sworn and enrolled will result in dismissal of the petition.

Amended effective February 21, 1984; August 23, 1984, effective January 1, 1985; April 1, 1986, effective May 1, 1986; March 26, 1997, effective July 1, 1997; May 6, 1997, effective June 2, 1997; December 20, 2000, effective March 1, 2001; April 1, 2009, effective July 1, 2009; June 10, 2010, effective July 1, 2010; November 7, 2017, effective March 1, 2018.

Section 7. Bar Examiners' Rules

7.1 The Board of Bar Examiners may, subject to the approval of the Supreme Judicial Court, make rules consistent with these rules.

Amended effective November 7, 2017, effective March 1, 2018.

Section 8. Subpoenas

8.1 Any member of the Board of Bar Examiners may summon witnesses to appear before the Board of Bar Examiners.

Amended effective November 7, 2017, effective March 1, 2018.

Section 9. Immunity

9.1 The Board of Bar Examiners, and its members, employees, and agents are immune from all civil liability for conduct and communications occurring in the performance of their official duties relating to the examination, character and fitness qualification, and licensing of persons seeking to be admitted to the practice of law.

9.2 Records, statements of opinion and other information regarding a petitioner for admission to the bar communicated by any entity, including any person, firm, or institution, without malice, to the Board of Bar Examiners, or to its members, employees or agents are privileged, and civil suits predicated thereon may not be instituted.

Amended November 7, 2017, effective March 1, 2018.

RULES OF THE BOARD OF BAR EXAMINERS

Rule I. Petitions and Certificates

Every petitioner for admission to the bar who desires to take a written law examination in Massachusetts or a concurrent written exam in another Uniform Bar Examination jurisdiction shall file a petition with the Clerk for the Supreme Judicial Court of the County of Suffolk at least 75 days before the law examination which he/she intends to take, together with such certificates as the Board of Bar Examiners shall prescribe, giving information as to age, residence, character, and general and legal education and proof of passing the Multistate Professional Responsibility Examination. For good cause shown, the Board of Bar Examiners may recommend that the Court allow petitions or certificates to be filed after the time fixed.

Rule II. Time and Place of Law Examinations

Law examinations shall be held at least twice a year in Boston or in surrounding city or town within 50 miles of Boston, and in such other place or places, if any as the Board of Bar Examiners shall designate. The exact times and places shall be fixed by the Board of Bar Examiners and due notice thereof shall be given.

Rule III. Subjects under Rule 3:01, § 3

Petitioners will be expected to be familiar with the law in the fields as determined by the National Conference of Bar Examiners, as published from time to time at www.ncbex.org.

The examinations will be conducted in part by written questions to be answered in writing and in part by printed questions to be answered by selections from answers supplied.

Rule IV. Petitioners under Rule 3:01, § 6

Every petitioner for admission as an attorney under Rule 3:01, § 6 of the Rules of the Supreme Judicial Court shall obtain at his/her own expense and furnish to the Board of Bar Examiners a report by the National Conference of Bar Examiners of an investigation made by it of the moral character and professional experience and standing of such petitioner. The Board of Bar Examiners may waive this requirement in any case in which it deems such a report to be unnecessary.

Rule V. Character and Fitness Standards for Admission

V.1 Report On Character & Fitness: Pursuant to Supreme Judicial Court Rule 3:01, the Board of Bar Examiners shall report to the Court as to the character, acquirements and qualifications of each candidate for admission who has passed the written bar examination in Massachusetts, or a concurrent written exam in another Uniform Bar Examination jurisdiction, or has transferred a qualifying Uniform Bar Examination score earned previously in another jurisdiction, or who has filed a petition for admission by motion.

The Board of Bar Examiners considers good character to embody that degree of honesty, integrity and discretion that the public and members of the bench and the bar have the right to demand of a lawyer. The Board of Bar Examiners considers sufficient acquirements and qualifications to be those that are necessary to demonstrate a lawyer's fitness to practice law. In evaluating character and fitness, the Board of Bar Examiners takes into consideration all available pertinent information as to past conduct of the candidate. A record manifesting a significant deficiency in the honesty, trustworthiness, diligence or reliability of a candidate may constitute a basis for denial of a recommendation for admission. Engaging in any conduct which would have subjected the candidate to discipline if he/she had already been a member of the bar will weigh strongly against a determination of good character and fitness. There shall be a rebuttable presumption that nondisclosure of a material fact on the candidate's application(s) to the bar, law school or undergraduate school is prima facie evidence of the lack of good character.

The Board of Bar Examiners considers the following attributes to be essential for all petitioners seeking admission to the Massachusetts bar:

- The ability to reason, recall complex factual information and integrate that information with complex legal theories;

- The ability to communicate with clients, attorneys, courts, and others with a high degree of organization and clarity;

- The ability to use good judgment on behalf of clients and in conducting one's professional business;

- The ability to conduct oneself with respect for and in accordance with the law;

- The ability to avoid acts which exhibit disregard for the rights or welfare of others;

- The ability to comply with the requirements of the Rules of Professional Conduct, applicable state, local, and federal laws, regulations, statutes and any applicable order of a court or tribunal;

- The ability to act diligently and reliably in fulfilling one's obligations to clients, attorneys, courts, and others;

- The ability to use honesty and good judgment in financial dealings on behalf of oneself, clients, and others; and

- The ability to comply with deadlines and time constraints.

V.1.1 Relevant Conduct: The standards listed below should be used as guidance for candidates rather than a finite list of subjects considered by the Board of Bar Examiners. The revelation or discovery of information on any of the following will be treated as cause for further inquiry before the Board of Bar Examiners in deciding whether the candidate possesses the character and fitness to practice law:

- Unlawful conduct
- Academic misconduct
- Making of false statements, including omissions
- Misconduct in employment
- Acts involving dishonesty, fraud, deceit or misrepresentation
- Abuse of legal process
- Neglect of financial responsibilities
- Neglect of professional obligations
- Violation of a court order
- Evidence of mental or emotional instability
- Evidence of drug or alcohol dependency
- Denial of admission to the bar in another jurisdiction on character and fitness grounds
- Disciplinary action by a lawyer disciplinary agency or other professional disciplinary agency of any jurisdiction

The Board of Bar Examiners shall determine whether the current character and fitness of a candidate qualifies the candidate for admission. In considering the factors listed above, the Board of Bar Examiners will consider the following:

- The candidate's age at the time of the conduct
- The amount of time since the conduct
- The reliability of the information concerning the conduct
- The seriousness of the conduct
- The cumulative effect of conduct or information
- The evidence of rehabilitation
- The candidate's positive social contributions since the conduct
- The candidate's candor in the admissions process
- The materiality of any omissions or misrepresentations

V.1.2 Other Relevant Information: Until the attorney oath has been administered, candidates have a continuing duty to disclose promptly any changes that occur with respect to information given in response to questions in the petition.

A candidate's failure or refusal to supply information deemed relevant by the Board of Bar Examiners or otherwise to cooperate with the Board of Bar Examiners may be grounds for denial of a recommendation for admission. Failure to respond in a timely manner, without good cause, to inquiries by the Board of Bar Examiners, or to make a timely request for an extension of time to respond, may be grounds for the Board of Bar Examiners to seek dismissal of the petition.

V.1.3 Informal Oral Interview: When a candidate's record contains information that may cast doubt on his/her good character, he/she will be asked via written notice to appear before a member or members of the Board of Bar Examiners for an informal oral interview. The candidate will be given the opportunity to respond to the information and to demonstrate current good character and fitness. Following the interview, the Board of Bar Examiners will render a decision to either a) recommend the candidate for admission, or b) request additional information/action from the candidate, or c) request that the candidate appear for a formal hearing before the Board of Bar Examiners.

If the Board of Bar Examiners' decision is to recommend the candidate to the Court for admission, the Board of Bar Examiners will issue a report of qualification to the Court and notify the candidate. No further action will be taken on the petitions of those whom the Board of Bar Examiners requests to supply additional information or take corrective action until after the Board of Bar Examiners' requests have been fulfilled. If the Board of Bar Examiners is unable to recommend the candidate to the Court for admission, the Board of Bar Examiners will provide the candidate with an opportunity for a formal hearing before the Board of Bar Examiners; establish the date, time, and place of the hearing; and so notify the candidate.

V.2 Formal BBE Hearing Procedures: Formal hearings shall take place before members of the Board of Bar Examiners and be recorded by a stenographer. The candidate has the burden to convince the Board of Bar Examiners that it should recommend him or her to the Supreme Judicial Court for admission to the bar.

V.2.1 Notice of Hearing: A written notice shall be sent to the candidate requesting his or her appearance at a hearing before the Board of Bar Examiners. The notice shall contain the date, time, and place of the hearing as well as the reason for the hearing. All hearings will take place at the offices of the Board of Bar Examiners unless otherwise designated.

V.2.2 Burden of Proof: The candidate shall have the burden to establish by clear and convincing evidence his or her current good character and fitness to be admitted to the practice of law in the Commonwealth.

Factors such as incarceration, probation, restrictions of parole still in effect, current unsatisfied judgments or unfulfilled sentences, while not determinative, generally are considered to indicate that the rehabilitation process has not been completed.

V.2.3 Investigation: Prior to a hearing, the Board of Bar Examiners may conduct a detailed investigation of facts and circumstances bearing on a candidate's character and fitness to practice law. A copy of any investigative report prepared for the Board of Bar Examiners shall be given to the candidate and his/her counsel.

V.2.4 Witnesses: The Board of Bar Examiners may authorize witness summonses either for counsel, for the Board of Bar Examiners or for the candidate.

V.2.5 Evidence: The candidate and counsel for the Board of Bar Examiners shall be provided the opportunity to present testimonial and documentary evidence at the hearing. Conformity to the legal rules of evidence shall not be necessary. The Board of Bar Examiners shall determine the admissibility, relevance and materiality of the evidence offered. Counsel for the Board of Bar Examiners and the candidate (or his/her counsel) have the right to call witnesses, request the issuance of witness summonses in accordance with V.2.4 and cross-examine witnesses. The Board of Bar Examiners shall have the discretion to question witnesses directly. The Board of Bar Examiners has the discretion to vary this procedure; provided that the parties are treated with equality and that each party has the right to be heard and is given a fair opportunity to present its case.

V.2.6 Testimony: All testimony shall be given under oath.

V.2.7 Report and Recommendation: Following the conclusion of the formal hearing, the Board of Bar Examiners shall make its findings of fact and recommendation for or against the admission of the candidate. If the Board of Bar Examiners determines that it will recommend a candidate for admission, it shall file a report of qualification with the Clerk of the Supreme Judicial Court for Suffolk County and so notify the candidate. If the Board of Bar Examiners determines that it will not recommend a candidate for admission, it shall file a report of non-qualification with the Clerk of the Supreme Judicial Court for the County of Suffolk and notify the candidate.

V.2.8 Non–Qualified Candidates: Any candidate who is dissatisfied with the Board of Bar Examiners' recommendation concerning his or her character and fitness may, within 60 days after the Board of Bar Examiners' recommendation, request that the Chief Justice of the Supreme Judicial Court order a hearing on the matter. See S.J.C. Rule 3:01, Sec. 5.3.

V.3 Qualification:

The attorney oath will not be administered to any candidate prior to the Board of Bar Examiners' report of qualification to the court. In addition, qualification of a candidate may be revoked by the Board of Bar Examiners at any time prior to the administration of the oath on the receipt of information warranting further review.

The following are noteworthy Supreme Judicial Court decisions relevant to character and fitness:

Matter of Hiss, 368 Mass. 447 (1975)
Matter of Prager, 422 Mass. 86 (1996)
In Re Admission to Bar of Commonwealth, 431 Mass. 678 (2000)
In Re Admission to Bar of Commonwealth, 444 Mass. 393 (2005)

Rule VI. Foreign Law School Graduates

VI.1 Foreign law School Graduates—Requirements for Examination and Admission by Motion:

Graduates of law schools in foreign countries may be permitted to petition for admission by sitting for the written bar examination in Massachusetts or a concurrent written exam in another Uniform Bar Examination jurisdiction, petition for admission by transfer of a previously earned Uniform Bar Examination score, or petition for admission by motion upon obtaining a prior determination of their education sufficiency from the Board of Bar Examiners. (See VI.7 below for a special rule on Canadian law schools)

VI.2 Request for Advanced Determination on Education:

Except for those qualified by VI.7, at least four months prior to making petition all foreign educated attorneys who wish to obtain a determination of their eligibility to petition for admission either by written examination in Massachusetts or a concurrent written exam in another Uniform Bar Examination jurisdiction, petition for admission by transfer of a previously earned Uniform Bar Examination score, or petition for admission by motion must submit a cover letter that describes the action sought from the Board of Bar Examiners, the reason for the request, and the following documentation:

Documentation Required:

In order for the Board of Bar Examiners to determine sufficiency, each foreign educated attorney shall supply the Board of Bar Examiners with the following documents written in or translated into English:

1.   Official Transcripts: An official transcript from every college, university and law school (foreign or American) attended; this must include the courses taken, the grade for each course, the degree and date awarded, and the dates of attendance;

2.   Diploma: Copies of all diplomas or degree certificates;

3.   Course Descriptions: Descriptions of all courses, if not included in the transcripts, along with the method of study, i.e. classroom or long distance learning, etc.;

4.   Certificate(s) of Admission: An official Certificate of Admission and Certificate of Good Standing from each jurisdiction to which the attorney is admitted; and

5.   Résumé: A résumé detailing work history.

This documentation will not be returned to the petitioner.

VI.3 Determination of Educational Sufficiency:

VI.3.1 In General. In malting a determination of educational sufficiency, the Board of Bar Examiners takes into consideration the following:

● The jurisprudence in the country of the foreign law school

● The course of study that was completed at the foreign law school as compared to that offered in a law school approved by the American Bar Association (ABA)

● The attorney's pre-legal education as compared to that offered in a US college or university

● The attorney's license to practice law in either a foreign or American jurisdiction

● The length and nature of prior legal practice or teaching, if any

● The petitioner's familiarity with the American constitutional, common-law and statutory legal systems

● The petitioner's successful completion of additional legal studies.

VI.3.2 Safe Harbor. A graduate of a foreign law school who meets the standards set forth below will be deemed to have satisfied the educational sufficiency requirement of Rule VI.1 above, and will not be required to take further legal studies. For purposes of this section VI.3.2, "foreign law school" does not include an institution whose program of study consists primarily of distance study, correspondence study or an on-line program.

i). *Standards for Graduates of Law Schools in Countries with Common–Law Tradition:*

1. The petitioner is admitted to the practice of law in a foreign country;

2. The petitioner is in good standing at the bar in all jurisdictions where he or she is admitted; and

3. The petitioner has successfully completed fifteen credit hours of courses in the categories listed below in Section VI.3.2.iii at a law school that is ABA accredited or authorized by a Massachusetts statute to grant the degree of bachelor of laws or juris doctor. The required credit hours must include a course in basic constitutional law and a course in professional responsibility. Distance study, correspondence study and on-line programs are not acceptable.

ii). *Standards for Graduates of Law Schools in Countries with Civil–Law Tradition:*

1. The petitioner is admitted to the practice of law in a foreign country;

2. The petitioner is in good standing at the bar in all jurisdictions where he or she is admitted; and

3. The petitioner has successfully completed an LLM program of at least twenty four credit hours at a law school that is ABA accredited or authorized by a Massachusetts statute to grant the degree of LLM, which program includes a course in basic constitutional law, a course in professional responsibility, and a minimum of one course from at least three of the **other** categories listed below in Section VI.3.2.iii. Distance study, correspondence study and on-line programs are not acceptable.

iii). *List of Categories for Additional Courses:* The categories listed below represent a consolidation of the subjects tested on the bar examination. They encompass a range of courses falling within the category.

1. Business Organization: including, for example, Agency, Business Organizations

2. Commercial Law: including, for example, Contracts and Uniform Commercial Code (articles 1–9)

3. Constitutional Law

4. Criminal Justice: including, for example, Criminal Law

5. Property and Estate Planning: including, for example, Estates, Real Property, Trusts and Wills

6. Domestic Relations

7. Procedural Law: including, for example, Federal Rules of Evidence, Federal Jurisdiction, Federal Rules of Civil Procedure

8. Professional Responsibility

9. Torts

VI.4 Method of Evaluation:

Each file is reviewed individually on its own merits. Upon completion of its review, the Board of Bar Examiners issues a determination that the foreign educated attorney a) must take further legal studies as the Board of Bar Examiners may

designate at a law school accredited by the ABA or authorized by a Massachusetts statute to grant the degree of bachelor of laws or juris doctor; or b) is eligible to petition to sit for the bar examination; or c) is eligible to petition for admission by motion provided all other requirements are met.

VI.5 Burden of Proof:

The petitioner has the burden to demonstrate that he or she has obtained an education similar in nature and quality to that of a graduate of a law school accredited by the American Bar Association.

VI.6 Appeals:

Petitioners who are dissatisfied with the Board of Bar Examiners' determination concerning their petition may write a letter to the Board of Bar Examiners requesting a reconsideration of its decision.

Information regarding the process of appeal to the Supreme Judicial Court may be obtained by contacting an assistant clerk in the Clerk's Office of the Supreme Judicial Court for Suffolk County.

VI.7 Canadian Law Schools:

Graduates of common law studies at Canadian law schools that are members of the Law School Admissions Council shall be permitted to petition for admission by sitting for the written bar examination in Massachusetts, or a concurrent written exam in another Uniform Bar Examination jurisdiction, petition for admission by transfer of a previously earned Uniform Bar Examination score, or petition for admission by motion on the same basis as graduates of law schools approved by the American Bar Association. A list of such law schools appears below:

Dalhousie University	University of Ottawa
McGill University	University of Saskatchewan
Queen's University	University of Toronto
University of Alberta	University of Victoria
University of British Columbia	University of Western Ontario
University of Calgary	University of Windsor Faculty of Law
University of Manitoba	York University–Osgoode Hall Law School
University of New Brunswick	

The following are Supreme Judicial Court decisions concerning foreign education equivalency:

Wei Jia v. Board of Bar Examiners, 427 Mass. 777(1998)
Osakwe v. Board of Bar Examiners, 448 Mass. 85 (2006)
Yakah v. Board of Bar Examiners, 448 Mass. 740 (2006)

Amended November 7, 2017, effective March 1, 2018.

Rule 3:02. Administration of Justice

(1) A corporation or association shall not be represented under G.L. c. 221, § 46, by a disbarred attorney.

(2) All clerks of court, registers of probate, the recorder of the Land Court and their assistants and employees in their offices are prohibited from engaging in the practice of law during the time they hold such office or employment.

Rule 3:03. Legal Assistance to the Commonwealth and to Indigent Criminal Defendants, and to Indigent Parties in Civil Proceedings

(1) A senior law student in an accredited law school, or a law school authorized by statute of the Commonwealth to

grant the degree of bachelor of laws or juris doctor, who has successfully completed or is enrolled in a course for credit in evidence or trial practice, with the written approval by the dean of such school of his character, legal ability, and training, may appear without compensation (a) on behalf of the Commonwealth (including a subdivision of the Commonwealth or an agency of the Commonwealth or of a subdivision) in proceedings in any division of the District Court, Juvenile Court, Probate and Family Court or Housing Court Departments or in the Boston Municipal Court Department, provided that the conduct of the case is under the general supervision of a member of the bar of the Commonwealth who is a regular or special assistant district attorney, a regular or special assistant attorney general, an agency counsel or assistant agency counsel, or a corporation counsel, city solicitor, town counsel, assistant municipal counsel or assistant solicitor; (b) on behalf of indigent defendants in criminal proceedings in any division of the District Court, Juvenile Court or Housing Court Departments or in the Boston Municipal Court Department, or in the Supreme Judicial Court or the Appeals Court, provided that the conduct of the case is under the general supervision of a member of the bar of the Commonwealth assigned to the case by the Committee for Public Counsel Services or employed by a non-profit program of legal aid, legal assistance or defense or a law school clinical instruction program; and (c) on behalf of indigent parties in civil proceedings in any division of the District Court, Juvenile Court, Probate and Family Court or Housing Court Departments or in the Boston Municipal Court Department, provided that the conduct of the case is under the general supervision of a member of the bar of the Commonwealth assigned by the Committee for Public Counsel Services or employed by a non-profit program of legal aid, legal assistance or defense or a law school clinical instruction program.

(2) The expression "general supervision" shall not be construed to require the attendance in court of the supervising member of the bar. The term "senior student" or "senior law student" shall mean students who have completed successfully their next to the last year of law school study.

(3) The written approval described in paragraph (1), for a student or group of students, shall be filed with the clerk of the Supreme Judicial Court for the county of Suffolk and shall be in effect, unless withdrawn earlier, until the date of the first bar examination following the student's graduation, and as to a student taking that examination, until the announcement of the results thereof. For any student who passes that examination, the approval shall continue in effect for six months after the date of examination or until the date of his or her admission to the bar, whichever is sooner, unless otherwise ordered by the Supreme Judicial Court.

(4) A justice of the Superior Court Department may, in his discretion, permit a senior law student, qualified and supervised as provided in paragraphs (1) through (3) above, to appear without compensation on behalf of the Commonwealth or on behalf of an indigent defendant in a criminal proceeding:

(a) on a motion for a new trial in that court seeking post-conviction relief after the time for direct appeal has expired, or (if such an appeal has been taken) after the appeal has been decided by the Supreme Judicial Court, or

(b) on an appeal for review of sentence in the Appellate Division of that court under G.L. c. 278, §§ 28A–28D, or

(c) on a petition heard in that court, under G.L. c. 276, § 58, as amended, for review of District Court refusal to authorize pretrial release of defendant on personal recognizance.

(5) A justice of the Superior Court or the Land Court Departments may, in his discretion, permit a senior law student, qualified and supervised as provided in paragraphs (1) through (3) above, to appear without compensation on behalf of the Commonwealth or indigent persons in civil proceedings.

(6) If an appearance by a senior law student is not permitted as of right by this rule, a justice of the Supreme Judicial Court or of the Appeals Court may, in his discretion, permit a senior law student, qualified and supervised as provided in paragraphs (1) through (3) above, to appear in those courts without compensation on behalf of the Commonwealth or indigent persons. Successful completion of or enrollment in a course for credit in appellate practice in an accredited law school, or a law school authorized by statute of the Commonwealth to grant the degree of bachelor of laws or juris doctor, may, in the discretion of an appellate justice, be deemed a substitute for the course requirement provision of paragraph (1) of this rule.

(7) A senior law student, qualified and supervised as provided in paragraphs (1) through (3) above, may appear without compensation on behalf of the Commonwealth or indigent persons before any administrative agency, provided such appearance is not inconsistent with its rules.

(8) A student who has begun his next to the last year of law study in an accredited law school, or a law school authorized by statute of the Commonwealth to grant the degree of bachelor of laws or juris doctor, qualified and supervised as provided in paragraphs (1) through (3) above, may appear in civil proceedings under the same conditions as a senior law student, provided that the written approval referred to in paragraphs (1) and (3) states that he is currently participating in a law school clinical instruction program.

(9) Rule 3:03 applies only to a student whose right to appear commenced at least three months prior to graduation from law school. Subject to the time limitations expressed in paragraph (3) of this rule, such a student may make appearances after graduation under the same or any other non-profit program of legal aid, legal assistance, prosecution or defense, or law school clinical instruction.

Amended May 29, 1986, effective July 1, 1986; October 24, 1989, effective January 1, 1990; November 21, 1989, effective December 1, 1989; January 6, 1993, effective February 1, 1993; September 29, 1993, effective November 1, 1993; amended effective October 7, 1994; amended April 16, 2008, effective June 1, 2008; November 30, 2009, effective January 1, 2010; September 7, 2012, effective October 15, 2012.

Order Implementing Supreme Judicial Court Rule 3:03

As a result of the order of this court dated June 26, 1980, previous orders implementing former Supreme Judicial Court Rule 3:11 must be revised. Therefore, effective January 1, 1981, it is hereby ordered that the January 17, 1975 order, as amended by order dated July 18, 1979, implementing former Supreme Judicial Court Rule 3:11 is repealed and replaced by the following order:

1. That part of Rule 3:03(1)(a) allowing a senior student to appear on behalf of the Commonwealth in criminal proceedings in specified courts, provided the conduct of the case is under the general supervision of a regular or special assistant district attorney or a regular or special assistant attorney general, shall be construed to permit such a student to appear on behalf of a municipality under the general supervision of the latter's corporation counsel, city solicitor or town counsel, or an assistant municipal counsel or assistant solicitor.

2. Before a senior student shall act or appear for any person (client) under Rule 3:03, he shall: (a) disclose to the client his status as a law student, (b) obtain from the client a signed document in which the client acknowledges that he has been informed of the student's status and authorizing the named student to appear for and represent him in the litigation or proceedings identified in the document, (c) have the document approved by the supervising attorney, and (d) file the document and the written appearance of the supervising attorney with the court or administrative agency in which the litigation or proceedings are pending.

3. The rules of law and of evidence relating to privileged communications between attorney and client shall govern communications made or received by any student acting under the provisions of Rule 3:03.

4. A student acting under Rule 3:03 shall comply with the standards of professional conduct set out in S.J.C. Rules 3:07 and 3:08. Failure of an attorney supervising students to provide proper training or supervision may be ground for disciplinary action or revocation or restriction of the attorney's authority to supervise students.

5. The appearance of law school students in behalf of clients in cases or proceedings pending before administrative agencies or in any court of the Commonwealth shall be governed by S.J.C. Rule 3:03 and any orders from time to time issued by this court in implementation of that rule, notwithstanding any opinion or dictum contained in *Opinion of the Justices*, 289 Mass. 607, 615 (1935).

6. S.J.C. Rule 3:03 does not require that a law student shall be approved by the dean of a law school or be a senior student in order to participate in litigation lawfully conducted by another, when the participation consists of such activities as interviewing parties or witnesses, investigating facts or law, or writing briefs or memoranda. The name of a student so participating may appear on a brief or memorandum submitted in such litigation.

7. The expression 'without compensation' used in paragraphs (1), (4), (5), (6) and (7) of Rule 3:03 shall not be construed to prohibit the receipt of a fixed compensation paid regularly by a governmental agency or legal assistance program acting as the employer of a law student. It shall, however, be construed to prohibit the receipt of a fee by a law student from a client for work on a particular case.

8. Deleted.

Adopted June 26, 1980, effective January 1, 1981; amended June 7, 1985, effective July 1, 1985; May 29, 1986, effective July 1, 1986.

Rule 3:04. Limited Practice by Attorneys From Other Jurisdictions Who Are Engaged in Certain Graduate Law Studies or Programs of Legal Assistance

(1) A person (a) who is enrolled in a graduate criminal law or poverty law and litigation program in an approved Massachusetts law school or who, after graduation from an approved law school, is employed by or associated with an organized nonprofit legal services program providing legal assistance to indigents in civil or criminal matters, and (b) who is a member of the bar of the highest judicial court of any state, district, or territory of the United States (or in the case of the District of Columbia, of the District Court of the United States for the District of Columbia), may engage in practice before the courts of the Commonwealth in all causes in which he is associated with such graduate program or with an organized nonprofit defender association or an organized nonprofit legal services program. Practice under this rule shall be limited to the above causes. The permission granted by this rule shall become effective upon filing with the clerk of this court for Suffolk County a certificate of any such court of another jurisdiction certifying that the attorney is a member in good standing at the bar of that court, and also (a) a statement signed by a representative of the law school that the attorney is enrolled in the specified graduate program or (b) a statement signed by a representative of the organized legal services program that the attorney is currently associated with such program. An attorney engaging in practice under this rule shall be subject to the provisions of Chapter Four of these rules, and the permission granted by this rule shall be conditioned on compliance by the attorney with the requirements of Rules 4:02 and 4:03.

(2) Practice under this rule shall cease whenever that attorney ceases to be enrolled in or associated with such a program. When an attorney ceases to be so enrolled or associated, a statement to that effect shall be filed with the clerk of this court for Suffolk County by a representative of the law school or legal services program. In no event shall an attorney engage in practice under this rule for more than two years.

RULE 3:05. LICENSING OF FOREIGN LEGAL CONSULTANTS

Adopted July 28, 1999, effective January 1, 2000.

Table of Contents

[This Table of Contents is for convenience of reference and is not part of the Licensing of Foreign Legal Consultants or the adopting order.]

Section 1. General Regulation as to Licensing

1.1 *Petitions.* A person desiring to be licensed to practice in this Commonwealth as a foreign legal consultant shall apply by filing an application for such license with the Clerk of the Supreme Judicial Court for the County of Suffolk on such form as the Clerk may prescribe for this purpose. Upon the recommendation of the Board of Bar Examiners, the Supreme Judicial Court may, in its discretion, grant such application.

1.2 *General Qualifications.* A person will be considered eligible for licensing as a foreign legal consultant only if such person:

(a) is a member in good standing of a recognized legal profession in a foreign country, the members of which are admitted to practice as attorneys or counselors at law or the equivalent and are subject to effective regulation and discipline by a duly constituted professional body or a public authority;

(b) for at least five years immediately preceding his or her application has been a member in good standing of such legal profession and has been engaged in the practice of law in such foreign country or elsewhere substantially involving or relating to the rendering of advice or the provision of legal services concerning the law of the said foreign country;

(c) possesses the good moral character and general fitness requisite for a member of the bar of this Commonwealth; and

(d) intends to practice as a foreign legal consultant in this Commonwealth and to maintain an office in this Commonwealth for that purpose.

Adopted July 28, 1999, effective January 1, 2000.

Section 2. Proof Required

Every applicant for a license as a foreign legal consultant shall file with the application to the Clerk:

(a) a certificate from the professional body or public authority in such foreign country having final jurisdiction over profession discipline, certifying as to the applicant's admission to practice and the date thereof, and as to his or her good standing as such attorney or counselor at law or the equivalent;

(b) a letter of recommendation from one of the members of the executive body of such professional body or public authority or from one of the judges of the highest law court or court of original jurisdiction of such foreign country;

(c) a duly authenticated English translation of such certificate and such letter if, in either case, it is not in English;

(d) affidavits as to the applicant's good moral character and fitness from three reputable persons residing in this Commonwealth and not related to the applicant, one of whom shall be a member of the bar of the Commonwealth; and

(e) such other evidence as to the nature and extent of the applicant's educational and professional qualifications, good moral character and general fitness, and compliance with the requirements of Section 1 of this Rule as the Board of Bar Examiners may require.

Adopted July 28, 1999, effective January 1, 2000. Amended December 2, 1999, effective January 1, 2000.

Section 3. Reciprocal Treatment of Members of the Board of the Commonwealth

In considering whether to recommend an applicant to practice as a foreign legal consultant, the Board of Bar Examiners may in its discretion take into account whether a member of the bar of this Commonwealth would have a reasonable and practical opportunity to establish an office for the giving of legal advice to clients in the applicant's country of admission. Any member of the bar who is seeking or has sought to establish an office in that country may request the Board of Bar Examiners to consider the matter, or the Board may do so *sua sponte.*

Adopted July 28, 1999, effective January 1, 2000.

Section 4. Disposition of Applications

4.1 *Qualified Applicants.* The applications of those who are found by the Board of Bar Examiners to have satisfied the requirements for licensing as foreign legal consultants may be allowed by the Supreme Judicial Court and the applicants may be licensed upon (i) the taking of such oaths as the Supreme Judicial Court shall prescribe, (ii) paying the prescribed registration fee,* and (iii) fulfilling all other requirements set forth in this Rule or otherwise promulgated by the Supreme Judicial Court.

4.2 *Non-Qualified Applicants.* The applications of those who are not recommended by the Board of Bar Examiners for licensing as foreign legal consultants shall be denied, subject to the right of the applicant to request a hearing on the matter before the Supreme Judicial Court.

Adopted July 28, 1999, effective January 1, 2000.

Section 5. Scope of Practice

5.1 *Limitations.* A person licensed to practice as a foreign legal consultant under this Rule may render legal services in this Commonwealth subject, however, to the limitations that he or she shall not:

(a) appear for a person other than himself or herself as attorney in any court, or before any magistrate or other judicial officer, in this Commonwealth (other than upon admission *pro hac vice* pursuant to G. L. c. 221, § 39);

(b) prepare any instrument effecting the transfer or registration of title to real estate located in the United States of America;

(c) prepare:

(i) any will or trust instrument effecting the disposition on death of any property located in the United States of America and owned by a resident thereof, or

(ii) any instrument relating to the administration of a decedent's estate in the United States of America;

(d) prepare any instrument in respect of the marital or parental relations, rights or duties of a resident of the United States of America, or the custody or care of the children of such a resident;

(e) render professional legal advice on the law of this Commonwealth or of the United States of America (whether rendered incident to the preparation of legal instruments or otherwise);

(f) be, or in any way hold himself or herself out as, a member of the bar of this Commonwealth unless duly admitted as such; or

(g) carry on his or her practice under, or utilize in connection with such practice, any name, title or designation other than one or more of the following:

(i) his or her own name;

(ii) the name of the law firm with which he or she is affiliated;

(iii) his or her authorized title in the foreign country of his or her admission to practice, which may be used in conjunction with the name of such country; and

(iv) the title "foreign legal consultant," which may be used in conjunction with the words "admitted to the practice of law in [name of the foreign country of his or her admission to practice]."

5.2 *Not Unauthorized Practice of Law.* A duly licensed foreign legal consultant acting in accordance with the foregoing limitations shall not be considered engaged in the unauthorized practice of law for purposes of G.L. c. 221, § 46A (or any successor provision).

Adopted July 28, 1999, effective January 1, 2000.

Section 6. Rights and Obligations

6.1 *Rules of Professional Conduct.* Subject to the limitations set forth in Section 5 of this Rule, a person licensed to practice as a foreign legal consultant under this Rule shall be entitled and subject to the rights and obligations set forth in Rule 3:07 (Massachusetts Rules of Professional Conduct) or arising from the other conditions and requirements that apply to a member of the bar of this Commonwealth under the rules of the Supreme Judicial Court.

6.2 *Affiliation.* A person licensed to practice as a foreign legal consultant under this Rule may affiliate with one or more members of the bar of this Commonwealth, including by:

(a) employing one or more members of the bar of this Commonwealth;

(b) being employed by one or more members of the bar of this Commonwealth or by any partnership or professional corporation which includes members of the bar of this Commonwealth or which maintains an office in this Commonwealth; or

(c) being a partner in any partnership or shareholder in any professional corporation which includes members of the bar of this Commonwealth or which maintains an office in this Commonwealth.

6.3 *Privilege.* A person licensed to practice as a foreign legal consultant under this Rule shall enjoy the same attorney-client privilege, work-product privilege and similar professional privileges as members of the bar of this Commonwealth.

Adopted July 28, 1999, effective January 1, 2000.

Section 7. Service of Process

7.1 *Appointment of Clerk as Agent for Service of Process.* Every person licensed to practice as a foreign legal consultant under these Rules shall execute and file with the Supreme Judicial Court, in such form and manner as such court may prescribe, an instrument, in writing, setting forth his or her address in this Commonwealth and designating the Clerk of the Supreme Judicial Court for Suffolk County as his or her agent upon whom process may be served, with like effect as if served personally upon him or her, in any action or proceeding thereafter brought against him or her and arising out of or based upon any legal services rendered or offered to be rendered by him or her within the Commonwealth or to residents of this Commonwealth, whenever after due diligence service cannot be made upon him or her at such address or at such new address in this Commonwealth as he or she shall have filed in the office of such Clerk by means of a supplemental instrument in writing.

7.2 *Effect of Service on Clerk.* Service of process on such Clerk, pursuant to the designation filed as aforesaid, shall be made by personally delivering to and leaving with such Clerk, or with a deputy or assistant authorized by him or her to receive such service, at his or her office, duplicate copies of such process together with a fee of $10. Service of process shall be complete when such Clerk has been so served. Such

Clerk shall promptly send one of such copies to the foreign legal consultant to whom the process is directed, by certified mail, return receipt requested, addressed to such foreign legal consultant at the address specified by him or her as aforesaid.

Adopted July 28, 1999, effective January 1, 2000.

Section 8. Revocation of License

In the event that the Supreme Judicial Court determines that a person licensed as a foreign legal consultant under this Rule no longer meets the requirements for licensure set forth in Section 1 of this Rule, it shall revoke the license granted to such person hereunder.

Adopted July 28, 1999, effective January 1, 2000.

Section 9. Admission to the Bar

In the event that a person licensed as a foreign legal consultant under this Rule is subsequently admitted as a member of the bar of this Commonwealth under the provisions of the Rules governing such admission, the license granted to such person hereunder shall be deemed superseded by the license granted to such person to practice law as a member of the bar of this Commonwealth.

Adopted July 28, 1999, effective January 1, 2000.

Section 10. Application for Waiver of Provisions

The Supreme Judicial Court, upon application, may in its discretion vary the application of or waive any provision of this Rule where strict compliance will cause undue hardship to the applicant. Such application shall be in the form of a verified petition setting forth the applicant's name, age and residence address, the facts relied upon and a prayer for relief.

Adopted July 28, 1999, effective January 1, 2000.

RULE 3:06—USE OF LIMITED LIABILITY ENTITIES

(1) As used in this rule, the term "entity" shall mean a professional corporation, a limited liability company, or a limited liability partnership organized to practice law pursuant to the laws of any state or other jurisdiction of the United States and which practices law in the Commonwealth. The provisions of such laws shall be applicable to attorneys practicing law in the Commonwealth subject to the terms and conditions of this rule. Such terms and conditions are necessary and appropriate for the purpose of making the provisions of those laws applicable to attorneys. As used in this rule, the term "owner" shall mean a shareholder of a professional corporation, a member of a limited liability company, or a partner of a limited liability partnership.

(2) In addition to other provisions required by law, the articles of organization or similar organizational document ("Charter") of each entity shall contain provisions to assure compliance with the following requirements:

(a) All owners shall be persons who are duly licensed by this court to practice law in the Commonwealth, if they are actively engaged in the practice of law in the Commonwealth, or duly licensed by the licensing authority of the jurisdiction in which they are actively engaged in the practice of law. All owners shall be in good standing before this court or before the licensing authority of the jurisdiction in which they are actively engaged in the practice of law, and all owners of the entity shall own their shares or other ownership interests in their own right. All owners shall be individuals who, except for temporary absence due to illness or accident, time spent in the Armed Services of the United States, vacations, and leaves of absence not to exceed two years, are actively engaged in the practice of law as employees or owners of the entity. Notwithstanding the foregoing, an owner may be an entity rather than an individual, provided that the owners of such entity are individuals who satisfy all of the other conditions of this rule.

(b) Any owner who ceases to be eligible to be an owner and the executor, administrator, or other legal representative of a deceased owner shall be required to dispose of his or her shares or other ownership interests as soon as reasonably possible either to the entity or to an individual or entity duly qualified to be an owner of the entity.

(c) The name of the entity shall contain words or abbreviations that indicate that it is a limited liability entity and shall also conform to the requirements of Mass.R.Prof.C. 7.5

(d) All owners of the entity shall, by becoming owners, agree to the provisions of this rule, including without limitation paragraph (3) of this rule.

(e) All directors of a professional corporation and managers of a limited liability company, as the case may be, shall be owners.

(3) The following provisions are established with respect to the liability of the owners of an entity with respect to damages which arise out of the performance of legal services by the entity, such provisions to be in addition to any statutory or common law rules of general application which deal with the liability of entities and their owners:

(a) Each owner of the entity shall be personally liable for damages which arise out of the performance of legal services on behalf of the entity and which are caused by his or her own negligent or wrongful act, error, or omission. Owners of the entity whose acts, errors, or omissions did not cause the damages shall not be personally liable therefor, whether or not they have agreed with any owners or employees or other persons to contribute to the payment of the liability, except to the extent provided in subparagraphs (b), (c), and (d).

(b) All the owners of an entity which is a professional corporation at the time of any negligent or wrongful act, error, or omission of any owner or employee of said entity which occurs in the performance of legal services by said entity and which results in damages to the person or persons for whom the services were being performed shall be jointly and severally liable for such damages, but only to the extent of the excess, if any, of (1) the sum of $50,000 plus the product of $15,000 multiplied by the number of owners and employees of said entity at the time of such act, error, or omission who are duly licensed by this court to practice law in the Commonwealth, or duly licensed to practice law by the licensing authority in the jurisdiction in which they practice, and who are owners of or employed by said entity as lawyers, but not in excess of $500,000 in the aggregate, over (2) the sum of the assets of said entity and the proceeds of any insurance policy issued to it which are applied to the payment of such damages.

(c) Each entity which is not a professional corporation shall maintain at all times either (a) professional liability insurance covering negligence, wrongful acts, errors, and omissions of said entity and its owners and employees in connection with their performance of legal services in an amount per claim and in an annual aggregate limit, exclusive of any deductible or retention, not less than the Designated Amount, or (b) a specifically designated and segregated fund for the satisfaction of judgments against said entity or its owners or employees based on their professional negligence, wrongful acts, errors, or omissions in connection with their performance of legal services in not less than the Designated Amount, maintained as (i) a deposit in trust or a bank escrow of cash, bank certificates of deposit, or United States Treasury obligations, or (ii) a bank letter of credit or an insurance company bond. As used herein the term "Designated Amount" shall mean $50,000 plus the product of $15,000 multiplied by the number of owners and employees of said entity who are licensed to practice law in the Commonwealth or another jurisdiction, but not in excess of $500,000 in the aggregate. If such an entity fails to maintain insurance or a fund in the Designated Amount in compliance with this rule, its owners at the time when a professional liability claim is asserted shall be jointly and severally liable to the claimant for an amount not to exceed the Designated Amount applicable at that time, less the sum of the assets of said entity and the proceeds of any professional liability insurance policy issued to it which are applied to the payment of said liability.

(d) If an entity is an owner (an "ownership entity") or a partner in a general partnership, the provisions of subparagraphs (a), (b), and (c) shall apply to each of the individual owners of such ownership entity or such partners, and the formulas in subparagraphs (b) and (c) shall be based on all of the individual owners, partners, and employees of the entity or general partnership and of each ownership entity and partner thereof who is licensed to practice law.

(4) The entity shall at all times comply with all applicable standards of professional conduct which may be established by this court or by the licensing authority of any jurisdiction in which the entity practices law. Any violation of such standards shall be grounds for this court, after hearing and if it deems the circumstances appropriate, to terminate or suspend the right of the entity to practice law in the Commonwealth.

(5) Nothing in this rule shall be deemed to diminish or change the obligation of each attorney who is an owner of or who is employed by the entity or an ownership entity to conduct the practice of law in accordance with generally recognized standards of professional conduct and in accordance with any specific standards which may be promulgated by this court or the licensing authority of the jurisdiction in which the attorney practices. Any attorney who by act or omission causes the entity to act or fail to act in a way which violates any applicable standard of professional conduct, including any provision of this rule, shall be personally responsible for such act or omission and shall be subject to discipline therefor.

(6) Nothing in this rule shall be deemed to modify, abrogate, or reduce the attorney-client privilege or any comparable privilege or relationship whether statutory or deriving from the common law.

(7) Nothing in this rule shall prohibit the use of a voting trust to hold stock of a professional corporation. For all purposes under this rule, a person who holds a beneficial interest in such a voting trust shall be treated as a shareholder of the corporation, and, additionally, shall be deemed to own in his or her own right a percentage of shares in the corporation equal to his or her percentage of beneficial interest in the shares held by the voting trust.

(8) An entity which is a limited liability partnership or a limited liability company shall not be deemed to be an "association" pursuant to G.L. c. 221, § 46.

Amended effective January 29, 1987; July 1, 1994; November 1, 1994; January 1, 1996; July 1, 1996; July 11, 1996; amended August 31, 1999, effective October 1, 1999.

RULE 3:07. MASSACHUSETTS RULES OF PROFESSIONAL CONDUCT AND COMMENTS

Adopted June 9, 1997, effective January 1, 1998.

Table of Contents

[This Table of Contents is for convenience of reference and is not part of the Massachusetts Rules of Professional Conduct or the order adopting such rules.]

[Pub. Note: Each rule is followed by an official Comment section. The Supreme Judicial Court order adopting this new rule refers to "new Rule 3:07 (Massachusetts Rules of Professional Conduct and Comments)".]

PREAMBLE AND SCOPE

Preamble: A Lawyer's Responsibilities

1. A lawyer is a representative of clients, an officer of the legal system, and a public citizen having special responsibility for the quality of justice.

2. As a representative of clients, a lawyer performs various functions. As advisor, a lawyer provides a client with an informed understanding of the client's legal rights and obligations and explains their practical implications. As advocate, a lawyer zealously asserts the client's position under the rules of the adversary system. As negotiator, a lawyer seeks a result advantageous to the client but consistent with requirements of honest dealing with others. A lawyer acts as evaluator by examining a client's legal affairs and reporting about them to the client or to others.

3. In all professional functions a lawyer should be competent, prompt, and diligent. A lawyer should maintain communication with a client concerning the representation. A lawyer should keep in confidence information relating to representation of a client except so far as disclosure is required or permitted by the Rules of Professional Conduct or other law.

4. A lawyer's conduct should conform to the requirements of the law, both in professional service to clients and in the lawyer's business and personal affairs. A lawyer should use the law's procedures only for legitimate purposes and not to harass or intimidate others. A lawyer should demonstrate respect for the legal system and for those who serve it, including judges, other lawyers, and public officials. While it is a lawyer's duty, when necessary, to challenge the rectitude of official action, it is also a lawyer's duty to uphold legal process.

5. As a public citizen, a lawyer should seek improvement of the law, the administration of justice, and the quality of service rendered by the legal profession. As a member of a learned profession, a lawyer should cultivate knowledge of the law beyond its use for clients, employ that knowledge in reform of the law, and work to strengthen legal education. A lawyer should be mindful of deficiencies in the administration of justice and of the fact that the poor, and sometimes persons who are not poor, cannot afford adequate legal assistance, and should therefore devote professional time and civic influence in their behalf. A lawyer should aid the legal profession in pursuing these objectives and should help the bar regulate itself in the public interest.

6. Many of a lawyer's professional responsibilities are prescribed in the Rules of Professional Conduct, as well as in substantive and procedural law. However, a lawyer is also guided by personal conscience and the approbation of professional peers. A lawyer should strive to attain the highest level of skill, to improve the law and the legal profession, and to exemplify the legal profession's ideals of public service.

7. A lawyer's responsibilities as a representative of clients, an officer of the legal system, and a public citizen are usually harmonious. Thus, when an opposing party is well represented, a lawyer can be a zealous advocate on behalf of a client and at the same time assume that justice is being done. So also, a lawyer can be sure that preserving client confidences ordinarily serves the public interest because people are more likely to seek legal advice, and thereby heed their legal obligations, when they know their communications will be private.

8. In the nature of law practice, however, conflicting responsibilities are encountered. Virtually all difficult ethical problems arise from conflict between a lawyer's responsibilities to clients, to the legal system, and to the lawyer's own interest in remaining an upright person while earning a satisfactory living. The Rules of Professional Conduct prescribe terms for resolving such conflicts. Within the framework of these Rules, many difficult issues of professional discretion can arise. Such issues must be resolved through the exercise of sensitive professional and moral judgment guided by the basic principles underlying the Rules.

9. The legal profession is largely self-governing. Although other professions also have been granted powers of self-government, the legal profession is unique in this respect because of the close relationship between the profession and the processes of government and law enforcement. This connection is manifested in the fact that ultimate authority over the legal profession is vested largely in the courts.

10. To the extent that lawyers meet the obligations of their professional calling, the occasion for government regulation is obviated. Self-regulation also helps maintain the legal profession's independence from government domination. An independent legal profession is an important force in preserving government under law, for abuse of legal authority is more readily challenged by a profession whose members are not dependent on government for the right to practice.

11. The legal profession's relative autonomy carries with it special responsibilities of self-government. The profession has a responsibility to assure that its regulations are conceived in the public interest and not in furtherance of parochial or self-interested concerns of the bar. Every lawyer is responsible for observance of the Rules of Professional Conduct. A lawyer should also aid in securing their observance by other lawyers. Neglect of these responsibilities compromises the independence of the profession and the public interest which it serves.

12. Lawyers play a vital role in the preservation of society. The fulfillment of this role requires an understanding by lawyers of their relationship to our legal system. The Rules of Professional Conduct, when properly applied, serve to define that relationship.

Scope

[1] The Rules of Professional Conduct are rules of reason. They should be interpreted with reference to the purposes of legal representation and of the law itself. Some of the Rules are imperatives, cast in the terms "shall" or "shall not." These define proper conduct for purposes of professional discipline. Others, generally cast in the term "may" are permissive and define areas under the Rules in which the lawyer has professional discretion. No disciplinary action should be taken when the lawyer chooses not to act or acts within the bounds of such discretion. Other Rules define the nature of relationships between the lawyer and others. The Rules are thus partly obligatory and disciplinary and partly constitutive and descriptive in that they define a lawyer's

professional role. Many of the Comments use the term "should." Comments do not add obligations to the Rules but provide guidance for practicing in compliance with the Rules.

[2]   The Rules presuppose a larger legal context shaping the lawyer's role. That context includes court rules and statutes relating to matters of licensure, laws defining specific obligations of lawyers, and substantive and procedural law in general. Compliance with the Rules, as with all law in an open society, depends primarily on understanding and voluntary compliance, secondarily on reinforcement by peer and public opinion, and, finally, when necessary, on enforcement through disciplinary proceedings. The Rules do not, however, exhaust the moral and ethical considerations that should inform a lawyer, for no worthwhile human activity can be completely defined by legal rules. The Rules simply provide a framework for the ethical practice of law.

[3]   Furthermore, for purposes of determining the lawyer's authority and responsibility, principles of substantive law external to these Rules determine whether a client-lawyer relationship exists. Most of the duties flowing from the client-lawyer relationship attach only after the client has requested the lawyer to render legal services and the lawyer has agreed to do so. But there are some duties, such as that of confidentiality under Rule 1.6, that may attach when the lawyer agrees to consider whether a client-lawyer relationship shall be established. Whether a client-lawyer relationship exists for any specific purpose can depend on the circumstances and may be a question of fact.

[4]   Under various legal provisions, including constitutional, statutory, and common law, the responsibilities of government lawyers may include authority concerning legal matters that ordinarily reposes in the client in private client-lawyer relationships. For example, a lawyer for a government agency may have authority on behalf of the government to decide upon settlement or whether to appeal from an adverse judgment. Such authority in various respects is generally vested in the Attorney General, and Federal counterparts, and the same may be true of other government law officers. Also, lawyers under the supervision of these officers may be authorized to represent several government agencies in intragovernmental legal controversies in circumstances where a private lawyer could not represent multiple private clients. They also may have authority to represent the "public interest" in circumstances where a private lawyer would not be authorized to do so. These rules are not meant to address the substantive statutory and constitutional authority of the Attorney General when appearing for the Commonwealth to assume primary control over the litigation and to decide matters of legal policy on behalf of the Commonwealth.

[5]   Failure to comply with an obligation or prohibition imposed by a Rule is a basis for invoking the disciplinary process. The Rules presuppose that disciplinary assessment of a lawyer's conduct will be made on the basis of the facts and circumstances as they existed at the time of the conduct in question and in recognition of the fact that a lawyer often has to act on uncertain or incomplete evidence of the situation. Moreover, the Rules presuppose that whether or not discipline should be imposed for a violation, and the severity of a sanction, depend on all the circumstances, including the wilful-

ness and seriousness of the violation, extenuating factors, and whether there have been previous violations.

[6]   "A violation of a canon of ethics or a disciplinary rule . . . is not itself an actionable breach of duty to a client." *Fishman* v. *Brooks*, 396 Mass. 643, 649 (1986). The Rules are designed to provide guidance to lawyers and to provide a structure for regulating conduct through disciplinary agencies. The fact that a Rule is just a basis for a lawyer's self-assessment, or for sanctioning a lawyer under the administration of a disciplinary authority, does not necessarily mean that an antagonist in a collateral proceeding or transaction may rely on a violation of a Rule. "As with statutes and regulations, however, if a plaintiff can demonstrate that a disciplinary rule was intended to protect one in his position, a violation of that rule may be some evidence of the attorney's negligence." Id. at 649.

[7]   Moreover, these Rules are not intended to govern or affect judicial application of either the attorney-client or work product privilege. Those privileges were developed to promote compliance with law and fairness in litigation. In reliance on the attorney-client privilege, clients are entitled to expect that communications within the scope of the privilege will be protected against compelled disclosure. The attorney-client privilege is that of the client and not of the lawyer. The fact that in exceptional situations the lawyer under the Rules has a limited discretion to disclose a client confidence does not vitiate the proposition that, as a general matter, the client has a reasonable expectation that information relating to the client will not be voluntarily disclosed and that disclosure of such information may be judicially compelled only in accordance with recognized exceptions to the attorney-client and work product privileges.

[8]   [RESERVED]

[9]   The Comment accompanying each Rule explains and illustrates the meaning and purpose of the Rule. The Preamble and this note on Scope provide general orientation. The Comments are intended as guides to interpretation, but the text of each Rule is authoritative.

Adopted June 9, 1997, effective January 1, 1998.

Rule 1.0.   Terminology

The following definitions are applicable to the Rules of Professional Conduct:

(a)   "Bar association" includes an association of specialists in particular services, fields, and areas of law.

(b)   "Belief" or "believes" denotes that the person involved actually supposed the fact in question to be true. A person's belief may be inferred from circumstances.

(c)   "Confirmed in writing," when used in reference to the informed consent of a person, denotes informed consent that is given in writing by the person or a writing that a lawyer promptly transmits to the person confirming an oral informed consent. See paragraph (f) for the definition of "informed consent." If it is not feasible to obtain or transmit the writing at the time the person gives informed consent, then the lawyer must obtain or transmit it within a reasonable time thereafter.

(d)   "Firm" or "law firm" denotes a lawyer or lawyers in a law partnership, professional corporation, limited liability entity, sole proprietorship or other association authorized to practice law; or lawyers employed in a legal services organization or the legal department of a corporation, government entity, or other organization.

(e) "Fraud" or "fraudulent" denotes conduct that is fraudulent under substantive or procedural law and has a purpose to deceive.

(f) "Informed consent" denotes the agreement by a person to a proposed course of conduct after the lawyer has communicated adequate information and explanation about the material risks of and reasonably available alternatives to the proposed course of conduct.

(g) "Knowingly," "known," or "knows" denotes actual knowledge of the fact in question. A person's knowledge may be inferred from circumstances.

(h) "Partner" denotes a member of a partnership, a shareholder in a law firm organized as a professional corporation, or a member of an association authorized to practice law.

(i) "Person" includes a corporation, an association, a trust, a partnership, and any other organization or legal entity.

(j) "Qualified legal assistance organization" means a legal aid, public defender, or military assistance office; or a bona fide organization that recommends, furnishes or pays for legal services to its members or beneficiaries, provided the office, service, or organization receives no profit from the rendition of legal services, is not designed to procure financial benefit or legal work for a lawyer as a private practitioner, does not infringe the individual member's freedom as a client to challenge the approved counsel or to select outside counsel at the client's expense, and is not in violation of any applicable law.

(k) "Reasonable" or "reasonably" when used in relation to conduct by a lawyer denotes the conduct of a reasonably prudent and competent lawyer.

(l) "Reasonable belief" or "reasonably believes" when used in reference to a lawyer denotes that the lawyer believes the matter in question and that the circumstances are such that the belief is reasonable.

(m) "Reasonably should know" when used in reference to a lawyer denotes that a lawyer of reasonable prudence and competence would ascertain the matter in question.

(n) "State" includes the District of Columbia, Puerto Rico, and federal territories or possessions.

(o) "Substantial" when used in reference to degree or extent denotes a material matter of clear and weighty importance.

(p) "Tribunal" denotes a court, an arbitrator in a binding arbitration proceeding, or a legislative body, administrative agency or other body acting in an adjudicative capacity. A legislative body, administrative agency or other body acts in an adjudicative capacity when a neutral official, after the presentation of evidence or legal argument by a party or parties, will render a binding legal judgment directly affecting a party's interests in a particular matter.

(q) "Writing" or "written" denotes a tangible or electronic record of a communication or representation, including handwriting, typewriting, printing, photostating, photography, audio or videorecording and electronic communications. A

"signed" writing includes an electronic sound, symbol or process attached to or logically associated with a writing and executed or adopted by a person with the intent to sign the writing.

(r) These Rules shall be known and cited as the Massachusetts Rules of Professional Conduct (Mass. R. Prof. C.).

Adopted March 26, 2015, effective July 1, 2015.

Comment

Confirmed in Writing

[1] If it is not feasible to obtain or transmit a written confirmation at the time the client gives informed consent, then the lawyer must obtain or transmit it within a reasonable time thereafter. If a lawyer has obtained a client's informed consent, the lawyer may act in reliance on that consent so long as it is confirmed in writing within a reasonable time thereafter.

Firm

[2] Whether two or more lawyers constitute a firm within paragraph (d) can depend on the specific facts. For example, two practitioners who share office space and occasionally consult or assist each other ordinarily would not be regarded as constituting a firm. However, if they present themselves to the public in a way that suggests that they are a firm or conduct themselves as a firm, they should be regarded as a firm for purposes of the Rules. The terms of any formal agreement between associated lawyers are relevant in determining whether they are a firm, as is the fact that they have mutual access to information concerning the clients they serve. Furthermore, it is relevant in doubtful cases to consider the underlying purpose of the Rule that is involved. A group of lawyers could be regarded as a firm for purposes of the Rule that the same lawyer should not represent opposing parties in litigation, while it might not be so regarded for purposes of the Rule that information acquired by one lawyer is attributed to another.

[3] With respect to the law department of an organization, including the government, there is ordinarily no question that the members of the department constitute a firm within the meaning of the Rules of Professional Conduct. There can be uncertainty, however, as to the identity of the client. For example, it may not be clear whether the law department of a corporation represents a subsidiary or an affiliated corporation, as well as the corporation by which the members of the department are directly employed. A similar question can arise concerning an unincorporated association and its local affiliates.

[4] Similar questions can also arise with respect to lawyers in legal aid and legal services organizations. Depending upon the structure of the organization, the entire organization or different components of it may constitute a firm or firms for purposes of these Rules.

Fraud

[5] When used in these Rules, the terms "fraud" or "fraudulent" refer to conduct that is characterized as such under the substantive or procedural law of the applicable jurisdiction and has a purpose to deceive. This does not include merely negligent misrepresentation or negligent failure to apprise another of relevant information. For purposes of these Rules, it is not necessary that anyone has suffered damages or relied on the misrepresentation or failure to inform.

Informed Consent

[6] Many of the Rules of Professional Conduct require the lawyer to obtain the informed consent of a client or other person (*e.g.*, a former client or, under certain circumstances, a prospective client) before accepting or continuing representation or pursuing a course of conduct. See, *e.g.*, Rules 1.2(c), 1.6(a) and 1.7(b). The communication necessary to obtain such consent will vary according to the Rule involved and the circumstances giving rise to the need to obtain informed consent. The lawyer must make reasonable efforts to ensure that the client or other person possesses information reason-

ably adequate to make an informed decision. Ordinarily, this will require communication that includes a disclosure of the facts and circumstances giving rise to the situation, any explanation reasonably necessary to inform the client or other person of the material advantages and disadvantages of the proposed course of conduct and a discussion of the client's or other person's options and alternatives. In some circumstances it may be appropriate for a lawyer to advise a client or other person to seek the advice of other counsel. A lawyer need not inform a client or other person of facts or implications already known to the client or other person; nevertheless, a lawyer who does not personally inform the client or other person assumes the risk that the client or other person is inadequately informed and the consent is invalid. In determining whether the information and explanation provided are reasonably adequate, relevant factors include whether the client or other person is experienced in legal matters generally and in making decisions of the type involved, and whether the client or other person is independently represented by other counsel in giving the consent. Normally, such persons need less information and explanation than others, and generally a client or other person who is independently represented by other counsel in giving the consent should be assumed to have given informed consent.

[7] Obtaining informed consent will usually require an affirmative response by the client or other person. In general, a lawyer may not assume consent from a client's or other person's silence. Consent may be inferred, however, from the conduct of a client or other person who has reasonably adequate information about the matter. A number of Rules require that a person's consent be confirmed in writing. See Rules 1.7(b) and 1.9(a). For a definition of "writing" and "confirmed in writing," see paragraphs (q) and (c). Other Rules require that a client's consent be obtained in a writing signed by the client. See, *e.g.*, Rules 1.8(a) and (g). For a definition of "signed," see paragraph (q).

[8] The final category of qualified legal assistance organization requires that the organization "receives no profit from the rendition of legal services." That condition refers to the entire legal services operation of the organization; it does not prohibit the receipt of a court-awarded fee that would result in a "profit" from that particular lawsuit. An award of attorney's fees that leads to an operating gain in a fiscal year does not create a "profit" for purposes of this subparagraph.

CLIENT–LAWYER RELATIONSHIP

Rule 1.1. Competence

A lawyer shall provide competent representation to a client. Competent representation requires the legal knowledge, skill, thoroughness, and preparation reasonably necessary for the representation.

Adopted June 9, 1997, effective January 1, 1998. Amended March 26, 2015, effective July 1, 2015.

Comment

Legal Knowledge and Skill

[1] In determining whether a lawyer employs the requisite knowledge and skill in a particular matter, relevant factors include the relative complexity and specialized nature of the matter, the lawyer's general experience, the lawyer's training and experience in the field in question, the preparation and study the lawyer is able to give the matter and whether it is feasible to refer the matter to, or associate or consult with, a lawyer of established competence in the field in question. In many instances, the required proficiency is that of a general practitioner. Expertise in a particular field of law may be required in some circumstances. See Rule 7.4.

[2] A lawyer need not necessarily have special training or prior experience to handle legal problems of a type with which the lawyer is unfamiliar. A newly admitted lawyer can be as competent as a practitioner with long experience. Some important legal skills, such as the analysis of precedent, the evaluation of evidence and legal drafting, are required in all legal problems. Perhaps the most fundamental legal skill consists of determining what kind of legal problems a situation may involve, a skill that necessarily transcends any particular specialized knowledge. A lawyer can provide adequate representation in a wholly novel field through necessary study. Competent representation can also be provided through the association of a lawyer of established competence in the field in question.

[3] In an emergency a lawyer may give advice or assistance in a matter in which the lawyer does not have the skill ordinarily required where referral to or consultation or association with another lawyer would be impractical. Even in an emergency, however, assistance should be limited to that reasonably necessary in the circumstances, for ill-considered action under emergency conditions can jeopardize the client's interest.

[4] A lawyer may accept representation where the requisite level of competence can be achieved by reasonable preparation. This applies as well to a lawyer who is appointed as counsel for an unrepresented person. See also Rule 6.2.

Thoroughness and Preparation

[5] Competent handling of a particular matter includes inquiry into and analysis of the factual and legal elements of the problem, and use of methods and procedures meeting the standards of competent practitioners. It also includes adequate preparation. The required attention and preparation are determined in part by what is at stake; major litigation and complex transactions ordinarily require more extensive treatment than matters of lesser complexity and consequence. An agreement between the lawyer and the client regarding the scope of the representation may limit the matters for which the lawyer is responsible. See Rule 1.2(c).

Retaining or Contracting With Other Lawyers

[6] Before a lawyer retains or contracts with other lawyers outside the lawyer's own firm to provide or assist in the provision of legal services to a client, the lawyer should ordinarily obtain informed consent from the client and must reasonably believe that the other lawyers' services will contribute to the competent and ethical representation of the client. See also Rules 1.2 (allocation of authority), 1.4 (communication with client), 1.5(e) (fee sharing), 1.6 (confidentiality), and 5.5(a) (unauthorized practice of law). The reasonableness of the decision to retain or contract with other lawyers outside the lawyer's own firm will depend upon the circumstances, including the education, experience and reputation of the nonfirm lawyers; the nature of the services assigned to the nonfirm lawyers; and the legal protections, professional conduct rules, and ethical environments of the jurisdictions in which the services will be performed, particularly relating to confidential information.

[7] When lawyers from more than one law firm are providing legal services to the client on a particular matter, the lawyers ordinarily should consult with each other and the client about the scope of their respective representations and the allocation of responsibility among them. See Rule 1.2. When making allocations of responsibility in a matter pending before a tribunal, lawyers and parties may have additional obligations that are a matter of law beyond the scope of these Rules, such as in the context of discovery.

Maintaining Competence

[8] To maintain the requisite knowledge and skill, a lawyer should keep abreast of changes in the law and its practice, including the benefits and risks associated with relevant technology, and engage in continuing study and education.

Rule 1.2. Scope of Representation and Allocation of Authority Between Client and Lawyer

(a) A lawyer shall seek the lawful objectives of his or her client through reasonably available means permitted by law and these Rules. A lawyer does not violate this Rule, however, by acceding to reasonable requests of opposing counsel which do not prejudice the rights of his or her client, by being punctual in fulfilling all professional commitments, by avoiding offensive tactics, or by treating with courtesy and consideration all persons involved in the legal process. A lawyer shall abide by a client's decision whether to accept an offer of settlement of a matter. In a criminal case, the lawyer shall abide by the client's decision, after consultation with the lawyer, as to a plea to be entered, whether to waive jury trial, and whether the client will testify.

(b) A lawyer's representation of a client, including representation by appointment, does not constitute an endorsement of the client's political, economic, social, or moral views or activities.

(c) A lawyer may limit the scope of the representation if the limitation is reasonable under the circumstances and the client gives informed consent.

(d) A lawyer shall not counsel a client to engage, or assist a client, in conduct that the lawyer knows is criminal or fraudulent, but a lawyer may discuss the legal consequences of any proposed course of conduct with a client and may counsel or assist a client to make a good faith effort to determine the validity, scope, meaning, or application of the law.

Adopted June 9, 1997, effective January 1, 1998. Amended March 26, 2015, effective July 1, 2015.

Comment

Allocation of Authority between Client and Lawyer

[1] Paragraph (a) confers upon the client the ultimate authority to determine the purposes to be served by legal representation, within the limits imposed by law and the lawyer's professional obligations. The decisions specified in paragraph (a), such as whether to settle a civil matter, must also be made by the client. See Rule 1.4(a)(1) for the lawyer's duty to communicate with the client about such decisions. With respect to the means by which the client's objectives are to be pursued, the lawyer shall consult with the client as required by Rule 1.4(a)(2) and may take such action as is impliedly authorized to carry out the representation.

[2] On occasion, however, a lawyer and a client may disagree about the means to be used to accomplish the client's objectives. Clients normally defer to the special knowledge and skill of their lawyer with respect to the means to be used to accomplish their objectives, particularly with respect to technical, legal and tactical matters. Conversely, lawyers usually defer to the client regarding such questions as the expense to be incurred and concern for third persons who might be adversely affected. Because of the varied nature of the matters about which a lawyer and client might disagree and because the actions in question may implicate the interests of a tribunal or other persons, this Rule does not prescribe how such disagreements are to be resolved. Other law, however, may be applicable and should be consulted by the lawyer. The lawyer should also consult with the client and seek a mutually acceptable resolution of the disagreement. If such efforts are unavailing and the lawyer has a fundamental disagreement with the client, the lawyer may withdraw from the representation. See Rule 1.16(b)(4). Conversely, the client may resolve the disagreement by discharging the lawyer. See Rule 1.16(a)(3).

[3] At the outset of a representation and subject to Rule 1.4, the client may authorize the lawyer to take specific action on the client's behalf without further consultation. Absent a material change in circumstances, a lawyer may rely on such an advance authorization. The client may, however, revoke such authority at any time.

[4] In a case in which the client appears to be suffering diminished capacity, the lawyer's duty to abide by the client's decisions is to be guided by reference to Rule 1.14.

Independence from Client's Views or Activities

[5] Legal representation should not be denied to people who are unable to afford legal services, or whose cause is controversial or the subject of popular disapproval. By the same token, representing a client does not constitute approval of the client's views or activities.

Agreements Limiting Scope of Representation

[6] The scope of services to be provided by a lawyer may be limited by agreement with the client or by the terms under which the lawyer's services are made available to the client. When a lawyer has been retained by an insurer to represent an insured, for example, the representation may be limited to matters related to the insurance coverage. A limited representation may be appropriate because the client has limited objectives for the representation. In addition, the terms upon which representation is undertaken may exclude specific means that might otherwise be used to accomplish the client's objectives. Such limitations may exclude actions that the client thinks are too costly or that the lawyer regards as repugnant or imprudent.

[7] Although this Rule affords the lawyer and client substantial latitude to limit the representation, the limitation must be reasonable under the circumstances. If, for example, a client's objective is limited to securing general information about the law the client needs in order to handle a common and typically uncomplicated legal problem, the lawyer and client may agree that the lawyer's services will be limited to a brief telephone consultation. Such a limitation, however, would not be reasonable if the time allotted was not sufficient to yield advice upon which the client could rely. Although an agreement for a limited representation does not exempt a lawyer from the duty to provide competent representation, the limitation is a factor to be considered when determining the legal knowledge, skill, thoroughness and preparation reasonably necessary for the representation. See Rule 1.1.

[8] All agreements concerning a lawyer's representation of a client must accord with the Rules of Professional Conduct and other law. See, *e.g.*, Rules 1.1, 1.5, 1.8 and 5.6. Although paragraph (c) does not require that the client's informed consent to a limited representation be in writing, the specification of the scope of representation as well as the rate or basis of the lawyer's fee is generally required to be communicated to the client in writing by Rule 1.5(b).

Criminal, Fraudulent and Prohibited Transactions

[9] Paragraph (d) prohibits a lawyer from knowingly counseling or assisting a client to commit a crime or fraud. This prohibition, however, does not preclude the lawyer from giving an honest opinion about the actual consequences that appear likely to result from a client's conduct. Nor does the fact that a client uses advice in a course of action that is criminal or fraudulent of itself make a lawyer a party to the course of action. There is a critical distinction between presenting an analysis of legal aspects of questionable conduct and recommending the means by which a crime or fraud might be committed with impunity.

[10] When the client's course of action has already begun and is continuing, the lawyer's responsibility is especially delicate. The lawyer is required to avoid assisting the client, for example, by drafting or delivering documents that the lawyer knows are fraudulent or by suggesting how the wrongdoing might be concealed. A lawyer may not continue assisting a client in conduct that the lawyer originally supposed was legally proper but then discovers is criminal or fraudulent. The lawyer must, therefore, withdraw from the representation of the client in the matter. See Rule 1.16(a). But see Rule

347

3.3(e). In some cases, withdrawal alone might be insufficient. It may be necessary for the lawyer to give notice of the fact of withdrawal and to disaffirm any opinion, document, affirmation or the like. See Rule 4.1.

[11] Where the client is a fiduciary, the lawyer may be charged with special obligations in dealings with a beneficiary.

[12] Paragraph (d) applies whether or not the defrauded party is a party to the transaction. Hence, a lawyer must not participate in a transaction to effectuate criminal or fraudulent avoidance of tax liability. Paragraph (d) does not preclude undertaking a criminal defense incident to a general retainer for legal services to a lawful enterprise. The last clause of paragraph (d) recognizes that determining the validity or interpretation of a statute or regulation may require a course of action involving disobedience of the statute or regulation or of the interpretation placed upon it by governmental authorities.

[13] If a lawyer comes to know or reasonably should know that a client expects assistance not permitted by the Rules of Professional Conduct or other law or if the lawyer intends to act contrary to the client's instructions, the lawyer must consult with the client regarding the limitations on the lawyer's conduct. See Rule 1.4(a)(5).

Rule 1.3. Diligence

A lawyer shall act with reasonable diligence and promptness in representing a client. The lawyer should represent a client zealously within the bounds of the law.

Adopted June 9, 1997, effective January 1, 1998. Amended March 26, 2015, effective July 1, 2015.

Comment

[1] A lawyer should pursue a matter on behalf of a client despite opposition, obstruction or personal inconvenience to the lawyer, and take whatever lawful and ethical measures are required to vindicate a client's cause or endeavor. A lawyer must also act with commitment and dedication to the interests of the client and with zeal in advocacy upon the client's behalf. A lawyer is not bound, however, to press for every advantage that might be realized for a client. For example, a lawyer may have authority to exercise professional discretion in determining the means by which a matter should be pursued. See Rule 1.2. The lawyer's duty to act with reasonable diligence does not require the use of offensive tactics or preclude the treating of all persons involved in the legal process with courtesy and respect.

[2] A lawyer's work load must be controlled so that each matter can be handled competently.

[3] Perhaps no professional shortcoming is more widely resented than procrastination. A client's interests often can be adversely affected by the passage of time or the change of conditions; in extreme instances, as when a lawyer overlooks a statute of limitations, the client's legal position may be destroyed. Even when the client's interests are not affected in substance, however, unreasonable delay can cause a client needless anxiety and undermine confidence in the lawyer's trustworthiness. A lawyer's duty to act with reasonable promptness, however, does not preclude a lawyer from agreeing to a reasonable request for a postponement that will not prejudice the lawyer's client.

[4] Unless the relationship is terminated as provided in Rule 1.16, a lawyer should carry through to conclusion all matters undertaken for a client. If a lawyer's employment is limited to a specific matter, the relationship terminates when the matter has been resolved. If a lawyer has served a client over a substantial period in a variety of matters, the client sometimes may assume that the lawyer will continue to serve on a continuing basis unless the lawyer gives notice of withdrawal. Doubt about whether a client-lawyer relationship still exists should be clarified by the lawyer, preferably in writing, so that the client will not mistakenly suppose the lawyer is looking after the client's affairs when the lawyer has ceased to do so. For example, if a

lawyer has handled a judicial or administrative proceeding that produced a result adverse to the client and the lawyer and the client have not agreed that the lawyer will handle the matter on appeal, the lawyer must consult with the client about the possibility of appeal before relinquishing responsibility for the matter. See Rule 1.4(a)(2). Whether the lawyer is obligated to prosecute the appeal for the client may depend on the scope of the representation the lawyer has agreed to provide to the client. See Rule 1.2.

[5] To prevent neglect of client matters in the event of a sole practitioner's death or disability, the duty of diligence may require that each practitioner prepare a plan, in conformity with applicable rules, that designates another competent lawyer to review client files, notify each client of the lawyer's death or disability, and determine whether there is a need for immediate protective action. See S.J.C. Rule 4:01, § 14.

Rule 1.4. Communication

(a) A lawyer shall:

(1) promptly inform the client of any decision or circumstance with respect to which the client's informed consent, as defined in Rule 1.0(f), is required by these Rules;

(2) reasonably consult with the client about the means by which the client's objectives are to be accomplished;

(3) keep the client reasonably informed about the status of the matter;

(4) promptly comply with reasonable requests for information; and

(5) consult with the client about any relevant limitation on the lawyer's conduct when the lawyer knows that the client expects assistance not permitted by the Rules of Professional Conduct or other law.

(b) A lawyer shall explain a matter to the extent reasonably necessary to permit the client to make informed decisions regarding the representation.

Adopted June 9, 1997, effective January 1, 1998. Amended March 26, 2015, effective July 1, 2015.

Comment

[1] Reasonable communication between the lawyer and the client is necessary for the client effectively to participate in the representation.

Communicating with Client

[2] If these Rules require that a particular decision about the representation be made by the client, paragraph (a)(1) requires that the lawyer promptly consult with and secure the client's consent prior to taking action unless prior discussions with the client have resolved what action the client wants the lawyer to take. For example, a lawyer who receives from opposing counsel an offer of settlement in a civil controversy or a proffered plea bargain in a criminal case must promptly inform the client of its substance unless the client has previously indicated that the proposal will be acceptable or unacceptable or has authorized the lawyer to accept or reject the offer. See Rule 1.2(a) and Comment 3 thereto.

[3] Paragraph (a)(2) requires the lawyer to reasonably consult with the client about the means to be used to accomplish the client's objectives. In some situations—depending on both the importance of the action under consideration and the feasibility of consulting with the client—this duty will require consultation prior to taking action. In other circumstances, such as during a trial when an immediate decision must be made, the exigency of the situation may require the lawyer to act without prior consultation. In such cases the lawyer must nonetheless act reasonably to inform the client of actions the lawyer has taken on the client's behalf. Additionally, paragraph (a)(3)

requires that the lawyer keep the client reasonably informed about the status of the matter, such as significant developments affecting the timing or the substance of the representation.

[4] A lawyer's regular communication with clients will minimize the number of occasions on which a client will need to request information concerning the representation. When a client makes a reasonable request for information, however, paragraph (a)(4) requires prompt compliance with the request, or if a prompt response is not feasible, that the lawyer, or a member of the lawyer's staff, acknowledge receipt of the request and advise the client when a response may be expected. A lawyer should promptly respond to or acknowledge client communications.

Explaining Matters

[5] The client should have sufficient information to participate intelligently in decisions concerning the objectives of the representation and the means by which they are to be pursued, to the extent the client is willing and able to do so. Adequacy of communication depends in part on the kind of advice or assistance that is involved. For example, when there is time to explain a proposal made in a negotiation, the lawyer should review all important provisions with the client before proceeding to an agreement. In litigation a lawyer should explain the general strategy and prospects of success and ordinarily should consult the client on tactics that are likely to result in significant expense or to injure or coerce others. On the other hand, a lawyer ordinarily will not be expected to describe trial or negotiation strategy in detail. The guiding principle is that the lawyer should fulfill reasonable client expectations for information consistent with the duty to act in the client's best interests, and the client's overall requirements as to the character of representation.

[6] Ordinarily, the information to be provided is that appropriate for a client who is a comprehending and responsible adult. However, fully informing the client according to this standard may be impracticable, for example, where the client is a child or suffers from diminished capacity. See Rule 1.14. When the client is an organization or group, it is often impossible or inappropriate to inform every one of its members about its legal affairs; ordinarily, the lawyer should address communications to the appropriate officials of the organization. See Rule 1.13. Where many routine matters are involved, a system of limited or occasional reporting may be arranged with the client.

Withholding Information

[7] In some circumstances, a lawyer may be justified in delaying transmission of information when the client would be likely to react imprudently to an immediate communication. Thus, a lawyer might withhold a psychiatric diagnosis of a client when the examining psychiatrist indicates that disclosure would harm the client. Ordinarily, a lawyer may not withhold information to serve the lawyer's own interest or convenience or the interests or convenience of another person. Rules or court orders governing litigation may provide that information supplied to a lawyer may not be disclosed to the client. Rule 3.4(c) directs compliance with such rules or orders.

[8] There will be circumstances in which a lawyer should advise a client concerning the advantages and disadvantages of available dispute resolution options in order to permit the client to make informed decisions concerning the representation.

Rule 1.5.   Fees

(a) A lawyer shall not enter into an agreement for, charge, or collect an illegal or clearly excessive fee or collect an unreasonable amount for expenses. The factors to be considered in determining whether a fee is clearly excessive include the following:

(1) the time and labor required, the novelty and difficulty of the questions involved, and the skill requisite to perform the legal service properly;

(2) the likelihood, if apparent to the client, that the acceptance of the particular employment will preclude other employment by the lawyer;

(3) the fee customarily charged in the locality for similar legal services;

(4) the amount involved and the results obtained;

(5) the time limitations imposed by the client or by the circumstances;

(6) the nature and length of the professional relationship with the client;

(7) the experience, reputation, and ability of the lawyer or lawyers performing the services; and

(8) whether the fee is fixed or contingent.

(b)(1) Except as provided in paragraph (b)(2), the scope of the representation and the basis or rate of the fee and expenses for which the client will be responsible shall be communicated to the client in writing before or within a reasonable time after commencing the representation, except when the lawyer will charge a regularly represented client on the same basis or rate. Any changes in the basis or rate of the fee or expenses shall also be communicated in writing to the client.

(2) The requirement of a writing shall not apply to a single-session legal consultation or where the lawyer reasonably expects the total fee to be charged to the client to be less than $500. Where an indigent representation fee is imposed by a court, no fee agreement has been entered into between the lawyer and client, and a writing is not required.

(c) A fee may be contingent on the outcome of the matter for which the service is rendered, except in a matter in which a contingent fee is prohibited by paragraph (d) or other law. Except for contingent fee arrangements concerning the collection of commercial accounts and of insurance company subrogation claims, a contingent fee agreement shall be in writing and signed in duplicate by both the lawyer and the client within a reasonable time after the making of the agreement. One such copy (and proof that the duplicate copy has been delivered or mailed to the client) shall be retained by the lawyer for a period of six years after the conclusion of the contingent fee matter. The writing shall state the following:

(1) the name and address of each client;

(2) the name and address of the lawyer or lawyers to be retained;

(3) the nature of the claim, controversy, and other matters with reference to which the services are to he performed;

(4) the contingency upon which compensation will be paid, whether and to what extent the client is to be liable to pay compensation otherwise than from amounts collected for him or her by the lawyer, and if the lawyer is to be paid any fee for the representation that will not be determined on a contingency, the method by which this fee will be determined;

(5) the method by which the fee is to be determined, including the percentage or percentages that shall accrue to the lawyer out of amounts collected, and unless the parties otherwise agree in writing, that the lawyer shall be entitled

to the greater of (i) the amount of any attorney's fees awarded by the court or included in the settlement or (ii) the amount determined by application of the percentage or other formula to the recovery amount not including such attorney's fees;

(6) the method by which litigation and other expenses are to be calculated and paid or reimbursed, whether expenses are to be paid or reimbursed only from the recovery, and whether such expenses are to be deducted from the recovery before or after the contingent fee is calculated;

(7) if the lawyer intends to pursue such a claim, the client's potential liability for expenses and reasonable attorney's fees if the attorney-client relationship is terminated before the conclusion of the case for any reason, including a statement of the basis on which such expenses and fees will be claimed, and, if applicable, the method by which such expenses and fees will be calculated; and

(8) if the lawyer is the successor to a lawyer whose representation has terminated before the conclusion of the case, whether the client or the successor lawyer is to be responsible for payment of former counsel's attorney's fees and expenses, if any such payment is due.

Upon conclusion of a contingent fee matter for which a writing is required under this paragraph, the lawyer shall provide the client with a written statement explaining the outcome of the matter and, if there is a recovery, showing the remittance to the client and the method of its determination. At any time prior to the occurrence of the contingency, the lawyer shall, within twenty days after either 1) the termination of the attorney-client relationship or 2) receipt of a written request from the client when the relationship has not terminated, provide the client with a written itemized statement of services rendered and expenses incurred; except, however, that the lawyer shall not be required to provide the statement if the lawyer informs the client in writing that he or she does not intend to claim entitlement to a fee or expenses in the event the relationship is terminated before the conclusion of the contingent fee matter.

(d) A lawyer shall not enter into an arrangement for, charge, or collect:

(1) any fee in a domestic relations matter, the payment or amount of which is contingent upon the securing of a divorce or upon the amount of alimony or support, or property settlement in lieu thereof; or

(2) a contingent fee for representing a defendant in a criminal case.

(e) A division of a fee (including a referral fee) between lawyers who are not in the same firm may be made only if the client is notified before or at the time the client enters into a fee agreement for the matter that a division of fees will be made and consents to the joint participation in writing and the total fee is reasonable. This limitation does not prohibit payment to a former partner or associate pursuant to a separation or retirement agreement.

(f)(1) The following forms of contingent fee agreement may be used to satisfy the requirements of paragraphs (c) and (e) if they accurately and fully reflect the terms of the engagement.

(2) A lawyer who uses Form A does not need to provide any additional explanation to a client beyond that otherwise required by this rule. The form contingent fee agreement identified as Form B includes two alternative provisions in paragraphs (3) and (7). A lawyer who uses Form B shall show and explain these options to the client, and obtain the client's informed consent confirmed in writing to each selected option. A client's initialing next to the selected option meets the "confirmed in writing" requirement.

(3) The authorization of Forms A and B shall not prevent the use of other forms consistent with this rule. A lawyer who uses a form of contingent fee agreement that contains provisions that materially differ from or add to those contained in Forms A or B shall explain those different or added provisions or options to the client and obtain the client's informed consent confirmed in writing. For purposes of this rule, a fee agreement that omits option (i) in paragraph (3), and, where applicable, option (i) in paragraph (7) of Form B is an agreement that materially differs from the model forms. A fee agreement containing a statement in which the client specifically confirms with his or her signature that the lawyer has explained that there are provisions of the fee agreement, clearly identified by the lawyer, that materially differ from, or add to, those contained in Forms A or B meets the "confirmed in writing" requirement.

(4) The requirements of paragraphs (f)(1)—(3) shall not apply when the client is an organization, including a nonprofit or governmental entity.

CONTINGENT FEE AGREEMENT, FORM A

To be Executed in Duplicate

Date: _____, 20___

The Client _____

(Name) (Street & Number) (City or Town)

retains the Lawyer _____

(Name) (Street & Number) (City or Town)

to perform the legal services mentioned in paragraph (1) below. The lawyer agrees to perform them faithfully and with due diligence.

(1) The claim, controversy, and other matters with reference to which the services are to be performed are:

(2) The contingency upon which compensation is to be paid is recovery of damages, whether by settlement, judgment or otherwise.

(3) The lawyer agrees to advance, on behalf of the client, all out-of-pocket costs and expenses. The client is not to be liable to pay court costs and expenses of litigation, other than from amounts collected for the client by the lawyer.

(4) Compensation (including that of any associated counsel) to be paid to the lawyer by the client on the foregoing contingency shall be the following percentage of the (gross) (net) [indicate which] amount collected. [Here insert the percentages to be charged in the event of collection. These may be on a flat rate basis or in a descending or ascending scale in relation to the amount collected.] The percentage shall be applied to the amount of the recovery not including any attorney's fees awarded by a court or included in a

settlement. The lawyer's compensation shall be such attorney's fees or the amount determined by the percentage calculation described above, whichever is greater.

(5) [IF APPLICABLE] The client understands that a portion of the compensation payable to the lawyer pursuant to paragraph 4 above shall be paid to [Name of Attorney entitled to a share of compensation] and consents to this division of fees.

(6) [IF APPLICABLE] If the attorney-client relationship is terminated before the conclusion of the case for any reason, the attorney may seek payment for the work done and expenses advanced before the termination. Whether the lawyer will receive any payment for the work done before the termination, and the amount of any payment, will depend on the benefit to the client of the services performed by the lawyer as well as the timing and circumstances of the termination. Such payment shall not exceed the lesser of (i) the fair value of the legal services rendered by the lawyer, or (ii) the contingent fee to which the lawyer would have been entitled upon the occurrence of the contingency. This paragraph does not give the lawyer any rights to payment beyond those conferred by existing law.

(7) [USE IF LAWYER IS SUCCESSOR COUNSEL] The lawyer is responsible for payment of former counsel's reasonable attorney's fees and expenses and the cost of resolving any dispute between the client and prior counsel over fees or expenses.

This agreement and its performance are subject to Rule 1.5 of the Rules of Professional Conduct adopted by the Massachusetts Supreme Judicial Court.

WE EACH HAVE READ THE ABOVE AGREEMENT BEFORE SIGNING IT.

Witnesses to signatures	Signatures of client and lawyer
(To client) _____	_____
	(Signature of client)
(To lawyer) _____	_____
	(Signature of lawyer)

CONTINGENT FEE AGREEMENT, FORM B

To be Executed in Duplicate

Date: _____, 20___

The Client _____

(Name) (Street & Number) (City or Town)

retains the Lawyer _____

(Name) (Street & Number) (City or Town)

to perform the legal services mentioned in paragraph (1) below. The lawyer agrees to perform them faithfully and with due diligence.

(1) The claim, controversy, and other matters with reference to which the services are to be performed are:

(2) The contingency upon which compensation is to be paid is:

(3) Costs and Expenses. The client should initial next to the option selected.

(i) The lawyer agrees to advance, on behalf of the client, all out-of-pocket costs and expenses. The client is not to be liable to pay court costs and expenses of litigation, other than from amounts collected for the client by the lawyer; or

(ii) The client is not to be liable to pay compensation or court costs and expenses of litigation otherwise than from amounts collected for the client by the lawyer, except as follows:

(4) Compensation (including that of any associated counsel) to be paid to the lawyer by the client on the foregoing contingency shall be the following percentage of the (gross) (net) [indicate which] amount collected. [Here insert the percentages to be charged in the event of collection. These may be on a flat rate basis or in a descending or ascending scale in relation to the amount collected.] The percentage shall be applied to the amount of the recovery not including any attorney's fees awarded by a court or included in a settlement. The lawyer's compensation shall be such attorney's fees or the amount determined by the percentage calculation described above, whichever is greater. [Modify the last two sentences as appropriate if the parties agree on some other basis for calculation.]

(5) [IF APPLICABLE] The client understands that a portion of the compensation payable to the lawyer pursuant to paragraph 4 above shall be paid to [Name of Attorney entitled to a share of compensation] and consents to this division of fees.

(6) [IF APPLICABLE] If the attorney-client relationship is terminated before the conclusion of the case for any reason, the attorney may seek payment for the work done and expenses advanced before the termination. Whether the lawyer will be entitled to receive any payment for the work done before the termination, and the amount of any payment, will depend on the benefit to the client of the services performed by the lawyer as well as the timing and circumstances of the termination. Such payment shall not exceed the lesser of (i) the fair value of the legal services rendered by the lawyer, or (ii) the contingent fee to which the lawyer would have been entitled upon the occurrence of the contingency. This paragraph does not give the lawyer any rights to payment beyond those conferred by existing law.

(7) [USE IF LAWYER IS SUCCESSOR COUNSEL] Payment of any fees owed to former counsel. The client should initial next to the option selected.

(i) The lawyer is responsible for payment of former counsel's reasonable attorney's fees and expenses and the cost of resolving any dispute between the client and prior counsel over fees or expenses; or

(ii) The client is responsible for payment of former counsel's reasonable attorney's fees and expenses and the cost of resolving any dispute between the client and prior counsel over fees or expenses.

This agreement and its performance are subject to Rule 1.5 of the Rules of Professional Conduct adopted by the Massachusetts Supreme Judicial Court.

WE EACH HAVE READ THE ABOVE AGREEMENT BEFORE SIGNING IT.

Witnesses to signatures	Signatures of client and lawyer
(To client) _____	_____
	(Signature of client)
(To lawyer) _____	_____
	(Signature of lawyer)

Adopted June 9, 1997, effective January 1, 1998. Amended November 2, 2000, effective January 2, 2001. Amended December 22, 2010, effective March 15, 2011. Amended October 24, 2012, effective January 1, 2013. Comment amended March 26, 2015, effective July 1, 2015. *Comment* amended March 10, 2016, effective May 1, 2016. Amended June 7, 2018, effective September 1, 2018.

Comment

Basis or Rate of Fee

[1] When the lawyer has regularly represented a client, they ordinarily will have evolved an understanding concerning the basis or rate of the fee and the expenses for which the client will be responsible. In a new client-lawyer relationship, however, an understanding as to fees and expenses must be promptly established. It is not necessary to recite all the factors that underlie the basis of the fee, but only those that are directly involved in its computation. It is sufficient, for example, to state that the basic rate is an hourly charge or a fixed amount or an estimated amount, or to identify the factors that may be taken into account in finally fixing the fee. When developments occur during the representation that render an earlier estimate substantially inaccurate, a revised estimate should be provided to the client. A written statement concerning the fee reduces the possibility of misunderstanding.

[1A] Rule 1.5(a) departs from Model Rule 1.5(a) by retaining the standard of former DR 2–106(A) that a fee must be illegal or clearly excessive to constitute a violation of paragraph (a) of the rule. However, it does not affect the substantive law that fees must be reasonable to be enforceable against the client.

[1B] Paragraph (a) also requires that expenses for which the client will be charged must be reasonable. As such, the standard differs from that for fees, as described in Comment 1 A. A lawyer may seek reimbursement for the cost of services performed in-house, such as telephone charges, either by charging a reasonable amount to which the client has agreed in advance or by charging an amount that reasonably reflects the cost incurred by the lawyer.

[2] A written statement concerning the fee reduces the possibility of misunderstanding. Furnishing the client with a simple memorandum or a copy of the lawyer's customary fee schedule is sufficient if the scope of the representation and the basis or rate of the fee is set forth. Ordinarily, the lawyer should send the written fee statement to the client before any substantial services are rendered. Where the client retains a lawyer for a single-session consultation or where the total fee to the client is reasonably expected to be less than $500, a writing is not required, although the scope of the representation and the basis or rate of the fee and expenses for which the client will be responsible shall be communicated to the client.

[3] Contingent fees, like any other fees, are subject to the not-clearly-excessive standard of paragraph (a) of this rule. In determining whether a particular contingent fee is clearly excessive, or whether it is reasonable to charge any form of contingent fee, a lawyer must consider the factors that are relevant under the circumstances. Applicable law may impose limitations on contingent fees, such as a ceiling on the percentage allowable, or may require a lawyer to offer clients an alternative basis for the fee. Applicable law also may apply to situations other than a contingent fee, for example, government regulations regarding fees in certain matters. When there is doubt whether a contingent fee is consistent with the client's best interest, the lawyer should inform the client of alternative bases for the fee and explain their implications.

[3A] A lawyer must inform the client at the time representation is undertaken if there is a possibility that a legal fee or other payments will be owed under other circumstances. A lawyer may pursue a quantum meruit recovery or payment for expenses advanced only if the contingent fee agreement so provides.

[3B] The "fair value" of the legal services rendered by the attorney before the occurrence of a contingency in a contingent fee case is an equitable determination designed to prevent a client from being unjustly enriched if no fee is paid to the attorney. Because a contingent fee case does not require any certain amount of labor or hours worked to achieve its desired goal, a lodestar method of fee calculation is of limited use in assessing a quantum meruit fee. A quantum meruit award should take into account the benefit actually conferred on the client. Other factors relevant to determining "fair value" in any particular situation may include those set forth in Rule 1.5(a), as well as the circumstances of the discharge or withdrawal, the amount of legal work required to bring the case to conclusion after the discharge or withdrawal, and the contingent fee to which the lawyer would have been entitled upon the occurrence of the contingency. Unless otherwise agreed in writing, the lawyer will ordinarily not be entitled to receive a fee unless the contingency has occurred. Nothing in this Rule is intended to create a presumption that a lawyer is entitled to a quantum meruit award when the representation is terminated before the contingency occurs.

[3C] When the attorney-client relationship in a contingent fee case terminates before completion, and the lawyer makes a claim for fees or expenses, the lawyer is required to state in writing the fee claimed and to enumerate the expenses incurred, providing supporting justification if requested. In circumstances where the lawyer is unable to identify the precise amount of the fee claimed because the matter has not been resolved, the lawyer is required to identify the amount of work performed and the basis employed for calculating the fee due. This statement of claim will help the client and any successor attorney to assess the financial consequences of a change in representation.

[3D] A lawyer who does not intend to make a claim for fees in the event the representation is terminated before the occurrence of the contingency entitling the lawyer to a fee under the terms of a contingent fee agreement would not be required to use paragraph (6) of the model forms of contingent fee agreement specified in Rule 1.5(f)(1) and (2). However, if a lawyer expects to make a claim for fees if the representation is terminated before the occurrence of the contingency, the lawyer must advise the client of his or her intention to retain the option to make a claim by including the substance of paragraph (6) of the model form of contingent fee agreement in the engagement agreement and would be expected to be able to provide records of work performed sufficient to support such a claim.

Terms of Payment

[4] A lawyer may require advance payment of a fee, but is obliged to return any unearned portion. See Rule 1.16(d). A lawyer may accept property in payment for services, such as an ownership interest in an enterprise, providing this does not involve acquisition of a proprietary interest in the cause of action or subject matter of the litigation contrary to Rule 1.8(i). However, a fee paid in property instead of money may be subject to the requirements of Rule 1.8(a) because such fees often have the essential qualities of a business transaction with the client.

[5] An agreement may not be made whose terms might induce the lawyer improperly to curtail services for the client or perform them in a way contrary to the client's interest. For example, a lawyer should not enter into an agreement whereby services are to be provided only up to a stated amount when it is foreseeable that more extensive services probably will be required, unless the situation is adequately explained to the client. Otherwise, the client might have to bargain for further assistance in the midst of a proceeding or transaction. However, it is proper to define the extent of services in light of the client's ability to pay. A lawyer should not exploit a fee arrangement based primarily on hourly charges by using wasteful procedures.

Prohibited Contingent Fees

[6] Paragraph (d) prohibits a lawyer from charging a contingent fee in a domestic relations matter when payment is contingent upon the securing of a divorce or upon the amount of alimony or support or property settlement to be obtained. This provision does not preclude a contract for a contingent fee for legal representation in connection with the recovery of post-judgment balances due under support, alimony or other financial orders because such contracts do not implicate the same policy concerns.

Division of Fee

[7] A division of fee is a single billing to a client covering the fee of two or more lawyers who are not in the same firm. A division of fee facilitates association of more than one lawyer in a matter in which neither alone could serve the client as well, and most often is used when the fee is contingent and the division is between a referring lawyer and a trial specialist. Paragraph (e) permits the lawyers to divide a fee if the client has been informed that a division of fees will be made and consents in writing. A lawyer should only refer a matter to a lawyer whom the referring lawyer reasonably believes is competent to handle the matter. See Rule 1.1.

[7A] Unlike ABA Model Rule 1.5(e), Paragraph (e) does not require that the division of fees be in proportion to the services performed by each lawyer or require the lawyer to assume joint responsibility for the representation in order to be entitled to a share of the fee. The Massachusetts rule does not require disclosure of the fee division that the lawyers have agreed to, but if the client requests information on the division of fees, the lawyer is required to disclose the share of each lawyer.

[8] Paragraph (e) does not prohibit or regulate division of fees to be received in the future for work done when lawyers were previously associated in a law firm.

Disputes over Fees

[9] In the event of a fee dispute not otherwise subject to arbitration, the lawyer should conscientiously consider submitting to mediation or an established fee arbitration service. If such procedure is required by law or agreement, the lawyer shall comply with such requirement. Law may prescribe a procedure for determining a lawyer's fee, for example, in representation of an executor or administrator, a class or a person entitled to a reasonable fee as part of the measure of damages. The lawyer entitled to such a fee and a lawyer representing another party concerned with the fee should comply with the prescribed procedure. For purposes of paragraph 1.5(f)(3), a provision requiring that fee disputes be resolved by arbitration is a provision that differs materially from the forms of contingent fee agreement set forth in this rule and is subject to the prerequisite that the lawyer explain the provision and obtain the client's consent, confirmed in writing.

Form of Fee Agreement

[10] Paragraph (f) provides model forms of contingent fee agreements and identifies explanations that a lawyer must provide to a client, except where the client is an organization, including a non-profit or governmental entity.

[11] Paragraphs (f)(1) and (f)(2) provide two forms of contingent fee agreement that may be used. Because paragraphs (3) and (7) of Form A do not contain alternative provisions, a lawyer who uses Form A does not need to provide any special explanation to the client. Paragraphs (2), (3), and (7) of Form B differ from Form A. While in most contingency cases, the contingency upon which compensation will be paid is recovery of damages, paragraph (2) of Form B permits lawyers and clients to agree to other lawful contingencies. A lawyer is not required to provide any special explanation when using paragraph (2). Paragraphs (3) and (7) of Form B allow options for the payment of costs and expenses and the payment of reasonable attorney's fees and expenses to former counsel. To ensure that a client gives informed consent to the agreed-upon option, a lawyer who uses Form B must retain in the form both options contained in paragraphs (3) and, where

applicable, paragraph (7); show and explain these options to the client; and obtain the client's informed consent confirmed in writing to the selected option.

[12] Paragraph (f)(3) permits the lawyer and client to agree to modifications to Forms A and B, including modifications which are more favorable to the lawyer, to the extent permitted by this rule. However, a lawyer using a modified form of fee agreement must explain to the client any provisions that materially differ from or add to those contained in Forms A and B, and obtain the client's informed written consent. For purposes of this rule, an agreement that does not contain option (i) in paragraph (3) and, where applicable, option (i) in paragraph (7) of Form B is materially different, and a lawyer must explain those different or added provisions to the client, and obtain the client's informed written consent.

[13] When attorney's fees are awarded by a court or included in a settlement, a question arises as to the proper method of calculating a contingent fee. Rule 1.5(c)(5) and paragraph (4) of the form agreements contained in Rule 1.5(f) state the default rule, but the parties may agree on a different basis for such calculation, such as applying the percentage to the total recovery, including attorney's fees.

Rule 1.6. Confidentiality of Information

(a) A lawyer shall not reveal confidential information relating to the representation of a client unless the client gives informed consent, the disclosure is impliedly authorized in order to carry out the representation or the disclosure is permitted by paragraph (b).

(b) A lawyer may reveal confidential information relating to the representation of a client to the extent the lawyer reasonably believes necessary, and to the extent required by Rules 3.3, 4.1(b), 8.1 or 8.3 must reveal, such information:

(1) to prevent reasonably certain death or substantial bodily harm, or to prevent the wrongful execution or incarceration of another;

(2) to prevent the commission of a criminal or fraudulent act that the lawyer reasonably believes is likely to result in substantial injury to property, financial, or other significant interests of another;

(3) to prevent, mitigate or rectify substantial injury to property, financial, or other significant interests of another that is reasonably certain to result or has resulted from the client's commission of a crime or fraud in furtherance of which the client has used the lawyer's services;

(4) to secure legal advice about the lawyer's compliance with these Rules;

(5) to establish a claim or defense on behalf of the lawyer in a controversy between the lawyer and the client, to establish a defense to a criminal charge or civil claim against the lawyer based upon conduct in which the client was involved, or to respond to allegations in any proceeding concerning the lawyer's representation of the client;

(6) to the extent permitted or required under these Rules or to comply with other law or a court order; or

(7) to detect and resolve conflicts of interest arising from the lawyer's potential change of employment or from changes in the composition or ownership of a firm, but only if the revealed information would not compromise the attorney-client privilege or otherwise prejudice the client.

(c) A lawyer shall make reasonable efforts to prevent the inadvertent or unauthorized disclosure of, or unauthorized access to, confidential information relating to the representation of a client.

(d) A lawyer participating in a lawyer assistance program, as hereinafter defined, shall treat the person so assisted as a client for the purposes of this Rule. Lawyer assistance means assistance provided to a lawyer, judge, other legal professional, or law student by a lawyer participating in an organized nonprofit effort to provide assistance in the form of (a) counseling as to practice matters (which shall not include counseling a law student in a law school clinical program) or (b) education as to personal health matters, such as the treatment and rehabilitation from a mental, emotional, or psychological disorder, alcoholism, substance abuse, or other addiction, or both. A lawyer named in an order of the Supreme Judicial Court or the Board of Bar Overseers concerning the monitoring or terms of probation of another attorney shall treat that other attorney as a client for the purposes of this Rule. Any lawyer participating in a lawyer assistance program may require a person acting under the lawyer's supervision or control to sign a nondisclosure form approved by the Supreme Judicial Court. Nothing in this paragraph (d) shall require a bar association-sponsored ethics advisory committee, the Office of Bar Counsel, or any other governmental agency advising on questions of professional responsibility to treat persons so assisted as clients for the purpose of this Rule.

Adopted June 9, 1997, effective January 1, 1998. Amended December 30, 1997, effective March 1, 1998. Amended March 26, 2015, effective July 1, 2015. Amended March 10, 2016, effective May 1, 2016.

Comment

[1] This Rule governs the disclosure by a lawyer of confidential information relating to the representation of a client during the lawyer's representation of the client. See Rule 1.18 for the lawyer's duties with respect to confidential information provided to the lawyer by a prospective client, Rule 1.9(c)(2) for the lawyer's duty not to reveal confidential information relating to the lawyer's prior representation of a former client and Rules 1.8(b) and 1.9(c)(1) for the lawyer's duties with respect to the use of such information to the disadvantage of clients and former clients.

[2] A fundamental principle in the client-lawyer relationship is that, in the absence of the client's informed consent or as otherwise permitted by these Rules, the lawyer must not reveal confidential information relating to the representation. See Rule 1.0(f) for the definition of informed consent. This contributes to the trust that is the hallmark of the client-lawyer relationship. The client is thereby encouraged to seek legal assistance and to communicate fully and frankly with the lawyer even as to embarrassing or legally damaging subject matter. The lawyer needs this information to represent the client effectively and, if necessary, to advise the client to refrain from wrongful conduct.

[3] The principle of client-lawyer confidentiality established by this Rule is broader than the attorney-client privilege and the work-product doctrine. The attorney-client privilege and work-product doctrine apply in judicial and other proceedings in which a lawyer may be called as a witness or otherwise required to produce evidence concerning a client. The rule of client-lawyer confidentiality also applies in situations other than those where evidence is sought from the lawyer through compulsion of law.

[3A] "Confidential information" consists of information gained during or relating to the representation of a client, whatever its source, that is (a) protected by the attorney-client privilege, (b) likely to be embarrassing or detrimental to the client if disclosed, or (c) information that the lawyer has agreed to keep confidential. "Confidential information" does not ordinarily include (i) a lawyer's legal knowledge

or legal research or (ii) information that is generally known in the local community or in the trade, field or profession to which the information relates. A lawyer may not disclose confidential information except as authorized or required by the Rules of Professional Conduct or other law. See also Scope. Information that is "generally known in the local community or in the trade, field or profession to which the information relates" includes information that is widely known. Information about a client contained in a public record that has received widespread publicity would fall within this category. On the other hand, a client's disclosure of conviction of a crime in a different state a long time ago or disclosure of a secret marriage would be protected even if a matter of public record because such information was not "generally known in the local community." As another example, a client's disclosure of the fact of infidelity to a spouse is protected information, although it normally would not be after the client publicly discloses such information on television and in newspaper interviews. The accumulation of legal knowledge that a lawyer gains through practice ordinarily is not client information protected by this Rule. In addition, the factual information acquired about the structure and operation of an entire industry during the representation of one entity within the industry would not ordinarily prevent an attorney from undertaking a successive representation of another entity in a matter when the attorney had no other relevant confidential information from the earlier representation and there was no other conflict of interest at issue.

[3B] All these examples explain the addition of the word "confidential" before the word "information" in Rule 1.6(a) as compared to the comparable ABA Model Rule. It also explains the elimination of the words "or is generally known" in Rule 1.9(c)(1) as compared to the comparable ABA Model Rule. The elimination of such information from the concept of protected information in Rule 1.9(c)(1) has been achieved more generally throughout the Rules by the addition of the word "confidential" in this Rule.

[4] Paragraph (a) prohibits a lawyer from revealing confidential information relating to the representation of a client. This prohibition also applies to disclosures by a lawyer that do not in themselves reveal protected information but could reasonably lead to the discovery of such information by a third person. A lawyer's use of a hypothetical to discuss issues relating to the representation is permissible so long as there is no reasonable likelihood that the listener will be able to ascertain the identity of the client or the situation involved.

Authorized Disclosure

[5] Except to the extent that the client's instructions or special circumstances limit that authority, a lawyer is impliedly authorized to make disclosures about a client when appropriate in carrying out the representation. In some situations, for example, a lawyer may be impliedly authorized to admit a fact that cannot properly be disputed or to make a disclosure that facilitates a satisfactory conclusion to a matter. Lawyers in a firm may, in the course of the firm's practice, disclose to each other confidential information relating to a client of the firm, unless the client has instructed that particular confidential information be confined to specified lawyers. Before accepting or continuing representation on such a basis, the lawyers to whom such restricted confidential information will be communicated must assure themselves that the restriction will not contravene firm governance rules or prevent them from discovering disqualifying conflicts of interests.

Disclosure Adverse to Client

[6] Although the public interest is usually best served by a strict rule requiring lawyers to preserve the confidentiality of information relating to the representation of their clients, the confidentiality rule is subject to limited exceptions. Paragraph (b)(1) recognizes the overriding value of life and physical integrity and permits disclosure reasonably necessary to prevent reasonably certain death or substantial bodily harm. Such harm is reasonably certain to occur if it will be suffered imminently or if there is a present and substantial threat that a person will suffer such harm at a later date if the lawyer fails to take

action necessary to eliminate the threat. Thus, a lawyer who knows that a client has accidentally discharged toxic waste into a town's water supply may reveal this information to the authorities, even if the information is confidential information, if there is a present and substantial risk that a person who drinks the water will contract a life-threatening or debilitating disease and the lawyer's disclosure is necessary to eliminate the threat or reduce the number of victims.

[6A] The use of the term "substantial" harm or injury in paragraphs (b)(1), (b)(2) and (b)(3) of this Rule restricts permitted revelation by limiting the permission granted to instances when the harm or injury is likely to be more than trivial or small. The reference to bodily harm in paragraph (b)(1) is not meant to require physical injury as a prerequisite. Acts of statutory rape, for example, fall within the concept of bodily harm. Rule 1.6(b)(1) also permits a lawyer to reveal confidential information in the specific situation where such information discloses that an innocent person has been convicted of a crime and has been sentenced to imprisonment or execution. This language has been included to permit disclosure of confidential information in these circumstances where the failure to disclose may not involve the commission of a crime.

[7] Paragraph (b)(2) is a limited exception to the rule of confidentiality that permits the lawyer to reveal confidential information to the extent necessary to enable affected persons or appropriate authorities to prevent the commission of a crime or fraud that the lawyer reasonably believes is likely both to occur and to result in substantial injury to the interests or property of another. The lawyer should not ignore facts that would lead a reasonable person to conclude that disclosure is permissible. Although paragraph (b)(2) does not require the lawyer to reveal the misconduct, the lawyer may not counsel or assist the client in conduct the lawyer knows is criminal or fraudulent. See Rule 1.2(d). See also Rule 1.16 with respect to the lawyer's obligation or right to withdraw from the representation of the client in such circumstances, and Rule 1.13(c), which permits the lawyer, where the client is an organization, to reveal confidential information relating to the representation in limited circumstances.

[8] Paragraph (b)(3) addresses the situation in which the lawyer does not learn of the client's crime or fraud until after it has been consummated. Although the client no longer has the option of preventing disclosure by refraining from the wrongful conduct, there will be situations in which the loss suffered by the affected person can be prevented, rectified or mitigated. In such situations, the lawyer may disclose confidential information relating to the representation to the extent necessary to enable the affected persons to prevent or mitigate reasonably certain losses or to attempt to recoup their losses. Paragraph (b)(3) does not apply when a person who has committed a crime or fraud thereafter consults or employs a lawyer for the purpose of representation concerning that offense.

[8A] Paragraphs (b)(2) and (b)(3) each permit a lawyer to disclose client confidential information under certain circumstances to prevent or ameliorate harm caused by the commission of a crime or fraud. Disclosure is permitted only when the harm constitutes substantial injury to property, financial, or other significant interests of another. The modifier "significant" is added to emphasize that a substantial injury to an insignificant interest is not an adequate basis for disclosure. Unlike the corresponding ABA Model Rule, this rule permits disclosure to prevent or ameliorate harm to non-financial interests as well as to property or financial interests. For example, the kidnapping of a child by a non-custodial parent may result in substantial injury to the vital interest of the other parent in maintaining custody of or even contact with his or her child. A criminal trespasser might invade a significant privacy interest of another. A person by crime or fraud might deprive someone of the right to vote or some other significant right of participation in the political process. These interests are not financial interests, but are sufficiently important that lawyers should have the discretion to disclose client confidential information to prevent or ameliorate crimes and frauds that substantially injure those interests.

[9] A lawyer's confidentiality obligations do not preclude a lawyer from securing confidential legal advice about the lawyer's personal responsibility to comply with these Rules. In most situations, disclosing confidential information to secure such advice will be impliedly authorized for the lawyer to carry out the representation. Even when the disclosure is not impliedly authorized, paragraph (b)(4) permits such disclosure because of the importance of a lawyer's compliance with the Rules of Professional Conduct.

[10] Where a legal claim or disciplinary charge alleges complicity of the lawyer in a client's conduct or other misconduct of the lawyer involving representation of the client, the lawyer may respond to the extent the lawyer reasonably believes necessary to establish a defense. The same is true with respect to a claim involving the conduct or representation of a former client. Such a charge can arise in a civil, criminal, disciplinary or other proceeding and can be based on a wrong allegedly committed by the lawyer against the client or on a wrong alleged by a third person, for example, a person claiming to have been defrauded by the lawyer and client acting together. The lawyer's right to respond arises when an assertion of such complicity has been made. Paragraph (b)(5) does not require the lawyer to await the commencement of an action or proceeding that charges such complicity, so that the defense may be established by responding directly to a third party who has made such an assertion. The right to defend also applies, of course, where a proceeding has been commenced.

[11] A lawyer entitled to a fee is permitted by paragraph (b)(5) to prove the services rendered in an action to collect it. This aspect of the Rule expresses the principle that the beneficiary of a fiduciary relationship may not exploit it to the detriment of the fiduciary.

[12] Other law may require that a lawyer disclose confidential information about a client. Whether such a law supersedes Rule 1.6 is a question of law beyond the scope of these Rules. When disclosure of confidential information relating to the representation appears to be required by other law, the lawyer must discuss the matter with the client to the extent required by Rule 1.4. If, however, the other law supersedes this Rule and requires disclosure, paragraph (b)(6) permits the lawyer to make such disclosures as are necessary to comply with the law.

[13] Paragraph (b)(7) recognizes that lawyers in different firms may need to disclose limited confidential information to each other to detect and resolve conflicts of interest, such as when a lawyer is considering an association with another firm, two or more firms are considering a merger, or a lawyer is considering the purchase of a law practice. See Rule 1.17, Comment 7. Under these circumstances, lawyers and law firms are permitted to disclose limited confidential information, but only once substantive discussions regarding the new relationship have occurred. Any such disclosure should ordinarily include no more than the identity of the persons and entities involved in a matter, a brief summary of the general issues involved, the general extent of the lawyer's involvement in the matter, and information about whether the matter has terminated. Even this limited confidential information, however, should be disclosed only to the extent reasonably necessary to detect and resolve conflicts of interest that might arise from the possible new relationship. Moreover, the disclosure of any such information is prohibited if it would compromise the attorney-client privilege or otherwise prejudice the client (e.g., the fact that a corporate client is seeking advice on a corporate takeover that has not been publicly announced; that a person has consulted a lawyer about the possibility of divorce before the person's intentions are known to the person's spouse; or that a person has consulted a lawyer about a criminal investigation that has not led to a public charge). Under those circumstances, paragraph (a) prohibits disclosure unless the client or former client gives informed consent. A lawyer's fiduciary duty to the lawyer's firm may also govern a lawyer's conduct when exploring an association with another firm and is beyond the scope of these Rules.

[14] Any information received pursuant to paragraph (b)(7) may be used or further disclosed only to the extent necessary to detect and

resolve conflicts of interest. Paragraph (b)(7) does not restrict the use of information acquired by means independent of any disclosure pursuant to paragraph (b)(7). Paragraph (b)(7) also does not affect the disclosure of information within a law firm when the disclosure is otherwise authorized, see Comment 5, such as when a lawyer in a firm discloses confidential information to another lawyer in the same firm to detect and resolve conflicts of interest that could arise in connection with undertaking a new representation. See also Rule 1.16.

[15] A lawyer may be ordered to reveal confidential information relating to the representation of a client by a court or by another tribunal or governmental entity claiming authority pursuant to other law to compel the disclosure. Absent informed consent of the client to do otherwise, the lawyer should assert on behalf of the client all nonfrivolous claims that the order is not authorized by other law or that the confidential information sought is protected against disclosure by the attorney-client privilege or other applicable law. In the event of an adverse ruling, the lawyer must consult with the client about the possibility of appeal to the extent required by Rule 1.4. Unless review is sought, however, paragraph (b)(6) permits the lawyer to comply with the court's order.

[16] Paragraph (b) permits disclosure only to the extent the lawyer reasonably believes the disclosure is necessary to accomplish one of the purposes specified. Where practicable, the lawyer should first seek to persuade the client to take suitable action to obviate the need for disclosure. In any case, a disclosure adverse to the client's interest should be no greater than the lawyer reasonably believes necessary to accomplish the purpose. If the disclosure will be made in connection with a judicial proceeding, the disclosure should be made in a manner that limits access to the confidential information to the tribunal or other persons having a need to know it and appropriate protective orders or other arrangements should be sought by the lawyer to the fullest extent practicable. See also Rule 1.16, Comment 3.

[17] Paragraph (b) permits but does not require the disclosure of confidential information relating to a client's representation to accomplish the purposes specified in paragraphs (b)(1) through (b)(7). In exercising the discretion conferred by this Rule, the lawyer may consider such factors as: (1) the seriousness of the potential harm to others; (2) the degree of certainty that the harm will occur, including the attorney's assessment of the accuracy of the information; (3) the imminence of the harm; (4) the apparent absence of any other feasible way to prevent the potential harm; (5) the extent to which the client may be using or has used the lawyer's services to bring about the harm, or the lawyer's own involvement in the transaction; (6) the circumstances under which the lawyer acquired the confidential information, including if the information is protected by the attorney-client privilege; and (7) the nature of the lawyer's relationship with the client and with those who might be injured by the client. Some of these factors may also be relevant to the exercise of discretion under paragraphs (b)(4) through (b)(7). In any instance, disclosure should be no greater than the lawyer reasonably believes necessary to prevent the harm. A lawyer's decision not to disclose as permitted by paragraph (b) does not violate this Rule. Disclosure may be required, however, by other Rules. The reference to Rules 3.3, 4.1(b), 8.1 and 8.3 in the opening phrase of Rule 1.6(b) has been added to emphasize that Rule 1.6(b) is not the only provision of these Rules that deals with the disclosure of confidential information. Some Rules require disclosure only if such disclosure would be permitted by paragraph (b). See Rules 4.1(b), 8.1 and 8.3. Rule 3.3, on the other hand, requires disclosure in some circumstances regardless of whether such disclosure is permitted by this Rule. See Rule 3.3(c).

Notice of Disclosure to Client

[17A] Whenever these Rules permit or require the lawyer to disclose a client's confidential information, the issue arises whether the lawyer should, as a part of the confidentiality and loyalty obligation and as a matter of competent practice, advise the client beforehand of the plan to disclose. It is not possible to state an absolute rule to

govern a lawyer's conduct in such situations. In some cases, it may be impractical or even dangerous for the lawyer to advise the client of the intent to reveal confidential information either before or even after the fact. Indeed, such revelation might thwart the reason for creation of the exception. It might hasten the commission of a dangerous act by a client or it might enable clients to prevent lawyers from defending themselves against accusations of lawyer misconduct. But there will be instances, such as the intended delivery of whole files to prosecutors to convince them not to indict the lawyer, where the failure to give notice would prevent the client from making timely objection to the revelation of too much confidential information. Lawyers will have to weigh the various factors and make reasonable judgments about the demands of loyalty, the requirements of competent practice, and the policy reasons for creating the exception to confidentiality in order to decide whether they should give advance notice to clients of the intended disclosure.

Acting Competently to Preserve Confidentiality

[18] Paragraph (c) requires a lawyer to act competently to safeguard confidential information relating to the representation of a client against unauthorized access by third parties and against inadvertent or unauthorized disclosure by the lawyer or other persons who are participating in the representation of the client or who are subject to the lawyer's supervision. See Rules 1.1, 5.1 and 5.3. The unauthorized access to, or the inadvertent or unauthorized disclosure of, confidential information relating to the representation of a client does not constitute a violation of paragraph (c) if the lawyer has made reasonable efforts to prevent the access or disclosure. Factors to be considered in determining the reasonableness of the lawyer's efforts include, but are not limited to, the sensitivity of the information, the likelihood of disclosure if additional safeguards are not employed, the cost of employing additional safeguards, the difficulty of implementing the safeguards, and the extent to which the safeguards adversely affect the lawyer's ability to represent clients (*e.g.*, by making a device or important piece of software excessively difficult to use). A client may require the lawyer to implement special security measures not required by this Rule or may give informed consent to forgo security measures that would otherwise be required by this Rule. Whether a lawyer may be required to take additional steps to safeguard a client's information in order to comply with other law, such as state and federal laws that govern data privacy or that impose notification requirements upon the loss of, or unauthorized access to, electronic information, is beyond the scope of these Rules. For a lawyer's duties when sharing information with nonlawyers outside the lawyer's own firm, see Rule 5.3, Comments 3 and 4.

[19] When transmitting a communication that includes confidential information relating to the representation of a client, the lawyer must take reasonable precautions to prevent the confidential information from coming into the hands of unintended recipients. This duty, however, does not require that the lawyer use special security measures if the method of communication affords a reasonable expectation of privacy. Special circumstances, however, may warrant special precautions. Factors to be considered in determining the reasonableness of the lawyer's expectation of confidentiality include the sensitivity of the information and the extent to which the privacy of the communication is protected by law or by a confidentiality agreement. A client may require the lawyer to implement special security measures not required by this Rule or may give informed consent to the use of a means of communication that would otherwise be prohibited by this Rule. Whether a lawyer may be required to take additional steps in order to comply with other law, such as state and federal laws that govern data privacy, is beyond the scope of these Rules.

Former Client

[20] The duty of confidentiality continues after the client-lawyer relationship has terminated. See Rule 1.9(c)(2). See Rule 1.9(c)(1) for the prohibition against using such information to the disadvantage of the former client.

Rule 1.7. Conflict of Interest: Current Clients

(a) Except as provided in paragraph (b), a lawyer shall not represent a client if the representation involves a concurrent conflict of interest. A concurrent conflict of interest exists if:

(1) the representation of one client will be directly adverse to another client; or

(2) there is a significant risk that the representation of one or more clients will be materially limited by the lawyer's responsibilities to another client, a former client or a third person or by a personal interest of the lawyer.

(b) Notwithstanding the existence of a concurrent conflict of interest under paragraph (a), a lawyer may represent a client if:

(1) the lawyer reasonably believes that the lawyer will be able to provide competent and diligent representation to each affected client;

(2) the representation is not prohibited by law;

(3) the representation does not involve the assertion of a claim by one client against another client represented by the lawyer in the same litigation or other proceeding before a tribunal; and

(4) each affected client gives informed consent, confirmed in writing.

Adopted June 9, 1997, effective January 1, 1998. Amended March 26, 2015, effective July 1, 2015.

Comment

General Principles

[1] Loyalty and independent judgment are essential elements in the lawyer's relationship to a client. Concurrent conflicts of interest can arise from the lawyer's responsibilities to another client, a former client or a third person or from the lawyer's own interests. For specific Rules regarding certain concurrent conflicts of interest, see Rule 1.8. For former client conflicts of interest, see Rule 1.9. For the lawyer's duties with respect to information provided to the lawyer by a prospective client, see Rule 1.18. For definitions of "informed consent" and "confirmed in writing," see Rule 1.0(f) and (c).

[2] Resolution of a conflict of interest problem under this Rule requires the lawyer to (1) clearly identify the client or clients; (2) determine whether a conflict of interest exists; (3) decide whether the representation may be undertaken despite the existence of a conflict, i.e., whether the conflict is consentable; and (4) if so, consult with the clients affected under paragraph (a) and obtain their informed consent, confirmed in writing. The clients affected under paragraph (a) include both of the clients referred to in paragraph (a)(1) and the one or more clients whose representation might be materially limited under paragraph (a)(2).

[3] A conflict of interest may exist before representation is undertaken, in which event the representation must be declined, unless the lawyer obtains the informed consent of each client under the conditions of paragraph (b). To determine whether a conflict of interest exists, a lawyer should adopt reasonable procedures, appropriate for the size and type of firm and practice, to determine in both litigation and non-litigation matters the persons and issues involved. See also Comment to Rule 5.1. Ignorance caused by a failure to institute such procedures will not excuse a lawyer's violation of this Rule. As to whether a client-lawyer relationship exists or, having once been established, is continuing, see Comment to Rule 1.3 and Scope.

[4] If a conflict arises after representation has been undertaken, the lawyer ordinarily must withdraw from the representation, unless the lawyer has obtained the informed consent of the client under the conditions of paragraph (b). See Rule 1.16. Where more than one client is involved, whether the lawyer may continue to represent any of the clients is determined both by the lawyer's ability to comply with duties owed to the former client and by the lawyer's ability to represent adequately the remaining client or clients, given the lawyer's duties to the former client. See Rule 1.9. See also Comments 5 and 29.

[5] Unforeseeable developments, such as changes in corporate and other organizational affiliations or the addition or realignment of parties in litigation, might create conflicts in the midst of a representation, as when a company sued by the lawyer on behalf of one client is bought by another client represented by the lawyer in an unrelated matter. Depending on the circumstances, the lawyer may have the option to withdraw from one of the representations in order to avoid the conflict. The lawyer must seek court approval where necessary and take steps to minimize harm to the clients. See Rule 1.16. The lawyer must continue to protect the confidences of the client from whose representation the lawyer has withdrawn. See Rule 1.9(c).

Identifying Conflicts of Interest: Directly Adverse

[6] Loyalty to a current client prohibits undertaking representation directly adverse to that client without that client's informed consent. Paragraph (a) expresses that general rule. Thus, absent consent, a lawyer ordinarily may not act as an advocate in one matter against a person the lawyer represents in some other matter, even when the matters are wholly unrelated. The client as to whom the representation is directly adverse is likely to feel betrayed, and the resulting damage to the client-lawyer relationship is likely to impair the lawyer's ability to represent the client effectively. In addition, the client on whose behalf the adverse representation is undertaken reasonably may fear that the lawyer will pursue that client's case less effectively out of deference to the other client, i.e., that the representation may be materially limited by the lawyer's interest in retaining the current client. Similarly, a directly adverse conflict may arise when a lawyer is required to cross-examine a client who appears as a witness in a lawsuit involving another client, as when the testimony will be damaging to the client who is represented in the lawsuit. On the other hand, simultaneous representation in unrelated matters of clients whose interests are only economically adverse, such as representation of competing economic enterprises in unrelated litigation, does not ordinarily constitute a conflict of interest and thus may not require consent of the respective clients.

[7] Directly adverse conflicts can also arise in transactional matters. For example, if a lawyer is asked to represent the seller of a business in negotiations with a buyer represented by the lawyer, not in the same transaction but in another, unrelated matter, the lawyer could not undertake the representation without the informed consent of each client.

Identifying Conflicts of Interest: Material Limitation

[8] Even where there is no direct adverseness, a conflict of interest exists if there is a significant risk that a lawyer's ability to consider, recommend or carry out an appropriate course of action for the client will be materially limited as a result of the lawyer's other responsibilities or interests. For example, a lawyer asked to represent several individuals seeking to form a joint venture is likely to be materially limited in the lawyer's ability to recommend or advocate all possible positions that each might take because of the lawyer's duty of loyalty to the others. The conflict in effect forecloses alternatives that would otherwise be available to the client. The mere possibility of subsequent harm does not itself require disclosure and consent. The critical questions are the likelihood that a difference in interests will eventuate and, if it does, whether it will materially interfere with the lawyer's independent professional judgment in considering alternatives or foreclose courses of action that reasonably should be pursued on behalf of the client.

Lawyer's Responsibilities to Former Clients and Other Third Persons

[9] In addition to conflicts with other current clients, a lawyer's duties of loyalty and independence may be materially limited by responsibilities to former clients under Rule 1.9 or by the lawyer's responsibilities to other persons, such as fiduciary duties arising from a lawyer's service as a trustee, executor or corporate director.

Personal Interest Conflicts

[10] The lawyer's own interests should not be permitted to have an adverse effect on representation of a client. For example, if the probity of a lawyer's own conduct in a transaction is in serious question, it may be difficult or impossible for the lawyer to give a client detached advice. Similarly, when a lawyer has discussions concerning possible employment with an opponent of the lawyer's client, or with a law firm representing the opponent, such discussions could materially limit the lawyer's representation of the client. In addition, a lawyer may not allow related business interests to affect representation, for example, by referring clients to an enterprise in which the lawyer has an undisclosed financial interest. See Rule 1.8 for specific Rules pertaining to a number of personal interest conflicts, including business transactions with clients. See also Rule 1.10 (personal interest conflicts under Rule 1.7 ordinarily are not imputed to other lawyers in a law firm).

[11] When lawyers representing different clients in the same matter or in substantially related matters are closely related by blood or marriage, there may be a significant risk that client confidences will be revealed and that the lawyer's family relationship will interfere with both loyalty and independent professional judgment. As a result, each client is entitled to know of the existence and implications of the relationship between the lawyers before the lawyer agrees to undertake the representation. Thus, a lawyer related to another lawyer, e.g., as parent, child, sibling or spouse, ordinarily may not represent a client in a matter where that lawyer is representing another party, unless each client gives informed consent. The disqualification arising from a close family relationship is personal and ordinarily is not imputed to members of firms with whom the lawyers are associated. See Rule 1.10.

[12] The relationship between lawyer and client is a fiduciary one in which the lawyer occupies the highest position of trust and confidence. Because of this fiduciary duty to clients, combining a professional relationship with any intimate personal relationship raises concerns about conflict of interest, impairment of the judgment of both lawyer and client, and preservation of attorney-client privilege. These concerns are particularly acute when a lawyer has a sexual relationship with a client.

Interest of Person Paying for a Lawyer's Service

[13] A lawyer may be paid from a source other than the client, including a co-client, if the client is informed of that fact and consents and the arrangement does not compromise the lawyer's duty of loyalty or independent judgment to the client. See Rule 1.8(f). If acceptance of the payment from any other source presents a significant risk that the lawyer's representation of the client will be materially limited by the lawyer's own interest in accommodating the person paying the lawyer's fee or by the lawyer's responsibilities to a payer who is also a co-client, then the lawyer must comply with the requirements of paragraph (b) before accepting the representation, including determining whether the conflict is consentable and, if so, that the client has adequate information about the material risks of the representation.

Prohibited Representations

[14] Ordinarily, clients may consent to representation notwithstanding a conflict. However, as indicated in paragraph (b), some conflicts are nonconsentable, meaning that the lawyer involved cannot properly ask for such agreement or provide representation on the basis of the client's consent. When the lawyer is representing more than one client, the question of consentability must be resolved as to each client.

[15] Consentability is typically determined by considering whether the interests of the clients will be adequately protected if the clients are permitted to give their informed consent to representation bur-

dened by a conflict of interest. Thus, under paragraph (b)(1), representation is prohibited if in the circumstances the lawyer cannot reasonably conclude that the lawyer will be able to provide competent and diligent representation. See Rule 1.1 (competence) and Rule 1.3 (diligence).

[16] Paragraph (b)(2) describes conflicts that are nonconsentable because the representation is prohibited by applicable law. For example, under federal criminal statutes certain representations by a former government lawyer are prohibited, despite the informed consent of the former client. In addition, Chapter 268A of the General Laws may limit the ability of a lawyer to represent both a state, county or municipal government or governmental agency and a private party having a matter that is either pending before that government or agency or in which the government or agency has an interest, even when the interests of the government or agency and the private party appear to be similar.

[17] Paragraph (b)(3) describes conflicts that are nonconsentable because of the institutional interest in vigorous development of each client's position when the clients are aligned directly against each other in the same litigation or other proceeding before a tribunal. Whether clients are aligned directly against each other within the meaning of this paragraph requires examination of the context of the proceeding. Although this paragraph does not preclude a lawyer's multiple representation of adverse parties to a mediation (because mediation is not a proceeding before a "tribunal" under Rule 1.0(p)), such representation may be precluded by paragraph (b)(1).

Informed Consent

[18] Informed consent requires that each affected client be aware of the relevant circumstances and of the material and reasonably foreseeable ways that the conflict could have adverse effects on the interests of that client. See Rule 1.0(f) (informed consent). The information required depends on the nature of the conflict and the nature of the risks involved. When representation of multiple clients in a single matter is undertaken, the information must include the implications of the common representation, including possible effects on loyalty, confidentiality and the attorney-client privilege and the advantages and risks involved. See Comments 30 and 31 (effect of common representation on confidentiality).

[19] Under some circumstances it may be impossible to make the disclosure necessary to obtain consent. For example, when the lawyer represents different clients in related matters and one of the clients refuses to consent to the disclosure necessary to permit the other client to make an informed decision, the lawyer cannot properly ask the latter to consent. In some cases the alternative to common representation can be that each party may have to obtain separate representation with the possibility of incurring additional costs. These costs, along with the benefits of securing separate representation, are factors that may be considered by the affected client in determining whether common representation is in the client's interests.

Consent Confirmed in Writing

[20] Paragraph (b) requires the lawyer to obtain the informed consent of the client, confirmed in writing. Such a writing may consist of a document executed by the client or one that the lawyer promptly records and transmits to the client following an oral consent. See Rule 1.0(c). See also Rule 1.0(q) (writing includes electronic transmission). If it is not feasible to obtain or transmit the writing at the time the client gives informed consent, then the lawyer must obtain or transmit it within a reasonable time thereafter. See Rule 1.0(c). The requirement of a writing does not supplant the need for the lawyer to talk with the client, to explain the risks and advantages, if any, of representation burdened with a conflict of interest, as well as reasonably available alternatives, and to afford the client a reasonable opportunity to consider the risks and alternatives and to raise questions and concerns. Rather, the writing is required in order to impress upon clients the seriousness of the decision the client is being

asked to make and to avoid disputes or ambiguities that might later occur in the absence of a writing.

Revoking Consent

[21] A client who has given consent to a conflict may revoke the consent and, like any other client, may terminate the lawyer's representation at any time. Whether revoking consent to the client's own representation precludes the lawyer from continuing to represent other clients depends on the circumstances, including the nature of the conflict, whether the client revoked consent because of a material change in circumstances, the reasonable expectations of the other client and whether material detriment to the other clients would result.

Consent to Future Conflict

[22] Whether a lawyer may properly request a client to waive conflicts that might arise in the future is subject to the test of paragraph (b). The effectiveness of such waivers is generally determined by the extent to which the client reasonably understands the material risks that the waiver entails. The more comprehensive the explanation of the types of future representations that might arise and the actual and reasonably foreseeable adverse consequences of those representations, the greater the likelihood that the client will have the requisite understanding. Thus, if the client agrees to consent to a particular type of conflict with which the client is already familiar, then the consent ordinarily will be effective with regard to that type of conflict. If the consent is general and open-ended, then the consent ordinarily will be ineffective, because it is not reasonably likely that the client will have understood the material risks involved. On the other hand, if the client is an experienced user of the legal services involved and is reasonably informed regarding the risk that a conflict may arise, such consent is more likely to be effective, particularly if, *e.g.*, the client is independently represented by other counsel in giving consent and the consent is limited to future conflicts unrelated to the subject of the representation. In any case, advance consent cannot be effective if the circumstances that materialize in the future are such as would make the conflict nonconsentable under paragraph (b).

Conflicts in Litigation

[23] Paragraph (b)(3) prohibits representation of opposing parties in litigation, regardless of the clients' consent. On the other hand, simultaneous representation of parties whose interests in litigation may conflict, such as coplaintiffs or codefendants, is governed by paragraph (a)(2). A conflict may exist by reason of substantial discrepancy in the parties' testimony, incompatibility in positions in relation to an opposing party or the fact that there are substantially different possibilities of settlement of the claims or liabilities in question. Such conflicts can arise in criminal cases as well as civil. The potential for conflict of interest in representing multiple defendants in a criminal case is so grave that ordinarily a lawyer should decline to represent more than one codefendant, or more than one person under investigation by law enforcement authorities for the same transaction or series of transactions, including any grand jury proceeding. On the other hand, common representation of persons having similar interests in civil litigation is proper if the requirements of paragraph (b) are met.

[24] Ordinarily a lawyer may take inconsistent legal positions in different tribunals at different times on behalf of different clients. The mere fact that advocating a legal position on behalf of one client might create precedent adverse to the interests of a client represented by the lawyer in an unrelated matter does not create a conflict of interest. A conflict of interest exists, however, if there is a significant risk that a lawyer's action on behalf of one client will materially limit the lawyer's effectiveness in representing another client in a different case; for example, when a decision favoring one client will create a precedent likely to seriously weaken the position taken on behalf of the other client. Factors relevant in determining whether the clients need to be advised of the risk include: where the cases are pending, whether the issue is substantive or procedural, the temporal relation-

ship between the matters, the significance of the issue to the immediate and long-term interests of the clients involved and the clients' reasonable expectations in retaining the lawyer. If there is significant risk of material limitation, then absent informed consent of the affected clients, the lawyer must refuse one of the representations or withdraw from one or both matters.

[25] When a lawyer represents or seeks to represent a class of plaintiffs or defendants in a class-action lawsuit, unnamed members of the class are ordinarily not considered to be clients of the lawyer for purposes of applying paragraph (a)(1) of this Rule. Thus, the lawyer does not typically need to get the consent of such a person before representing a client suing the person in an unrelated matter. Similarly, a lawyer seeking to represent an opponent in a class action does not typically need the consent of an unnamed member of the class whom the lawyer represents in an unrelated matter.

Nonlitigation Conflicts

[26] Conflicts of interest under paragraphs (a)(1) and (a)(2) arise in contexts other than litigation. For a discussion of directly adverse conflicts in transactional matters, see Comment 7. Relevant factors in determining whether there is significant potential for material limitation include the duration and intimacy of the lawyer's relationship with the client or clients involved, the functions being performed by the lawyer, the likelihood that disagreements will arise and the likely prejudice to the client from the conflict. The question is often one of proximity and degree. See Comment 8.

[27] Conflict questions may also arise in estate planning and estate administration. A lawyer may be called upon to prepare wills for several family members, such as husband and wife, and, depending upon the circumstances, a conflict of interest may arise. In estate administration the lawyer should make clear his or her relationship to the parties involved.

[28] Whether a conflict is consentable depends on the circumstances. For example, a lawyer may not represent multiple parties to a negotiation whose interests are fundamentally antagonistic to each other, but common representation is permissible where the clients are generally aligned in interest even though there is some difference in interest among them. Thus, a lawyer may seek to establish or adjust a relationship between clients on an amicable and mutually advantageous basis; for example, in helping to organize a business in which two or more clients are entrepreneurs, working out the financial reorganization of an enterprise in which two or more clients have an interest or arranging a property distribution in settlement of an estate. The lawyer seeks to resolve potentially adverse interests by developing the parties' mutual interests. Otherwise, each party might have to obtain separate representation, with the possibility of incurring additional cost, complication or even litigation. Given these and other relevant factors, the clients may prefer that the lawyer act for all of them.

Special Considerations in Common Representation

[29] In considering whether to represent multiple clients in the same matter, a lawyer should be mindful that if the common representation fails because the potentially adverse interests cannot be reconciled, the result can be additional cost, embarrassment and recrimination. Ordinarily, the lawyer will be forced to withdraw from representing all of the clients if the common representation fails. In some situations, the risk of failure is so great that multiple representation is plainly impossible. For example, a lawyer cannot undertake common representation of clients where contentious litigation or negotiations between them are imminent or contemplated. Moreover, because the lawyer is required to be impartial between commonly represented clients, representation of multiple clients is improper when it is unlikely that impartiality can be maintained. Generally, if the relationship between the parties has already assumed antagonism, the possibility that the clients' interests can be adequately served by common representation is not very good. Other relevant factors are whether the lawyer subsequently will represent both parties on a

continuing basis and whether the situation involves creating or terminating a relationship between the parties.

[30] A particularly important factor in determining the appropriateness of common representation is the effect on client-lawyer confidentiality and the attorney-client privilege. With regard to the attorney-client privilege, the prevailing rule is that, as between commonly represented clients, the privilege does not attach. Hence, it must be assumed that if litigation eventuates between the clients, the privilege will not protect any such communications, and the clients should be so advised.

[31] As to the duty of confidentiality, continued common representation will almost certainly be inadequate if one client asks the lawyer not to disclose to the other client confidential information relevant to the common representation. This is so because the lawyer has an equal duty of loyalty to each client, and each client has the right to be informed of anything bearing on the representation that might affect that client's interests and the right to expect that the lawyer will use that information to that client's benefit. See Rule 1.4. The lawyer should, at the outset of the common representation and as part of the process of obtaining each client's informed consent, advise each client that confidential information will be shared and that the lawyer will have to withdraw if one client decides that some matter material to the representation should be kept from the other. In limited circumstances, it may be appropriate for the lawyer to proceed with the representation when the clients have agreed, after being properly informed, that the lawyer will keep certain information confidential. For example, the lawyer may reasonably conclude that failure to disclose one client's trade secrets to another client will not adversely affect representation involving a joint venture between the clients and agree to keep that information confidential with the informed consent of both clients.

[32] When seeking to establish or adjust a relationship between clients, the lawyer should make clear that the lawyer's role is not that of partisanship normally expected in other circumstances and thus that the clients may be required to assume greater responsibility for decisions than when each client is independently represented. Any limitations on the scope of the representation made necessary as a result of the common representation should be fully explained to the clients at the outset of the representation. See Rule 1.2(c).

[33] Subject to the above limitations, each client in the joint representation has the right to loyal and diligent representation and the protection of Rule 1.9 concerning obligations to a former client. The client also has the right to discharge the lawyer as stated in Rule 1.16.

Organizational Clients

[34] A lawyer who represents a corporation or other organization does not, by virtue of that representation, necessarily represent any constituent or affiliated organization, such as a parent or subsidiary. See Rule 1.13(a). Thus, the lawyer for an organization is not barred from accepting representation adverse to an affiliate in an unrelated matter, unless the circumstances are such that the affiliate should also be considered a client of the lawyer, there is an understanding between the lawyer and the organizational client that the lawyer will avoid representation adverse to the client's affiliates, or the lawyer's obligations to either the organizational client or the new client are likely to limit materially the lawyer's representation of the other client. As to lawyers representing governmental entities, see Scope [4].

[35] A lawyer for a corporation or other organization who is also a member of its board of directors should determine whether the responsibilities of the two roles may conflict. The lawyer may be called on to advise the corporation in matters involving actions of the directors. Consideration should be given to the frequency with which such situations may arise, the potential intensity of the conflict, the effect of the lawyer's resignation from the board and the possibility of the corporation's obtaining legal advice from another lawyer in such situations. If there is material risk that the dual role will compromise the lawyer's independence of professional judgment, the lawyer should not serve as a director or should cease to act as the corporation's lawyer when conflicts of interest arise. The lawyer should advise the other members of the board that in some circumstances matters discussed at board meetings while the lawyer is present in the capacity of director might not be protected by the attorney-client privilege and that conflict of interest considerations might require the lawyer's recusal as a director or might require the lawyer and the lawyer's firm to decline representation of the corporation in a matter.

Rule 1.8. Conflict of Interest: Current Clients: Specific Rules

(a) A lawyer shall not enter into a business transaction with a client or knowingly acquire an ownership, possessory, security or other pecuniary interest adverse to a client unless:

(1) the transaction and terms on which the lawyer acquires the interest are fair and reasonable to the client and are fully disclosed and transmitted in writing in a manner that can be reasonably understood by the client;

(2) the client is advised in writing of the desirability of seeking and is given a reasonable opportunity to seek the advice of independent counsel in the transaction; and

(3) the client gives informed consent, in a writing signed by the client, to the essential terms of the transaction and the lawyer's role in the transaction, including whether the lawyer is representing the client in the transaction.

(b) A lawyer shall not use confidential information relating to representation of a client to the disadvantage of the client or for the lawyer's advantage or the advantage of a third person, unless the client gives informed consent, except as permitted or required by these Rules.

(c) A lawyer shall not, for his own personal benefit or the benefit of any person closely related to the lawyer, solicit any substantial gift from a client, including a testamentary gift, or prepare for a client an instrument giving the lawyer or a person closely related to the lawyer any substantial gift, including a testamentary gift, unless the lawyer or other recipient of the gift is closely related to the client. For purposes of this Rule, a person is "closely related" to another person if related to such other person as sibling, spouse, child, grandchild, parent, or grandparent, or as the spouse of any such person.

(d) Prior to the conclusion of representation of a client, a lawyer shall not make or negotiate an agreement giving the lawyer literary or media rights to a portrayal or account based in substantial part on information relating to the representation.

(e) A lawyer shall not provide financial assistance to a client in connection with pending or contemplated litigation, except that:

(1) a lawyer may advance court costs and expenses of litigation, the repayment of which may be contingent on the outcome of the matter; and

(2) a lawyer representing an indigent client may pay court costs and expenses of litigation on behalf of the client.

(f) A lawyer shall not accept compensation for representing a client from one other than the client unless:

(1) the client gives informed consent;

(2) there is no interference with the lawyer's independence of professional judgment or with the client-lawyer relationship; and

(3) information relating to representation of a client is protected as required by Rule 1.6.

(g) A lawyer who represents two or more clients shall not participate in making an aggregate settlement of the claims of or against the clients, or in a criminal case an aggregated agreement as to guilty or nolo contendere pleas, unless each client gives informed consent, in a writing signed by the client. The lawyer's disclosure shall include the existence and nature of all the claims or pleas involved and of the participation of each person in the settlement.

(h) A lawyer shall not:

(1) make an agreement prospectively limiting the lawyer's liability to a client for malpractice unless the client is independently represented in making the agreement; or

(2) settle a claim or potential claim for such liability with an unrepresented client or former client unless that person is advised in writing of the desirability of seeking and is given a reasonable opportunity to seek the advice of independent legal counsel in connection therewith.

(i) A lawyer shall not acquire a proprietary interest in the cause of action or subject matter of litigation the lawyer is conducting for a client, except that the lawyer may:

(1) acquire a lien authorized by law to secure the lawyer's fee or expenses; and

(2) contract with a client for a reasonable contingent fee in a civil case.

(j) Reserved.

(k) While lawyers are associated in a firm, a prohibition in the foregoing paragraphs (a) through (i) that applies to any one of them shall apply to all of them.

Adopted June 9, 1997, effective January 1, 1998. Amended March 26, 2015, effective July 1, 2015.

Comment

Business Transactions Between Client and Lawyer

[1] A lawyer's legal skill and training, together with the relationship of trust and confidence between lawyer and client, create the possibility of overreaching when the lawyer participates in a business, property or financial transaction with a client, for example, a loan or sales transaction or a lawyer investment on behalf of a client. The requirements of paragraph (a) must be met even when the transaction is not closely related to the subject matter of the representation, as when a lawyer drafting a will for a client learns that the client needs money for unrelated expenses and offers to make a loan to the client. The Rule applies to lawyers engaged in the sale of goods or services related to the practice of law, for example, the sale of title insurance or investment services to existing clients of the lawyer's legal practice. See Rule 5.7. It also applies to lawyers purchasing property from estates they represent. It does not apply to ordinary fee arrangements between client and lawyer, which are governed by Rule 1.5, although its requirements must be met when the lawyer accepts an interest in the client's business or other nonmonetary property as payment of all or part of a fee. In addition, the Rule does not apply to standard commercial transactions between the lawyer and the client for products or services that the client generally markets to others, for example, banking or brokerage services, medical services, products manufactured or distributed by the client, and utilities' services. In

such transactions, the lawyer has no advantage in dealing with the client, and the restrictions in paragraph (a) are unnecessary and impracticable.

[2] Paragraph (a)(1) requires that the transaction itself be fair to the client and that its essential terms be communicated to the client, in writing, in a manner that can be reasonably understood. Paragraph (a)(2) requires that the client also be advised, in writing, of the desirability of seeking the advice of independent legal counsel. It also requires that the client be given a reasonable opportunity to obtain such advice. Paragraph (a)(3) requires that the lawyer obtain the client's informed consent, in a writing signed by the client, both to the essential terms of the transaction and to the lawyer's role. When necessary, the lawyer should discuss both the material risks of the proposed transaction, including any risk presented by the lawyer's involvement, and the existence of reasonably available alternatives and should explain why the advice of independent legal counsel is desirable. See Rule 1.0(f) (definition of informed consent).

[3] The risk to a client is greatest when the client expects the lawyer to represent the client in the transaction itself or when the lawyer's financial interest otherwise poses a significant risk that the lawyer's representation of the client will be materially limited by the lawyer's financial interest in the transaction. Here the lawyer's role requires that the lawyer must comply, not only with the requirements of paragraph (a), but also with the requirements of Rule 1.7. Under that Rule, the lawyer must disclose the risks associated with the lawyer's dual role as both legal adviser and participant in the transaction, such as the risk that the lawyer will structure the transaction or give legal advice in a way that favors the lawyer's interests at the expense of the client. Moreover, the lawyer must obtain the client's informed consent. In some cases, the lawyer's interest may be such that Rule 1.7 will preclude the lawyer from seeking the client's consent to the transaction.

[4] If the client is independently represented in the transaction, paragraph (a)(2) of this Rule is inapplicable, and the paragraph (a)(1) requirement for full disclosure is satisfied either by a written disclosure by the lawyer involved in the transaction or by the client's independent counsel. The fact that the client was independently represented in the transaction is relevant in determining whether the agreement was fair and reasonable to the client as paragraph (a)(1) further requires.

Use of Confidential Information Related to Representation

[5] Use of confidential information relating to the representation to the disadvantage of the client or for the lawyer's advantage or the advantage of a third person violates the lawyer's duty of loyalty. Paragraph (b) prohibits such use of client confidential information unless the client gives informed consent, except as permitted or required by these Rules. See Rules 1.2(d), 1.6, 1.9(c), 3.3, 4.1(b), 8.1, and 8.3. Paragraph (b) applies when such information is used to benefit either the lawyer or a third person, such as another client or business associate of the lawyer. For example, if a lawyer learns that a client intends to purchase and develop several parcels of land, the lawyer may not use that information to purchase one of the parcels in competition with the client or to recommend that another client make such a purchase.

Gifts to Lawyers

[6] A lawyer may accept a gift from a client, if the transaction meets general standards of fairness. For example, a simple gift such as a present given at a holiday or as a token of appreciation is permitted. If a client offers the lawyer a more substantial gift, paragraph (c) does not prohibit the lawyer from accepting it, although such a gift may be voidable by the client under the doctrine of undue influence, which treats client gifts as presumptively fraudulent. In any event, due to concerns about overreaching and imposition on clients, a lawyer may not suggest that a substantial gift be made to the lawyer or for the lawyer's benefit, except where the lawyer is related to the client as set forth in paragraph (c).

[7] If effectuation of a substantial gift to a lawyer or person closely related to the lawyer requires preparing a legal instrument such as a will or conveyance, the client should have the detached advice that another lawyer can provide. The sole exception to this Rule is where the client is a person closely related to the donee.

[8] Appointments as executor of a client's estate or other potentially lucrative fiduciary position will be subject to the general conflict of interest provision in Rule 1.7. The lawyer should advise the client concerning the nature and extent of the lawyer's financial interest in the appointment, as well as the availability of alternative candidates for the position.

Literary Rights

[9] An agreement by which a lawyer acquires literary or media rights concerning the conduct of the representation creates a conflict between the interests of the client and the personal interests of the lawyer. Measures suitable in the representation of the client may detract from the publication value of an account of the representation. Paragraph (d) does not prohibit a lawyer representing a client in a transaction concerning literary property from agreeing that the lawyer's fee shall consist of a share in ownership in the property, if the arrangement conforms to Rule 1.5 and paragraphs (a) and (i).

Financial Assistance

[10] Lawyers may not subsidize lawsuits or administrative proceedings brought on behalf of their clients, including making or guaranteeing loans to their clients for living expenses, because to do so would encourage clients to pursue lawsuits that might not otherwise be brought and because such assistance gives lawyers too great a financial stake in the litigation. These dangers do not warrant a prohibition on a lawyer advancing a client court costs and litigation expenses, including the expenses of medical examination and the costs of obtaining and presenting evidence, because these advances are virtually indistinguishable from contingent fees and help ensure access to the courts. Similarly, an exception allowing lawyers representing indigent clients to pay court costs and litigation expenses regardless of whether these funds will be repaid is warranted.

Person Paying for a Lawyer's Services

[11] Lawyers are frequently asked to represent a client under circumstances in which a third person will compensate the lawyer, in whole or in part. The third person might be a relative or friend, an indemnitor (such as a liability insurance company) or a co-client (such as a corporation sued along with one or more of its employees). Because third-party payers frequently have interests that differ from those of the client, including interests in minimizing the amount spent on the representation and in learning how the representation is progressing, lawyers are prohibited from accepting or continuing such representations unless the lawyer determines that there will be no interference with the lawyer's independent professional judgment and there is informed consent from the client. See also Rule 5.4(c) (prohibiting interference with a lawyer's professional judgment by one who recommends, employs or pays the lawyer to render legal services for another).

[12] Sometimes, it will be sufficient for the lawyer to obtain the client's informed consent regarding the fact of the payment and the identity of the third-party payer. If, however, the fee arrangement creates a conflict of interest for the lawyer, then the lawyer must comply with Rule 1.7. The lawyer must also conform to the requirements of Rule 1.6 concerning confidentiality. Under Rule 1.7(a), a conflict of interest exists if there is significant risk that the lawyer's representation of the client will be materially limited by the lawyer's own interest in the fee arrangement or by the lawyer's responsibilities to the third-party payer (for example, when the third-party payer is a co-client). Under Rule 1.7(b), the lawyer may accept or continue the representation with the informed consent of each affected client, unless the conflict is nonconsentable under that paragraph. Under Rule 1.7(b), the informed consent must be confirmed in writing.

Aggregate Settlements

[13] Differences in willingness to make or accept an offer of settlement are among the risks of common representation of multiple clients by a single lawyer. Under Rule 1.7, this is one of the risks that should be discussed before undertaking the representation, as part of the process of obtaining the client's informed consent. In addition, Rule 1.2(a) protects each client's right to have the final say in deciding whether to accept or reject an offer of settlement and in deciding whether to enter a guilty or nolo contendere plea in a criminal case. The rule stated in this paragraph is a corollary of both these Rules and provides that, before any settlement offer or plea bargain is made or accepted on behalf of multiple clients, the lawyer must inform each of them about all the material terms of the settlement, including what the other clients will receive or pay if the settlement or plea offer is accepted. See also Rule 1.0(f) (definition of informed consent). Lawyers representing a class of plaintiffs or defendants may not have a full client-lawyer relationship with each member of the class; nevertheless, such lawyers must comply with applicable rules regulating notification of class members and other procedural requirements designed to ensure adequate protection of the entire class. Similar considerations may apply in derivative actions.

Limiting Liability and Settling Malpractice Claims

[14] Agreements prospectively limiting a lawyer's liability for malpractice are prohibited unless the client is independently represented in making the agreement because they are likely to undermine competent and diligent representation. Also, many clients are unable to evaluate the desirability of making such an agreement before a dispute has arisen, particularly if they are then represented by the lawyer seeking the agreement. This paragraph does not, however, prohibit a lawyer from entering into an agreement with the client to arbitrate legal malpractice claims, provided such agreements are enforceable and the client is fully informed of the scope and effect of the agreement, including compliance with Rule 1.5(f) where applicable. Nor does this paragraph limit the ability of lawyers to practice in the form of a limited-liability entity, where permitted by law, provided that each lawyer remains personally liable to the client for his or her own conduct and the firm complies with any conditions required by law, such as provisions requiring client notification or maintenance of adequate liability insurance. Nor does it prohibit an agreement in accordance with Rule 1.2 that defines the scope of the representation, although a definition of scope that makes the obligations of representation illusory will amount to an attempt to limit liability.

[15] Agreements settling a claim or a potential claim for malpractice are not prohibited by this Rule. Nevertheless, in view of the danger that a lawyer will take unfair advantage of an unrepresented client or former client, the lawyer must first advise such a person in writing of the appropriateness of independent representation in connection with such a settlement. In addition, the lawyer must give the client or former client a reasonable opportunity to find and consult independent counsel.

Acquiring Proprietary Interest in Litigation

[16] Paragraph (i) states the traditional general rule that lawyers are prohibited from acquiring a proprietary interest in litigation. Like paragraph (e), the general rule has its basis in common law champerty and maintenance and is designed to avoid giving the lawyer too great an interest in the representation. In addition, when the lawyer acquires an ownership interest in the subject of the representation, it will be more difficult for a client to discharge the lawyer if the client so desires. The Rule is subject to specific exceptions developed in decisional law and continued in these Rules. The exception for certain advances of the costs of litigation is set forth in paragraph (e). In addition, paragraph (i) sets forth exceptions for liens authorized by law to secure the lawyer's fees or expenses and contracts for reasonable contingent fees. These may include liens granted by statute, liens originating in common law and liens acquired by contract with the client. When a lawyer acquires by contract a security interest in property other than that recovered through the lawyer's efforts in the litigation, such an acquisition is a business or financial transaction with

a client and is governed by the requirements of paragraph (a). Contracts for contingent fees in civil cases are governed by Rule 1.5.

[17] Reserved

[18] Reserved

[19] Reserved

Imputation of Prohibitions

[20] Under paragraph (k), a prohibition on conduct by an individual lawyer in paragraphs (a) through (i) also applies to all lawyers associated in a firm with the personally prohibited lawyer. For example, one lawyer in a firm may not enter into a business transaction with a client of another member of the firm without complying with paragraph (a), even if the first lawyer is not personally involved in the representation of the client.

Rule 1.9.   Duties to Former Clients

(a) A lawyer who has formerly represented a client in a matter shall not thereafter represent another person in the same or a substantially related matter in which that person's interests are materially adverse to the interests of the former client unless the former client gives informed consent, confirmed in writing.

(b) A lawyer shall not knowingly represent a person in the same or a substantially related matter in which a firm with which the lawyer formerly was associated had previously represented a client

(1) whose interests are materially adverse to that person; and

(2) about whom the lawyer had acquired information protected by Rules 1.6 and 1.9(c) that is material to the matter; unless the former client gives informed consent, confirmed in writing.

(c) A lawyer who has formerly represented a client in a matter or whose present or former firm has formerly represented a client in a matter shall not thereafter:

(1) use confidential information relating to the representation to the disadvantage of the former client or for the lawyer's advantage or the advantage of a third person, except as Rule 1.6, Rule 3.3 or Rule 4.1 would permit or require with respect to a client; or

(2) reveal confidential information relating to the representation except as Rule 1.6, Rule 3.3 or Rule 4.1 would permit or require with respect to a client.

Adopted June 9, 1997, effective January 1, 1998. Amended March 26, 2015, effective July 1, 2015.

Comment

[1] After termination of a client-lawyer relationship, a lawyer has certain continuing duties with respect to confidentiality and conflicts of interest and thus may not represent another client except in conformity with this Rule. Under this Rule, for example, a lawyer could not properly seek to rescind on behalf of a new client a contract drafted on behalf of the former client. So also a lawyer who has prosecuted an accused person could not properly represent the accused in a subsequent civil action against the government concerning the same transaction. Nor could a lawyer who has represented multiple clients in a matter represent one of the clients against the others in the same or a substantially related matter after a dispute arose among the clients in that matter, unless all affected clients give informed consent. See Comment 9. Current and former government lawyers must comply with this Rule to the extent required by Rule 1.11.

[2] The scope of a "matter" for purposes of this Rule depends on the facts of a particular situation or transaction. The lawyer's involvement in a matter can also be a question of degree. When a lawyer has been directly involved in a specific transaction, subsequent representation of other clients with materially adverse interests in that transaction clearly is prohibited. On the other hand, a lawyer who recurrently handled a type of problem for a former client is not precluded from later representing another client in a factually distinct problem of that type even though the subsequent representation involves a position adverse to the prior client. Similar considerations can apply to the reassignment of military lawyers between defense and prosecution functions within the same military jurisdictions. The underlying question is whether the lawyer was so involved in the matter that the subsequent representation can be justly regarded as a changing of sides in the matter in question.

[3] Matters are "substantially related" for purposes of this Rule if they involve the same transaction or legal dispute or if there otherwise is a substantial risk that confidential factual information as would normally have been obtained in the prior representation would materially advance the client's position in the subsequent matter. For example, a lawyer who has represented a business person and learned extensive private financial information about that person may not then represent that person's spouse in seeking a divorce. Similarly, a lawyer who has previously represented a client in securing environmental permits to build a shopping center would be precluded from representing neighbors seeking to oppose rezoning of the property on the basis of environmental considerations; however, the lawyer would not be precluded, on the grounds of substantial relationship, from defending a tenant of the completed shopping center in resisting eviction for nonpayment of rent. Information that has been disclosed to the public or to other parties adverse to the former client ordinarily will not be disqualifying. Information acquired in a prior representation may have been rendered obsolete by the passage of time, a circumstance that may be relevant in determining whether two representations are substantially related. In the case of an organizational client, general knowledge of the client's policies and practices ordinarily will not preclude a subsequent representation; on the other hand, knowledge of specific facts gained in a prior representation that are relevant to the matter in question ordinarily will preclude such a representation. A former client is not required to reveal the confidential information learned by the lawyer in order to establish a substantial risk that the lawyer has confidential information to use in the subsequent matter. A conclusion about the possession of such information may be based on the nature of the services the lawyer provided the former client and information that would in ordinary practice be learned by a lawyer providing such services.

Lawyers Moving Between Firms

[4] When lawyers have been associated within a firm but then end their association, the question of whether a lawyer should undertake representation is more complicated. There are several competing considerations. First, the client previously represented by the former firm must be reasonably assured that the principle of loyalty to the client is not compromised. Second, the Rule should not be so broadly cast as to preclude other persons from having reasonable choice of legal counsel. Third, the Rule should not unreasonably hamper lawyers from forming new associations and taking on new clients after having left a previous association. In this connection, it should be recognized that today many lawyers practice in firms, that many lawyers to some degree limit their practice to one field or another, and that many move from one association to another several times in their careers. If the concept of imputation were applied with unqualified rigor, the result would be radical curtailment of the opportunity of lawyers to move from one practice setting to another and of the opportunity of clients to change counsel.

[5] Paragraph (b) operates to disqualify the lawyer only when the lawyer involved has actual knowledge of information protected by Rules 1.6 and 1.9(c). Thus, if a lawyer while with one firm acquired no

knowledge or information relating to a particular client of the firm, and that lawyer later joined another firm, neither the lawyer individually nor the second firm is disqualified from representing another client in the same or a related matter even though the interests of the two clients conflict. See Rule 1.10(b) for the restrictions on a firm once a lawyer has terminated association with the firm.

[6] Application of paragraph (b) depends on a situation's particular facts, aided by inferences, deductions or working presumptions that reasonably may be made about the way in which lawyers work together. A lawyer may have general access to files of all clients of a law firm and may regularly participate in discussions of their affairs; it should be inferred that such a lawyer in fact is privy to all information about all the firm's clients. In contrast, another lawyer may have access to the files of only a limited number of clients and participate in discussions of the affairs of no other clients; in the absence of information to the contrary, it should be inferred that such a lawyer in fact is privy to information about the clients actually served but not those of other clients. In such an inquiry, the burden of proof should rest upon the firm whose disqualification is sought.

[7] Independent of the question of disqualification of a firm, a lawyer changing professional association has a continuing duty to preserve confidentiality of information about a client formerly represented. See Rules 1.6 and 1.9(c).

[8] Paragraph (c) provides that confidential information acquired by the lawyer in the course of representing a client may not subsequently be used or revealed by the lawyer to the disadvantage of the client or for the lawyer's advantage or the advantage of a third person unless the client gives informed consent, except as permitted or required by these Rules. However, the fact that a lawyer has once served a client ordinarily does not preclude the lawyer from using generally known information about that client when later representing another client. See Comment 3A to Rule 1.6.

[9] The provisions of this Rule are for the protection of former clients and can be waived if the client gives informed consent, which consent must be confirmed in writing under paragraphs (a) and (b). See Rule 1.0(f). With regard to the effectiveness of an advance waiver, see Comment 22 to Rule 1.7. With regard to disqualification of a firm with which a lawyer is or was formerly associated, see Rule 1.10.

Rule 1.10. Imputed Disqualification: General Rule

(a) While lawyers are associated in a firm, none of them shall knowingly represent a client when any one of them practicing alone would be prohibited from doing so by Rules 1.7 or 1.9, unless the prohibition is based on a personal interest of the prohibited lawyer and does not present a significant risk of materially limiting the representation of the client by the remaining lawyers in the firm. A lawyer employed by the Public Counsel Division of the Committee for Public Counsel Services and a lawyer assigned to represent clients by the Private Counsel Division of that Committee are not considered to be associated. Lawyers are not considered to be associated merely because they have each individually been assigned to represent clients by the Committee for Public Counsel Services through its Private Counsel Division.

(b) When a lawyer has terminated an association with a firm ("former firm"), the former firm is not prohibited from thereafter representing a person with interests materially adverse to those of a client represented by the formerly associated lawyer and not currently represented by the former firm, unless:

(1) the matter is the same or substantially related to that in which the formerly associated lawyer represented the client; and

(2) any lawyer remaining in the former firm has information protected by Rules 1.6 and 1.9(c) that is material to the matter.

(c) A disqualification prescribed by this Rule may be waived by the affected client under the conditions stated in Rule 1.7.

(d) When a lawyer becomes associated with a firm ("new firm"), the new firm may not undertake to or continue to represent a person in a matter that the firm knows or reasonably should know is the same or substantially related to a matter in which the newly associated lawyer (the "personally disqualified lawyer"), or the former firm, had previously represented a client whose interests are materially adverse to the new firm's client unless:

(1) the personally disqualified lawyer has no information protected by Rule 1.6 or Rule 1.9 that is material to the matter ("material information"); or

(2) the personally disqualified lawyer (i) had neither involvement nor information relating to the matter sufficient to provide a substantial benefit to the new firm's client and (ii) is screened from any participation in the matter in accordance with paragraph (e) of this Rule and is apportioned no part of the fee therefrom.

(e) For the purposes of paragraph (d) of this Rule and of Rules 1.11 and 1.12, a personally disqualified lawyer in a firm will be deemed to have been screened from any participation in a matter if:

(1) all material information possessed by the personally disqualified lawyer has been isolated from the firm;

(2) the personally disqualified lawyer has been isolated from all contact with the new firm's client relating to the matter, and any witness for or against the new firm's client;

(3) the personally disqualified lawyer and the new firm have been precluded from discussing the matter with each other;

(4) the former client of the personally disqualified lawyer or of the former firm receives notice of the conflict and an affidavit of the personally disqualified lawyer and the new firm describing the procedures being used effectively to screen the personally disqualified lawyer, and attesting that (i) the personally disqualified lawyer will not participate in the matter and will not discuss the matter or the representation with any other lawyer or employee of the new firm, (ii) no material information was transmitted by the personally disqualified lawyer before implementation of the screening procedures and notice to the former client; and (iii) during the period of the lawyer's personal disqualification those lawyers or employees who do participate in the matter will be apprised that the personally disqualified lawyer is screened from participating in or discussing the matter; and

(5) the personally disqualified lawyer and the new firm reasonably believe that the steps taken to accomplish the screening of material information are likely to be effective in preventing material information from being disclosed to the new firm and its client.

In any matter in which the former client and the new firm's client are not before a tribunal, the firm, the personally disqualified lawyer, or the former client may seek judicial review in a court of general jurisdiction of the screening procedures used, or may seek court supervision to ensure that implementation of the screening procedures has occurred and that effective actual compliance has been achieved.

(f) The disqualification of lawyers associated in a firm with former or current government lawyers is governed by Rule 1.11.

Adopted June 9, 1997, effective January 1, 1998. Amended March 26, 2015, effective July 1, 2015. *Comment* amended March 10, 2016, effective May 1, 2016.

Comment

Definition of "Firm"

[1] For purposes of the Rules of Professional Conduct, the term "firm" includes lawyers in a private firm, and lawyers in the legal department of a corporation or other organization, or in a legal services organization. Whether two or more lawyers constitute a firm within this definition can depend on the specific facts. For example, two practitioners who share office space and occasionally consult or assist each other ordinarily would not be regarded as constituting a firm. However, if they present themselves to the public in a way suggesting that they are a firm or conduct themselves as a firm, they should be regarded as a firm for the purposes of the Rules. The terms of any formal agreement between associated lawyers are relevant in determining whether they are a firm, as is the fact that they have mutual access to information concerning the clients they serve. Furthermore, it is relevant in doubtful cases to consider the underlying purpose of the Rule that is involved. A group of lawyers could be regarded as a firm for purposes of the rule that the same lawyer should not represent opposing parties in litigation, while it might not be so regarded for purposes of the rule that information acquired by one lawyer is attributed to the other.

[2] With respect to the law department of an organization, there is ordinarily no question that the members of the department constitute a firm within the meaning of the Rules of Professional Conduct. However, there can be uncertainty as to the identity of the client. For example, it may not be clear whether the law department of a corporation represents a subsidiary or an affiliated corporation, as well as the corporation by which the members of the department are directly employed. A similar question can arise concerning an unincorporated association and its local affiliates.

[3] Similar questions can also arise with respect to lawyers in legal aid. Lawyers employed in the same unit of a legal service organization constitute a firm, but not necessarily those employed in separate units. As in the case of independent practitioners, whether the lawyers should be treated as associated with each other can depend on the particular rule that is involved, and on the specific facts of the situation.

[4] Where a lawyer has joined a private firm after having represented the government, the situation is governed by Rule 1.11(a) and (b); where a lawyer represents the government after having served private clients, the situation is governed by Rule 1.11(d)(2)(i). The individual lawyer involved is bound by the Rules generally, including Rules 1.6, 1.7 and 1.9.

[5] Reserved.

Principles of Imputed Disqualification

[6] The rule of imputed disqualification stated in paragraph (a) gives effect to the principle of loyalty to the client as it applies to lawyers who practice in a law firm. Such situations can be considered from the premise that a firm of lawyers is essentially one lawyer for purposes of the rules governing loyalty to the client, or from the premise that each lawyer is vicariously bound by the obligation of loyalty owed by each lawyer with whom the lawyer is associated. Paragraph (a) operates only among the lawyers currently associated in a firm. When a lawyer moves from one firm to another, the situation is governed by Rules 1.9(b) and 1.10(b), (d) and (e).

[6A] The rule in paragraph (a) does not prohibit representation where neither questions of client loyalty nor protection of confidential information are presented. Where one lawyer in a firm could not effectively represent a given client because of strong political beliefs, for example, but that lawyer will do no work on the case and the personal beliefs of the lawyer will not materially limit the representation by others in the firm, the firm should not be disqualified.

[7] Rule 1.10(b) operates to permit a law firm, under certain circumstances, to represent a person with interests directly adverse to those of a client represented by a lawyer who formerly was associated with the firm. The Rule applies regardless of when the formerly associated lawyer represented the client. However, the law firm may not represent a person with interests adverse to those of a present client of the firm, which would violate Rule 1.7. Moreover, the firm may not represent the person where the matter is the same or substantially related to that in which the formerly associated lawyer represented the client and any other lawyer currently in the firm has material information protected by Rules 1.6 and 1.9(c).

[8] Paragraphs (d) and (e) of Rule 1.10 apply when a lawyer moves from a private firm to another firm ("new firm") and are intended to create procedures similar in some cases to those under Rule 1.11(b) for lawyers moving from a government agency to a private firm. Paragraphs (d) and (e) of Rule 1.10, unlike the provisions of Rule 1.11, do not permit a firm, without the consent of the former client of the disqualified lawyer or of the disqualified lawyer's former firm, to handle a matter with respect to which the personally disqualified lawyer was involved to a degree sufficient to provide a substantial benefit to the new firm's client or had confidential information relating to the matter sufficient to provide a substantial benefit to the new firm's client, as noted in Comment 11 below. Like Rule 1.11, however, Rule 1.10(d) can only apply if the lawyer no longer represents the client of the former firm after the lawyer arrives at the lawyer's new firm.

[9] If the lawyer has no information protected by Rule 1.6 or Rule 1.9 about the representation of the former client, the new firm is not disqualified and no screening procedures are required. This would ordinarily be the case if the lawyer did no work on the matter and the matter was not the subject of discussion with the lawyer generally, for example at firm or working group meetings. The lawyer must search his or her files and recollections carefully to determine whether he or she has confidential information. The fact that the lawyer does not immediately remember any details of the former client's representation does not mean that he or she does not in fact possess confidential information material to the matter.

[10] If the lawyer does have confidential information about the representation of the client of his former firm, the firm with which he or she is newly associated may represent a client with interests adverse to the former client of the newly associated lawyer only if the personally disqualified lawyer did not have involvement or confidential information relating to the matter sufficient to provide a substantial benefit to the new firm's client, the personally disqualified lawyer is apportioned no part of the fee, and all of the screening procedures are followed, including the requirement that the personally disqualified lawyer and the new firm reasonably believe that the screening procedures will be effective. For example, in a very small firm, it may be difficult to keep information screened. On the other hand, screening procedures are more likely to be successful if the personally disqualified lawyer practices in a different office of the firm from those handling the matter from which the personally disqualified lawyer is screened.

[11] In situations where the personally disqualified lawyer was involved in a matter to a degree sufficient to provide a substantial

benefit to the new firm's client or had confidential information relating to a matter sufficient to provide a substantial benefit to the new firm's client, the new firm will generally only be allowed to handle the matter if the former client of the personally disqualified lawyer or of the former law firm consents and the new firm reasonably believes that the representation will not be adversely affected, all as required by Rule 1.7. This differs from the provisions of Rule 1.11, in that Rule 1.11(a) permits a firm to handle a matter against a government agency, without the consent of the agency, with respect to which one of its associated lawyers was personally and substantially involved for that agency, provided that the procedures of Rule 1.11(a)(1) and (2) are followed. Likewise, Rule 1.11(b) permits a firm to handle a matter against a government agency, without the consent of the agency, with respect to which one of its associated lawyers had substantial material information even if that lawyer was not personally and substantially involved for that agency, provided that the lawyer is screened and not apportioned any part of the fee.

[12] The former client is entitled to review of the screening procedures if the former client believes that the procedures will not be or have not been effective. If the matter involves litigation, the court before which the litigation is pending would be able to decide motions to disqualify or to enter appropriate orders relating to the screening, taking cognizance of whether the former client is seeking the disqualification of the firm upon a reasonable basis or without a reasonable basis for tactical advantage or otherwise. If the matter does not involve litigation, the former client can seek judicial review of the screening procedures from a trial court.

Rule 1.11. Special Conflicts of Interest for Former and Current Government Officers and Employees

(a) Except as law may otherwise expressly permit, a lawyer who has formerly served as a public officer or employee of the government:

(1) is subject to Rule 1.9(c); and

(2) shall not otherwise represent a client in connection with a matter in which the lawyer participated personally and substantially as a public officer or employee, unless the appropriate government agency gives its informed consent, confirmed in writing, to the representation.

(b) When a lawyer is disqualified from representation under paragraph (a), no lawyer in a firm with which that lawyer is associated may knowingly undertake or continue representation in such a matter unless:

(1) the disqualified lawyer is timely screened from any participation in the matter and is apportioned no part of the fee therefrom; and

(2) written notice is promptly given to the appropriate government agency to enable it to ascertain compliance with the provisions of this Rule.

(c) Except as law may otherwise expressly permit, a lawyer having information that the lawyer knows is confidential government information about a person acquired when the lawyer was a public officer or employee, may not represent a private client whose interests are adverse to that person in a matter in which the information could be used to the material disadvantage of that person. As used in this Rule, the term "confidential government information" means information that has been obtained under governmental authority and which, at the time this Rule is applied, the government is prohibited by law from disclosing to the public or has a legal privilege not to disclose

and which is not otherwise available to the public. A firm with which that lawyer is associated may undertake or continue representation in the matter only if the disqualified lawyer is timely screened from any participation in the matter and is apportioned no part of the fee therefrom.

(d) Except as law may otherwise expressly permit, a lawyer currently serving as a public officer or employee:

(1) is subject to Rules 1.7 and 1.9; and

(2) shall not:

(i) participate in a matter in which the lawyer participated personally and substantially while in private practice or nongovernmental employment, unless the appropriate government agency gives its informed consent, confirmed in writing; or

(ii) negotiate for private employment with any person who is involved as a party or as lawyer for a party in a matter in which the lawyer is participating personally and substantially, except that a lawyer serving as a law clerk to a judge, other adjudicative officer, or arbitrator, may negotiate for private employment as permitted by Rule 1.12(b) and subject to the conditions stated in Rule 1.12(b).

(e) As used in this Rule, the term "matter" includes:

(1) any judicial or other proceeding, application, request for a ruling or other determination, contract, claim, controversy, investigation, charge, accusation, arrest or other particular matter involving a specific party or parties, and

(2) any other matter covered by the conflict of interest rules of the appropriate government agency.

Adopted June 9, 1997, effective January 1, 1998. Amended March 26, 2015, effective July 1, 2015.

Comment

[1] A lawyer who has served or is currently serving as a public officer or employee or is specially retained by the government is personally subject to the Rules of Professional Conduct, including the prohibition against concurrent conflicts of interest stated in Rule 1.7. In addition, such a lawyer may be subject to statutes and government regulations regarding conflict of interest. See G. L. c. 268A. Such statutes and regulations may circumscribe the extent to which the government agency may give consent under this Rule. See Rule 1.0(f) for the definition of informed consent.

[2] Paragraphs (a)(1), (a)(2) and (d)(1) restate the obligations of an individual lawyer who has served or is currently serving as an officer or employee of the government toward a former government or private client. Rule 1.10 is not applicable to the conflicts of interest addressed by this Rule. Rather, paragraph (b) sets forth a special imputation rule for former government lawyers that provides for screening and notice. Because of the special problems raised by imputation within a government agency, paragraph (d) does not impute the conflicts of a lawyer currently serving as an officer or employee of the government to other associated government officers or employees, although ordinarily it will be prudent to screen such lawyers.

[3] Paragraphs (a)(2) and (d)(2) apply regardless of whether a lawyer is adverse to a former client and are thus designed not only to protect the former client, but also to prevent a lawyer from exploiting public office for the advantage of another client. For example, a lawyer who has pursued a claim on behalf of the government may not pursue the same claim on behalf of a later private client after the lawyer has left government service, except when authorized to do so

by the government agency under paragraph (a). Similarly, a lawyer who has pursued a claim on behalf of a private client may not pursue the claim on behalf of the government, except when authorized to do so by paragraph (d). As with paragraphs (a)(1) and (d)(1), Rule 1.10 is not applicable to the conflicts of interest addressed by these paragraphs.

[4] This Rule represents a balancing of interests. On the one hand, where the successive clients are a public agency and another client, the risk exists that power or discretion vested in public authority might be used for the special benefit of another client. A lawyer should not be in a position where benefit to the other client might affect performance of the lawyer's professional functions on behalf of the government. Also, unfair advantage could accrue to the other client by reason of access to confidential government information about the client's adversary obtainable only through the lawyer's government service. On the other hand, the rules governing lawyers presently or formerly employed by a government agency should not be so restrictive as to inhibit transfer of employment to and from the government. The government has a legitimate need to attract qualified lawyers as well as to maintain high ethical standards. Thus a former government lawyer is disqualified only from particular matters in which the lawyer participated personally and substantially. The provisions for screening and waiver in paragraph (b) are necessary to prevent the disqualification rule from imposing too severe a deterrent against entering public service. The limitation of disqualification in paragraphs (a)(2) and (d)(2) to matters involving a specific party or parties, rather than extending disqualification to all substantive issues on which the lawyer worked, serves a similar function.

[5] When a lawyer has been employed by one government agency and then moves to a second government agency, it may be appropriate to treat that second agency as another client for purposes of this Rule, as when a lawyer is employed by a city and subsequently is employed by a federal agency. However, because the conflict of interest is governed by paragraph (d), the latter agency is not required to screen the lawyer as paragraph (b) requires a law firm to do. The question of whether two government agencies should be regarded as the same or different clients for conflict of interest purposes is beyond the scope of these Rules. See Rule 1.13 Comment 9.

[6] Paragraphs (b) and (c) contemplate a screening arrangement. These paragraphs do not prohibit a lawyer from receiving a salary or partnership share established by prior independent agreement. They prohibit directly relating the lawyer's compensation to the fee in the matter in which the lawyer is disqualified.

[7] Notice, including a description of the screened lawyer's prior representation and of the screening procedures employed, generally should be given as soon as practicable after the need for screening becomes apparent.

[8] Paragraph (c) operates only when the lawyer in question has knowledge of the information, which means actual knowledge; it does not operate with respect to information that merely could be imputed to the lawyer.

[9] Paragraphs (a) and (d) do not prohibit a lawyer from jointly representing a private party and a government agency when doing so is permitted by Rule 1.7 and is not otherwise prohibited by law.

[10] For purposes of paragraph (e) of this Rule, a "matter" may continue in another form. In determining whether two particular matters are the same, the lawyer should consider the extent to which the matters involve the same basic facts, the same or related parties, and the time elapsed.

Rule 1.12. Former Judge, Arbitrator, Mediator or Other Third-Party Neutral

(a) Except as stated in paragraph (d), a lawyer shall not represent anyone in connection with a matter in which the lawyer participated personally and substantially as a judge or other adjudicative officer, arbitrator, mediator, or other third-party neutral, or law clerk to such a person unless all parties to the current proceeding give informed consent, confirmed in writing.

(b) A lawyer shall not negotiate for employment with any person who is involved as a party or as lawyer for a party in a matter in which the lawyer is participating personally and substantially as a judge or other adjudicative officer or as an arbitrator, mediator or other third-party neutral. A lawyer serving as a law clerk to a judge or other adjudicative officer or an arbitrator, mediator or other third-party neutral may negotiate for employment with a party or lawyer involved in a matter in which the clerk is participating personally and substantially, but only after the lawyer has notified the judge or other adjudicative officer or an arbitrator, or mediator or other third-party neutral.

(c) If a lawyer is disqualified by paragraph (a), no lawyer in a firm with which that lawyer is associated may knowingly undertake or continue representation in the matter unless:

(1) the disqualified lawyer is timely screened from any participation in the matter and is apportioned no part of the fee therefrom; and

(2) written notice is promptly given to the parties and any appropriate tribunal to enable them to ascertain compliance with the provisions of this Rule.

(d) An arbitrator selected as a partisan of a party in a multimember arbitration panel is not prohibited from subsequently representing that party.

Adopted June 9, 1997, effective January 1, 1998. Amended March 26, 2015, effective July 1, 2015.

Comment

[1] This Rule generally parallels Rule 1.11. The term "personally and substantially" signifies that a judge who was a member of a multimember court, and thereafter left judicial office to practice law, is not prohibited by these Rules from representing a client in a matter pending in the court, but in which the former judge did not participate. So also the fact that a former judge exercised administrative responsibility in a court does not prevent the former judge from acting as a lawyer in a matter where the judge had previously exercised remote or incidental administrative responsibility that did not affect the merits. Compare the Comment to Rule 1.11. The lawyer should also consider applicable statutes and regulations, e.g. G. L. c. 268A. The term "adjudicative officer" includes such officials as magistrates, referees, special masters, hearing officers and other parajudicial officers. Canon 6A(2) of the Code of Judicial Conduct (S.J.C. Rule 3:09) provides that a retired judge recalled to active service "shall not, for a period of six months following the date of retirement, resignation, or most recent service as a retired judge pursuant to G. L. c. 32, §§ 65E–65G, perform court-connected dispute resolution services except on a pro bono publico basis, enter an appearance, or accept an appointment to represent any party in any court of the Commonwealth."

[2] Like former judges, lawyers who have served as arbitrators, mediators or other third-party neutrals may be asked to represent a client in a matter in which the lawyer participated personally and substantially. This Rule forbids such representation unless all of the parties to the proceedings give their informed consent, confirmed in writing. See Rule 1.0(f) and (c). Other law or codes of ethics governing third-party neutrals may impose more stringent standards of personal or imputed disqualification. See Rule 2.4.

[3] Although lawyers who serve as third-party neutrals do not have information concerning the parties that is protected under Rule 1.6, they typically owe the parties an obligation of confidentiality under law or codes of ethics governing third-party neutrals. Thus, paragraph (c) provides that conflicts of the personally disqualified lawyer will be imputed to other lawyers in a law firm unless the conditions of this paragraph are met.

[4] Requirements for screening procedures are stated in Rule 1.10(f). Paragraph (c)(1) does not prohibit the screened lawyer from receiving a salary or partnership share established by prior independent agreement, but that lawyer may not receive compensation directly related to the matter in which the lawyer is disqualified.

[5] Notice, including a description of the screened lawyer's prior representation and of the screening procedures employed, generally should be given as soon as practicable after the need for screening becomes apparent.

[6] Law clerks who serve before they are admitted to the bar are subject to the limitations stated in Rule 1.12(b). For purposes of this Rule, the term "law clerk" shall include judicial interns and others who provide similar legal assistance to a judge or other adjudicative officer or to an arbitrator, mediator, or other third-party neutral.

Rule 1.13.   Organization as Client

(a) A lawyer employed or retained by an organization represents the organization acting through its duly authorized constituents.

(b) If a lawyer for an organization knows that an officer, employee, or other person associated with the organization is engaged in action, intends to act or refuses to act in a matter related to the representation that is a violation of a legal obligation to the organization, or a violation of law that reasonably might be imputed to the organization, and that is likely to result in substantial injury to the organization, then the lawyer shall proceed as is reasonably necessary in the best interest of the organization. Unless the lawyer reasonably believes that it is not necessary in the best interest of the organization to do so, the lawyer shall refer the matter to higher authority in the organization, including, if warranted by the circumstances, to the highest authority that can act on behalf of the organization as determined by applicable law.

(c) Except as provided in paragraph (d), if

(1) despite the lawyer's efforts in accordance with paragraph (b) the highest authority that can act on behalf of the organization insists upon or fails to address in a timely and appropriate manner an action, or a refusal to act, that is clearly a violation of law, and

(2) the lawyer reasonably believes that the violation is reasonably certain to result in substantial injury to the organization,

then the lawyer may reveal information relating to the representation whether or not Rule 1.6 permits such disclosure, but only if and to the extent the lawyer reasonably believes necessary to prevent substantial injury to the organization.

(d) Paragraph (c) shall not apply with respect to information relating to a lawyer's representation of an organization to investigate an alleged violation of law, or to defend the organization or an officer, employee or other constituent associated with the organization against a claim arising out of an alleged violation of law.

(e) A lawyer who reasonably believes that he or she has been discharged because of the lawyer's actions taken pursuant to paragraphs (b) or (c), or who withdraws under circumstances that require or permit the lawyer to take action under either of those paragraphs, shall proceed as the lawyer reasonably believes necessary to assure that the organization's highest authority is informed of the lawyer's discharge or withdrawal.

(f) In dealing with an organization's directors, officers, employees, members, shareholders or other constituents, a lawyer shall explain the identity of the client when the lawyer knows or reasonably should know that the organization's interests are adverse to those of the constituents with whom the lawyer is dealing.

(g) A lawyer representing an organization may also represent any of its directors, officers, employees, members, shareholders or other constituents, subject to the provisions of Rule 1.7. If the organization's consent to the dual representation is required by Rule 1.7, the consent shall be given by an appropriate official of the organization other than the individual who is to be represented, or by the shareholders.

Adopted June 9, 1997, effective January 1, 1998. Amended December 30, 1997, effective March 1, 1998; November 28, 2007, effective January 1, 2008. Comment amended March 26, 2015, effective July 1, 2015.

Comment

The Entity as the Client

[1] An organizational client is a legal entity, but it cannot act except through its officers, directors, employees, shareholders and other constituents. Officers, directors, employees and shareholders are the constituents of the corporate organizational client. The duties defined in this Comment apply equally to unincorporated associations. "Other constituents" as used in this Comment means the positions equivalent to officers, directors, employees and shareholders held by persons acting for organizational clients that are not corporations.

[2] When one of the constituents of an organizational client communicates with the organization's lawyer in that person's organizational capacity, the communication is protected by Rule 1.6. Thus, by way of example, if an organizational client requests its lawyer to investigate allegations of wrongdoing, interviews made in the course of that investigation between the lawyer and the client's employees or other constituents are covered by Rule 1.6. This does not mean, however, that constituents of an organizational client are the clients of the lawyer. The lawyer may not disclose to such constituents information relating to the representation except for disclosures explicitly or impliedly authorized by the organizational client in order to carry out the representation or as otherwise permitted by Rule 1.6.

[3] When constituents of the organization make decisions for it, the decisions ordinarily must be accepted by the lawyer even if their utility or prudence is doubtful. Decisions concerning policy and operations, including ones entailing serious risk, are not as such in the lawyer's province. Paragraph (b) makes clear, however, that when the lawyer knows that the organization is likely to be substantially injured by action of an officer or other constituent that violates a legal obligation to the organization or is in violation of law that might be imputed to the organization, the lawyer must proceed as is reasonably necessary in the best interest of the organization. As defined in Rule 1.0(g), knowledge can be inferred from circumstances, and a lawyer cannot ignore the obvious.

[4] In determining how to proceed under paragraph (b), the lawyer should give due consideration to the seriousness of the violation and its consequences, the responsibility in the organization and the apparent motivation of the person involved, the policies of the organization

concerning such matters, and any other relevant considerations. Ordinarily, referral to a higher authority would be necessary. In some circumstances, however, it may be appropriate for the lawyer to ask the constituent to reconsider the matter; for example, if the circumstances involve a constituent's innocent misunderstanding of law and subsequent acceptance of the lawyer's advice, the lawyer may reasonably conclude that the best interest of the organization does not require that the matter be referred to higher authority. If a constituent persists in conduct contrary to the lawyer's advice, it will be necessary for the lawyer to take steps to have the matter reviewed by a higher authority in the organization. If the matter is of sufficient seriousness and importance or urgency to the organization, referral to higher authority in the organization may be necessary even if the lawyer has not communicated with the constituent. Any measures taken should, to the extent practicable, minimize the risk of revealing information relating to the representation to persons outside the organization. Even in circumstances where a lawyer is not obligated by Rule 1.13 to proceed, a lawyer may bring to the attention of an organizational client, including its highest authority, matters that the lawyer reasonably believes to be of sufficient importance to warrant doing so in the best interest of the organization.

[5] Paragraph (b) also makes clear that when it is reasonably necessary to enable the organization to address the matter in a timely and appropriate manner, the lawyer must refer the matter to higher authority, including, if warranted by the circumstances, the highest authority that can act on behalf of the organization under applicable law. The organization's highest authority to whom a matter may be referred ordinarily will be the board of directors or similar governing body. However, applicable law may prescribe that under certain conditions the highest authority reposes elsewhere, for example, in the independent directors of a corporation.

Relation to Other Rules

[6] The authority and responsibility provided in this Rule are concurrent with the authority and responsibility provided in other Rules. In particular, this Rule does not limit or expand the lawyer's responsibility under Rules 1.8, 1.16, 3.3, 4.1, or 8.3. Moreover, the lawyer may be subject to disclosure obligations imposed by law or court order as contemplated by Rule 1.6(b)(5). Paragraph (c) of this Rule supplements Rule 1.6(b) by providing an additional basis upon which the lawyer may reveal confidential information relating to the representation, but does not modify, restrict, or limit the provisions of Rule 1.6(b)(1)–(7). Under paragraph (c) the lawyer may reveal such information only when the organization's highest authority insists upon or fails to address threatened or ongoing action that is clearly a violation of law, and then only to the extent the lawyer reasonably believes necessary to prevent reasonably certain substantial injury to the organization. It is not necessary that the lawyer's services be used in furtherance of the violation, but it is required that the matter be related to the lawyer's representation of the organization. If the lawyer's services are being used by an organization to further a crime or fraud by the organization, Rule 1.6(b)(3) may permit the lawyer to disclose confidential information. In such circumstances Rule 1.2(d) may also be applicable, in which event, withdrawal from the representation under Rule 1.16(a)(1) may be required.

[7] Paragraph (d) makes clear that the authority of a lawyer to disclose confidential information relating to a representation in circumstances described in paragraph (c) does not apply with respect to information relating to a lawyer's engagement by an organization to investigate an alleged violation of law or to defend the organization or an officer, employee or other person associated with the organization against a claim arising out of an alleged violation of law. This is necessary in order to enable organizational clients to enjoy the full benefits of legal counsel in conducting an investigation or defending against a claim.

[8] A lawyer who reasonably believes that he or she has been discharged because of the lawyer's actions taken pursuant to paragraph (b) or (c), or who withdraws in circumstances that require or

permit the lawyer to take action under either of these paragraphs, must proceed as the lawyer reasonably believes necessary to assure that the organization's highest authority is informed of the lawyer's discharge or withdrawal. Nothing in these rules prohibits the lawyer from disclosing what the lawyer reasonably believes to be the basis for his or her discharge or withdrawal.

Government Agency

[9] The duty defined in this Rule applies to governmental organizations. Defining precisely the identity of the client and prescribing the resulting obligations of such lawyers may be more difficult in the government context and is a matter beyond the scope of these Rules. See Scope [4]. Although in some circumstances the client may be a specific agency, it may also be a branch of government, such as the executive branch, or the government as a whole. For example, if the action or failure to act involves the head of a bureau, either the department of which the bureau is a part or the relevant branch of government may be the client for purposes of this Rule. Moreover, in a matter involving the conduct of government officials, a government lawyer may have authority under applicable law to question such conduct more extensively than that of a lawyer for a private organization in similar circumstances. Thus, when the client is a governmental organization, a different balance may be appropriate between maintaining confidentiality and assuring that the wrongful act is prevented or rectified, for public business is involved. In addition, duties of lawyers employed by the government or lawyers in military service may be defined by statutes and regulation. This Rule does not limit that authority. See Scope.

Clarifying the Lawyer's Role

[10] There are times when the organization's interest may be or become adverse to those of one or more of its constituents. In such circumstances the lawyer should advise any constituent, whose interest the lawyer finds adverse to that of the organization of the conflict or potential conflict of interest, that the lawyer cannot represent such constituent, and that such person may wish to obtain independent representation. Care must be taken to assure that the individual understands that, when there is such adversity of interest, the lawyer for the organization cannot provide legal representation for that constituent individual, and that discussions between the lawyer for the organization and the individual may not be privileged.

[11] Whether such a warning should be given by the lawyer for the organization to any constituent individual may turn on the facts of each case.

Dual Representation

[12] Paragraph (g) recognizes that a lawyer for an organization may also represent a principal officer or major shareholder.

Derivative Actions

[13] Under generally prevailing law, the shareholders or members of a corporation may bring suit to compel the directors to perform their legal obligations in the supervision of the organization. Members of unincorporated associations have essentially the same right. Such an action may be brought nominally by the organization, but usually is, in fact, a legal controversy over management of the organization.

[14] The question can arise whether counsel for the organization may defend such an action. The proposition that the organization is the lawyer's client does not alone resolve the issue. Most derivative actions are a normal incident of an organization's affairs, to be defended by the organization's lawyer like any other suit. However, if the claim involves serious charges of wrongdoing by those in control of the organization, a conflict may arise between the lawyer's duty to the organization and the lawyer's relationship with the board. In those circumstances, Rule 1.7 governs who should represent the directors and the organization.

Rule 1.14.   Client With Diminished Capacity

(a) When a client's capacity to make adequately considered decisions in connection with a representation is diminished, whether because of minority, mental impairment or for some other reason, the lawyer shall, as far as reasonably possible, maintain a normal client-lawyer relationship with the client.

(b) When the lawyer reasonably believes that the client has diminished capacity that prevents the client from making an adequately considered decision regarding a specific issue that is part of the representation, is at risk of substantial physical, financial or other harm unless action is taken, and cannot adequately act in the client's own interest, the lawyer may take reasonably necessary protective action in connection with the representation, including consulting with individuals or entities that have the ability to take action to protect the client and, in appropriate cases, seeking the appointment of a guardian ad litem, conservator or guardian.

(c) Confidential information relating to the representation of a client with diminished capacity is protected by Rule 1.6. When taking protective action pursuant to paragraph (b), the lawyer is impliedly authorized under Rule 1.6(a) to reveal confidential information about the client, but only to the extent reasonably necessary to protect the client's interests.

Adopted June 9, 1997, effective January 1, 1998. Amended July 22, 2008, effective September 1, 2008. Amended March 26, 2015, effective July 1, 2015.

Comment

[1] The normal client-lawyer relationship is based on the assumption that the client, when properly advised and assisted, is capable of making decisions about important matters. When the client has diminished capacity, however, maintaining the ordinary client-lawyer relationship may not be possible in all respects. In particular, a severely incapacitated person may have no power to make legally binding decisions. Nevertheless, a client with diminished capacity often has the ability to understand, deliberate upon, and reach conclusions about matters affecting the client's own well-being. For example, children as young as five or six years of age, and certainly those of ten or twelve, are regarded as having opinions that are entitled to weight in legal proceedings concerning their custody. So also, it is recognized that some persons of advanced age can be quite capable of handling routine financial matters while needing special legal protection concerning major transactions.

[2] The fact that a client has diminished capacity does not lessen the lawyer's obligation to treat the client with attention and respect. Even if the person has a legal representative, the lawyer should as far as possible accord the represented person the status of client, particularly in maintaining communication.

[3] The client may wish to have family members or other persons participate in discussions with the lawyer. The lawyer may also consult family members even though they may be personally interested in the situation. Before the lawyer discloses confidential information of the client, the lawyer should consider whether it is likely that the person or entity to be consulted will act adversely to the client's interests. Decisions under Rule 1.14(b) whether and to what extent to consult or to disclose confidential information are matters of professional judgment on the lawyer's part.

[4] If a legal representative has already been appointed for the client, the lawyer should ordinarily look to the representative for decisions on behalf of the client. If the lawyer represents the guardian as distinct from the ward, and is aware that the guardian is acting adversely to the ward's interest, the lawyer may have an obligation to prevent or rectify the guardian's misconduct. See Rules 1.2(d), 1.6, 3.3 and 4.1.

Taking Protective Action

[5] If a lawyer reasonably believes that a client is at risk of substantial physical, financial or other harm unless action is taken, and that a normal client-lawyer relationship cannot be maintained as provided in paragraph (a) because the client lacks sufficient capacity to communicate or to make adequately considered decisions in connection with the representation, then paragraph (b) permits the lawyer to take protective measures deemed necessary. Such measures could include: consulting with family members, using a reconsideration period to permit clarification or improvement of circumstances, using voluntary surrogate decision-making tools such as durable powers of attorney or consulting with support groups, professional services, adult-protective agencies or other individuals or entities that have the ability to protect the client. In taking any protective action, the lawyer should be guided by such factors as the wishes and values of the client to the extent known, the client's best interests and the goals of intruding into the client's decision-making autonomy to the least extent feasible, maximizing client capacities and respecting the client's family and social connections.

[6] In determining whether a client has diminished capacity that prevents the client from making an adequately considered decision regarding a specific issue that is part of the representation, the lawyer should consider and balance such factors as: the client's ability to articulate reasoning leading to a decision, variability of state of mind and ability to appreciate consequences of a decision; the substantive fairness of a decision; and the consistency of a decision with the known long-term commitments and values of the client. In appropriate circumstances, the lawyer may seek guidance from an appropriate diagnostician.

[7] If a client is unable to make an adequately considered decision regarding an issue, and if achieving the client's expressed preferences would place the client at risk of a substantial harm, the attorney has four options. The attorney may:

i. advocate the client's expressed preferences regarding the issue;

ii. advocate the client's expressed preferences and request the appointment of a guardian ad litem or investigator to make an independent recommendation to the court;

iii. request the appointment of a guardian ad litem or next friend to direct counsel in the representation; or

iv. determine what the client's preferences would be if he or she were able to make an adequately considered decision regarding the issue and represent the client in accordance with that determination.

In the circumstances described in clause (iv) above where the matter is before a tribunal and the client has expressed a preference, the lawyer will ordinarily inform the tribunal of the client's expressed preferences. However, there are circumstances where options other than the option in clause (i) above will be impermissible under substantive law or otherwise inappropriate or unwarranted. Such circumstances arise in the representation of clients who are competent to stand trial in criminal, delinquency and youthful offender, civil commitment and similar matters. Counsel should follow the client's expressed preference if it does not pose a risk of substantial harm to the client, even if the lawyer reasonably determines that the client has not made an adequately considered decision in the matter.

Disclosure of the Client's Condition

[8] Disclosure of the client's diminished capacity could adversely affect the client's interests. For example, raising the question of diminished capacity could, in some circumstances, lead to proceedings for involuntary commitment. Confidential information relating to the representation is protected by Rule 1.6. Therefore, unless authorized to do so, the lawyer may not disclose such information. When taking protective action pursuant to paragraph (b), the lawyer is impliedly authorized to make the necessary disclosures, even when the client

directs the lawyer to the contrary. Nevertheless, given the risks of disclosure, paragraph (c) limits what the lawyer may disclose in consulting with other individuals or entities or seeking the appointment of a legal representative. At the very least, the lawyer should determine whether it is likely that the person or entity consulted with will act adversely to the client's interests before discussing matters related to the client. The lawyer's position in such cases is an unavoidably difficult one.

Emergency Legal Assistance

[9] In an emergency where the health, safety or a financial interest of a person with seriously diminished capacity is threatened with imminent and irreparable harm, a lawyer may take legal action on behalf of such a person even though the person is unable to establish a client-lawyer relationship or to make or express considered judgments about the matter, when the person or another acting in good faith on that person's behalf has consulted with the lawyer. Even in such an emergency, however, the lawyer should not act unless the lawyer reasonably believes that the person has no other lawyer, agent or other representative available. The lawyer should take legal action on behalf of the person only to the extent reasonably necessary to maintain the status quo or otherwise avoid imminent and irreparable harm. A lawyer who undertakes to represent a person in such an exigent situation has the same duties under these Rules as the lawyer would with respect to a client.

[10] A lawyer who acts on behalf of a person with seriously diminished capacity in an emergency should keep the confidences of the person as if dealing with a client, disclosing them only to the extent necessary to accomplish the intended protective action. The lawyer should disclose to any tribunal involved and to any other counsel involved the nature of his or her relationship with the person. The lawyer should take steps to regularize the relationship or implement other protective solutions as soon as possible. Normally, a lawyer would not seek compensation for such emergency actions taken.

Rule 1.15.   Safekeeping Property

(a) Definitions:

(1) "Trust property" means property of clients or third persons that is in a lawyer's possession in connection with a representation and includes property held in any fiduciary capacity in connection with a representation, whether as trustee, agent, escrow agent, guardian, executor, or otherwise. Trust property does not include documents or other property received by a lawyer as investigatory material or potential evidence. Trust property in the form of funds is referred to as "trust funds."

(2) "Trust account" means an account in a financial institution in which trust funds are deposited. Trust accounts must conform to the requirements of this Rule.

(b) Segregation of Trust Property. A lawyer shall hold trust property separate from the lawyer's own property.

(1) Trust funds shall be held in a trust account.

(2) No funds belonging to the lawyer shall be deposited or retained in a trust account except that:

(i) Funds reasonably sufficient to pay bank charges may be deposited therein, and

(ii) Trust funds belonging in part to a client or third person and in part currently or potentially to the lawyer shall be deposited in a trust account, but the portion belonging to the lawyer must be withdrawn at the earliest reasonable time after the lawyer's interest in that portion becomes fixed. A lawyer who knows that the right of the lawyer or law firm to receive such portion is disputed shall not withdraw the funds until the dispute is resolved. If the right of the lawyer or law firm to receive such portion is disputed within a reasonable time after notice is given that the funds have been withdrawn, the disputed portion must be restored to a trust account until the dispute is resolved.

(3) A lawyer shall deposit into a trust account legal fees and expenses that have been paid in advance, to be withdrawn by the lawyer only as fees are earned or as expenses incurred.

(4) All trust property shall be appropriately safeguarded. Trust property other than funds shall be identified as such.

(c) Prompt Notice and Delivery of Trust Property to Client or Third Person. Upon receiving trust funds or other trust property in which a client or third person has an interest, a lawyer shall promptly notify the client or third person. Except as stated in this Rule or as otherwise permitted by law or by agreement with the client or third person on whose behalf a lawyer holds trust property, a lawyer shall promptly deliver to the client or third person any funds or other property that the client or third person is entitled to receive.

(d) Accounting.

(1) Upon final distribution of any trust property or upon request by the client or third person on whose behalf a lawyer holds trust property, the lawyer shall promptly render a full written accounting regarding such property.

(2) On or before the date on which a withdrawal from a trust account is made for the purpose of paying fees due to a lawyer, the lawyer shall deliver to the client in writing (i) an itemized bill or other accounting showing the services rendered, (ii) written notice of amount and date of the withdrawal, and (iii) a statement of the balance of the client's funds in the trust account after the withdrawal.

(e) Operational Requirements for Trust Accounts.

(1) All trust accounts shall be maintained in the state where the lawyer's office is situated, or elsewhere with the consent of the client or third person on whose behalf the trust property is held, except that all funds required by this Rule to be deposited in an IOLTA account shall be maintained in this Commonwealth.

(2) Each trust account title shall include the words "trust account," "escrow account," "client funds account," "conveyancing account," "IOLTA account," or words of similar import indicating the fiduciary nature of the account.

(3) For each trust account opened, the lawyer shall submit written notice to the bank or other depository in which the trust account is maintained confirming to the depository that the account will hold trust funds within the meaning of this Rule. The lawyer shall retain a copy executed by the bank and the lawyer for the lawyer's own records. The notice shall identify the bank, account, and type of account, whether pooled, with interest paid to the IOLTA Committee (IOLTA account), or individual account with interest paid to the client or third person on whose behalf the trust property is held. For purposes of this Rule, one notice is sufficient

for a master or umbrella account with individual subaccounts.

(4) No withdrawal from a trust account shall be made by a check which is not prenumbered. No withdrawal shall be made in cash or by automatic teller machine or any similar method. No withdrawal shall be made by a check payable to "cash" or "bearer" or by any other method which does not identify the recipient of the funds.

(5) Every withdrawal from a trust account for the purpose of paying fees to a lawyer or reimbursing a lawyer for costs and expenses shall be payable to the lawyer or the lawyer's law firm.

(6) Each lawyer who has a law office in this Commonwealth and who holds trust funds shall deposit such funds, as appropriate, in one of two types of interest bearing accounts: either (i) a pooled account ("IOLTA account") for all trust funds which in the judgment of the lawyer are nominal in amount, or are to be held for a short period of time, or (ii) for all other trust funds, an individual account with the interest payable as directed by the client or third person on whose behalf the trust property is held. The foregoing deposit requirements apply to funds received by lawyers in connection with real estate transactions and loan closings, provided, however, that a trust account in a lending bank in the name of a lawyer representing the lending bank and used exclusively for depositing and disbursing funds in connection with that particular bank's loan transactions, shall not be required but is permitted to be established as an IOLTA account. All IOLTA accounts shall be established in compliance with the provisions of paragraph (g) of this Rule.

(7) Property held for no compensation as a custodian for a minor family member is not subject to the Operational Requirements for Trust Accounts set out in this paragraph (e) or to the Required Accounts and Records in paragraph (f) of this Rule. As used in this paragraph, "family member" refers to those individuals specified in Rule 7.3(a)(3).

(f) Required Accounts and Records: Every lawyer who is engaged in the practice of law in this Commonwealth and who holds trust property in connection with a representation shall maintain complete records of the receipt, maintenance, and disposition of that trust property, including all records required by this paragraph. Records shall be preserved for a period of six years after termination of the representation and after distribution of the property. Records may be maintained by computer subject to the requirements of subparagraph (1)G of this paragraph (f) or they may be prepared manually.

(1) *Trust Account Records.* The following books and records must be maintained for each trust account:

A. **Account Documentation.** A record of the name and address of the bank or other depository; account number; account title; opening and closing dates; and the type of account, whether pooled, with net interest paid to the IOLTA Committee (IOLTA account), or account with interest paid to the client or third person on whose behalf the trust property is held (including master or umbrella accounts with individual subaccounts).

B. **Check Register.** A check register recording in chronological order the date and amount of all deposits;

the date, check or transaction number, amount, and payee of all disbursements, whether by check, electronic transfer, or other means; the date and amount of every other credit or debit of whatever nature; the identity of the client matter for which funds were deposited or disbursed; and the current balance in the account.

C. **Individual Client Records.** A record for each client or third person for whom the lawyer received trust funds documenting each receipt and disbursement of the funds of the client or third person, the identity of the client matter for which funds were deposited or disbursed, and the balance held for the client or third person, including a subsidiary ledger or ledger for each client matter for which the lawyer receives trust funds documenting each receipt and disbursement of the funds of the client or third person with respect to such matter. A lawyer shall not disburse funds from the trust account that would create a negative balance with respect to any individual client.

D. **Bank Fees and Charges.** A ledger or other record for funds of the lawyer deposited in the trust account pursuant to paragraph (b)(2)(i) of this Rule to accommodate reasonably expected bank charges. This ledger shall document each deposit and expenditure of the lawyer's funds in the account and the balance remaining.

E. **Reconciliation Reports.** For each trust account, the lawyer shall prepare and retain a reconciliation report on a regular and periodic basis but in any event no less frequently than every sixty days. Each reconciliation report shall show the following balances and verify that they are identical:

(i) The balance which appears in the check register as of the reporting date

(ii) The adjusted bank statement balance, determined by adding outstanding deposits and other credits to the bank statement balance and subtracting outstanding checks and other debits from the bank statement balance.

(iii) For any account in which funds are held for more than one client matter, the total of all client matter balances, determined by listing each of the individual client matter records and the balance which appears in each record as of the reporting date, and calculating the total. For the purpose of the calculation required by this paragraph, bank fees and charges shall be considered an individual client record. No balance for an individual client may be negative at any time.

F. **Account Documentation.** For each trust account, the lawyer shall retain contemporaneous records of transactions as necessary to document the transactions. The lawyer must retain:

(i) bank statements.

(ii) all transaction records returned by the bank, including canceled checks and records of electronic transactions.

(iii) records of deposits separately listing each deposited item and the client or third person for whom the deposit is being made.

G. **Electronic Record Retention.** A lawyer who maintains a trust account record by computer must maintain the check register, client ledgers, and reconciliation reports in a form that can be reproduced in printed hard copy. Electronic records must be regularly backed up by an appropriate storage device.

(2) *Business Accounts.* Each lawyer who receives trust funds must maintain at least one bank account, other than the trust account, for funds received and disbursed other than in the lawyer's fiduciary capacity.

(3) *Trust Property Other than Funds.* A lawyer who receives trust property other than funds must maintain a record showing the identity, location, and disposition of all such property.

(4) *Dissolution of a Law Firm.* Upon dissolution of a law firm, the partners shall make reasonable efforts to ensure the maintenance of client trust account records specified in this Rule.

(g) Interest on Lawyers' Trust Accounts.

(1) The IOLTA account shall be established with any bank, savings and loan association, or credit union authorized by Federal or State law to do business in Massachusetts and insured by the Federal Deposit Insurance Corporation or similar State insurance programs for State chartered institutions. At the direction of the lawyer, funds in the IOLTA account in excess of $100,000 may be temporarily reinvested in repurchase agreements fully collateralized by U.S. Government obligations. Funds in the IOLTA account shall be subject to withdrawal upon request and without delay.

(2) Lawyers creating and maintaining an IOLTA account shall direct the depository institution:

(i) to remit interest or dividends, net of any service charges or fees, on the average monthly balance in the account, or as otherwise computed in accordance with an institution's standard accounting practice, at least quarterly, to the IOLTA Committee;

(ii) to transmit with each remittance to the IOLTA Committee a statement showing the name of the lawyer who or law firm which deposited the funds; and

(iii) at the same time to transmit to the depositing lawyer a report showing the amount paid, the rate of interest applied, and the method by which the interest was computed.

(3) Lawyers shall certify their compliance with this Rule as required by S.J.C. Rule 4:02, § 2.

(4) This court shall appoint members of a permanent IOLTA Committee to fixed terms on a staggered basis. The representatives appointed to the committee shall oversee the operation of a comprehensive IOLTA program, including:

(i) the receipt of all IOLTA funds and their disbursement, net of actual expenses, to the designated charitable entities, as follows: sixty seven percent (67%) to the Massachusetts Legal Assistance Corporation and the remaining thirty three percent (33%) to other designated charitable entities in such proportions as the Supreme Judicial Court may order;

(ii) the education of lawyers as to their obligation to create and maintain IOLTA accounts under this Rule;

(iii) the encouragement of the banking community and the public to support the IOLTA program;

(iv) the obtaining of tax rulings and other administrative approval for a comprehensive IOLTA program as appropriate;

(v) the preparation of such guidelines and rules, subject to court approval, as may be deemed necessary or advisable for the operation of a comprehensive IOLTA program;

(vi) establishment of standards for reserve accounts by the recipient charitable entities for the deposit of IOLTA funds which the charitable entity intends to preserve for future use; and

(vii) reporting to the court in such manner as the court may direct.

(5) The Massachusetts Legal Assistance Corporation and other designated charitable entities shall receive IOLTA funds from the IOLTA Committee and distribute such funds for approved purposes. The Massachusetts Legal Assistance Corporation may use IOLTA funds to further its corporate purpose and other designated charitable entities may use IOLTA funds either for (a) improving the administration of justice or (b) delivering civil legal services to those who cannot afford them.

(6) The Massachusetts Legal Assistance Corporation and other designated charitable entities shall submit an annual report to the court describing their IOLTA activities for the year and providing a statement of the application of IOLTA funds received pursuant to this Rule.

(h) Dishonored Check Notification.

All trust accounts shall be established in compliance with the following provisions on dishonored check notification:

(1) A lawyer shall maintain trust accounts only in financial institutions which have filed with the Board of Bar Overseers an agreement, in a form provided by the Board, to report to the Board in the event any properly payable instrument is presented against any trust account that contains insufficient funds, and the financial institution dishonors the instrument for that reason.

(2) Any such agreement shall apply to all branches of the financial institution and shall not be cancelled except upon thirty days notice in writing to the Board.

(3) The Board shall publish annually a list of financial institutions which have signed agreements to comply with this Rule, and shall establish rules and procedures governing amendments to the list.

(4) The dishonored check notification agreement shall provide that all reports made by the financial institution shall be identical to the notice of dishonor customarily forwarded to the depositor, and should include a copy of the dishonored instrument, if such a copy is normally provided to depositors. Such reports shall be made simultaneously with the notice of dishonor and within the time provided by law for such notice, if any.

(5) Every lawyer practicing or admitted to practice in this Commonwealth shall, as a condition thereof, be conclusively

deemed to have consented to the reporting and production requirements mandated by this Rule.

(6) The following definitions shall be applicable to this subparagraph:

(i) "Financial institution" includes (a) any bank, savings and loan association, credit union, or savings bank, and (b) with the written consent of the client or third person on whose behalf the trust property is held, any other business or person which accepts for deposit funds held in trust by lawyers.

(ii) "Notice of dishonor" refers to the notice which a financial institution is required to give, under the laws of this Commonwealth, upon presentation of an instrument which the institution dishonors.

(iii) "Properly payable" refers to an instrument which, if presented in the normal course of business, is in a form requiring payment under the laws of this Commonwealth.

Adopted June 9, 1997, effective January 1, 1998. Amended September 5, 2003, effective July 1, 2004. Amended March 26, 2015, effective July 1, 2015.

Comment

[1] A lawyer should hold property of others with the care required of a professional fiduciary. Securities should be kept in a safe deposit box, except when some other form of safekeeping is warranted by special circumstances. Separate trust accounts are warranted when administering estate monies or acting in similar fiduciary capacities.

[2] In general, the phrase "in connection with a representation" includes all situations where a lawyer holds property as a fiduciary, including as an escrow agent. For example, an attorney serving as a trustee under a trust instrument or by court appointment holds property "in connection with a representation". Likewise, a lawyer serving as an escrow agent in connection with litigation or a transaction holds that property "in connection with a representation". However, a lawyer serving as a fiduciary who is not actively practicing law does not hold property "in connection with a representation."

[2A] Legal fees and expenses paid in advance that are to be applied as compensation for services subsequently rendered or for expenses subsequently incurred are trust property and are required by paragraphs (b)(1) and (b)(3) to be deposited to a trust account. These fees and expenses can be withdrawn by a lawyer only as fees are earned or expenses incurred. The Rule does not require flat fees to be deposited to a trust account, but a flat fee that is deposited to a trust account is subject to all the provisions of this Rule, including paragraphs (b)(2) and (d)(2). A flat fee is a fixed fee that an attorney charges for all legal services in a particular matter, or for a particular discrete component of legal services, whether relatively simple and of short duration, or complex and protracted. For the obligation to refund an unearned fee in the event of a discharge or withdrawal, see Rule 1.16(d).

[3] Lawyers often receive funds from third parties from which the lawyer's fee will be paid. If there is risk that the client may divert the funds without paying the fee, the lawyer is not required to remit the portion from which the fee is to be paid. However, a lawyer may not hold funds to coerce a client into accepting the lawyer's contention. The disputed portion of the funds must be kept in trust and the lawyer should suggest means for prompt resolution of the dispute, such as arbitration. The undisputed portion of the funds shall be promptly distributed.

[4] Third parties, such as a client's creditors, may have just claims against funds or other property in a lawyer's custody. A lawyer may have a duty under applicable law to protect such third party claims against wrongful interference by the client, and accordingly may refuse to surrender the property to the client. However, a lawyer should not unilaterally assume to arbitrate a dispute between the client and the third party.

[5] The obligations of a lawyer under this Rule are independent of those arising from activity other than rendering legal services. For example, a lawyer who serves as an escrow agent is governed by the applicable law relating to fiduciaries even though the lawyer does not render legal services in the transaction.

[6] How much time should elapse between the receipt of funds by the lawyer and notice to the client or third person for whom the funds are held pursuant to paragraph (c) depends on the circumstances. By example, notice must be furnished immediately upon receipt of funds in settlement of a disputed matter, but a lawyer acting as an escrow agent or trustee routinely collecting various items of income may give notice by furnishing a complete statement of receipts and expenses on a regular periodic basis satisfactory to the client or third person. Notice to a client or third person is not ordinarily required for payments of interest and dividends in the normal course, provided that the lawyer properly includes all such payments in regular periodic statements or accountings for the funds held by the lawyer.

[6A] Paragraph (d)(2) provides that, on or before the date of any withdrawals from a trust account to pay fees due, the lawyers must provide the client in writing with, among other information, an itemized bill or other accounting showing the services rendered. Because the definition of "trust property" in paragraph (a)(1) includes funds held in a fiduciary capacity, lawyers who represent themselves as fiduciaries(such as personal representatives, executors, conservators, guardians or trustees) must comply with paragraph (d)(2) by creating, prior to or contemporaneous with any withdrawal of fees, the bills or accountings required by the rule to justify payment. Such accountings may consist of itemized written time records, formal written bills, or other contemporaneous written accountings that show the services rendered and the method for calculating the fees. The lawyer is also required to maintain all trust account records specified in paragraphs (e) and (f) of this rule.

[7] Paragraph (e)(3) requires attorneys to provide a written notice to the bank or other depository when opening any account that is a trust account within the meaning of this Rule, regardless of whether the account is an IOLTA account or an individual trust account. The notice must be acknowledged in writing by the bank and an executed copy retained for the lawyer's own records. Forms for opening an IOLTA account (called an Attorney's Notice of Enrollment) may be found on the IOLTA Committee website or obtained by contacting the IOLTA Committee directly. See the IOLTA Guidelines for additional procedures to be used when opening IOLTA accounts. Forms for notice to a bank when opening an individual (i.e., non-IOLTA) trust account may be obtained online from the website of the Board of Bar Overseers. The use of these forms shall not prevent the use of other forms consistent with this Rule.

[8] Paragraph (e)(4) states the general rule that all withdrawals and disbursements from trust account must be made in a manner which permits the recipient or payee of the withdrawal to be identified. It does not prohibit electronic transfers or foreclose means of withdrawal which may be developed in the future, provided that the recipient of the payment is identified as part of the transaction. When payment is made by check, the check must be payable to a specific person or entity. A prenumbered check must be used, except that starter checks may be used for a brief period between the opening of a new account and issuance of numbered checks by the bank or depository.

[9] Paragraph (f) lists records that a lawyer is obliged to keep in order to comply with the requirement that "complete records" be maintained. Additional records may be required to document financial transactions with clients or third persons. Depending on the circumstances, these records could include retainer, fee, and escrow agreements and accountings, including RESPA or other real estate closing statements, accountings in contingent fee matters, and any other statement furnished to a client or third person to document receipt and disbursement of funds.

[10] The "Check Register," "Individual Client Ledger" and "Ledger for Bank Fees and Charges" required by paragraph (f)(1) are all chronological records of transactions. Each entry made in the check register must have a corresponding entry in one of the ledgers. This requirement is consistent with manual record keeping and also comports with most software packages. In addition to the data required by paragraph (f)(1)(B), the source of the deposit and the purpose of the disbursement should be recorded in the check register and appropriate ledger. For non-IOLTA accounts, the dates and amounts of interest accrual and disbursement, including disbursements from accrued interest to defray the costs of maintaining the account, are among the transactions which must be recorded. Check register and ledger balances should be calculated and recorded after each transaction or series of related transactions.

[11] Periodic reconciliation of trust accounts is also required. Generally, trust accounts should be reconciled on a monthly basis so that any errors can be corrected promptly. Active, high-volume accounts may require more frequent reconciliations. A lawyer must reconcile all trust accounts at least every sixty days.

The three-way reconciliation described in paragraph (f)(1)(E) must be performed for any account in which funds related to more than one client matter are held. The reconciliation described in paragraph (f)(1)(E)(iii) need not be performed for accounts which only hold the funds of a single client or third person, but the lawyer must be sure that the balance in that account corresponds to the balance in the individual ledger maintained for that client or third person.

The method of preparation and form of the periodic reconciliation report will depend upon the volume of transactions in the accounts during the period covered by the report and whether the lawyer maintains records of the account manually or electronically. By example, for an inactive single-client account for which the lawyer keeps records manually, a written record that the lawyer has reconciled the account statement from the financial institution with the check register maintained by the lawyer may be sufficient.

[12] Lawyers who maintain records electronically should back up data on a regular basis. For moderate to high-volume trust accounts, weekly or even daily backups may be appropriate.

[13] Paragraph (f)(4), along with Rule 1.17(e), provides for the preservation of a lawyer's client trust account records in the event of dissolution or sale of a law practice. These provisions reflect the supervisory responsibilities of partners under Rule 5.1. Regardless of the arrangements the partners make among themselves for maintenance of the client trust records, each partner can be held responsible for ensuring the availability of these records. For the definition of "law firm," "partner," and "reasonable," see Rules 1.0(d), (h), and (k).

Rule 1.15A. Client Files

(a) For purposes of this Rule, the client's file consists of the following physical and electronically stored materials:

(1) all papers, documents, and other materials, whether in physical or electronic form, that the client supplied to the lawyer;

(2) all correspondence relating to the matter, whether in physical or electronic form;

(3) all pleadings and other papers filed with or by the court or served by or upon any party relevant to the client's claims or defenses;

(4) all investigatory or discovery documents, including but not limited to medical records, photographs, tapes, disks, investigative reports, expert reports, depositions, and demonstrative evidence;

(5) all intrinsically valuable documents of the client; and

(6) copies of the lawyer's work product.

Paragraph (a) does not impose an obligation to preserve documents that a lawyer following customary practices would not normally preserve in the client's file. For purposes of subparagraph (5), documents are intrinsically valuable where they constitute trust property as defined in Rule 1.15 or have legal, operative, personal, historical or other significance in themselves, including wills, trusts and other executed estate planning documents, deeds, securities, negotiable instruments, and official corporate or other records. For purposes of this Rule, work product shall consist of documents and tangible things prepared in the course of the representation of the client by the lawyer or at the lawyer's direction by the lawyer's employee, agent, or consultant, and not described in subparagraphs (2), (3), (4) or (5) above. Examples of work product include without limitation legal research, closing binders, records of witness interviews, and reports of negotiations.

(b) A lawyer must make the client's file available to a client or former client within a reasonable time following the client's or former client's request for his or her file, provided however, that:

(1) the lawyer may at the lawyer's own expense retain copies of documents turned over to the client;

(2) the client may be required to pay (i) any copying charges for copying the material described in subparagraphs (a)(3) and (a)(6), consistent with the lawyer's actual copying cost, unless the client has already paid for such material, and (ii) the lawyer's actual cost for the delivery of the file;

(3) the lawyer is not required to turn over to the client investigatory or discovery documents for which the client is obligated to pay under the fee agreement but has not paid; and

(4) unless the lawyer and the client have entered into a contingent fee agreement, the lawyer is only required to turn over copies of the lawyer's work product for which the client has paid.

Notwithstanding anything in this paragraph (b) to the contrary, a lawyer may not refuse, on grounds of nonpayment, to make available materials in the client's file when retention would unfairly prejudice the client.

(c) Except for materials governed by paragraphs (d), (e) and (f), a lawyer shall take reasonable measures to retain a client's file in a matter until at least six years have elapsed after completion of the matter or termination of the representation in the matter unless (i) the lawyer has transferred the file or items to the client or successor counsel, or as otherwise directed by the client, or (ii) the client agrees in writing to an alternative arrangement for the file's custody or destruction, provided, however, that files relating to the representation of a minor shall be retained until at least six years after the minor reaches the age of majority. If the client has not requested the file within six years after completion or termination of the representation or within six years after a minor reaches the age of majority, the file may be destroyed except as provided in paragraphs (d), (e), and (f) below.

(d) Intrinsically valuable documents that constitute trust property of the client must be delivered to the client as provided in Rule 1.15(c). All other intrinsically valuable documents must be appropriately safeguarded and delivered in accordance with paragraph (b) above, or retained until such time as the documents no longer possess intrinsic value. If the client cannot be found, the lawyer shall securely retain such documents or, where applicable, deliver such items to an appropriate governmental repository.

(e) A lawyer shall not destroy a client's file if the lawyer knows or reasonably should know that:

(1) a lawsuit or other legal claim related to the client matter is pending or anticipated;

(2) a criminal or other governmental investigation related to the client matter is pending or anticipated; or

(3) a disciplinary investigation or proceeding related to the client matter or a claim before the Client Security Board is pending or anticipated.

(f) Criminal defense counsel and defense counsel in delinquency cases shall retain a client's files as follows:

(1) for the life of the client if the matter resulted in a conviction and a sentence of death or life imprisonment with or without the possibility of parole; and

(2) in all other criminal or delinquency matters, for ten years after the latest of the completion of the representation, the conclusion of all direct appeals, or the running of an incarcerated defendant's maximum period of incarceration, but in no event longer than the life of the client.

(g) A lawyer shall take reasonable measures to ensure that the destruction of all or any portion of a client file shall be carried out in a manner consistent with all applicable confidentiality obligations.

Adopted June 7, 2018, effective September 1, 2018.

Comment

[1] In order to represent clients competently in a matter, lawyers customarily maintain a file of papers and electronically stored information that will in the lawyers' judgment aid in the representation. This Rule governs lawyers' obligations with respect to the custody and destruction of client files. A lawyer's obligations with respect to client funds are governed by Rule 1.15 and, with specific respect to trust property such as jewelry and other valuables entrusted to the lawyer by the client, by Rule 1.15(b)(4). Lawyers are encouraged to address disposition of client files in the written engagement letter required by Rule 1.5(b)(1) and, in instances where particular arrangements for disposition or transfer have not been made, in the lawyer's final communication to the client at the conclusion of a matter.

[2] The client's file in a given matter consists of those items that must be made available upon the client's direction to the client or successor counsel to provide a reasonably complete record of the services provided and, if the matter is unfinished, to give successor counsel what is needed to complete the representation. Thus, the client file for a litigation matter would include the pleadings and court filings, rulings and other documents issued by the court, all correspondence including with the client and opposing counsel, deposition transcripts, documents produced or received in discovery (subject to applicable protective orders), investigatory materials and expert reports, the trial record, memorialized legal research and analysis, and any settlement documents. In a case with a limited number of parties, the pleadings would include all the material pleadings. In a large case with many parties, such as a large bankruptcy proceeding, the pleadings would only include those directly relevant to the client's claims and defenses. The client file for a transactional matter would include all correspondence, including with the client and counterparties and the exchange of drafts, contracts and other documents establishing the terms of the transaction (often gathered into a "closing binder"), and memorialized legal research and analysis.

[3] Multiple copies or drafts of the same document ordinarily do not constitute part of the client's file unless the matter is unfinished, and the client and successor counsel must have the drafts to complete the representation. Similarly, a lawyer's personal notes ordinarily do not constitute part of the client's file unless the notes are the only record of a witness interview, a settlement negotiation, a meeting with regulators or prosecutors, or some similar event. Once a document is finalized or personal notes of an event are memorialized, this Rule does not require preservation of the drafts or notes. However, documents that are part of the client's file at the time of a request for the file must thereafter be preserved and produced. Except as provided in Comment 4, this Rule does not require preservation of any physical documents that have been converted to electronic form.

[4] Unless other applicable law requires a particular document to be physically preserved for its legal effectiveness, a lawyer may maintain a client's file in electronic form, provided, however, that, for documents stored only in electronic form, the lawyer must make reasonable efforts to store such electronic files in a form that can be read with available technology for any period during which the file must be retained. If the original form of the document is important, however, it should not be destroyed without the client's permission.

[5] The client's file does not include a lawyer's administrative files such as conflict checks, billing and accounting records, and communications within a law firm concerning matters of administration such as account creation, billing and collections, logistics, and the assignment and evaluation of personnel assigned to the matter. Such documents may be subject to discovery in a dispute concerning the representation, but ordinarily do not need to be provided to the client or successor counsel at the client's direction.

[6] Rule 1.15A does not supersede obligations imposed by court order, rules of a tribunal, or other law including discovery rules in civil cases, subpoenas and other mandatory process, and the law of spoliation and obstruction of justice. Similarly, Rule 1.15A does not supersede specific retention requirements imposed by other rules of professional conduct. *See, e.g.,* Rule 1.5(c). The maintenance of records required for trust property and trust accounts is governed exclusively by Rule 1.15. A document may be subject to more than one retention requirement, in which case the lawyer should retain the document for the longest applicable period.

[7] Under paragraphs (c) and (f) of this Rule, the nature of the underlying case dictates the minimum time period that a file must be retained before it may be destroyed without client agreement. In addition, a lawyer may not destroy the files under paragraph (e) if the lawyer knows that there are legal or disciplinary proceedings pending or anticipated that relate to the matter for which the lawyer created the files, if the materials at issue are intrinsically valuable documents under paragraph (d), or if the lawyer has agreed otherwise. If the conditions imposed by this Rule are satisfied, the lawyer may destroy the files in a manner consistent with the lawyer's obligation to maintain the confidentiality of information relating to the representation under Rules 1.6 and 1.9 and other applicable law such as the Massachusetts Privacy Act, Mass. Gen. Laws c. 93H, and the HIPAA Privacy Rule, 45 C.F.R. Parts 160 and 164. *See* Rule 1.6(c). A lawyer may destroy a client's file in accordance with this Rule notwithstanding the possibility that there could be further proceedings after the expiration of the time limits set forth in this Rule (such as a motion for a new trial or for relief from a judgment in light of changes in the law or the discovery of additional evidence), so long as such proceedings are not pending or anticipated at the time of the destruction.

[8] The lawyer's obligations under this Rule to retain and return files to the client are not excused because the lawyer forwarded papers to the client from time to time during the course of the representation.

[9] Nothing in this Rule is intended to mandate that a lawyer destroy a file. A lawyer appropriately may decide to retain certain types or portions of files, or portions of files for longer than six years, such as files relating to a structured settlement or other matters creating long-term obligations to or by the client. Unless the lawyer and the client have otherwise agreed, a lawyer may retain a copy of the file or any document in the file.

Rule 1.16. Declining or Terminating Representation

(a) Except as stated in paragraph (c), a lawyer shall not represent a client or, where representation has commenced, shall withdraw from the representation of a client if:

(1) the representation will result in violation of the rules of professional conduct or other law;

(2) the lawyer's physical or mental condition materially impairs the lawyer's ability to represent the client; or

(3) the lawyer is discharged.

(b) Except as stated in paragraph (c), a lawyer may withdraw from representing a client if:

(1) withdrawal can be accomplished without material adverse effect on the interests of the client;

(2) the client persists in a course of action involving the lawyer's services that the lawyer reasonably believes is criminal or fraudulent;

(3) the client has used the lawyer's services to perpetrate a crime or fraud;

(4) the client insists upon taking action that the lawyer considers repugnant or with which the lawyer has a fundamental disagreement;

(5) the client fails substantially to fulfill an obligation to the lawyer regarding the lawyer's services and has been given reasonable warning that the lawyer will withdraw unless the obligation is fulfilled;

(6) the representation will result in an unreasonable financial burden on the lawyer or has been rendered unreasonably difficult by the client; or

(7) other good cause for withdrawal exists.

(c) If permission for withdrawal from employment is required by the rules of a tribunal, a lawyer shall not withdraw from employment in a proceeding before that tribunal without its permission.

(d) Upon termination of representation, a lawyer shall take steps to the extent reasonably practicable to protect a client's interests, such as giving reasonable notice to the client, allowing time for employment of other counsel, surrendering papers and property to which the client is entitled, and refunding any advance payment of fee or expense that has not been earned or incurred.

Adopted June 9, 1997, effective January 1, 1998. Amended March 26, 2015, effective July 1, 2015. Amended June 7, 2018, effective September 1, 2018.

Comment

[1] A lawyer should not accept representation in a matter unless it can be performed competently, promptly, without improper conflict of interest and to completion. Ordinarily, a representation in a matter is completed when the agreed-upon assistance has been concluded. See Rules 1.2(c) and 6.5. See also Rule 1.3, Comment 4.

Mandatory Withdrawal

[2] A lawyer ordinarily must decline or withdraw from representation if the client demands that the lawyer engage in conduct that is illegal or violates the Rules of Professional Conduct or other law. The lawyer is not obliged to decline or withdraw simply because the client suggests such a course of conduct; a client may make such a suggestion in the hope that a lawyer will not be constrained by a professional obligation.

[3] When a lawyer has been appointed to represent a client, withdrawal ordinarily requires approval of the appointing authority. See also Rule 6.2. Similarly, court approval or notice to the court is often required by applicable law before a lawyer withdraws from pending litigation. Difficulty may be encountered if withdrawal is based on the client's demand that the lawyer engage in unprofessional conduct. The court may request an explanation for the withdrawal, while the lawyer may be bound to keep confidential the facts that would constitute such an explanation. If a lawyer's withdrawal is mandatory under these Rules, the lawyer's statement to that effect should ordinarily be accepted as sufficient. Lawyers should be mindful of their obligations to both clients and the court under Rules 1.6 and 3.3.

Discharge

[4] A client has a right to discharge a lawyer at any time, with or without cause, subject to liability for payment for the lawyer's services. Where future dispute about the withdrawal may be anticipated, it may be advisable to prepare a written statement reciting the circumstances.

[5] An appointed lawyer should advise a client seeking to discharge the appointed lawyer of the consequences of such an action, including the possibility that the client may be required to proceed pro se.

[6] If the client has severely diminished capacity, the client may lack the legal capacity to discharge the lawyer, and in any event the discharge may be seriously adverse to the client's interests. The lawyer should make special effort to help the client consider the consequences and may take reasonably necessary protective action as provided in Rule 1.14.

Optional Withdrawal

[7] A lawyer may withdraw from representation in some circumstances. The lawyer has the option to withdraw if it can be accomplished without material adverse effect on the client's interests. Withdrawal is also justified if the client persists in a course of action that the lawyer reasonably believes is criminal or fraudulent, for a lawyer is not required to be associated with such conduct even if the lawyer does not further it. Withdrawal is also permitted if the lawyer's services were misused in the past even if that would materially prejudice the client. The lawyer may also withdraw where the client insists on taking action that the lawyer considers repugnant or with which the lawyer has a fundamental disagreement.

[8] A lawyer may withdraw if the client refuses to abide by the terms of an agreement relating to the representation, such as an agreement concerning fees or court costs or an agreement limiting the objectives of the representation.

Assisting the Client upon Withdrawal

[9] Even if the lawyer has been unfairly discharged by the client, a lawyer must take all reasonable steps to mitigate the consequences to the client.

[10] Rule 1.15(c) specifies the lawyer's obligation to return funds and other property to which the client is entitled, and Rule 1.15A(b) details the lawyer's obligation to make client files available to a client or former client at the client's request.

Rule 1.17.　Sale of Law Practice

A lawyer or law firm may sell, and a lawyer or law firm may purchase, with or without consideration, a law practice, including good will, if the following conditions are satisfied:

(a) Reserved

(b) Reserved

(c) The seller gives written notice to each of the seller's clients regarding:

(1) the proposed sale;

(2) the client's right to retain other counsel or to take possession of the file; and

(3) the fact that the client's consent to the transfer of that client's representation will be presumed if the client does not take any action or does not otherwise object within ninety (90) days of receipt of the notice.

If a client cannot be given notice, the representation of that client may be transferred to the purchaser only upon entry of an order so authorizing by a court having jurisdiction. The seller may disclose to the court in camera confidential information relating to the representation only to the extent necessary to obtain an order authorizing the transfer.

(d) The fees charged clients shall not be increased by reason of the sale. The purchaser may, however, refuse to include a particular representation in the purchase unless the client consents to pay the purchaser fees at a rate not exceeding the fees charged by the purchaser for rendering substantially similar services prior to the initiation of the purchase negotiations.

(e) Upon the sale of a law practice, the seller shall make reasonable arrangements for the maintenance of property and records specified in Rule 1.15.

Adopted June 9, 1997, effective January 1, 1998. Amended March 26, 2015, effective July 1, 2015.

Comment

[1] The practice of law is a profession, not merely a business. Clients are not commodities that can be purchased and sold at will. Pursuant to this Rule, when a lawyer or an entire firm ceases to practice and another lawyer or firm takes over the representation, the selling lawyer or firm may obtain compensation for the reasonable value of the practice as may withdrawing partners of law firms. See Rules 5.4 and 5.6.

[2] Reserved

[3] Reserved

[4] Reserved

[5] Reserved

[6] Reserved

Client Confidences, Consent and Notice

[7] Negotiations between seller and prospective purchaser prior to disclosure of information relating to a specific representation of an identifiable client no more violate the confidentiality provisions of Rule 1.6 than do preliminary discussions concerning the possible association of another lawyer or mergers between firms, with respect to which client consent is not required. See Rule 1.6(b)(7). Providing the purchaser access to detailed confidential information relating to the representation, such as the client's file, however, requires client consent. The Rule provides that before such information can be disclosed by the seller to the purchaser the client must be given actual written notice of the contemplated sale, including the identity of the purchaser, and must be told that the decision to consent or make other arrangements must be made within 90 days. If nothing is heard from the client within that time, consent to the sale is presumed.

[8] A lawyer or law firm ceasing to practice cannot be required to remain in practice because some clients cannot be given actual notice of the proposed purchase. Since these clients cannot themselves consent to the purchase or direct any other disposition of their files, the Rule requires an order from a court having jurisdiction authorizing their transfer or other disposition. The Court can be expected to determine whether reasonable efforts to locate the client have been exhausted, and whether the absent client's legitimate interests will be served by authorizing the transfer of the file so that the purchaser may continue the representation. If necessary to preserve client confidences, the lawyer shall request that the petition for a court order be considered *in camera*.

[9] All the elements of client autonomy, including the client's absolute right to discharge a lawyer and transfer the representation to another, survive the sale of the practice.

Fee Arrangements Between Client and Purchaser

[10] The sale may not be financed by increases in fees charged the clients of the practice. Existing agreements between the seller and the client as to fees and the scope of the work must be honored by the purchaser. The purchaser may, however, refuse to include a particular representation in the purchase unless the client consents to pay the purchaser fees at a rate not exceeding the fees charged by the purchaser for rendering substantially similar services prior to the initiation of the purchase negotiations.

Other Applicable Ethical Standards

[11] Lawyers participating in the sale of some or all of a law practice or a practice area are subject to the ethical standards applicable to involving another lawyer in the representation of a client. These include, for example, the seller's obligation to exercise competence in identifying a purchaser qualified to assume the practice and the purchaser's obligation to undertake the representation competently (see Rule 1.1); the obligation to avoid disqualifying conflicts, and to secure the client's informed consent for those conflicts that can be agreed to (see Rule 1.7 regarding conflicts and Rule 1.0(f) for the definition of informed consent); and the obligation to protect confidential information relating to the representation (see Rules 1.6 and 1.9).

[12] If approval of the substitution of the purchasing lawyer for the selling lawyer is required by the rules of any tribunal in which a matter is pending, such approval must be obtained before the matter can be included in the sale (see Rule 1.16).

Applicability of the Rule

[13] This Rule applies to the sale of a law practice of a deceased, disabled or disappeared lawyer. Thus, the seller may be represented by a non-lawyer representative not subject to these Rules. Since, however, no lawyer may participate in a sale of a law practice that does not conform to the requirements of this Rule, the representatives of the seller as well as the purchasing lawyer can be expected to see to it that they are met.

[14] Admission to or retirement from a law firm, retirement plan and similar arrangements, and a sale of tangible assets of a law practice, do not constitute a sale or purchase governed by this Rule.

[15] This Rule does not apply to the transfers of legal representation between lawyers when such transfers are unrelated to the sale of a practice.

[16] This Rule does not require the seller to cease to engage in the practice of law in a geographical area. This is a matter for agreement between the parties to the transfer.

[17] Under Rule 1.17, a lawyer may sell all or part of the practice.

[18] A law practice may be transferred and acquired without the necessity of consideration, and the client's consent referred to in Rule 1.17(c)(3) is only to the transfer of that client's representation.

[19] The Rule permits the estate or representative of a lawyer to make a transfer of the lawyer's practice to one or more purchasers.

[20] Paragraph (e) provides for the preservation of a lawyer's client trust account records in the event of the sale of a law practice and is the counterpart to Rule 1.15(f)(4), which applies when the law practice is dissolved. Comment 13 to Rule 1.15 is also applicable to paragraph (e) of this Rule.

Rule 1.18. Duties to Prospective Client

(a) A person who consults with a lawyer about the possibility of forming a client-lawyer relationship with respect to a matter is a prospective client.

(b) Even when no client-lawyer relationship ensues, a lawyer who has learned confidential information from a prospective client shall not use or reveal that information, except as Rule 1.9 would permit with respect to confidential information of a former client.

(c) A lawyer subject to paragraph (b) shall not represent a client with interests materially adverse to those of a prospective client in the same or a substantially related matter if the lawyer received confidential information from the prospective client that could be significantly harmful to that person in the matter, except as provided in paragraph (d). If a lawyer is disqualified from representation under this paragraph, no lawyer in a firm with which that lawyer is associated may knowingly undertake or continue representation in such a matter, except as provided in paragraph (d).

(d) When the lawyer has received disqualifying information as defined in paragraph (c), representation is permissible if:

(1) both the affected client and the prospective client have given informed consent, confirmed in writing, or:

(2) the lawyer who received the information took reasonable measures to avoid exposure to more disqualifying information than was reasonably necessary to determine whether to represent the prospective client; and

(i) the disqualified lawyer is timely screened, as defined in Rule 1.10(e), from any participation in the matter and is apportioned no part of the fee therefrom; and

(ii) written notice is promptly given to the prospective client.

Adopted March 26, 2015, effective July 1, 2015.

Comment

[1] Prospective clients, like clients, may disclose information to a lawyer, place documents or other property in the lawyer's custody, or rely on the lawyer's advice. A lawyer's consultations with a prospective client usually are limited in time and depth and leave both the prospective client and the lawyer free (and sometimes required) to proceed no further. Hence, prospective clients should receive some but not all of the protection afforded clients.

[2] A person becomes a prospective client by consulting with a lawyer about the possibility of forming a client-lawyer relationship with respect to a matter. Whether communications, including written, oral, or electronic communications, constitute a consultation depends on the circumstances. For example, a consultation is likely to have occurred if a lawyer, either in person or through the lawyer's advertising in any medium, specifically requests or invites the submission of confidential information about a potential representation without clear and reasonably understandable warnings and cautionary statements that limit the lawyer's obligations, and a person provides confidential information in response. See also Comment 4. In contrast, a consultation does not occur if a person provides confidential information to a lawyer in response to advertising that merely describes the lawyer's education, experience, areas of practice, and contact information, or provides legal information of general interest. Such a person communicates uninvited confidential information unilaterally to a lawyer, without any reasonable expectation that the lawyer is willing to discuss the possibility of forming a client-lawyer relationship, and is thus not a "prospective client." Moreover, a person who communicates with a lawyer for the purpose of disqualifying the lawyer is not a "prospective client."

[3] It is often necessary for a prospective client to reveal confidential information to the lawyer during an initial consultation prior to the decision about formation of a client-lawyer relationship. The lawyer often must learn such information to determine whether there is a conflict of interest with an existing client and whether the matter is one that the lawyer is willing to undertake. Paragraph (b) prohibits the lawyer from using or revealing that information, except as permitted by Rule 1.9, even if the client or lawyer decides not to proceed with the representation. The duty exists regardless of how brief the initial conference may be.

[4] In order to avoid acquiring disqualifying information from a prospective client, a lawyer considering whether or not to undertake a new matter should limit the initial consultation to only such information as reasonably appears necessary for that purpose. Where the information indicates that a conflict of interest or other reason for nonrepresentation exists, the lawyer should so inform the prospective client or decline the representation. If the prospective client wishes to retain the lawyer, and if consent is possible under Rule 1.7, then consent from all affected present or former clients must be obtained before accepting the representation.

[5] A lawyer may condition a consultation with a prospective client on the person's informed consent that no confidential information disclosed during the consultation will prohibit the lawyer from representing a different client in the matter. See Rule 1.0(f) for the definition of informed consent. If the agreement expressly so provides, the prospective client may also consent to the lawyer's subsequent use of confidential information received from the prospective client.

[6] Even in the absence of an agreement, under paragraph (c), the lawyer is not prohibited from representing a client with interests adverse to those of the prospective client in the same or a substantially related matter unless the lawyer has received from the prospective client confidential information that could be significantly harmful if used in the matter.

[7] Under paragraph (c), the prohibition in this Rule is imputed to other lawyers as provided in Rule 1.10, but, under paragraph (d)(1), imputation may be avoided if the lawyer obtains the informed consent, confirmed in writing, of both the prospective and affected clients. In the alternative, imputation may be avoided if the conditions of paragraph (d)(2) are met and all disqualified lawyers are timely screened and written notice is promptly given to the prospective client. See Rule 1.10(e) (requirements for screening procedures). Paragraph (d)(2)(i) does not prohibit the screened lawyer from receiving a salary or partnership share established by prior independent agreement, but that lawyer may not receive compensation directly related to the matter in which the lawyer is disqualified.

[8] Notice, including a general description of the subject matter about which the lawyer was consulted, and of the screening procedures employed, generally should be given as soon as practicable after the need for screening becomes apparent.

[9] For the duty of competence of a lawyer who gives assistance on the merits of a matter to a prospective client, see Rule 1.1. For a

lawyer's duties when a prospective client entrusts valuables or papers to the lawyer's care, see Rule 1.15.

COUNSELOR

Rule 2.1. Advisor

In representing a client, a lawyer shall exercise independent professional judgment and render candid advice. In rendering advice, a lawyer may refer not only to law but to other considerations such as moral, economic, social and political factors, that may be relevant to the client's situation.

Adopted June 9, 1997, effective January 1, 1998. Amended March 26, 2015, effective July 1, 2015.

Comment

Scope of Advice

[1] A client is entitled to straightforward advice expressing the lawyer's honest assessment. Legal advice often involves unpleasant facts and alternatives that a client may be disinclined to confront. In presenting advice, a lawyer endeavors to sustain the client's morale and may put advice in as acceptable a form as honesty permits. However, a lawyer should not be deterred from giving candid advice by the prospect that the advice will be unpalatable to the client.

[2] Advice couched in narrow legal terms may be of little value to a client, especially where practical considerations, such as cost or effects on other people, are predominant. Purely technical legal advice, therefore, can sometimes be inadequate. It is proper for a lawyer to refer to relevant moral and ethical considerations in giving advice. Although a lawyer is not a moral advisor as such, moral and ethical considerations impinge upon most legal questions and may decisively influence how the law will be applied.

[3] A client may expressly or impliedly ask the lawyer for purely technical advice. When such a request is made by a client experienced in legal matters, the lawyer may accept it at face value. When such a request is made by a client inexperienced in legal matters, however, the lawyer's responsibility as advisor may include indicating that more may be involved than strictly legal considerations.

[4] Matters that go beyond strictly legal questions may also be in the domain of another profession. Family matters can involve problems within the professional competence of psychiatry, clinical psychology or social work; business matters can involve problems within the competence of the accounting profession or of financial specialists. Where consultation with a professional in another field is itself something a competent lawyer would recommend, the lawyer should make such a recommendation. At the same time, a lawyer's advice at its best often consists of recommending a course of action in the face of conflicting recommendations of experts.

Offering Advice

[5] In general, a lawyer is not expected to give advice until asked by the client. However, when a lawyer knows that a client proposes a course of action that is likely to result in substantial adverse legal consequences to the client, the lawyer's duty to the client under Rule 1.4 may require that the lawyer offer advice if the client's course of action is related to the representation. Similarly, when a matter is likely to involve litigation, it may be necessary under Rule 1.4 to inform the client of forms of dispute resolution that might constitute reasonable alternatives to litigation. See Comment 8 to Rule 1.4. A lawyer ordinarily has no duty to initiate investigation of a client's affairs or to give advice that the client has indicated is unwanted, but a lawyer may initiate advice to a client when doing so appears to be in the client's interest.

Rule 2.2. Intermediary [Reserved]

Reserved June 9, 1997, effective January 1, 1998.

Comment

[1]   ABA Model Rule 2.2 sets forth circumstances in which a lawyer may act as an intermediary between clients. The court concluded that a lawyer representing more than one client should be governed by the conflict of interest principles stated in Rule 1.7. Specific Massachusetts Comments 12 through 12F to Rule 1.7 provide guidance concerning the joint representation of clients.

Special Massachusetts Comment. See Special Massachusetts Comment to Rule 1.7 concerning joint representation.

Rule 2.3. Evaluation for Use by Third Persons

(a) A lawyer may provide an evaluation of a matter affecting a client for the use of someone other than the client if:

(1) the lawyer reasonably believes that making the evaluation is compatible with other aspects of the lawyer's relationship with the client; and

(2) the client gives informed consent or providing the evaluation is impliedly authorized to carry out the representation.

(b) Reserved.

(c) Except as disclosure is authorized in connection with a report of an evaluation, information relating to the evaluation is otherwise protected by Rule 1.6.

Adopted June 9, 1997, effective January 1, 1998. Amended March 26, 2015, effective July 1, 2015.

Comment

Definition

[1] An evaluation may be performed at the client's direction but for the primary purpose of establishing information for the benefit of third parties; for example, an opinion concerning the title of property rendered at the behest of a vendor for the information of a prospective purchaser, or at the behest of a borrower for the information of a prospective lender. In some situations, the evaluation may be required by a government agency; for example, an opinion concerning the legality of the securities registered for sale under the securities laws. In other instances, the evaluation may be required by a third person, such as a purchaser of a business.

[1A] Where the person receiving the evaluation is also a client of the lawyer, the propriety of providing the evaluation is governed by Rule 1.7 and not this Rule. The propriety of a lawyer's use of the client's confidential information in preparing the evaluation is governed by Rule 1.6.

[2] A legal evaluation should be distinguished from an investigation of a person with whom the lawyer does not have a client-lawyer relationship. For example, a lawyer retained by a purchaser to analyze a vendor's title to property does not have a client-lawyer relationship with the vendor. So also, an investigation into a person's affairs by a government lawyer, or by special counsel employed by the government, is not an evaluation as that term is used in this Rule. The question is whether the lawyer is retained by the person whose affairs are being examined. When the lawyer is retained by that person, the general rules concerning loyalty to client and preservation

of confidences apply, which is not the case if the lawyer is retained by someone else. For this reason, it is essential to identify the person by whom the lawyer is retained. This should be made clear not only to the person under examination, but also to others to whom the results are to be made available.

Duties Owed to Third Person and Client

[3] When the evaluation is intended for the information or use of a third person, a legal duty to that person may or may not arise. That legal question is beyond the scope of this Rule. However, since such an evaluation involves a departure from the normal client-lawyer relationship, careful analysis of the situation is required. The lawyer must be satisfied as a matter of professional judgment that making the evaluation is compatible with other functions undertaken in behalf of the client. For example, if the lawyer is acting as advocate in defending the client against charges of fraud, it would normally be incompatible with that responsibility for the lawyer to perform an evaluation for others concerning the same or a related transaction. Assuming no such impediment is apparent, however, the lawyer should advise the client of the implications of the evaluation, particularly the lawyer's responsibilities to third persons and the duty to disseminate the findings.

Access to and Disclosure of Information

[4] The quality of an evaluation depends on the freedom and extent of the investigation upon which it is based. Ordinarily a lawyer should have whatever latitude of investigation seems necessary as a matter of professional judgment. Under some circumstances, however, the terms of the evaluation may be limited. For example, certain issues or sources may be categorically excluded, or the scope of search may be limited by time constraints or the noncooperation of persons having relevant information. Any such limitations that are material to the evaluation should be described in the report. If after a lawyer has commenced an evaluation, the client refuses to comply with the terms upon which it was understood the evaluation was to have been made, the lawyer's obligations are determined by law, having reference to the terms of the client's agreement and the surrounding circumstances. In no circumstances is the lawyer permitted to knowingly make a false statement of material fact or law in providing an evaluation under this Rule. See Rule 4.1.

[5] Reserved.

Financial Auditors' Requests for Information

[6] When a question concerning the legal situation of a client arises at the instance of the client's financial auditor and the question is referred to the lawyer, the lawyer's response may be made in accordance with procedures recognized in the legal profession. Such a procedure is set forth in the American Bar Association Statement of Policy Regarding Lawyers' Responses to Auditors' Requests for Information, adopted in 1975.

Rule 2.4. Lawyer Serving as Third–Party Neutral

(a) A lawyer serves as a third-party neutral when the lawyer assists two or more persons who are not clients of the lawyer to reach a resolution of a dispute or other matter that has arisen between them. Service as a third-party neutral may include service as an arbitrator, a mediator or in such other capacity as will enable the lawyer to assist the parties to resolve the matter.

(b) A lawyer serving as a third-party neutral shall inform unrepresented parties that the lawyer is not representing them. When the lawyer knows or reasonably should know that a party does not understand the lawyer's role in the matter, the lawyer shall explain the difference between the lawyer's role as a third-party neutral and a lawyer's role as one who represents a client.

Adopted June 8, 2005, effective July 1, 2005. Comment amended March 26, 2015, effective July 1, 2015.

Comment

[1] Alternative dispute resolution has become a substantial part of the civil justice system. Aside from representing clients in dispute-resolution processes, lawyers often serve as third-party neutrals. A third-party neutral is a person, such as a mediator, arbitrator, conciliator or evaluator, who assists the parties, represented or unrepresented, in the resolution of a dispute or in the arrangement of a transaction. Whether a third-party neutral serves primarily as a facilitator, evaluator or decisionmaker depends on the particular process that is either selected by the parties or mandated by a court.

[2] The role of a third-party neutral is not unique to lawyers, although, in some court-connected contexts, only lawyers are allowed to serve in this role or to handle certain types of cases. In performing this role, the lawyer may be subject to court rules or other law that apply either to third-party neutrals generally or to lawyers serving as third-party neutrals. Lawyer-neutrals may also be subject to various codes of ethics, such as the Code of Ethics for Arbitration in Commercial Disputes prepared by a joint committee of the American Bar Association and the American Arbitration Association or the Model Standards of Conduct for Mediators jointly prepared by the American Bar Association, the American Arbitration Association and the Society of Professionals in Dispute Resolution. In particular, lawyers in Massachusetts may be subject to the Uniform Rules of Dispute Resolution set forth in Supreme Judicial Court Rule 1:18.

[3] Unlike nonlawyers who serve as third-party neutrals, lawyers serving in this role may experience unique problems as a result of differences between the role of a third-party neutral and a lawyer's service as a client representative. The potential for confusion is significant when the parties are unrepresented in the process. Thus, paragraph (b) requires a lawyer-neutral to inform unrepresented parties that the lawyer is not representing them. For some parties, particularly parties who frequently use dispute-resolution processes, this information will be sufficient. For others, particularly those who are using the process for the first time, more information will be required. Where appropriate, the lawyer should inform unrepresented parties of the important differences between the lawyer's role as third-party neutral and a lawyer's role as a client representative, including the inapplicability of the attorney-client evidentiary privilege. The extent of disclosure required under this paragraph will depend on the particular parties involved and the subject matter of the proceeding, as well as the particular features of the dispute-resolution process selected.

[4] A lawyer who serves as a third-party neutral subsequently may be asked to serve as a lawyer representing a client in the same matter. The conflicts of interest that arise for both the individual lawyer and the lawyer's law firm are addressed in Rule 1.12. See also Uniform Rule of Dispute Resolution 9(e) set forth in S.J.C. Rule 1.18.

[5] Lawyers who represent clients in alternative dispute-resolution processes are governed by the Rules of Professional Conduct. When the dispute-resolution process takes place before a tribunal, as in binding arbitration (see Rule 1.0(p)), the lawyer's duty of candor is governed by Rule 3.3. Otherwise, the lawyer's duty of candor toward both the third-party neutral and other parties is governed by Rule 4.1.

ADVOCATE

Rule 3.1.   Meritorious Claims and Contentions

A lawyer shall not bring, continue, or defend a proceeding, or assert or controvert an issue therein, unless there is a basis in law and fact for doing so that is not frivolous, which includes a good faith argument for an extension, modification or reversal of existing law. A lawyer for the defendant in a criminal proceeding, or the respondent in a proceeding that could result in incarceration, may nevertheless so defend the proceeding as to require that every element of the case be established.

Adopted June 9, 1997, effective January 1, 1998. Amended March 26, 2015, effective July 1, 2015.

Comment

[1] The advocate has a duty to use legal procedure for the fullest benefit of the client's cause, but also a duty not to abuse legal procedure. The law, both procedural and substantive, establishes the limits within which an advocate may proceed. However, the law is not always clear and never is static. Accordingly, in determining the proper scope of advocacy, account must be taken of the law's ambiguities and potential for change.

[2] The filing of an action or defense or similar action taken for a client is not frivolous merely because the facts have not first been fully substantiated or because the lawyer expects to develop vital evidence only by discovery. What is required of lawyers, however, is that they inform themselves about the facts of their clients' cases and the applicable law and determine that they can make good faith arguments in support of their clients' positions. Such action is not frivolous even though the lawyer believes that the client's position ultimately will not prevail. The action is frivolous, however, if the client desires to have the action taken primarily for the purpose of harassing or maliciously injuring a person, or if the lawyer is unable either to make a good faith argument on the merits of the action taken or to support the action taken by a good faith argument for an extension, modification or reversal of existing law.

[3] The lawyer's obligations under this Rule are subordinate to federal or state constitutional law that entitles a defendant in a criminal matter to the assistance of counsel in presenting a claim or contention that otherwise would be prohibited by this Rule. The principle underlying the provision that a criminal defense lawyer may put the prosecution to its proof in all circumstances often will have equal application to proceedings in which the involuntary commitment of a client is in issue.

[4] The option granted to a criminal defense lawyer to defend the proceeding so as to require proof of every element of a crime does not impose an obligation to do so. Sound judgment and reasonable trial tactics may reasonably indicate a different course.

Rule 3.2.   Expediting Litigation

A lawyer shall make reasonable efforts to expedite litigation consistent with the interests of the client.

Adopted June 9, 1997, effective January 1, 1998. Comment amended March 26, 2015, effective July 1, 2015.

Comment

[1] Dilatory practices bring the administration of justice into disrepute. Although there will be occasions when a lawyer may properly seek a postponement for personal reasons, it is not proper for a lawyer to routinely fail to expedite litigation solely for the convenience of the advocates. Nor will a failure to expedite be reasonable if done for the purpose of frustrating an opposing party's attempt to obtain rightful redress or repose. It is not a justification that similar conduct is often

tolerated by the bench and bar. The question is whether a competent lawyer acting in good faith would regard the course of action as having some substantial purpose other than delay. Realizing financial or other benefit from otherwise improper delay in litigation is not a legitimate interest of the client.

Rule 3.3.   Candor Toward the Tribunal

(a) A lawyer shall not knowingly:

(1) make a false statement of fact or law to a tribunal or fail to correct a false statement of material fact or law previously made to the tribunal by the lawyer;

(2) fail to disclose to the tribunal legal authority in the controlling jurisdiction known to the lawyer to be directly adverse to the position of the client and not disclosed by opposing counsel; or

(3) offer evidence that the lawyer knows to be false, except as provided in Rule 3.3(e). If a lawyer, the lawyer's client, or a witness called by the lawyer, has offered material evidence and the lawyer comes to know of its falsity, the lawyer shall take reasonable remedial measures, including if necessary, disclosure to the tribunal. A lawyer may refuse to offer evidence, other than the testimony of a defendant in a criminal matter, that the lawyer reasonably believes is false.

(b) A lawyer who represents a client in an adjudicative proceeding and who knows that a person intends to engage, is engaging or has engaged in criminal or fraudulent conduct related to the proceeding shall take reasonable remedial measures, including, if necessary, disclosure to the tribunal.

(c) The duties stated in paragraphs (a) and (b) continue to the conclusion of the proceeding including all appeals, and apply even if compliance requires disclosure of information otherwise protected by Rule 1.6.

(d) In an ex parte proceeding, a lawyer shall inform the tribunal of all material facts known to the lawyer that will enable the tribunal to make an informed decision, whether or not the facts are adverse.

(e) In a criminal case, defense counsel who knows that the defendant, the client, intends to testify falsely may not aid the client in constructing false testimony, and has a duty strongly to discourage the client from testifying falsely, advising that such a course is unlawful, will have substantial adverse consequences, and should not be followed.

(1) If a lawyer discovers this intention before accepting the representation of the client, the lawyer shall not accept the representation.

(2) If, in the course of representing a defendant prior to trial, the lawyer discovers this intention and is unable to persuade the client not to testify falsely, the lawyer shall seek to withdraw from the representation, requesting any required permission. Disclosure of privileged or prejudicial information shall be made only to the extent necessary to effect the withdrawal. If disclosure of privileged or prejudicial information is necessary, the lawyer shall make an application to withdraw ex parte to a judge other than the judge who will preside at the trial and shall seek to be heard

in camera and have the record of the proceeding, except for an order granting leave to withdraw, impounded. If the lawyer is unable to obtain the required permission to withdraw, the lawyer may not prevent the client from testifying.

(3) If a criminal trial has commenced and the lawyer discovers that the client intends to testify falsely at trial, the lawyer need not file a motion to withdraw from the case if the lawyer reasonably believes that seeking to withdraw will prejudice the client. If, during the client's testimony or after the client has testified, the lawyer knows that the client has testified falsely, the lawyer shall call upon the client to rectify the false testimony and, if the client refuses or is unable to do so, the lawyer shall not reveal the false testimony to the tribunal. In no event may the lawyer examine the client in such a manner as to elicit any testimony from the client the lawyer knows to be false, and the lawyer shall not argue the probative value of the false testimony in closing argument or in any other proceedings, including appeals.

Adopted June 9, 1997, effective January 1, 1998. Amended March 26, 2015, effective July 1, 2015.

Comment

[1] This Rule governs the conduct of a lawyer who is representing a client in the proceedings of a tribunal. See Rule 1.0(p) for the definition of "tribunal." It also applies when th e lawyer is representing a client in an ancillary proceeding conducted pursuant to the tribunal's adjudicative authority, such as a deposition. Thus, for example, paragraph (a)(3) requires a lawyer to take reasonable remedial measures if the lawyer comes to know that a client who is testifying in a deposition has offered evidence that is false.

[2] This Rule sets forth the special duties of lawyers as officers of the court to avoid conduct that undermines the integrity of the adjudicative process. A lawyer acting as an advocate in an adjudicative proceeding has an obligation to present the client's case with persuasive force. Performance of that duty while maintaining confidences of the client, however, is qualified by the advocate's duty of candor to the tribunal. Consequently, although a lawyer in an adversary proceeding is not required to present an impartial exposition of the law or to vouch for the evidence submitted in a cause, the lawyer must not allow the tribunal to be misled by false statements of law or fact or evidence that the lawyer knows to be false.

Representations by a Lawyer

[3] An advocate is responsible for pleadings and other documents prepared for litigation, but is usually not required to have personal knowledge of matters asserted therein, for litigation documents ordinarily present assertions by the client, or by someone on the client's behalf, and not assertions by the lawyer. Compare Rule 3.1. However, an assertion purporting to be on the lawyer's own knowledge, as in an affidavit by the lawyer or in a statement in open court, may properly be made only when the lawyer knows the assertion is true or believes it to be true on the basis of a reasonably diligent inquiry. There are circumstances where failure to make a disclosure is the equivalent of an affirmative misrepresentation. The obligation prescribed in Rule 1.2(d) not to counsel a client to commit or assist the client in committing a fraud applies in litigation. Regarding compliance with Rule 1.2(d), see the Comment to that Rule. See also the Comment to Rule 8.4(b).

Legal Argument

[4] Legal argument based on a knowingly false representation of law constitutes dishonesty toward the tribunal. A lawyer is not required to make a disinterested exposition of the law, but must recognize the existence of pertinent legal authorities. Furthermore, as stated in paragraph (a)(2), an advocate has a duty to disclose directly adverse authority in the controlling jurisdiction that has not been disclosed by the opposing party. The underlying concept is that legal argument is a discussion seeking to determine the legal premises properly applicable to the case.

Offering Evidence

[5] Paragraph (a)(3) requires that the lawyer refuse to offer evidence that the lawyer knows to be false, regardless of the client's wishes, except as provided in Rule 3.3(e). This duty is premised on the lawyer's obligation as an officer of the court to prevent the trier of fact from being misled by false evidence. A lawyer does not violate this Rule if the lawyer offers the evidence for the purpose of establishing its falsity.

[6] When false evidence is offered by the client, however, a conflict may arise between the lawyer's duty to keep the client's revelations confidential and the duty of candor to the court. Upon ascertaining that material evidence is false, the lawyer should seek to persuade the client that the evidence should not be offered or, if it has been offered, that its false character should immediately be disclosed. If the persuasion is ineffective, the lawyer must take reasonable remedial measures.

[7] Reserved.

[8] The prohibition against offering false evidence only applies if the lawyer knows that the evidence is false. A lawyer's reasonable belief that evidence is false does not preclude its presentation to the trier of fact. A lawyer's knowledge that evidence is false, however, can be inferred from the circumstances. See Rule 1.0(g). Thus, although a lawyer should resolve doubts about the veracity of testimony or other evidence in favor of the client, the lawyer cannot ignore an obvious falsehood. For issues raised by perjury by a criminal defendant, see Comments 11A–11E.

[9] Although paragraph (a)(3) only prohibits a lawyer from offering evidence the lawyer knows to be false, it permits the lawyer to refuse to offer testimony or other proof that the lawyer reasonably believes is false. Offering such proof may reflect adversely on the lawyer's ability to discriminate in the quality of evidence and thus impair the lawyer's effectiveness as an advocate. Because of the special protections historically provided criminal defendants, however, Rule 3.3(e) separately addresses issues that arise in that context.

Remedial Measures

[10] Having offered material evidence in the belief that it was true, a lawyer may subsequently come to know that the evidence is false. Or, a lawyer may be surprised when the lawyer's client, or another witness called by the lawyer, offers testimony the lawyer knows to be false, either during the lawyer's direct examination or in response to cross-examination by the opposing lawyer. In such situations or if the lawyer knows of the falsity of testimony elicited from the client during a deposition, the lawyer must take reasonable remedial measures. In such situations, the advocate's proper course is to remonstrate with the client confidentially, advise the client of the lawyer's duty of candor to the tribunal and seek the client's cooperation with respect to the withdrawal or correction of the false statements or evidence. If that fails, and except as provided for in Rule 3.3(e), the advocate must take further remedial action. Except as provided in Rule 3.3(e), if withdrawal from the representation is not permitted or will not undo the effect of the false evidence, the advocate must make such disclosure to the tribunal as is reasonably necessary to remedy the situation, even if doing so requires the lawyer to reveal information that otherwise would be protected by Rule 1.6. It is for the tribunal then to determine what should be done—making a statement about the matter to the trier of fact, ordering a mistrial or perhaps nothing.

[11] The disclosure of a client's false testimony can result in grave consequences to the client, including not only a sense of betrayal but also loss of the case and perhaps a prosecution for perjury. But the alternative is that the lawyer cooperate in deceiving the court, thereby subverting the truth-finding process which the adversary system is designed to implement. See Rule 1.2(d). Furthermore, unless it is

clearly understood that the lawyer will act upon the duty to disclose the existence of false evidence, the client can simply reject the lawyer's advice to reveal the false evidence and insist that the lawyer keep silent. Thus the client could in effect coerce the lawyer into being a party to fraud on the court.

Perjury by a Criminal Defendant

[11A] In the defense of a criminally accused, the lawyer's duty to disclose the client's intent to commit perjury or offer of perjured testimony is complicated by state and federal constitutional provisions relating to due process, right to counsel, and privileged communications between lawyer and client. Rule 3.3(e) accommodates these special constitutional concerns in a criminal case by providing specific procedures and restrictions to be followed in the rare situations in which the client states his intention to, or does, offer testimony the lawyer knows to be perjured in a criminal trial.

[11B] Rule 3.3(e) requires that a lawyer know that the client intends to present false testimony before the lawyer proceeds under paragraph (e). This standard requires that the lawyer, before invoking the Rule, act in good faith and have a firm basis in objective fact. Conjecture or speculation that the defendant intends to testify falsely is not enough. Inconsistencies in the evidence or in the defendant's version of events are also not enough to trigger the Rule, even though the inconsistencies, considered in light of the Commonwealth's proof, raise concerns in the lawyer's mind that the defendant is equivocating and not an honest person. Similarly, the existence of strong physical and forensic evidence implicating the defendant would not be sufficient. Lawyers may rely on facts made known to them, and are under no duty to conduct an independent investigation.

[11C] In cases to which Rule 3.3(e) applies, it is the clear duty of the lawyer first to seek to persuade the client to refrain from testifying perjuriously. That persuasion should include, at a minimum, advising the client that such a course of action is unlawful, may have substantial adverse consequences, and should not be followed. If that persuasion fails, and the lawyer has not yet accepted the case, the lawyer must not agree to the representation. If the lawyer learns of this intention after the lawyer has accepted the representation of the client, but before trial, and is unable to dissuade the client of his or her intention to commit perjury, the lawyer must seek to withdraw from the representation. The lawyer must request the required permission to withdraw from the case by making an application ex parte before a judge other than the judge who will preside at the trial. The lawyer must request that the hearing on this motion to withdraw be heard in camera, and that the record of the proceedings, except for an order granting a motion to withdraw, be impounded.

[11D] Once the trial has begun, the lawyer may seek to withdraw from the representation but is not required to do so if the lawyer reasonably believes that withdrawal would prejudice the client. If the lawyer learns of the client's intention to commit perjury during the trial, and is unable to dissuade the client from testifying falsely, the lawyer may not stand in the way of the client's absolute right to take the stand and testify. If, during a trial, the lawyer knows that his or her client, while testifying, has made a perjured statement, and the lawyer reasonably believes that any immediate action taken by the lawyer will prejudice the client, the lawyer should wait until the first appropriate moment in the trial and then attempt to persuade the client confidentially to correct the perjury.

[11E] In any of these circumstances, if the lawyer is unable to convince the client to correct the perjury, the lawyer must not assist the client in presenting the perjured testimony and must not argue the false testimony to a judge, or jury or appellate court as true or worthy of belief. Except as provided in this Rule, the lawyer may not reveal to the court that the client intends to perjure or has perjured himself or herself in a criminal trial.

Preserving Integrity of Adjudicative Process

[12] Lawyers have a special obligation to protect a tribunal against criminal or fraudulent conduct that undermines the integrity of the adjudicative process, such as bribing, intimidating or otherwise unlawfully communicating with a witness, juror, court official or other participant in the proceeding, unlawfully destroying or concealing documents or other evidence or failing to disclose information to the tribunal when required by law to do so. Thus, paragraph (b) requires a lawyer to take reasonable remedial measures, including disclosure if necessary, whenever the lawyer knows that a person, including the lawyer's client, intends to engage, is engaging or has engaged in criminal or fraudulent conduct related to the proceeding.

Duration of Obligation

[13] A practical time limit on the obligation to rectify false evidence or false statements of law and fact has to be established. The conclusion of the proceeding is a reasonably definite point for the termination of the obligation. A proceeding has concluded within the meaning of this Rule when a final judgment in the proceeding has been affirmed on appeal or the time for review has passed.

Ex Parte Proceedings

[14] Ordinarily, an advocate has the limited responsibility of presenting one side of the matters that a tribunal should consider in reaching a decision; the conflicting position is expected to be presented by the opposing party. However, in any ex parte proceeding, such as an application for a temporary restraining order, there is no balance of presentation by opposing advocates. The object of an ex parte proceeding is nevertheless to yield a substantially just result. The judge has an affirmative responsibility to accord the absent party just consideration. The lawyer for the represented party has the correlative duty to make disclosures of material facts known to the lawyer and that the lawyer reasonably believes are necessary to an informed decision. Rule 3.3(d) does not change the rules applicable in situations covered by specific substantive law, such as presentation of evidence to grand juries, applications for search or other investigative warrants and the like.

[14A] When adversaries present a joint petition to a tribunal, such as a joint petition to approve the settlement of a class action suit or the settlement of a suit involving a minor, the proceeding loses its adversarial character and in some respects takes on the form of an ex parte proceeding. The lawyers presenting such a joint petition thus have the same duties of candor to the tribunal as lawyers in ex parte proceedings and should be guided by Rule 3.3(d).

Withdrawal

[15] Normally, a lawyer's compliance with the duty of candor imposed by this Rule does not require that the lawyer withdraw from the representation of a client whose interests will be or have been adversely affected by the lawyer's disclosure. The lawyer may, however, be required by Rule 1.16(a) to seek permission of the tribunal to withdraw if the lawyer's compliance with this Rule's duty of candor results in such an extreme deterioration of the client-lawyer relationship that the lawyer can no longer competently represent the client. Also see Rule 1.16(b) for the circumstances in which a lawyer will be permitted to seek a tribunal's permission to withdraw. In connection with a request for permission to withdraw that is premised on a client's misconduct, a lawyer may reveal confidential information relating to the representation only to the extent reasonably necessary to comply with this Rule or as otherwise permitted by Rule 1.6.

Rule 3.4. Fairness to Opposing Party and Counsel

A lawyer shall not:

(a) unlawfully obstruct another party's access to evidence or unlawfully alter, destroy, or conceal a document or other material having potential evidentiary value. A lawyer shall not counsel or assist another person to do any such act;

(b) falsify evidence, counsel or assist a witness to testify falsely, or offer an inducement to a witness that is prohibited by law;

(c) knowingly disobey an obligation under the rules of a tribunal except for an open refusal based on an assertion that no valid obligation exists;

(d) in pretrial procedure, make a frivolous discovery request or fail to make reasonably diligent effort to comply with a legally proper discovery request by an opposing party;

(e) in appearing before a tribunal on behalf of a client:

(1) state or allude to any matter that the lawyer does not reasonably believe is relevant or that will not be supported by admissible evidence;

(2) assert personal knowledge of facts in issue except when testifying as a witness; or

(3) assert a personal opinion as to the justness of a cause, the credibility of a witness, the culpability of a civil litigant or the guilt or innocence of an accused, but the lawyer may argue, upon analysis of the evidence, for any position or conclusion with respect to the matters stated herein;

(f) request a person other than a client to refrain from voluntarily giving relevant information to another party unless:

(1) the person is a relative or an employee or other agent of a client; and

(2) the lawyer reasonably believes that the person's interests will not be adversely affected by refraining from giving such information;

(g) pay, offer to pay, or acquiesce in the payment of compensation to a witness contingent upon the content of his or her testimony or the outcome of the case. But a lawyer may advance, guarantee, or acquiesce in the payment of:

(1) expenses reasonably incurred by a witness in preparing, attending or testifying;

(2) reasonable compensation to a witness for loss of time in preparing, attending or testifying; and

(3) a reasonable fee for the professional services of an expert witness;

(h) present, participate in presenting, or threaten to present criminal or disciplinary charges solely to obtain an advantage in a private civil matter; or

(i) in appearing in a professional capacity before a tribunal, engage in conduct manifesting bias or prejudice based on race, sex, religion, national origin, disability, age, or sexual orientation against a party, witness, counsel, or other person. This paragraph does not preclude legitimate advocacy when race, sex, religion, national origin, disability, age, or sexual orientation, or another similar factor is an issue in the proceeding.

Adopted June 9, 1997, effective January 1, 1998. Amended March 26, 2015, effective July 1, 2015.

Comment

[1] The procedure of the adversary system contemplates that the evidence in a case is to be marshalled competitively by the contending parties. Fair competition in the adversary system is secured by prohibitions against destruction or concealment of evidence, improperly influencing witnesses, obstructive tactics in discovery procedure, and the like.

[2] Documents and other items of evidence are often essential to establish a claim or defense. Subject to evidentiary privileges, the right of an opposing party, including the government, to obtain evidence through discovery or subpoena is an important procedural right. The exercise of that right can be frustrated if relevant material is altered, concealed or destroyed. Applicable law in many jurisdictions makes it an offense to destroy material for purpose of impairing its availability in a pending proceeding or one whose commencement can be foreseen. Falsifying evidence is also generally a criminal offense. Paragraph (a) applies to evidentiary material generally, including computerized information. Applicable law may permit a lawyer to take temporary possession of physical evidence of client crimes for the purpose of conducting a limited examination that will not alter or destroy material characteristics of the evidence. In such a case, applicable law may require the lawyer to turn the evidence over to the police or other prosecuting authority, depending on the circumstances.

[3] With regard to paragraph (b), it is not improper to pay a witness as provided in paragraph (g).

[4] Paragraph (f) permits a lawyer to advise employees of a client to refrain from giving information to another party, for the employees may identify their interests with those of the client. See also Rule 4.2.

[5] Paragraph (g) concerns the payment of funds to a witness. Compensation of a witness may not be based on the content of the witness's testimony or the result in the proceeding. A lawyer may pay a witness reasonable compensation for time lost and for expenses reasonably incurred in preparing for or attending the proceeding. A lawyer may pay a reasonable fee for the professional services of an expert witness.

[6] Paragraph (h) prohibits filing or threatening to file disciplinary charges as well as criminal charges solely to obtain an advantage in a private civil matter. The word "private" makes clear that a government lawyer may pursue criminal or civil enforcement, or both criminal and civil enforcement, remedies available to the government. This Rule is never violated by a report under Rule 8.3 made in good faith because the report would not be made "solely" to gain an advantage in a civil matter.

[7] Paragraph (i) concerns conduct before a tribunal that manifests bias or prejudice based on race, sex, religion, national origin, disability, age, or sexual orientation of any person. When these factors are an issue in a proceeding, paragraph (i) does not bar legitimate advocacy.

Rule 3.5. Impartiality and Decorum of the Tribunal

A lawyer shall not:

(a) seek to influence a judge, juror, prospective juror or other official by means prohibited by law;

(b) communicate ex parte with such a person during the proceeding unless authorized to do so by law or court order;

(c) communicate with a juror or prospective juror after discharge of the jury if:

(1) the communication is prohibited by law or court order;

(2) the juror has made known to the lawyer, either directly or through communications with the judge or otherwise, a desire not to communicate with the lawyer; or

(3) the communication involves misrepresentation, coercion, duress or harassment; or

(4) the communication is initiated by the lawyer without the notice required by law; or

(d) engage in conduct intended to disrupt a tribunal.

Adopted June 9, 1997, effective January 1, 1998. Amended March 26, 2015, effective July 1, 2015; November 16, 2017, effective December 1, 2017.

Comment

[1] Many forms of improper influence upon a tribunal are proscribed by criminal law. Others are specified in S.J.C. Rule 3:09, the Code of Judicial Conduct, with which an advocate should be familiar. A lawyer is required to avoid contributing to a violation of such provisions.

[2] During a proceeding a lawyer may not communicate ex parte with persons serving in an official capacity in the proceeding, such as judges, masters or jurors, unless authorized to do so by law or court order.

[3] A lawyer may on occasion want to communicate with a juror or prospective juror after the jury has been discharged. Subject to the notice requirements discussed below, the lawyer may do so unless the communication is prohibited by law or a court order. For example, in most cases common-law principles bar inquiry into the contents of jury deliberations and the thought processes of jurors, but not into extraneous influences. The lawyer must respect the desire of the juror not to talk with the lawyer. Where a juror makes known to the judge a desire not to communicate with the lawyer, and the judge so informs the lawyer, the lawyer may not initiate contact with that juror, directly or indirectly. The lawyer may not engage in improper conduct during the communication.

[3A] If the lawyer wishes to initiate the communication with a juror or prospective juror after discharge of the jury, the lawyer must send notice of the lawyer's intent to initiate such contact to counsel for the opposing party or parties (or directly to the opposing party or parties, if not represented by counsel) five business days before contacting any juror. The notice must include a description of the proposed manner of contact and the substance of any proposed inquiry to the jurors, and, where applicable, a copy of any letter or other form of written communication the lawyer intends to send. The preferred method of initiating contact with a juror is by written letter, and the letter must include a statement that the juror may decline any contact with the lawyer or terminate contact once initiated. If the lawyer seeks to initiate contact through an oral conversation (whether in person, by telephone, or otherwise), the lawyer is nonetheless required to provide opposing counsel or opposing parties with prior notice of the substance of the intended communication five business days before the contact is initiated. See *Commonwealth v. Moore*, 474 Mass. 541, 551-52 (2016).

[3B] If the juror initiates the communication with the lawyer and seeks to communicate about permissible subjects, such as the existence of extraneous influences on the jury deliberation process or the lawyer's performance during the trial, the lawyer is permitted to communicate with that juror after discharge of the jury without following these notice requirements.

[4] The advocate's function is to present evidence and argument so that the cause may be decided according to law. Refraining from abusive or obstreperous conduct is a corollary of the advocate's right to speak on behalf of litigants. A lawyer may stand firm against abuse by a judge but should avoid reciprocation; the judge's default is no justification for similar dereliction by an advocate. An advocate can present the cause, protect the record for subsequent review and preserve professional integrity by patient firmness no less effectively than by belligerence or theatrics.

[5] The duty to refrain from disruptive conduct applies to any proceeding of a tribunal, including a deposition. See Rule 1.0(p).

Rule 3.6.   Trial Publicity

(a) A lawyer who is participating or has participated in the investigation or litigation of a matter shall not make an extrajudicial statement that the lawyer knows or reasonably should know will be disseminated by means of public communication and will have a substantial likelihood of materially prejudicing an adjudicative proceeding in the matter.

(b) Notwithstanding paragraph (a), a lawyer may state:

(1) the claim, offense, or defense involved, and, except when prohibited by law, the identity of the persons involved;

(2) the information contained in a public record;

(3) that an investigation of the matter is in progress;

(4) the scheduling or result of any step in litigation;

(5) a request for assistance in obtaining evidence and information necessary thereto;

(6) a warning of danger concerning the behavior of a person involved, when there is reason to believe that there exists the likelihood of substantial harm to an individual or to the public interest; and

(7) in a criminal case, in addition to subparagraphs (1) through (6):

(i) the identity, residence, occupation, and family status of the accused;

(ii) if the accused has not been apprehended, information necessary to aid in apprehension of that person;

(iii) the fact, time, and place of arrest; and

(iv) the identity of investigating and arresting officers or agencies and the length of the investigation.

(c) Notwithstanding paragraph (a), a lawyer may make a statement that a reasonable lawyer would believe is required to protect a client from the substantial undue prejudicial effect of recent publicity not initiated by the lawyer or the lawyer's client. A statement made pursuant to this paragraph shall be limited to such information as is necessary to mitigate the recent adverse publicity.

(d) No lawyer associated in a firm or government agency with a lawyer subject to paragraph (a) shall make a statement prohibited by paragraph (a).

(e) This rule does not preclude a lawyer from replying to charges of misconduct publicly made against him or her or from participating in the proceedings of a legislative, administrative, or other investigative body.

Adopted June 9, 1997, effective January 1, 1998. Amended March 26, 2015, effective July 1, 2015.

Comment

[1] It is difficult to strike a balance between protecting the right to a fair trial and safeguarding the right of free expression. Preserving the right to a fair trial necessarily entails some curtailment of the information that may be disseminated about a party prior to trial, particularly where trial by jury is involved. If there were no such limits, the result would be the practical nullification of the protective effect of the rules of forensic decorum and the exclusionary rules of evidence. On the other hand, there are vital social interests served by the free dissemination of information about events having legal consequences and about legal proceedings themselves. The public has a right to know about threats to its safety and measures aimed at assuring its security. It also has a legitimate interest in the conduct of judicial proceedings, particularly in matters of general public concern. Furthermore, the subject matter of legal proceedings is often of

direct significance in debate and deliberation over questions of public policy.

[2] Special rules of confidentiality may validly govern proceedings in juvenile, domestic relations and mental disability proceedings, and perhaps other types of litigation. Rule 3.4(c) requires compliance with such rules.

[3] The Rule sets forth a basic general prohibition against a lawyer's making statements that the lawyer knows or should know will have a substantial likelihood of materially prejudicing an adjudicative proceeding. Recognizing that the public value of informed commentary is great and the likelihood of prejudice to a proceeding by the commentary of a lawyer who is not involved in the proceeding is small, the Rule applies only to lawyers who are, or who have been involved in the investigation or litigation of a case, and their associates.

[4] Paragraph (b) identifies specific matters about which a lawyer's statements would not ordinarily be considered to present a substantial likelihood of material prejudice, and should not in any event be considered prohibited by the general prohibition of paragraph (a). Paragraph (b) is not intended to be an exhaustive listing of the subjects upon which a lawyer may make a statement, but statements on other matters may be subject to paragraph (a).

[5] There are, on the other hand, certain subjects that are more likely than not to have a material prejudicial effect on a proceeding, particularly when they refer to a civil matter triable to a jury, a criminal matter, or any other proceeding that could result in incarceration. These subjects relate to:

(1) the character, credibility, reputation or criminal record of a party, suspect in a criminal investigation or witness, or the identity of a witness, or the expected testimony of a party or witness;

(2) in a criminal case or proceeding that could result in incarceration, the possibility of a plea of guilty to the offense or the existence or contents of any confession, admission, or statement given by a defendant or suspect or that person's refusal or failure to make a statement;

(3) the performance or results of any examination or test or the refusal or failure of a person to submit to an examination or test, or the identity or nature of physical evidence expected to be presented;

(4) any opinion as to the guilt or innocence of a defendant or suspect in a criminal case or proceeding that could result in incarceration;

(5) information that the lawyer knows or reasonably should know is likely to be inadmissible as evidence in a trial and that would, if disclosed, create a substantial risk of prejudicing an impartial trial; or

(6) the fact that a defendant has been charged with a crime, unless there is included therein a statement explaining that the charge is merely an accusation and that the defendant is presumed innocent until and unless proven guilty.

[6] Another relevant factor in determining prejudice is the nature of the proceeding involved. Criminal jury trials will be most sensitive to extrajudicial speech. Civil trials may be less sensitive. Non-jury hearings and arbitration proceedings may be even less affected. The Rule will still place limitations on prejudicial comments in these cases, but the likelihood of prejudice may be different depending on the type of proceeding.

[7] Finally, extrajudicial statements that might otherwise raise a question under this Rule may be permissible when they are made in response to statements made publicly by another party, another party's lawyer, or third persons, where a reasonable lawyer would believe a public response is required in order to avoid prejudice to the lawyer's client. When prejudicial statements have been publicly made by others, responsive statements may have the salutary effect of lessening any resulting adverse impact on the adjudicative proceeding. Such responsive statements should be limited to contain only such information as is necessary to mitigate undue prejudice created by the statements made by others.

[7A] In making the statements permitted by paragraph (e), a lawyer must safeguard confidential information relating to the representation of a client as required by Rule 1.6.

[8] See Rule 3.8(f) for additional duties of prosecutors in connection with extrajudicial statements about criminal proceedings.

Rule 3.7. Lawyer as Witness

(a) A lawyer shall not act as advocate at a trial in which the lawyer is likely to be a necessary witness unless:

(1) the testimony relates to an uncontested issue;

(2) the testimony relates to the nature and value of legal services rendered in the case; or

(3) disqualification of the lawyer would work substantial hardship on the client.

(b) A lawyer may act as advocate in a trial in which another lawyer in the lawyer's firm is likely to be called as a witness unless precluded from doing so by Rule 1.7 or Rule 1.9.

Adopted June 9, 1997, effective January 1, 1998. Amended March 26, 2015, effective July 1, 2015.

Comment

[1] Combining the roles of advocate and witness can prejudice the tribunal and the opposing party and can also involve a conflict of interest between the lawyer and client.

Advocate–Witness Rule

[2] The trier of fact may be confused or misled by a lawyer serving as both advocate and witness. The combination of roles may also prejudice another party's rights in the litigation. A witness is required to testify on the basis of personal knowledge, while an advocate is expected to explain and comment on evidence given by others. It may not be clear whether a statement by an advocate-witness should be taken as proof or as an analysis of the proof.

[3] To protect the tribunal, paragraph (a) prohibits a lawyer from simultaneously serving as advocate and necessary witness except in those circumstances specified in paragraphs (a)(1) through (a)(3). Paragraph (a)(1) recognizes that if the testimony will be uncontested, the ambiguities in the dual role are purely theoretical. Paragraph (a)(2) recognizes that where the testimony concerns the extent and value of legal services rendered in the action in which the testimony is offered, permitting the lawyers to testify avoids the need for a second trial with new counsel to resolve that issue. Moreover, in such a situation the judge has firsthand knowledge of the matter in issue; hence, there is less dependence on the adversary process to test the credibility of the testimony. This Rule does not prohibit the lawyer from acting as a witness if the lawyer is a party to the action and is appearing pro se.

[4] Apart from these two exceptions, paragraph (a)(3) recognizes that a balancing is required between the interests of the client and those of the tribunal and the opposing party. Whether the tribunal is likely to be misled or the opposing party is likely to suffer prejudice depends on the nature of the case, the importance and probable tenor of the lawyer's testimony, and the probability that the lawyer's testimony will conflict with that of other witnesses. Even if there is risk of such prejudice, in determining whether the lawyer should be disqualified, due regard must be given to the effect of disqualification on the lawyer's client. It is relevant that one or both parties could reasonably foresee that the lawyer would probably be a witness.

[5] Because the tribunal is not likely to be misled when a lawyer acts as advocate in a trial in which another lawyer in the lawyer's firm

will testify as a necessary witness, paragraph (b) permits the lawyer to do so except in situations involving a conflict of interest.

Conflict of Interest

[6] In determining if it is permissible to act as advocate in a trial in which the lawyer will be a necessary witness, the lawyer must also consider that the dual role may give rise to a conflict of interest that will require compliance with Rules 1.7 or 1.9. For example, if there is likely to be substantial conflict between the testimony of the client and that of the lawyer the representation involves a conflict of interest that requires compliance with Rule 1.7. This would be true even though the lawyer might not be prohibited by paragraph (a) from simultaneously serving as advocate and witness because the lawyer's disqualification would work a substantial hardship on the client. Similarly, a lawyer who might be permitted to simultaneously serve as an advocate and a witness by paragraph (a)(3) might be precluded from doing so by Rule 1.9. The problem can arise whether the lawyer is called as a witness on behalf of the client or is called by the opposing party. Determining whether or not such a conflict exists is primarily the responsibility of the lawyer involved. If there is a conflict of interest, the lawyer must secure the client's informed consent, confirmed in writing. In some cases, the lawyer will be precluded from seeking the client's consent. See Rule 1.7. See Rule 1.0(c) for the definition of "confirmed in writing" and Rule 1.0(f) for the definition of "informed consent."

[7] Paragraph (b) provides that a lawyer is not disqualified from serving as an advocate because a lawyer with whom the lawyer is associated in a firm is precluded from doing so by paragraph (a). If, however, the testifying lawyer would also be disqualified by Rule 1.7 or Rule 1.9 from representing the client in the matter, other lawyers in the firm will be precluded from representing the client by Rule 1.10 unless the client gives informed consent under the conditions stated in Rule 1.7.

Rule 3.8. Special Responsibilities of A Prosecutor

The prosecutor in a criminal case shall:

(a) refrain from prosecuting where the prosecutor lacks a good faith belief that probable cause to support the charge exists, and refrain from threatening to prosecute a charge where the prosecutor lacks a good faith belief that probable cause to support the charge exists or can be developed through subsequent investigation;

(b) make reasonable efforts to assure that the accused has been advised of the right to, and the procedure for obtaining, counsel and has been given reasonable opportunity to obtain counsel;

(c) not seek to obtain from an unrepresented accused a waiver of important pretrial rights, such as the right to a preliminary hearing, unless a court first has obtained from the accused a knowing and intelligent written waiver of counsel;

(d) make timely disclosure to the defense of all evidence or information known to the prosecutor that tends to negate the guilt of the accused or mitigates the offense, and, in connection with sentencing, disclose to the defense and to the tribunal all unprivileged mitigating information known to the prosecutor, except when the prosecutor is relieved of this responsibility by a protective order of the tribunal;

(e) not subpoena a lawyer in a grand jury or other criminal proceeding to present evidence about a past or present client unless:

(1) the prosecutor reasonably believes:

(i) the information sought is not protected from disclosure by any applicable privilege;

(ii) the evidence sought is essential to the successful completion of an ongoing investigation or prosecution; and

(iii) there is no other feasible alternative to obtain the information; and

(2) the prosecutor obtains prior judicial approval after an opportunity for an adversarial proceeding;

(f) except for statements that are necessary to inform the public of the nature and extent of the prosecutor's action and that serve a legitimate law enforcement purpose:

(1) refrain from making extrajudicial comments that have a substantial likelihood of heightening public condemnation of the accused and from making an extrajudicial statement that the prosecutor would be prohibited from making under Rule 3.6 or this Rule; and:

(2) take reasonable steps to prevent investigators, law enforcement personnel, employees or other persons assisting or associated with the prosecutor in a criminal case from making an extrajudicial statement that the prosecutor would be prohibited from making under Rule 3.6 or this Rule;

(g) not avoid pursuit of evidence because the prosecutor believes it will damage the prosecution's case or aid the accused; and

(h) refrain from seeking, as a condition of a disposition agreement in a criminal matter, the defendant's waiver of claims of ineffective assistance of counsel or prosecutorial misconduct.

(i) When, because of new, credible, and material evidence, a prosecutor knows that there is a reasonable likelihood that a convicted defendant did not commit an offense of which the defendant was convicted, the prosecutor shall within a reasonable time:

(1) if the conviction was not obtained by that prosecutor's office, disclose that evidence to an appropriate court or the chief prosecutor of the office that obtained the conviction, and

(2) if the conviction was obtained by that prosecutor's office,

(i) disclose that evidence to the appropriate court;

(ii) notify the defendant that the prosecutor's office possesses such evidence unless a court authorizes delay for good cause shown;

(iii) disclose that evidence to the defendant unless a court authorizes delay for good cause shown; and

(iv) undertake or assist in any further investigation as the court may direct.

(j) When a prosecutor knows that clear and convincing evidence establishes that a defendant, in a case prosecuted by that prosecutor's office, was convicted of an offense that the defendant did not commit, the prosecutor shall seek to remedy the injustice.

(k) A prosecutor's independent judgment, made in good faith, that the new evidence is not of such nature as to trigger the obligations of sections (i) and (j), though subsequently determined to have been erroneous, does not constitute a violation of this Rule.

Adopted June 9, 1997, effective January 1, 1998. Amended December 9, 1998, effective January 1, 1999; January 7, 2016, effective April 1, 2016.

Comment

[1] A prosecutor has the responsibility of a minister of justice and not simply that of an advocate. This responsibility carries with it specific obligations to see that the defendant is accorded procedural justice, that guilt is decided upon the basis of sufficient evidence, and that special precautions are taken to prevent and to rectify the conviction of innocent persons. Competent representation of the government may require a prosecutor to undertake some procedural and remedial measures as a matter of obligation. Applicable law may require other measures by the prosecutor and knowing disregard of those obligations or a systematic abuse of prosecutorial discretion could constitute a violation of Rule 8.4.

[1A] While a prosecutor may not threaten to prosecute a charge that the prosecutor knows is not supported by probable cause, this rule does not prohibit a prosecutor from declaring the intention to prosecute an individual for as yet uncharged criminal conduct if the prosecutor has a good faith belief that probable cause to support the charge can be developed through subsequent investigation.

[2] Paragraph (c) permits a prosecutor to seek a waiver of pretrial rights from an accused if the court has first obtained a knowing and intelligent written waiver of counsel from the accused. The use of the term "accused" means that paragraph (c) does not apply until the person has been charged. Paragraph (c) also does not apply to an accused appearing pro se with the approval of the tribunal. Nor does it forbid the lawful questioning of an uncharged suspect who has knowingly waived the rights to counsel and silence.

[3] The exception in paragraph (d) recognizes that a prosecutor may seek an appropriate protective order from the tribunal if disclosure of information to the defense could result in substantial harm.

[3A] The obligations imposed on a prosecutor by the rules of professional conduct are not coextensive with the obligations imposed by substantive law. Disclosure is required when the information tends to negate guilt or mitigates the offense without regard to the anticipated impact of the information. The obligations imposed under paragraph (d) exist independently of any request for the information. However, regardless of an individual's right to disclosure of exculpatory or mitigating information in criminal proceedings, a prosecutor violates paragraph (d) only if the information required to be disclosed is known to the prosecutor as tending to be exculpatory or mitigating.

[4] Paragraph (e) is intended to limit the issuance of lawyer subpoenas in grand jury and other criminal proceedings to those situations in which there is a genuine need to intrude into the client-lawyer relationship.

[5] Paragraph (f) supplements Rule 3.6, which prohibits extrajudicial statements that have a substantial likelihood of prejudicing an adjudicatory proceeding. In the context of a criminal prosecution, a prosecutor's extrajudicial statement can create the additional problem of increasing public condemnation of the accused. Although the announcement of an indictment, for example, will necessarily have severe consequences for the accused, a prosecutor can, and should, avoid comments which have no legitimate law enforcement purpose and have a substantial likelihood of increasing public opprobrium of the accused. Nothing in this Comment is intended to restrict the statements which a prosecutor may make which comply with Rule 3.6(b) or 3.6(c).

[6] Like other lawyers, prosecutors are subject to Rules 5.1 and 5.3, which relate to responsibilities regarding lawyers and nonlawyers who work for or are associated with the lawyer's office. Paragraph (f) reminds the prosecutor of the importance of these obligations in connection with the unique dangers of improper extrajudicial statements in a criminal case. In addition, paragraph (f) requires a prosecu-

tor to take reasonable steps to prevent all those assisting or associated with the prosecution team, but not under the direct supervision or control of the prosecutor, including law enforcement personnel, from making improper extrajudicial statements. A prosecutor's issuing the appropriate cautions to such persons will ordinarily satisfy the obligations of paragraph (f).

[7] Consistent with the objectives of Rules 4.2 and 4.3, disclosure under paragraph (i) to a represented defendant must be made through the defendant's counsel, and, in the case of an unrepresented defendant, would ordinarily be accompanied by a request to a court for the appointment of counsel to assist the defendant in taking such legal measures as may be appropriate. Paragraph (i) applies to new, credible, and material evidence regardless of whether it could previously have been discovered by the defense. The disclosures required by paragraph (i) should ordinarily be made promptly.

[8] Under paragraph (j), once the prosecutor knows that clear and convincing evidence establishes that the defendant, in a case prosecuted by that prosecutor's office, was convicted of an offense that the defendant did not commit, the prosecutor must seek to remedy the injustice. Necessary steps may include disclosure of the evidence to the defendant, requesting that the court appoint counsel for an unrepresented indigent defendant, and notifying the court that the prosecutor has knowledge that the defendant did not commit the offense of which the defendant was convicted.

Rule 3.9. Advocate in Nonadjudicative Proceedings

A lawyer representing a client before a legislative body or administrative agency in a nonadjudicative proceeding shall disclose that the appearance is in a representative capacity and shall conform to the provisions of Rules 3.3(a) through (c), 3.4(a) through (c), and 3.5.

Adopted June 9, 1997, effective January 1, 1998. Amended March 26, 2015, effective July 1, 2015.

Comment

[1] In representation before bodies such as legislatures, municipal councils, and executive and administrative agencies acting in a rule-making or policy-making capacity, lawyers present facts, formulate issues and advance argument in the matters under consideration. The decision-making body, like a court, should be able to rely on the integrity of the submissions made to it. A lawyer appearing before such a body must deal with it honestly and in conformity with applicable rules of procedure. See Rules 3.3(a) through (c), 3.4(a) through (c) and 3.5.

[2] Lawyers have no exclusive right to appear before nonadjudicative bodies, as they do before a court. The requirements of this Rule therefore may subject lawyers to regulations inapplicable to advocates who are not lawyers. However, legislatures and administrative agencies have a right to expect lawyers to deal with them as they deal with courts.

[3] This Rule only applies when a lawyer represents a client in connection with an official hearing or meeting of a governmental agency or a legislative body to which the lawyer or the lawyer's client is presenting evidence or argument. It does not apply to representation of a client in a negotiation or other bilateral transaction with a governmental agency or in connection with an application for license or other privilege or the client's compliance with generally applicable reporting requirements, such as filing of income tax returns. Nor does it apply to the representation of a client in connection with an investigation or examination of the client's affairs conducted by government investigators or examiners. Representation in such matters is governed by Rules 4.1 through 4.4.

[4] Unless otherwise expressly prohibited, ex parte contacts with legislators and other persons acting in a legislative capacity are not prohibited.

TRANSACTIONS WITH PERSONS OTHER THAN CLIENTS

Rule 4.1.   Truthfulness in Statements to Others

In the course of representing a client a lawyer shall not knowingly:

(a) make a false statement of material fact or law to a third person; or

(b) fail to disclose a material fact to a third person when disclosure is necessary to avoid assisting a criminal or fraudulent act by a client, unless disclosure is prohibited by Rule 1.6.

Adopted June 9, 1997, effective January 1, 1998. Comment amended March 26, 2015, effective July 1, 2015.

Comment

Misrepresentation

[1] A lawyer is required to be truthful when dealing with others on a client's behalf, but generally has no affirmative duty to inform an opposing party of relevant facts. A misrepresentation can occur if the lawyer incorporates or affirms a statement of another person that the lawyer knows is false. Misrepresentations can also occur by partially true but misleading statements or omissions that are the equivalent of affirmative false statements. For dishonest conduct that does not amount to a false statement or for misrepresentations by a lawyer other than in the course of representing a client, see Rule 8.4.

Statements of Fact

[2] This Rule refers to statements of fact. Whether a particular statement should be regarded as one of fact can depend on the circumstances. Under generally accepted conventions in negotiation, certain types of statements ordinarily are not taken as statements of material fact. Estimates of price or value placed on the subject of a transaction and a party's intentions as to an acceptable settlement of a claim are ordinarily in this category, and so is the existence of an undisclosed principal except where nondisclosure of the principal would constitute fraud. Lawyers should be mindful of their obligations under applicable law to avoid criminal and tortious misrepresentation.

Crime or Fraud by Client

[3] Under Rule 1.2(d), a lawyer is prohibited from counseling or assisting a client in conduct that the lawyer knows is criminal or fraudulent. Paragraph (b) states a specific application of the principle set forth in Rule 1.2(d) and addresses the situation where a client's crime or fraud takes the form of a lie or misrepresentation. Paragraph (b) recognizes that substantive law may require a lawyer to disclose certain information to avoid being deemed as having assisted the client's crime or fraud. In paragraph (b) the word "assisting" refers to that level of assistance which would render a third party liable for another's crime or fraud, *i.e.*, assistance sufficient to render one liable as an aider or abettor under criminal law or as a joint tortfeasor under principles of tort and agency law. The requirement of disclosure in this paragraph is not intended to broaden what constitutes unlawful assistance under criminal, tort or agency law, but instead is intended to ensure that these Rules do not countenance behavior by a lawyer that other law marks as criminal or tortious.

[4] Paragraph (b) requires a lawyer in certain circumstances to disclose material facts to a third person "unless disclosure is prohibited by Rule 1.6." Rule 1.6(a) prohibits disclosure of confidential information relating to the representation of a client unless the client consents or the disclosure is impliedly authorized to carry out the representation. Rule 1.6(b), however, gives the lawyer permission to disclose confidential information without client consent in certain circumstances. For example, under Rule 1.6(b)(2), a lawyer may reveal confidential information to prevent a criminal or fraudulent act that is likely to result in substantial injury to the property of another.

If Rule 1.6(b) gives a lawyer permission to make disclosure, then disclosure is not prohibited by Rule 1.6, and disclosure under paragraph (b) of this Rule is mandatory. If Rule 1.6(b) does not give permission to disclose—as in the previous example when the injury from a criminal or fraudulent act is not "substantial"—then the disclosure requirement of Rule 4.1(b) does not apply. See Rule 1.6, Comment 6A. Even if Rule 1.6 prohibits disclosure, the lawyer may have other duties, such as a duty to withdraw from the representation. See Rule 1.2(d) and Rule 1.16(a)(1).

Rule 4.2.   Communication with Person Represented by Counsel

In representing a client, a lawyer shall not communicate about the subject of the representation with a person the lawyer knows to be represented by another lawyer in the matter, unless the lawyer has the consent of the other lawyer or is authorized to do so by law or a court order.

Adopted June 9, 1997, effective January 1, 1998. Amended effective June 5, 2002. Amended March 26, 2015, effective July 1, 2015.

Comment

[1] This Rule contributes to the proper functioning of the legal system by protecting a person who has chosen to be represented by a lawyer in a matter against possible overreaching by other lawyers who are participating in the matter, interference by those lawyers with the client-lawyer relationship and the uncounselled disclosure of confidential information relating to the representation.

[2] This Rule applies to communications with any person who is represented by counsel concerning the matter to which the communication relates.

[3] The Rule applies even though the represented person initiates or consents to the communication. A lawyer must immediately terminate communication with a person if the lawyer learns that the person is one with whom communication is not permitted by this Rule.

[4] This Rule does not prohibit communication with a represented person, or an employee or agent of such a person, concerning matters outside the representation. For example, the existence of a controversy between a government agency and a private party, or between two organizations, does not prohibit a lawyer for either from communicating with nonlawyer representatives of the other regarding a separate matter. Nor does this Rule preclude communication with a represented person who is seeking advice from a lawyer who is not otherwise representing a client in the matter. Parties to a matter may communicate directly with each other, and a lawyer is not prohibited from advising a client concerning a communication that the client is legally entitled to make. A lawyer may not, however, make a communication prohibited by this Rule through the acts of another. See Rule 8.4(a). Also, a lawyer having independent justification or legal authorization for communicating with a represented person is permitted to do so. For example, counsel could prepare and send written default notices and written demands required by such laws as Chapter 93A of the General Laws.

[5] Communications authorized by law may include communications by a lawyer on behalf of a client who is exercising a constitutional or other legal right to communicate with the government. Communications authorized by law may also include investigative activities of lawyers representing governmental entities, directly or through investigative agents, prior to the commencement of criminal or civil enforcement proceedings. When communicating with the accused in a criminal matter, a government lawyer must comply with this Rule in addition to honoring the constitutional rights of the accused. The fact that a communication does not violate a state or federal constitutional

right is insufficient to establish that the communication is permissible under this Rule.

[6] A lawyer who is uncertain whether a communication with a represented person is permissible may seek a court order. A lawyer may also seek a court order in exceptional circumstances to authorize a communication that would otherwise be prohibited by this Rule, for example, where communication with a person represented by counsel is necessary to avoid reasonably certain injury.

[7] In the case of a represented organization, this Rule prohibits communications by a lawyer for another person or entity concerning the matter in representation only with those agents or employees who exercise managerial responsibility in the matter, who are alleged to have committed the wrongful acts at issue in the litigation, or who have authority on behalf of the organization to make decisions about the course of the litigation. Consent of the organization's lawyer is not required for communication with a former constituent. If a constituent of the organization is represented in the matter by his or her own counsel, the consent by that counsel to a communication will be sufficient for purposes of this Rule. Compare Rule 3.4(f). In communicating with a current or former constituent of an organization, a lawyer must not use methods of obtaining evidence that violate the legal rights of the organization. See Rule 4.4.

[8] The prohibition on communications with a represented person only applies in circumstances where the lawyer knows that the person is in fact represented in the matter to be discussed. This means that the lawyer has knowledge of the fact of the representation; but such knowledge may be inferred from the circumstances. See Rule 1.0(g). Thus, the lawyer cannot evade the requirement of obtaining the consent of counsel by closing eyes to the obvious.

[9] In the event the person with whom the lawyer communicates is not known to be represented by counsel in the matter, the lawyer's communications are subject to Rule 4.3.

Rule 4.3. Dealing With Unrepresented Person

In dealing on behalf of a client with a person who is not represented by counsel, a lawyer shall not state or imply that the lawyer is disinterested. When the lawyer knows or reasonably should know that the unrepresented person misunderstands the lawyer's role in the matter, the lawyer shall make reasonable efforts to correct the misunderstanding. The lawyer shall not give legal advice to an unrepresented person, other than the advice to secure counsel, if the lawyer knows or reasonably should know that the interests of such a person are or have a reasonable possibility of being in conflict with the interests of the client.

Adopted June 9, 1997, effective January 1, 1998. Amended March 26, 2015, effective July 1, 2015.

Comment

[1] An unrepresented person, particularly one not experienced in dealing with legal matters, might assume that a lawyer is disinterested in loyalties or is a disinterested authority on the law even when the lawyer represents a client. In order to avoid a misunderstanding, a lawyer will typically need to identify the lawyer's client and, where necessary, explain that the client has interests opposed to those of the unrepresented person. For misunderstandings that sometimes arise when a lawyer for an organization deals with an unrepresented constituent, see Rule 1.13(f).

[2] The Rule distinguishes between situations involving unrepresented persons whose interests may be adverse to those of the lawyer's client and those in which the person's interests are not in conflict with the client's. In the former situation, the possibility that the lawyer will compromise the unrepresented person's interests is so great that the Rule prohibits the giving of any advice, apart from the

advice to obtain counsel. This Rule does not prohibit a lawyer from negotiating the terms of a transaction or settling a dispute with an unrepresented person. So long as the lawyer has explained that the lawyer represents an adverse party and is not representing the person, the lawyer may inform the person of the terms on which the lawyer's client will enter into an agreement or settle a matter, prepare documents that require the person's signature and explain the lawyer's own view of the meaning of the document or the lawyer's view of the underlying legal obligations.

Rule 4.4. Respect for Rights of Third Persons

(a) In representing a client, a lawyer shall not use means that have no substantial purpose other than to embarrass, delay, or burden a third person, or use methods of obtaining evidence that violate the legal rights of such a person.

(b) A lawyer who receives a document or electronically stored information relating to the representation of the lawyer's client and knows or reasonably should know that the document or electronically stored information was inadvertently sent shall promptly notify the sender.

Adopted June 9, 1997, effective January 1, 1998. Amended March 26, 2015, effective July 1, 2015.

Comment

[1] Responsibility to a client requires a lawyer to subordinate the interests of others to those of the client, but that responsibility does not imply that a lawyer may disregard the rights of third persons. It is impractical to catalogue all such rights, but they include legal restrictions on methods of obtaining evidence from third persons and unwarranted intrusions into privileged relationships, such as the client-lawyer relationship.

[2] Paragraph (b) recognizes that lawyers sometimes receive a document or electronically stored information that was mistakenly sent or produced by opposing parties or their lawyers. A document or electronically stored information is inadvertently sent when it is accidentally transmitted, such as when an email or letter is misaddressed or a document or electronically stored information is accidentally included with information that was intentionally transmitted. If a lawyer knows or reasonably should know that such a document or electronically stored information was sent inadvertently, then this Rule requires the lawyer to promptly notify the sender in order to permit that person to take protective measures. Whether the lawyer is required to take additional steps, such as returning or deleting the document or electronically stored information, is a matter of law beyond the scope of these Rules, as is the question of whether the privileged status of a document or electronically stored information has been waived. Similarly, this Rule does not address the legal duties of a lawyer who receives a document or electronically stored information that the lawyer knows or reasonably should know may have been inappropriately obtained by the sending person. For purposes of this Rule, "document or electronically stored information" includes paper documents, email and other forms of electronically stored information, including embedded data (commonly referred to as "metadata"), that is subject to being read or put into readable form. Metadata in electronic documents creates an obligation under this Rule only if the receiving lawyer knows or reasonably should know that the metadata was inadvertently sent to the receiving lawyer.

[3] Some lawyers may choose to return a document or delete electronically stored information unread, for example, when the lawyer learns before receiving it that it was inadvertently sent. Where a lawyer is not required by applicable law to do so, the decision to voluntarily return such a document or delete electronically stored information is a matter of professional judgment ordinarily reserved to the lawyer. See Rules 1.2 and 1.4.

LAW FIRMS AND ASSOCIATIONS

Rule 5.1.　Responsibilities of Partners, Managers and Supervisory Lawyers

(a) A partner in a law firm, and a lawyer who individually or together with other lawyers possesses comparable managerial authority in a law firm, shall make reasonable efforts to ensure that the firm has in effect measures giving reasonable assurance that all lawyers in the firm conform to the Rules of Professional Conduct.

(b) A lawyer having direct supervisory authority over another lawyer shall make reasonable efforts to ensure that the other lawyer conforms to the Rules of Professional Conduct.

(c) A lawyer shall be responsible for another lawyer's violation of the Rules of Professional Conduct if:

　(1) the lawyer orders or, with knowledge of the specific conduct, ratifies the conduct involved; or

　(2) the lawyer is a partner or has comparable managerial authority in the law firm in which the other lawyer practices, or has direct supervisory authority over the other lawyer, and knows of the conduct at a time when its consequences can be avoided or mitigated but fails to take reasonable remedial action.

Adopted June 9, 1997, effective January 1, 1998. Amended March 26, 2015, effective July 1, 2015.

Comment

[1] Paragraph (a) applies to lawyers who have managerial authority over the professional work of a firm. See Rule 1.0(d). This includes members of a partnership, the shareholders in a law firm organized as a professional corporation, and members of other associations authorized to practice law; lawyers having comparable managerial authority in a legal services organization or a law department of an enterprise or government agency; and lawyers who have intermediate managerial responsibilities in a firm. Paragraph (b) applies to lawyers who have supervisory authority over the work of other lawyers in a firm.

[2] Paragraph (a) requires lawyers with managerial authority within a firm to make reasonable efforts to establish internal policies and procedures designed to provide reasonable assurance that all lawyers in the firm will conform to the Rules of Professional Conduct. Such policies and procedures include those designed to detect and resolve conflicts of interest, identify dates by which actions must be taken in pending matters, account for client funds and property and ensure that inexperienced lawyers are properly supervised.

[3] Other measures that may be required to fulfill the responsibility prescribed in paragraph (a) can depend on the firm's structure and the nature of its practice. In a small firm of experienced lawyers, informal supervision and periodic review of compliance with the required systems ordinarily will suffice. In a large firm, or in practice situations in which difficult ethical problems frequently arise, more elaborate measures may be necessary. Some firms, for example, have a procedure whereby junior lawyers can make confidential referral of ethical problems directly to a designated senior partner or special committee. See Rule 5.2. Firms, whether large or small, may also rely on continuing legal education in professional ethics. In any event, the ethical atmosphere of a firm can influence the conduct of all its members, and the partners may not assume that all lawyers associated with the firm will inevitably conform to the Rules.

[4] Paragraph (c) expresses a general principle of personal responsibility for acts of another. See also Rule 8.4(a).

[5] Paragraph (c)(2) defines the duty of a partner or other lawyer having comparable managerial authority in a law firm, as well as a lawyer who has direct supervisory authority over performance of specific legal work by another lawyer. Whether a lawyer has supervisory authority in particular circumstances is a question of fact. Partners and lawyers with comparable authority have at least indirect responsibility for all work being done by the firm, while a partner or manager in charge of a particular matter ordinarily also has supervisory responsibility for the work of other firm lawyers engaged in the matter. Appropriate remedial action by a partner or managing lawyer would depend on the immediacy of that lawyer's involvement and the seriousness of the misconduct. A supervisor is required to intervene to prevent avoidable consequences of misconduct if the supervisor knows that the misconduct occurred. Thus, if a supervising lawyer knows that a subordinate misrepresented a matter to an opposing party in negotiation, the supervisor as well as the subordinate has a duty to correct the resulting misapprehension.

[6] Professional misconduct by a lawyer under supervision could reveal a violation of paragraph (b) on the part of the supervisory lawyer even though it does not entail a violation of paragraph (c) because there was no direction, ratification or knowledge of the violation.

[7] Apart from this Rule and Rule 8.4(a), a lawyer does not have disciplinary liability for the conduct of a partner, associate or subordinate. Whether a lawyer may be liable civilly or criminally for another lawyer's conduct is a question of law beyond the scope of these Rules.

[8] The duties imposed by this Rule on managing and supervising lawyers do not alter the personal duty of each lawyer in a firm to abide by the Rules of Professional Conduct. See Rule 5.2(a).

Rule 5.2.　Responsibilities of a Subordinate Lawyer

(a) A lawyer is bound by the Rules of Professional Conduct notwithstanding that the lawyer acted at the direction of another person.

(b) A subordinate lawyer does not violate the Rules of Professional Conduct if that lawyer acts in accordance with a supervisory lawyer's reasonable resolution of an arguable question of professional duty.

Adopted June 9, 1997, effective January 1, 1998.

Comment

[1] Although a lawyer is not relieved of responsibility for a violation by the fact that the lawyer acted at the direction of a supervisor, that fact may be relevant in determining whether a lawyer had the knowledge required to render conduct a violation of the Rules. For example, if a subordinate filed a frivolous pleading at the direction of a supervisor, the subordinate would not be guilty of a professional violation unless the subordinate knew of the document's frivolous character.

[2] When lawyers in a supervisor-subordinate relationship encounter a matter involving professional judgment as to ethical duty, the supervisor may assume responsibility for making the judgment. Otherwise a consistent course of action or position could not be taken. If the question can reasonably be answered only one way, the duty of both lawyers is clear and they are equally responsible for fulfilling it. However, if the question is reasonably arguable, someone has to decide upon the course of action. That authority ordinarily reposes in the supervisor, and a subordinate may be guided accordingly. For example, if a question arises whether the interests of two clients conflict under Rule 1.7, the supervisor's reasonable resolution of the

question should protect the subordinate professionally if the resolution is subsequently challenged.

Corresponding ABA Model Rule. Identical to Model Rule 5.2.

Corresponding Former Massachusetts Rule. None.

Rule 5.3. Responsibilities Regarding Nonlawyer Assistance

With respect to a nonlawyer employed or retained by or associated with a lawyer:

(a) a partner, and a lawyer who individually or together with other lawyers possesses comparable managerial authority in a law firm, shall make reasonable efforts to ensure that the firm has in effect measures giving reasonable assurance that the person's conduct is compatible with the professional obligations of the lawyer;

(b) a lawyer having direct supervisory authority over the nonlawyer shall make reasonable efforts to ensure that the person's conduct is compatible with the professional obligations of the lawyer; and

(c) a lawyer shall be responsible for conduct of such a person that would be a violation of the Rules of Professional Conduct if engaged in by a lawyer if:

(1) the lawyer orders or, with the knowledge of the specific conduct, ratifies the conduct involved; or

(2) the lawyer is a partner or has comparable managerial authority in the law firm in which the person is employed, or has direct supervisory authority over the person, and knows of the conduct at a time when its consequences can be avoided or mitigated but fails to take reasonable remedial action.

Adopted June 9, 1997, effective January 1, 1998. Amended March 26, 2015, effective July 1, 2015.

Comment

[1] Paragraph (a) requires lawyers with managerial authority within a law firm to make reasonable efforts to ensure that the firm has in effect measures giving reasonable assurance that nonlawyers in the firm and nonlawyers outside the firm who work on firm matters act in a way compatible with the professional obligations of the lawyer. See Comment 6 to Rule 1.1 (retaining lawyers outside the firm) and Comment 1 to Rule 5.1 (responsibilities with respect to lawyers within a firm). Paragraph (b) applies to lawyers who have supervisory authority over such nonlawyers within or outside the firm. Paragraph (c) specifies the circumstances in which a lawyer is responsible for the conduct of such nonlawyers within or outside the firm that would be a violation of the Rules of Professional Conduct if engaged in by a lawyer.

Nonlawyers Within the Firm

[2] Lawyers generally employ assistants in their practice, including secretaries, investigators, law student interns, and paraprofessionals. Such assistants, whether employees or independent contractors, act for the lawyer in rendition of the lawyer's professional services. A lawyer must give such assistants appropriate instruction and supervision concerning the ethical aspects of their employment, particularly regarding the obligation not to disclose confidential information relating to representation of the client, and should be responsible for their work product. The measures employed in supervising nonlawyers should take account of the fact that they do not have legal training and are not subject to professional discipline.

Nonlawyers Outside the Firm

[3] A lawyer may use nonlawyers outside the firm to assist the lawyer in rendering legal services to the client. Examples include retaining an investigative or paraprofessional service, hiring a document management company to create and maintain a database for complex litigation, sending client documents to a third party for printing or scanning, and using an Internet-based service to store client information. When using such services outside the firm, a lawyer must make reasonable efforts to ensure that the services are provided in a manner that is compatible with the lawyer's professional obligations. The extent of this obligation will depend upon the circumstances, including the education, experience and reputation of the nonlawyer; the nature of the services involved; the terms of any arrangements concerning the protection of client information; and the legal and ethical environments of the jurisdictions in which the services will be performed, particularly with regard to confidentiality. See also Rules 1.1 (competence), 1.2 (allocation of authority), 1.4 (communication with client), 1.6 (confidentiality), 5.4(a) (professional independence of the lawyer), and 5.5(a) (unauthorized practice of law). When retaining or directing a nonlawyer outside the firm, a lawyer should communicate directions appropriate under the circumstances to give reasonable assurance that the nonlawyer's conduct is compatible with the professional obligations of the lawyer.

[4] Where the client directs the selection of a particular nonlawyer service provider outside the firm, the lawyer ordinarily should agree with the client concerning the allocation of responsibility for monitoring as between the client and the lawyer. See Rule 1.2. When making such an allocation in a matter pending before a tribunal, lawyers and parties may have additional obligations that are a matter of law beyond the scope of these Rules.

Rule 5.4. Professional Independence of a Lawyer

(a) A lawyer or law firm shall not share legal fees with a nonlawyer, except that:

(1) an agreement by a lawyer with the lawyer's firm, partner, or associate may provide for the payment of money, over a reasonable period of time after the lawyer's death, to the lawyer's estate or to one or more specified persons;

(2) a lawyer who purchases the practice of a deceased, disabled, or disappeared lawyer may, pursuant to the provisions of Rule 1.17, pay to the estate or other representative of that lawyer the agreed-upon purchase price;

(3) a lawyer or law firm may include nonlawyer employees in a compensation or retirement plan, even though the plan is based in whole or in part on a profit-sharing arrangement; and

(4) a lawyer or law firm may agree to share a statutory or tribunal-approved fee award, or a settlement in a matter eligible for such an award, with a qualified legal assistance organization that referred the matter to the lawyer or law firm, if the client consents, after being informed that a division of fees will be made, to the sharing of the fees and the total fee is reasonable.

(b) A lawyer shall not form a partnership or other business entity with a nonlawyer if any of the activities of the entity consist of the practice of law.

(c) A lawyer shall not permit a person who recommends, employs, or pays the lawyer to render legal services for another to direct or regulate the lawyer's professional judgment in rendering such legal services.

(d) A lawyer shall not practice with or in the form of a limited liability entity authorized to practice law for a profit, if:

(1) a nonlawyer owns any interest therein, except that a fiduciary representative of the estate of a lawyer may hold the stock or interest of the lawyer for a reasonable time during administration;

(2) a nonlawyer is a corporate director or officer thereof or occupies the position of similar responsibility in any form of association other than a corporation including a limited liability company; or

(3) a nonlawyer has the right to direct or control the professional judgment of a lawyer.

Adopted June 9, 1997, effective January 1, 1998. Amended August 31, 1999, effective October 1, 1999. Amended March 26, 2015, effective July 1, 2015. Amended March 10, 2016, effective May 1, 2016. *Comment* amended June 20, 2016, effective August 1, 2016.

Comment

[1] The provisions of this Rule express traditional limitations on sharing fees. These limitations are to protect the lawyer's professional independence of judgment. Where someone other than the client pays the lawyer's fee or salary, or recommends employment of the lawyer, that arrangement does not modify the lawyer's obligation to the client. As stated in paragraph (c), such arrangements should not interfere with the lawyer's professional judgment.

[2] This Rule also expresses traditional limitations on permitting a third party to direct or regulate the lawyer's professional judgment in rendering legal services to another. See also Rule 1.8(f) (lawyer may accept compensation from a third party as long as there is no interference with the lawyer's independent professional judgment and the client gives informed consent).

[3] Rule 5.4(a)(4) explicitly permits a lawyer, with the client's consent, to share certain fees with a qualified legal assistance organization that has referred the matter to the lawyer. The financial needs of these organizations, which serve important public ends, justify a limited exception to the prohibition against fee-sharing with nonlawyers. Should abuses occur in the carrying out of such arrangements, they may constitute a violation of Rule 5.4(c) or Rule 8.4(d) or (h). The permission to share fees granted by this Rule is not intended to restrict the ability of those qualified legal assistance organizations that engage in the practice of law themselves to receive a share of another lawyer's legal fees pursuant to Rule 1.5(e).

Rule 5.5. Unauthorized Practice of Law; Multijurisdictional Practice of Law

(a) A lawyer shall not practice law in a jurisdiction in violation of the regulation of the legal profession in that jurisdiction, or assist another in doing so.

(b) A lawyer who is not admitted to practice in this jurisdiction shall not:

(1) except as authorized by these Rules or other law, establish an office or other systematic and continuous presence in this jurisdiction for the practice of law; or

(2) hold out to the public or otherwise represent that the lawyer is admitted to practice law in this jurisdiction.

(c) A lawyer admitted in another United States jurisdiction, and not disbarred or suspended from practice in any jurisdiction, may provide legal services on a temporary basis in this jurisdiction that:

(1) are undertaken in association with a lawyer who is admitted to practice in this jurisdiction and who actively participates in the matter;

(2) are in or reasonably related to a pending or potential proceeding before a tribunal in this or another jurisdiction, if the lawyer, or a person the lawyer is assisting, is authorized by law or order to appear in such proceeding or reasonably expects to be so authorized;

(3) are in or reasonably related to a pending or potential arbitration, mediation, or other alternative dispute resolution proceeding in this or another jurisdiction, if the services arise out of or are reasonably related to the lawyer's practice in a jurisdiction in which the lawyer is admitted to practice and are not services for which the forum requires pro hac vice admission; or

(4) are not within paragraphs (c)(2) or (c)(3) and arise out of or are reasonably related to the lawyer's practice in a jurisdiction in which the lawyer is admitted to practice.

(d) A lawyer admitted in another United States jurisdiction or in a foreign jurisdiction, and not disbarred or suspended from practice in any jurisdiction or the equivalent thereof, may provide legal services through an office or other systematic and continuous presence in this jurisdiction that:

(1) are provided to the lawyer's employer or its organizational affiliates and are not services for which the forum requires pro hac vice admission; or

(2) are services that the lawyer is authorized to provide by federal law or other law or rule of this jurisdiction.

(e) For purposes of paragraph (d), the foreign lawyer must be a member in good standing of a recognized legal profession in a foreign jurisdiction, the members of which are admitted to practice as lawyers or counselors at law or the equivalent, and are subject to effective regulation and discipline by a duly constituted professional body or a public authority.

Adopted June 9, 1997, effective January 1, 1998. Amended effective January 1, 2007. Amended March 26, 2015, effective July 1, 2015. Amended March 10, 2016, effective May 1, 2016.

Comment

[1] A lawyer may practice law in this jurisdiction only if admitted to practice generally or if authorized by court rule or order or by law to practice for a limited purpose or on a restricted basis. Paragraph (a) applies to unauthorized practice of law by a lawyer, whether through the lawyer's direct action or by the lawyer assisting another person. For example, a lawyer may not assist a person in practicing law in violation of the rules governing professional conduct in that person's jurisdiction.

[2] Limiting the practice of law to members of the bar protects the public against rendition of legal services by unqualified persons. This Rule does not prohibit a lawyer from employing the services of paraprofessionals and delegating functions to them, so long as the lawyer supervises the delegated work and retains responsibility for their work. See Rule 5.3.

[3] A lawyer may provide professional advice and instruction to nonlawyers whose employment requires knowledge of law; for example, claims adjusters, employees of financial or commercial institutions, social workers, accountants and persons employed in government agencies.

[4] Other than as authorized by law or this Rule, a lawyer who is not admitted to practice generally in this jurisdiction violates paragraph (b)(1) if the lawyer establishes an office or other systematic and continuous presence in this jurisdiction for the practice of law. Presence may be systematic and continuous, for example by placing a name on the office door or letterhead of another lawyer without

qualification, even if the lawyer is not physically present here. A lawyer not admitted to practice in this jurisdiction must not hold out to the public or otherwise represent that the lawyer is admitted to practice law in this jurisdiction. See also Rules 7.1(a) and 7.5(b).

[5] There are occasions in which a lawyer admitted to practice in another United States jurisdiction, and not disbarred or suspended from practice in any jurisdiction, may provide legal services on a temporary basis in this jurisdiction under circumstances that do not create an unreasonable risk to the interests of the lawyer's clients, the public or the courts. Paragraph (c) identifies four such circumstances. The fact that conduct is or is not so identified does not imply that the conduct is or is not authorized. With the exception of paragraphs (d)(1) and (d)(2), this Rule does not authorize a U.S. or foreign lawyer to establish an office or other systematic and continuous presence in this jurisdiction without being admitted to practice generally here.

[6] There is no single test to determine whether a lawyer's services are provided on a "temporary basis" in this jurisdiction, and may therefore be permissible under paragraph (c). Services may be "temporary" even though the lawyer provides services in this jurisdiction on a recurring basis, or for an extended period of time, as when the lawyer is representing a client in a single lengthy negotiation or litigation.

[7] Paragraphs (c) and (d) apply to lawyers who are admitted to practice law in any United States jurisdiction, which includes the District of Columbia and any state, territory or commonwealth of the United States. Paragraph (d) also applies to lawyers admitted in a foreign jurisdiction. The word "admitted" in paragraphs (c), (d) and (e) means the lawyer is authorized to practice in the jurisdiction in which the lawyer is admitted and excludes a lawyer who while technically admitted is not authorized to practice, because, for example, the lawyer is on inactive status.

[8] Paragraph (c)(1) recognizes that the interests of clients and the public are protected if a lawyer admitted only in another jurisdiction associates with a lawyer licensed to practice in this jurisdiction. For this paragraph to apply, however, the lawyer admitted to practice in this jurisdiction must actively participate in and share responsibility for the representation of the client.

[9] Lawyers not admitted to practice generally in this jurisdiction may be authorized by law or order of a tribunal or an administrative agency to appear before the tribunal or agency. This authority may be granted pursuant to formal rules governing admission pro hac vice or pursuant to informal practice of the tribunal or agency. Under paragraph (c)(2), a lawyer does not violate this Rule when the lawyer appears before a tribunal or agency pursuant to such authority. To the extent that a court rule or other law of this jurisdiction requires a lawyer who is not admitted to practice in this jurisdiction to obtain admission pro hac vice before appearing before a tribunal or administrative agency, this Rule requires the lawyer to obtain that authority.

[10] Paragraph (c)(2) also provides that a lawyer rendering services in this jurisdiction on a temporary basis does not violate this Rule when the lawyer engages in conduct in anticipation of a proceeding or hearing in a jurisdiction in which the lawyer is authorized to practice law or in which the lawyer reasonably expects to be admitted pro hac vice. Examples of such conduct include meetings with the client, interviews of potential witnesses, and the review of documents. Similarly, a lawyer admitted only in another jurisdiction may engage in conduct temporarily in this jurisdiction in connection with pending litigation in another jurisdiction in which the lawyer is or reasonably expects to be authorized to appear, including taking depositions in this jurisdiction.

[11] When a lawyer has been or reasonably expects to be admitted to appear before a court or administrative agency, paragraph (c)(2) also permits conduct by lawyers who are associated with that lawyer in the matter, but who do not expect to appear before the court or administrative agency. For example, subordinate lawyers may con-

duct research, review documents, and attend meetings with witnesses in support of the lawyer responsible for the litigation.

[12] Paragraph (c)(3) permits a lawyer admitted to practice law in another jurisdiction to perform services on a temporary basis in this jurisdiction if those services are in or reasonably related to a pending or potential arbitration, mediation, or other alternative dispute resolution proceeding in this or another jurisdiction, if the services arise out of or are reasonably related to the lawyer's practice in a jurisdiction in which the lawyer is admitted to practice. The lawyer, however, must obtain admission pro hac vice in the case of a court-annexed arbitration or mediation or otherwise if court rules or law so require.

[13] Paragraph (c)(4) permits a lawyer admitted in another jurisdiction to provide certain legal services on a temporary basis in this jurisdiction that arise out of or are reasonably related to the lawyer's practice in a jurisdiction in which the lawyer is admitted but are not within paragraphs (c)(2) or (c)(3). These services include both legal services and services that nonlawyers may perform but that are considered the practice of law when performed by lawyers.

[14] Paragraphs (c)(3) and (c)(4) require that the services arise out of or be reasonably related to the lawyer's practice in a jurisdiction in which the lawyer is admitted. A variety of factors evidence such a relationship. The lawyer's client may have been previously represented by the lawyer, or may be resident in or have substantial contacts with the jurisdiction in which the lawyer is admitted. The matter, although involving other jurisdictions, may have a significant connection with that jurisdiction. In other cases, significant aspects of the lawyer's work might be conducted in that jurisdiction or a significant aspect of the matter may involve the law of that jurisdiction. The necessary relationship might arise when the client's activities or the legal issues involve multiple jurisdictions, such as when the officers of a multinational corporation survey potential business sites and seek the services of their lawyer in assessing the relative merits of each. In addition, the services may draw on the lawyer's recognized expertise developed through the regular practice of law on behalf of clients in matters involving a particular body of federal, nationally-uniform, foreign, or international law.

[15] Paragraph (d) identifies two circumstances in which a lawyer who is admitted to practice in another United States or foreign jurisdiction, and is not disbarred or suspended from practice in any jurisdiction or the equivalent thereof, may establish an office or other systematic and continuous presence in this jurisdiction for the practice of law. Pursuant to paragraph (c) of this Rule, a lawyer admitted to any U.S. jurisdiction may also provide legal services in this jurisdiction on a temporary basis. Except as provided in paragraphs (d)(1) and (d)(2), a lawyer who is admitted to practice law in another jurisdiction and who establishes an office or other systematic or continuous presence in this jurisdiction must become admitted to practice law generally in this jurisdiction.

[16] Paragraph (d)(1) applies to a lawyer who is employed by a client to provide legal services to the client or its organizational affiliates, i.e., entities that control, are controlled by, or are under common control with the employer. This paragraph does not authorize the provision of personal legal services to the employer's officers or employees that are unrelated to their employment. The paragraph applies to in-house corporate lawyers, government lawyers and others who are employed to render legal services to the employer. The nature of the relationship between the lawyer and client provides a sufficient safeguard that the lawyer is competent to advise regarding the matters for which the lawyer is employed.

[17] If an employed lawyer establishes an office or other systematic presence in this jurisdiction for the purpose of rendering legal services to the employer, the lawyer may be subject to registration or other requirements, including assessments for appropriate fees and charges.

[18] Paragraph (d)(2) recognizes that a U.S. or foreign lawyer may provide legal services in this jurisdiction even though not admitted

when the lawyer is authorized to do so by federal or other law, which includes statute, court rule, executive regulation or judicial precedent.

[19] A lawyer who practices law in this jurisdiction pursuant to paragraphs (c) or (d) or otherwise is subject to the disciplinary authority of this jurisdiction. See Rule 8.5(a).

[20] In some circumstances, a lawyer who practices law in this jurisdiction pursuant to paragraphs (c) or (d) may have to inform the client that the lawyer is not admitted to practice law in this jurisdiction. For example, that may be required when the representation occurs primarily in this jurisdiction and requires knowledge of the law of this jurisdiction. See Rule 1.4(b).

[21] Paragraphs (c) and (d) do not authorize communications advertising legal services in this jurisdiction by lawyers who are admitted to practice in other jurisdictions. Whether and how lawyers may communicate the availability of their services in this jurisdiction is governed by Rules 7.1 to 7.5.

Rule 5.6. Restrictions on Right to Practice

A lawyer shall not participate in offering or making:

(a) a partnership, shareholders, operating, employment, or other similar type of agreement that restricts the right of a lawyer to practice after termination of the relationship, except an agreement concerning benefits upon retirement; or

(b) an agreement in which a restriction on the lawyer's right to practice is part of the settlement of a client controversy.

Adopted June 9, 1997, effective January 1, 1998. Amended March 26, 2015, effective July 1, 2015.

Comment

[1] An agreement restricting the right of lawyers to practice after leaving a firm not only limits their professional autonomy but also limits the freedom of clients to choose a lawyer. Paragraph (a) prohibits such agreements except for restrictions incident to provisions concerning retirement benefits for service with the firm.

[2] Paragraph (b) prohibits a lawyer from agreeing not to represent other persons in connection with settling a claim on behalf of a client.

[3] This Rule does not apply to prohibit restrictions that may be included in the terms of the sale of a law practice pursuant to Rule 1.17.

Rule 5.7. Responsibilities Regarding Law–Related Services

(a) A lawyer shall be subject to the Rules of Professional Conduct with respect to the provision of law-related services, as defined in paragraph (b), if the law-related services are provided:

(1) by the lawyer in circumstances that are not distinct from the lawyer's provision of legal services to clients; or

(2) in other circumstances by an entity controlled by the lawyer individually or with others if the lawyer fails to take reasonable measures, which shall include notice in writing, to assure that a person obtaining the law-related services knows that the services are not legal services and that the protections of the client-lawyer relationship do not exist.

(b) The term "law related services" denotes services that might reasonably be performed in conjunction with and in substance are related to the provision of legal services, and

that are not prohibited as unauthorized practice of law when provided by a nonlawyer.

Adopted June 9, 1997, effective January 1, 1998. Amended March 26, 2015, effective July 1, 2015.

Comment

[1] When a lawyer performs law-related services or controls an organization that does so, there exists the potential for ethical problems. Principal among these is the possibility that the person for whom the law-related services are performed fails to understand that the services may not carry with them the protections normally afforded as part of the client-lawyer relationship. The recipient of the law-related services may expect, for example, that the protection of client confidences, prohibitions against representation of persons with conflicting interests, and obligations of a lawyer to maintain professional independence apply to the provision of law-related services when that may not be the case.

[2] Rule 5.7 applies to the provision of law-related services by a lawyer even when the lawyer does not provide any legal services to the person for whom the law-related services are performed and whether the law-related services are performed through a law firm or separate entity. The Rule identifies the circumstances in which all of the Rules of Professional Conduct apply to the provision of law-related services. Even when those circumstances do not exist, however, the conduct of a lawyer involved in the provision of law-related services is subject to those Rules that apply generally to lawyer conduct, regardless of whether the conduct involves the provision of legal services. See, *e.g.*, Rule 8.4.

[3] When law-related services are provided by a lawyer under circumstances that are not distinct from the lawyer's provision of legal services to clients, the lawyer in providing the law-related services must adhere to the requirements of the Rules of Professional Conduct as provided in paragraph (a)(1). Even when the law-related and legal services are provided in circumstances that are distinct from each other, for example through separate entities or different support staff within the law firm, the Rules of Professional Conduct apply to the lawyer as provided in paragraph (a)(2) unless the lawyer takes reasonable measures, which shall include notice in writing, to assure that the recipient of the law-related services knows that the services are not legal services and that the protections of the client-lawyer relationship do not apply.

[4] Law-related services also may be provided through an entity that is distinct from that through which the lawyer provides legal services. If the lawyer individually or with others has control of such an entity's operations, the Rule requires the lawyer to take reasonable measures, which shall include notice in writing, to assure that each person using the services of the entity knows that the services provided by the entity are not legal services and that the Rules of Professional Conduct that relate to the client-lawyer relationship do not apply. A lawyer's control of an entity extends to the ability to direct its operation. Whether a lawyer has such control will depend upon the circumstances of the particular case.

[5] When a client-lawyer relationship exists with a person who is referred by a lawyer to a separate law-related service entity controlled by the lawyer, individually or with others, the lawyer must comply with Rule 1.8(a).

[6] In taking the reasonable measures referred to in paragraph (a)(2) to assure that a person using law-related services understands the practical effect or significance of the inapplicability of the Rules of Professional Conduct, the lawyer should communicate to the person receiving the law-related services, in a manner sufficient to assure that the person understands the significance of the fact, that the relationship of the person to the business entity will not be a client-lawyer relationship. The communication must be made before entering into an agreement for provision of or providing law-related services, and must be in writing.

[7] The burden is upon the lawyer to show that the lawyer has taken reasonable measures under the circumstances to communicate the desired understanding. For instance, a sophisticated user of law-related services, such as a publicly held corporation, may require a lesser explanation than someone unaccustomed to making distinctions between legal services and law-related services, such as an individual seeking tax advice from a lawyer-accountant or investigative services in connection with a lawsuit.

[8] Regardless of the sophistication of potential recipients of law-related services, a lawyer should take special care to keep separate the provision of law-related and legal services in order to minimize the risk that the recipient will assume that the law-related services are legal services. The risk of such confusion is especially acute when the lawyer renders both types of services with respect to the same matter. Under some circumstances the legal and law-related services may be so closely entwined that they cannot be distinguished from each other, and the requirement of disclosure and consultation imposed by paragraph (a)(2) of the Rule cannot be met. In such a case a lawyer will be responsible for assuring that both the lawyer's conduct and, to the extent required by Rule 5.3, that of nonlawyer employees in the distinct entity which the lawyer controls complies in all respects with the Rules of Professional Conduct.

[9] A broad range of economic and other interests of clients may be served by lawyers' engaging in the delivery of law-related services. Examples of law-related services include providing title insurance, financial planning, accounting, trust services, real estate counseling, legislative lobbying, economic analysis social work, psychological counseling, tax preparation, and patent, medical or environmental consulting.

[10] When a lawyer is obliged to accord the recipients of such services the protections of those Rules that apply to the client-lawyer relationship, the lawyer must take special care to heed the proscriptions of the Rules addressing conflict of interest (Rules 1.7 through 1.11, especially Rules 1.7(a)(2) and 1.8(a),(b) and (f)), and to scrupulously adhere to the requirements of Rule 1.6 relating to disclosure of confidential information. The promotion of the law-related services must also in all respects comply with Rules 7.1 through 7.5, dealing with advertising and solicitation.

[11] When the full protections of all of the Rules of Professional Conduct do not apply to the provision of law-related services, principles of law external to the Rules, for example, the law of principal and agent, govern the legal duties owed to those receiving the services. Those other legal principles may establish a different degree of protection for the recipient with respect to confidentiality of information, conflicts of interest and permissible business relationships with clients. See also Rule 8.4 (Misconduct).

PUBLIC SERVICE

Rule 6.1.   Voluntary Pro Bono Publico Service

A lawyer should provide annually at least 25 hours of *pro bono publico* legal services for the benefit of persons of limited means. In providing these professional services, the lawyer should:

(a) provide all or most of the 25 hours of *pro bono publico* legal services without compensation or expectation of compensation to persons of limited means, or to charitable, religious, civic, community, governmental, and educational organizations in matters that are designed primarily to address the needs of persons of limited means. The lawyer may provide any remaining hours by delivering legal services at substantially reduced compensation to persons of limited means or by participating in activities for improving the law, the legal system, or the legal profession that are primarily intended to benefit persons of limited means; or,

(b) contribute from $250 to 1% of the lawyer's annual taxable, professional income to one or more organizations that provide or support legal services to persons of limited means.

Adopted January 4, 1999, effective February 1, 1999. Comment amended March 26, 2015, effective July 1, 2015.

Comment

[1] Every lawyer, regardless of professional prominence or professional work load, should provide legal services to persons of limited means. This Rule sets forth a standard which the court believes each member of the Bar of the Commonwealth can and should fulfill. Because the Rule is aspirational, failure to provide the *pro bono publico* services stated in this Rule will not subject a lawyer to discipline. The Rule calls on all lawyers to provide a minimum of 25 hours of *pro bono publico* legal services annually. Twenty-five hours is one-half of the number of hours specified in the ABA Model Rule 6.1 because this Massachusetts rule focuses only on legal activity that benefits those unable to afford access to the system of justice. In some years a lawyer may render greater or fewer than 25 hours, but during the course of his or her legal career, each lawyer should render annually, on average, 25 hours. Also, it may be more feasible to act

collectively, for example, by a firm's providing through one or more lawyers an amount of *pro bono publico* legal services sufficient to satisfy the aggregate amount of hours expected from all lawyers in the firm. Services can be performed in civil matters or in criminal or quasi-criminal matters for which there is no government obligation to provide funds for legal representation.

[2] The purpose of this Rule is to make the system of justice more open to all by increasing the *pro bono publico* legal services available to persons of limited means. Because this Rule calls for the provision of 25 hours of *pro bono publico* legal services annually, instead of the 50 hours per year specified in ABA Model Rule 6.1, the provision of the ABA Model Rule regarding service to non-profit organizations was omitted. This omission should not be read as denigrating the value of the voluntary service provided to non-profit community and civil rights organizations by many lawyers. Such services are valuable to the community as a whole and should be continued. Service on the boards of non-profit arts and civic organizations, on school committees, and in local public office are but a few examples of public service by lawyers. Such activities, to the extent they are not directed at meeting the legal needs of persons of limited means, are not within the scope of this Rule. While the American Bar Association Model Rule 6.1 also does not credit general civic activities, it explicitly provides that some of a lawyer's *pro bono publico* obligation may be met by legal services provided to vindicate "civil rights, civil liberties and public rights." Such activities, when undertaken on behalf of persons of limited means, are within the scope of this Rule.

[2A] Paragraph (a) describes the nature of the *pro bono publico* legal services to be rendered annually under the Rule. Such legal services consist of a full range of activities on behalf of persons of limited means, including individual and class representation, the provision of legal advice, legislative lobbying, administrative rule making, community legal education, and the provision of free training or mentoring to those who represent persons of limited means.

[3] Persons eligible for *pro bono publico* legal services under this Rule are those who qualify for publicly-funded legal service programs and those whose incomes and financial resources are above the guidelines used by such programs but who, nevertheless, cannot afford counsel. Legal services can be rendered to individuals or to organizations composed of low-income people, to organizations that serve those of limited means such as homeless shelters, battered women's centers,

and food pantries or to those organizations which pursue civil rights, civil liberties, and public rights on behalf of persons of limited means. Providing legal advice, counsel and assistance to an organization consisting of or serving persons of limited means while a member of its board of directors would be *pro bono publico* legal services under this Rule.

[4] In order to be *pro bono publico* services under the first sentence of Rule 6.1(a), services must be provided without compensation or expectation of compensation. The intent of the lawyer to render free legal services is essential for the work performed to fall within the meaning of this paragraph. Accordingly, services rendered cannot be considered pro bono if an anticipated fee is uncollected. The award of statutory attorney's fees in a case accepted as a pro bono case, however, would not disqualify such services from inclusion under this Rule.

[5] A lawyer should perform *pro bono publico* services exclusively or primarily through activities described in the first sentence of paragraph (a). Any remaining hours can be provided in the ways set forth in the second sentence of that paragraph, including instances in which an attorney agrees to receive a modest fee for furnishing legal services to persons of limited means. Acceptance of court appointments and provision of services to individuals when the fee is substantially below a lawyer's usual rate are encouraged under this sentence.

[6] The variety of activities described in Comment 3 should facilitate participation by government and corporate attorneys, even when restrictions exist on their engaging in the outside practice of law. Lawyers who by the nature of their positions are prohibited from participating in the activities described in the first sentence of paragraph (a) may engage in the activities described in the second sentence of paragraph (a) or make a financial contribution pursuant to paragraph (b).

[7] The second sentence of paragraph (a) also recognizes the value of lawyers engaging in activities, on behalf of persons of limited means, that improve the law, the legal system, or the legal profession. Examples of the many activities that fall within this sentence, when primarily intended to benefit persons of limited means, include: serving on bar association committees, serving on boards of pro bono or legal services programs, taking part in Law Day activities, acting as a continuing legal education instructor, a mediator or an arbitrator, and engaging in legislative lobbying to improve the law, the legal system, or the profession.

[8] Lawyers who choose to make financial contributions pursuant to paragraph (b) should contribute from $250 to 1% of the lawyer's adjusted net Massachusetts income from legal professional activities. Each lawyer should take into account his or her own specific circumstances and obligations in determining his or her contribution.

[9] Reserved

[10] Reserved

[11] Law firms should act reasonably to enable and encourage all lawyers in the firm to provide the pro bono legal services called for by this Rule.

Rule 6.2. Accepting Appointments

A lawyer shall not seek to avoid appointment by a tribunal to represent a person except for good cause, such as:

(a) representing the client is likely to result in violation of the Rules of Professional Conduct or other law;

(b) representing the client is likely to result in an unreasonable financial burden on the lawyer; or

(c) the client or the cause is so repugnant to the lawyer as to be likely to impair the client-lawyer relationship or the lawyer's ability to represent the client.

Adopted June 9, 1997, effective January 1, 1998. Comment amended March 26, 2015, effective July 1, 2015.

Comment

[1] A lawyer ordinarily is not obliged to accept a client whose character or cause the lawyer regards as repugnant. The lawyer's freedom to select clients is, however, qualified. All lawyers have a responsibility to assist in providing pro bono publico service. See Rule 6.1. An individual lawyer fulfills this responsibility by accepting a fair share of unpopular matters or indigent or unpopular clients. A lawyer may also be subject to appointment by a court to serve unpopular clients or persons unable to afford legal services.

Appointed Counsel

[2] For good cause a lawyer may seek to decline an appointment to represent a person who cannot afford to retain counsel or whose cause is unpopular. Good cause exists if the lawyer could not handle the matter competently, see Rule 1.1, or if undertaking the representation would result in an improper conflict of interest, for example, when the client or the cause is so repugnant to the lawyer as to be likely to impair the client-lawyer relationship or the lawyer's ability to represent the client. A lawyer may also seek to decline an appointment if acceptance would be unreasonably burdensome, for example, when it would impose a financial sacrifice so great as to be unjust.

[3] An appointed lawyer has the same obligations to the client as retained counsel, including the obligations of loyalty and confidentiality, and is subject to the same limitations on the client-lawyer relationship, such as the obligation to refrain from assisting the client in violation of the Rules.

Rule 6.3. Membership in Legal Services Organization

A lawyer may serve as a director, officer, or member of a legal services organization, apart from the law firm in which the lawyer practices, notwithstanding that the organization serves persons having interests adverse to a client of the lawyer. The lawyer shall not knowingly participate in a decision or action of the organization:

(a) if participating in the decision or action would be incompatible with the lawyer's obligations to a client under Rule 1.7; or

(b) where the decision or action could have a material adverse effect on the representation of a client of the organization whose interests are adverse to a client of the lawyer.

Adopted June 9, 1997, effective January 1, 1998.

Comment

[1] Lawyers should be encouraged to support and participate in legal service organizations. A lawyer who is an officer or a member of such an organization does not thereby have a client-lawyer relationship with persons served by the organization. However, there is potential conflict between the interests of such persons and the interests of the lawyer's clients. If the possibility of such conflict disqualified a lawyer from serving on the board of a legal services organization, the profession's involvement in such organizations would be severely curtailed.

[2] It may be necessary in appropriate cases to reassure a client of the organization that the representation will not be affected by conflicting loyalties of a member of the board. Established, written policies in this respect can enhance the credibility of such assurances.

Corresponding ABA Model Rule. Identical to Model Rule 6.3.

Corresponding Former Massachusetts Rule. None.

Rule 6.4. Law Reform Activities Affecting Client Interests

A lawyer may serve as a director, officer, or member of an organization involved in reform of the law or its administration notwithstanding that the reform may affect the interests of a client of the lawyer. When the lawyer knows that the interests of a client may be materially benefitted by a decision in which the lawyer participates, the lawyer shall disclose that fact but need not identify the client.

Adopted June 9, 1997, effective January 1, 1998.

Comment

[1] Lawyers involved in organizations seeking law reform generally do not have a client-lawyer relationship with the organization. Otherwise, it might follow that a lawyer could not be involved in a bar association law reform program that might indirectly affect a client. See also Rule 1.2(b). For example, a lawyer specializing in antitrust litigation might be regarded as disqualified from participating in drafting revisions of rules governing that subject. In determining the nature and scope of participation in such activities, a lawyer should be mindful of obligations to clients under other Rules, particularly Rule 1.7. A lawyer is professionally obligated to protect the integrity of the program by making an appropriate disclosure within the organization when the lawyer knows a private client might be materially benefitted.

Corresponding ABA Model Rule. Identical to Model Rule 6.4.

Corresponding Former Massachusetts Rule. None. But see G.L. c. 211D, § 1, as to members of the Committee for Public Counsel Services.

Rule 6.5. Nonprofit and Court–Annexed Limited Legal Services Programs

(a) A lawyer who, under the auspices of a program sponsored by a nonprofit organization or court, provides short-term limited legal services to a client without expectation by either the lawyer or the client that the lawyer will provide continuing representation in the matter:

(1) is not subject to Rule 1.5(b);

(2) is subject to Rules 1.7 and 1.9(a) only if the lawyer knows that the representation of the client involves a conflict of interest; and

(3) is subject to Rule 1.10 only if the lawyer knows that another lawyer associated with the lawyer in a law firm is disqualified by Rule 1.7 or 1.9(a) with respect to the matter.

(b) Except as provided in paragraph (a)(3), Rule 1.10 is inapplicable to a representation governed by this Rule.

Adopted June 8, 2005, effective July 1, 2005. Amended October 24, 2012, effective January 1, 2013.

Comment

[1] Legal services organizations, courts and various nonprofit organizations have established programs through which lawyers provide short-term limited legal services — such as advice or the completion of legal forms — that will assist persons to address their legal problems without further representation by a lawyer. In these programs, such as legal-advice hotlines, advice-only clinics or pro se counseling programs, a client–lawyer relationship is established, but there is no expectation that the lawyer's representation of the client will continue beyond the limited consultation. Such programs are normally operated under circumstances in which it is not feasible for a lawyer to systematically screen for conflicts of interest as is generally required before undertaking a representation. See, e.g., Rules 1.7, 1.9 and 1.10.

[2] A lawyer who provides short-term limited legal services pursuant to this Rule must secure the client's informed consent to the limited scope of the representation. See Rule 1.2(c). If a short-term limited representation would not be reasonable under the circumstances, the lawyer may offer advice to the client but must also advise the client of the need for further assistance of counsel. Except as provided in this Rule, the Rules of Professional Conduct, including Rules 1.6 and 1.9(c), are applicable to the limited representation.

[3] Because a lawyer who is representing a client in the circumstances addressed by this Rule ordinarily is not able to check systematically for conflicts of interest, paragraph (a) requires compliance with Rules 1.7 or 1.9(a) only if the lawyer knows that the representation presents a conflict of interest for the lawyer, and with Rule 1.10 only if the lawyer knows that another lawyer in the lawyer's firm is disqualified by Rules 1.7 or 1.9(a) in the matter.

[4] Because the limited nature of the services significantly reduces the risk of conflicts of interest with other matters being handled by the lawyer's firm, paragraph (b) provides that Rule 1.10 is inapplicable to a representation governed by this Rule except as provided by paragraph (a)(3). Paragraph (a)(3) requires the participating lawyer to comply with Rule 1.10 when the lawyer knows that the lawyer's firm is disqualified by Rules 1.7 or 1.9(a). By virtue of paragraph (b), however, a lawyer's participation in a short-term limited legal services program will not preclude the lawyer's firm from undertaking or continuing the representation of a client with interests adverse to a client being represented under the program's auspices. Nor will the personal disqualification of a lawyer participating in the program be imputed to other lawyers participating in the program.

[5] If, after commencing a short-term limited representation in accordance with this Rule, a lawyer undertakes to represent the client in the matter on an ongoing basis, Rules 1.7, 1.9(a) and 1.10 become applicable.

INFORMATION ABOUT LEGAL SERVICES

Rule 7.1. Communications Concerning a Lawyer's Services

A lawyer shall not make a false or misleading communication about the lawyer or the lawyer's services. A communication is false or misleading if it contains a material misrepresentation of fact or law, or omits a fact necessary to make the statement considered as a whole not materially misleading.

Adopted June 9, 1997, effective January 1, 1998. Amended August 31, 1999, effective October 1, 1999. Comment amended March 26, 2015, effective July 1, 2015.

Comment

[1] This Rule governs all communications about a lawyer's services, including advertising permitted by Rule 7.2. Whatever means are used to make known a lawyer's services, statements about them should be truthful.

[2] Truthful statements that are misleading are also prohibited by this Rule. A truthful statement is misleading if it omits a fact necessary to make the lawyer's communication considered as a whole not materially misleading. A truthful statement is also misleading if there is a substantial likelihood that it will lead a reasonable person to

formulate a specific conclusion about the lawyer or the lawyer's services for which there is no reasonable factual foundation.

[3] An advertisement that truthfully reports a lawyer's achievements on behalf of clients or former clients may be misleading if presented so as to lead a reasonable person to form an unjustified expectation that the same results could be obtained for other clients in similar matters without reference to the specific factual and legal circumstances of each client's case. Similarly, an unsubstantiated comparison of the lawyer's services or fees with the services or fees of other lawyers may be misleading if presented with such specificity as would lead a reasonable person to conclude that the comparison can be substantiated. The inclusion of an appropriate disclaimer or qualifying language may preclude a finding that a statement is likely to create unjustified expectations or otherwise mislead the public.

[4] See also Rule 8.4(e) for the prohibition against stating or implying an ability to influence improperly a government agency or official or to achieve results by means that violate the Rules of Professional Conduct or other law.

Rule 7.2. Advertising

(a) Subject to the requirements of Rules 7.1 and 7.3, a lawyer may advertise services through written, recorded or electronic communication, including public media.

(b) A lawyer shall not give anything of value to a person for recommending the lawyer's services, except that a lawyer may:

(1) pay the reasonable costs of advertisements or communications permitted by this Rule;

(2) pay the usual charges of a legal service plan, not-for-profit lawyer referral service, or qualified legal assistance organization;

(3) pay for a law practice in accordance with Rule 1.17;

(4) refer clients to another lawyer or a nonlawyer professional pursuant to an agreement not otherwise prohibited under these Rules that provides for the other person to refer clients or customers to the lawyer, if

(i) the reciprocal referral agreement is not exclusive, and

(ii) the client is informed of the existence and nature of the agreement; and

(5) pay fees permitted by Rule 1.5(e) or Rule 5.4(a)(4).

(c) Any communication made pursuant to this Rule shall include the name of the lawyer, group of lawyers, or firm responsible for its content.

Adopted June 9, 1997, effective January 1, 1998. Amended December 8, 1997, effective January 1, 1998; amended August 31, 1999, effective October 1, 1999. Amended March 26, 2015, effective July 1, 2015.

Comment

[1] To assist the public in learning about and obtaining legal services, lawyers should be allowed to make known their services not only through reputation but also through organized information campaigns in the form of advertising.

[2] [Reserved]

[3] [Reserved]

[3A] The advertising and solicitation rules can generally be applied to computer-accessed or other similar types of communications by analogizing the communication to its hard-copy form. Thus, because it is not a communication directed to a specific recipient, a website or home page would generally be considered advertising subject to this Rule, rather than solicitation subject to Rule 7.3. For the distinction between advertising governed by this Rule and solicitations governed by Rule 7.3, see Comment 1 to Rule 7.3.

[4] Neither this Rule nor Rule 7.3 prohibits communications authorized by law, such as notice to members of a class in class action litigation.

Paying Others to Recommend a Lawyer

[5] Except as permitted under paragraphs (b)(1)–(b)(5), lawyers are not permitted to pay others for recommending the lawyer's services or for channeling professional work in a manner that violates Rule 7.3. A communication contains a recommendation if it endorses or vouches for a lawyer's credentials, abilities, competence, character, or other professional qualities. Paragraph (b)(1), however, allows a lawyer to pay for advertising and communications permitted by this Rule, including the costs of print directory listings, on-line directory listings, newspaper ads, television and radio airtime, domain-name registrations, sponsorship fees, banner ads, Internet-based advertisements, and group advertising. A lawyer may compensate employees, agents and vendors who are engaged to provide marketing or client development services, such as publicists, public-relations personnel, business-development staff and website designers. See also Rule 5.3 (duties of lawyers and law firms with respect to the conduct of nonlawyers; Rule 8.4(a) (duty to avoid violating the Rules through the acts of another).

[6] A lawyer may pay the usual charges of a legal service plan, not-for-profit lawyer referral service, or qualified legal assistance organization. A legal service plan is a prepaid or group legal service plan or a similar delivery system that assists people who seek to secure legal representation. A lawyer referral service is a consumer-oriented organization that provides unbiased referrals to lawyers with appropriate experience in the subject matter of the representation and affords other client protections, such as complaint procedures or malpractice insurance requirements. A qualified legal assistance organization is defined by Rule 1.0(j).

[7] A lawyer who accepts assignments or referrals from a legal service plan or referrals from a lawyer referral service must act reasonably to assure that the activities of the plan or service are compatible with the lawyer's professional obligations. See Rules 5.3 and 8.4(a). Legal service plans and lawyer referral services may communicate with the public, but such communication must be in conformity with these Rules. Thus, advertising must not be false or misleading, as would be the case if the communications of a group advertising program or a group legal services plan would mislead the public to think that it was a lawyer referral service sponsored by a state agency or bar association. Nor could the lawyer allow in-person, telephonic, or real-time contacts that would violate Rule 7.3.

[8] A lawyer also may agree to refer clients to another lawyer or a non-lawyer professional, in return for the undertaking of that person to refer clients or customers to the lawyer. Such reciprocal referral arrangements must not interfere with the lawyer's professional judgment as to making referrals or as to providing substantive legal services. See Rules 2.1 and 5.4(c). Except as provided in Rule 1.5(e), a lawyer who receives referrals from a lawyer or nonlawyer professional must not pay anything for the referral, but the lawyer does not violate paragraph (b) of this Rule by agreeing to refer clients to the other lawyer or nonlawyer professional, so long as the reciprocal referral agreement is not exclusive and the client is informed of the referral agreement. Such arrangements are governed by Rule 1.7, and therefore require the client's informed consent in writing. Reciprocal referral agreements should not be of indefinite duration and should be reviewed periodically to determine whether they comply with these Rules. This Rule does not restrict referrals or divisions of revenues or net income among lawyers within firms comprised of multiple entities.

Rule 7.3. Solicitation of Clients

(a) A lawyer shall not by in-person, live telephone or real-time electronic contact solicit professional employment for a fee, unless the person contacted:

(1) is a lawyer;

(2) has a prior professional relationship with the lawyer;

(3) is a grandparent of the lawyer or the lawyer's spouse, a descendant of the grandparents of the lawyer or the lawyer's spouse, or the spouse of any of the foregoing persons; or

(4) is (i) a representative of an organization, including a non-profit or government entity, in connection with the activities of such organization, or (ii) a person engaged in trade or commerce as defined in G. L. c. 93A, § 1 (*b*), in connection with such person's trade or commerce.

(b) A lawyer shall not solicit professional employment by written, recorded or electronic communication or by in-person, telephone or real-time electronic contact even when not otherwise prohibited by paragraph (a), if:

(1) the target of the solicitation has made known to the lawyer a desire not to be solicited by the lawyer;

(2) the solicitation involves coercion, duress or harassment; or

(3) the lawyer knows or reasonably should know that the physical, mental, or emotional state of the target of the solicitation is such that the target cannot exercise reasonable judgment in employing a lawyer, provided, however, the prohibition in this clause (3) only applies to solicitations for a fee.

(c) [Reserved]

(d) Notwithstanding the prohibitions in paragraph (a), a lawyer may request referrals from a lawyer referral service operated, sponsored, or approved by a bar association or other non-profit organization, and cooperate with any other qualified legal assistance organization.

Adopted June 9, 1997, effective January 1, 1998. Amended August 31, 1999, effective October 1, 1999; October 27, 1999, effective December 1, 1999; amended effective, April 3, 2000; March 26, 2015, effective July 1, 2015.

Comment

[1] A solicitation is a targeted communication initiated by the lawyer that is directed to a specific person and that offers to provide, or can reasonably be understood as offering to provide, legal services. In contrast, a lawyer's communication typically does not constitute a solicitation if it is directed to the general public, such as through a billboard, an Internet banner advertisement, a website or a television commercial, or if it is in response to a request for information or is automatically generated in response to Internet searches.

[2] This Rule allows lawyers to conduct some form of solicitation of employment, except in a small number of very special circumstances, and hence permits the public to receive information about legal services that may be useful to them. At the same time it recognizes the possibility of undue influence, intimidation, and overreaching presented by personal solicitation in the circumstances prohibited by this Rule and seeks to limit them by regulating the form and manner of solicitation by rules that reach no further than the danger that is perceived. Lawyers are also required to comply with other applicable laws that govern solicitations.

[3] Paragraph (a) applies to in-person, live telephone, and real-time electronic contact by a lawyer. Paragraph (b) applies to all forms of solicitation, including both the realtime solicitation covered by paragraph (a) and solicitation by written, recorded or other forms of electronic communication such as email. In determining whether a contact is permissible under Rule 7.3(b)(3), it is relevant to consider the times and circumstances under which the contact is initiated. For example, a person undergoing active medical treatment for traumatic injury is unlikely to be in an emotional state in which reasonable judgment about employing a lawyer can be exercised. The reference to the "physical, mental, or emotional state of the target of the solicitation" is intended to be all-inclusive of the condition of such person and includes anyone who for any reason lacks sufficient sophistication to be able to select a lawyer. A proviso in subparagraph (b)(3) makes clear that it is not intended to reduce the ability possessed by nonprofit organizations to contact the elderly and the mentally disturbed or disabled. Abuse of the right to solicit such persons by non-profit organizations may constitute a violation of paragraph (b)(2) of the Rule or Rule 8.4(c) or (d). The references in paragraph (a) and (b)(3) of the Rule to solicitation "for a fee" are intended to exempt solicitations by non-profit organizations. Where such an organization is involved, the fact that there may be a statutory entitlement to a fee is not intended by itself to bring the solicitation within the scope of the Rule. There is no blanket exemption from regulation for all solicitation that is not done "for a fee." Non-profit organizations are subject to the general prohibitions of subparagraphs (b)(1) and (b)(2).

[4] The use of general advertising and written, recorded or electronic communications to transmit information from lawyer to the public, rather than direct in person, live telephone or real-time electronic contact, will help to assure that the information flows cleanly as well as freely. The contents of advertisements and communications permitted under Rule 7.2 can be permanently recorded so that they cannot be disputed and may be shared with others who know the lawyer. This potential for informal review is itself likely to help guard against statements and claims that might constitute false and misleading communications, in violation of Rule 7.1. The contents of direct in person, live telephone or real-time electronic contact can be disputed and may not be subject to third party scrutiny. Consequently, they are much more likely to approach (and occasionally cross) the dividing line between accurate representations and those that are false and misleading.

[5] While paragraph (b) permits written and other nondirect solicitation of any person, except under the special circumstances set forth in subparagraphs (1) through (3), paragraph (a) prohibits solicitation in person or by live telephone or real-time electronic communication, except in the situations described in subparagraphs (1) through (4). See also Comment 3A to Rule 7.2, discussing prohibited personal solicitation through computer-accessed or similar types of communications. The prohibitions of paragraph (a) do not of course apply to in-person solicitation after contact has been initiated by a person seeking legal services.

[6] Subparagraphs (1) through (4) of paragraph (a) acknowledge that there are certain situations and relationships in which concerns about overreaching and undue influence do not have sufficient force to justify banning all in-person solicitation. The risk of overreaching and undue influence is diminished where the target of the solicitation is a former client or a member of the lawyer's immediate family. The word "descendant" is intended to include adopted and step-members of the family. Similarly, other lawyers and those who manage commercial, nonprofit, and governmental entities generally have the experience and judgment to make reasonable decisions with respect to the importunings of trained advocates soliciting legal business Subparagraph (a)(4) permits in-person solicitation of organizations, whether the organization is a non-profit or governmental organization, in connection with the activities of such organization, and of individuals engaged in trade or commerce, in connection with the trade or commerce of such individuals.

[7] Paragraph (d) permits a lawyer to request referrals from described organizations.

Rule 7.4.   Communication of Fields of Practice

(a) A lawyer may communicate the fact that the lawyer does or does not practice in particular fields of the law.

(b) Lawyers may hold themselves out publicly as specialists in particular services, fields, and areas of law if the communication is not false or misleading. Such holding out includes a statement that the lawyer concentrates in, specializes in, is certified in, has expertise in, or limits practice to a particular service, field, or area of law. Lawyers who hold themselves out as specialists shall be held to the standard of performance of specialists in that particular service, field, or area.

(c) A lawyer shall not state or imply that a lawyer is certified as a specialist in a particular field of law unless the name of the certifying organization is clearly identified in the communication and:

(1) the lawyer has been certified as a specialist by an organization that has been approved by an appropriate state authority or accredited by the American Bar Association, or

(2) the communication states that the certifying organization is "a private organization, whose standards for certification are not regulated by a state authority or the American Bar Association."

Adopted June 9, 1997, effective January 1, 1998. Amended December 8, 1997, effective January 1, 1998; August 31, 1999, effective October 1, 1999; March 26, 2015, effective July 1, 2015.

Comment

[1] Paragraphs (a) and (b) of this Rule permit a lawyer to indicate areas of practice in communications about the lawyer's services. Lawyers are generally permitted to hold themselves out as specialists in a particular service, field or area of law but the definition of what is included in the term "holding out" is broad and the examples in paragraph (b) are not intended to be exclusive. Any such claims of specialization are subject to the "false and misleading" standard applied in Rule 7.1 to communications concerning a lawyer's services.

[2] Paragraph (c) identifies the circumstances under which lawyers may state that they are certified as specialists in a field or area of law. Certification signifies that an objective entity has recognized an advanced degree of knowledge and experience in the specialty area greater than is suggested by general licensure to practice law. Certifying organizations may be expected to apply standards of experience, knowledge and proficiency to insure that a lawyer's recognition as a specialist is meaningful and reliable. In order to insure that consumers can obtain access to useful information about an organization granting certification, the name of the certifying organization must be included in any communication regarding the certification.

Rule 7.5.   Firm Names and Letterheads

(a) A lawyer shall not use a firm name, letterhead, or other professional designation that violates Rule 7.1. A trade name may be used by a lawyer in private practice if it does not imply a connection with a government agency or with a public or charitable legal services organization and is not otherwise in violation of Rule 7.1.

(b) A law firm with offices in more than one jurisdiction may use the same name or other professional designation in each jurisdiction, but identification of the lawyers in an office of the firm shall indicate the jurisdictional limitations on those not licensed to practice in the jurisdiction where the office is located.

(c) The name of a lawyer holding a public office shall not be used in the name of a law firm, or in communications on its behalf, during any substantial period in which the lawyer is not actively and regularly practicing with the firm.

(d) Lawyers may state or imply that they practice in a partnership or other organization only when that is the fact.

Adopted June 9, 1997, effective January 1, 1998. Amended March 26, 2015, effective July 1, 2015.

Comment

[1] A firm may be designated by the names of all or some of its members, by the names of deceased or retired members where there has been a continuing succession in the firm's identity or by a trade name such as the "ABC Legal Clinic." A lawyer or law firm may also be designated by a distinctive website address or comparable professional designation. Use of such names, including trade names, in law practice is acceptable so long as it is not misleading. If a private firm uses a trade name that includes a geographical name such as "Springfield Legal Clinic," an express disclaimer that it is a public legal aid agency may be required to avoid a misleading implication. It may be observed that any firm name including the name of a deceased or retired partner is, strictly speaking, a trade name. The use of such names to designate law firms has proven a useful means of identification. However, it is misleading to use the name of a lawyer not associated with the firm or a predecessor of the firm, or the name of a nonlawyer.

[2] With regard to paragraph (d), lawyers who are not in fact partners, such as those who are only sharing office facilities, may not denominate themselves as, for example, "Smith and Jones," or "Smith and Jones, A Professional Association," for those titles, in the absence of an effective disclaimer of joint responsibility, suggest partnership in the practice of law or that they are practicing law together in a firm. Likewise, the use of the term "associates" by a group of lawyers implies practice in either a partnership or sole proprietorship form and may not be used by a group in which the individual members disclaim the joint or vicarious responsibility inherent in such forms of business in the absence of an effective disclaimer of such responsibility.

[3] S.J.C. Rule 3:06 imposes further restrictions on trade names for firms that are professional corporations, limited liability companies or limited liability partnerships.

MAINTAINING THE INTEGRITY OF THE PROFESSION

Rule 8.1.   Bar Admission and Disciplinary Matters

An applicant for admission to the bar, or a lawyer in connection with a bar admission application or in connection with a disciplinary matter, shall not:

(a) knowingly make a false statement of material fact; or

(b) fail to disclose a fact necessary to correct a misapprehension known by the person to have arisen in the matter, or knowingly fail to respond to a lawful demand for information from an admissions or disciplinary authority, except that this

Rule does not require disclosure of information otherwise protected by Rule 1.6.

Adopted June 9, 1997, effective January 1, 1998. Amended March 26, 2015, effective July 1, 2015.

Comment

[1] The duty imposed by this Rule extends to persons seeking admission to the bar as well as to lawyers. Hence, if a person makes a material false statement in connection with an application for admission, it may be the basis for subsequent disciplinary action if the person is admitted, and in any event may be relevant in a subsequent admission application. The duty imposed by this Rule applies to a lawyer's own admission or discipline as well as that of others. Thus, it is a separate professional offense for a lawyer to knowingly make a misrepresentation or omission in connection with a disciplinary investigation of the lawyer's own conduct. Paragraph (b) of this Rule also requires correction of any prior misstatement in the matter that the applicant or lawyer may have made and affirmative clarification of any misunderstanding on the part of the admissions or disciplinary authority of which the person involved becomes aware.

[2] This Rule is subject to the provisions of the Fifth Amendment of the United States Constitution and Article 12 of the Massachusetts Declaration of Rights. A person relying on such a provision in response to a question, however, should do so openly and not use the right of nondisclosure as a justification for failure to comply with this Rule.

[3] A lawyer representing an applicant for admission to the bar, or representing a lawyer who is the subject of a disciplinary inquiry or proceeding, is governed by the rules applicable to the client-lawyer relationship, including Rule 1.6 and, in some cases, Rule 3.3.

Rule 8.2.   Judicial and Legal Officials

A lawyer shall not make a statement that the lawyer knows to be false or with reckless disregard as to its truth or falsity concerning the qualifications or integrity of a judge or a magistrate, or of a candidate for appointment to judicial or legal office.

Adopted June 9, 1997, effective January 1, 1998. Comment amended March 26, 2015, effective July 1, 2015.

Comment

[1] Assessments by lawyers are relied on in evaluating the professional or personal fitness of persons being considered for appointment to judicial or legal offices. Expressing honest and candid opinions on such matters contributes to improving the administration of justice. Conversely, false statements by a lawyer can unfairly undermine public confidence in the administration of justice. A lawyer violates this Rule by impugning the integrity of a judge or magistrate either by making an intentionally false statement or by making a false statement when the lawyer has no reasonably objective basis for the statement.

Rule 8.3.   Reporting Professional Misconduct

(a) A lawyer who knows that another lawyer has committed a violation of the Rules of Professional Conduct that raises a substantial question as to that lawyer's honesty, trustworthiness or fitness as a lawyer in other respects, shall inform the Bar Counsel's office of the Board of Bar Overseers.

(b) A lawyer who knows that a judge has committed a violation of applicable rules of judicial conduct that raises a substantial question as to the judge's fitness for office shall inform the Commission on Judicial Conduct.

(c) This Rule does not require disclosure of information otherwise protected by Rule 1.6.

Adopted June 9, 1997, effective January 1, 1998. Amended December 30, 1997, effective March 1, 1998. Amended March 26, 2015, effective July 1, 2015.

Comment

[1] This Rule requires lawyers to report serious violations of ethical duty by lawyers and judges. Even an apparently isolated violation may indicate a pattern of misconduct that only a disciplinary investigation can uncover. Reporting a violation is especially important where the victim is unlikely to discover the offense.

[2] A report about misconduct is not permitted or required where it would involve violation of Rule 1.6. However, a lawyer should encourage a client to consent to disclosure where prosecution would not substantially prejudice the client's interests.

[3] While a measure of judgment is required in complying with the provisions of the Rule, a lawyer must report misconduct that, if proven and without regard to mitigation, would likely result in an order of suspension or disbarment, including misconduct that would constitute a "serious crime" as defined in S.J.C. Rule 4:01, § 12(3). Precedent for determining whether an offense would warrant suspension or disbarment may be found in the Massachusetts Attorney Discipline Reports. Section 12(3) of Rule 4:01 provides that a serious crime is "any felony, and . . . any lesser crime a necessary element of which . . . includes interference with the administration of justice, false swearing, misrepresentation, fraud, willful failure to file income tax returns, deceit, bribery, extortion, misappropriation, theft, or an attempt or a conspiracy, or solicitation of another to commit [such a crime]." In addition to a conviction of a felony, misappropriation of client funds and perjury before a tribunal are common examples of reportable conduct. The term "substantial" refers to the seriousness of the possible offense and not the quantum of evidence of which the lawyer is aware. A lawyer has knowledge of a violation when he or she possesses supporting evidence such that a reasonable lawyer under the circumstances would form a firm opinion that the conduct in question had more likely occurred than not. A report should be made to Bar Counsel's office or to the Judicial Conduct Commission, as the case may be. Rule 8.3 does not preclude a lawyer from reporting a violation of the Massachusetts Rules of Professional Conduct in circumstances where a report is not mandatory.

[3A] In most situations, a lawyer may defer making a report under this Rule until the matter has been concluded, but the report should be made as soon as practicable thereafter. An immediate report is ethically compelled, however, when a client or third person will likely be injured by a delay in reporting, such as where the lawyer has knowledge that another lawyer has embezzled client or fiduciary funds and delay may impair the ability to recover the funds.

[4] The duty to report past professional misconduct does not apply to a lawyer retained to represent a lawyer whose professional conduct is in question. Such a situation is governed by the Rules applicable to the client-lawyer relationship.

Rule 8.4.   Misconduct

It is professional misconduct for a lawyer to:

(a) violate or attempt to violate the Rules of Professional Conduct, knowingly assist or induce another to do so, or do so through the acts of another;

(b) commit a criminal act that reflects adversely on the lawyer's honesty, trustworthiness or fitness as a lawyer in other respects;

(c) engage in conduct involving dishonesty, fraud, deceit or misrepresentation;

(d) engage in conduct that is prejudicial to the administration of justice;

(e) state or imply an ability (1) to influence improperly a government agency or official or (2) to achieve results by means that violate the Rules of Professional Conduct or other law;

(f) knowingly assist a judge or judicial officer in conduct that is a violation of applicable rules of judicial conduct or other law;

(g) fail without good cause to cooperate with the Bar Counsel or the Board of Bar Overseers as provided in S. J. C. Rule 4:01, § 3; or

(h) engage in any other conduct that adversely reflects on his or her fitness to practice law.

Adopted June 9, 1997, effective January 1, 1998. Amended effective March 5, 1998. Amended March 26, 2015, effective July 1, 2015.

Comment

[1] Lawyers are subject to discipline when they violate or attempt to violate the Rules of Professional Conduct, knowingly assist or induce another to do so or do so through the acts of another, as when they request or instruct an agent to do so on the lawyer's behalf. Paragraph (a), however, does not prohibit a lawyer from advising a client concerning action the client is legally entitled to take.

[2] Many kinds of illegal conduct reflect adversely on fitness to practice law, such as offenses involving fraud and the offense of willful failure to file an income tax return. However, some kinds of offenses carry no such implication. Traditionally, the distinction was drawn in terms of offenses involving "moral turpitude." That concept can be construed to include offenses concerning some matters of personal morality, such as adultery and comparable offenses, that have no specific connection to fitness for the practice of law. Although a lawyer is personally answerable to the entire criminal law, a lawyer should be professionally answerable only for offenses that indicate lack of those characteristics relevant to law practice. Offenses involving violence, dishonesty, breach of trust, or serious interference with the administration of justice are in that category. A pattern of repeated offenses, even ones of minor significance when considered separately, can indicate indifference to legal obligation.

[3] [Reserved]

[4] A lawyer may refuse to comply with an obligation imposed by law upon a good faith belief that no valid obligation exists. The provisions of Rule 1.2(d) concerning a good faith challenge to the validity, scope, meaning or application of the law apply to challenges of legal regulation of the practice of law.

[5] Lawyers holding public office assume legal responsibilities going beyond those of other citizens. A lawyer's abuse of public office can suggest an inability to fulfill the professional role of lawyers. The same is true of abuse of positions of private trust such as trustee, executor, administrator, guardian, agent and officer, director or manager of a corporation or other organization.

[6] Paragraph (e) prohibits the acceptance of referrals from a referral source, such as court or agency personnel, if the lawyer states or implies, or the client could reasonably infer, that the lawyer has an ability to influence the court or agency improperly.

[7] Paragraph (h) prohibits conduct that adversely reflects on a lawyer's fitness to practice law, even if the conduct does not constitute a criminal, dishonest, fraudulent, or other act specifically described in the other paragraphs of this Rule.

Rule 8.5.   Disciplinary Authority; Choice of Law

(a) Disciplinary Authority. A lawyer admitted to practice in this jurisdiction is subject to the disciplinary authority of this jurisdiction, regardless of where the lawyer's conduct occurs. A lawyer not admitted in this jurisdiction is also subject to the disciplinary authority of this jurisdiction if the lawyer provides or offers to provide any legal services in this jurisdiction. A lawyer may be subject to the disciplinary authority of both this jurisdiction and another jurisdiction for the same conduct.

(b) Choice of Law. In any exercise of the disciplinary authority of this jurisdiction, the rules of professional conduct to be applied shall be as follows:

(1) for conduct in connection with a matter pending before a governmental tribunal, the rules of the jurisdiction in which the tribunal sits, unless the rules of the tribunal provide otherwise; and

(2) for any other conduct, the rules of the jurisdiction in which the lawyer's principal office is located shall be applied, unless the predominant effect of the conduct is in a different jurisdiction, in which case the rules of that jurisdiction shall be applied. A lawyer shall not be subject to discipline if the lawyer's conduct conforms to the rules of a jurisdiction in which the lawyer reasonably believes the predominant effect of the lawyer's conduct will occur.

Adopted June 9, 1997, effective January 1, 1998. Amended May 26, 2009, effective July 1, 2009.

Comment

Disciplinary Authority

[1] It is longstanding law that the conduct of a lawyer admitted to practice in this jurisdiction is subject to the disciplinary authority of this jurisdiction. Extension of the disciplinary authority of this jurisdiction to other lawyers who provide or offer to provide legal services in this jurisdiction is for the protection of the citizens of this jurisdiction.

[1A] In adopting Rule 5.5, Massachusetts has made it clear that out-of-state lawyers who engage in practice in this jurisdiction are subject to the disciplinary authority of this state. A great many states have rules that are similar to, or identical with, Rule 5.5, and Massachusetts lawyers therefore need to be aware that they may become subject to the disciplinary rules of another state in certain circumstances. Rule 8.5 deals with the related question of the conflict of law rules that are to be applied when a lawyer's conduct affects multiple jurisdictions. Comments 2–7 state the particular principles that apply.

[1B] There is no completely satisfactory solution to the choice of law question so long as different states have different rules of professional responsibility. When a lawyer's conduct has an effect in another jurisdiction, that jurisdiction may assert that its law of professional responsibility should govern, whether the lawyer was physically present in the jurisdiction or not.

Choice of Law

[2] A lawyer may be potentially subject to more than one set of rules of professional conduct which impose different obligations. The lawyer may be licensed to practice in more than one jurisdiction with differing rules, or may be admitted to practice before a particular court with rules that differ from those of the jurisdiction or jurisdictions in which the lawyer is licensed to practice. Additionally, the lawyer's conduct may involve significant contacts with more than one jurisdiction.

[3] Paragraph (b) seeks to resolve such potential conflicts. Minimizing conflicts between rules, as well as uncertainty about which rules are applicable, is in the best interest of both clients and the profession (as well as the bodies having authority to regulate the profession). Accordingly, paragraph (b) provides that any particular act of a lawyer shall be subject to only one set of rules of professional conduct, makes the determination of which set of rules applies to particular conduct as straightforward as possible, consistent with recognition of the appropriate regulatory interests of relevant jurisdictions, and provides protection from discipline for lawyers who act reasonably in the face of uncertainty.

[4] Paragraph (b)(1) provides that as to a lawyer's conduct relating to a proceeding pending before a government tribunal, the lawyer shall be subject only to the rules of the government tribunal, if any, or of the jurisdiction in which the government tribunal sits unless the rules of that tribunal, including its choice of law rule, provide otherwise. By limiting application of the rule to matters before a government tribunal, e.g. a court or administrative agency, parties may establish which disciplinary rules will apply in private adjudications such as arbitration.

[4A] As to all other conduct, including conduct in anticipation of a proceeding not yet pending before a tribunal, the choice of law is governed by paragraph (b)(2). Paragraph (b)(2) creates a "default" choice of the rules of the jurisdiction in which the lawyer's principal office is located. There are several reasons for identifying such a default rule. First, the jurisdiction where the lawyer principally practices has a clear regulatory interest in the conduct of such lawyer, even in situations where the lawyer's conduct affects other jurisdictions. Second, lawyers are likely to be more familiar with the rules of the jurisdiction where they principally practice than with rules of another jurisdiction, even if licensed in that other jurisdiction. Indeed, most lawyers will be licensed in the jurisdiction where they principally practice, and familiarity with a jurisdiction's ethical rules is commonly made a condition of licensure. Third, in many situations, a representation will affect many jurisdictions, such as a transaction among multiple parties who reside in different jurisdictions involving performance in yet other jurisdictions. The selection of any of the jurisdictions that are affected by the representation will often be problematic.

[4B] There will be some circumstances, however, where the predominant effect of the lawyer's conduct will clearly be in a jurisdiction other than the jurisdiction in which the lawyer maintains his or her principal office. Accordingly, paragraph (b)(2) provides that when the predominant effect of the lawyer's conduct is in a jurisdiction other than the jurisdiction in which the lawyer's principal office is located, the ethical rules of such other jurisdiction apply to such conduct. For example, when litigation is contemplated but not yet instituted in another jurisdiction, a lawyer whose principal office is in this jurisdiction may well find that the rules of that jurisdiction govern the lawyer's ability to interview a former employee of a potential opposing party in that jurisdiction. Likewise, under Rule 8.5(b), when litigation is contemplated and not yet begun in this jurisdiction, a lawyer whose principal office is in another jurisdiction may well find that the rules of this jurisdiction govern the lawyer's ability to interview a former employee of a potential opposing party in this jurisdiction.

[4C] A lawyer who serves as in-house counsel in this jurisdiction pursuant to Rule 5.5, and whose principal office is in this jurisdiction will be subject to the rules of this jurisdiction unless the predominant effect of his or her conduct is clearly in another jurisdiction.

[5] The application of these rules will often involve the exercise of judgment in situations in which reasonable people may disagree. So long as the lawyer's conduct reflects an objectively reasonable application of the choice of law principles set forth in paragraph (b), the lawyer shall not be subject to discipline under this Rule.

[6] If this jurisdiction and another jurisdiction were to proceed against a lawyer for the same conduct, they should identify and apply the same governing ethics rules. Disciplinary authorities in this jurisdiction should take all appropriate steps to see that they do apply the same rule to the same conduct as authorities in other jurisdictions, and in all events should avoid proceeding against a lawyer on the basis of two inconsistent rules.

[7] The choice of law provision applies to lawyers engaged in transnational practice, unless international law, treaties or other agreements between competent regulatory authorities in the affected jurisdictions provide otherwise. Moreover, no lawyer should be subject to discipline in this jurisdiction for violating the regulations governing advertising or solicitation of a non–U.S. jurisdiction where the conduct would be constitutionally protected if performed in this jurisdiction.

IOLTA GUIDELINES

IOLTA Guidelines

July 2009

The IOLTA Committee ("Committee") provided for by Mass.R.Prof. C., 1.15(g)(4)(v)(Rule 3:07), adopts the following Guidelines, subject to the approval of the Court, to provide for the operation of the comprehensive IOLTA program set forth in amendments to SJC Rule 3:07 and 4:02 adopted by Orders of the Court dated September 26, 1989, October 1, 1992, April 6, 1993, July 26, 2006 and July 1, 2009.

* Pub. Note: The Massachusetts Rules of Professional Conduct and Comments are contained in Supreme Judicial Court Rule 3:07, supra.

A. Establishment and Maintenance of IOLTA Accounts.

1. *Method of Establishing IOLTA Accounts.* A lawyer or law firm shall establish an IOLTA account by completing an Attorney's Notice of Enrollment,* and mailing or delivering the original Notice to the financial institution where the account will be maintained and one copy of the Notice to the IOLTA Committee.

* Pub. Note: For a sample of this form, see Appendix A to these Guidelines, infra.

2. *Considerations Affecting Deposit in IOLTA Accounts.*

  (a) All client funds shall be deposited promptly in an IOLTA account unless they are deposited (1) in an interest bearing account for the benefit of the client; (2) in a conveyancing account as defined in paragraph A(3); or (3) as otherwise required by law.

  (b) All client funds which in the judgment of the lawyer are nominal in amount, or are to be held for a short period of time, shall be deposited in an IOLTA account. In determining whether to deposit funds into an IOLTA account or into an individual client account, a lawyer shall consider the amount of interest likely to be earned during the period the funds are expected to be deposited, as well as the estimated cost of establishing and administering a separate client fund account, including reasonable imputed overhead costs, and the estimated cost of preparing any tax or other reports required for interest accruing to a client's benefit.

3. *Conveyancing Accounts.* A conveyancing account is an account in the name of a lawyer in a lending bank used exclusively for depositing and disbursing funds in connection with that bank's loan transactions. A conveyancing account:

  (a) consists solely of funds which will be used in connection with transactions which the institution is financing; and

  (b) is used by the lawyer to disburse funds in connection with the institution's loan transactions; and

  (c) is used exclusively for the deposit and withdrawal of money related to the institution's loan transactions.

B. Characteristics of Accounts. Lawyers shall establish and maintain IOLTA accounts in eligible financial institutions which have the following characteristics:

1. *Interest Rates.* The financial institution pays interest comparable to the highest yield the financial institution offers to its non-IOLTA customers when the IOLTA account meets or exceeds the same minimum balance and other eligibility requirements.

(a) Comparability Options

A financial institution shall pay on IOLTA accounts the highest yield available among the following product option types (if the product option is available from the financial institution to other non-IOLTA customers) by either using the identified account option as an IOLTA account or paying the equivalent yield on the existing IOLTA account in lieu of actually using the highest yield bank product:

1. A business checking account with an automated investment feature, such as an overnight sweep and investment in repurchase agreements fully collateralized by U.S. government securities as described in Mass.R.Prof.C. 1.15 (g)(1).

2. A government (such as for municipal deposits) interest bearing checking account.

3. A checking account paying preferred interest rates, such as money market or indexed rates.

4. An interest bearing checking account such as a negotiable order of withdrawal (NOW) account, or business checking account with interest.

5. Any other suitable interest bearing deposit account offered by the institution to its non-IOLTA customers.

As an alternative, the financial institution may pay:

6. A "safe harbor" rate equal to 55% not yield of the Federal Funds Target Rate. *

7. A yield specified by the IOLTA Committee, if the Committee so chooses, which is agreed to by the financial institution. Such yield would be in effect for and remain unchanged during a period of no more than twelve months from the inception of the agreement between the financial institution and IOLTA.

* The IOLTA Committee will review and may revise the safe harbor rate from time to time based on changing market conditions.

(b) Implementation of Comparability

The following considerations will apply to determinations of comparability:

Accounts which have limited check writing capability required by law or government regulation may not be considered as comparable to IOLTA in Massachusetts. This, however, is distinguished from checking accounts which pay money market interest rates on account balances without the check writing limitations. Such accounts are included in the Option 3 class identified above. Additionally, rates that are not generally available to other account holders, such as special promotional rates used to attract new customers, are not considered for comparability in Massachusetts.

For the purpose of determining compliance with the above provisions, all participating financial institutions shall report in a form and manner prescribed by the IOLTA Committee the highest yield for each of the accounts they offer within the above listed account types. The IOLTA Committee will certify participating financial institutions compliance with these Guidelines on an annual basis.

(c) Definitions.

An "eligible financial institution" for IOLTA accounts is a financial institution that meets the requirements of Mass. R. Prof. C. 1.15 (g) (1), and has been certified by the Committee to be in compliance with these guidelines.

A "safe harbor" rate, as identified by the IOLTA Committee, is a rate which if paid by the financial institution on IOLTA accounts shall be deemed as a comparable return, regardless of the highest yield available at the financial institution. Such yield shall be calculated based on 55% net yield of the Federal Funds Target Rate as reported in the Wall Street Journal on the first business day of the calendar month.

"Net yield" is defined as the effective interest rate earned on the IOLTA account after considering any fees assessed by the financial institution against the interest earned. Allowable fees are defined at IOLTA Guidelines, B(3)(a) and (b).

2. *Minimum Balance.* The financial institution pays interest on all funds in the account. If a lawyer chooses to use for IOLTA purposes an account which requires a minimum balance to pay interest, the lawyer must maintain at least the minimum balance in the account at all times, even if to do so requires the deposit of the lawyer's own funds.

3. *Bank Charges.* The financial institution either waives all administrative and services charges on IOLTA accounts or imposes reasonable fees and charges as follows:

(a) IOLTA Fees. The only fees deducted from IOLTA interest are the reasonable costs of complying with the reporting requirements of the Guidelines.

(b) Normal Service Charges. The financial institution does not assess against the interest earned on an IOLTA account, fees and expenses which are normally imposed on business accounts. Such fees and expenses include but are not limited to check withdrawal and deposit fees, fees for wiring funds, costs of printing checks, charges for insufficient funds or check returns and a monthly service charge. Such fees and expenses are the responsibility of the lawyer or firm maintaining the account.

4. *Interest Remittance.* The financial institution complies with the following interest transmittal and reporting provisions:

(a) The financial institution remits all net interest monthly or quarterly to the IOLTA Committee. The financial institution deducts IOLTA fees from the interest earned on individual IOLTA accounts or aggregates all interest paid and deducts from the total interest earned for each interest remittance period the IOLTA fees imposed on all accounts. IOLTA fees which exceed the interest earned in one remittance period may be carried forward to succeeding remittance periods but may not be billed directly to the Committee, the lawyer or the firm maintaining the account or deducted from the principal in the account.

(b) Each remittance is accompanied by the information required by the Interest Remittance Report for each IOLTA account maintained in the financial institution whether or not any interest was earned on the account. The financial institution reports interest remittance informa-

tion in any format it chooses so long as the information required is conveyed in a reasonable manner.

(c) Remittances for multiple accounts are submitted through a single check or other payment and are accompanied by a single report containing the required information for each IOLTA account included in the report. The financial institution makes payments of interest (by check or otherwise) in the manner and to the address specified by the Committee.

(d) The financial institution mails or delivers interest remittance reports to the Massachusetts IOLTA Committee, 7 Winthrop Square, 3rd Floor, Boston, Massachusetts 02110–1245.

(e) In addition, the financial institution submits a copy of each interest remittance report at the time of remittance to the depositor.

(f) The financial institution either does not prepare W–9 forms and reports of income and IRS Forms 1099 or if the forms are prepared they reflect the Committee, not the lawyer or client, as the recipient and are forwarded to the Committee.

C. The Committee.

1. *Budgets.* Annually or more often, the Committee shall, in consultation with the charities, adopt a budget for the operation of the Committee which shall be funded by deducting from the amount received by the Committee on behalf of each charity that charity's proportionate share of the budget.

2. *Staff.* Staffing and general operational support for the Committee shall be provided by staff hired by the Committee for that purpose or by contract with one or more of the charities.

D. The Charities.

1. *Definition.* The charities shall be those organizations which are named by the Court as designated charitable entities from time to time to receive and disburse funds earned on IOLTA accounts.

2. *Additional Charities.* [At the direction of the Court, the Committee recommends the following criteria to the Court for use when considering the application of an organization for designation as a charity.] An organization applying to the Court for designation as a charity ("applicant"), shall demonstrate that it has satisfied the following criteria. An applicant must:

(a) be organized in Massachusetts as a non-profit corporation or trust, have § 501(c)(3) status under the Internal Revenue Code, and include among its purposes providing funds for delivering civil legal services to those who cannot afford them and/or for improving the administration of justice;

(b) have adopted and demonstrated its ability to administer competently a grants program including grant-making guidelines, proposal criteria, an appropriate grant selection process and the capacity to monitor the quality of the services delivered and the financial systems used by recipients; and,

(c) agree to adhere to these Guidelines and to cooperate with the Committee and the charities to ensure the smooth operation of the program.

3. *Expenses of Charities.* There shall be two permissible categories of IOLTA-related expenses which a charity may pay with or from IOLTA funds; (a) Committee expenses and (b) compliance and operating expenses.

(a) Committee expenses shall mean and include only the recipient's share of the Committee's expenses, as determined by the Committee from time to time. The Committee's expenses shall be shared according to the proportion of net IOLTA income received by the Committee on behalf of each charity.

(b) Compliance and operating expenses shall mean and include only the costs, including overhead, reasonably attributable to accounting for IOLTA funds, processing and evaluating grant requests, monitoring the quality of the services delivered and the financial systems used by recipients, preparing the reports required by Mass. R. Prof. C. 1.15(g)(6) or by the Committee, and handling and expending IOLTA funds for the charitable purposes of the IOLTA program.

(c) The maximum amount of compliance and operating expenses for which IOLTA funds may be used by any charity during or with respect to any calendar year shall be 5% of the IOLTA funds received by that recipient during that year; provided that, expenses in excess of such 5% limit may be authorized by the Committee with respect to any calendar year upon application and good cause shown by a charity.

4. *Record Keeping.* Each charity directly or by contract with another entity shall:

(a) Have its records of IOLTA receipts and disbursements audited annually by a Certified Public Accountant and file a copy of the audit report and the charity's last annual report with the annual report required by Mass R. Prof. C. 1.15(g);

(b) Prepare its IOLTA reports based on the charity's fiscal year; and

(c) Prepare annual financial statements in which all IOLTA funds (including interest, returns and prior year IOLTA receipts) are accounted for separately. This accounting shall report the entity's IOLTA fund balance at the end of its fiscal year as its "reserve" for that fiscal year.

5. *Stabilization Funds.* A charity may, in its discretion, reserve IOLTA funds from current distribution to stabilize the amounts available for distribution in future years.

(a) All reserved funds must be invested in, or fully collateralized by, United States Government securities including United States treasury obligations and obligations issued or guaranteed as to principal and interest by the United States or any agency or instrumentality thereof, or, deposited in fully insured bank accounts;

(b) Consistent with the preceding paragraph, reserved funds must be invested at competitive rates providing reasonable investment yield.

(c) Income from investment of reserved funds may be used only for the purposes approved by the Court for IOLTA funds.

(d) No more than 25% of the IOLTA income received by a charity during that charity's fiscal year may be added to that charity's reserve, provided however that in no event may the total reserve maintained by the charity exceed 50% of the average of the current fiscal year's IOLTA revenue to the entity (including interest) and the prior fiscal year's IOLTA revenue to the entity (including interest). Each charity has two years to comply with fluctuations that may occur as the average figure changes.

(e) If an entity's IOLTA reserve exceeds the amount allowed by these guidelines, the IOLTA Committee may withhold the distribution of further IOLTA revenue to the entity by the amount of the excess fund balance;

(f) The IOLTA Committee, in its sole discretion, may waive the provisions of sections (d) or (e) above if it determines that special circumstances warrant a waiver; and

(g) A charity establishing a stabilization fund shall adopt criteria regarding the amounts to be reserved and the uses of the reserved funds including the circumstances under which reserve may be expended.

E. Disclosure of Confidential Information Prohibited. The IOLTA Committee, the Board of Bar Overseers and the charities collect and retain confidential information on lawyers who have established IOLTA accounts. This information includes the name of the lawyer, the name of the client fund account established by or on behalf of the lawyer, the account number, the name of the bank in which the account is located and the amount of interest earned on each such account. Such confidential information, except as required by law or order of a court of competent jurisdiction, shall not be disclosed by any person who serves on or is employed by the IOLTA Committee, the charities and their governing boards. The governing bodies of the three charities shall adopt personnel policies and other policies and procedures which will effectuate this non-disclosure policy. The Board of Bar Overseers is requested to take such steps as it deems necessary and appropriate to insure the confidentiality of information received under the IOLTA program.

F. Annual Reports. The Committee shall annually, within 90 days following the end of each calendar year, submit to the Court a report containing the information required of the charities by Mass. R. Prof. C. 1.15(g)(6) and based on the information supplied to the Committee by the charities.

G. Interpretive Rulings. The Committee may from time to time issue rulings interpreting and explaining Mass. R. Prof. C. 1.15 (3:07) and 4:02 and these Guidelines.

H. Recommendations to the Board of Bar Overseers. Upon the request of a lawyer or the Board of Bar Overseers (Board), the Committee may make such recommendations to the Board as the Committee deems appropriate upon the facts presented including a recommendation that the Board take no action. Recommendations may be requested on any issue concerning the establishment or maintenance of an IOLTA account.

Adopted November 2, 1993, effective December 1, 1993. Amended December 12, 1997, effective January 1, 1998; July 26, 2006, effective January 1, 2007; May 26, 2009, effective July 1, 2009.

Appendix A. Attorney's Notice of Enrollment

ATTORNEY'S NOTICE OF ENROLLMENT

Notice to Financial Institution to Establish an IOLTA Account

ATTORNEY INFORMATION

INSTRUCTIONS TO ATTORNEYS: (1) COMPLETE THE "ATTORNEY INFORMATION" SECTION, (2) BRING THIS FORM TO THE FINANCIAL INSTITUTION OF YOUR CHOICE, (3) AFTER THE INSTITUTION HAS COMPLETED ITS SECTION BELOW, SEND THE PINK COPY TO THE IOLTA COMMITTEE ALONG WITH A DEPOSIT SLIP OR VOIDED CHECK.

Firm Name:_____

Attorney Name: _____

Mailing Address: _____

City: _____ State: _____ Zip Code: _____ Telephone: _____

The undersigned hereby enrolls in the comprehensive Interest on Lawyers' Trust Accounts (IOLTA) program established by the Massachusetts Supreme Judicial Court. Under this program, please open an account subject to negotiable orders of withdrawal (NOW, SuperNOW Account or other suitable interest-bearing account).

Authorized Signatories: _____

_____

_____

(Attach additional sheets for additional signatories)

FINANCIAL INSTITUTION INFORMATION

NOTE TO FINANCIAL INSTITUTIONS: PLEASE CALL (617) 723–9093 IF YOU RE-QUIRE ASSISTANCE IN SETTING UP THIS ACCOUNT.

Financial Institution Name:_____

Mailing Address: _____

City: _____ State: _____ Zip: _____ Telephone: _____

Date Opened: _____ By: _____   _____

(Financial Institution Representative)

Account Name: _____

Please attach a deposit slip or voided check to the IOLTA Committee copy

_____

Account Number: ☐☐☐☐☐☐☐☐☐☐☐☐☐☐ ☐☐☐☐☐☐☐

Interest as computed in accordance with your standard account disclosure should be remitted monthly or quarterly to the:

MASSACHUSETTS IOLTA COMMITTEE
18 Tremont Street, Suite 1010
BOSTON, MA 02108–2316
(617) 723–9093
TAXPAYER I.D. NO. 04–3168608

Remittance of interest may be made by your bank check via U.S. mail to the above address, or by Electronic Funds Transfer. Please call the IOLTA Committee for specific instructions on electronic payments. For each remittance, please submit a complete "Interest Remittance Report" and "IOLTA Summary Sheet".

For more complete instructions on opening and remitting interest on IOLTA accounts, contact the IOLTA Committee and request the "Operations Handbook for Financial Institutions".

Copies of this notice should be provided to

The IOLTA Committee, the financial institution, and for the attorneys own records.

RULE 3:08   DISCIPLINARY RULES APPLICABLE TO PRACTICE AS A PROSECUTOR OR AS A DEFENSE LAWYER [STRICKEN]

Stricken December 9, 1998, effective January 1, 1999.

RULE 3:09. CODE OF JUDICIAL CONDUCT

Table of Canons

Preamble

[1] An independent, fair, and impartial judiciary is indispensable to our system of justice. The United States legal system is based upon the principle that an independent, impartial, and competent judiciary, composed of persons of integrity, will interpret and apply the law that governs our society. Thus, the judiciary plays a central role in preserving the principles of justice and the rule of law. Inherent in all the Rules in this Code are the precepts that judges, individually and collectively, must respect and honor the judicial office as a public trust and must strive to maintain and enhance confidence in the legal system.

[2] Judges should maintain the dignity of judicial office at all times, and avoid both impropriety* and the appearance of impropriety* in their professional and personal lives. They should aspire at all times to conduct that ensures the greatest possible public confidence in their independence,* impartiality,* integrity,* and competence.

[3] The Code of Judicial Conduct establishes standards for the ethical conduct of judges. It is not intended as an exhaustive guide for the conduct of judges, who are governed in their judicial and personal conduct by general ethical standards as well as by the Code. The Code is intended, however, to provide guidance and to assist judges to maintain the highest standards of judicial and personal conduct, and to provide a basis for regulation of their conduct through disciplinary authorities.

Adopted October 8, 2015, effective January 1, 2016.

Scope

[1] The Code of Judicial Conduct consists of four Canons, numbered Rules under each Canon, and Comments that follow and explain each Rule. Scope and Terminology sections provide additional guidance in interpreting and applying the Code. An Application section establishes when the various Rules apply to a judge.

[2] The Canons state overarching principles of judicial ethics that all judges must observe. Although a judge may be disciplined only for violating a Rule, the Canons provide important guidance in interpreting the Rules. Where a Rule contains a permissive term, such as "may" or "should," the conduct being addressed is committed to the personal and

professional discretion of the judge, and no disciplinary action should be taken for action or inaction within the bounds of such discretion.

[3] The Comments that accompany the Rules serve two functions. First, they provide guidance regarding the purpose, meaning, and proper application of the Rules. They include explanatory material and, in some instances, provide examples of permitted or prohibited conduct. Comments neither add to nor subtract from the binding obligations set forth in the Rules. Therefore, when a Comment includes the term "must," it does not mean that the Comment itself is binding or enforceable; it signifies that the Rule in question, properly understood, is obligatory as to the conduct at issue.

[4] Second, the Comments identify aspirational goals for judges. To implement fully the principles of this Code as articulated in the Canons, judges should strive to exceed the standards of conduct established by the Rules, holding themselves to the highest ethical standards and seeking to achieve those aspirational goals, thereby enhancing the dignity of the judicial office.

[5] The Rules of the Code of Judicial Conduct are rules of reason that should be applied consistently with constitutional requirements, statutes, other court rules, and decisional law, and with due regard for all relevant circumstances. The Rules should not be interpreted to impinge upon the essential independence* of judges in making judicial decisions.

[6] Although the black letter of the Rules is binding and enforceable, it is not contemplated that every transgression will result in the imposition of discipline. Some conduct that literally may violate a Rule may not violate the policy behind the prohibition, or the violation may be de minimis. Whether discipline should be imposed should be determined through a reasonable and reasoned application of the Rules, and should depend upon factors such as the seriousness of the transgression, the facts and circumstances that existed at the time of the transgression, the extent of any pattern of improper activity, whether there have been previous violations, and the effect of the improper activity upon the judicial system or others.

[7] The Code is not designed or intended to be a basis for civil or criminal liability. Neither is it intended to be the basis for litigants to seek collateral remedies against each other or to obtain tactical advantages in proceedings before a court.

Adopted October 8, 2015, effective January 1, 2016.

Terminology

Whenever any term listed below is used in the Code, it is followed by an asterisk (*).

"Close personal friend" means a friend whose relationship to the judge is such that the friend's appearance or interest in a proceeding pending* or impending* before the judge would require disqualification of the judge. See Rule 3.13.

"Court personnel" means court employees subject to the judge's direction and control. See Rules 2.3, 2.5, 2.8, 2.9, 2.10, 2.11, 2.12, 2.13, and 3.5.

"Domestic partner" means a person with whom another person maintains a household and an intimate relationship,

other than a person to whom he or she is legally married. See Rules 2.11, 2.13, and 3.13.

"Economic interest" means ownership of more than a de minimis legal or equitable interest. Unless the judge participates in the management of such a legal or equitable interest, or the interest could be substantially affected by the outcome of a proceeding before a judge, it does not include:

(1) an interest in the individual holdings within a mutual or common investment fund;

(2) an interest in securities held by an educational, religious, charitable, fraternal, or civic organization in which the judge or the judge's spouse, domestic partner,* parent, or child serves as a director, an officer, an advisor, or other participant;

(3) a deposit in a financial institution or deposits or proprietary interests the judge may maintain as a member of a mutual savings association or credit union, or similar proprietary interests; or

(4) an interest in government securities held by the judge. See Rules 1.3, 2.11, and 3.2.

"Fiduciary" includes relationships such as executor, administrator, trustee, guardian, attorney in fact, or other personal representative. See Rules 2.11, 3.2, and 3.8.

"Fundraising event" means an event for which the organizers' chief objectives include raising money to support the organization's activities beyond the event itself. See Rule 3.7.

"Impartial," "impartiality," and **"impartially"** mean absence of bias or prejudice in favor of, or against, particular parties or classes of parties or their representatives, as well as maintenance of an open mind in considering issues that may come before a judge. See Rules 1.2, 2.2, 2.10, 2.11, 2.13, 3.1, 3.4, 3.6, 3.7, 3.12, 3.13, 3.14, and 4.1.

"Impending matter" is a matter that is imminent or expected to occur in the near future. A matter is impending if it seems probable that a case will be filed, if charges are being investigated, or if someone has been arrested although not yet charged. See Rules 2.9, 2.10, 3.2, and 3.13.

"Impropriety" means conduct that violates the law,* including provisions of this Code, conduct that constitutes grounds for discipline under G. L. c. 211C, § 2(5), and conduct that undermines a judge's independence,* integrity,* or impartiality.* See Rules 1.2, 2.10, and 3.13.

"Independence" means a judge's freedom from influences or controls other than those established by law.* See Rules 1.2, 2.7, 2.10, 3.1, 3.2, 3.4, 3.7, 3.12, and 3.13.

"Integrity" means probity, fairness, honesty, uprightness, and soundness of character. See Rules 1.2, 2.7, 2.10, 2.15, 3.1, 3.2, 3.4, 3.7, 3.12, and 3.13.

"Judicial applicant" means any person who has submitted an application for appointment as a judge in any court of the Commonwealth. See Rule 2.11.

"Judicial nominee" means any person who has been nominated by the Governor to judicial office but who has not assumed judicial office. See Rule 2.11.

"Knowingly," "knowledge," "known," and **"knows"** mean actual knowledge of the fact in question. A person's knowledge may be inferred from circumstances. See Rules 1.3, 2.5, 2.9, 2.11, 2.15, 2.16, 3.3, 3.5, and 3.6.

"Law" includes court rules and standing orders issued by the Supreme Judicial Court, the Appeals Court, the Chief Justice of the Trial Court, or a Chief Justice of a Trial Court Department, as well as statutes, constitutional provisions, and decisional law. Chapter 268A §§ 3 and 23(b)(2) provide that conduct explicitly recognized by another statute or regulation may supersede certain provisions of Chapter 268A. The Rules of the Supreme Judicial Court are considered regulations for this purpose. In several instances, provisions of this Code supersede provisions of Chapter 268A. See Rule 1.1.

"Member of the judge's family" means any of the following persons: a spouse or domestic partner*; a child, grandchild, parent, grandparent, or sibling, whether by blood, adoption, or marriage; or another relative or person with whom the judge maintains a close family-like relationship. Residence in the household of a judge may be relevant but is not dispositive when determining whether a judge maintains a close family-like relationship with another relative or person. See Rules 3.7, 3.8, 3.10, and 4.1.

"Member of the judge's family residing in the judge's household" means any of the following persons who resides in the judge's household: a relative by blood, adoption, or marriage; a domestic partner*; or a person with whom the judge maintains a close family-like relationship. See Rules 2.11 and 3.13.

"Nonpublic information" means information that is not available to the public. Nonpublic information includes information that is sealed or expunged by statute or court order, or information that is impounded or communicated in camera. See Rule 3.5.

"Pending matter" is a matter that has commenced. A matter continues to be pending through any appellate process until final disposition. See Rules 2.9, 2.10, 3.2, and 3.13.

"Political organization" means a political party or other group, the principal purpose of which is to further the election or appointment of candidates to political office or the passage or defeat of ballot questions. See Rule 4.1.

"Specialty court" means a specifically designated court session that focuses on individuals with underlying medical, mental health, substance abuse, or other issues that contribute to the reasons such individuals are before the courts. Specialty court sessions integrate treatment and services with judicial case oversight and intensive court supervision. Examples include drug courts, mental health courts, veterans' courts, and tenancy preservation programs. See Rule 2.9.

"Substantial value" means a dollar value determined by the State Ethics Commission in 930 C.M.R. 5.05. See Rules 3.13 and 3.15.

"Third degree of relationship" includes the following persons: great-grandparent, grandparent, parent, uncle, aunt, brother, sister, child, grandchild, great-grandchild, nephew, and niece. See Rule 2.11.

Adopted October 8, 2015, effective January 1, 2016.

Application

The Application section establishes when the various Rules apply to a judge.

I. APPLICABILITY OF THIS CODE

(A) Active Judges: The provisions of the Code apply to all judges of the Trial Court, the Appeals Court, and the Supreme Judicial Court until resignation, removal, or retirement, except as provided in Paragraph (B) below.

(B) Retired Judges: A judge whose name has been placed upon the list of retired judges eligible to perform judicial duties, pursuant to G. L. c. 32, §§ 65E—65G, shall comply with all provisions of this Code during the term of such eligibility.

II. TIME FOR COMPLIANCE

A person to whom this Code becomes applicable shall comply immediately with all its provisions except Rules 3.8 and 3.11(B), and shall comply with those sections as soon as reasonably possible and in any event within one year.

Adopted October 8, 2015, effective January 1, 2016.

COMMENT

[1] A judge who has retired or resigned from judicial office shall not, for a period of six months following the date of retirement, resignation, or most recent service as a retired judge pursuant to G. L. c. 32, §§ 65E—65G, perform dispute resolution services with a court-connected program except on a pro bono publico basis, or enter an appearance, or accept an appointment to represent any party, in any court of the Commonwealth.

[2] Judges should be aware that their conduct prior to assuming judicial office may have consequences under the law.* See, e.g., G. L. c. 211C, § 2(2), Rule 2.11(A)(4).

[3] This Code does not apply to judicial applicants* and judicial nominees.* Historically, by Executive Order, the Governor of the Commonwealth has created a code of conduct for judicial applicants* and judicial nominees.*

[4] An active judge who becomes an applicant or candidate for a different judicial office, state or federal, must comply with the requirements of any appointing authority in addition to this Code.

CANON 1. A JUDGE SHALL UPHOLD AND PROMOTE THE INDEPENDENCE,* INTEGRITY,* AND IMPARTIALITY* OF THE JUDICIARY, AND SHALL AVOID IMPROPRIETY* AND THE APPEARANCE OF IMPROPRIETY*

Rule 1.1. Compliance With the Law

A judge shall comply with the law,* including the Code of Judicial Conduct.

Adopted October 8, 2015, effective January 1, 2016.

* For definition of term, see S.J.C. Rule 3:09, Code of Jud. Conduct, Terminology.

COMMENT

[1] A judge's obligation to comply with the law* ordinarily includes the obligation to comply with the State conflict of interest law, G. L. c. 268A and c. 268B. However, the unique role of judges requires that

judges on occasion follow rules that may be more or less restrictive than those followed by other public employees. In many instances, this Code imposes more stringent restrictions on judges' activities because of their obligation to act at all times in a manner that promotes public confidence in the judiciary. Thus, for example, the Code regulates aspects of a judge's personal conduct, including a judge's participation in extrajudicial activities unrelated to the law,* and prohibits judges from political and campaign activities open to many other public employees. See, e.g., Rules 3.7 and 4.1. However, in a few instances, this Code creates exemptions from particular restrictions imposed by G. L. c. 268A §§ 3 and 23(b)(2) so that judges may more fully participate in activities related to the law,* the legal system, and the administration of justice. See, e.g., Rules 3.1(E) and 3.13(D)—(E).

* For definition of term, see S.J.C. Rule 3:09, Code of Jud. Conduct, Terminology.

Rule 1.2.   Promoting Confidence in the Judiciary

A judge shall act at all times in a manner that promotes public confidence in the independence,* integrity,* and impartiality* of the judiciary, and shall avoid impropriety* and the appearance of impropriety.*

Adopted October 8, 2015, effective January 1, 2016.

COMMENT

[1] Public confidence in the judiciary is eroded by improper conduct and conduct that creates the appearance of impropriety.* This principle applies to both the professional and personal conduct of a judge.

[2] A judge should expect to be the subject of public scrutiny that might be viewed as burdensome if applied to other citizens, and must accept the restrictions imposed by the Code.

[3] Conduct that compromises or appears to compromise the independence,* integrity,* or impartiality* of a judge undermines public confidence in the judiciary. Because it is not practicable to list all such conduct, the Rule is necessarily cast in general terms.

[4] A judge is encouraged to participate in activities that promote ethical conduct among judges and lawyers, support professionalism within the judiciary and the legal profession, and promote access to justice for all.

[5] Improprieties include violations of law* or this Code, or other conduct for which the judge could be disciplined pursuant to G. L. c. 211C, § 2(5). The test for appearance of impropriety* is whether the conduct would create in reasonable minds a perception that the judge violated this Code or engaged in other conduct that reflects adversely on the judge's honesty, impartiality,* temperament, or fitness to serve as a judge.

[6] A judge is encouraged to initiate and participate in appropriate community outreach activities for the purpose of promoting public understanding of and confidence in the administration of justice. In conducting such activities, the judge must act in a manner consistent with this Code. See, e.g., Rules 3.1 and 3.7.

Rule 1.3.   Avoiding Abuse of the Prestige of Judicial Office

A judge shall not abuse the prestige of judicial office to advance the personal or economic interests* of the judge or others, or allow others to do so.

Adopted October 8, 2015, effective January 1, 2016.

COMMENT

[1] It is improper for a judge to use or attempt to use the judge's position to gain personal advantage or preferential treatment of any kind. For example, a judge must not refer to the judge's judicial status to gain favorable treatment in encounters with traffic officials. Similarly, a judge must not use judicial letterhead to gain an advantage in conducting personal business.

[2] A judge may provide an educational or employment reference or recommendation for an individual based on the judge's personal knowledge.* The judge may use official letterhead and sign the recommendation using the judicial title if the judge's knowledge* of the applicant's qualifications arises from observations made in the judge's judicial capacity. The recommendation may not be accompanied by conduct that reasonably would be perceived as an attempt to exert pressure on the recipient to hire or admit the applicant. Where a judge's knowledge* of the applicant's qualifications does not arise from observations made in the judge's judicial capacity, the judge may not use official letterhead, court email, or the judicial title, but the judge may send a private letter stating the judge's personal recommendation. The judge may refer to the judge's current position and title in the body of the private letter only if it is relevant to some substantive aspect of the recommendation.

Court hiring policies may impose additional restrictions on recommendations for employment in the judicial branch, and the law* may impose additional restrictions on recommendations for employment in state government. See, e.g., G. L. c. 66, § 3A; G. L. c. 276, § 83; G. L. c. 211B, § 10(D). See also Trial Court Personnel Policies and Procedures Manual, § 4.000, et seq. See Rule 3.3 for instances when a judge is asked to provide a character reference on behalf of a bar applicant or provide information for a background investigation in connection with an application for public employment or for security clearance.

[3] Judges may participate in the process of judicial selection by cooperating with screening, nominating, appointing, and confirming authorities. Judges may make recommendations to and respond to inquiries from such entities concerning the professional qualifications of a person being considered for judicial office. Judges also may testify at confirmation hearings.

[4] Special considerations arise when judges write or contribute to publications of for-profit entities, whether related or unrelated to the law.* A judge should not permit anyone associated with the publication of such materials to exploit the judge's office in a manner that violates this Rule or other applicable law.* In contracts for publication of a judge's writing, the judge should retain sufficient control over the advertising to avoid such exploitation.

CANON 2.   A JUDGE SHALL PERFORM THE DUTIES OF JUDICIAL OFFICE IMPARTIALLY,* COMPETENTLY, AND DILIGENTLY

Rule 2.1.   Giving Precedence to the Duties of Judicial Office

The duties of judicial office, as prescribed by law,* shall take precedence over all of a judge's personal and extrajudicial activities.

Adopted October 8, 2015, effective January 1, 2016.

COMMENT

[1] To ensure that judges are available to fulfill their judicial duties, judges must conduct their personal and extrajudicial activities to minimize the risk of conflicts that would result in frequent disqualification. See Canon 3.

[2] Although it is not a duty of judicial office unless prescribed by law,* judges are encouraged to participate in activities that promote

public understanding of and confidence in the justice system. See Rule 3.7.

[3] With respect to time devoted to personal and extrajudicial activities, this Rule must be construed in a reasonable manner. Family obligations, illnesses, and emergencies may require a judge's immediate attention. Attending to those obligations and situations is not prohibited by this Rule.

Rule 2.2. Impartiality and Fairness

A judge shall uphold and apply the law,* and shall perform all duties of judicial office fairly and impartially.*

Adopted October 8, 2015, effective January 1, 2016.

COMMENT

[1] To ensure impartiality* and fairness to all parties, a judge must be objective and open-minded.

[2] Although each judge comes to the bench with a unique background and personal philosophy, a judge must interpret and apply the law* without regard to whether the judge approves or disapproves of the law* in question.

[3] When applying and interpreting the law,* a judge sometimes may make good-faith errors of fact or law.* Errors of this kind do not violate this Rule. In the absence of fraud, corrupt motive, or clear indication that the judge's conduct was in bad faith or otherwise violates this Code, it is not a violation for a judge to make findings of fact, reach legal conclusions, or apply the law as the judge understands it.

[4] It is not a violation of this Rule for a judge to make reasonable accommodations to ensure self-represented litigants are provided the opportunity to have their matters fairly heard. See Rule 2.6(A).

Rule 2.3. Bias, Prejudice, and Harassment

(A) A judge shall perform the duties of judicial office, including administrative duties, without bias, prejudice, or harassment.

(B) A judge shall not, in the performance of judicial duties, by words or conduct manifest bias or prejudice or engage in harassment, including bias, prejudice, or harassment based upon a person's status or condition. A judge also shall not permit court personnel* or others subject to the judge's direction and control to engage in such prohibited behavior.

(C) A judge shall require lawyers in proceedings before the court to refrain from manifesting bias or prejudice or engaging in harassment against parties, witnesses, lawyers, or others, including bias, prejudice, or harassment based upon a person's status or condition.

(D) This rule does not preclude judges or lawyers from making legitimate reference to a person's status or condition when it is relevant to an issue in a proceeding.

Adopted October 8, 2015, effective January 1, 2016.

COMMENT

[1] A judge who manifests bias or prejudice or engages in harassment in a proceeding impairs the fairness of the proceeding and brings the judiciary into disrepute. A judge must avoid words or conduct that may reasonably be perceived as manifesting bias or prejudice or engaging in harassment.

[2] As used in this Rule, examples of status or condition include but are not limited to race, color, sex, gender identity or expression, religion, nationality, national origin, ethnicity, citizenship or immigra-

tion status, ancestry, disease or disability, age, sexual orientation, marital status, socioeconomic status, or political affiliation.

[3] As used in this Rule, examples of manifestations of bias or prejudice include but are not limited to epithets; slurs; demeaning nicknames; negative stereotyping; attempted humor based upon stereotypes; threatening, intimidating, or hostile acts; improper suggestions of connections between status or condition and crime; and irrelevant references to personal characteristics. Even facial expressions and body language can convey an appearance of bias or prejudice to parties and lawyers in the proceeding, jurors, the media, and others.

[4] As used in this Rule, harassment is verbal or physical conduct that denigrates or shows hostility or aversion toward a person on bases such as those listed in Comment [2].

[5] Sexual harassment includes but is not limited to sexual advances, requests for sexual favors, and other verbal or physical conduct of a sexual nature that is unwelcome.

Rule 2.4. External Influences on Judicial Conduct

(A) A judge shall not be swayed by partisan interests, public clamor, or fear of criticism.

(B) A judge shall not permit family, social, political, financial, or other interests or relationships to influence the judge's judicial conduct or judgment.

(C) A judge shall not convey or permit others to convey the impression that any person or organization is in a position to influence the judge.

Adopted October 8, 2015, effective January 1, 2016.

COMMENT

[1] An independent judiciary requires that judges decide cases according to the law* and facts, without regard to whether particular laws* or litigants are popular or unpopular with the public, the media, government officials, or the judge's friends or family. Confidence in the judiciary is eroded if judicial decision-making is perceived to be subject to inappropriate outside influences.

Rule 2.5. Competence, Diligence, and Cooperation

(A) A judge shall perform judicial and administrative duties competently, diligently, and in a timely manner.

(B) A judge shall cooperate with other judges and court officials in the administration of court business.

Adopted October 8, 2015, effective January 1, 2016.

COMMENT

[1] Competence in the performance of judicial duties requires the legal knowledge,* skill, thoroughness, and preparation reasonably necessary to perform a judge's responsibilities of judicial office.

[2] A judge should seek the necessary resources to discharge all adjudicative and administrative responsibilities.

[3] Timely disposition of the court's business requires a judge to devote adequate time to judicial duties, to be punctual in attending court and expeditious in determining matters under advisement, and to take reasonable measures to ensure that court personnel,* litigants, and lawyers cooperate with the judge to that end.

[4] In disposing of matters efficiently and in a timely manner, a judge must demonstrate due regard for the rights of parties to be heard and to have issues resolved without unnecessary cost or delay. A judge should monitor and supervise cases in ways that reduce or eliminate dilatory practices, avoidable delays, and unnecessary costs.

Rule 2.6.   Ensuring the Right to be Heard

(A) A judge shall accord to every person who has a legal interest in a proceeding, or that person's lawyer, the right to be heard according to law.*   A judge may make reasonable efforts, consistent with the law,* to facilitate the ability of all litigants, including self-represented litigants, to be fairly heard.

(B) A judge may encourage parties and their lawyers to resolve matters in dispute and, in accordance with applicable law,* may participate in settlement discussions in civil proceedings and plea discussions in criminal proceedings, but shall not act in a manner that coerces any party into settlement or resolution of a proceeding.

Adopted October 8, 2015, effective January 1, 2016.

COMMENT

[1] The right to be heard is an essential component of a fair and impartial* system of justice.   Substantive rights of litigants can be protected only if procedures protecting the right to be heard are observed.

[1A] The judge has an affirmative role in facilitating the ability of every person who has a legal interest in a proceeding to be fairly heard.   In the interest of ensuring fairness and access to justice, judges may make reasonable accommodations that help self-represented litigants to understand the proceedings and applicable procedural requirements, secure legal assistance, and be heard according to law.*   The judge should be careful that accommodations do not give self-represented litigants an unfair advantage or create an appearance of judicial partiality.   In some circumstances, particular accommodations for self-represented litigants are required by decisional or other law.*   In other circumstances, potential accommodations are within the judge's discretion.   By way of illustration, a judge may: (1) construe pleadings liberally; (2) provide brief information about the proceeding and evidentiary and foundational requirements; (3) ask neutral questions to elicit or clarify information; (4) modify the manner or order of taking evidence or hearing argument; (5) attempt to make legal concepts understandable; (6) explain the basis for a ruling; and (7) make referrals as appropriate to any resources available to assist the litigants.   For civil cases involving self-represented litigants, the Judicial Guidelines for Civil Hearings Involving Self–Represented Litigants (April 2006) provides useful guidance to judges seeking to exercise their discretion appropriately so as to ensure the right to be heard.

[2] A judge may encourage parties and their lawyers to resolve matters in dispute.   A judge's participation in settlement discussions in civil proceedings and plea discussions in criminal proceedings must be conducted in accordance with applicable law.*   Judicial participation may play an important role, but the judge should be careful that the judge's efforts do not undermine any party's right to be heard according to law.*   The judge should keep in mind the effect that the judge's participation may have not only on the judge's own views of the case, but also on the perceptions of the lawyers and the parties if these efforts are unsuccessful and the case remains with the judge.   Other factors that a judge should consider when deciding upon an appropriate practice for a case include: (1) whether the parties have requested or voluntarily consented to a certain level of participation by the judge; (2) whether the parties and their counsel are relatively sophisticated in legal matters; (3) whether the case will be tried by the judge or a jury; (4) whether the parties participate with their counsel in the discussions; (5) whether any parties are self-represented; (6) whether the matter is civil or criminal; and (7) whether there is a history of physical or emotional violence or abuse between the parties.   See Rule 2.9(A)(4).

[3] Judges must be mindful of the effect settlement or plea discussions can have not only on their objectivity and impartiality,* but also on the appearance of their objectivity and impartiality.*   Despite a judge's best efforts, there may be instances when information obtained during such discussions could influence a judge's decision-making during trial, and, in such instances, the judge should consider whether disqualification may be appropriate.   See Rule 2.11.

Rule 2.7.   Responsibility to Decide

A judge shall hear and decide matters assigned to the judge, except when disqualification is required by Rule 2.11 or other law.*

Adopted October 8, 2015, effective January 1, 2016.

COMMENT

[1] Although there are times when disqualification is necessary to protect the rights of litigants and preserve public confidence in the independence,* integrity,* and impartiality* of the judiciary, judges must be available to decide matters that come before the court.   Unwarranted disqualification may bring public disfavor to the court and to the judge personally.   The dignity of the court, the judge's respect for fulfillment of judicial duties, and a proper concern for the burdens that may be imposed upon the judge's colleagues require that a judge not use disqualification to avoid cases that present difficult, controversial, or unpopular issues.

Rule 2.8.   Decorum, Demeanor, and Communication with Jurors

(A) A judge shall require order and decorum in proceedings before the court.

(B) A judge shall be patient, dignified, and courteous to litigants, jurors, witnesses, lawyers, court personnel,* and others with whom the judge deals in an official capacity, and shall require similar conduct of lawyers, court personnel,* and others subject to the judge's direction and control.

(C) A judge shall not commend or criticize jurors for their verdict other than in a court order or opinion in a proceeding but may express appreciation to jurors for their service to the judicial system and the community.

Adopted October 8, 2015, effective January 1, 2016.

COMMENT

[1] The duty to conduct all proceedings with patience and courtesy is not inconsistent with the duty imposed in Rule 2.5 to dispose promptly of the business of the court.   Judges can be efficient and businesslike while being patient and deliberate.

[2] Commending or criticizing jurors for their verdict, other than in a court order or opinion, may imply a judicial expectation in future cases and may impair a juror's ability to be fair and impartial* in a subsequent case.   Such commendations or criticisms of verdicts could also be perceived as calling into question the judge's ability to rule impartially* on any post-trial motions, or on remand, in the same case.

[3] A judge who is not otherwise prohibited by law* from doing so may meet with jurors who choose to remain after trial but should be careful not to discuss the merits of the case.

Rule 2.9.   Ex Parte Communications

(A) A judge shall not initiate, permit, or consider ex parte communications, or consider other communications made to the judge outside the presence of the parties or their lawyers, concerning a pending* or impending matter,* except as follows:

(1) When circumstances require it, ex parte communication for scheduling, administrative, or emergency purposes, which does not address substantive matters, is permitted, provided:

(a) the judge reasonably believes that no party will gain a procedural, substantive, or tactical advantage as a result of the ex parte communication; and

(b) the judge makes provision promptly to notify all other parties of the substance of the ex parte communication, and gives the parties an opportunity to respond.

(2) A judge may engage in ex parte communications in specialty courts,* as authorized by law.*

(3) A judge may consult with court personnel* whose function is to aid the judge in carrying out the judge's adjudicative responsibilities, or with other judges, subject to the following:

(a) a judge shall take all reasonable steps to avoid receiving from court personnel* or other judges factual information concerning a case that is not part of the case record. If court personnel* or another judge nevertheless brings information about a matter that is outside of the record to the judge's attention, the judge may not base a decision on it without giving the parties notice of that information and an opportunity to respond. Consultation is permitted between a judge, clerk-magistrate, or other appropriate court personnel* and a judge taking over the same case or session in which the case is pending with regard to information learned from prior proceedings in the case that may assist in maintaining continuity in handling the case;

(b) when a judge consults with a probation officer, housing specialist, or comparable court employee about a pending* or impending* matter, the consultation shall take place in the presence of the parties who have availed themselves of the opportunity to appear and respond, except as provided in Rule 2.9(A)(2);

(c) a judge shall not consult with an appellate judge, or a judge in a different Trial Court Department, about a matter that the judge being consulted might review on appeal; and

(d) no judge shall consult with another judge about a pending matter* before one of them when the judge initiating the consultation knows* the other judge has a financial, personal or other interest that would preclude the other judge from hearing the case, and no judge shall engage in such a consultation when the judge knows* he or she has such an interest.

(4) A judge may, with the consent of the parties, confer separately with the parties and their lawyers in an effort to settle civil matters pending before the judge.

(5) A judge may initiate, permit, or consider any ex parte communication when authorized by law* to do so.

(B) If a judge inadvertently receives an unauthorized ex parte communication bearing upon the substance of a matter, the judge shall make provision promptly to notify the parties of the substance of the communication.

(C) A judge shall consider only the evidence presented and any adjudicative facts that may properly be judicially noticed, and shall not undertake any independent investigation of the facts in a matter.

(D) A judge shall make reasonable efforts, including providing appropriate supervision, to ensure that this Rule is not violated by court personnel.*

Adopted October 8, 2015, effective January 1, 2016.

COMMENT

[1] To the extent reasonably possible, all parties or their lawyers shall be included in communications with a judge.

[1A] "Ex parte communication" means a communication pertaining to a proceeding that occurs without notice to or participation by all other parties or their representatives between a judge (or court personnel* acting on behalf of a judge) and (i) a party or a party's lawyer, or (ii) another person who is not a participant in the proceeding.

[2] Whenever the presence of a party or notice to a party is required by this Rule, it is the party's lawyer, or if the party is self-represented, the party, who is to be present or to whom notice is to be given, unless otherwise required by law.* For example, court rules with respect to Limited Assistance Representation may require that notice be given to both the party and the party's limited assistance attorney.

[3] The proscription against ex parte communications concerning a proceeding includes communications with lawyers, law teachers, and other persons who are not participants in the proceeding, except to the limited extent permitted by this Rule.

[4] Paragraph (A)(2) permits a judge to engage in ex parte communications in conformance with law,* including court rules and standing orders, governing operation of specialty courts.*

[4A] Ex parte communications with probation officers, housing specialists, or other comparable court employees are permitted in specialty courts* where authorized by law.* See Paragraph (A)(2) and Comment [4]. Where ex parte communications are not permitted, a judge may consult with these employees ex parte about the specifics of various available programs so long as there is no discussion about the suitability of the program for a particular party.

[5] A judge may consult with other judges, subject to the limitations set forth by this Rule. This is so whether or not the judges serve on the same court. A judge must avoid ex parte communications about a matter with a judge who has previously been disqualified from hearing the matter or with an appellate judge who might be called upon to review that matter on appeal. The same holds true with respect to those instances in which a judge in one department of the trial court may be called upon to review a case decided by a judge in a different department; for example, a judge in the Superior Court may be required to review a bail determination made by a judge in the District Court. The appellate divisions of the Boston Municipal Court and of the District Court present a special situation. The judges who sit as members of these appellate divisions review on appeal cases decided by judges who serve in the same court department. However, the designation of judges to sit on the appellate divisions changes quite frequently; every judge on the Boston Municipal Court will, and every judge on the District Court may, serve for some time as a member of that court's appellate division. Judges in the same court department are not barred from consulting with each other about a case, despite the possibility that one of the judges may later review the case on appeal. However, when a judge is serving on an appellate division, the judge must not review any case that the judge has previously discussed with the judge who decided it; disqualification is required. Consultation between or among judges, if otherwise permitted, is appropriate only if the judge before whom the matter is pending* does not abrogate the responsibility personally to decide it.

[6] The prohibition in Paragraph (C) against a judge independently investigating adjudicative facts applies equally to information available in all media, including electronic media.

[7] A judge may consult the Committee on Judicial Ethics, the State Ethics Commission, outside counsel, or legal experts concerning the judge's compliance with this Code.

Rule 2.10.　Judicial Statements on Pending and Impending Cases

(A) A judge shall not make any statement that might reasonably be expected to affect the outcome or impair the fairness of a matter pending* or impending* in any Massachusetts court.

(B) A judge shall not, in connection with cases, controversies, or issues that are likely to come before any Massachusetts court, make pledges, promises, or commitments that are inconsistent with the impartial* performance of the duties of judicial office.

(C) A judge shall require court personnel* to refrain from making statements that the judge would be prohibited from making by Paragraphs (A) and (B).

(D) Subject to the restrictions in Paragraphs (A) and (B), a judge may make statements that explain the procedures of the court, general legal principles, or what may be learned from the public record in a case. A judge may comment on any proceeding in which the judge is a litigant in a personal capacity.

(E) Subject to the restrictions in Paragraphs (A) and (B), a judge may respond directly or through a third party to public criticisms of the judge's behavior, but shall not respond to public criticisms of the substance of the judge's rulings other than by statements consistent with Paragraph (D).

(F) Subject to the restrictions in Paragraphs (A) and (B), a judge may speak, write, or teach about issues in pending* or impending* matters, but not matters pending* or impending* before that judge, when such comments are made in legal education programs and materials, scholarly presentations and related materials, or learned treatises, academic journals, and bar publications.

Adopted October 8, 2015, effective January 1, 2016.

COMMENT

[1] This Rule's restrictions on judicial speech are essential to the maintenance of the independence,* integrity,* and impartiality* of the judiciary.

[2] Paragraph (A) does not apply to any oral or written statement or decision by a judge in the course of adjudicative duties. A judge is encouraged to explain on the record at the time decisions are made the basis for those decisions or rulings, including decisions concerning bail and sentencing. By helping litigants to understand the basis for decisions in cases, the judge also promotes public understanding of judicial proceedings.

[3] "[A]ny Massachusetts court" for purposes of this Rule means any state or federal court within the Commonwealth of Massachusetts.

[4] The requirement that a judge abstain from statements regarding a pending* or impending* matter continues throughout the appellate process and until final disposition.

[5] This Rule does not prohibit a judge from commenting on proceedings in which the judge is a litigant in a personal capacity.

However, even in such instances, a judge must act in a manner that promotes public confidence in the independence,* integrity,* and impartiality* of the judiciary, and shall avoid impropriety* and the appearance of impropriety.*

[6] Paragraph (D) permits the dissemination of public information to educate and inform the public, while assuring the public that cases are tried only in the judicial forum devoted to that purpose. A judge may explain to the media or general public the procedures of the court and general legal principles such as the procedures and standards governing a "dangerousness hearing" under G. L. c. 276, § 58A, or restraining orders under G. L. c. 209A. A judge may also explain to the media or the general public what may be learned from the public record in a particular case. For example, a judge may respond to questions from a reporter about a judicial action that was taken and may correct an incorrect media report by referring to matters that may be learned from pleadings, documentary evidence, and proceedings held in open court. Paragraph (D) permits similar responsive comments or explanations by a judge acting in accordance with the judge's administrative duties.

[7] As used in Paragraph (E), "behavior" does not include the substance of a judge's rulings. For example, a judge may respond to criticism that the judge is disrespectful to litigants, but may not respond to criticism that the judge made an incorrect ruling other than by statements allowed by Paragraph (D).

[8] The authorizations to comment in this Rule are permissive, not suggestive. A judge is not required to respond to statements in the media or elsewhere. Depending on the circumstances, the judge should consider the timing of any response and whether it may be preferable for a third party, rather than the judge, to respond.

[9] When speaking, writing, or teaching about issues in cases or matters, a judge must take care that the judge's comments do not impair public confidence in the independence,* integrity,* or impartiality* of the judiciary.

[10] When a judge orally renders a decision and intends to explain the judge's reasons in a written memorandum, the judge should simultaneously inform the parties that an explanatory memorandum will be forthcoming. When a judge has not indicated at the time the judge issues the underlying order that a written explanatory comment will be forthcoming and such a memorandum has not been requested by a party or by an appellate single justice or court, a judge has the discretion to issue an explanatory memorandum. The exercise of that discretion should be informed by the following guidance:

(i) A judge should weigh, at a minimum, the following factors:

• the importance of avoiding or alleviating the parties' or the public's misunderstanding or confusion by supplementing the record to reflect in more detail the reasons in support of the judge's earlier decision;

• the amount of time that has elapsed since the order was issued and the extent to which the judge's reasons for the decision remain fresh in the judge's mind;

• the risk that an explanatory memorandum may unfairly affect the rights of a party or appellate review of the underlying order; and

• the danger that the issuance of an explanatory memorandum would suggest that judicial decisions are influenced by public opinion or criticism voiced by third parties, and would not promote confidence in the courts and in the independence,* integrity,* and impartiality* of judges.

(ii) An explanatory memorandum is appropriate only if issued within a reasonable time of the underlying order and if the judge clearly recalls the judge's reasons for the decision. An explanatory memorandum should not rely on any information that was not in the record before the judge at the time of the underlying order.

(iii) A judge may not issue an explanatory memorandum if the court no longer has authority to alter or amend the underlying order. For example, a judge may not issue an explanatory memorandum when:

- the underlying order is the subject of an interlocutory appeal, report, or other appellate proceeding that has already been docketed in the appellate court, unless such a memorandum has been requested by an appellate single justice or court;

- the case has been finally adjudicated in the trial court, no timely-filed post-judgment motions are pending,* and the time within which the court may modify its orders and judgments on its own initiative has passed; or

- an appeal has been taken from a final order or judgment, and the appeal has been docketed in the appellate court.

Rule 2.11.   Disqualification

(A) A judge shall disqualify himself or herself in any proceeding in which the judge cannot be impartial* or the judge's impartiality* might reasonably be questioned, including but not limited to the following circumstances:

(1) The judge has a personal bias or prejudice concerning a party or a party's lawyer, or personal knowledge* of facts that are in dispute in the proceeding.

(2) The judge knows* that the judge, the judge's spouse or domestic partner,* or a person within the third degree of relationship* to either of them, or the spouse or domestic partner* of such a person is:

(a) a party to the proceeding, or an officer, director, general partner, managing member, or trustee of a party;

(b) acting as a lawyer in the proceeding;

(c) a person who has more than a de minimis financial or other interest that could be substantially affected by the proceeding; or

(d) likely to be a material witness in the proceeding.

(3) The judge knows* that he or she, individually or as a fiduciary,* or the judge's spouse, domestic partner,* parent, or child, or any other member of the judge's family residing in the judge's household,* has an economic interest* in the subject matter in controversy or is a party to the proceeding.

(4) The judge, while a judge or a judicial applicant* or judicial nominee,* has made a public statement, other than in a court proceeding, judicial decision, or opinion, that commits or appears to commit the judge to reach a particular result or rule in a particular way in the proceeding or controversy.

(5) The judge:

(a) served as a lawyer in the matter in controversy, or was associated with a lawyer who participated substantially as a lawyer in the matter during such association;

(b) served in governmental employment, and in such capacity participated personally and substantially as a lawyer or public official concerning the proceeding, or has publicly expressed in such capacity an opinion concerning the merits of the particular matter in controversy;

(c) was a material witness concerning the matter; or

(d) previously presided as a judge over the matter in another court.

(B) A judge shall keep informed about the judge's personal and fiduciary* economic interests,* and make a reasonable effort to keep informed about the personal economic interests* of the judge's spouse or domestic partner* and minor children residing in the judge's household.

(C) A judge subject to disqualification under this Rule, other than for bias or prejudice under Paragraph (A)(1), may disclose on the record the basis of the judge's disqualification and may ask the parties and their lawyers to consider, outside the presence of and without participation by the judge and court personnel,* whether to waive disqualification. If, following a consultation that is free from coercion, express or implied, the parties and lawyers agree that the judge should not be disqualified, the judge may participate in the proceeding. The agreement shall be incorporated into the record of the proceeding.

Adopted October 8, 2015, effective January 1, 2016.

COMMENT

[1] A judge is disqualified from any matter if the judge cannot satisfy both a subjective and an objective standard. The subjective standard requires disqualification if the judge concludes that he or she cannot be impartial.* The objective standard requires disqualification whenever the judge's impartiality* might reasonably be questioned by a fully-informed disinterested observer, regardless of whether any of the specific provisions of Paragraphs (A)(1) through (5) apply. By way of example, a judge must disqualify himself or herself from any proceeding in which the judge is a client of a party's lawyer or the lawyer's firm. Whether a judge must continue to disqualify himself or herself after this attorney-client relationship has concluded should be determined by considering all relevant factors, including the terms on which the lawyer provided representation, the length of time since the representation concluded, the nature and subject matter of the representation, and the extent of the attorney-client relationship, including the length of the relationship and the frequency of contacts between the judge and the lawyer. A judge must also bear in mind that social relationships may contribute to a reasonable belief that the judge cannot be impartial.

[2] A judge's obligation not to hear or decide matters in which disqualification is required applies regardless of whether a motion to disqualify is filed.

[3] The rule of necessity may override the rule of disqualification. For example, a judge might be required to participate in judicial review of a judicial salary statute, or might be the only judge available in a matter requiring immediate judicial action, such as a hearing on probable cause or a temporary restraining order. In matters that require immediate action, the judge must disclose on the record the basis for possible disqualification and make reasonable efforts to transfer the matter to another judge as soon as practicable.

[4] The fact that a lawyer in a proceeding is affiliated with a law firm with which a relative of the judge is affiliated does not itself disqualify the judge. If, however, under the circumstances, the judge's impartiality* might reasonably be questioned under Paragraph (A), then the judge's disqualification is required.

[5] A judge should disclose on the record information that the judge believes the parties or their lawyers might reasonably consider relevant to a possible motion for disqualification, even if the judge believes there is no basis for disqualification.

[6] The filing of a judicial discipline complaint during the pendency of a matter does not necessarily require disqualification of the judge presiding over the matter. The judge's decision to disqualify in such circumstances must be resolved on a case-by-case basis.

Rule 2.12.   Supervisory Duties

(A) A judge shall require court personnel* and others subject to the judge's direction and control to act in a manner consistent with the judge's obligations under this Code.

(B) A judge with supervisory authority for the performance of other judges shall take reasonable measures to ensure that those judges properly discharge their judicial responsibilities, including the prompt disposition of matters before them.

Adopted October 8, 2015, effective January 1, 2016.

COMMENT

[1] A judge may not direct court personnel* to engage in conduct on the judge's behalf or as the judge's representative when such conduct would violate the Code if undertaken by the judge.

[2] Public confidence in the judicial system depends upon timely justice. To promote the efficient administration of justice, a judge with supervisory authority must take the steps needed to ensure that those under the judge's supervision administer their workloads promptly.

Rule 2.13.   Administrative Appointments

(A) In making administrative appointments, a judge shall:

(1) exercise the power of appointment impartially* and on the basis of merit; and

(2) avoid nepotism, favoritism, and unnecessary appointments.

(B) A judge shall not approve compensation of appointees beyond the fair value of services rendered.

Adopted October 8, 2015, effective January 1, 2016.

COMMENT

[1] Appointees of a judge may include assigned counsel, guardians ad litem, special masters, receivers, and any court personnel* subject to appointment by a judge. Consent by the parties to an appointment or an award of compensation does not relieve the judge of the obligation prescribed by this Rule. Compliance with court rules pertaining to fee-generating appointments satisfies the judge's obligations under Paragraph (A). See SJC Rule 1:07.

[2] Unless otherwise defined by law,* nepotism is the appointment or hiring of any relative within the third degree of relationship* of either the judge or the judge's spouse or domestic partner,* or the spouse or domestic partner* of such relative. See also Trial Court Personnel Policies and Procedures Manual, § 4.304.

Rule 2.14.   Disability and Impairment

A judge having a reasonable belief that the performance of a lawyer or another judge is impaired by drugs or alcohol, or by a mental, emotional, or physical condition, shall take appropriate action, which may include a confidential referral to a lawyer or judicial assistance program.

Adopted October 8, 2015, effective January 1, 2016.

COMMENT

[1] Taking appropriate action to address disability or impairment pursuant to this Rule is part of a judge's judicial duties. This Rule requires a judge to take appropriate action even if the disability or impairment has not manifested itself in a violation of the Rules of Professional Conduct or the Code of Judicial Conduct. See Rule 2.15,

which requires a judge to take action to address violations of the Rules of Professional Conduct or the Code of Judicial Conduct.

[2] Appropriate action means action intended and reasonably likely to help the judge or lawyer in question address the problem and prevent harm to the justice system. Depending upon the circumstances, appropriate action may include but is not limited to speaking directly to the impaired person, notifying an individual with supervisory responsibility over the impaired person, or making a referral to an assistance program. If the lawyer is appearing before the judge, a judge may defer taking action until the matter has been concluded, but must do so as soon as practicable thereafter. However, immediate action is compelled when a lawyer is unable to provide competent representation to the lawyer's client.

[3] Taking or initiating corrective action by way of referral to an assistance program may satisfy a judge's responsibility under this Rule. Assistance programs have many approaches for offering help to impaired judges and lawyers, such as intervention, counseling, or referral to appropriate health care professionals. Depending upon the gravity of the conduct that has come to the judge's attention, however, the judge may be required to take other action. See Rule 2.15.

Rule 2.15.   Responding to Judicial and Lawyer Misconduct

(A) A judge having knowledge* that another judge has committed a violation of this Code that raises a substantial question regarding the judge's honesty, integrity,* trustworthiness, or fitness as a judge in other respects shall inform the Chief Justice of the Supreme Judicial Court, the Chief Justice of the court on which the judge sits, and if the judge is a Trial Court judge, the Chief Justice of the Trial Court.

(B) A judge having knowledge* that a lawyer has committed a violation of the Rules of Professional Conduct that raises a substantial question regarding the lawyer's honesty, integrity,* trustworthiness, or fitness as a lawyer in other respects shall inform the Office of Bar Counsel.

(C) A judge having knowledge* of or receiving credible information indicating a substantial likelihood that another judge has otherwise violated this Code shall take appropriate action.

(D) A judge having knowledge* of or receiving credible information indicating a substantial likelihood that a lawyer has otherwise violated the Rules of Professional Conduct shall take appropriate action.

Adopted October 8, 2015, effective January 1, 2016.

COMMENT

[1] Taking action to address known* misconduct is part of a judge's duties. Paragraphs (A) and (B) impose an obligation on the judge to report to the appropriate authority the known* misconduct of another judge or a lawyer that raises a substantial question regarding the honesty, integrity,* trustworthiness, or fitness of that judge or lawyer. Ignoring or denying known* misconduct among one's judicial colleagues or members of the legal profession undermines a judge's responsibility to participate in efforts to ensure public respect for the justice system. This Rule limits the reporting obligation to those offenses that an independent judiciary must vigorously endeavor to prevent. If the lawyer is appearing before the judge, a judge may defer making a report until the matter has been concluded, but the report should be made as soon as practicable thereafter. However, an immediate report is compelled when a person will likely be injured by a delay in reporting, such as where the judge has knowledge* that a

lawyer has embezzled client or fiduciary* funds and delay may impair the ability to recover the funds.

[2] A judge who has knowledge* or receives credible information indicating a substantial likelihood that a judge has otherwise violated this Code, or that a lawyer has otherwise violated the Rules of Professional Conduct, is required to take appropriate action under Paragraph (C) or (D). Appropriate action pursuant to Paragraph (C) may include communicating directly with the judge, reporting to the first justice or regional administrative justice of the court where the violation occurred or where that judge often sits, reporting to the Chief Justice of that judge's court, and/or calling the judicial hotline maintained by Lawyers Concerned for Lawyers. Appropriate action pursuant to Paragraph (D) may include communicating directly with the lawyer, reporting to the lawyer's supervisor or employer, and/or reporting to the Office of Bar Counsel. These lists of actions are illustrative and not meant to be limiting. If the lawyer is appearing before the judge, a judge may defer taking action until the matter has been concluded, but action should be taken as soon as practicable thereafter. Reporting a violation is especially important where the

victim is unlikely to discover the offense, and an immediate report is compelled when a person will likely be injured by a delay in reporting.

Rule 2.16. Cooperation With Disciplinary Authorities

(A) A judge shall cooperate and be candid and honest with judicial and lawyer disciplinary authorities.

(B) A judge shall not retaliate, directly or indirectly, against a person known* or suspected to have assisted or cooperated with an investigation of a judge or a lawyer.

Adopted October 8, 2015, effective January 1, 2016.

COMMENT

[1] Cooperation with investigations and proceedings of judicial and lawyer discipline authorities, as required in Paragraph (A), instills confidence in judges' commitment to the integrity* of the judicial system and the protection of the public.

CANON 3. A JUDGE SHALL CONDUCT THE JUDGE'S PERSONAL AND EXTRAJUDICIAL ACTIVITIES TO MINIMIZE THE RISK OF CONFLICT WITH THE OBLIGATIONS OF JUDICIAL OFFICE

Rule 3.1. Extrajudicial Activities in General

A judge may engage in extrajudicial activities, except as prohibited by law * or this Code. However, when engaging in extrajudicial activities, a judge shall not:

(A) participate in activities that are reasonably likely to interfere with the proper performance of the judge's judicial duties;

(B) participate in activities that are reasonably likely to lead to recurrent disqualification of the judge;

(C) participate in activities that would appear to a reasonable person to undermine the judge's independence,* integrity,* or impartiality *;

(D) engage in conduct that would appear to a reasonable person to be coercive; or

(E) make use of court premises, staff, stationery, equipment, or other resources, except for use that is reasonable in scope, not prohibited by law,* and incidental to activities that concern the law,* the legal system, or the administration of justice.

Adopted October 8, 2015, effective January 1, 2016.

* For definition of term, see S.J.C. Rule 3:09, Code of Jud. Conduct, Terminology.

COMMENT

[1] To the extent that time permits, and judicial independence * and impartiality * are not compromised, judges are encouraged to engage in appropriate extrajudicial activities. Judges are uniquely qualified to engage in extrajudicial activities that concern the law,* the legal system, and the administration of justice. In addition, judges are permitted and encouraged to engage in educational, religious, charitable, fraternal or civic extrajudicial activities not conducted for profit, even when the activities do not involve the law.* Participation in both law-related and other extrajudicial activities helps integrate judges into their communities, and furthers public understanding of and respect for courts and the judicial system. See Rule 3.7.

[2] This Rule emphasizes that when engaging in any extrajudicial activity, a judge must consider the obligations of judicial office and

avoid any activities that are reasonably likely to interfere with those obligations.

[3] Discriminatory actions and expressions of bias or prejudice by a judge, even outside the judge's official or judicial actions, are likely to appear to a reasonable person to call into question the judge's independence,* integrity,* or impartiality.* Examples include jokes or other remarks that demean individuals based upon their race, color, sex, gender identity or expression, religion, nationality, national origin, ethnicity, citizenship or immigration status, ancestry, disease or disability, age, sexual orientation, marital status, socioeconomic status, or political affiliation. For the same reason, a judge's extrajudicial activities must not be conducted in connection or affiliation with an organization that practices invidious discrimination. See Rule 3.6.

[4] While engaged in permitted extrajudicial activities, judges must not coerce others or take action that would reasonably be perceived as coercive. For example, a judge's urging a lawyer who appears in the judge's court to assist on a time-consuming extrajudicial project would create the risk that the person solicited would feel obligated to respond favorably, or would do so to curry favor with the judge.

[5] Paragraph (E) recognizes that reasonable use of public resources to support a judge's law-related activities advances the legitimate interests of the public and the court system.

* For definition of term, see S.J.C. Rule 3:09, Code of Jud. Conduct, Terminology.

Rule 3.2. Appearances Before Governmental Bodies and Consultation With Government Officials

A judge shall not appear voluntarily at a public hearing before, or otherwise consult with, an executive or a legislative body or official, except:

(A) in connection with matters concerning the law,* the legal system, or the administration of justice; or

(B) when the judge is acting pro se in a matter involving the judge's legal or economic interests,* or when the judge is acting in a fiduciary* capacity pursuant to Rule 3.8.

Adopted October 8, 2015, effective January 1, 2016.

COMMENT

[1] Judges possess special expertise in matters of law,* the legal system, and the administration of justice, and may properly share that expertise with governmental bodies and executive or legislative branch officials by, for example, proposing new legislation, commenting on new legislation proposed by others, or proposing or commenting on amendments to existing law.* The types of topics that a judge may address include but are not limited to court facilities, funding, staffing, resources, and security; terms of employment, compensation, and other benefits of judges and court personnel*; personal safety of judges and court personnel*; court jurisdiction and procedures; the work of specialty courts*; the admissibility or inadmissibility of evidence; judicial discretion in sentencing; funding for the legal representation of indigents; access to justice; and similar matters.

[2] In appearing before governmental bodies or consulting with government officials, judges must be mindful that they remain subject to other provisions of this Code, such as Rule 1.3, which prohibits judges from abusing the prestige of office to advance their own or others' interests; Rule 2.10, which governs public comment on pending* and impending matters*; and Rule 3.1(C), which prohibits judges from engaging in extrajudicial activities that would appear to a reasonable person to undermine the judge's independence,* integrity,* or impartiality.*

[3] In general, it would be an unnecessary and unfair burden to prohibit judges from appearing before governmental bodies or consulting with government officials on matters that are likely to affect them as private citizens, such as zoning proposals affecting their real property. In engaging in such activities, however, judges must not refer to their judicial positions, and must otherwise exercise caution to avoid abusing the prestige of judicial office.

Rule 3.3. Testifying as a Character Witness

A judge shall not testify as a character witness in a judicial, administrative, or other adjudicatory proceeding or otherwise vouch for the character of a person in a legal proceeding, except when duly summoned.

Adopted October 8, 2015, effective January 1, 2016.

COMMENT

[1] A judge who, without being subpoenaed, testifies as a character witness lends the prestige of judicial office to advance the interests of another. See Rule 1.3. Except in unusual circumstances where the demands of justice require, a judge should discourage a party from requiring the judge to testify as a character witness.

[2] This Rule does not preclude a judge from voluntarily testifying or otherwise vouching for the qualifications, including the character, of an applicant or nominee for judicial or court-related office, as long as the judge's observations are based on the judge's personal knowledge.* See Rule 1.3.

[3] This Rule does not preclude a judge from providing a character reference based on personal knowledge* for an applicant to the bar of any state.

[4] This Rule does not preclude a judge from responding based on personal knowledge* to an inquiry from any state or federal entity, or a contractor for such an entity, conducting a background investigation in connection with an application for public employment or for security clearance.

Rule 3.4. Appointments to Governmental Positions

A judge shall not accept appointment to a governmental committee, board, commission, or other governmental position, unless it is one that concerns the law,* the legal system, or the administration of justice.

Adopted October 8, 2015, effective January 1, 2016.

COMMENT

[1] This Rule implicitly acknowledges the value of judges accepting appointments to entities that concern the law,* the legal system, or the administration of justice. However, a judge must assess the appropriateness of accepting an appointment, paying particular attention to the subject matter of the appointment, see Rule 3.2, and the availability and allocation of judicial resources, including the judge's time commitments, and giving due regard to the importance of respecting the separation of powers, upholding the independence,* integrity,* and impartiality* of the judiciary, and minimizing judicial disqualification. Furthermore, acceptance of extrajudicial appointments is subject to applicable restrictions relating to multiple office holding set forth in the Constitution of the Commonwealth. See Part 2, Chapter 6, Article II and Article VIII of the Amendments to the Constitution. A judge should regularly reexamine the propriety of continuing in the appointed position, as the composition and/or mission of any such committee, board, or commission may change.

[2] A judge may represent the United States, the Commonwealth of Massachusetts, or the judge's county, city or town on ceremonial occasions or in connection with historical, educational, or cultural activities. Such representation does not constitute acceptance of a government position.

Rule 3.5. Use of Nonpublic Information

A judge shall not knowingly* disclose or use nonpublic information* acquired in a judicial capacity for any purpose unrelated to the judge's judicial duties.

Adopted October 8, 2015, effective January 1, 2016.

COMMENT

[1] In the course of performing judicial duties, a judge may acquire information of commercial or other value that is unavailable to the public. The judge must not reveal or use such information for personal gain or for any purpose unrelated to the performance of judicial duties.

[2] This Rule is not intended to affect a judge's ability to act on information as necessary to protect the health or safety of the judge or a member of the judge's family,* court personnel,* or any other person if consistent with other provisions of this Code.

Rule 3.6. Affiliation With Discriminatory Organizations

(A) A judge shall not hold membership in any organization that practices invidious discrimination.

(B) A judge shall not use the benefits or facilities of an organization if the judge knows* or should be aware that the organization practices invidious discrimination. A judge's attendance at an event in a facility of such organization is not a violation of this Rule when the judge's attendance is an isolated event that could not reasonably be perceived as an endorsement of the organization's practices.

Adopted October 8, 2015, effective January 1, 2016.

COMMENT

[1] A judge's public manifestation of approval of invidious discrimination diminishes public confidence in the integrity* and impartiality* of the judiciary. A judge's membership in an organization that

practices invidious discrimination similarly diminishes public confidence in the integrity* and impartiality* of the judiciary.

[2] Whether an organization practices invidious discrimination is a complex question to which judges must be attentive. The answer cannot be determined from a mere examination of an organization's current membership rolls, but depends upon how the organization selects members, as well as other relevant factors, such as whether the organization is dedicated to the preservation of religious, ethnic, or cultural values of legitimate common interest to its members that do not stigmatize any excluded persons as inferior and therefore unworthy of membership. The purpose of this Rule is to prohibit judges from joining organizations practicing invidious discrimination, whether or not an organization's membership practices are constitutionally protected. When a judge learns that an organization to which the judge belongs engages in invidious discrimination, the judge must resign immediately from the organization.

[3] Whether an organization engages in invidious discrimination is a threshold issue but not the end of the judge's inquiry. Even an organization that does not engage in invidious discrimination may engage in practices such that a judge's membership in the organization might erode public confidence in the impartiality* of the judiciary. Before holding membership in any organization, a judge must consider whether membership would appear to undermine the judge's impartiality* in the eyes of a reasonable litigant. See Rules 3.1 and 3.7.

[4] A judge's membership in a religious organization as a lawful exercise of the freedom of religion is not a violation of this Rule.

[5] This Rule does not apply to national or state military service.

Rule 3.7. Participation in Legal, Educational, Religious, Charitable, Fraternal, or Civic Organizations and Activities

(A) Subject to the requirements of Rule 3.1, a judge may participate in activities of or sponsored by or on behalf of (i) legal, educational, religious, charitable, fraternal, or civic organizations, which are not conducted for profit, or (ii) governmental entities concerned with the law,* the legal system, or the administration of justice. Permitted participation includes but is not limited to the following:

(1) A judge may serve as a member of the organization.

(2) A judge may plan and attend events and activities of the organization.

(3) A judge may participate in internal discussions related to fundraising. However, a judge shall not otherwise participate in fundraising, and shall not manage or invest funds belonging to or raised by the organization unless the organization is composed entirely or predominantly of judges and exists to further the educational or professional interests of judges.

(4) A judge shall not solicit contributions or members for the organization, except that a judge may solicit contributions or members from members of the judge's family* or from judges over whom the judge does not exercise supervisory or appellate authority.

(5) A judge may serve as an officer, director, trustee, or nonlegal advisor of the organization, unless it is likely that the organization:

(a) will be engaged in proceedings that would ordinarily come before the judge; or

(b) will frequently be engaged in adversary proceedings in the court of which the judge is a member, or in any court subject to the appellate jurisdiction of the court of which the judge is a member.

(6) A judge may serve as a keynote or featured speaker at, receive an award or other comparable recognition at, be featured on the program of, and permit the judge's title to be used in connection with the promotion of an organization's event that is not a fundraising event,* but shall not do so at a fundraising event* except as permitted in Paragraph (6A).

(6A) A judge may serve as a keynote or featured speaker at, receive an award or other comparable recognition at, be featured on the program of, and permit the judge's title to be used in connection with the promotion of a fundraising event* only if the event is sponsored by an organization concerned with the law,* the legal system, or the administration of justice, and that organization promotes the general interests of the judicial branch of government or the legal profession, including enhancing the diversity and professionalism of the bar.

(7) A judge may make recommendations to public or private fund-granting organizations or agencies for programs and projects, but only on behalf of organizations that are concerned with the law,* the legal system, or the administration of justice.

(B) A judge may encourage lawyers to provide pro bono publico legal services.

(C) A judge may, as a parent or guardian, assist minor children in their fundraising activities if the procedures employed are not coercive and the sums solicited are modest.

Adopted October 8, 2015, effective January 1, 2016.

COMMENT

[1] This Rule governs a judge's participation in a variety of activities sponsored by organizations not conducted for profit, whether public or private, and by governmental entities (collectively referred to as "organizations"). Paragraph (A) identifies the types of organizations covered by this Rule. Examples include bar associations, other not-for-profit private organizations, and court-created commissions. The first clause of Paragraph (A), "subject to the requirements of Rule 3.1," emphasizes that even with respect to activities that are explicitly permitted by Rule 3.7, a judge must always consider whether participation would violate Rule 3.1.

[1A] In considering whether participation in any extrajudicial activity would violate Rule 3.1, a judge should consider all relevant factors, including the membership and purposes of the organization, the nature of the judge's participation in or association with the organization or event, whether the organization or its members typically advocate on one side of issues before or likely to come before the court of which the judge is a member or any court subject to the appellate jurisdiction of the court of which the judge is a member, and the number, diversity, and identity of the financial supporters of the organization or sponsors of a particular event. Although activities permitted under this Rule must be of or sponsored by an organization not conducted for profit, this requirement does not preclude the judge from participating in events of an organization that receives sponsorship or financial support from for-profit entities. A judge must avoid giving the impression that the organization, its members, or an event's sponsors are in a special position to influence the judge, and, where appropriate, a judge must avoid giving the impression that the judge favors the organization's mission.

[1B] The Code explicitly encourages certain activities where the nature of a judge's participation will promote public understanding of and confidence in an independent* judiciary, foster collegiality among the bar and communication and cooperation between the judiciary and the bar, enhance the judge's ability to perform judicial or administrative duties, or otherwise further the goals of the courts. See, e.g., Rule 1.2, Comments [4] and [6]. So, for example, judges are encouraged to speak about the administration of justice to not-for-profit groups, including business and community groups and bar associations. Such speaking engagements ordinarily will not raise an issue under Rule 3.1 even when an event or program is held in space provided by a law firm or is financially supported or sponsored by one or more for-profit entities, such as law firms or legal vendors, that do substantial business in the court on which the judge sits. If, however, fundraising is a chief objective of the event or program, Paragraph (A)(6A) governs whether a judge may be a keynote or featured speaker. Giving a presentation at an educational conference where the judge's involvement would help to further the goals of the court system is another example of encouraged participation. Such participation would not ordinarily raise an issue under Rule 3.1 even when the conference is financially supported or sponsored by organizations or vendors that do business in the court on which the judge sits.

[2] The restrictions in Paragraph (A)(4) are necessary because, depending on the circumstances, a judge's solicitation of contributions or members for an organization might create the risk that the person solicited would feel obligated to respond favorably or would do so to curry favor with the judge. However, a judge may be identified by name and title as an organization's officer, director, trustee, non-legal advisor, or member on websites, emails, letterhead, and any other communication materials created and issued by others within the organization to solicit or accept donations or to enroll members so long as comparable designations are used for other persons.

[3] As used in Paragraphs (A)(6) and (A)(6A), a fundraising event* is one for which the organizers' chief objectives include raising money to support the organization's activities beyond the event itself. Unless that is the case, an event is not a fundraising event,* even if the revenues ultimately exceed the cost. A judge may attend a fundraising event* but may not participate in additional activities except as permitted by Paragraph (A)(6A). However, a judge who attends a fundraising event* is not in violation of this Rule merely because a laudatory reference to or about the judge, not announced in advance, is made at the event.

[4] Paragraph (A)(6A) permits a judge to participate in additional activities (e.g., being a featured speaker or receiving an award) at fundraising events* of or sponsored by organizations concerned with the law,* the legal system, or the administration of justice that serve the general interests of the judicial branch of government and the legal profession, including organizations that enhance the diversity and professionalism of the bar. The nature of such organizations makes it unlikely that a judge's involvement would reflect adversely upon that judge's independence,* integrity,* or impartiality.* Organizations concerned with the general interests of the judicial branch of government and the legal profession include general purpose and affinity bar associations (e.g., county bar associations, bar associations composed exclusively or primarily of members of an ethnic group, bar associations specializing in particular practice areas but whose members take positions on both sides of disputed issues), organizations dedicated to enhancing the professionalism of the judicial branch (e.g., the National Center for State Courts), and organizations composed entirely or primarily of judges (e.g., the Massachusetts Judges Conference, the Flaschner Judicial Institute), but exclude organizations composed exclusively or primarily of lawyers who typically take one side of contested issues (e.g., plaintiffs' personal injury bar associations, insurance defense bar associations), organizations dedicated to influencing opinion on contested legal or constitutional issues, or organizations that represent one constituency (e.g., prosecutors, criminal defense counsel).

[5] In addition to the types of participation expressly contemplated by this Rule, a judge's permissible extrajudicial activities often involve teaching or writing on law-related subjects and, on occasion, non-law-related subjects. See Rule 1.3 for special considerations that arise when a judge writes or contributes to publications of a for-profit entity. Similar considerations also may arise if a judge teaches for a for-profit entity.

[6] In addition to appointing lawyers to serve as counsel for indigent parties in individual cases as authorized by law,* a judge may promote broader access to justice by encouraging lawyers to provide pro bono publico or reduced fee legal services, if in doing so the judge does not employ coercion or abuse the prestige of judicial office. Such encouragement may take many forms, including providing lists of available programs, training lawyers to do pro bono publico legal work, and participating in events recognizing lawyers who have done pro bono publico work.

[7] Paragraph (C) is intended to allow a judge to participate in a child's normal, daily activities. Thus, for example, a judge may accompany the judge's child while the child sells Girl Scout cookies or collects UNICEF donations, or may work at a refreshment stand at a school-sponsored sports event intended to raise money to finance a class trip. On the other hand, this provision does not permit a judge to participate in fundraising activities for the primary or exclusive benefit of the judge's own child, such as raising funds so that the judge's child may participate in a school-sponsored trip. The word "assist" is intended to convey that a judge should not engage in direct solicitations on behalf of the child other than from members of the judge's family.* A judge may not, for example, sell Girl Scout cookies in the workplace.

Rule 3.8. Appointments to Fiduciary Positions

(A) A judge shall not accept appointment to serve in a fiduciary* position, except for the estate, trust, or person of a member of the judge's family,* and then only if such service will not interfere with the proper performance of judicial duties.

(B) A judge shall not serve in a fiduciary* position if the judge as fiduciary* will likely be engaged in proceedings that would ordinarily come before the judge, or if the estate, trust, or ward becomes involved in adversary proceedings in the court on which the judge serves, or one under its appellate jurisdiction.

(C) A judge acting in a fiduciary* capacity shall be subject to the same restrictions on engaging in financial activities that apply to a judge personally.

(D) If a person who is serving in a fiduciary* position becomes a judge, he or she must comply with this Rule as soon as reasonably possible and in any event within one year.

Adopted October 8, 2015, effective January 1, 2016.

COMMENT

[1] A judge should recognize that other restrictions imposed by this Code may conflict with a judge's obligations as a fiduciary.* In such circumstances, a judge should resign as fiduciary* as soon as reasonably possible and in any event within one year. For example, serving as a fiduciary* might require frequent disqualification of a judge under Rule 2.11 because a judge is deemed to have an economic interest* in shares of stock held by a trust if the amount of stock held is more than de minimis.

Rule 3.9. Service as Arbitrator or Mediator

A judge shall not act as an arbitrator or a mediator or perform other judicial functions apart from the judge's official duties unless expressly authorized by law.*

Adopted October 8, 2015, effective January 1, 2016.

[1] This Rule does not prohibit a judge from participating in mediation, conciliation, or settlement conferences performed as part of judicial duties. Rendering dispute resolution services apart from those duties, whether or not for economic gain, is prohibited unless it is expressly authorized by law.*

Rule 3.10.   Practice of Law

A judge shall not practice law,* except that:

(A) A judge may act pro se and may, without compensation, give legal advice to and draft or review documents for a member of the judge's family,* but is prohibited from serving as the family member's lawyer in any forum, and

(B) A judge may serve as a judge advocate general in the context of a judge's service in the United States Armed Forces, the reserve components of the United States Armed Forces, or the National Guard.

Adopted October 8, 2015, effective January 1, 2016.

COMMENT

[1] A judge may act pro se in all legal matters, including matters involving litigation and matters involving appearances before or other dealings with governmental bodies.

[2] A judge must not use the prestige of office to advance the judge's personal or family interests. See Rule 1.3.

[3] While performing legal services in the context of a judge's military service, the judge must confine that conduct to authorized activities.

Rule 3.11.   Financial, Business, or Remunerative Activities

(A) A judge may hold and manage investments of the judge and members of the judge's family.*

(B) A judge shall not serve as an officer, director, manager, general partner, advisor, or employee of any business entity except that a judge may manage or participate in a business entity primarily engaged in investment of the financial resources of the judge or members of the judge's family.*

(C) A judge shall not engage in financial activities permitted under Paragraphs (A) and (B) if they will:

(1) interfere with the proper performance of judicial duties;

(2) lead to frequent disqualification of the judge;

(3) involve the judge in frequent transactions or continuing business relationships with lawyers or other persons likely to come before the court on which the judge serves; or

(4) result in violation of other provisions of this Code.

Adopted October 8, 2015, effective January 1, 2016.

COMMENT

[1] As soon as practicable without serious financial detriment, the judge must divest himself or herself of investments and other financial interests that might require frequent disqualification or otherwise violate this Rule.

[2] Under this Rule, a judge must consider the difference between the permitted management of an investment and the prohibited management of a business. For example, a judge who owns residential or commercial properties as investments may establish policy and participate in decisions regarding the purchase, sale, and use of land, but must leave the actual day-to-day management to others.

Rule 3.12.   Compensation for Extrajudicial Activities

A judge may accept reasonable compensation for extrajudicial activities permitted by this Code or other law* unless such acceptance would appear to a reasonable person to undermine the judge's independence,* integrity,* or impartiality.*

Adopted October 8, 2015, effective January 1, 2016.

COMMENT

[1] A judge is permitted to accept wages, salaries, royalties, or other compensation for teaching, writing, and other extrajudicial activities, provided the compensation is commensurate with the task performed and the judge's qualifications to perform that task. A judge must ensure, however, that no conflicts are created by the arrangement. A judge must not appear to trade on the judicial position for personal advantage. See Rule 1.3. In addition, the source, amount, and timing of the payment, alone or in combination, must not raise any question of undue influence or undermine the judge's ability to act independently,* impartially,* and with integrity.* The judge should also be mindful that judicial duties must take precedence over other activities. See Rule 2.1.

[2] A teaching activity may include lecturing in educational programs sponsored by non-profit organizations and associations including but not limited to educational institutions, bar associations, professional associations, providers of continuing legal education, and governmental entities concerned with the law,* the legal system, or the administration of justice. A judge is not permitted to accept an honorarium or fee for a speaking engagement other than a teaching activity, but may accept reimbursement of expenses. See Rule 3.14.

[3] Compensation derived from extrajudicial activities may be subject to public reporting. See Rule 3.15.

Rule 3.13.   Acceptance and Reporting of Gifts, Loans, Bequests, Benefits, or Other Things of Value

(A) A judge shall not accept any gifts, loans, bequests, benefits, or other things of value ("gifts" or "benefits") if acceptance is prohibited by law* or would appear to a reasonable person to undermine the judge's independence,* integrity,* or impartiality.*

(B) Unless otherwise prohibited by Paragraph (A), a judge may accept the following gifts or benefits provided that they are not given for or because of the judge's official position or action, without publicly reporting them:

(1) gifts or benefits not of substantial value* as that term is defined by the State Ethics Commission, see 930 C.M.R. 5.05;

(2) gifts or benefits from close personal friends* or relatives whose appearance or interest in a matter pending* or impending* before the judge would in any event require disqualification of the judge under Rule 2.11;

(3) ordinary social hospitality;

(4) gifts or benefits given in connection with a judge's participation in the organizations described in Rule 3.7, so long as the same gifts, benefits, and opportunities are made

available on the same terms to similarly situated persons who are not judges;

(5) commercial or financial opportunities and benefits, including special pricing and discounts, and loans from lending institutions in their regular course of business, if the same opportunities and benefits or loans are made available on the same terms to similarly situated persons who are not judges;

(6) rewards and prizes given to competitors or participants in random drawings, contests, or other events that are open to persons who are not judges;

(7) scholarships, fellowships, and similar benefits or awards, if they are available to similarly situated persons who are not judges, based upon the same terms and criteria; and

(8) gifts or benefits associated with the business, profession, or other separate activity of a spouse, a domestic partner,* or other family member of a judge residing in the judge's household,* but that incidentally benefit the judge.

(C) Unless otherwise prohibited by Paragraph (A), a judge may accept any other gift or benefit provided that it is not given for or because of the judge's official position or action, but the judge must publicly report the gift or benefit in the manner required under Rule 3.15.

(D) Unless otherwise prohibited by Paragraph (A), a judge may accept the following gifts or benefits given for or because of the judge's official position or action, without publicly reporting them:

(1) a gift, award, or other benefit incident to public recognition of the judge, provided the gift is not of substantial value* as that term is defined by the State Ethics Commission, see 930 C.M.R. 5.05;

(2) invitations to the judge to attend without charge a luncheon, dinner, reception, award ceremony, or similar event, held in Massachusetts, of a bar association or other non-profit organization concerned with the law, the legal system, or the administration of justice;

(3) discounted or free membership to a bar association or other nonprofit organization concerned with the law,* the legal system, or the administration of justice; and

(4) books, magazines, journals, and other resource materials supplied by publishers on a complimentary basis for official use.

(E) Unless otherwise prohibited by Paragraph (A), a judge may accept the following gifts or benefits given for or because of the judge's official position or action, but the judge must publicly report the gift or benefit in the manner required under Rule 3.15:

(1) a gift, award, or other benefit incident to public recognition of the judge, if the gift is of substantial value* as that term is defined by the State Ethics Commission, see 930 C.M.R. 5.05; and

(2) a complimentary invitation for a spouse or domestic partner,* or other guests, to attend an event of a bar association or other non-profit organization concerned with

the law, the legal system, or the administration of justice where a judge is being honored.

Adopted October 8, 2015, effective January 1, 2016.

COMMENT

[1] This Rule addresses whether and in what circumstances a judge may accept gifts or other items of value ("gifts" or "benefits") without paying fair market value. Judges, like other public employees, are governed by the conflict of interest laws set forth in G. L. c. 268A and c. 268B and by associated regulatory exemptions that establish exclusions for certain situations that do not present a genuine risk of a conflict of interest or the appearance of a conflict of interest. This Code is largely consistent with c. 268A and regulations adopted by the State Ethics Commission. However, Rule 3.13 differs from those provisions in two important respects. First, because judges are always obligated to uphold and promote the independence,* integrity,* and impartiality* of the judiciary, a judge may not accept any gift or benefit, even if available to other public employees and unrelated to the judge's official position or action, if acceptance would appear to a reasonable person to undermine the judge's independence,* integrity,* and impartiality.* Second, this Rule carves out a few limited exceptions where a judge may accept a gift or benefit given for or because of the judge's official position or action even if such gift or benefit would ordinarily be prohibited by G. L. c. 268A, §§ 3 and 23(b)(2). See Rule 1.1. These exceptions are intended to allow judges to participate more fully in activities and organizations dedicated to the law,* the legal system, and the administration of justice.

[2] Paragraph (A) recognizes that whenever a judge accepts a gift without paying fair market value, even one not given for or because of a judge's official position or action, there is a risk that the public may regard the gift as an attempt to influence the judge in the performance of judicial duties. Paragraph (A) therefore requires a judge to reject any gift if acceptance would appear to a reasonable person to undermine the judge's independence,* integrity,* or impartiality.* Paragraphs (B) and (C) address instances when a gift is not given for or because of a judge's official position or action. Paragraph (B) identifies limited circumstances in which a gift may be accepted and not disclosed, while Paragraph (C) allows for additional instances when a judge may accept but must publicly report a gift. Paragraphs (D) and (E) identify limited instances where, after making a threshold determination that acceptance of a gift or benefit would not appear to a reasonable person to undermine the judge's independence,* integrity,* or impartiality,* a judge may accept a gift or benefit given for or because of the judge's official position or action. Paragraph (D) identifies instances when the judge may accept such a gift or benefit without public disclosure while Paragraph (E) identifies instances when public reporting is required to foster public confidence in the judiciary.

[3] A judge's acceptance of a gift from a lawyer or law firm who is appearing before the judge is an example of a gift prohibited by Paragraph (A), as such a gift would appear to a reasonable person to undermine the judge's independence,* integrity,* or impartiality.* A judge's acceptance of a gift or other thing of value from a party when the party's interests are before the judge raises the same concerns. The same concerns also are raised when the lawyer or law firm has appeared before, or the party's interests have come before, the judge in the reasonably recent past or are likely to come before the judge in the future.

[4] Paragraph (B)(1) provides that a judge may accept and not publicly report a gift or benefit not of substantial value* if it is not prohibited by Paragraph (A) and is not given because of a judge's official position or action.

[5] Gift-giving between close personal friends* and relatives is a common occurrence, and ordinarily does not create an appearance of impropriety* or cause a reasonable person to believe that the judge's independence,* integrity,* or impartiality* has been compromised even when the close personal friend* or relative is a lawyer. In

addition, because the appearance of close personal friends* or relatives in a case would require the judge's disqualification under Rule 2.11, there would be no opportunity for a gift or other thing of value to influence the judge's decision making; nor would a reasonable person believe that the gift was given due to the judge's official position. Paragraph (B)(2) places no restrictions upon the ability of a judge to accept gifts or other things of value from friends or relatives under these circumstances and does not require public reporting.

[6] "Ordinary social hospitality" consists of those social events and routine amenities, gifts, and courtesies which are normally attended by or exchanged between friends, colleagues, and acquaintances, and which would not create an appearance of impropriety* to a reasonable, objective observer. The test is objective, not subjective. Paragraph (B)(3) permits that type of social event or gift which is so common among people in the judge's community that no reasonable person would believe that: (i) the host/giver was intending to or would obtain any advantage; or (ii) the guest/recipient would believe that the host/giver intended to obtain any advantage.

[7] Paragraph (B)(4) recognizes that a judge's participation in organizations and activities, such as those permitted under Rule 3.7, may lead to the judge's being offered a gift or benefit. A judge may accept such a gift or benefit so long as the same gift or benefit is made available on the same terms to similarly situated persons who are not judges. For example, a local professional performer may offer the members of a neighborhood chorus complimentary tickets of substantial value* to attend a concert. A judge who sings in the chorus may accept a ticket because the gift is offered on the same terms to all of the members.

[8] Businesses and financial institutions frequently make available special pricing, discounts, and other benefits, either in connection with a temporary promotion or for preferred customers, based upon longevity of the relationship, volume of business transacted, and other factors. Paragraphs (B)(5)—(B)(7) provide that a judge may freely accept such benefits if they are available to the general public, or if the judge qualifies for the special price or discount according to the same criteria as are applied to persons who are not judges. As an example, loans provided at generally prevailing interest rates are not gifts, but a judge could not accept a loan from a financial institution at a below-market interest rate unless the same rate was being made available to the general public for a certain period of time or to borrowers with specified qualifications that the judge also possesses.

[9] This Rule applies only to acceptance of gifts or benefits by a judge. Nonetheless, if a gift or benefit is given to the judge's spouse, domestic partner,* or member of the judge's family residing in the judge's household,* it may be viewed as an attempt to evade this Rule and influence the judge indirectly. Where the gift or benefit is being made primarily to such other persons, and the judge is merely an incidental beneficiary, this concern is reduced and Paragraph (B)(8) does not require disclosure. A judge should remind family and household members of the restrictions imposed upon judges, and urge them to take these restrictions into account when making decisions about accepting such gifts or benefits.

[10] Paragraph (C) allows a judge to accept any other gift of substantial value* that is not given because of the judge's official position or action and is not prohibited by Paragraph (A), provided that the judge publicly reports the gift.

[11] In general, the receipt by a judge of free or discounted legal services carries a significant risk that such a gift would appear to a reasonable person to be given because of the judge's official position or action and to undermine the judge's independence,* integrity,* or impartiality.* There are, however, certain circumstances when that risk is sufficiently abated that a judge may accept and not disclose a gift of free or discounted legal fees pursuant to Paragraphs (B)(2) or

(B)(5) or may accept but must disclose the gift pursuant to Paragraph (C).

Paragraph (B)(2) permits a judge to accept and not disclose free or discounted legal services from a relative or close personal friend* whose appearance in a matter would require the judge's disqualification if the lawyer is a sole practitioner or at a firm where all the lawyers are relatives or close personal friends* of the judge (e.g., a firm composed of two siblings who are both close personal friends* of the judge). Because a gift of legal services is always a gift from both the lawyer providing the services and that lawyer's firm, Paragraph (B)(2) does not apply if the lawyer providing the services is a sole practitioner but not a relative or close personal friend* of the judge, or if that lawyer works at a firm where not all of the lawyers are relatives or close personal friends* of the judge.

Paragraph (B)(5) permits a judge to accept and not disclose free or discounted legal services when a lawyer or law firm has offered special pricing or a discount as part of a commercial opportunity or marketing strategy to a group of similarly situated persons who are not judges. For example, a law firm may have different rate structures for individual and corporate clients. Another example is a law firm that offers a reduced rate for estate planning services to all persons over 65. Paragraph (B)(5) does not apply if the special pricing is offered as a professional courtesy only to judges.

Paragraph (C) provides for instances when a judge may accept but must disclose free or discounted legal services. A reasonable person would not believe the gift or benefit undermines the judge's independence,* integrity,* or impartiality* when the same discount is extended to non-judges in comparable circumstances, and the lawyer, the lawyer's firm, and their interests are not before the judge, have not come before the judge in the reasonably recent past, and are not likely to come before the judge in the reasonably near future. Examples of comparable circumstances include the following: a law firm's policy is to extend professional courtesies to all former partners, and the judge is a former partner; a law firm's policy is to extend professional courtesies to the relatives of partners, and the judge's sibling is a partner at the firm; a lawyer's policy is to offer discounted legal services both to lawyers facing proceedings before the Board of Bar Overseers and to judges facing proceedings before the Commission on Judicial Conduct. Nevertheless, disclosure is necessary to maintain public confidence in the judiciary by making readily identifiable any potential for compromise to the judge's independence,* integrity,* or impartiality.*

[11A] Where a judge retains legal representation due to a matter before the Commission on Judicial Conduct, a judge may be entitled to the payment of reasonable attorneys' fees by the Commonwealth with the approval of the Supreme Judicial Court as provided by G. L. c. 211C, § 7(15). See SJC Standing Order Regarding Procedure for Judges Seeking a Determination Concerning Attorneys' Fees for Representation in a Matter Before the Commission on Judicial Conduct.

[11B] A judge may accept free or discounted legal representation due to a matter before the Commission on Judicial Conduct upon a determination by the Supreme Judicial Court that such representation would serve the public interest. See SJC Standing Order Regarding Procedure for Judges Seeking a Determination Concerning Attorneys' Fees for Representation in a Matter Before the Commission on Judicial Conduct.

[12] Paragraphs (D) and (E) identify limited instances when, after making a threshold determination that, in the particular circumstances, acceptance of a gift or benefit would not appear to a reasonable person to undermine the judge's independence,* integrity,* or impartiality,* a judge may accept a gift or benefit given for or because of the judge's official position or action. Paragraph (D) identifies instances where the risk of the appearance of a conflict of interest is

so slight that public reporting is not required, while Paragraph (E) identifies instances in which public reporting is required.

[13] Paragraph (D)(1) permits a judge to accept gifts not of substantial value* that are incident to public recognition of the judge. Examples might include plaques, trophies, and certificates. Gifts that are inscribed or personalized may have little market value.

[14] Paragraphs (D)(2) and (D)(3) are intended to encourage judicial participation in the activities of bar associations and other non-profit organizations concerned with the law,* the legal system, and the administration of justice. Judicial participation in such activities promotes professionalism within the legal profession and public confidence in the administration of justice. See, e.g., Rules 1.2, 3.1, and 3.7.

Paragraph (D)(2) encourages judicial participation in bar association activities by permitting judges to attend without charge luncheons, dinners, receptions, award ceremonies, or similar events held in Massachusetts. Unlike the invitations addressed in Rule 3.14, invitations under Paragraph (D)(2) may be accepted without obtaining a determination by the Chief Justice of the court on which the judge sits that acceptance will serve a legitimate public purpose, and that such public purpose outweighs any non-work related benefit to the judge or to the organization providing the waiver of expenses. That is because the judge's attendance at these types of events is presumed to serve such a public purpose.

[15] Paragraph (D)(4) provides that a judge may accept for official use books and other electronic and non-electronic resource materials supplied by publishers on a complimentary basis.

[16] Paragraph (E)(1) permits a judge to accept a gift of substantial value* incident to public recognition of the judge, but requires the judge to publicly report the gift.

[17] Paragraph (E)(2) recognizes that there are instances when it may be appropriate for a judge to accept complimentary invitations for family members or guests so long as the judge publicly reports the gift. For example, a judge receiving an award from a bar association may accept an offer of complimentary tickets to be used by the judge's spouse and children.

Rule 3.14. Reimbursement of Expenses and Waivers of Fees or Charges

(A) Unless otherwise prohibited by Rules 3.1 and 3.13(A) or other law,* a judge may accept reimbursement of necessary and reasonable expenses for travel, food, lodging, or other incidental expenses, or a waiver or partial waiver of fees or charges for registration, tuition, and similar items, from sources other than the judge's employing entity, if the expenses or charges are associated with the judge's participation in extrajudicial activities permitted by this Code.

(B) Reimbursement of expenses for necessary travel, food, lodging, or other incidental expenses shall be limited to the actual costs reasonably incurred by the judge.

(C) If the invitation to the judge is connected to the judge's official position or official action and is not covered by Rule 3.13(D)(2), a judge is required to notify the Chief Justice of the court on which the judge sits and obtain a determination that acceptance of the reimbursement or waiver serves a legitimate public purpose and such purpose outweighs any non-work

related benefit to the judge or to the person or organization providing the payment or waiver of expenses.

Adopted October 8, 2015, effective January 1, 2016.

COMMENT

[1] This Rule applies specifically to a judge's attendance at tuition-waived and expense-paid seminars and similar events that may be sponsored by law-related organizations or by educational, civic, religious, fraternal, and charitable organizations, and is intended to apply to events not described in Rule 3.13(D)(2).

[2] Not infrequently, sponsoring organizations invite certain judges to attend seminars or other events on a fee-waived or partial-fee-waived basis, and sometimes include reimbursement for necessary travel, food, lodging, or other incidental expenses. A judge's decision whether to accept reimbursement of expenses or a waiver or partial waiver of fees or charges in connection with these or other extrajudicial activities must be based upon an assessment of all the circumstances. The judge must undertake a reasonable inquiry to obtain the information necessary to make an informed judgment about whether acceptance would be consistent with the requirements of this Code.

[3] A judge must assure himself or herself that acceptance of reimbursement or fee waivers would not appear to a reasonable person to undermine the judge's independence,* integrity,* or impartiality.* This decision involves consideration of the totality of circumstances, including but not limited to the nature of the sponsor, the source of the funding, whether the sponsor or source of the funding frequently takes positions on issues before or likely to come before the court where the judge sits, and the content of the program or event, including whether differing viewpoints are presented. Where the invitation is associated with any of the judge's non-law-related activities, including educational, religious, fraternal, or civic activities, the judge may accept reimbursement or fee waiver only if the same invitation is offered to similarly-situated non-judges who are engaged in similar ways as the judge.

[4] Paragraph (C) is intended to ensure that a judge obtains a determination from the Chief Justice of the court on which the judge sits that a legitimate public purpose is served by the judge's acceptance of the reimbursement or waiver when the invitation is connected to the judge's official position or official action. In contrast, no such determination is required in the circumstances covered by Rule 3.13(D)(2) because a legitimate public purpose is presumed.

Rule 3.15. Reporting Requirements

(A) A judge shall annually complete the Public Report of Extra–Judicial Income in the form promulgated by the Supreme Judicial Court and the Statement of Financial Interests in the form promulgated by the Massachusetts State Ethics Commission.

(B) The Public Report of Extra–Judicial Income shall require the public reporting of the following items if they are of substantial value*:

(1) compensation received for extrajudicial activities permitted under Rule 3.12; and

(2) gifts and other things of value where disclosure is required by Rule 3.13.

Adopted October 8, 2015, effective January 1, 2016.

CANON 4. A JUDGE SHALL REFRAIN FROM POLITICAL ACTIVITY INCONSISTENT WITH THE INDEPENDENCE,* IMPARTIALITY,* OR INTEGRITY,* OF THE JUDICIARY

Rule 4.1. Political and Campaign Activities

(A) A judge shall not:

(1) act as a leader in, or hold an office in, a political organization*;

(2) make speeches on behalf of a political organization* or candidate;

(3) publicly endorse or oppose a candidate for any public office;

(4) solicit funds for, pay an assessment to, or make a contribution to a political organization* or a candidate for public office; or

(5) attend or purchase tickets for dinners or other events sponsored by a political organization* or a candidate for public office or intended to raise money or gather support for or against a political organization* or candidate.

(B) A judge may engage in activity in support or on behalf of measures to improve the law,* the legal system, or the administration of justice, provided that the judge complies with the other provisions of this Code.

(C) On assuming a judicial office, a judge shall resign any elective public office then held.

Adopted October 8, 2015, effective January 1, 2016.

COMMENT

[1] While judges have the right to participate as citizens in their communities and not be isolated from the society in which they live, judges must at all times act in a manner that promotes public confidence in their independence,* integrity,* and impartiality.* This Rule imposes restrictions on a judge's political activities because public confidence in the judiciary is eroded if judges are perceived to be subject to political influence or give the impression of favoring the interests of a political organization* or candidate.

[2] The restrictions in Paragraph (A) prohibit a judge from engaging in any public display in support of or opposition to a political candidate, including displaying a bumper sticker on an automobile the judge regularly uses, posting a campaign sign outside the judge's residence, signing nomination papers for a political candidate or ballot issue, carrying a campaign sign, distributing campaign literature, or encouraging people to vote for or give money to a particular candidate or political organization.*

[3] A judge may not avoid the restrictions imposed by this Rule by making contributions or endorsements through a spouse, domestic partner,* or other member of the judge's family.* Political contributions by the judge's spouse or domestic partner* must result from that person's independent choice, and checks by which contributions are made must not include the name of the judge.

[4] Although members of the judge's family* are free to engage in their own political activity, including running for public office, a judge must not endorse, appear to endorse, become involved in, or publicly associate with any family member's political activity or campaign for public office.

[5] A judge may register as a member of a political party. A judge may also attend non-partisan events, such as a forum that is open to all candidates and is intended to inform the public.

Rule 4.2. Activities of Judges Who Become Candidates for Nonjudicial Office

(A) Upon becoming a candidate in a primary or general election for elective office, a judge shall resign from judicial office.

(B) Upon becoming a candidate for a nonjudicial appointive office, a judge is not required to resign from judicial office, provided that the judge complies with the other provisions of this Code.

Adopted October 8, 2015, effective January 1, 2016.

COMMENT

[1] The "resign to run" rule set forth in Paragraph (A) ensures that a judge cannot use the judicial office to promote his or her candidacy. When a judge is seeking appointive nonjudicial office, however, the dangers are not sufficient to warrant imposing the "resign to run" rule.

[2] Upon being appointed to any nonjudicial office except as permitted by Rule 3.4, a judge must resign from judicial office.

Rule 3:10. Assignment of Counsel

Section 1. Definitions. The following definitions apply in this rule:

(a) **Available funds**—A party's liquid assets and disposable net monthly income calculated after providing for the party's bail obligations. A party's available funds shall include the liquid assets and disposable net monthly income of the party's spouse (or person in substantially the same relationship), provided that person lives in the same residence as the party and contributes substantially towards the household's basic living costs, unless that person has an adverse interest in the proceeding (e.g. is the victim, complainant, or petitioning party, is a prospective prosecution witness, or, in a civil matter, is a party) or unless the inclusion of the income of the party's spouse would be contrary to the interests of justice.

(b) **Basic living costs**—The average monthly amount spent for reasonable payments toward living costs, such as shelter, food, utilities, health care, transportation, clothing, education, child care, alimony and child support payments, and payments and interest on loans for such living costs.

(c) **Child welfare proceeding**—Where the party is a juvenile, a care and protection proceeding, termination of parental rights proceeding, child requiring assistance proceeding, adoption, guardianship of a minor, or permanency hearing. Where the party is a young adult, a permanency hearing.

(d) **Contribution fee**—A fee imposed by a judge pursuant to Section 10 on a party who has been determined to be indigent but able to contribute. The contribution fee shall not include the indigent counsel fee, but shall be an amount above and beyond the indigent counsel fee that the party is able to pay without substantial financial hardship for the cost of any attorney appointed to represent the party.

(e) **Disposable net monthly income**—The income remaining each month after deducting income taxes, social security and Medicare taxes, ordinary retirement contributions, union dues, and basic living costs.

(f) **Income**—Salary, wages, interest, dividends, rental income, and other earnings and regular cash payments, such as amounts received from pensions, annuities, social security, alimony, and child support. Irregular or infrequent income (e.g., earnings from day labor, seasonal, or on-call work) that a party can reasonably be expected to receive shall count as income under this rule. Irregular or infrequent income that cannot reasonably be anticipated to continue shall not count as income.

(g) **Indigency verification process**—The attempt by probation to verify a claim of indigency, in accordance with G. L. c. 211D, § 2A(c), by a party or, where appropriate, a parent or guardian, by accessing wage, tax, and asset information in the possession of the Department of Revenue, information regarding benefits received from the Department of Transitional Assistance, and any information relevant to the determination of indigency in the possession of the Registry of Motor Vehicles.

(h) **Indigent**—A party who is:

(i) receiving one of the following types of public assistance: Transitional Aid to Families with Dependent Children (TAFDC), Emergency Aid to Elderly, Disabled and Children (EAEDC), need-based veterans' benefits, Supplemental Nutrition Assistance Program (SNAP) benefits, Refugee Cash Assistance, or SSI State Supplemental Program;

(ii) receiving an annual income, after taxes, of one hundred twenty-five percent or less of the current poverty guidelines referred to in G. L. c. 261, § 27A(b);

(iii)(1) residing in a tuberculosis treatment center, a mental health facility or a facility for individuals with intellectual or developmental disabilities, including the Bridgewater State Hospital and Massachusetts Treatment Center; or (2) the subject of a proceeding regarding admission or commitment to such a center or facility, a proceeding to make a substituted judgment determination concerning treatment, a proceeding under G. L. c. 190B, § 5–309(g) to admit to a nursing facility defined in G. L. c. 190B, § 5–101(15), or a civil commitment proceeding under G. L. c. 123, § 35; provided, however, that when the judge has reason to believe that the party is not indigent, a determination of indigency shall be made in accordance with Section 5 and other applicable provisions of this rule; or

(iv) a juvenile, a child who is in the care or custody of the Department of Children and Families, or a young adult provided, however, that when a judge has reason to believe that the juvenile or young adult is not indigent, a determination of indigency shall be made in accordance with Section 5 and other applicable provisions of this rule.

(i) **Indigent but able to contribute**—A party who is:

(i) has an annual income, after taxes, of more than one hundred twenty five percent and less than two hundred fifty percent of the current poverty guidelines referred to in G. L. c. 261, § 27A(b), or

(ii)(1) is charged with a felony solely within the jurisdiction of the Superior Court or is the parent, guardian, or custodian of a juvenile or young adult who is the subject of a child welfare proceeding, subject to the exception in Section 6A for a parent or guardian who has had custody of the juvenile removed by a court of competent jurisdiction, or who has an interest adverse to the juvenile or young adult, and (2) has an annual income, after taxes, of more than two hundred fifty percent of the current poverty guidelines referred to in G. L. c. 261, § 27A(b); and (3) whose available funds are insufficient to pay the anticipated cost of counsel for this representation, but are sufficient to pay part of that cost. The anticipated cost of counsel shall be the cost of retaining private counsel for, as applicable, the defense of a felony charge within the jurisdiction of the Superior Court, or a child welfare proceeding, as estimated and published from time to time by the Committee for Public Counsel Services; or

(iii) is over the age of eighteen and is claimed as a dependent for tax purposes by a parent or guardian who is not indigent.

(j) **Indigent counsel fee**—A fee assessed on a person provided counsel pursuant to G. L. c. 211D, § 2A(f).

(k) **Intake report**—The report provided to the judge by probation regarding the party's or, where appropriate, the party's parents' or guardians', responses to biographical and financial questions asked by probation.

(*l*) **Juvenile**—A child under the age of 18 who is the subject of a child welfare proceeding or a delinquency or youthful offender proceeding.

(m) **Juvenile legal fee**—The fee assessed on a parent or guardian to pay for the cost of any attorney appointed to represent a party under the age of 18. The fee shall not exceed the fee set forth in G.L. c. 119, § 29A or G.L. c. 119, § 39F.

(n) **Liquid assets**—Cash, savings accounts, bank accounts, stocks, bonds, certificates of deposit, equity in real estate, and equity in a motor vehicle or other tangible property, provided that any equity in real or personal property is reasonably convertible to cash. Any motor vehicle necessary to maintain employment, including travel to and from the party's employment, shall not be considered a liquid asset. Expenses associated with the liquidation of assets, including penalties for early withdrawal and tax burdens, shall not be included as available funds.

(o) **Party**—Any person who may be entitled to the appointment of counsel in relation to any court proceeding on the basis of indigency under the law of the Commonwealth.

(p) **Probation**—The Office of the Commissioner of Probation or any member of its staff.

(q) **Young adult**—A person between the ages of 18 and 22 who is the subject of a child welfare proceeding.

Section 2. Advice as to Right to Counsel.

If any party to a proceeding appears in court without counsel where the party has a right to be represented by counsel under the law of the Commonwealth, the judge shall advise the party or, if the party is a juvenile, the party and a parent or legal guardian, where appropriate, that: (a) the party may be entitled to the appointment of counsel at public expense; and (b) the Committee for Public Counsel Services will provide counsel to the party at no cost or at a reduced cost if the court finds that the party wants but cannot afford counsel.

Section 3. Waiver of Counsel.

If the party elects to proceed without counsel, the party shall sign a written waiver and the judge shall certify in writing that the party executed the waiver in the judge's presence after the judge informed the party of the right of counsel. If the party elects to proceed without counsel but refuses to sign the written waiver, the judge shall so certify in writing.

Before allowing a waiver of counsel, the judge, after conducting a colloquy with the party, shall make written findings that the party is competent to waive counsel and that the party has knowingly and voluntarily elected to proceed without counsel.

Section 4. Standby Counsel.

Notwithstanding a party's waiver of counsel, where the interests of justice so require, the judge may assign standby counsel to assist the party in the course of the proceedings regardless of whether the party is indigent.

Section 5. Determination of Indigency Status.

(a) If the party requests appointment of counsel, or if counsel is appointed under Section 6 or 6A of this rule, or if the judge for any reason finds that the party has not knowingly and voluntarily elected to proceed without counsel, probation shall provide the judge with an intake report. Probation shall attempt to verify the self-reported information on the intake report through the indigency verification process.

(b) Unless the party is a juvenile, or is a person over eighteen who is claimed as a dependent for tax purposes, probation shall make a recommendation as to the indigency of the party. Where the party is a juvenile, probation shall make a recommendation as to the indigency of the parents or guardian in accordance with Sections 1, 6 and 6A of this rule and G.L. c. 119, §§ 29A and 39F. Where a person over eighteen is claimed as a dependent for tax purposes, probation shall make a recommendation as to the indigency of the parents or guardian.

(c) After reviewing the intake report and recommendation and questioning the party, as appropriate, the judge shall make a determination that:

  (i) the party is indigent,

  (ii) the party is indigent but able to contribute, or

  (iii) the party is not indigent.

The clerk shall enter the judge's determination on the court docket.

(d) In order to determine a party's current financial status, the judge shall evaluate (1) the party's income in the current calendar quarter (i.e., January–March, April–June, July–September, October–December), and (2) the party's income in the three preceding calendar quarters.

(e) Any party seeking appointment of counsel shall bear the burden of proving indigency by a preponderance of the evidence.

(f) Even where a party meets or fails to meet the definitions of "indigent" or "indigent but able to contribute," the judge retains the discretion to determine that the interests of justice require a different determination based on the party's available funds in relation to the party's basic living costs, or special circumstances, or both. A judge may consider, for example, receipt of Medicaid benefits as one factor in assessing whether the interests of justice would require a different determination. Where a judge exercises this discretion, the judge shall set forth on the record the reason for doing so.

Section 6. Assignment of Counsel/Notice of Assignment.

If under Section 5 the judge finds that a party is indigent or indigent but able to contribute, the judge shall assign the Committee for Public Counsel Services to provide representation for the party, unless exceptional circumstances, supported by written findings, necessitate a different procedure that is consistent with G. L. c. 211D and the rules of the Supreme Judicial Court. The clerk or register shall promptly notify the party of the assignment of counsel.

If a judge has determined that a party is not indigent, and the party after a reasonable time has not waived counsel, procured counsel, or petitioned for the appointment of counsel on the ground that, despite reasonable efforts, the party has been unable to afford the cost of counsel, the case may be ordered to proceed without appointed counsel. In proceedings where there is an entitlement to the appointment of counsel pursuant to General Laws, chapter 111, §§ 94C and 94G, chapter 123, chapter 123A, and chapter 190B, the judge shall appoint counsel immediately upon the filing of a petition and entry of any requisite findings. If, before the hearing, the judge determines that the party is not indigent, assigned counsel may be dismissed, and the party shall be advised to retain private counsel without delay; provided, however, that the judge shall authorize the continued services of appointed counsel at public expense where the interests of justice so require. The interests of justice may require such appointment if, for example, the party is incompetent to obtain counsel, unable to access funds, or unable to retain counsel. If, after the hearing has commenced, the judge determines that the party is not indigent, appointed counsel shall continue to represent the party and the judge may order the party to reimburse the Commonwealth for the cost of counsel.

Section 6A. Assignment of Counsel for Juveniles.

All juveniles, regardless of the financial status of their parents or guardians, shall be entitled to the appointment of counsel. Unless the juvenile is represented by retained private counsel, the judge shall assign the Committee for Public Counsel Services to represent the juvenile in accordance with Section 6. If the juvenile is provided with appointed counsel and the judge determines that the juvenile's parent or legal guardian is not indigent, the judge shall assess the juvenile legal fee against the parent or guardian as payment toward the cost of counsel supplied by the Committee for Public Counsel Services. If the parent or guardian is determined to be indigent but able to contribute, the court shall order the parent or guardian to pay a reasonable amount toward the cost of appointed counsel, provided that the amount shall not exceed the juvenile legal fee and shall not cause substantial financial hardship. This section shall not apply to a parent or guardian who has had custody of the juvenile removed by a court of competent jurisdiction, or who has an interest adverse to the juvenile. The failure of a juvenile's parent or guardian to pay any fee assessed under this Section shall not be grounds for withholding or revoking the juvenile's appointed counsel.

Section 7.   Review of Indigency Determination.

(a) The judge may review indigency status at any stage of a proceeding if information regarding a change in financial circumstances is obtained by probation through the indigency verification process or from some other source, including the party.

(b) There shall be a right to an evidentiary hearing to reconsider the judge's findings and determination as to the party's entitlement to appointed counsel. The judge shall schedule the evidentiary hearing promptly after it is requested. If requested by the party, the judge shall appoint counsel to represent the party at the evidentiary hearing. Before the hearing, the judge shall provide the party with a copy of probation's intake report and recommendation described in Section 5(a) and any records in the court's possession relating to the party's financial status. The judge may issue any protective orders needed to protect the privacy of the party or any third parties. The party shall have the opportunity to introduce any relevant evidence and to call witnesses to testify. The party shall bear the burden of proving indigency by a preponderance of the evidence. At the conclusion of the hearing, the judge shall make written findings regarding whether the party is entitled to appointed counsel. These findings shall be part of the case record and maintained in the official file of the case.

Section 8. Inadmissibility of Information Obtained from a party.

(a) No information provided by a party pursuant to this rule may be used in any proceeding against the party except in a prosecution for perjury or contempt committed in providing such information or at an evidentiary hearing conducted under Section 7(b).

(b) No party shall be asked or required to provide any information regarding his or her immigration or citizenship status as part of intake, indigency determination, or verification.

Section 9.   Counsel for parties who are indigent or indigent but able to contribute.

(a) **Appearance of Counsel.** Counsel assigned by the Committee for Public Counsel Services to represent a party pursuant to this rule shall file an appearance within forty-eight hours after receipt of notification of the assignment.

(b) **Withdrawal of Appearance.** If counsel assigned by the Committee for Public Counsel Services has filed an appearance and is unable or unwilling to represent a party, counsel shall move to withdraw the appearance. If the judge allows the motion for withdrawal, the clerk or register shall immediately notify the Committee for Public Counsel Services to make a new assignment of counsel.

Section 10.   Contribution toward Cost of Counsel.

(a) If a judge determines that a party is indigent, the judge may not order, require, or solicit the party to make any payment toward the cost of counsel, except for an indigent counsel fee. The indigent counsel fee shall be waived where a judge, after the indigency verification process, determines that the party is unable without substantial financial hardship to pay the indigent counsel fee within 180 days. Where the indigent counsel fee is not waived, the judge may authorize the party to perform community service in lieu of payment of the indigent counsel fee in accordance with G. L. c. 211D, § 2A(g). The clerk shall enter the judge's determination on the court docket.

(b) If a judge determines that a party is indigent but able to contribute, the judge shall order the party to pay the indigent counsel fee plus a contribution fee based on the financial circumstances of the party, provided that the amount of the contribution fee shall not cause substantial financial hardship. The party shall be given an opportunity to be heard and to present information, including witness affidavits or testimony, regarding whether the contribution fee would cause substantial financial hardship.

(c) If a party over the age of eighteen is determined to be indigent but able to contribute under Section 1(h)(iii) because the party is claimed as a dependent for tax purposes by a parent or guardian who is not indigent, the contribution fee shall be based on the financial circumstances of the parent or guardian. The parent or guardian shall be solely responsible for paying any contribution fee assessed under this subsection.

Section 11.   Collection of Fees and Contributions.

(a) All payments toward the cost of counsel, including the indigent counsel fee, the contribution fee, and the juvenile legal fee, shall be made to the office of the clerk of court and shall be deposited with the State Treasurer in accordance with law.

(b) The clerk shall inform the judge at each court event for a case whether the party has failed to pay an indigent counsel fee or contribution fee. If the party has failed to pay an indigent counsel fee or contribution fee within sixty days of appointment of counsel, the clerk, unless otherwise ordered by the judge, shall report the unpaid amount to the Department of Revenue, the Department of Transitional Assistance, and the Registry of Motor Vehicles as required by G. L. c. 211D, § 2A.

(c) The failure of a party, parent, or guardian to pay an indigent counsel fee, a contribution fee, or a juvenile legal fee shall not be grounds for withholding or revoking appointed counsel.

(d) Probation shall not be responsible for monitoring or enforcing payment of any indigent counsel fee, contribution fee, or juvenile legal fee.

(e) No party may be subject to incarceration for failing to pay an indigent counsel fee or a contribution fee.

Amended July 1, 1993, effective October 1, 1993; July 20, 2016, effective November 1, 2016.

Rule 3:11. Committee On Judicial Ethics

(1) **Structure.** There shall be a Committee on Judicial Ethics (Committee) to render opinions concerning the Code of Judicial Conduct, S. J. C. Rule 3:09. The Committee shall consist of five persons appointed by this court at least three of whom shall be active or retired judges. No Justice currently serving on this court shall be a member of the Committee. This court shall designate one member as Chairperson and one court employee to serve as the staff counsel to the Committee.

Committee members shall be appointed to three-year terms, but the length of a member's initial term may be shorter to create staggered terms among the members. Members may be reappointed to the Committee, but no member shall be appointed to more than two successive full terms. The members of the Committee shall serve without compensation but shall be reimbursed for necessary expenses incurred in the performance of their official duties. A member whose term has expired shall remain on the Committee pending appointment of his or her successor, and until the successor's term begins.

(2) **Requests By Individual Judges.**

A. The Committee shall render Informal Opinions and Letter Opinions with respect to the interpretation of the Code of Judicial Conduct. The Committee shall provide opinions with respect to conduct contemplated by judges, but shall not render opinions on hypothetical questions, questions relating solely to past conduct, questions relating to the conduct of persons other than the requestor, or on issues pending before a court, agency, or commission, including the Commission on Judicial Conduct. The Committee may decline to render an opinion for any reasons that it deems sufficient. The Committee may also issue Emergency Opinions to offer guidance to judges faced unexpectedly with questions within the Committee's jurisdiction that require an immediate response.

B. *Who May Request.* A request for an Informal Opinion, a Letter Opinion, or an Emergency Opinion may be made by a judge, a person who has been nominated to be a judge, or a former judge to whom provisions of the Code of Judicial Conduct apply.

C. *Confidentiality.* All requests for advice and all of the Committee's proceedings thereon, shall be strictly confidential unless the Supreme Judicial Court requires disclosure or the Committee determines that disclosure is necessary to prevent or remedy a serious injury to person, property or the administration of justice. Published Informal and Letter Opinions shall not include the name of the judge requesting the opinion and any other identifying information without the judge's consent.

D. *Procedure for Requesting Informal Opinions, Letter Opinions, and Emergency Opinions.*

i. Informal Opinions. A judge may request an Informal Opinion by making an oral or written request to the Committee's staff counsel. Upon making a request for an Informal Opinion, the requesting judge shall be told that in contrast to a Letter Opinion, an Informal Opinion does not carry with it the protection from discipline described in paragraph 2(D)(ii). However, a judge's reliance on an Informal Opinion would be considered as a mitigating factor in any disciplinary proceeding, so long as the judge did not omit or misstate any material fact in the request for an opinion. The Committee may provide an Informal Opinion if the answer to the judge's request may be found in a previously published Informal or Letter Opinion or an Ethics Advisory or is otherwise reasonably clear. An Informal Opinion may be given orally or in writing. If the Committee determines that the answer is unsettled, the Committee shall inform the requestor, and indicate that the Committee will act only in response to a written request for a Letter Opinion. The Committee may publish an Informal Opinion if the Committee concludes that the advice contained in the Informal Opinion will be useful to other judges, but shall redact the name of the judge and any other identifying information unless the judge has consented to its inclusion.

ii. Letter Opinions. A judge may request a Letter Opinion by making a written request to the Committee's staff counsel. The written request shall set forth fully all facts bearing on the question or questions on which the judge seeks advice. A Letter Opinion requires agreement among a majority of the Committee. Each Letter Opinion shall contain a statement of the facts and a discussion of the application of the relevant rules to the facts. If the judge did not omit or misstate any material fact in the request for an opinion, the judge may rely on a Letter Opinion until and unless revised or revoked. A judge shall not be disciplined for conduct undertaken in reasonable reliance on a Letter Opinion issued to that judge pursuant to this rule. The Committee shall publish Letter Opinions, but shall redact the name of the judge and any other identifying information unless the judge has consented to its inclusion.

iii. Emergency Letter Opinions. Where a judge seeks the protection of a Letter Opinion but is faced unexpectedly with questions within the committee's jurisdiction that require an immediate response, staff counsel with the approval of at least two members of the Committee may give advice on an emergency basis. The request for advice shall set forth fully all facts bearing on the question or questions on which the judge seeks advice, and whenever possible, shall be in writing. The emergency advice will be given in writing. Emergency advice shall be submitted to the full Committee for action. If the Committee agrees with the advice given, it will issue a confirming Letter Opinion to the requestor. If it disagrees, it will issue a Letter Opinion to the requestor setting forth the emergency advice that was given so that the judge will have the benefit of the protection of a Letter Opinion given by this rule as to conduct undertaken in reliance on that advice, but it will also set forth the view of the full Committee on the issue presented. A Letter Opinion will supersede all inconsistent emergency advice.

(3) **Requests by Organizations or Associations of Judges or Lawyers.** An organization or association composed of judges or lawyers (e.g., Massachusetts Judges Conference, Flaschner Judicial Institute, bar associations) may request an Informal Opinion concerning contemplated conduct by making an oral or written request to the Committee's staff counsel. The request may not pose a question on behalf of a specific

judge. The Committee may decline to render an opinion for any reasons that it deems sufficient. The Committee may give an Informal Opinion orally or in writing. All requests for advice, and all of the Committee's proceedings thereon, shall be strictly confidential unless the Supreme Judicial Court requires disclosure or the Committee determines that disclosure is necessary to prevent or remedy a serious injury to person, property or the administration of justice. The Committee may publish an Informal Opinion if the Committee concludes that the advice contained in the Informal Opinion will be useful to judges or lawyers, but shall redact the name of the requestor unless the requestor consents to its publication.

(4) **Ethics Advisories.** The Justices of the Supreme Judicial Court may on their own initiative or when a request is made issue an Ethics Advisory to clarify the meaning and application of any provision of the Code of Judicial Conduct, and to expound upon provisions of the Code that are of broad interest and application. An Ethics Advisory may be requested by any judge, lawyer, or organization or association of judges or lawyers (e.g., Massachusetts Judges Conference, Flaschner Judicial Institute, and bar associations). Prior receipt of an Informal or Letter Opinion does not preclude a request for an Ethics Advisory. A request for an Ethics Advisory may pose questions related to past or hypothetical conduct. The court may decline to render an Ethics Advisory for any reasons that it deems sufficient. An Ethics Advisory supersedes all inconsistent Informal Opinions and Letter Opinions, but a judge shall not be disciplined for conduct undertaken in reasonable reliance on a Letter Opinion issued to that judge before the issuance and publication of an Ethics Advisory.

(5) **Other Duties.** The Committee shall adopt Rules of the Committee as necessary, subject to the approval of this court, to implement this rule. Each year, the Committee shall submit to the court a report of its activities, together with any recommendations for amendments to the Code of Conduct or the Committee's rules.

Adopted March 31, 1988, effective September 1, 1988. Amended effective February 1, 1991; amended May 3, 2002, effective May 20, 2002; November 5, 2002, effective December 2, 2002; December 17, 2008, effective January 1, 2009; October 20, 2015, effective January 1, 2016; amended effective November 21, 2016.

RULES OF THE COMMITTEE ON JUDICIAL ETHICS

1. **Requests for Opinions and Informal Advice.** A judge seeking advice from the Committee on Judicial Ethics should contact Supreme Judicial Court Senior Attorney Barbara F. Berenson, counsel to the Committee, at Barbara.Berenson@sjc.state.ma.us or 617-557-1048.

A request for an Informal Opinion may be made via email or phone. A request for a Letter Opinion (formerly known as an Advisory Opinion) must be in writing (email preferred, but a judge may alternatively send a letter to Attorney Barbara Berenson, Supreme Judicial Court, John Adams Courthouse, One Pemberton Square, Boston, MA 02108). A judge or any other person or organization seeking an Ethics Advisory from the Supreme Judicial Court should also contact Barbara Berenson.

2. **Form of Request for Advisory Opinion.** The letter should be signed by the judge (or nominee) requesting the advice and should set forth fully all facts bearing on the question or questions on which he requests advice. Because Supreme Judicial Court Rule 3:11(2) precludes the committee from rendering opinions "on issues pending before a court, agency, or commission, including the Judicial Conduct Commission," the request should contain an affirmation that, to the best of the information and belief of the judge (or nominee) requesting the opinion, no issue raised thereby, whether in reference to himself or to any other person, is presently pending before any court, agency, or commission.

3. **Scope of Question.** Under Supreme Judicial Court Rule 3:11, advisory opinion requests must relate "to the interpretation of rules of court relating to the ethical and professional conduct of judges." The committee will not render opinions on hypothetical questions nor upon questions relating to the conduct of persons other than the requesting judge (or nominee).

4. **Advisory Opinions.** Opinions of the committee require the affirmative vote of at least three members and, except for emergency opinions, will be rendered in writing. The committee may publish its opinions but the name of the judge (or nominee) requesting the opinion and any other identifying information shall not be included in a published opinion unless the requester consents to such inclusion. Pursuant to Supreme Judicial Court Rule 3:11(3), if "the judge did not omit or misstate any material fact in his request for an opinion, the judge may rely on a written opinion until and unless revised or revoked."

5. **Emergency Opinions.** To offer guidance to judges faced unexpectedly with questions within the committee's jurisdiction that require an immediate response, the secretary with the approval of two members of the committee, or the chairperson or vice-chairperson with the concurrence of one other member of the committee, may give advice on an emergency basis. Whenever possible, the request for advice shall be in writing. The emergency advice will be given orally or in writing, as seems appropriate. Emergency advice shall be submitted to the full committee for action. If the committee agrees with the advice given, it will issue a written confirming opinion to the inquirer. If it disagrees, it will issue a written opinion to the inquirer setting forth the emergency advice that was given so that the judge will have the benefit of the protection given by S.J.C. Rule 3:11(3) as to conduct undertaken in reliance on that advice, but it will also set forth the view of the full committee on the issue presented. The view of the full committee will supersede all inconsistent emergency advice.

6. **Informal Advice.** To provide informal guidance to judges (or nominees) who orally request advice, the committee may also give advice as follows: (A) Upon receiving an oral request for advice, the secretary shall tell the requesting judge (or nominee) that informal, unwritten advice from the committee does not carry with it the protection described in S.J.C. Rule 3:11(3), and that the judge (or nominee) is free to submit to the committee a written request for an opinion. If the

judge (or nominee) elects to proceed with a request for informal advice, the secretary shall present the request to the committee. (B) If the committee concludes that the answer to the request can be found in one of its previously published opinions or is otherwise reasonably clear, the committee, through the secretary, may respond orally to the requesting judge (or nominee) with informal advice, and shall remind the judge (or nominee) that such advice does not come with the protection described in Rule 3:11(3). If the committee determines that the answer is unclear, the committee, through the secretary, shall so inform the requesting judge (or nominee) and shall indicate that the committee will act only in response to a written request for an opinion. (C) The secretary shall maintain a record of all requests for informal advice and committee responses thereto. (D) The committee may elect to treat any request for informal advice as a request for an emergency opinion and may proceed in accordance with rule 5.

7. Decision to Refuse Opinion or Advice. In addition to the reasons stated in rules 1, 2, 3 and 6, the committee may decline to render an opinion or provide informal advice for any other reason which it deems sufficient.

8. Confidentiality. All requests to the committee for advisory opinions, emergency opinions, and informal advice, and all committee proceedings thereon, shall be confidential as provided by S.J.C. Rule 3:11(6).

RULE 3:12.   CODE OF PROFESSIONAL RESPONSIBILITY FOR CLERKS OF THE COURTS

Table of Canons

Canon 1.   Purpose and Applicability

This Code shall be known as the "Code of Professional Responsibility for Clerks of the Courts of the Commonwealth of Massachusetts." Its purpose is to define norms of conduct and practice appropriate to persons serving in the positions covered by the Code and thereby to contribute to the preservation of public confidence in the integrity, impartiality, and independence of the courts.

The word "Clerk-Magistrate" in this Code, unless otherwise expressly provided, shall mean anyone serving in the position of Clerk-Magistrate, Clerk, Register, Recorder, Assistant Clerk-Magistrate, Assistant Clerk, Assistant Register, or Deputy Recorder, Judicial Case Manager or Assistant Judicial Case Manager in the Supreme Judicial Court, the Appeals Court, or a Department of the Trial Court of the Commonwealth, whether elected or appointed, and whether serving in a permanent or temporary capacity. The words "elected Clerk-Magistrate" shall also include a person who is appointed to complete the term of an elected Clerk-Magistrate. The word "court" in this Code shall mean the Supreme Judicial Court, the Appeals Court, a particular division of a Department of the Trial Court, or a particular Department of the Trial Court if the Department does not have divisions.

Adopted February 9, 1990, effective April 1, 1990. Amended December 17, 2012, effective January 1, 2013.

Canon 2.   Compliance With Statutes and Rules of Court

A Clerk-Magistrate shall comply with the laws of the Commonwealth, rules of court, and lawful directives of the several judicial authorities of the Commonwealth. The words "judicial authorities" in this Code, unless otherwise expressly provided, shall mean the Justices of the Supreme Judicial Court and Appeals Court, the Chief Administrative Justice of the Trial Court, the Administrative Justices of the several Departments of the Trial Court, or Associate Justices of the Trial Court, as is appropriate under the circumstances. A Clerk Magistrate shall also comply with the lawful directives of the Court Administrator.

Adopted February 9, 1990, effective April 1, 1990. Amended December 17, 2012, effective January 1, 2013.

Canon 3.   Performance of Duties

A Clerk-Magistrate shall devote the entire time during normal court hours to the duties of his or her office, but may, according to established procedures, participate during that time in law-related educational and public service activities. An elected Clerk-Magistrate may participate during ordinary court hours in activities reasonably related to his or her duties as an elected Clerk-Magistrate. A Clerk Magistrate shall not engage in the practice of law, except that a Clerk Magistrate may act pro se and may, without compensation, give legal advice to and draft or review documents for a member of the Clerk Magistrate's family, but may not serve as the family member's lawyer in any forum. Also, a Clerk Magistrate may serve as a judge advocate general in the context of service in the United States Armed Forces, the reserve components of the United States Armed Forces, or the National Guard.

(A) Adjudicative and Administrative Responsibilities. In the performance of adjudicative and administrative responsibilities, the following additional standards shall apply:

(1) A Clerk-Magistrate shall be faithful to the law and maintain professional competence in it as it relates to the performance of his or her duties. A Clerk-Magistrate shall not be swayed by partisan interests, public clamor, or fear of criticism.

(2) A Clerk-Magistrate should seek to maintain order and decorum in proceedings.

(3) A Clerk-Magistrate should be patient, dignified, and courteous to litigants, jurors, witnesses, lawyers, and others in official dealings, and should require similar conduct of those subject to his or her direction and control.

(4) A Clerk-Magistrate shall accord to every person who is legally so entitled the right to be heard in a proceeding in person or through his or her lawyer. A Clerk Magistrate may make reasonable efforts to facilitate the ability of all litigants, including self-represented litigants, to be fairly heard.

(5) A Clerk-Magistrate should diligently carry out his or her responsibilities and should dispose of them promptly.

(6) A Clerk-Magistrate shall facilitate public access to court records that, by law or court rule, are available to the public and shall take appropriate steps to safeguard the security and confidentiality of court records that are not open to the public.

(7) A Clerk-Magistrate may explain his or her own decisions made in the course of his or her official duties and may explain for public information the procedures of the court and the applicability of those procedures in particular circumstances. A Clerk-Magistrate should otherwise abstain from public comment about any pending or impending proceeding in any court, and should require similar abstention by subordinate court personnel.

(B) Administrative Responsibilities. A Clerk-Magistrate should diligently discharge administrative responsibilities, maintain professional competence in judicial administration, and facilitate the performance of the administrative responsibilities of other court officials. In so doing, a Clerk-Magistrate should be cognizant of the need to employ efficient, businesslike methods and sound practices. A Clerk-Magistrate should organize and manage the business of the Clerk-Magistrate's Office with a view to the prompt and convenient dispatch of the business of the court. A Clerk-Magistrate should supervise subordinate personnel and arrange for their training. A Clerk-Magistrate shall make personnel appointments on the basis of merit, and in compliance with applicable personnel standards.

Adopted February 9, 1990, effective April 1, 1990. Amended January 24, 2018, effective March 1, 2018.

Canon 4. Impartiality and Disqualification

A Clerk-Magistrate shall perform the duties of Clerk-Magistrate impartially and should act at all times in a manner that promotes public confidence in the integrity and impartiality of the judicial branch of government.

(A) Appearance of Impartiality. A Clerk-Magistrate shall not convey the impression that any person is in a special position to influence the Clerk-Magistrate, and the Clerk-Magistrate should discourage others from suggesting that they are in a position to exert such influence.

(B) Personal Affairs. A Clerk-Magistrate shall conduct personal affairs in such a way as not to cause public disrespect for the court and the judicial system. A Clerk-Magistrate shall not engage in activities nor incur obligations which would tend to detract from the dignity of the Clerk-Magistrate's office or interfere or appear to interfere with official duty. A Clerk-Magistrate shall not engage in outside activities which would cast doubt on his or her capacity to decide impartially any issue that may come before the Clerk-Magistrate in any official capacity.

(C) Business Activities. A Clerk-Magistrate shall not enter into any business relationship which reasonably might create a conflict with the proper performance of his or her official duty or detract from the dignity of the office. A Clerk-Magistrate shall not use the influence of the office to promote his or her business interests or those of others.

(D) Activities to Improve the Law. A Clerk-Magistrate may use his or her title to engage in activity to improve the law, the legal system, or the administration of justice. A Clerk-Magistrate may appear at public hearings and may otherwise consult with governmental bodies or officials on such matters.

(E) Disqualification. A Clerk-Magistrate should disqualify himself or herself from serving in an adjudicative capacity in a proceeding in which the Clerk-Magistrate's impartiality might reasonably be questioned. A Clerk-Magistrate who would be so disqualified may, instead of withdrawing from the proceeding, disclose on the record the basis of disqualification. If, based on such disclosure, the parties, individually or through counsel, after consultation independent of the Clerk-Magistrate, agree in writing that the Clerk-Magistrate need not be disqualified, the Clerk-Magistrate may participate in the proceeding. The agreement, signed by all parties, shall be incorporated in the record of the proceeding.

Adopted February 9, 1990, effective April 1, 1990.

Canon 5. Outside Activities

A Clerk-Magistrate shall regulate outside and personal activities to minimize the risk of conflict with official duties:

(A) Personal Conduct. A Clerk-Magistrate should not engage in activities which might detract from the dignity of the office of Clerk-Magistrate or interfere with the performance of the duties of the office.

(B) Civic and Charitable Activities. A Clerk-Magistrate may participate in civic and charitable activities that do not reflect adversely on the Clerk-Magistrate's impartiality or interfere with the performance of his or her official duties. A Clerk-Magistrate may serve as an officer, director, trustee, or non-legal advisor of an educational, religious, charitable, fraternal, or civic organization not conducted for the economic or political advantage of its members, subject to the following limitations:

(1) A Clerk-Magistrate shall not participate if there is a substantial likelihood that the organization, or a significant number of members of the organization, will be engaged in proceedings that would ordinarily come before the Clerk-Magistrate or the court in which the Clerk-Magistrate serves.

(2) A Clerk-Magistrate may solicit funds for any educational, religious, charitable, fraternal, or civic organization, but shall not use or permit the use of the prestige of the office for that purpose or solicit his or her staff for that purpose. A Clerk-Magistrate, however, may call his or her employees' attention to a general fund raising campaign such as the Commonwealth of Massachusetts Employees Campaign. Except as provided in paragraph (3), a Clerk Magistrate may attend but, except for an elected Clerk Magistrate, shall not be a speaker or the guest of honor at an organization's fund raising event. A Clerk-Magistrate may be listed as an officer, director, or trustee of such an organization.

(3) A Clerk Magistrate may serve as a keynote or featured speaker at, receive an award or other comparable recognition at, be featured on the program of, and permit the Clerk Magistrate's title to be used in connection with the promotion of a fundraising event only if the event is sponsored by an organization concerned with the law, the legal system, or the administration of justice, and that organization promotes the general interests of the judicial branch of government or the legal profession, including enhancing the diversity and professionalism of the bar.

(C) Financial Activities.

(1) A Clerk-Magistrate shall not conduct outside business activities in the courthouse at any time nor shall a Clerk-

Magistrate conduct any outside business activities anywhere during normal court hours. A Clerk-Magistrate shall refrain from financial and business dealings that tend to reflect adversely on the Clerk-Magistrate's impartiality, interfere with the proper performance of the position of Clerk-Magistrate, or involve the Clerk-Magistrate in transactions with lawyers or other persons likely to come before the court in which the Clerk-Magistrate is serving.

(2) Subject to the limitations of subsection 5(C)(1) and subsection 4(C) of this Code, a Clerk-Magistrate may hold and manage investments, including real estate, and engage in other remunerative activity.

(D) Fiduciary Activities.

(1) A Clerk-Magistrate shall not serve as an executor, administrator, trustee, guardian, or other fiduciary, except for the estate, trust, or person of a member of his or her family, and then only if such service will not interfere with the proper performance of the Clerk-Magistrate's duties. "Member of his or her family" includes a spouse, child, grandchild, parent, grandparent, or other relative or person with whom the Clerk-Magistrate maintains or maintained a close familial relationship. As a family fiduciary, a Clerk-Magistrate is subject to the following restrictions:

(a) A Clerk-Magistrate shall not serve in any fiduciary capacity if it is likely that as a fiduciary the Clerk-Magistrate will be engaged in proceedings that would ordinarily come before the Clerk-Magistrate in a decision-making capacity and shall resign as a fiduciary if the estate, trust, or ward becomes involved in adversary proceedings in the court in which he or she is serving.

(b) While acting as a fiduciary, a Clerk-Magistrate is subject to the same restrictions on financial activities that apply to the Clerk-Magistrate in his or her personal capacity.

(2) A Clerk-Magistrate may serve as an executor, administrator, trustee, guardian, or other fiduciary for the estate, trust, or person of one who is not a member of his or her family provided that the Clerk-Magistrate was acting in the fiduciary position prior to April 1, 1990, or that, in the case of a will designating the Clerk-Magistrate as a fiduciary, the testator or testatrix died prior to April 1, 1990. Such fiduciary activity shall not be permitted if it interferes with the proper performance of the Clerk-Magistrate's duties and shall be subject to the provisions of subsections 5(D)(1)(a) and (b) of this Code.

(E) Appointments. Except for activities to improve the law, the legal system, or the administration of justice, as permitted by Canon 4(D), a Clerk-Magistrate shall not accept appointment within the geographical jurisdiction of the court in which he or she serves to a governmental committee, commission or other governmental position if there is a substantial likelihood that matters involving that committee, commission or other governmental position will come before the Clerk-Magistrate or the court in which the Clerk-Magistrate serves. A Clerk-Magistrate may, however, represent the United States, the Commonwealth of Massachusetts, or a locality on ceremonial occasions or in connection with historical, educational, armed services and cultural activities.

(F) Free or Discounted Legal Services. A Clerk-Magistrate may accept free or discounted legal services: 1) from a relative or close personal friend whose appearance in a matter would require the Clerk Magistrate's disqualification if the lawyer is a sole practitioner or at a firm where all the lawyers are relatives or close personal friends of the Clerk Magistrate; 2) when a lawyer or law firm has offered special pricing or a discount as part of a commercial opportunity or marketing strategy to a group of similarly situated persons who are not Clerk Magistrates; and 3) when the same discount is extended to non-Clerk Magistrates in comparable circumstances, and the lawyer, the law firm and their interests are not likely to come before the Clerk Magistrate in the reasonably near future.

Adopted February 9, 1990, effective April 1, 1990. Amended May 30, 1990, effective April 1, 1990; January 24, 2018, effective March 1, 2018.

Canon 6.   Political Activity and Elective Office

A Clerk-Magistrate, other than an elected Clerk-Magistrate, shall refrain from political activity and, in particular, shall not:

(1) act as a leader or hold any office in a political organization;

(2) make speeches for a political organization or candidate or publicly endorse a candidate for public office;

(3) solicit funds for a political organization or candidate; or

(4) hold or seek an elective public office if there is a substantial likelihood that matters involving that office will come before the Clerk-Magistrate or the court in which the Clerk-Magistrate serves. An appointed Clerk-Magistrate may become a candidate for an elected Clerk-Magistrate position. An appointed Clerk-Magistrate who holds elective office at the time of the adoption of this Code may continue to serve consecutive terms in that office.

Adopted February 9, 1990, effective April 1, 1990.

Canon 7.   Education

A Clerk-Magistrate should seek to improve his or her own magisterial and administrative capabilities. The Clerk-Magistrate should also seek to maintain and improve the knowledge, abilities, and skills of all personnel in his or her office.

Adopted February 9, 1990, effective April 1, 1990.

Canon 8.   Non–Discrimination

A Clerk Magistrate shall not discriminate based on sex, race, color, gender identity or expression, religion, nationality, national origin, ethnicity, citizenship or immigration status, ancestry, disease or disability, political affiliation, sexual orientation, age, marital status or socioeconomic status.

Adopted February 9, 1990, effective April 1, 1990. Amended effective January 1, 1992. Amended January 24, 2018, effective March 1, 2018.

Canon 9.   Compliance With the Code of Professional Responsibility for Clerks of the Courts

A Clerk-Magistrate who has retired or resigned from the judicial branch shall not perform court-connected dispute resolution services except on a pro bono publico basis in any court of the Commonwealth for a period of six months following the date of retirement or resignation.

Adopted May 1, 1998, effective June 1, 1998. Amended effective January 1, 2013.

Rule 3:13. Committee on Professional Responsibility for Clerks of the Courts

(1) Complaints against a court Clerk, Clerk Magistrate, Register or Recorder (hereinafter Clerk), and against an Assistant Clerk, Assistant Clerk–Magistrate, Assistant Register, Deputy Recorder, Judicial Case Manager, and Assistant Judicial Case Manager (hereinafter Assistant Clerk), involving the following actions shall be addressed as set forth in this rule: (a) conviction of a crime, (b) wilful misconduct in office, (c) wilful misconduct that, although not related to duties as a Clerk or Assistant Clerk, brings the office of Clerk or Assistant Clerk into disrepute, (d) conduct prejudicial to the administration of justice or conduct unbecoming a Clerk or Assistant Clerk, whether conduct in office or outside of duties of the office, that brings the office into disrepute, or (e) any conduct that constitutes a violation of S.J.C. Rule 3:12.

(2) Complaints involving trial court Clerks shall be referred to their respective Chief Justice who shall investigate and impose discipline as appropriate, except as provided in paragraphs (4)(B) and (C).

(3) Complaints involving trial court Assistant Clerks shall be governed by the provisions of the Trial Court Personnel Policies and Procedures Manual. Complaints involving appellate court Clerks and Assistant Clerks shall be addressed as directed by the Justices of the appropriate court.

(4) There shall be a Trial Court Committee on Professional Responsibility for Clerks of the Courts (hereinafter Committee) with the following authority:

(A) Upon appeal by a Clerk, the Committee shall review discipline of a Clerk imposed by a trial court Chief Justice that includes a suspension without pay of any length or a recommendation for removal of a Clerk. Discipline imposed on a Clerk by a trial court Chief Justice that does not include any suspension without pay or recommendation for removal may not be appealed to the Committee.

(B) Upon referral from a trial court Chief Justice, the Committee shall address a complaint of misconduct against a Clerk in the first instance. Such referral by the Chief Justice shall be made in accordance with guidelines established by the Chief Justice of the Trial Court and the Court Administrator in consultation with representatives of the Clerks. Upon such referral, the Committee may receive information, conduct investigations and hearings, dismiss, informally resolve, issue formal charges, impose any form of discipline except for removal, or otherwise dispose of complaints, and make recommendations to the Supreme Judicial Court concerning removal of a Clerk.

(C) Upon referral from a trial court Chief Justice, the Committee shall investigate information involving allegations that a Clerk is unable adequately to perform as a Clerk because of a mental or physical disability. Upon such referral, the Committee may receive information, investigate, and take appropriate action relative to any mental or physical disability of a Clerk.

(5) The Committee shall consist of three members. The Chief Justice of the Trial Court and the Court Administrator shall be permanent members of the Committee unless recused or disqualified in a particular matter pursuant to the Committee's rules. The third member of the Committee shall be selected for each proceeding in accordance with the Committee's rules.

(6) The rules of the Committee shall be as established by the Supreme Judicial Court.

Adopted February 9, 1990, effective April 1, 1990. Amended February 25, 2015, effective March 23, 2015.

RULES OF THE TRIAL COURT COMMITTEE ON PROFESSIONAL RESPONSIBILITY FOR CLERKS OF THE COURTS

Table of Rules

Scope and Title

These rules govern the procedures of the Trial Court Committee on Professional Responsibility for Clerks of the Courts (hereinafter Committee) in the exercise of its jurisdiction pursuant to Supreme Judicial Court Rule 3:13. They may be known and cited as the Rules of the Committee on Professional Responsibility for Clerks of the Courts.

Adopted February 25, 2015, effective March 23, 2015.

Rule 1. Definitions

A. In these rules, unless otherwise provided, the term Chief Justice shall mean the Chief Justice of a Department of the Trial Court.

B. Clerk means anyone serving in the position of Clerk, Clerk–Magistrate, Register or Recorder in the Trial Court, whether elected or appointed and whether serving in a permanent or temporary capacity.

C. Committee means the Trial Court Committee on Professional Responsibility for Clerks of the Courts.

D. Complaint means a written statement, or an oral statement memorialized in writing, that alleges misconduct of a Clerk, or a mental or physical disability of a Clerk.

E. Hearing Officer means a person appointed by the Committee for the purpose of presiding over a hearing.

F. Special Counsel means an attorney appointed by the Committee to conduct investigations, to make recommendations to the Committee, and to present evidence at a hearing, with respect to charges against a Clerk, and to take any other action related thereto which the Committee may direct.

Adopted February 25, 2015, effective March 23, 2015.

Rule 2. Composition of the Committee

A. The Chief Justice of the Trial Court and the Court Administrator shall be permanent members of the Committee, and the Chief Justice of the Trial Court shall be the Chair. A third member of the Committee shall be selected for each proceeding. The third member shall be chosen by the association of Clerks or Registers to which the Clerk who is the subject of the proceeding may belong.

B. A member of the Committee shall not participate in any proceeding in which the impartiality of that member might reasonably be questioned. Recusal and disqualification pursuant to this section shall be by a member him- or herself or at the request of the two other members. In case of recusal or disqualification of a member, an alternate member shall be appointed by the remaining two members, except that if the recused or disqualified member was appointed by an association of Clerks or Registers, the association shall select the alternate member. If the Chief Justice of the Trial Court and the Court Administrator are both recused or disqualified, the Chief Justice of the Supreme Judicial Court shall select their replacements.

C. An affirmative vote of at least two members of the Committee is required to affirm or modify discipline imposed by a Chief Justice. An affirmative vote of at least two members also is required to dismiss, informally resolve or otherwise dispose of a complaint, to issue formal charges, impose discipline or make recommendations to the Supreme Judicial Court regarding removal of a Clerk. A meeting may be held and a vote may be taken by telephone unless any member objects.

Adopted February 25, 2015, effective March 23, 2015.

Rule 3. Jurisdiction of the Committee

Complaints against a Clerk shall be referred to a Chief Justice for investigation and resolution. As provided in S.J.C. Rule 3:13, the Committee is authorized:

A. upon appeal by a Clerk, to review discipline imposed by a Chief Justice that includes a suspension without pay of any length or a recommendation that a Clerk be removed;

B. upon referral of a Chief Justice, to address a complaint against a Clerk in the first instance. Such referral by the Chief Justice shall be made in accordance with guidelines established by the Chief Justice of the Trial Court and the Court Administrator in consultation with representatives of the Clerks. Upon such referral, the Committee may receive information, conduct investigations and hearings, dismiss, informally resolve, issue formal charges, impose discipline except for removal, or otherwise dispose of complaints, and make recommendations to the Supreme Judicial Court concerning removal of a Clerk.

C. upon referral from a Chief Justice, to receive information, investigate, and take appropriate action relative to any mental or physical disability of a Clerk.

Adopted February 25, 2015, effective March 23, 2015.

Rule 4.   Confidentiality

All Committee proceedings prior to the filing of formal charges shall be confidential. Prior to formal charges, records, files and reports of the Committee shall be confidential, and no disclosure shall be made except as follows: (1) upon written waiver of the Clerk; (2) upon inquiry by a state or federal agency conducting an investigation on behalf of the Commonwealth or the United States government after seven days' notice to the Clerk in writing; or (3) upon inquiry by the Supreme Judicial Court or on appeal by the Clerk to the Supreme Judicial Court.

The Committee may issue public statements and release general information concerning the nature of its jurisdiction and the procedure for filing complaints. In cases where the subject matter has become public, the Committee may issue public statements as it deems appropriate to confirm the pendency of the investigation, clarify procedural aspects and correct misinformation. The Committee may issue public statements and release information concerning its proceedings and reports at the direction of the Supreme Judicial Court and may provide whatever records, files, reports or other information is necessary in an appeal of a decision by the Clerk to the Supreme Judicial Court. If, in the course of its proceedings, the Committee becomes aware of credible evidence that any person has committed a crime, the Committee shall report such evidence to the appropriate law enforcement agency.

Formal charges become public ten days after issuance or upon the filing of the Clerk's response, whichever occurs first. In the case of formal proceedings, only the formal charges, the answer thereto, the evidentiary hearings, the report of the hearing officer, and the final action by the Committee shall become public.

Adopted February 25, 2015, effective March 23, 2015.

Rule 5.   General Procedures of the Committee

A.   Upon request for good cause, or on its-own motion, the Committee may extend any time limit set forth herein.

B.   At any stage of the process, the Committee may place a Clerk on paid administrative leave, or with the consent of the Clerk, specially assign the Clerk pending the final disposition of a complaint. The Committee may specially assign a Clerk pending the final disposition of a complaint without the Clerk's consent only with the approval of the Supreme Judicial Court.

C.   At any stage of the process, the Committee may consult with any appropriate judicial or administrative officer. At any stage of the process, the Committee and the Clerk may reach a negotiated settlement of the case that may include any terms and conditions agreeable to both parties, including discipline up to and including resignation. The Committee shall promptly notify the appropriate Chief Justice of any settlement or informal resolution.

D.   At any stage of the process, the Committee may appoint Special Counsel.

E.   At any time prior to the issuance of formal charges, the Committee may conduct interviews, whether or not under oath and whether or not such statements are memorialized.

F.   In the event that the Clerk resigns after formal charges have been issued, the Committee may, upon a finding that the integrity of the judicial branch and the interest of the administration of justice would be served, continue its investigation in order to make a report to the Supreme Judicial Court.

G.   The Committee shall keep a record of all proceedings concerning a Clerk. The Committee's findings, conclusions and recommendations shall be entered in the Committee's record.

Adopted February 25, 2015, effective March 23, 2015.

Rule 6.   Matters Referred to the Committee in the First Instance

When a Chief Justice refers a matter directly to the Committee, the Committee may assign an investigator to undertake a discreet and confidential investigation and evaluation. The Committee shall notify the Clerk involved when it receives a referral from a Chief Justice. The notice shall include a summary of the allegations. If the investigator determines that the matter referred by the Chief Justice does not set forth allegations that, if true, would constitute misconduct or disability, the investigator shall recommend that the complaint be dismissed. If the Committee accepts the investigator's recommendation, the matter shall be dismissed and the appropriate Chief Justice and the Clerk shall be notified.

If the investigator, after an initial investigation and evaluation, determines that the matter referred by the Chief Justice sets forth facts that, if true, would constitute misconduct and recommends to the Committee that it proceed further, the Committee shall decide whether there is adequate reason to proceed to the preparation of formal charges. If the Committee decides that further investigation is necessary before making this determination, the Committee may continue the investigation. If the Committee finds that there is sufficient cause to proceed, the Committee shall issue formal charges against the Clerk pursuant to Rule 8. If the Committee finds that there is insufficient cause to proceed, the matter shall be dismissed and the Chief Justice and the Clerk shall be notified.

Adopted February 25, 2015, effective March 23, 2015.

Rule 7.   Matters on Appeal From a Decision of a Chief Justice

A Clerk may appeal to the Committee from a disciplinary sanction imposed by a Chief Justice that includes a recommendation of removal or a suspension without pay of any length by submitting a written request for appeal to the Committee within ten days of receipt of the decision of the Chief Justice. An appeal shall stay any suspension imposed by the Chief Justice unless the Committee determines otherwise. A Chief Justice may place a Clerk on paid administrative leave or, with the consent of the Clerk, specially assign the Clerk pending the final disposition of a complaint. A Chief Justice may specially assign a Clerk pending the final disposition of a complaint without the Clerk's consent only with the approval of the Supreme Judicial Court.

Any discipline imposed by the Committee that does not include a suspension without pay or a recommendation for removal shall be final with no further appeal.

A. Suspension without pay of fewer than three days

If the Chief Justice imposes a suspension without pay of fewer than three days, and the Clerk appeals, the Chief Justice shall provide the Committee with written findings and conclusions that support the discipline, and the Clerk may submit written objections to the findings and conclusions according to a schedule established by the Committee. The appeal shall consist of a hearing before the Committee at which the Clerk and the Chief Justice or their representatives may appear. The Clerk and the Chief Justice may also submit memoranda in support of their positions. After hearing and review of the memoranda, the Committee may affirm, increase or decrease the suspension. If the Committee affirms the suspension or imposes any suspension without pay that is fewer than three days, the Clerk may appeal the Committee's decision in accordance with the provisions of Rule 9. If the Committee decides to consider imposing a suspension without pay of three days or more, the Committee shall issue formal charges in accordance with Rule 8A.

B. Suspension without pay of three days or more

If the Chief Justice imposes a suspension without pay of three days or more and the Clerk appeals, the appeal shall constitute a formal proceeding before the Committee, commencing with the issuance of formal charges by the Committee in accordance with Rule 8A.

Adopted February 25, 2015, effective March 23, 2015.

Rule 8.   Formal Proceedings

A. Formal charges

Formal charges issued under Rules 6 or 7 shall be in the form of a detailed, signed complaint that includes a clear statement of the allegations against the Clerk and the alleged facts forming their basis. Where more than one act of misconduct is alleged, each act should be clearly set forth in the complaint. The Committee shall promptly serve the Clerk with a copy of the formal charges, and the Clerk shall have ten days to respond. The appropriate Chief Justice shall be notified of the filing of formal charges. After issuance and before a hearing commences, formal charges may be substantively amended, provided that the Clerk is given notice of the amended charges, twenty one days to respond, and adequate time before the hearing to prepare a defense regarding the amended charges.

Upon the filing of the Clerk's written response to the formal charges or the expiration of the time for its filing, the formal charges shall become public. The Committee shall designate both a Special Counsel to prepare and present the case and a Hearing Officer to take evidence and report thereon to the Committee. Special Counsel who has been designated at an earlier stage may continue to serve in that capacity.

B. Discovery

1. Within ten days after service of the formal charges, the Committee shall make available for inspection to the Clerk all books, papers, records, documents, electronic recordings, and other tangible things within the custody and control of the Committee relevant to any issues in the case, and any written or electronically recorded statement within the custody and control of the Committee that is relevant to the issues in the case.

2. Within thirty days after service of the formal charges, the Special Counsel and the Clerk

a. May, upon written request to the other party prior to the hearing:

(i) Inspect and copy within a reasonable period of time all books, papers, records, documents, electronic recordings, and other tangible things which the other party intends to present at a hearing.

(ii) Obtain the names and addresses of witnesses to the extent known to a party in the proceeding, including an identification of those intended to be called to testify at the hearing.

(iii) Inspect and copy within a reasonable period of time any written or electronically recorded statements made by witnesses who may be called to give testimony at the hearing.

b. May, upon such terms and conditions as the Hearing Officer may impose:

(i) Depose within or without the Commonwealth persons who may have relevant testimony. The complete record of the testimony so taken shall be made and preserved by stenographic record or electronic recording. The written application to the Hearing Officer shall state the name and post office address of the witness, the subject matter concerning which the witness is expected to testify, the time and place of taking the deposition, and the reason why such deposition should be taken. Unless notice is waived, no deposition shall be taken except after at least seven days' notice to the other parties. Unless otherwise directed by the Committee, the deponent may be examined regarding any matter, not privileged, which is relevant to the subject matter of the proceedings. Parties shall have the right of cross-examination and objection. In making objections to questions or evidence, the grounds relied upon shall be stated briefly, but no recording filed in the proceeding shall include argument or debate. Objections to questions or evidence shall be noted in the record, but the stenographer or recorder shall not have the power to decide on the competency, materiality or relevancy of evidence. Objections to the competency, relevancy, or materiality of the testimony are not waived by failure to make them before or during the taking of the deposition.

(ii) Subpoena relevant witnesses and documents to the hearing.

(iii) Seek any limitation or protection for any discovery permitted by this Rule.

3. In granting discovery the Hearing Officer shall protect against disclosure the mental impressions, conclusions,

opinions, and legal theories of an attorney or other representative of a witness or party in these proceedings.

4. Other issues relative to discovery that are not covered in these Rules shall be addressed or resolved by the Hearing Officer in accordance with the comparable provisions of the Massachusetts Rules of Civil Procedure.

C. Hearing

1. The Committee shall schedule a hearing to take place in not fewer than thirty nor more than sixty days from the date a written answer is due to the Committee. The Hearing Officer shall immediately notify the Clerk and all counsel of the time and place for the hearing. The Special Counsel and the Clerk may jointly agree to delay the commencement of the hearing. Also, at the request of Special Counsel or the Clerk, the hearing officer may extend the date for the hearing.

2. The hearing shall be conducted by a Hearing Officer chosen by the Committee. The hearing shall be open to the public and recorded. The rules of evidence applicable to civil proceedings in Massachusetts shall apply, and all testimony shall be under oath. Both the Clerk and Special Counsel shall be permitted to introduce evidence and produce and cross-examine witnesses. The Clerk and Special Counsel shall be entitled to compel the attendance and testimony of witnesses, and the production of papers, books, accounts, documents, electronic recordings, other tangible things, and any other relevant evidence or testimony. Formal charges may be amended after the commencement of a hearing only if the amendment is technical in nature and if the Clerk and counsel are given adequate time to prepare a response.

D. Decision of the Committee

1. Within thirty days after the conclusion of the hearing, the Hearing Officer shall submit to the Committee, Special Counsel, and the Clerk a report which shall contain findings, the recording of testimony, all exhibits, and a recommendation on discipline.

2. Unless there is good cause for delay, within sixty days of receipt of the Hearing Officer's report, the Committee shall render a decision on discipline based upon the report of the Hearing Officer. In its discretion, the Committee may allow the Clerk and Special Counsel to submit written objections to the Hearing Officer's findings and recommendation on discipline. The Clerk and Special Counsel may file a request to be heard by the Committee and if either participant so requests, the Committee shall schedule a hearing and give notice to both as to the time and place at least seven days in advance of the hearing. The hearing shall be public but the deliberations of the Committee shall be conducted in executive session. In rendering its decision, the Committee is not required to accept the recommended discipline of the Hearing Officer. The Committee's decision shall contain its reasons, and it may adopt all or part of the findings and conclusions of the Hearing Officer as support for its decision. The Committee shall immediately provide a copy of its decision to the Clerk and to Special Counsel.

3. The Committee shall not impose any discipline unless the charges have been proven by clear and convincing evidence in the record of the hearing.

Adopted February 25, 2015, effective March 23, 2015.

Rule 9. Appeal to the Supreme Judicial Court

The Clerk may appeal any recommendation for removal or suspension without pay imposed by the Committee to the Supreme Judicial Court within ten days of receiving the decision of the Committee. An appeal shall stay any suspension imposed by the Committee unless the Supreme Judicial Court determines otherwise. If a suspension is fewer than three days, the appeal shall be requested in a writing directed to the Chief Justice of the Supreme Judicial Court and will consist of a review of the record of the Committee's proceedings by the Justices of the Supreme Judicial Court in their administrative capacity. If a suspension is three or more days, the matter shall be filed in the Office of the Clerk for the Commonwealth and proceed in such manner as the Court may direct. The decision of the Justices shall be public. The Clerk may not appeal to the Supreme Judicial Court from any discipline imposed by the Committee that does not include a suspension without pay or a recommendation for removal.

Adopted February 25, 2015, effective March 23, 2015.

Rule 10. Cases Involving Allegations of Mental or Physical Disability

In considering allegations that a Clerk is unable adequately to perform as a Clerk because of mental or physical disability, the Committee shall, insofar as applicable and except as provided below, follow procedures established by these Rules.

A. If in a matter relating to an allegation of mental or physical disability the Clerk is not represented by counsel, the Committee may appoint an attorney to represent the Clerk at public expense.

B. If a complaint or statement of allegations involves the mental or physical health of a Clerk, and the Clerk denies the alleged disability, the Committee may upon good cause shown require the examination of the Clerk by qualified medical experts selected by the Committee.

C. If a complaint or statement of allegations involves the mental or physical health of a Clerk, the Committee shall investigate whether a Clerk's mental or physical condition may, even with a reasonable accommodation, adversely affect the Clerk's ability to serve as Clerk.

Adopted February 25, 2015, effective March 23, 2015.

Rule 3:14. Advisory Committee on Ethical Opinions for Clerks of the Courts

The Supreme Judicial Court may establish a committee to render advisory opinions with respect to the interpretation of rules of court relating to the ethical and professional conduct of Clerk-Magistrates, as defined in Rule 3:12. The committee shall consist of at least five persons, none of whom shall be a Justice of the Supreme Judicial Court, at least one of whom shall be a currently elected Clerk-Magistrate and at least one of whom shall be an appointed Clerk-Magistrate. Except in emergency situations, a request for an advisory opinion must be in writing and shall be signed by the Clerk-Magistrate requesting the opinion.

The request must set forth fully all facts bearing on the question or questions on which the Clerk-Magistrate requests advice. The committee shall not render opinions on hypothetical questions, on issues pending before or under consideration by a judicial authority, unless that authority so requests, or by a court, agency, or commission. The committee may decline to render an opinion for any other reason which it deems sufficient.

Each opinion shall be in writing and shall contain a statement of the facts and a discussion of the application of the relevant rules to the facts. The committee shall publish its opinions, but the name of the Clerk-Magistrate requesting the opinion and other identifying information shall not be included in published opinions unless the concerned Clerk-Magistrate consents to such inclusion. If a Clerk-Magistrate did not omit or misstate any material fact in the request for an opinion, the Clerk-Magistrate may rely on the written opinion until and unless revised or revoked by the committee or this court or superseded by law. The Supreme Judicial Court will not impose sanctions in any disciplinary proceeding involving an ethical violation if the Clerk-Magistrate's conduct was undertaken in reasonable reliance on an opinion issued to the Clerk-Magistrate pursuant to this provision.

Adopted February 9, 1990, effective April 1, 1990.

RULES OF ADVISORY COMMITTEE ON ETHICAL OPINIONS FOR CLERKS OF COURT

Table of Rules

Rule 1. Opinion Requests

Requests for advisory opinions should be made by letter, addressed to Christine Burak, Esquire, Secretary, Advisory Committee on Ethical Opinions for Clerks of Court, 1350 New Courthouse, Boston, Massachusetts 02108. A request may only be made by a Clerk–Magistrate or a person who has been nominated to be a Clerk–Magistrate as that term is defined in Canon I of Supreme Judicial Court Rule 3:12.

Effective June, 1990.

Rule 2. Form of Request

The letter should be signed by the Clerk-Magistrate requesting the advice and should set forth fully all facts bearing on the question or questions on which the Clerk-Magistrate requests advice. Because Supreme Judicial Court Rule 3:14(2) precludes the committee from rendering opinions "on issues pending before or under consideration by a judicial authority, unless that authority so requests, or by a court, agency, or commission," the request should contain an affirmation that, to the best of the information and belief of the Clerk-Magistrate requesting the opinion, no issue raised thereby, whether in reference to the Clerk-Magistrate or to any other person, is presently pending before or under consideration by any judicial authority, court, agency, or commission.

Effective June, 1990.

Rule 3. Scope of Question

Under Supreme Judicial Court Rule 3:14, advisory opinion requests must relate "to the interpretation of rules of court relating to the ethical and professional conduct of Clerk-Magistrates." The committee will not render opinions on hypothetical questions, questions relating solely to past conduct or questions relating to the conduct of persons other than the requesting Clerk-Magistrate.

Effective June, 1990.

Rule 4. Opinion

Opinions of the committee require the affirmative vote of at least three members and, except for emergency opinions, will be rendered in writing. The committee shall publish its opinions but the name of the Clerk-Magistrate requesting the opinion and any other identifying information shall not be included in a published opinion unless the requester consents to such inclusion. Pursuant to Supreme Judicial Court Rule 3:14, if "a Clerk-Magistrate did not omit or misstate any material fact in the request for an opinion, the Clerk-Magistrate may rely on the written opinion until and unless revised or revoked" by the committee or by the Supreme Judicial Court or superseded by law.

Effective June, 1990.

Rule 5. Emergency Opinions

To offer guidance to Clerk-Magistrates faced unexpectedly with questions within the committee's jurisdiction that require an immediate response, the secretary, with the approval of the chairperson of the committee (or if the chairperson is unavailable, of one other member of the committee), or the chairperson, with the concurrence of one other member of the committee, may give advice on an emergency basis. Whenever possible, the request for advice shall be in writing. The emergency advice will be given orally or in writing, as seems appropriate. Emergency advice shall be submitted to the full committee for action. If the committee agrees with the advice given, it will issue a written confirming opinion to the inquirer. If it disagrees, it will issue a written opinion to the inquirer setting forth the emergency advice that was given so that the Clerk-Magistrate will have the benefit of the protection given by S.J.C. Rule 3:14 as to conduct undertaken in reliance on that advice, but it will also set forth the view of the full committee on the issue presented. The view of the full committee will supersede all inconsistent emergency advice.

Effective June, 1990.

Rule 6. Decision to Refuse Opinion

In addition to the reasons stated in rules 1, 2, and 3, the committee may decline to render an opinion for any other reason which it deems sufficient.

Effective June, 1990.

Rule 3:15. *Pro Hac Vice* Registration Fee

1.   Each attorney not admitted to practice in this Commonwealth who seeks to be admitted *pro hac vice* in the Superior Court, Land Court, or any appellate court (not including the Appellate Division of the District Court or of the Boston Municipal Court) shall pay a non-refundable *pro hac vice* registration fee of $355 per case to the Board of Bar Overseers (Board), except when the attorney is providing *pro bono publico* legal assistance to an indigent client. Each attorney not admitted to practice in this Commonwealth who seeks to be admitted *pro hac vice* in any other court shall pay a non-refundable *pro hac vice* registration fee of $101 per case to the Board, except when the attorney is providing *pro bono publico* legal assistance to an indigent client. For purposes of this Rule, a case shall include an appeal. However, where an attorney has paid the appropriate registration fee of $355 or $101 and the case is removed, transferred, appealed or further appellate review is sought, no additional fee need be paid. Only individual attorneys, not law firms, may seek such admission.

A.   Payment may be made by check, money order or online pursuant to policies established by the Board.

B.   Payment will be accompanied by a form prescribed by the Board including at least the following information:

(1) The name, business address, telephone number, email address and attorney license number and states in which the attorney is licensed;

(2) The court in which the motion for *pro hac vice* admission is to be made, the name of the party to be represented, and the docket number if it is known; and

(3) a statement, made under the penalties of perjury, that the attorney is admitted to practice and in good standing in every jurisdiction where the attorney is admitted, and an acknowledgment that the attorney is subject to discipline by the Supreme Judicial Court and the Board.

C.   Within seven days of receipt of a *pro hac vice* registration fee the Board will send an acknowledgment to the attorney seeking admission.

D.   An attorney who is exempt from paying a registration fee because the attorney will provide *pro bono publico* legal assistance to an indigent client must complete and submit to the Board the form required by paragraph B, along with a statement that the attorney will be providing services *pro bono publico* to an indigent client.

2.   Motions to a court for admission *pro hac vice* shall be made by a member of the bar of the Commonwealth of Massachusetts and must aver that the registration fee required by Rule 3:15 has been paid or include, as an attachment, a copy of the Board acknowledgment. An attorney who is exempt from paying a registration fee because the attorney will provide *pro bono publico* legal assistance to an indigent client must aver that the attorney will provide such assistance.

3.   The Board may retain a portion of each *pro hac vice* registration fee to cover its costs in administering the fee and will pay the balance to the IOLTA Committee on a quarterly basis. The IOLTA Committee shall disburse the fees in the same manner as other IOLTA funds are disbursed in accordance with Rule 1.15(g)(4) and (5) of Rule 3:07, Massachusetts Rules of Professional Conduct.

Adopted April 12, 2012, effective September 4, 2012. Amended June 27, 2018, effective January 1, 2019.

Rule 3:16. Practicing with Professionalism Course for New Lawyers

1.   **Practicing with Professionalism Course Requirement.** All persons who are admitted to the bar of the Commonwealth, whether admitted after passing the law examination pursuant to S.J.C. Rule 3:01, Section 5, or by motion pursuant to Section 6, shall, by no later than eighteen months after admission to the Massachusetts bar, complete a mandatory Practicing with Professionalism Course approved by the Supreme Judicial Court or its designee. The course shall be presented as needed to accommodate the number of lawyers admitted in Massachusetts annually.

2.   **Course Offering.** The course shall be offered by one or more continuing legal education providers, bar associations, law schools, other educational institutions, or other providers approved by the Supreme Judicial Court or its designee. The course curriculum shall be subject to standards issued by the Supreme Judicial Court or its designee.

3.   **Proof of Compliance.** The course provider(s) shall submit documentation of course completion to the Massachusetts Board of Bar Overseers and the attendees in accordance with procedures established by the Supreme Judicial Court or its designee.

4.   **Failure to Comply.** Any attorney who fails to complete the course described in Section 1 within eighteen months after admission to practice in Massachusetts shall receive a written notice of noncompliance from the Board of Bar Overseers, sent by e-mail or first-class mail to the e-mail or home address furnished by the attorney on the last registration statement filed as required by S.J.C. Rule 4:02. If the attorney fails to complete the course described in Section 1 within ninety days from the date of the mailing of the notice, the Board of Bar Overseers shall file a petition for the attorney's suspension with the Clerk of this court for Suffolk County.

5.   **Suspension.** Any attorney suspended under the provisions of Section 4 above shall become subject to the provisions of Rule 4:01, Section 17(4), upon entry of the suspension order, and if not reinstated within thirty days after entry shall become subject to the other provisions of said Section 17.

6.   **Reinstatement.** Any attorney otherwise in good standing who is suspended for failure to complete the course described in Section 1 may be reinstated to practice in Massachusetts by filing with the court and serving upon the Board of Bar Overseers (a) documentation of course completion; (b) an affidavit on a form provided by the Board of Bar Overseers showing that the attorney has fully complied with the requirements of the suspension order and with the applicable provisions of Rule 4:01, Section 17, has registered pursuant to Rule 4:02, and paid all arrears in bar registration fees due from the date of the last payment to the date of his or her request for reinstatement, including any late assessments required under Rule 4:03; and (c) paid the Board of Bar Overseers an assessment of $100.

7. Fees. Fees for the course shall be approved by the Supreme Judicial Court.

8. Annual Evaluation. Each approved provider shall report annually to the Supreme Judicial Court or its designee. The report shall include the agenda, faculty, fee, attendance, curriculum, and course evaluation. The Board of Bar Overseers shall report annually the number of attorneys suspended for noncompliance.

9. Application. This Rule 3:16 shall apply to all attorneys admitted to the Massachusetts bar on or after the effective date of the rule.

Adopted November 20, 2012, effective September 1, 2013. Amended December 19, 2018, effective January 1, 2019.

CHAPTER FOUR. BAR DISCIPLINE AND CLIENTS' SECURITY PROTECTION

Rule 4:01. Bar Discipline

Section 1. Jurisdiction.

(1) Any lawyer or foreign legal consultant admitted to, or engaging in, the practice of law in this Commonwealth shall be subject to this court's exclusive disciplinary jurisdiction and the provisions of this rule as amended from time to time.

(2) Any Information, report, or other pleading filed in the Supreme Judicial Court pursuant to this rule shall be filed with the clerk of this court for Suffolk County. It shall be presented to the chief justice, who shall designate a justice to hear the matter.

Section 2. Venue of Disciplinary Hearings.

Unless the Board Chair or the Chair's designee specifies a different venue, a hearing on a petition for discipline shall take place at the offices of the Board. The Board Chair or the Chair's designee shall consider the convenience of the complainant, witnesses, the respondent and hearing committee in selecting a hearing location.

Section 3. Grounds for Discipline.

(1) Each act or omission by a lawyer, individually or in concert with any other person or persons, which violates any of the Massachusetts Rules of Professional Conduct (see Rule 3:07), shall constitute misconduct and shall be grounds for appropriate discipline even if the act or omission did not occur in the course of a lawyer-client relationship or in connection with proceedings in a court. A violation of this Chapter 4 by a lawyer, including without limitation the failure without good cause (a) to comply with a subpoena validly issued under section 22 of this rule; (b) to respond to requests for information by the Bar Counsel or the Board made in the course of the processing of a complaint; (c) to comply with procedures of the Board consistent herewith for the processing of a petition for discipline or for the imposition of public reprimand or admonition (see section 4 of this rule); or (d) to comply with a condition of probation or diversion to an alternative educational, remedial, or rehabilitative program shall constitute misconduct and shall be grounds for appropriate discipline.

(2) Failure to comply with (a) or (b) of subsection (1) or failure to file an answer as required by section 8(3) of this rule or to appear at a hearing before a hearing committee, special hearing officer, or panel of the Board shall result in the entry of an order of administrative suspension upon the bar counsel's filing with this court of a petition for administrative suspension which sets forth the violation of this section and an affidavit of the bar counsel affirming that the lawyer was served with the request for information, the subpoena, the petition for discipline, or the notice of hearing in accordance with the provisions of section 21 of this rule; that the lawyer was afforded a reasonable period of time for compliance with the request for information or the subpoena, or to answer the petition, or with reasonable notice of the hearing and had failed to comply, to answer, or to appear; and that the request for information, subpoena, petition, or notice of hearing was accompanied by a statement advising the respondent-lawyer that failure to comply with the request for information or subpoena, or to answer timely the petition, or to appear at the hearing would result in administrative suspension without further hearing.

(3) Any suspension under the provisions of subsection (2) above shall be effective forthwith upon entry of the suspension order and shall be subject to the provisions of section 17(4) of this rule. If not reinstated within thirty days after entry, the lawyer shall become subject to the other provisions of section 17 of this rule. As a condition precedent to reinstatement, such lawyer shall file with the Board and with the bar counsel an affidavit stating the extent to which he or she has complied with subsection (1) of this section and with the applicable provisions of section 17 of this rule. The lawyer shall also as a condition of reinstatement pay all expenses incurred by the Office of Bar Counsel and the Board in obtaining compliance with this section and in seeking suspension, including an administrative fee of twenty-five dollars.

Section 4. Types of Discipline.
Discipline of lawyers may be (a) by disbarment, resignation pursuant to section 15 of this rule, or suspension by this court; (b) by public reprimand by the Board; or (c) by admonition by the bar counsel.

Section 5. The Board of Bar Overseers.

(1) This court shall appoint a Board of Bar Overseers (Board) to act, as provided in this Chapter Four, with respect to the conduct and discipline of lawyers and in such matters as may be referred to the Board by any court or by any judge or justice. The Board shall consist of such number of members as the court may determine from time to time. The court, by order, shall request the submission of nominations to fill vacancies in such manner as it may determine. The Massachusetts Bar Association and each county bar association (including, for the purposes of this section, the Boston Bar Association as the bar association for Suffolk County) may submit to this court in writing the names of two nominees for each vacancy in the Board. Any lawyer may submit in writing the names of nominees. The court may, but need not, make appointments to the Board from the nominees so submitted

and, in making appointments, shall give appropriate consideration to a reasonable geographical distribution of appointees among disciplinary districts. The court shall from time to time designate one member of the Board as Chair and another as Vice Chair. The Vice Chair shall perform the duties of the Chair in the Chair's absence or incapacity to act.

(2) Appointments to the Board shall be for a term of four years. No member shall be appointed to more than two consecutive full terms but (a) a member appointed for less than a full term (originally or to fill a vacancy) may serve two full terms in addition to such part of a full term, and (b) a former member shall again be eligible for appointment after a lapse of one or more years. A member whose term has expired shall continue in office until a successor is appointed and, in any event, shall continue to serve on any hearing or appeal panel to which he or she has been appointed until the panel completes its duties and may be recalled to serve on the panel in the event of a remand by the Board or the court.

(3) The Board of Bar Overseers

(a) may consider and investigate the conduct of any lawyer within this court's jurisdiction either on its own motion or upon complaint by any person;

(b) shall appoint a chief Bar Counsel (the Bar Counsel) who shall, with the concurrence of the Board, hire such assistants to the Bar Counsel as may be required, all to serve at the pleasure of the court, the appointment of the Bar Counsel to be with the approval of the court; and may employ and compensate such other persons as may be required or appropriate in the performance of the Board's duties;

(c) shall appoint one or more hearing committees, each committee to consist of three or more individuals, to perform such functions as may be assigned by the Board with reference to charges of misconduct; provided, however, that each hearing committee shall be chaired by a lawyer and no hearing committee shall consist of more than one nonlawyer;

(d) may appoint a special hearing officer, who shall be a lawyer, to hear charges of misconduct when, in view of the anticipated length of the hearing or for other reasons, the Board determines that a speedy and just disposition would be better accomplished by such appointment than by referring the matter to a hearing committee or panel of the Board;

(e) may, through its Chair, refer charges to an appropriate hearing committee, to a special hearing officer, or to a hearing panel of the Board;

(f) shall review, and may revise, the findings of fact, conclusions of law, and recommendations of hearing committees, special hearing officers, or hearing panels. The Board in its discretion may refer an appeal taken pursuant to section 8(5) of this rule to a panel of its own members for its recommendation;

(g) may issue a public reprimand to lawyers for misconduct, and in any case where disbarment or suspension of a lawyer is to be sought or recommended, or where the Bar Counsel or the Respondent-lawyer appeals pursuant to section 8(6) of this rule, shall file an Information with this court;

(h) with the approval of this court, may adopt and publish rules of procedure and other regulations not inconsistent with this rule;

(i) may lease office space and make contracts and arrangements for the performance of administrative and similar services required or appropriate in the performance of the Board's duties;

(j) may, but need not, consult with local bar associations in the several counties and their officers concerning any appointments which it is herein authorized to make;

(k) may invest or direct the investment of the fees or any portion thereof, paid pursuant to Rule 4:03, section (1), and may cause funds to be deposited in any bank, banking institution, savings bank, or federally insured savings and loan association in this Commonwealth provided, however, that the Board shall have no obligation to cause these fees or any portion thereof to be invested; and

(*l*) may perform other acts necessary or proper in the performance of the Board's duties.

(4) For any action requiring a vote of the Board, the Board shall act only with the concurrence of a majority of the Board who are present and voting, provided, however, that a quorum shall be present. A quorum shall consist of a majority of the Board, including members who are recused or abstain.

Section 6. Hearing Committees.

(1) Hearing committee members shall be appointed for a term of three years, and no member shall serve for more than two successive three-year terms. A member whose term has expired shall continue in office until a successor is appointed, and, in any event, shall continue to serve on any committee to which he or she has been appointed until the committee completes its duties and may be recalled to serve on the committee in the event of a remand by the Board or the court. A former member may be again appointed after the expiration of one year from his or her last service.

(2) The Board shall designate one member of each committee, who shall be a lawyer, to serve as chair. The committee shall act only with a concurrence of a majority of its members who are present, provided, however, that two members shall constitute a quorum.

(3) Hearing committees

(a) shall conduct hearings on formal charges of misconduct upon reference by the Board or its chair, and

(b) may recommend that the matter be concluded by dismissal, admonition, public reprimand, suspension, or disbarment.

(4) If a special hearing officer is appointed to hear disciplinary charges, that officer shall perform all the duties imposed upon a hearing committee by this rule or by the rules of the Board. Unless otherwise provided herein, the words "hearing committee" used throughout this rule shall also mean a special hearing officer or hearing panel.

Section 7. The Bar Counsel.

The Bar Counsel

(1) shall investigate all matters involving alleged misconduct by a lawyer coming to his or her attention from any source,

except matters involving alleged misconduct by the Bar Counsel, assistant Bar Counsel, or any member of the Board, which shall be forwarded to the Board for investigation and disposition, provided that Bar Counsel need not entertain any allegation that Bar Counsel in his or her discretion determines to be frivolous, to fall outside the Board's jurisdiction, or to involve conduct that does not warrant further action;

(2) shall dispose of all matters involving alleged misconduct by a lawyer in accordance with this rule and any rules and regulations issued by the Board for his or her guidance which may provide

(a) that Bar Counsel need not pursue or may close a complaint whenever the matter complained of is frivolous, falls outside the jurisdiction of the Board, or involves allegations of misconduct that do not warrant further action,

(b) for adjustment of complaints found by the Bar Counsel to be of a minor character by informal conference, admonition, or by diversion to an alternative educational, remedial, or rehabilitative program, and

(c) for disposition by recommending to the Board the institution of formal proceedings in which the Bar Counsel seeks public discipline,

but, except as to a complaint that is closed by Bar Counsel or that Bar Counsel determines need not be pursued, no disposition shall be recommended or undertaken by the Bar Counsel until the accused lawyer shall have been afforded opportunity to state his or her position with respect to the allegations against him or her;

(3) shall prosecute all disciplinary proceedings before hearing committees, special hearing officers, the Board, and this court;

(4) shall appear, with full rights to participate as a party, at hearings conducted with respect to petitions for reinstatement by suspended or disbarred lawyers, lawyers who have resigned, or lawyers on disability inactive status;

(5) shall maintain permanent records of all matters presented to him or her and the disposition thereof, except that (a) the Board may provide by rule for the expunction of the records of a complaint against a lawyer which has been docketed solely on account of a report made by a financial institution that has dishonored an instrument presented against a lawyer's trust account when the instrument was dishonored solely due to the error of the financial institution, and (b) the Bar Counsel shall destroy and expunge the records of a complaint against a lawyer which has been closed and not subsequently reopened within six years of the date of closing unless a complaint has been filed in the intervening six-year period. In the event a complaint is so filed or reopened, the records shall not be destroyed and expunged until the expiration of six years from the date on which all complaints have been closed and not reopened and all complaints have been dismissed and not reopened;

(6) shall, with the concurrence of the Board, hire such assistants to the Bar Counsel as may be required; and

(7) may delegate any duties or functions to a duly appointed assistant acting under his or her general supervision.

Section 8. Procedure.

(1) **Investigation.** In accordance with any rules and regulations of the Board, investigations (whether upon complaint or otherwise) shall be conducted by the Bar Counsel, except as otherwise provided by section 7(1) of this rule. Following completion of any investigation, or of a determination pursuant to section 7(1) that an investigation is not warranted, the Bar Counsel shall take further action, which may include, among others,

(a) closing or declining to pursue a complaint and informing the complainant in writing of the reasons for not investigating a complaint or for closing the file and of the complainant's right to request review by a member of the Board;

(b) closing a matter after adjustment, informal conference, or diversion to an alternative educational, remedial, or rehabilitative program;

(c) recommending to the Board that

(i) an admonition of the lawyer be administered;

(ii) formal proceedings be instituted; or

(iii) public discipline be imposed by agreement.

Except in the case of a recommendation that public discipline be imposed by agreement, a designated Board member may approve, reject, or modify the recommended action, but the Bar Counsel may appeal to the Board Chair from any modification or rejection of a recommendation that an admonition be administered, or that formal proceedings be instituted. The Board Chair may approve or modify the recommended action. A recommendation that formal discipline be imposed by agreement shall be submitted directly to the full Board.

(2) **Admonition.**

(a) On appeal by Bar Counsel pursuant to subsection (1), the decision of the Board Chair to approve, modify, or reject the recommendation of an admonition shall be final.

(b) If an admonition is approved by either the designated Board member or the Board Chair on appeal, the Bar Counsel shall make service of the admonition on the Respondent-lawyer together with a summary of the basis for the admonition. Bar Counsel shall also provide written notice to the Respondent-lawyer of the right to demand in writing within fourteen days of the date of service that the admonition be vacated and a hearing provided; the requirement that the Respondent-lawyer submit with the demand a written statement of objections to the factual allegations and disciplinary violations set forth in the summary and all matters in mitigation; that failure of the Respondent-lawyer to demand within fourteen days after service that the admonition be vacated and to submit a statement of objections constitutes consent to the admonition; and that failure to set forth matters in mitigation constitutes a waiver of the right to present evidence in mitigation at the hearing.

(c) In the event of a demand that the admonition be vacated, the matter shall be disposed of in accordance with the procedure set forth in section 8(4) for expedited hearings.

(d) Eight years after the administration of an admonition, it shall be vacated, and the complaint which gave rise to it dismissed, unless during such period another complaint has resulted in the imposition of discipline or is then pending.

(3) Formal Proceedings.

(a) As to matters for which formal proceedings have been approved pursuant to section 8(1) of this rule, disciplinary proceedings shall be instituted by the Bar Counsel's filing a petition for discipline with the Board setting forth specific charges of alleged misconduct. A copy of the petition shall be served, together with a notice from the Board, setting a time for answer which shall not be less than twenty days after such service upon the Respondent-lawyer and advising the Respondent-lawyer that the failure to file an answer shall be grounds for administrative suspension pursuant to section 3(2) of this rule. The Respondent-lawyer shall file his or her answer with the Board and serve a copy thereof on the Bar Counsel. In the event the Respondent-lawyer fails to file a timely answer to the petition, the charges shall be deemed admitted. Averments in the petition are admitted when not denied in the answer.

(b) The matter shall be assigned to a hearing committee, to a special hearing officer, or to the Board or a panel of the Board, and the Board shall give notice to the Bar Counsel, and to the Respondent-lawyer's counsel, if any, and, if not, to the Respondent-lawyer of the date and place set for hearing. The notice of hearing shall be served at least fifteen days in advance thereof. The notice shall advise the Respondent-lawyer that the failure to appear for hearing will be grounds for administrative suspension pursuant to section 3(2) of this rule.

(c) In the event the Respondent-lawyer files an answer admitting the charges and does not request the opportunity to be heard in mitigation, the Bar Counsel and the Respondent-lawyer may jointly recommend to the Board that the Respondent-lawyer receive a public reprimand or a suspension. If the Board accepts a joint recommendation for a public reprimand, it shall issue such reprimand. If the Board accepts a joint recommendation for suspension, the Board shall file with the clerk of this court for Suffolk County an Information, together with the record of its proceedings. If the parties do not make such a joint recommendation, or if the Board rejects such recommendation, the matter shall be assigned to an appropriate hearing committee, to a special hearing officer, or to the Board or a panel of the Board, for hearing. A tie vote of the Board on such a recommendation shall constitute a rejection of the recommendation.

(d) The hearing committee, special hearing officer, or panel of the Board shall file promptly with the Board a written report containing its findings of fact, conclusions of law, and recommendations, together with a record of the proceedings before it.

(4) Expedited Hearing

(a) When the Respondent-lawyer has requested a hearing within fourteen days of service of an admonition in accordance with the requirements of section 8(2) of this rule, Bar Counsel shall file the admonition summary with the Board, along with the Respondent-lawyer's demand for hearing and statement of objections and matters in mitigation, if any, and the matter shall be assigned to a special hearing officer.

After hearing, the special hearing officer shall file with the Board a report containing his or her written findings of fact and conclusions of law, and shall recommend that: (1) the Respondent-lawyer receive an admonition, (2) the charges be dismissed, or (3) the matter warrants a more substantial sanction than admonition and should be remanded for formal proceedings in accordance with section 8(3) of this rule.

(b) Respondent-lawyer and Bar Counsel shall have the right to seek review by the Board of the decision by the special hearing officer in accordance with the procedure set forth in subsection (5)(a) of this rule, but any such review shall be on the briefs only and there shall be no oral argument. In the event the Board determines that the matter shall be remanded for formal proceedings, it shall assign the matter to a hearing committee or special hearing officer other than the one who heard the case initially. The Board's decision shall otherwise be final and there shall be no right by either Bar Counsel or the Respondent-lawyer to demand after conclusion of an expedited hearing that an Information be filed.

(5) Review by the Board

(a) Upon receipt of a hearing committee's, special hearing officer's, or hearing panel's report after formal proceedings, if there is objection by the Respondent-lawyer or by the Bar Counsel to the findings and recommendations, the Board shall set dates for submission of briefs and for any further hearing which the Board in its discretion deems necessary. The Board shall review, and may revise, the findings of fact, conclusions of law and recommendation of the hearing committee, special hearing officer, or hearing panel, paying due respect to the role of the hearing committee, the special hearing officer, or the panel as the sole judge of the credibility of the testimony presented at the hearing.

(b) In the event that the Board determines that the proceedings should be dismissed, it shall so notify the Respondent-lawyer.

(c) In the event that the Board determines that the proceedings should be concluded by admonition or public reprimand, it shall so notify the Respondent-lawyer.

(6) Review by the Supreme Judicial Court.
The Board shall file an Information whenever it shall determine that formal proceedings should be concluded by suspension or disbarment; or whenever either the Bar Counsel or the Respondent-lawyer objects to having formal proceedings concluded by dismissal, admonition or by public reprimand, by filing a written demand with the Board for the filing of an Information within twenty days after the date of the notice of the Board's action, which time limit shall be jurisdictional. The subsidiary facts found by the Board and contained in its report filed with the Information shall be upheld if supported by substantial evidence, upon consideration of the record, or such portions as may be cited by the parties.

(7) Disbarment by Consent.
A lawyer accused of professional misconduct who does not wish to contest the charges may waive the foregoing provisions of this section and consent to the entry of a judgment of disbarment. Upon satisfying itself that the lawyer has given such consent freely and voluntarily, with full awareness of the implications of consenting to disbarment, and has acknowledged under oath that the

material facts upon which the charges are based are true or can be proved by a preponderance of the evidence, the court may enter a judgment disbarring the lawyer from the practice of law.

Section 9. Immunity.

(1) Complaints submitted to the Board or to the bar counsel shall be confidential and absolutely privileged. The complainant shall be immune from civil liability based upon his or her complaint; provided, however, that such immunity from suit shall apply only to communications to the Board or the bar counsel and shall not apply to public disclosure of information contained in or relating to the complaint.

(2) The complainant and each witness giving sworn testimony or otherwise communicating with the Board or the bar counsel during the course of any investigation or proceedings under this rule shall be immune from civil liability based on any such testimony or communications; provided, however, that such immunity from suit shall apply only to testimony given or communications made to the Board or the bar counsel and shall not apply to public disclosure of information attested to or communicated during the course of the investigation or proceedings.

(3) The Board, members of the Board and its staff, members of hearing committees, special hearing officers, and the bar counsel and members of his or her staff shall be immune from liability for any conduct in the course of their official duties.

Section 10. Refusal of Complainant to Proceed; Compromise; or Restitution.
Abatement of an investigation into the conduct of a lawyer or other related proceedings shall not be required by the unwillingness or neglect of the complainant to cooperate in the investigation, or by any settlement, compromise or restitution. A lawyer shall not, as a condition of settlement, compromise or restitution, require the complainant to refrain from filing a complaint, to withdraw the complaint, or to fail to cooperate with the bar counsel.

Section 11. Matters Involving Related Pending Civil, Criminal, or Administrative Proceedings.
The investigation or prosecution of complaints involving material allegations which are substantially similar to the material allegations of pending criminal, civil, administrative, or bar disciplinary proceedings in this or another jurisdiction shall not be deferred unless the Board or a single member designated by the Chair, in its discretion, or the court, for good cause shown, shall authorize such deferment, as to which either the court or the Board may impose conditions. The acquittal of the Respondent-lawyer on criminal charges, or a verdict, judgment, or ruling in the lawyer's favor in civil, administrative, or bar disciplinary proceedings shall not require abatement of a disciplinary investigation predicated upon the same or substantially similar material allegations.

Section 12. Lawyers Convicted of Crimes.

(1) The term "conviction" shall include any guilty verdict or finding of guilt and any admission to or finding of sufficient facts and any plea of guilty or nolo contendere which has been accepted by the court, whether or not sentence has been imposed.

(2) A conviction of a lawyer for any crime shall be conclusive evidence of the commission of that crime in any disciplinary proceeding instituted against that lawyer based upon the conviction.

(3) The term "serious crime" shall include (a) any felony, and (b) any lesser crime a necessary element of which, as determined by the statutory or common law definition of such crime, includes interference with the administration of justice, false swearing, misrepresentation, fraud, willful failure to file income tax returns, deceit, bribery, extortion, misappropriation, theft, or an attempt or a conspiracy, or solicitation of another, to commit a "serious crime."

(4) Upon the filing with this court of a certificate establishing a lawyer's conviction of a serious crime, this court shall enter an order to show cause why the lawyer should not be immediately suspended from the practice of law, regardless of the pendency of an appeal, pending final disposition of any disciplinary proceeding commenced upon such conviction. The court or a justice, after affording the lawyer opportunity to be heard, may make such order of suspension or restriction as protection of the public may make appropriate. The court shall also refer the matter to the Board to take appropriate action, which may include investigation by the bar counsel or the institution of a formal proceeding. A disciplinary proceeding so instituted need not be brought to hearing until all appeals from the conviction are concluded.

(5) Upon receipt of a notice of a conviction of a lawyer for a crime not constituting a serious crime, this court may refer the matter to the Board to take appropriate action, which may include investigation by the bar counsel or the institution of a formal proceeding. This court need make no reference with respect to convictions for minor offenses.

(6) A lawyer suspended under the provisions of subsection (4) above will be reinstated immediately upon the filing of a certificate that the underlying conviction for a serious crime has been reversed or set aside, but the reinstatement need not terminate any formal proceedings then pending against the lawyer.

(7) The clerk of any court within the Commonwealth in which a lawyer is convicted shall transmit a certificate thereof to this court and to the Board within ten days of said conviction.

(8) Within ten days of a lawyer's conviction of a crime, as defined in subsection 12(1) of this rule, the lawyer shall notify the bar counsel of the conviction.

(9) Upon being advised that a lawyer has been convicted of (a) a crime within this Commonwealth and that no certificate has been filed under subsection (7) above, or (b) a crime in another jurisdiction, the bar counsel shall obtain a certificate of the conviction and transmit it or a copy to the court and to the Board.

Section 12A. Lawyer Constituting Threat of Harm to Clients.
Upon the filing with this court of a petition by the bar counsel alleging facts showing that a lawyer poses a threat of substantial harm to clients or prospective clients, or that the lawyer's whereabouts are unknown, this court shall enter an order to show cause why the lawyer should not be immediately suspended from the practice of law pending final disposition of any disciplinary proceeding commenced by the bar counsel.

The court or a justice, after affording the lawyer opportunity to be heard, may make such order of suspension or restriction as protection of the public may make appropriate. In the interest of justice, the court, upon application of the lawyer, may terminate such suspension at any time after affording the bar counsel an opportunity to be heard.

Section 13. Disability Inactive Status.

(1) *Involuntary Commitment, Adjudication of Incompetence, or Transfer to Disability Inactive Status.* Where a lawyer has been judicially declared incompetent or committed to a mental hospital after a judicial hearing, or where a lawyer has been placed by court order under guardianship or conservatorship, or where a lawyer has been transferred to disability inactive status in another jurisdiction, the court, upon proper proof of the fact, shall enter an order transferring the lawyer to disability inactive status. A copy of such order shall be served, in the manner the court may direct, upon the lawyer, his or her guardian or conservator, and the director of the institution to which the lawyer is committed.

(2) *Investigation of Incapacity.* The bar counsel shall investigate information that a lawyer's physical or mental condition may adversely affect his or her ability to practice law, except information involving the physical or mental condition of the bar counsel, assistant bar counsel, or any member of the Board, which shall be forwarded to the Board for investigation and disposition. In the event that the lawyer admits that he or she is incapacitated, the court may, upon petition of the bar counsel, enter an order placing the lawyer on disability inactive status, accepting the lawyer's resignation, or temporarily suspending the lawyer from the practice of law. With the approval of the Board chair or a member of the Board designated by the chair, the bar counsel may initiate formal proceedings pursuant to subsection (4) of this section to determine whether the lawyer shall be transferred to disability inactive status.

(3) *Inability to Assist in Defense.* If during the course of a disciplinary investigation or proceeding under this rule the respondent-lawyer alleges an inability to assist in the defense due to mental or physical incapacity, the court, upon petition by the bar counsel or the respondent-lawyer, shall immediately transfer the respondent-lawyer to disability inactive status until further order of the court. If the bar counsel contests the respondent-lawyer's allegation, then a determination shall be made concerning the incapacity pursuant to subsection (4) of this section.

(4) *Proceedings to Determine Incapacity.*

(a) Proceedings to adjudicate contested allegations of disability or incapacity shall be held before a hearing committee, special hearing officer, or a panel of the Board and shall be commenced upon petition by the bar counsel. The proceedings shall be conducted in the same manner as disciplinary hearings and shall be open to the public as provided in section 20.

(b) The court, Board, hearing committee, special hearing officer, or hearing panel may require the examination of the respondent-lawyer by qualified medical experts designated by them.

(c) The court or the Board may appoint a lawyer to represent the respondent-lawyer if the lawyer is without adequate representation.

(d) The hearing committee, special hearing officer, or panel of the Board shall report promptly to the Board its findings and recommendations, together with a record of the proceedings before it. The lawyer and the bar counsel shall have the rights of appeal provided for in section 8 of this rule. The Board shall file an Information with the clerk of this court for Suffolk County together with its recommendation and the record of the proceedings before it.

(e) If, after hearing and upon due consideration of the record including the recommendation of the Board as provided in subsection (6) of section 8 of this rule, the court concludes that the respondent is incapacitated from continuing to practice law, it shall enter an order transferring the respondent to disability inactive status until further order of the court.

(f) Disciplinary proceedings shall not be stayed unless the court finds that the respondent-lawyer is so incapacitated by reason of mental or physical infirmity that he or she is incapable of assisting in his or her defense as provided in subsection (3) of this section. If the court determines the respondent-lawyer's claim of incapacity to defend to be invalid, the disciplinary investigation or proceedings shall resume, and the court shall immediately temporarily suspend the respondent-lawyer from the practice of law pending final disposition of the matter. The court may direct that the expense of the independent examinations be paid by the lawyer.

(5) *Public Notice of Transfer to Disability Inactive Status.* The Board shall cause a notice of transfer to disability inactive status to be published in the same manner as a disciplinary sanction imposed under section 8 of this rule is published.

(6) *Reinstatement from Disability Inactive Status.*

(a) Reinstatements from disability inactive status shall be subject to the provisions of section 18 of this rule except as herein provided.

(b) A lawyer shall be entitled to petition for transfer to active status from disability inactive status once a year or at such intervals as this court may direct in the order transferring the respondent to disability inactive status or any modifications thereof.

(c) The Board, upon referral from the court, may direct an examination of the lawyer by qualified medical experts designated by the Board.

(d) Where a lawyer placed on disability inactive status under subsection (1) of this section has been judicially declared to be competent or returned to active status by the other jurisdiction, this court, after hearing, may dispense with referring the matter to the Board pursuant to subsection (5) of section 18 for the taking of further evidence that his or her disability has been removed and may immediately direct the lawyer's reinstatement to active status upon such terms as are deemed proper and advisable.

(e) A lawyer seeking reinstatement under this section shall have the burden of demonstrating that his or her physical or mental condition does not adversely affect the lawyer's ability to practice law and that he or she has the competency and learning in law required for admission to practice.

(7) *Waiver of Privilege.* A lawyer who files for reinstatement pursuant to the provisions of subsection (6) of this section or who alleges incapacity to defend himself or herself in a disciplinary investigation or proceedings pursuant to the provisions of subsection (3) shall be required to disclose the name of each medical provider, hospital, or other institution by whom or in which the lawyer has been examined or treated since the time of transfer to disability inactive status or during the period of the alleged incapacity. The lawyer shall furnish to this court and to the bar counsel written consent to the release of information and records relating to the disability upon request by the court or Board, court- or Board-appointed medical experts, or the bar counsel.

Section 14. Appointment of Commissioner to Protect Clients' Interests When Lawyer Disappears or Dies, or is Placed on Disability Inactive Status.

(1) Whenever a lawyer is placed on disability inactive status, or disappears or dies, and no partner, executor, or other responsible party capable of conducting the lawyer's affairs is known to exist, this court, after giving the bar counsel an opportunity to be heard and upon proper proof of the fact, may appoint a lawyer or lawyers as commissioner to make an inventory of the files of the inactive, disappearing, or deceased lawyer and to take appropriate action to protect the interests of clients of the inactive, disappearing, or deceased lawyer, as well as such lawyer's interest.

(2) The commissioner so appointed shall not disclose any information contained in any files listed in such inventory without the consent of the client to whom such file relates except as necessary to carry out the order of this court to make such inventory. The commissioner shall be reimbursed for reasonable expenses and may be awarded fair compensation. The commissioner's expenses and fees shall be paid by the lawyer unless otherwise ordered by the court.

Section 15. Resignations by Lawyers under Disciplinary Investigation.

(1) A lawyer who is the subject of an investigation under this Chapter Four may submit a resignation by delivering to the Board an affidavit stating that he or she desires to resign, and that:

(a) the resignation is freely and voluntarily rendered; the lawyer is not being subjected to coercion or duress and is fully aware of the implications of submitting the resignation;

(b) the lawyer is aware that there is currently pending an investigation into allegations that he or she has been guilty of misconduct, the nature of which shall be specifically set forth; and

(c) the lawyer acknowledges that the material facts, or specified material portions of them, upon which the complaint is predicated are true or can be proved by a preponderance of the evidence.

(d) the lawyer waives the right to hearing as provided by this rule.

(2) Upon receipt of the required affidavit, the Board shall file it, together with its recommendation thereon, with this court which may enter an order.

(3) All proceedings under this section shall be public as provided in section 20 of this rule.

(4) Any lawyer whose resignation under this section has been accepted must comply with the provisions of section 17 of this rule regarding notice.

Section 16. Reciprocal Discipline.

(1) Upon receipt of a certified copy of an order that a lawyer admitted to practice in this Commonwealth has been suspended or disbarred from the practice of law in another jurisdiction (including any federal court and any state or federal administrative body or tribunal) or has resigned during the pendency of a disciplinary investigation or proceeding, this court shall issue a notice directed to the respondent-lawyer containing: (a) a copy of the order from the other jurisdiction; and (b) an order directing that the respondent-lawyer inform the court within thirty days from service of the notice of any claim that the imposition of the identical or other discipline in this Commonwealth would be unwarranted and the reasons therefor. The bar counsel shall cause this notice to be served on the respondent-lawyer in accordance with this rule.

(2) In the event that the discipline imposed in the other jurisdiction has been stayed there, any reciprocal discipline imposed in the Commonwealth may (but need not) be deferred.

(3) Upon the expiration of thirty days from service of the notice under subsection (1) above, the court, after hearing, may enter such order as the facts brought to its attention may justify. The judgment of suspension or disbarment shall be conclusive evidence of the misconduct unless the bar counsel or the respondent-lawyer establishes, or the court concludes, that the procedure in the other jurisdiction did not provide reasonable notice or opportunity to be heard or there was significant infirmity of proof establishing the misconduct. The court may impose the identical discipline unless (a) imposition of the same discipline would result in grave injustice; (b) the misconduct established does not justify the same discipline in this Commonwealth; or (c) the misconduct established is not adequately sanctioned by the same discipline in this Commonwealth.

(4) Upon receipt of a certified copy of an order that a lawyer admitted to practice in this Commonwealth has been subjected to public discipline other than suspension or disbarment in another jurisdiction (including any federal court and any state or federal administrative body or tribunal), the Board and the clerk of this court for Suffolk County shall file it and make it available to the public to the extent that the record of any other public disciplinary proceeding would be made available.

(5) A final adjudication in another jurisdiction that a lawyer has been guilty of misconduct or an admission in connection with a resignation in another jurisdiction may be treated as establishing the misconduct for purposes of a disciplinary proceeding in the Commonwealth.

(6) A lawyer subject to public or private discipline in another jurisdiction (including any federal court and any state or federal administrative body or tribunal), or whose right to practice law has otherwise been curtailed or limited in such other jurisdiction, shall provide certified copies of the order imposing such discipline or other disposition to the Board and

to the bar counsel within ten days of the issuance of such order.

(7) A lawyer admitted to practice in this Commonwealth who is denied admission to the bar of another jurisdiction (including any federal court and any state or federal administrative body or tribunal), for reasons other than failure to pass the bar examination, shall provide certified copies of any such decision, notice or order to the Board and the bar counsel within ten days of its issuance.

Section 17. Action by Attorneys after Disbarment, Suspension, Resignation or Transfer to Disability Inactive Status.

(1) In every case where a lawyer has been disbarred, suspended, temporarily suspended, or placed on disability inactive status, or where a lawyer has resigned pursuant to the provisions of section 15 of this rule, the lawyer shall, within fourteen days of the date of entry of the disbarment, suspension, temporary suspension, transfer to disability inactive status, or resignation, take the following actions:

(a) file a notice of withdrawal as of the effective date thereof with every court, agency, or tribunal before which a matter is pending, together with a copy of the notices sent pursuant to paragraphs (c) and (d) of this subsection, the client's or clients' place of residence, and the case caption and docket number of the client's or clients' proceedings;

(b) resign as of the effective date thereof all appointments as guardian, executor, administrator, trustee, attorney-in-fact, or other fiduciary, attaching to the resignation a copy of the notices sent to the wards, heirs, or beneficiaries pursuant to paragraphs (c) and (d) of this subsection, the place of residence of the wards, heirs, or beneficiaries, and the case caption and docket number of the proceedings, if any;

(c) provide notice to all clients and to all wards, heirs, and beneficiaries that the lawyer has resigned or that the lawyer has been disbarred, suspended, temporarily suspended, or transferred to disability inactive status; that he or she is disqualified from acting as a lawyer after the effective date thereof; and that, if not represented by co-counsel, the client, ward, heir, or beneficiary should act promptly to substitute another lawyer or fiduciary or to seek legal advice elsewhere, calling attention to any urgency arising from the circumstances of the case;

(d) provide notice to counsel for all parties (or, in the absence of counsel, the parties) in pending matters that the lawyer has resigned, been disbarred, suspended, or transferred to disability inactive status and, as a consequence, is disqualified from acting as a lawyer after the effective date thereof;

(e) make available to all clients being represented in pending matters any papers or other property to which they are entitled, calling attention to any urgency for obtaining the papers or other property;

(f) refund any part of any fees paid in advance that have not been earned;

(g) close every IOLTA, client, trust or other fiduciary account and properly disburse or otherwise transfer all client and fiduciary funds in his or her possession, custody or control.

(h) give such other notice of the court's action as the court may direct in the public interest.

Unless otherwise ordered by the court, all notices required by this section shall be served by certified mail, return receipt requested, in a form approved by the Board.

(2) Whenever the court deems it necessary, it may appoint a commissioner to take appropriate action in lieu of, or in addition to, the action directed in subsection (1) of this section. The appointment of the commissioner shall be at the expense of the lawyer unless otherwise ordered by the court.

(3) Orders imposing temporary suspension shall be immediate and forthwith, and orders imposing disbarment or suspension or accepting the resignation of the lawyer or placing a lawyer on disability inactive status shall be effective thirty days after entry, unless otherwise ordered by the court. After entry of such order, the lawyer shall not accept any new retainer or engage as lawyer for another in any new case or matter of any nature. During the period between the entry date of the order and its effective date, however, the lawyer may wind up and complete, on behalf of any client, all matters which were pending on the entry date.

(4) The Board shall promptly transmit a copy of the order of temporary suspension, suspension, disbarment, resignation, or transfer to disability inactive status to the clerk of each court in the Commonwealth, state or federal, in which it has reason to believe the disciplined lawyer has been engaged in practice.

(5) Within twenty-one days after the entry date of the disbarment, suspension, temporary suspension, resignation, or disability inactive status order, the lawyer shall file with the Office of the Bar Counsel an affidavit certifying that the lawyer has fully complied with the provisions of the order and with bar disciplinary rules. Appended to the affidavit of compliance shall be

(a) a copy of each form of notice, the names and addresses of the clients, wards, heirs, beneficiaries, attorneys, courts and agencies to which notices were sent, and all return receipts or returned mail received up to the date of the affidavit. Supplemental affidavits shall be filed covering subsequent return receipts and returned mail. Such names and addresses of clients shall remain confidential unless otherwise requested in writing by the lawyer or ordered by the court.

(b) a schedule showing the location, title and account number of every bank account designated as an IOLTA, client, trust or other fiduciary account and of every account in which the lawyer holds or held as of the entry date of the order any client, trust or fiduciary funds;

(c) a schedule describing the lawyer's disposition of all client and fiduciary funds in the lawyer's possession, custody or control as of the entry date of the order or thereafter;

(d) such proof of the proper distribution of such funds and the closing of such accounts as has been requested by the bar counsel, including copies of checks and other instruments;

(e) a list of all other state, federal and administrative jurisdictions to which the lawyer is admitted to practice;

(f) the residence or other street address where communications to the lawyer may thereafter be directed.

The lawyer shall retain copies of all notices sent and shall maintain complete records of the steps taken to comply with the notice provisions of this rule.

(6) Within twenty-one days after the entry date of the disbarment, suspension, temporary suspension, resignation, or disability inactive status order, the lawyer shall file with the clerk of this court for Suffolk County:

(a) a copy of the affidavit of compliance required by subsection 5, above.

(b) a list of all other state, federal and administrative jurisdictions to which the lawyer is admitted to practice;

(c) the residence or other street address where communications to the lawyer may thereafter be directed.

(7) Except as provided in section 18(3) of this rule, no lawyer who is disbarred or suspended, or who has resigned or been placed on disability inactive status under the provisions of this rule shall engage in legal or paralegal work, and no lawyer or law firm shall knowingly employ or otherwise engage, directly or indirectly, in any capacity, a person who is suspended or disbarred by any court or has resigned due to allegations of misconduct or who has been placed on disability inactive status.

(8) Any lawyer who is disbarred, suspended for a definite or an indefinite period, or who has resigned and who is found by the court to have violated the provisions of this rule by engaging in legal or unauthorized paralegal work prior to reinstatement under this rule may not be reinstated until after the expiration of a specified term determined by the court after a finding that the lawyer has violated the provisions of this rule. A lawyer on disability inactive status who knowingly violates the provisions of this rule by engaging in legal or paralegal work shall be removed from disability inactive status and temporarily suspended pending the outcome of the disciplinary investigation and proceedings.

Section 18. Reinstatement.

(1) Eligibility for Reinstatement—Short-term suspensions.

(a) A lawyer who has been suspended for six months or less pursuant to disciplinary proceedings shall be reinstated at the end of the period of suspension by filing with the court and serving upon the Bar Counsel an affidavit stating that the lawyer (i) has fully complied with the requirements of the suspension order, (ii) has paid any required fees and costs, and (iii) has repaid the Clients' Security Board any funds awarded on account of the lawyer's misconduct.

(b) A lawyer who has been suspended for more than six months but not more than one year pursuant to disciplinary proceedings shall be reinstated at the end of the period of suspension by filing with the court and serving upon the Bar Counsel an affidavit stating that the lawyer (i) has fully complied with the requirements of the suspension order, (ii) has taken the Multi–State Professional Responsibility Examination during the period of suspension and received a passing grade as established by the Board of Bar Examiners, (iii) has paid any required fees and costs, and (iv) has

repaid the Clients' Security Board any funds awarded on account of the lawyer's misconduct.

(c) Reinstatement under this subsection (1) will be effective automatically ten days after the filing of the affidavit unless the Bar Counsel, prior to the expiration of the ten-day period, files a notice of objections with the court. In such instances, the court shall hold a hearing to determine if the filing of a petition for reinstatement and a reinstatement hearing as provided elsewhere in this section 18 shall be required.

(d) The right to automatic reinstatement under this subsection (1) shall not apply to any lawyer who fails to file the required affidavit within six months after the original term of suspension has expired. In such a case the lawyer must file a petition for reinstatement under paragraph (2) of this section.

(2) Eligibility for Reinstatement—Disbarment, Resignation, and Long-term Suspensions.

(a) Except as the court by order may direct, a lawyer who has been disbarred, or whose resignation has been allowed under section 15 of this rule, may not petition for reinstatement until three months prior to the expiration of at least eight years from the effective date of the order of disbarment or allowance of resignation.

(b) Except as the court by order may direct, a lawyer who has been suspended for an indefinite period may not petition for reinstatement until the expiration of at least three months prior to five years from the effective date of the order of suspension.

(c) Except as the court by order may direct, a lawyer who has been suspended for a specific period of more than one year may not petition for reinstatement until three months prior to the expiration of the period specified in the order of suspension.

(3) Employment as Paralegal.

At any time after the expiration of the period of suspension specified in an order of suspension, or after the expiration of four years in a case in which an indefinite suspension has been ordered, or after the expiration of seven years in a case in which disbarment has been ordered or a resignation has been allowed under section 15 of this rule, a lawyer may move for leave to engage in employment as a paralegal. When the term of suspension or disbarment or resignation has been extended pursuant to the provisions of section 17(8) of this rule, the lawyer may not petition to be employed as a paralegal until the expiration of the extended term. The court may allow such motion subject to whatever conditions it deems necessary to protect the public interest, the integrity and standing of the bar, and the administration of justice.

(4) Petitions for Reinstatement.

Petitions for reinstatement required under this section 18 and those required under section 13 of this rule shall be filed with the clerk of this court for Suffolk County and

(a) shall state whether the petitioner has complied with all the terms and conditions of the order imposing suspension or disbarment, accepting a resignation, or placing the petitioner on disability inactive status, as the case may be;

(b) shall state whether the petitioner has paid any costs assessed by the court under section 23 of this rule;

(c) shall state the extent to which the petitioner has made restitution to, or otherwise made whole, all clients or others injured by the petitioner's misconduct;

(d) shall state whether the petitioner has repaid the Clients' Security Board any funds awarded on account of the petitioner's misconduct;

(e) shall state that the petitioner has taken the Multi–State Professional Responsibility Examination after entry of the order of suspension, disbarment, or acceptance of resignation, and has received a passing grade as established by the Board of Bar Examiners;

(f) shall state that the petitioner has posted with the Board any bond it has required under paragraph 6 of this section 18; and

(g) shall state that the petitioner has filed with the Board and served upon the Bar Counsel copies of the petition and the completed questionnaire required by the Board under its rules.

(5) Procedure on Petitions for Reinstatement.

The clerk shall transmit a copy of the petition for reinstatement to the Board within three days after filing. Except with the written consent of the Board or the Bar Counsel, no hearing upon the merits of such a petition shall be held prior to the expiration of the full term of suspension, indefinite suspension, disbarment, or resignation pursuant to section 15 of this rule and in no event earlier than sixty days after transmittal of the petition to the Board or such further time as the court may allow to permit reasonable consideration of the petition by the Board. Upon receipt of such a petition the Board may hear the petition itself or may refer it to an appropriate hearing committee, to a special hearing officer, or to a panel of the Board designated by the Chair. On any petition the Board, the hearing committee, special hearing officer, or panel shall promptly hear the petitioner who shall have the burden of demonstrating that he or she has the moral qualifications, competency and learning in law required for admission to practice law in this Commonwealth, and that his or her resumption of the practice of law will not be detrimental to the integrity and standing of the bar, the administration of justice, or to the public interest. On any petition referred, the hearing committee, special hearing officer, or panel shall transmit to the Board its findings and recommendations, together with any record. The Board shall file the Board's recommendations and findings with the court, together with any record. The subsidiary facts found by the Board shall be upheld if supported by substantial evidence, upon consideration of the record, or such portions as may be cited by the parties.

(6) Costs and Expenses.

The court in its discretion may direct that the petitioning lawyer pay all necessary expenses incurred in connection with a petition for reinstatement, and the Board may require the posting of a reasonable bond to cover such expenses before acting on any petition assigned for hearing under this section 18.

(7) Waiver of Hearing.

The court may, on motion of the Bar Counsel, assented to by the Board and the petitioner, waive hearing under this section and allow the petition for reinstatement.

(8) Further Petitions for Reinstatement.

Except as the court by order may direct, no lawyer shall be permitted to reapply for reinstatement or readmission within one year following the final disposition of an adverse judgment upon a petition for reinstatement or readmission.

Section 19. Expenses. The salary of the bar counsel, the bar counsel's expenses, the expenses of the Board, hearing committees, and special hearing officers, and other expenses incurred in the administration of this rule, may be paid by the Board out of the funds collected under the provisions of Rule 4:03, or, where the court deems that appropriate, from state funds as the court may order. The Board shall annually obtain an independent audit by a certified public accountant of the funds entrusted to it and their disposition, and shall file a copy of such audit with this court.

Section 20. Confidentiality and Public Proceedings.

(1) Except as the court shall otherwise order or as otherwise provided in this rule, the Board and the bar counsel shall keep confidential all information involving allegations of misconduct by a lawyer and all information that a lawyer's physical or mental condition may adversely affect his or her ability to practice law until the occurrence of one of the following events:

(a) Submission of a resignation pursuant to section 15 of this rule;

(b) Submission of a recommendation that formal discipline be imposed by agreement;

(c) Service upon the respondent-lawyer of a petition for discipline instituting formal charges against the lawyer or of a petition seeking to place the lawyer on disability inactive status.

This section shall not prevent the members of the Board or the bar counsel from disclosing such information to this court or as they deem necessary to carry out their duties under this rule.

(2) Notwithstanding subsection (1) of this section, the bar counsel or the Board may disclose the pendency, subject matter, and status of an investigation if:

(a) the respondent-lawyer has formally waived confidentiality or made the matter public;

(b) the investigation is predicated upon a conviction of the respondent-lawyer for a serious crime as defined in section 12 herein;

(c) the investigation is based upon allegations that have become generally known to the public; or

(d) there is a need to notify another person or organization in order to protect the public, the administration of justice, or the legal profession.

(3) Upon the submission of an affidavit of resignation pursuant to section 15 of this rule or upon the submission of a stipulation between the bar counsel and the respondent-lawyer which recommends public discipline or after the service upon the respondent-lawyer of a petition for discipline instituting

formal disciplinary charges or of a petition seeking to place the lawyer on disability inactive status, the proceedings are open to the public except for:

(a) deliberations of the hearing committee, the special hearing officer, the hearing panel, the appeal panel, the Board, or this court;

(b) information with respect to which the Board has issued a protective order under subsection (4) hereof;

(c) information with respect to which this court has issued a protective order on appeal from a Board decision denying such order under subsection (4) hereof; or

(d) further proceedings following the recommendation by a hearing committee, a special hearing officer, a hearing panel, or an appeal panel, or following an order of the Board or this court, that an admonition be imposed or that a petition for discipline be dismissed. In such event, the record shall be sealed and the proceedings shall be closed until and unless the Board or this court orders otherwise.

(4) In order to protect the interests of a complainant, witness, third party, or respondent-lawyer, the Board may, upon application of the bar counsel or any affected person and for good cause shown, issue a protective order prohibiting the public disclosure of specific information otherwise privileged or confidential and direct that the proceedings be conducted so as to implement the order, including requiring that the hearing be conducted in such a way as to preserve the confidentiality of the information that is the subject of the application. If bar discipline or other professional discipline has been imposed on the respondent-lawyer on a prior occasion, in this Commonwealth or elsewhere, the fact that the discipline imposed is or has been confidential shall not constitute good cause for the issuance of a protective order. The bar counsel or any affected person may appeal from an order granting or denying an application for a protective order by filing a notice of appeal with the clerk of this court for Suffolk County within seven days after the date of the notice of the Board's action, which time limit shall be jurisdictional. The pendency of such an appeal shall not be grounds to stay proceedings before a hearing committee, a special hearing officer, or any panel of the Board.

(5) The provisions of this section shall not be construed to prohibit the Board from notifying a complainant concerning the Board's disposition of the complaint and the reasons therefor, or to deny access to relevant information to the Clients' Security Board, or to authorized agencies investigating the qualifications of judicial candidates, or to other jurisdictions investigating qualifications for admission to practice or considering reciprocal disciplinary action, or to law enforcement agencies investigating qualifications for government employment where discipline under this Chapter Four has been imposed, or, except as the court may direct, where the proceedings are pending and the Board in its discretion believes disclosure is warranted. In addition, the clerk of this court for Suffolk County shall transmit notice of all public discipline imposed by this court to the National Discipline Data Bank maintained by the American Bar Association.

(6) When an investigation by the bar counsel or the Board concerns allegations of a serious crime as defined in section 12 herein, or disciplinary charges in another jurisdiction, the bar counsel or the Board may disclose information not otherwise public under this rule to the appropriate agency responsible for criminal or disciplinary enforcement and exchange such information with such agency during the course of its investigation of the same lawyer. When requested by an appropriate disciplinary agency investigating disciplinary charges in another jurisdiction, the bar counsel or the Board may also disclose the existence of any prior discipline.

Section 21. Service. Any notice or pleading required to be served under this Chapter Four may be served upon the respondent-lawyer in hand or by addressing it by certified, registered or first class mail to the address furnished in the last registration statement filed by the respondent-lawyer in accordance with Rule 4:02. Service by mail is complete upon mailing.

Section 22. Subpoena Power.

(1) Upon request by the bar counsel or a respondent-lawyer for testimony or the production of evidence at a hearing, or upon request by the bar counsel for testimony or the production of evidence at any stage of an investigation, witnesses may be summoned by subpoenas issued at the direction of a Board member, the chair of a hearing committee, or a special hearing officer. Witnesses shall be examined under oath or affirmation. Testimony may be taken by a hearing committee, a special hearing officer, or a hearing panel outside the Commonwealth if the ends of justice so require. Where appropriate, testimony may be taken within or without the Commonwealth by deposition or by Commission. So far as practicable a stenographic, electronic, or videotape record shall be made and preserved for a reasonable time.

(2) Whenever a subpoena is sought in this state pursuant to the law of another jurisdiction for use in lawyer discipline or disability proceedings, and where the issuance of a subpoena has been duly approved under the law of the other jurisdiction, a member of the Board may issue a subpoena as provided in this section to compel the attendance of witnesses and production of documents.

Section 23. Costs. The court, in its discretion, may direct that a respondent-lawyer pay the costs incurred in connection with the processing of a disciplinary proceeding and information, as well as the costs incurred by the bar counsel and the Board in attempting to gain information from the respondent-lawyer in connection with the processing of a complaint against said lawyer.

Section 24. Restitution. The court or the Board, in its discretion, may order a respondent-lawyer to make restitution to those persons financially injured by his or her conduct and to reimburse the Clients' Security Fund for any payments made on account of misappropriation.

Adopted June 3, 1974, effective September 1, 1974. Amended September 17, 1975, effective January 1, 1976; amended effective April 20, 1976; amended July 28, 1976, effective September 1, 1976; amended effective October 11, 1977; amended August 10, 1978, effective September 1, 1978; December 22, 1978, effective January 1, 1979; amended effective April 12, 1979; amended May 15, 1979, effective July 1, 1979; June 26, 1980, effective January 1, 1981; July 29, 1980, effective September 1, 1980; April 13, 1982, effective April 30, 1982; August 4, 1982, effective August 30, 1982; January 2, 1985, effective March 1, 1985; April 1, 1986, effective May 1, 1986; March 29, 1988, effective July 1, 1988; amended effective September 3, 1991; January 6, 1993;

July 1, 1993; amended December 3, 1993, effective December 6, 1993; amended effective July 1, 1997; amended June 9, 1997, effective January 1, 1998; amended effective December 2, 1997; amended July 28, 1999, effective January 1, 2000; amended effective October 27, 1999; amended December 15, 1999, effective January 3, 2000; November 2, 2000, effective January 2, 2001; November 29, 2001, effective January 1, 2002; November 5, 2002, effective December 2, 2002; April 9, 2009, effective September 1, 2009.

Rule 4:02. Periodic Registration of Attorneys

(1) Registration Statement Required. Every attorney admitted to, or engaging in, the practice of law in this Commonwealth, within three months of becoming subject to this chapter and annually thereafter, shall file with the Board a registration statement setting forth his or her current residence and office addresses, and a business email address, and such other information as this court may from time to time direct, including the date of his or her admission to the bar of this court and of each admission to practice in each other jurisdiction, including each Federal court and each administrative body. The statement shall disclose whether the attorney is in good standing in each such jurisdiction, and, if not in good standing in any jurisdiction, it shall contain an explanation of the circumstances. The Board may adopt rules and regulations establishing a system of staggered annual registrations, and in order to implement such a system may provide for a transition period during which different attorneys may be required to file registration statements at different times and with different expiration dates, so that thereafter all annual registrations will not expire on the same date. In addition to such registration statement, every attorney shall file a supplemental statement of any change in the information previously submitted, including residential address, office address, and business email address, within fourteen days of such change. Within twenty days of the receipt of a registration statement or supplement thereto filed by an attorney, the Board shall acknowledge receipt thereof in order to enable the attorney on request to demonstrate compliance with the requirement of this rule.

(1A) Foreign Legal Consultants. Every person licensed to practice in this Commonwealth as a foreign legal consultant pursuant to Rule 3:05, within three months of becoming subject to this chapter and annually thereafter, shall file with the Board a registration statement setting forth his or her current residence and office addresses, and a business email address, and such other information as this court may from time to time direct, including the date of his or her license to practice as a foreign legal consultant and of each admission to practice in each other jurisdiction including each foreign court. The original statement and each annual statement shall provide a document establishing that the foreign legal consultant is in good standing in each such jurisdiction, and, if not in good standing in any jurisdiction, it shall contain an explanation of the circumstances. In addition to such registration statement, every foreign legal consultant shall file a supplemental statement of any change in the information previously submitted, including residential address, office address, and business email address, within fourteen days of such change. Foreign legal consultants shall be subject to the provisions of Rule 4:03 and subsections (2), (3), (4), and (5) of this Rule.

Designation of IOLTA Account. Each attorney shall, as part of the annual filing required by subsection (1) of this rule and on forms provided by the Board for this purpose, specify the name, account number and depository of his or her IOLTA account. The Board shall transmit information regarding attorneys' IOLTA accounts to the Supreme Judicial Court and to the IOLTA Committee established by the Court.

(2A) Professional Liability Insurance Disclosure.

(a) Each attorney shall, as part of the annual filing required by subsection (1) of this rule and on forms provided by the Board for this purpose, certify whether he or she is currently covered by professional liability insurance. Each attorney currently registered as active in the practice of law in this Commonwealth who reports being covered by professional liability insurance shall notify the Board in writing within thirty days if the insurance policy providing coverage lapses or terminates for any reason without immediate renewal or replacement with substitute coverage.

(b) The foregoing shall be certified by each attorney in such form as may be prescribed by the Board. The information submitted pursuant to this subsection will be made available to the public by such means as may be designated by the Board.

(c) Any attorney who fails to comply with this subsection may, upon petition filed by the bar counsel or the Board, be suspended from the practice of law until such time as the attorney complies. Supplying false information or failure to notify the Board of lapse or termination of insurance coverage as required by this subsection shall subject the attorney to appropriate disciplinary action.

(3) Failure to File. Any attorney who fails to file the statement or any supplement thereto in accordance with the requirements of subsections (1), (1A), (2), and (2A) above shall be subject to suspension in accordance with the procedures set forth in Rule 4:03.

(4) Inactive Status.

(a) Any attorney may advise the Board in writing that he or she desires to assume inactive status and to discontinue the practice of law in this Commonwealth. Upon the filing of such notice, the attorney shall continue to file annual registration statements for as long as he or she remains on inactive status, but shall no longer be eligible to practice law in this Commonwealth, except to provide pro bono publico legal services in accordance with Rule 4:02(8)(a). Any inactive attorney shall pay the fee imposed pursuant to Rule 4:03 for inactive attorneys.

(b) Upon the filing of a notice that he or she wishes to assume inactive status, an attorney shall be removed from the rolls of those classified as active until and unless he or she requests reinstatement to the active rolls and pays for the year of reinstatement the fee imposed pursuant to Rule 4:03 for active attorneys.

(5) Retirement.

(a) Any attorney may advise the Board in writing that he or she desires to retire from the bar and to discontinue the practice of law in this Commonwealth. Upon the filing of such notice, the attorney shall no longer be eligible to practice law in this Commonwealth but shall continue to file registration statements for three years thereafter in order that he or she can be located in the event complaints are made about his or her conduct while he or she was engaged in practice in this Commonwealth. A retired attorney may provide pro bono publico legal services in accordance with Rule 4:02(8)(b). A retired attorney providing such services shall file annual registration statements as provided in that Rule. Any retired attorney will be relieved from the payment of the fees imposed pursuant to Rule 4:03.

(b) Upon the filing of a notice that he or she wishes to retire from the bar, an attorney shall be removed from the rolls of those classified as active until and unless he or she requests reinstatement to the active rolls and pays the fee imposed pursuant to Rule 4:03 for active attorneys for each of the years during which he or she was retired from the bar.

(6) Judicial Status.

(a) Any attorney who sits as a judge of any state or Federal court may advise the Board in writing that he or she is a sitting judge and desires to discontinue the practice of law in this Commonwealth. Upon the filing of such a notice, the attorney will be placed on judicial status and will be relieved from the payment of the fees imposed pursuant to Rule 4:03.

(b) Upon the filing of a notice that he or she has left the bench and wishes to be reinstated to the active rolls and upon payment for the year of reinstatement of the fee imposed pursuant to Rule 4:03 for active attorneys, an attorney on judicial status shall be so reinstated.

(7) Clerk Status.

(a) Any "clerk-magistrate," as defined in Canon 1 of Supreme Judicial Court Rule 3:12, and any Federal clerk of court, chief deputy clerk and deputy clerk may advise the Board in writing that he or she is a clerk. Upon the filing of such a notice, the attorney will be placed on clerk status and will be relieved from the payment of the fees imposed pursuant to Rule 4:03.

(b) Upon the filing of a notice that he or she is no longer a clerk and wishes to be reinstated to the active rolls and upon payment for the year of reinstatement of the fee imposed pursuant to Rule 4:03 for active attorneys, an attorney on clerk status shall be so reinstated.

(8) Pro Bono Status.

(a) Any attorney admitted to the practice of law in the Commonwealth who has assumed inactive status in accordance with Rule 4:02(4) but who wishes to provide pro bono publico legal services without compensation or expectation of compensation as described in Rule 6.1 of the Massachusetts Rules of Professional Conduct (S.J.C. Rule 3:07) may advise the Board by filing an appropriate annual registration statement that he or she will limit his or her legal practice to providing pro bono publico legal services under the auspices of an approved legal services organization, as defined below. The annual registration statement shall indicate whether the attorney is, or was at the time he or she assumed inactive status, the subject of any pending grievance or disciplinary charge and shall be signed by an authorized representative of the approved legal services organization under whose auspices the attorney will provide services. Unless the Board of Bar Overseers objects, the attorney may begin providing pro bono services after filing such a statement.

(b) Any attorney admitted to the practice of law in the Commonwealth who has retired from the bar and discontinued the practice of law in this Commonwealth in accordance with Rule 4:02(5) may advise the Board by filing an appropriate annual registration statement that he or she will limit his or her legal practice to providing pro bono publico legal services without compensation or expectation of compensation as described in Rule 6.1 of the Massachusetts Rules of Professional Conduct (S.J.C. Rule 3:07) under the auspices of an approved legal services organization, as defined below. The annual registration statement shall indicate whether the attorney is, or was at the time he or she retired, the subject of any pending grievance or disciplinary charge and shall be signed by an authorized representative of an approved legal services organization under whose auspices the attorney will provide services. Unless the Board of Bar Overseers objects, the attorney may begin providing pro bono services after filing such a statement.

(c) For purposes of this Rule, an approved legal services organization shall include a pro bono publico legal services program sponsored by a court-annexed program, a bar association, a Massachusetts law school, or a not-for-profit organization that provides legal services to persons of limited means and that receives funding from the federal Legal Services Corporation, the Massachusetts Legal Assistance Corporation, the Massachusetts Bar Foundation, the Boston Bar Foundation, or the Women's Bar Foundation, and in addition, shall include any not-for-profit legal services organization designated as an approved legal services organization after petition to the Supreme Judicial Court.

(9) In–House Counsel Status.

(a) Any attorney who is admitted in another United States jurisdiction or in a foreign jurisdiction, and not disbarred or suspended from practice in any jurisdiction, and who wishes to engage in the practice of law as in-house counsel in the Commonwealth of Massachusetts shall advise the Board by (i) filing an appropriate annual registration statement that he or she will limit legal practice in Massachusetts to engaging in the practice of law as in-house counsel, and (ii) identifying the organization on whose behalf the legal services are provided. The initial annual registration statement shall be accompanied by a certificate of good standing from each jurisdiction in which the attorney is licensed to practice law. The initial annual registration statement and all later annual registration statements shall disclose whether the attorney is in good standing in each jurisdiction to which he or she is admitted, and, if not in good standing in any jurisdiction, it shall contain an explanation of the circumstances. The initial annual registration statement and all later annual registration statements shall be signed by an authorized representative of the organization on whose behalf the attorney seeks to engage in the practice of law as in-house counsel. Unless the Board of Bar Overseers objects, after filing such initial statement the attorney may engage in the practice of law as in-house counsel in the Commonwealth of Massachusetts as described in the filing under this Rule.

(b) As used in this section 9, "to engage in the practice of law as in-house counsel" means to provide on behalf of a single organization (including, for attorneys admitted in a United States jurisdiction, a governmental entity) or its organizational affiliates any legal services that constitute the practice of law. Notwithstanding this limitation, in-house counsel who are admitted in another United States jurisdiction may provide pro bono publico legal services without compensation or expectation of compensation as described in Rule 6.1 of the Massachusetts Rules of Professional Conduct (S.J.C. Rule 3:07) under the auspices of either (1) an approved legal services organization (as defined in paragraph (8)(c) above), or (2) a lawyer admitted to practice and in good standing in the Commonwealth of Massachusetts.

(c) Any attorney registered under this section who changes or terminates his or her employment shall be required to file a supplemental statement of change in information under Rule 4:02(1) regardless of whether he or she wishes to continue to engage in the practice of law in the Commonwealth of Massachusetts as in-house counsel for another organization.

(d) Nothing in this section shall be deemed to affect any definition, limitation or explanation under rule, by decision, or otherwise, of what constitutes engaging in the practice of law in this Commonwealth, as used in section 4:02(1).

(e) Nothing in this section permits an attorney registered under this section to provide services for which the forum requires pro hac vice admission.

(f) As used in this section, "organization" does not include a corporation, partnership, limited liability company or other entity that itself engages in the practice of law by providing legal services to others.

(10) **Residential Addresses Confidential.** Residential addresses disclosed on registration statements, except those designated as the registrant's place of business, shall be treated as confidential and shall be used by the Board and by Bar Counsel only for the purpose of communicating with registrants or otherwise in the course of the business of the Board or Bar Counsel. Other than in the course of such business, neither the Board nor Bar Counsel shall disclose any such residential address to any third party unless directed to do so by order of this Court for Suffolk County.

(11) **Use by courts of attorneys' business physical and electronic mailing addresses.** On a regular basis, the courts will access the data base of the board to obtain attorneys' business physical and electronic mailing addresses. The courts may use the attorneys' business physical and electronic mailing addresses for the courts' business purposes.

Adopted June 3, 1974, effective September 1, 1974. Amended July 28, 1976, effective September 1, 1976; August 10, 1978, effective September 1, 1978; amended effective July 18, 1979; amended September 26, 1989, effective January 1, 1990; May 25, 1993, effective September 1, 1993; December 3, 1993, effective September 1, 1993; July 28, 1999, effective January 1, 2000; July 21, 2004, effective January 1, 2005; June 28, 2006, effective September 1, 2006; February 4, 2008, effective June 1, 2008; June 22, 2011, effective September 1, 2011; January 30, 2013, effective March 1, 2013; January 30, 2014, effective July 1, 2014; January 25, 2017, effective February 1, 2017.

Rule 4:03.   Periodic Assessment of Attorneys

(1)(a) Every attorney required to register in accordance with Rule 4:02, other than a retired attorney, sitting judge, clerk-magistrate as defined in Canon 1 of Supreme Judicial Court Rule 3:12, Federal clerk of court, chief deputy clerk and deputy clerk, or suspended attorney, shall pay an annual fee * as established by the court from time to time, which shall be paid to the Board with the registration statement required under Rule 4:02. The fee so paid subject to any applicable orders of this court shall be used to defray the costs of attorney registration and disciplinary enforcement, to provide funds for the operation of the Clients' Security Board and Fund established under Rule 4:04, to provide funds for the operation of the Massachusetts lawyers assistance programs provided by Lawyers Concerned for Lawyers, Inc. (LCL), and for such other purposes as the Board, with the approval of the court, from time to time shall determine.

(b) The registration statement required under Rule 4:02 shall provide for a voluntary annual fee of $51, or such amount as established by the court from time to time, for use in the administration of justice and provision of civil legal services to those who cannot afford them. The registration statement shall further provide that any attorney who does not wish to pay the voluntary fee under this subsection shall so indicate and shall not be required to make the payment. An attorney's decision as to whether to pay this voluntary fee shall be confidential.

(c) The Board shall remit, at least quarterly, to the IOLTA Committee the fees collected under subsection (b), which shall disburse the fees in the same manner as other IOLTA funds are disbursed in accordance with Rule 1.15(g)(4) and (5) of Rule 3:07, Supreme Judicial Court Rules of Professional Conduct. The Massachusetts Legal Assistance Corporation and other designated charitable entities receiving these funds shall describe their distribution of these funds for use in the administration of justice and provision of civil legal services to those who cannot afford them in the annual report required under Rule 1.15(g)(6) of Rule 3:07.

(2) To any attorney who, without permission from the Board, fails to pay the fee required under subsection (1) above within thirty days, the Board shall mail a letter by first-class mail to the addresses furnished on the last registration statement filed as required by Rule 4:02, notifying the attorney of his or her failure to pay the required fee and that, if within fifteen days from the date of the mailing of the letter the attorney shall fail to pay the fee, there shall be added to the fee a late assessment of fifty dollars. If within forty-five days from the date of the mailing of the letter, he or she shall fail to pay the fee, the Board shall mail a certified or registered letter to the last known business address and a letter by first-class mail to the last known residential address, notifying the attorney of his or her failure to pay, and shall file a petition for the attorney's suspension with the Clerk of this court for Suffolk County.

(3) Any attorney suspended under the provisions of subsection (2) above shall become subject to the provisions of Rule 4:01, Section 17(4), upon entry of the suspension order, and if not reinstated within thirty days after entry shall become subject to the other provisions of said Section 17. As a condition precedent to reinstatement, such attorney shall file with the Board an affidavit stating the extent to which he or she has complied with applicable provisions of Rule 4:01, Section 17, and shall pay all arrears due from the date of the last payment to the date of his or her request for reinstatement, including the late assessment of fifty dollars required

under subsection (2) above, and shall also pay to the Board a penalty of one hundred dollars.

Adopted June 3, 1974, effective September 1, 1974. Amended September 17, 1975, effective January 1, 1976; July 28, 1976, effective September 1, 1976; September 23, 1977, effective September 1, 1977; August 10, 1978, effective September 1, 1978; July 29, 1980, effective September 1, 1980; amended effective February 1, 1993; amended May 25, 1993, effective September 1, 1993; December 3, 1993, effective September 1, 1993; amended effective October 2, 1995; amended June 29, 2010, effective September 1, 2010.

* See Clerk of Court for current fee information.

Rule 4:04. Clients' Security Board and Fund

Section 1. The full court shall appoint a Clients' Security Board (Board). This Board shall consist of seven members of the Massachusetts bar to serve as public trustees to receive, hold, manage, and distribute the funds allocated to the Board from the annual fees assessed under Rule 4:03(1)(a). The Board shall hold such funds in trust as the Clients' Security Fund (Fund). The purpose of the Fund is to discharge, as far as practicable and in a reasonable manner, the collective professional responsibility of the members of the Massachusetts bar for actual losses caused by the theft of client funds or property by attorneys, acting either as attorneys or as fiduciaries (except to the extent to which such losses are otherwise reimbursed).

Section 2.

(A) The Massachusetts Bar Association, each county bar association (including the Boston Bar Association as the county bar association for Suffolk County) and other appropriate organizations may submit to the full court not more than three nominees for each vacancy on the Board. The full court shall select from these nominees or from any other members of the bar a person to fill each vacancy, and shall designate a Chair and a Vice Chair to act in the absence of the Chair.

(B) All terms (except to fill an unexpired term) shall be for five years. No member shall serve more than two consecutive full terms, in addition to any term of less than five years, either by original appointment or to complete an unexpired term. A member shall be eligible, however, for reappointment for further terms after a lapse of one or more years. A member whose term has expired shall continue in office until the full court appoints a successor.

Section 3. The Chair or a majority of the members may call meetings of the Board. The Board shall meet at least quarterly, upon reasonable notice to the Board members. A majority of members shall constitute a quorum. A majority of the members present at a duly constituted meeting may exercise any powers held by the Board.

Section 4. The Board, members of the Board, and the staff of the Board shall be immune from liability for any conduct in the course of their official duties.

Adopted June 3, 1974, effective September 1, 1974. Amended September 17, 1975, effective January 1, 1976; May 25, 1982, effective September 1, 1982; amended effective August 3, 1982; February 1, 1991; October 14, 1997; amended October 1, 1998, effective November 2, 1998; June 26, 2019, effective September 1, 2019.

Rule 4:05. Claims by Clients

Section 1. The Board may consider a client's claim for reimbursement of losses caused by an attorney who had been a member of the Massachusetts bar and who has been disbarred, suspended, has resigned from the bar, or has died. The Board may allow or deny such claims in whole or in part to the extent that funds are available and in accordance with all applicable rules and principles, especially the provisions of this Chapter Four.

Section 2. All reimbursements shall be a matter of grace, not right, and no client, beneficiary, employer, organization, or other person shall have any right or interest in the Fund. No decision to allow or deny reimbursement shall be subject to judicial review in a court of either appellate or original jurisdiction.

Section 3. In exercising its discretion whether to allow any claim for reimbursement from the Fund, the Board shall attempt to establish fair, reasonable, and consistent principles for the allowance and denial of claims. To the extent possible, the Board shall attempt to fully reimburse claimants for their actual losses consistent with the Board's role as public trustee of the Fund and considering the following and other factors as the Board may deem appropriate and relevant:

(A) The amounts available and likely to become available to the Fund for payment of claims;

(B) The size and number of claims likely to be presented in the future;

(C) The amount of the claimant's loss as compared with the amount of the losses sustained by other claimants who may merit reimbursement from the Fund;

(D) The unreimbursed amounts of claims recognized by the Board as meriting reimbursement but for which complete reimbursement has not been made;

(E) The degree of hardship suffered by the claimant as compared with that suffered by other claimants; and

(F) Any negligence or conduct of the claimant that may have contributed to the loss.

Section 4. The Board may require any claimant, as a condition of any payment from the Fund, to execute such instruments, to take such action, and to enter into such agreements as the Board may direct, including assignments, subrogation agreements, trust agreements, and promises to cooperate with the Board in making and prosecuting claims or charges against any person.

Section 5. The Board may issue a subpoena requiring the attendance and testimony of a witness, including the disbarred or suspended attorney, to appear before the Board or its counsel at a specified date and time. The subpoena shall specify any evidence relating to the Board investigation that the witness shall produce to the Board, including but not limited to books, records, correspondence, or documents. The Board may record testimony electronically or otherwise. The Board shall use the recording for its own administrative purposes.

Section 6. The Board shall keep confidential all claim forms, proceedings, investigations, claimants' and respondents' financial information, and reports involving specific claims received and payments made from the Fund. The Board and its staff shall maintain the confidentiality of the claim forms, investigations, and proceedings. This provision shall not be construed to:

(A) deny relevant information to the Board of Bar Overseers, to a court or investigative agency of proper jurisdiction, to an authorized agency investigating the qualifications of a judicial candidate, or applicant for governmental employment;

(B) prohibit the release of statistical or summary information that does not disclose the identity of the parties; or

(C) prohibit the release of publicity in a manner that is consistent with the provisions of this section.

Adopted June 3, 1974, effective September 1, 1974. Amended effective September 14, 1977; April 15, 1996; amended December 11, 2003, effective January 1, 2004; June 26, 2019, effective September 1, 2019.

Rule 4:06.   Miscellaneous Powers and Duties of Clients' Security Board

Section 1.   In addition to other powers the Board may:

(A) adopt, with the approval of this court, rules that are consistent with these rules;

(B) enforce, in its discretion, claims for restitution arising by subrogation, assignment, or otherwise;

(C) invest or direct the investment of the Fund, or any portion thereof, in such investments as the Board may deem appropriate, and may cause funds to be deposited in any bank, banking institution, savings bank, or federally insured savings and loan association in this Commonwealth provided, however, that the Board shall have no obligation to cause the Fund or any portion thereof to be invested;

(D) employ and compensate consultants, agents, legal counsel, and employees;

(E) enter into contracts for goods and services as are necessary for the Board to carry out its duties;

(F) obtain surety bond or insurance coverage useful or appropriate in providing protections to clients of attorneys;

(G) assign for administrative purposes its duties under subsections (D) and (E) to the Executive Director of the Board of Bar Overseers, in accordance with the Board's written directions, which the Board may amend or rescind at any time;

(H) sue in the name of the Board without joining any or all of its individual members; and

(I) perform other acts necessary or proper for the efficient administration of the Fund.

Section 2.   The Board shall authorize disbursement of money from the Fund only after issuing a written order pursuant to this Chapter Four.

Section 3.   At least once each year, and at such additional times as the court may order, the Board shall file with this court a written report of its administration of the Fund. The written report shall include a list of any material written contracts into which the Board entered, including the name of the contracting party, the amount of the contract, the beginning and end date of the contract, and the scope of work to be accomplished.

Section 4.   The Board shall annually, and at such other times as this court may direct, obtain an independent audit by a certified public accountant of funds received and paid out in connection with the administration of the Fund. The Fund shall pay the cost of any such audit.

Adopted June 3, 1974, effective September 1, 1974. Amended October 1, 1998, effective November 2, 1998; June 26, 2019, effective September 1, 2019.

Rule 4:07.   Lawyers Concerned for Lawyers Fund and Oversight Committee

Section 1.   Lawyers Concerned for Lawyers, Inc. (LCL) provides programs to assist lawyers, judges, other legal professionals and law students who may be impaired in their ability to function as a result of the disease of addiction, including but not limited to alcoholism or other chemical dependency. In addition, LCL provides assessment and referral services with respect to other psychological, emotional and physical impairments that might interfere with an individual's capacity to function as a lawyer. The Board shall bill and collect the portion of the annual registration fee designated by the court for LCL to provide funds for the operation of the lawyers assistance programs and, upon receipt, shall hold the funds collected in trust as a separate fund for LCL. The court shall appoint an LCL Oversight Committee (hereinafter the Committee) to oversee the appropriate use of the fund so set apart for the operation of LCL. The court shall appoint to the Committee a representative from LCL, a present or former member of the Board of Bar Overseers, a present or former member of the Clients' Security Board, and three or more members of the Massachusetts bar.

Section 2.

(1) The Committee, as initially constituted, shall consist of such members as the court may determine, to be selected by the court as soon as reasonably practicable after the adoption of this rule. Thereafter the court, by order, shall request the submission of nominations to fill vacancies in such manner as it may determine. LCL, the Board of Bar Overseers, the Clients' Security Board, the Massachusetts Bar Association, and each county bar association (including the Boston Bar Association as the bar association for Suffolk County) may nominate a person to fill a vacancy in the Committee. Any attorney may also submit in writing the names of nominees. The court may, but need not, make appointments to the Committee from the nominees so submitted. The court shall from time to time designate one member of the Committee as Chair and another as Vice Chair to act in the absence, for any cause, of the Chair.

(2) When the Committee is first selected, approximately one-third of the members shall be appointed for a term of three years, one-third for a term of two years, and one-third for a term of one year. Subsequent appointments to the Committee shall be for a term of four years. No member shall be appointed to more than two consecutive full terms but (a) a member appointed for less than a full term (originally or to fill a vacancy) may serve two consecutive full terms in addition to such part of a full term, and (b) a former member shall again be eligible for appointment after a lapse of at least one year. The Committee shall act only with the concurrence of a majority of the members who are present provided,

however, that a quorum shall be constituted of a majority of the Committee. A member whose term has expired shall continue in office until a successor is appointed.

Section 3.

(1) LCL shall annually, and at such additional times as the court may order, cause to be performed an independent audit of its books by a certified public accountant. Further, LCL shall annually, and at such additional times as the court may order, file with the court a written report of its operations. Copies of such audit and report will be furnished to the Committee.

(2) At least annually, LCL shall prepare and submit to the Committee for approval a budget of its financial requirements for the period covered by such budget. Upon approval of such budget, the Committee shall authorize in writing disbursement for such period from the funds held by the Board for LCL's account. Pursuant to such authority, disbursement shall be made at such times and in such manner as LCL may from time to time request of the Board in writing.

Section 4. Members of LCL and its staff shall be immune from liability for any good faith conduct in the course of their official duties.

Section 5. Pursuant to the provisions of Mass. R. Prof. C. 1.6(c) (Rule 3:07), a lawyer participating in an LCL program to provide lawyer assistance, as defined in Mass. R. Prof. C. 1.6(c), may require a person acting under the lawyer's supervision or control to sign a non-disclosure form approved by the Supreme Judicial Court.

Adopted effective February 1, 1993, with former Rules 4:07 and 4:08 renumbered as Rules 4:08 and 4:09. Amended effective November 15, 1995; January 1, 1997; amended June 9, 1997, effective January 1, 1998.

Rule 4:08. Interpretation of Chapter Four of These Rules

Section 1. The Board of Bar Overseers or the Clients' Security Board may request this court for an interpretation of any portion of this Chapter Four, and for advice and instructions as to their powers and duties. Either of these boards may submit to the court suggestions or proposals for revisions, modifications, or improvement of this Chapter Four, including proposals for affording protection to clients by surety bonds, group insurance of attorneys, or other means of insurance or indemnity coverage.

Section 2. Except where powers are expressly given to the full court, or the context indicates clearly that the full court alone is to have the power, the powers of this court may be exercised by a justice, subject to any appropriate review.

Adopted as Rule 4:07 June 3, 1974, effective September 1, 1974. Renumbered as Rule 4:08 effective February 1, 1993. Amended June 26, 2019, effective September 1, 2019.

Rule 4:09. Amendment, Modification, Repeal

This court may amend, modify, or repeal this Chapter Four of these rules at any time without prior notice and, in its discretion, may provide for the dissolution and winding up of the Fund.

Adopted as Rule 4:08 June 3, 1974, effective September 1, 1974. Renumbered as Rule 4:09 effective February 1, 1993. Amended June 26, 2019, effective September 1, 2019.

AFFIDAVIT OF INDIGENCY

AFFIDAVIT OF INDIGENCY AND REQUEST FOR WAIVER, SUBSTITUTION OR STATE PAYMENT OF FEES & COSTS

Commonwealth of Massachusetts

AFFIDAVIT OF INDIGENCY

AND REQUEST FOR WAIVER, SUBSTITUTION
OR STATE PAYMENT OF FEES & COSTS

*(Note: If you are **currently confined in a prison or jail** and are not seeking immediate release under G.L. c. 248 § 1, but you are suing correctional staff and wish to request court payment of "normal" fees (for initial filing and service), **do not use this form**. Obtain separate forms from the clerk.)*

_____   _____
       Court   Case Name and Number (if known)

Name of applicant: _____

Address: _____
      (Street and number)   (City or town)   (State and Zip)

SECTION 1:   Under the provisions of General Laws, Chapter 261, Sections 27A–27G, I swear (or affirm) as follows: **I AM INDIGENT** in that *(check only one)*:

☐ (A) I receive public assistance under *(check form of public assistance received)*:
       ☐ Transitional Aid to Families with ☐ Medicaid (MassHealth)
          Dependent Children (TAFDC)
       ☐ Emergency Aid to Elderly, Dis- ☐ Supplemental Security Income
          abled or Children (EAEDC)   (SSI)
       ☐ Massachusetts Veterans Benefits
          Programs; **or**

☐ (B) My income, less taxes deducted from my pay, is $ _____ per ☐ week ☐ biweekly ☐ month ☐ year
     (check the period that applies) for a household of _____ persons, consisting of myself and _____ dependents; which income is at or below the court system's poverty level; *(Note: The court system's poverty levels for households of various sizes must be posted in this courthouse. If you cannot find it, ask the clerk or check online at:* http:// www.mass.gov/courts/sjc/docs/povertyguidelines.pdf. *The court system's poverty level is updated each year.)*

     (List any other available household income for the checked period on this line: $ _____); **or**

☐ (C) I am unable to pay the fees and costs of this proceeding, or I am unable to do so without depriving myself or my dependents of the necessities of life, including food, shelter and clothing.

IF YOU CHECKED (C), YOU MUST ALSO COMPLETE THE <u>SUPPLEMENT</u>
<u>TO THE AFFIDAVIT OF INDIGENCY</u>.

SECTION 2:   (*Note: In completing this form, please be as specific as possible as to fees and costs known at the time of filing this request. A supplementary request may be filed at a later time, if necessary.*)

I request that the following **NORMAL FEES AND COSTS** be waived (not charged) by the court, or paid by the state, or that the court order that a document, service or object be substituted at no cost (or a lower cost, paid for by the state): (*Check all that apply and, in any "$ _____" blank, indicate your best guess as to the cost, if known.*)

☐ Filing fee and any surcharge. $ _____

☐ Filing fee and any surcharge for appeal. $ _____

☐ Fees or costs for serving court summons, witness subpoenas or other court papers. $ _____

☐ Other fees or costs of $ _____ for (*specify*): _____

_____

☐ Substitution (*specify*): _____

_____

SECTION 3:   I request that the following **EXTRA FEES AND COSTS** either be waived (not charged), substituted or paid for by the state:

☐ Cost, $ _____, of expert services for testing, examination, testimony or other assistance (*specify*):

_____

☐ Cost, $ _____, of taking and/or transcribing a deposition of (*specify name of person*):

_____

☐ Cassette copies of tape recording of trial or other proceeding, needed to prepare appeal for applicant **not** represented by Committee for Public Counsel Services (CPCS–public defender).

☐ Appeal bond

☐ Cost, $ _____, of preparing written transcript of trial or other proceeding

☐ Other fees and costs, $ _____, for (*specify*): _____

_____

☐ Substitution (*specify*) _____

_____
Date signed   Signed under the penalties of perjury

x _____

By order of the Supreme Judicial Court, all information in this affidavit is
CONFIDENTIAL. Except by special order of a court, it shall not be disclosed
to anyone other than authorized court personnel, the applicant, applicant's
counsel or anyone authorized in writing by the applicant.

This form prescribed by the Chief Justice of the SJC pursuant to G.L. c. 261,
§ 27B. Promulgated March   , 2003. Fillable PDF created August 2013.

SUPPLEMENT TO AFFIDAVIT OF INDIGENCY AND REQUEST FOR WAIVER, SUBSTITUTION OR STATE PAYMENT OF FEES & COSTS

Commonwealth of Massachusetts

SUPPLEMENT TO AFFIDAVIT OF INDIGENCY

AND REQUEST FOR WAIVER, SUBSTITUTION
OR STATE PAYMENT OF FEES & COSTS

(Note: If you checked (C) on the AFFIDAVIT OF INDIGENCY, you must complete this form.)

_____   _____
        Court   Case Name and Number (if known)

Name of applicant: _____

Address: _____
    (Street and number)   (City or town)   (State and Zip)

Under the provisions of General Laws, Chapter 261, Sections 27A–27G, I swear or affirm as follows:

1. **PERSONAL INFORMATION**

    (a) Date of Birth: _____

    (b) Highest Grade in School: _____

    (c) Special Training: _____

    (d) List any physical or mental disabilities which you wish to reveal and which affect your earning capacity or living expenses:

        _____

    (e) Number of Dependents: _____

2. **INCOME AFTER TAXES (monthly)**

    (a) If from employment, list your occupation and employer's name and address:

    (b) Sources of income, if not from employment:

    (c) My gross annual income for the past twelve months was: $ _____

    (d) Gross Income (monthly): $ _____

    (e) Taxes Deducted (monthly):

        Federal Tax $ _____

        State Tax $ _____

        Social Security $ _____

Medicare $ _____

Other Taxes *(specify)* _____ $ _____

Total Taxes Deducted $ _____

(f)   Total Income After Taxes *(subtract 2(e) from 2(d)):* $ _____

(g)   If any other member of your household is employed, list occupation and name and address of his/her employer and monthly income after taxes:

_____

3. **NET INCOME (monthly)**

(a)   Income After Taxes *(from line 2(f)):* $ _____

(b)   Expenses (monthly):

Rent or Mortgage	$ _____	Uninsured Medical Expenses	$ _____
Food	$ _____	Child Care	$ _____
Electricity	$ _____	Education Expenses for Children	$ _____
Gas	$ _____	Child Support	$ _____
Oil	$ _____	Clothing	$ _____
Water	$ _____	Laundry/Cleaning	$ _____
Telephone	$ _____	Car Insurance	$ _____
Health Insurance	$ _____	Transportation Expenses	$ _____

Other *(specify)*: _____ $ _____

_____

Total Expenses $ _____

(c)   Income After Taxes Minus Expenses (monthly) *(subtract 3(b) from 3(a)):* $ _____

4. **ASSETS**

(a)   Own Home?   Yes ☐ No ☐   Market Value $ _____   Balance Owed $ _____

(b)   Own Car?   Yes ☐ No ☐   Year & Make _____

     Market Value $ _____   Balance Owed $ _____

(c)   Bank Accounts (specify type and balance)

_____

(d)   Other Property including Real Estate (specify type and value)

_____

5. **DEBTS**

    (a)   Specify:

          _____

6. **MISCELLANEOUS**

    (a)   Other facts which may be relevant to your ability to pay fees and costs?

          _____

Signed under the penalties of perjury: Signature: x_____

                                               Type/Printed Name: _____

                                               Address: _____

                                               City: _____ State: _____ Zip Code: _____

                                             Date signed: _____

POVERTY THRESHOLD GUIDELINES

Poverty Guidelines for Affidavit of Indigency—2019

125% of Current Poverty Guidelines Applicable under G. L. c. 261, § 27A.

Size of Family Unit	125% of Poverty Guidelines
1	$15,612.50
2	$21,137.50
3	$26,662.50
4	$32,187.50
5	$37,712.50
6	$43,237.50
7	$48,762.50
8	$54,287.50

For family units with more than 8 members add $5,525 for each additional member.

DETERMINATION REGARDING FEES AND COSTS

DETERMINATION REGARDING FEES AND COSTS

_____   _____

Court   Case Name and Number (if known)

Name of applicant _____

Address _____

       (Street and number)   (City or town)   (State and Zip)

FORTHWITH DETERMINATION BY CLERK (Register, Recorder)

☐   **ALLOWED FORTHWITH.** The applicant's affidavit appears regular and complete on its face, indicates that the applicant is indigent, and requests waiver, substitution or payment by the Commonwealth of normal fees and costs only. Pursuant to G. L. c. 261, § 27C(2), the application is therefore **ALLOWED** forthwith without hearing, and the normal fees and costs indicated in the application are:

☐   waived in full   ☐ to be paid by the Commonwealth in the amount of $

☐   **REFERRED TO A JUDGE.** The applicant's affidavit does not satisfy all the conditions of § 27C(2), and is therefore referred to a judge pursuant to § 27C(3), because:

☐   The affidavit is not regular and complete on its face.

☐   The affidavit does not indicate that the applicant is indigent within the meaning of § 27A.

☐   The affidavit requests waiver, substitution or payment by the Commonwealth of **extra** fees and costs.

Comments:

Describe fees and costs waived:

Date   Clerk–Magistrate/ Assistant Clerk (register, recorder/assistant)

_____ X _____

       DETERMINATION BY JUDGE ☐ **after hearing** ☐ **without hearing**

NORMAL FEES AND COSTS

☐   The application is **ALLOWED** with respect to the normal fees and costs indicated in the application, and they are ordered:

     ☐ waived in full. ☐ to be paid by the Commonwealth in the amount of $ _____.

     ☐ waived in part. I find that it is within the applicant's limited financial means to pay a reduced amount of $ _____.

     ☐ to be avoided by the provision of _____ to the applicant, pursuant to § 27F, as an alternative which is available at lower or no cost, is substantially equivalent and does not materially impair the rights of any party.

☐   The application is **DENIED** with respect to the normal fees and costs indicated in the application, because I find that:

☐ The applicant is not indigent within the meaning of § 27A.

☐ Other:

Describe normal fees and costs waived:

EXTRA FEES AND COSTS

☐   The application is **ALLOWED** with respect to the extra fees and costs indicated in the application, and they are ordered:

    ☐ waived in full. ☐ to be paid by the Commonwealth in the amount of $ ____.

    ☐ waived in part. I find that it is within the applicant's limited financial means to pay a reduced amount of $ ___.

☐   to be avoided by the provision of _____ to the applicant, pursuant to § 27F, as an alternative which is available at lower or no cost, is substantially equivalent and does not materially impair the rights of any party.

☐   The application is **DENIED** with respect to the extra fees and costs indicated in the application, because I find that:

    ☐ The applicant is not indigent within the meaning of § 27A.

    ☐ The document, service or object is not reasonably necessary to assure the applicant as effective a prosecution, defense or appeal as if the applicant were financially able to pay.

    ☐ Other:

Describe extra fees and costs waived:

Date   Judge

           X

The applicant may appeal denial of this application by filing a notice of appeal with the clerk (register, recorder) of this court within 7 days from notice of denial.

INMATE'S AFFIDAVIT OF INDIGENCY

IMPOUNDED—CONFIDENTIAL

COMMONWEALTH OF MASSACHUSETTS

_____ Court

NO. _____

INFORMATION FOR THE INMATE/APPLICANT: You have requested that the _____ Court waive the filing fees and (normal) costs and allow you to proceed as an indigent plaintiff. You are required to provide the court with information about your finances so that the court can determine whether you are unable to pay the fee or to make partial payments. You are required to sign this affidavit form under the penalties of perjury. This includes a statement that no action has been taken to hide assets. The court can dismiss the complaint if it finds that the claim of indigency is untrue. In addition, the court may impose costs on an inmate who intentionally files an affidavit that contains false information or that omits material information. You are also subject to loss of up to 60 days of good time earned or to be earned under G. L. c. 127, § 129C (for blood donation) or under c. 127, § 129D (for work, education or rehabilitation programs) if the court finds that the affidavit is frivolous and filed in bad faith in order to abuse the judicial process. See G. L. c. 261, § 29.

_____,   Plaintiff(s)

v.

_____,   Defendant(s)

INMATE'S AFFIDAVIT OF INDIGENCY AND REQUEST FOR WAIVER OF NORMAL FEES AND COSTS IN COMPLIANCE WITH GENERAL LAWS c. 261, § 29

Pursuant to General Laws c. 261, § 29, the applicant, _____, swears (or
(NAME)

affirms) that the following information is true.

SOCIAL SECURITY #: _____

DATE OF BIRTH: _____

INMATE IDENTIFICATION #: _____

CORRECTIONAL FACILITY: _____

ASSETS:

    CASH: _____

    MONIES IN BANK ACCOUNTS:

        INMATE CANTEEN ACCOUNT: _____

        OTHER INSTITUTIONAL ACCOUNT: _____

        NON–PRISON ACCOUNT(S): _____

        REAL ESTATE: _____

    OTHER INVESTMENTS: _____

ACCESSIBLE ASSETS OF A SPOUSE: _____

INCOME:

LAST SIX MONTHS' INCOME: _____

INCOME EXPECTED IN NEXT SIX MONTHS: _____

LIABILITIES (for example, any debts you owe, including Victim/Witness fees, restitution fees, child support, other court-imposed costs, and costs assessed for incarceration and pre-release programs):

_____

MONTHLY EXPENSES:

NECESSARY CANTEEN PURCHASES (for example, stamps, envelopes, soap, toothpaste and other toiletries, medications and clothing):

_____

OTHER EXPENSES: _____

I state under penalties of perjury that the statements made in this affidavit are true, that I have not omitted any assets that are available to me to pay filing fees or court costs, that I have not transferred any assets to avoid payment of filing fees and costs, and that I have not taken any action nor has any action been taken on my behalf relative to any assets in order to avoid having such assets used for payment of filing fees and costs.

Signature of applicant: _____

DATE: _____

ALL INFORMATION CONTAINED HEREIN IS CONFIDENTIAL. EX-CEPT BY SPECIAL ORDER OF A COURT, IT SHALL NOT BE DISCLOSED TO ANYONE OTHER THAN AUTHORIZED COURT PERSONNEL, PARTIES TO THIS LITIGATION OR THEIR COUNSEL, AND AN AUTHORIZED (IN WRITING) REPRESENTATIVE OF THE APPLICANT.

INSTRUCTIONS FOR USERS OF AFFIDAVIT OF INDIGENCY AND ITS SUPPLEMENT

A state statute provides that if you cannot pay for court fees or costs, you may be able to have the state pay for them. These instructions describe who is eligible and how to use this law.

Who Is Eligible? - You are eligible for a waiver, substitution or state payment of fees and costs if any one of the following applies to you:

Category (A) You receive public assistance under one of the following programs: Massachusetts Transitional Aid to Families With Dependent Children; Massachusetts Emergency Aid to Elderly, Disabled & Children; Federal Supplemental Security Income; Massachusetts MassHealth (formerly Medicaid) or Massachusetts Veterans Benefits; or

Category (B) Your income, after taxes, does not exceed 125% of the current Federal Poverty Line. This Poverty Line is revised annually, and the current chart should be posted in your local courthouse. If you do not find it there, please ask the Clerk's office where it is or for a copy; or

Category (C) You cannot pay the court fees or costs without depriving yourself or those who are dependent on you of the necessities of life, including food, shelter and clothing.

If you are *currently* confined in prison or jail and do not seek your immediate release but are suing a "state or county agency, official or employee" about something "arising out of or resulting from a condition of or occurrence during confinement," *and* you are seeking court payment of "normal" costs (see definition below), please get from the Clerk's office separate forms for prisoners which you must complete in order to qualify for a waiver. You can use the general forms for nonprisoners if you are asking the court to pay for "extra" fees. Regardless of which forms you use you might find the information below useful.

What Fees And Costs are Covered?—All fees and costs (other than attorneys fees) involved in the prosecution or defense of "any civil, criminal or juvenile proceeding or appeal in any court" are eligible for waiver, substitution or payment by the Commonwealth. When you prepare your application, please identify those costs which you need waived or paid for the initial or next steps of your court case. For example, if you are filing a case in court and you need a waiver of the court filing fee, prepare an application for waiver of that fee. If, in addition, you need to have a sheriff or other officer serve court process, or you need publication of notice, include your estimates of these costs also. If, at a later time, you need waiver or payment of other court costs (such as costs for subpoenas of witnesses to hearings, costs of taking depositions of witnesses, etc.) you should make a separate application at that time.

The fees and costs which can be waived or paid by the state are divided into two categories:

(1) **Normal** fees and costs are those that "a party normally is required to pay in order to prosecute or defend the particular type of proceeding." They include, for example:

• Court filing fees and surcharges, and also appeal fees and surcharges

• Other court fees for issuing or certifying papers or for photocopies.

• Constable or sheriff fees for serving court process, witness subpoenas, or other court papers.

• Costs of publishing notices relating to a court action.

If you are requesting only normal fees and costs, and your affidavit appears regular and complete on its face and indicates that you are indigent, the Clerk will allow your request immediately "without hearing and without the necessity of appearance of any party or counsel." The Clerk will waive the fees or costs completely, order them to be paid by the Commonwealth, or substitute "an alternative means at lower or no cost [that] is substantially equivalent and . . . does not materially impair the rights of any party." If your affidavit is not regular and complete or you do not appear to be indigent, the clerk-magistrate will promptly present your request to a Judge for decision within 5 days. The Judge will either grant your request without a hearing or you will be notified of a hearing date.

If you are a prisoner, a Judge will need to act on your application after first ordering the facility where you are confined to produce a copy of your canteen account for the last six months. You may ask the court to order payment of the cost of serving the summons and complaint in the meantime, however, so your case can begin.

(2) **Extra** fees and costs are those that are "in addition to those a party is normally required to pay in order to prosecute or defend [the] case, which result when a party employs or responds to a procedure not necessarily required in the particular type of proceeding." They include, for example:

• Costs of expert testing, examination or testimony

• Cassette copies for indigent parties not represented by a public defender

• Appeal bonds

If you are requesting any extra fees and costs, the Clerk will promptly present your request to a Judge for decision within 5 days. The Judge may allow your request without a hearing, but will not deny your request without holding a hearing. In reviewing a request for extra fees or costs, the Judge will decide whether the document, service or object is reasonably necessary to assure you as effective a prosecution, defense or appeal as you would have if you were financially able to pay.

"Normal" and "extra" fees and costs do not include attorneys' fees.

How Do I Apply?—You should complete the Affidavit of Indigency form that applies to you. If you claim eligibility under Category (C) above, you must also complete the Supplement to Affidavit of Indigency form. File your papers with the Clerk of the court where your case has been filed (or where you are seeking to file it). Court Clerks must accept your initial court papers when you present them, even if you have not then obtained a waiver of the filing fee. If the fee is later waived, the date of filing your court papers will be the day you first presented them to the Clerk.

What is the Federal Poverty Line?—If you want to qualify under Category (B) above (income, after taxes, which is less than 125% of the Federal Poverty Line), you should consult a chart of these income limits which should be posted in your local courthouse. If you cannot find this chart, go to the Clerk's office and find out where it is or ask to be given or to read a copy. This Poverty Line is increased every year in February or March, and so the court should have an up-to-date schedule.

How Do I Estimate the Costs?—There are places on the form where you can give the cost (if you know it) or give your best estimate of the cost of the particular fee or service that you need. If you do not know what the cost will be, give your best description of what you need. The court should approve your application, if you are otherwise eligible, even though you have not filled in complete information about the costs.

What Are the Situations in Which I Can Get a Substitution of a Service?—Under the law, a court can order that a different (or substitute) method of performing a certain act or service be allowed, rather than a less convenient or more expensive one. For example, in some situations a court might order that notice of filing a court action be made by posting in certain locations rather than by publishing the notice in a newspaper. In other situations you may be able to take depositions using tape recorders rather than using a more expensive stenographer. If you have a request for a substitute method, please ask for it in your application. The court may, itself, order a less expensive or easier substitution. However, the judge may order you to pay a partial fee or cost rather than to waive it if you are otherwise eligible for waiver or state payment.

If you are a prisoner bringing an action in Superior Court, you will receive a summons and be instructed to serve it with your complaint by certified mail. You can ask for permission to use regular mail if paying the cost of certified mail presents a hardship. If you are filing a case in another court, you can ask for permission to serve by certified or regular mail.

Can I Appeal A Denial?—Yes. If you disagree with any decision of the Clerk or Assistant Clerk, you can request a review by the judge. If you disagree with a decision of a Judge, you can appeal to the next court level. There are short deadlines for doing this, so you must act quickly. Consult the Clerk's office for information about how to do this.

Are the Indigent Court Costs Papers That I File in Court Confidential?—Yes, these papers are not available to the general public or to any other party in the case, but are only available to authorized court personnel and to you and your attorney or your other authorized representative. If you want an authorized representative other than your attorney to see or get copies of these documents, you should prepare a written consent so that a designated individual will have authority to do that. Any other party to the case, or their authorized representative, does not have access to these records unless that party gets a court order giving permission. Also, when you file an application or an appeal under the indigent court costs law, you are not required to give copies of any of these documents to any other party in the case.

INTERIM ELECTRONIC FILING RULES
FOR PILOT COURTS [REPEALED]

The Interim Electronic Filing Rules for Pilot Courts were repealed effective September 1, 2018. See, now, Supreme Judicial Court Rule 1:25, Massachusetts Electronic Filing Rules.

STANDING ORDERS OF THE
SUPREME JUDICIAL COURT

Table of Standing Orders

Matters Not Disposed of in the County Court for More Than Three Months*

1. It is ORDERED that in February, May, August and November of each year there shall be a call, in the county court (single justice session), of all petitions and suits which have remained for more than three months upon the docket of the county court, without final disposition. The clerk of the Supreme Judicial Court for Suffolk County shall, without further order of the court, prepare lists for such calls, and shall give seasonable and appropriate notice by mail to all interested parties or their attorneys of record. The notice in each case shall state that the matter is being called for dismissal or other appropriate order, and that failure of a party or his attorney to answer may result in dismissal of the matter.

2. A copy of this order shall be filed with the clerk of the Supreme Judicial Court for Suffolk County.

Adopted February 8, 1972. Amended April 5, 2007.

Record of Proceedings in the Supreme Judicial Court of Suffolk County*

Unless a justice shall otherwise direct, all proceedings in the Supreme Judicial Court for the county of Suffolk shall be recorded electronically, subject to the availability and functioning of the appropriate recording devices. Cassette or similar tape recordings of the original recording shall be available to counsel through the clerk's office on the payment of a reasonable fee and notice of the making of such request to all parties.

If a transcript of the proceedings is required by statute or is requested by a justice, unless an official stenographer has been appointed, a transcript of the proceedings shall be made under the direction of the clerk and certified by him.

A certified copy of any transcript prepared under the direction of the clerk shall be available to counsel on the payment of a reasonable fee. In his discretion, a justice of the court may order a party or parties to bear the cost of the preparation of a transcript for use of the court.

Adopted August 18, 1976.

* Suggested title added by Publisher.

Time Within Which Cases May Be Determined by the Appellate Courts*

WHEREAS the Chief Justice and the Justices of the Supreme Judicial Court recognize the necessity for reasonably expeditious disposition of appealed cases, and appreciate the Court's duty of public accountability in this matter; and

WHEREAS the Justices of the Appeals Court have expressed their agreement with those views by adopting today such portions of this order as relate to the Appeals Court,

Now therefore it is ORDERED:

The following standards are adopted as administrative goals establishing a time within which cases can be expected to be determined by the appellate courts of Massachusetts. Variation from the 130-day standard set out in paragraph 2 should be permitted by vote of the quorum when necessary to accommodate special problems in individual cases. Docket entries will be made as to any such action.

1. Oral argument, or the decision conference in cases not orally argued, should be held promptly after the appellee's brief is filed or should have been filed. Cases in which the appellee's brief is due on or before February 1 should be heard or made the subject of a decision conference during that court year. (Court year: September 1 through August 31.)

2. Cases should be decided within 130 days after argument or after submission without argument.

3. Paragraphs one and two shall be applicable in the Supreme Judicial Court forthwith, and paragraph two shall be applicable in the Appeals Court for all cases argued or submitted for decision after the date of this order. Paragraph one shall be applicable in the Appeals Court as soon as possible after the additional justices authorized by St. 1978, c. 478, § 104, have assumed their duties, with a tentative goal of full applicability not later than the close of the 1979-1980 court year.

Adopted October 2, 1978. Amended January 24, 1983.

* Suggested title added by Publisher.

Storage of Documents at State Archives*

ORDERED: That any papers, records, exhibits and artifacts which have been filed or deposited in or which are located in any court of the Commonwealth may be moved to the State Archives at Columbia Point in Boston, Massachusetts provided that the Administrative Assistant (G.L. c. 211, § 3A) to the Supreme Judicial Court approves. G.L. c. 221, § 27A. The State Archivist shall be the custodian of all court papers, records, exhibits and artifacts maintained at the State Archives. The Supreme Judicial Court shall retain control of such papers, records, exhibits and artifacts under such conditions as shall be agreed to by the State Archivist and the Supreme Judicial Court.

* Suggested title added by Publisher.

Agreement Between the Supreme Judicial
Court and the State Archivist

Pursuant to the provisions of the order of the Supreme Judicial Court dated January 17, 1984, the State Archivist and the Administrative Assistant to the Supreme Judicial Court hereby agree to the following terms and conditions with respect to all judicial papers, records, exhibits and artifacts to be moved to the State Archives at Columbia Point in Boston, Massachusetts:

(1) Consistent with the Separation of Powers Clause (Article 30) of the Constitution of the Commonwealth, there shall be a separate judicial archives located within the space occupied by the State Archives. The Supreme Judicial Court acting through the Administrative Assistant to the Supreme Judicial Court, and the Judicial Records Committee of the Supreme Judicial Court, shall maintain control of all court papers, records, exhibits and artifacts moved to the State Archives. The State Archivist, as a member ex officio of the Judicial Records Committee of the Supreme Judicial Court, shall be the physical custodian of all court papers, records, exhibits and artifacts stored at the State Archives.

(2) Subject to appropriation, there shall be a curator of judicial records at the State Archives who shall be responsible for the administration of the judicial archives. The curator of judicial records shall be an employee of the Office of the Secretary of the Commonwealth. The job description of the curator of judicial records shall be subject to the approval of the Supreme Judicial Court.

In addition to the curator of judicial records, employees of the State Archivist shall be authorized to administer the judicial archives in a manner consistent with the policies established by the Supreme Judicial Court.

The State Archivist shall periodically report to the Administrative Assistant to the Supreme Judicial Court.

(3) The procedures for processing judicial records for entry into the State Archives shall be established by the Supreme Judicial Court in consultation with the State Archivist.

Upon the completion of construction of the State Archives and Records Center at Columbia Point, the State Archivist shall designate a single location in the State Archives portion of the building consisting of approximately 12,000 cubic feet of shelving space to be occupied by the judicial archives. The space shall be discrete and continuous. It shall be distinct from the non-judicial archival collections with adequate access to the public research room of the State Archives. If at some time in the future additional space is necessary for expansion of the judicial archives, the State Archivist shall make reasonable attempts to designate such additional space as may be necessary consistent with the need to maintain a separate judicial collection. To the extent possible, the State Archivist shall attempt to designate the additional space at a single location with discrete and continuous shelving as close to the initial judicial archives space as is feasible.

(4) The judicial archives initially shall consist of the following records:—(1) pre-1860 records of the predecessors of the Superior Court; (2) pre-1860 Supreme Judicial Court records and records of special courts such as admiralty; (3) cases of unique historical interest (e.g. the Sacco-Vanzetti records). Some of these records will be treated in the Supreme Judicial Court records preservation laboratory in the Suffolk County Courthouse prior to deposit in the State Archives. Other records will first be shipped to the State Archives to be stored prior to later treatment either in the Supreme Judicial Court laboratory or in the laboratory of the State Archives.

There shall be no prohibition on maintaining closed shelved materials in the judicial archives. Such materials, if any, shall be closed by direction of the Supreme Judicial Court.

The facilities of the State Archives, including the fumigation laboratory and special treatment facilities, shall be open to the judicial archives, subject to the control of the State Archivist. However, all conservation procedures performed on judicial records shall be subject to the approval of the Administrative Assistant to the Supreme Judicial Court. Endangered judicial records which cannot be treated in a timely fashion in the Supreme Judicial Court laboratory shall be given status in the State Archives laboratory consistent with the status given endangered non-judicial records.

(5) The State Archives shall maintain all judicial records in its custody with the same care and security as is provided for other archival documents held at the State Archives.

(6) This agreement may be amended by written agreement of the State Archivist and the Administrative Assistant to the Supreme Judicial Court. The Secretary of the Commonwealth and the Chief Justice of the Supreme Judicial Court shall be notified of any proposed amendment to the agreement prior to the effective date of the amendment. The Secretary of the Commonwealth and the Supreme Judicial Court may prohibit or nullify any such change in the agreement or may otherwise jointly revise the terms of the agreement.

Adopted January 17, 1984.

* Suggested title added by Publisher.

Time Standards for Civil Cases*   [Repealed]

Repealed effective October 4, 2004.

Authority of Appellate Clerks to Make Microforms of Transcripts in Their Custody*

ORDERED: It is hereby authorized that the clerks of the appellate courts may make microform copies of transcripts in their custody. Such microform copies shall be made in accordance with standards and procedures established by the Chief Justice of the Supreme Judicial Court. After the completion of a microform copy which accurately reproduces the transcript and forms a durable medium for its retention, the clerk may destroy the original transcript in the regular course of business.

Adopted July 28, 1987.

Advisory Committee to the Judicial Training Institute *

I. (a) Consistent with the provisions of G.L. c. 211, § 3G, as inserted by St. 1987, c. 199, § 142, there is hereby established the Advisory Committee (hereinafter "Committee") of the Judicial Training Institute (hereinafter "Institute") for assisting the Justices of the Supreme Judicial Court in matters pertaining to the policies and activities of the Institute and for assisting the Institute's Executive Director and staff in the performance of their statutory duties and of such other duties as may be assigned to the Institute from time to time by rule or order of the Supreme Judicial Court.

II. (a) The Committee shall consist of an Associate Justice of the Appeals Court designated by the Chief Justice of that court; an Associate Justice of the Superior Court Department of the Trial Court designated by the Chief Justice of that department; an Associate Justice of the Family and Probate Court Department of the Trial Court designated by the Chief Justice of that department; an Associate Justice of the District Court Department of the Trial Court designated by the Chief Justice of that department; two Associate Justices of the Boston Municipal Court, Housing Court, Juvenile Court or Land Court Departments of the Trial Court, but not both from the same department, who shall be appointed by the Justices of the Supreme Judicial Court acting upon four nominations, one for each such department, made by the Chief Administrative Justice after consultation with the Chief Justices of those departments; the Chief Administrative Justice of the Trial Court, or his designee; the Commissioner of Probation, or his designee; two members designated by the Chief Administrative Justice of the Trial Court who shall each be a Clerk or Assistant Clerk, Register or Assistant Register, or a Recorder or Deputy Recorder of a department of the Trial Court; and three members who shall be appointed by the Justices of the Supreme Judicial Court.

(b) When the Committee is first selected, the Justices of the Supreme Judicial Court shall assign approximately one-third of its members to a term of three years, one-third to a term of two years, and one-third to a term of one year. Subsequent appointments to the Committee shall be for a term of four years.

(c) The Justices of the Supreme Judicial Court shall from time to time designate a member of the Committee to serve as chairman and another as vice chairman.

(d) The Committee may appoint a judge or other officer or employee of the judicial department to serve, at its pleasure, as its secretary.

(e) The Committee may invite other persons, including but not limited to judges and members of the bar, (a) to participate in any one or more projects, studies, meetings, or other activities, or (b) to prepare and present studies, analyses, recommendations, and comments upon matters concerning which the Committee desires information.

(f) The members of the Committee and the secretary shall serve without compensation but shall be reimbursed for necessary expenses incurred incidental to the performance of their duties.

III. (a) The Committee shall prepare a statement of the qualifications, functions, and responsibilities of the Executive Director of the Institute to be appointed by the Justices of the Supreme Judicial Court and, upon the approval of such statement, shall assist the Justices in recruiting and selecting a qualified Executive Director for the Institute.

(b) Upon the appointment of an Executive Director, the Committee shall confer with him or her as to the organization and duties of the Institute's staff.

(c) The Committee shall also confer with the Executive Director with respect to the policies and programs of the Institute, and the priorities among them, and shall assist the Executive Director and the Justices of the Supreme Judicial Court in matters relating to the activities of the Institute, including the preparation of the comprehensive training needs assessment and program plan required by the provisions of St. 1987, c. 199, § 2, Account No. 0321–0002.

Adopted January 26, 1988.

* Suggested title added by Publisher.

Dismissals of Appeals and Reports Pending in the Supreme Judicial Court for Lack of Prosecution*

It is ORDERED that, except in cases in which there has been a conviction of first degree murder, whenever the clerk of this court (clerk) shall not have received the brief and appendix of an appellant (including in that term a party treated as an appellant under Rule 5 of the Massachusetts Rules of Appellate Procedure [Rules]) within the time required or permitted by Rules 11(g), 13(a), 18(a) and 19(a) (unless said time shall previously have been enlarged or unless, in the case of an appendix, the filing shall have been deferred or dispensed with under Rule 18[c] or [f]), the clerk shall send a copy of this order by first class mail to the attorney of record for such appellant (and to such appellant at his last known address in a criminal case or if he is not represented by such an attorney in a civil case) and to all other parties or to their attorneys of record, together with notice in writing that the appeal of such appellant or the report, as the case may be, will be dismissed as to him for lack of prosecution unless, within twenty-one days of the date of such notice in a civil case or within thirty days of the date of such notice in a criminal case, the clerk shall receive (a) a motion by such appellant to enlarge to a date certain set forth therein the time for serving and filing such brief and appendix and (b) an affidavit of such appellant (or his attorney) which shall set forth all the facts which such appellant wishes to have considered by the single justice of this court, who will act on such motion in accordance with the provisions of Rule 15(b) and (c). If no such motion and affidavit are received by the clerk within such period, the clerk shall forthwith dismiss such appeal or report for lack of prosecution and shall note such dismissal on the docket. The clerk shall take like action whenever a particular appellant has failed to serve and file his brief or appendix (when an appendix is required) within an enlargement of time previously granted. The sending of every notice required by this order shall be noted on the docket. Unless a dismissal shall have been vacated by a single justice within twenty-one days from the docketing thereof, the clerk shall notify the clerk of the trial court that the appeal or report has been dismissed as to the particular appellant for lack of prosecution. A dismissal in a criminal case may be vacated by a single justice of this court after the expiration of said twenty-one days upon a showing of the existence of a meritorious case.

Adopted May 17, 1988, effective July 1, 1988.

* Suggested title added by Publisher.

Matters Pending in the Supreme Judicial Court for More Than Six Months Without Activity*

It is ORDERED that in January and July of each year there shall be a call of all cases pending in the Supreme Judicial Court for the Commonwealth (other than cases which are ready for hearing or have been argued, but including cases in which a stay of appellate proceedings has been ordered) in which there has been no activity reflected on the docket (other than clerk's requests for status) for more than six months. For purposes of this standing order, ready for hearing shall mean that the appellant's brief and, if any is required, appendix, have been filed and no stay of appellate proceedings has been ordered. The clerk of the Supreme Judicial Court for the Commonwealth shall, after consultation with the single justice who will be sitting in January or July regarding cases which appropriately might be excluded from such calls, prepare lists for such calls, and shall give seasonable and appropriate notice by mail to all interested parties or their attorneys of record. The notice in each case shall state that the matter is being called for dismissal or other appropriate order, and that failure of a party or his attorney to answer may result in dismissal of the matter. A copy of this order shall be included with the notice.

Adopted May 17, 1988, effective July 1, 1988.

* Suggested title added by Publisher.

Applications For Stays Pending U.S. Supreme Court Consideration Of Applications For Certiorari

Pursuant to Mass. R.A.P. 15(c), applications for stays pending the United States Supreme Court's consideration of applications for writs of certiorari shall be considered upon the filing of a motion with the Clerk of the Supreme Judicial Court for the Commonwealth. Reasonable notice of the motion shall be given to all parties. The motion may be decided with or without a hearing by the panel whose decision is sought to be reviewed. At its discretion, the court may order a hearing by a single justice who was a member of that panel either for the justice's recommendation or decision. Relief available under this order, or denial of such relief, may be conditioned on such reasonable terms as the panel or single justice may impose, including appropriate conditions for the security of the adverse party.

Adopted effective July 1, 1988.

Applications to a Single Justice Pursuant to Mass.R.Crim.P. 15(a)(2)

(a) **Contents of Application.** An application to a single justice for leave to appeal an order determining a motion to suppress evidence prior to trial pursuant to Mass. R. Crim. P. 15(a)(2) shall contain the following information and supporting documents: (1) the docket number of the trial court case and current docket sheet; (2) the findings and rulings by the trial court; (3) a brief memorandum of law, including an explanation of how the administration of justice would be facilitated by the grant of leave to appeal; (4) an estimate of the length of the trial; (5) the scheduled trial date or next scheduled trial court event; (6) an affirmative representation whether the application and notice of appeal are timely under Mass. R. Crim. P. 15(b)(1); (7) if the application or notice of appeal is untimely, a motion to enlarge the time for filing with a supporting affidavit setting forth in meaningful detail the reasons for the delay; and (8) in an application by the Commonwealth, a statement whether the Commonwealth has a viable case without the suppressed evidence, and the strength of that case, if viable. A transcript shall not accompany the application unless oral findings and rulings were placed on the record by the trial court. The caption of the case shall remain the same as in the trial court.

(b) **Time for Filing Notice of Appeal and Application.** A notice of appeal shall be filed in the trial court and an application for leave to appeal under Mass. R. Crim. P. 15(a)(2) shall be filed in the Supreme Judicial Court for the County of Suffolk within the time prescribed by Mass. R. Crim. P. 15(b)(1).

(c) **Time for Filing Opposition.** Within fourteen days after the date of entry of the application for leave to appeal, or within such time as the single justice may direct, the other party or parties to the case may, but need not, file and serve a brief memorandum in opposition setting forth reasons why the application should not be granted. If the other party or parties determine not to file an opposition, a notice shall be served and filed within the time provided in this paragraph stating that no such opposition will be filed.

(d) Filing by Mail. The application for leave to appeal and any opposition shall be docketed on the date of receipt and shall be deemed timely filed if (i) received within the time fixed for filing or (ii) accompanied by an affidavit signed by counsel of record attesting that the day of mailing was within the time fixed for filing.

(e) Service. One copy of the application and supporting documents and one copy of each memorandum in opposition shall be served on all parties in the case, the chief of the appellate department for the prosecuting office, and any other interested parties. A certificate of service shall be filed for all documents setting forth the method of service and the names, addresses, telephone numbers, and e-mail addresses if any of all those upon whom service has been made.

(f) Hearing. The single justice will consider the application on the papers submitted pursuant to this order unless he or she otherwise orders.

Adopted effective February 1, 1997. Amended June 8, 2016, effective August 1, 2016.

In Re: Limited Assistance Representation [Repealed]

Repealed November 29, 2018, effective February 1, 2019. See, now. Uniform Trial Court Rule XVI: Limited Assistance Representation.

Order Re: Protection of Personal Information

Introduction. Massachusetts General Laws c. 93H provides that the judicial branch shall adopt rules or regulations to safeguard certain nonpublic personal information relating to residents of the Commonwealth, the improper or inadvertent disclosure of which could create a substantial risk of identity theft or fraud. This Order governs the security and confidentiality of personal information as defined by c. 93H in the Judicial Branch. It is designed to safeguard the personal information of all individuals, including nonresidents. It shall apply to the appellate courts, trial courts, court administrative offices and court affiliates, which shall be in compliance by September 1, 2010.

Definition. Under G. L. c. 93H, personal information consists of a resident's "first name and last name, or first initial and last name, in combination with any one or more of the following data elements that relate to such resident:

a. Social Security number;

b. driver's license number or state-issued identification card number;

c. financial account number, or credit or debit card number, with or without any required security code, access code, personal identification number or password, that would permit access to a resident's financial account.

Chapter 93H provides that personal information "shall not include information that is lawfully obtained from publicly available information, or from federal, state or local government records lawfully made available to the general public."

Information Security Program. Each appellate court, the Trial Court and any court affiliate that owns, stores or maintains personal information about an individual shall develop, implement, maintain and monitor a comprehensive, written information security program applicable to any records containing such personal information. The information security program shall govern the collection, use, dissemination, storage, retention and destruction of personal information. The program shall ensure that courts and court affiliates collect the minimum quantity of personal information reasonably needed to accomplish the legitimate purpose for which the information is collected; securely store and protect the information against unauthorized access, destruction, use, modification, disclosure or loss; provide access to and disseminate the information only to those who reasonably require the information to perform their duties; and destroy the information as soon as it is no longer needed or required to be maintained. Such information security program shall contain administrative, technical, and physical safeguards to ensure the security and confidentiality of such records.

Every information security program shall include:

(1) A requirement for notice to the Chief Justice for Administration and Management in the case of a trial court, and to the appropriate Chief Justice in the case of an appellate court, in the event of any incident involving a breach of security [1] of personal information.

(2) Regular monitoring to ensure that the information security program is operating in a manner reasonably calculated to prevent unauthorized access to or unauthorized use of personal information; and upgrading information safeguards as necessary to limit risks.

(3) A regular review, at least annually, of the scope of the security measures. Such review also must be conducted whenever there is an incident involving a breach of security and when there is a material change in business practices that may reasonably implicate the security or integrity of records containing personal information.

(4) Documentation of responsive actions taken in connection with any incident involving a breach of security, and actions taken, if any, to make changes in practices relating to protection of personal information.

Departmental reviews. Each appellate court, court department and court entity shall review the type of personal information it collects and maintains with the goal of identifying any personal information that need not be collected or maintained. Each department will report the results of this review to the Chief Justice for Administration and Management, or, in the case of the appellate courts and affiliated agencies, to the Chief Justice of the Supreme Judicial Court, within six months.

Computer systems. If personal information is stored electronically, the information security program shall include provisions that relate to the protection of personal information stored or maintained in electronic form. Such provisions shall be developed with the Courts' Chief Information Officers.

Contracts. All contracts entered into by the Judicial Branch shall contain provisions requiring contractors to notify the court of any incident involving a breach of security of personal information, and to certify that they have read this Order, that they have reviewed and will comply with all information security programs and policies that apply to the work they will be performing, that they will communicate these provisions to and enforce them against their subcontractors, and that they will implement and maintain any other reasonable and appropriate security procedures and practices necessary to protect personal information to which they are given access as part of the contract from unauthorized access, destruction, use, modification, disclosure or loss.

Adopted effective January 7, 2010.

Order Regarding Procedure for Judges Seeking a Determination Concerning Attorney's Fees for Representation in a Matter Before the Commission on Judicial Conduct

Where a judge retains legal representation due to a matter before the Commission on Judicial Conduct, the Supreme Judicial Court may authorize the payment of reasonable attorneys' fees by the Commonwealth, or authorize the judge to accept free or discounted legal fees, in the following circumstances:

1. "With the approval of the Supreme Judicial Court, a judge shall be entitled to the payment of reasonable attorneys' fees by the Commonwealth in any case where the matter is dismissed by the commission at any stage after the filing of a sworn complaint or statement of charges, where the Supreme Judicial Court determines despite a commission recommendation for discipline that no sanction is justified, or where the Supreme Judicial Court determines that justice will be served by the payment of such fees." G. L. c. 211C, § 7(15). See S.J.C. Rule 3:09, Code of Judicial Conduct, Rule 3.13, Comment [11A].

2. "A judge may accept free or discounted legal representation due to a matter before the Commission on Judicial Conduct upon a determination by the Supreme Judicial Court that such representation would serve the public interest." See S.J.C. Rule 3:09, Code of Judicial Conduct, Rule 3.13, Comment [11B].

A judge seeking a determination under paragraph 1 or 2 shall file an application, supported by affidavit, with the clerk of the Supreme Judicial Court for the Commonwealth, setting forth with particularity the reasons why the Court should make the requested determination. The application may be accompanied by a motion to impound. The clerk shall transmit the application to the Justices, and shall notify the judge of their determination. A judge awarded payment of reasonable attorneys' fees or permitted to accept free or discounted legal services shall publicly report in the manner required under Rule 3.15 of the Code of Judicial Conduct.

Adopted October 8, 2015, effective January 1, 2016.

Order Regarding Electronic Filing Pilot Projects

To advance efficiency in the Massachusetts courts and thereby better serve the public and the bar, the Justices hereby authorize the trial and appellate courts to conduct pilot projects on electronic filing and electronic service of court documents. The attached Interim Massachusetts Electronic Filing Rules that will govern the pilot projects are also approved. Therefore,

IT IS ORDERED THAT:

1. Electronic filing pilot projects are hereby authorized for the trial and appellate courts. Trial court pilot courts shall be approved by the Chief Justice of the Trial Court and the Court Administrator. The Justices of the appellate courts shall approve the pilot projects in those courts.

2. The attached [1] Interim Massachusetts Electronic Filing Rules are approved for use in the pilot projects. These rules shall remain in effect throughout the pilot projects, unless otherwise ordered by this Court. The rules may be amended by order of this Court.

3. If there is any conflict between the Interim Massachusetts Electronic Filing Rules and the Massachusetts Rules of Appellate Procedure, the Massachusetts Rules of Civil Procedure, or the rules of any appellate court or trial court department, the terms of the Interim Massachusetts Electronic Filing Rules shall govern the pilot projects.

4. Each pilot court shall issue an order describing the scope of its pilot project and any additional requirements that are not set forth in the Interim Massachusetts Electronic Filing Rules.

5. The pilot projects shall begin in March, 2015, or as soon after as practicable and shall continue until further order of the Court.

Adopted February 25, 2015.

[1] See Interim Electronic Filing Rules for Pilot Courts following the Rules of the Supreme Judicial Court.

Sampling of Case Records Pursuant to Section 6 of Supreme Judicial Court Rule 1:11, Rule Relative to the Disposal of Court Papers and Records G.L. c. 221, § 27A, as amended

Case records not required to be retained pursuant to S.J.C. Rule 1:11 may be destroyed after they are sampled pursuant to this Order, which sets forth the sampling requirements for case records in all departments of the Trial Court.

All case record samples retained pursuant to this Order shall be stamped so as to be clearly visible on the front, "SAMPLED." All containers for such case records shall be labeled so as to be clearly visible on the front, "SAMPLED – SEE SELECTION CRITERIA IN CLERK'S OFFICE." Copies of the selection criteria shall be available on the court's website, in the storage area containing records, in the clerk's office, and in the State Archives.

Boston Municipal Court, District Court, Housing Court and Juvenile Court: Case records under the custody of the clerks of these departments not required to be retained pursuant to S.J.C. Rule 1:11 may be destroyed as long as the following samples are retained:

Minor violation records: [1] a random selection of 20 case records for each type of case record for each year of case records to be destroyed.

All other records: a systematic sample of case records consisting of

● 5% (docket numbers ending in "00," "20," "40," "60," and "80") of case records for the period from 1800 to 1969, and

● 2% (docket numbers ending in "00" and "50") of case records starting in 1970 [2].

Land Court: Case records under the custody of the recorder of the Land Court not required to be retained pursuant to S.J.C. Rule 1:11 may be destroyed as long as the following samples are retained:

Case records from proceedings to foreclose a mortgage pursuant to the federal Servicemembers Civil Relief Act may be destroyed ten years after final disposition of the case as long as a random sample of twenty case records is retained for each year of records to be destroyed.

All other records: a systematic sample of case records in all permit sessions and miscellaneous cases within the jurisdiction of the Land Court consisting of

● 5% (docket numbers ending in "00," "20," "40," "60," and "80") of case records for the period prior to 1970, and

● 2% (docket numbers ending in "00" and "50") of case records starting in 1970.

Probate and Family Court: [RESERVED]

Superior Court: Case records under the custody of the clerks of the Superior Court not required to be retained pursuant to S.J.C. Rule 1:11 may be selectively retained as long as the following are retained:

In Barnstable, Dukes, Essex, and Nantucket counties: all case records.

In Berkshire, Franklin and Hampshire counties, a systematic sample of case records consisting of

● 10% (docket numbers ending in "0") of case records for the period from 1860 to 1968, and

● 2% (docket numbers ending in "00" and "50") of case records starting in 1969.

In all other counties, [3] a systematic sample of case records consisting of

● 20% (docket numbers ending in "0" and "5") of case records from 1860 to 1889,

● 10% (docket numbers ending in "0") of case records from 1890 to 1919.

● 5% (docket numbers ending in "00," "20," "40," "60," and "80") of case records from 1920 to 1969, and

● 2% (docket numbers ending in "00" and "50") starting in 1970.

Adopted September 26, 2018, effective October 1, 2018.

1 Section 2 of Rule 1:11 defines "minor violation records" as "case records, other than dockets, filed in or relating to a proceeding involving civil motor vehicle infractions, parking, littering, bicycles, pedestrians, municipal dog control, the decriminalized disposition of violations of municipal ordinances or by-laws or other decriminalized regulatory offenses."

2 If a case included within the samples has no papers but has a card indicating that it was filed separately or was sent to the Superior Court, the card shall be retained as part of the sampled file.

3 In the period when law and equity files are separate, a 30% (docket numbers ending in "3," "6," and "9") sample of equity files shall be retained for the following years:

● Bristol County: entered 1897 – June 30, 1974, and

● Middlesex and Suffolk Counties: entered 1892 to June 30, 1974.

Order Regarding Amount–in–Controversy Requirement Under G.L. c. 218, § 19 and G.L. c. 212, § 3

Under G.L. c. 218, § 19, civil actions for money damages may proceed in the District and Boston Municipal Court departments "only if there is no reasonable likelihood that recovery by the plaintiff will exceed $25,000, or an amount ordered from time to time by the supreme judicial court." The Court hereby exercises its authority to order that the amount be increased from $25,000 to $50,000.

Under G.L. c. 212, § 3, a reciprocal $25,000 amount requirement applies to civil actions for money damages commenced in the Superior Court. Under this statute, such actions may proceed in the Superior Court "only if there is no reasonable likelihood that recovery by the plaintiff will be less than or equal to $25,000 or an amount ordered from time to time by the supreme judicial court." The Court hereby exercises its authority to order that this amount also be increased from $25,000 to $50,000.

This Order shall be effective on January 1, 2020, and applicable to civil actions for money damages commenced on or after that date.

Adopted effective January 1, 2020.

Order Governing Appeals from Convictions of Murder in the First Degree

General Laws c. 278, § 33E, is intended to provide defendants with a comprehensive review of their convictions and to ensure that their appeals are finally adjudicated without undue delay. The dual goals of rendering justice and achieving finality are documented in the statute's legislative history.

After a direct appeal from a conviction of murder in the first degree has been entered in the Supreme Judicial Court, the statute requires motions for a new trial to be filed in the Supreme Judicial Court. The court has, in the past, typically stayed the direct appeal for an indefinite time while a defendant investigates, prepares, and files a new trial motion, and thereafter until the motion has been heard and decided, typically after referral by this court to the Superior Court. Consequently, direct appeals of convictions of murder in the first degree have sometimes remained on this court's docket for five, ten, fifteen, or more years.

So that direct appeals and any appeals from the rulings on the new trial motions may be heard and decided without undue delay, this ORDER sets forth the following protocol:

(a) Special master or single justice. The court shall appoint a special master to oversee the progress of first degree murder appeals and motions for a new trial and to implement and enforce the terms of this Order. Alternatively, the court may designate one of the Justices to perform that role. All references in this Order to "the special master" shall mean either the special master or any Justice who has been designated by the court for these purposes.

(b) Time for filing motions for a new trial. In any case in which the defendant contemplates filing a motion for a new trial in this court after the direct appeal has been entered and having the ruling on that motion considered in conjunction with the direct appeal, the defendant must file the motion as soon as reasonably practicable, but no later than eighteen months after the entry of the direct appeal. Extensions may be granted by the special master, on a case-by-case basis, based on a substantial showing of need. Review of the denial of a motion for a new trial filed within eighteen months or within the period of any authorized extension will be considered with the direct appeal. Review of the denial of a motion for a new trial filed after eighteen months (or after the extended deadline) will not presumptively be considered with the direct appeal.

(c) Status conferences. An initial status conference with counsel for the defendant and counsel for the Commonwealth shall be held before the special master within six months of the date of entry of the direct appeal. Further status conferences presumptively shall be held at nine, twelve, and fifteen months after the direct appeal has been entered, or at such other intervals as determined by the special master. The special master, in consultation with the clerk, will set the specific dates for these conferences.

(1) Within four months after entry of the direct appeal, the defendant shall file a status report stating whether all transcripts necessary for review under G. L. c. 278, § 33E, have been received by the clerk for the full court.

(2) At the six-month status conference, the defendant's counsel will be required to report whether the defendant does or does not intend to file a motion for a new trial. If no motion will be filed, the briefing schedule for the direct appeal will begin to run and will follow the time periods set forth in Mass. R.A.P. 19(c)(1).

(3) Unless the defendant will not be filing a motion for a new trial, at each status conference following the filing of the four-month status report, the defendant's counsel shall report on (i) the progress that has been made in investigating and pursuing the motion for a new trial; (ii) the next steps that are planned; and (iii) any difficulties that have been encountered or are anticipated that might affect the timely filing of the motion for a new trial. The report may be given orally, unless the special master requires it to be in writing.

(4) At the twelve-month status conference, if a motion for a new trial has not been filed, the defendant's counsel shall report whether a motion for a new trial will be filed. If counsel reports that a motion will be filed, counsel will then have up to six additional months to file the motion. If no motion will be filed, the briefing schedule for the direct appeal will begin to run and will follow the time periods set forth in Mass. R.A.P. 19(c)(1).

(5) If, at any point after the initial status conference, it becomes apparent to counsel that a motion for a new trial will not be filed, counsel shall so advise the clerk and counsel for the Commonwealth immediately, in which case the briefing schedule for the direct appeal will begin to run and will follow the time periods set forth in Mass. R.A.P. 19(c)(1).

(6) The special master may adjust the schedule for these periodic status conferences, and the time for the ultimate filing of a motion for a new trial, on a case-by-case basis.

(d) Action on motions. When a motion for a new trial is filed during the pendency of a direct appeal, G. L. c. 278, § 33E, authorizes the Supreme Judicial Court either to rule on the motion or to remand it to the Superior Court for hearing and determination there. If a motion is timely filed in accordance with this Order and is remanded to the Superior Court, the Supreme Judicial Court, in the absence of extraordinary circumstances, will not require briefs to be filed for the direct appeal until the motion has been decided in the Superior Court.

(e) Time for filing briefs. As stated in paragraph (b) above, the denial of a motion for a new trial filed within eighteen months or within the period of any authorized extension will be considered with the direct appeal. When a motion for a new trial has been decided in the Superior Court, after the appeal from the ruling on the motion is entered in this court, the time for filing briefs addressing both the direct appeal and the ruling on the new trial motion (in a situation where the motion has been denied), or for filing briefs on the new trial ruling alone (in a situation where the motion has been allowed), will be set by the clerk as required by Mass. R.A.P. 19(c)(2); presumptively, the briefing schedule will be ninety days for the appellant's brief, ninety days thereafter for the appellee's brief, and thirty days for any reply brief.

(f) Changes of counsel. If, during the pendency of an appeal, new counsel is appointed or has been retained to represent the defendant, counsel shall file a notice of appearance in this court immediately. The deadlines previously set forth in this Order and by the special master shall remain in effect despite the change in counsel, but the special master may adjust the time for status conferences and for the filing of briefs and new trial motions for good cause.

(g) Review after eighteen months. This Order will be reviewed by the court eighteen months from the date of this Order.

This Order shall be effective on September 4, 2019, and applicable to appeals entered on or after that date.

Adopted August 6, 2019, effective September 4, 2019.

MASSACHUSETTS APPEALS COURT RULES FOR THE REGULATION OF APPELLATE PRACTICE

Approved November 10, 1972

RULES FOR THE REGULATION OF APPELLATE PRACTICE

THE RECORD

Rule 1:01. [Repealed]
Repealed effective July 1, 1981.

Rules 1:02 to 1:05. [Repealed]
Repealed effective February 27, 1975.

Rule 1:06. [Repealed]
Repealed effective July 1, 1981.

Rules 1:07, 1:08. [Repealed]
Repealed effective February 27, 1975.

Rules 1:09, 1:10. [Repealed]
Repealed effective July 1, 1981.

ENTRY IN THIS COURT

Rule 1:11. [Repealed]

Repealed effective July 1, 1981.

BRIEFS AND ARGUMENTS

Rule 1:12. [Repealed]
Repealed effective February 27, 1975.

Rules 1:13 to 1:16. [Repealed]
Repealed effective July 1, 1981.

Rule 1:17. [Repealed]

Repealed effective February 27, 1975.

QUORUM

Rules 1:18 and 1:19. [Repealed]

Repealed effective July 1, 1981

ORAL ARGUMENTS

RULE 1:20. [REPEALED]

Repealed effective July 1, 1981.

Rule 1:21. [Repealed]

Repealed effective February 27, 1975.

OUTLINE BILL OF EXCEPTIONS

Rule 1:22. [Repealed]

Repealed effective July 1, 1981.

FELONY APPEALS

Rule 1:23. [Repealed]

Repealed effective July 1, 1981.

Rules 1:24, 1:25. [Rule Numbers Reserved]

SITTINGS

Rule 1:26. Sittings for Hearing Questions of Law

(Applicable to all cases.)

Sittings of this court pursuant to G.L. c. 211A, § 4, shall be held at Boston on the second and third Mondays of October, November, December, January, February, March, April, and May, and at such other places or times as the chief justice of this court from time to time may order.

Amended November 27, 1972; amended February 26, 1975, effective February 27, 1975.

Rule 1:27. [Repealed]

Repealed effective July 1, 1981.

Rule 1:28. Summary Disposition

(Applicable to all cases.)

At any time following the filing of the appendix (or the filing of the original record) and the briefs of the parties on any appeal in accordance with the applicable provisions of Rules 14(b), 18 and 19 of the Massachusetts Rules of Appellate Procedure, a panel of the justices of this court may determine that no substantial question of law is presented by the appeal or that some clear error of law has been committed which has injuriously affected the substantial rights of an appellant and may, by its written order, affirm, modify or reverse the action of the court below. The panel need not provide an opportunity for oral argument before disposing of cases under this rule. Any order entered under this rule shall be subject to the provisions of Rules 27 and 27.1 of the Massachusetts Rules of Appellate Procedure. If, in a brief or other filing, a party cites to an order issued under this rule, the party shall cite the case title, a citation to the Appeals Court Reports where issuance of the order is noted, and a notation that the order was issued pursuant to this rule; in addition, a party citing such an order shall include the full text of the order as an addendum to the brief or other filing. No such order issued before February 26, 2008, may be cited.

Adopted June 25, 1975, effective September 8, 1975. Amended February 28, 1978, effective March 2, 1978; amended effective September 25, 1980; amended April 28, 1998, effective September 1, 1998; amended November 25, 2008, effective January 1, 2009.

RULES FOR THE REGULATION OF PRACTICE
BEFORE A SINGLE JUSTICE

Rule 2:01. Practice Before A Single Justice

(General.)

Any matter which is within the jurisdiction of this court, whether originally entered or transferred to this court under the provisions of G.L. c. 211, § 4A, and which might otherwise be disposed of by a single justice of the Supreme Judicial Court, shall be filed with the clerk of this court and shall be heard and determined by a single justice of this court in accordance with the same rules, practices and procedures which would govern if the same matters were heard and determined by a single justice of the Supreme Judicial Court. The Massachusetts Rules of Civil or Appellate Procedure shall apply to any matter which would be subject thereto if it were being heard and determined by a single justice of the Supreme Judicial Court; and any other matter shall be heard and determined in accordance with the rules, practices and procedures of the Supreme Judicial Court which would be applicable thereto if it were being heard and determined by a single justice of that court.

A determination of any of the foregoing matters by a single justice of this court may be reviewed by a panel of other justices of this court in the same manner and to the same extent that the determination of a like matter by a single justice of the Supreme Judicial Court may be reviewed by the full court of the Supreme Judicial Court. As to such review in civil matters, see paragraphs (a) and (b) of Rule 1 of the Massachusetts Rules of Appellate Procedure.

Amended February 26, 1975, effective February 27, 1975.

Rule 2:02. Review Under Rule 15(c) of the Massachusetts Rules of Appellate Procedure

(Applicable to civil cases.)

The review of the action of a single justice which is afforded by the last sentence of paragraph (c) of Rule 15 of the Massachusetts Rules of Appellate Procedure shall be by a panel of other justices of this court, shall be claimed by an appeal to such a panel, and shall be prosecuted in the same manner as if the single justice were the "lower court" within the meaning of paragraph (c) of Rule 1 of said Rules. See paragraphs (a) and (b) of Rule 1 of said Rules.

Adopted February 26, 1975, effective February 27, 1975.

Rule 2:03. Special Masters and Commissioners

(Applicable to all cases.)

A majority of the justices of this court may designate special masters and commissioners to deal with specified cases or with such matters as may be referred to them by a written order of a single justice or of a panel of the justices. The acts of such special master and commissioner, when confirmed or approved by a single justice or by a panel of the justices, as the case may be, shall have all the force and effect of a decision by a single justice or by a panel of the justices.

Adopted April 30, 1976, effective May 5, 1976.

Rule 2:04. [Repealed]

Repealed May 1 2006, effective July 1, 2006.

STANDING ORDERS OF THE APPEALS COURT

Table of Standing Orders

Standing Order Concerning Dismissal of Appeals and Reports in All Cases for Lack of Prosecution

Whenever the clerk of this court (clerk) shall not have received the brief and appendix of an appellant (including in that term a party treated as an appellant under Rule 5 of the Massachusetts Rules of Appellate Procedure [Rules]) within the time required or permitted by Rules 13(a), 18(f) and 19(a)(1), 19(b)(1), or 19(b)(2) (unless said time shall previously have been enlarged), the clerk shall send a copy of this standing order to the attorney of record for such appellant (and to such appellant at the last known address in a criminal case or if such appellant is not represented by an attorney in a civil case) and to all other parties or to their attorneys of record, together with notice in writing that the appeal of such appellant or the report, as the case may be, will be dismissed as to that appellant for lack of prosecution unless, within fourteen days of the date of such notice in a civil case or within thirty days of the date of such notice in a criminal case, the clerk shall receive (a) a motion by such appellant to enlarge to a date certain set forth therein the time for serving and filing such brief and appendix and (b) an affidavit of such appellant (or that appellant's attorney) which shall set forth all the facts which such appellant wishes to have considered by the single justice of this court, who will act on such motion in accordance with the provisions of Rule 15(b) and (c). If no such motion and affidavit are received by the clerk within such period, the clerk shall forthwith dismiss such appeal or report for lack of prosecution and shall note such dismissal on the docket. The clerk shall take like action whenever a particular appellant has failed to serve and file a brief or appendix (when an appendix is required) within an enlargement of time previously granted. The sending of every notice required by this order shall be noted on the docket. Unless a dismissal shall have been vacated by a single justice within fourteen days from the docketing thereof, the clerk shall notify the clerk of the trial court that the appeal or report has been dismissed as to the particular appellant for lack of prosecution. A dismissal of an appeal in a criminal case may be vacated by a panel of the justices after the expiration of said fourteen days upon a showing either (a) of the existence of a meritorious case or (b) that the defendant was deprived of the right of direct appeal as a result of an act or omission of counsel after the appeal had been entered in this court.

Amended September 18, 2008, effective October 1, 2008. Amended March 27, 2019, effective May 1, 2019.

Standing Order Concerning Petitions to the Single Justice Pursuant to G.L. C. 231, § 118 (First Paragraph) or Rule 12(a) of the Uniform Rules on Impoundment Procedure

(a) Contents of Petition for Relief; Form. A petition for relief pursuant to G. L. c. 231, § 118 (first paragraph), or Rule 12(a) of the Uniform Rules on Impoundment Procedure, shall include, in the following order:

(1) a request for review, which shall state briefly the nature of the order or action of the trial court from which review is sought, the entry date of such order or action, and the name of the judge who entered it;

(2) a statement of the issues of law raised by the petition;

(3) a statement as to whether a party has filed, served, or intends to file a motion for reconsideration in the trial court;

(4) a statement of the specific relief requested; and

(5) an addendum containing a copy of the order or action of the trial court (a draft order for the single justice may be attached).

References to the parties in the petition shall be by designation of the party in the trial court (e.g., "plaintiff," "defendant," "third-party defendant," etc.). The petition shall not exceed five pages of text in monospaced font or 1,000 words in proportional font compliant with Mass. R.A.P. 20(a)(4)(A)–(C) without leave of the court.

(b) Supporting Memorandum of Law and Record Appendix. The petition shall, unless otherwise ordered, be accompanied by a memorandum of law (not to exceed fifteen pages of text in monospaced font or 3,500 words in proportional font compliant with Mass. R.A.P. 20[a][4][A]–[C] unless leave of the court has been obtained) in support of the petitioner's position, with citations to appropriate authorities and a statement addressing why relief is appropriate. The argument shall make reference to those portions of the record which are directly relevant to the issues raised by the petition. Relevant portions of the record shall be filed as a record appendix, and include a current copy of the trial court docket entries and all relevant papers filed in the trial court, including those filed by the other party or parties. The record appendix shall be consecutively numbered starting with the cover or first page as page 1 followed by a table of contents that lists each document contained therein and the page on which it appears. Only those pleadings, exhibits, and papers which were before the trial court when the order appealed from was entered, and which are necessary for an adjudication of the issues raised, may be submitted.

(c) Response; Form. Within seven days (ten days if the petitioner's certificate of service required under [d] hereof shows service by first-class mail) after the filing of the petition, or such other time as the court may direct, the other party or parties to the case may, but need not, file and serve a response thereto (not to exceed fifteen pages of text in monospaced font or 3,500 words in proportional font compliant with Mass. R.A.P. 20[a][4][A]–[C] unless leave of court has been obtained) setting forth reasons why the petition should or should not be granted. The response shall not restate matters contained in the petition unless the responding party is dissatisfied with the statement thereof contained in the petition. The response may be accompanied by a supplemental record appendix containing such additional portions of the record as were before the trial court and are necessary for adjudication, and which the petitioner failed to include in its record appendix.

(d) Filing; Service; Required Certificate(s). The petition, memorandum, record appendix, and any subsequently filed response and supplemental record appendix, shall be filed electronically if the filing party is represented by counsel. Self-represented litigants may file electronically, or may file a single paper original or duplicate in the office of the Clerk of the Appeals Court. Any document required to be e-filed may be filed on paper upon allowance of a motion to waive the e-filing requirement, preferably filed in advance or with the document. The motion must contain a showing of undue hardship, significant prejudice, exigency, or other good cause.

Whether filed electronically or on paper, all filings shall include a certificate of service on all other parties in the case, including the service and filing of a copy in the appropriate trial court clerk's office from which the matter arose. The certificate of service shall set forth the name, address, email address, and telephone number of counsel or other persons upon whom service has been made, and specify the date and manner of service. The certificate of service shall identify the name of each party represented by counsel and specify the counsel who represents each party.

Service may be personal, by first class mail, or electronically with the consent of the person served. Personal service includes delivery of the copy to a clerk or other responsible person at the office of counsel. Service by first class mail is complete on mailing. Registration for and use of the electronic filing system constitutes consent to electronic service, and such service is complete upon e-filing.

If a petition and supporting memorandum of law or a response is produced in a proportional font, an additional certificate of compliance with the length limit(s) is required and must include the name and size of the proportionally spaced font used, the number of non-excluded words, and the name and version of the word-processing program used.

(e) Impounded or confidential information. In any case in which the trial court entered an order impounding, sealing, or excluding from public access all or any portion of the trial court records, or there is material or information in a party's petition, addendum, response, or any appendix that is automatically impounded or deemed confidential by statute or court rule, the parties shall comply with Mass. R.A.P. 16(d), 16(m), and 18(d). The parties shall comply with Supreme Judicial Court Rule 1:24, Protection of Personal Identifying Information in Publicly Accessible Court Documents in all filings to the Appeals Court.

(f) Hearing. The single justice has discretion to determine whether a hearing shall be held.

Adopted effective September 1, 1989, with strict enforcement delayed until March 1, 1990. Amended effective January 1, 2002. Amended April 20, 2011, effective June 1, 2011; September 24, 2015, effective October 1, 2015; September 28, 2016, effective November 1, 2016; July 27, 2018, effective September 1, 2018; March 27, 2019, effective May 1, 2019.

Standing Order Governing Appeals From the Industrial Accident Reviewing Board [Repealed]

Repealed effective July 1, 2005.

Standing Order of the Appeals Court Concerning Conferences in Civil Appeals [Repealed]

Adopted effective October 19, 1992. Amended December 15, 1993; August 19, 1999; December 2, 1999. Repealed March 27, 2019, effective May 1, 2019.

Standing Order Governing the Filing of an Appendix Consisting of Three or More Volumes [Rescinded]

Rescinded effective March 2, 2009.

Standing Order Requiring the Electronic Filing of All Motions and Letters Filed After Panel Assignment [Rescinded]

Adopted March 31, 2010, effective May 1, 2010; Amended April 20, 2011, effective June 1, 2011. Rescinded effective September 1, 2018.

Standing Order Governing Motions to Stay a Judgment or Execution of Sentence Filed Pursuant to Mass. R.A.P. 6

(a) Contents of a Motion for a Stay; Form. A motion for a stay pursuant to Mass.R.A.P. 6 shall include in the following order:

(1) a request for a stay, which shall state briefly the nature of the judgment or sentence entered by the trial court for which a stay is sought, the entry date of such judgment or conviction, and the name of the judge who entered it;

(2) the text of the order and rationale of the trial court denying the motion for stay or, if no such motion was filed in the trial court, a showing why filing the motion in the trial court was not practicable;

(3) a statement of the issues of law raised by the motion;

(4) a statement of the specific relief requested; and

(5) an addendum containing copies of the judgment, notice of appeal, and the trial court's order denying the prior motion for a stay.

References to the parties in the motion shall be by the designation of the party in the trial court. The motion shall not exceed five pages of text in monospaced font or 1,000 words in proportional font compliant with Mass. R.A.P. 20(a)(4)(A)–(C) without leave of the court.

(b) Supporting Memorandum of Law and Record Appendix. The motion shall, unless otherwise ordered, be accompanied by a memorandum of law (not to exceed fifteen pages of text in monospaced font or 3,500 words in proportional font compliant with Mass. R.A.P. 20[a][4][A]–[C] unless leave of the court has been obtained) in support of the movant's position, with citations to appropriate authorities and a statement addressing why a stay is appropriate. The argument shall make reference to those portions of the record which are directly relevant to the issues raised by the motion. Relevant portions of the record shall be filed as a record appendix, and include a current copy of the trial court docket entries and all relevant papers filed in the trial court, including those filed by the other party or parties. The record appendix shall be consecutively numbered starting with the cover or first page as page 1 followed by a table of contents that lists each document contained therein and the page on which it appears.

(c) Response, Form. The non-moving party or parties to the case may, but need not, file and serve a response thereto (not to exceed fifteen pages of text in monospaced font or 3,500 words in proportional font compliant with Mass. R.A.P. 20[a][4][A]–[C] unless leave of court has been obtained) setting forth reasons why the motion should or should not be granted. The response shall not restate matters contained in the motion unless the responding party is dissatisfied with the statement thereof contained in the motion. The response may be accompanied by a supplemental record appendix containing such additional portions of the record as were before the trial court and are necessary for adjudication, and which the movant failed to include in its record appendix.

(d) Response, Timing.

(1) For motions filed in all civil matters and for criminal matters entered in the Appeals Court's single justice session (i.e., prior to the entry of an appeal pursuant to Mass. R.A.P. 10[a][1] or [2]), the other party or parties to the case may, but need not, file and serve a response thereto within seven days after the service of the motion (ten days if the movant's certificate of service required under [e] hereof shows service by first-class mail), or such other time as the court may direct.

(2) For motions filed in criminal appeals subsequent to the entry of and during the pendency of a direct or collateral appeal in the Appeals Court, the time limit for a response is governed by the provisions of Mass. R.A.P. 6(b)(2)(B)–(C).

(3) For motions filed in civil appeals entered pursuant to Mass. R.A.P. 10(a)(1) the other party or parties to the case may, but need not, file and serve a response thereto within seven days after the service of the motion (ten days if the movant's certificate of service required under [e] hereof shows service by first-class mail), or such other time as the court may direct.

(e) Filing; Service; Required Certificate(s). The motion, memorandum, record appendix, and any subsequently filed response and supplemental record appendix, shall be filed electronically if the filing party is represented by counsel. Self-represented litigants may file electronically, or may file a single paper original or duplicate in the office of the Clerk of the Appeals Court. Any document required to be e-filed may be filed on paper upon allowance of a motion to waive the e-filing requirement, preferably filed in advance or with the document. The motion must contain a showing of undue hardship, significant prejudice, exigency, or other good cause.

Whether filed electronically or on paper, all filings shall include a certificate of service on all other parties in the case, including the service and filing of a copy in the appropriate trial court clerk's office from which the matter arose. The certificate of service shall set forth the name, address, email address, and telephone number of counsel or other persons upon whom service has been made, and specify the date and manner of service. The certificate of service shall identify the name of each party represented by counsel and specify the counsel who represents each party.

Service may be personal, by first class mail, or electronically with the consent of the person served. Personal service includes delivery of the copy to a clerk or other responsible person at the office of counsel. Service by first class mail is complete on mailing. Registration for and use of the electronic filing system constitutes consent to electronic service, and such service is complete upon e–filing.

If a petition and supporting memorandum of law or a response is produced in a proportional font, an additional certificate of compliance with the length limit(s) is required and must include the name and size of the proportionally spaced font used, the number of non-excluded words, and the name and version of the word-processing program used.

(f) Impounded or confidential information. In any case in which the trial court entered an order impounding, sealing, or excluding from public access all or any portion of the trial court records, or there is material or information in a party's motion, addendum, memorandum, or any appendix that is automatically impounded or deemed confidential by statute or court rule, the parties shall comply with Mass.R.A.P. 16(d), 16(m), and 18(d). See G. L. c. 265, § 24C. The parties shall comply with Supreme Judicial Court Rule 1:24, Protection of Personal Identifying Information in Publicly Accessible Court Documents in all filings to the Appeals Court.

(g) Hearing. The single justice has discretion to determine whether a hearing shall be held.

Adopted April 20, 2011, effective June 1, 2011. Amended September 28, 2016, effective November 1, 2016. Amended July 27, 2018, effective September 1, 2018. Amended March 27, 2019, effective May 1, 2019.

Standing Order Governing Electronic Notification of Court Orders, Notices, and Decisions in Lieu of Paper Notice

A. Registration.

(1). All counsel of record and self-represented litigants may register with the Appeals Court to receive only electronic (i.e., e-mail) notification of all actions, orders, judgments, rescripts, and decisions entered by the Appeals Court, including the scheduling of an oral argument, in an appeal in which they are participating. Persons who register to receive electronic notification will not receive any paper notice by first-class U.S. mail. Persons who do not register to receive electronic notification will receive only paper notice by first-class U.S. mail.

(2). Registration is performed by signing and filing the "Consent to Electronic Notification Form" (Consent Form). The Consent Form is available on the Appeals Court's website. The completed Consent Form can be filed with the Clerk's Office either as an original paper by hand delivery or by first-class mail, or by scanning it, with the required written signature, in portable document format (PDF) and emailing the PDF to enoticesignup@appct.state.ma.us with the subject header "E–Notice Consent Registration."

(3). Registrations for attorneys will be applied to all pending and future notifications entered in the Appeals Court involving that attorney. Once the Consent Form has been registered for an attorney, there is no need to register separately for each appeal. Self-represented litigants must register separately in each appeal for which they seek to receive electronic notice by identifying the docket number of each appeal in their Consent Form.

(4). Only one e-mail address per attorney or self-represented litigant can be used at a time. Each attorney can designate a second person employed at the same law firm or office (e.g., co-counsel, secretary, assistant district attorney, etc.) to receive a copy of all electronic notifications sent to the attorney.

(5). Persons who previously registered to receive electronic notices prior to the effective date of this standing order and who wish to continue to receive electronic notices must file a Consent Form. Persons who previously registered and who do not file a Consent Form will no longer receive electronic notices.

B. Transmission of Orders, Notices, and Decisions.

The clerk will serve and give notice of actions, orders, judgments, rescripts, and decisions entered by the Appeals Court, including the scheduling of oral argument, by electronic notification to all attorneys and self-represented litigants who have properly registered to receive electronic notification.

C. Transmission of Orders, Notices, and Decisions to Self–Represented Litigants.

If during the course of the appeal, a self-represented litigant who has registered to receive electronic notification retains an attorney who enters an appearance, the clerk shall stop serving notice to the former self-represented litigant.

D. Clerk's Functions and Entry of Court–Issued Documents.

(1). The court may issue orders through the creation of a docket entry and the issuance of notice thereof to the parties. Any order or document electronically issued by the court without the original signature of a judge or authorized court personnel has the same force and effect as if the judge or clerk had signed a paper copy of the order. Actions or orders also may be issued as "text-only" entries on the docket, without a separate paper copy of the action or order. Such orders are official and binding.

(2). Upon the entry of an action, order, judgment, rescript, or decision, the clerk will electronically transmit to registered recipients in the case a Notice of Docket Entry or Decision that contains the court's order, action, notice, or judgment. The full text of a rescript or decision will not accompany the notice because that information is available at the Reporter of Decisions website and will be so noted in the electronic notification.

(3). Electronic notification of the Notice of Docket Entry or Decision constitutes the notice and service of the action, order, judgment, rescript, or decision required by Mass.R.A.P. 31(c). The clerk shall provide notice in paper form by first-class mail only to a person who has not consented and registered for electronic notification.

E. Recipient's Responsibilities and Undeliverable Electronic Notification.

(1). It is the responsibility of counsel and the self-represented litigant to maintain a current e-mail address with the court, to verify that their e-mail inbox is working properly and receiving incoming electronic notifications at all times from the court, and to file a Change of Electronic Mail Address Form within three business days of a change of e-mail address.

(2). If service is made to the recipient's most current electronic mail address on file with the court and returned to the court as undeliverable, the notice will then be served by first-class mail; provided, however, any time period countable from the completion of service of notice shall be based upon the service of the electronic notice. The recipient's e-mail address will be deactivated until the recipient provides written notice to the court that the address is again receiving electronic notifications.

F. Application.

The clerk's issuance of electronic notifications pursuant to this standing order shall be deemed to be in compliance with the requirements concerning the clerk's service or mailing of paper notice by conventional or first-class mail, as required by Mass.R.A.P. 1, 10(a)(3), 23, and 31(c).

Adopted April 20, 2011, effective June 1, 2011.

Standing Order. Docketing Statement for All Appeals (Civil and Criminal)

(a) **Filing.** Each appellant or cross-appellant, other than a self-represented person who is incarcerated, shall complete and file a docketing statement for each appeal or cross-appeal. The docketing statement is due within fourteen days after the Appeals Court issues the "Notice of Entry" of the appeal.

(b) **Content and Form.** The docketing statement shall contain such information as required on the form located on the Appeals Court's website. The filer shall comply with the instructions on the docketing statement form.

(c) **Multiple Appellants or Cross–Appellants.** Each separately represented appellant or cross-appellant shall file a separate docketing statement. Counsel representing multiple appellants or cross-appellants shall file one docketing statement on behalf of all appellants or cross-appellants represented by that counsel. Each appellant or cross-appellant who is not represented by counsel shall file one docketing statement.

(d) **Failure to File Docketing Statement.** The court may take such action as necessary to ensure the filing of the docketing statement, including denying without prejudice any motion to enlarge time to file a brief or motion to stay appellate proceedings until the appellant has filed the docketing statement.

Adopted December 16, 2015, effective January 1, 2016.

Order Concerning Electronic Filing Pilot Project [Rescinded]

Adopted March 30, 2016, effective March 31, 2016. Rescinded effective September 1, 2018.

Standing Order Governing Number of Copies of Brief and Record Appendix to be Filed [Rescinded]

Adopted July 29, 2016, effective August 1, 2016. Rescinded effective September 1, 2018.

Standing Order Concerning Electronic Filing

Consistent with Rule 1 of S.J.C. Rule 1:25, Massachusetts Rules of Electronic Filing ("E–Filing Rules"), the Appeals Court hereby adopts this standing order concerning its electronic filing program.

A. Governing Rules and Orders.

1. Filers who submit documents electronically through the e-filing service provider ("Provider"), on the Massachusetts Court System Odyssey File and Serve Site ("EfileMA.com") shall comply with the E–Filing Rules,[1] the Massachusetts Rules of Appellate Procedure, the Appeals Court electronic filing format requirements found on the Appeals Court website,[2] and all other applicable Appeals Court rules and standing orders.

2. To the extent that any court rule or standing order is inconsistent with this Order concerning electronic filing in the Appeals Court, the E–Filing Rules, or the Appeals Court electronic filing format requirements found on the Appeals Court website, then the E–Filing Rules, this Order, and the Appeals Court electronic filing format requirements shall control.

B. Mandatory Attorney Registration for Electronic Filing and Service. All law firms and attorneys with cases pending in the Appeals Court shall register for electronic filing at eFileMA.com. Registration shall not constitute a notice of appearance in any particular case. Attorney registrants are required to use their business email address on file with the Board of Bar Overseers and to maintain their name and business email address on the eFileMA.com "Public List." If such email address is different from the email address previously registered with the Appeals Court for receipt of electronic court notices, the filer shall file a change of email address with the Appeals Court.

C. Mandatory Attorney Electronic Filing. Except as provided in Section E(l) (which provides there is no requirement to e-file an impounded document), the following documents filed by an attorney representing a party to a case shall be filed electronically using eFileMA.com. Use of the eFileMA.com system constitutes "e-filed" as used herein. The Appeals Court designates each case docket as either: (i) "public" meaning all data and documents are publicly accessible; (ii), "partially impounded," meaning some information or documents are publicly accessible and other data or document(s) are not publicly accessible; or, (iii) "impounded," meaning no case information or records are publicly accessible.

1. *All filings in criminal panel cases.* All documents in public and partially impounded criminal panel cases (on the court's "P" docket) must be e-filed.

2. *Briefs and appendices in civil panel cases.* All briefs and appendices in public and partially impounded civil panel cases (on the court's "P" docket) must be e-filed.

3. *All docketing statements.* All docketing statements, in public and partially impounded civil and criminal panel cases, must be e-filed pursuant to the Appeals Court Standing Order Concerning Docketing Statements for All Appeals (Civil and Criminal). Filers may request a waiver of the Provider convenience fee using a waiver account.

4. *All motions and letters filed after panel assignment.* After the Appeals Court assigns a case to a panel of justices for consideration on the merits, either with or without oral argument, all subsequent filings in the case must be e-filed. This requirement applies in all public and partially impounded civil and criminal panel cases. Filers may request a waiver of the Provider convenience fee using a waiver account.

5. *All filings on the Single Justice docket.* All documents in public and partially impounded single justice cases (on the court's "J" docket) must be e-filed.

Except upon motion and order as provided in paragraph F, the Court may decline to docket any of the foregoing documents submitted on paper.

D. Voluntary Electronic Filing by Attorneys and Self–Represented Litigants.

1. *Voluntary e-filing.* Any document that is not identified as mandatory in paragraph C may nonetheless be e-filed voluntarily by the attorney or party. The Appeals Court encourages all attorneys and self-represented liti-

gants in public, partially impounded, and impounded cases, to e-file every document submitted to the court.

2. *Self-represented litigants.* Self-represented litigants may register for electronic filing at eFileMA.com.

3. *Public Access Scanner and Terminal.* A public access computer terminal and scanner are located in the Clerk's Office of the Appeals Court, which may be used by any party to e-file a paper document without payment of the Provider convenience fee.

E. Electronic Filing of Impounded Documents.

1. *Voluntary e-filing.* Impounded documents may be e-filed through EfileMA.com, but there is no requirement to e-file an impounded document.

2. *Marking impounded documents.* Prior to e-filing, the filer shall mark any impounded document as impounded on the cover or first page of the document, as required by E–Filing Rule 11, Mass. R. App. P. 16(m) and 18(d).

3. *Designation of impounded documents on Efile-MA.com.* The filer shall also designate the document as impounded using the appropriate field on EfileMA.com, which shall satisfy the requirement of providing written notice to the clerk of a document's impounded status. Impounded documents may otherwise be e-filed in the same manner as non-impounded documents.

4. *Confidentiality.* The confidentiality of an electronic record or an electronic or paper copy thereof is equivalent to that of a paper record. Access may be permitted only to the extent provided by law. E–notices from the eFile-MA.com system containing hyperlinks to impounded documents shall be treated as confidential.

F. Waiver of Mandatory Electronic Filing and Permission to File Paper Original and Copies. Any document required to be e-filed under paragraph C may be filed on paper upon allowance of a motion to waive the e-filing requirement, preferably filed in advance or with the document. The motion must contain a showing of undue hardship, significant prejudice, exigency, or other good cause. For self-represented litigants who are confined in an institution, the requirement of Mass. R. App. P. 20(a)(6)(A) that a paper brief must have a color cover is suspended and no color cover is required.

G. Format. All e-filed documents shall comply with the formatting requirements of the Massachusetts Rules of Appellate Procedure except as modified by the Appeals Court's electronic filing format requirements found on the Appeals Court website. See generally E–Filing Rule 1.

H. No Paper Duplicates. All documents that are e-filed shall be submitted electronically only. Neither a paper original nor duplicate shall be filed unless specifically requested by the Court.

I. Electronic Service of E–Filed Documents.

1. *Service of Documents E–Filed in the Appeals Court.* Pursuant to E–Filing Rule 3(d), the filer's registration with EfileMA.com constitutes consent to receive electronic service in all cases. All documents submitted electronically through EfileMA.com may be electronically served through EfileMA.com pursuant to E–Filing Rule 7 and such service shall be considered compliant with Mass. R. App. P. 13,

provided the other party or party's attorney has registered with EfileMA.com. Registered filers must maintain their name and email address on the eFileMA.com "Public List." If a party's representative has not registered with EfileMA.com, service should be made by the conventional methods (e.g., paper copies and regular mail).

2. *No Copies of Applications, Responses, or Oppositions Filed in the Supreme Judicial Court.* A party is not required to file or serve a copy in the Appeals Court of any application, response, or opposition that is filed in the Supreme Judicial Court pursuant to Mass. R. App. P. 11 and 27.1.

J. Mandatory Electronic Notice.

1. *Notice from Provider.* The eFileMA.com system will transmit electronic notifications (i) when an e-filed document is submitted, (ii) when the Clerk's Office accepts or rejects the document, and (iii) possibly at other times during an e-filing transaction.

2. *Notice from the Appeals Court.* All attorneys will receive electronic notifications in lieu of paper notices of the court's actions, orders, judgments, rescripts, and decisions. The Court will use the business email addresses on file with the Board of Bar Overseers pursuant to S.J.C. Rule 4:02(11). Attorneys must ensure that their business email address registered with the Board of Bar Overseers is up to date. A self-represented litigant may authorize the Court to send electronic notice in lieu of paper notices.

K. Support. All technical support shall be provided by Provider. The Appeals Court's Clerk's Office may be contacted with procedural questions or with questions regarding the application of this Order.

L. Cessation of Appeals Court's "emotions" email filings. The Appeals Court will no longer accept emails and PDFs of filings at its "emotions@appct.state.ma.us" address. All electronic filings shall be submitted via the eFileMA.com system.

M. Prior Orders Rescinded. The following prior orders of the Appeals Court are hereby rescinded by this Order and no longer in effect:

1. Appeals Court Order Concerning Electronic Filing Pilot Project, adopted March 30, 2016.

2. Appeals Court Order Concerning Number of Copies of Brief and Record Appendix to be Filed, adopted July 29, 2016.

3. Appeals Court Standing Order Requiring the Electronic Filing of All Motions and Letters Filed After Panel Assignment, adopted May 1, 2010, and amended June 1, 2011.

N. Future Changes and Updates. This order may be superseded or amended, in writing, at any time.

O. Effective Date. This Order shall become effective on September 1, 2018.

Adopted July 27, 2018, effective September 1, 2018. Amended March 27, 2019, effective May 1, 2019.

1See https://www.mass.gov/supreme-judicial-court-rules/supreme-judicial-court-rule-125-massachusetts-rules-of-electronic

2See https://www.mass.gov/guides/electronic–filing–at–the–appeals–court

TRIAL COURT RULES

Summary of Contents

I. UNIFORM SUMMARY PROCESS RULES

Effective September 1, 1980

I. UNIFORM SUMMARY PROCESS RULES

Rule 1. Scope and Applicability of Rules

These rules govern procedure in all summary process actions in the Trial Court of the Commonwealth. Procedures in such actions that are not prescribed by these rules shall be governed by the Massachusetts Rules of Civil Procedure insofar as the latter are not inconsistent with these rules, with applicable statutory law or with the jurisdiction of the particular court in which they would be applied.

These rules and, where applicable, the Massachusetts Rules of Civil Procedure, shall be construed and applied to secure the just, speedy, and inexpensive determination of every summary process action.

Any procedural steps taken in a summary process action before the effective date of these rules which conform to then-effective rules will be regarded as valid during the pendency of that action. All procedure after the effective date of these rules with respect to a pending summary process action will be governed by these rules.

Commentary

Four Departments of the Massachusetts Trial Court have jurisdiction over summary process actions (Superior Court, District Court, Boston Municipal Court and Housing Court). This set of rules replaces the disparate sets of preexisting rules in order to establish uniformity of procedure in the Trial Court.

These rules seek to reconcile two competing principles. The first is that time is of the essence in eviction cases. This is based on the

501

notion that real estate constitutes unique property and that because it generates income, time lost in regaining it from a party in illegal possession can represent an irreplaceable loss to the owner. The Legislature clearly recognized these factors in creating a special chapter of the General Laws establishing a "summary" procedure. The other principle involved is the unique and fundamental need of tenants for dwellings that are habitable and secure. Recognition of this need has resulted in extensive changes through case law in the legal relationship between tenants and landlords and a host of legislative enactments providing tenants with new rights and remedies. These changes have made the legality of possession an often difficult and complex judicial question.

The need, then, is for rules that will ensure expeditious proceedings and yet comprehend all potential substantive and procedural complexities. It is believed that these rules meet that need by addressing specifically the basic procedural steps in summary process actions, by adopting by reference the Massachusetts Rules of Civil Procedure to cover any unusual procedural questions that may arise, and by stating in Rule 1 that the rules are to be construed and applied so as "to secure the just, speedy, and inexpensive determination" of summary process actions.

Rule 2.　Form of Summons and Complaint; Entry of Action; Scheduling of Trial Date; Service of Process

(a) Form of Summons and Complaint. The form of Summary Process Summons and Complaint, as promulgated by the Chief Administrative Justice of the Trial Court, shall be the only form of summons and complaint used in summary process actions. This form of Summary Process Summons and Complaint shall be considered a writ in the form of an original summons as required by G.L. c. 239, § 2. This form shall be available in blank at each of the courts at which summary process actions may be commenced.

(b) Service of Process. Service of a copy of a properly completed Summary Process Summons and Complaint shall be made on the defendant no later than the seventh day nor earlier than the thirtieth day before the entry day, provided, however, that service shall not be made prior to the expiration of the tenancy by notice of termination or otherwise except as permitted by statute. Service shall be made in accordance with Rule 4(d) of the Massachusetts Rules of Civil Procedure, provided that if service is not made in hand, the person making such service shall mail, first-class, to the defendant, at the address indicated on the Summary Process Summons and Complaint, a copy of the Summary Process Summons and Complaint; and provided further that return of service, including a statement of mailing where the latter was required, shall be made to the plaintiff only and shall be made in the appropriate space provided on the Summary Process Summons and Complaint. The date of service pursuant to this paragraph shall be deemed the date of commencement of the action subject to proper entry in accordance with the provisions of Rule 2(d).

Service shall be made by those authorized to make service by Rule 4(c) of the Massachusetts Rules of Civil Procedure, provided that such service shall be made as required by this section.

(c) Entry Date; Scheduling of Trial Date. Entry dates for summary process actions shall be each Monday and cases shall be placed on the list for hearing on the second Thursday following the entry date without any further notice to the parties. Subject to the prior approval of the Administrative Justice of his or her Department, the First Justice of any Division may designate Friday, Monday, Tuesday, and Wednesday as summary process trial days either as alternatives to Thursday or in addition to Thursday. The cases shall be placed on the list for hearing on the second Friday, the second Monday, the third Tuesday, or the third Wednesday after the Monday entry day without any further notice to the parties when such day is designated as a summary process trial day. Summary process actions originally commenced in the Superior Court Department shall be added to the next non-jury list for assignment for trial.

(d) Entry of Action. Summary process actions shall be entered by filing with the clerk of the court in which the action is to be heard the following documents:

(1) the original of the properly completed form of Summary Process Complaint and Summons, a copy of which has been served on the defendant, with return of service recorded thereon;

(2) a copy of any applicable notice(s) of termination of the defendant's tenancy of the premises upon which the plaintiff(s) relies where such notice is required by law and any proof of delivery of such notice upon which the plaintiff(s) plans to rely at trial;

(3) in jurisdictions wherein rent control is in effect a copy of a certificate of eviction granted by the appropriate rent control agency, or an affidavit of exemption;

(4) in jurisdictions wherein local laws governing condominium conversion evictions are in effect, a copy of any applicable affidavit of compliance with such local laws;

(5) any entry fee prescribed by law unless waived.

On the appropriate portion of the Summary Process Summons and Complaint the reason(s) for eviction shall be indicated by the plaintiff(s) in concise, untechnical form and with sufficient particularity and completeness to enable a defendant to understand the reasons for the requested eviction and the facts underlying those reasons.

(e) Method and Time for Filing. Filing of the Summary Process Summons and Complaint and necessary accompanying documents, if any, shall be by delivery in hand or by first-class mail to the clerk. Filing by mail is complete upon receipt by the clerk. Papers and documents required in accordance with the preceding paragraph shall be filed together no later than the close of business on the scheduled Monday entry day. Late filing of the summons and complaint shall not be permitted without the written assent of the defendant or the defendant's attorney.

Amended effective February 1, 1982; January 28, 1986; February 1, 1993.

Commentary

The procedure for commencing a summary process action under this rule can be summarized in the following three steps:

First, a plaintiff wishing to institute an action must secure and complete the required form. One item he must indicate on the form is the date of the hearing. In order to determine this, the plaintiff must choose an entry day (any Monday) prior to which he can get effective service on the defendant and return of service. The hearing date will be on the second Thursday following the Monday entry day selected (unless Friday, Monday, Tuesday, or Wednesday, as a day other than or in addition to Thursday, is approved for that court). Although cases originally commenced in the Superior Court Department are at first scheduled for a hearing on the second Thursday after the entry day, it is likely that such Superior Court cases would have to be rescheduled as provided in section (c).

Second, the plaintiff must have a copy of the completed Summary Process Summons and Complaint properly served on the defendant and get the original of this form back from the process server showing a return of service. Service must be made not later than the seventh day nor earlier than the thirtieth day before the Monday entry day chosen. Therefore, service could be made on the Monday of the week prior to a Monday entry day. Note that Rule 2(b) provides that service is not to be made prior to the expiration of the tenancy except as permitted by law. See G.L. c. 186, §§ 11, 12; G.L. c. 239, § 1; see also, Hodgkins v. Price, 137 Mass. 13.

Third, the plaintiff must file with the court the original of the completed Summary Process Summons and Complaint (showing return of service), the entry fee and possible certain other documents. This Filing constitutes entry of the action. Filing must be made no later than the close of business on the Monday entry day. Note that if filing is by mail, the documents must arrive in court by the Monday entry day. The hearing will be on the second Thursday (or second Friday, second Monday, third Tuesday, or third Wednesday, if so designated) following the Monday entry day.

This three-step procedure is required to allow flexibility in the time for commencing these actions yet at the same time to provide an automatic hearing date that can be predetermined and communicated to the defendant with the summons and complaint. Commencement of the summary process action under these rules occurs when proper service of the Summary Process Summons and Complaint is completed, subject, however, to the proper entry of the action.

It should be noted that the clerk should not refuse to accept a summons and complaint for failure to file documents which may be required by Rules 2(d)(2), (3) or (4). It is a matter for the determination of the court as to whether such documents are required. It should be noted further that the requirement in Rule 2(d)(3) that a certificate of eviction, if any is necessary, be filed and served with the Summary Process Summons and Complaint satisfies the requirement of District Court Administrative Regulation No. 3-73 and the statutory law it reflects. That regulation requires that a certificate of eviction, issued before the commencement of the action, be filed with the court before any judgment will be entered.

Rule 2(d) requires that the plaintiff state the reason(s) for eviction on the summons and complaint. While the substantive law of the Commonwealth may not always require a reason for termination of a tenancy, it does require a reason for eviction. That reason might be simply that a tenant is holding against the right of the landlord after the tenancy has been terminated. When the termination of the tenancy itself requires some reason—e.g. breach of lease, termination in a rent control jurisdiction, nonpayment of rent—the reason for the termination must be provided. See G.L. c. 239, §§ 1, 1A.

It should be noted that the provisions of Mass.R.Civ.P. 6(a), concerning holidays, are applicable to summary process actions. Therefore, if the entry day or the day for filing answers is a holiday, the entry or filing day would be the next day on which the court is open for business. However, if the plaintiff selects a hearing date which is a holiday, the hearing would be scheduled either the next business day after the holiday or one week later on the following Thursday (or Friday or Monday, if applicable).

In rent control jurisdictions, a certificate of eviction is a prerequisite to the commencement of a summary process action. The granting of a certificate of eviction by a rent control board is subject to judicial review. In Gentile v. Rent Control Board of Somerville, 365 Mass. 343, 350 f.n. 7, the Supreme Judicial Court stated that, if a complaint

is filed challenging the issuance of the certificate of eviction, in many instances that complaint and any related summary process action may be consolidated for trial. Therefore, the court should consider the possibility of consolidation in such cases in order to avoid piecemeal litigation.

Amended effective January 28, 1986; February 1, 1993.

Rule 3. Answer

The defendant shall prepare a written answer containing at the top of the page the caption "Summary Process Answer" with the trial date set forth below the caption. The answer shall deny every statement in the complaint which is in dispute. The defendant shall also state in the answer any affirmative defense which may be asserted and may state any counterclaim permitted by Rule 5 of these rules. The answer shall be filed with the clerk and served on the plaintiff no later than the first Monday after the Monday entry day. The answer shall be filed by mailing first-class or by delivering a copy of it to the clerk. Service of the answer shall be made upon the plaintiff or plaintiff's attorney by first-class mail or delivery pursuant to the provisions of Mass.R.Civ.P. 5(b), except that service by mail is complete upon receipt. Filing by mail also is complete upon receipt. Forms of answer, as promulgated by the Chief Administrative Justice of the Trial Court, shall be made available in each clerk-magistrate's office.

Amended effective February 1, 1982; February 1, 1993.

Commentary

Default for failure to answer properly is dealt with in Rule 10 of these rules.

By operation of Rule 1 of these rules, questions regarding service by "delivery" to the plaintiff, proof of service, the effect of failure to file, etc., are governed by the provisions of Mass.R.Civ.P. 5; however, service by mail is complete upon receipt rather than upon mailing.

The requirement that answers be filed and served no later than the first Monday after the Monday entry day establishes that day as the last day for filing and service of the answer.

An answer form, as promulgated by the Chief Administrative Justice of the Trial Court, may be obtained in the offices of the clerks of the Housing Court, District Court, Boston Municipal Court and Superior Court Departments.

The requirement of a caption and hearing date on the answer was inserted to assist the clerks in identifying summary process papers. Because of the commencement provisions in Rule 2, a clerk may choose not to assign docket numbers to answers until after the entry day. Except for the answer, however, all papers filed with the clerk must contain the docket number. See Rules 6 and 7; see also, Mass.R.Civ.P. 10(a).

Clerks should not refuse to accept answers filed before the entry date.

Amended effective January 28, 1986; February 1, 1993.

Rule 4. Transfer of Action

A party wishing to transfer a summary process action pending in another department to a division of the Housing Court Department pursuant to law shall do so by filing in both departments a completed transfer form provided by the clerk of the court where the action was commenced. The form shall be filed in both courts no later than the day before the commencement of the trial. The clerk of the court from which the case is transferred shall forward to the clerk of the appropriate Housing Court division all relevant papers within four business days from the receipt of the transfer form. No entry fee shall be charged upon such transfer. Upon receipt of a copy of this form, the clerk of the Housing Court division shall insure that the case is scheduled forthwith and shall notify the parties in any practical way thereof. A demand for jury trial, if any, pursuant to Rule 8 of these rules, shall be made with the request for transfer.

Failure of a party to make a timely transfer as provided above shall not prohibit the court in which the action has been commenced from allowing such transfer on motion for cause shown at any time during the proceedings.

Amended effective February 1, 1982.

Commentary

This rule refers to transfer of summary process actions from the Superior, District and Boston Municipal Court Departments to the Housing Court Department at the request of any party, as permitted by G.L. c. 185C, § 20. The clerk of the Housing Court division should insure that the transferred case is scheduled for trial on a date that is convenient to the court and the parties and reasonably consistent with the time limitations in these rules; however, the clerk is not required to choose a Thursday, Friday, or Monday hearing date.

A party may transfer an action even though an answer was not timely filed.

Amended effective January 28, 1986.

Rule 5.   Counterclaims

Counterclaims shall be permitted in accordance with the provisions of G.L. c. 239, § 8A. Counterclaims shall be set forth in the defendant's answer and shall be expressly designated as counterclaims. The right to counterclaim shall be deemed to be waived as to the pending action if such a claim is not filed with the answer pursuant to Rule 3, unless the court shall otherwise order on motion for cause shown. Counterclaims shall not be considered compulsory; that is, they shall not be considered waived for the purpose of a separate civil action or actions if not asserted in a summary process action. No responsive pleading to a counterclaim is necessary.

Commentary

This rule recognizes the statutory right of summary process defendants to assert counterclaims. Counterclaims must be asserted with the defendant's answer. A plaintiff against whom a counterclaim is asserted is not required to answer; but an answer to a counterclaim may be filed prior to or at the time of the trial. The court may, of course, in its discretion grant a motion for a continuance in order to grant a party time to prepare a defense to a counterclaim. Because counterclaims are not compulsory, the court retains discretion to sever a counterclaim which cannot appropriately be heard as part of the summary process action. It would, however, appear to be contrary to the law to sever a counterclaim which is being relied upon as a defense under G.L. c. 239, § 8A.

It should be noted that the counterclaim provisions of G.L. c. 239, § 8A apply to premises "rented or leased for dwelling purposes".

Rule 6.   Motions

All pretrial motions shall be made in writing containing the docket number of the case, shall state with particularity the grounds therefor, shall include a brief written statement of reasons in support, shall set forth the relief or order sought, and, except as otherwise provided in this rule, shall be filed with the court and served on the opposing party or that party's attorney, if any, no later than the first Monday after the Monday entry day. A pretrial motion shall be filed with the court by mailing first-class or by delivering a copy of it to the clerk. A pretrial motion shall be served on the opposing party by mailing first-class or by delivering a copy of it to that party or that party's attorney. Filing or service by mail is complete upon receipt.

Unless the court otherwise orders, the hearing on pretrial motions shall be without further notice at the time and on the date the case is originally scheduled for trial. If, however, a motion to dismiss is filed and served on or before the entry date and if the defendant so requests after notice to the plaintiff, the motion shall be heard on the Thursday (or Friday or Monday or second Tuesday or second Wednesday) following the entry date. If the motion is denied, continued, or taken under advisement at the hearing, the defendant's answer shall continue to be due as provided in Rule 3 and the schedule for trial shall not be affected, unless the court otherwise orders.

All other motions, including motions to allow late filing of pretrial motions, shall be made in such manner, at such time, and with such notice as the court may permit or direct.

Amended effective February 1, 1982; January 28, 1986; February 1, 1993.

Commentary

This rule establishes the general requirement that all previously filed motions shall be heard by the court on the originally scheduled trial day (i.e. the second Thursday, or the second Friday, the second Monday, the third Tuesday, or the third Wednesday in some courts, after the entry day) unless the court otherwise orders. The rule also establishes an alternative procedure if the defendant wishes to seek resolution of a motion to dismiss before the trial date. The motion to dismiss would be heard on the first Thursday (or first Friday or first Monday or second Tuesday or second Wednesday) after the entry day; and, unless the motion is allowed or the court otherwise orders, the regular schedule for summary process cases (answer, trial date, etc.) would not be changed.

Pretrial motions, other than motions to dismiss filed pursuant to the alternative procedure (supra), must be filed by the first Monday after the Monday entry day. As to any other motions, the court has complete discretion concerning the manner of filing, notice, and hearing.

Service of pretrial motions is made in the same manner as service of answers pursuant to Rule 3.

Amended effective January 28, 1986; February 1, 1993.

Rule 7.   Discovery

(a) General. Either party may obtain discovery by serving on the opposing party a demand therefor and filing a copy of such demand with the court. Such service and filing shall be made no later than the first Monday after the Monday entry day. A discovery demand, in the form provided in this section, shall be served on the opposing party by mailing first-class or by delivering a copy of it to that party or that party's attorney. A discovery demand shall be filed with the court by mailing first-class or by delivering a copy of it to the clerk. Filing or service by mail is complete upon receipt.

Discovery may be demanded in any of the following forms:

(1) written interrogatories;

(2) request(s) for admission;

(3) request(s) for the production of documents.

Neither written interrogatories nor requests for admissions shall exceed 30 in number including any interrogatories or requests subsidiary or incidental to other interrogatories or requests, however grouped or combined.

Requests for discovery or further discovery not made in compliance with the requirements of this rule shall not be allowed unless on motion and for good cause shown. A request for discovery in response to an answer or counterclaim shall be deemed to establish good cause.

All papers relating to discovery which are filed with the clerk shall contain the docket number of the case.

(b) Postponement of Trial Date. Upon proper service and filing of a demand for discovery as required in section (a) above, hearing of the action shall be automatically postponed and rescheduled for the date two weeks from the original trial date. With the service of the discovery demand, the party demanding discovery shall notify the opposing party of the automatic two week postponement, the newly scheduled trial date, and the requirement in Rule 7(c) as to filing and service of responses no later than ten days after receipt of the request.

(c) Response to Demand for Discovery; Relief or Objection. The party of whom discovery is demanded shall respond by filing and serving answers to the interrogatories and/or responses to the requests for admission, and/or by producing the documents no later than ten days after receipt of the requests. The response shall be completed upon its receipt.

Each interrogatory shall be answered separately and fully in writing under the penalties of perjury, unless it is objected to, in which event the reasons for objection shall be stated in lieu of an answer. The answers are to be signed by the person making them, and the objections by the attorney or person making them. The scope and procedure for requests for production of documents and responses thereto shall be made as permitted and as required by Mass.R.Civ.P. 34(a)(1) and (b); provided, however, that the time limits specified in this rule shall govern. The scope and effect of and the procedure for requests for admission and responses thereto shall be made as permitted and as required by Mass.R.Civ.P. 36; provided, however, that the time limitations specified in this rule shall govern.

A party or the party's attorney objecting to or seeking relief from a discovery request may do so by a motion for protective orders or other relief which shall be filed within five days after receipt of such discovery request.

(d) Enforcement of Discovery Demand. The fact of a party's failure to respond to a demand for discovery as required by this rule and within the time specified by this rule shall be brought to the attention of the court by the party aggrieved thereby or the party's attorney within five days after such failure by a motion for an order compelling discovery as permitted by Mass.R.Civ.P. 37(a) or by an application for final judgment for relief or dismissal.

If a party willfully fails to respond to a discovery demand, on motion heard on the rescheduled trial date the court may make such orders in regard to the failure as are just, and among others the following:

(1) an order that matters regarding which discovery is sought shall be taken to be established for the purposes of the action in accordance with the claim of the moving party;

(2) an order refusing to allow the party failing to respond to support or oppose designated claims or defenses or prohibiting the party from introducing designated matters in evidence;

(3) an order striking out pleadings or parts thereof or staying further proceedings until the discovery demand is satisfied or dismissing the action or any part thereof, or rendering a judgment by default against the party failing to respond.

(e) Further Postponement of Trial Date. Upon proper service and filing of a motion for a protective order against a demand for discovery, or upon proper service and filing of a motion to compel response to a demand for discovery or for final judgment for failure to respond, the rescheduled trial date may be postponed and may be rescheduled, if needed, by the court following the hearing and ruling on such motion.

Amended effective February 1, 1982; February 1, 1993.

Commentary

This rule establishes a limited right to discovery in summary process actions.

In keeping with the need for expeditious procedure, an automatic postponement of the trial date for two weeks from the originally scheduled date results from the timely service and filing of a discovery demand. This two-week postponement allows a reasonable time prior to the rescheduled trial date for a response to the demand and for action permitted by the rule, should a timely response not be made. The party demanding discovery must notify the opposing party of the automatic two-week postponement and of the requirements of Rule 7(c).

It is noteworthy that demands for discovery must be filed and served no later than the first Monday after the Monday entry day. Because the answer and discovery deadlines fall on the same day, a plaintiff will often not know in time whether discovery is desirable because of the answer and any possible counterclaim. Therefore, section (a) provides that the plaintiff's request for discovery in response to an answer or counterclaim should be allowed on motion. In most cases, the defendant (tenant) will probably not object to any additional delay caused by the plaintiff's request for discovery. See Rule 6 [hearing on pretrial motions on date case is originally scheduled for trial].

In section (d), the sanctions listed for failure to respond to a discovery demand are based on Mass.R.Civ.P. 37(b)(2)(A), (B), and (C).

For the requirements of service, see Rule 3 and Mass.R.Civ.P. 5.

Amended effective February 1, 1993.

Rule 8. Jury Trial

The provisions of Mass.R.Civ.P. 38 shall apply insofar as jury trial is available in the court where the action is pending, provided that:

(1) in cases commenced in a court where jury trial is available, a demand for jury trial shall be filed with the court no later than the date on which the defendant's answer is due;

(2) in cases transferred from a court in which jury trial is not available to one in which jury trial is available, such demand shall be filed with the transfer form pursuant to Rule 4 of these rules; and

(3) in cases appealed to the Superior Court Department, such demand shall be filed within ten days of entry in the Superior Court.

Commentary

Jury trials are available in summary process actions in the Superior Court Department (whether the action was commenced there or is there on an appeal from the District Court Department or the Boston Municipal Court Department) and in the Housing Court Department (whether the action has been commenced there or has been transferred there). This rule governs the time for filing the demand for jury trial in each such situation.

Determination of the issues in which jury trial is available and the procedures therefor are governed by Mass.R.Civ.P. 38, adopted by reference in this rule.

It should be noted that jury trials in summary process actions are available in the Worcester Division and the Northern Essex Division (Haverhill) of the District Court Department pursuant to G.L. c. 218, §§ 19A and 19B, respectively.

Rule 9. Equitable Relief

The appointment of receivers and the issuance of restraining orders and injunctions shall be governed by applicable statutes and by Rule 65 and 66, respectively, of the Massachusetts Rules of Civil Procedure; provided, however, that the court may modify the time periods and notice requirements of those rules and otherwise fashion the relief it orders as it deems appropriate.

Commentary

This rule, in effect, permits the court to analogize to the procedures for equitable relief required in regular civil actions. Thus the rules referred to can serve as a guide to the court in fashioning the equitable relief it may order in a summary process action.

Rule 9 reflects the expanded scope of summary process. For several years, the District Court Department has had equitable power in housing cases under G.L. c. 186, § 14 (injunctions against interference with utilities, etc.) and G.L. c. 218, § 19C (injunctive relief to order sanitary code compliance similar to the powers given to the Superior Court Department in G.L. c. 111, § 127H). Under G.L. c. 239, § 8A, the court, in its discretion, may order that funds paid into court by a tenant be expended for repair of the premises at issue; the court may appoint a receiver to supervise this procedure. Other forms of equitable relief appear to be available to a defendant by way of counterclaim. For example, a counterclaim under G.L. c. 186, § 14 could involve equitable relief. In short, all courts have the authority to issue injunctive relief in appropriate cases.

Rule 10. Entry of Default, Entry of Dismissal; Removal of Default or Dismissal; Entry of Judgment After Trial, Default, or Dismissal; Notice

(a) **Entry of Default.** If a defendant fails to answer and also fails to appear for trial, said defendant shall be defaulted at the call of the trial list on the day set for hearing, provided that the plaintiff appears at the call of the list. If a defendant has filed an answer but fails to appear for trial, said defendant shall also be defaulted provided that the plaintiff appears. If the plaintiff also fails to appear, the case shall be dismissed seven days after the trial date unless either party requests a new trial date within the seven day period. If the defendant appears but has failed to file a timely answer, no default shall enter and the court shall postpone the trial date one week from the original trial date, unless the plaintiff consents in writing to an immediate trial. If the defendant appears but has failed to file a timely answer and the plaintiff fails to appear, the court shall postpone the trial date one week from the original trial date and notice shall be sent to the plaintiff. If the plaintiff fails to appear after being notified of the new trial date, the case shall be dismissed.

(b) **Entry of Dismissal.** Dismissal shall be entered when a plaintiff fails to appear for trial, provided that the defendant has filed a timely answer and appears for trial. If the defendant files a timely answer but neither party appears for trial, the case shall be dismissed seven days after the trial date unless either party requests a new trial date within the seven day period.

(c) **Removal of Dismissal or Default.** A default or a dismissal may be removed at the court's discretion, on its own initiative or on motion of either party in writing, at any time prior to the entry of judgment on such default or dismissal.

(d) **Entry of Judgment.** All judgments shall be entered at 10:00 a.m. on the next business day following the court's decision after hearing or trial, or following the entry of default or dismissal, as the case may be, provided that (1) in the case of a default, said default is not removed prior thereto, (2) in the case of a finding pursuant to G.L. c. 239, § 8A that the tenant owes rent, judgment shall be entered in accordance with that statute, and (3) where a default is pending no judgment shall be entered unless the following prerequisites are met:

(i) The plaintiff shall file an affidavit made by a competent person, on the affiant's own knowledge, setting forth facts showing that the defendant is not a person in military service as defined in Article I of the "Soldiers' and Sailors' Civil Relief Act" of 1940, as amended, except upon order of the court in accordance with the Act.

(ii) Where the complaint sets forth a claim for rent and/or use and occupation, the plaintiff shall file an affidavit stating the aggregate amount of payments, if any, which have been made subsequent to the date of the commencement of the action on account of such amount claimed.

(iii) The clerk shall review the documents filed with the court. No judgment by default shall enter against any defendant where it appears from such review that the summons was not properly completed, served or returned, that the complaint was not properly completed or served, or that the other documents required to be filed with the court pursuant to Rule 2(d) have not been filed.

(e) **Notice.** Notice of judgment shall be sent to all parties forthwith upon entry of judgment.

Amended effective February 1, 1982. Amended January 20, 2004, effective March 1, 2004.

Commentary

This rule deals with two related but distinct subjects: (1) the entry of defaults and dismissals and (2) the entry of judgment after entry of default or dismissal, and after trial.

Entry of default or dismissal can depend on two considerations, namely, whether defendant has filed a timely answer and appeared for trial, and whether plaintiff appears for trial. Paragraphs (a) and (b) cover all situations involving failure of the parties to fulfill either one of these requirements.

Note, for example, that upon failure of the defendant to file a timely answer and appear, entry of default is in order if the plaintiff or his attorney appears. Under section (a), if a defendant who has not answered appears, plaintiff has the option of obtaining an automatic one week postponement or proceeding to trial forthwith. The plaintiff, therefore, could have an attorney present to answer the list and obtain defaults while avoiding unnecessary personal appearances. If default ultimately is entered and not removed prior to entry of judgment under paragraph (d), the defendant is left to his rights to relief from judgment under Rule 11 and to appeal under Rule 12.

The provisions of G.L. c. 239, §§ 9 and 10, whereby a tenant can apply for a stay of judgment and execution, are relevant here.

Rule 11.   Relief From Judgment

(a) District and Boston Municipal Court Departments. In the District Court and Boston Municipal Court Departments, Rules 60 and 62(b) and (d) of the Massachusetts Rules of Civil Procedure, which deal with relief from judgment and stay of execution, respectively, shall apply to summary process actions; provided that relief under Rule 60(b) shall be available only in cases where the judgment has been entered on default or dismissal. In cases that have been heard on the merits, relief under Rule 60(b) shall not be available.

(b) Superior and Housing Court Departments. In the Superior Court and Housing Court Departments, Rules 60 and 62 of the Massachusetts Rules of Civil Procedure shall apply to summary process actions.

Commentary

Section (a) of Rule 11 applies only to the District Court and Boston Municipal Court Departments. The right of an aggrieved party to a new trial on appeal provides the rationale for limiting the availability of relief under Rule 60 in those two Departments. See G.L. c. 231, § 97.

Section (b) applies to the Superior Court and Housing Court Departments. An aggrieved party in those departments does not have a right to a new trial; instead the appeal is heard in the Appeals Court. See G.L. c. 239, § 5.

It must be noted that the running of time for appeal in summary process actions is not affected by the filing of a motion under Rule 60.

Rule 62(b) allows the court to stay execution under certain conditions upon filing of a motion under Rule 60. Stay of execution pending appeal is governed by G.L. c. 239, § 5.

Rule 12.   Appeals

Any judgment in a summary process action, except a default judgment, may be appealed by an aggrieved party in accordance with the provisions of law. Upon receipt of notice of appeal and request for setting of bond within the time prescribed by G.L. c. 239, § 5, the clerk shall forthwith schedule a hearing before the court on whether an appeal bond shall be required and on the form and amount of such appeal bond. The hearing shall be held within three business days of said receipt.

Amended effective February 1, 1982. Amended January 20, 2004, effective March 1, 2004.

Commentary

The subject of appeals in summary process actions is directly governed by G.L. c. 239, §§ 3 and 5. Section 3 requires that appeals from cases heard in the District Court Department be taken to the Superior Court Department and that appeal may be on either or both of the issues of possession or rent claimed. Section 5 sets forth the procedural mechanism for claiming and prosecuting appeals. No direct reference is made in either statute to a right on the part of a plaintiff to claim an appeal in a summary process action. However, the general terms of G.L. c. 231, § 97 do confer upon plaintiffs in the District Court Department the right to appeal summary process actions to the Superior Court and, more specifically, to "take" such appeals "within the time limits specified" in G.L. c. 239, § 5.

Read together, the provisions of G.L. c. 231, § 97 and G.L. c. 239, § 5 seem to require that just as a defendant, a plaintiff in the District Court or Boston Municipal Court Departments aggrieved by a judgment on the issue of possession or rent, or both, must file a notice of appeal with the court issuing the judgment within ten days of the judgment being entered.

Detailed provisions regarding the appeal in summary process cases including bond requirements for an appealing defendant and appeal of the bond decision, are set forth in G.L. c. 239, § 5. This statute should be consulted directly on questions relating to these procedures.

Relief from a default judgment is subject to the provisions of Rules 11 and 12.

It should be noted that the indigent court costs statute, G. L. c. 261, § 27A *et seq.* places appeals bonds into the "extra fees and costs" category. The court can waive the appeals bond upon a determination of indigency pursuant to these sections of the General Laws or for such other reasons as the court deems proper.

Rule 13.   Execution

Execution shall issue upon application, but not prior to the termination of the time limits imposed by applicable law and by the relevant provisions of Rules 60 and 62 of the Massachusetts Rules of Civil Procedure.

Commentary

Section 5 of Chapter 239 of the General Laws prohibits the issuance of execution in a summary process action prior to the expiration of ten days after the entry of judgment. If appeal is claimed, Mass.R.Civ.P. 62(d) stays execution pending appeal.

When the defendant moves for a waiver of appeal bond, section 5 of Chapter 239 also prohibits the issuance of execution prior to the expiration of six days from the court's decision on the motion, or prior to the expiration of the time specified for the taking of appeal, whichever is later.

The statute also provides that where a defendant seeks review of the court's ruling on the motion for waiver of appeal bond, no execution may issue until the expiration of five days from the date defendant receives notice of the decision of the reviewing court. Of course, if the defendant posted bond after losing an appeal of the trial court's denial of waiver of that bond, execution would continue to be unavailable pending the completion of the appeal of the underlying judgment under Rule 62(d), cited above.

Note should also be made of the special provision regarding execution in G.L. c. 239, § 1A (recovery of possession before termination of a lease), and the provisions of G.L. c. 239, §§ 9 and 10 regarding application for stay for judgment and execution.

FORMS

Summary Process Summons and Complaint

Commonwealth of Massachusetts
SUMMARY PROCESS (EVICTION) SUMMONS AND COMPLAINT

_____ Department

☐ Residential

_____ Division

☐ Commercial

Docket No._____

(To be added by clerk's office)

Entry Date:_____

_____ ss

NOTICE OF A COURT CASE TO EVICT YOU - PLEASE READ IT CAREFULLY

ESTA ES UNA NOTIFICACION DE UN CASO EN CORTE PARA DESALOJARLE - FAVOR DE LEER EL MISMO CON CUIDADO

TO DEFENDANT(S)/TENANT(S)/OCCUPANT(S):_____

ADDRESS: _____CITY/TOWN:_____ ZIP:_____

You are hereby summonsed to appear at a hearing before a Judge of the Court at the time and place listed below:

DAY:_____DATE:_____ TIME:_____COURT NAME:_____

COURT ADDRESS: _____ **ROOM**:_____

to defend against the complaint of PLAINTIFF/LANDLORD/OWNER:_____

_____ of

STREET _____CITY/TOWN:_____ ZIP:_____

that you occupy the premises at _____,

being within the judicial district of this court, unlawfully and against the right of said Plaintiff/Landlord/Owner

because:_____

_____

and further, that $_____ rent is owed according to the following account:

WITNESS:

ACCOUNT ANNEXED (itemize)

_____
First or Chief Justice

_____
Printed Name of Plaintiff or Attorney

_____
Signature of Plaintiff or Attorney

_____
Date of Signature of Plaintiff or Attorney

_____
_____
_____
_____

_____
Address of Plaintiff or Attorney

_____
Telephone Number of Plaintiff or Attorney

NOTICE TO EACH DEFENDANT/TENANT/OCCUPANT: At the hearing on _____
you (or your attorney) must appear in person to present your defense. You (or your attorney) must also file a written answer to this complaint. An answer is your response stating the reason(s) why you should not be evicted and may, in residential cases, include any claims you have against the Landlord. (An Answer Form is available in the **clerk's office whose telephone number is** _____.) You must file (deliver or mail) the answer with the court clerk and serve (deliver or mail) a copy on the landlord (or landlord's attorney) at the address shown above. **The Answer must be received by the court clerk and received by the landlord (or the landlord's attorney) no later than Monday,** _____, which is the first Monday after the "entry date" listed above. The entry date is the day by which your landlord must file this complaint with the court clerk.

NOTICE TO EACH DEFENDANT/TENANT/OCCUPANT: IF YOU DO NOT FILE AND SERVE AN ANSWER, OR IF YOU DO NOT DEFEND AT THE TIME OF THE HEARING, JUDGMENT MAY BE ENTERED AGAINST YOU FOR POSSESSION AND THE RENT AS REQUESTED IN THE COMPLAINT.

SI USTED NO REGISTRA O NOTIFICA UNA CONTESTA, O SI USTED NO PRESENTA UNA DEFENSA A LA HORA DE LA AUDIENCIA, UNA SENTENCIA PUEDE SER REGISTRADA EN SU CONTRA PARA POSECCION Y POR LA RENTA REQUERIDA EN EL RECLAMO.

To the Sheriffs of our several counties, or their Deputies, or any Constable of any City or Town within said Commonwealth, GREETINGS: We command you to summon the within named defendant(s)/ tenant(s)/occupant(s) to appear as herein ordered.

_____
Clerk-Magistrate

Officer's Return

_____, ss   City/Town:_____   Date:_____

By virtue of this Writ, I this day served the within-named tenant or occupant, and summonsed him/her as herein

directed, by giving in hand to_____

or leaving it at _____ the last and usual place of abode.

A copy of this summons was mailed first class to each tenant/occupant at the address on:_____ .

Fees for Service:

Service	$_____	
Copy/Attest	_____	
Travel	_____	
Use of Car	_____	
Mailing	_____	

TOTAL $_____

_____
Signature of Officer

_____
Printed Name of Officer

_____
Address of Officer

_____
Telephone Number of Officer

NOTICE TO PLAINTIFF/LANDLORD/OWNER: Have the Officer complete and return above. Service must be made on the defendant(s) no later than the seventh day and not earlier than the thirtieth day before the Monday entry date. This form must be filed in court no later than the close of business on the scheduled Monday entry date. In appropriate cases, proper evidence of notice to quit must be provided to this court upon the filing of this complaint. See Uniform Summary Process Rule 2(d). According to Uniform Summary Process Rule 2(c), the hearing date is the second Thursday after the entry date. In some courts, the hearing date is the second Monday, third Tuesday, third Wednesday, or second Friday.

Amended effective February 1, 1982; July 1, 1986; September 1, 2005.

Summary Process Answer

COMMONWEALTH OF MASSACHUSETTS
THE TRIAL COURT
SUMMARY PROCESS ANSWER

_____
(trial date)

(select county), ss: Housing Court Department

_____ Division

SUMMARY PROCESS
ACTION DOCKET
NO. / / / / / /

_____

Plaintiff(s) – Landlord(s)

versus

_____

Defendant(s) – Tenant(s)

INSTRUCTIONS TO DEFENDANT (TENANT)—PLEASE READ CAREFULLY:

Listed below for you to check and fill in as applicable are possible defenses you might have to the Plaintiff's (Landlord's) Complaint which has been served on you. (A defense is a legal reason for not evicting you.) If one or more of these defenses apply to your case, check the appropriate box(es). If you check a defense which has blank lines after it, you must write in facts in support of that defense. Use additional pages if necessary.

In addition, space is provided for you to counterclaim against your landlord if you wish to do so. (A counterclaim means asking that the amount of rent you owe be reduced or that your landlord pay you money because he or she has violated your rights.) If you wish to counterclaim, fill in the appropriate blank lines. Use additional pages if necessary, and please be as specific as possible.

You should be aware that there may be possible defenses and counterclaims which are not listed below, and that some are rather technical in nature. You are permitted to fill out and file this answer, and to appear in court without a lawyer; but if you can and wish to, you should obtain the services of a lawyer for advice and/or representation in court.

YOU MUST FILE THIS ANSWER OR ANOTHER LEGALLY SUFFICIENT ANSWER, WITH THE CLERK AND SEND A COPY TO THE PLAINTIFF OR PLAINTIFF'S ATTORNEY TO BE RECEIVED NO LATER THAN THE MONDAY BEFORE THE DATE SCHEDULED FOR TRIAL, AS INDICATED ON THE SUMMONS, OR YOU MAY LOSE BY DEFAULT. YOU MUST ALSO BE IN COURT FOR TRIAL OR YOU WILL LOSE BY DEFAULT.

ANSWER TO COMPLAINT
(Please type or print)

( ) I specifically deny the following facts stated in the Complaint: _____

( ) I am legally withholding my rent because: _____ _____ _____

( ) The landlord is trying to evict me for my exercising my rights as follows: _____ _____ _____

( ) I have a written lease which has not expired and the landlord has not given me notice that he/she is terminating my lease.

( ) I have not received a notice from the landlord telling me to leave the premises, and I do not have a written lease.

( ) If I have ever owed the landlord any rent, I have paid it all or have paid it within the time required by law.

( ) I was not properly notified of this court action: _____

( ) The landlord's Complaint fails to state facts which would allow him/her to evict me: _____ _____

( ) There is another person against whom this action should be brought: _____ _____

( ) I have not been properly named in the Complaint: _____

( ) There is another Summary Process action pending against me.

( ) I am a tenant in a public housing program and my landlord did not get the required permission before beginning this eviction case.

( ) I have other defenses as follows: _____

IMPORTANT: In some cases, the court has the power to give you time to find a new place to live even if you do not have any of the listed defenses. If you wish the court to determine whether you are entitled to it, please check below:

☐   I wish time to move because I cannot find another residence.

COUNTERCLAIM

If you believe that you are entitled to a return of part of your rent payment or other damages from the landlord, complete the statement below:

I hereby counterclaim in the amount of $_____. I feel that I am entitled to this amount for the following reasons: _____ _____ _____

_____

(Name of Defendant(s) or Attorney)

_____

(Signature of Defendant(s) or
Attorney)

_____

(Address)

Amended effective February 1, 1982.

II. UNIFORM MAGISTRATE RULES

Table of Rules

Rule 1. Scope and Applicability of Rules

These rules govern the exercise of power by magistrates pursuant to the provisions of G.L. c. 221, §§ 62B and 62C.

These rules shall be applicable in every Department of the Trial Court except the Land Court Department.

The rules shall be construed and applied to secure the just, speedy and inexpensive determination of proceedings in the Trial Court.

Rule 2. Uncontested Non–Evidentiary Motions

(a) Civil Cases. Magistrates may hear and rule on the following motions in civil actions provided that such motions are uncontested or assented to in writing and provided further that neither party is proceeding pro se:

(1) For Entry of Default

(2) For Entry of Default Judgment under Mass.R.Civ.P. 55(b)(1) or Dist./Mun.Cts.R.Civ.P., 55(b)(1)

(3) To Amend any Pleading

(4) To File a Responsive Pleading Late

(5) For Order of Notice

(6) To Strike Out and Answer Over Interrogatories

(7) To Compel Answers to Interrogatories

(8) For Consolidation of Cases Pending in One Court

(9) To Remove Default Entered by a Magistrate

(10) To Permit Marriage Without Delay (Probate and Family Court Department)

(11) To Waive the Thirty-Days Living Apart Requirement (Probate and Family Court Department)

(12) To Extend or Shorten Time or Continue a Hearing on a Motion.

Within a Department of the Trial Court, The Administrative Justice of that Department may delete or make additions to the motions enumerated in this section.

(b) Criminal Cases. Magistrates may hear and either grant or deny a pretrial motion to correct defects in a criminal complaint, criminal process or supporting documents in criminal cases, provided that such a motion is uncontested or assented to in writing and the defendant is represented by counsel.

(c) General. If the motion before the magistrate is uncontested based on the fact that the party who would be in a position to contest it has not filed a timely response, the magistrate shall be satisfied that the motion was duly served on that party prior to making a ruling. Also, the fact that a party failed to appear for a hearing on a motion shall be stated in writing by the magistrate.

A magistrate acting on a motion must indicate that the action was taken by the magistrate and not by the justice. Any person aggrieved by the action of a magistrate on any motion may be reheard by a justice provided that a motion for rehearing is filed within five days of the giving of notice of the action of the magistrate.

In no event shall a ruling be made pursuant to this rule if that ruling would affect the date of a court appearance previously set in accordance with the caseflow management policies of a Department or division.

Rule 3. Pretrial Conferences

(a) Civil Cases. In each Department, the Administrative Justice, may establish policies and procedures for the scheduling and conduct before a magistrate of pretrial conferences in civil cases. This rule shall not apply to small claims cases. Among the procedures that may be required at such pretrial conferences are: (1) ascertaining trial readiness of the parties; (2) if a court appearance is necessary on a subsequent day, setting the date and specific purpose of such court appearance; (3) filing of stipulations agreed upon by the parties; (4) filing of agreements by the parties as to which motions may be filed; (5) filing of agreements by the parties as to the amendment of pleadings; (6) filing of agreements by the parties as to settlement possibilities; (7) filing of agreements by the parties as to discovery procedures; and (8) identification and simplification of factual and legal issues.

At the conclusion of the conference the magistrate shall enter a report on a form approved by the Chief Administrative Justice of the Trial Court containing the results of the conference.

The civil pretrial conference policy that is adopted by each Department may also govern the scheduling of such conferences in relation to a proposed trial date and in relation to the daily calendar and whether such conferences will be mandatory or voluntary in all or certain types of civil cases.

Notice for all such conferences may include a statement that counsel are to attend with the parties and with authorization for the terms for possible settlement. Where public officials are sued in their official capacity, they shall not be required to attend the pretrial conference. Upon failure of any party to appear for a scheduled pretrial conference, the magistrate may order dismissal or default against the absent party or parties.

The court may, upon motion therefor, award costs against the party or attorney whose unjustified absence or lack of preparation prevented the conduct of a pretrial conference.

Trial dates established at a pretrial conference shall be subject to the control of the court.

This rule shall be construed so as to be consistent with Mass.R.Civ.P. 16, Mass.R.Dom.Rel.P. 16, and Dist./ Mun.Cts.R.Civ.P. 16. The aforementioned rule 16 shall be read to apply pretrial conferences held before a judge.

(b) Criminal Cases. In appropriate Departments the Administrative Justice may establish policies and procedures for the scheduling and conduct before a magistrate of pretrial conferences in criminal cases. Such policy may include a procedure whereby the court may, at the time of arraignment, schedule cases for pretrial conference before a magistrate.

Among the procedures that may be required at such pretrial conferences are: (1) ascertaining trial readiness of the parties; (2) if a court appearance is necessary on a subsequent day, reporting the case to a judge for the setting of a date for such court appearance; (3) filing of stipulations and admissions between the prosecution and the defense; (4) filing of agreements between the prosecution and the defense as to which motions may be filed; (5) filing of agreements between the prosecution and defense as to the amendment of pleadings; and (6) filing of agreements between the prosecution and defense as to discovery procedures.

At the conclusion of the conference the magistrate shall enter an appropriate report on a form approved by the Chief Administrative Justice of the Trial Court containing the results of the conference.

Other aspects of the pretrial conference policy that may be considered by each appropriate Department are the scheduling of such conferences in relation to a proposed trial date and in relation to the daily calendar and whether such conferences will be mandatory or voluntary in all or certain types of criminal cases for which they are permitted under this rule.

The magistrate shall not take part in plea negotiations.

No pretrial conference policy established pursuant to this rule shall permit the disposition of any case without appearance before a judge.

This rule shall be construed so as to be consistent with Mass.R.Crim.P. 11.

Rule 4. Mediation of Small Claims Actions

(District Court, Boston Municipal Court and Housing Court Departments)

(a) Scope of Rule. This rule governs procedure by which magistrates act as mediators in small claims actions pursuant to G.L. c. 218, s. 22 and G.L. c. 185C, s. 3. The rule shall apply to the District Court, Boston Municipal Court and Housing Court Departments.

(b) Informing Plaintiff and Defendant. All plaintiffs in small claims actions shall be informed upon the filing of their complaints that such actions may be submitted to a magistrate of the court for mediation and resolution at the request of either party and with the agreement of all parties. Such information shall be contained in a written notice to be given to the plaintiff personally or by mail at the time of the filing of the action. Such written notice shall be in the form approved by the Chief Administrative Justice of the Trial Court. If the plaintiff indicates to the court within ten days after this notice is given or sent that he desires mediation, the summons sent to the defendant or a notice included with the summons sent to the defendant shall indicate this fact and the fact that the defendant may consent to mediation on the date for which the case is scheduled.

(c) Mediation Procedures. Mediation sessions may be conducted in courtrooms or in any other room in the courthouse deemed appropriate for the purpose by the magistrate, including the magistrate's office. The mediation process shall consist of a discussion of the dispute by the parties, guided by the magistrate, with the goal of achieving a voluntary resolution of the dispute on terms mutually agreeable to the parties. Procedures governing the order in which the parties may speak, their opportunity to speak, and the participation of lawyers and witnesses, shall be as the magistrate shall determine, consistent with the achievement of a voluntary resolution of the dispute. Mediation sessions are not to be recorded and participants are not to be sworn.

(d) Termination of Mediation. If at any time prior to the agreement of the parties the magistrate for any reason determines that the procedures have reached an impasse or are not leading to a voluntary and equitable resolution, he or she may so inform the parties and terminate the mediation procedure. Upon such termination, the magistrate shall schedule the action for the small claims session and may attempt to obtain from the parties stipulations and agreed facts. Such stipulations and statements of agreed facts, if any, shall be submitted to the court when the case comes on for hearing in the small claims session.

(e) Judgment After Mediation. Upon the achievement of a voluntary resolution by mediation, the magistrate shall cause such resolution to be reduced to writing, including all the terms thereof on a memorandum in a form approved by the Chief Administrative Justice of the Trial Court. The parties shall sign this written memorandum of their agreement and be given copies thereof. The magistrate shall thereupon enter judgment in the case in accordance with said agreement and shall likewise enter any agreed-upon order for payment.

(f) Enforcement. Satisfaction and enforcement of monetary judgments entered on mediated agreements and of the terms of payment thereof shall be by the same supplementary process procedures as are applicable to small claims judgments generally.

(g) Review. The action of a magistrate pursuant to this rule shall be reviewable by a justice provided that a request for said review is made within five days of the giving of notice of the action of the Magistrate.

Rule 5. Petitions for Review of Dog Orders

(District Court and Boston Municipal Court Departments)

Petitions for review of dog orders and their disposition pursuant to G.L. c. 140, § 157 shall be set forth on forms prescribed by the Chief Justice of the District Court Department. The statutory filing fee shall be paid upon the filing of a petition in the District Court or Boston Municipal Court Departments.

Hearings held by magistrates on petitions for review of dog orders shall be conducted in courtrooms whenever feasible. The rules of evidence shall not apply at such hearings. All evidence shall be given such weight as deemed appropriate by the magistrate. All witnesses shall be placed under oath by the magistrate and both the petitioner and respondent shall be allowed to cross-examine adverse witnesses. Proceedings shall be electronically recorded if equipment necessary for such recording is available.

Pursuant to G.L. c. 140, § 157, the magistrate shall review the action of the body or person having issued the order, shall hear any witnesses and shall affirm the order unless it shall appear that it was made without proper cause or in bad faith, in which case the order shall be reversed. The magistrate's decision shall be entered promptly and notice of the decision showing the date of entry shall be sent to the parties immediately upon entry.

A request for a de novo hearing before a justice must be received within 10 days after the entry of the decision of the magistrate. The de novo hearing shall be held promptly.

Rule 6. Preliminary Probation Revocation Hearings

(District Court, Boston Municipal Court and Superior Court Departments)

(a) **Applicability of Rule.** This rule governs procedures for the scheduling and conduct of preliminary hearings held before magistrates for the purpose of determining whether there is probable cause to believe a probationer has violated the terms of his probation in the District Court, Boston Municipal Court and Superior Court Departments. Such preliminary hearings are required by law to be conducted as a prerequisite to holding the probationer in custody pending the full probation revocation hearing and only when the basis for such custody, if any, will be the charge of probation violation.

(b)(1) *Surrender on Warrant.* If a probationer is surrendered by means of a warrant, no preliminary hearing shall be held until the probationer is given written notice of the factual allegations on which the surrender was based. Upon such surrender a justice or magistrate shall set the date and time of such hearing and shall decide the terms of release pending such hearing, which may include modification of the pending recognizance.

(2) *Voluntary Surrender.* If a probationer surrenders in response to a written notice of surrender, no preliminary hearing shall be held until the magistrate is satisfied that the written notice fully describes the factual allegations on which the surrender was based and that the probationer is aware of these allegations. Such written notice of probation surrender shall be on the form provided by the Commissioner of Probation or such other form as may be promulgated by the Chief Administrative Justice of the Trial Court. Such form shall be completed and sent by the probation officer wishing to effect the surrender, provided that said probation officer consults with the magistrate regarding the date and time of hearing that are to appear on such notice and the decision on whether a preliminary hearing will be necessary.

(c) **Counsel.** If a preliminary probation revocation hearing is held, the probationer shall have the right to be assisted by counsel. The magistrate conducting the hearing shall follow the procedures as to the assignment of counsel established in G.L. c. 211D and Supreme Judicial Court Rule 3:10.

(d) **Procedure.** Preliminary probation revocation hearings shall be conducted in courtrooms whenever feasible. If not feasible, such hearings shall take place in any other room in the courthouse in which the public has access. Only when no courtroom or public room is available shall a magistrate's office or any other room to which the public generally has limited access be used for such hearings. In those instances when a magistrate's office or other private room must be used in accordance with this rule, the magistrate shall explain to the probationer and his counsel, if any, the reason for the use of such room.

Such hearings shall be stenographically or electronically recorded unless neither a stenographer nor electronic recording equipment is available.

All witnesses at such hearings shall be placed under oath.

The probationer or, if he is represented by counsel, his counsel, shall be allowed to question any witnesses he may present and shall be allowed to cross-examine witnesses testifying against him.

The rules of evidence shall not apply at such hearings. All evidence shall be given such weight as deemed appropriate by the magistrate.

The minimum quantum of evidence necessary for a finding that there is probable cause to believe a probationer has violated the terms of his probation shall be sworn testimony setting forth facts substantiating such allegations. If such testimony of itself is satisfactory to the magistrate to establish that the allegations are probably correct, and if this probability is not overcome by testimony by the probationer or his witnesses or by documentary evidence submitted by the probationer, then probable cause may be found by the magistrate. In cases when the surrender is based on an allegation that there has been a criminal conviction or finding of probable cause entered against the probationer subsequent to the probation order of which revocation is sought, and there is a dispute on the validity of this allegation, a certified copy of such conviction or probable cause finding or the original of the record thereof shall be requested from the prosecuting probation officer by the magistrate. However, the submission of such records or copies shall not be indispensable to a finding of probable cause.

When available, a court officer shall be present at such hearings.

If probable cause is found, a probation violation hearing shall be scheduled, the probationer shall thereupon be served in hand with a notice of said hearing, and the magistrate may order the probationer to be held in custody pending the conduct and completion of the scheduled final violation hearing. The magistrate's decision whether to release the probationer pending the conduct and completion of the final probation violation hearing, notwithstanding a finding of probable cause on an alleged violation, shall include, but not necessarily be limited to:

i. The probationer's criminal record;

ii. The nature of the offense for which the probationer is on probation;

iii. The nature of the current offense or offenses with which the probationer is newly charged, if any;

iv. The nature of any other pending alleged probation violations;

v. The likelihood of probationer's appearance at the final probation violation hearing if not held in custody; and

vi. The likelihood of incarceration if a violation is found following the final probation violation hearing.

If no probable cause is found, a probation violation hearing may be scheduled and the probationer thereupon served with notice thereof, but the probationer may not be held in custody pending said hearing based on the alleged probation violation.

(e) Summary of Proceedings. The magistrate shall, upon the completion of such hearing, prepare a written memorandum summarizing the proceedings and stating the reasons for the finding made. Such summary and statement of reasons shall be made on the form provided for this purpose by the Commissioner of Probation or such other form as may be promulgated by the Chief Administrative Justice of the Trial Court. When completed, one copy of such form shall be placed with the case papers, one copy shall be given to the probation officer and one copy shall be given to the probationer.

(f) Bail: Upon a finding of probable cause and an order of custody, the magistrate shall not consider or impose any terms of release such as bail, personal recognizance or otherwise as an alternative to such custody. Notwithstanding such order of probation custody, if release terms have not yet been set by a judge on any newly charged offense, the probationer shall be brought before a judge if the court is then in session, and the judge shall proceed to determine release terms and any issue of pretrial detention ("dangerousness") on such newly charged offense, as provided by law and the Massachusetts Rules of Criminal Procedure. If the court is not then in session, the magistrate shall set release terms on such newly charged offense until the probationer can be brought before a judge at the next sitting of the court.

Amended effective July 1, 1986; September 6, 2001, effective October 1, 2001.

Rule 7.   [Deleted effective July 1, 1986]

III. UNIFORM SMALL CLAIMS RULES

Table of Rules

Rule 1. Scope and Applicability of Rules; Definitions

Pursuant to G.L. c. 218, §§ 21–25, these rules govern procedures in all small claims actions in the Trial Court of the Commonwealth. They shall be construed and applied to secure the just, speedy and inexpensive determination of every small claim action. Other civil rules of court shall not be applicable in small claims.

As used herein the singular shall include the plural.

In these rules, the following terms shall have the following meanings:

"Clerk" shall mean the Clerk–Magistrate of the division or a person assigned by him or her to perform the required function.

"Court" shall mean the magistrate or judge presiding over the hearing of a small claim action.

"Magistrate" shall mean a clerk-magistrate or assistant clerk-magistrate authorized by G.L. c. 218, §§ 21–23 to hear and determine small claims actions.

"Trade" and "commerce" shall have the same meaning as in G.L. c. 93A, § 1, but shall not include the lease or rental of residential property that is the plaintiff's primary residence and that consists of three units or less, provided the plaintiff does not own, manage or have other involvement in the lease or rental of other residential property.

"Assigned debt" shall mean a claim or judgment where the right to collect the debt has been assigned by the creditor to another person or entity.

"Plaintiff" in Rules 7 through 10, shall include a defendant with respect to any counterclaim or any claim against a third party brought by him or her, and the word "defendant" shall include a plaintiff or a third party with respect to any counterclaim or any third-party claim brought against him or her.

"He" or "she" shall include any entity that may sue or be sued.

The Chief Justice for Administration and Management shall promulgate the Statement of Small Claim form, the Verification of Defendant's Address form, and the Agreement for Judgment form provided for in these rules.

Amended October 1, 2001, effective January 1, 2002; July 22, 2009, effective October 1, 2009.

Commentary to 2001 Amendments

Most of these amendments are proposed to conform the Uniform Small Claims Rules to the statutory changes enacted by St. 1992, c. 379. The reasons for other proposed changes are noted under each rule.

The former second paragraph of Rule 1 has been rendered unnecessary by the passage of time since the 1983 promulgation of the Uniform Small Claims Rules.

The newly-added definition of "magistrate" reflects the statutory change contained in St. 1992, c. 379 and intends that small claims matters generally be heard in the first instance by a clerk-magistrate or an assistant clerk-magistrate. No magistrate who is not qualified by education or training should preside over small claims since these matters are to be determined "according to the rules of substantive law." G.L. c. 218, § 21. The Trial Court will provide training pursuant to criteria approved by the Chief Justice for Administration and Management.

The newly-added definitions of "plaintiff" and "defendant" reflect the holdings of *Most v. Fitzgerald,* 417 Mass. 1001 (1994), and *Bischof v. Kern,* 33 Mass. App. Ct. 45 (1992), that small claims plaintiffs may appeal from an adverse decision on a counterclaim brought by the defendant. The addition of these definitions permits simple, consistent use of the terms "plaintiff" and "defendant" throughout these rules.

Commentary to 2009 Amendments

The authority formerly granted by Rule 1 to vary the notice requirements of these rules has been deleted because of the addition of mandatory address verification requirements in Rule 2(b). The court continues to have authority under Rule 3(a) to vary the manner in which notice is served. The definitions of "trade" and "commerce" and of "assigned debt" were added to implement the new address verification and pleading requirements of Rule 2(b). The definitions of "trade" and "commerce" refer to the Consumer Protection Act, G.L. c. 93A, but contain an exclusion for rentals of landlord-occupied multiple dwellings of three units or less. Case law further defining trade or commerce in the context of c. 93A cases is intended to be applicable here.

Rule 2. Filing A Statement of Claim

(a) **Statement of Claim.** Each small claim action shall be begun on a Statement of Small Claim form. The claim shall be stated in concise, untechnical language, but with particularity and comprehensiveness. A statement shall not be insufficient merely because the plaintiff has failed to allege all the elements of a prima facie case. The plaintiff shall state specifically any amounts sought for damages, for multiple damages or statutory penalties, for attorney's fees, and for costs, as well as the total amount being sought, exclusive of any prejudgment interest being sought from the court pursuant to G.L. c. 231, §§ 6B or 6C. If requested by the plaintiff or if otherwise feasible and appropriate to facilitate the filing of a legible and complete claim that conforms to the requirements of this rule, the clerk shall provide assistance to the plaintiff in completing the form. The clerk shall provide necessary and helpful procedural information to small claim litigants if requested.

(b) Additional Requirements for plaintiffs in trade or commerce or pursuing assigned debt. Any plaintiff pursuing a claim incurred in the course of plaintiff's trade or commerce, or pursuing a claim for assigned debt, shall file along with the Statement of Small Claim form the Verification of Defendant's Address form, certifying that he or she has verified the defendant's mailing address in the manner set forth therein. The form need not be served on the defendant.

Any such plaintiff shall include the following information in the description of claim in the Statement of Small Claim form when the claim is filed with the court:

(1) The name of the original creditor (if different from plaintiff's);

(2) The last four digits of the account number assigned by the original creditor, if any; and

(3) The amount and date of the defendant's last payment, if any.

If the plaintiff fails to comply with this section and the defendant does not appear at the scheduled trial, no default judgment shall be entered for the plaintiff and the claim shall be dismissed without prejudice.

(c) Filing with the Clerk. A claim may be filed in person or by mail. In either case, except where waived by the clerk of the court under the Indigent Court Costs Law (G.L. c. 261, §§ 27A–29), the claim shall be accompanied by the entry fee required by G.L. c. 218, § 22 and the surcharge required by G.L. c. 262, § 4C. The clerk shall provide a copy of the Statement of Small Claim form to the plaintiff as soon as is practicable, which copy shall show the date and time of trial. The date the Statement of Small Claim form is received by the clerk shall constitute the date of commencement of the claim.

Amended November 22, 1989, effective November 30, 1989; October 1, 2001, effective January 1, 2002; July 22, 2009, effective October 1, 2009.

Commentary to 2001 Amendments

The change in the first paragraph is intended to encourage court personnel to provide procedural information and to assist claimants in the preparation of forms.

Commentary to 2009 Amendments

Section (a) has been amended to require the plaintiff to state specifically any amounts sought for damages, for multiple damages or statutory penalties, for attorney's fees, and for costs, as well as the total amount sought, exclusive of any statutory prejudgment interest. This provides the defendant with a breakdown of the amount being claimed and assists the court in determining the amount of any award. It does not limit the amount of the court's award except for default judgments. Such a breakdown of the elements of the plaintiff's claim is already required in regular civil cases by Dist./Mun. Cts. Supp. R. Civ. P. 106(B).

Section (b) introduces two additional requirements for plaintiffs in trade or commerce or pursuing assigned debt. Such plaintiffs must

verify the defendant's current address in one of several specified ways and certify this when filing the Statement of Small Claim. This enhanced filing requirement is intended to increase the likelihood that the defendant will receive notice of the claim when it is mailed.

Such plaintiffs must also provide three items of basic information which will help the defendant to identify the debt that is the basis of the claim. Such information may be particularly important when the plaintiff is an assignee rather than the original creditor. For privacy reasons, only the last four digits of the original creditor's account number are to be given.

If the defendant fails to appear for trial, the plaintiff's failure to comply with this section will result in denial of a default judgment and in dismissal of the claim without prejudice.

Rule 3. Notice to Defendant; Answer to Claim

(a) Notice. The clerk shall promptly send to the defendant by first class mail, at the address or addresses supplied by the plaintiff, a copy of the Statement of Small Claim form. Such first class mail notice shall be sufficient, provided that it is not returned to the court undelivered. Service on out-of-state defendants shall be made pursuant to the provisions of G.L. c. 223A. The court may provide for any other means of service in individual cases as is deemed necessary.

(b) Answer. The Statement of Small Claim form shall instruct the defendant that he or she may, if he or she wishes, submit a written answer to the claim in the form of a letter to the court, with a copy mailed to the plaintiff, signed by the defendant and setting out in clear and simple language the reason(s) why the plaintiff should not prevail. The answer should state fully and specifically what parts of the claim are contested. However, the filing of an answer is optional, and the failure to file an answer shall not result in the defendant's default. If the defendant's failure to submit a written answer, or to send a copy of it to the plaintiff in a timely manner, has prejudiced the presentation of the plaintiff's case, the court shall grant a continuance at the plaintiff's request.

(c) Defendant's Counterclaim. In the answer, or in a separate writing filed with the court, the defendant may set forth any claim which he or she has against the plaintiff within the jurisdiction of the court in small claims cases, without incurring any filing fee or surcharge. Both the plaintiff's claim and the defendant's claim shall be deemed one case if the defendant mails notice of his claim to the plaintiff at least ten days in advance of the scheduled trial date. The court may also permit the defendant to bring such a claim in writing at any time. Such claims shall not be compulsory. No written answer to the defendant's claim is required. If the defendant's presentation of a counterclaim, or failure to send timely notice to the plaintiff, has prejudiced the presentation of the plaintiff's case, the court shall grant a continuance at the plaintiff's request.

(d) Third–Party Practice. The defendant may bring a claim against any third party who may be liable to him or her for all or part of the plaintiff's claim if the defendant's claim is within the jurisdiction of the court in small claims cases and notice is mailed to the third party in the manner provided in Rule 2 at least ten days in advance of the scheduled trial date. The court may also permit the defendant to bring such a claim in writing at any time. There shall be no filing fee or surcharge for such a claim. When a counterclaim is asserted against the plaintiff, he or she may bring a claim against a third party in the same manner.

Amended effective July 1, 1986; amended November 22, 1989, effective November 30, 1989; October 1, 2001, effective January 1, 2002; November 29, 2004, effective January 1, 2005; July 22, 2009, effective October 1, 2009.

Commentary to 2001 Amendments

The change to paragraph (a) codifies the holding of *Schreiber v. Hoyusgaard*, 1989 Mass. App. Div. 138 (S. Dist.), that in the case of an out-of-state defendant the service provisions of the long-arm statute (G.L. c. 223A, § 6) prevail over those in this rule. The practical significance of this change is that mail service on an out-of-state defendant is valid only if there is a signed receipt for the certified mail.

The procedure embodied in the proposed amendment to paragraph (b) would give plaintiffs a guarantee of protection from surprise defenses, but it would not require an answer to be filed in all cases. The amendment to paragraph (c) would also protect plaintiffs from surprise.

Commentary to 2004 Amendments

The change to paragraph (a) reflects the amendment of G.L. c. 218, § 22 by St. 2004, c. 149, § 199. This amendment abolishes the earlier statutory requirement of notice by registered mail. Notice by first class mail is now sufficient.

Rule 4.   Transfer

(a) To Regular Civil Docket. The court may, upon request of a party or upon its own motion, transfer a claim or counterclaim begun under the small claims procedure to the regular civil docket pursuant to G.L. c. 218, § 24. Any such request shall be made prior to the date when trial is scheduled before a magistrate with notice to the other party. If the court orders such a transfer: (i) the claim shall be entered on the court's regular docket for hearing and determination as though it had been begun under the Massachusetts Rules of Civil Procedure, but no entry fee shall be charged upon such transfer; (ii) the defendant shall serve and file an answer to the plaintiff's claim within twenty days of the date of such transfer, if the defendant has not already done so in the small claims action; (iii) in the order of transfer or thereafter the court may direct any party to file specific additional or substitute pleadings pursuant to the Massachusetts Rules of Civil Procedure; and, (iv) the court may impose any terms upon the transfer as the interests of justice may require.

(b) To Housing Court under c. 185C. Any small claims action within the jurisdiction of the Housing Court Department may be transferred to the Housing Court Department pursuant to G.L. c. 185C, § 20 by filing a notice of removal with the clerk of the division where such action is pending, and serving a copy thereof on the other parties. The clerk shall thereupon transfer such action to the Housing Court Department, where it shall be entered on the regular small claims docket. Thereafter, the court may, upon request of a party or upon its own motion, transfer a claim or counterclaim to the regular civil docket pursuant to G.L. c. 218, § 24, but no entry fee shall be charged upon such transfer.

(c) To Medical Malpractice Tribunal. Prior to trial by a magistrate, any small claims action for malpractice, error or mistake against a provider of health care shall be referred for the convening of a medical malpractice tribunal pursuant to G.L. c. 231, § 60B.

Amended October 1, 2001, effective January 1, 2002; July 22, 2009, effective October 1, 2009.

Commentary to 2001 Amendments

The change to paragraph (a) clarifies that when a small claim is transferred to the regular civil docket the defendant must file an answer within twenty days, if no answer was previously filed in the small claim. This eliminates the present uncertainty as to the next procedural step where no answer has been filed in such transferred cases. The court is also authorized to require additional or substitute pleadings where appropriate to clarify the issues in the transferred case—for example, requiring the plaintiff to file a formal complaint or an answer to a defendant's counterclaim. The former generalized reference to the "civil rules of court applicable to the department in which the case is pending" is no longer necessary because of the July 1, 1996 merger of the District/Municipal Courts Rules of Civil Procedure into the Massachusetts Rules of Civil Procedure.

The change to paragraph (b) clarifies that removal of a small claims action to the Housing Court Department under G.L. c. 185C, § 20 is a matter of right, requiring only a notice of removal, and not a motion that involves any exercise of discretion by the court from which the small claim is being removed.

Paragraph (c) has been added as a reminder to litigants and court personnel that occasionally medical malpractice claims (usually in the form of billing disputes) are brought as small claims, and they remain subject to the statutory procedures in G.L. c. 231, § 60B. Administrative arrangements for such medical malpractice tribunals are currently made through the Superior Court's administrative office.

Commentary to 2004 Amendment

The addition to paragraph (a) clarifies that any request to transfer a small claim to the regular civil docket must be made prior to the initial trial and may not be made for the first time when an appeal is pending for trial before a judge or jury.

Commentary to 2009 Amendments

The change to paragraph (a) clarifies that any party seeking to transfer a small claim action must do so prior to the day of trial before the magistrate, thereby avoiding any undue inconvenience to the non-moving party.

Rule 5.   Amendments and Discovery

The court may at any time allow any claim or answer to be amended as justice may require. No discovery shall be allowed except upon good cause shown. Service of witness summonses shall be in accordance with the Massachusetts Rules of Civil Procedure.

Amended October 1, 2001, effective January 1, 2002.

Commentary to 2001 Amendment

The former generalized reference to the "civil rules of court applicable to the department in which the case is pending" is no longer necessary because of the July 1, 1996 merger of the District/Municipal Courts Rules of Civil Procedure into the Massachusetts Rules of Civil Procedure.

Rule 6.   Attachments

Pre-trial attachment shall not be permitted. Post-trial attachment shall be in accordance with applicable statutory provisions and with the Massachusetts Rules of Civil Procedure.

Amended October 1, 2001, effective January 1, 2002.

Commentary to 2001 Amendment

The former generalized reference to the "civil rules of court applicable to the department in which the case is pending" is no longer necessary because of the July 1, 1996 merger of the District/Municipal Courts Rules of Civil Procedure into the Massachusetts Rules of Civil Procedure.

Rule 7. Trials and Judgments

(a) **Agreement for Judgment.** The parties may at any time file with the court, in person or by mail, an agreement for judgment, which may include an agreement for a payment order, on the Agreement for Judgment form promulgated by the court. The clerk shall not accept for filing, and the court shall not approve, any agreement for judgment or for a payment order that is not set out on such form.

If the Agreement for Judgment form is filed prior to the scheduled trial date, neither party need appear on the scheduled trial date unless directed otherwise by the court.

If the Agreement for Judgment form is proffered when the parties are present, the court shall review the agreement and, if it includes a payment order, inquire of the defendant to ascertain that he or she is able to pay the payment order and understands the consequences of not complying with the payment order.

Unless justice would not be served thereby, the court shall enter such agreement as the judgment and payment order of the court and notify the parties in writing that it has done so. The court shall not enter a payment order or otherwise approve any payment agreement that relies on exempt sources of income.

(b) **Continuances.** Where the defendant has been given notice as provided in these rules, trial shall not be continued to another date unless by agreement of the parties with the approval of the court, or unless there is a showing of good cause. Any motion for continuance shall be in writing unless the court permits an oral application. Except as provided in Rule 3(b), the defendant's appearing ready for trial and requiring the plaintiff to prove his or her case is not good cause for granting the plaintiff a continuance.

(c) **Plaintiff's Failure to Appear or Proceed to Trial.** If the defendant appears for trial on the scheduled trial date and the plaintiff fails to appear or is not prepared to proceed to trial, judgment shall be entered for the defendant. If neither the plaintiff nor the defendant appears for trial, a judgment of dismissal shall be entered.

(d) **Defendant's Failure to Appear for Trial.** If the plaintiff appears for trial and the defendant fails to appear, the court may render judgment for the plaintiff and make an order for payment to the plaintiff. Prior to entering such judgment the court shall review the Statement of Small Claim to determine whether further inquiry or an assessment of damages is required. Normally these should be done on the scheduled trial date. The court shall examine any of the following circumstances:

(1) *Uncertain Jurisdiction.* If the court's subject matter jurisdiction or proper service of the Statement of Small Claim is uncertain, the court shall inquire into the matter.

(2) *Uncertain Claim.* If the facts alleged, taken as true, do not appear to constitute a claim on which relief may be granted, the court shall inquire into the matter.

(3) *Uncertain Liability.* If the facts alleged, taken as true, do not establish each essential element of a claim, the court shall inquire into the matter and may elicit additional facts to determine if such element or elements are established.

(4) *Uncertain Damages.* If the Statement of Small Claim requests damages that are not a sum certain or a sum which can by computation be made certain, the court shall conduct an assessment of damages. The court shall inquire into any amounts sought which do not appear to be supported by the facts as alleged.

(5) *Discretionary Awards.* If the law requires an exercise of discretion in awarding multiple damages, a statutory penalty, or discretionary attorney's fees or court costs, the court shall inquire into the matter and exercise such discretion.

(6) *When Review for Reasonableness Required.* The court shall review any amounts that the law requires be examined for reasonableness, such as contractual attorney's fees or collection costs. In such matters, the court's function is not to substitute its own discretion for the parties' agreement, but to avoid court enforcement of a clearly unjust result.

(7) *Inconclusive Military Affidavit.* If the plaintiff is unable to file the affidavit required by the Servicemembers Civil Relief Act, 50 U.S.C. App. § 501 et seq., stating that the defaulting defendant is not in military service and showing necessary facts to support the affidavit, the court shall inquire into the matter. If it appears that the defendant is in military service, the court shall not enter any default judgment without first appointing an attorney for the defendant, and under certain circumstances staying the entry of any default judgment, as required by the Act. If the court cannot determine from the affidavit whether the defendant is in military service, the court may exercise the discretion granted by the Act to require an indemnity bond, to stay execution, or to make such other orders as the court deems necessary to protect the rights of the defendant, or the court may dismiss the claim without prejudice.

(8) *Plaintiff in trade or commerce or pursuing assigned debt.* Where the claim involves a plaintiff in trade or commerce or pursuing assigned debt and the plaintiff has not complied with Rule 2(b), the court shall not enter a default judgment for the plaintiff, and shall dismiss the claim without prejudice.

(e) **Appearance as Substitute Counsel.** An attorney who is not current counsel of record for a party shall not appear in court to answer for that party until he or she has filed with the court a written notice of appearance. An attorney appearing as substitute counsel for another attorney must file a written appearance, which may indicate that the attorney is appearing as substitute counsel solely for that day's proceedings. Any such notice of appearance shall be entered on the docket and filed with the case papers. The clerk need not notify counsel who has filed a time-limited appearance of any future events or proceedings in that case.

(f) Trial. A small claim action shall generally be tried, and pretrial and post-judgment motions relating to such trials shall generally be determined, by a magistrate. Judges may hear such matters when deemed necessary by the court, provided that the defendant has first acknowledged in writing that, by electing to proceed with an initial trial by a judge, the defendant will waive the right to appeal for a subsequent trial by a judge or before a jury. Magistrate hearings shall be conducted in a courtroom, if one is available, and if not, in an area of the courthouse which is open and available to the public. Whenever possible, a court officer shall be in attendance. A magistrate shall sit at the clerk-magistrate's bench and not at the judge's bench, and shall not wear a robe. At the beginning of the small claims session, a magistrate shall identify himself or herself as such to those present. A magistrate who has acted as a mediator pursuant to Uniform Magistrate Rule 4 shall not thereafter rule on any motion, nor preside over any trial or enforcement proceeding, in the same small claim.

(g) Conduct of Trials. All small claim proceedings shall be recorded in accordance with applicable rules of court. The parties and witnesses testifying shall be sworn. The court shall conduct the trial in such order and form and with such methods of proof as it deems best suited to discover the facts and do justice in the case. The participation by attorneys representing parties may be limited in a manner consistent with the simple and informal adjudication of the controversy. Non-attorneys shall be allowed to assist parties in the presentation or defense of their cases when, in the judgment of the court, such assistance would facilitate the presentation or defense. When an oral motion has been made, the clerk shall note in the docket any action taken on the motion.

(h) Judgments. Judgment shall be entered forthwith upon the decision of the court. The date of judgment shall be the date the judgment is entered in the docket. The clerk shall promptly complete and send to each party by first class mail the Notice of Judgment and Order form.

(i) Payment Hearing and Orders to Pay. If the decision of the court is for the plaintiff, the court shall, except where justice will not be served thereby, also order payment to the plaintiff, or to the court on behalf of the plaintiff, of the amount of the judgment and costs, as the case may be, on or by a date stated or in specified installments. If the defendant has appeared and is before the court at the time of decision and if the defendant does not pay the amount of the judgment and costs or agree to a payment schedule acceptable to the plaintiff, the court shall conduct a payment hearing, including requiring the defendant to complete a written financial statement signed under the penalties of perjury. The financial statement shall be kept separate from other papers in the case and shall not be available for public inspection, but shall be available to the court, to attorneys whose appearances are entered in the case and to the parties to the case. If the defendant is not before the court at the time of decision or the defendant has not appeared, the order shall be for the full amount of the judgment and costs, payable in full in thirty days, unless the court orders otherwise. The provisions of an order to pay shall be stated on the Notice of Judgment and Order form. Unless a payment hearing is waived by the plaintiff, the court shall also schedule the matter for a payment hearing thirty days from the date of judgment or shortly thereafter. The Notice of Judgment and Order form shall advise the parties that, unless the defendant timely appeals from the judgment or makes payment as ordered, the defendant is required to complete a written financial statement under the penalties of perjury, to provide the plaintiff with a copy of the statement prior to the payment hearing, and to appear in court on that date. The Notice shall further state that any such financial statement shall be kept separate from other papers in the case and shall not be available for public inspection, but shall be available to the court, to attorneys whose appearances are entered in the case and to the parties to the case. The Notice shall further state that if the defendant fails to appear on that date and the plaintiff does appear and states under oath or in writing under the penalties of perjury that payment has not been made as ordered, the court may immediately issue a capias to bring the defendant before the court without the need for prior service of an Order to Show Cause pursuant to Rule 9(a). The Notice of Judgment and Order form shall also advise the parties that they are not required to appear in court on that date if payment has been made as ordered. Following the payment hearing the court may amend its previous order to pay or issue a new order.

(j) Costs. If the decision of the court is for the plaintiff, the plaintiff's actual cash disbursements for the entry fee and surcharge shall be allowed as costs. Witness fees and other costs shall be allowed only by special order of court. The court may, in its discretion, award additional costs in a sum not exceeding one hundred dollars against any party who has set up a frivolous or misleading claim or answer, or has otherwise sought to hamper a speedy and fair determination of the claim. The court may at any time amend the judgment to add the cost of service of any post-judgment process that was necessary to enforce the judgment.

(k) Execution. Execution shall issue to the plaintiff upon written request after the payment hearing, or if no payment hearing is scheduled, thirty days after the entry of judgment. Execution shall be in accordance with the statutory requirements for execution on civil judgments generally; provided, however, that execution shall in no way affect the procedure for enforcement of judgments under Rule 9 of these rules, except that double satisfaction of judgments shall not be allowed.

Amended October 1, 2001, effective January 1, 2002; July 22, 2009, effective October 1, 2009.

Commentary to 2001 Amendments

New paragraph (a) encourages the parties to file agreements for judgment or payment orders whenever they are able to reach such agreement.

New paragraph (d) is necessary to conform this Rule to the intent of the small claims amendments enacted by St. 1992, c. 379 that small claims matters generally be heard in the first instance by a magistrate. The new paragraph recognizes the authority of judges to adjudicate small claims cases in the first instance when needed in a particular court. The language of the paragraph responds to the Supreme Judicial Court's decision in *Trust Ins. Co. v. Bruce at Park Chiropractic Clinic*, 430 Mass. 607 (January 20, 2000) which holds that, by proceeding with an initial hearing by a judge, a defendant, including a plaintiff or a third party with respect to any counterclaim or any third-party claim brought against him, waives his right to appeal for a subsequent trial by a judge or before a jury. The language also responds to the Supreme Judicial Court's acknowledgment in *Trust Ins. Co. v. Bruce at Park Chiropractic Clinic, supra* at 610, that magistrates may determine contested motions in small claims actions, thereby in effect overruling the decision of the Appellate Division of the Boston Municipal Court in *Acentech, Inc. v. Cecconi,* 1994 Mass. App. Div. 44. (Note: On October 25, 2000, the Appeals Court decided *Boat Maintenance & Repair Co. v. Lawton,* 50 Mass. App. Ct. 329, in which that court determined that a clerk-magistrate had no authority to hear and decide a contested motion in a small claim action. However, in so deciding, the Appeals Court did not acknowledge the Supreme Judicial Court's earlier decision in *Trust Ins. Co. v. Bruce at Park Chiropractic Clinic, supra*).

Paragraph (d) also states that magistrates who have mediated a small claim be disqualified from ruling on motions or presiding over any trial on the merits. It also requires recusal from any enforcement proceedings in the same small claim, because it seems inappropriate for one person to exercise both mediation and enforcement functions in the same case, even at different stages of the proceedings. The requirement that a court officer be in attendance whenever possible is strongly recommended by the Trial Court Committee on Small Claims Practices and Procedures. The remaining amendments in paragraphs (d) and (e) codify the procedural directives promulgated in the Policy Statement of Chief Justice for Administration and Management John E. Fenton, Jr., "Policies Regarding Hearing Small Claims under the Court Reorganization Act, Chapter 379 of the Acts of 1992" (February 19, 1993). Those involving the use of a courtroom and an appropriate bench, and involving the recording of proceedings, were also supported by the Trial Court Committee on Small Claims Practices and Procedures.

Paragraph (g) introduces an automatic payment hearing. The Trial Court Committee on Small Claims Practices and Procedures has found that frustration with the current system for collecting judgments is the principal source of citizen dissatisfaction with the small claims process. Presently the burden falls to the prevailing party to initiate collection proceedings and to get the defendant before the court. The new payment hearing mandates a more active role for the courts. As the Committee has noted:

"this streamlined approach to collections would be less costly for the prevailing party because an automatically scheduled hearing would eliminate the need, in the first instance, for service of a Notice to Show Cause. In addition, the parties would more clearly recognize that they have thirty days to work out payment in a non-adversarial manner."

The provisions in Paragraph (g) for the filing of a financial statement also require that any such financial statement is to be protected from public inspection in terms similar to those of Rule 401(d) of the Supplemental Rules of the Probate Court.

The Committee secured the cooperation of three District Courts and one Housing Court and ran the payment hearing system as described in paragraph (g) on an experimental basis. The results not only supported the Committee's belief that more judgments would be satisfied at an early date with less cost to the plaintiff, but court staff also found that the new procedure was less time consuming for them.

Since no appeal lies from the entry of a default judgment, a defendant against whom a default judgment has been entered must, upon receipt of a Notice of Judgment and Order form, complete a written financial statement, provide a copy of that statement to the plaintiff, and appear in court on the date specified in the Notice and Order form in accordance with the provisions of Rule 7(g) if payment has not been made as ordered.

The amendment to paragraph (h) provides authority for the long-standing practice of requiring the defendant to reimburse the plaintiff for the costs of service of any post-judgment Order to Show Cause or *capias* that is necessary to enforce the judgment.

Commentary to 2009 Amendments

New paragraph (a) requires use of the official Agreement for Judgment form, which includes the list of statutory exemptions. This insures that the court does not order or otherwise endorse any private payment agreement that relies on exempt sources of income. General Laws c. 224, § 16 (made applicable to small claims by G.L. c. 218, § 22) prohibits the court from ordering a defendant to make any payment from exempt income. Likewise it is not appropriate for the court to endorse any voluntary payment agreement that relies on exempt sources of income.

The amendment to paragraph (b) makes clear that a defendant's appearance for trial does not automatically result in prejudice to the plaintiff sufficient to trigger grounds for a continuance pursuant to Rule 3(b).

The amendment to paragraph (c) provides that judgment is to be entered for the defendant when a plaintiff is unable to proceed to trial and there is no good cause basis for a continuance.

Paragraph (d) now lists specific matters that must be considered by the court before a default judgment may be entered, in order to determine legal liability, correctly calculate an award, and avoid any misuse of the small claims court. These are obligations that are entirely consistent with the court's obligation in an adversarial proceeding to maintain his or her neutrality and include the following:

(d)(1) Uncertain Jurisdiction. When the court's jurisdiction is questionable (e.g., a claim that appears to fall under the Massachusetts Tort Claims Act), then the matter must be reviewed by the court for a determination as to whether jurisdiction exists.

(d)(2) Uncertain Claim. By defaulting, a defendant admits any facts alleged in the Statement of Small Claim, but does not admit legal liability. If there is uncertainty, the court must determine whether the Statement of Small Claim sets forth a cognizable cause of action on which relief may be granted. While Rule 2 does not require the allegations of facts, only facts alleged are admitted by a defendant's default.

(d)(3) Uncertain Liability. If the facts alleged do not include all essential elements of the claim, then the court must elicit these additional facts before a default judgment may enter. Since a defaulting defendant is deemed to have admitted the facts set forth in the Statement of Small Claim, the court may not require the plaintiff to offer evidence of a prima facie case, except as to any element of the claim that is not covered by the facts set forth in the statement. A default judgment may enter only if the facts alleged in the Statement of Small Claim and any additional facts elicited and established by evidence provide a prima facie case on a recognized claim for which relief may be granted. This does not require the court to raise potential matters of defense not raised by the defendant. There are differing views as to the appropriateness of doing so, given the tension between the special nature of small claim proceedings and the court's ethical obligations to maintain his or her neutrality.

(d)(4) Uncertain damages. The court must conduct an assessment of damages whenever the Statement of Small Claim requests damages that are not a sum certain or in instances where the amount claimed appears to be inflated or unrelated to the claim. No assessment of damages should be conducted except as indicated in this rule.

(d)(5) Discretionary awards. A small claim must be reviewed by the court whenever an exercise of discretion is required in awarding multiple damages (e.g., in G.L. c. 93A consumer protection claims), statutory damages (e.g., for bad checks and shoplifting claims), or discretionary attorney fees or court costs.

(d)(6) Review for reasonableness. Some items that are not considered discretionary must still be reviewed by the court for reasonableness (e.g., contractual attorney fees or collection costs).

(d)(7) Inconclusive military affidavit. Where the plaintiff is unable to file the required affidavit, the court cannot enter a default judgment without further inquiry and compliance with the requirements of the Servicemembers Civil Relief Act, 50 U.S.C. App. § 501 et seq.

(d)(8) Plaintiff in trade or commerce or pursuing assigned debt. Before entering a default judgment, the court must review the Statement of Small Claim to determine whether the plaintiff is required to comply with Rule 2(b) and if so whether the plaintiff has properly done so.

When the court must conduct such a review or assessment, normally it should be done on the scheduled trial date.

Paragraph (e) now requires that substitute or "covering" counsel file an appearance. The rule permits substitute counsel to file a time limited appearance, thereby acknowledging a common practice in small claim proceedings while permitting the court to maintain an accurate record of all attorneys who appear before the court. As the rule applies exclusively to litigants who are already represented by counsel, it does not implicate the terms of the Supreme Judicial Court order, effective May 1, 2009, regarding Limited Assistance Representation.

Paragraph (k) now delays the issuance of an execution until after the payment hearing or, if no payment hearing is scheduled, until the expiration of the usual 30–day payment order. This avoids any unfair surprise to the defendant by delaying any levy on the judgment until the defendant has had an opportunity to pay as ordered or to attend a payment hearing.

Please note that due to the insertion of new paragraphs d and e in Rule 7 of the 2009 Amendments, paragraphs f–k were formerly paragraphs d–i.

Rule 8.   Relief From Judgment or Order

Within one year of the date of judgment the court may, upon a party's application and after notice to the other party in such form as the court deems appropriate, vacate or grant relief from any judgment or order, including an order for a judgment of dismissal under Rule 7, entered under these Rules for any cause that the court may deem sufficient, and may supersede execution.

At any time after judgment, with notice to the other party, a party may apply to vacate or grant relief from any judgment or order, including an order for a judgment of dismissal under Rule 7, if it is alleged that the party did not receive actual notice of the claim and the date of trial. If the court determines that no notice was received, the court shall vacate or grant relief from any judgment or order entered under these rules.

The court may also order the repayment of any amount collected under such judgment or order, and any action by the court may be made conditional upon the performance of any reasonable condition, including payment of or reimbursement for any reasonable expenses incurred by the other party.

Amended October 1, 2001, effective January 1, 2002; July 22, 2009, effective October 1, 2009.

Commentary to 2001 Amendment

These amendments clarify two ambiguities in the text of Rule 8. The first makes clear that relief from judgment may not be granted on ex parte application. The form, but not the obligation, of giving notice to the other parties is meant to be discretionary with the court. The second makes clear that the court, in vacating an order of dismissal or a default judgment, may, in appropriate circumstances, award reasonable expenses such as lost wages to the other party if the party was present on the day the case was dismissed or the defendant defaulted.

Commentary to 2009 Amendment

This amendment requiring relief without regard to the time within which the relief is sought, reflects the due process requirements embodied in Mass. R. Civ. P. 60(b)(4) that a judgment may be challenged and must be voided at any time for lack of notice. See, e.g., *Bowers v. Board of Appeals of Marshfield*, 16 Mass. App. Ct. 29, 31 (1983). The one-year limitation applies to all other grounds for relief from judgment.

Rule 9.   Enforcement of Judgments

(a) Order to Show Cause. On an order issued after the payment hearing, or if there was no payment hearing, upon being informed by the plaintiff that a defendant who has been ordered to pay has failed to obey the order, the clerk shall schedule the matter before the court for enforcement proceedings and shall issue a Notice to Show Cause to the plaintiff, who must arrange for the Notice to Show Cause to be served by an officer duly qualified to serve it. The court may provide for any other means of service in individual cases as is deemed appropriate. The Notice to Show Cause shall indicate the date and time of hearing.

(b) Enforcement Proceedings. Upon hearing, the court shall take such action, permitted by law, as it deems appropriate to the end that orders of payment are complied with promptly and satisfaction of the judgment in the case is not frustrated. Such enforcement proceedings may be conducted either by a judge or by a magistrate, but a magistrate shall have no authority to enter an adjudication of civil contempt or to issue an order of incarceration. When enforcement proceedings are conducted by a magistrate and it appears that such action may be required, the magistrate shall refer the matter to a judge, who shall make an independent determination whether to enter an adjudication of civil contempt and may issue an order of incarceration or such other order as may be appropriate to enforce payment of the judgment. If a judge is available at the time of such referral, the matter may immediately be placed before the judge

(c) Inability to Pay. Unless the court orders otherwise, a defendant who asserts that he or she is presently unable to pay the amount of the judgment in full shall complete a financial statement on a form provided by the court and signed under the penalties of perjury prior to being examined by the court. The financial statement shall be kept separate from other papers in the case and shall not be available for public inspection, but shall be available to the court, to attorneys whose appearances are entered in the case, and to the parties in the case. If the court previously determined that at that time the defendant was financially able to comply with the court's payment order, the burden of proof shall be on the defendant to establish that he or she is currently unable to comply with the court's payment order.

(d) Defendant's Move to Another District. If, after a small claim is filed, the defendant moves out of the judicial district where the action was brought, the court may, on request of the plaintiff, transfer the action to the division of the court in the judicial district to which the defendant has moved. If the court orders such a transfer, the docket entries and the original papers in the case shall be forwarded to said court, without payment of an entry fee, and the case shall proceed in that court as though originally entered therein.

(e) Acknowledgment of Satisfaction of Judgment. Within ten days of full payment of a judgment, the plaintiff shall file an Acknowledgment of Satisfaction of Judgment with the court. Upon the filing of such acknowledgment, the clerk shall recall any outstanding execution.

(f) Court Determination of Satisfaction of Judgment. At the request of the defendant, and upon notice to the plaintiff, a judge or magistrate may order the entry of a docket notation indicating full satisfaction of the judgment if the defendant files an affidavit stating that he or she has made full payment of the judgment, and that the plaintiff has been requested to file an acknowledgment of satisfaction of the judgment and refuses to do so, or that the present address of the plaintiff is unknown. The defendant shall accompany such affidavit with canceled checks or money orders for the full amount of the judgment written by the defendant and made payable to and endorsed by the plaintiff, or cash receipts for the full amount of the judgment made out to the defendant and signed by the plaintiff, or other documents demonstrating the plaintiff's receipt of full payment of the judgment. Any such docket notation shall establish a rebuttable presumption of full payment of the judgment.

Amended October 1, 2001, effective January 1, 2002; July 22, 2009, effective October 1, 2009.

Commentary to 2001 Amendments

Paragraph (a) is amended to eliminate the directive to the clerk to "make such inquiry into the matter [of non-payment], if any, as he deems useful." Since a clerk may later preside over enforcement proceedings as a magistrate, such informal contacts are best avoided since they might well involve ex parte discussions that would be inconsistent with a magistrate's responsibilities under S.J.C. Rule 3:12, Canon 3.

Paragraph (b) reflects the recommendation of the Trial Court Committee on Small Claims Practices and Procedures that magistrates be authorized to preside over proceedings to enforce small claims judgments, but not to enter adjudications of civil contempt or to make orders of incarceration. When such steps appear necessary, the matter is to be transferred to a judge "immediately," which assumes no need for rescheduling or further notice if a judge is then available.

While it is expected that most proceedings to enforce small claims judgments will be conducted by magistrates, paragraph (b) preserves the authority of judges to preside over such enforcement hearings ab initio.

New paragraph (c) makes it a matter of routine for a defendant who claims to be unable to pay the judgment in full to complete a sworn financial statement. The specific assignment of the burden of proof in paragraph (c) restates current case law. *Roy v. Leventhal*, 5 Mass. App. Ct. 792 (1977). See also G.L. c. 215, § 34 (in Probate Court contempt proceedings, "the defendant shall have the burden of proving his or her inability to comply with the pre-existing order or judgment of which the complaint alleges violation"). The defendant's financial statement shall be treated as confidential information in terms similar to those of Rule 401(d) of the Supplemental Rules of the Probate Court. See Rule 7(g) and the Commentary thereto.

Commentary to 2009 Amendments

Paragraph (d) now authorizes transfer to the appropriate court when the defendant moves from the original court's geographical jurisdiction, whether before or after judgment.

Paragraph (e) requires for the first time in Massachusetts that the plaintiff file an acknowledgment of satisfaction with the court once a judgment is paid in full. Paragraph (f) provides a remedy to the defendant where plaintiff fails to file an acknowledgment. These additional provisions are necessitated by the difficulty that defendants increasingly experience in proving that a judgment that appears in a credit report was satisfied, sometimes years before.

Rule 10. Appeal

(a) Claim of Appeal. A defendant's claim of appeal for trial by a judge or before a jury of six persons shall be made in writing, shall comply with the requirements of G.L. c. 218, § 23, and shall specify whether the defendant claims trial by a judge or before a jury. The defendant shall mail a copy of the claim of appeal to the plaintiff. Upon the defendant's filing of a claim of appeal, the clerk shall forthwith note on the docket of the case the receipt of the claim of appeal, the filing fee for the appeal required by section 23, and any appeal bond required by section 23 or an equivalent cash deposit in lieu thereof. If each of these items has been timely received, the clerk shall schedule the matter for trial. If a jury trial is to be held at another division, the clerk shall transmit the original docket entries and the original papers in the case, or an attested copy of the original docket entries and the original papers in the case, to the clerk of the appropriate jury session. The court may waive the filing fee if the applicant is indigent and may waive the bond requirement if it finds that the applicant has insufficient funds to furnish the bond and that the appeal is not frivolous. Prior to the case being tried in the division from which the case is appealed or transmitted to the jury session at another division, any judge of the division from which the case is appealed may hear and determine any question raised by a party concerning the defendant's compliance with the statutory requirements for appeal. The clerk of the division from which the case is appealed shall retain custody of any appeal bond posted pursuant to section 23 or any equivalent cash deposit in lieu thereof, and shall deposit with the State Treasurer the filing fee and surcharge for the appeal.

If any required item has not been timely received, the clerk shall so notify both parties, shall return any filing fee, surcharge, appeal bond or cash deposit in lieu thereof forwarded by the defendant, and shall note such action, and the reasons therefor, on the docket. The clerk's notice shall inform the defendant that he may have the issue of his compliance with the statutory prerequisites for appeal determined by a judge, upon motion filed within ten days of receiving the notice.

(b) Conduct of Trials. Trials by a judge or before a jury shall be conducted in accordance with the provisions of Rule 7, and, in the case of a trial before a jury, in accordance with the provisions of law applicable to jury trials in the Superior Court Department. In a trial before a jury, the judge may direct that any provisions of the Massachusetts Rules of Civil Procedure be utilized, if not inconsistent with Rule 7. A counterclaim or third-party claim may not be raised for the first time on appeal.

(c) Judgments and Orders to Pay. Judgment shall be entered forthwith upon the decision of the judge or the verdict of the jury. Subject to any continuance granted pursuant to Rule 7(b), a judgment for the plaintiff shall be entered forthwith if the defendant fails to appear for trial or is not prepared to proceed to trial and the plaintiff does appear, or if the defendant withdraws the claim of appeal. Subject to any continuance granted pursuant to Rule 7(b), a judgment for the defendant shall be entered forthwith if the plaintiff fails to appear for trial or is not prepared to proceed to trial and the defendant does appear. Subject to any continuance granted pursuant to Rule 7(b), a judgment dismissing the claim shall be entered forthwith if both the plaintiff and the defendant fail to appear for trial. Except where justice will not be served thereby, the judge shall, after holding a payment hearing, forthwith order payment to the plaintiff, in accordance with Rule 7(i). Otherwise the judge must schedule a payment hearing in accordance with Rule 7(i) in the division from which the case was appealed. Any order for payment shall grant the party no less than thirty days within which to pay. The clerk shall promptly furnish each party with written notice of the court's judgment, any order for payment, and any payment hearing. When judgment is entered in the jury session, such notice shall be given by the clerk of the jury session.

(d) Post-judgment Proceedings in Jury Session at Another Division. When a small claims action has been tried on appeal in the jury session at another division, any post-trial motions filed within ten days after the entry of judgment shall be filed with the clerk of the jury session and heard by the judge who presided over the trial. If justice will be served thereby, the judge may stay, modify, or supersede any order for payment already made.

Unless the judge orders otherwise, upon the expiration of ten days after judgment, the case shall be retransferred to the division from which it was appealed for any further enforcement proceedings pursuant to Rule 7 and Rule 9, except that a case shall not be retransferred until any motion filed, or any appeal claimed, within ten days after entry of judgment has been decided. The clerk of the jury session shall transmit original or attested copies of the judgment, any order for payment, any order deciding a post-trial motion, and any rescript of an appellate court, to the clerk of the division to which the case is being re-transferred.

Any motions which are filed after the case has been re-transferred shall be filed with the clerk of the division to which the claim has been re-transferred. The clerk shall transmit any such motion that affects the judgment to the judge who presided over the trial in the jury session, who may determine such motion, with or without hearing, wherever the judge is then sitting. Other motions that affect only an order for payment or proceedings to enforce the judgment may be heard by any judge or magistrate sitting in the division to which the claim has been re-transferred.

(e) Appeal from the Housing Court Department to the Appeals Court. Any claim of appeal from the Housing Court Department to the Appeals Court from the judgment in a small claims action tried by a judge or before a jury shall be filed with the clerk of the division or the jury session where the case was tried within ten days after entry of judgment. If justice will be served thereby, the judge who presided over the trial may stay, modify, or supersede any order for payment

already made. Further procedures on appeal shall be governed by the Massachusetts Rules of Appellate Procedure. Amended February 10, 1987, effective April 1, 1987; November 22, 1989, effective November 30, 1989; October 1, 2001, effective January 1, 2002; July 22, 2009, effective October 1, 2009.

Commentary to 2001 Amendments

Most of these amendments are necessary because an appealing party must now elect between trial by a judge and trial before a jury. Jury session procedures are amended to permit the increasingly frequent practice of sending original case papers to the jury session (while retaining copies at the primary court). The authority granted the Chief Justice of the District Court Department to designate where trials are to be heard in G.L. c. 218, § 23, permits the retention of jury-waived cases in the court where the case originated regardless of whether that court has a jury session. The purpose is to take caseload pressure away from busy jury sessions.

Unlike the District Court and Housing Court Departments, the Boston Municipal Court Department of the Trial Court does not consist of separate geographical divisions. Accordingly, all appeals from a small claims session of the Boston Municipal Court are to a jury session of that same court and all papers related to such appeals are processed within the Office of the Clerk of the Boston Municipal Court for Civil Business.*

In paragraph (a), the reference to the surcharge required by G.L. c. 262, § 4C for new entries "to which a separate docket number is assigned" has been deleted since virtually all courts no longer assign a new docket number when a magistrate's decision in a small claim is appealed to a judge or a jury.

The deletion in paragraph (b) of the reference to the District/Municipal Courts Rules of Civil Procedure reflects their July 1, 1996 consolidation with the Massachusetts Rules of Civil Procedure.

The limitation in paragraph (e) of appeals to the Appeals Court to those deriving from cases tried by a judge or before a jury in the Housing Court Department reflects the decision of the Supreme Judicial Court in *Trust Ins. Co. v. Bruce at Park Chiropractic Clinic*, 430 Mass. 607, 610 n.9 (2000). There, in a case involving a motion heard initially by a District Court judge, the Supreme Judicial Court stated:

"To the extent that Rule 10(e) of the Uniform Small Claims Rules (1999) provides for an appeal to the Appeals Court from the jury session, it is in conflict with G.L. c. 218, § 23, which provides for the report of questions of law to the appellate division in certain circumstances. General Laws Chapter 211A, § 10 provides for an appeal from the appellate division to the Appeals Court."

However, there is no appellate division in the Housing Court Department, thereby necessitating, in order to provide for appellate review, an appeal to the Appeals Court from cases heard by a judge or before a jury in the Housing Court Department.

Commentary to 2009 Amendments

Paragraph (c) is amended to provide that when either the plaintiff or defendant fails to appear for trial, or appears but is not prepared to proceed with trial and there is not a good cause basis for a continuance, judgment is to be entered in favor of the party appearing and ready to proceed.

2009 Note

*On July 1, 2003 the Boston Municipal Court Department was expanded to include eight former divisions of the District Court located in Suffolk County.

SMALL CLAIMS STANDARDS

January 1, 2002

Table of Standards

FORWARD

The Administrative Office of the Trial Court issues these Standards to assist judges, clerk-magistrates and other personnel of the District Court, Boston Municipal Court, and Housing Court Departments in implementing recently amended Trial Court Rule III, Uniform Small Claims Rules (effective January 1, 2002). The long delayed amendments to the Uniform Small Claims Rules were necessitated by amendments to G.L.c. 218, §§ 21–25, especially those authorizing clerk-magistrates to hear and decide small claims in the first instance, and by appellate decisions effecting procedural changes in small claims actions.

The goal of the Standards is two fold:

1. To expedite, consistent with applicable statutory and decisional law and court rules, the fair and efficient disposition of small claims in all Trial Court departments having jurisdiction of such actions; and

2. To promote confidence among litigants that their small claims will be processed expeditiously and impartially by the courts according to applicable rules and statutes and recognized Standards.

The Standards were carefully constructed by the Trial Court Committee on Small Claims Procedures to mesh with the amended Uniform Small Claims Rules and applicable appellate decisions. That Committee brought to its task a wealth of experience and insights gained from a variety of perspectives. In developing the Standards, the Committee also drew heavily upon the District Court Department's earlier Standards of Judicial Practice: Small Claims (1984).

The Standards not only reflect statutory amendments to the small claims process and recent appellate decisions, but they also emphasize those procedural improvements adopted as part of the recently amended Uniform Small Claims Rules. The most significant of these improvements is the provision for automatic payment hearings in place of the former cumbersome, expensive, and often time-consuming process for collecting on small claims judgments. In tests concluded prior to the amendment of the rules, this provision garnered enthusiastic support from judicial personnel as well as from practitioners and representatives of consumer advocacy and legal services programs.

I wish to thank all who have contributed to the adoption of the amended Uniform Small Claims Rules and to these companion Standards. Their contributions are of invaluable assistance to the administration of justice by the Trial Court and to the tens of thousands of litigants who resort annually to the Trial Court for the fair and expeditious resolution of their small claims.

/s/_____

Barbara A. Dortch–Okara
Chief Justice for Administration and
Management

_____
Date
November 30, 2001

GENERAL
Standards 1:00 through 1:01

1:00. Purpose of the Standards

These standards represent recommended practices for the small claims procedure in the Boston Municipal Court, District Court, and the housing court departments of the Trial Court. Their purpose is:

1. To increase the efficiency and effectiveness of the small claims procedure;

2. To improve the process by which small claims judgments are satisfied while respecting the due process rights of defendants;

3. To make small claims procedures uniform throughout the Commonwealth and more accessible to all;

4. To expand community awareness and understanding of the small claims process.

Amended effective January 1, 2002.

Commentary

The stated goal of Massachusetts small claims procedure is to provide a simple, prompt, informal, and inexpensive mechanism for the resolution of monetary disputes in which damages do not exceed a specific dollar value. G. L. c. 218, s. 21; McLaughlin v. Levenbaum, 248 Mass. 170, 175–176, (1924). In Fiscal Year 1996, small claims related filings comprised 44% of all civil filings in the Boston Municipal Court, the District Court, and the Housing Court Departments of the Trial Court, the courts with jurisdiction over small claims. Annual Report on the State of Massachusetts Court System, Fiscal Year 1996. For many citizens, the only direct contact with the courts may be their participation in a small claims case. For these individuals, their perception of the fairness and efficiency of the court system will be shaped by the quality of their experience in the small claims session. If small claims litigants find the process understandable and the court personnel helpful and courteous, and if they achieve a result without spending too much time or money, they are likely to think well of the courts and feel they have received justice even if they may not prevail. If, on the other hand, litigants find the small claims process difficult to comprehend and seemingly arbitrary and capricious, if they are not treated with dignity and courtesy, if they wait months for hearings and have to spend more time and effort than the case is worth to collect a judgment, they will think ill of the courts and buy into the most negative stereotypes about a broken judicial system.

Small claims court is intended to be "The People's Court," to borrow the title of the popular television show. It is the responsibility of the Trial Court to make this so. The small claims experience is different from other court proceedings because litigants, other than commercial litigants, generally appear without lawyers and therefore do not benefit from the mediating function attorneys perform in the judicial process. Trial Court personnel should recognize this fact and make every effort to assist small claims litigants as they try to navigate the unfamiliar territory of the clerk-magistrate's office and the courtroom on their own.

These Standards are recommendations intended to implement the small claims statute, G.L. c. 218, ss. 21–25 (reproduced as Appendix A) and the Uniform Small Claims Rules (Trial Court Rule III, reproduced as Appendix B).

1:01. Definitions

A. Court: except where used to refer to a particular division of a department of the Trial Court, the term means the adjudicator, and is inclusive of clerk–magistrate, assistant clerk–magistrate, and judge.

B. Appeal: refers to the subsequent trial before a jury
    of six or a judge without a jury guaranteed by G.L.
    c. 218, s. 23.

Added effective January 1, 2002.

COURT STRUCTURE
Standards 2:00 through 2:06

2:00. Accessibility of the Court

Court personnel should facilitate the use of the small claims procedure by the public.

Added effective January 1, 2002.

Commentary

Courts are encouraged to explore means of publicizing the small claims process. The use of simple and inexpensive measures (such as a letter from the presiding justice or the clerk-magistrate to local public service agencies and public institutions describing the procedure) will help overcome the lack of public awareness and enhance the effectiveness of the small claims procedure.

Conspicuous signs should be posted near courthouse entrances directing the small claims litigant to the proper office. See Standard 2:01. On days when small claims sessions are held, signs should be posted to direct small claims litigants to the appropriate courtroom. The small claims section of the clerk-magistrate's office should make copies of the Uniform Small Claims Rules and other relevant instructions and/or information available for public reference.

Court employees should provide general guidance and information to potential small claims litigants, but should take care not to place themselves in the position of advocating or appearing to advocate a particular litigant's position on the merits of the small claims case. *Opinion No. 95–6 of the Advisory Committee on Ethical Opinions for Clerks of Courts,* Supreme Judicial Court, November 8, 1995, reproduced as Appendix C; Uniform Small Claims Rule 2, as recently amended. Court personnel in the clerk-magistrate's office may, in appropriate situations, suggest that a potential plaintiff or complainant consider a small claim as a "simple, informal and inexpensive" (G.L. c. 218, s. 21) alternative to a full-fledged lawsuit or criminal complaint, but should leave the decision to the litigant. Standard court procedures may be summarized in written form and made available to litigants.

Court personnel have special statutorily-mandated responsibilities regarding accessibility for non–English speaking litigants and litigants with disabilities. See Standards 2:05 and 2:06 for a full discussion of these issues. Court personnel should make every effort to be helpful to non–English speaking litigants or litigants with disabilities, but should take care that in their effort to be helpful they do not advocate, or appear to advocate, a particular litigant's position on the merits of the claim. Court personnel should be aware that some litigants may mistake courtesy in providing information as support for the litigant's claim.

2:01. Organization of the Clerk–Magistrate's Office

Each court should establish a well–marked small claims section.

Amended effective January 1, 2002.

Commentary

Those of us who work daily with legal terminology and routinely deal with members of the bar and law enforcement personnel may not fully appreciate the confusion, uncertainty, and uneasiness a first experience with a court may evoke in a lay litigant. Since the clerk-

magistrate's office is generally the first point of contact with the courts for those who use the small claims procedure, the importance of providing a customer-friendly atmosphere in that office cannot be overstated.

One way the clerk-magistrate's office can be more responsive to the needs of lay litigants is to locate the personnel responsible for processing small claims actions in office space apart from the civil, criminal, and cashier sections. In those courts where funds and facilities permit, a separate space within the clerk-magistrate's office or a separate room for the small claims section, apart from the main clerk-magistrate's office, is suggested. Signs indicating the location of the small claims section should be conspicuously posted.

If space and resources do not permit a separate small claims area, signs should be posted that clearly identify the court employee(s) in charge of small claims and the appropriate line for the small claims litigant to stand in. Small claims litigants should not have to endure a lengthy wait at a front counter only to be referred elsewhere. Since the hurried atmosphere of a front counter is only likely to increase the confusion and frustration of lay litigants, they should be referred to a knowledgeable person in the small claims section for any but the simplest questions. In those courts that employ a single counter person to furnish general information and forms, that employee may distribute small claims forms as well.

The small claims section should maintain an index of small claims actions, arranged alphabetically by name of defendant. This index should be available to the public upon request, but a procedure should be established that allows public access without unduly disrupting the orderly operation of the clerk-magistrate's office. Persons who routinely request access to large numbers of cases at a time should be required to make prior arrangements with the small claims assistant clerk-magistrate or the small claims supervisor. At no time should these persons be allowed behind the counter to search the index files, as such liberties may create the impression of one party having an unfair advantage over another.

2:02. Specialized Personnel

The small claims sections should be supervised by an assistant clerk–magistrate or small claims supervisor and should be staffed by specially designated clerical personnel where possible.

Amended effective January 1, 2002.

Commentary

Where numbers of personnel permit, one assistant clerk-magistrate should be given administrative responsibility for the operation of the small claims section. If numbers do not permit, one clerical employee of appropriate title and experience should be designated as the small claims supervisor. The small claims assistant clerk-magistrate or small claims supervisor should supervise any clerical personnel involved in small claims matters and oversee the general processing of small claims cases. Other court personnel should direct all inquiries and complaints regarding small claims to the small claims assistant clerk-magistrate or the small claims supervisor.

The small claims assistant clerk-magistrate or the small claims supervisor, if qualified, should routinely act as courtroom clerk for the small claims session. This person should be responsible for reviewing the list of scheduled cases, calling the small claims list in the court-room, and otherwise assisting the clerk-magistrate, assistant clerk-magistrate, or judge assigned to adjudicate small claims cases.

In those courts with available funds and sufficient small claims business, one or more clerical employees should be designated to work primarily with small claims. These employees should be afforded whatever small claims training is available and should be regularly apprised of changes in small claims procedures and practices. In those courts with insufficient small claims business to justify a clerical employee assigned solely to small claims, the responsibility for dealing with telephone or in-person inquiries about small claims should be designated to a specific employee whenever possible. This arrangement will provide continuity of contact for litigants and will also allow the designated employee to develop expertise in small claims.

All courts should have back-up clerical employees who are trained in small claims practices and are capable of assuming responsibility for the processing of small claims should the "primary" small claims employee be on vacation, out sick, or otherwise unavailable.

To avoid any problems that may arise in the handling of money, court personnel should not accept any payments from small claims debtors for transmittal to creditors *unless* a judge or a clerk-magistrate or an assistant clerk-magistrate has issued an order stating that payment must be made through the court. Uniform Small Claims Rule 7(g).

2:03.　Adjudication

Clerk–magistrates who are qualified by education or training should be primarily responsible for the adjudication of small claims matters, including payment hearings and motions. judges may hear these matters when deemed necessary by the court and the defendant elects to waive the right to appeal for a subsequent trial by a judge or before a jury.

Added effective January 1, 2002.

Commentary

Small claims matters should primarily be heard in the first instance by clerk-magistrates and assistant clerk-magistrates. Judges however, may adjudicate cases when needed in any particular court but only in cases where the defendant (including a defendant in counterclaim or in any third party claim) elects to proceed with an initial trial by a judge and thereby agrees to waive any right to appeal for a subsequent trial by a judge or before a jury. Uniform Small Claims Rule 7(d); Trust Insurance Company v. Bruce at Park Chiropractic Clinic, 403 Mass. 607 (1/20/00). The court should have the defendant sign a written waiver of appeal rights before the case is assigned to a judge. Clerk–magistrates and assistant clerk-magistrates have the authority to try and to decide cases, to preside at payment hearings, and to decide motions. Uniform Small Claims Rule 7(d), as recently amended; Trust Ins. Co., supra, at 608, n.2, and 610. Hearings on contempt should be referred to a judge whenever there is the possibility of incarceration. Uniform Small Claims Rule 9(b). (Note: On October 25, 2000, the Appeals Court decided Boat Maintenance & Repair Co. v. Lawton, _____ Mass. App. Ct. _____, in which that court determined that a clerk-magistrate had no authority to hear and decide a contested motion in a small claims action. However, in so deciding, the Appeals did not acknowledge the Supreme Judicial Court's earlier decision in Trust Ins. Co. v. Bruce at Park Chiropractic Clinic, supra.).

When there is no clerk-magistrate or assistant clerk-magistrate qualified to adjudicate small claims for a particular Trial Court division, either a judge sitting in that division, if the defendant has waived appellate rights, or a clerk-magistrate or assistant clerk-magistrate from another division should be assigned to hear small claims in that division.

Because it is important that small claims actions be decided according to substantive law, clerk-magistrates and assistant clerk-magistrates should attend an educational program addressing both procedural and substantive law. See G.L. c. 218, s. 21; Canon 7 of the Code of Professional Responsibility for Clerks of the Courts. This program will be developed and provided by the Judicial Institute of the Trial Court and approved by the Chief Justice for Administration and Management. The education and training requirements are not meant to limit the inherent powers of the Chief Justice for Administration and Management, departmental chief justices, first justices, or clerk-magistrates to assign any clerk-magistrate or assistant clerk-magistrate to adjudicate small claims matters even though qualified by education or training.

2:04.　Periodic Review of the Small Claims Procedure

Each division of the trial court hearing small claims shall regularly review the operation of the small claims procedure and shall make a quarterly report to its departmental chief justice.

Amended effective January 1, 2002.

Commentary

The first justice and the clerk-magistrate of each division of the Trial Court hearing small claims should meet regularly to discuss the overall operation of the small claims procedure. The small claims assistant clerk-magistrate and/or the small claims supervisor should also attend these meetings and a mechanism should be developed to ensure their input in the event that they are unable to attend.

The agenda of this meeting should include, among other things (1) a discussion of whether any backlog in hearings and/or paperwork is developing and, if so, what should be done to alleviate it; and (2) a consideration of whether scheduling changes for the small claims session are desirable. In addition, any complaints and suggestions received from litigants regarding the small claims process should be reviewed. While *ex parte* contacts between interested parties and the judges or clerk-magistrates or assistant clerk-magistrates who have adjudicated their cases are not appropriate, courts should develop some mechanism to solicit feedback from those who have experienced the small claims session firsthand. The small claims assistant clerk-magistrate or small claims supervisor should be encouraged to record complaints and suggestions from litigants and to share these comments, as well as their own day-to-day observations of the problems and successes they have encountered while administering small claims, with their departmental Administrative Office.

Each division of the Trial Court hearing small claims shall make a quarterly report to their departmental chief justice, and where applicable, to the regional administrative justice. This report should state the average time elapsed between the filing of a small claim and a first hearing, and the average time elapsed between a judgment and any payment hearing. The period of elapsed time should not exceed 8 *weeks* from the filing to hearing or 6 *weeks* from judgment to payment hearing.

If the averages in any particular court exceed 8 weeks from the filing to hearing or 6 weeks from judgment to payment hearing, or if the departmental chief justice or regional administrative justice learns that a particular court is having problems processing or disposing of small claims cases expeditiously, the departmental chief justice or regional administrative justice should require the presiding justice and clerk-magistrate of that court to submit a case flow management plan.

The case flow management plan should outline steps for bringing the court within the acceptable time periods and include a timetable for compliance. It should propose specific measures, such as increasing the number of days each week that small claims are heard, increasing the number of cases scheduled per day, or using judges or clerk-magistrates from other courts until the court can conform to the average time periods. The plan should also address the court's management structure as it relates to small claims, including issues of accountability and the training and cross-training of clerical employees. (In some courts, for example, one factor contributing to a backlog is the lack of back-up employees who can process small claims when the employee designated to handle small claims is absent. See Standard 2:02.)

As individual courts review and respond to problems they have encountered in the small claims process, particular care should be taken not to vary those practices and forms that the Uniform Small Claims Rules and G.L. c. 218, ss. 21–25 intend to be universal throughout the Trial Court. While individual courts will differ in their needs and resources, variations in basic procedures, forms, and fees should be avoided.

2:05. Provision of Interpreters

The court must take the necessary steps to provide qualified interpreters to participants in small claims matters who are not fully conversant in English or who are hearing–impaired.

Added effective January 1, 2002.

Commentary

Section 2 of G.L. c. 221C accords participants in small claims cases who are not fully conversant in English the right to the assistance of a qualified interpreter throughout the proceedings. Under G.L. c. 221, s. 92A, a deaf or hearing-impaired person who is a party or a witness in a small claims case is entitled to the assistance of a person (or persons) qualified to interpret the proceedings. In addition to the state statutory right to the assistance of an interpreter, deaf or hearing-impaired people are also entitled to reasonable accommodations under the Americans with Disabilities Act. See Standard 2:06 for further discussion.

At whatever stage of a case court personnel become aware of the need for an interpreter, the court should grant a continuance and order an interpreter for the next scheduled date. The court should not require any litigant who is not fully conversant in English or any hearing-impaired litigant to go forward at a trial or any other significant event without a qualified interpreter. The court should not assume that friends or family members accompanying the litigant are proficient enough in English or sign language to serve as translators or interpreters.

In ordering interpreters for small claims cases, the court should follow the same procedures used to order interpreters for other cases.

Any court that routinely deals with persons of a particular language group should consider obtaining and dispensing translated versions of the instructions found on the small claims forms.

2:06. Reasonable Accommodations for Persons With Disabilities

The court must make reasonable accommodations to make the small claims procedure accessible to persons with disabilities.

Added effective January 1, 2002.

Commentary

The Massachusetts Trial Court is subject to the Americans with Disabilities Act. Accordingly, all participants in small claims cases are entitled to equal access to the court and to the services of the court, without regard to disability.

It is the responsibility of the Trial Court to provide reasonable accommodations in order to assure access. Reasonable accommodations include, but are not limited to, sound-amplifying devices for hearing-impaired litigants and tape recordings of small claims filing instructions for visually-impaired litigants.

It is the responsibility of each court to prominently display written material that will allow disabled persons to make their needs known. Such information should also be accessible to the visually-impaired in a taped format.

The Supreme Judicial Court has designated Ms. Marge Brown to coordinate all Trial Court efforts to comply with the Americans with Disabilities Act. Inquiries, requests, and complaints should be directed to:

Marge Brown, Deputy Commissioner of Probation
One Ashburton Place
Room 405
Boston, MA 02108
(617) 727–0260

COMMENCING THE ACTION
Standards 3:00 through 3:04

3:00. Advising Small Claims Litigants

Personnel in the clerk–magistrate's office should provide necessary and helpful procedural information to small claims litigants in a prompt and courteous manner.

Amended effective January 1, 2002.

Commentary

The only contact many individuals have with the courts may be a small claims experience. Their attitude toward the entire court system may depend in large part on the manner in which they are received by small claims personnel. The importance of dealing with small claims litigants in a prompt and courteous fashion cannot be overemphasized.

Court personnel should be sensitive to the fact that for many litigants filing or responding to a small claim is an emotionally difficult experience. Many small claims arise from personal or business dealings that have soured. Some litigants are highly emotional about their claim and may transfer their anger and frustration to court personnel.

These situations call for great patience and tact. Techniques for defusing confrontations are recommended subjects for staff conferences and training sessions.

Court personnel should also realize that while they are intimately familiar with court practice and are accustomed to dealing with legal procedures on a day-to-day basis, many small claims litigants will find the most elementary legal matters to be bewildering. Court personnel should make every effort to answer all small claims inquiries in a helpful and patient manner.

Courts can facilitate the small claims experience by providing clear instructions to litigants. If time permits, the small claims assistant clerk-magistrate or appropriate clerical personnel should describe the small claims procedure. At the very least, small claims personnel should direct litigants to the general instructions on the claim form and be available for questions.

Plaintiffs should be informed that they must be prepared to prove their cases by a fair preponderance of the evidence. Both parties should be reminded of the importance of producing all witnesses, documents, pictures, or other evidence in support of their position at trial. Plaintiffs should also be made aware that they have no appeal from the decision of the court if their claims are not successful.

Court personnel should administer help in an even-handed manner and provide guidance and assistance in a way that is equitable to all parties to the proceeding. Court personnel may assist parties with procedural aspects of their small claims, but should not advise litigants as to the merits of a claim or defense or its likelihood of success or give any other legal advice. Court personnel should be aware that dispensing advice about the proper content and wording of claims and answers or offering litigants help in choosing the proper party to sue may inadvertently turn into inappropriate advocacy-oriented assistance. Such assistance violates Canons 4 and 5 of the Code of Professional Responsibility for Clerks of Court and raises the risk that the litigant may incorrectly believe that he or she may rely upon such advice as if it were the advice of an attorney. See *Opinion No. 95–6 of the Advisory Committee on Ethical Opinions for Clerks of Courts*, Supreme Judicial Court, November 8, 1995, reproduced in Appendix C, and recently amended Uniform Small Claims Rule 2.

Small claims personnel may advise litigants that many public libraries have books on small claims practice and that many consumer agencies and groups offer assistance in filing small claims.

If the plaintiff or the court has doubts about the probable effectiveness of mailed service in a particular case, the plaintiff should be advised to contact the clerk-magistrate's office before the date of trial to learn whether service has been effected. See Standard 4:04.

3:01. Statement of Small Claim: Contents

All small claims must be filed on the uniform "Statement of Small Claim and Notice of Trial" form. Small claims personnel should assist the claimant in completing this form.

Amended effective January 1, 2002.

Commentary

Small claims personnel should instruct the claimant that they must utilize the uniform Statement of Small Claim and Notice of Trial form to file their small claim. The uniform form is designed to be usable in all departments and divisions of the Trial Court with small claims jurisdiction. Individual courts should not "personalize" their stock copies, and no claim presented on the uniform form should be rejected because it is not accompanied by any locally-developed "pre-application" or supplementary form.

Plaintiffs should not be charged for copies of the Statement of Small Claim and Notice of Trial form. Courts should not hesitate when asked to distribute a reasonable supply of forms to community organizations and large commercial plaintiffs. (Courts should anticipate requests for such distributions in determining the quantity of forms to requisition from the Administrative Office of the Trial Court.)

Small claims personnel should assist plaintiffs in correctly filling out the Statement of Small Claim and Notice of Trial form. Since the multi-part form serves as notice to the defendant, it should be stressed that all copies must be legible. Plaintiffs should be encouraged to state their claim in "concise, untechnical language, but with particularity and comprehensiveness." Uniform Small Claims Rule 2. Plaintiffs should be advised that their statement of claim must be specific enough to place the defendant on fair notice as to what allegations he or she is required to defend.

Small claims personnel should advise plaintiffs that the defendant be identified as correctly as possible on the claim form, and that such identification must include the following information:

● In the case of an individual defendant, the full name and address of the defendant.

● In the case of a corporate defendant, its full legal name, and if known, the name and address of a corporate officer or agent, to aid in the enforcement of any payment order. Exact corporate names can be obtained from the Corporate Records Division of the Secretary of the Commonwealth, Room 1712, One Ashburton Place, Boston, MA 02114, (617) 727–9640.

● In the case of an unincorporated business (for example, a partnership), the name(s) of its owner(s) as well as the name under which business is conducted. The owner(s) of an unincorporated business can be learned from the city or town clerk where the company's offices are located. Local consumer groups will often assist consumer plaintiffs with this task.

● In the case of a trust, the full name and address of the trustee.

Small claims plaintiffs are not allowed to divide a single claim into multiple causes of action in order to get around the statutory limit on recovery or for any other reason. Bougiokas v. Moore, 58 Mass. App. Dec. 74 (N. Dist. 1976). The rule against claim-splitting, however, does not prevent a plaintiff from bringing multiple similar small claims, each within the statutory limit, where the basis of each is legally a separate claim. Boyd v. Jamaica Plain Co-operative Bank, 7 Mass. App. Ct. 153, 163–167, 386 (1979).

A 1995 amendment to G.L. c. 218, s. 23 provides, however, that a judgment in a small claims motor vehicle property damage case "shall not have a *res judicata*, collateral estoppel, or other preclusive effect on any other action arising out of the same cause of action."

3:02. Statement of Small Claim: Filing

The clerk-magistrate's office shall accept all claims for filing. the plaintiff should be informed if a claim exceeds the statutory maximum or if venue is improper. Filing by mail should be encouraged.

Amended effective January 1, 2002.

Commentary

Any person of legal age may file a claim in his or her own name as plaintiff. An attorney may file a claim for a client. In the spirit of small claims practice, one of a number of partners or joint plaintiffs acting for all should be permitted to file a claim for all, and an officer, manager, or local manager of a corporation acting for the corporation should be permitted to file a claim in the corporation's behalf. A person who represents that he or she is authorized to do so should be permitted to file a claim on behalf of another, but the identity of any surrogate should be noted on the Statement of Small Claim. See Standard 6:09.

Court personnel should appreciate that trips to the courthouse may be inconvenient, time-consuming, and costly for litigants. Telephone callers inquiring about the initiation of a claim should be informed that a claim may be filed by mail. Uniform Small Claims Rule 2. The court should only return mailed-in forms to the sender if necessary information is missing or if there is a serious deficiency in the Statement of Small Claim, i.e. not for minor drafting faults.

Claims in excess of the statutory limit may be accepted, but the plaintiff should be informed that bringing the matter as a small claim will waive any claim to such excess. A surrogate should not be permitted to waive another's excess claim. There is no statutory limit in automobile property damage tort claims brought under the procedure. For cases under the consumer protection statute, G.L. c. 93A, or the security deposit statute, G.L. c. 186, s.15B, only the base amount of the claim must be within the statutory limit. Hampshire Village v. District Court, 381 Mass. 148 (1980).

No small claim should be rejected for what the clerk-magistrate's office perceives as venue/jurisdictional problems. In the District Court and the Boston Municipal Court, venue is proper in the court where the *plaintiff* or *defendant* lives or has his or her usual place of business or employment. (Previously, venue was proper only where the *defendant* lived or had his or her usual place of business or employment.) Where a claim is against a residential landlord for a matter arising out of a tenancy, venue also exists where the property is located. G.L. c. 218, s. 21. The venue for the Housing Court is limited to where the property that is the subject of the small claim is located. G.L. c. 185C, s.3. If a defendant will not waive a defect in venue, G.L. c. 218, s. 21 permits a court to cure improper venue by transferring a small claim to the appropriate court, but obviously it is preferable to have proper venue initially. Accordingly, unless there is reason to believe the defendant will waive venue or if immediate filing is necessary to toll the statute of limitations, the clerk-magistrate's office should normally refer a plaintiff who has the wrong venue to the proper court and suggest that the claim be filed there.

If an inmate of a correctional facility seeks to file a claim, the Statement of Small Claim should be accepted, thereby tolling the statute of limitations. The prisoner should be informed that the matter will be heard when he or she notifies the court of his or her release. The defendant should be served and notified of the court's action. In appropriate circumstances, however, the court may permit the issuance of a writ of *habeas corpus* pursuant to G.L. c. 248, s. 25.

A claim against multiple defendants made out on separate Statement of Small Claim forms should be accepted for filing as a single claim even if that court's usual practice is to use a single form.

Small claims clerical personnel should prepare a docket form and index card for each small claim filed.

3:03. Filing Fees

The plaintiff shall pay the statutory filing fee and surcharge unless found to be indigent.

Amended effective January 1, 2002.

Commentary

The plaintiff, unless found to be indigent, shall pay the filing fee established by G.L. c. 218, s. 22 and the surcharge imposed by G.L. c. 262, s. 4(c) to the appropriate clerk-magistrate's office. The plaintiff should not be charged any fee for the blank Statement of Small Claim form itself, nor should a plaintiff who files a small claim by mail be charged for postage to send out his or her own copy of the Statement of Small Claim by return mail.

Just as with other civil actions, multiple plaintiffs should be charged a single filing fee if they are seeking joint relief. Multiple plaintiffs should be charged a single surcharge. If they file simultaneously, they may be asked to divide the surcharge; otherwise the first plaintiff to file must pay the entire surcharge. Regardless of whether a division normally advises plaintiffs to file a claim against multiple defendants on a single Statement of Small Claim (photocopying extra copies as needed for giving notice) or on separate Statement of Small Claim forms for each defendant, the plaintiff should pay only a single filing fee and surcharge.

Upon request, or when otherwise indicated, a plaintiff should be referred to the clerk-magistrate or a designated assistant clerk-magistrate for a determination as to whether entry fees should be waived pursuant to the Indigent Court Costs Law. G.L. c. 261, ss. 27A–27G and Uniform Small Claims Rule 2.

3:04. Scheduling the Case

Small claims should be scheduled for prompt trial, with concern for the convenience of the parties. Small claims sessions should be separate from criminal sessions and all other civil sessions. When possible, separate sessions or starting times should be scheduled for consumer and commercial small claims plaintiffs.

Amended effective January 1, 2002.

Commentary

Prompt trial dates are crucial to the success of the small claims process. Small claims trials should be scheduled no later than 4–8 weeks from filing of the initial claim. Trial dates beyond that time severely undermine the statutory goal of a prompt, efficient procedure. Conversely, scheduling a trial earlier than 4 weeks from filing generally does not allow sufficient time for the notices to the defendant to have been returned by the postal service if undeliverable. Also, if the trial date is set too soon, it may be unfair to one or both of the parties, as they may have to arrange for the appearance of witnesses, set up child care, schedule time off from work, and manage other details. In addition, while the plaintiff may have all of his or her facts and witnesses marshaled before filing the claim, the defendant may be unaware of the claim until he or she receives the notice from the court. If requested by one party to move up or postpone the trial date, court personnel should explain that adhering to a set date generally results in a fundamentally fair and evenhanded treatment of parties as they prepare for trial. See Standard 6:03 concerning continuances.

Small claims sessions should be conducted at times distinct and apart from busy criminal days or times. These times should be devoted solely to small claims matters and payment hearings. Courts are encouraged to be innovative and flexible in the scheduling of small claims sessions. The time of day and the day of the week for holding small claims sessions should be the subject of experimentation in keeping with the needs of the community. If deemed appropriate, small claims hearings may be divided into commercial and consumer sessions, with each category of plaintiff accorded a different starting time. Where volume requires it, sessions should be held more often than once per week. Small claims sessions should not be discontinued during the summer months. See Dist. Ct. Special Rule 202 which indicates that when so ordered by the justice of any court, small claims sittings may be held bi-weekly during the summer months.

NOTICE OF TRIAL
Standards 4:00 through 4:05

4:00. Purpose of Notice of Trial

Notice of trial serves four main purposes:

1. To inform defendants that a claim has been made against them;

2. To explain to defendants what their rights and responsibilities are as they respond to the claim;

3. To warn defendants of the probable consequences should they fail to appear at the trial; and

4. To notify all parties of the date set for trial.

Amended effective January 1, 2002.

Commentary

The Notice of Trial is probably the defendant's first contact with the court and the first indication that an action has been brought. The typical small claims defendant may not have any idea of what is involved in a court proceeding. The Notice of Trial tells the defendant the name of the plaintiff bringing the claim and describes the nature of the claim. It also briefly instructs the defendant as to what the small claims process is and states his or her obligation to appear at trial and his or her opportunity to make an answer to the claim.

4:01. Form of Notice

The appropriate copies of the multi–part "Statement of Small Claim and Notice of Trial" form should be used to notify the defendant of the claim.

Amended effective January 1, 2002.

Commentary

The court gives notice to the defendant by mailing copies of the Statement of Small Claim and Notice of Trial form promulgated by the Chief Justice for Administration and Management. Uniform Small Claims Rule 3(a). Court personnel should encourage plaintiffs to state their claims as clearly and specifically as they can, since small claims defendants, unlike most other civil defendants, are usually not represented by counsel and have limited discovery mechanisms available should they need to clarify an issue prior to the date of the hearing.

Plaintiffs who are willing to submit their claim to mediation may indicate this on the face of the Statement of Small Claim and Notice of Trial form. No separate form of notice is required to comply with the Notice of Mediation provisions of G.L. c. 218, s.22 and Uniform Magistrate Rule 4(b). See Standards 6:04 and 6:05.

4:02. When Notice to Issue

The court should issue notice of a claim to the parties within five court days of the filing of the claim.

Amended effective January 1, 2002.

Commentary

Pursuant to Uniform Small Claims Rule 2, a claim is commenced upon filing. The clerk-magistrate's office should issue notice to the defendant within five court days after receipt of the claim. Inordinate delay in issuing notice may hinder the defendant's ability to prepare adequately for trial and may not allow sufficient time for undeliverable notices to be returned by the postal service.

Prompt issuance of notice reflects the court's regard for the defendant's due process rights and demonstrates to both parties that the administration of justice is operating efficiently. See Uniform Small Claims Rule 3(a).

4:03. How Notice Served

Initial service on the defendant should be by first class mail.

Amended effective January 1, 2002; amended November 29, 2004, effective January 1, 2005.

Commentary

The Massachusetts Rules of Civil Procedure regarding service of process are not applicable to small claims. In–state defendants should be served by first class mail. First class mail notice is sufficient provided that it is not returned to the court undelivered. Uniform Small Claims Rule 3 (a).

If the plaintiff indicates that the defendant has more than one address, the court should mail additional photocopies of the front *and back* of the Statement of Small Claim and Notice of Trial to each of the defendant's addresses at no additional cost to the plaintiff.

If the plaintiff is not satisfied with the first class mail method of serving notice and requests another method, he or she may obtain initial service of notice by a deputy sheriff or constable, although this option is entirely at the plaintiff's expense. The constable or deputy

sheriff should serve one of the two defendant's copies of the Statement of Small Claim and Notice of Trial, upon the defendant, and return the second copy to the court with his or her return of service. If "last and usual" constable service is made, the constable or deputy sheriff must obtain a photocopy of the notice to be mailed to the defendant in order to comply with G.L. c. 223, s. 31. If served by constable or sheriff, the defendant should receive the notice at least fourteen days before trial to enable him or her to prepare for the case.

In cases where the defendant is a corporation or trust, notice should be delivered to an appropriate officer, agent, or trustee. If service is mistakenly made on an officer personally when service on a corporation or trust was intended, the plaintiff should be permitted to amend the notice by naming or adding the intended entity. If the defendant has appeared in court despite the initial inaccurate notice, further service should not ordinarily be required, but the defendant should, if necessary, have the benefit of a continuance. If the defendant has not appeared, the court should order the amended claim to be served again.

4:04. If Notice Not Served

If the first class mail notice has not been returned undelivered and the defendant does not appear for trial, he or she may be defaulted. If notice is insufficient under Uniform Small Claims Rule 3 to permit a default to be entered, the plaintiff should be told what further service is necessary.

Amended effective January 1, 2002; amended November 29, 2004, effective January 1, 2005.

Commentary

Unless the first class mail notice is returned undelivered to the court, an inquiring plaintiff should be advised that he or she must still appear at court on the scheduled trial date.

If the first class mail notice is returned to the court undelivered, the plaintiff should be informed. If the plaintiff believes that the defendant may be located at another address, new service should be made to that address by first class mail. As with initial notice, there should be no charge to the plaintiff. If the new address creates venue issues, see Standard 3:02.

If additional service by mail is not advisable, the plaintiff should be instructed how to arrange for a different method of service. The form of that service is to be as "[t]he Court may provide . . . in individual cases as is deemed necessary" (Uniform Small Claims Rule 3[a]) and is not limited by the rules of service in other civil cases, although reference to service in other civil cases will provide guidance to the court in determining other means of service. See Uniform Small Claims Rule 1. This is an area appropriate for local experimentation. The following considerations are suggested to guide such experimentation:

- The goal is to ensure actual notice to the defendant. That goal must, within constitutional limits, be balanced with the recognition that some defendants consciously avoid service, and that expense or delay to the plaintiff are particularly to be avoided in small claims.

- Where first class mail notice has failed, further mail service of any sort to the same address may be futile. Nevertheless, consideration might be given to attempting service of notice by registered mail, return receipt requested.

- Requiring in-hand service by a constable or deputy sheriff, while more certain, may add considerably to expense and delay. If cost is an important concern to a small claims plaintiff, the court may wish to consider appointing someone nominated by the plaintiff as an unpaid special process server. If the plaintiff selects this option, the court should make the plaintiff aware that in-hand service by someone other than a constable or deputy sheriff may be difficult to effect, may increase the opportunity for a reluctant defendant to avoid service, and may even invite a physical confrontation between the defendant and the server.

• If a defendant's residence or workplace is known with some certainty, "last and usual" service delivered by a process server appears to be an appropriate solution in many cases.

• When a constable or deputy sheriff is to make service on the defendant, he or she should be encouraged to file the return at least three days before the scheduled trial date, so that the plaintiff will be able to ascertain in advance whether service has been made. When anyone other than a constable or deputy sheriff is permitted to effect in-hand or "last and usual" service, his or her return should be in the form of an affidavit filed at least three days before trial. The clerk-magistrate's office shall make available copies of the customary sheriff's return as an exemplar of such an affidavit.

If service cannot be effected prior to the scheduled trial date, the plaintiff should not be required to appear in order to obtain a continuance date. A court's case management policies should permit the clerk-magistrate's office to assign a further date in such cases.

If it is determined that the defendant cannot be served within the court's jurisdiction but his or her whereabouts are known, the plaintiff should be advised as to the proper court in which to continue the action. Upon the plaintiff's request, the small claim should be transferred to that other court with an appropriate note of its status. See G.L. c. 218, s. 21.

4:05. Service On Out-Of-State Defendants

Service on out-of-state defendants must be made in accordance with the provisions of G.L. c. 223A, s. 6.

Added effective January 1, 2002.

PRETRIAL MATTERS
Standards 5:00 through 5:06

5:00. Answers

The purpose of notice in a small claim is to bring the parties before the court so that the dispute may be heard and resolved. An answer may be filed at any time prior to trial.

Amended effective January 1, 2002.

Commentary

The Statement of Small Claim and Notice of Trial form sent to the defendant indicates that a written answer may be filed prior to trial by sending a letter to the court stating simply and clearly why the plaintiff should not prevail. The answer should state fully and specifically what parts of the claim are contested. The notice also informs the defendant that he or she should send a copy of the answer to the plaintiff. The plaintiff should be advised that he or she must appear at the scheduled trial even if no answer has been filed. Pursuant to Rule 3, the failure to file an answer will not result in the default of an action or otherwise delay the proceedings.

If the defendant does not file an answer, or does file one but fails to give the plaintiff timely notice, the court shall continue the case if the plaintiff requests and can demonstrate prejudice in going forward on the trial date. Uniform Small Claims Rule 3(b), as recently amended.

5:01. Counterclaims

Counterclaims may be made at any time in the proceeding but are not compulsory. If necessary, a defendant in counterclaim may be permitted additional time to prepare for trial.

Amended effective January 1, 2002.

Commentary

A defendant may raise any counterclaim against the plaintiff that is within the small claim procedure's jurisdiction. Uniform Small Claims Rule 3(c) defines a counterclaim very broadly as "any claim which [the defendant] has against the plaintiff" and therefore a small claims counterclaim need not arise out of the same incident as the original claim. Although under Rule 3 counterclaims are not compulsory, the court should accept all counterclaims from the same incident before or at the trial of the original claim, so that all matters arising from the same incident may be adjudicated at one time. A defendant should be informed that by bringing a counterclaim in the small claims session, he or she waives the right to a subsequent jury or bench trial with respect to that counterclaim.

Rule 3 requires that a counterclaim be set forth in writing, but specifically permits a defendant to do so at any time during the course of the proceedings. A defendant should not be required to file a counterclaim on a separate Statement of Small Claim and Notice of Trial form as if it were a separate claim. The defendant may file the counterclaim within his or her answer to the original claim or may write a separate letter to the court stating the counterclaim.

Rule 3 does not require that an answer or counterclaim be served upon the plaintiff, but it does provide that "the plaintiff's claim and the defendant's claim shall be deemed one case if the defendant mails notice of his claim to the plaintiff at least ten days in advance." As the rule permits the defendant to file a counterclaim in writing during the course of the proceedings, failure to serve a counterclaim before the trial date should not be automatic grounds for granting the plaintiff a continuance unless the plaintiff is genuinely surprised by the counterclaim at trial to the extent that he or she is prejudiced in his or her presentation. In general, if court personnel are in communication with the defendant, they should point out the importance of giving the plaintiff notice of the answer and/or counterclaim. If the defendant requests the court to do so, the court should mail the answer and/or counterclaim to the plaintiff at no cost to the defendant. The court should always permit the plaintiff to read or photocopy an answer or counterclaim filed by the defendant.

5:02. Discovery

Discovery is not routinely available in a small claim.

Amended effective January 1, 2002.

Commentary

Discovery is not available in a small claim except by leave of court "for good cause shown." Uniform Small Claims Rule 5. The court may allow discovery if it would provide material assistance to the court in deciding the case. See G.L. c. 231, ss. 61–69. If the court permits discovery, it should closely monitor the process in order to prevent confusion or possible harassment of an unrepresented party.

5:03. Transfers to the Civil Docket

The court should inquire into the underlying purpose of a motion for transfer to the civil docket. The motion should be scrutinized carefully to ensure that its allowance would not frustrate the overall purpose of the small claims procedure.

Amended effective January 1, 2002.

Commentary

Motions for transfer of a small claim to the regular civil docket are permissible under G.L. c. 218, s. 24 and Uniform Small Claims Rule 4. Since transfer to the civil docket eliminates the simplified procedures available under small claims practice, such motions should be carefully scrutinized. The court should require the party making the motion to demonstrate the need for the transfer. The court should be alert for any indication that the motion is interposed for delay or for strategic advantage, particularly where the opposing party is unrepresented by counsel. Adequate reasons for transfer would include:

- the presence of a counterclaim arising from the same incident in excess of the small claims limits;

- other pending civil cases with the same or related parties;

- an artificial division of the claim to bring it within the small claims limits;

- the requirement of a compulsory counterclaim in a related case on the civil docket; or

- numerous witnesses or extensive discovery requirements.

- the preservation of appellate rights when there are issues of law. See Standard 8:05; Trust Insurance Company v. Bruce at Park Chiropractic Clinic, 430 Mass. 607, 610 (2000).

There is, however, one set of circumstances where the court has little or no discretion to deny such a motion, i.e. where a defendant moves to transfer on the grounds that his or her right to a jury trial under Article 15 of the Declaration of Rights of the Constitution of the Commonwealth, and to due process and equal protection under the Constitution of the Commonwealth and the United States Constitution would be impaired by the statutory provision giving *prima facie* effect to the court's decision on appeal in a jury or bench trial. Daum v. Delta Airlines, Inc., 396 Mass. 1013 (1986); Gozzo v. Anglin, 31 Mass. App. Ct. 936 (1991). In such cases, the motion to transfer must explicitly raise these rights. In addition, the court has discretion to scrutinize such a motion to determine whether the motion is in fact based on grounds other than the constitutional claims. In Lyons v. Kinney Sys., Inc., 27 Mass. App. Ct. 386, 389, 390. (1989), the court determined that a judge properly denied a motion to transfer a small claim to the regular civil docket where the basis of the motion, despite an invocation of Daum, was to obtain discovery.

The court, therefore, if presented with a motion for transfer, should analyze whether the motion before it is truly based upon Daum grounds. If the court so finds, the motion may be denied only if the plaintiff agrees in advance to waive the *prima facie* effect of a favorable finding by the magistrate in any later retrial before a jury. See Newgent v. Colonial Contractors & Builders, Inc., 348 Mass. 582 (1965) wherein the Supreme Judicial Court suggested such an approach in an analogous context.

If transfer seems appropriate, the court may wish to advise unrepresented parties of the complexity of regular civil actions.

If the court in its discretion orders a transfer from the small claim to the civil docket, the case should be entered on the court's civil docket pursuant to Rule 4 without payment of an additional entry fee, as if the cause of action had been begun in the first instance under the Massachusetts Rules of Civil Procedure. The defendant must file an answer within twenty days of the transfer unless the defendant has already answered in the small claims case. The court may, in the order of transfer or thereafter, direct any party to file specific additional or substitute pleadings pursuant to the Massachusetts Rules of Civil Procedure or impose such other terms as may appear just. G.L. c. 218, s. 24; Uniform Small Claims Rule 4, as recently amended.

If a claim for motor vehicle property damage is transferred to the civil docket at the request of the insurer, any judgment against the insurer must incorporate the other party's costs and reasonable attorney's fees. G.L. c. 218, s. 23.

5:04. Third–Party Impleader

The defendant may join as third–party defendants others who are asserted to be liable for all or part of the plaintiff's claim.

Amended effective January 1, 2002.

Commentary

If a defendant informs the court that someone else is responsible for all or part of the claim against him or her, the court may inform the defendant that he or she may implead the other person as a third-party defendant.

The filing and notice procedure for impleading a party is the same as that required for initiating a claim. The defendant should not be charged a new filing fee or surcharge.

If the court becomes aware at trial that impleader is proper, the court may so inform the parties. The court may then decide the merits of the claim before it and suggest that the defendant bring another small claim to resolve any third-party liability that is asserted to exist. Alternatively, the court could continue the case to allow for service upon the impleaded party.

5:05. Amendments

Amendments should be liberally allowed.

Added effective January 1, 2002.

Commentary

Amending a Statement of Small Claim and Notice of Trial should be liberally permitted "as justice may require" at any time before judgment, so that claims may be resolved on their merits rather than on technical considerations. Uniform Small Claims Rule 5; G.L. c. 231, ss. 51, 71.

5:06. Settlement

The court should encourage settlements between parties to a small claim.

Amended effective January 1, 2002.

Commentary

Settlement saves both parties the inconvenience of further court appearances and often provides a speedier resolution that is reasonably acceptable to both parties. The court should encourage settlement, particularly if the parties appear to exhibit a willingness to compromise. The clerk-magistrate's office should take advantage of its close contact with the parties to discuss the possibility of settlement.

If the parties do reach a settlement, the clerk-magistrate's office should inform the parties that it is advisable for them to reduce their agreement to writing and present it to the court for recording prior to entry of judgment, unless the interests of justice would not be served thereby, so that the court will have the power to enforce the agreement should it be violated. See recently amended Uniform Small Claims Rule 7(a). If the parties notify the court by mail prior to the trial date that the matter has been settled without reducing it to writing or requesting it to be entered as an order of the court, the court should place that letter in the file of the case. In these circumstances, there is no judgment, and no further action is required by the court.

TRIALS AND OTHER RESOLUTIONS SHORT OF TRIAL
Standards 6:00 through 6:10

6:00. Calling the List

The small claims session should begin promptly at the scheduled time. Before calling the list, the court should instruct the litigants as to the meaning of court terminology and explain the actions they may be required to take.

Amended effective January 1, 2002.

Commentary

The time and location of the small claims session should be clearly posted in the courthouse lobby. See Standard 2:00. The proceedings should begin promptly at the scheduled time. The court should understand that beginning the small claims session later than the appointed time may significantly inconvenience litigants who have appeared on time and who may have employment or family obligations to return to. If the court is running behind schedule (or if the court decides to briefly delay the call of the list in order to accommodate tardy litigants) an announcement should be made at the scheduled starting time out of courtesy to those who have arrived on time.

Court personnel should be sensitive to the fact that the calling of the list, though routine to them, may seem incomprehensible to an unrepresented litigant. A simple set of instructions, read loudly, clearly, and slowly by the court before the call of the list should obviate much of the confusion and uncertainty that may arise in the minds of litigants. The extent and contents of these instructions will vary with local practice. The court may wish to utilize the sample instructions provided as Appendix D.

If the court does not intend to hear cases immediately after the call of the list, an announcement should be made to inform litigants as to the amount of time they will have available before they must be present in the courtroom. Small courtesies such as this will be appreciated by litigants who need to tend to parking, make a telephone call, or take care of other personal matters.

6:01. Dismissals

If the plaintiff fails to appear at the calling of the list, the court should dismiss the claim.

Amended effective January 1, 2002.

Commentary

If the plaintiff does not appear at the calling of the list, the court should dismiss the claim. Uniform Small Claims Rule 7(c). If the defendant has appeared, the docket should reflect this fact.

If the plaintiff telephones the court in advance of the trial date to inquire whether the defendant has answered, the plaintiff should be informed that he or she must appear on the scheduled trial date even if the defendant has not filed an answer.

Whenever the court dismisses a small claim, it should utilize the Notice of Judgment form to give notice of the dismissal to both parties.

See Standard 7:06 when a plaintiff wishes to reactivate a claim that has been dismissed for failure to appear.

6:02. Defaults; Military Affidavits

If the defendant fails to appear at the calling of the list, the court should issue a default against the non–appearing defendant and should routinely order judgment and a payment order for the plaintiff. A separate military affidavit is necessary only if the appropriate box has not been completed on the statement of small claim.

Amended effective January 1, 2002.

Commentary

If the defendant has defaulted by not appearing at the call of the list and the plaintiff is present, the court should routinely enter judgment for the plaintiff. Uniform Small Claims Rule 7(c),(f), and (g) contemplates a largely automatic process and does not require that the court hear a *prima facie* case. It is advisable, however, for the court to briefly review the claim, and, if necessary, to conduct a hearing in cases where the damages are uncertain or the claim itself appears to be totally without merit or beyond the jurisdiction of the court. Courts should analyze the amount of damages sought in order to make sure that the plaintiff's loss is not overstated. Examples of situations where reductions would be appropriate include: unprovable damages; instances of partial payment or partial performance; inflated claims; depreciated value; lower actual cost to the plaintiff; uncertain estimates; and instances where collection expenses or interest or other costs (e.g., lost wages for attending court) have been improperly included.

Once the amount of the judgment has been established, the court should immediately enter a thirty day payment order.

A military affidavit is required before entry of a default judgment. The Federal Soldiers' and Sailors' Relief Act of 1940 (54 Stat. 1178, 50 U.S.C. App. s. 520 [1]) requires that before a default judgment is entered, "the plaintiff ... shall file in the court an affidavit setting forth facts showing that the defendant is not in military service." Except in special circumstances, a separate form of military affidavit should not be required for a small claim. Because speedy trials are the norm for small claims, the plaintiff's verified statement that the defendant is not in the military in the Statement of Small Claim and Notice of Trial is sufficiently contemporaneous with the entry of judgment to fulfill the requirements of the Act. The filing of a military affidavit does not prevent a default judgment from being voidable upon a showing of a meritorious defense if the defendant was in military service when the judgment was rendered. 50 U.S.C. App. s. 520 (4).

See Standard 7:06 concerning removal of a default judgment.

6:03. Continuances

The court should only grant continuances upon a showing of good cause unless both parties voluntarily agree to the continuance.

Amended effective January 1, 2002.

Commentary

A court's case management policies should permit continuances that are agreed to by both parties provided that the parties request the continuance sufficiently in advance of the scheduled trial date. Inasmuch as small claims trials are scheduled within a short time period (eight weeks or less) from the date of the filing of a claim, parties often need additional time either to reach out-of-court settlements or to accommodate their work or personal schedules. The parties should not be required to appear in person in order to obtain a mutually agreed upon continuance.

Continuances that are requested by only one party should be granted for good cause only. The court must determine each case on an individual basis. The court should routinely grant motions for continuances that are filed well in advance of the date of trial unless there is prejudice to the other party. The court should allow requests for continuances that are filed close to the date of trial only in exceptional circumstances. Uniform Small Claims Rule 3, as recently amended, provides for two such circumstances: when a plaintiff is prejudiced by the circumstances of (1) a defendant's answer or (2) a defendant's counterclaim. In all cases, the court should give speedy notice to the other side of an allowance of a continuance, by telephone if the trial date is near, in order to minimize inconvenience to the other party.

On the date of the trial, when only a judge is available to hear the case, the court should grant a continuance to a defendant who declines to elect to waive the right to appeal for a subsequent trial by a judge or before a jury. The new trial date should be one when the court expects a clerk-magistrate to be available to hear the case. See Standard 2:03.

6:04. Mediation: the Purpose

The courts should provide mediation services and encourage small claims litigants to take advantage of mediation as a possible substitute for trial.

Amended effective January 1, 2002.

Commentary

Crucial to the fair resolution of a small claim is the determination whether the parties need the services of a mediator or that of an adjudicator, whether they can reach a solution together with some assistance and prodding or whether nothing but an "outside umpire's" call will end the matter. Clerk–magistrates and designated assistant clerk-magistrates are encouraged by statute and rule to make their services as mediators available. See G.L. c. 218, s. 22; G.L. c. 221, ss. 62B, 62C (d); Uniform Magistrate Rule 4.

Clerk-magistrates and assistant clerk-magistrates who offer their services as mediators should first complete basic mediation training. A magistrate who has acted as a mediator should not thereafter rule on any motion or preside over any trial or enforcement proceeding in the same small claim. In the Housing Court, housing specialists can assist parties to identify areas of dispute and resolve their differences through the process of dispute intervention. Housing specialists, clerk-magistrates and assistant clerk-magistrates who conduct mediation sessions must receive approval as a dispute resolution program from the chief justice of the applicable department. See Supreme Judicial Court Rule 1:18, Uniform Rules on Dispute Resolution, Rule 2 (definition of "program"), 4(a) and 6(a).

It is obvious that successful mediation and dispute intervention help the court by reducing the number of small claims requiring a contested trial, but mediation and dispute intervention have many positive benefits to litigants as well. Because mediation and dispute intervention allow parties to retain control over the outcome of the dispute, they often produce more satisfying results than adjudication and a greater commitment to maintaining the agreement. Mediation is even more informal than a small claims adjudicatory hearing and often allows parties to resolve their disputes with greater privacy and speed than adjudication. It allows parties to avoid all-or-nothing solutions, and, if offered in the courthouse on the day of trial, makes it clear to parties that they have the option to proceed directly to a trial if they are unable to reach agreement in mediation or dispute intervention. Finally, mediation teaches people who are in an ongoing relationship (such as families, landlords and tenants, and business associates) techniques that will assist them in maintaining the relationship and in dealing with future conflicts.

A clerk-magistrate who provides mediation is bound by ethical standards for neutrals set forth in Supreme Judicial Court Rule 1:18, Uniform Rules on Dispute Resolution, Rule 9. A clerk-magistrate has very limited authority or ability to redress unequal bargaining power between the parties because of financial means, education, or other social factors, but a clerk-magistrate and must terminate mediation if he or she believes that continuation of the process would violate any of the ethical standards. See Supreme Judicial Court Rule 1:18, Uniform Rules on Dispute Resolution, Rule 9(i).

Although mediation of small claims is strongly encouraged, courts must bear in mind the statutory limits of their mediation authority. A small claim may be submitted to mediation or dispute intervention only "with the agreement of both parties" and any action "which is not resolved by agreement may, at the request of any party, be heard" for adjudication. G.L. c. 218, s. 22. The statutory scheme provides for mediation at the option of the parties, not for a system which is mandatory. See Supreme Judicial Court Rule 1:18, Uniform Rules on Dispute Resolution, Rule 6(d).

Although not specifically provided for by statute, many courts successfully utilize the services of qualified unpaid volunteer mediators. A volunteer who understands the role and the limitations of the mediator function can render an important service to the court and the community. Courts may attempt to obtain the services of volunteer mediators through a community mediation program, the Massachusetts Office of Dispute Resolution, a university-run mediation program, or some other comparable group. Before accepting the services of a volunteer mediator, the court must ensure that any such volunteer mediator is affiliated with a program which has been approved by the chief justice of the applicable department. See Supreme Judicial Court Rule 1:18, Uniform Rules on Dispute Resolution, Rules 4(a) and 6(a).

6:05. Mediation: the Procedure

Mediation of small claims should be done in an informal manner that permits the parties to express their disagreements and then guides them beyond that point to explore possible solutions.

Amended effective January 1, 2002.

Commentary

The District Court Special Committee to Study Alternative Means of Dispute Resolution has offered some suggestions for mediation in the courts. Similar considerations apply to dispute intervention:

When disputants elect to mediate their dispute, their choice should be an informed one. They should understand the mediation process, its purpose, and the details of the judicial alternative for resolving their dispute. The impact of their decision should also be explained. They should be notified that, irrespective of their initial decision to mediate their dispute, they may have a court hearing . . .

At the commencement of a mediation session, the mediator should explain that he is not a Judge . . . and that the proceeding differs from a trial. Throughout the process, he should not find fault with any of the disputants, but should assume the role of an objective third party in assisting the disputants to reach an agreement. He should not accept as accurate any disputant's version of a contested issue and should never take sides. Further, he should act as a referee, controlling . . . outbursts and directing the parties to discuss the disputed issues.

As the mediation session progresses, the mediator's role changes. At first, the mediator serves as a confidant. He listens to each disputant relate his version of the controversy and tries to control interruptions and interjections by the other disputant. The rendition of the cause of the quarrel is beneficial for two reasons. The disputants have a need to tell a neutral third party why they have been wronged . . . In addition, the mediator needs to learn some background information about the controversy.

Once disputants have aired their grievance, the mediator must assume a more active role in trying to isolate the areas of agreement and disagreement. Some specific questions may be asked to clarify the nature of the dispute . . . Once the contested issues are discerned, the mediator should encourage the disputants to discuss them further.

Next, the mediator must play an active part in discerning whether a mutually acceptable solution can be reached. The mediator may ask each disputant how the dispute may be resolved. If that tactic proves ineffective, it may be necessary for the mediator to speak with each disputant privately. The use of the caucus technique will enable the mediator to learn each party's "bottom line." Privy to this information, the mediator may guide parties to reach a mutually acceptable agreement when the disputants reconvene . . .

The mediator may make suggestions and describe alternatives. The disputants may demonstrate an unwillingness to compromise. Symbolic gestures . . . as well as verbal expressions of dissatisfaction may indicate that an impasse has been reached . . .

Frequently the disputants will continue discussing their differences and will reach an agreement . . . At the conclusion of the mediation session, disputants should be notified of the follow-up procedure and their options should there be a breakdown in the agreement.

Special Committee Report at 19–21.

It should be noted that the "caucus" technique, i.e. discussing the matter separately with each party, is a sensitive one. It may lead to an impression of favored treatment. As a rule, when caucusing is done, it should be done with both parties.

Mediation and dispute intervention sessions should not be recorded or participants sworn. Other procedures are in the magistrate's discretion, "consistent with the achievement of a voluntary resolution of the dispute." Uniform Magistrate Rule 4 (c).

It is normally appropriate for a mediator to communicate the results of mediation in writing to the clerk of the small claims session. Supreme Judicial Court Rule 1:18, Uniform Rules on Dispute Resolution, Rule 7(g). If the mediation attempt has been unsuccessful, however, the mediator may not report agreed facts or stipulations which the parties have reached, in order to simplify issues for trial, unless both parties give their permission. Supreme Judicial Court Rule 1:18, Uniform Rules on Dispute Resolution, Rule 6(f) and 9(h). At the conclusion of a dispute intervention, the housing specialist may communicate to the court his or her recommendations, a list of those issues which are and are not resolved, and the housing specialist's assessment of whether the case will go to trial or settle, provided the parties are informed in advance of the session that such communication will occur. Supreme Judicial Court Rule 1:18, Uniform Rules on Dispute Resolution, Rule 6(f)(iv). If the mediation or dispute intervention has resulted in a voluntary agreement, it should be reduced to writing and signed by the parties. Unless the interests of justice would not be served thereby, the clerk of the small claims session then enters judgment and a payment order in the case in accordance with the agreement. Uniform Magistrate Rule 4 (e). Each party must be given a copy of the written agreement inasmuch as the agreement "frequently serves as a reminder to the disputants and demonstrates their good faith," Special Committee Report at 21. A successfully settled case should always be reduced to an agreed-upon judgment and payment order as this will facilitate enforcement proceedings should they become necessary. Uniform Magistrate Rule 4 (e) and (f).

If a matter shows promise for resolution by mediation or dispute intervention, but final agreement cannot be obtained in a single session, it may be continued for further sessions in compliance with the court's case management policies. With the agreement of the parties, a court may also schedule mediation sessions before the date set for trial if both parties' willingness to mediate is known in advance. Repeated court appearances should be minimized, however, and therefore courts should routinely schedule mediation or dispute intervention sessions on the same day as the small claims session. A simple claim that cannot be successfully mediated or resolved through dispute intervention should normally proceed to trial immediately.

6:06. Settlement

In appropriate cases, the court may facilitate a settlement short of trial.

Added effective January 1, 2002.

Commentary

Even when the parties have not requested mediation, the court must initially make a determination, similar to the exercise undertaken by a mediator, as to whether the parties are actually demanding a judgment or are essentially utilizing the small claims session as a place to discuss disagreements and arrive at informal solutions. Often the parties may not be able to immediately articulate what they are asking of the court; the clerk-magistrate or judge must help them clarify their positions.

Obviously, settlement and adjudication involve two very different processes, and the court should clearly understand its role in each. In a settlement, the court's primary goal is to help the parties reach a conciliation and agree to a specific, mutually acceptable result. If, on the other hand, the court is adjudicating a dispute, its goals are to provide due process and to render a decision that is correct under substantive rules of law. The court may wish to point out to the parties that there are at least three essential aspects of adjudication that are dramatically different from the mediation and settlement processes:

● a third party, the adjudicator, is given coercive power;

● each party usually obtains only a "win or lose" decision; and

● decision making is focused narrowly on the immediate matter at issue, as distinguished from a concern with the underlying relationship between the parties.

Where it becomes clear that the parties will not, or will no longer, work towards a settlement, the court must consciously change roles from conciliator to fact finder. To prevent misunderstanding, it is important that the parties note this change of function. The court must explicitly communicate to the parties that once the case moves into an adjudication phase their roles also change. The parties must understand that they are now operating within an adversarial context, and that they must marshal whatever evidence and arguments they wish to present to the court.

The societal importance attached to criminal matters and civil cases of a higher dollar amount should not diminish the allocation of attention and time spent in achieving a full and fair hearing for small claims litigants who are insistent upon trial rather than negotiation.

Unless the interests of justice would not be served thereby, any settlement agreement should be entered as a judgement, with a payment order, if appropriate. Uniform Small Claims Rule 7(a), as recently amended.

6:07. Trial: the Purpose

The purpose of a trial of a small claim is to obtain an adjudication of an issue between the parties that is based upon information presented by the parties and the application of substantive law. The court should give the parties sufficient opportunity to present their cases and should recognize that the case is important to the parties despite the relatively small monetary amount involved.

Amended effective January 1, 2002.

Commentary

Even though a small claims trial dispenses with much of the customary legal procedures, forms, and terminology, the parties should understand that the concept of an adversary hearing, basic to our jurisprudence, remains intact. Indeed, for some small claims litigants the opportunity merely to present arguments in this forum is almost as important as the actual decision in the case. The trial may be the culmination of months of frustration and tension. Their opportunity to present their respective positions to an impartial arbiter who has the authority to resolve their disputes according to substantive law is their "day in court."

6:08. Trial: the Procedure

Before a trial begins, the court should explain the procedure to the litigants. the court should conduct small claims trials in an informal manner while maintaining order and protecting the due process rights of the parties.

Amended effective January 1, 2002.

Commentary

The attractiveness of small claims procedure is a direct reflection of the atmosphere in which it is conducted and the quality of justice that is perceived to be available. While small claims sessions are apt to be busy and sometimes emotional, the court must insist that litigants do not use the informality to debase the forum. It is also important that the court be perceived as giving equal consideration and impartiality to the hearing of small claims as it does to more complex trials.

Small claims trials should be conducted in open court and on the record. Tape recording of trials is necessary for accountability purposes and so that the court will have a record of evidence to consult if the small claim is taken under advisement. At least one court officer should attend all small claims sessions. Uniform Small Claims Rule 7(d) and (e), as recently amended.

Before trials begin, the court should instruct parties as to how they are to proceed. (See Appendix E for sample instructions.) To save time, the instructions should be given to all the litigants waiting for trials rather than individually.

Before commencing a trial, the court should determine whether any party has a language barrier that inhibits full understanding of the proceedings. A continuance may be in order if there is not a qualified interpreter present. See Standard 2:05.

The court should conduct the trial in whatever order and form and with such methods of proof as it deems best suited to discover the facts and do justice in the case. Uniform Small Claims Rule 7(c). The Supreme Judicial Court has commented on the implications of this Rule.

Rule 7 ... provid[es] ... that a judge shall have wide discretion in conducting the hearing as to "order and form" and "methods of proof" in matters that in formal procedure are governed by fixed rules or principles ... The statute would fail of its purpose if it merely substituted for established rules or principles applicable to ordinary procedure another set of detailed rules for the trial of cases under the small claims procedure. The informality that is to characterize a hearing under the small claims procedure imports that the judge may be permitted by rule to exercise a wide discretion ... Even under formal procedure the judge "ought to be always the guiding spirit and the controlling mind at a trial" ... [and] may put proper questions to witnesses ... The statute relating to small claims procedure, however, contemplates, if necessary, more active participation of the judge in the conduct of the hearing than is usual under formal procedure. Obviously it was intended by the statute to provide a form of hearing in which assistance of parties by counsel would not be required ... [and] in such cases active participation by the judge in the examination of witnesses ordinarily would be essential for discovery of the facts and determination of the justice of the case ..." McLaughlin v. Municipal Court of the Roxbury Dist., 308 Mass. 397, 403–405 (1941), citations omitted.

Informalities may thus be permitted in order to encourage ease. Parties and other witnesses must be sworn when testifying (see Uniform Small Claims Rule 7 [e]) but the parties may stand or sit at the counsel tables rather than take the witness stand. They may use conversational tones and present facts in narrative form; they may be permitted to alternate speaking when such order of evidence appears warranted.

When an oral motion is made, the court should note on the docket sheet whatever action the court takes on the motion. Uniform Small Claims Rule 7 (e). Motions to amend pleadings should be liberally allowed so that claims are determined on their merits rather than on technical considerations. Uniform Small Claims Rule 5.

Despite the informality of the proceedings, the plaintiff must, as in any civil action, prove each of the elements of his or her cause of action by a preponderance of the evidence and according to the rules of substantive law. G.L. c. 218, s. 21.

6:09. Role of Participants

Small claims litigants may utilize attorneys to assist in the presentation of their claim or to appear in their behalf. The role of the attorney may be limited, but not eliminated, by the court. Small claims litigants may also utilize non–attorneys to assist them or, at the court's discretion, to appear in their behalf.

Amended effective January 1, 2002.

Commentary

Attorneys may represent parties at small claims trials. A party represented by counsel should not be required to appear personally unless the party is a necessary witness. Although attorneys are permitted in small claims sessions, the forum was "obviously" intended to provide a form of hearing that did not require assistance of counsel. See McLaughlin v. Municipal Court of the Roxbury Dist., 308 Mass. 397, 405 (1941). Thus, the court should carefully control the proceedings to insure that the presence of an opposing attorney does not inhibit a full presentation by the unrepresented litigant. One party cannot, "by being represented by counsel, change the essential nature of the hearing [and] by being so represented relieve the judge of his duty under the statute." Uniform Small Claims Rule 7 (e). The court has wide discretion as to the extent of participation by counsel in a hearing, and, in appropriate circumstances, may refuse to permit uncooperative counsel to examine witnesses. McLaughlin at 406. Limitations imposed on particular attorneys should stem from inappropriate tactics or style rather than from the merits of their client's cases.

Non-attorneys closely connected to a party, such as spouses, family members, or employees, may be permitted to appear in place of the party if the court, in its discretion, is satisfied that the person is authorized to appear for the party and that substantial justice can be accomplished with the use of a surrogate. If it should have been obvious that the personal presence of a party was necessary to determine the issues, the court may refuse to credit the testimony of a surrogate party. In such circumstances, a continuance should be denied and/or appropriate costs may be imposed under Uniform Small Claims Rule 7(h). In reaching its decision as to whether a particular individual is a legitimate surrogate, a distinction may appropriately be made between those parties who are necessary to a fair trial because they are percipient actors in, or witnesses to, the disputed matter, and those (such as officers of corporate plaintiffs) whose testimony is unlikely to be valuable.

The court may permit spouses, family members, employees, and others to assist an appearing party in the presentation of his or her evidence. Uniform Small Claims Rule 7(h). In this area there is no "bright line" rule, and the court must balance its desire to maintain the informality of the small claims procedure with the need to limit formal representation of others to those subject to the discipline of the court.

The court may impose reasonable limitations on the presentation of evidence and argument, but this must not be done summarily or arbitrarily. Procedural due process, albeit simplified, must always be adhered to. O'Farrell v. Dubin, 16 Mass. App. Dec. 100 (N. Dist. 1958).

6:10. Rules of Evidence

The court should not require strict adherence to the rules of evidence in small claims trials.

Amended effective January 1, 2002.

Commentary

The small claims procedure has from its inception been intended to give

... an opportunity to the parties to come directly before the judge, tell him their story, answer his questions, and let him settle it, and that is what most people in such small matters want ...

[T]he extent to which rules of practice shall be applied may well be left to the discretion of the courts. The judge is dealing directly with parties who are not lawyers and do not understand the rules of evidence. The judge can sift the evidence. He is left free to get at the facts. When he gets them, he applies the law and decides the case.

Report of the Judicature Commission 12, 14, 1920 House Doc. No. 597.

The court should not require adherence to technical rules of evidence except those relating to privileged communications. Evidence, including hearsay evidence, may be admitted and given probative effect if it is the kind of evidence that reasonable persons are accustomed to rely upon in the conduct of serious affairs. In keeping with the nature of the small claims procedure, the court may restrict the form of cross-examination and may exclude unduly repetitious evidence.

Although the rules of evidence are relaxed, the court should not overlook its duty to assure the relevance and reliability of the evidence admitted.

This Standard is also applicable to trials on appeal. See Standard 8:02.

JUDGMENTS AND PAYMENT ORDERS
Standards 7:00 through 7:07

7:00. Rendering of Decision

The court should favor announcing the decision of a small claim at the end of the trial.

Amended effective January 1, 2002.

Commentary

Clerk-magistrates and judges have varied opinions as to the advantages and disadvantages of announcing a decision in a small claim at the conclusion of the trial as compared with taking a case under advisement and then rendering a decision at a later time. The practice of rendering a decision immediately at the end of the trial has certain advantages that would make this practice preferable.

By announcing a decision immediately at the end of the trial, finality is brought to the process. The court also has the opportunity to state briefly to the parties the reasoning behind the decision. To some people, understanding the reasoning behind the decision is as important as the decision itself. Since the court appearance is often the finale of a long disagreement between the parties where each party may have extensively planned and worried over its presentation and taken time from work to be in court, an immediate decision and explanation is preferable to simply having the case taken under advisement and subsequently rendering a decision in the mail without any explanation.

In cases where the plaintiff prevails and the defendant does not wish to claim a jury trial or bench trial, another very important advantage of rendering a decision at the conclusion of the trial while the parties are still before the court is to enter into an immediate discussion of the defendant's ability to pay. This avoids additional delay and the need for a further court appearance to attend a subsequent payment hearing. See Standard 7:03. A full payment hearing can and should be entered into immediately upon rendering a decision. Occasionally the court may need to grant a short continuance in order to gather additional information necessary to evaluate a defendant's ability to pay, but such continuances should be the exception and not the rule. If, for any reason, a payment hearing is not commenced immediately upon the rendering of a decision, then a full payment hearing shall be scheduled no later than thirty days from the time judgment is entered or shortly thereafter.

Those in favor of reserving decision emphasize that small claim sessions may be volatile, and sometimes the rendering of an immediate decision might provoke emotional outbursts, taxing the court's patience as well as its time. For this reason, all small claim sessions should have appropriate court officers assigned to the session just as they are to all other court sessions.

There are times when further research is necessary in order to render a just decision. In those circumstances, the court should take the appropriate time.

Regardless of which approach is utilized by the court, a written decision with a brief statement of findings where possible should be issued by the court immediately after a decision is made even if the decision is made orally at the end of the trial. The court's comments at the time of trial or at the time of rendering a decision serve to assist the litigants in understanding the reasoning behind each other's position and controlling their emotional reaction to the decision. All decisions should be reasoned and based upon substantive law. A final decision must be just and not based upon "a flip of the coin" or a splitting of a decision equally between the parties without any basis in fact or substantive law. Although all clerk-magistrates and judges have discretion in rendering decisions, when decisions are made without the application of logic, reasoning, or pertinent mathematical calculations, there exists the possibility of the public losing faith in the decision-making process. This is not to suggest that there are not cases where the court must render a decision without any precise logical or mathematical guides. There are, obviously, cases that require the best decision of the fact finder that is devoid of mathematical certainties.

Any orders for payment should be included in the decision and mailed to the parties promptly.

7:01. Promptness of Decision

If the court does not announce a decision at the end of the trial, it should tell the parties when they may expect a decision. unless special circumstances necessitate further delay, the decision should be made within five court days of trial.

Amended effective January 1, 2002.

Commentary

The court's obligation after trial is to render a decision. Although an immediately-rendered judgment is generally preferable, invariably there will be times when the court will take the case under advisement. In these instances, the court should make every effort to reach its decision within five court days of the trial. If special circumstances preclude this—e.g. the court is awaiting receipt of further evidence or time consuming research is required—the court should give the parties some indication of when they may expect a decision.

7:02 Remedies

The court has the power to enter money judgments and equitable relief.

Added effective January 1, 2002.

Commentary

Although the original action brought must include a claim for money damages, the court may order equitable remedies such as specific performance, instead of, or in addition to, damages. The court has all equity powers and jurisdictions conferred by G.L. c. 218, s. 21 and G.L. c. 214, ss. 1, 1A, 2, 3 (1).

7:03. Payment Orders When Decision Announced

If a decision for the plaintiff is announced at the end of trial, the defendant should be examined as to ability to pay, and a payment order should be made contemporaneously with the judgment.

Amended effective January 1, 2002.

Commentary

A plaintiff who has prevailed should not, if at all possible, have to make additional court appearances in order to obtain a payment order. Uniform Small Claims Rule 7(g) requires that a payment order be entered immediately upon decision "except where justice will not be served thereby." Therefore, unless there is a compelling reason—e.g. additional information is needed to properly evaluate a defendant's ability to pay—the court should conduct a full payment hearing immediately after announcing its decision.

Prior to the commencement of any payment hearing, the defendant must be advised of his or her right to appeal the court's judgment on the small claim. See Standard 8:00. If the defendant indicates he or she will appeal, the court shall not conduct a payment hearing.

Payment orders should be issued for the amount of the judgment plus allowable costs and should require payment by a definite date or on a definite schedule, unless the court finds an inability to pay or that the defendant's income is exempt from judgment. See Uniform Small Claims Rule 7(g) and 7(h) and Standard 7:04. If the defendant requests time to pay and the schedule of periodic payment proposed by the defendant is unacceptable to the prevailing party, the court shall require the defendant to complete a written financial statement on a form prescribed by the Chief Justice for Administration and Management. The financial statement should provide information sufficient to determine the source of the defendant's income and ability to pay and to allow the court to order specific and suitable payment installments. In making an order to pay, the court should observe all relevant statutory exemptions, such as those in G.L. c. 235, s. 34. See G.L. c. 224, s. 16, made applicable to small claims by G.L. c. 218, s. 23. The court should recognize that unrepresented defendants may not be aware of such exemptions. If the defendant's income is exempt or the defendant is unable to pay, the court should continue the payment hearing date to a further date to see if the defendant's financial status has changed.

The provisions of a payment order should be entered on the Notice of Judgment form. In unusual circumstances, the court may order the defendant to make payments through the court rather than directly to the prevailing party. Uniform Small Claims Rule 7(g).

A payment order against a corporation is made by naming its president, treasurer, cashier, or other officer or agent in charge of the payment of corporate debts. A payment order against a trust with transferable shares is made against the trustee or agent in charge of payment of its debts. See G.L. c. 224, ss. 2, 15, made applicable to small claims by G.L. c. 218, s. 23. In such situations, the person should be named in her representative capacity, i.e. "Jane H. Jones, as President of ABC, Inc."

In the rare cases where the court is unable to conduct a payment hearing upon decision, that hearing may be continued for a period of time not to exceed thirty days or shortly thereafter.

The court must inform the defendant that failure to comply with a payment order could result in his or her or her being held in contempt.

See Standard 7:07 as to modification of payment orders.

7:04. Payment Orders When Decision Reserved or the Defendant Defaults; Automatic Payment Hearings

If the court finds for the plaintiff after decision has been reserved, or if the defendant defaults at the hearing, an order to pay in full within thirty days should be entered and a prompt payment hearing scheduled.

Amended effective January 1, 2002.

Commentary

In cases where the decision is not announced at trial or in default situations, a payment order should routinely be entered for the full amount of the judgment and costs, payable in full in thirty days unless the court specifically orders a longer period. The making of such orders is essential to expeditious small claims processing. When the court informs the small claims assistant clerk-magistrate or small claims supervisor of his or her decision in a reserved case, the assistant clerk-magistrate or small claims supervisor should confirm with the clerk-magistrate or judge that a thirty day payment order should also enter. In an exceptional case where the court consciously declines to issue a payment order at the time of judgment because "justice will not be served thereby," (see Uniform Small Claims Rule 7 [g]) or the defendant has no present ability to pay, the court should direct the small claims assistant clerk-magistrate or small claims supervisor to note that ruling on the docket sheet as a guide in subsequent hearings on the matter.

A payment order against a corporation is made by naming its president, treasurer, cashier, or other officer or agent in charge of the payment of corporate debts. A payment order against a trust with transferable shares is made against the trustee or agent in charge of payment of its debts. See G.L. c. 224, ss. 2, 15, made applicable to small claims by G.L. c. 218, s. 23. In such situations, the person should be named in her representative capacity, i.e. "Jane H. Jones, as President of ABC, Inc."

Pursuant to the new Uniform Small Claims Rule 7 (g), the court should automatically schedule a payment hearing at the time of the judgment and payment order. In most cases, the automatic payment hearing should obviate the need for a show cause hearing. Historically, a show cause hearing took weeks and months to schedule. This new rule was promulgated in order to obtain a quick determination as to whether the defendant has exempt income or is unable to pay and to eliminate the need for the plaintiff to obtain and pay for service of process and thus save the plaintiff additional frustration in those cases where the defendant's financial status precludes the judgment from being satisfied.

The payment hearing must be scheduled for the thirtieth day following judgment or shortly thereafter. The court must send to the parties a Notice of Payment Hearing as well as the Notice of Judgment. The defendant is afforded several options within the thirty day period. First, the defendant in a case that went to trial may claim an appeal within ten days of receipt of Notice of Judgment, in which case the payment hearing would be canceled. Second, the defendant can simply pay the successful party and satisfy the judgment. (A form should be provided for the plaintiff and the defendant to file with the court as evidence of payment.) Third, the defendant can appear at the payment hearing and the burden would then fall upon him or her to show why payment should not be made in full. For the defendant to avail himself of this option, however, he or she would have to fill out a Trial Court-approved financial disclosure form and provide a copy to the plaintiff in advance of the payment hearing. The court should be mindful of the statutory exemptions for certain types and amounts of income, such as those in G.L. c. 235, s. 34. See G.L. c. 224, s. 16, made applicable to small claims by G.L. c. 218, s. 23. The court should recognize that unrepresented defendants may not be aware of such exemptions.

If the defendant fails to appear at the payment hearing, this failure to appear shall constitute a default and subject the defendant to arrest. If the defendant appears but has failed to provide a financial statement, the court should direct the defendant to do so forthwith. If the defendant refuses to fill out a financial statement, then the matter should be referred to a judge on the issue of contempt. The court, in addition to reviewing the defendant's financial statement, may require additional financial information including, but not limited to, income tax returns, payroll information, and investment information.

The court must inform the defendant that failure to comply with a payment order could result in his or her being held in contempt of court. In most cases, the court should schedule review dates to ensure compliance with any orders entered for payment or to review the ability to pay of a defendant who is currently judgment proof or unable to pay. These review dates allow the court to become more pro-active with respect to the satisfaction of judgments entered and orders made.

A successful small claims litigant should never be required to initiate formal supplementary process proceedings under G.L. c. 224 to obtain a payment order. Similarly, the Uniform Small Claims Rules no longer require that the losing party be summonsed (by the procedure formerly referred to as "small claims supplementary process") merely for the court to issue a payment order. If, inadvertently, a payment order was not made at the time of judgment, upon inquiry by the prevailing party, the small claims assistant clerk-magistrate or small claims supervisor should bring the omission to the attention of a clerk-magistrate or judge in order to have a payment order entered and a payment hearing scheduled.

7:05. Costs

The actual cash disbursements of the prevailing party for entry fee and surcharge should be assessed as costs. Witness fees and other costs may be allowed only by court order. The court should examine carefully all claims for discretionary costs.

Amended effective January 1, 2002.

Commentary

The prevailing party should receive his or her actual cash disbursements for filing and services fees. The court may tax other costs, such as witness fees or fees for experts, only by special order. Any specific statutory provisions regarding the costs of civil proceedings are applicable to such special situations. Additional costs not exceed-

ing $100.00 may be assessed against any party who has set up a frivolous or misleading claim or answer, or otherwise sought to hamper a speedy and fair resolution of the dispute at hand. See Uniform Small Claims Rule 7(h).

Attorney's fees should not be added to the judgment unless there is a written provision for such in the contract upon which the claim is based. See G.L. c.186, s. 20 with respect to contractual attorney's fees in actions involving residential leases. Attorney's fees may also be awarded where expressly authorized by statute, but the court should weigh such awards carefully in the light of the "obvious" legislative intent that small claims procedure should not require assistance of counsel. McLaughlin v Municipal Court of the Roxbury Dist., 308 Mass. 397, 405 (1941).

7:06. Relief From Judgment

The court should exercise with caution the discretion to grant relief from judgment, including vacating dismissals and removing defaults.

Amended effective January 1, 2002.

Commentary

Within one year of the date of judgment, the court may grant relief from judgment or from any order "for want of actual notice to a party, for error, or for any other cause that the court may deem sufficient," and may condition relief upon any reasonable condition. See amended Uniform Small Claims Rule 8. The court may not grant such relief *ex parte*. The opposing party must be given an opportunity to be heard in opposition to a request for relief from judgment. Although Mass. R. Civ. P. 59 (New Trials) and 60 (Relief from Judgment or Order) do not apply to small claims, case law applying Rules 59 and 60 may appropriately guide a clerk-magistrate or judge's discretion in granting relief from judgment in a small claim.

A plaintiff seeking to vacate a dismissal for failure to appear for trial (see Standard 6:01) or a defendant seeking to remove a default judgment (see Standard 6:02) must file a motion for relief from the judgment pursuant to Rule 8 within the one year period. The court must require a showing of sufficient cause before permitting a plaintiff to bring the claim again or vacating a defendant's default. The court must be wary not to permit simplified small claims procedures and the nominal filing fee to be used by a negligent or ill-willed plaintiff to harass a defendant or abuse the process itself. McLaughlin v. Levenbaum, 248 Mass. 170, 176 (1924). Likewise, the fact that a small claims defendant may have a meritorious excuse why he or she did not appear in court as required, is not, of itself, sufficient reason to require the removal of a default. Younis v. Mario Musto Corp., 1979 Mass. App. Dec. 240, 243 (S. Dist.) See also, Maguire v. Quality Foreign Cars, Inc. 54 Mass. App. Dec. 76, 81, 82 (N. Dist. 1974) wherein refusal to remove default was upheld where judge found that defendant's attorney intentionally harassed the plaintiff by phoning the court to ask that case be held until later.

Even if a party can show sufficient cause for the failure to appear, the court may consider an award of costs for lost wages and other out-of-pocket expenses to the opposing party who appeared in good faith at the initially scheduled court date. See amended Uniform Small Claim Rule 8.

7:07. Modification of Payment Orders

The court may modify a payment order at any time based on new evidence or changed circumstances.

Added effective January 1, 2002.

Commentary

Either party may request the court to modify the terms of any payment order if the defendant's financial circumstances change or if the plaintiff becomes aware of newly discovered evidence that effects the defendant's financial ability to satisfy the judgment. All requests for modification of a payment order must be done through the court and proper notice shall be sent to the parties by the court. At any

hearing on the modification of the payment order, the court may require additional financial statements by the defendant or other evidence sufficient to establish the need for modification of a previously entered payment order.

APPEALS
Standards 8:00 through 8:05

8:00. Appealing From the Judgment

A defendant against whom a judgment has been rendered (including the defendant in a counterclaim or third party claim), may appeal for a trial by a judge or before a jury of six persons, unless the defendant elected to have the case tried initially by a judge, in which instance there is no opportunity for another trial.

The defendant must first:

1. file an affidavit setting forth questions of law and fact in the case requiring a trial and stating that such trial is intended in good faith;

2. pay an entry fee unless found indigent; and

3. post a bond, unless waived or not required.

Added effective January 1, 2002.

Commentary

Within ten days of receipt of the court's judgment after a trial, the defendant (including a defendant in a counterclaim or third party claim) may file a notice that he or she claims a trial by a judge or before a jury of six persons unless the defendant has waived the right to appeal by electing to have the case tried initially by a judge. There is no right to another trial if there has been such an election. See Standard 2:03. There is also no right to another trial if the judgment is due to the defendant's default. See Standards 6:02 and 7:06 regarding the defendant's course of action to remove a default. The statute limits an appeal to matters where there was a "finding" by the court "where the cause was determined". G.L. c.218, s. 23. Interpreting a similar statute, the Appeals Court has indicated that a dismissal or default is not an appealable "decision or finding." H. Sandbar & Son, Inc. v. Clerk of the Dist. Court of N. Norfolk, 12 Mass. App. Ct. 686 (1981).

The claim does not need to be on a Trial Court form but must be in writing and must comply with the requirements of G.L. c. 218, s. 23 and shall specify whether the defendant claims a trial by a judge or by a jury. The appeal must also be accompanied by:

● an affidavit that specifies the questions of law and fact in the case requiring a trial by judge or jury of six and that states that such trial is intended in good faith;

● a $25.00 entry fee that the court may waive if the applicant is indigent; and

● a bond in a penal sum of $100.00, with such sureties as may be approved by the plaintiff or the clerk-magistrate or an assistant clerk-magistrate, payable to the other party to satisfy any judgment and costs that may be entered against that party. The bond is not required for municipal and county bodies and officials, from defendants who have already posted bond to dissolve an attachment, or to appeal from a judgment secured by a motor vehicle insurance policy. A residential landlord's appeal from an adverse small claim decision involving a security deposit requires a higher bond, details of which are set out in G.L. 218, s. 23. The court may waive the $100.00 bond requirement if it finds that the defendant has insufficient funds to furnish the bond and that the appeal is not frivolous.

Personnel in the clerk-magistrate's office should provide litigants who wish to appeal with information regarding the procedure consistent with Standards 2:00 and 3:00. Personnel shall ascertain whether the defendant elects a jury trial or claims a trial before a judge and shall note that decision on the papers if it is not set forth in the defendant's claim. After the appeal and appropriate bond are filed, if the defendant claims a jury trial, the clerk-magistrate's office must promptly transmit the papers to the jury session designated to hear small claims for that court.

8:01. Scheduling the Case for Trial

The court should schedule the case for prompt trial. A District Court that does not have a jury session is responsible for scheduling bench trials in that division.

Added effective January 1, 2002.

Commentary

Small claims trials before a jury or judge are designated as "speedy trial[s]" by statute and therefore the court must give them priority. G.L. c. 218, s. 23. The statutory goals of a simple, informal, and inexpensive procedure are frustrated when the litigants on appeal are not given a trial date that is within two or three months from filing or are subjected to many continuances because their cases are treated as secondary to the criminal docket. The court must therefore schedule a prompt trial upon receiving the appeal claim and make sure that small claims cases are not set down for days with a heavy volume of criminal trials.

Although it is always appropriate for the court to encourage settlement (see Standards 5:06 and 6:06), the court should not place undue pressure on the parties to settle or to waive a jury trial because of a crowded docket.

If a court has separate jury and jury-waived trial lists, the clerk's office should note carefully whether the defendant has requested a jury trial or a trial before a judge and place each case on the appropriate list. A District Court that does not have a jury session must try jury-waived cases in that division; those cases should not be sent to the court designated for jury trials. Uniform Small Claims Rule 7(a).

Pursuant to G.L. c. 218, s. 23, the court may require pleadings pursuant to the Massachusetts Rules of Civil Procedure, but the court should rarely exercise this power so as not to frustrate the goals of the small claims procedure. The court should not entertain motions for summary judgment. Todino v. Arbella Mutual Ins. Co., 415 Mass. 298 (1993) (summary judgment not available to defendant).

8:02. Conduct of the Trial

The court should conduct the trial consistent with standards 6:07–6:10 except for:

1. the prima facie effect of the judgment of the first trial;

2. the applicability of the provisions of law concerning jury trials in the Superior Court; and

3. a prohibition on counterclaims and third party claims being raised for the first time.

Added effective January 1, 2002.

Commentary

Standards 6:07—6:10 apply to trials on appeal. Strict adherence to the rules of evidence in a jury trial or trial before a judge should not be required as it would be confusing and unfair to litigants to be governed by relaxed rules of evidence in the original trial and then later be subjected to strictly enforced evidentiary rules at the trial on appeal. Uniform Small Claims Rule 10(b). Pursuant to Uniform Small Claims Rule 7, which is applicable to appeals, "(t)he Court shall conduct the trial in such order and form and with such methods of proof as it deems best suited to discover the facts and do justice in the case." See Standard 6:10, which states that although the rules of evidence are relaxed, the court should not overlook its duty to assure the relevance and reliability of the evidence admitted.

The judge should advise the parties and at a jury trial instruct the jury that judgment was entered in the plaintiff's favor in the original trial, and that the *prima facie* effect of such judgment will require a finding in favor of the plaintiff unless the defendant introduces some credible contradictory evidence during the trial. The judge should also make clear that the earlier judgment will be evidence for the plaintiff even when the defendant does introduce contradictory evidence.

In a jury trial, all of the provisions of law governing jury trials in Superior Court, such as required *voir dire* questions and the manner of taking a verdict, apply, except that peremptory challenges are limited to two for each side. G.L. c.218, s.23; Rule 10(b). Pretrial Superior Court procedures such as summary judgment should not be used in small claims cases. Uniform Small Claims Rule 1. See also Todino v. Arbella Mutual Ins. Co., 415 Mass. 298 (1993).

A counterclaim or third party claim may not be raised for the first time on appeal.

8:03. Judgments and Payment Orders

Judgment should be entered immediately on a jury verdict or a judge's decision. On a verdict, or if the judge announces a decision at the end of trial, the judge should enter a contemporaneous payment order after a payment hearing.

Added effective January 1, 2002.

Commentary

A judgment shall be entered forthwith upon the decision of the judge or the verdict of the jury. On a verdict, or on a judge's decision announced at the conclusion of a bench trial that requires payment of damages, the judge should hold a payment hearing and order payment to the prevailing party unless the defendant is "judgment proof" or unable to pay. See Standard 7:03. The court should also address the disposition of any bond posted by the appealing party. The court shall promptly furnish each party with written notice of the court's judgment and order of payment along with the scheduled date of a hearing to measure compliance or ability to pay.

If, after a jury-waived trial, the judge decides that the interests of justice require reserving decision, the judge, upon reaching a decision, should, pursuant to Standard 7:04, order payment and schedule a payment hearing within thirty days or shortly thereafter. The payment hearing should take place in the court where the original small claim was filed unless the judge retains jurisdiction in his or her court.

8:04. Motions to Allow Apparently Late Filed Appeals

The court shall permit appeals to proceed only if the appealing party can demonstrate that the appeal was filed within ten days from actual receipt of notice.

Added effective January 1, 2002.

Commentary

The clerk-magistrate's office must accept for docketing any notice of a claim for a trial by judge or jury of six, even if it appears that the appealing party is filing after the deadline of ten days from receipt of judgment has expired. Morales v. Commonwealth, 424 Mass. 1010 (1997); Davis v. Tabachinick, 425 Mass. 1010 (1997). The clerk-magistrate shall return to the appealing party who appears to be filing late the filing fees and appeal bond, and the clerk-magistrate shall inform the party that he or she must file a motion, with notice to the opposing party, to allow the appeal to go forward. A judge must hear the motion. Uniform Small Claims Rule 10(a).

The court should allow an appeal to proceed only if the appealing party can demonstrate that the appeal was filed within ten days from actual receipt of notice. There is no authority to enlarge the time for filing beyond ten days.

8:05. Further Appellate Rights

In the District Court or Boston Municipal Court, the case may be appealed to the Appellate Division if the judge, in the judge's discretion, submits a question of law to the Appellate Division, but only in the form of a report of a case stated. In the Housing Court, further appeal is to the appeals court.

Added effective January 1, 2002.

Commentary

After a jury trial or a jury-waived trial in the Housing Court, the losing party may appeal to the Appeals Court as in any Superior Court civil jury trial. Uniform Small Claims Rule 10(e). There is no such option in the District Court or the Boston Municipal Court. G.L. c. 218, § 23; Trust Insurance Company v. Bruce at Park Chiropractic Clinic, 430 Mass. 607, 610 (2000).

In the District Court or the Boston Municipal Court neither party has a right to a report of a question of law to the Appellate Division, but the judge may report a question to the Appellate Division in the form of a case stated. G.L. c.218, s. 23. Such reports are limited to questions of law only. Questions of fact or discretion may not be reported.

In the Housing Court, the notice of appeal must be filed within ten days of judgment. Uniform Small Claims Rule 10(e).

ENFORCEMENT OF JUDGMENTS
Standards 9:00 through 9:05

9:00. Enforcement of Judgments—General

In order for the small claims procedure to be effective, the parties must have some assurance that the judgment will be satisfied unless the defendant is judgment proof or unable to pay. To that end, the court should take an active role in the enforcement of judgments. Institution of supplementary proceedings should not be required to satisfy a small claims judgment.

Amended effective January 1, 2002.

Commentary

Probably the most frequent complaint of small claims plaintiffs who have had judgments rendered in their favor is the difficulty they encounter in enforcing that judgment. After devoting substantial time, effort, and out-of-pocket expense to the prosecution of their cases, successful plaintiffs too often find themselves unable to collect payment. Historically, the courts have required these plaintiffs to activate each step in the enforcement proceedings. In many respects, this requirement has proven to be too complex for the average plaintiff. Given the relatively small amount of money that is usually involved in small claims, many plaintiffs become discouraged and decide that it is not worth the further time and effort needed to continue to pursue payment from the defendant.

The court therefore should assume a more active role in the enforcement process. The recent amendments to the Uniform Small Claims Rules intend that more active role and eliminate the necessity of formal show cause or supplementary process hearings in most cases. Although there will inevitably be some judgments that will ultimately prove to be uncollectible (e.g. because the person's source of income is not subject to execution), there are specific things that the court may do to speed up the enforcement process and make it more effective. These include:

• requiring strict compliance with the automatic payment hearing procedure sent with the Notice of Payment Hearing;

• scheduling a compliance hearing or hearings after entering a payment order so that the burden is not on the plaintiff to get the case back on the list;

• requiring strict compliance in completing the financial disclosure form and requiring additional financial information when warranted, including, but not limited to, income tax returns, payroll stubs, production of bank books, contributions to retirement funds, and payments to creditors; and

• holding the defendant in contempt after a hearing before a judge.

If the defendant moves to the jurisdiction of another court at any time during the process of enforcing a payment order, the small claim may be transferred at the request of the plaintiff to the court in the judicial district to which the defendant has moved for further enforcement actions. This matter should not automatically be transferred but may be transferred if requested by the plaintiff. Uniform Small Claims Rule 9 (b).

9:01. Compliance Review Hearings

If the court has entered a payment order after holding a payment hearing, it should in most instances schedule review hearings to monitor compliance with its order.

Added effective January 1, 2002.

Commentary

In most cases where payment orders have been entered after a payment hearing, the court should schedule a compliance review hearing or a series of hearings. The court should play this pro-active role rather than placing the burden on the plaintiff to have the case placed back on the list. At the time of scheduling the review, the court can inform the plaintiff that he or she can cancel the hearing if payment is made prior to the scheduled date.

If the defendant fails to appear at any compliance review hearing, the court should invoke the procedures for a *capias* or order to show cause set forth in Standard 9:02. If both parties are present and the

court determines there is noncompliance with the payment order, the court may consider one or more of the following steps:

• requiring the defendant to fill out a new financial statement to determine ability to pay and whether any of the defendant's income is now exempt;

• revising the payment order and setting a new review date;

• referring the case immediately, or, where justice so requires, at a later date, to a judge for a contempt hearing.

9:02. Arrest and Show Cause Procedures

When a defendant fails to appear at a payment hearing or a compliance review hearing or the court receives information from the plaintiff that the defendant has not complied with a payment order, the court should take immediate steps to bring the defendant before the court.

Added effective January 1, 2002.

Commentary

Should a party who has the ability to pay fail to satisfy a payment order, the principal tool available to the court is contempt proceedings. In all instances, once an order for payment has been made, the defendant should be informed that failure to make payment may result in the defendant being held in contempt of court for failure to comply, and, that upon a finding of contempt, he or she may be fined or imprisoned. No contempt proceedings should be commenced within the ten day appeal period.

If the defendant fails to appear at a scheduled payment hearing, then the court may issue a *capias* for the defendant's arrest. If the court is satisfied that the defendant received the notice of payment hearing in the mail, the court has authority to order the *capias* if the defendant fails to appear; more formal notice, including in-hand service, is not required. In certain circumstances, the court may schedule a show cause hearing in lieu of issuing a *capias*. This procedure should only be utilized if and when the court, after appropriate inquiry, is uncertain as to whether the defendant may be in contempt of court and therefore arrest would be inappropriate or where the court believes there may be deficiencies in the notice to the defendant. Service of a notice to show cause must comply with Uniform Small Claims Rule 9.

Since a sheriff has no means of determining who is an officer of a corporation and thus may be liable for arresting the wrong person, a *capias* issued against a corporation or trust should state the name of the specific officer, trustee, or agent against whom the payment order was made and whom the law treats as the contemnor. (See G.L. c. 224, ss. 15,16, and Standard 7:02.) In such situations, the contemnor should be named in the *capias* in his representative capacity—e.g. "Jane H. Jones, as President of ABC, Inc."

Once the court has ordered a *capias*, the clerk-magistrate's office should issue it immediately. The small claims form of *capias* should expire in all courts after one year. This period of time should be sufficient for the sheriff or constable to bring the defendant before the court. Historically, shorter periods of time have proven insufficient and have required additional pleadings and court appearances to obtain a new *capias*. This one year period should eliminate additional court appearances and delays in bringing the defendants before the court.

If a plaintiff presents the court with *ex parte* evidence that the defendant has not complied with a payment order, the court should schedule a compliance hearing with written notice to the defendant, or, if the noncompliance appears willful, the court may schedule at the plaintiff's request a show cause hearing.

9:03. Contempt

Once the defendant is before the court on a *capias* or order to show cause, the court should expeditiously hold a contempt hearing. Only a judge may fine or imprison a defendant.

Added effective January 1, 2002.

Commentary

When the defendant comes before the court on a *capias* or order to show cause, a contempt hearing shall be held and the court shall take such action permitted by law as it deems appropriate to the end that orders for payment are complied with promptly and satisfaction of the judgment in the case is not frustrated. Uniform Small Claim Rule 9 (a). The defendant should understand the serious point to which the proceedings have progressed. Thus, when the debtor is before the court on arrest, the fact that he or she is under arrest should be made clear to the debtor. The court should hear the matter even if the debtor is brought in on a day other than one scheduled for small claims or enforcement of judgments. This procedure is recommended because, if chronic debtors are aware that they will be arrested only on that day, they may make themselves unavailable. If the court cannot, or in the interest of justice should not, hear the case that day, the court has the power to set bail.

Only a judge can find contempt, fine, and imprison a defendant; remedies short of imprisonment or punitive fine may be administered by a clerk-magistrate or assistant clerk-magistrate. Uniform Small Claim Rule 9(b), as recently amended. A judge considering incarceration as the remedy for contempt has two options. The first is to issue a traditional civil contempt ruling whereby the defendant is held in jail only so long as the court's order for payment or other terms set by the judge to purge the contempt are not complied with. In a civil contempt proceeding, due process requires that the court advise the defendant of the particulars of the charge against him or her, that the defendant have a reasonable opportunity to be heard in reply, including offering testimony and calling witnesses, and that the defendant has the right to have retained counsel represent him or her. Petition of Crystal, 330 Mass. 583 (1933). There is no right to trial by jury. Matter of DeSaulnier, 360 Mass. 769 (1971).

The judge's second option is to proceed under the quasi-criminal provisions of G.L. c. 224, s. 18. Under this procedure, the defendant may be punished by not more than thirty days in the common jail or a fine of not more than $200.00. Because of the punitive nature of the sanction, more extensive due process is required.

9:04. Attachment

Pretrial attachment is not available in small claims actions. Post-judgment attachment may be permitted where necessary to secure satisfaction of the judgment.

Amended effective January 1, 2002.

Commentary

Pretrial attachment is not permitted for a small claim. Attachment after judgment may be granted by the court in accordance with statutory provisions and applicable civil rules. Uniform Small Claims Rule 6. This apparently means that in lieu of levy of execution (see Standard 9:04), a judgment creditor may, as part of a civil action brought on the small claims judgment (see G.L. c. 235, s. 14), obtain an attachment (see G.L. c. 223, ss. 42–132) or trustee process (see G.L. c. 246) to secure the amount of the judgment.

In small claims, a real estate attachment may not be granted to secure a judgment of $20.00 or less. G.L. c. 223, s. 42.

9:05. Execution

An execution shall be issued only when requested.

Amended effective January 1, 2002.

Commentary

Executions obtained in small claims can be very useful to a judgment creditor in realizing its judgment against the defendant. When an execution is requested by a judgment creditor, the execution shall be issued by the court without inquiry as to the reason why the judgment creditor is requesting the execution. Executions are not needed for the payment hearing nor for the issuance of a *capias*. A small claim action need not be dismissed when the judgment creditor requests an execution. Execution shall issue fifteen court days after the date of judgment (Uniform Small Claims Rule 7 [f]) unless the case is appealed for jury trial. G.L. c. 235, s. 16. A plaintiff who has obtained an execution need not surrender it to enforce a payment order, but may not obtain a double satisfaction. Uniform Small Claims Rule 7(i).

Most often, executions in small claims are needed for extrajudicial purposes. The Registry of Motor Vehicles requires an execution to suspend a defendant's license for an unpaid property damage judgment. G.L. c. 90, s. 22A. Motor vehicle insurance companies often require an execution before they will pay a contested claim. In these cases, the plaintiff should be informed to request an execution.

APPENDICES

Appendix A: The Small Claims Statute

218:21. Power to establish rules of procedure; venue; jurisdictional amount; hearings; damages and penalties.

Section 21. There shall be within the district court department and the Boston municipal court department a simple, informal and inexpensive procedure, hereinafter called the procedure, for the determination, according to the rules of substantive law, of claims in the nature of contract or tort, other than slander and libel, in which the plaintiff does not claim as debt or damages more than $7,000; provided, however, that a city or town may bring an action under section 35 of chapter 60 for the collection of unpaid taxes on personal property or an action which shall not exceed $15,000; and provided further, that said dollar limitation shall not apply to an action for property damage caused by a motor vehicle, and for a review of judgments upon such claims when justice so requires. The procedure shall not be exclusive, but shall be alternative to the formal procedure for civil actions begun by summons and complaint.

The chief justice for the district court department shall make uniform rules with respect to the procedure applicable to all the courts within said department, and the chief justice for the Boston municipal court department shall make rules for the Boston municipal court department, all such rules being subject to the approval of the supreme judicial court.

Actions under this section and sections twenty-two to twenty-five inclusive, shall be brought, at the option of the plaintiff, in the judicial district where either the plaintiff or the defendant lives or has his usual place of business or employment; provided, however, that actions brought against a landlord or lessor of land or tenements rented for residential purposes, and arising out of such property or rental, may also be brought in the judicial district in which the property is located.

Notwithstanding the foregoing, each court within the district court department shall have civil jurisdiction of such actions commenced in such court which should have been brought in some other court, to the extent that the action may be heard and disposed of by the court in which it was begun, if the venue of said action is waived or, if venue requirements are not waived, the court may, on motion of any party, order the action, with all papers relating thereto, transferred for hearing and disposition to the court in which the action should have been commenced. Said action shall thereupon be entered and prosecuted in such court as if it had originally commenced therein, and all prior proceedings otherwise regularly taken shall thereafter be valid. An action may be commenced under this section if the initial amount of damages claimed is $7,000 or less or is an action by a city or town under said section 35 of said chapter 60 for the collection of unpaid taxes on personal property or an action by a city or town which shall not exceed $15,000 for property damage caused by a motor vehicle regardless of the amount of the claims notwithstanding that the court may award double or treble damages in accordance with the provisions of any general or special law.

Actions brought under sections twenty-one to twenty-five, inclusive, may be heard in the first instance by a clerk-magistrate of the district court department or the Boston municipal court department. For the purpose of hearing such property damage claims caused by a motor vehicle the procedure established shall provide for all such claims to be heard on one evening every other week, and on one Saturday on the alternative week, unless otherwise agreed to by all parties in such actions in accordance with the provisions of section thirty-four O of chapter ninety.

In the hearing and disposition of any claim for money damages within the jurisdiction of such procedure, the Boston municipal and district court departments shall have all equity powers and jurisdiction conferred by sections one, one A and two, and clause (1) of section three of chapter two hundred and fourteen.

218:22. Procedure.

Section 22. The procedure shall include the beginning of actions with an entry fee of $20 for claims of $500 or less and $30 for claims of greater than $500, plus the surcharge required by section four C of chapter two hundred and sixty-two, but without summons and complaint and without requirement, except by special order of court, of any pleading other than a concise written statement of the claim. The procedure shall include notice by registered mail instead of the mode of service heretofore required, and shall include provisions for early hearing. The procedure may include the modification of any or all rules of pleading and practice, anything contained in other chapters, sections or acts notwithstanding, and may include a stay of the entry of judgment or of the issue of execution and authority in the court, in its discretion, after proper inquiry, to order payment to the prevailing party of the amount found due on or before a day stated or by instalments, to modify, extend or vacate such order and, in its discretion, to enforce such order by contempt proceedings, substantially in the manner provided in chapter two hundred and twenty-four, and to provide therefor in the rules for the procedure. Said rules for the procedure may provide for the elimination of any or all fees and costs, and that costs shall be in the discretion of the court. In causes begun under the procedure, the court may on application for cause shown issue writs of attachment of property.

At the commencement of an action under the procedure the plaintiff shall be informed that such action may be submitted for mediation and resolution at the request of either party and with the agreement of both parties. The clerk-magistrate shall make appropriate note of any agreement so reached, and entry of judgment shall be made by the court. Any action which is not resolved by agreement may, at the request of any party, be heard by a clerk-magistrate under the provisions of sections twenty-one to twenty-five, inclusive; provided, however, that cases heard before a jury of six must be heard by a justice.

The procedure shall include the beginning of actions with an entry fee of $30 for claims of $500 or less, $40 for claims of greater than $500 but less than or equal to $2000, $90 for claims of greater than $2000 but less than or equal to $5000, and $140 for claims greater than $5000, plus the surcharge required by section four C of chapter two hundred and sixty-two, but without summons and complaint and without requirement, except by special order of court, of any pleading other than a concise written statement of the claim.

218:23. Initial determination of cause; removal; claim for trial by jury; bond or deposit; finding as evidence; report to appellate division.

Section 23. Every cause begun under the procedure shall be determined initially in the district court department. No such cause may be removed for trial in the superior court department. In any action for property damage caused by a motor vehicle where the action is transferred to the regular civil docket in the district court department by the insurer and the unpaid party recovers a judgment for any amount due and payable by the insurer, the court shall assess against the insurer in addition thereto, costs and reasonable attorney's fees.

A plaintiff beginning a cause under the procedure shall be deemed to have waived a trial by jury and any right of appeal to a jury of six session in the district court department. If, however, said cause shall be appealed to a jury of six session in the district court department by the defendant as hereinafter provided, the plaintiff shall have the same right to claim a trial by a jury of six.

The defendant may, within ten days after receipt of the magistrate's finding, file in the court where the cause was determined a claim of trial by jury, or in the alternative for a trial before a single justice and shall file his affidavit that there are questions of law and fact in the cause requiring a trial by jury or a single justice, with the specifications thereof, and that such trial is intended in good faith.

Trials by jury of six in the district court department shall proceed in accordance with the provisions of law applicable to trials by jury in the superior court department, except that each party shall be entitled to two preemptory challenges. Jurors shall be drawn from the pool of jurors available for the jury sessions in civil cases in the superior court department.

The chief justice of the district court department shall designate at least one court in each region for the purpose of hearing cases where a claim for trial by a jury of six or by a single justice is entered. Claims for trial by a jury of six or by a single justice from courts within Suffolk county shall be held in the Boston municipal court department or district courts in Suffolk county or, with the approval of the chief justice of the district court department, may be held in those district courts whose judicial districts adjoin Suffolk county as are designated by said chief justice. Notwithstanding the foregoing, the chief justice for administration and management may designate the facilities of any other department of the trial court for trial by jury of six or by a single justice in the district court department or the Boston municipal court department. The Boston municipal court department shall be authorized to hear such appeals for the district courts in Suffolk county.

A defendant's claim for trial by jury or by a single justice shall be accompanied by twenty-five dollars for the entry of the cause in the court of the department to which the case has been appealed, and a bond in the penal sum of one hundred dollars, with such surety or sureties as may be approved by the plaintiff or the clerk or an assistant clerk of the district court department, payable to the other party or parties to the cause, conditioned to satisfy any judgment and costs which may be entered against him in the jury of six proceeding or a proceeding before a single justice in said cause waiting thirty days after the entry thereof. Notwithstanding the foregoing, in any action brought by a tenant of residential premises pursuant to the provisions of section fifteen B of chapter one hundred and eighty-six, bond shall be given in an amount equal to three times the amount of the security deposit or balance thereof to which the tenant is entitled, plus interest at the rate of five percent from the date when such payment became due, together with court costs and an amount equal to a reasonable attorney's fee for service which had been performed by an attorney, if any, or which may be expected to be performed by an attorney during the pendency of the appeal.

The clerk shall forthwith transmit such original papers or attested copies thereof as the rules for the procedure may provide, and the court of the department to which the case has been appealed may require pleadings pursuant to the District/Municipal Courts Rules of Civil Procedure, but the cause may be marked for trial on the list of causes advanced for speedy trial by jury. A finding for the plaintiff in the district court department shall be prima facie evidence for the plaintiff in the trial by jury of six or before a single justice. At such trial the plaintiff may, but need not, introduce evidence.

No bond shall be required of a county, town or other municipal corporation, or of a board, officer or employee thereof represented by the city solicitor, town counsel or other officer having similar duties, or of a political subdivision, or of a party who has given bond according to law to dissolve an attachment or of a defendant in an action of tort arising out of the ownership, operation, maintenance, control or use of a motor vehicle or trailer as defined in section one of chapter ninety if the payment of any judgement for costs which may be entered against him is secured, in whole or in part, by a motor vehicle liability bond or policy or a deposit as provided in section thirty-four D of chapter ninety.

The court shall waive the requirement of a bond in the amount of one hundred dollars if it is satisfied that the defendant has insufficient funds available to him to furnish the necessary bond and that the defendant's appeal is not frivolous.

No party to a cause under the procedure shall be entitled to a report. If the court is of the opinion that a question of law requires review, it may submit the matter, in the form of a report of a case stated, to the appellate division.

A judgment in an action for property damage caused by a motor vehicle commenced under the procedure shall not have a res judicata, collateral estoppel or other preclusive effect on any other action arising out of the same cause of action.

218:24. Transfer to regular docket.

Section 24. The court may, in its discretion, transfer a cause begun under the procedure to the regular civil docket for formal hearing and determination as though it had been begun by summons and complaint, and may impose terms upon such transfer.

218:25. Costs; discretion of court.

Section 25. In any civil action begun by summons and complaint which might have been begun under the procedure, the rules for the procedure may provide, or the court may by special order direct, that the costs to be recovered by the plaintiff, if he prevails, shall be eliminated in whole or in part.

Appendix B: The Uniform Small Claims Rules

Trial Court Rule III
Uniform Small Claims Rules
(Effective January 1, 2002)

Publishers Note: See Uniform Small Claims Rules 1 to 10 which precede the Small Claims Standards

Appendix C: SJC Advisory Committee Opinion

SUPREME JUDICIAL COURT

ADVISORY COMMITTEE ON ETHICAL OPINIONS
FOR CLERKS OF THE COURTS
1350 COURTHOUSE
BOSTON, MASSACHUSETTS 02108

617–557–1161

95–6

November 8, 1995

Dear Register

This is in response to your letter of September 8, 1995, in which you request advice from the Committee on a number of questions concerning the practice of law. You are the Register of Probate in the Division of the Probate and Family Court Department. You refer the Committee to S.J.C. Rule 3:02(2) which prohibits all Clerks of Court, Registers of Probate and the Land Court Recorder, and their assistants and employees from "engaging in the practice of law during the time they hold such office or employment."

Your employees, clerks and assistant registers have asked you to define what constitutes the practice of law pursuant to the rule. You ask this Committee: "1) Should this rule be interpreted to preclude any Clerk, Register, Recorder and their assistants and employees who are attorneys from engaging in the private practice of law;

or

2) should we read it in a broader context to apply to all the identified employees, regardless of whether they are attorneys, in their daily interactions with the members of the Bar and the general public in their roles as providers of access to the judicial system."

You further ask that, if the prohibition is interpreted in the broader context, the Committee provide guidance on the parameters of what constitutes legal practice. You describe five scenarios concerning which you request specific guidance. The scenarios, which we set forth below, are examples of situations which occur daily at the divisions in your department. With respect to each of the examples, you ask whether the Committee's interpretation of the "practice of law" would differ if the registry employee were responding to an attorney rather than a pro se litigant.

The five scenarios follow.

I. In response to a litigant's inquiry, a registry employee will suggest "the best" or "preferred" manner in which the litigant can proceed in the action.

Scenario 1: A grandmother comes to the counter to ask for help; she wants her grandson to come and live with her because the child's mother is addicted to drugs and unable to care for the son. The child's father is dead and has left money for the child but mother is spending it quickly on drugs. The registry employee tells the grandmother what the possibilities are with regard to filing a petition for guardianship of a minor of the person and the estate, or just the person and explains the need for filing a bond and the various types of sureties on the bond. After asking a few more questions of the grandmother, the registry employee suggests she file a guardianship of minor of the person and the estate, and a bond with sureties.

II. In response to a litigant's inquiry, the registry employee will advise the litigant of the options available to them and procedures which the litigant should follow.

Scenario 2: A husband calls the court to ask for no-fault divorce forms and when the registry employee asks which type of no-fault divorce, the husband responds he didn't know there was more than one. The registry employee distinguishes the Joint Petition for Divorce, Irretrievable Breakdown pursuant to c. 208, § 1A, and the Complaint for Divorce used for Irretrievable Breakdown pursuant to c. 208, § 1B, as well as the fault divorces. The registry employee further enumerates the forms and materials required for each type and outlines the process and time lines for the two Irretrievable Breakdown actions.

III. In a typical incident of "counter assistance," the registry employee may do any or all of the following: explain terminology used in forms and the descriptions of the legal process; advise how to complete the form; actually complete the form; or explain a registry practice, i.e., marking up motions, or making service.

Scenario 3: A pro se litigant arrives at the counter saying her former husband is not paying the medical bills for her children as he was ordered in the divorce judgment. She has no money, speaks with an accent, and says the collection agency is threatening to bring her to court. She asks what she can do to make her former husband pay these bills. The registry employee gives her a complaint for contempt form and tells her to fill it out. The litigant begins to ask questions about the form, and the registry employee recognizes the litigant is illiterate. The registry employee reads the information requests on the form and fills it out quoting the plaintiff. The registry employee files the complaint and gives a copy of it along with a summons to the litigant and tells her how it should be served.

Scenario 4: A Vietnamese mother comes to the counter with bandages on her arms and face, two children bearing bruises on their arms and legs, and another woman. The mother wants to file a Complaint for Protection from Abuse, and to keep her address secret from her boyfriend. She speaks no English, and the woman with her speaks English but can not write it. The registry employee, through the English-speaking friend, asks the questions on the form and completes the form. Again, through the interpreter, the registry employee asks for a description of the incident of violence, and completes the affidavit based upon what the interpreter states.

Scenario 5: Pro se parties have come to the court for a wife's motion for temporary support in a Complaint for Civil Support action. The judge had referred them to the Family Service Office asking that financial statements be completed for each party. The Probation Officer learns that the wife has previously paid all the bills and kept the accounts because the husband cannot add and subtract. The Probation Officer asks the husband the questions on the financial statement, writes the answers, and gives the completed financial statement to the husband for signature.

We note at the beginning of our discussion, that although you refer the Committee to the prohibition on the practice of law contained in S.J.C. Rule 3:02, this Committee is only empowered and charged with interpreting the Code of Professional Responsibility for Clerks of Court. Canon 3 of that Code, however, provides similarly that "[A] Clerk–Magistrate shall not engage in the practice of law".

The Committee reads Canon 3's primary purpose as assuring that court employees do not practice law for private clients, whether or not for a fee, either during or after their normal hours of employment by the Court. Such a prohibition both assures that court employees devote their full time to their duties, see Canon 3, and that they avoid private business dealings which could suggest a lack of impartiality in their role as court employees. See Canons 4(C) and 5(C)(1). It is, in the Committee's view, an integral part of a court employee's mandate to be sufficiently skilled and qualified to provide service to litigants and their attorneys in their dealings with the Courts, and we do not read this Canon to suggest or require otherwise.

We do recognize that the Canons, in particular Canons 4 and 5, require clerks to remain impartial, and we can conceive of situations where the degree of advocacy-oriented assistance provided to a litigant would not only call these Canons into operation but possibly raise the risk that the litigant would unjustifiably rely upon a clerk's advice as he or she might that of an attorney, potentially implicating Canon 3 under a far narrower construction directed at preventing this type of consequence. As with questions regarding the "unauthorized practice of law" in other contexts, such determinations are necessarily made on the facts of each case. See In the Matter of the Shoe Manufacturers Protective Assn., Inc., 295 Mass. 369, 372 (1936).

With these interpretations in mind, we have reviewed the five scenarios. Each involves court employees being asked for assistance in the context of their jobs. In general, the assistance needed is advice concerning court procedures. In several scenarios, the assistance involves the completion of forms for a pro se litigant. In our opinion, the employees providing the assistance described in scenarios 2, 4, and 5 would not constitute the practice of law in violation of Canon 3 (or S.J.C. Rule 3:02). Our response on this issue would not differ if the requests for assistance were made by an attorney rather than a pro se litigant.

Under a literal reading of scenario 1, we perceive potential problems. In your description of this scenario, the clerk not only identifies and describes options and provides appropriate forms and assistance in completing them, but recommends or chooses the specific manner in which the litigant should proceed. We recommend that court employees provide such guidance and information as allows the litigant to make an informed choice among procedures, leaving however, the decision to the litigant.

Portions of scenario 3 are also troublesome for similar reasons. In that scenario, in response to an inquiry from a pro se litigant, the "registry employee gives her a complaint for contempt form and tells her to fill it out." Again, in our view, it is not the role of a court employee to advise a litigant to bring a problem before the court or to suggest the specific manner of proceeding. The litigants must decide for themselves whether and how to proceed. Prior to making these decisions, however, they are entitled to receive a wide range of assistance and guidance from court employees.

You should be aware that other provisions of the Code may also be implicated in these scenarios and in other circumstances when assistance is requested from court employees. One of the principal themes underlying the canons of the Code of Professional Responsibility for Clerks of the Courts is the principle of impartiality. Your employees should be reminded that in providing help they must be evenhanded. Under Canon 4, they must be and appear to be impartial at all times. They must provide guidance and assistance in an equitable way to all parties to a proceeding.

In the opinion of the Committee, providing assistance with filling out forms and offering procedural advice clearly do not run afoul of the prohibition on the practice of law. Drafting documents, taking over a case and becoming an advocate on behalf of a litigant would clearly violate the prohibition. Other situations may need to be addressed on a case by case basis.

CPB:pg

Appendix D: Sample Instructions to Litigants Before Calling the List.

Introductory Remarks.

This is the small claims session of this court. Please listen to these instructions so that you will know what to do when your case is called. Please answer "here" when I call your name or the name of your business. The plaintiff is the person or business that brought the small claim. The defendant is the one being sued.

If Both Litigants are Present.

First, I will give instructions on what to do if both sides are here. Essentially, you may settle the case without a trial, or you may have a trial.

Settlement or Mediation. If the defendant admits owing what is claimed, or if you think you can settle the matter between yourselves, you should talk outside the courtroom after your names are called. If you cannot reach an agreement by yourselves, but both sides feel an agreement is possible with outside assistance, the court has mediators available for this purpose. If a voluntary settlement is reached, a form will be provided and your written agreement will be the court's order in this case. As soon as the settlement is approved by the court, you will be given a copy and may depart.

Trial. If you cannot settle the case, you should return to the courtroom and wait for your trial. When your case is called for trial, you will be given instructions as to how to proceed by the adjudicator. Your case will either be decided today or will be "taken under advisement". If it is taken under advisement, you will be notified of the decision by mail.

If Only One Side is Present.

Defaults. If, when I call your case, the plaintiff is here but the defendant is not, the plaintiff will win automatically by default. The court will review your complaint before deciding what the amount of the judgment should be. The defendant will be ordered to pay you within thirty days, and if this is not done, both parties will be required to attend a payment hearing that will be set by the court. You will receive a written judgment in the mail with additional instructions as to what will happen if you do not receive payment.

Dismissals. If, when I call your case, the defendant is here but the plaintiff is not, the case will be dismissed. You will receive a written judgment of the dismissal in the mail. Oftentimes parties who did not appear request, at a later date, that the court "vacate" the default or dismissal because they had a good excuse for not being present. The court will listen to both sides before allowing or denying these requests.

Other Matters.

If you are here for other small claims matters (motions, payment hearings, review, etc.) you should remain in the courtroom until your case has been heard by the court. Please listen carefully for your name or the name of your business. If you do not hear your name, please let me know at the end.

Appendix E: Sample Instructions to Litigants Before Trial.

For those of you who have never before been in small claims court, let me explain our procedures. My name is _____, and I am _____ of this court.

When your case is called for trial, you will be sworn in. The plaintiff—the party who is suing—will then tell me his or her story, as you would tell it to a friend. If either side has photographs or anything in writing that you wish to show the court, such as receipts, leases, or contracts, please show such evidence as you tell me your story.

Though the rules of evidence are relaxed in small claims, my sworn duty, nevertheless, is to follow the law. The most important rule of law here is that the plaintiff must prove the claim by a preponderance—a majority—of the evidence. This is like a set of balance scales: the plaintiff's proof is put on one side and the defendant's on the other. If the defendant's side is heavier, or if the scales are evenly balanced, the plaintiff loses. It does not matter how honestly and certainly the plaintiff believes he or she is right—the law says you must *prove* the claim in order to win.

Please be brief if you can, but take as much time as you need to tell me your side of the case. When you think you are through, I will ask if there is anything else you wish to tell me that you have not already told me—and please, that is the time you should tell me anything else you wish to add. After this, you then must remain quiet while this same procedure is repeated with the defendant, the person being sued.

After both sides are finished, a decision and a payment order will be entered. I may announce my decision from the bench, but you will still receive a written confirmation in the mail. If I announce that I will take the case under advisement, that means that I want to give the case some more thought, and you will be notified of my decision by mail.

Remember, when your case is called, please come forward and bring all witnesses you have here with you today. Everyone will be sworn in, and we will be ready to try your case.

(Taken from National Conference of Special Court Judges, American Bar Association, Small Claims Form Guide Book s. 28 [E.A. Rissman ed.].)

IV. UNIFORM RULE REQUIRING DISCLOSURE OF PENDING AND CONCLUDED CARE OR CUSTODY MATTERS

Uniform Rule Requiring Disclosure of Pending and Concluded Care or Custody Matters

Applicable to Boston Municipal, District, Juvenile, Probate and Family and Superior Court Departments

Upon the filing or issuance of any petition or complaint involving the care, custody, visitation, or change of name of a child, pursuant to G.L. c. 119 (except delinquency actions under G.L. c. 119), G.L. c. 190B, G.L. c. 207, G.L. c. 208, G.L. c. 209, G.L, c. 209A, G.L. c. 209C, G.L. c. 210, or any other provision of law concerning the care or custody of a child, the plaintiff shall file an affidavit. Such affidavit shall contain relevant information concerning such child including, but not limited to, a list of all other known proceedings involving the care or custody of said child which are pending or have been concluded in any court in the Commonwealth of Massachusetts or in any court in any other state or foreign country. All other parties appearing in the action shall likewise file such affidavit. No pleading shall be accepted for filing without such affidavit unless the plaintiff or other party has already filed an affidavit, or unless the court, on written motion for good cause shown, extends the time for filing such affidavit. No such extension shall exceed 30 days. A copy of the affidavit shall be furnished by the plaintiff or other party filing it to all other parties to the action. Upon the discovery of new information subsequent to the filing of such affidavit, the plaintiff or other party shall file a revised affidavit.

The plaintiff shall attach to the affidavit certified copies of each pleading and of any determination entered in any care or custody proceeding which the plaintiff knows of, or has participated in, involving the child in any court in any state other than the Commonwealth of Massachusetts or in any foreign country, unless the court, on written motion for good cause shown, extends the time for filing such pleadings and determinations. No such extension shall exceed 30 days, unless the court, on written motion for good cause shown, finds an extension in excess of 30 days is warranted. All other parties shall attach to the affidavit certified copies of each pleading and of any determination entered in any care or custody proceeding as required above, unless previously filed by the plaintiff or unless the plaintiff has been granted an extension for filing such pleadings and determinations.

The court, upon written motion of any party, or upon its own motion, may order the impoundment of an affidavit which discloses the adoption of a child. Impounded affidavits shall not be available for public inspection, but shall be available to the court and its employees, attorneys whose appearances are entered in a case, the parties, the Department of Social Services or its licensed adoption agencies, and such other persons whom the court, upon written motion, may permit.

The affidavit shall be on a form prescribed by the Chief Administrative Justice of the Trial Court, which upon its filing, shall be deemed in compliance with the provisions of G.L. c. 209B, the Massachusetts Child Custody Jurisdiction Act.

Amended effective July 1, 1984; amended July 1, 1993, effective September 1, 1993; amended effective August 1, 1995; amended June 24, 2009, effective July 1, 2009.

Form OCAJ-1. Affidavit Disclosing Care or Custody Proceedings

BEFORE COMPLETING, READ INSTRUCTIONS ON BACK OF PART 2
TYPE OR PRINT WITH A BALLPOINT PEN—PRESS HARD

AFFIDAVIT DISCLOSING CARE OR CUSTODY PROCEEDING Pursuant to Trial Court Rule IV	TRIAL COURT OF MASSACHUSETTS Name of Case _____	DOCKET NUMBER

BMC	District Court	Juvenile Court	Prob & Family Court	Superior Court
Division	Division	Division	Division	Division

Section 1 — I, _____ hereby declare, to the best of my knowledge, information, and belief that all information on this form is true and complete:

Section 2 — The name(s) of the child(ren) whose care or custody is at issue in this case are:

A. _____ B. _____ C. _____
(LAST, FIRST)   (LAST, FIRST)   (LAST, FIRST)

Use only the letter appearing in front of the child's name above when referring to the child in completing the remaining sections.

Section 3 — The party filing this affidavit may request certain addresses to be kept confidential if the address is a shelter for battered persons and their dependent child(ren), or the party filing this affidavit believes that he/she or the child(ren) are in danger of physical or emotional abuse, or the party is filing an action under G.L. c. 209A. **If you believe that this provision applies to you, check the box at right, complete sections 10 and 11 on the reverse side of this page and DO NOT complete sections 4 and 5 below.** ☐

Section 4 — The address(es) of the above-named child(ren) whose care and custody is at issue in this case is/are:
Address(es):   Address
CHILD A _____
CHILD B _____
CHILD C _____

Section 5 — My address is: _____

Section 6 — I ☐ have ☐ have not participated in and I ☐ know ☐ do not know of other care or custody proceedings involving the above-named child(ren) in Massachusetts or in any state or country.

Certified copies of any pleadings or determinations in care a or custody proceeding outside of Massachusetts listed in Sections 7 and 8 must be filed with this affidavit unless already filed with this court or an extension for filing these documents has been granted by this court.

Section 7 — The following is a list of all pending or concluded proceedings I have participated in or know of involving the care or custody of the above-named child(ren):

Letter of Child	Court	Docket No.	Status	[W]itness [P]arty [O]ther [N]one
CHILD _____	_____	_____	_____	[ ]
CHILD _____	_____	_____	_____	[ ]
CHILD _____	_____	_____	_____	[ ]

Section 8 — The names and addresses of parties to care or custody proceedings involving any of the above-named child(ren) or those claiming a legal right to these child(ren) during the last two years (not including myself) are:

Letter of Child	Name of Party/Claimant	Current (or last known) Address of Party/Claimant
CHILD _____	_____	_____
CHILD _____	_____	_____
CHILD _____	_____	_____

Section 9 — If the box at the right is checked, this affidavit discloses the adoption of one or more of the above-named child(ren) and I am requesting the court to impound this affidavit. See instructions. ☐

This affidavit must be personally signed by the party listed in section 1 above, unless he/she is under 18 years of age or has been adjudged incompetent in which case the attorney of record must sign. A revised affidavit must be filed with the court if new information is discovered subsequent to this filing.

Signed this _____ day of _____, 20 _____ under the penalties of perjury.

X _____
SIGNATURE OF PARTY OR ATTORNEY OF RECORD FOR JUVENILE/INCOMPETENT   PRINTED NAME OF PERSON SIGNING

_____
ADDRESS OF ATTORNEY OF RECORD FOR JUVENILE/INCOMPETENT

THE PARTY FILING THIS AFFIDAVIT MUST FURNISH A COPY OF IT TO ALL OTHER PARTIES TO THIS ACTION.

OCAJ-1 TRC IV (07/95)

A D D R E S S E S   T O   B E   K E P T   C O N F I D E N T I A L

The party filing this affidavit may request certain address(es) to be kept confidential if the address is a shelter for battered persons and their dependent child(ren), **or** the party filing this affidavit believes that he/she or the child(ren) are in danger of physical **or** emotional abuse, **or** the party is filing an action under G.L. c. 209A. **If you checked the box in section 3 indicating that you believe the above provision applies to you, complete sections 10 and 11 below, and DO NOT complete sections 4 and 5.**

Section 10

The address(es) of the child(ren) listed in section 2 whose care or custody is at issue in this case are:

Child(ren)	Address(es)	Address(es) During Last 2 Years, If Different
Child A.	_____	_____
	Street Address	Street Address
	_____	_____
	City, State, Zip Code	City, State, Zip Code
Child B.	_____	_____
	Street Address	Street Address
	_____	_____
	City, State, Zip Code	City, State, Zip Code
Child C.	_____	_____
	Street Address	Street Address
	_____	_____
	City, State, Zip Code	City, State, Zip Code

Section 11

My address is: _____
Street Address, City, State, Zip Code

A D D R E S S E S   T O   B E   K E P T   C O N F I D E N T I A L

LIST OF ATTORNEYS AND GUARDIANS AD LITEM/INVESTIGATORS

Please list the names of all attorneys and guardians ad litem involved in the pending proceedings listed in section 7.

Section 12

1. ☐ _____
   Attorney(s) for child(ren). (Please specify if each child is represented by a different attorney.)
   ☐ _____
   ☐ _____

2. ☐ _____
   GAL(s)/Investigator(s) (Please indicate if a GAL has been appointed to represent a specific child.)
   ☐ _____
   ☐ _____

3. ☐ _____
   Attorney(s) for mother
   ☐ _____

4. ☐ _____
   Attorney(s) for father

(Fill Out Below If Applicable)

I, _____ , attorney for D.C.F. or its agent have ascertained from the above checked off attorney(s) and guardian(s) ad litem/investigators a willingness to accept an appointment from the court to represent the same party should the court elect to make such appointment.

_____
(Signature)

READ BEFORE COMPLETING THE AFFIDAVIT

A. WHAT IS AN "AFFIDAVIT DISCLOSING CARE OR CUSTODY PROCEEDING"?

It is a document signed under the penalties of perjury which lists information required by Trial Court Rule IV concerning children involved in a care or custody proceeding.

B. WHO MUST FILE THIS AFFIDAVIT?

The party to a petition (including a modification petition) or complaint involving the care, custody, visitation, or change of name of a child pursuant to G.L. c. 119 (except delinquency actions under G.L. c. 201, G.L. c. 207, G.L. c. 208, G.L. c. 209, G.L. c. 209A, G.L. c. 209C, G.L. c. 210, or any other provision of law concerning the care or custody of a child must file this affidavit.

This affidavit **must be signed by the party** unless the party is under 18 years of age or has been adjudged incompetent in which case the attorney of record must sign this affidavit on behalf of the juvenile or incompetent party.

C. WHEN MUST THIS AFFIDAVIT BE FILED?

The person filing the petition or complaint must file this affidavit at the time of filing and the other party must file this affidavit with the first pleading.

This affidavit should be submitted upon the filing of an application for a Child Requiring Assistance (CRA) pursuant to G.L. c. 119.

This affidavit need not be filed if the petition or complaint is for **support only.**

D. WHERE MUST THIS AFFIDAVIT BE FILED?

The completed affidavit must be filed, in person or by mail, with the Clerk-Magistrate or Register of Probate in the court in which this action is being brought.

E. WHEN MUST A REVISED AFFIDAVIT BE FILED?

A revised affidavit must be filed with the Clerk-Magistrate or Register of Probate if new information is discovered subsequent to the filing of this affidavit.

F. WHAT MUST BE FILED AS PART OF THIS AFFIDAVIT?

Certified copies of each pleading and of any determination entered in a foreign country or in a state other than Massachusetts must be filed with this affidavit unless these documents are on file with the court in this case, or an extension has been granted by the court for filing these documents.

INSTRUCTIONS FOR COMPLETING AFFIDAVIT

When completing this affidavit if additional space is needed for any of the sections, attach a separate sheet which includes your name (printed), the docket number and the sections to which you are referring. You must also sign and date the sheet.

The party filing this affidavit must complete the section entitled "Name of Case" and indicate the Court Department and Division in which the case is being brought. The docket number should also be listed, if known.

DO NOT COMPLETE SECTIONS 2, 3, 4, 8 AND 10 IF THIS AFFIDAVIT IS BEING FILED WITH A PETITION FOR ADOPTION.

Section 1	You must print your first and last name. If this affidavit is filed by an attorney on behalf of an incompetent person or a juvenile, the name of the party on which behalf this affidavit is being completed must be listed.
Section 2	List the names of all child(ren) involved in this care or custody proceeding. All future references to the child(ren) listed in this section should be with the letter in front of the child's name (e.g. If John Smith is listed next to the letter A, all references to John Smith will be as Child A).
Section 3	Check the box if this section applies to you. If this box is checked, do not complete Sections 4 and 5. You must complete Sections 10 and 11 on the reverse side of page 1.
Sections 4 & 5	List the present and all prior addresses during the last two years of the above-named child(ren) and your present address. If legal custody of a child has been awarded to a social service agency, list the name and address of the agency with legal custody.
Section 6	Check the appropriate box.
Section 7	List all pending or concluded proceedings which you have participated in or know of involving the care or custody of the child(ren) named in this affidavit. Indicate the letter of the child; the court in which the case was heard, the docket number, the person(s) to whom custody was awarded, and the date of the award, and the nature of your participation in the proceeding by listing "W" for witness, "P" for party, "O" for other or "N" for none. If specific information required in this section is not known, you or your attorney should contact the court where the case was heard to obtain such information . **In the case of a petition for adoption, list all information except the person(s) to whom custody was awarded, the date of the award and the nature of your participation. Under the heading "Status of Case", indicate type of case.**
Section 8	List the name(s) and current residential address(es), if known, otherwise the last known address(es) of parties to care or custody proceedings or persons claiming a legal right to the above-named child(ren) during the last two years. Do not include yourself.
Section 9	Check this box if this affidavit discloses the adoption of a child and you are requesting the court to impound this affidavit. If this provision is applicable, you should contact the Clerk-Magistrate or Register of Probate for assistance concerning the appropriate motion to be filed.
Sections 10 & 11	**COMPLETE ONLY IF YOU CHECKED THE BOX IN SECTION 3.** List the present and all prior addresses during the last two years of the child(ren) listed in Section 2 of this affidavit and your present address. If legal custody of a child has been awarded to a social service agency, list the name and address of the agency with legal custody.
Section 12	List the attorneys and guardians ad litem/investigators previously appointed in Section 7.
Signature	The party listed in Section 1 must date and sign this affidavit except for an incompetent or juvenile, in which case the attorney of record on behalf of the juvenile or incompetent party must date and sign this affidavit and print his/her name and address.

THIS AFFIDAVIT MUST BE FILED WITH THE COURT AND A COPY FURNISHED BY THE PARTY FILING IT TO ALL OTHER PARTIES TO THIS ACTION.

Amended July 1995.

V. PROCEDURE REGULATING THE ISSUANCE OF STANDING ORDERS

Procedure Regulating the Issuance of Standing Orders

The following procedure regulating the issuance of Standing Orders is hereby promulgated for use in all Departments of the Trial Court. The procedure establishes general requirements which are applicable to all Departments. If necessary, additional procedures to regulate matters of concern to individual departments may be promulgated on a departmental basis.

1. Effective forthwith, all Standing Orders, except those issued by the Administrative Justices of the Departments of the Trial Court, are hereby vacated and shall have no further effect.

2. Standing Orders presently in effect issued by the Administrative Justices shall be submitted to Lawyers' Weekly for publication and shall be forwarded to the office of each Clerk-Magistrate and Register in the Department.

3. No Standing Order shall be issued by a Justice of the Trial Court unless it has been submitted to and approved in writing by the Administrative Justice of that Department.

4. All proposed Standing Orders shall be submitted by the Administrative Justices for review by the Chief Administrative Justice no later than 30 days before their proposed effective date. The Chief Administrative Justice shall review the pro-

posed Standing Orders to ensure that they do not conflict with the Orders of other Departments.

5. When circumstances require immediate action, Standing Orders may be issued with the oral approval of the Administrative Justice, with subsequent compliance with the provisions of paragraphs 3 and 4.

6. Standing Orders shall be numbered sequentially, the number of each Standing Order to include the year in which the order becomes effective.

7. Unless circumstances require immediate action, all Standing Orders shall be submitted for publication in Massachusetts Lawyers Weekly and posted in all Clerk-Magistrates' or Registers' offices in the Department not less than fifteen days prior to their effective date. The Administrative Justices shall provide the Clerk-Magistrates and Registers with copies of each Standing Order.

8. Each Clerk-Magistrate, Register and the office of each Administrative Justice shall keep a file of all Standing Orders currently in effect in the Department. An index of the Standing Orders shall also be maintained. The index and Standing Orders shall be available to the public.

9. All Standing Orders shall also be filed in the Office of the Chief Administrative Justice. The Office of the Chief Administrative Justice shall keep an index and file of all Standing Orders issued in all Departments of the Trial Court.

VI. UNIFORM RULES FOR PERMANENCY HEARINGS

Effective July 1, 1985

Table of Rules

Rule 1. Purpose

The Uniform Rules for Permanency Hearings provide a consistent procedure for hearings conducted, pursuant to G.L. c. 119, § 29B. This procedure is intended to encourage meaningful participation by the parties. Permanency hearings provide the child or young adult an important opportunity to have individual needs addressed by the court to ensure that the child or young adult is receiving the necessary supports to timely reach a permanent, safe, and healthy home and a successful adulthood.

Amended June 28, 2000, effective September 5, 2000; January 10, 2018, effective March 1, 2018.

Rule 2. Scope of Rules and Definitions

(a) Scope. These rules govern the procedure for hearings conducted pursuant to G.L. c. 119, § 29B in the Juvenile, District, and Probate and Family Court Departments. Procedures not addressed by these rules shall be governed by the rules of procedure applicable to the court in which the matter is heard.

(b) Definitions. The following definitions apply in this Rule:

(1) *"APPLA"* — another permanent planned living arrangement or an alternative planned permanent living arrangement in which the Department maintains care and custody or responsibility of a child age 16 or older or of a young adult and arranges a stable living situation for that child or young adult when it continues not to be in the best interest of the child or young adult to pursue another permanency option.

(2) *"Child"* — a person under the age of eighteen.

(3) *"Clerk's Office"*— the office of the Clerk–Magistrate or Register of Probate of the court where the permanency hearing is scheduled.

(4) *"Department"*— the Department of Children and Families, or its successor agency.

(5) *"Indian Child"* — an unmarried child who either is a member of a federally recognized Indian tribe or is eligible for membership in a federally recognized Indian tribe and a biological child of a member pursuant to the Indian Child Welfare Act, 25 U.S.C. § 1903.

(6) *"Kin"*— any person to whom a child and/or the child's parent(s) and family members ascribe a "family" relationship. Such individual may be related by blood, marriage or adoption or a person to whom the child and/or parent(s) ascribe the role of family based on cultural and affectional ties or individual family values.

(7) *"Parent"*— a child's biological, adoptive, or legal mother or father.

(8) *"Party"* — a person who is a party in the underlying case, except the parent of a young adult or a parent whose parental rights have been terminated under G.L. c. 119, § 26 or G.L. c. 210, § 3 or who has signed a voluntary surrender under G.L. c. 119, § 23(a)(2) or G.L. c. 210, § 2.

(9) *"Permanency Hearing"* — a hearing conducted pursuant to G.L. c. 119, § 29B and as described in these Rules.

(10) *"Permanency Plan* — a plan for the child as determined by the court pursuant to G.L. c. 119, § 29B and Rule 9, that addresses whether, and if applicable when, the child or young adult will be: (i) returned to the parent: (ii) placed for adoption and the steps the Department will take to free the child for adoption: (iii) referred for legal guardianship: (iv) placed in permanent care with kin: or (v) placed in APPLA.

(11) *"Permanency Report"* — a written document prepared by the Department and reviewed by the court at the permanency hearing regarding a child in the care or custody or under the responsibility of the Department or a young adult, which sets forth the Department's proposed permanency plan and the efforts it has made and will make to implement the permanency plan in a timely manner as detailed in Rule 4.

(12) *"Transition Plan"* — a plan which includes the components listed in Rule 4(c), approved by the court pursuant to G.L. c. 119, § 29B(c) for a child who is age 17 years and 9 months or older or for a young adult who will be leaving care within the next 90 days.

(13) *"Young Adult"* — a person between the ages of 18 and 22 under the responsibility of the Department pursuant to G.L. c. 119, § 23(f).

Amended June 28, 2000, effective September 5, 2000; January 10, 2018, effective March 1, 2018.

Commentary

Rule 2(b)(1) APPLA. Federal law uses the term another planned permanent living arrangement. 42 U.S.C. § 675a. State law uses the term another permanent planned living arrangement. G.L. c. 119, § 29(a)(v). The Department of Children and Families (DCF) uses the term alternative planned permanent living arrangement. DCF *Permanency Planning Policy #2013-01* (July 1, 2013) at 22, 51. For purposes of this Rule, the terms are interchangeable and expressed as APPLA.

Rule 2(b)(12) Transition Plan. Federal law also describes the components of a transition plan. See 42 U.S.C. § 675(5)(H).

Rule 3. Scheduling the Permanency Hearing

(a) Scheduling. The committing court shall schedule the first permanency hearing at the original commitment grant of care or custody, or transfer of responsibility of a child or young adult to the Department by order of a court of competent jurisdiction, and at each permanency hearing, the court shall schedule the next permanency hearing. Except, however, if the underlying case is a child requiring assistance petition, the court shall schedule a permanency hearing at the first dispositional review hearing. Nothing in this rule shall be read to prevent the parties from requesting, or the court from scheduling, a permanency hearing more frequently than required.

(1) The court shall conduct the first permanency hearing within twelve (12) months of the date the child or young adult first entered the care, custody, or responsibility of the Department. Subsequent permanency hearings shall be held no less frequently than every twelve (12) months thereafter, while the child or young adult remains in the care or custody or under the responsibility of the Department.

(2) If the court has determined that reasonable efforts to preserve and reunify the family are not required pursuant to G.L. c. 119, § 29C, a permanency hearing shall be held within thirty (30) days of the court's determination that no reasonable efforts are required.

(b) Announcement. The court shall announce the date on which the permanency report is due and the date of the permanency hearing in open court at each court event until the permanency hearing is held. Failure of the court to announce the date of the permanency hearing shall not preclude the court from proceeding with the permanency hearing.

(c) Hearing on the Permanency Report and the Transition Plan. Upon the request of any party, the court shall schedule and/or hold a hearing on the Department's permanency report, particularly the proposed transition plan, for a child in the care and custody or under the responsibility of the Department who has attained the age of 17 years 9 months or for a young adult who plans to leave the responsibility of the Department in the next 90 days.

Adopted January 10, 2018, effective March 1, 2018.

Commentary

Rule 3(a). In order to encourage the participation of a child or a young adult in his or her permanency hearing, the parties may request and the court shall make every effort to schedule a hearing day and time that accommodates the schedule of the child or young adult and that is within the prescribed timeframes.

Rule 3(a)(1). For a child or young adult who has experienced interruptions in care or custody, responsibility, or placement with the Department, a permanency hearing may still be required. See 45 C.F.R. § 1356.21(e) (describing a trial home visit). For example, if a child in the care or custody or under the responsibility of the Department or a young adult has been placed at home for less than six months, a permanency hearing is still required for that child or young adult. U.S. Department of Health and Human Services Administration for Children and Families. Children's Bureau, *Child Welfare Policy Manual* Tit. IV–E 8.3C.5, available at https://www.acf.hhs.gov/cwpm/programs/cb/laws_policies/laws/cwpm/policy (last accessed May 24, 2016).

Rule 4. Permanency Reports

(a) Permanency Reports for All Children and Young Adults. Permanency reports for all children and young adults shall be in writing and shall include the following:

(1) identifying information about the child or young adult and biological family including siblings as well as the Department's efforts to identify whether the child is an Indian Child and the result of those efforts;

(2) a brief history of the legal and clinical case, including placement history;

(3) the efforts the Department has made to engage and include the family in the development of the permanency plan, including the child, as appropriate, or young adult.

(4) the proposed permanent plan for the child or young adult, including:

i. when the plan will be accomplished.

ii. what steps the Department has taken and will take to implement the permanency plan for the child or young adult, and

iii. if the plan is APPLA, the compelling reason for proposing that plan, and why it continues to not be in the best interests of the child to return home: be placed for adoption; be placed with a legal guardian; or be placed with fit and willing kin.

(5) services and other assistance provided, currently and in the past, to safely reunify the child with his or her parent or guardian, or, if the court has previously determined a plan other than reunification, to further that permanency plan, and the engagement of all parties with those services. The report shall include any services and needed assistance provided to accommodate a parent, child, or young adult's disability, and how the services and assistance provided are specifically tailored to meet the parent, child, or young adult's cultural background and language needs:

(6) information about the current placement including: how it meets the child's or young adult's current needs and furthers the permanency plan; if the child is not placed in family foster care, the reasons the Department determined the child is in need of special care, treatment or education, and if the child is placed in foster care outside the state in which the child's parents' home is located, why the out-of-

state placement continues to be appropriate and in the child's best interests:

(7) medical information about the child or young adult, including ongoing treatment and medications being provided to the child or young adult, and, if the child or young adult is medically needy, a description of his or her individualized health care plan;

(8) the plan for visits and/or contact with parents and among siblings;

(9) results of any internal reviews by the foster care review unit;

(10) a description of the child's or the young adult's educational history, needs, and current status, including efforts made to maintain school stability;

(11) information about the regular, ongoing opportunities the child or young adult has had to engage in age and developmentally appropriate activities; and

(12) if the proposed permanency plan for the child or young adult is APPLA:

i. the intensive, ongoing, and, as of the date of the report, unsuccessful efforts made by the Department to return the child or young adult home or secure a placement for the child or young adult with kin, a legal guardian, or an adoptive parent, including efforts that utilize search technology to find biological family members, and

ii. what steps the Department has taken to ensure that the foster care provider of the child or young adult is following the reasonable and prudent parent standard.

(b) Permanency Reports for Children Age 14 or Older and Young Adults. For a child age 14 or older or a young adult, the permanency report shall include the information required under Rule 4(a) as well as information about any additional or specialized services provided to the child or young adult to assist with the transition to successful adulthood. Such services include those designed to help the child or young adult:

(1) build relationships with other caring adults, particularly with life-long connections;

(2) make an education plan;

(3) find vocational, employment, and career counseling and placement;

(4) secure stable housing;

(5) develop expertise in daily living skills;

(6) maintain physical and mental health care and health insurance;

(7) learn how to access community resources and public benefits and services;

(8) connect with other state agencies; and

(9) develop financial skills including receiving, understanding, and correcting, if applicable, his/her consumer credit report.

(c) Permanency Reports for Children who are Age 17 Years and 9 Months or Older and for Young Adults. For a child in the care or custody or under the responsibility of the Department who is age 17 years and 9 months or older or for a young adult, the permanency report shall include the information required under Rule 4(a) and Rule 4(b) as well as a proposed transition plan. Proposed transition plans shall be personalized at the direction of the child or young adult, be as detailed as the child or young adult shall elect, and include specific options on:

(1) stable housing;

(2) health insurance;

(3) physical and mental health care including the designation of a health care proxy:

(4) educational services;

(5) long–term connections with mentors and caring adults;

(6) continuing support services including state agencies;

(7) workforce supports and employment services; and

(8) maintaining contact with siblings still in DCF custody or care.

Adopted January 10, 2018, effective March 1, 2018.

Commentary

Rule (4)(a)(3). Permanency plan options include: reunification, adoption, guardianship, permanent care with kin, and APPLA. See 42 U.S.C. § 675(5)(C)(i): G.L. c. 119, § 29(a)(v); DCF *Permanency Planning Policy* #2013–01 (July 1, 2013) at 22, 29–51.

Rule 4(a)(5). Information about the placement may include: (i) the type and level of placement (ii) whether the child is placed with kin and, if not, the reasons why not; (iii) whether the child is placed with siblings and, if not, the reasons why the department determined placement with siblings is not in the child's best interests; (iv) if the child is not placed in family foster care, the reasons why the child requires a more restrictive setting; (v) if an Indian child is placed in a non-preferred placement as described in Rule 9(c)(3), why the department determined there was "good cause" to not follow the placement preferences required by 25 U.S.C. § 1915(b).

Rule 4(a)(11)(ii). See 42 U.S.C. § 675(10)(A) (definition of the reasonable and prudent parent standard). The reasonable and prudent parent standard means the standard a caregiver shall use to ensure that children are participating in age and developmentally appropriate extracurricular, enrichment, cultural, and social activities.

Rule 4(b). For a child who is age 14 or older or for a young adult, the Department may already have developed a Youth Readiness Assessment Tool, which identifies and prioritizes the skill development needed to prepare the child or young adult for the transition to adulthood.

Rule 4(b)(5). Examples of daily living skills include driving, navigating public transportation, maintaining healthy relationships, opening a bank account, and budgeting. The child or young adult may need, and the Department is required to provide, certain personal documents in order to develop these skills, such as a birth certificate, social security card, other identification, a credit report (annually), and a document that describes the right of the child or young adult to education, health care, visitation, and court participation.

Rule 5. Notice

The Department shall provide notice of the scheduled permanency hearing date to the foster parent, pre-adoptive parent or relative providing care for the child who is the subject of the petition pursuant to G.L. c. 119, § 29D. The Department shall provide notice of the scheduled permanency hearing date to the Department of Youth Services if the child or young adult is committed to the care or custody of the Department of Youth Services. Failure of the Department to comply with this section shall not preclude the court from proceeding with the permanency hearing.

Adopted January 10, 2018, effective March 1, 2018.

Rule 6. Submission of Report and Response or Objections

(a) Filing of the Permanency Report. For a child in the care or custody or under the responsibility of the Department or for a young adult, no less than thirty (30) days prior to the scheduled permanency hearing date the Department shall file the permanency report with the clerk's office and shall send copies to all parties or, if the parties are represented by counsel, to the counsel of record.

(b) Filing of the Permanency Report for an Expedited Permanency Hearing. If the court has determined that reasonable efforts to reunify the family are not required pursuant to G.L. c. 119, § 29C, the Department shall file the permanency report and send copies as provided above within ten (10) days of entry of the "no reasonable efforts required" order.

(c) Filing of Response or Objection to the Permanency Report. Any party may file a response or objection to the permanency report no less than ten (10) days prior to the scheduled permanency hearing date.

Adopted January 10, 2018, effective March 1, 2018.

Rule 7. Counsel

(a) Right to Counsel. All parties have the right to be represented by counsel at the permanency hearing.

(b) Attendance of Counsel. All counsel of record shall attend the permanency hearing. Failure of counsel to attend, without good cause, shall not require that the hearing be postponed unless the interests of justice so require..

Amended June 28, 2000, effective September 5, 2000. Renumbered and amended January 10, 2018, effective March 1, 2018.

Rule 8. The Permanency Hearing

(a) Purpose of the Permanency Hearing. The purpose of the Permanency Hearing shall be to:

(1) determine the permanency plan for the child or young adult and when the plan will be implemented;

(2) aid in the timely implementation of such plan; and

(3) determine whether the Department has made reasonable efforts to safely reunify the child or young adult with his or her parent or guardian, or if the court has previously determined under Rule 9(c) a plan other than reunification, to implement the previously determined plan.

(b) Parties and Non–Parties.

(1) Any child or young adult who is a party has a right to attend the permanency hearing. There shall be a presumption that the child who is age 14 or older or the young adult will attend the permanency hearing. If the child age 14 or older or the young adult is not present at the hearing, the court will inquire of counsel for the child or young adult as to the reason his or her client is not present.

(2) Pursuant to G.L. c. 119, § 29D, foster parents, pre-adoptive parents or relatives providing care for the child have the right to attend the permanency hearing and be heard. Nothing in this provision shall be construed to provide that such foster parent, pre-adoptive parent or relative shall be made a party to the proceeding by exercising his/her right to attend and be heard.

(3) Failure of one or more parties or non-parties to appear shall not preclude the court from proceeding with the permanency hearing.

(c) The Hearing.

(1) The permanency hearing, including the hearing as described in Rule 3(c), shall be conducted in the same manner as any other hearing unless otherwise stated in these Rules. At the hearing, the judge will review the permanency report, any objections and responses, and make the determinations required by these Rules.

(2) The author of the Department's permanency report shall be available for cross-examination by each of the parties.

(3) The judge who entered the adjudication, or if there has not been an adjudication, who entered the original order of commitment, grant of custody, or transfer of responsibility of a child or young adult to the Department shall conduct the hearing unless impractical or would cause undue delay.

(4) The court shall consult with the child or young adult in an age-appropriate manner about the permanency report and the permanency plan. Counsel for the child or young adult shall be prepared to provide the court with the child's position regarding the permanency report and the permanency plan.

(5) The permanency hearing, including the hearing as described in Rule 3(c), may be held simultaneously with a trial, review and redetermination, other hearing, or other proceeding in the matter, but no later than the scheduling requirements contained in Rule 3(a)(1).

Amended June 28, 2000, effective September 5, 2000. Renumbered and amended January 10, 2018, effective March 1, 2018.

Rule 9. Orders

(a) Permanency Plan. The court shall determine the permanency plan for the child or young adult going forward and when that plan will be implemented.

(1) Permanency plan options include: reunification, adoption, guardianship, permanent care with kin, and APPLA.

(2) In determining the permanency plan, the health and safety of the child or young adult shall be of paramount, but not exclusive, concern.

(3) If the child is an Indian child, the court shall determine and document in writing whether the placement preferences required by 25 U.S.C. § 1915 have been applied in any foster care, pre-adoptive, or adoptive placement, unless it determines that good cause exists to not apply those placement preferences.

(4) If the court determines the permanency plan for a child or young adult to be APPLA, the court shall make findings regarding why APPLA is the best permanency plan for the child or young adult and the compelling reasons why it continues to not be in the best interests of the child or young adult to return home, be placed for adoption, be placed with a legal guardian, or be placed with a fit and willing relative.

(b) Reasonable Efforts pursuant to G.L. c. 119, §§ 29B, 29C. The court shall determine whether the Department has made reasonable efforts to safely reunify the child or young adult with his or her parent or guardian, or, if the court has previously determined under Rule 9(c) a permanency plan other than reunification, to implement the previously determined permanency plan. The court is not required to make a reasonable efforts determination at an expedited permanency hearing as described in Rule 3(a)(2). A determination by the court that the Department has not made reasonable efforts does not preclude the court from entering any appropriate order as may be in the child or young adult's best interests.

(c) Services Needed for Children age 14 or Older or Young Adults. For a child age 14 or older and for a young adult, the court shall determine whether the services the child or young adult needs are in place to assist him or her to make a transition from foster care to a successful adulthood.

(d) Satisfactory Transition Plan. After a hearing conducted pursuant to Rule 3(c), the court shall determine whether the proposed transition plan is satisfactory and shall retain jurisdiction of the matter until it finds that a satisfactory transition plan has been provided for the child or young adult.

(e) Orders in the Best Interest of the Child or Young Adult. At a permanency hearing, including at a hearing conducted pursuant to Rule 3(c), the court may make any appropriate order in the child's or young adult's best interest, including but not limited to orders with respect to the child's or young adult's care or custody or that will aid in the implementation of the permanency plan.

(f) Findings. The court need not enter findings absent an appeal from its order with the exception of those findings required by law or this Rule.

Amended June 28, 2000, effective September 5, 2000. Renumbered and amended January 10, 2018, effective March 1, 2018.

Commentary

Rule 9(a)(3). "Good cause" is defined pursuant to 25 C.F.R. § 23.132 (effective December 12, 2016). There are two sets of placement preferences. In adoptive placements, where the Indian child's tribe has not established a different order of preference, placement preferences for the child must descend as follows: 1) a member of the Indian child's extended family; 2) other members of the Indian child's Tribe: or 3) other Indian families. 25 C.F.R. § 23.130(a). If the Indian child's Tribe has established by resolution a different order of preference than that specified in ICWA, the Tribe's placement preferences apply. 25 C.F.R. § 23.130(b). The court must, where appropriate, also consider the placement preference of the Indian child or Indian child's parent. 25 C.F.R. § 23.130(c)(effective December 12, 2016). In any foster care or pre-adoptive placement, including changes in foster-care or pre-adoptive placement, the child must be placed in the least restrictive setting that most approximates a family, taking into consideration sibling attachment: that allows the Indian child's special needs (if any) to be met: and is in reasonable proximity to the Indian child's home, extended family, or siblings. In any foster care or pre-adoptive placement, including changes in foster care or pre-adoptive placement, where the Indian child's Tribe has not specified a different order, placement preferences for the child must descend as follows: 1) a member of the Indian child's extended family; 2) a foster home licensed, approved or specified by the Tribe; 3) an Indian foster home licensed or approved by an authorized, non–Indian licensing authority; and 4) an Indian institution. The court must, where appropriate, also consider the preference of the Indian child or the Indian child's parent. See Indian Child Welfare Act 25 U.S.C. § 1915: 25 C.F.R. §§ 23.130134 (effective December 12, 2016).

Rule 9(e). See G.L. c. 119, § 29B(c) ("the court shall retain jurisdiction until it finds, after a hearing at which the person is present unless the person chooses otherwise, that a satisfactory transition plan has been provided for the person").

Rule 10.   Appeals

(a) Timing. Any party may appeal the court's determination(s) and/or order(s) to the Appeals Court by filing a notice of appeal in the clerk's office no later than thirty (30) days following the entry of such determination(s) and/or order(s) on the court's docket.

(b) Notice to the Judge. The clerk's office shall inform the judge within five (5) days from the filing of the notice of appeal that the determination(s) and /or order(s) have been appealed.

(c) Findings. The judge shall file written findings within sixty (60) days from the filing of the notice of the appeal.

Amended June 28, 2000, effective September 5, 2000. Renumbered and amended January 10, 2018, effective March 1, 2018.

VII. UNIFORM RULE ON CIVIL MOTOR VEHICLE INFRACTIONS

Effective July 1, 1986

Table of Forms

Form

DC–MV–4. Primary Court.

DC–MV–4. Appellate Division Notice.

DC–MV–4. Appellate Division Finding.

DC–MV–4. Prosecutor Copy.

Form

DC–MV–4. Appellant.

DC–MV–5. Court Copy.

DC–MV–5. Violator Copy.

DC–MV–5. Police Copy.

DC–MV–5. Return of Service.

(a) Scope of Rule. This rule shall be applicable in the Boston Municipal Court, District Court and Juvenile Court Departments. This rule governs (1) the procedure for the determination of responsibility for civil motor vehicle infractions, in accordance with G.L. c. 90C, § 3, at hearings conducted by clerk-magistrates, de novo hearings conducted by judges, and hearings held by judges where the civil motor vehicle infraction has arisen from the same occurrence as a criminal automobile law violation cognizable under G.L. c. 90C, § 3(B); (2) the procedure for civil contempt in civil motor vehicle infraction cases; and (3) appeal under G.L. c. 90C, § 3(A) of issues of law arising from the decisions of judges in civil motor vehicle infraction cases. Such appeal is available following adjudication by judges in cases heard on appeal following a clerk-magistrate's finding and disposition, and in cases where the civil motor vehicle infraction arose from the same occurrence as a criminal motor vehicle violation cognizable under G.L. c. 90C, § 3(B). This rule shall be construed and applied to secure the prompt and informal determination of civil motor vehicle infractions.

(b) Hearings.

(1) *General.* When conducted by a clerk-magistrate, hearings on civil motor vehicle infractions, other than in juvenile proceedings, shall take place in a room to which the public has access. When conducted by a judge on appeal or in conjunction with a criminal violation, such hearings shall be held in a courtroom. The judge or clerk-magistrate shall inform the parties that he is conducting a non-criminal hearing on an alleged civil motor vehicle infraction. Counsel may participate in such hearings.

All witnesses shall be placed under oath. The rules of evidence shall not apply at such hearings. The evidence shall be given such weight as the judge or clerk-magistrate deems appropriate. Questioning and cross-examination of witnesses shall proceed to the extent and in the manner determined appropriate by the judge or clerk-magistrate, provided, however, that a party shall not be denied the opportunity to present relevant evidence or cross-examine witnesses.

Hearings on civil motor vehicle infractions shall not be delayed or postponed except for good and sufficient reason.

(2) *Finding and Disposition.* At the conclusion of the hearing, the judge or clerk-magistrate shall announce a finding and disposition of "not responsible" or "responsible". The judge or clerk-magistrate shall enter a finding of "not responsible" if he determines that it was not shown, by a preponderance of the credible evidence, that the alleged violator committed the infraction charged. If the judge or magistrate determines by a preponderance of the credible evidence that the alleged violator did commit the infraction charged, he shall enter a finding of "responsible" and impose an assessment which shall be within the range permitted by law and in accordance with any applicable guidelines that have been promulgated pursuant to law. No other disposition shall be permitted. No disposition may be suspended and no costs shall be assessed, except that after a finding of "responsible" the judge or clerk-magistrate may continue the proceeding for a limited time to permit the violator to pay the assessment imposed. No case shall be continued without a finding or filed, and no person shall be subject to any terms of probation or any other requirement; provided, however, that if the violator has been found guilty and is simultaneously being sentenced upon a criminal motor vehicle violation that arose from the same occurrence as one or more civil motor vehicle infractions, the judge may order any other civil motor vehicle infractions to be filed without imposition of an assessment.

(3) *Appeal of Clerk-Magistrate's Finding and Disposition.* Claim of appeal to a judge from a clerk-magistrate's finding and disposition shall be made upon the clerk-magistrate's announcement of the finding and disposition, and shall be noted on the citation. There shall be no filing fee for such appeal.

(c) Complaint for Contempt.

(1) *General.* Upon (1) failure of a person who has received a citation for a civil motor vehicle infraction to either make timely payment of the appropriate civil assessment or notify the court that he wishes to contest the infraction in accordance with G.L. c. 90C, or (2) failure or refusal of such person to pay such assessment after being found responsible, within the time allowed, or (3) failure of such person, without good cause, to appear for a hearing on a civil motor vehicle infraction, a judge of the court may issue, at the request of the District Attorney

or police prosecutor or clerk-magistrate, or sua sponte, a complaint for civil contempt against such person. Such complaint shall be on a form prescribed therefor, and shall indicate the failure or refusal that is the basis for the contempt charge.

(2) *Summons.* Upon the signing of the complaint by the District Attorney, by the officer involved or by a designated officer of the police department involved, or, in the case of a complaint requested by the clerk-magistrate or ordered issued by a judge, by the clerk-magistrate, the court shall forthwith issue a summons to the person so charged, together with a copy of the complaint, requiring said person to appear before the court on a date certain to explain the reasons for such failure or refusal as set forth in the complaint.

(3) *Service.* The summons and copy of complaint shall be served by first-class mail or by any officer authorized to serve criminal process, as provided by law. Service by said officer shall be made in hand or by leaving a copy at the defendant's last and usual place of abode.

(4) *Arrest Warrant.* If the person fails, without good cause, to appear in response to the summons, and the court has satisfactory proof of service of said summons, an arrest warrant may be issued, and shall be served by any officer authorized to serve criminal process. Upon appearance in court on said warrant, the hearing on the civil contempt shall proceed.

(5) *Hearing.* Proceedings for civil contempt under this rule shall be prosecuted by the District Attorney or police prosecutor, pursuant to G.L. c. 90C, § 3(A), and heard by a judge. At the hearing in such cases, testimony shall be taken under oath. If the court determines by a preponderance of the credible evidence that the person's failure or refusal as alleged in the complaint did occur and is without good cause, the court shall adjudicate the defendant to have committed an act of civil contempt. If the court finds that the defendant did not commit an act of civil contempt, it shall forthwith proceed to make such order as is necessary for the disposition of the pending civil motor vehicle infraction.

(6) *Disposition and Adjudication of Contempt.* Upon entry of a finding that the defendant has committed an act of civil contempt, the court may, consistent with the court's determination of the defendant's ability to pay, order payment of an amount, in addition to any other sum then owed, to reimburse the Commonwealth or the appropriate political subdivision thereof for the reasonable expense related to the person's failure or refusal to act that constituted the contempt, together with an amount for the reasonable expense involved in prosecuting the contempt action, including cost of service. If necessary, the court, consistent with the court's determination of the defendant's ability to pay, shall commit such person so adjudicated in civil contempt to the county jail or house of correction until all amounts owed are paid or shall order such commitment and stay its execution for a reasonable time to allow such payment; provided, however, that juveniles shall be committed to the Department of Youth Services and incarcerated as provided by law. Such contempt shall be considered purged upon payment of all amounts owed.

(7) *Other Actions.* Procedure under this rule shall not be construed to exclude any other remedy otherwise available by law.

(8) *Appeal of Contempt.* Parties may appeal matters of law arising in a contempt proceeding to the appropriate Appellate Division.

(d) Appeal.

(1) *Claim of Appeal.* Claim of appeal to the appropriate Appellate Division shall be filed with the clerk-magistrate of the court in which the civil motor vehicle infraction was heard. Such claim of appeal shall be set forth in writing on the form provided therefor and shall state specifically the issue of law for which appellate review is sought. Such claim of appeal shall be filed no later than ten days following the entry of the court's determination of responsibility in the civil motor vehicle infraction case.

(2) *Transmission of Papers to the Appellate Division.* Upon receipt of a claim of appeal, the clerk shall promptly transmit a copy of it, together with copies of all papers in the case then on file, including the citation, front and back, to the appropriate Appellate Division.

(3) *Notice From Appellate Division.* Upon receipt of the case, the Appellate Division shall notify the parties of the right to submit written briefs on the legal issue or issues presented for review, and the date by which such briefs must be submitted. Said notice shall also indicate, where deemed necessary by the Appellate Division, that a review of the tape recordings of the proceedings, if such recording is available, will be required for proper appellate review, and in such cases, shall instruct the appellant to obtain a cassette copy of the tape in accordance with the applicable procedures and provide it to the Appellate Division by a date certain.

(4) *Appellate Division Review.* Appeals shall be reviewed and decided by the Appellate Division without oral argument unless the Appellate Division shall otherwise allow, and this shall also be indicated to the parties in the aforementioned notice. When oral argument is allowed, the parties shall be informed reasonably in advance of the date, time, and place of such proceedings, and the time to be allowed for argument, which shall be in the discretion of the Appellate Division.

(5) *Disposition by the Appellate Division.* If, as a result of its resolution of a legal issue presented for appeal, the Appellate Division concludes that prejudicial error occurred in the civil motor vehicle infraction proceeding, it shall order the court's finding and disposition vacated, and shall order a new hearing held, consistent with its rulings on the legal issues that were the subject of the appeal, or the case dismissed or the violator found not responsible, whichever disposition it deems appropriate.

If the Appellate Division finds that no issue of law is presented or that no prejudicial error occurred, it shall affirm the adjudication of the court below.

Failure by the appellant to comply with these rules may be grounds for dismissal of the appeal.

The Appellate Division shall communicate its findings and its order, if any, to the parties and the clerk-magistrate of the court from which the appeal was taken. Upon receipt of said finding and order, said clerk shall take all other necessary action, including collection of any assessment or other charge the payment of which was stayed pending the appeal.

FORMS
FORMS
FORM DC-MV-4. PRIMARY COURT

[Pub. Note: This Form is composed of five documents which should be filed together, viz., Primary Cou
Appellate Division Notice, Appellate Division Finding, Prosecutor Copy, and Appellant.]

CIVIL MOTOR VEHICLE INFRACTION—CLAIM OF APPEAL	Trial Court of Massachusetts
	District Court Department

1. DATE APPEAL FILED	2. DATE OF DISPOSITION	3. POLICE DEPARTMENT	
4. DOCKET NUMBER(S)	5. OFFENSE(S)		6. COURT DIVISION

7. NAME, ADDRESS AND ZIP CODE OF APPELLANT

8. APPELLANT'S ATTORNEY

NAME   ADDRESS

To the District Court Appellate Division:

I, the above named Appellant, having been found responsible for the civil motor vehicle infraction(s) described above, hereby claim appellate review of this matter in the Appellate Division. The issue(s) of law upon which appellate review is sought is/are described below:

9. Issue(s) of law upon which review is sought:

ATTACH ADDITIONAL SHEETS IF NECESSARY

X _____   _____
SIGNATURE OF APPELLANT   DATE

INSTRUCTIONS FOR PERSONS FILING A CLAIM OF APPEAL

1. Please type or print clearly with a ball point pen. Press hard—you are making 5 copies.

2. You must complete items numbered 1–9 of this form.
   No. 1   "Date Appeal Filed"—This is the date you file the appeal form with the Clerk-Magistrate of the court.
   No. 2   "Date of Disposition"—This is the date on which the District Court judge found you responsible for the motor vehicle infraction. You must file your appeal within 10 days of this date.
   No. 3   "Police Department"—This is the name of the police agency that issued the citation that is basis of this appeal.
   No. 4   "Docket Number(s)"—This is the case control number that the District Court has assigned to this case. You must inquire of the court to obtain this number.
   No. 5   "Offense(s)"—This is the infraction or infractions which is the basis of your appeal.
   No. 6   "Court Division"—This is the name of the court at which you were found responsible for the motor vehicle infraction.
   No. 7   "Name and Address of Appellant"—The person filing this appeal is the Appellant. Give your complete name, address and zip code.
   No. 8   "Appellant's Attorney"—The appellant must indicate the name and address of his or her attorney, if any.
   No. 9   "Issue(s) of Law"—An issue of law is the legal error you claim was committed in the hearing of this case. The alleged legal error must be stated specifically. A general disagreement with the judge's finding is not an issue of law.

3. The Appellant must sign his or her name in the space provided, and indicate the date of signing.

4. Detach and keep the last part (Appellant Copy) for your records. Return the rest of this form with the remaining parts intact to the Clerk-Magistrate of the court in which you were found responsible.

5. The Clerk-Magistrate will forward the necessary papers to the Appellate Division. The Appellate Division will then contact you.

DC-MV-4(2-99)

PRIMARY COURT

FORM DC–MV–4. APPELLATE DIVISION NOTICE

[Pub. Note: This Form is composed of five documents which should be filed together, viz., Primary Court, Appellate Division Notice, Appellate Division Finding, Prosecutor Copy, and Appellant.]

NOTICE FROM APPELLATE DIVISION	APPELLATE DIVISION DOCKET NO.	Trial Court of Massachusetts District Court Department
DATE APPEAL FILED	DATE OF DISPOSITION	POLICE DEPARTMENT	
DOCKET NUMBER(S)	OFFENSE(S)		COURT DIVISION FROM WHICH APPEAL CLAIMED
			NAME AND ADDRESS OF APPELLATE DIVISION

NAME, ADDRESS AND ZIP CODE OF APPELLANT

APPELLANT'S ATTORNEY

NAME   ADDRESS

To the parties to the civil motor vehicle infraction appeal described above:

This notice is to inform you of the following:

1. The Appellate Division is in receipt of the civil motor vehicle infraction appeal described above. The docket number that the Appellate Division has assigned to this case is indicated in the shaded area.

2. Parties to this action have the right to submit written briefs on the legal issue(s) presented for review.

   Briefs must be submitted on or before: _____
   DATE

3. ☐ A review of the tape recording of the trial proceedings is not necessary in this case. However, if a review of the tape recording is later determined to be necessary, you will be notified.

   ☐ A review of the tape recording is necessary in this case. The appellant is instructed to obtain a cassette copy of the District Court proceeding. The appellant must contact the Clerk–Magistrate of the District Court about the procedures to be followed. The Appellant must provide the cassette copy to the Appellate Division on or before _____
   DATE

4. Appeals are reviewed and decided by the Appellate Division without oral argument unless the Appellate Division shall otherwise allow.

   ☐ Oral argument will not be allowed in this case. However, if it is later determined that oral argument will be permitted, you will be notified.

   ☐ Oral argument will be allowed in this case. The date, time, place and the amount of time allowed for oral argument is indicated below:

   _____

   _____

X _____
APPELLATE DIVISION CLERK   DATE

DC–MV–4(2–89)

APPELLATE DIVISION NOTICE

FORM DC–MV–4.   APPELLATE DIVISION FINDING

[Pub. Note: This Form is composed of five documents which should be filed together, viz., Primary Court, Appellate Division Notice, Appellate Division Finding, Prosecutor Copy, and Appellant.]

CIVIL MOTOR VEHICLE INFRACTION	APPELLATE DIVISION DOCKET NO.	Trial Court of Massachusetts
APPELLATE DIVISION FINDING AND ORDER		District Court Department

DATE APPEAL FILED	DATE OF DISPOSITION	POLICE DEPARTMENT	
DOCKET NUMBER(S)	OFFENSE(S)		COURT DIVISION FROM WHICH APPEAL CLAIMED
			NAME AND ADDRESS OF APPELLATE DIVISION

NAME, ADDRESS AND ZIP CODE OF APPELLANT

APPELLANT'S ATTORNEY

NAME   ADDRESS

APPELLANT'S CLAIM OF ERROR

I, the above named Appellant, having been found responsible for the civil motor vehicle infraction(s) described above, hereby claim appellate review of this matter in the Appellate Division. The issue(s) of law upon which appellate review is sought is/are described below:

Issue(s) of law upon which review is sought:

X _____   _____
SIGNATURE OF APPELLANT   DATE

APPELLATE DIVISION FINDING AND ORDER

Justices hearing this matter: _____

☐ No issue of law presented. Adjudication affirmed.

☐ No prejudicial error occurred. Adjudication affirmed.

☐ Appeal dismissed for failure of appellant to comply with procedural rules, specifically:

☐ Prejudicial error found, specifically:

Judgment of the trial court is vacated, and ☐ the case is dismissed ☐ the violator is found not responsible ☐ the case is remanded to the trial court for rehearing consistent with this ruling.

☐ Opinion attached.

☐ Other:

A true copy, attest: _____   _____
APPELLATE DIVISION CLERK   DATE

DC-MV-4(2-88)

APPELLATE DIVISION FINDING

FORM DC–MV–4. PROSECUTOR COPY

[Pub. Note: This Form is composed of five documents which should be filed together, viz., Primary Court, Appellate Division Notice, Appellate Division Finding, Prosecutor Copy, and Appellant.]

CIVIL MOTOR VEHICLE INFRACTION—CLAIM OF APPEAL			Trial Court of Massachusetts
1. DATE APPEAL FILED	2. DATE OF DISPOSITION	3. POLICE DEPARTMENT	District Court Department
4. DOCKET NUMBER(S)	5. OFFENSE(S)		6. COURT DIVISION

7. NAME, ADDRESS AND ZIP CODE OF APPELLANT

8. APPELLANT'S ATTORNEY

NAME   ADDRESS

To the District Court Appellate Division:

I, the above named Appellant, having been found responsible for the civil motor vehicle infraction(s) described above, hereby claim appellate review of this matter in the Appellate Division. The issue(s) of law upon which appellate review is sought is/are described below:

9. Issue(s) of law upon which review is sought:

X
_____
SIGNATURE OF APPELLANT   DATE

DC–MV–4 (2–86)

PROSECUTOR COPY

FORM DC–MV–4. APPELLANT

[Pub. Note: This Form is composed of five documents which should be filed together, viz., Primary Court, Appellate Division Notice, Appellate Division Finding, Prosecutor Copy, and Appellant.]

CIVIL MOTOR VEHICLE INFRACTION—CLAIM OF APPEAL   Trial Court of Massachusetts

District Court Department

1. DATE APPEAL FILED	2. DATE OF DISPOSITION	3. POLICE DEPARTMENT

4. DOCKET NUMBER(S)	5. OFFENSE(S)

6. COURT DIVISION

7. NAME, ADDRESS AND ZIP CODE OF APPELLANT

8. APPELLANT'S ATTORNEY

NAME   ADDRESS

To the District Court Appellate Division:

I, the above named Appellant, having been found responsible for the civil motor vehicle infraction(s) described above, hereby claim appellate review of this matter in the Appellate Division. The issue(s) of law upon which appellate review is sought is/are described below:

9. Issue(s) of law upon which review is sought:

ATTACH ADDITIONAL SHEETS IF NECESSARY

X _____   _____

SIGNATURE OF APPELLANT   DATE

INSTRUCTIONS FOR PERSONS FILING A CLAIM OF APPEAL

1. Please type or print clearly with a ball point pen. Press hard—you are making 5 copies.

2. You must complete items numbered 1–9 of this form.
   - No. 1   "Date Appeal Filed"—This is the date you file the appeal form with the Clerk-Magistrate of the court.
   - No. 2   "Date of Disposition"—This is the date on which the District Court judge found you responsible for the motor vehicle infraction. You must file your appeal within 10 days of this date.
   - No. 3   "Police Department"—This is the name of the police agency that issued the citation that is basis of this appeal.
   - No. 4   "Docket Number(s)"—This is the case control number that the District Court has assigned to this case. You must inquire of the court to obtain this number.
   - No. 5   "Offense(s)"—This is the infraction or infractions which is the basis of your appeal.
   - No. 6   "Court Division"—This is the name of the court at which you were found responsible for the motor vehicle infraction.
   - No. 7   "Name and Address of Appellant"—The person filing this appeal is the Appellant. Give your complete name, address and zip code.
   - No. 8   "Appellant's Attorney"—The appellant must indicate the name and address of his or her attorney, if any.
   - No. 9   "Issue(s) of Law"—An issue of law is the legal error you claim was committed in the hearing of this case. The alleged legal error must be stated specifically. A general disagreement with the judge's finding is not an issue of law.

3. The Appellant must sign his or her name in the space provided, and indicate the date of signing.
4. Detach and keep the last part (Appellant Copy) for your records. Return the rest of this form with the remaining parts intact to the Clerk-Magistrate of the court in which you were found responsible.
5. The Clerk-Magistrate will forward the necessary papers to the Appellate Division. The Appellate Division will then contact you.

DC-MV-4 (2-89)   APPELLANT

FORM DC–MV–5. COURT COPY

[Pub. Note: This Form is composed of four documents which should be filed together, viz., Court Copy, Violator Copy, Police Copy, and Return of Service.]

CIVIL MOTOR VEHICLE INFRACTION COMPLAINT FOR CIVIL CONTEMPT	DOCKET NUMBER	Trial Court of Massachusetts District Court Department	
NAME, ADDRESS AND ZIP CODE OF VIOLATOR		NAME AND ADDRESS OF COURT DIVISION	← A CIVIL CONTEMPT HEARING WILL BE HELD AT THIS COURT ON THE DATE AND TIME SPECIFIED ←
DATE OF BIRTH CITATION NUMBER POLICE DEPARTMENT		DATE OF HEARING TIME AT .M.	

To any Justice of the District Court Department:

The undersigned complainant, on behalf of the Commonwealth, on oath complains that the above named person did fail or refuse to comply with the provisions of Chapter 90C of the General Laws, as indicated more fully below, and did therefore commit an act of civil contempt.

Basis of contempt charge: It is alleged that the above named person:

☐ After receiving the citation, indicated above for one or more civil motor vehicle infractions, did fail to either make payment of the appropriate civil assessment or notify the court of a desire to contest the infractions within 20 days, in accordance with G.L. c. 90C, s. 3(A).

☐ After being found responsible for one or more civil motor vehicle infractions charged in the citation indicated above, did fail or refuse to pay the imposed motor vehicle infraction assessment(s) by _____, 19___, as ordered.

☐ Did fail, without good cause, to appear on _____, 19___, for a hearing on one or more civil motor vehicle infractions charged in the citation indicated above.

SIGNATURE OF COMPLAINANT	SWORN TO BEFORE CLERK–MAGISTRATE/ASST. CLERK
X	X
FIRST JUSTICE	DATE SWORN TO
WITNESS	

DC–MV–5 (2/88)

COURT COPY

FORM DC–MV–5.   VIOLATOR COPY

[Pub. Note: This Form is composed of four documents which should be filed together, viz., Court Copy, Violator Copy, Police Copy, and Return of Service.]

CIVIL MOTOR VEHICLE INFRACTION CONTEMPT COMPLAINT AND SUMMONS	DOCKET NUMBER	Trial Court of Massachusetts District Court Department	
NAME, ADDRESS AND ZIP CODE OF VIOLATOR		NAME AND ADDRESS OF COURT DIVISION	< A CIVIL CONTEMPT HEARING WILL BE HELD AT THIS COURT ON THE DATE AND
DATE OF BIRTH CITATION NUMBER POLICE DEPARTMENT		DATE OF HEARING TIME AT .M.	TIME SPECIFIED <

To the person named above:

The undersigned complainant, on behalf of the Commonwealth, on oath complains that the above named person did fail or refuse to comply with the provisions of Chapter 90C of the General Laws, as indicated more fully below, and did therefore commit an act of civil contempt.

You are therefore ordered to appear in this court to answer to the charge of civil contempt on the date and time indicated above.

Failure to appear as ordered without good cause may result in the issuance of a warrant for your arrest.

Basis of contempt charge: It is alleged that the above named person:

☐ After receiving the citation, indicated above for one or more civil motor vehicle infractions, did fail to either make payment of the appropriate civil assessment or notify the court of a desire to contest the infractions within 20 days, in accordance with G.L. c. 90C, s. 3(A).

☐ After being found responsible for one or more civil motor vehicle infractions charged in the citation indicated above, did fail or refuse to pay the imposed motor vehicle infraction assessment(s) by _____, 19___, as ordered.

☐ Did fail, without good cause, to appear on _____, 19___, for a hearing on one or more civil motor vehicle infractions charged in the citation indicated above.

SIGNATURE OF COMPLAINANT X	SWORN TO BEFORE CLERK–MAGISTRATE/ASST. CLERK X
FIRST JUSTICE WITNESS	DATE SWORN TO

ATENCIÓN. ESTE ES UN AVISO OFICIAL DE LA CORTE. SI USTED NO SABE LEER INGLÉS, OBTENGA UNA TRADUCCIÓN.
ATTENTION. CECI EST UNE ANNONCE OFFICIELLE DU PALAIS DE JUSTICE. SI VOUS ÊTES INCAPABLE DE LIRE ANGLAISE, OBTENEZ UNE TRADUCTION.
ATTENZIONE. IL PRESENTE È UN AVVISO UFFICIALE DAL TRIBUNALE. SE NON SAPETE LEGGERE IN INGLESE, OTTENETE UNA TRADUZIONE.
ATENÇÃO. ESTE É UM AVISO OFICIAL DO TRIBUNAL. SE NÃO SABE LER INGLÊS, OBTENHA UMA TRADUÇÃO.
LƯU Ý: ĐÂY LÀ THÔNG BÁO CHÍNH THỨC CỦA TÒA-ÁN. NẾU BẠN KHÔNG ĐỌC ĐƯỢC TIẾNG ANH, HÃY TÌM NGƯỜI DỊCH HỘ.

注意：此份表格你官方文件，如果你不致英文认识，可向法庭管理室取中文翻译。

DC–MV–5 (2/88)

VIOLATOR COPY

FORM DC–MV–5. POLICE COPY

[Pub. Note: This Form is composed of four documents which should be filed together, viz., Court Copy, Violator Copy, Police Copy, and Return of Service.]

CIVIL MOTOR VEHICLE INFRACTION COMPLAINT FOR CIVIL CONTEMPT	DOCKET NUMBER	Trial Court of Massachusetts District Court Department	
NAME, ADDRESS AND ZIP CODE OF VIOLATOR		NAME AND ADDRESS OF COURT DIVISION	←——— A CIVIL CONTEMPT HEARING WILL BE HELD AT THIS COURT ON THE DATE AND
DATE OF BIRTH CITATION NUMBER POLICE DEPARTMENT		DATE OF HEARING TIME AT .M.	TIME SPECIFIED ←———

To any Justice of the District Court Department:

The undersigned complainant, on behalf of the Commonwealth, on oath complains that the above named person did fail or refuse to comply with the provisions of Chapter 90C of the General Laws, as indicated more fully below, and did therefore commit an act of civil contempt.

Basis of contempt charge: It is alleged that the above named person:

☐ After receiving the citation, indicated above for one or more civil motor vehicle infractions, did fail to either make payment of the appropriate civil assessment or notify the court of a desire to contest the infractions within 20 days, in accordance with G.L. c. 90C, s. 3(A).

☐ After being found responsible for one or more civil motor vehicle infractions charged in the citation indicated above, did fail or refuse to pay the imposed motor vehicle infraction assessment(s) by _____ 19___, as ordered.

☐ Did fail, without good cause, to appear on _____, 19___, for a hearing on one or more civil motor vehicle infractions charged in the citation indicated above.

SIGNATURE OF COMPLAINANT	SWORN TO BEFORE CLERK–MAGISTRATE/ASST. CLERK
X	X
FIRST JUSTICE	DATE SWORN TO
WITNESS	

DC–MV–5 (2/86)

POLICE COPY

FORM DC–MV–5. RETURN OF SERVICE

[Pub. Note: This Form is composed of four documents which should be filed together, viz., Court Copy, Violator Copy, Police Copy, and Return of Service.]

CIVIL MOTOR VEHICLE INFRACTION SUMMONS AND RETURN OF SERVICE	DOCKET NUMBER	Trial Court of Massachusetts District Court Department	
NAME, ADDRESS AND ZIP CODE OF VIOLATOR		NAME AND ADDRESS OF COURT DIVISION	<— A CIVIL CONTEMPT HEARING WILL BE HELD AT THIS COURT ON THE DATE AND

DATE OF BIRTH	CITATION NUMBER	POLICE DEPARTMENT	DATE OF HEARING	TIME	TIME SPECIFIED
				AT .M.	<—

To the person named above:

The undersigned complainant, on behalf of the Commonwealth, on oath complains that the above named person did fail or refuse to comply with the provisions of Chapter 90C of the General Laws, as indicated more fully below, and did therefore commit an act of civil contempt.

You are therefore ordered to appear in this court to answer to the charge of civil contempt on the date and time indicated above.

Failure to appear as ordered without good cause may result in the issuance of a warrant for your arrest.

Basis of contempt charge: It is alleged that the above named person:

☐ After receiving the citation, indicated above for one or more civil motor vehicle infractions, did fail to either make payment of the appropriate civil assessment or notify the court of a desire to contest the infractions within 20 days, in accordance with G.L. c. 90C, s. 3(A).

☐ After being found responsible for one or more civil motor vehicle infractions charged in the citation indicated above, did fail or refuse to pay the imposed motor vehicle infraction assessment(s) by _____, 19___, as ordered.

☐ Did fail, without good cause, to appear on _____, 19___, for a hearing on one or more civil motor vehicle infractions charged in the citation indicated above.

SIGNATURE OF COMPLAINANT	SWORN TO BEFORE CLERK–MAGISTRATE/ASST. CLERK
X	X
FIRST JUSTICE	DATE SWORN TO
WITNESS	

SERVICE BY MAIL (BY CLERK–MAGISTRATE'S OFFICE)

☐ Complaint and summons mailed by regular mail on: _____ by: _____
☐ Complaint and summons mailed by certified mail on: _____ by: _____

RETURN OF SERVICE (IF OFFICER SERVICE REQUIRED)

I certify that I served this complaint and summons by:
☐ Delivering a copy of it personally to the defendant
☐ Leaving a copy of it at the defendant's last and usual place of abode.
☐ I was unable to make service because:

DATE OF SERVICE	SIGNATURE OF PERSON MAKING SERVICE	TITLE OF PERSON MAKING SERVICE

DC–MV–5 (2/88)   RETURN OF SERVICE

VIII.   UNIFORM RULES ON IMPOUNDMENT PROCEDURE

Effective September 1, 1986

Table of Rules

Rule 1.   Applicability and Definitions

(a) Applicability. The Uniform Rules on Impoundment Procedure (URIP) govern impoundment of otherwise public case records that are filed in civil and criminal proceedings in each Department of the Trial Court. Case records are presumed to be open to the public, unless they are impounded or sealed as a matter of law, or impounded by a court order. These rules are inapplicable to case records that are required to be impounded by statute, court rule, standing order, or case law, except as otherwise provided in Rules 9, 11, and 13. These rules shall not be construed to deprive a person of any rights or remedies regarding impoundment that are otherwise available under law.

(b) Definitions. As used herein:

(1) "Case" shall include any matter that has been entered in any Department of the Trial Court. Each case shall always have a case caption and an assigned case number visible on the court's docket and index, even if a pseudonym must be used for a party whose identity is impounded.

(2) "Case Caption" shall mean the official title of the case. For example, *Commonwealth v. Smith, Jones v. Jones*, or *Impounded Plaintiff v. Jones*.

(3) "Case record" shall mean all or any portion of court papers, documents, exhibits, orders, and other records, including an audio recording or official transcript of a proceeding, that are made, entered, or filed and maintained by the clerk in connection with a transaction of court business.

(4) "Case law" shall mean appellate decisions that are binding precedent for a Massachusetts court.

(5) "Clerk" shall mean Clerk, Clerk–Magistrate, Register of Probate, Recorder of the Land Court, their assistants, and designated court personnel.

(6) "Court" shall mean a judge or justice.

(7) "Docket" shall mean the paper or electronic list of case information maintained by the clerk that contains the case caption, case number, and a chronological entry identifying the date and title of each paper, document, exhibit, order, or judgment filed in a case, and the scheduling and occurrence of events in the case.

(8) "Final Disposition" shall mean, in a civil or criminal proceeding, when (i) a final judgment, sentence, decree, or order of dismissal has entered as to all claims, counts, and parties, (ii) any timely post-judgment motions have been disposed, and (iii) any appeal has been concluded and the rescript entered.

(9) "Impoundment" shall mean the act of keeping some or all of the case record separate and unavailable for public inspection. Impounded records are not accessible to anyone other than the court, clerk, authorized court personnel, attorneys of record, and the parties to the case, unless otherwise ordered. Any order of impoundment shall not restrict the clerk, as keeper of the records, from accessing information sufficient to file the impounded documents and carry out the clerk's duties required under URIP Rule 9. "Impounded" information includes material that a statute, court rule, standing order, case law, or court order designates must be withheld as "impounded," "withheld from public inspection," "not available for public inspection," "segregated," or "confidential," though these terms are not exhaustive. "Sealed" records are distinct from "impounded" records, in that sealed records are available to the court only, unless otherwise ordered.

(10) "Index" or "indices" shall mean the clerk's list of cases, whether maintained alphabetically or chronologically.

(11) "Interested nonparty" shall mean a person who is not or was not a party to the underlying matter in which an impoundment issue has arisen, but who nevertheless expresses to the court (through a motion, an appearance limited to impoundment, filing, or otherwise) an interest in the impoundment proceeding, or who has been named by the court as a person who shall receive notice.

(12) "Party" shall mean a person who is a litigant in the civil or criminal matter in which the impoundment proceeding has arisen.

(13) "Person" shall mean any natural person or any business, legal, or government entity.

(14) "Public record" or "public case record" shall mean a record that is accessible to any and all persons.

(c) Impoundment and Discovery.

(1) Where impoundment is sought in connection with discovery, these rules shall be applied in a manner consistent with the provisions of Rule 26(c) of the Massachusetts Rules of Civil Procedure, Rule 26(c) of the Massachusetts Rules of Domestic Relations Procedure, or Rule 14(a)(6) of the Massachusetts Rules of Criminal Procedure.

(2) In civil and criminal proceedings, material received by the clerk directly from a third person or nonparty in response to a subpoena, summons, or court order for discovery purposes is not available for public inspection until either a party files the material as an attachment to a pleading or motion, introduces the material as evidence, or the court so orders. The clerk shall make a notation on the docket indicating that impounded materials were filed in response to court order or discovery request.

Amended April 24, 2015, effective October 1, 2015.

Rule 2. Motion for Impoundment

(a) Content of Motion.

(1) *Motion.* Any party or interested nonparty may file a written motion for impoundment of a portion or all of the case record in any judicial proceeding. The motion shall describe with particularity (i) the material sought to be impounded, (ii) the duration for which impoundment is sought, (iii) the reasons impoundment is necessary, and (iv) the reasons other alternatives to impoundment will not afford adequate protection. The movant shall include proposed findings and a proposed order, conforming to URIP Rule 8, with the motion.

(2) *Affidavit.* A motion for impoundment shall be accompanied by affidavit in support thereof. Unless otherwise provided herein, the rules governing motions and affidavits in civil or criminal proceedings generally shall apply to requests for impoundment.

(3) *Public Nature of Motion and Affidavit.* The clerk shall enter the motion and affidavit on the case docket. Unless the court impounds the motion and affidavit by separate order, they remain publicly available documents.

(b) Submission of the Material Sought to Be Impounded.

(1) *Material Outside of the Case Record.* A motion for impoundment must be filed and ruled upon prior to submission of the actual material sought to be impounded. The clerk shall not accept any document that the movant seeks to be impounded until the court has ruled on the motion or ordered otherwise.

(2) *Materials for in camera Review.* If the court orders the movant to file the materials sought to be impounded for the court's *in camera* review, the movant shall first place them in an envelope bearing the case caption and a prominent notation that the documents within are "PROVISIONALLY IMPOUNDED PENDING COURT ORDERED *IN CAMERA* REVIEW." The clerk shall withhold the submission from public inspection until there is a ruling on the motion. If the court allows the motion, the allowance shall

be noted on the envelope and the materials shall be impounded for the duration of the order. If the court denies the motion, within fourteen days, the movant must retrieve the materials from the clerk or notify the clerk that the materials should be filed in their entirety. Should the same materials be filed, they will be placed in the public case record. The clerk will destroy any materials that have not been retrieved or filed by the fifteenth day.

(3) *Materials Previously Filed in the Case Record.* A motion may be made for impoundment of information that is currently contained in the case record. Upon receipt of such a motion, the clerk shall remove the subject material from the case record and withhold it from public dissemination pending the court's ruling on the motion. A hearing on the motion shall be held within three days unless otherwise agreed by the parties or ordered by the court.

Amended April 24, 2015, effective October 1, 2015.

Rule 3. *Ex Parte* Impoundment

(a) Motion and How Allowed.
An *ex parte* order of impoundment may be issued by the court without prior notice only upon either the filing of a written motion supported by affidavit in the manner provided in URIP Rule 2, or by the court *sua sponte*, and only upon a showing that immediate and irreparable injury may result before a party or interested third person can be heard in opposition. The court may conduct an *ex parte* hearing prior to issuing an order.

(b) Limited Duration of *Ex Parte* Impoundment Order.
An *ex parte* order of impoundment shall include the date of issuance and the clerk shall record the filing of the order on the docket, if one is maintained for that case type, and store the order with the underlying materials. An *ex parte* order of impoundment shall expire ten days from the date of issuance unless otherwise ordered by the court for good cause shown.

(c) Notice.
After the court has ruled on the *ex parte* motion for impoundment, the movant, unless the ruling was *sua sponte* by the court, shall serve a copy of the motion, supporting affidavit, and any other related documents, on the parties and any interested nonparty. The clerk shall provide notice of the *ex parte* order or the *sua sponte* order and the scheduling of any subsequent hearing. The court has discretion to order that certain notice requirements be withheld for good cause shown.

(d) Motion to Modify or Terminate *Ex Parte* Impoundment Order.
Any party or interested nonparty aggrieved by an *ex parte* order may file a written motion to vacate or modify the *ex parte* order. The motion may request a hearing not fewer than two days from the date of filing. Any motion to modify or terminate an *ex parte* order shall be accompanied by a certificate of service that notice has been provided to all parties, any interested nonparty, and any other person named by the court.

(e) Search Warrants.

(1) *Ex Parte Motion for Impoundment, Order, and Notice.* An *ex parte* motion to impound materials related to the issuance and/or execution of a search warrant may be filed and allowed in conformance with Rule 3(a). The court may enter, contemporaneously with or subsequent to the issuance of a search warrant, an *ex parte* order that the

search warrant application and any related materials be impounded upon their return to the court. An *ex parte* order of impoundment shall expire ten days from the date of issuance unless otherwise ordered by the court for good cause shown. The clerk shall record the filing of any order on the docket or, if a docket for search warrants is not maintained, on the clerk's application folder. The court has discretion to order that the notice requirements of Rule 3(c) be withheld for good cause shown.

(2) *Motion to Modify or Terminate an Ex Parte Order Related to a Search Warrant.* After an order to impound a search warrant or related materials has issued, any motion for relief from the impoundment order shall be filed in the court or division where the search warrant was returned. A judge in the court or division where the search warrant was returned may request the transfer of a hearing on a motion to impound a search warrant or motion for relief of an impoundment to a different court department or division (i) if the impoundment order was ordered by a judge of a different court department or division or (ii) if a criminal case relating to the search warrant is pending in a different court department or division.

Amended April 24, 2015, effective October 1, 2015.

Rule 4. Service

(a) **Service.** Except as otherwise provided by these rules, a movant shall serve any motion or opposition related to impoundment, or motion to modify or terminate impoundment, and any supporting materials on all parties, interested nonparties, and any other person named by the court, by mailing or delivering a copy to counsel for any represented person and to any self-represented person. Service on a represented person shall be made on the person's attorney unless service on the represented person is ordered by the court. Service shall be made in the manner provided by Rule 5 of the Massachusetts Rules of Civil Procedure or by any alternative means ordered by the court. In the event an order of impoundment is sought at the time of, or prior to, service of the original complaint, service shall be made in accordance with Rule 4 of the Massachusetts Rules of Civil Procedure. The time periods for hearing shall be as set forth in Rule 6 of the Massachusetts Rules of Civil Procedure.

(b) **Service on Parties Prior to, or Simultaneously with, Service of Complaint in Civil Proceedings.** When an order of impoundment is sought at the time of, or prior to, service of the original complaint in a civil proceeding, service shall be made in the manner provided by Rule 4 of the Massachusetts Rules of Civil Procedure.

(c) **Service on Interested Nonparty.** The court may, prior to hearing, order notice to be given to any interested nonparty. Notice to such interested nonparty shall be given in such manner as the court may direct. If a person who receives notice under this subsection seeks to participate in the impoundment proceedings, the person must comply with URIP Rule 6.

(d) **Service on the Office of the Attorney General by Interested Nonparty in Criminal Cases.** The movant shall serve notice on the Office of the Attorney General, in addition to the parties to the case, of any motion filed in any court by an interested nonparty to obtain access to impounded documents in a criminal case. The Office of the Attorney General shall have an opportunity to be heard on the motion. The movant shall also notify the court of that office's right to be heard on the motion.

(e) **Affidavit of Service.** Service shall be proved by an affidavit containing a particular statement thereof, including the names and addresses of all parties, their counsel, and all interested nonparties who have been given notice, and the method and date of service. The affidavit shall be served and filed with the motion.

(f) **Timing.** The motion for impoundment and supporting materials shall be served before or at the same time as such documents are mailed or delivered to the court.

Amended April 24, 2015, effective October 1, 2015.

Rule 5. Opposition

Any party or interested nonparty may serve and file an opposing affidavit not later than one day before any hearing, if scheduled, unless otherwise ordered. Service of any opposing affidavit shall be made in accordance with the procedures provided in URIP Rule 4 unless otherwise ordered.

Amended April 24, 2015, effective October 1, 2015.

Rule 6. Involvement of Interested Nonparties

(a) **Motion and Appearance in Pending Civil or Criminal Cases.** An interested nonparty who seeks, pursuant to URIP Rules 2, 3, 5, or 10, to request, oppose, modify, or terminate an order of impoundment pertaining to the case record of a pending civil or criminal case shall file a motion for such relief with the court and shall serve the motion in accordance with URIP Rule 4 and subsection (c) of this rule. Such a motion shall (i) specify the relief requested, (ii) specify the grounds therefor, (iip be accompanied by an affidavit setting forth the nature of the movant's interest in the matter of impoundment and any facts on which the motion relies, and (iv) be accompanied by a notice of appearance for the limited purpose of participating in the impoundment proceeding, but without making the person a party to the case for other purposes. Proceedings on the motion shall be in accordance with the procedures described in URIP Rules 2, 3, 5, or 10, as applicable.

(b) **Cases in Which a Final Disposition Has Entered.** An interested nonparty who seeks, pursuant to URIP Rules 2, 3, 5, or 10, to request, oppose, modify, or terminate an order of impoundment pertaining to the case record of a prior civil or criminal case in which a final disposition has been entered shall file a separate civil action in the court where the prior action commenced, specifying the relief sought. The civil action shall name, as defendants, the clerk of court in his or her official capacity and (1) if the prior case was a civil case, all parties to the prior case, or (2) if the prior case was a criminal case, the defendant(s) in the prior case, the Office of the Attorney General, and the Office of the District Attorney of the county where the case commenced.

(c) **Service on the Office of the Attorney General by Interested Nonparty in Criminal Cases.** The interested nonparty movant shall serve notice on the Office of the Attorney General, in addition to the parties to the case, of any motion filed in any court to obtain access to impounded documents in a criminal case in accordance with the provisions of URIP Rule 4(d).

Amended April 24, 2015, effective October 1, 2015.

Rule 7. Hearing

(a) **Hearing Required.** The court may enter an order of impoundment for good cause shown and in accordance with applicable law only after a hearing, except as provided in URIP Rule 2(b)(3), URIP Rule 3(a), or URIP Rule 7(e). During the hearing, those present shall preserve the confidentiality of the material that is at issue. A record of the proceedings, including the record of any *in camera* hearing, shall be preserved stenographically or by a recording device.

(b) **Good Cause.** In determining good cause, the court shall consider all relevant factors. including, but not limited to, (i) the nature of the parties and the controversy, (ii) the type of information and the privacy interests involved, (iii) the extent of community interest, (iv) constitutional rights, and (v) the reason(s) for the request. Agreement of all parties, interested nonparties, or other persons in favor of impoundment shall not, in itself, be sufficient to constitute good cause.

(c) **Interested Nonparties.** The court may, in its discretion, permit an interested nonparty who files a notice of appearance limited to participation in the impoundment proceeding to be heard at any impoundment hearing.

(d) *In Camera* **Hearing.** Where a public hearing may risk disclosure of the information sought to be impounded, the court may, upon a written finding of good cause, conduct *in camera* only that portion of the hearing that would risk disclosure. The record of any *in camera* hearing shall be impounded until a court orders otherwise.

(e) **Trade Secret Exception.** The court may, upon a written finding of good cause under URIP Rule 7(b), allow a motion for impoundment without a hearing when (1) the reason for the impoundment is to protect trade secrets or other confidential research, development, or business information, (2) the motion is by agreement or the motion is unopposed, (3) no party or other person has requested a hearing, and (4) the information does not involve an alleged or potential public hazard or risk to public safety.

Amended April 24, 2015, effective October 1, 2015.

Rule 8. Order of Impoundment

(a) **Good Cause.** An order of impoundment, whether *ex parte* or after notice, may be entered only upon a written finding of good cause.

(b) **Specificity.** An order of impoundment shall specifically state what material is to be impounded, and, where appropriate, may specify how impoundment is to be implemented. An order of impoundment shall include the date of issuance and shall specify the duration of the order with a date certain for expiration of the order.

(c) **Narrow Tailoring.** The court shall tailor the scope of the impoundment order so that it does not exceed the need for impoundment. The court may order that the movant or the filer of any material submit a redacted copy of the impounded document to the clerk for public inspection.

(d) **Public Inspection.** The order shall be entered on the docket, kept in the public file, and made available for public inspection. The order shall provide sufficient information for the public to identify the case caption, the case number, and to ascertain the grounds, duration, and scope of the impoundment. All information stating or disclosing the impounded material shall be omitted or redacted from the order prior to public inspection. A copy of the order shall be affixed to the envelope or other receptacle containing the court's copy of the impounded materials.

Amended April 24, 2015, effective October 1, 2015.

Rule 9. Clerk's Duties

Upon entry of an order of impoundment, or pursuant to an impoundment designation set forth in a statute, court rule, standing order, or case law, the clerk shall make a notation in the docket indicating what material has been impounded and the duration of its impoundment status. All impounded material shall be clearly marked, and kept separate and unavailable for public inspection. The impounded material shall be available to the court, the clerk and designated court personnel, the attorneys of record, the parties to the case, and other persons designated by the court, unless otherwise ordered by the court. Upon expiration or other termination of the order of impoundment, the material shall be returned to the public case record, unless other arrangements have been made, and the docket marked accordingly.

Amended April 24, 2015, effective October 1, 2015.

Rule 10. Modification or Termination
of Order of Impoundment

A party or interested nonparty may, by motion supported by affidavit, seek to modify or terminate an order of impoundment. The motion shall be served in accordance with URIP Rule 4 and 6(c).

No order of impoundment may be modified or terminated, except upon an order of the court and upon written findings in support thereof.

Amended April 24, 2015, effective October 1, 2015.

Rule 11. Material Impounded by Statute, Court
Rule, Standing Order, or Case Law

Any party or interested nonparty may file a motion supported by affidavit for relief from impoundment or for release of material required to be impounded pursuant to a statute, court rule, standing order, or case law, except where a different procedure is otherwise provided. The procedures set forth in these rules shall govern requests for relief from impoundment to the extent practicable.

Relief from impoundment shall be granted by the court only upon written findings.

Amended April 24, 2015, effective October 1, 2015.

Rule 12. Review

(a) Review of Orders Entered in Ongoing Proceedings.
A party or interested nonparty aggrieved by an order impounding or refusing to impound material or vacating, modifying, or refusing to modify a prior order of impoundment in an ongoing proceeding, may enter in the Appeals Court, within thirty days of the entry of such order, a petition for review by the single justice. The single justice's review shall proceed in accordance with the law and procedures governing petitions to the single justice.

(b) Review of Orders Entered in Proceedings Which Have Concluded. Upon the entry of judgment, including in an action commenced pursuant to URIP Rule 6(b), or other final disposition of the proceeding, any appeal of an impoundment order proceeds pursuant to the Massachusetts Rules of Appellate Procedure.

(c) Notice to the Clerk. In any matter entered or pending in an appellate court, the filer of any document shall provide written notice to the clerk of the appellate court of any document that contains impounded information. Such notification shall accompany the document and specify those papers, documents, or exhibits, or portions thereof, that are impounded and shall include a copy of the order of impoundment, if any, or a reference to other authority for the impoundment. Unless otherwise ordered, material impounded in the Trial Court shall remain impounded in the appellate court.

Amended April 24, 2015, effective October 1, 2015.

Rule 13. Maintaining Confidentiality of Impounded Material

(a) Duty to Identify Impounded Material. The filer of any document in a case or court proceeding shall first ascertain whether any information contained within the document is subject to a court order of impoundment, or contains information designated as "impounded" by statute, court rule, standing order, or case law. Unless it is necessary to do so, a filer shall not include impounded information in documents filed with the court

(b) Notice to the Clerk. The filer of a document containing impounded information shall simultaneously file a notice that shall (i) notify the clerk that impounded information is included within the document being filed; (ii) identify the specific legal authority requiring impoundment of the identified information; and (iii) identify the precise location of the impounded information within the document being filed. The clerk shall docket the notice and designate the referenced document as impounded. The cover page of the document containing the impounded information shall identify that it is impounded.

(c) Duty to Protect Confidentiality. All persons shall protect the confidentiality of the impounded material. During any hearing or trial in public sessions, a filer shall not disclose impounded material, provided that in cases where such disclosure is necessary, a filer shall notify the clerk in advance and shall, in appropriate cases, make such disclosures in a manner which protects the confidentiality of the impounded material.

(d) Inadvertent Filing. Any inadvertent filing of a document that contains impounded information, without the required accompanying notice, does not waive the confidentiality of the information. In such instances, any party may file a motion to strike such material from the record, or the court may act *sua sponte*. The court may order the material struck and to be refiled, with the appropriate notice and any necessary redaction.

Adopted April 24, 2015, effective October 1, 2015.

IX. UNIFORM RULES ON SUBPOENAS TO COURT OFFICIALS

Adopted Effective September 1, 1992

Table of Rules

Rule 1.   Subpoena to a Justice, Magistrate or Probation Officer

A subpoena to compel a justice, magistrate or probation officer of the Trial Court to testify concerning actions taken in her or his official capacity shall not be served without the prior approval of the court in which the underlying matter is pending. The party shall seek the necessary order of approval by written motion which shall specify the purpose(s) for which the testimony is sought. Except for good cause shown, a copy of such motion shall be served on the justice, magistrate or probation officer whose testimony the party seeks to compel. If the court grants its approval, the party shall serve the subpoena and a copy of the court order approving the subpoena on the justice, magistrate or probation officer. A justice, magistrate or probation officer shall not be required to respond to a subpoena served on her or him unless it is accompanied by a copy of the court order approving the subpoena.

Adopted effective September 1, 1992; amended effective July 1, 1995.

Rule 2.   Subpoena Duces Tecum to Court Officials

(1) A party shall not be entitled to serve a subpoena on a clerk-magistrate, register, recorder, or other official keeper of records of the Trial Court to compel the production of court records [1] or administrative records [2] which said court official holds in his or her official capacity and said court official shall not be required to respond to such a subpoena.

(2) In accordance with the applicable rules of procedure,[3] a clerk-magistrate, register, recorder, or other official keeper of records of the Trial Court shall provide an attested copy of court records or administrative records to a party who requests an attested copy of such records unless the records have been sealed or impounded by statute, court rule, standing order, administrative directive, or order of impoundment. Access to sealed or impounded court records or administrative records shall be governed by the applicable statute, court rule, standing order, administrative directive, or Trial Court Rule VIII, Uniform Rules on Impoundment Procedure in the case of orders of impoundment.

(3) Notwithstanding the provisions of subsection (2), a clerk-magistrate, register, recorder, or other official keeper of records of the Trial Court may deny a request for an attested copy of administrative records if she or he determines that production of such records either may unduly impair the Trial Court's ability to perform its necessary functions or may constitute an unwarranted invasion of personal privacy.

(4) A party whose request for an attested copy of court records or administrative records is denied shall be entitled to ask the court in which the underlying matter is pending to order the clerk-magistrate, register, recorder, or other official keeper of records who denied the request to provide the party with an attested copy of the records provided said records have not been sealed or impounded. The party shall request the order by written motion and shall specify the purpose(s) for which the records are sought. Except for good cause shown, a copy of the motion shall be served on the court official who denied the request. Said official shall be entitled to provide the court with a brief written statement of his or her reasons for denying the request. Where it would assist an appropriate determination, the justice before whom the motion is pending may order the clerk-magistrate, register, recorder, or other official keeper of records to provide to the court a copy of the records for inspection in camera.

(5) A party who receives an attested copy of court records or administrative records of the Trial Court pursuant to the provisions of this rule shall be required to pay the clerk-magistrate, register, recorder, or other official keeper of records the regular fee for an attested copy of such records unless the requesting party is a court, the Office of the Attorney General, an office of a district attorney, any other agency of the Commonwealth, a police prosecutor, or a party represented by an attorney provided by the Committee for Public Counsel Services. Massachusetts General Laws c. 261, §§ 27A–27G shall apply to any request on behalf of an indigent party who is not represented by an attorney provided by the Committee for Public Counsel Services and in such case the cost of attested copies shall be deemed an "extra cost" as defined in § 27A.

Adopted effective September 1, 1992; amended September 6, 2001, effective October 1, 2001.

1 For purposes of this rule the term "court records" shall include, but is not limited to, indexes, dockets, case papers, pleadings, records, reports, exhibits, electronic and stenographic recordings of court proceedings, created by, filed with, or kept and maintained by a clerk-magistrate, register, recorder, or other official keeper of court records in connection with any civil or criminal proceeding in any communicable form including, but not limited to, written, typed or printed records, microfiche records, microfilm records, audio and video recordings, and electronic or computerized records.

2 For purposes of this rule "administrative records" shall mean those records related to the administrative rather than the judicial functions of the Trial Court. Such records shall include, but are not limited to, audit forms and records, budget forms and records, MMARS/accounting forms and records, payroll forms and records, procurement forms and records, personnel records, and correspondence.

3 Mass.R.Civ.P. 44 and Mass.R.Crim.P. 40.

Rule 3. Subpoena Duces Tecum for Records of the Office of the Commissioner of Probation

(1) A party shall not be entitled to serve a subpoena duces tecum on the official keeper of records * for the Office of the Commissioner of Probation and said official shall not be required to respond to such a subpoena.

(2) A party shall be entitled to access to records of the Office of the Commissioner of Probation only as provided by statute or court order. A party seeking a court order permitting access to records of the Office of the Commissioner of Probation shall request such an order from the court in which the underlying matter is pending by written motion which shall specify the purpose(s) for which access to such records is sought. Except for good cause shown, a copy of such motion shall be served on the official keeper of records for the Office of the Commissioner of Probation.

(3) A court order granting a party access to records of the Office of the Commissioner of Probation shall (1) require the party to supply to the Office of the Commissioner of Probation sufficient personal identifiers (e.g. name, address, date of birth) for each record requested so that probation central file personnel can narrow each request down to one record, (2) direct the official keeper of records for the Office of the Commissioner of Probation to provide the party with attested copies of said records, and (3) specifically limit the party's use of the attested copies of such records and the information contained therein to the purpose(s) for which access was granted.

Adopted effective September 1, 1992.

X. UNIFORM RULE REQUIRING DISCLOSURE OF PRESENT OR PAST RECEIPT OF PUBLIC ASSISTANCE BENEFITS BY MINOR CHILDREN

Adopted Effective February 1, 1993

Upon the filing or issuance of any petition or complaint pursuant to G.L. c. 190B, G.L. c. 208, G.L. c. 209, G.L. c. 209A, G.L. c. 209C or G.L. c. 209D or any other provision of law concerning the support and maintenance of a minor child, the plaintiff in the action, should any minor child who is named in the petition or complaint be either a past or present recipient of public assistance through Aid to Families With Dependent Children, General Assistance, Medicaid, or Foster Care or any other program established pursuant to G.L. c. 117A, G.L. c. 118, or G.L. c. 118E, shall notify the Child Support Enforcement Division of the Department of Revenue of the pendency of the petition or complaint within three (3) days of its filing. The moving party must thereafter serve notice on the Child Support Enforcement Division of each hearing or trial date with respect to any such petition or complaint.

Notice in compliance with this rule shall be served upon the Department of Revenue at the Office of the Child Support Enforcement Division for the county in which the petition or complaint is pending.

Said notice shall identify the division and department of the Trial Court in which the action has been filed, the title and docket number of the action, the name of the parents of any such child, the Social Security number of each parent and the name or names of any such child or children.

Amended effective December 27, 1995; amended June 24, 2009, effective July 1, 2009.

XI. UNIFORM RULE FOR PROBABLE CAUSE DETERMINATIONS FOR PERSONS ARRESTED WITHOUT A WARRANT

Effective July 1, 1994

(a) Definitions. In this rule the following words and phrases shall have the following meanings:

(1) "Judicial officer" means a clerk-magistrate, assistant clerk, temporary clerk-magistrate or temporary assistant clerk. In emergency circumstances, a judge of any department of the Trial Court may act as a judicial officer under this rule.

No judicial officer shall receive a fee for admitting a person to bail or recognizance in a case in which such judicial officer makes the determination provided for in this rule.

(2) "Local Court" means, the Boston Municipal Court Department, or the division of the District Court Department, the Housing Court Department, or the Juvenile Court Department, with jurisdiction over such offense.

(3) "Police" means the officer in charge of the place of detention, or his or her designee.

(4) "Weekday" means the period beginning at 8:30 A.M. on Monday and ending at 4:30 P.M. on the following Friday, exclusive of legal holidays.

(5) "Weekend" means the period beginning at 4:30 P.M. on Friday and ending at 8:30 A.M. on the following Monday.

(6) "Holiday" means the period beginning at 4:30 P.M. on the day before a legal holiday and ending at 8:30 A.M. on the day after a legal holiday.

(b) Right to Probable Cause Determination. A person who has been arrested for an offense for which no warrant has issued, if not released on bail or recognizance, shall be entitled prior to any extended pretrial detention to a determination by a judicial officer of whether there is probable cause to believe that such person has committed such offense, except where such person's detention is otherwise authorized by a warrant or other judicial process.

(c) Time for Determination. The police shall request such determination from a judicial officer as soon as reasonably possible after such person's arrest. Such request and determination must be made no later than twenty-four hours after arrest, absent exigent circumstances.

(1) *On Weekdays.* If such determination is requested on a weekday, such determination shall be made by a judicial officer of the local court as soon as reasonably possible. If no judicial officer is in attendance at the local court during normal court hours, such determination shall be made by a judge, or shall be made by a judicial officer of such other division of that court department as has been designated by the chief justice of that department.

(2) *On Weekends and Holidays.* If such determination is requested on a weekend or holiday, such determination shall be made by a judicial officer of the Boston Municipal, District, Housing, Juvenile or Superior Court Departments. The Trial Court's Chief Justice for Administration and Management shall establish a procedure to make available one or more such judicial officers to make such determinations each weekend and holiday during such hours as the Chief Justice for Administration and Management shall determine. All clerk-magistrates, assistant clerks, temporary clerk-magistrates and temporary assistant clerks of such departments, who are determined necessary to the implementation of the procedure by the Chief Justice for Administration and Management, shall participate in such procedure unless exempted by the Chief Justice for Administration and Management because of illness or other personal hardship.

(d) Nature of Determination. A judicial officer shall make such determination prior to arraignment in an ex parte, non-adversary and informal proceeding at which the arrestee has no right to be present or to be represented by counsel. Such determination shall be governed by the same legal standards that govern determinations of probable cause to support the issuance of an arrest warrant. In making such determination, the judicial officer shall consider all relevant information that is alleged to constitute probable cause for each offense for which such person has been arrested without a warrant, submitted under oath or affirmation, or under the pains and penalties of perjury, whether or not such information was known at the time of arrest. Such information, if presented in writing, may be transmitted to a judicial officer by facsimile transmission.

A judicial officer's liability for any determination made under this rule shall be governed by the legal standards concerning immunity for legal decisions made by judges and magistrates.

(e) Results of Determination. The judicial officer shall promptly reduce to writing his or her determination as to each offense and notify the police of each determination. A copy of such written determination shall be transmitted to the police as soon as possible. Such copy may be transmitted by facsimile transmission.

(1) *Probable Cause Found by Judicial Officer of Local Court.* If a judicial officer of the local court determines that there is probable cause to believe that such arrestee committed one or more of the offenses for which he or she was arrested, the judicial officer shall file with such court copies of his or her written determination and of any written statement of facts submitted to him or her. Such determination, and any such written statement of facts, shall be filed and docketed with the record of such case, and shall be a public record.

(2) *Probable Cause Found by Other Judicial Officer.* If a judicial officer other than a judicial officer of the local court determines that there is probable cause to believe that such arrestee committed one or more of the offenses for which he or she was arrested, the judicial officer shall direct the police to file with the local court, together with the application for complaint for such offense, copies of the judicial officer's written determination and of any written statement of facts submitted to him or her. Such determination, and such written statement of facts, shall be filed and docketed with the record of such case, and shall be a public record.

(3) *No Probable Cause Found.* If a judicial officer determines that there is no probable cause to believe that the arrestee committed any of the offenses for which he or she was arrested, the police shall promptly release such arrestee from pretrial detention for such offenses. The judicial officer shall file with the local court copies of his or her written determination and of any written statement of facts submitted to him or her. Such determination, and any such written statement of facts, shall be filed separately from the records of criminal and delinquency cases, but shall be a public record.

Amended effective July 1, 1994.

XII.   REQUESTS FOR INTERDEPARTMENTAL JUDICIAL ASSIGNMENTS

Adopted Effective December 2, 1996

This Rule governs the method for requesting interdepartmental judicial assignments. Pursuant to G.L. c. 211B, section 9, the Chief Justice for Administration and Management of the Trial Court (hereafter, "CJAM") is authorized to assign a judge appointed to any Department of the Trial Court to sit in any other Department of the Trial Court for such period or periods of time as will best promote the speedy dispatch of judicial business.

The assignments may authorize a judge to sit simultaneously as a judge of several Departments for the purpose of reducing delay and duplication in actions pending in the Trial Court.

As used herein, the term "party" shall mean the attorney of record for a party, if represented by counsel, or, if a party is not represented by counsel, the party acting pro se.

1.   Interdepartmental Assignment and Consolidation of Cases—Purpose and Procedure.   If two or more actions are pending in different departments of the Trial Court, and if a judge, Clerk–Magistrate, register, or party determines that the separate actions are related actions involving substantially the same or similar issues and parties, the judge, Clerk–Magistrate, register, or party may request that the Chief Justice for Administration and Management make an appropriate interdepartmental assignment so that one judge may hear all related matters.   The requests should be directed to the CJAM, with copies to the Chief Justice of each Department in which the related actions are pending.

Such assignments shall be made to accomplish one or more of the following purposes:

- to promote speedy disposition of cases, reduce duplication of hearings and promote judicial economy when each pending action will require a hearing or trial;
- to afford complete and permanent relief which might not be obtained unless the actions are consolidated for hearing and heard by one judge;
- to effectuate a proposed settlement of one case through the filing of a subsequent action in another court department; or
- where there is some other reason, consistent with the speedy and efficient dispatch of judicial business, why the cases should be assigned to and heard by one judge.

2.   Content and Timing of Request.   If a request for an interdepartmental assignment is made by one or more parties, the request shall be made in a letter to the CJAM and the Chief Justices of the Departments in which the actions are pending.   The letter should identify by title, name of court division, and docket number each of the related cases; list all parties and counsel of record, with addresses; describe the nature of the cases; and include a specific, individualized statement of reasons why the separate actions are deemed related and an interdepartmental assignment would be appropriate, with particular attention to the latter in situations in which at least one of the related cases will *not* require a hearing or trial.   Every request must be accompanied by a copy of the current docket entries in the related cases, with the most recent court activity listed thereon.   Requests which

are submitted without *current* docket sheets need not be considered.

A party making a request pursuant to this Rule shall at the same time send a copy of such request to all parties in the related cases, and to any judge who has been specially assigned to any of the cases, and, as to any case to which no judge has been specially assigned, to the first justice of the court in which that case is pending.   Any party opposing the request will have seven days from receipt of the request to submit to the CJAM and Chief Justices of the respective Departments a letter in opposition with a statement of the reasons therefor.

Except for good cause shown and described in the request, a request for an interdepartmental judicial assignment will not be considered if made within 60 days prior to an established trial date.   Cases shall not be removed from a trial list solely because a request for an interdepartmental judicial assignment is pending.

3.   Applicable Considerations.   Factors to be considered in determining whether actions are related include the following:

- whether the actions involve the same parties (including children) and the same attorneys;
- whether, in child welfare cases in which all parties are not identical, the person who is not a party to one of the cases sought to be consolidated is a parent, foster parent, guardian, relative or caretaker who seeks custody, visitation, or related orders regarding the child;
- whether the actions involve common, or substantially the same or similar, questions of law and fact;
- whether the witnesses and the evidence to be presented in the separate actions will be the same or similar;   and
- whether the requested forms of relief are similar or related.

Factors to be considered in determining whether allowance of the request would tend to promote the speedy dispatch of court business and to reduce delay and duplication include the following:

- whether the actions are in similar stages of readiness;
- whether either action has an established trial date;
- whether the request was made to take advantage of an existing trial date in one case for use in the other case(s);
- whether allowance of the request might require that an established trial date for one of the cases be rescheduled to afford additional time for preparation or for trial of the other, unscheduled case(s);   and
- whether, notwithstanding the provisions of this Rule, a party already has caused a case to be removed from a trial list by informing the court that a request for an interdepartmental judicial assignment was or will be made.

Additional factors to be considered may include the following:

- whether, if the request is allowed, there will be a continuing or long-term need for a judge of one court Department to exercise the powers normally vested within another court Department, or whether the assignment only will be needed for one hearing;

- especially in cases involving child welfare, whether, due to special assignment to, or continuing familiarity with, one of the cases, it would be appropriate for the same judge to hear the related matter(s) to promote case continuity or permanency planning;
- whether the request should have been made earlier in order to reduce resulting delay; and
- any other special considerations that are not apparent from the docket entries or other portions of the written request.

4. Action by Chief Justices. Upon receipt of a complete request, the Chief Justices will review the request and any letters in opposition to determine whether the cases are related and whether the efficient administration of judicial business would be served by having the several actions heard by one judge. The Chief Justices will then forward their recommendations to the CJAM. When possible, the recommendations shall be forwarded to the CJAM within 30 days of receipt of a complete request.

5. Action by CJAM. The CJAM will review the request and the recommendations of the Chief Justices, and, if the interests of the Trial Court and of the parties would be served thereby, may make an appropriate order of assignment which would allow one judge to hear the related actions. When possible, the order of assignment or disallowance of the request shall be made by the CJAM within 45 days of receipt of a complete request. In cases with an established trial date, the decision on the request shall be made prior to the trial date. The CJAM will notify the Chief Justices and all parties of his decision on each request. Notwithstanding the provisions of this paragraph, in no event shall the pendency of a request be the sole cause for a case to be removed from a trial list.

6. Presumption in Certain Cases. There shall be a presumption in favor of allowance of the request if the parties to all the actions sought to be consolidated are identical, if each case will require a hearing or trial, and if the issues are substantially related. This presumption shall not apply with respect to the consolidation of hearings or reviews conducted pursuant to G.L. c. 119, § 29B with post-decree reviews of G.L. c. 210, § 3 matters.

7. Authority of CJAM in Absence of a Request. The CJAM may make such assignments in the absence of a request by a judge, Clerk–Magistrate, register, or party.

8. This rule shall not apply to a request by a party for the interdepartmental judicial assignment of a justice of the Superior Court Department to hear related actions pending in the Superior Court Department, the District Court Department and/or the Boston Municipal Court Department nor shall it apply to a joint request by all the principal parties for an interdepartmental assignment of a justice of the District Court Department or the Boston Municipal Court Department to hear related actions pending in the Superior Court Department, the District Court Department and/or the Boston Municipal Court Department. A party or parties seeking to have such related actions heard by a single justice shall file a motion to transfer in the Superior Court Department pursuant to G.L. c. 223, § 2B and then a motion to consolidate pursuant to Mass.R.Civ.P. 42 (a) in the court to which the transfer is made.

Adopted effective December 2, 1996. Amended May 3, 2005, effective July 1, 2005.

XIII. UNIFORM TRIAL COURT RULES FOR CIVIL COMMITMENT PROCEEDINGS FOR ALCOHOL AND SUBSTANCE USE DISORDERS G.L. c. 123 § 35

Table of Rules

Rule 1. Commencement of Proceedings

(a) Proceedings under the provisions of G.L. c. 123, § 35 in the District Court, Boston Municipal Court, and Juvenile Court Departments shall be commenced by the filing of a written petition, signed under the penalties of perjury, by a police officer, physician, spouse, blood relative, guardian, or court official seeking the issuance of an order of commitment of a person (hereinafter the "respondent") who the petitioner has reason to believe is an individual with an alcohol or substance use disorder, as those terms are defined in G.L. c. 123, § 35. Such a petitioner, including a court official, may petition on behalf of the respondent.

(b) Proceedings may be commenced in any Division of any of the three Departments without regard to the age, residence, or location of the respondent, but the age, residence, or location of the respondent may determine to which Division or Department any warrant or summons will be returnable pursuant to Rule 3.

(c) Following commencement, a petition may not be withdrawn without leave of court.

Adopted July 22, 2015, effective February 1, 2016. Amended July 20, 2016, effective September 6, 2016.

Commentary—2015

These rules implement the provisions of G.L. c. 123, § 35, clarifying and facilitating the conduct of the proceedings that the statute requires. Although section 35 appears within chapter 123, *Mental Health*, its provisions are confined to commitment for alcohol and substance use. The purpose of these rules is to provide a procedural groundwork for the orderly processing of section 35 petitions.

Rule 1(a) regulates the existing practice in the courts of allowing persons to seek their own commitment for substance use treatment. The statute requires that a police officer, physician, spouse, blood relative, guardian, or court official act as petitioner. As a result, a substance user desiring his own commitment will need to obtain the assistance of a statutorily-authorized petitioner. In many courts, a police prosecutor or a probation officer or other court official will be available to serve as petitioner when a substance user seeks the assistance of the court in addressing the addiction. Such a police officer or court official would be expected to determine whether there is a reasonable basis to believe that the substance user meets the statutory requirements for commitment and that voluntary treatment resources are unavailable or inadequate for the substance user's needs. The rule specifically permits this useful procedure.

Section 35 permits a qualified petitioner to initiate a petition in "any district court or any division of the juvenile court department." Unlike with harassment prevention orders, *see* G.L. c. 258E, § 2, section 35 imposes no venue requirements and does not differentiate jurisdiction by the age of the respondent. Accordingly, Rule 1(b) recognizes that there is no basis for denying a petitioner the right to file a petition in the Division or Department of the petitioner's choice. *Cf. M.B. v. J.B.*, 86 Mass. App. Ct. 108, 114–15 (2014) (venue requirements in G.L. c. 209A, § 2 are not jurisdictional and must be raised by the respondent or are waived). A petition for the commitment of a juvenile may be filed in Boston Municipal Court or a District Court, and a petition for the commitment of an adult may be filed in Juvenile Court. Similarly, a petition for commitment may be filed in a Division that is not the usual residence of the respondent. There is no statutory basis for prohibiting a petitioner from a choice of Department and Division and, in light of the usual emergency nature of section 35 petitions, requiring a petitioner to travel to another court could impose unnecessary risks to the safety of the respondent and others. Nonetheless, as provided in Rule 3(d), where the respondent is not present, the court may direct that the case ultimately be adjudicated in a more appropriate location or Department while respecting the petitioner's choice of where to initiate the petition.

Rule 1(c) recognizes that a section 35 proceeding is not an ordinary civil case terminable by the parties at will, but rather an invocation of the court's statutory power to protect the respondent, petitioner, and society at large. For this reason, once the petitioner has filed the petition by signing it and providing it to the court, withdrawal of a petition must be approved by a judge and should not be allowed unless the judge is satisfied that such withdrawal will not jeopardize the safety of the respondent, petitioner, or any other person.

Commentary—2016 Amendments

General Laws c. 123, § 35 was amended in 2016 by An Act Relative *to* Civil Commitments for Alcohol and Substance Use Disorders, St. 2016, c. 8, requiring revisions to the Uniform Rules. The Act was effective April 24, 2016.

Among other things, the 2016 legislation deleted the outdated terms "alcoholic" and "substance abuser," and replaced them with "alcohol use disorder" and "substance use disorder." St. 2016, c. 8, §§ 1–2, 4. This exemplary change reflects the desirability of removing stigma from persons suffering from these disorders, with the beneficial effects of increasing the willingness of persons to seek treatment for these disorders, both for themselves or for others. All participants in G.L. c. 123, § 35 commitment proceedings should remain focused on the goals of protecting persons suffering from these disorders and the community from the likelihood of serious harm and of providing necessary treatment to such persons.

The 2016 legislation reformatted G.L. c. 123, § 35, most notably by collapsing the first and second paragraphs into one paragraph and by replacing the fourth and fifth paragraphs with three paragraphs (now the third, fourth, and fifth paragraphs). Accordingly, some of the citations in the original commentary are now citing to an incorrect paragraph.

Rule 2.   Review of Petition

Upon the filing of a petition and any sworn statements the court may request from the petitioner at the time of such filing, the case shall be brought expeditiously before a judge who shall review the petition on the record in court. If the judge determines that either (1) the petitioner is statutorily unqualified to file a petition under the provisions of G.L. c. 123, § 35; or (2) the petitioner's allegation that the respondent is an individual with an alcohol or substance use disorder has no reasonable basis, the judge shall dismiss the case. Otherwise, if the respondent is present, the court shall immediately proceed in accordance with Rules 4 and 5. If the respondent is not present, the court shall immediately proceed in accordance with Rule 3.

Adopted July 22, 2015, effective February 1, 2016. Amended July 20, 2016, effective September 6, 2016.

Commentary—2015

Rule 2 contemplates that the judge may be able to determine that a petition lacks merit prior to the issuance of a summons or a warrant. The judge, in the exercise of discretion, may inquire further of a petitioner in making this preliminary decision. If the petitioner is statutorily unqualified but appears to have a strong case for the respondent's commitment, the judge may choose to refer the petitioner to a qualified petitioner, who would then decide whether to file a new petition for commitment. The absence of the petitioner, because the petitioner is a physician still at a hospital or for any other reason, would not be by itself grounds for dismissing the petition.

The last two sentences of Rule 2 recognize the importance of prompt action when addressing section 35 petitions. When the respondent is present at the time of the petition, the court must proceed expeditiously to the appointment of counsel and no consideration is given to whether a different Division or Department would have been preferable. When the respondent is not present, the court must expeditiously decide whether to issue a summons or a warrant.

Rule 3.   Issuance of Warrant or Summons; Execution of Warrant

(a) If the judge determines that there are reasonable grounds to believe that the respondent will not appear at the hearing and that any further delay in the proceeding would present an immediate danger to the physical well-being of the respondent, the court may issue a warrant for the apprehension and appearance of the respondent.

(b) If the court does not issue a warrant pursuant to Rule 3(a), the court shall cause a summons and a copy of the petition to be served on the respondent in the manner provided in G.L. c. 276, § 25. Following such service, if the respondent fails to appear at the time summoned, the court may issue a warrant for the apprehension and appearance of the respondent. The issuance of such a warrant shall not require a determination of immediate danger to the physical well-being of the respondent.

(c) The judge shall determine how long the warrant shall be effective, but shall not make any warrant effective for more than five business days. A warrant issued under this rule shall provide that it may be executed only when the respondent may be presented immediately after apprehension before a judge pursuant to Rule 4 or Rule 10.

(d) If the judge determines that the case should be heard in another Division or Department, because of the respondent's age or location or for other good reason, the judge may, in the exercise of discretion, make the warrant or summons returnable to an appropriate court in another Division or Department. The clerk shall notify the return court of the warrant or summons and transmit the papers listed in Rule 10(a) to the return court.

Adopted July 22, 2015, effective February 1, 2016. Amended July 20, 2016, effective September 6, 2016.

Commentary—2015

The standard for a warrant in Rule 3(a) is taken directly from G.L. c. 123, § 35, ¶ 3. It is important to note that immediate danger to the physical well-being of the respondent is a statutory prerequisite for issuing a warrant of apprehension at the time of the petition.

The last sentence in Rule 3(b) is based on the fact that a finding of "immediate danger" is not a statutory prerequisite for the issuance of a warrant after a respondent has failed to appear on a summons.

Rule 3(c) provides that the judge must determine how long a warrant of apprehension may be effective, but must choose a length of time no longer than three business days. Because of the emergency nature of section 35 petitions, the information supporting the petition is likely to become stale with the passage of time. The judge should make the warrant effective for a period of time less than three business days if the nature of the petition suggests that the information will become stale sooner than that. If the warrant expires without the respondent's apprehension, the petitioner would be able to initiate a new petition after providing fresh information or confirming the continued need for apprehension.

The provisions of Rule 3(d) balance the advisability of having section 35 petitions adjudicated by courts accustomed to determining the rights of persons the age of the respondent and the need for prompt disposition of any section 35 petition. Accordingly, when the respondent is present and no warrant or summons is necessary, the court should adjudicate the petition regardless of the age of the respondent to avoid the delays and possible loss of the respondent's presence that moving the proceeding would cause. Similarly, requiring the initial review and the determination whether to issue a warrant or a summons to be conducted by the court in which the petitioner files avoids unnecessary delays and risks. By contrast, issuing a warrant or summons returnable to another Department does not pose the same risks. Whether to do so in a particular case is a matter entrusted to the judge's discretion. It may be prudent for a Juvenile Court to retain a case involving a young adult or other person with whom the court has experience.

Similarly, a judge may decide that the filing court is a poor venue to adjudicate the petition because the respondent is expected to be located far from the court or because witnesses and information might be available in a different venue, such as one that contains the respondent's school or place of employment. In such cases, the judge may choose to make the warrant or summons returnable to the preferred venue.

Commentary—2016 Amendments

General Laws c. 123, § 35 was amended in 2016 by An Act Relative to Substance Use, Treatment, Education, and Prevention, St. 2016, c. 52, § 40. This amendment provides that "the warrant shall continue day after day for up to 5 consecutive days, excluding Saturdays,

Sundays and legal holidays, or until such time as the person is presented to the court, whichever is sooner; provided, however that an arrest on such warrant shall not be made unless the person may be presented immediately before a judge." The act was effective March 14, 2016.

Rule 4. Appointment of Counsel

Unless the respondent is represented by counsel, the court shall appoint counsel pursuant to Supreme Judicial Court Rule 3:10(1)(f)(iii) before or upon the respondent's appearance before the court.

Adopted July 22, 2015, effective February 1, 2016. Amended July 20, 2016, effective September 6, 2016.

Commentary—2015

Rule 4 provides the court with flexibility to determine the appropriate time to appoint counsel for an unrepresented respondent. It may be convenient to appoint counsel upon a respondent's arrest, or even before then, to allow consultation before the respondent is brought before a judge. In any event, however, counsel must be appointed before the court-ordered examination, pursuant to G.L. c. 123, § 35, ¶ 3, and the attorney should be allowed to consult with the respondent before the examination begins.

Rule 5. Order for Examination

The judge shall order an examination of the respondent to be conducted by a qualified physician, a qualified psychologist, or a qualified social worker.

Adopted July 22, 2015, effective February 1, 2016. Amended July 20, 2016, effective September 6, 2016.

Commentary—2015

Section 35 provides that "[t]he court shall order examination by a qualified physician, qualified psychologist or a social worker." Rule 5 clarifies that the social worker must be qualified to opine on substance abuse matters. See 104 C.M.R. § 33.06 (setting forth the process for designating social workers to opine on section 35 matters); accord 104 C.M.R. § 33.04 (process for designating physicians and psychologists).

As there is no statutory provision for holding a respondent overnight pending a hearing, the examination (and the hearing) must occur as soon as practical and, in any event, no later than the end of the day on which the respondent is brought to court. Prior to the examination, a psychologist or social worker clinician must provide the respondent with the warnings required by Commonwealth v. Lamb, 365 Mass. 265, 270 (1974), regarding the unprivileged nature of communications during the examination, and the respondent must knowingly and voluntarily waive the privilege otherwise afforded by G.L. c. 233, § 20B or G.L. c. 112, § 135B. See In re Laura L., 54 Mass. App. Ct. 853, 858–61 (2002). In deciding whether to waive the privilege and participate in the examination, the respondent may consult with counsel. See Seng v. Commonwealth, 445 Mass. 536, 548–49 (2005). As provided in Rule 7(b), if the respondent declines to participate in the examination, the clinician may nevertheless render an opinion and, in testifying at the commitment hearing, may report the respondent's refusal to participate. The judge, however, may not draw an adverse inference from the respondent's refusal to participate in the examination.

Commentary—2016 Amendments

The 2016 legislation amended G.L. c. 123, § 35 to add the word "qualified" before "social worker" in the list of persons who may conduct an examination. St. 2016, c. 8, § 3. The original Rule 5 already had this requirement.

Rule 6. Conduct of the Hearing; Standard of Proof

(a) After the completion of the examination ordered under Rule 5, the judge shall hold a hearing expeditiously to determine whether there is clear and convincing evidence that (1) the respondent is an individual with an alcohol or a substance use disorder, as defined in G.L. c. 123, § 35; and (2) there is a likelihood of serious harm, as defined in G.L. c. 123, § 1, as a result of the respondent's alcohol or substance use disorder, to the respondent, the petitioner, or any other person.

(b) The judge may inquire of the petitioner and may accept testimony or other evidence from the petitioner or any other person, including a court official.

(c) The respondent shall have the right to cross-examine witnesses, present independent expert evidence, call witnesses, and submit documents or other evidence.

(d) All testimony shall be taken under oath and shall be recorded or transcribed.

Adopted July 22, 2015, effective February 1, 2016. Amended July 20, 2016, effective September 6, 2016.

Commentary—2015

Among the provisions in these rules that are not set forth in the statute are the applicable standard of proof, the admissibility of hearsay, and the impermissibility of an inference to be drawn by the court from a respondent's refusal to speak with a clinician. These three topics were mentioned as matters requiring clarification in In re Jennifer Henley, Supreme Judicial Court Single Justice Opinion (July 23, 2014) (section 35 hearings involve "several important unresolved issues" regarding evidentiary standards). These issues are addressed in Rules 6 and 7.

Rule 6(a) imposes a "clear and convincing" standard of proof for these cases because this is the standard required for other temporary detention orders, specifically pretrial detention based on "dangerousness" under G.L. c. 276, § 58A. See Mendonza v. Commonwealth, 423 Mass. 771, 782–84 (1996). The Supreme Judicial Court has explained that the reason that proof beyond a reasonable doubt is required in the G.L. c. 123A and G.L. c. 123, § 8 contexts is because "civil commitment of those who are mentally ill and dangerous to themselves or others is 'potentially indefinite and even lifelong,' although the first order of commitment expires after six months and all subsequent commitments expire after one year." Abbott A. v. Commonwealth, 458 Mass. 24, 40 (2010) (quoting Mendonza, 423 Mass. at 783) (citation omitted); accord Querubin v. Commonwealth, 440 Mass. 108, 120 n.9 (2003). Shorter–term civil commitments under G.L. c. 123, § 12 and § 15, by contrast, do not require proof beyond a reasonable doubt. Mendonza, 423 Mass. at 783 n.5. A commitment order under section 35 cannot be extended beyond 90 days for any reason. Contrast Abbott A., 458 Mass. at 36–40 (pretrial detention for dangerousness under G.L. c. 276, § 58A may be extended under certain, limited circumstances). Accordingly, proof beyond a reasonable doubt is not required to satisfy the requirements of due process in section 35 proceedings.

Rule 6(b) recognizes that, after the amendment of section 35 in St. 2011, c. 142, § 18, nonmedical testimony may be presented to the court in support of a section 35 petition, in addition to the medical testimony of the clinician. Accordingly, the judge may inquire of the petitioner (or the nonqualified petitioner who brought the matter to the attention of a court official) to determine whether the petitioner has relevant evidence to present on the petition. Similarly, the judge may accept testimony or evidence from other witnesses as well. Where court officials, especially probation officers, have had contact with a respondent, they may well have useful information for the court.

Section 35 provides that the respondent "may present independent expert or other testimony." Rule 6(c) expands this right to include cross-examination and the submission of nontestimonial evidence.

Commentary—2016 Amendments

As discussed in the commentary to Rule 1, the 2016 legislation deleted the terms "alcoholic" and "substance abuser" and replaced them with "alcohol use disorder" and "substance use disorder." St. 2016, c. 8, §§ 1–2, 4.

In addition, after the promulgation of the original Uniform Rules, the Supreme Judicial Court approved the standard of proof in Rule 6(a) in *In re G.P.*, 473 Mass. 112, 118–20 (2015). The Court also provided detailed guidance on assessing the likelihood of serious harm when adjudicating section 35 commitments proceedings. *G.P.*, 473 Mass. at 124–29.

Rule 7. Evidence

(a) The rules of evidence shall not apply in proceedings under G.L. c. 123, § 35, except that privileges and statutory disqualifications shall apply. Hearsay evidence shall be admissible, but may be relied upon only if the judge finds that it is substantially reliable.

(b) The judge shall not draw any adverse inference from a respondent's refusal to testify or to speak during the examination ordered pursuant to Rule 5 or at any other time during the proceedings. This shall not prohibit the clinician from offering an opinion despite such refusal and reporting such refusal to the court.

(c) The court shall base its findings on credible and competent evidence, including medical testimony and such other evidence as may be admitted.

Adopted July 22, 2015, effective February 1, 2016. Amended July 20, 2016, effective September 6, 2016.

Commentary—2015

Rule 7(a) permits the admission of hearsay in section 35 proceedings. The Supreme Judicial Court has consistently permitted the admission of hearsay in appropriate proceedings "even where deprivation of liberty is at stake as is the case here." *Mendonza v. Commonwealth*, 423 Mass. 771, 785 (1996) (dangerousness hearing under G.L. c. 276, § 58A); *accord Commonwealth v. Bukin*, 467 Mass. 516, 519–20 (2014) (hearsay is admissible in probation violation proceedings); *Querubin v. Commonwealth*, 440 Mass. 108, 118 (2003) (decision whether to admit a defendant to bail). Pretrial commitment on the basis of dangerousness or unlikelihood to appear at trial is viewed as sufficiently analogous to section 35 proceedings to provide the appropriate basis, consistent with due process requirements, for the provisions in Rule 7(a) regarding the admissibility and use of hearsay evidence. Although most evidentiary rules are relaxed for section 35 proceedings, all privileges and statutory disqualifiers apply. Accordingly, for example, strict compliance with rules regarding the waiver of privileges from the clinician-patient relationship, particularly those set forth in *Commonwealth v. Lamb*, 365 Mass. 265, 270 (1974), is necessary. Despite the relaxed evidentiary rules, the judge may rely only upon evidence, whether hearsay or otherwise, that is substantially reliable. Substantially reliable hearsay has been held to be a proper basis for other detention decisions, such as detention for dangerousness, *Abbott A. v. Commonwealth*, 458 Mass. 24, 34–36 (2010), and revocation of probation, *Bukin*, 467 Mass. at 522.

Although there is no constitutional prohibition on drawing an adverse inference from a civil respondent's invocation of a right against self-incrimination or other refusal to talk, *Soe v. Sex Offender Registry Bd*, 466 Mass. 381, 388–89 & n.8 (2013), the probative value of such refusal in the context of a respondent alleged to be an alcoholic or

substance abuser is minimal. *Cf. Commonwealth v. Gagnon*, 408 Mass. 185, 197–98 (1990) (invocation of privilege against self-incrimination before the jury by a witness in a criminal case would invite uninformed speculation). Rule 7(b), therefore, bars drawing such an inference. These rules, however, are not intended to interfere with a qualified clinician's exercise of the clinician's medical judgment. Accordingly, the clinician may offer an opinion despite a respondent's refusal to speak and may report that refusal to the court, so as to provide the judge with an understanding of the basis of the clinician's opinion. Although the judge may not independently draw an adverse inference from the respondent's failure to cooperate, a clinician's opinion should not be rejected or discounted because the clinician considered the respondent's failure to cooperate, assuming that such consideration was medically sound.

Rule 7(c) recognizes that, since St. 2011, c. 142, § 18 amended G.L. c. 123, § 35, ¶ 4, a judge must hear medical testimony but may base a decision on other testimony and evidence. In light of the legislative provisions for examination by a psychologist, St. 1989, c. 352, or by a social worker, St. 2014, c. 165, § 155, the meaning of "medical testimony" extends beyond expert testimony by a medical doctor. *Cf. Ortiz v. Examworks, Inc.*, 470 Mass. 784, 788 (2015) (usual and accepted meaning of "physician" extends beyond medical doctors to all "who engage in the healing arts"). It may include the opinion of a qualified psychologist or social worker, or even lay testimony about medical matters by persons with personal knowledge of such matters. *See Commonwealth v. Gaudette*, 441 Mass. 762, 771 (2004) (lay person may testify about the extent of a family member's injuries and length of recovery); *Moore v. Fleet Refrigeration & Air Conditioning Co.*, 28 Mass. App. Ct. 971, 972 (1990) (error to categorically exclude a social worker's testimony on psychological matters on the ground that she was not a medical doctor).

Commentary—2016 Amendments

After the promulgation of the original Uniform Rules, the Supreme Judicial Court approved the inapplicability of the rules of evidence in Rule 7(a) in *In re G.P.*, 473 Mass. 112, 120–22 (2015).

Rule 8. Findings and Issuance of Commitment Order

(a) If the judge makes the findings required by Rule 6(a), the court may then issue an order of commitment consistent with the terms and requirements set forth in G.L. c. 123, § 35, which shall be for a period not to exceed 90 days. The order shall specify whether the commitment is based on a finding of alcohol use disorder, substance use disorder, or both. The commitment shall be to a facility designated by the department of public health. The order shall specify that the receiving facility, or any facility to which the respondent is transferred, is responsible for providing and maintaining custody of the respondent until expiration or termination of the order, as provided by law.

(b) The judge shall include a provision in the order requiring the facility, or any facility to which the respondent is transferred, to provide the clerk of the committing court with notice, in the manner directed by the court, of the release, the transfer, or of any escape by the respondent.

(c) The commitment shall be made to a facility approved by the department of public health for the care and treatment of individuals with an alcohol or substance use disorder. If (i) the judge finds that the only appropriate setting for the treatment of the respondent is a secure facility or (ii) the department of public health informs the court that there are no suitable facilities available for treatment licensed or approved by the department of public health or the department of mental health, the judge may commit the respondent to the Massachusetts correctional institution at Bridgewater, for an adult male respondent, or to a secure facility for women approved by the department of public health or the department of mental health, for an adult female respondent.

(d) Upon issuance of a commitment order, the court shall notify the respondent that the respondent is prohibited from being issued a firearm identification card pursuant to G.L. c. 140, § 129B, or a license to carry pursuant to G.L. c. 140, §§ 131 and 131F, unless a petition for relief pursuant to G.L. c. 123, § 35 is subsequently granted.

Adopted July 22, 2015, effective February 1, 2016. Amended July 20, 2016, effective September 6, 2016.

Commentary—2015

Rule 8 does not set forth the specific terms required to be included in commitment orders issued under G.L. c. 123, § 35. Those terms are set forth in the official commitment order form. Regarding those terms, the statute provides as follows:

[T]he court may order such person to be committed for a period not to exceed 90 days, followed by the availability of case management services provided by the department of public health for up to 1 year; provided, however, that a review of the necessity of the commitment shall take place by the superintendent on days 30, 45, 60 and 75 as long as the commitment continues. A person so committed may be released prior to the expiration of the period of commitment upon written determination by the superintendent that release of that person will not result in a likelihood of serious harm. Such commitment shall be for the purpose of inpatient care in public or private facilities approved by the department of public health under chapter 111B for the care and treatment of alcoholism or substance abuse. The person may be committed to the Massachusetts correctional institution at Bridgewater, if a male, or at Framingham, if a female, if there are not suitable facilities available under said chapter 111B; provided, however, that the person so committed shall be housed and treated separately from convicted criminals. Such person shall, upon release, be encouraged to consent to further treatment and shall be allowed voluntarily to remain in the facility for such purpose. The department of mental health, in conjunction with the department of public health, shall maintain a roster of public and private facilities available, together with the number of beds currently available, for the care and treatment of alcoholism or substance abuse and shall make the roster available to the district courts on a monthly basis.

Rule 8(a) also includes a provision intended to eliminate any doubt that a commitment order issued under Section 35 requires that the receiving facility must hold the respondent in custody for the duration of the commitment, unless terminated by the facility's superintendent pursuant to the procedure set forth in G.L. c. 123, § 35, ¶ 4.

Rule 8(b) requires the judge to include a provision in a commitment order requiring the receiving facility to provide notice to the court of the release of the respondent. Such notice may be useful to the court in addressing future issues concerning the respondent or petitioner. In the case of any escape, such notification permits the court to determine whether further action is advisable, such as the issuance of a warrant for apprehension.

Rule 8(c) requires that commitment to the Department of Correction be limited to situations in which there is no facility approved by the Department of Public Health that is suitable and available. As Rule 8(c) reflects, commitment of a juvenile to the Department of Correction is never appropriate and may violate the Prison Rape Elimination Act. *See* 28 C.F.R. § 115.14(a).

Particular care is necessary when a respondent is subject to other criminal process, such as an unsatisfied order of bail. Commitment under section 35 may be advisable for criminal defendants, especially where the respondent might otherwise be able to post bail before completing treatment in pretrial detention. In such circumstances, it is necessary that the respondent be returned to court upon release from the facility so that the court may ensure that the criminal process is respected and revisit the criminal process if necessary. When a criminal defendant is committed under section 35, the judge should make a bail determination at the time of arraignment and not defer the bail determination until after release from the section 35 commitment. Any changes to the bail order after successful completion of treatment can be addressed as a matter of course after treatment without visiting upon the respondent and the Commonwealth the uncertainty of unaddressed bail.

Rule 8(d) addresses the firearm warning required by St. 2014, c. 284, § 15.

Commentary—2016 Amendments

The 2016 legislation made several changes to the options available to committing courts and to how respondents are handled after commitment, all necessitating changes to the Uniform Rules.

The amendments to Rule 8(a) and 8(b) recognize that the 2016 legislation granted the superintendents of treatment facilities plenary authority to transfer respondents between and among approved facilities. St. 2016, c. 8, § 4. Accordingly, Rule 8(a) now extends the requirement for maintaining custody of the respondent to the superintendent of any facility to which the respondent is transferred. The means by which custody is provided, maintained, and described is exclusively within the discretion of the appropriate Executive Branch authority. It remains the case that no facility may release the respondent prior to ninety days absent a written determination that release of the respondent will not result in a likelihood of serious harm.

Rule 8(b) has been amended so that the commitment order shall include a provision that facilities notify the court of any transfers, as required by the amended G.L. c. 123, § 35. The rule continues the requirement that facilities notify the committing court of any release or escape, specifically providing that this duty falls upon the facility receiving a transferred respondent. The rule now clarifies that the notice must be made to the clerk of the committing court, and in the manner directed by the court in the commitment order.

The amendments to Rule 8(c) implement the 2016 legislation's prohibition on committing female respondents to the Department of Correction. St. 2016, c. 8, § 4. The amended Rule 8(c) recognizes that adult females may be committed to a secure facility for women approved by the department of public health or the department of mental health. The amended Rule 8(c) also reflects the new statutory standard for commitment to the new secure facilities or, for adult men, to the Department of Correction. Finally, in light of the new transferability of section 35 respondents, it is no longer necessary that the commitment order specify a facility, although it may be convenient for the judge to specify to which facility a respondent will initially be sent.

Rule 9. Security of Respondent

The court shall take such action and issue such orders as may be necessary to secure the presence of the respondent after the respondent's arrival at the court, prior to or during the hearing, and while awaiting transport following the issuance of a commitment order, as the circumstances may require.

Adopted July 22, 2015, effective February 1, 2016. Amended July 20, 2016, effective September 6, 2016.

Commentary—2015

Rule 9 is intended to address those situations in which a respondent may present a risk of flight or harm, given the fact that the respondent may be before the court unwillingly and may be suffering from the effects of alcohol or drugs resulting in unpredictable, aggressive, or violent behavior.

The law provides the court, as a matter of its inherent power, with broad discretion regarding security in the courtroom, including controlling the behavior of those before the court, when necessary. The Supreme Judicial Court has stated:

> Of necessity, a judge's inherent powers must encompass the authority to exercise "physical control over his courtroom." *Chief Admin. Justice of the Trial Court v. Labor Relations Comm'n*, 404 Mass. 53, 57 (1989). As we noted in *Chief Admin. Justice of the Trial Court v. Labor Relations Comm'n* "[t]he power of the judiciary to control its own proceedings, the conduct of participants, the actions of officers of the court and the environment of the court is a power absolutely necessary for a court to function effectively and do its job of administering justice." *Id.* at 57, quoting *State v. LaFrance*, 124 N.H. 171, 179–180 (1983).

Commonwealth v. O'Neil, 418 Mass. 760, 764 (1994).

Rule 10. Proceedings When a Respondent Appears Before a Court Other Than the Court That Issued the Warrant or Summons

(a) When (1) a warrant or summons is issued pursuant to Rule 3(d) or (2) a warrant is executed where it is impractical to transport the respondent to the return court, the respondent may be brought before a court having jurisdiction of cases under G.L. c. 123, § 35 (hereinafter the "new court"). The new court shall immediately contact the issuing court and obtain copies of (1) the docket in the case; (2) the petition; and (3) any other documents in the case file.

(b) The new court shall open a new case file for the matter and make reasonable efforts to notify the petitioner of the location of the new court. The new court, in its discretion, may wait a reasonable time for the petitioner to arrive.

(c) The new court shall proceed to adjudicate the case in accordance with Rules 4 through 9. The new court shall promptly inform the issuing court of its disposition by transmitting to the issuing court a copy of its docket entries.

Adopted July 22, 2015, effective February 1, 2016. Amended July 20, 2016, effective September 6, 2016.

Commentary—2015

Rule 10 governs the procedure when a respondent is apprehended far enough away from the issuing court that transportation to that court before court closes is not practical. In such circumstances, law enforcement may bring the respondent to another court, and the matter will be adjudicated there as if the case had arisen there. This may cause issues with the petitioner's ability to arrive at the new court in a reasonable amount of time, and the use of remote testimony or the receipt of hearsay evidence may be appropriate to balance the need for dispatch with the desire for the petitioner's participation.

Rule 11. Appeal

(a) Any person aggrieved by a decision of the District Court Department or the Boston Municipal Court Department may appeal to the Appellate Division of such Department within seven days. Upon request, the Appellate Division shall expedite consideration of any appeal.

(b) Any person aggrieved by a decision of the Juvenile Court Department may appeal to the Appeals Court within seven days. Upon request, the Appeals Court shall expedite consideration of any appeal.

(c) The clerk shall serve notice of the filing of the appeal to any adverse party and to the facility to which a respondent was committed, if any.

Adopted July 22, 2015, effective February 1, 2016. Amended July 20, 2016, effective September 6, 2016.

Commentary—2015

Rule 11 provides a direct appellate remedy for section 35 determinations to the appropriate Appellate Division or, in the case of the Juvenile Court, to the Appeals Court. *See Hunt v. Appeals Ct.*, 444 Mass. 460, 463–66 (2005) (where a statute does not expressly provide an appellate remedy, rules may provide an appropriate avenue of appeal). Because a section 35 commitment cannot last longer than ninety days, a short time limit for filing a notice of appeal and a requirement of expediting the appeal upon request are necessary to avoid the appeal becoming moot.

Although the appellee ordinarily will be the petitioner (in the case of an appeal by the respondent) or the respondent (in the case of an appeal by the petitioner), Rule 11(c) requires the clerk to notify the facility to which the respondent was committed. Knowledge of the appeal may require alterations to the respondent's treatment, and the facility may seek to be heard by the appellate court, either in support of or in opposition to continued commitment, in certain cases.

Helpful information regarding the conduct of Section 35 commitment proceedings can be found in the Benchbook for District Court Judges, Proceedings Under Massachusetts General Laws Chapter 123 (2011), published by the Judicial Institute, at pages 228–234. The Benchbook provides sources of clinical information relevant to the definitions of "alcoholic" and "substance abuser" and clinical criteria relevant to the determination of the "likelihood of serious harm." It also provides information on the availability of placements to assist the court when a commitment order is issued. It should be noted that the version of G.L. c. 123, § 35 that appears in the Benchbook was amended following its publication.

Commentary—2016 Amendments

After the promulgation of the original Uniform Rules, the Supreme Judicial Court approved the appellate review procedures in Rule 11. *In re G.P.*, 473 Mass. 112, 123–24 (2015).

XIV. UNIFORM RULES ON PUBLIC ACCESS TO COURT RECORDS

Table of Rules

Rule 1. Scope and Definitions

(a) **Purpose.** These rules are intended to provide public access to court records and information while protecting the security and privacy of litigants and non-litigants.

(b) **Scope.** These rules govern access to the court records of the Trial Court. These rules apply to all court records, regardless of the physical form, method of recording, or method of storage, subject to these rules and the technological capacity of the Trial Court to make such a court record available. Administrative records of the Trial Court are not within the scope of these rules.

(c) **General Policy.** Publicly available court records in the custody of a Clerk and located in a courthouse shall be available to any member of the public for inspection and/or copying during the regular business hours of the court, consistent with these rules. Electronic court records may be made available in part or in their entirety at the courthouse consistent with Rule 2, as compiled data consistent with Rule 3, or by remote access consistent with Rule 5.

(d) **Types of access.** Access to court records may be courthouse access or remote access. Courthouse access includes requests to the Clerk at the counter and access through a computer kiosk. Remote access includes both an internet-based portal for the public and an Internet-based Attorney's Portal for registered Massachusetts attorneys.

(e) **Definitions.**

"Access" means the ability to inspect and obtain a copy of a court record.

"Administrative record" means any record pertaining to the management, supervision, or administration of the Trial Court, including any court department, committee, or board appointed by or under the direction of the Trial Court or any department thereof, the Office of the Commissioner of Probation, Office of the Jury Commissioner, or the office of any Clerk.

"Bulk data" means electronic court records as originally entered in Trial Court case management database(s), not aggregated or compiled by computerized searches intended to retrieve specific data elements.

"Compiled data" means electronic court records that have been generated by computerized searches of Trial Court case management database(s) resulting in the compilation of specific data elements.

"Clerk" means a Clerk, Clerk–Magistrate, Register of Probate, Recorder of the Land Court, and their assistants or designees.

"Court" means any department of the Trial Court.

"Court record" means all or any portion of court papers, documents, exhibits, orders, recordings, dockets, and other records that are made, entered, filed, and/or maintained by the Clerk in connection with a case or proceeding.

"Docket" means the paper or electronic list of case information maintained by the Clerk that contains the case caption, case number, and a chronological entry identifying the date and title of each paper, order, or judgment filed in a case, and the scheduling and occurrence of events in the case.

"Electronic court record" means the whole or partial information content of court records, stored in an electronic database. This shall include an audio or video recording, analog or digital, of a proceeding, to the extent permitted by these rules and subject to the Trial Court's technological capacities.

"Prohibited from public disclosure" means any court record, or portion thereof, to which public access is restricted pursuant to any Federal or state statute, court rule, standing order, case law, or court order.

"Public" or "member of the public" means any person and any business or non-profit entity, association, or government entity, or organization, including the media, who seeks access to a court record. The term "public" does not include (1) Judicial Branch staff, acting in their official capacities; (2) authorized persons or entities, private or governmental, who assist the court in providing court services; (3) public agencies or law enforcement departments whose access to court records is defined by statute, court rule, standing order, case law, or court order; and (4) the parties to a case, their lawyers, victims as authorized by G.L. c. 258B, § 3, or their authorized representatives requiring access to the court record in a specific case.

"Publicly available court record" means any court record that is not prohibited from public disclosure.

"Remote access" means accessing court records through electronic means from outside a courthouse.

Adopted July 20, 2016, effective November 1, 2016.

NOTES

Rule 1(a), Purpose. These rules are intended to provide public access to designated publicly available court records and information, while protecting the security and privacy of litigants and non-litigants.

Rule 1(b), Scope. These rules govern access by the public to the court records maintained by a Clerk in a court, whether the court record is maintained in paper or electronic form.

These rules apply only to access to court records by the public. The rules do not limit access to court records by a party to an action or proceeding, by the attorney or authorized representative of such party, by Judicial Branch staff or those entities which assist the Judicial Branch in providing services, or any other persons or entities entitled to access by Federal or state law, statute or rule, unless otherwise required by law or court order.

Rule 1(c), General Policy. Court records in the custody of a Clerk shall be available for public access during normal business hours consistent with these rules, unless otherwise prohibited by law or court order. A judge has the authority to impound an otherwise public court record. See Trial Court Rule VIII, Uniform Rules on Impoundment Procedure (as amended effective October 1, 2015).

Massachusetts has long recognized that the public has a common law right of access to certain court records. *New England Internet Café, LLC v. Clerk of the Super. Ct. for Criminal Bus, in Suffolk Cnty.*, 462 Mass. 76, 82–83 (2012), citing *Republican Co. v. Appeals Ct.*, 442 Mass. 218, 222 (2004). See also Massachusetts Body of Liberties, art. 48 (1641) ("Every inhabitant of the Country shall have free liberty to search and review any rolls, records or registers of any Court or office"). Therefore, most court records are presumptively public documents, unless required to be withheld from public inspection by statute, court rule, standing order, case law, or court order. *New England Internet Cafe. LLC*, 462 Mass. at 83, citing *Republican Co.*, 442 Mass. at 222–223. See also *Boston Herald, Inc.*, 432 Mass. at 608; *Newspapers of New England*, 403 Mass. at 631–632, 637. This right of public access has been described as the "general principle of publicity", applicable to court records and court proceedings. *Ottaway Newspapers, Inc. v. Appeals Ct.*, 372 Mass. 539, 546 (1977). The general principle of publicity is enhanced by a qualified First Amendment right of access in criminal proceedings. See *Newspapers of New England, Inc. v. Clerk-Magistrate of the Ware Div. of the Dist. Ct. Dep't*, 403 Mass. 628, 635 (1988) (stating that there is "a two-part test for determining whether a First Amendment right of access applies to any particular proceeding. First, the proceeding must have an historic tradition of openness, and second the public's access must play 'a significant positive role in the functioning of the particular process in question.'"). The Supreme Judicial Court recognizes the qualified right of public access to court records in criminal proceedings. See *Boston Herald, Inc. v. Sharpe*, 432 Mass. 593, 606–08 (2000) ("balancing the public's right to inspect documents against a defendant's rights guaranteed by the Sixth Amendment to a fair trial.").

However, while the public has a right to obtain a copy of a court record, subject to the procedures described in Rule 2, the presumption of public access is not absolute. *Commonwealth v. Winfield*, 464 Mass. 672, 674 (2013). See also *Commonwealth v. Pon*, 469 Mass. 296, 312 (2014) ("Although this common-law presumption [of public access to judicial records] is of paramount importance, like its constitutional counterpart, it is not absolute") (alterations added); *Nixon v. Warner Communications, Inc.*, 435 U.S. 589, 597 (1978) ("It is uncontested . . . that the right to inspect and copy judicial records is not absolute. Every court has supervisory power over its own records and files, and access has been denied where court files might have become a vehicle for improper purposes."). The public's qualified right of access includes the right to view or "inspect" a *non-impounded record* free of charge during the court's regular business hours. A limitation of this right exists in the court's "inherent equitable power to impound its files in a case and to deny public inspection of them when justice so requires." *George W. Prescott Pub. Co. v. Reg, of Probate for Norfolk Cnty.*, 395 Mass. 274, 277 (1985), quoting *Sanford v. Boston Herald-Traveler Corp.*, 318 Mass. 156, 158 (1945). Such a restriction on public access to records requires a showing of good cause. "[A] judge must balance the rights of the parties based on the particular facts of each case and take into account all relevant factors, including but not

limited to the nature of the parties and the controversy, the type of information and the privacy interests involved, the extent of community interest, and the reason for the request." *New England Internet Café, LLC*, 462 Mass. at 83 (citations omitted).

Clerk's Responsibilities. Pursuant to S.J.C. Rule 3:12, Canon 3(A)(6), the "Clerk-Magistrate shall facilitate public access to court records that, by law or court rule, are available to the public and shall take appropriate steps to safeguard the security and confidentiality of court records that are not open to the public." A Clerk "shall have responsibility for the internal administration of his office, including personnel, staff services and record keeping." *State Bd. of Retirement v. Bulger*, 446 Mass. 169, 176 (2006), quoting G.L. c. 218, § 8. Clerk-magistrates maintain "all records, books and papers" filed in "their respective offices", G.L. c. 218, § 12, and must make available public documents on request and protect impounded documents. *In re Powers*, 465 Mass. 63, 67 (2013). Essential to these duties is the Clerk's responsibility for the integrity of court records by protecting such records from any unauthorized alteration, mutilation, or theft.

Record Retention. The retention and eventual destruction of court records in the Trial Court are governed by Supreme Judicial Court Rule 1:11. The Massachusetts public records statute, G.L. c. 66, § 10, and its Federal counterpart, the Freedom of Information Act, 5 U.S.C. §§ 551 and 552, do not apply to records of the Judicial branch. See G.L. c. 4, § 7, Twenty-sixth; G.L. c. 66, § 10; *Kettenbach v. Board of Bar Overseers*, 448 Mass. 1019, 1020 (2007); *Lambert v. Executive Dir. of the Judicial Nominating Council*, 425 Mass. 406, 409 (1997); *New Bedford Standard-Times Pub. Co. v. Clerk of the Third Dist. Ct. of Bristol*, 377 Mass. 404, 407 (1979); *Ottaway Newspapers, Inc. v. Appeals Ct.*, 372 Mass. 539, 545–546 (1977); *Sanford v. Boston Herald-Traveler Corp.*, 318 Mass. 156, 157 (1945); *Peckham v. Boston Herald. Inc.*, 48 Mass. App. Ct. 282, 286 n.6 (1999). See also G.L. c. 66A, § 1 (Fair Information Practices Act limited to executive branch agencies and legislatively-created authorities); 801 Code Mass. Regs. § 3.01(3) ("Freedom of Information" regulations [801 Code Mass. Regs. § 3.00 et seq.] limited to executive branch agencies); 950 Code Mass. Regs. § 32.03 (2015) (public records regulations inapplicable to judicial branch).

Rule 1(d), Types of Access. The Trial Court offers several different methods of access to publicly available court records. The traditional and most common method is through a request at the counter of a Clerk's office for the assistance of court personnel in obtaining a case file. Because many court records are now maintained in electronic case management databases, all courts also maintain in the Clerk's office a public computer kiosk at which members of the public may search and access court information. These types of access are governed by Rule 2. In addition, remote access through the Internet is available in two forms. The first is a Public Internet Portal through which members of the public may search and access electronic records. The second is the so-called Attorney Portal, which allows registered Massachusetts attorneys access to information and calendar events. These types of access are governed by Rule 5. Finally, in circumstances described in Rule 3, the Court Administrator may provide data compiled from the electronic case management databases.

Rule 1(e), Definitions. Rule 1(e) contains the definition of terms used in the rules. "Administrative record" as defined in Rule 1(e) includes any information maintained by the Trial Court that is not a court record. This definition includes records kept by the Trial Court that are not filed in relation to the litigation or resolution of a specific case or proceeding (e.g., court e-mail, inter-office memoranda, personnel information, travel vouchers, etc.); administrative and management reports of the Trial Court; and information gathered, maintained, or stored by a governmental agency or other entity to which the court has access but which is not part of the court record.

"Court record" means all or any portion of court papers, documents, exhibits, orders, recordings, dockets, and other records that are made, entered, filed, and/or maintained by the Clerk in connection with a case or proceeding. The definition of a "court record" includes an audio recording or official transcript of a proceeding, and any electronic duplicate or original court record. *Commonwealth v. Winfield*, 464 Mass. 672, 678–679 (2013), and cases cited therein; *Commonwealth v. Silva*, 448 Mass. 701, 706 n.8 (2007), quoting *Boston Herald. Inc. v. Superior Court Dep't of the Trial Court*, 421 Mass. 502, 505 (1995). A "court record" also includes a list identifying the names of jurors who have been empaneled and rendered a verdict in a criminal case. *Commonwealth v. Fujita*, 470 Mass. 484, 486 (2015). "Court record" does not include court papers, documents, exhibits, orders, dockets, and other records that are not filed with the court or otherwise created in connection with the case file. *Commonwealth v. Winfield*, 464 Mass. at 679. Discovery documents, interrogatories, backup room recordings, and other documents and recordings not filed with the court are not part of the "court record."

Court records do not include judicial work product related to the deliberative process, including confidential communications among judges and between judges and court staff made in the course of and related to their deliberative processes in particular cases. See *Matter of the Enforcement of a Subpoena*, 463 Mass. 162, 174–175, 178 (2012) (recognizing absolute judicial privilege protects confidential communications among judges and court staff).

As used in these rules, "court records" is the equivalent of "judicial record" as that term is used in the case law. See, e.g., *Commonwealth v. Fujita*, 470 Mass. 484, 487 (2015); *Republican Co. v. Appeals Court*, 442 Mass. 218, 222 (2004). These Rules, however, use the term "court record" instead of "judicial record" in order to be consistent with other Rules of the Trial Court and the notes thereto. See, e.g., Trial Court Rule IX, Rule 2; Notes to Mass. R. Civ. P. and Mass. R. Dom. Rel. 12, 19, 41, 60, 63, 64; Notes to Mass. R. Crim. P. 4, 8, 12.

Prior Trial Court Administrative Orders. To the extent any preexisting administrative order of the Trial Court or the Chief Justice of the Trial Court are inconsistent with these rules, the rules control and govern future procedures and access to court records.

Rule 2. Access to Court Records in a Courthouse

(a) Scope. This rule governs the procedure for access to publicly available court records in a courthouse.

(b) Request. Any member of the public may submit to the Clerk at a courthouse a request to access a court record. The Chief Justice of each Trial Court Department may determine whether to require a written form for all requests. Such written request shall be in the form prescribed by the Chief Justice of the Trial Court and provide sufficient specificity to enable the Clerk to identify the requested court record. The requester shall not be required to disclose the reason for the request.

(c) Reasonable Limits. The Clerk may set reasonable limits on the time, location, volume, and manner of access to protect the integrity of the court record and to prevent undue disruption to the operations of the Clerk's office. Only the Clerk may add, remove, and replace records in the court's files.

(d) Production.

(1) The Clerk is responsible for providing access to all publicly available court records. The Clerk shall first determine whether the requested court record, or any portion thereof, is prohibited from public disclosure. The Clerk shall provide the record in the form requested by the public if practicable. The Clerk shall respond promptly upon receipt of a request for access to a court record.

(2) If the court record is stored outside the courthouse, is under review by a judge, or is otherwise not readily accessible by the Clerk, the Clerk will procure the court record or a duplicate in a reasonably timely manner and notify the requester when the court record may be accessed.

(e) Exhibits. The Clerk shall provide access, including reproduction, to documentary exhibits entered at a trial or hearing and retained by the court, unless the exhibits are contraband or are otherwise prohibited from public access, except where such access would pose a threat of deterioration or destruction of the exhibits. The Clerk may allow the public to view and photograph non-documentary exhibits, except where such access would pose a threat of deterioration, contamination, or destruction of the exhibits. The Clerk shall not allow the public to handle non-documentary exhibits without leave of court.

(f) Computer Kiosk. All publicly available electronic docket information shall be viewable at a computer kiosk or terminal located in the courthouse. There shall be no fee to access the kiosk. The Clerk may set reasonable limits on the time and volume of kiosk access to protect the Clerk's office from undue disruption and to promote access to the kiosk for all users.

(g) Impounded Records. A party or attorney who has entered an appearance in a case shall be allowed to access an impounded record in that case, except as prohibited by law or court order. The Clerk shall verify the requester's identity and participation in the case before permitting access to any impounded court record.

(h) Available Formats for Reproduction.

(1) *Paper copy.* The Clerk shall produce a paper copy of any court record upon request.

(2) *Printout.* To the extent that publicly available court records are maintained in electronic form, upon request the Clerk shall provide a printout.

(3) *Reproduction by court-provided machine.* If the Clerk or the court makes a copy machine available for public use, the requester may make a copy of the court record for whatever cost is required by that machine.

(4) *Audio or audiovisual recording.* To the extent the Clerk or the court department maintains an audio or audiovisual recording of a public hearing or trial, the Clerk shall provide a copy upon request, subject to any statute, court rule, standing order, case law, or court order.

(5) *Electronic document.* If the court maintains a court record in electronic form (e.g., portable document format ["PDF"]), the Clerk may provide an electronic copy of the document upon request.

(6) *Additional formats.* If technologically feasible, the Clerk may provide a court record on a CD or DVD or other media, and may transmit the reproduction electronically.

(i) Fee. The Clerk shall charge a fee for its duplication or provision of any court record as prescribed in the Trial Court's Uniform Schedule of Fees. No fee shall be charged to view a court record without reproduction.

(j) Requester's Self–Service Duplication of a Court Record.

(1) *Handheld device.* The Clerk shall allow a member of the public to use a personal handheld electronic imaging device (e.g., personal scanner, or, if permitted at the court location, a camera on a cell phone) to make a copy of a court record, subject to limitations set forth in Rule 2(c) and use of such devices being permitted in the courthouse. A fee shall not be charged for such reproduction.

(2) *Sheet-fed or flatbed scanner.* The Clerk may allow a member of the public to use a sheet-fed or flatbed scanner or imaging device to make a copy of a court record, subject to space limitations and the limitations set forth in Rule 2(c). A fee shall not be charged for such reproduction.

Adopted July 20, 2016, effective November 1, 2016.

NOTES

Rule 2(a), Scope. This rule governs the procedure for the public to obtain access to publicly available court records in a courthouse. Access to publicly available court records in a courthouse shall be provided in paper form and through a computer kiosk.

Rule 2(b), Request. Any member of the public may submit to the Clerk at a courthouse a request to access a court record. Each Department of the Trial Court may determine whether to require a written form for all requests or to permit oral and written requests. All written requests shall be submitted on a uniform form prescribed by the Chief Justice of the Trial Court. A written request form is not required to be retained by the Clerk after the court record has been returned. Each Clerk may elect to dispose or retain completed forms, but if retained, the forms should not be maintained in the court record or case file.

For security and record keeping purposes, the best practice, where feasible, is for the Clerk to require the requester to fill out a written form (or submit an electronic request) providing the requester's name and address and specifying the case name, case number, and document(s) requested. Neither the Clerk nor any request form may demand or require a reason for the request. Nonetheless, the Clerk may ask for such information because often such a simple inquiry enables the Clerk to assist the requester in focusing a request. The reason for a request might also inform a Clerk's use of discretion in determining the form in which the Clerk provides the record or any reasonable limits that should apply. Where a requester desires a copy, it may be prudent for the request form to allow the requester to express a preference for a paper copy or a scanned, PDF electronic copy, as the Clerk should provide a copy in the form desired by the requester if practical. The Clerk shall charge and collect a fee for copying or scanning and providing a PDF as provided in the Uniform Schedule of Fees.

Rule 2(c), Reasonable Limits. The Clerk may set reasonable limits on the time, location, volume, and manner of access to protect the integrity of the court record and to protect the Clerk's office from undue disruption. See *Globe Newspaper Co. v. Pokaski*, 868 F.2d 497, 505 (1989). In exercising the discretion contemplated in this rule, for example, the Clerk may reasonably limit the public's use of the Clerk's office lobby or space for the purposes of copying court records. The Clerk may also reasonably limit the devices used and the number of court records requested during a certain time period. In both of these circumstances, the Clerk may be guided by considerations including whether the use of the space or the number of requests negatively affects the Clerk's office staff's ability to perform other essential work, or whether the public's requests are negatively affecting the ability of other members of the public to access court records.

An original court record should not be taken from the Clerk's office without the Clerk's express permission or an order of the court. Transfer of the case file for the purposes of a judge's rotation, interdepartmental transfer, consolidation, or for an appeal, does not constitute the taking or removal of the court record. An order of the court is not required for the court record, including information protected from public disclosure, to be transferred or sent to another court.

Rule 2(d), Production. To further the policy of general public access, the Clerk should accede to the requester's choice of format unless doing so imposes a significant, unrecoverable cost or other burden on the Clerk or the court. For example, when requested, the Clerk should provide a copy as a PDF instead of as paper.

Rule 2(e), Exhibits. Documentary exhibits submitted to, and accepted by, a court in the course of adjudicatory proceedings are documents which the public shall be allowed to access and duplicate, unless the exhibits are contraband or are otherwise prohibited from public disclosure. In addition, a Clerk may withhold access to documentary exhibits if access poses a threat of deterioration or destruction of those exhibits.

Non-documentary exhibits pose special challenges, both logistical and pursuant to the Clerk's statutory duty in criminal cases to "prevent . . . destruction or deterioration" of evidence. G.L. c. 278A, § 16(a). Accordingly, a Clerk may allow the public to view non-documentary exhibits in the Clerk's possession, at least where such viewing would not pose a threat of deterioration or destruction of the exhibits. The Clerk shall not allow the public to handle non-documentary exhibits without leave of court.

The Clerk can allow access only to exhibits retained in the possession of the Clerk. In civil cases, the Clerk is not obligated to retain trial exhibits and such exhibits are routinely returned to the offering party once the appeal period has ended or earlier, if authorized by a judge. Business records produced pursuant to G.L. c. 233, § 79J, and hospital records under G.L. c. 233, § 79, are to be returned "upon the completion of such trial or hearing."

In criminal cases, pursuant to the Trial Court's Exhibit Retention Policy in Criminal Cases, which is available on the Trial Court's website, controlled substances and currency subject to civil forfeiture are returned to the Commonwealth at the completion of a trial or hearing. Other exhibits are retained by the Clerk for the period of time that the defendant remains incarcerated or under parole or probation supervision. The Clerk, however, has the discretion to return exhibits to the offering party whenever retention is impracticable, and the judge also has the discretion to order earlier return of exhibits. Because the Clerk has the statutory duty to "retain all such evidence or biological material in a manner that is reasonably designed to preserve the evidence and biological material and to prevent its destruction or deterioration", G.L. c. 278A, § 16(a), public access to physical exhibits may be limited or impossible.

Rule 2(f), Computer Kiosk. This rule requires the Trial Court to provide the public with a computer kiosk or terminal for accessing electronic court records. Such electronic access may lead to requests for particular paper records, which will be handled as any such request would be handled. The Clerk may set reasonable restrictions on the amount of time that any one person may use a computer kiosk, the number of searches, or the number of documents viewed, to ensure that the computer kiosk is not monopolized or misused.

Rule 2(g), Impounded Records. Only parties to and attorneys of record with an active appearance in a restricted case shall be granted access to the impounded court records in that case, unless the records are sealed or access is ordered otherwise.

Rule 2(h), Available Formats for Reproduction. This rule recognizes the variety of formats in which a court record exists and may be purchased, including a paper copy produced by a Clerk, a printout by the Clerk, reproduction by a machine made available for public use, audio or audiovisual recording, electronic form (e.g., portable document format ("PDF")), and on a CD or DVD or other device. For computer security reasons, the Clerk will not store electronic documents on a person's self-provided flash drive, CD, DVD, or other media.,

Rule 2(h)(3), Reproduction by Court–Provided Machine. Some courts and Clerk's offices provide for public use a copy machine. In such locations, the public has the option to use the machine or request the Clerk to produce the copy. The cost for the public to use the machine is usually less than the fee required for the Clerk to produce the copy. No additional fee beyond the machine's fee should be charged for a copy.

Rule 2(h)(4), Audio or audiovisual recording. To the extent the Clerk or the court department maintains an audio or audiovisual recording of a public hearing or trial, upon request the Clerk shall provide a copy, subject to any statute, court rule, standing order, case law, or court order. See *Bledsoe v. Commissioner of Correction,* 470 Mass. 1017, 1018 (2014) ("[W]e would expect that, if a DVD or other official record of a video conference exists, a litigant would be allowed to purchase it at his or her own expense. An official video record of a hearing would be no less of a judicial record than a transcript or audio cassette."); *Commonwealth v. Winfield,* 464 Mass. 672, 679–680 (2013) ("Where an electronic recording of a proceeding is made in the absence of a court reporter, the court file contains either the recording itself or a log entry that would allow the public to know the beginning and end points of the proceeding so that they may obtain a copy of the recording."); see also id. at 679 ("The First Amendment right of access to court trials includes the right to purchase a transcript of the court proceeding that was open to the public").

Rule 2(i), Fee. Pursuant to G.L. c. 262, § 4B, the Clerk shall charge a fee as set forth in the Trial Court's Uniform Schedule of Fees. The Uniform Schedule of Fees is available on the Trial Court's website

Rule 2(i), Requester's Self–Service Duplication of a Court Record. This subsection is consistent with Supreme Judicial Court Rule 1:19(3), which states: "A judge may permit the use of electronic or photographic means for . . . the perpetuation of a record when authorized by law, for other purposes of judicial administration . . ."

(1) Handheld Device. A member of the public may use a cellular telephone or other electronic imaging device to photograph or generate an image of a court record in a Clerk's office provided doing so does not unreasonably interfere with the operation of the Clerk's office or make an audio or video recording.

A "personal handheld scanner or electronic imaging device" includes a device held in one's hand that is moved by hand across the document being scanned. This includes a battery operated electronic scanning device that does not leave marks on the court record or unreasonably interfere with the Clerk's operations. The Clerk may exercise discretion not to permit any handheld device in order to maintain the integrity and format of the court records.

The Trial Court has adopted a Policy on Possession and Use of Cameras and Personal Electronic Devices (effective August 14, 2015). Under the policy, some Trial Court facilities do not permit the public to bring cellular telephones and other personal electronic devices into a court facility. The Trial Court's policy and a list of the Trial Court facilities that have banned the public's use of cellular telephones and PEDs is available on the Trial Court's website. Rule 2(j) does not supersede a particular courthouse's security regulations. If the court facility does not permit cell phones within the building, the requester may obtain a copy through other means identified in this rule.

(2) Sheet–Fed or Flatbed Scanner. A sheet-fed scanner or a flatbed scanner is a portable scanner that rests on a flat surface and requires pages to be fed through the machine. It is similar to a copier. A document is typically placed onto the transparent glass of the scanner, where a scanner head assembly moves underneath the glass to capture the image contained on the document. To obtain a legible scan of a record contained in a bound volume using a flatbed scanner, it is necessary to press the volume against the glass until the page lies flat. Pressing a bound volume against the glass may leave a mark or impression on the original record. Similarly, separation of a document's binding may be necessary. For reasons including poten-

tial harm to the original records, the Clerk may limit or prohibit scanning on a sheet-fed or flatbed scanner, and may condition such use on the person's restoration of the binding to secure the document's original condition.

Rule 3.   Requests for Compiled Data

(a) Procedure for Making Requests. Requests for compiled data may be made by any member of the public for scholarly, educational, journalistic, or governmental purposes. Such requests shall be made to the Court Administrator in such form as the Court Administrator may prescribe. Each request must (i) identify what compiled data is sought, and (ii) describe the purpose for requesting the compiled data.

(b) Determination. The Court Administrator, in consultation with the Chief Justice of the Trial Court, shall have discretion to grant or deny any request or part thereof for compiled data. The Court Administrator shall consider (i) whether the request is consistent with the purpose of these rules and (ii) whether the requested data may be compiled by the court without undue burden or expense. The Court Administrator shall not grant a request for data that is prohibited from public disclosure or for data where the electronic record is not an accurate representation of the official court record. The Court Administrator's decision shall be communicated to the requester with the reasons therefor.

(c) Fees. Upon allowance of a request, the Court Administrator may require the payment of a reasonable fee for staff time and resources to compile and provide the requested compiled data.

(d) Conditions. The Court Administrator may condition approval of a request for compiled data on the requester agreeing in writing to certain limitations on the use of the data, such as that it not be used for a commercial purpose.

Adopted July 20, 2016, effective November 1, 2016.

NOTES

"Compiled data" is defined in Rule 1(e). Although the Trial Court seeks to provide access to electronic court records for purposes of transparency and accountability, it is also concerned about the potential for unwarranted harm to litigants, victims, witnesses and jurors that can come with unfettered access. Much of the information obtained by the court from litigants and non-parties is not provided voluntarily, but is required by the court both to provide fair and timely resolution of cases and to enhance public safety. The Trial Court's case management databases, which result in electronic records, are created to support those functions. Further the manner of collection and the definition of certain data may not result in an accurate representation of the underlying cases. The discretion vested in the Court Administrator under this rule is intended to address these concerns.

Regular Compiled Reports. The Trial Court provides a list on its website of publicly available reports, including annual and quarterly reports. The Trial Court may provide some reports to the public at no charge and other reports may be provided upon payment of a fee or subscription.

Rule 3(a), Procedure for Making Requests. In making a request for compiled data, a requestor shall describe the scholarly, educational, journalistic, or governmental purpose of the request. It is within the discretion of the Court Administrator to deny requests that do not fit these purposes.

Rule 3(d), Conditions. The Court Administrator may condition the provision of compiled information on a requester signing an agreement limiting the use of the information. For example, the Court Administrator may require that such information not be resold or used for a commercial purpose, except journalistic purposes.

Rule 4. Requests for Bulk Data

Requests for bulk distribution of court record information shall not be granted except where explicitly required by law, court rule, or court order.

Adopted July 20, 2016, effective November 1, 2016.

NOTES

"Bulk data" is defined in Rule 1(e). It is the policy of the Trial Court not to provide bulk distribution of electronic court data. An attempt to duplicate in whole or substantial part any of the case management databases would be burdensome to court personnel and could cause unwarranted harm to litigants, victims, witnesses, and jurors. The need for information from court databases for scholarly, educational, journalistic, or governmental purposes can be satisfied by the tailored provision of compiled data under Rule 3.

Rule 5. Remote Access to Electronic Court Records

(a) Remote Accessibility to Information in Electronic Form Through the Public Internet Portal. The following information in a publicly available court record shall be made remotely accessible to the public unless access is otherwise restricted or exempted under these rules or by terms and conditions for use of the public portal website to be set by the Chief Justice of the Trial Court after notification to the Supreme Judicial Court:

(1) *Civil cases.*

(i) Generally. Except as exempted in Rule 5(a)(*l*)(iii), the following information shall be viewable remotely in civil court records:

(A) The full name of each party and the related case or case number(s) by court department and division;

(B) The name and mailing address of each attorney who has entered an appearance for a party and of each self-represented litigant;

(C) The docket of a specific case; and

(D) Calendar information.

(ii) Search. Civil cases may be searched by party name, case number, or other criteria as set by the Chief Justice of the Trial Court.

(iii) Exemption of certain civil case types. Abuse prevention and harassment orders and proceedings, and sexually dangerous person proceedings, shall not be available by remote access. Each Department of the Trial Court may by a Standing Order approved by the Chief Justice of the Trial Court after notification to the Supreme Judicial Court exempt certain additional civil case types or categories of information from remote access. A list of the approved exemptions shall be available on the Trial Court's website.

(2) *Criminal cases.*

(i) Generally. Except as exempted in Rule 5(a)(2)(iii), the following information shall be viewable remotely in criminal court records:

(A) The full name of each defendant and the related case or case number(s) by court department and division;

(B) The name and mailing address of each attorney who has entered an appearance and of each self-represented litigant;

(C) The docket of a specific case; and

(D) Calendar information.

(ii) Search. Criminal cases may be searched by case number.

(iii) Exemption of certain criminal case types. Each appropriate Department of the Trial Court may by a Standing Order approved by the Chief Justice of the Trial Court after notification to the Supreme Judicial Court exempt certain criminal case types or categories of information from remote access. A list of the approved exemptions shall be available on the Trial Court's website.

(b) Remote Accessibility to Information in Electronic Form through the Attorney Portal. Attorneys who are licensed to practice in Massachusetts and have registered with the Massachusetts Trial Court shall have access to a portal providing remote access to all non-exempt cases, and a calendar of scheduled events in the cases in which they have entered an appearance. Civil and criminal cases may be searched by party name or other criteria as set by the Chief Justice of the Trial Court. Access is subject to terms and conditions set by the Chief Justice of the Trial Court, and an attorney's access may be suspended or revoked for violation of those terms. The portable document format (PDF) version of certain publicly available court records, if so maintained by the court, may be made available on the Attorney Portal. Each appropriate Department of the Trial Court may request permission from the Chief Justice of the Trial Court to exempt certain criminal or civil case types or categories of information from remote access.

(c) Nonparty Information. Information that specifically identifies an individual who in that case is a witness in a criminal case, victim of a criminal or delinquent act, or juror shall not be stated in the caption of a filing.

(d) Availability of Additional Records. The Chief Justice of the Trial Court may determine that additional electronic court records or information may be made remotely accessible to the public.

(e) No Creation of Rights. This rule does not provide the public a right of access to any court record prohibited from public disclosure or to the provision of remote access to all content of publicly available court records. The right of the public to access court records at a Clerk's office pursuant to Rule 2 shall not be limited by concurrent remote access.

Adopted July 20, 2016, effective November 1, 2016. Amended June 7, 2018, effective July 1, 2018.

NOTES

Rule 5(a), Remote Accessibility of Information in Electronic Form Through the Public Internet Portal. All publicly available docket information in civil and criminal proceedings, except those exempted pursuant to Rule 5(a)(1)(iii) and Rule 5(a)(2)(iii), shall be made available electronically to the extent that the public shall be able to search and view the information designated in this rule. At this time, this rule does not encompass remote access to audio, audiovisual, or electronic images, including portable document format ("PDF") by the general public. The Chief Justice of the Trial Court has authority to expand remote access to include audio, audiovisual, or electronic images when technology and policy allow.

Rule 5(a)(1), Remote Accessibility of Civil Case Types. All civil case types not exempted by statute, rule, court order, standing order, or determination of the Chief Justice of the Trial Court shall be made available.

Exempted Civil Case Types. A list of exempted case types shall be maintained on the Trial Court's website. A non-exhaustive list of exempted case types can also be found in Addendum A, "Records Excluded From Public Access."

Notwithstanding amendments to the list of exempted case types, the following case types shall always remain exempted from the Public Internet portal:

Harassment and Domestic Abuse Records. The Federal Violence Against Women Act (VAWA) prevents the courts from displaying harassment and domestic abuse case types on the Internet. See 18 U.S.C. § 2265(d)(3) ("A State ... shall not make available publicly on the Internet any information regarding the registration, filing of a petition for, or issuance of a protection order, restraining order or injunction, restraining order, or injunction in either the issuing or enforcing State, tribal or territorial jurisdiction, if such publication would be likely to publicly reveal the identity or location of the party protected under such order."). Thus, cases and orders entered under G.L. c. 208, § 18, G.L. c. 209, § 32, G.L. c. 209A, G.L. c. 209C, § 15, or G.L. c. 258E, as well as any similar order, shall not be made available through remote access.

Sexually Dangerous Person Proceedings. The court record in these proceedings conducted pursuant to G.L. c. 123A, § 1, et seq., often involves voluminous records identifying the names of victims of sexual assault and their families. Pursuant to G.L. c. 265, § 24C, the portion of the records of a court which contains the name of the victim in an arrest, investigation, or complaint for rape or assault with intent to rape in certain specified offenses, shall be withheld from public inspection, except with the consent of a justice of such court where the complaint is or would be prosecuted. Under section 24C, except as otherwise provided, it shall be unlawful to publish, disseminate or otherwise disclose the name of any individual identified as a victim of the specified offenses. The public may contact the Sex Offender Registry Board and the Department of Criminal Justice Information Services for information regarding sex offenders and persons with a criminal history.

Rule 5(a)(1)(i)(B), Address of Self-represented Litigants. The current mailing addresses for all attorneys or self-represented litigants is required to allow parties and the court to promptly and effectively serve notice, filings, and decisions on all necessary parties. Self–represented litigants may provide a "preferred" address, such as a United States post office box number, if they do not want their home address viewable on the Trial Court's Public Internet Portal.

Rule 5(a)(1)(ii), Search. As the technical capabilities of the Public Internet Portal change, the Chief Justice of the Trial Court may expand the available search fields for civil cases. Future possibilities include searching by date or by case type.

Rule 5(a)(2), Criminal Cases. All criminal case types not exempted by statute, rule, court order, standing order, or determination of the Chief Justice of the Trial Court shall be made available on the Public Internet Portal. However, as a matter of policy, the committee has determined that criminal case searches will be limited to case number. Therefore, search by defendant name shall not be permitted on the internet portal for criminal cases.

Each court should provide in the Clerk's office a kiosk for the public to use to view court records of criminal cases that are not otherwise prohibited from public disclosure. Searches of court records on the court kiosk will not be limited to case number.

The Criminal Offender Record Information (CORI) statute, G.L. c. 6, §§ 167–178B (CORI) governs the dissemination of criminal offender record information. The legislative history to the 2010 amendments to the CORI statute provides that the intent was to strike "a great balance ... between providing information that the public has a right to know and protecting people's privacy." State House News Service, Nov. 18, 2009 (statement of Sen. Creem on Senate Doc. No. 2210). If the Trial Court were to provide the public with the ability to remotely search criminal cases by a defendant's last name, which could essentially reveal a defendant's entire criminal history, it could thwart the careful balance between access and privacy struck by the Legislature in enacting the CORI statute.

The 2010 CORI reform enacted by the Legislature includes enhanced online access to a record subject's criminal history record and expanded the group of people who could receive this information. G. L. c. 6 § 172(a); see generally Gregory I. Massing, "CORI Reform Providing Ex–Offenders with Increased Opportunities Without Compromising Employers' Needs", 55 Boston B.J., no. 1, 2011, at 21, 22, 24. However, the Legislature also gave record subjects the ability, free of charge, to obtain a list of everyone, other than a criminal justice agency, who has accessed their CORI. Id. at 21, 24. This provides a check on CORI access and usage. The CORI law also provides for review and issuance of penalties for improper usage of CORI information. G.L. c. 6, § 178 1/2. Given these numerous protections and limitations, the Legislature instituted a system that included accountability for CORI access and use. Such limitations and accountability could not reasonably be maintained if a defendant's criminal history could be pieced together through a search on the Trial Court's website. For members of the public seeking a criminal offender record on an individual, the Department of Criminal Justice Information Services ("DCJIS") has created a website ("iCORI") for registered users to request and obtain criminal offender record information. See 803 Code Mass. Regs. § 2.00 et seq.

Further, allowing remote access to court records in certain criminal cases implicates the concerns identified by the Supreme Judicial Court in *Commonwealth v. Pon*, 469 Mass. 296, 307 (2014), namely that access to criminal records negatively affects a defendant's future employment prospects, which, in turn, makes rehabilitation more difficult. The Court's decision in *Pon* was limited to closed criminal proceedings that resulted in a dismissal or an entry of nolle prosequi and also possibly to acquittals and findings of no probable cause. Id. at 316 & n. 24. All of these would be viewable on the Trial Court's Public internet portal; such access runs against the specific concerns enunciated in *Pon*. For court records not implicated in *Pon*, there is nonetheless a concern that permitting a broad criminal record search through the internet portal would frustrate the privacy and rehabilitation concerns identified and protected by the Legislature and Supreme Judicial Court.

The committee concluded that allowing the public to view the progress and resolution of individual proceedings by case number allows for "the contemporaneous review [of judicial proceedings] in the forum of public opinion", *Commonwealth v. Cohen*, 456 Mass. 94, 106 (2010), quoting *In re Oliver*, 333 U.S. 257, 270 (1948), without allowing for criminal offender record information to be easily assembled from the Internet Portal. Public access to criminal records and proceedings in the courthouse shall not be affected or limited by this rule.

Rule 5(b), Access through the Attorney Portal. The Attorney Portal is intended as a convenience for attorneys to easily access their cases and other cases in which they have a legitimate interest. Attorneys may register to use the Attorney Portal by providing their business email address on file with the Board of Bar Overseers. Registered attorneys may log in to the portal upon certifying the attorney has read and agreed to comply with the Trial Court's "terms of use" agreement posted on the portal. Registered attorneys will have access to their calendar and cases and the ability to search other non-exempt cases throughout the portal by party name or other criteria as set by the Chief Justice of the Trial Court. The "terms of use" are intended to prevent misuse, tampering, and criminal behavior, including any activity that would seek to violate the intent of the CORI law.

Access to the Attorney Portal should be available to both attorneys licensed in Massachusetts and attorneys licensed in other jurisdictions who enter an appearance pro hac vice and have complied with S.J.C. Rule 3:15.

Exempted Case Types. When feasible, otherwise exempted cases should be available for attorneys who have entered an appearance in that case to view through the Attorney Portal. However, impounded cases will not be available through the Attorney Portal. Each appropriate Department of the Trial Court may request permission from the Chief Justice of the Trial Court to exempt certain criminal or civil case types or categories of information from remote access.

Remote Accessibility of Case Documents through the Attorney Portal. Electronic access to portable electronic documents (PDFs) stored in the court's document management system may be through the Attorney Portal. The Chief Justice of the Trial Court may determine which documents and case types will be available through the Attorney Portal. Otherwise accessible documents may be restricted by the court if they include personal identifying information not redacted pursuant to S.J.C. Rule 1:24.

Rule 5(c), Nonparty Information. Information that specifically identifies an individual who is a witness in a criminal case, victim of a criminal or delinquent act, or juror shall not be stated in the caption of a filing. This subsection is intended to protect the privacy and safety of persons who are not litigants. Docket entries should not be created that use the full name of such individuals, for instance in conjunction with the title of a motion or notice relating to that person, except when required by law.

Rule 5(d), Availability of Additional Records. This subsection permits the Chief Justice of the Trial Court to determine that additional electronic court records may be, made remotely accessible to the public, which may include expanded availability of PDFs.

Rule 5(e), No Creation of Rights. The public has a qualified common law right to access court records in a courthouse. Although there is no constitutional or common law right to remote access of the same court records, the Trial Court recognizes that advances in technology provide the public and the court with additional means of access that benefit both the public and the court. This rule acknowledges the desirability of providing remote access to court information, and balances that access with the limits imposed by law and privacy concerns. Rule 5 does not provide the public a right of access to any court record prohibited from public disclosure (see Addendum A, "Records Excluded From Public Access"), nor to the provision of remote access to all content of publicly available court records. The right of the public to access to court records at a Clerk's office pursuant to Rule 2 shall not be limited because of concurrent remote access.

Attorney Portal Terms of Use

Users of the Attorney Portal agree to the following:

• You may use the Attorney Portal to access information in civil cases and criminal cases, and to access calendar events. You may access information in criminal cases only in connection to your representation of a client in a criminal or disciplinary matter. However, you may not use your access to criminal cases to obtain criminal offender record information (CORI) for purposes that violate the CORI law, G. L. c. 6, §§ 167 *et seq.*, to provide CORI to individuals who are not your clients in a criminal matter, or otherwise to provide CORI in violation of the CORI law.

• You may not use the Attorney Portal to access information in a manner that knowingly risks the integrity or security of the Trial Court's case management system; or for any purpose prohibited by law or court rule. Nor may you engage in "data scraping". For purposes of these Terms of Use, "data scrapping" refers to the use of a computer program or other automated process or technique to extract or collect data from the Trial Court's case management system".

• You may not sell information obtained from these records, directly or indirectly, to third parties and shall not use or allow others to use information obtained from these records for non-litigation purposes such as in connection with hiring or tenant screening.

• You must keep your user name and password (login credentials) confidential. You may allow persons under your supervision and direction to use your login credentials, but you will be fully responsible for all activity that occurs under your login credentials.

• Use of the Attorney Portal is subject to monitoring and auditing by the Trial Court at any time. If you (or persons who use your login credentials) use the Attorney Portal in any way that is prohibited by these Terms of Use, you may be denied future access to the Attorney Portal and will be subject to sanctions as provided by law or court rule. Any violation of the Terms of Use may be referred to the Board of Bar Overseers.

• The Trial Court reserves the right to amend, or discontinue any feature of the Attorney Portal, or amend the conditions of its use at any time. Absent unforeseen circumstances, any such changes will be announced in advance on the Attorney Portal.

• The Trial Court shall not be liable for any damages associated with use of the Attorney Portal.

I affirm that I have read and understand these Terms and Conditions, that I accept them, and that I agree to comply with them.

Rule 6.   Correction of Clerical Error in Electronic Docket Entry

Any party, nonparty, or their attorney may make a written request to correct a clerical error in an electronic docket. Such a request may be made using a form that shall be made available online at masscourts.org and at each Clerk's office. The completed form must be submitted to the Clerk's office where the court record in question is physically located and to all parties.

Adopted July 20, 2016, effective November 1, 2016.

NOTE

This Rule is intended to allow parties and nonparties to alert the Clerk to a potential clerical mistake or error, but does not apply to the correction of errors of substance. For further process see Mass. R. Civ. P. 60 and Mass. R. Crim. P. 42.

Addendum.   Records Excluded From Public Access

MASSACHUSETTS COURT SYSTEM LIST OF AUTHORITIES DESIGNATING MATERIAL AS IMPOUNDED, CONFIDENTIAL, OR NOT AVAILABLE FOR PUBLIC INSPECTION
(December 2015)

The following list is an overview of the material that a statute, court rule, or standing order designates must be withheld as "impounded," "withheld from public inspection," "not available for public inspection," "confidential," "segregated," or "sealed." The list is not an exhaustive compilation of such matters under Massachusetts law. Attorneys and self-represented litigants must conduct their own research prior to filing any papers to ensure full compliance with the law governing impoundment.

Abortion consent forms and materials ("Mary Moe" materials). "The said consent form and any other forms, transcript of evidence, or written findings and conclusions of a court, shall be confidential and may not be released to any person except by the pregnant woman's written informed consent or by a proper judicial order, other than to the pregnant woman herself, to whom such documents relate, the operating physician, or any person whose consent is required pursuant to this section, or under the law." (G.L. c. 112, § 12S)

Abuse Prevention Orders. If the plaintiff or defendant is a minor in an action arising under G.L. c. 209A, the records "shall be withheld from public inspection except by order of the court; provided, that such records shall be open, at all reasonable times, to the inspection of the minor, said minor's parent, guardian, attorney, and to the plaintiff and the plaintiff's attorney, or any of them." (G.L. c. 209A, § 8) The plaintiff's residential address, residential telephone number and workplace name, address, and telephone number "shall be confidential and withheld from public inspection" when pursuing an action under c. 209A. (G.L. c. 209A, § 8)

Address Confidentiality Program Affidavits. Affidavits giving the actual address of litigants who wish to employ in civil litigation the post office box address that has been assigned to them by the Secretary of State's Address Confidentiality Program. (S.J.C. Rule 1:20) The actual address of the program participant may be used by court personnel in the furtherance of their official duties, but such address shall not be used for purposes of mailing any documents, notices or orders. The affidavit shall be impounded by operation of this rule without any further judicial action. The Clerk shall segregate the impounded affidavit from the other papers and shall not make the information contained therein available to other parties. (G.L. c. 9A; 950 Code Mass. Regs. § 130)

Adoptions. "All petitions for adoption, all reports submitted there under and all pleadings, papers or documents filed in connection therewith, docket entries in the permanent docket and record books shall not be available for inspection, unless a judge of probate of the county where such records are kept, for good cause shown, shall otherwise order." (G.L. c. 210, § 5C)

Affidavits of Indigency. "[B]y order of the Supreme Judicial Court, as required by G.L. c. 261, § 27B, the financial information contained in an affidavit of indigency, pursuant to both G.L. c. 261, § 29 (inmate), and G.L. c. 261, § 27B (non-inmate), may not, except by order of the recipient court, be disclosed to anyone other than authorized court personnel, the applicant, the applicant's counsel or anyone authorized in writing by the applicant." *Kordis v. Superintendent, Souza Baronowski Correctional Ctr.*, 58 Mass. App. Ct. 902, 904 (2003). The affidavit of indigency form states that, "[b]y order of the Supreme Judicial Court, all information in this affidavit is CONFIDENTIAL. Except by special order of a court, it shall not be disclosed to anyone other than authorized court

personnel, the applicant, applicant's counsel or anyone authorized in writing by the applicant."

Alcohol and drug abuse program and treatment records. A party's release form and/or court order may be needed to access records. (42 U.S.C. § 1175, 290 dd–3)

Appeals from the Sex Offender Registry Board. "The court shall keep proceedings conducted pursuant to this paragraph and records from such proceedings confidential and such proceedings and records shall be impounded." (G.L. c. 6, § 178M)

Board of Bar Overseers proceedings. "Except as the Court shall otherwise order or as otherwise provided in this rule, the Board and the Bar Counsel shall keep confidential all information involving allegations of misconduct by a lawyer and all information that a lawyer's physical or mental condition may adversely affect his or her ability to practice law until the occurrence" of an enumerated event. (S.J.C. Rule 4:01, § 20(1))

Child Protection Orders. Any protection of children proceeding conducted pursuant to G.L. c. 119, § 1 to § 37 cannot be open to the general public and the name of the individual involved cannot be published. (G.L. c. 119, § 38)

Child in Need of Services/Child Requiring Assistance. Petitions seeking a determination that a child is in need of services or requiring assistance shall be confidential and not open to the public. (G.L. c. 119, § 39E to § 39I)

Civil Commitment and Mental Health Reports. Mental health examination and commitment records (G.L. c. 123, §§ 1–18, 35, 36A), other than ordinary entries on the criminal docket, except on a judge's order.

Commission on Judicial Conduct proceedings. "Except as provided in this section, all proceedings of the commission shall be confidential until there has been a determination of sufficient cause and formal charges have been filed with the supreme judicial court." (G.L. c. 211C, § 6)

Delinquency Proceedings. "The record of a youthful offender proceeding conducted pursuant to an indictment shall be open to public inspection in the same manner and to the same extent as adult criminal records. All other record of the court in cases of delinquency arising under sections fifty-two to fifty-nine, inclusive, shall be withheld from public inspection except with the consent of a justice of such court; provided however, that such records shall be open, at all reasonable times, to inspection by the child proceeded against . . ." (G.L. c. 119, § 60A)

Department of Workforce Development Hearings (unemployment hearings). All information "secured pursuant to this chapter is confidential and for the exclusive use and information of the department in the discharge of its duties. Such information is not a public record nor admissible in any action or proceeding, except as provided in this section. This information is absolutely privileged and shall not be made the subject matter or basis in any action of slander, libel or emotional distress." (G.L. c. 151 A, § 46)

Drug and Alcohol Treatment Records. Drug and alcohol treatment records are confidential under State and Federal law. See 42 U.S.C. § 290dd–2 (substance abuse treatment records); G. L. c. 111B, § 11 (alcoholism treatment records;

G. L. c. 111E, § 18 (drug rehabilitation treatment records). Such records may, however, be released to the parties by judicial order after application showing good cause therefor, including the need to avert a substantial risk of death or serious bodily harm, which specifically includes incidents of suspected child abuse and neglect. See 42 U.S.C. § 290dd–2.

Expunged Records. See *Commonwealth v. S.M.F.*, 40 Mass. App. Ct. 42, 43–45 (1996) (in certain circumstances where the sealing statutes are not applicable, a trial court may use its inherent judicial power to order expungement); *Commissioner of Probation v. Adams,* 65 Mass. App. Ct. 725 (2006) (expungement of 209A orders permissible where the order was obtained through fraud on the court).

Financial statements. Statements submitted by parties in the Probate and Family Court shall be impounded or kept separate from other papers in the case and shall not be available for public inspection, but shall be available to the courts, the attorneys (whose appearances are entered in the case), the parties to the case, the registers, assistant registers, members of the Probation Department of the Probate Courts and to employees of the Massachusetts Department of Revenue, where necessary. (Supplemental Probate and Family Court Rule 401(d)).

Grand Jury minutes or documents. "Any grand jury transcript or document citing or describing grand jury testimony filed with any court shall be filed and maintained under seal, unless the paper is filed in a criminal prosecution for perjury before a grand jury." (G.L. c. 268, § 13D(e))

Guardian ad Litem Reports. "Unless otherwise ordered by the court, all guardian ad litem reports except those filed in cases involving accounts, licenses to sell and estate plans are impounded." (Probate and Family Court Standing Order 2–08)

Harassment Prevention Orders. The records of cases arising out of actions in which the plaintiff or defendant is a minor shall be withheld from public inspection except by order of the court; provided, however, that such records shall be open, at all reasonable times, to the inspection of the minor, such minor's parent, guardian and attorney and to the plaintiff and the plaintiff's attorney. The plaintiff's residential address, residential telephone number and workplace name, address, and telephone number, contained within the court records shall also be withheld with the same exception. All confidential portions of the records shall be accessible at all reasonable times to the plaintiff and plaintiffs attorney, to others specifically authorized by the plaintiff to obtain such information and to prosecutors, victim-witness advocates as defined in section 1 of chapter 258B, sexual assault counselors as defined in section 20J of chapter 233 and law officers, if such access is necessary in the performance of their duties. (G.L. c. 258E, § 10)

Inquest Report and Transcript. See G.L. c. 38, § 10; *In re Globe Newspaper Co., Inc.,* 461 Mass. 113 (2011).

Juror Questionnaires. Jurors' confidential questionnaires or criminal records are not public records. (G.L. c. 234A, §§ 23, 33, 52)

Juvenile Trials. Juvenile trials must exclude the public. Courts shall designate a juvenile session with a separate docket and record for the hearing of cases of children under eighteen years of age. The session shall be separate from that for the trial of criminal cases. The court shall exclude the general public from juvenile sessions admitting only such persons as may have a direct interest in the case, except in cases where the Commonwealth has proceeded by indictment. (G.L. c. 119, §§ 52, 60A, 65; G.L. c. 276, § 100B). However, records of adults prosecuted for criminal offenses in the Juvenile Court shall be open to the public.

Mediator Records. "All memoranda, and other work product prepared by a mediator and a mediator's case files shall be confidential and not subject to disclosure in any judicial or administrative proceeding involving any of the parties to any mediation to which such materials apply. Any communication made in the course of and relating to the subject matter of any mediation and which is made in the presence of such mediator by any participant, mediator or other person shall be a confidential communication and not subject to disclosure in any judicial or administrative proceeding; provided, however, that the provisions of this section shall not apply to the mediation of labor disputes." (G.L. c. 233, § 23C)

Medical Certificates and Clinical Team Reports. These reports must be filed when seeking temporary guardianship on the grounds of mental illness or physical incapacity or for conservatorship on the grounds of mental weakness. These reports are impounded, held separate from the file, and not available for public inspection. Access to inspect the reports is limited to the court, attorneys of record, parties, guardians ad litem, and any probation officer assigned to the case. The order specifically prohibits use for any purpose other than consideration of the petition. The certificate, by the terms of this standing order, is substituted for records that are protected by the Health Insurance Portability and Accountability Act of 1996, Pub. L. 104–19 1 ("HIPAA") and would require a release form the person over whom guardianship is sought by the petition. (Probate and Family Court Standing Order 5–08)

Medical Health, and Hospital Records. A party's release form or court order is needed to access records. G.L. c. 111, §§ 70, 70E(b). HIPAA health providers may release personal health information only if the release signed by a party complies with the provisions of the federal law. Even if no statutory privilege applies to the information sought, the provider or keeper of other records (e.g., unlicensed support group leaders, batterer intervention programs) may also request a written release from their client.

Medical Peer Review Committee. "Except as otherwise provided in this section, the proceedings, reports and records of a medical peer review committee shall be confidential and shall be exempt from the disclosure of public records under G.L. c. 66, § 10 but shall not be subject to subpoena or discovery, or introduced into evidence, in any judicial or administrative proceeding." (G.L. c. 111, § 204)

Non–Adjudication of Party as Father. "In an action to establish paternity or in which paternity of a child is an issue, all complaints, pleadings, papers, documents or reports filed in connection therewith, docket entries in the permanent docket and record books shall be segregated and unavailable for inspection only if the judge of the court where such records are kept, for good cause shown, so orders or the person alleged to be the father is adjudicated not to be the father of the child; provided, however, that the child, the child's mother, the person adjudicated to be the father and the department of transitional assistance, the department of children and families, the division of medical assistance or any other public assistance program and the IV–D agency as set forth in chapter 119A, when the child who is or was the subject of the complaint is a recipient of public assistance of the attorney for any of them, and the department of children and families, when the child who is or was the subject of the complaint is within the care and protection of the department of children and families, is the subject of a petition for such care of protection pursuant to chapter 119 or is the subject of a petition to dispense with consent for adoption pursuant to subsection (b) of section 3 of chapter 210, shall have access to and the right to obtain copies of the papers, docket books and judgments in actions pursuant to this chapter." (G.L. c. 209C, § 13)

Office of the Jury Commissioner Records. These rules do not apply to the Office of the Jury Commissioner because it is not part of the Trial Court; it is a department within the Judicial Branch, supervised and controlled by the Supreme Judicial Court. (G.L. c. 211B, § 9A(viii); G.L. c. 234A, § 5). Therefore, juror attendance records, empanelment documents (e.g., case cover sheets, case information sheets, and courtroom panel worksheets), and grand juror financial questionnaires, among other documents created and/or maintained by the Office of the Jury Commissioner, are not subject to public access under these rules.

Pending or Denied Criminal Complaint Applications. Alphabetical indices, dockets, contents of case files, exhibits put in evidence, and tape recordings (if any) of proceedings should presumptively be closed to the public unless the Clerkmagistrate or a judge concludes that the legitimate interest of the public outweighs the privacy interests of the accused. District Court Standards of Judicial Practice, The Complaint Procedure §§ 3:15 and 5:02 (rev. 2008).

Personal Medical Information. See Probate and Family Court Standing Order 1–09, Article V of G.L. c. 190B.

Photographs of unsuspecting nude person. "A photograph, videotape or other recorded visual image, depicting a person who is nude or partially nude that is part of any court record arising from a prosecution under this section, shall not be open to public inspection and shall only be made available by court personnel to a law enforcement officer, prosecuting attorney, defendant's attorney, defendant, or victim connected to such prosecution for inspection, unless otherwise ordered by the court." (G.L. c. 272, § 105(g))

Presentence Probation Reports. "In extraordinary cases, the judge may except from disclosure parts of the report which are not relevant to a proper sentence, diagnostic opinion which might seriously disrupt a program of rehabilitation, sources of information obtained upon a promise of confidentiality, or any other information which, if disclosed, might result in harm, physical or otherwise, to the defendant or other persons." See Mass. R. Crim. P. 28(d)(3); *Commonwealth v. Martin*, 355 Mass 296 (1969).

Probation Records. The information obtained and recorded shall not be regarded as public records and shall not be open for public inspection but shall be accessible to the justices and probation officers of the courts, to the police commissioner for the city of Boston, to all chiefs of police and city marshals,

and to such departments of the state and local governments as the commissioner may determine. (G.L. c. 276, § 100)

Psychotherapist Treatment Records. See G.L. c. 112, § 129A, except as provided by G.L. c. 233, § 20(b).

Qualified Domestic Relation Orders. These reports are impounded, held separate from the file, and not available for public inspection. Access to inspect the reports is limited to the court, attorneys of record, and parties. (Probate and Family Court Standing Order 3–08)

Records deposited with the Clerk-magistrate as potential exhibits. Materials that are not yet introduced in evidence or filed as an attachment to a pleading or motion, including business records produced pursuant to G.L. c. 233, § 79J, hospital records produced pursuant to G.L. c. 233, § 79, and records produced pursuant to the protocol of *Commonwealth v. Dwyer*, 448 Mass. 122, 148–149 (2006).

Records and hearings related to court-ordered examinations in criminal proceedings. An examiner designated by the court for a court-ordered examination in a criminal proceeding may request records by filing a request with the court stating the records requested and the reason for the request. The defendant shall file objections to the production of the requested material and the judge may hold an ex parte hearing on those objection. "Records of such hearing shall be sealed until the report of the examiner is disclosed to the parties under Rule 14(b)(2)(B)(iii)." If a record request is granted, the files are subpoenaed by the Clerk and are kept under seal except as otherwise provided by rule. (Mass. R. Crim. P. 14(b)(2)(C)(iii))

Rights afforded victims, witnesses, or family members. "To provide victims a meaningful role in the criminal justice system, victims and witnesses of crime, or in the event the victim is deceased, the family members of the victim, shall be afforded the following basic and fundamental rights, to the greatest extent possible and subject to appropriation and to available resources, with priority for services to be provided to victims of crimes against the person and crimes where physical injury to a person results:

(h) for victims and witnesses, to be informed of the right to request confidentiality in the criminal justice system. Upon the court's approval of such request, no law enforcement agency, prosecutor, defense counsel, or parole, probation or corrections official may disclose or state in open court, except among themselves, the residential address, telephone number, or place of employment or school of the victim, a victim's family member, or a witness, except as otherwise ordered by the court. The court may enter such other orders or conditions to maintain limited disclosure of the information as it deems appropriate to protect the privacy and safety of victims, victims' family members and witnesses; . . ." (G.L. c. 258B, § 3(h))

Sealed Records. Records that have been properly sealed by a justice or by statute or the commissioner of probation, or in conjunction with a pardon granted by the Governor of the Commonwealth. See G.L. c. 276, §§ 100A, 100B and 100C.

School records. A party who has shared or sole legal custody may authorize release of records, except for a parent or party whose access is restricted by a Chapter 209A or other court order. (G.L. c. 71, § 34H; G.L. c. 208, § 31)

Search Warrants. Between issuance and return, a search warrant, the application for search warrant, and any supporting affidavits are not publicly available. (G.L. c. 276, § 2B)

Social Worker records. "All communications between a social worker licensed pursuant to the provisions of § 132 or a social worker employed in a state, county or municipal governmental agency, and a client are confidential." (G.L. c. 112, § 135A)

Trade secrets and other matters in connection with discovery. "Protective Orders. Upon motion by a party or by the person from whom discovery is sought, and for good cause shown, the court in which the action is pending or alternatively, on matters relating to a deposition, the court in the county or judicial district, as the case may be, where the deposition is to be taken may make any order which justice requires to protect a party or person from annoyance, embarrassment, oppression, or undue burden or expense, including one or more of the following: ... (7) that a trade secret or other confidential research, development, or commercial information not be disclosed or be disclosed only in a designated way" (Mass. R. Civ. P. 26(c)(7))

Victim's Name in Sexual Assault Record. The portion of the records of a court or any police department which contains the name of the victim in an arrest, investigation, or complaint for rape or assault with intent to rape in certain specified offenses, shall be withheld from public inspection, except with the consent of a justice of such court where the complaint is or would be prosecuted. Except as otherwise provided it shall be unlawful to publish, disseminate or otherwise disclose the name of any individual identified as an alleged victim of the specified offenses. (G.L. c. 265, § 24C). The sexual assault offenses referenced in § 24C include:

- Indecent assault and battery on a child under age 14 (G.L. c. 265, § 13B)

- Indecent assault and battery on a child under 14 during commission of certain offenses or by mandated reporters (G.L. c. 265, § 13B½)

- Indecent assault and battery on a child under 14 by certain previously convicted offenders (G.L. c. 265, § 13B¾)

- Rape or aggravated rape (G.L. c. 265, § 22)

- Forcible rape of a child (G.L. c. 265, § 22A)

- Rape of a child during commission of certain offenses or by force (G.L. c. 265, § 22B)

- Rape of a child through use of force by certain previously convicted offenders (G.L. c. 265, § 22C)

- Statutory rape (G.L. c. 265, § 23)

- Rape and abuse of a child aggravated by age difference between defendant and victim or by mandated reporters (G.L. c. 265, § 23A)

- Rape and abuse by certain previously convicted offenders (G.L. c. 265, § 23B)

- Assault with intent to rape (G.L. c. 265, § 24)

- Assault on a child under 16 with intent to commit rape (G.L. c. 265, § 24B)

- Trafficking of persons (G.L. c. 265, § 50)

Victim program locations. Locations of battered women's shelters, domestic violence, and rape crisis programs may not be disclosed by court order, or otherwise. (G.L. c. 233, §§ 20J, 20K)

Adopted July 20, 2016, effective November 1, 2016.

XVI. LIMITED ASSISTANCE REPRESENTATION

Table of Rules

Rule 1. Limited Assistance Representation

Limited Assistance Representation (LAR) permits an attorney to represent a party in a non-criminal action for discrete, limited purposes, if the limitation is reasonable under the circumstances and the client gives informed consent. LAR allows an attorney to withdraw from representation after s/he completes the agreed upon limited services. Before representing a client in an LAR matter, an attorney shall give a prospective client a written agreement that clearly and precisely states the scope of representation. The attorney shall review the written agreement with the client before it is signed and obtain the client's informed consent. Both the attorney and the client shall sign the agreement. An LAR attorney may appear on a compensated or an uncompensated basis.

Adopted November 29, 2018, effective February 1, 2019.

Rule 2. Applicability

This Rule applies to any Limited Assistance Representation of a party in a non-criminal action in any Trial Court department, provided it shall not apply to Juvenile Court unless adopted by Juvenile Court.

Adopted November 29, 2018, effective February 1, 2019.

Rule 3. Attorney Qualification

To qualify as an LAR attorney, an attorney must complete training, as provided for in the Uniform Protocol for Limited Assistance Representation Training in the Massachusetts Trial Court. An attorney must certify that s/he is LAR-qualified on the court-approved Notice of Limited Appearance.

Adopted November 29, 2018, effective February 1, 2019.

Rule 4. Notice of Limited Appearance

Before representing a client in an LAR matter, an LAR attorney must file a Notice of Limited Appearance on a form approved by the Chief Justice of the Trial Court and shall serve the Notice on all parties in compliance with applicable rules and paragraph 6 below. The Notice of Limited Appearance shall state precisely the discrete event(s) and/or discrete issue(s) for which the LAR attorney will represent the client. An LAR attorney may file a new or a revised Notice of Limited Appearance during or after the previously agreed upon events and/or issues. Both the LAR attorney and the client must sign each Notice of Limited Appearance. If an LAR attorney files a pleading, motion or other document and/or argues a legal issue outside the scope of a filed Notice of Limited Appearance, then the court may require the filing of a new Notice of Limited Appearance. If the LAR attorney thereafter fails to do so, the court may consider the LAR attorney to have entered a general appearance.

Adopted November 29, 2018, effective February 1, 2019.

Rule 5. Notice of Withdrawal of Limited Appearance

Upon completion of all events or issues for which an LAR attorney has filed a Notice of Limited Appearance, s/he shall serve and file a Notice of Withdrawal of Limited Appearance on a form approved by the Chief Justice of the Trial Court. A Notice of Withdrawal must be filed for each Notice of Limited Appearance. The attorney must sign the Notice of Withdrawal. A Notice of Withdrawal filed and served in compliance with this paragraph and paragraph 6 below is effective upon filing. No motion to withdraw under Mass. R. Civ. P. 11(c) is required. The Court may treat the attorney as appearing for the client until the attorney files a Notice of Withdrawal, even if the events or issues covered by the limited representation have concluded. In such instances, the Court also may order the attorney to file a Notice of Withdrawal. If any other party incurs costs or is otherwise prejudiced by the attorney's failure to file a Notice of Withdrawal, then upon motion the court for good cause may order a non-punitive remedy, including compensation for fees and costs reasonably incurred.

Adopted November 29, 2018, effective February 1, 2019.

Rule 6. Service

An LAR attorney who files a Notice of Limited Appearance, including a new or revised Notice of Limited Appearance, and/or Notice of Withdrawal of Limited Appearance shall serve a copy of each Notice, with a certificate of service, upon each opposing party's attorney or, if a party is not represented by an attorney, on that party.

Whenever service is required or permitted to be made upon a party who has an LAR attorney, for all matters within the scope of the Notice of Limited Appearance, service shall be made upon both the LAR attorney and the party. Service of the party should be made at the address listed for the party in the Notice of Limited Appearance. If the party's address has been impounded by court order or rule, service of the party shall be made as set out in the court order or rule. Service

606

upon an LAR attorney is not required for matters outside the scope of the Notice of Limited Appearance.

Adopted November 29, 2018, effective February 1, 2019.

Rule 7.   Filings Shall State LAR Appearance

An LAR attorney must comply with Mass. R. Civ. P. 11(a) when filing any pleading, motion or other document in the course of her/his limited appearance and shall state in bold type on the signature page of the document, **"Attorney of [party] for the limited purpose of [court event or issue]."**

Adopted November 29, 2018, effective February 1, 2019.

Rule 8.   Court Notice

Whenever a clerk, recorder, or register is required to provide notice where a party is represented by an LAR attorney, s/he shall provide notice to the party and to the LAR attorney unless the LAR attorney has filed a Notice of Withdrawal of Appearance.

Adopted November 29, 2018, effective February 1, 2019.

Rule 9.   Assisting a Party to Prepare Court Documents

An attorney may assist a party in preparing a pleading, motion or any other document that the party will sign and file in court. In assisting the preparation of any such pleading, motion or other document, the attorney shall insert the notation "prepared with assistance of counsel." Assisting a party with this type of document preparation does not constitute a general or limited appearance of the attorney. The party remains responsible to the court and other parties for all statements in any pleading, motion, or other document prepared but not signed by an attorney.

Adopted November 29, 2018, effective February 1, 2019.

STANDING ORDERS OF THE TRIAL COURT

Table of Standing Orders

Standing Order 1–16. Authority of the Judge with Respect to Communication with Specialty Court Teams

This Standing Order is promulgated by the Chief Justice of the Trial Court pursuant to G. L. c. 211B, Section 9 and shall constitute authorization by law as referenced in Rule 2.9 (A)(2) of the Code of Judicial Conduct (effective January 1, 2016).

For purposes of this Order:

Specialty Court means a specifically designated court session that focuses on individuals with underlying medical, mental health, substance abuse, or other issues that contribute to the reasons such individuals are before the courts. Specialty court shall also mean Veterans Treatment Court and Homelessness Court. Specialty court sessions integrate treatment and services with judicial case oversight and intensive court supervision. Examples include drug courts, mental health courts, veterans' courts, and tenancy preservation programs.

A Staffing shall refer to a regularly scheduled, informal conference not occurring in open court, the purpose of which is to permit the presiding judge and others, including counsel, to discuss a participant's progress in the specialty court, treatment recommendations, or responses to participant compliance issues.

IT IS THEREFORE ORDERED:

A judge presiding over a specialty court shall have the authority to initiate, permit or otherwise consider ex parte communications about defendants, juveniles or probationers with members of the specialty court team at a staffing or by written documents provided to all members of the specialty court team. The purpose of this authority is to allow judges in their role in presiding over specialty court sessions, and only in that capacity, to assume a more interactive role with parties, treatment providers, probation officers, social workers and others, than Rule 2.9 of the Code of Judicial Conduct would otherwise permit.

Adopted eff. Jan. 7, 2016.

Standing Order 2–16. Uniform Interdepartmental Procedures for Probation Violation Proceedings

This Standing Order is promulgated by the Chief Justice of the Trial court pursuant to G.L. c. 211B, Section 9 and stands effective October 3, 2016.

1. Application. This Order shall apply to the Superior Court, District Court, Boston Municipal Court and Juvenile Court Departments.

2. Purpose. This Order sets forth requirements regarding communication among the above-named departments of the Trial Court when an individual who is the subject of a probation order in one of these departments is charged with a new offense in another of these departments. Its purpose is to ensure that this required interdepartmental communication relating to the commencement of probation violation proceedings as a result of alleged new criminal behavior by a probationer, and the potential custody and transport of that probationer between different court departments, occur in a timely, informed and efficient manner. This Order does not apply to an individual who is the subject of a probation order issued prior to a trial or the formal submission and acceptance of a plea of guilty or an admission to sufficient facts, as provided in G.L. c. 276, § 87 ("pretrial probation").

3. Definition of Terms. As used in this Order, the terms below shall have the following meanings:

"Criminal:" includes delinquency or youthful offender.

"Criminal Court:" a court division of the Boston Municipal, District, or Juvenile Court or the Superior Court.

The terms used in this Order and the form promulgated by the Chief Justice of the Trial Court pursuant to Section 9 have been defined to include terminology associated with juvenile cases and proceedings and the Juvenile Court. They have been defined in this manner for the purposes of convenience and ease of reading and are applicable to this Order and form only. The terms as appearing in this Order and form do not change the meaning of the terminology used in adult and juvenile proceedings as defined and set forth by case law and statutes. Other than for the purposes of this Order and form, adult and juvenile terms are not interchangeable.

4. Intra–Departmental Communications. This Order does not apply to intra-departmental communications, transport of probationers, or use of the warrant management system, which may be the subject of rules or standing orders issued by and applicable within individual court departments.

5. Information to be Sent from the Criminal Court; Custody of Probationer. When an individual appears on a new criminal charge before a criminal court, and that individual is the subject of a probation order issued by a court in a different department of the Trial Court, the probation department of the criminal court shall transmit to the probation department of the court having responsibility for the supervision of the probationer (the "probation court") information and requests for information, including information regarding the possible service of a notice of violation on, and transport of, the probationer. This transmission shall be made by means of the form referred to in Section 9, below.

The transmission from the criminal court shall be sent electronically and promptly, to the probation officer in the probation court listed as the probation officer on duty in the probation court or, if there is no probation officer on duty, to the Chief Probation Officer of the probation court. The transmission shall be sent while the probationer is at the criminal court. When necessary, the criminal court may order the probationer held in custody until the procedures required by this Order are completed.

6. Information to be Returned by the Probation Court; Time Limit. The probation department of the probation court shall respond electronically, to the probation officer who transmitted the request for information from the criminal court. The response shall include information regarding service of a notice of violation on, and transport of, the probationer. This response shall be transmitted within two hours or within such time limit as extended, as provided in Section 7, such time limit to be measured from the time indicated on the transmission, and shall be set forth on the form referred to in Section 9, below.

If the probation department is requesting that the probationer be transported, the probation department shall request the issuance of an arrest warrant for a violation of probation ("warrant") from a judge in the probation court. If the judge issues such warrant, the clerk's office shall enter it promptly into the Warrant Management System and the probation department shall provide the criminal court with a notice of violation that cites the violation(s).

If the probation department is not requesting that the probationer be transported and is requesting that the probationer be served with a notice of violation, the probation department shall provide the probation department of the criminal court with a notice of violation that cites the violation(s) and indicates the date and time of the probationer's required appearance in the probation court.

7. Action by the Criminal Court. The criminal court shall await receipt of the information from the probation court for a period of two hours measured from the time of the transmission of the request for that information. This two-hour time limit may be extended by the criminal court.

Upon the timely receipt of the required information from the probation court and, if the probation court has issued a warrant, the criminal court shall serve on the probationer, in hand, a notice of violation on behalf of the probation court and shall either order transport of the probationer on such warrant or defer transport on the warrant until the termination of any custody ordered by the criminal court judge in the new criminal case. In the event that no warrant has been issued by the probation court, and the probation department has provided a notice of violation to the probation department of the criminal court, the criminal court shall serve such notice on the probationer, in hand, on behalf of the probation court.

If the probation department of the probation court does not provide the required information or a notice of violation to the probation department of the criminal court in the manner set forth in Section 6, the criminal court need not take any further action regarding the probation matter. In such instances, the probation department of the criminal court shall make an appropriate entry into its records.

8. Action by the Probation Court. Upon delivery of the probationer into the custody of the probation court on the warrant, and not withstanding any provision of this Order, the form promulgated pursuant to section 9, or the reason for the warrant as it may appear in the Warrant Management System, the probation court shall proceed on the violation of probation matter in accordance with applicable law and respective departmental rule or standing order.

9. Form to be Promulgated by the Chief Justice of the Trial Court. The transmittal of information between courts as required by this Order shall proceed by means of a form promulgated by the Chief Justice of the Trial Court. This form shall include such specific information requirements, data elements and attachments as the Chief Justice may deem appropriate, provided that nothing in this Order shall be construed to prohibit the use of telephone communication to supplement the use of such form and to achieve its purpose.

10. Probation Department Procedures and Record Keeping. Implementation of this Order by the Massachusetts Probation Service, including record keeping requirements, shall be as set forth in such instructions and regulations consistent with the provisions of this Order as may be deemed appropriate by the Commissioner of Probation.

Adopted eff. Oct. 3, 2016.

Standing Order 1–19. Promulgation of Mandatory Forms to be Used with Mass. Rule. Civ. P. 8.1 and 55.1

1. The following forms, copies of which are attached hereto, are hereby prescribed for use in the Trial Court in conjunction with Mass. R. Civ. P. 8.1 and 55.1:

- Affidavit Regarding Debt (Mass. R. Civ. P. 8.1(c))
- Affidavit Providing Documentation of Debt (Mass. R. Civ. P. 8.1(d))

- Affidavit of Address Verification (Mass. R. Civ. P. 8.1(e))

- Certification Regarding Statute of Limitations (Mass. R. Civ. P. 8.1(f))

- Affidavit of Compliance and Plaintiff's Entitlement to Judgement (Mass. R. Civ. P. 55.1(b)(1))

- Notice to Parties of Non–Entry of Default (Mass. R. Civ. P. 55.1(b)(2))

- Affidavit of Address Re–Verification Upon Request for Default Judgment (Mass. R. Civ. P. 55.1(d))

- Statement of Damages (G.L. c. 218, § 19A(a)) (for use in District Court and Boston Municipal Court)

- Civil Action Cover Sheet (for use in Superior Court)

2. These forms will be posted as PDF fillable forms on the mass.gov website.

AFFIDAVIT REGARDING DEBT
Mass. R. Civ. P. 8.1(c)

DOCKET NO.

Trial Court of Massachusetts

PLAINTIFF	DEFENDANT	COUNTY/COURT DIVISION

THIS FORM IS REQUIRED IN ALL CASES SUBJECT TO MASS. R. CIV. P. 8.1
(if additional space is needed, please include an attachment)

I. The affiant states that, to the best of the affiant's knowledge, the information provided below is accurate and complete:

1. The name, position, and employer of the affiant: _____

2. The name of the current owner of the debt: _____

3. The name of the original creditor, including the name under which the original creditor did business with the defendant, if different: _____

4. For debt arising from a credit card sponsored or co-sponsored by a retailer, the name of the sponsoring or co-sponsoring retailer: _____

5. The last four digits of the account number(s) assigned by the original creditor: _____

6. The amount and date of the defendant's last payment, if any, or a representation by the affiant that no payment has been made: _____

7. The date of charge-off: _____

8. The amount of the debt on the date of charge-off: _____

9. For the portion of the debt incurred after the date of charge-off, an itemization of the debt (broken down by principal, interest, fees, or other charges) and the method of calculating such principal, interest, fees, or other charges: _____

10. A chronological listing of the names of all prior owners of the debt and the date of each transfer of ownership of the debt, beginning with the original creditor: _____

II. The affiant has personally reviewed records sufficient to establish the information provided above.

SIGNED UNDER THE PENALTIES OF PERJURY

AFFIANT	DATE
X	

12.18

AFFIDAVIT PROVIDING DOCUMENTATION OF DEBT Mass. R. Civ. P. 8.1(d)	DOCKET NO.	Trial Court of Massachusetts
		COUNTY/COURT DIVISION
PLAINTIFF	DEFENDANT	

THIS FORM IS REQUIRED IN ALL CASES SUBJECT TO MASS. R. CIV. P. 8.1

The affiant states that the following documents are attached to this affidavit:

1. **DOCUMENTS ESTABLISHING THE EXISTENCE, AMOUNT, AND TERMS AND CONDITIONS APPLICABLE TO THE DEBT THAT IS THE SUBJECT OF THIS ACTION, INCLUDING:**

☐ A. A document provided to the defendant before the date of charge-off demonstrating the defendant incurred the debt and the amount owed.

☐ B. Documents establishing the terms and conditions applicable to the debt.

☐ C. The written document, if any, signed by the defendant evidencing the defendant's agreement to the terms and conditions described in the documents referenced in B above, or, if a signed copy of such document is not within the possession, custody, or control of the plaintiff, documents evidencing the defendant's acceptance of such terms and conditions (which may include the most recent monthly statement reflecting a purchase, payment, or balance transfer authorized by the defendant before the date of charge-off).

☐ Other document(s) establishing the existence, amount, and terms and conditions of the debt, if any:

_____

_____

2. **DOCUMENTS REGARDING OWNERSHIP OF DEBT:**

☐ Each bill of sale, assignment, or other document evidencing the transfer of ownership of the debt, beginning with the original creditor. (Such documentation must include a specific reference to the defendant or the defendant's account number.)

☐ Not Applicable - plaintiff is the original creditor.

The name, position, and employer of the affiant: _____

SIGNED UNDER THE PENALTIES OF PERJURY

AFFIANT	DATE
X	

12.18

AFFIDAVIT OF ADDRESS VERIFICATION Mass. R. Civ. P. 8.1(e)	DOCKET NO.	Trial Court of Massachusetts
		COUNTY/COURT DIVISION
PLAINTIFF	DEFENDANT	

THIS FORM IS REQUIRED IN ALL CASES SUBJECT TO MASS. R. CIV. P. 8.1

The affiant in this action states that the defendant's residential address was verified within three months prior to the commencement of this action by at least one of the following three methods, as indicated below *(check 1, 2 or 3)*:

☐ 1. Receipt of correspondence from the defendant with that return address OR other verification from the defendant within the three-month period that such address is current. Such other verification from defendant was obtained as follows:

_____

_____

Date of this verification: _____

☐ 2. Certified mail receipt signed by the defendant with that address within the three-month period.

Date of this verification: _____

☐ 3. Letter sent by first-class mail to that address for the defendant that has not been returned to sender by the postal service, AND verifying the same address as current using a paid subscriber-based commercial online database AND:

    ☐ A municipal record, such as a street list or tax records, namely:

    _____

    OR

    ☐ A state motor vehicle registry record, namely:

    _____

    ☐ Neither a municipal record nor a state motor vehicle registry record is available.

If any database or municipal or state record used shows more than one address for the defendant during the last 12 months, the basis for selecting the address(es) to be used for service is:

_____

Date of this verification: _____

The affiant also states that the documents reflecting the verification method(s) indicated above are attached to this affidavit.

The name, position, and employer of the affiant: _____

_____

SIGNED UNDER THE PENALTIES OF PERJURY

AFFIANT	DATE
X	

12.18

CERTIFICATION REGARDING STATUTE OF LIMITATIONS Mass. R. Civ. P. 8.1(f)	DOCKET NO.	Trial Court of Massachusetts
		COUNTY/COURT DIVISION
PLAINTIFF	DEFENDANT	

THIS FORM IS REQUIRED IN ALL CASES SUBJECT TO MASS. R. CIV. P. 8.1

Please provide the required information:

As required by Rule 8.1(f), the undersigned CERTIFIES that:

1. The terms and conditions applicable to the debt that is the subject of this action:

   ☐ DO NOT include a choice of law or limitation provision.

   ☐ DO include a choice of law or limitation provision, which states as follows:

   _____

   _____

2. The limitation period for the action is established by the following statute or other law:

   _____

3. The applicable limitations period is:

   _____

4. Based on plaintiff's reasonable inquiry, the applicable limitations period has not expired as of the date indicated below.

PLAINTIFF OR PLAINTIFF'S COUNSEL	DATE
X	

12.18

AFFIDAVIT OF COMPLIANCE AND PLAINTIFF'S ENTITLEMENT TO JUDGMENT Mass. R. Civ. P. 55.1(b)(1)	DOCKET NO.	Trial Court of Massachusetts
		COUNTY/COURT DIVISION
PLAINTIFF	DEFENDANT	

THIS FORM IS REQUIRED IN ALL CASES SUBJECT TO MASS. R. CIV. P. 8.1

Please check one:

☐ I am an unrepresented plaintiff

☐ I am counsel for the plaintiff

The undersigned hereby states that:

1. I have personally reviewed the documentation filed and served in this action pursuant to Rule 8.1;

2. The documentation meets all requirements of Rule 8.1(c)-(f) (with any exceptions specifically stated here):

_____

_____

AND

3. The documentation establishes the plaintiff's entitlement to judgment in the amount claimed.

CERTIFICATE OF SERVICE

I, _____ , attorney for the above-named plaintiff or unrepresented plaintiff, certify that

      name

on _____ I gave notice of the foregoing document to the defendant in the following manner:

    date

_____

_____

at the following address:

_____

     name

_____

     address

_____

     city/town/zip code

SIGNED UNDER THE PENALTIES OF PERJURY

PLAINTIFF OR PLAINTIFF'S COUNSEL	DATE
X	

12.18

NOTICE TO PARTIES OF NON-ENTRY OF DEFAULT Mass R. Civ. P. 55.1(b)(2)	DOCKET NO.	Trial Court of Massachusetts
		COUNTY/COURT DIVISION
PLAINTIFF	DEFENDANT	

THIS FORM IS REQUIRED IN ALL CASES SUBJECT TO MASS. R. CIV. P. 8.1

The parties in the above-captioned action are hereby NOTIFIED that the default against the defendant requested by the plaintiff has not been entered because the plaintiff failed to comply with the requirements of Mass. R. Civ. P. 8.1 and/or 55.1, and specifically as follows:

☐ No Affidavit Regarding Debt filed (Mass. R. Civ. P 8.1(c)).

☐ No Affidavit Providing Documentation of Debt filed (Mass. R. Civ. P 8.1(d)).

☐ No Affidavit of Address Verification filed (Mass. R. Civ. P. 8.1.(e)).

☐ No Certification Regarding Statute of Limitations filed (Mass. R. Civ. P 8.1(f)).

☐ No Affidavit of Compliance and Plaintiff's Entitlement to Judgment (Mass.R.Civ.P. 55.1(b)(1)).

☐ Address at which service made does not match verified address.

☐ Other: _____

_____

If the only basis, indicated above, for the non-entry of default is plaintiff's failure to file a completed Affidavit of Compliance and Plaintiff's Entitlement to Judgment, Rule 55.1(b)(1), dismissal will be avoided if the plaintiff submits the affidavit before the scheduled date of dismissal.

The parties are further NOTIFIED that this Court will ENTER A JUDGMENT OF DISMISSAL of the Complaint in this action, without prejudice, on or after the 30th day after the DATE OF THIS NOTICE, unless the plaintiff requests, in writing, prior to the expiration of the 30 day period, a hearing for the purpose of showing cause, with notice to the defendant, why the Complaint should not be dismissed.

CLERK MAGISTRATE/ASSISTANT CLERK MAGISTRATE	DATE
X	

12.16

AFFIDAVIT OF ADDRESS RE-VERIFICATION UPON REQUEST FOR DEFAULT JUDGMENT Mass. R. Civ. P. 55.1(d)	DOCKET NO.	Trial Court of Massachusetts
PLAINTIFF	DEFENDANT	COUNTY/COURT DIVISION

THIS FORM MAY BE REQUIRED IN CASES SUBJECT TO MASS. R. CIV. P. 55.1(d)

The affiant in this action states that the defendant's residential address was re-verified by within three months prior to the request for default judgment by at least one of the following three methods, as indicated below *(check 1, 2 or 3)*:

☐ 1. Receipt of correspondence from the defendant with that return address OR other verification from the defendant within the three-month period that such address is current. Such other verification from defendant was obtained as follows:

_____

_____

Date of this verification: _____

☐ 2. Certified mail receipt signed by the defendant with that address within the three-month period.

Date of this verification: _____

☐ 3. Letter sent by first-class mail to that address for the defendant that has not been returned to sender by the postal service, AND verifying the same address as current using a paid subscriber-based commercial online database AND:

☐ A municipal record, such as a street list or tax records, namely:

_____

OR

☐ A state motor vehicle registry record, namely:

_____

☐ Neither a municipal record nor a state motor vehicle registry record is available.

If any database or municipal or state record used shows more than one address for the defendant during the last 12 months, the basis for selecting the address(es) to be used for service is:

_____

Date of this verification: _____

The affiant also states that the documents reflecting the verification method(s) indicated above are attached to this affidavit.

The name, position, and employer of the affiant: _____

_____

SIGNED UNDER THE PENALTIES OF PERJURY

AFFIANT	DATE
X	

12.18

STATEMENT OF DAMAGES G.L. c. 218, § 19A(a)	DOCKET NO.	Trial Court of Massachusetts	
PLAINTIFF(s)	DEFENDANT(s)		DATE FILED

INSTRUCTIONS: THIS FORM MUST BE COMPLETED AND FILED WITH THE COMPLAINT OR OTHER INITIAL PLEADING IN ALL DISTRICT AND BOSTON MUNICIPAL COURT CIVIL ACTIONS SEEKING MONEY DAMAGES.	COURT DIVISION

TORT CLAIMS	AMOUNT
A. Documented medical expenses to date:	
1. Total hospital expenses:	$ _____
2. Total doctor expenses:	$ _____
3. Total chiropractic expenses:	$ _____
4. Total physical therapy expenses:	$ _____
5. Total other expenses (describe) _____	$ _____
_____	
SUBTOTAL:	$ _____
B. Documented lost wages and compensation to date:	$ _____
C. Documented property damages to date:	$ _____
D. Reasonably anticipated future medical and hospital expenses:	$ _____
E. Reasonable anticipated lost wages:	$ _____
F. Other documented items of damage (describe): _____	$ _____
_____	
G. Brief description of Plaintiff's injury, including nature and extent of injury:	
_____	
_____	
_____	
For this form, disregard double or treble damage claims; indicate single damages only. TOTAL:	$

CONTRACT CLAIMS	AMOUNT
☐ This action includes a claim involving collection of a debt incurred pursuant to a revolving credit agreement. Mass. R. Civ. P. 8.1(a)	
Provide a detailed description of the claim(s): _____	$ _____
_____	$ _____
_____	$ _____
For this form, disregard double or treble damage claims; indicate single damages only. TOTAL:	$

ATTORNEY FOR PLAINTIFF (OR UNREPRESENTED PLAINTIFF)	DEFENDANT'S NAME AND ADDRESS:
SIGNATURE DATE	
PRINT OR TYPE NAME B.B.O. #	
ADDRESS	

CERTIFICATION PURSUANT TO SJC RULE 1:18: I hereby certify that I have complied with requirements of Rule 5 of the Supreme Judicial Court Uniform Rules on Dispute Resolution (SJC Rule 1:18) requiring that I provide my clients with information about court-connected dispute resolution services and discuss with them the advantages and disadvantages of the various methods of dispute resolution.

Signature of Attorney on Record: Date:

12.18

CIVIL ACTION COVER SHEET	DOCKET NUMBER	Trial Court of Massachusetts The Superior Court

PLAINTIFF(S): _____

ADDRESS: _____

COUNTY _____

_____

DEFENDANT(S): _____

ATTORNEY: _____

ADDRESS: _____

ADDRESS: _____

BBO: _____

TYPE OF ACTION AND TRACK DESIGNATION (see reverse side)

CODE NO.	TYPE OF ACTION (specify)	TRACK	HAS A JURY CLAIM BEEN MADE?
_____	_____	____	☐ YES ☐ NO

*If "Other" please describe: _____

Is there a claim under G.L. c. 93A? ☐ YES ☐ NO   Is this a class action under Mass. R. Civ. P. 23? ☐ YES ☐ NO

STATEMENT OF DAMAGES PURSUANT TO G.L. c. 212, § 3A

The following is a full, itemized and detailed statement of the facts on which the undersigned plaintiff or plaintiff's counsel relies to determine money damages. For this form, disregard double or treble damage claims; indicate single damages only.

TORT CLAIMS
(attach additional sheets as necessary)

A. Documented medical expenses to date:
1. Total hospital expenses .... $ _____
2. Total doctor expenses .... $ _____
3. Total chiropractic expenses .... $ _____
4. Total physical therapy expenses .... $ _____
5. Total other expenses (describe below) .... $ _____
                                     Subtotal (A): $ _____

B. Documented lost wages and compensation to date .... $ _____
C. Documented property damages to date .... $ _____
D. Reasonably anticipated future medical and hospital expenses .... $ _____
E. Reasonably anticipated lost wages .... $ _____
F. Other documented items of damages (describe below) .... $ _____

G. Briefly describe plaintiff's injury, including the nature and extent of injury:

                             TOTAL (A-F):$ _____

CONTRACT CLAIMS
(attach additional sheets as necessary)

☐ This action includes a claim involving collection of a debt incurred pursuant to a revolving credit agreement. Mass. R. Civ. P. 8.1(a).
Provide a detailed description of claim(s):

                             TOTAL: $ _____

Signature of Attorney/ Unrepresented Plaintiff: X _____ Date: _____

RELATED ACTIONS: Please provide the case number, case name, and county of any related actions pending in the Superior Court.

CERTIFICATION PURSUANT TO SJC RULE 1:18

I hereby certify that I have complied with requirements of Rule 5 of the Supreme Judicial Court Uniform Rules on Dispute Resolution (SJC Rule 1:18) requiring that I provide my clients with information about court-connected dispute resolution services and discuss with them the advantages and disadvantages of the various methods of dispute resolution.

Signature of Attorney of Record: X _____ Date: _____

CIVIL ACTION COVER SHEET INSTRUCTIONS
SELECT CATEGORY THAT BEST DESCRIBES YOUR CASE

AC Actions Involving the State/Municipality *

AA1 Contract Action involving Commonwealth, Municipality, MBTA, etc. (A)
AB1 Tortious Action involving Commonwealth, Municipality, MBTA, etc. (A)
AC1 Real Property Action involving Commonwealth, Municipality, MBTA etc. (A)
AD1 Equity Action Involving Commonwealth, Municipality, MBTA, etc. (A)
AE1 Administrative Action involving Commonwealth, Municipality, MBTA, etc. (A)

CN Contract/Business Cases

A01 Services, Labor, and Materials (F)
A02 Goods Sold and Delivered (F)
A03 Commercial Paper (F)
A04 Employment Contract (F)
A05 Consumer Revolving Credit - M.R.C.P. 8.1 (F)
A06 Insurance Contract (F)
A08 Sale or Lease of Real Estate (F)
A12 Construction Dispute (A)
A14 Interpleader (F)
BA1 Governance, Conduct, Internal Affairs of Entities (A)
BA3 Liability of Shareholders, Directors, Officers, Partners, etc. (A)
BB1 Shareholder Derivative (A)
BB2 Securities Transactions (A)
BC1 Mergers, Consolidations, Sales of Assets, Issuance of Debt, Equity, etc. (A)
BD1 Intellectual Property (A)
BD2 Proprietary Information or Trade Secrets (A)
BG1 Financial Institutions/Funds (A)
BH1 Violation of Antitrust or Trade Regulation Laws (A)
A99 Other Contract/Business Action - Specify (F)

* Choose this case type if ANY party is the Commonwealth, a municipality, the MBTA, or any other governmental entity UNLESS your case is a case type listed under Administrative Civil Actions (AA).

† Choose this case type if ANY party is an incarcerated party, UNLESS your case is a case type listed under Administrative Civil Actions (AA) or is a Prisoner Habeas Corpus case (E97).

ER Equitable Remedies

D01 Specific Performance of a Contract (A)
D02 Reach and Apply (F)
D03 Injunction (F)
D04 Reform/ Cancel Instrument (F)
D05 Equitable Replevin (F)
D06 Contribution or Indemnification (F)
D07 Imposition of a Trust (A)
D08 Minority Shareholder's Suit (A)
D09 Interference in Contractual Relationship (F)
D10 Accounting (A)
D11 Enforcement of Restrictive Covenant (F)
D12 Dissolution of a Partnership (F)
D13 Declaratory Judgment, G.L. c.231A (A)
D14 Dissolution of a Corporation (F)
D99 Other Equity Action (F)

PA Civil Actions Involving Incarcerated Party †

PA1 Contract Action involving an Incarcerated Party (A)
PB1 Tortious Action involving an Incarcerated Party (A)
PC1 Real Property Action involving an Incarcerated Party (F)
PD1 Equity Action involving an Incarcerated Party (F)
PE1 Administrative Action involving an Incarcerated Party (F)

TR Torts

B03 Motor Vehicle Negligence - Personal Injury/Property Damage (F)
B04 Other Negligence - Personal Injury/Property Damage (F)
B05 Products Liability (A)
B06 Malpractice - Medical (A)
B07 Malpractice - Other (A)
B08 Wrongful Death - Non-medical (A)
B15 Defamation (A)
B19 Asbestos (A)
B20 Personal Injury - Slip & Fall (F)
B21 Environmental (F)
B22 Employment Discrimination (F)
BE1 Fraud, Business Torts, etc. (A)
B99 Other Tortious Action (F)

RP Summary Process (Real Property)

S01 Summary Process - Residential (X)
S02 Summary Process - Commercial/ Non-residential (F)

RP Real Property

C01 Land Taking (F)
C02 Zoning Appeal, G.L. c. 40A (F)
C03 Dispute Concerning Title (F)
C04 Foreclosure of a Mortgage (X)
C05 Condominium Lien & Charges (X)
C99 Other Real Property Action (F)

MC Miscellaneous Civil Actions

E18 Foreign Discovery Proceeding (X)
E97 Prisoner Habeas Corpus (X)
E22 Lottery Assignment, G.L. c. 10 §28 (X)

AB Abuse/Harassment Prevention

E15 Abuse Prevention Petition, G.L. c. 209A (X)
E21 Protection from Harassment, G.L. c. 258E (X)

AA Administrative Civil Actions

E02 Appeal from Administrative Agency, G.L. c. 30A (X)
E03 Certiorari Action, G.L. c.249 §4 (X)
E05 Confirmation of Arbitration Awards (X)
E06 Mass Antitrust Act, G. L. c. 93 §9 (A)
E07 Mass Antitrust Act, G. L. c. 93 §8 (X)
E08 Appointment of a Receiver (X)
E09 Construction Surety Bond, G.L. c. 149 §§29, 29A (A)
E10 Summary Process Appeal (X)
E11 Worker's Compensation (X)
E16 Auto Surcharge Appeal (X)
E17 Civil Rights Act, G.L. c.12 §11H (X)
E24 Appeal from District Court Commitment, G.L. c.123 §9(b) (X)
E25 Pleural Registry (Asbestos cases)
E95 Forfeiture, G.L. c.94C §47 (F)
E99 Other Administrative Action (X)
Z01 Medical Malpractice - Tribunal only, G.L. c. 231 §60B (F)
Z02 Appeal Bond Denial (X)

SO Sex Offender Review

E12 SDP Commitment, G.L. c. 123A §12 (X)
E14 SDP Petition, G.L. c. 123A §9(b) (X)

RC Restricted Civil Actions

E19 Sex Offender Registry, G.L. c.6 §178M (X)
E27 Minor Seeking Consent, G.L. c.112 §12S (X)

TRANSFER YOUR SELECTION TO THE FACE SHEET

EXAMPLE:

CODE NO.	TYPE OF ACTION (specify)	TRACK	HAS A JURY CLAIM BEEN MADE?
B03	Motor Vehicle Negligence-Personal Injury	F	☒ YES ☐ NO

STATEMENT OF DAMAGES PURSUANT TO G.L. c. 212, § 3A

DUTY OF THE PLAINTIFF - The plaintiff shall set forth, on the face of the civil action cover sheet (or attach additional sheets as necessary), a statement specifying the facts on which the plaintiff relies to determine money damages. A copy of such civil action cover sheet, including the statement as to the damages, shall be served with the complaint. **A clerk-magistrate shall not accept for filing a complaint, except as otherwise provided by law, unless it is accompanied by such a statement signed by the attorney or self-represented litigant.**

DUTY OF THE DEFENDANT - If the defendant believes that the statement of damages filed by the plaintiff is inadequate, the defendant may file with his/her answer a statement specifying the potential damages which may result if the plaintiff prevails.

A CIVIL COVER SHEET MUST BE FILED WITH EACH COMPLAINT.
FAILURE TO COMPLETE THIS COVER SHEET THOROUGHLY AND ACCURATELY
MAY RESULT IN DISMISSAL OF THIS ACTION.

Adopted Dec. 13, 2018, eff. Jan. 1, 2019.

Standing Order 2–19. Electronic Application for Criminal Complaint

I. Scope

(a) This standing order shall govern the Electronic Application for Criminal Complaint (EACC) in Massachusetts Trial Court departments that process criminal complaints.

(b) This standing order shall apply to all law enforcement agencies in Massachusetts that apply for criminal complaints.

II. Definitions

"Clerk" shall refer to a clerk-magistrate or any of his or her assistant clerk-magistrates.

"Conventional method" shall refer to the practice governing the application for a criminal complaint that would apply in the absence of EACC.

"Electronic Application for Criminal Complaint" or "EACC" shall refer to the electronic submission of an application for criminal complaint to a court clerk's office from a software program that is compatible with the Judicial Information Systems Department to a clerk's office through the Department of Criminal Justice Information Services ("DCJIS") information broker system.

"Law enforcement agency" shall mean a local police department, the office of environmental law enforcement, the University of Massachusetts, a state university, a community college, a Sheriff's Office, local hospital police departments the Department of Corrections, and state police or an officer appointed as a special state police officer under G.L. c. 22C, § 63.

III. Procedure

(a) All applications for criminal complaint and any supporting documents, including police reports, probable cause statements, shall be submitted to the clerk's office in the court having jurisdiction over the matter by EACC.

(b) During the court's business hours, the clerk shall promptly docket and process all applications for criminal complaint received by EACC.

If the clerk determines that an application submitted by EACC is incomplete or is otherwise unacceptable for filing, he or she shall alert the complaining officer or agency as soon as is practicable. The clerk shall have the discretion to permit the applicant to correct the already-filed incomplete or otherwise erroneous application or to submit a corrected application by EACC.

(c) Before a complaint is authorized, the complainant must subscribe to it under oath before an appropriate judicial officer, as required by G.L. c. 276, § 22, and Mass. R. Crim. P. 3(g)(1).

IV. Exceptions

(a) A law enforcement agency may request, for good reason, a waiver of compliance with this standing order from the Chief Justice of a Trial Court Department. An example that may constitute a good reason is that the law enforcement agency does not have access to the DCJIS broker system. Such request shall be in writing, and shall state the reasons for the request. The Chief Justice may waive the requesting agency's compliance with this standing order for a defined or indefinite period of time. If the Chief Justice approves a waiver of compliance with this standing order, the submitting law enforcement agency must submit all criminal complaints by the conventional method.

(b) In the event of a technical failure in a law enforcement agency's computer application software, the DCJIS broker system, or the Trial Court's electronic docketing system, which makes submission, docketing, and processing of the application by EACC impossible, a law enforcement agency may submit an application for criminal complaint by the conventional method.

(c) A law enforcement agency may submit a written request for a waiver of compliance with this standing order in an individual matter to the clerk of the court having jurisdiction over the matter upon a showing that deviation from the standing order is necessary. If the clerk determines that a waiver of compliance with this standing order is warranted, the clerk shall make a record of such a waiver on the docket.

(d) Any existing process beyond the procedures set forth in Standing Order 2–19 relative to the processing of an Electronic Application for Criminal Complaint that is in effect in a Trial Court Department as of the effective date of this standing order shall continue in effect at the discretion of the Departmental Chief Justice.

Adopted June 27, 2019, eff Dec. 1, 2019.

UNIFORM SCHEDULE OF FEES FOR THE TRIAL COURT AS PROVIDED FOR BY MASSACHUSETTS GENERAL LAWS CHAPTER 262, § 4B

Revised November 1, 2016

Effective November 1, 2016, the following fees, determined by the Chief Administrative Justice of the Trial Court pursuant to G.L. c. 262, § 4B, shall be charged in all Trial Court Departments:

For certificate of orders, decrees, rulings, judgments or other proceedings, twenty (20) dollars.

For an attested copy of court documents, records, including docket sheets, or other papers in possession and under the control of the clerk, register, or recorder, two (2) dollars and fifty (50) cents per page.

For an unattested copy or print out of court documents, records, or other papers in possession and under the control of the clerk, register, or recorder, five (5) cents per page.

For a blank summons, other than any summons in a small claims action or incident to a petition for victim compensation, or blank writ, except a writ of habeas corpus, five (5) dollars.

For a blank subpoena for one or more witnesses, five (5) dollars.

For a writ of habeas corpus, fifteen (15) dollars.

In the District, Probate and Family, and Boston Municipal Court Departments, for each order of notice, citation, or precept, fifteen (15) dollars.

For a transcript of judgment, fifty (50) dollars.

For recording of notarial commission, fifteen (15) dollars

For certification of a notarized document to be used in another state or a foreign country, five (5) dollars.

For taking and recording a recognizance under G.L. c. 256, twenty (20) dollars.

For approving or disapproving by the court of sureties on bonds or recognizances, but not for the approval of appeal or removal bonds filed in small claims or other civil actions, twenty (20) dollars.

For compact disc and tape cassette recordings of proceedings in all Departments of the Trial Court, fifty (50) dollars and fifty (50) cents plus postage per ninety (90) minutes of recording or part thereof.

For commissions to take depositions, twenty (20) dollars.

For waivers of notice of marriage in the Departments of the Trial Court where no statutory filing fee is applicable, fifty (50) dollars.

For utility company warrants under G.L. c. 164, § 116, fifteen (15) dollars.

For affidavit of creditor under G.L. c. 224, § 6, twenty-five (25) dollars.

For notice to creditor of debtor's desire for examination under G.L. c. 224, § 6, twenty (20) dollars.

For electronic access to audio recording of court case (hearing) per case, per day, ten (10) dollars. Multi day hearings are $10.00 per day.

For PDF or other electronically formatted document, five (5) dollars, (plus $4 if CD is mailed).

RULES OF THE DISTRICT COURTS OF MASSACHUSETTS AND THE MUNICIPAL COURT OF THE CITY OF BOSTON

Summary of Contents

DISTRICT/MUNICIPAL COURTS RULES OF CIVIL PROCEDURE

[Repealed July 1, 1996]

DISTRICT/MUNICIPAL COURTS FORMS

Publisher's Note

Former Dist./Mun. Cts. R. Civ. P. 84 provided that forms 1–30 and 32 appended to the Massachusetts Rules of Civil Procedure may be used in the District Court. The Supreme Judicial Court order of November 30, 2016, repealed Rule 84 and the related Appendix of Forms was deleted from the Massachusetts Rules of Civil Procedure effective January 1, 2017. The Reporter's Notes accompanying that order provided:

"Rule 84 was repealed and the related Appendix of Forms was deleted from the Massachusetts Rules of Civil Procedure effective January 1, 2017. Prior to repeal, Rule 84 provided in part: 'The forms contained in the Appendix of Forms are sufficient under the rules and are intended to indicate the simplicity and brevity of statement which the rules contemplate.'

"Many of the forms in the Appendix of Forms are out of date, and the Appendix is not widely used in its current form. In addition, the value of the Appendix of Forms has been diminished with the availability of a multiplicity of forms that are accessible on the website of the Massachusetts court system and from a variety of sources on-line.

"For similar reasons, Rule 84 of the Federal Rules of Civil Procedure and the federal Appendix of Forms were likewise repealed in 2015."

DISTRICT/MUNICIPAL COURTS SUPPLEMENTAL RULES OF CIVIL PROCEDURE

Table of Rules

Rule 100. Scope of Rules

These rules contain (1) rules supplementary to the District/Municipal Courts Rules of Civil Procedure and (2) rules governing particular civil proceedings not governed by the District/Municipal Courts Rules of Civil Procedure. They are applicable in the District Courts and the Municipal Court of the City of Boston. Every reference to the District Courts shall include within its meaning the Municipal Court of the City of Boston except as otherwise stated.

Unless a contrary intent appears, the word clerk as used in these rules shall include any assistant clerk, clerk pro tempore, or assistant clerk pro tempore; the word plaintiff shall include petitioner; the word defendant shall include respondent; and the word attorney or counsel shall include a party appearing or acting for himself.

Rule 101. Appearances

Appearances by a firm or by several attorneys shall at all times be accompanied by the designation of one as trial attorney.

Rule 102. Authority to Appear

The right of an attorney to appear for any party shall not be questioned by the opposite party, unless the objection be taken in writing within seven days after the appearance of such attorney, but the court may permit the objection to be taken later. When the authority of any attorney to appear for any party is demanded, if such attorney declares that he has been duly authorized to appear, by an application made directly to him by such party, or by some person whom he believes to have been authorized to employ him, such declaration shall be evidence of such authority.

Rule 102A. Statement of Damages

In all civil actions governed by the District/Municipal Courts Rules of Civil Procedure, a party seeking relief in the form of money damages in a complaint, crossclaim, or counterclaim shall state the amount of said money damages claimed on the form prescribed therefor by the Administrative Justice of the District Court Department or the Administrative Justice of the Boston Municipal Court Department, as the case may be. No clerk-magistrate shall accept for filing any complaint, crossclaim, or counterclaim unless it is accompanied by such form. A copy of the form, including the statement as to damages, shall be served on all other parties together with the complaint, crossclaim, or counterclaim.

Adopted July 16, 1987, effective July 20, 1987.

Rule 103. Special Costs and Terms

In allowing an amendment, removing a default or dismissal, granting a postponement, or making any other interlocutory order, costs may be awarded and terms imposed in the discretion of the court, in addition to any otherwise provided for by court rule.

Rule 104. Money Paid Into Court

Money paid into court shall be in the custody of the clerk, whose duty it shall be to receive it when paid under the authority of law or rule or order of the court. Any deposit of money in excess of one hundred dollars ($100.) paid into court shall be deposited in an interest bearing bank account. He shall pay it as directed by the court; but money paid into court upon tender or otherwise for the present and unconditional use of a party, shall be paid, on request, without special order, with any interest which has accrued thereon, to such party at whose risk it shall be from the time when it is paid into court. Money payable to a party may be paid to his attorney of record, if authorized by the court.

Rule 105. Motions and Other Interlocutory Matters

Motions and other interlocutory matters must be in writing and filed before being heard or placed on a list for hearing, unless otherwise ordered by the court. Notice of such hearings shall be as provided in Rule 6(c) of the District/Municipal Courts Rules of Civil Procedure. Hearing days for such matters may be established by the several district courts or by the Boston Municipal Court, respectively.

A motion for leave to amend pleadings shall contain, or have attached to it, the proposed amendment. An amendment of the pleadings agreed to in writing by all of the adverse parties shall take effect when filed, without any action by the court.

The court need not hear any motion, or opposition thereto, grounded on facts, unless the facts are verified by affidavit, or are apparent upon the record and files, or are agreed to and stated in writing signed by the attorneys for the parties interested.

Rule 106. Assessment of Damages

A. The clerk in assessing damages on a promissory note or other contract shall not allow interest at a rate in excess of six (6) per cent per annum, unless it shall be made to appear that the provisions of Section 206 of the Soldiers' and Sailors' Civil Relief Act as amended by amendment of 1942 are inapplicable.

B. In actions on bonds, and on all other contracts, when damages are to be assessed by the court or by the clerk, the plaintiff shall file an account or statement in writing of the particulars of his demand, unless the same are sufficiently apparent from the complaint or from the bond, note or other instrument on which the complaint is based. The party or his attorney shall also file a certificate setting forth (a) the amount, if any, paid to or in behalf of the plaintiff on account of his claim between the date of service of the complaint and the date on which damages are assessed, and (b) the net balance due the plaintiff from the defendant on the date of such certificate.

C. In any action in which a hearing for assessment of damages is required after default, a party desiring to place a case on the hearing list shall file with the clerk a request that the case be placed on such list and a certificate of service of notice thereof on all other parties entitled to such notice. The clerk shall give notice of such assessment of damages at least seven days before the hearing day.

Rule 107. Statutes, By–Laws, Ordinances, Rules, Orders, and Regulations

In every action wherein a party relies for ground of relief or defense upon any federal or state statute, by-law, ordinance, rule, order or regulation, he shall so state in his pleading and shall therein identify the same.

Rule 108. Trial Day and Trial Lists

A party desiring to place a case upon the trial list shall file with the clerk a request that the case be placed upon the trial list and a certificate of service of notice thereof on all other parties. The clerk shall give all parties entitled to be heard notice of such trial at least seven days before the trial day. No case shall be placed upon the trial list wherein issues have not been joined. The fact that interrogatories have not been answered or that a commission to take a deposition has not been returned or that a motion remains unheard, shall not prevent the placing of a case upon a trial or hearing list and shall not delay the trial or hearing, except by special order of the court.

Trial or hearing days for civil actions generally, or for particular matters, may be established by the several district courts or by the Boston Municipal Court, respectively.

The foregoing shall not be deemed to limit the authority of the court to assign matters for trial with such notice as the court may deem appropriate. Nothing in these rules shall prevent the court from postponing or specially assigning any case or continuing it to another day.

Causing a case to be placed upon a list for trial or hearing shall be representation that the party and counsel intends an actual trial or hearing and expects to be ready therefor when reached.

Rule 109. Copies for the Court

Copies of every account, schedule or statement containing more than three items of any matter of action or defense in each case on the trial list shall be handed to the clerk for the use of the court at the commencement of the trial; otherwise the action may be postponed or continued or such other terms imposed as the court may order.

Rule 110. Filing of Certain Papers Upon Judgments

Whenever judgment is rendered upon a bill of exchange, promissory note, check, trade acceptance, certificate of deposit or any negotiable instrument, the same shall be filed with the clerk. No execution shall issue nor other proceeding to enforce such judgment shall be maintained until such document is so filed with the clerk; provided that, if it shall be made to appear by satisfactory evidence that the paper or document necessary to be filed in order to complete the record has been lost or destroyed, the court may order issuance of execution upon the filing of a sufficient bond of indemnity, if so ordered by the court notwithstanding the foregoing provisions.

Such instrument shall not be withdrawn from the files except upon (1) order of court, (2) the making by the clerk of a memorandum on such instrument, if practicable, and otherwise on a paper attached thereto, showing the name of the court, the number of the case, the party or parties against whom judgment was rendered and the amount thereof, and (3) the filing of a copy of such instrument, attested by the clerk.

Rule 111. Applications Pertaining to Answers to Interrogatories

An application for dismissal or judgment for failure to serve timely answers to original interrogatories, as permitted by

Dist./Mun.Cts.R.Civ.P. 33(a), shall contain a statement showing the date on which such interrogatories were served and that the provisions of the applicable rules of civil procedure and of this court have been complied with; and such an application relating to failure to serve further answers shall set out the date on which the further answers should have been served. The application shall be verified by affidavit or as provided in Dist./Mun.Cts.R.Civ.P. Rule 33(a) or 43(d).

Rule 112.   Writs of Protection

A writ of protection shall issue only upon the application of the person for whom the writ of protection is to be issued, or some person in his behalf, and upon order of the court, and then only in case it is made to appear to the court, by affidavit and any other evidence that the court may require, (1) that the application is made in good faith and for the purpose of enabling such person to attend the court as a party or witness in some specified case pending, (2) if such person is a party, that such case has not been brought collusively to enable him to obtain a writ of protection, and (3) if such person is a witness, that he has not been required to attend as a witness by his own request or procurement to enable him to obtain a writ of protection.

Rule 113.   Attorney As Surety

No attorney shall be surety upon any bond which may be required in any civil suit or proceeding in this court, nor shall any special attorney be surety in any case in which he is or has been employed, except as endorser for costs, nor shall any attorney for the plaintiff in a trustee process appear or act for the party summoned therein as trustee.

Amended February 24, 1999, effective March 15, 1999.

Rule 114.   Sound Recording Devices

Recording of court proceedings is governed in the District Court Department by Rule 211 of the Special Rules of the District Court, and in the Boston Municipal Court Department by Rule 308 of the Special Rules of the Municipal Court of the City of Boston.

Amended June 19, 1975, effective July 1, 1975; amended effective May 1, 1986; amended December 31, 1987, effective February 1, 1988.

Rule 115.   Costs in Civil Actions Which Might Have Been Brought Pursuant to Small Claims Procedure

In a civil action begun pursuant to the District/Municipal Courts Rules of Civil Procedure in which the finding of debt or damages does not exceed the statutory limit for small claims proceedings in effect at the commencement of such civil action, no costs other than the taxable cash disbursements shall be recovered by the plaintiff, except by special order of the court for cause shown.

Rule 116.   [Repealed January 1, 2010]

Rules 117 to 129.   [Reserved]

Rule 130.   [Repealed November 26, 1980]

Rules 131 to 139.   [Reserved]

Rule 140.   [Repealed January 1, 2010]

Rules 141 to 149.   [Reserved]

Rule 150.   [Repealed January 1, 2010]

Rule 151.   Judicial Review of Determination of Claim of Victim of Crime Under Chapter 258C

Applicable to all claims filed on or after April 14, 1994

1. Applicability. This rule governs petitions filed by claimants seeking judicial review of the decisions of the Director of the Division of Victim Compensation and Assistance of the Office of the Attorney General (hereinafter "Director") pursuant to G.L. c. 258C, § 9. Except as indicated herein, no other rules shall govern such appeals.

2. Filing of Petition for Judicial Review. A claimant's petition for de novo judicial review shall be filed in the division of the District Court Department, or the Boston Municipal Court Department, for the judicial district in which the claimant resides. A nonresident claimant shall file the petition in the Boston Municipal Court Department. The petition must be filed within thirty days of the date of mailing of the notice of award or denial of a claim for compensation by the Director, or within twenty days from the date of mailing of the Director's decision on the claimant's request for reconsideration, whichever is later. If the claimant does not file a petition for de novo judicial review within the time allowed, then the decision of the Director shall become final. Filing may be accomplished either in person or by first class mail, either registered or unregistered. Filing by registered mail shall be considered timely if it is mailed within the aforementioned time limits; otherwise the filing must be received by the court within the applicable time limits to be considered timely filed. The petition must be accompanied by payment of the filing fee and surcharge prescribed by G.L. c. 262, §§ 2 and 4C unless waived pursuant to G.L. c. 261, §§ 27A–27G. The clerk-magistrate shall enter the petition upon the civil docket of the court and assign it a docket number.

3. Director's Return. The claimant shall promptly send a copy of the petition for judicial review to the Director by personal service or by first class mail. Within thirty days of receipt of a copy of the petition, the Director shall file with the court certified copies of the claim form filed by the complainant with the Division, the Director's decision on that claim, and the Director's decision on any request for reconsideration.

4. Notice and Scheduling of Hearing. Upon receipt of the requisite materials from the Director, the clerk-magistrate shall schedule the matter for hearing and shall notify the claimant and the Director of the date and time for the hearing.

5. Hearing. The judicial review of the finding and decisions of the Director shall be a de novo hearing of the original claim and shall be conducted without a jury. The hearing shall be conducted in such manner as to accomplish the just and speedy determination of the claim involved. Rules of evidence, other than those pertaining to privileges of parties and witnesses, need not be observed. Evidence may be admitted and given probative effect only if, in the judgment of the court, it is the kind of evidence on which reasonable persons are accustomed to rely in the conduct of serious affairs. The hearing shall be electronically recorded in accordance with Special Rule 211 of the District Court Department or Special Rule 308 of the Boston Municipal Court Department sitting for Civil Business.

6. Judgment. The court shall render a decision in writing in accordance with the requirements of G.L. c. 258C, § 9(e). The clerk-magistrate shall enter the decision on the docket as the judgment of the court and forthwith shall send copies of the judgment to the claimant and the Director. If the judgment is in favor of the claimant, upon expiration of ten days from the date of the entry of judgment, the clerk-magistrate shall send a certified copy of the judgment to the Treasurer of the Commonwealth, provided that if an appeal is claimed pursuant to paragraph (7) of this rule, the clerk-magistrate shall not send the certified copy of the judgment to the Treasurer until the conclusion of the appellate process.

7. Appeal. Within ten days after the date of the entry of judgment the claimant or the Director may appeal any error of law to the Appellate Division in accordance with the District/Municipal Courts Rules for Appellate Division Appeal. Any claim of appeal by the claimant shall be accompanied by payment of the Appellate Division filing fee prescribed by G.L. c. 262, § 2 unless waived pursuant to G.L. c. 261, §§ 27A–27G.

Adopted June 29, 1995 and applicable to claims filed on or after April 14, 1994.

Rules 152 to 159. [Reserved]

Rule 160. Repossession Hearings

Hearings to determine the rights of secured creditors to take possession of collateral under a consumer credit transaction entered into after January 1, 1974 subject to G.L. c. 255, 255B or 255D shall be subject to this rule.

(a) Where the request of the creditor for such determination is not ancillary to a pending legal proceeding in the same court, such a hearing shall be on petition filed by the creditor containing (a) a description of the parties, of the property involved and the place where the property is believed to be located, (b) a detailed statement of facts upon which the creditor claims a right of repossession, including facts as to compliance with statutory prerequisites, and (c) a copy of the contract under which the claim of a right of repossession is made. Venue shall be determined for such petition as in the case of a transitory action. If a determination of the right of repossession is sought in a pending legal proceeding between the creditor and debtor, such determination shall be made on motion of the creditor containing the data specified above. Such petition or motion, as the case may be, shall be verified under oath.

(b) The debtor shall be given notice in writing of the hearing on such petition or motion at least seven days in advance thereof. Said notice shall be served on the debtor by delivering the same to him personally or by mailing the same to him, postage prepaid, at his last address known to the creditor. Said notice shall include a copy of the petition or motion and a statement that failure to appear may result in a court order authorizing repossession of the property involved. The petition or motion and a copy of the notice shall be sent to the clerk at least seven days prior to the date of the hearing. A certificate of service by the person giving the notice shall be filed with the clerk.

(c) Before making a determination that the creditor has a right of repossession the court must be satisfied that the conditions of this Rule and the statutory conditions relative to the nature of the default, the notice of the default and all other statutory prerequisites have been met.

(d) In district courts, other than the Boston Municipal Court, hearings on such petitions or motions shall be held on the trial days for the hearing of civil actions, and on any additional days which the several courts may from time to time designate for such hearings.

(e) In the Boston Municipal Court, hearings on such petitions or motions shall be held in the motions session thereof, on motion days.

Rules 161 to 169. [Reserved]

RULES GOVERNING SMALL CLAIMS ACTIONS

Rules 170 to 174. [Repealed August 24, 1983, effective September 1, 1983]

Rule 174A. [Expired]

Rules 175 to 185. [Repealed August 24, 1983, effective September 1, 1983]

Rules 186 to 188. [Expired]

Publisher's Note

Rules 170–185 were superseded by the Uniform Small Claims Rules, effective September 1, 1983, which are located under the Trial Court Rules, III., supra. Rules 186–188 were interim clerk–magistrate rules which are now reflected in the Uniform Magistrate Rules, effective July 7, 1981, which are located under the Trial Court Rules, II., supra.

DISTRICT/MUNICIPAL COURTS RULES FOR APPELLATE DIVISION APPEAL

Table of Rules

Rule 1. Scope of Rules: Definitions

(a) Scope of Rules. These rules govern the procedures for appeals to the Appellate Division of the District Court and the Appellate Division of the Boston Municipal Court, as the case may be, of issues of law in civil actions, as provided by law.

(b) Rules Not to Affect Jurisdiction. These rules shall not be construed to extend or limit the jurisdiction of the Appellate Division as established by G.L. c. 231, ss. 108–110.

(c) Definitions. As used in these rules:

"appeal" means an appeal to the Appellate Division.

"Appellate Division" means the panel of judges appointed to exercise jurisdiction in accordance with G.L. c. 231, s. 108.

"civil action" means all District Court tort, contract and statutory actions seeking money damages or equitable relief, in which appeal to the Appellate Division is authorized by law.

"clerk" means the clerk-magistrate, or an assistant clerk, of the trial court in which the proceeding was heard.

"first class mail" means use of first class mail, postage prepaid, whether certified or uncertified.

"presiding justice" means a justice of the Appellate Division designated pursuant to G.L. c. 231, s. 108.

"trial court" means the judge or court whose judgment, ruling, finding or decision is the subject of an appeal.

(d) Construction. Words or phrases importing the singular number may extend and be applied to several persons or things, and words importing the plural number may include the singular. Any reference to counsel in these rules shall be deemed to apply to unrepresented parties. References to the District Court shall be deemed to include the Boston Municipal Court, except as otherwise noted.

Adopted effective July 1, 1994.

Commentary

These rules provide three procedural options for appeal to the Appellate Division. These three options replace the cumbersome and complicated process of requesting, preparing and filing a draft report, and then seeking to have the court settle the report in final form for the Appellate Division.

The first two options provide simplified and inexpensive means of framing the legal issues for Appellate Division review. The third option provides a more formal and detailed means of appeal, based on a transcript of the proceedings, with the transcript usually based on the electronic recording of the proceedings. This third option may be chosen at the outset, or only when one or both of the other procedures fails. It is based on the Mass.R.A.P. and adheres to those rules as closely as is feasible. Differences from the Mass.R.A.P., if any, are discussed in the commentary to each of the following rules.

Rule 1A. Applicability

These rules shall govern appeal to the Appellate Division in all civil actions commenced on or after July 1, 1994, and in civil actions pending on that date regarding any ruling, order, decision, judgment or other court action occurring on or after July 1, 1994 by which the appellant claims to be aggrieved. Appeals to the Appellate Division involving a ruling, order, decision, judgment or other court action occurring before July 1, 1994 shall be governed to conclusion by the rules governing such appeal in effect at the time of such ruling, order, decision, judgment or other court action.

Adopted effective July 1, 1994.

Rule 2. Suspension of Rules

In the interest of expediting decision, or for other good cause shown, the Appellate Division may, except as otherwise provided in Rules 4(c) and 14(b), suspend the requirements or provisions of any of these rules in a particular case on application of a party or on its own motion and may order proceedings in accordance with its direction. Such a suspension may be on reasonable terms.

Adopted effective July 1, 1994.

Commentary

This rule is identical to Mass.R.A.P. 2, except for the reference to the Appellate Division.

Rule 3. Appeal—How Taken

(a) **Filing the Notice of Appeal.** An appeal permitted by law from a trial court to the Appellate Division shall be taken by filing a notice of appeal together with the filing fee required by law with the clerk of the trial court within the time allowed by Rule 4. Such filing shall be in accordance with Rule 13(a). A copy of said notice of appeal shall be served on all other parties in accordance with Rule 13(b). Failure by an appellant to take any step other than the timely filing of a notice of appeal and payment of the filing fee shall not affect the validity of the appeal, but shall be ground only for such action as the Appellate Division deems appropriate, which may include dismissal of the appeal.

A party need not claim an appeal from an interlocutory ruling or order to preserve his or her right to have such order reviewed upon appeal from the final judgment; but for all purposes for which appeal from an interlocutory ruling or order has heretofore been necessary, it is sufficient that the party comply with the requirements of Dist./Mun.Cts.R.Civ.P. 46.

(b) **Joint or Consolidated Appeals.** If two or more persons are entitled to appeal from a judgment, ruling, finding or decision of a trial court and their interests are such as to make joinder practicable, they may file a joint notice of appeal, or may join in appeal after filing separate timely notices of appeal, and they may thereafter proceed on appeal as a single appellant. Appeals may be consolidated by order of the Appellate Division upon its own motion or upon motion of a party, or by stipulation of the parties to the several appeals.

(c) **Content of the Notice of Appeal.** The notice of appeal shall limit the scope of the appeal and shall contain:

(1) a designation of the party or parties taking the appeal,

(2) a concise statement of the issues of law presented for review,

(3) the judgment, ruling, finding, decision or part thereof being appealed, and,

(4) in the case of rulings, a copy of the motion, request for ruling or proof of evidence giving rise to such ruling, if any;

(5) the notice of appeal may also include a request that the clerk order a cassette copy of the electronic recording of the proceedings, set forth on the required form and accompanied by the required fee.

The statement of issues of law required in section (c)(2), above, shall not prevent the statement of additional or alternative issues for appeal as provided in Rule 8C, below.

(d) **Initial Duties of the Clerk.** Upon receipt of a timely filed notice of appeal that includes a request for a cassette copy of the electronic recording of the proceedings and the fee therefor, the clerk of the trial court shall forthwith order such cassette copy and shall notify the requesting party immediately upon its availability.

Adopted effective July 1, 1994.

Commentary

This rule governs the first steps an appellant must take. An appellant may decide which of the three types of appeal to select under Rules 8A, 8B or 8C *after* the notice of appeal has been filed.

This rule follows Mass.R.A.P. 3 with appropriate changes to refer to the Appellate Division. Also, the filing of the appropriate filing fee is added as a requisite of claiming appeal. Express references are also made to the rules governing the method of filing and service.

A major difference between this rule and Mass.R.A.P. 3 is that this rule requires the filing party to serve a copy of the notice of appeal on the other party or parties. This duty is left to the clerk under Mass.R.A.P. 3(d).

The second paragraph of section (a) is identical to its counterpart in Mass.R.A.P. 3(a) except that reference is made to Dist./Mun.Cts.R.Civ.P. 46. Note that under the terms of the latter no objection is needed to preserve for appeal rulings made by the court in response to requests for rulings under Dist./Mun.Cts.R.Civ.P. 64A.

Section (c) of Rule 3 is significantly different from its Mass.R.A.P. counterpart. The major differences involve the requirement of specificity when a particular ruling is being appealed and the option of including a request for a cassette copy of the tape recording of the proceedings. If the method of appeal chosen by the appellant is the one provided by Rule 8C, the appellant will not be limited to the issues set forth in the notice of appeal under this rule. Rather the issues for appeal will be those specified in the appendix to the appellant's brief. See Rule 18(a).

Section (d) of the rule sets out the duty of the court clerk when a request for a tape cassette is included in the notice of appeal.

Rule 4. Appeal—When Taken

(a) **Time for Filing.**

The notice of appeal required by Rule 3, together with the required filing fee, shall be filed with the clerk of the trial court within ten days after the date of the entry of the judgment in the case being appealed. If a notice of appeal and filing fee is mistakenly filed in the Appellate Division, the Appellate Division shall note the date on which they were received and transmit them to the clerk of the trial court from which the appeal was taken and they shall be deemed filed in the trial court on the date so noted. If a notice of appeal and filing fee are timely filed by a party, any other party may file a notice of appeal and filing fee within fourteen days of the date on which the first notice of appeal was filed, or within the time otherwise prescribed by this rule, whichever period last expires.

If a post-judgment motion under the Massachusetts Rules of Civil Procedure is timely served or filed in the trial court, as the case may be, by any party (1) under Rule 52(b) to amend or make additional findings of fact, whether or not an alteration of the judgment would be required if the motion is granted; (2) to alter or amend a judgment under Rule 59 or for relief from judgment under Rule 60, however titled, if either motion is served within ten days after entry of judgment; or (3) under Rule 59 for a new trial, the ten-day time for appeal for all parties shall run from the entry of the order denying a new trial or granting or denying any other such motion. A notice of appeal filed before the disposition of any of the above motions shall have no effect. A new notice of appeal must be filed within the prescribed time measured from the entry of the order disposing of the motion as provided above. No additional fees shall be required for such filing.

(b) [Reserved].

(c) Extension of Time for Filing Notice of Appeal. Upon a showing of excusable neglect or other good reason, the trial court may extend the time for filing the notice of appeal by any party for a period not to exceed ten days from the expiration of the time otherwise prescribed by this rule. Such an extension may be granted before or after the time otherwise prescribed by this rule has expired. A request for an extension shall be made by motion with such notice as the trial court shall deem appropriate, and in no event shall the court permit the filing of a notice of appeal later than 180 days after entry of the judgment or post-judgment order of which appeal is sought.

Adopted effective July 1, 1994. Amended March 22, 2013, effective May 1, 2013.

Commentary

This rule differs from Mass. R. A. P. 4 in that the notice of appeal (and filing fee) must be filed within ten, rather than thirty, days after entry of judgment, and this same time limit applies when the Commonwealth or an office or agency thereof is a party.

It should be noted that though this time limit is a brief one, the filing of the notice of appeal is essentially just "a foot in the door." Further time periods apply to allow the appellant to select and pursue the appropriate method of appeal. And extension of the ten-day period is allowable under section (c).

The last paragraph of section (a) of the rule provides the time limit for appeal when postjudgment motions are filed. A 2013 amendment to the last paragraph of section (a) added a reference in item (2) to Rule 60 motions, if served within ten days after entry of judgment, as extending the time period to claim an appeal from the underlying judgment. This conforms with a 2013 amendment to Mass. R. A. P. 4(a), which similarly recognized that a motion for relief from judgment under Rule 60 extends the time period to file a notice of appeal.

Section (c) of the rule varies from its Mass. R. A. P. counterpart by allowing the court to grant an extension of the time for filing for no more than ten, rather than thirty, days. It also imposes a maximum limit of 180 days to limit multiple successive extensions and the suspension of the time limits under Rules 2 and 14(b).

A 2013 amendment to this rule deleted the reference to the District/Municipal Court Rules of Civil Procedure, which were repealed in 1996, and replaced it with a reference to the Massachusetts Rules of Civil Procedure, which now govern civil proceedings in the District Court.

Rule 5. Report of a Case for Determination

Pursuant to G.L. c. 231, s. 108, a judge may, in his or her discretion, report a judgment, interlocutory or other ruling, finding or decision for determination by the Appellate Division. The judge's report shall for all purposes under these rules constitute a notice of appeal, and the filing of such report by

the judge shall be considered the filing of a notice of appeal for purposes of computing time under these rules. The court may, upon notice to the parties, conduct a hearing on the form and content of the report prior to filing. The report as filed shall contain all information necessary to permit a review and determination of the issues presented. The clerk of the trial court shall serve notice of the filing of the report by forthwith mailing a copy thereof to counsel of record for each party, and shall proceed as otherwise ordered by the court. Unless ordered otherwise by the court, the clerk shall transmit the report to the Appellate Division within 20 days after the filing thereof.

Adopted effective July 1, 1994.

Commentary

This rule differs significantly from Mass.R.A.P. 5. It refers to the applicable statute, expressly refers to the report of *interlocutory* rulings, and allows the court the option of conducting a hearing on the proposed report. The rule also requires the clerk to transmit the report to the Appellate Division within 20 days of its filing, though failure by the clerk to comply with this rule would not appear necessarily to result in prejudice to the report.

Rule 6. [Reserved]

(Mass.R.A.P. 6 is not adopted for appeals to the Appellate Division.)

Rule 7. Disability of the Trial Court Judge

If by reason of death, sickness, resignation, removal, retirement, or other disability, the judge or judges whose decision has been appealed is unable to perform the duties to be performed under these rules by the court in which the action was heard, then any other judge sitting in or assigned to such court may, on assignment by the Chief Justice of the District Court, or of the Municipal Court of the City of Boston, as the case may be, perform those duties.

Adopted effective July 1, 1994.

Commentary

This rule varies only slightly from Mass.R.A.P. 7 in its elimination of references to the "lower court" and allowance of assignment of a "new" judge by the Chief Justice of the appropriate department.

Rule 8A. Method of Appeal: Expedited Appeal

(a) Filing and Contents. Within twenty days after the filing of a notice of appeal, the appellant may file in the trial court an "Expedited Appeal," so captioned, in which shall be included, or to which shall be attached, the following:

(1) a copy of the notice of appeal referred to in Rule 3;

(2) the text of any rulings of law by which the appellant claims to be aggrieved and the related requests for ruling, if any;

(3) a description of the stage of the proceedings at which, and the manner in which, the issues presented for review in the notice of appeal arose;

(4) a summary of the undisputed facts and so much of the evidence, including copies of pleadings and other documents, as may be necessary to decide the questions of law presented;

(5) the text of any memorandum of decision and findings of fact issued by the trial court;

(6) official citations to the essential statutes, rules of court, administrative rules or regulations, municipal ordinances and town bylaws;

(7) proof of service upon the parties and the trial court of the expedited appeal, including all attachments, pursuant to Rule 13(d); and

(8) a certification that the expedited appeal contains all the evidence, facts and other material necessary for consideration of the appeal by the Appellate Division.

(b) Service; Objections. The appellant shall serve a copy of the expedited appeal in accordance with Rule 13(c) upon the other parties and upon the judge by whose action the appellant claims to be aggrieved. Such service shall be made no later than the date of filing. Such service on the judge shall be addressed to the court at which the judge is then sitting or is most likely to be sitting. If any party objects to the contents of the expedited appeal, said party, within ten days of filing, shall file in the trial court and serve upon the other parties a written statement of the objections. The timely filing of objections shall automatically terminate further proceedings under this rule. Such objections shall not be frivolous or made in bad faith. If, after appellee's objection, the appellant proceeds under Rule 8C, the issue of whether the objection was frivolous or made in bad faith may be the subject of a motion in the Appellate Division for costs as provided in Rule 26. Within the same ten days after the filing of the expedited appeal, the judge may enter an order terminating further proceedings under this rule upon a determination of noncompliance with the terms of this rule. In either event, further appellate procedures may proceed under either Rule 8B or 8C.

(c) Copies; Briefs; Transmission to Appellate Division. In the event that a party does not object to, or the judge does not terminate the proceedings as provided in section (b), above, the appellant shall file, within twenty-five days after the filing of the expedited appeal, six additional copies of the expedited appeal and six copies of its brief. One copy of its brief shall be served on each other party within the same time limit. The appellee shall serve one copy and file six copies of its brief within fifteen days after service of the appellant's brief. The appellant may serve one copy and file six copies of a reply brief within ten days after service of the appellee's brief. Briefs shall be in compliance with Rules 16 and 20 of these rules, except that no appendix shall be required. Upon expiration of sixty days from the filing of the expedited appeal, the clerk shall transmit to the Appellate Division six copies of the expedited appeal, six certified copies of the docket entries and six copies of the briefs of each party, if any, unless the court allows further time for the filing of briefs or any other reason. Said transmission shall not be delayed by the failure of any party to file a brief within the required time period or any extension thereof.

Adopted effective July 1, 1994.

Commentary

This rule provides the first of three optional methods of appeal to the Appellate Division. It has no equivalent under the Mass.R.A.P. It is appropriate when the issues are limited in number and fairly clearly defined. It allows an appellant promptly and specifically to describe the issue or issues for appeal. Unless the opposing party files a timely objection or the court enters a timely order, briefs must be filed and the case proceeds to the Appellate Division on those issues. If a timely objection is filed or order is entered, the expedited appeal is terminated. There is no hearing in the trial court on whether an objection is frivolous or made in bad faith. But if the appellant proceeds under Rule 8C, costs may be sought in the Appellate Division under Rule 26. Such costs may be appropriate if the issue on appeal is based solely on the pleadings, requiring no transcript under Rule 8C.

Note that service of the expedited appeal on the judge must be addressed to the court where that judge "is then sitting or is likely to be sitting." This could be a court other than the trial court. Counsel should check with the trial court or, where necessary, the appropriate Regional Administrative Office.

This method of appeal is "expedited" not only because it avoids the cumbersome process of filing and settling a report for the Appellate Division, but also because it requires briefs to be filed within a limited time in *the trial court.* The clerk must send the case to the Appellate Division after sixty days. This gives all parties a chance to file briefs in the trial court within the time limits allowed. Upon arrival in the Appellate Division, the case can be immediately scheduled for argument. See Rule 10.

It should be noted that the issues stated in the notice of appeal under Rule 3(c) may not be added to in an expedited appeal under this rule.

Given the limited time for filing the expedited appeal, an appellant wishing to first review the taped record may have to check to see that the request for the cassette filed with the notice of appeal is being promptly processed by the trial court. Rule 3(d) requires the clerk to "forthwith" process the order for the cassette copy. This consists of sending the order and the master tape to the District Court Administrative Office (or in some cases to the Trial Court Administrative Office) for duplication. The cassette and master is then sent back to the requesting court and the rule requires the clerk to immediately notify the requesting party of its availability. The "turn around" time for actually making the cassette copy is usually very short, no more than one or two days. Delay can occur if the master tape is not promptly sent out for duplication by the clerk or if notice of the availability of the cassette copy is not promptly given. Courts are not required to mail the cassettes to counsel, but some courts will make such mailing if provided with an addressed, postage-paid envelope by counsel.

If review of the tape is desired before filing an expedited appeal, but delay is encountered, a request for extension of the 20-day period for filing the expedited appeal may be necessary by motion under Rule 2.

Note that no appendix to the appellant's brief is required under this procedure. The contents of the expedited appeal fulfills this function.

Note also that when a party fails to file and serve a brief and the case is transmitted to the Appellate Division, the latter can permit late filing and service (Rule 19(a)) or impose sanctions, including dismissal of the appeal (Rule 19(c)).

Rule 8B. Method of Appeal: Agreed Statement of the Case

(a) In General. In lieu of the expedited appeal provided in Rule 8A or appeal on the record of proceedings as provided in Rule 8C, the parties may elect to submit an agreed statement of the case, which, upon approval by the trial court, shall constitute the record on appeal.

(b) Filing and Contents. Within thirty days after (1) the filing of a notice of appeal or (2) termination of an expedited appeal, the parties may prepare, sign and file in the trial court an agreed statement of the case. The agreed statement shall contain a copy of the notice of appeal, shall show how the issues presented by the appeal arose and were decided in the trial court and shall set forth only so many of the facts proved or sought to be proved as are essential to a decision of the issues presented.

(c) Approval by the Trial Court. The statement shall be deemed approved by the trial judge unless within fifteen days of its filing the trial judge, with or without a conference, enters an order of disapproval on the grounds that it does not accurately state the facts or how the issues arose. The trial judge may condition approval upon the inclusion of such additions or deletions as he or she considers necessary to present fully and accurately the issues raised by the appeal. The clerk shall serve notice on all parties of the approval or disapproval of the agreed statement which shall include any conditions, additions or deletions made by the trial judge.

If the agreed statement is disapproved, or approved on conditions or with additions or deletions that any party finds unacceptable, the agreed statement may thereupon be considered terminated and the party wishing to appeal may proceed under Rule 8C, or either party may move for a hearing on such revised agreement and the matter shall proceed as the judge may permit, within such times as the judge may permit. Failure to achieve an agreed statement that is acceptable to the parties and approved by the court shall result in a disapproval concluding the matter and the party wishing to appeal may proceed under Rule 8C.

(d) Copies; Briefs; Transmission to the Appellate Division. Within twenty-five days after receipt of notice of approval of the agreed statement from the clerk, as provided above, the appellant shall file six additional copies of the agreed statement and six copies of its brief. One copy of its brief shall be served on the other parties within the same time limit. The appellee shall serve one copy and file six copies of its brief within fifteen days after service of the appellant's brief. The appellant may serve one copy and file six copies of a reply brief within ten days after service of the appellant's brief. Such briefs shall be in compliance with Rules 16 and 20 of these rules, except that no appendix shall be required. After the expiration of sixty days from final approval of an agreed statement, the clerk shall transmit to the Appellate Division six copies of the agreed statement, six certified copies of the docket entries and six copies of the briefs of each party, if any, unless the court allows further time for the filing of briefs or any other reason. Said transmission shall not be delayed by the failure of any party to file a brief within the required period or any extension thereof, provided, however, that the consequences for failure to file a brief shall be governed by Rule 19(c).

Adopted effective July 1, 1994.

Commentary

This rule provides the second option for appeal to the Appellate Division. It has no equivalent under the Mass.R.A.P. It may be used instead of the other two or if the expedited appeal is tried but fails. It allows the appellant, with the agreement of the appellee and approval of the court, to frame the issues for appeal in a relatively brief form.

It can be in the appellee's interest to agree to an accurate statement of the issues and cooperate with this method of appeal because of the cost that will be incurred if appeal on the full record becomes necessary.

Once the agreed statement is timely filed and served, court approval is presumed unless an order of disapproval is entered by the court within fifteen days of the filing. If the court conditions its approval on changes, the appellant can terminate the process and proceed under Rule 8C or either party can request a hearing to resolve the matter and achieve an agreed statement in final form.

It should be noted that notice from the clerk of approval or disapproval of the agreed statement includes approval resulting from inaction by the trial judge. That is, if fifteen days passes from the filing of the agreed statement and the judge does not enter an order disapproving the statement, the clerk must send notice of approval to the parties. This notice triggers the next step, the filing of briefs in the trial court.

The clerk must transmit the case to the Appellate Division at the expiration of sixty days from approval of the agreed statement. This allows sufficient time for filing of briefs. If they are not filed, the case must be transmitted anyway. Note that when a party fails to file and serve a brief and the case is transmitted to the Appellate Division, the consequences of the failure are governed by Rule 19.

No appendix to the appellant's brief is required. The agreed statement itself fulfills that function.

When an agreed statement is "conditionally approved" by the court, the rule permits the court to schedule and hear argument as to the additions, deletions or changes involved, on its own timetable. If an acceptable agreement can be formulated and approved by the court, briefs can be filed and the matter transmitted to the Appellate Division. If an agreed statement cannot be formulated, the court will disapprove and the procedure is terminated, leaving the appellant with the Rule 8C avenue of appeal.

Rule 8C. Method of Appeal: Appeal on the Record of Proceedings

(a) In General. If an appeal is not claimed and perfected under Rule 8A or 8B, a party may appeal based on the record of proceedings as provided in this rule. The record of proceedings shall consist of a typewritten transcript of the electronic or stenographic recording of the proceedings or, where no such record is available, a statement of the evidence, as provided below. No transcript or statement of the evidence shall be required for appeal under this rule where the issue or issues presented is raised solely by the pleadings.

(b) Filing and Contents. Within thirty days after (1) filing the notice of appeal as required by Rule 3 or (2) termination of procedures under Rule 8A or 8B, an appellant appealing under this rule shall file and serve on all other parties a document captioned "Appeal on the Record of Proceedings." Such filing and service shall be in accordance with Rule 13.

The Appeal on the Record of Proceedings shall consist of a statement that the party intends to proceed under this rule, and, if a transcript will be necessary, shall also include a request for a cassette copy of the electronic recording of the trial proceedings made under the control of the court under Rule 114, Dist./Mun.Supp.R.Civ.P., unless such request was previously included with the notice of appeal. The request for the cassette copy shall be set forth on the required form and shall be accompanied by the appropriate fee.

Upon receipt of a request for cassette copy the clerk shall forthwith order the cassette and shall notify the requesting party immediately upon its availability.

(c) Obtaining Transcript of Cassette.

(1) *Cassette Designation Statement; Duties of Appellant.* Within fifteen days after receipt of notice from the clerk that the cassette is available, or if the cassette was previously obtained, within fifteen days after filing of the Appeal on the Record of Proceedings, the appellant shall file in court and serve on each appellee a document captioned "Designation for Transcription" which shall include the date of receipt of the cassette; a designation of the parts of the cassette the appellant desires to include in the transcript; and the name, address, and telephone number of the individual or firm selected to prepare the transcript, provided that the appellant and each appellee have agreed to this choice and the appellant so states. If the appellant and appellees have not so agreed, the designation shall also specifically notify the clerk to select the transcriber.

The designation of the parts of the cassette to be transcribed should be precise and include such details as the name of the witness whose testimony has been designated and the portions to be included giving an exact quote of the beginning words and concluding words of each designated portion.

If the selection of an individual or firm to prepare the transcript is not included, the clerk shall select the individual or firm in accordance with procedures promulgated by the Chief Administrative Justice. The clerk shall promptly notify all parties of the selection made by the clerk. Any individual or firm selected to transcribe the record pursuant to this rule is hereinafter called "the transcriber."

If the appellant has designated the entire cassette for transcription, then within the same fifteen days for filing and serving the designation, the appellant shall also send or deliver the cassette to the transcriber with a written order designating the entire cassette for transcription. If the appellant has not designated the entire cassette, then after twenty days have expired from the service upon the appellee of appellant's designation of transcript, the appellant shall send or deliver the cassette to the transcriber with a written order which states those parts of the cassette designated by the parties for transcription. In addition, the order, whether for all or part of the transcript, shall include a statement that the original of the designated portions of the transcript should be sent to the clerk of the trial court, and shall indicate the number of copies, if any, to be sent to the appellant. The appellant shall promptly file with the clerk and serve on the other parties a copy of the order placed with the transcriber.

The appellant shall cooperate with the transcriber by providing such information as is necessary to facilitate transcription, and make satisfactory arrangements with the transcriber to pay for the trial court's original of the designated portions of the transcript and any copies ordered by the appellant for the appellant's own use.

(2) *Duties of the Appellee.* If the appellee deems it necessary to have a cassette in order to consider counter-designating, or for any other purpose, the appellee shall, after receipt of the Appeal on the Record of Proceedings, promptly order the cassette from the clerk or promptly arrange with the appellant to use the appellant's cassette. If the appellant has not designated and ordered the entire transcript and if the appellee deems a transcript of other portions of the proceedings to be necessary, the appellee shall within fifteen days after receipt of the appellant's designation, file in court, and serve on the appellant, a designation of such additional parts. The designation of the parts of the cassette to be transcribed should be precise and include such details as the name of the witness whose testimony has been designated and the specific portions to be included, giving an exact quote of the beginning words and concluding words of each designated portion. If the appellant shall refuse to order such parts, the appellee shall either order the parts or apply to the trial court for an order requiring the appellant to do so upon such terms and costs as the court may direct. If the appellee desires a copy of designated portions of the transcript, the appellee shall promptly communicate to the transcriber the number of copies wanted and make satisfactory arrangements with the transcriber for payment for the appellee's own copies.

The appellee shall cooperate with the transcriber by providing such information as is necessary to facilitate transcription.

(3) *Duties of the Transcriber.* The transcriber shall prepare an original typed transcript of the designated portions and the requested number of copies in accordance with the designations, and shall deliver the original to the clerk, with the following certificate of accuracy:

I, _____, do hereby certify that the foregoing is a true and accurate transcript, prepared to the best of my ability, of the designated portions of the cassette provided to me by the appellant or appellee of a trial or hearing of the _____ Division of the _____ Court Department in the proceedings of _____ v. _____, case(s) no.(s) _____, before Justice _____ on _____.
(Day and Date)
　　Date: _____
　　　　　　　　　Transcriber's Signature

The transcriber shall deliver legible copies to all parties who have so requested.

(4) *Unintelligible Portions of the Cassette.* If portions of the cassette cannot be transcribed because they are unintelligible, the parties shall promptly use reasonable efforts to stipulate their content. If agreement cannot be reached, the parties shall promptly present their differences as to such portions to the trial judge who heard the testimony. The trial judge shall, if possible, settle the content of the unintelligible portions, which shall then be included in the transcript.

(d) Stenographic Record Available; Duty of Appellant; Notice to Appellee. A stenographic record is one made with the permission of the trial court pursuant to Massachusetts Rules of Civil Procedure 80(c) by a stenographer who, upon agreement of the parties, has been approved and designated as the "reporter" for that case by the trial judge.

Within ten days after filing the Appeal on the Record of Proceedings, the appellant shall order from the reporter a transcript of such parts of the proceedings not already on file as he or she deems necessary for inclusion in the record. If the appellant intends to urge on appeal that a finding or conclusion is unsupported by the evidence or is contrary to the evidence, he or she shall include in the record a transcript of all evidence relevant to such finding or conclusion. Unless the entire transcript is to be included, the appellant shall within the time above provided, file and serve on the appellee a designation of the parts of the transcript which he or she intends to include in the record. If the appellee deems a transcript of other parts of the proceedings to be necessary, he or she shall, within ten days after the service of the designation of the appellant, file and serve on the appellant a designation of additional parts to be included. If the appellant shall refuse to order such parts as the appellee has designated, the appellee shall apply to the trial court for an order requiring the appellant to do so or requiring the appellant to order a transcript of so much of the record as the trial judge deems appropriate, and upon such costs and terms as he or she may direct. At the time of ordering, a party shall make satisfactory arrangements with the reporter for payment of the cost of the transcript, and for transmission of the original transcript to the clerk.

(e) Statement of the Evidence or Proceedings When No Report Was Made or When the Transcript Is Unavailable. If no report of the evidence or proceedings at a hearing or trial was made, or if a transcript is unavailable, the appellant may, within thirty days after the Appeal on the Record of Proceedings is filed, file a statement of the evidence or proceedings from the best available means, including his or her recollection. The statement shall be served on the appellee, who may file objections or proposed amendments thereto within ten days after service. Thereupon the statement and any objections or proposed amendments thereto shall be submitted to the trial court for settlement and approval and as settled and approved shall be included in the case file and, as necessary, included in the appellant's appendix to the brief.

(f) Correction or Modification of the Record. If any difference arises as to whether the record truly discloses what occurred in the trial court, the difference shall be submitted to and settled by that court or, if necessary, the Appellate Division, and the record made to conform to the truth. If anything material to either party is omitted from the record by error or accident or is misstated therein, the parties by stipulation or the trial court or the Appellate Division, on proper suggestion or on its own motion, may direct that the omission or misstatement be corrected and if necessary that a supplemental record be certified and transmitted. All other questions as to the form and content of the record shall be presented to the Appellate Division.

(g) Copies, Transmission to the Appellate Division. Within thirty days after notice from the trial court clerk of receipt of the transcript from the transcriber, or within thirty days after settlement and approval of a statement of the evidence or proceedings, as the case may be, the appellant shall file six additional copies of the Appeal on the Record of Proceedings.

Upon receipt of said copies, the clerk shall transmit them along with six certified copies of the docket entries to the Appellate Division.

Adopted effective July 1, 1994. Amended March 22, 2013, effective May 1, 2013.

Commentary

This rule provides the third option for appeal to the Appellate Division. It can be used instead of the other two or after one or both of the other two have been tried but have failed.

Unlike the other two procedures, this procedure has a model in the Mass.R.A.P. and follows, for the most part, the cognate provisions in those rules. It is the most detailed and costly method of appeal to the Appellant Division, but may be necessary if the issues are complex or if there is a dispute as to what the issues are or how they arose.

In general, this rule differs from its counterpart, Mass.R.A.P. 8, in that it focuses on the electronic tape recording of the proceeding (which is required in the District Court) as the source of the transcript, rather than a stenographic record.

Section (a) of the rule differs greatly from its Mass.R.A.P. counterpart. Unlike the latter, this rule does *not* define a "record on appeal" consisting of the original papers, exhibits, transcript, if any, and certified docket entries. Providing those documents to the Appellate Division is addressed in various provisions of this rule, as necessary, most notably Rule 18(a). Rather this rule focuses on the "record of proceedings" i.e., the transcript (usually from the tape recording) or a statement of evidence or proceedings when no transcript is available.

As stated in section (a), no transcript will be necessary for appeal under Rule 8C if the issue on appeal is based solely on the pleadings. Such a case would appear appropriate for appeal under Rule 8A. If the appellant attempted a Rule 8A appeal but the appellee objected, such objection may be the subject of a motion for costs under Rule 26. See Rule 8A(b).

It should be noted that under section (b) of the rule the time limit for claiming this method of appeal is thirty days from filing the notice of appeal or from termination of either of the other methods of appeal. And the document by which appeal is claimed, the "Appeal on the Record of Proceedings" must include a proper request under section (c) for a cassette copy of the tape (unless such request was included with the notice of appeal).

The next step in the process under section (c) is for the appellant to file and serve a "designation" of those portions of the taped record to be transcribed. The designation must be filed and served (1) within fifteen days of the filing of the "Appeal on Record of Proceedings" if the tape was previously ordered and obtained, or (2) within fifteen days after the cassette copy is received, if it is ordered in the "Appeal on Record of Proceedings."

The requirements for the designation under section (c) are many and detailed. They closely follow the parallel provisions of the Mass. R.A.P. where a transcript must be obtained from a tape recording (Rule 8(b)(3)(ii)). As in the latter rule, if the appellant designates the entire cassette for transcript, he or she must send the cassette to the transcriber within the same fifteen days as for filing and serving the designation, with an order to transcribe the entire cassette. Note, however, that under this rule, the fifteen-day period may commence from the time the Appeal on Record of Proceedings was filed (if the cassette was not previously ordered in the notice of appeal) or from the time the cassette was made available (if it was requested in the Appeal on Record of Proceedings).

The time limit for sending an order for transcription of less than the entire cassette is the same as in the Mass.R.A.P.: The cassette and order must be promptly sent or delivered to the transcriber "after twenty days have expired from the service upon the appellee of appellant's designation of transcript." The appellee may designate additional portions under section (c)(2).

As in Mass.R.A.P. 8, the order to the transcriber must include the number of copies to be sent to the appellant and a copy of the order must be filed and served.

Note that under sections (c)(2) and (d) of the rule, the trial court can impose terms and costs if it has to order the appellant to order transcriptions of additional parts of the record that the appellee has designated.

Succeeding sections of the rule also follow parallel provisions of the Mass.R.A.P. regarding payment by the appellant to the transcriber, the duties of the appellee, the duties of the transcriber, unintelligible portions of the cassette, obtaining a "statement of the evidence or proceedings" when no transcript is available, and correcting or modifying the record of proceedings.

Section (d) provides the procedure to be followed in the unusual event that the proceedings were recorded by a court approved stenographer. It differs from the cognate rule in the Mass. R. A. P. (Rule 8(b)(1)) by measuring time limits from the filing of the "Appeal on the Record of Proceedings" and by allowing the court to decide what portions to transcribe if there is a dispute and impose terms and costs thereon. A 2013 amendment to this rule deleted the citation in section (d) to the District/Municipal Court Rules of Civil Procedure, which were repealed in 1996, and replaced it with a citation to the Massachusetts Rules of Civil Procedure, which now govern civil proceedings in the District Court.

Section (g) of the rule requires the appellant to file six copies of the Appeal on the Record of Proceedings after the original transcript has been received by the clerk from the transcriber and the parties so notified. When the clerk receives these six copies, the case is sent to the Appellate Division. This procedure differs substantially from the Mass.R.A.P., where the case cannot be transmitted to the Appellate Division until the clerk has completed the "assembly of the record." As discussed in the Commentary to Rule 9, below, assembly of the record is not required under these rules.

Also note that under this rule briefs are *not* filed in the trial court. Rather, briefs are filed in the Appellate Division after the case is received there. See Rule 19(a). This differs from appeal under Rules 8A or 8B where briefs must be filed in the trial court before the case is sent to the Appellate Division.

Rule 9.   Appeals Under Rule 8C: Transmission to the Appellate Division

Upon receipt from the appellant of six copies of the Appeal on Record of Proceedings, as provided in Rule 8C(g), the clerk shall promptly record such receipt on the docket and transmit the six copies and six certified copies of the docket to the Appellate Division.

Adopted effective July 1, 1994.

Commentary

This rule does not adopt the provisions of Mass.R.A.P. 9 requiring the clerk of the trial court to "assemble the record." Under that rule, the appeal cannot proceed until that assembly is complete. Yet the clerk is required to complete the assembly "as soon as may be," creating the potential for significant delay. Moreover, the assembled record is retained in the trial court unless and until needed in the appellate court and this appears to be a rare occurrence.

In contrast, the trial court clerk under these rules transmits the appeal to the Appellate Division as soon as the necessary acts are taken by the parties, culminating in the appellant filing six additional copies of the Appeal on Record of Proceeding.

This approach relieves the clerk's office of a task that can prove unnecessary to the disposition of the appeal and the cause of substantial delay. In the event that the Appellate Division needs all or any of the original documents on file in the case, it can obtain them directly from the trial court.

Rule 10.   Docketing the Appeal; Notice to the Parties

Upon receipt from the trial court of (1) the six copies of the Expedited Appeal, docket entries and briefs, if any, under Rule 8A; (2) the six copies of the Agreed Statement, docket entries and briefs under Rule 8B; or (3) the six copies of the Appeal on the Record of Proceedings and docket entries under Rule 8C, as the case may be, the Appellate Division shall make a record of said receipt and promptly serve notice of said receipt on the parties. In the case of appeal under Rule 8A or 8B, said notice may include notice of the date for oral argument.

Adopted effective July 1, 1994.

Commentary

This rule specifies clerical duties in the Appellate Division regarding receipt of the appeal from the trial court. It differs from Mass. R.Civ.P. 10 in several respects. For example, provisions in the latter are based on the filing fee being paid to the appellate court. In appeals to the Appellate Division, the filing fee is paid to the trial court along with the filing of the notice of appeal. See Rule 3(a). An appeal will not get to the Appellate Division unless the appropriate filing fee has been paid in the trial court.

With regard to the basic function of the rule, i.e. to provide for docketing of the appeal and notice thereof to the parties, this rule provides a simplified version of Mass.R.A.P. 10. For appeals under Rule 8A or 8B, the notice can specify the date for oral argument because in those cases briefs will already have been filed.

Failure of the parties to receive notice from the Appellate Division within a reasonable time after completion of procedures in the trial court can prompt an inquiry by the appellant to determine if the trial court has transmitted the appeal.

Although the caption of Rule 10 is identical to the caption of Mass.R.A.P. 10 in reference to "docketing" the appeal, the text of this rule uses the language "make a record of its receipt." This is because the Appellate Division is not a separate court, but rather an extension of the trial court whose case is on appeal. Thus, at least in a technical sense, it does not have its own docket. The only official docket in the case is that kept by the clerk of the trial court. On the other hand, the Appellate Division, or more accurately, each of the three "districts" of the Appellate Division, is its own administrative entity, and as such must make a record of all of its actions. When appropriate, that record should be deemed a continuation of the trial court docket.

Rule 11.   [Reserved]

(Mass.R.A.P. 11 is not adopted for appeals to the Appellate Division.)

Rule 12.   Proceeding in Forma Pauperis

(a) Leave to Proceed on Appeal In Forma Pauperis From Trial Court to Appellate Division. The trial court, in accordance with the relevant statutory procedures, may authorize an appeal to be prosecuted in forma pauperis.

(b) Form of Briefs, Appendices and Other Papers. Parties allowed to proceed in forma pauperis may file briefs, appendices and other papers in typewritten form, and may request that the appeal be heard on the original papers and exhibits on file without the necessity of reproducing parts thereof in any form.

Adopted effective July 1, 1994.

Commentary

This rule departs from Mass.R.A.P. 12 by making reference to relevant statutory requirements and by deleting a general reference to "cause shown" and "reasonable notice." Waiver of fees and costs on the basis of indigency is not a matter of the court's discretion but rather is governed by detailed procedures in G.L. c. 261, ss. 27A–27G. That statute defines "indigency," and permits waiver (or state payment) depending on the nature of the fee or cost involved. A specific form of affidavit of indigency is also required.

Rule 13. Filing and Service

(a) **Filing.** Papers required or permitted to be filed in connection with an appeal pursuant to these rules shall be filed with the clerk of the trial court and not at the court address where the Appellate Division sits, except as otherwise expressly provided. Filing may be accomplished by first class mail, either registered or unregistered, addressed to the clerk of the trial court, but filing shall not be timely unless the papers are received by the clerk within the time fixed for filing, except that briefs and appendices shall be deemed filed on the date of receipt if (i) received within the time fixed for filing or (ii) accompanied by an affidavit signed by counsel of record attesting that the day of mailing was within the time fixed for filing.

(b) **Service of All Papers Required.** Copies of all papers filed by any party and not required by these rules to be served by the clerk shall, at or before the time of filing, be served by a party or person acting for him or her on all other parties to the appeal. Service on a party represented by counsel shall be made on counsel.

(c) **Manner of Service.** Service may be personal or by first class mail. Personal service includes delivery of the copy to a responsible person at the office of counsel. Service by first class mail is complete on mailing.

(d) **Proof of Service.** Papers presented for filing shall contain an acknowledgment of service by the person served or proof of service in the form of a statement under the penalties of perjury of the date and manner of service and of the name of the person served, signed by the person who made service. Proof of service may appear on or be affixed to the papers filed. The clerk shall permit papers to be filed without acknowledgment or proof of service but shall require such acknowledgment of proof to be filed promptly thereafter.

(e) **Filing in the Appellate Division.** Where filing of documents in the Appellate Division is expressly allowed or required by these rules, such filing shall comply with the provisions of this rule, provided that such filings shall be addressed to the "Appellate Division" at the court address provided for the appropriate Appellate Division district involved in the appeal.

Adopted effective July 1, 1994.

Commentary

This rule is similar to Mass.R.A.P. 13 except that it is modified to reflect the fact that most filings relating to Appellate Division appeal are made in the *trial court* and not in the Appellate Division.

Section (e) has been added for those instances where a document must be filed in the Appellate Division. Each Appellate Division district has a mailing address, usually at the court in which the Presiding Justice of that district sits. This address can be obtained from the clerk of the trial court.

Rule 14. Computation and Extension of Time

(a) **Computation of Time.** In computing any period of time prescribed by these rules, by order of court, or by applicable statute, the day of the act, event, or default after which the designated period of time begins to run shall not be included. The last day of the period shall be included, unless it is a Saturday, Sunday or a legal holiday, in which event the period shall extend until the end of the next day which is not a Saturday, Sunday or a legal holiday. When the period of time prescribed or allowed is less than seven days, intermediate Saturdays, Sundays and legal holidays shall be excluded in the computation. As used in this rule "legal holiday" means those days specified in G.L. c. 4, s. 7 and any other day appointed as a holiday by the President or the Congress of the United States or so designated by the laws of the Commonwealth.

(b) **Enlargement of Time.** The trial court or Appellate Division for good cause shown may upon motion enlarge the time prescribed by these rules or by its order for doing any act, or may permit an act to be done after the expiration of such time; but the time for filing a notice of appeal may not be enlarged beyond 180 days from the date of entry of the judgment or order sought to be reviewed.

(c) **Additional Time After Service by Mail.** Whenever a party is required or permitted to do an act within a prescribed period after service of a paper upon him or her and the paper is served by mail, 3 days shall be added to the prescribed period.

Adopted effective July 1, 1994.

Commentary

This rule is identical to Mass.R.A.P. 14 except that the references to "appellate court" in section (b) are changed to "Appellate Division" and the reference in that section to a "one year" maximum enlargement of time for filing a notice of appeal is changed to "180" days. See Rule 4(c).

Also, section (b) refers to the authority of the trial court or Appellate Division to enlarge a required time period. Generally, the ruling on a request for an enlargement of time will be made by the trial court or Appellate Division depending on where the case is at the time the enlargement is sought. For example, where an appeal is transmitted to the Appellate Division under Rule 8A or 8B, without the timely filing of briefs in the trial court, an enlargement of time for filing must be sought in the Appellate Division. See Rule 19(d).

Rule 15. Motions

Unless another form is elsewhere prescribed by these rules, an application for an order or other relief shall be made by filing a motion for such order or relief with proof of service on all other parties. The motion shall contain or be accompanied by any matter required by a specific provision of these rules governing such a motion, shall state with particularity the grounds on which it is based, and shall set forth the order or relief sought. If a motion is supported by briefs, affidavits, or other papers, they shall be served and filed with the motion. Any party may file a response in opposition to a motion within seven days after service of the motion, but the trial court or Appellate Division in which the motion was filed may shorten or extend the time for responding to any motion.

Adopted effective July 1, 1994.

Commentary

Section (a) of this rule is substantially similar to section (a) of Mass.R.A.P. 15, except that references therein to section (b) and the special provision for Rule 6 motions (for stays and injunctions) are eliminated.

Sections (b)(c) and (d) of Mass.R.A.P. 15 have not been adopted.

See also Rules 13(e) and 20(b) regarding filing in the Appellate Division.

Rule 16. Briefs

(a) Brief of the Appellant. The brief of the appellant shall contain under appropriate headings and in the order here indicated:

(1) In all briefs of twenty pages or more, a table of contents, with page references, and a table of cases (alphabetically arranged), statutes and other authorities cited, with references to the pages of the brief where they are cited.

(2) A statement of the issues presented for review.

(3) A statement of the case, which shall first indicate briefly the nature of the case, the course of proceedings, and its dispositions in the trial court. There shall follow a statement of the facts relevant to the issues presented for review with appropriate references to the record (see subdivision (e)).

(4) The argument, which shall contain the contentions of the appellant with respect to the issues presented, and the reasons therefor, with citations to the authorities, statutes and parts of the record relied on. In a brief of more than twenty-four pages of argument, there shall be a short summary of argument, suitably paragraphed and with page references to later material in the brief dealing with the same subject matter, which should be a condensation of the argument actually made in the body of the brief and not a mere repetition of the headings under which the argument is arranged. The Appellate Division need not pass upon questions or issues not argued in the brief. Nothing argued in the brief shall be deemed to be waived by a failure to argue orally.

(5) A short conclusion stating the precise relief sought.

(6) In cases where geographical facts are of importance, unless appropriate plans are reproduced in the printed record or record appendix, an outline plan or chalk (preferably based on exhibits in evidence) shall be included. This outline plan should be suitable for reproduction on one page of the printed law reports.

(7) The names, addresses, and telephone numbers of individual counsel to which firm names may be added.

(b) Brief of the Appellee. The brief of the appellee shall conform to the requirements of subdivision (a)(1)–(4), (6) and (7), except that a statement of the issues or of the case need not be made unless the appellee is dissatisfied with the statement of the appellant.

(c) Reply Brief. The appellant may file a brief in reply to the brief of the appellee, and if the appellee has cross-appealed, the appellee may file a brief in reply to the response of the appellant to the issues presented by the cross appeal. No further briefs may be filed except with leave of the Appellate Division. Reply briefs shall comply with the requirements of Rule 16(a)(1).

(d) References in Briefs to Parties. Counsel will be expected in their briefs and oral arguments to keep to a minimum references to parties by such designations as "appellant" and "appellee." It promotes clarity to use the designations used in the lower court, or the actual names of the parties, or descriptive terms such as "the employee," "the injured person," "the taxpayer," "the landlord," etc.

(e) References in Briefs to the Record. References in the briefs to parts of the record reproduced in an appendix filed with a brief (see Rule 18(a)) shall be to the pages of the appendix at which those parts appear.

If the record is reproduced in accordance with the provisions of Rule 18(f), or if references are made in the briefs to parts of the record not reproduced, the references shall be to the pages of the parts of the record involved; e.g., Answer p. 1, Motion for Judgment p. 2, Transcript p. 231. Intelligible abbreviations may be used. If reference is made to evidence the admissibility of which is in controversy, reference shall be made to the pages of the appendix or of the transcript at which the evidence was identified, offered, and received or rejected. No statement of a fact of the case shall be made in any part of the brief without an appropriate and accurate record reference.

(f) Reproduction of Statutes, Rules, Regulations, etc. If determination of the issues presented requires consideration of constitutional provisions, statutes, rules, regulations, etc. or relevant parts thereof, they shall be reproduced in the brief or in an addendum at the end.

(g) Massachusetts Citations. Massachusetts Reports between 17 Massachusetts and 97 Massachusetts shall be cited by the name of the reporter. Any other citation shall include, wherever reasonably possible, a reference to any official report of the case or to the official publication containing statutory or similar material. References to decisions and other authorities should include, in addition to the page at which the decision or section begins, a page reference to the particular material therein upon which reliance is placed, and the year of the decisions; as, for example: 334 Mass. 593, 597–598 (1956). Quotations of Massachusetts statutory material shall include a citation to either the Acts and Resolves of Massachusetts or to the current edition of the General Laws published pursuant to a resolve of the General Court.

(h) Length of Briefs. Except by permission of the Appellate Division, principal briefs shall not exceed fifty pages of standard typographic printing, or seventy pages of reproduction by any other process of duplicating or copying, exclusive of pages containing the table of contents, tables of citations and any addendum containing statutes, rules, regulations, etc. Except by permission of the Appellate Division, reply briefs shall not exceed twenty-five pages of standard typographic printing or thirty-five pages or reproduction by any other process of duplicating or copying.

(i) Briefs in Cases Involving Cross Appeals. If a cross appeal is filed, the plaintiff in the trial court shall be deemed the appellant for purposes of this rule and Rules 18 and 19, unless the parties otherwise agree or the Appellate Division otherwise orders. The brief of the appellee shall contain the issues and argument involved in his or her appeal as well as the answer to the brief of the appellant.

(j) Brief in Cases Involving Multiple Appellants or Appellees. In cases involving more than one appellant or appellee, including cases consolidated for purposes of the appeal, any number of either may join in a single brief, and any appellant or appellee may adopt by reference any part of the brief of another. Parties may similarly join in reply briefs.

(k) Non-complying Briefs. A brief not in compliance with this rule may be struck from the files by the Appellate Division.

(*l*) Citation of Supplemental Authorities. When pertinent and significant authorities come to the attention of a party after his or her brief has been filed, or after oral argument but before decision, a party may promptly advise the Appellate Division, by letter, with a copy to all counsel, setting forth the citations. There shall be a reference either to the page of the brief or to a point argued orally to which the citations pertain, but the letter shall without argument state the reasons for the supplemental citations. Any response shall be made promptly and shall be similarly limited.

Adopted effective July 1, 1994.

Commentary

This rule is identical to Mass.R.A.P. 16, with the following exceptions: (1) all references in the latter to "appellate court", "court," and "appellate court or a single justice" have been changed to "Appellate Division;" (2) the second sentence of section (e) has been deleted; (3) references to "court below" in section (i) have been changed to "trial court"; and (4) references to "clerk of court" in section (*l*) have been changed to "Appellate Division."

Rule 17. Brief of an Amicus Curiae

A brief of an amicus curiae may be filed only (1) by leave of the Appellate Division or (2) at the request of the Appellate Division, except that consent or leave shall not be required when the brief is presented by the Commonwealth. The brief may be conditionally filed with the motion for leave. A motion for leave shall identify the interest of the applicant and shall state the reasons why a brief of an amicus curiae is desirable. Any amicus curiae shall file its brief within the time allowed the party whose position as to affirmance or reversal the amicus brief will support unless the Appellate Division for cause shown shall grant leave for later filing, and shall specify within what period an opposing party may answer. A motion of an amicus curiae to participate in the oral argument will be granted only for extraordinary reasons.

Adopted effective July 1, 1994.

Commentary

This rule is identical to Mass.R.A.P. 17, except that all references to "appellate court" and "appellate court or single justice" have been changed to "Appellate Division."

Rule 18. Appeals Under Rule 8C: Appendix to the Briefs

(a) Duty of Appellant to Prepare and File; Content of Appendix; Time for Filing; Number of Copies. In appeals under Rule 8C, the appellant shall prepare and file an appendix to the briefs. The appendix shall be filed and served with the brief. If separately bound, six copies of the appendix shall be filed with the trial court, and one shall be served on counsel for each party separately represented, unless the court shall order or direct the filing or service of a lesser number and except as otherwise provided in subdivision (e) of this rule.

The appendix shall contain: (1) the notice of appeal; (2) a copy of the docket entries in the trial court proceedings; (3) the findings, if any, and relevant portions of the pleadings; (4) the judgment, order, decision or rulings in question; (5) the transcript or relevant portions thereof; and (6) any other parts of the record for appeal which are necessary for the full understanding of the issues presented. Except where they have independent relevance, memoranda of law in the trial court should not be included in the appendix. The transcript need not be included where the issue or issues presented for appeal are raised solely by the pleadings.

The fact that parts of the record are not included in the appendix shall not prevent the parties or the Appellate Division from relying on such parts, provided that the Appellate Division may decline to permit the parties to refer to portions of the record omitted from the appendix unless leave be granted prior to argument.

(b) Determination of Contents of Appendix; Cost of Producing. The parties are encouraged to agree as to the contents of the appendix. In the absence of an agreement, the appellant shall, not later than ten days after receipt of notice from the Appellate Division of the receipt of the appeal, serve on the appellee, a designation of the parts of the record which he or she intends to include in the appendix. If the appellee deems it necessary to direct the particular attention of the Appellate Division to parts of the record not designated by the appellant, he or she shall, within ten days after receipt of the designation, serve upon the appellant, a designation of those parts. The appellant shall include in the appendix the parts thus designated. In designating parts of the record for inclusion in the appendix, the parties shall have regard for the fact that the entire record is always available to the Appellate Division for reference and examination and shall not engage in unnecessary designation.

Unless the parties otherwise agree, the cost of producing the appendix shall initially be paid by the appellant, but if the appellant considers that parts of the record designated by the appellee for inclusion are unnecessary for the determination of the issues presented he or she may so advise the appellee and the appellee shall advance the cost of including such parts. In the event of a dispute as to the parts to be included or the advance required to include them, the matter shall be settled by the Appellate Division on motion and notice. The cost of producing the appendix shall be taxed as costs in the case, but if either party shall cause matters to be included in the appendix unnecessarily, the Appellate Division may impose the cost of producing such parts on the party.

(c) [Reserved].

(d) Arrangement of the Appendix. The pages of the appendix shall be consecutively numbered and the parts of the record which are reproduced therein shall be set out in chronological order. The appendix shall commence with a chronologically ordered list of the parts of the record which it contains, with references to the pages of the appendix at which each part begins. When an appendix relates to two or more cases or to more than two parties, the appendix shall indicate the case to which each paper belongs and by whom it was filed. Unless the party filing the appendix reproduces the entire transcript of testimony, he or she shall, preceding each portion of testimony transcript reproduced, insert a concise statement identifying:

(1) the witness whose testimony is being reproduced;

(2) the party originally calling the witness;

(3) the party questioning the witness; and

(4) the classification of the examination (direct, cross, or other).

When matter contained in the transcript of proceedings is set out in the appendix, the page number of the original transcript at which such matter may be found may be indicated in brackets immediately before the matter which is set out, unless it already appears on the matter as set out. Omissions in the text of papers or of the transcript must be indicated by asterisks. Immaterial formal matters (captions, subscriptions, acknowledgments, etc.) may be omitted. A question and its answer may be contained in a single paragraph.

(e) Reproduction of Exhibits and Transcripts. Exhibits, and transcripts or portions thereof designated for inclusion in the appendix, may be contained in a separate volume, or volumes, suitably indexed. Six copies thereof shall be filed with the appendix and one copy shall be served on counsel for each party separately represented.

(f) Hearing of Appeals on the Original Record Without the Necessity of an Appendix. On motion, the Appellate Division may in specific cases dispense with the requirement of an appendix and permit appeals to be heard in whole or in part on the original record, with such copies of the record, or relevant parts thereof, as the Appellate Division may require. In such cases the Appellate Division shall order the clerk of the trial court to assemble and transmit to the Appellate Division the original record or parts thereof in such form and in such manner as it may direct.

Adopted effective July 1, 1994.

Commentary

This rule is limited in its application to appeals under Rule 8C, that is, appeals on the record of proceedings. No appendix to the briefs is required for appeals under Rule 8A or Rule 8B.

This rule differs from Mass.R.A.P. 18 in that the first paragraph of section (a) is added regarding filing, service and copies of the appendix. Also, the contents of the appendix are somewhat different under this rule.

Section (b) differs from its Mass.R.A.P. counterpart in that in this rule the time for service of the designation of parts of the record to be included in the appendix (assuming no agreement on this issue) is within ten days *after receipt of notice that the Appellate Division has received the appeal.* Another difference is that the appellant is *not* required under this rule to include in the designation a statement of issues for appeal.

This rule does not adopt section (c) of Mass.R.A.P. 18 allowing an alternate method of designating the contents of the appendix.

Section (d) is identical to the Mass.R.A.P. version, except reference is made to the "transcript of proceedings" rather than the "reporter's transcript of proceedings", since most District Court transcripts are based on the tape recording.

Under section (e), if exhibits or transcripts are contained in separate volumes or sets of volumes, six copies of the latter must be filed, that is, one with each copy of the appendix (rather than five as required in the Mass.R.A.P.)

Section (f) is identical to the Mass.R.A.P. version except the last sentence has been added to expressly authorize the Appellate Division to order the original record or any part thereof from the trial court clerk, as needed.

Rule 19.   Filing and Serving of Briefs

(a) Time for Serving and Filing Briefs. For appeals under Rules 8A and 8B, briefs shall be filed and served prior to transmittal of the case to the Appellate Division, pursuant to Rules 8A(c) and 8B(d), respectively.

For appeals under Rule 8C, the appellant shall serve and file his or her brief within thirty days after notice from the Appellate Division of receipt of the appeal from the trial court. The appellee shall serve and file his or her brief within twenty days after service of the brief of the appellant. The appellant may serve and file a reply brief within fourteen days after service of the brief of the appellee.

(b) Number of Copies to Be Filed and Served. Six copies of each brief shall be filed and one copy shall be served on each party or counsel.

(c) Consequences of Failure to File Briefs. If an appellant fails to file a brief within the time provided by these rules, or within the time as extended by the trial court or Appellate Division, an appellee may move for dismissal of the appeal, or the Appellate Division may sua sponte dismiss the appeal. If an appellee fails to file a brief, he or she will not be heard at oral argument except by permission of the Appellate Division.

(d) Late Filing and Service. For appeals filed under Rule 8A or Rule 8B, the Appellate Division may allow the late filing and service of briefs following receipt of said appeals from the trial court, as a matter of its discretion and upon the imposition of such terms and costs as it may deem appropriate.

Adopted effective July 1, 1994.

Commentary

Section (a) of the rule differs substantially from its counterpart in the Mass.R.A.P. For appeals under Rules 8A and 8B, it merely refers to the provisions under those rules whereby briefs must be filed in the trial court before the case is transmitted to the Appellate Division. For appeals under Rule 8C it provides specific time periods for the filing of briefs in the Appellate Division. (See Rule 13(e) and related commentary regarding filing in the Appellate Division.)

Section (b) requires six copies of briefs to be filed rather than fifteen under the Mass.R.A.P.

A new section (d) has been added specifically authorizing the Appellate Division to allow the late filing and service of briefs in appeals under Rules 8A and 8B. Those appeals must be transmitted to the Appellate Division by the trial court clerk regardless of whether briefs have been timely filed. The enlargement of a required time period may be allowed under the general authority of Rule 14(b).

Rule 20.   Forms of Briefs, Appendices and Other Papers

(a) Form of Briefs and Appendices. Except where a party is allowed to proceed in forma pauperis, or except on order of the Appellate Division, all briefs and appendices shall comply with (a)(1) or (2) below.

(1) *Form of Printed Briefs and the Appendix.* Briefs and appendices may be produced by standard typographic printing or by any duplicating or copying process which produces a clear black image on white paper. Carbon copies of briefs and appendices may not be submitted without permission of the Appellate Division, except as otherwise provided. All printed matter must be printed upon opaque paper having a dull

surface; the text shall be in clear type, not smaller than eleven-point, with three-point leads between lines; but indented quotations may be set without leads; and in footnotes ten-point type with one-point leads between lines may be used; the width of the type page shall not exceed five inches. All matter to be reproduced by Xerography or a similar process shall be typed in pica type, double-spaced. However produced, the page shall be eight and three-eighths or eight and one-half inches in width and ten and three-fourths or eleven inches in height. The width of the back margin, from the type page to the center fold, shall not be less than two inches. Pages shall be firmly bound at the left by saddle-wiring, side-wiring, stapling, or sewing. If side-wired or sewed, a strong paper cover shall be used. A transcript of testimony or a report of evidence may be printed as part of the appendix or may be reproduced by Xerography or a similar process.

The front covers of the briefs and/or appendices, if separately produced, shall contain: (1) a designation of the Appellate Division district; (2) the title of the case; (3) the nature of the proceeding in the Appellate Division (e.g., Appeal; Report by Trial Judge) and the name of the trial court and case and the trial court docket number; (4) the title of the document (e.g., Brief for Appellant, Appendix); and (5) the names, addresses and telephone numbers of counsel representing the party on whose behalf the document is filed.

(2) *Typewritten Briefs and Appendices.* Briefs and appendices may be typewritten upon opaque paper having a dull surface. The typewriting shall be double-spaced except for indented quotations which may be single-spaced, and appear on only one side of each page. The paper shall be eight and one-half inches in width and eleven inches in length. Briefs shall be signed by counsel. A transcript of testimony or a report of evidence may be typewritten as part of the appendix or may be reproduced by Xerography or a similar process.

(3) *Non-compliance.* Briefs or appendices not in substantial compliance with these rules shall not be received unless the court shall otherwise order.

(b) Form of Other Papers. Motions and other papers may be produced in the manner prescribed by subdivision (a)(1) or (2) above. Consecutive sheets shall be attached at the left margin. Carbon copies may be used for filing and service if they are legible.

A motion or other paper addressed to the Appellate Division shall contain a caption setting forth a designation of the Appellate Division district, the name of the trial court and case and the trial court docket number, and a brief descriptive title indicating the purpose of the paper; said caption shall appear on the first page, typed so as to be legible.

Adopted effective July 1, 1994.

Commentary

The contents of this rule are essentially the same as those of Mass.R.A.P. 20, except that a separate section, (a)(2), has been added to expressly provide for typewritten briefs and appendices.

The requirements for the form of "other papers" in section (b) have been simplified, with reference to the sections (a)(1) and (2) regarding the requirements for printing or typewriting, respectively.

Rule 21. Prehearing Conference

The Appellate Division may direct the attorneys for the parties to appear before the Appellate Division for a prehearing conference to consider the simplification of the issues and such other matters as may aid the disposition of the proceeding by the Appellate Division. The Appellate Division shall make an order which recites the action taken at the conference and the agreements made by the parties as to any of the matters considered and which limits the issues to those not disposed of by admissions or agreements of counsel, and such order when entered shall control the subsequent course of the proceeding, unless modified to prevent manifest injustice.

Adopted effective July 1, 1994.

Commentary

This rule is identical to Mass.R.A.P. 21, except that all references therein to "appellate court" and "appellate court or a single justice" have been changed to "Appellate Division."

Rule 22. Oral Argument

(a) Notice of Argument; Postponement. The Appellate Division shall advise all parties of the time and place at which oral argument will be heard. A request for postponement of the argument must be made by motion filed reasonably in advance of the date fixed for hearing.

(b) Time Allowed for Argument. Unless otherwise enlarged or limited by the Appellate Division, each side will be allowed fifteen minutes for argument. If counsel is of the opinion that additional time is necessary for the adequate presentation of his or her argument, such additional time may be requested, but such requests will rarely be granted. Requests may be made by letter to the Appellate Division reasonably in advance of the date fixed for the argument. The Appellate Division may terminate the argument whenever in its judgment further argument is unnecessary.

(c) Order and Content of Argument. The appellant will argue first and shall include a fair statement of the case. Counsel will not be permitted to read, except briefly, form briefs, records, prepared statements or authorities. The party making the opening argument on request may be allowed the opportunity to reply in writing to new matter in the arguments of his or her adversary.

(d) Cross and Separate Appeals. A cross or separate appeal shall be argued with the initial appeal at a single argument, unless the Appellate Division otherwise directs. If a case involves a cross appeal, the plaintiff in the action below shall be deemed the appellant for the purposes of this rule unless the parties otherwise agree or the Appellate Division otherwise directs. If separate appellants support the same argument, care shall be taken to avoid duplication of argument.

(e) Non-appearance of Parties. If the appellee fails to appear to present argument, the Appellate Division will hear argument on behalf of the appellant, if present. If the appellant fails to appear, the Appellate Division may hear argument on behalf of the appellee, if his or her counsel is present. If neither party appears, the case will be decided on the briefs unless the Appellate Division shall otherwise order.

(f) No Oral Argument by an Attorney Who Has Been a Witness Except by Leave of Appellate Division. No attorney shall be permitted to take part in the argument of a case in which that attorney has been a witness for his or her client, except by special leave of the Appellate Division.

(g) Submission on Briefs. By agreement of the parties, a case may at any time be submitted for decision on the briefs, but the Appellate Division may direct that the case be argued. At any time, any party may, by written notice filed and served, waive the right to oral argument.

(h) Use of Physical Exhibits at Argument; Removal. If physical exhibits other than documents or chalks are to be used at the argument, counsel shall arrange to have them placed in the court room before the Appellate Division convenes on the date of the argument. After the argument, the exhibits shall be left with the Appellate Division unless the Appellate Division otherwise directs. If exhibits are not reclaimed by counsel within a reasonable time after notice is given by the Appellate Division, they shall be destroyed or otherwise disposed of as the Appellate Division shall order.

Adopted effective July 1, 1994.

Commentary

This rule is identical to Mass.R.A.P. 22 except that all references in the latter to "clerk," "court" and "appellate court" have been changed to "Appellate Division."

Rule 23. [Reserved]

(Mass.R.A.P. 23, which governs the issuance and stay of "rescripts," has not been adopted for these rules. Procedures for the transmission of the Appellate Division decision and opinion, if any, to the trial court are provided in Rule 28.)

Rule 24. [Reserved]

Rule 25. Sanctions

If the Appellate Division shall determine that an appeal is frivolous, or that either party has acted in bad faith in proceeding under these rules, it may award to the aggrieved party just damages and single or double costs, and such interest on the amount of the judgment as may be allowed by law.

Adopted effective July 1, 1994.

Commentary

This rule follows Mass.R.A.P. 25, except that it has broader application, i.e., it is not limited to "damages" and costs against the appellant for a frivolous appeal, but rather includes monetary sanctions against either party for actions under these rules taken "in bad faith."

Rule 26. Costs

(a) To Whom Allowed. Except as otherwise provided by law, if an appeal is dismissed, costs shall be taxed against the appellant unless otherwise agreed by the parties or ordered by the Appellate Division; if a judgment is affirmed, costs shall be taxed against the appellant unless otherwise ordered; if a judgment is reversed, costs shall be taxed against the appellee unless otherwise ordered; if a judgment is affirmed or reversed in part, or is vacated, costs shall be allowed only as ordered by the Appellate Division. In assessing costs pursu-

ant to this rule, the Appellate Division may affirm, reverse, or modify an order, if any, for costs directed pursuant to Rule 8C(c)(2) or (d).

(b) Costs For and Against the Commonwealth. In cases involving the Commonwealth or an agency or officer thereof, if an award of costs against the Commonwealth is authorized by law, costs shall be awarded in accordance with the provisions of subdivision (a); otherwise, costs shall not be awarded for or against the Commonwealth.

(c) Costs of Briefs, Appendices, and Copies of Records. The costs of printing or otherwise producing necessary copies of briefs, appendices, or copies of records authorized by Rule 18(f) may be taxable in the trial court at rates not higher than those generally charged for such work in the Commonwealth. A party who desires such costs to be taxed shall state them in an itemized and verified bill of costs which he or she shall file with the clerk of the trial court, with proof of service, within fourteen days after the entry of judgment following the Appellate Division decision.

(d) Clerk to Insert Costs in Trial Court Judgment; Costs Taxable. The clerk of the trial court shall prepare and certify an itemized statement of costs for insertion in the trial court judgment following receipt of the Appellate Division decision. The statement shall include those costs taxable under subdivision (c) of this rule; costs incurred in the preparation and transmission of the record, the cost of the reporter's transcript, if necessary for the determination of the appeal, the premiums paid for cost of any bond to preserve rights pending appeal, and the fee for filing the notice of appeal shall be taxed as costs of the appeal in favor of the party entitled to costs under this rule.

Adopted effective July 1, 1994.

Commentary

Section (a) of this rule is identical to section (a) of Mass.R.A.P. 26, except the last sentence has been added with reference to costs imposed by the trial court.

Section (b) through (d) differ from the Mass.R.A.P. versions in that references to "lower court" in the latter have been changed to "trial court," and in section (c) language is added at the end to clarify when such costs are to be sought in the trial court. Similarly, section (d) has been changed to indicate that costs relating to appeal, which under section (c) must be sought after disposition of the appeal, are to be added to the judgment by the clerk of the trial court after the Appellate Division decision is received, assuming they are timely sought.

Rule 27. [Reserved]

(Mass.R.A.P. 27 regarding rehearing is not adopted for use in appeals to the Appellate Division.)

Rule 27.1. [Reserved]

(Mass.R.A.P. 27.1 regarding further appellate review in not adopted for use in appeals to the Appellate Division. The Mass R.A.P. themselves govern appeal from the Appellate Division to the Appeals Court.)

Rule 28.   Entry of Judgment Following Decision and Order

The Appellate Division shall promptly mail to the clerk of the trial court its decision and order, and its opinion, if any. Upon receipt of the decision and order from the Appellate Division, the clerk shall prepare, sign and enter judgment in accordance with said order. If the decision and order directs settlement of the form of the judgment in the trial court, the clerk shall sign and enter the judgment after settlement. Notation of a judgment in the trial court docket constitutes entry of the judgment. Following entry of judgment, the clerk shall forthwith send to the parties notice of entry of judgment in accordance with Dist./Mun.Cts.R.Civ.P. 77(d) together with a copy of the Appellate Division decision and order, and a copy of the opinion, if any.

Adopted effective July 1, 1994.

Commentary

This rule differs somewhat from the Mass.R.A.P. version. The primary difference is the addition of the last sentence requiring the clerk of the trial court to notify the parties of the entry of the Appellate Division judgment and send them copies of the decision and order, and opinion, if any.

Rule 29.   Voluntary Dismissal

(a) Dismissal in the Trial Court. If an appeal has not yet been transmitted to the Appellate Division, it may be dismissed by the trial court upon the filing in that court of a stipulation for dismissal signed by all the parties, or upon motion and notice by the appellant.

(b) Dismissal in the Appellate Division. An appeal that has been transmitted to the Appellate Division may be dismissed by the Appellate Division upon the filing in the Appellate Division of a stipulation for dismissal signed by all of the parties, or upon motion and notice by the appellant. The Appellate Division shall notify the clerk of the trial court of such judgment of dismissal as required by these rules.

(c) Settlement; Obligation of Appellant. In the event a case is settled or otherwise disposed of while an appeal is pending, it shall be the duty of counsel for the appellant to notify the Appellate Division forthwith.

Adopted effective July 1, 1994.

Commentary

Except for changed references to the "Appellate Division" and the "trial court," section (a) of this rule is virtually the same as section (a) of its Mass.R.A.P. counterpart.

Section (b) is somewhat different in that it does not require an order by the Appellate Division and does not require that the stipulation specify the terms as to payments of costs. Nor does this rule allow the Appellate Division to fix the terms of a dismissal as conditions of granting a motion therefor.

Rule 30.   Substitution of Parties

(a) Death of a Party. If a party dies after a notice of appeal is filed in the trial court or while a proceeding is pending in the Appellate Division, the personal representative of the deceased party may be substituted as a party on motion filed by the representative or by any party with the clerk.

The motion of party shall be served upon the representative in accordance with the provisions of Rule 13. If the deceased party has no representative, any party may suggest the death on the record and proceedings shall then be had as the Appellate Division may direct. If a party against whom an appeal may be taken dies after entry of a judgment or order in the trial court but before a notice of appeal is filed, an appellant may proceed as if death had not occurred. After the appeal has been transmitted to the Appellate Division substitution shall be effected in the Appellate Division in accordance with this subdivision. If a party entitled to appeal shall die before filing a notice of appeal, the notice of appeal may be filed by his or her personal representative, or, if he or she has no personal representative, by his or her attorney of record within the time prescribed by these rules. After the appeal has been transmitted to the Appellate Division, substitution shall be effected in the Appellate Division in accordance with this subdivision.

(b) Substitution for Other Causes. If substitution of a party in the Appellate Division is necessary for any reason other than death, substitution shall be effected in accordance with the procedure prescribed in subdivision (a).

(c) Public Officers; Death or Separation From Office.

(1) When a public officer is a party to an appeal or other proceeding in the Appellate Division in his or her official capacity and during its pendency dies, resigns, or otherwise ceases to hold office, the action does not abate and the successor is automatically substituted as a party. Proceedings following the substitution shall be in the name of the substituted party, but any misnomer not affecting the substantial rights of the parties shall be disregarded. An order of substitution may be entered at any time, but the omission to enter such an order shall not affect the substitution.

(2) When a public officer is a party to an appeal or other proceeding in his or her official capacity, that officer may be described as a party by his or her official title rather than by name; but the Appellate Division may require the name to be added.

Adopted effective July 1, 1994.

Commentary

This rule is virtually identical to Mass.R.A.P. 30. All references to "court" and "appellate court" have been changed to "Appellate Division" and all references to "lower court" have been changed to "trial court."

Rule 31.   Duties of the Presiding Justice of the Appellate Division District

As required by G.L. c. 231, § 108, the presiding justice of each Appellate Division district shall from time to time designate those Appellate Division justices who shall act on appeals in that district and direct the times and places of sittings.

Adopted effective July 1, 1994.

Commentary

This rule is totally different from Mass.R.A.P. 31. The latter deals with the duties of the appellate court clerk; there is no clerk, as such, in the District Court Appellate Division. Instead, this rule addresses the statutory duty of the Presiding Justice of each of the three Appellate Division districts to appoint the panels to hear cases and to schedule those hearings.

Rule 32. Title

These rules may be known and cited as the District/Municipal Courts Rules for Appellate Division Appeal (Dist./ Mun.Cts.R.A.D.A.).

Adopted effective July 1, 1994.

SPECIAL RULES OF THE DISTRICT COURTS OF MASSACHUSETTS

Table of Rules

Rule 200. Hour of Opening Court

In each District Court the hour of opening the daily session shall be 9:00 a.m.

Rule 201. Clerk's Office Hours

The office of the clerk shall be open in each District Court from 8:30 a.m. to 4:00 p.m. Monday through Friday; and 8:30 a.m. to 12:00 noon on Saturdays.

Rule 202. Sitting for Small Claims

In each District Court there shall be at least one sitting each week for the consideration of small claims, provided, however, that when so ordered by the justice of any court, such sittings may be held bi-weekly during the summer vacation period as established in said court.

RULES APPLICABLE TO JUVENILE PROCEEDINGS

Rule 203. Forms in Juvenile Cases

Forms for use in juvenile session prescribed on and after January 1, 1943 are hereby ordered to be continued in use.

Rule 204. Applicability of District Court Rules

Rules of the District Courts which are applicable to proceedings against adults shall, so far as pertinent, be applicable in proceedings against children between the ages of seven and seventeen, except as otherwise expressly provided.

Rule 205. Notice of Rights

A summons issued upon a complaint against a child alleged to be wayward or delinquent shall have attached thereto the following:

(1) A copy of the complaint.

(2) You have a right to legal counsel at all stages of the proceedings. If you are unable to afford counsel the court will appoint counsel for you.

(3) If you are of the opinion that all or any of the allegations contained in the complaint are not true, you have a right to deny the same and are entitled to a hearing before this court thereon.

(4) You have the privilege against self-incrimination and in consequence, you have a right to remain silent and to require the complainant to prove any and all charges made against you.

(5) You have the right to be confronted by the person making any accusation against you and to cross-examine that person and any other persons called to testify against you.

(6) You may produce witnesses in your own behalf at the hearing of the complaint.

(7) If there should be an adjudication or order of commitment against you, you have a right of appeal to the Superior Court of this county at the time thereof.

(8) You may, for cause, request a continuance of the hearing.

(9) Any questions relating to your rights may be submitted by you to the court at the hearing.

(10) Before the above mentioned hearing on the juvenile complaint the court, as provided by G.L. c. 119, s. 61, may hold a transfer hearing to determine whether you should be tried as an adult rather than a child and subject to adult criminal proceedings. If there will be such a transfer hearing, you will receive at least seven days notice of that hearing. See G.L. c. 119, s. 61 and Rule 208 of the Special Rules of the District Courts.

Said information in written form shall also be given to a child and his parent, guardian or other person or agency whose presence in court is or may be required by law when first appearing in court pursuant to such a complaint otherwise than upon a summons.

Amended May 10, 1976, effective June 1, 1976.

Rule 206. Copy of Complaint to Be Attached to Summons to Parent, Guardian or Agency

A summons to a parent, guardian or other person or agency whose presence in court is or may be required by law, shall have attached thereto a copy of the complaint.

Rule 207. Representation by Counsel

A child between seven and seventeen years of age against whom a complaint is made that he or she is a wayward or delinquent child, shall be represented by counsel at every stage of the proceedings if it shall appear to the court that such child may be committed to the custody of the Youth Service Board as the result of such complaint.

The court may require psychological testing and psychiatric examination whenever expedient.

Appointment of counsel, or an election to proceed without counsel, shall be governed by the provisions of Rule 3:10 of the General Rules of the Supreme Judicial Court and Rule 10 of the Initial Rules of Criminal Procedure of the District Courts.

Rule 208. Transfer Hearing
Under G.L. c. 119, s. 61

Publisher's Note

This Rule is no longer reflective of the current statute or actual practice. G.L. c. 119, § 61 was repealed by St.1996, c. 200, § 7, an emergency act, approved July 27, 1996, and by § 39 made effective October 1, 1996.

A transfer hearing shall be held (1) whenever requested by the Commonwealth or ordered by the court, on the basis that either condition denominated "a" or "b" in G.L. c. 119, s. 61, paragraph 1 exists, whether or not the same appears from the complaint; and (2) pursuant to court order in every case where the condition denominated "b" in said statute is met by reason of the fact that the offense is punishable by life imprisonment if committed by an adult. A request by the Commonwealth for a transfer hearing shall be filed in writing with the clerk not later than seven days after the arraignment on Uniform Form DCM–10, "Request for Transfer Hearing," promulgated herewith. Notice of the transfer hearing shall be given to the child or to his counsel, and to his parent or guardian, at least seven days prior to said transfer hearing upon Uniform Form DCM–11, "Notice of Transfer Hearing," promulgated herewith. If after the transfer hearing the court decides to dismiss the delinquency complaint it shall make a written finding and order upon Uniform Form DCM–12, "Finding and Order After Transfer Hearing," promulgated herewith.

Amended May 10, 1976, effective June 1, 1976.

Rule 209. Emergency Rule for Civil Support and Paternity Actions

(a) Scope and Applicability of Rule. This rule governs procedure in all actions for support and all actions for determination of paternity pursuant to G.L. c. 209, s. 32F and c. 209C in the District Court. It shall be construed and applied to secure the just, speedy and inexpensive determination of every such action. In appropriate cases, the court may direct that the procedures set forth in particular sections of the District/Municipal Courts Rules of Civil Procedures be utilized in these proceedings, when not inconsistent with this rule.

(b) Filing a Complaint. Each action for support or paternity shall be begun on a Complaint and Summons form. If requested by the plaintiff or if otherwise feasible and appropriate to facilitate the filing of a legible and complete complaint, the clerk shall provide assistance to the plaintiff in completing the form. The court shall not charge the plaintiff an entry fee or a fee for the cost of mailing or other method of service. The clerk shall provide a copy of the Complaint and Summons to the plaintiff at no cost upon filing.

(c) Notice to Defendant. The clerk shall promptly send to the defendant by certified mail, return receipt requested, and also by separate first class mail, at the address or addresses supplied by the plaintiff, a copy of the Complaint and Summons form. Such certified mail notice of the complaint shall be sufficient, although unclaimed or refused by the defendant, provided that the first class mail notice is not returned to the court undelivered. The court may provide for any other means of service in individual cases as is deemed necessary.

(d) Discovery. No depositions or interrogatories shall be permitted except upon good cause shown. Subpoenas for the attendance of witnesses or the production of documentary evidence shall be issued and served in accordance with the procedures set forth in Rule 45 of the District/Municipal Courts Rules of Civil Procedure.

(e) Trials and Judgments.

(1) *Time Goals for Orders and Judgments.* Whether or not the defendant appears for trial, it shall be the goal of the court to enter an order or a judgment for support in all cases within 45 days from the date of filing of the Complaint and Summons form, assuming valid service of the Complaint and Summons has been made; provided, however, that in any case in which blood or genetic marker testing is to be performed, the order or judgment for support should be entered as promptly as possible. Continuances which would frustrate the observance of the above goals shall not be granted except upon a showing of extreme circumstances.

(2) *Failure of a Defendant to Appear for Trial.* If valid service has been made and if the defendant fails to appear for trial and the plaintiff does appear, the court may adjudicate paternity, and may enter a temporary support order or judgment for support, including an income assignment as provided for in G.L. c. 119A; provided, however, that no order or judgment of support shall be made in a case filed pursuant to c. 209C unless the court has first found the defendant to be the parent of the child and chargeable with the support of said child.

(3) *Conduct of Trial.* The parties and witnesses testifying shall be sworn. Consistent with applicable statutes and the rules of evidence, the court shall conduct the trial in such order and form and with such methods of proof as it deems best suited to discover the facts and do justice in the case.

(4) *Judgments and Orders.* The clerk shall promptly enter the order, judgment, or adjudication of paternity on the docket, together with the date of such entry, and shall promptly complete and give a copy of such order, judgment or adjudication to each party. Such notice shall be given in-hand while the party is before the court, or by first class mail. In appropriate cases, including those in which an income assignment cannot be effectuated, the court may order an additional

or alternative method of notifying the defendant of the order, judgment or adjudication, including service by any person authorized to serve civil or criminal process, including police officers, as authorized by law.

The clerk shall keep such records of dates relative to the filing of complaints and the entry of orders and judgments under G.L. c. 209, s. 32F and c. 209C as may be prescribed by the administrative justice.

Adopted July 31, 1986, effective July 22, 1986.

Civil Contempt--Support Complaint and Summons

CIVIL CONTEMPT – SUPPORT COMPLAINT AND SUMMONS	DOCKET NUMBER	Trial Court of Massachusetts District Court Department
PLAINTIFF'S NAME, ADDRESS, ZIP CODE	WELFARE (DPW) OFFICE (IF PLAINTIFF RECEIVES WELFARE)	COURT DIVISION

THE DEFEN-DANT MUST APPEAR AT THIS COURT ADDRESS ON ON THE DATE AND TIME SPECIFIED HEREIN

	PLAINTIFF'S TELEPHONE NO.	DATE AND TIME OF HEARING
DEFENDANT'S NAME, ADDRESS, ZIP CODE		DEFENDANT'S TELEPHONE NO. HOME: WORK: EMPLOYER'S NAME AND ADDRESS (IF KNOWN)

TO ANY JUSTICE OF THE DISTRICT COURT DEPARTMENT

THE PLAINTIFF, PLAINTIFF'S REPRESENTATIVE AS AUTHORIZED BY LAW, OR DPW REPRESENTATIVE COMPLAINS THAT THE DEFENDANT HAS FAILED TO COMPLY WITH THE TERMS OF A COURT ORDER OR REGISTERED AGREEMENT, AS SPECIFIED BELOW, AFTER HAVING BEEN GIVEN NOTICE OF SAID ORDER BY SERVICE OR OTHERWISE, AND REQUESTS THAT THE DEFENDANT BE ORDERED TO APPEAR IN COURT TO SHOW CAUSE WHY HE OR SHE SHOULD NOT BE FOUND IN CONTEMPT AND PUNISHED.

1. BY COURT ORDER OR REGISTERED AGREEMENT DATED _____ THE DEFENDANT WAS REQUIRED:
   ☐ TO PAY $_____ PER ☐ WEEK ☐ MONTH SUPPORT FOR HIS OR HER ☐ SPOUSE ☐ MINOR CHILD(REN);
   ☐ TO PAY FOR OR PROVIDE ☐ MEDICAL ☐ DENTAL INSURANCE FOR HIS OR HER ☐ SPOUSE ☐ MINOR CHILD(REN);
   ☐ OTHER:

2. THE DEFENDANT HAS VIOLATED SAID ORDER OR AGREEMENT BY:
   ☐ FAILING TO MAKE PAYMENTS AS REQUIRED, AND THERE NOW REMAINS DUE AND UNPAID TO THE PLAINTIFF OR DPW THE SUM OF $_____ PLUS ANY FURTHER AMOUNTS AS MAY ACCRUE FROM THIS DATE.
   ☐ FAILING TO PAY FOR OR PROVIDE ☐ MEDICAL ☐ DENTAL INSURANCE AS REQUIRED.
   ☐ OTHER VIOLATION: _____

SIGNATURE OF
☐ PLAINTIFF OR AUTHORIZED REPRESENTATIVE (IF REPRESENTATIVE, GIVE TITLE)
☐ DPW REPRESENTATIVE

DATE

TO THE ABOVE NAMED DEFENDANT:

YOU ARE HEREBY ORDERED TO APPEAR AT THE DISTRICT COURT SHOWN ABOVE, ON THE DATE AND TIME NOTED, TO SHOW CAUSE WHY YOU SHOULD NOT BE HELD IN CIVIL CONTEMPT, THE PENALTY FOR WHICH MAY BE A JAIL SENTENCE. FAILURE TO APPEAR AS ORDERED MAY RESULT IN THE ISSUANCE OF A WARRANT FOR YOUR ARREST.

FIRST JUSTICE
WITNESS | SIGNATURE OF CLERK-MAGISTRATE OR DESIGNEE | DATE OF ISSUE

COURT USE ONLY:
SERVICE BY MAIL BY CLERK MAGISTRATE'S OFFICE:
☐ COMPLAINT AND SUMMONS MAILED BY REGULAR MAIL ON: _____
☐ COMPLAINT AND SUMMONS MAILED BY CERTIFIED MAIL ON: _____

IF OFFICER SERVICE REQUIRED:
I CERTIFY THAT I SERVED THIS COMPLAINT AND SUMMONS BY:
☐ DELIVERING A COPY PERSONALLY TO THE DEFENDANT.
☐ LEAVING A COPY AT THE DWELLING HOUSE OR USUAL PLACE OF ABODE OF THE DEFENDANT WITH A PERSON OF SUITABLE AGE AND DISCRETION RESIDING THEREIN.
☐ I WAS UNABLE TO MAKE SERVICE BECAUSE: _____

DATE OF SERVICE | SIGNATURE OF PERSON MAKING SERVICE | TITLE OF PERSON MAKING SERVICE

COMPLAINT AND SUMMONS FOR PATERNITY/SUPPORT: G.L. C. 209C

COMPLAINT AND SUMMONS FOR PATERNITY/SUPPORT: G.L. c. 209C	TRIAL COURT OF MASSACHUSETTS District Court Department	Docket No.

Court division: **Court address:**

Plaintiff's name, address, zip:

Phone (day):

If complaint is being filed/signed by DPW on behalf of plaintiff, list office below.

Defendant's name, address, zip:

Phone (home):   (work):
Social security number:
Employer's name and address (if known):

The above-named and undersigned plaintiff hereby states that: (Check #1 or 2, and/or 3)

1. ☐ paternity has been adjudicated;

2. ☐ the defendant is the father of the child(ren) named below; WHEREFORE the plaintiff requests an adjudication of paternity;

3. ☐ the child(ren) named below are in need of and entitled to support from the defendant under the provisions of c. 209C, and that the defendant has refused or neglected to provide fair and reasonable support; WHEREFORE the plaintiff requests an order for support and/or for reimbursement thereof directed to said defendant as shall be deemed fair and reasonable, and for such other and further relief as the law provides.

SIGNED: DATE:

LIST DEPENDENT CHILDREN FOR WHOM YOU SEEK PATERNITY FINDING, SUPPORT, OR INSURANCE:

Name   Date of birth   List any medical insurance in effect

NOTICE TO DEFENDANT: You are being sued for paternity and/or support by the plaintiff. You are directed to appear for trial of this matter on the date and time noted to the right. If you fail to appear, the court may issue a warrant for your arrest, or may proceed to hear the case and enter an order for you to pay support as requested by this complaint. You have the right to bring an attorney with you to the hearing.

DATE AND TIME OF TRIAL:

_____ at _____ AM PM
(Date)   (Time)

REPORT TO:

___ Probation department

___ Clerk's office

Both the plaintiff and defendant must appear at the court listed above the date and time specified to the left.

Justice:	Date of issue:	Clerk-magistrate or designee:

COMPLAINT AND SUMMONS FOR SUPPORT--G.L. C. 209C, § 32F

COMPLAINT AND SUMMONS FOR SUPPORT— G.L. c. 209, § 32F	TRIAL COURT OF MASSACHUSETTS District Court Department	Docket No.
Court division:	Court address:	

Plaintiff's name, address, zip: Phone (day): Do you have health insurance? ____ If complaint is being filed and/or signed by DPW on behalf of plaintiff, list office address below.	Defendant's name, address, zip: Phone (Home): (Work): Social security number: Employer's name and address (if known):

The above-named and undersigned plaintiff hereby states that the plaintiff and/or the dependent(s) named below are in need of and entitled to support from the above-named defendant under the provisions of G. L. c. 209, § 32F, and that the defendant has refused or neglected to provide fair and reasonable support; WHEREFORE, the plaintiff requests an order for support and/or for reimbursement thereof, directed to said defendant, as shall be deemed to be fair and reasonable, and for such other and further relief as the law provides.

SIGNED: DATE:

LIST DEPENDENT CHILDREN FOR WHOM YOU ARE SEEKING SUPPORT, OR MEDICAL INSURANCE:

Name	Date of birth	List any medical insurance in effect

NOTICE TO DEFENDANT: You are being sued for support by the above-named plaintiff. You are directed to appear for trial of this matter on the date and time noted to the right. If you fail to appear, the court may issue a warrant for your arrest, or may proceed to hear the case and enter an order for you to pay support as requested by this complaint. You have the right to bring an attorney with you to the hearing.	DATE AND TIME OF TRIAL: _____ at _____ AM (Date) (Time) PM REPORT TO: ____ Probation department ____ Clerk's office	Both the plaintiff and defendant must appear at the court listed above on date and time specified to the left.
Justice:	Date of issue:	Clerk–magistrate or designee:

Rule 210. Interim Rule for Incoming Interstate Income Withholding Actions

(a) Scope and Applicability of Rule. This rule governs procedure in all cases involving requests for interstate income withholding received by Massachusetts pursuant to G.L. c. 119A, s. 8, and c. 273A, s. 10, paragraph 4 in which a request for interstate income withholding has been made by a party in another state.

(b) Definitions. As used herein, the term "obligor" shall mean a person who has been ordered by a court or agency of competent jurisdiction in another state to pay support, and whose source of income in Massachusetts is the subject of a request for interstate income withholding under G.L. c. 273A, s. 10. The term "obligee" shall refer to a person or agency owed support pursuant to the terms of an existing order of another state and who has made a request for interstate income withholding pursuant to G.L. c. 119A, s. 8 or any other applicable provision of law. Any clear communication from another state which meets the requirements of c. 119A, s. 8 shall be deemed a request for interstate income withholding and shall be accepted for filing. As used herein, the term "IV–D agency" shall mean the Massachusetts Department of Revenue.

(c) Fees and Costs. The court shall not charge the obligee an entry fee or a fee for any other costs associated with the conduct of the matter.

(d) Notice to Obligor. Every obligor shall be notified of the filing of a request for interstate income withholding and of the date, time and place scheduled for the hearing, and shall receive a copy of the foreign order or judgment for support upon which the request is based, together with said notice.

Notice shall be sent by certified mail, return receipt requested, and also by separate first-class mail. Such certified mail notice shall be sufficient, although unclaimed or refused by the obligor, provided that the first-class mail notice is not returned to the sender undelivered. No additional service shall be required for any reason if notice by mail, in accordance with this section, appears to have been valid. In individual cases, if service by mail cannot be accomplished, the court may provide for any other means of service as is deemed necessary.

If the case was forwarded to the court by the IV–D agency pursuant to G.L. c. 119A, s. 8, the court shall provide the obligor's notice to the agency, to be served by the agency upon the obligor in accordance with G.L. c. 273A, s. 10 and the provisions of this rule. If the case was not forwarded by the IV–D agency, the clerk's office shall itself notify the obligor.

(e) Trials and Orders.

(1) *Time Goals for Orders.* Whether or not the obligor appears for the hearing, it shall be the goal of the court to conduct the hearing and to enter an order for support, if appropriate under the facts of the case pursuant to G.L. c. 273A, s. 10, para. 4 and if valid service has been made, within 45 days from the date of receipt by the court of the request for interstate income withholding.

(2) *Failure of an Obligor to Appear for the Hearing.* If it appears that valid notice of the hearing date was sent to the obligor in accordance with paragraph (d) and if the obligor fails to appear for the hearing, the court shall enter an order for income withholding if it finds that the factors and conditions set forth in G.L. c. 273A, s. 10, para. 4 obtain.

(3) *Orders.* The clerk shall promptly enter the income assignment order on the docket, together with the date of such entry, and shall promptly complete and give a copy of such order to each party. Such order shall be given to the obligor in-hand while the obligor is before the court, or, if the obligor does not appear, by first class mail. If the case was forwarded to the court by the IV–D agency pursuant to G.L. c. 119A, s. 8, the court shall provide the obligee's copy of the order to the agency. If the case was not forwarded by the IV–D agency, the clerk's office shall send a copy of the order directly to the obligee by first class mail.

(4) *Records.* The clerk shall perform such record-keeping relative to requests for interstate income withholding and the entry of orders under G.L. c. 273A, s. 10 as may be prescribed by the administrative justice.

Adopted July 28, 1987, effective January 1, 1987.

Rule 211. Recording of Court Proceedings

A. Official Recordings.

1. *When Required.* In all divisions of the District Court Department and in the Boston Municipal Court Department, all courtroom proceedings, including arraignments in criminal and juvenile delinquency cases, shall be recorded electronically, subject to the availability and functioning of appropriate recording devices, except that the following may but need not be recorded: (a) the call of the list and similar matters of an administrative nature; (b) proceedings that are being recorded by a court reporter appointed by the court; and (c) proceedings conducted by a magistrate other than a judge.

2. *Logging.* During every proceeding which is required to be recorded, the clerk shall: (a) announce clearly the name of the case and its docket number at the beginning of the proceeding; and (b) note on the case papers or in a separate log the number of the tape reel and the index numbers representing the beginning and end points of the proceeding.

3. *Counsel's Responsibility.* Counsel shall be responsible for assisting in the creation of an audible record by properly using the microphones provided. Counsel shall speak with sufficient clarity and in sufficient proximity to the microphones to ensure an audible record, and shall be responsible for requesting the judge, when necessary, to instruct other counsel, witnesses or others as to the proper use of the microphones in order to ensure an audible record.

4. *Preservation of Tapes.* The clerk-magistrate shall preserve for at least two and one-half years the original recording of: (a) any trial, evidentiary hearing, guilty plea or admission to sufficient facts in a criminal or juvenile delinquency case that was presided over by a judge; and (b) any trial or evidentiary hearing presided over by a judge in a care and protection matter. The clerk-magistrate shall preserve all other original recordings for at least one year.

When it appears to a party that an original recording should be preserved for a longer period for purposes of appeal, he or she shall be responsible for bringing a motion requesting any judge of the court to so order. Such a motion may be brought ex parte. The clerk-magistrate shall preserve an original recording for such longer period as a judge, acting upon motion or sua sponte, shall direct.

5. *Access to Cassette Copies.*

(a) Open Proceedings. Any person, whether or not a party, shall be permitted to obtain a cassette copy of an original recording, or any portion thereof, of any proceeding which was open to the public, unless the record of such proceeding has been sealed or impounded.

(b) Closed Proceedings. The original recording of a proceeding which was not open to the public, or of a proceeding whose record has been sealed or impounded, shall be deemed to be impounded and a cassette copy of the original recording, or any portion thereof, shall be made available only in accordance with the following provisions:

(i) Cassette Copies of Closed Proceedings for Purposes of Appeal. Counsel for any party, or any party who has entered an appearance pro se, shall be permitted to obtain a cassette copy of such a proceeding upon certifying that such cassette copy will be used solely for an appeal, or to determine whether to claim an appeal, in the same matter. Unless the judge who presided over the proceeding has ordered otherwise, the clerk-magistrate shall provide such cassette copy upon such certification without requiring a judge's approval of the request.

(ii) Cassette Copies of Closed Proceedings for Other Purposes. A cassette copy of such a proceeding may be made available to other persons or for other purposes only with the approval of the judge who presided over the proceeding or, if that judge is unavailable for an extended period or the proceeding was conducted by a magistrate other than a judge, any judge of the court. Any such request shall be accompanied by an affidavit, setting forth the reason for the request and the specific use to be made of the cassette copy, and shall be served on all parties to the proceeding. Any other party or interested person may file a statement in support of or in opposition to such a request. A judge may determine such a request with or without hearing wherever he or she is then sitting. A judge may permit access subject to appropriate restrictions upon the use and dissemination of the cassette copy of such proceeding.

(c) Ordering Cassette Copies. A request for a cassette copy shall be filed with the clerk-magistrate on a form prescribed by the Chief Justices of the District Court Department and the Boston Municipal Court Department for their respective departments. In order that multiple cassette copies may be made simultaneously whenever possible, any person making such a request regarding a proceeding that is presently pending on appeal shall certify that he has notified all other parties of his request.

The cost of a cassette copy shall be as established by the Chief Administrative Justice of the Trial Court pursuant to G.L. c. 262, s. 4B. The clerk-magistrate may require prepayment of all or some portion of such cost. There shall be no cost for a cassette copy produced for the use of the court, the Attorney General's office, a district attorney's office, any other agency of the Commonwealth, a police prosecutor, or a party represented by an attorney provided by the Committee for Public Counsel Services. General Laws c. 261, ss. 27A–27G shall apply to any request on behalf of an indigent party who is not represented by an attorney provided by the Committee for Public Counsel Services, and in such case the cost of a cassette copy shall be deemed an "extra cost" as defined in s. 27A.

6. *Impermissible Uses.* No cassette copy shall be used for a commercial purpose, for public or private entertainment or amusement, or for any other purpose detrimental to the administration of justice. No cassette copy shall be duplicated or tampered with. No cassette copy shall be erased, nor its labels removed or defaced, while the matter is pending in any court, or is subject to direct appellate review. Any cassette copy which is thereafter erased shall be erased in its entirety.

Any further dissemination of the cassette copy of a closed proceeding, or its contents, is permissible only: (a) for the purposes for which access was permitted; (b) subject to all provisions of law and court rules governing the records of such closed proceedings; and (c) subject to any additional restrictions with regard to its use which have been prescribed by the judge permitting access.

Any person requesting a cassette copy shall take all reasonable precautions to assure compliance with the requirements of this rule, including notifying anyone permitted to use the cassette copy of such requirements. Any person violating any such requirement shall be subject to appropriate sanctions, including contempt proceedings.

B. Unofficial Recordings.

1. *Covert Recording Forbidden.* No person shall make any electronic recording in any courtroom, hearing room, office, chambers or lobby of a judge or magistrate without prior authorization from a judge or magistrate then having immediate supervision over such place.

2. *Recording by a Party.* Upon application to the judge or magistrate presiding over a proceeding which is not being recorded by a sound recording device under the control of the court or by a court reporter appointed by the court, any party shall be permitted to record such proceeding electronically. Other parties to the proceedings shall be given reasonable access to review and copy any such recording.

3. *Recording by the News Media.* The recording by the news media of a proceeding open to the public is governed by the provisions of Supreme Judicial Court Rule [1.19].

Adopted December 31, 1987, effective February 1, 1988.

FORM DC–AO–2. CASSETTE COPY ORDER FORM

CASSETTE COPY ORDER FORM	COURT	ORDER NUMBER	Trial Court of Massachusetts District Court Department

PART I — TO BE COMPLETED BY PERSON PLACING ORDER

NAME, ADDRESS AND ZIP CODE OF PERSON PLACING ORDER

NAME OF CASE

DOCKET NUMBER OF CASE

NUMBER OF COPIES WANTED BY THIS PERSON ☐ 1 ☐ 2 ☐ OTHER

DATE(S) OF RECORDING(S) WANTED

MOST SERIOUS CHARGE, IF CRIMINAL, OTHERWISE, SUBJECT OF PROCEEDING

Copies are for: ☐ 2-Track Cassette Machine (1-7/8 IPS)

☐ 4-Track Cassette Machine (15/16 IPS)

Proceedings are recorded on 4 separate tracks. The enhanced track separation available on 4-track copies will facilitate more accurate transcription. However, 4-track copies require a special 4-track cassette machine, and cannot be played on an ordinary (2-track) cassette player. By Trial Court policy, copies made for transcription on appeal will automatically be made in 4-track.

NATURE OF PROCEEDING

☐ CRIMINAL BENCH TRIAL
☐ CRIMINAL JURY TRIAL
☐ PROBABLE CAUSE HEARING

☐ CRIMINAL SHOW CAUSE HEARING
☐ CMVI HEARING
☐ ABUSE PREVENTION ORDER

☐ DELINQUENCY
☐ CIVIL TRIAL
☐ OTHER (specify): _____

Is this proceeding presently pending on appeal? ☐ YES ☐ NO

If yes, in order that multiple cassette copies may be made simultaneously whenever possible,

☐ I certify that I have notified all other parties of this request. (The green copy of this form may be used for this purpose.)

If proceeding was not open to the public or its record has been sealed or impounded: I certify that I have entered an appearance in this matter as:

☐ counsel for_____, a party,

☐ a party appearing pro se,

and that this cassette copy will be used solely for an appeal, or to determine whether to appeal, in the same matter.
(Copies of closed proceedings are available to other persons or for other purposes only upon motion.)

I AGREE TO OBSERVE THE RESTRICTIONS ON THE USE OF SUCH CASSETTE COPIES FOUND IN DISTRICT COURT SPECIAL RULE 211 (see over).

X_____
SIGNATURE OF PERSON PLACING ORDER   DATE ORDER PLACED

PART II — TO BE COMPLETED BY CLERK-MAGISTRATE'S OFFICE

TAPE NO.	BEGINNING INDEX NO.	ENDING INDEX NO.	JUDGE PRESIDING	DATE RECORDED	SPECIAL INSTRUCTIONS OR COMMENTS
....	....	....	....	....	
....	....	....	....	....	
....	....	....	....	....	
....	....	....	....	....	
....	....	....	....	....	

Request will be returned if tape and index numbers are not supplied.

COURT EMPLOYEE RECEIVING ORDER

COMMENTS

DATE ORDER RECEIVED   DATE ORDER SENT TO AODC

COST WAIVED FOR:
☐ JUDGE ☐ D.A. ☐ POLICE PROSECUTOR
☐ ATTY. PROVIDED BY CPCS ☐ G.L. c. 261, §§ 27A-G
☐ OTHER (specify): _____
☐ If more than one copy requested: Person placing order has been informed that only one copy is provided cost-waived, and has agreed to pay for the additional copies desired.

PART III — TO BE COMPLETED BY THE ADMINISTRATIVE OFFICE OF THE DISTRICT COURT

AODC RECEIPT STAMP

COMMENTS

DATE RETURNED TO COURT   BY

COST
$, plus postage

DC-AO-2 (5-95)   SEE INSTRUCTIONS ON BACK OF THIS FORM

INSTRUCTIONS

Instructions to person placing order: Fill in Part I of this form. Use a separate form for each case and for each person requesting a cassette copy. If the proceeding is pending on appeal, you must notify all other parties of your request so that multiple copies may be made simultaneously whenever possible. (You may use the **green** copy of this form for that purpose, or photocopy it if there is more than one other party.) Present the other four parts of this form, with carbons intact, to the clerk-magistrate's office.

Instructions to clerk-magistrate's office: Check that Part I has been properly completed, and fill in Part II. Keep the **pink** copy of the form in your pending file, give the **blue** copy to the person placing the order, and discard the **green** copy if it is not needed to notify other parties. Send the **white** and the **yellow** copies, with the carbon between them intact, to the Administrative Office of the District Court, along with the original recording. Multiple requests for the same recording should be clipped together. The white copy will be returned to you with the cassette(s), and should then be filed with the case papers.

Excerpts from District Court Special Rule 211
RECORDING OF COURT PROCEEDINGS

(A)(3)   *Counsel's responsibility.* Counsel shall be responsible for assisting in the creation of an audible record by properly using the microphones provided. Counsel shall speak with sufficient clarity and in sufficient proximity to the microphones to ensure an audible record, and shall be responsible for requesting the judge, when necessary, to instruct other counsel, witnesses or others as to the proper use of the microphones in order to ensure an audible record.

(A)(5)(c)   *Open proceedings.* Any person, whether or not a party, shall be permitted to obtain a cassette copy of . . . any proceeding which was open to the public, unless the record of such proceeding has been sealed or impounded.

(A)(5)(b)   *Closed proceedings.* The original recording of a proceeding which was not open to the public, or of a proceeding whose record has been sealed or impounded, shall be deemed to be impounded and a cassette copy . . . shall be made available only in accordance with the following provisions: *(i) Cassette copies of closed proceedings for purposes of appeal.* Counsel for any party, or any party who has entered an appearance pro se, shall be permitted to obtain a cassette copy of such a proceeding upon certifying that such cassette copy will be used solely for an appeal, or to determine whether to claim an appeal, in the same matter. Unless the judge who presided over the proceeding has ordered otherwise, the clerk-magistrate shall provide such cassette copy upon such certification without requiring a judge's approval of the request. *(ii) Cassette copies of closed proceedings for other purposes.* A cassette copy of such a proceeding may be made available to other persons or for other purposes only with the approval of the judge who presided over the proceeding or, if that judge is unavailable for an extended period or the proceeding was conducted by a magistrate other than a judge, any judge of the court. Any such request shall be accompanied by an affidavit, setting forth the reason for the request and the specific use to be made of the cassette copy, and shall be served on all parties to the proceeding. Any other party or interested person may file a statement in support of or in opposition to such a request. A judge may determine such a request with or without hearing wherever he or she is then sitting. A judge may permit access subject to appropriate restrictions upon the use and dissemination of the cassette copy of such proceeding.

(A)(5)(c)   *Ordering cassette copies.* . . . In order that multiple cassette copies may be made simultaneously whenever possible, any person making such a request regarding a proceeding that is presently pending on appeal shall certify that he has notified all other parties of his request.

The cost of a cassette copy shall be as established by the Chief Administrative Justice of the Trial Court pursuant to G.L. c. 262, § 4B. The clerk-magistrate may require prepayment of all or some portion of such cost. There shall be no cost for a cassette copy produced for the use of the court, the Attorney General's office, a district attorney's office, any other agency of the Commonwealth, a police prosecutor, or a party represented by an attorney provided by the Committee for Public Counsel Services. General Laws c. 261, §§ 27A-27G shall apply to any request on behalf of an indigent party who is not represented by an attorney provided by the Committee for Public Counsel Services, and in such case the cost of a cassette copy shall be deemed an "extra cost" as defined in § 27A. . . .

(A)(6)   *Impermissible uses.* No cassette copy shall be used for a commercial purpose, for public or private entertainment or amusement, or for any other purpose detrimental to the administration of justice. No cassette copy shall be duplicated or tampered with. No cassette copy shall be erased, nor its labels removed or defaced, while the matter is pending in any court, or is subject to direct appellate review. Any cassette copy which is thereafter erased shall be erased in its entirety.

Any further dissemination of the cassette copy of a closed proceeding, or its contents, is permissible only: (a) for the purposes for which access was permitted; (b) subject to all provisions of law and court rules governing the records of such closed proceedings; and (c) subject to any additional restrictions with regard to its use which have been prescribed by the judge permitting access.

Any person requesting a cassette copy shall take all reasonable precautions to assure compliance with the requirements of this rule, including notifying anyone permitted to use the cassette copy of such requirements. Any person violating any such requirement shall be subject to appropriate sanctions, including contempt proceedings.

Rule 212. Care and Protection Cases

(a) Service of Summons. A summons to a party or a witness in a care and protection case filed pursuant to G.L. c. 119, § 24 may be served by any person authorized to serve civil or criminal process, either by delivering a copy thereof to the individual personally, or by leaving a copy thereof at the individual's last and usual place of abode. Alternatively, a judge may specially appoint a probation officer, court officer or any other person to serve a summons in such manner. Such a summons may also be served by the clerk-magistrate by mailing a copy thereof to the individual's last known address, if a judge has so directed.

(b) Service of Precept. A precept in a care and protection case may be served by any person authorized to serve civil or criminal process. In addition, or in the alternative, a judge may specially appoint a probation officer, court officer or any other person to serve a precept.

(c) Pretrial Conference. All parties shall participate in a pretrial conference, to be scheduled by the court, prior to the commencement of the adjudicatory hearing. At the conference, counsel shall be prepared to present an estimate of the time needed for trial, shall indicate the number and identity of all witnesses who are expected to testify, and shall also specify the nature of any exhibits which are expected to be offered into evidence. Counsel shall also be prepared to propose stipulations as to uncontested facts, admissibility of evidence, or legal conclusions which may be drawn by the judge.

(d) Adjudicatory Hearing. The parties shall be prepared to begin the adjudicatory hearing at any point after two weeks from the submission of the investigator's report, as directed by the court.

(e) Access to Records. In order to facilitate the trial and appeal of such matters, an attorney of record for any party may inspect and obtain a copy of any portion of the court record of the case (including the investigator's report), except for any portions of the court record which the judge has ordered impounded or otherwise restricted. In order to protect the privacy of the child and the parents, (1) the child's parents themselves and any other persons requesting access to the record of the case shall be granted such access only pursuant to an order by the court; (2) an attorney for a party may permit his or her client to view the attorney's copy, but shall not duplicate or distribute the copy to the client or to any other person, except upon court order; and (3) any other person (including a party) whom the court permits to receive a copy of any portion of the court record shall not further duplicate or distribute it, except upon court order.

Adopted May 30, 1990, effective August 1, 1990.

FORM DC–CP 1. CARE AND PROTECTION INTAKE SHEET

CARE AND PROTECTION INTAKE SHEET	Trial Court of Massachusetts District Court Department	COURT USE ONLY	DOCKET NUMBER

DATE	COURT DIVISION	☐ EMERGENCY C & P	☐ NON-EMERGENCY C & P

NAME, ADDRESS AND ZIP CODE OF PETITIONER (If filed on behalf of agency, use agency address.)   PETITIONER'S DAYTIME TELEPHONE NO.
(   )

NAME, ADDRESS, ZIP CODE OF MOTHER	NAME, ADDRESS, ZIP CODE OF FATHER

NAME, ADDRESS, ZIP CODE OF GUARDIAN OR CUSTODIAN (IF ANY)	NAME, ADDRESS, ZIP CODE OF ADDITIONAL INTERESTED PARTY (specify)

CHILD(REN) ALLEGED TO BE IN NEED OF CARE AND PROTECTION

CHILD'S FULL LEGAL NAME	ADDRESS	DATE OF BIRTH	SEX
A.			☐M ☐F
B.			☐M ☐F
C.			☐M ☐F
D.			☐M ☐F
E.			☐M ☐F
F.			☐M ☐F

INSTRUCTIONS TO PETITIONER

1. Please type or print all requested information. Do not complete shaded areas.
2. The "Court Division" is the name of the court in which you are filing this petition. **IMPORTANT:** Each child named in a Care and Protection petition must, **at the time of filing**, be physically present within the jurisdiction of the court.
3. Please list children in order of age, listing the youngest as "Child A," the next youngest as "Child B," etc.
4. Use the blank space above to list any additional children, parties or information relating to this petition. Use additional intake sheet, if necessary.
5. File this form, intact, with the Clerk-Magistrate of the court.
6. The Clerk's office will return Part 3 of this form to you with the docket number indicated at the top of the form.

DC-CP 1 (1/90)

CLERK'S COPY

INSTRUCTIONS TO CLERK-MAGISTRATE'S OFFICE FOR COMPLETING THIS FORM

After the petitioner has supplied all requested information, complete the shaded areas at the top of the form. Return Part 3 to the petitioner. Distribute Part 2 to the court-appointed investigator, together with the notice of the appointment (Part 4 of Form DC-CP-2), once an investigator has been appointed. Retain Part 1 in the case file.

FORM DC–CP 2. PETITION FOR CARE AND PROTECTION

PETITION FOR CARE AND PROTECTION	Trial Court of Massachusetts District Court Department	DOCKET NUMBER
NAME OF PETITIONER	AGENCY REPRESENTED	

I, the above-named petitioner, state under the penalties of perjury that I have reasonable cause to believe that the child(ren) named below, being under eighteen years of age, is (are) in need of care and protection, in that said child(ren) is (are) without necessary and proper physical, educational or moral care or discipline, or growing up under conditions or circumstances damaging to sound character development, or lacking proper attention of parent, guardian with care and custody, or custodian, or because said child(ren)'s parents, guardian or custodian is (are) unwilling, incompetent or unavailable to provide any such care, discipline or attention.

CHILD(REN) NAMED IN PETITION

CHILD'S FULL LEGAL NAME	ADDRESS	DATE OF BIRTH	SEX
A.			☐ M ☐ F
B.			☐ M ☐ F
C.			☐ M ☐ F
D.			☐ M ☐ F
E.			☐ M ☐ F
F.			☐ M ☐ F

WHEREFORE, the Petitioner requests that the court cause said child(ren) to be brought before this court, summons the person having custody and control of said child(ren) to appear, and determine whether said child(ren) should be committed to the custody of the Department of Social Services, or other appropriate order made.

SIGNATURE OF PETITIONER X	DATE AND TIME OF HEARING _____ AT _____ DATE TIME
SWORN TO BEFORE CLERK–MAGISTRATE/ASST. CLERK ON (DATE)	NAME AND ADDRESS OF COURT DIVISION
FIRST JUSTICE	

DC–CP 2 (1/90)

CLERK'S COPY

NOTIFICATION TO DSS OF CARE AND PROTECTION PETITION	Trial Court of Massachusetts District Court Department	DOCKET NUMBER
NAME OF PETITIONER	AGENCY REPRESENTED	

To the Department of Social Services:

You are hereby notified that a petition for care and protection has been filed in this court by the petitioner named above, on behalf of the child or children named below.

CHILD(REN) NAMED IN PETITION			
CHILD'S FULL LEGAL NAME	ADDRESS	DATE OF BIRTH	SEX
A.			☐ M ☐ F
B.			☐ M ☐ F
C.			☐ M ☐ F
D.			☐ M ☐ F
E.			☐ M ☐ F
F.			☐ M ☐ F

This case is scheduled for hearing on the date and time indicated below.

	DATE AND TIME OF HEARING
	_____ AT _____
	DATE TIME
	NAME AND ADDRESS OF COURT DIVISION
FIRST JUSTICE	

Additional Instructions: (if completed):

You are directed to bring the child(ren) named in this petition to this court for identification on _____ at _____.

DATE   TIME

BY THE COURT

X _____

SIGNATURE OF JUSTICE, CLERK-MAGISTRATE, OR ASST. CLERK

DC–CP 2 (1/90)   DSS NOTICE

CARE AND PROTECTION PRECEPT	Trial Court of Massachusetts District Court Department	DOCKET NUMBER
NAME OF PETITIONER	AGENCY REPRESENTED	

To any person authorized to serve civil or criminal process or specially appointed by the Court:

A petition for care and protection has been filed in this court by the above named petitioner, on behalf of the child or children under the age of eighteen named below.

THEREFORE, you are hereby commanded in the name of the Commonwealth of Massachusetts to take and bring said child or children before the juvenile session of this court.

CHILD(REN) TO WHOM PRECEPT APPLIES (Clerk–Magistrate: *Cross out names to whom precept does not apply*)

CHILD'S FULL LEGAL NAME	ADDRESS	DATE OF BIRTH	SEX
A.			☐ M ☐ F
B.			☐ M ☐ F
C.			☐ M ☐ F
D.			☐ M ☐ F
E.			☐ M ☐ F
F.			☐ M ☐ F

The child or children named above is or are required to appear at this court for identification or other proceeding:

☐ forthwith.
(or)
☐ on _____ at _____
　　　　　DATE　　　　　TIME

SIGNATURE OF CLERK-MAGISTRATE OR ASST. CLERK DATE	NAME AND ADDRESS OF COURT DIVISION
FIRST JUSTICE WITNESS:	

RETURN OF SERVICE

I have taken the above-named child or children and now have ☐ him ☐ her ☐ them in court as herein directed.

DATE	SIGNATURE OF PERSON SERVING PRECEPT	PRINTED NAME OF PERSON SERVING PRECEPT	DEPARTMENT

DC–CP 2 (1/90)

PRECEPT

AUTHORITY TO INVESTIGATE CARE AND PROTECTION MATTER	Trial Court of Massachusetts District Court Department	DOCKET NUMBER
NAME OF PETITIONER	AGENCY REPRESENTED	

NAME AND ADDRESS OF INVESTIGATOR

CHILD(REN) NAMED IN PETITION

CHILD'S FULL LEGAL NAME	ADDRESS	DATE OF BIRTH	SEX
A.			☐ M ☐ F
B.			☐ M ☐ F
C.			☐ M ☐ F
D.			☐ M ☐ F
E.			☐ M ☐ F
F.			☐ M ☐ F

To the Investigator Named Above:

Pursuant to the provisions of General Laws, chapter 119, section 24, you have been appointed to conduct an investigation into the conditions affecting the child(ren) named above and to make a report under oath to the court of such investigation.

All medical, hospital, educational and other relevant records of the above-named child(ren) shall be made available for your review. Your report must be filed at the Clerk-Magistrate's office on or before the report due date indicated below.

DATE OF APPOINTMENT	NAME AND ADDRESS OF COURT DIVISION
BY THE COURT:	
X_____	
SIGNATURE OF JUSTICE, CLERK-MAGISTRATE OR ASST. CLERK	

SPECIAL INSTRUCTIONS—The Court Has Ordered:

1. The investigator shall file the report on or before:_____
2. Upon filing of the investigator's report, the Clerk-Magistrate shall give copies of the report to the following: Counsel ☐ yes ☐ no;   Any party proceeding pro se ☐ yes ☐ no
3. Other:

DC–CP 2 (1/90)

INVESTIGATION

PETITION FOR CARE AND PROTECTION	Trial Court of Massachusetts District Court Department	DOCKET NUMBER
NAME OF PETITIONER	AGENCY REPRESENTED	

I, the above-named petitioner, state under the penalties of perjury that I have reasonable cause to believe that the child(ren) named below, being under eighteen years of age, is (are) in need of care and protection, in that said child(ren) is (are) without necessary and proper physical, educational or moral care or discipline, or growing up under conditions or circumstances damaging to sound character development, or lacking proper attention of parent, guardian with care and custody, or custodian, or because said child(ren)'s parents, guardian or custodian is (are) unwilling, incompetent or unavailable to provide any such care, discipline or attention.

CHILD(REN) NAMED IN PETITION

CHILD'S FULL LEGAL NAME	ADDRESS	DATE OF BIRTH	SEX
A.			☐ M ☐ F
B.			☐ M ☐ F
C.			☐ M ☐ F
D.			☐ M ☐ F
E.			☐ M ☐ F
F.			☐ M ☐ F

WHEREFORE, the Petitioner requests that the court cause said child(ren) to be brought before this court, summons the person having custody and control of said child(ren) to appear, and determine whether said child(ren) should be committed to the custody of the Department of Social Services, or other appropriate order made.

SIGNATURE OF PETITIONER	DATE AND TIME OF HEARING
X	_____ AT _____
SWORN TO BEFORE CLERK-MAGISTRATE/ASST. CLERK ON (DATE)	DATE TIME
	NAME AND ADDRESS OF COURT DIVISION
FIRST JUSTICE	

DC-CP 2 (1/90)

PROBATION COPY

INSTRUCTIONS TO CLERK–MAGISTRATE'S OFFICE FOR
COMPLETING THIS FORM

Part 1—Petition for Care and Protection. Use the information contained on the completed Care and Protection Intake Sheet (Form DC–CP–1) to complete the Petition for Care and Protection.

In an **emergency** situation in which the petitioner will be appearing immediately before a judge, complete the entire form **except for** the box which indicates the date and time of the next hearing before having the petitioner sign it. After the emergency hearing, fill in the date and time of the next hearing. If the judge has issued an emergency custody order, the next hearing should be held within 72 hours. If the judge has not issued an emergency custody order, the preliminary hearing should take place within 2 weeks.

In a **non-emergency** situation, complete the entire form, including the date and time of the preliminary hearing, before having the petitioner sign it.

Inform the petitioner of the next hearing date before the petitioner leaves the court.

Part 2—Notification to DSS of Care and Protection Petition. After the petition has been fully completed with the next hearing date indicated, distribute Part 2 to the Department of Social Services (DSS), either in-hand or by mail to the local DSS office.

If a DSS representative is to be responsible for bringing the child to court to be identified, this should be noted on the bottom of the form under "Additional Instructions."

Part 3—Care and Protection Precept. If a precept for the child is needed to bring the child before the court, complete the section on Part 3 which indicates when the child is to appear, and forward it to an appropriate process-server. If a precept is not needed, retain in case file for potential future use.

Part 4—Authority to Investigate Care and Protection Matter. Complete Part 4, including Items 1 and 2 under "Special Instructions," and give it to the Investigator upon appointment. Any additional instructions should be noted under Item 3 at the bottom of the page. In all cases, photocopy Part 4 before giving it to the Investigator, and retain the copy in the case file for future reference.

Part 5—Probation copy. Distribute this copy of the petition to the probation department.

SPECIAL RULES OF THE BOSTON MUNICIPAL COURT DEPARTMENT SITTING FOR CIVIL BUSINESS

Effective November 1, 1989

Table of Rules

Rule 300. Times for Holding Pre–Trial Conferences, Trials and Hearings

A. Civil Pre-trial Conferences.—Mondays through Thursdays, commencing at 8:45 a.m.

B. Civil Trials.—Mondays through Fridays, commencing at 9:00 a.m.

C. Summary Process.—Thursdays, commencing at 9:00 a.m.

D. Small Claims.—Mondays, Tuesdays, Thursdays and Fridays commencing at 2:00 p.m.

E. Assessments of Damages after Default Where Hearing Is Required. Wednesdays, commencing at 11:00 a.m.

F. Motions and Other Interlocutory Matters.—Mondays, Tuesdays, Thursdays and Fridays, commencing at 9:00 a.m. (except for motions for leave to make attachments or install keepers, to be heard on Mondays, Tuesdays, Wednesdays and Fridays at the conclusion of the Motion List.)

G. Supplementary Process.—Wednesdays, commencing at 2:00 p.m.

H. Small Claim Jury Appeals.—Mondays, Tuesdays and Thursdays, commencing at 11:00 a.m.

I. Support and Paternity Matters.—Wednesdays, commencing at 10:00 a.m.

For the convenience of the public, there shall be a recess each day between 1:00 p.m. and 2:00 p.m. except as otherwise provided by rule of court, or unless the court from time to time otherwise orders.

Amended effective January 8, 1997.

Rule 301. Pre–Trial Conference Lists, Trial Lists and Motion Lists

A. Civil Trials.

1. *Pre-trial Conferences.* All civil cases (except small claims, summary process and actions entered for the purpose of judicial review of the record), including those remanded from the Superior Court Department, shall be scheduled for pre-trial conference in compliance with Mass.R.Civ.P. 16. The parties must appear at the pre-trial conference with full authorization, including authority to resolve the case. The failure of an appearance by or on behalf of the plaintiff will result in dismissal. The failure of an appearance by or on behalf of the defendant will result in default. Failure of a party to cooperate in the preparation of the pre-trial memorandum will result in sanctions, including, where appropriate, dismissal or default. At the conclusion of each conference, the Conferencer will complete and file with the Clerk's office a Conference Report reciting the results of the pre-trial conference and establishing a firm trial date.

2. *Civil Trial Lists.* Notwithstanding the provisions of Rule 108 of the District/Municipal Courts Supplemental Rules of Civil Procedure, trial lists shall be prepared by the Clerk daily. Separate lists shall be prepared for actions remanded from the Superior Court Department and for actions entered originally in this court.

3. *Civil Actions Transferred for Trial by Superior Court.* All actions transferred for trial by the Superior Court to the Boston Municipal Court Department shall be entered on a docket to be known as the Remand Docket. A separate and distinct number shall be assigned to each action, and while such is being processed by the court, it shall always be referred to in the docket and on the trial list by said number.

4. *Summary Process Actions.* Such actions shall be placed on the general trial list (except during the summer suspension), pursuant to Rule 130 of the District/Municipal Courts Supplemental Rules of Civil Procedure, without notice and without a pre-trial conference.

B. Motion Lists.

1. In order to have a motion or other interlocutory matter placed on the list for hearing, the party requesting such assignment shall, no less than 7 days before the date of assignment so requested, file such motion or other pleading with the clerk, together with a certificate of service of notice thereof on the other party or parties.

2. Notwithstanding the foregoing provisions, the court may, at its discretion, hear motions or other interlocutory matters at such times and upon such notice, if notice is required, and upon such proof of notice, as it may deem reasonable and appropriate.

3. Any motion or other interlocutory matter on the list for hearing may be presented by the moving party or by any other party to the action.

Amended effective January 8, 1997.

Rule 302. Call of Trial and Motion Lists

A. Call of General Trial List. At the opening of court each day, the general trial list of actions assigned for trial on that day shall be called. If any party in such a case is not present, the court may, upon motion of the party or parties present, order the entry of default or dismissal of the action, as the case may be, and if none of the parties is present, the action may be continued generally, unless the court shall otherwise order.

B. Call of List of Remand Actions. At the opening of court each day, the special trial list of actions remanded to this court by the Superior Court pursuant to G.L. c. 231, § 102C shall be called in the session designated therefor. The failure of any party to appear on the date assigned for trial, without just cause, shall result in the immediate entry of (1) a judgment for the defendant where the plaintiff has failed to appear and the defendant has appeared; or (2) a default where the plaintiff has appeared and the defendant has failed to appear; or (3) a dismissal of the action where both parties have failed to appear; unless in any of said events, the court shall order a continuance. Such remanded actions shall not be continued generally. Continuances may be granted by special order of the court only for cause shown, and such continuances shall generally be for short periods, and on such terms as the court may specify.

C. Vacating of Dismissal or Default Entry. A dismissal or default entered pursuant to this rule shall not, unless the court otherwise order, be vacated after the day on which it is entered except (a) by the operation of some condition thereof, (b) by written consent of the parties filed with the clerk and approved by the court, or (c) upon motion supported by affidavit of the facts relied on in the prosecution or defense, notice to the adverse party, and such proof as the court may require that a prosecution or defense is intended in good faith. If judgment has been entered, it may be set aside in accordance with Rule 60(b) of the District/Municipal Courts Rules of Civil Procedure.

Rule 303. Appeals in Workmen's Compensation Cases

When an appeal is taken to this court in a Workmen's Compensation case pursuant to G.L. c. 152, sec. 11, notice thereof shall be mailed by the Clerk forthwith to all interested parties. The appeal shall be assigned for hearing in the 1st Civil Trial Session on the Thursday next following the expiration of seven days from the date of entry of such appeal, or if that Thursday falls on a legal holiday, the said appeal shall be heard on the next succeeding trial day. The date for hearing

of any such appeal shall be included in the notice sent by the Clerk to the interested parties pursuant hereto.

Immediately after the entry of any decree rendered by the Court in such proceedings, an attested copy of such decree shall be sent to all interested parties, including the Industrial Accident Board.

Rule 304. Appeals From Decisions of the Board of Appeal On Motor Vehicle Liability Policies and Bonds

Notice of filing of an appeal in this Court pursuant to G.L. c. 175, sec. 113D shall be mailed by the clerk forthwith to all parties and to the Registrar of Motor Vehicles. The appeal shall be in order for hearing in the Motion Session of this Court on the Friday next following the expiration of seven days from the entry of the appeal. If the date herein provided for hearing of such appeal shall fall on a legal holiday, said appeal shall be heard on the next day on which motions are heard in this Court. The hearing date shall be specified in the notice sent by the clerk pursuant to this rule.

After the hearing, the Court shall make a speedy disposition of the appeal. Within two days after the entry thereof, the clerk shall send an attested copy of the decree to each of the parties and the Commissioner of Insurance.

Rule 305. Clerk's Office

The office of the Clerk of this Court for the conduct of civil business shall be open from 8:30 A.M. to 4:30 P.M. Mondays through Fridays.

The Clerk shall be answerable for all records and papers filed in court or in his office. He shall not, except by specific order of the court, allow any pleadings, agreement of the parties, or any other writing which may be made part of the record, or which is part of any proceeding in this court, to be removed from the files of this court or from his custody by any person other than authorized personnel of the clerk's office subject to his control, and then only for purposes related to the functions of the court or the clerk's office thereof.

Rule 306. Emergency Rule for Civil Support and Paternity Actions

Rule 209 of the Special Rules of the District Court of Massachusetts governs procedure in the Boston Municipal Court.

Rule 307. Interim Rule for Incoming Interstate Income Withholding Actions

Rule 210 of the Special Rules of the District Court of Massachusetts shall govern the procedure in all cases involving requests for interstate income withholding received by Massachusetts pursuant to G.L. c. 119A, § 8 and c. 273A, § 10, paragraph 4 in which a request for interstate income withholding has been made by a party in another state.

Rule 308. Recording of Court Proceedings

A. Official Recordings.

1. *When Required.* In all divisions of the District Court Department and in the Boston Municipal Court Department, all courtroom proceedings, including arraignments in criminal and juvenile delinquency cases, shall be recorded electronical-

ly, subject to the availability and functioning of appropriate recording devices, except that the following may but need not be recorded: (a) the call of the list and similar matters of an administrative nature; (b) proceedings that are being recorded by a court reporter appointed by the court; and (c) proceedings conducted by a magistrate other than a judge.

2. *Logging.* During every proceeding which is required to be recorded, the clerk shall: (a) announce clearly the name of the case and its docket number at the beginning of the proceeding; and (b) note on the case papers or in a separate log the number of the tape reel and the index numbers representing the beginning and end points of the proceeding.

3. *Counsel's Responsibility.* Counsel shall be responsible for assisting in the creation of an audible record by properly using the microphones provided. Counsel shall speak with sufficient clarity and in sufficient proximity to the microphones to ensure an audible record, and shall be responsible for requesting the judge, when necessary, to instruct other counsel, witnesses or others as to the proper use of the microphones in order to ensure an audible record.

4. *Preservation of Tapes.* The clerk-magistrate shall preserve for at least two and one-half years the original recording of: (a) any trial, evidentiary hearing, guilty plea or admission to sufficient facts in a criminal or juvenile delinquency case that was presided over by a judge; and (b) any trial or evidentiary hearing presided over by a judge in a care and protection matter. The clerk-magistrate shall preserve all other original recordings for at least one year.

When it appears to a party that an original recording should be preserved for a longer period for purposes of appeal, he or she shall be responsible for bringing a motion requesting any judge of the court to so order. Such a motion may be brought ex parte. The clerk-magistrate shall preserve an original recording for such longer period as a judge, acting upon motion or sua sponte, shall direct.

5. *Access to Cassette Copies.*

(a) Open Proceedings. Any person whether or not a party, shall be permitted to obtain a cassette copy of an original recording, or any portion thereof, of any proceeding which was open to the public, unless the record of such proceeding has been sealed or impounded.

(b) Closed Proceedings. The original recording of a proceeding which was not open to the public, or of a proceeding whose record has been sealed or impounded, shall be deemed to be impounded and a cassette copy of the original recording, or any portion thereof, shall be made available only in accordance with the following provisions:

(i) Cassette Copies of Closed Proceedings for Purposes of Appeal. Counsel for any party, or any party who has entered an appearance pro se, shall be permitted to obtain a cassette copy of such a proceeding upon certifying that such cassette copy will be used solely for an appeal, or to determine whether to claim an appeal, in the same matter. Unless the judge who presided over the proceeding has ordered otherwise, the clerk-magistrate shall provide such cassette copy upon such certification without requiring a judge's approval of the request.

(ii) Cassette Copies of Closed Proceedings for Other Purposes. A cassette copy of such a proceeding may be

made available to other persons or for other purposes only with the approval of the judge who presided over the proceeding or, if that judge is unavailable for an extended period or the proceeding was conducted by a magistrate other than a judge, any judge of the court. Any such request shall be accompanied by an affidavit, setting forth the reason for the request and the specific use to be made of the cassette copy, and shall be served on all parties to the proceeding. Any other party or interested person may file a statement in support of or in opposition to such a request. A judge may determine such a request with or without hearing wherever he or she is then sitting. A judge may permit access subject to appropriate restrictions upon the use and dissemination of the cassette copy of such proceeding.

(c) Ordering Cassette Copies. A request for a cassette copy shall be filed with the clerk-magistrate on a form prescribed by the Chief Justices of the District Court Department and the Boston Municipal Court Department for their respective departments. In order that multiple cassette copies may be made simultaneously whenever possible, any person making such a request regarding a proceeding that is presently pending on appeal shall certify that he has notified all other parties of his request.

The cost of a cassette copy shall be as established by the Chief Administrative Justice of the Trial Court pursuant to G.L. c. 262, s. 4B. The clerk-magistrate may require prepayment of all or some portion of such cost. There shall be no cost for a cassette copy produced for the use of the court, the Attorney General's office, a district attorney's office, any other agency of the Commonwealth, a police prosecutor, or a party represented by an attorney provided by the Committee for Public Counsel Services. General Laws c. 261, ss. 27A–27G shall apply to any request on behalf of an indigent party who is not represented by an attorney provided by the Committee for Public Counsel Services, and in such case the cost of a cassette copy shall be deemed an "extra cost" as defined in s. 27A.

6. *Impermissible Uses.* No cassette copy shall be used for a commercial purpose, for public or private entertainment or amusement, or for any other purpose detrimental to the administration of justice. No cassette copy shall be duplicated or tampered with. No cassette copy shall be erased, nor its labels removed or defaced, while the matter is pending in any court, or is subject to direct appellate review. Any cassette copy which is thereafter erased shall be erased in its entirety.

Any further dissemination of the cassette copy of a closed proceeding, or its contents, is permissible only: (a) for the purposes for which access was permitted; (b) subject to all provisions of law and court rules governing the records of such closed proceedings; and (c) subject to any additional restrictions with regard to its use which have been prescribed by the judge permitting access.

Any person requesting a cassette copy shall take all reasonable precautions to assure compliance with the requirements of this rule, including notifying anyone permitted to use the cassette copy of such requirements. Any person violating any such requirement shall be subject to appropriate sanctions, including contempt proceedings.

B. Unofficial Recordings.

1. *Covert Recording Forbidden.* No person shall make any electronic recording in any courtroom, hearing room, office, chambers or lobby of a judge or magistrate without prior authorization from the judge or magistrate then having immediate supervision over such place.

2. *Recording by a Party.* Upon application to the judge or magistrate presiding over a proceeding which is not being recorded by a sound recording device under the control of the court or by a court reporter appointed by the court, any party shall be permitted to record such proceeding electronically. Other parties to the proceeding shall be given reasonable access to review and copy any such recording.

3. *Recording by the News Media.* The recording by the news media of a proceeding open to the public is governed by the provisions of Supreme Judicial Court Rule 3:09, Canon 3(A)(7).

DISTRICT/MUNICIPAL COURTS RULES OF CRIMINAL PROCEDURE

Adopted November 3, 1995, effective January 1, 1996

Table of Rules

Rule 1.   Applicability

Notwithstanding any other rule of court inconsistent herewith, the following rules shall govern procedure in all criminal cases commenced in the District Court and in the Boston Municipal Court on or after January 1, 1996. For the purpose of this provision, commencement of a criminal action shall occur on the date of arrest, or in cases not initiated by arrest, on the date of the issuance of a criminal complaint.

Adopted November 3, 1995, effective January 1, 1996.

Rule 2.   Issuance of Complaint; Police Statement

(a) Cases Commenced by Warrantless Arrest. Prior to the issuance of a criminal complaint in a case commenced by warrantless arrest, the clerk-magistrate shall obtain from the police department responsible for the arrest a written statement describing the facts constituting the basis for the arrest. This requirement may be satisfied by providing to the clerk-magistrate a copy of the arresting officer's police report at the time the Application for Complaint is filed or by setting forth the statement in the space provided on the Application for Complaint, with an additional sheet or sheets attached to the Application as may be needed.

(b) Cases Commenced by Issuance of a Criminal Complaint on Application by Police or Civilian. Prior to the issuance of a criminal complaint in a case commenced by an application therefor filed by a police officer, rather than by a warrantless arrest, the clerk-magistrate shall obtain from the police officer the police report, if any, relating to the alleged crime. In all cases, each police and civilian complainant shall, on the Application for Criminal Complaint, provide the information to support the issuance of the complaint.

Adopted November 3, 1995, effective January 1, 1996.

Rule 3.   Arraignment

(a) Defendant's Criminal Record and Police Statement. At or before arraignment, the court shall ensure (1) that a copy of the defendant's criminal record as compiled by the Commissioner of Probation pursuant to G.L. c. 276, s. 100, if any, is provided to the defense and to the prosecution, pursuant to Mass.R.Crim.P. 12(e), and (2) that a copy of the police

statement required by Rule 2 is provided to the defense by the prosecution.

(b) Notice of Probation Revocation Hearing. If a defendant against whom a criminal case is commenced in the Boston Municipal Court is on probation in that court, the defendant may be served at arraignment with a notice of a probation revocation hearing.

(c) Order for Pretrial Conference; Discovery; Pretrial Hearing. At arraignment in the District Court, the judge shall issue a written order to the attorney representing the defendant and to the prosecutor to (1) engage in a conference between themselves prior to a pretrial hearing in accordance with Mass.R.Crim.P. 11 and (2) appear before the court on a date certain for the conduct of the pretrial hearing on the results of that conference. If the parties agree to a date for the pretrial conference, said date shall be recorded on the order.

At arraignment in the Boston Municipal Court, the judge shall issue an order to the attorney representing the defendant and to the prosecutor to (1) appear for a conference between themselves under the supervision of an Assistant Clerk–Magistrate designated by the Clerk–Magistrate for Criminal Business and certified by the Chief Justice of the Boston Municipal Court, to be conducted in accordance with Mass.R.Crim.P. 11, in a designated courtroom and (2) appear before the court on a date certain for a hearing on the results of that pretrial conference.

Such order issued by the District Court or Boston Municipal Court shall also require the parties to provide, permit and obtain discovery in accordance with G.L. c. 218, s. 26A, and Mass.R.Crim.P. 14, in advance of the scheduled pretrial hearing and to be prepared to submit either a tender of plea or admission at said hearing or, in lieu thereof, a pretrial conference report, completed and signed by both parties. Discovery that is not provided, permitted or obtained in accordance with the arraignment order shall be the subject of a court order, a motion for relief, or sanctions at the pretrial hearing, as provided in Rule 4(b).

(d) Charges Not Within District Court Final Jurisdiction. In cases involving one or more charges not within District Court or Boston Municipal Court final jurisdiction, as the case may be, the order issued at arraignment shall allow

668

for a tender of plea, admission or other disposition on charges reduced by the prosecution so as to be within the court's final jurisdiction. The preliminary discovery required to be included in the arraignment order under section (c) of this rule shall apply only to cases within the court's final jurisdiction.

(e) Appearance of Defense Counsel; Lack of Counsel. Defense counsel, privately engaged or appointed on the basis of defendant's indigency, as the case may be, shall file an appearance at arraignment. If private or publicly provided defense counsel is not before the court at arraignment, if counsel is appointed "for bail only," or if the defendant indicates the intention to engage private counsel, the matter shall be continued for a brief period of time sufficient to permit the defendant to obtain counsel and to reappear for (1) either the assignment or waiver of counsel or the appearance of private counsel, and (2) completion of the arraignment, provided, however, that counsel "for bail only" may also be appointed "for arraignment only" in order to complete the arraignment.

If the arraignment is completed at defendant's first appearance, and the defendant indicates a desire to engage private counsel, the court may continue the matter for the next court event (namely, pretrial hearing in the District Court or pretrial conference in the Boston Municipal Court), set the date therefor and issue to the defendant to give to defense counsel the required arraignment order and other necessary documents. Such an approach shall be employed only when the court determines that the defendant will, in fact, secure private counsel sufficiently promptly for such counsel to prepare for and participate in any required pretrial conference and pretrial hearing.

Adopted November 3, 1995, effective January 1, 1996.

Rule 4. Pretrial Hearing

(a) Appearance of Parties. The parties shall appear as scheduled for a hearing on the results of their pretrial conference, in accordance with the terms of the order issued at arraignment under Rule 3(c). Cases in which the parties have not conferenced in accordance with the order shall be held so that said conference may be completed, and the pretrial hearing conducted, prior to the end of the court day, if possible.

(b) Discovery. Failure of either party to have provided, permitted or obtained discovery in accordance with the order issued at arraignment may subject that party to the sanctions provided in Mass.R.Crim.P. 14(c).

Where it is determined that discoverable material should have been produced but was not, the court may, in lieu of sanctions, order such discovery to be provided without further delay, including a brief continuance of the matter to allow the party responsible to secure the item at issue and bring it before the court that same day.

In the District Court, discovery that is not provided or permitted in accordance with the arraignment order and is not ordered at the pretrial hearing may be requested by motion filed at or prior to the conclusion of the pretrial hearing.

(c) Guilty Plea, Admission, or Other Disposition. At the pretrial hearing the defendant may tender to the court a plea, admission or other requested disposition conditioned on specific dispositional terms, with or without the agreement of the prosecutor. Such tender of plea, admission or other disposition shall be set forth on the form promulgated therefor by the Chief Justice of the District Court or the Chief Justice of the Boston Municipal Court, as the case may be. If the court rejects the dispositional terms agreed to by the parties, or requested by the defendant without the agreement of the prosecution, it shall so inform the defendant and the defendant shall be permitted to withdraw the plea or admission, in accordance with G.L. c. 278, s. 18. Prior to submission to the court of a tender of plea or admission or a request for other disposition, and if the proposed dispositional terms involve any probationary terms or conditions, the parties shall consult with the probation department, so as to enable the probation department to be heard as may be required by the court at the time the court considers the tendered plea or admission.

If the court rejects a tendered plea, admission or other disposition, the judge may indicate to the parties what disposition he or she would impose, as provided in Mass.R.Crim.P. 12(c)(6), and a pretrial disposition may be requested by the defendant on those terms.

(d) Pretrial Conference Report. If a pretrial disposition is not requested, or is requested but rejected by the court at the pretrial hearing, the parties shall submit a completed and signed pretrial conference report in accordance with the order issued at arraignment. Said report shall be set forth on the form promulgated therefor by the Chief Justice of the District Court or the Chief Justice of the Boston Municipal Court, as the case may be.

(e) Jury or Jury–Waived Trial. When the pretrial conference report is submitted, the court shall examine it for completeness, shall rule on any disputed discovery issues, and, unless discovery compliance is still pending, shall inquire if the defendant waives the right to jury trial.

The court shall not compel the defendant's decision on waiver of jury trial until all discovery issues have been resolved and compliance with any discovery orders has been completed. Compliance with discovery orders may require the scheduling of a "compliance/election hearing" as provided in Rule 5. However, the defendant may proceed to enter the decision on jury waiver and a trial date may be set prior to compliance with discovery orders, at the defendant's option.

A waiver of the right to jury trial shall be submitted by the defendant on the form promulgated therefor by the Supreme Judicial Court and shall be accepted only upon completion of the colloquy required by law and the certificate of counsel required by G.L. c. 218, s. 26A. The required certificate shall be submitted on the form promulgated therefor by the Chief Justice of the District Court or the Chief Justice of the Boston Municipal Court, as the case may be.

If a waiver of jury trial is accepted in a District Court in which jury trials are not available and in which only one judge regularly sits, and that judge has rejected defendant's tendered plea or admission, the defendant shall be asked if he or she waives the right to be tried by a different judge. If the right to be tried by a different judge is waived, the case shall be scheduled for jury-waived trial in that court. If the right to be tried by a different judge is not waived, the case shall be scheduled for jury-waived trial in the court in which a session has been designated for that purpose under G.L. c. 218, s. 27A.

If the right to jury trial is not waived when that issue is addressed by the court, the case shall be scheduled as follows: (1) in the District Court the case shall be scheduled for jury trial on a date certain, provided, however, that in the District Court such cases may be scheduled for a trial assignment date if that procedure is authorized by the Chief Justice of the District Court, and (2) in the Boston Municipal Court the case shall be scheduled for a date certain for trial assignment.

(f) Charges Outside District Court and Boston Municipal Court Final Jurisdiction. If the case involves one or more charges that are not within District Court or Boston Municipal Court final jurisdiction, as the case may be, or if the court declines final jurisdiction over the pending charges, the court shall schedule a probable cause ("bind-over") hearing in accordance with G.L. c. 218, s. 30 at the completion of the pretrial hearing.

If the prosecution reduces the charge to a crime within District Court or Boston Municipal Court final jurisdiction, but the case cannot be disposed of at the pretrial hearing in the District Court, or at the pretrial conference or pretrial hearing in the Boston Municipal Court, the court shall continue the matter for a further pretrial hearing on a date certain and shall issue such further discovery and pretrial conference orders as may be necessary.

Adopted November 3, 1995, effective January 1, 1996.

Rule 5. Hearing Date for Discovery Compliance and Jury Waiver Election

In those cases in the District Court wherein a discoverable item is not produced or is not deemed waived at the pretrial hearing and the court issues a discovery order, a subsequent court hearing shall be scheduled at the request of the party seeking discovery to ensure compliance with such order. In those cases in the Boston Municipal Court wherein a discoverable item is not produced or is not deemed waived at the pretrial hearing and the court issues a discovery order, a subsequent hearing may be scheduled by the court. If required, said hearing in the District Court or Boston Municipal Court shall be scheduled for a date on or after the compliance date and shall be limited to the following court actions:

(1) determining discovery compliance and, if necessary, ordering appropriate sanctions for non-compliance;

(2) receiving and acting on a tender of plea or admission in accordance with Rule 4(c); and

(3) obtaining defendant's decision on waiver of the right to jury and scheduling the trial date or trial assignment date, as required by Rule 4(e).

Adopted November 3, 1995, effective January 1, 1996.

Rule 6. Pretrial Motions

(a) In the District Court.

(1) *Discovery Motions.* Discovery motions shall be filed in accordance with Rule 4(b) and shall be heard and decided prior to the defendant's initial decision on waiver of jury trial, provided, however, that motions for discovery may be filed within twenty-one days after the defendant's initial decision on waiver of jury trial, or later, for good cause shown. Discovery motions filed within said twenty-one day period or later shall be entertained only upon a preliminary showing (1) that the items or information sought could not reasonably have been sought and obtained prior to the initial decision on waiver of jury trial or (2) of other grounds that the court determines reasonably justify the delay in having filed the discovery motion after completion of the pretrial hearing.

(2) *Non-discovery Pretrial Motions.* All pretrial motions other than those involving discovery may be filed before or after the defendant's initial decision on waiver of the right to jury trial.

Such motions filed before the defendant's initial decision on the waiver of jury trial shall be transmitted to the appropriate trial session and scheduled to be heard there on the trial date, provided, however, that the judge before whom any such motion is filed may, as a matter of his or her discretion, hear and decide said motion (1) prior to the trial date, or, (2) where the trial will be conducted in a different court, prior to transmission of the case to such other court.

Such motions filed after defendant's initial decision on waiver of jury trial shall be filed in the court wherein the trial is scheduled to be heard no later than twenty-one days after defendant's decision on waiver of jury trial, or later, for good cause shown. Notwithstanding the foregoing, the presiding justice of the court in which the pretrial hearing is conducted, if different from the court in which the trial will be conducted, may require that such motions be filed and heard in the former court. In such cases, transmission of the case file to the other court for trial should be deferred until after the motion is heard and decided.

Rulings on pretrial motions rendered prior to the transmission of a case to a trial session shall be final, as provided in G.L. c. 278, § 18.

(b) In the Boston Municipal Court.

(1) *Discovery Motions.* Discovery motions timely filed must be heard and decided prior to the scheduling of the trial session assignment date. Discovery motions filed after the scheduling of a trial session assignment date shall be allowed only:

(A) if the discovery being sought could not reasonably have been sought or obtained prior to the scheduling of the trial session assignment date; or

(B) if other good cause can be shown.

(2) *Non-discovery Pretrial Motions.* Pretrial motions other than those involving discovery may be filed at any time but no later than 21 days after the date of the filing of the Pretrial Conference Report.

Rulings on pretrial motions rendered prior to the transmission of a case to a trial assignment session shall be final, as provided in G.L. c. 278, § 18.

Adopted November 3, 1995, effective January 1, 1996.

Rule 7. Trials

Jury-waived trials and jury trials shall proceed in accordance with the provisions of law applicable to such trials in Superior Court, as provided by G.L. c. 218, §§ 26A and 27A(d) and (e), respectively.

Adopted November 3, 1995, effective January 1, 1996.

Rule 8. [Reserved]

Rule 9. Sanctions

The provisions of Mass.R.Crim.P. 48 regarding sanctions for willful violation of those rules shall apply to willful violations of these rules.

Adopted November 3, 1995, effective January 1, 1996.

Rule 10. Title

These rules may be known and cited as the District/Municipal Courts Rules of Criminal Procedure (Dist./Mun.Cts.R.Crim.P.).

Adopted November 3, 1995, effective January 1, 1996.

SPECIAL RULES OF THE BOSTON MUNICIPAL COURT DEPARTMENT SITTING FOR CRIMINAL BUSINESS

Effective November 1, 1989

Table of Rules

General Comments

These rules do not purport to be a comprehensive set of rules on criminal procedure. Most of them represent no innovations in what have been regarded heretofore as correct procedure. They are all drawn from approved practices which have heretofore been observed in this court, and while the rules herein promulgated represent in substance the general guide for the disposition of criminal business, it is the purpose of the justices of this court to continue consideration of the problems involved in the fair and efficient administration of criminal justice.

Publisher's Note

Rule captions have been editorially supplied for all but Rules 11, 13 and 15.

PROCEDURE

Rule 1.   Reading of Complaint

At arraignment each complaint, or the material portions thereof, shall be read aloud to the defendant by the session clerk or the judge. In the event codefendants are arraigned at the same time charged with the same offense, the complaint need be read only once with the stated identification of each defendant so complained against. Waiving of the reading shall not be permitted unless the defendant is represented at arraignment by counsel who shall make the waiver in open court.

Rule 2.   Entry of Plea

On any complaint charging an offense for which a sentence of imprisonment may be imposed, no plea other than "not guilty" shall be entered unless the defendant is represented by counsel who is present. (See Rule 4).

The assignment of counsel shall be governed by the provisions of G.L. c. 211D and Supreme Judicial Court Rule 3:10.

Rule 3.   Bail

No bail shall be set with respect to any defendant arraigned for trial unless the defendant has had an opportunity to confer with his counsel, except in cases where the defendant has waived counsel, in which case the court may set bail in its discretion without any further hearing.

Notice of the right to a speedy review of any grievance on account of the amount of bail set by the court shall be given to the defendant by the judge at the time bail is set.

Rule 4.   Guilty or Nolo Contendere Pleas by Pro Se Defendant

No plea of guilty or nolo contendere shall be accepted by the judge from any defendant who is not represented by counsel unless

(a) the judge is satisfied that the plea is made voluntarily;

(b) the judge is satisfied that the defendant understands the nature of the offense described in the complaint;

(c) the defendant understands that such a plea unless later withdrawn by leave of court will preclude his trial by jury on the question of guilt;

(d) the defendant has notice of the minimum and maximum sentence provided by the law therefor.

Rule 5. Refusal to Plead or Accept Guilty Plea

If the defendant refuses to plead or if the court refuses to accept a plea of guilty for any reason set forth in Rule 4, the court shall enter a plea of not guilty. The court shall not enter a judgment upon a plea of guilty nor make a finding of guilty upon the defendant admitting to a finding of facts sufficient to warrant the same, unless it is satisfied that there is a factual basis for such a plea or finding.

Rule 6. Recitation of Rights to Pro Se Defendant

An unrepresented defendant who has pleaded not guilty to any complaint shall be advised by the judge at the time of his hearing or trial that on any material matter pertaining to the offense charged he has the following rights:

(a) to cross-examine any witness offered by the prosecution; and

(b) subject to cross-examination to offer testimony by himself or any other witness.

The judge shall also then advise him of his rights not to testify and not to be prejudiced if he remains silent. If the prosecution offers an exhibit the judge shall allow the defendant to examine it.

Rule 7. Courtrooms

The court room regularly assigned for the trial of causes heard by the justices shall be used for the hearing of all causes adjourned to or called in such session unless at the discretion of the court it is advisable in the public interest that the parties be heard in a non-public session.

Rule 8. Consideration of Probation Department Records or Reports

During the trial on any complaint wherein the Municipal Court has, and does not decline final jurisdiction, no consideration of any probation department records or reports shall take place until the termination of the trial. If the judge then finds the defendant not guilty the session clerk shall so announce and notify the defendant that he is discharged of the offense set forth in that complaint. If the judge indicates a finding of guilty or facts sufficient to warrant such a finding, he shall only thereafter consider any probation department records or reports and instruct the session clerk to announce his decisions on adjudication, disposition or continuance, as the case may be.

Rule 9. Right to Appeal

In all cases where the defendant has a right to appeal to the Superior Court he shall be notified by the session clerk or the judge and shall be granted a reasonable time to make a decision after conferring with his counsel, or, if unrepresented, to make reasonable inquiry of the judge as to the procedures afforded him for this purpose.

ATTORNEYS

Rule 10. Appearance Slips

Attorneys must file an appearance slip for each defendant that they intend to represent, regardless of the number of complaints. Appearance slips must contain at least the following information: the printed name, address and office telephone number and signature of the attorney, the name of the defendant and the numbers of each case.

No attorney who has filed an appearance for a defendant may withdraw without the consent of the trial judge.

An attorney filing an appearance for a defendant corporation, except in parking violations, must file a written authorization signed by an officer of said corporation, unless waived by the trial justice.

PRELIMINARY MOTIONS

Rule 11. Motions for Return of Property and to Suppress Evidence
(Applicable to Criminal Cases)

Motions for the return of property and motions to suppress evidence shall be made in writing, shall specifically set forth the facts upon which the motions are based, shall be verified by affidavit, and shall be filed at least forty-eight hours in advance of trial unless the court for cause shown otherwise orders.

COMMITMENTS FOR MENTAL EXAMINATION

Rule 12. Mental Examination Commitments

Whenever it appears to the court that a serious question may exist with respect to the mental competence of a defendant appearing before it and the court has reasonable cause to believe that the defendant is incompetent to stand trial, the court may order the defendant committed for examination to an institution designated by public authority for such examina-tion, said examination to be for such period as in the opinion of court is necessary, but under no circumstances for a period exceeding 35 days, unless an extension of period is requested by the medical authorities in the institution to which said defendant has been committed.

In all cases where a commitment is made as provided above, the court before making such commitment shall require that a statement be made by the complainant as to the circumstances which resulted in the arraignment of defendant in court, and a summary of said statement shall be annexed to the papers providing for the commitment of said defendant.

HOURS OF BUSINESS

Rule 13. Time for Holding Criminal Trials

Unless otherwise ordered, the time for holding criminal trials shall be from 9:00 A.M. until 4:00 P.M. Mondays through Fridays. For the convenience of the public there shall be a recess each day between 1:00 P.M. and 2:00 P.M.

THE CLERK'S OFFICE

Rule 14. Business Hours of Clerk; Responsibility for Filed Records and Papers

The office of the Clerk of the Court for the conduct of criminal business shall be open from 8:30 A.M. to 4:30 P.M. Mondays through Fridays.

The Clerk shall be answerable for all records and papers filed in the court or in his office. He shall not allow any writ, petition, complaint, answer, agreement of parties or other writing which may be part of the record, or which is part of any proceeding in court, to be borrowed or taken from the files, and no other paper filed as aforesaid, shall be taken from the custody of the clerk without his consent, unless by order of the Court.

SOUND RECORDING DEVICES

Rule 15. Electronic Recordation of Proceedings

Recording of court proceedings is governed by Rule 308 of the Special Rules of the Boston Municipal Court Department Sitting for Civil Business.

DISTRICT COURT DEPARTMENT SUPPLEMENTAL RULES OF CRIMINAL PROCEDURE

Effective February 1, 1981

Table of Rules

Rule 1. Bail

If an assignment or appointment of counsel is made pursuant to Rule 8 of the Massachusetts Rules of Criminal Procedure, including a senior law school student pursuant to Supreme Judicial Court Rule 3:03, and the assignee or appointee is available during the same day within such time as the judge in his discretion shall permit, no determination of bail other than release on personal recognizance shall be made without a reasonable opportunity being given the assignee or appointee to confer with the defendant and to be heard on the question of bail. Notice of the right to a speedy review of any bail determination by a judge shall be given to the defendant by the judge at the time the determination is made, and a record of the giving of this notice shall be recorded by the session clerk.

Rule 2. Notice of Right to First–Instance Jury Trial; Waiver of Right

(A) **Notice of Right.** Every defendant appearing in the District Court Department in a case over which the court will exercise final jurisdiction shall be notified of his or her right to jury trial in the first instance. Such notice shall be given orally to the defendant by the judge or by the session clerk at arraignment, provided that the defendant is represented by counsel or has waived counsel. If the defendant does not have counsel or does not waive counsel at arraignment, the notice shall be given as soon as the defendant thereafter appears before the court with counsel or having waived counsel.

The oral notice of right to first-instance jury trial shall include a statement to the defendant that if he or she waives this right he or she will receive a trial before a judge and if not satisfied with the results of that trial will be able to appeal for a new trial before a jury.

The defendant shall decide whether or not he or she will waive this right to first-instance jury trial at the time the notice of that right is given to him or her unless the court allows further time.

(B) **Waiver of Right.** If the defendant decides to waive the right to first-instance jury trial, he or she shall so indicate on the form promulgated by the Chief Justice of the District Court Department.

Before the defendant signs this form the judge shall be satisfied that the waiver is voluntarily and knowingly made and to that end shall (1) advise the defendant and be sure the defendant understands that by waiving first-instance jury trial he or she is not losing the constitutional right to trial by jury, but that a trial by a jury will be available only after a trial without one, and (2) satisfy himself or herself that the defendant's waiver is not the product of pressure and that the defendant is not intoxicated or otherwise incapable of rational judgment.

When the judge feels it necessary, the judge should also inform the defendant of the essential elements of the jury trial, i.e. that the jury consists of members of the community; that the defendant may participate in their selection; that the jury verdict must be unanimous; that they decide guilt or innocence while the judge makes rulings of law and, when guilt is found, imposes sentence; and that when no jury is involved the judge alone decides guilt or innocence.

Rule 3. Refusal to Plead

The court shall not enter a judgment upon a plea of guilty nor make a finding of guilty upon the defendant admitting to a finding of facts sufficient to warrant the same, unless it is satisfied that there is a factual basis for such plea or finding.

Rule 4. Advice As to Rights

An unrepresented defendant who has pleaded not guilty to any complaint shall be advised by the judge at the time of his hearing or trial that on any material matter pertaining to the offense charged he has the following rights:

(a) to cross examine any witness offered by the prosecution; and

(b) subject to cross examination, to offer testimony by himself or any other witness.

The judge shall also then advise him of his rights not to testify and not to be prejudiced if he remains silent. If the prosecution offers an exhibit the judge shall allow the defendant to examine it.

Rule 5.   Place of Hearing

Except when in the discretion of the judge he shall deem it to be necessary or desirable in the interest of the defendant or the public,

(a) no room shall be used for a hearing or trial other than a room where a court session is customarily held; and

(b) no evidence shall be taken at any bench conference during a hearing or trial until the time of the judge's consideration of matters bearing on disposition.

Rule 6.   Probation Department Records or Reports

During the trial on any complaint wherein the District Court Department has and does not decline final jurisdiction, no consideration of any probation department records or reports shall take place until the termination of the trial. If the judge then finds the defendant not guilty, the session clerk shall so announce and notify the defendant that he is discharged of the offense set forth in the complaint. If the judge indicates a finding of guilty or facts sufficient to warrant such a finding, he shall only thereafter consider any probation department records or reports and instruct the session clerk to announce his decisions on adjudication, disposition or continuance, as the case may be.

Rule 7.   Appeal

In all cases where the defendant has a right to appeal to a jury session in the District Court Department he shall be notified by the session clerk or the judge and shall be granted a reasonable time to make a decision after conferring with his counsel, or, if unrepresented, to make reasonable inquiry of the judge as to the procedures afforded him for this purpose. This notice shall include a statement to the defendant that if he does not appeal he is waiving his right to jury trial. The court shall explain to the defendant the importance and procedure of trial by jury if it deems such explanation necessary for the defendant's knowledgeable decision on the question of appeal.

Notice of the right to appeal a finding of guilty and the defendant's decision on exercising that right shall be completed before the pronouncement of sentence. Regardless of whether the defendant claims appeal of the finding, the court shall proceed to pronounce sentence.

If the defendant has claimed appeal of the finding, notice of the right to appeal the sentence need not be given.

If the defendant has not claimed or is not entitled to claim appeal of the finding, notice must be given of the right to appeal the sentence. If the defendant then claims appeal of the sentence, he shall be entitled only to resentencing by the judge sitting in the jury session.

The session clerk shall indicate on the case papers whether the defendant has claimed appeal of the finding or of the sentence or of both.

Rule 8.   Appointment and Compensation of Attorneys

If it is necessary for the court to appoint private counsel at the Commonwealth's expense pursuant to the requirements of Rule 8 of the Massachusetts Rules of Criminal Procedure, other than counsel participating in bar-sponsored, approved indigent representation programs, such appointment shall be made in accordance with this rule.

(1) Every division shall maintain a list of attorneys who have offered to represent defendants pursuant to appointment by the court. Said list shall be part of the public records of the court open during regular business hours to public inspection. Any attorney may have his name placed on said list, whether or not he is a member of any bar association, provided that the court shall be satisfied that the attorney is geographically located so as to insure his reasonable availability to the court and to defendants brought before the court. Law firms shall not be listed as such.

(2) All appointments of attorneys shall be made from said list. The court shall, except in exceptional circumstances, appoint the attorney whose name next appears on said list, and may appoint said attorney to represent more than one defendant before proceeding to the next name. The court shall make appointments in such a way and for such periods of time as to insure the equal participation of all attorneys and to avoid favored treatment of any attorney.

(3) An attorney may withdraw his name from said list by communicating in writing with the Presiding Justice of the division. The name of an attorney may be removed from said list by the Presiding Justice of the division if he is satisfied that the appointment of said attorney under this rule would not be in the interest of justice.

(4) An attorney appointed to represent a defendant pursuant to this rule shall be personally responsible for the representation of said defendant at every stage of the District Court proceedings, except as may be otherwise provided in paragraph 7. Should new counsel subsequently be appointed by the District Court, the first appointed counsel shall respond cooperatively to any reasonable request for information by subsequently appointed counsel.

(5) An attorney appointed under this rule shall be entitled to compensation at a rate not to exceed thirty-five dollars ($35.00) per hour for time expended in court actually engaged in an evidentiary hearing or actual trial, and at a rate not to exceed twenty-five dollars ($25.00) per hour for other time reasonably expended with a maximum of one hour for any one court appearance and, unless authorized in advance by the court, a maximum of five hours for preparation or other services out of court. The amount of time billed shall not, as the result of counsel representing co-defendants, exceed the total amount of time actually expended. In addition, such counsel may be reimbursed for expenses reasonably incurred when authorized by the court before the expenses are incurred.

(6) Except as provided in paragraphs 7 and 8, compensation based on the nature of the offense or offenses charged, the number of offenses charged, a per diem rate or any formula other than that contained in paragraph 5, is expressly prohibited.

(7) In the event an insufficient number of attorneys come forward to offer to represent defendants in accordance with the foregoing provisions, the Presiding Justice of the division shall certify that fact to the Chief Justice of the District Court Department and shall recommend in writing an alternate plan which shall not require a greater expenditure of funds for implementation than would the plan outlined above. No such alternate plan shall be put into effect without the approval of the Chief Justice of the District Court Department and the Chief Administrative Justice.

(8) Notwithstanding the foregoing provisions of this rule, the court may enter into such arrangements as it deems appropriate to provide an organized system for the immediate representation of defendants at arraignment. Attorneys participating in such system may be compensated in a manner other than as provided in paragraph 5. This paragraph contemplates a plan whereby one attorney is assigned to represent all defendants at arraignment on a given day or days, said assignments to be distributed fairly among counsel wishing to participate. Appointment at arraignment of counsel who will not be trial counsel is not permitted except as provided in this paragraph.

(9) An attorney's bill for services shall be submitted to the clerk of the court within thirty days of termination of services. A separate bill shall be rendered for each defendant. Said bill shall be in the form prescribed by the Chief Justice of the District Court Department, but an attorney shall supply any additional information on the nature and extent of his services as the Presiding Justice of the court shall require. Failure to file a bill promptly shall be grounds for removal of the attorney from the list.

(10) No attorney appointed as counsel pursuant to this rule shall request or accept any payment or promise of payment from any other source for representing the defendant, except as ordered by the court.

Rule 9. Sound Recording Devices

Recording of court proceedings is governed by Rule 211 of the Special Rules of the District Court.

Amended effective May 1, 1986; amended December 31, 1987, effective February 1, 1988.

Rule 10. Special Procedures for Criminal Cases in Essex and Hampden Counties

(a) **Scope of Rule; Applicability of Rules 1 Through 9.** All criminal proceedings in the District Court primary courts and jury sessions in Essex and Hampden Counties shall be governed by Rules 1 through 9 of these rules, except as they are modified herein.

(b) **Notice of Right to Jury Trial; Waiver of Right.** Except as modified below, Rule 2 shall govern notice to the defendant of the right to jury trial and waiver of that right.

RULE 2. NOTICE OF RIGHT TO
JURY TRIAL; WAIVER OF RIGHT

(A) **Notice of Right; Decision on Waiver.** Every defendant appearing in the District Court Department in a case over which the court will exercise final jurisdiction shall be notified of his or her right to jury trial. Such notice shall be given orally to the defendant by the judge or by the session clerk at arraignment, provided that the defendant is represented by counsel or has waived counsel. If the defendant does not have counsel or does not waive counsel at arraignment, the notice shall be given as soon as the defendant thereafter appears before the court with counsel or having waived counsel.

The oral notice of right to jury trial shall include a statement to the defendant that, if he or she waives this right, he or she will receive a trial before a judge.

In the primary court the defendant shall decide whether or not he or she will waive the right to jury trial after completion of the pretrial conference and the hearing on the pretrial conference report, and after completion of the guilty plea or admission procedure, if any, and withdrawal of the plea or admission, if any. In the jury session, the defendant shall decide whether or not he or she will waive the right to jury trial no later than the commencement of trial. The defendant shall not be required to decide on waiver of the right to jury trial in either the primary court or jury session until disposition or withdrawal of any pretrial discovery motion filed in accordance with the Massachusetts Rules of Criminal Procedure and compliance with any court order issued in conjunction therewith.

(B) **Procedure for Waiver of Right.** If in the primary court the defendant decides to waive the right to jury trial and consents to be tried by the court, he or she shall so indicate on the form promulgated by the Chief Justice of the District Court Department.

Before the defendant signs this form the judge shall be satisfied that the waiver is voluntarily and knowingly made and to that end shall advise the defendant and be sure the defendant understands that by waiving jury trial he or she is losing the constitutional right to trial by jury, and satisfy himself or herself that the defendant's waiver is not the product of pressure and that the defendant is not intoxicated or otherwise incapable of rational judgment, and shall receive from defense counsel a properly executed certificate, signed by counsel, indicating that he or she has made all the necessary explanations and determinations regarding such waiver. Such certificate shall be set forth on the form prescribed therefor by the Chief Justice of the District Court Department.

When the judge determines it to be necessary, the judge should also inform the defendant of the essential elements of the jury trial, i.e. that the jury consists of members of the community; that the defendant may participate in their selection; that the jury verdict must be unanimous; that they decide guilt or innocence while the judge makes rulings of law and, when guilt is found, imposes sentence; and that when no jury is involved the judge alone decides guilt or innocence.

(C) **Appeal.** Rule 7 of the District Court Supplemental Rules of Criminal Procedure shall not apply to criminal cases in the District Court primary court and jury sessions in Essex and Hampden Counties. Appeals on issues of law in such cases shall be governed by the applicable statutes and the Massachusetts Rules of Appellate Procedure.

Adopted June 9, 1987, effective July 1, 1987.

DISTRICT/MUNICIPAL COURTS RULES FOR PROBATION VIOLATION PROCEEDINGS

Adopted December 2, 1999, effective January 3, 2000

Table of Rules

Rule 1. Scope and Purpose

These rules prescribe procedures in the Boston Municipal Court and the District Court to be followed upon the allegation of a violation of an order of probation issued in a criminal case after a finding of guilty or after a continuance without a finding. These rules do not apply to an alleged violation of pretrial probation, as the latter term is defined herein.

The purpose of these rules is to ensure that judicial proceedings undertaken upon the allegation of a violation of probation are conducted in full compliance with all applicable law, promptly and with an appropriate degree of procedural uniformity.

Adopted December 2, 1999, effective January 3, 2000. Amended February 25, 2015, effective September 8, 2015.

Commentary to District Court Rule 1—2000

Probation violation proceedings are among the most important matters within District Court jurisdiction. The timely and proper conduct of these proceedings is essential to protect the rights of probationers as set forth in federal and state law, as well as to maintain the credibility, and thus the effectiveness, of probation orders. Just as fundamentally, the proper and timely conduct of probation violation proceedings is necessary to vindicate the public trust. Failure of the court to take appropriate action when a convicted defendant who has been given the benefit of probation is then alleged to have violated that order erodes public confidence in the judicial system.

These rules are intended to codify the provisions of applicable case law and to provide clarity in areas of long-standing ambiguity. Their purpose is to provide a clear and predictable process whereby probation violation proceedings are to be commenced, conducted and completed.

One area of ambiguity involves terminology. These rules are entitled "Rules for Probation Violation Proceedings" and not "Rules for Probation Revocation Proceedings." This is an important distinction involving the essential difference between adjudication and disposition. Ambiguity concerning this distinction appears occasionally in the relevant case law, which almost uniformly refers to "probation revocation hearings." The problem is that when a probationer is alleged to have violated his or her probation order, the first purpose of the subsequent hearing is to adjudicate the factual question of whether that violation occurred. The decision to revoke probation, or order any other disposition, can proceed only if a violation is found. Most of the due process requirements that have evolved for these hearings relate to the process by which the court is to determine the factual issue. The nature of the alleged violation is essentially irrelevant to the factual determination of whether it occurred. In contrast, the issue of whether the probation order should be revoked (in many instances requiring the execution of a sentence of incarceration) focuses directly on the nature of the violation, among other factors. In addition, the issue of violation is essentially a *factual* matter whereas the dispositional decision of whether to revoke probation is essentially one of *discretion*.

Confusion on this distinction can affect proceedings significantly. For example, the preponderance of the evidence test at a probation violation hearing has nothing to do with the revocation decision; it is the evidentiary test by which the court must determine if a violation occurred. Conversely, the seriousness of the alleged violation has nothing to do with whether it occurred, but is an important consideration regarding revocation.

It is believed that often probation violation proceedings are not initiated because the Probation Department has no intention of recommending revocation and the incarceration it may require. As long as the proceeding is referred to, and believed to be for the purpose of, revocation and incarceration, there can be reluctance to allege a violation if the appropriate disposition is not revocation but rather the imposition of more stringent or intense probation requirements. The concept of a probation *revocation* hearing promotes a mistaken "all or nothing" perception. It implies that revocation is the purpose of the hearing and that if a violation is found, revocation must follow. In fact, the purpose of the hearing is to adjudicate the allegation, with the court having broad discretionary authority if a violation is found.

These rules seek to clarify the important difference between adjudicating the factual issue of whether a violation has occurred and the court's dispositional decision following such adjudication, not only by referring to the proceedings as "probation *violation* proceedings," but also by requiring a two-step procedure (Rule 5 [now Rule 6]) and expressly defining the different purpose and procedures required for each step (Rule 7 [now Rule 8]).

Throughout these rules the person who is the subject of probation violation proceedings is usually referred to as the "probationer" rather than the "defendant." With respect to the probation proceedings, such a person is *not* a defendant; he or she has either been convicted, after trial or based on a plea of guilty, or has formally submitted an admission to the facts of a criminal charge. Use of the term "probationer" is intended to underscore the legal status of the individual charged with a probation violation, which is fundamentally distinct from the status of a person who is a criminal defendant, particularly in terms of procedural rights.

Commentary to District/Municipal Courts Rule 1—2015

In recognition of the advisability of having uniform procedures, to the extent practical, within the Trial Court, a single set of Rules for Probation Violation Proceedings has been promulgated for use in both the Boston Municipal Court and the District Court. These rules are largely modeled on the District Court Rules for Probation Violation Proceedings, made effective in 2000, with changes made both to account for legal and technological developments since 2000 and to account for the respective needs of each department.

Rule 2. Definition of Terms

As used in these rules, the following terms shall have the following meanings:

"Continuance without a finding:" the order of a court, following a formal submission and acceptance of a plea of guilty or an admission to sufficient facts, whereby a criminal case is continued to a date certain without the formal entry of a guilty finding. A continuance without a finding may include conditions imposed in an order of probation (1) the violation of which may result in the revocation of the continuance, entry of a finding of guilty, and imposition of sentence, and (2) compliance with which will result in dismissal of the criminal case.

"District Attorney:" the criminal prosecuting authority including the Attorney General if the criminal case in which probation was ordered was prosecuted by the Office of the Attorney General.

"General conditions of probation:" the conditions of probation that are imposed as a matter of course in every order of probation, as set forth in the official form promulgated for such orders.

"Probation order:" the formal, written court order whereby a defendant is placed on probation and which expressly sets forth the conditions of probation. A probation order is not a contract.

"Pretrial probation:" the probationary status of a defendant pursuant to a probation order issued prior to a trial or the formal submission and acceptance of a plea of guilty or an admission to sufficient facts, as provided in G.L. c. 276, § 87.

"Revocation of probation:" the revocation by a judge of an order of probation as a consequence of a determination that a condition of that probation order has been violated.

"Special conditions of probation:" any condition of probation other than one of the general conditions of probation.

"Surrender:" the procedure by which a probation officer requires a probationer to appear before the court for a judicial hearing regarding an allegation of probation violation.

Adopted December 2, 1999, effective January 3, 2000. Amended February 25, 2015, effective September 8, 2015.

Commentary to District Court Rule 2—2000

This rule provides definitions for six terms that are important for a clear understanding of various provisions of these rules.

The definition of "continuance without a finding" is provided to make clear that, as used in these rules, the term presupposes that the defendant whose case has been so continued has formally submitted, and the court has accepted, a plea of guilty or an admission to sufficient facts. Thus there is no "continuance without a finding" unless a guilty plea or admission has been properly tendered and accepted.

This definition also makes clear that the conditions of the continuance may be set forth in an order of probation. Thus, upon violation of one or more conditions of probation, the court may proceed to enter a guilty finding and impose sentence, as provided in Rule 9. It may be possible for a court to continue a case without a finding *without* imposing the conditions of the continuance as probation conditions, but these rules have no application in such a circumstance. If the conditions of a continuance without a finding, whether or not imposed as conditions of probation, are *not* violated, the criminal case may be dismissed. *See Commonwealth v. Pyles*, 423 Mass. 717 (1996).

"Probation order" is defined as a written court order that specifies the conditions imposed. Fundamental fairness requires that if a probationer is to be subject to sanctions for failure to obey probation conditions, those conditions must be clearly specified. And proof of a violation will require evidence that the defendant was made aware of the conditions he or she allegedly violated. Conditions of probation must not be vague. *See Commonwealth v. Power*, 420 Mass. 410 (1995). A written order is conducive to clarity. The probation order also fulfills a statutory requirement for written conditions: "Every person released upon probation shall be given by the probation officer a written statement of the terms and conditions of the release." G.L. c. 276, § 85.

The definition of "pretrial probation" makes clear that this term includes probation orders issued before a trial, a plea or an admission. A defendant placed on pretrial probation under G.L. c. 276, § 87, is formally on probation, but violation of such probation would not appear to subject the probationer to any sanction other than the resumption of the criminal proceeding. Having not admitted guilt or been tried, and having waived no rights, such a probationer would not appear to be subject to any sentencing, let alone any loss of liberty, even if a violation of such probation were alleged and proved. As a result, the due process requirements that are the central focus of these procedural rules do not apply to an alleged violation of a pretrial probation order, and Rule 1 expressly so provides.

The definition of "revocation of probation" makes clear that this is an order that must be preceded by a judicial determination that a condition of a probation order has been violated.

Special conditions of probation are defined simply as any condition other than the "general conditions." A violation of such a special condition (or a general condition other than the prohibition against any violation of law) has traditionally, and perhaps unfortunately, been referred to as a "technical" violation.

"Surrender" is defined in accordance with *Commonwealth v. Durling*, 407 Mass. 108, 111 (1990):

When a violation is alleged, the probation officer "surrenders" the defendant to the court, subjecting the defendant to possible revocation of his probation.

This definition is intended to clarify that surrender is the process by which the Probation Department brings the probationer before the court to answer for an alleged violation. It may be effected by arrest with or without a warrant under G.L. c. 279, § 3, or by a notice requiring the defendant to appear before the court. If a defendant is already before the court on a separate matter (for example, following an arrest on a new alleged crime, with or without a warrant, or on a summons on a new alleged crime), he or she may be notified at that time of the probation violation and ordered to appear at, or held in custody until, a probation violation hearing. In such cases no actual surrender by the Probation Department is required, since the defendant is before the court for a different reason when violation proceedings are commenced.

This definition of "surrender" clarifies any confusion caused by the use of the term to mean the process following a revocation of probation where a sentence is executed or imposed. *See, e.g., Common-*

wealth v. Duro, No. 95–P–2186 (Appeals Court, March 28, 1997) (summary disposition) (court refers to "order revoking the defendant's probation and surrendering him to the custody of the State . . .").

Commentary to District/Municipal Courts Rule 2—2015

The "general conditions of probation" are set forth in standard probation forms, promulgated after consultation with the Office of the Commissioner of Probation. In the Boston Municipal Court, this is form BMCD–CR–104. In the District Court, this is form DC–CR–27.

A sentence has been added to the definition of "probation order" that existed in the 2000 District Court Rule to address the recurring error of probation orders being referred to as probation "contracts." A probation order is not a contract. *Commonwealth v. MacDonald*, 435 Mass. 1005, 1007(2001).

In the definition of "pretrial probation," a reference to the relevant statute has been added.

Rule 3. Commencement of Violation Proceedings: Charged Criminal Conduct

(a) **General.** This rule prescribes the procedures to be undertaken upon the issuance of a criminal complaint against a probationer.

(b) **When Probation Order and New Criminal Charge Involve Same Court Division.**

(i) *Issuance and Service of Notice of Violation; Termination of Proceedings; Withdrawal of Notice of Violation.* When a criminal complaint is issued by a court division against a defendant who is the subject of a probation order previously issued by that same court division, the Probation Department shall commence violation proceedings against that probationer. Such proceedings shall be commenced by the issuance by the Probation Department of a Notice of Probation Violation and Hearing at or before the arraignment on the criminal charge, or as soon thereafter as possible. The notice shall be served on the probationer in hand following the assignment of a date and time for a probation violation hearing, as provided in Rule 3(b)(ii), and such service shall be recorded on the case docket, provided that, if such in-hand service is not possible, the notice shall be served on the probationer by first-class mail, unless the court orders otherwise. Service of the notice by first-class mail shall be recorded on the case docket. Out-of–court service other than by mail shall require a written return of service. The Probation Department shall provide a copy of each notice of violation to the District Attorney forthwith upon its issuance.

At any time during violation proceedings, the court, upon review of the notice of violation and as a matter of its discretion, may order termination of the proceedings. A notice of violation may be withdrawn only with the permission of the court and such withdrawal and permission shall be set forth on the record and entered on the case docket.

(ii) *Contents of Notice of Violation.* The Notice of Probation Violation and Hearing shall set forth the criminal behavior alleged to have been committed by the probationer as indicated in the criminal complaint, and shall set forth any other conditions of the probation order that the Probation Department alleges have been violated with a description of each such alleged violation. The notice shall also state the date, time, and place of the hearing.

(iii) *Scheduling of Hearing.* The probation violation hearing shall be scheduled to be commenced on the date of the pretrial hearing for the criminal charge, unless the court expressly orders an earlier hearing. The hearing shall be scheduled for a date certain no less than seven days after service on the probationer of the notice of violation unless the probationer waives the seven-day notice period. The hearing date shall not be later than 30 days after service of the notice of violation, except in extraordinary circumstances. In scheduling the pretrial hearing on the new criminal charge together with the probation violation hearing, the court shall give primary consideration to the need for promptness in conducting the probation violation hearing.

(c) **When Probation Order and New Criminal Charge Involve Different Court Divisions within the Same Court Department.**

(i) *Issuance and Service of Notice of Violation.* When a criminal complaint is issued by a court division (hereinafter the "criminal court") against a defendant who is the subject of a probation order issued by a different division of the same court department (hereinafter a "probation court"), the Probation Department at the criminal court shall issue a Notice of Probation Violation and Hearing to the probationer at or before arraignment on the criminal charge, or as soon thereafter as possible. The notice shall be served on the probationer in hand and such service shall be recorded on the case docket. Nothing in this rule shall preclude the later issuance and service on the probationer of a notice of violation by the Probation Department of a probation court.

(ii) *Contents of Notice of Violation.* The notice of violation shall set forth the name of the court division at which the probationer is on probation and the criminal behavior alleged to have been committed by the probationer as indicated in the criminal complaint and shall order the probationer to appear at a specific date and time at the probation court for the express purpose of appointment of counsel, if necessary, and scheduling of a probation violation hearing.

(iii) *Transmission of Notice of Violation and Other Documents to Probation Court.* Prior to the service of the notice of violation on the probationer, the Probation Department at the criminal court shall send to the Chief Probation Officer at the probation court, by electronic transmission, copies of the following documents: the notice of violation; the criminal complaint and related police report on the new criminal charge that constitutes the alleged probation violation; and a request for the following information: whether the probation court recommends that the probationer to be transported in custody, and, if not, the date and time for the non-custodial appearance of the probationer at the probation court.

(iv) *Response by the Probation Court.* At the probation court, the Chief Probation Officer, an Assistant Chief Probation Officer, or a probation officer designated by either shall respond by electronic transmission to the request for information no later than one hour from receipt thereof. The response shall include a recommendation on whether the probationer should be transported to the probation court in custody, and, if not, the date and time for the probationer's non-custodial appearance at the probation court.

(v) *The Decision to Transport.* A judge at the criminal court shall decide whether the probationer is to be transported in custody to the probation court. The judge shall provide the probationer an opportunity to be heard and, unless exceptional circumstances require otherwise, shall wait at least one hour for receipt of the recommendation from the probation court before making such decision. If the criminal court orders custodial transport, it shall issue a probation warrant on behalf of the probation court, and the probation court shall be so notified. The probationer promptly shall be transported in accordance with the warrant, provided that, if the probationer is held in custody in the criminal proceeding, the warrant shall be lodged with custodial authority to ensure that the probationer will be detained and transported to the probation court. The Probation Department at the criminal court shall so notify the Probation Department at the probation court.

If the criminal court decides not to order custodial transport, it shall enter the probation court appearance date and other required information on the notice of violation and serve it on the probationer in accordance with Rule 3(c)(i). For good cause, the criminal court may hold the probationer in custody pending its decision regarding custodial transport. Nothing in this rule shall preclude the issuance of a probation warrant by the probation court to secure the appearance of a probationer for a probation violation proceeding.

(vi) *Probationer's Appearance at Probation Court; Service of a New Notice.* Upon appearance of the probationer at the probation court, that court shall appoint counsel, if necessary, and shall schedule a probation violation hearing for a date certain, the date to be no less than seven days later unless the defendant waives the seven-day period. The hearing date shall not be later than 30 days after the appearance, except in extraordinary circumstances. If the probation department at the probation court alleges additional violations, it shall prepare and serve on the probationer a new notice of violation which shall set forth all alleged violations. A new notice of violation shall also include the date, time, and place of the violation hearing, and shall be served on the probationer in hand while the probationer is before the court, or as soon thereafter as possible. Such service shall be recorded on the case docket. The Probation Department shall provide a copy of the notice of violation to the District Attorney at the time of, or before, such service on the probationer.

At any time during the proceedings, the probation court, upon review of the notice of violation and as a matter of its discretion, may order termination of the proceedings. A notice of violation may be withdrawn only with the permission of the court and such withdrawal and permission shall be set forth on the record and entered on the case docket.

(vii) *Procedure When a Defendant Is a Probationer at More than One Other Court Division within the Same Court Department.* When a defendant appearing in a court division on a new criminal charge is on probation at more than one other court division within the same court department, the criminal court shall select one of the latter divi-

sions to be the probation court and shall issue a notice of violation for that division. The criminal court shall interact as provided in this rule with the selected probation court. The other probation court or courts each shall be responsible for the issuance and service on the probationer of a notice of violation based on the new criminal charge, and for securing the presence of the probationer for a violation hearing by means of such notice or by means of a warrant or other process.

(viii) *Unified Proceedings Permitted by Standing Order.* Each department may provide, by standing order, for the hearing of probation violation matters pending in any of the several divisions of that department at any one division.

(d) When Probation Order and New Criminal Charge Involve Different Court Departments. When a criminal complaint is issued by a court against a defendant who is the subject of a probation order issued by a court in a different court department, the Probation Department at the criminal court shall notify the Probation Department at the probation court of the new complaint as soon as may be done, but in any event prior to the new matter being heard in the criminal court.

Adopted December 2, 1999, effective January 3, 2000. Amended February 25, 2015, effective September 8, 2015.

Commentary to District Court Rule 3—2000

This rule sets forth procedures for a specific circumstance, namely, where a probationer is charged with a crime by the issuance of a criminal complaint. It is based on the premise that when a formal criminal charge is issued against a person on probation, this constitutes a basis for an alleged violation of the first general condition of every probation order (that the probationer must obey all local, state and federal laws) and the court must address such an alleged violation.

Note that it makes no difference whether the criminal complaint was issued after an arrest, or after a hearing on a criminal complaint application with no arrest having occurred. Note also that the rule does not apply to alleged criminal conduct that has not yet resulted in a criminal complaint. Probation violation proceedings based on alleged criminal conduct where no criminal complaint has yet issued are governed by Rule 4.

Commencement of Proceedings in Every Case

The rule requires the commencement of a probation violation proceeding in *every* case where a criminal complaint is issued against a probationer. No attempt is made to discriminate between those criminal charges that are "serious enough" to warrant violation proceedings and those that are not. The charge of a crime against a person who has been given the benefit of probation is serious enough *per se* to require action by the Probation Department. If the violation is found to have occurred, it is important to document that finding. The seriousness of the violation is properly addressed by the court's *dispositional* discretion, which is extremely flexible: a serious violation may result in revocation; a minor violation may result in simply a warning. *See* Rule 7(d) [now Rule 8(d)]. Nor must an alleged minor violation require protracted proceedings. In appropriate cases, the defendant may admit to the probation violation resulting in a simple continuance of the current probation terms and consent to a disposition at arraignment on the new charge. Of course, a defendant's rights to oppose any alleged violation and to demand trial on any criminal charge remain inviolate.

Whenever a new crime is charged, commencement of probation violation proceedings may not be delayed solely to await the conclusion of the new criminal case. Rules 5(e) [now Rule 6(e)] and 7(a) [now Rule 8(a)] similarly preclude such "tracking" of the new criminal case as a basis for delaying the conduct and conclusion of probation violation proceedings. The commentary to Rules 5(e) [now Rule 6(e)] provides the rationale for the requirement. Continuances are available on specific grounds under Rule 5(e) [now Rule 6(e)].

Where the court "treats" a criminal charge as a civil infraction, as provided by G.L. c. 277, § 70C, the rule requiring the initiation of probation proceedings does not apply since the criminal charge, as such, can be considered no longer to exist. However, the underlying alleged behavior may constitute a violation of probation subject to possible violation proceedings under Rule 4.

Judicial Discretion to Terminate Proceedings After Commencement

It should be noted that the rule acknowledges the court's discretion to terminate a proceeding once it has been commenced. That is, the rule provides that proceedings are commenced "by the issuance by the Probation Department of a Notice of Probation Violation and Hearing at or before arraignment on the criminal charge." Usually such "issuance" will consist of the probation officer tendering the notice form to the court before the arraignment begins. (The notice will not be formally served on the probationer until and unless a hearing date is determined and recorded on the form.) At that time the judge is free as a matter of discretion to order that the proceedings be terminated. Such an order must be entered on the probation record and on the docket of the case in which probation was ordered to ensure accountability. While alleged probation violations based on new criminal charges, even minor ones, generally should proceed to a factual conclusion to vindicate the credibility of probation and to establish a proper record, there may be circumstances where, in the opinion of the court, the violation proceedings should be terminated at the outset.

Where the court at which the probationer is on probation is different from the court where the new criminal charge is brought, the judicial authority to order no further proceedings resides at the former court, and section (c)(iii) so states.

Same Court

There are two different circumstances in which proceedings under the rule can arise: where the criminal complaint is issued (1) by the same court that issued the probation order, or (2) by a different court. These situations are addressed separately in sections (b) and (c).

Section (b), the "same court" circumstance, requires the probationer to be served in hand with the Notice of Probation Violation and Hearing when he or she appears before the court for arraignment whenever possible. This requires administrative attention by the Probation Department at each court so as to ensure each day that all new arrestees and others appearing for arraignment are screened for probation status. Notices for all those who are on probation must be prepared for in-court service. Where necessary, these defendants can be scheduled last for arraignment to ensure preparation of the Notice and in-hand service. The issuance of the Notice constitutes "commencement" of action by the Probation Department. The prepared Notice should include any other violations that can properly be alleged in addition to the charged criminal conduct. For example, a probationer charged with a new crime may also have a history of failure to report as ordered. The date, time and place of the violation hearing should be left blank, to be recorded on the form when the hearing is scheduled along with the pretrial hearing on the criminal charge, as required in section (b)(iii). After this information is added, the Notice is to be served in hand on the probationer.

If the probationer defaults at arraignment, the Notice can be prepared and left in the case file.

When the court fails to make in-hand service at arraignment, the rule provides for other methods of service. In such cases, the goal should be to schedule the hearing on the same date as the pretrial hearing on the criminal charge, assuming this will not violate the seven-day minimum notice requirement.

There is no requirement that counsel in the original criminal case represent the probationer at the violation hearing. On the contrary, if appointment of counsel is required, it is appropriate to appoint the same attorney for the violation hearing and for the new criminal charge that also constitutes the alleged probation violation.

Different Courts

Section (c) of the rule addresses the circumstance where a person against whom a criminal complaint has issued is on probation in a different court. Under section (c)(i) the Probation Department of the court that issued the complaint must prepare and serve a Notice of Probation Violation and Hearing on the probationer in hand at arraignment, just as in the "same-court" situation. However, in addition to specifying the alleged violation, the Notice will order the probationer to appear on a date certain at the court where he or she is on probation. The purposes of that appearance will be to appoint counsel and schedule the violation hearing. The Probation Department of the court where the defendant is on probation may amend the notice to include additional violation allegations. Presumably the court where the probationer is on probation will schedule a prompt hearing date, consistent with the seven-day minimum notice period for the probationer. (See below.)

The requirement that copies of the Notice, criminal complaint and police report be sent "forthwith" to the probation court is most effectively satisfied by the use of facsimile ("fax") transmission.

Scheduling

Notice of the probation violation hearing "must be given sufficiently in advance of scheduled court proceedings so that reasonable opportunity to prepare will be afforded." *Commonwealth v. Odoardi*, 397 Mass. 28, 31–32 (1986), quoting *In re Gault*, 387 U.S. 1, 33 (1967). The rule provides a minimum of seven days notice in both the same-court and different-court situations. This is the minimum notice period previously provided by regulations of the Office of the Commissioner of Probation and should be minimally adequate in most cases given the narrow focus of these hearings. If either party desires more time than is allowed by the scheduled date, a continuance may be sought under Rule 5(e) [now Rule 6(e)].

The rule also provides that the hearing may not be scheduled for a date more than 30 days after service of the Notice if the probationer objects to such date. This is to protect the probationer from undue delay, which is a particular concern if the probationer is being held in probation detention. Finally, the rule provides that even if the hearing date is beyond the 30–day limit and the probationer objects, such delay may nonetheless be justified on the basis of "extraordinary circumstances."

The purpose of requiring the probation violation hearing to be scheduled along with the pretrial hearing on the new criminal case in the same-court situation (section (b)(iii)) is not only to avoid delay of the probation hearing, but also to create an opportunity for a disposition of the criminal case that takes into account the probation disposition. Most criminal cases, in fact, are disposed of by plea or admission. It is appropriate to provide the defendant an opportunity to consider whether to submit a plea or admission that may take into account the outcome of the probation violation hearing. The defendant's right to a trial on the new criminal charge remains unaffected.

The last sentence of section (b)(iii) is intended to indicate that the prompt scheduling of the probation violation hearing should drive the scheduling of the pretrial hearing on the new charge. Thus, in a court in which the next regularly available date for a pretrial hearing is not consistent with the need for a prompt hearing on the alleged probation violation in terms of public safety implications, a prompt date (even a minimum seven-day date where appropriate) should be given even if this means scheduling the pretrial hearing on the new criminal charge prior to the date it would otherwise receive.

In the different-court situation, the date of the Pretrial Hearing on the criminal charge should be indicated on the copy of the Notice sent to the probation court. This will allow the probation court to schedule the violation hearing before that date.

Under G.L. c. 258B, § 3(*o*), victims have a right to be notified by a probationer's supervising probation officer if a probationer "seeks to modify a restitution order." This does not appear to require a supervising probation officer to send a copy of the Notice of Probation Violation and Hearing to a victim, even if modification of a restitution order is a possible outcome of the hearing.

Notice to District Attorney

In both the same-court and the different-court situations, the rule requires that a copy of the Notice of Probation Violation and Hearing be provided to the District Attorney. The relevant law, G.L. c. 279, § 3, gives the District Attorney the right to receive a copy of the notice and appear at such hearings only where the original conviction for which the probationer is on probation involves at least one felony. However, the rule reflects the position that the District Attorney should be allowed to appear at all such hearings. It allows the District Attorney to decide which hearings to attend and provides as an alternative the submission of a written statement. (Rule 5(f) [now Rule 6(f)]) This is appropriate, given the fact that some misdemeanor charges may have greater public safety implications than felony charges, e.g., drunk driving, domestic assault and battery and violation of restraining orders. Also, the District Attorney has certain obligations to victims of crime regarding probation violation hearings that can be met only if the District Attorney is informed of the scheduling of such hearings. G.L. c. 258B, § 3. See Rule 5(f) [now Rule 6(f)] and related commentary.

Commentary to District/Municipal Courts Rule 3—2015

This rule involves cases in which an alleged probation violation consists of a new criminal charge against the probationer. Such cases can arise in two contexts: where the probationer is on probation at the same court division that issued the new criminal complaint (the "same court" situation), and where the criminal complaint was issued by a court division or department other than the one where the probationer is on probation (the "different court" situation).

For both situations, this rule contains a provision not included in the 2000 District Court Rules by which a Notice of Probation Violation and Hearing may be "withdrawn." Such withdrawals have been a method by which probation violation proceedings may be terminated. Withdrawal has been held to be within the discretion of a Probation Department. *Commonwealth v. Milton*, 427 Mass. 18, 21 (1998). There has been no requirement for court approval or permission. The new provision imposes two new requirements: (1) that such withdrawals must receive the permission of the court, and (2) that such permission and the fact of the withdrawal must be entered on the case docket. By requiring judicial permission and entry on the record, the new provision reflects the importance of a process by which a probation violation proceeding that has been formally commenced may be terminated without adjudication.

The new provision regarding withdrawal appears both in section (b)(i) (for the "same court" situation) and in section (c)(vi) (for the "different court" situation). Sections (b)(i) and (c)(vi) also now make clear that the Probation Department is responsible for providing a copy of the notice of violation to the District Attorney.

The last paragraph of section (b)(i) continues to authorize the termination of a probation violation proceeding as a matter of judicial discretion, on the court's own initiative or otherwise. The reference to such termination occurring "at arraignment" has been deleted because such termination may be ordered at any stage of the proceeding. A similar provision has been added to section (c)(vi) to address the "different court" situation.

New subsections (iii)—(v) have been added to section (c) of the rule that did not appear in the 2000 District Court Rule. Former section (iii) from the 2000 District Court Rule has been retained, but renumbered section (vi). See below. The purpose of the three new subsec-

tions is to provide a detailed process by which, in the "different court" situation, the "criminal court" must interact with the "probation court." The purpose of this interaction is to effect the transfer of the probation proceeding and, in some instances, the custodial transfer of the probationer, to the probation court.

Section (c)(iii) specifies the documents that must be sent by the criminal court to the probation court, including the request that the probation court make a recommendation on whether the probationer should be transported in custody. This section also provides that the criminal court may hold the probationer in custody pending this decision. This is important because, if not held on bail on the new criminal charge, the probationer may be otherwise free to leave the court. Such a departure would render moot the process of determining custody in the different-court situation. The legal bases for temporary custody of a probationer for good cause are set forth in the Commentary to Rule 6(h).

Section (c)(iv) describes the response required of the probation court to the criminal court. This response, including the recommendation regarding transport, is the responsibility of the Chief Probation Officer, an Assistant Chief Probation Officer, or a designated probation officer of the probation court and must be transmitted to the criminal court within one hour after receipt of the criminal court's request for information.

Section (c)(v) provides that the judge at the criminal court is responsible for the decision on whether the probationer will be transported to the probation court. The judge must give the probationer an opportunity to be heard and is not bound by the probation court's recommendation. The probation officer must provide the criminal court with a recommendation within one hour, and the judge must wait for that recommendation, absent exceptional circumstances. If a recommendation is not received within that hour, the judge at the criminal court may, but need not, wait longer before deciding whether to transport. If the decision is made to transport the probationer, the court will issue a probation warrant on behalf of the probation court. It is not necessary for the probation court to take any action in this regard. For this decision, the judge, for jurisdictional purposes, will be sitting at a session of the probation court held at the location of the criminal court, by designation of the Chief Justice of the relevant department under G.L. c. 211B, § 10 and G.L. c. 218, § 43A.

Under the former procedure, the decision to transport a probationer was to be made at the probation court and a warrant issued there and sent to the criminal court. This meant that a probation officer had to seek the issuance of a warrant by a judge of that court, a judge who was otherwise unaware of the matter and was usually engaged in that court's daily business. This would often delay the process, particularly in those cases where the judge at the probation court required a more detailed description of the underlying allegations before issuing the warrant.

This rule has been changed because the judge in the criminal court is in a superior position, both substantively and practically, to make the transport decision. That judge will be addressing an issue in a case that is before the court at that time, will be immediately aware of the criminal case which constitutes the alleged probation violation, and will have all relevant information regarding the probationer's criminal record and pending probation status.

Section (c)(vi) of the rule, corresponding to section (c)(iii) of the 2000 District Court Rule, has been amended to clarify and simplify the requirement that, if the probation court wishes to allege additional probation violations, it must issue and serve a new notice of violation.

Section (c)(vii) has been added to address a circumstance that the rules did not previously address, namely, where the defendant before the criminal court is currently on probation *in more than one other court division within the same court department*. It provides that in such cases the judge at the criminal court must decide the probation court with which the criminal court will interact. This decision will determine which of the probation courts will be "first in line" to address the probationer's alleged violation based on the new criminal charge. The rule provides that the other courts at which the individual is on probation are responsible for charging the new crime as an alleged violation, and initiating a violation proceeding by issuing a notice of violation and mailing it to the probationer or obtaining the appearance of the probationer by means of a probation warrant or other process such as a writ of habeas corpus.

Section (c)(viii) has been added to acknowledge the practice in Boston Municipal Court of allowing probation violation matters in several different divisions to be adjudicated in a single division. Each department may, by standing order, authorize and regulate such practices as will promote the orderly dispatch of probation matters in its department.

Section (d) addresses the circumstance where a defendant is on probation in one department (for example, the District Court or the Superior Court) and is arrested in another department (for example, the Boston Municipal Court). In such circumstances, the Probation Department in the criminal court must notify the Probation Department in the probation court as soon as possible and always before the case is heard in the criminal court. Such notification should ordinarily occur as soon as the Probation Department becomes aware that the defendant is on probation. Although the criminal court lacks the authority to issue a notice of violation or warrant for the probation court, the Probation Departments should coordinate, especially if the Probation Department in the probation court wishes to issue a warrant under G.L. c. 279, § 3.

Rule 4. Commencement of Violation Proceedings: Violations Other Than a New Criminal Complaint

(a) General. This rule prescribes the procedures to be undertaken regarding alleged violations of probation that do not involve or include criminal conduct charged in a criminal complaint.

(b) Issuance and Service of Notice; Termination of Proceedings; Withdrawal of Notice. When a probation officer of a court that has issued a probation order determines that a probationer has violated any condition of that order other than the alleged commission of a crime as charged in a criminal complaint, that probation officer shall decide whether to commence probation violation proceedings. Such decision shall be made in accordance with the rules and regulations of the Office of the Commissioner of Probation, provided, however, that probation violation proceedings shall be commenced (1) upon the issuance of an indictment, (2) when the judge issuing the probation order orders that such proceedings are to be commenced upon an alleged violation of one or more conditions of probation, or (3) when the commencement of such proceedings is required by statutory mandate. In any case, a judge of the court may order the commencement of violation proceedings.

Violation proceedings shall be commenced by the issuance by the Probation Department of a Notice of Probation Violation and Hearing, which shall be served on the probationer in hand or by first-class mail, unless the court orders otherwise. Service of the notice in hand or by first-class mail shall be noted in the court record. Out-of-court service other than by first-class mail shall require a written return of service. The Probation Department shall provide a copy of each notice of violation to the District Attorney forthwith upon its issuance.

If deemed appropriate, because of the seriousness of the alleged violation or for other good reason, the court may issue

a violation of probation warrant. The clerk shall forthwith enter such warrant in the warrant management system. Upon the probationer's first appearance before the court, the probationer shall be served in hand with the notice of violation.

At any time during the proceedings, the court, upon review of a notice of the violation and as a matter of its discretion, may order termination of the proceedings. A notice of violation maybe withdrawn only with the permission of the court and such withdrawal and permission shall be set forth on the record and entered on the case docket.

(c) Contents of Notice. The Notice of Probation Violation and Hearing shall set forth the conditions of the probation order that the Probation Department alleges have been violated and shall order the probationer to appear at a specific date and time for the express purpose of the appointment of counsel, if necessary, and the scheduling of a probation violation hearing.

(d) Scheduling of Hearing. Upon appearance of the probationer in accordance with the Notice required by Rule 4(c), the court shall appoint counsel, if necessary, and schedule a probation violation hearing for a date certain, the date to be no less than seven days later unless the probationer waives the seven-day notice period. The hearing date shall not be later than 30 days after the appearance, except in extraordinary circumstances.

Adopted December 2, 1999, effective January 3, 2000. Amended February 25, 2015, effective September 8, 2015.

Commentary to District Court Rule 4—2000

This rule provides the procedures to be followed when it is alleged that a probationer has violated any probation conditions that do not include criminal behavior as alleged in a criminal complaint, that is, any violation not governed by Rule 3. This includes allegations of criminal acts that are not the subject of a criminal complaint, allegations of a crime set forth in an indictment, any alleged violation of general probation conditions 2 (to report to the probation officer as required), 3 (to notify the probation officer of any change of employment or address) or 4 (to obtain permission to leave the Commonwealth), and any alleged violation of any special condition of probation.

Section (b) of the rule defers to the Rules and Regulations of the Office of the Commissioner of Probation (OCP) regarding the commencement of such proceedings. Unlike charged criminal acts, it is appropriate that other alleged violations be the subject of violation proceedings only in accordance with professional probation policies and standards. These policies provide an appropriate degree of discretion and also provide a procedure for administrative proceedings where the alleged violation does not warrant the commencement of court proceedings. Such policies require collaboration with the Presiding Justice at each court. Notwithstanding a probation officer's decision, in accordance with Probation Department regulations, not to commence proceedings in a particular case, a judge may order such proceedings to be commenced.

There are three exceptions to the reliance on OCP regulations and policies under section (b). The first requires commencement of proceedings upon the issuance of an indictment. The rationale for this is the same as for the required commencement of proceedings upon the issuance of a criminal complaint. See commentary to Rule 3. The second allows the sentencing judge to require in the probation order that upon certain alleged violations, a probation violation hearing must be commenced. The third exception is that a violation hearing must be commenced if required by law. Perhaps the most notable example of the last is G.L. c. 209A, § 7, which provides as follows:

If the defendant ordered to undergo treatment [after being convicted of a violation of a restraining order issued under G.L. c. 209A] has received a suspended sentence, the original sentence shall be reimposed if the defendant fails to participate in said program as required by the terms of his probation.

The statute would appear to require that probation violation proceedings be commenced upon an allegation of such a violation, and that revocation be ordered if the violation is found.

The rationale for providing a copy of each Notice of Probation Violation and Hearing to the District Attorney is the same as for notices in proceedings under Rule 3. It allows the District Attorney to decide which hearings to appear at and permits the District Attorney to fulfill certain legal obligations to victims and witnesses involved in the original criminal case in which the probation order was issued. See Rule 5(f) [now Rule 6(f)] and related commentary.

Sections (c) and (d) provide for notice to the probationer of the alleged violation and ordering him or her to appear in court on a specific date and time so that the issue of counsel may be addressed and the violation hearing scheduled. The minimum notice period for the hearing is seven days, unless waived.

In cases where custody of a probationer is warranted pending the hearing, the probationer may be arrested with or without a warrant pursuant to G.L. c. 279, § 3, and held if probable cause is found at a preliminary violation hearing following the arrest. See Rule 8 [now Rule 5].

Commentary to District/Municipal Courts Rule 4—2015

Section (b) differs from the 2000 District Court Rule in the addition of the last paragraph, which is identical to the last paragraph of Rule 3(b)(i) and (c)(vi). This paragraph refers to the authority of the court to terminate a violation proceeding and adds new requirements governing the withdrawal of a notice of violation by the Probation Department. This paragraph has been added to ensure that the same provisions that apply to violation proceedings involving charged criminal conduct (the subject of Rule 3), also apply to proceedings covered by Rule 4, i.e., proceedings that do *not* involve a new criminal complaint. The purpose of the new provisions governing the withdrawal of a notice of violation are discussed in the Commentary to the Rule 3 amendments.

Section (b) also makes clear that the Probation Department is responsible for providing a copy of the notice of violation to the District Attorney.

Section (b) specifies that the judge may issue a violation of probation warrant if the seriousness of the alleged violation or other good reason makes that advisable. For example, a probationer convicted of a sex crime may remove a global positioning system bracelet, demanding immediate action despite the absence of a new crime. Nothing in this grant of authority detracts from the statutory power of a probation officer to issue a violation of probation warrant without court approval under G.L. c. 279, § 3. The careful exercise of that power is essential to effective and efficient probation supervision.

The title of section (b) differs from the 2000 District Court Rule in referring to the two new topics that have been added to that section.

Rule 5. Probation Detention Hearings

(a) Purpose. A probation detention hearing maybe conducted to determine whether a probationer shall be held in custody pending the conduct of a probation violation hearing. The issues to be decided at a probation detention hearing are whether probable cause exists to believe that the probationer has violated a condition of the probation order, and, if so, whether the probationer should be held in custody.

(b) Notice of Hearing. The probationer shall be given a written notice indicating the purpose of the hearing and referring to the probation violations alleged in the notice of violation which is required to be served on the probationer under these rules. The detention proceeding shall be commenced by the service of such notice on the probationer. The court may, for good cause, order that the probationer be taken into custody pending the completion of the proceeding. The notice shall be served in hand when the probationer is before the court having been arrested on a new criminal charge, having been arrested for a probation violation, or for any other reason. The notice shall be prepared and served by the Probation Department at the discretion of a probation officer or as directed by the court.

(c) Conduct of Hearing. Probation detention hearings shall be conducted by a judge or, if there is no judge at the court, by a magistrate. When a magistrate conducts a probation detention hearing, a resulting custody order shall not extend beyond the date on which a judge will next be present at the court. On such date, the probationer shall be brought before the court and any further custody order will require the conduct of a detention hearing by a judge.

Probation detention hearings shall be conducted in a courtroom on the record. The probationer shall be entitled to counsel. Following service of notice, as provided in Rule 5(b), and the appointment of counsel, the appearance of private counsel, or the knowing and voluntary waiver of the right to counsel, the probationer shall be allowed a reasonable time to prepare for the hearing. At the hearing, the probation officer shall be required to present evidence to support a finding of probable cause. The District Attorney may assist in the presentation of such evidence. The probationer shall be entitled to be heard in opposition. Testimony, including testimony of a probation officer, shall be taken under oath. The court shall admit such evidence as it deems relevant and appropriate. The scope of the inquiry shall be limited to the issue of whether there is probable cause to believe that the alleged violation of probation has occurred.

If probable cause is found, the court may order the probationer to be held in custody pending the conduct and completion of the violation hearing. The court's decision whether to order such custody shall include, but not necessarily be limited to, consideration of the following:

i. the probationer's criminal record;

ii. the nature of the offense for which the probationer is on probation;

iii. the nature of the offense or offenses with which the probationer is newly charged, if any;

iv. the nature of any other pending alleged probation violations;

v. the likelihood of probationer's appearance at the probation violation hearing if not held in custody; and

vi. the likelihood of incarceration if a violation is found following the probation violation hearing.

If probable cause is found and the court does not order the probationer held in custody, the court may order the probationer released upon such conditions as maybe provided for in standing orders promulgated by that court's department.

If no probable cause is found, the court may terminate the proceedings or schedule a probation violation hearing, serving the probationer with notice thereof, but the probationer may not be held in custody pending the hearing based on the alleged probation violation.

Adopted December 2, 1999, effective January 3, 2000. Renumbered and amended February 25, 2015, effective September 8, 2015.

Commentary to District Court Rule 8—2000

Preliminary probation hearings are required only when the probationer is to be held in custody for an alleged probation violation pending the conduct of a full hearing.

The purpose of the preliminary hearing is to protect the rights of the ... probationer who, being at liberty, is taken into custody for alleged violation of his ... probation conditions, and detained pending a final revocation hearing.

Fay v. Commonwealth, 379 Mass. 498, 504 (1980) (citations omitted).

Thus, for example, there is no requirement of a preliminary hearing if the alleged probation violator already has received a probable cause hearing on the new crime and has been bound over to the grand jury. *Stefanik v. State Board of Parole*, 372 Mass. 726 (1977). *See also Commonwealth v. Odoardi*, 397 Mass. 28, 33, 34 (1986) (no preliminary hearing where probationer already incarcerated at the time of the proceeding on the alleged violation).

The issue of whether a probationer should be held in custody pending the conduct of a probation violation hearing can arise when a defendant is before the court on a separate matter (e.g., on arrest for a new criminal charge) or having been arrested with or without a warrant for a violation of probation. G.L. c. 279, § 3.

The probationer is entitled to a preliminary hearing "at the time of his arrest and detention ..." *Commonwealth v. Odoardi*, 397 Mass. 28, 33 (1986). That arrest can take place while the probationer is at liberty or when a probation officer takes custody of a probationer who is before the court on another matter, such as the charge of a new crime. Written notice must be given to the probationer at that time and the probationer and counsel must be given time to prepare for this hearing. If a continuance is requested and allowed, the custody resulting from the arrest will continue until the preliminary hearing (or a final hearing if the preliminary hearing is waived) is conducted.

The rule does not provide for notice of a preliminary probation violation hearing to be served on a probationer who is at liberty. If it is believed that a probationer who is at liberty has violated probation and should be in custody pending a hearing on that violation, custody should be effected by an arrest with or without a warrant, under G.L. c. 279, § 3. If it is believed that a probationer who is at liberty has violated probation, but there is no need to hold him or her in custody pending a final hearing, there is no need to serve a notice of a preliminary hearing. Rather, a notice of a final hearing should be served.

At the preliminary probation violation hearing, the question of revocation or other disposition is not at issue, only the question of probable cause for the alleged violation. Of course, the preliminary hearing can be transformed into a "final" hearing if the defendant waives the minimum seven-day notice period and both the probationer and the Probation Department are willing to proceed immediately with either an admission or a hearing. Only in such instances will the issue of revocation or other disposition be appropriately addressed.

The rule provides no qualifications on the evidence that may be admitted at preliminary hearings, other than to state that the court may hear such evidence as it deems appropriate. The rules of evidence do not apply. There appears to be no law categorically disqualifying a judge who has conducted a preliminary hearing from conducting the subsequent final hearing. When no judge is available, a magistrate may conduct the preliminary hearing. See G.L. c. 221, §§ 62B and 62C(g), and Uniform Magistrate Rule 6.

Section (c) of the rule also provides that upon a finding of probable cause, the court may order the probationer to be held in custody pending the final hearing. A finding of probable cause does not require a custody order. The rule lists six factors that the court must consider when deciding whether to release the probationer notwithstanding the finding of probable cause on the alleged violation. The list is not exclusive and the rule does not attempt to assign relative weight to the factors.

Section (d) makes clear that bail and other terms of pretrial release have no application regarding a probationer's custody pending the conduct and completion of a final probation violation hearing. Bail and other conditions of pretrial release, including pretrial detention based on "dangerousness," under G.L. c. 276, §§ 58 and 58A, have no legal or conceptual relevance to custody on an alleged probation violation. They relate solely to a newly alleged crime. If the court finds probable cause for a probation violation, it may order the defendant into custody pending the final hearing on the violation. If the court does *not* find probable cause, the probationer cannot be held in custody *on the alleged violation*. Even if the probationer *is* held on the probation allegation, if he or she is also before the court on a new criminal charge, the court must address the terms of pretrial release. This issue is unrelated to custody on the probation charge. The prosecutor may want to be heard on the issue of bail or dangerousness because if the probation matter is promptly resolved, the defendant may be released from custody on the probation matter well before the criminal case is concluded.

Conversely, the issue of probation custody should be addressed regardless of whether or not the prosecutor plans to ask for high bail or pretrial detention based on dangerousness.

There appears to be no basis in statutory or case law for Superior Court review of a District Court probable cause decision resulting in custody pending a final probation violation hearing.

Commentary to District/Municipal Courts Rule 5—2015

This rule differs from its antecedent, 2000 District Court Rule 8, both in its placement and the replacement throughout of the terms "preliminary probation hearing" and "final [or 'full'] probation hearing" with the terms "probation detention hearing" and "probation violation hearing," respectively. The purpose of these changes was to use terms that more accurately describe and clearly differentiate these proceedings.

Section (b) contains a new sentence indicating that a probation detention proceeding is commenced when the notice thereof is served on the probationer. Another new sentence indicates that the court has the authority to hold the probationer in custody pending the completion of the proceedings for good cause. The bases for the latter authority are the same as those set forth for the authority to hold a probationer in custody after the probationer's arrival at court pending the commencement and completion of a probation violation hearing. See the Commentary to Rule 6(h). Where an alleged probation violation consists of a new criminal charge, the probationer may already be in custody prior to the conduct of a detention hearing, e.g., while awaiting a bail hearing on that charge.

Section (b) contains a new, final sentence indicating that a probation detention hearing may be conducted at the direction of the court as well at the initiative of the Probation Department. In other words, the court may initiate a detention hearing.

The first paragraph of section (c) recognizes the authority of magistrates to conduct probation detention hearings. Such authority is specifically provided in G.L. c. 221, § 62C(g). The rule provides conditions for the exercise of this authority by requiring that it be used only when there is no judge at the court and by limiting the duration of any resulting custody order.

The first sentence of the second paragraph of section (c) corresponds to the first paragraph of section (c) in the 2000 District Court Rule 8. The second paragraph also contains a new, express reference to the requirement that a waiver by a probationer of the right to counsel at these hearings must be made knowingly and voluntarily.

The remainder of section (c) differs from its antecedent in the deletion of surplus language, especially references to the court's obligation to issue and serve a notice of violation and to schedule a violation hearing. These requirements are set forth in Rules 3 and 4.

One question that the rule does not address involves the effect, if any, on the *probation detention* probable cause determination when the alleged violation consists of a *new criminal charge*. In such cases, a probable cause determination will already have been made as a prerequisite for issuance of the criminal complaint for that charge. However, it would appear that a court conducting a probation detention hearing is not "bound" by the earlier probable cause ruling. While the same evidence that was considered for probable cause on the criminal complaint may also be presented to the court in the probation detention proceeding (e.g., a police report), a new probable cause ruling is nonetheless required. Under the principle of *res judicata* and the doctrine of "issue preclusion," an earlier ruling on a legal issue is binding in a subsequent proceeding only if several requirements are met. These requirements are not met in the situation at issue. For example, the issue must have involved a final judgment on the merits in the prior proceeding. *See Kobrin v. Bd. of Registration in Medicine*, 444 Mass. 837, 843–44 (2005), and cases cited therein. A probable cause ruling for the issuance of a criminal complaint is not a final judgment on the merits. Moreover, the party against whom preclusion would be asserted must have had a meaningful opportunity to have been heard in the prior proceeding. *Id.* In criminal cases, the accused is not entitled to be heard on the issue of probable cause (except in those cases where a criminal complaint hearing precedes an arrest).

The 2000 District Court Rule 8(d) prohibited conditions of release, including bail. This provision in not included in the District/Municipal Courts Rule. Instead, when probable cause is found, the court is authorized to impose conditions of release. Violation of such a condition would ordinarily result in detention until the violation hearing. Recognizing the differing needs of the various court departments in the orderly processing of probation detention matters, the rule permits each court department to specify the allowable conditions of release in a standing order applicable to that department. Although bail as authorized by G.L. c. 276, § 58 is not permissible, *see Commonwealth v. Puleio*, 433 Mass. 39, 42 (2000), a department, by standing order, may authorize release based on a monetary condition. A probationer released on a monetary condition would not be able to seek bail review under G.L. c. 276, § 58. *Puleio*, 433 Mass. at 42.

When the court does not find probable cause, the court must exercise its discretion whether to terminate proceedings or to schedule a probation violation hearing nonetheless. Because of the need for dispatch in conducting a detention hearing, the absence of evidence, witnesses, or assistance from the District Attorney may result in the probation officer's being unable to establish probable cause for the purpose of detention but still having a reasonable prospect of proving the probation violation at a full hearing. The court will decide whether further proceedings are in the interests of justice, but in no event may the probationer be held or subject to conditions of release on the probation matter pending a probation violation hearing.

Rule 6. Conduct of Violation Hearings

(a) In General. Probation violation hearings shall be conducted by a judge, in open court, on the record. All testimony, including that of a probation officer, shall be taken under oath. The presentation of the case against the probationer shall be the responsibility of the probation officer assigned by the Chief Probation Officer of the court. The probationer shall be entitled to the assistance of counsel, including the appointment of counsel for probationers determined by the

court to be indigent. A waiver by the probationer of the right to counsel shall be accepted by the court only if the court determines that such waiver is being made knowingly and voluntarily.

(b) Requirement of Two–Step Procedure. Probation violation hearings shall proceed in two distinct steps: the first to adjudicate the factual issue of whether the alleged violation or violations occurred, the second to determine the disposition of the matter if a violation of probation is found to have occurred.

(c) Adjudication of Alleged Violation. Probation violation hearings shall commence with a statement by the probation officer describing the violation or violations alleged in the notice of violation, and shall proceed with a presentation of the evidence supporting the allegations. The probationer shall be permitted to present evidence relevant to the issue of the alleged violation. Each party shall be permitted to cross-examine witnesses produced by the opposing party. Hearsay evidence shall be admitted by the court, in accordance with Rule 7, provided that the court shall enforce any statutory privileges and disqualifications. The probation officer shall have the burden of proving the alleged violations with or without the participation of the District Attorney as provided below. The standard of proof at such hearings shall be the preponderance of the evidence. After the presentation of evidence, both parties or their counsel shall be permitted to make a closing statement.

(d) Dispositional Decision. If the court finds that the probationer has violated one or more conditions of probation as alleged, the probation officer shall recommend to the court a disposition consistent with the dispositional options set forth in Rules 8(d) and 9(b) and may present argument and evidence in support of that recommendation. The probationer shall be permitted to present argument and evidence relevant to disposition and to propose a disposition.

(e) Continuances; "Tracking" Prohibited. Probation violation hearings shall be continued only by a judge and only for good cause shown. The reason for any continuance shall be stated by the judge and set forth on the record. No continuance shall be ordered other than to a date certain and for a specific purpose, and as provided in Rule 8(a). When a criminal charge is the basis for an alleged violation of probation, no continuance of the violation hearing or disposition shall be allowed solely to "track" or await the disposition of the criminal charge.

(f) Participation of the District Attorney.

(i) *In general.* The District Attorney may participate in probation violation hearings as provided in G.L. c. 279, § 3, and such participation shall be permitted in any such proceeding regardless of whether the criminal case in which the probation order was issued involved a felony charge.

(ii) *Coordination with the Probation Department.* If the District Attorney intends to appear at a probation violation hearing, he or she shall confer prior to the hearing with the probation officer responsible for presenting the matter to the court, for the purpose of coordinating the District Attorney's involvement in the hearing with the planned presentation of the probation officer.

(iii) *Presentation of Evidence.* The District Attorney may present and examine witnesses at the hearing, may examine witnesses presented by the probation officer, and may cross-examine witnesses presented by the probationer. The probationer may cross-examine all witnesses, whether presented by the District Attorney or the probation officer. The District Attorney shall be responsible for the attendance of every witness he or she wishes to present, and for the summoning of such witnesses.

(iv) *Finding and Disposition.* After the presentation of evidence, the District Attorney may be heard on the strength of that evidence in supporting a finding of violation. If the court finds that the probationer has violated one or more of the conditions of probation as alleged in the notice of violation, the District Attorney may be heard regarding the court's disposition of the matter. The District Attorney may present a recommendation on disposition orally or in writing.

(g) Admission to Violation and Waiver of Right to Hearing. The court may accept an admission to an alleged probation violation and a waiver of the right to a violation hearing only upon a determination that the admission and waiver have been made knowingly and voluntarily.

Such an admission and waiver shall not be accepted by the court subject to any condition regarding the disposition of such violation or the disposition of any other probation violation or any pending criminal charge. A probationer shall not be entitled to withdraw an admission as of right after it has been accepted by the court.

(h) Ensuring Probationer's Presence in Courtroom. For good cause, the court may order that the probationer be taken into custody pending the commencement and completion of the violation hearing.

Adopted December 2, 1999, effective January 3, 2000. Renumbered and amended February 25, 2015, effective September 8, 2015.

Commentary to District Court Rule 5—2000

Probation revocation hearings are not part of a criminal prosecution, and for this reason a probationer need not be provided with the full panoply of constitutional protections applicable at a criminal trial. *Gagnon v. Scarpelli*, 411 U.S. 778, 782 (1973). Indeed, case law has sought to preserve the flexible, informal nature of probation revocation hearings. *See Black v. Romano*, 471 U.S. 606 (1985).

On the other hand, the probationer's liberty is potentially at stake in violation proceedings, and therefore certain due process protections are required. As set forth for parole revocation in *Morrissey v. Brewer*, 408 U.S. 471 (1972), and made applicable to probation revocation by *Gagnon v. Scarpelli*, 411 U.S. 778 (1973), there are six such fundamental due process requirements: (1) written notice of the claimed violations of probation; (2) disclosure to the probationer of the evidence against him; (3) opportunity to be heard in person and to present witnesses and documentary evidence; (4) the right to confront and cross-examine adverse witnesses (unless a hearing officer specifically finds good cause for not allowing confrontation); (5) a neutral and detached hearing body, members of which need not be judicial officers or lawyers; and (6) a written statement by the fact finder as to the evidence relied on and reasons for revoking probation.

This rule is intended to provide an orderly, relatively informal and flexible procedure for probation violation hearings, but one in which all required and appropriate due process safeguards are ensured.

General Requirements

Section (a) requires several fundamental procedural elements: a judicial procedure in open court, testimony under oath and the cre-

ation of a record. With regard to the record, Rule 211 of the Special Rules of the District Courts of Massachusetts, "Recording of Court Proceedings," requires that such proceedings be electronically recorded. Any District Court judge may conduct the hearing; the original sentencing judge is not required.

One of the six fundamental due process requirements for probation violation hearings, as provided in *Gagnon v. Scarpelli*, 411 U.S. 778 (1973), is "a neutral and detached hearing body." This requirement would appear to preclude the model by which a judge would take the initiative in the proceeding, as in an inquest, and the probation officer remain essentially passive in the role of a witness. Accordingly, the rule requires the probation officer, who is the "accuser," to present the case, with the judge remaining in the traditional neutral role. This does not prevent the judge from asking appropriate questions, nor is it inconsistent with the role of the probation officer as witness. The probation officer must provide evidence under oath and is subject to cross-examination.

It should be noted that in probation violation hearings the exclusionary rule does not apply if the police were unaware that the defendant was a probationer. *Commonwealth v. Olsen*, 405 Mass. 491 (1989) (evidence seized in violation of Fourth Amendment was admissible in probation violation proceeding, where police who seized evidence neither knew nor had reason to know of probationary status of person whose property was seized). There is no Massachusetts decision on whether the exclusionary rule applies in these proceedings where police are aware that the person is on probation.

Regarding the right to counsel, the rule goes beyond current law by providing the right to counsel regardless of whether the probationer faces the possibility of imprisonment if probation is revoked. *See Commonwealth v. Faulkner*, 418 Mass. 352 (1994) (probationer at probation violation hearing has right to counsel if revocation might result in imprisonment).

Two-step Proceeding

Section (b) imposes the critical requirement of a two-stage proceeding. As observed by the Supreme Court of the United States,

the decision to revoke probation typically involves two distinct components: (1) a retrospective factual question whether the probationer has violated a condition of probation; and (2) a discretionary determination by the sentencing authority whether violation of a condition warrants revocation of probation.

Black v. Romano, 471 U.S. 606, 611 (1985), as quoted in *Commonwealth v. Marvin*, 417 Mass. 291, 295 (1994) (Liacos, C.J., dissenting).

This dichotomy is further reflected in Massachusetts law:

At the revocation hearing, the judge must determine, as a factual matter, whether the defendant has violated the conditions of his probation. If the judge determines that the defendant is in violation, he can either revoke the probation and sentence the defendant or, if appropriate, modify the terms of his probation.

Commonwealth v. Burling, 407 Mass. 108, 111 (1990).

This distinction is an important one. The factual decision that a probation violation has occurred in no way compels an order of revocation. The court has wide dispositional latitude if a violation is found. *See* Rule 7(d) [now Rule 8(d)]. However, even if an alleged violation is relatively minor and, in all likelihood will not warrant revocation, it is important that it be adjudicated. It is essential for effective probation that a record of compliance and noncompliance with probation orders be maintained.

In addition, the distinction between the factual determination and the disposition must be maintained because different legal requirements are invoked. For example, the factual issue of whether an alleged violation has occurred must be decided based on a preponderance of the evidence, *Commonwealth v. Holmgren*, 421 Mass. 224 (1995), while the dispositional decision is a matter of judicial discretion. *McHoul v. Commonwealth*, 365 Mass. 465, 469–70 (1974). Similarly, the "seriousness" of the alleged violation is irrelevant to whether it occurred, while it is relevant to the question of appropriate disposition.

Adjudication of Violation

Section (c) sets out the basic requirements for how the first step of the hearing, adjudication of the alleged violation, should proceed. It ensures both parties the right to present evidence and cross-examine adverse witnesses. The court has some discretion in limiting cross-examination involving irrelevant or redundant questioning. *See Commonwealth v. Odoardi*, 397 Mass. 28, 34 (1986). Section (c) also entitles both parties to make a closing statement. In *Commonwealth v. Marvin*, 417 Mass. 291, 295 (1994), the court declined "to impose a universal due process requirement that a defendant in a probation revocation hearing has an absolute right to make a closing argument." However, that case goes on to state that it would be a "better practice" to permit a probationer to present at least a brief closing argument. The provision in this rule is intended to ensure that this better practice is provided for both parties.

Disposition

Section (d) provides that both parties may be heard regarding disposition, assuming the court finds that one or more alleged violations was committed. The court's dispositional options are provided in Rule 7 [now Rule 8]. The probationer's right to be heard and present evidence regarding disposition implicate due process considerations. *See Commonwealth v. Odoardi*, 397 Mass. 28 (1986).

Continuances

Section (e) sets out certain requirements for continuances. It expressly eliminates "tracking," i.e., continuing a probation violation hearing to await disposition of the criminal case involving the charge that is also the alleged probation violation. The reason for this rule is that, on the one hand, there is no basis in law or in terms of fairness to the probationer for such a continuance, and, on the other hand, proceeding without delay on the alleged violation is of great importance in terms of the primary goals of probation, which are rehabilitation of the probationer and protection of the public. *Commonwealth v. LaFrance*, 402 Mass. 789, 795 (1988) (citations omitted). The rule does provide for continuances where good cause is shown and the reason for the continuance is stated by the judge and set forth on the record.

The Supreme Judicial Court has long made clear that there is no prerequisite that the probationer be convicted of a criminal charge to permit that criminal conduct to be used as the basis of a probation revocation.

> If the act alleged to be a violation of probation is made the subject of a criminal complaint, the commencement of the criminal prosecution does not preclude the revocation of the earlier probation nor does it require that the revocation proceedings be deferred until the completion of the new criminal proceeding.

Rubera v. Commonwealth, 371 Mass. 177, 181 (1976), and cases cited.

After analyzing the federal constitutional law relevant to the point and the precedents from other states, the Court in *Rubera* went on to explain the policy reasons that favor proceeding with revocation proceedings and not awaiting the outcome of the criminal case:

> We are aware that the practice which was followed in revoking the petitioner's probation in this case was not in accord with the procedure suggested by the ABA Project on Standards for Criminal Justice, Standards Relating to Probation § 5.3, at 62–63 (Approved Draft 1970), that "[a] revocation proceeding based solely upon commission of another crime ordinarily should not be initiated prior to the disposition of that charge." [citation omitted] That standard seems to impose an unreasonable and unfair burden on law enforcement authorities by placing them in the dilemma of having to decide between (a) having to forgo criminal prosecution of a person who is on probation and who appears to have committed another offense until they have first pursued steps to revoke his probation on the

basis of his conduct in ordinary proceedings without reliance on any subsequent criminal conviction, or (b) having to start criminal prosecution promptly on the later offense and then being prevented from trying to revoke his earlier probation until after the later prosecution has run its full course which, in the present state of our criminal dockets, would amount to arming the defendant with the weapon of potential delay with which he could forestall termination of the proceeding by endless appeals. We decline to impose the burden of such a choice on either probation officers or prosecutors.

Rubera v. Commonwealth, 371 Mass. at 184–85 (1976).

See also, Commonwealth v. Holmgren, 421 Mass. 224 (1995), which held that a probation violation hearing may proceed on a charge of a new crime, even if the defendant has been acquitted of that crime, because the standard of proof at a probation hearing is lower than the standard at a criminal trial. In other words, an acquittal, or the possibility of an acquittal, is irrelevant to a probation violation proceeding because failure to convict under the "reasonable doubt" standard neither precludes nor is inconsistent with a finding of a probation violation under the "preponderance of the evidence" standard.

The only legal relationship between a probation violation hearing and a criminal prosecution for the same alleged criminal conduct is that, if the criminal case *does* go forward before the probation hearing and results in a conviction, that conviction will be evidence of a probation violation and no independent finding of the underlying facts is required of the judge. *Commonwealth v. Maggio*, 414 Mass. 193 (1993).

District Attorney Participation

Section (f) addresses the subject of participation by the District Attorney. Rules 3 and 4 require the court to provide a copy of every Notice of Probation Violation and Hearing to the District Attorney. Section (f) of this rule is intended to clarify the involvement of the District Attorney in those cases where he or she decides to participate, consistent with the statutory provisions of G.L. c. 279, § 3.

It should be noted that as a constitutional matter, probation functions are within the judicial branch, and the office of the District Attorney is considered within the executive branch. *Commonwealth v. Tate*, 34 Mass. App. Ct. 446, 447–48 (1993), and cases cited. Under the Massachusetts Constitution, pt. 1, art. 30, the branches must maintain a separation of governmental powers.

> That separateness does not, however, lead to the conclusion that a district attorney's office may not assist the probation service in presenting evidence in support of a position that the probation service had decided upon.

> [P]robation officers are only aided, not interfered with, when district attorneys, upon invitation, conduct examination of witnesses and present evidence.

Id. at 448, and cases cited.

Thus the right of District Attorneys to present evidence and witnesses, and to examine and cross-examine witnesses at these proceedings would appear to be constitutionally acceptable as long as it does not fundamentally interfere with probation.

Commentary to District/Municipal Courts Rule 6—2015

Section (a) differs from its antecedent, 2000 District Court Rule 5, in the deletion of the last portion of the first sentence. This provision referred to the permissible "flexibility and informality" of violation hearings. While accurate, this reference was deemed unnecessary and the possible source of inappropriate informality.

Section (a) also contains a requirement that a waiver by a probationer of the right to counsel at a probation violation hearing requires a judicial determination that such waiver is being made knowingly and voluntarily.

Section (e) contains a different last sentence than the 2000 District Court Rule. The new sentence is meant to clarify and emphasize the prohibition in the rule against "tracking," i.e., the delay of a probation violation proceeding in order to await the disposition of a criminal charge when the criminal behavior involved constitutes the alleged probation violation. The disposition of an underlying criminal case is irrelevant to the issue at the probation violation hearing, that is, whether a violation can be proved by a preponderance of the evidence. The rationale for this prohibition and the case law on which it is based are set forth in the original commentary to this rule. The rule also has been amended to expressly prohibit "tracking" as a means of delaying dispositions as well as hearings. *See also* Rule 8(d). The caption of section (e) also is different.

Section (f) is modified from the 2000 District Court Rule to clarify its meaning.

Section (g) is new. It addresses the procedure whereby a probationer offers to admit to an alleged violation. The rule refers to the two components of such an admission. First, the probationer must admit to the commission of one or more of the violations charged in the notice of violation, and second, the probationer must waive the right to a violation hearing. *See Commonwealth v. Sayyid*, 86 Mass. App. Ct. 479, 489, *rev. denied*, 470 Mass. 1103 (2014). Although the term "stipulation" is commonly used, the rule uses the term "admission" because it more accurately and appropriately describes this legal event.

Section (g) also provides that, unlike a guilty plea or admission to sufficient facts to a *criminal* charge, an admission to a probation violation may not be accompanied by conditions which, if not accepted by the court, would allow the probationer to withdraw the admission. In other words, there is no equivalency to the "defendant-capped plea" which can be tendered in the context of a criminal proceeding. The court may *allow* a probationer to withdraw a probation violation admission based on the court's intended disposition as a matter of its discretion. The probationer may not withdraw an admission as a matter of right once an admission is submitted and accepted by the court. A defendant would be entitled to withdraw an admission that was not made knowing and voluntarily. *Sayyid*, 86 Mass. App. Ct. at 490–92.

The prohibition in section (g) against "conditioned" probation violation admissions also precludes admissions conditioned by proposed dispositions "agreed to" by the probation department or by a prosecutor. Such an agreement does not bind the court or permit the withdrawal of the admission if the court's disposition is other than that "agreed upon" by a probation officer or prosecutor. The court may consult with probation regarding the disposition after finding a probation violation. *See* Rule 8(d). But for probation violation admissions there is no equivalent to the tender of criminal guilty pleas which may include dispositional terms agreed to by the prosecution.

It should also be noted that section (g) does not require the conduct of a specific colloquy as the means by which the court is to determine that a probationer's admission to a violation is being made knowingly and voluntarily. The colloquy required for the acceptance of a *guilty plea to a criminal charge* is not required for the acceptance of a probation violation admission. *See Sayyid*, 86 Mass. App. Ct. at 488–89, 492–93. Rather, the court is left to conduct such questioning of the probationer and his or her counsel as it deems adequate for this determination. *See Sayyid*, 86 Mass. App. Ct. at 489, 492–93.

Section (g) does not require that a probationer's admission to a violation and waiver of the right to a hearing be set forth on a particular form. However, an approved form is available for this purpose on the internet at www.mass.gov/courts/courtsandjudges/courts/districtcourt/forms.html. At a minimum, the court's questioning of a probationer on this issue and the probationer's responses should be memorialized on the audio recording of the proceedings, and the facts that the questioning occurred and that the court accepted the admission and waiver should be entered on the court's written record.

Section (h) is new. It refers to the court's authority to secure the presence of a probationer pending the commencement and completion

of a probation violation hearing. This rule addresses the problem of a probationer who, having arrived in court for a violation hearing while not in custody (in response to a notice of violation or otherwise), simply decides to exit the courtroom and the court house. This can occur if a probationer, while awaiting his or her hearing, observes a hearing that results in a finding of violation, revocation, and immediate execution of sentence.

The basis of the court's authority to secure the presence of a probationer, which includes custody, if necessary, pending the conduct of his or her hearing is threefold:

1. First, as a matter of constitutional law, a person on probation has a conditional liberty interest. The restricted scope of this liberty interest is perhaps best illustrated by the statutory authority of a probation officer *to issue an arrest warrant or to arrest a probationer without a warrant* to bring him or her before the court to answer to a possible probation violation. G.L. c. 279, § 3. If a probationer may be arrested by a probation officer without a warrant to be brought to court on an alleged violation, then it would appear to follow that a probationer charged with a violation may be held by the court for good cause upon his or her non-custodial arrival in court for a hearing on that alleged violation.

2. Such a custody order merely enforces the existing order requiring the probationer's presence at the court. A probationer who has arrived in court in response to a notice of violation has been formally accused in that notice of one or more specific probation violations and ordered to appear in court. The notice informs the probationer that he or she is "HEREBY ORDERED AS FOLLOWS: YOU MUST APPEAR IN THIS COURT" on a specific date at a specific time. Thus, the probationer is under court order to be in court for the conduct of the violation hearing. He or she is not free to leave. Custody of the probationer pending the conduct and completion of the hearing ensures compliance with that court order.

3. The authority of the court to secure the presence of a probationer for the conduct of a scheduled hearing also has a constitutional basis in the court's inherent power. "Of necessity, a judge's inherent power must encompass the authority to exercise 'physical control over his courtroom.'" *Commonwealth v. O'Neil*, 418 Mass. 760, 764 (1994) (quoting *Chief Admin. Justice of the Trial Ct. v. Labor Relations Comm'n*, 404 Mass. 53, 57 (1989)); *see id.* ("'[t]he power of the judiciary to control its own proceedings, the conduct of participants, the actions of officers of the court and the environment of the court is a power absolutely necessary for a court to function effectively and do its job of administering justice'") (quoting *Chief Admin. Justice of the Trial Ct.*, 404 Mass. at 57). Perhaps nothing could be viewed as more fundamental or essential to the court's ability to function than the power to prevent a probationer who has been ordered to appear for a hearing on an alleged violation from simply leaving the court prior to the conduct of that hearing.

In order to secure the presence of the probationer, the rule requires that the court have "good cause," that is, some reason to believe that the probationer may attempt to leave the courtroom to avoid the proceeding (e.g., the probationer's in-court behavior, history of defaults, and history of previous probation violations; the seriousness of the underlying crime; the potential sentence if revocation is ordered; etc.).

The custody provision in this rule is relevant only when the violation hearing will proceed that same day. If a probationer arrives at court and is seen as a flight risk, but the actual hearing will be scheduled for a later date, the probation department may immediately request a detention hearing under Rule 5 (formerly Rule 8). That rule also provides for custody of a probationer prior to the conduct of such a hearing. If detention is ordered, it will result in the probationer's continued custody until the conduct and completion of the violation hearing.

Rule 7. Hearsay Evidence

(a) Admissibility of Hearsay Evidence. Hearsay evidence shall be admissible at probation violation hearings.

(b) Legal Sufficiency of Hearsay Evidence. The court may rely on hearsay as evidence of a probation violation only if the court finds in writing that the hearsay is substantially reliable. In determining if hearsay evidence is substantially reliable, the court may consider, among any other relevant factors, whether that evidence

(1) is based on personal knowledge and/or direct observation, rather than on other hearsay;

(2) involves observations recorded close in time to the events in question;

(3) is factually detailed, rather than generalized and conclusory;

(4) is internally consistent;

(5) is corroborated by any evidence provided by the probationer;

(6) was provided by a disinterested witness; or

(7) was provided under circumstances that support the veracity of the source (e.g., was provided under the pains and penalties of perjury or subject to criminal penalties for providing false information).

Adopted December 2, 1999, effective January 3, 2000. Renumbered and amended February 25, 2015, effective September 8, 2015.

Commentary to District Court Rule 6—2000

Probation violation hearings often involve evidence in the form of records, documents and statements that constitute hearsay, that is, "an extrajudicial statement offered to prove the truth of the matter asserted." *Commonwealth v. Keizer*, 377 Mass 264, 269 n.4 (1979). Common examples of hearsay evidence used at these hearings are police reports used as evidence of the probationer's criminal behavior, and correspondence from programs such as batterers' treatment programs used as evidence of the probationer's failure to complete the program in compliance with the probation order.

This rule is based almost exclusively on the opinion in *Commonwealth v. Durling*, 407 Mass. 108 (1990), the leading case on the use of hearsay evidence at probation violation hearings. It is divided into separate sections, one on the *admissibility* of hearsay, the other on the *sufficiency of hearsay as a matter of law* when it is the only evidence presented against the probationer.

<u>Admissibility</u>

Section (a) states simply that hearsay is admissible at probation violation hearings. The Supreme Judicial Court "has always allowed the use of hearsay at probation revocation hearings." *Commonwealth v. Durling*, 407 Mass. at 114. The admissibility of hearsay is based on the principles set forth in Morrissey and Gagnon. The revocation process "should be flexible enough to consider evidence including letters, affidavits, and other material that would not be admissible in an adversary criminal trial." *Morrissey v. Brewer*, 408 U.S. 471, 489 (1972). Similarly, the Supreme Court has sanctioned the "use where appropriate of the conventional substitutes for live testimony including affidavits, depositions and documentary evidence." *Gagnon v. Scarpelli*, 411 U.S. 778, 782 n.5 (1973).

It has been held that if hearsay evidence qualifies under any of the legal exceptions to the hearsay rule (e.g., business record, excited utterance, dying declaration) it is presumptively reliable. *Durling*, 407 Mass. at 118. However, in keeping with the informal nature of these hearings and the fact that the case against the probationer is the

responsibility of a probation officer rather than a trained criminal prosecutor, it would appear that the court should make a determination of the reliability of any hearsay, rather than engage in an argument on whether the hearsay qualifies as an exception to the hearsay rule so as to merit presumptively reliable status. In other words, if the court determines that a record of a drug treatment center is reliable, it is irrelevant as to whether it qualifies as a "business record." An example of hearsay that might be found unreliable, and thus not worthy of the court's consideration, would be a second- or third-hand out-of-court statement, or a statement that is vague or internally contradictory or inconsistent.

<u>Sufficiency</u>

Section (b) of the rule addresses an issue quite different from admissibility, namely, the legal sufficiency of hearsay evidence where hearsay is the only evidence of the probationer's alleged violation. In such cases, the probationer has no opportunity to confront a witness with personal knowledge and test the reliability of that evidence by cross-examination. This deprivation of the right to confrontation of witnesses implicates due process considerations. However, the Supreme Court in *Durling* made clear that since a probationer's liberty interest is conditional, so too is the probationer's right to confront witnesses, and that right can be denied for "good cause."

The court's description of "good cause," in *Durling* is somewhat unclear. On the one hand, the court indicates that "good cause" for denying the probationer the right to confront witnesses "has thus far been defined in terms of difficulty and expense of procuring witnesses *in combination* with 'demonstrably reliable' or 'clearly reliable' evidence." *Durling*, 407 Mass. at 120 (emphasis added).

In fact, the court defines the question in *Durling* in terms of this two-pronged issue:

> The judge in this case relied solely on hearsay in revoking the defendant's probation. The judge did not make any express determination that there was good cause for denying the defendant the right to confront a witness with personal knowledge. Nor did the judge make any determination whether the proffered hearsay was reliable.

Durling, supra, at 115.

However, in contrast to this two-pronged definition, the *Durling* court also defines "good cause" solely in terms of the reliability of the hearsay evidence:

> In our view, a showing that the proffered evidence bears substantial indicia of reliability and is substantially trustworthy is a showing of good cause obviating the need for confrontation.

Durling, supra, at 118.

Despite this apparent conflict, the opinion appears to settle on the two-pronged definition of good cause:

> On the whole, the resolution of the confrontation issue depends on the totality of the circumstances in each case ... If the Commonwealth has "good cause" for not using a witness with personal knowledge, *and* instead offers reliable hearsay or other evidence, then the requirements of due process are satisfied.

Durling, supra, at 118–19 (emphasis added).

Also,

> The substantial reliability of the police reports in this case, *coupled with* the practical difficulty of presenting live testimony, discussed earlier, convinces us that the District Court judge could properly base his order of revocation on the evidence presented.

Durling, supra, at 122 (emphasis added).

In *Commonwealth v. Calvo*, 41 Mass. App. Ct. 903 (1996) (rescript), the Appeals Court interpreted *Durling* to require only a showing that hearsay evidence bears substantial indicia of reliability and is substantially trustworthy in order to meet the "good cause" test, obviating the right to confrontation. In *Calvo*, "good cause" was held not to require any showing that a live witness was unavailable.

This rule takes a middle ground, requiring that in *all* cases where the only evidence of an alleged probation violation is hearsay there must be a finding that the hearsay is substantially trustworthy and demonstrably reliable, and requiring a showing of why a live witness is unavailable when the alleged probation violation is based on charged or uncharged criminal behavior.

Trustworthiness and Reliability of Hearsay

There are at least five criteria for the court's determination of whether a given piece of hearsay evidence is "substantially trustworthy" and "demonstrably reliable," namely, whether the out-of-court statement:

(1) is factually detailed, rather than generalized and conclusory;

(2) is based on personal knowledge and direct observation by the source;

(3) is corroborated by evidence submitted by the probationer;

(4) was provided under circumstances that support the veracity of the source (e.g., was provided under the pains and penalties of perjury or subject to criminal penalties for providing false information);

(5) was provided by a disinterested witness.

This list of factors for determining reliability is taken directly from *Durling*, except item (5), which is taken from *Commonwealth v. Delaney*, 36 Mass. App. Ct. 930, 932 n.4 (1994) (rescript), a case applying the *Durling* test.

Good Cause for Absence of Witness

There are three factors mentioned in *Durling* for determining good cause for the absence of a live witness, namely,

(1) the distance a witness would have to travel to get to court,

(2) the costs the witness (or his or her public or private employer) would have to incur if the witness were compelled to appear, and

(3) the difficulty in scheduling the probation violation hearing at a time convenient to the witness and all other participants.

Hearsay Test Where the Alleged Violation Is Criminal Conduct

One of the most common alleged violations of probation is alleged criminal conduct. In many of these cases, evidence of the alleged violation will be a police report. Under the rule, there are two issues if the police report is the only evidence presented: reliability of the report and the reason for the absence of a live witness.

In establishing the requisite reliability of the police reports in *Durling*, the Court stressed that the two police reports related facts observed by the officers personally, and were factually detailed rather than general statements or conclusions. "We think the factual detail is indicative of reliability." *Durling, supra*, at 121 (citation omitted). The Court also mentioned the similarity of the two reports and the fact that the two officers were from different departments. Thus, in *Durling*, the police reports corroborated each other.

The *Durling* Court also stressed that in determining "good cause" to justify a finding of violation solely on hearsay, the court had to balance the interests of the probationer and those of the Commonwealth and look to the "totality of the circumstances." It would appear that such balancing includes the concept that the more reliable the hearsay evidence, the less stringent the test regarding the practical reasons for absence of a live witness. Conversely, where the reliability of the hearsay is not as high as it was in *Durling*, (which involved the unusual circumstance of two separate police reports) it would appear that the justification for the absence of a witness would have to be that much stronger.

Hearsay Test Where the Alleged Violation Is Something Other Than Criminal Conduct

The rule does not require a showing of why the live witness is unavailable where the alleged violation is something other than criminal conduct. Thus, for example, if the alleged violation were failure to attend a rehabilitation program, a report from the program, though hearsay, would be sufficient evidence if it met the reliability test of *Durling*, without regard to why the live witness were not present.

For cases applying the *Durling* test, see *Commonwealth v. Delaney*, 36 Mass. App. Ct. 930 (1994) (finding of violation based on hearsay statement reversed; statement did not meet reliability standard comparable to police reports in *Durling* and witness was available to testify); and *Commonwealth v. Joubert*, 38 Mass. App. Ct. 943 (1995) (revocation order reversed because hearsay statements of a child were not sufficiently reliable and findings indicate judge may have relied on them as the basis of decision).

Commentary to District/Municipal Courts Rule 7—2015

Section (a) is the same as the 2000 District Court Rule 6(a). It provides that hearsay evidence "shall be admissible" in Boston Municipal Court and District Court probation violation hearings. In *Commonwealth v. Durling*, 407 Mass. 108, 114 (1990), the Supreme Judicial Court stated that only "reliable" hearsay is admissible in these proceedings. The rule does not impose reliability as a formal precondition to admission, but rather requires that, in effect, hearsay evidence be admitted *de bene*. This avoids the potential bifurcation of each proceeding into a preliminary "suppression" hearing followed, if necessary, by a separate hearing on the factual issue of the alleged violation. Instead, the court commences the violation hearing and receives all proffered evidence, including hearsay. As set forth in section (b), any hearsay challenged as, and found by the court to be, unreliable may not be used as evidence of a violation. Moreover, if the court finds hearsay to be reliable it must provide written reasons. After resolving any issue of hearsay reliability, the court then rules on the alleged violation based on any competent evidence. Thus, the rule provides appropriate procedural clarity and simplicity while ensuring compliance with the constitutionally-based limitation on the use of hearsay in these proceedings, as set forth in *Durling*.

Nothing in these Rules precludes the judge from allowing a continuance to give either party an opportunity to summons witnesses if the judge deems it necessary to resolve facts in dispute.

Section (b) has been amended to conform to case law decided after the rule was initially promulgated. That case law has made it clear that there is a "one-pronged" test for determining whether hearsay evidence is legally sufficient as proof of a violation. Specifically, such evidence must be found by the court, in writing, to be "substantially reliable." *Commonwealth v. Maggio*, 414 Mass. 193 (1993); *see also Commonwealth v. Negron*, 441 Mass. 685 (2004).

The previous version of this rule imposed a two-pronged test, namely, for evidence to be legally adequate as a basis for finding a probation violation the rule required that it be both "substantially reliable," and, when the alleged violation was new criminal behavior, there had to be "good cause" for the absence of the percipient witness, i.e., the source of the hearsay. Current case law holds that where the hearsay is substantially reliable, this satisfies the good cause requirement. This paragraph and the previous paragraph of this Commentary were cited with approval by the Supreme Judicial Court in *Commonwealth v. Bukin*, 467 Mass. 516, 522 n.10 (2014).

The new rule also makes it clear that the single "substantial reliability" test applies regardless of whether the alleged violation consists of a new criminal charge.

Section (b) and its caption require that hearsay be found by the court to be "substantially reliable" before it can serve as evidence of a violation, *even when the court also has relied on non-hearsay evidence*. The previous rule imposed the substantial reliability test only when hearsay was the only evidence relied upon by the court. In doing so it followed case law, *Commonwealth v. Durling*, 407 Mass. 108 (1990). Under the rule as amended, the court need not attempt to distinguish between hearsay that is "reliable" (and thus may be used if other, non-hearsay evidence is also relied upon by the court), and hearsay that is "substantially reliable" (and thus may be used when it is the *only* evidence of a violation). *See Commonwealth v. Durling*, 407 Mass. 108, 117–19 (1990).

Finally, section (b) lists the seven indicia set forth in case law that the court may consider in determining whether the "substantial reliability" test has been met.

It should be noted that, even if the court finds that hearsay is "substantially reliable" and thus may be used as evidence of an alleged violation, this is not conclusive on the issue whether a violation has occurred. The court's finding on an alleged violation must be based on whether, based on all the competent evidence submitted by both parties, the violation has been proved by a preponderance of that evidence.

Rule 8.   Finding and Disposition

(a) Requirement of Finding. Upon the completion of the presentation of evidence and closing arguments on the issue of whether the probationer has violated one or more conditions of a probation order, as alleged, the court shall make a determination of that issue. The court shall decide the matter promptly and shall not continue the proceeding generally.

(b) Finding of No Violation. If the court determines that probation has failed to prove by a preponderance of the evidence that the probationer committed a violation alleged in the notice of violation, the court shall expressly so find and the finding shall be entered on the record.

(c) Finding of Violation; Written Finding of Fact. If the court determines that probation has proved by a preponderance of the evidence that the probationer has violated a condition of probation as alleged in the notice of violation, or if the probationer waives the hearing and admits such violation and the court accepts such admission in accordance with Rule 6(g), the court shall expressly so find, and such finding shall be entered on the record. In a contested proceeding, the court shall make written findings of fact to support the finding of violation, stating the evidence upon which the court relied. A finding of violation based on an admission may be recorded as such.

(d) Disposition After Finding of Violation. After the court has entered a finding that a violation of probation has occurred, the court may order any of the following dispositions set forth below, as it deems appropriate. These dispositional alternatives shall be the exclusive options available to the court. The court shall proceed to determine disposition promptly following the entry of a finding of violation. General continuances are prohibited. Awaiting the disposition of an underlying criminal charge shall not constitute such good cause for any continuance. In determining its disposition, the court shall give such weight as it may deem appropriate to the recommendation of the Probation Department, the probationer, and the District Attorney, if any, and to such factors as public safety; the circumstances of any crime for which the probationer was placed on probation; the nature of the probation violation; the occurrence of any previous violations; and the impact of the underlying crime on any person or community, as well as any mitigating factors.

(i) *Continuance of Probation.* The court may decline to modify or revoke probation and, instead, issue to the proba-

tioner such admonition or instruction as it may deem appropriate.

(ii) *Termination.* The court may terminate the probation order.

(iii) *Modification.* The court may modify the conditions of probation. Such modification may include the addition of reasonable conditions and the extension of the duration of the probation order.

(iv) *Revocation; Statement of Reasons.* The court may order that the order of probation be revoked. If the court orders revocation, it shall state the reasons therefor in writing.

(e) Execution of Suspended Sentence; Stay of Execution. Upon revocation of a probation order, any sentence that was imposed for the crime involved, the execution of which was suspended, shall be ordered executed forthwith; provided, however, that such execution may be stayed (1) pending appeal in accordance with Mass. R. Crim. P. 31, or (2) at the court's discretion, and upon the probationer's motion, to provide a brief period of time for the probationer to attend to personal matters prior to commencement of a sentence of incarceration. The execution of such sentence shall not be otherwise stayed.

(f) Imposition of Sentence Where No Sentence Previously Imposed. Upon revocation of probation in a case where no sentence was imposed following conviction, the court shall impose a sentence or other disposition as provided by law.

Adopted December 2, 1999, effective January 3, 2000. Renumbered and amended February 25, 2015, effective September 8, 2015.

Commentary to District Rule 7—2000

Requirement of a Finding

This rule addresses the court's two separate tasks upon completion of the violation hearing. Section (a) requires the court to adjudicate the factual issue of whether a violation has occurred. It expressly eliminates as an option a "general continuance."

The requirement that a finding be made on the issue of violation is based on several considerations. First, and most important, it is essential for the credibility of the probation order that the issue raised by the alleged violation be resolved. Even if the alleged violation involves a relatively minor matter, the likelihood of successful change in the probationer's behavior is diminished if the court temporizes in its role as finder of fact. If a violation has occurred, the probationer should be confronted with that fact. If no violation is found, the probationer is entitled to that finding on the record. No useful judicial or probation purpose is served by failure to adjudicate after the evidence has been presented. A failure by the court to decide the issue can foster the perception on the part of the probationer that if the court does not take the matter seriously, neither should he or she.

Second, adjudication of the violation charge does not limit the court's wide discretion regarding disposition. As addressed further in the rule, if a violation is found, the court's options range from a simple warning with the current terms of probation continued, to a revocation of probation, which in many instances will result in incarceration.

Third, the adjudication of a violation will establish an appropriate record of the probationer's non-compliance, which can be essential to an appropriate disposition if a subsequent violation occurs. Minor violations, even if they do not warrant significant sanctions in themselves, may provide important information in any subsequent proceedings.

It should be noted that the "seriousness" of the violation, its impact or lack of impact on any victim and the nature of the underlying crime are irrelevant to whether the alleged violation occurred. Those matters relate solely to the court's disposition if a violation is found.

In referring to the situation where the court finds no violation, section (b) of the rule reiterates three important points: the probation officer bears the burden of proof, the standard of proof is a preponderance of the evidence, and only a violation that has been formally alleged in the Notice of Probation Violation and Hearing may be found.

Section (c) of the rule repeats these three points regarding the finding of a violation and adds that a violation may be found based on the probationer's admission. It also adds the requirements of findings of fact and a statement of the evidence relied on, which are due process requirements. *Morrissey v. Brewer*, 408 U.S. 471, 489 (1972). Failure to make findings and a statement of the evidence relied on appears to be reversible error. *See Fay v. Commonwealth*, 379 Mass. 498, 504–05 (1980). The Court in *Fay* also ruled that written findings were not required as a matter of due process, where such findings were announced orally on the record in the presence of the probationer and the probationer subsequently obtained a written copy in the form of a transcript. *Fay v. Commonwealth*, 379 Mass. at 504–05 (1980). The rule, however, requires that the findings and evidence relied on be stated in writing.

Disposition

Section (d) of the rule sets out four specific types of dispositions that are available to the court if a violation is found. These are expressly described as an exclusive list of the court's options, though they provide a comprehensive range of sanctions. The rule also provides factors that the court should consider on disposition, namely:

- the recommendation of the Probation Department.

- public safety.

- seriousness of the crime of which the probationer was found guilty.

- nature of the violation.

- record of any previous violation.

- impact on a victim of the underlying crime.

Counsel is free to argue, and the court is free to consider, any relevant mitigating factors.

Regarding the choice of disposition, two factors are essential: (1) disposition is a matter of the court's discretion. *McHoul v. Commonwealth*, 365 Mass. 465, 469–70 (1974); *Commonwealth v. Durling*, 407 Mass. 108, 111 (1990); and (2) disposition is not a punishment for the new crime, but rather relates to the underlying offense. *Commonwealth v. Odoardi*, 397 Mass. 28, 30 (1986).

Section (d)(i) provides for continuance of probation. This may be appropriate where the violation is minor and the probationer has no history of previous violations. It can be completely appropriate for a probation officer to commence and successfully prosecute a probation violation proceeding and then recommend that the current probation terms merely be continued. This may reflect the probation officer's judgment that, though minor, the offense should be adjudicated to impress upon the probationer the importance of compliance, that a warning from the court is necessary to prevent more serious violations and that the violation should be a matter of record. The continuance of current probation terms despite a finding of violation is sometimes referred to as "reprobating" the probationer.

Section (d)(ii), provides for termination of probation. This outcome can be appropriate where the offense is minor and the court determines that the purpose of probation has been accomplished. It can also be appropriate in conjunction with the disposition of a new offense, where the probationer is already serving a sentence, and where the probationer is on probation in another court.

Under section (d)(iii), the court has the dispositional option of modifying the probationary terms after a finding of violation. It has

been held that it is "a matter of well-established common law, that courts do possess [the authority to modify probation conditions], and that conditions of probation may be amended to serve 'the ends of justice and the best interests of both the public and the defendant.'" *Buckley v. Quincy Division of the District Court Dept.*, 395 Mass. 815, 817 (1985), citing *Burns v. United States*, 287 U.S. 216, 221 (1932).

The addition of reasonable conditions to an individual's probation does not constitute a revision or revocation of a sentence under Mass. R. Crim. P. 29. *Buckley, supra*, at 818–19. The Court did not "define that point at which the modification is so drastic that it becomes the revision of a sentence subject to the requirements of rule 29," noting that the modification in *Buckley* was a nonpunitive rehabilitative measure, designed to facilitate the successful reintegration of the plaintiff into the community. *Buckley, supra*, at 818–19 n.5.

It should be noted that the Court in *Buckley* was addressing a situation where conditions were added to a probation order without any finding of a violation, but rather based on an assessment by a probation officer. The Court ruled that a *supervising* court (as distinguished from a *sentencing* court) may not modify the conditions of probation without a material change in circumstances such as a violation of probation. It also indicated that a violation of probation is a material change in circumstances:

> Our holding does not limit whatever authority is held by the supervisory court to modify conditions where there has been a material change in circumstances (such as a violation of a condition of probation). Nor need we outline those situations in which the sentencing court might modify the terms of probation.

Buckley v. Quincy Div. of Dist. Court Dept., supra, at 820.

Section (d)(iii) addresses issues left unaddressed in *Buckley* by affirmatively authorizing the court conducting a probation violation hearing to modify the conditions of probation upon a finding of violation.

Revocation: Stay after Revocation

Section (d)(iv) provides for the most serious sanction upon a finding of probation violation, namely, revocation of probation. Under *Commonwealth v. Holmgren*, 421 Mass. 224 (1995), any sentence that was imposed, but its execution suspended pending probation, must be ordered executed in its entirety upon revocation of probation. This ruling was based on an unambiguous statutory requirement in G.L. c. 279, § 3.

The requirement of executing a suspended sentence upon revocation of probation is reflected in section (e), which also provides two specific bases for a stay of execution. This provision precludes any stay other than for (1) appeal or (2) a brief time for a probationer to attend to personal matters. A stay simply to avoid the execution of sentence, with or without the addition of new terms, is not allowed under the rule. There are several reasons for this. First, there appears to be no established legal basis for such a stay. Second, such a stay is inconsistent with the plain language of *Holmgren*. Third, the terms of such a stay are unenforceable. Conditions on the person's behavior during the stay cannot be ordered as probation—probation has been revoked. On the other hand, the court cannot condition the stay on unstated or vague conditions (e.g., "stay out of further trouble"), since a termination of the stay presumably requires incarceration, which, in turn, requires an opportunity for the person to be notified and heard regarding the factual issue of whether he or she violated the stay. One element of such a process would be specificity of the alleged violation. Even if conditions on such a stay were expressly stated in writing, they could not be enforced without a due process procedure similar to the same probation revocation procedure that has just been concluded. Since the person would not be on probation, there would be no one with authority to "prosecute" the alleged violation of the stay conditions. Perhaps most important, such a stay is impermissible because it implies that if the person successfully completes the stay, on whatever terms are imposed, written or unwritten, the sentence that had to be ordered executed pursuant to *Holmgren* somehow disappears.

Section (d)(iv) requires that, if the court decides to revoke probation, it must provide the reasons for that decision. A statement of reasons for deciding to revoke probation is a requirement of due process. *Gagnon v. Scarpelli*, 411 U.S. 778 (1973). While the reasons need not be put in writing to ensure due process, *Fay v. Commonwealth*, 379 Mass. 498 (1980), the rule requires them in writing to ensure a clear and accessible record.

Disposition Where No Sentence Originally Imposed

Section (f) addresses the situation where the probationer was sentenced with "straight probation" on the underlying conviction. On the one hand, this means that upon a revocation of probation, there is no suspended sentence to be executed. On the other hand, the probationer is subject to any sentence for the underlying crime that is provided by law. Though it may appear illogical, this would appear to include a sentence involving probation, even though the triggering event for the imposition of such a sentence is a violation and revocation of the "straight" probation originally ordered. Presumably, if such post-revocation probation is imposed, the conditions and the consequences for any violation will take into account the fact that probation has already been violated.

Commentary to District/Municipal Courts Rule 8—2015

Section (c) differs from its antecedent, 2000 District Court Rule 7(c), in the addition of a reference to a probationer's waiver *of the violation hearing* as being part of the violation admission procedure. The sentence also differs in the deletion of the term "stipulates." Although an admission of a violation is often referred to as a "stipulation," it was concluded that the latter term inadequately describes the legal event at issue, and that the term "admission" is preferable. These amendments are consistent with Rule 6(g), which specifically addresses the violation admission procedure. Section (c) includes a reference to Rule 6(g).

Section (c) makes it clear that written findings stating the evidence relied upon are not required when a finding of violation is based on an admission.

Section (d) differs from its antecedent in the addition of its third sentence, which prohibits the "continuance for disposition" without good cause, and expressly eliminates delay to await the outcome of an underlying new criminal charge as constituting such good cause. The latter provision is intended to eliminate the possibility of post-finding "tracking." Delay in the form of "tracking" at the *outset* of a violation proceeding, before a violation is found, is expressly prohibited by Rule 6(e).

Section (d) contains some minor improvements in terminology that are of no critical legal or procedural significance.

Section (f) reflects the addition of the phrase "or other disposition" in recognition of the fact that, following the revocation of probation, the court's options where no sentence was imposed at the time probation was ordered are not limited to the imposition of a sentence. For example, where straight probation (which is not a "sentence") had been ordered, the court, after finding violation and revoking probation, may once again order straight probation.

Rule 9. Violation of Conditions of A "Continuance Without A Finding"

(a) Notice, Conduct of Hearing, Adjudication. The procedures set forth in these rules regarding notice for, and the conduct and adjudication of, probation violation hearings shall also apply where the Probation Department alleges a violation of one or more conditions of probation imposed together with a continuance without a finding.

(b) Disposition. The dispositional options available to the court following a determination that one or more conditions of probation imposed together with a continuance without a finding have been violated shall be as follows:

(i) *Termination of Probation.* The court may terminate the order of probation and the continuance without a finding and enter a dismissal on the underlying criminal case.

(ii) *Continuation of the Continuance Without a Finding With No Probation Modification.* The court may continue the continuance without a finding and issue to the probationer such admonition or instruction as it may deem appropriate.

(iii) *Continuation of the Continuance Without a Finding With Modification of Probation.* The court may continue the continuance without a finding and modify the conditions of probation including the duration of the continuance.

(iv) *Termination of the Continuance Without a Finding and No Revocation of Probation.* The court may terminate the continuance without a finding without revoking probation and, if a finding of sufficient facts was entered at the time the continuance without a finding was ordered, shall proceed to enter a guilty finding. The order of probation, with or without modifications, may thereupon constitute the disposition on the guilty finding if the probationer consents.

(v) *Termination of the Continuance Without a Finding and Revocation of Probation.* The court may terminate the continuance without a finding and revoke the order of probation. If the court orders revocation, it shall state the evidence relied upon in writing, and, if a finding of sufficient facts was entered at the time the continuance without a finding was ordered, the court shall enter a guilty finding and impose a sentence or other disposition as provided by law.

Adopted December 2, 1999, effective January 3, 2000. Amended February 25, 2015, effective September 8, 2015.

Commentary to District Court Rule 9—2000

Continuance Without a Finding with Probation

This rule addresses the situation where the allegation of a probation violation involves a probation order issued together with a continuance without a finding. In such cases, the conditions of probation are also the conditions whereby the underlying criminal case has been continued without the entry of a finding of guilty, following submission and acceptance of a formal plea or admission.

The rule makes clear that the procedure in these cases for commencing, conducting and disposing of probation violation proceedings is the same as in cases where a finding of guilty has been entered following a plea, admission or trial. The only differences from the latter involve the court's dispositional options if a probation violation is found.

Specifically, if the court finds a probation violation and decides as a matter of its discretion to revoke probation, the continuance is thereby terminated, a finding of guilty must be entered and sentence must be imposed. The court will be bound by whatever dispositional terms were set by the probationer and accepted by the court as formal conditions of his or her plea or admission, if any.

The rule takes the position that upon revocation of probation in a case continued without a finding, a sentence that was conditioned on probation compliance should be ordered executed in its entirety. This is parallel to the ruling in *Commonwealth v. Holmgren*, 421 Mass. 224

(1995), a case which involved execution of a suspended sentence upon violation of probation.

In cases where the defendant submitted his or her plea or admission conditioned only by a requirement that the case be continued without a finding, with no sentencing terms specified in the tender of plea or admission, the court may have indicated what sentence should be imposed if probation is violated and revoked (sometimes referred to as "a *Duquette* alternative"). Such a sentence should be given great deference but is not binding on the judge who enters the guilty finding and then imposes sentence. This parallels the "straight probation" situation. That is, if a violation is found and the court decides to revoke probation, the sentence to be imposed following entry of the guilty finding may be any sentence provided by law.

Continuance Without a Finding Without Probation

This rule does not address the situation where the court has ordered a case continued without a finding, but has not placed the defendant on probation, that is, where the conditions of the continuance are not conditions of probation.

In *Commonwealth v. Rivera*, No. SJ–96–0578 (Supreme Judicial Court, Single Justice Decision, November 29, 1996), the Single Justice held that

> like the procedure for probation revocation, the procedure for revocation of a continuance without a finding may result in the loss of the defendant's liberty, [thus] for purposes of due process it is appropriate to analyze the revocation of a continuance without a finding the same as this court does a revocation of probation.

Apparently, in *Rivera* the defendant's case had been continued without a finding, but he had not been placed on probation.

One problem with such cases involves the need for conditions of the continuance to be set forth in writing and given to the defendant. Where a case is continued without a finding, but the defendant not placed on probation, it is not clear how and by whom those conditions are reduced to writing and given to the defendant. Similarly, if the defendant is not on probation, it is not clear who presents the allegation of an alleged violation of the conditions of the continuance. In any event, the Court in *Rivera*, applying the due process requirements of probation violation proceedings, found that the proceedings were inadequate in terms of notice of the alleged violation, time to prepare for the hearing, and the reliability of the hearsay evidence submitted, and vacated the revocation of the continuance.

Commentary to District/Municipal Rule 9—2015

The order of sections (b)(i) and (b)(ii) differs from the 2000 District Rule to more accurately reflect the increasingly severe "hierarchy" of this list of dispositional options. Other, minor changes exist as well.

Section (b)(iii) reflects the fact that, where a probation order is modified after a finding of violation, there is no need to mention in the rule that a "material change of circumstance" is a prerequisite to such modification. This is so because a violation of probation constitutes per se sufficient grounds for a modification. See *Buckley v. Quincy Div. of the Dist. Ct. Dep't*, 395 Mass. 815, 820 (1985).

New section (b)(iv) has been added to acknowledge the court's option of terminating a CWOF, *but not revoking probation*. In such cases, the court, if a finding of sufficient facts had been made at the time the CWOF was ordered, may enter a guilty finding with the probation order, with or without modification, serving as the criminal sentence.

Section (b)(v) is based on the 2000 District Court Rule 9(b)(iv) and includes the requirement that when the court orders a revocation of probation it *must state in writing the evidence relied upon*. This has been held to be a requirement of fundamental due process. *Morrissey v. Brewer*, 408 U.S. 471, 488–89 (1972) (due process requirements for parole revocation hearings); *accord Gagnon v. Scarpelli*, 411 U.S. 778, 782 (1973) (same due process rights apply in probation revocation hearings).

Section (b)(v) also indicates that, if a violation of probation is found in the context of a continuance without a finding and probation is then revoked, the entry of a guilty finding and sentencing in the underlying case is possible only if the court that ordered the CWOF had entered a finding of sufficient facts.

Section (b)(v) also reflects the addition of a reference to the court's obligation to "impose a sentence or other disposition as provided by law" when it finds a violation and orders revocation in the context of a CWOF. This phrase formerly appeared in 2000 District Court Rule 9(d), which has been deleted, as explained below.

Section (c) of the 2000 District Court Rule has been deleted. It limited stays of execution following the imposition of sentence upon revocation of probation and entry of a guilty finding. The only stays permitted by the rule were those provided by the rule (stay pending appeal, Mass. R. Crim. P. 31) and stays to allow a defendant to attend to personal matters prior to commencement of an incarceration sentence, as provided under common law. It was concluded that, since there is no other legal ground for such stays, the express limitation in the rule was unnecessary.

Section (d) of the 2000 District Court Rule has also been deleted. It involved admissions to sufficient facts seeking a CWOF tendered by defendants and accepted by the court with no sentencing conditions included in the tender. In such cases, the court that later revokes probation is free to impose any sentence provided by law. The implication in this provision was that, if sentencing terms *had been included* with the tender, the court that later found a violation of the CWOF and revoked probation would be limited to imposing a sentence consistent with the terms set forth in the tender. It was concluded that this provision was unnecessary because such conditioned tenders seeking CWOFs are, in fact, not made, or, if made, are not accepted by the courts. In any event, Rule 9(b)(v) adequately addresses the issue in general terms: when the court terminates a CWOF and revokes probation, "the court must impose a sentence or other disposition *as provided by law*." (Emphasis added.) This obviates the need for these rules to resolve the question of whether the tender of a plea or admission seeking a CWOF may be conditioned on specific sentencing terms, and, if accepted by the sentencing court, whether such sentencing terms are "binding" on the court that subsequently revokes probation and terminates the CWOF.

STANDING ORDERS OF THE DISTRICT COURT

Table of Standing Orders

Standing Order 1–83.   Civil Pretrial Procedure

Applicable to the Clinton Division

All civil cases, including those remanded from the Superior Court Department, shall be scheduled for pretrial conference in compliance with Dist./Mun.Cts.R.Civ.P. 16.

At the conclusion of each conference, the court will enter an order reciting the results of the conference, and will set a trial date. Arrangements for a trial date cannot be made in any other manner. In accordance with Rule 16, the order will control the subsequent course of the case.

Counsel must appear at the pretrial conference with full authorization in all respects. The court may award costs against any party or attorney whose unjustified absence or lack of preparation prevented the conduct of a pretrial conference. See *Beit v. Probate & Family Court Dep't*, 385 Mass. 854, 434 N.E.2d 642 (1982).

Adopted effective December 1, 1983.

Standing Order 2–83.   Calendaring of Civil Cases

Applicable to the Fall River Division

1. A general call of the civil list will be conducted in a civil assignment session held at 2:00 P.M. on the first Monday of each month. If the first Monday is a holiday, the assignment session will be held on the next business day. Counsel or parties will be notified at least 7 days in advance that a case is on the monthly assignment session list.

2. A case may be added to the monthly assignment session list by filing a request for trial pursuant to District/Municipal Courts Supplementary Rules of Civil Procedure 108 at least ten days before the first Monday of the month. The Court may, on its own motion, add cases to the monthly assignment session list pursuant to District/Municipal Courts Rules of Civil Procedure 41(b)(1).

3. Attorneys for both sides must appear, prepared to advise the Court as to the nature of the case, the number of witnesses, and the approximate duration of trial. Requests for pretrial conferences should be made at this time. Failure to appear will result in the entry of a dismissal or default.

4. Counsel may avoid the necessity of appearing at the assignment session by submitting a written request for trial on a day and at a time certain, assented to by all attorneys or parties to the action. Such requests will be honored, subject to scheduling availability.

5. Cases will be assigned for trial throughout the month at a time and date certain. Cases may be assigned for any weekday at the convenience of the parties, subject to the availability of a Judge and courtroom. No further notice of the day and time of trial will be given other than the oral notice in the assignment session.

6. Once a case is scheduled for trial, the Court will enforce a strict continuance policy. When in extraordinary circumstances the Court grants a continuance, the case will be continued to the next monthly assignment session for rescheduling.

7. Motions will be heard on Tuesdays and Thursdays at 10:00 A.M. Motions which will be argued by conference call may be marked for any day of the week at a mutually agreeable time.

Adopted effective December 1, 1983.

Standing Order 3–83. Petitions for Review in Cambridge Rent Control Cases (Pursuant to St.1976, C. 36, § 10)

Applicable to the Cambridge Division

REVOCATION OF STANDING ORDER 3–83

Effective November 14, 1985, the standing order with respect to petitions for review in rent control cases previously in effect as of December 1, 1983, is and shall be revoked. Petitions for review shall be governed by Chapter 36 of the Acts of 1976, as amended by Chapter 399 of the Acts of 1985.

Adopted November 6, 1985, effective November 14, 1985.

Standing Order 4–83. Summonsing Breathalyzer Operators

Applicable to the Westborough Division

Whenever defense counsel in a trial for operating a motor vehicle under the influence of alcohol desires to have the testimony of the police breathalyzer operator at trial, a request must be made to the district attorney's office at least 48 hours in advance of the trial date, or a summons issued as for any other witness.

Because the Commonwealth can establish a prima facie case without the breathalyzer operator, a continuance will not be granted because of his or her absence unless this procedure has been followed.

Adopted effective December 1, 1983.

Standing Order 5–83. Case Management Procedures in Criminal Cases

Applicable to the Pittsfield Division

The following procedures are applicable to all primary court criminal cases:

I. Procedures for the Criminal Session.

1. Criminal sessions are held each weekday at 9 a.m., holidays excepted.

2. The list of continued cases is called first, in docket number sequence.

3. The arraignment list is called, in docket number sequence, after continued cases.

(a) Defendants facing possible imprisonment will be scheduled for pretrial conference sessions.

(b) Other defendants will have their cases continued for trial and/or disposition to a 9 a.m. criminal session, within two weeks of arraignment if possible.

(c) Submissions to sufficient facts may be offered at the second call of the arraignment list, and will be taken prior to scheduled trials.

(d) A waiver of first instance jury trial and of double jeopardy claims shall be filed at arraignment by any defendant represented by counsel or not facing possible imprisonment.

4. Attorneys shall be prepared to go forward with all scheduled matters except by leave of the court.

5. Pretrial motions shall be filed with the Clerk–Magistrate's office in compliance with Mass.R.Crim.P. 13.

6. The trial of co-defendants will be severed only upon written motion allowed by the court. See Mass.R.Crim.P. 9(c), 9(d) and 19. The case folders of co-defendants will be marked with a blue dot and a cross-reference to the co-defendant's case number.

7. No defendant will be brought before the court from any jail or correctional institution except by mittimus or writ of habeas corpus upon order of the court.

8. The Chief Probation Officer, or in his or her absence a Probation Officer designated by the Chief Probation Officer, will maintain the scheduled calendar of trials and conferences.

II. Procedures for the Conference Session.

1. Pretrial conference sessions are scheduled each Tuesday and Thursday, holidays excepted, at 1 p.m.

2. Defense attorneys are encouraged to conference cases with the district attorney's office prior to the scheduled conference. Cases that have been conferenced in advance and for which a conference report has been completed will be called first.

3. Defendants and defense attorneys must appear for the call of the conference list.

4. Except by leave of the court, a defendant's election or waiver of first instance jury trial must be filed no later than the first scheduled conference session.

5. Continuances for further conference will be allowed only with the approval of the conference session Judge upon written motion signed by the defendant, defense counsel and the prosecutor.

III. Conference Reports.

1. A conference report shall be filed at the first scheduled conference. If there are subsequent conferences, an additional conference report shall be filed at each subsequent conference.

2. The conference report shall be signed by the defendant, defense counsel and the prosecutor.

3. The conference report may include any recommendation for disposition.

4. If the conference report indicates a submission to sufficient facts and the submission is not made at the conference session during which the report is filed, the submission shall be scheduled for and taken on the next available court date.

5. After filing a conference report, both defense counsel and the prosecutor shall be responsible for continued representation in that case except by motion to withdraw made in compliance with the Massachusetts Rules of Criminal Procedure and allowed by the court.

6. The session clerk shall file conference reports and appropriate waivers in the criminal complaint folders.

Adopted effective December 1, 1983.

Standing Order 6–83. Scheduling, Continuance and Administrative Policies

Applicable to the Northampton Division

I. Criminal Cases.

1. Defendants shall report to the Probation Office to complete required paperwork at or before 8:30 a.m. on the morning of arraignment and again after disposition. All defendants charged with imprisonable offenses who desire the services of the Bar Advocate shall complete the required application in the Probation Office prior to arraignment.

2. A defendant's application for appointment of the Bar Advocate will be acted upon, and the defendant notified of the court's decision, during arraignment. No plea except "not guilty" will be taken on the arraignment date from defendants charged with imprisonable offenses, unless represented by counsel or after signing a written waiver of counsel. All continued cases will be assigned a definite date for pretrial conference, trial or disposition. All cases will be scheduled for pretrial conference, except in certain minor motor vehicle matters.

3. On the day set for pretrial conference, defendants or defense counsel shall confer with the assigned prosecutor from the district attorney's office at 8:30 a.m. By 9:30 a.m., all cases scheduled for conference shall be ready for disposition, assignment for first instance jury trial, or scheduling for another date for motion hearing, bench trial or, in exceptional circumstances, for further pretrial conference. Pretrial conferences may be conducted with the district attorney's office in advance of the scheduled date, but all conferences shall be completed by 9:30 a.m. on the date scheduled for conference. Pretrial conference reports are required to be filed only in cases which are scheduled for trial. A case will not be scheduled for a motion hearing or trial until the pretrial conference has been completed.

4. Defense counsel shall file an appearance and have the defendant execute and file a waiver of first instance jury trial prior to the presentation of the case to the court for disposition or for scheduling of motions or trial.

5. All pretrial motions shall be filed on or after the date of pretrial conference and not before, and shall be in accordance with Mass.R.Crim.P. 13.

6. On the trial date, defendants or defense counsel shall confer with the assigned prosecutor from the district attorney's office at 9 a.m., prior to the commencement of trials at 9:30 a.m. All parties shall be prepared to commence trial promptly at 9:30 a.m. on the scheduled date and to continue without interruption until completion.

7. Arraignments, pretrial conferences and trials in criminal cases will be scheduled so that the period of time from the date of arrest, issuance of the citation or show cause hearing, whichever occurs first, to the date of adjudication or finding of sufficient facts, does not exceed 60 days.

8. Matters continued for payment of fines, restitution or court costs shall be scheduled on Fridays and will be considered by the court the following Monday at 2 p.m. Other matters continued after submission or trial, whether with or without probation, and also driving-under-the-influence and non-support matters for review, shall be scheduled on Mondays at 2 p.m. Defendants whose cases are continued after disposition, with or without probation, are not required to appear on the date scheduled for discharge from probation or for dismissal of the case.

II. Civil Cases. The trial of all civil cases, except those remanded by the Superior Court, shall be scheduled so that they are completed within 90 days from the date trial is requested.

III. Continuances.

1. Scheduling of cases for pretrial conference, motions, trial or disposition shall be the sole responsibility of the session clerk. The Clerk/Magistrate's office shall prepare the daily pretrial conference and trial lists.

2. In all criminal cases, unless the parties are present in court, the Commonwealth shall notify the complainant, and the Clerk/Magistrate's office shall notify the defendant, of the next scheduled court event.

3. In both civil and criminal cases, the parties shall be prepared to proceed to pretrial conference, trial or disposition on the assigned date, unless a motion for a continuance has been allowed pursuant to this standing order.

4. In both civil and criminal cases, a party shall file a motion for continuance with the Clerk/Magistrate's office as soon as the need for a continuance becomes apparent. A motion for continuance shall contain information as to:

(a) when the need for the continuance arose;

(b) what the grounds for the continuance are;

(c) the measures taken to avoid seeking a continuance; and

(d) the earliest date all parties will be ready to proceed.

When an oral motion for continuance is made to the court, it shall afterwards be reduced to writing and filed with the case.

5. Motions for continuance which are assented to by all parties shall be acted upon only by the Scheduling Coordinator (the Third Assistant Clerk, or in his absence, the Second Assistant Clerk) or by the Presiding Justice.

6. Motions for continuance which are not assented to by all parties shall be scheduled for hearing before the Presiding Justice, or in his absence by the Justice then presiding.

7. No continuance shall be allowed except for good cause shown. In determining whether to allow a motion for continuance, the Scheduling Coordinator and the Presiding Justice will apply the considerations set forth in Standards 3:00, 3:01, 3:02 and 3:03 of the Caseflow Management Standards of the District Court Department.

8. Reasonable costs may be assessed against a party or attorney who causes a case to be continued without good cause or adequate notice.

IV. Administrative Arrangements.

1. Ex parte motions of an emergency nature arising on Monday or Friday will be heard during the criminal session in Courtroom No. 1.

2. Arraignments and hearings in non-support cases will be scheduled for the Thursday criminal session in Courtroom No. 1.

3. Attorneys shall not pass beyond the counter into the work areas of the Clerk/Magistrate's or Probation offices, or use telephones, typewriters or other equipment of those offices, without prior permission from a staff member of those offices.

4. Attorneys appointed under Mass.R.Crim.P. 8 and Dist. Ct.Supp.R.Crim.P. 8 to represent criminal defendants shall submit the appropriate form completely filled out, including the date of appointment, appointing Judge, name of client, docket number(s), and the attorney's name, address, telephone number, social security number, and signature.

5. Attorneys shall not contact personnel of the Clerk/Magistrate's office for assistance that could be readily obtained from the General Laws, the District/Municipal Courts Rules of Civil Procedure, or the Massachusetts Rules of Criminal Procedure.

Adopted effective December 1, 1983.

Standing Order 7–83. Pretrial Conference and Continuance Policies

Applicable to the Wareham Division

I. Pretrial Conferences. All civil cases (except small claims and summary process) and all criminal cases in which a jail sentence is possible will be assigned for pretrial conference, normally on a Monday. Attorneys and parties are required to be present at the pretrial conference.

If a case is not disposed of after conference, it will be assigned a day-certain for trial or transferred to the jury-of-six session. Any trial date may be requested and will be assigned if acceptable to the court and not previously fully committed. At the time of assignment for trial, the parties or attorneys shall inform the court of the number of witnesses for each side and the expected length of trial. In a criminal case, a jury waiver shall be filed before a trial date is assigned, and the Judge will make a finding as to whether such waiver is voluntarily and intelligently made.

Any case assigned for trial will be reached and tried on the day assigned.

The failure without just cause of any party or attorney to appear at the call of an assignment list, pretrial conference list, or trial list may result in a default or dismissal being entered against the offending party, the denial of any request for continuance, or, in appropriate cases, the assessment of costs against either the party or attorney at fault.

II. Continuances. In accordance with this court's stringent continuance policy, a case once assigned for trial will not be continued except for good cause. "Good cause" is construed to mean cause which compels the court in good conscience to grant a continuance, and includes actual engagement in trial before another court. Agreement of counsel or parties is not itself sufficient grounds to continue a case scheduled for trial. Failure to prepare for trial adequately and diligently, including advance arrangement for necessary witnesses, is not a sufficient reason to continue a case.

Once committed to a trial date in this court, parties and attorneys are expected to protect that commitment and the time of witnesses by informing any Judge before whom they subsequently appear of that commitment. This court will make every effort to coordinate its trial schedule with that of any other trial court faced with an extraordinary scheduling problem.

Any lawyer or party who cannot be present at a pretrial conference may protect himself or herself with respect to scheduling by arranging with the Judge's office before the conference date several acceptable open dates to which the attorney or party will commit himself or herself if one of those dates is assigned by the court.

This court will not order civil cases "off the list" or "continued generally." Any case once assigned for a day-certain will be continued only for a purpose-certain (i.e. for trial, review, status, further pretrial conference or assignment).

Adopted effective December 1, 1983.

Standing Order 1–84. Appearances

Applicable to Edgartown Division

The Court will not take any action on matters before it, requested by any attorney, until such time as an appearance in writing is submitted to it.

Adopted effective June 1, 1984.

Standing Order 2–84. Continuances

Applicable to Edgartown Division

Any matter scheduled for Trial shall not be continued unless forty-eight (48) hours before the scheduled date, a request for continuance in writing has been received in the office of the Clerk/Magistrate.

Failure to abide by this rule will result in the imposition of costs. The Court will waive the sanctions of this rule should unforeseen or extraordinary circumstances prevent compliance.

Adopted effective June 1, 1984.

Standing Order 1–85. Consolidation of Related Civil Cases Pending in More Than One Division (Pursuant to G.L. C. 223, § 2A)

Applicable to All Divisions

General Laws c. 223, s. 2A, as amended by St.1985, c. 221, assigns to the administrative justice of each department of the Trial Court the power to consolidate related civil cases pending in more than one division of that department. Section 2A formerly provided for such consolidations only within the

District Court, and gave such authority to the Appellate Division of the District Court, established pursuant to G.L. c. 231, s. 108.

In order to expedite the judicial business of the District Court, and in accordance with the authority granted by G.L. c. 211B, s. 10, I hereby delegate severally to the presiding justices of the districts of the Appellate Division of the District Court and to their successors as presiding justices, or to any justice of the Appellate Division of the District Court designated by such presiding justices, the responsibilities and powers assigned to me as Administrative Justice of the District Court by G.L. c. 223, s. 2A, as amended by St.1985, c. 221.

The procedure for such motions to consolidate is contained in Dist./Mun.Cts.R.Civ.P. 42(a).

Adopted November 18, 1985.

Standing Order 2–85.   Civil Pretrial Procedure

Applicable to the Natick Division

All civil cases, including those remanded from the Superior Court Department, shall be scheduled for pretrial conference in compliance with Dist./Mun.Cts.R.Civ.P. 16.

The Court will make a record of the results of each conference as well as of any Orders made pursuant thereto and, at the conclusion of each conference, will set a trial date. Arrangements for a trial date cannot be made in any other manner. In accordance with Rule 16, the record and Orders will control the subsequent course of the case.

Counsel must appear at the pretrial conference with full authority in all respects. The Court may award costs against any party or attorney whose unjustified absence or lack of preparation prevented the conduct of a pretrial conference. See *Beit v. Probate and Family Court Department*, 385 Mass. 854, 434 N.E.2d 642 (1982).

Adopted effective December 1, 1985.

Standing Order 1–88.   Superseded by Joint Standing Order 1–04

Publisher's Note

Standing Order 1–04, in Section I., provides: "This Order applies to all tort and contract actions in which money damages are sought ('civil actions') and which have been commenced in the Boston Municipal Court Department and the District Court Department on or after August 31, 2004. In the District Court Department, this Order shall also apply to all civil actions previously governed by District Court Standing Order 1–98 regarding any procedures occurring on or after that date. Sections VI (Motion Practice) and VII (Continuances) of this Order shall also apply to all civil actions pending in the divisions of the Boston Municipal Court Department and in the divisions of the District Court Department in Plymouth, Suffolk and Worcester Counties, regardless of the date of commencement of such actions." Standing Order 1–04 in Section I., further provides: "This Order supersedes Boston Municipal Court Department Standing Order 1–88 and District Court Department Standing Orders 1–88 and 1–98 with respect to all civil actions and all procedures to which this Order applies."

Standing Order 2–88.   Caseflow Management of Juvenile Cases

Applicable to All Divisions With Juvenile Jurisdiction

I. Authority. This Order is promulgated by the Administrative Justice of the District Court pursuant to his statutory responsibility over caseflow management, G.L. c. 211B, s. 10, and uniform practices, G.L. c. 218, s. 43A.

II. Purpose. The purpose of this Order is to facilitate compliance with the standards for juvenile cases issued by the Supreme Judicial Court on April 7, 1986.

III. Juvenile Delinquency Cases.

1. *Bail Hearings.* As required by Mass. R. Crim. P. 7(a)(1), the court shall provide for each juvenile who has been arrested and not released a hearing on the issue of detention and bail on the same day as the arrest, if the court is then in session, and if not, at the next court session.

2. *Non–jury Trials and Transfer Hearings.* Non–jury trials for the adjudication of delinquency and juvenile transfer hearings should be scheduled by the court as follows:

Juvenile in detention: Hearing date within 30 days of issuance of complaint.

Juvenile not in detention: Hearing date within 60 days of issuance of complaint.

The periods listed in Mass. R. Crim. P. 36(b)(2) shall be excluded from the 30– or 60–day period.

IV. Care and Protection Cases.

1. *Preliminary Stages.* In care and protection cases (G.L. c. 119, §§ 24, 26), the following time standards shall be adhered to. In non-emergency situations, the preliminary hearing shall be conducted within two weeks of the filing of the petition. In all cases, the investigator's report shall be filed no later than eight weeks after the filing of the petition, except upon leave of court. A pretrial conference shall be held within two weeks after the filing of the investigator's report. Except for investigators' reports, all written reports of any type which are to be submitted to the court shall be filed with the Clerk–Magistrate's office at least three days in advance of the court date for which it has been prepared, unless the court directs otherwise.

2. *Adjudicatory Hearing.* The adjudicatory hearing shall not begin sooner than two weeks after the submission of the investigator's report unless all parties agree to a shorter period of time. The adjudicatory hearing should be heard in its entirety with as few interruptions as possible, preferably with day-to-day hearings if the other business of the court permits. In any event, "[o]nce a trial begins it should proceed expeditiously to completion. All parties involved then benefit from increased continuity. Efficiency is increased when delays between hearings are kept to a minimum." *Care and Protection of Three Minors*, 392 Mass. 704, 705 n. 3, 467 N.E.2d 851, 854 n. 3 (1984). The adjudicatory hearing shall be completed no later than six months from the filing of the petition.

3. *Judgment.* After completing the adjudicatory hearing, the court should promptly render its judgment as to whether the child is in need of care and protection. This judgment

shall be entered no later than 30 days after completion of the evidentiary hearing. By law, the judge must file written findings and conclusions of law within ten days after entry of judgment. (G.L. c. 119, § 27.) "Continuances without a finding" and "general continuances" should not be utilized instead of entering a judgment.

4. *Disposition.* Following adjudication, the court should determine all dispositional issues and issue the necessary orders, temporary and permanent, without delay.

The Supreme Judicial Court has indicated that "[n]o cases of any kind have a greater claim for expedition *at all stages* than those involving care and custody of children" (emphasis supplied). *Custody of a Minor*, 389 Mass. 755, 764 n. 2, 452 N.E.2d 483, 489 n. 2 (1983).

Adopted May 31, 1988, effective July 1, 1988. Amended July 6, 1990, effective August 1, 1990.

Standing Order 1–90. Scheduling of Civil Motions

Applicable to the Orleans Division

Due to the pressure of business, it is necessary to take certain measures to limit the number of motions to be heard on Mondays, our regular motion session.

Until further notice, it is ordered that the clerk-magistrate will limit accepting and marking of motions for a particular Monday to 15 motions. Any motions sought to be marked in excess of 15 in number will be placed on the list for hearing on the next available civil motion day by the clerk-magistrate, with notice to the parties.

Exempted from this order are motions for dissolution of attachments granted ex parte.

Adopted effective February 23, 1990.

Standing Order 2–90. Scheduling, Continuance and Administrative Policies

Applicable to the Greenfield Division

I. Criminal Cases.

1. All defendants shall report to the Probation Office to complete intake on the morning of arraignment and after disposition.

Any defendant charged with an offense which carries a possible sentence of imprisonment shall complete an application for court appointed counsel before arraignment.

2. A defendant's application for court appointed counsel will be acted upon and defendant notified at arraignment. No plea except "not guilty" will be accepted on the arraignment date. All cases will be continued to a definite date for pretrial conference, trial or disposition, except certain minor motor vehicle matters.

3. On the date set for pretrial conference defendants or defense counsel shall confer with the assigned prosecutor from the District Attorney's Office. All cases scheduled for conference shall be ready for disposition, assignment for first instance jury trial, or scheduled for another date for motion hearing, bench trial or, in exceptional circumstances, for further pretrial conference. If a further pretrial conference is requested, this must be done in writing and for good cause.

Pretrial conference reports are required to be filed in all cases. A case will not be scheduled for motion or trial until the pretrial conference report has been completed and filed with the court.

4. Defense counsel shall file an appearance and have the defendant execute a waiver of first instance jury trial prior to presentation to the court for disposition or for scheduling of motions or trial.

5. All pretrial motions will be filed on or after the pretrial conference and not before, and shall be in accordance with Mass.R.Crim.P. 13.

6. On the trial date defendants, defendants' counsel and prosecutors shall be prepared to commence trial and to continue said trial to completion.

7. Arraignments, pretrial conferences, and trials in criminal cases will be scheduled so that the period of time from the date of arrest, issuance of the citation or show cause hearing, whichever occurs first, to the date of adjudication or finding of sufficient facts will not exceed 60 days.

II. Civil Cases.

1. The trial of all civil cases, except those remanded by the Superior Court, shall be scheduled so that they will be completed within 90 days from the trial date.

III. Continuances.

1. In all criminal cases, unless the parties are in court, the Commonwealth shall notify the complainant, and the Clerk-Magistrate's Office shall notify the defendant, of the next scheduled court event.

2. In both criminal and civil cases, the parties shall be prepared to proceed to pretrial conference, trial or disposition on the assigned date, unless a motion to continue has been allowed pursuant to this standing order.

3. In both criminal and civil cases a party shall file a motion for continuance with the Clerk-Magistrate's Office as soon as the need for a continuance becomes apparent. Motions for continuance shall contain information as to:

(a) when the need for the continuance arose;

(b) what the grounds for the continuance are;

(c) the measures taken to avoid seeking a continuance;

(d) the earliest date all parties will be ready to proceed.

4. Motions for continuances assented to by all parties must be acted upon by the court.

5. Motions for continuances not assented to by all parties will be scheduled for hearing before the court.

6. No continuance will be allowed except for good cause shown. Reasonable costs may be assessed against an attorney or party who causes a case to be continued without good cause or adequate notice.

Adopted effective November 1, 1990.

Standing Order 1–92. Case Management and Procedures

Applicable to the Charlestown Division

I. Case Management.

A. *Criminal Cases.*

1. Hours. The Clerk–Magistrate's Office is open from 8:30 A.M. until 4:30 P.M. from Monday through Friday. Defense counsel should advise defendants to report to the Probation Department at or before 8:30 A.M. on the morning of arraignment or on the day of their first appearance in court.

Criminal cases are heard on Monday, Wednesday and Friday of each week of the year and are called in the first session courtroom at 9:00 A.M. If Monday or Wednesday is a legal holiday, the court will hear cases on Tuesday or Thursday, respectively, of that week, and may hear criminal cases at other times and in other places by special assignment.

2. Daily Lists. The daily list of cases is available for inspection at 9:00 A.M. each day. Only a judge sitting in the Charlestown court is authorized to excuse a defendant from his or her appearance in court, or to reschedule or continue a case which has been scheduled for a particular day. When a judge is sitting, a defendant who is in custody may not be released until presented to the judge.

3. Call of the List. The first call of the list is scheduled for 9:00 A.M. If counsel is required to be in another court on the same day as his or her appearance in Charlestown, every effort will be made to reach such cases first if counsel brings the matter to the attention of the clerk prior to 9:00 A.M.

4. When a Judge Is Unavailable. Whenever during normal court business hours a judge is unavailable, the Clerk–Magistrate or a designated Assistant Clerk–Magistrate may set terms of release and assign a trial date, and may exercise the Court's authority to appoint counsel pursuant to Supreme Judicial Court Rule 3:10. A party aggrieved by any action of the Clerk–Magistrate or Assistant Clerk–Magistrate may obtain review of that action at the next scheduled sitting of the court.

5. Scheduling Cases for Trial. Generally, criminal cases will be scheduled for trial or other disposition following arraignment. In appropriate circumstances (e.g., seriousness or complexity of the charge), a case may be scheduled for pretrial conference. Default removals, probation reviews, and probation surrenders are generally scheduled for the afternoon session.

6. Election. Except by leave of Court, the defendant's election or waiver of first instance trial by jury must be filed at the defendant's first appearance following arraignment.

7. Pretrial Motions. The Court will not hear any pretrial motions in a case unless and until the defendant makes an election and waives the right to jury trial in the first instance. Pretrial motions, including requests for a continuance, must be in writing and must comply with the provisions of the Massachusetts Rules of Criminal Procedure. Costs may be assessed under Mass.R.Crim.P. 10(b) against a party who requests a continuance that is not in compliance with the rules. In all but the most extraordinary circumstances, a case marked "no further continuances" will be dismissed if the Commonwealth is not prepared for trial on the scheduled date. Costs may be assessed against a defendant or defense counsel if the defense is not prepared for trial on the scheduled date.

8. Special Disposition Session. On the second Monday of each month, or on the second Tuesday if the second Monday is a legal holiday, the court will conduct a Special Disposition Session at 8:00 A.M. in the first session courtroom. This session is designed for the convenience of counsel and litigants in criminal and civil matters in which the parties have reached agreement in all respects and in which the presence of witnesses (other than a defendant in a criminal case who has been released on recognizance) is not required. Matters will be heard in the Special Disposition Session only by prearrangement. In order to schedule a matter for the Special Disposition Session, the parties must prepare and file an Agreement for Disposition Form on or before the close of business on the Wednesday preceding the Special Disposition Session.

9. Defaults. A defendant seeking to remove a default in a criminal case shall be directed to report to the Probation Department and to the Clerk–Magistrate's Office before he or she comes before the Court. In any case in which there is an entry of a defendant's default, the Court may impose costs under Mass.R.Crim.P. 6(d) and G.L. c. 280, § 6.

10. Interpreter. A Spanish speaking interpreter is scheduled to be present on the second Wednesday of each month. Counsel who are aware of the need for an interpreter are requested to advise the Clerk–Magistrate's Office as soon as possible.

B. *Emergency Relief Under G.L. c. 209A.*

1. Priority Attention. Requests for protection and relief from abuse under G.L. c. 209A shall take precedence over all non-emergency matters before the court. The Chief Probation Officer and a victim/witness advocate are available to assist anyone seeking relief under G.L. c. 209A.

2. Relief After Hours. The court will hear requests for relief from abuse under G.L. c. 209A at any time when a judge is present in the courthouse. On weekdays when the court is not sitting in Charlestown (usually Tuesdays and Thursdays), a person may secure relief under G.L. c. 209A during business hours by coming to the Clerk–Magistrate's Office, which will contact a judge by telephone. At other times, a party in need of assistance should be directed to contact local police to request assistance from the Trial Court's emergency response system.

C. *Juvenile Matters.*

1. Schedule. Juvenile cases are scheduled for hearing or trial in the second session courtroom on Wednesday afternoons at 2:00 P.M., or at any other time that may be designated by the Presiding Justice. Defense counsel should advise juveniles to report to the Probation Department no later than 1:30 P.M. on the day their cases are scheduled, unless directed by the Probation Department to report at another time. Juvenile arraignments will be scheduled as soon as possible following the arrest of a juvenile.

D. *Civil Matters.*

1. Schedule. Scheduling of cases for motion, hearing, trial, or disposition should be arranged with the Assistant Clerk–Magistrate for Civil Business. Unless otherwise ordered by the Court or permitted by law, the Clerk–Magistrate's Office must be notified no later than the close of business on Tuesday in order for a civil matter to be scheduled for hearing or trial on Friday of that week. With the approval of the Court, a civil case may be scheduled for a time certain on any other day.

2. Call of the List. On Friday afternoons at 1:30 P.M., there will be a call of the civil list in the second session courtroom for previously scheduled Small Claims, Summary Process, Trustee Process, Supplementary Process, tort, contract or other civil matters. The order in which civil cases are called is within the discretion of the court. Generally, matters in which the parties are in agreement or as to which no opposition has been filed will be called first.

3. List. A Civil List will be available on Thursday of each week for the session scheduled for the next day.

4. Conference. All civil cases, including those remanded from the Superior Court Department, shall be scheduled for a pretrial conference for consideration of the matters referred to in Dist./Mun.Cts.R.Civ.P. 16. Counsel shall appear at the pretrial conference with full authority in all respects, or shall make advance arrangements for the client to be available for consultation during the course of the pretrial conference. The Court may enter an order summarizing the actions taken at the conference and setting a date for trial, which will control the subsequent course of the action unless modified at trial to prevent manifest injustice.

II. Special Procedures and Programs.

A. *Probation Surrender.* The Charlestown District Court follows a strict policy regarding compliance with the terms of court ordered probation. Unless specified otherwise by the sentencing judge, a sentence of probation is a sentence to "supervised probation" subject to the statutory probation supervision fee in G.L. c. 276, § 87A. Probationers are subject to periodic reviews by the assigned probation officer in every case. Terms of probation shall be in writing and signed by the probationer. Failure to honor any of the terms of the probation supervision may result in an administrative review by the Chief Probation Officer. Any substantial deviation from the terms of the probation will result in the issuance of a surrender notice followed by a prompt hearing to determine whether probation should be revoked.

B. *Payment of Fines, Fees, Costs, and Restitution.* The fee required by G.L. c. 211D, § 2A for the cost of appointed counsel is required to be paid at the defendant's next appearance in court following the appointment of counsel unless otherwise ordered by the Court. Unless otherwise ordered by the Court, the Probation Department is authorized to schedule payment of fines, fees, costs, and restitution over the period of time that the offender is on probation or subject to a continuance without a finding.

C. *Substance Abuse Evaluation.* It is a standing order of the Court in any case in which a person is placed on probation as part of the sentence in a criminal case or prior to trial under G.L. c. 276, § 87 that the probation is to be supervised and may include a requirement of outpatient evaluation for any substance abuse problem which may exist. The Chief Probation Officer may require such evaluation at any time in his or her discretion if the defendant consents; if the defendant refuses such consent, the Chief Probation Officer may recommend that the Court require such an evaluation.

D. *Community Service.* The Probation Department of the Charlestown District Court supervises an active program of community service. It is a standing order of the Court that any person who is ordered to pay a fine, assessment or cost, other than restitution, and is found to be indigent or is otherwise unable to pay shall satisfy the financial obligation by performing community service at the rate of $6.00 per hour unless disqualified by a verified disability.

E. *Diversion Program.* Appropriate first time offenders are eligible for the court's Juvenile Diversion Program. For further details, contact the Chief Probation Officer.

F. *Mediation.*

1. General Rule. The court strongly encourages the informal resolution of civil cases and other appropriate matters, and will assist the parties with the possibility of settlement by providing mediation services whenever requested by a party or a lawyer. Parties or lawyers who wish to explore a resolution of their dispute by a method other than the traditional court process should contact the Assistant Clerk–Magistrate for Civil Business.

2. Small Claims. All small claims cases will be screened for voluntary participation in a court sponsored mediation session at the courthouse prior to the presentation of the case to the court.

G. *Probation Department Services.* The Charlestown District Court Probation Department sponsors and supports a variety of community based programs for persons who are victims of crime, for offenders, and for the families and friends of those affected by crime, including in particular support groups, counselling, and mental health services. Particular emphasis is given to persons and families affected by alcohol and drug abuse. For more information, contact Chief Probation Officer Dr. Barbara Burke.

Adopted effective September 1, 1992.

Standing Order 1–98. Superseded by Joint Standing Order 1–04

Publisher's Note

Standing Order 1–04, in Section I., provides: "This Order applies to all tort and contract actions in which money damages are sought ('civil actions') and which have been commenced in the Boston Municipal Court Department and the District Court Department on or after August 31, 2004. In the District Court Department, this Order shall also apply to all civil actions previously governed by District Court Standing Order 1–98 regarding any procedures occurring on or after that date. Sections VI (Motion Practice) and VII (Continuances) of this Order shall also apply to all civil actions pending in the divisions of the Boston Municipal Court Department and in the divisions of the District Court Department in Plymouth, Suffolk and Worcester Counties, regardless of the date of commencement of such actions." Standing Order 1–04 in Section I., further provides: "This Order supersedes Boston Municipal Court Department Standing Order 1–88 and District Court Department Standing Orders 1–88 and 1–98 with respect to all civil actions and all procedures to which this Order applies."

Joint Standing Order 1–04. Civil Case Management

I. PURPOSE AND APPLICABILITY

The purpose of this Joint Order is to establish case management procedures that will facilitate the prompt and efficient disposition of civil cases and reduce the expense and delay of civil litigation in the Boston Municipal Court Department and the District Court Department.

This Order applies to all tort and contract actions in which money damages are sought ("civil actions") and which have been commenced in the Boston Municipal Court Department and the District Court Department on or after August 31, 2004. In the District Court Department, this Order shall also apply to all civil actions previously governed by District Court Standing Order 1–98 regarding any procedures occurring on or after that date. Sections VI (Motion Practice) and VII (Continuances) of this Order also apply to all civil actions pending in the divisions of the Boston Municipal Court Department and in the divisions of the District Court Department in Plymouth, Suffolk and Worcester Counties, regardless of the date of commencement of such actions.

This Order supersedes Boston Municipal Court Department Standing Order 1–88 and District Court Department Standing Orders 1–88 and 1–98 with respect to all civil actions and all procedures to which this Order applies.

II. GENERAL PRETRIAL SCHEDULE

It shall be the responsibility of counsel to complete the preparation of his or her case by the date of the pretrial conference as scheduled in accordance with Section IV A, unless the court orders otherwise. Discovery and pretrial motions, including motions pursuant to Mass. R. Civ. P. 12, 15, 19, 20 and 56, and such other motions as may be prescribed by the court, shall be filed, marked and caused to be heard by such date unless the court permits otherwise for good cause shown.

III. CASE MANAGEMENT CONFERENCE

A. Scheduling. Upon the filing of an answer by any defendant, the court shall immediately give notice to all parties in the action of a Case Management Conference pursuant to Mass. R. Civ. P. 16 to be held on a date certain within four months of the date of filing of such answer, or sooner if directed by the court or jointly requested by all parties. Such notice shall inform the parties of the purposes of the conference and the desirability of addressing any discovery issues prior to the conference. Counsel or pro se litigants shall appear in person at the Case Management Conference. The court may impose sanctions, including dismissal, default and assessment of costs, for failure to attend the conference without good cause.

B. Purpose. The purpose of the Case Management Conference shall be to (1) discuss settlement progress and opportunities for settlement, and offer early intervention alternative dispute resolution; (2) consider case management orders proposed by any party, or by the court, regarding limitation or sequencing of discovery events, disclosure or limitation of expert witnesses, motion briefing, and other matters that would reduce expense and delay of litigation, and enter appropriate orders; (3) enter judgment for relief or dismissal, and schedule hearing for assessment of damages if necessary; and (4) assign a firm date for pretrial conference for all cases which are not yet ready for trial; (5) assess the trial-readiness of cases; (6) assign a firm trial date for cases that are ready for trial.

Among the orders that a Judge may impose at the Case Management Conference under item (2), above, is an "Order for Early Disclosure," requiring compliance with the terms set forth in Section III D.

Notice of the date of trial or Pretrial Conference shall be given to the parties at the Case Management Conference after consultation with counsel.

In all cases scheduled for trial, the person conducting the Case Management Conference shall prepare a Pretrial Conference report. In all cases scheduled for Pretrial Conference, the person conducting the Case Management Conference shall prepare a Case Management Conference report summarizing the results of the conference.

C. Judicial officer. The Case Management Conference shall be conducted by a Judge or, if a Judge is unavailable, by a Clerk–Magistrate or Assistant Clerk–Magistrate designated by the Chief Justice of the Boston Municipal Court Department or the Chief Justice of the District Court Department in accordance with G.L. § 221, § 62C and Trial Court Rule II(3)(a) to conduct such conferences. Only a Judge may issue or approve any orders arising from the Case Management Conference.

D. Mandatory Early Disclosure. If ordered by the court at the Case Management Conference as provided above in section III B, each party shall provide the discovery specified below without a request by any opposing party. Unless otherwise agreed by the parties or ordered by the court, such disclosure shall be completed no later than 90 days after completion of the Case Management Conference.

1. Actions Involving Tort Claims.

(a) Plaintiff. A party asserting a tort claim shall provide to all other parties copies of medical bills and medical records in its possession, custody, or control, or provide written authorizations signed by the patient to permit opposing counsel to obtain such documents; all accident reports, sketches and photographs of the accident scene; property damage or injury reports; an itemized list of special damages and non-medical damages known to counsel; admissions by the opposing party; names and addresses of witnesses; reports of all government agencies or officials which investigated the event giving rise to the claim; personal injury protection (PIP) applications and documents; the identity of any person, firm or entity who may be responsible for the plaintiff's injury; and any documents that counsel agree to disclose without formal discovery.

(b) Defendant. A party defending against a tort claim shall provide to all other parties copies of all primary and excess insurance policies that may be available to satisfy a judgment; copies of all documents reserving an insurer's right to deny coverage; all accident reports, sketches and photographs of the accident scene; property damage or injury reports; medical examination reports of the plaintiff (which the defendant intends to introduce as evidence at trial); admissions by the opposing party; names and addresses of witnesses; reports of government agencies or officials which investigated the event giving rise to the claim; and any documents that counsel agree to disclose without formal discovery.

2. Actions Involving Contract Claims.

(a) Plaintiff. A party asserting a contract claim shall provide to all other parties copies of the contracts or written agreements that give rise to the claim, including warranties, notes, and guaranties; names and addresses of witnesses; an itemized list of special damages; admissions by the opposing party; and any documents that counsel agree to disclose without formal discovery.

(b) Defendant. A party defending a contract claim shall provide to all other parties copies of all primary and excess insurance policies that may be available to satisfy a judgment; copies of all documents reserving an insurer's right to deny coverage; any contracts or written agreements that give rise to the claim, including warranties, notes and guaranties; names and addresses of witnesses; admissions by the opposing party; and any documents that counsel agree to disclose without formal discovery.

3. Expert Witnesses.

A party shall identify any person who may be used as an expert witness at trial in advance of the pretrial hearing date. Except as otherwise stipulated or directed by the court, this disclosure shall be accompanied by a written report prepared by the witness. The report shall contain a complete statement of all opinions to be expressed and the basis and reasons therefor; the data or other information considered by the witness in forming the opinions; any exhibits to be used as a summary of or support for the opinions; the qualifications of the witness, including a list of all publications authored by the witness within the preceding five years; the compensation to be paid for the study and testimony; and a listing of any cases in which the witness has testified as a witness at trial or by deposition within the preceding three years.

4. Contested Discovery.

Before filing any discovery motion, including any motion for sanctions or for a protective order, counsel for each of the parties shall confer in good faith to narrow the areas of disagreement to the greatest possible extent. It shall be the responsibility of counsel for the moving party to arrange for the conference. Any motion to compel discovery shall include a certificate of counsel filed by the moving party certifying that he has conferred with opposing counsel as required by this section.

IV. PRETRIAL CONFERENCE

A. Scheduling and pretrial memorandum. All cases not disposed or assigned a trial date at the Case Management Conference shall be assigned a firm date for Pretrial Conference when they are expected to be ready for trial, such date to be not later than the end of the tenth month after the month in which the action was filed, or such later date as the court may order for good cause shown. Upon scheduling an action for Pretrial Conference, the court shall issue a notice of Pretrial Conference requiring the parties to prepare a joint pretrial memorandum for use at the Pretrial Conference. Failure of any party to attend the Pretrial Conference or prepare a joint pretrial memorandum may result in sanctions, including dismissal, default and assessment of costs.

B. Agenda, report and Trial Order. The purpose of the Pretrial Conference is to discuss settlement opportunities and to achieve settlement or, for cases which do not settle, to assign a firm trial date. The person conducting the Pretrial Conference shall thereafter prepare a pretrial conference report. For actions requiring a trial date, notice of such date shall be given to all parties at the Pretrial Conference after consultation with counsel. Upon scheduling a case for trial, the court shall issue a Trial Order requiring the parties to prepare for trial. Failure of any party to prepare for trial as required by such order may result in preclusion of evidence or other sanctions in the discretion of the trial judge.

C. Judicial officer. The Pretrial Conference shall be conducted by a Judge or, if a Judge is unavailable, by a Clerk–Magistrate or Assistant Clerk–Magistrate who has been designated by the Chief Justice of the Boston Municipal Court Department or the Chief Justice of the District Court Department in accordance with G.L. c. 221, § 62C and Trial Court Rule II(3)(a) to conduct such conferences, or by alternative dispute resolution personnel approved by the court. Only a Judge may issue or approve any orders arising from the Pretrial Conference.

V. DISMISSAL FOR LACK OF SERVICE OR FAILURE TO ACT ON DEFAULT

All actions in which there is no timely service of the complaint or no timely action upon default shall be dismissed as follows:

A. Dismissal for lack of service. After commencement of each action, the Clerk–Magistrate shall review the docket to determine whether the plaintiff has complied with the time limits for service pursuant to Mass. R. Civ. P. 4(j), together with any extensions allowed by the court pursuant to Mass. R. Civ. P. 6. Upon determining noncompliance, the Clerk–Magistrate shall issue notice of dismissal of the action as provided by Rule 4(j).

B. Dismissal nisi for failure to act on default. Where an action has remained on the docket for eight months without an answer or defensive motion having been filed by any defendant, the Clerk–Magistrate shall enter an Order Nisi for Dismissal advising the plaintiff that a Judgment of Dismissal will be entered 30 days from the date of the Order unless the plaintiff either (1) requests entry of default and moves for default judgment in accordance with Mass. R. Civ. P. 55, or (2) reports in writing that the case is active and requests that it not be dismissed.

VI. MOTION PRACTICE

A. General. Pursuant to Mass. R. Civ. P. 6 and 78, all motions shall be accompanied by an affidavit of notice setting forth the date and time of hearing on the motion. All motions shall be scheduled by counsel for the moving party on the court's usual civil motion hearing day as published by the court, or on the date the case is scheduled for Case Management Conference or Pretrial Conference, or as otherwise ordered by the court.

B. Agreed Upon Motions. Motions filed by the parties jointly or where the moving party avers that all other parties agree with the outcome sought by the motion may be submitted for a ruling on the papers without the presence of the parties. Such motions shall be accompanied by an express request that the court rule without a hearing. This procedure shall be available only in cases where all parties are represented by counsel.

C. Discovery and summary judgment motions. All discovery motions filed pursuant to Mass. R. Civ. P. 26 or 37 shall include copies of the discovery requests and responses which are the subject of the motion. Motions for summary judgment which rely on any pleading or discovery shall include copies of such pleadings or discovery with the motion. Any discovery or summary judgment motions which do not include such copies may be denied without prejudice.

D. Opposition procedure. In actions where all parties are represented by counsel, motions may be acted upon by the court without a hearing in the following manner.

1. **Designation by moving party.** A moving party who chooses to use this procedure shall state on the caption of the motion and on the affidavit of notice, "SUBJECT TO OPPOSITION PROCEDURE," and file and serve such motion at least 14 days before the motion hearing date. If no other party timely files and serves an "OPPOSITION TO MOTION" as described below, the motion will be considered by the court without a hearing or the attendance of any counsel.

2. **Opposition by other party.** If any other party opposes the motion or otherwise seeks to be heard, such party shall file and serve a document captioned "OPPOSITION TO MOTION" at least five days before the motion hearing date. If any party timely files and serves such an "OPPOSITION TO MOTION," all counsel shall be required to attend the scheduled hearing, unless in such "OPPOSITION TO MOTION" the party expressly waives the right to such hearing, in which case the motion will be considered by the court without a hearing or the attendance of any counsel.

3. **Exempted motions.** This opposition procedure shall not apply to the following motions: motions to continue Case Management Conference, Pretrial Conference or trial; ex parte motions; petitions for approval of settlement by a minor; motions seeking sanctions of any kind; motions for preliminary and permanent injunction; motions for a receiver; motions to vacate a default judgment; motions for relief from judgment; motions for a new trial; motions for reconsideration; and any motion ordered by a Judge to be decided after hearing.

4. **Notice of decision.** When a motion is considered under the opposition procedure, the court shall act upon, and send written notice of such action to all parties, within 14 days after the hearing date.

VII. CONTINUANCES

A. General. Continuances of Case Management Conferences, Pretrial Conferences and trials shall be disfavored because of the advance notice to, and the participation of

counsel in, the scheduling of these events. Continuances of these events will be allowed for good cause only, and any continuance shall be to a date and event certain. No action shall be "continued generally" or taken off the schedule for any reason.

B. Form of motions. Requests for continuances shall be made only by written motion supported by an affidavit of counsel, and counsel shall send a copy of the continuance request to his or her client(s) by first-class mail. All motions for continuance shall include a list of any days within the next 30 days that counsel for any party is unavailable for the continued event.

C. Joint requests to continue case management conference or pretrial conference. The Clerk-Magistrate or an Assistant Clerk designated by the Clerk-Magistrate may allow a joint request to continue a Case Management Conference or Pretrial Conference after review of the motion without hearing, provided that the event shall be continued not more than once and for not more than 30 days.

D. Trial continuances, opposed continuances and repeat continuances. Motions to continue a trial, whether or not agreed to by the parties, may be allowed only by a Judge assigned to the civil trial session or, in the absence or unavailability of such Judge, by the Presiding Justice or other Judge designated by the Presiding Justice. Motions to continue a Case Management Conference or Pretrial Conference which are opposed by any party, as well as motions to continue an event previously continued pursuant to Section VII C above, shall be marked and heard as motions before a Judge. Counsel and pro se litigants shall not be excused from attending the scheduled event unless notified by the court that the event has been continued. No employee or officer of the court shall be authorized to allow continuances of trials or conferences, except as provided in this section.

/s/CHARLES R. JOHNSON   /s/LYNDA M. CONNOLLY

_____   _____

Charles R. Johnson, Chief Justice   Lynda M. Connolly, Chief Justice

Boston Municipal Court Department   District Court Department

Adopted August 23, 2004, effective August 31, 2004.

Order of Suspension

District Court Order of March 21, 2011, provided:

"Effective April 1, 2011, a pilot program will be conducted for civil money damage actions at the Springfield Division of the District Court Department, in those actions where all parties are represented by counsel, under which parties and their counsel may avoid appearance in court for the conduct of a Case Management Conference upon the timely filing of a joint certification that the purposes of such conference have been achieved by the parties without such appearance.

"The pilot program will be implemented and administered by Honorable William J. Boyle, First Justice of the Springfield District Court.

"The provisions of Paragraph III of Joint Standing Order No. 1-04 regarding the scheduling, conduct and attendance at Case Management Conferences that are inconsistent with the terms and requirements of the pilot program as established by Judge William J. Boyle are hereby suspended for the duration of said program.

"The pilot shall remain in effect until further order of the Chief Justice of the District Court."

Joint Standing Order 2–04. Time Standards for Civil Cases

I. INTRODUCTION

These time standards are promulgated to provide judges and clerk-magistrates with specific maximum time periods within which civil cases (1) should progress between court events and (2) should be disposed. The purpose of these time standards is to promote timely disposition of civil cases and to provide a basis for assessing the movement of civil cases from commencement to disposition in each division of the two departments in which they apply.

The time standards are divided into three categories, each comprised of specific types of civil actions ("casetypes") and each governed by a specific standard for a maximum time to disposition.

In general, these three time standard categories reflect the complexity (or potential complexity) of the casetypes each includes, with the least complex in Category A, the more complex in Category B, and the most complex (or potentially complex) in Category C.

The casetypes in Category A consist mainly of actions that by law must be disposed well within the two-month maximum. For these cases the time standard will provide a basis for periodically confirming that no cases are unaccounted for or overlooked.

Two casetypes in Category B, summary process and small claims, have "staircased" time standards to reflect the fact that significant numbers of these cases should be disposed well before their overall maximum time to disposition.

Category C, which consists of tort and contract actions, also has "staircased" time standards to reflect the fact that most of these cases should be disposed well before the overall maximum time limit.

II. THE TIME STANDARDS

CATEGORY A—Time to Disposition: Upon Filing or <u>Not more than 2 months</u> from commencement

- Abuse Restraining Orders (c.209A)
- Landlord Failures to Provide Utilities (c. 186 § 14)
- Landlord Interference with Quiet Enjoyment (c. 186 § 14)
- Landlord Unlawfully Entering/Repossessing Land (c. 184 § 18)
- Lead Poisoning Prevention Actions (c. 111 § 198)
- License Suspension for Chemical Test Refusal Appeals (c.90 § 24[1][g])
- Marriage Age Waivers (c.207 § 25)
- Marriage Waiting Period Waivers (c.207 § 30)
- Mental Health Proceedings (c. 123)
- Sanitary Code Enforcement Actions (c. 111 § 127C)

CATEGORY B—Time to Disposition: <u>Not more than 4 months</u> from commencement

- Summary Process: 50% NMT 1 month; 90% NMT 2 months; 100% NMT 4 months
- Small Claims: 75% NMT 2 months; 100% NMT 4 months (5 months if de novo appeal claimed)
- Civil Motor Vehicle Infractions (5 months if de novo appeal claimed)
- Non–Motor Vehicle Civil Infractions (5 months if de novo appeal claimed) (see attached list)
- Supplementary Process
- Judicial Review of Administrative Decisions (see attached list)
- Other Specialized Civil Actions (see attached list)

CATEGORY C—Tort and Contract Actions

C–1	Time to Disposition: <u>Not more than 6 months</u> from commencement
75% of Total Dispositions	• Cases dismissed for plaintiff's failure to make timely service • Cases disposed by default judgment

	• Cases disposed by voluntary dismissal, agreement for judgment or other consensual disposition
C–2 20% of Total Dispositions	Time to Disposition: <u>Not more than 12 months</u> from commencement • Cases disposed by bench trial • Cases disposed by voluntary dismissal, agreement for judgment or other consensual disposition • Cases dismissed for plaintiff's failure to seek default judgment
C–3 5% of Total Dispositions	Time to Disposition: <u>Not more than 18 months</u> from commencement • Cases disposed by jury trial • Cases disposed by bench trial after having been scheduled for jury trial • Cases disposed by voluntary dismissal, agreement for judgment or other consensual disposition after having been scheduled for trial

Maximum Intervals Between Court Events:
- From Answer to Case Management Conference Date: Not More Than 4 Months
- From Case Management Conference to Pretrial Conference Date: Not More Than 7 Months
- From Pretrial Conference to Trial: Not More Than 3 Months

Originally Promulgated: October 1, 2004, to be effective November 1, 2004

Amended: July 1, 2008 for cases filed on and after January 1, 2008

APPENDIX

Non–Motor Vehicle Civil Infractions (Category B) include

- Bicycle Civil Infractions (c.85 § 11C)
- Dog Control Civil Infractions (c. 140 § 173A)
- Environmental Civil Infractions (c.21A §§ 10G–10H)
- MBTA Smoking Civil Infractions (c. 161A § 42)
- Motorboat Civil Infractions (c.90B § 14[a])
- Municipal Ordinance/Bylaw Civil Infractions (c.40 § 21D)
- Pedestrian Civil Infractions (c.90 § 18A)
- Rubbish Disposal Civil Infractions (c.270 § 16A)
- State Building Code or Fire Code Civil Infractions (c. 148A)
- State Park / Forest / Recreation Area Civil Infractions (c. 132A § 7A)

Judicial Review of Administrative Decisions (Category B) includes

- Abandoned Property Appeals (c.200A § 10[d])
- Ammunition Dealer License Appeals (c. 140 § 122B)
- County Employee Discharge Appeals (c.35 § 51)
- Dog Order Appeals (c. 140, § 157)
- Farm Nuisance Abatement Order Appeals (c. 111 § 125A)
- Fence Viewer Certiorari Actions (c.249 § 4)
- Firearms Identification Card Appeals (c. 140 § 129B[5])
- Firearms License Appeals (c. 140 § 131[h])
- Funeral Director License Appeals (c. 112 § 84A)
- Historic District Commission Appeals

• Home Improvement Contractor Arbitration Appeals (c. 142A § 4[e])

• MCAD Housing Discrimination Award Appeals (c. 151B § 5)

• Raffle/Bazaar Permit Appeals (c.271 § 7A)

• Retirement Board/PERA Appeals (c.32 § 16[c][3][a])

• Unemployment Compensation Appeals (c. 151A § 42)

• Used Car Lemon Law Arbitration Appeals (c.90 § 7N¼)

• Victim of Violent Crime Compensation Appeals (c.258C § 9)

• Zoning Appeals (c.40A § 17)

Other Specialized Civil Actions (Category B) include:

• Auto/Boat Forfeiture Actions based on Fourth or Subsequent OUI (c.90 § 24W)

• Beach Free Passage Actions (St. 1991 c. 176 § 4)

• Child Labor Citation Enforcement Actions (c. 149 § 78A[d])

• Condominium Conversion Violation Actions (St. 1983 c.527 § 5 & St. 1989, c.709 § 20)

• Discovery in Foreign Proceeding (c.223A § 11)

• Election Violation Inquest (c.55 § 35)

• Explosives/Inflammables Forfeiture Actions (c. 148 §§ 50–51)

• Forfeiture of Property Seized in Criminal Offense (c.257 §§ 2–7)

• Juror Wage Denial Actions (c.234A § 60)

• Lien Enforcement Actions (c.254 § 5; 255 § 26)

• Livestock Disease Control Actions (c. 129 § 37)

• Medical Provider Overpayment Recovery Actions (c. 118E § 38)

• Municipal Tax Collection Proceedings (c.60 § 29)

• Replevin (c.247)

• Repossession of Secured Goods (c.255 § 13J; c.255B § 20B; c.255D § 22)

• Security Actions for Impounded Animal (c.272 § 104[c])

• Settlement Approval for Personal Injury to Minor/Incompetent (c.231 § 140C½)

• State Fire Marshal Investigations (c. 148 § 3)

• Structured Settlement Transfer Approvals (c.231C § 2)

• Tenant Illegal Activity Declaratory Judgments (c. 139 § 19)

• Tuberculosis Commitments/Discharges (c. 111, §§ 94C or 94G)

• Unemployment Compensation Actions against Employer by DET (c. 151A § 15)

Adopted October 1, 2004, effective November 1, 2004. Amended effective July 1, 2008 for cases filed on and after January 1, 2008.

Joint Standing Order 3–04. Time Standards for Criminal Cases

1. AUTHORITY

This Standing Order is jointly promulgated by the Chief Justice of the Boston Municipal Court Department and the Chief Justice of the District Court Department pursuant to their statutory responsibility for case management under G.L. c. 211B, § 10 and uniform practices under G.L. c. 218, § 43A.

2. PURPOSE

These time standards are intended to reaffirm the goals of "simplicity in procedure, fairness in administration, and the elimination of expense and delay," as provided by Mass. R. Crim. P. 2(a). Recognizing that excessive delay can undermine public confidence in the delivery of justice in our courts, the following time standards have been established to advance the expeditious and just disposition of all criminal matters.

3. TIME STANDARDS

There shall be two track designations for criminal cases commenced within the final jurisdiction of the Boston Municipal and District Court Departments. Track A shall include all criminal offenses which provide a maximum period of incarceration of six months or less, including all criminal offenses which carry no term of imprisonment and are punishable only by fine. Track B shall include all criminal offenses punishable by a period of incarceration longer than six months.

The maximum time to disposition for Track A cases shall be five months. The maximum time to disposition for Track B cases shall be twelve months. If a defendant is charged with one or more Track A and Track B offenses in a single complaint, the case shall be treated as Track B for all purposes. Cases may be transferred from Track A to Track B, or the maximum time period allowable between court events may be extended, only by a judge for demonstrated good cause stated on the record. Requests to alter the track designation of cases or to extend a maximum time period within a track shall be evaluated consistent with the purposes of this Order set forth in paragraph 2. Nothing in this Order shall be construed to deter resolution of cases prior to the maximum time limits set forth herein.

Consistent with the applicable provisions of the Mass. R. Crim. P. and the Dist./Mun. Cts. R. Crim. P., the time between court events in criminal cases shall be as follows:

Track A:

• From Arraignment to Pretrial Hearing date: Not more than 45 days;

• From Pretrial Hearing to Motion/Compliance/Election date: Not more than 45 days;

• From Motion/Compliance/Election date to Trial date: Not more than 45 days.

Track B:

• From Arraignment to Pretrial Hearing date: Not more than 45 days;

• From Pretrial Hearing to Motion/Compliance/Election date: Not more than 60 days;

• From Motion/Compliance/Election to Trial date: Not more than 90 days.

4. CRIMINAL CASE MANAGEMENT

Performance goals for criminal case management in the Boston Municipal Court Department shall be determined by the Chief Justice of the Boston Municipal Court Department.

Criminal case management in the District Court Department shall be assessed in accordance with District Court Standing Order No. 4-04, Performance Goals for Criminal Case Management.

Computation of the time periods set forth above shall exclude any time during which the defendant is legally unavailable to proceed with the criminal case; e.g., time during which the defendant is in default and periods of time during which the defendant is under a term of involuntary civil commitment pursuant to the provisions of G.L. c. 123.

/s/CHARLES R. JOHNSON	/s/LYNDA M. CONNOLLY
Charles R. Johnson, Chief Justice	Lynda M. Connolly, Chief Justice
Boston Municipal Court Department	District Court Department

Promulgated:

Effective:

Adopted effective November 1, 2004.

Standing Order 4-04. Performance Goals for Criminal Case Management

In the District Court Department criminal case management in each division will be assessed from time to time in terms of overall time to disposition for the court's entire criminal caseload.

The performance goals will be as follows:

Dispositions	Maximum time from arraignment to disposition
80–90%	Not more than four months
92–98%	Not more than six months
100%	Not more than twelve months

In determining time to disposition under this Order, any time during which the defendant is legally unavailable to proceed with a case (e.g., time during which a defendant is in default or under civil commitment) will not be included.

/s/LYNDA M. CONNOLLY

Lynda M. Connolly, Chief Justice

District Court Department

Promulgated: _____

Effective: _____

Adopted effective November 1, 2004.

Commentary

The Criminal Time Standards in Joint Standing Order 3-04 provide two tracks for time-to-disposition and standards for intervals between court events. They are intended to provide specific time limits at the outset of each case to enable the judge to avoid delay as that case moves forward. Factors can emerge in any case that will determine whether these limits are unnecessarily long (e.g., "driving uninsured" cases normally should be disposed of quickly, despite being on Track B) or unreasonably brief (e.g., despite being on Track A, a minor case may require more than four months if the defendant demands a jury trial or if the case involves significant economic consequences). In any event, the Joint Criminal Time Standards provide that the track limit in any particular case may be extended for good cause stated on the record.

The District Court criminal case management goals set forth in *this* Standing Order focus on each court's actual criminal dispositions, rather than governing cases as they proceed. They assess performance in terms of the court's entire criminal caseload, irrespective of tracks.

This assessment approach avoids subdividing actual dispositions in terms of the penalties available by statute for each case, and thus simplifies the assessment process. This approach also appropriately accounts for cases that should be disposed of quickly, though they have been placed initially on the twelve-month track.

This assessment approach also provides flexibility to reflect the different types of caseloads in the District Court divisions. A court with relatively few time-consuming criminal cases (generally rural or suburban courts with high proportions of motor vehicle offenses and other minor, non-violent crimes) may have a higher percentage of dispositions within the four-month limit and fewer within the six-to-twelve month limit. For case management assessment purposes the breakdown for such a court might be 90%, 98%, 100%.

By comparison, an urban court with a higher proportion of crimes involving violence, drug charges and repeat offenders would be expected to have a higher percentage of dispositions in the six-to-twelve-month range and proportionately fewer within the four-month limit. Such a court may have a breakdown for case management assessment purposes of 80%, 92%, 100%.

The point is that both courts will be within the performance goals.

The assessment will take into account cases commenced in one court but disposed in a jury session that is provided in another court.

It is important to note that when the case management of individual courts is assessed, the process will allow court personnel—judges, clerk-magistrates, chief probation officers, and staff—to review court practices and procedures and identify strengths and any weaknesses. Regional and Administrative Office personnel will be available to assist in appropriate circumstances. It is anticipated that this comprehensive, coordinated approach, which is an approach followed by the American Bar Association in its caseflow management recommendations, will provide a meaningful opportunity for all court components to effectively collaborate in the timely movement of criminal cases to disposition.

Standing Order 1-08. Petitions for Judicial Review of License Suspension for Chemical Test Refusal

(Applicable to All Divisions)

1. Applicability. This Order governs the orderly processing of petitions pursuant to G.L. c. 90, § 24(1)(g), first paragraph, for judicial review of a decision of the Registrar of Motor Vehicles upholding the suspension of a motorist's license, permit or right to operate a motor vehicle based upon an alleged refusal to submit to a chemical test or analysis of the motorist's breath or blood at the time of arrest for operating a motor vehicle while under the influence of intoxicating liquor. Such petitions shall be filed and determined in accordance with the following procedures.

2. Filing of petition. Such petitions for judicial review shall be timely filed in the appropriate court on the form provided therefor, along with the filing fee and surcharge required by G.L. c. 262, §§ 2 and 4C, unless waived pursuant to G.L. c. 261, §§ 27A–27G. Such forms shall be available in each clerk-magistrate's office and on the District Court's internet website. Such petitions shall be docketed as a separate civil case, and not as part of the underlying criminal case. The clerk-magistrate shall immediately send a copy of any such petition to the Suspension Department of the Registry of Motor Vehicles by facsimile transmission.

3. Scheduling. The clerk-magistrate shall schedule such petition for hearing at least 15 days from the filing of the petition. As required by G.L. c. 90, § 24(1)(g), the hearing shall be scheduled as soon as possible thereafter and not more than 30 days from the filing of the petition, unless the petitioner consents to a later date. No pre-hearing motion or memorandum shall be required, unless specifically ordered by the Court. The petitioner may waive oral argument and submit on written argument, or without argument, by so notifying the clerk-magistrate in writing prior to the scheduled hearing date.

4. Filing of RMV record. Within 15 days after receiving a copy of the petition by facsimile transmission, the Registry of Motor Vehicles shall, by way of appearance and answer, file with the clerk-magistrate a copy of the entire record established at the hearing before the Registrar or the Registrar's designee, certified in accordance with G.L. c. 233, § 76 as a true and complete copy of such record. The Registry shall simultaneously serve a copy of such record upon the petitioner by mail to the petitioner's current mailing address as established pursuant to G.L. c. 90, § 26A. The Registry shall not be required to file an appearance of counsel nor appear at the hearing, but if the Registry chooses to so appear by counsel it shall give written notice of such intent to the court and the petitioner when filing such record.

5. Hearing. Since § 24(1)(g) limits the Court's review to the record that was established at the Registry hearing, the court's hearing shall be limited to oral argument concerning such record, and no additional testimony or other evidence shall be presented.

6. Decision. Pursuant to G.L. c. 90, § 24(1)(g), the Court may reverse the Registrar's decision if the Registry exceeded its constitutional or statutory authority, made an erroneous interpretation of the law, acted in an arbitrary and capricious manner, or made a determination which is unsupported by the evidence in the record. The Court's determination shall be recorded in the appropriate section of the petition form, and the clerk-magistrate shall then provide the petitioner with a copy of that determination and send a copy to the Registry by facsimile transmission.

The Court's decision is not appealable to the Appellate Division. *Simon v. Registry of Motor Vehs.*, 1995 Mass. App. Div. 129 (N. Dist.)

Adopted February 7, 2008, effective April 1, 2008.

Standing Order 1–11. Limited Assistance Representation and Substitute Counsel

(Applicable to All Divisions)

This Standing Order is promulgated by the Chief Justice of the District Court Department pursuant to the provisions of G.L. c. 211B, § 10 and G.L. c. 218, § 43. This Standing Order addresses two issues concerning the representation of parties by counsel in non-criminal proceedings in the District Court Department of the Trial Court. Part A of the Standing Order addresses the "unbundling" of legal services and implements the Order In Re: Limited Assistance Representation issued by the Massachusetts Supreme Judicial Court, effective May 1, 2009. The Standing Order provides the parameters for limited assistance representation in the District Court Department.

Part B of the Standing Order addresses court proceedings where an attorney substitutes or "covers" for an attorney who has already filed a general appearance on behalf of the litigant but is not present at that particular court proceeding. The Standing Order requires substitute counsel to file an appearance. The Order permits a time limited appearance, thereby acknowledging a common practice in certain civil proceedings in the court while permitting the court to maintain an accurate record of all attorneys who appear before the court. This part of the Order applies exclusively to those litigants who are already represented by counsel, and not to the unbundling of legal services, which is addressed by the first part of this Standing Order. The Standing Order does not address the legal or ethical requirements applicable to such representation, which are governed by the Code of Professional Conduct, S.J.C. Rule 3:07.

PART A: LIMITED ASSISTANCE REPRESENTATION

Publisher's Note: Part A. Limited Assistance Representation, was rescinded effective February 1, 2019, the date upon which Trial Court Rule XVI Limited Assistance Representation becomes effective.

PART B: SUBSTITUTE COUNSEL

15. Substitute Counsel. The term "substitute counsel," shall mean one attorney standing in or "covering" for another attorney who has already filed a general appearance on behalf of a litigant.

16. Notice of Appearance. In cases where a party is already represented by counsel who has filed a general appearance in the case, an attorney who is not current counsel of record shall not appear in court to answer for that party until he or she has filed with the court a written notice of appearance as substitute counsel. Such appearance may be time-limited and may indicate that the attorney is appearing as substitute counsel solely for that day's proceedings. The scope of an appearance as substitute counsel may not otherwise be limited, and substitute counsel must be authorized and prepared to proceed with all matters before the court at that time. Any such notice of appearance as substitute counsel shall be entered on the docket and filed with the case papers.

17. Notice to Substitute Counsel. The clerk need not notify counsel who has filed an appearance as substitute counsel of any orders, future events or proceedings in that case.

Adopted January 25, 2011, effective for one year. Amended and made permanent effective January 25, 2012. Amended January 29, 2019, effective February 1, 2019.

Standing Order 1–15. Provision of Respondents' Non-Clinical Identifying Information in Commitment Proceedings Under G. L. c. 123, §§ 7, 8, and 12(e), or G. L. c. 123, § 35

The purpose of this Joint Order is to provide for the collection of non-clinical identifying information in commitment proceedings in the Boston Municipal Court Department and the District Court Department necessary to comply with the courts' reporting requirements pursuant to Chapter 284, Acts of 2014 , An Act Relative to the Reduction of Gun Violence.[1]

IT IS THEREFORE ORDERED:

An applicant seeking a court order to commit a respondent to a mental health facility pursuant to G.L. c. 123, § 12(e) , a petitioner seeking a court order to commit or retain a respondent for inpatient care pursuant to G.L. c. 123, §§ 7 and 8 , and a petitioner seeking a court order to commit a respondent for treatment for alcoholism and/or substance abuse pursuant to G.L. c. 123, § 35 , shall provide the respondent's date of birth and social security number, if available, to the court.

Adopted May 20, 2015, effective June 1, 2015.

1 Although commitment matters are also brought under G.L. c. 123, §§ 15(b), 16(b) or (c), or 18 that arise out of criminal proceedings, the respondent's or defendant's date of birth and social security number is obtained and provided to the court through the Defendant Identification Information System in those cases.

Joint Standing Order 2–15. Verification of Defendant's Address for Claims Incurred in Trade or Commerce or Pursuing Assigned Debt

[Suspended effective January 1, 2019.]

This standing order is issued pursuant to the authority of Chief Justices of the Boston Municipal Court and of the District Court under G.L. c. 211B, § 10 and G.L. c. 218, § 43A to address the verification of a defendant's address in civil actions in the regular civil dockets in the Boston Municipal Court and the District Court, in cases in which the plaintiff is pursuing a claim incurred in the course of the plaintiff's trade or commerce, or pursuing a claim for assigned debt. Its purpose is to assure notice to the defendant and to provide the defendant with an opportunity to be heard prior to any default judgment.

1. Definitions. As used in this standing order, the following terms shall have the following meanings: "Assigned debt" shall mean a claim or judgment where the right to collect the debt has been assigned by the creditor to another person or entity. "Trade" and "commerce" shall have the same meaning as in G.L. c. 93A, § 1, but shall not include the lease or rental of residential property that is the plaintiff's primary residence and that consists of three units or less, provided the plaintiff does not own, manage, or have other involvement in the lease or rental of other residential property.

2. Verification of Address. Unless otherwise authorized by the court upon motion, a plaintiff commencing an action in the Boston Municipal Court or the District Court against one

or more individual defendants for a claim incurred in the course of plaintiff's trade or commerce, or a claim for assigned debt, shall file along with the complaint a Verification of Defendant's Address (District Court Form file size 1MB / Boston Municipal Court Form file size 1MB), certifying that the plaintiff has verified the defendant's residential address in the manner set forth herein. The Verification of Defendant's Address shall be signed by the plaintiff or plaintiff's counsel under the penalties of perjury and upon personal knowledge and state that the defendant's residential address has been verified as follows:

a. by at least one of the following methods:

    i. address listed in a municipal record, such as a street list or tax records, verified within twelve months prior to the commencement of the action, with the date of verification;

    ii. address listed with the Registry of Motor Vehicles, verified within twelve months prior to the commencement of the action, with the date of verification;

    iii. receipt of correspondence from the defendant with that return address within twelve months prior to the commencement of the action, with the date the correspondence was received;

    iv. other verification from the defendant within twelve months prior to the commencement of the action that the address is current, followed by a description of such verification; or

b. by at least two of the following methods:

    i. a letter having been sent to the defendant at the address by first-class mail on a date within six months prior to the commencement of the action and at least four weeks prior to the commencement of the action, with the letter not having been returned to the sender by the postal service, with a specification of the date of mailing;

    ii. using an online database (other than the white pages or other unpaid general telephone directory) within six months prior to the commencement of the action, specifying the name and source of the database;

    iii. using an additional source, with an identification of the source.

3. Description of Claim. The following information shall be set forth in the complaint:

    (1) the name of the original creditor (if different from plaintiff's);

    (2) the nature of any debt claimed (for example, credit card, educational loans, medical debt);

    (3) the last four digits of the account number assigned by the original creditor, if any; and

    (4) the amount and date of the defendant's last payment, if any.

4. Service of Process. If the summons and complaint are served upon the defendant by leaving copies thereof at the defendant's last and usual place of abode pursuant to Mass. R. Civ. P. 4(d), the place of abode must be the address as verified in section 2, and the return of service shall set forth the address.

5. Service of Other Papers. Except where the defendant has provided an address to the court in the case, if a pleading or other paper is served on a defendant by mailing it to the defendant at the defendant's last known address pursuant to Mass. R. Civ. P. 5(b), the last known address must be the address as verified in section 2, and any certification of service shall set forth the address.

6. Change of Address. If the plaintiff or plaintiff's counsel learns that the defendant has changed address, the plaintiff shall verify same and file a new Verification of Defendant's Address Form.

7. Sanctions. If the plaintiff fails to comply with this order and the defendant does not file an answer or responsive pleading or otherwise appear at trial or other scheduled court events, no default or default judgment shall be entered for the plaintiff, and the complaint may be dismissed by the court without prejudice.

Adopted June 23, 2015, effective October 1, 2015.

Standing Order 3–15. Electronic Filing Pilot Project Applicable to the Worcester District Court

I. Purpose and Applicability

The purpose of this Standing Order is to establish a pilot process within a single division of the District Court Department that will permit litigants to electronically file and serve certain documents by electronic means. The goal of the pilot court site shall be to facilitate the prompt and efficient disposition of civil cases, to provide enhanced service to the public, and to increase efficiency in the Massachusetts courts by reducing the expense and delay of civil litigation in the District Court Department. To achieve this end the Worcester Division of the District Court Department is designated as the pilot site for electronic filing and as of the effective date of this Standing Order will be authorized to receive and send documents, orders, and judgments through electronic filing under the Interim Electronic Filing Rules/or Pilot Courts (2015).

II. Designation of Pilot Site

The designated pilot site to implement electronic filing for the District Court Department will be the Worcester Division, located at 225 Main Street, Worcester, MA 01608–1203. Unless otherwise ordered by the Chief Justice of the District Court Department, the electronic filing pilot project will continue for one year from the date of this Standing Order.

III. Scope of the Pilot Project

The initial scope of the Worcester Electronic Filing Pilot Project will include all Civil Actions for money damages under Tort and Contract (G.L. c. 231, §§ 103—104), and the following specific Civil actions:

- Arbitrator's Award Confirmation (G.L. c. 251, §§ 11, 14)
- Condominium Conversion Violation (St. 1983, c. 527, § 5 & St. 1989, c. 709, § 20)
- Interpleader of Money deposited in Court (Mass. R. Civ. P. 67)
- Lien Enforcement Action (G.L. c. 254, § 5; c. 255, § 26)

- Landlord Failure to Provide Utilities (G.L. c. 186, § 14)
- Landlord Interference with Quiet Enjoyment (G.L. c. 186, § 14)
- Lead Poisoning Prevention (G.L. c. 111, §§ 196—198)
- Repossession of Secured Goods (G.L. c. 255, § 13J; c. 255B, § 20B; c. 255D, § 22)
- Settlement Approval for a Minor/Incompetent (G.L. c. 231, § 140C 1/2)
- Suit on a Foreign Judgment (G.L. c. 235, §§ 14, 23A; 28 U.S.C. § 1738)
- Structured Settlement Transfer Approval (G.L. c. 231C, § 2)
- Unemployment Compensation Action against Employer by DET (G.L. c. 151A, § 15)
- Used Car Lemon Law Arbitration Appeal (G.L. c. 90, § 7N)
- Unlawful Entry (Trespass)/Repossession of Land (G.L. c. 184, § 18)

As set forth in the Interim Electronic Filing Rules/or Pilot Courts (2015), registered electronic filers participating in the Worcester pilot project will be eligible to use the electronic filing system for any cause of action listed above, for the purpose of filing new claims, subsequent pleadings, discovery requests, responsive pleadings, and motions and notices promulgated pursuant to the Massachusetts Rules of Civil Procedure. Service of the initial process or summons to gain jurisdiction over persons or property may not be made by electronic service; only the conventional method for service of process will be permitted during the pilot project.

IV. Participants

Eligibility and conditions of registration to participate in electronic filling shall be in accordance with Rule 3 of the Interim Electronic Filing Rules/or Pilot Courts (2015). For the initial implementation of the Worcester Electronic Filing Pilot Project, the following law firms have opted to participate:

- Law Office of Joseph J. Cariglia, PC—188 Lincoln Street, Worcester, MA 01605
- Law Offices of Gary H. Kreppel, PC—33 Post Road West, Suite 590, Marlborough, MA 01752
- Law Offices Howard Lee Schiff, PC—25 Southbridge Street, Building 2, Suite 2, Auburn, MA 01501

The Worcester Electronic Filing Pilot Project will be available to all additional eligible participants after completion of the registration process set forth in the Interim Electronic Filing Rules/or Pilot Courts (2015).

V. Additional Provisions

In the event that certain filing activities cannot be completed by electronic filing, because of the technical limitations of either the E–Filing vendor or the Trial Court's Case Management System, the Worcester Electronic Filing Pilot Project reserves the right to require an otherwise eligible participant to file a document or notice by conventional means. Such filing activity may include, but shall not be limited to, any request for waiver of filing fees, a request for appointment of an interpreter, a request to purchase miscellaneous copies or forms, or other filing activity as defined by the pilot court site.

Adopted June 24, 2015, effective September 1, 2015.

Joint Standing Order 3–15.   Notice and Docketing of Impounded Materials

This standing order is issued pursuant to the authority of the Chief Justices of the Boston Municipal Court and of the District Court under G.L. c. 211B, § 10; G.L. c. 218, § 43A; and Uniform Rule on Impoundment Procedure 13(b) of Trial Court VIII to regulate clerk records of impounded materials in the Boston Municipal Court and District Court pursuant to Uniform Rule on Impoundment Procedure 13. The requirement in Rule 13(b) that the filer of a document containing impounded information file a separate notice notifying the clerk of the impounded material is intended to "enable[] the clerk and court staff to properly identify and set aside protected material." Committee Notes. Accordingly, the application of this requirement should be waived where the nature of the material impounded renders a separate notice not useful to the clerk.

1. **Purpose and applicability.** To advance efficiency in the Boston Municipal Court and the District Court and to better serve the public and the bar, this standing order shall provide for exceptions to the notice of impounded filing requirements contained in Uniform Rule on Impoundment Procedure 13.

2. **Exempted documents.** The notice provisions contained in Uniform Rule on Impoundment Procedure 13(b) shall not apply to the following:

   a.   Affidavit of indigency

   b.   Allegation of domestic abuse under G.L. c. 276, § 56A

   c.   Search warrant applications and supporting documents impounded pursuant to Rule on Impoundment Procedure 3(e)(1)

   d.   Plaintiff's residential address, residential telephone number, workplace name, workplace address, and workplace telephone number in abuse prevention and harassment prevention proceedings, see G.L. c. 209A, § 8; G.L. c. 258E, § 10

   e.   All reports, petitions, and other documents filed pursuant to and as provided in G.L. c. 123, including but not limited to mental health and substance abuse reports, petitions, and dockets.

   f.   Financial statement of judgment debtor

   g.   Name of the victim in investigations or prosecutions for sexual assault offenses listed in G.L. c. 265, § 24B

   h.   All documents in cases that are or have been impounded in their entirety

   i.   All other documents that are impounded in their entirety by statute, court rule, standing order, or case law.

Adopted effective October 1, 2015.

Standing Order 4–15.   Conditions of Release at a Probation Detention Hearing

1. This standing order is issued pursuant to Dist./Mun. Cts. R. Prob. Viol. P. 5(c) to set forth the only permissible conditions of release that may be imposed after a court finds probable cause at a probation detention hearing to believe that a probationer has violated a condition of probation. Such conditions are intended to be of limited duration, applying only until the probation violation hearing, which shall be within thirty days, absent "extraordinary circumstances." Dist./Mun. Cts. R. Prob. Viol. P. 3(b)(iii), 3(c)(vi), 4(d). Conditions may be set only when the court, in the exercise of discretion, decides not to detain the probationer. Conditions of release shall be set forth in writing and a copy thereof served in hand to the probationer.

2. Upon a finding of probable cause that a probationer has violated a condition of probation, the court may impose only nonmonetary conditions of release, including but not limited to any one or a combination of the following conditions:

   a.   **No contact.** The probationer shall have no contact with a specified person or persons, in person, by telephone, in writing, electronically, or otherwise, either directly or through someone else.

   b.   **Stay away.** The probationer shall stay a defined distance away from a specified person, persons, business, or location.

   c.   **Report as directed.** In addition to any preexisting reporting requirements, the probationer shall report to the probation department as ordered by the court or, with the court's authorization, as directed by the probation department.

   d.   **Electronic monitoring.** The probationer shall submit to electronic monitoring, which may include

      i.   house arrest, with such exceptions as the court may allow;

      ii.   curfew, requiring the probationer to be at a specified address between specified hours; and/or

      iii.   exclusion zones, as set by the court.

   e.   **Required residence.** The probationer shall reside at a specified address, which may be verified by unannounced home visits by probation.

   f.   **Abstinence and testing.** The probationer shall abstain from the consumption of illegal and non-prescribed narcotics, alcohol, and/or non-medical marijuana, with testing to verify such abstinence.

   g.   **Motor vehicle restrictions.** The probationer shall not operate a motor vehicle, with such exceptions as the court may allow.

3. If the court or a probation officer has reasonable grounds to believe that a probationer has violated a condition of release, the court or probation officer may summons the probationer for a hearing or, if there is probable cause, issue an arrest warrant. A probation officer, if there is probable cause, may arrest the probationer without a warrant. The court shall then hold a hearing as soon as practicable to determine whether there is probable cause to believe that the probationer has violated a condition of release. The rules of

evidence shall not apply, and this determination may be "decided based on documents (e.g., police reports) and the representations of counsel." *Paquette v. Commonwealth*, 440 Mass. 121, 133 (2003). The court may, in its discretion, allow the presentation of testimonial evidence and cross-examination "when the circumstances of a particular case warrant." *Id.* If the court determines that there is probable cause that a probationer has violated such a condition of release, the court shall have the authority, in the exercise of discretion, to order the probationer detained until the completion of the probation violation hearing. *See id.* at 126 ("if the person violates the explicit condition of his release, then his liberty can be curtailed"). When granted conditional release, a person's "continued freedom [i]s entirely within his own control, and the deprivation thereof [i]s an inevitable consequence of his alleged failure to conform his conduct ... to the explicit condition of his earlier release." *Id.* at 129.

4. Conditions of release imposed under Rule 5(c) are not conditions of probation. A violation of a condition of release shall not itself be the basis for a finding of a violation of probation, although the judge may consider such violation in determining a proper disposition under Dist./Mun. Cts. R. Prob. Viol. P. 8(d) and 9(b).

Adopted effective September 8, 2015. Amended effective December 1, 2019.

Joint Standing Order 1–16. Authority of the Judge with Respect to Communication with Specialty Court Teams

This Standing Order is promulgated by the chief Justice of the Trial Court pursuant to G. L, c. 211B, Section 9 and shall constitute authorization by law as referenced in Rule 2.9 (A)(2) of the Code of Judicial Conduct (effective January 1, 2016).

For purposes of this Order:

Specialty Court means a specifically designated court session that focuses on individuals with underlying medical, mental health, substance abuse, or other issues that contribute to the reasons such individuals are before the courts. Specialty court shall also mean Veterans Treatment Court and Homelessness Court. Specialty court sessions integrate treatment and services with judicial case oversight and intensive court supervision. Examples Include drug courts, mental health courts, veterans' courts, and tenancy preservation programs.

A Staffing shall refer to a regularly scheduled, informal conference not occurring in open court, the purpose of which is to permit the presiding judge and others, including counsel, to discuss a participant's progress in the specialty court, treatment recommendations, or responses to participant compliance issues.

IT IS THEREFORE ORDERED:

A judge presiding over a specialty court shall have the authority to initiate, permit or otherwise consider ex parte communications about defendants, juveniles or probationers with members of the specialty court team at a staffing or by written documents provided to all members of the specialty court team, The purpose of this authority is to allow judges in their role in presiding over specialty court sessions, and only in that capacity, to assume a more interactive role with parties,

treatment providers, probation officers, social workers and others, than Rule 2.9 of the Code of Judicial Conduct would otherwise permit.

Adopted effective January 7, 2016.

Standing Order 1–16. Norfolk County Pilot Program for Civil Money Damage Actions

(Applicable to Norfolk County)

I. The Pilot Program; Effective Date.

A Pilot Program shall be implemented in accordance with the provisions of this Order applicable to civil money damage actions in the five District Courts in Norfolk County:

- The Municipal Court of Brookline (Brookline)
- The District Court of Northern Norfolk (Dedham)
- The District Court of East Norfolk (Quincy)
- The District Court of Southern Norfolk (Stoughton)
- The District Court of Western Norfolk (Wrentham)

The Pilot Program shall consist of (1) the division of civil money damage cases into two separate categories, each with differing procedural requirements, and (2), for cases in one such category, the establishment of Designated Civil Sessions (DCSs) dedicated exclusively to the conduct of all necessary proceedings in such cases, including jury and jury-waived trials.

The Pilot Program shall be implemented effective May 31, 2016, and shall apply to actions commenced on and after that date, as provided in Section V, below, provided that it shall also apply to cases commenced as small claims action which, on or after May 31, 2016 are transferred to the regular civil docket pursuant to G.L. c. 218, s. 24.

II. Purpose of the Program

The purpose of the Pilot Program is to determine whether the procedures it requires are feasible and effective in reducing costs and delay in the disposition of civil money damage actions in the District Court.

III. Applicability of Existing Procedural Orders

The procedures required in this Standing Order shall supersede the otherwise applicable provisions in court orders, including District Court and Boston Municipal Court Joint Standing Order 1-04, with which they conflict. In all matters not affected by the procedures required in this Standing Order, the otherwise applicable procedural requirements shall continue to govern.

IV. Establishment of Designated Civil Sessions

Two Designated Civil Sessions (DCSs) shall be established: One at the Quincy District Court for cases commenced at that court; and one at the Dedham District Court to which cases may be transferred pursuant to Section V below following commencement at the Dedham, Brookline, Stoughton and Wrentham District Courts.

Each DCS shall be devoted exclusively to the disposition of the civil actions transferred to it. Likewise, the judge assigned to each DCS shall devote his or her attention, during the term of that assignment, exclusively to the management and disposition of the civil cases transferred to that session.

V. Actions Commenced On and After May 31, 2016

A. Division of cases into two categories; Identification of category by Plaintiff

Civil money damage cases shall be divided into the following two categories to which different procedures shall apply:

1. Actions involving only a claim or claims based on alleged consumer credit debt, and

2. All other actions, including tort and statutory money damage claims and other types of contract money damage claims (hereinafter "DCS" cases).

"Consumer credit debt actions" shall be defined as those cases in which the defendant is an individual, and in which the claimed debt involves the purchase of consumer goods or services by the defendant based on credit extended to the defendant by the plaintiff or by the entity whose ownership of the rights regarding said debt have been obtained by the plaintiff by assignment.

The plaintiff in each money damage case shall indicate the category of the case, as provided above, on the Statement of Damages form, in the version of that form amended for use in cases governed by this Standing Order. The Statement of Damages form must be filed and served with the complaint, as provided by G.L. c. 218, § 19A(a). Failure to properly categorize a case on the Statement of Damages form shall not be grounds for dismissal or other sanction.

B. Procedures in Consumer Credit Debt Actions

Consumer credit debt actions shall proceed in accordance with otherwise applicable procedural requirements, except as follows:

1. *Proceedings*

Consumer credit debt actions shall proceed to disposition in the court in which the case was commenced, or, where necessary, in the appropriate jury session, in accordance with the same procedures in effect prior to the effective date of this order, except as provided below regarding discovery.

2. *Notice of Case Management; Discovery*

The Notice of Case Management Conference shall include:

(a) a provision requiring the Plaintiff to serve on the Defendant, no later than 14 days prior to the date of the Case Management Conference, copies of any documents constituting evidence of the debt and of the assignment of the debt to the Plaintiff, if any, and requiring the Plaintiff to bring copies of such documents to the Case Management Conference, and

(b) a provision requiring the Defendant to serve on the Plaintiff, no later than 14 days prior to the date of the Case Management Conference, copies of any documents constituting evidence that the debt is not owed by the Defendant, or that Defendant has paid the alleged debt in part or in full, and requiring the Defendant to bring copies of such documents to the Case Management Conference.

C. Procedures in DCS Cases

All other actions commenced on or after May 31, 2016, shall proceed in accordance with otherwise applicable procedural requirements, except as follows:

1. *Cases in which an Answer or Pre-Answer Motion by defendant is filed; Notice of Pretrial Conference or Notice of Hearing*

Upon the filing of an Answer or Pre-Answer Motion by the defendant, the court shall promptly issue to the parties a Notice of Pretrial Conference or Notice of Hearing on Motion, as appropriate, which shall indicate that the next court event will proceed in the DCS. No Case Management Conferences, as would otherwise be required by Joint Standing Order No. 1-04, shall be scheduled or conducted in these cases.

The Notice of Pretrial Conference shall include the location of the DCS, the date and time of the conference, and the courtroom in which it will be conducted, and shall include a provision requiring discovery to be completed no later than 14 days prior to the Pretrial Conference. The Pretrial Conference shall be scheduled on a date no earlier than six months from the date on which the Answer was filed by the Defendant.

The Notice of Hearing on a Pre-Answer Motion shall include the location of the DCS and the courtroom in which the hearing will be conducted. As necessary, the court shall contact the parties to confirm the date for which the hearing has been marked up or to adjust the date.

Upon issuance of a Notice of Pretrial Conference or a Notice of Hearing on a Pre-Answer Motion, the case shall be transferred to the DCS. Following such transfer, all further proceedings in the case shall be conducted at the DCS, up to and including the order for entry of judgment.

2. *Post-judgment proceedings*

The DSC Court shall enter judgment on each case transferred to the DCS. After the entry of judgment is made the case shall be returned to the court in which the action was commenced. Post-judgment matters, including motions for relief from judgment, appeal and issuance of execution that arise after the entry of judgment shall be the responsibility of the court in which the action was commenced.

3. *Cases in which No Answer or Pre-Answer Motion is filed*

Cases in which an Answer or Pre-Answer Motion is not filed by the Defendant shall proceed to disposition in the court in which they were commenced, provided that if a default or default judgment is entered, but later set aside or vacated, and the Defendant allowed to file and serve a late Answer or Pre-Answer Motion, the case shall be transferred to the appropriate DCS as provided above in Section V. 1. All proceedings relating to the entry of default and default judgment and any proceedings involving relief therefrom shall be conducted in the court in which the action was commenced.

VI. DCS Actions Commenced Before May 31, 2016

The judge assigned to a DCS, may, as a matter of his or her discretion, order any DCS case commenced before May 31, 2016 to proceed in the DCS.

VII. Jury Trials; Attorney Voir Dire

In jury trials conducted in a DCS under the provisions of this Standing Order, the court, upon motion of any party, may allow counsel for such party to examine prospective jurors, subject to reasonable limitations imposed by the court upon the questions and the time allowed during such examination, including, but not limited to, requiring pre-approval of the questions.

Adopted effective May 31, 2016.

Joint Standing Order 2–16.   Uniform Interdepartmental Procedures for Probation Violation Proceedings

This Standing Order is promulgated by the Chief Justice of the Trial Court pursuant to G. L, c. 211B, Section 9 and stands effective October 3, 2016.

1. Application

This Order shall apply to the Superior Court, District Court, Boston Municipal Court and Juvenile Court Departments.

2. Purpose

This Order sets forth requirements regarding communication among the above-named departments of the Trial Court when an individual who is the subject of a probation order in one of these departments is charged with a new offense in another of these departments. Its purpose is to ensure that this required interdepartmental communication relating to the commencement of probation violation proceedings as a result of alleged new criminal behavior by a probationer, and the potential custody and transport of that probationer between different court departments, occur in a timely, informed and efficient manner. This Order does not apply to an individual who is the subject of a probation order issued prior to a trial or the formal submission and acceptance of a plea of guilty or an admission to sufficient facts, as provided in G.L. c. 276, § 87 ("pretrial probation").

3. Definition of Terms

As used in this Order, the terms below shall have the following meanings:

"Criminal:" includes delinquency or youthful offender.

"Criminal Court:" a court division of the Boston Municipal, District, or Juvenile Court or the Superior Court.

The terms used in this Order and the form promulgated by the Chief Justice of the Trial Court pursuant to Section 9 have been defined to include terminology associated with juvenile cases and proceedings and the Juvenile Court. They have been defined in this manner for the purposes of convenience and ease of reading and are applicable to this Order and form only. The terms as appearing in this Order and form do not change the meaning of the terminology used in adult and juvenile proceedings as defined by case law and statutes. Other than for the purposes of this Order and form, adult and juvenile terms are not interchangeable.

4. Intra-Departmental Communications

This Order does not apply to intra-departmental communications, transport of probationers, or use of the warrant management system, which may be the subject of rules or standing orders issued by and applicable within individual court departments.

5. Information to be Sent from the Criminal Court; Custody of Probationer

When an individual appears on a new criminal charge before a criminal court, and that individual is the subject of a probation order issued by a court in a different department of the Trial Court, the probation department of the criminal court shall transmit to the probation department of the court having responsibility for the supervision of the probationer (the "probation court") information and requests for information, including information regarding the possible service of a notice of violation on, and transport of, the probationer. This transmission shall be made by means of the form referred to in Section 9, below.

The transmission from the criminal court shall be sent electronically and promptly, to the probation officer in the probation court listed as the probation officer on duty in the probation court or, if there is no probation officer on duty, to the Chief Probation Officer of the probation court. The transmission shall be sent while the probationer is at the criminal court. When necessary, the criminal court may order the probationer held in custody until the procedures required by this Order are completed.

6. Information to be Returned by the Probation Court; Time Limit

The probation department of the probation court shall respond electronically, to the probation officer who transmitted the request for information from the criminal court. The response shall include information regarding service of a notice of violation on, and transport of, the probationer. This response shall be transmitted within two hours or within such time limit as extended, as provided in Section 7, such time limit to be measured from the time indicated on the transmission, and shall be set forth on the form referred to in Section 9, below.

If the probation department is requesting that the probationer be transported, the probation department shall request the issuance of an arrest warrant for a violation of probation ("warrant") from a judge in the probation court. If the judge issues such warrant, the clerk's office shall enter it promptly into the Warrant Management System and the probation department shall provide the criminal court with a notice of violation that cites the violation(s).

If the probation department is not requesting that the probationer be transported and is requesting that the probationer be served with a notice of violation, the probation department shall provide the probation department of the criminal court with a notice of violation that cites the violation(s) and indicates the date and time of the probationer's required appearance in the probation court.

7. Action by the Criminal Court

The criminal court shall await receipt of the information from the probation court for a period of two hours measured from the time of the transmission of the request for that information. This two-hour time limit may be extended by the criminal court.

Upon the timely receipt of the required information from the probation court and, if the probation court has issued a warrant, the criminal court shall serve on the probationer, in hand, a notice of violation on behalf of the probation court and shall either order transport of the probationer on such warrant or defer transport on the warrant until the termination of any custody ordered by the criminal court judge in the new criminal case. In the event that no warrant has been issued by the probation court, and the probation department has provided a notice of violation to the probation department of the criminal court, the criminal court shall serve such notice on the probationer, in hand, on behalf of the probation court.

If the probation department of the probation court does not provide the required information or a notice of violation to the probation department of the criminal court in the manner set forth in Section 6, the criminal court need not take any further action regarding the probation matter. In such instances, the probation department of the criminal court shall make an appropriate entry into its records.

8. Action by the Probation Court

Upon delivery of the probationer into the custody of the probation court on the warrant, and not withstanding any provision of this Order, the form promulgated pursuant to section 9, or the reason for the warrant as it may appear in the Warrant Management System, the probation court shall proceed on the violation of probation matter in accordance with applicable law and respective departmental rule or standing order.

9. Form to be Promulgated by the Chief Justice of the Trial Court

The transmittal of information between courts as required by this Order shall proceed by means of a form promulgated by the Chief Justice of the Trial Court. This form shall include such specific information requirements, data elements and attachments as the Chief Justice may deem appropriate, provided that nothing in this Order shall be construed to prohibit the use of telephone communication to supplement the use of such form and to achieve its purpose.

10. Probation Department Procedures and Record Keeping

Implementation of this Order by the Massachusetts Probation Service, including record keeping requirements, shall be as set forth in such instructions and regulations consistent with the provisions of this Order as may be deemed appropriate by the Commissioner of Probation.

Adopted August 18, 2016, effective October 3, 2016.

Standing Order 1–18.   Voir Dire Protocol

Preamble

Subject to applicable statutes, rules, and controlling authority, the trial judge in each case has discretion to determine a procedure for examining and selecting jurors designed to maintain juror privacy and dignity, identify explicit and implicit bias, and foster efficiency in the session and among sessions using the same jury pool. This standing order provides a standard procedure for each civil and criminal case unless otherwise ordered by the trial judge, while permitting attorneys and self-represented parties a fair opportunity to participate in voir dire through individual voir dire, panel voir dire, or a combination of the two so as to identify inappropriate bias.

I.   Requests for Attorney or Party Voir Dire.

In civil and criminal cases, the parties shall submit in writing: any requests for attorney/party voir dire; motions in limine concerning the method of jury selection; proposed subject matters or questions for inquiry by the parties or judge; any proposed preliminary legal instructions to the venire or juror panels; the location within the courtroom where jurors and parties will stand or sit during voir dire; and any other matter setting forth the party's position regarding impanelment.

In a civil case, all voir dire related requests shall be filed in accordance with the Trial Order issued pursuant to District Court Joint Standing Order 1–04 as may be amended from time to time, but not later than (5) business days before trial.

In a criminal case, all voir dire related requests shall be filed by a date set by the Court, but not later than five (5) business days before trial.

A judge may order, or an attorney or party may request, a hearing in advance of the trial date. The attorney or party shall request such a hearing in time for a pre-trial ruling by the trial judge if the attorney or party is requesting extensive participation in voir dire (e.g., panel voir dire or to be allowed to ask a substantial number of questions).

Upon hearing any written request for attorney/party voir dire, consideration should be given to procedural issues including:

    a.   a statement of the case to be read to the venire;

    b.   the number of jurors to be seated;

    c.   the extent of any pre-charge on significant legal principles;

    d.   the method and content of the judge's intended voir dire of jurors;

    e.   the method and content of any attorney or party participation in voir dire;

    f.   judicial approval or disapproval of subject matter or proposed questions;

    g.   any time limits on attorney or party voir dire;

    h.   the number of peremptory challenges;

    i.   the order and timing of the parties' assertions of challenges for cause and peremptory challenges;

    j.   any agreement to allow deliberation by fewer jurors in a civil case if seated jurors are dismissed post-impanelment.

II.   Scope and Subject Matter of Permissible Attorney or Party Voir Dire.

A.   General Matters. The trial judge shall allow attorney or party voir dire if properly requested according to the time as set forth in paragraph I above. The trial judge has discretion regarding the scope and manner of voir dire.

The judge should, at a minimum, allow the attorneys or parties to ask reasonable follow-up questions seeking elaboration or explanation concerning juror responses to the judge's questions, or concerning any written questionnaire.

A trial judge should allow a reasonable number of questions that: (i) seek factual information about the prospective juror's background and experience pertinent to the issues expected to arise in the case; (ii) may reveal preconceptions or biases, explicit or implicit, relating to the identity of the parties or the nature of the claims or issues expected to arise in the case; (iii) inquire into the prospective jurors' willingness and ability to accept and apply pertinent legal principles as instructed; (iv) are meant to elicit information on subjects that controlling authority has identified as preferred subjects of inquiry, even if not absolutely required; and (v) are appropriate in quantity to the anticipated length and complexity of the trial.

A trial judge may impose reasonable restrictions on the subject matter, time, number of questions, or method of attorney or party voir dire. The judge may utilize individual voir dire, panel voir dire, or any combination of the two. If employing panel voir dire, the trial judge shall determine the procedure and may elect to follow the method set forth in Addendum A to this Order or adopt variations thereof.

A party objecting to a question posed by another party shall state, 'objection,' without elaboration or argument. The judge may rule on the objection in, or outside of, the juror's presence. The trial judge may *sua sponte* strike or rephrase a party's question. The judge may interrupt or supplement a party's questioning to provide the juror(s) with an explanation of the law or the jury trial process. The judge may ask additional questions to assist the judge in determining a juror's impartiality.

An attorney or party may ask questions about the law if approved by the trial judge. The judge may require the questioner to use specific words or phrases and may give an instruction on the law beforehand or at the time the question is asked. If a juror asks a question to clarify an aspect of the law, the questioner shall respond by requesting the judge to answer the question.

If intending to challenge a juror for cause as a result of attorney or party voir dire, the questioner ordinarily should lay an adequate foundation showing that, in light of the information or viewpoint expressed, the juror may not be fair and impartial and decide the case solely on the facts and law presented at trial. A juror's "yes" or "no" answer to a question about a viewpoint or experience may not, by itself, support a challenge for cause. An attorney or party challenging a juror for cause shall state the reason and the court may inquire further, or may decide without further questioning if the judge believes that the existing record is sufficient to resolve the challenge for cause.

B. Prohibited and Disfavored Subjects.

1. No attorney or party may inquire into the following prohibited subjects:

a. questions framed in terms of how the juror would decide this case (prejudgment), including hypotheticals that are close/specific to the facts of this case (any hypotheticals that may trigger this rule must be presented to the judge before trial);

b. questions that seek to commit juror(s) to a result, including, without limitation, questions about what evidence would cause the juror(s) to find for the attorney's client or the party;

c. questions having no substantial purpose other than to argue an attorney's or party's case or indoctrinate any juror(s);

d. questions about the outcome in prior cases where the person has served as a juror, including the prior vote(s) of the juror or the verdict of the entire jury;

e. questions in the presence of other jurors that specifically reference what is written on a particular juror's confidential juror questionnaire.

2. No attorney or party may inquire into any of the following disfavored subjects absent the trial judge's prior express approval:

a. the juror's political views, voting patterns or party preferences;

b. the juror's religious beliefs or affiliation.

To obtain approval, an attorney or party must at a minimum explain how the inquiry is relevant to the issues, may affect the juror's impartiality, or may assist the proper exercise of peremptory challenges.

C. Procedural Matters.

1. *Mandatory Voir Dire.* The trial judge shall ask all voir dire questions specifically required by statute, court rule, or controlling authority, but retains discretion as to when and how to do so.

2. *Individual Voir Dire.*

a. Questioning shall occur through individual voir dire if: (i) required by statute, rule, or controlling authority; (ii) inquiry concerns private or potentially embarrassing information; or (iii) questioning would specifically reference what is written on a particular juror's confidential juror questionnaire.

b. The trial judge should conduct an individual voir dire in all cases to: (i) determine whether any juror has any issues concerning hearing, vision, language, mental health, or comprehension, and to determine whether a reasonable accommodation can enable a juror to serve; (ii) address any private or embarrassing information not disclosed in public portions of the voir dire; or (iii) identify any other impediment to jury service that the trial judge and parties might not observe without personal contact with the juror.

3. *Timing of Challenges.* The judge may require exercise of peremptory challenges after filling the jury box with jurors found to stand indifferent, after completion of side bar inquiry of an individual juror, or at some other time after the judge's finding of indifference or, if employing panel voir dire, after the attorneys have completed questioning the panel.

4. *Maintaining the Record.* Counsel and the parties must ensure an accurate record of attorney or party voir dire. During panel voir dire, an attorney or a party must refer to the juror seat number (or juror number) of any individual juror who is questioned individually or who responds audibly. Failure to do so may constitute a waiver of any claim of error

arising from any inaudible or unattributed portions of the record.

ADDENDUM A
PANEL VOIR DIRE

I. Pretrial Procedure

Any attorney or self-represented party who requests panel voir dire shall serve and file a motion requesting leave to do so in accordance with District Court Standing Order 1–18: Voir Dire Protocol. The motion shall identify the general areas of panel inquiry by topic, recognizing some topics must be raised with each juror individually.[1] The trial judge may, in the exercise of discretion, require attorneys and self-represented parties to submit the specific language of the proposed questions for pre-approval. The motion and any responsive filing shall also include a concise description of the case, along with any proposed language for brief preliminary instructions on principles of law to be given pursuant to paragraph 2(b) below.

The trial judge should inform the parties of any reasonable time limit the trial judge has set for examination of each panel of prospective jurors by attorneys or self-represented parties, giving due regard to: (a) the objective of identifying explicit and implicit bias in fairness to all parties; (b) the interests of the public and of the parties in reasonable expedition, in proportion to the nature and seriousness of the case and the extent of the anticipated evidence; and (c) the needs of cases scheduled in other sessions drawing on the same jury pool for access to prospective jurors.

II. Venire Examination

Before any questioning of a juror panel by attorneys or self-represented parties, or at such other time as the trial judge deems most appropriate, the trial judge should:

a. provide the venire with a brief description of the case, including the nature of the facts alleged and of the claims or charges;

b. provide the venire with brief, preliminary instructions on significant legal principles pertinent to the case. Such instructions should include a brief recitation of the burden and standard of proof, the elements of at least the primary civil claim or at least the most serious criminal charge, if appropriate to the case and requested by counsel or a self-represented party, the elements of any affirmative defense that will be presented to the jury, and, in criminal cases, the defendant's right not to testify or to present any evidence;

c. explain the impanelment process and inform the jurors that any juror who finds either a particular question or the process of questioning by attorneys or self-represented parties intrusive on the juror's privacy may request that steps be taken to protect the privacy of any information disclosed;

d. ask all questions required by statute or case law and any additional questions the trial judge deems appropriate in light of the nature of the case and the issues expected to be raised;

e. conduct individual voir dire of those jurors who will be part of the panel voir dire

The trial judge should then hear challenges for cause based upon the initial questioning of the venire and individual voir dire.

III. Panel Examination

After the initial questions are asked, and individual voir dire is conducted, the judge shall seat the jurors found preliminarily indifferent as a panel. There are various versions of panel voir dire that may be employed in the District Court. The judge may employ multiple panels or a single panel depending upon recording capabilities, the size and physical layout of a courtroom, jury box, or jury venire, and the number of court officers. If more than one panel is used, the judge should consider whether the jurors who remain qualified should be temporarily excused from the courtroom while the next panel is seated and questioned.

a. The parties shall then proceed with questioning the panel. Parties with the burden of proof shall conduct their questioning first. In cases with multiple parties on a side, the parties on each side shall agree as to an order in which to proceed. In the absence of agreement, the judge shall assign an order. The attorney or party may pose questions to the entire panel or to individual members.

b. Throughout the proceedings, attorneys and self-represented parties at the trial are responsible for correcting any misstatement as to juror numbers and seat numbers being read for the record.

c. If the trial judge has not already done so, he or she shall remind the jurors that during such questioning a juror may request to respond to a question outside the presence of other jurors.

d. The trial judge and the attorneys participating shall at all times during panel questioning take reasonable steps to ensure that the identity of each juror speaking is adequately maintained on the record, by reference to juror number or seat number. In particular:

    I. In an electronically recorded courtroom, the attorney or party shall stand near a microphone; and

    II. When posing questions to, or receiving a response from, any specific juror(s), the attorney or party must identify each such juror(s) by juror seat number (or, less ideally, by juror number). They shall not refer to any juror by name.

e. The trial judge may intervene at any time to ensure an accurate record (including recording of seat numbers of jurors who respond to questions), to clarify or instruct on a point of law, or to ensure that panel voir dire proceeds in an orderly, fair, and efficient manner.

f. The trial judge may at any time bring an individual juror to sidebar for questioning out of the hearing of other jurors about any potential bias revealed by panel questioning. If a juror is brought to sidebar, the judge may direct all other parties to do their own questioning on the same subject matter at that time to avoid a need to return to sidebar for later questioning on that subject matter. If the juror's responses to such questioning at sidebar result in a challenge for cause, the judge may rule on the challenge at that time or at the conclusion of all panel questioning. If time limits on panel questioning have been set, the judge may decide whether to exclude all or part of the time spent at side bar from the questioning party's time.

g. Any party may object to a question posed by another party by stating "objection," without elaboration or argument. The judge may rule on the objection in the presence of the juror or jurors, or may hear argument and rule on the objection outside the presence or hearing of the juror or jurors.

h. Unless the judge specifically allows, there shall be no follow-up questioning of a panel by attorneys or self-represented parties once each has taken his or her turn.

IV.   Challenges for Cause and Peremptory Challenges

a. After panel examination by all parties, the trial judge shall hear any further challenges for cause as to any panel members at sidebar.

b. Unless the trial judge decides to postpone exercise of peremptory challenge until after voir dire of additional panels, the parties shall then exercise at sidebar any peremptory challenges they have as to any jurors remaining on the panel. The party with the burden shall proceed first, using all peremptory challenges the party seeks to use with that panel. All other parties shall then proceed, using all peremptory challenges each seeks to use with that panel. In civil cases, the judge may alternate sides. The jurors remaining after challenge may then be directed to a separate location, possibly outside the courtroom.

c. Upon any challenge for cause, the judge may ask additional questions, with or without further instructions on the law, and may allow counsel further opportunity to question the juror.

V.   Additional Panels of Jurors

The same procedures shall apply for all subsequent panels required to seat a full jury, except:

a. the judge may seat a different number of jurors in a subsequent panel;

b. the judge may allow a different amount of time for attorney or party voir dire of second and subsequent panels;

c. if, after the final panel, more than the necessary number of jurors have been declared indifferent and remain unchallenged at the conclusion of those procedures, the jurors shall be seated for trial in the order in which they were originally seated for panel, and the remaining jurors shall be excused; and

d. the judge has discretion to vary panel voir dire procedures after the first panel in any lawful manner the judge deems fair and efficient.

Adopted effective May 1, 2018.

1 Individual voir dire is required in cases involving alleged sexual assault of a minor, lack of criminal responsibility defense, and certain cases involving interracial violence, see District Court model jury instruction 1.100 n 2, as well as those areas identified in § II.C.2.a of District Court Standing Order 1–18: Voir Dire Protocol.

STANDING ORDERS OF THE BOSTON MUNICIPAL COURT

Table of Standing Orders

Standing Order 1–83. Stenographers in the Jury–Of–Six Session

In all cases in the jury-of-six sessions in which the defendant desires to have a stenographer, a written request for the same shall be made in writing and filed with the Court at least forty-eight hours prior to the hearing or trial at which the stenographer is required.

In the event that the hearing or trial is continued, it shall be the obligation of the defendant to renew the request for stenographer in the same manner prescribed in the foregoing paragraph.

Failure to comply with this Order will be deemed to be a waiver of a defendant's right to request a stenographer.

This Order is made in accordance with M.G.L. c. 218, § 27A(h).

Adopted October 17, 1983.

Standing Order 2–83. Interpreters

In all cases in which the services of an interpreter are required, it shall be the obligation of the litigants to file with the Court a request, in writing, seeking the appointment of the interpreter at least forty-eight hours prior to the hearing or trial at which said services are required. Such request shall specify the language for which the interpreter is required.

In the event that the hearing or trial is continued, it shall be the obligation of the litigants to renew the request for an interpreter in the same manner prescribed in the foregoing paragraph.

This Order is made in accordance with Rule 43(f) of the Massachusetts Rules of Civil Procedure and Rule 41 of the Massachusetts Rules of Criminal Procedure.

Adopted October 17, 1983.

Standing Order 1–84. Abuse Prevention, G.L. c. 209A

The attached form entitled "Complaint for Protection from Abuse" will be used by any applicant seeking a protective order or relief under the provisions of G.L. c. 209A, as amended, until a permanent form is promulgated in accordance with the statute.

The attached form promulgated in accordance with the statute, entitled "(Temporary) Order Pursuant to G.L. c. 209A, as amended" will be used until a permanent form is promulgated in accordance with the statute.

Prior and pending Care or Custody Actions shall be disclosed in accordance with Trial Court Rule IV.

Complaints for relief under G.L. c. 209A shall be filed with the Clerk–Magistrate for Civil Business during regular court hours.

The justice assigned to the BMC Motion Session is designated to hear all applications for temporary orders and other remedies as provided in G.L. c. 209A. The Motion Session Justice will set these matters for hearing on Mondays and Fridays at 2:00 p.m., or at such other times within the statutory five day period as the Motion Session Justice may determine.

Complaints and applications for temporary orders must be filed with the Clerk–Magistrate for Civil Business on the next business day following issuance of an emergency order. Hearings on same will be scheduled within five business days of the date they are filed with the Clerk–Magistrate for Civil Business. Notice to the defendant of such hearings will be made in accordance with the provisions of the statute.

The Clerk–Magistrate for Civil Business shall maintain a separate docket for complaints sought under G.L. c. 209A, and shall make the necessary provisions for custody of these records as provided by the statute.

Adopted January 21, 1984.

Standing Order 1–88. Superseded by Order 1–04

Publisher's Note

Standing Order 1–04, in Section I., provides: "This Order applies to all tort and contract actions in which money damages are sought ('civil actions') and which have been commenced in the Boston Municipal Court Department and the District Court Department on or after August 31, 2004. In the District Court Department, this Order shall also apply to all civil actions previously governed by District Court Standing Order 1–98 regarding any procedures occurring on or after that date. Sections VI (Motion Practice) and VII (Continuances) of this Order shall also apply to all civil actions pending in the divisions of the Boston Municipal Court Department and in the divisions of the District Court Department in Plymouth, Suffolk and Worcester Counties, regardless of the date of commencement of such actions." Standing Order 1–04 in Section I., further provides: "This Order supersedes Boston Municipal Court Department Standing Order 1–88 and District Court Department Standing Orders 1–88 and 1–98 with respect to all civil actions and all procedures to which this Order applies."

Joint Standing Order 1–04. Civil
Case Management

I. PURPOSE AND APPLICABILITY

The purpose of this Joint Order is to establish case management procedures that will facilitate the prompt and efficient disposition of civil cases and reduce the expense and delay of civil litigation in the Boston Municipal Court Department and the District Court Department.

This Order applies to all tort and contract actions in which money damages are sought ("civil actions") and which have been commenced in the Boston Municipal Court Department and the District Court Department on or after August 31, 2004. In the District Court Department, this Order shall also apply to all civil actions previously governed by District Court Standing Order 1–98 regarding any procedures occurring on or after that date. Sections VI (Motion Practice) and VII (Continuances) of this Order also apply to all civil actions pending in the divisions of the Boston Municipal Court Department and in the divisions of the District Court Department in Plymouth, Suffolk and Worcester Counties, regardless of the date of commencement of such actions.

This Order supersedes Boston Municipal Court Department Standing Order 1–88 and District Court Department Standing Orders 1–88 and 1–98 with respect to all civil actions and all procedures to which this Order applies.

II. GENERAL PRETRIAL SCHEDULE

It shall be the responsibility of counsel to complete the preparation of his or her case by the date of the pretrial conference as scheduled in accordance with Section IV A, unless the court orders otherwise. Discovery and pretrial motions, including motions pursuant to Mass. R. Civ. P. 12, 15, 19, 20 and 56, and such other motions as may be prescribed by the court, shall be filed, marked and caused to be heard by such date unless the court permits otherwise for good cause shown.

III. CASE MANAGEMENT CONFERENCE

A. Scheduling. Upon the filing of an answer by any defendant, the court shall immediately give notice to all parties in the action of a Case Management Conference pursuant to Mass. Civ. P. 16 to be held on a date certain within four months of the date of filing of such answer, or sooner if directed by the court or jointly requested by all parties. Such notice shall inform the parties of the purposes of the conference and the desirability of addressing any discovery issues prior to the conference. Counsel or pro se litigants shall appear in person at the Case Management Conference. The court may impose sanctions, including dismissal, default and assessment of costs, for failure to attend the conference without good cause.

B. Purpose. The purpose of the Case Management Conference shall be to (1) discuss settlement progress and opportunities for settlement, and offer early intervention alternative dispute resolution; (2) consider case management orders proposed by any party, or by the court, regarding limitation or sequencing of discovery events, disclosure or limitation of expert witnesses, motion briefing, and other matters that would reduce expense and delay of litigation, and enter appropriate orders; (3) enter judgment for relief or dismissal, and schedule hearing for assessment of damages if necessary; and (4) assign a firm date for pretrial conference for all cases which are not yet ready for trial; (5) assess the trial-readiness of cases; (6) assign a firm trial date for cases that are ready for trial.

Among the orders that a Judge may impose at the Case Management Conference under item (2), above, is an "Order for Early Disclosure," requiring compliance with the terms set forth in Section III D.

Notice of the date of trial or Pretrial Conference shall be given to the parties at the Case Management Conference after consultation with counsel.

In all cases scheduled for trial, the person conducting the Case Management Conference shall prepare a Pretrial Conference report. In all cases scheduled for Pretrial Conference, the person conducting the Case Management Conference shall prepare a Case Management Conference report summarizing the results of the conference.

C. Judicial officer. The Case Management Conference shall be conducted by a Judge or, if a Judge is unavailable, by a Clerk–Magistrate or Assistant Clerk–Magistrate designated by the Chief Justice of the Boston Municipal Court Department or the Chief Justice of the District Court Department in accordance with G.L. § 221, § 62C and Trial Court Rule II(3)(a) to conduct such conferences. Only a Judge may issue or approve any orders arising from the Case Management Conference.

D. Mandatory Early Disclosure. If ordered by the court at the Case Management Conference as provided above in section III B, each party shall provide the discovery specified below without a request by any opposing party. Unless otherwise agreed by the parties or ordered by the court, such disclosure shall be completed no later than 90 days after completion of the Case Management Conference.

1. Actions Involving Tort Claims.

(a) Plaintiff. A party asserting a tort claim shall provide to all other parties copies of medical bills and medical records in its possession, custody, or control, or provide written authorizations signed by the patient to permit opposing counsel to obtain such documents; all accident reports, sketches and photographs of the accident scene; property damage or injury reports; an itemized list of special damages and non-medical damages known to counsel; admissions by the opposing party; names and addresses of witnesses; reports of all government agencies or officials which investigated the event giving rise to the claim; personal injury protection (PIP) applications and documents; the identity of any person, firm or entity who may be responsible for the plaintiff's injury; and any documents that counsel agree to disclose without formal discovery.

(b) Defendant. A party defending against a tort claim shall provide to all other parties copies of all primary and excess insurance policies that may be available to satisfy a judgment; copies of all documents reserving an insurer's right to deny coverage; all accident reports, sketches and photographs of the accident scene; property damage or injury reports; medical examination reports of the plaintiff (which the defendant intends to introduce as evidence at trial); admissions by the opposing party; names and addresses of witnesses; reports of government agencies or officials which investigated the event giving rise to the claim; and any documents that counsel agree to disclose without formal discovery.

2. Actions Involving Contract Claims.

(a) Plaintiff. A party asserting a contract claim shall provide to all other parties copies of the contracts or written agreements that give rise to the claim, including warranties, notes, and guaranties; names and addresses of witnesses; an itemized list of special damages; admissions by the opposing party; and any documents that counsel agree to disclose without formal discovery.

(b) Defendant. A party defending a contract claim shall provide to all other parties copies of all primary and excess insurance policies that may be available to satisfy a judgment; copies of all documents reserving an insurer's right to deny coverage; any contracts or written agreements that give rise to the claim, including warranties, notes and guaranties; names and addresses of witnesses; admissions by the opposing party; and any documents that counsel agree to disclose without formal discovery.

3. Expert Witnesses.

A party shall identify any person who may be used as an expert witness at trial in advance of the pretrial hearing date. Except as otherwise stipulated or directed by the court, this disclosure shall be accompanied by a written report prepared by the witness. The report shall contain a complete statement of all opinions to be expressed and the basis and reasons therefor; the data or other information considered by the witness in forming the opinions; any exhibits to be used as a summary of or support for the opinions; the qualifications of the witness, including a list of all publications authored by the witness within the preceding five years; the compensation to be paid for the study and testimony; and a listing of any cases in which the witness has testified as a witness at trial or by deposition within the preceding three years.

4. Contested Discovery.

Before filing any discovery motion, including any motion for sanctions or for a protective order, counsel for each of the parties shall confer in good faith to narrow the areas of disagreement to the greatest possible extent. It shall be the responsibility of counsel for the moving party to arrange for the conference. Any motion to compel discovery shall include a certificate of counsel filed by the moving party certifying that he has conferred with opposing counsel as required by this section.

IV. PRETRIAL CONFERENCE

A. Scheduling and pretrial memorandum. All cases not disposed or assigned a trial date at the Case Management Conference shall be assigned a firm date for Pretrial Conference when they are expected to be ready for trial, such date to be not later than the end of the tenth month after the month in which the action was filed, or such later date as the court may order for good cause shown. Upon scheduling an action for Pretrial Conference, the court shall issue a notice of Pretrial Conference requiring the parties to prepare a joint pretrial memorandum for use at the Pretrial Conference. Failure of any party to attend the Pretrial Conference or prepare a joint pretrial memorandum may result in sanctions, including dismissal, default and assessment of costs.

B. Agenda, report and Trial Order. The purpose of the Pretrial Conference is to discuss settlement opportunities and to achieve settlement or, for cases which do not settle, to assign a firm trial date. The person conducting the Pretrial Conference shall thereafter prepare a pretrial conference report. For actions requiring a trial date, notice of such date shall be given to all parties at the Pretrial Conference after consultation with counsel. Upon scheduling a case for trial, the court shall issue a Trial Order requiring the parties to prepare for trial. Failure of any party to prepare for trial as required by such order may result in preclusion of evidence or other sanctions in the discretion of the trial judge.

C. Judicial officer. The Pretrial Conference shall be conducted by a Judge or, if a Judge is unavailable, by a Clerk–Magistrate or Assistant Clerk–Magistrate who has been designated by the Chief Justice of the Boston Municipal Court Department or the Chief Justice of the District Court Department in accordance with G.L. c. 221, § 62C and Trial Court Rule II(3)(a) to conduct such conferences, or by alternative dispute resolution personnel approved by the court. Only a Judge may issue or approve any orders arising from the Pretrial Conference.

V. DISMISSAL FOR LACK OF SERVICE OR FAILURE TO ACT ON DEFAULT

All actions in which there is no timely service of the complaint or no timely action upon default shall be dismissed as follows:

A. Dismissal for lack of service. After commencement of each action, the Clerk–Magistrate shall review the docket to determine whether the plaintiff has complied with the time limits for service pursuant to Mass. R. Civ. P. 4(j), together with any extensions allowed by the court pursuant to Mass. R. Civ. P. 6. Upon determining noncompliance, the Clerk–Magistrate shall issue notice of dismissal of the action as provided by Rule 4(j).

B. Dismissal nisi for failure to act on default. Where an action has remained on the docket for eight months without an answer or defensive motion having been filed by any defendant, the Clerk–Magistrate shall enter an Order Nisi for Dismissal advising the plaintiff that a Judgment of Dismissal will be entered 30 days from the date of the Order unless the plaintiff either (1) requests entry of default and moves for default judgment in accordance with Mass. R. Civ. P. 55, or (2) reports in writing that the case is active and requests that it not be dismissed.

VI. MOTION PRACTICE

A. General. Pursuant to Mass. R. Civ. P. 6 and 78, all motions shall be accompanied by an affidavit of notice setting forth the date and time of hearing on the motion. All motions shall be scheduled by counsel for the moving party on the court's usual civil motion hearing day as published by the court, or on the date the case is scheduled for Case Management Conference or Pretrial Conference, or as otherwise ordered by the court.

B. Agreed Upon Motions. Motions filed by the parties jointly or where the moving party avers that all other parties agree with the outcome sought by the motion may be submitted for a ruling on the papers without the presence of the parties. Such motions shall be accompanied by an express request that the court rule without a hearing. This procedure shall be available only in cases where all parties are represented by counsel.

C. Discovery and summary judgment motions. All discovery motions filed pursuant to Mass. R. Civ. P. 26 or 37 shall include copies of the discovery requests and responses which are the subject of the motion. Motions for summary judgment which rely on any pleading or discovery shall include copies of such pleadings or discovery with the motion. Any discovery or summary judgment motions which do not include such copies may be denied without prejudice.

D. Opposition procedure. In actions where all parties are represented by counsel, motions may be acted upon by the court without a hearing in the following manner.

1. **Designation by moving party.** A moving party who chooses to use this procedure shall state on the caption of the motion and on the affidavit of notice, "SUBJECT TO OPPOSITION PROCEDURE," and file and serve such motion at least 14 days before the motion hearing date. If no other party timely files and serves an "OPPOSITION TO MOTION" as described below, the motion will be considered by the court without a hearing or the attendance of any counsel.

2. **Opposition by other party.** If any other party opposes the motion or otherwise seeks to be heard, such party shall file and serve a document captioned "OPPOSITION TO MOTION" at least five days before the motion hearing date. If any party timely files and serves such an "OPPOSITION TO MOTION," all counsel shall be required to attend the scheduled hearing, unless in such "OPPOSITION TO MOTION" the party expressly waives the right to such hearing, in which case the motion will be considered by the court without a hearing or the attendance of any counsel.

3. **Exempted motions.** This opposition procedure shall not apply to the following motions: motions to continue Case Management Conference, Pretrial Conference or trial; ex parte motions; petitions for approval of settlement by a minor; motions seeking sanctions of any kind; motions for preliminary and permanent injunction; motions for a receiver; motions to vacate a default judgment; motions for relief from judgment; motions for a new trial; motions for reconsideration; and any motion ordered by a Judge to be decided after hearing.

4. **Notice of decision.** When a motion is considered under the opposition procedure, the court shall act upon, and send written notice of such action to all parties, within 14 days after the hearing date.

VII. CONTINUANCES

A. General. Continuances of Case Management Conferences, Pretrial Conferences and trials shall be disfavored because of the advance notice to, and the participation of counsel in, the scheduling of these events. Continuances of these events will be allowed for good cause only, and any continuance shall be to a date and event certain. No action shall be "continued generally" or taken off the schedule for any reason.

B. Form of motions. Requests for continuances shall be made only by written motion supported by an affidavit of counsel, and counsel shall send a copy of the continuance request to his or her client(s) by first-class mail. All motions for continuance shall include a list of any days within the next 30 days that counsel for any party is unavailable for the continued event.

C. Joint requests to continue case management conference or pretrial conference. The Clerk–Magistrate or an Assistant Clerk designated by the Clerk–Magistrate may allow a joint request to continue a Case Management Conference or Pretrial Conference after review of the motion without hearing, provided that the event shall be continued not more than once and for not more than 30 days.

D. Trial continuances, opposed continuances and repeat continuances. Motions to continue a trial, whether or not agreed to by the parties, may be allowed only by a Judge assigned to the civil trial session or, in the absence or unavailability of such Judge, by the Presiding Justice or other Judge designated by the Presiding Justice. Motions to continue a Case Management Conference or Pretrial Conference which are opposed by any party, as well as motions to continue an event previously continued pursuant to Section VII C above, shall be marked and heard as motions before a Judge. Counsel and pro se litigants shall not be excused from attending the scheduled event unless notified by the court that the event has been continued. No employee or officer of the court shall be authorized to allow continuances of trials or conferences, except as provided in this section.

/s/CHARLES R. JOHNSON	/s/LYNDA M. CONNOLLY
Charles R. Johnson, Chief Justice	Lynda M. Connolly, Chief Justice
Boston Municipal Court Department	District Court Department

Adopted August 23, 2004, effective August 31, 2004.

Standing Order 2–04. Probation Violation Proceedings [Repealed].

Repealed and replaced by District/Municipal Courts Rules for Probation Violation Proceedings effective September 8, 2015.

Joint Standing Order 2–04. Time Standards for Civil Cases

I. INTRODUCTION

These time standards are promulgated to provide judges and clerk-magistrates with specific maximum time periods within which civil cases (1) should progress between court events and (2) should be disposed. The purpose of these time standards is to promote timely disposition of civil cases and to provide a basis for assessing the movement of civil cases from commencement to disposition in each division of the two departments in which they apply.

The time standards are divided into three categories, each comprised of specific types of civil actions ("casetypes") and each governed by a specific standard for a maximum time to disposition.

In general, these three time standard categories reflect the complexity (or potential complexity) of the casetypes each includes, with the least complex in Category A, the more complex in Category B, and the most complex (or potentially complex) in Category C.

The casetypes in Category A consist mainly of actions that by law must be disposed well within the two-month maximum. For these cases the time standard will provide a basis for periodically confirming that no cases are unaccounted for or overlooked.

Two casetypes in Category B, summary process and small claims, have "staircased" time standards to reflect the fact that significant numbers of these cases should be disposed well before their overall maximum time to disposition.

Category C, which consists of tort and contract actions, also has "staircased" time standards to reflect the fact that most of these cases should be disposed well before the overall maximum time limit.

II. THE TIME STANDARDS

CATEGORY A—Time to Disposition: Upon Filing or Not more than 2 months from commencement

- Abuse Restraining Orders (c.209A)
- Landlord Failures to Provide Utilities (c. 186 § 14)
- Landlord Interference with Quiet Enjoyment (c. 186 § 14)
- Landlord Unlawfully Entering/Repossessing Land (c. 184 § 18)
- Lead Poisoning Prevention Actions (c. 111 § 198)
- License Suspension for Chemical Test Refusal Appeals (c.90 § 24[1][g])
- Marriage Age Waivers (c.207 § 25)
- Marriage Waiting Period Waivers (c.207 § 30)
- Mental Health Proceedings (c. 123)
- Sanitary Code Enforcement Actions (c. 111 § 127C)

CATEGORY B—Time to Disposition: Not more than 4 months from commencement

- Summary Process: 50% NMT 1 month; 90% NMT 2 months; 100% NMT 4 months
- Small Claims: 75% NMT 2 months; 100% NMT 4 months (5 months if de novo appeal claimed)
- Civil Motor Vehicle Infractions (5 months if de novo appeal claimed)
- Non–Motor Vehicle Civil Infractions (5 months if de novo appeal claimed) (see attached list)
- Supplementary Process
- Judicial Review of Administrative Decisions (see attached list)
- Other Specialized Civil Actions (see attached list)

CATEGORY C—Tort and Contract Actions

C–1 75% of Total Dispositions	Time to Disposition: Not more than **6 months** from commencement • Cases dismissed for plaintiff's failure to make timely service • Cases disposed by default judgment • Cases disposed by voluntary dismissal, agreement for judgment or other consensual disposition
C–2 20% of Total Dispositions	Time to Disposition: Not more than **12 months** from commencement • Cases disposed by bench trial • Cases disposed by voluntary dismissal, agreement for judgment or other consensual disposition • Cases dismissed for plaintiff's failure to seek default judgment
C–3 5% of Total Dispositions	Time to Disposition: Not more than **18 months** from commencement • Cases disposed by jury trial • Cases disposed by bench trial after having been scheduled for jury trial • Cases disposed by voluntary dismissal, agreement for judgment or other consensual disposition after having been scheduled for trial

Maximum Intervals Between Court Events:
- From Answer to Case Management Conference Date: Not More Than 4 Months
- From Case Management Conference to Pretrial Conference Date: Not More Than 7 Months
- From Pretrial Conference to Trial: Not More Than 3 Months

Originally Promulgated: October 1, 2004, to be effective November 1, 2004

Amended: July 1, 2008 for cases filed on and after January 1, 2008

APPENDIX

Non–Motor Vehicle Civil Infractions (Category B) include

- Bicycle Civil Infractions (c.85 § 11C)
- Dog Control Civil Infractions (c. 140 § 173A)
- Environmental Civil Infractions (c.21A §§ 10G–10H)
- MBTA Smoking Civil Infractions (c. 161A § 42)
- Motorboat Civil Infractions (c.90B § 14[a])
- Municipal Ordinance/Bylaw Civil Infractions (c.40 § 21D)
- Pedestrian Civil Infractions (c.90 § 18A)
- Rubbish Disposal Civil Infractions (c.270 § 16A)
- State Building Code or Fire Code Civil Infractions (c. 148A)
- State Park / Forest / Recreation Area Civil Infractions (c. 132A § 7A)

Judicial Review of Administrative Decisions (Category B) includes

- Abandoned Property Appeals (c.200A § 10[d])
- Ammunition Dealer License Appeals (c. 140 § 122B)
- County Employee Discharge Appeals (c.35 § 51)
- Dog Order Appeals (c. 140, § 157)
- Farm Nuisance Abatement Order Appeals (c. 111 § 125A)
- Fence Viewer Certiorari Actions (c.249 § 4)
- Firearms Identification Card Appeals (c. 140 § 129B[5])
- Firearms License Appeals (c. 140 § 131[h])
- Funeral Director License Appeals (c. 112 § 84A)
- Historic District Commission Appeals
- Home Improvement Contractor Arbitration Appeals (c. 142A § 4[e])
- MCAD Housing Discrimination Award Appeals (c. 151B § 5)
- Raffle/Bazaar Permit Appeals (c.271 § 7A)
- Retirement Board/PERA Appeals (c.32 § 16[c][3][a])
- Unemployment Compensation Appeals (c. 151A § 42)
- Used Car Lemon Law Arbitration Appeals (c.90 § 7N¼)
- Victim of Violent Crime Compensation Appeals (c.258C § 9)
- Zoning Appeals (c.40A § 17)

Other Specialized Civil Actions (Category B) include:

- Auto/Boat Forfeiture Actions based on Fourth or Subsequent OUI (c.90 § 24W)
- Beach Free Passage Actions (St. 1991 c. 176 § 4)
- Child Labor Citation Enforcement Actions (c. 149 § 78A[d])
- Condominium Conversion Violation Actions (St. 1983 c.527 § 5 & St. 1989, c.709 § 20)
- Discovery in Foreign Proceeding (c.223A § 11)
- Election Violation Inquest (c.55 § 35)
- Explosives/Inflammables Forfeiture Actions (c. 148 §§ 50–51)
- Forfeiture of Property Seized in Criminal Offense (c.257 §§ 2–7)
- Juror Wage Denial Actions (c.234A § 60)
- Lien Enforcement Actions (c.254 § 5; 255 § 26)
- Livestock Disease Control Actions (c. 129 § 37)
- Medical Provider Overpayment Recovery Actions (c. 118E § 38)
- Municipal Tax Collection Proceedings (c.60 § 29)
- Replevin (c.247)
- Repossession of Secured Goods (c.255 § 13J; c.255B § 20B; c.255D § 22)
- Security Actions for Impounded Animal (c.272 § 104[c])

- Settlement Approval for Personal Injury to Minor/Incompetent (c.231 § 140C½)
- State Fire Marshal Investigations (c. 148 § 3)
- Structured Settlement Transfer Approvals (c.231C § 2)
- Tenant Illegal Activity Declaratory Judgments (c. 139 § 19)
- Tuberculosis Commitments/Discharges (c. 111, §§ 94C or 94G)
- Unemployment Compensation Actions against Employer by DET (c. 151A § 15)

Adopted October 1, 2004, effective November 1, 2004. Amended effective July 1, 2008 for cases filed on and after January 1, 2008.

Joint Standing Order 3–04. Time Standards for Criminal Cases

1. AUTHORITY

This Standing Order is jointly promulgated by the Chief Justice of the Boston Municipal Court Department and the Chief Justice of the District Court Department pursuant to their statutory responsibility for case management under G.L. c. 211B, § 10 and uniform practices under G.L. c. 218, § 43A.

2. PURPOSE

These time standards are intended to reaffirm the goals of "simplicity in procedure, fairness in administration, and the elimination of expense and delay," as provided by Mass. R. Crim. P. 2(a). Recognizing that excessive delay can undermine public confidence in the delivery of justice in our courts, the following time standards have been established to advance the expeditious and just disposition of all criminal matters.

3. TIME STANDARDS

There shall be two track designations for criminal cases commenced within the final jurisdiction of the Boston Municipal and District Court Departments. Track A shall include all criminal offenses which provide a maximum period of incarceration of six months or less, including all criminal offenses which carry no term of imprisonment and are punishable only by fine. Track B shall include all criminal offenses punishable by a period of incarceration longer than six months.

The maximum time to disposition for Track A cases shall be five months. The maximum time to disposition for Track B cases shall be twelve months. If a defendant is charged with one or more Track A and Track B offenses in a single complaint, the case shall be treated as Track B for all purposes. Cases may be transferred from Track A to Track B, or the maximum time period allowable between court events may be extended, only by a judge for demonstrated good cause stated on the record. Requests to alter the track designation of cases or to extend a maximum time period within a track shall be evaluated consistent with the purposes of this Order set forth in paragraph 2. Nothing in this Order shall be construed to deter resolution of cases prior to the maximum time limits set forth herein.

Consistent with the applicable provisions of the Mass. R. Crim. P. and the Dist./Mun. Cts. R. Crim. P., the time between court events in criminal cases shall be as follows:

Track A:

- From Arraignment to Pretrial Hearing date: Not more than 45 days;
- From Pretrial Hearing to Motion/Compliance/Election date: Not more than 45 days;
- From Motion/Compliance/Election date to Trial date: Not more than 45 days.

Track B:

- From Arraignment to Pretrial Hearing date: Not more than 45 days;
- From Pretrial Hearing to Motion/Compliance/Election date: Not more than 60 days;
- From Motion/Compliance/Election to Trial date: Not more than 90 days.

4. CRIMINAL CASE MANAGEMENT

Performance goals for criminal case management in the Boston Municipal Court Department shall be determined by the Chief Justice of the Boston Municipal Court Department.

Criminal case management in the District Court Department shall be assessed in accordance with District Court Standing Order No. 4–04, Performance Goals for Criminal Case Management.

Computation of the time periods set forth above shall exclude any time during which the defendant is legally unavailable to proceed with the criminal case; e.g., time during which the defendant is in default and periods of time during which the defendant is under a term of involuntary civil commitment pursuant to the provisions of G.L. c. 123.

Adopted effective November 1, 2004.

Standing Order 1–06. Establishment of Specialized Sessions Boston Municipal Court Department

I. Authority

This amended Standing Order 1–06 is promulgated by the Chief Justice of the Boston Municipal Court Department pursuant to the provisions of G. L. c. 211B, § 10 and G. L. c. 218, § 51A, and in compliance with the Trial Court Policy for Specialty Court Sessions issued by the Executive Office of the Trial Court on June 5, 2014 ("SC Policy") *and* revised S.J.C. Rule 3:09 Code of Judicial Conduct effective on January 1, 2016 ("revised CJC"), which are incorporated herein by reference.

II. Purpose and Applicability

The Boston Municipal Court Department has long recognized the benefits of providing specialized sessions to address specific public health and safety issues presented by individuals appearing in criminal or civil matters brought before our court divisions. In order to achieve consistency, accountability, and the efficient use of existing resources, Standing Order 1–06 originally promulgated uniform procedures for the establishment or continued operation of specialized sessions in this Department. With the issuance of a formal Trial Court Policy for Specialty Court Sessions and the revision of the Code of Judicial Conduct effective on January 1, 2016, Standing Order 1–06 is hereby amended to conform to the provisions of both the SC Policy and the revised CJC, and to formally adopt the Trial Court designation and definition of "specialty court sessions". Using evidence-based practices, specialty court sessions target individuals with underlying medical, mental health, substance use disorders and other issues in an effort to reduce recidivism and improve public safety. A hallmark of a specialty court session is the integration of treatment and services with judicial case oversight and intensive court supervision.

III. Written Plan Requirement

A. *For Establishment of New Specialty Court Session*

Any court division of this Department seeking to establish a new specialty court session shall fully comply with all provisions of the SC Policy, including the submission of a written plan as described in Section I of the SC Policy. Said written plan shall be submitted for initial review to the Director of Specialty Courts prior to final approval by the Chief Justice of the Boston Municipal Court Department.

B. *For Continued Operation of Existing Specialty Court Session(s)*

Within forty-five (45) days of the effective date of this amended Standing Order 1–06, and then biannually, the First Justice of each court division of this Department with existing specialty court session(s) shall submit a written plan for its/their continued operation as described below in subsection C to the Director of Specialty Courts.

C. *Issues to be Addressed in Written Plan for Continued Operation of Existing Specialty Court Session(s)*

After consultation with the Clerk Magistrate, Chief Probation Officer and Chief Court Officer, the First Justice of each court division of this Department seeking to continue operating specialty court session(s) shall submit a written plan to the Director of Specialty Courts for each specialty court session addressing the following issues: (1) the continued need for and benefit(s) of the existing specialty court session; (2) the continued availability of resources in terms of court staff and workload, court security, and community treatment providers; (3) the protocol outlining the eligibility, operating procedures and frequency of the scheduled specialty court session; (4) the need for any additional training of court personnel; (5) the performance standards expected of individuals participating in the existing specialty court session; (6) the methodology being used to collect and report data; and (7) all foreseeable operational issues or concerns with proposed resolutions.

IV. Additional Provisions

A. *Ex Parte Communications in Court Proceedings*

Pursuant to the revised CJC, a judge may exercise his/her discretion to engage in ex parte communications in specialty courts as authorized by law.

B. *Statistical Data Requirements*

Each specialty court session shall maintain statistical data, including the number of referrals to each specialty court session, the status of each case, a description of all case activity, and the next scheduled event. Specialty court sessions must comply with all applicable time standards as provided by Boston Municipal/District Court Joint Standing Orders 2–04 and 3–04.

C. *Judicial Assignment*

All departmental judges are eligible for and subject to assignment to any specialty court session, and must familiarize themselves with all provisions and requirements contained in this amended Standing Order, the SC Policy and the revised CJC.

V. Duration and Periodic Review of Each Specialty Court Session

Unless otherwise ordered by the Chief Justice, authorization to establish a new specialty court session will expire two (2) years from the date of approval. A written plan as described in Section III. C. for the continued operation of an approved specialty court session must be submitted to the Director of Specialty Courts by the First Justice within sixty (60) days of expiration. The periodic review of all existing specialty court sessions as provided for in this Standing Order is independent of and shall not be replaced by the certification process described in the Adult Drug Court Manual issued by the Executive Office of the Trial Court.

Adopted June 5, 2006. Amended January 5, 2016, effective January 15, 2016.

Standing Order 1–09. For the Sealing of Three or More Dismissals and Non–Conviction Criminal Records

I. Authority

This permanent Standing Order is promulgated and revised by the Chief Justice of the Boston Municipal Court Department pursuant to G. L. c. 211B, § 10 and G. L. c. 218, § 51A.

II. Purpose and Applicability

In recognition of the hardships faced by individuals of limited economic resources with criminal records, and the burdens they face when seeking to seal their criminal records at the various court divisions in this Department, and in an effort to alleviate these hardships and burdens while promoting judicial economy, this Standing Order was originally promulgated by the Boston Municipal Court Department to allow for the filing of a single petition to seal three or more dismissals and non-conviction criminal records pursuant to the provisions of G. L. c. 276, § 100C. This Standing Order established the procedures to be followed by all court divisions of this Department in those instances when a person seeks to seal three or more criminal records from two or more court divisions within this Department where a dismissal or nolle prosequi or finding of no probable cause has been entered, or the defendant was found not guilty. However, in light of the recent Supreme Judicial Court decision in *Commonwealth v. Pon*, SJC–11542 (August 15, 2014), 469 Mass. _____ (2014), this Standing Order is being revised as of the effective date below to conform to the new legal standard and analysis established by the SJC in *Pon*.

III. Required Protocols and Procedures

A. *Petition to Seal Multiple Criminal Records; Venue; Filing.* As of the effective date of this revised Standing Order, a person who resides within the territorial jurisdiction of the court divisions of the Boston Municipal Court Department, with three or more dismissals and/or non-conviction criminal records in the court divisions of this Department, may request that these criminal records be sealed in a single petition filed in the court division in whose territory the person resides. If a person with three or more dismissals and/or non-conviction criminal records in the court divisions of this Department does not reside within the territorial jurisdiction of this Department, then these criminal records may be sealed in a single petition filed in the court division of the most recent applicable criminal record. A person seeking to seal multiple criminal records in a single petition pursuant to this amended Standing Order should be sure to list all applicable criminal cases with docket numbers from all court divisions of the Boston Municipal Court Department. A modified petition form that conforms to the *Pon* decision is available on the Trial Court website.

The Clerk–Magistrate who receives for filing the original petition to seal multiple criminal records shall docket and file the petition in the corresponding criminal case(s) within three (3) business days, and shall provide a copy of the petition with notice of the preliminary hearing to the Probation Department.

B. *Hearing.* In *Pon*, the Supreme Judicial Court determined that a court has the discretion either to conduct a preliminary hearing and then a final hearing, or to conduct a single final hearing.

1. *Preliminary hearing:* Upon the filing of a petition for sealing multiple criminal records, a preliminary hearing may be held to determine whether the petitioner has made out a prima facie case in favor of sealing said records. The new legal standard for the petitioner's prima facie case was established by the SJC in *Commonwealth v. Pon*, SJC–11542 (August 15, 2014), 469 Mass. _____ (2014), and is specifically incorporated by this revised Standing Order. In his discretion, a judge hearing a petition for sealing multiple criminal records may request additional information or document(s) regarding the criminal case(s) listed in the petition from the Clerk–Magistrate and/or the Probation Department.

2. *Final hearing:* If a judge finds that the petitioner has shown a prima facie case for sealing, whether at the preliminary hearing described above or upon review of the petition and/or other papers submitted by the petitioner, a final hearing shall be scheduled for no earlier than thirty (30) days, but no later than forty-five (45) days, from the date of the preliminary hearing or the filing of the petition. The Clerk–Magistrate of the court division ordering a final hearing shall notify the Probation Department of said final hearing.

C. *Public Notice of Final Hearing.* The Clerk–Magistrate of the court division conducting the final hearing shall post for a minimum of seven (7) days public notice of the date, time, and location of the final hearing.

D. *Notice to District Attorney of Final Hearing; Objection to Venue.* The petitioner is required to send a copy of the petition to seal multiple criminal records to the Suffolk County District Attorney's Office at least thirty (30) days before the final hearing so as to permit the District Attorney's Office to notify the victim(s), if any, of the scheduled final hearing. Unless the petitioner has complied with this provision, or said District Attorney's Office has waived the full thirty (30) day notice, no criminal record(s) from other court division(s) shall be sealed at the final hearing.

The victim(s), if any, and/or the Assistant District Attorney(s) of criminal case(s) from other court division(s) shall have the right to object to venue. Upon the receipt or articulation of any such objection, a judge in the court division in which the petition was filed may for good cause decline to hear the petition to seal for those criminal case(s) from other court division(s), without prejudice to the petitioner's filing of a separate petition to seal in the court division(s) in which those criminal case(s) originated.

E. *Order on Petition to Seal Multiple Criminal Records.* The Clerk–Magistrate of the court division that issues an order on the original petition to seal multiple criminal records shall promptly docket and file said order in the corresponding criminal case(s), shall transmit a copy of said order to the Probation Department, and shall transmit a copy of said order to the Clerk–Magistrate(s) of the other court division(s) with criminal case(s) listed on the petition.

F. *Notice to Office of the Commissioner of Probation.* The Chief Probation Officer of the Probation Department of the court division that enters an order to seal criminal record(s) is responsible for notifying the Office of the Commissioner of Probation of the court's order.

Adopted April 10, 2009, effective May 15, 2009 to May 14, 2010; extended May 20, 2010 through May 14, 2011; amended and made permanent May 9, 2012, effective May 14, 2012; amended August 27, 2014, effective September 2, 2014.

Standing Order 1–10. Limited Assistance Representation in Civil Matters Only [Rescinded]

Adopted March 23, 2010, effective May 3, 2010. Rescinded January 3, 2019, effective February 1, 2019. See, now, Uniform Trial Court Rule XVI. Limited Assistance Representation.

Joint Standing Order 1–15. Provision of Respondents' Non-Clinical Identifying Information in Commitment Proceedings Under G. L. c. 123, §§ 7, 8, and 12(e), or G. L. c. 123, § 35

The purpose of this Joint Order is to provide for the collection of non-clinical identifying information in commitment proceedings in the Boston Municipal Court Department and the District Court Department necessary to comply with the courts' reporting requirements pursuant to Chapter 284, Acts of 2014 , An Act Relative to the Reduction of Gun Violence.[1]

IT IS THEREFORE ORDERED:

An applicant seeking a court order to commit a respondent to a mental health facility pursuant to G.L. c. 123, § 12(e) , a petitioner seeking a court order to commit or retain a respondent for inpatient care pursuant to G.L. c. 123, §§ 7 and 8 , and a petitioner seeking a court order to commit a respondent for treatment for alcoholism and/or substance abuse pursuant to G.L. c. 123, § 35 , shall provide the respondent's date of birth and social security number, if available, to the court.

Adopted May 20, 2015, effective June 1, 2015.

1 Although commitment matters are also brought under G.L. c. 123, §§ 15(b), 16(b) or (c), or 18 that arise out of criminal proceedings, the respondent's or defendant's date of birth and social security number is obtained and provided to the court through the Defendant Identification Information System in those cases.

Standing Order 1–15. Initial Limited Electronic Filing Pilot Project in the Brighton Division of the Boston Municipal Court Department for Designated Civil Matters Only

I. Authority

This Standing Order 1–15 is promulgated by the Chief Justice of the Boston Municipal Court Department pursuant to the provisions of G. L. c. 211B, § 10 and G. L. c. 218, § 51A, and in compliance with the Order Re: Electronic Filing Pilot Projects issued by the Massachusetts Supreme Judicial Court effective February 25, 2015.

II. Purpose and Applicability

In order to advance efficiency in the Massachusetts courts and better serve the public and the bar, the Supreme Judicial Court has authorized electronic filing pilot projects for the trial and appellate courts and approved Interim Massachusetts Electronic Filing Rules effective February 25, 2015. By this Standing Order 1–15, the Boston Municipal Court Department hereby designates the Brighton Division, located at 52 Academy Hill Avenue, Brighton, MA, for its department pilot project permitting electronic filing and electronic service of court documents (the "Brighton Pilot Project") for designated civil matters only, as set forth below in section III. B.

Standing Order 1–15 shall incorporate by reference the Interim Massachusetts Electronic Filing Rules (the "Interim Rules"), and, for the duration of the Brighton Pilot Project, shall establish additional procedures for the implementation and operation of electronic filing and electronic service of court documents in designated civil matters commenced after the effective date of this Standing Order, notwithstanding any provision to the contrary in any rule of court or other standing order. This is an initial limited Standing Order to establish the parameters of the implementation of the Brighton Pilot Project; this Standing Order shall be amended and revised by this Department as necessary during the course of the electronic filing pilot projects generally, and the Brighton Pilot Project specifically.

III. Designations

A. **Lawyers/Law Firms.** In this initial implementation stage, two designated law firms have agreed to participate in the Brighton Pilot Project: Kream & Kream of Weymouth, MA, and Alford & Bertrand, LLC of Watertown, MA. The designated lawyers/law firms shall be given training and access to the Provider's electronic filing system, and shall participate in the Brighton Pilot Project as properly registered users in compliance with the Interim Rules. Additional lawyers/law firms may be approved by this Department to participate in the Brighton Pilot Project without further amendment of this Standing Order.

B. **Civil Case Types.** The following civil case types are specifically designated for electronic filing and electronic service of court documents in the Brighton Pilot Project:

• Interpleader of Money Deposited in Court (Mass. R. Civ. P. 67)

- Landlord Failure to Provide Utilities (G. L. c. 186, § 14)

- Landlord Interference with Quiet Enjoyment (G. L. c. 186, § 14)

- Lead Poisoning Prevention (G. L. c. 111, §§ 196—198)

- Lien Enforcement Action (G. L. c. 254, § 5; G. L. c. 255, § 26)

- Money Action (under both Tort and Contract) (G. L. c. 231, §§ 103—104)

- Replevin (G. L. c. 247)

- Repossession of Secured Goods (G. L. c. 255, § 13J; G. L. c. 255B, § 20B; G. L. c. 255D, § 22)

- Service in Foreign Proceeding (G. L. c. 223A, § 9)

- Settlement Approval for Personal Injury to Minor/Incompetent (G. L. c. 231, § 140C1/2;)

- Structured Settlement Transfer Approval (G. L. c. 231C, § 2)

- Suit on a Foreign Judgment (G. L. c. 235, §§ 14, 23A; 28 U.S.C. § 1738)

IV. Additional Provisions

A. Limited Assistance Representation. For purposes of the Brighton Pilot Project, Standing Order 1–10 of the Boston Municipal Court Department authorizing Limited Assistance Representation in Civil Matters Only is hereby incorporated by reference where applicable. Because there currently are no filing codes that correspond to Limited Assistance Representation (LAR) in the electronic filing system, an attorney must enter the term "LAR" into either the Filing Description field or the Filing Comment field when electronically filing an LAR Notice of Appearance or LAR Notice of Withdrawal of Appearance.

B. Technical Limitations. In the event certain filing activities cannot be completed by electronic filing because of technical limitations of either the Provider, the Provider's electronic filing system, or the Trial Court's case management system, the Brighton Pilot Project and this Department reserve the right to require a party to submit these documents or requests to the Brighton Division Clerk's Office in the conventional manner, but shall permit said party to electronically file the remainder of his/her civil case pursuant to the Interim Rules. These filing activities may include, but shall not be limited to, a request for a fee waiver/ indigency determination, a request for an interpreter, or a request to purchase miscellaneous copies or forms, or other filing activities as defined/designated by the Brighton Pilot Project or this Department.

V. Duration

The Brighton Pilot Project described herein shall expire one year from the effective date of this Standing Order, and Standing Order 1–15 may be superseded or amended, in writing, at any time during this period.

Adopted November 24, 2015, effective December 4, 2015.

Joint Standing Order 2–15. Verification of Defendant's Address for Claims Incurred in Trade or Commerce or Pursuing Assigned Debt

[Suspended effective January 1, 2019]

This standing order is issued pursuant to the authority of Chief Justices of the Boston Municipal Court and of the District Court under G.L. c. 211B, § 10 and G.L. c. 218, § 43A to address the verification of a defendant's address in civil actions in the regular civil dockets in the Boston Municipal Court and the District Court, in cases in which the plaintiff is pursuing a claim incurred in the course of the plaintiff's trade or commerce, or pursuing a claim for assigned debt. Its purpose is to assure notice to the defendant and to provide the defendant with an opportunity to be heard prior to any default judgment.

1. Definitions. As used in this standing order, the following terms shall have the following meanings: "Assigned debt" shall mean a claim or judgment where the right to collect the debt has been assigned by the creditor to another person or entity. "Trade" and "commerce" shall have the same meaning as in G.L. c. 93A, § 1, but shall not include the lease or rental of residential property that is the plaintiff's primary residence and that consists of three units or less, provided the plaintiff does not own, manage, or have other involvement in the lease or rental of other residential property.

2. Verification of Address. Unless otherwise authorized by the court upon motion, a plaintiff commencing an action in the Boston Municipal Court or the District Court against one or more individual defendants for a claim incurred in the course of plaintiff's trade or commerce, or a claim for assigned debt, shall file along with the complaint a Verification of Defendant's Address (District Court Form file size 1MB Boston Municipal Court Form file size 1MB), certifying that the plaintiff has verified the defendant's residential address in the manner set forth herein. The Verification of Defendant's Address shall be signed by the plaintiff or plaintiff's counsel under the penalties of perjury and upon personal knowledge and state that the defendant's residential address has been verified as follows:

a. by at least one of the following methods:

i. address listed in a municipal record, such as a street list or tax records, verified within twelve months prior to the commencement of the action, with the date of verification;

ii. address listed with the Registry of Motor Vehicles, verified within twelve months prior to the commencement of the action, with the date of verification;

iii. receipt of correspondence from the defendant with that return address within twelve months prior to the commencement of the action, with the date the correspondence was received;

iv. other verification from the defendant within twelve months prior to the commencement of the action that the address is current, followed by a description of such verification; or

b. by at least two of the following methods:

i. a letter having been sent to the defendant at the address by first-class mail on a date within six months prior to the commencement of the action and at least four weeks prior to the commencement of the action, with the letter not having been returned to the sender by the postal service, with a specification of the date of mailing;

ii. using an online database (other than the white pages or other unpaid general telephone directory) within six months prior to the commencement of the action, specifying the name and source of the database;

iii. using an additional source, with an identification of the source.

3. Description of Claim. The following information shall be set forth in the complaint:

(1) the name of the original creditor (if different from plaintiff's);

(2) the nature of any debt claimed (for example, credit card, educational loans, medical debt);

(3) the last four digits of the account number assigned by the original creditor, if any; and

(4) the amount and date of the defendant's last payment, if any.

4. Service of Process. If the summons and complaint are served upon the defendant by leaving copies thereof at the defendant's last and usual place of abode pursuant to Mass. R. Civ. P. 4(d), the place of abode must be the address as verified in section 2, and the return of service shall set forth the address.

5. Service of Other Papers. Except where the defendant has provided an address to the court in the case, if a pleading or other paper is served on a defendant by mailing it to the defendant at the defendant's last known address pursuant to Mass. R. Civ. P. 5(b), the last known address must be the address as verified in section 2, and any certification of service shall set forth the address.

6. Change of Address. If the plaintiff or plaintiff's counsel learns that the defendant has changed address, the plaintiff shall verify same and file a new Verification of Defendant's Address Form.

7. Sanctions. If the plaintiff fails to comply with this order and the defendant does not file an answer or responsive pleading or otherwise appear at trial or other scheduled court events, no default or default judgment shall be entered for the plaintiff, and the complaint may be dismissed by the court without prejudice.

Adopted June 23, 2015, effective October 1, 2015.

Standing Order 2–15. Conditions of Release Pursuant to Rule 5(c) of the District/Municipal Courts Rules for Probation Violation Proceedings

I. Authority

This Standing Order 2–15 is promulgated by the Chief Justice of the Boston Municipal Court Department pursuant to the provisions of G. L. c. 211B, § 10 and G. L. c. 218, § 51A, pursuant to the provisions of Rule 5 (c) of the District/Municipal Courts Rules for Probation Violation Proceedings approved by the Massachusetts Supreme Judicial Court effective September 8, 2015, and approved by the Chief Justice of the Trial Court pursuant to Trial Court Rule V.

II. Purpose and Applicability

In order to advance uniformity and efficiency in the Massachusetts courts and better serve the public and the bar, the Boston Municipal Court and District Court Departments collaborated to develop joint rules for probation violation proceedings. The Supreme Judicial Court has approved the District/Municipal Courts Rules for Probation Violation Proceedings effective September 8, 2015, to supersede District Court Rules for Probation Violation Proceedings and Boston Municipal Court Standing Order 2–04.

Standing Order 2–15 shall incorporate by reference the 2015 District/Municipal Courts Rules for Probation Violation Proceedings, and, pursuant to Rule 5 (c), shall provide for the conditions of release within the Boston Municipal Court Department as described below.

III. Conditions of Release

Rule 5 of the 2015 District/Municipal Courts Rules for Probation Violation Proceedings provides for a probation detention hearing to be conducted to determine whether a probationer shall be held in custody pending the conduct of a probation violation hearing. Pursuant to Rule 5 (c), following a judicial determination that (1) probable cause exists that a probationer has violated a condition of probation, and (2) that the probationer shall be released from custody pending the probation violation hearing, the court, in its discretion, may impose the following condition(s) of release:

(a) In its discretion, the court may order any condition(s) of release it deems necessary and appropriate to ensure the safety of a particular individual or the community, and/or the probationer's presence at the probation violation proceeding.

(b) *Monetary Condition.* The court may condition the probationer's release upon the deposit of a sum of money with the Clerk Magistrate. The amount of money deposited will either be returned after a disposition of the probation violation hearing, or may, upon order of the court, be forfeited in the event the probationer fails to appear at the probation violation hearing. A monetary condition of release shall not be considered bail under G. L. c. 276, § 58.

IV. Additional Provisions

A. Probation Detention Hearing Finding and Order Form. All conditions of release, if any, must be specified in writing on the form prescribed by the departmental Chief Justice, and a copy shall be served in-hand to the probationer at the conclusion of the probation detention hearing.

B. Violation of Condition of Release. If a court or a probation officer has reasonable grounds to believe that a probationer has violated a condition of release, the court or probation officer may summons the probationer for a hearing or, if there is probable cause, the court may issue an arrest warrant. A probation officer, if there is probable cause, may arrest the probationer without a warrant. The court shall then hold a hearing as soon as practicable to determine whether there is probable cause to believe that the probationer has violated a condition of release.

C. Conditions of release imposed under Rule 5 (c) are not conditions of probation. A violation of a condition of release shall not itself be the basis for a finding of a violation of probation, although the judge may consider such violation of a condition of release in determining a proper disposition under Rules 8 (d) and 9 (b) of the 2015 District/Municipal Courts Rules for Probation Violation Proceedings.

Adopted August 20, 2015, effective September 8, 2015.

Joint Standing Order 3–15.　Notice and Docketing of Impounded Materials

This standing order is issued pursuant to the authority of the Chief Justices of the Boston Municipal Court and of the District Court under G.L. c. 211B, § 10; G.L. c. 218, § 43A; and Uniform Rule on Impoundment Procedure 13(b) of Trial Court VIII to regulate clerk records of impounded materials in the Boston Municipal Court and District Court pursuant to Uniform Rule on Impoundment Procedure 13. The requirement in Rule 13(b) that the filer of a document containing impounded information file a separate notice notifying the clerk of the impounded material is intended to "enable[] the clerk and court staff to properly identify and set aside protected material." Committee Notes. Accordingly, the application of this requirement should be waived where the nature of the material impounded renders a separate notice not useful to the clerk.

1. **Purpose and applicability.** To advance efficiency in the Boston Municipal Court and the District Court and to better serve the public and the bar, this standing order shall provide for exceptions to the notice of impounded filing requirements contained in Uniform Rule on Impoundment Procedure 13.

2. **Exempted documents.** The notice provisions contained in Uniform Rule on Impoundment Procedure 13(b) shall not apply to the following:

　　a.　Affidavit of indigency

　　b.　Allegation of domestic abuse under G.L. c. 276, § 56A

　　c.　Search warrant applications and supporting documents impounded pursuant to Rule on Impoundment Procedure 3(e)(1)

　　d.　Plaintiff's residential address, residential telephone number, workplace name, workplace address, and workplace telephone number in abuse prevention and harassment prevention proceedings, see G.L. c. 209A, § 8; G.L. c. 258E, § 10

　　e.　All reports, petitions, and other documents filed pursuant to and as provided in G.L. c. 123, including but not limited to mental health and substance abuse reports, petitions, and dockets.

　　f.　Financial statement of judgment debtor

　　g.　Name of the victim in investigations or prosecutions for sexual assault offenses listed in G.L. c. 265, § 24B

　　h.　All documents in cases that are or have been impounded in their entirety

　　i.　All other documents that are impounded in their entirety by statute, court rule, standing order, or case law.

Adopted effective October 1, 2015.

Joint Standing Order 1–16.　Authority of the Judge with Respect to Communication with Specialty Court Teams

This Standing Order is promulgated by the chief Justice of the Trial Court pursuant to G. L, c. 211B, Section 9 and shall constitute authorization by law as referenced in Rule 2.9 (A)(2) of the Code of Judicial Conduct (effective January 1, 2016).

For purposes of this Order:

Specialty Court means a specifically designated court session that focuses on individuals with underlying medical, mental health, substance abuse, or other issues that contribute to the reasons such individuals are before the courts. Specialty court shall also mean Veterans Treatment Court and Homelessness Court. Specialty court sessions integrate treatment and services with judicial case oversight and intensive court supervision. Examples Include drug courts, mental health courts, veterans' courts, and tenancy preservation programs.

A Staffing shall refer to a regularly scheduled, informal conference not occurring in open court, the purpose of which is to permit the presiding judge and others, including counsel, to discuss a participant's progress in the specialty court, treatment recommendations, or responses to participant compliance issues.

IT IS THEREFORE ORDERED:

A judge presiding over a specialty court shall have the authority to initiate, permit or otherwise consider ex parte communications about defendants, juveniles or probationers with members of the specialty court team at a staffing or by written documents provided to all members of the specialty court team, The purpose of this authority is to allow judges in their role in presiding over specialty court sessions, and only in that capacity, to assume a more interactive role with parties, treatment providers, probation officers, social workers and others, than Rule 2.9 of the Code of Judicial Conduct would otherwise permit.

Adopted effective January 7, 2016.

Joint Standing Order 2–16.　Uniform Interdepartmental Procedures for Probation Violation Proceedings

This Standing Order is promulgated by the Chief Justice of the Trial Court pursuant to G. L, c. 211B, Section 9 and stands effective October 3, 2016.

1. Application

This Order shall apply to the Superior Court, District Court, Boston Municipal Court and Juvenile Court Departments.

2. Purpose

This Order sets forth requirements regarding communication among the above-named departments of the Trial Court when an individual who is the subject of a probation order in one of these departments is charged with a new offense in another of these departments. Its purpose is to ensure that this required interdepartmental communication relating to the commencement of probation violation proceedings as a result of alleged new criminal behavior by a probationer, and the potential custody and transport of that probationer between different court departments, occur in a timely, informed and efficient manner. This Order does not apply to an individual who is the subject of a probation order issued prior to a trial or the formal submission and acceptance of a plea of guilty or an admission to sufficient facts, as provided in G.L. c. 276, § 87 ("pretrial probation").

3. Definition of Terms

As used in this Order, the terms below shall have the following meanings:

"Criminal:" includes delinquency or youthful offender.

"Criminal Court:" a court division of the Boston Municipal, District, or Juvenile Court or the Superior Court.

The terms used in this Order and the form promulgated by the Chief Justice of the Trial Court pursuant to Section 9 have been defined to include terminology associated with juvenile cases and proceedings and the Juvenile Court. They have been defined in this manner for the purposes of convenience and ease of reading and are applicable to this Order and form only. The terms as appearing in this Order and form do not change the meaning of the terminology used in adult and juvenile proceedings as defined and set forth by case law and statutes. Other than for the purposes of this Order and form, adult and juvenile terms are not interchangeable.

4. Intra-Departmental Communications

This Order does not apply to intra-departmental communications, transport of probationers, or use of the warrant management system, which may be the subject of rules or standing orders issued by and applicable within individual court departments.

5. Information to be Sent from the Criminal Court; Custody of Probationer

When an individual appears on a new criminal charge before a criminal court, and that individual is the subject of a probation order issued by a court in a different department of the Trial Court, the probation department of the criminal court shall transmit to the probation department of the court having responsibility for the supervision of the probationer (the "probation court") information and requests for information, including information regarding the possible service of a notice of violation on, and transport of, the probationer. This transmission shall be made by means of the form referred to in Section 9, below.

The transmission from the criminal court shall be sent electronically and promptly, to the probation officer in the probation court listed as the probation officer on duty in the probation court or, if there is no probation officer on duty, to the Chief Probation Officer of the probation court. The transmission shall be sent while the probationer is at the criminal court. When necessary, the criminal court may order the probationer held in custody until the procedures required by this Order are completed.

6. Information to be Returned by the Probation Court; Time Limit

The probation department of the probation court shall respond electronically, to the probation officer who transmitted the request for information from the criminal court. The response shall include information regarding service of a notice of violation on, and transport of, the probationer. This response shall be transmitted within two hours or within such time limit as extended, as provided in Section 7, such time limit to be measured from the time indicated on the transmission, and shall be set forth on the form referred to in Section 9, below.

If the probation department is requesting that the probationer be transported, the probation department shall request the issuance of an arrest warrant for a violation of probation ("warrant") from a judge in the probation court. If the judge issues such warrant, the clerk's office shall enter it promptly into the Warrant Management System and the probation department shall provide the criminal court with a notice of violation that cites the violation(s).

If the probation department is not requesting that the probationer be transported and is requesting that the probationer be served with a notice of violation, the probation department shall provide the probation department of the criminal court with a notice of violation that cites the violation(s) and indicates the date and time of the probationer's required appearance in the probation court.

7. Action by the Criminal Court

The criminal court shall await receipt of the information from the probation court for a period of two hours measured from the time of the transmission of the request for that information. This two-hour time limit may be extended by the criminal court.

Upon the timely receipt of the required information from the probation court and, if the probation court has issued a warrant, the criminal court shall serve on the probationer, in hand, a notice of violation on behalf of the probation court and shall either order transport of the probationer on such warrant or defer transport on the warrant until the termination of any custody ordered by the criminal court judge in the new criminal case. In the event that no warrant has been issued by the probation court, and the probation department has provided a notice of violation to the probation department of the criminal court, the criminal court shall serve such notice on the probationer, in hand, on behalf of the probation court.

If the probation department of the probation court does not provide the required information or a notice of violation to the probation department of the criminal court in the manner set forth in Section 6, the criminal court need not take any further action regarding the probation matter. In such instances, the probation department of the criminal court shall make an appropriate entry into its records.

8. Action by the Probation Court

Upon delivery of the probationer into the custody of the probation court on the warrant, and not withstanding any provision of this Order, the form promulgated pursuant to section 9, or the reason for the warrant as it may appear in the Warrant Management System, the probation court shall proceed on the violation of probation matter in accordance with applicable law and respective departmental rule or standing order.

9. Form to be Promulgated by the Chief Justice of the Trial Court

The transmittal of information between courts as required by this Order shall proceed by means of a form promulgated by the Chief Justice of the Trial Court. This form shall include such specific information requirements, data elements and attachments as the Chief Justice may deem appropriate, provided that nothing in this Order shall be construed to prohibit the use of telephone communication to supplement the use of such form and to achieve its purpose.

10. Probation Department Procedures and Record Keeping

Implementation of this Order by the Massachusetts Probation Service, including record keeping requirements, shall be as set forth in such instructions and regulations consistent with the provisions of this Order as may be deemed appropriate by the Commissioner of Probation.

Adopted August 18, 2016, effective October 3, 2016.

Standing Order 1–17. Pilot Initiative Pursuant to G. L. c. 123, § 35 and Uniform Trial Court Rules for Civil Commitment Proceedings for Alcohol and Substance Use Disorders

I. Authority

This Standing Order is promulgated by the Chief Justice of the Boston Municipal Court Department pursuant to G. L. c. 211B, § 10 and G. L. c. 218, § 51A.

II. Purpose and Applicability

The opioid epidemic has created a public health crisis that has resulted in all branches of government devoting greater efforts and increased resources to combat this crisis, including the Trial Court, which promulgated the Uniform Trial Court Rules for Civil Commitment Proceedings for Alcohol and Substance Use Disorders G. L. c. 123 § 35, effective September 6, 2016 ("Uniform Commitment Rules"). In recognition of this valuable tool, and in an effort to alleviate the burden and time constraints faced by police officers and physicians seeking to petition for an order of commitment, the Boston Municipal Court Department has promulgated Standing Order 1–17 for a one year pilot initiative in the West Roxbury Division, establishing the procedures to be followed by a police officer or physician seeking to file a petition for an order of civil commitment without having to appear in person as permitted by statute and rule.

III. Required Procedures and Forms

A. Venue. G. L. c. 123, § 35, amended effective April 24, 2016, permits any qualified petitioner to petition in writing any district court [1] for an order of commitment, and Uniform Commitment Rules 1(b) specifically provides that "[p]roceedings may be commenced in any Division of any of the three Departments [District Court, Boston Municipal Court, and Juvenile Court Departments] without regard to the age, residence, or location of the respondent, ..." Therefore, any police officer or physician may file a petition for an order of commitment in the West Roxbury Division regardless of the location of the hospital or the age or location of the patient or person in need.

B. Petitioner. As used in this Standing Order, and solely for purposes of this one year pilot initiative, the term "petitioner" shall apply only to a police officer or physician as provided for in G. L. c. 123, § 35, third par. [2] and Uniform Commitment Rule 1(a).

C. Required Forms/Documents. Although the statute and rules do not require a petitioner to appear at the courthouse to file a petition seeking the issuance of an order of commitment of a respondent, to ensure that the Court has sufficient information to make the necessary determinations, in order to file a petition pursuant to this Standing Order, a police officer or physician shall submit the following completed forms [3] to the Clerk's Office of the West Roxbury Division:

(1) Petition for Commitment for Alcohol or Substance Use Disorder;

(2) Respondent Information Form as Provided by Petitioner; and

(3) Petitioner's Supplemental Information Affidavit (attached hereto) https://www.mass.gov/files/documents/2017/04/zp/petitioner-supplemental-information-affidavit.pdf.

D. Respondent Information Form. To the extent possible, the petitioner should provide the specific location where the person/respondent may be found in the event the Court issues a warrant of apprehension, and should include the full name, date of birth or approximate age, and last known address of the person/respondent.

E. Petitioner's Supplemental Information Affidavit. The petitioner is required to provide specific information or data regarding the likelihood of serious harm to the person/respondent by reason of alcohol or substance use disorder. The petitioner should also include information of said person's/respondent's history of harmful behaviors, including overdoses, recent hospitalizations, diagnoses, lab results, and medications.

When the person/respondent is a patient in a medical hospital, a physician shall also include the reasons why the medical hospital is unable to meet the patient's treatment needs, as well as a statement that the patient is detoxed and medically stable for discharge from the hospital.

When the person/respondent is a patient in a psychiatric hospital, a physician shall include the person's/respondent's history of harmful behaviors, including overdoses, recent hospitalizations, diagnoses, lab results, and medications, along with the admission and discharge notes, as well as a statement that the person is psychiatrically stable for discharge.

If applicable, this form must also include a written statement of facts supporting the reasons why the petitioner believes that the person/respondent will not appear if a summons were to issue for a later date and why any further delay in the proceedings would present an immediate danger to the physical well-being of the person/respondent or to other members of the community.

F. Submission of Completed Forms. Once the required forms are completed, and signed and dated as necessary, the forms shall be faxed to Clerk-Magistrate Sean P. Murphy, Clerk's Office, West Roxbury Division at (617) 983-0243.

G. Court Review; Dismissal; Summons; Warrant. Upon receipt of the completed forms, the Clerk-Magistrate shall expeditiously present the matter to a judge "who shall review the petition on the record in court." Uniform Commitment Rule 2. Upon review, the judge may dismiss petition, or determine whether to issue a summons or a warrant of apprehension. Uniform Commitment Rules 2 and 3 and G. L. c. 123, § 35, third par. If the judge determines there are reasonable grounds to believe that the person/respondent will not appear at the hearing provided below and that any further delay in the proceedings would present an immediate danger to the physical well-being of the person/respondent, the Court will issue a warrant for the person's/respondent's apprehension and appearance in Court. Uniform Commitment Rule 3 and G. L. c. 123, § 35, third par. The petitioner will be notified by the Clerk-Magistrate of the Court's decision.

H. Appointment of Counsel; Examination; Hearing. After the person/respondent is detained and brought to the Court, an attorney shall be appointed to represent the respondent and the court clinician or other qualified physician, psychologist or social worker will conduct an assessment. See G. L. c. 123, § 35, third par. and Uniform Commitment Rules 4 and 5. A judge shall then conduct a hearing to determine whether there is clear and convincing evidence that the person/respondent is an individual with an alcohol or substance use disorder and there is a likelihood of serious harm to the respondent, petitioner, or any other person as a result of the respondent's alcohol or substance use disorder. Uniform Commitment Rule 6(a) and G. L. c. 123, § 35, fourth par. In some limited circumstances, the presence of the petitioner may be necessary at this hearing. See Uniform Commitment Rule 6(b). The police officer or physician will be notified by the Clerk-Magistrate if his/her presence is necessary at this hearing.

I. Duration. This pilot initiative in the West Roxbury Division shall expire one year from the effective date set forth below.

Adopted April 10, 2017, effective May 1, 2017.

1 Although the Boston Municipal Court Department is not explicitly named in G. L. c. 123, § 35, the reference in this statute to "any district court" would also include any division of the BMCD by statutory construction as set forth in G. L. c. 4, § 7 (1) clause Seventh, which provides " 'District', when applied to courts or the justices or other officials thereof, shall include municipal."

2 Although the amendment to G. L. c. 123, § 35 effective April 24, 2016 essentially deleted the second paragraph, the paragraph references used in the statute prior to the amendment were retained in the amended statute and are cited accordingly.

3 The Petition for Commitment form and Respondent Information Form are available on the Boston Municipal Court Department's website at http://mass.gov/courts/forms. The Petitioner's Supplemental Information Affidavit is promulgated specifically for use in the pilot initiative established by this Standing Order and is attached hereto: https://www.mass.gov/files/documents/2017/04/zp/petitioner-supplemental-information-affidavit.pdf.

| PETITIONER'S SUPPLEMENTAL INFORMATION AFFIDAVIT pursuant to G. L. c. 123, § 35 Page 1 of 2 | COURT DEPARTMENT Boston Municipal Court COURT DIVISION West Roxbury | TRIAL COURT OF MASSACHUSETTS |

As a qualified Petitioner pursuant to G. L. c. 123, § 35, and as required pursuant to BMCD Standing Order 1-17, I hereby submit this Supplemental Information Affidavit together with the Petition and Respondent Information Form requesting an order of commitment for the following Respondent/Patient.

DATE:

Name of Petitioner: | Police District:

Contact Number* (cell phone or pager): | Hospital:

* Although your physical presence at the preliminary hearing for the issuance of the warrant of apprehension and subsequent hearing is not required, the clinician and court may need to contact you for additional information.

Name of Respondent/Patient: | Date of Birth, if known, or Approximate Age

Last Known Address or Whereabouts: | Telephone Number

City/Town | State | Zip Code

How long have you known the person? Describe the nature of your relationship, the frequency of your interactions, and any behaviors you have observed that cause you concern for the health and welfare of the person.

_____

_____

_____

_____

REASON(S) FOR THE PETITION (please check all that apply and provide specific details):

☐ Likelihood of serious harm to this person or harm to others within the community due to his/her use of drugs and/or alcohol. Please provide a detailed explanation below.

_____

_____

_____

_____

☐ Person needs emergency care and treatment due to the following recent event(s) as explained below.

☐ Overdose   ☐ Self-destructive behavior   ☐ Criminal activity   ☐ Hospitalization   ☐ Other

_____

_____

_____

_____

[Petitioner's Supplemental Information Affidavit G. L. c. 123, § 35 (BMCD 04-10-17 ly)]

PETITIONER'S SUPPLEMENTAL INFORMATION AFFIDAVIT pursuant to G. L. c. 123, § 35 Page 2 of 2	COURT DEPARTMENT Boston Municipal Court COURT DIVISION West Roxbury	TRIAL COURT OF MASSACHUSETTS

DATE:

Name of Petitioner:

Name of Respondent/Patient: Date of Birth, if known, or Approximate Age

☐ Prior suicide attempts or a history of mental health commitments or treatment. Please provide a detailed explanation including when, where, and how recently.

☐ Person has a history of violence or threats to commit violence. Please provide a detailed explanation below.

☐ Drugs and/or alcohol are contributing factors. Please provide a detailed explanation below.

☐ Person's use of drugs and/or alcohol present a substantial threat to the public safety and the community where he/she resides. Please provide a detailed explanation.

Please attach any police reports, medical reports or other documentation concerning the respondent/patient that will assist the court in determining whether the respondent/patient is an individual with an alcohol or substance use disorder, whether the respondent/patient needs emergency hospitalization and treatment, and whether there is a likelihood of serious harm to respondent, petitioner or any other person. **After printing and signing this form, please fax this form with all attachments, along with the Petition and Respondent Information Form, to Office of Clerk-Magistrate, Attention: Clerk-Magistrate Sean Murphy, at Fax No. (617) 983-0243.**

SIGNED UNDER THE PAINS AND PENALTIES OF PERJURY,

SIGNATURE

X_____

Printed or Typed Name:

[Petitioner's Supplemental Information Affidavit G. L. c. 123, § 35 (BMCD 04-10-17 ly)]

Standing Order 1–18. Voir Dire Protocol

Preamble

Subject to applicable statutes, rules, and controlling authority, the trial judge in each civil or criminal jury case has discretion to allow for a procedure for examining and selecting jurors designed to maintain juror privacy and dignity, identify explicit and implicit bias, and foster efficiency in our jury sessions and among sessions using the same jury pool. If allowed by the trial judge, this rule provides a uniform procedure for each civil and criminal case unless otherwise ordered by the trial judge, while permitting attorneys and self-represented parties a fair opportunity to participate in voir dire so as to identify inappropriate bias.

1. Requests for Attorney or Party Voir Dire. In civil and criminal cases, the parties shall submit in writing any requests for attorney/party voir dire; motions in limine concerning the method of jury selection; proposed subject matters or questions for inquiry by the parties or judge; any proposed preliminary legal instructions to the venire or juror panels; the location within the courtroom where jurors and parties will stand or sit during voir dire; and any other matter setting forth the party's position regarding impanelment.

In a civil case, all voir dire related requests shall be filed no later than at the final pretrial conference scheduled pursuant to Joint Standing Order 1–04, Civil Case Management, as may be amended from time to time.

In a criminal case, all voir dire related requests shall be filed by a date set by the Court, but not later than five (5) business days before trial.

A judge may order, or an attorney or party may request, a hearing in advance of the trial date. The attorney or party shall request such a hearing in time for a pre-trial ruling by the trial judge if the attorney or party is requesting extensive participation in voir dire (e.g., panel voir dire or to be allowed to ask a substantial number of questions).

Upon hearing any written request for attorney/party voir dire, consideration should be given to procedural issues including:

    a. a statement of the case to be read to the venire;

    b. the number of jurors to be seated;

    c. the extent of any pre-charge jury instructions on significant legal principles;

    d. the method and content of the judge's intended voir dire of jurors;

    e. the method and content of any attorney or party participation in voir dire;

    f. judicial approval or disapproval of proposed questions or subject matter;

    g. any time limits on attorney or party voir dire;

    h. the number of peremptories;

    i. the order and timing of the parties' assertions of challenges for cause and peremptory challenges;

    j. any agreement to allow deliberation by fewer jurors in a civil case if seated jurors are dismissed post-impanelment.

2. Scope and Subject Matter of Permissible Attorney or Party Voir Dire.

A. *General Matters.* The trial judge may allow attorney or party voir dire if properly requested according to the time as set forth in Section 1 above. The trial judge has discretion regarding the scope and manner of voir dire.

If allowed by the judge:

1. The judge should, at a minimum, allow reasonable questions seeking elaboration or explanation concerning juror responses.

2. A trial judge should allow a reasonable number of questions that: (i) seek factual information about the prospective juror's background and experience pertinent to the issues expected to arise in the case; (ii) may reveal preconceptions or biases relating to the identity of the parties or the nature of the claims or issues expected to arise in the case; (iii) inquire into the prospective jurors' willingness and ability to accept and apply pertinent legal principles as instructed; (iv) are meant to elicit information on subjects that controlling authority has identified as preferred subjects of inquiry, even if not absolutely required; and (v) are proportional in quantity to the anticipated length and complexity of the trial.

3. A trial judge may impose reasonable restrictions on the subject matter, time, number of questions, or method of attorney or party voir dire. The judge may utilize individual voir dire, panel voir dire, or any combination of the two. If employing panel voir dire, the trial judge shall determine

the procedure and may elect to follow the method set forth in Addendum A or adopt variations thereof. (Addendum A)

4. A party objecting to a question posed by another party shall state, "objection," without elaboration or argument. The judge may rule on the objection in, or outside of, the juror's presence. The trial judge may *sua sponte* strike or rephrase a party's question. The judge may interrupt or supplement a party's questioning to provide the juror(s) with an explanation of the law or the jury trial process. The judge may ask additional questions to assist in the determination of a juror's impartiality.

5. An attorney or party may ask questions about the law if approved by the trial judge. The judge may require the questioner to use specific words or phrases and may give an instruction on the law beforehand or at the time the question is asked. If a juror asks a question to clarify an aspect of the law, the questioner shall defer to the judge to answer the question.

6. If intending to challenge a juror for cause as a result of attorney or party voir dire, the questioner ordinarily should lay an adequate foundation showing that, in light of the information or viewpoint expressed, the juror may not be fair and impartial and decide the case solely on the facts and law presented at trial. A juror's "yes" or "no" answer to a question about a viewpoint or experience may not, by itself, support a challenge for cause. An attorney or party challenging a juror for cause shall state the reason and the court may inquire further, or may decide without further questioning if the judge believes that the existing record is sufficient to resolve the challenge for cause.

B. *Prohibited and Disfavored Subjects.*

1. No attorney or party may inquire into the following prohibited subjects:

    a. questions framed in terms of how the juror would decide the outcome of the case (prejudgment), including hypotheticals that are close/specific to the facts of the case (any hypotheticals that may trigger this rule must be presented to the judge before trial);

    b. questions that seek to commit juror(s) to a result, including, without limitation, questions about what evidence would cause the juror(s) to find for the attorney's client or the party;

    c. questions having no substantial purpose other than to argue an attorney's or party's case or indoctrinate any juror(s);

    d. questions about the outcome in prior cases where the person has served as a juror, including the prior vote(s) of the juror or the verdict of the entire jury;

    e. questions in the presence of other jurors that specifically reference what is written on a particular juror's confidential juror questionnaire.

2. No attorney or party may inquire into any of the following disfavored subjects absent the trial judge's prior express approval:

    a. the juror's political views, voting patterns or party preferences;

    b. the juror's religious beliefs or affiliation.

To obtain approval, an attorney or party must at a minimum explain how the inquiry is relevant to the issues, may affect a juror's impartiality, or may assist the proper exercise of peremptory challenges.

C. *Procedural Matters.*

1. Mandatory Voir Dire. The trial judge shall ask all voir dire questions specifically required by statute, court rule, or controlling authority, but retains discretion as to when and how to do so.

2. Individual Voir Dire.

a. Questioning shall occur through individual voir dire if: (i) required by statute, rule, or controlling authority; (ii) inquiry concerns private or potentially embarrassing information; or (iii) questioning would specifically reference what is written on a particular juror's confidential juror questionnaire.

b. The trial judge should conduct an individual voir dire in all cases to: (i) determine whether any juror has any issues concerning hearing, vision, language, mental health, or comprehension, and to determine whether a reasonable accommodation can enable a juror to serve; (ii) address any private or embarrassing information not disclosed in public portions of the voir dire; or (iii) identify any other impediment to jury service that the trial judge and parties might not observe without personal contact with the juror.

3. Timing of Challenges. After the trial judge finds that each juror stands indifferent, the parties shall exercise their peremptory challenges. The judge may require exercise of peremptory challenges after filling the jury box with jurors found to stand indifferent, after completion of side bar inquiry of an individual juror, or at some other time after the judge's finding of indifference.

4. Maintaining the Record. Counsel and the parties must ensure an accurate record of attorney or party voir dire. During panel voir dire, an attorney or a party must refer to the juror seat number (or juror number) of any individual juror who is questioned individually or who responds audibly. Failure to do so may constitute a waiver of any claim of error arising from any inaudible or unattributed portions of the record.

ADDENDUM A TO BOSTON MUNICIPAL COURT DEPARTMENT STANDING ORDER 1–18 PANEL VOIR DIRE

1. **Pretrial Procedure.** Any attorney or self-represented party who requests panel voir dire shall serve and file a motion requesting leave to do so in accordance with Boston Municipal Court Department Standing Order 1–18: Panel Voir Dire. The motion shall identify the general areas of panel inquiry by topic, recognizing some topics must be raised with each juror individually.[1] The trial judge may, in the exercise of discretion, require attorneys and self-represented parties to submit the specific language of the proposed questions for pre-approval. The motion and any responsive filing shall also include a concise description of the case, along with any proposed language for brief preliminary instructions on principles of law to be given pursuant to paragraph 2(b) below.

The trial judge should inform the parties of any reasonable time limit the trial judge has set for examination of each panel of prospective jurors by attorneys or self-represented parties, giving due regard to (a) the objective of identifying inappropriate bias in fairness to all parties; (b) the interests of the public and of the parties in reasonable expedition, in proportion to the nature and seriousness of the case and the extent of the anticipated evidence; and (c) the needs of cases scheduled in other sessions drawing on the same jury pool for access to prospective jurors.

2. **Venire Examination.** Before any questioning of a juror panel by attorneys or self-represented parties, or at such other time as the trial judge deems most appropriate, the trial judge should:

(a) provide the venire with a brief description of the case, including the nature of the facts alleged and of the claims or charges;

(b) provide the venire with brief, preliminary instructions on significant legal principles pertinent to the case. Such instructions should include a brief recitation of the burden and standard of proof, the elements of at least the primary civil claim or at least the most serious criminal charge, if appropriate to the case and requested by counsel or a self-represented party, the elements of any affirmative defense that will be presented to the jury, and, in criminal cases, the defendant's right not to testify or to present any evidence;

(c) explain the empanelment process and inform the jurors that any juror who finds either a particular question or the process of questioning by attorneys or self-represented parties intrusive on the juror's privacy may request that steps be taken to protect the privacy of any information disclosed;

(d) ask all questions required by statute or case law and any additional questions the trial judge deems appropriate in light of the nature of the case and the issues expected to be raised; and

(e) conduct individual voir dire of those jurors who will be part of the panel voir dire. The trial judge should then hear challenges for cause based upon the initial questioning of the venire and individual voir dire.

3. **Panel Examination.** After the initial questions are asked, and individual voir dire is conducted, the judge shall seat the jurors found preliminarily indifferent as a panel. There are various versions of panel voir dire that may be employed by the Boston Municipal Court Department. The judge may employ multiple panels or a single panel depending upon recording capabilities, the size and physical layout of a courtroom, jury box, or jury venire, and the number of court officers. If more than one panel is used, the judge should consider whether the jurors who remain qualified should be temporarily excused from the courtroom while the next panel is seated and questioned.

(a) The parties shall then proceed with questioning the panel. Parties with the burden of proof shall conduct their questioning first. In cases with multiple parties on a side, the parties on each side shall agree as to an order in which to proceed. In the absence of agreement, the judge shall assign an order. The attorney or party may pose questions to the entire panel or to individual members.

(b) Throughout the proceedings, attorneys and self-represented parties at the trial are responsible for correcting any misstatement as to juror numbers and seat numbers being read for the record.

(c) If the trial judge has not already done so, he or she shall remind the jurors that during such questioning a juror may request to respond to a question outside the presence of other jurors.

(d) The trial judge and the attorneys participating shall at all times during panel questioning take reasonable steps to ensure that the identity of each juror speaking is adequately maintained on the record, by reference to juror number or seat number. In particular:

    i. In an electronically recorded courtroom, the attorney or party shall stand near a microphone; and

    ii. When posing questions to, or receiving a response from, any specific juror(s), the attorney or party must identify each such juror(s) by juror seat number (or, less ideally, by juror number). They shall not refer to any juror by name.

(e) The trial judge may intervene at any time to ensure an accurate record (including recording of seat numbers of jurors who respond to questions), to clarify or instruct on a point of law, or to ensure that panel voir dire proceeds in an orderly, fair, and efficient manner.

(f) The trial judge may at any time bring an individual juror to sidebar for questioning out of the hearing of other jurors about any potential bias revealed by panel questioning. If a juror is brought to sidebar, the judge may direct all other parties to do their own questioning on the same subject matter at that time to avoid a need to return to sidebar for later questioning on that subject matter. If the juror's responses to such questioning at sidebar result in a challenge for cause, the judge may rule on the challenge at that time or at the conclusion of all panel questioning. If time limits on panel questioning have been set, the judge may decide whether to exclude all or part of the time spent at side bar from the questioning party's time.

(g) Any party may object to a question posed by another party by stating "objection," without elaboration or argument. The judge may rule on the objection in the presence of the juror or jurors, or may hear argument and rule on the objection outside the presence or hearing of the juror or jurors.

(h) Unless the judge specifically allows, there shall be no follow-up questioning of a panel by attorneys or self-represented parties once each has taken his or her turn.

4. Challenges for Cause and Peremptories.

(a) After panel examination by all parties, the trial judge shall hear any further challenges for cause as to any panel members at sidebar.

(b) Unless the trial judge decides to postpone exercise of peremptories until after voir dire of additional panels, the parties shall then exercise at sidebar any peremptory challenges they have as to any jurors remaining on the panel. The party with the burden shall proceed first, using all peremptories the party seeks to use with that panel. All other parties shall then proceed, using all peremptories each seeks to use with that panel. In civil cases, the judge may alternate sides. The jurors remaining after challenge may then be directed to a separate location, possibly outside the courtroom.

(c) Upon any challenge for cause, the judge may ask additional questions, with or without further instructions on the law, and may allow opposing counsel further opportunity to question the juror.

5. Additional Panels of Jurors.

The same procedures shall apply for all subsequent panels required to seat a full jury, except:

(a) the judge may seat a different number of jurors in a subsequent panel;

(b) the judge may allow a different amount of time for attorney or party voir dire of second and subsequent panels;

(c) if, after the final panel, more than the necessary number of jurors have been declared indifferent and remain unchallenged at the conclusion of those procedures, the jurors shall be seated for trial in the order in which they were originally seated for panel questioning, and the remaining jurors shall be excused; and

(d) the judge has discretion to vary panel voir dire procedures after the first panel in any lawful manner the judge deems fair and efficient.

Adopted effective November 20, 2018.

1 Individual voir dire is required in cases involving alleged sexual assault of a minor, lack of criminal responsibility defense, and certain cases involving interracial violence. See District Court model jury instruction 1.100 fn 2.

RULES OF THE WESTERN DIVISION OF THE HOUSING COURT DEPARTMENT

Publisher's Note

The Rules of the Western Division of the Housing Court Department were promulgated in 1974, which pre-dates the enactment of G.L. c. 185C establishing the Housing Court Department in its present form. See St.1978, c. 478, § 92. As a result of the 1978 legislation, the Rules of the Western Division of the Housing Court Department have been repealed.

HOUSING COURT DEPARTMENT
SUMMARY PROCESS ACTION FORMS

Publisher's Note

Massachusetts Housing Court Forms may be found on the Official Website of the Massachusetts Judicial Branch: http://www.mass.gov/courts/forms/.

STANDING ORDERS OF THE HOUSING COURT

Table of Standing Orders

Standing Order 1–83. Filing Briefs On Motions for Further Answers

It is ORDERED BY THE COURT that the moving party shall file a supporting brief by a minimum of three days prior to any hearing on a motion for further answers to interrogatories. Such brief, relating to interrogatories, shall set forth the nature of the case, the interrogatory, the answer thereto, and a concise statement of the *reasons* for the motion.

This Order shall remain in effect until further Order of the Court.

Adopted December 1, 1983.

Standing Order 1–96. Filing Written Discovery Materials in Civil Cases

Counsel are reminded that the 1989 amendments to Mass. R.Civ.P. 5(d)(2) provide that written discovery materials should be served but not filed.

The rule expressly mentions deposition notices, transcripts, document requests, and documents produced under Rule 34.

This court construes Mass.R.Civ.P. 5(d)(2) to dispense with the need to file any written discovery materials in civil cases, unless and until, and then only to the extent that there is a need to do so.

Therefore, the following materials need not be filed when served, but may be referred to by affidavit, or exhibited, as appropriate, to discovery motions and to re-applications for final judgment under Rule 33(a):

R. 29	discovery stipulations
R. 30	deposition notices deposition transcripts and exhibits
R. 30A	audio-visual stipulations audio-visual recordings
R. 31	depositions on written questions
R. 33	written interrogatories

	answers and objections initial applications for judgment
R. 34	document requests documents produced responses and objections
R. 34	requests to inspect responses and objections
R. 35	requests to examine responses and objections examination reports
R. 36	requests to admit responses and objections
R. 45	witness subpoenas

It should be observed that discovery materials, especially those that are not expressly mentioned in Mass.R.Civ.P. 5(d)(2) will not be rejected for filing, only that the need to file such materials will be dispensed with and indefinitely postponed until the need to file arises.

It should also be observed that because of the automatic rescheduling requirements of Uniform Summary Process Rule 7, discovery requests in summary process cases should continue to be filed when served.

The cooperation of the bar in minimizing the time and expense for clerical filing in this court is greatly appreciated.

Adopted effective June 1, 1996.

Standing Order 1–01. [Lawyer For a Day Program]

A Lawyer for a Day Program ("LDP") is a program in which attorneys, acting pro bono, provide limited legal advice to pro se litigants in the Housing Court on a first-come, first-served basis. It is hereby ORDERED that LDP programs shall be permitted in any Housing Court under the following guidelines:

1. The LDP shall be sponsored and administered by a state or local bar association or legal services organization, in conjunction with the Housing Court.

2. The LDP shall provide advice to *all pro se litigants* in the Housing Court, *tenant or landlord*, on a first-come, first-served basis.

3. Attorneys participating in the LDP shall follow all applicable guidelines and provisions of the Massachusetts Rules of Professional Conduct.

4. No attorney providing advice to a pro se litigant as part of the LDP shall, by reason of providing that advice, be required to enter an appearance in any action in the Housing Court.

5. Attorneys participating in the LDP shall be permitted to assist or represent pro se litigants in mediation in connection with an action in the Housing Court. No attorney assisting or representing a pro se litigant in such mediation as part of the LDP shall, by reason of such assistance or representation, be required to enter an appearance in any action in the Housing Court. If the LDP attorney assisting or representing a pro se litigant in mediation does not enter an appearance in that litigant's action, the LDP attorney may assist the litigant in preparing a Motion for Continuance of Trial. Such a motion shall be allowed if good cause is shown. If the LDP attorney assisting or representing a pro se litigant in mediation does enter an appearance in that litigant's action, the litigant shall be entitled to a two (2) week continuance of trial.

Adopted effective September 10, 2001.

Standing Order 1–04.   Time Standards for Cases Filed in the Housing Court Department

I. ADOPTION OF STANDING ORDER

The Housing Court Department recognizes that the fair and efficient administration of justice requires that all cases that come before the Housing Court receive the timely attention necessary to secure a just and expeditious determination of each claim. It is for this reason that these time standards have been promulgated as a standing order of the Housing Court. [1]

Each case is unique and each judge and clerk-magistrate (as to cases over which the clerk-magistrate presides) must, consistent with applicable statutes and the rules of court, exercise sound judgment in a manner that affords the parties a fair opportunity to develop and present their claims to the court. These time standards preserve some discretion for judges to schedule individual cases according to the particular needs of the parties or the public. The Court shall continue to support and encourage the use of mediation and other Alternative Dispute Resolution programs whenever appropriate.

ACCORDINGLY:

1. The Housing Court Department hereby adopts these time standards and case management procedures as **Housing Court Standing Order No. 1–04.**

2. This Standing Order applies to all actions filed in the Housing Court.

3. This Standing Order applies to all divisions of the Housing Court.

4. The provisions of **Housing Court Standing Order No. 1–04** shall supercede rules promulgated by any Housing Court Division to the extent such rules differ from or are inconsistent with **Standing Order No. 1–04.**

5. The timing for the completion of the case, from filing to trial, settlement, or dismissal, shall be calculated from the date of filing the application or Complaint.

II. AUTHORITY

This standing order is promulgated by the Chief Justice of the Housing Court Department pursuant to his statutory authority and responsibility for case flow management. G.L. c. 211B, § 10 and G.L. c. 185C, § 8A.

III. IMPLEMENTATION OF STANDING ORDER

● All civil and criminal cases filed in the Housing Court on or after **September 1, 2004**, shall be subject to the provisions of this Standing Order.

● All civil and criminal cases pending in the Housing Court as of **August 31, 2004,** shall be subject to the provisions of this Standing Order only to the extent a judge incorporates specific provisions in a supplemental scheduling order.

● The Housing Court shall schedule case management status conferences, pre-trial conferences, motion hearings and trials on its own initiative, or as reasonably requested by the parties, consistent with this Standing Order.

IV. TRACK DESIGNATION

At the time of filing, all cases shall be assigned to one of the following tracks according to the type of case:

● **SP Track** (Summary Process Action)

● **CV–F Track** (Civil Action–Fast)

● **CV–A Track** (Civil Action–Average)

● **CV–X Track** (Civil Action–Accelerated)

● **CV–AAP Track** (Civil Action–Administrative Agency Proceeding)

● **SC Track** (Small Claims Action)

● **SU Track** (Supplementary Process/Collection Action)

● **CR Track** (Criminal Action)

V. SCHEDULING ORDER PREPARATION AND NOTIFICATION

While the Court will endeavor to provide notice, the ultimate responsibility for obtaining information from the Court about the designation of the case and the corresponding scheduling order shall rest with each party. The parties and counsel shall receive notice as follows:

Civil Actions (CV–F, CV–A, CV–X, CV–AAP Tracks)

o The Clerk will prepare a Scheduling Order for each civil action in accordance with the provisions of this Standing Order.

o Upon the filing of any civil complaint initiating a new action (but not including a pleading that seeks as relief only a temporary restraining order), the Clerk shall, simultaneously with the filing of the Complaint, issue to the plaintiff a

Scheduling Order, to be served upon the defendant(s) together with the Complaint and Summons.

o A party or counsel who appears in the action after the issuance of the Scheduling Order shall have the responsibility of obtaining a copy of the Order. The Clerk shall make copies of the Order available to the parties and counsel of record as requested by them, at any time.

o If a civil action is transferred to the Housing Court from another court, or if a summary process claim or counterclaim is transferred from the Housing Court's summary process docket to the civil docket, or if a criminal action is transferred from the Housing Court's criminal docket to the civil docket, the Clerk shall schedule a Case Management Conference before a judge within thirty (30) days of said transfer. The judge shall issue an individualized Scheduling Order at the conclusion of the conference.

Criminal Actions (CR Track)

o At the time a criminal summons and complaint issues, the Clerk shall prepare a Scheduling Order in accordance with the provisions of this Standing Order.

o At the time a criminal summons and complaint issues, the clerk shall provide the commonwealth, city or plaintiff with a Scheduling Order. The Commonwealth, city or plaintiff shall be required to serve the Scheduling Order on the defendant(s) with the criminal summons and complaint. [2]

Summary Process Actions (SP Track)

o Because the time deadlines for pleadings, motions, discovery and trial are governed by and set forth in the Uniform Rules of Summary Process, the Clerk will not issue a Scheduling Order upon the filing of a Summary Process Complaint. However, the Court may issue a Scheduling Order when appropriate due to the nature and complexity of a case.

o Each party must refer to the Uniform Rules of Summary Process.

Small Claims Actions (SC Track)

o Because the time deadlines for pleadings, motions, discovery and trial are governed by and set forth in the Uniform Small Claims Rules, the Court will not issue a Scheduling Order for each small claims case.

o Each party must refer to the Uniform Small Claims Rules.

Supplementary Process/Collection Actions (SU Track)

o Because collection actions rarely require motions, discovery or trials, the Court will not issue a Scheduling Order for each supplementary process action.

o The Clerk shall provide the parties with written notice of all hearing and status hearing dates in accordance with this Standing Order.

VI. SCHEDULING ORDERS

The following schedules shall be mandatory except upon written waiver, amendment or modification granted by a Judge or a Clerk–Magistrate (as to cases over which a Clerk–Magistrate presides). Documents filed outside the established time limitations without the Court's approval shall have no binding effect on the Court or the parties.

Summary Process (SP) (governed by Uniform Rules of Summary Process)

o The Housing Court recognizes that a significant number of litigants appear in court pro se and are unfamiliar with the Uniform Rules of Summary Process. Housing Court judges shall apply the rules in a fair, reasonable and practical manner consistent with the legitimate interests of all parties. Housing Court judges may allow late-filed motions, answers and other pleadings in the exercise of their sound discretion. Housing Court judges may reschedule hearings in the exercise of their sound discretion.

o The provisions of **Housing Court Standing Order 1–01** (Lawyer for a Day Program) shall continue to apply to summary process cases. Specifically, "if the LDP attorney assisting or representing a pro se litigant in mediation does enter an appearance in that litigant's action, the litigant shall be entitled to a two (2) week continuance of trial."

o The Clerk shall schedule a **Case Management Conference** in a summary process action only as directed by a judge.

Pre–trial motions (Rule 6)

• Filed and served in accordance with Rule 6 by the first Monday after the entry day.

• Heard on the date the case is originally scheduled for trial (however, if the defendant requests, motions to dismiss, if filed by the entry day, shall be heard on the Thursday [or other day designated by the division] following the entry date).

• All late filed motions shall be made and heard only in such manner, at such time, and with such notice as the court may, in its discretion, permit or direct.

• **Motions to Strike Discovery as of Right for Untimely Service**, if filed by the original trial day, shall be heard on the Thursday (or other day designated by the division) following the original trial day. If the motion is denied, the plaintiff shall at that time elect one of two options to complete discovery. Either (1) the plaintiff shall serve answers to discovery upon the defendant by the Monday before the rescheduled trial date and the trial will commence as scheduled, or (2) the plaintiff shall serve answers to discovery upon the defendant by the Monday after the rescheduled trial date and the trial will be rescheduled to the next Thursday.

Discovery (Rule 7)

• All discovery must be filed and served by the first Monday after the Monday entry day (unless otherwise permitted by the Court). [3]

• Responses to discovery must be served no later than ten (10) days after receipt (unless otherwise permitted by the Court).

Trial (Rule 2(c) and 7b)

Non–Jury

o Trial is automatically scheduled for hearing on the **second Thursday** after the entry date (Divisions may designate an alternate or additional day for trials).

o If discovery is properly filed and served, the trial is automatically postponed and rescheduled for the date **two (2) weeks** from the original trial date.

o If trial is continued by Court Order, the trial shall be rescheduled to commence as soon as the trial calendar allows, but no later than **sixty (60) days** from the date of the Order.

Jury

o Trial shall be rescheduled to commence as soon as the trial calendar allows, but no later than **ninety (90) days** from the original trial date. [4]

Findings of Fact and Ruling of Law (non–jury)

In all summary process actions tried upon the facts without jury, the Court shall find the facts and state its conclusions of law thereon as follows:

Possession at issue with no counterclaims (or counterclaims filed with no evidence produced at trial):

● Within **thirty (30) days** from the date the case is taken under advisement.

Possession and counterclaims at issue:

● Within **sixty (60) days** from the date the case is taken under advisement.

Possession moot, but other claims and counterclaims at issue:

● Within one hundred and **twenty (120) days** from the date the case is taken under advisement.

CIVIL ACTIONS–F (CV–F) [5]

(governed by Massachusetts Rules of Civil Procedure)

● Within **three months (90 days)** from date Complaint filed:

● Service completed by all parties.

● All returns of service filed.

● If service is not made upon any defendant, the action shall be dismissed as to that defendant, without prejudice unless otherwise ordered by the First Justice upon request filed within 90 days after the Complaint is filed. [6]

● Within **two months (60 days)** from date Complaint filed:

● Case Management Status Conference held before a judge. [7]

● Within **five months (150 days)** from date Complaint filed:

● Rule 12, 19 and 20 motions served and heard. [8]

● Within **seven months (210 days)** from date Complaint filed:

● All discovery requests served.

● Within **nine months (270 days)** from date Complaint filed:

● All discovery and depositions completed. [9]

● Within **eleven months (330 days)** from date Complaint filed:

● Rule 56 motions served and heard. [10]

● Within **twelve months (360 days)** from date Complaint filed:

● Date set for final pretrial conference and for submission of joint Rule 16 pretrial memorandum.

● Firm trial date set for trial to commence within **one (1) month** from date of pretrial conference.

Findings of Fact and Ruling of Law (non–jury)

In all civil actions on the CV–F track tried upon the facts without jury, the Court shall find the facts and state its conclusions of law thereon **within 120 days** from the date the case is taken under advisement.

CIVIL ACTION–AVERAGE [11] (CV–A)

(governed by Massachusetts Rules of Civil Procedure)

● Within **three months (90 days)** from date Complaint filed:

● Service completed by all parties.

● All returns of service filed.

● If service is not made upon any defendant, the action shall be dismissed as to that defendant, without prejudice unless otherwise ordered by the First Justice upon request filed within **90 days** after the Complaint is filed. [12]

● Within **four months (120 days)** from date Complaint filed:

● Case Management Status Conference held before a Judge. [13]

● Within **five months (150 days)** from date Complaint filed:

● Rule 12, 19 and 20 motions served and heard. [14]

● Within **fifteen months (450 days)** from date Complaint filed:

● Rule 15 motions served and heard.

● Within **twenty–six months (790 days)** from date complaint filed:

● All discovery and depositions completed. [15]

● Within **twenty–eight months (840 days)** from date complaint filed:

● Rule 56 motions served and heard. [16]

● Within **thirty–two months (960 days)** from date complaint filed:

● Date set for final pretrial conference and for submission of joint Rule 16 pretrial memorandum.

● Firm trial date set for trial to commence within **four (4) months** from date of pretrial conference.

Findings of Fact and Ruling of Law (non–jury)

In all civil actions on the CV–A track tried upon the facts without jury, the court shall find the facts and state its conclusions of law thereon within 120 days from the date the case is taken under advisement.

CIVIL ACTIONS—ACCELERATED [17] (CV–X)

(governed by Massachusetts Rules of Civil Procedure) [18]

● **Order of Notice issued at time Complaint filed:**

- Service completed within **ten (10) days** from date Complaint filed.

- All returns of service filed prior to preliminary injunction hearing or within **thirty (30) days** from date Complaint filed, whichever is earlier.

- Preliminary injunction hearing conducted within **twenty-one (21) days** from date complaint filed.

- Within **twenty (20) days** from date Complaint served:

- All discovery requests served.

- Within **sixty-five (65) days** from date Complaint served:

- All discovery and depositions completed. [19]

- Date set for final pretrial conference and for submission of joint Rule 16 pretrial memorandum.

- Firm trial date set for trial to commence within one month from date of pretrial conference.

- Within **three months (90 days)** from date Complaint filed:

- If service is not made upon any defendant, the action shall be dismissed as to that defendant, without prejudice unless otherwise ordered by the First Justice upon request filed within **90 days** after the Complaint is filed. [20]

Findings of Fact and Ruling of Law (non–jury)

In all civil actions on the CV–E track tried upon the facts without jury, the court shall find the facts and state its conclusions of law thereon within 30 days from the date the case is taken under advisement.

CIVIL ACTIONS–ADMINISTRATIVE AGENCY APPEALS (CV–AAA)

Claims filed seeking judicial review of administrative agency proceedings on the administrative record pursuant to the standards set forth in G.L. c. 30A, § 14, G.L. c. 249, § 4, or similar statutes, whether joined with a claim for declaratory relief under G.L. c. 231A, or any other claim, shall be heard in accordance with the following procedure.

- Within **thirty (30) days** after service of the Complaint:

- Party seeking review must request a copy of the transcript or portion thereof, and such transcript or portion thereof shall be made part of the record. [21]

- Within **three months (90 days)** from date complaint served on administrative agency:

- Administrative agency shall by way of answer, file the original or certified copy of the record of the proceeding under review (the record). [22]

- Within **twenty (20) days** after record filed:

- Rule 12(b) or 12(e) motions filed.

- Motions for leave to present testimony of alleged irregularities in procedure before agency, not shown in record filed.

- Motions for leave to present additional evidence filed.

- Within **90 days** after service of the record filed:

- All pre-trial motions heard and decided.

- Within **thirty (30) days** after record filed or after the Court's decisions on all pre-trial motions, whichever is later:

- Plaintiff's **Motion for Judgment on the Pleadings** and supporting memorandum filed (Mass. R. Civ. P. 12(c)). [23]

- Within **thirty (30) days** after Plaintiff's **Motion for Judgment on the Pleadings** filed:

- Defendant's response to motion and supporting memorandum filed.

- Within **120 days** after **Motion for Judgment on the Pleadings** filed:

- **Motion for Judgment on the Pleadings** scheduled and heard. [24]

o Ruling on Motion for Judgment on the Pleadings:

- The Court shall render a written decision within **120 days** from the date the case is taken under advisement.

SMALL CLAIMS ACTIONS

(governed by Uniform Small Claims Rules)

o **Magistrate Hearings**

- Trial before Clerk–Magistrate to be scheduled to commence within **60 days** from the date the Complaint is filed.

- Decision rendered by Clerk–Magistrate within **30 days** from the date the case is taken under advisement.

o **Appeals**

- **Non–jury trial:**

o Trial to be scheduled to commence within **60 days** from date appeal filed.

o The Court shall find the facts and state its conclusions of law thereon within **60 days** from the date the case is taken under advisement.

- **Jury Trial:**

o Trial to be scheduled to commence within **90 days** from date appeal filed.

SUPPLEMENTARY PROCESS/COLLECTION ACTIONS

o Hearing to be scheduled and held within **60 days** from date Complaint is filed.

o The Court shall render a decision and issue appropriate orders within **seven (7) days** from hearing date.

o Status hearing to be scheduled and held within **six months (180 days)** from initial hearing date, and every **six months (180 days)** thereafter, until case is dismissed. [25]

CRIMINAL ACTIONS [26]

o **Show Cause Determination**

- Hearing to be scheduled and commenced within **one month (30 days)** from date application for Criminal Complaint filed. The Clerk–Magistrate shall have the discretion to continue the hearing for a reasonable period at the request of either party for good cause shown.

- Clerk–Magistrate to render show cause determination within **seven (7) days** of completion of hearing.

- Summons and criminal complaint to issue within 7 days of show cause determination. The judge shall have the discretion to continue the hearing for a reasonable period at the request of either party for good cause shown.

o Arraignment

• Arraignment to be scheduled and completed within one month (30 days) from date criminal summons and complaint issues. The judge shall have the discretion to continue the arraignment for a reasonable period at the request of either party for good cause shown (such as the work is in progress with completion expected within a reasonable period, and there is no substantial continuing risk to health or safety).

o Discovery

• Discovery to be completed within three months (90 days) from date of arraignment.

o Pre–trial Conference

• Pre-trial conference to be scheduled and held within four months (120 days) from date of arraignment.

o Trial

• Firm date to be set for trial to commence within six months (180 days) from date of arraignment.

VII. DISPOSITION OF INACTIVE CASES

Matters Pending for More than One Year Without Docket Activity

During the first quarter of each year there shall be a call in each Division of the Housing Court of all cases pending in which there has been no activity reflected on the docket for more than 12 months. The Clerk–Magistrate shall, after consultation with the First Justice regarding cases which appropriately might be excluded from such calls, prepare lists for such calls, and shall give seasonable and appropriate notice by mail to all interested parties or their attorneys of record. The notice in each case shall state that the matter is being called for dismissal or other appropriate order, and that failure of a party or his attorney to answer may result in dismissal of the matter.

Appeals Pending for More than Three (3) Months Without Assembly of Record

In each calendar quarter there shall be a call in each Division of the Housing Court of all appeals pending for more than 3 months in which the record has not been assembled. The Clerk–Magistrate shall, after consultation with the First Justice regarding cases which appropriately might be excluded from such calls, prepare lists for such calls, and shall give seasonable and appropriate notice by mail to all interested parties or their attorneys of record. The notice in each case shall state that the matter is being called for dismissal or other appropriate order, and that failure of a party or his attorney to answer may result in dismissal of the appeal.

VIII. AMENDMENT, MODIFICATION OR WAIVER OF ORDERS

Scheduling Orders

Amendments, extensions or other modifications of any of a scheduling order may be ordered by the Court on its own motion as the interests of justice require, but otherwise may be requested by a party only upon motion and for good cause shown. A **Motion to Amend or Modify the Scheduling**

Order shall be in writing and set forth in detail the facts upon which the moving party relies in support of said motion. **Motions to Continue Trials** are disfavored, and may be allowed only for good cause shown. Hearings on scheduling order motions shall be held only if deemed necessary by the assigned judge.

Standing Order

Nothing in this standing order shall limit the Housing Court's authority, in appropriate cases where the interests of justice require, or other good reasons appear, to stay, waive or alter provisions of this Standing Order, or to order that a particular case not be or not remain subject to the time standards set forth in this standing order.

Adopted effective September 1, 2004.

1 As used herein, the term "the Court" and "Court Order" shall encompass an Order issued by a judge, an Order issued by the Clerk–Magistrate at the direction of a judge, an Order issued by a Clerk–Magistrate pertaining to a judicial matter over which the Clerk–Magistrate presides and a scheduling, continuance or other Notice/Order issued by a Clerk–Magistrate within the scope of the Clerk–Magistrate's ministerial functions.

2 In those divisions where the clerk sends the criminal summons and complaint to the defendant by first class mail, the clerk shall include a copy of the Scheduling Order with the criminal summons and complaint sent to the defendant.

3 If the Monday falls on a holiday when the Court is closed, all discovery must be filed and served by the next day.

4 See footnote 2, supra.

5 Except as to cases specifically assigned to a different track in accordance with this Standing Order, all civil actions shall be placed on the CV–F track. A judge, acting on a motion filed by any party, may for good cause shown transfer a civil action from the CV–F track to the CV–A or CV–X track.

6 The dismissal will be entered automatically by the clerk-magistrate under the authority of this Standing Order and notices given as required.

7 At the Case Management Status Conference, the case shall be reviewed, the possibility of an Alternative Dispute Resolution (ADR) referral to a court mediator or other court approved mediation program shall be considered and, if appropriate, a case-specific scheduling order shall be established which may or may not follow exactly the presumptive guidelines of the scheduling order issued when the case was filed. All parties shall appear in person or through counsel at the Case Management Status Conference. All counsel attending are required to be fully familiar with the case. Clients shall attend the conference or be available to their counsel via telephone, and shall be prepared to discuss all aspects of the conduct of the litigation, including the settlement or compromise of the claims. Any party who does not appear at the conference in person or through counsel shall be defaulted or nonsuited.

8 If a party who has been served has not filed a response to the complaint, that party shall be defaulted and notification of default shall be forwarded to the other parties. Where appropriate, cases shall be ordered for assessment of damages.

9 A party may not have responded to timely filed requests for discovery at this juncture and accordingly a motion to compel production of that discovery would be appropriate. All such motions must be filed within a reasonable period, and further discovery responses shall be served in accordance with the court's order and not later than the date that the joint pre-trial memorandum is filed. This Standing Order does not change the duty of a party to supplement under the provisions of Mass.R.Civ.P. 26(e).

10 Certain summary judgment motions may be sufficiently complex to require additional judicial time to render a decision. The case should nonetheless continue on track. The status of the summary judgment motion should be brought to the attention of the judge at the pre-trial conference for his or her consideration and action.

11 All toxic tort actions, including mold, lead and asbestos exposure claims, shall be placed on the CV–A track. A judge, acting on a motion filed by any party, may for good cause shown transfer a civil action from the CV–A track to the CV–F or CV–X track.

12 The dismissal will be entered automatically by the clerk-magistrate under the authority of this Standing Order and notices given as required.

13 See Footnote 5, supra.

14 If a party who has been served has not filed a response to the complaint, that party shall be defaulted and notification of default shall be forwarded to the other parties. Where appropriate, cases shall be ordered for assessment of damages.

15 A party may not have responded to timely filed requests for discovery at this juncture and accordingly a motion to compel production of that discovery would be appropriate. All such motions must be filed within a reasonable period, and further discovery responses shall be served in accordance with the court's order and not later than the date that the joint pre-trial memorandum is filed. This Standing Order does not change the duty of a party to supplement under the provisions of Mass.R.Civ.P. 26(e).

16 Certain summary judgment motions may be sufficiently complex to require additional judicial time to render a decision. The case should nonetheless continue on track. The status of the summary judgment motion should be brought to the attention of the judge at the pre-trial conference for his or her consideration and action.

17 All G.L. c. 139, § 19 and G.L. c. 121B, § 32 actions shall be placed on the CV–X track. A judge, acting on a motion filed by any party, may for good cause shown transfer a civil action that involves only injunctive relief from the CV–F to the CV–X track.

18 Because of the accelerated schedule, the Court will not automatically schedule a Case Management Conference for a case placed on the CV–X track.

19 A party may not have responded to timely filed requests for discovery at this juncture and accordingly a motion to compel production of that discovery would to be appropriate. All such motions must be filed within a reasonable period, and further discovery responses shall be served in accordance with the court's order and not later than the date that the joint pretrial memorandum is filed. This Standing Order does not change the duty of a party to supplement under the provisions of Mass.R.Civ.P. 26(e).

20 The dismissal will be entered automatically by the Clerk–Magistrate under the authority of this Standing Order and notices given as required.

21 Any party seeking to defend the agency's decision as supported by the substantial evidence or as not arbitrary or capricious, or is not an abuse of discretion shall have an affirmative obligation to provide the court with a copy of the transcript or portion thereof in support of its position.

22 Such record "shall consist of (a) the entire proceedings, or (b) such portions thereof as the agency and the parties may stipulate, or (c) a statement of the case agreed to by the agency and the parties. G.L. c. 30A, § 14. A judge may enlarge the time for filing the record, for good cause shown, upon allowance of an appropriate motion.

23 A claim for judicial review shall be resolved through a motion for judgment on the pleadings, Mass.R.Civ.P 12(c), unless the court's decision on a pre-trial motion has made such resolution unnecessary.

24 No pre-trial conference will be held, and no pre-trial memorandum filed, unless specifically ordered by the Court.

25 If the plaintiff does not appear at the status hearing, the case will be dismissed.

26 The Massachusetts Rules of Criminal Procedure do not explicitly govern criminal proceedings in the Housing Court. See, Mass.R.Crim.P., Rule 1(b). Nevertheless, the Housing Court looks to those rules for guidance where appropriate. The time standard pertaining to criminal actions shall be applied with due consideration of the fact that as to criminal matters that come before it, the Housing Court's principal objective is to insure that residential property is brought into compliance with applicable health, building, sanitary, fire or other safety codes. The primary purpose of code enforcement is to protect the public health and safety rather than to punish past violations as criminal offenses, *Commonwealth v. Hadley, 351 Mass. 439, 442, 222 N.E.2d 681, 683 (1966)*. However, the full range of criminal sanctions set forth in the applicable statutes, including fines and incarceration, are available to the Court in appropriate cases. If it is found that the criminal offense charged was not willful, intentional, reckless or repeated, the proceeding shall not be deemed criminal and no record of the case shall be entered in the probation records. G.L. c.185C, § 19; *Commonwealth v. Olivo, 369 Mass. 62, 66–68, 337 N.E.2d 904, 908 (1975)*. The time standards pertaining to criminal actions shall be applied by the court with due consideration for the above stated principles, and with due consideration to the possibility that certain code enforcement cases should be deemed civil and made subject to the civil action time standards provisions.

Standing Order 1–10. Limited Assistance Representation [Rescinded]

Adopted effective November 1, 2010. Rescinded January 16, 2019, effective February 1, 2019. See, now, Uniform Trial Court Rule XVI. Limited Assistance Representation.

Standing Order 1–15. Application of Rule 13 (b) of Trial Court Rule VIII, the Uniform Rules on Impoundment Procedure ("URIP"), in the Housing Court Department

I. APPLICABILITY

The Uniform Rules on Impoundment Procedure (URIP) govern impoundment of otherwise public case records that are filed in civil and criminal proceedings in each Department, including the Housing Court Department of the Trial Court. Case records are presumed to be open to the public, unless they are impounded or sealed as a matter of law, or impounded by a court order.

These rules are inapplicable to case records that are required to be impounded by statute, court rule, standing order, or case law, except as otherwise provided in URIP. *See* URIP Rule 1(a). These rules shall not be construed to deprive a person of any rights or remedies regarding impoundment that are otherwise available under law. *See* URIP Rule 1(a). It is for these reasons that the Housing Court incorporates by reference URIP and specifically promulgates the application of Rule 13 (b) of the URIP within the Housing Court.

II. AUTHORITY

This standing order is promulgated by the Chief Justice of the Housing Court Department pursuant to his statutory authority and responsibility of the administration of justice. *See* G.L. c. 211B, § 10 and G.L. c. 185C, § 8A.

III. IMPLEMENTATION OF STANDING ORDER

Consistent with the URIP, all documents filed in civil and criminal cases in the Housing Court on or after October 1, 2015, shall be subject to the provisions of Standing Order No. 1–15.

IV. APPLICATION OF STANDING ORDER

The Housing Court Department, with the approval of the Chief Justice for Trial Court, hereby adopts Housing Court Standing Order No. 1–15, to implement the application of Rule 13 (b) of the URIP within the Housing Court.

Notwithstanding any provisions to the contrary in any court rule or standing order, it is hereby ORDERED that the following procedures shall apply in the Housing Court Department with respect to the application of Rule 13 (b) of the URIP.

Rule 13 (b) of the URIP provides as follows:

Notice to the Clerk. The filer of a document containing impounded information shall simultaneously file a notice that shall:

(i) notify the clerk that impounded information is included within the document being filed;

(ii) identify the specific legal authority requiring impoundment of the identified information; and

(iii) identify the precise location of the impounded information within the document being filed.

The clerk *shall* docket the notice and designate the referenced document as impounded. The cover page of the document containing the impounded information shall identify that it is impounded.

As required in Rule 13 (b) of the URIP, the filer of a document *shall* file the notice even if the information or document is impounded by statute, court rule, standing order, or case law.

However, by operation of this standing order, in the Housing Court, the filer of the documents listed below is exempt from filing the Rule 13 (b) notice:

a) affidavit of indigency

b) financial statement

The exemption applies only when the documents are filed in the Housing Court. If any of the documents listed above are filed in connection to a case in another court department, the Rule 13 (b) notice is required, unless that court department has a standing order exempting the filer.

Adopted effective October 1, 2015

Joint Standing Order 1–16. Authority of the Judge with Respect to Communication with Specialty Court Teams

This Standing Order is promulgated by the chief Justice of the Trial Court pursuant to G. L, c. 211B, Section 9 and shall constitute authorization by law as referenced in Rule 2.9 (A)(2) of the Code of Judicial Conduct (effective January 1, 2016).

For purposes of this Order:

Specialty Court means a specifically designated court session that focuses on individuals with underlying medical, mental health, substance abuse, or other issues that contribute to the reasons such individuals are before the courts. Specialty court shall also mean Veterans Treatment Court and Homelessness Court. Specialty court sessions integrate treatment and services with judicial case oversight and intensive court supervision. Examples Include drug courts, mental health courts, veterans' courts, and tenancy preservation programs.

A Staffing shall refer to a regularly scheduled, informal conference not occurring in open court, the purpose of which is to permit the presiding judge and others, including counsel, to discuss a participant's progress in the specialty court, treatment recommendations, or responses to participant compliance issues.

IT IS THEREFORE ORDERED:

A judge presiding over a specialty court shall have the authority to initiate, permit or otherwise consider ex parte communications about defendants, juveniles or probationers with members of the specialty court team at a staffing or by written documents provided to all members of the specialty court team, The purpose of this authority is to allow judges in their role in presiding over specialty court sessions, and only in that capacity, to assume a more interactive role with parties, treatment providers, probation officers, social workers and others, than Rule 2.9 of the Code of Judicial Conduct would otherwise permit.

Adopted effective January 7, 2016.

Standing Order 1–20.   Implementation of Mandatory Electronic Filing for Attorneys in Summary Process and Small Claims Cases in the Housing Court Department

Consistent with Rule 1 of S.J.C. Rule 1:25, Massachusetts Rules of Electronic Filing ("E–Filing Rules"), the Housing Court Department of the Massachusetts Trial Court hereby adopts this Standing Order implementing mandatory electronic filing for attorneys in the civil cases identified in Section B. As additional electronic filing capabilities become available, this Standing Order will be amended to implement those additional capabilities.

A.   Governing Rules and Orders.

1. Filers who submit documents electronically through the e-filing service provider ("Provider"), on the Massachusetts Court System Odyssey File and Serve Site ("efileMA.com") shall comply with the E–Filing Rules, the Massachusetts Rules of Civil Procedure, the rules governing time standards and case management, and all other applicable Trial Court and department rules and standing orders.

2. To the extent that any Massachusetts Court Rules and Orders, as defined in the E–Filing Rules, are inconsistent with this Standing Order, the E–Filing Rules and this Standing Order shall control. *See generally* E–Filing Rules, Rules 1(a) & 2.

B.   Applicability of Standing Order. This Standing Order applies to all **Summary Process** and **Small Claims** cases in any division of the Housing Court Department on and after the effective date of this Standing Order, as set forth in Section M. For any party whose Summary Process or Small Claims case was filed before this Standing Order's effective date and who is represented by an attorney, the attorney must register for electronic filing at eFileMA.com and, thereafter, electronically file any documents according to the E–Filings Rules and this Standing Order. Anyone who is a party to a Summary Process or Small Claims case who is not represented by an attorney may register for electronic filing at eFileMA.com and, thereafter, electronically file case documents as permitted by the E–Filings Rules and this Standing Order.

C.   Mandatory Attorney Registration for Electronic Filing and Service. All attorneys representing parties in any division of the Housing Court Department after the effective date of this Standing Order shall register for electronic filing at eFileMA.com. Please see E–Filing Rules, Rule 3(d)(1) for the effect that registering for e-filing will have on cases in court departments other than the Housing Court Department. Registration shall not constitute a notice of appearance in any case. During the registration process, each attorney must provide the attorney's Board of Bar Overseers Number and email address. Each attorney registrant must maintain the attorney's contact information, including email address, on the eFileMA.com "Service Contacts Public List."

D.   Mandatory Attorney Electronic Filing in the Housing Court. Except as set forth in Section E and H, all documents filed by an attorney in Summary Process or Small Claims cases shall be filed electronically using eFileMA.com. A document filed using the eFileMA.com system exclusively constitutes "e-filed" as used herein.

E.   Exemption from Mandatory Attorney Electronic Filing and Permission to File Paper Original.

1. An attorney who is required to file documents electronically under this Standing Order may request to be excused from these requirements. If a party files a request for exemption from mandatory E-filings by "conventional methods," as defined in E–Filing Rules, Rule 2, and makes a showing of undue hardship, significant prejudice, exigency, or other good cause, the Clerk Magistrate in the respective Division of the Housing Court Department may grant that party an exemption from the mandatory e-filing requirements under the E–Filing Rules and this Standing Order. A showing of undue hardship, significant prejudice, exigency, or other good cause does not include the inability to pay fees for electronic filing, as fee waivers may be requested if the party otherwise qualifies for, or has been granted, a fee waiver in accordance with Massachusetts law or court rules. A Clerk Magistrate's decision on an exemption request made pursuant to this section shall be final.

2. The exemption from the mandate of electronic filing applies only to the case in which the request for exemption from mandatory E-filings was allowed. An attorney whose request for exemption from mandatory E-filings was allowed shall file documents by conventional methods and shall deliver and receive copies of filed documents to and from other parties by conventional methods. An attorney whose request for exemption from mandatory E-filings has been allowed must

provide a copy of the Clerk Magistrate's decision granting the request to all parties in that case.

F. Requests to Waive Provider Fees. Pursuant to S.J.C. Rule 1:25, upon request, the Housing Court shall waive the e-filing fees in a Summary Process or Small Claims case where an attorney demonstrates that he or she represents an indigent party, as set forth in G. L. c. 261, §§ 27A–27G. In requesting such waiver, the attorney shall file an "Affidavit of Indigency and Request for Waiver, Substitution or State Payment of Fees & Costs", and a "Supplement to Affidavit of Indigency and Request for Waiver, Substitution or State Payment of Fees & Costs," if required, through eFileMA.com, on behalf of the client, and select the "waiver" Payment Account in the Fees section of eFileMA.com.

G. Impounded Documents in eFileMa.com. All attorneys who use the eFileMA.com system to file impounded documents in Summary Process and Small Claims cases in the Housing Court shall comply with S.J.C. Rule 1:25 and Housing Court Standing Order 1–15.

H. No Paper Duplicates; In–Court Filings.

1. All documents that are e-filed shall be submitted electronically only. Neither a paper original nor duplicate shall be filed unless specifically requested by the Court.

2. In all electronically filed Summary Process cases in the Housing Court, an original Summons and Complaint, as required by the Affidavit of Compliance, shall be filed with the Court by "conventional methods" as defined in E–Filing Rules, Rule 2.

3. Documents that are filed during a court proceeding that is being held after the case has been initiated do not have to be electronically filed. An attorney who files a document during a court proceeding must bring paper copies of the document for delivery to the other parties during the court proceeding. When documents are filed during a court proceeding the Clerk Magistrate, or his or her designee, must scan those documents into an electronic format.

I. Service. All electronically filed documents shall be served on the other party (parties) by "conventional methods" as defined in E–Filing Rules, Rule 2.

J. Notice from Provider. The eFileMA.com system will transmit electronic notifications (i) when an e-filed document is submitted, (ii) when the Clerk's Office accepts or rejects the document, and (iii) possibly at other times as determined by the Provider.

K. Support. All technical support shall be rendered by the Provider. The appropriate Clerk's Office may be contacted with procedural questions.

L. Transfers under G. L. c. 185C, § 20. If an attorney seeks to transfer a Summary Process or Small Claims case into the Housing Court pursuant to G. L. c. 185C, § 20, that attorney must file by conventional methods a Notice of Transfer in the appropriate division of the Housing Court. Except as provided in Section E, once the Housing Court receives the case from the originating court and assigns it a Housing Court docket number, all subsequent filings made therein by an attorney shall be electronically filed.

M. Effective Date. This Standing Order shall become effective on January 27, 2020.

N. Future Changes and Updates. This Standing Order may be rescinded, superseded, or amended, in writing, at any time.

Adopted effective January 27, 2020.

JUVENILE COURT RULES FOR THE CARE
AND PROTECTION OF CHILDREN

Publisher's Note

These rules repeal and replace all prior Juvenile Court Rules in their entirety. The Supreme Judicial Court's Notice of Approval adopting the Juvenile Court Rules for the Care and Protection of Children contained the following statement: "Effective January 1, 2007, the Juvenile Court Rules, effective April 15, 1996 and the Interim Supplemental Rules of Appellate Procedure in Care and Protection Cases, effective September 3, 1991, are hereby repealed."

Table of Rules

JUVENILE COURT RULES FOR THE CARE AND PROTECTION OF CHILDREN

Rule 1. Scope of Rules

These rules apply to all actions in the Juvenile Court Department for the care and protection of children, including actions for guardianship of minors, child support, parentage, name change and actions seeking to dispense with parental consent to adoption, custody, guardianship or any other disposition of the child pursuant to G. L. c. 119 and c. 210.

Adopted July 27, 2018, effective November 5, 2018.

Note

Throughout these rules "paternity" has been replaced by the gender-neutral term "parentage." *See Partenan v. Gallagher*, 475 Mass. 632 (2016).

See G. L. c. 119, § 24 (care and protection), c. 190B, §§ 1–401 and 5–101 (guardianship of minors), c. 209C, § 3(c) (parentage and support), c. 119, § 28 (temporary support), and c. 210, § 1 (authority of the Juvenile Court to hear cases pursuant to c. 210 with respect to pending proceedings in the Juvenile Court). Proceedings that seek equitable relief are governed by the Massachusetts Rules of Civil Procedure, including proceedings pursuant to G. L. c. 210, § 6D (enforcement of post-adoption agreements). *See* G. L. c. 218, § 59 and Mass. R. Civ. P., Rule 1. Permanency Hearings are governed by the Massachusetts Trial Court Rule VI Uniform Rules for Permanency Hearings.

Rule 2. Definition of Terms

For these rules the terms below shall have the following definitions:

"Child" means the person who is the subject of the petition or complaint.

"Department" means the Department of Children and Families or its successor.

"Order or Decree Dispensing with Consent to Adoption" means an order or decree dispensing with the need for consent to adoption, guardianship or any other disposition of the child, commonly referred to as "termination of parental rights."

"Precept" means an order of the court to take and bring the child who is the subject of the care and protection petition before the court.

Adopted July 27, 2018, effective November 5, 2018.

Rule 3. Precepts

A. Procedure. The court may order a precept sua sponte or upon the request of the petitioner or the Department. The precept shall be served by a court officer, constable, deputy sheriff, sheriff, police officer, or other person designated by the court and shall be on a form approved by the Chief Justice of the Juvenile Court.

B. Service. The precept shall be served forthwith. The child shall be brought to the court within court hours and identified. Nothing in this rule limits the authority or responsibility of the Department regarding the care and custody of children as set forth in statutes, case law and Department regulations.

C. Return of Service. The officer or other person making service in accordance with this rule shall make a return of service on the precept and file it promptly with the court.

Adopted July 27, 2018, effective November 5, 2018.

Note

If the precept is served and the child cannot be brought before the court the same day, the Department shall bring the child to the court for identification as soon thereafter as practicable. If available and with prior arrangement, the child may be identified by way of video-conference. *See* Executive Office Transmittal 14–4 Trial Court Video-conferencing Policy. The child should be identified by a judge from the court that issued the precept. However, if necessary and with prior arrangement, the child may be identified by a judge from a different Juvenile Court. *See* Order of Assignment dated February 12, 2014 authorizing justices appointed to a particular division of the Juvenile Court Department and circuit justices appointed to the Juvenile Court Department to sit and act as justices in all divisions of the Juvenile Court Department.

Rule 4. Appointment of Counsel

Counsel shall be appointed in accordance with the provisions of G. L. c. 119, § 29 and c. 211D, the Massachusetts Rules of the Supreme Judicial Court, Rule 3:10, and applicable case law.

Adopted July 27, 2018, effective November 5, 2018.

Note

See Dept. of Pub. Welfare v. J.K.B., 379 Mass. 1 (1979) (indigent parent entitled to court-appointed counsel in termination of parental rights proceedings pursuant to G. L. c. 210, § 3), *Guardianship of V. V.*, 470 Mass. 590 (2015) (indigent parent entitled to court-appointed counsel on a guardianship petition pursuant to G. L. c. 190B) and *L.B. v. Chief Justice of the Probate and Family Court Dept.*, 474 Mass. 231 (2016) (indigent parent entitled to court-appointed counsel in petitions to remove guardian and/or seek visits with the child under the guardianship provided the parent presents a meritorious claim for removal and/or modification of visitation).

Rule 5. Process

A. Summons to Parent/Guardian; Service of Process by Publication

1. *Care and Protection Cases.* After the filing of the care and protection petition, the petitioner shall cause a summons or order of notice and a copy of the petition to be served by a court officer, constable, deputy sheriff, sheriff, police officer, or other person approved by the court on each of the parents of the child, the legal guardian, if any, the legal custodian, if any, and the Department, if the legal custodian. The summons or order of notice shall be on a form approved by the Chief Justice of the Juvenile Court and shall be served on each of the above in the following manner:

(a) If the place of residence or whereabouts of the persons above is known, service shall be accomplished by delivery in hand. Service shall be accomplished on the Department by delivering the summons or order of notice to the appropriate Office of the Regional Counsel.

(b) Personal service may be accomplished the first time the matter comes before the judge or at the temporary custody hearing on persons above, if present, and upon a representative of the Department

(c) If the Department is not the legal custodian, the petitioner shall provide notice to the Department of the filing of the petition by certified or registered mail, return receipt requested, to the appropriate Office of Regional Counsel, attention to the Regional Counsel.

(d) If the place of residence or whereabouts of persons above, except the parent(s), is known but the petitioner has been unable to accomplish in-hand service despite diligent efforts to do so, on the petitioner's written motion for alternate manner of service setting forth the diligent efforts made to accomplish in-hand service, the court may order that service be accomplished by certified or registered mail, return receipt requested, to the last known place of residence, the mailing to be at least twenty-one days before the date of the pretrial conference, unless the court otherwise orders.

(e) If the place of residence or whereabouts of a parent is known but the petitioner has been unable to accomplish in-hand service despite diligent efforts to do so, or the place of residence or whereabouts of a parent cannot be found after diligent efforts, on the petitioner's written motion for alternate manner of service setting forth the diligent efforts made to accomplish in-hand service or ascertain the place of residence or whereabouts, the court may order that service be accomplished on that parent, either within or outside of the Commonwealth, by:

(i) certified or registered mail, return receipt requested, to the last known place of residence of the parent, the mailing to be at least twenty-one days before the date of the pretrial conference, unless the court otherwise orders, and

(ii) publication in accordance with subsection (g), below.

(f) If the identity of a parent is not known, service shall be accomplished on that parent by publication in accordance with subsection (g), below.

(g) Whenever service by publication is required in a care and protection case, the court shall, upon motion of the petitioner, other party, or sua sponte, issue an Order for Service by Publication. The petitioner shall cause notice to be published in accordance with the order in the newspaper or newspapers designated by the court once in each of three successive weeks, the final publication to appear no later than the pretrial conference date unless the court otherwise orders. Whenever the court orders service by publication the court shall also require the petitioner to file a Military Affidavit on a form approved by the Chief Justice of the Juvenile Court as to the parent to be served by publication.

(h) If, after the petitioner has perfected service of process in accordance with this rule, no parent has appeared or can be found, and the legal guardian, if any, has not appeared and the legal custodian, if any, has not appeared, a summons shall be issued to the person with whom such child last resided, if known

2. *Guardianship of a Minor Cases.* Except as provided for in subsection (i), after the filing of a guardianship petition, the petitioner shall cause notice and a copy of the petition to be served by a court officer, constable, deputy sheriff, sheriff, police officer, or other person approved by the court on the person(s) set forth in G. L. c. 190B, § 5–206. The notice shall be on a form approved by the Chief Justice of the Juvenile Court and shall be served with a copy of the petition in the following manner:

(a) If the place of residence or whereabouts of persons entitled to notice pursuant to G. L. 190B, § 5–206 is known, service shall be accomplished by delivery in hand on the:

(i) parent(s);

(ii) child if age fourteen or older and not the petitioner;

(iii) person given care or custody of the child by court order and with whom the child has resided within sixty days prior to the filing of the petition, excluding foster parent(s);

(iv) current guardian or conservator for the child; and

(v) the Department, if the legal custodian. In-hand service shall be accomplished on the Department by delivering the notice to the appropriate Office of the Regional Counsel.

(b) Personal service may be accomplished on person(s) entitled to in-hand service pursuant to paragraph (a), if present, and upon a representative of the Department, if the legal custodian, when the matter comes before the judge.

(c) Service shall be accomplished on all others entitled to notice pursuant to G. L. c. 190B, § 5–206 by certified or registered mail, return receipt requested, to the last known place of residence or whereabouts, if known. Service shall be accomplished on the Department, if not the legal custodian, by certified or registered mail, return receipt requested, to the appropriate Office of Regional Counsel, attention to the Regional Counsel.

(d) If the place of residence or whereabouts of a person, except the parents, entitled to in-hand service pursuant to paragraph (a) is known but the petitioner has been unable to accomplish in-hand service despite diligent efforts to do so, on the petitioner's written motion for alternate manner of service setting forth the diligent efforts made to accomplish in-hand service, the court may order that service be accomplished by certified or registered mail, return receipt requested, to the last known place of residence, the mailing to be at least fourteen days before the petition for guardianship is heard, unless the court otherwise orders.

(e) If the place of residence or whereabouts of a parent is known but the petitioner has been unable to accomplish in-hand service despite diligent efforts to do so or the place of residence or whereabouts of a parent cannot be found after diligent efforts, on the petitioner's written motion for alternate manner of service setting forth the diligent efforts made to accomplish in-hand service or ascertain the place of residence or whereabouts, the court may order that service

be accomplished on that parent, either within or outside of the Commonwealth, by:

(i) certified or registered mail, return receipt requested, to the last known place of residence of the parent, the mailing to be at least fourteen days before the petition for guardianship is heard, unless the court otherwise orders, and

(ii) publication in accordance with subsection (g), below.

(f) If the identity of a parent is not known, service shall be accomplished on that parent by publication in accordance with subsection (g), below.

(g) Whenever service by publication is required in a guardianship case the court shall, upon motion of the petitioner, other party, or sua sponte, issue an Order for Service by Publication. The petitioner shall cause notice to be published in accordance with the order at least once in the newspaper or newspapers designated by the court, the publication to appear at least seven days before the petition for guardianship is heard, unless the court otherwise orders. Whenever the court orders service by publication the court shall also require the petitioner to file a Military Affidavit on a form approved by the Chief Justice of the Juvenile Court, as to the parent to be served by publication.

(h) If the minor is entitled to any benefit, estate, or income paid or payable through the United States Veterans. Administration or its successor, service shall be made on the Veterans Administration or its successor by certified or registered mail, return receipt requested, unless the court otherwise orders.

(i) No notice need be given in the following circumstances: (1) to a person entitled to notice under this rule who has assented in writing to the allowance of the petition if the assent is filed in court; (2) to a parent who executes an adoption surrender in conformance with G. L. c. 210, § 2; or (3) if the court has terminated parental rights pursuant to G. L. c. 119, § 26 or c. 210, § 3.

(j) A motion for the appointment of a temporary guardian may not be filed unless a guardianship petition has been filed. If service of the notice of the guardianship petition has not been made in accordance with this rule, a copy of the motion for the appointment of temporary guardian and written notice of its hearing shall be served with the notice of the guardianship petition, unless the court otherwise orders.

3. *Parentage and Child Support Cases.* After the filing of a complaint for parentage or an order of child support, or both, the plaintiff shall cause notice and a copy of the complaint to be served by a court officer, constable, deputy sheriff, sheriff, police officer, or other person approved by the court on each of the parents of the child unless a parent has assented to the filing of the complaint, on the child, if the child is age fourteen years or older, on the Department, if the legal custodian, and on the person entitled to notice pursuant to G.L. c. 209C, § 6. The notice shall be on a form approved by the Chief Justice of the Juvenile Court and shall be served with a copy of the complaint in the following manner:

(a) If the place of residence or whereabouts of a parent is known, service shall be accomplished on that parent by delivery in hand to the parent. If the child is age fourteen years or older, service shall be made in the same manner on the child. Service shall be accomplished on the Department by delivering the notice to the appropriate Office of the Regional Counsel, attention to the Regional Counsel.

(b) Personal service may be accomplished on the parent or child who is age fourteen years or older, if present, and on a representative of the Department, if the legal custodian, when the matter comes before the judge.

(c) If the Department is not the legal custodian of the child, the plaintiff shall provide notice to the Department of the filing of the complaint by certified or registered mail, return receipt requested, to the appropriate Office of Regional Counsel, attention to the Regional Counsel.

(d) If the place of residence or whereabouts of a parent is known but the plaintiff has been unable to accomplish in-hand service despite diligent efforts to do so or the place of residence or whereabouts of a parent cannot be found after diligent efforts, on the plaintiffs written motion for alternate manner of service setting forth the diligent efforts made to accomplish in-hand service or ascertain the place of residence or whereabouts, the court may order that service be accomplished on that parent, either within or outside of the Commonwealth, by:

(i) certified or registered mail, return receipt requested, to the last known place of residence of the parent, the mailing to be at least fourteen days before the complaint for parentage or support is heard, unless the court otherwise orders, and

(ii) publication in accordance with subsection (e), below.

(e) Whenever service by publication is required in a parentage or child support case the court shall, upon motion of the plaintiff, other party, or sua sponte, issue an Order for Service by Publication. The plaintiff shall cause notice to be published in accordance with the order at least once in the newspaper or newspapers designated by the court, the publication to appear at least seven days before the complaint for parentage or support is heard, unless the court otherwise orders. Whenever the court orders service by publication the court shall also require the plaintiff to file a Military Affidavit on a form approved by the Chief Justice of the Juvenile Court as to the person to be served by publication.

4. *Change of Name Cases.* Except as provided in subsection (e), after the filing of a change of name petition, the petitioner shall serve notice on each of the parents of the child and upon the Department if the legal custodian or if there is a care and protection case pending, in accordance with an order of notice. An order of notice shall be on a form approved by the Chief Justice of the Juvenile Court and shall be served with a copy of the petition in the following manner:

(a) Service shall be accomplished by certified or registered mail, return receipt requested, on the parent to the last known place of residence of the parent and on the Department to the appropriate Office of the Regional Counsel, attention to the Regional Counsel, the mailing to be at least fourteen days before the petition for change of name is heard, unless the court otherwise orders.

(b) Service may be accomplished by a court officer on the parent, if present, and on a representative of the Department when the matter comes before the judge.

(c) If the place of residence or whereabouts of a parent is known but the petitioner has been unable to accomplish service by certified or registered mail despite diligent efforts to do so or if the place of residence or whereabouts of a parent cannot be found after diligent efforts, on the petitioner's written motion for alternate manner of service setting forth the diligent efforts made to accomplish service or ascertain the place of residence or whereabouts, the court may order that service be accomplished on that parent, either within or outside of the Commonwealth, by publication in accordance with subsection (d), below.

(d) Whenever service by publication is required in a change of name case the court shall, upon motion of the petitioner, or sua sponte, issue an Order for Service by Publication. The petitioner shall cause notice to be published in accordance with the order at least once in the newspaper or newspapers designated by the court, the publication to appear at least seven days before the petition is heard, unless the court otherwise orders. Whenever the court orders service by publication the court shall also require the petitioner to file a Military Affidavit on a form approved by the Chief Justice of the Juvenile Court, as to the parent to be served by publication.

(e) No notice need be given in the following circumstances: (1) to a person entitled to notice under this rule who has assented in writing to the allowance of the petition if the assent is filed in court; (2) to a parent who executes an adoption surrender in conformance with G. L. c. 210, § 2; or (3) if the court has terminated parental rights pursuant to G. L. c. 210, § 3.

B. Filing Proof of Publication. Following publication in accordance with the order, counsel for the petitioner or plaintiff shall promptly complete and file in the Clerk's office an Affidavit of Notice of Publication on a form approved by the Chief Justice of the Juvenile Court and shall file a completed Military Affidavit as to the person served by publication.

C. Joint Publication. In a case involving two or more children who have the same parents, the petitioner or plaintiff may accomplish service by joint publication. In all other cases, there shall be a separate publication for each child who is a subject of a case.

D. Filing of Return of Service. The officer or other person making service in accordance with this rule shall make a return of service on a copy of the summons or order of notice that the petitioner or plaintiff shall promptly file with the court

Adopted July 27, 2018, effective November 5, 2018.

Note

See Trial Court Rules, Rule IV Uniform Rule Requiring Disclosure of Pending and Concluded Care or Custody Matters and Rule X Uniform Rule Requiring Disclosure of Present or Past Receipt of Public Assistance Benefits by Minor Children. Current Juvenile Court forms are available online on the Juvenile Court website.

Subsection A. Service on the Department. When providing service in hand or by certified or registered mail on the Department, the address to be used is that of the Office of the Regional Counsel for the region in which the case is filed.

Subsection A.3. See G.L. c. 209C, § 6, relative to persons who must be joined as a party and the manner of notice required.

Subsection A. 4. Petitions for change of name pursuant to G. L. c. 210, § 12 are for name changes other than those that occur in the context of adoption cases or, in some instances, parentage cases. After the petition for change of name is allowed, the clerk may, upon request, issue a Certificate of Name Change. Allowance of the petition for change of name will not result in an amendment of the birth certificate. The birth name remains the same. The new name is considered an alias or an "also known as" ("aka"). *See* G. L. c. 210, §§ 12 –14.

Rule 6.   Filing of Birth Certificates

A.   Care and Protection Cases. The petitioner shall file, within sixty days of commencement of the action, a certified copy of the birth certificate issued after the date of the filing of the petition, of each child named in the petition. In rare circumstances and for good cause shown, the judge may extend the time or waive the filing of the birth certificate. The petitioner may request an order from the court to produce a birth certificate pursuant to G. L. c. 46, § 2A if the petitioner does not have custody of the child.

B.   Guardianship, Parentage and Change of Name Cases. The petitioner or plaintiff shall file along with the petition or complaint, a certified copy of the birth certificate for each child named in the petition or complaint. For good cause shown, the judge may extend the time or waive the filing of the birth certificate. The certified birth certificate shall have been issued within sixty days of filing the petition or complaint. The petitioner or plaintiff may request an order from the court to produce a birth certificate pursuant to G. L. c. 46, § 2A if the petitioner or plaintiff does not have custody of the child. If there is a certified copy of the child's birth certificate on file in the care and protection case, the clerk may copy and file it in the guardianship, parentage or change of name case provided that it was filed in the care and protection case within sixty days of the filing of the guardianship petition, parentage complaint or change of name petition.

Adopted July 27, 2018, effective November 5, 2018.

Note

A.   The importance of having a recent certified copy of the child's birth certificate to determine parentage in order to provide parents with notice and the opportunity to be heard cannot be overstated. "Good cause" should be construed narrowly and constitute more than mere inconvenience; however, there may be circumstances in which a certified copy of the birth certificate cannot be obtained or obtaining it would cause unreasonable delay in the disposition of the case. In such circumstances, including but not limited to instances in which a foreign birth certificate cannot be obtained, a judge may waive the filing of a certified copy of a birth certificate. In the event a foreign birth certificate is obtained, the burden is on the petitioner to provide an English translation of a foreign birth certificate.

B.   There may be circumstances in which the certified copy of the birth certificate in the care and protection case does not satisfy the requirements of this rule and cannot be used when filing a guardianship, change of name petition, or a parentage complaint. In those instances, if the petitioner or the plaintiff does not have custody of the child and cannot otherwise obtain a certified copy of the birth certificate, he/she may file a motion in the underlying care and protection case for a court order to produce the birth certificate for filing with

the petition or complaint. The person seeking such an order may be permitted to appear in the care and protection case for the sole purpose of filing such a motion. An appearance for this limited purpose does not make the person a party to the care and protection case.

Rule 7.   Service and Form of Papers

A.   Form of Motion. Every motion or other document filed with the court, other than documents offered in evidence, shall be on 8 ½″ × 11″ paper, or in an electronic or digital manner approved by the court, and shall have a heading which includes the name, division and county of the court, the docket number, the title of the action and a designation of the nature of the motion or document. Every such motion or document shall set forth the name, address, telephone number and email address of the attorney or pro se party filing it, the Board of Bar Overseers registration number of the attorney, and the date on which the motion or other document was filed with the court.

B.   Requirement of Affidavit. Unless a motion, other than a motion to dismiss as provided in paragraph C, is made during a hearing or trial, any request for a court order shall be made by written motion accompanied by an affidavit signed by the person with personal knowledge of the factual basis of the motion, and shall state with particularity the grounds therefor, and shall set forth the relief or order sought, provided howeverer, that the following types of motions are not required to be accompanied by an affidavit: motions in limine, motions to strike, motions for discovery, motions for appointment of appellate counsel, motions to correct a name on the petition and motions for continuance or change of court date. Whenever a motion is supported by an affidavit or memorandum, the affidavit or memorandum shall be served with the motion.

C.   Motions to Dismiss. All motions to dismiss shall be in writing accompanied by an affidavit signed by the person with personal knowledge of the factual basis of the motion and shall state with particularity the grounds therefor.

D.   Notice. All motions other than those which do not require a hearing shall be scheduled by the court in accordance with procedures established by the court division. A written motion, other than one that may be heard ex parte, and notice of the hearing of the motion, shall be served pursuant to paragraph E of this rule, no later than seven days prior to the hearing. When service is made by mail, the motion and notice of the hearing shall be served no later than ten days prior to the hearing. An application for ex parte relief from the seven day notice requirement shall be made by motion for a short order of notice and supported by affidavit setting forth the nature of the emergency.

E.   Manner of Service. Every motion, except an ex parte motion, or document filed in court shall be served by the attorney or party filing it by mailing or delivering a copy or electronically in accordance with court procedure, to each attorney of record, and each party appearing pro se.

Adopted July 27, 2018, effective November 5, 2018.

Rule 8.   Appearances

All counsel, including court-appointed counsel, shall file a notice of appearance in the Clerk's Office by hand delivery or mail that shall include the name of the attorney, address, telephone number, email address and Board of Bar Overseers registration number. A copy of the appearance shall be served on all parties.

Adopted July 27, 2018, effective November 5, 2018.

Note

This rule applies to all private and court-appointed counsel and to attorneys employed by state agencies, including but not limited to, the Department and the Committee for Public Counsel Services.

Rule 9. Temporary Custody Hearing and Waiver

The temporary custody hearing pursuant to G. L. c. 119, § 24 or § 25 may be waived by a parent, guardian, custodian or child. The waiver of the parent, guardian or custodian shall be in writing signed by the parent, guardian or custodian and, unless such person is self-represented, accompanied, by a certification by his/her attorney. The certification shall include a statement that the attorney has discussed the waiver with his/her client and advised the client that he/she is giving up the right to object and present evidence at the hearing in opposition to the court's orders, including orders regarding his/her child's custody, and the right to appeal the court's orders. The waiver and the certification shall be on a form approved by the Chief Justice of the Juvenile Court. The court shall conduct a colloquy with the parent, guardian or custodian and determine whether the waiver was intelligently and voluntarily made. The attorney for the child may waive the temporary custody hearing by signing a waiver and certification form on behalf of his/her client.

Adopted July 27, 2018, effective November 5, 2018.

Note

This temporary custody hearing may be held pursuant to one of two mutually exclusive statutory provisions, G. L. c. 119, § 24 (so-called "72 hour" hearing) or § 25 (non-emergency temporary custody hearing). At the temporary custody hearing, the judge must determine whether custody should be removed from the child's parent, guardian or custodian, or whether the initial temporary custody order should be, continued, depending on the circumstances. The judge must consider any nomination by the child or the parents of a relative or other individual to become the temporary legal custodian pending the hearing on the merits. *See Care and Protection of Manuel*, 428 Mass. 527 (1998). The judge must also make the written certification and determinations required by G. L. c. 119, § 29C (contrary to the welfare certification and reasonable efforts determination). *See Care and Protection of Walt*, 478 Mass. 212 (2017).

This rule addresses waiver of a parent, guardian, custodian or child of either a § 24 or § 25 temporary custody hearing. By waiving the temporary custody hearing, the parent, guardian, custodian or child is relinquishing his/her right to be heard, to object to the court's orders and to appeal the orders. A parent, guardian, custodian or child may waive the hearing by formal action as provided in this rule or may forfeit the hearing by failure to appear or participate after having received notice of such hearing. Waiver or forfeiture of the hearing is distinguished from the circumstance in which a parent, guardian, custodian or child agrees to a temporary transfer of custody but seeks to nominate a relative or other individual to be appointed the child's temporary custodian pending the hearing on the merits or be heard on the issue of reasonable efforts. Although that party may have acknowledged or stipulated that there is sufficient evidence to support a temporary transfer of custody, he/she has not waived the opportunity to be heard on the issue of a third party temporary custody order or the issue of reasonable efforts. There may be situations in which a parent, guardian, custodian or child requests a reasonable amount of time beyond the scheduled 72 hour hearing to nominate another individual or family member, or more time is necessary to complete a home study of the proposed nominee. In those cases, after the hearing has commenced, the judge may continue the temporary custody hearing to another date for this purpose.

A temporary custody hearing held pursuant to either G. L. c. 119, § 24 or § 25 is not a so called "placement hearing". Placement decisions are within the discretionary powers of the legal custodian as one of the usual incidents of custody. *See* G. L. c. 119, § 21. Decisions related to the normal incidents of custody generally are committed to the Department or third party legal custodian and are reviewable only under § 21 for abuse of discretion or error of law. The court does not have authority to subject the Department to conditions regarding placement. *See Care and Protection of Isaac*, 419 Mass. 602 (1995), *Care and Protection of Jeremy*, 419 Mass. 616 (1995) but *see Care and Protection of Walt*, 478 Mass. 212. In contrast, if the court grants custody to a third party, it may subject the grant of custody to conditions, including conditions that restrict the third party custodian from changing the child's placement.

Rule 10. Written Reports by the Department

The Department shall file a written report with the court each time the case is before a judge for hearing or report. The report shall be filed in the Clerk's Office at least two days in advance of the scheduled court date and shall contain relevant information regarding the child, the parents, caregivers, the services being offered and provided and the progress towards the permanency goal. The failure of the Department to provide the report in advance of the scheduled court date shall not preclude the judge from proceeding with the hearing.

Adopted July 27, 2018, effective November 5, 2018.

Rule 11. Investigator's Report in Care and Protection Cases

In a care and protection case, including a case in which the need for parental consent to adoption is an issue, the report of the court-appointed investigator required by G. L. c. 119, §§ 21A and 24 shall be filed in the Clerk's Office within sixty days after the appointment of the investigator, unless the court otherwise orders. A request for extension of time to file the court investigator's report shall be made by motion on a form approved by the Chief Justice of Juvenile Court, signed by the court investigator and approved by a justice of the Juvenile Court. Any motion for extension of time shall be filed no later than fourteen days prior to the date the report is due, provided however, that the court may permit the filing of a motion for an extension of time at some other time in the interests of justice. If the court approves a motion for extension of time, the court investigator shall provide a copy of the approved motion to all counsel of record and to any party who is not represented by counsel.

Adopted July 27, 2018, effective November 5, 2018.

Note

Counsel of record may obtain from the Clerk's Office a copy of the court investigator's report without filing a motion to do so. Standing Order 1–84 applies to all court-appointed investigator reports.

Rule 12.   Assignment of Care and Protection Cases

At the conclusion of the temporary custody hearing in a care and protection case, if not before, a judge shall be assigned to that case in accordance with procedures established by the Chief Justice of the Juvenile Court. Nothing in this rule shall preclude changing the assignment of a case to, or matters being heard by, a different judge for good cause.

Adopted July 27, 2018, effective November 5, 2018.

Rule 13.   Discovery

A.   Department or Licensed Placement Agency. In any care and protection case in which the Department or a licensed placement agency is or becomes a party, the Department or the licensed placement agency shall produce for each party a copy of its entire social services file, including reports made pursuant to G. L. c. 119, § 51A and § 51B, within sixty days from the date the case is commenced, or within sixty days from the date the Department or the licensed placement agency becomes a party, whichever is later. No party receiving material produced pursuant to this rule shall further duplicate or divulge the material to any person not a party to the case unless by order of court, except that counsel for a party may disclose the material to an expert retained by counsel. The expert shall not further duplicate or divulge the material and shall return the material to the counsel that retained him/her.

When producing a copy of its social services file in compliance with this rule, the Department or the licensed placement agency may withhold privileged material and work product of its attorney, and may withhold the names, and other reasonable, identifying data, of past or present foster parents of a child who is a subject of the case or of an adoptive parent or prospective adoptive parent of a child who is a subject of the case or of the reporter on reports made pursuant to G. L. c. 119, § 51A, subject to orders for further production.

The attorney for the Department or the licensed placement agency shall produce with the copy of the file a list of the materials and information withheld. The attorney for the Department or the licensed placement agency shall have an ongoing duty to produce for each other party on a timely basis any additions to the social services file made after initial production required in this subsection.

B.   Other Discovery. Other discovery may be had only by court order on such terms as the court prescribes. A court order shall be requested by motion in accordance with Rule 7.

Adopted July 27, 2018, effective November 5, 2018.

Note

Section A. *See* Juvenile Court Standing Order 1–84, Juvenile Court Case Records and Reports.

Rule 14.   Status Hearing

There shall be a status hearing within ninety days after the commencement of a care and protection case, provided however, that it shall be scheduled to occur after the court investigator's report has been filed. All parties are required to be present with counsel at the status hearing, except that counsel for the child may appear without his/her client. Failure of one or more parties to appear shall not preclude the court from proceeding with the status hearing.

A.   Summons to the Court Investigator. The court may issue, or one or more of the parties may request, a summons to the court investigator to attend the status hearing. When so summoned, the court investigator shall attend the status hearing to respond to any questions regarding the process of the investigation or the report filed in accordance with Rule 11 and G. L. c. 119, §§ 21A and 24. Failure of the court investigator to be present without good cause or the report to be available shall not preclude the court from proceeding with the status hearing.

B.   Issues to be Addressed. Unless previously addressed and resolved, at the status hearing the court shall address but is not limited to addressing: the process of the court investigation or the report; service of process in accordance with Rule 5; discovery motions; child identification; the Indian Child Welfare Act; any special evidentiary issues; the Department's plan to achieve permanence; any issues regarding services being offered or delivered to the family pending trial; the scheduling of a pretrial conference; and compliance with the standing order regarding time standards. Nothing in this rule shall preclude the court from hearing motions, including discovery motions, at other times in the interests of justice.

C.   Court Investigator's Report. The court shall attach the court investigator's report to the petition at the status hearing, or at the next court date after the filing of the report. The report shall then become a part of the record in accordance with G. L. c. 119, § 24.

D.   Orders. At the conclusion of the status hearing, the court shall issue any necessary and appropriate orders to resolve the matters before the court.

Adopted July 27, 2018, effective November 5, 2018.

Note

The purpose of the status hearing is to address any matters that may impact the timely resolution of the case and permanency for the child.

This rule differs from the prior rule in that it provides a uniform procedure to secure the presence of the court investigator and addresses how the court investigator's report becomes part of the record and evidence in the case.

When summoned to attend the status hearing by the Clerk's Office, the court investigator is present to answer any questions from the parties, their attorneys or the court regarding the process of the investigation and to identify sources of information. It is not the purpose of the attendance of the court investigator at the status hearing to address the factual content of the investigator's report, or assess the credibility of the investigator or the reliability of the information in the report When the court investigator is summoned to attend the status hearing, the court should make every effort to conduct the hearing as early as possible on the scheduled date in order to avoid and/or reduce the wait time for the court investigator.

This rule makes it clear that the court investigator's report automatically becomes part of the record in accordance with G. L. c. 119, § 24. The court investigator's report becomes part of the record and evidence not by its physical "attachment" to the petition but by operation of law. General Laws c. 119, § 24, requires that "the court shall appoint a person qualified under section 21A to investigate the conditions affecting the child and to make a report under oath to the court, which shall be attached to the petition *and be a part of the record.*" (emphasis added). Accordingly, the Appeals Court has held that there is "no question that § 24 anticipates use of the report by the trial judge." *In re Zita*, 455 Mass. 272, 281 (2009) (citing *Custody of Two Minors*, 19 Mass. App. Ct. 552, 559 (1985)). See also *Custody of Michel*, 28 Mass. App. Ct. 260, 267 (1990). ("Primary reliance concerning the family picture will be on the § 24 report. Such is the import of the statutory language ...")

Because the investigator's report is part of the record of the case, there can be no objection in general to the receipt or use of the investigator's report in arriving at decisions in care and protection cases. *Custody of Michel*, 28 Mass. App. Ct. at 265. The report may contain hearsay statements from a wide variety of sources and the cases do not distinguish between levels of hearsay. *Id.* at 266. Parties have a fair opportunity to rebut allegations in the report by cross examining the court investigator and his/her sources or by other means at trial, so it is vital that all sources of statements and information in the report be clearly identified. Specific objections may be made by motions in limine. *Custody of Tracy*, 31 Mass. App. Ct., 481 (1991) and *Custody of Michel* . See also Mass. G. Evid. § 1115(c)(1) and (e)(6) regarding court investigator reports in general.

Rule 15. Pretrial Conference in Care and Protection Cases

A pretrial conference shall be scheduled to occur no later than thirty days before the trial on the merits, except for good cause shown provided however, that it shall be scheduled to occur after the date upon which the court investigator's report is due. All parties are required to be present with counsel at the pretrial conference, except that counsel for the child may appear without his/her client. Failure of one or more parties to appear shall not preclude the court from proceeding with the pretrial conference.

A. Witness and Exhibit Lists. The parties shall file written witness and exhibit lists with the court at the pretrial conference. As a matter of discretion in a particular case, the trial judge may order the parties to submit a written joint or individual pretrial memorandum that covers any or all of the issues set forth below in subsection B of this rule. Parties shall be bound by the witness and exhibit lists filed separately or set forth in a pretrial memorandum, except by court order for good cause shown.

B. Issues to be Addressed. At the pretrial conference, the court shall address the matters set forth below:

1. Whether parents have been served by the petitioner and the date(s) of service

2. Whether discovery has been completed; and if discovery has not been completed, a list of discovery items not yet provided and the compliance date

3. Relief sought, including whether or not there will be a request for a decree dispensing with the need for parental consent to the adoption, custody, guardianship or other disposition of the child named in the petition

4. Identification of the specific contested issues to be litigated at trial

5. A stipulation of all uncontested facts and issues

6. A list of proposed exhibits to be introduced at trial

7. A list of proposed witnesses which shall include the names of any expert witnesses, a delineation of the issues to which the expert is expected to testify, and a copy of his or her curriculum vitae

8. Issues regarding the admissibility of evidence at trial

9. Scheduling a date for the submission of motions in limine, if any, and scheduling a hearing thereon, if necessary

10. Any unaddressed motions

11. Whether a writ of habeas corpus will be required to ensure attendance of a party or witness, or whether a witness needs to participate telephonically or by other means

12. Whether an interpreter is required

13. Whether a child witness needs an accommodation to testify

14. Whether, if the Indian Child Welfare Act (ICWA) applies, the tribe has been notified and has responded and whether other legal requirements under ICWA have been satisfied

15. An estimate of trial time

16. Any other matters that may aid in the disposition of the action

The court shall address, where applicable:

17. Whether the possibility of settlement has been discussed

18. Whether counsel for the parties have discussed mediation with their client(s) pursuant to Rule 5 of Rule 1:18 of the Supreme Judicial Court

19. The Department's plan to provide timely notice of the trial to the foster parent, pre-adoptive parent or relative providing care.

C. Scheduling the Hearing on the Merits. At the pretrial conference, unless previously scheduled, the court shall schedule a hearing on the merits to be heard within twelve months of the filing of the petition unless a later date is necessary in the interests of justice.

Adopted July 27, 2018, effective November 5, 2018.

Note

This rule differs from the prior 2007 rule in that it retains the pretrial conference and written witness and exhibit lists but removes the requirement of a written pretrial conference memorandum unless ordered by the trial judge. Pretrial memoranda that contain mere boilerplate paragraphs relative to the issues to be addressed or a list of all possible witnesses are of no value to the court.

In some divisions, proposed exhibits are marked for identification at various stages of the proceedings. In those divisions, when listing exhibits marked for evidence under Rule 15 B. 6, counsel should use the same numbers used by the court to mark the exhibits for identification.

If a date has not been set for the submission of, or to hear, motions in limine, the trial judge should schedule said date(s) at the pretrial conference.

Rule 16. Notice to Foster Parent, Pre-adoptive Parent, or Relative Providing Care for a Child

The Department shall file a certification with the court that the Department has provided notice and informed the foster parent, pre-adoptive parent or relative providing care for a child, who is the subject of a care and protection petition, of his/her right to attend and be heard at a hearing held pursuant to G. L. c. 119, §§ 26 and 29B. The certification shall be on a form approved by the Chief Justice of the Juvenile Court. In the event the foster parent, pre-adoptive parent or relative chooses to exercise his/her right to be heard, he/she shall testify in court under oath. Failure by the Department to provide timely notice does not preclude the judge from proceeding with the hearing.

Adopted July 27, 2018, effective November 5, 2018.

Note

General Laws c. 119, § 29D requires the Department to provide notice and inform the foster parent, pre-adoptive parent or relative providing care of a child who is the subject of a care and protection petition of the right to attend and be heard at hearings pursuant to G. L. c. 119, §§ 26 and 29B. This includes hearings on the merits, (including the termination or so called "best interests" hearing) review and redetermination hearings, and permanency hearings. The statute expressly provides that the foster parent, pre-adoptive parent or relative does not become a party to the case by exercising his/her right to attend and be heard. Although the rule provides that the hearing may proceed in the absence of timely notice by the Department, the court may provide an opportunity for the foster parent, pre-adoptive parent or relative to be heard on another date. The rule does not require the foster parent, pre-adoptive parent or relative to inform the court in advance of the hearing of his/her intention to attend and be heard but he/she may do so. *See Adoption of Sherry*, 435 Mass. 331 (2001) (usual rules of evidence apply; testimony of foster parent must be under oath and subject to cross examination; unsworn written statement is inadmissible.)

Rule 17.   Sanctions and Contempt

A.   Sanctions. If a party, or an attorney, or both, engages in conduct that either delays the progress of litigation, wastes judicial resources or causes an unnecessary increase in expenses on a party, or otherwise impedes the full and effective administration of justice, without sufficient justification as determined by the court, the court may order the party, or the attorney, or both to pay reasonable costs and expenses. The court shall provide notice and a hearing before final imposition of costs or expenses. The court shall articulate, in writing, the reasons for the imposed sanctions.

B.   Contempt. Enforcement of compliance with court orders may be sought by means of civil contempt, which shall proceed in accordance with the provisions of Mass. R. Civ. P. 65.3 (b)—(h). Proceedings for summary contempt shall be held in accordance with the provisions of Mass. R. Crim. P. 43. Prosecutions for criminal contempt shall proceed in accordance with the provisions of Mass. R. Crim. P. 44.

Adopted July 27, 2018, effective November 5, 2018.

Rule 18.   Subpoenas

Subpoenas shall be served and enforced as provided by Mass. R. Civ. P. 45 and may be issued by the Clerk's Office or as otherwise provided in Mass. R. Civ. P. 45.

Adopted July 27, 2018, effective November 5, 2018.

Rule 19.   Trial Judge's Order, Findings of Fact and Conclusions of Law and Notification by Clerk of Issuance of Findings of Fact and Conclusions of Law

A.   Entry of Adjudication, Order of Commitment, Order Dispensing with the Need for Consent to Adoption, Allowance or Denial of Guardianship Petition. Upon adjudication, order of commitment, or order dispensing with the right of the parents to receive notice of or consent to the adoption, custody, or guardianship or any other disposition of the child or an allowance or denial of a guardianship petition, the clerk shall forthwith enter that adjudication, order, allowance or denial on the court's docket. If the court issues a permanent mittimus or grants permanent custody of a child to the Department, the court shall schedule the case for review which shall be no later than six months from the date of the mittimus or custody order and every six months thereafter until permanency has been achieved for the child.

B.   Notice. Immediately following the clerk's entry of the above adjudication, order, allowance or denial on the docket, the clerk shall notify all attorneys of record and parties who are self-represented by mail or electronically, of the entry of that adjudication, order, allowance or denial. The clerk shall note on the docket, or otherwise record electronically, the names of the persons to whom the notice was sent, with the date notified. This notice shall include: 1) a copy of the adjudication, order, allowance or denial; 2) the date of the clerk's entry; and 3) notice that each party has thirty (30) days from the date of entry within which to file a claim of appeal.

C.   Order or Decree Dispensing with Consent to Adoption. In all cases in which the court issues an order dispensing with the right of the parents to receive notice of or consent to the adoption, custody, or guardianship or any other disposition of the child, the court shall enter the order or decree on a document separate from any findings of fact and conclusions of law.

D.   Trial Judge's Findings of Fact and Conclusions of Law. The trial judge, upon making an adjudication or issuing an order of commitment or an order dispensing with the right of the parents to receive notice of or consent to the adoption, custody, or guardianship or any other disposition of the child, shall file with the clerk, consistent with time standards promulgated by the Chief Justice of the Juvenile Court, findings of fact and conclusions of law to support the order and/or adjudication.

E.   Notification to All Parties by Clerk. Immediately upon the filing of the findings of fact and conclusions of law, the clerk shall mail or transmit a copy to each attorney of record and party who is self-represented.

Adopted July 27, 2018, effective November 5, 2018.

Note

After an adjudication, the judge may make any appropriate dispositional order including conditions and limitations relative to the care and custody of the child. The dispositional order may include, but is not limited to, reunification with the parent, guardian, or other custodian found by the court to be qualified to care for the child; custody to any agency or private organization licensed or otherwise authorized to provide care for the child; or custody to the Department G. L. c. 119, § 26(b).

Although issuance of a permanent mittimus or grant of permanent custody to the Department is a permissible post-adjudication order under § 26(b), these alternatives are not considered to be permanent plans for children under Rule 9(a)(1) of Trial Court Rule VI Uniform Rules for Permanency Hearings. Accordingly, this rule requires the court to schedule a review of these cases no later than six months after the date of the issuance of a permanent mittimus or order of permanent custody to the Department and every six months thereafter until the child is returned to his/her parents, is adopted, is placed with a third party custodian, a permanent guardian is appointed, or the child ages out of the system.

While an alternative planned permanent living arrangement ("AP-PLA") is considered to be a possible permanency plan for a child sixteen years of age or over under Rule 9(a)(1) of the Uniform Rules for Permanency Hearings, it does not achieve legal permanency for the child. Therefore, if APPLA is approved by the court as the permanency plan, the court must schedule a review of the case every six months thereafter until the child is returned to his/her parents, is adopted, is placed with a third party custodian, a permanent guardian is appointed, or the child ages out of the system. The review required in section A of this rule is different from the right of review and redetermination under G. L. c. 119, § 26(c); rather it is established by

this rule to permit the court to assess progress toward permanency in keeping with the best practices for achieving legal permanency for children.

Rule 20. Appeal

A. Claim of Appeal. An appeal, as permitted by G. L. c. 119, § 27, shall be governed by the Massachusetts Rules of Appellate Procedure. The claim of appeal shall be on a form approved by the Chief Justice of the Juvenile Court and shall be taken to constitute the "notice of appeal" for the purposes of complying with the Massachusetts Rules of Appellate Procedure. The claim of appeal and any request for a transcript, if required, shall be signed by the appealing party or parties unless the appellant is the child; a claim of appeal that is not so signed by the party or parties shall not be accepted for filing by the clerk.

B. Record on Appeal. In addition to the requirements of the Rules of Appellate Procedure, the record on appeal as assembled shall include a copy of the trial judge's findings of fact and conclusions of law.

Adopted July 27, 2018, effective November 5, 2018.

STANDING ORDERS OF THE JUVENILE COURT

Table of Standing Orders

Standing Order 1–82.   Court Hours

The hours during which the Divisions of the Juvenile Court Department shall be open for business to the general public shall be 8:30 a.m. to 4:30 p.m., Monday through Friday.

Adopted Feb. 3, 1982.

Standing Order 1–84.   Juvenile Court Case Records and Reports

Applicable to All Divisions

All juvenile court case records and reports are confidential and are the property of the court.

Reports loaned to or copied for attorneys of record, or such other persons as the court may permit, shall be returned to the court after their use or at the conclusion of the litigation, whichever occurs first.

Said reports shall not be further copied or released without permission of the court.

Adopted May 8, 1984.

Standing Order 1–88.   Time Standards [Superseded]

(Superseded by 1–04)

Standing Order 1–93.   Procedures for Care and Protection Cases Under St.1992, c. 303 [Repealed]

(Repealed January 1, 2007)

Standing Order 1–04.   Time Standards [Superseded]

(Superseded by 2–07)

Standing Order 2–04.   Electronic Recording of Court Proceedings

A.   Official Recordings.

1.   When required.   In all divisions of the Juvenile Court Department all courtroom proceedings shall be recorded electronically, subject to the availability and functioning of appropriate recording devices, except that the following may but need not be recorded: (a) the call of the list and similar matters of an administrative nature; and (b) proceedings conducted by a magistrate other than a judge.   Said recording shall take place whether or not a court stenographer is present in the courtroom.

2.   Logging.   During every proceeding which is required to be recorded, the clerk shall: (a) announce clearly the name of the case and its docket number at the beginning of the proceeding; and (b) note, whenever practicable, on the case papers or in a separate log the cassette number and the index numbers representing the beginning and end points of the proceeding.

3.   Counsel's responsibility.   Counsel shall be responsible for assisting in the creation of an audible record by properly using the microphones provided.   Counsel shall speak with sufficient clarity and in sufficient proximity to the microphones to ensure an audible record, and shall be responsible for requesting the judge, when necessary, to instruct other counsel, witnesses or others as to the proper use of the microphones in order to ensure an audible record.

4.   Preservation of tapes.   The clerk-magistrate shall preserve for at least three years the original recording of any trial, evidentiary hearing, guilty plea or admission to sufficient facts that was presided over by a judge.

5.   Access to cassette copies.

(a) Open proceedings. Any person whether or not a party, shall be permitted to obtain a cassette copy of an original recording, or any portion thereof, of any proceeding which was open to the public, unless the record of such proceeding has been sealed or impounded.

(b) Closed proceedings. The original recording of a proceeding which was not open to the public, or of a proceeding whose record has been sealed or impounded, shall be deemed to be impounded and a cassette copy of the original recording, or any portion thereof, shall be made available only in accordance with the following provisions:

(i) Cassette copies of closed proceedings for purposes of appeal. Counsel for any party, or any party who has entered an appearance *pro se*, shall be permitted to obtain a cassette copy of such a proceeding upon certifying that such cassette copy will be used solely for an appeal, or to determine whether to claim an appeal, in the same matter. Unless the judge who presided over the proceeding has ordered otherwise, the clerk-magistrate shall provide such cassette copy upon such certification without requiring a judge's approval of the request.

(ii) Cassette copies of closed proceedings for other purposes. A cassette copy of such a proceeding may be made available to other persons or for other purposes only with the approval of the judge who presided over the proceeding or, if that judge is unavailable for an extended period or the proceeding was conducted by a magistrate other than a judge, any judge of the court. Any such request shall be accompanied by an affidavit, setting forth the reason for the request and the specific use to be made of the cassette copy, and shall be served on all parties to the proceeding. Any other party or interested person may file a statement in support of or in opposition to such a request. A judge may determine such a request with or without hearing wherever he or she is then sitting. A judge may permit access subject to appropriate restrictions upon the use and dissemination of the cassette copy of such proceeding.

(c) Ordering cassette copies. A request for a cassette copy shall be filed with the clerk-magistrate on a form prescribed by the Chief Justice of the Juvenile Court. In order that multiple cassette copies may be made simultaneously whenever possible, any person making such a request regarding a proceeding that is presently pending on appeal shall certify that he has notified all other parties of his request.

The cost of a cassette copy shall be as established by the Chief Administrative Justice of the Trial Court pursuant to G.L. c. 262, s. 4B. The clerk-magistrate may require prepayment of all or some portion of such cost. There shall be no cost for a cassette copy produced for the use of the court, the Attorney General's office, a district attorney's office, any other agency of the Commonwealth, a police prosecutor, or a party represented by an attorney provided by the Committee for Public Counsel Services. General Laws c. 261, ss. 27A–27G shall apply to any request on behalf of an indigent party who is not represented by an attorney provided by the Committee for Public Counsel Services, and in such case the cost of a cassette copy shall be deemed an "extra cost" as defined in s. 27A.

6. Impermissible uses. No cassette copy shall be used for a commercial purpose, for public or private entertainment or amusement, or for any other purpose detrimental to the administration of justice. No cassette copy shall be duplicated or tampered with. No cassette copy shall be erased, nor its labels removed or defaced, while the matter is pending in any court, or is subject to direct appellate review. Any cassette copy which is thereafter erased shall be erased in its entirety.

Any further dissemination of the cassette copy of a closed proceeding, or its contents, is permissible only: (a) for the purposes for which access was permitted; (b) subject to all provisions of law and court rules governing the records of such closed proceedings; and (c) subject to any additional restrictions with regard to its use which have been prescribed by the judge permitting access.

Any person requesting a cassette copy shall take all reasonable precautions to assure compliance with the requirements of this rule, including notifying anyone permitted to use the cassette copy of such requirements. Any person violating any such requirement shall be subject to appropriate sanctions, including contempt proceedings.

B. Unofficial recordings.

1. Covert recording forbidden. No person shall make any electronic recording in any courtroom, hearing room, office, chambers or lobby of a judge or magistrate without prior authorization from the judge or magistrate then having immediate supervision over such place.

2. Recording by the news media. The recording by the news media of a proceeding open to the public is governed by the provisions of Supreme Judicial Court Rule 1:19.

Adopted October 13, 2004, effective November 1, 2004.

Standing Order 1–07. Violation of Probation Proceedings [Superseded]

Superseded by Standing Order 1-17 effective September 25, 2017.

Standing Order 2–07. Time Standards [Superseded]

[See, now, Standing Order 2–18.]

Standing Order 1–09. Application of G.L. c. 190B, Article V to Guardianship of a Minor Cases Pending on July 1, 2009 or with a Decree Issued Prior Thereto

On July 1, 2009, certain provisions of the Massachusetts Uniform Probate Code, G.L. c. 190B (Code), become effective. The provisions are primarily contained in Article V of the Code, Protection of Persons under Disability and Their Property. The Code significantly reforms the practice of guardianship law.

The Massachusetts Uniform Probate Code applies to any guardianship case:

(a) where a permanent decree has previously entered and the guardianship has not terminated;

(b) pending on July 1, 2009 without a permanent decree having entered; or

(c) commenced on or after July 1, 2009.

Accordingly:

1. PENDING CASES WITH NO PERMANENT DE-CREE

Any Petition for Guardianship of the Minor pending before July 1, 2009 does not require amendment or the filing of a new petition.

2. CASES WHERE A GUARDIAN OF THE MINOR WAS APPOINTED BEFORE JULY 1, 2009

A. Issuance of Letters of Appointment.

When any party seeks a certified copy of the Decree appointing the guardian of the minor, Letters of Appointment of Guardian shall issue in accordance with the prior Decree and encompass duties and responsibilities set forth in the Code.

B. Reporting Requirements

Guardians of minors are required, at a minimum, to file a report on the condition of the minor and the condition of the estate of the minor within one year following the anniversary date of their appointment, but no later than July 1, 2010, whichever comes first. Whenever any guardian of the minor is before the court, the court shall ensure the timely filing and review of any and all reports.

Adopted June 22, 2009, effective July 1, 2009.

Standing Order 2–09. Sound Recording of Court Proceedings

A. Definitions.

1. *Sound recording:* a recording, such as but not limited to a cassette tape or compact disc, used to store recorded sound.

B. Official Recordings.

1. *When Required.* In all divisions of the Juvenile Court Department all courtroom proceedings shall be recorded, subject to the availability and functioning of appropriate recording devices, except that the following may but need not be recorded: (a) the call of the list and similar matters of an administrative nature; and (b) proceedings conducted by a magistrate other than a judge. Said recording shall take place whether or not a court stenographer is present in the courtroom.

2. *Logging.* During every proceeding which is required to be recorded, the clerk shall: (a) announce clearly the name of the case and its docket number at the beginning of the proceeding; and (b) log, whenever practicable, the sound recording number and the index numbers or dates representing the beginning and end points of the proceeding.

3. *Counsel's Responsibility.* Counsel shall be responsible for assisting in the creation of an audible record by properly using the microphones provided. Counsel shall speak with sufficient clarity and in sufficient proximity to the microphones to ensure an audible record, and shall be responsible for requesting the judge, when necessary, to instruct other counsel, witnesses or others as to the proper use of the microphones in order to ensure an audible record.

4. *Preservation of Recordings.* The clerk-magistrate shall preserve for at least three years the original recording of any trial, evidentiary hearing, guilty plea or admission to sufficient facts that was presided over by the judge.

5. *Access to copies of sound recordings.*

(a) *Open proceedings.* Any person whether or not a party, shall be permitted to obtain a sound recording copy of an original recording, or any portion thereof, of any proceeding which was open to the public, unless the record of such proceeding has been sealed or impounded.

(b) *Closed proceedings.* The original recording of a proceeding which was not open to the public, or of a proceeding whose record has been sealed or impounded, shall be deemed to be impounded and a sound recording copy of the original recording, or any portion thereof, shall be made available only in accordance with the following provisions:

(i) *Sound recording copies of closed proceedings for purposes of appeal.* Counsel for any party, or any party who has entered an appearance *pro se*, shall be permitted to obtain a sound recording copy of the original recording of such a proceeding upon certifying that such sound recording copy will be used solely for an appeal, or to determine whether to claim an appeal, in the same matter. Unless the judge who presided over the proceeding has ordered otherwise, the clerk-magistrate shall provide such sound recording copy upon such certification without requiring a judge's approval of the request.

(ii) *Sound recording copies of closed proceedings for other purposes.* A sound recording copy of such a proceeding may be made available to other persons or for other purposes only with the approval of the judge who presided over the proceeding or, if that judge is unavailable for an extended period or the proceeding was conducted by a magistrate other than a judge, any judge of the court. Any such request shall be accompanied by an affidavit, setting forth the reason for the request and the specific use to be made of the sound recording copy, and shall be served on all parties to the proceeding. Any other party or interested person may file a statement in support of or in opposition to such a request. A judge may determine such a request with or without hearing wherever he or she is then sitting. A judge may permit access subject to appropriate restrictions upon the use and dissemination of the sound recording copy of such proceeding.

(c) *Ordering sound recording copies.* A request for a sound recording copy shall be filed with the clerk-magistrate on a form prescribed by the Chief Justice of the Juvenile Court. In order that multiple sound recording copies may be made simultaneously whenever possible, any person making such a request regarding a proceeding that is presently pending on appeal shall certify that he has notified all other parties of his request. The cost of a sound recording copy shall be as established by the Chief Administrative Justice of the Trial Court pursuant to G.L. c. 262, s. 4B. The clerk-magistrate shall require prepayment of all or some portion of such cost. There shall be no cost for a sound recording copy produced for the use of the court, the Attorney General's office, a district attorney's office, any other agency of the Commonwealth, a police prosecutor, or a party represented by an attorney provided by the Committee for Public Counsel Services.

General Laws c. 261, ss. 27A–G shall apply to any request by a party who is not represented by an attorney provided by the Committee for Public Counsel Services, and in such case the cost of a sound recording copy shall be deemed an "extra cost" as defined in s. 27A.

6. *Impermissible uses.* No sound recording copy shall be used for a commercial purpose, for public or private entertainment or amusement, or for any other purpose detrimental to the administration of justice. No sound recording copy shall be duplicated or tampered with. No sound recording copy shall be erased, nor its labels removed or defaced, while the matter is pending in any court, or is subject to direct appellate review. Any sound recording copy which is thereafter erased shall be erased in its entirety.

Any further dissemination of the sound recording copy of a closed proceeding, or its contents, is permissible only: (a) for the purposes for which access was permitted; (b) subject to all provisions of law and court rules governing the records of such closed proceedings; and (c) subject to any additional restrictions with regard to its use which have been prescribed by the judge permitting access.

Any person requesting a sound recording copy shall take all reasonable precautions to assure compliance with the requirements of this rule, including notifying anyone permitted to use the sound recording copy of such requirements. Any person violating any such requirement shall be subject to appropriate sanctions, including contempt proceedings.

C. Unofficial recordings.

1. *Covert recording forbidden.* No person shall make any recording in any courtroom, hearing room, office, chambers or lobby of a judge or magistrate without prior authorization from the judge or magistrate then having immediate supervision over such place.

2. *Recording by the news media.* The recording by the news media of a proceeding open to the public is governed by the provisions of Supreme Judicial Court Rule 1:19.

Adopted effective November 1, 2009.

Standing Order 1–10. Scheduling Care and Protection and Termination of Parental Rights Trials

1. **Purpose.** The purpose of this Standing Order is to establish procedures and standards and promote uniformity to ensure that care and protection and termination of parental rights trials are completed within a reasonable time after commencement of trial.

2. **Applicability.** This Standing Order is applicable to all Divisions of the Juvenile Court and to all care and protection and termination of parental rights trials.

3. **Definitions.** *Commencement of Trial*—the date when testimonial evidence is presented by witnesses called to testify before the court; the date that a document is submitted to the court, accepted and admitted into evidence as an exhibit. *Close of Evidence*—the date when all parties have completed the submission of all evidence.

4. **Length of Trial.** All care and protection and termination of parental rights trials will conclude no later than thirty (30) calendar days after commencement of trial. Trial dates should be scheduled for consecutive days, whenever possible. Potential exhibits should be "marked for identification" prior to the commencement of trial whenever possible.

5. **Cases Under Advisement.** An adjudication that a child is, or is not, in need of care and protection, or an order terminating, or a decision not to terminate, parental rights shall be made no later than thirty (30) days after the close of evidence.

6. **Emergency Extension for Trial or Cases Under Advisement.** In extraordinary circumstances, the justice presiding over the trial may request approval from the Chief Justice to extend the time for trial, or extend the time for adjudication, order or decision, for an additional fifteen (15) calendar days. Such request should be submitted in writing, should identify the extraordinary circumstances that necessitated the request and should be submitted no later than ten (10) calendar days prior to the expiration of the thirty (30) day period, except when the request for additional time is due to unforeseen circumstances which occur subsequent to the ten (10) calendar day period.

8. **Dedicated Trial Sessions.** Dedicated trial sessions for care and protection and termination of parental rights cases are encouraged where there are available judicial resources, sufficient attorneys to represent the parties and where multiple demands upon court time do not make such sessions impractical and inefficient.

9. **Effective Date.** This Standing Order and the procedures and standards contained herein shall apply to all care and protection and termination of parental rights trials commenced on or after September 1, 2010.

Adopted effective September 1, 2010.

Standing Order 1–15. Provision of Respondents' Non-Clinical Identifying Information in Commitment Proceedings Under G. L. c. 123, §§ 7, 8, and 12(e), or G. L. c. 123, § 35

The purpose of this Order is to provide for the collection of non-clinical identifying information in commitment proceedings in the Juvenile Court Department necessary to comply with the courts' reporting requirements pursuant to Chapter 284, Acts of 2014 , An Act Relative to the Reduction of Gun Violence.[1]

IT IS THEREFORE ORDERED:

An applicant seeking a court order to commit a respondent to a mental health facility pursuant to G.L. c. 123, § 12(e) , a petitioner seeking a court order to commit or retain a respondent for inpatient care pursuant to G.L. c. 123, §§ 7 and 8 , and a petitioner seeking a court order to commit a respondent for treatment for alcoholism and/or substance abuse pursuant to G.L. c. 123, § 35 , shall provide the respondent's date of birth and social security number, if available, to the court.

Adopted May 20, 2015, effective June 1, 2015.

1 Although commitment matters are also brought under G.L. c. 123, §§ 15(b), 16(b) or (c), or 18 that arise out of criminal proceedings, the respondent's or defendant's date of birth and

social security number is obtained and provided to the court through the Defendant Identification Information System in those cases.

Standing Order 2–15. Relief from Notification Requirements of Rule 13(b) of the Trial Court Rule VIII, Uniform Rules of Impoundment Procedure

Any party or interested nonparty filing materials in a Juvenile Court case that is impounded by statute, caselaw, court rule or standing order, is not required to file a notice identifying the case and/or the material as 'impounded' as required by Rule 13(b) of the Uniform Rules of Impoundment Procedure. In the Juvenile Court, any cases or case records that are confidential or not available for public inspection are considered to be impounded by statute, caselaw, court rule or standing order. These cases include but are not limited to care and protection and delinquency cases. Rule 13(b) of the Uniform Rules of Impoundment Procedure applies only to Juvenile Court cases and case records that are open to the public and to public inspection, such as Youthful Offender and adult criminal cases.

Adopted effective October 1, 2015.

Joint Standing Order 1–16. Authority of the Judge with Respect to Communication with Specialty Court Teams

This Standing Order is promulgated by the chief Justice of the Trial Court pursuant to G. L, c. 211B, Section 9 and shall constitute authorization by law as referenced in Rule 2.9 (A)(2) of the Code of Judicial Conduct (effective January 1, 2016).

For purposes of this Order:

Specialty Court means a specifically designated court session that focuses on individuals with underlying medical, mental health, substance abuse, or other issues that contribute to the reasons such individuals are before the courts. Specialty court shall also mean Veterans Treatment Court and Homelessness Court. Specialty court sessions integrate treatment and services with judicial case oversight and intensive court supervision. Examples Include drug courts, mental health courts, veterans' courts, and tenancy preservation programs.

A Staffing shall refer to a regularly scheduled, informal conference not occurring in open court, the purpose of which is to permit the presiding judge and others, including counsel, to discuss a participant's progress in the specialty court, treatment recommendations, or responses to participant compliance issues.

IT IS THEREFORE ORDERED:

A judge presiding over a specialty court shall have the authority to initiate, permit or otherwise consider ex parte communications about defendants, juveniles or probationers with members of the specialty court team at a staffing or by written documents provided to all members of the specialty court team, The purpose of this authority is to allow judges in their role in presiding over specialty court sessions, and only in that capacity, to assume a more interactive role with parties, treatment providers, probation officers, social workers and others, than Rule 2.9 of the Code of Judicial Conduct would otherwise permit.

Adopted effective January 7, 2016.

Joint Standing Order 2–16. Uniform Interdepartmental Procedures for Probation Violation Proceedings

This Standing Order is promulgated by the Chief Justice of the Trial Court pursuant to G. L, c. 211B, Section 9 and stands effective October 3, 2016.

1. Application

This Order shall apply to the Superior Court, District Court, Boston Municipal Court and Juvenile Court Departments.

2. Purpose

This Order sets forth requirements regarding communication among the above-named departments of the Trial Court when an individual who is the subject of a probation order in one of these departments is charged with a new offense in another of these departments. Its purpose is to ensure that this required interdepartmental communication relating to the commencement of probation violation proceedings as a result of alleged new criminal behavior by a probationer, and the potential custody and transport of that probationer between different court departments, occur in a timely, informed and efficient manner. This Order does not apply to an individual who is the subject of a probation order issued prior to a trial or the formal submission and acceptance of a plea of guilty or an admission to sufficient facts, as provided in G.L. c. 276, § 87 ("pretrial probation").

3. Definition of Terms

As used in this Order, the terms below shall have the following meanings:

"Criminal:" includes delinquency or youthful offender.

"Criminal Court:" a court division of the Boston Municipal, District, or Juvenile Court or the Superior Court.

The terms used in this Order and the form promulgated by the Chief Justice of the Trial Court pursuant to Section 9 have been defined to include terminology associated with juvenile cases and proceedings and the Juvenile Court. They have been defined in this manner for the purposes of convenience and ease of reading and are applicable to this Order and form only. The terms as appearing in this Order and form do not change the meaning of the terminology used in adult and juvenile proceedings as defined and set forth by case law and statutes. Other than for the purposes of this Order and form, adult and juvenile terms are not interchangeable.

4. Intra-Departmental Communications

This Order does not apply to intra-departmental communications, transport of probationers, or use of the warrant management system, which may be the subject of rules or standing orders issued by and applicable within individual court departments.

5. Information to be Sent from the Criminal Court; Custody of Probationer

When an individual appears on a new criminal charge before a criminal court, and that individual is the subject of a probation order issued by a court in a different department of the Trial Court, the probation department of the criminal court shall transmit to the probation department of the court having responsibility for the supervision of the probationer (the "probation court") information and requests for information, including information regarding the possible service of a notice of violation on, and transport of, the probationer. This transmission shall be made by means of the form referred to in Section 9, below.

The transmission from the criminal court shall be sent electronically and promptly, to the probation officer in the probation court listed as the probation officer on duty in the probation court or, if there is no probation officer on duty, to the Chief Probation Officer of the probation court. The transmission shall be sent while the probationer is at the criminal court. When necessary, the criminal court may order the probationer held in custody until the procedures required by this Order are completed.

6. Information to be Returned by the Probation Court; Time Limit

The probation department of the probation court shall respond electronically, to the probation officer who transmitted the request for information from the criminal court. The response shall include information regarding service of a notice of violation on, and transport of, the probationer. This response shall be transmitted within two hours or within such time limit as extended, as provided in Section 7, such time limit to be measured from the time indicated on the transmission, and shall be set forth on the form referred to in Section 9, below.

If the probation department is requesting that the probationer be transported, the probation department shall request the issuance of an arrest warrant for a violation of probation ("warrant") from a judge in the probation court. If the judge issues such warrant, the clerk's office shall enter it promptly into the Warrant Management System and the probation department shall provide the criminal court with a notice of violation that cites the violation(s).

If the probation department is not requesting that the probationer be transported and is requesting that the probationer be served with a notice of violation, the probation department shall provide the probation department of the criminal court with a notice of violation that cites the violation(s) and indicates the date and time of the probationer's required appearance in the probation court.

7. Action by the Criminal Court

The criminal court shall await receipt of the information from the probation court for a period of two hours measured from the time of the transmission of the request for that information. This two-hour time limit may be extended by the criminal court.

Upon the timely receipt of the required information from the probation court and, if the probation court has issued a warrant, the criminal court shall serve on the probationer, in hand, a notice of violation on behalf of the probation court and shall either order transport of the probationer on such warrant or defer transport on the warrant until the termination of any custody ordered by the criminal court judge in the new criminal case. In the event that no warrant has been issued by the probation court, and the probation department has provided a notice of violation to the probation department of the criminal court, the criminal court shall serve such notice on the probationer, in hand, on behalf of the probation court.

If the probation department of the probation court does not provide the required information or a notice of violation to the probation department of the criminal court in the manner set forth in Section 6, the criminal court need not take any further action regarding the probation matter. In such instances, the probation department of the criminal court shall make an appropriate entry into its records.

8. Action by the Probation Court

Upon delivery of the probationer into the custody of the probation court on the warrant, and not withstanding any provision of this Order, the form promulgated pursuant to section 9, or the reason for the warrant as it may appear in the Warrant Management System, the probation court shall proceed on the violation of probation matter in accordance with applicable law and respective departmental rule or standing order.

9. Form to be Promulgated by the Chief Justice of the Trial Court

The transmittal of information between courts as required by this Order shall proceed by means of a form promulgated by the Chief Justice of the Trial Court. This form shall include such specific information requirements, data elements and attachments as the Chief Justice may deem appropriate, provided that nothing in this Order shall be construed to prohibit the use of telephone communication to supplement the use of such form and to achieve its purpose.

10. Probation Department Procedures and Record Keeping

Implementation of this Order by the Massachusetts Probation Service, including record keeping requirements, shall be as set forth in such instructions and regulations consistent with the provisions of this Order as may be deemed appropriate by the Commissioner of Probation.

Adopted August 18, 2016, effective October 3, 2016.

Standing Order 1–17. Violation of Probation Proceedings

I. SCOPE AND PURPOSE

This standing order prescribes procedures in the Juvenile Court to be followed upon the allegation of a violation of an order of probation issued in a delinquency, youthful offender or criminal case after a finding of delinquency, youthful offender, or guilty, or after a continuance without a finding. This standing order does not apply to an alleged violation of pretrial probation, as the latter term is defined herein.

The purpose of this standing order is to ensure that judicial proceedings undertaken upon the allegation of a violation of probation are conducted in a manner consistent with the Commonwealth's policy regarding children as set forth in G. L. c. 119 and in full compliance with all applicable law, promptly and with an appropriate degree of procedural uniformity.

This standing order supersedes Standing Order 1–07 Violation of Probation Proceedings.

Commentary

The first purpose of the violation hearing is to adjudicate the factual question of whether a probationer has violated his or her probation order. The second purpose is to revoke probation or order any other disposition. The issue of violation is essentially a *factual* matter whereas the dispositional decision of whether to revoke probation is essentially a matter of *discretion*.

Throughout this standing order the person who is the subject of probation violation proceedings is usually referred to as the "probationer" rather than the "defendant." With respect to the probation proceedings, such a person is not a defendant; he or she has either been adjudicated or convicted, after trial or based on a plea of delinquent, youthful offender or guilty, or has formally submitted an admission to the facts of a criminal charge. Use of the term "probationer" is intended to underscore the legal status of the person charged with a probation violation, which is fundamentally distinct from the status of a person who is a defendant on a delinquency, youthful offender or criminal case, particularly in terms of procedural rights.

II. DEFINITION OF TERMS

In construing this standing order, the following terms shall have the following definitions:

"Continuance without a finding" is the order of a court, following a formal submission and acceptance of a plea of guilty or an admission to sufficient facts in a youthful offender case or criminal case; or, in a delinquency case, following a formal submission and acceptance of a plea of delinquency or an admission to sufficient facts or after a trial in which the allegations are proven beyond a reasonable doubt, whereby the case is continued to a date certain without the formal entry of a delinquency, youthful offender, or guilty finding. A continuance without a finding may include conditions imposed in an order of probation (1) the violation of which may result in the revocation of the continuance, entry of a finding of guilty, youthful offender or delinquency and imposition of sentence or commitment to the Department of Youth Services and (2) compliance with which will result in dismissal of the case.

"Defendant" is a juvenile adjudged delinquent or youthful offender or an adult convicted of a crime.

"District Attorney" is the criminal prosecuting authority and includes the Attorney General if the delinquency, youthful offender, or criminal case in which probation was ordered was prosecuted by the Office of the Attorney General.

"General conditions of probation" are the conditions of probation that are imposed as a matter of course in every order of probation, as set forth in the official form promulgated by the Chief Justice of the Juvenile Court for such orders.

"Probation order" is the formal, written court order whereby a defendant is placed on probation and which expressly sets forth the conditions of probation. A probation order is not a contract.

"Pretrial probation" is the probationary status of a defendant pursuant to a probation order issued prior to a trial or prior to the formal submission and acceptance of a plea of delinquent, youthful offender or guilty, or prior to an admission to sufficient facts, as provided in G. L. c. 276, § 87.

"Revocation of probation" is the revocation by a judge of an order of probation as a consequence of a determination that a condition of that probation order has been violated.

"Special conditions of probation" are any condition of probation other than one of the general conditions of probation.

"Surrender" is the procedure by which a probation officer requires a probationer to appear before the court for a judicial hearing regarding an allegation of a probation violation.

III. COMMENCEMENT OF VIOLATION PROCEEDINGS: CHARGED CRIMINAL CONDUCT

(a) General. This standing order prescribes the procedures to be undertaken upon the issuance of a delinquency or criminal complaint or youthful offender indictment against a probationer.

(b) Where Probation Order and Delinquency or Criminal Complaint or Youthful Offender Indictment Involve Same Court Division.

(i) *Issuance and Service of Notice of Violation; Termination of Proceedings; Withdrawal of Notice of Violation.* When a delinquency or criminal complaint is issued by a court division or a youthful offender indictment is returned by a grand jury and remitted to a court division of the Juvenile Court against a defendant who is the subject of a probation order previously issued by that same court division, the Probation Department shall commence violation proceedings against that probationer. Such proceedings shall be commenced by the issuance by the Probation Department of a Notice of Probation Violation/Hearing at or before the arraignment on the delinquency or criminal complaint or youthful offender indictment, or as soon thereafter as possible. The Notice shall be served on the probationer in hand following the assignment of a date and time for a probation violation hearing as provided in Section III(b)(ii) and such service shall be entered in the case docket, provided that if such in-hand service is not possible, the Notice shall be served on the probationer by first-class mail, unless the court orders otherwise. Service of the Notice by first-class mail shall be entered in the case docket. Out of court service other than by mail shall require a written return of service. The Probation Department shall provide a copy of each Notice of Probation Violation/Hearing to the District Attorney forthwith upon its issuance.

At any time during violation proceedings, the court, upon review of the Notice and as a matter of its discretion, may order termination of the proceedings. A Notice of Probation Violation may be withdrawn only with the permission of the court and such withdrawal and permission shall be entered in the case docket.

(ii) *Contents of Notice of Violation.* The Notice of Probation Violation/Hearing shall set forth the criminal conduct alleged to have been committed by the probationer as indicated in the delinquency or criminal complaint or youthful offender indictment, and shall set forth any other specific conditions of the probation order that the Probation Department alleges have been violated with a description of each such alleged violation. The Notice shall also state the date, time, and place of the probation violation hearing.

(iii) *Scheduling of Hearing.* The probation violation hearing shall be scheduled to commence on the date of the pretrial hearing for the new delinquency or criminal complaint or youthful offender indictment, unless the court expressly orders an earlier hearing. The hearing shall be scheduled for a date certain no less than seven days after service on the probationer of the Notice of Violation/Hearing unless the probationer waives said seven day notice period. The hearing date shall not be later than fifteen days after service of the Notice of Violation/Hearing without the probationer's consent if he or she is held pursuant to Section V of this standing order. In any case, the hearing shall not be later than thirty days after service of the Notice of Violation/Hearing, except in extraordinary circumstances. In scheduling the pretrial hearing on the new delinquency or criminal complaint or youthful offender indictment together with the probation violation hearing, the court shall give primary consideration to the need for promptness in conducting the probation violation hearing.

(c) Where Probation Order and Delinquency or Criminal Complaint or Youthful Offender Indictment Involve Different Divisions.

(i) *Issuance and Service of Notice of Violation.* When a delinquency or criminal complaint is issued by a court division of the Juvenile Court or a youthful offender indictment is returned by a grand jury (hereinafter the "criminal court") against a defendant who is the subject of a probation order issued by a different court division of the Juvenile Court Department (hereinafter the "probation court"), the Probation Department in the criminal court shall issue a Notice of Probation Violation/Hearing to the probationer at or before arraignment on the new delinquency or criminal complaint or youthful offender indictment, or as soon thereafter as possible. The Notice, as provided in paragraph (c)(ii) below, shall be served on the probationer in hand and such service shall be entered in the case docket. Nothing in this section shall preclude the later issuance and service on the probationer of a Notice of Probation Violation/Hearing by the Probation Department of the probation court.

(ii) *Contents of Notice of Violation.* The Notice of Probation Violation/Hearing shall set forth the name of the probation court and criminal conduct alleged to have been committed by the probationer as indicated in the delinquency or criminal complaint or youthful offender indictment and shall order the probationer to appear at a specific date and time at the probation court for the express purpose of appointment of counsel, if necessary, and scheduling of a probation violation hearing.

(iii) *Transmission of Notice of Violation and Other Documents to Probation Court.* Prior to the service of the Notice of Violation/Hearing on the probationer, the Probation Department at the criminal court shall send to the probation officer on duty in the probation court or, if there is no probation officer on duty, to the Chief Probation Officer at the probation court, by electronic transmission, copies of the following documents: the notice of violation; the delinquency or criminal complaint or youthful offender indictment and related police report on the new criminal charge that constitutes the alleged probation violation; and a request for the following information: whether the probation court recommends that the probationer be transported

in custody, and, if not, the date and time for the non-custodial appearance of the probationer at the probation court.

(iv) *Response by the Probation Court.* At the probation court, the probation officer on duty, the Chief Probation Officer, an Assistant Chief Probation Officer, or a probation officer designated by either shall respond by electronic transmission to the request for information no later than one hour from receipt thereof. The response shall include a recommendation on whether the probationer should be transported to the probation court in custody, and, if not, the date and time for the probationer's non-custodial appearance at the probation court.

(v) *The Decision to Transport.* A judge at the criminal court shall decide whether the probationer is to be transported in custody to the probation court. The judge shall provide the probationer an opportunity to be heard and, unless exceptional circumstances require otherwise, shall wait at least one hour for receipt of the recommendation from the probation court before making such decision. If the criminal court orders custodial transport, it shall issue an arrest warrant for a violation of probation ("probation warrant") on behalf of the probation court, and the probation court shall be so notified. The clerk's office in the criminal court shall enter it promptly into the Warrant Management System. The probationer shall be transported in accordance with the probation warrant, provided that, if the probationer is held in custody in the criminal proceeding, the criminal court will defer transport on the probation warrant and it shall be lodged with custodial authority to ensure that the probationer will be detained and transported to the probation court. The Probation Department at the criminal court shall so notify the Probation Department at the probation court.

If the criminal court decides not to order custodial transport, it shall enter the probation court appearance date and other required information on the Notice of Probation Violation/Hearing and serve it on the probationer in accordance with Section III(c)(i) above. For good cause, the criminal court may hold the probationer in custody pending its decision regarding custodial transport. Nothing in this rule shall preclude the issuance of a probation warrant by the probation court to secure the appearance of a probationer for a probation violation proceeding.

(vi) *Probationer's Appearance at the Probation Court; Service of a New Notice.* Upon appearance of the probationer at the probation court, the court shall appoint counsel, if necessary, and shall schedule a probation violation hearing for a date certain, the date to be no less than seven days later unless the probationer waives said seven-day period. The hearing date shall not be later than fifteen days after said appearance without the probationer's consent if he or she is held pursuant to Section V of this standing order, or in any case no later than thirty days after said appearance, except in extraordinary circumstances. If the Probation Department at the probation court alleges additional violations, it shall prepare and serve on the probationer a new Notice of Probation Violation/Hearing which shall set forth all alleged violations. The Notice shall also include the date, time and place of the violation hearing and shall be served on the probationer in hand while he or she is before the court, or as soon thereafter as possible. Such service shall be entered in the case docket. The Probation Department shall provide a copy of the new Notice to the District Attorney at the time of, or before such service on the probationer.

At any time during the proceeding, the probation court, upon review of the Notice and as a matter of its discretion, may order termination of the proceedings The Notice may be withdrawn only with the permission of the court and such withdrawal and permission shall be set forth on the record and entered in the case docket.

(vii) *Procedure When a Defendant Is a Probationer at More than One Other Court Division within the Juvenile Court.* When a defendant appearing in a court division on a new delinquency, youthful offender or criminal charge is on probation at more than one other court division within the Juvenile Court, the criminal court shall select one of the latter divisions to be the probation court and shall issue a Notice of Violation/Hearing for that division. The criminal court shall interact as provided in this section with the selected probation court. The other probation court or courts each shall be responsible for the issuance and service on the probationer of a Notice of Violation/Hearing based on the new criminal conduct, and for securing the presence of the probationer for a violation hearing by means of such Notice or by means of a probation warrant or other process.

(d) When Probation Order and New Criminal Charge Involve Different Court Departments. When a criminal complaint is issued by a court or an indictment is returned against a defendant who is the subject of a probation order issued by a court in a different court department, the criminal and probation court personnel shall proceed in accordance with Trial Court Standing Order 2–16, Uniform Interdepartmental Procedures for Probation Violation Proceedings.

Commentary

This section involves cases in which an alleged probation violation consists of new criminal conduct charged against the probationer. Such cases can arise in two contexts: where the probationer is on probation at the same court division that issued the new charges (the "same court" situation), and where the new charges were issued by a court division or department other than the one where the probationer is on probation (the "different court" situation).

For both situations, this section contains a provision by which a Notice of Probation Violation/Hearing may be "withdrawn." Such withdrawals have been a method by which probation violation proceedings may be terminated. There has been no requirement for court approval or permission. The provision imposes two new requirements: (1) that such withdrawals must receive the permission of the court, and (2) that such permission and the fact of the withdrawal must be entered on the case docket. By requiring judicial permission and entry on the record, the provision reflects the importance of a process by which a probation violation proceeding that has been formally commenced may be terminated without adjudication.

New subsections (c)(iii)–(v) have been added to provide a detailed process by which, in the "different court" situation, the "criminal court" must interact with the "probation court." The purpose of this interaction is to effect the transfer of the probation proceeding and, in some instances, the custodial transfer of the probationer, to the probation court.

Under the former procedure, the decision to transport a probationer was made at the probation court, a warrant issued there and was sent to the criminal court. This meant that a probation officer had to seek the issuance of a warrant by a judge of that court, a judge who was otherwise unaware of the matter and was usually engaged in that court's daily business. This would often delay the process, particularly in those cases where the judge at the probation court required a more detailed description of the underlying allegations before issuing the warrant.

This standing order has been changed because the judge in the criminal court will be addressing an issue in a case that is before the court at that time, will be immediately aware of the criminal case which constitutes the alleged probation violation, and will have all relevant information regarding the probationer's criminal record and pending probation status.

Section (c)(vii) has been added to address a circumstance not previously addressed, namely, where the defendant before the criminal court is currently on probation in more than one other court division within the Juvenile Court. It provides that in such cases the judge at the criminal court must decide the probation court with which the criminal court will interact. This decision will determine which of the probation courts will be "first in line" to address the probationer's alleged violation based on new charged criminal conduct. The standing order provides that the other courts at which the individual is on probation are responsible for charging the new criminal conduct as an alleged violation, and initiating a violation proceeding by issuing a Notice of Violation/Hearing and mailing it to the probationer or obtaining the appearance of the probationer by means of a probation warrant or other process such as a writ of habeas corpus.

IV. COMMENCEMENT OF VIOLATION PROCEEDINGS: VIOLATIONS OTHER THAN NEW CHARGED CRIMINAL CONDUCT

(a) General. This section prescribes the procedures to be undertaken regarding alleged violations of probation that do not involve or include criminal conduct charged in a new delinquency or criminal complaint or youthful offender indictment.

(b) Issuance and Service of Notice; Termination of Proceedings, Withdrawal of Notice. When a probation officer of a court division that has issued a probation order determines that a probationer has violated any condition of that order other than alleged criminal conduct as charged in a new delinquency or criminal complaint or youthful offender indictment, that probation officer shall decide whether to commence probation violation proceedings. Such decision shall be made in accordance with the rules and regulations of the Office of the Commissioner of Probation, provided, however, that probation violation proceedings shall be commenced (1) upon the issuance of a criminal complaint or indictment, (2) when the judge issuing the probation order orders that such proceedings are to be commenced upon an alleged violation of one or more conditions of probation, or (3) when the commencement of such proceedings is required by statutory mandate. In any case, a judge of the court division may order the commencement of violation proceedings.

Violation proceedings shall be commenced by the issuance by the Probation Department of a Notice of Probation Violation/Hearing which shall be served on the probationer in hand or by first-class mail, unless the court orders otherwise. Service of the Notice in hand or by first-class mail shall be entered in the case docket. Out-of-court service other than by first-class mail shall require a written return of service. The Probation Department shall provide a copy of each Notice of Probation Violation/Hearing to the District Attorney forthwith upon its issuance.

If deemed appropriate, because of the seriousness of the alleged violation or for other good reason, the court may issue an arrest warrant for a violation of probation. The clerk shall forthwith enter such warrant in the Warrant Management System. Upon the probationer's first appearance before the court, the probationer shall be served in hand with the Notice of Violation/Hearing.

At any time during the proceedings, the court, upon review of the Notice and as a matter of its discretion, may order termination of the proceedings. The Notice may be withdrawn only with the permission of the court and such withdrawal and permission shall be set forth on the record and entered in the case docket.

(c) Contents of Notice. The Notice of Probation Violation/Hearing shall set forth the conditions of the probation order that the Probation Department alleges have been violated and shall order the probationer to appear at a specific date and time for the express purpose of the appointment of counsel, if necessary, and the scheduling of a probation violation hearing.

(d) Scheduling of Hearing. Upon appearance of the probationer in accordance with the Notice required by paragraph (c) above, the court shall appoint counsel, if necessary, and schedule a probation violation hearing for a date certain, said date to be no less than seven days later unless the probationer waives said seven-day notice period. The hearing date shall not be later than fifteen days after said appearance without the probationer's consent if he or she is held pursuant to Section V of this standing order, or in any case no later than thirty days after said appearance, except in extraordinary circumstances.

V. PROBATION DETENTION HEARINGS

(a) Purpose. A probation detention hearing may be conducted to determine whether a probationer shall be held in custody pending the conduct of a probation violation hearing. The issues to be decided at a probation detention hearing are whether probable cause exists to believe that the probationer has violated a condition of the probation order, and, if so, whether the probationer should be held in custody.

(b) Notice of Hearing. The probationer shall be given a written notice of probation detention hearing indicating the purpose of the hearing and referring to the probation violations alleged in the Notice of Violation/Hearing which is required to be served on the probationer under this standing order. The probation detention proceeding shall be commenced by the service of such notice on the probationer. The court may, for good cause, order that the probationer be taken into custody pending the completion of the proceeding. The notice of probation detention hearing shall be served in hand when the probationer is before the court having been arrested on a new delinquency or criminal complaint or youthful offender indictment, having been arrested for a probation violation, or for any other reason. The notice of probation detention hearing shall be prepared and served by the Probation Department at the discretion of a probation officer or as directed by the court.

(c) Conduct of Hearing. Probation detention hearings shall be conducted by a judge or, if a judge is not available, by a clerk-magistrate. When a clerk-magistrate conducts a pro-

bation detention hearing, a resulting custody order shall not extend beyond the date on which a judge will next be available at the court. On such date, the probationer shall be brought before the court and any further custody order will require the conduct of a detention hearing by a judge.

Probation detention hearings shall be conducted in a courtroom on the record. The probationer shall be entitled to counsel. Following service of notice as provided in paragraph (b) above, the appointment of counsel, the appearance of private counsel or the knowing and voluntary waiver of the right to counsel in accordance with G. L. c. 119, § 55A, the probationer shall be allowed a reasonable time to prepare for the hearing. At the hearing, the probation officer shall be required to present evidence to support a finding of probable cause. The District Attorney may assist in the presentation of such evidence. The probationer shall be entitled to be heard in opposition. Testimony, including the testimony of the probation officer, shall be taken under oath. The court shall admit such evidence as it deems relevant and appropriate. The scope of the inquiry shall be limited to the issue of whether there is probable cause to believe that the alleged violation of probation has occurred.

If probable cause is found, the court may order the probationer to be held in custody pending the conduct and completion of the violation hearing. The court's decision whether to order such custody, shall include, but not necessarily be limited to consideration of the following:

   i. the probationer's criminal or juvenile record;

   ii. the nature of the offense for which the probationer is on probation;

   iii. the nature of the offense or offenses with which the probationer is newly charged, if any;

   iv. the nature of any other pending alleged probation violations;

   v. the likelihood of probationer's appearance at the probation violation hearing if not held in custody; and

   vi. the likelihood of incarceration or commitment if a violation is found following the probation violation hearing.

If probable cause is found and the court does not order the probationer held in custody, the court may order the probationer released upon such terms it deems necessary and appropriate to insure the safety of an individual or the community. In the case of a juvenile, the court may impose terms of release that balance the issues of public safety and the best interests of the juvenile. These terms may include, but are not limited to, an earlier curfew, restrictions on the juvenile's activities, or terms that permit a juvenile to attend school and/or receive services available only in the community. Terms of release shall be set forth in writing and served in hand on the probationer. Terms of release imposed under this section are not conditions of probation. A violation of a term of release shall not itself be the basis for a finding of a violation of probation, although the judge may consider such violation of a term of release in determining a proper disposition under section VIII(d) and IX(b).

If no probable cause is found, the court may terminate the proceedings or schedule a probation violation hearing serving the probationer with notice thereof, but the probationer may not be held in custody nor shall an order with terms of release be issued pending the hearing based on the alleged probation violation.

(d) Bail. Bail and other conditions of pretrial release pursuant to G. L. c. 276, §§ 58 and 58A do not apply to a probation detention hearing. However, the court shall proceed to determine the issues of bail and pretrial detention ("dangerousness") on any new delinquency or criminal complaint or youthful offender indictment, as provided by law.

Commentary

This section differs from its antecedent, in its replacement throughout of the terms "preliminary probation hearing" and "final [or 'full'] probation hearing" with the terms "probation detention hearing" and "probation violation hearing," respectively. The purpose of these changes is to use terms that more accurately describe and clearly differentiate these proceedings.

Paragraph (b) contains a new sentence indicating that a probation detention proceeding is commenced when the notice thereof is served on the probationer. Another new sentence indicates that the court has the authority to hold the probationer in custody pending the completion of the proceedings for good cause.

Paragraph (b) contains a new, final sentence indicating that a probation detention hearing may be conducted at the direction of the court as well at the initiative of the Probation Department.

When probable cause is found and the court does not order the probationer held in custody, Section V authorizes the court to impose terms of release. Authorizing the court to impose terms of release is consistent with the Juvenile Court's mission to further the best interests of children who appear before the court by offering a course of rehabilitation rather than punishment, consistent with the provisions of G. L. c 119. See also *Jake J. v. Commonwealth*, 433 Mass. 70, 75 (2000). If a probationer fails to comply with the order of terms of release, the probationer may be subject to arrest and brought before the court for a review of custody status.

When the court does not find probable cause, the court must exercise its discretion whether to terminate proceedings or to schedule a probation violation hearing nonetheless. Because of the need for dispatch in conducting a detention hearing, the absence of evidence, witnesses, or assistance from the District Attorney may result in the probation officer's being unable to establish probable cause for the purpose of detention but still having a reasonable prospect of proving the probation violation at a full hearing. The court will decide whether further proceedings are in the interests of justice, but in no event may the probationer be held or subject to terms of release on the probation matter pending a probation violation hearing.

Paragraph (d) makes clear that bail and other terms of pretrial release have no application to a probationer's custody pending the conduct and completion of a violation hearing. Bail and other conditions of pretrial release, including pretrial detention based on "dangerousness" under G. L. c. 276, § 58 and 58A, relate solely to a newly alleged crime. If the court finds probable cause for a probation violation, it may order the defendant into custody pending the violation hearing. If the court does not find probable cause, the probationer cannot be held in custody on the alleged violation. Even if the probationer is held on the probation allegation, if he or she is also before the court on a new delinquency, youthful offender or criminal charge, the court must address the terms of pretrial release on the new charge(s). This issue is unrelated to custody on the probation charge. The prosecutor may want to be heard on the issue of bail or dangerousness because if the probation matter is promptly resolved, the defendant may be released from custody on the probation matter well before the new delinquency, youthful offender or criminal case is concluded.

Conversely, the issue of probation custody should be addressed regardless of whether or not the prosecutor plans to ask for high bail or pretrial detention based on dangerousness on the new charge(s).

VI. CONDUCT OF HEARINGS

(a) In General. Probation violation hearings shall be conducted by a judge, on the record. All testimony, including that of a probation officer, shall be taken under oath. The presentation of the case against the probationer shall be the responsibility of the probation officer assigned by the Chief Probation Officer of the court. The probationer shall be entitled to the assistance of counsel, including the appointment of counsel for probationers determined by the court to be indigent. A waiver by the probationer of the right to counsel shall be accepted by the court only if the court determines that such waiver is being made knowingly and voluntarily and in accordance with G. L. c. 119, § 55A.

(b) Requirement of Two Step Procedure. Probation violation hearings shall proceed in two distinct steps, the first to adjudicate the factual issue of whether the alleged violation or violations occurred, the second to determine the disposition of the matter, if a violation of probation is found to have occurred.

(c) Adjudication of Alleged Violation. Probation violation hearings shall commence with testimony by the probation officer describing the violation or violations alleged in the Notice of Violation/Hearing, and shall proceed with a presentation of the evidence supporting the allegations. The probationer shall be permitted to present evidence relevant to the issue of the alleged violation. Each party shall be permitted to cross-examine witnesses produced by the opposing party. Hearsay evidence shall be admitted by the court in accordance with section VII of this standing order, provided that the court shall enforce any statutory privileges unless waived and any legally required disqualifications. The probation officer shall have the burden of proving the alleged violations with or without the participation of the District Attorney as provided below. The standard of proof at such hearings shall be the preponderance of the evidence. After the presentation of evidence, both parties or their counsel shall be permitted to make a closing statement.

(d) Dispositional Decision. If the court finds that the probationer has violated one or more conditions of probation as alleged, the probation officer shall recommend to the court a disposition consistent with the dispositional options set forth in sections VIII(d) and IX(b), and may present argument and evidence in support of that recommendation. The probationer shall be permitted to present argument and evidence relevant to disposition and to propose a disposition.

(e) Continuances. Probation violation hearings shall be continued only by a judge and only for good cause shown. No continuance shall be ordered other than to a date certain and for a specific purpose, and as provided in section VIII(a). The pendency of a delinquency or criminal complaint or youthful offender indictment which also constitutes an alleged violation of probation shall not be grounds for a continuance of the probation violation hearing unless a judge determines the interests of justice require it. The reason of any continuance shall be stated by the judge and entered in the case docket.

(f) Participation of the District Attorney.

(i) *In General.* The District Attorney may participate in probation violation hearings as provided in G. L. c. 279, § 3, and such participation shall be permitted in any such proceeding regardless of whether the delinquency or criminal or youthful offender case in which the probation order was issued involved a felony charge.

(ii) *Coordination with the Probation Department.* If the District Attorney intends to appear at a probation violation hearing, he or she shall confer prior to the hearing with the probation officer responsible for presenting the matter to the court, for the purpose of coordinating the District Attorney's involvement in the hearing with the planned presentation of the probation officer.

(iii) *Presentation of Evidence.* The District Attorney may present and examine witnesses at the hearing and may examine witnesses presented by the probation officer, and may cross- examine witnesses presented by the probationer. The probationer may cross-examine witnesses presented by the District Attorney. The District Attorney shall be responsible for the attendance of every witness he or she wishes to present, and for the summoning of such witnesses.

(iv) *Finding and Disposition.* After the presentation of evidence, the District Attorney may be heard on the strength of that evidence in supporting a finding of violation. If the court finds that the probationer has violated one or more of the conditions of probation as alleged in the Notice of Violation/Hearing, the District Attorney may be heard regarding the court's disposition of the matter. The District Attorney may present a recommendation on disposition orally or in writing.

(g) Admission to Violation and Waiver of Right to Hearing. The court may accept an admission to an alleged probation violation and a waiver of the right to a violation hearing only upon a determination that the admission and waiver have been made knowingly and voluntarily.

Such an admission and waiver shall not be accepted by the court subject to any condition regarding the disposition of such violation or the disposition of any other probation violation or any pending delinquency or criminal complaint or youthful offender indictment. A probationer shall not be entitled to withdraw an admission as of right after it has been accepted by the court.

(h) Ensuring Probationer's Presence in Courtroom. For good cause, the court may order that the probationer be taken into custody pending the commencement and completion of the violation hearing.

Commentary

District Attorney Participation

Section (f) addresses participation by the District Attorney. Sections III and IV of this standing order require the probation officer to provide a copy of every Notice of Probation Violation and Hearing to the District Attorney. Section (f) is intended to clarify the involvement of the District Attorney in those cases where he or she decides to participate, consistent with the statutory provisions of G. L. c. 279, § 3.

It should be noted that as a constitutional matter, probation functions are within the judicial branch, and the office of the District Attorney is considered within the executive branch. *Commonwealth v. Tate,* 34 Mass.App.Ct. 446 (1993). Under the Massachusetts Constitution, Pt. 1 Art. 30, the branches must maintain a separation of governmental powers. That separateness does not, however, lead to the conclusion that a district attorney's office may not assist the probation service in presenting evidence in support of a position that the probation service had decided upon. Probation officers are only aided, not interfered with, when district attorneys, upon invitation, conduct examination of witnesses and present evidence. *Commonwealth v. Tate* at 448 and cases cited.

Thus the right of District Attorneys to present evidence and witnesses, and to examine and cross-examine witnesses at these proceedings would appear to be constitutionally acceptable as long as it does not fundamentally interfere with probation.

VII. HEARSAY EVIDENCE

(a) Admissibility of Hearsay Evidence. Hearsay evidence shall be admissible at probation violation hearings.

(b) Legal Sufficiency of Hearsay Evidence. The court may rely on hearsay as evidence of a probation violation only if the court finds in writing that the hearsay is substantially reliable. In determining if hearsay is substantially reliable, the court may consider, among any other relevant factors, whether that evidence

(1) is based on personal knowledge and/or direct observation, rather than on other hearsay;

(2) involves observations recorded close in time to the events in question;

(3) is factually detailed, rather than generalized and conclusory;

(4) is internally consistent;

(5) is corroborated by any evidence provided by the probationer;

(6) was provided by a disinterested witness; or

(7) was provided under circumstances that support the veracity of the source (e.g., was provided under the pains and penalties of perjury or subject to criminal penalties for providing false information).

VIII. FINDING AND DISPOSITION

(a) Requirement of Finding. Upon the completion of the presentation of evidence and closing arguments on the issue of whether the probationer has violated one or more conditions of a probation order, as alleged, the court shall make a determination of that issue. The court shall decide the matter promptly and shall not continue the proceeding generally.

(b) Finding of No Violation. If the court determines that the probation officer has failed to prove by a preponderance of the evidence that the probationer committed a violation alleged in the Notice of Probation Violation/Hearing, the court shall expressly so find and said finding shall be entered in the case docket.

(c) Finding of Violation; Written Findings of Fact. If the court determines that the Probation Department has proved by a preponderance of the evidence that the probationer has violated a condition of probation as alleged in the Notice of Probation Violation/Hearing, or if the probationer waives the hearing and admits such violation and the court accepts such admission in accordance with section VI(g), the court shall expressly so find, and said finding shall be entered in the case docket. In a contested proceeding, the court shall make written findings of fact to support the finding of violation, stating the evidence upon which the court relied. A finding of violation based on an admission may be recorded as such.

(d) Disposition After Finding of Violation. After the court has entered a finding that a violation of probation has occurred, the court may order any of the following dispositions set forth below, as it deems appropriate. These dispositional alternatives shall be the exclusive options available to the court. The court shall proceed to determine disposition promptly following the entry of a finding of violation. General continuances are prohibited. In determining its disposition, the court shall give such weight as it may deem appropriate to the recommendation of the Probation Department, the probationer, and the District Attorney, if any, and to such factors as public safety; the seriousness of any offense of which the probationer was placed on probation; the nature of the probation violation; the occurrence of any previous violations and the impact of the underlying offense on any person or community, as well as any mitigating factors.

(i) *Continuance of Probation.* The court may decline to modify or revoke probation and, instead, issue to the probationer such admonition or instruction as it may deem appropriate.

(ii) *Termination.* The court terminate the probation order.

(iii) *Modification.* The court may modify the conditions of probation. Such modification may include the addition of reasonable conditions and the extension of the duration of the probation order.

(iv) *Revocation.* The court may order that the order of probation be revoked. If the court orders revocation, it shall state the reasons therefor in writing.

(e) Execution of Suspended Sentence or Commitment; Stay of Execution. Upon revocation of a probation order, any sentence or commitment that was imposed for the offense involved, the execution of which was suspended, shall be ordered executed forthwith; provided, however, that such execution may be stayed (1) pending appeal in accordance with Mass.R.Crim.P. 31, or (2) at the court's discretion, and upon the probationer's motion, to provide a brief period of time for the probationer to attend to personal matters prior to commencement of a sentence of incarceration or commitment to the Department of Youth Services. The execution of such sentence or commitment shall not be otherwise stayed.

(f) Imposition of Sentence or Commitment Where No Sentence or Commitment Previously Imposed. Upon revocation of probation in a case where no sentence or commitment was imposed following conviction or adjudication, the court shall impose a sentence, commitment, or other disposition as provided by law.

IX. VIOLATION OF CONDITIONS OF A CONTINUANCE WITHOUT A FINDING

(a) Notice, Conduct of Hearing, Adjudication. The procedures set forth in this standing order regarding notice for, and the conduct and adjudication of, probation violation hearings shall also apply where the Probation Department alleges a violation of one or more conditions of probation imposed together with a continuance without a finding.

(b) Disposition. The dispositional options available to the court following a determination that one or more conditions of probation imposed together with a continuance without a finding have been violated shall be as follows:

(i) *Termination of Probation.* The court may terminate the order of probation and the continuance without a finding and enter a dismissal on the underlying criminal case.

(ii) *Continuation of the Continuance Without a Finding With No Probation Modification.* The court may continue the continuance without a finding and issue to the probationer such admonition or instruction as it may deem appropriate.

(iii) *Continuance of the Continuance Without a Finding With Modification of Probation.* The court may continue the continuance without a finding and modify the conditions of probation including the duration of the continuance.

(iv) *Termination of the Continuance Without a Finding and No Revocation of Probation.* The court may terminate the continuance without a finding without revoking probation and, if a finding of sufficient facts was entered at the time the continuance without a finding was ordered, shall proceed to enter a guilty, delinquency or youthful offender finding. The order of probation, with or without modifications, may thereupon constitute the disposition on the finding if the probationer consents.

(v) *Termination of the Continuance Without a Finding and Revocation of Probation.* The court may terminate the continuance without a finding and revoke the order of probation. If the court orders revocation, it shall state the evidence relied upon in writing, and, if a finding of sufficient facts was entered at the time the continuance without a finding was ordered, the court shall enter a guilty, delinquency or youthful offender finding and impose a sentence, commitment or other disposition as provided by law.

Adopted effective September 25, 2017.

Standing Order 1-18 Notification Requirements and Counsel Appointment Procedures for Permanency Hearings Held Pursuant to G.L. c. 119, § 29B and Trial Court Rule VI, Uniform Permanency Hearings

1. Purpose. The purpose of this Standing Order is to establish procedures for notification to parties and attorneys and for appointment of counsel for permanency hearings held pursuant to G.L. c. 119, § 29B and Trial Court Rule VI.

2. Applicability. This Standing Order is applicable to all Divisions of the Juvenile Court and to all matters where a permanency hearing is required pursuant to G.L. c. 119, § 29B.

3. Scheduled Hearing List. (a). No less than ninety (90) days prior to the required scheduled hearing date in accordance with G.L. c. 119, § 29B and Rule 3 of Trial Court Rule VI, the clerk's office of the court wherein the hearing is to be convened shall send a list of cases scheduled for permanency hearings to the Department of Children and Families ('Department'). (b). The Department shall, within thirty (30) days of receipt of the list, advise the court in writing of the name of any child or young adult on the list who is no longer in the care or custody of the Department and therefore no longer requires a permanency hearing. In addition, the Department shall advise the court in writing whether the parents' rights to consent or receive notice of any petition for adoption, custody, guardianship or other disposition have been dispensed with pursuant to G.L. c. 119, § 26 or G.L. c. 210, § 3, whether the parents have signed voluntary surrenders under G.L. c. 119, § 23(a) or G.L. c. 210, § 2 or whether the young adult or the Department terminated the agreement to continue responsibility for the young adult under G.L c. 119, § 23(f).

4. Notice. No less than forty-five (45) days prior to the hearing date, the clerk's office shall send notice of the hearing to the Department, to the petitioner, if different from the Department, to the child or young adult's attorney, and unless the parents' rights to consent or receive notice of any petition for adoption, custody, guardianship or other disposition of the child have been dispensed with, or the parents have signed voluntary surrenders or the subject of the hearing is a young adult, to the parents, by mailing to their last known addresses, or if the parents are represented by counsel, to their attorney(s) of record. Such notice shall inform the parties of the date, time, and location of the hearing, of their right to counsel pursuant to G.L. c. 119, § 29, and of the right to file objections pursuant to Rule 6. If a case is scheduled for permanency hearing and the child or young adult is no longer in the care or custody of the Department, the Department shall notify the court and all parties, or if the parties are represented by counsel, the attorneys of record, and the court will take the case off the hearing list. The time for notice provided in this paragraph shall not apply if the court has determined that reasonable efforts to reunify the family are not required pursuant to G.L. c. 119, § 29C.

5. Appointment of Counsel. (a). All parties have the right to counsel. If a party was represented by counsel at the trial, that counsel shall continue to represent the party until the court permits him/her to withdraw his/her appearance or until an appearance is filed by successor counsel. If trial counsel wishes to withdraw his/her appearance, and if the party has been determined to be indigent, a motion for withdrawal requesting appointment of successor counsel shall be filed. Any motion under this paragraph shall be scheduled for hearing no later than seven (7) days after filing. Counsel wishing to withdraw shall ensure that the motion to withdraw and appoint successor counsel is scheduled for hearing no less than thirty (30) days prior to the date of the scheduled permanency hearing. A permanency hearing shall not be taken off a court calendar to accommodate a motion to withdraw.

(b). If the attorney of record is no longer available to represent the child or young adult, the court shall remove the attorney and appoint successor counsel. The clerk's office shall send notice of the permanency hearing as set forth in section 4 of this Standing Order to the newly appointed counsel.

(c). If the attorney of record is no longer available to represent a parent and if the parent is indigent and their rights have not been dispensed with or the parent has not signed a voluntary surrender, the court shall remove the attorney and appoint successor counsel. The clerk's office shall send notice of the permanency hearing as set forth in section 4 of this Standing Order to the newly appointed counsel.

6. Effective Date. This Standing Order is effective on March 1, 2018.

Adopted effective March 1, 2018.

Standing Order 2–18. Time Standards

The Juvenile Court Department has jurisdiction over a variety of criminal and civil case types including delinquency and youthful offender proceedings, child requiring assistance proceedings (CRA) and care and protection/termination of parental rights proceedings. The vast majority of cases addressed by the Juvenile Court fall within the parameters of these four case types. The Juvenile Court has jurisdiction, by statute, of matters ancillary to these four case types including guardianship petitions, parentage complaints, change of name petitions and adoption petitions.

The work of the Juvenile Court often reflects shifting community expectations and social science theory regarding children. Those shifts in expectations often unpredictably alter Juvenile Court caseloads.

The purpose of the time standards is to provide guidelines for application in the great majority of cases; it being understood that, as a matter of discretion in specific situations, a judge may extend time periods and vary requirements in the interest of justice. The time standards set forth below for the trial, settlement or other disposition of cases are applicable to cases filed in any division of the Juvenile Court Department on or after November 5, 2018. The benchmarks are not part of the time standards but are provided to offer guidance in achieving compliance with the standards.

I. DELINQUENCY AND YOUTHFUL OFFENDER PROCEEDINGS (G.L. c. 119, §§ 52–74, MA Rules of Criminal Procedure)

A. Filing of complaint or indictment to adjudication/disposition (bench trial): Six months (180 days).

Indictment of a juvenile as a Youthful Offender proceeds only at the option of the District Attorney for whom there are no time requirements for the exercise of that option.

B. Filing of complaint or indictment to adjudication/disposition jury trial): Eight months (240 days).

Benchmarks:

1. *Arraignment:* within fifteen (15) days from the issuance of the complaint, unless the juvenile has been referred to diversion.

2. *Pre-trial Conference:* within thirty (30) days from the arraignment.

The prosecuting attorney and defense counsel shall confer prior to the scheduled pretrial hearing in order to conference the case and to prepare a written pretrial conference report. In addition to those matters set forth in the Rules of Criminal Procedure, counsel shall also discuss whether the case can be disposed of by means of a plea and, if so, shall propose a date for a change of plea within the conference report. Special circumstances should be identified, including but not limited to: unavailability of victim or essential witness; information relating to the victim's capacity to testify at trial within the time frame established by the standards; existence of multiple defendants; anticipated delays occasioned by necessary forensic or scientific testing (e.g. DNA testing, drug analysis, etc.); delays due to issues related to the juvenile's competency, or the necessity for extended pretrial hearings such as those relating to the pretrial inspection of third party records or similar proceedings but not including motions to dismiss or motions to suppress statements, evidence, search warrants, or identifications.

II. CHILD REQUIRING ASSISTANCE PROCEEDINGS (G.L. c. 119, §§ 39E–I)

A. Filing of application to preliminary hearing: Fifteen (15) days.

B. Acceptance of application to determination/disposition: Six (6) months.

Numerous reasons may delay the final disposition of cases, such as an outstanding warrant, the unavailability or inappropriateness of a home to which the child can return, and frequently, serious mental health issues which defy easy and quick resolution. In addition, the preliminary hearing may result in a referral to informal assistance which is not to exceed ninety (90) days and which may, with the agreement in writing of the parents and child, last an additional ninety (90) days for a total of one hundred and eighty (180) days.

III. CARE AND PROTECTION/TERMINATION OF PARENTAL RIGHTS PROCEEDINGS (G.L. c. 119, §§ 24–29D, G.L. c. 210, § 3 and Juvenile Court Rules on Care and Protection Cases, Standing Order 1–10, Scheduling Care and Protection and Termination of Parental Rights Trials)

A. Filing of petition to final order of adjudication and permanent disposition: Fifteen (15) months, which may be extended once for a period not to exceed 3 months.

Benchmarks:

1. *Temporary custody hearing:* within seventy-two (72) hours of *ex parte* transfer of custody except by agreement of parties for good cause shown.

2. *Filing of court investigator report:* within sixty (60) days after the appointment of the investigator unless the court otherwise orders.

3. *Status Hearing:* within ninety (90) days after filing of the petition.

4. *Pre-trial Conference:* no later than thirty (30) days before trial.

5. *Permanency hearings for children in the custody of the Department of Children and Families:* twelve (12) months from the transfer of custody and annually thereafter.

B. Trial: Twelve (12) to fifteen (15) months after filing of the petition.

C. Decision and Written Findings: within ninety (90) days from the close of evidence. See Standing Order 1–10, requiring that an adjudication, termination of parental rights or decision not to terminate parental rights shall be made no later than thirty (30) days after the close of evidence.

D. Permanency Review: Following the entry of an order granting permanent custody of the child to the Department of Children and Families, the court shall hold a permanency review every six (6) months until legal permanency is achieved for the child. Legal permanency is achieved upon the closure of the case to reunification, adoption, guardianship or third party custody.

E. Legal Permanency: within 24 months after filing of the petition.

Adopted October 5, 2018, effective November 5, 2018.

RULES OF THE LAND COURT

Effective July 1, 2005

[These Rules supersede and replace all prior Land Court Rules in their entirety.]

Table of Rules

Rule 1. Applicability of Rules

The following rules apply to all cases pending on the effective date of these rules, unless ordered by the court in a particular case.

Rule 2. Fees and Deposits

Parties to any action, at such times and in such amounts as are ordered by the court or required by statute, shall pay or deposit those sums into court for application to the fees and expenses payable under applicable statutes or by order of the court.

In addition, a plaintiff who files a complaint for registration or confirmation shall make a deposit for the assurance fund required under G. L. 185, § 99, to be applied to that fund.

Deposits paid into court shall be held in the custody of the recorder who, if practicable, shall return any surplus which remains at the conclusion of the case to the party who paid the surplus. Otherwise, the surplus shall be delivered to the state treasurer.

Rule 3. Exhibits

Unless a longer time is required under Mass. R. A. P. 9(c), exhibits offered as evidence and chalks shall be retained by the recorder for three years after the trial or hearing at which they were used, subject to an order of confiscation or destruction, unless sooner delivered to the parties or counsel by whom they were presented or introduced. Unless otherwise ordered, jointly submitted exhibits will be considered to belong to the plaintiff. If in doubt as to the party or counsel entitled to delivery, the recorder may require an agreement of parties or counsel or an order of the court before delivery. After the expiration of three years from such trial or hearing, the recorder may destroy or discard such exhibits after giving thirty days' notice to the parties, if practicable.

Rule 4. Motions Under Mass. R. Civ. P. 12(b)(1), 12(b)(6), 12(c) or 56

A party moving under Mass. R. Civ. P. 12(b)(1), 12(b)(6), 12(c) or 56, or opposing such a motion, shall file with the motion or opposition a brief containing: (1) a statement of the issue or issues presented, (2) a statement of the legal elements, with citations to supporting law, of each claim upon which judgment is sought or opposed, (3) an argument in summary form, and (4) a short conclusion stating precisely the relief or order sought; otherwise the court may decline to act on the motion or consider the opposition, as the case may be.

Each motion under Rules 12(b)(1) or 56 shall be accompanied by a concise statement, in consecutive numbered paragraphs, of the material facts upon which the moving party relies, with page or paragraph references to supporting pleadings, depositions, answers to interrogatories, admissions and affidavits. If the motion is brought under Rule 56, the material facts in the statement must be those as to which the moving party contends there is no genuine issue to be tried.

Each opposition to a motion under Rules 12(b)(1) or 56 shall include: (1) a response, using the same paragraph numbers, to the moving party's statement of facts, and (2) in consecutive numbered paragraphs, a concise statement of any additional material facts which the opposing party deems relevant and necessary to the motion. Any response other than "admitted" to a statement of fact made by the moving party, and any statement of additional material fact, must include page or paragraph references to supporting pleadings, depositions, answers to interrogatories, admissions and affidavits, or else the facts described by the moving party as undisputed shall be deemed to have been admitted.

The statements filed by the moving party and the opposing party shall each be accompanied by an appendix, appropriately indexed, composed of: (1) all cited portions of the documents or other materials referenced in those statements, and (2) copies of all legal and other authorities cited in the briefs with the exception of the Massachusetts General Laws and cases reported in the official Massachusetts Reports, the Massachusetts Appeals Court Reports, or the Land Court Reporter. The opposing party's appendix need not duplicate any materials contained in the moving party's appendix so long as the cross-referencing is clear. The court need not look in the record or take judicial notice beyond the materials brought to its attention by the parties.

A copy of the motion, brief and (in the case of Rule 12(b)(1) and 56 motions) the statement of material facts and the appendix containing copies of supporting materials, shall be served upon all other parties and filed with the court within the time limits set forth in Land Court Standing Order No. 1–04, if applicable.[1] Cross-motions must follow the same procedures and timeframes as motions, and must likewise be served and filed in accordance with Standing Order 1–04, if applicable. Responses to motions or cross-motions, including any controverting statements and the materials supporting those statements (including any counter or Rule 56(e) affidavits), must be served upon all other parties and filed with the court within thirty (30) days after service of the motion or cross-motion. A hearing date shall be set by the court. Reply briefs, affidavits and other materials in support of the reply (if any) must be served on the parties and filed with the court no later than ten (10) days prior to the date the court first set for hearing; any rescheduling of the hearing date shall not change this deadline. Affidavits and other materials in support of the reply which, in the opinion of the court, are not responsive to the opposition or cross-motion, may be stricken. An opposing party's failure to file a cross-motion shall not preclude the court from granting dispositive relief to the opposing party if such relief is appropriate (see Rule 56(c)). Extensions or other modifications of the dates set forth above may be ordered by the court on its own motion for good reason and as the interests of justice require, or upon motion and for good cause shown.

The court need not act on any motion or cross-motion unless the parties have complied with the requirements of this rule and may deny any such motion or cross-motion which fails to comply.

1 Standing Order No. 1–04 applies to certain cases filed on or after October 4, 2004.

Rule 5. All Other Motions

All motions not covered by Rule 4 must be filed with the court and marked by the moving party for hearing on at least seven (7) days' notice (the number of days to be calculated as provided in Mass. R. Civ. P. 6(a)) at such dates and times for the hearing of motions as shall be established and published by the court from time to time. It is the responsibility of the moving party to determine whether a motion must be heard by a particular judge and, if so, the motion must be marked for hearing before that judge at an appropriate date and time. The motion shall contain a statement of reasons, including supporting authorities, why the motion should be granted and a statement of the precise relief sought; otherwise the court may deny or decline to act on the motion. Unless the court, in its discretion, grants permission, all affidavits and other materials in support of the motion must be filed and served with

the motion. Oppositions to such motions, and all materials in support of that opposition along with any cross-motions (including motions to strike), must be served and filed with the court so they are received by all other parties and by the court no later than noon one (1) business day prior to the date marked for the motion's hearing. Any papers not served and filed with the motion or opposition and in timely fashion may be filed only with leave of court.

Rule 6. Matters Which May Not Require Oral Argument

The court in its discretion may decide matters on submitted papers without oral argument, but only after having received written statements of reasons in support and opposition from all interested parties, or having given those parties fair opportunity to submit written statements.

Rule 7. Settlement of Discovery Disputes

The parties shall confer in advance of filing any motion under Mass. R. Civ. P. 26 or 37 in a good faith effort to narrow areas of disagreement to the fullest possible extent. The party who intends to file the motion shall be responsible for initiating the conference. All such motions shall contain a certificate stating that the conference required by this rule was held, together with the date and time of the conference and the names of all participating parties. Motions unaccompanied by such certificate may be denied without prejudice to renewal when accompanied by the required certificate.

Rule 8. Motions for Discovery Orders

All motions arising out of a party's response (or non–response) to an interrogatory, request for admission, deposition question, or arising out of a party's response to, or asserted failure to comply with, a request for production of documents, shall be accompanied by a brief. With respect to each interrogatory, deposition question, or request at issue, the brief shall set forth separately and in the following order: (1) the text of the interrogatory, deposition question, or request, (2) the opponent's response, and (3) an argument. Alternatively, the text of the interrogatory, deposition question or request and the opponent's response may be contained in an appendix to the brief.

Rule 9. Motions for Reconsideration

Motions for reconsideration, and all briefs and affidavits or other supporting materials filed by the moving party in support thereof, shall be filed with the court and served on all parties. The words "MOTION FOR RECONSIDERATION" shall appear clearly in the title to the motion. Upon filing, the recorder shall transmit the motion and supporting papers to the judge who decided the original motion or matter. No response to the motion for reconsideration shall be required, and no hearing shall be marked or scheduled, unless the judge so requests, and the judge may deny the motion without the need of such a response or hearing. No motion to reconsider shall be granted without giving the opposing party an opportunity to respond.

Rule 10. Agreements for Judgment

A written agreement for judgment for a sum certain or that all relief shall be denied shall be accepted by the recorder for filing, and upon filing shall constitute the judgment of the court for all purposes as provided in Mass. R. Civ. P. 58(a). Any other agreement for judgment (including, without limitation, those for declaratory or injunctive relief, requiring the parties to enter into agreements or perform any acts, or ordering any official or board to take any action), whether or not accepted for filing by the recorder, shall not constitute the judgment of the court unless and until the court, either on its own motion or on motion of one or more parties, endorses or otherwise approves the agreement for judgment. Motions for approval of agreements for judgment may be decided by the court without hearing, but the court may in its discretion order a hearing.

Rule 11.   Identification of Judge On Court Filings

After a party receives written notice from the recorder that a case has been assigned to one of the judges of the court, or otherwise becomes aware of such a notice, all pleadings thereafter filed in that case shall include, prominently in the case caption immediately following or underneath the case number, the surname or initials of that judge.

Rule 12.   Forms

The use of the court's forms in the case of complaints for registration, confirmation, tax foreclosure, or pursuant to the Servicemembers' Relief Act, is mandatory. The use of such other forms as the court may publish from time to time is not mandatory; however, those forms should be consulted, where appropriate, for guidance as to the content of alternative submissions.

Rule 13.   Rules Applicable to Partition Proceedings

The Rules of Civil Procedure, and these Rules, shall apply to all partition proceedings.

Rule 14.   Binding Summary Decision Following Bench Trial: Waiver by Parties of Detailed Findings of Fact and Rulings of Law

(a) Court May Approve Waiver. To make speedy and efficient the decision of matters tried to the court on the facts, the court, in its discretion, and with the consent of all interested parties, may, following a trial or evidentiary hearing, render its decision without detailed written findings of fact and rulings of law. No matter shall be so decided, however, unless the parties shall have submitted to the court, and the court shall have approved, a voluntary stipulation of the interested parties which waives all rights they may have to have the court find the facts specially and to state conclusions of law separately, including rights pursuant to Mass. R. Civ. P. 52(a).

(b) Form of Decision. The court shall render its decision in writing or shall lay the decision upon the record orally from the bench, in a form comparable to a jury verdict within the meaning of Mass. R. Civ. P. 49. In rendering a decision under this Rule, the judge shall, at a minimum, answer special questions on the elements of each claim, at a level of detail comparable to a special jury verdict form pursuant to Mass. R. Civ. P. 49(a). The court may, in cases it considers appropriate, in its decision under this Rule also return special or subsidiary findings on some or all of the issues of fact tried to the court; the court's decision in such a case shall be comparable to the general verdict form of a jury accompanied by answer to interrogatories in a case submitted to a jury as provided in Mass. R. Civ. P. 49(b).

(c) Stipulations of the Parties. The court, after hearing the parties if they request or the court orders, shall settle in advance of trial the form of the stipulation the parties shall submit pursuant to this Rule, and the form of any particular questions of fact which the parties would have the court answer in its decision. In the stipulation the parties file, they may waive their rights of appeal in whole or in part, but in any event shall stipulate that (i) they waive all arguments in the trial court or on appeal that require or depend upon the existence of detailed written findings of fact, and (ii) in the event of appeal, they waive all arguments that appellate review of the court's decision and of the judgment entered, be based upon a standard of review other than that which would apply to a verdict by a jury in a case tried to a jury and to the judgment entered thereon.

(d) Procedure Discretionary with Court. In no case shall the court be required to dispense with the requirements of Mass. R. Civ. P. 52(a) to have the court find the facts specially and to state conclusions of law separately. The court in its discretion may at any time before, during, or after the trial of the case, determine to find the facts specially and to state conclusions of law separately, notwithstanding any contrary stipulation of the parties or previous order of the court. However, once the court has accepted the parties' stipulation, the court shall not, contrary to that stipulation, proceed to find the facts specially and to state conclusions of law separately over the objection of any party to the stipulation, without first having given the parties opportunity to be heard.

Adopted October 26, 2016, effective January 1, 2017.

STANDING ORDERS OF THE LAND COURT

Table of Standing Orders

Standing Order 1–88. Electronic Recordation of Proceedings [Deleted]

Deleted with the adoption of Standing Order 1–06, adopted December 29, 2005, effective January 3, 2006.

Standing Order 2–88. Time Standards [Deleted]

Deleted with the adoption of Standing Order 1–04, adopted effective October 4, 2004.

Standing Order 1–97. Notice Under G.L. c. 185, § 39

Whenever the plaintiff in a complaint for registration of title or for confirmation of title without registration requests to have the line of a public way determined, the Recorder is hereby ordered to give notice of the complaint by mailing a certified letter, including a copy of the complaint, to the mayor of the city or to one of the selectmen of the town or towns where the land lies, or, if the way is a highway, to one of the county commissioners of the county or counties where the land lies.

Whenever the land involved in a complaint for registration of title or for confirmation of title without registration borders on a river, navigable stream or shore, or on an arm of the sea where a river or harbor line has been established, or on a great pond, or if it otherwise appears from the complaint or the proceedings that the commonwealth may have a claim adverse to that of the plaintiff, notice shall be given by the Recorder by mailing a certified letter, including a copy of the complaint, to the attorney general.

Adopted November 12, 1996, effective February 1, 1997.

Standing Order 1–04. Time Standards for Cases Filed in the Land Court Department.

A. General Considerations

To "secure the just, speedy and inexpensive determination of every action," as required by Mass. R. Civ. P. 1, the Land Court Department ("Court") hereby adopts these time standards and procedures relating to an individual calendar system as a Standing Order of the Court ("Standing Order" or "Order"), superceding Standing Order 2–88, adopted May 1, 1988. This Order is intended to provide the Court with recognized goals for the management and timely disposition of cases. The Order also preserves some discretion in the judges of the Court to schedule individual cases according to the particular needs of the parties or the public.

An integral part of case management and judicial supervision is an individual calendar system, which the Court hereby adopts as set forth below. Generally within three months from entry date, all appropriate cases will be examined by the judge assigned to the case and appropriate orders may be entered notwithstanding any previously assigned presumptive tracking schedule.

ACCORDINGLY:

1. All miscellaneous, tax foreclosure, registration, confirmation, and contested "S" cases ("Cases") filed in the Court on or after the effective date of this Order, shall be subject to the provisions of this Standing Order. Cases filed under the Servicemembers Civil Relief Act under chapter 57 of the Acts of 1943, as amended, are not subject to this Standing Order.

2. Cases entered prior to the effective date of this Order shall be incorporated into this Order, when appropriate.

3. The timing for the completion of various steps of litigation will be calculated from the date of filing of the Complaint, except for original registration and confirmation cases (see E(1) below).

4. At or shortly after the time of filing of the Complaint or other initial pleading, each case (other than tax foreclosure cases) shall be assigned to one of the judges. All tax foreclosure cases shall be assigned to the Recorder.

5. The Court shall schedule case management conferences and pre-trial conferences on its own, or as reasonably requested by the parties, consistent with this Order.

B. Individual Calendar System

In its operation the Court shall use an individual calendar system. The basic elements of the system are: a single judge, assigned to a case from beginning to end, who participates with the lawyers and pro se litigants in the management of the case as it proceeds to resolution. Ordinarily, the judge assigned to the case will hold all hearings and preside at the trial of the case. In case of an emergency, circumstances may require that another judge handle a hearing if the assigned judge is unavailable. Except in tax foreclosure cases, as soon as practicable after a Complaint is filed and served, the assigned judge shall schedule and conduct a Case Management Conference. At the conference, the case shall be reviewed and, if appropriate, a case-specific tracking order shall be established.

The Court has historically set firm dates for trial, and the Court will continue to do so under this Order. The fact that cases are assigned firm trial dates dictates a strict approach to continuances. When the Court has given the parties an exclusive trial date which the parties themselves have participated in selecting, any change threatens not only to affect all parties to that particular case, but also to leave the judge without a case for trial on that date. Accordingly, no continuances will be given without leave of the Court, for good cause shown. The assent of all parties will not constitute per se good cause.

C. Track Designation

1. At time of filing, all Cases shall be assigned to one of the following tracks: fourteen (14) months to trial (Tax or "T" Track); sixteen (16) months to trial (Fast or "F" Track); or thirty-one (31) months to trial (Average or "A" Track).

2. Initial designation to a particular track shall be determined by the main cause of action indicated by the plaintiff on the civil action cover sheet.

3. For good cause shown, a party may request that a case be assigned to a track other than the track in which the main cause of action falls or to a special accelerated track (the "X" Track). The request shall be made by filing a motion with the Court prior to (or in exceptional circumstances, after) the Case Management Conference.

4. At any time, the judge to whom the action has been assigned may, at his or her discretion, and after the parties have had a chance to be heard, change the track which governs the case.

5. Parties must first file their cases in the "A", "F", or "T" Track. To be considered for reassignment to the "X" Track, any party may file a motion. Such motion shall be filed jointly or contain a certification that the motion has been discussed with all other parties. Once filed with the Court, the case is then sent to the judge assigned to the case for review and a hearing for determination as to whether the case properly may be accommodated in the "X" Track. Because assignment to the "X" Track will require a significantly higher level of judicial resources, "X" Track designation will be made infrequently, and only when the case's prompt disposition will serve a demonstrated public interest, different in kind from most "F" Track cases. The need for special case management is the touchstone of the "X" Track. Every motion for "X" Track consideration shall include a proposed schedule of events and counsel's certification that the schedule is realistic.

6. Amendments to the designation or tracking order of a case, or an extension or other modification of any of the tracking order dates, may be ordered by the Court on its own motion, for good reasons and as the interests of justice require, but otherwise may be requested and granted only upon motion and for good cause shown. A motion to amend or modify the tracking order shall be in writing and set forth in detail the facts upon which the moving party relies in support of said motion. Motions to continue a trial are strictly disfavored. Hearings on motions under this paragraph shall only be held if deemed necessary by the assigned or emergency judge.

D. Notification To Parties

While the Court will endeavor to provide notice, the ultimate responsibility for obtaining information from the Court about the track designation of the case and the corresponding tracking order shall rest with each party. Notification shall occur as follows:

1. At or shortly after the time of filing of the Complaint, the plaintiff(s) will be provided with a judge designation and a general Track Assignment and Scheduling Notice ("Track Assignment"), which shall reflect the assigned judge, the assigned track, and the initial presumptive tracking order. All cases filed shall be accompanied by a self-addressed stamped envelope, which shall be used by the Court to mail the Track Assignment to the plaintiff. It is then the responsibility of the plaintiff to mail or deliver the Track Assignment to all parties, which shall be accomplished within ten (10) days after the plaintiff's receipt of the Track Assignment. The plaintiff has the continuing responsibility as the case progresses to mail or deliver the Track Assignment to all subsequently added parties.

2. It shall be the obligation of the plaintiff to effectuate service of the Complaint on the defendant(s) in a timely fashion so that all parties have adequate time to prepare for the Case Management Conference. Approximately one month prior to the scheduling of the Case Management Conference, a specific date shall be sent by the Court to all parties. The date established for the Case Management Conference does not preclude the earlier filing of a motion, or the marking for earlier hearing of a motion, where appropriate. Discovery and all other aspects of the case may proceed amongst the parties, in accordance with applicable rules and the initial presumptive tracking order, pending the Case Management Conference.

3. All documents and motions filed with the Court within designated time standards under this Order shall contain a certification on the signature page that they are being served within the designated time or by leave of the judge to whom the matter has been assigned.

4. All pleadings and appearances submitted by counsel of record shall be accompanied by counsel's Board of Bar Overseers (BBO) Number. The BBO Number shall appear immediately after counsel's name. It is the responsibility of all counsel of record to ensure that the BBO has their correct and current address.

E. Assignment To Tracks

At filing, all Cases shall be assigned to a track according to the following chart. Assignment to a track indicates the maximum amount of time in which a case should be completed. Some cases may be completed before the maximum time period of the track. All cases transferred to the Court from other courts shall be assigned to a track at the time of transfer.

1. Average ("A") Track

All cases not otherwise assigned to the Fast Track or Tax Track. Original registration and confirmation cases under G. L. c. 185, are included within the "A" Track commencing on the date when the citation issues.

2. Fast ("F") Track

a. All cases afforded priority by statute, including G. L. c. 40A, § 17; c. 40B; and c. 41, § 81BB.

b. Specific performance under G. L. c. 185, § (1)(k).

c. Partition under G. L. c. 241.

3. Tax ("T") Track

All cases filed under G. L. c. 60, § 65.

4. Accelerated ("X") Track

Upon motion and by leave of the assigned judge.

F. Track Assignment and Scheduling Notice

The Court will issue a Track Assignment for each appropriate case, in accordance with the provisions of this Order. A later notice issued by the assigned judge will reflect the specific date for the Case Management Conference. A specific tracking order shall be established at the Case Management Conference. A specific trial date shall be established at the pre-trial conference. The Court may require the parties to file written status reports on or before major milestone dates as set forth below.

The following steps and limitations shall be mandatory except upon special written waiver or modification, for good cause shown and supported by appropriate documentation, granted by the judge to whom the matter has been assigned. Failure to comply with this Order may result in the imposition of any available sanctions, including, but not limited to, the entry of judgments of dismissal or default. Documents filed outside the established time limitations without such a waiver shall not be considered or acted upon by the Court, even if filed by agreement between the parties, unless the Court in its discretion otherwise allows.

The initial presumptive tracking order shall be as follows:

(i) After Designation To Average ("A") Track:

1. Three months (90 days):

• Service completed on all parties. (If a party who has been served has not timely filed a response to the Complaint, that party shall be defaulted by the Court).

• If service is not made upon any defendant, the action shall be dismissed without prejudice as to that defendant.

• Case Management Conference held (all pro se parties shall appear in person and all other parties shall be represented by counsel with decision-making authority and parties may be defaulted or nonsuited if they do not appear). The Court reserves the right to require all parties to appear at the Case Management Conference. All counsel attending are required to be fully familiar with the case and have complete authority regarding all aspects of the conduct of the litigation. A discovery schedule shall be discussed and implemented. If any party has not received notice of the

Case Management Conference by the ninetieth (90th) day following the filing of the Complaint, that party shall request in writing that the Court proceed to schedule the Case Management Conference.

• If not held earlier, an early intervention event shall be held pursuant to Supreme Judicial Court Uniform Rules on Dispute Resolution, Rule 1:18, at which the case may be assigned for alternative dispute resolution screening.

2. Sixteen months (480 days):

• All discovery requests served and answered, and all depositions completed.

• All requests for admissions served and answered.

3. Eighteen months (540 days):

• Dispositive motions (filed under Mass. R. Civ. P. 12(b)(1); 12(b)(6); 12(c); and 56)("Dispositive Motions") filed and served (including supporting memoranda and affidavits).

4. Nineteen months (570 days):

• Dispositive Motions responses filed.

5. Twenty months (600 days):

• Dispositive Motions reply briefs filed ten (10) days prior to hearing.

• Dispositive Motions heard.

6. Twenty–seven months (810 days):

• Case assigned for pre-trial conference and joint pre-trial memorandum must be filed. Parties not filing a joint pre-trial memorandum may be sanctioned.

7. Twenty–eight months (840 days):

• Pre-trial conference held (mandatory attendance or party may be sanctioned).

• Firm trial date, generally within the next three months, set.

8. Thirty–one months (930 days):

• Trial held.

9. Thirty–three months (990 days):

• Transcripts filed with the Court and all parties.

10. Thirty–four months (1020 days):

• Post trial briefs filed with the Court within thirty (30) days of receipt of transcript.

(ii) After Designation to Fast ("F") Track:

1. Three months (90 days):

• Service completed on all parties. (If a party who has been served has not timely filed a response to the Complaint, that party shall be defaulted by the Court).

• If service is not made upon any defendant, the action shall be dismissed without prejudice as to that defendant.

• Case Management Conference held (all pro se parties shall appear in person and all other parties shall be represented by counsel with decision-making authority and parties may be defaulted or nonsuited if they do not appear). The court reserves the right to require all parties to appear at the Case Management Conference. All counsel attending are required to be fully familiar with the case and have complete authority regarding all aspects of the conduct of the litigation. A discovery schedule shall be discussed and implemented. If any party has not received notice of the Case Management Conference by the nineteenth day following the filing of the Complaint, that party shall request in writing that the Court proceed to schedule the Case Management Conference.

• If not held earlier, an early intervention event shall be held pursuant to Supreme Judicial Court Uniform Rules on Dispute Resolution, Rule 1:18, at which the case may be assigned for alternative dispute resolution screening.

2. Six months (180 days):

• All discovery requests served and answered, and all depositions completed.

• All requests for admissions served and answered.

3. Seven months (210 days):

• Dispositive Motions filed and served (including supporting memoranda and affidavits).

4. Eight months (240 days):

• Dispositive Motions responses filed.

5. Nine months (270 days):

• Dispositive Motions reply briefs filed ten (10) days prior to hearing.

• Dispositive Motions heard.

6. Thirteen months (390 days):

• Case assigned for pre-trial conference and a joint pre-trial memorandum must be filed. Parties not filing a joint pre-trial memorandum may be sanctioned.

7. Fourteen months (420 days):

• Pre-trial conference held (mandatory attendance or party may be sanctioned).

• Firm trial date, generally within the next two months, set.

8. Sixteen months (480 days):

• Trial held.

9. Eighteen months (540 days):

• Transcripts filed with the Court and all parties.

10. Nineteen months (570 days):

• Post-trial briefs filed with the Court within thirty (30) days of receipt of transcript.

(iii) After Designation to Tax ("T") Track:

1. Three months (90 days):

• Title report completed and submitted to Land Court examiner (reference to examiner automatically revoked for failure to submit report with reference assigned to another examiner). Title report should include names and addresses of all interested persons, including condominium trustees.

2. Four months (120 days):

• Title report docketed and reviewed.

• Citation issued or request for additional information sent by the Court to plaintiff's counsel. (Failure to provide additional information within time specified by the Court may result in dismissal).

3. Five months (150 days):

• Return day. Pleadings closed unless special notice issued.

4. Six months (180 days):

• Military affidavit and motion for general default submitted.

• Request made for additional service.

• Request made for hearing in any contested case.

5. Seven months (210 days):

• Special notice issued where required.

• Finding entered after hearing.

6. Eight months (240 days):

• Return day on special notices. Pleadings close.

7. Nine months (270 days):

• Military affidavit and motion for general default submitted in cases with completed special notice.

• Hearing request in contested cases with special notice.

8. Ten months (300 days):

• If terms of redemption established in Finding are not satisfied, motion for judgment submitted and marked for hearing.

• Finding entered in any contested case with special notice.

9. Eleven months (330 days):

• Motion for judgment heard and allowed if finding unsatisfied.

10. Twelve months (360 days):

• Final judgment entered after allowance of motion for judgment.

11. Thirteen months (390 days):

• If terms of redemption established in Finding in any contested case with special notice are not satisfied, motion for judgment submitted and marked for hearing.

• Final judgment entered after allowance of motion for judgment in contested cases with special notice.

G. Decisions

Trial decisions should be decided within one hundred twenty (120) days from the date cases are taken under advisement.[1]

/s/KARYN F. SCHEIER

Karyn F. Scheier

Chief Justice

Land Court Department

Adopted effective October 4, 2004.

1 Section G shall apply to all cases taken under advisement on or after October 1, 2005.

Standing Order 1–06.   Electronic Recordation of Proceedings [Superseded]

Adopted December 29, 2005, effective January 3, 2006. Superseded by Standing Order 1–18, adopted effective December 17, 2018.

Standing Order 2–06.   Processing and Hearing of Claims for Judicial Review of Matters on the Administrative Record

1.   Claims filed in the Land Court seeking judicial review of administrative agency or other proceedings on the administrative record pursuant to the standards set forth in G.L. c. 30A, § 14, G.L. c. 249, § 4, or similar statutes, whether joined with a claim for declaratory relief under G.L. c. 231A, or any other claim, shall be heard in accordance with the following procedures.[1]

2.   The administrative agency or other body whose proceedings are to be judicially reviewed in this manner (the agency) shall, by way of answer to such claims, file the original or certified copy of the record of the proceeding under review (the record) within ninety (90) days after service upon it of the Complaint. Such record "shall consist of (a) the entire proceedings, or (b) such portions thereof as the agency and the parties may stipulate, or (c) a statement of the case agreed to by the agency and the parties." G.L. c. 30A, § 14 (4). Upon service of the Complaint, the agency shall notify all parties of procedures for acquiring a transcript of the hearing testimony. The agency shall also inform the parties of their obligation to provide a transcript, or the stipulated portions thereof, to the court if alleging that the agency's decision is not supported by substantial evidence or is arbitrary or capricious, or is an abuse of discretion. A request for a copy of the transcript must be made by a party within thirty (30) days after service of the Complaint, and such transcript, or the stipulated portions thereof, shall be made a part of the record. Any party seeking to challenge the agency's decision as not supported by substantial evidence or as arbitrary or capricious, or an abuse of discretion, shall have an affirmative obligation to obtain a copy of the transcript, or the stipulated portions thereof, in support of its position, and to ensure that it is timely included in the record submitted to the court.

The court may assess the expense of preparing the record, including the cost of the transcript, as part of the costs of the case. G.L. c. 30A, § 14 (4). Additionally, "the court may, regardless of the outcome of the case, assess any one unreasonably refusing to stipulate to limit the record, for the additional expenses of preparation caused by such refusal." G.L. c. 30A, § 14 (4). The court may require or permit subsequent corrections or additions to the record when deemed desirable. G.L. c. 30A, § 14 (4). The time for filing the record may be shortened or enlarged, for good cause shown, upon allowance of an appropriate motion.

3.   The following motions raising preliminary matters must be served on the parties and filed with the court not later than twenty (20) days after service of the record:

(a) Motions authorized by Mass. R. Civ. P. 12 (b) or 12 (e).

(b) Motion for leave to present testimony of alleged irregularities in procedure before the agency, not shown in the record (G.L. c. 30A, § 14 (5)).

(c) Motion for leave to present additional evidence (G.L. c. 30A, § 14 (6)).

Any party failing to serve and file such a motion within the prescribed time limit, or within any court-ordered extension, shall be deemed to have waived any such motion (unless related to jurisdiction) and the case shall proceed solely on the basis of the record. Responses to such motions shall be served and filed not later than seven (7) days after service of the motion (the number of days to be calculated as provided in Mass. R. Civ. P. 6 (a)), and the court, in its discretion, may either schedule the motion for hearing or decide it on the submitted papers. If the motion specified in (c) is allowed, all further proceedings shall be stayed until the agency has complied with the provisions of G. L. c. 30A, § 14 (6).

4.   A claim for judicial review on the administrative record shall be resolved through a motion for judgment on the pleadings, Mass. R. Civ. P. 12 (c), unless the court's decision on any motion specified in part 3 above has made such a resolution inappropriate. All Rule 12 (c) motions and supporting memoranda shall be served and filed within thirty (30) days of the service of the record or of the court's decision on any motion specified in part 3 above, whichever is later. The responses to such motions shall be served and filed within thirty (30) days after service of the motion and memorandum. The court may grant an extension of time for good cause shown. Memoranda shall include specific page citations to matters in the record.

5.   The Recorder or her/his designee will schedule a hearing date after receiving the motion materials. No pre-trial conference will be held, and no pre-trial memorandum filed, unless specifically ordered by the court. No testimony or other evidence shall be presented at the hearing, and the review shall be confined to the record. A party may waive oral argument and submit on the brief by filing a written notice. Failure to appear at the time and place scheduled for hearing shall also be deemed such a waiver. Such waiver by a party shall not affect the right of any other party to appear and present oral argument.

[1] If the Complaint also raises claims subject to *de novo* or other type of review, those claims shall be addressed and resolved in the manner required by the applicable statute and the Massachusetts Rules of Civil Procedure.

Standing Order 1–12.   Limited Assistance Representation [Rescinded]

Adopted January 2, 2013. Rescinded January 16, 2019, effective February 1, 2019. See, now, Uniform Trial Court Rule XVI. Limited Assistance Representation.

Standing Order 1–15.   Exceptions to the Notice Requirement of Trial Court Rule VIII, Uniform Rules of Impoundment Procedure

Effective October 1, 2015, in the Land Court Department of the Trial Court, all G.L. c. 261, s. 27B Affidavits of Indigency and Request for Waiver, Substitution or State Payment of Fees or Costs filed with the court are exempted from the notice requirement of Rule 13(b) of the Uniform Rules of Impoundment Procedure because they are automatically CON-

FIDENTIAL and no additional notice form is required to be filed with the Recorder's Office.

Adopted effective October 1, 2015.

Joint Standing Order 1–16. Authority of the Judge with Respect to Communication with Specialty Court Teams

This Standing Order is promulgated by the chief Justice of the Trial Court pursuant to G. L, c. 211B, Section 9 and shall constitute authorization by law as referenced in Rule 2.9 (A)(2) of the Code of Judicial Conduct (effective January 1, 2016).

For purposes of this Order:

Specialty Court means a specifically designated court session that focuses on individuals with underlying medical, mental health, substance abuse, or other issues that contribute to the reasons such individuals are before the courts. Specialty court shall also mean Veterans Treatment Court and Homelessness Court. Specialty court sessions integrate treatment and services with judicial case oversight and intensive court supervision. Examples Include drug courts, mental health courts, veterans' courts, and tenancy preservation programs.

A Staffing shall refer to a regularly scheduled, informal conference not occurring in open court, the purpose of which is to permit the presiding judge and others, including counsel, to discuss a participant's progress in the specialty court, treatment recommendations, or responses to participant compliance issues.

IT IS THEREFORE ORDERED:

A judge presiding over a specialty court shall have the authority to initiate, permit or otherwise consider ex parte communications about defendants, juveniles or probationers with members of the specialty court team at a staffing or by written documents provided to all members of the specialty court team, The purpose of this authority is to allow judges in their role in presiding over specialty court sessions, and only in that capacity, to assume a more interactive role with parties, treatment providers, probation officers, social workers and others, than Rule 2.9 of the Code of Judicial Conduct would otherwise permit.

Adopted effective January 7, 2016.

Land Court Standing Order 1–18. Electronic Recordation of Proceedings

1) All Land Court courtroom proceedings shall be recorded by a digital audio recording system. Recording shall take place whether or not a court stenographer is present in the courtroom. Unless the Court on its own motion or that of one or more of the parties shall by order direct otherwise, the official record of the proceedings shall be the digital audio recording made by the Court whether or not a court stenographer is present.

2) **Access to audio recordings**

a) For courtroom proceedings that took place on or before June 30, 2016, and recorded on the CourtSmart system:

A copy of the original recording or any portion thereof may be requested. Pursuant to the procedures prescribed by the Chief Justice of the Trial Court, the copy shall consist of a compact disc of the original recording, or such portion as is requested. The request for a compact disc of the original recording shall be filed with the Recorder of the Land Court on the form prescribed by the Trial Court. These forms are available at the Land Court and on the Trial Court web site.

b) For courtroom proceedings that took place after June 30, 2016, and recorded on the For the Record system:

A digital audio file copy of the original recording or any portion thereof is available via an online request to the audio vendor, "For the Record" (FTR), at the website us.court.fm.

c) *Costs.* The costs for a compact disc or an on-line digital audio file are set forth in the Uniform Schedule of Fees for the Trial Court, adopted pursuant to Massachusetts G. L. c. 262, § 4B. The Court deems Massachusetts G. L. c. 261, §§ 27A through 27G applicable to requests by or on behalf of parties determined to be indigent, and deems the cost of a compact disc or digital audio file to be an "extra cost" as defined in § 27A.

This Standing Order 1–18, supersedes Standing Order 1–06, dated January 3, 2006.

Adopted November 26, 2018, effective December 17, 2018.

Land Court Standing Order 2–18. Initial Limited Electronic Filing Project

I. Authority. This Standing Order 2–18 is promulgated by the Chief Justice of the Land Court Department pursuant to the provisions of G. L. c. 211B, § 10 and G. L. c. 185, § 1, and in compliance with the Order Re: Electronic Filing Pilot Projects issued by the Massachusetts Supreme Judicial Court effective February 25, 2015.

II. Purpose and Applicability. To advance efficiency in the Massachusetts courts and better serve the public and the bar, the Supreme Judicial Court has authorized electronic filing pilot projects for the trial and appellate courts. By this Standing Order 2–18, the Land Court Department hereby designates its pilot project permitting electronic filing and electronic service of court documents for Servicemembers Civil Relief Act cases (the "Pilot Project").

Effective September 1, 2018, the Supreme Judicial Court adopted SJC Rule 1:25 Massachusetts Rules of Electronic Filing (the "Electronic Filing Rules"). For the duration of the Pilot Project, these Electronic Filing Rules shall govern the general procedures of electronic filing and electronic service of court documents in designated matters commenced after the effective date of this Standing Order, notwithstanding any provision to the contrary in any rule of court or other standing order. All terms used in this Standing Order shall have the meanings defined in the Electronic Filing Rules.

Except insofar as the Electronic Filing Rules effective September 1, 2018 supersede the "Interim Massachusetts Electronic Filing Rules," previously adopted on February 25, 2015, the Supreme Judicial Court's Order regarding Electronic Filing Pilot Projects shall govern the conduct of the Pilot Project. This is an initial limited Standing Order to establish the parameters of the Pilot Project, and may be amended and revised by this Department as necessary during the course of the Pilot Project.

III. Designations.

A. *Participants.* The following law firms are participating during the Pilot Project: Harmon Law Offices, PC of Newton, MA; Korde & Associates, PC of Lowell, MA; Brock & Scott, PLLC of Pawtucket, RI; and Orlans PC of Waltham, MA. The designated lawyers/law firms shall be given training and access to the Provider's electronic filing system, and shall participate in the Pilot Project as properly registered Users in compliance with the Electronic Filing Rules. Additional lawyers/law firms will be approved by this Department to participate in the Pilot Project without further amendment of this Standing Order as the Pilot Project proceeds.

B. *Scope of the Pilot Project.* The Servicemembers case type (cases brought pursuant to the Servicemembers Civil Relief Act as set forth in 50 U.S.C. § 3901 (et seq.) and Chapter 57 of the Acts of 1943, as amended) is specifically designated for electronic filing and electronic service of court documents in this Pilot Project.

IV. Additional Provisions.

A. *Limited Assistance Representation.* For purposes of the Pilot Project, Trial Court Rule XVI: Uniform Rule on Limited Assistance Representation is hereby incorporated by reference where applicable. Because there currently are no filing codes that correspond to Limited Assistance Representation (LAR) in the electronic filing system, an attorney must enter the term "LAR" into either the Filing Description field or the Filing Comment field when electronically filing an LAR Notice of Appearance or LAR Notice of Withdrawal of Appearance.

B. *Technical Limitations.* In the event certain filing activities cannot be completed by electronic filing because of technical limitations of either the Provider, the Provider's electronic filing system, or the Trial Court's case management system, the Land Court Department reserves the right to require a party to submit such filings to the Land Court Recorder's Office in the conventional method, but shall permit that party to file electronically the remainder of the case pursuant to the Electronic Filing Rules. These filing activities may include, but shall not be limited to, requests for a fee waiver/indigency determination, requests for an interpreter, requests to purchase miscellaneous copies or forms, or other filing activities as defined or designated by this Department.

C. *Electronic Signatures.* In accordance with Rules 13 and 14 of the Electronic Filing Rules, filed documents, orders, and judgments in cases within the scope of this Pilot Project may be signed electronically. Electronic signatures have the force of conventional signatures. In addition, a digital stamp of the Land Court Recorder shall be accepted for the issuance of all court documents and to certify an electronic copy of any document associated with this Pilot Project.

V. Duration. The Land Court Servicemembers case e-filing Pilot Project described herein shall continue until further order of the Court, and this Standing Order 2–18 may be superseded or amended, in writing, at any time during the duration of the pilot.

Adopted November 26, 2018, effective December 17, 2018. Amended effective December 16, 2019.

MASSACHUSETTS RULES OF DOMESTIC RELATIONS PROCEDURE

Table of Rules

I. SCOPE OF RULES—ONE FORM OF ACTION

Rule 1. Scope of Rules

These rules govern the procedure in the Probate and Family Court Department in all proceedings for divorce, separate support, and custody of minor children, annulment or affirmation of marriage, an action for spousal and/or child support, an action to determine paternity and/or support for a child born out of wedlock, modification thereof, contempt and abuse prevention as enumerated in General Laws, Chapters 207, 208, 209, 209A, 209C, 215 and 209D. They shall be construed to secure the just, speedy and inexpensive determination of every action they govern.

Amended effective January 1, 1976; amended June 25, 1979, effective July 19, 1979; July 31, 1986, effective July 22, 1986; January 6, 1995, effective February 1, 1995; amended effective July 26, 1995.

Rule 2. One Form of Action

There shall be one form of action to be known as "civil action". *Identical to Mass.R.Civ.P. Rule 2.*

II. COMMENCEMENT OF ACTION; SERVICE OF PROCESS, PLEADINGS, MOTIONS AND ORDERS

Rule 3. Commencement of Action

A civil action is commenced by (1) mailing to the clerk of the proper court by certified or registered mail a complaint and an entry fee prescribed by law, or (2) filing such complaint and an entry fee with such clerk. Actions brought pursuant to G.L. c. 185 for registration or confirmation shall be commenced by filing a surveyor's plan and complaint on a form furnished by the Land Court. *Identical to Mass.R.Civ.P. Rule 3.*

Rule 4. Process

(a) Summons: Issuance. Upon commencing the action the plaintiff or his attorney shall deliver a copy of the complaint and a summons for service to the sheriff, deputy sheriff, or special sheriff; any other person duly authorized by law; a person specifically appointed to serve them; or as otherwise provided in subdivision (c) of this rule. Upon request of the plaintiff separate or additional summons shall issue against any defendant. The summons may be procured in blank from the clerk, and shall be filled in by the plaintiff or the plaintiff's attorney in accordance with Rule 4(b). *Identical to Mass. R.Civ.P. Rule 4(a).*

(b) Same: Form. The summons shall bear the signature or facsimile signature of the clerk; be under the seal of the court; be in the name of the Commonwealth of Massachusetts; bear teste of the first justice of the court to which it shall be returnable who is not a party; contain the name of the court and the names of the parties; be directed to the defendant; state the name and address of the plaintiff's attorney, if any, otherwise the plaintiff's address, and the time within which these rules require the defendant to appear and defend; and shall notify him that in case of his failure to do so judgment by default may be rendered against him for the relief demanded in the complaint. *Identical to Mass.R.Civ.P. Rule 4(b).*

(c) By Whom Served. Except as otherwise permitted by paragraph (h) of this rule, service of all process shall be made by a sheriff, by his deputy, or by a special sheriff; by any other disinterested person; by any other person duly authorized by law; by some person specially appointed by the court for that purpose; or in the case of service of process outside the Commonwealth, by an individual permitted to make service of process under the law of this Commonwealth or under the law of the place in which the service is to be made, or who is designated by a court of this Commonwealth. A subpoena may be served as provided in Rule 45. Notwithstanding the provisions of this paragraph (c), wherever in these rules service is permitted to be made by certified or registered mail, the mailing may be accomplished by the party or his attorney.

(d) Summons: Personal Service Within the Commonwealth. The summons and a copy of the complaint shall be served together. The plaintiff shall furnish the person making service with such copies as are necessary. Service shall be made as follows:

(1) The defendant, whether within or without the Commonwealth, may accept personal service by written endorsement of his duly notarized acceptance of service on the summons or other process. In the event that service is not so accepted, service shall be made as set forth hereafter:

(2) Upon an individual by delivering a copy of the summons and of the complaint to him personally.

In complaints seeking establishment of paternity or for support of a child born out of wedlock, complaints for support of a spouse or child under Chapter 209, § 32F, for actions under Chapter 209D, for contempt and complaints for modification only, upon an individual:

(i) by delivering a copy of the summons and complaint to him personally, or

(ii) by leaving a copy of the summons and complaint at his last and usual place of abode and by mailing copies thereof to the defendant. Notice under this subsection shall be proved by affidavit containing a particular statement thereof.

(3) If the person authorized to serve process makes return that after diligent search he cannot find the defendant, or if it appears that a defendant resides outside of the Commonwealth or is of parts unknown, the court may on application of the plaintiff issue an order of notice in the manner and form prescribed by law.

(4) If personal service shall not be made as aforesaid, such notice in the form ordered by the court shall be served by publishing a copy of the said notice once in some newspaper designated by the Register or the court and by mailing a copy of such notice by registered or certified mail, if practicable, to the defendant at his last known address. The defendant shall file his answer or other responsive pleading within the time periods allowed under these rules computed as if the date of last publication were the date on which personal service was made.

(5) Service of publication and mailing shall be proved by affidavit containing a particular statement thereof, accompanied by a copy of the advertisement (or tear sheet) of the newspaper containing the publication and, if practicable, by the return receipt showing receipt of a copy sent by registered or certified mail.

(6) The court shall require proof of actual notice when practicable. If such notice is not shown to have been received by the defendant, the complaint shall not be assigned for hearing until the expiration of three months after the publication date, date of service at a last and usual place of abode, or date of a mailing to the last known address of the defendant if such service has been ordered by the court. Nothing in this rule shall prevent hearing of a motion for temporary orders or issuance of temporary orders prior to the expiration of three months, provided notice of the motion and hearing has been mailed to the defendant's last and usual place of abode in accordance with Rules 5 and 6.

(7) [Deleted].

(e) Same. Personal Service Outside the Commonwealth. When any statute or law of the Commonwealth authorizes service of process outside the Commonwealth, the service shall be made by delivering a copy of the summons and of the complaint: (1) in any appropriate manner prescribed in subdivision (d) of this Rule; or (2) in the manner prescribed by the law of the place in which the service is made for service in that place in an action in any of its courts of general jurisdiction; or (3) by any form of mail addressed to the person to be served and requiring a signed receipt; or (4) as directed by the appropriate foreign authority in response to a letter rogatory; or (5) as directed by order of the court. *Identical to Mass.R.Civ.P.Rule 4(e).*

(f) Return. The person serving the process shall make proof of service thereof in writing to the court promptly and in any event within the time during which the person served must respond to the process. The person making return of service shall state in his return of service that a copy of the summons and complaint was delivered by him in hand to the defendant and shall further state the date on which and the place where such service was made. If service is made by a person other than a sheriff, deputy sheriff, or special sheriff, he shall make affidavit thereof. Proof of service outside the Commonwealth may be made by affidavit of the individual who made the service or in the manner prescribed by the law of the Commonwealth, or the law of the place in which the service is made for proof of service in an action in any of its courts of general jurisdiction. When service is made by mail, proof of service shall include a receipt signed by the addressee or such other evidence of personal delivery to the addressee as may be satisfactory to the court. Failure to make proof of service does not affect the validity of the service.

(g) Amendment. At any time in its discretion and upon such terms as it deems just, the court may allow any process or proof of service thereof to be amended, unless it clearly appears that material prejudice would result to the substantial rights of the party against whom the process is issued. *Identical to Mass.R.Civ.P. 4(g).*

(h) Certain Actions in Probate Courts: Service. Notwithstanding any other provision of these rules, in actions in the Probate Courts in the nature of petitions for instructions or for the allowance of accounts, service may be made in accordance with G.L. c. 215, § 46, in such manner and form as the court may order. *Identical to Mass.R.Civ.P. 4(h).*

(i) [Deleted].

(j) Summons: Time Limit for Service. If a service of the summons and complaint is not made upon a defendant within 90 days after the filing of the complaint and the party on whose behalf such service was required cannot show good cause why such service was not made within that period, the action shall be dismissed as to that defendant without prejudice upon the court's own initiative with notice to such party or upon motion. *Identical to Mass.R.Civ.P. 4(j).*

Amended effective January 1, 1976; March 8, 1976; amended January 16, 1979, effective February 12, 1979; November 16, 1979, effective December 17, 1979; amended effective January 1, 1983; amended June 27, 1983, effective July 1, 1983; July 18, 1988, effective August 1, 1988; August 5, 1992, effective September 1, 1992; January 6, 1995, effective February 1, 1995; amended effective July 26, 1995; amended October 10, 1997, effective December 1, 1997; June 5, 2003, effective September 2, 2003; amended April 1, 2009, effective May 1, 2009.

Reporter's Notes—1997

Rule 4(d)(7) was deleted in order to eliminate the requirement of an identifying witness in service of process.

Reporter's Notes—2003

Rule 4(d)(6) was amended to clarify the misunderstanding that the court is prohibited from entering a temporary order prior to the expiration of three (3) months if there is not proof of actual notice.

Reporter's Notes—2009

Rule 4(d)(4) was amended to reduce the number of times notice must be published. This change is consistent with the probate rule requirement and will be more cost effective for litigants.

Rule 4.1. Attachment

(a) Availability of Attachment. Subsequent to the commencement of any action under these rules, real estate, goods and chattels and other property may, in the manner and to the extent provided by law, but subject to the requirements of this rule, be attached and held to satisfy the judgment for damages and costs which the plaintiff may recover. *Identical to Mass. R.Civ.P 4.1(a).*

(b) Writ of Attachment: Form. The writ of attachment shall bear the signature or facsimile signature of the clerk, be under the seal of the court, be in the name of the Commonwealth, contain the name of the court, the names and residences (if known) of the parties and the date of the complaint, bear teste of the first justice of the court to which it is returnable who is not a party; state the name and address of the plaintiff's attorney (if any), be directed to the sheriffs of the several counties or their deputies, or any other person duly authorized by law, and command them to attach the real estate or personal property of the defendant to the value of an amount approved by the court, and to make due return of the writ with their doings thereon. The writ of attachment shall also state the name of the justice who entered the order approving attachment of property and the date thereof. *Identical to Mass.R.Civ.P 4.1(b).*

(c) Same: Service. The writ of attachment may be procured in blank from the clerk and shall be filled out by the plaintiff or plaintiff's attorney as provided in subdivision (b) of this rule, either of whom shall deliver to the officer making the attachment the original writ of attachment upon which to make his return and a copy thereof.

No property may be attached unless such attachment for a specified amount is approved by order of the court. Except as provided in subdivision (f) of this rule, the order of approval may be entered only after notice to the defendant and hearing and upon a finding by the court that there is a reasonable likelihood that the plaintiff will recover judgment, including interest and costs, in an amount equal to or greater than the amount of the attachment over and above any liability insurance shown by the defendant to be available to satisfy the judgment.

An action in which attachment of property is sought may be commenced only by filing the complaint with the court, together with a motion for approval of the attachment. The motion shall be supported by affidavit or affidavits meeting the requirements set forth in subdivision (h) of this rule. Except as provided in subdivision (f) of this rule, the motion and affidavit or affidavits with the notice of hearing thereon shall be served upon the defendant in the manner provided by Rule 4, at the same time the summons and complaint are served upon him.

Inclusion of a copy of the complaint in the notice of hearing shall not constitute personal service of the complaint upon the defendant. The notice shall inform the defendant that by appearing to be heard on the motion for approval of an attachment he will not thereby submit himself to the jurisdiction of the court nor waive service of the complaint and summons upon him in the manner provided by law.

Except as provided in subdivision (e) of this rule, any attachment of property shall be made within 30 days after the order approving the writ of attachment. When attachments of any kind of property are made subsequent to service of the summons and complaint upon the defendant, a copy of the writ of attachment with the officer's endorsement thereon of the date or dates of the attachments shall be promptly served upon the defendant in the manner provided by Rule 5. *Identical to Mass.R.Civ.P 4.1(c).*

(d) Attachment on Counterclaim, Cross–Claim or Third–Party Complaint. An attachment may be made by a party bringing a counterclaim, a cross-claim, or a third-party complaint in the same manner as upon an original claim. *Identical to Mass.R.Civ.P 4.1(d).*

(e) Subsequent Attachment. Either before or after expiration of the applicable period prescribed in subdivision (c) of this rule for making attachments, the court may, subject to the provisions of subdivision (f) of this rule, order another or an additional attachment of real estate, goods, and chattels or other property. *Identical to Mass.R.Civ.P 4.1(e).*

(f) Ex Parte Hearings on Property Attachments. An order approving attachment of property for a specific amount may be entered ex parte upon findings by the court that there is a reasonable likelihood that the plaintiff will recover judgment in an amount equal to or greater than the amount of the attachment over and above any liability insurance known or reasonably believed to be available, and that either (i) the person of the defendant is not subject to the jurisdiction of the court in the action, or (ii) there is a clear danger that the defendant if notified in advance of attachment of the property will convey it, remove it from the state or will conceal it, or (iii) there is immediate danger that the defendant will damage or destroy the property to be attached. The motion for such ex parte order shall be accompanied by a certificate by the plaintiff or his attorney of the amount of any liability insurance which he knows or has reason to believe will be available to satisfy any judgment against the defendant in the action. The motion, in the filing of which the plaintiff's attorney shall be subject to the obligations of Rule 11, shall be supported by affidavit or affidavits meeting the requirements set forth in subdivision (h) of this rule. *Identical to Mass.R.Civ.P 4.1(f).*

(g) Dissolution or Modification of Ex Parte Attachments. On two days' notice to the plaintiff or on such shorter notice as the court may prescribe, a defendant whose real or personal property has been attached pursuant to an ex parte order entered under subdivision (f) of this rule may appear without thereby submitting his person to the jurisdiction of the court, and move the dissolution or modification of the attachment, and in that event the court shall proceed to hear and determine such motion as expeditiously as the ends of justice require. At such hearing the plaintiff shall have the burden of justifying any finding in the ex parte order which the defendant has challenged by affidavit. Nothing herein shall be construed to abolish or limit any means for obtaining dissolution, modification or discharge of an attachment that is otherwise available by law. *Identical to Mass.R.Civ.P 4.1(g).*

(h) Requirements for Affidavits. Affidavits required by this rule shall set forth specific facts sufficient to warrant the required findings and shall be upon the affiant's own knowledge, information or belief; and, so far as upon information and belief, shall state that he believes this information to be true. *Identical to Mass.R.Civ.P 4.1(h).*

(i) Form of Hearing. At any hearing held under this rule, either party may adduce testimony and may call witnesses (including any opposing party). The court, for cause shown on the evidence so adduced, may make such interlocutory orders concerning disposition of the property sought to be attached as justice may require. *Identical to Mass.R.Civ.P 4.1(i).*

Rule 4.2.   Trustee Process

(a) Availability of Trustee Process. Subsequent to the commencement of any personal action under these rules, except actions only for specific recovery of goods and chattels, for malicious prosecution, for slander or libel, or for assault and battery, trustee process may be used, in the manner and to the extent provided by law, but subject to the requirements of this rule, to secure satisfaction of the judgment for damages and costs which the plaintiff may recover, provided, however, that no person shall be adjudged trustee for any amount due from him to the defendant for wages or salary for personal labor or services of the defendant except on a claim that has first been reduced to judgment or otherwise authorized by law; and in no event shall the attachment exceed the limitations prescribed by law. *Identical to Mass.R.Civ.P 4.2(a).*

(b) Summons to Trustee: Form. The summons to a trustee shall bear the signature or facsimile signature of the clerk, be under the seal of the court, be in the name of the Commonwealth, contain the name of the court, the names and residences (if known) of the parties and the date of the filing of the complaint, bear teste of the first justice of the court to which it is returnable who is neither a party nor a trustee; state the name and address of the plaintiff's attorney (if any), be directed to the trustee, shall notify him that the goods, effects or credits of the defendant in the hands of the trustee have been attached to the value of the amount authorized by the court, shall state the time within which these rules require the trustee to answer, shall notify him that in case of his failure to do so he will be defaulted and adjudged trustee as alleged, and, if wages, a pension, or a bank account is sought to be attached, shall notify him of such amount of wages, pension, or bank account as are by law exempt from attachment and shall direct him to pay over to the defendant the exempted amount. The summons to the trustee shall also state the name of the justice who entered the order approving the trustee attachment and the date thereof. *Identical to Mass.R.Civ.P 4.2(b).*

(c) Same: Service. The trustee summons may be procured in blank from the clerk and shall be filled out by the plaintiff or the plaintiff's attorney as provided in subdivision (b) of this rule, either of whom shall deliver to the person who is to make service the original trustee summons upon which to make his return and a copy thereof.

No trustee summons may be served unless attachment on trustee process for a specified amount has been approved by order of the court. Except as provided in subdivision (g) of this rule, the order of approval may be entered only after notice to the defendant and hearing and upon a finding by the court that there is a reasonable likelihood that the plaintiff will recover judgment, including interest and costs, in an amount equal to or greater than the amount of the trustee process over and above any liability insurance shown by the defendant to be available to satisfy the judgment.

An action in which trustee process is sought may be commenced only by filing the complaint with the court, together with a motion for approval of attachment on trustee process. The motion shall be supported by affidavit or affidavits meeting the requirements set forth in Rule 4.1(h). Except as provided in subdivision (g) of this rule, the motion and affidavit or affidavits with the notice of hearing thereon shall be served upon the defendant in the manner provided by Rule 4, at the same time the summons and complaint are served upon him; and the defendant shall also be served with a copy of the trustee summons in cases where attachment has been approved ex parte as provided in subdivision (g) of this rule. Inclusion of a copy of the complaint in the notice of hearing shall not constitute personal service of the complaint upon the defendant. The notice shall inform the defendant that by appearing to be heard on the motion for approval of an attachment on trustee process he will not thereby submit himself to the jurisdiction of the court nor waive service of the complaint and summons upon him in the manner provided by law.

Except as provided in subdivision (f) of this rule, any trustee process shall be served within 30 days after the date of the order approving the attachment. Promptly after the service of the trustee summons upon the trustee or trustees, a copy of the trustee summons with the officer's endorsement thereon of the date or dates of services shall be served upon the defendant in the manner provided by Rule 5. *Identical to Mass. R.Civ.P 4.2(c).*

(d) Answer by Trustee; Subsequent Proceedings. A trustee shall file, but need not serve, his answer, under oath, or signed under the penalties of perjury, within 20 days after the service of the trustee summons upon him, unless the court otherwise directs. The answer shall disclose plainly, fully, and particularly what goods, effects or credits, if any, of the defendant were in the hands or possession of the trustee when the trustee summons was served upon him. The proceedings after filing of the trustee's answer shall be as provided by law. *Identical to Mass.R.Civ.P 4.2(d).*

(e) Trustee Process on Counterclaim, Cross–Claim or Third–Party Complaint. Trustee process may be used by a party bringing a counterclaim, a cross-claim, or a third-party complaint in the same manner as upon an original claim. Such party may use trustee process, even though the trustee does not reside or maintain a usual place of business in the county where the action is pending. *Identical to Mass.R.Civ.P 4.2(e).*

(f) Subsequent Trustee Process. Either before or after expiration of the applicable period prescribed in subdivision (c) of this rule for serving trustee process, the court may, subject to the provisions of subdivision (g) of this rule, order another or an additional service of the trustee summons upon the original trustee. *Identical to Mass.R.Civ.P 4.2(f).*

(g) Ex Parte Hearings on Trustee Process. An order approving trustee process for a specific amount may be entered ex parte upon findings by the court that there is a reasonable likelihood that the plaintiff will recover judgment in an amount equal to or greater than the amount of the trustee process over and above any liability insurance known or reasonably believed to be available, and that either (i) the person of the defendant is not subject to the jurisdiction of the court in the action, or (ii) there is a clear danger that the defendant if notified in advance of the attachment on trustee process will withdraw the goods or credits from the hands and possession of the trustee and remove them from the state or will conceal them, or (iii) there is immediate danger that the defendant will dissipate the credits, or damage or destroy the goods to be attached on trustee process. The motion for an ex parte order shall be accompanied by a certificate by the plaintiff or his attorney of the amount of any liability insurance which he knows or has reason to believe will be available to satisfy any judgment against the defendant in the action. The motion, in the filing of which the plaintiff's attorney shall be subject to the obligations of Rule 11, shall be supported by affidavit or affidavits meeting the requirements set forth in Rule 4.1(h). *Identical to Mass.R.Civ.P 4.2(g).*

(h) Dissolution or Modification of Ex Parte Trustee Process. On two days' notice to the plaintiff or on such shorter notice as the court may prescribe, a defendant whose goods or credits have been attached on trustee process pursuant to an ex parte order entered under subdivision (g) of this rule may appear, without thereby submitting his person to the jurisdiction of the court, and move the dissolution or modification of the trustee process, and in that event the court shall proceed to hear and determine such motion as expeditiously as the ends of justice require. At such hearing the plaintiff shall have the burden of justifying any finding in the ex parte order which the defendant has challenged by affidavit. Nothing herein shall be construed to abolish or limit any means for obtaining dissolution, modification or discharge of an attachment that is otherwise available by law. *Identical to Mass. R.Civ.P 4.2(h).*

(i) Form of Hearing. At any hearing held under this rule, either party may adduce testimony and may call witnesses (including any opposing party). The court, for cause shown on the evidence so adduced, may make such interlocutory orders concerning disposition of the goods or credits sought to be subject to trustee process as justice may require. *Identical to Mass.R.Civ.P 4.2(i).*

Rule 4.3. Arrest: Supplementary Process: Ne Exeat

(a) Arrest; Availability of Remedy. Except in cases of civil contempt or as specifically authorized by law, no civil arrest shall be permitted in connection with any action under these rules, except as provided in section (c) of this rule. *Identical to Mass.R.Civ.P 4.3(a).*

(b) [Deleted].

(c) Ne Exeat. An order of arrest may be entered upon motion with or without notice when the plaintiff has obtained a judgment or order requiring the performance of an act, the neglect or refusal to perform which would be punishable by the court as a contempt, and where the defendant is not a resident of the Commonwealth or is about to depart therefrom, by reason of which nonresidence or departure there is danger that such judgment or order will be rendered ineffectual. The motion shall be accompanied by an affidavit showing that the plaintiff is entitled to the relief requested. The court may fix such terms as are just, and shall in any event afford the defendant an opportunity to obtain his release by the giving of an appropriate bond. In this rule the words "plaintiff" and "defendant" mean respectively the party who has obtained the judgment or order and the person whose arrest is sought. *Identical to Mass.R.Civ.P 4.3(c).*

Rule 5. Service and Filing of Pleadings and Other Papers

(a) Service: When Required. Except as otherwise provided in these Rules, or unless the court on motion with or without notice or of its own initiative otherwise orders, every order required by its terms to be served, every pleading subsequent to the original complaint, every paper relating to discovery required to be served upon a party, every written motion other than one which may be heard ex parte, and every written notice, notice of change of attorney, appearance, demand, brief or memorandum of law, offer of judgment, designation of record on appeal, and similar paper shall be served upon each of the parties. No service need be made on any

party in default for failure to appear except that any pleading asserting new or additional claims for relief against him shall be served upon him in the manner provided for service of summons in Rule 4. *Identical to Mass.R.Civ.P. 5(a).*

(b) Same: How Made. Whenever under these rules service is required or permitted to be made upon a party represented by an attorney the service shall be made upon the attorney unless service upon the party himself is ordered by the court. Service upon the attorney or upon a party shall be made by delivering a copy to him or by mailing it to him at his last known address or, if no address is known, by leaving it with the register of probate. Delivery of a copy within this rule means: handing it to the attorney or to the party; or leaving it at his office with his clerk or other person in charge thereof; or, if there is no one in charge, leaving it in a conspicuous place therein; or if the office is closed or the person to be served has no office, leaving it at his dwelling house or usual place of abode with some person of suitable age and discretion then residing therein. Service by mail is complete upon mailing. If notice of a hearing is given by service in hand delivered after 4 p.m., an additional day shall be added for purposes of computation of time under Rule 6(c). The time when the in hand service was made shall be reflected on the Certificate of Service.

(c) Same: Multiple Defendants. The court, on motion with or without notice or of its own initiative, may order that service of the pleadings of the defendants and replies thereto need not be made as between the defendants and that any cross-claim, counterclaim, or matter constituting an avoidance or affirmative defense contained therein shall be deemed to be denied or avoided by all other parties and that the filing of any such pleading and service thereof upon the plaintiff constitutes due notice of it to the parties. A copy of every such order shall be served upon the parties in such manner and form as the court directs. *Identical to Mass.R.Civ.P. 5(c).*

(d) Filing Generally, and Nonfiling of Discovery Materials.

(1) Except as otherwise provided in Rule 5(d)(2), all papers after the complaint required to be served upon a party shall be filed with the court either before service or within a reasonable time thereafter. Such filing by a party's attorney shall constitute a representation by him, subject to the obligations of Rule 11, that a copy of the paper has been or will be served upon each of the other parties as required by Rule 5(a). No further proof of service is required unless an adverse party raises a question of notice. In such event, prima facie proof of service shall be made out by a statement signed by the person making service, or by a written acknowledgment signed by the party or attorney served; and such statement or acknowledgment shall be filed within a reasonable time after notice has been questioned. Failure to make proof of service does not affect the validity of service.

(2) Unless the court, generally or in a specific case, on motion ex parte by any party or concerned citizen, or on its own motion shall otherwise order, the following shall not be presented or accepted for filing: notices of taking depositions, transcripts of depositions, interrogatories under Rule 33, answers and objections to interrogatories under Rule 33, requests under Rule 34, and responses to requests under Rule 34. The party taking a deposition or obtaining material

through discovery is responsible for its preservation and delivery to court if needed or so ordered. Notwithstanding anything in this Rule 5(d)(2), any party pressing or opposing any motion or other application for relief may file any document pertinent thereto. *Identical to Mass.R.Civ.P. 5(d).*

(e) Filing with the Court Defined. The filing of pleadings and other papers with the court as required by these rules shall be made by filing them with the clerk of the court, except that a judge may permit the papers to be filed with him, in which event he shall note thereon the filing date and forthwith transmit them to the office of the clerk. *Identical to Mass. R.Civ.P. 5(e).*

(f) Effect of Failure to File. If any party fails within five days after service to file any paper required by this rule to be filed, the court on its own motion or the motion of any party may order the paper to be filed forthwith; if the order be not obeyed, it may order the paper to be regarded as stricken and its service to be of no effect. *Identical to Mass.R.Civ.P. 5(f).*

(g) Information Required. On any pleading or other paper required or permitted by these rules to be filed with the court, there shall appear the name of the court and the county, the title of the action, the docket number, the designation of the nature of the pleading or paper, and the name and address of the person or attorney filing it. In any case where an endorsement for costs is required, the name of any attorney of this Commonwealth appearing on the complaint filed with the court shall constitute such an endorsement in absence of any words used in connection therewith showing a different purpose. *Identical to Mass.R.Civ.P. 5(g).*

Amended June 8, 1989, effective July 1, 1989; October 10, 1997, effective December 1, 1997; June 5, 2003, effective September 2, 2003.

Reporter's Notes—1997

The amendment to Rule 5(b) allows for an additional day to be added for the purpose of computation of time if service is delivered in hand after 4 p.m. The amendment also provides that if service is made by in hand service it will be reflected on the Certificate of Service.

Reporter's Notes—2003

The amendment to Rule 5(d) is in response to the amendment to Mass.R.Civ.P. Rule 5(d) Service and Filing of Pleadings and Other Papers. The amendment is intended to relieve the parties and court personnel of the burdens involved with the filing of interrogatories and answers with the court.

Rule 6.   Time

(a) Computation. In computing any period of time prescribed or allowed by these rules, by order of court, or by any applicable statute or rule, the day of the act, event, or default after which the designated period of time begins to run shall not be included. The last day of the period so computed shall be included, unless it is a Saturday, a Sunday, or a legal holiday, in which event the period runs until the end of the next day which is not a Saturday, a Sunday, or a legal holiday. When the period of time prescribed or allowed is less than 7 days, intermediate Saturdays, Sundays, and legal holidays shall be excluded in the computation. As used in this rule and in Rule 77(c), "legal holiday" includes those days specified in Mass. G.L. c. 4, § 7 and any other day appointed as a holiday by the President or the Congress of the United States or

designated by the laws of the Commonwealth. *Identical to Mass.R.Civ.P. 6(a).*

(b) Enlargement. When by these rules or by a notice given thereunder or by order or rule of court an act is required or allowed to be done at or within a specified time, the court for cause shown may at any time in its discretion (1) with or without motion or notice order the period enlarged if request therefor is made before the expiration of the period originally prescribed or as extended by a previous order; or (2) upon motion made after the expiration of the specified period permit the act to be done where the failure to act was the result of excusable neglect; or (3) permit the act to be done by stipulation of the parties; but it may not extend the time for taking any action under Rules 50(b), 52(b), 59(b), (d), and (e), and 60(b), except to the extent and under the conditions stated in them. *Identical to Mass.R.Civ.P. 6(b).*

(c) For Motions–Affidavits–Proposed Orders. A written motion, other than one which may be heard ex parte, and notice of the hearing thereof shall be served not later than seven (7) days before the time specified for the hearing, unless a different period is fixed by these rules or by order of the court. Such an order may be made on ex parte application when an emergency justifies the same. An application for ex parte relief from the seven (7) day notice requirement shall be by motion and supported by affidavit setting forth the nature of the emergency. On allowance of the motion, the court shall make a written finding that the emergency exists and setting forth the nature of the emergency. Whenever a motion is supported by a memorandum or affidavit, the memorandum or affidavit shall be served with the motion; and except as provided in Rule 59(c), opposing memoranda or affidavits must be served not later than one (1) business day before the hearing, unless the court permits them to be served at some other time. Every motion shall be accompanied by a proposed order, which shall be served with the motion. The proposed order shall set forth in detailed itemized paragraphs the relief sought from the court. The proposed order should not be docketed or included in the permanent file if the order is not adopted by the court and may be destroyed after the hearing on the motion. The service and the content of all motions, affidavits, and supporting papers shall be subject to the sanctions of Rule 11 of these rules.

(d) Additional Time After Service by Mail. Whenever a party has the right or is required to do some act or take some proceedings within a prescribed period after the service of a notice or other papers upon him and the notice or paper is served upon him by mail, 3 days shall be added to the prescribed period. *Identical to the Mass.R.Civ.P. 6(d).*

Amended October 10, 1997, effective December 1, 1997; October 27, 1999, effective January 1, 2000; June 5, 2003, effective September 2, 2003.

Reporter's Notes—1997

This amendment to Rule 6(c) changes the time requirements for service of a motion from three (3) to seven (7) days, unless it is a motion that may be heard *ex parte*. All *ex parte* motions must be accompanied by an affidavit setting forth the nature of the emergency. If the motion is allowed, the court must make written findings that an emergency exists and set forth the nature of the emergency.

The amendment also provides that if a motion is supported by an affidavit it must be served with the motion, except as provided in Rule

59(c). The service of opposing affidavits is no longer optional. If a motion is accompanied by an affidavit, then an opposing affidavit must also be served. The amendment to the rule changes the time requirement for service of the opposing affidavit from not later than one (1) day before the hearing, to not later than two (2) full business days before the hearing.

All motions must now be accompanied by a proposed order which sets forth, in itemized detail, the relief sought from the court. In addition, Rule 6(c) explicitly states that the service and content of motions are subject to the sanctions of Rule 11.

Reporter's Notes—2000

Rule 6(c) requires every motion to be accompanied by a proposed order. The amendment to rule 6(c) makes clear that the proposed order should not be docketed or included in the permanent case file and may be destroyed after a hearing on the motion.

Reporter's Notes—2003

The amendment to Rule 6(c) requires that any pleadings, whether an affidavit or a memorandum in support or in opposition to a motion, be served prior to the time fixed for hearing on the motion.

III. PLEADINGS AND MOTIONS

Rule 7. Pleadings Allowed: Form of Motions

(a) Pleadings. There shall be a complaint and (except as provided by law) an answer, and a trustee's answer under oath if trustee process is used; a reply to a counterclaim denominated as such; an answer to a cross-claim, if the answer contains a cross-claim; a third-party complaint, if a person who was not an original party is summoned under the provisions of Rule 14; and a third-party answer, if a third-party complaint is served. No other pleading shall be allowed, except that the court may order a reply to an answer or a third-party answer. In the Land Court, answers in actions for registration, confirmation, or tax foreclosure shall conform to G.L. c. 185, § 41, and G.L. c. 60, § 68, where applicable. *Identical to Mass.R.Civ.P. 7(a).*

(b) Motions and Other Papers.

(1) An application to the court for an order shall be by motion which, unless made during a hearing or trial, shall be made in writing, shall state with particularity the grounds therefor, and shall set forth the relief or order sought.

(2) The rules applicable to captions, signing, and other matters of form of pleadings apply to all motions and other papers provided for by these rules. *Identical to Mass. R.Civ.P. 7(b).*

(c) Demurrers, Pleas, Etc., Abolished. Demurrers, pleas, and exceptions for insufficiency of a pleading shall not be used. *Identical to Mass.R.Civ.P. 7(c).*

Rule 8.   General Rules of Pleading

(a) Claims for Relief. A pleading which sets forth a claim for relief, whether an original claim, counterclaim, cross-claim, or third-party claim shall contain (1) a short and plain statement of the claim showing that the pleader is entitled to relief, and (2) a demand for judgment for the relief to which he deems himself entitled. Relief in the alternative or of several different types may be demanded. *Identical to Mass.R.Civ.P. 8(a).*

(b) Defenses: Form of Denials. A party shall state in short and plain terms his defenses to such claim asserted and shall admit or deny the averments upon which the adverse party relies. If he is without knowledge or information sufficient to form a belief as to the truth of an averment, he shall so state and this has the effect of a denial. Denials shall fairly meet the substance of the averments denied. When a pleader intends in good faith to deny only a part or a qualification of an averment, he shall specify so much of it as is true and material and shall deny only the remainder. Unless the pleader intends in good faith to controvert all the averments of the preceding pleading, he may make his denials as specific denials of designated averments or paragraphs, or he may generally deny all the averments except such designated averments or paragraphs as he expressly admits; but, when he does so intend to controvert all its averments, he may do so by general denial subject to the obligations set forth in Rule 11. The signature to an instrument set forth in any pleading shall be taken as admitted unless a party specifically denies its genuineness. An allegation in any pleading that a place is a public way shall be taken as admitted unless a party specifically denies such allegation. *Identical to Mass.R.Civ.P. 8(b).*

(c) Affirmative Defenses. In pleading to a preceding pleading, a party shall set forth affirmatively accord and satisfaction, arbitration and award, assumption of risk, contributory negligence, discharge in bankruptcy, duress, estoppel, failure of consideration, fraud, illegality, injury by fellow servant, laches, license, payment, release, res judicata, statute of frauds, statute of limitations, waiver, and any other matter constituting an avoidance or affirmative defense. When a party has mistakenly designated a defense as a counterclaim or a counterclaim as a defense, the court on terms, if justice so requires, shall treat the pleading as if there had been a proper designation. *Identical to Mass.R.Civ.P. 8(c).*

(d) [Deleted].

(e) Pleading to be Concise and Direct; Consistency.

(1) Each averment of a pleading shall be simple, concise, and direct. No technical forms of pleading or motions are required.

(2) A party may set forth two or more statements of a claim or defense alternatively or hypothetically, either in one count or defense or in separate counts or defenses. When two or more statements are made in the alternative and one of them if made independently would be sufficient, the pleading is not made insufficient by the insufficiency of one or more of the alternative statements. A party may also state as many separate claims or defenses as he has regardless of consistency and whether based on legal or equitable grounds. All statements shall be made subject to the obligations set forth in Rule 11. *Identical to Mass.R.Civ.P. 8(e).*

(f) Construction of Pleadings. All pleadings shall be so construed as to do substantial justice. *Identical to Mass. R.Civ.P. 8(f).*

Rule 9. Pleading Special Matters

(a) Capacity. It is not necessary to aver the capacity of a party to sue or be sued or the authority of a party to sue or be sued in a representative capacity or the legal existence of an organized association of persons that is made a party. When a party desires to raise an issue as to the legal existence of any party or the capacity of any party to sue or be sued or the authority of a party to sue or be sued in a representative capacity, he shall do so by specific negative averment, which shall include such supporting particulars as are peculiarly within the pleader's knowledge. *Identical to Mass.R.Civ.P. 9(a).*

(b) Fraud, Mistake, Duress, Undue Influence, Condition of the Mind. In all averments of fraud, mistake, duress or undue influence, the circumstances constituting fraud, mistake, duress or undue influence shall be stated with particularity. Malice, intent, knowledge, and other condition of mind of a person may be averred generally. *Identical to Mass.R.Civ.P. 9(b).*

(c) Conditions Precedent. In pleading the performance or occurrence of conditions precedent, it is sufficient to aver generally that all conditions precedent have been performed or have occurred. A denial of performance or occurrence shall be made specifically and with particularity. *Identical to Mass. R.Civ.P. 9(c).*

(d) Official Document or Act. In pleading an official document or official act it is sufficient to aver that the document was issued or the act done in compliance with law. *Identical to Mass.R.Civ.P. 9(d).*

(e) Judgment. In pleading a judgment or decision of a domestic or foreign court, judicial or quasi-judicial tribunal, or of a board or officer, it is sufficient to aver the judgment or decision without setting forth matter showing jurisdiction to render it. *Identical to Mass.R.Civ.P. 9(e).*

(f) Time and Place. For the purpose of testing the sufficiency of a pleading, averments of time and place are material and shall be considered like all other averments of material matter. *Identical to Mass.R.Civ.P. 9(f).*

(g) Special Damage. When items of special damage are claimed, they shall be specifically stated. *Identical to Mass. R.Civ.P. 9(g).*

Rule 10. Form of Pleadings

(a) Caption; Names of Parties. Every pleading shall contain a caption setting forth the name of the court, the county, the title of the action, the docket number, and a designation as in Rule 7(a). In the complaint the title of the action shall include the names of all the parties, but in other pleadings it is sufficient to state the name of the first party on each side with an appropriate indication of other parties. *Identical to Mass.R.Civ.P. 10(a).*

(b) Paragraphs; Separate Statements. All averments of claim or defense shall be made in numbered paragraphs, the contents of each of which shall be limited as far as practicable to a statement of a single set of circumstances; and a paragraph may be referred to by number in all succeeding pleadings. Each claim founded upon a separate transaction or occurrence and each defense other than denials shall be stated in a separate count or defense whenever a separation facili-

tates the clear presentation of the matters set forth. *Identical to Mass.R.Civ.P. 10(b).*

(c) Adoption by Reference; Exhibits. Statements in a pleading may be adopted by reference in a different part of the same pleading or in another pleading or in any motion. A copy of any written instrument which is an exhibit to a pleading is a part thereof for all purposes. *Identical to Mass.R.Civ.P. 10(c).*

(d) Parties' Residence or Place of Business. The complaint, and any subsequent pleading stating a claim against a person not originally a party to the action, shall state the respective residences or usual places of business of the party stating a claim and of each person against whom a claim is stated, if known to the pleader; if unknown, the complaint or pleading shall so state. *Identical to Mass.R.Civ.P. 10(d).*

(e) Two–Sided Documents. The text of any document may appear on both sides of the page. *Identical to Mass. R.Civ.P. 10(e).*

Amended January 24, 1978, effective February 21, 1978; March 5, 2010, effective May 1, 2010.

Reporter's Notes—2010

Rule 10(e) was added in 2010 to recognize the existing practice by which some attorneys include text on both the front and back of a page. The language of Rule 10(e) is similar to a 1999 amendment to Appellate Rule 20(a)(4) regarding briefs and other documents filed in the appellate courts.

Although the two-sided document language has been added to Rule 10, which governs the form of pleadings, the provisions of Rule 7, including the two-sided document language, are also applicable to motions and other papers filed under the Massachusetts Rules of Civil Procedure. See Rule 7(b)(2).

Rule 11. Appearances and Pleadings

(a) Signing. Every pleading of a party represented by an attorney shall be signed in his individual name by at least one attorney who is admitted to practice in this Commonwealth. The address of each attorney, telephone number, and e-mail address if any shall be stated. A party who is not represented by an attorney shall sign his pleadings and state his address, telephone number, and e-mail address if any. Except when otherwise specifically provided by rule or statute, pleadings need not be verified or accompanied by affidavit. The signature of an attorney to a pleading constitutes a certificate by him that he has read the pleading; that to the best of his knowledge, information, and belief there is a good ground to support it; and that it is not interposed for delay. If a pleading is not signed, or is signed with intent to defeat the purpose of this Rule, it may be stricken and the action may proceed as though the pleading had not been filed. For a wilful violation of this rule an attorney may be subjected to appropriate disciplinary action. Similar action may be taken if scandalous or indecent matter is inserted. *Identical to Mass. R.Civ.P. 11(a).*

(b) Appearances.

(1) The filing of any pleading, motion, or other paper shall constitute an appearance by the attorney who signs it, unless the paper states otherwise.

(2) An appearance in a case may be made by filing a notice of appearance, containing the name, address, and telephone number of the attorney or person filing the notice.

(3) No appearance shall, of itself, constitute a general appearance. *Identical to Mass.R.Civ.P. 11(b).*

(c) Withdrawals. An attorney may, without leave of court, withdraw from a case by filing written notice of withdrawal, together with proof of service on his client and all other parties, provided that (1) such notice is accompanied by the appearance of successor counsel; (2) no motions are then pending before the court; and (3) no trial date has been set. Under all other circumstances, leave of court, on motion and notice, must be obtained. *Identical to Mass.R.Civ.P. 11(c).*

(d) Change of Appearance. In the event an attorney who has heretofore appeared, ceases to act, or a substitute attorney or additional attorney appears, or a party heretofore represented by attorney appears without attorney, or an attorney appears representing a heretofore unrepresented party, or a heretofore stated address or telephone number is changed, the party or attorney concerned shall notify the court and every other party (or his attorney, if the party is represented) in writing, and the clerk shall enter such cessation, appearance, or change on the docket forthwith. Until such notification the court, parties, and attorneys may rely on action by, and notice to, any attorney previously appearing (or party heretofore unrepresented), and on notice, at an address previously entered. *Identical to Mass.R.Civ.P. 11(d).*

(e) Verification Generally. When a pleading is required to be verified, or when an affidavit is re-quired or permitted to be filed, the pleading may be verified or the affidavit made by the party, or by a person having knowledge of the facts for and on behalf of such party. *Identical to Mass.R.Civ.P. 11(e).*

Amended March 5, 2010, effective May 1, 2010.

Reporter's Notes—2010

Rule 11(a) has been amended to require attorneys and unrepresented parties to include their e-mail addresses, if any, on pleadings. The requirement of e-mail addresses already exists in the Federal Rules of Civil Procedure (Rule 11(a), as amended in 2007) and in the Rules of the Superior Court (Rule 9A(6)), effective March 2, 2009).

The Advisory Committee Notes to the 2007 amendment to the Federal Rules of Civil Procedure state that "[p]roviding an e-mail address is useful, but does not of itself signify consent to filing or service by e-mail." Likewise, the 2010 amendment to Rule 11(a) "does not of itself signify consent to filing or service by e-mail" in civil actions in Massachusetts.

Rule 12. Defenses and Objections—When and How Presented—by Pleading or Motion

(a) When Presented

(1) After service upon him of any pleading requiring a responsive pleading, a party shall serve such responsive pleading within 20 days unless otherwise directed by order of the court.

(2) The service of a motion permitted under this rule alters this period of time as follows, unless a different time is fixed by order of the court:

(i) if the court denies the motion or postpones its disposition until the trial on the merits, the responsive pleading

shall be served within 10 days after notice of the court's action;

(ii) if the court grants a motion for a more definite statement, the responsive pleading shall be served within 10 days after the service of the more definite statement. *Identical to Mass.R.Civ.P. 12(a).*

(b) How Presented. Every defense, in law or fact, to a claim for relief in any pleading, whether a claim, counterclaim, cross-claim, or third-party claim, shall be asserted in the responsive pleading thereto if one is required, except that the following defenses may at the option of the pleader be made by motion:

(1) Lack of jurisdiction over the subject matter;

(2) Lack of jurisdiction over the person;

(3) Improper venue;

(4) Insufficiency of process;

(5) Insufficiency of service of process;

(6) Failure to state a claim upon which relief can be granted;

(7) Failure to join a party under Rule 19;

(8) Misnomer of a party;

(9) Pendency of a prior action in a court of the Commonwealth.

A motion making any of these defenses shall be made before pleading if a further pleading is permitted. No defense or objection is waived by being joined with one or more other defenses or objections in a responsive pleading or motion. If a pleading sets forth a claim for relief to which the adverse party is not required to serve a responsive pleading, he may assert at the trial any defense in law or fact to that claim for relief. If, on any motion asserting the defense numbered (6), to dismiss for failure of the pleading to state a claim upon which relief can be granted, matters outside the pleading are presented to and not excluded by the court, the motion shall be treated as one for summary judgment and disposed of as provided in Rule 56, and all parties shall be given reasonable opportunity to present all material made pertinent to such a motion by Rule 56. A motion, answer, or reply presenting the defense numbered (6) shall include a short, concise statement of the grounds on which such defense is based. *Identical to Mass.R.Civ.P. 12(b).*

(c) [Deleted]. (Motion for Judgment on the Pleadings.)

(d) Preliminary Hearings. The defenses specifically enumerated (1)–(9) in subdivision (b) of this rule, whether made in a pleading or by motion shall be heard and determined before trial on application of any party, unless the court orders that the hearing and determination thereof be deferred until the trial.

(e) Motion for More Definite Statement. If a pleading to which a responsive pleading is permitted is so vague or ambiguous that a party cannot reasonably be required to frame a responsive pleading, he may move for a more definite statement before interposing his responsive pleading. The motion shall point out the defects complained of and the details desired. If the motion is granted and the order of the court is not obeyed within 10 days after notice of the order or within such other time as the court may fix, the court may strike the pleading to which the motion was directed or make such order as it deems just. *Identical to Mass.R.Civ.P. 12(e).*

(f) Motion to Strike. Upon motion made by a party before responding to a pleading or, if no responsive pleading is permitted by these rules, upon motion made by a party within 20 days after the service of the pleading upon him or upon the court's own initiative at any time, the court may after hearing order stricken from any pleading any insufficient defense, or any redundant, immaterial, impertinent, or scandalous matter. *Identical to Mass.R.Civ.P. 12(f).*

(g) Consolidation of Defenses in Motion. A party who makes a motion under this rule may join with it any other motions herein provided for and then available to him. If a party makes a motion under this rule but omits therefrom any defense or objection then available to him which this rule permits to be raised by motion, he shall not thereafter make a motion based on the defense or objection so omitted.

(h) Waiver or Preservation of Certain Defenses.

(1) A defense of lack of jurisdiction over the person, improper venue, insufficiency of process, insufficiency of service of process, misnomer of a party, or pendency of a prior action is waived (A) if omitted from a motion in the circumstances described in subdivision (g), or (B) if it is neither made by motion under this rule nor included in a responsive pleading or an amendment thereof permitted by Rule 15(a) to be made as a matter of course.

(2) [Deleted].

(3) Whenever it appears by suggestion of a party or otherwise that the court lacks jurisdiction of the subject matter, the court shall dismiss the action.

Rule 13.   Counterclaim and Cross–Complaint

(a) Compulsory Counterclaims. A pleading shall state as a counterclaim any claim for relief the court has power to give which at the time of serving the pleading the pleader has against any opposing party, if it arises out of the transaction or occurrence that is the subject matter of the opposing party's claim and does not either require for its adjudication the presence of third parties over whom the court cannot acquire jurisdiction or constitute an action required by law to be brought in a county other than the county in which the court is sitting. But the pleader need not state the claim if (1) at the time the action was commenced the claim was the subject of another pending action or (2) the opposing party brought suit upon his claim by attachment or other process by which the court did not acquire jurisdiction to render a personal judgment on that claim, and the pleader is not stating any counterclaim under this Rule 13.

(b) Permissive Counterclaims. A pleading may state as a counterclaim any claim against an opposing party. *Identical to Mass.R.Civ.P. 13(b).*

(c) Counterclaim Exceeding Opposing Claim. A counterclaim may or may not diminish or defeat the recovery sought by the opposing party. It may claim relief exceeding in amount or different in kind from that sought in the pleading of the opposing party. *Identical to Mass.R.Civ.P. 13(c).*

(d) Counterclaim Against the Commonwealth. These rules shall not be construed to enlarge beyond the limits now fixed by law the right to assert counterclaims or to claim credits against the Commonwealth of Massachusetts or a political subdivision thereof, or any of their officers and agencies. *Identical to Mass.R.Civ.P. 13(d).*

(e) Counterclaim Maturing or Acquired After Pleading. A claim which either matured or was acquired by the pleader after serving his pleading may, with the permission of the court, be presented as a counterclaim by supplemental pleading. *Identical to Mass.R.Civ.P. 13(e).*

(f) Omitted Counterclaim. When a pleader fails to set up a counterclaim through oversight, inadvertence, or excusable neglect, or when justice requires, he may by leave of court set up the counterclaim by amendment. *Identical to Mass. R.Civ.P. 13(f).*

(g) Cross–Claim Against Co–Party. A pleading may state as a cross-claim any claim by one party against a co-party arising out of the transaction or occurrence that is the subject matter either of the original action or of a counterclaim therein or relating to any property that is the subject matter of the original action. Such cross-claim may include a claim that the party against whom it is asserted is or may be liable to the cross-claimant for all or part of a claim asserted in the action against the cross-claimant. *Identical to Mass.R.Civ.P. 13(g).*

(h) Joinder of Additional Parties. Persons other than those made parties to the original action may be made parties to a counterclaim or cross-claim in accordance with the provisions of Rules 19 and 20. *Identical to Mass.R.Civ.P. 13(h).*

(i) Separate Trials; Separate Judgments. If the court orders separate trials as provided in Rule 42(b), judgment on a counterclaim or cross-claim may be rendered in accordance with the terms of Rule 54(b) when the court has jurisdiction so to do, even if the claims of the opposing party have been dismissed or otherwise disposed of. *Identical to Mass. R.Civ.P. 13(i).*

(j) Cross–Complaint. In a contested action for divorce if the defendant upon payment of the proper entry fee and at any time prior to the conclusion of the hearing shall cause to be entered his or her cross-complaint for divorce, the court shall allow the entry of said cross-complaint after giving of such notice or service to the new defendant as the court, in its discretion, shall order.

Amended January 16, 1979, effective February 12, 1979.

Rule 14.   Third–Party Practice [Deleted]

[Deleted].

Rule 15.   Amended and Supplemental Pleadings

(a) Amendments. A party may amend his pleading once as a matter of course at any time before a responsive pleading is served and prior to entry of an order of dismissal or, if the pleading is one to which no responsive pleading is permitted and the action has not been placed upon the trial calendar, he may so amend it at any time within 20 days after it is served. Otherwise a party may amend his pleading only by leave of court or by written consent of the adverse party; and leave shall be freely given when justice so requires. A party shall plead in response to an amended pleading within the time remaining for response to the original pleading or within 10 days after service of the amended pleading, whichever period may be the longer, unless the court otherwise orders. *Identical to Mass.R.Civ.P. 15(a).*

(b) Amendments to Conform to the Evidence. When issues not raised by the pleadings are tried by express or implied consent of the parties, they shall be treated in all respects as if they had been raised in the pleadings. Such amendment of the pleadings as may be necessary to cause them to conform to the evidence and to raise these issues may be made upon motion of any party at any time, even after judgment; but failure so to amend does not affect the result of the trial of these issues. If evidence is objected to at the trial on the ground that it is not within the issues made by the pleadings, the court may allow the pleadings to be amended and shall do so freely when the presentation of the merits of the action will be subserved thereby and the objecting party fails to satisfy the court that the admission of such evidence would prejudice him in maintaining his action or defense upon the merits. The court may grant a continuance to enable the objecting party to meet such evidence. *Identical to Mass. R.Civ.P. 15(b).*

(c) Relation Back of Amendments. Whenever the claim or defense asserted in the amended pleading arose out of the conduct, transaction, or occurrence set forth or attempted to be set forth in the original pleading, the amendment (including an amendment changing a party) relates back to the original pleading. *Identical to Mass.R.Civ.P. 15(c).*

(d) Supplemental Pleadings. Upon motion of a party the court may, upon reasonable notice and upon such terms as are just, permit him to serve a supplemental pleading setting forth transactions or occurrences or events which have happened since the date of the pleading sought to be supplemented.

Permission may be granted even though the original pleading is defective in its statement of a claim for relief or defense. If the court deems it advisable that the adverse party plead to the supplemental pleading it shall so order, specifying the time therefor. *Identical to Mass.R.Civ.P. 15(d).*

Rule 16. Pre–Trial Procedure: Formulating Issues

In any action, the court may in its discretion direct the attorneys for the parties to appear before it for a conference to consider:

1. The simplification of the issues;

2. The necessity or desirability of amendments to the pleadings;

3. The possibility of obtaining admissions of fact and of documents which will avoid unnecessary proof;

4. The limitation of the number of expert witnesses;

5. The advisability of a preliminary reference of issues to a master;

6. The possibility of settlement;

7. Agreement as to damages; and

8. Such other matters as may aid in the disposition of the action.

The court shall make an order which recites the action taken at the conference, the amendments allowed to the pleadings, and the agreements made by the parties as to any of the matters considered, and which limits the issues for trial to those not disposed of by admissions or agreements of counsel; and such order when entered controls the subsequent course of the action, unless modified at the trial to prevent manifest injustice.

IV. PARTIES

Rule 17. Parties Plaintiff and Defendant: Capacity

(a) Real Party in Interest. Except for any action brought under General Laws, chapter 152, section 15, every action shall be prosecuted in the name of the real party in interest. An executor, administrator, guardian, conservator, bailee, trustee of an express trust, a party with whom or in whose name a contract has been made for the benefit of another, or a party authorized by statute may sue in his own name without joining with him the party for whose benefit the action is brought; and when a statute so provides, an action for the use or benefit of another shall be brought in the name of the Commonwealth. An insurer who has paid all or part of a loss may sue in the name of the assured to whose rights it is subrogated. No action shall be dismissed on the ground that it is not prosecuted in the name of the real party in interest until a reasonable time has been allowed after objection for ratification of commencement of the action by, or joinder or substitution of, the real party in interest; and such ratification, joinder, or substitution shall have the same effect as if the action had been commenced in the name of the real party in interest. *Identical to Mass.R.Civ.P. 17(a).*

(b) Infant or Incompetent Persons. Whenever an infant or incompetent person, or an incapacitated person as defined in G.L. c.190B has a representative, such as a guardian, conservator, or other like fiduciary, the representative may sue or defend on behalf of the infant or incompetent person, or an incapacitated person as defined in G.L. c.190B. If an infant or incompetent person, or an incapacitated person as defined in G.L. c.190B does not have a duly appointed representative, he may sue by his next friend or by a guardian ad litem. The court may appoint a guardian ad litem for an infant or incompetent person, or an incapacitated person as defined in G.L. c.190B not otherwise represented in an action or may make such other order as it deems proper for the protection of the infant or incompetent person, or an incapacitated person as defined in G.L. c.190B.

Amended June 24, 2009, effective July 1, 2009; November 30, 2009, effective December 1, 2009.

Rule 18. Joinder of Claims and Remedies [Deleted]

[Deleted].

Rule 19. Joinder of Persons Needed for Just Adjudication

(a) Persons to be Joined if Feasible. A person who is subject to service of process shall be joined as a party in the action if (1) in his absence complete relief cannot be accorded among those already parties, or (2) he claims an interest relating to the subject of the action and is so situated that the disposition of the action in his absence may (i) as a practical matter impair or impede his ability to protect that interest or (ii) leave any of the persons already parties subject to a substantial risk of incurring double, multiple, or otherwise inconsistent obligations by reason of his claimed interest. If he has not been so joined, the court shall order that he be made a party. If he should join as a plaintiff but refuses to do so, he may be made a defendant. *Identical to Mass.R.Civ.P. 19(a).*

(b) Determination by Court Whenever Joinder Not Feasible. If a person as described in subdivision (a)(1)—(2) hereof cannot be made a party, the court shall determine whether in equity and good conscience the action should proceed among the parties before it, or should be dismissed, the absent person being thus regarded as indispensable. The factors to be considered by the court include: first, to what extent a judgment rendered in the person's absence might be prejudicial to him or those already parties; second, the extent to which, by protective provisions in the judgment, by the shaping of relief, or other measures, the prejudice can be lessened or avoided; third, whether a judgment rendered in the person's absence will be adequate; fourth, whether the plaintiff will have an adequate remedy if the action is dismissed for nonjoinder. *Identical to Mass.R.Civ.P. 19(b).*

(c) Pleading Reasons for Nonjoinder. A pleading asserting a claim for relief shall state the names, if known to the pleader, of any persons as described in subdivision (a)(1)—(2) hereof who are not joined, and the reasons why they are not joined. *Identical to Mass.R.Civ.P. 19(c).*

(d) [Deleted].

Rule 20. Permissive Joinder of Parties [Deleted]

[Deleted].

Rule 21. Misjoinder and Non–Joinder of Parties [Deleted]

[Deleted].

Rule 22. Interpleader [Deleted]

[Deleted].

Rule 23. Class Actions [Deleted]

[Deleted].

Rule 23.1. Derivative Actions by Shareholders [Deleted]

[Deleted].

Rule 23.2. Actions Relating to Unincorporated Associations [Deleted]

[Deleted].

Rule 24. Intervention

(a) Intervention of Right. Upon timely application anyone shall be permitted to intervene in an action: (1) when a statute of the Commonwealth confers an unconditional right to intervene or (2) when the applicant claims an interest relating to the property or transaction which is the subject of the action and he is so situated that the disposition of the action may as a practical matter impair or impede his ability to protect that interest, unless the applicant's interest is adequately represented by existing parties. *Identical to Mass.R.Civ.P. 24(a).*

(b) Permissive Intervention. Upon timely application anyone may be permitted to intervene in an action: (1) when a statute of the Commonwealth confers a conditional right to intervene; or (2) when an applicant's claim or defense and the main action have a question of law or fact in common. When a party to an action relies for ground of claim or defense upon any statute or executive order administered by a federal or state governmental officer or agency or upon any regulation, order, requirement, or agreement issued or made pursuant to the statute or executive order, the officer or agency upon timely application may be permitted to intervene in the action. In exercising its discretion the court shall consider whether the intervention will unduly delay or prejudice the adjudication of the rights of the original parties. *Identical to Mass. R.Civ.P. 24(b).*

(c) Procedure. A person desiring to intervene shall serve a motion to intervene upon the parties as provided in Rule 5. The motion shall state the grounds therefor and shall be accompanied by a pleading setting forth the claim or defense for which intervention is sought. *Identical to Mass.R.Civ.P. 24(c).*

(d) Intervention by the Attorney General. When the constitutionality of an act of the legislature or the constitutionality or validity of an ordinance of any city or the by-law of any town is drawn in question in any action to which the Commonwealth or an officer, agency, or employee thereof is not a party, the party asserting the unconstitutionality of the act or the unconstitutionality or invalidity of the ordinance or by-law shall notify the attorney general within sufficient time to afford him an opportunity to intervene. *Identical to Mass. R.Civ.P. 24(d).*

Rule 25. Substitution of Parties

(a) [Deleted].

(b) Incompetency or Incapacity. If a party becomes incompetent or incapacitated as defined in G.L. c.190B, the court upon motion served, may allow the action to be continued by or against his representative.

(c) [Deleted].

(d) [Deleted].

Amended June 24, 2009, effective July 1, 2009.

V. DEPOSITIONS AND DISCOVERY

Rule 26. General Provisions Governing Discovery

(a) Discovery Methods. Parties may obtain discovery by one or more of the following methods except as otherwise provided in Rule 30(a) and Rule 30A(a), (b): depositions upon oral examination or written questions; written interrogatories; production of documents or things or permission to enter upon land or other property, for inspection and other purposes; physical and mental examinations; and requests for admission. Unless the court orders otherwise, or unless otherwise provided in these rules, the frequency of use of these methods is not limited. *Identical to Mass.R.Civ.P. 26(a) (as amended January 1, 1981).*

(b) Scope of Discovery. Unless otherwise limited by order of the court in accordance with these rules, the scope of discovery is as follows:

(1) *In General.* Parties may obtain discovery regarding any matter, not privileged, which is relevant to the subject matter involved in the pending action, whether it relates to the claim or defense of the party seeking discovery or to the claim or defense of any other party, including the existence, description, nature, custody, condition and location of any books, documents, or other tangible things and the identity and location of persons having knowledge of any discoverable matter. It is not ground for objection that the information sought will be inadmissible at the trial if the information sought appears reasonably calculated to lead to the discovery of admissible evidence.

(2) *Insurance Agreements.* A party may obtain discovery of the existence and contents of any insurance agreement under which any person carrying on an insurance business may be liable to satisfy part or all of a judgment which may be entered in the action or to indemnify or reimburse for payments made to satisfy the judgment. Information concerning the insurance agreement is not by reason of disclosure admissible in evidence at trial. For purposes of this paragraph, an application for insurance shall not be treated as part of an insurance agreement.

(3) *Trial Preparation: Materials.* Subject to the provisions of subdivision (b)(4) of this rule, a party may obtain discovery of documents and tangible things otherwise discoverable under subdivision (b)(1) of this rule and prepared in anticipation of litigation or for trial by or for another party or by or for that other party's representative (including his attorney, consultant, surety, indemnitor, insurer, or agent) only upon a showing that the party seeking discovery has substantial need of the materials in the preparation of his case and that he is unable without undue hardship to obtain the substantial equivalent of the materials by other means. In ordering discovery of such materials when the required showing has been made, the court shall protect against disclosure of the mental impressions, conclusions, opinions, or legal theories of an attorney or other representative of a party concerning the litigation.

A party may obtain without the required showing a statement concerning the action or its subject matter previously made by that party. Upon request, a person not a party may obtain without the required showing a statement concerning the action or its subject matter previously made by that person. If the request is refused, the person may move for a court order. The provisions of Rule 37(a)(4) apply to the award of expenses incurred in relation to the motion. For purposes of this paragraph, a statement previously made is (A) a written statement signed or otherwise adopted or approved by the person making it, or (B) a stenographic, mechanical, electrical, or other recording, or a transcription thereof, which is a substantially verbatim recital of an oral statement by the person making it and contemporaneously recorded.

(4) *Trial Preparation: Experts.* Discovery of facts known and opinions held by experts, otherwise discoverable under the provisions of subdivision (b)(1) of this rule and acquired or developed in anticipation of litigation or for trial, may be obtained only as follows:

(A)(i) A party may through interrogatories require any other party to identify each person whom the other party expects to call as an expert witness at trial, to state the subject matter on which the expert is expected to testify, and to state the substance of the facts and opinions to which the expert is expected to testify and a summary of the grounds for each opinion. (ii) Upon motion, the court may order further discovery by other means, subject to such restrictions as to scope and such provisions, pursuant to subdivision (b)(4)(C) of this rule, concerning fees and expenses as the court may deem appropriate.

(B) A party may discover facts known or opinions held by an expert who has been retained or specially employed by another party in anticipation of litigation or preparation for trial and who is not expected to be called as a witness at trial, only as provided in Rule 35(b) or upon a showing of exceptional circumstances under which it is impracticable for the party seeking discovery to obtain facts or opinions on the same subject by other means.

(C) Unless manifest injustice would result, (i) the court shall require that the party seeking discovery pay the expert a reasonable fee for time spent in responding to discovery under subdivisions (b)(4)(A)(ii) and (b)(4)(B) of this rule; and (ii) with respect to discovery obtained under subdivision (b)(4)(A)(ii) of this rule the court may require, and with respect to discovery obtained under subdivision (b)(4)(B) of this rule the court shall require, the party seeking discovery to pay the other party a fair portion of the fees and expenses reasonably incurred by the latter party in obtaining facts and opinions from the expert.

(5) *Claims of Privilege or Protection of Trial Preparation Materials: Privilege Log.* When a party withholds information otherwise discoverable under these rules by claiming that it is privileged or subject to protection as material prepared in anticipation of litigation or for trial, the party shall make the claim expressly and, without revealing information that is privileged or protected, shall prepare a privilege log containing the following information: the respective author(s) and sender(s) if different; the recipient(s); the date and type of document, written communication or thing not produced; and in general terms, the subject matter of the withheld information. By written agreement of the party seeking the withheld

information and the party holding the information or by court order, a privilege log need not be prepared or may be limited to certain documents, written communications, or things.

(c) Protective Orders. Upon motion by a party or by the person from whom discovery is sought, and for good cause shown, the court in which the action is pending or alternatively, on matters relating to a deposition, the court in the county or judicial district, as the case may be, where the deposition is to be taken may make any order which justice requires to protect a party or person from annoyance, embarrassment, oppression, or undue burden or expense, including one or more of the following: (1) that the discovery not be had; (2) that the discovery may be had only on specified terms and conditions, including a designation of the time or place; (3) that the discovery may be had only by a method of discovery other than that selected by the party seeking discovery; (4) that certain matters not be inquired into, or that the scope of the discovery be limited to certain matters; (5) that discovery be conducted with no one present except persons designated by the court; (6) that a deposition after being sealed be opened only by order of the court; (7) that a trade secret or other confidential research, development, or commercial information not be disclosed or be disclosed only in a designated way; (8) that the parties simultaneously file specified documents or information enclosed in sealed envelopes to be opened as directed by the court.

If the motion for a protective order is denied in whole or in part, the court may, on such terms and conditions as are just, order that any party or person provide or permit discovery. The provisions of Rule 37(a)(4) apply to the award of expenses incurred in relation to the motion.

(d) Sequence and Timing of Discovery. Unless the court upon motion, for the convenience of parties and witnesses and in the interests of justice, orders otherwise, methods of discovery may be used in any sequence and the fact that a party is conducting discovery, whether by deposition or otherwise, shall not operate to delay any other party's discovery. *Identical to Mass.R.Civ.P. 26(d)*.

(e) Supplementation of Responses. A party who has responded to a request for discovery with a response that was complete when made is under no duty to supplement his response to include information thereafter acquired, except as follows:

(1) A party is under a duty seasonably to supplement his response with respect to any question directly addressed to (A) the identity and location of persons having knowledge of discoverable matters, and (B) the identity of each person expected to be called as an expert witness at trial, the subject matter on which he is expected to testify, and the substance of his testimony.

(2) A party is under a duty seasonably to amend a prior response if he obtains information upon the basis of which (A) he knows that the response was incorrect when made, or (B) he knows that the response though correct when made is no longer true and the circumstances are such that a failure to amend the response is in substance a knowing concealment.

(3) A duty to supplement responses may be imposed by order of the court, agreement of the parties, or at any time prior to trial through new requests for supplementation of prior responses. *Identical to Mass.R.Civ.P. 26(e)*.

(f) Format of Discovery Motions. A motion to compel (1) further responses to interrogatories, (2) answers to a request for admissions, (3) answers to questions propounded at a deposition, or (4) production of documents or tangible things shall be submitted with a separate document setting forth each separate interrogatory, item or category of items, request, question, document or tangible thing to which further response, answer or production is requested. Said separate document shall include the response given, and the factual and legal reasons that the court should compel the specific item. Materials may not be incorporated by reference in the documents accompanying the motion. If pleadings or other documents in the court file are relevant to the motion, the party relying on such pleadings or other documents shall clearly identify and summarize each relevant document in a separate paragraph in any papers submitted to the court regarding the discovery motion. The motion must include a sworn statement by the moving party setting forth the specific steps taken in an attempt to obtain the desired discovery responses. The responding party shall submit to the court and to the moving party a written statement setting forth the reasons for non-compliance and/or a denial, in whole or in part, of the allegations of the motion to compel and its supporting documentation. Said written statement shall be served not later than two (2) business days before the hearing.

(g) Mandatory Pre–Motion Conference. Prior to seeking judicial resolution of a discovery or procedural dispute, the attorneys for the affected parties or non-party witness shall confer in good faith in person or by telephone in an effort to resolve the dispute.

(h) Certification of Discovery Motions. All discovery motions shall contain a certificate by the party filing same that efforts to resolve the discovery dispute without the necessity of court intervention have been attempted and failed. The certification shall be included in the statement required of the moving party under Rule 26(f) supra.

(i) No–Contact Order. Where there is no-contact order in effect, the parties shall be exempted from the requirements of Rule 26(f) and (g). There shall be no requirement that they confer in order to resolve the discovery dispute.

(j) Special Master. The court, on its own motion or at the request of either party, may appoint a special master to control the extent of discovery, including the scheduling and oversight of depositions as more fully set out in Rule 30(c), the time for completion of discovery and to resolve any discovery disputes which may arise during the course of the litigation. Prior to the appointment of said special master, the court may inquire whether the parties can agree upon a special master. The court may appoint the person agreed upon or such other suitable person.

The special master shall be appointed by a written order of reference. Said order shall set the terms and conditions under which the special master is to proceed and may specify or limit the special master's powers. The fees and costs of the special master including a reasonable retainer shall be borne equally by the parties unless the special master determines that a different allocation of the fees and costs is appropriate.

Subject to the specifications and limitations stated in the order of reference, the special master has and shall exercise the power to regulate all matters before him and to do all acts and take all measures necessary or proper for the efficient performance of his duties under the order, including the authority to grant sanctions limited to reasonable counsel fees and/or special master fees if a party takes an unreasonable position, in accordance with the standards established pursuant to rule 37.

If a party disagrees with a decision of the special master, the matter may be brought before the court. Each party and the special master shall submit proposed orders to the court. A party who has acted arbitrarily or in bad faith in bringing the matter before the court may be subject to sanctions as the court deems appropriate, including counsel fees and/or special master fees.

Amended effective September 1, 1981; amended October 10, 1997, effective December 1, 1997; October 27, 1999, effective January 1, 2000; February 27, 2008, effective April 1, 2008.

Reporter's Notes—1997

Rule 26 was expanded by adding section (f), (g) and (h) and (i). Section (f) of the rule sets forth the specific format for motions to compel discovery. Sections (g) and (h) requires that parties confer in an effort to resolve the discovery dispute, and then certify to the court that efforts to resolve the dispute have been tried and failed. Section (i) exempts parties from the requirement of section (g) and (h) where there is a no-contact order in effect.

Reporter's Notes—2000

Rule 26(j) was added to provide for the appointment of a special master on motion of the court or on motion of either party. The special master may be appointed to control discovery including scheduling and oversight of depositions, the time for completion of discovery and to resolve any discovery disputes which may arise during the course of litigation. If a party disagrees with a decision of the special master, the matter may be brought before the court. However, if a party has acted arbitrarily or in bad faith in bringing the matter before the court, they may be subject to sanctions. The fees and costs of the special master, including a reasonable retainer, shall be borne equally by the parties unless the special master determines that a different allocation of the fees and costs is appropriate.

Rule 27. Depositions Before Action or Pending Appeal

(a) Before Action.

(1) *Petition.* A person who desires to perpetuate his own testimony or that of another person regarding any matter that may be cognizable in any court where these rules apply may file a verified petition in the Superior Court in the county or District Court in the judicial district, as the case may be, of the residence of any expected adverse party. The petition shall be entitled in the name of the petitioner and shall show: 1, that the petitioner expects to be a party to an action cognizable in a court where these rules apply but is presently unable to bring it or cause it to be brought, 2, the subject matter of the expected action and his interest therein, 3, the facts which he desires to establish by the proposed testimony and his reasons for desiring to perpetuate it, 4, the names or a description of the persons he expects will be adverse parties and their addresses so far as known, and 5, the names and addresses of the persons to be examined and the substance of the testimony which he expects to elicit from each, and shall ask for an order authorizing the petitioner to take the depositions of the persons to be examined named in the petition, for the purpose of perpetuating their testimony.

(2) *Notice and Service.* The petitioner shall thereafter serve a notice upon each person named in the petition as an expected adverse party, together with a copy of the petition, stating that the petitioner will apply to the court, at a time and place named therein, for the order described in the petition. At least 20 days before the date of hearing the notice shall be served either within or without the Commonwealth in the manner provided in Rule 4 for service of summons; but if such service cannot with due diligence be made upon any expected adverse party named in the petition, the court may make such order as is just for service by publication or otherwise, and shall appoint, for persons not served in the manner provided in Rule 4, an attorney who shall represent them, and, in case they are not otherwise represented, shall cross-examine the deponent. If any expected adverse party is a minor or incompetent the provisions of Rule 17(b) apply.

(3) *Order and Examination.* If the court is satisfied that the perpetuation of the testimony may prevent a failure or delay of justice, it shall make an order designating or describing the persons whose depositions may be taken and specifying the subject matter of the examination and whether the depositions shall be taken upon oral examination or written interrogatories. The depositions may then be taken in accordance with these rules; and the court may make orders of the character provided for by Rules 34 and 35. For the purpose of applying these rules to depositions for perpetuating testimony, each reference therein to the court in which the action is pending shall be deemed to refer to the court in which the petition for such deposition was filed.

(4) *Use of Deposition.* If a deposition to perpetuate testimony is taken under these rules or if, although not so taken, it would be admissible in evidence in the courts of the Commonwealth, it may be used in any action involving the same subject matter subsequently brought in such a court, in accordance with the provisions of Rule 32(a). *Identical to Mass.R.Civ.P. 27(a).*

(b) Pending Appeal.

If an appeal has been taken from a judgment of a court of this Commonwealth or before the taking of an appeal if the time therefor has not expired, the court in which the judgment was rendered may allow the taking of the depositions of witnesses to perpetuate their testimony for use in the event of further proceedings in that court. In such case the party who desires to perpetuate the testimony may make a motion in that court for leave to take the depositions, upon the same notice and service thereof as if the action was pending in that court. The motion shall show (1) the names and addresses of persons to be examined and the substance of the testimony which he expects to elicit from each; (2) the reasons for perpetuating their testimony. If the court finds that the perpetuation of the testimony is proper to avoid a failure or delay of justice, it may make an order allowing the depositions to be taken and may make orders of the character provided for by Rules 34 and 35, and thereupon the depositions may be taken and used in the same manner and under the same conditions as are prescribed in these rules for depositions taken in pending actions. _Identical to Mass. R.Civ.P. 27(b)._

(c) **Perpetuation by Action.** This rule does not limit the power of a court to entertain an action to perpetuate testimony. _Identical to Mass.R.Civ.P. 27(c)._

Amended May 3, 1996, effective July 1, 1996.

Rule 28. Persons Before Whom Depositions May Be Taken

(a) **Within the United States.** Within the United States or within a territory or insular possession subject to the jurisdiction of the United States, depositions shall be taken before an officer authorized to administer oaths by the laws of the United States or of the place where the examination is held, or before a person appointed by the court in which the action is pending. A person so appointed has power to administer oaths and take testimony. The term officer as used in Rules 30, 31 and 32 includes a person appointed by the court or designated by the parties under Rule 29. _Identical to Mass.R.Civ.P. 28(a)._

(b) **In Foreign Countries.** In a foreign country, depositions may be taken (1) on notice before a person authorized to administer oaths in the place in which the examination is held, either by the law thereof or by the laws of the United States, or (2) before a person commissioned by the court, and a person so commissioned shall have the power by virtue of his commission to administer any necessary oath and take testimony, or (3) pursuant to a letter rogatory. A commission or a letter rogatory shall be issued on application and notice and on terms that are just and appropriate. It is not requisite to the issuance of a commission or a letter rogatory that the taking of the deposition in any other manner is impracticable or inconvenient; and both a commission and a letter rogatory may be issued in proper cases. A notice or commission may designate the person before whom the deposition is to be taken either by name or descriptive title. A letter rogatory may be addressed "To the Appropriate Authority in [here name the country]." Evidence obtained in response to a letter rogatory need not be excluded merely for the reason that it is not a verbatim transcript or that the testimony was not taken under oath or for any similar departure from the requirements for depositions taken within the United States under these rules. _Identical to Mass.R.Civ.P. 28(b)._

(c) **Disqualification for Interest.** No deposition shall be taken before a person who is a relative or employee or attorney or counsel of any of the parties, or is a relative or employee of such attorney or counsel, or is financially interested in the action. _Identical to Mass.R.Civ.P. 28(c)._

Amended October 27, 1981, effective January 1, 1982.

Rule 29. Stipulations Regarding Discovery Procedure

Unless the court orders otherwise, the parties may by written stipulation (1) provide that depositions may be taken before any person, at any time or place, upon any notice, and in any manner and when so taken may be used like other depositions; and (2) modify the procedures provided by these rules for other methods of discovery. _Identical to Mass. R.Civ.P. 29._

Rule 30. Depositions Upon Oral Examination

(a) **When Depositions May Be Taken.** After commencement of the action, any party may take the testimony of any person, including a party, by deposition upon oral examination. Leave of court, granted with or without notice, must be obtained only if: (i) the plaintiff seeks to take a deposition prior to the expiration of 30 days after service of the summons and complaint upon any defendant or service made under Rule 4(e) (except that leave is not required (1) if a defendant has served a notice of taking deposition or otherwise sought discovery, or (2) if special notice is given as provided in subdivision (b)(2) of this rule); (ii) (deleted); (iii) (deleted); (iv) there has been a hearing before a master; or (v) (deleted). The attendance of witnesses may be compelled by subpoena as provided in Rule 45. The deposition of a person confined in prison or a minor child may be taken only by leave of court on such terms as the court prescribes.

(b) **Notice of Examination: General Requirements; Special Notice; Non-stenographic Recording; Production of Documents and Things; Deposition of Organization:**

(1) A party desiring to take the deposition of any person upon oral examination shall give at least seven days' notice in writing to every other party to the action. The notice shall state the time and place for taking the deposition and the name and address of each person to be examined, if known, and, if the name is not known, a general description sufficient to identify him or the particular class or group to which he belongs. If a subpoena duces tecum is to be served on the person to be examined, the designation of the materials to be produced as set forth in the subpoena shall be attached to or included in the notice. _Identical to Mass.R.Civ.P. 30(b)(1)._

(2) Leave of court is not required for the taking of a deposition by plaintiff if the notice (A) states that the person to be examined is about to go out of the county where the action is pending and more than 100 miles from the place of trial, or is about to go out of the United States, or is bound on a voyage abroad, and will be unavailable for examination unless his deposition is taken before expiration of the 30–day period, and (B) sets forth facts to support the statement. The plaintiff's attorney shall sign the notice, and his signature constitutes a certification by him that to the best of his knowledge, information, and belief the statement and supporting facts are true. The sanctions provided by Rule 11 are applicable to the certification. If a party shows that when he was served with notice under this subdivision (b)(2) he was unable through the exercise of diligence to obtain counsel to represent him at the taking of the deposition, the deposition may not be used against him. _Identical to Mass.R.Civ.P. 30(b)(2)._

(3) The court may for cause shown enlarge or shorten the time for taking the deposition. _Identical to Mass.R.Civ.P. 30(b)(3)._

(4) By leave of court upon motion with notice and an opportunity to be heard in opposition, or by stipulation in writing of all parties, a party taking an oral deposition may have the testimony recorded by other than stenographic means. The stipulation or order shall designate the person

before whom the deposition shall be taken, the manner of recording, preserving and filing the deposition, and may include other provisions to assure that the recorded testimony will be accurate and trustworthy. A party may arrange to have a stenographic transcription made at his own expense. Any objections under subdivision (c), any changes made by the witness, his signature identifying the deposition as his own or the statement of the officer that is required if the witness does not sign, as provided in subdivision (e), and the certification of the officer required by subdivision (f) shall be set forth in a writing to accompany a deposition recorded by non-stenographic means. In any event, however, where testimony is to be recorded by audio-visual means, the provisions of Rule 30A shall apply. *Identical to Mass.R.Civ.P. 30(b)(4) as amended January 1, 1981.*

(5) The notice to a party deponent may be accompanied by a request made in compliance with Rule 34 for the production of documents and tangible things at the taking of the deposition. The procedure of Rule 34 shall apply to the request and, notwithstanding the provisions of subdivision (b)(1) of this Rule, the party making the request shall give at least 30 days' notice in writing to every other party to the action. The court may on motion with or without notice allow a shorter or longer time. *Identical to Mass.R.Civ.P. 30(b)(5).*

(6) A party may in his notice and in a subpoena name as the deponent a public or private corporation or a partnership or association or governmental agency and describe with reasonable particularity the matters on which examination is requested. The organization so named shall designate one or more officers, directors, or managing agents, or other persons who consent to testify on its behalf, and may set forth, for each person designated, the matters on which he will testify. A subpoena shall advise a non-party organization of its duty to make such a designation. The persons so designated shall testify as to matters known or reasonably available to the organization. This subdivision (b)(6) does not preclude taking a deposition by any other procedure authorized in these rules. *Identical to Mass.R.Civ.P. 30(b)(6).*

(c) Examination and Cross–Examination; Record of Examination; Oath; Objections. Examination and cross-examination of witnesses may proceed as permitted at the trial under the provisions of Rule 43(b). The officer before whom the deposition is to be taken shall put the witness on oath and shall personally, or by someone acting under the officer's direction and in the officer's presence, record the testimony of the witness. The testimony shall be taken stenographically or by voice writing or recorded by any other means ordered in accordance with subdivision (b)(4) of this rule. If requested by one of the parties, the testimony shall be transcribed. In lieu of participating in the oral examination, parties may serve written questions in a sealed envelope on the party taking the deposition and such party shall transmit them to the officer, who shall propound them to the witness and record the answers verbatim.

All objections made at the time of the examination to the qualifications of the officer taking the deposition, or to the manner of taking it, or to the evidence presented, or to the conduct of any party, and any other objection to the proceedings, shall be noted by the officer upon the deposition; but the examination shall proceed. Any objection to testimony during a deposition shall be stated concisely and in a non-argumentative and non-suggestive manner. Testimony to which objection is made shall be taken subject to the objections. Counsel for a witness or a party may not instruct a deponent not to answer except where necessary to assert or preserve a privilege, a disqualification pursuant to G.L. c. 233, § 20, or protection against disclosure, to enforce a limitation on evidence directed by the court or stipulated in writing by the parties, or to terminate the deposition and present a motion to the court pursuant to Rules 30(d) or 37(d).

Pursuant to Rule 26(j), a special master may be appointed to oversee the deposition practice and procedure. The court may order or the special master may decide to attend the deposition. A party may request the attendance of the special master at a deposition, if a party reasonably believes it is necessary. In addition to the powers enumerated in Rule 26(j) and subject to the specifications and limitations stated in the order of reference, the special master may decide the time, date and place for the deposition, the length of the deposition and who may be present at the deposition.

(d) Motion to Terminate or Limit Examination. At any time during the taking of the deposition, on motion of any party or of the deponent and upon a showing that the examination is being conducted in bad faith or in such manner as unreasonably to annoy, embarrass, or oppress the deponent or party, the court in which the action is pending or the court in the county or judicial district, as the case may be, where the deposition is being taken may order the officer conducting the examination to cease forthwith from taking the deposition, or may limit the scope and manner of the taking of the deposition as provided in Rule 26(c). If the order made terminates the examination, it shall be resumed thereafter only upon the order of the court in which the action is pending. Upon demand of the objecting party or deponent, the taking of the deposition shall be suspended for the time necessary to make a motion for an order. The provisions of Rule 37(a)(4) apply to the award of expenses incurred in relation to the motion. *Identical to Mass.R.Civ.P. 30(d).*

(e) Submission to Witness; Changes; Signing. When the testimony is fully transcribed the deposition shall be submitted to the witness for examination and shall be read to or by him, unless such examination and reading are waived by the witness and by the parties. Any changes in form or substance which the witness desires to make shall be entered upon the deposition by the officer with a statement of the reasons given by the witness for making them. The deposition shall then be signed by the witness, unless the parties by stipulation waive the signing or the witness is ill or cannot be found or refuses to sign. If the deposition is not signed by the witness within 30 days of its submission to him, the officer shall sign it and state on the record the fact of the waiver or of the illness or absence of the witness or the fact of the refusal to sign together with the reason, if any, given therefor; and the deposition may then be used as fully as though signed, unless on a motion to suppress under Rule 32(d)(4) the court holds that the reasons given for the refusal to sign require rejection of the deposition in whole or in part. *Identical to Mass.R.Civ.P. 30(e).*

(f) Certification and Delivery by Officer; Exhibits; Copies; Notice of Receipt.

(1) The officer shall certify on the deposition that the witness was duly sworn by him and that the deposition is a true record of the testimony given by the witness. Unless otherwise ordered by the court generally or in a specific case or stipulated by the parties, he shall then securely seal the deposition in an envelope endorsed with the title of the action and marked "Deposition of [here insert name of witness]" and shall promptly deliver or send it to the party taking the deposition. Documents and things produced for inspection during the examination of the witness, shall, upon the request of a party, be marked for identification and annexed to the deposition and may be inspected and copied by any party, except that if the person producing the material desires to retain them he may (A) offer copies to be marked for identification and annexed to the deposition and to serve thereafter as originals if he affords to all parties fair opportunity to verify the copies by comparison with the originals, or (B) offer the originals to be marked for identification, after giving to each party an opportunity to inspect and copy them, in which event the materials may then be used in the same manner as if annexed to the deposition. Any party may move for an order that the original be annexed to and returned with the deposition to the court, pending final disposition of the case.

(2) Upon payment of reasonable charges therefor, the officer shall furnish a copy of the deposition to any party or to the deponent.

(3) The party taking the deposition shall give prompt notice of its receipt to all other parties. Identical to Mass.R.Civ.P. 30(f)(1)—(3)

(g) Failure to Attend or to Serve Subpoena; Expenses.

(1) If the party giving the notice of the taking of a deposition fails to attend and proceed therewith and another party attends in person or by attorney pursuant to the notice, the court may order the party giving the notice to pay to such other party the amount of the reasonable expenses incurred by him and his attorney in so attending, including reasonable attorney's fees.

(2) If the party giving the notice of the taking of a deposition of a witness fails to serve a subpoena upon him and the witness because of such failure does not attend, and if another party attends in per-son or by attorney because he expects the deposition of that witness to be taken, the court may order the party giving the notice to pay to such other party the amount of the reasonable expenses incurred by him and his attorney in so attending, including reasonable attorney's fees. *Identical to Mass.R.Civ.P. 30(g).*

Amended effective September 1, 1981; amended January 30, 1989, effective March 1, 1989; June 8, 1989, effective July 1, 1989; October 10, 1997, effective December 1, 1997; October 27, 1999, effective January 1, 2000.

Reporter's Notes–1997

Rule 30(a) was amended to eliminate the requirement that leave of court be obtained before the taking of oral deposition in actions in which the relief sought is the custody of minor children, or the affirmance or annulment of marriage.

The amendment to Rule 30(f) makes it identical to Mass.R.Civ.P. 30(f) by including (f)(2) which requires the officer to furnish a copy of the deposition to any party or to the deponent upon payment of reasonable charges.

Reporter's Notes—2000

The purpose of the amendment to rule 30(c), modeled after the 1998 amendment to rule 30(c) of the Massachusetts Rules of Civil Procedure, is to address the problem created by objections during a deposition and by directions to a deponent by counsel not to answer a question.

Under Mass.R.Civ.P. 30(c), it would appear that counsel could instruct a deponent not to answer a question that comes within the disqualification of G.L. c. 233, § 20, since the latter would constitute a "protection against disclosure." However, in light of the frequency in which this issue occurs in domestic relations cases, it was deemed advisable to add the Domestic Relations Rules a specific reference to this statutory disqualification.

The revised rule references Mass.R.Dom.Rel.P. 26(j) regarding the appointment of a special master to oversee the deposition practice and procedure. In addition to the powers enumerated in rule 26(j), the amendment to rule 30(c) allows for the special master to decide the time, date and place for the deposition, the length of the deposition and who may be present.

Rule 30A.   Audiovisual Depositions

(a) Authorization of Audio–Visual Depositions. By leave of court upon motion with notice and an opportunity to be heard in opposition, or by stipulation of all parties, a party taking an oral deposition may have the testimony recorded by audio-visual means by complying with the provisions of this rule. Except as otherwise provided by this rule, the rules governing the practice and procedure in depositions and discovery shall apply. At the taking of any such deposition, unless the parties otherwise stipulate, or the court for good cause otherwise orders, there shall also be prepared a simultaneous stenographic record of the deposition.

(b) Notice. Except by leave of court, granted after notice and opportunity to be heard in opposition, a notice for the taking of an audio-visual deposition shall not be served sooner than six (6) months after the action has been commenced. Every notice for the taking of an audio-visual deposition and the subpoena for attendance at that deposition shall state that it is to be recorded by audio-visual means and the name and address of the person whose deposition is to be taken. If the operator is an employee of the attorney taking the deposition, the notice shall so indicate.

(c) Procedure. The party taking the audio-visual deposition shall be responsible for assuring that the necessary equipment for making an audio-visual recording of the deposition is present at the time the deposition is taken. The following procedure shall be observed in recording an audiovisual deposition:

(1) *Opening of Deposition.* The deposition shall begin with an oral or written statement on camera which includes:

(i) the operator's name and business address;

(ii) the name and address of the operator's employer;

(iii) the date, time and place of the deposition;

(iv) the caption of the case;

(v) the name of the witness-deponent;

(vi) the name of the party on whose behalf the deposition is being taken; and

(vii) any stipulation by the parties.

The opening statement, if oral, shall be made by the officer before whom the deposition is to be taken, unless counsel agree that one of counsel will make the statement.

(2) *Counsel.* Counsel shall identify themselves on camera by stating their names, their addresses, and the names of the parties or persons for whom they appear at the deposition, and nothing more.

(3) *Oath.* The officer before whom the deposition is taken shall then identify himself and swear or affirm the witness on camera.

(4) *Multiple Units.* When the length of the deposition requires the use of more than one recording unit, the end of each recording unit and the beginning of each succeeding recording unit shall be announced on camera by the operator.

(5) *Closing of Deposition.* At the conclusion of the deposition, a statement shall be made on camera that the deposition is concluded. A statement may be made on camera setting forth any stipulation made by counsel concerning the custody of the audio-visual recording and exhibits and other pertinent matters.

(6) *Index.* The deposition shall be timed by a digital clock on camera which shall show continually each hour, minute and second of each recording unit of the deposition or otherwise suitably indexed by a time generator. The date(s) on which the deposition is taken shall be shown.

(7) *Objections.* An objection shall be made as in the case of depositions taken solely by stenographic means.

(8) *Interruption of Recording.* No party shall be entitled to cause the operator to interrupt or halt the recording of the audio-visual deposition without the assent of all other parties present.

(9) *Submission to Witness; Changes; Signing.* Unless the parties have stipulated that a simultaneous stenographic record of the deposition not be prepared, the provisions of Rule 30(e) shall apply to the stenographic record of the deposition. Except upon order of the court and upon such terms as may be provided, the witness shall have no right to examine and view the audio- visual recording.

(10) *Certification.* The officer before whom the audio-visual deposition is taken shall attach to the original audio-visual recording a certificate stating that the witness was sworn or affirmed by him and that the audio-visual recording is a true record of the testimony given by the witness.

(d) Recording Officer; Use of Camera; Copies. The officer before whom an audio-visual deposition is taken shall be subject to the provisions enumerated in Rule 28(a)—(c). During the taking of the audio-visual deposition, the officer shall assure that the audio-visual tape records the witness in a standard fashion at all times during the deposition, unless all counsel agree otherwise, or unless on motion be-fore the court, the court directs otherwise. In no event shall the officer use, or permit the use of, audio-visual tape camera techniques to vary the view which is being recorded for presentation in the courtroom unless agreed upon or ordered by the court as recited above. As an exception to the foregoing, the officer shall, at the request of the attorney questioning the witness, cause a close-up view of a deposition exhibit or visual aid to be taken while the witness is being questioned concerning the exhibit. Upon the request of any of the parties, the officer shall provide, at the cost of the party making the request, a copy of the deposition in the form of a videotape or other form of audio-visual recording, an audio recording, or a written transcription.

(e) Custody; Filing; Notice of Filing. Unless the parties have otherwise stipulated, the officer shall take custody of each recording unit upon its completion and shall retain custody of all completed units throughout the deposition. When a deposition is to be completed on another day, the officer shall also take custody of any uncompleted recording unit during the interval. Upon completion of a deposition, unless the parties have otherwise stipulated, the original audio-visual recording and the typewritten transcript of the deposition shall be filed forthwith by the officer with the clerk of the trial court in accordance with subdivision (1) of Rule 30(f) and notice of its filing shall be given as provided in subdivision (3) of that rule.

(f) Inspection and Release of Audio-Visual Recordings. Except upon order of the court and upon such terms as may be provided, the audio-visual recordings on file with the clerk of the court in which the action is pending shall not be available for inspection or viewing after their filing and prior to their use at the trial of the case or their disposition in accordance with this rule. The clerk may release the audio-visual recording to the officer taking the deposition, without an order of court, for the purpose of preparing a copy at the request of a party as provided in subdivisions (a) and (d) of this rule.

(g) Rulings on Objections; Editing of Recording. If any party has any objections to the audio-visual deposition which would otherwise be made at trial, pursuant to Rule 32(b), such objections shall if practicable, be submitted to the trial judge prior to commencement of the trial or hearing for the purpose of obtaining rulings on such objections. An audio copy of the sound track or the transcript may be submitted in lieu of the audio-visual recording for this purpose. For the purpose of ruling on the objections, the trial judge may view the entire audio-visual recording, or view only those parts of the audio-visual recording pertinent to the objections made, or he may listen to an audio-tape recording submitted in lieu of the audio-visual recording, or he may read the transcript. The trial judge shall, if practicable, rule on the objections prior to the commencement of the trial or hearing and shall return the recording to the party who took the audio-visual deposition, with notice to all parties of his rulings and of his instructions as to editing. The editing shall reflect the rulings of the trial judge and shall then remove all references to the objections. After making a copy of the audio-visual recording, the officer shall cause said copy to be edited in accordance with the court's instructions. He shall then cause both the original audio-visual recording and the edited version thereof, each clearly identified, to be returned to the trial judge for use during the trial or hearing. The original audio-visual recording shall be preserved intact and unaltered.

(h) Transcribing of Audio Portion; Marking for Identification. At a trial or hearing, that part of the audio portion of an audio-visual deposition which is offered in evidence and admitted, or which is excluded on objection, shall be transcribed in the same manner as the testimony of other witnesses. Both the original unedited audio-visual recording and the edited version shall be marked for identification.

(i) Use of Audio–Visual Deposition and Responsibility for Assuring Necessary Equipment at Time of Use. An audio-visual deposition may be used for any purpose and under any circumstances in which a stenographic deposition may be used. The party desiring to use the audio-visual deposition for any purpose shall be responsible for assuring that the necessary equipment for playing the audio-visual recording back is available when the audio-visual deposition is to be used. When an audio-visual deposition is used during a hearing, a trial, or any other court proceeding, the party first using such audio-visual deposition in whole or in part shall assure the availability of the same or comparable videotape playback equipment to any other party for such other party's use in further showing such audio-visual deposition during the hearing, the trial, or other court proceeding or at any rehearing, recess, or continuation thereof.

(j) Discrepancy Between Audio–Visual Deposition and Stenographic Deposition. Upon the claim of a party that a discrepancy exists between the audio-visual deposition and the stenographic deposition, the trial judge shall determine: (i) whether such discrepancy reasonably appears; and (ii) whether the relevant part of the audio-visual deposition is intelligible. If the relevant part of the audio-visual deposition is not intelligible, the stenographic deposition controls. If the relevant part of the audio-visual deposition is intelligible and the trial judge rules that a discrepancy reasonably appears, the jury, in a jury action, shall determine from the audio-visual deposition the deponent's testimony. The trial judge, in his discretion, may permit the jury to be aided in its determination by the stenographic deposition.

(k) Evidence by Audio-Visual Recording.

(1) *Authorization of Audio–Visual Testimony or Other Evidence.* Upon motion with notice and an opportunity to be heard, or by stipulation of all parties approved by the court, or upon the court's motion, the court may order, in the interest of justice and with due regard to the importance of presenting the testimony of witnesses orally in open court, that all or part of the testimony, and such other evidence as may be appropriate, may be presented at trial by audio-visual means. The provisions of Rule 30A shall govern such audio-visual recordings.

(2) *Introduction as Evidence.* Notwithstanding Rule 30A(i) or Rule 32(a)(3), but subject to rulings on objections pursuant to Rule 30A(k)(3), any party may introduce any such audio-visual recording, that has been authorized under Rule 30A(k)(1), at trial if the court finds its introduction to be in the interest of justice.

(3) *Objections.* Before such audio-visual recording is admitted at trial, the trial judge shall rule upon any objection to any portion thereof and the recording shall be edited to reflect the rulings. The objections shall be presented to the trial judge and the editing to reflect the rulings shall be accomplished, each in accordance with the provisions of Rule 30A(g).

(4) *Part of the Record; Not an Exhibit.* Any portion of the audio-visual recording so introduced shall be part of the record, and subject to the provisions of Rule 30A(h), but not an exhibit.

(*l*) Costs. The reasonable expense of recording, editing, and using an audio- visual deposition may be taxed as costs, pursuant to the provisions of Rule 54(e).

(m) Audio–Visual Depositions of Treating Physicians and Expert Witnesses for Use at Trial.

(1) *Authorization and Definitions.* Unless the court upon motion orders otherwise, any party intending to call a treating physician or expert witness at trial as that party's own witness may take the oral deposition of any such treating physician or expert witness by audio-visual means for the purpose of its being used as evidence at trial in lieu of oral testimony. Such depositions shall be known as "audio-visual expert witness depositions for trial." This rule 30A(m) does not apply to another party's treating physician or expert, discovery from whom is subject to the provisions of rule 26(b)(4)(A) or 26(b)(4)(B). A "treating physician" is a physician who has provided medical treatment to a party or other person involved in the lawsuit, and who will be questioned about such treatment and matters related thereto. An "expert witness" is a person qualified as an expert by knowledge, skill, experience, training, or education to testify in the form of an opinion or otherwise.

(2) *Timing, Curriculum Vitae, and Report.* Except by leave of court, a notice for the taking of an audio-visual expert witness deposition for trial shall not be served (i) sooner than six (6) months after the action has been commenced, and (ii) until thirty (30) days after a written report of that witness has been furnished to all parties. Such report shall contain a curriculum vitae of that witness, shall cover the subjects described in rule 26(b)(4)(A)(i), and, in the case of a treating physician, a description of the treatment and its costs. Any party may move for further discovery of that witness, to take place prior to the audio-visual expert witness deposition for trial, in accordance with Rule 26(b)(4)(A)(ii).

(3) *Notice; Opposition.* In addition to the requirements of rule 30A(b), every notice for the taking of an audio-visual expert witness deposition for trial shall state that it is to be recorded by audio-visual means with the purpose of its being used as evidence at trial in lieu of oral testimony. Any motion in opposition to the taking of an audio-visual expert witness deposition for trial must be filed within fourteen (14) days of receipt of the notice or on or before the specified time for taking of the audio-visual expert witness deposition for trial, if such time is less than fourteen (14) days from receipt of the notice. The audio-visual expert witness deposition shall not occur until the court rules on the motion opposing the deposition.

(4) *Ruling on Objections; Editing of Recording.* When an audio-visual expert witness deposition for trial is taken, all evidential objections shall, to the extent practicable, be made during the course of the deposition. If any party has made objections during the course of the audio-visual expert witness deposition for trial, or has any objections to such deposition which would otherwise be made at trial, pursuant to rule 32(b), such objections shall be filed with the trial judge or a motion judge, if the trial judge has not yet been designated, no later than twenty-one (21) days before the commencement of the trial. Objections not so submitted shall be deemed waived, except to the extent that events at the trial, which could not have reasonably been foreseen by the objecting party, necessi-

tate an objection at trial. The nonobjecting party shall file a response to the submissions by the objecting party within fourteen (14) days of the receipt of the objecting party's submissions. Failure to respond to an objection shall constitute a waiver with respect thereto. The party making the objection shall be responsible for providing the judge with a stenographic record of the deposition, unless it is already on file at the court, and, if the judge requests, with the audio-visual recording or an audio copy of the sound track. For the purpose of ruling on the objections, the judge may utilize the entire stenographic record, audio-visual recording, or audio-tape recording, or those portions that are pertinent to the objections made. The judge shall rule on the objections prior to the commencement of trial or hearing and give notice to all parties of the rulings and instructions as to editing. The editing shall reflect the rulings of the judge and shall remove all references to the objections. The officer shall cause a copy of the audio-visual recording to be edited in accordance with the court's instructions. The officer shall then cause copies of the edited version thereof to be delivered to the parties who ordered them, and to the court, if so instructed by the court. The stenographic record, and the original audio-visual recording and the edited version thereof, if any, shall be preserved intact and unaltered.

(5) *Use at Trial.* Unless the court upon motion orders otherwise, an audio- visual expert witness deposition for trial may be used by any party for any purpose and under any circumstances in which a stenographic deposition may be used and, in addition, may be used at trial in lieu of oral testimony whether or not such witness is available to testify.

(6) *Applicability of Rule 30A(a)—(l).* Except as altered by rule 30A(m), the provisions of rule 30A(a)—(*l*) shall apply to audio-visual expert witness depositions for trial. *Identical to Mass.R.Civ.P. 30A which was effective January 1, 1981.*

Adopted effective September 1, 1981.

Rule 31. Depositions of Witnesses Upon Written Questions

(a) **Serving Questions; Notice.** After commencement of the action, any party may take the testimony of any person, including a party, by deposition upon written questions. The attendance of witnesses may be compelled by the use of subpoena as provided in Rule 45. The deposition of a person confined in prison may be taken only by leave of court on such terms as the court prescribes. A party desiring to take a deposition upon written questions shall serve them upon every other party with a notice stating (1) the name and address of the person who is to answer them, if known, and if the name is not known, a general description sufficient to identify him or the particular class or group to which he belongs, and (2) the name or descriptive title and address of the officer before whom the deposition is to be taken. A deposition upon written questions may be taken of a public or private corporation or a partnership or association or governmental agency in accordance with the provisions of Rule 30(b)(6).

Within 30 days after the notice and written questions are served, a party may serve cross questions upon all other parties. Within 10 days after being served with cross questions, a party may serve redirect questions upon all other parties. Within 10 days after being served with redirect questions, a party may serve recross questions upon all other parties. The court may for cause shown enlarge or shorten the time. *Identical to Mass.R.Civ.P. 31(a).*

(b) **Officer to Take Responses and Prepare Record.** A copy of the notice and copies of all questions served shall be delivered by the party taking the deposition to the officer designated in the notice, who shall proceed promptly, in the manner provided by Rule 30(c), (e), and (f), to take the testimony of the witness in response to the questions and to prepare, certify, and deliver or send the deposition to the party taking the deposition, attaching thereto the copy of the notice and questions received by him. *Identical to Mass. R.Civ.P. 31(b).*

(c) **Notice of Receipt.** When the deposition is received the party taking it shall promptly give notice thereof to all other parties. *Identical to Mass.R.Civ.P. 31(c).*

Amended Jan. 30, 1989, effective Mar. 1, 1989; Amended June 8, 1989, effective July 1, 1989.

Rule 32. Use of Depositions in Court Proceedings

(a) **Use of Depositions.** At the trial or upon the hearing of a motion or an interlocutory proceeding, any part or all of a deposition, so far as admissible under the rules of evidence applied as though the witness were then present and testifying, may be used against any party who was present or represented at the taking of the deposition or who had due notice thereof, in accordance with any one of the following provisions:

(1) Any deposition may be used by any party for the purpose of contradicting or impeaching the testimony of deponent as a witness.

(2) The deposition of a party or of any one who at the time of taking the deposition was an officer, director, or managing agent, or a person designated under Rule 30(b)(6) or 31(a) to testify on behalf of a public or private corporation, partnership or association or governmental agency which is a party may be used by an adverse party for any purpose.

(3) The deposition of a witness, whether or not a party, may be used by any party for any purpose if the court finds: (A) that the witness is dead; or (B) that the witness is out of the Commonwealth, unless it appears that the absence of the witness was procured by the party offering the deposition; or (C) that the witness is unable to attend or testify because of age, sickness, infirmity, or imprisonment; or (D) that the party offering the deposition has been unable to procure the attendance of the witness by subpoena; or (E) upon application and notice, that such exceptional circumstances exist as to make it desirable, in the interest of justice and with due regard to the importance of presenting the testimony of witnesses orally in open court, to allow the deposition to be used.

(4) If only part of a deposition is offered in evidence by a party, an adverse party may require him to introduce any other part which ought in fairness to be considered with the part introduced, and any party may introduce any other parts. Substitution of parties pursuant to Rule 25 does not affect the right to use depositions previously taken; and when an action has been brought in any court of the United States or of any

state and another action involving the same subject matter is afterward brought between the same parties or their representatives or successors in interest, all depositions lawfully taken and duly filed in the former action may be used in the latter as if originally taken therefor. *Identical to Mass. R.Civ.P. 32(a).*

(b) Objections to Admissibility. Subject to the provisions of Rules 28(b) and subdivision (d)(3) of this rule, objection may be made at the trial or hearing to receiving in evidence any deposition or part thereof for any reason which would require the exclusion of the evidence if the witness were then present and testifying. *Identical to Mass.R.Civ.P. 32(b).*

(c) Effect of Taking or Using Depositions. A party does not make a person his own witness for any purpose by taking his deposition. The introduction in evidence of the deposition or any part thereof for any purpose other than that of contradicting or impeaching the deponent makes the deponent the witness of the party introducing the deposition, but this shall not apply to the use by an adverse party of a deposition under subdivision (a)(2) of this rule. At the trial or hearing any party may rebut any relevant evidence contained in a deposition whether introduced by him or by any other party. *Identical to Mass.R.Civ.P. 32(c).*

(d) Effect of Errors and Irregularities in Depositions.

(1) *As to Notice.* All errors and irregularities in the notice for taking a deposition are waived unless written objection is promptly served upon the party giving the notice.

(2) *As to Disqualification of Officer.* Objection to taking a deposition because of disqualification of the officer before whom it is to be taken is waived unless made before the taking of the deposition begins or as soon thereafter as the disqualification becomes known or could be discovered with reasonable diligence.

(3) *As to Taking of Deposition.*

(A) Objections to the competency of a witness or to the competency, relevancy, or materiality of testimony are not waived by failure to make them before or during the taking of the deposition, unless the ground of the objection is one which might have been obviated or removed if presented at that time.

(B) Errors and irregularities occurring at the oral examination in the manner of taking the deposition, in the form of the questions or answers, in the oath or affirmation, or in the conduct of parties, and errors of any kind which might be obviated, removed, or cured if promptly presented, are waived unless seasonable objection thereto is made at the taking of the deposition.

(C) Objections to the form of written questions submitted under Rule 31 are waived unless served in writing upon the party propounding them within the time allowed for serving the succeeding cross or other questions and within 5 days after service of the last questions authorized.

(4) *As to Completion and Return of Deposition.* Errors and irregularities in the manner in which the testimony is transcribed or the deposition is prepared, signed, certified, sealed, indorsed, transmitted, filed, or otherwise dealt with by the officer under Rules 30 and 31 are waived unless a motion to suppress the deposition or some part thereof is made with

reasonable promptness after such defect is, or with due diligence might have been, ascertained. *Identical to Mass. R.Civ.P. 32(d).*

Rule 33. Interrogatories to Parties

(a) Availability: Procedures for Use. Any party may serve upon any other party written interrogatories to be answered by the party served or, if the party served is a public or private corporation or a partnership or association or governmental agency, by any officer or agent, who shall furnish such information as is available to the party. Interrogatories may without leave of court, be served upon the plaintiff after commencement of the action and upon any other party with or after service of the summons and complaint upon that party.

No party shall serve on any other party as of right more than one set of interrogatories, unless the total number of all interrogatories in all sets combined does not exceed thirty, including interrogatories, subsidiary or incidental to, or dependent upon, other interrogatories, and however the same may be grouped or combined. The court, on a showing of good cause, or upon agreement of the parties, may allow service of additional interrogatories.

Each interrogatory shall be answered separately and fully in writing under the penalties of perjury, unless it is objected to, in which event the reasons for objection shall be stated in lieu of an answer; each answer or objection shall be preceded by the interrogatory to which it responds. The answers are to be signed by the person making them, and the objections signed by the attorney making them. The party upon whom the interrogatories have been served shall serve the answers and objections, if any, within 30 days after the service of the interrogatories, except that a defendant may serve answers or objections within 45 days after service of the summons and complaint upon the defendant. The court may allow a shorter or longer time. The party submitting the interrogatories may move for an order under Rule 37(a) with respect to any objection or other failure to answer an interrogatory. In addition, for failure to serve timely answers or objections to interrogatories (or further answers, as the case may be), the interrogating party may serve a final request for answers, specifying the failure. All sanctions available to a party under Rule 37 and any other sanction that the court may deem appropriate shall be available to compel compliance with this rule and such sanctions shall be ordered by the court except for good cause shown.

(b) Scope: Use at Trial. Interrogatories may relate to any matters which can be inquired into under Rule 26(b), and the answers may be used to the extent permitted by the rules of evidence. An interrogatory otherwise proper is not necessarily objectionable merely because an answer to the interrogatory involves an opinion or contention that relates to fact or the application of law to fact, but the court may order that such an interrogatory need not be answered until after designated discovery has been completed, or until a pretrial conference, or other later time. *Identical to Mass.R.Civ.P. 33(b).*

(c) Option to Produce Business Records. Where the answer to an interrogatory may be derived or ascertained from the business records of the party upon whom the interrogatory has been served or from an examination, audit or inspection of such business records, including a compilation, abstract or summary thereof, and the burden of deriving or ascertaining the answer is substantially the same for the party serving the interrogatory as for the party served, it is a sufficient answer to such interrogatory to specify the records from which the answer may be derived or ascertained and to afford to the party serving the interrogatory reasonable opportunity to examine, audit or inspect such records and to make copies, compilations, abstracts or summaries. A specification shall be in sufficient detail to permit the interrogating party to locate and to identify, as readily as can the party served, the records from which the answer may be ascertained. *Identical to Mass.R.Civ.P. 33(c).*

Amended June 5, 2003, effective September 2, 2003.

Reporter's Notes—2003

The non-filing requirement of amended Rule 5(d) necessitated changes in the Rule 33(a) procedure by which a party who has served interrogatories seeks to have judgment entered against a party for failure to respond to the interrogatories. Since a default judgment is not permissible under the Rules of Domestic Relations procedure, all sanctions available to a party under Rule 37 and any other sanction that the court may deem appropriate shall be available to compel compliance with this rule and such sanctions shall be ordered by the court except for good cause shown. In addition, the amendment brings the Probate and Family Court into conformity with the Rules of Civil Procedure by requiring that each answer or objection shall be preceded by the interrogatory to which it responds.

Rule 34. Production of Documents and Things and Entry Upon Land for Inspection and Other Purposes

(a) Scope. Any party may serve on any other party a request (1) to produce and permit the party making the request, or someone acting on his behalf, to inspect and copy, any designated documents (including writings, drawings, graphs, charts, photographs, phono-records, and other data compilations from which information can be obtained, translated, if necessary, by the respondent through detection devices into reasonably usable form), or to inspect and copy, test, or sample any tangible things which constitute or contain matters within the scope of Rule 26(b) and which are in the possession, custody or control of the party upon whom the request is served; or (2) to permit entry upon designated land or other property in the possession or control of the party upon whom the request is served for the purpose of inspection and measuring, surveying, photographing, testing or sampling the property or any designated object or operation thereon, within the scope of Rule 26(b).

(b) Procedure. The request may, without leave of court, be served upon the plaintiff after commencement of the action and upon any other party with or after service of the summons and complaint upon that party. The request shall set forth the items to be inspected either by individual item or by category, and describe each item and category with reasonable particularity.

The request shall specify a reasonable time, place, and manner of making the inspection and performing the related acts. The party upon whom the request is served shall serve a written response within 30 days after the service of the request, except that a defendant may serve a response within 45 days after service of the summons and complaint upon that defendant. The court may allow a shorter or longer time. The response shall state, with respect to each item or category, that inspection and related activities will be permitted as requested, unless the request is objected to, in which event the reasons for objection shall be stated. If objection is made to part of an item or category, the part shall be specified. The party submitting the request may move for an order under Rule 37(a) with respect to any objection to or other failure to respond to the request or any part thereof, or any failure to permit inspection as requested. A party who produces documents for inspection shall produce them as they are kept in the usual course of business or shall organize and label them to correspond with the categories in the request.

(c) Persons Not Parties. This rule does not preclude an independent action against a person not a party for production of documents and things and permission to enter upon land.

Rule 35. Physical and Mental Examination of Persons

(a) Order for Examination. When the mental or physical condition (including the blood group) of a party, or of a person in the custody or under the legal control of a party, is in controversy, the court in which the action is pending may order the party to submit to a physical or mental examination by a physician or to produce for examination the person in his custody or legal control. The order may be made only on motion for good cause shown and upon notice to the person to be examined and to all parties and shall specify the time, place, manner, conditions, and scope of the examination and the person or persons by whom it is to be made. *Identical to Mass.R.Civ.P. 35(a).*

(b) Report of Examining Physician.

(1) If requested by the party against whom an order is made under Rule 35(a) or the person examined, the party causing the examination to be made shall deliver to him a copy of a detailed written report of the examining physician setting out his findings, including results of all tests made, diagnoses and conclusions, together with like reports of all earlier examinations of the same condition. After delivery the party causing the examination shall be entitled upon request to receive from the party against whom the order is made a like report of any examination, previously or thereafter made, of the same condition, unless, in the case of a report of examination of a person not a party, the party shows that he is unable to obtain it. The court on motion may make an order against a party requiring delivery of a report on such terms as are just, and if a physician fails or refuses to make a report the court may exclude his testimony if offered at the trial.

(2) By requesting and obtaining a report of the examination so ordered or by taking the deposition of the examiner, the party examined waives any privilege he may have in that action or any other involving the same controversy, regarding the testimony of every other person who has examined or may thereafter examine him in respect of the same mental or physical condition; but he does not otherwise waive his right to object at the trial to the introduction into evidence of the report or any part thereof.

(3) This subdivision applies to examinations made by agreement of the parties, unless the agreement expressly provides

otherwise. This subdivision does not preclude discovery of a report of an examining physician or the taking of a deposition of the physician in accordance with the provisions of any other rule. *Identical to Mass.R.Civ.P. 35(b).*

Rule 36. Requests for Admission

(a) Request for Admission. A party may serve upon any other party a written request for admission, for purposes of the pending action, only, of the truth of any matters within the scope of Rule 26(b) set forth in the request that relate to statements or opinions of fact or of the application of law to fact, including the genuineness of any documents described in the request. Copies of documents shall be served with the request unless they have been or are otherwise furnished or made available for inspection and copying. The request may, without leave of court, be served upon the plaintiff after commencement of the action and upon any other party with or after service of the summons and complaint upon that party.

Each matter of which an admission is requested shall be separately set forth. The matter is admitted unless, within 30 days after service of the request, or within such shorter or longer time as the court may allow, the party to whom the request is directed serves upon the party requesting the admission either (1) a written statement signed by the party under the penalties of perjury specifically (i) denying the matter or (ii) setting forth in detail why the answering party cannot truthfully admit or deny the matter; or (2) a written objection addressed to the matter, signed by the party or his attorney, but, unless the court shortens the time, a defendant shall not be required to serve answers or objections before the expiration of 45 days after service of the summons and complaint upon him. If objection is made, the reasons therefor shall be stated. A denial shall fairly meet the substance of the requested admission, and when good faith requires that a party qualify his answer or deny only a part of the matter of which an admission is requested, he shall specify so much of it as is true and qualify or deny the remainder. An answering party may not give lack of information or knowledge as a reason for failure to admit or deny unless he states that he has made reasonable inquiry and that the information known or readily obtainable by him is insufficient to enable him to admit or deny. A party who considers that a matter of which an admission has been requested presents a genuine issue for trial may not, on that ground alone, object to the request; he may, subject to the provisions of Rule 37(c), deny the matter or set forth reasons why he cannot admit or deny it. Each admission, denial, objection, or statement shall be preceded by the request to which it responds. The party who has requested the admissions may move to determine the sufficiency of the answers or objections. Unless the court determines that an objection is justified, it shall order that an answer be served. If the court determines that an answer does not comply with the requirements of this rule, it may order either that the matter is admitted or that an amended answer be served. The court may, in lieu of these orders, determine that final disposition of the request be made at a pre-trial conference or at a designated time prior to trial. The provisions of Rule 37(a)(4) apply to the award of expenses incurred in relation to the motion. *Identical to Mass.R.Civ.P. 36(a).*

(b) Effect of Admission. Any matter admitted under this rule is conclusively established unless the court on motion permits withdrawal or amendment of the admission. Subject to the provisions of Rule 16 governing amendment of a pretrial order, the court may permit withdrawal or amendment when the presentation of the merits of the action will be subserved thereby and the party who obtained the admission fails to satisfy the court that withdrawal or amendment will prejudice him in maintaining his action or defense on the merits. Any admission made by a party under this rule is for the purpose of the pending action only and is not an admission by him for any other purpose nor may it be used against him in any other proceeding. *Identical to Mass.R.Civ.P. 36(b).*

Rule 37. Failure to Make Discovery: Sanctions

(a) Motion for Order Compelling Discovery. Upon reasonable notice to other parties and all persons affected thereby, a party may apply for an order compelling discovery as follows:

(1) *Appropriate Court.* An application for an order to a party may be made to the court in which the action is pending, or on matters relating to a deposition, to the court in the county where the deposition is being taken. An application for an order to a deponent who is not a party shall be made to the court in the county where the deposition is being taken.

(2) *Motion.* If a deponent fails to answer a question propounded or submitted under Rules 30 or 31, or a corporation or other entity fails to make a designation under Rule 30(b)(6) or 31(a), or a party fails to answer an interrogatory submitted under Rule 33, or if a party, in response to a request for inspection submitted under Rule 34, fails to respond that inspection will be permitted as requested or fails to permit inspection as requested, the discovering party may move for an order compelling an answer or a designation or an order compelling inspection in accordance with the request. When taking a deposition on oral examination, the proponent of the question may complete or adjourn the examination before he applies for an order. If the court denies the motion in whole or in part, it may make such protective order as it would have been empowered to make on a motion made pursuant to Rule 26(c).

(3) *Evasive or Incomplete Answer.* For purposes of this subdivision an evasive or incomplete answer is to be treated as a failure to answer.

(4) *Award of Expenses of Motion.* If the motion is granted, the court may, after opportunity for hearing, require the party or deponent whose conduct necessitated the motion or the party or attorney advising such conduct or both of them to pay to the moving party the reasonable expenses incurred in obtaining the order, including attorney's fees, unless the court finds that the opposition to the motion was substantially justified or that other circumstances make an award of expenses unjust.

If the motion is denied, the court may, after an opportunity for a hearing, require the moving party or the attorney advising the motion or both of them to pay to the party or deponent who opposed the motion the reasonable expenses incurred in opposing the motion, including attorney's fees, unless the court finds that the making of the motion was substantially justified or that other circumstances make an award of expenses unjust.

If the motion is granted in part and denied in part, the court may apportion the reasonable expenses incurred in relation to the motion among the parties and persons in a just manner.

(b) Failure to Comply with Order.

(1) *Sanctions by Court in County Where Deposition Is Taken.* If a deponent wilfully fails to be sworn or to answer a question after being directed to do so by the court in the county in which the deposition is being taken, the failure may be considered a contempt of that court.

(2) *Sanctions by Court in Which Action Is Pending.* If a party or an officer, director, or managing agent of a party or a person designated under Rule 30(b)(6) or 31(a) to testify on behalf of a party or a person interrogated under Rule 33 wilfully fails to obey an order to provide or permit discovery, including an order made under subdivision (a) of this rule or Rule 35, the court in which the action is pending may make such orders in regard to the failure as are just, and among others the following:

(A) An order that the matters regarding which the order was made or any other designated facts shall be taken to be established for the purposes of the action in accordance with the claim of the party obtaining the order;

(B) An order refusing to allow the disobedient party to support or oppose designated claims or defenses, or prohibiting him from introducing designated matters in evidence;

(C) An order striking out pleadings or parts thereof, or staying further proceedings until the order is obeyed, or dismissing the action or proceeding or any part thereof;

(D) In lieu of any of the foregoing orders or in addition thereto, an order treating as a contempt of court the wilful failure to obey any orders except an order to submit to a physical or mental examination;

(E) Where a party has wilfully failed to comply with an order under Rule 35(a) requiring him to produce another for examination, such orders as are listed in paragraphs (A), (B) and (C) of this subdivision, unless the party failing to comply shows that he is unable to produce such person for examination.

In lieu of any of the foregoing orders or in addition thereto, the court may require the party failing to obey the order or the attorney advising him or both to pay the reasonable expenses, including attorney's fees, caused by the failure.

(c) Expenses on Failure to Admit. If a party fails to admit the genuineness of any documents or the truth of any matters as requested under Rule 36, and if the party requesting the admissions thereafter proves the genuineness of the document or the truth of the matter, he may apply to the court for an order requiring the other party to pay him the reasonable expenses incurred in making that proof, including reasonable attorney's fees. The court shall make the order unless it finds that (1) the request was held objectionable pursuant to Rule 36(a), or (2) the admission sought was of no substantial importance, or (3) the party failing to admit had reasonable grounds to believe that he might prevail on the matter, or (4) there was other good reason for the failure to admit. *Identical to Mass.R.Civ.P. 37(c).*

(d) Failure of Party to Attend at Own Deposition or Serve Answers to Interrogatories or Respond to Request of Inspection. If a party or an officer, director, or a managing agent of a party or a person designated under Rule 30(b)(6) or 31(a) to testify on behalf of a party wilfully fails (1) to appear before the officer who is to take his deposition, after being served with a proper notice, or (2) to serve answers or objections to interrogatories submitted under Rule 33, after proper service of the interrogatories, or (3) to serve a written response to a request for inspection submitted under Rule 34, after proper service of the request, the court in which the action is pending on motion may make such orders in regard to the failure as are just, and among others it may take any action authorized under paragraphs (A), (B), (C) and (D) of subdivision (b)(2) of this rule. In lieu of any order or in addition thereto, the court may require the party failing to act or the attorney advising him or both to pay the reasonable expenses, including attorney's fees, caused by the failure.

The failure to act described in this subdivision may not be excused on the ground that the discovery sought is objectionable unless the party failing to act has applied for a protective order as provided by Rule 26(c).

(e) Expenses Against Commonwealth. Except to the extent permitted by statute, expenses and fees may not be awarded against the Commonwealth under this rule.

VI. TRIALS

Rule 38. Jury Trial of Right [Deleted]
[Deleted].

Rule 39. Trial by Jury or by the Court

(a)–(b) [Deleted].

(c) Framing Jury Issues. In all actions not triable of right by a jury, the court, except where otherwise provided by law, may upon motion frame issues of fact to be tried by a jury. *Identical to Mass.R.Civ.P. 39(c).*

Rule 40. Assignment of Cases for Trial: Continuances

(a) Assignment of Cases for Trial. Cases may be assigned to the appropriate calendar or list for trial or other disposition by order of the court including general rules and orders adopted for the purpose of assignment. Precedence shall be given to actions entitled thereto by statute. *Identical to Mass.R.Civ.P. 40(a).*

(b) Continuances. Continuances shall be granted only for good cause, in accordance with general rules and orders which the court may from time to time adopt. *Identical to Mass. R.Civ.P. 40(b).*

(c) Affidavit or Certificate in Support of Motion. The court need not entertain any motion for a continuance based on the absence of a material witness unless such motion be supported by an affidavit which shall state the name of the witness and, if known, his address, the facts to which he is expected to testify and the basis for such expectation, the efforts which have been made to procure his attendance or deposition, and the expectation which the party has of procuring his testimony or deposition at a future time. Such motion may, in the discretion of the court, be denied if the adverse party will admit that the absent witness would, if present, testify as stated in the affidavit. The same rule shall apply, with the necessary changes in points of detail, when the motion is grounded on the want of any material document, thing, or other evidence. *Identical to Mass.R.Civ.P. 40(c).*

Rule 41. Dismissal of Actions

(a) Voluntary Dismissal: Effect Thereof.

(1) *By Plaintiff; By Stipulation.* Subject to the provisions of these rules and of any statute of this Commonwealth, an action may be dismissed by the plaintiff without order of court (i) by filing a notice of dismissal at any time before service by the adverse party of an answer or (ii) that after a judgment nisi has been entered, upon the filing of a stipulation of dismissal signed by all the parties who have appeared in the action, the same shall be presented forthwith to a judge of the Court who shall thereupon enter an order of dismissal. Unless otherwise stated in the notice of dismissal or stipulation, the dismissal is without prejudice, except that a notice of dismissal operates as an adjudication upon the merits when filed by a plaintiff who has once dismissed in any court of the United States or of this or any other state an action based on or including the same claim.

(2) *By Order of Court.* Except as provided in paragraph (1) of this subdivision (a), an action shall not be dismissed at the plaintiff's instance save upon order of the court and upon such terms and conditions as the court deems proper. If a counterclaim has been pleaded by a defendant prior to the service upon him of the plaintiff's motion to dismiss, the action shall not be dismissed against the defendant's objection unless the counterclaim can remain pending for independent adjudication by the court. Unless otherwise specified in the order, a dismissal under this paragraph is without prejudice. *Identical to Mass.R.Civ.P. 41(a)(2).*

(b) Involuntary Dismissal: Effect Thereof.

(1) *On Court's Own Motion.* The court may on notice as hereinafter provided at any time, in its discretion, dismiss for lack of prosecution any action which has remained upon the docket for three years preceding said notice without activity shown other than placing upon the trial list, marking for trial, being set down for trial, the filing or withdrawal of an appearance, or the filing of any paper pertaining to discovery. The notice shall state that the action will be dismissed on a day certain, (not less than one year from the date of the notice) unless before that day the case has been tried, heard on the merits, otherwise disposed of, or unless the court on motion with or without notice shall otherwise order. The notice shall be mailed to the plaintiff's attorney of record, or, if there be none, to the plaintiff if his address be known. Otherwise such notice shall be published as directed by the court. Dismissal under this paragraph shall be without prejudice.

(2) *On Motion of the Defendant.* On motion of the defendant, with notice, the court may, in its discretion, dismiss any action for failure of the plaintiff to prosecute or to comply with these rules or any order of court. After the plaintiff, in an action tried by the court without a jury, has completed the

presentation of his evidence, the defendant, without waiving his right to offer evidence in the event the motion is not granted, may move for a dismissal on the ground that upon the facts and the law the plaintiff has shown no right to relief. The court as trier of the facts may then determine them and render judgment against the plaintiff or may decline to render any judgment until the close of all the evidence. If the court renders judgment on the merits against the plaintiff the court shall make findings as provided in Rule 52(a).

(3) *Effect.* Unless the dismissal is pursuant to paragraph (1) of this subdivision (b), or unless the court in its order for dismissal otherwise specifies, a dismissal under this subdivision (b) and any dismissal not provided for in this rule, other than a dismissal for lack of jurisdiction, for improper venue, or for failure to join a party under Rule 19, operates as an adjudication upon the merits.

Identical to Mass.R.Civ.P. 41(b).

(c) Dismissal of Counterclaim, Cross–Claim, or Third–Party Claim.
The provisions of this rule apply to the dismissal of any counterclaim, cross-claim, or third-party claim. A voluntary dismissal by the claimant alone pursuant to paragraph (1) of subdivision (a) of this rule shall be made before a responsive pleading or a motion for summary judgment is served, whichever first occurs, or, if there is none, before the introduction of evidence at the trial or hearing. *Identical to Mass.R.Civ.P. 41(c).*

(d) Costs of Previously–Dismissed Action.
If a plaintiff who has once dismissed an action in any court commences an action based upon or including the same claim against the same defendant, the court may make such order for the payment of costs of the action previously dismissed as it may deem proper and may stay the proceedings in the action until the plaintiff has complied with the order. *Identical to Mass. R.Civ.P. 41(d).*

Amended January 24, 1978, effective February 21, 1978; amended June 7, 1979.

Rule 42. Consolidation: Separate Trials

(a) Courts Other Than District Court: Consolidation.
When actions involving a common question of law or fact are pending before the court, in the same county or different counties, it may order a joint hearing or trial of any or all the matters in issue in the actions; it may order all the actions consolidated; and it may make such orders concerning proceedings therein as may tend to avoid unnecessary costs or delay. *Identical to Mass.R.Civ.P. 42(a).*

(b) Courts Other Than District Court: Separate Trials.
The court, in furtherance of convenience or to avoid prejudice, or when separate trials will be conducive to expedition and economy, may order a separate trial in the county where the action is pending or in a different county of any claim, cross-claim, counterclaim, or third-party claim, or of any separate issue or of any number of claims, cross-claims, counterclaims, third-party claims, or issues, always preserving inviolate the right of trial by jury as declared by the constitution of this Commonwealth or as set forth in a statute. *Identical to Mass.R.Civ.P. 42(b).*

Rule 43.   Evidence

(a) Form and Admissibility. In all trials the testimony of witnesses shall be taken orally in open court, or such other place as the judge may in his discretion determine, unless otherwise provided by these rules. All evidence shall be admitted which is admissible under the statutes of this Commonwealth or under the rules of evidence applied in this Commonwealth. The competency of a witness to testify shall be determined in like manner.

(b) Scope and Examination and Cross–Examination. A party may interrogate any unwilling or hostile witness by leading questions. A party may call an adverse party and interrogate him by leading questions and contradict and impeach him in all respects as if he had been called by the adverse party, except by evidence of bad character, and the witness thus called may be contradicted and impeached by or on behalf of the adverse party also, and may be cross-examined by the adverse party only upon the subject matter of his examination in chief. Any other witness may be cross-examined without regard to the scope of his testimony on direct, subject only to the trial judge's sound discretion.

(c) Record of Excluded Evidence. If an objection to a question propounded to a witness is sustained by the court, the examining attorney may make a specific offer of what he expects to prove by the answer of the witness, except that the court, when there is a stenographer appointed or when a stenographer has been appointed, upon request shall take and report evidence in full, unless it clearly appears that the evidence is not admissible on any ground or that the witness is privileged.

(d) Affirmation in Lieu of Oath. Whenever under these rules an oath is required to be taken, a solemn affirmation under the penalties of perjury may be accepted in lieu thereof. *Identical to Mass.R.Civ.P. 43(d).*

(e) Evidence on Motions. When a motion is based on facts not appearing of record the court may hear the matter on affidavits presented by the respective parties, but the court may direct that the matter be heard wholly or partly on oral testimony or depositions. *Identical to Mass.R.Civ.P. 43(e).*

(f) Interpreters. The court may appoint an interpreter of its own selection and may fix his reasonable compensation. The compensation shall be paid out of funds provided by law or by one or more of the parties as the court may direct, and may be taxed ultimately as costs, in the discretion of the court. *Identical to Mass.R.Civ.P. 43(f).*

(g) Examination of Witnesses. Unless otherwise permitted by the court, the examination and cross-examination of any witness shall be conducted by one attorney only for each party. The attorney shall stand while so examining or cross-examining unless the court otherwise permits. *Identical to Mass.R.Civ.P. 43(g).*

Rule 44.   Proof of Official Records

(a) Authentication.

(1) *Domestic.* An official record kept within the Commonwealth, or an entry therein, when admissible for any purpose, may be evidenced by an official publication thereof or by a copy attested by the officer having legal custody of the record, or by his deputy. If the record is kept in any other state, district, commonwealth, territory or insular possession of the United States, or within the Panama Canal Zone, the Trust Territory of the Pacific Islands, or the Ryukyu Islands, any such copy shall be accompanied by a certificate that such custodial officer has the custody. This certificate may be made by a judge of a court of record of the district or political subdivision in which the record is kept, authenticated by the seal of the court, or may be made by any public officer having a seal of office and having official duties in the district or political subdivision in which the record is kept, authenticated by the seal of his office.

(2) *Foreign.* A foreign official record, or an entry therein, when admissible for any purpose, may be evidenced by an official publication thereof; or a copy thereof, attested by a person authorized to make the attestation, and accompanied by a final certification as to the genuineness of the signature and official position (i) of the attesting person, or (ii) of any foreign official whose certificate of genuineness of signature and official position relates to the attestation or is in a chain of certificates of genuineness of signature and official position relating to the attestation. A final certification may be made by a secretary of embassy or legation, consul general, consul, vice consul, or consular agent of the United States, or a diplomatic or consular official of the foreign country assigned or accredited to the United States. If reasonable opportunity has been given to all parties to investigate the authenticity and accuracy of the documents, the court may, for good cause shown, (i) admit an attested copy without final certification, or (ii) permit the foreign official record to be evidenced by an attested summary with or without a final certification. *Identical to Mass.R.Civ.P. 44(a).*

(b) Lack of Record. A written statement that after diligent search no record or entry of a specified tenor is found to exist in the records designated by the statement, authenticated as provided in subdivision (a)(1) of this rule in the case of a domestic record, or complying with the requirements of subdivision (a)(2) of this rule for a summary in the case of a foreign record, is admissible as evidence that the records contain no such record or entry. *Identical to Mass.R.Civ.P. 44(b).*

(c) Other Proof. This rule does not prevent the proof, by any other method authorized by law, of the existence of, or the lack of, an official record, or of entry, or lack of entry therein. *Identical to Mass.R.Civ.P. 44(c).*

Rule 44.1   Determination of Foreign Law

A party who intends to raise an issue concerning the law of the United States or of any state, territory or dependency thereof or of a foreign country shall give notice in his pleadings or other reasonable written notice. The court, in determining such law, may consider any relevant material or source, including testimony, whether or not submitted by a party or admissible under Rule 43. The court's determination shall be treated as a ruling on a question of law. *Identical to Mass.R.Civ.P. 44.1.*

Rule 45.   Subpoena

(a) For Attendance of Witnesses; Form; Issuance. Every subpoena shall be issued by the clerk of court, by a notary public, or by a justice of the peace, shall state the name of the court and the title of the action, and shall command each person to whom it is directed to attend and give testimony at a time and place therein specified. The clerk, notary public, or justice of the peace shall issue a subpoena, or a subpoena for the production of documentary evidence, signed but otherwise in blank, to a party requesting it, who shall fill it in before service.

(b) For Production of Documentary Evidence. A subpoena may also command the person to whom it is directed to produce the books, papers, documents, or tangible things designated therein; but the court, upon motion made promptly and in any event at or before the time specified in the subpoena for compliance therewith, may (1) quash or modify the subpoena if it is unreasonable and oppressive or (2) condition denial of the motion upon the advancement by the person in whose behalf the subpoena is issued of the reasonable cost of producing the books, papers, documents, or tangible things.

(c) Service. A subpoena may be served by any person who is not a party and is not less than 18 years of age. Service of a subpoena upon a person named therein shall be made by delivering a copy thereof to such person, or by exhibiting it and reading it to him, or by leaving a copy at his place of abode; and by tendering to him the fees for one day's attendance and the mileage allowed by law. When the subpoena is issued on behalf of the United States or the Commonwealth or a political subdivision thereof, or an officer, or agency of either, fees and mileage need not be tendered.

(d) Subpoena for Taking Deposition; Place of Examination.

(1) No subpoena for the taking of a deposition shall be issued prior to the service of a notice to take the deposition.

The subpoena may command the person to whom it is directed to produce and permit inspection and copying of designated books, papers, documents, or tangible things which constitute or contain evidence relating to any of the matters within the scope of the examination permitted by these rules, but in that event the subpoena will be subject to the provisions of Rule 26(c) and subdivision (b) of this rule.

A deposition subpoena upon a party which commands the production of documents or things must give the party deponent at least thirty days for compliance after service thereof. Such subpoena shall not require compliance of a defendant within 45 days after service of the summons and complaint on that defendant. The court may allow a shorter or longer time.

The person to whom the subpoena is directed may within 10 days after the service thereof or on or before the time specified in the subpoena for compliance if such time is less than 10 days after service, serve upon the attorney designated in the subpoena written objection to inspection or copying of any or all of the designated materials. If objection is made, the party serving the subpoena shall not be entitled to inspect and copy the materials except pursuant to an order of the court from which the subpoena was issued. The party serving the subpoena may if objection has been made, move upon notice to the deponent for an order at any time before or during the taking of the deposition.

(2) Unless the court orders otherwise, a resident of this Commonwealth shall not be required to attend an examination at a place more than 50 airline miles distant from either his residence, place of employment, or place of business, whichev-

er is nearest to the place to which he is subpoenaed. A nonresident of the Commonwealth when served with a subpoena within the Commonwealth may be required to attend only in that county wherein he is served, or within 50 airline miles of the place of service, or at such other convenient place as is fixed by an order of court.

(e) Subpoena for a Hearing or Trial. At the request of any party subpoenas for attendance at a hearing or trial shall be issued by any of the persons directed in subdivision (a) of this rule. A subpoena requiring the attendance of a witness at a hearing or trial may be served at any place within the Commonwealth.

(f) Contempt. Failure by any person without adequate excuse to obey a subpoena served upon him may be deemed a contempt of the court in which the action is pending.

Rule 46. Exceptions Unnecessary

Formal exceptions to rulings or orders of the court in cases in which a stenographer is present or a recording is made are unnecessary; but for all purposes for which an exception has heretofore been necessary it is sufficient that a party, at the time the ruling or order of the court is made or sought, makes known to the court the action which he desire the court to take or his objection to the action of the court and his grounds therefor; and, if a party has no opportunity to object to a ruling or order at the time it is made, the absence of an objection does not thereafter prejudice him.

Rule 47. Jurors [Deleted]

[Deleted].

Rule 48. Juries of Less Than Twelve— Majority Verdict [Deleted]

[Deleted].

Rule 49. Special Verdicts and Interrogatories [Deleted]

[Deleted].

Rule 50. Motion for A Directed Verdict and for Judgment Notwithstanding the Verdict [Deleted]

[Deleted].

Rule 51. Argument

(a) Time for Argument. Counsel for each party shall be allowed thirty minutes for argument; but before the argument commences, the court, on motion or sua sponte, may reasonably reduce or extend the time. When two or more attorneys are to be heard on behalf of the same party, they may divide their time as they elect. *Identical to Mass.R.Civ.P. 51(a).*

(b) [Deleted].

Rule 52. Findings by the Court

(a) Effect. In actions tried upon the facts without a jury, except as provided herein for judgments entered pursuant to G.L. ch. 208, sec. 34, the court shall upon written motion made prior to final argument, providing either party or the court has requested appointment of a stenographer pursuant to Rule 202 or the trial was recorded electronically, find the facts specially and state separately its conclusions of law thereon, and judgment shall be entered pursuant to Rule 58. Where the court enters judgment pursuant to G.L. ch. 208, sec. 34 it shall issue findings of fact and conclusions of law thereon within sixty (60) days of the filing of a notice of appeal. Request for findings are not necessary for purposes of review. Findings of fact shall not be set aside unless clearly erroneous, and due regard shall be given to the opportunity of the trial court to judge of the credibility of the witnesses. The findings of a master, to the extent that the court adopts them, shall be considered as the findings of the court. If an opinion or memorandum of decision is filed, it will be sufficient if the findings of fact and conclusions of law appear therein. Findings of fact and conclusions of law are unnecessary on decisions of motions except as provided in Rule 41(b)(2).

(b) Amendment. Upon motion of a party made not later than 10 days after entry of its findings the court may amend its findings or make additional findings and may amend the judgment accordingly. The motion may be made with a motion for a new trial pursuant to Rule 59. When findings of fact are made in actions tried by the court without a jury, the question of the sufficiency of the evidence to support the findings may thereafter be raised whether or not the party raising the question has made in the trial court an objection to such findings or has made a motion to amend them or a motion for judgment.

(c) Transcript of Proceedings Upon Request for Special Findings. Upon a written motion under paragraph (a) of this rule, the party making such request shall order from the stenographer and file with the court the original of a transcript of such parts of the proceedings not already on file as the court may determine material to any facts essential to a determination of the case. At the time of ordering, a party shall make satisfactory arrangements with the stenographer for payment of the cost of the transcript.

Amended effective July 1, 1984; amended December 15, 1986, effective January 2, 1987.

Rule 53. Masters

(a) Definition. The following words, as used in this rule, shall mean:

(i) "master" shall mean any person, however designated, who is appointed by the court to hear evidence in connection with any action and report facts.

(ii) "stenographer" shall mean a stenographer appointed by the master before commencement of the hearing. *Identical to Mass.R.Civ.P 53(a).*

(b) Appointment.

(1) *Member of Bar.* The court in which an action is pending may appoint a master therein subject however, to a standing order, if any, of the Administrative Justice designating classes of cases not to be tried to a master, and provided further that in the District Court, no master may be appointed without the assent of all parties. No master shall be appointed who is not a member in good standing of the bar of one of the United States or of the District of Columbia.

(2) *Selection by Agreement.* Prior to the appointment of a master, the court may inquire whether the parties can agree

upon a master. The court may appoint the person agreed upon or such other suitable person.

(3) Deleted.

(4) *Objection to Master Selected.* If an objection is made by any party to the appointment of a master selected by the court, whether from the official standing list, if any, or otherwise, the objecting party shall file with the court within five (5) days of notice of such appointment a written objection to such appointment, and notice of such filing shall be forwarded forthwith by the clerk of court to the referring justice. The grounds for such objection shall not be included within such written objection but shall be furnished to the referring justice upon his request and in the form that the referring justice shall order.

(5) *Inability to Serve.* Upon receipt of an order of reference as herein provided, a person appointed a master shall notify the referring justice immediately if he is unable or unwilling to serve as master in the case. No person shall accept appointment as master in any case in which he cannot be impartial. If there are circumstances known to the master, which may give the appearance of partiality, including the existence of any pending matter between the master and any party to the litigation or any party's counsel, the master must make full written disclosure to the referring justice and all parties immediately after receipt of the order of reference.

(c) Compensation. The compensation allowed to a master may be charged in whole or in part upon the parties, or out of any fund or subject matter of the action which is in the custody or control of the court, or, when authorized by law, upon the Commonwealth, as the court may direct. The rate of compensation to be paid by the parties or out of any fund or subject matter of the action shall be fixed by the court; the rate of compensation to be paid by the Commonwealth shall be fixed from time to time by rule of each department. Where compensation is to be paid by the Commonwealth, no additional compensation shall be accepted from the parties, unless approved by the court and stated in the order of reference. When a party ordered to pay the compensation allowed by the court does not pay it after notice and within the time prescribed by the court, the master is entitled to a writ of execution against the delinquent party. *Identical to Mass. R.Civ.P 53(c).*

(d) Order of Reference. A master shall be appointed by a written order of reference. Said order: (i) shall either fix definite times for the hearings or fix the time when or before which hearings shall be begun and the time within which they shall be ended; (ii) shall fix the time for the filing of the master's report; (iii) may specify or limit the master's powers and may direct him to report only upon particular issues or to do or perform particular acts. *Identical to Mass.R.Civ.P 53(d).*

(e) Powers. Subject to the specifications and limitations stated in the order of reference, the master has and shall exercise the power to regulate all proceedings in every hearing before him and to do all acts and take all measures necessary or proper for the efficient performance of his duties under the order. He may require the production before him of evidence upon all matters embraced in the reference, including the production of all books, papers, vouchers, documents, and writings applicable thereto. He may rule upon the admissibility of evidence unless otherwise directed by the order of reference and he shall have the authority to put witnesses on oath and may himself examine them and may call the parties to the action and examine them upon oath. *Identical to Mass. R.Civ.P 53(e).*

(f) Proceedings.

(1) *Hearings.* When a reference is made, the clerk shall forthwith furnish the master with a copy of the order of reference. Upon receipt thereof the master shall forthwith notify the parties or their attorneys of the time, date and place of the first hearing. The order of reference may require that the hearings proceed from day to day, Saturdays, Sundays and holidays excepted, until completed. If the court does not order the master to proceed from day to day, nevertheless he shall proceed as nearly as possible on consecutive days, and shall grant no adjournment for a longer period than three (3) days except by order of the court. Either party, on notice to the parties and master, may apply to the court for an order requiring the master to speed the proceedings and to make his report. The court may change or extend the time for hearings.

(2) *Evidence.* Rules 43(a), (b), (d) and (g) will govern hearings before masters. If an objection to a question propounded to a witness is sustained by the master, and there is a stenographer present, upon request the master shall take the proffered evidence as an offer of proof unless the master finds that the proffered evidence is privileged.

(3) *Interpreters.* The master may appoint an interpreter whose compensation shall be fixed by the court. The compensation shall be paid out of funds provided by law or by one or more of the parties as the court may direct, and may be taxed ultimately as costs in the discretion of the court.

(4) *Stenographers.* No master shall, without prior approval of the court, appoint a stenographer to be paid by the Commonwealth.

(5) *Statement of Accounts.* When matters of accounting are in issue before the master, he may prescribe the form in which the accounts shall be submitted and in any proper case may require or receive in evidence a statement by a certified public accountant who is called as a witness. Upon objection of a party to any of the items thus submitted or upon showing that the form of statement is insufficient, the master may require a different form of statement to be furnished, or the accounts or specific items thereof to be proved by oral examination of the accounting parties or upon written interrogatories or in such other manner as he directs.

(6) *Failure to Appear.* If all parties fail to appear at a hearing without showing good cause, the master shall report forthwith to the clerk of the court in which the action is pending, and the clerk shall bring such report forthwith to the attention of the referring justice, if practicable, otherwise to any justice of the court. If a party fails to appear at the time and place appointed, the master may proceed ex parte or, in his discretion, adjourn the proceedings to a future day, giving notice to the absent party of the adjournment, or apply to the court, with notice to the parties, for the imposition of sanctions.

(7) *Witnesses.* The parties may procure the attendance of witnesses before the master by the issuance and service of subpoenas as provided in Rule 45. If without adequate excuse a witness fails to appear or give evidence, he may be punished by the court as for a contempt.

(g) Master's Report.

(1) *Contents.* The master shall prepare a report upon the matters submitted to him by the order of reference, and, if required by the order of reference to make findings of fact and conclusions of law, he shall set them forth in the report. The master's report will contain the master's general finding upon each issue that is within the order of reference and will include and clearly identify the subsidiary findings upon which each general finding is based. No general findings will be presumed by the court to be supported by subsidiary findings which are not stated in the report as the basis therefor. Any party, at the conclusion of the evidence may file with the master requests for findings of fact and conclusions of law.

(2) *Filing.* At least ten (10) days before filing his report, the master shall submit a draft thereof to counsel for all parties. Counsel for any party may submit to the master suggested amendments in writing, copies of which must be contemporaneously submitted to counsel for all of the parties. The master may, in his discretion, allow a hearing on any suggested amendments. If any suggested amendment is adopted by the master, he shall furnish counsel for all parties with copies of said amendment contemporaneously with the filing of his report. Within thirty (30) days after the close of the evidence, unless the court, on motion or otherwise, for good cause shown, shall alter the time, the master shall file his report and the original exhibits with the clerk of the court. The clerk shall forthwith mail to all parties notice of the filing.

(h) Master's Report in Non-jury Cases.

(1) *Status of Report.* In an action to be tried without a jury, the court shall accept the master's subsidiary findings of fact unless they are clearly erroneous, mutually inconsistent, unwarranted by the evidence before the master as a matter of law or are otherwise tainted by error of law. Any party who contends that the master's subsidiary findings are clearly erroneous, mutually inconsistent, unwarranted by the evidence before the master or are otherwise tainted by error of law must make such contentions by objection as hereinafter provided. The court may draw its own inferences from the master's subsidiary findings. The court may make findings in accordance with Rule 52, which are in addition to the master's findings and not inconsistent therewith, based either on evidence presented to the court or evidence before the master which was recorded by means approved by the master before commencement of the hearing.

(2) *Objections to Report.* Within ten (10) days after service of notice of the filing of the report or such other time as the court may allow, any party may serve written objections thereto upon every other party making any of the contentions referred to in paragraph (1) of this section, clearly stating the grounds for each objection and the relief sought. At any time after the filing of objections or the expiration of the time therefor, any party may move the court, with notice to all other parties, to act upon the report and upon any objections thereto, provided, however, the court may so act upon its own motion after notice to all parties.

(3) *Limitations on Review.* The court will not review a question of law dependent upon evidence before the master unless the evidence was recorded by a stenographer and a transcript of so much of the proceedings before the master as is necessary to dispose of the objections adequately is served, together with the objections, upon every other party. Any party may designate additional portions of the transcript for submission to the court by the service of notice within 10 days after service of the objections. The objecting party shall serve such additional portions upon every other party; but if the objecting party shall refuse to do so, the party designating such additional portions shall either serve them upon every other party or shall move the court to require the objecting party to do so. At the time of ordering a transcript from the stenographer, a party shall make satisfactory arrangements with the reporter for payment of the cost of any transcript ordered. The parties are encouraged to agree as to the portions of the transcript that will accompany the objections.

(4) *Action on Report.* The court may adopt the report, strike it in whole or in part, modify it, recommit it to the master with instructions or take any other action that justice requires. Any motion to adopt a report shall be deemed to include a motion to enter judgment and shall be accompanied by a proposed form of judgment.

(i) Master's Report in Jury Cases. Deleted.

Amended effective July 1, 1982; amended October 10, 1997, effective December 1, 1997.

Reporter's Notes—1997

Rule 53(b)(2) was added which allows the court to inquire as to whether the parties can agree upon a master. The court would have the discretion to appoint the mutually agreed upon master or another suitable person.

VII. JUDGMENT

Rule 54. Judgments: Costs

(a) Definition; Form. The terms "judgment" and "final judgment" include a decree and mean the act of the trial court finally adjudicating the rights of the parties affected by the judgment, including:

(1) judgments entered under Rule 50(b) and Rule 52(a) and (b);

(2) judgments entered under Rule 58 upon a general verdict of a jury, or upon a decision by the court that a party shall recover only a sum certain or costs or that all relief shall be denied, or upon a special verdict under Rule 49(a) or a general verdict accompanied by answers to interrogatories under Rule 49(b). A judgment shall not contain a recital of pleadings, the report of a master or the record of prior proceedings. *Identical to Mass.R.Civ.P. 54(a).*

(b) Judgment Upon Multiple Claims or Involving Multiple Parties. When more than one claim for relief is presented in an action, whether as a claim, counterclaim, cross-claim, or third-party claim, or when multiple parties are involved, the court may direct the entry of a final judgment as to one or more but fewer than all of the claims or parties only upon an express determination that there is no just reason for delay and upon an express direction for the entry of judgment. In the absence of such determination and direction, any order or other form of decision, however designated, which adjudicates fewer than all the claims or the rights and liabilities of fewer than all the parties shall not terminate the action as to any of the claims or parties, and the order or other form of decision is subject to revision at any time before the entry of judgment adjudicating all the claims and the rights and liabilities of all the parties. *Identical to Mass.R.Civ.P. 54(b).*

(c) [Deleted].

(d) [Deleted].

(e) Costs on Depositions. The taxation of costs in the taking of depositions, including audio-visual depositions, shall be subject to the discretion of the court, but in no event shall costs be allowed unless the court finds that the taking of the deposition was reasonably necessary, whether or not the deposition was actually used at the trial. Taxable costs may include the cost of service of subpoena upon the deponent, the reasonable fees of the officer before whom the deposition is taken, the fees and mileage allowances of the witnesses, the stenographer's reasonable fee for attendance, and the cost of the transcript of the testimony or such part thereof as the court may fix. When an audio-visual deposition is taken, taxable costs may include a reasonable fee for the use of the audio-visual equipment and for the services of the operator both in recording the deposition and editing it. *Identical to Mass.R.Civ.P. 54(e) as amended January 1, 1981.*

Amended effective Sept. 1, 1981.

Comments—Mass.R.Dom.Rel.P.

Rule 54(c) (demand for judgment) and Rule 54(d) (costs) have been deleted as inapplicable to Domestic Relations practice.

Comment—Mass.R.Dom.Rel.P.–1981

(Present comment unchanged.) Rule 54(e) was amended in 1981 to incorporate an amendment to the Massachusetts Rules of Civil Procedure by reference.

Rule 55. Default [Deleted]

[Deleted].

Rule 56. Summary Judgment

(a) Motions for Summary Judgment. A party may move for summary judgment subsequent to the commencement of any proceeding under these rules except in actions for divorce or in actions for custody or visitation or for criminal contempt. Each motion for summary judgment shall be accompanied by an "Affidavit of Undisputed Facts" which shall enumerate discretely each of the specific material facts relied upon in support of the motion and cite the particular portions of any pleading, affidavit, deposition, answer to interrogatories, admission or other document relied upon to establish that fact. The motion shall be served at least ten (10) days before the time fixed for the hearing. The moving party shall be responsible for filing with the Court all evidentiary documents cited in the moving papers. The motion for summary judgment shall be denied if the moving party fails to file and serve the affidavit required by this paragraph.

(b) Opposition. Any party opposing a motion for summary judgment shall file and serve no later than three (3) days before the time fixed for the hearing, unless the court otherwise orders, an affidavit using the same paragraph numbers as in the "Affidavit of Undisputed Facts" and admit those facts which are undisputed and deny those which are disputed, including with each denial a citation to the particular portions of any pleading, affidavit, deposition, answers to interrogatories, admission or other document relied upon in support of the denial. The opposing party may also file a concise "Affidavit of Disputed Facts," and the source thereof in the record, of all additional material facts as to which there is a genuine issue precluding summary judgment. The opposing party shall be responsible for the filing with the court of all evidentiary documents cited in the opposing papers. If a need for discovery is asserted as a basis for denial of the motion, the party opposing the motion shall provide a specification of the particular facts on which discovery is to be had or the issues on which discovery is necessary.

(c) Stipulated Facts. All interested parties may jointly file a stipulation setting forth a statement of stipulated facts to which all interested parties agree. As to any stipulated facts, the parties so stipulating may state that their stipulations are entered into only for the purposes of the motion for summary judgment and are not intended to be otherwise binding.

    (1) In any pending motion for summary judgment, the assigned judge may order the parties to meet, confer and submit, on or before a date set the assigned judge, a joint statement of undisputed facts.

(d) [deleted] [Case Not Fully Adjudicated on Motion].

(e) Form of Affidavits; Further Testimony; Defense Required. Supporting and opposing affidavits shall be made on personal knowledge, shall set forth such facts as would be admissible in evidence, and shall show affirmatively that the affiant is competent to testify to the matters stated therein. Sworn or certified copies of all papers or parts thereof referred to in any affidavits shall be attached thereto or served therewith. The court may permit affidavits to be supplemented or opposed by depositions, answers to interrogatories, or further affidavits. When a motion for summary judgment is made and supported as provided in this rule, an adverse party may not rest upon the mere allegations or denials of his pleading, but his response, by affidavits or as otherwise provided in this rule, must set forth specific facts showing that there is a genuine issue for trial. If he does not so respond, summary judgment, if appropriate, shall be entered against him.

(f) When Affidavits Are Unavailable. Should it appear from the affidavits of a party opposing the motion that he cannot for reasons stated present by affidavit facts essential to justify his opposition, the court may refuse the application for judgment or may order a continuance to permit affidavits to be obtained or depositions to be taken or discovery to be had or may make such other order as is just.

(g) Affidavits Made in Bad Faith. Should it appear to the satisfaction of the court at any time that any of the affidavits presented pursuant to this rule are presented in bad faith or solely for the purpose of delay, the court shall forthwith order the party employing them to pay to the other party the amount of the responsible expenses which the filing of the affidavits caused him to incur, including reasonable attorney's fees, and any offending party or attorney may be adjudged guilty of contempt.

(h) Judgment. The judgment sought shall be rendered forthwith if the pleadings, depositions, answers to interrogatories, and responses to requests for admission under Rule 36, together with the affidavits, if any, show that there is no genuine issue as to any material fact and that the moving party is entitled to a judgment as a matter of law. Summary judgment, when appropriate, may be rendered against the moving party.

Adopted October 10, 1997, effective December 1, 1997. Amended October 27, 1999, effective January 1, 2000; June 5, 2003, effective September 2, 2003; April 1, 2009, effective May 1, 2009.

Reporter's Notes—1997

Rule 56 introduces summary judgment for the first time to domestic relations procedure. The rule allows a party to move for summary judgment in actions for modification and actions to modify or enforce a foreign judgment. Rule 56(h) allows summary judgment only if there is "no genuine issue as to any material fact and that the moving party is entitled to a judgment as a matter of law."

Rule 56(a) requires that each motion for summary judgment be accompanied by an "Affidavit of Undisputed Facts" which sets forth the material facts relied upon in support of the motion. If the moving party fails to file and serve the affidavit, the summary judgment motion will be denied.

The party opposing the motion for summary judgment shall reproduce the "Affidavit of Undisputed Facts" and shall admit those facts which are undisputed and deny those which are disputed. The opposing party has the option of filing an "Affidavit of Disputed Facts" enumerating all additional material facts where there is a genuine issue which would preclude summary judgment.

Rule 56 allows parties to jointly file a statement of stipulated facts. If they do so, they may state that the stipulation is only for the purpose of the motion for summary judgment and is not intended to be otherwise binding. The rule also allows the judge to order the parties to meet and submit a joint statement of undisputed facts.

Sections (e), (f) and (g) of Rule 56 address the form of the affidavits, when an affidavit is not available, and sanctions for falsely made affidavits.

Reporter's Notes—2000

As originally promulgated, rule 56(b) did not require the party opposing a motion for summary judgment to file an affidavit. Rather, it required the opposing party to reproduce the itemized facts contained in the "Affidavit of Undisputed Facts" and admit those facts which were undisputed and deny those which were disputed. The amendment to rule 56(b) rectifies this problem by requiring the party opposing the motion for summary judgment to file and serve, no later than three (3) days before the time fixed for the hearing, an affidavit reproducing the itemized facts contained in the "Affidavit of Undisputed Facts."

Reporter's Notes—2003

The amendment to Rule 56(h) deletes the phrase "on file" from the first sentence in recognition that discovery documents are generally no longer filed separately with the court. See Rule 5(d)(2). The previous reference to admissions has also been replaced by a reference to "responses to requests for admission under Rule 36."

Reporter's Notes—2009

The amendment will allow for summary judgment in all cases exclusive of divorce actions, actions for custody or visitation or actions for criminal contempt.

Rule 57.   Declaratory Judgment

The procedure for obtaining a declaratory judgment pursuant to General Laws c. 231A shall be in accordance with these rules, and the right to trial by jury may be demanded under the circumstances and in the manner provided in Rules 38 and 39.   The existence of another adequate remedy does not preclude a judgment for declaratory relief in cases where it is appropriate.   The court may order a speedy hearing of an action for a declaratory judgment and may advance it on the calendar.

Rule 58.   Entry of Judgment

(a) **After Trial or Hearing or by Agreement.**   Subject to the provisions of Rule 54(b): (1) Upon a decision by the court that a party shall recover only a sum certain or costs or that all relief shall be denied, or upon a written agreement for judgment for a sum certain or denying relief, the court shall forthwith prepare, sign and enter judgment; (2) upon a decision by the court granting other relief, the court shall promptly approve the form of the judgment.   Every judgment shall be set forth on a separate document.   A judgment is effective only when so set forth and when entered as provided in Rule 79(a).   Entry of the judgment shall not be delayed for the taxing of costs.   Attorneys shall submit forms of judgment upon direction of the court.

(b) **Upon Order of Supreme Judicial Court.**   The clerk shall enter any judgment specifically directed by the Supreme Judicial Court.   *Identical to Mass.R.Civ.P. 58(b).*

(c) **Nisi Judgment.**   At any time before the expiration of ninety days from the entry of a judgment of divorce nisi, the defendant, or any other person interested, may file in the Registry of Probate a statement of objections to the judgment becoming absolute, which shall set forth specifically the facts on which it is founded and shall be verified by affidavit.   Notice of the filing of said objections shall be given to the plaintiff or defendant or his attorney, not later than the day of filing said objections.   The portion of the judgment to which any objection is filed, but only that portion, shall not become absolute until such objections have been disposed of by the court.   If said petition to stay the judgment absolute is subsequently dismissed by the court, the judgment shall become absolute as of ninety days from the date of the judgment nisi.

Amended effective July 1, 1984; amended December 15, 1986, effective January 2, 1987; July 18, 1988, effective August 1, 1988; June 8, 1989, effective July 1, 1989; October 6, 2004, effective November 1, 2004.

Reporter's Note–2004

The amendment to Rule 58 is necessitated by the implementation of the revised Time Standards Standing Order, Section 19.

Rule 59.   New Trials: Amendment of Judgments

(a) **Grounds.**   A new trial may be granted to all or any of the parties and on all or part of the issues for any of the reasons for which rehearings have heretofore been granted in suits in equity in the courts of the Commonwealth.   On a motion for a new trial, the court may open the judgment if one has been entered, take additional testimony, amend findings of fact and conclusions of law or make new findings and conclusions, and direct the entry of a new judgment.

(b) **Time for Motion.**   A motion for a new trial shall be served not later than 10 days after the entry of judgment.   *Identical to Mass.R.Civ.P. 59(b).*

(c) **Time for Serving Affidavits.**   When a motion for new trial is based upon affidavits they shall be served with the motion.   The opposing party has 10 days after such service within which to serve opposing affidavits, which period may be extended for an additional period not exceeding 20 days either by the court for good cause shown or by the parties by written stipulation.   The court may permit reply affidavits.   *Identical to Mass.R.Civ.P. 59(c).*

(d) **On Initiative of Court.**   Not later than 10 days after entry of judgment the court of its own initiative may order a new trial for any reason for which it might have granted a new trial on motion of a party.   After giving the parties notice and an opportunity to be heard on the matter, the court may grant a motion for a new trial, timely served, for a reason not stated in the motion.   In either case, the court shall specify in the order the grounds therefor.   *Identical to Mass.R.Civ.P. 59(d).*

(e) **Motion to Alter or Amend a Judgment.**   A motion to alter or amend the judgment shall be served not later than 10 days after entry of the judgment.   *Identical to Mass.R.Civ.P. 59(e).*

Rule 60.   Relief From Judgment or Order

(a) **Clerical Mistakes.**   Clerical mistakes in judgments, orders or other parts of the record and errors therein arising from oversight or omission may be corrected by the court at any time of its own initiative or on the motion of any party and after such notice, if any, as the court orders.   During the pendency of an appeal, such mistakes may be so corrected before the appeal is docketed in the appellate court, and thereafter while the appeal is pending may be so corrected with leave of the appellate court.   *Identical to Mass.R.Civ.P. 60(a).*

(b) **Mistake; Inadvertence; Excusable Neglect; Newly Discovered Evidence; Fraud, etc.**   On motion and upon such terms as are just, the court may relieve a party or his legal representative from a final judgment, order, or proceeding for the following reasons: (1) mistake, inadvertence, surprise, or excusable neglect; (2) newly discovered evidence which by due diligence could not have been discovered in time to move for a new trial under Rule 59(b); (3) fraud (whether heretofore denominated intrinsic or extrinsic), misrepresentation, or other misconduct of an adverse party; (4) the judgment is void; (5) the judgment has been satisfied, released, or discharged, or a prior judgment upon which it is based has been reversed or otherwise vacated, or it is no longer equitable that the judgment should have prospective application; or (6) any other reason justifying relief from the operation of the judgment.   The motion shall be made within a reasonable time, and for reasons (1), (2), and (3) not more than one year after the judgment, order or proceeding was entered or taken.   A motion under this subdivision (b) does not affect the finality of a judgment or suspend its operation.

This rule does not limit the power of a court to entertain an independent action to relieve a party from a judgment, order, or proceeding, or to set aside a judgment for fraud upon the court. Writs of review, of error, of audita querela, and petitions to vacate judgment are abolished, and the procedure for obtaining any relief from a judgment shall be by motion as prescribed in these rules or by an independent action. *Identical to Mass.R.Civ.P. 60(b).*

Rule 61. Harmless Error

No error in either the admission or the exclusion of evidence and no error or defect in any ruling or order or in anything done or omitted by the court or by any of the parties is ground for granting a new trial or for setting aside a verdict or for vacating, modifying or otherwise disturbing a judgment or order, unless refusal to take such action appears to the court inconsistent with substantial justice. The court at every stage of the proceeding must disregard any error or defect in the proceeding which does not affect the substantial rights of the parties. *Identical to Mass.R.Civ.P. 61.*

Rule 62. Stay of Proceedings to Enforce a Judgment

(a) Automatic Stay; Exceptions–Injunctions and Receiverships. Except as stated herein, no execution shall issue upon a judgment nor shall proceedings be taken for its enforcement until the time for appeal from the judgment has expired. In the District Court, in the case of a default judgment, no execution shall issue until 10 days after entry of such judgment. Unless otherwise ordered by the court, an interlocutory or final judgment in an action for an injunction or in a receivership action shall not be stayed during the period after its entry and until an appeal is taken or during the pendency of an appeal. The provisions of subdivision (c) of this rule govern the suspending, modifying, restoring, or granting of an injunction during the pendency of an appeal. *Identical to Mass.R.Civ.P. 62(a).*

(b) Stay on Motion to Vacate Judgment. In its discretion and on such conditions for the security of the adverse party as are proper, the court may stay the execution of or any proceedings to enforce a judgment pending the disposition of a motion for relief from a judgment or order made pursuant to Rule 60. *Identical to Mass.R.Civ.P. 62(b).*

(c) Injunction Pending Appeal. When an appeal is taken from an interlocutory or final judgment granting, dissolving, or denying an injunction, the court in its discretion may suspend, modify, restore, or grant an injunction during the pendency of the appeal upon such terms as to bond or otherwise as it considers proper for the security of the rights of the adverse party. *Identical to Mass.R.Civ.P. 62(c).*

(d) [Deleted].

(e) Power of Appellate Court Not Limited. The provisions in this rule do not limit any power of the appellate court or of a single justice thereof to stay proceedings during the pendency of an appeal or to suspend, modify, restore, or grant an injunction during the pendency of an appeal or to make any order appropriate to preserve the status quo or the effectiveness of the judgment subsequently to be entered. *Identical to Mass.R.Civ.P. 62(e).*

(f) Stay of Judgment as to Multiple Claims or Multiple Parties. When a court has ordered a final judgment under the conditions stated in Rule 54(b), the court may stay enforcement of that judgment until the entering of a subsequent judgment or judgments and may prescribe such conditions as are necessary to secure the benefit thereof to the party in whose favor the judgment is entered. *Identical to Mass. R.Civ.P. 62(f).*

(g) Stay of Nisi Period in Divorce Cases. The filing of an appeal shall stay the running of the nisi period as provided by Rule 58(c) only if the claim of appeal is from that portion of the judgment nisi which dissolved the marriage. If the appeal is subsequently dismissed by the appellate court, the judgment shall become absolute as of ninety days from the date of the judgment nisi. Unless the court otherwise orders, the filing of an appeal shall not stay the operation:

(i) of any other aspect of a divorce judgment; or

(ii) of any other order or judgment of the court relative to custody, visitation, alimony, support, or maintenance.

Amended December 15, 1986, effective January 2, 1987; June 8, 1989, effective July 1, 1989; April 29, 1992, effective June 1, 1992.

Comments—Mass.R.Dom.Rel.P.

Rule 62(g) has been added to clarify the difference between the stay of the nisi period pending an appeal from the permissive stay of any other terms of a judgment pending an appeal.

Rule 63. Disability of a Judge

If by reason of death, sickness, resignation, removal or other disability, a judge before whom an action has been tried is unable to perform the duties to be performed by the court under these rules after findings of facts and conclusions of law are filed, then any other judge regularly sitting in or assigned to the court in which the action was tried may, on assignment by the Chief Judge, or in case of disability of such Chief Judge, by the senior judge of the Administrative Committee present and qualified to act, perform those duties; but if such other judge is satisfied that he cannot perform those duties because he did not preside at the trial or for any other reason, he may in his discretion grant a new trial.

Comments—Mass.R.Dom.Rel.P.

Rule 63 has been amended to delete jury references and correct nomenclature appropriate to Probate Court.

VIII. PROVISIONAL AND FINAL REMEDIES AND SPECIAL PROCEDURES

Rule 64. Report of Case

(a) **Courts Other Than District Court.** The court, after verdict or after a finding of facts under Rule 52, may report the case for determination by the appeals court. If the trial court is of opinion that an interlocutory finding or order made by it so affects the merits of the controversy that the matter ought to be determined by the appeals court before any further proceedings in the trial court, it may report such matter, and may stay all further proceedings except such as are necessary to preserve the rights of the parties. The court, upon request of the parties, in any case where the parties agree in writing as to all the material facts, may report the case to the appeals court for determination without making any decision thereon. In an action commenced before a single justice of the supreme judicial court, the court may report the case in the circumstances above described to either the appeals court or the full supreme judicial court; provided further that a single justice of the supreme judicial court may at any time reserve any question of law for consideration by the full court, and shall report so much of the case as is necessary for understanding the question reserved.

(b) **District Court.** Report of a case or a ruling by the court to the Appellate Division shall be governed by District/Municipal Courts Rules for Appellate Division Appeal 5.

Rule 65. Injunctions

(a) **Temporary Restraining Order; Notice; Hearing; Duration.** A temporary restraining order may be granted without written or oral notice to the adverse party or his attorney only if it clearly appears from specific facts shown by affidavit or by the verified complaint that immediate and irreparable injury, loss or damage will result to the applicant before the adverse party or his attorney can be heard in opposition. On two days' notice to the party who obtained the temporary restraining order without notice or on such shorter notice to that party as the court may prescribe, the adverse party may appear and move its dissolution or modification and in that event the court shall proceed to hear and determine such motion as expeditiously as the ends of justice require.

(b) [Deleted].

(c) **Security.** Unless the court, for good cause shown, shall otherwise order, no restraining order except an order restraining any restriction on the personal liberty of a person, shall issue except upon the giving of security by the applicant, in such sum as the court deems proper, for the payment of such costs and damages as may be incurred or suffered by any party who is found to have been wrongfully enjoined or restrained. The provisions of Rule 65.1 apply to a surety upon a bond or undertaking under this rule.

(d) **Form and Scope of Injunction or Restraining Order.** Unless the court, for good cause shown, otherwise orders, an injunction or restraining order shall be specific in terms; shall describe in reasonable detail, and not by reference to the complaint or other document, the act or acts sought to be restrained; and is binding only upon the parties to the action, their officers, agents, servants, employees, and attorneys, and upon those persons in active concert or participation with them who receive actual notice of the order by personal service or otherwise. *Identical to Mass.R.Civ.P. 65(d).*

(e) [Deleted].

Comments—Mass.R.Dom.Rel.P.

Rule 65(a) has been amended to delete reference to the automatic expiration at the end of ten (10) days. The most widespread use of restraining orders in domestic relations cases related to interference with the personal liberty of the parties. Retention of such an automatic expiration of the order would prove cumbersome in such cases.

Rule 65.1. Security: Proceedings Against Sureties

Whenever these rules require or permit the giving of security by a party, and security is given in the form of a bond or stipulation or other undertaking with one or more sureties, each surety submits himself to the jurisdiction of the court and irrevocably appoints the clerk of the court as his agent upon whom any papers affecting his liability on the bond or undertaking may be served. His liability may be enforced on motion without the necessity of an independent action. The motion and such notice of the motion as the court prescribes may be served on the clerk of the court, who shall forthwith mail copies to the sureties if there addresses are known. *Identical to Mass.R.Civ.P. Rule 65.1.*

Rule 66. Receivers [Deleted]

[Deleted].

Rule 67. Deposit in Court

In an action in which any part of the relief sought is a judgment for a sum of money or the disposition of a sum of money or the disposition of any other thing capable of delivery, a party, upon notice to every other party, and by leave of court, may deposit with the court all or any part of such sum or thing. Money paid into court under this rule shall be deposited and withdrawn in accordance with the provisions of any applicable statute or rule. *Identical to Mass.R.Civ.P. 67.*

Rule 68. Offer of Judgment [Deleted]

[Deleted].

Rule 69. Execution

Process to enforce a judgment for the payment of money shall be a writ of execution, unless the court directs otherwise. The procedure on execution, in proceedings on and in aid of execution shall be in accordance with applicable statutes. In aid of the judgment or execution, the judgment creditor or his successor in interest when that interest appears of record, may obtain discovery from any person, including the judgment debtor, in the manner provided in these rules. *Identical to Mass.R.Civ.P. 69.*

Rule 70. Judgment for Specific Acts: Vesting Title

If a judgment directs a party to execute a conveyance of land or to deliver deeds or other documents or to perform any other specific act and the party fails to comply within the time specified, the court may direct the act to be done at the cost of the disobedient party by some other person appointed by the court and the act when so done has like effect as if done by the party. On application of the party entitled to performance, the clerk shall issue a writ of attachment against the property of the disobedient party to compel obedience to the judgment. The court may also in proper cases adjudge the party in contempt. If real or personal property is within the Commonwealth, the court in lieu of directing a conveyance thereof may enter a judgment divesting the title of any party and vesting it in others and such judgment has the effect of a conveyance executed in due form of law. When any order or judgment is for the delivery of possession, the party in whose favor it is entered is entitled to a writ of execution upon application to the clerk. *Identical to Mass.R.Civ.P. 70.*

Rule 71. Process in Behalf of and Against Persons Not Parties [Deleted]

[Deleted].

Rules 72 to 76. [Reserved]

IX. COURTS AND CLERKS

Rule 77. Courts and Registers

(a) Courts Always Open. Unless otherwise provided by law, the courts shall be deemed always open for the purpose of filing any pleading or other proper paper, of issuing and returning process, and of making and directing all interlocutory motions, orders, and rules. *Identical to Mass.R.Civ.P. 77(a).*

(b) Register's Office. The register's office for each county with a register or assistant register in attendance shall be open during business hours on all days except Saturdays, Sundays and legal holidays.

(c) Filing Date of All Papers Received by Clerk. The clerk shall date-stamp all papers whatsoever received by him, whether by hand or by mail. Any paper so received, whether stamped or not, shall be deemed to have been filed as of the date of receipt. If at any subsequent time, any party disputes the fact of such filing, the court shall determine the question, taking whatever evidence it deems appropriate. Proof of mailing shall constitute prima facie proof of receipt. *Identical to Mass.R.Civ.P. 77(c).*

(d) Notice of Orders or Judgments. Unless an order or judgment is entered in open court in the presence of the parties or their counsel, the register shall immediately upon the entry of an order or judgment serve a notice of the order including the terms of any order of custody, support or alimony by mail in the manner provided for in Rule 5 upon each party and shall make a note in the docket of the mailing. Such mailing is sufficient notice for all purposes for which notice of the entry of an order is required by these rules; but any party may in addition serve a notice of such entry in the manner provided in Rule 5 for the service of papers. Lack of notice of the entry by the register does not affect the time to appeal or relieve or authorize the court to relieve a party for failure to appeal within the time allowed, except as permitted in Rule 4 of the Massachusetts Rules of Appellate Procedure.

(e) Transmittal of Papers. At the direction of the Chief Judge, the registers of the several counties shall transmit the papers in any action from one county to another when a matter has been duly set down for hearing in a county other than that in which the action is pending. Pleadings, motions and papers to be filed in such case shall be filed in the office of the register for the county in which the case is pending. The register for the county in which the case is heard shall certify the proceedings had in his county to the Chief Judge of the Probate Courts and, at the direction of any judge of the court, shall return to the register for the county in which the case is pending all the papers, to be kept there on file.

Rule 78. Motion Day

The court shall establish regular times and places, at intervals sufficiently frequent for the prompt dispatch of business, at which motions requiring notice and hearing may be heard and disposed of; but a judge at any time or place and on such notice, if any, as he considers reasonable may make orders for the advancement, conduct, and hearing of such motions. To expedite its business, the court may provide by order for the submission and determination of motions without oral hearing upon brief written statements of reasons in support and opposition. The court may require the filing of briefs, in such form and within such time as it may direct. *Identical to Mass.R.Civ.P. 78.*

Rule 79. Books and Records Kept by the Clerk and Entries Therein

(a) Civil Docket. The clerk shall keep the civil docket and shall enter therein each civil action to which these rules are made applicable. Actions shall be assigned consecutive file numbers. The file number of each action shall be noted on the folio of the docket whereon the first entry of the action is made. All papers filed with the clerk, all process issued and returns made thereon, all appearances, orders, verdicts, and judgments shall be entered chronologically in the civil docket on the folio assigned to the action and shall be marked with its file number. These entries shall be brief but shall show the nature of each paper filed or writ issued and the substance of each order or judgment of the court and of the returns showing execution of process. The entry of an order or judgment shall show the date the entry is made. When in an action trial by jury has been properly demanded or ordered the clerk shall enter the word "jury" on the folio assigned to that action. *Identical to Mass.R.Civ.P. 79(a)*

(b) Indices; Calendars. Suitable indices of the civil docket shall be kept by the clerk according to law under the direction of the court. *Identical to Mass.R.Civ.P. 79(b).*

(c) Other Books and Records of the Clerk. The clerk shall also keep such other books and records as may be required by law or by direction of the court. *Identical to Mass.R.Civ.P. 79(c).*

Rule 80. Stenographic Report or Transcript

(a) Courts Other Than District Court: Evidence in Subsequent Trial. Whenever the testimony of a witness at a trial or hearing which was officially stenographically reported is admissible in evidence at a later trial, it may be proved by the transcript thereof duly certified by the person who reported the testimony. *Identical to Mass.R.Civ.P. 80(a).*

(b) Courts Other Than District Court: Part of Record on Appeal. A transcript, duly certified by the person officially reporting the testimony, shall be considered part of the record on appeal. The trial court need not appoint said person a commissioner to report the evidence. *Identical to Mass. R.Civ.P. 80(b).*

X.   GENERAL PROVISIONS

Rule 81. Applicability of Rules

(a) Applicability in General. These rules apply to all civil proceedings in courts whose proceedings they govern except:

(1) proceedings pertaining to the writ of habeas corpus;

(2) [Deleted];

(3) proceedings pertaining to the disciplining of an attorney;

(4)–(8) [Deleted].

In respects not governed by statute, the practice in the enumerated proceedings shall follow the course of the common law, as near to these rules as may be, except that depositions shall not be taken, nor interrogatories served, save by order of the court on motion, with notice, for good cause shown.

(b) Writs Abolished. The following writs are abolished: audita querela; certiorari; entry; error; mandamus; prohibition; quo warranto; review; and scire facias. In any action seeking relief formerly obtainable under any such writ, procedure shall follow these rules. *Identical to Mass.R.Civ.P. 81(b).*

(c) [Deleted].

(d) Terminology in Statutes. In applying these rules to any proceedings to which they apply, the terminology of any statute which also applies shall, if inconsistent with these rules, be taken to mean the analogous device or procedure proper under these rules. *Identical to Mass.R.Civ.P. 81(d).*

(e) Procedure Not Specifically Prescribed. When no procedure us specifically prescribed, the court shall proceed in any lawful manner not inconsistent with the Constitution of this Commonwealth, these rules, or any applicable statute. *Identical to Mass.R.Civ.P. 81(e).*

(f) [Deleted].

(g) [Deleted].

(h) The following definitions for purposes of these rules apply to terms as appearing in Mass.R.Civ.P.:

(1) *Clerk* includes Register of Probate.

(2) *Justice* includes Judge of Probate Court.

(3) *Chief Justice* includes the Chief Judge of Probate Court.

(4) *Superior Court* includes Probate Court.

(5) The word *"complaint"* includes "petition" and "libel."

(6) The words *"jury"* and *"verdict"* and Rules applicable to jury cases apply only to courts having jurisdiction of jury trials.

(7) *Third-party actions* shall not be applicable to Domestic Relations matters.

(8) References in Mass.R.Civ.P. to actions including remanded cases and/or defenses and the capacity of parties not recognized in Domestic Relations practice as set out in Rule 1 shall be inapplicable to Domestic Relations cases.

(9) In Domestic Relations matters in the Probate Court forms, where prescribed, will be required in lieu of pleadings.

Comments—Mass.R.Dom.Rel.P.

Rule 81(a), (c), (f) and (g) have been amended by deleting proceedings not applicable to Domestic Relations Courts. Rule 81(h) has been added to broaden the definitions of some terms as appearing in Mass.R.Civ.P.

Rule 82. Jurisdiction and Venue Unaffected

These rules shall not be construed to extend or limit the jurisdiction of the courts or the venue of actions therein. *Identical to Mass.R.Civ.P.Rule 82.*

Rule 83. Supplemental Rules

Any court whose procedure is regulated in whole or in part by these rules may from time to time make and amend supplemental rules, or continue in force existing rules, governing its procedure not inconsistent with these rules. In instances not provided for by rule, each said court may regulate its practice in a manner not inconsistent with these rules and the said supplemental rules. *Identical to Mass.R.Civ.P. 83.*

Rule 84. Forms

Rule 84 has been reserved pro tem. NOTE: Separate forms to be drafted which in Domestic Relations practice in Probate Court shall be mandatory.

Rule 85. Title

These rules may be known and cited as the Massachusetts Rules of Domestic Relations Procedure (Mass.R.Dom.Rel.P.).

CHILD SUPPORT GUIDELINES

Table of Guidelines

CHILD SUPPORT GUIDELINES

Preamble

These child support guidelines shall take effect on September 15, 2017, as amended on June 15, 2018, and shall be applied to all child support orders and judgments entered as of the amended date. In recognition of the priority of the interests of the children of the Commonwealth, these guidelines are formulated to be used by all of the justices of the Trial Court. There shall be a rebuttable presumption that these guidelines apply in all cases establishing or modifying a child support order, regardless of whether the parents of the child are married or unmarried, the order is temporary or final, or the Court is deciding whether to approve an agreement for child support. There shall also be a rebuttable presumption that the amount of the child support order calculated under these guidelines is the appropriate amount of child support to be ordered. These guidelines are based on various considerations, including, but not limited to, each parent's earnings, income, and other evidence of ability to pay. These guidelines are intended to be of assistance to attorneys and to litigants in determining what level of payment would be expected given the relative income levels of the parties. In all cases where an order for child support may be established or modified, a guidelines worksheet must be filled out, regardless of the income of the parties.

Commentary 2017—Preamble

The Child Support Guidelines Task Force for the 2016–2017 review ("Task Force") was convened by Chief Justice of the Trial Court Paula M. Carey in the spring of 2016 to undertake the quadrennial review of the Massachusetts child support guidelines ("guidelines") as required by federal regulations. See 45 C.F.R. § 302.56. In January 2017, amendments to § 302.56 became effective. The Task Force for this quadrennial review was not required to implement the January 2017 amendments, and thus did not do so in this review. However, where appropriate and constructive, the Task Force considered the policies underlying the 2017 amendments when making its recommendations.

The comprehensive review of the Task Force included reviewing each section of the guidelines, line by line, as a whole and in subcommittees. In formulating its recommendations, the Task Force considered public comments, relevant research, information from economic consultants, and the comments and experience of Task Force members. The Task Force was cognizant that child support in Massachusetts seeks to reflect the incremental cost of raising a child, separate and distinct from expenses of other household members. The Task Force recommended edits for simplification, clarification, and policy considerations. These guidelines include commentary to indicate the reasoning and intent behind the recommendations of the Task Force. Trial Court departments, litigants and attorneys may use the commentary to resolve questions of interpretation or application of the guidelines.

The changes made in the Preamble reflect that the guidelines apply to child support orders entered as of September 15, 2017. The fifth sentence of the Preamble was added for clarification and is consistent with the January 2017 changes to 45 C.F.R. § 302.56 (c). The Task Force further clarified that the guidelines worksheet must be completed in all cases where a child support order may be established or modified. A guidelines worksheet is necessary for the Court to determine whether there is a deviation from the presumptive child support order such that findings must be completed. See Section IV.

Commentary 2018—Preamble

After the promulgation of the Child Support Guidelines in September 2017, the Trial Court reviewed two issues on which it received questions: the application of the adjustment factors for children 18 years of age or older, and the adjustment for child care, health care coverage, and dental/vision insurance costs when parents share financial responsibility and parenting time approximately equally. In the June 2018 amendments, the Trial Court revised the age adjustment factors in the worksheet to eliminate counterintuitive outcomes in support orders for four or five children, at least one being 18 years of age or older. The Trial Court also redesigned the worksheet so that one worksheet can be used regardless of whether the parenting plan is shared, split, or approximately 2/3 and 1/3. It is no longer necessary to use multiple worksheets to determine the child support amount where there is shared or split parenting plans. The June 2018 amendments do not address the 2018/2019 changes to the federal tax code with regard to alimony and dependency exemptions.

Principles

In establishing these guidelines, due consideration has been given to the following principles:

1. promoting parental financial responsibility for children;

2. meeting the child's survival needs in the first instance, but, to the extent either parent enjoys a higher standard of living, allowing the child to enjoy that higher standard;

3. minimizing negative changes to the child's standard of living;

4. protecting a basic subsistence level of income of parents;

5. recognizing that deviations should be used when appropriate to tailor a child support order to the unique circumstances of a particular family;

6. recognizing that parents should bear any additional expenses resulting from the maintenance of two separate households;

7. recognizing the non-monetary contributions and involvement of both parents;

8. recognizing the monetary and/or in-kind contributions of both parents in addition to the child support order;

9. recognizing the importance, availability, and cost of health care coverage for the child;

10. promoting simplicity and consistency in establishing and modifying child support orders; and

11. streamlining administration and minimizing problems of proof.

Commentary 2017—Principles

The Task Force refined and reorganized the Principles section for clarification. The Task Force included Principle 5 regarding deviation to highlight that, where appropriate, the Court should deviate from the presumptive child support order amount and that attorneys and litigants should offer reasons as to why a deviation may be warranted. In making this change, the Task Force acknowledged the sentiments expressed by attorneys and litigants that there may be hesitation by the Court to deviate from the presumptive child support order. The Principles section has also been revised to reflect the January 2017 changes to 45 C.F.R. § 302.56 (c) by adding "basic" in Principle 4 of the Principles and changing "health insurance coverage" to "health care coverage" in Principle 9 of the Principles.

I. INCOME DEFINITION

A. Sources of Income. For purposes of these guidelines, income is defined as gross income from whatever source, regardless of whether that income is recognized by the Internal Revenue Code or reported to the Internal Revenue Service or state Department of Revenue or other taxing authority. However, income derived from a means-tested public assistance program (for example: TAFDC, SNAP, veterans' benefits and SSI benefits) shall not be counted as income for either parent.

Sources of income include, but are not limited to, the following:

1. salaries, wages, overtime and tips,

2. income from self-employment;

3. commissions;

4. severance pay;

5. royalties;

6. bonuses;

7. interest and dividends;

8. income derived from businesses/partnerships;

9. social security excluding any benefit due to a child's own disability;[1]

10. non means-tested veterans' benefits;

11. military pay, allowances and allotments;

12. insurance benefits, including those received for disability and personal injury, but excluding reimbursements for property losses;

13. workers' compensation;

14. unemployment compensation;

15. pensions;

16. annuities;

17. distributions and income from trusts;

18. capital gains in real and personal property transactions to the extent that they represent a regular source of income;

19. spousal support received from a person not a party to this order;

20. contractual agreements;

21. perquisites or in-kind compensation to the extent that they represent a regular source of income;

22. unearned income of children, in the Court's discretion;

23. income from life insurance or endowment contracts;

24. income from interest in an estate, either directly or through a trust;

25. lottery or gambling winnings received either in a lump sum or in the form of an annuity;

26. prizes or awards;

27. net rental income;

28. funds received from earned income credit; and

29. any other form of income or compensation not specifically itemized above.

B. Overtime and Secondary Jobs

1. The Court may consider none, some, or all overtime income or income from a secondary job. In determining whether to disregard none, some or all income from overtime or a secondary job, due consideration must first be given to the history of the income, the expectation that the income will continue to be available, the economic needs of the parties and the children, the impact of the overtime or secondary job on the parenting plan, and whether the overtime work is a requirement of the job.

2. If after a child support order is entered, a payor or recipient begins to work overtime or obtains a secondary job, neither of which was worked prior to the entry of the order, there shall be a presumption that the overtime or secondary job income should not be considered in a future child support order.

C. Self–Employment and Other Business Income. Income from self-employment, rent, royalties, proprietorship of a business, or joint ownership of a partnership or closely-held corporation is defined as gross receipts minus ordinary and necessary expenses required to produce income. In general, income and expenses from self-employment or operation of a business should be carefully reviewed to determine the appropriate level of gross income available to the parent to satisfy a child support obligation. In many cases, this amount will differ from a determination of business income for tax purposes.

D. Imputation of Income

1. When the Court finds that a parent has, in whole or in part, undocumented or unreported income, the Court may reasonably impute income to the parent based on all the evidence submitted, including, but not limited to, evidence of the parent's ownership and maintenance of assets, and the parent's lifestyle, expenses and spending patterns.

2. Expense reimbursements, in-kind payments or benefits received by a parent, personal use of business property, and payment of personal expenses by a business in the course of employment, self-employment, or operation of a business may be included as income if such payments are significant and reduce personal living expenses.

3. In circumstances where the Court finds that a parent has unreported income, the Court may adjust the amount of income upward by a reasonable percentage to take into account the absence of income taxes that normally would be due and payable on the unreported income.

E. Attribution of Income

1. Income may be attributed where a finding has been made that either parent is capable of working and is unemployed or underemployed.

2. If the Court makes a determination that either parent is earning less than he or she could earn through reasonable effort, the Court should consider potential earning capacity rather than actual earnings in making its child support order.

3. The Court shall consider the age, number, needs and care of the children covered by the child support order. The Court shall also consider the specific circumstances of the parent, to the extent known and presented to the Court, including, but not limited to, the assets, residence, education, training, job skills, literacy, criminal record and other employment barriers, age, health, past employment and earnings history, as well as the parent's record of seeking work, and the availability of employment at the attributed income level, the availability of employers willing to hire the parent, and the relevant prevailing earnings level in the local community.

F. Non–Parent Guardian.

The income of a non-parent guardian shall not be considered for purposes of calculating a child support obligation.

Commentary 2017—Section I.—Income Definition

A. Sources of Income

Although the Task Force did not recommend any substantive changes to Section I. A., Sources of Income, it considered whether to do so in light of emerging areas of income-producing activities such as transportation networking companies, crowd funding, domain site flipping, and inconsistent, short-term home rentals. The Task Force determined that these income-producing activities were encompassed by the existing list of sources of income.

The Task Force received public comment regarding means-tested and non means-tested veterans' benefits and, in response, clarified that means-tested veterans' benefits are a type of income that is not included as income for child support calculation purposes. Due to the complexity of determining whether a veteran's benefit is means-tested, the Task Force strongly recommended that the Court should inquire regarding the benefit.

If the Court determines that there has been misrepresentation of income to a taxing authority or on a court-filed financial statement and/or guidelines worksheet, the Court may be required to report the information to the appropriate authority. See Rule 2.15(B) of SJC Rule 3:09: Code of Judicial Conduct.

B. Overtime and Secondary Jobs

The Task Force recommended continuation of the presumptive exclusion of certain overtime and secondary job income from the calculation of gross income for child support purposes. The Task Force rewrote and moved for clarification the sentence that previously read, "The Court may consider none, some, or all overtime income even if overtime was earned prior to the entry of the order." The Task Force also determined that the language in this section applies to payors and recipients since the income of both parents is considered in setting a child support order.

C. Self–Employment and Other Business Income

The Task Force renamed, reorganized and refined this section to focus on issues related to self-employment and the operation of a business. The Task Force moved the language regarding imputing income to the newly created Section I. D. entitled, "Imputation of Income". Because the Task Force felt it was redundant, it deleted from the guidelines the sentence, "The calculation of income for purposes of this section may increase gross income by certain deductions or other adjustments taken for income tax purposes.". The Appeals Court noted in *Whelan v. Whelan*, 74 Mass. App. Ct. 616, 626–27 (2009), "in determining income from self-employment, a judge must determine whether claimed business deductions are reasonable and necessary to the production of income, without regard to whether those deductions may be claimed for Federal or State income tax purposes." As further direction, the Appeals Court noted in an unpublished decision, *Zoffreo v. Zoffreo*, 76 Mass. App. Ct. 1105 (2010), "[t]he fact that [a parent] is permitted under the tax laws to deduct an amount for depreciation does not mean that those funds, which are not out of pocket expenses, are not available to pay child support."

For additional decisional guidance regarding calculating gross income, the Supreme Judicial Court held "that a determination whether and to what extent the undistributed earnings of an S corporation should be deemed available income to meet a child support obligation must be made based on the particular circumstances presented in each case." *J.S. v. C.C.*, 454 Mass. 652, 662–63 (2009). The Supreme Judicial Court included a non-exhaustive list of relevant factors to consider when making this determination, such as "a shareholder's level of control over corporate distributions", "the legitimate business interests justifying corporate earnings", the "affirmative evidence of an attempt to shield income by means of retained earnings", and "the allocation of burden of proof in relation to the treatment of an S corporation's undistributed earnings for purposes of determining income available for child support[.]" *J.S. v. C.C.*, 454 Mass. 652, 662–65 (2009).

In *Fehrm–Cappuccino v. Cappuccino*, 90 Mass. App. Ct. 525 (2016), the Appeals Court addressed the appropriateness of including rental income when determining income for child support purposes. The decision notes that "there is no risk of double counting, where 'neither the value of [the father's interest in [the asset]] nor the [father's] ability to earn income is diminished by treating the [father's interest in [the asset]] as a marital asset as well as a source of income by which [the father] can meet his support obligations.'" *Fehrm–Cappuccino v. Cappuccino*, 90 Mass. App. Ct. 525, 528 (2016) (quoting *Champion v. Champion*, 54 Mass. App. Ct. 215, 221 (2002)).

D.   Imputation of Income

The Task Force renamed, reorganized and refined the section previously entitled, "Unreported Income" to focus on issues related to the imputation of income. Income may be imputed when there are actual resources available to the parent that are not reported for tax purposes.

In general terms, undocumented income is income that does not result in the issuance of a tax reporting form. Unreported income is any income that is received and required to be reported that the taxpayer does not report on his or her taxes.

The Appeals Court decision in *Crowe v. Fong*, 45 Mass. App. Ct. 673 (1988) is instructional regarding Section I. D. 2. In Crowe, the payor earned $275 per week working at a business owned by his mother, lived rent-free in a home owned by his father, and had use of a vehicle. The Appeals Court upheld the trial judge's "characterization of [the payor's] free use of the home as 'perquisite or in-kind income' for purposes of calculating his support obligation under the guidelines[.]" *Crowe v. Fong*, 45 Mass. App. Ct. 673, 680–81 (1988).

E.   Attribution of Income

The Task Force reorganized and refined this section for clarification and to distinguish attributed income from imputed income. Income is attributed to a parent when the Court determines a parent is capable of earning more than is currently being earned and assigns a hypothetical amount of income to the parent. The Task Force, in consideration of the January 2017 changes to 45 C.F.R. § 302.56 (c) (2017), revised the factors to be considered when attributing income to a parent.

In *P.F. v. Department of Revenue*, 90 Mass. App. Ct. 707 (2016), the Appeals Court addressed attribution of income where the payor is incarcerated. "'Income may be attributed where a finding has been made that [the payor] is capable of working and is unemployed or underemployed,' ... or where the payor owns 'substantial assets.'" *P.F. v. Department of Revenue*, 90 Mass. App. Ct. 707, 710 (2016) (quoting *Wasson v. Wasson*, 81 Mass. App. Ct. 574, 581 (2012), quoting from *Flaherty v. Flaherty*, 40 Mass. App. Ct. 289, 291 (1996)). However, where there is "no income or assets from which to pay child support", the Court may not attribute income to the payor based on the payor's prior earning capacity, even if the payor is incarcerated due to committing a crime against the child for whom child support is being paid. *P.F. v. Department of Revenue*, 90 Mass. App. Ct. 707, 710–11 (2016).

F.   Non–Parent Guardian

The Task Force did not recommend any changes to this section.

II.   FACTORS TO BE CONSIDERED IN SETTING THE CHILD SUPPORT ORDER

A.   Relationship to Alimony or Separate Maintenance Payments

1.   These guidelines were developed with the understanding that alimony is for the support of a spouse, while child support is for the support of children.

2.   These guidelines were developed with the understanding that child support is nondeductible by the payor and non-taxable to the recipient. These guidelines do not preclude the Court from deciding that any support order be designated in whole or in part as alimony or unallocated support without it being deemed a deviation, provided that the tax consequences are considered in determining the support order and the after-tax support received by the recipient is not diminished. The parties have the responsibility to present to the Court the tax consequences of proposed orders.

3.   Chapter 124 of the Acts of 2011, entitled, "An Act Reforming Alimony in the Commonwealth", amended G. L. c. 208 and prohibits the use of gross income which the Court has already considered in making a child support order from being used again in determining an alimony order. See G. L. c. 208, § 53 (c) (2). The parties may consider preparing alternate calculations of alimony and child support to determine the most equitable result for the children and the parties. Depending upon the circumstances, alimony may be calculated first, and in other circumstances child support may be calculated first. Judicial discretion is necessary and deviations shall be considered.

B.   Claims of Personal Exemptions for Child Dependents.   In setting a support order, the Court and the parties shall consider the allocation of personal exemptions for child dependents between the parties to the extent permitted by law.

C.   Minimum and Maximum Levels

1.   These guidelines are intended to protect a minimum subsistence level for those parents obligated to pay child support whose gross income is $115 per week or less. However, it is the obligation of all parents to contribute to the support of their children. To that end, a minimum order of $25 per week should enter. This minimum should not be construed as limiting the Court's discretion to set a higher or lower order, should circumstances warrant, as a deviation from the guidelines. See Section IV.

2.   These guidelines are calculated up to a maximum combined available annual gross income of the parties of $250,000. In cases where combined available income is over $250,000, the guidelines should be applied on the first $250,000 in the same proportion as the recipient's and payor's actual income as provided on Line 2h of the guidelines worksheet. In cases where income exceeds this limit, the Court should consider the award of support at the $250,000 level as the minimum presumptive order. The child support obligation for the portion of combined available income that exceeds $250,000 shall be at the discretion of the Court.

D.   Parenting Time

1.   These guidelines recognize that children should enjoy parenting time with both parents to the greatest extent possible consistent with the children's best interests. The basic calculations under these guidelines are based upon the children having a primary residence with one parent and

spending approximately one-third of the time with the other parent.

2. These guidelines apply to all types of parenting plan schedules. Information regarding whether the parents share financial responsibility and parenting time for the children approximately equally (shared), whether the children reside primarily with one parent for approximately 2/3 of the time, and whether, in a family with more than one child covered by the order, each parent provides a primary residence for at least one child (split) is entered directly into the worksheet. The worksheet will calculate the presumptive child support order based on the information entered into the worksheet.

3. Where parenting time is substantially less than one-third for the parent who is not the residential parent, the Court may consider deviation by an upward adjustment to the amount calculated under the guidelines worksheet. See Section IV.B.8.

E. Child Care Costs

1. Reasonable child care costs for the children covered by the child support order and due to gainful employment of either parent are to be deducted from the gross income of the parent who pays the cost. The guidelines worksheet makes an adjustment so that the parents share the burden of the cost proportionately. The adjustment involves a two-step calculation. First, a parent who is paying the child care deducts the out-of-pocket cost from his or her gross income. Second, the parties share the total child care costs for both parents in proportion to their income available for support. The combined adjustment for child care and health care costs is capped at fifteen percent of the child support order.

2. In appropriate circumstances, child care costs may include those due to training or education reasonably necessary to obtain gainful employment or enhance earning capacity. The Court may consider a deviation where the child care cost is disproportionate to income. See Section IV.B.7.

F. Child Support for Children Between the Ages of 18 and 23

1. By statute, the Court has discretion either to order or to decline to order child support for children age 18 or older. If the Court exercises its discretion to order child support for children age 18 or older, the guidelines formula reduces the amount of child support in accordance with Table C of the guidelines worksheet. For the guidelines calculation to account for families with children both under age 18 and age 18 or older, the guidelines worksheet requires the input of information regarding the number of children age 18 or older and under age 18.

2. A child age 18 or older who is enrolled in and attending high school shall be deemed to be under age 18 for purposes of the guidelines and Table C, absent deviation.

3. In determining whether to order child support for a child age 18 or older, the Court shall consider the reason for the child's continued residence with and principal dependence on the recipient, the child's academic circumstances, the child's living situation, the available resources of the parents, and each parent's contribution to the costs of post-secondary education for the child and/or other children of

the family. The Court may also consider any other relevant factors.

G. Contribution to Post-secondary Educational Expenses

1. By statute, the Court has discretion either to order or to decline to order a parent to contribute to post-secondary educational expenses. Contribution to post-secondary educational expenses is not presumptive.

2. In determining whether to order contribution to post-secondary educational expenses, the Court shall consider the cost of the post-secondary education, the child's aptitudes, the child's living situation, the available resources of the parents and child, and the availability of financial aid. The Court may also consider any other relevant factors.

3. No parent shall be ordered to pay an amount in excess of fifty percent of the undergraduate, in-state resident costs of the University of Massachusetts–Amherst, unless the Court enters written findings that a parent has the ability to pay a higher amount. Costs for this purpose are defined as mandatory fees, tuition, and room and board for the University of Massachusetts–Amherst, as set out in the "Published Annual College Costs Before Financial Aid" in the College Board's Annual Survey of Colleges. This section applies to all orders requiring parental contribution to post-secondary educational expenses, regardless of where the child resides or attends school.

4. When exercising its discretion to order child support for a child over age 18 and contribution to the child's post-secondary educational expenses, the Court shall consider the combined amount of both orders.

H. Health Care Coverage

1. a. Each parent may deduct from gross income the reasonable cost of individual or family health care coverage actually paid by that parent. If there is an additional cost to insure a person not covered by this order, and the Court determines that such additional cost would unreasonably impact the amount of child support, then some or all of such additional cost shall not be deducted.

b. The guidelines worksheet makes an adjustment so that the parents share the burden of the cost proportionately. The adjustment involves a two-step calculation. First, a parent who is paying the health care deducts the out-of-pocket cost from his or her gross income. Second, the parties share the total health care costs for both parents in proportion to their income available for support. The combined adjustment for child care and health care costs is capped at fifteen percent of the child support order.

2. When the Court makes an order for child support, the order shall include an order of health care coverage unless the payor and recipient agree in writing that such coverage will be provided by other means.

3. a. The Court shall determine whether health care coverage that may be extended to cover the child is available through an employer or otherwise available at a reasonable cost. Health care coverage shall be deemed available to the payor at reasonable cost if it is available through an employer.

b. If health care coverage is available at a reasonable cost, the Court shall then determine whether the cost of such coverage creates an undue hardship on the payor, and, if that determination is made, the payor shall not be required to provide such coverage. In determining whether the cost of health care coverage creates an undue hardship for the payor, the Court may consider whether the cost of maintaining health care coverage would prevent payment of some or all of the child support order, whether the available coverage lacks the comprehensiveness to meet the health care needs of the child such that significant uninsured medical expenses will be incurred, whether the payor's gross income is less than 300% of the federal poverty guidelines for the payor's household, and any other relevant factors.

c. When such health care coverage is available at a reasonable cost and does not cause an undue hardship, the Court shall include in the child support order a requirement that such insurance for the child be obtained or maintained.

d. If the Court determines that health care coverage is not available at a reasonable cost or that ordering health care coverage creates an undue hardship for the payor and the IV–D agency is providing services, the Court shall enter an order requiring the payor to notify the IV–D agency if access to health care coverage for the child becomes available. If the Court determines that health care coverage is not available at a reasonable cost or that ordering health care coverage creates an undue hardship for the payor and the IV–D agency is not providing services, the Court shall enter an order requiring the payor to notify the recipient if access to health care coverage for the child becomes available.

I. Dental/Vision Insurance

1. Each parent may deduct from gross income the reasonable cost actually paid by that parent of dental/vision insurance insuring the children covered by this order.

2. If there is an additional cost to insure a person not covered by this child support order, and the Court determines such additional cost would unreasonably reduce the amount of child support, then some or all of such additional cost shall not be deducted from gross income.

3. The cost of dental/vision insurance insuring the children covered by this order is included on the guidelines worksheet in the combined child care and health care costs adjustment.

J. Routine Uninsured Medical and Dental/Vision Expenses and Extraordinary Uninsured Medical and Dental/Vision Expenses

1. The recipient shall be responsible for payment of the first $250 each year in combined routine uninsured medical and dental/vision expenses for all the children covered by this child support order. For amounts above that limit, at the time of entry of an order establishing or modifying the child support order, the Court shall allocate expenses between the parties without adjustment to the child support order.

2. The payment of extraordinary uninsured medical and dental/vision expenses incurred for the children, absent agreement of the parties, shall be treated on a case-by-case basis (for example: orthodontia, psychological/psychiatric counseling, etc.). Where the Court makes a determination that such medical and dental/vision services are necessary and are in the best interests of the children, the Court shall allocate such expenses between the parties.

K. Existing Support Obligations and Responsibility for Children Not in the Case under Consideration

1. When an initial order or a modification of an existing order is sought for a child covered by the order in the case under consideration, the amount actually paid by a parent pursuant to a pre-existing support order for a child or spouse not in the case under consideration shall be deducted from the gross income of that parent where that parent provides sufficient proof of the order and payments made. Payments on arrearages shall not be deducted from gross income.

2. When an initial order or a modification of an existing order is sought for a child covered by the order in the case under consideration, the amount of voluntary payments actually paid to support a child not in the case under consideration and with whom the parent does not reside shall be deducted from the gross income of that parent, but only to the extent the Court determines the payments to be reasonable. The parent who seeks the deduction must provide sufficient proof of the legal obligation to support the child and of actual payments made to the other parent or guardian.

3. When an initial order or a modification of an existing order is sought for a child covered by the order in the case under consideration, a hypothetical amount of child support for a child with whom the parent resides but for whom no child support order exists shall be deducted from the gross income of the parent. The parent seeking the deduction must provide sufficient proof of the legal obligation to support the child and of the gross income of that child's other parent. The hypothetical child support amount shall be calculated according to the guidelines worksheet using the gross incomes of both parents of the child for whom the hypothetical child support amount is being calculated.

4. Obligations to a subsequent family may be used as a defense to a request to modify an order seeking an increase in the existing order, but such obligations should not be considered a reason to decrease an existing order.

L. Families with More than Five Children. The guidelines formula applies to families with one to five children. For more than five children, the order should be at least the amount ordered for five children.

M. Contribution to Other Child–Related Expenses. In cases where the Court makes a determination that there are additional child-related expenses such as extra-curricular activities, private school, or summer camps, which are in the best interest of the child and which are affordable by the parties, the Court may allocate costs to the parties on a case-by-case basis.

Commentary 2017—Section II.—Factors To Be Considered In Setting The Child Support Order

A. Relationship to Alimony or Separate Maintenance Payments

The Task Force discussed the challenges related to the tax consequences of unallocated support. The Task Force recommended that the Court, especially in cases involving parties with disparate levels of income, consider an unallocated support order. By designating some, or all, of a payor's support obligation as tax-deductible to the payor and a taxable payment to the recipient, a significant tax benefit may be achieved.

Under *Fechtor v. Fechtor*, 26 Mass. App. Ct. 859 (1989), it is the responsibility of the parties to bring the tax implications of a support order to the attention of the Court. Parties and attorneys should familiarize themselves with the applicable provisions of I.R.C. § 71, which provides specific rules that must be followed in order to fashion support orders that will be deemed tax-deductible under the Internal Revenue Code.

The relationship between alimony and child support remained an issue during this review as it was during the 2012 review. When issuing an alimony order, "the court shall exclude from its income calculation gross income which the court has already considered for setting a child support order." G. L. c. 208, § 53 (c) (2). However, the converse is not stated in the statute.

Since the 2012 review and report, the Massachusetts appellate courts have not issued any decisions on point, nor has there been a statutory change. The Task Force discussed this conundrum and determined that, despite the desire to provide more instruction, no changes to this section were recommended at this time. The Task Force recommended that this issue be reviewed again during the next quadrennial review.

B. Claims of Personal Exemptions for Child Dependents

The Task Force refined this section to emphasize the importance of considering the allocation of the dependency exemptions.

C. Minimum and Maximum Levels

The Task Force considered whether the minimum support order required adjustment. The minimum support order has not changed since 2002 when it was established at $18.46 per week. After discussion, the Task Force recommended that the minimum support order be increased to $25 per week. This increase is consistent with economic data on the increase in the overall cost of living in Massachusetts since 2002. The guidelines chart has been adjusted to reflect that the minimum support order applies to combined available income up to $115 per week.

For informational assistance with regard to child support when the parents' combined gross income is over $250,000, section 6 of the guidelines worksheet calculates the amount by which each parent's available income exceeds $250,000. Child support based on income above $250,000 is discretionary. The excess income information in section 6 of the guidelines worksheet may be considered on a case-by-case basis.

D. Parenting Time

The Task Force discussed at length the consequences of the changes that were incorporated by the 2012 Task Force with regard to when parenting time is more than one-third but less than fifty percent. The Task Force agreed that the provision relating to these circumstances needed to be eliminated. The Task Force considered public comment, attorney and judicial experience, the 2008 Report of the Child Support Guidelines Task Force, and the Final Report of the 2012 Task Force when making this determination. The 2012 change increased litigation and acrimony between parents, shifted the focus from a parenting plan that is in the best interests of the children to a contest about a parenting plan that attempts to reduce a child support order, and failed to create the consistency in child support orders that it sought to create.

The Task Force suggested that the first step in determining a child support order is actually creating a parenting plan that is best for the children, recognizing that children should enjoy parenting time with both parents to the greatest extent possible consistent with the children's best interests. Child support should not be driving the parenting plan. Once the parenting plan is established, then calculations may occur. It is important to note again here that the Task Force specifically created a principle regarding the appropriate use of a deviation where the circumstances of a family require one. See Principles, Principle 5.

The Task Force recommended deleting the provisions inserted in the 2009 guidelines that limited the deduction of other support orders from gross income when making certain calculations related to parenting time. This Task Force was unable to determine why the provisions were included, and thus determined that equity required their deletion.

E. Child Care Costs

The Task Force discussed at length how to address the concerns raised by many people regarding the significant costs of child care. The Task Force recommended a proportional adjustment to the child support order based on child care and health care costs. The proportional adjustment for the costs is not dollar-for-dollar because the significant costs of child care and health care coverage could unfairly skew a child support order. Instead, the adjustment is capped, either up or down, at fifteen percent of the child support order.

F. Child Support for Children Between the Ages of 18 and 23

The Task Force renamed and restructured the section previously entitled, "Age of the Children". The Task Force clarified that these guidelines apply in all cases where a child support order is established or modified and not just in cases involving children under age 18. See 45 C.F.R. § 302.56 (a) (2017). That Massachusetts by statute allows for, but does not require, child support until age 23 does not negate the federal requirement that the guidelines must apply in all cases. However, the C.F.R. does not mandate that the guidelines be identical for children of all ages. For dependent children between 18 and 21, child support may be ordered if the dependent child is domiciled with a parent and is principally dependent on that parent. See G. L. c. 208, § 28, G. L. c. 209C, § 9 and G. L. c. 209, § 37.

For dependent children between 21 and 23, child support may be ordered if the dependent child is domiciled with a parent and is principally dependent on that parent due to enrollment in an educational program, as long as the program is not beyond an undergraduate degree. *See id.* Although the Task Force received public comment suggesting that child support end at age 18, the Task Force did not amend the provision retaining discretion in entering child support orders for children between the ages of 18 and 23 because this discretion is statutory. The Task Force strongly recommended that, until or unless the Massachusetts

Legislature amends the child support statutes to clarify that child support is mandatory through graduation of high school, the Court consider child support orders for those children who have turned 18 but are still in high school as mandatory rather than permissive.

Because these guidelines apply to all child support orders, including those for children up to age 23, the Task Force discussed whether the application of the guidelines through the guidelines worksheet should result in a reduction in the base amount of child support for children who are age 18 or older and not attending high school, but nevertheless eligible for child support pursuant to Massachusetts law. The Task Force agreed that a twenty-five percent reduction is appropriate as it takes into consideration factors typical of this age group. For example, the child may be living away at school thereby reducing some of the household expenses for the recipient or the child may be living at home and is not enrolled in a post-secondary educational program and should be working and contributing to the household expenses. The reduction balances the requirement imposed by federal regulation that all child support orders are the product of a formula established by guidelines, while also considering important factors unique to children between the ages of 18 and 23. See *M.C. v. T.K.*, 463 Mass. 226, 231 (2012) ("The Chief Justice of the Trial Court is authorized to promulgate guidelines establishing presumptive child support awards, based on articulated principles and calculated according to specified mathematical formulas.") Nothing in this section limits the ability of the Court to deviate from the presumptive order where appropriate. For example, the child may be living at home and commuting to a post-secondary educational program.

This section shall not be construed to change the rule set forth in *Feinberg v. Diamant*, 378 Mass. 131 (1979) allowing the Court to require a financially able parent to "contribute to the support of an adult child who by reason of mental or physical infirmity incurs expenses that he or she is unable to meet." *Feinberg v. Diamant*, 378 Mass. 131, 134 (1979). These matters are addressed in equity actions.

G. Contribution to Post-secondary Educational Expenses

The Task Force created a new section to address the complexity of contributions to post-secondary educational expenses. Post-secondary educational expenses have increased exponentially since 1976 when the Massachusetts Legislature amended statutes to permit the Court to order parents to pay for educational expenses. Overall, both public and private four-year college expenses for fees, tuition, room and board, have increased approximately 250%, as adjusted for inflation. See College Board, Annual Survey of Colleges, 2017. The Task Force shared the pervasive concern that many parents cannot pay post-secondary educational expenses from their income, while meeting other expense obligations. The Task Force intended to discourage orders requiring parents to incur liability for loans in excess of state university costs unless the parents agree to accept such liabilities. The Task Force also intended an expense limitation to provide general uniformity in court-ordered, post-secondary educational expenses contributions.

The limitation on post-secondary educational expenses orders is recommended for most cases, but it is not mandatory. The Task Force does not intend the limitation to apply to children already enrolled in post-secondary education before the effective date of these guidelines or to parents who are financially able to pay educational expenses using assets or other resources.

The University of Massachusetts–Amherst was designated as the benchmark for maximum orders because it was the flagship, and most expensive, Massachusetts state college when these guidelines became effective.

H. Health Care Coverage

The Task Force renamed, reorganized, and revised this section. The phrase "health care coverage" was changed from "health insurance" to reflect recent changes in federal law, which now references both private and public health care coverage. Under federal regulations, child support guidelines must "[a]ddress how the parents will provide for the child's health care needs through private *or public health care* coverage and/or through cash medical support." 45 C.F.R. § 302.56 (c) (2) (2017) (emphasis added). Under 45 C.F.R. § 303.31 (a) (3), "[c]ash medical support or the cost of health insurance is considered reasonable in cost if the cost to the parent responsible for providing medical support does not exceed five percent of his or her gross income or, at State option, a reasonable alternative income-based numeric standard defined in State law, regulations or court rule having the force of law or State child support guidelines adopted in accordance with § 302.56(c) of [Chapter 45]." The Massachusetts Legislature has not amended G. L. c. 119A to reflect the federal definition of reasonableness or to grant the authority to order cash medical support. Nor does G. L. c. 119A allow the Court to order either parent to provide health care coverage. See G. L. c. 119A, § 12 (b) (5). The Task Force strongly recommended that the Massachusetts Legislature amend G. L. c. 119A to be consistent with the federal regulations.

The Task Force also made revisions that more clearly reflect the statutory requirements relating to orders for health care coverage. Before requiring a payor to obtain health care coverage, the Court must determine that such coverage is available at reasonable cost, "provided that the cost of such coverage does not create an undue hardship upon the [payor]." G. L. c. 119A, § 12 (b) (5). Because "undue hardship" is not defined by statute or case law, factors relating to determining whether an order of health care coverage creates an undue hardship on the payor are included in these guidelines. There are circumstances where the combined child support order and the cost to the payor for obtaining and maintaining health care coverage exceed the amount allowed under law to be ordered withheld from a payor's income. If health care coverage is ordered in these circumstances, and the costs for the health care coverage are deducted from the payor's income before the child support order is paid, the child support order is not paid in full and the payor accrues child support arrears. For purposes of this section, an undue hardship may occur if the combined health care coverage and child support order exceeds statutory garnishment limits. The Task Force determined that it was appropriate to adopt the percentage of poverty level that MassHealth's Children's Health Insurance Program (CHIP) uses for eligibility screening. See http://children.massbudget.org/masshealth. The Court retains the discretion to consider other relevant factors in making the determination regarding undue hardship.

If health care coverage is not currently available at a reasonable cost or the payment of health care coverage causes an undue hardship, the Task Force removed the requirement that the Court enter an order requiring the payor to obtain and maintain health care coverage for the child if and when the parent has access to such coverage. Instead, the Task Force added a provision that requires the payor to notify the IV–D agency or the recipient if health care coverage becomes available. If health care coverage becomes available, a modification of the child support order may be appropriate to reflect the cost of such coverage, as well as to determine whether there is any undue hardship.

In addition to child care costs, the Task Force also discussed at length how to address the concerns raised by many people regarding the significant costs of health care coverage. The Task Force recommended a proportional adjustment to the child support order based on child care and health care costs. The proportional adjustment for the costs is not dollar-for-dollar because the significant costs of child care and health care coverage could unfairly skew a child support order. Instead, the adjustment is capped, either up or down, at fifteen percent of the child support order.

The Task Force recommended that, where appropriate, the Court should examine whether the parent who seeks to deduct the total amount of health care coverage is including in that total amount the cost for covering persons not covered by the order under consideration. In that circumstance, the Court may determine that some or all of the additional cost should not be deducted from gross income on the guidelines worksheet.

I. Dental/Vision Insurance

The Task Force reorganized this section. The Task Force determined that the costs of the dental and vision insurance covering children under this order shall be included as a component of the child care and health care adjustment.

J. Routine Uninsured Medical and Dental/Vision Expenses and Extraordinary Uninsured Medical and Dental/Vision Expenses

The Task Force reorganized the sections previously entitled, "Routine Uninsured Medical and Dental Expenses" and "Uninsured Extraordinary Medical and Dental Expenses" into one section without any substantive changes.

K. Existing Support Obligations and Responsibility for Children Not in the Case under Consideration

The Task Force recommended changes to this section to clarify the different circumstances that may result in a deduction from gross income when a parent has a legal responsibility to support a child not part of the case currently being considered. The Task Force clarified that where applicable either parent may seek the deductions from gross income and that sufficient proof must be provided. The Task Force reviewed language from the New Jersey, North Carolina, Ohio, and Tennessee child support guidelines to assist in drafting the clarifications.

In *Department of Revenue v. Mason M.,* the Supreme Judicial Court endorsed the use of deducting a hypothetical support order from a parent's gross income where that parent had multiple children to support. *Department of Revenue v. Mason M.,* 439 Mass. 665, 671–72 (2003). However, to calculate a hypothetical amount of child support, the gross incomes of both parents of that child must be used. This calculation can be difficult to compute because the Court does not have the non-party parent's gross income. The burden is on the parent who seeks to deduct a hypothetical amount to provide to the Court the information necessary for calculating the hypothetical amount, including the non-party parent's gross income.

L. Families with More than Five Children

The Task Force did not recommend any substantive changes to this section.

M. Contribution to Other Child–Related Expenses

The Task Force renamed this section for consistency. "Post-secondary education" was deleted from this section only because the Task Force created a new section that addresses contribution to post-secondary educational expenses. See Section II. G.

Commentary 2018—Section II.—Factors To Be Considered In Setting The Child Support Order

D. Parenting Time

This section was amended to eliminate the directions on how the guidelines should be calculated based on the type of parenting plan. The directions are no longer necessary because of the newly-designed worksheet effective on June 15, 2018. This section now reflects that one worksheet is used to calculate the presumptive child support order for shared, split and approximately 2/3 and 1/3 parenting plans.

F. Child Support for Children Between the Ages of 18 and 23

This section was amended to reflect the changes in Table B and Table C in the June 2018 amendments. In the June 2018 amendments, the September 2017 Table B was split into two separate tables. Table B now lists the adjustment factors for the number of children, and Table C lists the adjustment percentages for children's ages.

The application of the adjustment percentages in this section was revised by the Trial Court to eliminate counterintuitive outcomes in support orders for four or five children, at least one being 18 years of age or older. The age adjustments in the September 2017 Table B were based on applying the 25 percent discount listed in the guidelines in equal proportion to the number of children 18 years of age or older. The age adjustment percentages in the June 2018 Table C are based on applying the 25 percent discount to the oldest children last. That is, the 25 percent discount is applied only to the increases in child support for additional children, rather than to the overall amount of support. The children 18 years of age or older are accounted for last in this calculation to fully preserve the increases in child support for additional younger children.

III. MODIFICATION

A. A child support order may be modified if any of the circumstances listed below exist.

1. There is an inconsistency between the amount of the existing order and the amount that would result from the application of the guidelines.

2. Previously ordered health care coverage is no longer available.

3. Previously ordered health care coverage is still available but no longer at a reasonable cost or without an undue hardship.

4. Access to health care coverage not previously available to a parent has become available.

5. Any other material and substantial change in circumstances has occurred.

B. Upon a request for modification of an order that deviated from the guidelines at the time it was entered, the Court shall apply the existing deviation to the modification action if:

1. the facts that gave rise to deviation still exist; and

2. deviation continues to be in the child's best interest; and

3. the guidelines amount would be unjust or inappropriate under the circumstances.

C. Section III. B. does not preclude deviations based on other grounds set forth in Section IV. or grounds for modification as set forth in Section III. A.

Commentary 2017—Section III.—Modification

The Task Force deleted Paragraph B of the 2013 guidelines because it was premised on the assumption that Massachusetts law provides for a separate standard to be used by the Court when the Department of Revenue is providing IV–D services in a case where the order is less than three years old. While the Department of Revenue is not required to use the inconsistency standard when determining whether to provide IV–D services to seek a modification of an order that is less than three years old, the Court must apply the inconsistency standard once any complaint for modification is filed and is before the Court. See 57 Fed. Reg. 61559, 61577 (1992). See also G. L. c. 208, § 28, G. L. c. 209C, § 20 and G. L. c. 209, § 37.

The Department of Revenue's review process does not prohibit an individual from filing a complaint for modification on his or her own, regardless of whether the case is receiving IV–D services.

The Task Force refined the language to clarify that if circumstances that resulted in a deviation are still in existence during a modification action, those circumstances shall be considered to remain even though it may be appropriate to modify the existing order. For example, a child may have a medical condition that results in ongoing, extraordinary medical expenses and the existing child support order deviates from the guidelines amount. The recipient is now unemployed and files a complaint for modification. The underlying circumstances for the existing deviation remains; however, the Court also considers the additional circumstances.

IV. DEVIATION

A. The Court, or the parties by agreement approved by the Court, may deviate from these guidelines and overcome the presumptive application of these guidelines, provided the Court enters specific written findings stating:

1. the amount of the order that would result from application of the guidelines;

2. that the guidelines amount would be unjust or inappropriate under the circumstances;

3. the specific facts of the case which justify departure from the guidelines; and

4. that such departure is consistent with the best interests of the child.

B. Circumstances which may support deviating, above or below the presumptive guidelines amount, including the minimum order amount, are as follows:

1. the parties agree and the Court determines the agreement to be fair and reasonable and approves their agreement;

2. a child has ongoing special needs or aptitudes with financial consequences;

3. a child has ongoing extraordinary mental, physical, or developmental needs with financial consequences;

4. a parent has ongoing extraordinary mental, physical, or developmental needs with financial consequences;

5. a parent has extraordinary expenses for health care coverage;

6. a parent has extraordinary travel or other expenses related to parenting;

7. a parent is absorbing a child care cost that is disproportionate in relation to his or her income;

8. a parent provides substantially less than one-third of the parenting time for a child or children;

9. the payor is incarcerated and has insufficient financial resources to pay support;

10. application of the guidelines, particularly in low income cases, leaves a parent without the ability to self support;

11. application of the guidelines would result in a gross disparity in the standard of living between the two households such that one household is left with an unreasonably low percentage of the combined available income;

12. application of the guidelines may adversely impact reunification of a parent and child where the child has been temporarily removed from the household in accordance with G. L. c. 119; and

13. absent deviation, application of the guidelines would lead to an order that is unjust, inappropriate or not in the best interests of the child, considering the Principles of these guidelines.

Commentary 2017—Section IV.—Deviation

The Task Force refined and clarified the circumstances where deviation may be appropriate. The Task Force reordered this section for clarification purposes only and not to prioritize any one factor over another. The Task Force emphasized that a deviation may be appropriate for a family and encourages the Court to deviate where circumstances require it.

The Task Force clarified in the first phrase of Section IV.B. that it is permissible to deviate to an amount below the presumptive guidelines amount. Because the deviation circumstances affect an ongoing child support award, rather than a one-time or occasional allocation, the Task Force emphasized that certain circumstances must be ongoing and with financial consequences for them to be considered appropriate for a deviation. In Section IV.B.8., the Task Force added "substantially" to emphasize as it did it Section II.D. that a parenting plan that is in the best interest of the child is the first step in determining a child support order. The inclusion of "substantially" provides a parameter with the goal of reducing acrimony and litigation between parents regarding the interaction of the parenting plan and the amount of the child support order.

Amended June 12, 2013, effective August 1, 2013; amended July 18, 2017, effective September 15, 2017; amended effective June 15, 2018.

1If a parent receives social security benefits or SSDI benefits and the children of the parties receive a dependency benefit derived from that parent's benefit, the amount of the dependency benefit shall be added to the gross income of that parent. This combined amount is that parent's gross income for purposes of the child support calculation.

If the dependency benefit derives from the payor's benefit and the amount of the dependency benefit exceeds the child support obligation calculated under the guidelines, then the payor shall not have responsibility for payment of current child support in excess of the dependency benefit. However, if the guidelines are higher than the dependency benefit that derives from the payor's benefit, the payor must pay the difference between the dependency benefit and the weekly child support amount under the guidelines. See *Rosenberg v. Merida*, 428 Mass. 182 (1998); *Schmidt v. McColluch–Schmidt*, 86 Mass. App. Ct. 902 (2014).

INSTRUCTIONS FOR CHILD SUPPORT GUIDELINES WORKSHEET

INSTRUCTIONS FOR COMPLETING THE GUIDELINES WORKSHEET
FOR THE 2017 CHILD SUPPORT GUIDELINES

General Information
The "recipient" is the person who will receive child support.
The "payor" is the person who will pay child support.
Enter all income and expense amounts as weekly amounts.
To change a yearly amount to a weekly amount, divide the yearly amount by 52.
To change a monthly amount to a weekly amount, multiply the monthly amount by 12 and then divide that number by 52.
To change a semi-monthly (twice per month) amount to a weekly amount, multiply the semi-monthly amount by 24 and then divide that number by 52.
To change a bi-weekly (every other week) amount to a weekly amount, divide the bi-weekly amount by 2.
Round all amounts to the nearest dollar or whole percentage.
The only official electronic version of the Child Support Guidelines and the Guidelines Worksheet ("Worksheet") can be found at www.mass.gov/courts. Any other version of the Worksheet is not endorsed by the Massachusetts Trial Court. It is **STRONGLY** recommended to fill out the electronic version of the Worksheet on the mass.gov/court website rather than manually, as the electronic version automatically calculates most numbers in the Worksheet and is easier to complete.

		Detailed Instructions	
		Calculation	
Line	Instruction	Manual Version	Electronic Version
Heading	At the top of the Worksheet, enter the Case Name (the names of the plaintiff/petitioner and defendant/respondent) and the Docket Number assigned by the Court. Also enter the Date Prepared and the Name of the Preparer (self, attorney, IV-D agency, etc.).	No calculation necessary. Input data only.	No calculation necessary. Input data only.
Line 1(a)	Enter the number of children under age 18 to be covered by this order. If there is a child who is 18 or older but still attending high school, that child should be included in this line and not in Line 1(b). See the Child Support Guidelines, Section II. F.	No calculation necessary. Input data only.	No calculation necessary. Input data only.
Line 1(b)	Enter the number of children who are age 18 or older who may be eligible to be covered by this order. See the Child Support Guidelines, Section II. F.	No calculation necessary. Input data only.	No calculation necessary. Input data only.
Line 1(c)	Total number of children to be covered by this order.	Add Lines 1(a) and 1(b) and enter that number on Line 1(c).	Fills in automatically.

Detailed Instructions			
		Calculation	
Line	Instruction	Manual Version	Electronic Version
Line 2(a)	Enter the total gross (before tax) weekly income in the first column for the recipient and In the second column for the payor. Do not include means-tested benefits in gross income. See the Child Support Guidelines, Section I.	No calculation necessary. Input data only.	No calculation necessary. Input data only.
Line 2(b)	Enter the actual amounts paid for work-related child care costs for the children covered by this order. Enter the amount paid by the recipient in the first column and the amount paid by the payor in the second column. See the Child Support Guidelines, Section II. E.	No calculation necessary. Input data only.	No calculation necessary. Input data only.
Line 2(c)	Enter the actual amounts paid for the cost of individual or family health care coverage. Enter the amount paid by the recipient in the first column and the amount paid by the payor in the second column. The Court may change the amounts included here for health coverage for a person not covered by the order. See the Child Support Guidelines, Section II. H.	No calculation necessary. Input data only.	No calculation necessary. Input data only.
Line 2(d)	Enter the actual amounts paid for the cost of dental/vision insurance for the children covered by this order. Enter the amount paid by the recipient in the first column and the amount paid by the payor in the second column. The Court may change the amounts included here for dental/vision coverage for a person not covered by the order. See the Child Support Guidelines, Section II. I.	No calculation necessary. Input data only.	No calculation necessary. Input data only.
Line 2(e)	Enter the actual amounts paid to support a spouse or a child not covered by this order or the amount of a hypothetical order to support a child not covered by this order. Enter amounts for the recipient in the first column and amounts for the payor in the second column. See the Child Support Guidelines, Section II. K.	No calculation necessary. Input data only.	No calculation necessary. Input data only.
Line 2(f)	Available income	For each column, subtract Lines 2(b), 2(c), 2(d) and 2(e) from Line 2(a) and enter that amount in Line 2(f).	Fills in automatically.
Line 2(g)	Combined available income	Add the amount in each column of Line 2(f) and enter that amount in Line 2(g).	Fills in automatically.

		Detailed Instructions	
		Calculation	
Line	Instruction	Manual Version	Electronic Version
Line 2(h)	Share of combined available income	For each column, divide Line 2(f) by Line 2(g). Then to get the percentage for each column, multiply that number by 100 and round to the nearest whole number. Enter that final number in Line 2(h).	Fills in automatically.
Line 3(a)	Applicable available income	Enter the amount from Line 2(g), unless the amount in Line 2(g) is more than $4,808. If the amount in Line 2(g) is more than $4,808, enter $4,808 in Line 3(a).	Fills in automatically.
Line 3(b)	The support amount for one child can be found in the Guidelines Chart or calculated manually. To use the Guidelines Chart, find the amount in Line 3(a). If that amount falls between two rows in the Guidelines Chart, use the row for the lower amount. Enter the bold "Combined Support Amount" in that row in Line 3(b) of the Worksheet.	To manually calculate the combined support amount for one child, use the amounts and percentages in Table A: CHILD SUPPORT OBLIGATION SCHEDULE. Enter the resulting amount in Line 3(b).	Fills in automatically.
Line 3(c)	The adjustment for number and ages of children covered by this order is found in Table B: ADJUSTMENT FOR NUMBER AND AGES OF CHILDREN. See Child Support Guidelines, Section II. F. and Section II. L.	In the left-hand column of Table B, find the row listing the number in Line 1(a). Then follow across to the right, to the column listing the number in Line 1(b). Enter the number from the corresponding row and column in Line 3(c).	Fills in automatically.
Line 3(d)	Combined support amount	Multiply the amount in Line 3(b) by the number in Line 3(c) and enter that amount in Line 3(d).	Fills in automatically.
Line 3(e)	Recipient's share of support	Multiply the amount in Line 3(d) by the percentage in the first column of Line 2(h) and enter that amount in Line 3(e).	Fills in automatically.
Line 3(f)	Payor's share of support	Subtract Line 3(e) from Line 3(d). If the amount is $25 or more, enter that amount in Line 3(f). If the amount is less than $25, enter $25 in Line 3(f).	Fills in automatically.
Line 4(a)	Child care and health care costs paid	For each column, add Lines 2(b), 2(c), and 2(d) and enter that amount in Line 4(a). Enter the amount for the recipient in the first column and the amount for the payor in the second column.	Fills in automatically.
Line 4(b)	Payor's share of recipient's cost	Multiply the amount in the first column of Line 4(a) (the recipient's child care and health care costs paid) by the percentage in the second column of Line 2(h) (the payor's share of combined available income) and enter that amount in Line 4(b).	Fills in automatically.

	Detailed Instructions		
		Calculation	
Line	Instruction	Manual Version	Electronic Version
Line 4(c)	Recipient's share of payor's cost	Multiply the amount in the second column of Line 4(a) (the payor's child care and health care costs paid) by the percentage in the first column of Line 2(h) (the recipient's share of combined available income) and enter that amount in Line 4(c). This amount could be a negative number.	Fills in automatically.
Line 4(d)	Payor's net cost	Subtract Line 4(c) from Line 4(b) and enter that amount in Line 4(d).	Fills in automatically.
Line 4(e)	Maximum adjustment amount	If the amounts in Line 4(a) total more than $0, multiply Line 3(f) by 0.15 and enter that amount in Line 4(e). Otherwise, enter $0.	Fills in automatically.
Line 4(f)	Adjustment applied to order	If the amount in Line 4(d) is $0 or higher, enter the lesser of the amounts in Line 4(d) or Line 4(e). If the amount in Line 4(d) is a negative number, enter zero.	Fills in automatically.
Line 4(g)	Adjustment applied to order	If Line 4(d) is a positive number, enter zero in Line 4(g). If Line 4(d) is a negative number, enter the value of Line 4(d) as a positive number or the value of Line 4(e), whichever is less.	Fills in automatically.
Line 4(h)	Payor's net cost	Add Lines 3(f) and 4(f) then subtract Line 4(g) from that amount. If that amount is $25 or more, enter that amount in Line 4(h). If that amount is less than $25, enter $25.	Fills in automatically.
Line 5(a)	Support as a % of Recipient income	If the amount in the first column of Line 2(f) (the recipient's available income) equals $0, enter 100 in Line 5(a). Otherwise, divide Line 4(h) by the amount in the first column of Line 2(f) (the recipient's available income). Then to get the percentage, multiply that number by 100 and round to the nearest whole number. Enter that final number in Line 5(a).	Fills in automatically.

		Calculation	
Line	Instruction	Manual Version	Electronic Version
Line 5(b)	In most cases, the adjustment in Line 5(b) will not change the weekly support amount shown in Line 4(g). The adjustment in Line 5(b) changes the payor's weekly support amount only in cases with relatively high-income recipients and low-income payors.	If Line 5(a) is 10% or more, enter the amount from Line 4(h) or $25, whichever is higher. If Line 5(a) is less than 10%, add 10% to the percentage in Line 5(a) and multiply that percentage by the payor's available income in the second column of Line 2(f). If that amount is equal to or greater than $25 but less than the amount in Line 4(h), enter it in Line 5(b). Otherwise, enter the amount from Line 4(h) or $25, whichever is less.	Fills in automatically.
Line 6(a)	This line is purely informational. It shows the amount of combined available income beyond the $4,808 per week maximum amount of income considered under the Child Support Guidelines. See the Child Support Guidelines, Section C.	If the amount of combined available income in Line 2(g) is less than $4,808, leave Lines 6(a) and 6(b) blank. If the amount of combined available income in Line 2(g) is greater than $4,808, subtract $4,808 from the amount in Line 2(g) and enter that amount in Line 6(a).	Fills in automatically.
Line 6(b)	This line is purely informational. It shows the shares of available income for the Payor and Recipient beyond the $4,808 per week maximum considered under the Guidelines. See the Child Support Guidelines, Section C.	Multiply Line 6(a) by each column of Line 2(h) and enter those amounts in each of the same columns of Line 6(b).	Fills in automatically.

Detailed Instructions

Amended effective September 15, 2017.

CHILD SUPPORT GUIDELINES WORKSHEET

Case Name _____   Date Prepared _____

Docket Number _____   Name of Preparer _____

CHILD SUPPORT GUIDELINES WORKSHEET

All dollar amounts are weekly. Round all numbers to the nearest whole dollar or percentage.

1. AGE, NUMBER, AND PARENTING OF CHILDREN

a. Number of children who may be eligible to be covered by this order

b. Check the box that applies to the children listed in 1(a) (check **one** box only):

The parents share financial responsibility and parenting time approximately equally (shared)	Box 1	☐
The children primarily reside with one parent for approximately 2/3 of the time	Box 2	☐
There is more than one child covered by the order and each parent provides a primary residence for at least one child (split)	Box 3	☐

c. Enter each parent's name

If you checked Box 2 above, enter the name of the parent with whom the children primarily reside in the column for Parent A, and the other parent's name as Parent B; otherwise, enter either parent's name in either column

                       Parent A   Parent B

Enter the number and age of children for whom each parent may be eligible to receive support

If you checked Box 1 above (shared), enter the number of children from 1(a) in the columns for both parents

If you checked Box 2 above, enter the number of children from 1(a) in the column for Parent A, and enter 0 in the column for Parent B

If you checked Box 3 above (split), enter the number of children primarily residing with each parent in each column

d. Number of children under age 18

e. Number of children 18 years or older

f. Total number of children

2. INCOME

a. Gross weekly income

b. *Minus*   Child care cost paid

c. *Minus*   Health care cost paid

d. *Minus*   Dental/vision insurance cost paid

e. *Minus*   Other support obligations paid

f. Available income   *2(a) - Sum of 2(b) through 2(e), but not less than $0*

g. Combined available income   *Parent A 2(f) + Parent B 2(f)*

h. Share of combined available income   *2(f) ÷ 2(g) (Min 0%, Max 100%)*

3. GROSS SUPPORT AMOUNTS

a. Applicable available income   *2(g) or $4,808, whichever is less*

b. Support amount for one child   *From Table A or Guidelines Chart for 3(a)*

c. Adjustment for the number of children in 1(f)   *From Table B*

d. Combined support amount   *3(b) x 3(c)*

4. ADJUSTMENT FOR CHILDREN 18 YEARS OR OLDER

a. Adjustment percentage for the ages of the children listed in 1(d) and 1(e)   *From Table C*

b. Adjustment for children 18 years or older   *3(d) x 4(a)*

c. Adjusted combined support amount   *3(d) - 4(b)*

CJD 304 (6/15/18) CSG   page 1 of 2

Case Name _____

Docket No. _____

	Parent A	Parent B

5. PROPORTIONAL SUPPORT AMOUNTS

a. *Minus* Each parent's share of support   2(h) x 4(c)

b. Other parent's share of support   4(c) - 5(a)

c. Support as % of each parent's available income

   If you checked Box 2 in 1(b), enter N/A
   If you checked Box 1 or Box 3 in 1(b), enter 5(b) ÷ 2(f)   *(If 2(f) = $0, enter 100%)*

d. Other parent's adjusted share of support

   If 5(c) is N/A, enter 5(b) or $25, whichever is more, for Parent A and $0 for Parent B
   If 5(c) is ≥ 10%, enter 5(b) or $25, whichever is more
   If 5(c) is < 10%, enter 5(b) or ((5(c) + 10%) x the other parent's 2(f)), whichever is less, but not less than $25

e. Recipient and Payor

   Enter "Recipient" in the column where 5(d) is higher and "Payor" in the other column
   If 5(d) is the same in both columns, enter "Recipient" in either column and "Payor" in the other

f. Payor's net share of support   Recipient 5(d) - Payor 5(d)

6. ADJUSTMENT FOR CHILD CARE AND HEALTH CARE COSTS

a. Child care and health care cost paid   2(b) + 2(c) + 2(d)

b. Payor's share of Recipient's cost   Payor 2(h) x Recipient 6(a)

c. *Minus* Recipient's share of Payor's cost   Recipient 2(h) x Payor 6(a)

d. Payor's net cost   6(b) - 6(c)

e. Maximum adjustment amount

   If 6(a) = $0 for both parents, enter $0; otherwise enter 5(f) x 0.15

   Adjustment applied to this order

f.   *If 6(d) < $0, enter $0; otherwise enter 6(d) or 6(e), whichever is less*

g.   *If 6(d) ≥ $0, enter $0; otherwise enter the positive value of 6(d) or 6(e), whichever is less*

h. Payor's adjusted net share of support   5(f) + 6(f) - 6(g)

7. PAYOR'S NET SUPPORT OBLIGATION

a. Support as % of Recipient's available income

   If you checked Box 1 or Box 3 in 1(b), enter N/A
   If you checked Box 2 in 1(b), enter 6(h) ÷ Recipient 2(f)   *(If Recipient 2(f) = 0, enter 100%)*

b. Payor's final support obligation

   If 7(a) is N/A, enter 6(h)
   If 7(a) ≥ 10%, enter 6(h) or $25, whichever is more
   If 7(a) < 10%, enter 6(h) or ((7(a) + 10%) x Payor 2(f)), whichever is less, but not less than $25

   Payor pays Recipient

8. ADDITIONAL INCOME ABOVE $4,808

a. Combined additional income   2(g) - $4,808 or $0, whichever is more

b. Share of combined additional income   8(a) x 2(h)

TABLE A: CHILD SUPPORT OBLIGATION SCHEDULE		
All dollar amounts are weekly and rounded to the nearest dollar		
INCOME FROM LINE 2(g) Minimum Maximum	CHILD SUPPORT AMOUNT (1 CHILD)	
$0 $115	$25 per week, unless the court deviates	
$116 → $750	22%	
$751 → $1250	$165 + 21%	above $750
$1251 → $2000	$270 + 19%	above $1250
$2001 → $3000	$413 + 15%	above $2000
$3001 → $4000	$563 + 12%	above $3000
$4001 → $4808	$683 + 11%	above $4000

TABLE B: ADJUSTMENT FOR NUMBER OF CHILDREN	
NUMBER OF CHILDREN	ADJUSTMENT FACTOR
0	0.00
1	1.00
2	1.25
3	1.38
4	1.45
5	1.48

TABLE C: ADJUSTMENT FOR CHILDREN 18 YEARS OR OLDER						
CHILDREN UNDER 18	CHILDREN 18 OR OLDER					
	0	1	2	3	4	5
0	0%	25%	25%	25%	25%	25%
1	0%	5%	8%	9%	9%	
2	0%	3%	4%	4%		
3	0%	1%	2%			
4	0%	1%				
5	0%					

CJD 304 (6/15/18) CSG

Amended effective September 15, 2017; June 15, 2018.

CHILD SUPPORT GUIDELINES CHART

2017 Child Support Guidelines Chart

All dollar amounts are weekly, for one child under 18 years old, rounded to the nearest dollar.
If combined available income falls between two numbers, use the lower combined support amount.
Enter the combined support amount on Line 3(b) of the Child Support Guidelines Worksheet.

Combined available income	Combined support amount	Combined available income	Combined support amount	Combined available income	Combined support amount	Combined available income	Combined support amount	Combined available income	Combined support amount
$0	$25	$340	$75	$567	$125	$796	$175	$1,034	$225
$116	$26	$344	$76	$572	$126	$800	$176	$1,039	$226
$121	$27	$349	$77	$576	$127	$805	$177	$1,043	$227
$125	$28	$354	$78	$581	$128	$810	$178	$1,048	$228
$130	$29	$358	$79	$585	$129	$815	$179	$1,053	$229
$135	$30	$363	$80	$590	$130	$820	$180	$1,058	$230
$139	$31	$367	$81	$594	$131	$824	$181	$1,062	$231
$144	$32	$372	$82	$599	$132	$829	$182	$1,067	$232
$148	$33	$376	$83	$604	$133	$834	$183	$1,072	$233
$153	$34	$381	$84	$608	$134	$839	$184	$1,077	$234
$157	$35	$385	$85	$613	$135	$843	$185	$1,081	$235
$162	$36	$390	$86	$617	$136	$848	$186	$1,086	$236
$166	$37	$394	$87	$622	$137	$853	$187	$1,091	$237
$171	$38	$399	$88	$626	$138	$858	$188	$1,096	$238
$175	$39	$404	$89	$631	$139	$862	$189	$1,100	$239
$180	$40	$408	$90	$635	$140	$867	$190	$1,105	$240
$185	$41	$413	$91	$640	$141	$872	$191	$1,110	$241
$189	$42	$417	$92	$644	$142	$877	$192	$1,115	$242
$194	$43	$422	$93	$649	$143	$881	$193	$1,120	$243
$198	$44	$426	$94	$654	$144	$886	$194	$1,124	$244
$203	$45	$431	$95	$658	$145	$891	$195	$1,129	$245
$207	$46	$435	$96	$663	$146	$896	$196	$1,134	$246
$212	$47	$440	$97	$667	$147	$900	$197	$1,139	$247
$216	$48	$444	$98	$672	$148	$905	$198	$1,143	$248
$221	$49	$449	$99	$676	$149	$910	$199	$1,148	$249
$225	$50	$454	$100	$681	$150	$915	$200	$1,153	$250
$230	$51	$458	$101	$685	$151	$920	$201	$1,158	$251
$235	$52	$463	$102	$690	$152	$924	$202	$1,162	$252
$239	$53	$467	$103	$694	$153	$929	$203	$1,167	$253
$244	$54	$472	$104	$699	$154	$934	$204	$1,172	$254
$248	$55	$476	$105	$704	$155	$939	$205	$1,177	$255
$253	$56	$481	$106	$708	$156	$943	$206	$1,181	$256
$257	$57	$485	$107	$713	$157	$948	$207	$1,186	$257
$262	$58	$490	$108	$717	$158	$953	$208	$1,191	$258
$266	$59	$494	$109	$722	$159	$958	$209	$1,196	$259
$271	$60	$499	$110	$726	$160	$962	$210	$1,200	$260
$275	$61	$504	$111	$731	$161	$967	$211	$1,205	$261
$280	$62	$508	$112	$735	$162	$972	$212	$1,210	$262
$285	$63	$513	$113	$740	$163	$977	$213	$1,215	$263
$289	$64	$517	$114	$744	$164	$981	$214	$1,220	$264
$294	$65	$522	$115	$749	$165	$986	$215	$1,224	$265
$298	$66	$526	$116	$753	$166	$991	$216	$1,229	$266
$303	$67	$531	$117	$758	$167	$996	$217	$1,234	$267
$307	$68	$535	$118	$762	$168	$1,000	$218	$1,239	$268
$312	$69	$540	$119	$767	$169	$1,005	$219	$1,243	$269
$316	$70	$544	$120	$772	$170	$1,010	$220	$1,248	$270
$322	$71	$549	$121	$777	$171	$1,015	$221	$1,253	$271
$326	$72	$554	$122	$781	$172	$1,020	$222	$1,258	$272
$331	$73	$558	$123	$786	$173	$1,024	$223	$1,264	$273
$335	$74	$563	$124	$791	$174	$1,029	$224	$1,269	$274

2017 Child Support Guidelines Chart

All dollar amounts are weekly, for one child under 18 years old, rounded to the nearest dollar.

If combined available income falls between two numbers, use the lower combined support amount.

Enter the combined support amount on Line 3(b) of the Child Support Guidelines Worksheet.

Combined available income	Combined support amount	Combined available income	Combined support amount	Combined available income	Combined support amount	Combined available income	Combined support amount	Combined available income	Combined support amount
$1,274	$275	$1,537	$325	$1,800	$375	$2,077	$425	$2,410	$475
$1,279	$276	$1,543	$326	$1,806	$376	$2,084	$426	$2,417	$476
$1,285	$277	$1,548	$327	$1,811	$377	$2,090	$427	$2,424	$477
$1,290	$278	$1,553	$328	$1,816	$378	$2,097	$428	$2,430	$478
$1,295	$279	$1,558	$329	$1,822	$379	$2,104	$429	$2,437	$479
$1,300	$280	$1,564	$330	$1,827	$380	$2,110	$430	$2,444	$480
$1,306	$281	$1,569	$331	$1,832	$381	$2,117	$431	$2,450	$481
$1,311	$282	$1,574	$332	$1,837	$382	$2,124	$432	$2,457	$482
$1,316	$283	$1,579	$333	$1,843	$383	$2,130	$433	$2,464	$483
$1,322	$284	$1,585	$334	$1,848	$384	$2,137	$434	$2,470	$484
$1,327	$285	$1,590	$335	$1,853	$385	$2,144	$435	$2,477	$485
$1,332	$286	$1,595	$336	$1,858	$386	$2,150	$436	$2,484	$486
$1,337	$287	$1,600	$337	$1,864	$387	$2,157	$437	$2,490	$487
$1,343	$288	$1,606	$338	$1,869	$388	$2,164	$438	$2,497	$488
$1,348	$289	$1,611	$339	$1,874	$389	$2,170	$439	$2,504	$489
$1,353	$290	$1,616	$340	$1,879	$390	$2,177	$440	$2,510	$490
$1,358	$291	$1,622	$341	$1,885	$391	$2,184	$441	$2,517	$491
$1,364	$292	$1,627	$342	$1,890	$392	$2,190	$442	$2,524	$492
$1,369	$293	$1,632	$343	$1,895	$393	$2,197	$443	$2,530	$493
$1,374	$294	$1,637	$344	$1,900	$394	$2,204	$444	$2,537	$494
$1,379	$295	$1,643	$345	$1,906	$395	$2,210	$445	$2,544	$495
$1,385	$296	$1,648	$346	$1,911	$396	$2,217	$446	$2,550	$496
$1,390	$297	$1,653	$347	$1,916	$397	$2,224	$447	$2,557	$497
$1,395	$298	$1,658	$348	$1,922	$398	$2,230	$448	$2,564	$498
$1,400	$299	$1,664	$349	$1,927	$399	$2,237	$449	$2,570	$499
$1,406	$300	$1,669	$350	$1,932	$400	$2,244	$450	$2,577	$500
$1,411	$301	$1,674	$351	$1,937	$401	$2,250	$451	$2,584	$501
$1,416	$302	$1,679	$352	$1,943	$402	$2,257	$452	$2,590	$502
$1,422	$303	$1,685	$353	$1,948	$403	$2,264	$453	$2,597	$503
$1,427	$304	$1,690	$354	$1,953	$404	$2,270	$454	$2,604	$504
$1,432	$305	$1,695	$355	$1,958	$405	$2,277	$455	$2,610	$505
$1,437	$306	$1,700	$356	$1,964	$406	$2,284	$456	$2,617	$506
$1,443	$307	$1,706	$357	$1,969	$407	$2,290	$457	$2,624	$507
$1,448	$308	$1,711	$358	$1,974	$408	$2,297	$458	$2,630	$508
$1,453	$309	$1,716	$359	$1,979	$409	$2,304	$459	$2,637	$509
$1,458	$310	$1,722	$360	$1,985	$410	$2,310	$460	$2,644	$510
$1,464	$311	$1,727	$361	$1,990	$411	$2,317	$461	$2,650	$511
$1,469	$312	$1,732	$362	$1,995	$412	$2,324	$462	$2,657	$512
$1,474	$313	$1,737	$363	$2,000	$413	$2,330	$463	$2,664	$513
$1,479	$314	$1,743	$364	$2,004	$414	$2,337	$464	$2,670	$514
$1,485	$315	$1,748	$365	$2,010	$415	$2,344	$465	$2,677	$515
$1,490	$316	$1,753	$366	$2,017	$416	$2,350	$466	$2,684	$516
$1,495	$317	$1,758	$367	$2,024	$417	$2,357	$467	$2,690	$517
$1,500	$318	$1,764	$368	$2,030	$418	$2,364	$468	$2,697	$518
$1,506	$319	$1,769	$369	$2,037	$419	$2,370	$469	$2,704	$519
$1,511	$320	$1,774	$370	$2,044	$420	$2,377	$470	$2,710	$520
$1,516	$321	$1,779	$371	$2,050	$421	$2,384	$471	$2,717	$521
$1,522	$322	$1,785	$372	$2,057	$422	$2,390	$472	$2,724	$522
$1,527	$323	$1,790	$373	$2,064	$423	$2,397	$473	$2,730	$523
$1,532	$324	$1,795	$374	$2,070	$424	$2,404	$474	$2,737	$524

2 of 3

849

2017 Child Support Guidelines Chart

All dollar amounts are weekly, for one child under 18 years old, rounded to the nearest dollar.
If combined available income falls between two numbers, use the lower combined support amount.
Enter the combined support amount on Line 3(b) of the Child Support Guidelines Worksheet.

Combined available income	Combined support amount	Combined available income	Combined support amount	Combined available income	Combined support amount	Combined available income	Combined support amount	Combined available income	Combined support amount
$2,744	$525	$3,096	$575	$3,513	$625	$3,930	$675	$4,360	$723
$2,750	$526	$3,105	$576	$3,521	$626	$3,938	$676	$4,369	$724
$2,757	$527	$3,113	$577	$3,530	$627	$3,946	$677	$4,378	$725
$2,764	$528	$3,121	$578	$3,538	$628	$3,955	$678	$4,387	$726
$2,770	$529	$3,130	$579	$3,546	$629	$3,963	$679	$4,396	$727
$2,777	$530	$3,138	$580	$3,555	$630	$3,971	$680	$4,405	$728
$2,784	$531	$3,146	$581	$3,563	$631	$3,980	$681	$4,414	$729
$2,790	$532	$3,155	$582	$3,571	$632	$3,988	$682	$4,423	$730
$2,797	$533	$3,163	$583	$3,580	$633	$3,996	$683	$4,432	$731
$2,804	$534	$3,171	$584	$3,588	$634	$4,005	$684	$4,441	$732
$2,810	$535	$3,180	$585	$3,596	$635	$4,014	$685	$4,450	$733
$2,817	$536	$3,188	$586	$3,605	$636	$4,023	$686	$4,460	$734
$2,824	$537	$3,196	$587	$3,613	$637	$4,032	$687	$4,469	$735
$2,830	$538	$3,205	$588	$3,621	$638	$4,041	$688	$4,478	$736
$2,837	$539	$3,213	$589	$3,630	$639	$4,050	$689	$4,487	$737
$2,844	$540	$3,221	$590	$3,638	$640	$4,060	$690	$4,496	$738
$2,850	$541	$3,230	$591	$3,646	$641	$4,069	$691	$4,505	$739
$2,857	$542	$3,238	$592	$3,655	$642	$4,078	$692	$4,514	$740
$2,864	$543	$3,246	$593	$3,663	$643	$4,087	$693	$4,523	$741
$2,870	$544	$3,255	$594	$3,671	$644	$4,096	$694	$4,532	$742
$2,877	$545	$3,263	$595	$3,680	$645	$4,105	$695	$4,541	$743
$2,884	$546	$3,271	$596	$3,688	$646	$4,114	$696	$4,550	$744
$2,890	$547	$3,280	$597	$3,696	$647	$4,123	$697	$4,578	$747
$2,897	$548	$3,288	$598	$3,705	$648	$4,132	$698	$4,587	$748
$2,904	$549	$3,296	$599	$3,713	$649	$4,141	$699	$4,596	$749
$2,910	$550	$3,305	$600	$3,721	$650	$4,150	$700	$4,605	$750
$2,917	$551	$3,313	$601	$3,730	$651	$4,160	$701	$4,614	$751
$2,924	$552	$3,321	$602	$3,738	$652	$4,169	$702	$4,623	$752
$2,930	$553	$3,330	$603	$3,746	$653	$4,178	$703	$4,632	$753
$2,937	$554	$3,338	$604	$3,755	$654	$4,187	$704	$4,641	$754
$2,944	$555	$3,346	$605	$3,763	$655	$4,196	$705	$4,650	$755
$2,950	$556	$3,355	$606	$3,771	$656	$4,205	$706	$4,660	$756
$2,957	$557	$3,363	$607	$3,780	$657	$4,214	$707	$4,669	$757
$2,964	$558	$3,371	$608	$3,788	$658	$4,223	$708	$4,678	$758
$2,970	$559	$3,380	$609	$3,796	$659	$4,232	$709	$4,687	$759
$2,977	$560	$3,388	$610	$3,805	$660	$4,241	$710	$4,696	$760
$2,984	$561	$3,396	$611	$3,813	$661	$4,250	$711	$4,705	$761
$2,990	$562	$3,405	$612	$3,821	$662	$4,260	$712	$4,714	$762
$2,997	$563	$3,413	$613	$3,830	$663	$4,269	$713	$4,723	$763
$3,005	$564	$3,421	$614	$3,838	$664	$4,278	$714	$4,732	$764
$3,013	$565	$3,430	$615	$3,846	$665	$4,287	$715	$4,741	$765
$3,021	$566	$3,438	$616	$3,855	$666	$4,296	$716	$4,750	$766
$3,030	$567	$3,446	$617	$3,863	$667	$4,305	$717	$4,760	$767
$3,038	$568	$3,455	$618	$3,871	$668	$4,314	$718	$4,769	$768
$3,046	$569	$3,463	$619	$3,880	$669	$4,323	$719	$4,778	$769
$3,055	$570	$3,471	$620	$3,888	$670	$4,332	$720	$4,787	$770
$3,063	$571	$3,480	$621	$3,896	$671	$4,341	$721	$4,796	$771
$3,071	$572	$3,488	$622	$3,905	$672	$4,350	$722	$4,805	$772
$3,080	$573	$3,496	$623	$3,913	$673	$4,560	$745	$4,808	$772
$3,088	$574	$3,505	$624	$3,921	$674	$4,569	$746		

Amended June 12, 2013, effective August 1, 2013; amended effective September 15, 2017.

FINDINGS AND DETERMINATIONS FOR CHILD SUPPORT AND POST–SECONDARY EDUCATION

FINDINGS AND DETERMINATIONS FOR CHILD SUPPORT AND POST-SECONDARY EDUCATION	Docket No.	Commonwealth of Massachusetts The Trial Court Probate and Family Court

Case name: _____

Payor is _____   _____ Division

Recipient is _____

MINIMUM AND MAXIMUM LEVELS - Section II. C. of the 2017 Child Support Guidelines

☐ The combined gross income of the parties exceeds $250,000.

IMPUTATION OF INCOME - Section I. D. of the 2017 Child Support Guidelines

☐ The Court finds that **the payor** has gross income that is undocumented or unreported. Accordingly, the Court imputes

income of $ _____ per _____ based on:

☐ The Court finds that **the recipient** has gross income that is undocumented or unreported. Accordingly, the Court imputes

income of $ _____ per _____ based on:

ATTRIBUTION OF INCOME - Section I. E. of the 2017 Child Support Guidelines

☐ The Court finds that **the payor** is capable of working and is unemployed or underemployed.

☐ The Court determines that **the payor** is earning less than could be earned through reasonable effort.

Accordingly, the Court attributes income of $ _____ per _____ based on:

☐ The Court finds that **the recipient** is capable of working and is unemployed or underemployed.

☐ The Court determines that **the recipient** is earning less than could be earned through reasonable effort.

Accordingly, the Court attributes income of $ _____ per _____ based on:

CHILD SUPPORT FOR CHILDREN BETWEEN AGES 18 AND 23 - Section II. F. of the 2017 Child Support Guidelines

☐ The Court finds that the _____ is 18 or older and attending high school, but shall not be
                                    (first born, second born, etc.)
considered to be under age 18 for purposes of the guidelines and Table B because:

☐ The Court finds that the _____ is 18 or older and attending high school, but shall not be
                                    (first born, second born, etc.)
considered to be under age 18 for purposes of the guidelines and Table B because:

CJ-D 305 9/15/17   page   1   of   4

Case Name: _____	Docket No.

CONTRIBUTION TO POST-SECONDARY EDUCATION - Section II. G. of the 2017 Child Support Guidelines

☐ The Court finds that **the payor** has the ability to pay an amount higher than 50% of the undergraduate, in-state resident costs of the University of Massachusetts - Amherst because:

☐ The Court finds that **the recipient** has the ability to pay an amount higher than 50% of the undergraduate, in-state resident costs of the University of Massachusetts - Amherst because:

HEALTH CARE COVERAGE - Section II. H. of the 2017 Child Support Guidelines

☐ The Court determines that the additional cost paid by **the payor** to insure a person not covered by the child support order unreasonably reduces the amount of child support. The Court allows $ _____ per week to be deducted from gross income on the guidelines worksheet.

☐ The Court determines that the additional cost paid by **the recipient** to insure a person not covered by the child support order unreasonably reduces the amount of child support. The Court allows $ _____ per week to be deducted from gross income on the guidelines worksheet.

☐ Health care coverage is available to **the payor** through employment or other means at a reasonable cost. However, the cost of such coverage creates an undue hardship on **the payor** because:

DENTAL/VISION INSURANCE - Section II. I. of the 2017 Child Support Guidelines

☐ The Court determines that the additional cost paid by **the payor** to insure a person not covered by the child support order unreasonably reduces the amount of child support. The Court allows $ _____ per week to be deducted from gross income on the guidelines worksheet.

☐ The Court determines that the additional cost paid by **the recipient** to insure a person not covered by the child support order unreasonably reduces the amount of child support. The Court allows $ _____ per week to be deducted from gross income on the guidelines worksheet.

CJ-D 305 9/15/17

Case Name: _____	Docket No.

DEVIATION - Section IV. of the 2017 Child Support Guidelines

The guidelines are applicable in this case. The amount of the child support order that would result from the application of the

guidelines is $ _____ ☐ Weekly ☐ Bi-weekly ☐ Monthly ☐ Other(specify) _____

However, the Court finds the presumptiveness of the guidelines has been rebutted because, after considering the best interests of the child, the application of the guidelines would be unjust or inappropriate.

The specific circumstance of the case which justify departure from the guidelines are:

☐ the parties agree and the Court has reviewed and approved their agreement dated _____

☐ a child has ongoing special needs or aptitudes with financial consequences

☐ a child has ongoing extraordinary mental, physical, or developmental needs with financial consequences

☐ a parent _____ has ongoing extraordinary mental, physical, or
                     Name
developmental needs with financial consequences

☐ a parent _____ has extraordinary expenses for health care
                     Name
coverage

☐ a parent _____ has extraordinary travel or other expenses
                     Name
related to parenting

☐ a parent _____ is absorbing a child care cost that is
                     Name
disproportionate in relation to his or her income

☐ a parent _____ provides substantially less than one-third of the
                     Name
parenting time for a child or children

☐ the payor is incarcerated and has insufficient financial resources to pay support

☐ application of the guidelines, particularly in low income cases, leaves a parent _____
                                                              Name
without the ability to self support

☐ application of the guidelines would result in a gross disparity in the standard of living between the two households such that one household is left with an unreasonably low percentage of the combined available income

☐ application of the guidelines may adversely impact reunification of a parent and child where the child has been temporarily removed from the household in accordance with G. L. c. 119

☐ absent deviation, application of the guidelines would lead to an order that is unjust, inappropriate or not in the best interests of the child, considering the Principles of the 2017 Child Support Guidelines

☐ this is a modification of an order that deviated from the guidelines at the time it entered and the facts that gave rise to the deviation still exists, deviation continues to be in the child's best interest, and the guidelines amount would be unjust or inappropriate under the circumstances

☐ other:

CJ-D 305 9/15/17   page   3   of   4

Case Name:	Docket No.

FOR COURT USE ONLY

After hearing, at which _____ and/ or _____
_____Name_____   _____Name_____

was present, the Court entered an order dated _____.

_____ was ordered to pay child support in the amount of
_____Name_____

$ _____ ☐Weekly ☐Bi-weekly ☐Monthly ☐Other(specify) _____

Date _____

_____
Judge of the Probate and Family Court

THIS FORM MUST BE FILED AND DOCKETED WITH THE CASE

Amended effective September 15, 2017.

SUPPLEMENTAL RULES OF THE PROBATE AND FAMILY COURT

Publisher's Note

The General Rules of the Probate Court were combined with the Supplemental Rules of the Probate Court by order of the Supreme Judicial Court dated December 14, 2011, effective January 2, 2012, and renamed the Supplemental Rules of the Probate and Family Court.

Table of Rules

Rule 1.   Effect of Rules

The provisions of these rules shall apply to all proceedings in the Probate Court unless a contrary intent appears.

Whenever a Supplemental Rule of the Probate and Family Court refers to a rule in the Massachusetts Rules of Civil Procedure, or to a rule in the Massachusetts Rules of Domestic Relations Procedure, it shall mean the rule in the Massachusetts Rules of Civil Procedure or in the Massachusetts Rules of Domestic Relations Procedure as it may be amended from time to time.

Amended December 14, 2011, effective January 2, 2012.

Reporter's Notes–2012

The Court's name is corrected.

Rule 2.   Appearances

In all cases not governed by the Mass.R.Dom.Rel.P., appearances and pleadings shall be governed by Mass.R.Civ.P. 11.

If the person appearing is an attorney-at-law, the written appearance shall also include the person's Board of Bar Overseers number.

Except for joint petitions for divorce, petitions for grandparent visitation and joint petitions for modification of child support, no appearance in a case commenced by petition shall be filed after 10:00 a.m. on the return day except by leave of court or in substitution or addition of attorneys.

An appearance may specify that it is not an objection to the petition, and such an appearance may be filed after 10:00 a.m. on the return day without leave of court.

Amended December 14, 2011, effective January 2, 2012.

Reporter's Notes–2012

Appearances are generally covered by Mass.R.Civ.P. 11. Not covered by Rule 11 is an appearance after 10:00 a.m. on return days of citations, which is added to this rule.

Rule 2A.   [Repealed]

Repealed effective January 2, 1987.

Rule 3.   Giving Service of Notice

In all cases not governed by the Mass.R.Dom.Rel.P., service and filing of pleadings and other papers shall be governed by Mass.R.Civ.P. 5. Wherever the word "complaint" appears in said rule, it shall also mean, where applicable, "petition."

When notice of a petition has been given by service of a citation, notice of any pleading asserting new or additional claims for relief not asserted in the original petition shall be given by service of a new citation.

Amended December 14, 2011, effective January 2, 2012.

Reporter's Notes–2012

Rule 5 of the Mass.R.Civ.P. sufficiently addresses the topic, so there is no need for a different rule.

Rule 4.   Copies to Adverse Parties [Repealed]

Repealed December 14, 2011, effective January 2, 2012.

Reporter's Notes–2012

Answers to interrogatories are no longer to be filed, see Mass. R.Civ.P. 5(d)(2) and Mass.R.Dom.Rel.P. 5(d)(2). Mass.R.Dom.Rel.P. 5 and Mass.R.Civ.P. 5, made applicable by Rule 3 of these rules, cover this, so a separate rule is unnecessary.

Rule 5.   Guardians Ad Litem

In addition to making appointments of guardians ad litem in cases required by statute, whenever it shall appear that a minor, intellectually disabled person, a person under disability, an incapacitated person, a person to be protected or a person not ascertained or not in being is interested in any matter pending, a guardian ad litem for said person may be appointed by the court at its discretion. No Judge of the Probate and Family Court shall be appointed a guardian ad litem.

Amended June 24, 2009, effective July 1, 2009; amended December 14, 2011, effective January 2, 2012.

Reporter's Notes–2012

The requirement of waiting until the return day to make an appointment is eliminated. This rule supplements MUPC § 1–404 which calls for appointment of such a GAL "upon the representation of any party . . ., or of any person interested," but not on the sole initiative of the judge.

Rule 6.   Citations: Return Days; Service; Publication

A.   Return Days. All citations shall be made returnable not later than three months after the date of such citation except as otherwise provided by statute. Every day when a court session is scheduled in the city or town where the registry is located shall be a return day for probate citations. A return day is not a hearing date, but a date by which an interested person must file his or her appearance to contest a probate proceeding.

B.   Extension of the Return Day. There shall be only one return day outstanding, and no return day shall be changed or extended before the return day unless it is certified in writing by the party or his or her attorney that no service has been made on the original citation. Notwithstanding the foregoing, if counsel is appointed to represent an alleged incapacitated person, incapacitated person, person to be protected, protected person, minor or ward at any point prior to the entry of a decree on the petition, the court may provide a separate date by which said counsel may file an appearance and objection.

C.   Service within the Commonwealth. Except where otherwise required by statute or ordered by the court, service of a citation within the Commonwealth shall be given by delivering in hand or by mailing by certified, registered or ordinary first class mail at least fourteen (14) days before the return day.

D.   Service outside the Commonwealth. Except where otherwise required by statute or ordered by the court, if it shall appear from the petition that there is anyone interested who is outside the Commonwealth in any part of the United

States, its Commonwealths or territories, service of the citation shall be given by delivering in hand or by mailing by certified, registered or ordinary first class mail at least fourteen (14) days before the return day; if in other parts, one (1) month.

E. Service When Whereabouts Unknown. Except where otherwise required by statute or ordered by the court, if it shall appear from the petition that there is anyone interested who is of parts unknown, service of the citation shall be given by delivery or mailing to the last known address at least one (1) month before the return day.

F. Service by Publication. Except where otherwise required by statute or ordered by the court, and in addition to the service requirements above, publication shall be required if any interested person's whereabouts, address or identity is unknown. Publication shall also be required in all formal testacy and appointment proceedings. A copy of the citation shall be published once in a newspaper designated by the register of probate having general circulation in the county where the proceeding is pending at least seven (7) days before the return date.

Amended December 15, 1986, effective January 2, 1987; amended June 24, 2009, effective July 1, 2009; amended December 14, 2011, effective January 2, 2012.

Reporter's Notes–2012

The rule was amended as a result of the enactment of the Massachusetts Uniform Probate Code, G.L. c. 190B and clarifies service within and without the Commonwealth as well as when publication is required.

Rule 7. Amendments

In all cases not governed by the Mass.R.Dom.Rel.P., amended and supplemental pleadings shall be governed by Mass. R.Civ.P. 15. In all cases commenced by petition, except for joint petitions for divorce, petitions for grandparent visitation and joint petitions for modification of child support, a "responsive pleading" shall include an appearance filed before 10:00 a.m. on the return day.

Amended December 14, 2011, effective January 2, 2012.

Reporter's Notes–2012

Mass.R.Civ.P. 15 already addresses this issue. A different rule is not needed.

Rule 7A. Time

In cases not governed by the Mass.R.Dom.Rel.P., the time for acts to be performed shall be governed by Mass.R.Civ.P. 6.

Adopted December 14, 2011, effective January 2, 2012.

Reporter's Notes–2012

This rule replaces the second paragraph of the former Probate Court Rule 7.

Rule 8. Further Notice

If a notice, given in accordance with the forms approved as provided by General Laws Chapter 215, Section 30, General Laws Chapter 217, Section 8, or otherwise provided by these

rules, is held by the judge to be insufficient, the judge may order such further notice as the case requires.

Amended December 14, 2011, effective January 2, 2012.

Reporter's Notes–2012

Language from the otherwise identical Rule 102 of the Supplemental Probate Court Rules is added. Rule 102 of the Supplemental Probate Court Rules is now repealed.

Rule 9. Depositions and Commissions [Repealed]

Repealed December 14, 2011, effective January 2, 2012.

Reporter's Notes–2012

The subject matter of this rule is covered by Mass.R.Civ.P. 28. and made applicable under Rule 27A of these rules.

Rule 10. Depositions, Manner of Taking [Repealed]

Repealed December 14, 2011, effective January 2, 2012.

Reporter's Notes–2012

See Rule 27A. Rule 27A of these rules made this obsolete in 2000.

Rule 11. Depositions, Filing and Use [Repealed]

Repealed December 14, 2011, effective January 2, 2012.

Reporter's Notes–2012

Rule 27A of these rules makes this obsolete, Mass.R.Civ.P. 5(d)(2) contradicts the rule and states that "[u]nless the court ... shall otherwise order, the following shall not be presented or accepted for filing: notices of taking depositions, transcripts of depositions, interrogatories ..."

Rule 12. Depositions of Witnesses to Will [Repealed]

Repealed December 14, 2011, effective January 2, 2012.

Reporter's Notes–2012

See discovery under Rule 27A of these rules in a case for probate of a will.

Rule 13. Examination of Witnesses

In cases not governed by the Mass.R.Dom.Rel.P., the examination of witnesses shall be governed by Mass.R.Civ.P. 43(g).

Amended December 14, 2011, effective January 2, 2012.

Reporter's Notes–2012

Mass.R.Dom.Rel.P. 43(g) and Mass.R.Civ.P. 43(g) are identical to the present Rule 13, with the addition of the words "unless the court otherwise permits."

Rule 14. Writ of Protection

A writ of protection shall issue only upon the application of the person for whom such writ is to be issued, or some person in his behalf, and upon order of the court, and then only if it is made to appear to the court, by affidavit and any other evidence that the court may require, (1) that the application is made in good faith and for the purpose of enabling such person to attend this court as a party or witness in some specified proceeding pending, (2) if such person is a party, that such proceeding has not been brought collusively to enable him to obtain a writ of protection, and (3) if such person is a witness, that he has not been required to attend as a witness by his own request or procurement, to enable him to obtain a writ of protection.

Amended December 14, 2011, effective January 2, 2012.

Rule 15. Interlocutory Hearings

The court may hear motions and other interlocutory matters in chambers or in open court at such times, and upon such notice as may be otherwise required by law provided the proceedings are recorded as required by Rule 201.

Amended January 24, 1978, effective February 21, 1978; amended December 14, 2011, effective January 2, 2012.

Reporter's Notes–2012

Requirement for recording of the proceedings is added.

Rule 16. Will Contests

Neither the filing nor hearing of a motion to strike objections is a prerequisite to the filing or hearing of a motion for summary judgment.

Amended December 15, 1986, effective January 2, 1987; amended December 14, 2011, effective January 2, 2012.

Reporter's Notes–2012

The MUPC, at G. L. c. 190B, § 1–401(e)–(f), makes the original Rule 16 unnecessary. The remaining language is added in response to *O'Rourke* v. *Hunter* decided by the SJC on May 31, 2006.

Rule 17. Foreign Law

In cases not governed by the Mass.R.Dom.Rel.P., the determination of foreign law shall be governed by Mass.R.Civ.P. 44.1. In addition, it shall be the duty of counsel to call to the attention of the court such authorities or other material relating to the question as they wish the court to consider.

Amended December 14, 2011, effective January 2, 2012.

Reporter's Notes–2012

The provisions of Mass.R.Civ.P. 44.1 (which is identical to Mass.R.Dom.Rel.P. 44.1) are added to the existing rule.

Rule 18. Appointment of Stenographers

Request for the appointment of a stenographer to take the testimony at a trial for the purpose of reporting the testimony on appeal to the Appeals Court or the Supreme Judicial Court shall be given to the register in writing not later than forty-eight hours before trial. If trial is cancelled at the request of either party, cost of the stenographer may be assessed by the presiding judge unless twenty-four hours notice in writing is given to the register to cancel the request for the stenographer.

Amended December 14, 2011, effective January 2, 2012.

Reporter's Notes–2012

The rule is updated now that we have an Appeals Court.

Rule 19. Report of Evidence

Upon an appeal, where the court under General Laws Chapter 215, Section 18, has appointed a stenographer to take the evidence to be reported to the Appeals Court or the Supreme Judicial Court, the appellant, unless he files with the appeal a disclaimer of any right to rely upon the transcript of the evidence, shall, within sixty days of the date of the appeal, file with the register for the use of the court and for use in the preparation of the record on appeal one certified transcript of the stenographic notes taken by the stenographer. The court, at any time, may extend the time for filing the transcript. The transcript shall be subject to the right of the court, before copies thereof are prepared for the use of the Appeals Court or the Supreme Judicial Court, to direct that the transcript be submitted to it for such correction as it may direct after hearing.

When decree or judgment after rescript has been entered or after dismissal of appeal, the register shall notify the persons supplying the transcript to call for the same within ten days, and, if not so called for, the transcript may be destroyed.

Amended December 14, 2011, effective January 2, 2012.

Reporter's Notes–2012

The rule is updated now that we have an Appeals Court.

Rule 20. Appointment and Compensation of Masters

In all cases not governed by the Mass.R.Dom.Rel.P., appointment and compensation of masters shall be governed by Mass.R.Civ.P. 53(a) and (c) and SJC Rule 1:07.

Amended July 31, 1978, effective November 16, 1978; amended effective July 1, 1985; amended December 14, 2011, effective January 2, 2012.

Reporter's Notes–2012

Eliminates reference to court appointed auditors, assessors or arbitrators, which no longer exist. The rule is changed to be consistent with the Probate and Family Court Department's SJC Rule 1:07 procedures which permit an attorney to be on the list for Master appointments in up to four divisions at once.

The rule is also changed to reflect the usual practice by which the parties pay a discovery master at an hourly rate that has not been approved by a judge, and the master may re-allocate the payments if one party runs up the costs.

Rule 21. Hearings Before Masters

In all cases not governed by the Mass.R.Dom.Rel.P., hearings before masters shall be governed by Mass.R.Civ.P. 53.

Amended December 14, 2011, effective January 2, 2012.

Reporter's Notes–2012

Eliminates reference to court appointed auditors, assessors or arbitrators, which no longer exist.

Rule 22. Auditors Whose Findings of Fact Are Not Final [Repealed]

Repealed December 14, 2011, effective January 2, 2012.

Reporter's Notes–2012
There are no longer auditors appointed by the court.

Rule 23. Auditors Whose Findings of Fact Are Final [Repealed]

Repealed December 14, 2011, effective January 2, 2012.

Reporter's Notes–2012
There are no longer auditors appointed by the court.

Rule 24. Masters

In all cases not governed by the Mass.R.Dom.Rel.P., proceedings involving masters shall be governed by Mass.R.Civ.P. 53.

Amended December 14, 2011, effective January 2, 2012.

Reporter's Notes–2012
Applies Mass.R.Civ.P. 53 and Mass.R.Dom.Rel.P. 53.

Rule 25. Recording of Papers

The Registers of Probate shall record the following documents:

Wills—when allowed

Agreement to Compromise Will

All licenses to Sell Real Estate: (Where no License Issues Record Decree)

Leave to Mortgage—Decree

Sale—Mortgage of Real Estate—Subject to Remainder—Decree

Partition cases—Warrant—Report—Decree only

Affidavits—re: Sales—if Public Auction

Adoption—Decree (To be recorded in Special Adoption Volume)

Change of Name—Decree (On petition to Change Name only)

Trusts Inter Vivos—Unless Recorded in another Registry

Waiver of Will

It is suggested that docket entries be made in regard to the following:

Total of Schedules in Account

Divorce and Separate Support Judgments

Modification Judgments

Custody Decrees and Judgments

All Orders for Execution

The register shall, however, record on request of any person in interest at such person's cost, to be estimated by the register and paid in advance within a designated time, any paper or instrument not herein required to be recorded relating to any probate proceeding on file in the registry, but not

including interrogatories, depositions and similar discovery matters, and papers impounded by order of the court.

Amended December 14, 2011, effective January 2, 2012.

Reporter's Notes–2012
Reference to dower or curtesy have been removed. Updates decree to judgment where appropriate.

G.L. c. 215, § 36, appears to require a rule which instructs the Registers which papers to scan. The statute provides that:

"The registers shall record in books kept therefor such judgments, decrees, orders and other proceedings in said courts and such instruments, as shall be determined by rules made from time to time under section thirty, by entering the same upon the pages thereof in fair and legible handwriting, printing, typewriting, or by photographic process, or by any combination of any two or more of such methods. They may also direct the recording of any judgments, decrees, orders, instruments and other proceedings in their offices, irrespective of the time when such judgments, decrees, orders, instruments or other proceedings were made, received or held, by means of microphotography or other similar photographic process, and, in such case need not maintain books for such records, but shall provide such filing equipment therefor as they deem proper, the cost of which shall be paid by the county. When such recording is by photographic process, registers shall keep an alphabetical index thereof, or other appropriate description of and reference to the film upon which such recording may be found."

Rule 26. Exhibits

Exhibits which are placed in the custody of the register shall be retained by him for one year after the trial or hearing at which they were used, unless sooner delivered to the parties or counsel to whom they respectively belong or by whom they were respectively presented or introduced. If in doubt as to the party or counsel entitled to delivery, the register may require an agreement of parties or counsel or order of the court, before delivery. The register may destroy or discard such exhibits, but not earlier than thirty days after notice by him to the party presenting or introducing such exhibits, requesting him to remove them, nor earlier than one year after such trial or hearing.

Amended December 14, 2011, effective January 2, 2012.

Rule 27. [Repealed]

Repealed effective January 1, 2000.

Rule 27A. Depositions and Discovery

In all cases not governed by the Mass.R.Dom.Rel.P., depositions and discovery shall be governed by Rules 26 through 37 of the Mass.R.Civ.P.

Adopted October 27, 1999, effective January 1, 2000; amended December 14, 2011, effective January 2, 2012.

Reporter's Notes—2000
The adoption of rule 27A works a major change in probate discovery practice. Formerly, the discovery rules of the Massachusetts Rules of Civil Procedure were only applicable to probate accounts. Other contested probate proceedings required prior court approval for obtaining discovery which is clearly inconsistent with modern civil discovery rules. Now depositions and discovery in all probate matters shall be governed by the Massachusetts Rules of Civil Procedure.

Reporter's Notes–2012

Added clarification that the Mass.R.Civ.P. do not override the Mass.R.Dom.Rel.P.

Rule 27B. Summary Judgment

In all cases not governed by the Mass.R.Dom.Rel.P., summary judgment may be granted in accordance with the provisions of Rule 56 of the Mass.R.Civ.P.

Adopted October 27, 1999, effective January 1, 2000; amended December 14, 2011, effective January 2, 2012.

Reporter's Notes—2000

Rule 27B makes summary judgment under Rule 56 of the Massachusetts Rules of Civil Procedure available in probate proceedings.

Reporter's Notes–2012

Reference to Mass.R.Dom.Rel.P. added as summary judgment in those cases is limited to modifications.

Rule 27C. Summary Judgment Procedure

(a) Form of Motions for Summary Judgment and Oppositions Thereto.

(1) *Motions.* A moving party shall serve with the motion for summary judgment a separate memorandum stating the reasons, including supporting authorities, why the motion should be granted. Affidavits and other documents setting forth or offering evidence of facts on which the motion is based shall be served with the motion.

(2) *Oppositions to Motions.* A party opposing a motion for summary judgment may serve a memorandum in opposition. The memorandum in opposition may include a statement of reasons, with supporting authorities, why the motion should not be allowed and may include a request for a hearing. Affidavits and other documents setting forth or offering evidence of facts on which the opposition is based shall be served with the memorandum in opposition.

(3) *Reply and Sur-reply Memoranda.* A reply memorandum may be filed only with leave of court. Such leave must be sought within 5 days of service of a memorandum in opposition. A reply memorandum shall be limited to addressing matters raised in the opposition that were not and could not reasonably have been addressed in the moving party's initial memorandum. In view of the limitations upon a reply memorandum, a sur-reply is strongly disfavored and may not be filed without leave of court sought within 5 days of service of the reply. To request leave of court, a party shall file and serve a motion setting forth the grounds to support the request and shall have the motion scheduled for hearing. If the motion is allowed granting leave, the requesting party shall serve notice of the grant of leave with its reply memorandum or sur-reply.

(4) *Facts Verified by Affidavit.* The court need not consider any motion for summary judgment or opposition thereto unless the facts are verified by affidavit, are apparent upon the record, or are agreed to in writing, signed by interested parties or their counsel.

(5) *Format and Length.* All motions, memoranda of law and other papers, except for exhibits, filed pursuant to this rule shall be filed on 8 ½″ by 11″ paper and, except for exhibits, shall be typed in no less than 12–point type and double-spaced, provided that the title of the case, footnotes and quotations may be single spaced. The title of each document shall appear on the first page thereof. Unless leave of court has been obtained in advance by motion with notice, all memoranda of law and the oppositions thereto shall not exceed 20 pages, and any reply memoranda shall not exceed 10 pages. Any document package permitted by paragraph b(2) of this rule shall not be included in the page limit. To request leave of court, a party shall file and serve a motion stating the number of pages the party desires, and why the party's objective cannot be achieved within the applicable page limit. The party shall have the motion scheduled for hearing. Any leave of court obtained by a moving party shall apply to all opposing parties. The moving party shall serve notice of the grant of leave of court with the moving party's memorandum.

(6) *Email Addresses.* Each party or attorney filing a motion for summary judgment or opposition papers shall include his or her email address on the papers, unless he or she does not have an email address.

(b) Procedure for Serving and Filing Motions for Summary Judgment.

(1) *General.* All motions for summary judgment and oppositions shall be served on all parties and filed with the register in accordance with the procedure set forth in this paragraph (b). Compliance with this paragraph is compliance with the "reasonable time" provisions of the first sentence of Mass. R. Civ. P. 5(d)(1) or Mass. R. Dom. Rel. P. 5(d)(1).

(2) *Service and Filing of Motions for Summary Judgment and Oppositions.* The moving party shall serve a copy of the motion and the other documents specified by this rule on every other party. Every opposing party shall serve on the moving party an original and a copy, and on every other party a copy, of the opposition and the other documents specified by this rule. The opposition to a motion shall be served within (A) 21 days after service of a motion for summary judgment or (B) such additional time as is allowed by statute or order of the court. Upon receipt of the opposition and associated documents, if any, the moving party shall attach the original of the opposition and associated documents to the original motion and associated documents and within 10 days shall file with the register the combined documents ("the document package"), unless within the same 10–day period the moving party notifies all counsel that the motion has been withdrawn. If leave to file a reply memorandum is allowed, the reply shall be served and filed within 10 days of the allowance, unless the court orders otherwise. If leave to file a reply has been allowed, or, if a motion to strike has been served in response to the opposition to a motion or a cross-motion, the period for filing the document package is extended to the time granted for serving the reply or the opposition to the motion to strike. If the party opposing a summary judgment motion serves an additional statement of material facts under paragraph (b)(5)(iv), the moving party shall have 21 days to file the document package or to notify all counsel that the motion has been withdrawn. If the moving party does not receive an opposition within 3 business days after expiration of the time permitted for service of an opposition, then the moving party shall file with the register the motion and other documents initially served on the other parties with an affidavit reciting

compliance with this rule and receipt of no opposition in timely fashion, unless the moving party has notified all parties that the motion has been withdrawn. The moving party shall give prompt notice of the filing of the document package to all other parties by serving thereon a copy of a certificate of notice of filing on a separate document. A separate document accompanying the filing shall list the title of each document in the document package.

(3) *Cross–Motions.* A cross-motion for summary judgment, accompanied by the other documents specified in paragraph (a)(1) of this rule, shall be served on the moving party with the opposition to the original motion. A party opposing a cross-motion may serve a memorandum in opposition within (A) 21 days after service of a cross-motion for summary judgment or (B) such additional time as is allowed by statute or order of the court.

(4) *Motions to Strike.*

(i) A motion to strike brought in response to a motion for summary judgment shall be served along with the opposition to the original motion. An opposition to the motion to strike shall be served within 10 days of service of the motion to strike. The motion to strike and the opposition thereto shall be filed with the document package relating to the original motion in the manner specified in Paragraph (b)(2) of this rule.

(ii) A motion to strike brought in response to the opposition to the original motion shall be served within 10 days of service of the opposition. An opposition to the motion to strike shall be served within 10 days of service of the motion to strike. The motion to strike and the opposition thereto shall be filed with the document package relating to the original motion in the manner specified in paragraph (b)(2) of this rule. Compliance with the times for service contained herein shall extend the time for filing prescribed in paragraph (b)(2) of this rule.

(iii) A motion to strike brought in response to a cross-motion shall be served along with the opposition to the cross-motion. An opposition to the motion to strike shall be served within 10 days of service of the motion to strike. The motion to strike and the opposition thereto shall be filed with the document package relating to the original motion and the cross-motion in the manner specified in paragraph (b)(2) of this rule. Compliance with the times for service contained herein shall extend the time for filing prescribed in paragraph (b)(2) of this rule.

(5) *Statement of Material Facts and Response.*

(i) A motion for summary judgment shall be accompanied by a statement of the material facts as to which the moving party contends there is no genuine issue to be tried, set forth in consecutively numbered paragraphs, with page or paragraph references to supporting pleadings, depositions, answers to interrogatories, responses to requests for admission, affidavits, or other evidentiary documents. Failure to include the foregoing statement shall constitute grounds for denial of the motion. In addition to the service specified in Paragraph (b)(2) of this rule, the statement of material facts shall be *contemporaneously* sent in electronic form by email to all parties against whom summary judgment is sought in order to facilitate the requirements of the following para-

graph. The statement of material facts in electronic form shall be sent as an attachment to an email and shall be in Rich Text Format (RTF) unless the parties agree to use another word processing format. The requirement to email the statement of material facts to the opposing party does not alter the date or method of service, which continues to be governed by Mass. R. Civ. P. 5(b) or Mass. R. Dom. Rel. P. 5(b). The requirement for transmission by email of the statement of material facts in electronic form shall be excused if (A) the moving or any opposing party is appearing *pro se,* (B) the attorney for the moving party certifies in an affidavit that he or she does not have access to email, or (C) the attorney for the moving party certifies in an affidavit that an opposing party's attorney has no email address or has not disclosed his or her email address.

(ii) An opposition to a motion for summary judgment shall include a response to the moving party's statement of facts as to which the moving party claims there is no genuine issue to be tried. To permit the court to have in hand a single document containing the parties' positions as to material facts in easily comprehensible form, in preparing this response the opposing party shall reprint the moving party's statement of material facts and shall set forth a response to each directly below the appropriate numbered paragraph. Where the obligation to send the statement of material facts in electronic form has been excused, the response to the statement of material facts may be in a separate document. For purposes of summary judgment, the moving party's statement of a material fact shall be deemed to have been admitted unless controverted as set forth in this paragraph.

(iii) Neither the statement of material facts as to which there is no genuine issue to be tried nor the response thereto shall be subject to the 20–page limitation in paragraph (a) (5) of this rule.

(iv) An opposing party, with the response to the moving party's statement of facts, may assert an additional statement of material facts with respect to the claims on which the moving party seeks summary judgment, each to be supported with page or paragraph references to supporting pleadings, depositions, answers to interrogatories, responses to requests for admission, affidavits, or other evidentiary documents. Such an additional statement shall be a continuation of the opposing party's response described in paragraph (b)(5)(ii), with an appropriate heading, and shall not be a separate document. In addition to the service specified in paragraph (b)(2) of this rule, where the party opposing summary judgment includes such an additional statement in its response, the response, including the additional statement, also shall be sent in electronic form by email to the moving party, unless excused as provided in paragraph (b)(5)(I). The moving party shall respond to the opposing party's additional statement of material facts within the time prescribed by paragraph (b)(2)(A), resulting in a single document for the court's consideration, unless the obligation to send the additional statement of material facts in electronic form has been excused. For purposes of summary judgment, the opposing party's additional statement of a material fact shall be deemed to have been admitted unless controverted as set forth in this paragraph.

(v) Cross-motions for summary judgment and oppositions thereto shall comply with the requirements of paragraph (b)(5), with the result that there shall be a single consolidated document containing the respective statements of material facts and responses thereto, unless excused as provided in paragraph (b)(5)(I).

(vi) All exhibits referred to in a motion, a cross-motion, or opposition thereto shall be filed as a joint appendix, which shall include an index of the exhibits. The initial moving party, with the cooperation of each opposing party, shall be responsible for assembling the joint appendix and the index. Unless all the pages of the joint appendix are consecutively numbered, each exhibit shall be separated by an off-set tab divider. Where such dividers are used, the exhibits in the joint appendix shall be numbered consecutively. The moving party shall serve a copy of its exhibits to each opposing party with the motion. If a party opposing the initial motion designates additional exhibits, the additional exhibits shall begin with the next consecutive designation following the last designation by the initial moving party. Where an opposing party relies upon any evidence contained in the exhibits supporting the motion for summary judgment, the opposing party in its memorandum shall cite to that evidence using the form of designation of the moving party. Where the opposing party relies upon evidence not contained in such exhibits, the opposing party shall treat such additional evidence as new exhibits. Such new exhibits, as well as an index of the new exhibits, shall be served with the opposition. The initial moving party shall certify that the joint appendix includes all exhibits served upon the initial moving party with the opposition to the summary judgment motion. If the initial moving party does not receive with the opposition an exhibit designated by the opposing party, then the moving party shall file with the register the joint appendix of exhibits without that designated exhibit, with the certification required by this rule. The burden will then rest with the opposing party to move to file any designated exhibit not timely submitted.

(vii) The initial moving party, upon filing a motion for summary judgment, shall serve upon the opposing parties, in paper and electronic form, unless electronic form is excused, the consolidated statement of material facts and responses filed with the register, unless the response is filed as a separate document in accordance with this rule. The moving party shall also serve upon the opposing parties the joint appendix of exhibits, including the index of the exhibits, filed with the register, unless the parties otherwise agree. If the joint appendix of exhibits, including the index, is in electronic form, an electronic copy shall also be sent, unless the parties otherwise agree.

(6) *Sanctions for Noncompliance.* The court need not consider any motion for summary judgment or opposition that fails to comply with the requirements of this rule.

(7) *Applicability.* This rule applies to all actions in the Probate and Family Court in which motions for summary judgment are permitted.

(8) *Hearing.* It is the responsibility of the moving party to obtain a hearing date for the motion for summary judgment and any cross motions.

Adopted April 1, 2009, effective May 1, 2009; amended December 14, 2011, effective January 2, 2012.

Reporter's Notes—2009

The adoption of this new Rule specifies the mandatory format to be used for supporting documents in summary judgment proceedings in the Probate and Family Court.

Reporter's Notes–2012

The language of Rule 27C, for summary judgment motions, is now consistent with the most recent version of Superior Court Rule 9A.

Rule 28. Signatures to Pleadings

In all cases not governed by the Mass.R.Dom.Rel.P., any matter that is not required to be signed under oath or under penalties of perjury by the petitioner or an interested party may be signed by counsel of record, and Mass.R.Civ.P. 11(a) shall apply to such signings.

Returns of service and military affidavits may be signed by counsel of record, and Mass.R.Civ.P. 11(a) shall apply to such signings.

Amended December 14, 2011, effective January 2, 2012.

Reporter's Notes–2012

Makes Rule 11 certification applicable. Mass.R.Civ.P. 11 is worded differently from, but essentially makes the same provision as the MUPC at G.L. c. 190B, § 1–310.

Rule 28A. Certificates of Service

The last page of every paper served in accordance with Mass.R.Civ.P. 5(a) or Mass.R.Dom.Rel.P. 5(a) shall contain a brief statement showing the date on which and manner in which service of the paper was made on each other party, with the name and address of each person served. The statement may be in the following form:

I hereby certify under the penalties of perjury that a true copy of the above document was served upon the following people at the following addresses by mail (by hand) on (date): (Names and addresses), (Signature).

Adopted December 14, 2011, effective January 2, 2012.

Reporter's Notes–2012

Although most attorneys include a certificate of service with each motion or other paper served, neither the Mass.R.Civ.P. nor the Mass.R.Dom.Rel.P. require one unless service is challenged. This proposed rule is similar to Superior Court Rule 9B and so should already be familiar to most attorneys.

Rule 29. Service and Giving of Notice

In all cases not governed by the Mass.R.Dom.Rel.P., time for service and giving of notice shall be governed by Mass. R.Civ.P. 5 and 6. Wherever the word "complaint" appears in said rule, it shall also mean, where applicable, "petition."

Amended January 16, 1979, effective February 12, 1979; amended December 14, 2011, effective January 2, 2012.

Reporter's Notes–2012

The subject of this Rule is covered in Mass.R.Civ.P. 5 and 6. They eliminate the need for a written certificate of service or affidavit of notice unless service or notice is questioned. But see proposed new Rule 28A which will require a certificate of service.

Rule 29A. Probate Accounts [Repealed]

Repealed December 14, 2011, effective January 2, 2012.

Reporter's Notes–2012

This rule is repealed with changes recommended by the MUPC working group and renumbered as Rule 72A.

Rule 29B. Temporary Conservatorships and Guardianships

Written notice of a hearing on a petition for a temporary conservatorship or guardianship shall be given at least seven (7) days in advance of said hearing, as follows:

(1) Temporary Guardianship of a Minor.

a. To the minor, if he is fourteen or more years of age; and

b. To all persons named in said petition.

(2) Temporary Guardianship of an Incapacitated Person and Temporary Conservatorship.

a. To the person alleged to be incapacitated or the person to be protected and his or her spouse and children, or, if none, parents, brothers and sisters, or, if none, heirs apparent or presumptive;

b. To any person who is serving as guardian, conservator, or who has the care or custody of the person or with whom the person has resided during the sixty (60) days (exclusive of any period of hospitalization or institutionalization) preceding the filing of the petition;

c. In case no other person is notified under paragraph (a), to at least one of the nearest adult relatives, if any can be found;

d. To all other persons named in the petition;

e. If the person is alleged to be intellectually disabled, to the Department of Developmental Services;

f. To the United States Veteran's Administration or its successor, if the person is entitled to any benefit, estate or income paid or payable by or through said Administration or its successor; and

g. To any other person as directed by the court.

Notice shall be given to the respondent in hand and to all other interested persons by delivery or mail.

No extension of a temporary appointment of a conservator will be allowed unless an inventory and bond of the temporary fiduciary has been filed.

Amended effective February 1, 1982; amended June 24, 2009, effective July 1, 2009; amended December 14, 2011, effective January 2, 2012.

Rule 29C. Uniform Forms

The Chief Justice of the Probate and Family Court shall prescribe and promulgate uniform probate and domestic relations forms, and shall designate the specifications under which such forms may be printed or computer generated.

Amended December 14, 2011, effective January 2, 2012.

Reporter's Notes–2012

The language of the rule is updated.

Rule 29D. Notice Regarding Appointment of Counsel

A) In all guardianship of an incapacitated person and in all conservatorship matters, all notices and all citations shall include the following language in the following format:

IMPORTANT NOTICE

The outcome of this proceeding may limit or completely take away the above—named person's right to make decisions about personal affairs or financial affairs or both. The above—named person has the right to ask for a lawyer. Anyone may make this request on behalf of the above—named person. If the above—named person cannot afford a lawyer, one may be appointed at State expense.

B) In all other guardianship of minor matters, all notices and all citations shall include the following language in the following format:

IMPORTANT NOTICE

The minor or another person on his or her behalf may ask for a lawyer for the minor. If the minor cannot afford a lawyer, one may be appointed at State expense.

Adopted June 24, 2009, effective July 1, 2009; amended December 14, 2011, effective January 2, 2012.

Rule 30. Dismissal of Abandoned Appeals

If the appellant has failed to (i) file the transcript of the proceedings or the designated portions thereof or the statement of certification within the time required by Rule 8(b)(1) and Rule 9(d)) of the Massachusetts Rules of Appellate Procedure (unless such time shall previously have been enlarged as permitted by Rule 10(c)); (ii) docket the appeal within the time required by Rule 10(a)(1) of the Massachusetts Rules of Appellate Procedure (unless such time shall previously have been enlarged or the late docketing allowed as permitted by Rule 10(a)(3)); or (iii) failed to file the transcript of the proceedings or the designated portion thereof within six (6) months of filing the statement of certification, the register shall send written notice by first class mail that the appeal will be dismissed for lack of prosecution to the attorney of record for each party, or to the party at his last known address if he is not represented by an attorney. A copy of this rule shall accompany said written notice. The sending of every notice required by this rule shall be noted on the docket.

Fourteen (14) days after the date of such notice, the register shall forthwith dismiss such appeal for lack of prosecution and shall note said dismissal on the docket, unless the register receives a) a motion to enlarge to a date certain set forth therein the time for complying with this rule and the requirements of said Rule 8(b)(1) and Rule 9(d) and/or Rule 10(a)(1) or (3) which has been marked for hearing and b) an affidavit of the movant which shall set forth all the facts which such movant wishes to have considered by the court which will act on such motion in accordance with the provisions of this rule and Rule 10(c).

Adopted July 18, 1988, effective August 1, 1988; amended October 27, 1999, effective January 1, 2000; amended December 14, 2011, effective January 2, 2012; amended October 4, 2019, effective November 1, 2019.

Reporter's Notes—2000

Rule 30 was amended to facilitate the dismissal of abandoned appeals. Pursuant to Rule 9(c)(2) of the Massachusetts Rules of Appellate Procedure, the appellant in a civil case shall deliver to the clerk of the lower court either a transcript of those portions of the transcript of the lower court proceedings which the appellant deems necessary for determination of the appeal or a signed statement certifying that the appellant has ordered such portions from the court reporter. Upon receiving the transcript, the appellant is to deliver it forthwith to the clerk of the lower court.

Under the prior version of rule 30, the appeal could not be dismissed for lack of prosecution if the appellant filed a signed statement certifying that they have ordered the transcript, despite the fact that the transcript is never produced. With the amended version of rule 30, if the appellant fails to file the transcript within six (6) months of filing the statement of certification, the appeal shall be dismissed.

Another problem with the prior version of the rule is that it allowed the appellant to stop the dismissal by filing a motion to enlarge. However, the rule required no further action on the motion. The amendment to rule 30 requires that the motion to enlarge be marked for hearing.

Rule 30 was also amended to reference Massachusetts Rule of Appellate Procedure 8(b)(3) in addition to rule 9(c) in order to include electronically recorded proceedings.

Reporter's Notes—2019

Rule 30 was amended to correct the prior reference to Rule 8(b)(3) of the Massachusetts Rules of Appellate Procedure to state now Rule 8(b)(1), and the prior reference to Rule 9(c) of the Massachusetts Rules of Appellate Procedure to state now Rule 9(d), as a result of amendments to the Massachusetts Rules of Appellate Procedure effective March 1, 2019.

Rule 31.   Pre–Trial Procedure

In all cases not governed by the Mass.R.Dom.Rel.P., pretrial procedure shall be governed by Mass.R.Civ.P. 16.

Adopted December 14, 2011, effective January 2, 2012.

Reporter's Notes–2012

Establishes a rule calling for pre-trial conferences in probate and other matters commenced by petition. Pre-trial conferences are now required by the standing order establishing Time Standards.

Rule 40.   Assignment of Cases for Trial: Continuances

In all cases not governed by the Mass.R.Dom.Rel.P., assignment of cases for trial and granting of continuances shall be governed by Mass.R.Civ.P. 40.

Adopted December 14, 2011, effective January 2, 2012.

Reporter's Notes–2012

Establishes a continuance rule for probate cases. Mass.R.Civ.P. 40 and Mass.R.Dom.Rel.P. 40 are identical.

Rule 43.   Evidence

In all cases not governed by the Mass.R.Dom.Rel.P., taking of evidence shall be governed by Mass.R.Civ.P. 43. A judge may, in the judge's discretion, take evidence at a place other than a courthouse.

Adopted December 14, 2011, effective January 2, 2012.

Reporter's Notes–2012

Cases heard in hospitals, for example, require the exception, which also appears in Mass.R.Dom.Rel.P. 43.

Rule 44.   Proof of Official Records

In all cases not governed by the Mass.R.Dom.Rel.P., proof of official records shall be governed by Mass.R.Civ.P. 44.

Adopted December 14, 2011, effective January 2, 2012.

Reporter's Notes–2012

Mass.R.Civ.P. 44 and Mass.R.Dom.Rel.P. 44 are identical.

Rule 45.   Subpoena

In all cases not governed by the Mass.R.Dom.Rel.P., subpoenas shall be governed by Mass.R.Civ.P.45.

Adopted December 14, 2011, effective January 2, 2012.

Reporter's Notes–2012

Mass.R.Civ.P. 45 and Mass.R.Dom.Rel.P. 45 are identical.

Rule 46.   Exceptions Unnecessary

In all cases not governed by the Mass.R.Dom.Rel.P., exceptions shall be unnecessary as provided in Mass.R.Civ.P. 46.

Adopted December 14, 2011, effective January 2, 2012.

Reporter's Notes–2012

Mass.R.Civ.P. 46 and Mass.R.Dom.Rel.P. 46 are identical except that Mass. R.Dom.Rel.P. 46 applies only when a stenographer is present or the proceedings are recorded.

Rule 52.   Findings by the Court

In all cases not governed by the Mass.R.Civ.P.,

(a) Effect. Except in actions to which G.L. c. 208, § 34, applies, the court shall upon written motion made prior to final argument, providing either party or the court has requested appointment of a stenographer pursuant to Rule 18 or the trial was recorded electronically, find the facts specially and state separately its conclusions of law thereon. Where the court enters judgment pursuant to G.L. c. 208, § 34 it shall issue findings of fact and conclusions of law thereon within sixty (60) days of the filing of a notice of appeal. Requests for findings are not necessary for purposes of review. Findings of fact shall not be set aside unless clearly erroneous, and due regard shall be given to the opportunity of the Trial Court to judge the credibility of the witnesses. The findings of a master, to the extent that the court adopts them, shall be considered as the findings of the court. If an opinion or memorandum of decision is filed, it will be sufficient if the findings of fact and conclusions of law appear therein. Findings of fact and conclusions of law are unnecessary on decisions of motions except as provided in Mass.R.Civ.P. 41(b)(2).

(b) Amendment. Upon motion of a party made not later than 10 days after entry of its findings the court may amend its findings or make additional findings and may amend the judgment accordingly. The motion may be made with a motion for a new trial. When findings of fact are made in actions tried by the court without a jury, the question of the sufficiency of the evidence to support the findings may thereafter be raised whether or not the party raising the question has made in the trial court an objection to such findings or has made a motion to amend them or a motion for judgment.

(c) Transcript of Proceedings Upon Request for Special Findings. Upon a written motion under paragraph (a) of this rule, the party making such request shall order from the stenographer and file with the court the original of a transcript of such parts of the proceedings not already on file as the court may determine material to any facts essential to a determination of the case. At the time of ordering, a party shall make satisfactory arrangements with the stenographer for payment of the cost of the transcript.

Adopted December 14, 2011, effective January 2, 2012.

Reporter's Notes–2012

The amended rule makes Mass.R.Dom.Rel.P. 52 applicable in cases not governed by Mass.R.Civ.P.

Rule 59.   New Trials: Amendment of Judgments

In all cases not governed by the Mass.R.Dom.Rel.P., new trials and amendment of judgments shall be governed by Mass.R.Civ.P. 59.

Adopted December 14, 2011, effective January 2, 2012.

Reporter's Notes–2012

Mass.R–Civ.P. 59 has language about cases tried to a jury and about damages which is not in Mass.R.Dom.Rel.P. 59. The language will do no harm.

Rule 60.   Relief From Judgment or Order

In all cases not governed by the Mass.R.Dom.Rel.P., motions for relief from judgment or order shall be governed by Mass.R.Civ.P. 60.

Adopted December 14, 2011, effective January 2, 2012.

Reporter's Notes–2012

Mass.R.Civ.P. 60 and Mass.R.Dom.Rel.P. 60 are identical.

Rule 61.   Harmless Error

In all cases not governed by the Mass.R.Dom.Rel.P., harmless error shall be governed by Mass.R.Civ.P. 61.

Adopted December 14, 2011, effective January 2, 2012.

Reporter's Notes–2012

Mass.R.Civ.P. 61 and Mass.R.Dom.Rel.P. 61 are identical.

Rule 70.   MUPC Magistrates; Scope of Delegable Duties; Effect of Decree and Orders Entered in Formal Proceedings

This rule shall govern the designation and duties of magistrates pursuant to the provisions of G.L.C. 190B.

a) Magistrates' Designation. The first justice of each division of the Probate and Family Court may, with the approval of the Chief Justice of the Probate and Family Court, designate one or more qualified officials of the court to act as magistrate pursuant to G.L. c. 190B, § 1–307, by a written order filed and recorded in the registry of the court.

A register of the Probate and Family Court shall be designated as magistrate pursuant to G.L. c. 190B, § 1–307, by the first justice of the division in which he or she serves, upon his or her written request to the first justice, and with the approval of the Chief Justice of the Probate and Family Court.

A first assistant register, assistant register or deputy assistant register, may be designated as magistrate, pursuant to G.L. c. 190B, § 1–307, by the first justice of the division in which he or she serves, subject to specific authorization by the register, and with the approval of the Chief Justice of the Probate and Family Court.

An official designated as magistrate by the first justice may not delegate the power, responsibilities or duties without the prior approval of the first justice.

b) Magistrates' Removal. An individual designated as magistrate pursuant to section (a) may be removed from that office by the first justice of the division, with the approval of the Chief Justice of the Probate and Family Court, by a written order revoking the order of designation filed and recorded in the registry of the court.

c) Scope of Delegable Duties. A magistrate designated pursuant to section (a) may perform the acts and issue orders as specified in G.L. c. 190B, including, but not limited to, informal proceedings and the following administrative duties, all as exercised under the supervision of the first justice of the division where he or she serves, unless otherwise ordered by the court:

1.   To approve any bond of a personal representative in an informal proceeding;

2.   To approve the bond of a guardian or conservator;

3.   To admit a valid and unrevoked will to formal probate under § 3–409 and determine heirs, if uncontested or assented to in writing, or if there is no objection to such admission or determination by any interested person;

4.   To appoint a personal representative with priority for appointment in an unsupervised administration, determine heirs and approve any bond of the personal representative in a formal proceeding, if uncontested or assented to in writing, or if there is no objection to such appointment by any interested person;

5.   To enter orders and decrees on accounts, including a decree and order for complete settlement of the estate in formal proceedings, if uncontested or assented to in writing, or if there is no objection to the entering of such order by any interested person;

6. To perform such other acts as the court may authorize as necessary or incidental to the conduct of informal and uncontested formal proceedings.

d) Effect of Decree and Orders Entered in Formal Proceedings. A magistrate acting on an unopposed petition in a formal proceeding must indicate that the action was taken by the magistrate and not by a justice. Any interested person aggrieved by the action of a magistrate in a formal proceeding may be heard by a justice provided that a motion for a hearing is filed within five days of the date of the entry of the formal decree.

Adopted December 14, 2011, effective January 2, 2012.

Reporter's Notes–2012

This rule is adopted as a result of the enactment of the Massachusetts Uniform Probate Code, G. L. c. 190B. Sections 62B and 62C of Chapter 221 of the General Laws, inserted by St.1978, c. 478, § 250, established the office of magistrate in all departments of the Trial Court and gave to that official certain quasi-judicial powers. This rule is not intended to expand or contract the powers which such statutory Trial Court magistrates may exercise in the Probate and Family Court, but rather to create the new and separate position of MUPC magistrate in that court.

Section (d) of this Rule, Effect of Decree and Orders Entered in Formal Proceedings, is intended to clarify the difference between an order entered by a magistrate in an informal proceeding and a decree or order entered by a magistrate in an unopposed formal proceeding under the Code. The denial of a petition for informal probate or appointment by a magistrate is not an adjudication and cannot be appealed. Any person aggrieved by the action of a magistrate in an informal proceeding may initiate a formal proceeding, within the time limits, so that the matter may be brought before a justice following the procedure for contested formal petitions.

Rule 72. Allowance of Accounts

(a) Scope and Applicability of Rule. This rule shall govern the procedure for the allowance of all accounts filed in the Probate and Family Court except those for which allowance is sought pursuant to G.L. c. 215, § 6.

(b) Accounts With Written Assent. If a fiduciary files his or her interim or final account with: (1) the proper petition; (2) the filing fee(s); (3) the written assent or waiver of every person interested in the account; and (4) all tax receipts or tax waivers required by law, the court or magistrate may allow the account without further notice. If any interested person is, as defined in G.L. c. 190B, an incapacitated person, a protected person or a minor, then the person's conservator, or if none, the person's guardian, shall sign any assent, unless the account is the conservator's own account.

(c) Accounts Without Written Assent.

(1) *Notice: Form.* If the interim or final account of a fiduciary is filed for allowance with the proper petition, filing fee(s) and all tax receipts or tax waivers required by law, but without the written assent or waiver of every person interested in the account, notice of the proceeding for allowance of a fiduciary account or the account of a common trust fund shall be served in accordance with the procedure set forth in G.L. c. 190B, § 1–401 on all interested persons, including the Veterans Administration, Department of Developmental Services or Attorney General, if interested. An account is deemed to be filed for allowance when it has been filed with the court along with the proper petition, filing fee(s) and a citation, as described below, has been issued by the court. The notice, in the form of a citation issued by the court, shall specify a return date as set forth in Rule 6 of the Supplemental Rules of the Probate and Family Court and shall provide that any person having an interest affected by the account:

(A) may file an appearance and objection to oppose the account in accordance with the procedure set forth in G.L. c. 190B, § 1–401;

(B) may, except in a proceeding to allow an account of a common trust fund, obtain, at no cost to himself or herself, a copy of the account by sending a written request, by certified or registered mail, to the petitioner, accountant (fiduciary) or counsel. In a proceeding for the allowance of an account of a common trust fund, the notice, in the form of a citation issued by the court, shall provide that any person so requesting may obtain without cost to himself or herself a copy of the annual report of said common trust fund for the period of the account, and may obtain a copy of the account on request, subject to such terms, if any, as to costs, which the court may determine upon application of the accountant.

(2) *Guardian Ad Litem.* If the court appoints a guardian ad litem to represent an individual or class interested in the account, the petitioner or accountant shall serve forthwith upon the guardian ad litem a copy of the petition, account and the citation. Such copies shall be without cost to the guardian ad litem. The guardian ad litem shall file his or her report within sixty days following the return date, or as otherwise allowed by the court, and shall serve a copy of the report upon the petitioner, accountant, and any person interested who has filed an appearance in the proceeding. The court may, upon ex parte application or such notice as the court may require, extend the time for the filing such report.

(3) *Objection: Effect.* If, at any time, there shall have been filed either: (A) an appearance and objection pursuant to par. (c)(1)(A) of this rule; or (B) a guardian ad litem's report containing an objection, the account shall thereafter be regarded as contested and further proceedings shall be governed, in addition to this rule, by the Supplemental Rules of the Probate and Family Court and any other rule as provided by law.

(4) *Objection: Withdrawal.* Any objection filed, whether by an interested person or a guardian ad litem, may be withdrawn by filing a statement to that effect, signed by the person or the guardian ad litem, or counsel, and served on any person (including, as necessary, the guardian ad litem) whose appearance is then on file. The conservator or if there is no conservator, the guardian of an interested person shall sign any withdrawal for the ward, incapacitated or protected person.

(5) *Objection: Striking.* Objections may be stricken by the court, if appropriate.

(6) *Contested Accounts: Hearings.* The petitioner, accountant, any person whose appearance and objection is then on file, or the guardian ad litem may request that the court assign a hearing date or the court may, on its own motion, assign a hearing date.

A Decree and Order entered after hearing shall be subject to the provisions of Rule 60 of the Supplemental Rules of the Probate and Family Court (except that the standard governing any relief under Rule 60(b) shall be fraud or manifest error and Rule 60(b)(3) shall not apply).

(7) *Uncontested Accounts.* An account shall be regarded as uncontested if:

(A) It has been filed pursuant to par. (b) of this rule; or

(B) After 10:00 a.m. on the return day (i) either no appearance and objection is filed to oppose the proceeding or any appearance and objection previously filed shall have been withdrawn or stricken; and (ii) the report of the guardian ad litem, if any, is on file and contains no objection.

A Decree and Order on any uncontested account may be entered forthwith subject only to the provisions of Rule 60 of the Supplemental Rules of the Probate and Family Court (except that the standard governing any relief under Rule 60(b) shall be fraud or manifest error and Rule 60(b)(3) shall not apply).

Adopted December 14, 2011, effective January 2, 2012.

Reporter's Notes–2012

Rule 72 has been added to the Supplemental Rules of the Probate and Family Court and is intended to replace former Rule 72 of the Massachusetts Rules of Civil Procedure. Supplemental Rule 72 was drafted to be consistent with the provisions of the Massachusetts Uniform Probate Code, G.L. c. 190B ("Code"). Supplemental Rule 72 shall be applicable to all actions in the Probate and Family Court seeking the allowance of an account, except actions filed pursuant to G.L. c. 215, § 6, which shall continue to be governed by Mass.R.Civ.P. For proceedings involving the allowance of an account of a common trust fund, Supplemental Rule 72 incorporates and makes applicable the procedures set forth in Code section 1–401. Rule 72 of the Supplemental Rules eliminates the prior references to specific Rules of Civil Procedure applicable in contested account proceedings, as those specific references are no longer necessary due to the adoption of the Supplemental Rules of the Probate and Family Court making the Rules of Civil Procedure more broadly applicable to probate proceedings.

Rule 72A. Content of Accounts

Accounts of conservators or trustees with accounting periods terminating after January 1, 1974, shall include real estate.

A personal representative, executor, administrator, conservator or trustee, with respect to assets with readily ascertainable market value shall include in his or her account, if the accounting period terminates after January 2, 1973, such market value as of the end of the accounting period or as of such date as may be chosen by the accountant prior to and not more than six months before the end of the accounting period. Market value shall be in addition to book or accounting values. Market values may be furnished by double column on schedule C or by separate schedule. For assets without readily ascertainable market values, such as real estate, patent and copyright interests, oil well interests, close corporation stock and the like, the basis of the valuation used shall be stated (e.g., appraisal on a specified date, assessed value, tax value, book value, nominal value, etc.). Such appraisal may be provided by separate schedule or in juxtaposition to book values of assets held at the end of the accounting period.

Each item or entry within the schedules of accounts shall be numbered sequentially within the schedule.

Adopted December 14, 2011, effective January 2, 2012.

Reporter's Notes–2012

Rule 29A is changed to Rule 72A to keep the account related rules together. "Content" is added to distinguish the rule from Rule 72 which deals with allowance of accounts.

Rule 90. Resignation of Personal Representative

A justice of the Probate and Family Court may accept the resignation of a personal representative when it appears proper to do so.

Adopted December 14, 2011, effective January 2, 2012.

Reporter's Notes–2012

This rule will replace G.L. c. 195, § 13, which was repealed.

Rule 101. Interlocutory Hearings [Repealed]

Repealed December 14, 2011, effective January 2, 2012.

Reporter's Notes–2012

See Rules 15 and 29. The first paragraph of this rule is identical to Rule 15, so it does not need to be repeated here. The second paragraph of this rule has contradicted Mass.R.Dom.Rel.P. 6(c) since that rule was amended in 1997 to require 7 days notice (plus 3 for mailing), unless the motion is brought *ex parte.*

Rule 102. Further Notice [Repealed]

Repealed December 14, 2011, effective January 2, 2012.

Reporter's Notes–2012

Rule 8 of these rules is identical to this rule.

Rule 103. Writ of Protection [Repealed]

Repealed December 14, 2011, effective January 2, 2012.

Reporter's Notes–2012

Rule 14 of these rules is identical to this rule.

Rule 201. Recording of Court Proceedings

(1) In all Probate and Family Court divisions, all proceedings shall be held in a courtroom and recorded electronically, subject to the availability and functioning of appropriate recording devices. Said recording shall take place whether or not a court stenographer is present in the courtroom. Uncontested adoption hearings may be held in the lobby and need not be recorded. Proceedings, if recorded, may be held in a hospital or other location when a litigant is, for health reasons, unable to come to the courthouse or in other exigent circumstances.

(2) A copy of the original recording, or any portion thereof, may be requested by counsel or by litigants or by an agency party to the proceedings within one year of the date the proceedings are recorded, provided that failure to request said copy seasonably shall not be grounds for the delay of subsequent proceedings. Upon motion for good cause shown, the court may extend the time period within which a copy may be requested. The copy shall consist of a cassette or disk copy of the original recording, or such portion thereof as is requested, which copy shall be produced pursuant to such process and procedure as is prescribed by the Chief Justice for Adminis-

tration and Management of the Trial Court and the Chief Justice of the Probate and Family Court, and which shall be playable on standard cassette or disk devices designed for home or office use. Said request for a cassette or disk copy of an original court proceeding shall be filed with the Register of the Probate and Family Court in the division in which the case was heard. Such request shall be on a form prescribed by the Chief Justice of the Probate and Family Court. Any person making such a request shall, in advance, notify all parties of the intention to make said request, to the end that multiple requests shall be made simultaneously wherever possible. The cost of said cassette or disk copy, which shall be prepaid, shall be determined by the Chief Administrative Justice pursuant to G.L. c. 262, § 4B, plus postage, except that there shall be no cost for a cassette or disk copy produced for the use of the court. Sections 27A through 27G of Chapter 261 of the General Laws shall be deemed applicable to a request by or on behalf of an allegedly indigent party and the cost of a cassette or disk copy shall be deemed an "extra cost" as defined in said section 27A.

(3) A cassette or disk copy shall, upon request as aforesaid, be made available to any party to a proceeding so recorded or to his counsel of record. A cassette or disk copy may be made available to any other interested person or interested agency in the discretion of the judge who presided over the proceedings. After the submission by said person or agency of a request in writing setting forth the basis of the request and the specific use to be made of the cassette or disk copy, said request is to be acted upon promptly, and any denial thereof or undue delay in obtaining a copy may be referred to the Chief Justice of the Probate and Family Court.

(4) A cassette or disk shall not be erased or tampered with nor its labels removed or defaced as long as the matter recorded is pending in any court or is subject to or the subject of appellate review. A cassette or disk which is thereafter erased shall be erased in its entirety. No cassette or disk shall be erased until a period of three years has expired from the date of the original recording. Duplication of a cassette or disk is expressly prohibited except where specifically authorized by the presiding justice of a Probate and Family Court, the Chief Justice of the Probate and Family Court, or the Chief Justice for Administration and Management of the Trial Court, as the case may be.

(5) A copy of a cassette or disk or a copy of any portion of the material contained in a cassette or disk shall not be used for a commercial purpose, for the purpose of public or private entertainment or amusement or for any other purpose detrimental to the administration of justice. A cassette or disk copy of an original recording of a proceeding from which the public was excluded shall be deemed confidential and subject to such additional restrictions with regard to its use as may be prescribed by the judge who presided over the session so recorded.

(6) All persons receiving a cassette or disk copy shall comply with the provisions of sections (4), (5) and (6) of this rule and shall be subject to the imposition of appropriate sanctions for non-compliance, including contempt proceedings. It shall be the responsibility of a person requesting a copy of a cassette or disk from the register of probate to take all necessary and reasonable precautions to prevent any incident of non-compliance with said sections, including but not necessarily limited to notifying persons who are permitted to use said copy of the provisions of said sections.

Adopted effective July 1, 1981. Amended effective July 1, 1983; amended April 29, 1992, effective June 1, 1992; amended December 14, 2011, effective January 2, 2012.

Reporter's Notes—1981

Supplemental Rule 201 was reserved when the Massachusetts Rules of Domestic Relations Procedure and the Supplemental Rules of the Probate and Family Court Department were promulgated in 1975.

Reporter's Notes–2012

Adds references to disks as new recording systems make copies to disks, not to cassettes.

Eliminates option of lobby conferences or other proceedings outside of a courtroom absent exigent circumstances. Eliminates the sub-title "Under the Control of the Court." That line in that position did not add anything to the rule.

Rule 202. Appointment of Stenographers [Repealed]

Repealed December 14, 2011, effective January 2, 2012.

Reporter's Notes–2012

Rule 18 of these rules is identical to this rule.

Rule 203. Exhibits [Repealed]

Repealed December 14, 2011, effective January 2, 2012.

Reporter's Notes–2012

Rule 26 of these rules is identical to this rule.

Rule 204. Printing of Forms [Repealed]

Repealed December 14, 2011, effective January 2, 2012.

Reporter's Notes–2012

Rule 29C of these rules is identical to this rule.

Rule 401. Financial Statement

(a) Except as otherwise ordered by the court, each party to a divorce or separate support action or any other domestic relations action where financial relief is requested, shall file with the court and shall deliver to the other party within 45 days from the date of the service of the summons, a complete and accurate financial statement showing, insofar as possible, the assets, liabilities and current income and expenses of both parties and children involved in the case. The form of the financial statement which each party must complete is dependent upon his or her income. Except as otherwise ordered by the court, a party whose income equals or exceeds $75,000.00 must complete the long form financial statement. A party whose income is less than $75,000.00 must complete the short form financial statement.

(b) In the event a hearing on a motion for temporary orders, or a pretrial conference is scheduled by either party prior to the expiration of the 45 day period, financial statements by both parties shall be filed with the court and exchanged between the parties no later than two (2) business days prior to the hearing or the conference without the necessity of a request for such statements.

(c) The form of the financial statement shall be determined from time to time by the Probate and Family Court judges of the Commonwealth. The judges of the Probate and Family Court may require from time to time during the pendency of a separate support or divorce action, or in any action involving a financial order, a new financial statement containing current information as to the assets, liabilities, current income and expenses of the parties and any children involved in the litigation.

(d) The financial statement or new financial statement, as the case may be, shall be impounded or kept separate from other papers in the case and shall not be available for public inspection, but shall be available to the court, the attorneys (whose appearances are entered in the case), the parties to the case, the registers, assistant registers, members of the Probation Department of the probate and family courts and to employees of the Massachusetts Department of Revenue, where necessary.

(e) All financial statements shall be signed by the party filing the same and shall be subject to the penalties of perjury.

(f) Either party in a contested matter may request the other party, upon ten (10) days notice, in the form of a separate request titled "Request for a Financial Statement" to furnish a signed, current financial statement to the court with a copy of the financial statement to the requesting party. No further request may be made within ninety (90) days of a prior request except by order of the court.

(g) All sanctions available to a party under Rule 37 of the Massachusetts Rules of Domestic Relations Procedure and any other sanction that the court may deem appropriate shall be available to compel compliance with this rule and such sanctions shall be ordered by the court except for good cause shown.

Amended November 16, 1979, effective December 17, 1979; October 10, 1997, effective December 1, 1997; amended December 14, 2011, effective January 2, 2012.

Comment—1979

Presently we do not have available specific sanctions for failure to file financial statements. This rule change will remedy that problem.

Reporter's Notes—1997

The amended Rule 401 requires financial statements to be exchanged automatically between the parties within forty-five (45) days from the date of the service of the summons or when the matter first comes before the court. The amended rule also provides that in the event a hearing or conference is scheduled by either party before the expiration of the forty-five (45) day period, then both parties must file and exchange financial statements no later than two (2) business days prior to the hearing or conference.

The form of the financial statement which each party must complete is now dependent upon each party's level of income. If a party's income is less than $75,000.00, they would complete the short form financial statement. If the party's income equals or exceeds $75,000.00 they would complete the long form financial statement. The income is based on each individual's income, and not the combined income of the parties.

The amendment to Rule 401 also requires that requests for financial statements be made through a separate pleading entitled "Request for

a Financial Statement". The time allowed to produce a financial statement on demand was expanded from 48 hours to ten (10) days. Sanctions for failure to comply with the rule are now mandatory, except for good cause shown.

Reporter's Notes–2012

Added limitation to "domestic relations" actions to make it clear the requirement is not automatic in equity or probate actions in which financial relief is requested. The name of the court is updated.

Rule 402. Assignment of Counsel

If any party appears in court in a matter in which the laws of the Commonwealth or the rules of the Supreme Judicial Court establish a right to be represented by counsel, the judge shall follow the procedures established in G.L. c. 211D and in Supreme Judicial Court Rules 1:07 and 3:10.

Amended December 15, 1986, effective January 2, 1987; amended December 14, 2011, effective January 2, 2012.

Reporter's Notes–2012

Adds reference to SJC Rule 1:07.

Rule 403. Waiver of Fees, Expenses and Other Provisions for Indigent Litigants [Repealed]

Repealed December 14, 2011, effective January 2, 2012.

Reporter's Notes–2012

See G.L. c. 261, § 27A *et seq.* The determination of indigency for purposes of state payment of costs is established in G.L. c. 261, §§ 27A–G. It happens in the Registry and only comes to a judge if the indigent status is not granted in the Registry.

Rule 404. Charges of Adultery or Criminal Acts

Whenever adultery, any specific criminal act with a third person or allegations derogatory to the character or reputation of a third person are charged in a complaint, cross-complaint, answer, statement of objections, or other pleading, it shall be stated therein that the name of the person, hereinafter called the co-defendant, charged with committing adultery with one of the parties, is known or is not known to the pleader, but such person shall not be named.

If the name of the co-defendant is stated as known, the party making such allegation, upon the filing of such pleading, shall deliver to the register a motion to amend the pleading by inserting the name of the co-defendant, and his residence, if known, and he shall also deliver to the register at least one affidavit, other than those of counsel, or a duly certified court record, with an affidavit of identity, supporting the allegation, or he shall present such motion to a judge at an ex parte hearing, as provided by statute.

The motion with the affidavit or affidavits and certificates shall be sealed up by the register until presented by him or by counsel to a judge, who shall inspect the same and hold such ex parte hearing, if any, as he may deem proper, and shall grant the motion if he finds probable cause has been shown that the allegation is true.

If the motion is allowed, it shall be filed and an entry shall be made on the docket, "Motion to insert name of co-defendant allowed," and the affidavit or affidavits and certificates shall be sealed and returned to the register to be held for the inspection of parties, including the co-defendant and counsel of record, but for no others except by order of the court.

If the motion is denied, it shall be sealed by the judge with the affidavit or affidavits and certificates and returned to the register, to be held subject to the order of the court, and the register shall enter upon the docket, "Motion to insert name of co-defendant denied."

If the co-defendant is unknown at the time of filing the complaint or other pleading, but becomes known while the matter is pending, a motion shall thereupon be delivered to the register and further proceedings had as hereinbefore provided.

This rule shall be applicable to separate support and divorce proceedings.

Amended December 14, 2011, effective January 2, 2012.

Rule 405. Notice to Person Charged With Adultery or Criminal Act

When a complaint, cross-complaint, answer, or statement of objections to an absolute judgment charges adultery, any criminal act with a third person or allegations derogatory to the character or reputation of a third person, a notice of such complaint, cross-complaint, answer or statement of objections shall be mailed by registered or certified mail, return receipt requested, to such person at his last known address at least fourteen (14) days before the answer is due on such complaint, or forthwith upon the filing of such answer or cross-complaint or statement of objections, or forthwith upon the amendment of the complaint so as to name such persons after the issuance of process. Such service by mailing shall be proved by affidavit containing a particular statement thereof, accompanied if practicable by the return receipt showing receipt of the copy sent by registered or certified mail. Such person shall be entitled to appear within twenty (20) days after such return day or after the day of mailing such copy.

Amended December 14, 2011, effective January 2, 2012.

Reporter's Notes–2012

The proposed change would replace the obsolete reference to a divorce "return day of process" with reference to when the answer is due.

Rule 406. Allowance for Fees, Costs, and Expenses

An application by a party for an allowance from the other party to prosecute or defend a complaint shall contain a statement that the party intends in good faith to defend or prosecute such complaint, and shall be accompanied by a certificate of the party's attorney that the attorney believes such statement to be true. The judge shall review the financial statements of the parties and other relevant evidence, including affidavits, and shall order an allowance, if appropriate, for counsel fees and necessary expenses. If such allowance is granted, it shall be paid as the court may direct.

Amended October 29, 1992, effective January 1, 1993; amended December 14, 2011, effective January 2, 2012.

Rule 407. [Deleted]

Deleted effective February 12, 1979.

Rule 408. Dismissal of Inactive Cases

(1) Not less often than twice each year, once in January and once in July, a report shall be prepared listing cases of any nature for which there has been no activity reflected on the docket for more than six (6) months and there is no next event scheduled.

(2) The register of probate shall mail notice to all persons who have entered an appearance in any matter listed as having no activity reflected on the docket for more than six (6) months. The notice in each case shall state that the matter shall be dismissed by the court in sixty (60) days unless within sixty (60) days of the sending of the notice:

(a) there are further proceedings in the case; or

(b) a motion to avoid the proposed dismissal is filed and presented to the court with an explanation of what steps will be taken for the case to proceed. The motion may be presented administratively.

(3) Unless a motion to avoid the dismissal has been allowed by the court, after the sixtieth day following the sending of the notice, the register shall enter a judgment of dismissal without prejudice and send the judgment to all parties who have entered an appearance in the matter.

(4) For cause shown the court may dismiss cases at other times.

Amended December 14, 2011, effective January 2, 2012.

Reporter's Notes–2012

The rule is amended to provide for dismissal of any inactive case, not just divorces. The dismissal process is to be done at least twice a year. The procedure to avoid dismissal is detailed.

Rule 409. Case Management Conference [Repealed]

Repealed effective November 1, 2004.

Reporter's Notes–2004

The repeal of Rule 409 is necessitated by the implementation of the revised Standing Order on Time Standards in an effort to consolidate all case management related policies and procedures in one place.

Reporter's Notes–2012

See Standing Order 1–06.

Rule 410. Mandatory Self Disclosure

(a) Initial Disclosures.

(1) Except as otherwise agreed by the parties or ordered by the court, each party to a divorce action, each party to a complaint for separate support, and each parent who is a party to an action under Chapter 209C that includes a claim for child support where paternity has already been adjudicated or where the parents have completed a notarized voluntary acknowledgment of paternity shall deliver to the other party or parties within 45 days from the date of service of the summons the following documents:

(a) The parties' federal and state income tax returns and schedules for the past three (3) years and any non-public, limited partnership and privately held corporate returns for any entity in which either party has an interest together with all supporting documentation for tax returns, including but not limited to w-2's, 1099's 1098's, K-1, Schedule C and Schedule E.

(b) The four (4) most recent pay stubs from each employer for whom the party worked.

(c) Documentation regarding the cost and nature of available health insurance coverage.

(2) Except as otherwise agreed by the parties or ordered by the court, each party to a divorce action and each party to a complaint for separate support shall also deliver to the other party within 45 days from the date of service of the summons the following documents:

(a) Statements for the past three (3) years for all bank accounts held in the name of either party individually or jointly, or in the name of another person for the benefit of either party, or held by either party for the benefit of the parties' minor child(ren).

(b) Statements for the past three (3) years for any securities, stocks, bonds, notes or obligations, certificates of deposit owned or held by either party or held by either party for the benefit of the parties' minor child(ren), 401K statements, IRA statements, and pension plan statements for all accounts listed on the 401 financial statement.

(c) Copies of any loan or mortgage applications made, prepared or submitted by either party within the last three (3) years prior to the filing of the complaint.

(d) Copies of any financial statement and/or statement of assets and liabilities prepared by either party within the last three (3) years prior to the filing of the complaint.

(b) Additional Disclosures.

(1) Except as otherwise agreed by the parties or ordered by the court, each party to an action under Chapter 209C that includes a claim for child support where paternity has already been adjudicated or where the parents have completed a notarized voluntary acknowledgment of paternity may serve on a parent who is a party to the action a separate written request entitled "Request for Additional Rule 410 Documents," and the parent served shall, within 45 days from the date of service of the request, deliver to the other party or parties the documents set out in (a)(2)(a)-(d) above.

(2) When a request for child support is first added to an action under Chapter 209C by counterclaim or by amendment of the complaint, a party may serve on a parent who is a party to the action a separate written request entitled "Request for Rule 410 Documents," and the parent served shall, within 45 days from the date of service of the request, deliver to the other; party or parties the documents set out in (a)(1)(a)-(c) above.

(3) The parties shall supplement all disclosures as material changes occur during the progress of the case. No party required to deliver documents under this rule shall be permitted to file any discovery motions prior to making the initial disclosure as described herein, and no party to a divorce or separate support action shall be permitted to file any discovery

motions prior to making both the initial and the additional disclosures as described herein.

(c) Unavailability of Documents. In the event that any party required to deliver documents under this rule does not have any of the documents required pursuant to this rule or has not been able to obtain them in a timely fashion, he or she shall state in writing, under the penalties of perjury, the specific documents which are not available, the reasons the documents are not available, and what efforts have been made to obtain the documents. As more information becomes available there is a continuing duty to supplement.

Adopted October 10, 1997, effective December 1, 1997. Amended June 5, 2003, effective September 2, 2003; amended April 1, 2009, effective May 1, 2009; amended December 14, 2011, effective January 2, 2012.

Reporter's Notes—2003

The amendment to Rule 410(a)(1) clarifies that the Rule applies to parties to a divorce action and to complaints for separate support.

Reporter's Notes—2009

The amendment provides for two prongs of document disclosure. The first prong requires automatic exchange of pay stubs, tax returns and health insurance information within 45 days of service of a complaint or counterclaim for establishment of child support. Second prong documents are produced only upon the serving of a Rule 410 notice for request of these documents.

Rule 411. Automatic Restraining Order

(a) The following automatic restraining order shall apply to both parties to a complaint for divorce or separate support. This automatic restraining order shall be effective with regard to the plaintiff upon the filing of the complaint by the plaintiff or the plaintiff's counsel and with regard to the defendant upon service of the summons and complaint or any other acceptance of service by the defendant.

After service of the complaint for divorce or separate support, on two (2) days notice to the other party or on such shorter notice as the court may prescribe, a party may appear without thereby submitting his person to the jurisdiction of the court, and move to modify or dissolve the automatic restraining order and in that event the court shall proceed to hear and determine such motion as expeditiously as the ends of justice require.

The following restraining order shall remain in effect during the pendency of the action, unless it is modified by agreement of the parties or by further order of the court.

(1) Neither party shall sell, transfer, encumber, conceal, assign, remove or in any way dispose of any property, real or personal, belonging to or acquired by, either party, except: (a) as required for reasonable expenses of living; (b) in the ordinary and usual course of business; (c) in the ordinary and usual course of investing; (d) for payment of reasonable attorney's fees and costs in connection with the action; (e) written agreement of both parties; or (f) by order of the court.

(2) Neither party shall incur any further debts that would burden the credit of the other party, including but not limited to further borrowing against any credit line secured by the marital residence or unreasonably using credit cards or cash advances against credit or bank cards.

(3) Neither party shall directly or indirectly change the beneficiary of any life insurance policy, pension or retirement plan, or pension or retirement investment account, except with the written consent of the other party or by order of the court.

(4) Neither party shall directly or indirectly cause the other party or the minor child(ren) to be removed from coverage under an existing insurance policy, including medical, dental, life, automobile, and disability insurance. The parties shall maintain all insurance coverage in full force and effect.

(b) The provisions of this automatic restraining order shall be issued over the signature of the Chief Justice of the Probate and Family Court Department and a copy thereof shall be served with every complaint to which it applies, except if personal service is not made as provided in Rule 4 and service is made by publication, said notice shall include a statement that an automatic restraining order has been issued pursuant to this rule. The provisions of this automatic restraining order need not be reprinted in said public notice.

(c) The automatic restraining order provided for under this rule is automatically vacated upon the entry of a judgment of divorce or separate support.

Adopted October 27, 1999, effective January 1, 2000; amended December 14, 2011, effective January 2, 2012.

Reporter's Notes—2000

Rule 411 provides for the automatic issuance of a restraining order which is applicable to both parties to a complaint for divorce or separate support. The restraining order is effective with regard to the plaintiff upon the filing of the complaint by the plaintiff or plaintiff's counsel and with regard to the defendant upon service of the summons and complaint or any other acceptance of service by the defendant.

Said restraining order remains in effect during the pendency of the action for divorce, unless it is modified by agreement of the parties or by further order of the court. The restraining order is automatically vacated upon the entry of judgment of divorce or separate support. A party may appear on two (2) days notice to the other party or such shorter notice as the court may prescribe and move to modify or dissolve the automatic restraining order.

A copy of this automatic restraining order must be served with every complaint to which it applies, except where service is made by publication. In which case, a statement that an automatic restraining order has been issued will be included in said public notice.

Rule 412. Uncontested Actions to Modify a Judgment or Order

In order to facilitate uncontested actions to modify a judgment or order, including, but not limited to, actions to modify child support consistent with the Child Support Guidelines, the following uniform procedure is to be followed:

(a) The parties shall file with the court a joint petition to modify a judgment or a joint motion to modify an order, on a form approved by the Probate and Family Court. The petition or motion shall be accompanied by a copy of the judgment or order to be modified and:

(1) an agreement setting forth the agreed upon modification(s), which must be notarized if modifying a judgment. If a child's primary residence or custody is being modified, the agreement must specifically state whether any terms in a prior judgment or order related to child support, health, dental, vision or life insurance coverage are also modified, or if they

remain in effect. If child support is being modified and the parties deviate from the guidelines amount, the agreement must include specific facts that justify departure from the guidelines, and if the parties agreement terminates child support upon the age of 18, the agreement must acknowledge that G.L. c. 208, § 28 or G.L. c. 209C, § 9 is not applicable;

(2) complete and accurate financial statements signed by each party, and counsel, if any, pursuant to Supplemental Probate and Family Court Rule 401, with supporting documentation (attach W- 2, and 1099 forms for prior year), if financial issues are being modified;

(3) a complete and accurate Child Support Guidelines Worksheet, if child support or medical, dental or vision insurance is being modified;

(4) a written assent from the Department of Revenue Child Support Enforcement Division as the IV–D agency when a party, and/or a dependent child, is a current recipient of public assistance or owes a past-due child support debt assigned to the Commonwealth, and any term relating to child support or medical insurance is being modified;

(5) a proposed Child Support Findings form, if child support is being modified and the parties deviate from the guidelines amount;

(6) an Affidavit Disclosing Care or Custody Proceeding form by each party, pursuant to Trial Court Rule IV, if the care, custody or visitation of a child is being modified;

(7) any other assent or document required by statute or court rule; and

(8) a proposed judgment or order on a form approved by the Probate and Family Court.

(b) Formal notice or service shall not be required.

(c) Neither party shall mark the joint petition or joint motion for hearing. In the event that the court believes that a hearing is necessary or helpful to a disposition of the matter, the court will set the time and date for the hearing and will notify the parties within twenty-one (21) days of the filing of the petition or motion. If the pleadings are deficient or incomplete, an in-person hearing will be required.

(d) A joint petition or joint motion that is not scheduled for a hearing will be decided on the papers filed in accordance with this rule within thirty (30) days of such filing.

(e) A judgment or order entered on a joint petition or joint motion involving child support will be entered in the State Case Registry pursuant to G.L. c. 119A, § 4.

(f) This rule cannot be applied to actions governed by G.L. c. 209A.

Adopted June 5, 2003, effective September 2, 2003; amended December 14, 2011, effective January 2, 2012; June 25, 2013, effective August 1, 2013.

Reporter's Notes—2003

This new Rule allows for a simplified process by which parties may agree to modify a judgment for child support consistent with the Child Support Guidelines. Entry of the case in the State Case Registry pursuant to section (d) necessitates the filing of a State Case Registry form if the parties have not previously filed the form.

Reporter's Notes—2013

The Rule is expanded to allow parties to jointly request modification of a judgment or order of the Probate and Family Court where the parties are in agreement, the agreement is in writing, and all other requirements of this Rule are met. The 2013 amendments to the Rule will allow the court to handle more cases administratively. Section (d), as referenced in the 2003 Reporter's Notes, is now section (e).

Section (f) allows a modification of child support to be brought under this Rule when there is an active c. 209A order, but custody or visitation changes that require the modification of a c. 209A order are prohibited. The joint pleadings approved for use by the Probate and Family Court under section (a) shall require the parties to disclose any past or present c. 209A order, or DCF involvement, in order to highlight cases that might be able to use this Rule but require additional scrutiny by the court.

PROBATE AND FAMILY COURT DEPARTMENT
UNIFORM FEE SCHEDULE

Uniform Fee Schedule

Probate and Family Court Department Uniform Fee Schedule – Effective July 9, 2012
(revised as of May 15, 2015)

NOTE: The fees listed below do NOT include the fee for a citation or summons. Each citation is an additional $15 and each summons is an additional $5. Costs for publication, if applicable, are the responsibility of the petitioner/plaintiff. If there is no initial filing fee, other fees and costs associated with the action, including, but not limited to, a citation, summons or copies, still apply and shall be charged.

Any party entering a complaint, petition or other civil action in which an initial filing fee is payable, and to which a separate docket number is assigned shall pay to the Register a surcharge of $15 in addition to the fee otherwise required. See G. L. c. 262, § 4C. Adding a suffix does not create a separate docket number that requires a surcharge.

Category	Type of Pleading (in alphabetical order)	Filing Fee	Surcharge (if applicable)
Abuse Prevention	Abuse Prevention/Abuse Protection	No Fee	
	Disabled Abuse Petition	No Fee	
	Elderly Abuse Petition	No Fee	
Accounts	Allowance of Account, Petition	$75	$15
	Amended/Substituted Account	$75	
	Render an Inventory or Account, Petition	$75	
	Where the gross value accounted for in Schedule A of the Account is $1,000 or less	No Fee	
	Where the gross value accounted for is more than $1,000 but not more than $10,000, provided, however, that the fees shall not exceed $170 regardless of the time covered by such account	$75	
	Where the gross value accounted for is $10,000 or more than $10,000 but not more than $100,000 (per year or fraction thereof covered by such account)	$100	
	Where the gross value accounted for is more than $100,000 but not more than $500,000 (per year or fraction thereof covered by such account)	$150	
	Where the gross value accounted for is more than $500,000 but not more than $1,000,000 (per year or fraction thereof covered by such account)	$200	
	Where the gross value accounted for is more than $1,000,000 but not more than $2,000,000 (per year or fraction thereof covered by such account)	$400	
	Where the gross value accounted for is more than $2,000,000 but not more than $5,000,000 (per year or fraction thereof covered by such account)	$750	
	Where the gross value accounted for is more than $5,000,000 but not more than $7,500,000 (per year or fraction thereof covered by such account)	$1500	
	Where the gross value accounted for is more than $7,500,000 but not more than $10,000,000 (per year or fraction thereof covered by such account)	$2500	
	Where the gross value accounted for is more than $10,000,000 (per year or fraction thereof covered by such account)	$3500	

Category	Type of Pleading (in alphabetical order)	Filing Fee	Surcharge (if applicable)
Adoption	Dispense with consent to adoption, Petition	No Fee	
	Complaint/Petition	No Fee	
Bonds/ Surety	Filing of a Subsequent Bond	$75	
	Leave to Bring suit on a bond	No Fee	
	New Bond, Petition	$75	
	Demand for Sureties	$75	
	Discharge of Surety, Petition	$75	
	Modification of Bond, Petition	$75	
	Reduction of Bond, Petition	$75	
Change of Name	Motion – in divorce actions only, during Nisi period	$100	
	Petition	$150	$15
Guardian/ Conservator *(Note: There is NO separate fee for the initial appointment bond of a fiduciary or the initial Letters of appointment).*	Appointment of Conservator or for Single Transaction, Petition	$240	$15
	Appointment of a Guardian, Petition	No Fee	
	Expand, Modify, Limit Powers of a Conservator, Petition	$150	
	Expand, Modify, Limit Powers of a Guardian, Petition	No Fee	
	Foreign Conservator Sworn Statement	$75	$15
	Removal of a Fiduciary	$100	
	Resignation of Conservator or Guardian, Petition	No Fee	
	Termination of Conservator or Guardian, Petition	No Fee	
Domestic Relations and Paternity	Affirmation of Marriage, Complaint	$200	$15
	Alimony, Complaint	$100	$15
	Annulment, Complaint	$200	$15
	Complaint for Custody-Support-Parenting Time	$100	$15
	Complaint for Paternity	$100	$15
	Complaints to establish paternity or for custody-support-parenting time and modifications filed by the IV-D agency	No Fee	
	Convey land as if sole	$150	
	Divorce, Complaint	$200	$15
	Enforcement of Foreign Decree – Alimony only	$100	$15
	Grandparent visitation, Petition	No Fee	
	Marriage of a minor	$180	$15
	Marriage without delay	$180	$15
	Modification of all non-child related issues	$150	

Category	Type of Pleading (in alphabetical order)	Filing Fee	Surcharge (if applicable)
	Modification of Foreign Custody or Support Decree, G. L. c. 208, s. 29 – except for those actions filed by the IV-D agency for which there is no filing fee	$100	
	Modification relative to child support, custody and parenting time – except for those actions filed by the IV-D agency for which there is no filing fee	$50	
	Registration of Foreign Custody Decree	No Fee	
	Removal, Post-Judgment	$50	
	Separate Support	$100	$15
	Support of spouse or child pursuant to G. L. c. 209, § 32F, Complaint	No Fee	
	Temporary restraining order against a spouse related to a complaint for divorce or separate support	No Fee	
Equity	Complaint	$240	$15
	Complaint related to separate support or the custody or support of minors	$100	$15
	Complaint to Correct Birth Record	$240	$15
	Partition, Petition	$240	$15
	Restrain a Personal Representative, Complaint	$240	
	Specific Performance, Petition	$240	$15
	Temporary Restraining Order/Injunction	$100	
Letters	Subsequent Letter	$25	
Probate *(Note: There is NO separate fee for the initial appointment bond of a fiduciary or the initial Letters of appointment).*	Appointment of a Receiver of the Estate of an Absentee, Petition	$200	$15
	Appointment of Special Personal Representative, Petition	$375	$15
	Appointment of a Trustee, Petition	$375	$15
	Approval of Compromise, Petition	$75	
	Care of Burial Lot	$60	
	Closing Statement	$75	
	Counsel Fees, Petition	$150	
	Determination of Value, Petition	$75	
	Erection of Monument	$60	
	Filing a will for Safekeeping – except that no additional fee shall be charged for filing a will in substitution for a will previously filed and withdrawn	$75	
	Filing of a Declaration of Common Trust Fund	$400	$15
	Foreign Personal Representative Sworn Statement	$75	$15
	Formal Probate of Will, Adjudication of Intestacy and Appointment of Personal Representative, Petition	$375	$15
	Formal Appointment of Successor Personal Representative, Petition	$375	$15
	Formal Removal of Personal Representative, Petition	$100	
	General Petition, Probate	$150	$15
	General Petition, Trust	$375	$15
	Informal Probate of Will and/or Appointment of Personal Representative, Petition	$375	$15
	Informal Appointment of Successor Personal Representative, Petition	$375	$15
	Leave to Deposit Certain Funds	$200	

Category	Type of Pleading (in alphabetical order)	Filing Fee	Surcharge (if applicable)
	Order of Complete Settlement, Petition	$75	
	Payment of Deposits, Petition	No Fee	
	Public Administration, Petition	$100	$15
	Removal of a Fiduciary	$100	
	Resignation of a Fiduciary	No Fee	
	Representation of Insolvency	$150	
	Small Estate Closing Statement	$75	
	Supervised Administration, Petition	$375	$15
	Termination of Trust, Petition	$240	$15
	Vacate a Formal Order, Petition	$150	
	Voluntary Administration, Statement	$100	$15
Sale, Lease or Mortgage of Real or Personal Estate by any fiduciary:	Leave to Lease real estate	$75	
	Leave to Mortgage real estate	$75	
	Sale where the gross value accounted for is $100,000 or less	$100	
	Sale where the gross value accounted for is more than $100,000 but not more than $250,000	$250	
	Sale where the gross value accounted for is more than $250,000 but not more than $500,000	$500	
	Sale where the gross value accounted for is more than $500,000 but not more than $1,000,000	$750	
	Sale where the gross value accounted for is more than $1,000,000	$1,000	
Miscellaneous	Amendment of record – except as relates to separate support, adoption or the custody or support of minors	$60	
	Certificate of Orders, Decrees, Rulings, Judgments or Other Proceedings	$20 + $1 per page for each page except the first	
	Citation, order of notice or precept	$15	
	Commission to take Depositions	$20	
	Copy, Attested – of court documents and records, including docket sheets or other papers in possession and under the control of the Register	$2.50 per page	
	Copy Unattested – of court documents, records or other papers in possession and under the control of the Register	$1 per page	
	Exemplified copies	$50 + $1 per page for each page except the first	
	General Petition – except as relates to custody or support of minors	$150	$15
	Summons	$5	
	Summons for Contempt	$5	

Category	Type of Pleading (in alphabetical order)	Filing Fee	Surcharge (if applicable)
	Tape Cassette or CD recordings of proceedings	$50.50 + postage per 90 minutes of recording or part thereof	
	Transcript of a Judgment	$50 + $1 per page for each page except the first	

Adopted effective July 1, 2003; Amended effective November, 2007; July 1, 2009; July 9, 2012; October 17, 2012; May 15, 2015.

UNIFORM PRACTICES OF PROBATE AND FAMILY COURTS

Table of Practices

Practice I. Certification of Securities Held by Corporate Fiduciary, Custodian or Agent

Guardians ad litem shall where applicable attach to their report to be filed with the register of probate the certification of the corporate fiduciary, custodian or agent described in G.L. c. 167G, § 3, para. 5, in substantially the following form, that securities filed by issue, held in bulk, or deposited in a securities depository, clearing corporation or federal reserve bank are, in fact, held by the corporate fiduciary, custodian or agent. Such certification shall relieve the guardian ad litem of any further duty to verify the existence of such securities.

FORM OF CERTIFICATION

In accordance with Massachusetts G.L. c. 167G, § 3, para. 5, we hereby certify that the securities contained on the attached list of assets are held by us in our capacity as _____, for the amount of _____.

We agree to hold harmless any interested party, or fiduciary or guardian representing such party for loss arising from reliance upon this certificate.

Bank and Trust Company
By _____
Title _____

Amended December 4, 1979, effective December 17, 1979; December 15, 1986, effective January 2, 1987.

Practice II. Necessity of Corroborating Witness(es) in Uncontested Divorce and Annulment Matters

Corroborating witness(es) shall not be required except where necessary, *e.g.*, in adultery cases (where plaintiff does not have personal knowledge), in imprisonment cases where the plaintiff was not present in court when defendant was sentenced, and in any other case when the court so requires.

Practice III. Petitions for Temporary Guardianship and Conservatorship

Uniform Practice III has been superseded by Probate Court Rule 29B and, therefore, is no longer in effect.

Practice IV. Petitions for Contempt

Upon a hearing for contempt, the judge may, when notice has been given of the intention to assess any arrearage to the date of the hearing, order the defendant to make payment of all arrearages outstanding on the date of the hearing, and upon failure to make such payment make such order as is authorized by G.L. Chapter 215, Section 34.

Practice V. Temporary Restraining Orders in Equity Cases

See Rule 65, Massachusetts Rules of Civil Procedure, which is similar to this Practice.

Practice VI. Temporary Restraining Orders in Probate Divorce and Separate Support Matters

Uniform Practice VI is superseded by Rule 6(c) and 65(a) of Domestic Relations Procedure.

Practice VII. Support Orders Against Non–Residents [Repealed]

Repealed effective October 30, 1996.

Practice VIII. Uniform Fees

Pursuant to Chapter 684, of the Acts of 1972, each Registry of Probate is required, unless otherwise waived by rule of court, to receive all fees therein enumerated.

"Amendment of record" as listed therein shall uniformly be interpreted to include such motions as may require any amendment of any document recorded pursuant to Rule 25.

Practice IX. Stenographers

The register of probate, unless otherwise ordered by a probate judge, pursuant to Rule 18, or Mass.R.Dom.Rel.P. 202, shall assess the full costs of a stenographer against the party marking such case for trial where the trial is cancelled, unless twenty-four hours' notice, in writing, is given to the register to cancel the request for the stenographer.

Practice X. Plan of Adoption Required in Petitions to Establish Consent

In an uncontested adoption, filed pursuant to Chapter 210, Section 3, requiring the submission of a plan, the Department of Social Services or other agency shall submit to the Court at the time of allowance a written report. The report shall consist of:

1. a. The name, date of birth and age of the child who is the subject of the proceeding.

b. The name(s), current address(es), and age(s) of the biological/legal parents, to the extent the information is available.

c. History of legal actions including the present action; Date of petition, Return date, how notice was accomplished, if a valid surrender was filed and by whom, that the petition was uncontested.

d. Brief background on the fitness, availability, capacity and readiness of parents to assume parental responsibility for the child; Acts of neglect, emotional/physical/sexual abuse, psychiatric/psychological evaluations, interactions and attachments between parents and child, and the timetable, if any, when parent(s) will be able to assume the care and custody of the child and the effect of this change on the minor.

e. The needs of the child.

2. The agency's plan for the child upon the release of the required parental consent. A plan that elaborates in detail what steps the agency plans to employ to find a suitable adoptive parent may be deemed sufficient without further specificity.

Amended December 14, 1979, effective January 28, 1980; amended effective July 1, 1989.

Comment—1989 Amendment

The amendment to Uniform Practices X requires a detailed plan be submitted to the court in *uncontested* matters.

Practice XA. Tracking System and Procedures for Termination Petitions Filed Pursuant to M.G.L. Ch. 210, Sec. 3 [Repealed]

Repealed effective September 10, 2004.

Reporter's Notes

The repeal of Uniform Practice Xa is necessitated by the implementation of the revised Standing Order on Time Standards in an effort to consolidate all case management related policies and procedures in one place.

Practice XB. Tracking System and Procedures for Petitions Filed Pursuant to M.G.L. Ch. 119, Sec. 23C and Ch. 201, Sec. 5 by the Department of Social Services or Other Child Welfare Agency [Repealed]

Repealed effective September 10, 2004.

Reporter's Notes—2004

The repeal of Uniform Practice Xb is necessitated by the implementation of the revised Standing Order on Time Standards in an effort to consolidate all case management related policies and procedures in one place.

Practice XI. Trial Assignments [Repealed]

Repealed effective September 10, 2004.

Reporter's Notes—2004

The repeal of Uniform Practice XI is necessitated by the implementation the revised Standing Order on Time Standards in an effort to consolidate all case management related policies and procedures in one place.

Practice XII. Notices of Divorce Decrees

Upon the entry of a temporary order or a judgment of divorce nisi, separate support, or annulment or any modification thereof, the register of probate shall give notice to the defendant and all attorneys at the last known address of record of the entry of such order or judgment, including as part of said notice any order for support or alimony.

(Note: This practice has been amended to delete the requirement of giving notice of the entry of a divorce judgment absolute.)

Practice XIII. Domestic Relations—Acceptance of Service—Summons Form

When service of a complaint is accepted in accordance with Dom.Rel.P. Rule 4(d)(1), such acceptance shall be as prescribed on the Domestic Relations Summons form.

Amended October 31, 1978, effective November 16, 1978; June 25, 1979, effective July 19, 1979.

Practice XIV. Conveyance of Real Estate

No conveyance of real estate pursuant to General Laws, Chapter 208, sec. 34A or Chapter 209, secs. 30, 32 and 32D shall be entered in any order or judgment of divorce or separate support unless a specific demand therefor has been made in the complaint of which the defendant has received actual notice; or unless an affidavit of notice stating that the defendant has been notified by certified mail, return receipt requested, and returned signed by the defendant, of the intention of the plaintiff to request the conveyance of specific real estate is filed in the Registry of Probate at least seven days prior to the hearing of said case.

No conveyance of real estate may be ordered in any judgment against a non-resident unless personal service of a complaint and affidavit, as above-described, has been made in accordance with General Laws Chapter 208, sec. 8 and Rule 4 of the Massachusetts Rules of Domestic Relations Procedure.

Amended February 2, 1981, effective March 2, 1981.

Practice XV. Probate Accounts [Repealed]

Repealed effective January 2, 2012.

Reporter's Notes—2012

Uniform Practice XV is repealed in light of Probate Court Rule 29A which has been revised and renumbered as Rule 72A of the Supplemental Rules of the Probate and Family Court. *See also* Rule 72A of the Supplemental Rules of the Probate and Family Court.

Practice XVI. Allowance of Probate Accounts Pursuant to Rule 72 of the Massachusetts Rules of Civil Procedure [Repealed]

Repealed effective January 2, 2012.

Reporter's Notes—2012

Uniform Practice XVI is repealed in light of the adoption of Rule 72 of the Supplemental Rules of the Probate and Family Court. *See also* Rule 72 of the Supplemental Rules of the Probate and Family Court.

Practice XVIA. Co–Fiduciary Accounts— Appointment of G.A.L.

If a non-accounting co-fiduciary of an accountant, who has received or waived notice relating to the allowance of the account(s), currently represents the interests of a person or persons, the court may waive the appointment of a guardian ad litem for such person or persons upon motion of the accountant brought ex parte.

Such motion shall be accompanied by an affidavit representing:

1. that such co-fiduciary has received or waived notice relating to the allowance of the pending account(s);

2. that such co-fiduciary is not aware of any conflict of interest which would prevent him from representing the person or persons whose interest would otherwise require appointment of a G.A.L.;

3. that such co-fiduciary has a duty to account in his capacity as a fiduciary;

4. that such co-fiduciary recognizes that he has a fiduciary duty to review such pending accounts with due care and has done so; and

5. that such fiduciary assents to the allowance of the pending account(s).

Such motion may be allowed without a hearing in the discretion of the court; provided, however, that the accountant shall be given an opportunity to be heard before such motion is denied.

Adopted effective May 1, 1984.

Practice XVIB. Power of Appointment—Waiver of Guardian Ad Litem [Repealed]

Repealed effective January 2, 2012.

Reporter's Notes—2012

The repeal of Uniform Practice XVIB is necessitated by the repeal of G.L. c. 206, § 24, which formed the basis for the uniform practice. *See also* G.L. c. 190B, §§ 1–403 and 1–404.

Practice XVII. Accounts—Time for Allowance

(a) Estates of Decedents Dying Prior to January 1, 1990. An account of a personal representative may be presented for allowance after the expiration of nine months from the date upon which the personal representative's bond was approved.

(b) Estates of Decedents Dying On or After January 1, 1990. An account of a personal representative may be presented for allowance upon the expiration of one year from the date of death of the decedent.

(c) Any account which shows a zero balance in Schedule C may be labeled "final."

Amended effective January 1, 1992; January 2, 2012.

Reporter's Notes (2012)

Practice updated to reflect terminology changes introduced by the Massachusetts Uniform Probate Code, G. L. c. 190B.

Practice XVIII. Annulment

A petition for annulment or affirmation of marriage shall be presented on a general petition.

Practice XIX. Dismissal of Appeals

Appeals shall be dismissed only upon a written motion to dismiss and seven days' notice of such motion must be given by certified mail.

Practice XX.　Assents

A fiduciary need only sign a petition once if all the individual capacities in which he signs or assents are indicated under his signature.

Practice XXI.　Marking Ex Parte Lists

Matters may be placed upon the motion and ex parte list only by written request or by personal entry by the party or his attorney at the Registry.

Practice XXII.　Medical Certificate (Guardian–Conservator)

When accepted by the Court, a Medical Certificate shall be completed by a physician, a certified psychiatric nurse clinical specialist, a licensed psychologist, or a nurse practitioner, professionally competent to complete a medical certificate.

Amended effective April 21, 2008; amended effective July 1, 2009; November 16, 2010.

Reporter's Notes–2010

The title and practice were amended to allow a nurse practitioner to complete a Medical Certificate. The requirement that the medical certificate be dated and the examination have taken place within thirty (30) days prior to the entry of the decree is deleted since it is required by G.L. c. 190B, 5–306(b)(4).

Reporter's Notes–2009

The title and practice were amended to conform with the new Medical Certificate issued by the Probate and Family Court Administrative Office.

Reporter's Notes–2008

The Practice was amended to conform with the new Medical Certificate issued by the Probate and Family Court Administrative Office.

Practice XXII(A).　Clinical Team Report (Guardian–Conservator of Mentally Retarded) [Deleted]

Deleted effective July 1, 2009.

Practice XXIII.　Modification of Temporary Orders [Repealed]

Repealed June 5, 2003, effective September 2, 2003.

Reporter's Notes–2003

The repeal of Uniform Practice XXIII reflects that the Practice was inconsistent with the time standards of Rule 6(c).

Practice XXIV.　[Deleted]

Deleted effective January 9, 1978.

Practice XXV.　Military Affidavits

If there has not been an answer or other appearance (as defined in Rule 11(b) of the Massachusetts Rules of Civil Procedure) filed in a matter by each defendant, respondent or other interested person, after the time for filing the answer or other appearance has expired, after diligent inquiry a military affidavit certifying the military status of each defendant, respondent or other interested person who has not appeared or answered must be filed before the earliest of:

(1) any subsequent request for a court hearing; or

(2) the date of the next event scheduled by the court; or

(3) a temporary order in the case.

A subsequent military affidavit must be filed before a final judgment or decree may be entered in a case when more than three (3) months have expired from the filing of the prior military affidavit and the prior military affidavit states that each defendant, respondent, or interested person is not currently in military service or military status cannot be determined.

A military affidavit shall not be required to be filed when it appears that all interested persons have filed a written assent to the allowance or judgment.

Amended effective January 2, 2012; June 1, 2018.

Reporter's Notes—2012

The Practice is amended to apply generally to all matters in the Probate and Family Court.

Reporter's Notes—2018

The Practice is amended to clarify when a military affidavit is required to be filed in all matters in the Probate and Family Court. The Servicemembers Civil Relief Act, 50 U.S.C. § 3931, requires that in cases in which the defendant does not make an appearance, the plaintiff must file an affidavit as to military service before the court may enter judgment—temporary or final. If it appears from the military affidavit that the defendant is in military service, no judgment (temporary or final) may be entered until the court appoints an attorney to represent the non-appearing defendant.

Practice XXVI.　Probate of Will— Incompetent Heir [Repealed]

Repealed effective January 2, 2012.

Reporter's Notes—2012

The repeal of Uniform Practice XXVI is necessitated by the enactment of G.L. c. 190B, § 1–404(d), which mandates the appointment of a guardian ad litem in certain proceedings

Practice XXVII.　Contempt Summons

Whenever an original summons for contempt shall be caused to be issued, the day set for court appearance shall be no less than fifteen days from the date that the court causes the summons to be issued unless a different period is fixed by order of the court. The summons shall indicate that service must be made upon the defendant at least seven days prior to the return date unless the court otherwise orders. If service is not made within seven days said summons shall be returned to the court.

Adopted January 10, 1978, effective January 17, 1978.

Practice XXVIII.　Masters—Periodic Reports

In all cases Masters shall give a written progress report to the appointing justice at least every thirty days. This practice shall be typed or printed on every reference to a Master.

Failure to observe this practice may be cause for revocation of the reference to the Master.

Adopted October 31, 1978, effective November 16, 1978.

Practice XXIX. Special Administrators— Limitation on Appointments [Repealed]

Repealed effective January 2, 2012.

Practice XXX. Filing of Financial Statements

No complaint for divorce brought pursuant to G.L. c. 208, secs. 1, 1A or 1B, nor complaint for separate support under G.L. c. 209, nor complaint for any modification thereof shall be marked for a hearing unless a financial statement of each party is on file with the court.

This requirement may be waived:

1.) by the court, sua sponte;

2.) on the motion of either party asserting non-compliance with Supplemental Rule 401 by the other party which is accompanied by a request for sanctions pursuant to Dom. Rel. P. Rule 37, or

3.) on an affidavit asserting unavailability of the opposing party which precludes compliance with Rule 401 and this practice.

A previously filed financial statement shall be deemed acceptable for the purposes of this practice if a sworn statement is filed stating that there has been no change in the party's finances since the last statement was filed.

Adopted December 4, 1979, effective December 17, 1979. Amended effective August 1, 1982.

Practice XXXI. Income Assignments in Uncontested Matters

An executed income assignment form shall be prepared by counsel and filed with the court prior to hearing in all actions or motions seeking support or alimony in which an assent, agreement or stipulation is filed with the court relative to the support or alimony issue. This practice shall not prohibit the scheduling of such matter prior to the filing of the assignment.

Adopted effective May 1, 1984.

Practice XXXII. Compensation of Guardians Ad Litem: Limitation On Hours

A. 1. Guardians ad litem appointed by justices of the Probate and Family Court Department in cases in which the cost will be borne by the Commonwealth, except as otherwise provided herein, shall be compensated at the rate of $50.00 per hour including expenses. This rate does not apply in cases in which the G.A.L. is paid by a party or from an estate unless specifically ordered by the court.

2. Guardians ad litem appointed to serve process pursuant to MGL 215:56 B shall be compensated at the rate of $17.00 per hour, plus expenses, excluding travel.

B. The appointment of any guardian ad litem in cases in which the cost will be borne by the Commonwealth shall be limited to ten hours. An extension of time may be authorized by the court for additional hours upon motion of the guardian ad litem. The guardian ad litem shall be advised by the Register of this limitation in writing.

C. No payment for services shall be authorized and approved by the court until the guardian ad litem has filed a report and surrendered his or her appointment except where the Court orders otherwise.

D. The Court shall examine the financial ability of the parties to pay for all or a portion of the fees of the guardian ad litem so appointed and the parties shall be notified by the Court of its intention to assess the cost of the service of the guardian ad litem against either or both of them.

Adopted effective January 1, 1988.

Practice XXXIII. Standards for Computer Generated Forms

Preamble: This Uniform Practice governs the use of computer-generated forms by counsel and parties.

Definition: For the purposes of this Uniform Practice XXXIII, the "official form" shall be defined as either: (i) the paper form promulgated and distributed by the Administrative Office of the Probate and Family Court or (ii) the electronic form most recently posted on the Massachusetts Judiciary web site, www.mass.gov/courts and approved by the Administrative Office of the Probate and Family Court.

I. Use. The use of computer-generated forms is hereby permitted, except where the Court blank ("official form") is a multi-part form, such as the G.L. c. 209A Complaint For Protection From Abuse form.

II. Specifications.

A. *Paper.* 8 ½ × 11 inch, acid free paper shall be used for all computer-generated forms. Acid free paper is specified to ensure archival quality and permanence.

B. *Paper and Ink Color.* A computer-generated form shall be printed with black ink on white paper except for forms CJ–D 301 S Financial Statement (short form) and CJ–D 301 L Financial Statement (long form), which shall be printed with black ink on pink colored paper, and form CJ–D 304 Child Support Guidelines Worksheet shall be printed with black ink on light-blue colored paper.

C. *Printing.* All computer-generated forms shall be printed with "letter quality" or "near letter quality" output. "Draft" quality output is not acceptable.

III. Consequences of Failing to Follow These Standards. The Register of Probate may reject any form that fails to comply with these standards. In the event that a Register deems a submitted form to be outside these standards, such determination may be reviewed by the Chief Justice of the Probate and Family Court at the request of the submitting counsel or party. It is the responsibility of the submitting party to ensure that the form adheres to the above standards. If the form is rejected, the submitting party shall forfeit the filing fee. The submitting party's attorney shall not be allowed to pass this cost on to his/her client, but shall bear the financial burden personally. Accordingly, the submitting party's attorney shall either reimburse the client for the forfeited fee or the attorney shall personally pay the filing fee when he/she refiles the form.

Adopted effective January 1, 1992. Amended effective September 4, 2007; effective April 7, 2008; effective January 1, 2009.

Reporter's Notes—2008

The 2008 amendment to Uniform Practice XXXIII requires that forms CJ-D 301 S Financial Statement (short form) and CJ-D 301 L Financial Statement (long form), be printed with black ink on pink colored paper and that form CJ-D 304 Child Support Guidelines Worksheet be printed with black ink on yellow colored paper.

The December 2008 amendment to Uniform Practice XXXIII requires that form CJ-D 304 Child Support Guidelines Worksheet be printed with black ink on light-blue colored paper. The change was necessitated by the amendments to the Child Support Guidelines effective January 1, 2009.

Practice XXXIV. Charitable Interests

A. When Notice to the Attorney General Is Required.

1. In connection with a petition for informal probate or appointment pursuant to G.L. c. 190B, § 3–306 or in formal testacy proceedings pursuant to § 3–403, notice to the Office of the Attorney General, Division of Public Charities, is required if:

  a. There is no spouse or heir of the decedent; or

  b. Any devisee is a charity; or

  c. A will contains a devise to the trustee(s) of an inter vivos trust, where the trust instrument provides for one or more charitable gifts; and the personal representative(s) and the trustee(s) are the same persons or entities or the trustee or one of the trustees has a beneficial interest in the estate or trust.

Where notice is required because of a charitable interest, the initial notice shall be accompanied by a copy of the will and, where the charitable interest is through a trust, either a copy of the trust instrument or a summary of the charitable gifts contained therein certified to be accurate by the trustee or his or her representative.

2. With respect to any estate as to which notice is required under Paragraph A1 above, notice shall also be given to the Office of the Attorney General, Division of Public Charities, of any subsequent filing by the personal representative(s) of such estate relating to a matter which will affect the charitable interest, including without limitation the allowance of accounts, the sale of an asset, the compromise of a claim, the removal of a fiduciary, and the appointment of a successor fiduciary. A notice relating to the allowance of an account shall be accompanied by a copy of the account.

3. Notice to the Office of the Attorney General, Division of Public Charities, is required in connection with a petition or complaint filed by (a) the trustee(s) of a trust, created either by written instrument or by will, under which there are present or future charitable interests; (b) a charitable corporation; and (c) any other entity holding property in a fiduciary capacity for the benefit of a charitable entity or purpose. The notice shall be accompanied by a copy of the petition or complaint and a copy of the governing instrument(s) unless provided previously.

B. Attorney General as a Necessary Party to an Action.

In matters before the court as set forth below, the Attorney General shall be a necessary party. The plaintiff shall not present to the court any request for affirmative action with respect to the relief being requested unless the Attorney General has been made a party with proper service. The matters to which this section applies are:

1. A complaint by a fiduciary for cy pres relief or for authority to deviate from the terms of a governing instrument which deviation may affect a charitable interest.

2. A complaint by a fiduciary for instructions or a declaratory judgment in which the relief sought may affect a charitable interest.

3. Compromise of a will which compromise may affect a charitable interest.

4. A complaint by a fiduciary for a license to sell an asset in circumstances in which a charitable interest may be affected by the sale.

5. A complaint by a fiduciary for authority to consolidate or terminate a trust pursuant to G.L. c. 190B or otherwise, which consolidation or termination may affect a charitable interest.

C. Attorney General as an Interested Party.

In all other matters before the court or magistrate where the Attorney General is not a necessary party, as described above in Paragraph B, but is an interested party entitled to notice of the proceedings and an opportunity to be heard, the matter, provided notice is given and the notice period has expired, may be presented to the court or magistrate, in an informal or uncontested formal proceeding, without regard to whether the Attorney General has assented thereto or indicated that he or she does not wish to be heard.

Adopted effective December 1, 1996. Amended effective January 2, 2012.

Reporter's Notes (2012)

The Practice is amended as a result of the enactment of the Massachusetts Uniform Probate Code, G. L. c. 190B.

Practice XXXV. Change of Name Actions

(a) Scope. Pursuant to G. L. c. 210, § 12, a petition for the change of name of a resident of Massachusetts may be heard by the division of the Probate and Family Court (hereinafter "the Court") in the county where the petitioner resides. If the petition for the change of name is for a minor child, the minor child shall be listed as the petitioner. The minor child's legal parent(s) or any court-appointed guardian(s) as next friend will present the petition to the Court.

(b) Separate Petition Required. To seek a name change, a petition for a change of name must be filed unless:

(1) A party in a divorce case seeks to resume that party's birth surname or that of a former spouse prior to the issuance of the judgment of divorce (G. L. c. 208, § 23); or

(2) An individual seeks to change the name of the person to be adopted as part of an adoption proceeding (G. L. c. 210, § 6); or

(3) A parentage judgment includes an order to amend the name of the child in an Order to Amend Birth Certificate (G. L. c. 209C, § 8; see also G. L. c. 46, § 13(d)(4)).

(c) Proper Filing. A properly filed name change request includes:

(1) A Petition to Change Name of Adult or Petition to Change Name of Minor on a form issued and approved by the Court;

(2) A certified copy of the birth certificate of the person whose name is to be changed. Any birth certificate containing foreign language must be accompanied by a professional English language translation. The translator must provide a notarized statement of the accuracy of the translation and self-certification of their ability to translate;

(3) A Court Activity Record Information (CARI) and Warrant Management System (WMS) Release Request form (CJP 34) (for the name change of any person 12 years of age or older);

(4) A certified copy of any prior name change (i.e., marriage certificate, divorce decree, court order changing name);

(5) The filing fee, including the fee for any citation (unless the filing fee is waived by the Court pursuant to G. L. c. 261; see also section (d) and section (f)(4) of this Uniform Practice); and

(6) If the petition seeks to change the name of a minor, the following additional requirements:

(A) The notarized assent of any minor 12 years of age or older;

(B) The death certificate of any deceased legal parent; and

(C) The Affidavit Disclosing Care or Custody Proceedings form.

(d) Joint Filing Fee. If an entire family seeks a name change or two or more children who have the same legal parents seek a name change, a separate petition must be filed for each person whose name is seeking to be changed, but the filing fee shall be assessed on one petition only (unless the filing fee is otherwise waived by the Court pursuant to G. L. c. 261).

(e) CARI and WMS Check. The Probation Department shall conduct a Court Activity Record Information (CARI) and Warrant Management System (WMS) check for any person 12 years of age or older who is the subject of a petition for a change of name.

(f) Notice Requirements. After the filing of a petition and payment or waiver of the filing fees, the Court shall set a return date and issue a citation. Rule 6 of the Supplemental Rules of the Probate and Family Court applies to such citations, except as changed below.

The petitioner, or the next friend in the case of a petition to change the name of a minor, shall cause citation notice to be made as follows:

(1) *Notice by Publication.* In all cases, pursuant to the requirement of G. L. c. 210, § 13, service shall be made to the public by publication unless the publication requirement is waived by the Court on motion for good cause shown.[1]

(2) *Additional Notice in Certain Cases Whether an Adult or Minor.* Before the Court may grant a change of name for any person who is incarcerated, on probation or parole, or who is committed to the Massachusetts Treatment Center as a sexually dangerous person, the petitioner must serve a copy of the petition and the citation by certified mail, return receipt requested, on the following:

(A) The Massachusetts Department of Correction, or the Massachusetts Parole Board, respectively; and

(B) The office of the prosecuting official (District Attorney, Attorney General, or United States Attorney) and the Sheriff's Office(s) in the jurisdiction where the conviction(s) or delinquency adjudication(s) occurred.

(C) For a person who is required, pursuant to G. L. c. 6, § 178C to register as a sexual offender, the petitioner must serve a copy of the petition and the citation on the Sex Offender Registry Board and the prosecuting official by certified mail, return receipt requested.

(3) *Additional Notice in Cases Involving Minors.* In addition to the notice requirements in (f)(1) and (f)(2) above, notice must be given to any legal parent who has not assented to the petition and to any court-appointed guardian who has not assented to the petition. Exceptions to the additional notice required under this section are as provided for in section (D) below. The citation shall be served with a copy of the petition, in the following manner:

(A) Service Within Massachusetts. Service within Massachusetts shall be made by mailing the citation and petition by certified or registered mail, return receipt requested.

(B) Service Outside of Massachusetts. If it appears from the petition that a person is outside of Massachusetts in any part of the United States, its Commonwealths or territories, or outside the United States, service of the citation shall be made by mailing the citation and petition by certified or registered mail, return receipt requested.

(C) Service When Address or Whereabouts Is Unknown or Service Cannot be Accomplished. If it appears from the petition that the address or whereabouts of a legal parent or court-appointed guardian is unknown or if the address or whereabouts is known but service by certified or registered mail cannot be accomplished despite diligent efforts, on written motion setting forth the diligent efforts made to ascertain their address or whereabouts (see form CJP 31, Motion for Alternate Service and Affidavit of Diligent Search), the Court may order that service shall be made, either within or outside Massachusetts, by publication only or by any other manner approved by the Court. Whenever the Court orders alternate service under this subsection, the Court shall also require that a military affidavit be filed as to the person to be served by publication or other manner.

(D) When Additional Notice is Not Required. The additional notice required under section (3)(A), (3)(B) or (3)(C) above does not need to be given when: (i) the legal parent(s) and any court-appointed guardian(s) have assented in writing to the allowance of the petition and the notarized assents are filed with the Court (see form CJP 25, Petition to Change Name of Minor or form CJP 30, Assent to Petition to Change Name of Minor); (ii) a legal parent executes an adoption surrender in conformity with G. L. c. 210, § 2; (iii) a court has terminated parental rights; or (iv) the Court on motion for good cause has otherwise ordered or waived notice. This section does not impact the notice required by section (f)(1), *Notice by Publication*, or (f)(2), *Additional Notice in Certain Cases Whether an Adult or Minor*.

(4) *Joint Citation.* If an entire family seeks a name change or two or more children who have the same legal parents seek a name change, the Court shall issue one citation for purposes of publication or for any other notice requirements.

(5) *Proof of Notice.* Proof of notice, including proof of publication and certified or registered mailing shall be filed with the Court prior to allowance of the petition. When service is made by mail, proof of notice shall include a receipt signed by the addressee or other evidence of personal delivery to the addressee satisfactory to the Court.

(g) Objecting to a Petition. Any person may appear for purposes of objecting to the petition by filing an appearance prior to the return date listed on the citation and such appearances may not be stricken. Any person appearing in a proceeding for change of name has a right to be heard on the merits of the petition.

(h) Hearing Not Required. If no objections to the petition are filed, the Court, in its discretion, may act upon the petition without a hearing.

(i) Proof of Change of Name. If the Court grants the petition for the change of name, a certified copy of the decree shall issue. If requested, a Certificate of Name Change, under seal of the Court, may be issued by the registry upon payment of the proper fee (unless fees have been waived by the Court pursuant to G. L. c. 261).

(j) Statutory Notification of Changes of Name. Each register of probate shall, at a minimum, make an annual return in December of each year, or as otherwise may be required by G. L. c. 210, § 14, to the Commonwealth's Registry of Vital Records and Statistics under the supervision of the Commissioner of Public Health, and to the Commissioner of Probation of all changes of name which have been granted during that year in the division.

Adopted June 5, 2018, effective August 1, 2018.

1Examples of good cause shown may include that (a) the petitioner seeks to change a first/middle name only; (b) the change of name of a minor child is assented to by all persons interested; (c) publication poses a safety risk to an adult or minor child; and (d) the petitioner seeks to resume a former legal name.

Reporter's Notes—2018

Practice XXXV governs change of name actions filed in the Probate and Family Court for which a separate petition is required. The Practice is adopted to clarify procedural omissions in the controlling statute, G. L. c. 210, § 12 *et seq.* The Practice, *inter alia*, makes clear the notice requirements in change of name actions for both adults and minors, including the statutory requirement to provide notice to the public by publication in all cases.

STANDING ORDERS OF THE PROBATE AND FAMILY COURT

Table of Standing Orders

Standing Order 1–83. Pre–Trial Conferences [Repealed]

Repealed by Standing Order 2–88, adopted March 31, 1988, effective May 1, 1988.

Standing Order 2–83. Individual Calendar Sessions

No division of the Probate & Family Court Department currently utilizing a master calendar system, so-called, shall implement an individual calendar system for any justice without the prior written approval of the Chief Justice of this department.

Divisions currently utilizing individual calendar systems may continue to do so, provided, however, that no such system shall be modified to include any judgeship established after July 1, 1982 without prior written approval of the Chief Justice of this department.

Adopted December 1, 1983.

Standing Order 1–88. Time Standards [Deleted]

Deleted with the adoption of Standing Order 1–04, adopted effective October 4, 2004.

Standing Order 2–88. Pre–Trial Conferences [Deleted]

Deleted with the adoption of Standing Order 1–04, adopted effective October 4, 2004.

Standing Order 1–94. Assignment of Cases to the Middlesex Satellite Sessions At Concord and Marlborough [Repealed]

Repealed effective January 16, 2004.

Standing Order 1–95. Parent Education Program Attendance [Deleted]

Applicable to the Berkshire, Hampshire, Norfolk and Worcester Divisions

Deleted with the adoption of Standing Order 1–97, adopted May 22, 1997, effective July 1, 1997.

Standing Order 1–97. Parent Education Program Attendance [Deleted]

(APPLICABLE TO THE BERKSHIRE, FRANKLIN, HAMPSHIRE, HAMPDEN, NORFOLK, PLYMOUTH AND WORCESTER DIVISIONS)

Deleted with the adoption of Standing Order 1–03, adopted effective August 1, 2003.

Standing Order 2–97. Service

Service by facsimile or other electronic or telephonic transmittal is not service within the meaning of Mass.R.Dom.Rel.P. 5 unless expressly permitted by a specific rule for a specific purpose, by order of the court for cause shown, or pursuant to a written stipulation of the parties allowing for service by facsimile.

Adopted effective November 1, 1997.

Standing Order 1–98. Parent Education Program Attendance [Deleted]

Deleted with the adoption of Standing Order 1–03, adopted effective August 1, 2003.

Standing Order 2–98. Tracking of Appointments of Guardians *Ad Litem* and Probation Officers to Conduct Investigations in Domestic Relations* and Child Welfare† Matters

It is ordered that the Probation Department of each Division shall track all appointments of Guardians *Ad Litem* and Probation Officers to conduct investigations in Domestic Relations* and Child Welfare† matters.

The following procedure will be followed:

1. When a Judge appoints a Guardian *Ad Litem* (G.A.L.) or a Probation Officer (P.O.) to conduct an investigation in Domestic Relations or Child Welfare matters, the person preparing the appointment form will provide the Probation Department with a copy of the completed form.

2. Upon receipt of the copy of the appointment form the Probation Department will prepare a tracking system which will record, at a minimum, the following:

a. Docket number;

b. Name of the case;

c. Date of appointment;

d. Name of the Judge making the appointment;

e. Whether the appointing judge wants to be notified when the Report is filed;

f. Name(s) of Attorney(s) of record;

g. Name of G.A.L. or P.O.;

h. Due date of the Report;

i. Extension date, if any, granted by the judge;

j. Date Report is received;

k. Date Parties are notified of receipt of Report;

l. Pre-trial date; and

m. Trial date.

3. The G.A.L. will file his/her report with the Probation Department on or before the due date. In situations where the G.A.L. has not filed his/her report in a timely fashion, the Probation Department will contact the G.A.L., either by telephone or in writing, to notify him/her of the need to file the Report and determine if an extension is necessary. If the G.A.L. fails to respond or fails to meet the agreed upon due date, the Probation Department shall notify the Judge who made the appointment of this fact and seek further instruction. It is expected that the Probation Department has in place a mechanism to ensure the timeliness of Reports on investigations performed by its Probation Officers in accordance with the Standards of the Office of the Commissioner of Probation.

4. Once the Report is filed, the Probation Department will notify in writing the attorney(s) of record, if any, or the litigant(s) if *pro se* that the Report has been filed and is available for inspection; how to inspect the Report; and that it is required that counsel or a party, within thirty (30) days from the date of the notice, request the hearing of the matter as an uncontested matter or the scheduling of a pre-trial conference. In its notice the Probation Department shall give a brief description of the process for requesting an uncontested hearing or pre-trial conference. For *pro se* litigants, a Trial Request Form shall be sent with the notice.

5. Once the Probation Office has recorded the receipt of the G.A.L. Report, the Report shall be filed and stored in accordance with the directions of the First Justice.

6. After thirty (30) days from the date of notice to counsel or the parties the Probation Department will contact the Trial Department to establish whether a Trial Request Form has been received requesting an uncontested hearing or a pre-trial conference. If no request has been received, the Trial Assignment Clerk shall schedule a pre-trial conference.

7. On the first day of each month, the Probation Department will supply each judge with a status report on his/her outstanding G.A.L. and/or Probation Officer investigations and a report to the First Justice as to the status of all Guardian *Ad Litem* and Probation Officer investigations in the Division.

The court shall provide a copy of this protocol to the Guardian *Ad Litem* with each appointment.

Adopted September 22, 1998, effective October 1, 1998.

Standing Order 1–99.   Parent Education Program Attendance [Deleted]

Deleted with the adoption of Standing Order 1–03, adopted effective August 1, 2003.

Standing Order 2–99.   Procedure for Submission and Disposition of Certain Post-Hearing Motions

Pursuant to Rule 78 of the Rules of Civil Procedure and Domestic Relations Procedure, the provisions of this Standing Order shall apply to the following post-hearing motions:

i) to Amend Findings of Fact (Rule 52)

ii) to Amend Conclusions of Law (Rule 52)

iii) for New Trial (Rule 59)

iv) to Amend Judgments (Rule 59 (e))

v) for Relief from Judgment and Order (Rule 60)

The purpose of this Standing Order is to set out the procedures by which relief pursuant to subparagraphs i) through v) above, is sought. This Standing Order does not create any substantive right to relief, other than as set forth above.

Motions for post-hearing relief should be titled to reference the rule the moving party asserts is applicable to the relief requested. Even if the rule is not specifically identified, the motion shall be disposed of by the Court in accordance with the factors and time limitations set out in the applicable Rule specified in subparagraphs i) through v) above, since no other relief is available. The provisions of this Standing Order shall not apply to the following:

i) Objections to a Judgment of Divorce Nisi- pursuant to Rule 58(c) of the Rules of Domestic Relations Procedure

ii) Motions to Stay Proceedings to Enforce a Judgment (Rule 62)

(a) Submission of the Motion and Opposition Thereto.

(1) *Submission of Motion.* The moving party shall serve with the motion a copy of the order or judgment at issue and a concise statement of facts and law in support of why the motion should be granted. The statement shall be no longer than five (5) pages and shall be signed under the penalties of perjury. All documents required to be served with the motion shall be filed with the court on the date of service or within five (5) days after service. Compliance with this paragraph is compliance with the "reasonable time" provisions of Mass. R.Civ.P. 5(d)(1) and Mass.R.Dom. Rel.P. 5(d)(1).

(2) *Submission of Statement in Opposition or Support of the Motion.* Except by leave of court, upon motion, within ten (10) days after service of the motion, the non-moving party(ies) opposing or supporting the motion may file and serve a concise statement of facts and law in opposition to or in support of the motion. Said statement shall be no longer than five (5) pages, should explain why the motion should or should not be allowed, and shall be signed under the penalties of perjury.

(3) *Additional Papers.* With the exception of the certificate of service or, when applicable, the motion to extend the time for filing the statement in opposition or support of the motion

provided for under paragraph (a)(2) of this rule, papers not served with the motion or statement in opposition or support may be filed only with leave of court.

(4) *Form of the Motion.* The moving party shall indicate in the title of the motion the name of the Justice who decided the original order or judgment and identify the applicable rule.

(5) *Filing the Motion and Statement in Opposition or Support by Mail.* If the motion and/or the statement in opposition or support is filed by mail, the bottom left-hand corner of the envelope should clearly indicate "Post–Hearing Motion".

(b) Hearing on Motion.

(1) *Marking.* No party shall mark the motion for hearing. No later than twenty (20) days from the date the motion is filed, the motion, supporting papers and any statement(s) of opposition or support shall be transmitted to the justice who decided the original order or judgment, unless the court has extended the time for filing the statement in opposition or support of the motion. In such case, the motion and supporting papers shall be transmitted to the justice who decided the original order or judgment within five (5) days from the date the certificate of service is filed with the court on the statement in opposition or support of the motion. In the event the court believes that a hearing is necessary or helpful to the disposition of the motion, the court will set the time and date for the hearing and will notify the parties of that date and time.

(2) *Request for Hearing.* If a party wishes to request a hearing on the motion, said request shall be filed and served with the motion or the statement in opposition or support of the motion. A request for a hearing shall set forth any statute, rule of court or case law which, in the opinion of the submitting party, mandates a hearing on the motion. After reviewing the motion, the statement in opposition or support of the motion, and the request for hearing, the court will determine whether a hearing should be held and, if a hearing is to be held, will notify the parties of that date and time. Failure to request a hearing shall be deemed a waiver of any right to a hearing afforded by statute, court rule or case law.

(c) Disposition of Motion.

Motions which are not set down for hearing shall be decided on the written submissions filed in accordance with this order.

(d) Sanction for Noncompliance.

Failure to comply with any and all of the provisions of this order may result in the Court's refusal to entertain the motion and/or the imposition of sanctions and/or costs against a party or his/her counsel.

Adopted effective October 1, 1999. Amended May 23, 2012, effective July 2, 2012.

Standing Order 1–03.   Parent Education Program Attendance [Superseded]

Superseded by Standing Order 4–08, adopted April 7, 2008.

Standing Order 1–04. Time Standards for Cases Filed in the Probate and Family Court Department [Deleted]

Deleted with the adoption of Standing Order 1–06, adopted effective April 3, 2006.

Standing Order 1–05. Standards for Guardians Ad Litem/Investigators

1. The Standards for Category F, Guardians ad Litem/Investigators in actions involving: Domestic Relations or Custody/Visitation/Adoption G.L. c. 215, § 56A; c. 208, § 16, (hereinafter "Standards") are effective January 24, 2005.

2. The purpose of these Standards is to:

• provide accountability related to guardian ad litem/investigations;

• improve custody, visitation, and other outcomes for children;

• promote uniformity and consistency in guardian ad litem/investigations; and,

• promote respect for the rights of parties and their children, including their safety.

3. It is ordered that all guardians ad litem/investigators appointed pursuant to G.L. c. 215, § 56A, c. 208, § 16 utilize the Standards in conducting these investigations. Guardians ad litem/investigators who are certified by the Probate and Family Court Administrative Office to receive appointments under Supreme Judicial Court Rule 1:07, and those persons not on the list who are appointed in accordance with Section (4) of Rule 1:07, are governed by this Order and shall conduct their investigations in accordance with the Standards.

STANDARDS FOR CATEGORY F

GUARDIAN AD LITEM

INVESTIGATORS

Table of Contents

INTRODUCTION

A Category F Guardian ad Litem investigator (GAL) is appointed by the Probate and Family Court to investigate facts in cases involving the care and custody of minor children and other matters that implicate the interests or rights of children.

G.L. c. 215, § 56A; G.L. 208, § 16. A GAL is often appointed in cases that raise questions about:

• a child's best interests as related to custody and visitation;

• advantages or disadvantages of removing a child from the Commonwealth;

• changes in circumstances that might warrant modification of a judgment;

• existence of a de facto parent-child relationship;

• parental fitness as related to termination of parental rights or guardianship;

• paternity of a minor child; or

• other matters implicating the rights and interests of a minor child.

The purpose of these standards is to:

• provide accountability related to GAL investigations;

• improve custody, visitation, and other outcomes for children;

• promote uniformity and consistency in GAL investigations; and

• promote respect for the rights of parties and their children, including their safety.

These standards apply to all Category F guardian ad litem investigators.

1. THE ROLE OF THE GAL INVESTIGATOR

The GAL performs duties that are within the scope of the court order of appointment.

1.1 The GAL Shall Gather and Report Factual Data to the Court.

The role of the Category F GAL investigator is to gather and report factual information that will assist the court in making custody, visitation, or other decisions related to the welfare of a child. Unless the appointing judge specifies otherwise, the GAL investigator's role is limited to gathering and reporting information to the court. The GAL may include recommendations in the report if the order of the court authorizes inclusion of such recommendations.

Commentary. The court, not the GAL, decides legal issues and ultimately makes credibility determinations and factual findings when facts are in dispute. The GAL reports on facts and avoids providing legal conclusions or legal analysis.

Inappropriate analysis: "This case presents a legal question of first impression as to whether the mother is entitled to relief from judgment. The national trend is to deny relief in this situation and in a recent case, the SJC hinted that it also would reject a claim based on weak facts such as those in this case."

A. The GAL Investigator is Not a Clinical Evaluator and Shall Not Perform Clinical Assessments or other Clinical Functions.

The GAL should provide descriptive information without clinical interpretations, even if the GAL is a mental health professional.

Example of a descriptive statement: "Mr. Jones said that he has felt very sad since his separation with his wife; he said he has trouble sleeping, has no appetite, and has missed numerous days of work because he is too depressed to get up."

Example of improper clinical interpretation: "Mr. Jones appears to be clinically depressed."

B. The GAL Shall Investigate Only those Areas Specified by the Court.

If the GAL sees a need to broaden the scope of the investigation, the GAL shall seek authority from the court before broadening the investigation. For example, a GAL appointed to investigate the issue of visitation discovers that the major conflict between the parties involves a parent's plan to remove the child out of state. The GAL must file a motion with the court before expanding the investigation to encompass fact gathering relating to the removal issue. Copies of any and all motions filed by a GAL must be sent to counsel of record and any pro se parties.

Commentary. This standard does not preclude a GAL from investigating factual issues that were not identified at the time of the appointment if they are relevant to the legal issues identified in the appointment.

1.2 The GAL's Role Requires Participation in the Trial and Discovery.

After conducting the investigation and writing a report, the GAL shall be available for trial and for possible deposition. If the parties do not reach an agreement about their case, the GAL may be subpoenaed by a party or the court may request that the GAL be present for trial.

Commentary. Absent a protective order of the court, the GAL shall appear for deposition as required under the applicable rules and statutes as part of his or her responsibilities as the GAL.

1.3 The GAL Shall Serve as an Impartial Investigator and Reporter.

The GAL is an impartial investigator and reporter in all cases.

A. The GAL Shall Decline or Withdraw from the Appointment if a Conflict of Interest Exists, or the GAL has Information or Personal Relationships that Will Bias the Process or Outcome of the Investigation.

If the GAL has any prior or existing direct or indirect relationships with parties, their families, their attorneys, material witnesses, or someone else connected with the family, the GAL must consider whether the GAL's impartiality is compromised as a result of these relationships. The GAL shall decline the appointment if:

• The GAL or the GAL's law firm previously advised or acted as counsel for a party, child, or other person closely aligned to a party, including but not limited to a party's spouse, non-marital partner, or a material witness;

• The GAL has or had a dating or intimate relationship with any counsel of record, or a close personal relationship with any counsel of record that will impact the GAL's ability to be unbiased;

• The GAL provided counseling or other services to a party or members of the family, or a material witness;

• The GAL was married to or had a personal relationship with a party, a member of the party's family, a material witness, or another person closely aligned to a party;

• The GAL has or had pecuniary interests or financial involvement with a party, the party's spouse or non-marital partner, a material witness, counsel for a party or other person closely aligned to a party;

• The GAL's concerns about reprisal or adverse personal consequences if the report is unfavorable to a party will impede the GAL's candor or ability to be impartial and render an unbiased report;

• The GAL is aware of other circumstances that will impede the GAL's candor or ability to be impartial and render an unbiased report.

Commentary. If a GAL is aware of circumstances that indicate that the GAL may have a conflict of interest or other circumstances that may make it inappropriate for the GAL to serve as the investigator, the GAL shall disclose the information to counsel of record and any pro se parties. The GAL also shall immediately file a motion for instructions from the appointing judge as appropriate with notice to counsel and any pro se parties.

B. The GAL Engages in Nondiscriminatory Practices.

The GAL shall not engage in conduct manifesting bias or prejudice based on race, gender, religion, ethnicity, disability, age, socioeconomic status, marital status or sexual orientation against a party, witness, counsel, or other persons involved in the case.

Commentary. The GAL must be aware of how societal and personal biases may interfere with an objective investigation and recommendations. The GAL recognizes and strives to overcome any such biases. If the GAL is not able to do so, he or she must promptly decline or withdraw from the appointment. If the GAL considers factors related to race, gender, religion, ethnicity, disability, age, sexual orientation, marital status or socioeconomic status concerning a party in the investigation or report, the GAL must explain the relevance of these factors to the issues before the court.

C. The GAL Investigator Shall Not Act as an Attorney or Legal Advocate for the Child.

The GAL is an objective and even-handed reporter. The GAL shall not give legal advice or act as advocate or attorney for the child. In some cases, the child's wishes may be contrary to the child's best interests.

Commentary. A GAL is not a party to the case. A GAL is a witness to the case. A GAL shall not engage in direct or cross examinations of witnesses or conduct depositions. The GAL shall not file motions except as related to performance of the GAL's responsibilities and as provided in these standards.

D. The GAL Does Not Represent Parties or Give Them Legal Advice.

The GAL refrains from giving legal advice to parties, including but not limited to advice about how the law applies to the facts of their case, how to obtain or modify court orders, or how to draft legal documents. The GAL refers parties to their attorneys for legal advice. If a party is pro se, the GAL suggests that the party seek legal advice from an attorney.

Commentary. Many courts have "Lawyer of the Day" programs for indigent parties and many bar associations have lawyer-referral panels. Non–profit "legal aid" (a/k/a "legal services") programs may be able to provide free legal advice and representation to low income or indigent parties.

The GAL shall refrain from giving a party legal advice that he or she should drop a restraining order so that the parties may meet together with the GAL or engage in mediation pertaining to the restraining order. See G.L. c. 209A, § 3.

1.4 The GAL Avoids Dual or Multiple Roles.

The GAL shall not provide legal, mental health, mediation or other professional services to any party or the child during the investigation or pendency of the case.

Commentary. To provide such services during the investigation or pendency of the case is inconsistent with the GAL's role as an impartial investigator and reporter. The GAL, however, may provide information to the parties, the court, and counsel about community resources available to the parties, such as but not limited to substance abuse treatment programs or other professional services that may be helpful to the parties and their children.

1.5 The GAL Adheres to Applicable Ethical and Professional Standards.

The GAL shall adhere to the ethical guidelines and standards for his or her profession to the extent that these guidelines apply. An attorney must remain in good standing as a member of the bar and adhere to the Rules of Professional Conduct that apply to lawyers. See Mass. R. S. Ct. Rule 3:07. Likewise, mental health professionals must adhere to ethical and professional standards that govern their respective professions.

Commentary. There is no attorney-client confidentiality when an attorney serves as a GAL investigator because the investigator does not represent any party. If an attorney or mental health professional serving as a GAL is unable to perform his or her investigatory responsibilities because of a conflict with applicable professional standards, the GAL shall promptly file a motion to withdraw as the GAL with notice to counsel and any pro se parties.

2. COMPENSATION

GAL investigator's fees paid by the Commonwealth are set by the Administrative Office of the Trial Court. If the court order lacks clarity about who will pay for GAL services, the GAL shall file a motion for clarification by the appointing judge with notice to counsel and any pro se party. If the order specifies that compensation will be paid by the Commonwealth, the GAL is prohibited from charging additional fees to the parties. The GAL files the report in a timely fashion whether or not compensation has been paid.

Commentary. At present, Category F Guardian ad litem investigators paid by the Commonwealth are compensated in accordance with Memo No. 14 (February 28, 1997, Fiscal Year 1997) issued by the Administrative Office of the Trial Court. The GAL also may file a motion with notice to counsel and any pro se party for an extension of hours beyond the number of

hours set forth in the order of appointment for approval by the judge who appointed the GAL.

3. UPON RECEIVING THE APPOINTMENT

The GAL carefully reviews the order of appointment to determine the scope of the investigation and the duties to be performed.

3.1 The GAL Clarifies the Scope of the Appointment and Duties as Necessary.

If the GAL is uncertain about the areas to be investigated or the GAL's responsibilities, the GAL shall file a motion for clarification for hearing before the appointing judge with notice to counsel and pro se parties.

Commentary: A Category F investigative appointment should indicate that the GAL shall "investigate" certain issues, rather than "evaluate" the issues. If the order includes both mandates, the GAL should file a motion for clarification for hearing before the appointing judge with notice to counsel and any pro se party.

3.2. The GAL Determines Whether he or she has the Requisite Expertise and Competence in the Areas to be Investigated.

If the GAL lacks the necessary experience, expertise or competence to conduct an investigation of the issues, the GAL shall decline the appointment.

3.3 The GAL Determines Whether the GAL's Personal and Professional Schedule Permit a Timely Report.

The GAL reviews the areas to be investigated and the tasks to be performed. If the GAL will not be able to complete a report by the designated deadline, the GAL shall promptly decline the appointment.

Commentary. If the GAL determines after commencement of the investigation that additional time will be needed to complete the investigation, the GAL may file a motion to extend the deadline with notice to counsel and any pro se party. The motion shall include a new proposed due date for the report so that the judge may determine whether the deadline should be extended or the appointment should be vacated.

3.4 The GAL Promptly Accepts or Rejects any Appointment.

The GAL shall promptly accept or reject the appointment no later than twenty days after the GAL receives it, or earlier if requested by the court. The GAL accepts or rejects the appointment by returning the completed form to the court.

4. THROUGHOUT THE CASE

4.1 The GAL Maintains an Attitude of Respect.

The GAL shall approach all family members and parties with an attitude of respect and openness to hear their account of the relevant facts regardless of any allegations that have been made. The GAL shall be patient, courteous, and dignified in his or her interactions with litigants, witnesses, attorneys, and others with whom the GAL deals in this official capacity.

Commentary. The GAL may limit the number of telephone calls and contacts made by a party or attorney as is reasonable given the particular circumstances. The GAL may seek assistance from the court on issues related to the GAL's safety or to address inappropriate conduct by a party related to the investigation. In such instances, a motion must be filed with the court with a copy sent to counsel of record and any pro se parties.

4.2 The GAL is Diligent and Adheres to Time Deadlines.

The GAL shall adhere to all time frames set forth in the order of appointment as applicable.

Commentary. If the report is not filed on time, the Probation Office notifies the judge and seeks further instruction from the court. Probate and Family Court Standing Order 2–98. If the GAL needs more time to complete the report, the GAL shall file a motion with notice to counsel and pro se parties to extend the deadline prior to the date when it is due. The motion shall indicate the proposed due date for the report. The GAL shall complete the report even if a party declines to participate or an attorney indicates that the case may settle.

4.3 The GAL Maintains Safety.

The GAL shall make every reasonable effort to ensure the safety of all parties and their children. To implement this requirement, the GAL shall:

    A. Arrange joint parent-child interviews, home visits, or observations of a party with the children only when such processes are safe.

    B. Arrange interview schedules so that parties do not come into contact during the interview process when domestic violence is alleged or identified as a possible issue.

    C. Inquires about and refrains from disclosing, directly or indirectly, residential, telephone, work, or other location information that a party has kept confidential for safety reasons.

    D. Refrain from recommending visitation or other arrangements that bring the parties into contact when an abuse prevention order is in effect, or when the investigator has reasonable cause to believe that such contact may be dangerous or harmful for either party or the child.

    E. Warn the party, the party's attorney and contact police as appropriate if the GAL believes that a party or child is in danger of imminent physical harm from the other party in the case.

Commentary. To ensure the safety of the parties and their children, the GAL should screen for previously undisclosed safety issues in separate interviews with the partes early in the investigation. Depending on the circumstances, the other party, the child, the GAL, or others may be at risk if there are issues of mental illness, domestic violence, child abuse, or substance abuse. The GAL should attempt to gather and communicate information in ways that avoid harm to parties, the child or children, or others involved in the case. The GAL shall consider the safety of the parties and other family members when he or she makes recommendations and determines how the information he or she has collected will be reported to the court.

4.3.1 The GAL Files Mandatory "51A" Reports When Required and as Appropriate.

In cases of suspected child maltreatment, many mental health professionals are required to file a "51A" report. G.L.

c. 119, § 51A. However, a lawyer or mental health professional, who is not a mandated reporter, may still report suspected abuse or neglect as necessary if a child is at risk. If the GAL has reasonable cause to believe a child is in imminent danger, the GAL should report this information to the police department and should also report the information to the Court through an emergency motion for instructions with the required notice to counsel and pro se parties.

4.4 The GAL Shall Use a Process for Communication and Collection of Information that is Conducive to Disclosure of Information and Fair to the Parties.

The GAL shall provide each party with a separate interview so that each party may speak with candor. The GAL encourages parties and their attorneys to provide additional relevant information and documents. The process for communications must be even-handed and provide each party with the opportunity to present relevant information and respond to relevant allegations by the opposing party. The GAL also affords a pro se party the same procedural protections that the GAL affords a party with an attorney.

4.4.1 The GAL Shall Conduct All Oral and Written Communications with Attorneys and Pro Se Parties in a Manner that Avoids the Question of Bias.

The GAL shall send counsel of record and pro se parties copies of any motions and other documents filed by the GAL in court, except for the GAL report. If the GAL sends a substantive written communication to one counsel or a pro se party, the GAL shall send a copy of the communication to the opposing counsel or pro se party.

Commentary. A GAL's written communications to one party or attorney about administrative or scheduling matters, such as arranging a time for an interview or signing releases, are not substantive matters. While it is not required by any statute or rule, attorneys may agree to send copies of all written correspondence addressed to the guardian ad litem to the opposing counsel.

4.4.2 The GAL Arranges for a Qualified Interpreter if a Party or Child is Unable to Understand or Use the English language.

The need for an interpreter goes beyond the courtroom if a party is not completely fluent or comfortable in using the English language. The party, child or child's guardian should be interviewed to determine the communication system to be used and the party's or child's comfort with it. In the case of a deaf or hard-of-hearing person, this communication system could be oral, cued-speech, finger spelling, sign language, or a combination of all of them. People may prefer to use their native language. Using a child as an interpreter is not appropriate, and using relatives or friends may have a chilling effect on what is disclosed. If the child or a party has limited or no English language skills and the GAL does not speak the language, every effort should be made to ensure that only qualified interpreters are used. Any authorizations for release of information and other forms should be translated for such parties. Likewise, a party or child may have a need for a sign language interpreter.

Commentary. If a party does not supply a qualified interpreter, the GAL may file a motion in court for appointment of a qualified interpreter that includes a request that the Commonwealth pay for the interpreter's services if a party is indigent, or that a party or parties who are not indigent pay for the interpreter. Counsel and pro se parties shall be given notice of the motion. If the GAL desires payment from or reimbursement from the Commonwealth for the cost of using an interpreter, the GAL must receive approval from the court before incurring the expense. Bias or incompetence of an interpreter can lead to omitted and inaccurate communications with the GAL. The interpreter should not have a conflict of interest or a relationship with a party or other person that will bias the interpretation. The Supreme Judicial Court has promulgated standards for court interpreter services and qualifications which are available on the internet at: http://www.state.ma.us/courts/formsandguidelines/index.html.

Certain cases may require that the GAL possess or utilize cross-cultural competence and expertise. For example, if the parents dispute whether a certain religious ritual was integral to a certain faith and whether the ritual should be performed on the child. The role of the interpreter, however, is to facilitate communication rather than serve as a substitute for an expert on a particular culture.

4.5 The GAL Answers Appropriate Questions about the GAL's Credentials or Role.

The GAL answers appropriate questions about the GAL's education, training, experience, practice areas, professional affiliations, and the process of the GAL investigation.

Commentary. If requested by counsel or a pro se party, the GAL shall provide a copy of his or her curriculum vitae to said counsel or party. However, questions pertaining to the GAL's personal life need not be answered.

4.6 The GAL Maintains Confidentiality.

The information gathered by the GAL for the court is confidential. The GAL shall not disclose confidential and personally identifiable information about the parties, their children, or the services rendered by the GAL to a person who is not a party or counsel in the case, except as necessary to gather information to complete the investigation and report, or to perform responsibilities related to the order of appointment. This prohibition is permanent and applies to the GAL's writings, lectures, or other media communications.

Commentary. If a GAL has questions regarding release of information pertaining to the parties, child, or the investigation and report, the GAL may file a motion for instructions with the court with notice to counsel and any pro se party.

4.6.1 The GAL Obtains Appropriate Release Forms or Court Orders before Obtaining Privileged and Confidential Information about the Parties and their Children.

Many of the most common and relevant records that are subject to statutory privileges or other restrictions can be obtained with an appropriate authorization for release of the information or a court order.

- Department of Social Services (DSS) records. A party's release form or court order is needed to access records. The GAL can obtain the DSS file with a release from a party but privileged information must be redacted. 10 C.M.R. § 12.09(1)–(3).

- Medical, health and hospital records. A party's release form or court order is needed to access records. G.L. c. 111

§ 70, § 70E(b); The Health Insurance Portability and Accountability Act of 1996, Pub. L. 104–19 1 (HIPAA).

- Psychotherapist records. A party's release form or court order is needed to access records pertaining to an adult from a psychotherapist whose communications are privileged. G.L. c. 112, § 8GB; Commonwealth v. Bernard, 424 Mass. 32, 673 N.E.2d 1220 (1996). G.L. c. 233, § 20B.

- Social Worker records. A party's release form or court order is needed to access records. G.L. c. 112, §§ 135A, 135B.

- Alcohol and drug abuse programs records. A party's release form and/or court order may be needed to access records. 42 U.S.C. §§ 1175, 290 dd–3.

- School records. If a party has shared or sole legal custody, he or she may authorize release of records, except for a parent or party whose access is restricted by a Chapter 209A or other court order. G.L. c. 71, § 34H; G.L. c. 208, § 31.

- Criminal Offender Record Information (CORI and CARI). The GAL can most easily review these records with a court order through the Probation Department, or request the records through the Criminal History Systems Board.

- Prior GAL reports, Probation Office or Court Clinic reports involving the parties. The GAL must file a motion with the court with notice to the parties to access these records.

- Domestic Violence or Sexual Assault Victim–Counselor records. Confidential communications cannot be disclosed in civil actions by court order and are not discoverable without the victim's prior consent. G.L. c. 233, §§ 20J, 20K.

- Victim program locations. Locations of battered women's shelters, domestic violence, and rape crisis programs may not be disclosed by court order, or otherwise to the GAL. G.L. c. 233, §§ 20J, 20K.

- Mediator Records. Communications made during mediation with a mediator are privileged and the court cannot order disclosure. G.L. c. 233, § 23C.

- Alternative dispute resolution information. The Probation Department of the Probate and Family Court may release the information to the GAL if the court orders release of the information or the parties consent to the release of information.

The Health Insurance Portability and Accountability Act of 1996, Pub. L. 104–19 1 (HIPAA) requires that health providers may only release personal health information if the release signed by a party complies with the provisions of the federal law. Even if no statutory privilege applies to the information sought by the GAL, the provider or keeper of other records (e.g. unlicensed support group leaders, batterer intervention programs) may also request a written release from their client. In some instances, the order for appointment of the GAL will provide that the GAL is permitted to access certain records and information; this obviates the need for a party's authorization for release of the information.

Commentary. Some third parties or providers may be unaware of protections that apply to records or confidential information relating to the parties or the children. The GAL, however, shall only review the information after appropriate releases or court orders for access to the information have been provided to the holder of the information. If a privilege is not properly waived, a judge may allow a motion to strike reference to the information from the GAL report.

4.6.2 The GAL Recognizes that Children's Rights to Confidentiality are Different than Other Parties' Rights to Confidentiality.

The GAL shall obtain authorizations for release of information pertaining to children from the children's parents or legal guardians. A parent, however, cannot waive a child's psychotherapy or social worker privilege. If the counseling information is needed but protected by a privilege, the GAL or counsel must return to the appointing judge and present a motion for appointment of another guardian ad litem to investigate whether waiver of the child's psychotherapy privilege is in the child's best interest. Adoption of Diane, 400 Mass. 196, 201 (1987); G.L. c. 233, § 20B. The motion should indicate the scope of the information sought and the GAL's reason for seeking the information. Counsel and pro se parties must have notice of the motion. If the court later waives the privilege, the GAL may access the information.

Commentary. A parent or parents with legal custody of the child, or a party granted legal guardianship of the child, may authorize access to most other records of the child. If a parent or parents refuse to authorize release of information that is important to the investigation, the GAL may file a motion for access to the information with notice to counsel and pro se parties.

5. COMMENCEMENT OF THE INVESTIGATION

After the GAL accepts the appointment, he or she promptly schedules initial investigatory contacts with each of the parties and their attorneys if they are represented.

Commentary. If a party has an attorney, the GAL should first make contact with the attorney. The GAL may find it helpful to send a letter of introduction to counsel and pro se parties outlining the investigative process. The GAL should use additional means of communication, however, if a party's primary language is not English, or there are literacy or other barriers impacting written communication. The GAL can determine more easily if a party understands what is communicated in a face-to-face interview.

5.1 The GAL Provides an Explanation of the GAL's Role and a Lamb-type Warning at the Commencement of the Investigation.

The GAL must explain the GAL's role and the purpose of the investigation to the parties. The GAL shall inform the parties how the information gathered by the GAL will be used. The GAL must provide a "Lamb warning" that explains there are no "off the record" discussions and any information collected by the GAL may appear in the GAL report, be disclosed in court or to the other party, Commonwealth v. Lamb, 1 Mass. App. Ct. 530 (1973), or otherwise disclosed as required or permitted by law. As appropriate based on the child's level of maturity, the GAL should provide a similar explanation of the investigative process and a Lamb warning to a child, but modified to reflect the child's age and level of understanding. If the GAL interviews other witnesses, they also must receive a Lamb warning.

Commentary. To ensure a person understands the Lamb warning, the GAL should ask the person to summarize it for the GAL. The parties or witnesses should be informed that while they are encouraged to provide information, they may decline to answer a question and have an attorney present during any interview. Increasingly, parties represent themselves in court. Therefore, the GAL should avoid use of professional jargon or legalese that a party may not understand. The GAL should strive to explain things in simple language and terms as appropriate so that a party with a limited educational background or language ability can better understand what the GAL is communicating.

5.2 The GAL Inquires if the Parties have Relevant Safety Concerns.

The GAL shall inquire at the outset of the investigation about any safety risks related to the investigation for either party, the child, or others because of any party's mental illness, substance abuse, domestic violence, child abuse, or history of violence against others. The GAL should attempt to conduct the investigation in such a manner as appropriate to avoid likely harm to the child, a party, the GAL, or others.

5.3 The GAL Explains the Limits on Confidentiality and Complies with Legal and Ethical Standards Governing Disclosure of Privileged Communications.

The GAL shall obtain information or review records after appropriate authorizations for release of information are executed or the court orders release of the information. The GAL shall respect the parties' and their children's right to confidentiality. Before obtaining an authorization for release of records or other information from a party, the GAL should inform the party how the information will be used. The GAL should also disclose that any information obtained by the GAL could appear in the GAL report, be disclosed to the other party, put into evidence during court proceedings or depositions, or disclosed to others as necessary to complete the investigation, discovery, or trial of the case. The authorization for release of information form given to a party by the GAL shall include but is not limited to who the information is sought from and the duration of the authorization of the release. A party should also be informed that he or she has a right to seek legal advice before signing a release and may decline to sign an authorization for release of information. A party may direct that all release forms be sent directly to counsel of record. If a party consents to release of information, the GAL should use forms for release of information that comply with applicable laws and that are acceptable to providers. The Health Insurance Portability and Accountability Act of 1996, Pub. L. 104–19 1 (HIPAA) requires that health providers may only release personal health information if the release form complies with the provisions of the federal law.

Commentary. The GAL should not seek confidential information unless it is necessary. If a party objects to release of certain information, the GAL may file a motion to obtain this information. G.L. c. 233, § 20B; G.L. c. 112, § 135B; Commonwealth v. Bernard, 424 Mass. 32 (1996). A parent cannot consent to release of a child's psychotherapy information. See Section 4.9. 2.

6. INVESTIGATION SOURCES AND METHODS

The GAL shall conduct the investigation in a fair and balanced manner. The GAL should obtain similar types of information about each party. If the case involves more than one child, each child's best interests must be addressed unless the court orders otherwise. If the GAL is unable to report on all of the children, the GAL shall indicate why in the report.

Commentary. Depending on the circumstances, the GAL may need to spend more time investigating facts that relate only to one party, especially if such facts are disputed, difficult to investigate, or new information arises about that parent. The GAL may have satisfactory information about one parent, but incomplete data about the other parent. For example, further investigation of alleged drug use might be needed if a party's drug testing results are unreliable because the facility did not monitor how samples from the party were collected, or new sources indicate that the party has used drugs since the time of the last testing.

6.1 The GAL Spends Sufficient Time Interviewing Parties and Investigating their Concerns as Necessary to Gather Relevant Information.

The GAL conducts an initial interview with each party and additional interviews with each party and other witnesses as necessary to gather relevant information. In addition, the GAL may gather information by telephone, email, and or other means.

Commentary. A party is permitted to have counsel present during an interview, but the GAL controls the interview and conducts the questioning. If counsel directs a party to refuse to answer a question or plead the Fifth Amendment against self-incrimination, the GAL moves on to other questions, noting the objection. Such objections do not prohibit the GAL from using other sources to obtain the information. If the GAL does not meet with any party, the GAL explains why in the report.

6.2 The GAL Asks Each Party about Relevant Witnesses and Documents and Investigates these Sources of Information as Appropriate.

As a starting point, the GAL invites counsel and parties to provide relevant information, including a fact summary, procedural history, relevant documents, and a list of witnesses and professionals who can provide relevant information. In deciding what records to review or witnesses to interview, the GAL considers the likelihood that relevant information will be obtained, with reasonable convenience, efficiency, cost, and physical safety of a party, child or informant. The order of appointment also may direct the GAL to contact certain witnesses or sources.

Commentary. In determining what witnesses to interview, the GAL may also consider: the number of witnesses suggested, whether the witness directly witnessed important events or the aftermath of important events, the potential bias of the witness, the importance of the interview to a party, and other relevant considerations. At the beginning of each collateral witness or party interview, it is important that the GAL explain the GAL's role and the limits of confidentiality. The GAL shall access information after appropriate release forms are provided to professionals. In addition to oral communications, the GAL may provide written questions and accept additional written responses from witnesses or collateral sources.

6.3 The GAL Accesses Original Sources When Possible.

To increase the reliability of reported information, the GAL investigates original sources of information.

For example: John Jones says that Jane Doe saw the parties' son drinking beer at a soccer game. The GAL speaks with Jane Doe to ascertain what she observed.

For example: a police report indicates that the child told his soccer coach that the child's parent supplied the beer. The GAL speaks with the coach and the child.

6.4 The GAL Uses Multiple Fact Sources When Possible.

If certain events or facts are disputed, the GAL should investigate more than one source of information relating to the events or allegations when possible. The parties should be encouraged to provide names of witnesses who were present, written reports, or other relevant evidence related to the event or allegation.

Commentary. For example, the husband disputes the wife's claim that the husband told her that he was treated at Cambridge Hospital after he attempted suicide by taking an overdose of sleeping pills and cocaine. The GAL contacts the hospital and interviews any other witnesses with direct knowledge about the disputed event or his statements about it. Hospital records in the case lead to other relevant sources of information such as "911" call records, a police report, and an ambulance report, including a copy of a suicide note found in the ambulance. The GAL reports all the relevant facts collected about the disputed allegation.

6.5 The GAL Conducts a Home Visit When Appropriate.

Ordinarily, home visits can yield valuable information, but on occasion a home visit is not indicated. Factors to consider in deciding whether to conduct home visits include: whether issues or problems with either home are alleged, cost and time involved, location, and the likelihood of obtaining relevant information not accessible in other ways. If no home visit is conducted, the GAL shall explain why that decision was made in the report.

Commentary. If home visits are conducted, care must be exercised so that inequality in housing conditions or perceived wealth do not lead to bias. A person, who is a fit parent and caretaker for the child, also may experience transitional or temporary housing difficulties as a result of separation from the other party, nonpayment of support, inadequate financial support, or relocation related to domestic violence or loss of income.

6.6 The GAL Meets with the Children.

The GAL meets with the children as part of the investigation. Children can offer useful information and should be offered the opportunity to provide information about themselves and their family. The conditions under which children are interviewed must be carefully considered, including what conditions will put the child most at ease and yield the most useful information. The GAL shall explain the reasons for not meeting with any of the children in the GAL report.

Commentary. Some children may be much less candid in the interview if a parent or the parents are present during the child's interview, or are visible or able to hear the interview.

6.7 The GAL Observes Children with Each Parent When Appropriate.

The GAL should observe the child with each parent when appropriate. This often provides valuable information about the parent-child relationship.

Commentary. The GAL has a duty to avoid further harm to children when possible. If concerns are raised that a child will be traumatized or at risk by contact with a parent (e.g. due to severe neglect or abuse, exposure to domestic violence, traumatic or unpredictable absence, or other inappropriate behavior) a parent-child observation may not be indicated. The GAL explains the reasons for not observing children with each parent in the report.

6.8 The GAL Considers the Need for any Further Information Necessary to Complete the GAL investigation and Provide a Comprehensive Report.

The GAL shall collect and review documents as well as conduct additional interviews of the parties, each of the children and other witnesses until the necessary information is fully gathered.

7. SCOPE AND CONTENT OF THE INVESTIGATION

A comprehensive history creates a context for understanding the current issues in dispute. The nature and extent of the family history obtained, through both interviews as well review of documents depends on the particular family's circumstances and the directives contained in the order of appointment. However, it is commonplace to obtain the:

A. History of legal proceedings and prior investigations.

● The nature of the case, including the parties and children involved, relevant procedural history, current orders, and the relief sought by each party;

● History of other cases involving the parties, including prior cases pertaining to parties or the children including, but not limited to Probate and Family Court, Juvenile Court, criminal, abuse prevention, or other relevant cases;

● Prior custody related investigations and evaluations, including GAL, Court Clinic, Probation, Department of Social Services, or other evaluations or assessments;

B. Facts designated by court order and the applicable law.

● The issues that the court specifies for investigation in the order of appointment;

● Facts relevant to the legal standard that applies to the case for:

1. modification of custody or visitation;
2. termination of parental rights;
3. guardianship of a minor;
4. removal of the child from the Commonwealth;
5. custody or visitation by a parent.

C. Relevant concerns raised in the case by each parent, including facts related to how each parent's proposed outcome serves or conflicts with the child's best interests.

D. Parenting history.

● With whom have the children lived and for how long;

● What parenting tasks have each parent performed, when, for how long;

● The competence with which each parent carried out parenting tasks;

● History of parents' past joint decision- making regarding children;

● Parent's present ability to communicate or make joint decisions;

● Whether a third party or either party is or was a primary caretaker;

● History and impact of a parent's substance abuse, mental illness, or domestic violence on the children and the parent's parenting ability;

● History of physical, sexual or emotional abuse of the children;

● History of past restraining orders and violence against others;

● Each parent's past and present parenting skills and deficits;

● The strength and quality of the parent-child relationships, emotional closeness, attachment, and perceptions of each other;

● Each parent's or potential caretaker's knowledge of the children, knowledge of parenting techniques, disciplinary practices, ability to distinguish his or her own needs from the needs of the children, and to understand and respond to the children's needs;

● The ability of the parent to promote and support appropriate social, emotional, and educational development in the children, and to provide a stable home environment for the children;

● Each parent's or potential caretaker's ability to support the children's relationship with the other parent as appropriate;

● Each party's ability to communicate and cooperate with the other parent regarding the children as appropriate, including the impact of substance abuse, mental illness or domestic violence on that ability.

E. The family history.

● History of parents' relationship, including if and for how long the parties lived together as a family;

● Parties' accounts of how difficulties began, how they were disclosed, or if they persist;

● Prior Department of Social Services involvement with family members;

● Children's present and past school functioning;

● Criminal history of both parties (CORI (Criminal Offender Record Information) or CARI (Court Activity Record Information);

● Sexual offense history (Sexual Offender Registry Information, or SORI);

● Substance abuse and substance use history of family members;

• Mental health treatment and history of family members;

• Relevant medical history or problems of family members;

• Presence of new relationships, partners or their children;

• Relationships with significant caretakers, grandparents, relatives, child care providers;

• Each parent's relationship with family of origin and partner's family;

• Education and employment history of parents;

• If relevant, ethnic, cultural, lifestyle, and religious factors.

F. Developmental status and parenting needs of the children.

• Each child's developmental history, functioning in school, peer relationships, medical and mental health history, activities, schedules;

• Special needs of each child: medical, learning or developmental problems;

• Assessment of each child's adjustment to school, friends, community, and extended families;

• Child's temperament and response to transitions;

• Impact of change on child's routines, attachments, familiar environs;

• Child's exposure to, understanding of or concerns about a parent's needs, wishes, concerns, safety, or problems;

• Quality of relationship between siblings;

• Particular challenges for either parent or the child with each other.

8. REPORT WRITING

The report should address and relate to the areas of investigation designated by the order of appointment. The report should provide accurate, detailed and balanced information about the parties and their children.

8.1 The Report Should Appear Professional in Appearance, Format and Writing Style.

The report should be typed, well-written and neat in appearance. Pages must be numbered. The GAL shall attempt to avoid spelling, grammar or typographical errors in the report. The GAL should write the report in a way that is concise in words, yet able to encompass all the relevant facts and provide detailed information. The language used in the report should be understandable to the average layperson and avoid jargon that may be confusing. The GAL should prepare a report that is well-organized. Use of headings, bold type, or underlining to separate sections or topics in the report may make a report easier to comprehend. The report shall be dated and signed by the GAL with the GAL's name typed below the signature. The report shall include the GAL's mailing or office address and telephone number.

8.2 The Report Should be Accurate, Objective and Unbiased.

When writing the report, the GAL provides a balanced view of the parties that includes all of their relevant strengths and weaknesses. The information contained in the report should be accurate. It also should be as factual and detailed as possible. The GAL report should:

A. Use descriptive statements rather than evaluative statements.

Evaluative statement: "Michael is a cruel and aggressive boy."

Descriptive statements: "In his interview, Michael said he punches his younger brother, Joseph, almost every day. Michael's father reports that he had to interfere three times last week when Michael hit the family dog with a hockey stick."

B. Provide ample details, but avoid inflammatory characterizations if possible.

Derogatory statement: "Mr. Jones is well-known to the courts as a drunk."

Descriptive statement: "Mr. Jones was convicted in Somerville District Court of driving under the influence of alcohol in 1986, 1996, 2001, and in July, 2003."

C. Provide past and present relevant facts relating to both parties and the children.

1. Include all relevant facts that address the court's directives.

2. Include all relevant facts collected from all sources, including facts that are consistent and inconsistent with other reported facts.

3. Provide balanced and similar information about both parties;

4. Provide relevant and detailed information about all of the children.

5. Include facts that do not support the GAL's recommendations or conclusions.

6. Disclose what important information may be missing and why it missing.

D. Include specific information and provide dates and pinpoint time frames if at all possible.

Avoid use of vague phrases or time frames such as "in the past" or "occasionally" or "sometimes" if a more precise time frame is available. The GAL should provide detailed information.

Vague: "John says he used heroin in the past."

Specific: "John says he used heroin in May, 1996 and June, 1998."

Vague: "Mary states that John occasionally uses drugs."

Specific: "Mary states that she saw John use cocaine twice in August, 1998."

Vague: "The child has health problems."

Specific: "The child has diabetes."

8.3 The GAL Identifies the Sources of Information.

Sources should be easily identified in the report. The GAL must list every person interviewed and the records reviewed with any relevant information about the informant or source.

• Date and Name of each person interviewed (e.g. Dr. Tom Jones on 9/5/03),

● Position, profession, place of employment (psychiatrist, General Hospital);

● Description of record reviewed (Dr. Jones' records regarding mother);

● Date the record was made and period it encompasses (July, 2002 to July, 2003);

● How information was obtained (e.g. in person, telephone call, written request);

● Date records were reviewed or obtained by the GAL (9/5/03);

● Informant or record author's relationship to the parties, child or family (Dr. Jones is mother's psychiatrist, but also saw her and the husband for marriage counseling in May, 2001).

If a source is not clearly identified, a party can move to strike the statement from the report.

Example of improper attribution: "Hospital staff said that Drew Smith was hospitalized there for three months last year." (Names of the staff and hospital are missing).

Use of hearsay statements is permitted in the report, but the GAL should always attempt to contact and also quote the original source in the report if possible.

8.4 If a Party Fails or Refuses to Participate, the GAL Includes the Information that the GAL has Obtained in the Report.

The GAL encourages parties to participate in the investigation. If a party does not participate, the GAL is still permitted to file a report and to disclose whatever information has been collected about that party from other sources. The report should disclose that such a party has not participated or declined to provide information.

Commentary. The GAL shall refrain from drawing conclusions about a party without a factual basis.

8.5 Facts Shall be Separated in the Report from Recommendations or Conclusions.

Only facts should be contained in the body of the investigation. The investigator's inferences, conclusions or recommendations based on the facts shall be confined to separate summary or recommendations sections of the report. Such material is then easier to redact if it is later excluded from evidence at trial and stricken from the report.

Commentary. The GAL's conclusions or recommendations should be consistent with the information that is collected; the GAL shall set forth the connection between the facts and the conclusions or recommendations. The trial judge is the ultimate fact finder. Thus, the GAL's conclusions as to whether a party has met his or her burden of proof should be avoided.

8.6 The GAL Files a Timely Report and Informs Counsel and Pro Se Parties.

The GAL should inform counsel and pro se parties when the report is filed at the court so that the parties can read the report. The GAL should inform parties requesting a copy of the report that the report is property of the court; it cannot be given out or shown to anyone, except the parties or their counsel. A court order may be required for any distribution of the report, even to parties or their counsel. The GAL shall not distribute copies of the report to the parties, counsel of record or anyone else unless the court orders that the GAL may release copies to such individuals.

Commentary. If information or recommendations in the GAL report have the potential of exposing a party or the child to danger, the GAL should consider advising the endangered parent or party about the date that he or she expects to file the report in court.

8.7 THE GAL SHALL RETAIN ANY MATERIALS GATHERED OR CREATED DURING THE INVESTIGATION

The GAL shall retain any notes, records, documents, taped recordings, videos, or other material gathered or created during the investigation so that these materials are available for trial, discovery, appeal and remand of the case.

Commentary. Notes or other materials created or obtained by a GAL may be sought by a party through discovery. The GAL's notes, written observations, or other materials created during interviews or telephone conversations should be descriptive, factual, and respectful in tone. Note taking should be objective and include quotations of witnesses and parties when possible.

Adopted effective January 24, 2005.

Standing Order 2–05. Hampshire Division Parent Education Program for Never Married Parents

"FOR THE CHILDREN"

This Court finds that the interests of the minor children of never-married parents appearing before it would be well served by educating the parents about children's emotional needs and the effects of family-related litigation on child behavior and development.

IT IS HEREBY ORDERED THAT:

1. In the Hampshire Division of the Probate and Family Court Department, all parties to a Complaint to Establish Paternity, a Complaint for Custody/Support/Visitation, a Complaint for Modification or Contempt in any case involving visitation, custody or support of minor children of never-married parents filed on or after September 1, 2005, shall attend and participate in a three (3) hour education program known as *"For the Children"*. Complaints filed by the Department of Revenue shall be exempt from this requirement.

2. Attendance at the program is mandatory unless waived by the Court. Parties must register within sixty (60) days of service of the complaint and attend the next available session.

3. No Pre-Trial Conference or Trial will be held by the Court until the Court receives a certificate of attendance from the program or waives the attendance requirement. Nothing herein shall limit the judge or his or her designee from waiving this requirement.

4. The Court may waive the attendance requirement upon motion, with notice, for one or both parties. Waivers will be granted only upon a showing of chronic and severe violence which negates safe parental communication, language barriers, institutionalization or other unavailability of a party, or where justice otherwise indicates.

5. Sanctions may be imposed by the Court for a party's failure to register with "For the Children" within sixty days of service of the complaint.

6. A pamphlet describing "For the Children" and including a copy of this Order shall be given to the plaintiff or his/her attorney upon the filing of a complaint involving minor children as set forth above. The plaintiff or his/her attorney shall serve a copy of the pamphlet along with the complaint and summons to the person authorized to make service according to Mass.R.Dom.Rel.P.4(c)

7. The parties shall each pay $50.00 to "For the Children" in advance of the program to offset the cost of materials and facilitators.

8. A party may pay a reduced fee of $5.00 to "For the Children" if that party has submitted and had allowed an "Affidavit of Indigency and Request for Waiver, Substitution or State Payment of Fees and Costs." This form is prescribed by the Chief Justice of the Supreme Judicial Court pursuant to G.L. c. 261, sec. 27B, promulgated March, 2003 and is available at the Registry of the Probate and Family Court. The party must submit a copy of the allowed form to "For the Children" when registering at a reduced fee of $5.00.

9. Nothing herein shall be construed to limit the authority of any Probate and Family Court Justice sitting in the Hampshire Division to order parties to attend a parent education program in any case involving visitation, custody or support of minor children.

10. All information and materials submitted in conjunction with "For the Children" shall not be discoverable.

11. The parties to a particular case are prohibited from attending the same program session.

November 22, 2005 /s/SEAN M. DUNPHY
Date   Sean M. Dunphy, Chief Justice

Adopted effective December 1, 2005.

Standing Order 1–06. Case Management and Time Standards for Cases Filed in the Probate and Family Court Department

PREAMBLE

The fair and efficient administration of justice requires that all cases and actions before the Probate and Family Court receive timely attention and action from the court. This requires that the judicial system dispose of cases as expeditiously as is consistent with care, fairness and sound decisions. It is the responsibility of the court to manage the process and disposition of the cases before the court. These time standards are intended to provide the Probate and Family Court with recognized goals for the timely disposition of cases.

These time standards represent aspirational goals to measure the movement of cases in the Probate and Family Court. Each case is unique and the Judges must, consistent with the rules of court and statutes, exercise sound judgment in such a manner as to provide the parties with a fair opportunity to be heard and to allow the court to achieve a reasoned disposition. Those individuals who appear before our courts have distinct needs that must be addressed on an individual basis, case by case. These time standards preserve discretion for judges to schedule individual cases according to the particular needs of the individuals involved.

These time standards recognize that there are many factors that determine the flow of cases in the Probate and Family Court which are not within the control of the court. These standards also recognize that the cases heard in the Probate and Family Court require consideration of the individual needs of the families who come before the court.

Accordingly:

1. GENERAL PROVISIONS

This Standing Order applies to all actions filed in the Probate and Family Court.

This Standing Order applies to all Divisions of the Probate and Family Court.

The timing for the completion of the case, from filing to trial, settlement, or dismissal, shall be calculated from the date of filing the petition or complaint.

At time of filing, all cases shall be assigned to a caseflow track according to the type of case. Most cases shall be assigned to one of the following tracks; 3–6 months to trial, 8 months to trial, or 14 months to trial.

2. TRACK ASSIGNMENT AND CASE MANAGEMENT

a. Track Assignment

At filing each case is assigned to a track.

The Plaintiff/Petitioner shall be provided with a Track Assignment Notice except as set forth below. The Plaintiff/Petitioner shall serve the Track Assignment Notice upon the Defendant/Respondent along with the summons or notice (citation). No service of the Track Assignment Notice will be required in cases where service is by publication.

No Track Assignment Notice shall be issued for cases in the 3–6 month track: Probate of Will, Administration, Accounts, Real Estate Sales, and Change of Name. No Track Assignment Notice shall be issued for cases described in sections 10 through 17 of this Standing Order. No Track Assignment Notice shall be issued at the time of filing for any case filed by the Department of Revenue, Child Support Enforcement Division.

The goals for completion of all cases filed in the Probate and Family Court are outlined in the chart in section 7(a) and in sections 10 through 17 of this Standing Order. A Judge, at any time, may change the track designation for a case and issue a new Track Assignment Notice.

b. Next Event Scheduling

At the conclusion of every court event, until a judgment has issued or the complaint has been dismissed, or until a permanent decree has issued or the petition has been dismissed, the Court shall schedule the next court event for the case.

Once a motion hearing, conference, or any other court event has been scheduled and placed on a court list, whether at the request of a party, a party's lawyer, the Register, or the Court, it can be removed from the list or continued only if a next court event is scheduled.

c. Case Management Conferences: Generally

Case Management Conferences will be scheduled by the court for the case types set forth in sections 2(d),(e), and (f) below, when a return of service, answer, objection, or counterclaim is filed and there is no future court event scheduled for the case.

In scheduling a case management conference, the Register shall issue a Case Management Conference Notice and Order in the format specified by the Chief Justice of the Probate and Family Court.

The purpose of the Case Management Conference is to establish the Court's control of the progress of the case, to provide early intervention by the Court, to offer Alternative Dispute Resolution processes, to establish discovery limitations and deadlines, to discuss settlement progress and opportunities for settlement, and to assign a date for the pre-trial conference, if needed.

d. Case Management Conference: Equity, Petition to Partition, and Domestic Relations, including Paternity (except Joint Petitions for Divorce, Joint Petitions for Modification and Complaint for Divorce filed under G.L. c. 208, § 1B).

Upon the filing of the return of service, answer, objection, or counterclaim, the Register shall review the case to determine if a future court event has been scheduled in the case. If no future court event has been scheduled, the Register shall schedule a Case Management Conference on the next available date, but no sooner than thirty (30) days from the filing of the return of service, answer, objection, or counterclaim. The Register shall send the Case Management Conference Notice and Order to all parties.

e. Case Management Conference: 1B Divorce, Guardianship and Conservatorship

All G.L. c. 208, § 1B Divorce Cases

The Register shall review the case one hundred twenty (120) days after the case is filed. If no return of service has been filed, and no answer, appearance, motion, or other paper has been filed by a defendant, the Register shall mail to the plaintiff a written notice of dismissal in accordance with section 3 of this Standing Order. If the return of service or an answer, objection, or counterclaim has been filed, but no future court event has been scheduled, a Case Management Conference shall be scheduled on the next available date, but no sooner than thirty (30) days from the filing of the return of service. The Register shall send the Case Management Conference Notice and Order to all parties.

Guardianship and Conservatorship Cases

The Register shall review the case one hundred twenty (120) days after the case is filed. If no future court event has been scheduled, the Register shall schedule a Case Management Conference on the next available date. The Register shall send the Case Management Conference Notice and Order to all parties. All temporary guardianships shall include an expiration date and a further hearing date. All guardianships with approval and authorization of an antipsychotic medication treatment plan shall include an expiration date and a review date, which may be the same date. All guardianships with authority to approve other extraordi-

nary medical treatment shall include an expiration date for the authority.

f. Case Management Conference for Certain Probate Matters

A Track Assignment Notice shall not be issued at the time of filing for the cases assigned to the 3–6 Month Track: Probate of Will, Administration, Accounts, Real Estate Sales, and Change of Name. If a timely appearance in opposition or objection is filed in a case initially assigned to the 3–6 Month Track, the Register shall reassign the case to the 8 Month Track and issue to all parties a Track Assignment Notice. The Register shall also issue a Pre–Trial Notice and Order in the form specified by the Chief Justice of the Probate and Family Court with an established date for a Pre–Trial Conference unless another future court event has been scheduled. The date for the Pre–Trial Conference shall be after the return date, but no more than forty-five (45) days after the return date.

g. Case Management Conference conducted at Motion Hearing

If a motion, or other hearing, is scheduled and held prior to the date of the Case Management Conference, the Judge may conduct a Case Management Conference in connection with the motion hearing, even if there has been no notice of a Case Management Conference for that day, and may cancel any previously scheduled Case Management Conference, making sure to schedule a next event in the order on the motion or the order after Case Management Conference.

Motions shall not be heard at a scheduled Case Management Conference without prior approval of the Court. As a general rule, the discovery schedule and deadline and a Pre–Trial Conference date should be assigned the first time the case is before a Judge with both parties or counsel present.

h. Joint Stipulation on Case Management Conference

Counsel and pro se parties may, at any time after a complaint is filed, file a Joint Stipulation signed by counsel for each represented party and by each pro se party which, at a minimum, requests a pre-trial conference date and agrees to a specific date to be the discovery deadline for that case. The discovery deadline date shall be not more than 180 days after the date of filing of the complaint.

Counsel and pro se parties may, after receiving notice that a Case Management Conference has been scheduled, file, on or before the date of the Case Management Conference, a Joint Stipulation signed by counsel for each represented party and by each pro se party which, at a minimum, requests a pre-trial conference date and agrees to a specific date to be the discovery deadline for that case. The discovery deadline date shall be not more than 120 days after the date of filing of the Joint Stipulation. If the Joint Stipulation is filed prior to the time scheduled for the Case Management Conference, no one need appear for the Case Management Conference.

Upon the filing of such a Joint Stipulation, the Register shall schedule a pre-trial conference for the next available date not sooner than 14 days after the discovery deadline and issue a Pre–Trial Notice and Order in the form specified by the Chief Justice of the Probate and Family Court. The scheduled pre-trial conference is a "future court event" so that a Case Management Conference will not be automatically scheduled upon the 120 day review or upon the filing of a return of service, answer, objection or counterclaim.

i. Joint Requests to Continue Case Management Conference

Parties engaged in alternative dispute resolution may request an extension of a scheduled Case Management Conference date by filing a joint or assented to motion which attests that the parties are engaged in alternative dispute resolution and includes:

▲ the name of the alternative dispute resolution provider;

▲ the dates and number of sessions held and;

▲ the dates and number of future sessions scheduled.

All other joint requests to continue shall be by written motion stating detailed and specific reasons for the request. All motions shall include proposed dates for the rescheduling of the Case Management Conference. Joint or assented to motions shall be considered without an in person hearing, unless otherwise ordered by the Court. If the motion is allowed, the court shall reschedule the Case Management Conference and send notice to all parties.

j. Citations in Probate, Guardianship, Child Welfare, and Adoption Petitions

Unless all required assents are filed with a probate petition, including guardianship petitions, custody petitions under c.119, and adoption petitions, the Register shall issue a citation no later than three (3) court days after the date of filing.

k. General Provisions

Nothing in this Standing Order precludes the marking of an earlier hearing date for a motion or other case event when appropriate.

The Court may schedule conferences, including Case Management, Pre–Trial and Status Conferences, as well as Trials, in its discretion.

Any party to any matter filed in the Probate and Family Court may request a Case Management Conference or Pre–Trial Conference after service of the complaint or petition, with notice to the other side of such request.

When a Case Management Conference is held, the conference will include discussion of all actions pending between the named parties. Other pending actions shall be scheduled for a future court event or shall be dismissed.

3. DISMISSAL FOR LACK OF SERVICE

The Register shall review all Domestic Relations and Equity cases 120 days after filing of the complaint to determine whether a return of service has been filed. If a return of service has not been filed, and no future court event has been scheduled, the Register shall issue a notice in a format specified by the Chief Justice of the Probate and Family Court. The notice shall inform the plaintiff that, because no return of service has been filed to show that service was made within 90 days of filing as required by Mass.R.Civ.P./Mass.R.Dom.Rel.P. 4(j), the case will be dismissed 21 days after the date of the notice unless the plaintiff files the return of service showing that service was made within ninety (90) days after the filing of the complaint or unless within those twenty-one (21)days, the plaintiff files and has scheduled a motion for extension of time which shows good cause why service was not made within ninety (90) days after the filing of the complaint.

4. CONDUCT of CASE MANAGEMENT CONFERENCE

a. Counsel and/or Parties Encouraged to Confer.

Prior to the Case Management Conference, counsel and/or parties are encouraged to confer for the purpose of agreeing on a proposed schedule of deadlines and dates through trial.

If a domestic violence restraining order (G.L. c. 209A) or a domestic violence protective order (G.L. c. 208) has been issued for one party against the other, then the parties are not expected to confer. The Case Management Conference shall still be held.

b. At a Case Management Conference the Court may:

(1) explore the possibility of settlement including but not limited to exploring the use of Alternate Dispute Resolution (ADR) processes;

(2) identify or formulate (or order attorneys or parties to formulate) the principal issues and disputes;

(3) prepare (or order attorneys or parties to prepare) a discovery schedule including discovery parameters and deadlines;

(4) establish deadlines for filing motions, including but not limited to motions for summary judgment and a time frame for their disposition;

(5) explore any other matters that the court determines appropriate for the fair and efficient management of the litigation;

(6) hear the case on an uncontested basis if settlement has been achieved, or if no appearance or answer is filed after service and return of service and there is no opposition; or

(7) dismiss the case if no parties are present for the Case Management Conference or if the plaintiff or petitioner is not present.

c. Next Event Scheduling

At the Case Management Conference, the next court date shall be assigned unless a judgment or permanent decree is issued or the case is dismissed.

d. Requirement to Appear

Counsel and parties, or parties alone if not represented by counsel, shall be required to appear at the Case Management Conference, except as provided in section 2(h) above. The Court, in its discretion, may waive the requirement for the appearance of the parties if they are represented by counsel. The Court may conduct Case Management Conferences by telephone, in its discretion.

e. Sanctions for Failure to Appear.

The court may impose sanctions for failure to attend the Case Management Conference without good cause, including dismissal, or may hear the case as if it were uncontested.

5. ALTERNATE DISPUTE RESOLUTION SERVICES

When appropriate, cases may be referred to:

a. Probation Officers for dispute intervention services in contested matters at any court event; or

b. Other approved providers of court connected dispute resolution services as defined in S.J.C. Rule 1:18, Uniform Rules on Dispute Resolution.

6. CHANGES TO TRACK ASSIGNMENT and RESCHEDULING OF SCHEDULED EVENTS

a. A party may file and serve a motion requesting a change in track assignment or rescheduling of scheduled events. Changes in track assignment or rescheduling of scheduled events shall be allowed only at the discretion of the Judge. A Probation Officer, in connection with an investigation, may file and serve on all parties a motion requesting a change in track assignment or rescheduling of scheduled events.

b. Motions to continue a trial may be allowed, only for good cause shown, with notice and hearing, in accordance with Mass.R.Dom.Rel.P. 40(b) and Mass.R.Civ.P.40(b).

c. All requests for rescheduling shall include proposed future dates. No action shall be "continued generally." Any rescheduling shall be to a date and event certain.

d. In cases involving allegations or a history of domestic violence, or a prior or current abuse prevention order, the Judge shall take into account the safety of alleged victims and victims and the reduction of conflict when considering any requests for changes in track assignment or rescheduling of scheduled events.

7. ASSIGNMENT TO TRACKS:

a. At filing, all Probate, Equity, Domestic Relations (including Paternity) cases (except Joint Petitions for Divorce, Joint Petitions for Modification of Child Support, and Complaints for Contempt, which shall be heard as outlined in sections 10 through 12) shall be assigned to a track according to the chart below:

3–6 Month Track[1]	8 Month Track	14 Month Track
Probate of Wills and Administration of Estates	Complaint to Establish Paternity	Complaint for Divorce
Accounts	Complaint for Custody, Visitation, and Support (Paternity)	Complaints in Equity
All Other "Probate" except Guardianships and Conservatorships	Complaint for Modification (except Joint Petition for Modification of Child Support)	Petitions to Partition
Real Estate Sales	Probate–Guardianships Conservatorships	Other "Divorce" Case Types (except Joint Petition for Divorce)
Change of Name	Complaint for Separate Support	
	Other Paternity Case Types	

b. G.L. c. 209A Complaints and G.L. c.19A Petitions for Protection from Abuse, cases concerning the custody of children under G.L. c. 119, § 23A, G.L. c. 119, § 23C, and G.L. c. 210, § 3, and Adoptions shall be heard as outlined below in sections 13 through 17.

c. Assignment to a track indicates the maximum amount of time in which a case should be tried, settled, or dismissed. Most cases should be tried, settled, or dismissed before the maximum time period of the track.

d. There may be extraordinary cases which cannot be disposed of within the time frames set forth in their track designations.

e. The Register shall issue a Track Assignment Notice for each case in the 8 month and 14 month tracks, except as outlined in section 2 (a) of this Standing Order, in a format specified by the Chief Justice of the Probate and Family Court. The Track Assignment Notice shall reflect the time requirements for each track.

8. CONDUCT OF PRE–TRIAL CONFERENCES

a. The Pre–Trial Conference shall be conducted in accordance with Rule 16 of the Massachusetts Rules of Domestic Relations Procedure or the Massachusetts Rules of Civil Procedure.

b. In scheduling a Pre–Trial Conference the court shall issue a Pre–Trial Notice and Order in a format specified by the Chief Justice of the Probate and Family Court.

c. If a case is not resolved at the Pre–Trial Conference, an Order After Pre–Trial Conference shall be issued which include provisions specified by the Chief Justice of the Probate and Family Court, and may also include additional provisions at the discretion of the Judge conducting the Pre–Trial Conference.

9. SEQUENTIAL TRIAL DAYS

When trial dates are originally assigned, they shall be scheduled on days as close to sequential trial days as the calendar of the trial Judge permits. When trials are not completed in the number of days originally scheduled, the Court shall schedule the remaining trial days as soon as possible using the earliest available trial days, with the goal of minimizing intervals between trial days.

10. TRACK FOR COMPLAINTS FOR CONTEMPT

At time of filing, a summons shall issue with the date for the contempt hearing. The hearing date shall be set for no later than twenty-eight (28) days from the date of filing.

11. JOINT PETITIONS FOR DIVORCE UNDER G.L. c. 208, § 1A

All Joint Petitions for Divorce shall be scheduled for hearing within thirty (30) days of filing of all required documents.[2]

12. JOINT PETITION FOR MODIFICATION OF CHILD SUPPORT

Pursuant to Probate and Family Court Supplemental Rule 412 and Protocol, these cases shall be decided on the pleadings without hearing, within fourteen (14) days of filing, unless otherwise ordered by the Court. If a hearing is ordered by the Court, the Court shall set the time and date for the hearing and shall notify the parties within fourteen (14) days of the filing of the joint petition.

13. G.L. c. 209A COMPLAINT FOR PROTECTION FROM ABUSE

All proceedings pursuant to G.L. c. 209A shall be processed in accordance with the existing statutory time requirements and each order shall specifically state the next hearing date and expiration date of the order, unless the order is permanent. If the order is permanent, it shall so specify.

14. COMPLAINTS FOR PROTECTION FROM ELDER AND DISABLED ABUSE, G.L. c. 19A, § 20, G.L. c. 19C, § 7

An initial hearing shall be held within fourteen (14) days of the filing of a petition. Emergency hearings may be held with at least twenty-four (24) hours notice to the elderly or disabled person. The court may dispense with notice upon finding that immediate and foreseeable physical harm to the individual or others will result from the twenty-four (24) hour delay and that reasonable attempts have been made to give notice.

15. TRACK FOR PETITIONS FILED PURSUANT TO G.L. c. 210, § 3 AND PETITIONS FILED PURSUANT TO G.L. c. 119, § 23C

a. If the Petition is uncontested, due to the assent of all parties or completion of proper notice, with no appearance in opposition filed, the Register shall, within fourteen (14) days of the return date, notify the petitioners that the case is uncontested, and schedule an uncontested hearing within 30 days of the return date. For cases filed under G.L. c. 210, § 3, an adoption plan shall be filed, in accordance with Uniform Probate Court Practice X prior to the hearing date.

b. If, by virtue of an appearance the case is contested, the Register shall issue a Track Assignment and Scheduling Notice for a Case Management Conference to be held not more than thirty (30) days after the return date.[1]

c. At the Case Management Conference, referral to Permanency Mediation shall be considered and a Pre–Trial Conference shall be scheduled for a date within seventy-five (75) days of the Case Management Conference. At the Pre–Trial Conference, a trial date shall be set for no later than one hundred twenty (120) days from the date of the Pre–Trial Conference.

d. If a sua sponte or ex parte custody order under c.119, § 23C is issued, the Court shall schedule a hearing within 72 hours of the sua sponte or ex parte custody order, unless a prior evidentiary hearing has been held. Notice shall be given to all parties and counsel.

16. TRACK FOR ADOPTION PETITIONS

a. If a Petition is filed as uncontested, due to the filing of necessary surrenders or termination decrees, and notice is not required, a hearing shall be scheduled within thirty (30) days of the filing of the Petition.[3]

b. If a timely appearance is filed, a Case Management Conference shall be scheduled for not more than thirty (30) days after the return date.

c. At the Case Management Conference, a Pre–Trial Conference shall be scheduled for a date within seventy-five (75) days of the Case Management Conference. At the Pre–Trial Conference, a trial date shall be set for no later than one hundred twenty (120) days from the date of the Pre–Trial Conference.

17. PETITIONS FILED PURSUANT TO G.L. c. 119, § 23(A), VOLUNTARY PLACEMENT WITH DEPARTMENT OF SOCIAL SERVICES

At time of filing, all petitions filed pursuant to G.L. c. 119, § 23(A) shall be scheduled for hearing within thirty (30) days.

18. ISSUANCE OF TEMPORARY ORDERS

Temporary orders shall be issued as expeditiously as possible, but in no event more than fourteen (14) days from the conclusion of the hearing, or the receipt by the court of all written submissions. On motions for summary judgment, orders shall be issued within thirty (30) days of the conclusion of the hearing, or the receipt by the court of all written submissions.

19. ISSUANCE OF JUDGMENT OR DECREE

Except as otherwise indicated in this Standing Order, or with notice to the Chief Justice of the Probate and Family Court, and counsel or parties, the judgment or decree shall be issued as follows:

Trial Time	Entry of Judgment or Decree
One day or less	Within 30 days of the conclusion of the trial
Two days	Within 60 days of the conclusion of the trial
Three to Seven days	Within 90 days of the conclusion of the trial
Exceeds Seven days	Within 120 days of the conclusion of the trial

Adopted effective April 3, 2006.

1 As described in section 2(f) above, if a case assigned to this track becomes contested due to the filing of an appearance and, if required, objections, the Register shall change the track designation to an 8 month track.

2 If a case is ready for hearing at time of filing, a hearing shall be scheduled within 30 days. If a case is uncontested at time of filing, but incomplete, the case shall be scheduled for hearing within thirty (30) days of the date of filing all required documents.

3 If a case is ready for hearing at time of filing, a hearing shall be scheduled within 30 days. If a case is uncontested at time of filing, but incomplete, the case shall be scheduled for hearing within thirty (30) days of the date of filing all required documents.

Standing Order 1–08. Standards for Guardians ad Litem/Evaluators

1. The Standards for Category E, Guardians ad Litem/Evaluators in actions involving: Domestic Relations or Custody/Visitation/Adoption G.L. c. 215, § 56A; c. 208, § 16, (hereinafter "Standards") are effective January 15, 2008.

2. The purpose of these Standards is to:

• provide accountability related to guardian ad litem/evaluations;

• improve custody, visitation, and other outcomes for children;

• promote uniformity and consistency in guardian ad litem/evaluations; and

• promote respect for the rights of parties and their children, including their safety.

3. It is ordered that all guardians ad litem/evaluators appointed pursuant to G.L. c. 215, § 56A, c. 208, § 16 utilize the Standards in conducting these evaluations. Guardians ad litem/evaluators who are certified by the Probate and Family Court Administrative Office to receive appointments under Supreme Judicial Court Rule 1:07, and those persons not on the list who are appointed in accordance with Section (4) of Rule 1:07, are governed by this Order and shall conduct their evaluations in accordance with the Standards.

STANDARDS FOR CATEGORY E GUARDIANS AD LITEM/EVALUATORS

INTRODUCTION

A Category E Guardian ad Litem/Evaluator (GAL) is appointed by the Probate and Family Court to investigate and evaluate facts in cases involving the care and custody of minor children and other matters that implicate the interests or rights of children. G.L. c. 215, § 56A; G.L. c. 208, § 16. A GAL is often appointed in cases that raise questions about:

• a child's best interests as related to custody and visitation;

• advantages or disadvantages of removing a child from the Commonwealth;

• changes in circumstances that might warrant modification of a judgment;

• existence of a de facto parent-child relationship;

• parental fitness as related to termination of parental rights or guardianship;

• paternity of a minor child; or

• other matters implicating the rights and interests of a minor child.

The purpose of these standards is to:

• provide accountability related to GAL evaluations;

• improve custody, visitation, and other outcomes for children;

• promote uniformity and consistency in GAL evaluations; and

• promote respect for the rights of parties and their children, including their safety.

These standards apply to all Category E Guardians ad Litem/Evaluators.

1. THE ROLE OF THE GAL EVALUATOR

The GAL performs duties that are within the scope of the court order of appointment.

1.1 The GAL Shall Gather and Report Factual Data to the Court, and, when Competent to do so, Offer Clinical Opinions.

The role of the Category E GAL evaluator is to gather and report factual information, use clinical knowledge to interpret that data, and formulate clinical opinions to assist the court in making custody, visitation, or other decisions related to the welfare of a child. Unless the appointing judge specifies otherwise, the GAL's role it limited to gathering and evaluating information and reporting it to the court. The GAL may include recommendations in the report if the order of the court authorizes inclusion of such recommendations. The GAL shall not offer clinical assessment or conclusions unless the GAL has the requisite expertise to offer such opinions.

Commentary. The court, not the GAL, decides legal issues and ultimately makes credibility determinations and factual findings when facts are in dispute. The GAL reports on facts and avoids providing legal conclusions or legal analysis.

A. The GAL Shall Investigate and Evaluate Only those Areas Specified by the Court.

If the GAL sees a need to broaden the scope of the evaluation, the GAL shall seek authority from the court before broadening the evaluation. Copies of any and all motions filed by a GAL must be sent to counsel of record and any pro se parties.

Commentary: This standard does not preclude a GAL from investigating and evaluating factual issues that were not identified at the time of the appointment if they are relevant to the legal issues identified in the appointment.

1.2 The GAL's Role Requires Participation in the Trial and Discovery.

After conducting the evaluation and writing a report, the GAL shall be available for trial and for possible deposition. If the parties do not reach an agreement about their case, the GAL may be subpoenaed by a party or the court may request that the GAL be present for trial.

Commentary. Absent a protective order of the court, the GAL shall appear for deposition as required under the applicable rules and statutes as part of his or her responsibilities as the GAL.

1.3 The GAL Serves as an Impartial Investigator, Evaluator and Reporter.

The GAL is an impartial investigator, evaluator and reporter in all cases.

A. The GAL Shall Decline or Withdraw from the Appointment if a Conflict of Interest Exists, or the GAL has Information or Personal Relationships that Will Bias the Process or Outcome of the Evaluation.

If the GAL has any prior or existing direct or indirect relationships with parties, their families, material witnesses, or someone else connected with the family, the GAL must consider whether the GAL's impartiality is compromised as a result of these relationships. The GAL shall decline the appointment if:

• The GAL has or had a dating or intimate relationship with any counsel of record, or a close personal relationship with any counsel of record that will impact the GAL's ability to be unbiased;

• The GAL provided counseling or other services to a party or members of the family, or a material witness;

• The GAL, by virtue of a professional relationship with a colleague (e. g. members of the same practice, members of a peer review/case review/professional development group, supervisory/consulting relationship), has or has had access to information about the parties, children, material witnesses, that would otherwise not be available to the GAL in the normal course of the evaluation;

- The GAL was married to or had a personal relationship with a party, a member of the party's family, a material witness, or another person closely aligned to a party;

- The GAL has or had pecuniary interests or financial involvement with a party, the party's spouse or non-marital partner, a material witness, counsel for a party or other person closely aligned to a party;

- The GAL's concerns about reprisal or adverse personal consequences if the report is unfavorable to a party will impede the GAL's candor or ability to be impartial and render an unbiased report;

- The GAL is aware of other circumstances that will impede the GAL's candor or ability to be impartial and render an unbiased report.

Commentary. If a GAL is aware of circumstances that indicate that the GAL may have a conflict of interest or other circumstances that may make it inappropriate for the GAL to serve as the evaluator, the GAL shall disclose the information to counsel of record and any pro se parties. The GAL also shall immediately file a motion for instructions from the appointing judge as appropriate with notice to counsel and any pro se parties.

B. The GAL Engages in Nondiscriminatory Practices

The GAL shall not engage in conduct manifesting bias or prejudice based on race, gender, religion, ethnicity, disability, age, socioeconomic status, marital status or sexual orientation against a party, witness, counsel, or other persons involved in the case.

Commentary. The GAL must be aware of how societal and personal biases may interfere with an objective evaluation and recommendations. The GAL recognizes and strives to overcome any such biases. If the GAL is not able to do so, he or she must promptly decline or withdraw from the appointment. If the GAL considers factors related to race, gender, religion, ethnicity, disability, age, sexual orientation, marital status or socioeconomic status concerning a party in the evaluation or report, the GAL must explain the relevance of these factors to the issues before the court.

C. The GAL Evaluator Shall Not Act as an Attorney or Legal Advocate for the Child.

The GAL is an objective and even-handed reporter. The GAL shall not give legal advice or act as advocate or attorney for the child. In some cases, the child's wishes may be contrary to the child's best interests.

Commentary. A GAL is not a party to the case. A GAL is a witness to the case. The GAL shall not file motions except as related to performance of the GAL's responsibilities and as provided in these standards.

D. The GAL Does Not Give Legal Advice or Act as Either Party's Legal Advocate.

The GAL refrains from giving legal advice to parties including but not limited to advice about how the law applies to the facts of their case, how to obtain or modify court orders, or how to draft legal documents. The GAL refers parties to their attorneys for legal advice. If a party is pro se, the GAL suggests that the party seek legal advice from an attorney.

Commentary. Many courts have "Lawyer of the Day" programs for indigent parties as well as family law facilitators and many bar associations have lawyer-referral panels. Nonprofit "legal aid" (a/k/a "legal services") programs may be able to provide free legal advice and representation to low income or indigent parties.

The GAL shall refrain from giving a party legal advice that he or she should drop a restraining order so that the parties may meet together with the GAL or engage in mediation pertaining to the restraining order. See G.L. c. 209A, § 3.

1.4 The GAL Avoids Dual or Multiple Roles.

The GAL shall not provide legal, mental health, parent coordination, mediation or other professional services to any party or the child during the evaluation or pendency of the case.

Commentary. To provide such services during the Evaluation or pendency of the case is inconsistent with the GAL's role as an impartial evaluator and reporter. The GAL, however, may provide information to the parties, the court, and counsel about community resources available to the parties, such as but not limited to substance abuse treatment programs or other professional services that may be helpful to the parties and their children.

1.5 The GAL Adheres to Applicable Ethical and Professional Standards.

The GAL shall adhere to the ethical guidelines and standards for his or her profession to the extent that these guidelines apply.

Commentary. If the mental health professional serving as a GAL is unable to perform his or her evaluative responsibilities because of a conflict with applicable professional standards, the GAL shall file a motion to withdraw as the GAL with notice to counsel and any pro se parties.

2. COMPENSATION

GAL evaluator's fees paid by the Commonwealth are set by the Administrative Office of the Trial Court. If the court order lacks clarity about who will pay for GAL services, the GAL shall file a motion for clarification by the appointing judge with notice to counsel and any pro se party. If the order specifies that compensation will be paid by the Commonwealth, the GAL is prohibited from charging additional fees to the parties. The GAL files the report in a timely fashion whether or not compensation has been paid.

Commentary. At present, Category E Guardians ad Litem/Evaluators paid by the Commonwealth are compensated in accordance with Memo No. 14 (February 28, 1997, Fiscal Year 1997) issued by the Administrative Office of the Trial Court. The GAL also may file a motion with notice to counsel and any pro se party for an extension of hours beyond the number of hours set forth in the order of appointment for approval by the judge who appointed the GAL.

3. UPON RECEIVING THE APPOINTMENT

The GAL carefully reviews the order of appointment to determine the scope of the evaluation and the duties to be performed.

3.1 The GAL Clarifies the Scope of the Appointment and Duties as Necessary.

If the GAL is uncertain about the areas to be evaluated, or the GAL's responsibilities, the GAL shall file a motion for clarification for hearing before the appointing judge with notice to counsel and pro se parties.

3.2 The GAL Determines Whether he or she has the Requisite Expertise and Competence in the Areas to be Evaluated.

If the GAL lacks the necessary experience, expertise or competence to conduct an evaluation of the issues, the GAL shall decline the appointment.

3.3 The GAL Determines Whether the GAL's Personal and Professional Schedule Permit a Timely Report.

The GAL reviews the areas to be evaluated and the tasks to be performed. If the GAL will not be able to complete a report by the designated deadline, the GAL shall decline the appointment.

Commentary. If the GAL determines after commencement of the evaluation that additional time will be needed to complete the evaluation, the GAL may file a motion to extend the deadline with notice to counsel and any pro se party. The motion shall include the reasons for the proposed extension and a new proposed due date for the report so that the judge may determine whether the deadline should be extended or the appointment should be vacated.

3.4 The GAL Promptly Accepts or Rejects any Appointment.

The GAL shall promptly accept or reject the appointment no later than twenty days after the GAL receives it, or earlier if requested by the court. The GAL accepts or rejects the appointment by returning the completed form to the court.

4. THROUGHOUT THE CASE

4.1 The GAL Maintains an Attitude of Respect.

The GAL shall approach all family members and parties with an attitude of respect and openness to hear their account of the relevant facts regardless of any allegations that have been made. The GAL shall be patient, courteous, and dignified in his or her interactions with litigants, witnesses, attorneys, and others with whom the GAL deals in this official capacity.

Commentary. The GAL may limit the number of telephone calls and contacts made by a party or attorney as is reasonable given the particular circumstances. The GAL may seek assistance from the court on issues related to the GAL's safety or to address inappropriate conduct by a party related to the evaluation. In such instances, a motion must be filed with the court with a copy sent to counsel of record and any pro se parties.

4.2 The GAL is Diligent and Adheres to Time Deadlines.

The GAL shall adhere to all time frames set forth in the order of appointment as applicable.

Commentary. If the report is not filed on time, the Probation Office notifies the judge and seeks further instruction from the court in accordance with Probate and Family Court Standing Order 2–98. If the GAL needs more time to complete the report, the GAL shall file a motion with notice to counsel and pro se parties to extend the deadline prior to the date when it is due. The motion shall indicate the proposed due date for the report. The GAL shall complete the report even if a party declines to participate or an attorney indicates that the case may settle. A party or GAL may file a motion to terminate the GAL appointment with notice to the parties or GAL as applicable if a case settles and the GAL's services are no longer necessary.

4.3 The GAL Maintains Safety.

The GAL shall make every reasonable effort to ensure the safety of all parties and their children. To implement this requirement, the GAL shall:

A. Arrange joint parent and child interviews, home visits, or observations of a party with the children

B. Avoid interview strategies which put the child(ren) at risk of physical or psychological harm from one or both parents after the interview.

C. Arrange interview schedules so that parties do not come into contact during the interview process when domestic violence is alleged or identified as a possible issue.

D. Inquire about and refrains from disclosing, directly or indirectly, residential, telephone, work, or other location information that a party has kept confidential for safety reasons.

E. Refrain from recommending visitation or other arrangements that bring the parties into contact when an abuse prevention order is in effect, or when the evaluator has reasonable cause to believe that such contact may be dangerous or harmful for either party or the child.

F. Warn the party, the party's attorney and contact police as appropriate if the GAL believes that a party or child is in danger of imminent physical harm from the other party in the case.

Commentary. To ensure the safety of the parties and their children, the GAL should screen for previously undisclosed safety issues in separate interviews with the parties early in the evaluation. Depending on the circumstances, the other party, the child, the GAL, or others may be at risk if there are issues of mental illness, domestic violence, child abuse, or substance abuse. The GAL should attempt to gather and communicate information in ways that avoid harm to parties, the child or children, or others involved in the case. The GAL shall consider the safety of the parties and other family members when he or she makes recommendations and determines how the information he or she has collected will be reported to the court.

4.3.1 The GAL Files Mandatory "51A" Reports When Required.

In cases of suspected child maltreatment, many mental health professionals are required to file a "51A" report. G.L.

c. 119, § 51A. However, a mental health professional who is not a mandated reporter may still report suspected abuse or neglect as necessary if a child is at risk. If the GAL has reasonable cause to believe a child is in imminent danger, the GAL should also report the information to the police department and should also report the information to the Court through an emergency motion for instructions with the required notice to counsel and pro se parties.

Commentary. If a GAL files a 51A report, the GAL should assess whether he or she can remain neutral and complete his or her duties free of bias.

4.4 The GAL Shall Use a Process for Communication and Collection of Information that is Conducive to Disclosure of Information and Fair to the Parties.

The GAL provides each party with a separate interview so that each party may speak with candor. The GAL encourages parties and their attorneys to provide additional relevant information and documents. The process for communications must be even-handed and provide each party with the opportunity to present relevant information and respond to relevant allegations by the opposing party. The GAL also affords a pro se party the same procedural protections that the GAL affords a party with an attorney.

4.4.1 The GAL Shall Conduct All Oral and Written Communications with Attorneys and Pro Se Parties in a Manner that Avoids the Question of Bias.

The GAL shall send counsel of record and pro se parties copies of any motions and other documents filed by the GAL in court, except for the GAL report. If the GAL sends a substantive written communication to one counsel or a pro se party, the GAL shall send a copy of the communication to the opposing counsel or pro se party.

Commentary. A GAL's written communications to one party or attorney about administrative or scheduling matters, such as arranging a time for an interview or signing releases, are not substantive matters. While it is not required by any statute or rule, attorneys may agree to send copies of all written correspondence addressed to the guardian ad litem to the opposing counsel.

4.4.2 The GAL Arranges for a Qualified Interpreter if a Party or Child is Not Fluent in the English language or a Sign Language Interpreter is Needed.

The need for an interpreter goes beyond the courtroom if a party is not completely fluent or comfortable in using the English language or needs an American Sign Language interpreter. Using a child as the interpreter is not appropriate, and using relatives or friends may have a chilling effect on what is disclosed. If the child or a party has limited or no English language skills and the GAL does not speak the language, a qualified interpreter should be used. Any authorizations for release of information and other forms should be translated for such parties. Likewise, a party or child may have a need for a sign language interpreter.

Commentary. If a party does not supply a qualified interpreter, the GAL may file a motion in court for appointment of a qualified interpreter that includes a request that the Commonwealth pay for the interpreter's services if a party is indigent, or that a party or parties who are not indigent pay

for the interpreter. Counsel and pro se parties shall be given notice of the motion. If the GAL desires payment from or reimbursement from the Commonwealth for the cost of using an interpreter, the GAL must receive approval from the court before incurring the expense. Bias or incompetence of an interpreter can lead to omitted and inaccurate communications with the GAL. The interpreter should not have a conflict of interest or a relationship with a party or other person that will bias the interpretation. The Supreme Judicial Court has promulgated standards for court interpreter services and qualifications which are available on the internet at: http://www.state.ma.us/courts/formsandguidelines/index.html. Certain cases may require that the GAL possess or utilize cross-cultural competence and expertise. For example, if the parents dispute whether a certain religious ritual was integral to a certain faith and whether the ritual should be performed on the child. The role of the interpreter, however, is to facilitate communication rather than serve as a substitute for an expert on a particular culture.

4.5 The GAL Answers Appropriate Questions about the GAL's Credentials or Role.

The GAL answers appropriate questions about the GAL's education, training, experience, practice areas, professional affiliations, and the process of the GAL evaluation.

Commentary. If requested by counsel or a pro se party, the GAL shall provide a copy of his or her curriculum vitae to said counsel or party. However, questions pertaining to the GAL's personal life need not be answered.

4.6 The GAL Maintains Confidentiality.

The information gathered by the GAL for the court is confidential. The GAL shall not disclose confidential and personally identifiable information about the parties, their children, or the services rendered by the GAL to a person who is not a party or counsel in the case, except as necessary to gather information to complete the evaluation and report, or to perform responsibilities related to the order of appointment. This prohibition is permanent and applies to the GAL's writings, lectures, or other media communications.

Commentary. If a GAL has questions regarding release of information pertaining to the parties, child, or the evaluation and report, the GAL may file a motion for instructions with the court with notice to counsel and any pro se party.

4.6.1 The GAL Obtains Appropriate Release Forms or Court Orders before Obtaining Privileged and Confidential Information about the Parties and their Children.

Many of the most common and relevant records that are subject to statutory privileges or other restrictions can be obtained with an appropriate authorization for release of the information or a court order.

● Department of Social Services (DSS) records. A party's release form or court order is needed to access records. The GAL can obtain the DSS file with a release from a party but privileged information must be redacted. 10 C.M.R. § 12.09(1)–(3).

● Medical, health and hospital records. A party's release form or court order is needed to access records. G.L. c. 111 § 70, § 70E(b); The Health Insurance Portability and Accountability Act of 1996, Pub. L. 104–19 1 (HIPAA).

• Psychotherapist records. A party's release form or court order is needed to access records pertaining to an adult from a psychotherapist whose communications are privileged. G.L. c. 112, § 8GB; Commonwealth v. Bernard, 424 Mass. 32, 673 N.E.2d 1220 (1996). G.L. c. 233, § 20B.

• Social Worker records. A party's release form or court order is needed to access records. G.L. c. 112, §§ 135A, 135B.

• Alcohol and drug abuse programs records. A party's release form and/or court order may be needed to access records. 42 U.S.C. §§ 1175, 290 dd–3.

• School records. If a party has shared or sole legal custody, he or she may authorize release of records, except for a parent or party whose access is restricted by a Chapter 209A or other court order. G.L. c. 71, § 34H; G.L. c. 208, § 31.

• Criminal Offender Record Information (CORI and CARI). The GAL can most easily review these records with a court order through the Probation Department, or request the records through the Criminal History Systems Board.

• Prior GAL reports, Probation Office or Court Clinic reports involving the parties. The GAL must file a motion with the court with notice to the parties to access these records.

• Domestic Violence or Sexual Assault Victim–Counselor records. Confidential communications cannot be disclosed in civil actions by court order and are not discoverable without the victim's prior consent. G.L. c. 233, §§ 20J, 20K.

• Victim program locations. Locations of battered women's shelters, domestic violence, and rape crisis programs may not be disclosed by court order, or otherwise to the GAL. G.L. c. 233, §§ 20J, 20K.

• Mediator Records. Communications made during mediation with a mediator are privileged and the court cannot order disclosure. G.L. c. 233, § 23C.

• Alternative dispute intervention information. The Probation Department of the Probate and Family Court may release the information to the GAL if the court orders release of the information or the parties consent to the release of information.

The Health Insurance Portability and Accountability Act of 1996, Pub. L. 104–19 1 (HIPAA) requires that health providers may only release personal health information if the release signed by a party complies with the provisions of the federal law. Even if no statutory privilege applies to the information sought by the GAL, the provider or keeper of other records (e.g. unlicensed support group leaders, batterer intervention programs) may also request a written release from their client. In some instances, the order for appointment of the GAL will provide that the GAL is permitted to access certain records and information; this obviates the need for a party's authorization for release of the information.

Commentary. Some third parties or providers may be unaware of protections that apply to records or confidential information relating to the parties or the children. The GAL, however, shall review the information only after appropriate releases or court orders for access to the information have been provided to the holder of the information. If a privilege is not properly waived, a judge may allow a motion to strike reference to the information from the GAL report.

4.6.2 The GAL Recognizes that Children's Rights to Confidentiality are Different than Other Parties' Rights to Confidentiality.

The GAL shall obtain authorizations for release of information pertaining to children from the children's parents or legal guardians. A parent, however, cannot waive a child's psychotherapy or social worker privilege. If the counseling information is needed but protected by a privilege, the GAL or counsel must return to the appointing judge and present a motion for appointment of another guardian ad litem to evaluate whether waiver of the child's psychotherapy privilege is in the child's best interest. Adoption of Diane, 400 Mass. 196, 201 (1987); G.L. c. 233, § 20B. The motion should indicate the scope of the information sought and the GAL's reason for seeking the information. Counsel and pro se parties must have notice of the motion. If the privilege is waived, the GAL may access the information.

Commentary. A parent or parents with legal custody of the child, or a party granted legal guardianship of the child, may authorize access to most other records of the child. If a parent or parents refuse to authorize release of information that is important to the evaluation, the GAL may file a motion for access to the information with notice to counsel and pro se parties.

5. COMMENCEMENT OF THE EVALUATION

After the GAL accepts the appointment, he or she promptly schedules initial contacts with each of the parties and their attorneys if they are represented.

Commentary. If a party has an attorney, the GAL should first make contact with the attorney. The GAL may find it helpful to send a letter of introduction to counsel and pro se parties outlining the evaluation process. The GAL should use additional means of communication, however, if a party's primary language is not English, or there are literacy or other barriers impacting written communication. The GAL can determine more easily if a party understands what is communicated in a face-to-face interview.

5.1 The GAL Provides an Explanation of the GAL's Role and a Lamb-type Warning at the Commencement of the Evaluation.

The GAL must explain the GAL's role and the purpose of the evaluation to the parties. The GAL shall inform the parties how the information gathered by the GAL will be used. The GAL must provide a "Lamb warning" that explains there are no "off the record" discussions and any information collected by the GAL may appear in the GAL report, be disclosed in court or to the other party, Commonwealth v. Lamb, 1 Mass. App. Ct. 530 (1973), or otherwise disclosed as required or permitted by law. As appropriate based on the child's level of maturity, the GAL should provide a similar explanation of the evaluative process and a Lamb warning to a child, but modified to reflect the child's age and level of understanding. If the GAL interviews other witnesses, they also must receive a Lamb warning.

Commentary. To ensure a person understands the Lamb warning, the GAL should ask the person to summarize it for the GAL. The parties or witnesses should be informed that while they are encouraged to provide information, they may decline to answer a question and have an attorney present during any interview. Increasingly, parties represent themselves in court. The GAL should avoid use of professional jargon or legalese that a party may not understand. The GAL should strive to explain things in simple language and terms as appropriate so that a party with a limited educational background or language ability can better understand what the GAL is communicating.

5.2 The GAL Inquires if the Parties have Relevant Safety Concerns.

The GAL shall inquire at the outset of the evaluation about any safety risks related to the evaluation for either party, the child, or others because of any party's mental illness, substance abuse, domestic violence, child abuse, or history of violence against others. The GAL should attempt to conduct the investigation and evaluation in such a manner as appropriate to avoid likely harm to the child, a party, the GAL, or others.

5.3 The GAL Explains the Limits on Confidentiality and Complies with Legal and Ethical Standards Governing Disclosure of Privileged Communications.

The GAL shall obtain information or review records after appropriate authorizations for release of information are executed or the court orders release of the information. The GAL shall respect the parties' and their children's right to confidentiality. Before obtaining an authorization for release of records or other information from a party, the GAL should inform the party how the information will be used. The GAL should also disclose that any information obtained by the GAL could appear in the GAL report, be disclosed to the other party, put into evidence during court proceedings or depositions, or disclosed to others as necessary to complete the evaluation, discovery, or trial of the case. The authorization for release of information form given to a party by the GAL should include who the information is sought from and the duration of the authorization of the release. A party should also be informed that he or she has a right to seek legal advice before signing a release and may decline to sign an authorization for release of information. A party may direct that all release forms be sent directly to counsel of record.

If a party consents to release of information, the GAL should use forms for release of information that comply with applicable laws and that are acceptable to providers. The Health Insurance Portability and Accountability Act of 1996, Pub. L. 104–19 1 (HIPAA) requires that health providers may only release personal health information if the release form complies with the provisions of the federal law.

Commentary. The GAL should not seek confidential information unless it is necessary. If a party objects to release of certain information, the GAL may file a motion to obtain this information. G.L. c. 233, § 20B; G.L. c. 112, § 135B; Commonwealth v. Bernard, 424 Mass. 32 (1996). A parent cannot consent to release of a child's psychotherapy information. See Section 4.6.2.

6. EVALUATION SOURCES AND METHODS

The GAL shall conduct the evaluation in a fair and balanced manner. The GAL should obtain similar types of information about each party. If the case involves more than one child, each child's best interests must be addressed unless the court

orders otherwise. If the GAL is unable to report on all of the children, the GAL shall indicate why in the report.

Commentary. Depending on the circumstances, the GAL may need to spend more time investigating facts or evaluating issues that relate only to one party, especially if such facts are disputed, difficult to investigate, or new information arises about that parent. The GAL may have satisfactory information about one parent, but incomplete data about the other parent. For example, further investigation of alleged drug use might be needed if a party's drug testing results are unreliable because the facility did not monitor how samples from the party were collected, or new sources indicate that the party has used drugs since the time of the last testing.

6.1 The GAL Shall be Familiar with Applicable Legal Standards and Procedures.

The GAL shall be familiar with the law and the legal standards applicable to the questions the GAL has been appointed to evaluate.

Commentary. A GAL who is not an attorney, shall nonetheless have a sufficient understanding of the law to provide the judge with the facts that the judge will need to apply the applicable legal standard.

6.2 The GAL Spends Sufficient Time Interviewing Parties and Investigating their Concerns as Necessary to Gather Relevant Information.

The GAL conducts an initial interview with each party and additional interviews with each party and other witnesses as necessary to gather relevant information. In addition, the GAL may gather information by telephone, email, and or other means.

Commentary. A party is permitted to have counsel present during an interview, but the GAL controls the interview and conducts the questioning. If counsel directs a party to refuse to answer a question or plead the Fifth Amendment against self-incrimination, the GAL moves on to other questions, noting the objection. Such objections do not prohibit the GAL from using other sources to obtain the information. If the GAL does not meet with any party, the GAL explains why in the report.

6.3 The GAL Asks Each Party about Relevant Witnesses and Documents and Investigates these Sources of Information as Appropriate.

As a starting point, the GAL invites counsel and parties to provide relevant information, including a fact summary, procedural history, relevant documents, and a list of witnesses and professionals who can provide relevant information. In deciding what records to review or witnesses to interview, the GAL considers the likelihood that relevant information will be obtained, with reasonable convenience, efficiency, cost, and physical safety of a party, child or informant. The order of appointment also may direct the GAL to contact certain witnesses or sources.

Commentary. In determining what witnesses to interview, the GAL may also consider: the number of witnesses suggested, whether the witness directly witnessed important events or the aftermath of important events, the potential bias of the witness, the importance of the interview to a party, and other relevant considerations. At the beginning of each collateral witness or party interview, it is important that the GAL explain the GAL's role and the limits of confidentiality. The GAL shall access information after appropriate release forms are provided to professionals. In addition to oral communications, the GAL may provide written questions and accept additional written responses from witnesses or collateral sources. If a GAL declines to interview some or all of suggested witnesses, the GAL shall provide an explanation why the witnesses were not interviewed.

6.4 The GAL Shall Use Methods Designed to Assess the Accuracy of Information Gathered.

The GAL uses interview and fact gathering techniques designed to test the factual accuracy and reliability (i.e. objective truth) of the information gathered. The GAL compares sources of information, looks for consistencies and inconsistencies in reports, and appraises the value of the information gathered.

6.4.1 The GAL Uses Multiple Fact Sources When Possible.

If certain events or facts are disputed, the GAL should investigate more than one source of information relating to the events or allegations when possible. The parties should be encouraged to provide names of witnesses who were present, written reports, or other relevant evidence related to the event or allegation.

Commentary. For example, the husband disputes the wife's claim that the husband told her that he was treated at Cambridge Hospital after he attempted suicide by taking an overdose of sleeping pills and cocaine. The GAL contacts the hospital and interviews any other witnesses with direct knowledge about the disputed event or his statements about it. Hospital records in the case lead to other relevant sources of information such as "911" call records, a police report, and an ambulance report, including a copy of a suicide note found in the ambulance. The GAL reports all the relevant facts collected about the disputed allegation.

6.4.2 The GAL Accesses Original Sources When Possible.

To increase the reliability of reported information, the GAL investigates original sources of information.

For example: John Jones says that Jane Doe saw the parties' son drinking beer at a soccer game. The GAL speaks with Jane Doe to ascertain what she observed.

For example: a police report indicates that the child told his soccer coach that the child's parent supplied the beer. The GAL speaks with the coach and the child.

6.5 The GAL Conducts a Home Visit When Appropriate.

Ordinarily, home visits can yield valuable information, but on occasion a home visit is not indicated. Factors to consider in deciding whether to conduct home visits include: whether issues or problems with either home are alleged, cost and time involved, location, and the likelihood of obtaining relevant information not accessible in other ways. If no home visit is conducted, the GAL shall explain why that decision was made in the report.

Commentary. If home visits are conducted, care must be exercised so that inequality in housing conditions or perceived wealth do not lead to bias. A person, who is a fit parent and

caretaker for the child, also may experience transitional or temporary housing difficulties as a result of separation from the other party, nonpayment of support, inadequate financial support, or relocation related to domestic violence or loss of income.

6.6 The GAL Meets with the Children and Interviews them in a Developmentally Appropriate Manner.

The GAL meets with the children as part of the investigation. Children can offer useful information and should be offered the opportunity to provide information about themselves and their family. The GAL uses developmentally appropriate techniques to observe, interview and evaluate each child in the family. The conditions under which children are interviewed must be carefully considered, including what conditions will put the child most at ease and yield the most useful information. The GAL shall explain the reasons for not meeting with any of the children in the GAL report.

Commentary. Some children may be much less candid in the interview if a parent or the parents are present during the child's interview, or are visible or able to hear the interview.

6.7 The GAL Observes Children with Each Parent When Appropriate.

The GAL should observe the child with each parent when appropriate. This often provides valuable information about the parent-child relationship.

Commentary. The GAL has a duty to avoid further harm to children when possible. If concerns are raised that a child will be traumatized or at risk by contact with a parent (e.g. due to severe neglect or abuse, exposure to domestic violence, traumatic or unpredictable absence, or other inappropriate behavior) a parent-child observation may not be indicated. The GAL explains the reasons for not observing children with each parent in the report.

6.8 The GAL Considers the Need for any Further Information Necessary to Complete the GAL Evaluation and Provide a Comprehensive Report.

The GAL shall collect and review documents as well as conduct additional interviews of the parties, each of the children and other witnesses until the necessary information is fully gathered.

The GAL may consider the usefulness of specialized evaluation tools such as behavioral information surveys; psychological and neuropsychological testing of mental health, adaptive functioning and/or medication needs; evaluations of substance abuse, sexual offending behavior, domestic violence, educational/learning needs; or clinical determinations of child sexual abuse.

7. USE OF SPECIALIZED CLINICAL METHODS IN THE FORENSIC CONTEXT

Specialized methods include primarily psychological testing and sexual abuse evaluations. Other specialized methods such as educational or medical evaluations are subject to the same general requirements as those set forth here.

7.1 The GAL Shall use Specialized Methods Only when Doing so is Likely to Produce Necessary, Relevant and Useful Information to Evaluate the Forensic Questions in the Case.

The GAL must evaluate the merits of using a specialized method and consider the costs (e.g. financial and time) to the parties or to the Court. If the GAL chooses to use a specialized method, the GAL explains the reasons to the parties and counsel, and documents those reasons in the report.

Psychological Testing

Psychological testing is not required in most cases. The GAL shall obtain an order of the court before performing psychological testing unless previously authorized to do so by the court. In each case the GAL must balance likelihood of obtaining relevant and reliable information against the financial costs, the time involved and the potential invasiveness of the testing. Testing may be necessary when the psychological health or functioning of a party or child is directly relevant to the issues the GAL has been appointed to evaluate, or when psychological limitations of the parties make it difficult to obtain relevant information without psychological testing. When considering psychological testing, the GAL should first determine whether the information sought by the testing could be obtained in other ways.

When selecting a particular psychological test, the GAL ensures and is prepared to explain how any chosen test measures factors relevant to the issues before the court. The GAL shall consider and be prepared to articulate for the Court the reliability and validity of any chosen test. (See Daubert v. Merrell Dow Pharmaceuticals, Inc. 509 U.S. 579 (1993) and Commonwealth v. Lanigan, 413 Mass. 154 (1994). Elements of reliability and validity include: commercial availability of the test or measure including a comprehensive test manual; relevant measures of reliability for the test or measure; relevant measures of validity for the test or measure; appropriateness of use with the examinee (e.g. relevance of race, ethnicity, primary language, reading level); peer reviews of the test or measure; relevant error rates of the test or measure or of components (e.g. index or scale) of the test or measure; method of scoring and interpreting including the published system (e.g. Rorschach Comprehensive System); appropriateness of use in the context for which it is being used.

Sexual Abuse Evaluations

In determining the appropriateness of conducting a sexual abuse evaluation, the GAL shall first consider the nature and extent of the alleged sexual abuse, the context in which the sexual abuse allegations were raised (e.g. custody conflict) and the relationship of potential findings from the sexual abuse evaluation to the questions that the GAL has been appointed to evaluate

As with psychological testing, the GAL takes reasonable steps to ensure the relevance, reliability, and validity of the sexual abuse evaluation procedure the GAL uses. The GAL shall consider and be prepared to articulate for the Court the reliability and validity of the sexual abuse evaluation procedure.

7.2 The GAL shall Only use those Specialized Methods that the GAL is Competent to use in the Forensic Context.

The GAL adheres to relevant standards of ethics and conduct including those which govern psychological testing and other specialized methods, and does not practice outside his or her areas of competence. The GAL shall also be competent to use these specialized methods in a forensic context.

Commentary: The GAL or designee does not succumb to pressure by legal actors to overstate or inaccurately represent tests, test interpretations, or the results of sexual abuse evaluations or other specialized methods.

Psychological Testing

The GAL must be qualified to administer and interpret each test instrument used, or ensure that his or her designee is qualified to perform these functions. In addition, the GAL or designee must be familiar with applicable testing standards such as the current American Psychological Association's Standards for Educational and Psychological Testing. The GAL must also be knowledgeable about psychological testing in the forensic context, and must be able to link the data, hypotheses and interpretations generated by testing to the forensic questions the GAL has been appointed to evaluate, and must be able to articulate to the Court the limitations of the each test used and its role in the comprehensive GAL evaluation.

Sexual Abuse Evaluations

The GAL or designee must be qualified to perform sexual abuse evaluations. Qualifications include: training in child and adolescent psychology; supervised training and practice in conducting sexual abuse evaluations in the forensic context, knowledge of the literature of sexual abuse as it pertains to the family court context and knowledge of the relevant practice guidelines and standards (an example of one well known set of standards is the American Professional Society on the Abuse of Children [APSAC] Standards). In addition, the GAL must be able to link the evaluation data, hypotheses and interpretations generated by the sexual abuse evaluation to the forensic questions before the evaluator, and to articulate to the Court the limitations of the sexual abuse evaluation and its role in the comprehensive GAL evaluation.

7.2.1 If the GAL is not Competent to Perform Psychological Testing or a Sexual Abuse Evaluation, the GAL shall make a Referral to, or Obtain a Consultation with, an Appropriate Clinical Evaluator (henceforth, the "Designee.").

The GAL seeks a Court order to have an additional professional conduct the specialized evaluation. The GAL takes reasonable steps to ensure the designee is competent to perform psychological testing or a sexual abuse evaluation.

Before making a referral to a designee for psychological testing or a sexual abuse evaluation, a GAL should consider obtaining a consultation from an appropriate professional. The purpose of this consultation is to determine whether or not psychological testing or a sexual abuse evaluation would provide useful information to the Court.

The GAL shall inform the designee that the designee is subject to the requirements of these standards where applicable.

7.2.2 If the GAL is Competent to Perform Psychological Testing or a Sexual Abuse Evaluation, the GAL shall Consider Whether it is Nevertheless Useful or Necessary to have Another Professional Conduct the Testing or Sexual Abuse Evaluation.

If the Court has not already clarified whether the GAL or another professional should conduct the testing or sexual abuse evaluation, factors for the GAL to consider in making that determination include: the clinical appropriateness of having the GAL conduct the evaluation. (e.g. an eight year old female alleged sexual abuse victim might feel frightened or uncomfortable with a male evaluator.); the need for consultation from another professional, whether performing the overall GAL evaluation biases, or appears to bias, the GAL's interpretation of testing/sexual abuse evaluation data.

7.3 The GAL Shall Only Interpret the Results of Psychological Testing and Sexual Abuse evaluations in the Context of Multiple Sources of Data.

The GAL should not use psychological testing data as the sole source of information from which to draw conclusions about a party or child. The GAL should consider psychological tests as a means of supporting, disconfirming or generating hypotheses that are to be further investigated and confirmed or disconfirmed through clinical interviews, collateral interviews, document reviews, observations and other available data. If test data conflicts with other sources of data, the GAL is obliged to explain how the GAL understands the discrepancies.

It is particularly important that the GAL be knowledgeable about the ways in which specialty issues (such as Domestic Violence, Child Abuse and Substance Abuse) may contribute to the interpretation of test data.

The results of a sexual abuse evaluation are not, by themselves, determinative of parenting capacity. The sexual abuse evaluation data must be reviewed in the context of the broader forensic question that the GAL has been appointed to evaluate.

7.4 The GAL Avoids Offering Psychiatric Diagnoses, Except when Special Circumstances Require the GAL to do so.

The role of the GAL in most Probate and Family Court matters does not require or warrant the formulation of psychiatric diagnoses. The GAL does gather information relevant to the psychological functioning and mental health histories (both directly and through collateral sources) of both parties and the child(ren). The GAL recognizes that a diagnostic label is not determinative of parenting capacity. Rather than making diagnoses, the GAL describes the impact of clinical symptoms or known diagnoses on the functional abilities of a parent or child and the relationship between the parent and child.

Commentary. In the unusual circumstance where formulating a new diagnosis might be appropriate, the GAL considers the potential risks and benefits of making the diagnosis, and the relevance of such a diagnosis to the referral question. The GAL assures that s/he has all the information necessary to make such a diagnosis and is competent to do so. The GAL is particularly sensitive to the potentially pejorative and prejudicial aspects of a diagnosis in the legal context. The GAL provides the rationale for making the diagnosis in the report.

8.0. SPECIALTY EVALUATION TOPICS

In the context of disputed Probate and Family Court matters, some allegations require specialized investigation and evaluation. Examples of such specialty topics which frequently arise in Category E GAL evaluations include: substance abuse, domestic violence, mental illness, and child abuse. Specialty evaluation topics demand both process and content considerations.

8.1 The GAL Asks the Parties about Key Issues which Might Warrant Specialized Attention.

As part of the comprehensive evaluation, the GAL gathers a background history of each party designed to screen for specialty concerns (see 9.1E). The GAL is also attentive to allegations raised by all parties. The GAL should phrase questions about the specialized topics in non-judgmental language, and ask them in multiple ways. This affords the parties the greatest opportunity to answer openly and accurately.

8.2 The GAL Considers Whether the GAL is Competent to Evaluate Questions that Require Specialized Expertise.

The GAL assesses his or her competence to address the specialty issues that are present in the case. The GAL makes this assessment at the outset of the case, and throughout the case.

If the GAL is not competent to evaluate the specialized questions, the GAL considers:

- Referring the specialized assessment component of the comprehensive GAL evaluation to a competent mental health professional with specialized expertise,

- Seeking consultation and/or supervision from a professional with specialized expertise,

- Withdrawing from the case because the specialized issue warrants that a person with specialized expertise conduct the comprehensive GAL evaluation.

Commentary: The GAL also considers the level of attention required to appropriately address the concerns or allegations. In making decisions about whether to refer or seek consultation with a person with specialized expertise, the GAL takes reasonable steps to ensure that the professional to whom the referral is made is competent as per standard 8.2 and does not have a conflict of interest or role conflict as per 1.3 A or 1.4. Finally, the GAL considers the issues of cost, inefficiency, and delay in assigning such assessments to other professionals.

8.3 The GAL Shall be Competent to Evaluate Specialized Topics Within a Forensic Context.

- The GAL or designee must have the education or training, knowledge and experience necessary to evaluate a specialty topic within the forensic context.

- The GAL or designee must be knowledgeable about any relevant laws, legal standards or rules particular to specialty topics.

- The GAL or designee must be aware of any relevant standards of practice relevant to the evaluation of specialty topics. These include the Massachusetts Standards on Substance Abuse by the Justices of the Supreme Judicial Court in collaboration with the Massachusetts Trial Court (1998) at: http://www.mass.gov/courts/forms andguidelines/substancev.html, and the Standards on Judicial Practice, Abuse Prevention Guidelines by the Administrative Office of the

Trial Court (2000) at: http://www.mass.gov/courts/formsandguidelines/domestic/dvtoc.html

- The GAL or designee must be knowledgeable about ways that specialty topics might present in the forensic context.

- The GAL must be able to access and interpret collateral sources relevant to each specialty topic.

- The GAL or designee must maintain a current knowledge of the literature and critical issues in specialty topics in the forensic context.

8.4 The GAL Incorporates the GAL's Conclusions from the Specialty Areas with all other Data Gathered in the Evaluation to Complete a Functional Assessment of Parenting as it Relates to the Forensic Questions to be Addressed.

A. **Substance abuse and Mental Illness**—Conclusions about a party related to his/her substance abuse, mental illness, are not dispositive on the question of parenting capacity. The applicable case law states that a determination that one party has or had an active substance abuse problem or mental illness does not constitute unfitness, in and of itself. (See, for example, Adoption of Katharine, 674 N.E. 2d 256 (Mass. App.Ct. (1997)).

B. **Domestic violence**—Conclusions that a party has been a victim of domestic violence are not dispositive of parenting capacity. Conclusions that a party has been the perpetrator of domestic violence are considered direct indicia of parenting capacity, but do not predetermine the answer to the forensic question (e.g. the specifics of a custody/visitation plan). Some conclusions by the GAL about domestic violence may lead to findings by the Court which trigger the requirements of the custodial presumption in favor of custody to the non-perpetrating parent. (G.L. c.208, § 31a)

C. **Child Abuse**—Conclusions that a party has perpetrated abuse against a child are direct indicia of parenting capacity. As above, however, such conclusions do not dictate the answer to the forensic question to be addressed.

Commentary: The GAL recognizes that an adequate assessment of any of these specialized topics involves consideration of co-existing issues that may complicate the resolution of the problem, or mitigate the importance of the problem. For example, resolving a substance dependence problem does not necessarily resolve the other mental health problems, nor does it automatically improve parenting. On the other side, a mentally ill parent may have a support and resource network which allows adequate caretaking of the children even when flagrantly ill or incapacitated.

8.5 In Cases Involving but not Limited to Domestic Violence, Substance Abuse, Child Abuse and Mental Illness, the GAL Should Identify the Types of Supportive Services Believed Necessary to Successfully Implement a Custody and Access Plan.

Examples. Such resources may include: substance abuse assessment and treatment, mental health evaluation and treatment, sexual abuse or certified batterers' treatment; supervised visitation; counseling; parenting education; educational assessment for the child(ren); medication assessment; recreational or social services; housing or public benefits advocacy; regular payment of court ordered child support; DSS provided in-home services.

Commentary. Standard VII of the Massachusetts Substance Abuse Standards promulgated by the Supreme Judicial Court and the Trial Court requires prompt screening to alert the court to the possible need for an immediate substance abuse assessment or treatment program. The Substance Abuse Standards depend to some extent on resources that are not yet fully available to the Court. This may limit the GAL's ability to perform the tasks set out in the standards. It is nonetheless important that the GAL be aware of the standards and consider which elements the GAL has the resources to perform.

8.6 In Cases Where it is Appropriate that a Party's Access to Children Proceeds in Stages, the GAL may Suggest a Process for Monitoring Such Access.

In some cases involving domestic violence, child abuse, substance abuse or mental illness, it may be appropriate that access to the child on the part of the "visiting" party proceed in stages. When appropriate, the GAL may suggest, a process for monitoring a plan built on access increasing in stages.

Commentary. The Massachusetts Substance Abuse Standards require a monitoring plan in cases where a party's substance abuse problem is a factor in behavior related to the case. Specifically, Standard XII requires that the Court monitor compliance and Standard XIII requires the Court to implement strategies to prevent relapse. (But see commentary to 8.5 above).

Planning for shifts in access requires many considerations including the recognition that predicting behavior over lengthy time frames has serious potential for inaccuracy. The following is a non-inclusive list of considerations: Whether a parent can comply with the recommendations; How likely is it that compliance with recommended interventions will translate into changes related to parenting?; How important it is that the child have access to the parent even if the parent is non-compliant?; What conditions need to be required of the parent without the problem (e.g. substance abuse, mental illness, etc.) in order for a child to better benefit from contact with the parent with the problem?

9. SCOPE AND CONTENT OF THE EVALUATION

A comprehensive history creates a context for understanding the current issues in dispute. The nature and extent of the family history obtained, through both interviews as well as review of documents depends on the particular family's circumstances and the directives contained in the order of appointment. However, it is commonplace to obtain the following information unless it is not relevant:

A. History of legal proceedings and prior investigations and evaluations.

- The nature of the case, including the parties and children involved, relevant procedural history, current orders, and the relief sought by each party;

- History of other cases involving the parties, including prior cases pertaining to parties or the children including, but not limited to Probate and Family Court, Juvenile Court, criminal, abuse prevention, or other relevant cases;

- Prior custody related investigations and evaluations, including GAL, Court Clinic, Probation, Department of Social Services, or other evaluations or assessments;

B. Facts designated by court order and the applicable law.

- The issues that the court specifies for investigation and evaluation in the order of appointment;

- Facts relevant to the legal standard that applies to the case for:

1. modification of custody or visitation;
2. termination of parental rights;
3. guardianship of a minor;
4. removal of the child from the Commonwealth;
5. custody or visitation by a parent.

C. Relevant concerns raised in the case by each parent, including facts related to how each parent's proposed outcome serves or conflicts with the child's best interests.

D. Parenting history.

- With whom have the children lived and for how long;
- What parenting tasks have each parent performed, when, for how long;
- Each parent's past and present parenting capacities including both skills and deficits;
- The competence with which each parent carried out parenting tasks; History of parents' past joint decision- making regarding children;
- Parent's present ability to communicate or make joint decisions;
- Whether a third party or either party is or was a primary caretaker;
- History and impact of a parent's substance abuse, mental illness, or domestic violence on the children and the parent's parenting ability;
- History of physical, sexual or emotional abuse of the children;
- History of past restraining orders and violence against others;
- Each parent's past and present parenting skills and deficits;
- The strength and quality of the parent-child relationships, emotional closeness, attachment, and perceptions of each other;
- Each parent's or potential caretaker's knowledge of the children, knowledge of parenting techniques, disciplinary practices, ability to distinguish his or her own needs from the needs of the children, and to understand and respond to the children's needs;
- The ability of the parent to promote and support appropriate social, emotional, and educational development in the children, and to provide a stable home environment for the children;

- Each parent's or potential caretaker's ability to support the children's relationship with the other parent as appropriate;
- Each party's ability to communicate and cooperate with the other parent regarding the children as appropriate, including the impact of substance abuse, mental illness or domestic violence on that ability;
- Each parent's ability to recognize his or her own and the other parents strengths and weaknesses as parent.

E. The family history.

- History of parents' relationship, including if and for how long the parties lived together as a family;
- Parties' accounts of how difficulties began, were disclosed, or persist;
- Prior Department of Social Services involvement with family members;
- Children's present and past school functioning;
- Criminal history of both parties (CORI (Criminal Offender Record Information) or CARI (Court Activity Record Information);
- Sexual offense history (Sexual Offender Registry Information, or SORI);
- Substance abuse and substance use history of family members;
- Mental health treatment and history of family members;
- Relevant medical history or problems of family members;
- Presence of new relationships, partners or their children;
- Relationships with significant caretakers, grandparents, relatives, child care providers;
- Each parent's family history and current relationship with family of origin and partner's family;
- Education and employment history of parents;
- If relevant, ethnic, cultural, lifestyle, and religious factors.

F. Developmental status and parenting needs of the children.

The child's preferences for custody and access.

- Each child's developmental history, functioning in school, peer relationships, medical and mental health history, activities, schedules;
- Special needs of each child: medical, learning or developmental problems;
- Assessment of each child's adjustment to school, friends, community, and extended families;
- Child's temperament and response to transitions;
- Impact of change on child's routines, attachments, familiar environs;

- Impact of the divorce or separation on the child, if any.

- Child's exposure to, understanding of or concerns about a parent's needs, wishes, concerns, safety, or problems;

- Quality of relationship between siblings;

- Particular challenges for either parent or the child with each other.

10. REPORT WRITING AND ANALYSIS

The report should address and relate to the areas of investigation and evaluation designated by the order of appointment. The report should provide accurate, detailed and balanced information about the parties and their children.

10.1 The Report Should Appear Professional in Appearance, Format and Writing Style.

The report should be typed, well-written and neat in appearance. Pages must be numbered. The GAL shall attempt to avoid spelling, grammar or typographical errors in the report. The GAL should write the report in a way that is concise in words, yet able to encompass all the relevant facts and provide detailed information. The language used in the report should be understandable to the average layperson and avoid jargon that may be confusing. The GAL should prepare a report that is well-organized. Use of headings, bold type, or underlining to separate different sections or topics in the report may make a report easier to comprehend. The report shall be dated and signed by the GAL with the GAL's name typed below the signature. The report shall include the GAL's mailing or office address and telephone number.

10.2 The Report Should be Accurate, Objective and Unbiased.

When writing the report, the GAL provides a balanced view of the parties that includes all of their relevant strengths and weaknesses. The information contained in the report should be accurate. It also should be as factual and detailed as possible. The GAL report should:

A. Use descriptive statements and provide ample details, but avoid inflammatory characterizations if possible.

Inflammatory characterization: "Mr. Jones is well-known to the courts as a drunk." Descriptive statement: "Mr. Jones was convicted in Somerville District Court of driving under the influence of alcohol in 1986, 1996, 2001, and in July, 2003."

B. Provide past and present relevant facts relating to both parties and the children.

1. Include all relevant facts that address the court's directives.

2. Include all relevant facts collected from all sources, including facts that are consistent and inconsistent with other reported facts.

3. Provide balanced and similar information about both parties;

4. Provide relevant and detailed information about all of the children.

5. Include facts that do not support the GAL's recommendations or conclusions.

6. Disclose what important information may be missing and why it is missing.

C. Include specific information and provide dates and pinpoint time frames if at all possible.

Avoid use of vague phrases or time frames such as "in the past" or "occasionally" or "sometimes" if a more precise time frame is available. The GAL should provide detailed information.

Vague: "John says he used heroin in the past."

Specific: "John says he used heroin in May, 1996 and June, 1998."

Vague: "Mary states that John occasionally uses drugs."

Specific: "Mary states that she saw John use cocaine twice in August, 1998."

Vague: "The child has health problems."

Specific: "The child has diabetes."

10.3 The GAL Identifies the Sources of Information.

Sources should be easily identified in the report. The GAL must list every person interviewed and the records reviewed with any relevant information about the informant or source.

- Date and Name of each person interviewed (e.g. Dr. Tom Jones on 9/5/03),

- Position, profession, place of employment (psychiatrist, General Hospital);

- Description of record reviewed (Dr. Jones' records regarding mother);

- Date the record was made and period it encompasses (July, 2002 to July, 2003);

- How information was obtained (e.g. in person, telephone call, written request);

- Date records were reviewed or obtained by the GAL (9/5/03);

- Informant or record author's relationship to the parties, child or family (Dr. Jones is mother's psychiatrist, but also saw her and the husband for marriage counseling in May, 2001).

If a source is not clearly identified, a party can move to strike the statement from the report.

Example of improper attribution: "Hospital staff said that Drew Smith was hospitalized there for three months last year." (Names of the staff and hospital are missing).

Use of hearsay statements is permitted in the report, but the GAL should always attempt to contact and also quote the original source in the report if possible.

10.4 If a Party Fails or Refuses to Participate, the GAL Includes the Information that the GAL has Obtained in the Report.

The GAL encourages parties to participate in the evaluation. If a party does not participate, the GAL is still permitted to file a report and to disclose whatever information has been collected about that party from other sources. The report should disclose that such a party has not participated or declined to provide information.

Commentary. The GAL shall refrain from drawing conclusions about a party without a factual basis.

10.5   Facts Shall be Separated in the Report from Recommendations or Conclusions.

The investigative and evaluative information shall be separated from the GAL's conclusions and recommendations. The report shall include a section on the facts of the case in the body of the evaluation.

10.6   The GAL's Conclusions or Recommendations Shall Follow Clearly from the Data Gathered and the Analysis of that Data.

The GAL shall set forth the connection between the facts, the analysis of the facts, and the GAL's conclusions and recommendations. The GAL shall explain the basis for any opinions or conclusions drawn.

Commentary. This includes stating in the report: alternative explanations the GAL considered, how conflicting data was reconciled, and the clinical or theoretical framework, if any, which informed the GAL's opinions.

10.7   The GAL shall Identify any Limits of the Completed GAL Evaluation.

The GAL shall list any important sources of information that were not obtained and why. The GAL shall articulate any limits to the usefulness of the report's final conclusions. The GAL shall not draw any conclusions for which s/he does not have the adequate supporting data.

Example: The GAL discovers that a party's medical records from a particular hospital have been lost. The records were alleged to be evidence of mother's injuries due to domestic violence. The GAL documents the attempts to acquire these records, and that without them mother's allegations of physical injury cannot be confirmed.

10.8   The GAL Files a Timely Report and Informs Counsel and Pro Se Parties.

The GAL should inform counsel and pro se parties when the report is filed at the court so that the parties can read the report. The GAL should inform parties requesting a copy of the report that the report is property of the court; it cannot be given out or shown to anyone, except the parties or their counsel. A court order is required for any distribution of the report, even to parties or their counsel. The GAL shall not distribute copies of the report to the parties, counsel of record or anyone else unless the court orders that the GAL may release copies to such individuals.

Commentary. If information or recommendations in the GAL report have the potential of exposing a party or the child to danger, the GAL should consider advising the endangered parent or party about the date that he or she expects to file the report in court.

11. THE GAL SHALL RETAIN ANY MATERIALS GATHERED OR CREATED DURING THE EVALUATION

The GAL shall retain any notes, records, documents, taped recordings, videos, or other material gathered or created during the evaluation so that these materials are available for trial, discovery, appeal and remand of the case.

Commentary. Notes or other materials created or obtained by a GAL may be sought by a party through discovery. The GAL's notes, written observations, or other materials created during interviews or telephone conversations should be descriptive, factual, and respectful in tone. Note taking should be objective and include quotations of witnesses and parties when possible.

Adopted effective January 14, 2008.

Standing Order 2–08.   Impoundment of Guardian Ad Litem Reports

Unless otherwise ordered by the court, all guardian ad litem reports except those filed in cases involving accounts, licenses to sell and estate plans are impounded. As used herein, "impounded" shall mean the act of keeping the guardian ad litem report separate and unavailable for public inspection. The reports shall be kept in the Registry of Probate unless otherwise determined by the First Justice. The following procedure will be followed:

1. Upon filing with the court, guardian ad litem reports shall be kept separate from the case file and unavailable for public inspection. Access to inspect the impounded reports shall be limited to the court, the attorney(s) of record, if any, and the party(ies), unless otherwise ordered by the court. Where appropriate, the court may instruct the guardian ad litem to send a copy of a report to the attorney(s) of record or the parties.

2. Unless otherwise ordered by the court, the attorney(s) of record, if both parties are represented by counsel, shall be entitled to receive a copy of a report. If a party wishes to obtain a copy of the report, the party or their attorney must file a Motion with the Court. If a party is unrepresented by counsel and wishes to obtain a copy of the report, they must file a Motion with the Court. The attorney(s) of record or the party(ies) who are authorized to have a copy of the guardian ad litem report:

   a. Shall make no further copies of the report for use outside of counsel's office except as provided below;

   b. Shall not show the report to any person except, to his or her client or, to an expert engaged or consulted regarding the case;

   c. Shall, in the case of an attorney, return the copy of the report to the court upon withdrawal or conclusion of the case, and in the case of a party, return the copy of the report to the court at the conclusion of the case,

   d. Shall comply with such conditions as the Trial Judge may impose.

   e. May provide a copy to an expert engaged or consulted on the case, provided the expert certifies in writing that he or she will be bound by this Standing Order, and;

   f. Shall not provide a copy to his or her client except upon the allowance of a motion.

3. In accordance with Trial Court Rule IX, Rule 2, Uniform Rules on Subpoenas to Court Officials, the Register shall not provide a copy of an impounded guardian ad litem report to a person who is not a party to the case.

4. Relief from impoundment may be sought by Motion supported by affidavit, and may be granted after notice by the court only upon written findings.

5. Service of the Motion for Relief from Impoundment and affidavit shall be made on all parties in accordance with Rule 5 of the Massachusetts Rules of Domestic Relations Procedure. The time periods for hearing shall be as set forth in Rule 6 of the Massachusetts Rules of Domestic Relations Procedure.

6. The attorney(s) of record, if any, or the party(ies) if unrepresented by counsel, shall receive a copy of this Standing Order when they are notified in writing by the Court in accordance with Standing Order 2–98 that a report has been filed and is available for inspection.

Adopted effective March 10, 2008.

Standing Order 3–08. Impoundment of Qualified Domestic Relations Orders, Domestic Relations Orders and Orders Commonly Known as *Mangiacotti* Orders

Unless otherwise ordered by the court, all qualified domestic relations orders, domestic relations orders and orders issued pursuant to *Contributory Retirement Board of Arlington v. Mangiacotti*, 406 Mass.184, (1989) are impounded. As used herein, "impounded" shall mean the act of keeping the orders separate and unavailable for public inspection. The following procedure will be followed:

1. Upon filing with the court, the orders shall be kept separate from the case file and unavailable for public inspection. Access to inspect the impounded orders is limited to the court, the attorney(s) of record, if any, and the party(ies), unless otherwise ordered by the court.

2. In accordance with Trial Court Rule IX, Rule 2, Uniform Rules on Subpoenas to Court Officials, the Register shall not provide a copy of the impounded orders to a person who is not a party to the case.

3. Relief from impoundment may be sought by Motion supported by affidavit, and may be granted after notice by the court only upon written findings.

4. Service of the Motion for Relief from Impoundment and affidavit shall be made on all parties in accordance with Rule 5 of the Massachusetts Rules of Domestic Relations Procedure. The time periods for hearing shall be as set forth in Rule 6 of the Massachusetts Rules of Domestic Relations Procedure.

Adopted effective March 10, 2008.

Standing Order 4–08. Parent Education Program Attendance [Repealed]

Repealed effective May 1, 2016. See Standing Order 2–16.

Standing Order 5–08. Medical Certificates and Clinical Team Reports [Deleted]

Deleted with the adoption of Standing Order 1–09, adopted effective July 1, 2009.

Standing Order 6–08. Parent Education Program for Never Married Parents *"For the Children"*

This Court finds that the interests of the minor children of never-married parents appearing before the Court would be well served by educating the parents about children's emotional needs and the effects of family-related litigation on child behavior and development.

IT IS HEREBY ORDERED THAT:

1. In the Hampshire, Essex and Suffolk Divisions of the Probate and Family Court Department, all parties to Complaint to Establish Paternity, a Complaint for Custody/Support/Visitation, and in any case involving visitation or custody of minor children of never-married parents filed on or after July 1, 2008, may be ordered by a judge of this court to attend and participate in a education program known as *"For the Children"*. Nothing herein shall limit the judge or his or her designee from waiving this requirement.

2. Attendance at the program is mandatory unless waived by the Court. Parties must register within sixty (60) days of service of the complaint and attend the next available session. The Court may waive the attendance requirement upon motion, with notice, for one or both parties. Waivers will be granted upon a showing of chronic and severe violence which negates safe parental communication, language barriers, institutionalization or other unavailability of a party, or where justice otherwise indicates.

3. Sanctions may be imposed by the Court for a party's failure to register with *"For the Children"* within sixty days of service of the complaint.

4. A pamphlet describing *"For the Children"* and including a copy of this Order shall be given to the plaintiff or his/her attorney upon the filing of a complaint involving minor children as set forth above. The plaintiff or his/her attorney shall serve a copy of the pamphlet along with the complaint and summons to the person authorized to make service according to Mass.R.Dom.Rel.P.4(c)

5. Nothing herein shall be construed to limit the authority of any Probate and Family Court Justice sitting in the Hampshire, Essex and Suffolk Divisions to order parties to attend a parent education program in any case involving visitation, custody or support of minor children.

6. All information and materials submitted in conjunction with *"For the Children"* shall not be discoverable.

7. The parties to a particular case are prohibited from attending the same program session.

Adopted effective November 1, 2008.

Standing Order 1–09. Impoundment of Personal Medical Information

1. Whenever a Medical Certificate or Clinical Team Report is required to be filed under Article V of G.L. c. 190B, it must be in the possession of the Court or accompany the petition or motion. The Medical Certificate must be dated and an examination must have taken place within 30 days of the filing of the petition or motion or, in the case of a person alleged to be

mentally retarded, the Clinical Team Report must be dated and an examination must have taken place within 180 days of the filing of the petition or motion.

2. The Court may waive or postpone the requirement of filing of a Medical Certificate or Clinical Team Report upon the filing of a statement that it is **impossible** to obtain a Medical Certificate or Clinical Team Report. Such a statement of impossibility shall be supported by an affidavit or affidavits meeting the requirements set forth in Massachusetts Rules of Civil Procedure 4.1(h).

3. All Medical Certificates, Clinical Team Reports, treatment plans and medical affidavits shall be impounded and kept separate from other papers in the case and shall not be available for public inspection. These documents shall be available for inspection to authorized Court personnel, the Respondent, the attorneys who have filed an appearance in the case, all persons named in the petition who make a written request, and any Guardian *ad litem* appointed in the case. They may not be copied without further order of the Court, but Registry staff may scan them into an impounded computer file.

4. Authorized Court personnel, parties, attorneys, and Guardians *ad litem* with access to a Medical Certificate, Clinical Team Report, treatment plan or medical affidavit are prohibited from using or disclosing the information on the form for any purpose other than the Guardianship or Conservatorship case for which it was filed.

Adopted effective July 1, 2009.

Standing Order 2–09. Application of G.L. c. 190B, Article V to Guardianship and/or Conservatorship Cases Pending on July 1, 2009 or With a Decree Issued Prior Thereto

On July 1, 2009, certain provisions of the Massachusetts Uniform Probate Code, G.L. c. 190B ("the Code"), become effective. The provisions are primarily contained in Article V of the Code, Protection of Persons under Disability and Their Property. The Code significantly reforms the practice of Guardianship and Conservatorship law.

The Probate and Family Court interprets the Massachusetts Uniform Probate Code to apply to any Guardianship and Conservatorship case:

(a) pending on July 1, 2009 without a permanent decree having entered;

(b) where a permanent decree has previously entered and the Guardianship or Conservatorship has not terminated; or

(c) commenced on or after July 1, 2009.

Accordingly:

1. PENDING CASES WITH NO PERMANENT DECREE

Any Petition for Guardianship of the person and/or estate or Conservatorship filed prior to and pending as of July 1, 2009 generally does not need to be amended. If the petitioner seeks authority to admit the alleged incapacitated person to a nursing facility and such authorization was not explicitly requested on the petition, the petition must be amended to include a request for such authorization and a new citation must issue.

Any citation issued before July 1, 2009 shall be accepted by the Court after July 1, 2009 as sufficient even if the return date is after July 1, 2009. Any citation issued after July 1, 2009 must be served in accordance with the notice requirements of the applicable MUPC sections.

Any Petition for Guardianship of the person and/or estate or Conservatorship filed prior to and pending as of July 1, 2009 must be accompanied by the new Medical Certificate or Clinical Team Report form.

Any Petition requesting the appointment of a Guardian of the estate pending as of July 1, 2009 shall be treated as a Petition for the Appointment of a Conservator. At the time of allowance, an Order and Decree of Appointment of Conservator shall be issued (in addition to an Order and Decree of Appointment of Guardian if appointment of a Guardian of the person was also requested) and docketed in a Conservator file. The Conservator case file shall include a copy of the Petition for Guardianship docket sheet up to the time of appointment. There shall be no fee charged when a new Conservator case initiation is required. Thereafter, the Conservator shall file any and all required Financial Plan, Inventory and Accounts in the Conservator file.

2. CASES WHERE A GUARDIAN OF THE PERSON AND/OR ESTATE OR A CONSERVATOR WAS APPOINTED PRIOR TO JULY 1, 2009

a. **Issuance of Letters of Appointment.**

When any party seeks a certified copy of the Decree appointing the Guardian of the person, a Letter of Appointment of Guardian shall be issued in accordance with the prior Decree and the Code.

When any party seeks a certified copy of the Decree appointing the Guardian of the estate or the Conservator, a Letter of Appointment of Conservator shall be issued indicating all powers vested in the Conservator in accordance with the prior Decree and the Code and a new Conservator file opened.

The Letter of Conservatorship shall be placed in the new case file. The new case file shall include a copy of the Petition for Guardianship docket sheet up to the time of the issuance of the Letter of Conservatorship. There shall be no fee charged if a new Conservator case initiation is required.

b. **Reporting Requirements**

Guardians of Incapacitated Persons are required to file a Care Plan/Report within 60 days following their appointment. All Guardians of Incapacitated Persons and Guardians of Wards, regardless of the date of appointment, must file a Report annually thereafter. G.L. c. 190B, § 5–309(b). Whenever any Guardian of the person is before the Court, the Court shall insure the timely filing and review of any and all Care Plans/Reports. If Care Plans/Reports have not been filed, the Court shall order the filing of a Care Plan/Report.

A Conservator may be required to file a Conservator Financial Plan for managing, expending and distributing the assets of the estate. G.L. c. 190B, § 5–416(c). Whenever any Guardian of the estate or Conservator is before the

Court, the Court may order the filing of a Conservator Financial Plan.

c. Accounting Requirements

Any Guardian of the estate or Conservator is subject to the accounting requirements of G.L. c. 190B, § 5–418 of the Code. Whenever any Guardian of the estate or Conservator is before the Court, the Court shall insure the timely filing and review of any and all required Inventory and Accounts.

d. Nursing Facility Admissions

Any nursing facility admission made by a Guardian before July 1, 2009 shall continue to be considered a valid admission after July 1, 2009 without the need for further Court authorization. If the incapacitated person is temporarily hospitalized, the Guardian may readmit the incapacitated person to the nursing facility the incapacitated person was in immediately before being hospitalized, without further authorization, notwithstanding the fact that this admission may be considered a new admission due to the length of hospitalization and/or loss of the prior bed. However, if the incapacitated person is being admitted to a nursing facility other than one the incapacitated person was in immediately before being hospitalized or, if it is a first-time admission after July 1, 2009, Court authorization for admission must be sought by the filing of a General Petition.

e. Previous Authority to Admit/Commit

Beginning July 1, 2009, the Probate and Family Court no longer has the authority to authorize a Guardian to admit or commit an incapacitated person to a mental health facility or a mental retardation facility as defined in the regulations of the department of mental health. G.L. c. 190B, § 5–309(f). In addition, beginning July 1, 2009, the Probate and Family Court will no longer have the authority to review or extend an admit/commit order previously authorized by the Court. An initial commitment order is generally valid for six months, and subsequent commitment orders are valid for one year. G.L. c. 123, § 8(d). Guardianship of Weedon, 409 Mass. 196 (1991).

If the authority to admit/commit is in an existing decree allowed before July 1, 2009, but the incapacitated person is not admitted/committed before July 1, 2009, this authority shall be considered to have expired on July 1, 2009 and the authority to admit/commit may not be relied upon after July 1, 2009. A new order must be sought through the appropriate District Court proceeding.

If the authority to admit/commit is in an existing decree allowed before July 1, 2009, and the incapacitated person is admitted/committed before July 1, 2009, this authority shall continue to be valid, but will expire six months after the date of admission/commitment.

If the authority to admit/commit issued before July 1, 2009 has expired, it cannot be relied upon nor can the Probate and Family Court review or extend the prior authorization. Any such order must now be sought through the appropriate District Court proceeding.

3. STANDBY OR EMERGENCY GUARDIANSHIP PROXY

The current provisions of G.L. c. 201, § 2(A)–(H) regarding Standby or Emergency Guardianship Proxies will be repealed as of July 1, 2009. Under G.L. c. 190B, § 5–202(a) and (b), a parent or a current Guardian may appoint a Guardian for any minor child in a writing that must be attested to by at least two witnesses. This requirement is similar to the requirements of G.L. c. 201, § 2B, which provides that the standby Guardianship proxy must be in writing, designate an adult and be "witnessed by two or more persons, at least eighteen years of age, neither of whom is to be designated as the proxy." Therefore, the Court shall deem designations executed in accordance with G.L. c. 201, § 2B valid parental or Guardian appointments under G.L. c. 190B, § 5–202 regardless of the date of execution.

Adopted effective July 1, 2009.

Standing Order 3–09. Notice in Guardianship of Incapacitated Persons and Conservatorship Matters

In all Guardianship of incapacitated person and Conservatorship matters, notice pursuant to G.L. c. 190B, § 1–401(c) will be presumed insufficient unless:

1.) Proof of mailing is provided for all notice given by first-class mail; and

2.) Proof of publication is provided for all cases where there are interested persons whose address or identity is not known or cannot be ascertained with reasonable diligence.

This Standing Order does not preclude the Court from requiring additional proof of notice as the case requires.

Adopted effective July 1, 2009.

Standing Order 4–09. Notice in Guardianship of Minors Matters

(Amended effective February 8, 2010)

Pursuant to G.L. c. 190B, § 1–401 (b) of the Massachusetts Uniform Probate Code, to promote the well-being of the children of the Commonwealth who are the subjects of Guardianship proceedings, the Probate and Family Court establishes the following order for notice to parties in all Petitions for Appointment of Guardian of a Minor proceedings.

Petition for Appointment of Guardian of a Minor

Notice to Interested Parties

Definitions:

Interested Parties under G.L. c. 190B, § 5–206:

(1) The minor, if the minor is 14 or more years of age and is not the petitioner;

(2) Any person who has been awarded care or custody of the minor by a Court of competent jurisdiction, who is alleged to have had the principal care or custody of the minor, or with whom the minor has resided during the 60 days preceding the filing of the petition, excluding foster parents. If the Department of Children and Families has custody of the minor, it must be served;

(3) Any living parent of the minor, excluding a parent whose parental rights have been terminated or a parent who has signed a voluntary surrender or, if none, brothers and sisters 18 years or older or, if none, heirs apparent or presumptive;

(4) The spouse if the minor is married;

(5) Any person nominated as Guardian by the minor if the minor has attained 14 years of age;

(6) Any parental or Guardian appointee whose appointment has not been prevented or terminated under G.L. c. 190B, § 5–203;

(7) Any Guardian or Conservator currently acting for the minor in this Commonwealth or elsewhere; and

(8) The United States Veterans Administration or its successor if the minor is entitled to any benefit, estate or income paid or payable by or through said administration or its successors.

Order:

Upon the filing of the Petition for Appointment of Guardian of a Minor, the Court shall establish a date for hearing on the Petition and enter this date on the "Order and Notice." For Petitions that also include a request for the appointment of a temporary Guardian (either with notice or *ex parte*), the date for hearing on the Petition shall be on or before the expiration of the temporary Guardianship. For all other Petitions, the date for hearing on the Petition shall be at least twenty-one (21) days after the filing of the Petition, but no more than forty-five (45) days after the filing of the Petition.

Except as provided for in subsection "c" of this order, following the filing of Petition, the petitioner shall cause an "Order and Notice" and a copy of the Petition to be served by a constable, deputy sheriff, sheriff or other person approved by the Court on all interested parties. The Order and Notice shall be on a form issued or approved by the Court and shall be served with a copy of the Petition in the following manner:

(a) If the place of residence or whereabouts of an interested party is known, service shall be accomplished on the interested party by:

(i) Delivery in hand to the party at least fourteen days before the date of hearing for the Petition. If the minor is above the age of fourteen years and has not nominated the Guardian proposed in the petition in conformance with the requirements of G.L. c. 190B, § 5–207, then service shall be made in the same manner on the minor; or

(ii) Written and duly notarized endorsement of the party's acceptance of service on the Order and Notice of hearing, whether within or without the Commonwealth.

(b) If the place of residence or whereabouts of an interested party is known, but the petitioner has been unable to accomplish service by delivery despite efforts to do so, the Petitioner may accomplish service on that interested party, either within or without the Commonwealth, by leaving a copy of the Petition and Order and Notice at his or her last and usual place of residence, and by mailing by first-class mail copies to the interested party at least fourteen (14) days before the date of the hearing for the Petition, or by some other method as ordered by the Court.

(c) If the place of residence or whereabouts of an interested party is not known or cannot be ascertained with reasonable diligence, the Court shall order that service be accomplished on that interested party, either within or without the Commonwealth, by mailing by first-class mail to the interested party at his or her last known address, at least fourteen (14) days before the date of the hearing for the Petition, or by some other method as ordered by the Court. In addition, the Court shall issue an Order for Service by Publication, and the petitioner shall cause notice to be published at least one time in the newspaper or newspapers designated by the Register of Probate having general circulation in the county where the proceeding is pending, the publication to appear at least seven days before the date of the hearing for the Petition, unless otherwise directed by the Court.

(d) If the identity of an interested party is not known, service shall be accomplished on that interested party by publication as follows: the Court shall issue an Order for Service by Publication, and the petitioner shall cause notice to be published at least one time in the newspaper or newspapers designated by the Register of Probate having general circulation in the county where the proceeding is pending, the publication to appear at least seven days before the date of the hearing for the Petition, unless otherwise ordered by the Court.

(e) If the minor is entitled to any benefit, estate, or income paid or payable through the United States Veterans Administration or its successor, service shall be made on the Veterans Administration by regular first-class mail at least seven days before the date of the hearing for the Petition.

(f) If the minor is in the custody of the Department of Children and Families, service shall be made on the Department of Children and Families by regular first-class mail at least seven days before the date of the hearing for the Petition.

(g) No notice need be given in the following circumstances:

(1) to a person entitled to notice under this rule who has consented in writing to the allowance of the Petition, if the consent is filed in Court;

(2) to a parent who signed a voluntary surrender in conformance with G.L. c. 210, § 2, or

(3) if the Court has terminated parental rights pursuant to G.L. c. 210, § 3.

(h) The officer or other person making service in accordance with this rule shall make a return of service on a copy of the Order and Notice, which the petitioner shall promptly file with the Court. The return of service shall indicate the method of service. If service is made by leaving at last and usual address and first class mail, the officer or other person making service shall describe the efforts made to complete in-hand service.

APPLICABILITY OF ORDER TO OTHER PROCEEDINGS

This order for notice shall apply to all petitions relating to the Guardianship of a Minor, including, but not limited to, Petitions to Resign as Guardian of a Minor, Petitions for Removal of Guardian of a Minor, Petitions for Visitation, and Petitions for Support.

Adopted effective July 1, 2009. Amended effective February 8, 2010.

Standing Order 5–09. Medical Certificates in Conservatorship of Minor Matters

No Medical Certificate or Clinical Team Report shall be required in proceedings for Conservatorship of a minor filed pursuant to G.L. c. 190B, § 5–401(b) unless ordered by the Court.

Adopted effective July 1, 2009.

Standing Order 1–10. Special Procedures for Cases Involving Children

Preamble

The Hampshire Division of the Probate and Family Court is committed to a child-focused procedural model for all cases involving children and has developed a pilot project for this purpose.

This Standing Order applies to all cases involving children filed in the Hampshire Division and will be liberally construed and applied to establish, ensure and support child-focused parenting and care giving, professional conduct and court procedures by and for families served by this Court.

The purposes of the child-focused model are as follows:

- to provide early opportunities for parents and care givers to learn the effects of hostile litigation on children;
- to provide early opportunities for non-adversarial planning of all unresolved issues;
- to establish a problem-solving environment in which each parent, care giver and attorney is expected to be a problem solver; and
- to establish an atmosphere in which parents and care givers are encouraged to experiment responsibly with multiple child care models as they observe children's adjustment to parenting in two households.

A. Application of the Rule

This Standing Order applies:

1. to all cases involving children filed in the Hampshire Division, including Divorce, Separate Support, Paternity, Support/Custody/Visitation, Modification, Contempt, Guardianship and Termination of Parental Rights; and

2. to all attorneys, parents and care givers involved in each such case. A "care giver" is a party to a case who is either a guardian, potential guardian, grandparent seeking visitation, de facto parent or person seeking de facto parent status.

B. Domestic Violence and Application of the Rule

Parents, care givers and attorneys will not be expected to adhere to the requirements of Paragraph E of this Standing Order if there is an abuse prevention order in effect.

C. Introductory Letter

1. After the commencement of an action, the Court will send an Introductory Letter to each parent, care giver or to the attorney representing each parent or care giver.

2. The attorney, upon receipt of the Introductory Letter, shall provide the original letter to his or her client.

D. Duties of Attorneys, Parents, Care Givers and the Court

1. Problem solving

Attorneys, parents and care givers shall make all efforts to solve problems before seeking the decision making intervention of the Court and shall seek that intervention only as needed.

2. Conduct

Parents, care givers, attorneys and the Court shall consistently observe the following conduct:

a. consistent, focused attention on each child's needs including maintaining an awareness that children suffer when their parents or care givers fight about them;

b. consistent, focused attention on each parent or care giver's needs, including maintaining an awareness

i. that children will be well served if each parent or care giver's ability to provide safe, healthy and responsible parenting time with the children is supported by each parent or care giver;

ii. that children will be well served if there is reasonable financial security in each household; and

iii. that children will be well served if parents or care givers are able to resolve conflicts in a constructive manner.

3. Resources

a. Attorneys shall inform their clients about resources available for counseling, mediation, conciliation or other assistance to help parents, care givers and children improve their relationships and functioning, and to adjust to the realities of parenting or care giving in two households.

b. The Court shall maintain and make available to the public information about the following court-related resources, which parents are encouraged (and may be ordered) to use:

i. Parenting websites
- www.uptoparents.org
- www.proudtoparent.org

ii. Mediation/Conciliation
- Hampshire Introductory Mediation Program
- Hampshire Conciliation Program

iii. Referrals to bar association lawyer referral services and the Massachusetts Justice Project.

4. Planning

Parents, care givers, attorneys and the Court shall engage in consistent and, if necessary, repeated attempts to improve the circumstances of the children by cooperative planning on each relevant issue at each stage of the court process.

5. Administrative Efficiency

The Court shall establish an administrative process to accept full written agreements for temporary orders without the necessity of a hearing.

E. Introductory Meeting

1. General Requirement

All parties and attorneys shall schedule and participate in an Introductory Meeting at a time and place to be agreed upon by the attendees which shall take place as set forth below and, except in an emergency, no less than two days prior to a motion hearing.

The Introductory Meeting shall take place no later than forty-five days after the filing of an Answer or other relevant responsive pleading.

2. Content and Process of the Introductory Meeting

Attendees at the Introductory Meeting shall:

a. explore whether the parents or care givers need assistance gaining access to resources that could help them resolve the open issues or improve relevant relationships or functioning, and adjust to the realities of parenting or care giving in two households;

b. confirm, if applicable, whether the parents or care givers have completed their website work, and if so, discuss the Agreed Commitments reached;

c. work on a parenting or care giving plan;

d. identify

i. issues that require immediate resolution;

ii. issues that require additional planning prior to resolution;

iii. tasks to be performed as to each issue;

iv. person(s) responsible for completing each task; and

v. the completion date for each task.

e. attempt to resolve all issues that require resolution by the parties;

f. confirm that each parent has complied with the parent education program required of them; and

g. write, for presentation in court, any agreements or partial agreements achieved by the parties in the Introductory Meeting.

3. Facilitation Services

The family service resources of the Probation Department of the Court are available to assist in (a) facilitating the Introductory Meeting or any follow-up meeting, (b) suggesting resources available to the parents and care givers, and (c) writing any agreements or partial agreements reached in any meeting. In order to make use of these resources, the parents or care givers or counsel shall, in sufficient time to be in compliance with the scheduling requirements of this Standing Order, make an appointment with the Probation Department for assistance on a day before the date on which a motion or Case Management Conference is scheduled to be heard.

4. Non-Compliance

If parents or care givers and/or attorneys representing each parent or care giver fail to comply with the requirements of the Introductory Meeting, they shall be prepared to report to the Court the reasons therefor. In the event of an unexcused non-compliance, the Court has the discretion to refuse to hear the motion, alter the Case Management Order and issue sanctions, including but not limited to attorney's fees.

5. Follow Up Meetings

A follow-up meeting shall be held upon the request of any attorney or self-represented parent or care giver at any time, and at least two days prior to any hearing on each subsequently filed motion. Such a follow-up meeting may be held in person or by conference call, and shall, as applicable, address the same issues addressed in the Introductory Meeting.

6. Summary of Cooperative Efforts

Parents, care givers and attorneys, in compliance with the Pre-Trial Notice and Order, shall present at the Pre-Trial Conference a summary of the steps they have taken under this Standing Order toward the cooperative resolution of the unresolved issues.

F. Training

The Court, in collaboration with the Hampshire County Bar Association, shall offer training to attorneys on such topics as:

- representing children, parents and care givers in the context of this Standing Order;

- special skills needed to represent children, parents and care givers in the context of this Standing Order;

- processes developed in this Court and other Courts to carry out the purposes of the Standing Order; and

- ethical considerations in representing children, parents and care givers.

4/7/10

_____

Date   Paula M. Carey, Chief Justice

Adopted effective May 5, 2010.

Standing Order 2-10.   Medical Certificate Affidavit

A court-promulgated Medical Certificate Affidavit Form (Medical Certificate Affidavit) may be used prior to a determination of incapacity or disability, or, in limited circumstances at a hearing for a final determination of incapacity or disability for a person who has been and continues to be medically stable as indicated on the most recently filed Medical Certificate Form (Medical Certificate), particularly Part I, A, B & C. A Medical Certificate Affidavit may be used at the time of a final determination of incapacity or disability in the limited circumstances where counsel for the Incapacitated or Protected Person has been appointed and does not object to its use. A Medical Certificate Affidavit shall be completed by a registered physician, a licensed psychologist, a certified psychiatric nurse clinical specialist or a nurse practitioner and must be dated and the examination must have taken place within thirty (30) days prior to the entry of each decree, temporary or permanent. This Standing Order does not preclude the Court from requiring additional medical information, including a Medical Certificate, as the case requires.

Adopted effective November 16, 2010.

Standing Order 1-11. Probate and Family Court's Use of Information Contained in the Court Activity Record Information (CARI) Report

1. The Probation Department shall obtain Court Activity Record Information (CARI) and Warrant Management system information (WMS) for all parties referred by a judge of the Probate and Family Court for probation services. Such services include, but are not limited to, dispute intervention, short-term investigation, full investigation, supervision and case intervention.

2. CARI includes Criminal Offender Record Information (CORI), juvenile records and civil restraining order information.

3. The Court has an obligation to obtain CARI in all cases pertaining to abuse prevention orders pursuant to Chapter 209A and domestic relations protective orders pursuant to Chapters 208, 209 or 209C. Nothing in this Standing Order is intended to restrict access that the Court would otherwise have to CORI/CARI records.

4. Prior to the delivery of any probation services, the Probation Department shall disclose to a party who is the subject of a CARI record, and his or her counsel, that the party's CARI record has been reviewed by the Probation Department.

5. In a dispute intervention where all parties and their counsel, if any, are present, the Probation Department shall advise all of the parties, and their counsel, whether CARI information of any party has been considered. If safety concerns are raised by either party, the CARI information shall be discussed separately.

6. The Probation Department shall inform each party who is the subject of a CARI record, and his or her counsel, of the information in his or her CARI record that has been considered by the Probation Department in the context of completing the referred service. The Probation Department shall provide the party and his or her counsel the opportunity to review the CARI record.

7. A party may consent to the disclosure to the other party of the information contained in his or her CARI record in order to complete the referred services. Absent such consent, a party seeking disclosure of CARI information may request an order from the judge for disclosure of the CARI information. Subject to the judge's discretion, including the entry of appropriate protective orders, CARI information may be disclosed pursuant to a court order to adverse counsel and/or the adverse litigant, in order to complete the referred services, including, but not limited to, dispute interventions and court hearings.

8. The Probation Department is authorized to provide the CARI record to the judge. If the judge reviews the CARI record, the judge shall explain on the record or by written findings the information relied upon and any inferences or conclusions made as a result of the review of the CARI information.

9. The judge shall afford a party a reasonable and meaningful opportunity to rebut any adverse information that might appear in the party's CARI record, and to otherwise respond to the CARI record. Upon request, additional time to rebut such adverse information may be allowed in the judge's discretion. The Court shall enter an order if necessary to protect the interests of a party or the child or children involved prior to the continued hearing.

10. Upon receipt of information that an outstanding warrant exists for either party, a member of the Probation Department shall notify the judge.

11. No CARI/WMS information shall be stored in the court case file. All CARI/WMS information shall be shredded unless a party or the judge requests that it be returned to the Probation Department and kept in the Probation file.

12. No dissemination or use of any CARI information obtained under this order may be used outside the context and purpose for which it was sought without further order of the court unless otherwise permitted by law.

COMMONWEALTH OF MASSACHUSETTS

TRIAL COURT

PROBATE AND FAMILY COURT DEPARTMENT

_____ DIVISION　　　　　　Docket No. _____

_____
Plaintiff

v.

_____
Defendant

NOTICE, CONSENT and/or REQUESTS RELATING TO PROBATE AND FAMILY COURT'S USE OF CARI RECORDS

Standing Order 1-11

Notice to Parties

Standing Order 1-11 is about Court Activity Record Information (CARI).

CARI includes all Criminal Offender Record Information (CORI), as well as juvenile court records and civil restraining order information.

The Court is required to review CARI in all cases about abuse prevention orders and domestic relations protective orders.

Before delivering any probation services, the Probation Department shall inform you if your CARI has been reviewed.

The Probation Department will inform you of the information included in your CARI that they have considered in this case.

You shall have the opportunity to review your CARI record.

The Probation Department shall inform both parties, together, whether any CARI information has been considered. If you have safety concerns, the Probation Department will discuss the information separately.

You may consent to the disclosure of your CARI information to the other party.

Absent your consent, the other party may ask the Court for an order disclosing your CARI information, and the Court may order its disclosure.

A member of the Probation Department may provide the CARI record to the Court.

If the Court reviews the CARI record, the Court shall explain on the record or describe by written findings what CARI information was relied on and any conclusions that were made as a result of the review the CARI.

You shall have a reasonable and meaningful opportunity to rebut or otherwise respond to the CARI record.

You may request additional time to prepare your rebuttal.

The Probation Department will notify the Court if there is an outstanding warrant for either party.

Adopted effective June 1, 2011.

Standing Order 2–11. Probate and Family Court's Use of Information Obtained by the Department of Children and Families

1. Whenever the Probate and Family Court determines that it requires information from the Department of Children and Families (DCF) in order to make a determination relating to the care and custody of a child, the Court shall either obtain the written, informed consent of the party(ies), after identifying the documents requested on the form entitled "Consent and/or Order for Production of Department of Children and Families Documents", and/or issue an order identifying the documents to be produced. Such orders may, in the judge's sound discretion, be made under G.L. c. 119, §§ 51E and 51F, or any other applicable provision of law. Any written, informed consent and/or order shall be docketed. Parties may request a hearing on the issue of the need for DCF documents.

2. Circumstances where documents may be requested include, but are not limited to, where (a) a party's "Affidavit Disclosing Care or Custody Proceedings (Trial Court Uniform Rule IV)" or other filing reveals a pending child welfare case; (b) a Probation or guardian ad litem report reveals a party's past or pending child welfare case, past or present DCF involvement, or history of child abuse or neglect; (c) witness testimony reveals a party's past or pending child welfare case, past or present DCF involvement, or history of child abuse or neglect; or (d) a party discloses his or her own, or alleges another party's, past or pending child welfare case, past or present DCF involvement, or history of child abuse or neglect.

3. The Court shall provide DCF with a copy of the written, informed consent or order, which identifies the requested documents.

4. The parties and counsel shall be given the opportunity to review all documents obtained from DCF prior to the hearing, and be provided with an adequate and meaningful opportunity to respond. Upon the request of counsel or a party for additional time to rebut or respond to the DCF documents, the matter may be continued for up to 7 days for hearing. Leave to continue shall be freely granted. The Court shall enter an order if necessary to protect the interests of the child or children prior to the continued hearing. At the hearing, the DCF documents shall be available to the Court and to the parties and shall be admissible in accordance with applicable rules of evidence.

5. Upon its own initiative, or upon the request of any party, or upon the request of DCF, the Court may issue an order allowing a representative of DCF to present oral testimony at a hearing or trial by electronic means. The phrase "electronic means" shall include communication by telephone, video teleconference, or the Internet. Testimony presented by electronic means shall be admissible in accordance with the applicable rules of evidence.

6. The Court shall afford a party the opportunity to object to and rebut information about the party that appears in the DCF documents and otherwise to respond to the DCF documents or information presented in person by DCF.

7. Parties and counsel shall have the right to view the DCF documents as often as they wish, upon reasonable request. Handwritten notes may be taken, however, no electronic reproductions shall be allowed. This restriction includes, but is not limited to, scanning and photography, by mobile device or otherwise.

8. Unless otherwise ordered by the court, the attorney(s) of record, if both parties are represented by counsel, shall be entitled to copies of the DCF documents. In the event only one party, or neither party, is represented by counsel and a party wishes to obtain a copy of the DCF documents, the party or his/her attorney must file a motion with the Court. Service of the motion and the time periods for hearing shall be in accordance with the Massachusetts Rules of Domestic Relations Procedure, or the Massachusetts Rules of Civil Procedure, as applicable.

9. In order to protect the privacy of the parties and the children involved, all documents received from DCF will be segregated by the Court and will be made available to parties, counsel and any other individual who would otherwise be authorized to have access to such information, who shall treat such information as confidential. Any individual who views DCF documents, including counsel, is prohibited from disclosing an impounded address or using information in the DCF documents except as allowed by order of the Court. Any DCF documents produced pursuant to the procedures set forth in this Standing Order will be maintained in the Probation Department of each division of the Probate and Family Court. In the event DCF records are subpoenaed for trial or evidentiary hearing, the records shall be kept in the Registry of Probate, in the customary manner.

10. This Standing Order shall be construed to authorize a judge to issue such other or additional orders or rulings as are necessary and appropriate under the circumstances and consistent with due process.

11. Once the Court has placed a child with DCF pursuant to G.L. c. 119, § 23(a)(3), the provisions of this Standing Order no longer apply and the protections and procedures of Chapter 119 apply.

COMMONWEALTH OF MASSACHUSETTS
TRIAL COURT
PROBATE AND FAMILY COURT DEPARTMENT

———— DIVISION   Docket No. ————

————————
Plaintiff

v.

————————
Defendant

CONSENT and/or ORDER FOR PRODUCTION OF DEPARTMENT OF CHILDREN AND FAMILIES DOCUMENTS

Standing Order 2–11

Notice to Parties

Your signature below permits the Department of Children and Families (DCF) to produce the specific documents listed below to the Probate and Family Court.

You will have an adequate and meaningful opportunity to review all documents received by the Court before the judge sees them.

If you do not sign this Consent for Production, the judge may issue an order requesting DCF to produce the specific documents.

You may request a hearing on the issue of the need for DCF documents.

The Court may use the documents produced as evidence in the case.

You will have the opportunity to object to the judge considering the documents as evidence in the case.

You will have the opportunity to rebut, address, and respond to the information contained in the documents.

At your request the judge will grant you a continuance of up to 7 days if you need additional time in order to object, rebut, address, or respond to the documents. However, the Court shall enter an order, if necessary, to protect the interests of the child or children prior to the continued hearing.

Neither your consent nor the judge's order requires or permits DCF to disclose information contained in the documents that DCF is prohibited by law from disclosing.

Documents to be Produced

[ ] Records or reports of investigations or assessments of allegations of child abuse or neglect pursuant to G.L. c. 119, § 51B during the period _____ to _____.

[ ] Reports of child abuse or neglect pursuant to G.L. c. 119, § 51A which are currently being investigated.

[ ] _____
_____
_____
_____

covering the period _____ to _____.

Personal Information to be Removed from Produced Documents

I request that DCF remove from its records any occurrence of:

[ ] my residential address and telephone number

[ ] my workplace address and telephone number

[ ] the school name, address and telephone number of myself and/or child(ren) because:

_____

_____

_____   _____
Signature of Party   Date

Order for Production

The Court requests that the above referenced documents be produced by _____. Such release shall be made notwithstanding G.L. c. 119, §§ 51E and 51F, G.L. c. 66A, and G.L. c. 112, §§ 135–135B.

_____   _____
Date   Justice
                                            Probate and Family Court

Adopted effective June 1, 2011.

Standing Order 3–11. Modification Pilot Program for IV–D Cases Filed in the Probate and Family Court

In an effort to explore the possibility of streamlining the modification process in the Probate and Family Court, the following procedures will be implemented for all IV–D cases that seek a modification of child support and/or medical support.

A. Application

These procedures apply to all IV–D cases filed in the Probate and Family Court, including those filed by private counsel, parties on a pro se basis and/or by DOR, that involve a request for modification of child and/or medical support only.

These procedures do not apply to complaints for modification that seek a change in custody and/or visitation, nor can these procedures be used to address the issues of custody and/or visitation.

B. Forms and Procedures

For cases that have previously gone to judgment:

1. A unified, one-page form that combines a complaint for modification and motion for temporary orders for child or medical support only may be filed. The unified complaint and temporary motion form will be accompanied by a summons establishing a hearing date on the return day. The hearing date will be set by the Court when issuing the summons.

OR

2. A complaint for modification of child or medical support only (no motion) may be filed. Those parties who choose not to use the unified form, may use the simplified complaint form. The summons for this complaint will establish a date for a case management conference. The date of the case management conference will be no earlier than 45 days from the date the complaint was filed. The case management conference date will be set by the Court when issuing the summons.

For cases where there is an open complaint and a support order has previously been established:

1. A simplified form for a motion for further temporary orders is available. The hearing date will be set by the Court and included on the motion.

C. Service

Notwithstanding the form filed, service by first-class mail will be used on a routine basis for all IV–D cases seeking a modification of child or medical support only. When serving a Complaint for Modification with Motion for Temporary Orders form or a Complaint for Modification form, service shall be made on the party no later than 10 days prior to the date of the hearing or case management conference. When serving a motion for further temporary orders, service shall be made on the party, or attorney, if applicable.

D. Proof of Notice for Complaint for Modification with Motion for Temporary Orders and Complaint for Modification only

1. A certificate of service must be filed with the Court on or before the date of the hearing or case management conference. The certificate of service shall include who was served, the address to which service was mailed, and the date service was mailed. If the defendant is served in hand, the certificate of service must also be filed. The certificate of service shall include who was served, and the date, time and place service was made.

2. If the defendant does not appear for the hearing or case management conference in response to first-class mail service, a judge may still proceed if there is proof of actual notice. Proof of actual notice, includes, but is not limited to, (a) the responding party filed an answer to the complaint for modification; (b) the responding party called DOR to inquire about the upcoming hearing/matter; or (c) the filing party testifies that the responding party contacted him or her in response to the complaint. A judge may decline to go forward and hear the case if not satisfied that actual notice occurred.

3. If proof of actual notice is not established at the hearing or case management conference, the Court shall then require service under the existing Massachusetts procedures for domestic relations cases. See Mass. R. Dom. Rel. P. 4 (d). A new summons shall be issued on the date of the hearing or case management conference by the Registry or a judicial case manager.

E. Effect of Non–attendance

1. If one party does not attend the hearing or case management conference, and the other party does attend but the matter cannot go forward, upon receipt of information verifying the amounts, the judge may require the non-attending party to pay the costs and/or lost wages of the attending party.

2. If the plaintiff/requesting party or, after proof of actual notice, the responding party does not attend the hearing or case management conference, the judge may enter a default support and/or medical support order.

3. If, in a case where the Department of Revenue is not providing assistance with the modification to the plaintiff, the plaintiff does not attend the hearing or case management conference but the defendant does, and the plaintiff has not filed a Motion to Continue, the Court may dismiss the Complaint for Modification with Motion for Temporary Orders or Complaint for Modification.

4. If, in a case where the Department of Revenue is not providing assistance with the modification to the plaintiff, neither party appears for the hearing or case management conference, and neither party has filed a Motion to Continue, the Court may dismiss the Complaint for Modification with Motion for Temporary Orders or Complaint for Modification.

F. Reissuance of Initial Summons

There may be circumstances where judicial or Registry staff may determine that it is appropriate to reissue an initial summons that may be mailed. These circumstances include, but are not limited to, if (a) the plaintiff did not have the defendant's correct address and now has it, and/or (b) the plaintiff requests a new hearing or case management conference date, prior to the scheduled date.

G. Implementation Dates

These procedures, as revised, will remain in effect in the Bristol Division.

As of May 15, 2013, these procedures will be implemented in the Barnstable Division.

As of July 1, 2013, these procedures will be implemented in the Hampshire and Norfolk Divisions.

As of August 1, 2013, these procedures will be implemented in the Dukes, Franklin, Nantucket and Plymouth Divisions.

As of September 3, 2013, these procedures will be implemented in the Berkshire, Middlesex, and Worcester Divisions.

As of October 1, 2013, these procedures will be implemented in the Essex and Hampden Divisions.

As of November 1, 2013, these procedures will be implemented in the Suffolk Division.

BRISTOL PILOT PROJECT

Commonwealth of Massachusetts
The Trial Court
Probate and Family Court Department

Bristol Division   Docket No._____

COMPLAINT FOR MODIFICATION OF CHILD SUPPORT AND/OR MEDICAL SUPPORT
WITH MOTION FOR TEMPORARY ORDERS

_____, Plaintiff   v. _____, Defendant

COMPLAINT FOR MODIFICATION

1. Plaintiff resides at _____
   (Street Address)   (City/Town)   (County)   (State) (Zip Code)
   Defendant resides at _____
   (Street Address)   (City/Town)   (County)   (State) (Zip Code)

2. This Court on _____, ordered that _____, pay $_____, per _____
   (Date)   (Name)   (Amount)   (week/month)
   as child support and/or ordered that _____ provide health insurance coverage.
                                          (Name)

3. There is a difference between the amount of the existing order/judgment and the amount that would result from application of the Child Support Guidelines for the following reason(s):

   *Check all that apply **and** explain below*

   ☐ **My income and ability to pay child support has substantially decreased due to:**
      ( ) job loss or pay cut   ( ) injury or disability
   ☐ **The other parent's income and ability to pay has substantially increased.**
   ☐ **Change in health insurance.**
   ☐ **Order needs to be terminated/adjusted due to:**
      ( ) emancipation of the child(ren)   ( ) reconciliation with other parent
   ☐ **Other**

   Explanation: _____
   _____
   _____
   _____

4. Plaintiff requests that this Court order that the above referenced Judgment be modified.

MOTION FOR TEMPORARY ORDERS

Plaintiff requests that this Court enter a temporary order for the reason(s) stated in Paragraph 3 above, and incorporated herein.
                     SEE SUMMONS FOR DATE OF HEARING

Signature of Plaintiff (if pro se) or Attorney
Print Name: _____
Address: _____
_____

Date: _____
Telephone Number: _____
BBO Number: _____

The within motion is hereby [ ] **ALLOWED** [ ] **DENIED**
_____
_____
_____
_____
Date   Justice of the Probate and Family Court

For use only in Bristol Division of Probate and Family Court

BRISTOL PILOT PROJECT

Commonwealth of Massachusetts
The Trial Court
Probate and Family Court Department

Bristol Division   **Docket No.**_____

SUMMONS AND NOTICE
on
COMPLAINT FOR MODIFICATION OF CHILD SUPPORT AND/OR MEDICAL SUPPORT
WITH MOTION FOR TEMPORARY ORDERS

_____, Plaintiff

v.

_____, Defendant

To _____, the above named Defendant:

- You are **required** to appear at the Bristol Division of the Probate and Family Court located in _____ on _____, 2011, at _____ a.m./p.m. for a hearing in connection with the attached Complaint for Modification of Child Support and/or Medical Support with Motion for Temporary Orders.

- You are **not required** to serve or file a written answer to the attached Complaint for Modification of Child Support and/or Medical Support with Motion for Temporary Orders.

- You must bring everything that you have that may help to resolve the child support issues. In particular, remember to bring:

-photo identification (driver's license)   -current paycheck stubs
-most recent tax return with W-2 and 1099 forms   -the enclosed Financial Statement
-copies of other child support orders if you have them   -proof of child support already paid or being
-documentation of your health insurance costs   paid even if there is no order

- On the day you are scheduled to appear, the matter may, with the agreement of the parties, go to judgment.

- If you fail to appear, the Court may still enter a modified child and/or medical support order.

Witness _____, Esquire, First Justice

of said Court at _____, this _____ day of _____, 2011.

_____
Register of Probate
For use only in Bristol Division of Probate and Family Court

BRISTOL PILOT PROJECT

Commonwealth of Massachusetts
The Trial Court
Probate and Family Court Department

Bristol Division   Docket No._____

SECOND SUMMONS AND NOTICE
on
COMPLAINT FOR MODIFICATION OF CHILD SUPPORT AND/OR MEDICAL SUPPORT
WITH MOTION FOR TEMPORARY ORDERS

_____, Plaintiff

v.

_____, Defendant

To _____, the above named Defendant:

- You are **required** to appear at the Bristol Division of the Probate and Family Court located in _____on _____, 2011, at _____ a.m./p.m. for a hearing in connection with the attached Complaint for Modification of Child Support and/or Medical Support with Motion for Temporary Orders.

- You are **not required** to serve or file a written answer to the attached Complaint for Modification of Child Support and/or Medical Support with Motion for Temporary Orders.

- You must bring everything that you have that may help to resolve the child support issues. In particular, remember to bring:

  -photo identification (driver's license)   -current paycheck stubs
  -most recent tax return with W-2 and 1099 forms   -the enclosed Financial Statement
  -copies of other child support orders if you have them   -proof of child support already paid or being
  -documentation of your health insurance costs   paid even if there is no order

- On the day you are scheduled to appear, the matter may, with the agreement of the parties, go to judgment.

- If you fail to appear, the Court may still enter a modified child and/or medical support order.

Witness _____, Esquire, First Justice

of said Court at _____, this _____ day of _____, 2011.

_____
Register of Probate

For use only in Bristol Division of Probate and Family Court

BRISTOL PILOT PROJECT

Commonwealth of Massachusetts
The Trial Court
Probate and Family Court Department

Bristol Division   Docket No._____

CERTIFICATE OF SERVICE ON SECOND SUMMONS

_____, Plaintiff

v.

_____, Defendant

ACCEPTANCE OF SERVICE

I, _____, the above named Defendant, hereby accept service of this summons and understand that judgment may be rendered against me in accordance with the complaint, a copy of which I have received this day.

Date: _____   _____
                                                     Signature of Defendant

NOTARIZATION

_____ ss   Date: _____

Then personally appeared the above named _____ who made oath that the foregoing acceptance was his free act and deed.

             Signature of Notary Public: _____

                          Print Name: _____

             My Commission Expires: _____

PROOF OF SERVICE

I hereby certify and return that on _____ I served a copy of the within summons, together
                                     (date)
with a copy of the complaint in this action upon the within named defendant by:

_____
                       (method of service)

Date: _____   Signed under the penalties of perjury

Date of Service: _____   _____

For use only in Bristol Division of Probate and Family Court

BRISTOL PILOT PROJECT

Commonwealth of Massachusetts
The Trial Court
Probate and Family Court Department

Bristol Division   Docket No._____

COMPLAINT FOR MODIFICATION OF CHILD SUPPORT AND/OR MEDICAL SUPPORT

_____, Plaintiff   v.   _____, Defendant

1. Plaintiff resides at _____
                           (Street Address)   (City/Town)   (County)   (State) (Zip Code)
    Defendant resides at _____
                           (Street Address)   (City/Town)   (County)   (State) (Zip Code)

2. This Court on _____, ordered that _____, pay $_____, per _____
                       (Date)   (Name)   (Amount)   (week/month)
    as child support and/or ordered that _____ provide health insurance coverage.
                                             (Name)

3. There is a difference between the amount of the existing order/judgment and the amount that would result from
    application of the Child Support Guidelines for the following reason(s):

*Check all that apply **and** explain below*

☐ **My income and ability to pay child support has substantially decreased due to:**
       ( ) job loss or pay cut   ( ) injury or disability
☐ **The other parent's income and ability to pay has substantially increased.**
☐ **Change in health insurance.**
☐ **Order needs to be terminated/adjusted due to:**
       ( ) emancipation of the child(ren)   ( ) reconciliation with other parent
☐ **Other**

Explanation: _____
_____
_____
_____

4.   Plaintiff requests that this Court order that the above referenced Judgment be modified.

_____
Signature of Plaintiff (if pro se) or Attorney

Print Name:_____

Address: _____
_____

Date: _____

Telephone Number: _____

BBO Number: _____

For use only in Bristol Division of Probate and Family Court

Commonwealth of Massachusetts
The Trial Court
Probate and Family Court Department

Bristol Division   Docket No._____

SUMMONS
on
COMPLAINT FOR MODIFICATION OF CHILD SUPPORT AND/OR MEDICAL SUPPORT

_____, Plaintiff

v.

_____, Defendant

To _____, the above named Defendant:

- You are **required** to appear at the Bristol Division of the Probate and Family Court located in _____ on _____, 2011, at _____ a.m./p.m. for a case management conference in connection with the attached Complaint for Modification of Child Support and/or Medical Support.

- You must bring everything that you have that may help to resolve the child support issues. In particular, remember to bring:

-photo identification (driver's license)	-current paycheck stubs
-most recent tax return with W-2 and 1099 forms	-the enclosed Financial Statement
-copies of other child support orders if you have them	-proof of child support already paid or being
-documentation of your health insurance costs	paid even if there is no order

- On the day you are scheduled to appear, the matter may, with the agreement of the parties, go to judgment.

- If you fail to appear, the Court may still enter a modified child and/or medical support order.

Witness _____, Esquire, First Justice

of said Court at _____, this _____ day of _____, 2011.

_____
Register of Probate

For use only in Bristol Division of Probate and Family Court

Commonwealth of Massachusetts
The Trial Court
Probate and Family Court Department

Bristol Division   Docket No._____

SECOND SUMMONS
on
COMPLAINT FOR MODIFICATION OF CHILD SUPPORT AND/OR MEDICAL SUPPORT

_____, Plaintiff

v.

_____, Defendant

To _____, the above named Defendant:

- You are **required** to appear at the Bristol Division of the Probate and Family Court located in _____ on _____, 2011, at _____ a.m./p.m. for a case management conference in connection with the attached Complaint for Modification of Child Support and/or Medical Support.

- You must bring everything that you have that may help to resolve the child support issues. In particular, remember to bring:

-photo identification (driver's license)   -current paycheck stubs
-most recent tax return with W-2 and 1099 forms   -the enclosed Financial Statement
-copies of other child support orders if you have them -proof of child support already paid or being
-documentation of your health insurance costs   paid even if there is no order

- On the day you are scheduled to appear, the matter may, with the agreement of the parties, go to judgment.

- If you fail to appear, the Court may still enter a modified child and/or medical support order.

Witness _____, Esquire, First Justice

of said Court at _____, this _____ day of _____, 2011.

_____
Register of Probate

For use only in Bristol Division of Probate and Family Court

Commonwealth of Massachusetts
The Trial Court
Probate and Family Court Department

Bristol Division   Docket No._____

CERTIFICATE OF SERVICE ON SECOND SUMMONS

_____, Plaintiff

v.

_____, Defendant

ACCEPTANCE OF SERVICE

I, _____, the above named Defendant, hereby accept service of this summons and understand that judgment may be rendered against me in accordance with the complaint, a copy of which I have received this day.

Date: _____   _____

                                                        Signature of Defendant

NOTARIZATION

_____ ss   Date: _____

Then personally appeared the above named _____ who made oath that the foregoing acceptance was his free act and deed.

Signature of Notary Public: _____

Print Name: _____

My Commission Expires: _____

PROOF OF SERVICE

I hereby certify and return that on _____ I served a copy of the within summons, together
                                                        (date)
with a copy of the complaint in this action upon the within named defendant by:

_____
                            (method of service)

Date: _____   Signed under the penalties of perjury

Date of Service: _____   _____

For use only in Bristol Division of Probate and Family Court

BRISTOL PILOT PROJECT

Commonwealth of Massachusetts
The Trial Court
Probate and Family Court Department

Bristol Division   **Docket No._____**

MOTION FOR FURTHER TEMPORARY ORDERS
TO CHANGE CHILD SUPPORT AND/OR MEDICAL SUPPORT

_____, Plaintiff   v.   _____, Defendant

_____, ☐ Plaintiff ☐ Defendant, requests that the
               (Name)

Court enter a further temporary order to change child support and/or medical support for the following reason (s):

*Check all that apply **and** explain below*

☐ **My income and ability to pay child support has substantially decreased due to:**
     ( ) job loss or pay cut   ( ) injury or disability
☐ **The other parent's income and ability to pay has substantially increased.**
☐ **Change in health insurance.**
☐ **Order needs to be terminated/adjusted due to:**
     ( ) emancipation of the child(ren)   ( ) reconciliation with other parent
☐ **Other**

Explanation:_____

_____

_____

_____

Date: _____   _____
                                            (signature of Plaintiff (if pro se) or Attorney)

NOTICE OF HEARING	
This motion will be heard at the Probate & Family Court	_____
	(Print name)
in _____	
(city)	_____
on _____	(street address)
(month/day/year)	
at _____	(city or town) (state) (zip code)
(time of hearing)	Tel No. _____
	B.B.O. # _____

The within motion is hereby   **ALLOWED**   **DENIED**

_____

_____

_____   _____
Date   Justice of the Probate and Family Court

For use only in Bristol Division of Probate and Family Court

Adopted effective May 11, 2011. Amended effective May 15, 2013.

Standing Order 4–11. Administrative Process for Uncontested *Rogers* Reviews and Extensions

In order to provide for the orderly and efficient administration of uncontested *Rogers* review cases and extensions, and for the convenience of Incapacitated Persons (hereinafter "IP") and other interested parties, all requests for review and/or extension of court orders authorizing the use of antipsychotic medications may be submitted to the Court for administrative allowance without a hearing where the requests are uncontested.

Unless otherwise ordered by the Court and subject to the terms and conditions stated below, uncontested requests for reviews and extensions of *Rogers* Orders shall be considered by Judicial Case Managers, Assistant Judicial Case Managers, or other designees of the First Justice of each Probate and Family Court Division (hereinafter collectively referred to as "judicial designees"). See *Rogers v. Commissioner of the Department of Mental Health*, 390 Mass. 489 (1983).

Initial petitions for guardianship seeking authority to administer antipsychotic medication to an IP shall be heard by a judge. Initial petitions and all annual reviews for wards (minors) shall also be heard by a judge.

The Administrative Process for Uncontested Rogers Reviews and Extensions shall be as follows:

1. An uncontested Motion to Extend and/or Amend an existing Treatment Order for a period not to exceed twelve (12) months may be allowed without a judicial hearing provided the following court-approved pleadings and documents have been filed, and are in proper order. The documents listed below shall constitute a completed package.

a. Motion to Extend and/or Amend Treatment Plan.

b. Motion to Waive Appearance of the IP brought by counsel for the IP.

c. Clinician's Affidavit and Treatment Plan completed by the IP's treating physician, certified psychiatric nurse clinical specialist, or other person(s) so authorized by law. The Clinician's Affidavit shall include any proposed changes in medication or dosage, the reasons therefore, and any possible side effects. No more than four (4) alternative and different class antipsychotic medications shall be permitted absent judicial approval. The affidavit must indicate that the examination of the IP was completed within sixty (60) days of the filing of the pleadings for administrative review.

d. *Rogers* Monitor's Report in accordance with the terms of the Appointment of *Rogers* Monitor. The *Rogers* Monitor is to meet with the IP a reasonable time prior to the review date. The *Rogers* Monitor is to provide a copy of the report to Petitioner and/or counsel, and to the IP's counsel, at least thirty (30) days prior to the review date.

e. Representations of Respondent's (IP's) Counsel indicating that counsel has met with the Respondent, reviewed the Clinician's Affidavit and the Monitor's Report, and that Respondent does not object to the proposed Order and Treatment Plan. Respondent's counsel shall list the date(s) s/he has seen the IP within the last 12 months. The lack of objection by Respondent's counsel to a proposed Treatment Plan shall not constitute a waiver or partial waiver of the attorney-client privilege.

f. A proposed Review Order which shall include the new treatment plan.

g. A Motion for Fees pursuant to *Rudow v. Commissioner of the Division of Medical Assistance*, 429 Mass. 218 (1999) may be presented for services, provided there is an Affidavit supporting the fees, and provided the Motion is assented to by Counsel for the IP.

2. Proposed changes to medication or dosage that offer increased treatment options for the IP, and that are assented to by the IP's counsel, may be considered by the judicial designee at the time of the extension of the Order without a judicial hearing.

3. If no changes to the original Treatment Plan are proposed other than those permitted in this standing order, and there is no contest, the treatment plan may be allowed as amended, or the previous treatment plan may be extended administratively, for up to twelve (12) months. The review date shall be the same as the expiration date of the Order. The newly approved Treatment Plan will expire twelve (12) months from the date of allowance, unless extended before then.

4. Upon completion of the review by the judicial designee, the filings will be submitted to the judge with a recommendation for allowance, or a recommendation that the matter be scheduled for a hearing before a judge.

5. If a completed uncontested package is filed within sixty (60) days of the expiration of a Treatment Plan Order, the matter may be considered for administrative allowance.

6. Any requests for renewal, extension, or amendment of a Treatment Plan Order filed more than sixty (60) days after the review date set in the most recent Order may be initiated by a Motion to Reinstate *Rogers* Authority, and must be presented to a judge.

7. Any interested party may seek judicial review at any time should circumstances warrant a hearing.

8. When deemed appropriate to do so, Orders may be entered *nunc pro tunc*; however, *nunc pro tunc* Orders shall only be issued at the discretion of a judge.

Adopted effective July 1, 2011.

Standing Order 5–11. Regarding the Application of G.L. c. 190B, Articles I–IV, VI & VII to Estate Cases Pending on March 31, 2012 or with a Decree Issued Prior Thereto

This Amended Standing Order addresses how the estate administration and trust provisions of the Massachusetts Uniform Probate Code, G.L. c. 190B ("MUPC"), will apply to proceedings pending after March 31, 2012. For the purposes of this Amended Standing Order, "pending" shall mean any petition which will be governed by the MUPC after March 31, 2012 ("Petition") which has been docketed, filed, or date stamped as received by any Division of the Probate and Family Court ("the Court") on or before March 30, 2012:

A. where a permanent decree has not entered; or

B. where a permanent decree has entered, but other proceedings may be pending in the matter.

Any petition which is not pending as defined herein shall be returned to the petitioner and an appropriate MUPC petition and filing fee shall be required. If the Court has received after March 31, 2012 a petition for probate of will accompanied by an original will, the original will (and death certificate) shall be retained by the Court and filed as a "Will File" and the remaining documents shall be returned to petitioner.

This Standing Order shall not apply to Public Administrators pursuant to G.L. c. 194 or to Receivers pursuant to G.L. c. 200.

A. Where a Permanent Decree has not Entered

1. Citations

Citations issued by the Court on or before March 30, 2012 ("Pre–MUPC Citations") on pending Petitions shall be served in accordance with the Order of Notice therein, including filing the Return of Service with the Court.

a. Any Pre–MUPC Citation with a return date after March 31, 2012 issued on a Petition that seeks the appointment of a fiduciary SHALL be accompanied by a supplemental notice form ("MUPC Supplemental Notice") stating information about changes in the obligations of a

Court appointed fiduciary pursuant to the MUPC. The MUPC Supplemental Notice shall be served on all interested parties in accordance with the Order of Notice in the Pre- MUPC Citation.

b. If a Pre–MUPC Citation that has a return day on or before March 30, 2012 has been issued, but an additional Pre–MUPC Citation ("Additional Pre-MUPC Citation") that has a return date after March 31, 2012 is issued by the Court for any reason (i.e., due to failure to serve all parties with the Pre–MUPC Citation, or amendment of the Petition), the Additional Pre–MUPC Citation SHALL be accompanied by the MUPC Supplemental Notice, which shall be served on all interested parties in accordance with the Order of Notice in the Pre–MUPC Citation.

c. A Pre–MUPC Citation or an Additional Pre–MUPC Citation with a return date after January 2, 2012 but on or before March 30, 2012 issued on a Petition requesting the appointment of a fiduciary MAY be accompanied by the MUPC Supplemental Notice, which shall be served on all interested parties in accordance with the Order of Notice in the Pre–MUPC Citation.

d. If publication of the Pre–MUPC Citation was required, publication of the MUPC Supplemental Notice also is required.

After March 31, 2012, if an Additional Citation on a Petition is required for any reason or the Petition requires amendment for any reason, the Petitioner must file a Motion to Substitute accompanied by the appropriate MUPC petition, and a MUPC citation will be issued by the Court which must be served on all interested person in accordance with the Order of Notice therein. There will be no new filing fee for the substitute Petition or the MUPC citation issued thereon.

2. Allowance of Decree and Appointment of Fiduciary

a. Probate of Will

A Petition for probate of will shall proceed as a formal petition for probate of the will presented and appointment of a personal representative ("PR") except that it shall not determine heirs pursuant to MUPC section 3–402. A Decree entered on a Petition for probate of will that has not been amended to seek a determination of heirs shall not determine heirs.

To request a determination of heirs, after March 31, 2012 a Petitioner shall file a Motion to Substitute accompanied by an appropriate MUPC petition ("Substitute Petition"), and a MUPC Citation will be issued by the Court which must be served on all interested persons in accordance with the Order of Notice therein. There will be no new filing fee for the Substitute Petition or the MUPC citation issued thereon.

If service of a Pre–MUPC Citation with a return day on or before March 30, 2012 has been completed timely, and the Petition is presented for allowance to the Court on or before September 28, 2012, the appropriate pre-MUPC Decree for probate of will shall be used and the pre-MUPC bond shall be required. No such uncontested Petition shall be amended or presented for allowance after September 28, 2012 and shall be dismissed by the Court without further notice.

If service of a Pre–MUPC Citation or Additional Pre–MUPC Citation with a return day after March 31, 2012 and of the MUPC Supplemental Notice have been completed timely, and the Petition is presented for allowance on or before September 28, 2012, the appropriate pre-MUPC Decree for probate of will shall be used and the MUPC bond shall be required. No such uncontested Petition shall be amended or presented for allowance after September 28, 2012 and the Petition shall be dismissed by the Court without further notice.

b. Administration

A Petition for administration shall proceed as a formal petition for appointment of a PR except that it shall not determine heirs or intestacy pursuant to MUPC section 3–402. A Decree entered on a Petition for administration that has not been amended to seek a determination of heirs or intestacy shall not determine heirs or intestacy.

To request a determination of heirs and/or intestacy, after March 31, 2012 a Petitioner shall file a Motion to Substitute accompanied by an appropriate Substitute Petition and a MUPC Citation will be issued by the Court which must be served on all interested persons in accordance with the Order of Notice therein. There will be no new filing fee for the Substitute Petition or the MUPC citation issued thereon.

If service of a Pre–MUPC Citation with a return day on or before March 30, 2012 has been completed timely, and the Petition is presented for allowance to the Court on or before September 28, 2012, the appropriate pre-MUPC Decree for administration shall be used and the pre-MUPC bond shall be required. No such uncontested Petition shall be amended or presented for allowance after September 28, 2012 and shall be dismissed by the Court without further notice.

If service of a Pre–MUPC citation or Additional Pre–MUPC Citation with a return day after March 31, 2012 and of the MUPC Supplemental Notice have been completed timely, and the Petition is presented for allowance on or before September 28, 2012, the appropriate pre-MUPC Decree for administration shall be used and the MUPC bond shall be required. No such uncontested Petition shall be amended or presented for allowance after September 28, 2012 and shall be dismissed by the Court without further notice.

If no citation is necessary for a Petition, the appropriate pre-MUPC Decree for administration shall be used and the pre-MUPC bond shall be required. No such uncontested Petition shall be amended or presented for allowance after September 28, 2012 and shall be dismissed by the Court without further notice.

c. Other Pending Matters

i. Testamentary Trusts

The procedure for a Petition to establish a testamentary trust or a Petition to fill a vacancy in a previously established testamentary trust or other instrument shall follow section A. 2. b above.

ii. License to Sell

A petition for License to Sell that is pending on or filed after March 31, 2012 shall continue to be governed by G.L. c. 202. If a fiduciary is required to file an additional bond pursuant to G.L. c. 205, § 13, the type of bond filed by the fiduciary at the time of appointment shall determine the type of bond filed by the fiduciary at the time of the Decree authorizing sale.

iii. All other Petitions

If no citation is necessary for the Petition, the appropriate pre-MUPC Decree shall be used, and the pre-MUPC Bond, if applicable, shall be required. No such uncontested Petition shall be amended or presented for allowance after September 28, 2012 and shall be dismissed by the Court without further notice.

If a citation is necessary for the Petition, the procedure shall follow section A. 2. b above.

iv. Allowance of Accounts

Account(s) on which a pre-MUPC citation has been issued by the Court with a return date on or before March 30, 2012 shall be governed after January 2, 2012 by Rule 72 of the Supplemental Rules of the Probate Court and a Decree and Order, rather than a Judgment, shall be used.

Any appearance that is filed timely in response to a Pre–MUPC Citation issued by the Court on or before December 30, 2011 that has a return date after January 2, 2012 shall be considered an appearance for the purpose of opposing the allowance of the Account(s) pursuant to MUPC section 1–401 unless otherwise stated and MUPC section 1–401 and Rule 72 of the Supplemental Rules of the Probate and Family Court shall apply.

Any appearance to object filed in response to a Pre–MUPC Citation issued after January 2, 2012 shall be filed pursuant to MUPC section 1–401 and Rule 72 of the Supplemental Rules of the Probate and Family Court.

The appropriate petition for the allowance of Account(s) filed after January 2, 2012 and on or before March 30, 2012 pursuant Rule 72 of the Supplemental Rules of the Probate and Family Court shall be a general petition. Allowance of Account(s) filed after March 31, 2012 shall be by appropriate MUPC petition and citation.

B. Where a Temporary or Permanent Decree has Entered

A person who has undertaken to act as a voluntary executor or voluntary administrator on or before March 30, 2012 shall be treated after March 31, 2012 as a voluntary personal representative ("VPR") and shall have all the powers of a VPR pursuant to MUPC section 3–1201.

A fiduciary, other than a trustee, whose appointment is temporary on or before March 30, 2012 shall be treated after March 31, 2012 as a special personal representative ("SPR") pursuant to MUPC section 3–617 until the expiration of the appointment, except that until the appointment expires, the temporary fiduciary shall have only those powers enumerated in the temporary decree of appointment or in G.L. c. 193, § 11 (which although repealed, will be treated as incorporated by

reference into the decree). After March 31, 2012, a temporary fiduciary may request additional powers available to a SPR pursuant to MUPC section 3–617(b) and/or MUPC section 3–715(b) by filing a Motion for same, and may seek an extension of his or her appointment by filing a Motion to Extend and a MUPC bond shall not be required.

A fiduciary, other than a trustee, whose appointment is permanent on or before March 30, 2012 shall be treated after March 31, 2012 as a personal representative ("PR") pursuant to MUPC section 3–701 et seq and shall have all the powers designated by the MUPC pursuant to MUPC section 3–715(a) unless expressly limited by the terms of the appointment. Such fiduciary shall continue to be obligated to make and return to the Court an Inventory within three months from the date of his or her appointment and shall continue to be obligated to file Account(s) with the Court.

A fiduciary appointed on or before March 30, 2012 ("Pre–MUPC Fiduciary") shall use a pre-MUPC bond to qualify. All Pre–MUPC Fiduciaries, including trustees, shall continue to have the obligations of their pre-MUPC bonds unless modified after March 31, 2012.

If the MUPC Supplemental Notice WAS SERVED with a Pre–MUPC Citation or an Additional Pre–MUPC Citation issued on the Petition seeking the appointment of the Pre–MUPC Fiduciary, then after March 31, 2012, the Pre–MUPC Fiduciary may substitute a MUPC Bond without further notice.

If the MUPC Supplemental Notice WAS NOT SERVED with a Pre–MUPC Citation or an Additional Pre–MUPC Citation issued on the Petition seeking the appointment of the Pre–MUPC Fiduciary, then after March 31, 2012, the Pre–MUPC Fiduciary may seek to file a MUPC Bond by petition served pursuant to section 1–401.

Adopted effective December 29, 2011.

Standing Order 1–15. Application of Rule 13 (b) of the Uniform Rules of Impoundment Procedure to the Probate and Family Court

Rule 13 (b) of the Uniform Rules of Impoundment Procedure provides as follows:

Notice to the Clerk. The filer of a document containing impounded information shall simultaneously file a notice that shall (i) notify the clerk that impounded information is included within the document being filed; (ii) identify the specific legal authority requiring impoundment of the identified information; and (iii) identify the precise location of the impounded information within the document being filed. The clerk shall docket the notice and designate the referenced document as impounded. The cover page of the document containing the impounded information shall identify that it is impounded.

As written, the filer of a document shall file the notice even if the information or document is impounded by statute, court rule, standing order, or case law.

In the Probate and Family Court, the filer of the documents listed below is exempt from filing the Rule 13 (b) notice:

a. affidavit of indigency—by order of the SJC;

b. financial statement—Supplemental Probate and Family Court Rule 401 (d);

c. qualified domestic relations order, domestic relations order, and *Mangiacotti* order—Probate and Family Court Standing Order 3–08;

d. guardian ad litem report—Probate and Family Court Standing Order 2–08;

e. medical certificate, clinical team report, treatment plan and medical affidavit—Probate and Family Court Standing Order 1–09 and G.L. c. 190B;

f. all filings in an adoption case—G.L. c. 210, § 5C;

g. all filings in a child welfare case—G.L. c. 119; and

h. all filings in a paternity case after there has been a judgment of non-paternity—G.L. c. 209C, § 13.

The exemption applies only when the documents are filed in the Probate and Family Court. If any of the documents listed above are filed in connection to a case in another court department, the Rule 13 (b) notice is required, unless that court department has a standing order exempting the filer.

Adopted effective October 1, 2015.

Joint Standing Order 1–16. Authority of the Judge with Respect to Communication with Specialty Court Teams

This Standing Order is promulgated by the chief Justice of the Trial Court pursuant to G. L. c. 211B, Section 9 and shall constitute authorization by law as referenced in Rule 2.9 (A)(2) of the Code of Judicial Conduct (effective January 1, 2016).

For purposes of this Order:

Specialty Court means a specifically designated court session that focuses on individuals with underlying medical, mental health, substance abuse, or other issues that contribute to the reasons such individuals are before the courts. Specialty court shall also mean Veterans Treatment Court and Homelessness Court. Specialty court sessions integrate treatment and services with judicial case oversight and intensive court supervision. Examples Include drug courts, mental health courts, veterans' courts, and tenancy preservation programs.

A Staffing shall refer to a regularly scheduled, informal conference not occurring in open court, the purpose of which is to permit the presiding judge and others, including counsel, to discuss a participant's progress in the specialty court, treatment recommendations, or responses to participant compliance issues.

IT IS THEREFORE ORDERED:

A judge presiding over a specialty court shall have the authority to initiate, permit or otherwise consider ex parte communications about defendants, juveniles or probationers with members of the specialty court team at a staffing or by written documents provided to all members of the specialty court team, The purpose of this authority is to allow judges in their role in presiding over specialty court sessions, and only in that capacity, to assume a more interactive role with parties, treatment providers, probation officers, social workers and others, than Rule 2.9 of the Code of Judicial Conduct would otherwise permit.

Adopted effective January 7, 2016.

Standing Order 1–16. Initial Limited Electronic Filing Pilot Project in the Essex Division of the Probate and Family Court Department for Designated Estate Matters Only

I. Purpose

In order to advance efficiency in the Massachusetts courts and better serve the public and the bar, the Supreme Judicial Court has authorized electronic filing pilot projects for the trial and appellate courts and approved Interim Massachusetts Electronic Filing Rules effective February 25, 2015. By this Standing Order 1–16, the Probate and Family Court Department hereby designates the Essex Division as the department pilot project permitting electronic filing and electronic service of court documents (the "Essex Electronic Filing Pilot Project") for designated estate matters only, as set forth below in section II. A. As of the effective date of this Standing Order, the Essex Division will be authorized to receive and send documents, orders, and judgments through electronic filing under the *Interim Electronic Filing Rules for Pilot Courts (2015)*.

Standing Order 1–16 shall incorporate by reference the interim Massachusetts Electronic Filing Rules (the "Interim Rules"), and, for the duration of the Essex Electronic Filing Pilot Project, shall establish additional procedures for the implementation and operation of electronic filing and electronic service of court documents in designated estate matters commenced after the effective date of this Standing Order, notwithstanding any provision to the contrary in any rule of court or other standing order. This is an initial Standing Order to establish the parameters of the implementation of the Essex Pilot Project; this Standing Order will be amended and revised by this Department as necessary during the course of the electronic filing pilot projects generally, and the Essex Electronic Filing Pilot Project specifically.

II. Designations

A. Participants and Case Types

Eligibility and conditions of registration to participate in electronic filing shall be in accordance with Rule 3 of the *Interim Electronic Filing Rules for Pilot Courts (2015)*. For the initial pilot, designated lawyers/law firms shall be given training and access to the electronic filing program known as Odyssey File & Serve, and shall participate in the Essex Electronic Filing Pilot Project as properly registered users in compliance with the Interim Rules. The Essex Electronic Filing Project will be available to add additional eligible participants after completing the registration process set forth in the *Interim Electronic Filing Rules for Pilot Courts (2015)*.

The following estate case types are specifically designated for electronic filing and electronic service of court documents in the Essex Electronic Filing Pilot Project:

- Informal Probate of Will
- Informal Probate of Will with appointment of Personal Representative

- Informal Appointment of Personal Representative
- Informal Appointment of Successor Personal Representative
- Formal Adjudication of intestacy and Appointment of Personal Representative
- Formal Adjudication of Intestacy
- Formal Appointment of Personal Representative
- Formal Probate of Will
- Formal Probate of Will with appointment of Personal Representative
- Supervised Administration
- Public Administration
- Modify Bond
- Formal Removal of Personal Representative
- Formal Appointment of Successor Personal Representative
- Voluntary Administration Statement

III. Additional Procedures

A. No Fee Waiver Requests, Interpreter Requests

Because the Odyssey File & Serve program is not yet able to electronically process a request for a fee waiver/ indigency determination or a request for an interpreter, a party seeking these options must continue to submit these requests to the Essex Probate and Family Court Registry of Probate in the conventional manner, but may proceed to electronically file his/her estate case pursuant to the Interim Rules.

B. Filing of Original Will

The filing of an original will is required pursuant to G. L. C.190B in many of the case types included in the Essex Electronic Filing Pilot Project. In these instances the following requirement will apply:

The original will must be mailed or delivered to the Essex Probate and Family Court no later than 5 business days after the electronic filing of the related Petition.

This requirement applies to the following case types and any pilot electronically filed case which requires the filing of an original will:

- Informal Probate of Will
- Informal Probate of Will with appointment of Personal Representative
- Formal Probate of Will
- Formal Probate of Will with appointment of Personal Representative
- May be required for Voluntary Administration Statement if decedent had will

C. Electronic Signatures

Pursuant to Rules 13 and 14 of the *Interim Electronic Filing Rules for Pilot Courts (2015)* orders and judgments in cases filed under the Essex Electronic Filing Pilot may be electronically signed. Electronic signatures have the force of conventional signatures. In addition, a digital stamp of the Register of Probate, Essex Probate and Family Court, shall be accepted to certify an electronic copy of any document issued pursuant to the Essex Electronic Filing Pilot. A digital stamp of the Register's signature shall be accepted for the issuance of letters associated with the Essex Electronic Filing Pilot case types.

IV. Duration

The Essex Electronic Filing Pilot Project described herein shall expire one year from the effective date of this Standing Order, and Standing Order 1–16 may be superseded or amended, in writing, at any time during this period.

Adopted February 9, 2016, effective March 8, 2016.

Standing Order 2–16. Parent Education Program Attendance

This Court finds that the best interests of the minor children of pat lies appearing before it would be well served by educating their parents about children's emotional needs and the effects of divorce on child behavior and development.

IT IS HEREBY ORDERED THAT:

1. All parties to a divorce action in which there are minor children are ordered to attend and participate in an approved Parent Education Program. In addition, a judge, in his or her discretion, of this Court may require the parties in an action to establish paternity, complaints for modification or contempt, or in any other case involving parenting time, custody, or support of minor children to attend a Parent Education Program.

2. All parties to a divorce action in which there are minor children must register with an approved program within thirty (30) days of service of the original complaint upon the original defendant. Other parties ordered to attend a parent education program must register for a program within thirty (30) days of the order. Sanctions for failure to register or complete a program may be imposed by the Court. Upon registering for a program, parties shall complete the "Affidavit Confirming Registration at Parent Education Program" and file with the Court.

3. For divorcing parents, and parents in other cases when specifically ordered by the Court, attendance at a program is mandatory unless waived. Parties must file their Certificates of Attendance with the Court no later than thirty (30) days after completing the program.

4. If a party seeks to waive attendance at a Parent Education Program, the party must file a "Motion to Waive Attendance at a Parent Education Program" with notice to the other party. The motion must include the reason the party is alleged to be unable to attend a Parent Education Program. Waivers may be granted upon a demonstrable showing of: chronic and severe violence which negates safe parental communication; language barriers; institutionalization or other unavailability of a party; or where justice otherwise indicates. The Court may elect to deny the "Motion to Waive Attendance at a Parent Education Program" and may, instead, permit use of a five-hour DVD or online program entitled *KidCare for Co-Parents: An Educational Program for Divorcing Families* to satisfy the Parent Education Program requirement. Waiver for one parent does not automatically apply to the other parent.

5. If a party is not able to attend an in person Parent Education Program, the party may file, with notice, a "Motion to Permit Completion of Parent Education Program via DVD". The motion must include the reason the party is alleged to be unable to attend a Parent Education Program in person. Approval to participate in a Parent Education Program through use of the DVD or online program may be granted upon a demonstrable showing of: significant health or financial issues, significant geographic and transportation issues, or other significant barriers to in person participation; or where justice otherwise indicates. If allowed, the party must complete the interactive program and obtain the Certificate of Attendance. This Certificate must be provided by the party to the Court no later than 30 days after completion of the program. Approval for one parent does not automatically apply to the other parent.

6. Unless the Court orders otherwise, the parties must attend programs currently approved by the Chief Justice of the Probate and Family Court. Program vendors will ensure that parties to an action do not attend the same session of any program unless the Court orders otherwise. Lists of currently approved programs (including *KidCare for Co-Parents: An Educational Program for Divorcing Families*) are available at http://www.mass.gov/courts/programs/parent-child/.

7. A copy of this Standing Order shall be provided by the Registry to the plaintiff or his/her attorney upon the filing of a complaint for divorce involving minor children. The plaintiff or his/her attorney shall serve a copy of this Standing Order along with the complaint and summons to the person authorized to make service pursuant to Mass.R.Dom.Re.I.P. 4(c).

8. The parties shall each pay $ 80.00 to the provider in advance of the program to offset cost of materials, facilitators, and program administration. The same fee applies to participation via DVD or online in the program entitled *KidCare for Co-Parents: An Educational Program for Divorcing Families*.

9. If a party is unable to afford the $80.00 course fee, the party may be eligible to pay a reduced fee of $5.00 to the provider. The party must submit to the Court an "Affidavit of Indigency and Request for Waiver, Substitution or State Payment of Fees and Costs." This form is promulgated by the Chief Justice of the Supreme Judicial Court pursuant to G.L. c. 261 sec. 27B and is available on the Court's website (mass. gov/courts) and at the Registries of the Probate and Family Court. If the waiver of the fee is allowed by the Court, the party must submit a copy of the approved waiver to the Parent Education provider when seeking to attend a program for the $5.00 reduced fee.

10. An uncontested divorce hearing may be scheduled pending attendance if the parties file an affidavit confirming their registration with the Court and so long as both parties complete the program prior to the hearing. A Pre-trial Conference in a contested case may be similarly scheduled so long as the parties complete the program prior to the Pre-trial Conference. No Trial will be held by the Court until the Court receives a Certificate of Attendance from an approved program for each party, or waives the requirement.

Changes enumerated in this Standing Order are effective as of May 1, 2016 and shall apply to all cases referenced in paragraph (1) filed thereafter.

Adopted April 11, 2016, effective May 1, 2016.

Standing Order 3–16.   Remote Access to Electronic Court Records for Probate and Family Records

Rule 5 (a) (iii) of the Trial Court Rule XIV, Uniform Rules on Public Access to Court Records, provides that each Department of the Trial Court, subject to the approval of the Chief Justice of the Trial Court after notification to the SJC, may exempt certain civil case types or categories of information from remote access.

Probate and Family Court Estate Administration electronic case information is currently available remotely. Effective November 1, 2016 electronic case information for Equity cases will be available remotely, with the exception of Paternity cases filed in equity pursuant to G.L. c. 215, § 6.

The following exemptions have been approved for these case types and types of information of the Probate and Family Court:

For all Divorce, Paternity, Guardianship, Conservatorship, Trust, Separate Support, Modification, Contempt, and Change of Name case types not restricted or impounded by other standing orders, rules or orders of the court, the following information shall be available through remote public access:

● Case Name

● Party Names

● Attorney Information

● Event Dates

● Subsequent Actions

● Case Disposition

For all Divorce, Paternity, Guardianship, Conservatorship, Trust, Separate Support, Modification, Contempt, and Change of Name case types not restricted or impounded by other standing orders, rules or orders of the court, the following information shall NOT be available through remote public access:

● Addresses for parties, whether represented by counsel or not

● Docket entries

Adopted effective November 1, 2016.

Standing Order 1–17.   Parenting Coordination

(1) Applicability

(a) This standing order applies to:

(i) the appointment of a parenting coordinator pursuant to an agreement by the parties to engage a parenting coordinator that is approved by the court and incorporated into an order or incorporated and merged into a judgment; and

(ii) the appointment of a parenting coordinator by a court order or judgment without agreement of the parties.

(b) This rule does not apply to an agreement to use a parenting coordinator that is not incorporated into an order or incorporated and merged into a judgment.

(c) A parenting coordinator may be appointed in cases filed pursuant to G.L. c. 208, 209, 209C and in other actions relating to the care and custody of a minor child or children, provided that there is an order or judgment establishing a parenting plan, custody and/or parenting time.

(d) A parenting coordinator shall not be appointed in actions filed pursuant to G.L. c. 209A.

(e) The appointment of a parenting coordinator does not divest the court of its exclusive jurisdiction to determine fundamental issues of care and custody and/or parenting time and support, and the authority to exercise management and control of the case, even where the parties have agreed to binding decision-making authority of the parenting coordinator.

(2) Definitions

In all sections of this standing order, the following definitions apply:

(a) "Parenting coordination" is a child-focused process in which the parties work with a parenting coordinator in an effort to reduce the effects or potential effects of conflict on the child or children involved in the parenting plan. Although parenting coordination may draw upon alternative dispute resolution techniques, parenting coordination is not governed by SJC Rule 1:18.

(b) "Parenting coordinator" means a court-appointed, third-party provider of parenting coordination services.

(c) "Related professional experience" includes direct or supportive professional work with families involved in custody or parenting time disputes, or family therapy or child therapy.

(3) Qualifications of a Parenting Coordinator

(a) To be approved by the court as a parenting coordinator, an individual shall:

(i) be an attorney who is licensed in Massachusetts, or be a licensed psychiatrist, licensed psychologist, licensed independent clinical social worker, licensed marriage and family therapist, or licensed mental health counselor who is licensed in Massachusetts; and

(ii) if an attorney, have at least four years of related professional experience undertaken after licensure in Massachusetts; if a licensed psychiatrist or licensed psychologist or licensed independent clinical social worker, have at least two years of related professional experience undertaken after licensure in Massachusetts; or if a licensed marriage and family therapist or licensed mental health counselor, have at least four years of related professional experience undertaken after licensure in Massachusetts; and

(iii) have professional liability insurance coverage of $100,000 or more.

(b) A parenting coordinator candidate shall complete the following training as approved by the Administrative Office of the Probate and Family Court prior to submitting an application:

(i) at least 30 hours of training in a mediation training program; and

(ii) at least 6 hours of training in intimate partner abuse and family violence dynamics to be established by the Probate and Family Court in conjunction with the Trial Court; and

(iii) at least 35 hours of accredited specialty training in topics related to parenting coordination, including, but not limited to, any mandatory training established by the Administrative Office of the Probate and Family Court, the role of the parenting coordinator in Massachusetts, the role of a parenting coordinator generally, communication, conflict management and dispute resolution skills, developmental stages of children, dynamics of high-conflict families, parenting skills, problem-solving techniques, and parenting in separate households.

(c) Within each calendar year, a parenting coordinator shall complete a minimum of six hours of continuing education approved by the Administrative Office of the Probate and Family Court in one or more of the topics listed in subsection 3 (b)(iii) of this standing order and in relevant domestic relations case law and statutes or in a training topic established by the Administrative Office of the Probate and Family Court. This continuing education requirement is separate and distinct from the continuing education requirements for other fee generating appointment categories.

(4) In accordance with SJC Rule 1:07, an individual who has the qualifications listed in section 3 of this standing order and seeks court appointment as a parenting coordinator shall submit an application to the Administrative Office of the Probate and Family Court to be included on the Category V—Parenting Coordination list. The application shall document that the individual meets the qualifications required in subsections 3 (a) and (b) of this standing order. If satisfied that the applicant meets the qualifications, the Administrative Office of the Probate and Family Court shall place the applicant's name on the list of qualified parenting coordinators.

(5) Approval of a Parenting Coordinator Engaged by Agreement of the Parties

(a) In any action in which the custody and/or parenting time of a child or children of the parties is or was at issue, the parties, by agreement, may engage a parenting coordinator to assist them in dealing with existing or future conflicts regarding their access to and responsibilities for their child or children.

(b) For the agreement to be enforceable by the court, the parties shall file a Joint Petition/Motion to Change a Judgment/Order (Form CJD 124) with the court to request that their agreement be incorporated into an order or incorporated and merged into a judgment. The court shall enter such an order or judgment if it finds that the parenting coordinator has the qualifications set forth in section 3 of this standing order, or is otherwise qualified to be the parenting coordinator, and that the agreement:

(i) is in writing and signed by the parties and the parenting coordinator; and

(ii) indicates whether the parenting coordinator is on the Category V list, and if not on the Category V list, how he or she is qualified to be the parenting coordinator; and

(iii) states the duties of the parenting coordinator, including whether the parties agree that the parenting coordinator shall have binding decision-making authority, and if so, the scope of said authority; and

(iv) states the period of time that the parenting coordinator will serve in the role; and

(v) states the amount or rate of compensation to be paid to the parenting coordinator, how the fees and expenses of the parenting coordinator are allocated between the parties, and the maximum expenditure for each party during the period of appointment as provided in subsection 5 (b)(iv) of this standing order; and

(vi) is otherwise consistent with the best interests of the child or children.

(c) Before incorporating the agreement into an order or incorporating and merging the agreement into a judgment, the judge shall inquire of the parties as to whether they understand that:

(i) if incorporated into an order, the agreement cannot be changed by the court without the filing of a motion and a showing of good cause and a showing that such change is in the best interests of the child or children; or

(ii) if incorporated into a judgment, cannot be modified by the court without the filing of complaint for modification and a showing of a material change in circumstances and a showing that such modification is in the best interests of the child or children; and

(iii) the parties have the right to access the court so that the court can determine fundamental issues of care and custody and/or parenting time and support, even where the parties have agreed to binding decision-making authority of the parenting coordinator; and

(iv) the court will not draw any adverse inference if the party does not agree to use a parenting coordinator.

(6) Appointment of a Parenting Coordinator by Court, Without Agreement of the Parties

(a) In any action in which the custody and/or parenting time of a child or children of the parties is or was at issue and the court determines that the level of conflict between the parties with respect to that issue so warrants, the court may appoint a parenting coordinator in accordance with this section if the court finds that:

(i) it is in the best interests of the child or children involved in the parenting plan; and

(ii) the parties have failed to successfully implement the parenting plan; or

(iii) the level of parental conflict is, or may become, detrimental to the child or children involved in the parenting plan.

(b) During the pendency of an action, by motion of a party or on the court's own initiative, and after notice and hearing, the court may appoint a parenting coordinator for the pendency of that action. Unless sooner terminated in accordance with this standing order, the appointment shall terminate upon the entry of a judgment in that action.

(c) Upon entry of a judgment establishing or modifying a parenting plan, custody and/or parenting time, the court, after notice and hearing, may appoint a parenting coordinator. The court may appoint the individual who served as a parenting coordinator during the pendency of the underlying action. Unless sooner terminated in accordance with this standing order, the appointment of a post-judgment parenting coordinator shall not exceed two years.

(d) An order or judgment appointing a parenting coordinator without the agreement of the parties shall include:

(i) written findings as to why a parenting coordinator is being appointed pursuant to subsection 6 (a) of this standing order;

(ii) the name, business address, e-mail address, and telephone number of the parenting coordinator; and

(iii) the duties of the parenting coordinator; and

(iv) the period of time that the parenting coordinator will serve in the role; and

(v) written findings regarding parenting coordination fees pursuant to subsection 15 (b) of this standing order and how the fees and expenses of the parenting coordinator are allocated between the parties.

(e) Notwithstanding any other provisions of this standing order, "a judge may not require the parties to use the services of a parent[ing] coordinator if the order would require one or both parents to pay for the services without his or her consent." Bower v. Bournay–Bower, 469 Mass. 690 (2014). If neither party agrees to pay to use the services of a parenting coordinator, the court is not permitted to enter an order or judgment requiring the use of a parenting coordinator.

(7) Permitted Duties of All Parenting Coordinators

As appropriate, and as determined by the order incorporating an agreement, the judgment incorporating and merging an agreement, an order or a judgment, a parenting coordinator may:

(a) assist the parties in amicably resolving disputes and in reaching agreements about the implementation of and compliance with the order regarding the child or children in their care including, but not limited to, the following types of issues:

(i) minor changes or clarifications of the existing parenting plan;

(ii) exchanges of the child or children including date, time, place, means of and responsibilities for transportation;

(iii) education or daycare including school choice, tutoring, summer school, before and after school care, participation in special education testing and programs, or other educational decisions;

(iv) enrichment and extracurricular activities including camps and jobs;

(v) the child or children's travel and passport arrangements;

(vi) clothing, equipment, and personal possessions of the child or children;

(vii) means of communication by a party with the child or children when they are not in that party's care;

(viii) role of and contact with significant others and extended families;

(ix) psychotherapy or other mental health care including substance abuse or mental health assessment or counseling for the child or children;

(x) psychological testing or other assessments of the children; and

(xi) religious observances and education.

(b) educate the parties about making and implementing decisions that are in the best interest of the child or children;

(c) assist the parties in developing guidelines for appropriate communication between them;

(d) suggest resources to assist the parties; and

(e) assist the parties, where appropriate, in identifying and addressing patterns of behavior and in developing parenting strategies to manage and reduce opportunities for conflict in order to reduce the impact of any conflict upon their child or children.

(8) Required Duty of All Parenting Coordinators

Whenever the parties come to an agreement with the assistance of the parenting coordinator that modifies an existing order or judgment, the parenting coordinator must inform the parties that the agreement is not enforceable unless it is submitted for approval and incorporated into an order or incorporated and merged into a judgment by the court.

(9) Duties Not Permitted of All Parenting Coordinators

A parenting coordinator may not:

(a) except as permitted by section 10 of this standing order, communicate orally or in writing with the court or any court personnel regarding the substance of the action;

(b) testify in the action as an expert witness;

(c) facilitate an agreement by the parties that would change legal custody from one party to the other or that would change the physical custody or parenting plan in a way that may result in a change of child support;

(d) offer legal advice, representation, therapy or counseling;

(e) delegate any portion of the parenting coordination process to anyone else, as the appointment is personal in nature; and

(f) make any binding decisions for the parties without the parties' express written agreement that has been incorporated into an order or judgment.

(10) Permissible Court Activities of All Parenting Coordinators

A parenting coordinator may:

(a) produce documents and testify in the action as a fact witness in response to a subpoena issued at the request of a party or an attorney for a child of the parties, or upon action of the court;

(b) if concerned that a party or child is in imminent physical or emotional danger, file a motion or complaint to request an immediate hearing; and

(c) file a motion or complaint for the appointment of a guardian to assert or waive a child's privilege.

(11) Confidential and Privileged Information

(a) The parenting coordinator shall have access to all non-impounded case records in the action. If a document or any information contained in a case record is impounded, the court shall determine whether the parenting coordinator may have access to it and shall specify any conditions to that access. Only the court may address access to an impounded document.

(b) A parenting coordinator may not require the parties or an attorney for the child to release any confidential or privileged information that is not included in the case record.

(c) Information acquired in the course of a parenting coordination appointment is confidential. The parenting coordinator shall use such information only for the benefit of the parties or the child or children involved in the parenting plan. Such information may be disclosed by the parenting coordinator to a party or parties, to an attorney for the child, to an attorney for a party, and in court pursuant to section 10 of this standing order.

(d) A party may release to the parenting coordinator his or her own educational, medical, and other third-party information and such information of the child or children involved in the parenting plan. However, a child's psychotherapy, counseling or social worker privilege may be waived only by a guardian appointed specifically by the court to investigate and assert or waive the child's privilege. A party or the parenting coordinator may at any time file a motion or complaint for the appointment of a guardian to assert or waive the child's privilege. The request shall specify the scope of the information sought and the reasons for seeking the waiver. The parties and all attorneys involved in the matter must be provided a copy of the request and notice of hearing.

(12) Conflict of Interest

The court may not appoint an individual as a parenting coordinator if the person has served or is serving in a professional capacity of any sort with either party, or both parties, or the child or children in the case, including, but not limited to, therapist, guardian ad litem, attorney or attorney for the child or children. After appointing a person pursuant to this standing order as a parenting coordinator in a case, the court may not subsequently appoint the person as a guardian ad litem or attorney for the child in the same case, or any other case, involving the parties or children.

(13) Domestic Violence

If there are credible allegations or findings of domestic violence committed by a party, against a party or a child or children involved in the action, the court:

(a) shall offer each party an opportunity to consult with an attorney or domestic violence advocate of his or her choosing before accepting an agreement pursuant to section 5 of this standing order; and

(b) shall not appoint a parenting coordinator over the objection of a party.

(14) Extension and Early Termination of Parenting Coordination Appointment During the Pendency of a Parenting Coordination Appointment; Replacement and Resignation of a Parenting Coordinator During the Pendency of a Parenting Coordination Appointment; Modification During the Pendency of a Parenting Coordination Appointment

(a) *Extension of Parenting Coordination Appointment During the Pendency of a Parenting Coordination Appointment*

(i) The parties and the parenting coordinator may agree in writing to an extension of the appointment. To be enforceable by the court, the agreement must be submitted for approval and incorporated into an order or judgment in accordance with the provisions of section 5.

(ii) If there is an action pending, a party may file a motion asking to extend the appointment. In making its determination, the court must consider the provisions of subsections 6 (a) and 15 (b) and enter the required findings. The court may extend the appointment for good cause shown and upon a showing that such extension is in the best interests of the child or children involved in the parenting plan. The first extension, and any subsequent extension, if allowed, shall not be for more than one year.

(iii) If there is no action pending, a party may file a complaint for modification asking to extend the appointment. In making its determination, the court must consider the provisions of subsections 6 (a) and 15 (b) and enter the required findings. The court may extend the appointment if there has been a material change in circumstances and upon a showing that such extension is in the best interests of the child or children involved in the parenting plan. The first extension, and any subsequent extension, if allowed, shall not be for more than one year.

(b) *Early Termination of Parenting Coordination Appointment During the Pendency of a Parenting Coordination Appointment*

(i) The parties may agree to terminate the parenting coordination appointment. To be enforceable by the court, the agreement must be submitted for approval and incorporated into an order or judgment in accordance with the provisions of section 5.

(ii) If there is an action pending, a party may file a motion asking to terminate the appointment. The court may terminate the appointment for good cause shown and upon a showing that such termination is in the best interests of the child or children involved in the parenting plan.

(iii) If there is no action pending, a party may file a complaint for modification asking to terminate the appointment. The court may terminate the appointment if there has been a material change in circumstances and upon a showing that such termination is in the best interests of the child or children involved in the parenting plan.

(c) *Replacement of a Parenting Coordinator During the Pendency of a Parenting Coordination Appointment*

(i) The parties may agree to replace the parenting coordinator with a different parenting coordinator. To be enforceable by the court, the agreement must be submitted for approval and incorporated into an order or judgment in accordance with the provisions of section 5.

(ii) If there is an action pending, a party may file a motion asking to replace the parenting coordinator with a different parenting coordinator. The court may order such replacement for good cause shown and upon a showing that such replacement is in the best interests of the child or children involved in the parenting plan.

(iii) If there is no action pending, a party may file a complaint for modification asking to replace the parenting coordinator with a different parenting coordinator. The court may order such replacement if there has been a material change in circumstances and upon a showing that such replacement is in the best interests of the child or children involved in the parenting plan.

(d) *Resignation of Parenting Coordinator During the Pendency of a Parenting Coordination Appointment*

(i) A parenting coordinator may resign at any time by written notice sent by first- class mail to each party and any attorney for the party, the child or children. The notice shall state the effective date of the resignation and inform the parties that they may ask the court to appoint a different parenting coordinator. The notice shall be sent at least 15 days before the effective date of the resignation. Promptly after mailing the notice, and at least seven days before the effective date of resignation, the parenting coordinator shall file a copy of the notice with the court.

(ii) The parties may agree to the appointment of a different parenting coordinator. To be enforceable by the court, the agreement must be submitted for approval and incorporated into an order or judgment in accordance with the provisions of section 5.

(iii) If an action is pending, a party may file a motion seeking the appointment of a different parenting coordinator. The court may order such appointment for good cause shown and upon a showing that such replacement is in the best interests of the child or children involved in the parenting plan.

(iv) If there is no action pending, a party may file a complaint for modification seeking the appointment of a different parenting coordinator. The court may order such appointment if there has been a material change in circumstances and upon a showing that such replacement is in the best interests of the child or children involved in the parenting plan.

(e) *Modification*

(i) For issues other than those listed in subsections 14 (a) through (d), during the pendency of a parenting coordination appointment, the parties may agree to modify the parenting coordination appointment. To be enforceable by the court, the agreement must be submitted for approval and incorporated into an order or judgment in accordance with the provisions of section 5.

(ii) For issues other than those listed in subsections 14 (a) through (d), during the pendency of a parenting coordination appointment, if an action is pending, a party may file a motion to change the provisions of a parenting coordination appointment. In making its determination, the court must consider the provisions of subsections 6 (a) and 15 (b) and enter the required findings. The court may order such change for good cause shown and upon a showing that such change is in the best interests of the child or children involved in the parenting plan.

(iii) For issues other than those listed in subsections 14 (a) through (d), during the pendency of a parenting coordination appointment, if there is no action pending, a party may file a complaint for modification to modify the provisions of a parenting coordination appointment. In making its determination, the court must consider the provisions of subsections 6 (a) and 15 (b) and enter the required findings. The court may order such modification upon a showing of material change in circumstances and a showing that such modification is in the best interests of the child or children involved in the parenting plan.

(15) Fees

(a) Where the parties have entered into an agreement that has been incorporated into an order or judgment pursuant to section 5 of this standing order, the agreement must include the amount or rate of compensation to be paid to the parenting coordinator and how the fees and expenses of the parenting coordinator are allocated between the parties.

(b) If the court orders parties to parenting coordination, the court must enter written findings that one or both of the parties consent to the allocation of fees and expenses of the parenting coordinator and the party or parties have the financial means to make such payment. The court shall enter an order allocating the fees and expenses of the parenting coordinator in accordance with the party's or parties' consent. "[A] judge may not require the parties to use the services of a parent[ing] coordinator if the order would require one or both parents to pay for the services without his or her consent." Bower v. Bournay–Bower, 469 Mass. 690 (2014). If neither party agrees to pay to use the services of a parenting coordinator, the court is not permitted to enter an order or judgment requiring the use of a parenting coordinator.

(16) Effect of Standing Order 1–17 on Existing Parenting Coordination Appointments

Section 14 applies to all parenting coordination appointments, regardless of whether the appointment was prior to the effective date of this standing order.

Adopted effective July 1, 2017.

Standing Order 2–17. Family-centered Case Resolution and Case Management in the Probate and Family Court Department

Preamble

The Probate and Family Court is committed to providing child-centered and family-centered opportunities for case resolution. Consistent research finds that children are harmed when they are exposed to conflict between their parents. The case resolution opportunities set forth below are designed to reduce conflict in the resolution of disputes between parents and other caregivers about children. In issuing this Standing Order, the Probate and Family Court affirms the importance of case resolution without a trial.

I. General Provisions

A. This Standing Order applies in all divisions of the Probate and Family Court Department. The mandatory provisions of this Standing Order apply to all contested custody divorce and contested custody divorce modification cases as defined below. The voluntary provisions apply to any divorce, divorce modification or separate support case.

B. Nothing in this Standing Order alters the requirement that all divorcing parents attend an approved Parent Education program as required by Standing Order 2-16: Parent Education Program Attendance.

C. A contested custody divorce case or contested custody divorce modification case is a case where the parties are not in agreement as to all terms of any parenting plan, including legal and physical custody, parenting time, as well as to the amount of a child support order.

D. The limited discovery provisions in Section III must be followed for all cases participating in the Early Case Settlement Process. Parties in any initial divorce or divorce modification or separate support case may, by written agreement, agree to follow the limited discovery provisions in Section III.

E. The case settlement conference provisions below must be followed for all cases participating in the Early Case Settlement Process. The case settlement conference provisions below must also be followed in all contested custody divorce cases and contested custody divorce modification cases, unless otherwise ordered by the Court or where an order prohibiting contact between the parties is in place. In any other action in which discovery is complete, at the request of both parties, the Court shall, except for good cause shown, direct the parties, and their attorneys, if any, to participate in a settlement conference or conferences before trial for the purpose of facilitating resolution on some or all of the contested issues in the case. If one party requests, the Court may schedule a settlement conference. The Court may also schedule a settlement conference on its own initiative.

II. Early Case Settlement Process

A. The Early Case Settlement Process is a voluntary process that parties to any divorce, divorce modification, or separate support case may elect to participate in by agreement. At any point in the Early Case Settlement Process, either party may "opt-out" of the process by filing a notice with the Court that includes a short summary of the status of the case and the date of the next scheduled event.

B. The Early Case Settlement Process includes three mandatory requirements:

1. Compliance with the limited discovery provisions of this Standing Order;

2. A limit of filing no more than two motions per party prior to the settlement conference; and

3. Participation in a case settlement conference.

C. To participate in the Early Case Settlement Process, the parties must complete the Early Case Settlement Process Opt-In form and file the form with the Court no later than 60 days after the filing of the divorce, divorce modification, or separate support complaint. The form requires that the parties acknowledge and understand that:

1. They have voluntarily agreed to participate in the Early Case Settlement Process;

2. They must complete all discovery required by Rule 410 of the Supplemental Rules of the Probate and Family Court and the limited discovery provisions in Section III;

3. No more than two motions per party may be filed prior to the settlement conference;

4. The Court will schedule a settlement conference no later than 60 days after the date set for discovery to be completed; and

5. As part of the settlement conference procedure, they must submit a completed settlement conference form to the Court and to the other party or his or her attorney if the other party is represented by an attorney.

III. Limited Discovery

The limited discovery provisions below must be followed for all cases participating in the Early Case Settlement Process. Parties in any initial or modification divorce or separate support case may, by written agreement, agree to follow the limited discovery provisions below.

A. In addition to the documents that are exchanged in accordance with Rule 410 of the Supplemental Rules of the Probate and Family Court, the parties shall exchange the following documents within 120 days of service of the summons:

1. Summary plan descriptions for qualified plans held by either party currently or at any time during the marriage;

2. All deeds and mortgages on which the name of either party currently appears or appeared at any time during the marriage;

3. Vehicle certificates of title and registration, and loan and lease documents on which the name of either party currently appears or appeared during the 12 months preceding the filing of the complaint;

4. All loan applications or personal financial statements submitted to any institution by either or both parties during the 5 years preceding the filing of the complaint;

5. All appraisals, valuations and opinions of value of all assets owned by either or both parties prepared during the 5 years preceding the filing of the complaint;

6. A complete copy of all credit card statements on which the name of either or both parties appears on which there has been any activity during any of the 12 months preceding the filing of the complaint;

7. Documentation and an inventory of the contents of any safe deposit box and/or vault on which the name of either party currently appears or appeared at any time during the marriage;

8. Copies of all insurance policies in effect at any point during the 3 years preceding the filing of the complaint, including without limitation, life insurance, homeowner's insurance, collectible or personal property insurance, personal liability insurance (umbrella), automobile insurance or any other insurance of any kind;

9. Documentation evidencing beneficiary designations and changes to beneficiary designations for all assets, IRAs, 401K plans, annuities, pension plans, profit sharing plans, insurance policies, etc., for either party during the 3 years preceding the filing of the complaint;

10. Documentation for any liability, debt, personal loan or charitable pledge in effect at any time during the 12 months preceding the filing of the complaint and the most recent statement evidencing the balance owed;

11. Documentation for any UTMA accounts, UPLAN, or 529 plans in existence during the 3 years preceding the filing of the complaint, including the most recent statement;

12. Documentation of any existing student loans for a child of the marriage;

13. The most recent credit report for each party;

14. Copy of the most recent Social Security Statement prepared by the Social Security Administration;

15. For self-employed parties filing a Schedule C, all documents evidencing business income and expenses for the 3 years preceding the filing of the complaint; and

16. Pay stubs or summaries of earnings of each party for the 12 months preceding the filing of the complaint.

B. In complaints for modification, parties shall exchange all documents listed above as they relate to the time period from the date of the judgment that is seeking to be modified to the filing of the complaint for modification, unless they agree otherwise.

C. Each party shall attach an "Affidavit of Full Disclosure" when submitting their discovery, signed under the penalties of perjury and signed by his or her attorney, if any.

D. No discovery outside of the provisions of Section III (A) is permitted, unless ordered by the Court upon motion of either party or by written agreement of the parties.

E. If any party required to deliver documents under the provisions of Section III (A) does not have any of the documents required or has not been able to obtain them in the required time frame, he or she shall state in writing, under the penalties of perjury, the specific documents which are not available, and what efforts have been made to obtain the documents. The statement shall be provided to other parties and/or their attorneys within 120 days of the service of the summons.

F. Each party has a continuing obligation to supplement discovery if and when such discovery becomes available.

IV. Settlement Conferences

The case settlement conference provisions below must be followed for all cases participating in the Early Case Settlement Process.

A. The case settlement conference provisions below must also be followed in all contested custody divorce cases and contested custody divorce modification cases, unless otherwise ordered by the Court or where an order prohibiting contact between the parties is in place.

B. In any other action in which discovery is complete, at the request of both parties, the Court shall, except for good cause shown, direct the parties, and their attorneys, if any, to participate in a settlement conference or conferences before trial for the purpose of facilitating settlement. If one party requests, the Court may schedule a settlement conference. The Court may also schedule a settlement conference on its own initiative.

C. A settlement conference is an in-person meeting with all parties, their attorneys, if any, and the judge on the case or another assigned judge. Attendance at a settlement conference must be in-person unless other arrangements have been approved by the Court in advance of the scheduled date for the settlement conference.

D. At the settlement conference, all parties shall make a good faith effort to fully discuss all unresolved issues in dispute.

E. In all contested custody divorce cases and contested custody divorce modification cases, the Court shall not schedule a pre-trial conference date or trial date until a settlement conference has been scheduled and held.

F. Unless scheduled by the Court on its own initiative, to obtain a date for a settlement conference, either party may file a "Request for Case Settlement Conference" form certifying that all interested parties have filed responses to the complaint, that all discovery requests and responses are completed, that the alternative dispute resolution (ADR) screening as required by Section V of this Standing Order has been attended or waived by the Court, and that the parent education class as required by the Court has been attended or waived. The Court shall assign the earliest available date for the settlement conference, but the date shall be no later than 60 days from the filing of the "Request for Case Settlement Conference" form.

G. At least 5 days prior to the settlement conference, each party shall provide the Court and the other party or his or her attorney, if any, a completed settlement conference form including:

1. An outline of agreed upon issues;

2. A general description of the contested issues, and the positions of each party with respect to each issue;

3. A brief, general description of the information that will be presented by each side with respect to each issue;

4. An assessment by each party of the length of trial; and

5. Any other information each party believes will be helpful to the settlement process.

H. The settlement conference form may not be submitted as evidence at trial.

I. If child support is a disputed issue, at least 5 days prior to the settlement conference, each party shall provide proposed child support guidelines worksheets, together with any required documents for determination of a deviation from the calculated amount of child support, including completed financial statements.

J. After settlement conference forms are provided, the parties are encouraged to negotiate and exchange any other necessary documents. Any party may file and serve supplemental settlement conference forms prior to the scheduled settlement conference if the party's analysis or proposal to resolve the issues has changed after reviewing the other party's settlement conference form. If the parties resolve all issues prior to the settlement conference, they should appear at the scheduled settlement conference prepared to submit their written agreement and place the settlement on the record and/or enter final orders resolving the action. If the parties resolve some, but not all, of the issues in dispute, they should be prepared to discuss the remaining contested issues at the settlement conference.

K. At the conclusion of the settlement conference, if the parties reach a full agreement and have executed the necessary paperwork, the Court shall hear the case for finalization at that time.

L. If the parties do not reach a complete agreement of all the issues in dispute, and the parties desire to continue discussing the issues, the Court may schedule a further settlement conference if warranted and time is available.

M. If the parties do not reach a complete agreement of all the issues in dispute and no further settlement conference dates are scheduled, the matter shall proceed to a pre-trial conference and then, if necessary, trial as to the issues remaining in dispute. As long as the parties participated in a settlement conference, no "four-way" meeting of the parties and any attorneys shall be required prior to the pre-trial conference. Up to the date of trial, the parties are encouraged to continue to resolve their disputes.

V. Alternative Dispute Resolution

A. All contested custody divorce cases and contested custody divorce modification cases will be referred by the Court for screening to an approved provider of court-connected dispute resolution services unless otherwise ordered by the Court, or when an order prohibiting contact between the parties is in place. See Rule 2 and Rule 6(b) of S.J.C. Rule 1:18: Uniform Rules on Dispute Resolution. The referral will be made prior to the scheduling of a settlement conference or pre-trial date. This requirement will begin in the Norfolk division on June 1, 2017 and in the remaining divisions on a schedule to be later promulgated by the Chief Justice of the Probate and Family Court.

B. When appropriate, any other disputed matters may be referred

1. To Probation Officers for dispute intervention services in contested matters at any court event; or

2. For screening to other approved providers of court-connected dispute resolution services as defined in Rule 2 of S.J.C. Rule 1:18: Uniform Rules on Dispute Resolution.

Adopted effective June 1, 2017.

Standing Order 3–17.   Fiduciary Litigation Session Pilot Project

1. Purpose. The purpose of this Standing Order is to establish a Fiduciary Litigation Session (hereinafter, "FLS") within the Probate and Family Court Department for certain complex probate litigation cases.

2. Goal. The goal of the FLS is to provide a specialized forum for the speedy resolution of complex probate litigation cases and to provide individualized and collaborative case management to reduce the costs associated with fiduciary litigation.

3. Location. The FLS will be held at the Norfolk Division of the Probate and Family Court and at the Marlborough District Court. The judges of the FLS have the authority to hear and decide matters reassigned to the FLS. Parties or attorneys of record who participate in the pilot project are encouraged to provide feedback so data may be gathered and analyzed to assess the efficacy of the project.

4. Applicable Divisions. The FLS may accept cases from all divisions of the Probate and Family Court.

5. Case Types. Cases that fall into any of the following categories may be accepted into the FLS based primarily on the complexity of the case and the need for substantial case management.

- Contested cases involving the probate of a will, determination of heirs, appointment or removal of a personal representative;

- Contested conservatorship, estate and trust accounts;

- Trust petitions which involve, *inter alia*, the removal of fiduciaries, reformation and modification of trust instruments, interpretation or construction of trust instruments, termination of trusts and allegations of breach of fiduciary duty by trustees;

- Equity complaints on issues involving estates and trusts, such as challenges to the validity of an instrument, removal of trustees, request for instructions, declaratory judgment actions, and breach of fiduciary duty allegations; and

- Removal of conservators.

(a) *No Jury Trial.* A jury trial is not available in any division of the Probate and Family Court, including the FLS. Any case requesting or requiring a jury trial will not be reassigned to the FLS.

6. Who May Request Reassignment. A request for reassignment to the FLS may be made by a Probate and Family Court judge before whom the case is originally assigned (hereinafter, "the assigned judge"), by a party's attorney, or by a self-represented party, in a new or pending matter.

7. Procedure to Request Reassignment. All new cases must continue to be filed in the division of proper venue. For new and pending cases, after the expiration of the answer period or return date, a *Request for Reassignment (MPC 304)* may be filed in the division where the matter is pending for consideration to reassign the case to the FLS.

(a) *Required Notice.* Upon filing, a copy of the *Request for Reassignment* must be sent contemporaneously to the Administrative Office of the Probate and Family Court, and to all attorneys and self-represented parties in the matter, by hand delivery, by United States mail or by email.

(b) *Contesting Reassignment.* Any party who wishes to contest reassignment must file a written response within ten (10) calendar days of the date of service of the *Request for Reassignment* in the division where the matter is pending. Notice must be sent as provided in section (a), above.

(c) *Initial Determination by the Assigned Judge.* A *Request for Reassignment* must first be approved or denied by the assigned judge. This determination may be made

without a hearing or, in the sole discretion of the assigned judge, a hearing may be scheduled. The assigned judge shall have final authority to approve or deny a request.

If the case is denied reassignment to the FLS, a copy of the denied *Request for Reassignment* shall be issued and the case shall proceed on the time standards established by Standing Order 1–06 and, if necessary, the next event shall be scheduled.

The initial determination is not an adjudication and cannot be appealed.

8. Acceptance into the FLS. If a case is approved for reassignment to the FLS by the assigned judge, after the objection period has expired, a copy of the approved *Request for Reassignment* shall be forwarded to the FLS judge, who will make a final determination within ten (10) business days of receipt whether to accept the case into the FLS.

If the case is accepted into the FLS, a *Notice of Reassignment to the Fiduciary Litigation Session (MPC 604)* shall be issued.

If the case is not accepted into the FLS, a *Notice of Denial of Reassignment to the Fiduciary Litigation Session (MPC 605)* shall be issued and the case shall proceed on the time standards established by Standing Order 1–06 and, if necessary, the next event shall be scheduled.

The final determination is not an adjudication and cannot be appealed.

9. Sua Sponte Reassignments to the FLS. *Sua sponte* requests for reassignment to the FLS by the assigned judge shall be made in the same manner as provided in 7 and 8 above.

10. Original Case File; Filing and Docketing Subsequent Documents. Once accepted into the FLS, the original case file shall be transferred to the FLS judge. Docketing shall be up to date and in proper order. All subsequent documents required to be filed shall be filed in the FLS and docketed by the FLS sessions clerk. After 45 days from the conclusion of the matter, the file shall be returned to the register of probate in the division of origin.

11. Case Management. Standing Order 1–06 [Case Management and Time Standards for Cases filed in the Probate and Family Court] shall not apply to cases reassigned to the FLS. Pre–trial procedure shall be governed by Mass.R.Civ.P. 16, any applicable rules of the Supplemental Rules of the Probate and Family Court, and the following.

12. Scheduling Conference. Within 30 days of acceptance into the FLS, attorneys and self-represented parties shall be required to appear at a scheduling conference for such purposes as:

- defining the issues and disputes;

- establishing early and continuing control of the case;

- discouraging wasteful pre-trial activities;

- facilitating settlement, including but not limited to, exploring the use of Alternative Dispute Resolution (ADR) processes; hearing the case on an uncontested basis if settlement has been achieved; and

• establishing a scheduling order appropriate to the case and expediting disposition of the action.

Parties represented by counsel are encouraged to attend the scheduling conference.

At least ten (10) days prior to the scheduling conference, attorneys and self-represented parties shall confer with each other in an attempt to agree upon, or narrow their differences as to a proposed scheduling order which must be filed with the court on or before the date of the scheduling conference.

(a) *Contents.* The scheduling order may set the time to join other parties, amend pleadings, complete discovery and file motions. It may also set a date for a pre-trial conference and set forth the format of the pre-trial memoranda.

(b) *Scheduling Order.* At the conclusion of the scheduling conference, the FLS judge shall issue a scheduling order. A scheduling order may be modified only for good cause and with the approval of the FLS judge.

13. Pre–trial Conference(s). The FLS judge may hold one or more pre-trial conferences following the scheduling conference.

(a) **Attendance.** All parties and attorneys are required to be present at the pre-trial conference, unless waived by motion. Failure of one or more parties to appear shall not preclude the court from proceeding with the pre-trial conference.

(b) *Trial Date(s).* By written order, the trial date(s) shall be set by the FLS judge at the pre-trial conference. Each attorney and self-represented party shall provide the court with a reasonably accurate estimate of the time required to try the case to completion. The FLS judge will impose a reasonable time limitation upon attorneys and self-represented parties to present their case, within the confines of due process, in order to ensure a timely and fair disposition from the court.

14. Motions in limine. Motions *in limine* shall be disposed of as follows:

• Unless a different schedule is ordered by the court, no later than 30 days before trial, attorneys and self-represented parties shall file all motions *in limine*. Prior to filing a motion *in limine*, attorneys and self-represented parties shall confer to identify disputed evidentiary issues that are anticipated to be the subject of motions *in limine*.

• Any opposition to a motion *in limine* shall be filed within ten (10) calendar days of the date of service of the motion. The moving party shall not file a reply to any opposition filed unless requested by the FLS judge.

• Motions *in limine* may be decided on the pleadings or scheduled for a hearing in the sole discretion of the FLS judge.

• All motions *in limine* submitted in accordance with this subsection shall be ruled upon before trial unless the court determines the particular issue of admissibility is better considered at trial.

• Motions *in limine* not filed in accordance with this subsection shall be deemed untimely.

15. Final Trial Management Conference. The FLS judge may hold a final trial management conference to formulate a trial plan, including a plan to facilitate the admission of evidence. The conference must be attended by any self-represented party and at least one attorney who will conduct the trial for each party. At least 24 hours prior to this conference, attorneys and self-represented parties shall exchange and file with the court a proposed judgment or decree.

16. Sanctions. On motion or *sua sponte*, the FLS judge may issue orders, including dismissal of the case and those authorized by Mass.R.Civ.P. 37, if a party or his/her attorney:

• fails to appear at a scheduling, pre-trial or final trial management conference;

• is substantially unprepared to participate in any conference; or

• fails to obey a scheduling, pre-trial, final trial management, or any other order.

17. Imposing Fees and Costs. Instead of or in addition to any other sanction, the FLS judge may order a party, his or her attorney, or both, to pay the reasonable expenses, including attorney's fees incurred because of any noncompliance with this Standing Order.

18. Next Event Scheduling. At the conclusion or cancellation of any court event, until a judgment or decree has issued, the court shall schedule the next court event for the case unless one has already been scheduled.

19. Issuance of Judgment or Decree. A judgment or decree shall issue after conclusion of the trial and receipt of any supplemental submissions ordered by the court.

20. Application. This Standing Order shall apply to all new cases filed on or after its effective date and to all cases pending on its effective date.

Adopted October 31, 2017, effective November 20, 2017. Amended December 4, 2018, effective *nunc pro tunc* November 20, 2018; amended April 18, 2019, effective April 23, 2019.

GUIDELINES FOR JUDICIAL PRACTICE; ABUSE PREVENTION PROCEEDINGS

Table of Guidelines

GENERAL

1:00 IN GENERAL

These Guidelines apply to proceedings under the Abuse Prevention Act, G.L. c. 209A, in the District Court, Boston Municipal Court, Probate and Family Court, and Superior Court departments of the Trial Court, to related criminal proceedings in the District Court, Boston Municipal Court and Superior Court departments and to related matters in the Probate and Family Court Department. These Guidelines also apply to protection orders issued by other jurisdictions. General Laws c. 209A, § 5A provides that "any protection order issued by another jurisdiction, as defined in section one, shall be given full faith and credit throughout the Commonwealth and enforced as if it were issued in the Commonwealth for as long as the order is in effect in the issuing jurisdiction." *See Guideline 8:00*, Venue; Territorial Jurisdiction for Criminal Prosecution of Violations of c. 209A Orders, and *Guideline 14:00*, Filing and Enforcement of Abuse Prevention Orders Issued by Other Jurisdictions. All such proceedings under c. 209A should be undertaken with sensitivity to safety, the need to ensure due process, and the personal and emotional nature of the issues involved.

Please note the word "Clerk" in these Guidelines, unless otherwise expressly provided, shall mean anyone serving in the position of Clerk Magistrate, Clerk of Courts, Clerk or Register. The words "clerk" or "clerk's office" shall mean any staff person working in the office of the Clerk Magistrate, Clerk of Courts, Clerk or Register

The Guidelines describe abuse prevention orders issued under c. 209A in three categories:

Emergency Orders. General Laws c. 209A, § 5 provides temporary relief, "[w]hen the court is closed for business or the plaintiff is unable to appear in court because of severe hardship due to the plaintiff's physical condition ...." When relief is granted under § 5 without the filing of a complaint, a complaint shall be filed in court on the next business day. Orders issued pursuant to § 5 are described in these Guidelines as "emergency" orders. *See Guideline 11:00*, Procedure for Response to Complaints When Court is Not in Session: Judicial Response System, and *Guideline 1:08*, Plaintiff Unable to Appear in Court. Emergency orders expire at the end of the next available court business day when a judge is sitting.

Ex Parte Orders. General Laws c. 209A, § 4 provides for the issuance of abuse prevention orders without notice to the defendant if the plaintiff comes before the court and "demonstrates a substantial likelihood of immediate danger of abuse ...." Orders obtained pursuant to c. 209A, § 4 have a maximum duration of ten court business days and are described in these Guidelines as "*ex parte*" orders. *See Guidelines* 3:00—4:07. They are initiated by the filing of a complaint. A hearing is held forthwith but with no notice to the defendant.

Orders After Notice. Abuse prevention orders issued under c. 209A that are not issued on an emergency or *ex parte* basis require the filing of a complaint, notice to the defendant and an opportunity for the defendant to be heard. Such orders are described in these Guidelines as "orders after notice." These orders may be issued in five different contexts: (1) after a hearing held within ten court business days after the issuance of an *ex parte* order; (2) when no *ex parte* order has been issued, but the defendant is present for the hearing (e.g., at an arraignment); (3) on motion for modification by either party during the life of an order; (4) on the expiration date of an order that was issued after notice; and (5) at a two-party hearing after notice to the defendant, with no prior *ex parte* order having been issued. Initial orders after notice have a maximum duration of one year. Orders issued on the expiration date of an existing order after notice may be issued for any additional time necessary to protect the plaintiff. This could include a permanent order.

Terminated Orders. Previous versions of the Guidelines, certain forms and case law have used the term "vacate" or "vacated order" to describe those orders that have been terminated upon motion of either party or because the plaintiff did not appear at a scheduled hearing. In contexts other than c. 209A, the word "vacate" carries the connotation that the order should not have been originally issued. In the instance of c. 209A orders, however, vacating an order merely terminates the order as of the date it was vacated, with the record of the order remaining in the Statewide Registry of Civil Restraining Orders. Therefore, to avoid confusion, both the

Guidelines and forms will henceforth use the word "terminated" to describe those orders that have been terminated upon motion of either party or because the plaintiff did not appear at a scheduled hearing. Please note, however, "vacate" will still be used when referring to specific language in a statute or case.

Expungement is inappropriate for terminated orders, other than orders obtained through the commission of fraud on the court. *See* Vaccaro v. Vaccaro, 425 Mass. 153, 157–159 (1997), Commissioner of Probation v. Adams, 65 Mass. App. Ct. 725 (2006).

COMMENTARY

The Abuse Prevention Act, G.L. c. 209A, is one of the most sensitive and potentially volatile areas of Trial Court jurisdiction. These Guidelines are intended to provide an analysis of the legal requirements of that law and to recommend particular interpretations in the many areas where the statute is vague or silent. The Guidelines also address the many unique practical, procedural and policy issues presented by c. 209A.

Although the Guidelines apply to c. 209A proceedings in four court departments, some of the Guidelines are not applicable to one or more of the departments because of the differences in jurisdiction on related matters. Nonetheless, all departments are encouraged to be aware of the Guidelines to promote a coordinated response by the Trial Court to domestic violence cases.

While the procedures in G.L. c. 258E for harassment prevention orders are largely parallel to abuse prevention orders under c. 209A, c. 258E permits anyone "suffering from harassment" to seek and obtain a harassment prevention order. Since there are many substantive differences in terms of eligibility, jurisdiction, and available relief, these Guidelines, while informative on procedural issues, are not intended to apply to orders issued under c. 258E.

1:01 PROTECTIVE PURPOSE OF C. 209A

The fundamental purpose of proceedings under c. 209A is to adjudicate the need for protection from abuse and, if that need is found to exist, to issue abuse prevention orders. Given this protective purpose, it is inappropriate for the court in c. 209A proceedings to attempt to reconcile the parties or to mediate disputes.

The court may provide information about domestic violence advocacy, counseling for substance abuse or certified batterer intervention programs, but such services are not a substitute for protective relief in the form of specific orders.

COMMENTARY

The protective purpose of proceedings under c. 209A can be jeopardized if the court attempts to resolve any perceived underlying conflict or problem in the relationship between the parties. While it might seem desirable for the court to play what it believes to be a helpful and constructive role, this is not the purpose of the proceedings. The plaintiff has a right to invoke the court's protective authority against abuse. More importantly, any attempt to explore the nature of the underlying relationship between the parties can inappropriately shift the focus of the proceedings away from the issue of whether the plaintiff requires the protection of the court in the form of an abuse prevention order under c. 209A. Such a shift of focus can weaken the plaintiff's resolve to seek protection and, if a defendant is a batterer, provide a context for a defendant's denial, domination and control. If the plaintiff desires counseling, it is available from professionals who are trained to provide it. The issues for the court before which a plaintiff brings a c. 209A complaint are limited in scope: is protection under the law warranted and, if so, what form should that protection take?

Judges, clerks and other court personnel should be aware that these proceedings often take place in times of great turmoil in the lives of the parties. Both plaintiffs and defendants sometimes come to court dressed differently from other litigants, or even dressed inappropriately, and they may display emotions infrequently observed in a courtroom. While overt disrespect for the court should not be tolerated, some sensitivity is called for. *See* Commonwealth v. Contach, 47 Mass. App. Ct. 247 (1999) (regarding the use of contempt power in an abuse prevention order hearing and citing this Commentary on the need for sensitivity in such matters).

See also Guideline 4:05, Reconciliation; *Guideline 6:01*, Referral for Treatment or Supportive Services; *Guideline 10:00*, Civil Commitment for Alcoholism or Other Substance Abuse; and *Guideline 12:05*, Proceedings in Probate and Family Court: Pre–Trial Conferences and Other Court Proceedings. For a list of certified batterer intervention programs go to www.mass.gov/dph/violence, click on Batterer Intervention Program Services, then click on Certified Batterer Intervention Programs and Services.

1:02　DUE PROCESS CONSIDERATIONS

The adjudication of cases by a neutral court is a fundamental element of due process. In c. 209A cases, as in all other court proceedings, the court is responsible for protecting the rights of the parties and adjudicating each complaint on a case-by-case basis.

Particular care is warranted regarding the following:

(A) An order should not issue unless the court is satisfied that it has jurisdiction, and that the facts alleged constitute abuse, or a substantial likelihood of abuse. *See Guideline 3:02*, Subject Matter Jurisdiction; *Guideline 3:03*, Venue; Territorial Jurisdiction for c. 209A Complaints; *Guideline 3:03A*, Personal Jurisdiction over a Non–Resident Defendant; and *Guideline 3:07*, Conduct of *Ex Parte* Hearings.

(B) The court should require evidence of notice to the defendant before issuing an order for longer than ten court business days. *See Guideline 5:05*, Failure of the Defendant to Appear.

(C) When possible (and when effective service can be made), the court should limit the duration of an *ex parte* order to fewer than the maximum ten days in order to minimize the deprivation of the defendant's rights before the defendant is given notice and an opportunity to be heard. *See Guideline 3:00, Ex Parte* Hearings: General; and *Guideline 5:00*, Scheduling Hearings After Notice.

(D) The plaintiff must prove, by a preponderance of the credible evidence, that the requested relief is legally warranted. *See Guideline 3:06*, Rules of Evidence and Standard and Burden of Proof; *Guideline 5:03*, Rules of Evidence; and *Guideline 5:04*, Standard and Burden of Proof.

(E) In appropriate circumstances, the court may decline to issue an *ex parte* order and delay action on the complaint until both parties have been given notice and an opportunity to be heard.

(F) Although the court should not permit harassment or intimidation, in contested proceedings each party must be given a meaningful opportunity to challenge the other party's evidence. *See Guideline 5:01*, Conduct of Hearings After Notice When Both Parties Appear: General.

(G) In determining whether to exercise jurisdiction under the emergency exception to the Uniform Child Custody Jurisdiction Act (G.L. c. 209B, § 2(a)(3)) in an interstate custody dispute, a judge must, at minimum, hear argument from and review the affidavits from both parents. Orchard v. Orchard, 43 Mass. App. Ct. 775, 781 n.11 (1997), citing Umina v. Malbica, 27 Mass. App. Ct. 351, 360 n.11 (1989).

COMMENTARY

As recognition that its scope and nature has increased, the issue of domestic violence has become the focus of legitimate and increasing public concern. However, that concern must not be permitted to affect or diminish the court's responsibility to remain neutral, to protect the rights of the parties in each case, and to address each case individually on its own merits. "Whether a defendant's constitutional rights have been violated [in a c. 209A proceeding] will depend on the fairness of a particular proceeding." Frizado v. Frizado, 420 Mass. 592, 598 (1995). *See also*, C.O. v. M.M., 442 Mass. 648, 656–659 (2004) (court found that defendant's right to due process had been denied where defendant was not given the opportunity to present or cross-examine witnesses during a hearing on the question of continuing a temporary order). *See Guideline 3:00, Ex Parte* Hearings: General.

Massachusetts's courts may issue an abuse prevention order under c. 209A against an out-of-state defendant even in cases where the court does not have personal jurisdiction over the defendant. Caplan v. Donovan, 450 Mass. 463, 463–64, (2008), *cert. denied*, Donovan v. Caplan, 553 U.S. 1018 (2008). However, such orders "cannot impose any personal obligations on a defendant, and [are] limited to prohibiting actions of the defendant." *Id.* at 469–471. *See Guideline 3:03A*, Personal Jurisdiction over a Non–Resident Defendant.

1:03　PROCEDURAL RULES; DISCOVERY

In the Probate and Family Court Department, the Massachusetts Rules of Domestic Relations Procedure apply to c. 209A actions. In the Boston Municipal Court, District Court and Superior Court departments, the provisions of the Massachusetts Rules of Civil Procedure may be applied.

Discovery orders are within the court's discretion and should be issued only after a hearing and only upon a showing that such discovery is necessary to provide specific information essential to the adjudication of the case or the issuance of particular abuse prevention orders.

COMMENTARY

With the exception of the Probate and Family Court Department, where the Massachusetts Rules of Domestic Relations Procedure specifically apply to c. 209A actions, none of the departments of the Trial Court with jurisdiction over c. 209A proceedings have formal procedural rules that specifically govern c. 209A proceedings. Chapter 209A sets out procedural requirements that must be followed. In addition, the Rules of Civil Procedure may be applied in the District Court, Boston Municipal Court and Superior Court departments, where the provisions of c. 209A itself leave a procedural question unanswered.

Discovery is not mentioned in c. 209A and should be considered a matter of the court's discretion, to be allowed only when determined by the court to be necessary for a particular purpose. Discovery should not be ordered if the information would be merely "relevant" or "interesting." The test should be one of necessity. Generally, the testimony of the parties and any witnesses will provide an adequate basis for the adjudication of domestic abuse cases and, when warranted, the issuance of abuse prevention orders.

1:04 COURT'S RELATIONSHIP WITH LOCAL ADVOCACY GROUPS

Courts should be open to contact from advocacy groups concerned with the issues of domestic violence. Meeting to discuss appropriate matters with representatives of such groups can be constructive for judges and other court personnel, as well as for the members of the groups themselves.

COMMENTARY

While the effectiveness of court procedures can be improved through open and constructive dialogue with all individuals and entities involved, it is essential that such meetings are open to all court personnel, the general public, and the defense bar, among others. The Supreme Judicial Court Committee on Judicial Ethics ("CJE") has issued two opinion letters on the subject of participation by judges in roundtable meetings with advocacy groups. *See* CJE Opinion 98–16, (Sept. 15, 1998) http://www.mass.gov/courts/sjc/cje/98–16h.html; CJE Opinion 01–7, (May 31, 2001) http://www.mass.gov/courts/sjc/cje/2001–7h.html

The opinion letters provide specific guidelines under which the propriety of judicial participation in roundtable meetings should be assessed. Judicial attendance at roundtables or other forums is only appropriate when invitations are extended to people representing a variety of perspectives so there is no appearance of being "exposed to an essentially one-sided format." CJE Opinion 01–7. *See also* CJE Opinion 98–16.

The occasional participation of the court with advocacy groups in a mutual exchange of appropriate information and a discussion of concerns, does not jeopardize the court's fundamental role as neutral finder of fact, as long as substantive matters and individual pending cases are not discussed. *See Guideline 2:08*, Role of Advocates in Assisting Parties; Guideline 3:09, Role of Advocates at *Ex Parte* Hearings; and *Guideline 5:02*, Role of Advocates at Hearings After Notice.

Providing essentially a two-part test to assess the propriety of judicial participation in roundtable meetings, the CJE indicated that it would focus on a consideration of the specific subject matter discussed at the meetings and the frequency of the judge's participation in those meetings. CJE Opinion 98–16. "Confidence in the judge's impartiality will not be undermined and any perception of favoritism will be sufficiently minimized if participation is occasional, and if the judge avoids repeated attendance at meetings when substantive issues are to be discussed in a one-sided fashion." *Id.* For example, the CJE determined that judicial participation in meetings at which procedural issues are addressed, such as logistical concerns regarding the processing of petitions, is not prejudicial to the interests of defendants and any perception of partiality would be mitigated by the beneficial nature of such meetings. *Id.* The opinion letters clearly state that a judge's frequent participation in roundtables or attendance at times when the discussion concerns issues not related to court administration is inappropriate. CJE Opinion 01–7. As such, in order to mitigate the risk of compromising the court's appearance of impartiality as a result of judicial participation in such meetings, "judges may consider notifying the private bar that they will be attending a meeting" or request that the organizers of an event make such notice. CJE Opinion 98–16. Judges may also consider "limiting attendance to a designated portion of the meeting, perhaps at the beginning, when matters related to court administration could be placed on the agenda," thereby allowing the judge to participate only in those neutral matters. *Id.*

1:05 PUBLIC ACCESS TO C. 209A CASE FILES

Public access to documents and case files in c. 209A proceedings is governed by c. 209A itself and by the law and procedures for court impoundment of court documents generally.

All records of cases in which the plaintiff and/or the defendant is a minor must be withheld from public inspection except by order of the court. *See* G.L. c. 209A, § 8; *Guideline 1:06*, Minors as Plaintiffs in c. 209A Actions; and *Guideline 1:06A*, Minors as Defendants in c. 209A Actions.

Pursuant to G.L. c. 209A, § 8, certain portions of all cases are "confidential" and shall be withheld from public inspection except by order of the court. The confidential information consists of the plaintiff's residential address, residential telephone number and workplace name, address, and telephone number. However, the plaintiff's residential address and workplace address shall appear on the order and be accessible to the defendant and the defendant's attorney unless the plaintiff specifically requests that the information be withheld from the order.

The confidential information is provided to the court by the plaintiff's completion of the Plaintiff Confidential Information Form (FA/HA–8). This form is kept by the court but is not part of the public record. Confidential information shall be accessible at all reasonable times to the plaintiff and plaintiff's attorney, to those specifically authorized by the plaintiff to obtain such information and, if necessary in the performance of their duties, to prosecutors, victim witness advocates, domestic violence victim counselors, sexual assault counselors, and law enforcement officers. Any authorized person who wishes to access the confidential information must complete a Request for Access to Plaintiff Confidential Information (FA/HA–7). The clerk's office should request identification from all individuals requesting confidential information.

The provisions of § 8 apply to any protection order issued by another jurisdiction that is filed with the court pursuant to G.L. c. 209A, § 5A. Confidential portions of the record are not deemed to be public records under the provisions of G.L. c. 4, § 7, clause 26. G.L. c. 209A, § 8.

COMMENTARY

Plaintiff safety is the most important aspect of the confidentiality requirements in c. 209A proceedings. In every case, § 8 prohibits public access to certain categories of information about the plaintiff. Section 8 also permits the plaintiff to request that the plaintiff's residential address and workplace address be withheld from the order so as to be inaccessible to the defendant and the defendant's attorney.

The confidential information is provided to the court by the plaintiff's completion of the Plaintiff Confidential Information Form (FA/HA–8). This form is kept by the court but is not part of the public record.

Before any confidential information is provided to a person authorized to receive it pursuant to G. L. c. 209A, § 8, the case file should be carefully reviewed to determine if the information has also been impounded. *See* Memorandum from Chief Justice for Administration and Management Barbara Dortch–Okara, November 10, 2000, "Amendments to the confidentiality provisions of c. 209A". http://www.mass.gov/courts/209a/docs/aotcconfidentiality-memo.pdf. The person requesting the information must complete a Request for Access to Plaintiff Confidential Information (FA/HA–7). The clerk's office should request identification from all individuals requesting confidential information.

The plaintiff may also request that other information be impounded, that is, kept confidential from the general public by court order. The plaintiff may use the Motion for Impoundment & Affidavit (FA/HA–8).

Except as noted above, judicial records of c. 209A proceedings are presumptively open to the public. The Boston Herald, Inc. v. Richard J. Sharpe, 432 Mass. 593, 608 (2000).

It should be noted that, pursuant to G.L. c. 6, § 172D, child support enforcement agencies may be granted access to records contained in the Statewide Registry of Civil Restraining Orders.

1:06   MINORS AS PLAINTIFFS IN C. 209A ACTIONS

Generally, if a minor (person under the age of 18) seeks an abuse prevention order, a parent or guardian should file the petition on behalf of the minor. If a minor plaintiff appears in court seeking an abuse prevention order against someone who is not a family member or a caretaker, the judge should attempt to secure the presence of a parent or guardian before proceeding with the hearing. If that is not practical, the judge may consider obtaining some form of authorization for the minor to proceed without a parent or guardian present. If neither is practical, the judge should consider appointing a or counsel for the minor before proceeding with the hearing. However, particularly in the case of a mature minor, the court should not refuse to issue an abuse prevention order simply because no adult is present.

Where a minor plaintiff appears in court, without a parent or guardian, seeking an abuse prevention order against a family member or caretaker, the judge should appoint a *guardian ad litem* or counsel for the minor before proceeding with the hearing. If the judge finds a basis to issue an order, the judge should direct that, pursuant to G.L. c. 119, § 51A, a report be filed by court personnel with the Department of Children and Families. In appropriate circumstances, it may be necessary to request that the Department respond to the court on an emergency basis to take custody of the minor.

Although by statute all case records of cases involving minor plaintiffs must be withheld from public inspection except by order of the court, *see* G.L. c. 209A, § 8, the courtroom should not be closed during c. 209A proceedings involving minors unless the strict requirements for closing the courtroom have been met. *See* Commentary to *Guideline 3:04*, Public Nature of *Ex Parte* Hearings.

COMMENTARY

The court should be conscious of the sensitive nature of a request for an abuse prevention order on behalf of a minor. Although proceedings in the Juvenile Court (or the Juvenile Sessions of the District Court in those courts that retain juvenile jurisdiction) are closed to the public, there is no similar provision allowing closure during proceedings under c. 209A involving minors. However, care should be taken to minimize, to the extent possible, disclosure of unnecessary identifying information about the minors involved in such proceedings. Cases involving minors may require involvement of other governmental agencies and the court should not hesitate to direct court personnel to notify the Department of Children and Families or any other agency where such notifications are required or advisable.

Although a petition under c. 209A on behalf of a minor should generally be made by a parent or guardian, in some circumstances the court can and should allow a minor to proceed without a parent or guardian. The court should not refuse to act solely because the court cannot secure the presence of a parent or guardian, particularly where the minor is mature (16 or 17), and where the defendant is an intimate partner or a family member who is not a parent or guardian or where there is an imminent threat of bodily injury. Authorization from a parent or guardian in writing or over the phone may, in appropriate circumstances, substitute for the presence of such a person.

The standard for issuance of an order under c. 209A is the same for minors as for adults. Abuse is defined as attempting to cause or causing physical harm, placing another in fear of imminent serious physical harm or causing another to engage involuntarily in sexual relations by force, threat or duress. G.L. c. 209A, § 1. Duress requires an immediate threat, no reasonable opportunity to escape, and no other choice in the circumstances. Smith v. Jones, 67 Mass. App. Ct. 129, 136–137 (2006), citing Commonwealth v. Perl, 50 Mass. App. Ct. 445, 446–450 (2000). Sexual contact between minors that is not accompanied by force, threat, or duress does not meet the definition of abuse, although it may constitute a criminal offense. *Id.*

1:06A   MINORS AS DEFENDANTS IN C. 209A ACTIONS

A parent or guardian should accompany a minor defendant (under the age of 18) at a hearing involving a request for an abuse prevention order by a plaintiff who is not a family member or caretaker. If a minor defendant appears alone, the judge should attempt to secure the presence of a parent or guardian before proceeding with the hearing. If that is not practical, the judge may consider obtaining some form of authorization from a parent or guardian for the minor to proceed alone. If neither is practical (or if the abuse prevention order is sought by a family member or caretaker), the judge should consider appointing a *guardian ad litem* for the minor.

Under c. 209A, the judge may order a minor defendant to refrain from abusing the plaintiff and to refrain from contacting the plaintiff. In some cases, this request might be made by a family member or caretaker in which case such an order might result in the defendant having to vacate and stay away from his or her residence. The statute does not explicitly provide that the judge may order a minor defendant to vacate and stay away from his or her residence, although this Guideline takes the position that such authority is inferred from the overall protective purpose of the statute. If a minor defendant is ordered to vacate or stay away from his or her home, the parent or guardian retains the responsibility to provide a safe residence for the minor. The parent or guardian should be required to identify where the minor defendant will reside. If no appropriate placement is identified, the judge should request, pursuant to G.L. c. 119, § 51A, that court personnel immediately file a report with the Department of Children and Families and that the Department respond to the court on an emergency basis to take custody of the minor.

If the plaintiff seeks an abuse prevention order against a minor defendant who is a family member, the judge should consider informing the plaintiff that the Juvenile Court can provide information about possible related actions, such as delinquency, criminal, mental health or child in need of services complaints. *See Guideline 10:03*, Care and Protection Proceedings; *Guideline 10:05*, Child in Need of Services (CHINS) Actions; and *Guideline 10:06*, Mental Health Actions. Providing this information should be in addition to, and not in lieu of, receiving, hearing and ruling on the c. 209A complaint. In appropriate circumstances, the judge may also consider requesting that court personnel file a report with the Department of Children and Families pursuant to G.L. c. 119, § 51A.

Although all records of cases involving minor defendants must be withheld from public inspection, except by order of the court, *see* G.L. c. 209A, § 8, the courtroom should not be closed unless the strict standards for closing the courtroom have been met. *See* Commentary to *Guideline 3:04*, Public Nature of *Ex Parte* Hearings.

COMMENTARY

The court should be conscious of the sensitive nature of a request for an abuse prevention order against a minor defendant. Although proceedings in the Juvenile Court (or the Juvenile Sessions of the District Court in those courts that retain juvenile jurisdiction) are closed to the public, there is no similar provision that permits closing the courtroom during proceedings under c. 209A involving minors. However, care should be taken to minimize, to the extent possible, disclosure of unnecessary identifying information about the minors involved in such proceedings.

Judges should be aware that orders that might otherwise be appropriate for adults might not be appropriate when dealing with minors. For example, an order for a minor defendant to vacate and remain away from the home might render a minor homeless. If the judge finds a basis to issue an abuse prevention order against a minor defendant at the request of a family member or caretaker that requires the defendant to vacate his or her residence, the parent or guardian remains responsible for providing a safe residence for the minor defendant. Often a family member or close friend can provide such a residence, but if no such placement is identified during the hearing, the court should request that the Department of Children and Families respond on an emergency basis to take custody of the minor defendant. The court should develop a working relationship with the Department that will facilitate such requests when they are necessary.

Similarly, an order to stay away from school might result in a truancy situation. Such an issue should be brought to the attention of parents, guardians or, if involved, the Department of Children and Families.

Cases involving minor defendants will often require involvement of other governmental agencies and the court should not hesitate to direct court personnel to notify the Department of Children and Families or other agencies where such notifications are required or advisable. Depending on the situation, care and protection, child in need of services, mental health or delinquency proceedings may provide needed services to the minor defendant and his or her family. *See Guideline 10:03*, Care and Protection Proceedings; *Guideline 10:05*, Child in Need of Services (CHINS) Actions; and *Guideline 10:06*, Mental Health Actions.

The standard for issuance of an order under c. 209A is the same for minors as for adults. Abuse is defined as attempting to cause or causing physical harm, placing another in fear of imminent serious physical harm or causing another to engage involuntarily in sexual relations by force, threat or duress. G.L. c. 209A, § 1. Duress requires an immediate threat, no reasonable opportunity to escape and no other choice in the circumstances. Smith v. Jones, 67 Mass. App. Ct. 129, 136–137 (2006) citing Commonwealth v. Perl, 50 Mass. App. Ct. 445, 446–450 (2000). Sexual contact between minors that is not accompanied by force, threat, or duress does not meet the definition of abuse, although it may constitute a criminal offense. *Id.*

1:07 NON-ENGLISH SPEAKING PARTIES IN C. 209A ACTIONS

Non–English speaking parties have a right to the assistance of a qualified interpreter in court proceedings. *See* G.L. c. 221C, § 2. The Office of Court Interpreter Services (OCIS) schedules and deploys spoken language interpreters to all departments of the Trial Court. Upon written request, OCIS will provide interpreters to appear in criminal or civil proceedings. In emergency situations, where it is not feasible to schedule interpreter services in advance, upon request from a court, OCIS will attempt to provide an interpreter, and, if none is available, will provide interpreter services via telephone.

The Massachusetts Commission for the Deaf and Hard of Hearing is statutorily responsible for providing interpreters for American (and other) sign languages. *See* G.L. c. 6, §§ 194 and 196. All requests for sign language interpreters, however, must be made through OCIS, which enters all requests directly into the Commission's scheduling database.

If no OCIS interpreter is available, either in person or via telephone, as a last resort, the court should determine whether any court personnel might be able to interpret for the parties. If no qualified interpreter is available, either in person or through the telephone, and there is no other option for obtaining interpreter services, individuals who have accompanied the plaintiff to court, or who happen to be in the court and speak the plaintiff's language may be asked to assist by interpreting for the plaintiff. Courts should never allow minor children to serve as interpreters, even in emergency situations. All interpreters should be sworn and should give their names for the record.

Courts should never permit the defendant in the c. 209A action, nor anyone accompanying the defendant to court, to interpret for the plaintiff, even if there are no other interpreter services available. Similarly, the plaintiff should never be permitted to interpret for the defendant.

COMMENTARY

Chapter 221C of the General Laws sets out a process by which interpreters are to be made available to every non-English speaker in a "legal proceeding." This chapter appears to apply to civil, as well as criminal, proceedings, and to everyone participating, whether as a witness or a party.

Interpreter services may be arranged by the court by contacting OCIS at (617) 878-0343. Guidelines for telephone interpreting are posted on the OCIS webpage of the Trial Court's intranet site at http://trialcourtweb/admin/planning/interpreters.html.

If an interpreter is assisting a non-English speaking plaintiff in completing an Affidavit, the plaintiff should write the affidavit in his or her language. The interpreter shall then provide a translation. The interpreter may use form entitled Translation of Affidavit (FA/HA–15). If the non-English speaking person is not literate, he or she should dictate the information to the interpreter, who will then also complete a translation of the Affidavit.

1:08 PLAINTIFF UNABLE TO APPEAR IN COURT

When a plaintiff is unable to appear in court because of severe hardship due to the plaintiff's physical condition, G.L. c. 209A, § 5 allows a representative of the plaintiff to appear in court on the plaintiff's behalf and file a complaint requesting an abuse prevention order. The plaintiff's representative must also file an affidavit describing the circumstances that prevent the plaintiff from personally appearing.

In such circumstances, any justice of the Superior Court, Probate and Family Court, District Court or Boston Municipal Court may grant an abuse prevention order, provided that the plaintiff is able to demonstrate a substantial likelihood of immediate danger of abuse.

COMMENTARY

General Laws c. 209A, § 5 provides that when "the plaintiff is unable to appear in court because of severe hardship due to the plaintiff's physical condition, any justice of the superior, probate and family, district or Boston municipal court departments may grant relief to the plaintiff as provided under section four if the plaintiff demonstrates a substantial likelihood of immediate danger of abuse."

In some cases, the plaintiff's physical condition may be only a temporary barrier to his or her ability to appear in court (e.g., a plaintiff may be hospitalized and unable to be present in court to request an abuse prevention order, but will be physically able to appear at future dates). In other cases, the plaintiff's physical disability may prevent him or her from being able to appear in court at any foreseeable point in the future (e.g., the plaintiff is elderly and bedridden).

In handling abuse prevention orders involving plaintiffs who cannot be physically present, it is essential that the court confirm the plaintiff's identity. The court must also be satisfied as to the identity of the plaintiff's representative and the representative's authority to act on behalf of the plaintiff. In many cases, the local police may be able to assist the court in making these determinations.

Where the plaintiff's inability to appear is only temporary, the court may issue a temporary order following the Guidelines established for conducting an *ex parte* hearing and issuing an *ex parte* order. *See Guidelines 3:00–3:09*, generally, and *Guidelines 4:00–4:07*, generally. The court should take the plaintiff's physical condition into consideration in scheduling the hearing after notice within ten court business days. In this circumstance, it is expected that the plaintiff would be able to be present for the hearing after notice.

Where the plaintiff's physical condition is expected to prevent him or her from appearing at the courthouse, either permanently or within the ten court business days in which the hearing after notice will occur, the court, in its discretion, may conduct the hearing by telephone. In this circumstance, the court should conduct the hearing in the courtroom using a speakerphone. In this way, the hearing will be recorded. This procedure can be utilized for the *ex parte* hearing as well as for the first hearing after notice and any subsequent hearings.

1:09   PLAINTIFF IN COURT WITHOUT TERRITORIAL JURISDICTION/PROPER VENUE

Proceedings under c. 209A shall be filed, heard and determined in the court having venue over the plaintiff's residence. If the plaintiff has fled a residence or household to avoid abuse, the plaintiff may commence the action either in the court with venue over the prior residence or in the court with venue over the present residence. *See G.L. c. 209A, § 2; Guideline 3:03*, Venue; Territorial Jurisdiction for c. 209A Complaints.

Occasionally, a plaintiff may mistakenly seek an abuse prevention order in a court that does not have venue over the plaintiff's prior or current residence. In that event, the court has two options. The primary issue for the court in making this decision is to ensure the safety of the plaintiff.

If the court is satisfied that the plaintiff can safely travel to the appropriate court, that it is early enough in the day, and the plaintiff has appropriate transportation, the court may send the plaintiff to that court. The court should notify the appropriate court of the plaintiff's impending arrival in order to ensure that the plaintiff may be heard that same day. If there is any question of the plaintiff's safety or the ability to be heard on the same day (whether due to scheduling issues in

the other court or the plaintiff's inability to travel, etc.), the court should not send the plaintiff to the other court.

If the judge makes the determination that it would not be appropriate to send the plaintiff to the court with venue for any reason, including, but not limited to, safety concerns, inability of the plaintiff to travel to the other court, or lateness of day, the judge may act for the appropriate court and conduct a hearing on the plaintiff's request.

This *ex parte* order should be issued for ten court business days or for such shorter duration as the court finds appropriate. The *ex parte* order should be returnable to the court with proper venue and the hearing after notice shall occur in that court.

COMMENTARY

Trial Court judges have been authorized by the Chief Justice for Administration and Management, pursuant to G.L. c. 211 § 9, to conduct a c. 209A hearing on behalf of the appropriate Trial Court Department and Division, when a plaintiff appears in a court location that does not have proper venue to hear the matter and the judge determines that it would not be appropriate to send the plaintiff to the court with venue for any reason, including, but not limited to, safety concerns, inability of the plaintiff to travel to the other court, or lateness of day.

When the plaintiff appears at a court without venue (Court A), and the judge determines to act on behalf of the court with venue (Court B), the following steps must be taken:

Court A:

1. The clerk's office in Court A shall open the case in Court A.

2. The clerk's office in Court A shall immediately contact the clerk's office in Court B to inform them of the judge's decision to hear the case and to determine an acceptable return date should an order issue.

3. The probation department in Court A shall obtain the criminal record and any record in the Statewide Registry of Civil Restraining Orders for the defendant.

4. The clerk's office in Court A shall check the Warrant Management System for the defendant's name to ascertain the existence of any warrants. If the matter is in the Probate and Family Court, the staff that currently checks the Warrant Management System for the defendant's name to ascertain the existence of any warrants shall conduct such a check.

5. The judge in Court A will conduct the hearing. The docket shall indicate that the session was conducted on behalf of Court B. All subsequent hearings, if any, will be held in Court B and any initial order will be returnable to Court B.

6. If an abuse prevention order is issued, the clerk's office in Court A shall immediately provide copies of the complaint and order to the appropriate police department for service on the defendant.

7. The clerk's office in Court A should clearly specify on all transmittals or copies provided to the police that the return of service must be delivered to Court B. Should the return of service be delivered in error to Court A, Court A shall immediately fax the return of service to Court B and mail the original return of service to Court B.

8. The probation department in Court A shall promptly enter any order issued into the CARI system for transmittal to the Statewide Registry of Civil Restraining Orders.

9. The clerk's office in Court A shall immediately notify the clerk's office in Court B by telephone whether or not an order has been issued and the date of return.

10. Court A will docket that the matter is being forwarded to Court B with the original papers and docket, that the matter will

proceed in Court B as if originally commenced therein, and will close its case.

11. The clerk's office in Court A must immediately transmit electronically or by facsimile a copy of the case file and docket, which docket shall include an indication of the location of the court recording of the hearing conducted in Court A.

12. By the end of the next business day, the clerk's office at Court A shall mail the original c. 209A case file and docket to Court B. Court A will retain a copy of the case file and docket.

Court B:

1. Court B shall open a case with its own docket number no later than the end of the next business day after the initial hearing and the matter shall proceed in Court B as if originally commenced therein.

2. The docket in Court B shall indicate that the matter has been transferred from Court A.

3. If Court B modifies or extends the original order, the clerk's office in Court B shall be responsible for providing copies of the modified or extended order to the appropriate police department for service on the defendant.

4. If Court B modifies or extends the original order, the probation department in Court B shall be responsible for entry of the modified or extended order into the GARI system for transmittal to the Statewide Registry of Civil Restraining Orders.

Referrals to Court with Venue: If the court refers the plaintiff to a court with venue, and the plaintiff already has completed an affidavit and/or Plaintiff Confidential Information Form and/or Defendant Information Form, the clerk's office should transmit the plaintiff's completed affidavit and forms to the proper court, so as to expedite the proceedings and to prevent the need for the plaintiff to complete an additional affidavit or forms. The papers may be sent by facsimile and/or given to the plaintiff to take to the court with venue.

Interdepartmental Transfers: There will be cases in which a plaintiff appears in a court without proper venue and the judge's determination to act on behalf of the court with venue will result in the judge acting on behalf of another Trial Court Department and returning the case to the court with venue in the other Trial Court Department.

It is anticipated that such cases will usually involve divisions of District Court Department and the Boston Municipal Court Department.

However, there may be instances where a plaintiff comes to a Probate and Family Court Division without venue. Before returning the matter to the Probate and Family Court with venue, the court should ascertain whether the plaintiff has the ability to travel to that Probate and Family Court or whether the District or Boston Municipal Court with venue might afford better access for the plaintiff.

In addition, there may be cases in which a plaintiff has come to a District or Boston Municipal Court without venue and the court learns that the parties in the c. 209A matter are also parties in a pending action in the Probate and Family Court involving issues of child custody or visitation. The District or Boston Municipal Court may consider having the matter returned to the Probate and Family Court with venue after determining the plaintiff's ability to travel to that court and whether the plaintiff consents to this decision.

1:10 PLAINTIFF IN A COURT WHERE THERE IS NO JUDGE SITTING

When a plaintiff seeking an abuse prevention order under c. 209A appears in a court where no judge is presently sitting, the clerk's office should assist the plaintiff in obtaining a hearing by telephone with a judge from the same department sitting in another location. If the court has jurisdiction over the plaintiff's residence, *see* G.L. c. 209A, § 2, the plaintiff

should not be sent to a different court or instructed to wait until the Judicial Response System goes into operation at 4:30 p.m.

An *ex parte* order issued over the telephone during court business hours should be for a duration of ten court business days or such shorter time as the court finds appropriate. The hearing after notice should be scheduled for hearing on a date on which a judge will be sitting in that court.

COMMENTARY

When the plaintiff appears at the court with venue over the plaintiff's residence and there is no judge available, the clerk's office should process the complaint for the abuse prevention order. The clerk's office in the original court (Court A) must gather all of the necessary paperwork, including a blank order with its docket number, the complaint and affidavit prepared by the plaintiff, the defendant's criminal record, if any, any record in the Statewide Registry of Civil Restraining Orders, and the results of a check of the Warrant Management System. These documents must then be transmitted by facsimile to the judge in the other court who will conduct the hearing (Court B).

The judge in Court B will, after reviewing the documents, telephone the clerk's office in Court A. The judge will conduct a hearing on the request for a c. 209A abuse prevention order. If possible, the judge should conduct the hearing with the plaintiff on speakerphone in a courtroom, thus ensuring that the hearing is preserved on the record.

If the judge determines that the plaintiff has met the burden for the issuance of the order, the order should be issued for ten court business days or a shorter duration at the discretion of the court. The hearing after notice should be scheduled for a date on which a judge will be present in Court A.

This situation is distinguishable from emergency orders issued when the court is not in session. Those orders should expire at the end of the next court day. *See* Commentary to *Guideline 11:00*, Procedure for Response to Complaints When Court is Not in Session.

Following the hearing, the judge in Court B should send a copy of the issued order to Court A. It is the responsibility of the clerk's office in Court A to transmit the order to the appropriate police department for service on the defendant and to the probation department in Court A for the immediate input of the order into the Statewide Registry of Civil Restraining Orders. The judge in Court B should also send the signed original documents to Court A by mail.

This procedure also may be used when the judge in a one-judge court must recuse him- or herself.

1:11 PLAINTIFF'S REQUESTED ORDER WILL CONTRADICT EXISTING PROBATE AND FAMILY COURT ORDER

At the beginning of each hearing, the judge should ask the plaintiff whether there are any outstanding court orders involving the same parties in the same or a different court. Except as noted below, the court should not order any relief that is inconsistent with any existing order in any other court. *See Guideline 13:00*, Assignment of Justices of the Probate and Family Court Department to Modify Inconsistent Orders, with regard to inconsistencies between an order issued by a District Court, the Boston Municipal Court or the Superior Court and a decision of a Probate and Family Court.

In emergency circumstances, the District Court, Boston Municipal Court, or Superior Court (including a judge on the Judicial Response System) may issue an order that conflicts with an existing custody or visitation order issued by a Probate and Family Court. These emergency circumstances are limited to those cases in which there is an allegation or threat of serious harm to the children who are the subject of an existing custody or visitation order and the plaintiff is unable to reach the Probate and Family Court. In such cases, the judge in the other court may issue the requested order for a short period of time (usually no more than 72 hours) to permit the plaintiff to go to the Probate and Family Court for relief, and should make findings of fact setting forth the reasons for that order. *See* Smith v. Joyce, 421 Mass. 520, 523–524 (1995).

COMMENTARY

If there is an existing Probate and Family Court custody and/or visitation order, the court in another department of the Trial Court (second court) may not issue custody or support orders. If a current Probate and Family Court order exists but the plaintiff seeks an order from a second court ordering the defendant to stay away from, or to have no contact with, the defendant's minor children because of allegation or threat of serious harm to the children, that court may enter a temporary order of protection (usually no more than 72 hours) and refer the plaintiff to the Probate and Family Court for an immediate review hearing. Since the Probate and Family Court has superseding jurisdiction in custody and support matters, its exclusive jurisdiction over visitation matters may be seriously hampered by a subsequent no-contact or stay-away order issued by a different court and made applicable to the defendant's minor children. *See Guideline 2:07*, Referral to and from Other Courts and Avoiding Inconsistent Orders; *Guideline 4:01*, Content of *Ex Parte* Orders; *Guideline 5:01*, Conduct of Hearings After Notice When Both Parties Appear: General; and *Guideline 6:00*, Orders After Notice: General. *See also Guideline 13:00*, Assignment of Justices of the Probate and Family Court Department to Modify Inconsistent Orders.

While the preferred practice is to avoid inconsistent or conflicting orders, and while the Probate and Family Court Department has

superseding jurisdiction over custody issues and exclusive jurisdiction for visitation orders, in emergency circumstances, a District Court, Boston Municipal Court, or Superior Court may issue an order which conflicts with an existing custody or visitation order issued by the Probate and Family Court. These emergency circumstances are limited to those cases in which there is an allegation or threat of serious harm to the children who are the subject of an existing custody or visitation order, and the plaintiff is unable to reach the Probate and Family Court. In such cases, the judge in the other court may issue the requested order for a short period of time (usually no more than 72 hours) to permit the plaintiff to go to the Probate and Family Court to seek the same relief. *See Guideline 2:07*, Referral to and from Other Courts and Avoiding Inconsistent Orders.

Where there is an existing c. 209A abuse prevention order in the second court and the judge in the second court determines to suspend the custody and/or visitation order of the Probate and Family Court for a short period of time, it is imperative that the judge in the second court carefully amend the order to provide the temporary relief while not changing the other preexisting terms of the order. In this regard, it is important that the original expiration date remains in effect and that the 72 hours or less period applies only to the custody and/or visitation terms.

Whenever a case is filed in the Probate and Family Court and there is an outstanding order issued by the District Court, Administrative Order 96–1 provides that the Boston Municipal Court or the Superior Court, the Probate and Family Court justice shall be temporarily assigned to the department that issued the outstanding order for the sole purpose of hearing and determining whether to modify, extend or vacate[1] the outstanding order to eliminate any conflict between the existing order and a decision of the Probate and Family Court. *See Guideline 13:00*, Assignment of Justices of the Probate and Family Court Department to Modify Inconsistent Orders.

1 Please note that Administrative Order 96–1 uses the term "vacate."

FILING OF THE COMPLAINT

2:00   DESIGNATION OF STAFF

The Clerk and the Chief Probation Officer in each court should designate particular personnel to respond to plaintiffs seeking relief under c. 209A.

COMMENTARY

The nature of c. 209A cases makes the selection of personnel to handle these actions particularly important. Personnel assignments should be made with an eye toward choosing people who will be sensitive to the safety concerns and the often intimate nature of the issues involved, as well as to the potential that the parties are unfamiliar with court procedures. Even in small courts, more than one person should be assigned to handle these cases to ensure that plaintiffs are assisted throughout the business day and when the primary employee is not available. Designated personnel should be thoroughly familiar with the procedures and forms involved in c. 209A cases and should receive regular training in domestic violence issues. Such training should include a thorough review of these Guidelines.

2:01   ASSISTING THE PLAINTIFF

The primary role of court personnel when a plaintiff seeks relief under c. 209A is to facilitate the filing of the complaint. The plaintiff should be questioned briefly about the nature of the case and then assisted in completing the complaint form, affidavit and other documents. Court personnel should proceed with patience, respect, professionalism and objectivity, but should not offer legal advice. In appropriate circum-

stances, court personnel should refer the plaintiff to the victim witness advocates who are permitted to offer additional assistance and advice to plaintiffs.

Only the judge should rule on the facts of a request for a c. 209A order. Court personnel should not attempt to "screen out" complaints or investigate the accuracy of allegations. Nor should they challenge a plaintiff's motives or intent or attempt to refer the plaintiff to service providers in lieu of filing the complaint.

COMMENTARY

The role of the clerk's office in processing c. 209A cases is to provide assistance. If it appears that the complaint is not one within the subject matter jurisdiction of c. 209A, or that the court does not have territorial jurisdiction over the action, the matter should be referred to the Clerk–Magistrate or an Assistant Clerk–Magistrate, or, in the Probate and Family Court, to the Register or an Assistant Register, Judicial Case Manager or Assistant Judicial Case Manager, who may determine and explain the jurisdictional prerequisites. No attempt should be made to "screen out" such cases. *See Guideline 2:05*, Processing the Complaint; *Guideline 3:00*, Venue; Territorial Jurisdiction for c. 209A Complaints; and *Guideline 3:03A*, Personal Jurisdiction over a Non–Resident Defendant. Staff members should also be prepared to assist those seeking to file a certified copy of a protection order issued by other jurisdictions, as well as the requisite affidavit attesting to the validity and effectiveness of the other jurisdiction's order. *See Guideline 14:00*, Filing and Enforcement of Abuse Prevention Orders Issued by Other Jurisdictions. Courts should encourage the involvement of victim assistance personnel or advocates in assisting the plaintiff with the complaint form. *See Guideline 2:08*, Role of Advocates in Assisting Parties. When no advocate is available, staff members may provide plaintiffs with information regarding community support services (e.g., shelters, advocacy groups, Al-Anon, etc.).

Finally, court personnel should provide information developed by the Massachusetts District Attorneys Association on behalf of all of the District Attorney's offices, pursuant to G.L. c. 209A, § 3A, regarding the options available for criminal prosecution. *See Guideline* 2:11, Check of the Court Activity Record Information System and the Warrant Management System; and *Guideline 8:01*, Issuance of Criminal Complaint.

2:02 ENSURING PRIVACY

A person requesting relief under c. 209A should be directed by the person designated to receive such requests to an area, preferably separate, where the matter can be discussed and the complaint form completed with as much privacy as possible. At a minimum, the matter should be discussed out of the hearing of all persons, court personnel and general public alike, who are not directly involved.

COMMENTARY

Despite the volume of activity in the typical clerk's office, efforts must be made to ensure privacy for the plaintiff seeking relief under c. 209A. Where a separate room or area is not available, the discussion should be conducted so as to protect the plaintiff's privacy (e.g., perhaps at one end of the counter.)

In the process of seeking relief under c. 209A a party may disclose information that is not known to family, friends, and associates. While no special procedures are required or recommended, it is important that court staff be aware that such disclosure might present concerns for a party and attempt to accommodate the privacy concerns of the individuals involved as much as possible.

2:03. COMPLETING THE COMPLAINT; OBTAINING REQUIRED INFORMATION

Staff members designated to assist plaintiffs seeking to file c. 209A complaints should explain, as necessary, the various sections of the complaint form that the plaintiff must fill out.

Each plaintiff should complete an affidavit describing the facts that form the basis for the relief sought. While not required by statute, requiring the affidavit in each case is highly recommended. *See Guideline 2:04*, Plaintiff's Affidavit. In the Probate and Family Court Department, a request for an *ex parte* order requires the filing of an affidavit or a verified complaint. *See* Mass. R. Dom. Rel. P. 65 (a).

The plaintiff should enter the appropriate information on the Plaintiff Confidential Information Form (FA/HA–6). The information provided on this form is accessible only by the plaintiff, those authorized by the plaintiff, those authorized by statute and by court order. *See Guideline 1:05*, Public Access to c. 209A Case Files.

Each plaintiff should also complete the Defendant Information Form (FA/HA–5), providing all of the available information about the defendant that is necessary for a check of the Statewide Registry of Civil Restraining Orders and for service of an order, should one be issued. If the case involves the care and custody of a child, the plaintiff should be assisted in completing the Affidavit Disclosing Care or Custody Proceedings that is required by Uniform Trial Court Rule IV, *Uniform Rule Requiring Disclosure of Pending and Concluded Care or Custody Matters*. http://www.mass.gov/courts/209a/docs/care-custody-affidavit.pdf

COMMENTARY

Court personnel who assist plaintiffs in completing the forms should be thoroughly familiar with those forms and with the instructions for their use which are printed on the back of the form. It is important that the Plaintiff Confidential Information Form (FA/HA–6) be completed in each case to ensure that "confidential" information is not provided to unauthorized persons.

In some cases, the plaintiff may not be able to provide all of the information requested on the Defendant Information Form. Even though the court might not have sufficient data to run a complete search of the Statewide Registry of Civil Restraining Orders or enter an order into the Registry, the case should proceed, as these steps are not prerequisites to issuing an order.

Plaintiffs should not be discouraged from filing a complaint because they may lack some particular piece of information requested on the complaint form. The Guideline recommends the use of the Defendant Information Form (FA/HA–5) to obtain information important for completing the record check and for locating the defendant for service, should an order issue. Court personnel should obtain as much identifying information as possible, including the defendant's date of birth, Social Security number, mother's maiden name, father's name, and alias for the record check. It is essential to have the defendant's date of birth for effective use of the Statewide Registry of Civil Restraining Orders and the Warrant Management System. Information necessary for service of an order is equally important, including the location where the defendant can be found, his or her physical appearance, whether the defendant has access to weapons, etc. This inquiry must be conducted with sensitivity. While plaintiffs should not be discouraged from seeking the court's protection because they cannot provide some of this information, they should be apprised that law enforcement efforts to protect them are considerably hampered if the defendant cannot be accurately identified or served with notice. Some plaintiffs may be able to obtain additional information from home or other sources. In such cases, the issuance of the order should not be delayed, but plaintiffs should be instructed to provide such information to the court, preferably through the victim witness advocate or to the police department later in the day, but as soon as reasonably possible.

When a plaintiff cannot complete an affidavit, due to limited proficiency in English, inability to read or write, or other language difficulties, an advocate or interpreter may assist the plaintiff by transcribing the plaintiff's statement in the affidavit. If an interpreter transcribes the statement, it should be done in the plaintiff's native language. The interpreter shall then translate the statement in writing for the court. In any of the above circumstances, the individual assisting the plaintiff must accurately transcribe the plaintiff's statement and must include his or her name and role in drafting the affidavit. The interpreter may use the form entitled Translation of Affidavit (FA/HA–15).

See Guideline 1:08, Plaintiff Unable to Appear in Court, regarding a complaint filed on behalf of a plaintiff seeking temporary relief who is unable to appear in court.

2:04. PLAINTIFF'S AFFIDAVIT

Plaintiffs should file a signed, sworn statement ("Affidavit") describing the factual basis of the complaint on the reverse side of the original court copy (top sheet) of the Complaint Form (FA–1). *See Guideline 2:03*, Completing the Complaint; Obtaining Required Information, regarding affidavits in *ex parte* cases in Probate and Family Court Department. Plaintiffs should be encouraged to provide as much information as possible about the allegations of abuse, including specific information about the most recent incident of abuse and the most serious incident, even if the most serious incident occurred some time ago. The plaintiff should be informed that the defendant will have access to the affidavit. If the plaintiff seeks an order that the defendant have no contact with or must stay away from the defendant's minor children, the grounds for that request should be set forth on Page 2 of the Complaint (FA–1A). The affidavit should also set forth the basis for such an order concerning the children.

COMMENTARY

The advantage of obtaining a signed statement, or affidavit, is that factual allegations are then preserved in the case file. This can also obviate the need for the judge to question the plaintiff extensively when the matter comes before the court at the *ex parte* hearing, saving time and embarrassment. However, the plaintiff's failure or inability to complete such a statement cannot be grounds for denial of the right to file a complaint and obtain a hearing. *See Guideline 2:05*, Processing the Complaint.

The plaintiff must establish a basis for requesting that the court order no contact with the defendant's minor children. "If there is to be a G.L. c. 209A order that a defendant stay away from and have no contact with his or her minor children, there must be independent support for the order." Smith v. Joyce, 421 Mass. 520, 523 (1995). Appropriate reasons for issuing such an order may include (but are not limited to) a finding that the children themselves have been abused; that they have witnessed the defendant's abuse of the plaintiff and are, therefore, afraid of the defendant and would be harmed by seeing him or her; or that no visitation can be arranged with the children in the plaintiff's custody without endangering the plaintiff. *See, e.g.*, Vittone v. Clairmont, 64 Mass. App. Ct. 479, 486–489 (2005), *rev. denied*, Vittone v. Clairmont, 445 Mass. 1106 (2005) (proper for court to issue abuse prevention order against father who abused mother and was convicted of sexually assaulting two of the parties' five children, where mother remained in reasonable fear of imminent serious physical harm to herself and one of the parties' children, who had not been abused by the defendant, once father was released from prison). If the plaintiff's children, or the children in the plaintiff's custody, are not the defendant's children, there need be no such showing. With respect to the effect of orders precluding contact between the defendant and his or her children, *see Guideline 1:11*, Plaintiff's Requested Order Will Contradict Existing Probate and Family Court Order; *Guideline 2:07*, Referral to and from Other Courts and Avoiding Inconsistent Orders; and *Guideline 12:00*, Visitation Proceedings in Probate and Family Court: Considered in Only Limited Circumstances.

2:05. PROCESSING THE COMPLAINT

Persons seeking to file complaints under c. 209A should not be denied the right to do so. Only when it is absolutely clear that the facts alleged by the plaintiff do not fall within the terms of c. 209A, or that the court lacks jurisdiction over the matter, should court personnel indicate that the court cannot grant the relief sought. Even in such cases, if the plaintiff continues to request an order, the form should be completed and the matter brought before the court.

COMMENTARY

Courts should not authorize or permit a step in the abuse prevention procedure similar to the "screening out" process that can occur in the complaint application stage in criminal cases. The only circumstance in which court personnel should attempt to dissuade a plaintiff is when a clear jurisdictional defect is apparent. Any such issue regarding jurisdiction should be brought to the attention of the Clerk–Magistrate

or an Assistant Clerk–Magistrate, or Register or Assistant Register, Judicial Case Manager or Assistant Judicial Case Manager in the Probate and Family Court, to ensure that it is correctly determined and explained, and that no "screening out" occurs. As stated above, if the plaintiff continues to request an order, the complaint form should be completed and the matter brought before the court for a formal ruling on jurisdiction. Where venue appears to be defective under G.L. c. 209A, § 2, refer to *Guideline 1:09*, Plaintiff in Court Without Territorial Jurisdiction/Proper Venue; *Guideline 3:03*, Venue; Territorial Jurisdiction for c. 209A Complaints; and *Guideline 3:03A*, Personal Jurisdiction over a Non–Resident Defendant.

2:06. CLERK'S RESPONSE TO THE FILING OF REPETITIOUS COMPLAINTS

No person seeking relief under c. 209A should be denied the right to file a complaint. Court personnel should treat a plaintiff with respect and courtesy, regardless of how many times the plaintiff has appeared before the court seeking relief and regardless of the outcome of any previous proceedings.

COMMENTARY

A plaintiff may initially seek relief, and then fail to follow up by not appearing at a subsequent hearing, by requesting to "drop" an order, or by deciding not to report violations of an order. Many complex dynamics contribute to this behavior. These can include the plaintiff's need for financial support, a desire to reconcile with the defendant, coercion or intimidation by the defendant, family pressures, children's issues, and a plaintiff's lack of self-esteem or sense of heightened danger at the time of separation.

It may seem frustrating to court personnel to go through the necessary procedures in processing a c. 209A action repeatedly. This Guideline, however, makes it clear that such past experience is not relevant to the question of whether the plaintiff needs protection in a new action, at least insofar as the right to file a new complaint is concerned. No plaintiff should be turned away based on the outcome of past efforts to seek and obtain abuse prevention orders.

2:07. REFERRAL TO AND FROM OTHER COURTS AND AVOIDING INCONSISTENT ORDERS

If the court has jurisdiction based on the facts as alleged by the plaintiff, the court should accept the complaint and proceed to hear and rule on the matter. However, the court should not order relief inconsistent with any existing order, except in the emergency circumstances described in *Guideline 1:11*, Plaintiff's Requested Order Will Contradict Existing Probate and Family Court Order. At the beginning of each hearing, whether an *ex parte* hearing or a hearing after notice, in order to avoid issuing inconsistent orders, the judge should ask the parties whether there are any outstanding court actions or orders in the same or a different court. The clerk's office should bring into the courtroom any related matters between the parties, including prior abuse prevention orders, complaints for abuse prevention orders, and any related criminal matters.

Plaintiffs seeking relief initially in the District Court, the Boston Municipal Court or the Superior Court Department should not be referred to the Probate and Family Court Department for any relief that is within the initial court's jurisdiction, regardless of marital status or the involvement of children. This includes the plaintiff's request for child support. *See Guideline 3:07*, Conduct of *Ex Parte* Hearings;

Guideline 4:02, Ex Parte Orders to Vacate; *Guideline 5:01,* Conduct of Hearings After Notice When Both Parties Appear: General; and *Guideline 6:00,* Orders After Notice: General.

A plaintiff who has been improperly referred to one court by another court within the same or a different department should not be sent back to the referring court, even if the latter had jurisdiction. Such actions should proceed in the referral court as though the plaintiff had come there originally.

COMMENTARY

If the court in which a person initially seeks protection under c. 209A has jurisdiction, the person should be heard as soon as possible in that court, and should not be sent to another court. Referring a plaintiff to another court may discourage the person from seeking the relief to which he or she is entitled under the law, and may expose the person to additional danger. This is particularly so where the other court is at some distance and may be inaccessible to the plaintiff.

Similarly, fragmenting the relief available in the initial court, such as refusing to deal with support orders even when they are necessary to assure a plaintiff's ability to live independently and free from abuse, denies the plaintiff rights which the law provides, and may discourage a victim of abuse from seeking any relief at all.

However, in order to avoid issuing orders inconsistent with those issued by another court, the judge should ask the parties about the existence of other court actions or orders; the parties are required to disclose this information under G.L. c. 209A, § 3, par. 8. Although this requirement appears to relate only to Massachusetts orders, the parties should also be asked to inform the court of any similar orders which may have been issued by other jurisdictions so that such orders can be given due consideration. *See Guideline 14:00,* Filing and Enforcement of Abuse Prevention Orders from Other Jurisdictions. The existence of other pending court orders may determine the type of relief available. For example, if there is an outstanding Probate and Family Court order involving custody or support for minor children, that order will prevent a District Court, Boston Municipal Court or Superior Court from issuing custody or support orders, except in emergency situations, (*see Guideline 1:11,* Plaintiff's Requested Order Will Contradict Existing Probate and Family Court Order), since the Probate and Family Court has superseding authority in those areas and exclusive authority over visitation.

Whenever a case is filed in the Probate and Family Court and there is an outstanding order issued by the District Court, the Boston Municipal Court or the Superior Court, the Probate and Family Court justice shall be temporarily assigned to the department that issued the outstanding order for the sole purpose of hearing and determining whether to modify, extend or vacate the outstanding order to eliminate inconsistencies between the existing order and a decision of the Probate and Family Court. *See Guideline 13:00,* Assignment of Justices of the Probate and Family Court Department to Modify Inconsistent Orders. For emergency situations, where the plaintiff alleges the likelihood of immediate harm to the children, *see* Commentary to *Guideline 2:04,* Plaintiff's Affidavit; *Guideline 3:07,* Conduct of *Ex Parte* Hearings, and related Commentary.

To the extent possible, the Probate and Family Court judge should specifically and clearly identify the modified provisions on the face of the c. 209A order. The modified order should not simply refer to an attached order or agreement, particularly with respect to modification of the provisions regarding the contact and stay-away orders between the parties and/or children.

In accordance with Administrative Order 96–1, the probation department in the modifying court will immediately transmit a copy of the order, including all additional pages of the order if there was inadequate space on the original order to include complete details of the modification, by facsimile to the issuing court. The issuing court must then enter the order into the Registry of Civil Restraining Orders, notify the appropriate police department of the modified

order, and update its case file. *See Guideline 13:00,* Assignment of Justices of the Probate and Family Court Department to Modify Inconsistent Orders.

2:08. ROLE OF ADVOCATES IN ASSISTING PARTIES

The court should support the participation of advocates at each stage of the c. 209A process, regardless of whether such persons are volunteers from a local advocacy group, law students, employees of the district attorney or of some other state, community or legal service agency, or friends or family members of either party. Where possible, such support should include providing an area of the courthouse where advocates can operate, allowing sufficient time in the complaint filing process for an advocate to speak to the party, individually or, if there are multiple parties, in a group setting, assisting the party in filing the complaint, and permitting the advocate to accompany the party, when so requested, to the courtroom. *See Guideline 1:04,* Court's Relationship With Local Advocacy Groups; *Guideline 3:09,* Role of Advocates at *Ex Parte* Hearings; and *Guideline 5:02,* Role of Advocates at Hearings After Notice. Advocates should coordinate their efforts with the appropriate staff in each court.

COMMENTARY

When parties in a c. 209A action come to court, the experience can be overwhelming.

Advocates can be helpful in directing a person seeking relief under c. 209A through the myriad of court procedures. In so doing, advocates should consult with the personnel in each court identified by the Clerk or Chief Probation Officer to promote efficiency and effectiveness in the processing of these matters. A victim of abuse may experience feelings of shock, fear, depression, shame and helplessness. Trained advocates can remind the plaintiff to provide the court with all the information necessary for the judge to make an informed decision, explain to a plaintiff the various questions which the judge may ask, and encourage the plaintiff to consider and to decide upon what relief to request.

An advocate may also be aware of potential problems which can be solved before the hearing (e.g., identifying the address, or other identifying information, of a defendant who does not live with the plaintiff), or can identify other problems of which the judge should be aware (e.g., the presence of weapons in the home which have been used in an abuse incident). An advocate may facilitate the service of the orders by acting as a liaison with the police department. Moreover, an advocate may be in a position to assist a plaintiff in developing a plan of action which will help to keep the plaintiff safe after the order is issued and in making referrals for other appropriate kinds of assistance, such as support groups, shelters, etc.

Other individuals, such as family members or friends, may also provide support for the parties, and such individuals should be encouraged to accompany parties at each stage of the proceedings.

The assistance of any advocate in any particular situation should not be permitted to interfere with the party's wishes or with the court's ability to conduct an orderly proceeding.

2:09. GUIDELINE INTENTIONALLY DELETED

2:10. CHECK OF THE COURT ACTIVITY RECORD INFORMATION SYSTEM, INCLUDING THE STATEWIDE REGISTRY OF CIVIL RESTRAINING ORDERS, AND OTHER PROBATION DEPARTMENT INVOLVEMENT AT THE COMPLAINT STAGE

As soon as the complaint is filed, the court's probation department must check the Court Activity Records Information (CARI) database, including the Statewide Registry of Civil Restraining Orders, and provide the judge with information on any criminal record which the defendant has in Massachusetts and any previous or current abuse prevention orders. When appropriate, the judge may request that the probation department obtain an out-of-state criminal record.

If the court issues an abuse prevention order, the probation department must, on the same day, record that order in the Statewide Registry of Civil Restraining Orders. Similarly, once a person files a certified copy of a protection order issued by another jurisdiction, along with an affidavit, the probation department must also record that order in the Statewide Registry of Civil Restraining Orders on the same day. *See Guideline 1:05*, Public Access to c. 209A Case Files; *Guideline 2:01*, Assisting the Plaintiff; *Guideline 2:04*, Plaintiff's Affidavit; *Guideline 2:12*, Referral for a Criminal Complaint; and *Guideline 14:00*, Fling and Enforcement of Abuse Prevention Orders Issued by Other Jurisdictions.

The probation department may assist in gathering information needed from the parties, such as identifying information. The probation department may also perform financial support guideline calculations. However, the parties should not be referred to the probation department, or elsewhere, for diversion of the c. 209A complaint or for mediation or couple's counseling of any kind. *See Guideline 1:01*, Protective Purposes of c. 209A; *Guideline 4:05*, Reconciliation; and *Guideline 6:01*, Referral for Treatment or Support Services.

COMMENTARY

General Laws c. 209A, § 7, states that the judge "shall cause a search to be made" of the Statewide Registry of Civil Restraining Orders and shall review the resulting data. The probation department is required to make this search. It must be completed as soon as possible after the complaint is received, so that the judge will have the results when the case proceeds in court. This search must be repeated before each subsequent hearing.

The purpose of the search is to provide the court with information about the defendant that can be essential to providing protection for the plaintiff, either in terms of immediate court action (where the defendant is on default or probation status, *see Guideline 3:05*, Court Action on the Defendant's Default, Probation, Parole or Warrant Status at *Ex Parte* Hearings; and *Guideline 5:07*, Court Action on Defendant's Warrant Status), or in terms of appropriately adjudicating or fashioning abuse prevention orders. The Statewide Registry of Civil Restraining Orders contains records of active, expired and terminated c. 209A orders.

The probation department may also be called upon by the court to perform other functions at later stages of the case. However, use of probation officers to "help resolve the parties' problem" or to mediate disputes is fundamentally inconsistent with the protective purpose of the c. 209A procedure.

A check of the Court Activity Records Information database (CARI), including the Statewide Registry of Civil Restraining Orders, may also reveal information pertinent to federal law regarding possession of guns by defendants convicted of "misdemeanor crimes of domestic violence." *See Guideline 4:04*, *Ex Parte* Orders to Surrender Guns, Licenses to Carry Firearms and FID Cards; and *Guideline 6:05*, Orders to Surrender Guns, Licenses to Carry Firearms and FID Cards.

2:11. CHECK OF THE COURT ACTIVITY RECORD INFORMATION (SYSTEM AND THE WARRANT MANAGEMENT SYSTEM

When the complaint is filed, the probation department must check the Court Activity Record Information System (CARI) system and the clerk's office must check the Warrant Management System (WMS) to see if there exists an outstanding warrant for the defendant's arrest. If so, that information must be provided to the judge at the time of the c. 209A hearing. These checks must be made each time the case is before the court.

COMMENTARY

These checks must be made before each abuse prevention order hearing so that the court can comply with c. 209A, § 7. "In all instances where an outstanding warrant exists, a judge shall make a finding, based upon all of the circumstances, as to whether a threat of bodily injury exists to the plaintiff. In all instances where such an imminent threat of bodily injury is found to exist, the judge shall notify the appropriate law enforcement officials of such finding . . . ." G.L. c. 209A, § 7. It is critical that the judge in the session have warrant information from both the probation computer (CARI) and the clerk's office computer (Warrant Management System) every time the case is before the court.

2:12. REFERRAL FOR A CRIMINAL COMPLAINT

Court personnel should inform the plaintiff that c. 209A proceedings are civil in nature and that certain violations of the orders issued under c. 209A are criminal in nature, as required by G.L. c. 209A, § 3A. Violations of orders (1) to refrain from abuse, (2) to vacate the household, or (3) to have no contact with and/or stay away from the plaintiff, are criminal violations. *See* Commonwealth v. Finase, 435 Mass. 310, 313–314 (2001). In addition, G.L. c. 209A, § 3B makes a violation of an order to surrender guns, ammunition, and gun licenses a criminal offense. *See Guideline 8:00*, Venue; Territorial Jurisdiction for Criminal Prosecution of Violations of c. 209A Orders.

In all cases, particularly those involving allegations of serious injury, court personnel should provide information developed by the District Attorney pursuant to G.L. c. 209A, § 3A regarding the options available for criminal prosecution. A plaintiff who wishes to pursue criminal charges should be referred to the District Attorney's office, the police, or advocates within the court to discuss the ramifications of that decision. Alternatively, a plaintiff may immediately file an application for a criminal complaint in the clerk's office in a District Court or Boston Municipal Court.

Providing information regarding procedures for a criminal complaint should be in addition to, and not in lieu of, receiving and processing the c. 209A complaint.

COMMENTARY

Many plaintiffs may not understand the difference between the civil relief provided by c. 209A and criminal penalties. The law requires that the plaintiff be advised that the abuse prevention order is civil in nature, but that certain violations of the order constitutes a criminal offense. The law requires that the information be given in the plaintiff's native language "whenever possible." G.L. c. 209A, § 3A.

In certain cases, the degree of harm, or threat of harm, is so great that protection under c. 209A alone may not be sufficient. Particularly in those cases, court personnel should inform the plaintiff about the availability of criminal prosecution and provide information developed by the Massachusetts District Attorneys Association on behalf of all of the District Attorney's offices, pursuant to G.L. c. 209A, § 3A, regarding the options available for criminal prosecution.

Referral to the police or to the District Attorney's office is often appropriate because it permits the prosecutor to assess, and to discuss with the plaintiff, the strength of a prospective criminal action, the level of participation required of the plaintiff in such an action, and the likely outcome. Referral to a court advocate may assist an undecided plaintiff in choosing a course of action that meets the plaintiff's needs.

EX *PARTE* HEARINGS

3:00 EX PARTE HEARINGS: GENERAL

A plaintiff applying for an abuse prevention order under c. 209A should be brought before the court for a possible *ex parte* hearing as soon as is practicable. The clerk's office should notify the judge when a plaintiff seeking a c. 209A protection order has entered the courtroom. *See Guideline 3:01*, Scheduling of *Ex Parte* Hearings.

Court personnel or others assisting the plaintiff in filing the complaint should not attempt to determine whether an *ex parte* hearing is appropriate. It is for the judge to decide whether the grounds are sufficient to conduct an *ex parte* hearing.

If a plaintiff is "unable to appear in court without severe hardship due to the plaintiff's physical condition," a representative of the plaintiff may, "appear in court on the plaintiff's behalf and file the requisite complaint with an affidavit setting forth the circumstances preventing the plaintiff from appearing personally." G.L. c. 209A, § 5. *See Guideline 1:08*, Plaintiff Unable to Appear in Court, and *Guideline 11:00*, Procedure for Response to Complaints When Court is Not in Session.

COMMENTARY

Just as non-judicial personnel should not attempt to screen out cases on jurisdictional or other grounds (*See Guideline 2:01*, Assisting the Plaintiff, and *Guideline 2:05*, Processing the Complaint), neither should they attempt to determine which cases do not warrant an *ex parte* hearing. This issue should be addressed by the court. In other words, all complaints should be brought promptly before the court.

In Commonwealth v. Gordon, 407 Mass. 340, 349 (1990), the Supreme Judicial Court found that the abuse required for the plaintiff to be put "in fear of imminent serious physical harm" under c. 209A is also consonant with the common law definition of assault, an act placing another in reasonable apprehension that force may be used. *Id.* In Commonwealth v. Matsos, 421 Mass. 391, 394–395 (1995), the Supreme Judicial Court, citing Gordon, held that placing a victim "in fear of bodily injury" approximates the common law definition of the crime of assault and the court should look to the words and actions of the defendant in light of the attendant circumstances to determine if the apprehension is reasonable. *Id.* Moreover, the "plaintiff's apprehension that force may be used" must be objectively, rather than subjectively, reasonable. Carroll v. Kartell, 56 Mass. App. Ct. 83, 87 (2002) (plaintiff's apprehension of imminent harm was not objectively reasonable, as defendant's persistent attempts to contact her, coupled with his criminal charges connected to the shooting death of his ex-wife's boyfriend, did not rise to the level of "abuse" for the purposes of c. 209A); *see also* Ginsberg v. Blacker, 67 Mass. App. Ct. 139 (2006) (where defendant's actions, which included flying into a rage at an "objectively trivial incident," arriving uninvited at plaintiff's home and screaming at her while gesticulating wildly, were sufficient to cause plaintiff to have had a reasonable fear of imminent serious physical harm constituting abuse). *Contrast* Keene v. Gangi, 60 Mass. App. Ct. 667 (2004) (plaintiff's testimony that defendant had placed a surveillance camera in her bedroom and her understanding that he possessed a firearms identification card and/or license to carry, even if true, were insufficient to justify the issuance of an abuse prevention order, as there was no history of violence or abuse between the parties and she had failed to show fear of imminent serious physical harm).

Proceeding with a hearing on a c. 209A complaint without prior notice to the defendant and a right to be heard constitutes an exception to fundamental due process. This exception, i.e., the right to proceed *ex parte*, is justified only when there is "a substantial likelihood of immediate danger of abuse." G.L. c. 209A, § 4. Past abuse alone, without plaintiff's present fear of imminent physical harm, is insufficient to justify the issuance of an abuse prevention order. Dollan v. Dollan, 55 Mass. App. Ct. 905 (2002).

3:01 SCHEDULING OF *EX PARTE* HEARINGS

Ex parte hearings should be held as soon as practicable after the complaint has been completed, signed, and the appropriate record checks are completed. Each court should hear c. 209A *ex parte* hearings expeditiously so as to minimize the time a plaintiff must wait.

The clerk's office must notify the judge immediately when an *ex parte* c. 209A complaint is brought to the courtroom. Without such notice from the clerk's office, it is possible that the c. 209A *ex parte* hearing will not be given the immediate preference it should be given, especially in those courts where the c. 209A case files do not have a distinctive color. This practice is particularly important when a c. 209A *ex parte* matter is brought into a courtroom where a visiting judge is sitting.

COMMENTARY

No plaintiff should be turned away, asked to make another trip to the courthouse (except in the circumstances described in *Guideline 1:09*, Plaintiff in Court Without Territorial Jurisdiction/Proper Venue), or required to wait an unreasonable period of time to be heard. Such delay could discourage a plaintiff in need of protection from remaining at the court or from returning to obtain necessary relief. Courts may adopt one, both, or a combination of the following approaches: (1) interrupt regularly scheduled court business and bring such cases before the court during "breaks" in the proceedings; or (2) schedule c. 209A hearings for a certain time of the day in a particular session. In choosing the time, the court should consult with victim witness personnel of the District Attorney's office, the police, and/or any participating advocacy groups, as appropriate. However, in cases where waiting until the assigned time would cause significant inconvenience to the plaintiff, the matter should be brought before the court as soon as possible.

In exceptional circumstances, where the presence of the defendant can be obtained easily, the court may briefly delay the hearing until the defendant is present, provided that doing so does not compromise the plaintiff's safety. The court must be cognizant that when a matter is scheduled for a two-party hearing without the issuance of an *ex parte* order, the plaintiff will not have the protection of a c. 209A order in the interim between the filing of the complaint and the subsequent two-party hearing. For this reason, such practice should be used only in situations in which it is clear that the delay will not present an elevated danger to the plaintiff.

Two examples of such situations are: (1) when the defendant is at the court being arraigned for the same conduct which is the basis for the c. 209A complaint, and (2) where the defendant may be available (e.g., at work) a short distance from the courthouse and can be notified of the hearing by telephone. *See Guideline 1:02*, Due Process Considerations. In light of the potential complications of such a practice, the court should employ it sparingly, and should consider other options for minimizing the delay between issuance of the order and the two-party hearing, including the issuance of an order with a return date of less than 10 days.

3:02   SUBJECT MATTER JURISDICTION

A court has subject matter jurisdiction to issue an abuse prevention order under c. 209A where the plaintiff and defendant:

(a) are or were married to each other;

(b) are or were residing in the same "household";

(c) are or were related by blood or marriage;

(d) have a child together, regardless of whether they have ever married or lived together;

(e) are or have been in a substantive dating or engagement relationship.

The basis for jurisdiction contained in section (e) does not extend to the Superior Court. Where there is no subject matter jurisdiction under c. 209A, the plaintiff may qualify for a harassment order pursuant to G.L. c. 258E.

COMMENTARY

Chapter 209A confers broad jurisdiction to issue abuse prevention orders regarding interpersonal violence. Current or previous marriage between the parties is only one basis of such jurisdiction. Unmarried persons who currently live together, or who did so in the past, are also within the court's jurisdiction under c. 209A, regardless of whether the relationship between them is sexual in nature. In addition, a substantive dating relationship between the parties confers jurisdiction on the District Court, Boston Municipal Court and Probate and Family Court departments, regardless of whether the parties ever lived together.

Under G.L. c. 209A, § 1(e), whether a "substantive" dating relationship does or did exist depends upon the following statutory factors:

(1) the length of time of the relationship;

(2) the type of relationship;

(3) the frequency of interaction between the parties; and,

(4) if the relationship has been terminated by either person, the length of time elapsed since the termination of the relationship.

In these cases, the court should give broad meaning to the term "substantive dating relationship" to assure that the protective purposes of the statute are achieved. The existence of a "substantive dating relationship" is to be determined on a case by case basis applying the factors set forth in G.L. c. 209A, § 1(e)(1)–(4), while keeping in mind the statute's protective purposes. C.O. v. M.M., 442 Mass. 648, 651 (2004). The plaintiff bears the burden of demonstrating by a preponderance of the evidence that such a relationship existed between the parties. *Id.* at 654. The lifestyles of the parties, e.g., unmarried cohabitation, or same-sex relationships, are not an appropriate subject for comment by anyone in the court. However, the court should make appropriate inquiry to ascertain that the relationship between the parties is one that is covered under the statute. The Superior Court Department does not appear to have jurisdiction over c. 209A cases in which the plaintiff seeks relief based on the statutory criterion of "substantive dating or engagement relationship." *See* G.L. c. 209A, § 1.

The court should give broad meaning to the words "related by blood or marriage." The test should be whether the relationship puts the parties into contact with one another, even though they might not otherwise seek or wish for such contact. For example, in Sorgman v. Sorgman, 49 Mass. App. Ct. 416 (2000), the Appeals Court found that an unadopted "stepdaughter," who had not lived in her "stepfather's" household for twenty years following her biological mother's divorce from him, had the requisite relationship for the purposes of the issuance of a c. 209A order against him. *Id.* at 417–418. The Court expressly rejected the defendant's argument that the statute did not apply to "'ex-stepchildren' . . . whose 'ex' status has persisted for so many years," on the basis of the "plain statutory language" of G.L. c. 209A, §§ 1 and 3, and the fact that "the parties continued to have contact and involvement with each other long after the marriage and living arrangement which initially gave rise to their relationship ended." *Id.* at 418. Similarly, in Turner v. Lewis, 434 Mass. 331, 334 (2001), the Court held that the paternal grandparent of a non-marital child was "related by blood" to the child's mother through the child and therefore able to invoke the protection of a c. 209A order. In reaching this conclusion, the Supreme Judicial Court explicitly noted the "social reality that the concept of 'family' is varied and evolving and, that as a result, different types of 'family' members will be forced into potentially unwanted contact with one another." *Id.* at 334–335.

In Sorgman v. Sorgman, 49 Mass. App. Ct. 416 (2000), the Appeals Court also considered the definition of "household member" and found that the "plain statutory language" of G.L. c. 209A, § 3 includes both past and present members of the household. *Id.* at 417–418. The Court found that, despite her having left the household approximately twenty years earlier, an unadopted "stepdaughter's" residence in the defendant's household for a period of ten years satisfied the "household" requirements of G.L. c. 209A, §§ 1 and 3. *Id.* at 417. However, the concept of how much time a person must spend in order to be considered a member of a household would appear to be a flexible one. The Appeals Court again considered the definition of "household member" in Aguilar v. Hernandez–Mendez, 66 Mass. App. Ct. 367 (2006). In that case, the defendant had lived with his father, the plaintiff, and her two teenage children for approximately two years before moving to a new residence, but still possessed keys to the apartment, received mail there, frequently used the premises to shower, and occasionally spent the night. The Appeals Court held that, in light of the broad interpretation of the statute, the defendant was a household member and the plaintiff could obtain an abuse prevention order under the statute. *Id.* at 370.

Harassment prevention orders under G.L. c. 258E are available from the District Court, Boston Municipal Court, Juvenile Court, and Superior Court departments. Unlike c. 209A, c. 258E does not require the plaintiff to have a familial, household, or substantive dating relationship with the defendant. Anyone "suffering from harassment" may seek to obtain a harassment prevention order under c. 258E.

In appropriate circumstances, the plaintiff may be referred to the District Attorney's office to obtain information about seeking a criminal complaint. *See Guideline 2:12*, Referral for a Criminal Complaint. The plaintiff should be provided information developed by the District Attorney pursuant to G.L. c. 209A, § 3A, regarding the options available for criminal prosecution.

Household resident status, for the purpose of determining jurisdiction, should not be applied to those who live in different apartments in multiple family dwellings. The provision in the law which refers to multiple family dwellings provides that vacate orders can extend to a defendant living in the same building (though in a different unit) as the plaintiff, where the court otherwise has jurisdiction, e.g., because the plaintiff and the defendant are family members or were dating.

Unless the parties meet the other statutory requirements for subject matter jurisdiction, c. 209A does not apply to landlord-tenant situations and should not be used as a substitute for the procedural requirements of summary process. *See Guideline 4:02, Ex Parte Orders to Vacate.* In addition, a defendant who is ordered to vacate the plaintiff's household may be ordered to stay away from the entire building, including apartments other than the one occupied by the plaintiff, if such an order is necessary to assure the plaintiff's safety.

3:03 VENUE; TERRITORIAL JURISDICTION FOR C. 209A COMPLAINTS

The requirements set forth in G.L. c. 209A, § 2 regarding where abuse prevention actions must be filed and heard should be considered jurisdictional. That is, if these requirements are not met, the court should be considered to have no authority to act on the complaint.

COMMENTARY

General Laws c. 209A, § 2 is entitled "Venue." However, the requirements set forth there appear to be jurisdictional.

Those requirements are that the action must be "filed, heard and determined" (1) in the court within whose judicial district the plaintiff resides, or (2) where the plaintiff has left a residence or household to avoid abuse, in the court within whose judicial district that prior residence or household is located or in the court within whose judicial district the plaintiff's current residence is located. *See* G.L. c. 209A, § 2. Since these appear to be prerequisites to the court's authority to act, they should be considered jurisdictional. Thus, inability to meet these requirements does not constitute a defect that may be waived by the defendant's failure to raise it. Rather, such defect renders the court without authority to act.

Jurisdiction, however, is personal. That is, once the court has jurisdiction over the parties, as described above, the court's order is valid anywhere in the Commonwealth. To determine whether the court has personal jurisdiction over a non-resident defendant, *see Guideline 3:03A*, Personal Jurisdiction over a Non–Resident Defendant. Thus the same court may order the defendant to stay away from the plaintiff's new residence, which is in the territorial jurisdiction of the court, and the plaintiff's parents' home, where the children stay regularly, and the plaintiff's workplace, even though the latter two locations are not within the territorial jurisdiction of the issuing court.

As indicated in *Guideline 2:05*, Processing the Complaint, where the initial interview with the plaintiff reveals that the case does not meet the requirements of territorial jurisdiction, this should be explained to the plaintiff and he or she should be directed to the proper court. If the plaintiff persists in the desire to file the complaint, however, this must be allowed, even if it is clear that the court will refuse to issue the order on jurisdictional grounds. If there are any factual questions concerning territorial jurisdiction, the complaint should be completed and the matter brought before the judge. *See Guideline 1:09*, Plaintiff in Court Without Territorial Jurisdiction/Proper Venue.

3:03A PERSONAL JURISDICTION OVER A NON-RESIDENT DEFENDANT

Exercise of personal jurisdiction over a non-resident defendant is proper when he or she acts directly or by an agent as to a cause of action in law or equity arising from the actions described in G.L. c. 223A, including causing a tortious injury (G.L. c. 223A, § 3(b)) or maintaining a domicile in the Commonwealth while a party to a personal or marital relationship out of which a claim is raised relating to divorce, alimony, property settlement, parentage of a child, child support or child custody (G.L. c. 223A, § 3 (g)). Even in the absence of personal jurisdiction over a non-resident defendant, a court may nevertheless issue an abuse protection order, provided that the order does not impose any affirmative duties on the defendant.

COMMENTARY

In Caplan v. Donovan, the Supreme Judicial Court held that "a court may issue . . . an order of prevention and protection even without personal jurisdiction over the defendant, but may not impose affirmative obligations on the defendant if there is no personal jurisdiction." Caplan v. Donovan, 450 Mass. 463, 463–464 (2008), *cert. denied*, Donovan v. Caplan, 553 U.S. 1018 (2008).

3:04 PUBLIC NATURE OF *EX PARTE* HEARINGS

All c. 209A hearings should be held in the courtroom and recorded. They should never be held in the judge's lobby or off the record.

As a general rule, *ex parte* hearings should not be conducted at sidebar. There are, however, specific circumstances in which sidebar may be appropriate, including cases involving sensitive issues such as sexual assault or abuse of children.

Although the hearings should presumptively be open to the public, in the most extraordinary circumstances, for good cause shown and based on specific findings indicated on the record, the court may close the courtroom.

COMMENTARY

All proceedings under c. 209A should be electronically recorded. In the Boston Municipal Court and the District Court, electronic recording is mandatory by Rule. *See* Rule 211, District Court Special Rules. Recording of court proceedings is required in the Probate and Family Court pursuant to the Supplemental Rules of the Probate and Family Court. *See* Suppl. Rule 201. *See also* Superior Court Standing Order 2–87.

Despite the emotional and volatile issues often involved in a c. 209A *ex parte* hearing, the matter should be treated like any other civil proceeding. The preferred practice is to conduct the hearing in open court. The judge always has discretion to hear from a party at sidebar when appropriate circumstances require.

A decision to close the courtroom in a c. 209A action should be made only in the most extraordinary circumstances. The party seeking to close the hearing has the burden of proving good cause, and good cause is established on a showing that disclosure will work a clearly defined and serious injury to the party seeking closure. Zenith Radio Corp. v. Matsushita Electrical Industrial Co., 529 F. Supp. 866, 890 (E.D. Pa. 1981). The injury must be shown with specificity. *Id*. The trial court, in closing a proceeding to the public, must both articulate the countervailing interest it seeks to protect and must make "findings specific enough that a reviewing court can determine whether the closure order was properly entered." *See* Press–Enterprise Co. v. Superior Court of California, Riverside County, 464 U.S. 501 (1984).

3:05 COURT ACTION ON DEFENDANT'S DEFAULT, PROBATION, PAROLE OR WARRANT STATUS AT EX PARTE HEARINGS

General Laws c. 209A, § 7 requires that the judge "shall review the defendant's criminal history and history of civil restraining orders." The clerk's office should also check the Warrant Management System.

If the judge receives information from either source that an outstanding warrant exists against the defendant, the judge "shall [(1)] order that the appropriate law enforcement officials be notified," (2) order that "any information regarding the defendant's most recent whereabouts . . . be forwarded to such officials," (3) "make a finding based on all of the circumstances, as to whether an imminent threat of bodily injury exists to the petitioner," and (4) if such a threat is found to exist, "notify the appropriate law enforcement officials of such finding and such officials shall take all necessary actions to execute any such outstanding warrant as soon as practicable." G.L. c. 209A, § 7.

Where the defendant is determined to be on probation, the judge should consider ordering that the supervising probation officer receive immediate notice of the issuance of the c. 209A order.

COMMENTARY

The defendant's criminal history and previous abuse prevention order history must be reviewed at the *ex parte* hearing for a variety of reasons. In addition to alerting the judge of outstanding warrants or other abuse prevention orders, this information is helpful in identifying situations in which the plaintiff may face a particularly heightened degree of danger.

The requirement that the judge notify the "appropriate law enforcement officials" about an outstanding warrant is triggered by the existence of any outstanding warrant. It is not clear from the statute who the "appropriate law enforcement officials" are, but they should be considered, at a minimum, to be the police department to which the c. 209A order is sent for service. Officers from that department will be attempting to serve the defendant with the order; they should be notified about outstanding warrants so that they can arrest the defendant on the warrants if and when they find him or her. In addition, such notice is important for the safety of the serving police officer. The Order provides a place to notify anyone reading it that a warrant exists, (section A.16, FA–2A), and completing this part of the order would seem to comply with the statute's notice requirement. It also provides the plaintiff with the warrant numbers so that, if the defendant violates the order, and the plaintiff calls the police for emergency assistance, he or she can give the warrant numbers to the responding police officers. (However, arrest in such circumstances does not usually require the existence of a warrant. *See Guideline 8:01*, Issuance of Criminal Complaint.)

Because the statute places the burden specifically on the judge, it is the judge who must review the record to ascertain the existence of any warrants.

In the District Court, Boston Municipal Court, and Superior Court departments, the printed copy of the defendant's criminal record should be returned to the defendant's probation file. In the Probate and Family Court, in accordance with Probate and Family Court Standing Order 1–11, no CARI/WMS information should be stored in the case file. http://www.mass.gov/courts/courtsandjudges/courts/probateandfamilycourt/standingorder1-11.pdf. The printed copy should not be placed in the case file since doing so could result in a violation of the CORI law if the criminal record is inadvertently revealed to one who has obtained public access to that file. *See Guideline 1:05*, Public Access to c. 209A Case Files. In addition, it is important that an up-to-date copy of the defendant's criminal record be obtained for each hearing; an old copy of the record may give inaccurate or incomplete information.

In some cases the judge may find that the nature of the warrant alone, or the nature of the warrant combined with the assertions of the party seeking c. 209A relief, presents an imminent threat of bodily injury to the plaintiff that goes beyond that required for the issuance of any c. 209A order. The judge may also find such an imminent threat of bodily injury exists based solely upon the assertions of the party seeking c. 209A relief. When the judge finds that such a threat exists, the judge should make the finding in the designated section on

page two of the c. 209A order (section A.17, FA–2A), and direct the clerk's office or the victim witness advocate or the district attorney's office to notify the appropriate law enforcement officials of the situation and the circumstances that give rise to the imminent threat of bodily injury. Those officials would include, at a minimum, the police department that is responsible for serving the c. 209A order on the defendant and/or the District Attorney's Office.

Probation departments are notified each day about the court activity of their probationers during the previous day. Therefore, each supervising probation officer should learn on the next court day about any c. 209A abuse prevention orders issued against his or her probationer and entered into the CARI system. In situations of particular danger or urgency, however, it may be appropriate for the judge to order that the probation officer supervising a c. 209A defendant be notified immediately. This notice can serve two purposes. First, the actions that constitute the basis for the c. 209A order may be sufficient to constitute a violation of the terms of the defendant's probation. The supervising probation department may wish to bring the allegations to the attention of the sentencing court, either by sending the defendant a notice of probation violation, or, in situations of particular danger, requesting an arrest warrant. The Commissioner of Probation has issued guidelines for the commencement of probation violation proceedings on the basis of the issuance of abuse prevention orders under c. 209A. *See* "Recommended Guidelines Regarding (1) 209A actions against active probationers and (2) Enforcement of stay-away orders" issued by Commissioner of Probation Donald Cochran on October 12, 1993. http://www.mass.gov/courts/209a/docs/probation-guidelines-probation-violation-proceedings.pdf *See also* District Court Transmittal No. 723, December 16, 1999, "New District Court Rules for Probation Violation Proceedings" (Rules not attached). http://www.mass.gov/courts/209a/docs/districtcourt-trans723-probation-violation-rules.pdf. Second, the supervising probation department can sometimes assist the court in notifying a defendant of the issuance of the *ex parte* order. This is particularly useful in situations where the plaintiff does not know where the defendant can be served.

3:06   RULES OF EVIDENCE AND STANDARD AND BURDEN OF PROOF

The common law rules of evidence, e.g., those regarding hearsay, authentication, and best evidence, should be applied with flexibility at the *ex parte* hearing, subject to considerations of fundamental fairness. The standard of proof is a preponderance of the evidence. The plaintiff has the burden of proof.

COMMENTARY

At the *ex parte* hearing, as at the hearing after notice in c. 209A proceedings, strict adherence to the common law rules of evidence is not expressly required by the statute. *See Guideline 5:03*, Rules of Evidence. For example, the court can properly receive testimony that would otherwise be hearsay (e.g., "the doctor said that I had a concussion"). "The rules of evidence need not be followed, provided there is fairness in what evidence is admitted and relied on." Frizado v. Frizado, 420 Mass. 592, 597–598 (1995).

The regular civil standard of proof, preponderance of the evidence, should be applied. *Id.* The plaintiff bears the burden of proof. Jones v. Gallagher, 54 Mass. App. Ct. 833, 890 (2002). *See Guideline 5:04*, Standard and Burden of Proof. Since the plaintiff is unopposed at the *ex parte* hearing, it is essential that the court be satisfied that the evidence submitted is credible, and sufficient as a matter of law, to justify the issuance of an order. The court should question the plaintiff, if necessary, to make this determination. In certain circumstances, inquiry beyond the face of the written affidavit or the plaintiff's oral statement is not only appropriate, but essential, to the proper exercise of the court's authority to decide these significant issues in the absence of the opposing party. *See Guideline 4:01*, Content of *Ex Parte* Orders; and *Guideline 4:05*, Reconciliation.

3:07 CONDUCT OF *EX PARTE* HEARINGS

The court should decide whether there is territorial and subject matter jurisdiction before proceeding with the *ex parte* hearing.

The *ex parte* hearing itself should consist of testimony by the plaintiff under oath as to the factual grounds for the complaint and the need for the relief sought. If the plaintiff has filed an affidavit that provides the court with substantive information supporting the complaint, the judge may incorporate the affidavit into the record to simplify the plaintiff's testimony. If the content of the affidavit alone does not provide sufficient evidence on the issue of abuse and the need for an abuse prevention order, the court may consider additional evidence, including further testimony, police reports or other documents, or observations of the plaintiff's visible physical injuries. The court may wish to memorialize this additional evidence and attach it to the affidavit or may wish to ask the plaintiff to add to the plaintiff's original affidavit additional facts that were set forth orally during the hearing. The court should question the plaintiff as necessary in order to obtain relevant information and assess credibility. The court should also hear the sworn testimony of any available witnesses offered by the plaintiff. The court may also consider applicable police reports provided by a party or otherwise available to the court.

The court should decide the facts and determine whether there is a statutory basis for relief before addressing the nature of the relief sought. This need not be a formal or time-consuming process, and the judge need not necessarily announce each finding on the record.

The court should not routinely refuse to grant particular types of relief available under c. 209A. For example, plaintiffs who are entitled to such relief as stay-away, no-contact, or vacate orders should not be referred to the Probate and Family Court Department for support or custody orders unless those issues are already the subject of a prior or pending order in that court. *See Guideline 2:07*, Referral to and from Other Courts and Avoiding Inconsistent Orders.

At the beginning of each hearing, the judge should ask the plaintiff whether there are any outstanding court orders involving the same parties in the same or a different court. The court should not order any relief that is inconsistent with any existing order in any other court, except in emergency circumstances. *See Guideline 1:11*, Plaintiff's Requested Order Will Contradict Existing Probate and Family Court Order. *See also Guideline 2:07*, Referral to and from Other Courts and Avoiding Inconsistent Orders, and *Guideline 13:00*, Assignment of Justices of the Probate and Family Court Department to Modify Inconsistent Orders, with regard to inconsistencies between an order issued by the District Court, the Boston Municipal Court or the Superior Court and a decision of the Probate and Family Court.

See Guideline 1:08, Plaintiff Unable to Appear in Court; *Guideline 3:00*, *Ex Parte* Hearings: General; and *Guideline 11:00*, Procedure for Response to Complaints When Court is Not in Session, regarding *ex parte* plaintiffs who are unable to appear to file a complaint.

COMMENTARY

The court should begin the *ex parte* hearing with a review of jurisdiction. If the court lacks subject matter or territorial/personal jurisdiction, the resulting order will be invalid and successful prosecution for a violation of that order will not be possible. *See Guidelines 3:02*, Subject Matter Jurisdiction; *Guideline 3:03*, Venue; Territorial Jurisdiction for c. 209A Complaints; and *Guideline 3:03A*, Personal Jurisdiction over a Non–Resident Defendant.

Harassment prevention orders under G.L. c. 258E are available from the District Court, Boston Municipal Court, Juvenile Court, and Superior Court departments. Unlike c. 209A, c. 258E does not require the plaintiff to have a familial, household, or substantive dating relationship with the defendant. Anyone "suffering from harassment" may seek to obtain a harassment prevention order under c. 258E.

If there is an existing Probate and Family Court custody, visitation and/or support order, the court in another department of the Trial Court may not issue custody or support orders. If such a current order exists but the plaintiff seeks an order from another court ordering the defendant to stay away from, or to have no contact with, the defendant's minor children, the court should refer the plaintiff to the Probate and Family Court for only that relief. While the other court has statutory authority to issue such an order, it is more appropriate that it be heard in the court where the parties have already appeared. The Probate and Family Court will also have superseding jurisdiction in custody and support matters: its exclusive jurisdiction over visitation matters may be seriously hampered by a subsequent no-contact or stay-away order issued by a different court and made applicable to the defendant's minor children. *See Guideline 2:07*, Referral to and from Other Courts and Avoiding Inconsistent Orders; *Guideline 4:01*, Content of *Ex Parte* Orders; *Guideline 5:00*, Scheduling Hearings After Notice; and *Guideline 6:00*, Orders After Notice: General. *See also Guideline 13:00*, Assignment of Justices of the Probate and Family Court Department to Modify Inconsistent Orders.

However, in an emergency situation, the District Court, Boston Municipal Court, or Superior Court (including a judge on the Judicial Response System) may issue an order that conflicts with an existing custody or visitation order issued by the Probate and Family Court. These emergency circumstances are limited to those cases in which there is an allegation or threat of serious harm to the children who are the subject of an existing custody or visitation order and the plaintiff is unable to reach the Probate and Family Court. In such cases, the judge in the other court may issue the requested order for a short period of time (usually no more than 72 hours) to permit the plaintiff to go to the Probate and Family Court for relief, and should make findings of fact setting forth the reasons for that order. *See* Smith v. Joyce, 421 Mass. 520, 523–524 (1995). *See Guideline 1:11*, Plaintiff's Requested Order Will Contradict Existing Probate and Family Court Order.

3:08 REPETITIOUS COMPLAINTS

The fact that a plaintiff has unsuccessfully sought relief previously, or has previously obtained abuse prevention orders but not sought to extend them, is not relevant to the decision on the need for relief in response to the new complaint. Each complaint must be evaluated on its own merits to determine whether evidence exists to support issuance of an abuse prevention order.

Court staff should provide the court with all prior related abuse prevention orders involving the parties presently before the court at the time of the hearing.

COMMENTARY

A plaintiff may initially seek relief, and then fail to follow up by not appearing at a subsequent hearing, by requesting to "drop" an order, or by deciding not to report violations of an order. Many complex dynamics contribute to this behavior. These can include the plaintiff's need for financial support, a desire to reconcile with the defendant, coercion or intimidation by the defendant, family pressures, children's issues, and a plaintiff's lack of self-esteem or sense of heightened danger at the time of separation.

Although the filing of repetitious complaints may be frustrating to the court and to the court staff, the plaintiff should be assured that the court's only concern is to adjudicate the new complaint on its merits and to provide any abuse prevention orders that are warranted by the evidence. *See Guideline 2:12*, Referral for a Criminal Complaint, and *Guideline 5:08*, Request by the Plaintiff or Defendant to Modify or Terminate the Abuse Prevention Order. If the same court where the current complaint is being heard issued a previously terminated protection order, it may be helpful for the judge to review that previous order.

3:09 ROLE OF ADVOCATES AT *EX PARTE* HEARINGS

Judges should permit advocates to stand with the parties whom they are assisting throughout the proceedings and to aid and support a party during the hearing to the extent that the party wishes it and the court deems it helpful.

COMMENTARY

Trained advocates and friends or relatives of the party can play an important role in supporting the party through what may be a difficult process and in reminding the party to provide the court with all relevant information. *See Guideline 1:04*, Court's Relationship With Local Advocacy Groups; *Guideline 2:08*, Role of Advocates in Assisting Parties; and *Guideline 5:02*, Role of Advocates at Hearings After Notice.

The role of the non-lawyer advocates in the courtroom should be limited to aiding the parties in their presentation to the court. Such aid may involve reminding the party of relevant factual information or pertinent circumstances that a party may have forgotten to state or, for whatever reason, did not bring to the court's attention. An advocate with personal knowledge pertaining to the allegations raised by the party may testify to such facts upon being sworn as a witness.

EX PARTE ORDERS

4:00 DURATION OF *EX PARTE* ORDERS

Orders entered after an *ex parte* hearing should have duration of no more than ten court business days. They should be effective through 4 p.m. on the date set for the hearing after notice.

COMMENTARY

It is a fundamental tenet of due process that one cannot be deprived of personal or property rights without advance notice and the right to be heard. Departures from this principle are allowed only on exceptional grounds. *Ex parte* orders in domestic abuse cases (e.g., requiring a defendant to leave the home with no right to be heard in opposition) are justified only insofar as the danger of physical abuse to the plaintiff is immediate and outweighs the defendant's right to be heard before the order issues. This exception to the defendant's due process rights can last only until the defendant can be notified and a hearing can be scheduled and conducted.

Accordingly, the *ex parte* orders should last only until the hearing after notice can be held, and that hearing should be scheduled for a date as soon as possible, consistent with service on the defendant, and, in any event, no more than "ten court business days" after the *ex parte* hearing. G.L. c. 209A, § 4, second par.

4:01 CONTENT OF *EX PARTE* ORDERS

If the plaintiff demonstrates a "substantial likelihood of immediate danger of abuse," as defined in the statute, the court should issue an *ex parte* order. The court may enter any order that it deems necessary to protect a plaintiff from further abuse, including, but not limited to, any of the orders expressly authorized by G.L. c. 209A, § 3. Such orders MUST include the surrender of guns, ammunition and gun licenses. *See Guideline 4:04, Ex Parte* Orders to Surrender Guns, Licenses to Carry Firearms and FID Cards. Judges should proofread the order before signing it and should review the relief ordered by reading the order aloud to the plaintiff.

COMMENTARY

The authority granted to the court under c. 209A is not limited to any specific type of relief. G.L. c. 209A, § 3. Nor is the court limited to the forms of relief originally requested by the plaintiff on the complaint form. The court should fashion its relief order in response to the need for protection shown by the facts presented at the hearing. For example, it may be determined that the defendant should be specifically ordered not to call or otherwise contact the plaintiff at the plaintiff's place of employment, despite the fact that this was not included on the complaint.

The protective purpose of *ex parte* orders may be interpreted broadly. For example, under appropriate circumstances, an *ex parte* order requiring the defendant to provide the keys to the family car to the plaintiff (e.g., by leaving them with police) might be deemed "protective," in the sense that it eliminates one reason for the plaintiff to contact the defendant during the duration of the *ex parte* order. When justified by the facts, the court has authority to order a defendant to stay away from a particular school or job site, even if the defendant attends the school or works at the same location. In such cases, the plaintiff should be provided with an additional copy of the order for the school or employer, so that responsible parties in those places will be notified of the court order, as well as of the possibility of danger to the plaintiff.

Judges should be mindful when crafting abuse prevention orders that, with respect to the terms "stay away" and "no contact", they are "not interchangeable." However, a "no contact" order includes a "stay away" order. Commonwealth v. Finase, 435 Mass. 310, 314 (2001) ("Pursuant to a 'stay away' order, the defendant may not come within a specified distance of the protected party, usually stated in the order, but written or oral contact between the parties is not prohibited. By contrast, a 'no contact' order mandates that the defendant not communicate by any means with the protected party, in addition to remaining physically separated. Thus, a 'no contact' order is broader than a 'stay away' order."). It may also be prudent to include a warning that intentional contact effectuated by the defendant through a third party may violate the no-contact provision of the order. *See, e.g.*, Commonwealth v. Consoli, 58 Mass. App. Ct. 734, 741 (2003), *rev. denied*, Commonwealth v. Consoli, 440 Mass. 1103 (2003) (a defendant cannot make comments to a third party that they intend or know will be heard by a plaintiff standing nearby).

No-contact orders can be violated through use of Facebook, Twitter, texting, or other use of social media. In cases where this may be an issue, judges may wish to specifically prohibit such use of social media to contact the plaintiff.

The terms of the orders must be reasonable. They must be clear in their language, so that the parties as well as the police know what has been ordered and what conduct violates the order. Plain language should be used (e.g., "100 yards," not "the length of a football field"). Conditional language should not be used (e.g., contact with the children should not be conditioned on the defendant's sobriety). In particular, an order which requires the defendant to stay a great distance, such as 1,000 yards, or even 500 or 200 yards, away from the plaintiff is difficult to enforce because it is almost impossible for such a defendant to know when he or she is in violation. Similarly, a District Court order that requires a defendant to stay more than 100 yards away from the plaintiff may make it difficult for the Probate and Family Court to craft an appropriate visitation order without amending the District Court order. *See Guideline 12:07* Custody and Visitation Proceedings in Probate and Family Court: Modifications of c. 209A Orders. Orders that require a defendant to stay from twenty to 100 yards away from the plaintiff are usually sufficient. An order requiring the defendant to stay "at least one hundred yards away" from the plaintiff and her job has been interpreted to require the defendant to stay one hundred yards away from "all of the property on which the workplace is located including the adjacent parking lot." Commonwealth v. O'Shea, 41 Mass. App. Ct. 115, 118 (1996), *overruled on other grounds*, Commonwealth v. Delaney, 425 Mass. 587 (1997). A defendant may be found guilty of a violation of an order to stay away from the protected person's workplace when he or she visits the plaintiff's workplace, even if the plaintiff is not at work at the time of the visit. *See* Commonwealth v. Habenstreit, 57 Mass. App. Ct. 785, 787 (2003), *rev. denied*, Commonwealth v. Habenstreit, 439 Mass. 785 (2003) (since the purpose of the abuse prevention order is to provide a safe haven for the victim and to lessen the chances for contact between the victim and the defendant, to interpret the order to apply only when the victim was physically present would "encourage a defendant to keep himself or herself informed about a protected person's schedule," a result that would be contrary to the intent of the order itself.)

In addition, as noted in *Guideline 3:07*, Conduct of Ex Parte Hearings, courts generally should avoid issuing inconsistent orders. However, in extraordinary circumstances, the District Court, Boston Municipal Court, or Superior Court may issue an order, which conflicts with an existing custody or visitation order issued by the Probate and Family Court. *See Guideline 1:11*, Plaintiff's Requested Order Will Contradict Existing Probate and Family Court Order.

Reading the terms of the order to the plaintiff before signing it allows the judge to make sure that the order is complete. For example, a no-contact order (sections A.2 or A.7, FA–2) should always include a reasonable distance in yards, which the defendant should observe in staying away from the plaintiff (A.2) or the children (A.7). Reading the order aloud also allows a plaintiff to bring to the judge's attention any requested relief that may have been forgotten or overlooked.

4:02 *EX PARTE* ORDERS TO VACATE

The court's decision to issue an *ex parte* order to the defendant to vacate the household residence should be based solely upon the plaintiff's need for such an order as a means of protection from abuse. The defendant's property interest in the household residence is irrelevant to the issuance of an order to vacate.

The court may also order the defendant not only to vacate an apartment, but also to stay away from the entire building or to stay away from a workplace. Implicit in an order to vacate is that the defendant remains away from the location while the abuse prevention order is in effect.

COMMENTARY

For an *ex parte* order to vacate, the only relevant issues are (1) whether the plaintiff shows, by a preponderance of the evidence, that there is "a substantial likelihood of immediate danger of abuse," and (2) whether an order to vacate is needed to protect the plaintiff from that abuse.

The defendant's property interest in the residence is not relevant to this inquiry. Thus, if the plaintiff and the defendant reside in the same household and there is a substantial likelihood of abuse to the plaintiff, then a vacate order is appropriate, irrespective of whether the defendant is the owner or lessee of the household premises. A defendant who is the owner or lessee of the premises might argue that the plaintiff's right to occupy the premises as an invitee has terminated and that the plaintiff is a trespasser. This is a separate issue. The defendant may seek relief in other forums, including summary process proceedings, but until the plaintiff leaves, the defendant's property interest in the household premises is subordinate to the protection afforded by the order to vacate. The defendant remains the owner or lessee, but this does not affect the court's authority to issue an order to vacate, especially for the brief duration of an *ex parte* order. This interpretation is consistent with the section of G.L. c. 209A, § 3, which states that "[n]o order shall in any manner affect title to real property."

Given the impact of a vacate order on the defendant, there is a particular need, when such an order is issued *ex parte*, to limit its duration to the minimum time consistent with notice to the defendant. Ten court business days is the maximum duration of such orders under the statute and should not be the presumptive or automatic term for scheduling the hearing after notice.

Under G.L. c. 209A, § 3(c), the court may order the defendant to vacate a multiple family dwelling (section A.3, FA–2) and to stay away from a workplace or school (sections A.4a and 4b, FA–2). Both orders require specific notation on the order form.

Unless the parties meet the other statutory requirements for subject matter jurisdiction, c. 209A does not apply to landlord-tenant situations. Chapter 209A should not be used as a substitute for the procedural requirements of summary process. *See Guideline 3:02*, Subject Matter Jurisdiction.

See Commonwealth v. Gordon, 407 Mass. 340, 347 (1990) regarding the "stay away" aspect of vacate orders, noting that "the Legislature intended the word 'vacate' to include the concept of 'remain away.'" See also Commonwealth v. Finase, 435 Mass. 310, 314 (2001) (with respect to the terms "stay away" and "no contact", they are "not interchangeable." However, a "no contact" order includes a "stay away" order.) The Finase Court noted that "[p]ursuant to a 'stay away' order, the defendant may not come within a specified distance of the protected party, usually stated in the order, but written or oral contact between the parties is not prohibited. By contrast, a 'no contact' order mandates that the defendant not communicate by any means with the protected party, in addition to remaining physically separated. Thus, a 'no contact' order is broader than a 'stay away' order." *Id.*

4:03 *EX PARTE* SUPPORT AND COMPENSATION ORDERS

Orders issued in the course of *ex parte* hearings should not ordinarily include terms of support or compensation for damages. Claims for such relief should be considered at the hearing after notice. The fact that the plaintiff is requesting such relief should be indicated on the complaint and also on the *ex parte* order so as to provide notice to the defendant that the issue will be addressed at the hearing after notice. The court should check the box in section 13 of the Order (FA–2) which notifies the defendant that at the next scheduled hearing testimony will be heard and evidence considered the issue of support for the plaintiff and/minor children and that the defendant is ordered to bring to that hearing any financial records that provide evidence of his or her current income.

COMMENTARY

There are several significant difficulties with ordering support and compensation on the *ex parte* order.

First, it is unlikely that the court will obtain adequate information in an *ex parte* hearing to make an informed decision in these matters, which can require substantial fact finding and testimony from both sides. The hearing after notice provides a more appropriate forum for such fact finding.

Second, even if an order for support or compensation were issued, it is not likely to be enforced prior to the expiration of the *ex parte* order. In fact, attempts by the plaintiff to demand payment from the defendant before the hearing after notice could be the occasion of further danger of abuse.

The plaintiff should never be discouraged from seeking support or compensation, but should be told that the court will consider these issues at the hearing after notice, when the defendant has an opportunity to be heard. *See Guideline 6:00*, Orders After Notice: General, and *Guideline 6:05B*, Support Orders. The complaint should indicate that the plaintiff is seeking restitution for damage done or support for minor children. The court should check the box in section 13 of the Order (FA–2) which notifies the defendant that at the next scheduled hearing testimony will be heard and evidence considered the issue of support for the plaintiff and/minor children and that the defendant is ordered to bring to that hearing any financial records that provide evidence of his or her current income.

Chapter 209A, § 3(e) requires that all orders of support "issued, reviewed or modified" under the statute also conform to and be enforced under the provisions of G.L. c. 119A, § 12 (pertaining to child support enforcement). *Guideline 6:05B*, Support Orders.

4:04 *EX PARTE* ORDERS TO SURRENDER GUNS, LICENSES TO CARRY FIREARMS AND FID CARDS

All *ex parte* orders MUST include (1) an order for the "immediate suspension and surrender of any license to carry firearms, and/or Firearm Identification Card which the defendant may hold" and (2) an order that the defendant surrender to the police "all firearms, rifles, shotguns, machine guns and ammunition which he then controls, owns or possesses." G.L. c. 209A, § 3B. Any license to carry firearms or firearms identification cards that the defendant may hold shall be surrendered to the appropriate law enforcement officials. G.L. c. 209A, § 3B. This provision MUST be included in any *ex parte* order regardless of whether there is any evidence presented that the defendant has a firearms identification card or license to carry or possesses any firearms or ammunition.

COMMENTARY

Since all *ex parte* orders issued under c. 209A must include an order that the defendant surrender any firearms or firearms licenses, the box in section A. 12 of the Order (FA–2) must be checked on all *ex parte* orders.

State and federal law prohibits possession of firearms, ammunition, firearms identification cards and licenses to carry firearms by individuals subject to c. 209A orders except in certain limited situations. Upon the issuance of a c. 209A order, any license to carry firearms

must be revoked or suspended by the licensing authority, (G.L. c. 140, § 131 (d)(vi); G.L. c. 140, § 131 (f)), and any firearms identification card must be revoked or suspended by the licensing authority. G.L. c. 140, § 129B (1) (viii); G.L. c. 140, § 129B (4).

Upon service of an order issued under c. 209A, law enforcement officials must immediately take possession of all firearms, rifles, shotguns, machine guns, ammunition, any license to carry firearms and any firearms identification cards. G.L. c. 209A, § 3B. When the judge learns from the plaintiff in the course of a hearing that the defendant possesses firearms or ammunition, any information regarding the number and type of firearms and the location where they are kept should be memorialized on the order itself and conveyed to the law enforcement officials responsible for serving the order on the defendant. This notation will assist police officers to implement the requirements of the order safely and effectively.

Each time an order issued under c. 209A is extended or modified the judge must determine if returning the defendant's firearms or firearm identification card would present a likelihood of abuse to the plaintiff. If the judge makes such a determination, the court shall continue the firearm surrender order and shall in sections C or D of the Order (FA–2a) by checking the box that provides, "Firearm surrender order continued. The items surrendered under section 12 will NOT be returned since doing so would present a likelihood of abuse to the plaintiff." *See Guideline 6:05*, Orders to Surrender Guns, Licenses to Carry Firearms and FID Cards. Enforcement of this provision in another state may be dependent upon whether the order contains such a finding.

Federal law prohibits possession of a firearm or ammunition by any person who is subject to a qualifying domestic violence protective order. 18 U.S.C. § 922 (g)(8). A protective order must meet certain requirements in order to qualify under that statute. The order must: (1) have been issued after a hearing of which the defendant received actual notice and had an opportunity to participate; (2) must restrain the defendant from harassing, stalking, or threatening an intimate partner or that partner's child or placing those individuals in reasonable fear of bodily injury; (3) must include a finding that the defendant represents a credible threat to the physical safety of the intimate partner or the partner's child; and (4) must prohibit the use, attempted use, or threatened use of physical force against the partner or child. There is an exception limited to only 18 U.S.C. 922 (g) (8) that permits law enforcement officers and military personnel in certain situations to possess an officially issued firearm while on duty even if they are currently subject to a qualifying protective order. 18 U.S.C. § 925 (a)(1).

Federal law also prohibits possession of a firearm or ammunition by any person who has a misdemeanor conviction for domestic violence. 18 U.S.C. § 922 (g) (9). Qualifying misdemeanors must have as an element the "use or attempted use of physical force, or the threatened use of a deadly weapon" and the named victim of the crime must be the current or former spouse of the defendant, a person with whom the defendant shared a child in common, a person who was cohabitating with or who had cohabitated with the defendant as a spouse, parent or guardian or a person who was similarly situated to a spouse, parent or guardian of the defendant.

4:05 RECONCILIATION

At the *ex parte* stage, the court should not attempt to compel or even suggest to the plaintiff that reconciliation be attempted. The sole issue is the alleged need for protection on an immediate basis. If that need is found to exist, an appropriate order or orders should issue. If not, the complaint should be denied or the matter deferred to the hearing after notice.

COMMENTARY

It is not appropriate for the court in a c. 209A proceeding to explore, or to ask the plaintiff to explore, the possibility of improving the underlying relationship. The issue presented is whether immediate protection is needed and, if so, what form it should take. *See* G.L. c. 209A, § 3; *Guideline 1:01*, Protective Purpose of c. 209A, and *Guideline 6:01*, Referral for Treatment or Support Services.

4:06   INFORMATION FOR THE PLAINTIFF

If an *ex parte* order issues, the plaintiff should be told:

(1) the contents of the order;

(2) that the police will serve the order on the defendant;

(3) the date and time of the hearing after notice;

(4) what will happen if either or both parties fail to appear at that hearing;

(5) that the order remains in effect until a judges changes the terms of or terminates the order;

(6) that the proceedings are civil in nature and certain violations of the order are criminal in nature; and

(7) that in the event that the defendant violates the order, the plaintiff should contact police immediately.

The Regional Administrative Justices of the Superior Court and the First Justices of the divisions of the Boston Municipal Court, District Court and the Probate and Family Court departments should coordinate with their staff to ensure that either court personnel or an advocate effectively communicates this information to the plaintiff.

COMMENTARY

For an *ex parte* order to be fully effective, its contents and meaning should be explained to the plaintiff. The plaintiff should be told that the police will attempt to serve the defendant with a copy of the order as issued. The plaintiff should contact the police immediately if the defendant violates the order.

The plaintiff should also be told that the order remains in effect until a judges changes or terminates the order. Any action by the defendant contrary to its terms will subject the defendant to immediate, warrantless arrest and possible criminal prosecution. *See Guideline 8:03*, Acquiescence by the Complainant to an Act Which May Violate the Terms of an Order.

The plaintiff should also be told that certain violations of c. 209A orders are criminal offenses. Violations of orders (1) to refrain from abuse, (2) to vacate the household, or (3) to have no contact with and/or stay away from the plaintiff, are criminal violations. *See* Commonwealth v. Finase, 435 Mass. 310, 313–314 (2001). In addition, G.L. c. 209A, § 3B makes a violation of an order to surrender guns, ammunition, and gun licenses a criminal offense.

4:07   TRANSMISSION OF *EX PARTE* ORDERS TO THE POLICE FOR SERVICE ON THE DEFENDANT

When an order under G.L. c. 209A is issued, the clerk's office must transmit two certified copies of the order and one copy of the complaint to "the appropriate law enforcement agency." G.L. c. 209A, § 7. The Defendant Information Form (FA/HA–5) should accompany these forms. The appropriate law enforcement agency should be the police department of the municipality wherein the defendant can be found. If the defendant's whereabouts or likely whereabouts are unknown, the clerk's office should transmit these documents to the police department of the city or town wherein the plaintiff resides.

Transmission of the papers for service on the defendant should take place immediately after the order is issued. Transmission should be accomplished in the manner best designed for speed and effectiveness. In many courts, this will be by facsimile. In other courts, arrangements are made to have police personnel pick up the order for service. In every case, the c. 209A order must be immediately transmitted by the court to the police, either by facsimile or being made available for pick up at the courthouse.

In no circumstances, however, should the order be given to the plaintiff to bring to the police station to effectuate service, nor should the order be mailed to the police station to effectuate service. If a plaintiff would like a copy of the order to bring directly to the police station, a copy of the order should be provided for that purpose. If a police department would like a "hard" copy of an order that has been faxed to it for service, the clerk's office may provide a copy by mail upon request.

The police must serve a copy of the order and a copy of the complaint on the defendant. Service should be made in hand, unless the court specifies otherwise. The police are required to make a return of service to the court. If the defendant is incarcerated and will be incarcerated at the time scheduled for the hearing after notice, a notice should accompany the order informing the defendant of his or her right to be present at the hearing and providing a mechanism for doing so. If the defendant asks to attend the hearing, the court should issue a writ of *habeas corpus* to produce the defendant for the scheduled hearing. *See* Commonwealth v. Henderson, 434 Mass. 155 (2001).

COMMENTARY

"Forthwith" transmission of the necessary papers to the police is specifically required by law. G.L. c. 209A, § 7, second par. The clerk's office is in the best position to determine the most expedient method of transmitting the documents to the appropriate police department for service on the defendant. A facsimile has the benefit of providing printed documentation that the transmission was made, when it was made and to whom it was made. The police department is then required to serve one copy of each order on the defendant, together with a copy of the complaint. The clerk's office should question the plaintiff if that would be helpful in determining which police department is the appropriate law enforcement agency to make service on the defendant. For example, when a defendant previously has been ordered to vacate the household by means of an emergency order, a plaintiff who does not know the location of the defendant's current residence may know where he or she works. In any event, all of the information which the plaintiff possesses about the defendant's whereabouts should be contained on the Defendant Information Form described in *Guideline 2:03*, Completing the Complaint; Obtaining Required Information (FA/HA–5).

In-hand service should be obtained if at all possible. Failure to make in-hand service may render the *ex parte* order ineffective. Further abuse will not be deterred if the defendant does not know that the order exists. Leaving the order and complaint at the "last and usual place of abode" may be ineffective if this is the address that the defendant was ordered to vacate in the emergency order.

In appropriate circumstances, the court may order an alternative method of service. Specifically, the Supreme Judicial Court has held, "when the appropriate law enforcement agency has made a conscientious and reasonable effort to serve the statutorily specified documents on the defendant, but has nevertheless failed, the agency should promptly notify the court so that a judge, if satisfied after a hearing that an appropriate effort has been made, may order that service be made by some other identified means reasonably calculated to reach the defendant. Where such substituted service appears unlikely to notify the defendant, the judge may excuse service." Zullo v. Goguen, 423 Mass. 679, 681 (1996). Alternative service may include service at last and usual address, leaving at an address a defendant is know to frequent (e.g., parent's home) and notice by publication. See also Commentary to Guideline 5:05, Failure of Defendant to Appear; and Guideline 6:03, Service of Orders on the Defendant. If alternative service is ordered, the judge should check the appropriate box in section B1 of the Order (FA2a).

The "necessary papers" to be served include a copy of the order and the complaint, but not the affidavit. See Flynn v. Warner, 421 Mass. 1002, 1002 (1995) (rescript). The statute also refers to service of a "summons," but this appears to be an error since the defendant is given an opportunity to appear at subsequent hearings, but is not required to do so. For this reason, summonses are not issued for defendants in c. 209A cases.

The police are required to "promptly" make a return of service. If the return is not made prior to the date of the hearing after notice, and there is no other evidence of notice to the defendant, an order after notice may not be issued at that time. See Guideline 5:05, Failure of the Defendant to Appear. Furthermore, successful prosecution for violation of an order of which the defendant is unaware is probably impossible. See Commentary to Guideline 5:05, Failure of the Defendant to Appear; and Guideline 6:03, Service of Orders on the Defendant, regarding service of orders after notice. If the case must be continued because there is no evidence that the defendant received notice, the same ten-day time limit as for ex parte orders should be observed.

Incarcerated defendants have the right to be heard on a requested extension of the ex parte order at a hearing after notice. The court should take steps to inform them of this right and to secure their presence in court if requested to do so. In the alternative, the court may issue a writ of habeas corpus sua sponte. While the court is under no obligation to issue a writ of habeas corpus absent a request by the defendant, Commonwealth v. Henderson, 434 Mass. 155, 163, n. 12 (2001), the issuance of a writ of habeas corpus is the preferred practice so that notice is clear in the event the defendant is subsequently charged with violating the restraining order.

In a prosecution for a violation of a c. 209A order, actual service of the order is unnecessary if the Commonwealth can prove beyond a reasonable doubt that the defendant had actual knowledge of the terms of the order. Commonwealth v. Delaney, 425 Mass. 587, 589–593 (1997), cert denied, Delaney v. Commonwealth, 522 U.S. 1058 (1998); Contrast Commonwealth v. Welch, 58 Mass. App. Ct. 408 (2003). In Delaney, the defendant was initially served with a 10–day abuse prevention order issued ex parte under c. 209A, which was left at his last and usual address and which warned him, in pertinent part, that if he failed to appear on the hearing date "an extended or expanded [o]rder may remain in effect for up to one year." Delaney, 425 Mass. at 588. The defendant failed to appear at the hearing, a 1–year order was issued, but not served, although there was evidence that the defendant had verbally acknowledged its existence. Delaney, 425 Mass. at 589. The court stated that "[i]n these circumstances the service of the extended order on the defendant was not a prerequisite to his prosecution for violating the terms of the order" since "the jury could have found that the defendant had actual and constructive notice of the order and that it continued in effect after the hearing date." Delaney, 425 Mass. at 591; see also Commonwealth v. Munafo, 45 Mass. App. Ct. 597, 601–602 (1998), rev. denied, Commonwealth v. Munafo, 428 Mass. 428 Mass. 1110 (1998) (concurring with Delaney that failure to serve an extended order was not fatal error). Failure to serve the order is, however "relevant to a determination as to whether the defendant possessed the knowledge required" for a conviction. Delaney, 425 Mass. at 593. Thus, where the victim testified that "once or twice maybe" she had spoken to the defendant about the existence of the abuse prevention order, there was insufficient evidence that the defendant knew of the order, and he could not be found guilty of a criminal violation. Commonwealth v. Welch, 58 Mass. App. Ct. 408, 410–411 (2003); compare Commonwealth v. Henderson, 434 Mass. 155, 161–164 (2001) (although the defendant was unaware that the protective order had been extended, he was given constructive notice thereof due to the inclusion of the scheduled hearing date on the initial order.); Commonwealth v. Melton, 77 Mass. App. Ct. 552, 555–556 (2010), rev. denied, Commonwealth v. Melton, 458 Mass. 1109 (2010) (where court found that a telephone conversation between the defendant and the victim, initiated by defendant, during which the victim asked the defendant why he was calling her and said "there's a restraining order," was sufficient for a jury to have found that the defendant was put on notice of the existence of a restraining order).

HEARINGS AFTER NOTICE

5:00　SCHEDULING HEARINGS AFTER NOTICE

A hearing after notice in a c. 209A case should be scheduled as soon as possible after an ex parte order is issued, but in no event later than ten court business days after the issuance of such an order. See Guideline 4:00, Duration of Ex Parte Orders.

However, hearings after notice may be held at any time within ten business days when both parties are present, including at the initial appearance or during the course of an arraignment on related criminal charges. See Guideline 8:06, Bail Procedures in Criminal Cases Involving Alleged Violation of an Abuse Prevention Order or Abuse: Dangerousness Hearings.

When scheduling the hearing after notice, the court should consider the plaintiff's ability to appear and the defendant's right to be heard within a minimum time following the issuance of an ex parte order.

COMMENTARY

Scheduling of the c. 209A hearing after notice should be expedited to the extent possible. If an ex parte order is issued, the hearing after notice must be held within "ten court business days" after the date of issuance. "Ten court business days" should be interpreted to mean ten days during which the court is open. Saturdays, Sundays and holidays are excluded. Courts should attempt to schedule hearings after notice sooner than the ten-day maximum if effective service of notice on the defendant and return of service can be made.

Nothing in the law requires two hearings, or a "cooling off period" between the ex parte and the hearing after notice. If both parties are present in court at the time of the plaintiff's initial contact with the court, or if the defendant's presence can be promptly obtained, there is no justification for proceeding ex parte.

If the judge is satisfied that notice of an order that was issued through the Judicial Response System was served on the defendant and that the notice informed the defendant of the date, time and place of the hearing, the court may hold the hearing on that date. See Guideline 11:00, Procedure for Response to Complaints When Court is Not in Session. Conducting a hearing after notice without a prior ex *parte* proceeding is particularly appropriate when the plaintiff is present and the defendant is before the court for arraignment, following arrest for an abuse related crime, and when no previously issued order is in effect. *See Guideline 8:06*, Bail Procedures in Criminal Cases Involving Alleged Violation of an Abuse Prevention Order or Abuse: Dangerousness Hearings.

5:01   CONDUCT OF HEARINGS AFTER NOTICE WHEN BOTH PARTIES APPEAR: GENERAL

The hearing after notice in a c. 209A action at which both parties appear is an adversarial proceeding in which both parties must be allowed to present evidence. The plaintiff bears the burden of proof.

The court should ensure an orderly proceeding and should be cognizant of safety issues. The court should address placement of participants in the courtroom with this in mind. All parties and witnesses should testify under oath.

Before the hearing begins, the judge should ask both parties whether there are any outstanding orders from any court involving the same parties. The response will govern the relief available. *See Guideline 2:07*, Referral to and from Other Courts and Avoiding Inconsistent Orders; *Guideline 3:07*, Conduct of *Ex Parte* Hearings; *Guideline 4:01*, Content of *Ex Parte* Orders; *Guideline 6:00*, Orders After Notice: General; *Guideline 6:07*, Mutual Abuse Prevention Orders; and *Guideline 13:00*, Assignment of Justices of the Probate and Family Court Department to Modify Inconsistent Orders.

Both parties have a general right to cross-examine witnesses, but the judge should not permit cross-examination to be used for harassment or intimidation or for discovery purposes. Each side must be given a meaningful opportunity to challenge the other's evidence. In some circumstances, it is appropriate for the judge to remind the parties of their rights under the Fifth Amendment. Neither the plaintiff nor the defendant should be compelled to provide incriminating information against him- or herself.

Both parties should be told that the defendant must comply with a no-contact or vacate order unless and until those specific orders are terminated in writing by the court. The plaintiff has no authority to "waive" the orders without going to court to ask to have them terminated, and the defendant is subject to mandatory warrantless arrest for violating these orders, notwithstanding the plaintiff's "consent."

The clerk's office should provide the court with all prior related abuse prevention orders involving the parties presently before the court at the hearing after notice. See *Guideline 3:08*, Repetitious Complaints.

COMMENTARY

A two-party hearing in a c. 209A matter is like any other contested civil proceeding. The plaintiff presents his or her evidence, the defendant presents his or her evidence, and the court decides if the plaintiff has proven the case by a preponderance of the credible evidence.

There are unique aspects to hearings under c. 209A. Most obvious are the interpersonal nature of these cases and the emotional and volatile issues involved. The court must control the hearing and address any hostility or safety issues that may emerge. As a general rule, two-party hearings should not be conducted at sidebar. The court should consider where each party is placed during the hearing in order to eliminate any possibility that either party will attempt to dominate the proceedings or to intimidate the other. As in any proceeding, the court must always exercise appropriate control. Orderly procedure requires, for example, that each participant, including the parties, witnesses, and counsel, address remarks only to the court. In cases where serious abuse has taken place, a plaintiff may be intimidated merely by the defendant's presence. While there are specific circumstances in which sidebar might be appropriate, such as sexual assault or abuse of children, the court should also consider the safety implications of having the parties in such close proximity to one another. Many courts position court officers and advocates between the parties during the hearing, particularly a hearing conducted at side bar, to prevent intimidation and any direct interaction between the parties.

These cases carry the potential for physical danger to court personnel as well as to the parties. It is important that each session be conducted with this consideration in mind, and at least one court officer be present at all times.

In many cases an *ex parte* hearing will have been held, and an *ex parte* order issued against the defendant. Nevertheless, the plaintiff still bears the burden of proof at the hearing after notice. *See, e.g.*, Jones v. Gallagher, 54 Mass. App. Ct. 883, 890 (2002). Fairness requires that the plaintiff's case be restated so that the defendant will know what has been alleged. This restatement may take the form of permitting the defendant to read the plaintiff's affidavit if one is contained within the file, and if the defendant is able to read English. Frizado v. Frizado, 420 Mass 592, 597 (1995). "A defendant or his counsel should be given adequate opportunity to consider any affidavit filed in the proceeding on which the judge intends to rely before being required to elect whether to cross-examine the complainant or any other witness." *Id.*

The defendant must then be given an opportunity to respond to the allegations bearing in mind that the defendant does not bear the burden of disproving the allegations or of proving that the *ex parte* order should not continue. "An inference adverse to a defendant may properly be drawn, however, from his or her failure to testify in a civil matter such as this even if criminal proceedings are pending or might be brought against the defendant." Frizado v. Frizado, 420 Mass. at 596 (1995). The plaintiff may then, in the court's discretion, be given an opportunity to supplement the allegations in the affidavit and respond to the defendant's statements.

"A defendant has a general right to cross-examine witnesses against him. There may be circumstances in which the judge may deny that right in a G.L. c. 209A hearing, and certainly a judge may limit cross-examination for good cause in an exercise of discretion." Frizado v. Frizado, 420 Mass. at 597 (1995). In a footnote, the Supreme Judicial Court agreed that cross-examination should not be permitted for harassment or discovery purposes in c. 209A actions, but also observed that the "judge's discretion in restricting cross-examination may not be unlimited in particular situations." *Id.* at 598, n.5. *See also* Silvia v. Duarte, 421 Mass. 1007 (1995). In that case, the Supreme Judicial Court upheld the trial judge's refusal to allow any cross examination where the parties were not married, shared no common domicile and no children, the defendant had served prison time for violence against the plaintiff, the plaintiff appeared *pro se* and the defendant was represented by counsel, the defendant asserted his Fifth Amendment privilege and declined to offer any evidence, and the only order entered was one to stay away from the plaintiff, an order that the court described as a "minimal intrusion." Silvia v. Duarte, 421 Mass. at 1008. *But see* C.O. v. M.M., 442 Mass. 648, 659–659 (2004) (court found that, absent grounds that would justify a limitation on the defendant's right to present evidence and cross-examine witnesses, the defendant's right to due process was denied him where the defendant was not given the opportunity to present and cross-examine witnesses).

5:02 ROLE OF ADVOCATES AT A HEARING AFTER NOTICE

At a hearing after notice, an advocate should be permitted to accompany a party in the courtroom, stand with the party throughout the proceedings, and assist and support the party to the extent that the party wishes it and the court deems it helpful. The court should allow an advocate to speak with the party in order to help the party to provide the court with relevant additional information.

COMMENTARY

The role of an advocate at a hearing after notice is essentially the same as at an *ex parte* hearing, whether or not the other party is represented by counsel. *See Guideline 1:04*, Court's Relationship With Local Advocacy Groups; *Guideline 2:08*, Role of Advocates in Assisting Parties; and *Guideline 3:09*, Role of Advocates at *Ex Parte* Hearings.

5:03 RULES OF EVIDENCE

The common law rules of evidence, e.g., those regarding hearsay, authentication, and best evidence, should be applied with flexibility, subject to considerations of fundamental fairness.

COMMENTARY

At the hearing after notice, as at the *ex parte* hearing in c. 209A proceedings, strict adherence to the common law rules of evidence is not required. Frizado v. Frizado, 420 Mass. 592, 597–598 (1995) (holding that "the rules of evidence need not be followed, provided that there is fairness in what evidence is admitted and relied on"). *See also Guideline 3:06*, Rules of Evidence and Standard and Burden of Proof. For example, the court can properly receive testimony that would otherwise be hearsay. ("The doctor said that I had a concussion.") Similarly, an answering machine message, voicemail, e-mail or other electronic transmission containing threats made by the defendant may be admitted without a formal authentication procedure, if the court is satisfied that it is reliable.

The spousal disqualification set forth in G.L. c. 233, § 20 does not extend "to words constituting or accompanying abuse, threats, or assaults of which the other spouse is the victim." Commonwealth v. Gillis, 358 Mass. 215, 218 (1970). "Even if induced by private conversation, such abusive or threatening words do not have any confidential aspect within the purpose of the protection" and may therefore be admitted. *Id.*

For a more detailed discussion of evidentiary issues, *see* Massachusetts Guide to Evidence, § 1106 (Supreme Judicial Court, 2011) http://www.mass.gov/courts/sjc/guide-to-evidence/

5:04 STANDARD AND BURDEN OF PROOF

The standard of proof in c. 209A hearings is the civil standard of preponderance of the evidence. The plaintiff has the burden of proof at both the *ex parte* hearing and any subsequent hearing after notice. Both sides have the right to introduce evidence.

COMMENTARY

Proceedings under c. 209A are not criminal. The usual civil standard of preponderance of the credible evidence should be applied in c. 209A actions, Frizado v. Frizado, 420 Mass. 592, 597 (1995), and the plaintiff bears the burden of proof. Jones v. Gallagher, 54 Mass. App. Ct. 883, 890 (2002). The standard and burden of proof for obtaining an extension are similar to the criteria for obtaining an initial order. *See,* Iamele v. Asselin, 444 Mass. 734, 734–735 (2005 ("A plaintiff seeking an extension of a protective order must make a showing similar to that of a plaintiff seeking an initial order.").

When requesting an extension of an abuse prevention order, the plaintiff need not make a showing of new abuse. *See* Rauseo v. Rauseo, 50 Mass. App. Ct. 911, 913 (2001), *rev. denied*, Rauseo v. Rauseo, 434 Mass. 1103 (2001) ("At a hearing on the plaintiff's request for an extension of an order ... the plaintiff is not required to re-establish facts sufficient to support that initial grant of an abuse prevention order."); *see also* G.L. c. 209A, § 3; Mitchell v. Mitchell, 62 Mass. App. Ct. 769, 774 (2005) ("[T]he fact abuse has not occurred during the pendency of an order shall not, in itself, constitute sufficient grounds for allowing an order to be vacated."); Doe v. Keller, 57 Mass. App. Ct. 776, 778 (2003). However, the threat of abuse that formed the basis for entry of the original abuse prevention order must continue to exist. *See* Pike v. Maguire, 47 Mass. App. Ct. 929 (1999) (rescript) ("The only criterion for extending the original [abuse prevention] order is a showing of continued need for the order.").

The appropriate inquiry at the extension hearing is "whether the plaintiff has shown by a preponderance of the evidence that an extension of the order is necessary to protect her from the likelihood of 'abuse' as defined in G.L. c. 209A, § 1. Typically, this inquiry will be whether a plaintiff has a reasonable fear of 'imminent serious physical harm'." (citation omitted). Iamele v. Asselin, 444 Mass. at 739–740.[1] "In evaluating whether the plaintiff has met her [or his] burden, a judge must consider the totality of the circumstances of the parties' relationship." *Id.* at 740. In considering the risk of future abuse should the existing order expire, the factors that the judge should examine include, but are not limited to: "the defendant's violations of protective orders, ongoing child custody or other litigation that engenders or is likely to engender hostility, the parties' demeanor in court, the likelihood that the parties will encounter one another in the course of their usual activities (e.g., residential or workplace proximity, attendance at the same place of worship), and significant changes in the circumstances of the parties." *Id.* at 740; *see also* Vittone v. Clairmont, 64 Mass. App. Ct. 479, 486–489 (2005), *rev. denied*, Vittone v. Clairmont, 445 Mass. 1106 (2005) (discussing factors for a judge to consider when deciding whether there was a continued need for an abuse prevention order where parties have not been in contact for eight years).

The court may not extend an *ex parte* abuse prevention order under c. 209A because of a subjective fear that allowing the parties to have contact with one another would lead to violence where plaintiff is unable to establish by a preponderance of the evidence that "abuse" within the definition of the statute occurred. Corrado v. Hedrick, 65 Mass. App. Ct. 477, 483–485 (2006). *See also* Banna v. Banna, 78 Mass. App. Ct. 34, 35–36 (2010) (where the only evidence at the hearing was the original affidavit, and the judge did not ascertain the nature of the interaction of the parties as it related to the likelihood of physical abuse in the future at the time of the hearing; merely asking the plaintiff if she wanted to extend the order was insufficient to extend the *ex parte* order).

---

1 The Court noted, however, that if the plaintiff were suffering from attempted or actual physical abuse or involuntary sexual relations, "there is no question than an extension should be granted." Iamele v. Asselin, 444 Mass. at 740, n. 3.

5:05 FAILURE OF THE DEFENDANT TO APPEAR

If the defendant fails to appear at the hearing after notice, and the plaintiff does appear, and if there is evidence of notice of the hearing to the defendant and no reason for excusing the defendant's absence, the court should consider the defendant to have forfeited his or her opportunity to be heard. In such cases the order after notice may issue as the court deems appropriate, and the existing terms of the *ex parte* order may be modified.

The defendant must be served with any order issued after notice, whether there has been a modification or not, and whether he has appeared or not.

If there is no return of service to the court, and no other acceptable evidence that the defendant has received notice of the hearing, or if the court is given an acceptable reason for the defendant's absence, the hearing should be continued for no more than ten court business days. The *ex parte* order may be extended during that time. New notice of the re-scheduled hearing should be provided to the defendant.

COMMENTARY

Due process requires that no order after notice be issued against a person without actual notice and the opportunity to be heard. If the defendant fails to appear, the court must have some basis on which to conclude that the defendant received notice, but, by ignoring the proceedings, waived the right to be heard. *See* Commonwealth v. Henderson, 434 Mass. 155, 163 (2001) (defendant waived opportunity to be heard by receiving actual notice of scheduled hearing date and failing to appear at hearing without good cause).

The best evidence that the defendant received notice is the return of service that the police are required to make. The court can take testimony from the plaintiff and/or from a police officer that they have verbally advised the defendant of the existence of the abuse prevention order, the terms of the order, and the date of the hearing. If the court finds such testimony credible, the court can make a finding that the defendant had notice. In-hand service of the order may not be required if the Commonwealth can establish that the defendant had actual notice of the terms of the order. *See* Commonwealth v. Delaney, 425 Mass. 587, 589–593 (1997), *cert denied*, Delaney v. Commonwealth, 522 U.S. 1058 (1998); *see also* Commentary to *Guideline 4:07*, Transmission of *Ex Parte* Orders to the Police for Service on the Defendant. If the case must be continued because there is no evidence that the defendant received notice, the same ten-day time limit as for *ex parte* orders should be observed.

To prevent a long series of extended *ex parte* orders where service of notice cannot be made because of lack of knowledge of the defendant's whereabouts or for any other reason, it should be kept in mind that notice can be given in several ways, including service at last and usual address, leaving at an address a defendant is know to frequent (e.g., parents' home) and notice by publication. *See* Commentary to *Guideline 4:07*, Transmission of *Ex Parte* Orders to the Police for Service on the Defendant; and *Guideline 6:03*, Service of Orders on the Defendant. When the court authorizes service by alternative means, the judge should check the appropriate box in section B1 of the Order (FA–2a). *See also* Zullo v. Goguen, 423 Mass. 679, 681 (1996), regarding court orders for alternative methods of service.

General Laws c. 209A, § 4, last par., provides that, "[i]f the defendant does not appear at such subsequent hearing [i.e. the hearing after notice], the temporary order shall continue in effect without further order of the court." However, case law is clear that an initial order "expires unless extended after a judicial determination, essentially, a new finding, that the plaintiff continues to require protection from 'abuse' as explicitly defined in c. 209A, § 1." Jones v. Gallagher, 54 Mass. App. Ct. 883, 889 (2002). Thus, even when the defendant does not appear, and there is evidence of notice, the court must be satisfied that sufficient grounds exist for extending or modifying the order. *See* Iamele v. Asselin, 444 Mass. 734, 739 (2005) ("The inquiry at the extension hearing is whether the plaintiff has shown by a preponderance of the evidence that an extension of the order is necessary to protect her from the likelihood of 'abuse' as defined in G.L. c. 209A, § 1."). The affidavit may be sufficient, but it may be supplemented by oral testimony. *See* Banna v. Banna, 78 Mass. App. Ct. 34, 35–36 (2010) (where the only evidence at the hearing was the original affidavit, and the judge did not ascertain the nature of the interaction of the parties as it related to the likelihood of physical abuse in the

future at the time of the hearing; merely asking the plaintiff if she wanted to extend the order was insufficient to extend the *ex parte* order).

5:06 FAILURE OF THE PLAINTIFF TO APPEAR

If the plaintiff fails to appear at the hearing after notice, and the defendant does appear, or if neither party appears, the order expires by its terms, unless the court is given an acceptable reason for the plaintiff's absence. If the court is given an acceptable reason, the hearing should be continued and the *ex parte* order extended. However, the new hearing date should be as soon as possible and no later than ten court business days from the original hearing date. The defendant must be provided with notice of the new hearing date, regardless of whether he or she appeared.

COMMENTARY

General Laws c. 209A, § 4, last paragraph, provides that:

[i]f the defendant does not appear at such subsequent hearing [i.e. the hearing after notice], the temporary order shall continue in effect without further order of the court.

This provision contains no requirement that the plaintiff appear in order for the order to be extended. However, as in any civil case, the failure of the plaintiff to appear may be grounds for dismissal. The court may elect to permit the order to expire by its terms when the plaintiff does not appear.

The court is not compelled to allow the order to expire on its own terms if the plaintiff does not appear. If there is an acceptable reason for plaintiff's absence, or some grounds to believe that such absence is not voluntary, the case and the order can be extended. This is true whether or not the defendant appears. In appropriate circumstances, the case may be held while an advocate or victim witness staff member contacts the plaintiff to determine the reason for the absence.

5:07 COURT ACTION ON DEFENDANT'S WARRANT STATUS

If, at the time of a hearing after notice, the court becomes aware, by means of the required check of the Statewide Registry of Civil Restraining Orders or the Warrant Management System or otherwise, that a warrant for the defendant's arrest is outstanding, and the defendant is present, the court should address the warrant before the end of the hearing. The District Court, Boston Municipal Court or Superior Court should release the defendant on personal recognizance, bail the defendant under G.L. c. 276, § 29–30, or hold the defendant without bail and order him transported to the court that issued the warrant under G.L. c. 37, § 24(a). The Probate and Family Court should arrange to have the defendant transported to the nearest court with jurisdiction to address the warrant.

COMMENTARY

Courts should not allow a defendant against whom a criminal default warrant is outstanding to leave the courthouse without addressing the warrant. If the defendant is not present, the court must note the existence of the warrant on the abuse prevention order. (section A.16, FA–2A).

5:08 REQUEST BY THE PLAINTIFF OR DEFENDANT TO MODIFY OR TERMINATE THE ABUSE PREVENTION ORDER

If the plaintiff appears on the date scheduled for the hearing after notice, or at any other time, and requests that the abuse prevention order be terminated, the judge should ask certain questions before acting on the request.[3] First, the court should ask about the reasons for the request. Such an inquiry is appropriate so that the reasons for the request appear on the record, and so that the plaintiff may be referred for supportive services, if needed. Second, the court should inquire whether any different or lesser order or component of the existing order (e.g., a refrain from abuse order) should be left in effect to accomplish the plaintiff's purpose. Third, the court should inquire whether vacating the order will place at risk any children living in the home. If the judge has reason to believe that terminating the abuse prevention order will place minor children in danger of physical harm or other abuse, the judge should advise the plaintiff that a report pursuant to G.L. c. 119, § 51A will be filed immediately. *See Guideline 10:03*, Care and Protection Proceedings.

[3] *See Guideline 1:00*, In General, for discussion of the current use of the term "terminated" instead of "vacated."

Nevertheless, a plaintiff who wishes to terminate the order should be permitted to do so, regardless of the reason given or the presence of children. *But see Guideline 10:03*, Care and Protection Proceedings. It is also important for the judge to state that terminating the order will not prevent a plaintiff suffering from abuse from seeking a new order or other protection from the court at any time in the future.

The request to terminate or modify the order should be done by written motion indicating the requested actions and stating the reasons therefore. The clerk's office should also request identification from all individuals seeking to modify or terminate an order.

A defendant may also request to modify or terminate an order. The request must be done by written motion, a hearing must be set and the plaintiff must be served with the motion and notified of the hearing date. *See Guideline* 6:04, Modification of Orders; Terminating Orders.

COMMENTARY

The courts alone cannot protect a victim of domestic violence from an abuser who is undeterred by the threat of arrest or incarceration. A victim of such abuse is in the best position to decide what course of action will provide more safety. At a given time, an abuse prevention order might exacerbate the plaintiff's danger. Similarly, a plaintiff may feel compelled for economic or family reasons to seek to terminate an abuse prevention order. Thus, the plaintiff's decision to terminate an order must be respected.

It is appropriate to refer plaintiffs who wish to terminate an abuse prevention orders to advocates who can review information about supportive services that might assist them. This information might include referrals to shelters and support groups for victims of battering, information about applying for public assistance or for obtaining support from the defendant through the court and the Department of Revenue (*See Guideline 6:05B*, Support Orders) and information about certified batterer intervention programs and any other appropriate services. For a list of certified batterer intervention programs go to www.mass.gov/dph/violence, click on Batterer Intervention Program Services, then click on Certified Batterer Intervention Programs and Services.

There are several instances in which a different order would serve the plaintiff's purpose as effectively as terminating the original order. For example, a plaintiff might wish to attend some function with the defendant, or to see him or her outside the home. In that case, it would be appropriate to terminate the "no-contact" part of the order, but to leave the "stay away from the residence" and "no abuse" orders in effect. Each time an order issued under c. 209A is extended or modified the judge must determine if returning the defendant's firearms or firearm identification card would present a likelihood of abuse to the plaintiff. If the judge makes such a determination, the court shall continue the firearm surrender order and shall check the box in sections C or D of the Order (FA–2a) that provides, "Firearm surrender order continued. The items surrendered under section 12 will NOT be returned since doing so would present a likelihood of abuse to the plaintiff." *See Guideline 6:05*, Orders to Surrender Guns, Licenses to Carry Firearms and FID Cards.

If the judge has reason to believe that terminating the abuse prevention order will place minor children in danger of physical harm or other abuse, the judge should advise the plaintiff that a report pursuant to G.L. c. 119, § 51A will be filed immediately. See *Guideline 10:03*, Care and Protection Proceedings.

Once a plaintiff has appeared before the court to terminate an order, the plaintiff may be reluctant to return no matter how great the danger. The judge should assure the plaintiff that he or she may always return to the court to seek a new order or, if the court is not open, secure an emergency order through the police utilizing the Judicial Response System.

It is recommended that the plaintiff's request to terminate or modify the order should be done by written motion indicating the requested actions and stating the reasons therefore. The Trial Court has promulgated a form for this purpose. Plaintiff's Motion to Modify or Terminate Abuse Prevention Order (FA–13). The signature on the form provides a record of the plaintiff's action and some means of assuring the plaintiff's identity. The clerk's office should also request identification from all individuals seeking to modify or terminate an order.

A motion by a defendant to terminate or modify the order must be done by written motion indicating the requested actions and stating the reasons therefore. The Trial Court has promulgated a form for this purpose. Defendant's Motion to Modify or Terminate Abuse Prevention Order Restraining Order (FA–14). The defendant must request that the motion be scheduled for a hearing. The plaintiff must be served with a copy of the motion and notice of the date and time of the hearing. In some courts, the practice is for the court schedule the hearing and notify both parties by mail. In other courts, the defendant must mail to the plaintiff a copy of the motion along with the information as to the date and time of the hearing.

ORDERS AFTER NOTICE

6:00 ORDERS AFTER NOTICE: GENERAL

Upon a finding of a substantial likelihood of an immediate danger of abuse in a hearing of which the defendant had notice (whether or not preceded by an *ex parte* or emergency order), the court may issue orders protecting the plaintiff from abuse, including but not limited to the following:

(a) ordering the defendant to refrain from abusing the plaintiff, whether the defendant is an adult or a minor;

(b) ordering the defendant to refrain from contacting the plaintiff, unless authorized by the court, whether the plaintiff is an adult or a minor;

(c) ordering the defendant to vacate forthwith and remain away from the household, multiple family dwelling, or workplace;

(d) awarding the plaintiff temporary custody of a minor child;

(e) ordering the defendant to pay temporary support for the plaintiff or any child in the plaintiff's custody or both, when the defendant has a legal obligation to support such a person;

(f) ordering the defendant to pay the plaintiff monetary compensation for losses suffered as a direct result of the abuse (compensatory losses may include, but not be limited to, loss of earnings or support, costs for restoring utilities, out-of-pocket losses for injuries sustained, replacement costs for locks or personal property removed or destroyed, medical and moving expenses and reasonable attorney's fees);

(g) ordering information in the case record to be impounded;

(h) ordering the defendant to refrain from abusing or contacting the plaintiff's child, or child in plaintiff's care or custody, unless such contact is authorized by the court; and

(i) recommending to the defendant that the defendant attend a batterer intervention program as certified by the Department of Public Health.

The court may issue mutual abuse prevention orders only if the court has made specific written findings of fact. *See Guideline 6:07*, Mutual Abuse Prevention Orders.

Plaintiffs should receive all of the relief to which the law and the facts entitle them. Judges should not, as a matter of practice, eliminate any option (e.g., support) from the relief statutorily available. *See Guideline 6:05B*, Support Orders.

However, in a court other than the Probate and Family Court, if the judge orders the defendant to stay away from or to have no contact with the defendant's minor children for more than a 10–day period, the judge should make written findings of fact that explain for the record the reason for the order. Such findings will serve as information for any Probate and Family Court judge who may hear the case at a later time and who may amend the order to eliminate inconsistent provisions pursuant to *Guideline 13:00*, Assignment of Justices of the Probate and Family Court Department to Modify Inconsistent Orders.

The Probate and Family Court judge will have superseding jurisdiction over custody and support and exclusive jurisdiction over visitation of minor children. Orders issued by the Probate and Family Court involving parents should indicate whether the non-custodial parent has sought and been denied shared legal custody based upon a threat to the safety of the child or custodial parent and whether the non-custodial parent is entitled to unsupervised visitation with the child. An order allowing, or not allowing, visitation affects a parent's access to information concerning a child. For example, G.L. c. 71, § 34H (amended by St. 2006, c. 62, § 1) provides that any parent without physical custody of his or her child may receive school information concerning said child unless: (a) the parent's access to same has been prohibited by a temporary or permanent protective order; (b) the parent has been denied visitation; or (c) based upon a threat to the child's safety, as specifically noted in the custody or visitation order, the parent has been denied legal custody, or has been restricted to supervised visitation only.

COMMENTARY

This Guideline lists the types of orders that are expressly authorized by law. However, the list is not exclusive. *See* G.L. c. 209A, § 3. The statute specifically provides that the court is not limited to the listed options and may issue any order warranted by the facts found. *See* Commentary to *Guideline 4:01*, Content of *Ex Parte* Orders ("[w]hen justified by the facts, the court has authority to order a defendant to stay away from a particular school or job site, even if the defendant attends the school or works at the same job."); *see also* Commonwealth v. Habenstreit, 57 Mass. App. Ct. 785 (2003), *rev. denied*, Commonwealth v. Habenstreit, 439 Mass. 1106 (2003).

Ordering a defendant to stay away from and to have no contact with his or her minor children is tantamount to extinguishing parental rights, at least for the duration of the order. Before issuing such an order, the judge should assess the danger of abuse to the children independently from the danger of abuse to the plaintiff. It is important that the plaintiff provide the court with a reason for ordering the defendant to have no contact with the defendant's minor children. "If there is to be a G.L. c. 209A order that a defendant stay from and have no contact with his or her minor children, there must be independent support for the order." Smith v. Joyce, 421 Mass. 520, 523 (1995). However, a defendant who abuses his or her child's other parent in the child's presence is likely abusing the child as well, by placing that child in fear of imminent serious physical harm and/or by causing emotional and psychological harm to the child. *See Guideline 2:04*, Plaintiff's Affidavit, regarding reasons to be set forth by plaintiff in an affidavit. Accordingly, it may be necessary and appropriate to issue a no-contact order concerning the defendant's minor children.

In certain cases, but particularly in a court other than the Probate and Family Court, the judge should make written findings to explain the reasons for the no-contact order. *See, e.g.*, Care and Protection of Lillith, 61 Mass. App. Ct. 132, 139–142 (2004), citing Custody of Vaughn, 422 Mass. 590, 599 (1996) (requirement of findings in custody cases when there has been evidence of domestic violence). Such findings will offer guidance to the Probate and Family Court in any later proceeding relating to custody of or visitation with the minor children, and will provide the best protection against the issuance of conflicting orders by the two courts. *Cf.*, Smith v. Joyce, 421 Mass. 520, 523 (1995). Appropriate reasons may include, but are not limited to, a finding that the children themselves have been abused, that they have witnessed the defendant's abuse of the plaintiff and are therefore afraid of the defendant, an would be harmed by seeing him or her, or that no visitation can be arranged with children in the plaintiff's custody without endangering the plaintiff.

General Laws c. 209A, § 3(e) requires that all orders of support "issued, reviewed or modified" under the statute must also conform to and be enforced under the provisions of G.L. c. 119A, § 12 (pertaining to child support enforcement). Any such orders of support should be issued in accordance with the Trial Court Child Support Guidelines (effective January 1, 2009) (available at http://www.mass.gov/courts/childsupport/guidelines.pdf). The child support worksheet may be accessed at http://www.mass.gov/courts/childsupport/worksheet-child-support-guidelines.pdf. *See 6:05B*, Support Orders.

6:01 REFERRAL FOR TREATMENT OR SUPPORTIVE SERVICES

In addition to including in the order terms necessary to ensure the safety of the plaintiff, the judge or court personnel may recommend and refer the parties to appropriate agencies for victims of violence, including but not limited to certified batterer intervention programs and counseling for substance abuse. The court should not recommend or suggest joint counseling or mediation. *See* G.L. c. 209A, § 3. For a list of certified batterer intervention programs go to www.mass.gov/ dph/violence, click on Batterer Intervention Program Services, then click on Certified Batterer Intervention Programs and Services.

The Probate and Family Court may issue orders contingent on the defendant's efforts to participate in and benefit from such services. The court should not attempt to order the plaintiff to participate in any such services.

COMMENTARY

In a case where social services can address some of the factors relating to abuse, such as alcohol or other substance abuse, the court may properly recommend or make referrals to such services, although these do not replace intervention to address the abuse. *See* Standards on Substance Abuse, Supreme Judicial Court, Approved April 28, 1998, Standard V, http://www.mass.gov/courts/formsandguidelines/ substancev.html. In addition, G.L. c. 209A, § 3 expressly authorizes the court to "recommend to the defendant that the defendant attend a batterer's intervention program that is certified by the department of public health." The Department of Public Health certifies batterer intervention programs. St. 1990, c. 403, § 16. Similarly, the court may recommend services helpful to the plaintiff. Such recommendations are not inconsistent with the protective purpose of c. 209A.

However, as discussed in *Guideline 1:01*, Protective Purpose of c. 209A, the purpose of c. 209A actions is to provide protection, when such is found to be warranted, and not to encourage reconciliation or joint counseling for the parties. Attempts by the court to require or even to promote reconciliation or joint counseling are inconsistent with the protective purpose of c. 209A. Such procedures can expose a plaintiff to further abuse and can provide an abuser with a forum for continued contact and domination. At the very least, such matters should be left to the plaintiff to decide. Moreover, the fear of being placed in such a situation may discourage or prevent a plaintiff from seeking the court's protection at all. Chapter 209A, § 3 provides specifically that:

No court shall compel parties to mediate any aspect of their case. Although the court may refer the case to the family service office of the probation department or victim/witness advocates for information gathering purposes, the court shall not compel the parties to meet together in such information gathering sessions.

In addition to including in the order terms necessary to ensure the safety of the plaintiff, the judge or court personnel may recommend and refer the parties to appropriate agencies for victims of violence and certified batterer intervention programs. Among these may be counseling for substance abuse. *See Guideline 10:00*, Civil Commitment for Alcoholism or Other Substance Abuse.

The Probate and Family Court alone may indicate that modification of the terms of its order may be contingent on the defendant's efforts to participate in and benefit from such services. G.L. c. 276, § 42A.

Further, regarding visitation (which is not within the jurisdiction of the District Court, Boston Municipal Court or Superior Court departments), G.L. c. 209A, § 3 provides:

[i]f ordering visitation to the abusive parent, the court shall provide for the safety and well-being of the child and the safety of the abused parent. The court may consider: . . . (c) ordering the abusive parent to attend and complete, to the satisfaction of the court, a certified batterer's treatment program as a condition of visitation; (d) ordering the abusive parent to abstain from possession or consumption of alcohol or controlled substances during the visitation and for 24 hours preceding visitation . . . (i) imposing any other condition that is deemed necessary to provide for the safety and well-being of the child and the safety of the abused parent . . . Nothing in this section shall

be construed to affect the right of the parties to a hearing under the rules of domestic relations procedure or to affect the discretion of the probate and family court in the conduct of such hearing.

G.L. c. 209A, § 3(d).

6:02   DURATION

Each order issued after notice (except permanent orders) should be for a minimum of one year, unless the plaintiff requests a lesser period or the court finds that a lesser period is warranted. The parties should be informed that the plaintiff must appear before the court on the date set for expiration of the order if the plaintiff wishes the order extended. The parties should be told that the order cannot be terminated prior to the termination date without an appearance in the same court. *See Guideline 4:06*, Information for the Plaintiff; and *Guideline 6:04*, Modification of Orders; Terminating Orders. If neither party appears on the expiration date, the order will expire by its own terms. *See also Guideline 6:09*, Extension of Orders for a Term of Years; Permanent Orders.

COMMENTARY

The court should not, as a matter of policy, routinely issue orders for less than a one-year period over the plaintiff's objection. Also, there is usually no reason for the civil order to track the schedule of a related criminal case. Nor is it appropriate to "see how the relationship goes" if the law and the facts support the issuance of an abuse prevention order and the plaintiff wishes it to be effective for a full year. If the defendant feels at some future point that an order should be terminated or its duration or terms limited, the defendant may move to modify the order. On the expiration date of an order after notice, the plaintiff may request a permanent order pursuant to G.L. c. 209A, § 3, which provides,

[i]f the plaintiff appears at the court at the date and time the order is to expire, the court shall determine whether or not to extend the order for any additional time reasonably necessary to protect the plaintiff or to enter a permanent order.

In Crenshaw v. Macklin, 430 Mass. 633, 635 (2000), the SJC affirmed a court's authority to issue a permanent order following a "renewal hearing. *See also* Commonwealth v. Leger, 52 Mass. App. Ct. 232, 239–241 (2001) (one-year time limitation for c. 209A orders applies only to initial hearing; judge may permanently extend order at subsequent hearing).

See Guideline 6:08, Further Extending an Order After Notice on Its Expiration, and Commentary thereto; *Guideline 6:09*, Extension of Orders for a Term of Years; Permanent Orders; and Commentary to *Guideline 12:10*, Issuance of Protective Orders: Divorce Proceedings; and *Guideline 12:11*, Issuance of Orders to Vacate Marital Residence: Divorce, Separate Support or Maintenance.

In some cases, at the expiration date of an order after notice it may be appropriate to issue an order for a period of time that is longer than an additional year but less than a permanent order. *See* Crenshaw v. Macklin, 430 Mass. 633, 635 (2000). In determining whether to issue a permanent order or an order for a particular period of years, the court may consider the severity and frequency of the violence involved, threats to do harm in the future and the ages of minor children, and any other relevant facts. For example, the court may determine that it is appropriate to extend an order until the youngest child of the parties reaches age 18. At the hearing, both parties should be informed that, as with all types of orders, the defendant must comply with a no-contact or vacate order unless and until those specific orders are terminated in writing by the court. The plaintiff has no authority to "waive" such orders, without going to court to ask to have them terminated, and the defendant who violates those orders is subject to mandatory warrantless arrest, regardless of the plaintiff's "consent."

6:03 SERVICE OF ORDERS
ON THE DEFENDANT

Service of the order after notice should be made in-hand by court personnel when the defendant is before the court for the hearing after notice or for any other purpose. This service should be recorded on the order form at section B.3. A copy of the order must also be sent to the appropriate police department.

If the defendant does not appear, the order must be transmitted to the police for service in accordance with G.L. c. 209A, § 7. The court should require that such service be made in the same manner as service of the *ex parte* order or in whatever manner is most likely to result in actual notice to the defendant.

A Defendant Information Form should always accompany the police copy and the service copies of the order.

COMMENTARY

General Laws c. 209A, § 7, second par., sets forth the required procedure for service of all orders issued under that law, including transmitting the documents to the appropriate police department, service by the police, and the filing of a return of service. However, if the defendant is before the court, direct in-hand service is appropriate and obviates the need for police service. Whenever it is possible, defendants should be instructed to remain in the courtroom until service is made. The plaintiff should receive a copy of the completed order before the defendant is served so that the plaintiff has the opportunity to leave the courthouse and avoid possible contact with the defendant. A copy of the order should nonetheless be sent to the appropriate police department for notification and enforcement purposes.

The judge and court personnel should be aware that a defendant subject to a recently issued abuse prevention order from that court may not yet have been served with a copy of that order. If a defendant is before the court at any other time, whether for related or unrelated criminal charges, or for subsequent c. 209A hearings, or for any other reason, he or she should be served with a copy of the order and such service should be reflected on the order.

If the defendant is not before the court when an order after notice is issued, service is required. *See* Commonwealth v. Griffen, 444 Mass. 1004 (2005) (service made via telephone is improper). If the *ex parte* order has been served on the defendant, the form itself notifies the defendant of the date for the hearing after notice and that, "[t]he Defendant may appear, with or without attorney, to oppose any extension or modification of this Order. If the Defendant does not appear, the Order may be extended or modified as determined by the Judge." (FA–2).

If the defendant is served with the *ex parte* order and fails to appear for the hearing after notice, the extended order will be valid, even if it is not subsequently served on the defendant. Commonwealth v. Delaney, 425 Mass. 587 (1997), *cert denied*, Delaney v. Commonwealth, 522 U.S. 1958 (1998). *See also* Commonwealth v. Henderson, 434 Mass. 155 (2001). In Delaney, the court stated that, "evidence that the *ex parte* order delivered to the defendant's last and usual address was actually received warrants the conclusion that the defendant had actual knowledge of the terms of the extended order, as does the defendant's testimony that, following his arrest after the [order was extended], he was aware that there was a protective order against him." *Id.* at 593. In addition, the court stated that this provision on the *ex parte* order form provides that, "the defendant, who with reasonable inquiry could have discovered that the temporary order had been extended, cannot be heard to complain that he was deprived of any opportunity to seek to have that extended order vacated." *Id.* at 592.

However, such constructive notice is not sufficient for successive orders issued after the one-year date. *See Guideline 6:08*, Further Extending an Order After Notice on Its Expiration Date, and the discussion regarding Commonwealth v. Delaney, *supra*, and Commonwealth v. Munafo, *supra*. Both Commonwealth v. Delaney, *supra*, and Commonwealth v. Munafo, *supra*, involve *ex parte* orders that were extended. In Commonwealth v. Molloy, 44 Mass. App. Ct. 306 (1998), *rev. denied*, Commonwealth v. Molloy, 427 Mass. 1107 (1998), the Appeals Court reversed a conviction for violation of an order that had been extended annually, distinguishing between service regarding extension of temporary orders and such "successive annual extensions." *Id.* at 308. The court stated, "the extension of an annual order pursuant to [c. 209A] § 3, in contrast to a § 4 continuation of a temporary order, is ... by no means automatic, even if a defendant fails to appear." *Id.* at 309. The court added that there was no evidence at trial, "that anyone made a 'conscientious and reasonable effort to serve ... the defendant' or that some alternative means of service was used to notify him." *Id.* at 309.

In Commonwealth v. Crimmins, 46 Mass. App. Ct. 489 (1999), the court affirmed a conviction for violation of an order extended annually where the serving officer signed the return of service but failed to check off the box on the order form to indicate the means of service. *Id.* at 492. The court stated that where a return of service of an extension of an annual order fails to indicate the manner in which service was achieved, "[t]he Commonwealth can meet that burden with evidence of proof of service of the order by means reasonably calculated to reach the defendant." *Id.* at 491. The court opined that the serving officer knew the defendant's address and that three and one-half hour period between issuance of the extended order and the officer's time of return of service suggests that there was no difficulty serving the defendant. Further, the court stated, the three and one-half hour time frame also precluded the seeking of an order for substituted service if the officer found it difficult to serve the order. *Id.* at 493 –494. *See also Guideline 6:08*, Further Extending an Order After Notice on Its Expiration Date, and Commentary thereto regarding standard of proof and service of extended orders and *Guideline 8:01*, Issuance of Criminal Complaint, regarding prosecution for violation of orders.

This guideline recommends in-hand service of each abuse prevention order issued by the court or service through whatever manner is most likely to result in actual notice to the defendant. Without such notice, the deterrent effect of the order is lost, and prosecution for a subsequent violation of the order is compromised.

In appropriate circumstances, the court may order an alternative method of service. Specifically, the Supreme Judicial Court has held, "when the appropriate law enforcement agency has made a conscientious and reasonable effort to serve the statutorily specified documents on the defendant, but has nevertheless failed, the agency should promptly notify the court so that a judge, if satisfied after a hearing that an appropriate effort has been made, may order that service be made by some other identified means reasonably calculated to reach the defendant. Where such substituted service appears unlikely to notify the defendant, the judge may excuse service." Zullo v. Goguen, 423 Mass. 679, 681 (1996). Alternative service may include service at last and usual address, leaving at an address a defendant is know to frequent (e.g., parent's home) and notice by publication. *See also* Commentary to *Guideline 4:07*, Transmission of *Ex Parte* Orders to the Police for Service on the Defendant, and *Guideline 5:05*, Failure of Defendant to Appear.

6:04 MODIFICATION OF ORDERS;
TERMINATING ORDERS

After a hearing, the court may modify or terminate an existing order upon motion by either party.[4] Such motions should be in writing and should be served on the opposing party and filed in court at least seven days in advance of the date requested for a hearing, unless the court otherwise permits. Where a plaintiff seeks to terminate an order in part or in its entirety, the court may hear that motion without advance notice to the defendant, since allowing the motion would reduce or eliminate the restrictions on the defendant. If a defendant seeks to modify an order and the plaintiff's address is inaccessible to the defendant as provided in G.L. c. 209A, § 8, the court is responsible for notifying the plaintiff. In no event shall the court disclose any such inaccessible address. G.L. c. 209A, § 3. Whenever a c. 209A order is modified or extended, the judge must determine if returning the license or guns or ammunition of the defendant would present "a likelihood of abuse to the plaintiff." G.L. c. 209A, § 3C. *See Guideline 6:05*, Orders to Surrender Guns, Licenses to Carry Firearms and FID Cards.

If the court modifies or terminates an order, it should transmit a copy of the modified or terminated order to the police department where the order is on file.

The police should be instructed to serve a copy of any modified order on the defendant, unless the defendant appeared in court at the hearing and was given a copy of the modified order at that time.

If an order is terminated, the court must notify the police in writing and direct the department to destroy all records of the terminated order. All changes should be entered promptly in the Statewide Registry of Civil Restraining Orders. Records of orders are not to be expunged from this record keeping system, except in the rare case when the order was obtained through the commission of fraud on the court. Comm'r of Probation v. Adams, 65 Mass. App. Ct. 725, 728–737 (2006). *See also* Commonwealth v. Boe, 456 Mass. 337, 347, n. 14 (2010).

4 *See Guideline 1:00*, In General, for discussion of the current use of the term "terminated" instead of "vacated."

COMMENTARY

Both parties have the right to ask the court to modify an existing order, by either increasing or decreasing the severity of the terms, or by terminating the order. Any motion to modify or terminate order by the Probate and Family Court must be filed with the court and served on the opposing party in compliance with Rule 6(c) of the Massachusetts Rules of Domestic Relations Procedures. *See Guideline 1:03*, Procedural Rules; Discovery, regarding application of rules of procedure.

Written notification from the court to the police directing them to destroy a vacated or terminated order, and compliance with such directive, are required by G.L. c. 209A, § 7, third par.[5] In most instances however, records of orders are not to be expunged from the Registry of Civil Restraining Orders, Vaccaro v. Vaccaro, 425 Mass. 153, 155–159 (1997), absent a showing that the order was obtained through the commission of fraud on the court. Comm'r of Probation v. Adams, 65 Mass. App. Ct. 725, 728–737 (2006). *See also* Commonwealth v. Boe, 456 Mass. 337, 347, n. 14 (2010).

In Vaccaro, "the Supreme Judicial Court held that the District Court has no authority to order that the name of a defendant in an abuse prevention proceeding under G.L. c. 209A be expunged from the Statewide Domestic Violence Registry." Vaccaro, 425 Mass. at 155–156. *But see* Faye v. Flemming, 48 Mass. App. Ct. 1113 (1999) (rescript) (ordering that a mutual *ex parte* order issued without sufficient factual support and without written findings of fact be vacated *nunc pro tunc*). The Appeals Court has modified the holding in Vaccaro, finding that a judge has the inherent authority to expunge an order issued under c. 209A in the "rare and limited circumstances"

that the party seeking the expungement can demonstrate by clear and convincing evidence that the order was obtained through commission of fraud on the court. *See* Adams, 65 Mass. App. Ct. at 737.

If, at the hearing on a motion by either party to modify an order, it is determined that there has been no prior service on the other party giving notice of the hearing, the court should defer action on the motion until service is made and adequate notice is given, at least when the new terms are adverse to the absent party. Action on a motion to modify filed by the plaintiff should not be deferred pending notice to the defendant if the grounds for an *ex parte* order are met, namely, the modification is needed because there is "a substantial likelihood of immediate danger of abuse." G.L. c. 209A, § 4. If the judge issues the modification *ex parte*, a hearing with notice to the other party should be scheduled within ten court business days. However, where a plaintiff seeks to terminate an order in part or in its entirety, the court may hear that motion without advance notice to the defendant. *See* Plaintiff's Motion to Modify or Terminate Abuse Prevention Order (FA–13) and Defendant's Motion to Modify or Terminate Abuse Prevention Order Restraining Order (FA–14).

The police must be given all modified and terminated orders and should be instructed to serve such orders on any defendant who was not given the modified order when before the court regardless of whether the defendant received notice of the hearing. Even if the defendant received notice of the hearing and failed to attend, service of the modified order is necessary to inform the defendant of any new protective restriction or requirement, and may be necessary for prosecutorial purposes should any new terms be violated.

Each time an order issued under c. 209A is extended or modified the judge must determine if returning the defendant's firearms or firearm identification card would present a likelihood of abuse to the plaintiff. If the judge makes such a determination, the court shall continue the firearm surrender order and shall in sections C or D of the order by checking the box that provides, "Firearm surrender order continued. The items surrendered under section 12.A will NOT be returned since doing so would present a likelihood of abuse to the plaintiff." *See Guideline 6:05*, Orders to Surrender Guns, Licenses to Carry Firearms and FID Cards.

See Guideline 5:08, Request by the Plaintiff or Defendant to Modify or Terminate the Abuse Prevention Order, and *Guideline 13:00*, Assignment of Justices of the Probate and Family Court Department to Modify Inconsistent Orders, regarding interdepartmental judicial assignments and modification of orders.

5 Please note that G.L. c. 209A, § 7 uses the term "vacated".

6:05 ORDERS TO SURRENDER GUNS, LICENSES TO CARRY FIREARMS AND FID CARDS

An order for the suspension of a license to carry a firearm and for the surrender of a gun, ammunition, license and FID card issued *ex parte* must be continued in any order after notice, if the court finds that the return of the license, FID card, gun or ammunition presents "a likelihood of abuse to the plaintiff." It appears that this requirement refers to a likelihood of abuse relating to the return of the license, gun or firearm.

In all other regards, the issuance of an order after notice requires proof, by a preponderance of the evidence, of a substantial likelihood of abuse.

COMMENTARY

All *ex parte* orders that are issued under c. 209A must contain orders that the defendant's firearms and any firearms licenses be surrendered to the police. G.L. c. 209A, § 3B. *See Guideline 4:04*, *Ex Parte* Orders to Surrender Guns, Licenses to Carry Firearms and FID Cards.

Each time an order issued under c. 209A is extended or modified the judge must determine if returning the defendant's firearms or firearm identification card would present a likelihood of abuse to the plaintiff. If the judge makes such a determination, the court shall continue the firearm surrender order and shall in sections C or D of the Order (FA–2a) by checking the box that provides, "Firearm surrender order continued. The items surrendered under section A.12 will NOT be returned since doing so would present a likelihood of abuse to the plaintiff." This determination must be made irrespective of whether the plaintiff requests it and the box indicating that the required finding has been made must be checked, even if the judge has indicated that the *ex parte* order will continue without modification. If the judge intends that the firearm restriction continue each time the order is modified or extended it must be made clear on the form. Enforcement of this provision in another state may be dependent upon whether the order contains such a finding.

Returning firearms while an abuse prevention order is in effect may place the defendant in violation of state and federal law. No firearms identification card may be issued to any person who is subject to a permanent or temporary protection order issued pursuant to c. 209A. *See* G.L. c. 140, § 129B(1)(viii)(b).

Similarly, no license to carry firearms may be issued to any person who is subject to a permanent or temporary protection order issued pursuant to c. 209A. G.L. c. 140, § 131(d)(vi)(B). *See* Commentary to *Guideline 4:04*, *Ex Parte* Orders to Surrender Guns, Licenses to Carry Firearms and FID Cards. Subject to certain exceptions, possession of a firearm and/or ammunition while subject to a qualifying abuse prevention order is a federal crime. *See* 18 U.S.C. § 922 (g)(8).

6:05A CUSTODY ORDERS

In a c. 209A proceeding brought in the Probate and Family Court Department, if the court finds by a preponderance of the credible evidence that a pattern or serious incident of abuse has occurred toward a parent or child, a rebuttable presumption is created that it is not in the best interest of the child to be placed in sole or shared custody with the abusive parent. If after so finding the court issues a temporary or permanent custody order, the court must within 90 days enter written findings as to the effects of the abuse on the child. These findings must demonstrate that the order is in the best interest of the child and provides for the child's safety and well-being.

COMMENTARY

General Laws c. 209A, § 3(d) provides that if the Probate and Family Court finds by a preponderance of the evidence that credible evidence was presented that a pattern or serious incident of abuse toward a parent or child has occurred, a rebuttable presumption is created that it is not in the best interest of the child to be placed in sole custody, shared legal custody or shared physical custody with the abusive parent. This presumption may be rebutted if the court finds that awarding custody to the abusive parent is in the best interests of the child.

"Abuse" as defined in G.L. c. 208, § 31A occurs when the defendant has engaged in one or more of the following acts: attempted to cause bodily injury to the other parent or to the child; has caused bodily injury to the other parent or to the child; or placed the other parent or the child in reasonable fear of imminent bodily injury. Section 31A defines a "serious incident of abuse" as engaging in action that: attempts to cause serious bodily injury to the other parent or to the child; causes serious bodily injury to the other parent or to the child; places the other parent or the child in reasonable fear of imminent serious bodily injury; or causes the other parent or the child to engage involuntarily in sexual relations by force, threat or duress.

"Bodily injury" and "serious bodily injury" are defined for purposes of G.L. c. 208, § 31A by G.L. c. 265, § 13K. Bodily injury is that which causes "substantial impairment of the physical condition, including, but not limited to, any burn, fracture of any bone, subdural hematoma, injury to any internal organ, or any injury which occurs as the result of repeated harm to any bodily function or organ, including human skin . . . ." G.L. c. 265, § 13K. Serious bodily injury is defined as "bodily injury which results in a permanent disfigurement, protracted loss or impairment of a bodily function, limb or organ, or substantial risk of death." *Id.*

For the purposes of G.L. c. 209A, § 3(d), the issuance of one or more orders pursuant to c. 209A does not in and of itself constitute a pattern or serious incident of abuse. In addition, an *ex parte* order or orders will not be admissible to show whether a pattern or serious incident of abuse has occurred. *Ex parte* orders may, however, be admissible for other purposes as the court may determine. Finally, the underlying facts upon which an order or orders issued pursuant to c. 209A was based may form the basis for a finding by the Probate and Family Court that a pattern or serious incident of abuse has occurred.

General Laws c. 209A, § 3(d) requires that the court enter findings within 90 days indicating the effects of the abuse on the child and that the order is in the best interests of the child and provides for the child's safety and well-being when issuing any temporary or permanent custody order when there has been a pattern or serious incident of abuse. These findings must be made in the following circumstances: 1) if there is a pre-existing custody order and the court finds by a preponderance of the evidence that a pattern or serious incident of abuse has occurred such that the court changes custody from the defendant to the plaintiff; or 2) if there is no custody order and the court finds by a preponderance of the evidence that a pattern or serious incident of abuse has occurred and the court grants custody to the plaintiff. The findings should not be made until the full hearing since the determination of a pattern or serious incident of abuse should not be made *ex parte*.

If a pre-existing custody order exists and it will not be modified by the c. 209A order, the custody presumption statute does not apply to the c. 209A order. If the court finds that the plaintiff has been the perpetrator of the abuse, then the c. 209A should be dismissed and the custody issue should be heard in another proceeding. *See Guideline 12:05A*, Custody Proceedings in Probate and Family Court: Custody Presumption Applicability.

6:05B SUPPORT ORDERS

Plaintiffs who are otherwise entitled to relief under c. 209A should be permitted to address the question of support for themselves and their minor children in the c. 209A hearing after notice. *See Guideline 3:07*, Conduct of *Ex Parte* Hearings, *Guideline 4:03*; *Ex Parte* Support and Compensation Orders; and *Guideline 6:00*, Orders After Notice: General. General Laws c. 209A, § 3(e) provides that the court may order "the defendant to pay temporary support for the plaintiff or any child in the plaintiff's custody or both, when the defendant has a legal obligation to support such a person." The court should refer plaintiffs who have an existing support order from the Probate and Family Court to that court for enforcement of the support order, or for any requested modifications.

The Trial Court Child Support Guidelines should be applied in determining the presumptive amount of child support. G.L. c. 209A, § 3(e). To determine an appropriate amount of child support based upon the Trial Court Child Support Guidelines, the judge should consider proof of income and expenses from both parties. Judges sitting in District Court, Boston Municipal Court and Superior Court can obtain this information by requiring the parties to complete the Plaintiff's Affidavit in Support of a Request for a Child Support Order (FA–11) and Defendant's Affidavit in Connection with Plaintiff's Request for a Child Support Order (FA12). Deviation from the presumptive amount of child support provided by the Guidelines may be appropriate in certain circumstances. *See* Trial Court Child Support Guidelines (effective January 1, 2009) (available at http://www.mass.gov/courts/childsupport/guidelines.pdf).

General Laws c. 209A, § 3(e) provides that child support orders must conform to and be enforced in compliance with the provisions of G.L. c. 119A, § 12. General Laws c. 119A, § 12 establishes that income withholding, commonly known as income assignment or wage garnishment, is the standard method for collecting child support. The Department of Revenue, Child Support Enforcement Division (DOR), is the agency designated to provide income withholding services for child support, either alone or in conjunction with support for the plaintiff. However, DOR does not provide income withholding services for support for the plaintiff, unless the court has ordered support for minor children.

To order the defendant to pay child support by income withholding, judges should check off the box in section 9 of the Order (FA–2), which orders the defendant to pay monthly or weekly payments of support to the child or children through the Department of Revenue, by income withholding. This also orders the defendant to send payments directly to DOR at P.O. Box 55144, Boston, Massachusetts, 02205, during the period of time (often several weeks) that DOR is setting up income withholding with the defendant's employer if any. All payments made directly to DOR should include the defendant's social security number. This type of order allows for child support to be collected with no contact between the parties.

General Laws c. 119A, § 12(c) allows a judge to "suspend" the income withholding and order child support to be paid directly to the plaintiff. Income withholding can be suspended if the parties agree in writing that the payment shall be made directly or if the judge finds good cause exists to order that the income withholding be suspended and makes written findings in support of suspension. "Such written findings shall include a determination by the court that immediate income withholding would not be in the best interests of the child and the reasons therefore and, in the case of a modification of a support order, shall include proof of timely payments made in compliance with the existing order." G.L. c. 119A, § 12(c).[6] If payment is to be made directly to the plaintiff, the judge must reconcile this order with any no-contact provision in the c. 209A order. For example, if the judge orders that the defendant have no contact with the plaintiff, and that support payments be mailed to the plaintiff, the order should state this as an exception to the no-contact provision for the limited purpose of mailing of support payments. *See Guideline 4:01*, Content of *Ex Parte* Orders, regarding no-contact orders. A judge may also choose to suspend income withholding but still direct payments be made through DOR.

6 G.L. c. 119A, § 12(c) also provides that the judge must, prior to a hearing on suspension, inform the defendant that the income withholding, even if suspended, will go into effect if there are two weeks of arrearages or if either party request, the withholding order go into effect.

COMMENTARY

The protective purpose of c. 209A is frustrated if the relief that it provides is not made available. Immediate support for the plaintiff and for any minor children may be a necessary precondition to the plaintiff's ability to seek other relief, e.g., the plaintiff may not be able to live away from a batterer unless he or she has enough money to feed the children or for a place to stay. Referring the plaintiff to the Probate and Family Court or to the Department of Revenue (DOR) to establish a child support order—a process that can take weeks or months—should not substitute for providing relief under c. 209A when the law and the facts warrant such relief.

Some courts, as a matter of course, provide the necessary Department of Revenue forms to c. 209A plaintiffs requesting child support. This makes beginning the process of enforcing a c. 209A support order easier for the plaintiff. While enforcing the c. 209A support order, DOR will typically pursue a child support order in the Probate and Family Court that will extend support until the minor children are emancipated. Thus, the DOR support process is one that may provide more long-term security for a plaintiff with minor children, along with the immediate relief that a c. 209A support order can bring. Upon request, DOR will provide any court with copies of the DOR forms.

The Trial Court Child Support Guidelines (effective January 1, 2009) (available at http://www.mass.gov/courts/childsupport/guidelines.pdf) should be applied in determining the amount of support. The child support worksheet may be accessed at http://www.mass.gov/courts/childsupport/worksheet-child-support-guidelines.pdf. The Guidelines are revised periodically, so the current version should be consulted. If a c. 209A support order is reviewed or modified, the judge should apply the Guidelines and construct an order that is consistent with G.L. c. 119A, § 12.

The court may order support payments in cases where there is not a current support order, even if the plaintiff is currently receiving cash benefits through Transitional Aid to Families with Dependent Children (TAFDC).

Violations of c. 209A support orders are punishable only by contempt actions and not as criminal violations of the c. 209A order. *See Guideline 8:00*, Venue; Territorial Jurisdiction for Criminal Prosecution of Violations of c. 209A Orders; *Guideline 8:01*, Issuance of Criminal Complaint; *Guideline 8:02*, Criminal Contempt; and *Guideline 8:02A*, Civil Contempt.

If legal paternity has not been established, and there is a dispute regarding paternity of the minor children, a judge cannot order c. 209A support. In most cases, legal paternity is established if the parties were married at the time the child was born, if defendant's name is listed on the birth certificate, or if the defendant has otherwise been adjudicated the father. The District Court, Boston Municipal Court and the Probate and Family Court can adjudicate paternity, but genetic marker testing to establish paternity is administered by DOR and is usually done in connection with an action in the Probate and Family Court.

6:06 VISITATION ORDERS AND OTHER COURTS

The District Court, Boston Municipal Court and Superior Court do not have jurisdiction to order visitation with minor children at the request of a defendant in a c. 209A action. Where either party seeks a court ordered visitation plan, the parties should be referred to the Probate and Family Court for consideration of such an order. Similarly, if the plaintiff asks that the defendant be permitted to visit with the children only if the defendant complies with certain conditions (substance abuse treatment, random drug or alcohol screens, counseling), the parties should be referred to the Probate and Family Court for that relief only.

In some cases, where the plaintiff requests a no-contact order and/or a stay-away order, and the court finds a basis to issue such an order, but the plaintiff wants the defendant to have contact with the minor children, the order may be drafted in a way that facilitates contact with those children. For example, telephone or e-mail contact or indirect contact through a third party may be authorized in order to facilitate contact with the minor children. Alternatively, the distance restriction may be drafted to permit curbside pick-up and drop-off of minor children. Any such orders should be crafted in a way that does not expose the plaintiff to harm or risk of harm.

Where the court has found an independent basis to issue an order prohibiting contact with minor children and the defendant seeks to have contact with those children, the Boston Municipal Court, District Court, or Superior Court should refer the defendant to the Probate and Family Court with regard to the visitation issues.

Both parties should be told that the Probate and Family Court has superseding jurisdiction regarding custody, support and contact with minor children and exclusive jurisdiction regarding visitation. See Guidelines 12:00–12:14 generally, regarding, related proceedings in Probate and Family Court.

There may be cases in which the Probate and Family Court issues a visitation order that is inconsistent with an existing order issued by the District Court, Boston Municipal Court or Superior Court. Consistent with Administrative Order 96–1, a judge in the Probate and Family Court may sit as a judge of the District Court, Boston Municipal Court, or Superior Court and modify, extend or vacate an abuse prevention order issued by the District Court, Boston Municipal Court, or Superior Court to eliminate conflict between said order and any order issued by the Probate and Family Court.[7] See Guideline 13:00, Assignment of Justices of the Probate and Family Court Department to Modify Inconsistent Orders. To the extent possible, the Probate and Family Court Judge should specifically and clearly identify the modified provisions on the face of the c. 209A order. The modified order should not simply refer to an attached order or agreement, particularly with respect to modification of the provisions regarding the contact and stay-away orders between the parties and/or children.

If the Probate and Family Court does not modify the existing order issued by the District Court, Boston Municipal Court, or Superior Court, any violation of the terms of the earlier order will expose the defendant to immediate arrest even if he or she is relying on the Probate and Family Court order.

[7] Please note that Administrative Order 96–1 uses the term "vacate."

COMMENTARY

District Court, Boston Municipal Court and Superior Court have no authority to order visitation for a defendant in a c. 209A action. Defendants seeking such orders should be referred to the Probate and Family Court.

However, the issue of contact with minor children arises frequently in the context of c. 209A proceedings in the District Court, Boston Municipal Court and Superior Court. In those circumstances where the court is satisfied that the requirements for issuing a c. 209A on behalf of the plaintiff have been met, but plaintiff or both parties want the defendant to continue to have contact with minor children, this guideline recommends that the court craft an order that accommo-

dates the plaintiff's desire that the defendant continue to have contact with the minor children. This Guideline recommends that the court do so only where the court is satisfied that such provisions do not expose the plaintiff (or the minor children) to harm or risk of harm. If the court finds an independent basis to issue an order that the defendant have no contact with his minor children, or if the parties do not agree on any provisions that would facilitate contact with minor children or if the court declines to craft an order that would facilitate that contact, the defendant should be told that visitation may be sought in the Probate and Family Court.

If the Probate and Family Court permits the defendant to have visitation or other contact with minor children, the Probate and Family Court can modify, extend, or vacate[8] any provisions of the original order to make them in order to eliminate any conflict between said order and the terms of the order issued by the Probate and Family Court. See Guideline 13:00, Assignment of Justices of the Probate and Family Court Department to Modify Inconsistent Orders. See also Administrative Order 96–1 reprinted at the end of Guideline 13:00, Assignment of Justices of the Probate and Family Court Department to Modify Inconsistent Orders. The Probate and Family Court should promptly provide a copy of the modified order and any Probate and Family Court visitation order to the court that issued the original order. Generally, this should be done via facsimile.

To the extent possible, the Probate and Family Court Judge should specifically and clearly identify the modified provisions on the face of the c. 209A order. The modified order should not simply refer to an attached order or agreement, particularly with respect to modification of the provisions regarding the contact and stay-away orders between the parties and/or children.

In accordance with Administrative Order 96–1, the probation department in the modifying court will immediately transmit a copy of the order, including all additional pages of the order if there was inadequate space on the original order to include complete details of the modification, by facsimile to the issuing court. The issuing court must then enter the order into the Registry of Civil Restraining orders, notify the appropriate police department of the modified order, and update its case file. See Guideline 13:00, Assignment of Justices of the Probate and Family Court Department to Modify Inconsistent Orders.

If the Probate and Family Court orders visitation but does not modify the court's original no-contact or stay-away order as it relates to the plaintiff, the Probate and Family Court order will not supersede the original court's no-contact or stay-away order. G.L. c. 209A, § 3 "does not provide for automatic supersession of the protective provisions of a 209A abuse prevention order upon the issuance of an inconsistent visitation order issued in, for example, a divorce or paternity action. Rather, to supersede the protective provisions of another court's 209A order, the Probate Court must modify that other court's abuse prevention order by entering the modification on the 209A form of order .... If orders entered in a 209A proceeding and another action in the Probate Court are inconsistent, the protections afforded by the 209A order will take precedence over orders for custody or visitation entered in the other proceeding." Commonwealth v. Rauseo, 50 Mass. App. Ct. 699, 709–710 (2001), rev. denied, Commonwealth v. Rauseo, 434 Mass 1102 (2001).

Where the Probate and Family Court has not modified the terms of the prior abuse prevention order, the parties may return to the court that issued the original order to seek a modification of the order to make it consistent with the Probate and Family Court visitation order. No "stipulation" of the parties in the Probate and Family Court will itself serve to modify any outstanding order of another court, or require the original court to modify its order. If the parties seek to modify the original no-contact order to make it consistent with a Probate and Family Court visitation order, the judge should ask the plaintiff if reduction in the terms of the abuse prevention order is what the plaintiff actually desires. If not, the original court order should not be modified, unless the evidence otherwise warrants a modification. If the original order is not modified (either because neither party seeks such modification or because the judge in the original court declines to modify the original order) the defendant is subject to immediate arrest for violation of the no-contact or stay-away provisions of the original order even though the defendant was acting in accordance with the Probate and Family Court visitation order.

The original court is responsible for the protection terms of the order (or the lack of such terms), notwithstanding discussions that may have occurred between the parties in proceedings before the Probate and Family Court. The issue of protection should not be confused with the issue of visitation, and the latter should be considered subordinate to the question of protection. If the plaintiff does agree to the modification of the abuse prevention order, the modification should ordinarily be allowed.

As in other instances where the parties to an order issued by one court seek relief in another court and there is the potential for mutual abuse prevention orders *Guideline 6:07*, Mutual Abuse Prevention Orders should be consulted.

It should be noted that even if the parties resolve the issue of visitation consensually, if the non-custodial parent's access to the child is restricted, the parent may be prohibited from contacting, and/or obtaining information from, the child's school. *See* G.L. c. 71, § 34H. *See also Guideline 6.00*, Orders After Notice: General.

For visitation matters before the Probate and Family Court Department, *see Guideline 12:00*, Visitation Proceedings in Probate and Family Court: Considered Only in Limited Circumstances.

8. Please note that Administrative Order 96–1 uses the term "vacate."

6:07 MUTUAL ABUSE PREVENTION ORDERS

Where the parties seek abuse prevention orders against one another, the court has a responsibility to decide who is in danger from whom, who needs the court's protection and whether one party is the primary aggressor. A mutual abuse prevention order should only be issued when both parties are suffering from abuse, having proved that circumstance by a preponderance of the evidence, and both are genuinely in need of protection from such abuse. "A court may issue a mutual restraining order or mutual no-contact order pursuant to any abuse prevention action only if the court has made specific written findings of fact." G.L. c. 209A, § 3. The findings of fact should provide the basis for the court's conclusion that each party has proved, by a preponderance of the evidence, that he or she is suffering abuse by the other party and that the resulting abuse prevention orders are warranted. "The court shall then provide a detailed order, sufficiently specific to apprise any law officer as to which party has violated the order, if the parties are in or appear to be in violation of the order." G.L. c. 209A, § 3. All mutual orders must include a reference to the other order by court department, division and case number.

Consecutive orders, where the same parties reverse roles in different courts are, also, mutual orders. Sommi v. Ayer, 51 Mass. App. Ct. 207, 209–210 (2001). If the second order is sought in the same court that issued the first, the court has three options, depending upon the court's findings: 1) if the standard for issuance of a order has not been met, decline to issue an order; 2) if the court finds a substantial likelihood of immediate danger and the hearing after notice on the first order has not yet been held, issue the order and either make it returnable on the date scheduled for the hearing in the first case or on a different date; or 3) if the standard for an *ex parte* hearing is not met, defer the hearing on the second order until a hearing with all parties is held. *See Guideline*

6:04, Modification of Orders; Terminating Orders. If, at the hearing, relief to both parties is warranted, mutual orders may be issued.

If the court in the second action is not the court that issued the first order, it has the following three options depending upon its findings: 1) if it finds that the standard for issuance of an order has not been met, decline to issue an order; 2) if it finds a substantial likelihood of immediate danger and the hearing after notice in the first court has not yet been held, the second court may issue the order and ask the departmental Chief Justice (or, if the courts are in different departments, the Chief Justice for Administration and Management) to transfer the second matter to the first court on the date scheduled for the hearing; or 3) the second court may schedule the complaint for a hearing in the second court after notice.

COMMENTARY

Mutual abuse prevention orders should be issued sparingly. *See Uttaro v. Uttaro*, 54 Mass. App. Ct. 871, 875 (2002). The law requires that the court issue specific written findings whenever mutual abuse prevention orders or mutual no-contact orders have issued. The purpose of these findings "is to ensure that the judge will carefully consider the evidence presented to determine who is the real victim and aggressor in an abusive relationship and if a mutual order is warranted." *Sommi v. Ayer*, 51 Mass. App. Ct. 207, 211 (2001). These findings should explain the basis for concluding that each party has abused the other and that the protective terms imposed against each party are warranted. "In issuing a mutual order, a judge is required to set forth the bases for concluding that mutual abuse occurred and, thus, a reciprocal order is warranted. The judge's failure to do so ... requires the order to be vacated." *Id.* at 211.

If such an order is issued, the police must have clear instructions about how it is to be enforced. For example, an order requiring A to stay away from B's address and B to stay away from A's address can be enforced. However, an order which orders both A and B to stay fifty yards away from one another cannot be enforced readily, because the responding officer often will not be able to say who approached whom.

The statute clearly appears to require that a single mutual order be issued, rather than separate orders in favor of each party. However, since this is not possible as a practical matter (each party is a plaintiff and each party is a defendant), the Guideline recommends cross-referencing each order in the other.

Consecutive orders from different courts involving the same parties in reverse roles are considered "mutual orders." The second court, considering a complaint filed by a party who is already the subject of a previous order, cannot amend or supersede the first order. Its order, if any, will run only in favor of the new plaintiff. Finally, the second court cannot change the first order.

Instead, if the second court has reason to believe that an order may be pending in another court against the plaintiff, in favor of the person now listed as defendant, the second judge should question the plaintiff about this and, if necessary, check the plaintiff's name on the State-wide Registry of Civil Restraining Orders. If the new plaintiff is the defendant listed in an existing order and does not appear to be in immediate danger, the court may suggest that he or she return to the court that issued that order and seek relief there by means of a motion to modify the existing order or issue a separate order in his or her favor. If the plaintiff in the second action declines to do so, the judge must rule on the second complaint.

If the plaintiff in the second action presents evidence that causes the judge to believe that there is a substantial likelihood of immediate danger of abuse and the hearing after notice has not yet been heard on the original order brought by the other party, the judge may issue an order *ex parte* and then, after receiving approval from the departmental Chief Justice (or, if the courts are in different departments, the Chief Justice for Administration and Management) to transfer the case, make it returnable to the first court for a joint hearing. The judge in the second court may obtain and consider the complaint, affidavit and, if necessary, the recording of the proceedings in the first court so as to assist in issuing the required written findings.

In those cases in which two different courts within the same department have jurisdiction over the different plaintiffs, the Chief Justice of that department may transfer the second case to the original court so that one judge can hear cases for both courts and decide which, if any, orders should issue. If two courts in different court departments have jurisdiction over the different plaintiffs, a request may be made to the Chief Justice for Administration and Management to transfer one of the cases to the other court so that one judge can hear both cases. In any of these instances, if the judge hearing both matters, after hearing, decides to issue mutual orders, that judge should be in a position to make the written findings required by the statute.

If the court hearing the second case, for whatever reason, does not refer the plaintiff back to the original court, any resulting order in favor of that new plaintiff cannot be inconsistent with the terms of the first order. The second order should also, in specific terms, acknowledge the existence of the first and specifically provide guidance on any enforcement issues that may arise.

If the plaintiff in the second case is seeking relief in the same court that issued the first order, the judge should consider whether the plaintiff is actually seeking to file a motion for modification in that pending case, or if the relief, if ordered, involves protection of that party and therefore must result in a mutual abuse prevention order.

6:08 FURTHER EXTENDING AN ORDER AFTER NOTICE ON ITS EXPIRATION DATE

If, subsequent to a hearing after notice, an order was issued for one year or some lesser period of time, that order may be extended further or made permanent at its expiration date regardless of whether there has been any new incident of abuse. The defendant must be served with a copy of the order that has been extended. Any such order should be entered in the Statewide Registry of Civil Restraining Orders immediately.

COMMENTARY

At the time scheduled for the order to expire, the plaintiff may seek to extend the order. No new application or complaint is required. However, the plaintiff should file a supplemental affidavit that explains the continued need for an abuse prevention order. Moreover, so long as the court had jurisdiction for issuing the original order, the fact that the plaintiff may have moved out of the jurisdiction is not a reason for denying the extension, or requiring the plaintiff to reapply in the court within whose jurisdiction he or she now lives.

No new incident of abuse is required for extending the order. General Laws c. 209A, § 3 states that "the fact that abuse has not occurred during the pendency of an order shall not, in itself, constitute sufficient ground for denying or failing to extend the order, or allowing an order to expire or be vacated, or for refusing to issue a new order." The statute also provides that a court "shall not deny any complaint filed under this chapter solely because it was not filed within a particular time period after the last alleged incident of abuse." The only criterion is a showing of continued need for the order. *See, e.g.,* Pike v. Maguire, 47 Mass. App. Ct. 929 (1999) (rescript); Mitchell v. Mitchell, 62 Mass. App. Ct. 769, 773–774 (2005) ("[T]he fact abuse has not occurred during the pendency of an order shall not, in itself, constitute sufficient grounds for allowing an order to be vacated.");

Doe v. Keller, 57 Mass. App. Ct. 776, 778 (2003); Rauseo v. Rauseo, 50 Mass. App. Ct. 911, 913 (2001), *rev. denied*, Rauseo v. Rauseo, 434 Mass. 1103 (2001) ("At a hearing on the plaintiff's request for an extension of an order … the plaintiff is not required to re-establish facts sufficient to support that initial grant of an abuse prevention order."). *Contrast* Banna v. Banna, 78 Mass. App. Ct. 34, 35–36 (2010) (where the only evidence at the hearing was the original affidavit, and the judge did not ascertain the nature of the interaction of the parties as it related to the likelihood of physical abuse in the future at the time of the hearing; merely asking the plaintiff if she wanted to extend the order was insufficient to extend the *ex parte* order). To obtain an extension of an abuse prevention order under c. 209A, the plaintiff must, by a preponderance of the evidence, demonstrate that an extension of the order is necessary to protect her from the likelihood of "abuse" as defined in G.L. c. 209A, § 1. Iamele v. Asselin, 444 Mass. 734, 739 (2005). "Typically, this inquiry will be whether a plaintiff has a reasonable fear or 'imminent serious physical harm'." (citation omitted). *Id.* at 739–740. [9][10]

Although the absence of abuse during the pendency of an order, by itself, will not bar the issuance of an extension of an abuse prevention order, Doe v. Keller, 57 Mass. App. Ct. 776, 778 (2003), the court should consider all of the evidence in determining whether the plaintiff's continuing fear is reasonable. Smith v. Jones, 75 Mass. App. Ct. 540, 543–546 (2009). In Smith, the Appeals Court held that since defendant had not attempted to contact the plaintiff in three years and there was no additional evidence supporting the plaintiff's fear of imminent physical harm, a permanent extension of the abuse prevention order was inappropriate. *Id.*

If the plaintiff appears in court seeking to extend the order "at the date and time the order is to expire," G.L. c. 209A, § 3, and the defendant was served with notice of that scheduled hearing in the order, no new notice need be sent, and the same order may be extended. The extended order must be served upon the defendant in the same manner as the prior order. The court should ask if the plaintiff knows of any new address for the defendant.

In prosecutions for violations of orders, actual service of an extended order may not be required if a defendant was served with a copy of the *ex parte* order. *See* Commonwealth v. Delaney, 425 Mass. 587, 591 (1997), *cert. denied*, Delaney v. Commonwealth, 522 U.S. 1058 (1998); Commonwealth v. Munafo, 54 Mass. App. Ct. 597, 600–602 (1998), *rev. denied*, Commonwealth v. Munafo, 428 Mass. 1110 (1998). Both Delaney and Munafo involved *ex parte* orders that were extended. On the other hand, service of a further extension of an order after notice is required. In Commonwealth v. Molloy, 44 Mass. App. Ct. 306 (1998), *rev. denied*, Commonwealth v. Molloy, 427 Mass. 1107 (1998), the Appeals Court reversed a conviction for violation of an order that had been extended annually, distinguishing between service of extension of temporary orders and such "successive annual extensions." *Id.* at 308. *See Guideline 6:08*, Further Extending an Order After Notice on Its Expiration Date. The court stated, "the extension of an annual order pursuant to [G.L. c. 209A] § 3, in contrast to a § 4 continuation of a temporary order, is … by no means automatic, even if a defendant fails to appear." *Id.* at 309. The court added that there was no evidence at trial, "that anyone made a 'conscientious and reasonable effort to serve … the defendant' or that some alternative means of service was used to notify him." *Id.* at 309. *See* Commentary to *Guideline 4:07*, Transmission of *Ex Parte* Orders to the Police for Service on the Defendant. For issues related to the length of an extension of an abuse prevention order, *see Guideline 6:09*, Extension of Orders for a Term of Years; Permanent Orders.

---

9 The court noted, however, that if the plaintiff were suffering from attempted or actual physical abuse or involuntary sexual relations, "there is no question that an extension should be granted." Iamele v. Asselin, 444 Mass. 734, 740, n.3.

10 Please note, in Iamele v. Asselin, the trial judge did not make findings and conclusions, and in absence of such findings the SJC was "unable to determine the standard the judge applied here" and remanded the case for a further hearing. *Id* at 741.

6:09 EXTENSION OF ORDERS FOR A TERM OF YEARS; PERMANENT ORDERS

Following a hearing after notice, an order can be issued for up to one year. When the plaintiff appears on that date, the court has three options: (1) the court can decline to extend the order; (2) the court can extend the order for "any time reasonably necessary" to protect the plaintiff, G.L. c. 209A, § 3(e); or (3) the court can make the order permanent.

COMMENTARY

In Crenshaw v. Macklin, 430 Mass. 633, 635 (2000), the Supreme Judicial Court affirmed a court's authority to issue a permanent order following a "renewal hearing." *See also* Doe v. Keller, 57 Mass. App. Ct. 776, 778–779 (2003) (permanently extending abuse prevention order may be appropriate even when there is no evidence of contact between plaintiff and defendant for a significant period of time). However, there is no presumption that an order be extended nor is there an entitlement that the order be made permanent. Jones v. Gallagher, 54 Mass. App. Ct. 883, 889 (2002). *See Guideline 6:08,* Further Extending an Order After Notice on Its Expiration Date, and Commentary thereto; *Guideline 6:09,* Extension of Orders for a Term of Years; Permanent Orders; Commentary to *Guidelines 12:10,* Issuance of Protective Orders: Divorce Proceedings; and *Guideline 12:11,* Issuance of Orders to Vacate Marital Residence: Divorce, Separate Support or Maintenance.

In some cases, at the expiration date of an order after notice it may be appropriate to issue an order for a period of time that is longer than an additional year but less than a permanent order. Lonergan–Gillen v. Gillen, 57 Mass. App. Ct. 746, 747–748 (2003). In determining whether to issue a permanent order or an order for a particular period of years, the court may consider the severity and frequency of the violence involved, threats to do harm in the future and the ages of minor children, and any other relevant facts. For example, the court may determine that it is appropriate to extend an order until the youngest child of the parties reaches age 18.

APPEAL

7:00 APPEAL

There is no provision in c. 209A for appeal by either party. However, the Supreme Judicial Court has ruled that litigants seeking appeals are directed to the Appeals Court.

COMMENTARY

The sole avenue for review of the issuance of an abuse prevention order is an appeal in the Appeals Court. Zullo v. Goguen, 423 Mass. 679, 681 (1996). *See also* Watson v. Walker, 447 Mass. 1014, 1015 (2006).

In Zullo, the Supreme Judicial Court held that, "[u]nless and until the Legislature decides otherwise, litigants seeking judicial review of an order made pursuant to c. 209A are directed to the Appeals Court."

Id. at 682. The Court found this determination necessary to ensure "uniform treatment of litigants" and "the development of a consistent body of law" on the subject.

If either party seeks to pursue an appeal, the clerk's office should be prompt in complying with Massachusetts Rules of Appellate Procedure 8 and 9 when assembling the record on appeal.

A defendant may appeal an order even if the order has expired. Such an appeal is not moot because the order has been entered in the Statewide Registry of Civil Restraining Orders and the defendant, "could be adversely affected by [the record] in the event of future applications for an order under G.L. c. 209A or in bail proceedings." Wooldridge v. Hickey, 45 Mass. App. Ct. 637, 638 (1998), citing Frizado v. Frizado, 420 Mass. 592, 593–594 (1995).

ENFORCEMENT OF ORDERS; CRIMINAL PROCEEDINGS; CRIMINAL AND CIVIL CONTEMPT

8:00 VENUE; TERRITORIAL JURISDICTION FOR CRIMINAL PROSECUTION OF VIOLATIONS OF C. 209A ORDERS

A violation of a c. 209A no-contact, stay-away, refrain from abuse, vacate or gun surrender order is a criminal offense and may be prosecuted in the court within whose territorial jurisdiction the act allegedly occurred, G.L. c. 218, § 26, or in the court that issued the order. G.L. c. 277, § 62A. A violation of such an order may also be prosecuted as criminal or civil contempt in the court that issued the order. *See Guideline 8:02,* Criminal Contempt, and Commentary thereto;, and *Guideline 8:02A,* Civil Contempt, respectively. Protection orders issued by other jurisdictions are to be enforced as though they were issued in the Commonwealth. *See* G.L. c. 209A, §§ 5A and 7; and *Guideline 14:00,* Filing and Enforcement of Abuse Prevention Orders Issued by Other Jurisdictions.

The violation of any other provisions of an abuse prevention order (e.g., support, custody or compensation) may be addressed only as a criminal or civil contempt in the court that issued the order.

If the no-contact, stay-away, refrain from abuse, vacate or gun surrender order was issued by the Probate and Family Court, the criminal complaint must be sought in the appropriate District Court, or Boston Municipal Court, depending on the location of the alleged violation. The Probate and Family Court or Superior Court that issued such an order or any other abuse prevention order may itself proceed on an alleged violation as a criminal or civil contempt.

COMMENTARY

General Laws c. 209A, § 7 provides that, while abuse prevention orders are civil in nature, violations of such orders are criminal. However, case law has interpreted this language to mean that only violations of orders (1) to refrain from abuse, (2) to vacate the household, (3) to have no contact with or (4) stay away from the plaintiff, are criminal violations. *See* Commonwealth v. Finase, 435 Mass. 310, 313–314 (2001). In addition, G.L. c. 209A, § 3B makes a violation of an order to surrender guns, ammunition, and gun licenses a criminal offense. Such offenses may be prosecuted in the court within whose territorial jurisdiction the alleged offense occurred, G.L. c. 218, § 26, or in the court that issued the c. 209A order. G.L. c. 277, § 62A. *See Guideline 6:05,* Orders to Surrender Guns, Licenses to Carry Firearms and FID Cards, and Commentary thereto. Alleged offenses by juveniles are handled as delinquency matters in the Juvenile Court. Violations of other provisions of the order, such as orders for support, custody, or compensation are punishable through civil contempt proceedings. G.L. c. 209A, § 7.

General Laws c. 209A, § 5A provides that "any protection order issued by another jurisdiction, as defined in section one, shall be given full faith and credit throughout the Commonwealth and enforced as if it were issued in the Commonwealth for as long as the order is in effect in the issuing jurisdiction." General Laws c. 209A, § 7 includes foreign orders in the list of orders the violation of which are subject to criminal prosecution. *See Guideline 14:00*, Filing and Enforcement of Abuse Prevention Orders Issued by Other Jurisdictions.

Consequently, orders issued by other states may be prosecuted in Massachusetts. Since such orders were issued by other jurisdictions, venue for prosecution for violations of such orders would lie in the jurisdiction where the violation occurred.

8:01 ISSUANCE OF CRIMINAL COMPLAINT[11]

When a violation of a vacate, refrain from abuse, no-contact, stay-away, or gun surrender order under c. 209A is alleged in an application for a criminal complaint, and the accused has not yet been arrested, the issuance of a criminal complaint should be sought and a hearing promptly held.

If a felony is also alleged or if there is an imminent threat of bodily injury or of the commission of a crime or flight by the accused from the Commonwealth, the hearing should be conducted immediately, with no notice to the accused. *See* G.L. c. 218, § 35A. The magistrate should record the statutory exception to the notice requirement on the application for the complaint.

[11] This Guideline applies only to the District Court and Boston Municipal Court.

COMMENTARY

Violation of a vacate, refrain from abuse, no-contact, or stay-away order issued under G.L. c. 209A, 3, 4 or 5, G.L. c. 209, § 32, G.L. c. 209C, §§ 15 or 20, and G.L. c. 208, §§ 18, 34B or 34C is a criminal offense punishable under G.L. c. 209A, § 7 by a fine of not more than $5,000 or by imprisonment for not more than 2 ½ years in a House of Correction, or both fine and imprisonment. Commonwealth v. Finase, 435 Mass. 310, 313–315 (2001). *See* G.L. c. 209A, § 5A and 7, and *Guideline 14:00*, Filing and Enforcement of Abuse Prevention Orders Issued by Other Jurisdictions. Violation of an order to surrender firearms, rifles, shotguns, machine guns, ammunition, licenses to carry firearms and firearms identification cards is a criminal offense, punishable under G.L. c. 209A, § 3B, by a fine of not more than $5,000, or by imprisonment for not more than 2 ½ years in the House of Correction, or both fine and imprisonment. Also, violation of a c. 209A vacate order is included under the specific crime of trespass. *See* G.L. c. 266, § 120). In addition, stalking in violation of certain court orders is a specific crime. *See* G.L. c. 265, § 43(b). *See also* Edge v. Commonwealth, 451 Mass. 74, 76–77 (2008) (violation of a c. 209A order is a lesser included offense of stalking in violation of that same c. 209A order). *But see* Commonwealth v. Kulesa, 455 Mass. 447, 452 (2009) (violation of a c. 209A order is not a lesser included offense of criminal harassment, G.L. c. 265, § 43A). *See also Guideline 8:06*, Bail Procedures in Criminal Cases Involving Alleged Violation of an Abuse Prevention Order or Abuse: Dangerousness Hearings, and *Guideline 14:00*, Filing and Enforcement of Abuse Prevention Orders Issued by Other Jurisdictions. A plaintiff who comes to court complaining of a violation of an order should be informed of the right to file a criminal complaint application for these crimes and any other crime that may have been committed.

It is important to note that the act that constituted the violation of the order may also itself be a separate crime (e.g., assault and battery). Charging both is not duplicative. In the alternative, all violations of the orders described above may be punished as contempt of court in the court that issued the order. Contempt is the only

avenue for punishing violations other than vacate, refrain from abuse, no-contact, stay-away and gun surrender orders (e.g., failure to pay support or restitution, to turn over keys, etc.). *See Guideline 8:02*, Criminal Contempt, and *Guideline 8:02A*, Civil Contempt.

Criminal violations of c. 209A orders issued by the Probate and Family Court must be prosecuted in the appropriate District Court or Boston Municipal Court because, under G.L. c. 209A, § 7, the Probate and Family Court does not have criminal enforcement authority except in cases of contempt. *See Guideline 8:02*, Criminal Contempt, and *Guideline 8:02A*, Civil Contempt.

The law provides that when the police are provided with probable cause to believe that a c. 209A refrain from abuse, no-contact, stay-away, or vacate order (or any such abuse prevention order issued under G.L. c. 209, § 32; G.L. c. 209C, §§ 15 or 20; G.L. c. 208, §§ 18, 34B or 34C) or a protection order issued by another jurisdiction has been violated, an immediate warrantless arrest is required. G.L. c. 209A, § 6(7). Such mandatory arrests are made possible without a warrant by G.L. c. 276, § 28. The failure to surrender guns, ammunition, licenses to carry firearms and firearms identification cards under G.L. c. 209A, §§ 3B and 3C also gives rise to mandatory, warrantless arrest, pursuant to G.L. c. 209A, § 6(7).

When the police confront a situation of alleged "abuse" as defined in G.L. c. 209A, § 1, with no c. 209A order then existing, they are instructed that, if they have probable cause to believe a crime has been committed, arrest is the preferred response. G.L. c. 209A, § 6(7). Under this law, they are free to make a warrantless arrest, even though they did not observe the offense and it is a misdemeanor, if it involves abuse as defined in G.L. c. 209A, § 1.

However, police may not make a warrantless arrest for the crime of threatening to commit a crime, G.L. c. 275, § 2, even though the threat involves abuse, because G.L. c. 275, § 3 contains specific requirements for issuing a warrant for "threats." Commonwealth v. Jacobsen, 419 Mass. 269, 273–274 (1995). When a defendant's words place the victim "in fear of imminent serious physical harm," the defendant may be charged instead with the crime of assault. G.L. c. 265, § 13A. In such a case, a warrantless arrest is permitted and, in fact, is the "preferred response" under G.L. c. 209A, § 6(7).

Where the police are provided with probable cause to believe that an existing refrain from abuse, no-contact, stay-away or vacate c. 209A order or a protection order issued by another jurisdiction has been violated, they are required to make a warrantless arrest. G.L. c. 209A, § 6(7). *See* G.L. c. 276, § 28. The authority to make such arrests is provided in G.L. c. 276, § 28, and the use of that authority is mandated by G.L. c. 209A, § 6(7). General Laws c. 209A, § 6(7) also states that when no abuse prevention order is in effect, arrest shall be the preferred response when a police officer witnesses or has probable cause to believe that a person either committed a felony, committed a misdemeanor involving abuse as defined G.L. c. 209A, § 1, or has committed an assault and battery in violation of G.L. c. 265, § 13A.

Victims of abuse are occasionally referred to court to file a complaint application. Rather than refer a complainant back to the police, this Guideline urges that the court should respond promptly to the complaint application.

If no arrest has occurred before an application is sought, a defendant accused of violating a c. 209A order is entitled to a hearing pursuant to G.L. c. 218, § 35A before the issuance of a misdemeanor complaint against him or her. Commonwealth v. Tripolone, 44 Mass. App. Ct. 23, 27–28 (1997) (dismissal of complaint affirmed). In Tripolone, the trial court judge found that the request for a hearing was denied on the basis of a policy issued by a First Justice, "directing the automatic issuance of a complaint without a prior hearing where there has been alleged a violation of a 209A order." *Id.* at 25. The Appeals Court found that this policy "conflicts directly with the statutory requirement that there be a hearing unless there is a showing sufficient to satisfy the judge that one of the statutory exceptions is available." *Id.* at 27. *See also* Commonwealth v. Irick, 58

Mass. App. Ct. 129, 132–133 (2003), *rev. denied*, Commonwealth v. Irick, 439 Mass. 1109 (2003) (show cause hearing required by statute, rather than by constitutional mandate). The statutory exemptions to the hearing requirement are imminent threat of bodily injury, the commission of a crime, or flight from the Commonwealth by the person who is the subject of the complaint. Tripolone, 44 Mass. App. Ct. at 27.

The court (usually the Clerk–Magistrate or an Assistant Clerk–Magistrate at this stage of proceedings) has discretion to issue a warrant rather than a summons. "The decision to issue a warrant may be based upon the representation of a prosecutor made to the court that the defendant may not appear unless arrested." Mass. R. Crim. P. 6(a)(2).

See Guideline 14:00, Filing and Enforcement of Abuse Prevention Orders Issued by Other Jurisdictions.

8:02   CRIMINAL CONTEMPT

Violation of provisions of c. 209A orders, other than orders to refrain from abuse, for no-contact, to vacate and/or stay-away from a household, multiple family dwelling or workplace, or to surrender guns, ammunition, and gun licenses, may not be prosecuted as criminal violations, but may be addressed through contempt proceedings.

Criminal contempt must be charged in the court that issued the order, regardless of where the alleged violation occurred. Criminal contempt can be alleged and prosecuted even when the alleged violation occurred in another state.

In many circumstances, civil rather than criminal contempt proceedings are preferred. The basic distinction lies, not in the contemnor's actions, but in the court's goal:

- if the court's purpose is ***solely coercive or remedial***, the contempt is *civil*;

- if the court has ***any punitive purpose*** (to punish the affront to the law or to deter others), the contempt must be treated as ***criminal***.

COMMENTARY

Only violations of orders to refrain from abuse, for no-contact, or to vacate and/or stay-away from a household, multiple family dwelling or workplace, or to surrender guns, ammunition, and gun licenses can be prosecuted as criminal violations of an abuse prevention order. Commonwealth v. Finase, 435 Mass. 310, 313–314 (2001). However, these violations can, as an alternative, be prosecuted as criminal contempt of court or be the subject of civil contempt proceedings. Violations of any other types of c. 209A orders (e.g., compensation, support or custody) can be prosecuted only as criminal or civil contempt.

In a case where the behavior constituting the violation of an order also gives rise to serious felony charges (e.g., assault with intent to murder, mayhem, rape, or kidnapping) or to an assault and battery with serious injuries, the court should proceed cautiously. Punishing the defendant for criminal contempt may preclude criminal prosecution on the underlying felonies or the assault and battery. *See* Mahoney v. Commonwealth, 415 Mass. 278, 283–287 (1993), and cases cited therein.

Suggested charging language to be set forth on a complaint charging criminal contempt is as follows:

Did commit an act of criminal contempt, to wit, [describe the act constituting the contempt], in violation of an order issued by this court pursuant to G.L. c. 209A on [date of issuance of order].

Prosecution of the criminal contempt case should proceed as any other criminal case. *See* Mass. R. Crim. P. 44.

Under certain circumstances, it may be preferable to initiate civil rather than criminal contempt proceedings, the key distinction being that criminal contempt must be used to punish the alleged contemnor, whereas civil contempt proceedings must be used where the object is to compel compliance to benefit the party in whose favor the order was issued. *See Guideline 8:02A*, Civil Contempt.

General Laws c. 209A, § 5A provides that "any protection order issued by another jurisdiction as defined in section one, shall be given full faith and credit throughout the commonwealth and enforced as if it were issued in the commonwealth for as long as the order is in effect in the issuing jurisdiction." *See Guideline 14:00*, Filing and Enforcement of Abuse Prevention Orders Issued by Other Jurisdictions. This may include enforcement through contempt proceedings. *See Guideline 8:02A*, Civil Contempt.

For an extensive analysis of contempt procedure, *see A Guide to Contempt Procedures in the District Court* (2009), available on the intranet at http://trialcourtweb.jud.state.ma.us/courtsandjudges/courts/districtcourt/contemptprocedures.pdf.

8:02A   CIVIL CONTEMPT

The court that issued a c. 209A order may enforce it by means of a proceeding for civil contempt in addition to, or in lieu of, criminal proceedings. The purpose of civil contempt is to coerce compliance with a court order, not to punish the defendant for violating an order.

Such proceedings should involve a civil complaint filed by the plaintiff, specifying the alleged violation, notice to the defendant and a hearing on the complaint. Actions for contempt filed in the Probate and Family Court should be on the pre-printed Complaint for Contempt form (CJ–D 103) and are governed by the Rules of Domestic Relations Procedure.

COMMENTARY

Civil contempt proceedings are expressly authorized in G.L. c. 209A, § 7. Since, by definition, civil contempt proceedings must be brought to coerce compliance with a court order for the benefit of the other party rather than to punish, they are appropriately used when the defendant has failed or refused to do something he or she has been ordered to do, rather than where the defendant has done something that has been forbidden. The most appropriate use of civil contempt (at least where the defendant is not before the court) is where some particular act, such as return of property, has been ordered but not accomplished by the defendant. In addition, civil contempt can be used for non-payment of child support and is particularly appropriate when standard methods of collection (e.g., income assignment) are unsuccessful. *See* G.L. c. 119A, § 12. Violations involving danger to the plaintiff will usually involve criminal charges or criminal contempt and prompt arrest with or without a warrant.

Commonly, if it is determined that the defendant knew of and understood the order, and has the present ability to take the required action but fails or refuses to do so, he or she is incarcerated until the act is accomplished. "[A] civil contempt finding [must] be supported by clear and convincing evidence of disobedience of a clear and unequivocal command." In re Birchall, 454 Mass. 837, 838–839 (2009).

A written complaint should be required from the victim, but may be informal. In the Probate and Family Court, plaintiffs should complete the Complaint for Contempt form (CJ–D 103). Reasonable notice and the opportunity to be heard must be provided to the defendant. There is no right to a jury trial in such proceedings. Presumably, appeal on issues of law would be available.

If the defendant in a civil contempt proceeding is not before the court when charged, he or she should be served with a complaint in hand, together with an order to show cause and notice of the date of the hearing. If the defendant fails to appear for the hearing, a capias should issue for the arrest of the defendant. The hearing would then proceed when the defendant is before the court. Service of process in civil contempt cases will require the plaintiff to pay the constable or deputy sheriff. If the plaintiff is indigent, it is not clear how service can be obtained, even if the court orders state assumption of the cost under the provisions of G.L. c. 261, §§ 27A *et seq.*

General Laws c. 209A, § 5A provides that "[a]ny protection order issued by another jurisdiction, as defined in section one, shall be given full faith and credit throughout the Commonwealth and enforced as if it were issued in the commonwealth for as long as the order is in effect in the issuing jurisdiction." *See Guideline 14:00*, Filing and Enforcement of Abuse Prevention Orders Issued by Other Jurisdictions. This may include enforcement through contempt proceedings.

For an extensive analysis of contempt procedure, *see A Guide to Contempt Procedures in the District Court* (2009), available on the intranet at http://trialcourtweb.jud.state.ma.us/courtsandjudges/courts/districtcourt/contemptprocedures.pdf.

8:03 ACQUIESCENCE BY THE COMPLAINANT TO AN ACT WHICH MAY VIOLATE THE TERMS OF AN ORDER

The court should instruct the parties that once a c. 209A order is issued, violation of certain of its terms constitute a criminal offense. *See Guideline 8:00*, Venue; Territorial Jurisdiction for Criminal Prosecution of Violations of c. 209A Orders and Commentary thereto. The court should further instruct the parties that the terms of the order remain in effect until the order is terminated by court order, expires by its own terms or until it is modified by the court. *See Guideline 4:06*, Information for the Plaintiff.

COMMENTARY

Abuse prevention orders under c. 209A can be terminated only by action of the court. Parties who appear before the court seeking such orders should be informed that the order remains in full force and effect until the order expires under its own terms or is modified or terminated by the court on motion of either party. *See Guideline 4:06*, Information for the Plaintiff; *Guideline 6:02*, Duration; and *Guideline 6:04*, Modification of Orders; Terminating Orders.

The plaintiff's acquiescence or consent to the violation is not a bar to criminal prosecution.

The issues of whether or why plaintiffs sometimes "acquiesce" in violations of c. 209A orders are complicated. They involve a variety of factual considerations, including a plaintiff's need for financial support or desire to reconcile with the defendant, possible intimidation or manipulation by either party, family pressures, children's issues, and others. For purposes of issuing a criminal complaint, however, these factors are not relevant to the question of whether the order was violated, although they may be relevant to disposition of the criminal charge.

8:04 BAIL PROCEDURES IN CRIMINAL CASES ALLEGING ABUSE OR VIOLATION OF AN ABUSE PREVENTION ORDER OR ABUSE: IN GENERAL[12]

Several statutes are applicable to the arraignment of a defendant charged with abuse (including assault and battery, assault and battery with a dangerous weapon, assault with a dangerous weapon, etc.), and/or violation of an abuse prevention order. G.L. c. 276, § 58 sets forth the standard for bail in all non-capital cases. General Laws c. 276, § 58A sets forth the standard by which a defendant may be held without bail or released on certain conditions if he or she is found to consti-

tute a danger to the community. General Laws c. 276, § 58 also permits the court to revoke the prior recognizance of a defendant who has previously been released pursuant to § 58 but has now been charged with a new offense committed during the period of release and who can be shown to be a danger to the community. General Laws c. 276, § 42A and § 58 permit the imposition of terms of release.

Each of these circumstances will be covered in a separate section of the Guidelines as follows:

- *Guideline 8:05*, Bail Procedures in Criminal Cases Involving Alleged Violation of an Abuse Prevention Order or Abuse: Release on Pretrial Probation or Personal Recognizance

- *Guideline 8:06*, Bail Procedures in Criminal Cases Involving Alleged Violation of an Abuse Prevention Order or Abuse: Dangerousness Hearings

- *Guideline 8:07*, Bail Warnings in Criminal Cases Involving Alleged Violation of an Abuse Prevention Order or Abuse: Revocation Due to New Charge

In addition to these statutes, c. 209A imposes other obligations on the arraigning court. (These factors are reviewed in *Guideline 2:10*, Check of the Court Activity Record Information System, Including the Statewide Registry of Civil Restraining Orders, and Other Probation Department Involvement at the Complaint Stage; *Guideline 3:05*, Court Action on the Defendant's Default, Probation, Parole or Warrant Status at *Ex Parte* Hearings; *Guideline 5:07*, Court Action on Defendant's Warrant; *Guideline 8:07*, Bail Procedures in Criminal Cases Involving Alleged Violation of an Abuse Prevention Order or Abuse: Dangerousness Hearings; and *Guideline 8:08*, Bail and Detention Hearing Procedures in Criminal Cases Involving Alleged Violation of an Abuse Prevention Order). These obligations include:

1. review of the defendant's Court Activity Record Information (CARI), including whether there are prior or pending abuse prevention orders (G.L. c. 209A, § 7);

2. review of the Warrant Management System;

3. issuance of a no-contact order as a condition of release if the named victim so requests (G.L. c. 209A, § 6); and

4. notice to the named victim if the defendant is going to be released (G.L. c. 209A, § 6).

12 This Guideline applies only to the District Court, the Boston Municipal Court, and to some extent, the Superior Court.

COMMENTARY

Under current law there are three types of bail/detention hearings and decisions. The first, pursuant to G.L. c. 276, § 58, involves only considerations of whether the defendant is likely to appear for trial. This has been the bail guideline for non-capital cases since 1970. In such a hearing the court shall admit the defendant to bail on his personal recognizance unless the judge decides, "in the exercise of his discretion, that such a release will not reasonably assure the appearance of the person before the court." G.L. c. 276, § 58, as amended, St. 2006, c. 48, § 8. If the judge decides that releasing the defendant on personal recognizance will not secure his presence, the court sets a bond amount reasonably calculated to assure the defendant's presence. Recent amendments to § 58 provide for the imposition of certain conditions of release, specifically, to impose "restrictions on personal associations or conduct including, but not limited to, avoiding all contact with an alleged victim of the crime and any potential witness or witnesses who may testify concerning the offense, as a condition of release." G.L. c. 276, § 58.

In the second type of hearing, pursuant to G.L. c. 276, § 58A, the question is whether the release of a defendant charged with certain specifically designated offenses, "will endanger the safety of any other person or the community." *Id.* This statute provides procedures by which a defendant may be held without bail, or released only on certain conditions, if he or she is found to pose such a danger. The statute has withstood constitutional challenge. Mendonza v. Commonwealth, 423 Mass. 771 (1996); *See Guideline 8:05,* Bail Procedures in Criminal Cases Involving Alleged Violation of an Abuse Prevention Order or Abuse: Release on Pretrial Probation or Personal Recognizance.

In the third type of hearing, pursuant to G.L. c. 276, § 58, the Commonwealth seeks to revoke the bail of a defendant who was earlier released pursuant to § 58 (the first type of hearing), but who has now been arrested for a new offense and who can be shown to be a danger to any person or the community.

This Guideline, *Guideline 8:05,* Bail Procedures in Criminal Cases Involving Alleged Violation of an Abuse Prevention Order or Abuse: Release on Pretrial Probation or Personal Recognizance, and *Guideline 8:07,* Bail Warnings in Criminal Cases Involving Alleged Violation of an Abuse Prevention Order or Abuse: Revocation Due to New Charge, apply to bail hearings pursuant to G.L. c. 276, § 58. *Guideline 8:06,* Bail Procedures in Criminal Cases Involving Alleged Violation of an Abuse Prevention Order or Abuse: Dangerousness Hearings, applies to detention or dangerousness hearings pursuant to § 58A. *Guideline 8:08,* Bail and Detention Hearing Procedures in Criminal Cases Involving Alleged Violation of an Abuse Prevention Order, and *Guideline 8:09,* Procedures where Defendant is Being Arraigned and Plaintiff is Requesting an Abuse Prevention Order, apply to hearings held pursuant to both statutes.

The law requires that for offenses punishable by more than one year imprisonment (which include assault and battery and violation of c. 209A orders), the probation department must present the defendant's criminal record to the court before such person is admitted to bail. G.L. c. 276, § 85. This includes violations of protection orders issued by other jurisdictions. *See* G.L. c. 209A, §§ 7 and 8; *see also Guideline 14:00,* Filing and Enforcement of Abuse Prevention Orders Issued by Other Jurisdictions. The bail law should be read to require the judge to review the defendant's probation record before any § 58 pretrial release decision is made in cases involving abuse or a c. 209A violation, irrespective of the prosecution's recommendations on the question of bail. It is the court's responsibility to determine whether the defendant is in default or already on recognizance on a previous charge and to review all available information relevant to the issue of the defendant's likelihood of appearing for trial. The court should also review the court case file on any c. 209A order that the defendant is accused of violating as well as any other c. 209A orders concerning the defendant, at least where those orders were issued by the same court in which the defendant is appearing.

Where the prosecutor is not familiar with the circumstances of the arrest or the nature of the alleged violation, and where neither the complaint application nor the police report nor the c. 209A file provides adequate information, the court should defer action on the case for a reasonable time until adequate information is obtained from the police or some other source.

8:05 BAIL PROCEDURES IN CRIMINAL CASES INVOLVING ALLEGED VIOLATION OF AN ABUSE PREVENTION ORDER OR ABUSE; RELEASE ON PRETRIAL PROBATION OR PERSONAL RECOGNIZANCE [13]

When releasing a defendant before trial, on bail or personal recognizance, the court should consider the addition of specific

terms that may reduce potential danger to the victim. General Laws c. 276, § 42A permits the imposition of "such terms as will insure the safety of the person allegedly suffering the physical abuse or threat thereof, and will prevent its recurrence. Such terms and conditions shall include reasonable restrictions on the travel, association or place of abode of the defendant as will prevent such person from contact with the person abused."

The issuance of a separate no-contact order as a condition of pretrial release is authorized by G.L. c. 209A, § 6, last par. "When any person charged with or arrested for a crime involving abuse . . . is released from custody," whether on personal recognizance or bail pursuant to G.L. c. 276, § 58 or on conditions after a detention or dangerousness hearing pursuant to G.L. c. 276, § 58A, the court must issue a no-contact order if the victim requests it. G.L. c. 209A, § 6, last par. When the victim is present at the arraignment or can be contacted, the victim should be asked about such an order.

13 Boston Municipal Court, and the Superior Court.

COMMENTARY

General Laws c. 276, § 42A provides an independent basis for the imposition of protective terms during the period of release. In addition, the issuance of a separate no-contact order under c. 209A is required by law, if requested by the victim. G.L. c. 209A, § 6, last par.

8:06 BAIL PROCEDURES IN CRIMINAL CASES INVOLVING ALLEGED VIOLATION OF AN ABUSE PREVENTION ORDER OR ABUSE: DANGEROUSNESS HEARINGS [14]

When the Commonwealth moves for a pretrial detention hearing, and the defendant is before the court charged with an offense enumerated in G.L. c. 276, § 58A, the court must hold such a hearing pursuant to § 58A (5). Among the offenses designated by the statute are felony offenses that have "as an element of the offense the use, attempted use, or threatened use of physical force against the person of another," violations of abuse prevention orders, misdemeanor or felony offenses involving abuse, or misdemeanor or felony offenses alleged to have been committed while a c. 209A abuse prevention order was in effect. G.L. c. 276, § 58A(1). If the court finds probable cause, the defendant must be detained pending the hearing.

If the court determines at such a hearing that personal recognizance "will endanger the safety of any other person or the community," the court may order pretrial custody of the defendant or may order the defendant released upon conditions. G.L. c. 276, § 58A(2). Such conditions must include the requirement that the person not commit a federal, state, or local crime during the period of release and may include other conditions that the court finds necessary to assure the defendant's appearance at trial or the safety of a particular person or of the community. In abuse cases, such conditions should always include an order to have no contact with the victim, if the victim requests such an order. If, after the hearing, the judge finds by clear and convincing evidence that no conditions of release will reasonably assure the safety of any other person or the community, the judge must order the defendant detained for a period not exceeding ninety days. G.L c. 276, § 58A(3).

If a defendant is ordered released on terms after a hearing on dangerousness under § 58A that order may be revoked if any of the terms are violated. The procedure for such revocation and for custody during any continuance of the revocation hearing is provided in G.L. c. 276, § 58B.

14 This Guideline applies only to the District Court, the Boston Municipal Court, and the Superior Court.

COMMENTARY

If the prosecution moves for a detention hearing pursuant to § 58A, the court must hold such a hearing, "immediately upon the person's first appearance before the court," unless the court allows a continuance of no more than three business days for the Commonwealth or seven days for the defendant. G.L. 276, § 58A(4). The court must make a determination that there is probable cause to believe that this defendant has committed a qualifying crime. A continuance of three business days may be granted to the Commonwealth only upon a showing of good cause. Mendonza v. Commonwealth and Commonwealth v. Callender, 423 Mass. 771, 773 (1996). A judge granting a three-day continuance to the Commonwealth "should then make a specific finding that such cause has been shown and what such cause is." Id. at 792. Both the Mendonza and Callender cases involve violation of an abuse prevention order (Mendonza included other criminal charges as well). In Mendonza, the Court rejected the defendant's numerous arguments and found that the challenged provisions of the preventive detention statute (G.L. c. 276, § 58A) pass constitutional muster on their face and as applied to the defendant. The statute has also been held to apply to juveniles. See Victor V. v. Commonwealth, 423 Mass. 793 (1996). The statute requires that the defendant be detained during a continuance, "upon a showing that there existed probable cause to arrest the person." G.L. 276, § 58A(4).

At the hearing, the defendant has the right to counsel, to testify, to present witnesses, to cross-examine witnesses who appear, and to present information. When the defendant seeks to call a particular witness, however, the court may request an offer of proof as to the relevance of the proposed testimony. If the testimony, even if accepted in its entirety, would be irrelevant to the issue of dangerousness, it may be possible for the court to exclude the witness's testimony or to accept a stipulation between the Commonwealth and the defendant for purposes of the detention hearing only. The rules concerning admissibility of evidence in a criminal case do not apply.

If the defendant is charged with violating a protection order issued by another jurisdiction, the Commonwealth moves for a pretrial detention hearing, and the defendant is before the court, the court should conduct the hearing as it would if the defendant were charged with violating an order issued by the Commonwealth. See G.L. c. 209A, § 5A (a protection order issued by other jurisdictions shall be given "full faith and credit" and "enforced as if it were issued in the commonwealth . . ."); see also Guideline 14:00, Filing and Enforcement of Abuse Prevention Orders Issued by Other Jurisdictions, regarding abuse prevention orders issued by other jurisdictions, generally.

For an analysis of proceedings under G.L. c. 276, § 58A to determine dangerousness, see District Court Transmittal No. 980, March 19, 2008, "Revised chart of predicate offenses for a § 58A dangerousness determination". http://www.mass.gov/courts/209a/docs/districtc ourttrans980-revised -chart-of-58a-predicate-offense

8:07 BAIL WARNINGS IN CRIMINAL CASES INVOLVING ALLEGED VIOLATION OF AN ABUSE PREVENTION ORDER OR ABUSE: REVOCATION DUE TO NEW CHARGE[15]

In all criminal cases, if the defendant is released pursuant to the provisions of G.L. c. 276, § 58, the court must advise the defendant that, should he or she be charged with any crime during the period of release, the defendant's bail may be revoked, and the defendant can be held without bail for a period not to exceed 60 days. The clerk's office must record on the court docket that this bail warning was given.

A defendant who is arrested while on release pending the adjudication of a prior charge may be held for a period not to exceed sixty days upon a showing of probable cause for the new arrest and a finding, in the judge's discretion, that "the release of said person will seriously endanger any person or the community." G.L. c. 276, § 58, as amended, St. 2006, c. 48, § 8.

15 The Guideline applies only to the District Court, the Boston Municipal Court, and the Superior Court.

COMMENTARY

General Laws c. 276, § 58, as amended by St. 2006, c. 48, § 8, provides that when any person is released on bail, the person authorized to admit the person to bail, "shall provide as an explicit condition of release . . . that, should said person be charged with a crime during the period of his release, his bail may be revoked . . . and the court shall enter in writing on the court docket that the person was so informed and the docket shall constitute prima facie evidence that the person was so informed." Bail warnings are required when a prisoner is released after being charged for any offense, not merely for violations of c. 209A orders or crimes constituting abuse. However, it is particularly important that the warning be given in cases involving abuse. If the warning is not given, the defendant may not know that his bail may be revoked if he commits a new offense while on release. A single justice has held that the failure to give the warning is also a factor for the judge to consider when deciding whether or not to revoke bail based on commission of a new offense (although the failure to advise does not preclude revocation, see Commonwealth v. Tice, No. SJ-98-0349 (Sup. Jud. Ct. for Suffolk Cty., July 7, 1998) (Marshall, J., single justice)).

8:08 BAIL AND DETENTION HEARING PROCEDURES IN CRIMINAL CASES INVOLVING ALLEGED VIOLATION OF AN ABUSE PREVENTION ORDER OR ABUSE: NOTIFYING THE VICTIM[16]

In criminal cases involving abuse, it is mandatory to notify the alleged victim when the defendant is released from custody. G.L. c. 209A, § 6. Any Clerk–Magistrate, Assistant Clerk Magistrate or Bail Commissioner who releases on bail or personal recognizance a defendant who has been charged with an offense under c. 209A or some other offense involving abuse, as defined in G.L. c. 209A, § 1, must make reasonable efforts to notify the alleged victim of that release. This provision applies to both in-court and out-of-court releases on bail that was set by a judge or a bail magistrate, or on personal recognizance that was ordered by a bail magistrate other than a judge. The Clerk–Magistrate or his or her designee should make such notification, unless the police, the prosecutor's office or the sheriff's office agrees to do so.

Any judge who releases on personal recognizance a criminal defendant who has been charged with an offense under c. 209A or some other offense involving abuse, as defined in G.L. c. 209A, § 1, must make reasonable efforts to notify the alleged victim of that release. During court hours this can be done by requesting that the police, the prosecutor's office, or the sheriff's office, inform the alleged victim or by directing the clerk's office or the probation department to notify the alleged victim.

16 This Guideline applies only to the District Court, the Boston Municipal Court, and the Superior Court.

COMMENTARY

General Laws c. 276, § 57 prohibits a clerk or bail commissioner from setting out-of-court bail for a defendant charged with violations of abuse prevention orders and other crimes involving abuse committed while an abuse prevention order is in effect against the defendant. The statute also prohibits setting an out-of-court bail in a case alleging commission of a felony or misdemeanor offense involving abuse and the defendant is a defendant in a current abuse protection case. Note that it appears that alleged victim of the new offense need not be the plaintiff in the current abuse prevention order.

The judge's responsibility to see that a reasonable effort is made to inform the alleged victim of a defendant's in-court release does not depend on whether the victim is in court or not. It is appropriate for a judge to instruct police, prosecutor, or victim witness advocate to attempt to contact the victim. In the alternative, the judge can request a probation officer or a staff member of the clerk's office to make such contact. In either case, such request should be made on the record.

Pursuant to a memorandum from Chief Justice John Irwin, February 21, 1995, "Judicial Response System—Release of Persons on Bail or Recognizance," justices assigned to the Judicial Response System "should not entertain any requests for release of persons on bail or recognizance during their term of service on the Judicial Response System." That policy remains in effect. http://www.mass.gov/courts/20 9a/docs/aotc-1995-bail-policy-memo.pdf

8:09 PROCEDURES WHERE DEFENDANT IS BEING ARRAIGNED AND PLAINTIFF IS RE-QUESTING AN ABUSE PREVENTION OR-DER[17]

If a defendant is arraigned for a crime involving alleged "abuse," as that term is defined in G.L. c. 209A, § 1, and there is no existing c. 209A order, and the victim is present in court seeking an abuse prevention order, the court should hold a hearing on the abuse prevention order at the same time as the arraignment. If the court decides to issue an abuse prevention order, because both parties are present, the order may be issued for up to one year.

If such order is issued, it should be served immediately on the defendant. If the defendant is arrested for a crime involving abuse and brought before the court for arraignment in the victim's absence, any abuse prevention order previously issued by the court and still in effect should be served on the defendant at that time, and such in-hand service recorded on the docket of the c. 209A action. In either case, the service should be noted on the order and the police should be notified that service has been accomplished. The order should still be provided to the police to effectuate the gun surrender ordered in the box in section 12 of the Order (FA–2). Any member of the court staff may serve the order.

17 This Guideline applies only to the District Court, the Boston Municipal Court, and, to some extent, the Superior Court.

COMMENTARY

If both parties are present in court, and the victim in the criminal case involving abuse also seeks civil relief as a plaintiff in a c. 209A action, there is no reason to require either the plaintiff or the defendant to return in ten days for another hearing. If both parties are present, the court should have a hearing after notice and issue any

appropriate order for a full year or such lesser time as the court decides. This obviates the need for another hearing on another day.

In-hand service of abuse prevention orders is critical to proper enforcement of those orders. Whenever a defendant appears in court, any current abuse prevention orders against the defendant in that court should be brought into the courtroom and a check should be done to determine whether in-hand service has been made on each order. If in-hand service has not been made, the defendant should be served with the order and such service should be documented in the court papers. Even when an abuse prevention order has previously been served on a defendant, such service may have been made at last and usual address or by alternate means. Serving the defendant in-hand while the defendant is before the court ensures that the defendant has actual notice of the terms of the order.

8:10 DEFAULT WARRANTS IN CRIMINAL CASES INVOLVING ALLEGED VIOLATION OF AN ABUSE PREVENTION ORDER OR ABUSE[18]

When a defendant charged with a violation of a c. 209A order, a protection order issued by another jurisdiction, or any crime involving "abuse," as defined in G.L. c. 209A, § 1, defaults on the terms of recognizance by failing to appear or otherwise, the court should promptly issue a default warrant. When the default warrant is issued, the clerk's office should promptly enter the warrant in the Warrant Management System for immediate execution by the police.

18 This Guideline applies only to the District Court, the Boston Municipal Court, and the Superior Court.

COMMENTARY

If a defendant fails to appear or otherwise violates the terms of pretrial release on a charge of violation of an abuse prevention order or any other crime involving abuse, the court should respond promptly. While default is not an uncommon occurrence in criminal cases, default in abuse cases can expose the victim to further danger. Accordingly, default warrants should be issued promptly and their priority communicated to police so that there is no confusion that such warrants are to be executed as soon as possible.

8:11. DISMISSAL OF A CRIMINAL CASE INVOLVING ALLEGED VIOLATION OF AN ABUSE PREVENTION ORDER OR ABUSE ON MOTION OF THE PROSECUTION[19]

If the prosecution moves for dismissal of a criminal case charging abuse or a violation of a c. 209A order, the court should require that the motion be in writing, setting forth the reasons therefore, in accordance with the requirements of Mass. R. Crim. P. 13.

Where the prosecution's reason for requesting the dismissal is that the alleged victim has failed to appear, the court, as a condition of granting the motion, should be satisfied concerning the efforts of the prosecution to obtain the attendance of the victim, and those efforts should be noted on the record.

The prosecution can terminate the proceeding without court permission or approval by means of a *nolle prosequi* under Mass. R. Crim. P. 16.

19 This Guideline applies only to the District Court, the Boston Municipal Court, and the Superior Court.

COMMENTARY

All pretrial motions in criminal cases in the District Court, Boston Municipal Court, and Superior Court are required to be in writing, setting forth the reasons therefore. Mass. R. Crim. P. 13. Enforcement of this rule is particularly important when the case that the prosecution is asking the court to dismiss is one involving an alleged violation of a c. 209A order, a protection order issued by another jurisdiction (pursuant to G.L. c. 209A, § 5A; *See Guideline 14:00,* Filing and Enforcement of Abuse Prevention Orders Issued by Other Jurisdictions), or a crime of domestic abuse, and the reason given is the reluctance or the refusal of the alleged victim to testify. There are a variety of reasons a prosecutor may request dismissal of the criminal charges, and the court may ask a prosecutor to provide an explanation on the record.

Where the prosecution intends to proceed notwithstanding the victim's reluctance or refusal to testify, the court should not attempt to terminate the case over the prosecution's objection. *See Guideline 8:12,* Dismissal of a Criminal Case Over the Prosecution's Objection.

However, the court is responsible for the decision to dismiss a case. If the court believes that dismissal may not be appropriate, it may deny the motion for dismissal. In such a case, the prosecution can terminate the case by filing a *nolle prosequi* under Mass. R. Crim. P. 16. If the prosecution will neither file a *nolle prosequi* nor proceed with the trial, the court should enter a dismissal on the record "for failure to prosecute." The court should not attempt to compel the prosecution to try the case.

8:12. DISMISSAL OF A CRIMINAL CASE OVER THE PROSECUTION'S OBJECTION[20]

The court should not dismiss any criminal case over the objection of the Commonwealth without a basis grounded in a violation of the defendant's constitutional rights or, in appropriate cases, as part of an accord and satisfaction. *See Guideline 8:12A,* Dismissal of a Case: Accord and Satisfaction. In order to support a dismissal, any violation of the defendant's constitutional rights must prejudice the defendant such that dismissal is the only sufficient remedy. The court may not dismiss a complaint because the court believes, as a matter of policy, that the case should not be prosecuted.

[20] This Guideline applies only to the District Court, the Boston Municipal Court, and the Superior Court.

COMMENTARY

There is no question that the court has the authority to dismiss a complaint over the objection of the prosecution based on a violation of the defendant's rights, such as a defective complaint or a violation of the right to speedy trial. Such dismissals must be requested by motion. Mass. R. Crim. P. 13.

A judge may not dismiss a criminal case because the judge has made a discretionary determination that the case should not be tried based upon the judge's view of the evidence. *See* Commonwealth v. Taylor, 428 Mass. 623, 628–630 (1999) (judge may not continue case for the sole purpose of a desire to see the case ultimately dismissed.)

"[P]retrial dismissal, over the Commonwealth's objection, of a valid complaint or indictment before a verdict, finding, or plea, and without an evidentiary hearing basically quashes or enters a *nolle prosequi* of the complaint or indictment." Commonwealth v. Pellegrini, 414 Mass. 402, 404 (1993). "A decision to *nolle prosequi* a criminal case rests with the executive branch of government and, absent a legal basis, cannot be entered over the Commonwealth's objection." *Id.* at 405; *see also* Shepard v. Attorney General, 409 Mass. 398, 401–402 (1991); Pineo v. Executive Counsel, 412 Mass. 31, 37 n. 9 (1992); Commonwealth v. Henderson, 411 Mass. 309, 310 (1991); Manning v. Municipal Court of Roxbury District, 372 Mass. 315, 318 (1977); Commonwealth v. Dascalakis, 246 Mass. 12, 18 (1923); Commonwealth v. Hart, 149

Mass. 7, 8 (1889); Commonwealth v. Wheeler, 12 Mass. 172, 173 (1806); Commonwealth v. Manning, 75 Mass. App. Ct. 829, 833 (2009).

Justice Morton stated in Commonwealth v. Tuck, 20 Pick. 356, 364–365 (1838), "the authority of the Attorney General [or District Attorney], when present, to conduct and manage all criminal prosecutions is unquestionable. It is his exclusive duty to do so." "The district attorney is the people's elected advocate for a broad spectrum of societal interests—from ensuring that criminals are punished for wrongdoing, to allocating limited resources to maximize public protection." Commonwealth v. Gordon, 410 Mass. 498, 500 (1991).

While the phrase "the victim wants to drop the charges" is sometimes used in these cases, it is important to remember that the named victim is not a party in a criminal case. A criminal prosecution is not intended to vindicate the interests of the named victim, but rather, the interests of the public as a whole, as represented by the prosecutor. "In American jurisprudence … a private citizen lacks a judicially cognizable interest in the prosecution or non-prosecution of another." Whitley v. Commonwealth, 369 Mass. 961, 962 (1975), quoting Linda R.S. v. Richard D., 410 U.S. 614, 619 (1973). Thus, the law is clear, and this Guideline emphasizes that it is inappropriate for a judge, over the Commonwealth's objection, to dismiss a criminal case because the judge has made a discretionary determination that the case should not be tried due to the alleged victim's reluctance or otherwise. This is a decision that the law leaves to the prosecutor. The prosecutor may have facts that are not known to the judge. These facts may include information concerning the defendant and the named victim, such as past history, mental status, and potential for danger.

8:12A. DISMISSAL OF A CASE: ACCORD AND SATISFACTION

General Laws c. 276, § 55 provides for dismissal of a charge of assault and battery or other misdemeanor for which the defendant could be liable in a civil action, except one committed upon a sheriff or other officer of justice or committed with intent to commit a felony, upon acceptance by the court of a written accord and satisfaction agreement signed by the victim named in the criminal complaint which acknowledges that the named victim has received satisfaction for the injury suffered. The nature of the satisfaction must be presented to the judge either in an affidavit or during a hearing.

The decision of whether or not to accept an accord and satisfaction in a particular case rests with the judge. The judge should make findings on the record regarding the reasons for accepting the accord and satisfaction to permit review of that decision.

COMMENTARY

A judge has discretion to determine whether or not to accept an accord and satisfaction. Commonwealth v. Guzman, 446 Mass. 344, 348 (2006). General Laws c. 276, § 55 requires the presence of the named victim in court at the time of the hearing and a written acknowledgement from the named victim that he or she has been satisfied. Credible evidence of the satisfaction involved must be set out in the accord and satisfaction agreement, or presented through an affidavit or it may be established at the hearing. *Id.*

An accord and satisfaction may be inappropriate in cases involving partner violence given the potential for coercion or intimidation. An accord and satisfaction may also be inappropriate in cases involving partner violence where the Commonwealth seeks to move forward with the prosecution using evidence other than the testimony of the named victim and/or where the defendant has a significant criminal history or history of prior abuse prevention orders.

8:13. SENTENCING FOR VIOLATION OF A C. 209A ORDER OR A CRIME INVOLVING ABUSE[21]

If the victim is present at sentencing on a charge of violation of a c. 209A order or a crime involving "abuse," as that term is defined in G.L. c. 209A, § 1, he or she has the right to be heard regarding "the effects of the crime on the victim and as to a recommended sentence." G.L. c. 258B, § 3(p). General Laws c. 279, § 4B provides that prior to the disposition in any case involving a guilty finding on a felony charge or a crime against a person or where physical injury to a person results, and where the victim is identified and his or her whereabouts are known, "the district attorney shall give the victim actual notice of the time and place of sentencing and of the victim's right to make a statement to the court, orally or in writing at the victim's option."

If the victim is not present at sentencing, the court should ask the prosecutor whether the victim has been consulted about the Commonwealth's recommendation on sentencing, if any, and, if so, what comments the victim made. If the victim has not been consulted, sentencing may be postponed to give the victim an opportunity to be heard.

If the sentence involves immediate release of the defendant from custody, and the victim is not present, the judge must make a reasonable effort to see that the victim is notified about the release. G.L. c. 209A, § 6, last par. The judge may direct the police, prosecutor, or victim witness advocate to make the contact. If one of these parties does not agree to do so, the judge should assign the task to a probation officer or member of the clerk's office.

[21] This Guideline applies only to the District Court, the Boston Municipal Court, and the Superior Court.

COMMENTARY

It is important that the court obtain information from the victim upon sentencing of a defendant for a violation of a c. 209A order, or in any case involving abuse.

The duty to attempt to notify the victim when a defendant is released from custody at sentencing is the same as when a defendant is released from custody at any other time. See Guideline 8:05, Bail Procedures in Criminal Cases Involving Alleged Violation of an Abuse Prevention Order or Abuse: Release on Pretrial Probation or Personal Recognizance. This requirement appears to apply when the charge is a violation of a c. 209A order or any other crime involving abuse.

8:14. SENTENCING CONSIDERATIONS WHERE DEFENDANT IS CONVICTED OF OR ADMITS TO SUFFICIENT FACTS FOR CONVICTION OF A VIOLATION OF AN ABUSE PREVENTION ORDER OR A PROTECTION ORDER ISSUED BY ANOTHER JURISDICTION OR A CRIME INVOLVING ABUSE[22]

The court has a variety of sentencing options for defendants who are convicted of or who admit to sufficient facts for conviction of violation of an abuse prevention order, or domestic assault and battery or other assaultive offences against an intimate partner or family or household member.

In addition to the usual sentencing considerations, there are several statutory requirements that are applicable to domestic violence cases.

As in any criminal case, the named victim has the right to provide a victim impact statement at sentencing or the disposition of the case against the defendant about the effects of the crime on the victim and as to a recommended sentence. See G.L. c. 258B, § 3(p); G.L. c. 279, § 4B. Victim input can be made orally in the courtroom or in writing, which can be read into the record by the prosecutor or other representative of the victim. As in a c. 209A hearing, the court should take appropriate steps whenever necessary to separate the victim from the defendant. See Guideline 5:01, Conduct of Hearings After Notice When Both Parties Appear: General.

Whenever a defendant is convicted of a violation of an abuse prevention order, or admits to sufficient facts and the case is continued without a finding, the sentencing judge must order that the defendant complete a certified batterer intervention program, unless the court makes specific written findings of good cause for not so ordering, or the certified batterer intervention program finds that the defendant is not a suitable candidate for the program. See G.L. c. 209A, § 7. In addition, G.L. c. 209A, § 7 mandates that the court shall not order a substance abuse program or an anger management program as a substitute for a certified batterer intervention program.

When the court imposes completion of a certified batterer intervention program as part of a sentence, G.L. c. 209A, § 10 imposes an assessment of $350.00, in addition to the cost of the certified batterer intervention program. This assessment can be waived or reduced when the defendant is indigent or when payment would cause the defendant and/or his/her dependents severe financial hardship.

When a defendant is convicted of violating an abuse prevention order, G.L. c. 209A, § 7(5), requires the imposition of a fine of $25.00.

Whenever a defendant is convicted of assault and battery in the jury session, G.L. c. 265, § 41 requires the court to make specific findings on the record for not imposing a sentence of incarceration.

In addition to the above statutory requirements, whenever a defendant is placed on probation[23] for violation of a c. 209A abuse prevention order or domestic assault and battery, the court has a wide range of options in ordering specific conditions of probation. These specific terms of probation can include:

1. abide by the terms of any c. 209A order or order of protection from another jurisdiction;

2. no abuse of and/or stay away from the named victim;

3. enter and complete a certified batterer intervention program (required as noted above for violation of a c. 209A abuse prevention order);

4. submit to a court clinic or other evaluation for substance abuse and comply with the recommendations of the evaluation, including inpatient or outpatient treatment;

5. submit to a court clinic or other evaluation for mental health issues, and comply with the recommendations of the evaluation, including inpatient or outpatient treatment;

6. abstain from drugs and/or alcohol with random testing; comply with the terms of a sobrietor;

7. comply with orders of the Probate and Family Court and/or the Department of Families and Children;

8. comply with the terms of global positioning system (GPS) monitoring.

22 This Guideline applies only to the District Court, the Boston Municipal Court, and the Superior Court.

23 The defendant may be placed on straight probation or may be given a split sentence in which there is a committed portion of the sentence followed by a term of probation.

COMMENTARY

Probation terms must be clear and strictly enforced in order to be effective. Substance abuse and mental health issues often contribute to the occurrence of violence in intimate partner relationships. Substance abuse and/or mental health treatment alone does not address violence in intimate partner relationships and should not be used as a substitute for completion of a certified batterer intervention program.

Consistent reporting by the defendant to the probation officer as well as ongoing contact with the named victim by the probation officer is critical to a reliable assessment of the efficacy of the terms of probation, including participation in the certified batterer intervention program, in eliminating violence in the relationship.

While the court may not impose probationary terms unrelated to the substance of the underlying offense, Commonwealth v. Gomes, 73 Mass. App. Ct. 857, 857–860 (2009), the court retains the authority to impose probationary conditions appropriate to the defendant's history, the interrelationship between the defendant and victim, and the abusive nature of the case. See also District Court Transmittal No. 1018, June 22, 2009, page 26, "Legal Update: New Cases and Statutes of Interest to the District Court No. 34." http://www.mass.gov/courts/209 a/docs/districtcourt-trans1018-legal-update -34.pdf

The Department of Public Health certifies batterer intervention programs for the Commonwealth. All offer sliding scales for their fees, and most permit participants to perform community service in lieu of fees. Certified batterer intervention programs are offered in a number of locations. Certified batterer intervention programs are conducted in a number of languages; and are available to persons of all sexual orientations. There are also programs specifically for juveniles. For a list of certified batterer intervention programs go to www.mass.gov/dph/violence, click on Batterer Intervention Program Services, then click on Certified Batterer Intervention Programs and Services.

As with any criminal case, it is important for the court to hear from all parties and to fashion a comprehensive and appropriate sentence. Advanced technical options, including GPS monitoring and sobrietors, have enhanced the ability of the probation department to monitor defendants and thus have enhanced the ability of the sentencing judge to fashion appropriate sentences utilizing these options.

GUIDELINE INTENTIONALLY DELETED

9:00. GUIDELINE INTENTIONALLY DELETED

Guideline 9:00 is now Guideline 8:02A.

OTHER COURT PROCEEDINGS RELATED TO ABUSE PREVENTION PROCEEDINGS

10:00. CIVIL COMMITMENT FOR ALCOHOLISM OR OTHER SUBSTANCE ABUSE

Where testimony in a c. 209A case reveals an underlying problem of serious alcohol or other substance abuse, the court should consider advising an appropriate person of the availability of procedures for petitioning a District Court for involuntary commitment on the ground of alcoholism or other substance abuse under G.L. c. 123, § 35. Such a referral should not take the place of a c. 209A order or criminal proceedings where the plaintiff is otherwise entitled to c. 209A relief and wishes to have an order issued.

COMMENTARY

Substance abuse frequently contributes to the violence in relationships, although the exact nature of the connection remains unclear. One means of addressing this aspect of the problem, in extreme circumstances, is involuntary commitment of a party to a c. 209A action for up to 30 days under G.L. c. 123, § 35. That statute defines an "alcoholic" as "a person who chronically or habitually consumes alcoholic beverages to the extent that (1) such use substantially injures his health or substantially interferes with his social or economic functioning, or (2) he has lost the power of self-control over the use of such beverages." A "substance abuser" is defined as a "person who chronically or habitually consumes or ingests controlled substances to the extent that (1) such use substantially injures his health, or substantially interferes with his social or economic functioning, or (2)

he has lost the power of self-control over the use of such controlled substances."

The persons who may file a petition under G.L. c. 123, § 35 include any police officer, physician, spouse, blood relative, guardian, or court official. The specific procedural requirements are set forth in the statute, and commitment is possible for up to 30 days.

In the Standards on Substance Abuse, Supreme Judicial Court (Approved April 28, 1998), Standard V recommends that:

[t]he court should take special precautions when dealing with orders of protection under G.L. c. 209A. When dealing with a batterer who is also a substance abuser, treatment for substance abuse should precede or be in conjunction with batterer's treatment or the batterer's treatment will be ineffective. Therefore, in cases involving batterers who are also substance abusers, the judge should order substance abuse treatment as well as a certified batterers' program.

Standards On Substance Abuse. http://www.mass.gov/courts/formsandguidelines/substancev.html

10:01. GUIDELINE INTENTIONALLY DELETED

Guideline 10:01 is now Guideline 6:05B.

10:02. ACTIONS FOR DIVORCE OR SEPARATE SUPPORT

Actions for divorce or separate support under G.L. c. 209 should be brought only in the Probate and Family Court. *See*

Guideline 12:10, Issuance of Protective Orders: Divorce Proceedings; *Guideline 12:11*, Issuance of Orders to Vacate Marital Residence: Divorce, Separate Support or Maintenance; and *Guideline 12:12*, Issuance of Protective Orders: Separate Support, regarding divorce and separate support in particular and *Guidelines 12:00—12:14*, generally, regarding related proceedings in Probate and Family Court.

Regarding referral of a c. 209A plaintiff to Probate and Family Court and avoidance of inconsistent orders, *see Guideline 1:11*, Plaintiff's Requested Order Will Contradict Existing Probate and Family Court Order; *Guideline 2:07*, Referral To and From Other Courts and Avoiding Inconsistent Orders; *Guideline 3:07*, Conduct of *Ex Parte* Hearings; *Guideline 4:01*, Content of *Ex Parte* Orders; *Guideline 5:01*, Conduct of Hearings After Notice When Both Parties Appear: General; and *Guideline 6:00*, Orders After Notice: General. *See also Guideline 13:00*, Assignment of Justices of the Probate and Family Court Department to Modify Inconsistent Orders.

COMMENTARY

The District Court, Boston Municipal Court, and Superior Court departments have no jurisdiction over divorce actions. The District Court and Boston Municipal Court have no jurisdiction over most actions for separate support, and the Superior Court has no jurisdiction over separate support. There is, however, a rarely used provision of G.L. c. 209, § 32F, which provides concurrent jurisdiction in the District Court, the Boston Municipal Court, and in the Probate and Family Court to grant a support order for married persons living apart.

10:03. CARE AND PROTECTION PROCEEDINGS

If, in the course of proceedings under G.L. c. 209A, court personnel or the judge learns that harm or substantial risk of harm may have occurred to a child under the age of 18 in the household, that information should be reviewed by the judge, Clerk, or a probation officer to determine if a report should be made to the Department of Children and Families for an investigation under G.L. c. 119, § 51A. *See Guideline 1:06*, Minors as Plaintiffs in c. 209A Actions.

In addition, if a minor defendant is ordered to vacate or stay away from his or her home, the parent or guardian retains the responsibility to provide a safe residence for the minor. The parent or guardian should be required to identify where the minor defendant will reside. If no appropriate placement is identified, the judge should request, pursuant to G.L. c. 119, § 51A, that court personnel immediately file a report with the Department of Children and Families and that the Department respond to the court on an emergency basis to take custody of the minor. *See Guideline 1:06A*, Minors as Defendants in c. 209A Actions.

COMMENTARY

Information may come to light in a c. 209A case regarding child abuse. In such an instance, the c. 209A case should continue, but, in addition, the issue of child abuse should be referred to the Clerk or a probation officer who is in the best position to file a "51A report" if such action is warranted. Probation officers and Clerk–Magistrates of the District Courts are mandated reporters of child abuse under G.L. c. 119, § 51A. Depending on the outcome of its investigation in response to the report, the Department of Children and Families may initiate a care and protection proceeding.

Similarly, in cases where the defendant is a minor and has been ordered to vacate or stay away from his or her home and the parent or guardian has not identified an appropriate place for the minor to reside, the judge should request that court personal file a "51A report" with the Department of Children and Families. Depending on the outcome of its investigation in response to the report, the Department of Children and Families may initiate a care and protection proceeding.

10:04. ELDER ABUSE ACTIONS

When abuse allegedly has been inflicted on a parent or grandparent or other person in the household who is 60 years of age or older, by a child or grandchild or other household member, the court, in addition to proceeding with the c. 209A action, should refer that person to a probation officer who should review the allegations and, if warranted, make a report of elder abuse to the Department of Elder Affairs in accordance with G.L. c. 19A, § 15(a).

COMMENTARY

Domestic abuse may also constitute elder abuse under G.L. c. 19A, where the person abused is 60 years old or older and the alleged abuser is a family or household member.

Probation officers are "mandated reporters" of elder abuse under G.L. c. 19A, § 15. Therefore, such matters should be referred to the probation department and the required elder abuse report procedures followed. The Department of Elder Affairs, acting itself or through a designated agency, may provide protective services to an elderly person, including petitioning the Probate and Family Court for appointment of a conservator or guardian or for emergency protective services.

The disposition of such a c. 209A case should be compatible with whatever protective services are eventually provided through the Department of Elder Affairs.

In addition, a criminal action may be brought against an adult child under G.L. c. 273, § 20 for failure to provide support and maintenance for a parent. Support could be ordered as part of the disposition in such a case.

10:05. CHILD IN NEED OF SERVICES (CHINS) ACTIONS

In appropriate cases, the court should consider informing parents of the availability of a Child in Need of Services (CHINS) petition against a minor defendant in a c. 209A action, in addition to the issuance of abuse prevention orders. *See Guideline 1:06A*, Minors as Defendants in c. 209A Actions.

COMMENTARY

One category of domestic abuse involves abusive conduct by a child against a parent, sibling, grandparent or other household member. In such cases, the conduct at issue may constitute grounds for a CHINS action under G.L. c. 119, §§ 39E and 39J. If it does, the court can refer the parent or other plaintiff to the appropriate Juvenile Court to file the required application for a petition to initiate the CHINS proceeding.

The filing of the CHINS petition is not meant to be a substitute for a c. 209A order. However, the initiation of a CHINS proceeding may offer a means of providing treatment and rehabilitative services to a child, while the c. 209A order ensures protection for the household members.

10:06. MENTAL HEALTH ACTIONS

In unusual circumstances, and in addition to considering the issuance of abuse prevention orders, the court before which a c. 209A complaint is pending may consider whether a party is a proper subject for involuntary civil commitment under the provisions of G.L. c. 123, § 12.

Consideration of the use of civil commitment procedures should be restricted to extreme cases, consistent with the requirements of applicable law. If civil commitment does appear warranted, the court may inform the appropriate person of the right to file the required petition.

COMMENTARY

On occasion, the behavior of a party involved in a c. 209A action is such that involuntary civil commitment may be appropriate. The standard for such commitment is: (1) the party suffers from a "mental illness," which for the purposes of involuntary commitment is defined as "a substantial disorder of thought, mood, perception, orientation, or memory which grossly impairs judgment, behavior, capacity to recognize reality or ability to meet the ordinary demands of life, but shall not include alcoholism or substance abuse which is defined in G.L. c. 123, § 35," 104 Code Mass. Regs. § 27.05(1) (promulgated by the Department of Mental Health); (2) poses a danger of serious harm, either to the person himself or to others; and (3) there is no less restrictive alternative to commitment available. If it does appear at a c. 209A hearing that these tests may be met, the court should consider advising the appropriate person of the right to file the necessary petition for commitment pursuant to G.L. c. 123, § 12(e). Given the nature and ramifications of the civil commitment procedure, it would appear that its use should be limited to unusual cases.

In any event, the use of this procedure should be seen as an additional step rather than an alternative to the issuance of abuse prevention orders under c. 209A.

10:07. ACTIONS INVOLVING DISABLED PERSONS

When it is alleged that abuse has been inflicted on a disabled person, the court, in addition to proceeding with the c. 209A action, should refer the disabled person to a probation officer. The probation officer should review the allegations and, if warranted, make a report to the Disabled Persons Protection Commission in accordance with G.L. c. 19C, §§ 1 and 10.

COMMENTARY

Domestic abuse may also involve abuse of a disabled person, and probation officers are "mandated reporters" of such abuse under G.L. c. 19C, § 1. A "disabled person" is defined in G.L. c. 19C, § 1 as "a person between the ages of eighteen to fifty-nine ... who is mentally retarded ... or who is otherwise mentally or physically disabled and as a result of such mental or physical disability is wholly or partially dependent on others to meet his daily living needs."

A "reportable condition" is a "serious physical or emotional injury resulting from abuse, including unconsented to sexual activity." *Id.* Section 10 of the statute requires that "mandated reporters shall notify the [Disabled Persons Protection] commission orally of any reportable condition immediately upon becoming aware of such condition and shall report in writing within forty-eight hours after such oral report."

The Disabled Persons Protection Commission refers complaints regarding individuals with physical disabilities to the Massachusetts Rehabilitation Commission and other complaints to the Department of Mental Retardation or Mental Health, depending on the disability of the individual being referred.

EMERGENCY RESPONSE

11:00. PROCEDURE FOR RESPONSE TO COMPLAINTS WHEN COURT IS NOT IN SESSION: JUDICIAL RESPONSE SYSTEM

During the hours when the court is not open for business, a judge is available through the Judicial Response System to assist parties seeking a c. 209A abuse prevention order. In conducting this hearing, the on-call judge should follow the Guidelines established for conducting an *ex parte* hearing and issuing an *ex parte* order. Usually these hearings are conducted by telephone, with the plaintiff relating the facts directly to the judge.

Under the Judicial Response System, the police department will contact the regional on-call judge. The judge should first ascertain that the police have taken the following steps:

(1) the plaintiff should have filled out a c. 209A complaint and affidavit, unless physically unable to do so;

(2) the police should have run the defendant's Court Activity Record Information (also referred to as Board of Probation record), including information from the Statewide Registry of Civil Restraining Orders, as to any current or prior abuse prevention orders; and

(3) the police should have run a Warrant Management System check of the defendant.

Once the police department has provided this information to the judge, the judge should speak directly to the plaintiff. The judge should ascertain the reasons for the plaintiff's request for an emergency abuse prevention order, the relation-

ship between the parties, and the requested relief sought by the plaintiff. The judge must determine whether or not a substantial likelihood of immediate danger of abuse exists. It may also be appropriate for the judge to consult with the police or any other person present concerning the need for an abuse prevention order. If the judge decides to issue an order, he or she should review the terms of the order with the plaintiff. The plaintiff should be told that the emergency order is only a temporary order, and will only be in effect until the close of business on the next available business day when a judge is sitting. The plaintiff should be told to appear in court on the next available business day when a judge is sitting at 9:00 A.M. for a hearing before the judge, and that the order will expire at the close of business on that day if the plaintiff does not appear. In determining the next available business day, the judge should consult with the police officer to ensure that the next hearing date is a day when a judge will be sitting in the return court, not merely when that court is open for business.

When serving on the Judicial Response System, the judge has the authority to make the order "returnable" to the most appropriate court. In most instances, the most appropriate court will be the division of the District Court or Boston Municipal Court in the jurisdiction in which the plaintiff resides. However, the judge issuing the order should consider instructing the police to deliver a copy of the order to the appropriate division of the Probate and Family Court (rather than to a division of the District Court or Boston Municipal Court) if the judge determines that:

(1) the parties in the domestic abuse action are also parties in a pending action in the Probate and Family Court in which the issue of child custody and/or child visitation/parenting time is disputed, or is likely to be disputed, as a result of the plaintiff's complaint for a protective order, and

(2) the plaintiff consents to this decision.

When appropriate and feasible, the judge should speak directly with the plaintiff in determining whether these two criteria are met.

Even if the two criteria listed above are met, emergency orders should not be returnable to a division of the Probate and Family Court if:

(1) the defendant in the domestic abuse action has also been arrested in connection with the abuse alleged in the c. 209A complaint, or a warrant for his/her arrest has issued or will be sought, or

(2) the appropriate division of the Probate and Family Court does not sit on a regular, full-time basis, or

(3) the plaintiff is unable to get to the division of the Probate and Family Court.

Any doubt regarding any of these three factors should be resolved in favor of making the order returnable to the appropriate division of the District Court or Boston Municipal Court Department.

The on-call judge should then review with the police officer the terms of the order form to ensure that it is properly filled out and that it accurately reflects the judge's decision. It is especially important that the date, time, and location of the next hearing date be noted accurately. If the defendant can be promptly served with a copy of the emergency order prior to the scheduled hearing, the hearing after notice can proceed on the next available business day when a judge is sitting. The emergency order should expire at the end of that day.

The police should deliver all of the paperwork, including the order, to the court where the order is returnable on the next business day when the clerk's office is open, whether or not there is a judge sitting in that court on that date. All emergency orders must be certified and docketed in the court that has jurisdiction over the c. 209A action on the next day when the clerk's office is open. The orders should also be entered that day into the Statewide Registry of Civil Restraining Orders. These orders should be entered into the Registry regardless of whether the plaintiff appears. It is particularly important in courts that do not have sessions every day that the order is docketed on the next day when the clerk's office is open, whether or not there is a court session so that the order is entered promptly into the Statewide Registry of Civil Restraining Orders.

If a plaintiff seeking temporary relief is unable to appear in court on the next court day to file the complaint without severe hardship due to a physical condition, a representative may appear and file the complaint with an affidavit that indicates the circumstances that prevent the plaintiff from appearing. *See G.L. c. 209A, § 5. See also Guideline 1:08*, Plaintiff Unable to Appear in Court.

COMMENTARY

The statewide Judicial Response System ensures that a judge is always available during non-court hours to handle a variety of emergency matters. The vast majority of calls to the Judicial Response System involve requests for the issuance of c. 209A abuse prevention orders. Virtually all of these c. 209A hearings are conducted over the telephone, although there is nothing to prevent a judge in a particular case from going to a police station or hospital or other location to conduct the hearing. Conducting these proceedings by telephone is expressly authorized by G.L. c. 209A, § 5. Often, the hearing may be conducted at a police station over a tape-recorded telephone line so that the substance of the hearing may be preserved.

The preferred practice in conducting emergency c. 209A abuse prevention order hearings by telephone is for the judge to speak directly to the plaintiff. By speaking directly to the plaintiff, the judge is in the best position to determine the appropriate terms and scope of the order, including the appropriate court to which to return the order. Direct contact with the plaintiff may also assist the judge in assessing the credibility of the plaintiff and in determining other actions that should be taken immediately, such as a report to the Department of Children and Families under G.L. c. 119, § 51A.

Occasionally, direct contact with the plaintiff is not possible, due to the plaintiff's physical condition or a language issue. Where the plaintiff is unable to communicate with the judge because of a physical disability, the judge may rely on information provided by the police, an eyewitness, and any other reliable sources. Where the plaintiff is unable to communicate with the judge due to a language issue, the judge may rely on information provided by the police or may utilize the assistance of a police officer or companion of the plaintiff for translation of the plaintiff's statements.

In appropriate circumstances, the judge may ask the police officer to provide other assistance to the plaintiff, such as reviewing the terms of the order with the plaintiff and making sure that the plaintiff has directions to the return court.

It is critical that the emergency order properly memorialize the terms of the order as well as the specific details about the date, time, and location of the next hearing. If the defendant is served with an order that clearly advises him or her of the date, time, and location of the next hearing, the court, at that hearing may conduct a hearing after notice and may issue an order for up to one year.

All emergency abuse prevention orders issued by the on-call judge, and any supporting documents, must be brought to the return court on the next working day after they are issued, whether or not a judge is sitting that day. This practice will ensure that the probation department will immediately enter the emergency order into the Statewide Registry of Civil Restraining Orders. General Laws c. 209A, § 5 requires the Clerk to certify orders issued by the on-call judge; these orders should be docketed in the clerk's office files as well, regardless of whether the plaintiff appears.

The on-call judge should always consider carefully which court is the most appropriate forum for hearing the petition on the next available business day when a judge is sitting. The judge should consider returning a case to the appropriate division of the Probate and Family Court if the parties have an ongoing case in the Probate and Family Court and the plaintiff consents to this decision. However, orders should not be made returnable to the Probate and Family Court if the defendant has been arrested on criminal charges (and will thus be arraigned in the District Court or Boston Municipal Court), the appropriate division of the Probate and Family Court does not sit on a regular or full-time basis, or the plaintiff is unable to travel to the Probate and Family Court. The on-call judge should obtain input from the plaintiff in determining if there is an ongoing case in the Probate and Family Court, whether or not the plaintiff consents to the matter being returned to that court and the plaintiff's ability to travel to that court. The judge should also advise the police where the order is to be returned so that both the plaintiff and the defendant are properly advised where to go for the hearing.

RELATED PROBATE AND FAMILY COURT MATTERS

12:00. VISITATION PROCEEDINGS IN PROBATE AND FAMILY COURT: CONSIDERED ONLY IN LIMITED CIRCUMSTANCES

Visitation should be considered only in limited circumstances in c. 209A proceedings.[24]

24 Although *Guidelines 12:00—12:14* are directed to the Probate and Family Court, they should also inform proceedings in the District Court, Boston Municipal Court and Superior Court when appropriate. *Guidelines 12:00—12:04*, regarding safety assessments, may be particularly instructive.

COMMENTARY

In the context of a c. 209A proceeding, the statute defines the relief available to the plaintiff. General Laws c. 209A, § 3 lists the remedies that the plaintiff may request, including but not limited to, the following: refrain from abuse; refrain from contact; vacate and stay away from household, multiple family dwelling, and workplace; an award of temporary custody of child(ren) to plaintiff; spousal or child support; monetary compensation for losses related to the abuse; impounding an address; and refrain from abusing or contacting plaintiff's child(ren).

The focus of a c. 209A proceeding is the protection of the victim(s). Orders should be made to maximize the safety of the plaintiff and the child(ren), when applicable. If the plaintiff has not requested that the court permit visitation or does not readily agree to amend the petition to include visitation, the court ordinarily should not issue a visitation order in the c. 209A proceeding. The preferred practice would be not to address a contentious visitation issue at the hearing after notice, but to assign the matter for hearing on the visitation issue at a later date.

If the parties agree to visitation, the court should still make a determination that the visitation proposed by the parties is not injurious to the child.

General Laws c. 209A, § 3, provides, *inter alia*, that if the Probate and Family Court orders visitation to the abusive parent, the court must provide for the safety and well-being of the child and the safety of the abused parent. The court may consider, but is not limited to, an order for supervised visitation, ordering the parent to attend and complete a certified batterer intervention program as a condition of visitation, ordering the abusive parent to abstain from possession or consumption of alcohol or controlled substances during the visitation and for twenty-four hours prior to visitation, or an order prohibiting overnight visitation. For a list of certified batterer intervention programs go to www.mass.gov/dph/violence, click on Batterer Intervention Program Services, then click on Certified Batterer Intervention Programs and Services.

An order allowing, or not allowing, visitation affects a parent's access to information concerning a child. For example, G.L. c. 71, § 34H (amended by St. 2006, c. 62, § 1) provides that any parent without physical custody of his or her child may receive school information concerning said child unless: (a) the parent's access to same has been prohibited by a temporary or permanent abuse prevention order; (b) the parent has been denied visitation; or (c) based upon a threat to the child's safety, as specifically noted in the custody or visitation order, the parent has been denied legal custody, or has been restricted to supervised visitation only.

See Guideline 6:00, Orders After Notice; *Guideline 6:06*, Visitation Orders and Other Courts; *Guideline 8:01*, Issuance of Criminal Complaint; and *Guideline 12:06*, Custody Proceedings in Probate and Family Court: Related Custody Issues in Domestic Relations Matters.

12.01. VISITATION PROCEEDINGS IN PROBATE AND FAMILY COURT: SAFETY ASSESSMENT PERTAINING TO THE PLAINTIFF IN ABUSE PREVENTION PROCEEDINGS

The risk of harm and potential for continuing abuse through the children must be considered when making visitation orders.

COMMENTARY

Faced with evidence of abuse between partners, entering an abuse prevention order requiring the defendant to stay away from the plaintiff is reasonably straightforward. When children are involved the proceeding becomes much more complicated. Determining whether or not a parent should have access to or custody of his or her child involves complex considerations. The "Supervised Visitation Risk Assessment" guide developed by the Probate and Family Court presents a protocol for the court to use to assess the safety needs of children and families and appropriate parental access orders in cases where the parents are, or have been, involved in partner violence.

In crafting visitation orders, the court should conduct a safety assessment of the family unit. Whenever possible, orders should be crafted to protect the emotional and physical well being of the child and the non-abusing parent, while preserving both parent-child relationships.

The following factors are among those to consider:

General Factors to Consider:[25]

1. **About the nature of the abuse**
   - What is the nature of the abuse?
   - Is there a history of controlling or abusive behavior, including emotional abuse, threats and/or intimidation as well as physical abuse?
   - Does the history include controlling or abusive behavior towards prior partner(s)?
   - What is the frequency? What is the most recent episode?
   - What is the most severe incident?
   - Was this an isolated incident?

2. **About the child**
   - Has the child witnessed, heard, seen the violence or aftermath?
   - Has the child been used to further control parent?
   - Has the child been hurt or neglected?
   - Is the Department of Children and Families involved with the family? If so, for what reason? Was a report of abuse/neglect supported? Abuse/neglect by which parent?

3. **About the abusive parent**
   - Is the abusive parent claiming to be the victim?
   - Is the abusive parent using systems like DCF, the police, or the courts to control or have contact with the victim?
   - Does the abusive parent have a history of restraining orders, criminal activity or violent behavior?
   - Is there information that the abusive parent has been able to accept limits?

4. **About the victim**
   - Is parent currently safe?

- Has parent sustained injuries?
- Can he/she separate his/her needs from those of children?
- Is there a history of prior victimization, mental illness, substance abuse?
- What is that parent's level of fear?

Factors to consider regarding each parent:

1. Takes responsibility for the situation.

A parent who is able to acknowledge his/her part in a situation is more likely to be able to consider the child's experience than a parent who projects blame onto others. Of greatest concern is a parent who believes that the child is responsible for the situation that led to a request for supervision. (This factor should not be read to mean that a victim of domestic violence should take responsibility for the abuser's behavior.)

2. Awareness of the impact of the negative behavior on the child

Unfortunately, many parents have difficulty imagining that their children's experience may be different than their own. The father who, when asked how he thought sexual abuse affected his 9 year old daughter, replied, "If I'm okay, she's okay," or the robber who could not understand his son's sense of shame, are examples of this. Parents who cannot empathize with their children, that is cannot see the world through their eyes, are less likely to be aware of their child's needs and present a greater risk of harm to the child.

Recognizing Patterns of Abuse[26]

Safe visitation is more likely to occur when the visitation order takes into account the specific patterns of domestic violence in the family. The following describe some of the different patterns of domestic violence and some of the considerations to take into account when ordering visitation in these circumstances.

Chronic pervasive control reinforced by severe violence is usually characterized by physical abuse that is intermittent or chronic over the course of the relationship or marriage. It is often associated with a more pervasive pattern of psychological and economic coercion and isolation, as well as more severe forms of violent acts. The prognosis for ceasing this pattern of violence is poor, even upon separation of the partners. Consideration should be given to a very strong response to any evidence of abuse prevention order violations, including referral for psychological evaluation and to certified batterer intervention programs. Consideration should be given to suspension of contact with children, or limiting contact to professionally supervised settings. Children will often exhibit signs of disturbed behavior. Exposure to the perpetrator may cause the child to be re-traumatized and contact should be suspended until the child feels, and is, safe.

Violence by a perpetrator who has psychiatrically impaired thinking. Illnesses such as psychosis or paranoia ordinarily stem from distorted or delusional thinking about the other person. In these cases the perpetrator may also experience serious bouts of depression with homicidal or suicidal thoughts. This may result in attempts or threats to harm self or others which may be very traumatic to the child(ren). It is difficult to predict what the prognosis is for cessation of the violence until there has been an adequate psychological evaluation of the perpetrating parent. Consider referral of the perpetrating parent for psychiatric evaluation to answer the specific question of the relationship of the possible mental illness to the violence in the relationship. Children may have been exposed to any number of violent incidents associated with the mental illness of the perpetrator. To protect and ensure the safety of the child, both physically and emotionally, consider suspension of visitation pending completion of a psychiatric assessment, particularly in cases where the perpetrator appears: (a) obsessed with the victim parent, (b) paranoid or delusional, or (c) suicidal or homicidal.

The next pattern is one that escalates until the more aggressive partner asserts control during disputes, either by physical intimidation or assault. These incidents may arise from mutual provocation that escalates until the more aggressive partner causes injury. It is not associated with brutal beatings, marital rape, sadistic infliction of pain or a pervasive pattern of coercion and control over the victim. The prognosis for the cessation of the violence between these parties may be good once the partners are physically separated. However, some perpetrators will require a clear signal that violations of an abuse prevention order will result in an imposition of external sanctions. Children have probably been exposed to a number of violent incidents in the course of the relationship of the adults. Violence is often the primary method of dispute resolution within the family. Children are not ordinarily directly at risk except at points of potential contact of the parents, such as at visitation exchanges. Children may need visitations supervised for a time to feel safe and to overcome fearfulness resulting from witnessing earlier conflicts. Evaluation of the child's functioning should be considered.

When the aggressor is the primary care giver, the court is presented with a more difficult decision. Such patterns of violence are categorized by an ordinarily passive partner who responds with defensive violence to extreme provocation, or actual assault, perpetrated by the aggressor. The relationship between the partners is unstable due to the volatility and potential for provocation or assault by the aggressor. Cessation of violence sometimes occurs following separation if there is no parental contact during visitation exchanges. Some perpetrators will need clear indications from the court that engaging in contact or provocative acts will receive sanctions from the court. In a significant number of such cases, the aggressor will continue the conflict through the children by actions such as the withholding of visitation. It is not uncommon for aggressors who initiate violence to possess underlying emotional problems that impact their parenting. In many such cases, the primary caretaker/aggressor and the child have an intense relationship that cannot be immediately severed without doing harm to the child. In addition to professional evaluation, the court should consider a gradual transition of custody to the passive parent unless the aggressor is able to contain his or her behavior. During the evaluation or transition process, orders should enter which restrict any contact between the parties.

In cases where the violence is restricted to isolated acts caused by separation, the onset and incidents of violence are substantially limited to periods of marital strain or transitions associated with the separation and divorce. This pattern is distinguished by uncharacteristic violent behavior. Violence tends to cease once the immediate strains associated with divorce and custody disputes settle.

These parents might benefit from a requirement that they complete an approved parent education program. Divorcing parents in Massachusetts are required to attend a mandatory parent education class pursuant to Probate and Family Court Standing Order 4–08 (effective April 7, 2008) (available at http://www.mass.gov/courts/courtsandjudges/courts/probateandfamilycourt/standing-order-4–08–parent-education-attendance.pdf) Where the court is considering waiver of the Parent Education requirement, an alternative option is available on a limited basis, whereby parents may participate in an educational DVD program in lieu of attending parenting classes.

With respect to actions involving never married parents filed in the Essex, Hampshire and Suffolk Divisions of the Probate and Family Court, parties to such actions are required to attend and participate in an educational pilot program designed to address parenting challenges unique to never married parents. (See Probate and Family Court Standing Order 6–08, effective November 1, 2008) (available at http://www.mass.gov/courts/courtsandjudges/courts/probateandfamilycourt/documents/standingorder608.pdf). With respect to all cases involving children filed in the Hampshire Division of the Probate and Family Court, attorneys, parents, and caregivers involved in such cases are required to participate in a child-focused procedural model pilot program. (See Probate and Family Court Standing Order 1–10, effective May 5, 2010) (available at http://www.mass.gov/courts/courtsandjudges/courts/probateandfamilycourt/documents/standingorder1-10.pdf).

See Guideline 6:06, Visitation Orders and Other Courts, regarding visitation orders and other Trial Court departments: Guideline 12:02, Visitation and Custody Proceedings in Probate and Family Court: Assessment of Impact on Children; Guideline 12:07, Custody and Visitation Proceedings in Probate and Family Court: Modifications of c. 209A Orders, and Commentaries thereto; and Guideline 13:00, Assignment of Justices of the Probate and Family Court Department to Modify Inconsistent Orders, regarding assignment of justices of the Probate and Family Court Department to modify inconsistent orders.

25 From Supervised Visitation Risk Assessment For Judges, Probate and Family Court, April 26, 2005, p. 20 http://www.mass.gov/courts/courtsandjudges/courts/probateandfami lycou rt/documents/supervisedvisita

26 See Peter G. Jaffe et al., Custody Disputes Involving Allegations of Domestic Violence: Toward a Differentiated Approach to Parenting Plans, 46 Fam.Ct.Rev. 500 (2008).

12:02. VISITATION AND CUSTODY PROCEEDINGS IN PROBATE AND FAMILY COURT: ASSESSMENT OF IMPACT ON CHILDREN

Children respond to domestic violence with a range of symptoms. The court must demonstrate in its findings that the effects of the violence have been considered and that the custody and visitation orders advance the best interest of the child.

COMMENTARY

G.L. c. 208, § 31A, § 3 provides:

In issuing any temporary or permanent custody order, the probate and family court shall consider evidence of past or present abuse toward a parent or child as a factor contrary to the best interest of the child. For the purposes of this section, 'abuse' shall mean the occurrence of one or more of the following acts between a parent and the other parent or between a parent and child: (a) attempting to cause or causing bodily injury; or (b) placing another in reasonable fear of imminent bodily injury. 'Serious incident of abuse' shall mean the occurrence of one or more of the following acts between a parent and the other parent or between a parent and child: (a) attempting to cause or causing serious bodily injury; (b) placing another in reasonable fear of imminent serious bodily injury; or (c) causing another to engage involuntarily in sexual relations by force, threat or duress . . .

A probate and family court's finding, by a preponderance of the evidence, that a pattern or serious incident of abuse has occurred shall create a rebuttable presumption that it is not in the best interests of the child to be placed in sole custody, shared legal custody or shared physical custody with the abusive parent. Such presumption may be rebutted by a preponderance of the evidence that such custody award is in the best interests of the child.

Where "the record raises sufficient concerns regarding domestic violence", the court is required to "make detailed and comprehensive findings of fact on the issues of domestic violence and its effect upon the child." Care and Protection of Lillith, 61 Mass. App. Ct. 132, 139 (2004), quoting Custody of Vaughn, 422 Mass. 590, 599 (1996) (additional quotation omitted). When making an order for visitation, the court should consider the symptomatology of the child. Research indicates that the range of reactions experienced by children when exposed to domestic violence varies with the age and gender of the child, the intensity and frequency of the violence, and the proximity of the child to the event(s). Very disruptive symptoms related to trauma can be exhibited by children even when they have not been personally subjected to direct physical or sexual abuse. Assessing and evaluating the impact of the violence on the particular child is required where credible evidence of physical abuse to a household member is perpetrated by a person seeking custody of or visitation with the child in a divorce proceeding. G.L. c. 208, § 31.

To assess the impact of the violence on the child the court should consider the following factors: has the child ever tried to intervene in a violent episode; has the child ever called the police to stop the violence or intervene in a violent episode; has the child ever been

threatened by the perpetrator; has the child ever been hit or physically hurt by inadvertent or intended violence; and has the child developed problems in school or with peer relationships? Other questions relating to the child's emotional, psychological and physical well-being should be asked to determine the need for further professional evaluation of the child. If there is credible evidence that the child exhibits troublesome symptoms, the court should consider ordering supervised visits or suspending visits until an evaluation can be completed.

See Guideline 6:06, Visitation Orders and Other Courts, regarding visitation orders, and other Trial Court departments and Guideline 13:00, Assignment of Justices of the Probate and Family Court Department to Modify Inconsistent Orders, regarding assignment of justices of the Probate and Family Court Department to modify inconsistent orders.

12:03. VISITATION PROCEEDINGS IN PROBATE AND FAMILY COURT: SAFETY ASSESSMENT AND TERMS OF VISITATION

The court shall provide for the safety and well being of the child and the safety of the abused parent when visitation is awarded to the perpetrator of the violence.

COMMENTARY

Although psychological research and clinical experience demonstrate that by and large children fare better if allowed an ongoing relationship with both parents, the risks of maintaining contact with an abusive parent must be weighed against the impact of disrupting the parent-child relationship. In any event, no contact should be allowed unless and until safety can be assured. If the court finds that visitation is appropriate under the circumstances, it must make "explicit findings" which demonstrate that it has considered "safety and well-being of the children" when ordering visitation. Maalouf v. Saliba, 54 Mass. App. Ct. 547, 551 (2002), citing G.L. c. 208, § 31A; Custody of Vaughn, 422 Mass. 590, 600. The court should order visitation that maximizes the safety and well-being of the child and the safety of the abused parent. When ordering visitation, the court should consider the following:

(a) ordering an exchange of the child to occur in a protected setting or in the presence of an appropriate third party;

(b) ordering visitation supervised by an appropriate third party, visitation center or agency;

(c) ordering the abusive parent to attend and complete, to the satisfaction of the court, an appropriate certified batterer intervention program as a condition of visitation;

(d) ordering the abusive parent to abstain from possession or consumption of alcohol or controlled substances during the visitation and for 24 hours preceding visitation;

(e) ordering the abusive parent to attend Alcoholics Anonymous (AA) or Narcotics Anonymous (NA) meetings as a condition of visitation;

(f) ordering the abusive parent to pay the costs of supervised visitation;

(g) prohibiting overnight visitation;

(h) requiring a bond from the abusive parent for the return and safety of the child;

(i) ordering an investigation, appointing a guardian ad litem, or attorney for the child; and

(j) imposing any other condition that is deemed necessary to provide for the safety and well-being of the child and the safety of the abused parent.

See G.L. c. 208, § 31A, which does not include (e) above, and Commentary to Guideline 12:02, Visitation and Custody Proceedings in Probate and Family Court: Assessment of Impact on Children.

For a list of certified batterer intervention programs go to www. mass.gov/dph/violence, click on Batterer Intervention Program Services, then click on Certified Batterer Intervention Programs and Services.

If supervised visitation is required, the visitation order should also delineate the reason for the supervision and the party or parties responsible for the cost of such supervision. The duties and obligations of an individual designated to supervise the visitation should also be clearly explained to the person. A probation officer or, if a *guardian ad litem* (GAL) has been involved in the case, the GAL should meet with the designated individual to explain the duties and obligations. A supervisor must have the authority and ability to stop a visit if inappropriate behavior occurs.

Although the facts of the c. 209A action may indicate a one year abuse prevention order between the parties would be appropriate, sometimes the court may need more information to determine an appropriate order relative to the child(ren). In such cases, the court should apply the conservative visitation principles generally applied to cases in which sexual abuse is alleged. Although a no-contact or supervised visitation order with the child(ren) may be appropriate at the outset, a review should be scheduled after an appropriate period of time.

See Guideline 6:06, Visitation Orders and Other Courts, regarding visitation orders and other Trial Court departments; *Guideline 12:01*, Visitation Proceedings in Probate and Family Court: Safety Assessment Pertaining to Plaintiff in Abuse Prevention Proceedings; *Guideline 12:02*, Visitation and Custody Proceedings in Probate and Family Court: Assessment of Impact on Children; *Guideline 12:07*, Custody and Visitation Proceedings in Probate and Family Court: Modifications of c. 209A Orders, and Commentaries thereto, regarding other visitation matters; and *Guideline 13:00*, Assignment of Justices of the Probate and Family Court Department to Modify Inconsistent Orders, regarding assignment of justices of the Probate and Family Court Department to modify inconsistent orders.

12:04. PROCEEDINGS IN PROBATE AND FAMILY COURT

Prior to the filing of an abuse prevention complaint pursuant to G.L. c. 209A, all the indices shall be checked to cross-reference other cases between the same parties.

COMMENTARY

When entering c. 209A orders, a judge should be aware of any existing orders. For example, a judge should determine whether there are in place support, custody, or visitation orders, a guardianship or other order giving custody to a third party, or temporary orders entered in connection with a currently pending divorce, or other, complaint. If an order exists in another action within the Probate and Family Court and the terms of the c. 209A order alter the prior order, a modification of the prior order should enter on the original action. Moreover, the timing of a prior order, i.e., a temporary order, might shed light on the petition under consideration.

A support or custody order which exists only by virtue of the abuse prevention order will not remain in effect beyond the life of the abuse prevention order. Particular attention should be paid to the c. 209A support order enforced through income assignments. Although the c. 209A support order is no longer valid when it lapses or is terminated, until a Support Order Termination Form is signed and transmitted, the obligor's wages will continue to be subject to income withholding.

The c. 209A complaint and the related action, whether it is a complaint for divorce, custody, separate support, or paternity, or a petition for the appointment of a guardian, should be filed under separate docket numbers, however, all actions should be cross-referenced and electronically linked on MassCourts, and all files should be pulled and brought into the courtroom together.

12:05. PROCEEDINGS IN PROBATE AND FAMILY COURT: PRE–TRIAL CONFERENCES AND OTHER COURT PROCEEDINGS

Where a no-contact order is in effect, the parties shall not be required to meet face to face outside the courtroom regarding any Probate and Family Court proceeding.

COMMENTARY

When the court hears temporary orders or other pre-trial matters in a divorce, separate support, or paternity action and an abuse prevention order is in effect, the court must be made aware of the abuse prevention order to avoid sending the parties to face-to-face dispute intervention. The probation department may conduct dispute interventions provided the parties have the opportunity to remain separate and apart and the plaintiff in the restraining order is made aware that such dispute intervention is not mandatory. Probation officers should ask whether or not an abuse prevention order is in effect, including any out-of-state orders, at the outset of every dispute intervention.

Attorneys may satisfy the pre-trial order requirement of a meeting between parties and any attorneys by alternate means such as keeping their clients on telephone contact while the attorneys meet.

12:05A. CUSTODY PROCEEDINGS IN PROBATE AND FAMILY COURT: CUSTODY PRESUMPTION APPLICABILITY

In a custody proceeding brought in the Probate and Family Court pursuant to G.L. c. 208, G.L. c. 209, or G.L. c. 209C, if the court finds by a preponderance of the credible evidence that a pattern of or a serious incident of abuse has occurred toward a parent or child, a rebuttable presumption is created that it is not in the best interest of the child to be placed in sole or shared custody with the abusive parent. If after so finding the court issues a temporary or permanent custody order, the court must, within 90 days, enter written findings as to the effects of the abuse on the child. These findings must demonstrate that the order is in the best interests of the child and provides for the child's safety and well-being.

COMMENTARY

In a custody proceeding brought pursuant to G.L. c. 208, G.L. c. 209, or G.L. c. 209C, respectively, if the Probate and Family Court finds by a preponderance of evidence that credible evidence was presented that a pattern or serious incident of abuse toward a parent or child has occurred, a rebuttable presumption is created that it is not in the best interest of the child to be placed in sole custody, shared legal custody or shared physical custody with the abusive parent. This presumption may be rebutted if the court finds that awarding custody to the abusive parent is in the best interests of the child.

"Abuse" as defined in G.L. c. 208, § 31A, occurs when the defendant has engaged in one or more of the following acts: attempted to cause bodily injury to the other parent or to the child; has caused bodily injury to the other parent or to the child; or placed the other parent or the child in reasonable fear of imminent bodily injury. Section 31A defines a "serious incident of abuse" as one that involves: attempting to cause serious bodily injury to the other parent or to the child; causing serious bodily injury to the other parent or to the child; placing the other parent or the child in reasonable fear of imminent serious bodily injury; or causing the other parent or the child to engage involuntarily in sexual relations by force, threat or duress.

"Bodily injury" and "serious bodily injury" are defined for purposes of G.L. c. 208, § 31A by G.L. c. 265, § 13K. "Bodily injury" is defined as "substantial impairment of the physical condition, including, but not limited to, any burn, fracture of any bone, subdural hematoma, injury to any internal organ, or any injury which occurs as the result of repeated harm to any bodily function or organ, including human skin . . ." "Serious bodily injury" is defined as "bodily injury which results in a permanent disfigurement, protracted loss or impairment of a bodily function, limb or organ, or substantial risk of death."

For the purpose of these sections, the issuance of one or more orders pursuant to c. 209A does not, in and of itself, constitute a pattern or serious incident of abuse. In addition, an *ex parte* order or orders will not be admissible to show whether a pattern or serious incident of abuse has occurred. *Ex parte* orders may, however, be admissible for other purposes as the court may determine. Finally, the underlying facts upon which an order or orders issued pursuant to c. 209A was based may form the basis for a finding by the Probate and Family Court that a pattern or serious incident of abuse has occurred.

When issuing any temporary or permanent custody order where there has been a pattern, or serious incident, of abuse, the court must, within 90 days thereafter, enter findings indicating: the effects of the abuse on the child; that the order is in the best interest of the child; and that the order provides for the child's safety and well-being.

Regardless of who is granted custody-the non-abusive or abusive parent-the court is required to make findings as to the effects of the abuse on the child. Effects of abuse on the child which might be noted include such things as: the child is afraid of the abusive parent; the child is having problems with his or her performance at school; the child has exhibited regressive behavior; the child has problems with peer or family relationships; the child has been experiencing nightmares and sleep disturbances; the child has frightening memories from witnessing the abuse; the child exhibited extreme distress at the time of the incident from witnessing the abuse; or, the child has exhibited hostile or aggressive behavior toward others.

There will be instances, however, when the child has been impacted by the pattern or serious incident of abuse, but notwithstanding these effects, the best interest and the safety and well being of the child necessitate that the court grant custody to the abusive parent. Some of these instances include: the child poses a threat to the safety of the non-abusive parent or the other children in the household of the non-abusive parent; the non-abusive parent's parenting ability is compromised such that the child is presently at risk of danger in his or her care; the child demonstrates a substantial emotional connection to the abusive parent; or custody to the non-abusive parent currently poses a serious risk to the child's psychological development.

If the court finds during a contested trial that a pattern or serious incident of abuse has occurred, findings in support of the judgment should be entered in specific detail. *See* Custody of Vaughn, 422 Mass. 590 (1996); *see also* Care and Protection of Lillith, 61 Mass. App. Ct. 132, 139 (2004) (where the record reveals "sufficient concerns" about abuse, the court must "make detailed and comprehensive findings of fact on the issues of domestic violence and its effect upon the child."), quoting Custody of Vaughn, 422 Mass. 590, 599 (1996) (additional quotation omitted).

12:06. CUSTODY PROCEEDINGS IN PROBATE AND FAMILY COURT: RELATED CUSTODY ISSUES IN DOMESTIC RELATIONS MATTERS

Shared legal or physical custody cannot be ordered absent an agreement, and without written findings pursuant to G.L. c. 208, §§ 31 and 31A, and G.L. c. 209C, § 10(a) when a c. 209A order is or has been issued. *See* Custody of Vaughn, 422 Mass. 590 (1996).

COMMENTARY

Shared legal or physical custody must be supported by written findings if there is a c. 209A order in effect, or if there had been a prior order. G.L. c. 208, § 31 provides that:

If, despite the prior or current issuance of an abuse prevention order against one parent pursuant to chapter two hundred and nine A, the court orders shared legal or physical custody either as a temporary order or at a trial on the merits, the court shall provide written findings to support such shared custody order.

Section 31A further provides, in part, that "[i]n issuing any temporary or permanent custody order, the probate and family court shall consider evidence of past or present abuse toward a parent or child as a factor contrary to the best interest of the child." G.L. c. 208, § 31A. There shall be no presumption either in favor of or against shared legal or physical custody at the time of the trial on the merits, except as provided for in § 31A.

The findings required by G.L. c. 208, § 31 must indicate that the court has evaluated the effects of domestic violence on the child and how such a custody order advances the best interest of the child. In Custody of Vaughn, 422 Mass. 590 (1996), the Supreme Judicial Court affirmed the Appeals Court's decision to reverse and remand the trial court's supplemental judgment, which granted primary physical custody to the father, for further consideration of evidence regarding domestic violence perpetrated by the father against the mother and the effect of the family violence on the child. *Id.* The Supreme Judicial Court found that, "the Probate Court had failed to give sufficient weight to the effects of domestic violence on women and their children." *Id.* at 596. In remanding the case, the Supreme Judicial Court stated that the Probate and Family Court shall make "explicit findings" in this regard. *Id.* at 600. *See also Adoption of Imelda, 72 Mass. App. Ct. 354, 364–365 (2008)*, rev. denied, *Adoption of Imelda, 452 Mass. 1105 (2008); Care and Protection of Lillith, 61 Mass. App. Ct. 132, 139–143 (2004).*

The Appeals Court has held that that "in order for joint custody or shared responsibility to work, both parents must be able mutually 'to agree on the basic issues in child rearing and want to cooperate in making decisions for [their] children'." Rolde v. Rolde, 12 Mass. App. Ct. 398, 404 (1981). The essence of shared custody is the ability to effectively communicate and to engage in joint decision-making. As such, if the parties are precluded from talking to each other or have a demonstrated history of an inability to communicate safely, then an award of joint custody would be inappropriate. Indeed, the express language of G.L. c. 209C provides that joint custody can be awarded "only if the parents have entered into an agreement pursuant to section eleven or the court finds that the parents have successfully exercised joint responsibility for the child prior to the commencement of the proceedings pursuant to this chapter and have the ability to communicate and plan with each other concerning the child's best interest." G.L. c. 209C, § 10(a) (emphasis added); *see also* Custody of Odette, 61 Mass. App. Ct. 904, 905 (2004) (award of joint custody, in the absence of positive findings entered by trial judge as to parents' demonstrated ability to communicate, constitutes reversible error). If such an award of custody is inconsistent with the no-contact provisions of a c. 209A order. *See Guideline 12:07*, Custody and Visitation Proceedings in Probate and Family Court: Modifications of c. 209A Orders.

Where the parties have reached an agreement on the issue of custody, the court should scrutinize the agreement to ensure that the best interest of the child has been promoted by the agreement, and that the agreement provides for the safety and well being of the child and the safety of the abused parent. The best interest of the child must be advanced in any award of custody or visitation to a perpetrator of domestic violence. If the court determines that the agreement of the parties is not in the best interest of the child, the court must make a specific finding to that effect. *See* G.L. c. 208, § 31 ("Where the parents have reached an agreement providing for the custody of the children, the court may enter an order in accordance with such agreement, unless specific findings are made by the court indicating that such an order would not be in the best interest of the children").

Custody determinations may also have other consequences, such as the ability of the non-custodial parent to access his or her child's school records. A statute pertaining to availability of school information to non-custodial parents, G.L. c. 71, § 34H, as amended by St. 2006, c. 62, § 1, provides:

(a) . . . For purposes of this section, any parent who does not have physical custody of a child shall be eligible for the receipt of information unless: (1) the parent's access to the child is currently prohibited by a temporary or permanent protective order, except where the protective order, or any subsequent order which modifies the protective order, specifically allows access to the information described in this section; or (2) the parent is denied visitation, or, based on a threat to the safety of the child, is currently denied legal custody of the child or is currently ordered to supervised visitation, and the threat is specifically noted in the order pertaining to custody or supervised visitation. All such documents limiting or restricting parental access to a student's records or information which have been provided to the school or school district shall be placed in the student's record.

Orders issued by the Probate and Family Court involving parents should indicate whether the non-custodial parent has sought and been denied shared legal custody based on a threat to the safety of the child or custodial parent and is entitled to unsupervised visitation with his child. *Id.* A non-custodial parent is not eligible for the receipt of school records if his or her access to the child or to the custodial parent has been restricted by a temporary or permanent abuse prevention order unless the abuse prevention order, or any subsequent order which modifies the abuse prevention order, specifically allows the non-custodial parent's access to the school records. G.L. c. 71, § 34H(a).

See Guideline 6:06, Visitation Orders and Other Courts, regarding visitation orders and other court departments; *Guideline 12:01*, Visitation Proceedings in Probate and Family Court: Safety Assessment Pertaining to the Plaintiff in Abuse Prevention Proceedings; *Guideline 12:02*, Visitation and Custody Proceedings in Probate and Family Court: Assessment of Impact on Children; *Guideline 12:03*, Visitation Proceedings in Probate and Family Court: Safety Assessment in Terms of Visitation; *Guideline 12:07*, Custody and Visitation Proceedings in Probate and Family Court: Modifications of c. 209A Orders, regarding visitation matters; and *Guideline 13:00*, Assignment of Justices of the Probate and Family Court Department to Modify Inconsistent Orders, regarding assignment of justices of the Probate and Family Court Department to modify inconsistent orders.

12:07. CUSTODY AND VISITATION PROCEEDINGS IN PROBATE AND FAMILY COURT: MODIFICATIONS OF C. 209A ORDERS

All orders must be consistent. Accordingly, a c. 209A order entered by the Probate and Family Court, or other court of competent jurisdiction, must be modified when the Probate and Family Court subsequently enters a custody or visitation order that conflicts with the c. 209A order.

COMMENTARY

A c. 209A no-contact order entered by the Probate and Family Court should be amended to reflect a subsequently entered visitation order in a divorce, paternity, or other custody proceeding. If the original c. 209A order is in a different Probate and Family Court division, the court entering the subsequent visitation order may telephone the Administrative Office of the Probate and Family Court to request a special assignment to amend the original c. 209A order. If the conflicting no-contact order was issued by a court in a different Department, it should be subject to interdepartmental assignment pursuant to *Guideline 13:00*, Assignment of Justices of the Probate

and Family Court Department to Modify Inconsistent Orders. Although only a Probate and Family Court can issue a visitation order, such an order does not override the no-contact or stay-away provision of the order entered by a court of another department, unless the Probate and Family Court modifies such provisions pursuant to an interdepartmental judicial assignment, under *Guideline 13:00*, Assignment of Justices of the Probate and Family Court Department to Modify Inconsistent Orders, thereby eliminating inconsistencies between the no-contact/stay-away provision of the order issued by the court of another department and the decision issued by the Probate and Family Court. (See Trial Court Administrative Order 96–1, effective October 16, 1996). Therefore, a Probate and Family Court judge should either amend the c. 209A order, sitting as a judge of the department that issued the c. 209A order, so that it is not inconsistent with the Probate and Family Court visitation order or issue a visitation order that conforms to and is not inconsistent with the existing c. 209A order.

To the extent possible, the Probate and Family Court Judge should specifically and clearly identify the modified provisions on the face of the c. 209A order. The modified order should not simply refer to an attached order or agreement, particularly with respect to modification of the provisions regarding the contact and stay-away orders between the parties and/or children.

In accordance with Administrative Order 96–1, the probation department in the modifying court will immediately transmit a copy of the order, including all additional pages of the order if there was inadequate space on the original order to include complete details of the modification, by facsimile to the issuing court. The issuing court must then enter the order into the Statewide Registry of Civil Restraining orders, notify the appropriate police department of the modified order, and update its case file. *See Guideline 13:00*, Assignment of Justices of the Probate and Family Court Department to Modify Inconsistent Orders.

See Guideline, Custody Proceedings in Probate and Family Court: Related Custody Issues in Domestic Relations Matters, regarding shared legal or physical custody; *Guidelines 12:01*, Visitation Proceedings in Probate and Family Court: Safety Assessment Pertaining to the Plaintiff in Abuse Prevention Proceedings; *Guideline 12:02*, Visitation and Custody Proceedings in Probate and Family Court: Assessment of Impact on Children; and *Guideline 12:03*, Visitation Proceedings in Probate and Family Court: Safety Assessment and Terms of Visitation, regarding visitation matters; and *Guideline 12:02*, Visitation and Custody Proceedings in Probate and Family Court: Assessment of Impact on Children; *Guideline 12:06*, Custody Proceedings in Probate and Family Court: Related Custody Issues in Domestic Relations Matters; *Guideline 12:08*, Custody Proceedings in Probate and Family Court: Interstate Custody Issues; and *Guideline 12:09*, Custody Proceedings in Probate and Family Court: Non–Parent Custody and No–Contact Orders, regarding custody.

12:08. CUSTODY PROCEEDINGS IN PROBATE AND FAMILY COURT: INTERSTATE CUSTODY ISSUES

General Laws c. 209B authorizes Massachusetts to enter emergency orders to protect the plaintiff and child from harm, notwithstanding the pendency of a custody proceeding in another state.

COMMENTARY

If there is a prior or pending action or an existing custody order from another state and that state continues to have jurisdiction under its own law(s), Massachusetts must defer to the jurisdiction of the other state unless that state relinquishes jurisdiction to Massachusetts. Even if a parent has fled from another jurisdiction to Massachusetts to avoid abuse, the state from which that parent fled will remain the child's home state for six months.

If a petition for protection from abuse is properly filed in Massachusetts, however, and another state has prior custody jurisdiction, G.L. c. 209B, § 2(a)(3)(ii) allows a Massachusetts court to enter a custody or visitation order on an emergency basis only. The issuance of a c. 209A order is a sufficient finding of an emergency to justify a temporary custody order. Any custody order is subject to the initial jurisdictional requirements of the Massachusetts Child Custody Jurisdiction Act (M.C.C.J.A.), pursuant to G.L. c. 209B, and the continuing jurisdiction of Parental Kidnapping Protection Act (P.K.P.A.), pursuant to 28 U.S.C. § 1738A (1988). *See* Umina v. Malbica, 27 Mass. App. Ct. 351, 358 (1989); Delk v. Gonzalez, 421 Mass. 525, 529 (1995).

If custody jurisdiction is contested, the judge should make specific findings relative to abuse and risk to the child that should be communicated to the court with primary custody jurisdiction, either through telephone communication or by providing a copy of the findings or both. If returning the child would create an undue risk of harm, the court may request that the other state consider bifurcating the proceeding with the Massachusetts court conducting a hearing or investigation for the benefit and use of the court with primary custody jurisdiction.

Child support awards in c. 209A orders may not conflict with awards in existence from another state. If there is a child support amount ordered by an out-of-state entity, the Uniform Interstate Family Support Act (U.I.F.S.A.) is applicable. *See* G.L. c. 209D.

See Guideline 12:02, Visitation and Custody Proceedings in Probate and Family Court: Assessment of Impact on Children; *Guideline 12:06*, Custody Proceedings in Probate and Family Court: Related Custody Issues in Domestic Relations Matters; *Guideline 12:07*, Custody and Visitation Proceedings in Probate and Family Court: Modifications of c. 209A Orders; and *Guideline 12:09*, Custody Proceedings in Probate and Family Court: Non–Parent Custody and No-Contact Orders, regarding other custody matters.

12:09. CUSTODY PROCEEDINGS IN PROBATE AND FAMILY COURT: NON–PARENT CUSTODY AND NO–CONTACT ORDERS

The court may enter a no-contact order relative to a child of the abuser who is not also a child of the victim, provided that they are all members of the same household. However, a guardianship petition should be filed if the court enters an order allowing a child of the abuser to remain with the victim.

COMMENTARY

When a child of the abuser is a member of the victim's household, or if an action is brought on behalf of that child, the court does not have authority pursuant to c. 209A to award custody to a third party. However, if the safety of the child necessitates allowing the child to remain with the non-parent plaintiff, a temporary custody order may be entered pursuant to a separate guardianship of a minor petition. Under c. 209A, there must be "independent support" for an order barring contact between the abuser and his or her child who is a member of the household. *See* Smith v. Joyce, 421 Mass. 520, 523 (1995).

12:10. ISSUANCE OF PROTECTIVE ORDERS: DIVORCE PROCEEDINGS

Protective orders may be entered pursuant to G.L. c. 208, § 18 during the pendency of a divorce to prohibit one spouse from imposing restraint on the personal liberty of the other spouse.

COMMENTARY

A request may be filed pursuant to G.L. c. 208, § 18 in the Probate and Family Court in which a divorce action is pending seeking that the other spouse be prohibited from imposing any restraint on her or his personal liberty.[27] Either spouse or his or her guardian may request additional orders to protect herself or himself, a ward, or their children, including an order to vacate the marital home. In some instances, parties may be required to seek protective orders pursuant to G.L. c. 208 because of the venue provisions of c. 209A.

Protective orders entered pursuant to § 18 are considered temporary orders and will be revoked by operation of law upon the entry of a final judgment of divorce unless incorporated in the judgment. If the court intends the order to be revoked, it must be vacated on the existing order, sent to the police, and entered in the Statewide Registry of Civil Restraining Orders. If the court intends to extend protection, after incorporating the temporary order in the final judgment, the order should be examined and extended for an appropriate duration. All changes must be served on the defendant and the police and entered in the Statewide Registry of Civil Restraining Orders.

The Supreme Judicial Court has ruled that the Probate and Family Court is authorized to issue permanent protective orders and incorporate them into judgments of divorce nisi, pursuant to the second sentence of G.L. c. 208, § 18. Champagne v. Champagne, 429 Mass. 324 (1999). *Cf.* Commonwealth v. Blessing, 43 Mass. App. Ct. 447 (1997). In Crenshaw v. Macklin, 430 Mass. 633, 635 (2000), the SJC affirmed a court's authority to issue a permanent order following a "renewal hearing."

When requesting an extension of a protective order, the plaintiff need not make a showing of new abuse. *See* Rauseo v. Rauseo, 50 Mass. App. Ct. 911, 913 (2001), *rev. denied*, Rauseo v. Rauseo, 434 Mass. 1103 (2001) ("At a hearing on the plaintiff's request for an extension of an order . . . the plaintiff is not required to re-establish facts sufficient to support that initial grant of an abuse prevention order."); *See also* G.L. c. 209A, § 3; Mitchell v. Mitchell, 62 Mass. App. Ct. 769, 773–774 (2005) ("[T]he fact abuse has not occurred during the pendency of an order shall not, in itself, constitute sufficient grounds for allowing an order to be vacated."); Doe v. Keller, 57 Mass. App. Ct. 776, 778 (2003). However, the threat of abuse which formed the basis for entry of the original protective order must continue to exist. *See* Pike v. Maguire, 47 Mass. App. Ct. 929 (1999) (rescript) ("The only criterion for extending the original [protective] order is a showing of continued need for the order.").

See Guideline 6:02, Duration and Commentaries thereto; *Guideline 6:08*, Further Extending an Order After Notice on Its Expiration Date; *Guideline 6:08*, Further Extending an Order After Notice on Its Expiration Date; and *Guideline 12:12*, Issuance of Protective Orders: Separate Support, regarding duration of orders. *See Guideline 6:05B*, Support Orders, regarding actions for divorce or separate support.

27 General Laws c. 208, § 18 "has come to serve two, somewhat different, purposes," as it not only authorizes judges to issue protective orders designed to prevent abuse, it also allows entry of protective orders designed to prevent harassing behaviors which do not rise to the level of abuse but nevertheless require temporary intervention during the pendency of the divorce proceedings. Hennessey v. Sarkis, 54 Mass. App. Ct. 152, 155 (2002). When G.L. c. 208, § 18 is "utilized for abuse prevention purposes akin to those of [G.L. c. 209A] . . . the serious consequences of such an order require that procedural formalities like those employed in 209A proceedings be observed." *Id.* at 155–156 (internal citations omitted). A protective order issued pursuant to G.L. c. 208, § 18 is considered akin to an order entered pursuant to G.L. c. 209A when violation thereof carries criminal penalties. *See* Sertel v. Kravitz, 54 Mass. App. Ct. 913, 914 (2002).

12:11. ISSUANCE OF ORDERS TO VACATE MARITAL RESIDENCE: DIVORCE, SEPARATE SUPPORT OR MAINTENANCE

An order to vacate a marital residence may be entered pursuant to G.L. c. 208, § 34B.

COMMENTARY

Orders to vacate the marital home may be entered during the pendency of divorce, separate support or maintenance actions. At the commencement, or during the pendency, of an action, the court may enter an order requiring the husband or wife to vacate the marital home for an initial period not to exceed 90 days, and an additional period upon further motion. Each order is predicated upon a showing of danger to the health, safety, or welfare of the moving party or any minor child(ren) residing with the parties. There is no requirement that the child(ren) be born of the marriage.

It should be noted that the standard for an order to vacate after notice to the alleged abuser is that "the health, safety, or welfare of the moving party or any minor child(ren) living with the parties would be endangered or substantially impaired." In a highly contested custody case, the court should consider the extent to which the conflict endangers the child(ren). Upon a showing of a substantial likelihood of immediate danger to the moving party or the child(ren) residing with them, the court may allow *ex parte* relief. In such case, the court shall schedule a second hearing no later than five days after the temporary order to vacate is entered. The time frames for the second hearing in this section differ from c. 209A. All other motions to vacate the marital home must be marked for hearing in compliance with the Massachusetts Rules of Domestic Relations Procedure, Rule 6(c) (seven days notice to the opposing party). An order to vacate may enter even if the opposing party is not residing in the marital home or if the moving party has vacated to protect her or his safety or the safety of any minor child(ren).

The court must be mindful that the order to vacate the marital residence must be properly extended prior to the expiration of its initial 90–day period, as a defendant could otherwise avoid a conviction for violating the order that has expired. *See, e.g.*, Commonwealth v. Blessing, 43 Mass. App. Ct. 447, 449–450 (1997). Additionally, a temporary order in a divorce action does not survive the judgment nisi and therefore there is no order in existence that the defendant could properly be convicted of violating. *Id. See* Commentary to *Guideline 12:10*, Issuance of Protective Orders: Divorce Proceedings, regarding duration of orders issued pursuant to G.L. c. 208, § 18; *Guideline 6:02*, Duration and Commentaries thereto; *Guideline 6:08*, Further Extending an Order After Notice on Its Expiration Date; *Guideline 12:10*, Issuance of Protective Orders: Separate Support, regarding duration of orders issued pursuant to c. 209A; and *Guideline 6:05B*, Support Orders, regarding actions for divorce or separate support. Protective orders may enter when a spouse is entitled to a decree of separate support pursuant to G.L. c. 209, § 32.

12:12. ISSUANCE OF PROTECTIVE ORDERS: SEPARATE SUPPORT

Protective orders may enter as part of an action for separate support pursuant to G.L. c. 209, § 32.

COMMENTARY

Orders prohibiting interference with the personal liberty of the other spouse may enter in a separate support action. A separate support judgment may issue when the court finds that a spouse failed without justifiable cause to provide suitable support, deserted the other spouse, or has justifiable cause for living apart. According to G.L. c. 209, § 32, the orders are governed by the Rules of Civil Procedure, notwithstanding Rule 1 of the Massachusetts Rules of Domestic Relations Procedure.

If the protective order is entered as a temporary order, it shall be revoked by operation of law upon entry of final judgment of separate support. Although revoked by operation of law, the temporary order must be vacated in the Statewide Registry of Civil Restraining Orders so that the law enforcement community will not still consider the order legally valid and enforceable. The final order may be prescribed for a time certain or until further order of the court.

Ex parte relief should be granted only upon a finding of a substantial likelihood of harm. If *ex parte* relief is granted, a further hearing, after notice, should be held within 10 days. Mitchell v. Mitchell, 62 Mass. App. Ct. 769 (2005). The service requirements are the same as those applicable to an order issued pursuant to c. 209A. If the order

is subsequently modified, the defendant must be served again, and provided with the modified order. Failure to properly serve the abuser may hamper criminal prosecution. *See* Commentary to *Guideline 8:01*, Issuance of Criminal Complaint, regarding proper notice.

12:13. ISSUANCE OF PROTECTIVE ORDERS: PATERNITY ACTIONS

Protective orders may be entered as part of a paternity action pursuant to G.L. c. 209C, §§ 15 and 20.

COMMENTARY

General Laws c. 209C was enacted more recently than the protective provisions of G.L. c. 208 and G.L. c. 209 and it includes comprehensive language which most closely mirrors the protections of c. 209A. Because the Appellate Courts have held that all parties, regardless of their marital status, and their children should be accorded equal protection of the law, the comprehensive rights under this section shall be accorded to all parties seeking protection pursuant to a divorce or separate support action. *See* Doe v. Roe, 32 Mass. App. Ct. 63, 65 (1992), *rev. denied*, Doe v. Roe, 412 Mass. 1103 (1992).

Pursuant to G.L. c. 209C, § 11(a), as amended by St. 2008, c. 176, § 113, a voluntary, written acknowledgment of parentage executed jointly by the mother and putative father of a child, whether a minor or not, and filed with the registrar of vital records and statistics or with the court shall be recognized as a sufficient basis for seeking an order of support, visitation or custody with respect to the child without further proceedings to establish paternity. G.L. c. 209C, § 11(a). Parties have 60 days during which to rescind such an acknowledgment by filing a petition with the Probate and Family Court, which then must order a genetic marker test for the purpose of determining parentage, although the rescission "shall constitute the proper showing required for an order to submit to such testing." *Id.* Further, following such a challenge to paternity, if the child is receiving public assistance, the court must provide notice of the rescission to the IV–D agency if that agency is not already a party to the matter. *Id. See also* G.L. c. 46, §§ 3A–3D.

The court may enter either temporary orders or a final judgment which includes a vacate, no-contact, or restraining provision. If the order is temporary, the statute provides that unless modified or revoked (pursuant to G.L. c. 209C, § 20) it shall continue in force and be incorporated in the final judgment. Notwithstanding the statute, a more prudent action would be that the court incorporate the order into the final judgment in order for the order to remain effective. If the court intends to revoke the order, it must be vacated, sent to the police, and entered in the Statewide Registry of Civil Restraining Orders. If the court intends to extend protection, after incorporating the temporary order in the final judgment, the order should be examined to determine the appropriateness of its duration. Any changes must be served on the defendant and the police and entered in the Statewide Registry of Civil Restraining Orders. Failure to properly serve the abuser may hamper criminal prosecution.

12:14. SERVICE OF DOMESTIC RELATIONS PROTECTIVE ORDERS

Protective orders issued pursuant to G.L. c. 208, §§ 18 and 34B; G.L. c. 209, § 32; or G.L. c. 209C, §§ 15 and 20 shall be served on the defendant by the appropriate law enforcement officials and shall otherwise be treated in a manner similar to c. 209A orders.

COMMENTARY

Protective orders may be requested by a party to a divorce, separate support or paternity action or anyone acting legally on his or her behalf, within the pending proceeding. Additionally, if the court becomes aware of the need for protective orders in the course of hearing a divorce, separate support or paternity, it may, on its own, enter such orders as it deems necessary to protect a party and/or any minor child(ren). A party needing protection shall be informed that any order will be civil in nature and that criminal proceedings may also be available. Although the Probate and Family Court Department cannot enforce its order by criminal process, all orders may be enforced in the Probate and Family Court through contempt proceedings, either civil or criminal. Protective orders are usually enforced, however, by criminal process in the District Court or Boston Municipal Court.

A search of the Statewide Registry of Civil Restraining Orders must be made before the matter can be heard. A judge shall review the alleged abuser's criminal record prior to the hearing to determine the existence of a history of domestic or other violence. If an outstanding warrant exists against the alleged abuser, the judge must make a finding as to whether or not an imminent threat of bodily injury exists to the victim. If such threat exists and the defendant is not present, the judge shall notify the appropriate law enforcement officials who are required to execute the warrant as soon as is practicable. In any event, the appropriate law enforcement officials shall be notified of any outstanding warrant. In cases where the defendant is present, courts

are referred to *Guideline 5:07*, Court Action on Defendant's Warrant Status.

Page two of the c. 209A order has a place to record information as to the existence of an outstanding warrant (section A.16, FA–2A) and a line for the judge to make a finding whether or not there is an imminent threat of bodily harm to the victim (section A.17, FA–2A). To assist the judge, it is preferable that the person who checks the record or a member of the probation department highlight any violent or domestic offenses and any outstanding warrants prior to the judge's review of the record.

Any protective order issued pursuant to G.L. c. 208, G.L. c. 209, or G.L. c. 209C shall be entered into the Statewide Registry of Civil Restraining Orders and shall be served in the same manner as orders entered pursuant to c. 209A. *See Guideline 4:07*, Transmission of *Ex Parte* Orders to the Police for Service on the Defendant; and *Guideline 6:03*, Service of Orders on the Defendant, regarding methods of service. Failure to properly serve the abuser may hamper criminal prosecution. *See* Commentary to *Guideline 8:01*, Issuance of Criminal Complaint, regarding proper notice.

INTERDEPARTMENTAL JUDICIAL ASSIGNMENTS

13:00. ASSIGNMENT OF JUSTICES OF THE PROBATE AND FAMILY COURT DEPARTMENT TO MODIFY INCONSISTENT ORDERS

Upon the appearance before a justice of the Probate and Family Court of a party or parties to an abuse prevention order issued by the District Court, Boston Municipal Court, or Superior Court, said justice shall be assigned to sit in the court department which issued the order to modify, extend or vacate the order so as to eliminate any conflict between said order and the terms of decisions issued by the Probate and Family Court in accordance with Trial Court Administrative Order 96–1.[28] These Guidelines apply to abuse prevention orders subject to Interdepartmental Judicial Assignment.

[28] Please note that Administrative Order 96–1 uses the term "vacate."

COMMENTARY

General Laws c. 209A, § 1 provides jurisdiction for issuing abuse prevention orders in the Probate and Family Court, District Court, Boston Municipal Court, or Superior Court. Parties who obtain relief in the District Court, Boston Municipal Court, or Superior Court may, for example, seek subsequent relief on family matters that affect the parties in the Probate and Family Court. To eliminate inconsistencies between orders issued by the District Court, the Boston Municipal Court, or the Superior Court and judgments issued by the Probate and Family Court in a timely manner, this Guideline refers to Trial Court Administrative Order 96–1, Procedure for Interdepartmental Determinations in Abuse Prevention Proceedings. The following memoranda were issued to implement Administrative Order 96–1: District Court Transmittal No. 623, December 4, 1996, "Procedures Regarding Probate and Family Court Action on District Court Domestic Abuse Orders" http://www.mass.gov/courts/209a/docs/districtcourt-trans623–admin-order–96–1.pdf, and a memorandum from Probate and Family Court Chief Justice Mary Fitzpatrick, November 25, 1996, "Administrative Order 96–1." http://www.mass.gov/courts/209a/docs/probateandfamilycourt-admin-order–96–1-memo.pdf The Boston Municipal Court has adopted the policy issued by the District Court.

Judges and court personnel should extend their cooperative efforts in order to implement interdepartmental judicial assignments under this Guideline and pursuant to Administrative Order 96–1 in a prompt and expeditious manner.

This Guideline makes it clear that orders subject to interdepartmental judicial assignment are also subject to the terms of these Guidelines. Application of appropriate provisions of *Guideline 6:04*, Modification of Orders; Terminating Orders, regarding modification of orders, and *Guideline 6:07*, Mutual Abuse Prevention Orders, regarding mutual orders, in particular, will help ensure consistent adjudication of related matters involving the same parties.

See Commentary to *Guidelines 3:07*, Conduct of *Ex Parte* Hearings, and *Guideline 5:01*, Conduct of Hearings After Notice When Both Parties Appear: General, regarding orders issued by different court departments and Commentary to *Guideline 6:04*, Modification of Orders; Terminating Orders, regarding gun license and gun surrender orders in modification proceedings. *See also Guideline 2:07*, Referrals To and From Other Courts: Avoiding Inconsistent Orders; *Guideline 3:07*, Conduct of *Ex Parte* Hearings; *Guideline 4:01*, Content of *Ex Parte* Orders; *Guideline 6:00*, Orders After Notice: General; *Guideline 6:06*, Visitation Orders and Other Courts; *Guideline 6:07*, Mutual Abuse Prevention Orders; *Guideline 10:02*, Actions for Divorce or Separate Support; and *Guideline 12:07*, Custody and Visitation Proceedings in Probate and Family Court: Modifications of c. 209A Orders.

Administrative Order 96–1

COMMONWEALTH OF MASSACHUSETTS
THE TRIAL COURT

ADMINISTRATIVE ORDER 96–1

PROCEDURE FOR
INTERDEPARTMENTAL DETERMINATIONS IN
ABUSE PREVENTION PROCEEDINGS

In order to coordinate the response of the Departments of the Trial Court in proceedings under G.L. c. 209A, involving the same parties, the following procedure is hereby established pursuant to the superintendence power of the Chief Justice of Administration and Management under G.L. c. 211B, § 9.

● Definitions. In this Administrative Order the following words and phrases shall have the following meanings:

● "Order" means an abuse prevention order issued by either the Boston Municipal Court Department, a Division of the District Court Department or a Division of the Superior Court Department pursuant to G.L. c. 209A.

• "Issuing Court" means the Boston Municipal Court Department, a Division of the District Court Department or a Division of the Superior Court Department that has issued an abuse prevention order pursuant to G.L. c. 209A.

• "Modifying Court" means a Division of the Probate and Family Court Department in which a justice of that court has modified, extended or vacated an abuse prevention order issued by the Boston Municipal Court Department, a Division of the District Court Department or a Division of the Superior Court Department, pursuant to G.L. c. 209A.

• "Modified Order" means an order issued by a justice of the Division of the Probate and Family Court Department pursuant to G.L. c. 209A which modifies, extends or vacates an order issued pursuant to the same statute by a justice of the Boston Municipal Court Department, a Division of the District Court Department or a Division of the Superior Court Department.

• "Registry" means the Domestic Violence Record Keeping System established pursuant to St. 1992, Chapter 188 and maintained by the Commissioner of Probation.

• Interdepartmental Judicial Assignment. The justices of the Probate and Family Court Department are hereby assigned to sit in the Boston Municipal Court Department, the District Court Department or the Superior Court Department whenever a party to an order issued by the Boston Municipal Court Department or a Division of the District Court Department or a Division of the Superior Court Department appears before a justice of the Probate and Family Court Department and the justice determines it is appropriate to modify, extend or vacate said order to eliminate any conflict between said order and the terms of decisions issued by the Probate and Family Court Department. No order shall be modified by the Probate and Family Court, pursuant to this Administrative Order, without notice and an opportunity to be heard being given to the parties to the order of the issuing court. A justice of the Probate and Family Court Department who so modifies, extends or vacates an order issued by the Boston Municipal Court Department or a Division of the District

Court Department or a Division of the Superior Court Department shall advise the party or parties appearing before said justice of the effects of the modified order and explain that the modified order shall be immediately returned to the issuing Court, subject to further modification, extension or vacating when a party to the order appears before the issuing court or the modifying court in future proceedings. An assignment shall expire immediately following the issuance of a modified order by a justice of the Probate and Family Court.

• Transmittal of Modified Order. The Probation department in the modifying court shall cause the modified order to be transmitted by facsimile to the Probation department of the issuing court promptly to enable the Probation staff of the issuing court to enter the order into the Registry on the day on which the modified order is issued. Upon receipt of the modified order, the Probation department in the issuing court shall promptly provide a copy of the modified order to the staff or the Clerk or Clerk–Magistrate of the issuing court, who shall promptly docket and file the modified order. The Register of Probate in the modifying court shall cause the modified order to be mailed to the Clerk or Clerk–Magistrate of the issuing court no later than three days after the modified order is issued.

• Docketing of Order. The Clerk or Clerk–Magistrate of the issuing court shall cause the modified order to be docketed in the appropriate case file of the issuing court in a timely manner.

• Entry of Order into Registry. The Probation department of the issuing court shall enter the modified order into the Registry on the day that the modified order is issued and follow the requirements of the Standard to Establish and Maintain a Domestic Violence Record Keeping System, Including a Registry of All Civil Vacate, Restraining, Protective and Abuse Prevention Orders established by the Commissioner of Probation with regard to entry of orders into the Registry.

John J. Irwin, Jr.
Chief Justice for
Administration and Management
Date: October 16, 1996

ORDERS FROM OTHER JURISDICTIONS

14:00.　FILING AND ENFORCEMENT OF ABUSE PREVENTION AND OTHER PROTECTIVE ORDERS ISSUED BY OTHER JURISDICTIONS

Abuse prevention and other protective orders issued by other jurisdictions outside of Massachusetts for the purpose of preventing violent or threatening acts against, or contact or communication with or physical proximity to another person, including *ex parte* and orders after notice issued by civil and criminal courts filed by or on behalf of a person seeking protection, shall be given full faith and credit throughout the Commonwealth and enforced as if they were issued in the Commonwealth for as long as they are in effect in the issuing jurisdiction.

A person entitled to protection under a protection order issued by another jurisdiction may file such order in the District Court, the Boston Municipal Court, the Probate and Family Court, or the Superior Court by filing with the court a certified copy of such order which shall be entered into the Statewide Registry of Civil Restraining Orders. Such person shall swear under oath in an affidavit that to the best of such person's knowledge such order is currently in effect as written. The Affidavit for Fling Out–Of–State Protective Order (FA/HA–9) may be used for this purpose. The clerk shall

provide a certified copy of the protection order issued by the other jurisdiction to a law enforcement agency upon request.

Statutory provisions pertaining to Massachusetts abuse prevention orders also apply to protection orders issued by other jurisdictions. Violations of orders from other jurisdictions shall be afforded the same treatment as violations of Massachusetts abuse prevention orders with respect to penalties and orders to pay damages. The exception to the rule of spousal disqualification (which bars a husband and wife from testifying about their private conversations), which applies, *inter alia*, to criminal proceedings in which one spouse is a defendant alleged to have committed a crime against the other spouse or to have violated a Massachusetts order, also applies to criminal proceedings in which one spouse is a defendant alleged to have violated a protection order issued by another jurisdiction. Persons who commit the crime of stalking in violation of an order issued by another jurisdiction are subject to the same penalty as those who commit the same crime in violation of a Massachusetts abuse prevention order.

COMMENTARY

General Laws c. 209A, § 5A provides that protection orders issued by another jurisdiction shall be given full faith and credit throughout the Commonwealth. General Laws. c. 209A, § 1 describes another jurisdiction as another state, territory or possession of the United

States, the Commonwealth of Puerto Rico, the District of Columbia or a tribal court. The statute apparently is intended to work in conjunction with the full faith and credit provisions of 18 U.S.C. § 2265.

Section 5A appears to include protection orders involving persons who may or may not be family or household members or who are in a substantive dating or engagement relationship, as provided by Massachusetts law. It is also worded to encompass orders restricting a broad variety of activities, including protection orders, the purpose of which is to prevent, in the alternative, violent or threatening acts, harassment, contact or communication with or physical proximity to another person. Such orders may be temporary or final and may have been issued by "civil and criminal courts." Court personnel should accept for filing any orders which fall into these categories in a manner reflecting the broad scope of the statute. The statute does not appear to include orders which contain other provisions, such as vacating the household, staying away from a multiple family dwelling and the workplace, awarding the plaintiff temporary custody of a minor child, and ordering the defendant to pay temporary support.

General Laws c. 265, § 43(b) provides that a person who commits the crime of stalking in violation of a protection order issued by another jurisdiction shall be punished the same as a person who committed the same crime in violation of a Massachusetts order. The crime of stalking may be "prosecuted and punished" in any jurisdiction of the Commonwealth where "an act constituting an element of the crime was committed." G.L. c. 277, § 62B.

Violations of orders issued by other jurisdictions are to be treated the same as violations of orders issued by Massachusetts courts. G.L. c. 209A, §§ 5A and 7. Law enforcement authorities are required to enforce foreign protection orders as they do Massachusetts orders. Specifically, police "may presume the validity of, and enforce . . . a copy of a protection order issued by another jurisdiction which has been provided to the law enforcement officer *by any source*; provided, however, that the officer is also provided with a statement by the person protected by the order that such order remains in effect. Law enforcement officers may rely on such statement by the person protected by such order." G.L. c. 209A, § 5A (emphasis added). These provisions appear to indicate that the filing of an order from another jurisdiction is not a prerequisite to enforcement in the Commonwealth. Protection orders from other jurisdictions are included among the types of orders the violation of which requires a police officer to make an arrest. G.L. c. 209A, § 6. Section 6 also authorizes police to make warrantless arrests if they have probable cause to believe that a firearms suspension and surrender provision of an order has been violated.

Memoranda and forms have been issued to facilitate filing of orders issued by other jurisdictions in the courts of the Commonwealth and logged onto the Registry of Civil Restraining Orders: a memorandum from Chief Justice for Administration and Management John Irwin, October 30, 1996, "Out-of-State Domestic Violence Restraining Orders," including a memorandum from Commissioner of Probation Donald Cochran, October 30, 1996, "Chapter 209A, Section 5A: Out-of-State Protective/Restraining Orders"; http://www.mass.gov/courts/209a/docs/aotc-out-of-state-orders-memo.pdf District Court Transmittal No. 622, November 6, 1996, "Out-of-State Domestic Violence Restraining Orders;" http://www.mass.gov/courts/209a/docs/districtcourt-trans 622-out-of -state-orders.pdf and a memorandum from Probate and Family Court Chief Justice Mary Fitzpatrick, November 5, 1996, "Registration of Foreign Protection Orders." http://www.mass.gov/courts/209a/docs/probateandfamilycourt-foreign-orders-memo.pdf

Persons who are protected by an order issued by another jurisdiction and who want to file a certified copy of it in a Massachusetts court with jurisdiction are required to file an affidavit stating that the out of state order is currently in effect as written. The Affidavit for Fling Out–Of–State Protective Order (FA/HA–9) may be used for this purpose. *See* G.L. c. 209A, § 5A. *See also Guideline 1:08*, Plaintiff Unable to Appear in Court; and *Guideline 2:03*, Completing the Complaint; Obtaining Required Information.

RULES OF THE SUPERIOR COURT

Table of Rules

GENERAL PROVISIONS

Rule 1.   Effect of These Rules

(Applicable to all cases)

The provisions of these rules, so far as they are the same as those of existing rules, shall be construed as a continuation thereof, and not as new provisions.

Unless a contrary intent appears, the word plaintiff shall include petitioner or libellant, and in criminal cases the Commonwealth, and the word defendant shall include respondent, libellee or co-respondent, and the word attorney or the word counsel shall include a party appearing or acting for himself.

Rule 2.   Appearances

(Applicable to all cases)

The name, address, and telephone number of the attorney for every party, or of the party if no attorney appears for him, shall be entered on the docket as they appear upon the paper or papers constituting the appearance, or some paper transmitted to the clerk therewith. Where no address or telephone number of the attorney or party, as the case may be, appears upon the docket, notice to such party may be given by posting the same publicly in the clerk's office or in a room, hall or passage adjacent thereto. The clerk upon request shall post the same.

Amended June 26, 1980, effective September 1, 1980.

Rule 3.   Authority to Appear

(Applicable to all cases)

The right of an attorney to appear for any party shall not be questioned by the opposite party, unless the objection be taken in writing within ten days after the appearance of such attorney, but the court may permit the objection to be taken later. When the authority of any attorney to appear for any party is demanded, if such attorney declares that he has been duly authorized to appear, by an application made directly to him by such party, or by some person whom he believes to have been authorized to employ him, such declaration shall be evidence of such authority.

Rule 4.   Postponement

(Applicable to all cases)

The court need not entertain any motion for postponement, grounded on the want of material testimony, unless supported by an affidavit, which shall state (1) the name, and, if known, the residence, of the witness whose testimony is wanted, (2) the particular testimony which he is expected to give, with the grounds of such expectation, and (3) the endeavors and means that have been used to procure his attendance or deposition; to the end that the court may judge whether due diligence has been used for that purpose. The party objecting to the postponement shall not be allowed to contradict the statement of what the absent witness is expected to testify, but may disprove any other fact stated in such affidavit. Such motion will not ordinarily be granted if the adverse party will admit that the absent witness would, if present, testify as stated in the affidavit, and will agree that the same shall be received and considered as evidence at the trial or hearing, as though the witness were present and so testified; and such agreement shall be in writing, upon the affidavit, and signed by such adverse party or his attorney. The same rule shall apply, *mutatis mutandis,* when the motion is grounded on the want of any material document, thing or other evidence. In all cases the granting or denial of a motion for postponement shall be discretionary, whether the foregoing provisions have been complied with or not.

The court will not ordinarily grant a motion for postponement grounded on the absence of a material witness whom it is in the power of the moving party to summon, unless such party has caused such witness to be regularly summoned and to be paid or tendered his travel and one day's attendance.

Rule 5.   Jurors

(Applicable to all cases)

Persons summoned as jurors, who are excused because of any statutory exemption, shall be entitled to their fees for travel and attendance; but if excused for any other cause, or if service is postponed, it shall be on condition that no fee shall be allowed where no service is rendered, unless in any special case the court otherwise directs.

When practicable, excuses of jurors shall be presented under oath to the presiding justice in the session to which such jurors are summoned, or, where jurors are held in a central pool, to the justice in charge thereof.

If it is necessary to present such excuses before the return day of the venire, they shall be submitted to the justice assigned to sit in said session, if available, or, where jurors are held in a central pool, to the justice in charge thereof, or to the chief justice; and, if unavailable, by jurors in Suffolk to the justice presiding in the first session without jury; and by jurors in other counties to a justice holding court or resident in such county or an adjoining county. If any juror is excused in any place other than in open court, the justice excusing him shall forthwith notify the clerk of his action and the ground thereof.

The word jurors in this rule shall include grand jurors.

Rule 6.   Jury Selection

(Applicable to all cases)

1. Subject to applicable statutes, rules, and controlling authority, the trial judge in each case has discretion to determine a procedure for examining and selecting jurors designed to maintain juror privacy and dignity, identify explicit and implicit bias, and foster efficiency in the session and among sessions using the same jury pool. This rule provides a standard procedure for each civil and criminal case unless otherwise ordered by the trial judge, while permitting attorneys and self-represented parties a fair opportunity to participate in voir dire so as to identify bias.

2. Conference With the Trial Judge

a. In civil cases, unless otherwise ordered, the court shall schedule a final trial conference in accordance with Standing Order 1–88, as may be amended from time to time.

In criminal cases, unless otherwise ordered, a final pretrial conference shall be scheduled in accordance with Standing Order 2–86. These conferences with the trial judge shortly before trial serve as the primary opportunity to discuss empanelment, including without limitation: the statement of the case to be read to the venire; the extent of any pre-charge on significant legal principles; the method and content of the judge's intended voir dire of jurors; the method and content of any attorney or party participation in voir dire; judicial approval or disapproval of proposed questions or subject matters; any time limits on attorney or party voir dire; the number of jurors to be seated; any agreement to allow deliberation by fewer jurors if seated jurors are dismissed post-empanelment; the content and method of employing any supplemental juror questionnaire; the number of peremptories; and the order and timing of the parties' assertions of challenges for cause and peremptory challenges.

b. If the court has not scheduled a final trial conference in a civil case or a final pre-trial conference in a criminal case, any party planning to submit a request, proposal, or motion regarding jury selection should request such a conference or submit a motion requesting voir dire procedures in time for a pretrial ruling by the trial judge. All parties shall avoid proposing jury selection procedures (including attorney/party voir dire) for the first time on the day of trial.

3. Voir Dire by Attorneys and Parties

a. On or before the final trial conference in a civil case or final pre-trial conference in a criminal case, or 5 business days before trial if no such conference is scheduled, the parties shall submit in writing any requests for attorney/party voir dire; motions in limine concerning the method of jury selection; proposed subject matters or questions for inquiry by the parties or trial judge; any proposed supplemental questionnaire; any proposed preliminary legal instructions to the venire or juror panels; the location within the courtroom where jurors and parties will stand or sit during voir dire; and any other matter setting forth the party's position regarding empanelment.

b. The trial judge shall allow attorney or party voir dire if properly requested at or before the time set forth in paragraph 3(a), above. The trial judge may deem any subsequent request for attorney or party voir dire untimely, but may in the judge's discretion allow the request in the absence of prejudice to any other party or significant impact on trial efficiency or on other sessions using the same jury pool.

c. When attorney or party voir dire is allowed, the trial judge shall, at a minimum, allow the attorneys or parties to ask reasonable follow-up questions seeking elaboration or explanation concerning juror responses to the judge's questions, or concerning any written questionnaire. After considering the goals set forth in paragraph 1 above, the trial judge should generally approve a reasonable number of questions that (i) seek factual information about the prospective juror's background and experience pertinent to the issues expected to arise in the case; (ii) may reveal preconceptions or biases relating to the identity of the parties or the nature of the claims or issues expected to arise in the

case; (iii) inquire into the prospective jurors' willingness and ability to accept and apply pertinent legal principles as instructed; and (iv) are meant to elicit information on subjects that controlling authority has identified as preferred subjects of inquiry, even if not absolutely required.

d. At the final trial conference in a civil case, or final pre-trial conference in a criminal case (or in a written submission in lieu of such conference), any attorney or party wishing to inquire into any of the following disfavored subjects must explain how the inquiry is relevant to the issues, may affect the juror's impartiality, or may assist the proper exercise of peremptory challenges:

i. The juror's political views, voting patterns or party preferences;

ii. The juror's religious beliefs or affiliation.

e. Counsel and Parties May Not Ask:

i. Questions framed in terms of how the juror would decide this case (prejudgment), including hypotheticals that are close/specific to the facts of this case (any hypotheticals that may trigger this rule must be presented to the judge before trial).

ii. Questions that seek to commit juror(s) to a result, including, without limitation, questions about what evidence would cause the juror(s) to find for the attorney's client or the party.

iii. Questions having no substantial purpose other than to argue an attorney's or party's case or indoctrinate any juror(s).

iv. Questions about the outcome in prior cases where the person has served as a juror, including the prior vote(s) of the juror or the verdict of the entire jury.

v. Questions in the presence of other jurors that specifically reference what is written on a particular juror's confidential juror questionnaire.

f. The trial judge may impose reasonable restrictions on the subject matter, time, or method of attorney or party voir dire and shall so inform the attorneys or parties before empanelment begins.

g. In approving or disapproving voir dire questions and procedures, the trial judge, on request, should consider whether questions or methods proposed by the attorneys or parties may assist in identifying explicit or implicit bias.

h. If employing panel voir dire, the trial judge shall determine the procedure and may elect to follow the method set forth in Addendum A or adopt variations thereof. The trial judge may also elect to use some of the methods set forth in Addendum A even if not employing panel voir dire. Nothing in Appendix A restricts the trial judge from selecting an alternative method of voir dire, including but not limited to:

i. Filling empty seats as they arise due to challenges for cause or the exercise of peremptories. The trial judge may do this by clearing additional prospective jurors or filling in from additional already cleared jurors;

ii. The "Walker method": Through panel voir dire or otherwise, the trial judge may clear as indifferent a number of prospective jurors that equals or exceeds the total number of jurors needed, plus alternates, plus the total number of peremptory challenges held by the parties. *See Commonwealth v. Walker*, 379 Mass. 297, 299 n.1 (1979). *But see Commonwealth v. Johnson*, 417 Mass. 498, 507–508 (1994).

4. Empanelment

a. The trial judge shall ask all voir dire questions specifically required by statute, court rule, or controlling authority, but retains discretion as to when and how to do so. The trial judge may allow individual voir dire, panel voir dire, or any combination.

b. Questioning shall occur through individual voir dire if (i) required by statute, rule, or controlling authority; (ii) inquiry concerns private or potentially embarrassing information; or (iii) questioning would specifically reference what is written on a particular juror's confidential juror questionnaire.

c. The trial judge should consider some individual voir dire in all cases to (i) determine whether any juror has an impediment concerning hearing, language or visual ability, mental health, or comprehension and to determine whether a reasonable accommodation would enable the juror to serve; (ii) address any private or embarrassing information not disclosed in public portions of the voir dire; or (iii) identify any other impediment to jury service that the trial judge and parties might not observe without personal contact with the juror.

d. Attorneys and parties shall limit their questioning of any juror(s) to such subject matters and methods as previously approved by the trial judge and shall avoid questions set forth in paragraph 3(e) above, even as follow-up, without court approval.

e. *Questions about the Law*

i. If the parties have obtained approval to ask voir dire questions about the law, the trial judge shall take appropriate measures to ensure that the jury is accurately and effectively instructed on the law. Such measures may include, but are not limited to: a brief pre-charge; requiring the questioner to use the words specifically approved by the judge; stating the law in a written supplemental questionnaire; or contemporaneous instructions by the trial judge at the time the question is asked.

ii. If a juror asks counsel a question to clarify an aspect of the law, counsel shall request that the trial judge answer the question; the trial judge may interrupt if counsel attempts to respond to a juror question by instructing on such a point of law.

f. Any party may object to a question posed by another party by stating "objection," without elaboration or argument. The trial judge may rule on the objection in, or outside of, the juror's presence. The trial judge may, on the judge's own motion, strike or rephrase a party's question and may interrupt or supplement a party's questioning to provide the juror(s) with an explanation of the law or the jury trial process, or to ask any additional questions that the trial judge believes will assist the trial judge in determining the juror's impartiality.

g. Counsel and the parties must ensure an accurate record of attorney or party voir dire. In an electronically recorded courtroom, counsel must stand near a microphone at all times. During panel voir dire in any courtroom, counsel must also call out the juror seat number (or juror number) of any individual juror who is questioned individually or who responds audibly. Failure to do so may constitute a waiver of any claim of error arising from any inaudible or unattributable portions of the record.

h. *Challenges for Cause*

i. The court will consider all its observations, including the juror's responses, to determine whether or not the juror will be fair, focus on the facts of the case and follow the law despite a particular viewpoint or experience.

ii. Whether at side bar or during panel inquiry, a juror's "yes" or "no" answer to a question about a viewpoint or experience may not, by itself, support a challenge for cause. If intending to challenge a juror for cause as a result of attorney or party voir dire, the questioner ordinarily should lay an adequate foundation showing that, in light of the information or viewpoint expressed, the juror may not be fair and impartial and decide the case solely on the facts and law presented at trial. The court may inquire further or may decide without further questioning, if the judge believes that the existing record is sufficient to resolve the challenge for cause.

i. *Peremptory Challenges*

i. After the trial judge finds that each juror stands indifferent, the parties shall exercise their peremptory challenges. The trial judge may require exercise of peremptory challenges after completion of side bar inquiry of an individual juror, after filling the jury box with jurors found to stand indifferent, or at some other time after the trial judge's finding of indifference.

ii. If the trial judge does not expressly rule on a juror's bias or impartiality, the trial judge's direction for the parties to exercise peremptory challenges constitutes an implicit finding that the juror stands indifferent. On request, made after the trial judge's direction but before exercise of a peremptory challenge, the trial judge shall make an explicit finding as to the juror's impartiality.

5. Supplemental Juror Questionnaires

Supplemental juror questionnaires are not protected by G.L. c. 234A, § 23 and cannot be kept confidential without complying with the impoundment procedures set forth in Trial Court Rule VIII. If using supplemental juror questionnaires, the judge shall consider methods to ensure the juror's personal privacy and to promote the candor of responses, including but not limited to asking jurors whether they wish to keep responses confidential, asking the grounds for any such request, and complying with applicable impoundment procedures.

Amended March 21, 1989, effective April 1, 1989. Amended July 26, 2017, effective September 1, 2017.

ADDENDUM A

SAMPLE PANEL VOIR DIRE PROTOCOL

1. Pretrial

The trial judge may permit counsel or self-represented parties to question jurors as a group, in a so-called "panel voir dire" procedure. Any attorney or self-represented party who seeks to examine the prospective jurors in panel format shall serve and file a motion requesting leave to do so in accordance with Superior Court Rule 6(3)(a). The motion shall identify generally the topics the moving party proposes to ask the prospective jurors and shall state whether each topic is for individual voir dire or for a panel of jurors. The trial judge may, in the exercise of discretion, require attorneys and self-represented parties to submit the specific language of the proposed questions for pre-approval. The motion and any responsive filing shall also include any proposed language for brief preliminary instructions on principles of law to be given pursuant to paragraph 2(b) below.

2. Initial Stages of Empanelment

Before any questioning of a juror panel by attorneys or self-represented parties, or at such other time as the trial judge deems most appropriate, the trial judge shall:

(a) provide the venire with a brief description of the case, including the nature of the facts alleged and of the claims or charges, including the date and location of the pertinent alleged event(s), and the identity of persons or entities significantly involved;

(b) provide the venire with brief, preliminary instructions on significant legal principles pertinent to the case. Such instructions should include a brief recitation of: the burden and standard of proof: the elements of at least the primary civil claim or at least the most serious criminal charge; if appropriate to the case and requested by counsel or a self-represented party, the elements of any affirmative defense that will be presented to the jury; and, in criminal cases, the defendant's right not to testify or to present any evidence;

(c) explain the empanelment process, describe the nature and topics of the questions that will be posed during panel examination, and inform the jurors that any juror who finds either a particular question or the process of questioning by attorneys or self-represented parties intrusive on the juror's privacy may request that steps be taken to protect the privacy of any information disclosed;

(d) ask all questions required by statute or case law, and any additional questions the trial judge deems appropriate in light of the nature of the case and the issues expected to be raised;

(e) if not previously established, inform the parties of any reasonable time limit the trial judge has set for examination of each panel of prospective jurors by attorneys or self-represented parties, giving due regard to (i) the objective of identifying bias in fairness to all parties; (ii) the interests of the public and of the parties in reasonable expedition, in proportion to the nature and seriousness of the case and the extent of the anticipated evidence; and (iii) the needs of cases scheduled in other sessions drawing on the same jury pool for access to prospective jurors;

(f) ask the clerk to direct into the jury box any juror who appears impartial, based upon initial questioning of the venire and individual voir dire, if any. The trial judge has discretion to seat a juror on a voir dire panel without making a preliminary determination of impartiality.

3. Panel Examination

(a) As the jury box is filled, and prior to any panel questioning, the clerk shall read into the record which juror, identified by juror number, is seated in which numbered seat in the jury box. All attorneys and self-represented parties at the trial are responsible for correcting any misstatement as to juror numbers and seat numbers being read for the record.

(b) If the trial judge has not already done so, he or she shall remind the jurors that during such questioning, if any juror seeks, due to privacy concerns, to respond to a question outside the presence of other jurors, the juror may alert the judge to that request.

(c) Upon request, the trial judge may permit each party to make a brief introductory statement to the venire limited to explaining the process and purpose of the questioning of jurors by attorneys or self-represented parties. During the introductory statement and subsequent questioning, counsel shall not refer to his or her own personal circumstances, personal history, or family, even by way of example. Any examples of what may or may not make a juror biased shall be phrased hypothetically.

(d) The parties shall then proceed with the panel portion of questioning. Parties with the burden of proof shall conduct their questioning first. In cases with multiple parties on a side, the parties on each side shall agree as to an order in which to proceed, In the absence of agreement, the judge shall assign an order. The attorney or party may pose questions to the entire panel, or to individual members.

(e) The trial judge and the attorneys participating shall at all times during panel questioning take reasonable steps to ensure that the identity of each juror speaking is adequately maintained on the record, by reference to juror number or seat number. In particular:

i. In an electronically recorded courtroom, the attorney or party shall stand near a microphone; and

ii. When posing questions to, or receiving a response from, any specific juror(s), the attorney or party must identify each such juror(s) by juror seat number (or, less ideally, by juror number). They shall not refer to any juror by name.

(f) The trial judge may intervene at any time to ensure an accurate record (including recording of seat numbers of jurors who respond to questions), to clarify or instruct on a point of law, or to ensure that panel voir dire proceeds in an orderly, fair, and efficient manner.

(g) The trial judge may at any time bring an individual juror to sidebar for questioning out of the hearing of other jurors about any potential bias revealed by panel questioning. If a juror is brought to sidebar, the judge may direct all other parties to do their own questioning on the same subject matter at that time to avoid a need to return to sidebar for later questioning on that subject matter. If the juror's responses to such questioning at sidebar result in a challenge for cause, the judge may rule on the challenge at that time or at the conclusion of all panel questioning. If time limits on panel questioning have been set, the judge may decide whether to exclude all or part of the time spent at side bar from the questioning party's time.

(h) Any party may object to a question posed by another party by stating "objection," without elaboration or argument. The judge may rule on the objection in the presence of the juror or jurors, or may hear argument and rule on the objection outside the presence or hearing of the juror or jurors.

(i) Unless the judge specifically allows, there shall be no follow-up questioning of a panel by attorneys or self-represented parties once each has taken his or her turn.

4. Challenges for Cause and Peremptories

(a) After panel examination by all parties, the trial judge shall hear any further challenges for cause as to any panel members at sidebar.

(b) Unless the trial judge decides to postpone exercise of peremptories until after voir dire of additional panels, the parties shall then exercise at sidebar any peremptory challenges they have as to any jurors remaining on the panel. The party with the burden shall proceed first, using all peremptories the party seeks to use with that panel. All other parties shall then proceed, using all peremptories each seeks to use with that panel. In civil cases, the judge may alternate sides. The jurors remaining after challenge shall then be directed to a separate location, usually outside the courtroom.

(c) Upon any challenge for cause, the judge may ask additional questions, with or without further instructions on the law, and may allow opposing counsel further opportunity to question the juror.

5. Additional Panels of Jurors

The same procedures shall apply for all subsequent panels required to seat a full jury, except:

(a) the judge may seat a different number of jurors in a subsequent panel;

(b) the judge may allow a different amount of time for attorney or party voir dire of second and subsequent panels;

(c) if, after the final panel, more than the necessary number of jurors have been declared indifferent and remain unchallenged at the conclusion of those procedures, the jurors shall be seated for trial in the order in which they were originally seated for panel questioning (generally in order of juror number), and the remaining jurors shall be excused; and

(d) the judge has discretion to vary panel voir dire procedures after the first panel in any lawful manner the judge deems fair and efficient.

Rule 7. Openings: Use of Pleadings

(Applicable to all cases as indicated)

The opening statement shall be limited to fifteen minutes, unless the court for cause shown shall extend the time.

The court in its discretion may permit, or in a civil action require, a defendant to make an opening statement of his defense before any evidence is introduced.

The court may order that the pleadings be summarized in an opening statement but not be read to the jury. Pleadings shall not go to the jury except by authorization of the court.

Amended September 24, 2015, effective January 1, 2016.

Rule 8. Objections to Evidence

(Applicable to all cases)

In civil actions, pursuant to the provisions of Mass.R.Civ.P. 46, and in criminal actions, pursuant to Mass.R.Crim.P. 22, if a party objects to the admission or exclusion of evidence, he may, if he so desires, state the precise grounds of his objection; but he shall not argue or further discuss such grounds unless the court then calls upon him for such argument or discussion.

Amended June 26, 1980, effective September 1, 1980.

Rule 8A. Notes by Jurors

(Applicable to all cases)

In any case where the court, in its discretion, permits jurors to make written notes concerning testimony and other evidence, the trial judge shall precede the announcement of permission to make notes with appropriate guidelines. Upon the recording of the verdict or verdicts, the notes of the jurors shall be destroyed by direction of the trial judge. Jurors may also be granted permission by the trial judge to make notes during summation by counsel and during the judge's instructions to the jury on the laws.

Adopted effective May 6, 1978.

Rule 9. Motions and Interlocutory Matters

(Applicable to all cases)

All civil motions shall be governed, where applicable, by Superior Court Rules 9A through 9E.

Any criminal motion must be in writing and filed before being placed upon a list for hearing, unless otherwise ordered by the court, or otherwise provided for under Superior Court Rule 61.

In criminal cases the court need not hear any motion, or opposition thereto, grounded on facts, unless the facts are verified by affidavit. No motion to suppress evidence, other than evidence seized during a warrantless search, and no motion to dismiss may be filed unless accompanied by a memorandum of law, except when otherwise ordered by the court.

Amended May 6, 1978, effective June 5, 1978; June 26, 1980, effective September 1, 1980; amended effective March 1, 1985; amended July 18, 1989, effective October 2, 1989; amended October 6, 2004, effective November 1, 2004.

Rule 9A. Civil Motions

(Applicable to civil cases)

(a) Motion Practice and Format of Papers.

(1) *Motions.* A moving party must serve with the motion, which shall contain a request for a hearing (if desired), (1) a separate memorandum stating the reasons, including supporting authorities, that the motion should be granted and (2) affidavits or other exhibits evidencing facts on which the motion is based. These papers are referred to below as the "Motion Papers." The moving party shall initiate a conference with the other parties for all dispositive and

discovery motions subject to Rule 9C. Motions for summary judgment must also comply with section (b)(5), below.

(2) *Oppositions to Motions.* A party opposing a motion may serve (1) a memorandum in opposition that includes a statement of reasons, with supporting authorities, that the motion should not be allowed, together with a request for a hearing (if desired) and (2) affidavits or other exhibits evidencing facts on which the opposition is based, as well as (3) any cross-motion (including but not limited to a motion to strike) and (4) memorandum and affidavits supporting the cross-motion. These papers are referred to below as the "Opposition."

(3) *Reply/Opposition to Motion to Strike.* The moving party may file a reply memorandum limited to matters raised in the opposition that were not and could not reasonably have been anticipated and addressed in the moving party's initial memorandum ("Reply"). The moving party may also file an opposition to any motion to strike or cross-motion. No other reply or surreply submission shall be filed without leave of court, which will be granted only in exceptional circumstances.

(4) *Facts Verified by Affidavit.* The court need not consider any motion, opposition, or reply based on facts unless the facts are verified by affidavit, are otherwise apparent in the record, or are agreed to in a writing signed by the interested parties or their counsel.

(5) *Format and Length of all Papers Except Exhibits.* All papers addressed by this Rule 9A, except exhibits, must conform to the following requirements:

(i) Paper size. Papers must be on 8 1/2″ by 11″ paper.

(ii) Typeface. Papers must be in 12–point, double-spaced type. The caption, footnotes, and indented quotations may be single-spaced in 12–point type.

(iii) Title. The title of each document must appear on the first page next to or below the caption.

(iv) Length. The memorandum supporting the motion or cross-motion and the memorandum in opposition may not exceed 20 pages, and the reply may not exceed 5 pages. Any appendix permitted by Superior Court Rule 9C(b) is not included in the page limit. Nor is an addendum that sets forth, verbatim and without argument, pertinent excerpts from key documents, statutes, regulations or the like.

(v) Email Addresses. Each attorney or self-represented party filing motion or opposition papers must include his or her email address on the papers, or certify in the filing that he or she does not have an email address.

(6) *Leave of court.* Advance leave of court is required to exceed the page limit or file a surreply. All requests for leave of court must: (1) be captioned as a pleading, (2) not exceed one page in length (not counting the caption and title), (3) state the grounds and specific relief sought (e.g., a specific proposed new page limit) and (4) include a certificate of service. The request must be sent directly to the session clerk, ATTN: Session Judge. The request must be served on all other parties, but the court need not await a response to such request before ruling. Any leave granted to the moving party for additional pages applies to the opposing party's memorandum as well, unless otherwise

ordered. The title of any surreply and any memorandum exceeding 20 pages must note the date on which leave was allowed.

(7) *No Automatic Extension of Time Pending Leave of Court.* A request for leave of court under Paragraph (a)(6) does not extend the date for filing the Rule 9A Package (See Rule 9A(b)(2)) to which it relates, unless the court orders otherwise or all parties agree.

(8) *Attorney Certifications.* All dispositive and discovery motions shall include the certificate required by Superior Court Rule 9C.

(b) Procedure for Serving and Filing Motions.

(1) *Service.*

(i) General: All Motion Papers, Oppositions, and Replies must be served on all parties and filed with the clerk in accordance with the procedure set forth in this Paragraph (b). Compliance with this Paragraph shall constitute compliance with the "reasonable time" provisions of the first sentence of Mass. R. Civ. P. 5(d)(1).

(ii) When Service on Non–Parties is Required: Papers must be served on specifically named non-parties in compliance with this Rule if (a) the Motion seeks to add the non-party as a party to the case; (b) the Motion seeks an order or other relief against the non-party; (c) the issues affect the personal information or other interests of the non-party. The non-party need not be served, however, if excused by a court order issued in advance for cause or if a statute or rule expressly authorizes ex parte relief.

(iii) Electronic Service: Motion and opposition papers may be served entirely electronically if the parties agree in writing to the method of service and the electronic format. The parties should note on their filings "served via email" so that scanned signatures are accepted by the court, except that all papers signed under penalties of perjury must bear original signatures when filed with the clerk. The agreement may be revoked only upon 10 days written notice to all parties. All 9A certifications must be filed in hard copy with original written signatures.

(2) *The Rule 9A Package.*

(i) The parties must cooperate in filing with the court a "Rule 9A Package." The Rule 9A Package consists of the original Motion Papers, the Opposition, and the Reply, any other papers for which leave of court is granted under Paragraph (a)(6), and any appendices or other papers permitted or required by this Rule, statute, or order of the court.

(ii) Time for Filing or Withdrawal of the Motion. Within 10 days of service of the Opposition, the moving party must either (1) file the Rule 9A Package with the court or (2) notify all parties that the motion has been withdrawn and will not be filed. If the moving party does not receive an Opposition within 3 business days after expiration of the time permitted for service of an Opposition, then the moving party must file with the clerk the Motion Papers together with an affidavit reciting compliance with this Rule and receipt of no Opposition in a timely fashion, unless the moving party withdraws the motion and has so notified all parties.

(iii) Notice of filing. The moving party must give prompt notice of the filing of a Rule 9A Package by serving all parties with a copy of a notice of filing in a separate document that lists the title of each document included in the Rule 9A Package, and by filing the notice with the Rule 9A Package.

(3) *Time Periods in General.* The time periods prescribed below apply unless a different time period is set by statute or order of the court. Where papers are served by mail, these time periods are extended by 3 days in accordance with Mass. R. Civ. P. 6(d).

(4) *Motions Except Motions for Summary Judgment.*

(i) Time for service of Opposition. All Oppositions must be served no later than 10 days after service of the Motion Papers.

(ii) Effect of cross-motion/motion to strike. The provisions of Paragraph (b)(4)(i) apply to cross-motions (including motions to strike) served with the Opposition to a motion. When a cross-motion is brought, the time for filing the Rule 9A Package for the original motion is extended to be coterminous with the date for filing the cross-motion. The Rule 9A Packages for the original motion and the cross-motion must be filed together by the original moving party.

(5) *Motions for Summary Judgment.*

(i) Statement of facts. A motion for summary judgment must be accompanied by a statement of the material facts as to which the moving party contends there is no genuine issue to be tried, set forth in consecutively numbered paragraphs, with page or paragraph references to supporting pleadings, depositions, answers to interrogatories, responses to requests for admission, affidavits, or other evidentiary documents ("Statement of Facts"). Only such facts as are material to deciding the motion shall be included in the Statement of Facts.

The Statement of Facts as served shall not exceed 20 pages in length and shall not include:

a. Background facts not material to decision of the motion. Such facts may be included in a party's memorandum of law even though they are not in the statement.

b. Quotations from any contract, trust, agreement, or other transactional document, or any characterizations of the document (except if admissible through percipient witnesses). The Statement of Facts may only establish the existence and authenticity of the document and the date it became effective.

c. Quotations from any statute, regulation or rule.

Quotations from material described in paragraphs b and c may be included, without argument or commentary, in an addendum to the party's memorandum of law.

This Statement of Facts must be a separately captioned document. Failure to include the Statement of Facts constitutes grounds for denial of the motion. The Court may disregard a Statement of Facts in whole or part if it is unnecessarily long or otherwise materially out of compliance with this rule.

(ii) Service of motion papers. The moving party must serve a copy of its Motion Papers, and the Moving Party's Statement of Facts, on every other party. The Moving Party's Statement of Facts must also be sent contemporaneously in electronic form by email to all parties in Rich Text Format (RTF) or such other format as to which the parties agree. The email transmission of the Moving Party's Statement of Facts is excused if (1) the moving or any opposing party is self-represented, (2) the attorney for the moving party certifies in an affidavit that he or she does not have access to email, or (3) the attorney for the moving party certifies in an affidavit that an opposing party's attorney has no email address or has not disclosed his or her email address.

(iii) Opposition. Within 21 days after service of the Motion Papers, any party opposing the motion must serve on the moving party the original and one copy of the Opposition, and must serve on all other parties one copy of the Opposition.

(A) Response to Moving Party's Statement of Facts. The Opposition may include a response to the Moving Party's Statement of Facts. The opposing party must reprint the Moving Party's Statement of Facts and set forth a response directly below the appropriate numbered paragraph, including, if the response relies on opposing evidence, page or paragraph references to supporting pleadings, depositions, answers to interrogatories, responses to requests for admission, affidavits, or other evidentiary documents. The response to the numbered paragraphs shall be limited to stating whether a given fact is disputed and, if so, cite to the specific evidence, if any, in the Joint Appendix that demonstrates the dispute. It shall not:

a. Deny a fact unless the party has a good faith basis for contesting it.

b. Include a statement that a fact is not supported by the materials cited by the moving party, unless the responding party has a good faith basis for contesting it.

c. Include commentary on whether the fact asserted is relevant or material to any issue raised in the case, although a responding party may indicate, where appropriate, that the fact is admitted only for the purposes of the summary judgment motion.

d. Assert any additional facts. Additional facts may be included in the response only in the manner provided in section (b)(5)(iii)(B) below.

e. Make legal arguments or advocacy-oriented characterizations concerning the sufficiency, relevance or materiality of the moving party's factual proffers.

Where the obligation to send the Moving Party's Statement of Facts in electronic form has been excused, the response thereto may be in a separate document. For purposes of summary judgment, each fact set forth in the moving party's statement of facts is deemed to have been admitted unless properly controverted in the manner forth in this Paragraph (b)(5)(iii)(A).

(B) Statement of additional facts. Opposing parties who argue that additional facts warrant denying summary judgment shall include those facts in the opposition memorandum, each to be supported with page or paragraph references to supporting pleadings, depositions, answers to interrogatories, responses to requests for admission, affidavits, or other evidentiary documents. They may not submit a separate statement of additional facts, except in support of a cross-motion for summary judgment.

(C) Service of response to statement of facts. The opposing party's response to the Moving Party's Statement of Facts must be served contemporaneously by email as described in (b)(5)(H) above, unless such service is excused.

(D) Exhibits for Joint Appendix. "Where the opposing party relies upon evidence not included in the exhibits served with the Motion Papers, the opposing party must serve the moving party with such evidence in the form of new exhibits for inclusion in the Joint Appendix, in accordance with Paragraph (b)(5)(v) below.

(E) Citation of evidence. The opposing party must cite to the Joint Appendix in accordance with Paragraph (b)(5)(v) below.

(iv) Filing of Rule 9A Package.

(A) Joint Appendix and Statement of Facts. The Rule 9A Package must also include the Joint Appendix and a Consolidated Statement of Facts, which must include the opposing party's responses to the Moving Party's Statement of Facts. Similarly, in cases with multiple parties, all parties moving or opposing summary judgment shall coordinate their statements and responses so that there shall be a single statement and response covering all motions. Unless the obligation to send the Moving Party's Statement of Facts or the response thereto in electronic form has been excused, only the Consolidated Statement of Facts (and not any intermediate versions thereof) may be filed so that the court has only a single document.

(B) Service of Statement of Facts and Joint Appendix. Upon filing the Rule 9A Package, the moving party must serve on the opposing parties the Notice of Filing described below and the following, in paper and electronic form, unless electronic form is excused: (1) the Consolidated Statement of Facts filed with the clerk; (2) the Joint Appendix, unless the parties otherwise agree

(C) Effect of cross-motion/motion to strike. The provisions of Paragraph (b)(5)(i)–(iv) apply to cross-motions for summary judgment and any other cross-motion (including a motion to strike) served with the Opposition to a motion for summary judgment. A separate Consolidated Statement of Facts must be served with any cross-motion for summary judgment. All parties moving for or opposing summary judgment shall coordinate their statements and responses so that there shall be a single consolidated document containing the respective statements of material facts and responses thereto. When a cross-motion (including motion to

strike) is brought, the time for filing the Rule 9A Package for the original motion is extended to be coterminous with the date for filing the cross-motion. The Rule 9A Packages for the original motion and the cross-motion must be filed together by the original moving party.

(v) Joint Appendix.

(A) Contents, Format, Citation, and Service. All exhibits referred to in the memoranda supporting or opposing a motion or cross-motion for summary judgment, or in the Consolidated Statement of Facts, must be filed as a single joint appendix, which must include an index of the exhibits ("Joint Appendix"). The initial moving party, with the cooperation of each opposing party, is responsible for assembling the Joint Appendix and index. Unless all the pages of the Joint Appendix are consecutively numbered by page, each exhibit must be separated by an off-set tab divider. The exhibits served by the moving party with its Motion Papers must include either the consecutive numbering or offset tabs. Where an opposing party relies upon any evidence included in the moving party's exhibits, the opposing party must cite to that evidence using the form of designation of the moving party. If the opposing party designates new exhibits in accordance with Paragraph (b)(5)(iii)(D), it must serve those new exhibits, together with an index of the new exhibits, on the moving party with the Opposition, and it must serve the index on the moving party in electronic form (unless electronic service is excused). Those new exhibits must begin with the next consecutive designation following the last designation by the initial moving party (whether consecutive page numbering or off-set tab dividers). The opposing party must serve the original and one copy of those new exhibits with its Opposition.

(B) Certification. The initial moving party must certify that the Joint Appendix includes all exhibits served with the Opposition, except for any exhibit(s) designated by the opposing party but not provided to the moving party. The burden is on the opposing party to move to file any designated exhibit not timely submitted. All memoranda of law filed in support of or in opposition to a motion for summary judgment shall reference the exhibit numbers as well as a paragraph in the statement of material facts.

(vi) Decision on Certain Motions Without A Hearing. The following types of summary judgment motions may, in the court's discretion, be denied on the papers without a hearing notwithstanding Rule 9A(c)(3) (but shall not be granted without a hearing unless the hearing is waived):

(1) Multiple summary judgment motions by a single party, or subsequent summary judgment motions by parties sharing similar interests and making the same arguments as those the court has already resolved.

(2) Motions for partial summary judgment that will save little or no trial time, will not simplify the trial and will not promote resolution of the case.

(3) Motions for summary judgment where a genuine dispute of material fact is obvious on the face of the papers.

(vii) *Sanctions for noncompliance.* The court need not consider any motion or opposition that fails to comply with the requirements of this Rule, may return non-compliant submissions to counsel with instructions for re-filing, and may impose other sanctions for flagrant violations of the Rule.

(c) Hearings on Motions.

(1) *Marking.* If the court believes that a hearing is necessary or helpful to a disposition of the motion, the court will set the time and date for the hearing and notify the parties.

(2) *Request for Hearing.* A request for a hearing must set forth any statute or rule of court which, in the judgment of the submitting party, requires a hearing on the motion, as well as any reason why the court should hold a hearing. After reviewing the motion, the court will decide whether a hearing should be held and, if a hearing is to be held, will notify the parties in accordance with Paragraph (c)(1). Failure to request a hearing shall be deemed a waiver of any right to a hearing afforded by statute or court rule.

(3) *Presumptive Right to, Hearing.* Requests for hearings on the following motions will ordinarily be allowed: Attachments (Rule 4.1), Trustee Process (Rule 4.2), Dismiss or Judgment on the Pleadings (Rule 12), Adopt Master's Report (Rule 53), Summary Judgment (Rule 56), Injunctions (Rule 65), Receivers (Rule 66), and Lis Pendens (G.L. c. 184, sec. 15). Motions that are not set down for hearing in accordance with Paragraph (c) will be decided on the papers filed in accordance with this Rule.

(d) Exceptions. The provisions of this Rule do not apply to the following motions:

(1) *Ex Parte, Emergency, and Other Motions.* A party filing an ex parte motion, emergency motion, or motion for appointment of a special process server is excused from compliance with Paragraph (b) of this rule. Ex parte motions must be served within 3 days of a ruling on the motion. Emergency motions, other than ex parte motions, must be served on all parties forthwith upon filing; provided, however, that a party filing an emergency motion shall certify in the motion that it has made a good faith effort to contact and confer with all parties regarding the subject of the motion, and shall set forth in the motion whether any party assents to or opposes the emergency motion.

(2) *Motions Involving Incarcerated Parties.* Administrative Directive No. 92–1, which governs civil actions filed by a plaintiff who is incarcerated, exempts that part of subdivision (b)(4)(i) of this Rule that requires the filing of the Rule 9A package. Such exemption also applies to motions in civil actions where a defendant is incarcerated and self-represented, but all parties, incarcerated or not, must serve copies upon all other parties in the case.

(3) *Motions governed by E-filing Rules:* A motion governed by a Statute or a Court rule or order for e-filing is exempt from any requirement of this Rule to the extent inconsistent with such e-filing requirements.

(4) *Review of Decision of Administrative Agency:* Motions governed by Standing Order 1–96, to the extent the standing order specifies alternate procedures.

Adopted July 21, 1988, effective October 3, 1988. Amended July 18, 1989, effective October 2, 1989; December 6, 1989, effective January 31, 1990; December 17, 1991, effective March 1, 1992; December 10, 1993, effective January 1, 1994; February 24, 1998, effective April 1, 1998; October 6, 2004, effective November 1, 2004; January 22, 2009, effective March 2, 2009; October 24, 2012, effective January 1, 2013; September 24, 2013, effective January 1, 2014; February 20, 2014, effective April 1, 2014; September 24, 2015, effective January 1, 2016; July 26, 2017, effective September 1, 2017; July 27, 2018, effective November 1, 2018.

Rule 9B. Certificates of Service

(Applicable to civil cases)

The last page of every paper served in accordance with Mass.R.Civ.P. 5(a) shall contain a brief statement showing the date on which and manner in which service of the paper was made on each other party. The statement may be in the following form:

I hereby certify that a true copy of the above document was served upon (each party appearing pro se and) the attorney of record for each (other) party by mail (by hand) on (date). (Signature).

Adopted July 18, 1989, effective October 2, 1989.

Rule 9C. Additional Requirements for Dispositive and Discovery Motions

(a) General Rule: Counsel for each of the parties shall confer in advance of serving any motion under Mass. R. Civ. P. 8(a), 12 (except Rule 12(c) motions in administrative appeals), 26, 37, 41(b)(2)(first sentence) or 56 and make a good faith effort to narrow areas of disagreement to the fullest extent. Counsel for the party who intends to serve the motion shall be responsible for initiating the conference, which conference shall be by telephone or in person. All such motions shall include a certificate stating that the conference required by this Rule was held, together with the date and time of the conference and the names of all participating parties, or that the conference was not held despite reasonable efforts by the moving party to initiate the conference, setting forth the efforts made to speak by telephone or in person with opposing counsel. Motions unaccompanied by such certificate will be denied without prejudice to renew when accompanied by the required certificate.

(b) Dispositive Motions: When conferring about any motion under Mass. R. Civ. P. 12, counsel for each of the parties shall make a good faith effort to narrow areas of disagreement that may be resolved through amendment of the pleading, curative action in respect to defective service, or other means related to the subject of the motion to dismiss. When conferring about any motion under Mass. R. Civ. P. 56 or 41(b)(2)(second sentence), counsel for each of the parties shall discuss whether the moving party should refrain from making any motion qualifying for decision without a hearing under Superior Court Rule 9A(b)(vi) and make a good faith effort to narrow areas of disagreement that may be resolved through amendment of the pleading, a stipulated dismissal of specified claims or parties, or otherwise.

(c) Discovery Disputes: All motions arising out of a party's response to an interrogatory or a request for admission or arising out of a party's response to, or asserted failure to comply with, a request for production of documents shall be accompanied by a brief. With respect to each interrogatory or request at issue, the brief shall set forth separately and in the following order (1) the text of the interrogatory or request, (2) the opponent's response and (3) an argument. Alternatively, the text of the interrogatory or request and the opponent's response may be provided in an appendix to the brief.

Adopted July 18, 1989, effective October 2, 1989. Amended October 6, 2004, effective November 1, 2004. Amended June 15, 2007, effective October 1, 2007; September 24, 2015, effective January 1, 2016; July 27, 2018, effective November 1, 2018.

Rule 9D. Motions for Reconsideration

(Applicable to all civil cases)

Motions for reconsideration shall be served and processed consistent with Rule 9A. Such motions seeking reconsideration of motions made pursuant to Mass. R. Civ. P. 50(b), 52(b), 59(b), 59(e) or 60(b) are considered made or served for purposes of those rules on the date of service pursuant to Rule 9A.

Additionally, the words "MOTION FOR RECONSIDERATION" shall appear clearly in the title of the motion. Upon filing, the clerk shall transmit the motion and supporting papers to the Justice who decided the original motion, but if that Justice has retired or is otherwise unavailable, the clerk shall transmit the motion to the Regional Administrative Justice for the region where the case is pending. If, upon reviewing the motion and supporting documents, the Justice who decided the original motion desires to hold a hearing on the motion for reconsideration, he or she may schedule a hearing thereon. Alternatively, he or she may refer the motion for reconsideration to the Regional Administrative Justice for the region where the case is pending.

Adopted December 6, 1989, effective January 31, 1990. Amended October 6, 2004, effective November 1, 2004; July 26, 2017, effective September 1, 2017.

Rule 9E. Motions to Dismiss and Post–Trial Motions

(Applicable to all civil cases)

Motions to dismiss pursuant to Mass. R. Civ. P. 12 are subject to Rule 9A. Because such motions often are the initial filing in response to a complaint, counterclaim or cross-claim, in order to avoid the entry of a default for failure to respond in a timely fashion, a party responding by a motion to dismiss must serve the motion on all parties pursuant to Superior Court Rule 9A(b)(2) and, in a timely manner, must also file with the court a simple "Notice of Motion to Dismiss" reciting the title of the motion and the date of its service on the parties.

Post-trial motions pursuant to Mass. R. Civ. P. 50, 52, 59 and 60 are subject to Rule 9A. A party serving any such motion must serve the motion on all parties pursuant to

Superior Court Rule 9A(b)(2) and, in a timely manner, must also file with the court a simple "Notice of Motion" reciting the title of the motion and the date of its service on the parties.

Adopted October 6, 2004, effective November 1, 2004.

Rule 10. Extra Charges by Officers

(Applicable to all cases)

When any officer claims extra compensation in serving a precept, the same shall not be allowed unless the officer return with his precept a bill of particulars of the expenses, with his affidavit that such expenses were actually incurred, and that the charges are reasonable.

Rule 11. Attorney Not to Become Bail or Surety

(Applicable to all cases)

No attorney shall become bail or surety in any criminal proceeding in which he is employed, or in any civil action or proceeding whatever in this court except as an endorser for costs.

Rule 12. Attorneys As Witnesses

(Applicable to all cases)

No attorney shall be permitted to take part in the conduct of a trial in which he has been or intends to be a witness for his client, except by special leave of the court.

Rule 13. Hospital Records

(First paragraph applicable to civil actions only; remainder of rule applicable to all cases)

Any party, or his attorney, in any action for personal injuries, may file an application for an order for a copy of any hospital records of a party, together with a copy of the proposed order and an affidavit that he has notified the other party, or his attorney, of his intention to file said application seven days at least prior to said filing and that he has not received any objections in writing thereto. The order shall issue as of course upon the receipt of such application.

In the event of an objection, no order shall issue unless the parties comply with Superior Court Rule 9A.

When a hospital record, or any part thereof, is received in evidence, the record shall be returned to the hospital upon the conclusion of the trial unless the court otherwise orders.

If the court orders the retention of the hospital record, it shall remain in the custody of the clerk, who shall give a receipt therefor. The record shall be released to the hospital, upon the giving of a receipt to the clerk.

Amended September 24, 2015, effective January 1, 2016.

Rule 14. Exhibits Other Than Hospital Records

(Applicable to all cases)

Exhibits other than hospital records, which are placed in the custody of the clerk shall be retained by him for three years after the trial or hearing at which they were used, subject to an order of confiscation or destruction, unless sooner delivered to the parties or counsel to whom they respectively belong or by whom they were respectively presented or introduced. If in doubt as to the party or counsel entitled to delivery, the clerk may require an agreement of parties or counsel or order of the court, before delivery. The clerk may destroy or discard such exhibits, but not earlier than thirty days after notice by the clerk to the party presenting or introducing such exhibits, requesting him to remove them, nor earlier than three years after such trial or hearing.

Rule 15. Eliminating Requirement for Verification by Affidavit

(Applicable to all cases)

No written statement in any proceeding in this court required to be verified by affidavit shall be required to be verified by oath or affirmation if it contains or is verified by a written declaration that it is made under the penalties of perjury.

Rule 16. Writ of Protection

(Applicable to all cases)

A writ of protection shall issue only upon the application of the person for whom the writ of protection is to be issued, or some person in his behalf, and upon order of the court, and then only in case it is made to appear to the court, by affidavit and any other evidence that the court may require, (1) that the application is made in good faith and for the purpose of enabling such person to attend this court as a party or witness in some specified case pending, (2) if such person is a party, that such case has not been brought collusively to enable him to obtain a writ of protection, and (3) if such person is a witness, that he has not been required to attend as a witness by his own request or procurement to enable him to obtain a writ of protection.

Rule 17. Recording Devices

(Applicable to all cases)

No person shall use or have in his possession or under his control in the chambers or lobby of a justice or justices of the court, or in any courtroom or other place provided for a hearing or proceeding of any kind on any action or matter pending before the court, or before any master, arbitrator, or any other person appointed by the court, any mechanical, electronic or other device, equipment, appliance or apparatus for recording, registering or otherwise reproducing sounds or voices, unless prior authorization for such use or possession is granted by the justice then having immediate supervision of such courtroom or other place. All recordings or transmissions must comply with Rule 1:19 of the Supreme Judicial Court ("Electronic Access to the Courts").

Amended September 24, 2015, effective January 1, 2016.

Rule 18. Impoundment and Personal Identifying Information

(Applicable to All Counties)

A. Impoundment

1. Impoundment in the Superior Court shall be governed by Trial Court Rule VIII (Uniform Rules on Impoundment Procedure ("URIP")), as supplemented by paragraph 2(b), below.

2. a. *Purpose.*

Paragraph 2(b) of this Rule makes exceptions to the notice requirement of URIP Rule 13(b), which ordinarily requires that when a person files impounded material, he or she also must file a notice alerting the clerk to that material.

b. *Exceptions to Notice Requirement of URIP Rule 13(b).*

Because the following materials are impounded by law, and the clerks' offices impound them in the normal course, no Rule 13(b) notice is necessary when filing any of them:

   1. an Affidavit of Indigency and Request for Waiver, Substitution or State Payment of Fees & Costs, on the form prescribed by the Chief Justice of the Supreme Judicial Court under G.L. c. 261, § 27B;

   2. a Petition for Abortion Authorization under G.L. c. 112, § 12S, or any materials in such matter;

   3. an action for judicial review of a decision of the Sex Offender Registry Board, under G.L. c. 6, § 178M, or any materials in such matter; or

   4. any confidential document or other material prepared especially for a pre-indictment judicial hearing concerning a grand jury proceeding.

c. *Duty of the Clerk.*

The clerk shall maintain the impounded material described above in accordance with the clerk's duties prescribed in URIP Rule 9.

B. Personal Identifying Information

3. Redaction and treatment of personal identifying information shall be governed by Supreme Judicial Court Rule 1:24, as supplemented by paragraph 4 below.

4. Pursuant to Section 5(c) of Supreme Judicial Court 1:24, personal identifying information contained in administrative records filed by agencies shall be treated as may be provided in Standing Order 1–96, as amended from time to time.

Adopted July 26, 2017, effective September 1, 2017.

SPECIAL PROVISIONS FOR CIVIL ACTIONS

Rule 19. Hearing in One Location, County or Region of Cases From Another

(Applicable to civil actions)

Unless otherwise ordered by the Chief Justice of the Superior Court, each Regional Administrative Justice ("RAJ") or

delegee shall have the authority to designate particular case(s) or categories of cases for hearing or trial in any location within the county (or for hearing, decision or non-jury trial within any multi-county Region), upon compliance with the statutory notice and posting requirements of G. L. c. 212, § 14A, and, if necessary to do so, shall serve as the Chief Justice's delegee for that limited purpose under G. L. c. 212, § 14A. With the advance approval of the Chief Justice of the Superior Court, a RAJ may also transfer a case or class of cases for hearing out of his or her region.

Adopted September 24, 2015, effective January 1, 2016.

Rule 20. Individual Case Management and Tracking

(Applicable to Civil Actions)

Any case may receive individual management or tracking so that the parties may secure a cost-effective means to resolve their dispute. To that end, the parties are encouraged to consider and propose options to achieve a less costly and more expeditious resolution of their dispute. This rule sets forth a non-exclusive mechanism to implement any such proposals, while reserving the parties' ability to exercise their full procedural and substantive rights if they so choose.

1. One or more parties may seek individual case management or tracking pursuant to this rule. If all parties agree, they shall have the right to individual case management to the extent provided in paragraph 2 below. In the absence of unanimity among the parties, any party may request that the judge exercise discretion to adopt individual case management or tracking in the interest of fair, timely, cost-effective and efficient resolution or litigation of the case.

2. All parties may agree to each of the following, unless the session judge specifically orders otherwise in writing for good cause:

    a. Immediate or early court conference for scheduling or case management (in person or by phone, as requested if feasible).

    b. Early, non-binding judicial assessment of the case. The judge who conducts any such assessment will consider whether disqualification as to subsequent matters in the case is appropriate.

    c. Immediate scheduling of a prompt and firm trial date (preferably agreed-upon), which the court will make every effort to accommodate.

    d. Scheduling of mediation, arbitration or other dispute resolution with a Superior Court approved alternative dispute resolution provider or a private alternative dispute resolution provider.

    e. Changes to standard pretrial deadlines, such as changes shortening the tracking order dates, the waiving of certain pre-trial motions such as motions made under Mass. R. Civ. P. 12 or Mass. R. Civ. P. 56 and, in medical malpractices cases, the waiver of the full statutory tribunal either in its entirety or so as to permit a prompt tribunal with the judge alone.

    f. Limits on discovery (by way of illustration: specific limitations on the subject matter of discovery, changes in the scope of discovery, procedures governing discovery disputes, limitations on eDiscovery, and the number or length of discovery events).

    g. Limits on oral arguments/court appearances not specifically ordered by the motion judge (by way of illustration: decision of categories of motions without argument; provid-ing for telephonic argument). Note that, on specific matters or motions, the judge may still schedule arguments or appearances that s/he anticipates will be necessary or helpful.

    h. Trial to a judge without a jury with or without additional conditions (by way of illustration: waiver of detailed written findings of fact and rulings of law; an agreement that expert testimony (in part, for example direct testimony, or in full) may be in writing; or agreement as to the number of witnesses, maximum trial time for each side's evidence and/or total length of trial).

    i. Limitations on a trial by jury (such as by way of illustration: agreement to a jury consisting of 6–8 people, waiver of attorney voir dire, or agreement to accept a verdict from fewer than 5/6 of the jurors, an agreement that expert testimony (in part, for example direct testimony, or in full) may be in writing, and agreement as to the number of witnesses, maximum trial time for each side's evidence and/or total length of trial).

    j. Waiver of, or limitations on, the rights to appeal and to file post-trial motions.

    k. Any other proposals acceptable to the parties and the court.

3. One or more parties may, without consent of all parties, move for any order granting the relief set forth in paragraph 2 and may make additional proposals for consideration by the court. Nothing in this rule, however, authorizes the court, over a party's objection, to restrict or deny any right that is protected by rule, statute or constitution.

4. Any party making a motion under this rule shall do so by serving and filing a Motion For Case–Specific Management ("Individual Case Management Form") pursuant to Superior Court Rule 9A. See Appendix of Forms to the Superior Court Rules, also available for download on the Superior Court's website.

5. No proposal may extend any deadline beyond the date otherwise provided in Standing Order 1–88, unless the tracking order for that case is itself amended.

6. Any matter stipulated pursuant to paragraph 2, or order entered pursuant to paragraph 3, may be revised or vacated on motion or by the court on its own motion, for good cause.

7. Nothing in this rule limits or precludes the right of any party to request a conference pursuant to Mass. R. Civ. P. 16 with or without completion of an Individual Case Management Form. Nor does it limit any party's right to request relief under any other statute, court rule, order or other law.

8. For purposes of Superior Court Rule 20(2)(h), the phrase "waiver of detailed written findings of fact" means waiver of written judicial findings with the level of detail required by Mass. R. Civ. P. 52(a). It does not mean waiver of findings that provide the equivalent of a jury verdict within the meaning of Mass. R. Civ. P. 49. See also Mass. R. Crim. P. 27 (by analogy only).

Therefore, when the parties agree to waive, in whole or part, detailed findings by the judge in a bench trial, the following rules shall apply:

    a. The judge shall, at a minimum, answer special questions on the elements of each claim, at a level of detail comparable to a special jury verdict form pursuant to Mass. R. Civ. P. 49(a), unless the parties explicitly choose, or the judge expressly orders, findings in the form provided by Mass. R. Civ. P. 49(b) (a general verdict accompanied by answer to interrogatories).

b. The parties waive all arguments in the trial court or on appeal that require or depend upon the existence of detailed written findings of fact. Any appellate review of the court's decision and of the judgment entered shall be according to the standard of review that would apply to a verdict by a jury in a case tried to a jury and to the judgment entered thereon. In addition, the parties may agree to waive their rights of appeal in whole or in part.

Adopted October 26, 2016, effective January 1, 2017. Amended February 28, 2018, effective March 1, 2018.

Rule 21.   Postponement.   Costs

(Applicable to civil actions)

When a case is postponed on the motion of one party, against the objection of the other, the granting of the motion may be upon the condition precedent that the moving party shall pay to the adverse party all his costs and such expenses as the court may allow incurred at the same session or upon the same short list in procuring the attendance of witnesses, unless (a) the motion is granted because of unfair or improper conduct of the adverse party, or (b) the moving party shall have given notice of such motion and the grounds thereof in such season as might have prevented the attendance of the witnesses, or (c) the moving party did not discover the grounds of the motion in season to give such notice. The costs and expenses thus paid shall not be included in the bill of costs of the party receiving them.

This rule shall not prevent an adverse party, receiving notice of such motion, from procuring the attendance of his witnesses, if he shall think fit to oppose the motion, or from including the costs for such witnesses in his bill of costs if he shall prevail in the case, even though such motion be granted.

Rule 22.   Money Paid Into Court

(Applicable to civil actions)

Money paid into court shall be in the custody of the clerk, whose duty it shall be to receive it when paid under the authority of law or rule or order of the court. Any deposit of money in excess of five thousand dollars ($5,000) paid into court shall be deposited in an interest bearing bank account. He shall pay it as directed by the court; but money paid into court upon tender or otherwise for the present and unconditional use of a party, shall be paid, on request, without special order, with any interest which has accrued thereon, to such party, at whose risk it shall be from the time when it is paid into court. Money payable to a party may be paid to his attorney of record, if authorized by the court.

If money paid into court, through interpleader or otherwise, goes unclaimed for 30 days after the claim(s) of every party to the funds has been eliminated by default or court order, the clerk shall schedule the matter for an assessment hearing, after which the session justice may enter a final judgment escheating the funds to the Commonwealth, provided that no such judgment shall provide for escheat sooner than three years after payment of the funds into court as provided in G. L. c. 200A, § 6.

Amended September 24, 2015, effective January 1, 2016.

Rule 23.   [Repealed]

Repealed effective January 1, 2015.

Rule 24.   [Repealed]

Repealed effective January 1, 2015.

Rule 25.   [Repealed]

Repealed effective January 1, 2015.

Rule 26.   [Repealed]

Repealed effective January 1, 2015.

Rule 27.   [Repealed]

Repealed effective January 1, 2015.

Rule 28.   Costs and Terms

(Applicable to civil actions)

In allowing an amendment, removing a default or dismissal, granting a postponement, or making any other interlocutory order, costs may be awarded and terms imposed in the discretion of the court, in addition to any otherwise provided for in these rules.

Formerly Rule 18. Renumbered July 26, 2017, effective September 1, 2017.

Rule 29.   Cover Sheet;   Statement As to Damages

(Applicable to civil actions)

1.   Cover Sheets. No Clerk-Magistrate shall accept for filing any Complaint or other pleading which commences a civil action unless accompanied by a civil action cover sheet completed and signed by the attorney or pro se party filing such pleading. The civil action cover sheet shall be in a form approved by the Chief Administrative Justice in consultation with the Chief Justice of the Superior Court.

2.   Duty of the Plaintiff. Upon the cover sheet provided for in paragraph one above, the plaintiff or his counsel shall set forth, where appropriate, a statement specifying in full and itemized detail the facts upon which the plaintiff then relies as constituting money damages. A copy of such civil action cover sheet, including the statement as to damages, shall be served on the defendant together with the complaint. If a statement of money damages, where appropriate is not filed, the Clerk-Magistrate shall transfer the action as provided in Rule 29(5)(c).

3.   Duty of the Defendant. Should the defendant believe the statement of damages filed by the plaintiff is in any respect inadequate, he or his counsel may file with the answer a statement specifying in reasonable detail the potential damages which may result should the plaintiff prevail. Such statement, if any, shall be served with the answer.

4. Limitation. A statement of money damages filed pursuant to this rule shall not constitute a judicial admission nor may it be admitted in evidence.

5. Power of the Court.

Should it appear from the statement(s) of damages filed as provided above, or from any subsequent amendments thereto, that there is no reasonable likelihood that recovery by the plaintiff will meet the amount necessary to proceed in the Superior Court under G.L. c. 212, §§ 3 and 3A, then the court, after receiving written responses from the parties and after a hearing, if requested by any party, may dismiss the case, in which case the clerk shall proceed as provided in G. L. c. 212, § 3A.

Amended effective November 1, 1974; May 8, 1976; amended January 9, 1979; amended effective August 1, 1984; March 25, 1986; November 17, 1986; September 24, 2015, effective January 1, 2016.

Rule 30. Interrogatories

(Applicable to civil actions)

Except as otherwise provided by special or standing order, interrogatories may be served within one year after the entry of an action or within such further time as the court may allow.

Each answer to an interrogatory, or objection thereto, shall be preceded by the interrogatory to which it responds.

An application for dismissal or judgment for failure to serve timely answers to original interrogatories, as permitted by Mass.R.Civ.P. 33(a), shall contain a statement showing the date on which such interrogatories were served and that the provisions of the applicable rules of civil procedure and of this court have been complied with; and such an application relating to failure to serve further answers shall set out the date on which the further answers should have been served. The application shall be verified by affidavit or as provided in Mass.R.Civ.P. 33(a) or 43(d).

Amended July 21, 1988, effective October 3, 1988.

Rule 30A. Written Discovery

(Applicable to Civil Actions)

1. Uniform definitions in discovery requests.

(a) *Incorporation by Reference and Limitations.* The full text of the definitions set forth in paragraph (*l*)(c) is deemed incorporated by reference into all discovery requests, but shall not preclude (i) the definition of other terms specific to the particular litigation; (ii) the use of abbreviations; or (iii) a narrower definition of a term defined in paragraph (1)(c).

(b) *Effect on Scope of Discovery.* This rule is not intended to broaden or narrow the scope of discovery permitted by the Massachusetts Rules of Civil Procedure.

(c) *Definitions.* The following definitions apply to all discovery requests, unless otherwise ordered by the court:

(1) *Communication.* The term "communication" means the transmittal of information (in the form of facts, opinions, ideas, inquiries, or otherwise).

(2) *Document.* The term "document" is defined to be synonymous in meaning and equal in scope to the usage of this term in Mass. R. Civ. P. 34(a). An earlier draft is a separate document within the meaning of this term.

(3) *Identify (With Respect to Persons).* When referring to a natural person, to "identify" means to give, to the extent known, the person's (a) full name, (b) present or last known address, and (c) the present or last known place of employment. Once a person has been identified in accordance with this subparagraph, only the name of that person need be listed in response to subsequent discovery requesting the identification of that person.

(4) *Identify (With Respect to Entities).* When referring to an entity, to "identify" means to give, to the extent known, (a) the entity's full name, including (when not apparent from the name) the nature of the entity, e.g. corporation, limited liability corporation, partnership, or professional corporation, (b) present or last known address of its headquarters or principal place of business, and (c) the state in which the entity is incorporated or otherwise created. Once an entity has been identified in accordance with this subparagraph, only the name of that entity need be listed in response to subsequent discovery requesting the identification of that entity.

(5) *Identify (With Respect to Documents).* When referring to documents, to "identify" means to give, to the extent known: (a) the type of document; (b) the general subject matter; (c) the date of the document; (d) the author or authors, according to the document; and (e) the persons to whom, according to the document, the document (or a copy) was to have been sent.

(6) *Parties.* The term "plaintiff" or "defendant," as well as a party's full or abbreviated name or a pronoun referring to a party, mean the party and, where applicable, its officers, directors, employees, partners, corporate parent, and subsidiaries. This definition is not intended to impose a discovery obligation on any person who is not a party to the litigation.

(7) *Person.* The term "person" means any natural person or any business, legal, or governmental entity.

(8) *Concerning.* The term "concerning" means referring to, describing, offering evidence of, or constituting.

(9) *State the Basis or State all Facts.* When an interrogatory calls upon a party to "state the basis" of or "state all facts" concerning a particular claim, allegation, or defense (or uses comparable language), the party shall provide a substantial summary of the factual basis supporting the claim, allegation, or defense at the time the interrogatory is answered. The summary shall: (a) identify the essential acts or failures to act forming the substance of the claim, allegation, or defense, (b) identify the persons and entities that, through firsthand information or possession of documents, are the sources of the party's information regarding the claim, allegation, or defense, and (c) when one or more documents is the basis of the claim, allegation, or defense, such as a written contract in a contractual claim or defense, or a written misrepresentation in a misrepresentation claim, identify (or provide as part of the interrogatory answer a copy of) each such document. In stating the basis, a party may not withhold information from the interrogatory answer because it derives from attorney work product or was

obtained in anticipation of litigation if the party intends to offer this information at trial.

2. Objections to Interrogatories.

General objections to interrogatories are prohibited. Each objection to an interrogatory shall be specific to that interrogatory and shall have a good faith basis. If a party refuses to answer an interrogatory, the party shall so state and identify each objection asserted to justify the refusal to answer. If a party, after having asserted an objection, answers the interrogatory, the answer shall state either: (a) notwithstanding the objection no information has been withheld from the answer, or (b) information has been withheld from the answer because of the objection. Where information has been withheld from the answer, the objecting party shall describe the nature of the information withheld and identify each objection asserted to justify the withholding.

3. Objections to Requests for the Production of Documents and Things.

(a) Where a party serves a response to a request for production of documents and things under Mass. R. Civ. P. 34 before production is completed, the response may include general objections. However, where general objections are made, the responding party shall prepare and serve a supplemental response no later than 10 days after the completion of production.

(b) Once production is completed, general objections to requests for production of documents and things are prohibited. As to each request, the supplemental response shall state either: (i) notwithstanding prior general objections, all responsive documents or things in the possession, custody, or control of the responding party have been produced; (ii) after diligent search no responsive documents or things are in the possession, custody, or control of the responding party; or (iii) the specific objection made to the request. When specific objection is made, the response shall describe the nature of all responsive documents or things in the possession, custody, or control of the responding party that have not been produced because of the objection. Where a privilege log is required by Mass. R. Civ. P. 26(b)(5) or court order, the log shall be served with the supplemental response, unless the requesting party waives entitlement to the log or agrees to a later date for service.

(c) In the initial written response, the responding party shall articulate with clarity the scope of the search conducted or to be conducted. If the scope of the search changes during production, the responding party in the supplemental written response shall articulate with clarity the change in scope. If the scope of the search does not include all locations, including electronic storage locations, where responsive documents or things reasonably might be found, the responding party shall explain why these locations have been excluded from the scope of the search.

Adopted September 24, 2015, effective January 1, 2016.

Rule 30B.   Expert Disclosures

(Applicable to Civil Actions)

(a) Timing. Unless the parties agree or the court in the interests of justice orders otherwise, each party shall set forth the following information in the pre-trial conference memorandum: the name, address, and qualifications of each expert a party intends to call, the subject matter on which the expert is expected to testify, the substance of all facts and opinions expected, and a summary of the grounds of each expert's opinion as detailed as would be expected in an answer to an expert interrogatory. The information as to any expert set forth in the pre-trial memorandum must be signed by that expert in accordance with Superior Court Rule 30B. A scanned or facsimile signature is sufficient. Any party who has previously made such disclosure in response to an expert interrogatory may satisfy this requirement by appending such response to the pre-trial memorandum. No party may reserve the right to make a later disclosure. A party who fails to comply substantially with the terms of this Rule shall not have the right to call an expert at trial, but the court in its discretion may permit that party to do so upon such additional terms, if any, that the court may require.

(b) Certification. In addition to the signature of the party, every disclosure called for by Mass. R. Civ. P. 26(b)(4)(A)(i) regarding any expert who is retained or specially employed to provide expert testimony in the case or one whose duties as the party's employee regularly involve giving expert testimony and whose testimony is to be presented at trial shall be signed by the expert so disclosed. The signature by the expert is a certification that the disclosure accurately states the subject matter(s) on which the expert is expected to testify, the substance of the facts and opinions to which the expert is expected to testify, and a summary of the grounds for each opinion to which the expert is expected to testify at trial.

Adopted October 24, 2012, effective January 1, 2013. Amended October 26, 2016, effective January 1, 2017.

Rule 31.   Consolidation of Superior Court Cases [1]

(Applicable to Civil Actions)

A motion to consolidate cases under Mass. R. Civ. P. 42(a) shall be served, in accordance with Superior Court Rule 9A, upon all parties in the cases proposed to be consolidated. The original motion, opposition(s), and other related documents shall be filed and the motion decided in the earliest-filed case. Notice of such filing, together with a copy of the documents filed, shall be filed in the later-filed case(s). A copy of the ruling on the motion to consolidate shall be filed in each of the cases proposed to be consolidated.

If the motion to consolidate is allowed, the cases will be consolidated in the session where the earliest-filed case is pending unless (a) the judge in that session orders, in the interest of justice or with the consent of all parties, that the cases be consolidated in a session where a later-filed case is pending, and (b) the judge in that other session agrees to accept the consolidated cases. The order for consolidation shall specify the session in which the cases will be consolidated ("the consolidating session").

Unless the judge of the consolidating session otherwise orders, the earliest-filed case in the session in which the cases are consolidated shall be designated the "lead case" and the other case(s) shall be designated the "consolidated case(s)." In documents filed in the lead or consolidated cases, the case caption shall identify the lead case first. Below the lead case caption shall be written the words, **"CONSOLIDATED WITH,"** in capital letters and in bold print. Below those words shall appear the case captions for the consolidated cases, in the order they were filed, with the earliest-filed case listed first. Regardless of the length of the case caption, the title of the document, identifying what it is, shall appear on the first page.

An order of consolidation is also an order of transfer. Once the cases are consolidated, the consolidating session is responsible for the lead case and all consolidated cases. If the lead case or any consolidated case(s) had been filed in different counties, the case file(s) shall be promptly transferred to the Clerk for the county in which the consolidating session is located. The Clerk shall then open a new case file in that county for each transferred consolidated case, shall assign a new docket number, and shall make all appropriate entries on the docket, including the entry reflecting the ultimate disposition of the case. The Clerk for the county in which any transferred case had been located shall reflect the transfer on the original docket and close the transferred case.

Unless the judge of the consolidating session otherwise orders, a party filing any document in either the lead case or any consolidated case shall file one set of original documents in the lead case, and a copy of each such document, clearly marked as a copy, in each consolidated case. The Clerk shall make appropriate entries on the docket of the lead case and each consolidated case.

Within thirty (30) days following entry of an order of consolidation, the judge of the consolidating session shall conduct a conference under Mass. R. Civ. P. 16 to establish a Tracking Order for the consolidated cases and to address other matters raised by the consolidation.

Adopted September 24, 2015, effective January 1, 2016.

1 This Rule applies only to the consolidation of Superior Court cases. The consolidation of a Superior Court case with a case from a different judicial department is governed by Trial Court Rule XII-Request for Interdepartmental Judicial Assignments. However, please note that Trial Court Rule XII does not apply when the related actions that are the subject of the consolidation request are in the Superior Court, the District Court, and/or the Boston Municipal Court. The appropriate procedure in such cases is for the parties to file a motion pursuant to G.L. c. 223, § 2B to transfer the case in the District Court or the Boston Municipal Court to the Superior Court and then to file a motion to consolidate under Mass. R. Civ. P. 42(a). See Trial Court Rule XII, ¶ 8.

Rule 32.   Certain Appearances Prohibited

(Applicable to civil actions)

The attorney for the plaintiff shall not appear or act for a trustee summoned in trustee process; or for a defendant in matters involving interpleader (Mass.R.Civ.P. 22) or in a proceeding to obtain a declaratory judgment or relief (Mass. R.Civ.P. 57).

Rule 33.   Continuances of Trial

(Applicable to Civil Actions)

The following procedure shall apply to requests for continuances of trial.

1.   No trial continuance shall be granted without the specific approval of the Justice in the session in which the case is pending or, in the event the session Justice is not available, of the Regional Administrative Justice (or designee thereof) in the County in which the case is pending.

2.   Any request for a trial continuance shall be in the form of a written motion, with notice to all parties.

3.   A motion for a trial continuance shall:

a.   identify the party or parties seeking the continuance, and state, if known, whether there is any opposition;

b.   state the grounds for the requested continuance; and

c.   state whether continuances have been sought previously by any party, and, if so, the number of times and the reasons therefor.

4.   If the grounds for the requested trial continuance include any ground identified in Rule 4 of the Rules of the Superior Court, the motion shall comply with that rule.

Adopted September 24, 2015, effective January 1, 2016.

Rule 34.   Engagements of Counsel

(Applicable to civil actions)

No party shall have a right to a postponement of a trial because of engagement of counsel or for the convenience of counsel or parties, but the court will grant a postponement if counsel is actually engaged before the Supreme Judicial Court or the Appeals Court and may grant a postponement because of engagement of counsel for not more than ten days or until said engagement is concluded.

No other postponement shall be granted to the same counsel except for good cause arising subsequent to the granting of the postponement.

Rule 35.   [Repealed]

Repealed effective January 1, 2015.

Rule 36.   [Repealed]

Repealed effective January 1, 2015.

Rules 37 to 42.   [Deleted]

Deleted July 21, 1988, effective October 3, 1988.

Rule 43.   [Repealed]

Repealed effective January 1, 2015.

Rule 44.   [Repealed]

Repealed effective January 1, 2015.

Rule 45.   [Repealed]

Repealed effective January 1, 2015.

Rule 46.   [Repealed]

Repealed effective January 1, 1981.

Rule 47.   Filing of Papers Upon Judgment

(Applicable to civil actions)

A bill of exchange, promissory note, check, trade acceptance, certificate of deposit or any negotiable instrument, shall be filed with the clerk before judgment thereon shall be entered or execution issued, unless the court otherwise orders.

Such instrument shall not be withdrawn from the files, except upon (1) order of the court, (2) the making of the clerk of a memorandum on such instrument, if practicable, and otherwise on a paper attached thereto, showing the name of the court, the county, the number of the case, the date of judgment, the party or parties against whom judgment was rendered, and the amount thereof, and (3) the filing of a copy of such instrument attested by the clerk.

Any person seeking enforcement of a lost or stolen negotiable instrument must provide sufficient proof in writing that the person required to pay the instrument is adequately protected against loss that might occur by reason of a claim by another person to enforce the instrument No judgment shall enter unless the court makes a finding to that effect pursuant to G. L. c. 106, § 3–309(b).

Amended July 27, 2018, effective November 1, 2018.

Rule 48. [Repealed]

Repealed effective January 1, 2015.

SPECIAL PROVISIONS RELATING TO MASTERS, RECEIVERS AND ARBITRATORS

Rule 49. Masters

(See Mass.R.Civ.P. 53)

1. Order of Reference. A master shall be appointed by an order of reference which, after the usual heading, shall be in substantially the following form, unless the court otherwise orders, and shall specifically refer the master to Section 4 of this Rule regarding forfeiture of compensation for failure to file his/her report seasonably.

NON–JURY ACTION

Order of Reference to Master

Ordered that this action be referred to _____ as Master for the conduct of proceedings pursuant to Mass.R.Civ.P. 53 and Superior Court Rule 49.

The Master shall make findings of fact and conclusions of law, and set them forth in his/her report, including all subsidiary findings of fact upon each issue.

He/she need not make findings on damages if he/she determines that there was no liability.

Hearings shall begin on or before _____, 19__, and:

a. shall end on or before _____, 19__, or

b. shall proceed from day to day, Saturdays, Sundays, and holidays excepted, until completed.

The report shall be filed on or before _____, 19__.

The Master is referred to Section 4 of Superior Court Rule 49 regarding forfeiture of compensation for failure to file his/her report seasonably.

By the Court (_____, J.)
Clerk

ENTERED:

JURY ACTION

Ordered that this action be referred to _____ as Master for the conduct of proceedings pursuant to Mass.R.Civ.P. 53 and Superior Court Rule 49.

The Master shall make findings of fact, with subsidiary findings of fact on each issue, including the issue of damages whatever the determination of liability.

Hearings shall begin on or before _____, 19__, and:

a. shall end on or before _____, 19__, or

b. shall proceed from day to day, Saturdays, Sundays, and holidays excepted, until completed.

The report shall be filed on or before _____, 19__.

The Master is referred to Section 4 of Superior Court Rule 49 regarding forfeiture of compensation for failure to file his/her report seasonably.

By the Court (_____, J.)
Clerk

ENTERED:

2. Compensation.

(a) Compensation of masters, for services performed after July 1, 1985 shall be allowed at the rate of fifty dollars ($50.00) an hour of attendance in a hearing room at the direction of the court, and of actual hearing and preparation of report. In the determination of the court a master may be allowed compensation not exceeding two hours at the rate specified above when an action is disposed of without the necessity of: attendance at court; or an actual hearing; or preparation of a report. Every master's bill shall be itemized as to dates, hours, and services and shall state the name of the justice who ordered the reference.

(b) If a master's report is not filed within the time provided by Mass. R. Civ. P. 53(g)(2) or any enlargement thereof, unless the court shall otherwise order, the appointment of the master shall be vacated automatically and the master shall be held to have forfeited his/her compensation.

3. Engagement. An engagement in actual hearing before a master shall have the same standing as an engagement in actual trial before the court, but no protective order for counsel or the master shall issue save by order of the Chief Justice of the Superior Court.

4. Filing of Master's Report; Enlargement of Time; Forfeiting Compensation.

(a) Pursuant to Mass. R. Civ. P. 53(g)(2), the court may enlarge the time for filing the master's report, but only if the master files a written statement of good and substantial reasons for such enlargement. The justice authorizing an enlargement shall forthwith file with the clerk a statement of his/her reasons for so doing.

(b) If a master's report is not filed within the time specified by Mass. R. Civ. P. 53(g)(2) or any enlargement thereof, the master's appointment shall, unless the court otherwise orders, lapse automatically, and the master shall be held to have forfeited his/her compensation.

5. Supervision of Master. The clerk shall keep a docket upon which shall be entered every case referred to a master. The court may call such docket or any part thereof at any time.

In cases referred to a master in which a statement by the referring or another justice is required by this Rule or Mass. R. Civ. P. 53, the clerk shall enter upon such docket the following:

(a) the statement by the referring justice as to the special reasons why the case was referred to a master not upon the Standing List.

(b) the statement by the objecting party containing the grounds for objecting to the persons appointed as master; and

(c) the statement by the justice granting an enlargement of time for the filing of the report of a master containing the reasons why the enlargement has been granted.

In each case referred to a master in which a justice or objecting party has filed a statement of reasons or objections in accordance with the provisions of this Rule or Mass. R. Civ. P. 53, the clerk shall report in summary written form to the Chief Justice, quarterly, the name of the case, the nature of the case, the name of the master appointed, and the statements of the referring or other justice or party which are of record.

The clerk shall place upon the list for hearing upon motions and other interlocutory matters, at the session for or including civil business without jury within the county to be held on or next after the first Monday of March and the first Monday of September in every year, every case in which the appointment of a master was made more than four months before such first Monday and his/her report has not been filed. The list shall state the name of such master, the date of his/her appointment, and the reason for placing the case upon said list. The clerk shall mail such list to the parties and such officer. Such cases shall be called at such session.

At any call of such docket or of such cases or at any other time, the court may make any order deemed proper to promote justice and prevent delay, including an order that the case proceed without regard to engagements of counsel, and an order removing such master.

6. Special Masters. The Chief Justice of the Superior Court or a justice of the court with the approval of the Chief Justice may appoint a special master to deal with administrative or other special matters. His/her compensation shall be paid at the rate provided in section 2 of this Rule.

Amended effective May 8, 1976; amended May 6, 1978, effective July 1, 1978; June 26, 1980, effective September 1, 1980; amended effective January 1, 1983; July 1, 1985.

Rule 50. Exhibits (Master's Cases)

(Applicable to civil actions)

The clerk's office shall accept into the care and custody of the clerk, all exhibits which have been offered before a master during the course of a hearing and duly marked at said hearing by said master.

Said exhibits must be presented in the clerk's office by said master personally. Appropriate notations and cross references will be made in the exhibit record book, and upon the docket to this effect.

The master will be required to fill out an exhibit record card in the clerk's office when depositing exhibits. Rule 14 shall govern.

Rule 51. Receivers

(Applicable to civil actions)

Every receiver, within thirty days after his appointment, shall file a detailed inventory of the property of which he has possession or the right to possession, with the estimated values thereof, together with a list of the encumbrances thereon; and also a list of the creditors of the receivership and of the party whose property is in the hands of the receiver, so far as known to him.

Every receiver shall file, not later than the fifteenth day of February of each year, a detailed account under oath of his receivership to and including the last day of the preceding year, substantially in the form required for an account by a conservator in the probate courts, together with a report of the condition of the receivership. He shall also file such further accounts and reports as the court may order.

When an attorney at law has been appointed a receiver, no attorney shall be employed by the receiver or receivers except upon order of court, which shall be made only upon the petition of a receiver, stating the name of the attorney whom he desires to employ and showing the necessity of such employment.

No order discharging a receiver from further responsibility will be entered until he has settled his final account.

Upon application for appointment of a receiver, the party seeking the receiver shall pay into Court the sum of $500.00, or such other amount as the Court may allow, for the use of the receiver when appointed to guarantee his or her expenses, disbursements and compensation. No process on the application for appointment of a receiver shall issue before payment of said sum. The Clerk shall pay said sum to the receiver when appointed and the receiver shall account for the disposition thereof in his or her required accountings. If the application for appointment of a receiver is denied, the Clerk shall repay to the plaintiff, or the plaintiff's attorney, the sum so deposited.

Amended effective September 3, 1991; amended June 24, 2009, effective July 1, 2009.

Rule 52. [Repealed]

Repealed effective January 1, 2015.

SPECIAL PROVISIONS FOR CRIMINAL CASES

Rule 53.   Assignment of Counsel

(Applicable to criminal cases)

1. All Cases. If any party appears in the court in a matter in which the laws of the Commonwealth or the rules of the Supreme Judicial Court establish a right to be represented by counsel, the judge shall follow the procedures established in Supreme Judicial Court Rule 3:10.

2. Murder Cases. Upon the determination by a judge that a person accused of murder in the first or second degree is to be provided counsel by the Committee for Public Counsel Services pursuant to Supreme Judicial Court Rule 3:10 and G.L. c. 211D, § 8, the clerk shall notify the chief counsel of the Committee for Public Counsel Services for purposes of the assignment of the case to either the Public Counsel Division or Private Counsel Division, subject to the approval of the justice making the determination of indigency.

Amended effective May 8, 1976; October 22, 1977; amended May 6, 1978, effective July 1, 1978; amended effective January 1, 1981; November 17, 1986.

Rule 54.   Experts in Criminal Cases

(Applicable to criminal cases)

The court will not allow compensation for the services of an expert or expert witness for the defense in a criminal case unless an order of the court or a justice, naming such expert or expert witness and authorizing his employment, was made before he was employed. Such order shall not be made without notice to the district attorney in charge of the case, and an opportunity to be heard.

Rule 55.   Experts in Criminal and Delinquent Children Cases

(Applicable to criminal cases and cases of delinquent children)

The court will not allow compensation as an expert witness to a salaried medical examiner or a salaried physician of a penal institution or place of detention, unless it appears by the certificate of the district attorney that he has testified as an expert.

The court will allow no fee to a salaried physician of a penal institution or place of detention for making an examination into the mental condition of a person held in custody therein or for a report or medical certificate as to such condition.

Rule 56.   Conditions of Probation

(Applicable to criminal cases)

The general conditions of probation shall be set forth in a standard form approved by the Justices of the Superior Court, which may be modified by the sentencing judge in his or her discretion.

Amended March 27, 2019, effective May 1, 2019.

Rule 57.   [Repealed]

Repealed March 27, 2019, effective May 1, 2019.

Rule 58.   [Repealed]

Repealed March 27, 2019, effective May 1, 2019.

Rule 59.   Waiver of Indictment

(Applicable to criminal cases)

The form for an application to waive indictment under the provisions of G.L. Chapter 263, § 4A shall be as follows:

COMMONWEALTH OF MASSACHUSETTS

_____ ss.   _____ 19__

COMMONWEALTH

v.

_____

APPLICATION TO WAIVE INDICTMENT

To the Honorable the Justices of the Superior Court:

Respectfully represents said defendant that on _____ 19___ he

was (committed   )
    (bound over   ) for trial in the Superior Court under the
    (complained of)

provisions of
(G.L. c. 218 § 30)   (_____ Court of _____
(   )   (Hon. _____, Trial
(G.L. c. 219 § 20) by the (Justice
(   )   (_____
(St.1934 c. 358)   (District Attorney for the
(   )   (_____ District

upon a complaint numbered _____ of 19__ charging him with a crime not punishable by death; that he desires to waive indictment upon said charge and now applies for leave to waive such indictment and for prompt arraignment on such complaint.

_____

I hereby consent to the foregoing application.

_____

District Attorney for the _____ District.

Approved

By the Court _____ Clerk.

Rule 60.   Plea of Not Guilty

(Applicable to criminal cases)

A plea of not guilty, whether voluntarily made by the defendant or entered by order of the court, shall not be deemed to be a waiver of matters in bar or abatement or an admission of the validity of the indictment or complaint. A defendant at the time of the entry of such plea, or within ten days thereafter or within such further time as the court may order, may file such motions and other pleadings relating to matters in bar or abatement or to the validity of the indictment or complaint as he may desire without at any time retracting the plea of not guilty.

Lack of jurisdiction or the failure of the indictment or complaint to charge an offense may be raised at any time during the pendency of the proceedings.

Rule 61.   Motions for Return of Property and to Suppress Evidence

(Applicable to criminal cases)

Motions for the return of property and motions to suppress evidence shall be in writing, shall specifically set forth the facts upon which the motions are based, shall be verified by affidavit, and shall otherwise comply with the requirements of Mass.R.Crim.P. 13.

Such motions shall be filed within seven days after the date set for the filing of the pre-trial conference report pursuant to Mass.R.Crim.P. 11(a)(2), or at such other time as the court may allow.

Amended June 26, 1980, effective September 1, 1980.

Rule 61A.   Motions for Post–Conviction Relief

(Applicable to criminal cases)

(A) Contents of the Motion. Motions for post-conviction relief filed under Mass. R. Crim. P. 30 shall contain (1) an identification by county and docket number of the proceeding in which the moving party was convicted, (2) the date the judgment of conviction entered, (3) the sentence imposed following conviction and (4) a statement of the facts and grounds on which the motion is based. The motion shall also contain (5) a statement identifying all proceedings for direct review of the conviction and the orders or judgment entered and (6) a statement identifying all previous proceedings for collateral review of the conviction and the orders or judgments entered.

(B) Docket of Proceedings and Transmission of Papers. After docketing, the Clerk shall attach to all such motions a copy of the docket of the proceedings that resulted in the conviction and shall forward the motion, and accompanying papers, to the Justice who presided at the trial from which the conviction resulted and to the office of the District Attorney or to the Attorney General responsible for prosecuting the case. If the Justice who presided at the trial has retired, or is otherwise unavailable, the Clerk shall forward the motion and accompanying papers to the Regional Administrative Justice for the county in which the conviction occurred.

(C) Action on Motions. Motions that do not comply with the requirements of paragraph (A) hereof may be summarily denied, without prejudice to renewal when filed in accordance with those requirements. For all motions that do comply with the requirements of paragraph (A), the court may direct the Commonwealth to file and serve an opposition, or may act thereon in the manner it deems appropriate and as authorized by Mass. R. Crim. P. 30.

Adopted February 9, 2001, effective March 1, 2001.

Rule 62.   Appearance

(Applicable to criminal cases)

An attorney who, before the return day, has entered an appearance in behalf of a defendant in a criminal case in the Superior Court, may withdraw his appearance within fourteen days after the return day, provided that the attorney who shall represent the defendant at trial files an appearance simultaneously with such withdrawal. An attorney shall not withdraw his appearance otherwise, except by express leave of court.

Amended June 26, 1980, effective September 1, 1980.

Rule 63.   Court Reporter in Grand Jury Proceedings

(Applicable to criminal cases)

Stenographic notes of all testimony given before any grand jury shall be taken by a court reporter, who shall be appointed by a justice of the superior court and who shall be sworn. Unless otherwise ordered by the court, the court reporter shall furnish transcripts of said notes only as required by the district attorney or attorney general.

Rule 64.   Appellate Division. Procedure and Forms

(Applicable to criminal cases)

Appeals to the appellate division, under G.L. Chapter 278, as amended, shall be signed by the person sentenced, on forms herein established to be furnished by the clerk.

Upon the imposition of a sentence which may be reviewed, the clerk shall forthwith advise the person sentenced of his right, within ten days to appeal to the appellate division for a review of the sentence or sentences imposed, notwithstanding that the execution of such sentence or sentences is stayed pending appeal or suspended with a term of probation, and shall make an entry on the docket that the person has been so advised.

The clerk shall forthwith notify the justice who imposed the sentence, of any appeal, and likewise shall notify the appellate division of any appeal.

If new process issues as a result of action by the appellate division, it shall recite the original sentence, sentences or disposition and set forth any amendment thereof.

The clerk of the appellate division shall send notice of the final action by the appellate division to the appellant, the superintendent of the correctional institution in which the appellant is confined, the clerk of the court in which judgment was rendered, the justice who imposed the sentence appealed from and the chief justice.

The appellate division shall hear appeals for the review of sentences only in those cases in which a claim of appeal has been filed within ten days after the date of the imposition of sentence.

The forms for appeal under the provisions of G.L. Chapter 278, Section 28B, shall be as follows:

COMMONWEALTH OF MASSACHUSETTS

_____ ss.   Superior Court

No. _____

COMMONWEALTH

v.

_____

APPEAL FROM SENTENCE TO
MASSACHUSETTS CORRECTIONAL
INSTITUTION, CEDAR JUNCTION

The defendant hereby appeals to the Appellate Division of the Superior Court for a review of a sentence to the Massachusetts Correctional Institution, Cedar Junction, imposed in the Superior Court sitting within and for the County of _____ by Justice _____ on the _____ day of _____, 20___.

_____
Signature of Defendant

_____, 20__

Note

This appeal must be filed within ten days of imposition of sentence.

In cases in which a sentence was imposed in accordance with a recommendation agreed to by or on behalf of the defendant, the Appellate Division will not normally hold a hearing but will consider the appeal solely on the basis of the record.

_____

COMMONWEALTH OF MASSACHUSETTS

_____ ss.   Superior Court
No. _____

COMMONWEALTH

v.

_____

APPEAL FROM SENTENCE OF MORE THAN
FIVE YEARS TO MASSACHUSETTS
CORRECTIONAL INSTITUTION,
FRAMINGHAM

The defendant hereby appeals to the Appellate Division of the Superior Court for a review of a sentence to the Massachusetts Correctional Institution, Framingham, imposed in the Superior Court sitting within and for the County of _____ by Justice _____ on the _____ day of _____, 20___.

_____
Signature of Defendant

_____, 20__

Note

This appeal must be filed within ten days of imposition of sentence.

In cases in which a sentence was imposed in accordance with a recommendation agreed to by or on behalf of the defendant, the Appellate Division will not normally hold a hearing but will consider the appeal solely on the basis of the record.

Amended effective July 1, 1986.

Rule 65.   Claim of Appeal

(Applicable to criminal cases)

After imposing judgment and sentence in a case which has gone to trial on a plea of not guilty, the judge or clerk shall forthwith advise the defendant of his right to appeal, and the clerk shall execute a statement in writing to that effect.

The clerk shall have no duty to advise the defendant of any right of appeal after sentence is imposed following a plea of guilty or nolo contendere.

Defendant's counsel shall be responsible for perfecting and prosecuting the appeal unless such counsel is relieved of that responsibility, after a hearing on counsel's motion to withdraw.

An appeal under General Laws Chapter 278, Section 28 shall be claimed within thirty days after the judgment from which the appeal is taken.

Amended October 22, 1977, effective January 1, 1978; May 30, 1990, effective July 1, 1990.

Rules 66 and 67.   [Repealed]

Repealed effective September 1, 1980.

Rule 68.   Arguments

(Applicable to criminal cases)

In trials of criminal cases the arguments of each party shall be limited to thirty minutes; but the court may reasonably reduce or extend the time.

Rule 69.   Examination of Witnesses

(Applicable to criminal cases)

Unless otherwise permitted by the court, the examination and cross-examination of each witness shall be conducted by one counsel only for each party, and the counsel shall stand while so examining or cross-examining.

Rule 70.   Requests for Instructions or Rulings

(Applicable to criminal cases)

Requests for instructions or rulings in trials or hearings with or without jury shall be made in writing before the closing arguments unless special leave is given to present requests later.

The question whether the court should order a verdict shall be raised by a motion, and not by a request for instructions.

Rule 71.   Depositions—Commissions

(Applicable to criminal cases so far as depositions may be taken by statute. See G.L. c. 277, §§ 76–77)

Publisher's Note

G.L. c. 277, §§ 76–77 were repealed by St.1979, c. 344, § 42, an emergency act, approved June 30, 1979, and by § 51 made effective July 1, 1979. For derivation and subject matter of the repealed sections, see M.G.L.A. c. 277, §§ 74–77.

Upon application by a defendant, the court will grant commissions to take the depositions of witnesses residing out of the Commonwealth. Such a defendant may, on application to the clerk, obtain a commission, directed to any commissioner appointed by the governor of the Commonwealth to take depositions in any other of the United States, or to any justice of the peace, notary public or other officer legally empowered to take depositions or affidavits in the state or country where the deposition is to be taken, or to such other person as the court may order. Unless otherwise ordered, such depositions shall be taken upon interrogatories filed by such defendant, and upon cross-interrogatories, if any, filed by the Commonwealth, which interrogatories and cross-interrogatories shall be annexed to the commission. Such defendant shall file his interrogatories in the clerk's office, give notice thereof to the Commonwealth, with a copy of the interrogatories, and file an affidavit of such notice in the clerk's office. The cross-interrogatories, if any, shall be filed within seven days after the giving of such notice, or within such further time as the court may order, and a copy shall be given to such defendant. When a deposition is taken and certified by any person as an officer or person to whom the commission was directed, if it shall be objected that such person was not the one to whom the commission was directed, the burden of proof shall be on the party so objecting. But if an objection be made to the authority of a person taking the deposition without such commission, the burden of proof of such authority shall be on the party producing the deposition.

Rule 72. Depositions—Manner of Taking

(Applicable to criminal cases so far as depositions may be taken by statute. See G.L. c. 277, §§ 76–77)

Publisher's Note

G.L. c. 277, §§ 76–77 were repealed by St.1979, c. 344, § 42, an emergency act, approved June 30, 1979, and by § 51 made effective July 1, 1979. For derivation and subject matter of the repealed sections, see M.G.L.A. c. 277, §§ 74–77.

Where a deposition is taken on interrogatories, the commissioner shall take such deposition in a place separate and apart from all other persons, and shall permit no person to be present during such examination except the deponent himself, and such disinterested person, if any, as he may think fit to appoint as a clerk or stenographer to assist him in reducing the deposition to writing. The commissioner shall permit no person to communicate by interrogatories or suggestions with the deponent while giving his deposition. The commissioner shall put the several interrogatories and cross-interrogatories to the deponent in their order, and shall take the answer of the deponent to each, fully and clearly, before proceeding to the next; and shall not read to the deponent, nor permit the deponent to read, a succeeding interrogatory, until the answer to the preceding has been fully taken down. The clerk, on issuing a commission to take a deposition on interrogatories, shall insert the substance of this rule therein; or shall annex this rule, or the substance thereof, to the commission, by way of notice and instruction to the commissioner.

Depositions shall be opened and filed by the clerk when received.

SPECIAL PROVISIONS FOR CERTAIN OTHER PROCEEDINGS

Rule 73. Medical Malpractice Cases

(Applicable to All Counties)

(applicable to all cases subject to G. L. c. 231, § 60B (medical malpractice))

1. Offer of Proof; Failure to File.

a. Within 15 days after each defendant's answer has been filed in a case subject to G.L. c. 231, § 60B, the plaintiff(s) shall file the offer of proof with the clerk and provide a copy to the defendant(s). The parties may agree to a different deadline, in a written stipulation filed with the court. For purposes of cases referred for a tribunal from other trial court departments, or the federal courts, the date of docketing of the referral in the Superior Court shall be substituted for the date of filing of the answer.

b. Upon a plaintiff's failure to file a timely offer of proof, the court may find, upon motion of a party or its own initiative, that the plaintiff has failed to present sufficient evidence to raise a legitimate question of liability appropriate for judicial inquiry as to the defendant who filed the answer. A plaintiff's failure to file a timely offer of proof shall waive the plaintiff's right to a tribunal before entry of such a finding by the court.

c. By motion, or on its own initiative, the court may schedule a prompt conference, in addition to, or in lieu of the procedures set forth in parts 2–6, below.

2. Demand for Tribunal; Notice to Massachusetts Medical Society; Duties of Party Demanding a Tribunal.

a. Any party who demands a tribunal under § 60B ("Filing Party") shall file a document entitled "Demand for Tribunal" within 30 days of the filing of the answer, after reviewing the offer of proof, if any. The Demand for Tribunal shall specify each respect, if any, in which the Filing Party claims that the offer of proof fails to raise a legitimate question of liability appropriate for judicial inquiry.

b. Any defendant's failure to file a timely Demand for Tribunal shall waive that defendant's right to a tribunal.

c. If the defendant is a licensed physician or a medical institution or facility:

   i. The Demand for Tribunal shall (A) specify the field of medicine in which the alleged injury occurred and (B) list each county where the defendant practices and each county where the defendant resides, or if the defendant is a medical institution or facility, shall list the county where the institution or facility is located. The Filing Party shall consult with all other parties, and if there is disagreement about the field of medicine or county, shall include all fields and counties identified by any party.

   ii. The Filing Party shall, simultaneously with filing, serve the Demand for Tribunal on all parties of record or their counsel and the Massachusetts Medical Society ("Society"). Any Demand for Tribunal sent to the Society shall state prominently that:

1. A medical malpractice tribunal will occur if the Society timely submits a case-specific list consisting of the name(s) of physicians representing the field of medicine in which the alleged injury occurred and licensed to practice medicine and surgery in the commonwealth under the provisions of section two of chapter one hundred and twelve; and that the list shall consist only of physicians who practice medicine outside the county where the defendant practices or resides or if the defendant is a medical institution or facility outside the county where said institution or facility is located; and

2. The Court considers a submission timely if the Society provides the information to the clerk, with copies to all parties or their counsel, within 30 days of receiving the Demand for Tribunal.

d. If the defendant is not a licensed physician, the Filing Party shall obtain a case-specific list from the pertinent licensing agency and provide it to the clerk within 90 days after the answer is filed, with advance notice to other parties, who may participate if they choose,

e. For purposes of this rule, a "case-specific list" means: (1) if the defendant is a physician, a list of physicians who meet the criteria appearing in par. 2.ii.1 or (2) if the defendant is not a physician, a list consisting of the name(s) of representatives of the field of medicine in which the alleged injury occurred who are licensed to practice in that field under the laws of the Commonwealth; provided that the list shall consist only of such representatives who practice outside the county where the defendant practices or resides.

3. Tribunal. The clerk shall schedule the tribunal as soon as practicable upon receipt from the Society (or the Filing Party under paragraph 2(d)) of the information required paragraph 2(c) or 2(d). The clerk shall send notice of the date and time of the tribunal hearing to all parties or their counsel, listing the panel members' names and contact information. The plaintiff shall send a copy of the offer of proof to each panel member at least 5 days before the tribunal hearing.

Until the clerk receives a case-specific list of eligible and available physicians or medical providers, the clerk has no statutory responsibility to schedule a tribunal, but may, in the exercise of discretion, choose to devote available resources in a timely manner to identify an eligible physician or medical provider member of the tribunal.

4. Delay in Providing The Case–Specific List of Physicians or Medical Providers to the Clerk. If the clerk does not receive a case-specific list of providers within 90 days after the answer is filed, the clerk shall schedule a hearing before a single judge to determine whether the offer of proof, if properly substantiated, is sufficient to raise a legitimate question of liability appropriate for judicial inquiry or whether the plaintiffs case is merely an unfortunate medical, result. Such determination shall be without prejudice to reconsideration by a full tribunal, consisting of medical member, attorney, and judge, as provided in part (2) of the next sentence hereof. If the clerk later receives a case-specific list of providers, then:

(1) if the hearing has not already occurred, it shall occur before a full tribunal; (2) if the hearing has already occurred, and if any party files a motion for reconsideration by a full tribunal, the court shall allow such motion unless it determines that allowing the motion would unduly delay the trial.

5. Voluntary Waiver of Tribunal. Any party may waive a right to a § 60B tribunal consisting of three members, without thereby waiving any other rights or arguments in the case. If the plaintiff waives the tribunal, the court shall require posting of a bond in the statutory amount, without prejudice to the right of either party to move to increase or reduce the amount of the bond. If the defendant waives the tribunal, the court may allow the plaintiff(s) to proceed without a bond and need not schedule any further § 60B Hearing with respect to that defendant. Upon waiver of the tribunal, the clerk shall send an informational copy of the complaint and offer of proof to the Board of Registration in Medicine with a clear disclaimer that no tribunal occurred under § 60B because the defendant waived the tribunal but reserved all rights to challenge the claims in the offer of proof at trial.

6. Stay.

a. No medical malpractice lawsuit is automatically stayed pending a tribunal decision, but a session judge may enter a stay, upon motion in compliance with Superior Court Rule 9A, if the Demand for Tribunal identifies a serious issue with the offer of proof and the plaintiff does not post a bond.

b. Notwithstanding subparagraph a, in the absence of a court order, no defendant is required, over objection, to take any action if the plaintiff does not timely post a bond (i) after failing to file a timely offer of proof or (ii) after a tribunal finding adverse to the plaintiff as to that defendant.

7. Trial Assignment Conference; Case–Specific Management.

a. Notwithstanding Standing Order 1–88, the parties in all medical malpractice cases shall appear at a trial assignment conference, to be scheduled by the court not later than 18 months after filing of the complaint. The parties shall be prepared to commit to a trial date within the tracking order, as well as to dates for expert disclosures. At the trial assignment conference, the court and parties will also select a date for a final pretrial conference at which they will file a pretrial memorandum and discuss the case's potential for resolution. The parties must discuss the potential for resolution with their clients and any other entity or individual with settlement authority, before the pretrial conference,

b. Any party who seeks to advance the case for earlier determination pursuant to G.L. c. 231, § 59C, may file a Motion For Case–Specific Management pursuant to Superior Court Rule 20 and Standing Order 1–88(B)(2), in compliance with Superior Court Rule 9A.

8. Judicial Discretion. After considering the impact on prompt resolution of the case and all other equities, the judge may waive any of these requirements or extend any of these deadlines. In ruling on a motion for waiver, the judge may require the moving party to demonstrate good cause and may impose conditions to facilitate timely resolution of the case or to protect the rights of any party opposing the waiver,

9. Other Rights. Nothing in this Rule shall be construed to limit the right of any party under generally applicable statutes, rules, orders, or other law to assert or oppose any dispositive or other motion, serve any discovery request, or request a conference under Rule 16 or otherwise at any time. For purposes of this rule, any plaintiff or defendant whose claim or liability is entirely vicarious or derivative has no separate right to a tribunal beyond that asserted by the principal(s), and shall, together with the principal(s), be considered as a single party.

Adopted November 7, 2017, effective January 1, 2018.

Rule 74.   [Repealed]

Repealed effective January 1, 2015.

Rule 75.   [Repealed]

Repealed effective January 1, 2015.

SPECIAL PROVISIONS FOR DIVORCE CASES

Rule 76.   Divorce Proceedings

(Includes cases of divorce and proceedings for the annulment or affirmation of marriage)

The applicable statutes and the rules of the Probate Court shall apply to divorce proceedings and proceedings for the annulment or affirmation of marriage brought in this court.

Rule 77.   Trial Lists of Divorce Cases in Suffolk

(Applicable to cases of divorce and proceedings for the annulment or affirmation of marriage in Suffolk)

The divorce list in Suffolk will be taken up in a divorce session at such times as the chief justice may designate, precedence being given to uncontested cases unless the court otherwise orders. Cases may be placed upon the list for the divorce session in Suffolk in the manner provided for the placing of cases on the list in counties other than Suffolk by Rule 37, and motions and other interlocutory matters in cases on the divorce docket in Suffolk may be placed upon the list for hearing thereon at the divorce session in Suffolk in the manner provided for the placing of such matters on the list in counties other than Suffolk by Rule 38.

APPENDIX OF FORMS

Table of Forms

Agreement for Judgment

COMMONWEALTH OF MASSACHUSETTS
COUNTY OF
THE SUPERIOR COURT

Docket No. _____

_____

VS.

_____

AGREEMENT FOR JUDGMENT SATISFIED

It is hereby agreed that the following entry shall be made in the above entitlted action:

* Judgment for Plaintiff(s)

_____

recover of the Defendant(s) _____

the amount of $ _____

* Judgment for Defendant(s) it is hereby agreed that the complaint of the (Plaintiff(s)

_____

against the defendant(s)

_____

is dismissed without prejudice, and the defendant(s) recover its costs of action.

(*Include all claims, cross claims, counterclaims and third party claims)

Signature: _____

Name _____

Address _____

City _____ State ____ Zip ____

Phone Number _____

Dated: _____

Signature _____

Name _____

Address _____

City _____ State ____ Zip ____

Phone Number _____

Civil Action Cover Sheet

CIVIL ACTION COVER SHEET	DOCKET NUMBER	Trial Court of Massachusetts The Superior Court

PLAINTIFF(S): _____

ADDRESS: _____

_____

COUNTY

DEFENDANT(S): _____

_____

ATTORNEY: _____

ADDRESS: _____

_____

ADDRESS: _____

_____

BBO: _____

TYPE OF ACTION AND TRACK DESIGNATION (see reverse side)

CODE NO.	TYPE OF ACTION (specify)	TRACK	HAS A JURY CLAIM BEEN MADE?
			☐ YES ☐ NO

*If "Other" please describe: _____

STATEMENT OF DAMAGES PURSUANT TO G.L. c. 212, § 3A

The following is a full, itemized and detailed statement of the facts on which the undersigned plaintiff or plaintiff counsel relies to determine money damages. For this form, disregard double or treble damage claims; indicate single damages only.

TORT CLAIMS
(attach additional sheets as necessary)

A. Documented medical expenses to date:
    1. Total hospital expenses .... $ _____
    2. Total doctor expenses .... $ _____
    3. Total chiropractic expenses .... $ _____
    4. Total physical therapy expenses .... $ _____
    5. Total other expenses (describe below) .... $ _____
                         Subtotal (A): $ _____

B. Documented lost wages and compensation to date .... $ _____
C. Documented property damages to dated .... $ _____
D. Reasonably anticipated future medical and hospital expenses ... $ _____
E. Reasonably anticipated lost wages .... $ _____
F. Other documented items of damages (describe below) .... $ _____

G. Briefly describe plaintiff's injury, including the nature and extent of injury:

                         TOTAL (A-F):$ _____

CONTRACT CLAIMS
(attach additional sheets as necessary)

Provide a detailed description of claims(s):

                         TOTAL: $ _____

Signature of Attorney/Pro Se Plaintiff: X _____   Date: _____

RELATED ACTIONS: Please provide the case number, case name, and county of any related actions pending in the Superior Court.

CERTIFICATION PURSUANT TO SJC RULE 1:18

I hereby certify that I have complied with requirements of Rule 5 of the Supreme Judicial Court Uniform Rules on Dispute Resolution (SJC Rule 1:18) requiring that I provide my clients with information about court-connected dispute resolution services and discuss with them the advantages and disadvantages of the various methods of dispute resolution.

Signature of Attorney of Record: X _____   Date: _____

CIVIL ACTION COVER SHEET INSTRUCTIONS
SELECT CATEGORY THAT BEST DESCRIBES YOUR CASE

AC Actions Involving the State/Municipality *

AA1 Contract Action involving Commonwealth, Municipality, MBTA, etc.	(A)
AB1 Tortious Action involving Commonwealth, Municipality, MBTA, etc.	(A)
AC1 Real Property Action involving Commonwealth, Municipality, MBTA etc.	(A)
AD1 Equity Action involving Commonwealth, Municipality, MBTA, etc.	(A)
AE1 Administrative Action involving Commonwealth, Municipality, MBTA,etc.	(A)

CN Contract/Business Cases

A01 Services, Labor, and Materials	(F)
A02 Goods Sold and Delivered	(F)
A03 Commercial Paper	(F)
A04 Employment Contract	(F)
A06 Insurance Contract	(F)
A08 Sale or Lease of Real Estate	(F)
A12 Construction Dispute	(F)
A14 Interpleader	(F)
BA1 Governance, Conduct, Internal Affairs of Entities	(A)
BA3 Liability of Shareholders, Directors, Officers, Partners, etc.	(A)
BB1 Shareholder Derivative	(A)
BB2 Securities Transactions	(A)
BC1 Mergers, Consolidations, Sales of Assets, Issuance of Debt, Equity, etc.	(A)
BD1 Intellectual Property	(A)
BD2 Proprietary Information or Trade Secrets	(A)
BG1 Financial Institutions/Funds	(A)
BH1 Violation of Antitrust or Trade Regulation Laws	(A)
A99 Other Contract/Business Action - Specify	(F)

* Choose this case type if ANY party is the Commonwealth, a municipality, the MBTA, or any other governmental entity UNLESS your case is a case type listed under Administrative Civil Actions (AA).

† Choose this case type if ANY party is an incarcerated party, UNLESS your case is a case type listed under Administrative Civil Actions (AA) or is a Prisoner Habeas Corpus case (E97).

ER Equitable Remedies

D01 Specific Performance of a Contract	(A)
D02 Reach and Apply	(F)
D03 Injunction	(F)
D04 Reform/ Cancel Instrument	(F)
D05 Equitable Replevin	(F)
D06 Contribution or Indemnification	(F)
D07 Imposition of a Trust	(A)
D08 Minority Shareholder's Suit	(A)
D09 Interference in Contractual Relationship	(F)
D10 Accounting	(A)
D11 Enforcement of Restrictive Covenant	(F)
D12 Dissolution of a Partnership	(F)
D13 Declaratory Judgment, G.L. c.231A	(A)
D14 Dissolution of a Corporation	(F)
D99 Other Equity Action	(F)

PA Civil Actions Involving Incarcerated Party †

PA1 Contract Action involving an Incarcerated Party	(A)
PB1 Tortious Action involving an Incarcerated Party	(A)
PC1 Real Property Action involving an Incarcerated Party	(F)
PD1 Equity Action involving an Incarcerated Party	(F)
PE1 Administrative Action involving an Incarcerated Party	(F)

TR Torts

B03 Motor Vehicle Negligence - Personal Injury/Property Damage	(F)
B04 Other Negligence - Personal Injury/Property Damage	(F)
B05 Products Liability	(A)
B06 Malpractice - Medical / Wrongful Death	(A)
B07 Malpractice - Other	(A)
B08 Wrongful Death, G.L. c.229 §2A	(A)
B15 Defamation	(A)
B19 Asbestos	(A)
B20 Personal Injury - Slip & Fall	(F)
B21 Environmental	(F)
B22 Employment Discrimination	(F)
BE1 Fraud, Business Torts, etc.	(A)
B99 Other Tortious Action	(F)

RP Real Property

C01 Land Taking	(F)
C02 Zoning Appeal, G.L. c. 40A	(F)
C03 Dispute Concerning Title	(F)
C04 Foreclosure of a Mortgage	(X)
C05 Condominium Lien & Charges	(X)
C99 Other Real Property Action	(F)

MC Miscellaneous Civil Actions

E18 Foreign Discovery Proceeding	(X)
E97 Prisoner Habeas Corpus	(X)
E22 Lottery Assignment, G.L. c. 10 §28	(X)

AB Abuse/Harassment Prevention

E15 Abuse Prevention Petition, G.L. c. 209A	(X)
E21 Protection from Harassment, G.L. c. 258E	(X)

AA Administrative Civil Actions

E02 Appeal from Administrative Agency, G.L. c. 30A	(X)
E03 Certiorari Action, G.L. c.249 §4	(X)
E05 Confirmation of Arbitration Awards	(X)
E06 Mass Antitrust Act, G. L. c. 93 §9	(X)
E07 Mass Antitrust Act, G. L. c. 93 §8	(X)
E08 Appointment of a Receiver	(X)
E09 Construction Surety Bond, G.L. c. 149 §§29, 29A	(A)
E10 Summary Process Appeal	(X)
E11 Worker's Compensation	(X)
E16 Auto Surcharge Appeal	(X)
E17 Civil Rights Act, G.L. c.12 §11H	(A)
E24 Appeal from District Court Commitment, G.L. c.123 §9(b)	(X)
E25 Pleural Registry (Asbestos cases)	
E94 Forfeiture, G.L. c265 §56	(X)
E95 Forfeiture, G.L. c.94C §47	(F)
E99 Other Administrative Action	(X)
Z01 Medical Malpractice - Tribunal only, G.L. c. 231 §60B	(F)
Z02 Appeal Bond Denial	(X)

SO Sex Offender Review

E12 SDP Commitment, G.L. c. 123A §12	(X)
E14 SDP Petition, G.L. c. 123A §9(b)	(X)

RC Restricted Civil Actions

E19 Sex Offender Registry, G.L. c.6 §178M	(X)
E27 Minor Seeking Consent, G.L. c.112 §12S	(X)

TRANSFER YOUR SELECTION TO THE FACE SHEET

EXAMPLE:

CODE NO.	TYPE OF ACTION (specify)	TRACK	HAS A JURY CLAIM BEEN MADE?
B03	Motor Vehicle Negligence-Personal Injury	F	☒ YES ☐ NO

STATEMENT OF DAMAGES PURSUANT TO G.L. c. 212, § 3A

DUTY OF THE PLAINTIFF - The plaintiff shall set forth, on the face of the civil action cover sheet (or attach additional sheets as necessary), a statement specifying the facts on which the plaintiff relies to determine money damages. A copy of such civil action cover sheet, including the statement as to the damages, shall be served with the complaint. **A clerk-magistrate shall not accept for filing a complaint, except as otherwise provided by law, unless it is accompanied by such a statement signed by the attorney or pro se party.**

DUTY OF THE DEFENDANT - If the defendant believes that the statement of damages filed by the plaintiff is inadequate, the defendant may file with his/her answer a statement specifying the potential damages which may result if the plaintiff prevails.

A CIVIL COVER SHEET MUST BE FILED WITH EACH COMPLAINT.
FAILURE TO COMPLETE THIS COVER SHEET THOROUGHLY AND ACCURATELY
MAY RESULT IN DISMISSAL OF THIS ACTION.

Military Affidavit

COMMONWEALTH OF MASSACHUSETTS

COUNTY OF THE SUPERIOR COURT

Civil Action No.

_____

_____

Plaintiff(s)

VS.

_____

Defendant(s)

MILITARY AFFIDAVIT

I, _____ on behalf of the Plaintiff, on oath depose and say that the defendant _____ in the above named action is/is not _____ the military service of the United States or any of its allies as defined in the federal Servicemembers Civil Relief Act of 2003, as set forth in 50 U.S.C. App. §§ 501 et seq., evidenced by the following facts:

Subscribed and sworn to under penalties of perjury

Dated: _____

Signature:

_____

Print name:

_____

Address:

_____

Address:

_____

City/State/
Zip

_____

Phone
Number

_____

** (State facts on which affidavit is based) _____

Notice of Appearance

COMMONWEALTH OF MASSACHUSETTS
COUNTY OF THE SUPERIOR COURT

Civil Action No. _____

_____

VS.

_____

NOTICE OF APPEARANCE

TO THE CLERK OF THE ABOVE NAMED COURT:

Please enter my appearance as attorney for_____

_____

in the above entitled action.

Date: _____

Signature:

_____

Print name: _____

Address: _____

Address: _____

City/State/Zip _____

BBO#   _____

Phone Number _____

Writ of Attachment

WRIT OF ATTACHMENT	DOCKET NUMBER	Trial Court of Massachusetts
		The Superior Court

CASE NAME:		
VS		Clerk of Courts
		County

TO:	COURT NAME & ADDRESS
THE SHERIFFS of our several counties or their deputies:	

DATE COMPLAINT WAS FILED	DATE ATTACHMENT APPROVED	ATTACHMENT AMOUNT	JUDGE APPROVING ATTACHMENT
		$	

Pursuant to Mass. R. Civ. P. 4.1, **WE COMMAND YOU** to attach the goods or estate of defendant

_____ of

to the value of $ _____ the amount authorized by the court and requested by the plaintiff

_____ of _____

whose attorney is _____

of _____

in an action brought by said plaintiff against the defendant in this court, and make due return of this writ with your doings thereon.

X _____
          Clerk

DATE ISSUED	WITNESS	CLERK	SESSION PHONE #
	Judith Fabricant, Chief Justice		

RETURN OF SERVICE

01/09/2015

APPENDIX OF ADMINISTRATIVE DIRECTIVES

*Suggested title added by Publisher

Administrative Directive No. 90–2. Non–Filing of Discovery Materials [Rescinded]

Effective December 3, 1990. Rescinded September 2, 2014, effective December 1, 2014.

Administrative Directive No. 91–1. Reapplications for Final Judgment for Relief or Dismissal [Rescinded]

Effective July 1, 1991. Rescinded effective October 4, 2010.

Administrative Directive No. 92–1. Inmate Civil Cases—Service of Process *

This administrative directive is implemented to address the unique problems that often accompany a civil action that is filed by someone who is incarcerated. Its aim is to promote a just and speedy resolution of these civil actions by ensuring:

1. That upon filing, the complaint is entered expeditiously and appropriate notice is sent.

2. That all named parties receive actual notice of the litigation.

3. That the cases proceed in a timely and cost effective manner.

Accordingly, it is ordered that upon the filing of the complaint, the Clerk is to pass upon the sufficiency of the affidavit of indigency (in almost all cases, the prisoner is indigent but has access to limited funds) and if indigent, to authorize service of process by certified mail on all named defendants—copy to the Attorney General. With notification of this action * * * the Clerk is to provide the plaintiff with the appropriate number of blank summonses. It is the obligation of the plaintiff to provide the requisite number of copies of the complaint and to complete the summons to perfect service. In those rare instances wherein the plaintiff has no access to funds (ex. not in the general population of the prison) service may be authorized by regular mail and the Court is to provide the appropriate number of blank summonses.

With the notice of the Court's action, the plaintiff is also to be notified of what is required in filing a return of service

* * * and of the waiving of that part of Superior Court Rule 9A which requires the packaging of motions and responses thereto. * * *

When a complaint filed by an inmate requests other than money damages, the complaint is to be reviewed by a justice for whatever action he or she deems appropriate. For example, it is in the discretion of the justice to decide a request for a preliminary injunction upon submissions and not require the presence of the inmate.

This administrative directive is to take effect forthwith.

Effective May 1, 1992.

Administrative Directive No. 03–1. Superior Court Business Litigation Session Extension and Expanded Venue [Rescinded]

Effective March 3, 2003. Rescinded with the adoption of Administrative Directive No. 09–1, effective January 19, 2009.

Administrative Directive No. 09–1. Superior Court Business Litigation Sessions [Superseded]

Effective January 19, 2009. Superseded with the adoption of Administrative Directive No. 17–1, effective March 1, 2017.

Administrative Directive No. 14–1. Preservation of Court Reporter Records and Recordings of Criminal Proceedings

Pursuant to G.L. c. 221, § 87, it is hereby ORDERED that all stenographers and court reporters (hereinafter "court reporter"), whether serving in an official, temporary or per diem capacity, shall preserve in perpetuity all original notes, tapes, discs, and other means used to record, electronically or by any other method, any criminal proceeding in the Superior Court.

Such materials shall be clearly labeled by date, court session, and parties. The court reporter shall advise the Administrative Office of the Superior Court, in writing, as to the method by which all such materials are preserved, the present location thereof, and the procedure and manner in which such materials shall be turned over to the court upon the death, disability, retirement, or termination of the court reporter.

Effective January 1, 2014.

Administrative Directive No. 14–2. Preservation of Court Reporter Records and Recordings of Civil Proceedings

Pursuant to G.L. c. 221, § 87, it is hereby ORDERED that all stenographers and court reporters (hereinafter "court reporter"), whether serving in an official, temporary or per diem capacity, shall preserve for a period of at least six years all original notes, tapes, discs, and other means used to record, electronically or by any other method, any civil proceeding in the Superior Court. Such materials shall be clearly labeled by case name, docket number, date and court session. The court reporter, upon request, shall advise the court, in writing, as to the method by which all of such materials are preserved, the present location thereof, and the procedure and manner in which such materials shall be turned over to the court upon the death, disability, retirement, or termination of the court reporter.

A court reporter storing such notes at one or more court locations shall maintain them at said location(s) only if such notes were generated within the six year retention period required by this regulation. Thereafter, such notes shall be stored and retained by the court reporter at a different location and for a term that the court reporter deems appropriate.

Effective July 1, 2014.

Administrative Directive No. 17–1. Superior Court Business Litigation Sessions

The Business Litigation Sessions of the Superior Court (BLS) are permanent sessions of the Superior Court located in the Suffolk County Superior Court. The Suffolk County Civil Clerk's Office is the clerk's office for the BLS.

Filing the Action

If a plaintiff seeks acceptance of a case into the BLS, the plaintiff shall file the complaint and *the BLS Civil Action Cover Sheet* with the Suffolk County Civil Clerk's Office. The Cover Sheet must articulate the reasons why the plaintiff believes the case should be accepted into the BLS. Failure to file a BLS Civil Action Cover Sheet will cause the case to be assigned to a Suffolk County civil session in accord with the Court's usual practice. A copy of the completed BLS Civil Action Cover Sheet shall be served on all defendants with the summons and complaint.

Venue Not a Bar to Requesting Acceptance into the BLS

A plaintiff may seek acceptance into the BLS even if venue does not lie in Suffolk County.

Although nothing in this Administrative Directive changes the statutory requirements for venue, because improper venue may be waived, the BLS Administrative Justice does not consider venue when determining whether to accept a case into the BLS.

The filing of a complaint in Suffolk County and its acceptance into the BLS does not prevent any party from moving to dismiss or transfer the case for improper venue. Upon such a motion and a determination that venue is improper, the case shall be transferred in accordance with G.L. c. 223. However, failure to file such a motion within the time limits prescribed by Mass. R. Civ. P. 12(h)(1) shall constitute a waiver of improper venue.

Acceptance into the BLS

Once a case has been filed, the clerk shall forthwith bring the complaint and BLS Civil Action Cover Sheet to the attention of the BLS Administrative Justice, who will determine whether to accept the case into the BLS. In the event that the plaintiff is seeking ex parte relief or a short order of notice, the BLS Administrative Justice will first decide if the case is accepted into the BLS and if it is, rule on the request. If the case is not accepted, then the case will be assigned to a regular Suffolk civil session and the request will be handled by the judge assigned to that session.

Cases that fall within any of the following categories may be accepted into the BLS in the sound discretion of the BLS Administrative Justice, based principally on the complexity of the case and the need for substantial case management:

a.1 claims relating to the governance and conduct of internal affairs of entities

a.2 claims relating to employment agreements

a.3 claims relating to liability of shareholders, directors, officers, partners, etc.

b.1 shareholder derivative claims

b.2 claims relating to or arising out of securities transactions

c.1 claims involving mergers, consolidations, sales of assets, issuance of debt, equity and like interests

d.1 claims to determine the use or status of, or claims involving, intellectual property

d.2 claims to determine the use or status of, or claims involving, confidential, proprietary or trade secret information

d.3 claims to determine the use or status of, or claims involving, restrictive covenants

e.1 claims involving breaches of contract or fiduciary duties, fraud, misrepresentation, business torts or other violations involving business relationships

f.1 claims under the U.C.C. involving complex issues

g.1 claims arising from transactions with banks, investment bankers and financial advisers, brokerage firms, mutual and money funds

h.1 claims for violation of antitrust or other trade regulation laws, including class actions

h.2 claims of unfair trade practices involving complex issues, including class actions that do not involve personal injury

i.1 professional malpractice claims other than claims for personal injury or death j.1   claims by or against a business enterprise to which a government entity is a party

k.1   other claims involving complex issues or that require close case management, including but not limited to insurance coverage or reinsurance, construction, commercial lease disputes, real estate and consumer matters.

If a case is accepted into the BLS, a Notice of Acceptance into the Business Litigation Session shall be issued and the case shall be assigned to either BLS1 or BLS2.

If a case is not accepted into the BLS, a Notice of Denial of Acceptance into the Business Litigation Session shall be issued and the case shall be assigned, or returned, to a regular civil session.

Transfers into the BLS

Requests to Transfer into the BLS from Another Suffolk County Superior Court Session

If a plaintiff files an action in Suffolk County and does not seek to have the case accepted into the BLS, any party may file a motion, in the manner provided by Superior Court Rule 9A, in the session to which the case is assigned, requesting a transfer to the BLS. If the motion is granted by the judge in the session, the clerk of that session shall promptly bring the case to the attention of the BLS Administrative Justice, who will decide whether to accept the case into the BLS in accordance with the procedure described above.

Requests to Transfer into the BLS from a Superior Court Session Outside of Suffolk County

If a plaintiff files an action outside of Suffolk County, any party may file in the session to which the case is assigned a motion requesting a transfer to the BLS. If no party opposes the motion, the failure to oppose shall be deemed a waiver of any defense of improper venue. If the motion is granted by the judge sitting in the session, the clerk of courts for that county shall promptly bring the case to the attention of the BLS Administrative Justice, who will decide whether to accept the case into the BLS in accordance with the procedure described above.

Sua Sponte Transfers into the BLS

A case filed in any Suffolk County session may be transferred to the BLS by a *sua sponte* order of: 1) the BLS Administrative Justice, or 2) the judge sitting in the session to which the case is assigned after that judge has consulted with the BLS Administrative Justice as to the propriety of a transfer. Transfer from a regular civil session shall be pursuant to a written Order of Referral coupled with an endorsement by the BLS Administrative Justice accepting or denying the transfer.

A case filed outside of Suffolk County may be transferred to the BLS by a *sua sponte* order of: 1) the BLS Administrative Justice, or 2) the judge sitting in the session to which the case is assigned after that judge has consulted with the BLS Administrative Justice as to the propriety of a transfer, as long as either venue lies in Suffolk County or, after consultation with the parties, no objection to venue is raised.

Rule 16 Conference Upon Acceptance into the BLS

When a case has been accepted into the BLS, either after filing there originally or via transfer, once each defendant has filed a responsive pleading or has been defaulted for failure to do so, the clerk of the assigned BLS session shall schedule a Rule 16 conference to establish a tracking order appropriate to the case. The parties shall confer with each other before the Rule 16 conference in an attempt to agree upon, or narrow their differences as to, a proposed tracking order.

This administrative directive supercedes Administrative Directive No. 09–1, dated January 19, 2009.

Effective March 1, 2017.

Administrative Directive No. 18–1.   Recording of Criminal Proceedings

All proceedings in criminal cases in the Superior Court shall be recorded by either an electronic recording system or a per diem court reporter. The means of recording a particular proceeding is an administrative matter, to be determined by the Chief Justice's designee within the Administrative Office of the Superior Court (AOSC).

Whenever feasible, criminal trials, except those identified pursuant to paragraph (1) or (2) herein, shall be recorded by an electronic recording system operated by an authorized monitor, who shall be responsible for ensuring that a complete, accurate and audible record is generated.

When a monitor is not available due to staffing or other constraints, the clerk, assistant clerk or other authorized employee of the clerk's office shall operate the electronic recording system in substantially the same manner as a monitor.

Whenever feasible, AOSC shall assign a per diem court reporter to record the following proceedings:

1.   Jury Trials of charges of homicide, rape, or sexual offenses against minors; in which a defense of lack of criminal responsibility is raised; or in which two or more defendants, represented by separate counsel, are joined for trial;

2.   Any other evidentiary proceeding, or portion thereof, if special circumstances relating to the particular proceeding raise a serious question as to whether electronic recording will provide an adequate record. A judge or clerk who identifies such a proceeding shall promptly bring it to the attention of the Regional Administrative Justice, who may make a request to AOSC for assignment of a per diem court reporter, identifying the special circumstances giving rise to the request.

A per diem court reporter's assignment shall be complete (1) in the case of a trial, at the end of the business day during which the case is submitted to the jury; (2) in the case of any other proceeding, upon conclusion of the proceeding for which the reporter was assigned. Per diem court reporters will not be assigned to attend a trial after a case has been submitted to a jury on a previous date.

For each proceeding for which assignment of a per diem court reporter is sought, the clerk shall submit a request to AOSC, in a form provided by AOSC, at least seven days prior to the scheduled date. When a per diem court reporter is assigned, the record produced by such court reporter shall be the official record. If the judge so directs, the clerk will also operate the electronic recording system for administrative purposes only.

This administrative directive does not affect any proceeding recorded by a temporary official court reporter appointed as such, upon motion of one or more parties and at their expense, pursuant to G. L. c. 221, § 83 (2nd para.). The record produced by such court reporter shall be the official record. If the judge so directs, the clerk will also operate the electronic recording system for administrative purposes only.

This administrative directive also does not affect the right of a criminal defendant to have a court reporter record a proceeding at the defendant's expense pursuant to G. L. c. 221,

§ 91B, if no per diem court reporter is assigned. In any such instance the proceeding shall also be recorded by the electronic recording system, and the record produced by the electronic recording system shall be the official record.

This administrative directive will take effect on or before July 1, 2018. It will be reviewed at quarterly intervals thereafter, and will be revised as the Court deems warranted in light of experience with transcripts produced from electronic recordings.

Effective July 1, 2018. Revised January 22, 2019, effective February 1, 2019.

RULES GOVERNING PERSONS AUTHORIZED TO ADMIT TO BAIL OUT OF COURT

Effective July 1, 2014

Rule 1. Definitions

A. **"Bail Magistrate"** is a person authorized to admit to bail out of court, including a clerk-magistrate or assistant clerk of the Superior Court, District Court, or Boston Municipal Court who has registered with the Office of Bail Administration, a bail commissioner inside or outside of Suffolk County, or, if appointed by the Governor in accordance with G.L. c. 221, § 53 or G.L. c. 218, § 36, a master in chancery or a justice of the peace, respectively.

B. **"Jurisdiction"** refers to the territory within which a bail magistrate may set or take bail or release on personal recognizance.

C. **"Division"** refers to the Brighton, Central, Charlestown, Dorchester, East Boston, Roxbury, South Boston, or West Roxbury Division of the Boston Municipal Court.

D. **"Home Court"**—with respect to bail commissioners, it refers to the district court or county listed in their commissions of appointment. With respect to Superior Court clerk-magistrates and assistant clerks, it refers to the superior courthouse in the county where their designated office is located. With respect to District or Boston Municipal Courts clerk-magistrates and assistant clerks, it refers to the district or division, respectively, listed in their commissions or the district or division to which they are regularly assigned.

E. **"Professional Bondsman"** refers to a person or agent for a corporation who acts as a bail or surety for a defendant in a criminal case and who has received, has been promised, or expects to receive a fee, pay, or reward for acting as bail or surety. Such person must be approved and registered as a professional bondsman by the Superior Court.

Rule 2

The Chief Justice of the Superior Court shall establish a Superior Court Committee on Bail for the purpose of appointing bail commissioners, drafting rules governing bail magistrates, overseeing the bail magistrates, and enforcing compliance by all bail magistrates with applicable statutes and rules.

Rule 3

The purpose of setting terms for any pre-trial release is to assure the presence at court of the person released. Any person charged with an offense other than an offense punishable by death, or for any offense on which a warrant of arrest has been issued by the Superior Court, is required by law to be released on his personal recognizance pending trial unless the person setting the terms of release determines, in the exercise of his discretion, that such a release will not reasonably assure the appearance of the person as required. In making a determination as to whether to release a person on personal recognizance or bail, the bail magistrate shall consider the factors set forth in G.L. c. 276, § 58. Each decision shall be reached on the basis of all available information pertaining to the factors set forth in the statute.

Rule 4

These rules shall apply only to out of court releases by bail magistrates on personal recognizance or bail. They shall apply even when the setting of bail was done by another if the taking of bail is done by them.

Rule 5

Bail magistrates shall comply with all laws governing their activities, including the provisions set forth in these rules. Failure to comply with such laws or rules may result in the suspension or termination of the power of the bail magistrate to admit persons to bail.

Rule 6

All bail magistrates shall comply with any training and educational requirements established by the Office of Bail Administration.

Rule 7

Clerk-magistrates and assistant clerks of the Superior, District, and Boston Municipal Courts who admit persons to bail must register with the Office of Bail Administration on a form approved by the Superior Court before exercising the authority of a bail magistrate. Any of the above who fails to so register shall not be authorized to admit persons to bail.

Clerk-magistrates and assistant clerks of the Superior, District, and Boston Municipal Courts and bail commissioners employed by the court shall not permit their out of court bailing activities to interfere with their regular court duties or attendance in court.

While clerk-magistrates must maintain the proper functioning of their offices, they shall not unreasonably restrict or exclude an assistant clerk from participating in out of court bailing.

Rule 8

The jurisdiction of clerk-magistrates and assistant clerks of the Superior Court shall be limited to the county in which they are elected or appointed, respectively. They may admit to bail any person held within their county even when such person is held on charges outside of that county.

Rule 9

The jurisdiction of clerk-magistrates or assistant clerks of the District and Boston Municipal Courts to admit a person to bail shall be limited to the district or division, respectively, to which they are appointed. They may admit to bail any person held within their district or division even when such person is held on charges outside of that district or division.

Rule 10

The jurisdiction of bail commissioners to admit a person to bail shall be limited to the geographical area contained in their commission. They may admit to bail any person held within their geographical area even when such person is held on charges outside of that geographical area.

Rule 11

The jurisdiction of masters in chancery and justices of the peace to admit a person to bail shall be limited to the county or judicial district, respectively, to which they are appointed. They may admit to bail any person held within their county or judicial district even when such person is held on charges outside of that county or judicial district.

Rule 12

The jurisdiction of clerk-magistrates or assistant clerks of the District and Boston Municipal Courts may be extended to any other judicial district or division, respectively, by written permission of the Chief Justice of their court. A copy of the application for such permission shall be sent to the Office of Bail Administration by the applicant, and if approved, a copy of the permission shall be forwarded to the Office of Bail Administration by the Chief Justice of such court.

Rule 13

The jurisdiction of bail magistrates may be temporarily extended to any other judicial district or division by a Justice of the Superior Court upon notification by the Office of Bail Administration that emergency coverage is required. Such coverage authorizations shall be for a specific period of time, but may be extended in the same manner as originally authorized.

Rule 14

The fee charged by a bail magistrate is governed by G.L. c. 262, § 24. The statute provides that such fee shall be received only by the bail magistrate who goes to the place of detention and completes the release. Fee splitting arrangements are prohibited.

This rule does not prohibit the taking of bail or releasing on personal recognizance for less than the maximum fee or without charge. However, if a fee is charged, payment shall be made in advance of the release.

The bail magistrate shall release a person without charging a fee if circumstances justify the release and the person is not able to pay the fee.

Clerk-magistrates and assistant clerks of the Superior, District, and Boston Municipal Courts and bail commissioners employed by the court shall not receive any fee or compensation, in addition to their salaries, for releasing a prisoner on bail or on personal recognizance during regular court hours.

Rule 15

A bail magistrate shall not receive anything other than the statutory fee for admitting a person to bail.

Rule 16

Unless restricted by the Superior Court or the Chief Justice of the District or Boston Municipal Courts, all bail magistrates are entitled to participate fairly in the out of court bailing activity in their jurisdiction, so long as they are willing and able to respond to all calls for their services with reasonable promptness.

In order to effectuate the purposes of this rule and to provide prompt out of court bailing services to all jails and holding facilities in a jurisdiction, the Justices of the Superior Court Committee on Bail may prepare and implement a plan for such coverage. All bail magistrates authorized in a jurisdiction affected by such a plan shall comply with it.

The bail magistrate shall not unduly delay the release of a defendant for the purpose of stacking or combining multiple defendants for release at a police holding facility or jail.

Rule 17

A bail magistrate shall not respond to calls for their services from a professional bondsman, surety agent, or money lender. A bail magistrate may only respond to calls from a defendant, someone calling on the defendant's behalf, a defendant's attorney, or the authorities at a jail or facility holding the defendant.

Rule 18

A bail magistrate shall only administer an oath or affirmation if the affiant is physically present. An oath or affirmation shall not be administered by telephone.

Rule 19

A bail magistrate shall not delegate the authority to admit a defendant to bail to a police officer, jail official, professional bondsman, or any other person.

Rule 20

A bail magistrate shall perform the duties impartially, with dignity and in a manner that befits the performance of a judicial act.

Rule 21

A bail magistrate shall administer an oath to a defendant admitted to bail, and to each person accepted as surety, that such person will perform the requirements of his recognizance or bond.

Oaths administered in the course of admitting a defendant to bail shall be given with solemnity and dignity.

Rule 22

A bail magistrate must ensure that each defendant has his own recognizance. Two or more defendants cannot be joined in one recognizance, even if they are jointly charged with the same crime. Each recognizance must be accompanied by a separate affidavit.

Rule 23

A bail magistrate shall not accept as surety a bondsman who has received, who has been promised, or who expects to receive pay or reward for acting as surety unless such proposed surety is at the time duly registered as a professional bondsman.

If the surety offered is an agent of a surety company, the bail magistrate shall, before accepting the surety, satisfy himself that the company is authorized to act as surety in criminal cases in the Commonwealth; that it is financially sound; that the agent purporting to bind the surety company in recognizance is properly authorized to do so; that the surety company will deal fairly with the defendant in all respects; and that there are no conditions indicating that the surety company is likely to lose interest in assuring a defendant's presence in court.

Rule 24

A bail magistrate shall verify that a professional bondsman has registered with the Superior Court, and that such bondsman has the necessary assets to satisfy his outstanding bail bond obligations.

Rule 25

A bail magistrate shall not accept as surety any professional bondsman if it appears that such bondsman's obligations as surety in criminal cases will be greater than the limit set by Rule 22 of the Superior Court's Rules Governing Professional Bondsmen (1991).

Rule 26

If the security offered is of the kind authorized by G.L. c. 276, § 79, a bail magistrate shall make careful inquiry as to the ownership of such property.

Rule 27

A bail magistrate shall not accept as surety any person who has previously been rejected as surety by any bail magistrate in the same proceeding.

Rule 28

A bail magistrate shall satisfy himself beyond a reasonable doubt that the person offered as surety is the person he claims to be.

Rule 29

The bail magistrate shall take all necessary steps to make certain that all persons admitted to bail and all sureties fully understand their obligations. This applies especially where such persons are not familiar with the English language. Bail magistrates must be equally certain that they understand the responses made by the persons admitted to bail or sureties under examination.

Rule 30

A bail magistrate shall not be a creditor of a defendant or a surety.

Rule 31

A bail magistrate shall not, directly or indirectly, provide substantive legal advice to a defendant whom he is admitting to bail as to any matter concerning the defendant's case. A bail magistrate may provide general procedural information to the defendant.

Rule 32

A bail magistrate shall not admit a person to bail in any proceeding in which he has acted or expects to act as counsel, nor shall he act as counsel in any proceeding in which he has at any time admitted such person to bail.

Rule 33

A bail magistrate shall not accept as surety any attorney or any such attorney's relative or employee if such attorney is directly or indirectly employed by the person being admitted to bail.

Rule 34

A bail magistrate shall not offer or give any gift, compensation, or reward to anyone for procuring or influencing the selection of a bail magistrate or for selecting any particular attorney or professional bondsman.

Rule 35

A bail magistrate is prohibited from taking or receiving any gift, commission, pay, or reward, tangible or intangible, from any person who lends money or offers bonds, bank books, or other securities to a person in custody or to any other person for the benefit of the defendant for use in depositing bail or security.

Rule 36

A bail magistrate is prohibited from procuring or recommending a particular professional bondsman or a person to lend the defendant money or property.

Rule 37

A bail magistrate is prohibited from referring a defendant to any attorney, a firm of attorneys, or other advisor, nor shall he, directly or indirectly, contact any such person on a defendant's behalf.

Rule 38

A bail magistrate shall not, directly or indirectly, lend or procure the lending of money, bonds, bank books, or other securities to a defendant or to any person for the benefit of the defendant for use in depositing as bail or security with himself or any other bail magistrate, or for use in paying, rewarding, or giving security to any professional bondsman, attorney, or other advisor.

Rule 39

A bail magistrate who releases an individual in custody on personal recognizance or on bail shall advise him of G.L. c. 276, § 82A, which provides that a person who fails to appear in court without sufficient excuse shall be punished by a fine of not more than $10,000 or by imprisonment in a house of correction for not more than one year, or both, in the case of a misdemeanor, and by a fine of not more than $50,000 and imprisonment in a state prison for not more than five years, or a house of correction for not more than two and one-half years, or by fine and imprisonment, in the case of a felony.

Rule 40

All bail magistrates shall maintain a dedicated checking account with the bail magistrate's name and the title "Bail

Magistrate" listed on numbered checks. It shall be used exclusively for depositing and transferring bail funds, and must be of a type where monthly statements include a page or pages showing copies of cancelled checks. A bail magistrate is prohibited from commingling personal funds with bail funds collected and deposited into the dedicated account. A bail magistrate may use personal funds to pay required bank fees. All bail funds not delivered to a court the following day shall be deposited into the dedicated checking account at the earliest feasible time. Bail funds to be delivered to courts outside of the bail magistrate's home court must be transferred using a check from the dedicated bail account and shall include on the check's memo line the defendant's name and docket number if available.

No later than five days after the dedicated bail account has been opened, the bail magistrate shall notify the Office of Bail Administration in writing of the name of the bank and the account number. A complete and accurate written register of account activity must be maintained at all times. The bail magistrate shall forward to the Office of Bail Administration copies of monthly statements from the dedicated bail account within seven days of receipt.

Separate checks must be used for each recognizance document transferred.

Rule 41

A bail magistrate may accept bail from a defendant or surety in the form of cash, a bank check, treasurer's or cashier's check, or U.S. Government money order made payable only to the bail magistrate authorizing the release.

Rule 42

The bail magistrate shall deliver all recognizances, certificates (affidavits) of sureties, other necessary documents, and all money, bank books, bonds and other security deposited with the bail magistrate to the clerk-magistrates' offices of the appropriate courts within the time frames established by this rule.

If the defendant is required to appear at the bail magistrate's home court, the bail magistrate shall deliver the recognizance, bail funds, and all other related items to the court no later than 8:30 a.m. on the next court day.

If the defendant is required to appear at a court outside the bail magistrate's home court, the bail magistrate shall deliver the recognizance, bail funds, and all other related items to the court by 4:30 p.m. on the third business day after the day on which the release was authorized. In addition, the bail magistrate must send by facsimile transmission or other electronic means a copy of the recognizance form to the appropriate court within 24 hours of the release. This responsibility may be satisfied where the jail or police authorities fax the recognizance, but the ultimate responsibility remains with the bail magistrate.

Rule 43

All certificates (affidavits) of sureties required by G.L. c. 276, § 61, and any amendments thereof that may be made, shall comply with all requirements of the statute. All sureties shall answer the following questions under an oath administered by the bail magistrate:

"Have you received or been promised pay or reward for acting as surety in this case?"

"Do you expect to receive pay or reward or a promise of pay or reward for your becoming surety in this case?"

"Are you approved and registered with the Superior Court as a professional bondsman?"

(This question is to be answered whether or not the other answers of the surety indicate that he is acting for hire.)

"Have you become bail or surety in criminal cases on five separate occasions during the now current calendar year?"

The surety, pursuant to G.L. c. 276, § 61, must complete an inventory of his net worth, including a full and detailed description of all personal and real property. A bail magistrate shall make careful inquiry as to the surety's ownership of such property. For example:

A. Motor vehicles, full information as to:

(a) mortgages, liens, and other encumbrances;

(b) engine number;

(c) make, type, mileage, and year of manufacture;

(d) nature of use being made of it;

(e) location of garage where it is usually kept; and

(f) assessed value, if any;

B. Shares of capital stock of corporations, full information as to:

(a) exact corporate name of corporation;

(b) name of state of incorporation;

(c) class of stock, whether common or preferred;

(d) par value of each share of stock;

(e) market value of the stock and whether listed on any stock exchange. If not listed, state where there is a market for the stock;

(f) whether or not the stock stands in the surety's name on the books of the corporation. If not in the surety's name, in whose name;

(g) whether or not the stock is subject to any existing pledge, mortgage, or other lien and, if it is, for how much and to whom and the nature of the obligation for which it is security; and

(h) whether or not dividends have been regularly paid on the stock and if so, how much in each of the last three years.

Rule 44

A bail magistrate shall submit a report on forms approved by the Superior Court, to the Office of Bail Administration by the second Monday of the month accounting for the total number of releases, i.e. cash bail releases, releases on personal recognizance, and releases for money owed to a court, that were authorized during the prior calendar month. Such report shall also include the totals of cash bail, bail fees, and other funds collected. The Superior Court may at any time amend such forms to require that additional information be reported.

The forms to be used for this purpose are the Bail Report Cover Sheet and the report page (yellow copy) from the recognizance form approved by the Court pursuant to G.L. c. 276, § 65. They are attached hereto and included by reference as part of these rules.

All bail magistrates on active status shall submit a report each month even if no releases have been authorized during that reporting period.

Rule 45

A bail magistrate may request to be placed on inactive status as a bail magistrate by submitting a written request for inactive status with the Office of Bail Administration. A bail magistrate on inactive status shall not be authorized to admit anyone to bail out of court. The Office of Bail Administration shall notify all police holding facilities and jails within a bail magistrate's jurisdiction of his inactive status.

A bail magistrate on inactive status may return to active status by submitting a written request to the Office of Bail Administration. A bail magistrate's inactive status will be reactivated upon acknowledgment in writing by the Office of Bail Administration. The Office of Bail Administration may require a bail magistrate to participate in training sessions before being returned to active status.

Footnote: Superior Court Rules Governing Professional Bondsmen, Rule 22

No bondsman shall become or at any time be surety in criminal cases for an amount of bail greater than the fair value of his property or the property of the company he represents, less encumbrances and liabilities, as stated in:

(a) His application for approval and registration, or

(b) If he has been required to make a statement under Rule 21, in the most recent statement so required and made.

BAIL REPORT COVER SHEET

Reports for the Month of:

_____, 19____

_____

_____

☐ C/M
☐ A/C
☐ B/C

1.   Bail Magistrate: _____

                                  (Please Print)

2.   Total Fees: $_____

3.   Total Releases Authorized: _____

     a.   Personal Recognizance: _____
     b.   Cash Bail: _____
     c.   Bail Bonds: _____

I certify that this report is a full and complete listing
of all the prisoner releases that I have authorized
during this reporting month.

Signed this _____ day of _____, 199___
under the penalties of perjury.

_____
(Person Authorized to Take Bail)

BAIL REPORT TO THE SUPERIOR COURT	COMMONWEALTH OF MASSACHUSETTS		DOCKET NUMBER

DEFENDANT'S NAME AND ADDRESS (INCLUDE ANY ALIAS) | **TERMS OF RELEASE** | **NAME AND ADDRESS OF COURT** | ← THE DEFENDANT MUST APPEAR AT THIS COURT ADDRESS ON THE DATE AND TIME SPECIFIED HEREIN ←

TERMS OF RELEASE:
- ☐ PERSONAL RECOGNIZANCE (Promise to Appear) $_____
- ☐ BAIL
  - ☐ CASH AS SURETY $_____
  - ☐ BOND AS SURETY $_____
  - ☐ OTHER SURETY $_____ (Please Specify)

DATE AND TIME OF APPEARANCE
_____ AT _____
DATE   TIME
☐ A.M. ☐ P.M.

SOCIAL SECURITY NUMBER | **DATE OF BIRTH**

SURETY/SURETIES NAME AND ADDRESS | **ARREST ON WARRANT** ☐ YES ☐ NO | **OFFENSE(S)**

I, as defendant, charged by complaint with the crime(s) listed above, understand that I am being released from custody according to the terms of release specified. I will personally appear before the above named court at the date and time indicated, and I will appear for any continuance until the final decree, sentence or order, and I will abide by it and not depart without leave. Further, I will appear before any court to which the charges may be transferred or appealed, or to any sitting of the Superior Court to which I may be bound over or indicted to answer to any indictment, and I will appear for any continuance until the final decree, sentence or order, and I will abide by it and not depart without leave.

I understand and acknowledge that if I fail without sufficient excuse to appear in accordance with the foregoing promise, I will be liable, jointly and severally if a surety has been required, to the Commonwealth of Massachusetts for the dollar amount specified in the terms of release.

SIGNED (DEFENDANT) X | **DATE**

I, as surety, understand and acknowledge that if the above named defendant fails to appear and abide by all orders of the court according to the foregoing promise, I will be liable, jointly and severally, with the defendant to the Commonwealth of Massachusetts for the dollar amount specified in the terms of release.

SIGNED (SURETY) X | **SIGNED (SURETY)** X

SIGNED (PERSON AUTHORIZED TO TAKE BAIL) X
☐ Clerk-Magistrate
☐ Assistant Clerk
☐ Bail Commissioner
Subscribed and sworn to before me, the defendant having been furnished a copy of this recognizance.

A. RELEASE AUTHORIZED FROM

B. JURISDICTION OF MAGISTRATE (Complete when appearance is being required outside of your jurisdiction)

BAIL FEE RECEIVED $_____

DATE AND TIME SIGNED ☐ A.M. ☐ P.M.

Notice to person taking bail or releasing on personal recognizance: Please complete the following information before submitting this copy to the Chief Justice of the Superior Court.

PLACE WHERE BAIL TAKEN	RELEASE TERMS SET BY	NAME AND ADDRESS OF AGENT FOR SURETY COMPANY	IS SURETY REGISTERED AT SUPERIOR COURT? ☐ YES ☐ NO
SUMMONED TO PLACE OF DETENTION BY	HOW SUMMONED?	OTHER SECURITY TAKEN BY SURETY	FEE OF SURETY

I certify that I have not received anything of value from anyone in addition to my fee for setting and or taking this bail. Subscribed and sworn to under the pains and penalty of perjury. | **SIGNED (PERSON AUTHORIZED TO TAKE BAIL)** X

RECEIPT-RECORD OF PAYMENT OF CASH BAIL ☐ NOT APPLICABLE

DATE	RECEIVED FROM SURETY (NAME AND ADDRESS)	DEFENDANT	AMOUNT
		CASE NUMBER	DISTRICT COURT

RECEIVED BY

DC-CR-S (6/95)
SC-1

SUPERIOR COURT COPY

GUIDELINES FOR PROBATION VIOLATION PROCEEDINGS IN THE SUPERIOR COURT

Effective February 1, 2016

Section One: Scope and Purpose

These guidelines prescribe procedures in the Superior Court to be followed upon the allegation of a violation of an order or condition of probation imposed in a criminal case after a finding of guilty or after a continuance without a finding. These guidelines do not apply to an alleged violation of pretrial probation or other conditions of pretrial release.

The purpose of the guidelines is to ensure that judicial proceedings undertaken on an allegation of a violation of probation are conducted in accordance with applicable law, and in a prompt, uniform and consistent manner.

Section Two: Definitions

In construing these guidelines, the following terms shall have the following meanings:

"Continuance without a finding" means the order of a court, following a formal submission and acceptance of a plea of guilty upon the defendant's agreement to the Commonwealth's evidence or a finding of sufficient facts, whereby a criminal case is continued to a date certain without formal entry of a guilty finding.[1] A court, in imposing a continuance without a finding, may include a term of probation with conditions, the violation of which may result in a revocation of the continuance and the entry of a finding of guilty and imposition of sentence.

"District Attorney" means the criminal prosecuting authority responsible for the criminal case in which a term of probation was imposed, to include the Attorney General.

"General conditions of probation" means those conditions of probation that are imposed as a matter of course in every probation order, as set forth in the official form promulgated for such orders.

"Notice of Surrender" means the written form issued by the Probation Department alleging a violation of probation and setting forth the precise grounds for a violation proceeding.

"Probation order" means the formal, written court order whereby a defendant is placed on probation and which expressly sets forth general and/or special conditions of probation.

"Pretrial Probation" means the probationary status of a defendant pursuant to a probation order issued prior to an adjudication of a criminal case.

"Revocation of probation" means the revocation of a probation order by a judge following an adjudication of a violation of a probation order.

"Special condition of probation" means any condition of probation imposed by a judge as part of a probation order in addition to general conditions of probation.

"Stipulation to violation" means a knowing and voluntary admission by a probationer that he/she has violated the probation order as alleged in the Notice of Surrender.

"Surrender" means the procedure, consistent with the instant Guidelines, by which a probation officer requires a probationer to appear before the court on an allegation of probation violation.

Section Three: Commencement of Violation Proceedings

A. Procedure. Violation Proceedings shall commence upon the filing, by a probation officer, of a written Notice of Surrender.[2] A Notice of Surrender shall be prepared in advance of Violation Proceedings except where the probationer has been arrested by the probation officer in accordance with G. L. c. 279, § 3, in which case the Notice of Surrender shall be prepared, filed with the court, and served on the probationer when the probationer first appears before the court. The Notice of Surrender shall be in a form promulgated by the Probation Department and shall identify the probationer by name, the offense or offenses for which the probationer was placed on probation, and the court and county where the offense was adjudicated and probation imposed. It shall specifically describe the basis for an alleged violation, shall include all alleged violations of the probation order known to the probation officer, and shall notify the probationer of the date and time of the Initial Hearing in the probation court.

B. Mandatory Commencement of Violation Proceedings. The probation officer shall issue a Notice of Surrender (1) when a probationer has been charged with a new criminal offense by way of complaint or indictment; (2) where the judge issuing the probation order directed that a Notice of Surrender is to issue upon any alleged violation of one or more conditions of probation; or (3) when the commencement of such proceedings is required by statute.

C. Discretionary Commencement of Violation Proceedings. Except as set forth above, the probation officer may issue a Notice of Surrender for an alleged violation of a general and/or special condition of probation if, in the discretion of the Probation Department, the alleged violation is unlikely to be successfully resolved through an administrative hearing or other intermediate interventions.

D. Amendment and Withdrawal. A Notice of Surrender may be amended at any reasonable time before a final surrender hearing, provided service is made in accordance with these guidelines. A Notice of Surrender may be withdrawn only with leave of court, provided, however, that a judge or magistrate may order the termination of the proceedings at any time in the exercise of discretion, after giving the Probation Department an opportunity to be heard.

Section Four: Service of a Notice of Surrender

A Notice of Surrender shall be served on the probationer by in-hand service or by first-class mail to the last known residential address that the probationer has provided to his probation officer. When a probationer is brought before the court where the probationer is under supervision as the result of his arrest by the probation officer pursuant to G. L. c. 279, § 3, or is in custody as the result of a separate criminal case, service shall be made in-hand and an initial hearing conducted. The manner of service of the Notice of Surrender shall be noted in the court docket. Out-of-court service other than by first-class mail shall require a written return of service. Where a probationer appears on a new criminal offense in a court other than the court that imposed or is supervising the probationer, the issuance and service of a Notice of Surrender shall be governed by Section Seven, Special Provisions For Commencement of Violation Proceedings based on a New Criminal Offense.

Section Five: Initial Violation Hearing

Except for good cause, an Initial Violation Hearing shall be scheduled not later than fourteen days after the issuance of a Notice of Surrender. Upon the probationer's initial appearance before the probation court based on the issuance of a Notice of Surrender, a judge or magistrate shall confirm that the probationer has received the written Notice of Surrender, shall appoint counsel in the event the probationer is indigent and the offense for which probation was imposed has a potential penalty of incarceration, shall schedule a date and time for a final Violation Hearing, and shall determine whether the probationer should be detained pending a final hearing, or whether bail or release on personal recognizance (with or without conditions) should be imposed.[3] The probationer shall have the right to counsel at the time any detention, bail or release determination is made. Nothing herein shall preclude a court, utilizing a HOPE/MORR model of probation supervision, from detaining a probationer for a discrete period of time in accordance with that model.

A probationer shall not be detained pending a final Violation Hearing unless a judge or magistrate finds probable cause to believe that the probationer has violated a condition of his probation.[4] A probationer shall be entitled upon request to a preliminary violation hearing, to be held not more than seven days after the initial appearance, unless the probationer consents to a later date. The issues to be determined at such hearing are whether probable cause exists to believe that the probationer has violated a condition of the probation order, and if so, whether the probationer should continue to be held on bail or without right to bail. Where the violation is based on the issuance of an indictment for a new criminal offense, the indictment shall constitute proof of probable cause.[5] The hearing shall be conducted by a judge or magistrate in open court and shall be recorded. At such hearing the probation officer shall present evidence to support a finding of probable cause, and the probationer or his counsel shall be entitled to be heard in opposition. The District Attorney may, upon request of the probation officer, assist the probation officer in the presentation of evidence. If probable cause is found, a final violation hearing shall be scheduled by the court and the probationer shall be given notice in open court of the final hearing date. If probable cause is not found, the judge or magistrate may terminate the proceedings or may schedule a final hearing, but the probationer shall not be held in custody pending the final hearing.

Section Six: Final Violation Hearing

A. Scheduling the Hearing. A final Violation Hearing shall be scheduled not earlier than seven days after the Initial Violation Hearing unless the probationer assents to an earlier hearing, and not later than thirty days thereafter unless good cause is shown. Where the probation surrender involves an alleged commission of a new criminal offense, a continuance to permit resolution of the case involving such new offense shall not ordinarily constitute good cause.[6]

B. Adjudicatory Determination. A final violation hearing shall consist of two parts: (1) an evidentiary hearing to adjudicate whether the alleged violation has occurred; and (2) upon a finding of violation, a dispositional hearing. The probationer shall be entitled to the assistance of counsel, but may waive counsel upon a determination by the court that such waiver is made knowingly and voluntarily.

The probation officer shall have the burden of proving that a probationer has violated one or more conditions of probation by a preponderance of evidence. At the request of a probation officer, or when required by G. L. c. 279, § 3, the District Attorney may participate in the presentation of evidence or examination of witnesses. Hearsay evidence shall be admissible at a Violation Hearing as permitted under Sections 802 through 804 of the Massachusetts Guide to Evidence, or when determined by the judge to be substantially reliable.[7] The probationer shall have the right to cross examine any witnesses called by the probation officer, including the probation officer; the right to call witnesses; the right to present evidence favorable to the probationer; the right to testify; and the right to make closing argument on the issue of whether a violation has been proved by a preponderance of evidence.

The court may accept a probationer's stipulation to a violation of probation as alleged in the Notice of Surrender if the judge finds after colloquy that the probationer is tendering a knowing and voluntary stipulation. However, the court shall not be bound by any agreement between the probationer and probation officer or District Attorney regarding the disposition to be imposed. A probationer shall not be entitled, as a matter of right, to withdraw a stipulation after it has been accepted by the court.

Upon the completion of the evidence and closing arguments, the court shall promptly determine whether a violation of probation has been proved by a preponderance of evidence. If the court finds that no violation has been proved, the probationer shall be restored to probation according to the terms and conditions previously imposed. If the court finds that a violation has been proved the judge shall make findings on the record as to the condition or conditions that have been violated and the facts found in making the determination.[8]

C. Dispositional Determination. Upon a finding that the probationer has violated one or more conditions of probation, the judge shall permit the probation officer and probationer, and where required by statute, the District Attorney, to make a recommendation regarding the appropriate sanction to be imposed by the court. Thereafter, the court shall impose a disposition based on the circumstances of the crime for which the probationer was placed on probation and its impact on any person or on the community, the occurrence of any prior violations of probation, the probationer's overall performance while on probation, the public safety, the effect of a sentence on the probationer's chances for rehabilitation, and any other mitigating or aggravating facts or circumstances. The court may consider information that was available to the judge who issued the probation order as well as information that has become available since the order was issued. The court, however, may not punish the probationer for criminal conduct which forms the basis of the violation.[9] The court may: (1) restore the probationer to his existing probationary term with such admonition or instruction as it may deem appropriate; (2) terminate the probation order and discharge the probationer; (3) extend the term of probation and modify the terms or conditions of probation; or (4) revoke probation in whole or in part.[10] Where probation is revoked on an offense for which a sentence had been imposed, the execution of which was suspended, the original sentence shall be ordered executed forthwith,[11] subject to a stay granted pending an appeal in accordance with Mass. R. Crim. P. 31, or at the court's discretion upon a probationer's request for a brief period of time to attend to personal affairs prior to the commencement of a sentence of incarceration. In the event probation is revoked on an offense for which no suspended sentence had previously been imposed, the court shall impose a sentence or other disposition as provided by law.[12]

Upon a finding of a violation of a probation order resulting from a continuance without a finding, the judge may terminate the probation order and the continuance without a finding and enter a dismissal on the underlying case, return the probationer to the same terms and conditions of probation with such admonitions or instructions as the judge deems appropriate, modify the continuance without a finding and modify the conditions of probation including the duration of the continuance, or terminate the continuance without a finding and enter a guilty finding and impose a sentence or other disposition as provided by law.

Section Seven: Special Provisions For Commencement of Violation Proceedings based on a New Criminal Offense.

Whenever a person on probation is charged with a new criminal offense, the probation officer in the criminal court where the new offense is pending ("criminal court") shall immediately notify the Probation Department in the court where the person is subject to probation supervision ("probation court"). Said notification shall be made in accordance with policies of the Commissioner of Probation, or any policy, administrative order or standing order of the Chief Justice of the Trial Court. In order to comply with the mandatory provisions of Section 3(B), the chief probation officer or his designee in the probation court may order the issuance of a

Notice of Surrender in the form set forth herein, to be served on the probationer by a probation officer in the criminal court, ordering the probationer to appear for an Initial Violation Hearing in the probation court at a fixed date and time.

Alternatively, the chief probation officer or his designee in the probation court may also seek the issuance of a warrant from the probation court pursuant to G.L. c. 279, § 3. In the event a warrant issued by the probation court is lodged at the criminal court or, where the probationer has been held in detention or in lieu of posted bail at a jail or house of correction, the clerk of the probation court shall, upon request, promptly issue process to bring the probationer before the probation court for an Initial Violation Hearing.

Adopted effective February 1, 2016.

1 *Commonwealth v. Powell*, 453 Mass. 320 (2009); G.L. c. 278, § 18.

2 *Commonwealth v. Wilcox*, 446 Mass. 61, 66 (2006); *Commonwealth v. Durling*, 407 Mass. 108, 111 (1990)("When a violation is alleged, the probation officer "surrenders" the defendant to the court, subjecting the defendant to possible revocation of his probation.")

3 No authority explicitly establishes that bail either may or may not be set in probation violation proceedings. But see *Commonwealth v. Ward*, 15 Mass. App. Ct. 388, 393 (1983); *Rubera v. Commonwealth*, 371 Mass. 177, 184 n.3 (1976) (both suggesting that the setting of bail is appropriate).

4 *Fay v. Commonwealth*, 379 Mass. 498, 504 (1980)(right to a hearing before detention pending a final hearing is ordered); *Commonwealth v. Odoardi*, 397 Mass. 28, 33 (1986).

5 *Stefanik v. State Board of Parole*, 372 Mass. 726 (1977).

6 The practice of a probation surrender proceeding "tracking" a new criminal case is discouraged by these guidelines. However, a judge or magistrate may decide that good cause exists to permit tracking, for example, when the new criminal case is particularly complex or sensitive, such that providing discovery or presenting evidence at a final hearing could compromise the integrity of the new case. Such a determination shall be made in open court and entered on the record.

7 *Commonwealth v. Durling*, 407 Mass. 108, 114–118 (1990); *Morrissey v. Brewer*, 408 U.S. 471, 489 (1972); *Gagnon v. Scarpelli*, 411 U.S. 778, 782 n.5 (1973).

8 *Fay v. Commonwealth*, 379 Mass. 498, 504–505 (1980)(findings of fact not required to be in writing provided that they are made and announced on the record in the probationer's presence).

9 *Commonwealth v. Doucette*, 81 Mass. App. Ct. 740, 745 (2012); *Commonwealth v. Rodriguez*, 52 Mass. App. Ct. 572, 577 n.8 (2001).

10 A partial revocation of probation occurs where the probationer has been placed on probation on multiple offenses and the court revokes probation and imposes a sentence as to one or more offenses, and continues probation as to other offenses, typically to run from and after the committed sentence.

11 *Commonwealth v. Holmgren*, 421 Mass. 224 (1995); see also, *Commonwealth v. Bruzese*, 437 Mass. 606 (2002)(where defendant was subject to multiple suspended sentences as part of a single sentencing structure, revoking probation on less than all charges violates double jeopardy principles)

12 A sentence imposed upon the finding of a violation shall not be imposed as punishment for any new crime, but rather as punishment for the offense(s) on which probation was imposed. *Commonwealth v. Odoardi*, 397 Mass. 28, 30 (1986). However, a judge may consider the conduct alleged in the new offense on the issue of the probationer's capacity for rehabilitation.

GUIDELINES FOR APPELLATE DIVISION PROCEEDINGS
(G.L. c. 278 §§ 28A–D)

The following practices, procedures and protocol will be followed in hearings conducted before the Appellate Division of the Superior Court (Division):

1. Date, Place and Time. The Division will convene on the first Mondays of May and November, and sit from day to day thereafter in those months until its current business has been completed. Unless otherwise designated by the Chief Justice, such hearing will take place in the County of Norfolk, at Dedham. Each daily session of the Division will commence promptly at 10:00 A.M. The hearings conducted by the Division shall be open to the public. Counsel will observe the usual courtroom protocol when addressing the justices of the Division.

2. (a) *Procedure.* The presiding justice will advise the defendant as to the nature of the proceedings and the jurisdiction and powers of the Division. The Division Clerk will then read the sentence(s) to be reviewed. The attorney for the defendant will then address the justices, followed by the district attorney. It shall be discretionary with the justices in each case whether to permit any statement by the defendant or the victim(s) (or representative thereof).

(b) *Probation Department.* The Probation Department will provide each of the justices with the following: (1) an Information Sheet, substantially in the form of, and containing the data set forth in Exhibit "A" attached hereto; and (2) Probation Intake Sheet; (3) Presentence Investigation Report; (4) any other social and background history, if supplied to the sentencing judge; (5) the Sentencing Guidelines, if available to or used by the sentencing judge. If a co-defendant was sentenced, a copy of the criminal record of the co-defendant will be of assistance to the Division.

(c) *District Attorney.* The district attorney will provide each of the justices with the following: (1) an Information Sheet substantially in the form of, and containing the data set forth in Exhibit "B" attached hereto; (2) a statement attached to the Information Sheet, setting forth the factual background of the case, a synopsis of the essential trial evidence, and the Commonwealth's view as to the appropriateness of the sentence(s) imposed; and (3) victim impact statement. The district attorney will make a copy of the statement specified in (2) above available to the attorney for the defendant seasonably before the hearing.

(d) *Counsel.*

(1) Trial Counsel. It is desirable that trial (or plea) counsel appear before the Division. Similarly, it is expected that the assistant district attorney who prosecuted the case will appear for the Commonwealth. The Division construes Mass.R.Crim.P. 7(c) ["An appearance (by an attorney) shall constitute a representation that the attorney shall represent the defendant for trial or plea . . ."] to include by necessary implication all of the dispositional aspects of a criminal case in the Superior Court including a review of sentence by the Division, whose proceedings are merely an extension of the earlier Superior Court disposition after trial or plea.

(2) Successor Counsel. If trial (plea) counsel for the defendant or the trial prosecutor does not appear before the Division, the defendant's attorney or district attorney who does appear shall consult with trial counsel or the trial prosecutor, as the case may be, so as to be fully informed as to all essential elements of the background of the sentence.

(3) Withdrawals. A motion for withdrawal of an appearance by an attorney for the defendant is to be filed with the Division Clerk, and not with the County Clerk-Magistrate.

(4) Continuances. A motion to continue to another session shall be in writing and seasonably filed with the Division Clerk. Normally, a motion seeking a continuance will be entertained only upon personal appearance of the attorney so moving, and oral argument.

(5) Conflicting Engagements. A prospective conflict in court engagements of defense counsel should be addressed and resolved before the date scheduled for hearing of the appeal of sentence so that counsel may be present and proceed promptly when that matter is reached on the daily hearing list. Counsel should immediately communicate with the Division Clerk when counsel learns that, for a substantial reason, counsel will be unavoidably delayed or unable to attend as scheduled.

3. Transcripts. Sentencing Memoranda. Where feasible, the Division will expect an official transcript of the sentencing proceedings. Defense counsel are encouraged to submit sentencing memoranda for the assistance of the Division.

4. Resentencing. When the defendant is returned for resentencing, it will not be mandatory for the district attorney or the probation officer to appear again before the Division. It will be expected that the attorney for the defendant will appear, to advise the defendant as to the consequences of the resentence.

5. Address. The address of the Clerk of the Division is 712 New Courthouse, Boston, MA 02108 (Tel.: 725–8165).

EXHIBIT A

PROBATION DEPARTMENT INFORMATION FOR THE APPELLATE DIVISION OF THE SUPERIOR COURT

NAME:

AGE:

DATE OF BIRTH:

BIRTHPLACE:

MARITAL STATUS:

CHILDREN:

EDUCATION:

AGE AT LEAVING SCHOOL:

LAST SCHOOL ATTENDED:

MILITARY HISTORY:

HEALTH HISTORY:

FINANCES:

LAST OCCUPATION:

EMPLOYMENT HISTORY:

PAROLE ELIGIBILITY DATE:

SENTENCING GUIDELINES USED BY OR MADE AVAILABLE TO SENTENCING JUDGE? YES: _____ NO: _____   (IF SO, COPY ATTACHED).

CO–DEFENDANT(S):

SENTENCE(S):

PRIOR CRIMINAL RECORD (ATTACHED).

EXHIBIT B

DISTRICT ATTORNEY'S INFORMATION SHEET FOR THE APPELLATE DIVISION OF THE SUPERIOR COURT

OFFENSE(S):

TRIAL JUDGE:

JURY TRIAL: ___; BENCH TRIAL: ___; PLEA: ___

AGREED RECOMMENDATION AS TO SENTENCE? YES ___ NO ___

COMMONWEALTH'S SENTENCE RECOMMENDATION(S):

SENTENCE(S) IMPOSED:

SIGNIFICANT PORTIONS OF DEFENDANT'S CRIMINAL HISTORY:

OTHER FACTORS PERTINENT TO SENTENCE APPEAL:

FACTUAL BACKGROUND AND EVIDENTIARY FACTS WHICH WERE PRESENTED AT TRIAL (to be Attached):

STANDING ORDERS OF THE SUPERIOR COURT

Table of Standing Orders

Standing Order 1–80. Notices of Appeal— Notification to Justices [Rescinded]

Rescinded September 2, 2014, effective December 1, 2014.

Standing Order 5–80. Trial Session Hours [Rescinded]

Rescinded September 2, 2014, effective December 1, 2014.

Standing Order 6–80. Complaints for Judicial Review of Surcharge Matters Under G.L. c. 175, § 113P; Notice to the Department of the Attorney General; Form Complaints [Rescinded]

Rescinded September 2, 2014, effective December 1, 2014.

Standing Order 9–80. Requests for Special Assignment of Justices to Civil Actions

Amended

(Applicable to All Counties)

APPLICABLE TO ALL CIVIL ACTIONS

In order to facilitate and clarify the orderly processing of requests by counsel for assignment of certain civil actions to a justice to be specially designated for pre-trial or trial proceedings or both, it is hereby **ORDERED** that the following uniform procedure is to be employed:

1. Definition. The term "party" shall mean the attorney of record for a party, if represented by counsel, or, if the party is not represented by an attorney, the party acting *pro se*.

2. If all of the parties agree that a particular civil action should be specially assigned to a justice of the Superior Court, designated by the Chief Justice of the Superior Court, they shall jointly complete and execute a "Request for Special Assignment of a Justice" in the form annexed hereto marked "Request *A*." Request *A* shall in each instance be accompanied by a copy of the current docket entries.

3. If a party (but not all of the parties) desires such a special assignment, the party(ies) seeking the assignment shall complete and execute a "Request for Special Assignment of a Justice" in the form annexed hereto marked "Request *B*." Request *B* shall in each instance be accompanied by a copy of the current docket entries.

4. Request *A*, fully completed, shall be submitted by the parties to the Chief Justice for his/her consideration and action thereon.

5. Request *B*, fully completed, shall be submitted by the requesting party(ies) to the Chief Justice for his/her consideration and action thereon. The submitting party(ies) shall notify all nonassenting parties of the submission to the Chief Justice; nonassenting parties will have **seven days from receipt** of the Request to submit a letter to the Chief Justice in opposition to the Request succinctly stating the grounds for the opposition thereto. Additionally, nonassenting parties may also recommend judges who would be acceptable for the special assignment should the request be approved by the Chief Justice.

6. Even if all parties have agreed, in his/her discretion the Chief Justice may require a conference with the parties before taking action on a Request. If so, the parties will be notified seasonably of time and place.

7. The Chief Justice will notify all parties of his/her decision on each Request submitted, and, if allowed, of the identity of the justice specially appointed.

This standing order supercedes Standing Order 9–80 dated August 25, 1988.

Adopted December 1, 1980. Amended August 25, 1988, effective October 1, 1988; amended January 17, 2000, effective February 28, 2000.

REQUEST A

COMMONWEALTH OF MASSACHUSETTS

————, ss.　　　　　**SUPERIOR COURT
CIVIL ACTION
NO.**

————————

vs

————————

JOINT REQUEST FOR SPECIAL ASSIGNMENT

[*Pursuant to Standing Order No. 9–80, as Amended*]

All of the parties to the above-entitled action jointly request that this case be assigned to a justice of the Superior Court to be specially designated by the Chief Justice to conduct proceedings herein. **A copy of the current docket entries is attached hereto.**

1. List **all** parties (including third-parties) and counsel of record.

Plaintiffs	Counsel
————————	————————
————————	————————

Defendants	Counsel
————————	————————
————————	————————

2. Please provide a brief description of the case.

---

3. Why should this case be specially assigned Are there any novel issues or questions of law? What is the expected length of the trial?

4. Counsel (parties) have conferred and all agree that the following judges would be acceptable for this special assignment [1]:

　1. ————————　　2. ————————
　3. ————————　　4. ————————
　5. ————————　　6. ————————

————————————　　————————————
————————————　　————————————

(Counsel for) All Plaintiffs　　(Counsel for) All Defendants

Dated:

[1] It is understood that the Chief Justice reserves the right, however, to designate <u>any</u> justice of the court.

REQUEST B

COMMONWEALTH OF MASSACHUSETTS

————, ss.　　　　　**SUPERIOR COURT
CIVIL ACTION
NO.**

————————

vs

————————

REQUEST (NON–JOINT) FOR SPECIAL ASSIGNMENT

[*Pursuant to Standing Order No. 9–80, as Amended*]

The following parties to the above-entitled action request that this case be assigned to a justice of the Superior Court to be specially designated by the Chief Justice to conduct the proceedings herein. **A copy of the current docket entries is attached hereto.**

1. List **all** parties (including third-parties) and counsel of record.

Plaintiffs	Counsel
————————	————————
————————	————————

Defendants	Counsel
————————	————————
————————	————————

2. Please provide a brief description of the case.

3. Why should this case be specially assigned? Are there any novel issues or questions of law? What is the expected length of the trial?

4. List the names of <u>all</u> parties opposing this request:

5. The requesting party suggests that the following judges would be acceptable for this special assignment [1]:

     1. _____   2. _____
     3. _____   4. _____
     5. _____   6. _____

     _____

     _____

         Attorneys for the requesting party(ies)

Dated:

Standing Order 1–81. Periodic Review, Call and Processing of Certain Non–Jury Civil Actions [Rescinded]

Rescinded effective October 4, 2010.

Standing Order 2–81. Periodic Review, Call and Processing of Certain Civil Actions With Jury Claims [Rescinded]

Rescinded effective October 4, 2010.

Standing Order 4–81. Pending Criminal Cases Subject to Dismissal Pursuant to the Provisions of Mass.R.Crim.P. 36 [Rescinded]

Rescinded effective October 4, 2010.

Standing Order 5–81. Uniform Procedures Regarding Petitions for Abortion Authorization Under G.L. c. 112, § 12S, Including Suggested Guidelines Originally Set Forth in *Planned Parenthood League of Massachusetts v. Bellotti*, No. 81–124 Civil (Supreme Judicial Court for Suffolk County; Liacos, J. Single Justice) (June 16, 1981)

Applicable to All Counties

(1) Upon the filing of a petition under G.L. c. 112, § 12S, the Clerk of Courts or Clerk–Magistrate (clerk) shall immediately bring the matter to the attention of the judge in any session assigned to hear emergency civil matters, or to the Regional Administrative Justice or designee, who will either hear the petition or, through the clerk, assign it for a hearing in another session.

The matter shall be given priority over all other cases then pending so "that the court may reach a decision promptly and without delay so as to serve the best interests of the pregnant woman." G. L. c. 112, § 12S. In this regard, a judge should not decline to decide a case brought under § 12S because of any pleading omissions or other technical defects. The Administrative Office of the Superior Court shall provide a form petition and form affidavit, to be available on the Trial Court's public website and in all clerks' offices for easy access by petitioners and their counsel.

If the petition is filed in a county in which no session is being held, the clerk who received the petition shall immediately notify the Regional Administrative Justice or the Administrative Office of the Superior Court by telephone of the pending petition. The Regional Administrative Justice or the Administrative Office of the Superior Court shall then take such action as is necessary to assign the petition for prompt hearing in a location accessible to the petitioner, so as to serve the best interests of the pregnant woman.

(2) The court shall appoint counsel for any petitioner who appears without counsel and requests representation, and shall waive costs and fees upon request, as provided by St. 1980, c. 539.

The court may appoint a guardian ad litem to represent the minor or may make such other orders as necessary pursuant to Mass. R. Civ. P. 17(b), but shall take care to avoid any delay that may result from such orders, and to ensure prompt determination of the petition.

(3) As provided by § 12S, all proceedings shall be confidential. All papers, other than the affidavit referred to herein, shall be designated anonymously in the name of Mary Moe. An affidavit bearing the minor's true name and her signature shall accompany the petition, and shall be kept in a sealed envelope or other container, identifiable by the docket number of the petition. All papers, recordings, transcripts, and any other records of the proceeding shall be impounded.

Each clerk shall undertake to insure that the minor's contact with the clerk's office is confidential and expeditious to the fullest extent practicable. For example, assistance in filing a petition should be provided in a confidential setting, such as a private office. Similarly, one or more persons in the clerk's office should be available at all times to answer questions asked by a minor or her counsel, either in person or by phone, and to assist the minor or her counsel in expeditiously presenting her petition to the court. Each clerk shall designate one or more persons to receive and process § 12S petitions, and shall ensure that one such person is available to ensure prompt treatment.

(4) All proceedings under § 12S, shall be conducted in the judge's lobby or other private setting, and shall be recorded electronically by means of a portable electronic recording device. In accord with the statute, the judge shall make specific factual findings and legal conclusions supporting the decision in writing, and shall order that the record of the proceeding, including the judge's findings and conclusions, be

maintained. The Administrative Office of the Superior Court shall provide a standard form for the making of such findings and order, which shall be available to all judges.

(5) Suggested guidelines, originally emanating from a memorandum of the Single Justice of the Supreme Judicial Court for Suffolk County in *Planned Parenthood League of Massachusetts v. Bellotti*, No. 81–124 Civil (Supreme Judicial Court for Suffolk County; Liacos, J. Single Justice) (June 16, 1981), are attached hereto.

Adopted July 31, 1981, effective August 1, 1981. Amended August 25, 1988, effective October 1, 1988; January 6, 2020, effective February 1, 2020.

SUGGESTED GUIDELINES

The following guidelines for handling § 12S petitions ("petitions"') are suggested to the Superior Court. These guidelines are intended to supplement amended Superior Court Standing Order No. 5–81 and not to replace it.

1. Petitions should ordinarily be heard on any day the court is in session.

2. Petitions should be heard as expeditiously as possible upon filing with the Clerk/Magistrate's office, and on the same day if practical.

3. All technical defects in the proceedings and in the pleadings and papers should ordinarily be disregarded by the Court and by the Clerk/Magistrate.

4. Hearings must be confidential and should be held in the judge's lobby except where physically impossible. The petitioner ('minor') should be permitted to have present any person she desires (social worker, counselor, parent, friend), but the judge should exclude all unnecessary court personnel or others. The minor should be free to choose whether to go forward without counsel.

5. The minor should not be required to state her true name. After explaining the impoundment procedures used to ensure confidentiality, the judge may wish to ask the minor her true first name in order to address her by it during the hearing. The transcript should not contain the minor's full true name since she will have previously stated her identity on a sealed affidavit held by the Clerk/Magistrate pursuant to Superior Court Standing Order 12–80.

6. It is contemplated that the judge will conduct the hearing on a 'two-tier' basis with 'maturity' determined first, and 'best interest' addressed only if maturity is not found.

7. As to the 'maturity' finding, inquiry may be appropriate in such areas as the minor's age and school and work experience, any history of mental illness or other treatment relating to mental competence, and whether the abortion decision is a personal decision and not one forced upon the minor by another and whether the minor has discussed her decision with other persons. In any inquiry as to the minor's maturity and her understanding of the nature, consequences and significance of her abortion choice, or in any inquiry as to her best interests, it is suggested that the judge should avoid the creation of the appearance of seeking to promote a particular set of moral values by inquiring into the minor's or her parents' views as to the morality of abortion; or into whether the minor considers a fetus to be an 'unborn child,' as to whether the minor believes she is in some way taking or destroying life.

8. Where the court finds a minor is not mature, it must make a determination of whether the abortion or childbirth alternative is in her 'best interest'. The court may be guided in making such a determination by the substantially coextensive doctrine of substituted judgment. That doctrine essentially requires a court to determine what an incompetent person would choose were she fully competent, while bearing in mind her expressed choice and partial competency. Various considerations may be relevant to a 'best interest' determination. As to this finding, the court may inquire into the minor's reasons for not seeking her parents' consent. Where the minor is accompanied by one parent who supports her petition, that support should be given great if not dispositive weight.

9. Where the court preliminarily concludes that the minor is mature, appointment of a guardian ad litem should ordinarily be unnecessary. Where the court preliminarily concludes that the minor is not fully mature, it should consider whether such an appointment is necessary to assure protection of the minor's best interest or whether it would lead to unnecessary delay, particularly if the minor is represented by counsel, or has been counseled by competent professionals, or is accompanied by a parent or other adult.

10. In view of the statutory mandate for expeditious decisions, petitions may be decided in chambers and should, in any event, be decided as promptly as possible, and ordinarily within twenty-four hours or less. The Clerk/Magistrate should inform the minor of the decision as soon as possible and in the manner which the minor requests.

11. The Judge or Clerk/Magistrate should give the minor a copy of an order under § 12S bearing the court's docket number, and a copy of her sealed affidavit bearing the same docket number. Where the decision can be made immediately, the Judge may choose to have the minor wait, deliver the order and a copy of the affidavit to her, and seal the original affidavit in her presence.

12. A petition should not be denied or a hearing delayed solely because the minor has not selected a particular clinic, hospital or doctor for performance of the abortion. If the judge authorizes an abortion for an immature minor on the 'best interest' basis, he may inquire into her contemplated plans in order to assure himself that the particular course of medical treatment she intends to follow will be in her best interests.

13. Appointed counsel in § 12S proceedings should be paid for in the same fashion as in criminal cases or in such other fashion as the Chief Administrative Justice of the Trial Court finds is best suited for such proceedings.

Standing Order 1–82. Chapter 231, Section 60B, of the General Laws—Medical Malpractice Action Against Provider of Health Care [Rescinded]

Rescinded November 21, 2017, effective January 1, 2018.

Standing Order 1–83.   Civil Action Cover Sheets

Applicable to All Counties

In order to facilitate court case data collection and the transfer procedure in the Superior Court Department in the several counties of the Commonwealth pursuant to G.L. c. 231, s. 102C and Rule 29 of the Superior Court Department (1974) as amended, it is hereby ORDERED that:

1.   The Clerk–Magistrate of the Superior Court Department in each county shall make available a "Civil Action Cover Sheet".   Form MTC 002 shall be used for that purpose.

2.   The Clerk–Magistrate not accept for filing any Complaint or other Pleading (hereafter "Complaint") which commences a civil action unless accompanied by a Civil Action Cover Sheet completed and signed by the attorney or pro se party filing such pleading.

3.   The Clerk–Magistrate, however, is authorized to accept for filing a Complaint without a Civil Action Cover Sheet submitted therewith if the Clerk–Magistrate is satisfied by representation of the offering counsel or pro se party, by averments in the Complaint, or otherwise, that the Statute of Limitations will run before the filing of the Civil Action Cover Sheet can be accomplished.   In such event, the Civil Action Cover Sheet shall be filed within ten (10) days thereafter.

4.   Failure to file the Civil Action Cover Sheet within that time will result in the imposition by the court of sanctions in the form of costs.

5.   The Clerk–Magistrate is further directed to report periodically, in writing, to the Administrative Justice of the Superior Court Department, actions in which there has been a failure to comply with the notice to file a Civil Action Cover Sheet.

6.   The Clerk–Magistrate is authorized to rely upon the representations contained in a Civil Action Cover Sheet as to the amount of damages claimed or expected in determining whether to transfer civil actions to the District Court Department.   The Clerk–Magistrate is further authorized to transfer to the District Court Department any Civil Action in which the Clerk–Magistrate finds that there is a willful failure to comply with the notice to file a Civil Action Cover Sheet.

Adopted December 1, 1983.

Standing Order 2–84.   Revocation of Standing Orders Nos. 2–78 and 3–78

Applicable to Civil Actions Pending in Suffolk County

Effective August 31, 1984, Standing Order No. 2–78 (Modification of Practice and Procedure as to Objection to and Revocation of Orders of Transfer) and Standing Order No. 3–78 (Modification of Transfer Procedure Pursuant to Rule 29 of the Rules of the Superior Court Department [1974], as amended) are hereby revoked.

Adopted effective August 31, 1984.

Standing Order 3–84.   Procedure in the Room List Session, Courtroom 6B, Middlesex County Only [Rescinded]

Rescinded effective October 4, 2010.

Standing Order 1–86.   Transfer Procedure Under G.L. c. 231, s. 102C and Superior Court Rule 29 [Rescinded]

Rescinded September 2, 2014, effective December 1, 2014.

Standing Order 2–86.   Criminal Case Management

[Applicable to All Counties to cases initiated by indictment on or after September 8, 2009.]

I.

PURPOSES

To improve procedures in criminal cases in the Superior Court.

To promote uniformity in practice throughout the Commonwealth.

To insure compliance with the provisions and aims of the Rules of Criminal Procedure and Rules of the Superior Court.

To recognize that a defendant's right to speedy trial, and the public, including victims and witnesses, interest in a timely, fair and just resolution of criminal cases, is best achieved by application of uniform and consistent time standards for the conduct of criminal cases in Superior Court.

To encourage the cooperation between the court, the prosecuting attorneys and the defense bar with a view towards a just and efficient disposition of criminal cases.

To provide guidelines for application in the great majority of cases, recognizing that a judge, in the exercise of discretion, may adjust or extend time periods in individual cases to insure a defendant's right to fair trial and the effective assistance of counsel, as well as, the protection of public safety.

To identify non-trial cases at the earliest stage so as to encourage their timely disposition with consequent savings of public and private resources.

II.

ARRAIGNMENTS

Arraignment will ordinarily take place in the first session by the judge presiding in that session, except in such counties utilizing a magistrate session pursuant to G. L. c. 221, §§ 62B and 62C in which case arraignment shall occur before the magistrate, or in a room list session in such counties utilizing a room list system for the assignment of cases.

An arraignment in Superior Court shall be conducted according to Mass. R. Crim. P. 7.   After entry of the defendant's plea to the charges, the judge or magistrate shall schedule dates for a mandatory pre-trial conference and a mandatory pre-trial hearing, the latter to occur within 90 days of arraignment for an "A" track case, 135 days of arraignment for a "B" track case, and 180 days of arraignment for a "C" track case.

At arraignment, the clerk shall issue a Notice of Presumptive Track Designation in the form of a Scheduling Order, setting forth dates at or before which certain events shall occur. The presumptive track designation shall be determined based solely on the lead indictment or charge unless a judge, for good cause shown, determines that a different track designation shall apply. In addition, the judge or clerk shall set forth dates for the filing and hearing of discovery motions and shall set a date for the filing of the Certificate of Compliance under Mass. R. Crim. P. 14(a)(3).

III.

CASE TRACK DESIGNATIONS

Cases shall be assigned a presumptive case track at arraignment that will establish a presumptive time period for disposition of the case. Cases shall be designated "A", "B", or "C" track cases based on the offense charged in the indictment, and on consideration of any extenuating or special circumstances raised by the parties. In the event more than one charge exists, the case track shall be the longest track determined by reference to the charges.

There shall be three criminal case tracks as follows:

"A"	"B"	"C"
Assaults and batteries (non-sexual)	Arson	Kidnapping
Breaking and entering	Embezzlement	Manslaughter
Burglary	Fraud	Murder
Civil rights offenses	Home invasion	Rape
Destruction of property	Larcenous scheme	
Firearms offenses	Robberies	
Larcenies	Sexual offenses other than rape	
Mayhem	Motor Vehicle Homicide	
Narcotics offenses (other than Trafficking/Subsequent Offenses)	Trafficking/Subsequent Offense Narcotics	
Operating under the influence		

Accessories to specific offenses, assaults with the specific intent to commit other offenses, attempts, cases carrying enhanced penalties, and conspiracies shall receive the same case track designations as provided for the underlying offenses.

The clerk shall enter the case track designation on the court's electronic docket, and shall enter the scheduled dates for pre-trial and trial proceedings in a Scheduling Order.

IV.

AUTOMATIC DISCOVERY

Automatic discovery, as defined by Mass. R. Crim. P. 14(a), shall be provided, or notice thereof given, at arraignment if possible, or thereafter at the earliest time possible, in the exercise of due diligence, in order to permit the Commonwealth and the defendant sufficient time in advance of the pretrial conference to evaluate the case and meaningfully participate in a pre-trial conference.

V.

THE PRE–TRIAL CONFERENCE

The prosecuting attorney and defense counsel shall confer prior to the scheduled pre-trial hearing in order to conference the case and to prepare a written pre-trial conference report. In accordance with Mass. R. Crim. P. 11(a), the defendant shall be available for attendance at the pre-trial conference. Further, the court may require the conference to be held at court under the supervision of a judge or magistrate. The pre-trial conference may occur on the same day as the pretrial hearing provided that the prosecution has furnished discovery to the defendant at least seven days prior to the pretrial hearing.

The parties shall discuss those matters set forth in Mass. R. Crim. P. 11(a)(1), and shall reflect the results of the conference in the written conference report filed in accordance with Mass. R. Crim. P. 11(a)(2). Counsel shall also discuss whether the case can be disposed of by means of a plea and, if so, shall propose a date for change of plea within the conference report. Except where the parties have tentatively reached an agreement to resolve the case by change of plea, counsel shall set forth within the conference report proposed dates for any anticipated pretrial events (motion filing and hearing dates, etc.) and a proposed trial date which shall be determined according to the designated case track for the lead charge of the indictment.

VI.

THE PRE–TRIAL HEARING

Counsel who are going to try the case <u>shall</u> attend the pretrial conference <u>and</u> pre-trial hearing and shall personally sign the conference report. In all cases the defendant shall be available for the pre-trial hearing in the courthouse, and shall sign the completed conference report when necessary to waive constitutional rights or when the report contains stipulations as to material facts. The conference report shall be tendered to the first session judge for his examination and approval before the clerk accepts it for filing.

The first session or room list judge shall personally meet with counsel and examine the proposed conference report so as to bring it into conformity with the spirit and language of Mass. R. Crim. P. 11. The judge shall determine the likelihood of trial, its length, and the issues in dispute. At this hearing the judge has the responsibility to foster plea negotiations within constitutional parameters and may, in her discretion, send the case to any available criminal session for a pretrial hearing, and the judge sitting in the receiving session shall conduct the pretrial hearing.

At the pre-trial hearing, the judge shall confirm the case track designation assigned at arraignment or designate a different track in accordance with Section III. In the event the parties are unable to resolve the case and seek further dates, the judge shall thereafter establish dates for the filing of any disputed motions, hearing dates, a final pre-trial conference, and a trial date. In the event that such dates are scheduled in a session other than the first or room list session, such dates shall be tentative until approved by the first session or room list judge.

VII.

FINAL CASE TRACK DESIGNATION

At the pre-trial hearing, the judge shall confirm the case track designation assigned at arraignment or designate a different track in accordance with Section III. In the event the parties are unable to resolve the case and seek further dates, the judge shall thereafter establish dates for the filing of any disputed motions, hearing dates, a final pre-trial conference, and a firm trial date. In the event that such dates are scheduled in a session other than the first session, such dates shall be tentative until approved by the first session or room list judge.

In confirming the final case track designation applicable to the case, the judge may consider whether any special circumstances exist to warrant placing the case on an alternate track. Special circumstances may be raised orally by counsel at the pre-trial hearing or may be set forth in a written submission to the court. Special circumstances include, but are not limited to: unavailability of a victim or essential witness; information relating to the victim's capacity to testify at trial within the time frame established by the case track; issues relating to a defendant's competency to stand trial or criminal responsibility; the need for a change of venue based on pretrial publicity; existence of multiple defendants; anticipated delays occasioned by necessary forensic or scientific testing (e.g. DNA testing, drug analysis of multiple samples, etc.); necessity for extended pre-trial hearings such as *Daubert/Lanigan*, *Dwyer/Lampron*, *Adjutant*, *Blaisdell*-type hearings, or similar proceedings; but not including motions to dismiss or motions to suppress statements, evidence, search warrants, or identifications. Counsel shall be afforded an opportunity to be heard regarding the existence of any special circumstance.

After consideration of special circumstances, the judge shall confirm the final case track designation applicable to the case and shall so designate on the record. Cases designated on the "A" Track shall presumptively be tried within 180 days of arraignment. Cases designated on the "B" Track shall presumptively be tried within 270 days of arraignment. Cases designated on the "C" Track shall presumptively be tried within 360 days of arraignment.

Following the court's determination of the final case track designation, the judge, in consultation with counsel, shall schedule a trial date, falling within the presumptive time periods set forth above. The judge shall also schedule dates for any contemplated pre-trial proceedings as reflected in the pre-trial conference report, and shall schedule a final pre-trial conference fourteen days prior to the assigned trial date. The selection of a trial date by trial counsel, either as reflected in the pre-trial conference report or following the pre-trial hearing, shall be deemed to be the equivalent of the district attorney placing the case on the trial list under G.L. c. 278, § 1, and in accordance with Mass. R. Crim. P. 11 (a)(1)(C), shall not be changed without express permission of the court.

VIII.

AMENDMENTS TO THE SCHEDULING ORDER

The court recognizes that there are cases which by their very nature and complexity require special tracking standards and, as well, that unanticipated events may delay the trial of a case or require that a previously determined date be extended or continued. Therefore, a Scheduling Order may, from time to time and for good cause shown, be amended upon oral motion of the parties. Special consideration for extending a Scheduling Order shall be given when the request is jointly made by the prosecutor and defense attorney and supported by good cause. All requests for an enlargement or limitation of a scheduled event shall in the first instance, be made by oral motion to the judge sitting in the session where the case is assigned. If the session judge hearing the motion denies the motion to enlarge or amend the Scheduling Order, the aggrieved party may file a motion for reconsideration with the session judge who heard the oral motion. The motion for reconsideration shall be in writing and set forth a statement specifying in detail the facts upon which the moving party then relies in support of said motion. The motion for reconsideration, and any opposition thereto, shall be submitted on the briefs without personal appearance or oral argument by counsel within seven days of the denial or the oral motion.

In the event the Scheduling Order is amended, the clerk shall enter the amended dates in the court's electronic docket and shall revise the Scheduling Order accordingly.

IX.

EARLY DISPOSITION PROCEDURE

At anytime within 45 days of the pre-trial conference, counsel may advance the case for an early disposition by notifying the first session or room list clerk who shall schedule the case for a hearing.

X.

FINAL PRE–TRIAL CONFERENCE

A final pre-trial conference shall be held fourteen days prior to the scheduled trial date. Trial counsel shall attend the final pre-trial conference. Prior to the conference, counsel shall meet for the purpose of preparing a Joint Pre-trial Memorandum, which shall be filed with the court at the time of said final pre-trial conference. Unless all counsel agree otherwise, counsel for the Commonwealth shall be responsible for preparing and circulating the first draft of the memorandum which shall contain the following component parts:

(1) Agreed statement of facts to be read to the jury during impanelment. (If counsel are unable to agree, each attorney shall submit a proposed statement of facts);

(2) Proposed stipulations of the parties;

(3) List of names of prospective witnesses;

(4) List of proposed exhibits;

(5) Statement of disputed legal issues, including but not limited to evidentiary issues (i.e. privilege, immunity, fresh complaint testimony, rape-shield, etc.);

(6) List of anticipated pre-trial or trial motions to be heard by the trial judge;

(7) Whether the defendant or any witness is in custody, and if so, where;

(8) Whether the defendant or any witness requires an interpreter or other similar needs and, if so, the language or service sought; and

(9) Estimated length of trial.

XI.

CONTINUANCES OF TRIAL DATE

A motion to continue a trial date, once set or confirmed by the court, shall be in writing and supported by good cause in conformity with Mass. R. Crim. P. Rule 10. Such motion shall include the following:

(a) whether the motion is a joint motion; and if not a joint motion, state, if known, whether there is opposition;

(b) the defendant's custody status;

(c) the specific grounds for the requested continuance, including when counsel learned of the grounds necessitating the request;

(d) the date when the case was first assigned a trial date;

(e) whether the trial date has been previously continued and, if so, the number of such continuances and the reasons therefor.

Special consideration for continuing a trial date shall be given when a motion to continue is jointly made by the prosecutor and defense attorney.

If the judge denies any motion to continue the trial, the judge shall state the reasons for such denial.

XII.

PROCEDURES APPLICABLE
TO THE FIRST SESSION

In counties utilizing a first session the following procedures shall apply. In counties utilizing a room list system of case assignments, the room list session shall perform the proceedings described below.

The first session shall receive all presentments by the grand jury, shall conduct all arraignments, bail reviews, dangerousness hearings, and other pre-trial hearings and proceedings. The first session judge may utilize a magistrate's session to conduct arraignments, bails and pretrial proceedings as assigned by the first session judge, and may also transfer cases to available criminal sessions for discrete events (e.g. a pre-trial conference or pre-trial hearing). All trial dates shall be set in the first session and all motions for continuance or amendment to the case track designation shall take place in the first session.

The first session judge shall assign cases scheduled for trial to the criminal trial sessions then sitting. Ordinarily, cases involving defendants in custody, defendants whose pre-trial liberty is reasonably believed to present unusual risks to society, and cases given priority by statute (i.e., criminal proceedings for sex crimes involving child victims or witnesses), shall be given priority.

Once in every two months, the Regional Administrative Justice or his/her designee shall conduct a tracking review of all cases that have been scheduled but not reached for trial within the presumptive time, as amended or extended by the court. All such cases shall be prioritized for trial at the earliest available date.

XIII.

MULTI–LOCATION, SINGLE SESSION, AND
SPECIALIZED SESSION COUNTIES

In those counties where from time to time there are only single judge criminal sessions or counties where there are specialized sessions, the duties imposed upon the first session judge by part XII may be modified as necessary.

XIV.

JUDICIAL DISCRETION

It is understood that specific situations may arise from time to time which require some variation from the procedures set forth above. In the interest of justice and to address specific concerns in unusual circumstances, and in the promotion of judicial efficiency, the first session judge, in his or her sound discretion, may extend the time periods and alter procedural requirements hereinbefore mandated.

XV.

EFFECT OF THIS STANDING ORDER

The procedures set forth herein are intended to facilitate the timely, fair and accurate resolution of criminal cases and to ensure the efficient use of court resources. They do not supplant any existing rule of criminal procedure or statute. A defendant's statutory right to a speedy trial is determined by Mass. R. Crim. P. 36 and not by reference to this Standing Order.

Adopted February 4, 1986. Amended, effective September 7, 2004. Amended June 1, 2009, effective September 8, 2009.

Standing Order 2–87. Electronic Recordation
of Proceedings [Rescinded]

Rescinded May 21, 2019 effective June 10, 2019.

Sixth Amended Standing Order
1–88. Time Standards

**[Sixth Amended Standing Order 1–88 applicable to all civil actions
filed in the Superior Court.]**

Applicable to all Counties

A. GENERAL CONSIDERATIONS. Responding to and complying with the directive of the Supreme Judicial Court for "... an attack on excessive delay and excessive cost of court proceedings ..." and in an effort to "secure the just, speedy and inexpensive determination of every action," Mass.R.Civ.P. 1, the Justices of the Superior Court, through our Chief Justice, hereby adopt these time standards as a standing order of the Superior Court ("Standing Order"). The Court recognizes that the litigation process is memory dependent. To the extent that memory dims or becomes unreliable over prolonged periods of time, a just determination may be jeopardized. The concept of early and continuous judicial supervision and control is intended to enhance the quality of litigation and ensure that justice is fairly rendered.

This Standing Order recognizes that there are viable alternative methods of dispute resolution that may avoid delay and reduce the expense inherent in court proceedings, such as mediation, arbitration, summary jury trials, mini-trials, and reference to masters. Such alternate methods of dispute resolution are compatible with the case management objectives of these time standards. Nothing in this Standing Order shall act as a bar to any form of early intervention by the Court to identify cases suitable for alternative dispute resolution.

The Court recognizes and is sensitive to the impact that this Standing Order will have on local legal culture. We have meticulously avoided intrusion into this rich culture except to the extent necessary to preserve to the Court its responsibility to manage the pace of litigation without disturbing the harmony of the trial bar.

Accordingly, it is hereby ORDERED that:

(1) All civil actions filed in the Superior Court shall be subject to the provisions of this Standing Order.

(2) This Standing Order is applicable to all counties.

(3) The Court will schedule trial dates for both jury and jury-waived cases on its own initiative.

B. TRACK DESIGNATIONS

1. *Tracks Based Upon the Nature of the Case*

(1) All civil actions shall be designated for purposes of this standing order as falling within one of three tracks based upon the nature of the case:

Fast Track ("F")

Average Track ("A")

Accelerated Track ("X")

A listing of case types by track is set forth in Schedules F, A, and X below.

(2) The plaintiff shall indicate the nature of the action and the appropriate track designation on the civil action cover sheet.[1]

(3) For good cause shown, a party may move that a case be designated to a track other than the track selected by the plaintiff on the civil action cover sheet. The motion shall comply with Superior Court Rule 9A, and shall be referred to the attention of the Session Judge.

2. *Individual Track*

(1) By order of the court, or stipulation of the parties, a civil action shall be assigned to its own individual track, which shall supersede the requirements of this standing order, provided that all deadlines in the individual track occur no later than the tracking order dates applicable to the case type, as established by the "Schedules of Case Types by Track," below.

(2) Any party wishing assignment to an individual track must complete and submit the form "Motion for Case-Specific Management" appearing in the Appendix of Forms to the Superior Court Rules and available for download on the Superior Court's website. See Superior Court Rule 20.

(3) The session judge assigned to the case will endorse the Motion in accordance with Superior Court Rules 9A and 20.

C. TRACKING ORDERS.

While the clerk shall provide notice to all parties and their counsel of the track designation and corresponding tracking deadlines, the final responsibility for obtaining information from the clerk about the designation of the case and the corresponding tracking order shall rest with each party. Notification shall occur as follows:

(1) The cover sheet will alert parties to the existence of this Standing Order and to the track designation.

(2) Upon the filing of an action and in accordance with the track designated by the plaintiff, the clerk shall issue a tracking order that establishes the tracking deadlines for completion of the stages of litigation. Specific dates for the tracking deadlines shall be included in the tracking order.

(3) After 90 days from the filing of the action, the clerk shall forward a copy of the tracking order to all counsel of record. Counsel who appear in the action after the expiration of 90 days shall be responsible to learn the tracking deadlines for completing the stages of the litigation.

(4) All motions shall be filed within the time prescribed by the tracking order unless the proponent of the motion first moves for and obtains leave of court to file beyond the designated tracking deadline.[2]

(5) All pleadings, appearances, and other papers filed by counsel of record shall be accompanied by counsel's Board of Bar Overseers (BBO) Number.[3] The BBO Number shall appear immediately after counsel's signature, address and telephone number.

D. AMENDMENTS TO TRACKING ORDERS.

This Standing Order anticipates that there will be instances when the designation of a case to a particular track is inappropriate or the tracking deadlines cannot reasonably be met. The court recognizes that there are cases which by their very nature require special tracking deadlines, and the system is sufficiently flexible to accommodate these cases as follows:

(1) Amendments to the tracking order of a case may be granted upon motion, filed in accordance with Superior Court Rule 9A, and for good cause shown.

(2) All motions to amend a tracking deadline shall be referred to the attention of the Session Judge for decision. Motions (or oppositions thereto) shall be submitted on the papers, without oral argument.

E. RULE 16 CONFERENCES.

This Standing Order also recognizes that the parties may benefit from a conference under Mass. R. Civ. P. 16 to address various matters that may aid in resolving a case or reducing the time or expense of litigation. Any party may ask the Court for a Rule 16 conference, and such requests will be honored if reasonable. The Court may also schedule a Rule 16 conference on its own initiative. Telephonic conferences may be arranged with the permission of the Court.

F. RESCINDED

G. TRACKING DEADLINES.

The following tracking deadlines shall be mandatory except as modified by order of the Session Judge or Regional Administrative Justice.[4] Documents filed outside the tracking deadlines without leave of court need not be acted upon by the Court, even if filed by agreement between the parties. The tracking deadlines for F and A Track cases will be calculated from the date of filing of the complaint.

(i) *After Designation to Fast ("F") Track:*

(1) Three months (90 days)

- Service shall be completed on all parties.

- All returns of service shall be filed.

- If service is not made upon a defendant within 90 days after filing of the complaint, the action shall be dismissed as to that defendant without prejudice unless the Court has found good cause to extend the time for service.[5]

(2) Four months (120 days)

- Rule 12, 15,[6] 19 and 20 motions shall be served.

- If no answer or motion to dismiss is filed by a defendant within 120 days of the filing of the complaint, the clerk shall issue a default as to that defendant and notify all parties of the default, unless the Court has found good cause to extend the time to file the answer or motion to dismiss.[7] Nothing in this Standing Order bars the earlier issuance of a default when legally appropriate. When appropriate, cases will be ordered for assessment of damages.

(3) Five months (150 days)

- Rule 12, 15, 19 and 20 motions shall be filed with the Court.

(4) Six months (180 days)

- Rule 12, 15, 19 and 20 motions shall be heard by the Court.

(5) Ten months (300 days)

- All discovery requests shall be served and non-expert depositions completed.[8] Requests for admissions are not included within this deadline but a party may not request of an adverse party the admission of more than thirty factual assertions after this deadline, except with leave of court.

(6) Eleven months (330 days)

- All motions for summary judgment shall be served. Nothing in this Standing Order bars summary judgment motions from being served earlier in the litigation.

(7) Twelve months (360 days)

- All motions for summary judgment shall be filed.

The remaining tracking deadlines assume that a motion for summary judgment has been filed. If no summary judgment motion is filed, earlier tracking deadlines may be set by the Court.

(8) Sixteen months (480 days)

- A pre-trial conference shall be conducted by the Court.[9] The joint pre-trial memorandum shall be filed with the Court no less than three business days prior to the pre-trial conference. A firm trial date shall be set by the pre-trial conference judge.

- The minimum requirements of the joint pre-trial order are attached to and made part of this Standing Order as Appendix B

(9) Twenty-two months (660 days)

- The case shall be resolved and judgment shall issue.

(ii) *After Designation to Average ("A") Track:*

(1) Three months (90 days)

- Service shall be completed on all parties.

- All returns of service shall be filed.

- If service is not made upon a defendant within 90 days after filing of the complaint, the action shall be dismissed as to that defendant without prejudice, unless the Court has found good cause to extend the time for service.

(2) Four months (120 days)

- Rule 12, 19 and 20 motions shall be served.

- If no answer or motion to dismiss is filed by a defendant within 120 days of the filing of the complaint, the clerk shall issue a default as to that defendant and notify all parties of the default, unless the Court has found good cause to extend the time to file the answer or motion to dismiss. Nothing in this Standing Order bars the earlier issuance of a default when legally appropriate. When appropriate, cases will be ordered for assessment of damages.

(3) Five months (150 days)

- Rule 12, 19 and 20 motions shall be filed with the Court.

(4) Six months (180 days)

- Rule 12, 19 and 20 motions shall be heard by the Court.

(5) Fourteen months (420 days)

- Rule 15 motions shall be served.

(6) Fifteen months (450 days)

- Rule 15 motions shall be filed and resolved, with or without hearing.

(7) Twenty-four months (720 days)

- All discovery requests served and non-expert depositions completed. Requests for admissions are not included within this deadline but a party may not request of an adverse party the admission of more than thirty factual assertions after this deadline, except with leave of court.

(8) Twenty-five months (750 days)

- All motions for summary judgment shall be served.

(9) Twenty-six months (780 days)

- All motions for summary judgment shall be filed.

The remaining Tracking Deadlines assume that a motion for summary judgment will be filed. If no summary judgment motion is filed, earlier tracking dates can be set by the Court.

(10) Thirty months (900 days)

- A pre-trial conference shall be conducted by the Court. The joint pre-trial memorandum shall be filed with the Court no less than three business days prior to the pre-trial conference. A firm trial date shall be set by the pre-trial conference judge.

• The minimum requirements of the joint pre-trial order are attached to and made part of this Standing Order as Appendix B

(11) Thirty-six months (1,080 days)

• The case shall be resolved and judgment shall issue.

(iii) *After Designation to Accelerated ("X") Track:*

• All X Track cases seeking judicial review of administrative agency proceedings on the administrative record pursuant to the standards set forth in G.L. c. 30A, § 14, G.L. c. 249, § 4, or similar statutes are governed by Standing Order 1–96, and the tracking deadlines set forth in that Order. Those tracking deadlines are as follows:

• No later than 90 days after service of the complaint, the administrative agency whose decision is at issue shall file a record of the proceeding.

• No later than 20 days after service of the record, all motions to dismiss or for a more definite statement under Mass. R. Civ. P. 12(b) or (e), all motions for leave to present testimony of alleged irregularities in the procedure before the agency that are not shown in the record under G.L. c. 30A, § 14(5), and all motions for leave to present additional evidence under G.L. c. 30A, § 14(6) shall be served.

• No later than 30 days after service of the record or the Court's decision on any motion specified above, whichever is later, the plaintiff shall serve a motion for judgment on the pleadings under Mass. R. Civ. P. 12(c).

• No later than 30 days after service of the motion for judgment on the pleadings, the defendant shall serve an opposition.

• All X Track cases under G.L. c. 123A, § 12 (SDP initial commitment) shall be governed by the deadlines set forth in G.L. c. 123A or otherwise established by law.

• Unless an earlier date is required by law, all disputes in X Track cases shall be resolved and judgment shall issue no later than 12 months (360 days) after the filing of the complaint.

H. CASES NOT REACHED FOR TRIAL. Any case not reached for trial or otherwise disposed of within the prescribed tracking deadline shall be referred to the attention of the Regional Administrative Justice who shall coordinate with the Session Judge to ensure a speedy disposition within the session or to reassign the case to another session.

A record shall be maintained by the Regional Administrative Justice of all cases not tried or otherwise not disposed of as required under this Standing Order setting forth the reason for the trial delay and the action taken to resolve the matter.

I. FINAL TRIAL CONFERENCE BEFORE JURY TRIAL

1. Shortly before each jury trial, the court shall hold a final trial conference unless otherwise ordered by the session judge or Regional Administrative Justice. The clerk shall schedule the final trial conference to occur before the trial judge whenever possible and shall notify all parties of the time, date and location of the final trial conference.

2. In cases to be tried by jury, the clerk's notice shall inform the parties that:

a. The purpose of the final trial conference is to discuss the matters set forth in Superior Court Rule 6(2)(a) and other matters that may arise at trial, without limitation those matters set forth in subparagraph 2(b) below, as well as the estimated length of the trial; any scheduling constraints affecting witnesses or other trial participants; any need for an interpreter for a party or witness, including the specific language involved and the date and time when interpretation is required; the number of jurors to be seated; any agreement to allow deliberation by fewer jurors if seated jurors are dismissed post-empanelment; the content and method of employing any supplemental juror questionnaire; the number of peremptories; the order and timing of the parties' assertions of challenges for cause and peremptory challenges; and any other matter affecting the efficiency and fairness of the trial.

b. At or before the final trial conference, the parties must submit the following unless otherwise ordered by the court:

i. a final joint witness list (if different from the final pretrial conference memo), showing each witness's city or town of residence except where doing so would endanger the witness's safety;

ii. a final joint statement of the case to read to the jury (if different from the final pretrial conference memo);

iii. a joint list of agreed exhibits (as required by Appendix B hereto);

iv. a list of contested exhibits (as required by Appendix B hereto);

v. a copy of any deposition transcript to be offered at trial, with objections highlighted for action by the court (as required by the last paragraph of Appendix B hereto);

vi. any proposed voir dire questions to be asked by the court;

vii. any motion requesting voir dire procedures, including proposed method and subject matter of any attorney or party voir dire and any proposed supplemental juror questionnaire;

viii. any requested pre-charge to be given by the judge before or during empanelment, or immediately after the jury is sworn;

ix. any motions in limine, specifically identifying motions in limine that affect empanelment or opening statements and stating whether each motion in limine is opposed, partially opposed, or unopposed;

x. any stipulation of fact to be read to the jury.

c. The parties must confer at least 48 hours before the final trial conference to discuss the matters set forth in subparagraphs 2(a) and 2(b) above.

* Excluding claims against the Commonwealth or a municipality, which are type E03 cases under Schedule 'A'(Average Track).

Adopted February 1, 1988. Amended December 22, 1989, effective January 15, 1990; April 25, 1990, effective September 1, 1990; amended effective December 5, 1994; December 1, 2003; December 26, 2006, effective March 1, 2007; December 2, 2016, effective January 1, 2017; August 14, 2017, effective September 1, 2017; Jan. 6, 2020.

[1] As a result of an amended complaint, crossclaim, counterclaim, or third party action, a case may change from a simple motor vehicle tort ("F" track) to a product liability case ("A" track) and warrant a motion to change the designation to the longer track.

[2] This provision places the responsibility of "timely filing" documents on the attorneys and relieves the clerks of the initial responsibility of determining if documents are filed in violation of time standards. The clerk's office does not have the responsibility to return improperly filed papers.

[3] This requirement will facilitate the generation of computer assisted notices and trial scheduling. During the past several years, the Trial Court has implemented a number of automated case management systems. The Superior Court civil case management system has been enhanced to support an attorney notice module which requires each attorney of record being assigned a unique code for purposes of computer sorting. The Board of Bar Overseers number provides that unique number and address.

[4] Wherever the term Regional Administrative Justice is used in this Standing Order, it shall include his or her designee.

[5] The dismissal will be entered automatically by the clerk under the authority of this Standing Order and notices given as required.

[6] This provision does not affect the power of the Court to allow amendments to pleadings where "justice appears to require such amendment." The party seeking to amend late must obtain leave from the Session Judge and make a good faith showing of inability to move in timely fashion.

[7] The default will be entered automatically by the clerk under the authority of this Standing Order and notices given as required.

[8] A party may not have responded to timely filed requests for discovery at this juncture and accordingly motions to compel production of that discovery continue to be appropriate. It is expected that all responses will be filed no later than the date that the joint pre-trial memorandum is filed. Non-expert depositions, however, must be held and completed on or before this date. This Standing Order does not change the duty of a party to supplement under the provisions of Mass.R.Civ.P. 26(e).

[9] Some summary judgment motions are sufficiently complex to require additional judicial time to render a decision. The case should nonetheless continue on track and be brought to the attention of the pre-trial conference Justice for his or her consideration and action.

CASE TYPES
AC Actions Involving the State/Municipality*

AA1	Contract Action involving Commonwealth, Municipality, MBTA, etc.	(A)
AB1	Tortious Action involving Commonwealth, Municipality, MBTA, etc.	(A)
AC1	Real Property Action involving Commonwealth, Municipality, MBTA etc.	(A)
AD1	Equity Action involving Commonwealth, Municipality, MBTA, etc.	(A)
AE1	Administrative Action involving Commonwealth, Municipality, MBTA, etc.	(A)

CN Contract/Business Cases

A01	Services, Labor, and Materials	(F)
A02	Goods Sold and Delivered	(F)
A03	Commercial Paper	(F)
A04	Employment Contract	(F)
A05	Consumer Revolving Credit—M.R.C.P. 8.1	(F)
A06	Insurance Contract	(F)
A08	Sale or Lease of Real Estate	(F)
A12	Construction Dispute	(A)
A14	Interpleader	(F)
BA1	Governance, Conduct, internal Affairs of Entities	(A)
BA3	Liability of Shareholders, Directors, Officers, Partners, etc.	(A)
BB1	Shareholder Derivative	(A)
BB2	Securities Transactions	(A)
BC1	Mergers, Consolidations, Sales of Assets, Issuance of Debt, Equity, etc.	(A)
BD1	Intellectual Property	(A)
BD2	Proprietary Information or Trade Secrets	(A)
BG1	Financial Institutions/Funds	(A)
BH1	Violation of Antitrust or Trade Regulation Laws	(A)
A99	Other Contract/Business Action—Specify	(F)

ER Equitable Remedies

D01	Specific Performance of a Contract	(A)
D02	Reach and Apply	(F)
D03	Injunction	(F)
D04	Reform/ Cancel Instrument	(F)
D05	Equitable Replevin	(F)
D06	Contribution or Indemnification	(F)
D07	Imposition of a Trust	(A)
D08	Minority Shareholder's Suit	(A)

D09 Interference in Contractual Relationship   (F)
D10 Accounting   (A)
D11 Enforcement of Restrictive Covenant   (F)
D12 Dissolution of a Partnership   (F)
D13 Declaratory Judgment, G.L. c.231A   (A)
D14 Dissolution of a Corporation   (F)
D99 Other Equity Action   (F)

PA Civil Actions Involving Incarcerated Party[†]

PA1 Contract Action involving an Incarcerated Party   (A)
PB1 Tortious Action involving an Incarcerated Party   (A)
PC1 Real Property Action involving an Incarcerated Party   (F)
PD1 Equity Action involving an Incarcerated Party   (F)
PE1 Administrative Action involving an Incarcerated Party   (F)

TR Torts

B03 Motor Vehicle Negligence—Personal Injury/Property Damage   (F)
B04 Other Negligence—Personal Injury/Property Damage   (F)
B05 Products Liability   (A)
B06 Malpractice—Medical   (A)
B07 Malpractice—Other   (A)
B08 Wrongful Death, —Non-medical   (A)
B15 Defamation   (A)
B19 Asbestos   (A)
B20 Personal Injury—Slip & Fall   (F)
B21 Environmental   (F)
B22 Employment Discrimination   (F)
BE1 Fraud, Business Torts, etc.   (A)
B99 Other Tortious Action   (F)

RP Summary Process [Real Property]

S01 Summary Process—Residential   (X)
S02 Summary Process—Commercial/Non-residential   (F)

RP Real Property

C01 Land Taking   (F)
C02 Zoning Appeal, G.L. c. 40A   (F)
C03 Dispute Concerning Title   (F)
C04 Foreclosure of a Mortgage   (X)
C05 Condominium Lien & Charges   (X)
C99 Other Real Property Action   (F)

MC Miscellaneous Civil Actions

E18 Foreign Discovery Proceeding   (X)
E97 Prisoner Habeas Corpus   (X)
E22 Lottery Assignment, G.L. c. 10 § 28   (X)

AB Abuse/Harassment Prevention

E15 Abuse Prevention Petition, G.L. c. 209A   (X)
E21 Protection from Harassment, G.L. c. 25SE   (X)

AA Administrative Civil Actions

E02 Appeal from Administrative Agency, G.L. c. 30A   (X)
E03 Certiorari Action, G.L. c.249 § 4   (X)
E05 Confirmation of Arbitration Awards   (X)
E06 Mass Antitrust Act. G. L. c. 93 § 9   (A)
E07 Mass Antitrust Act. G. L. c. 93 § 8   (X)
E08 Appointment of a Receiver   (X)
E09 Construction Surety Bond, G.L. c. 149 §§ 29, 29A   (A)
E10 Summary Process Appeal   (X)
E11 Worker's Compensation   (X)
E16 Auto Surcharge Appear   (X)

E17 Civil Rights Act, G.L. c.12 § 11H   (A)
E24 Appeal from District Court Commitment, G.L. c. 123 § 9(b)   (X)
E25 Pleural Registry (Asbestos cases)
E95 Forfeiture, G.L. c.94C § 47   (F)
E99 Other Administrative Action   (X)
Z01 Medical Malpractice—Tribunal only, G.L. c. 231 § 60B   (F)
Z02 Appeal Bond Denial   (X)

SO Sex Offender Review
E12 SDP Commitment, G.L. c. 123A§ 12   (X)
E14 SDP Petition, G.L. c. 123A § 9(b)   (X)

RC Restricted Civil Actions
E19 Sex Offender Registry, G.L. c.6 § 178M   (X)
E27 Minor Seeking Consent, G.L. c.112 § 12S   (X)

*Choose this case type if ANY party is the Commonwealth, a municipality, the MBTA, or any other governmental entity UNLESS your case is a case type listed under Administrative Civil Actions (AA).
†Choose this case type if ANY party is an incarcerated party, UNLESS your case is a case type listed under Administrative Civil Actions (AA) or is a Prisoner Habeas Corpus case (E97).

**APPENDIX A.   JOINT CASE MANAGEMENT STATEMENT
AND PROPOSED ORDER [Rescinded]**

APPENDIX B

NOTICE TO APPEAR FOR FINAL PRE-TRIAL CONFERENCE	DOCKET NUMBER	Trial Court of Massachusetts Superior Court Department

CASE NAME:

TO:

COURT NAME & ADDRESS

A final pre-trial conference in the above referenced case will be held on:

Date:

Time:

Event:

Session / Courtroom Location:

All <u>trial counsel are required to attend</u> and submit their joint pre-trial memorandum to the Court.

To facilitate orderly and efficient progress towards trial, counsel for all parties **shall confer** for the purpose of preparing a joint pre-trial memorandum. The joint pre-trial memorandum shall be submitted jointly and shall be filed with the court no less than three business days prior to the pre-trial conference. Unless all counsel agree otherwise, counsel for the plaintiff shall be responsible for preparing and circulating the first draft. Each party's lead counsel at trial is expected to attend the final pre-trial conference.

A. FOR JURY TRIAL

The joint pre-trial memorandum shall include the following component parts:

(1)   Agreed facts in a form suitable for submission as an exhibit at trial;

(2)   A brief statement by each party of what that party expects the evidence to show;

(3)   Agreed suggested description of the case to be read to the jury during impanelment;

(4)   Statement of all significant legal issues (including, particularly, any significant evidentiary issues), the position of the parties on these issues, and a statement of authorities. Provide a copy of all cases and other authorities relied upon other than reported Supreme Judical Court and Appeals Court cases.

(5)   The name and address of each witness to be called by each party. Failure to list a witness in the pre-trial memorandum may lead to an order precluding the testimony of that witness unless the need for the witness cannot reasonably be anticipated prior to trial or other good cause is shown. No party may reserve the right to add a witness after the pre-trial conference without leave of the Court. In addition, the parties shall identify any witness or party who needs an interpreter, as well as the language the interpreter needs to speak.

(6)   (a) The names, addresses and qualifications of each expert witness the parties intend to call, together with subject matter on which the expert is expected to testify, the substance of all facts and opinions to which the expert is expected to testify and a detailed summary of the grounds of each expert's opinion. If an expert witness's identity and expected testimony has previously been disclosed in response to expert interrogatories, this item may be covered by appending to the pre-trial memorandum a copy of the expert interrogatory responses. Failure to comply with this paragraph forfeits the party's ability to present an expert as of right. See Superior Court Rule 30B(a).

(b) Unless earlier resolved, whether any party moves to conduct any expert deposition under Mass. R. Civ. P. 26(b)(4). If so, unless the parties all agree to the expert deposition, a written motion to conduct the expert deposition and opposition shall be appended to the pre-trial memorandum so that the motion may be decided by the judge at the pre-trial conference.

NOTICE TO APPEAR FOR FINAL PRE-TRIAL CONFERENCE	DOCKET NUMBER	Trial Court of Massachusetts Superior Court Department

(c) Whether any party intends to serve any *Daubert-Lanigan* motion challenging the admissibility of expert testimony and, if so, when the party intends to serve and file such a motion and the anticipated basis for such a motion. Failure to inform the court in the pre-trial memorandum of a party's intent to file a *Daubert-Lanigan* motion may, in the discretion of the court, constitute a waiver of the motion. If the date proposed for the filing of a *Daubert-Lanigan* motion is deemed by the court to be too close to trial, the court may set an earlier deadline for the filing of the *Daubert-Lanigan* motion. At the pre-trial conference, the court will set a date for hearing on any *Daubert-Lanigan* motion.

NOTE: Inclusion of an expert witness' identity and expected testimony in the joint pre-trial memorandum does not waive any party's right to object to that expert's testimony on the ground that responses to expert discovery were untimely or inadequate.

(7) Estimated length of trial (please specify whether your estimate is based on half days or full days).

(8) An itemization of the special or liquidated damages alleged.

(9) A certification that counsel for all parties have conferred and discussed the possibility of settlement, and the amenability of the case to mediation or other forms of alternate dispute resolution. If alternative dispute resolution has commenced or will commence, the parties shall inform the Court of its status. The parties shall not disclose the contents of settlement demands or offers in the pre-trial memorandum.

(10) A statement whether the parties have consulted about provisions for case-specific management available under Superior Court Rule 20(h)-(i), and if so, which provisions are agreed or are still under consideration.

B. FOR BENCH TRIAL UPON WAIVER OF DETAILED WRITTEN FINDINGS:

If all parties have agreed to a bench trial with waiver of detailed findings (Superior Court Rule 20(h)), the joint pre-trial memorandum need not include items (1)-(3), and the parties will not be required to file proposed findings of fact. In the absence of such waiver, the joint pre-trial memorandum for a bench trial shall include all items listed in (A), above except item (3).

C. FUTURE FILINGS (All cases):

No later than five business days prior to the scheduled trial, counsel shall meet and review the exhibits proposed to be introduced by each party and all materials to be shown to the fact-finder. Based on that meeting and review of exhibits, counsel shall prepare a joint exhibit list identifying 1) stipulated exhibits (which shall be pre-marked and introduced at the commencement of trial) and 2) proposed exhibits of each party as to which there is no agreement on admissibility. The exhibit list is to be presented to the trial judge at the commencement of trial with a copy for the clerk or court reporter.

In the event deposition transcripts are to be offered at trial, and there are objections to any of the answers set forth in the transcript, the parties, not less than three days prior to the commencement of trial, are to supply to the court a transcript of the testimony with objections highlighted and, in the margin, a brief statement of the grounds of the objection and the response by the proponent of the testimony. Videotaped depositions are governed by Mass. R. Civ. P. 30A.

DATE ISSUED	ASSOCIATE JUSTICE	ASSISTANT CLERK	SESSION PHONE#

Date/Time Printed: 06-01-2017 11:32:53   SCV018-T/2017

Standing Order 1–96. Processing and Hearing of Complaints for Judicial Review of Administrative Agency Proceedings

(Applicable to Civil Actions in All Counties)

Processing and Hearing of Complaints for Judicial Review of Administrative Agency Proceedings

In order to facilitate and clarify the orderly processing and hearing of Complaints for Judicial Review of Administrative Agency Proceedings, it is hereby **ORDERED**, effective January 1, 2017 that:

1. Claims filed in the Superior Court seeking judicial review of administrative agency proceedings on the administrative record pursuant to the standards set forth in G. L. c. 30A, § 14, G. L. c. 249, § 4, or similar statutes, whether joined with a claim for declaratory relief under G. L. c. 231A, or any other claim, shall be heard in accordance with the following procedures.

2. The administrative agency whose proceedings are to be judicially reviewed shall, by way of answer, file the original or certified copy of the record of the proceeding under review (the record) within ninety (90) days after service upon it of the Complaint. Such record "shall consist of (a) the entire pro-

ceedings, or (b) such portions thereof as the agency and the parties may stipulate, or (c) a statement of the case agreed to by the agency and the parties." G. L. c. 30A, § 14(4). Upon service of a Complaint, the agency shall notify all parties of procedures for acquiring a transcript of the hearing testimony. The agency shall also inform the parties of their obligation to provide a transcript, or portions thereof, to the court if alleging that an agency's decision is not supported by substantial evidence or is arbitrary or capricious, or is an abuse of discretion. A request for a copy of the transcript must be made by a party within thirty (30) days after service of the Complaint, and such transcript or portion thereof shall be made part of the record. The Agency's certified record shall include any transcript that has been prepared but need not include a transcript of any untranscribed proceeding or portion thereof in the absence of a timely transcript request.

The court may assess the expense of preparing the record as part of the costs in the case. G. L. c. 30A, § 14(4). Additionally, "the court may, regardless of the outcome of the case, assess any one unreasonably refusing to stipulate to limit the record, for the additional expenses of preparation caused by such refusal." G. L. c. 30A, § 14(4). The court may require or permit subsequent corrections or additions to the record when deemed desirable. G. L. c. 30A, § 14(4). The time for filing the record may be enlarged, for good cause shown, upon allowance of an appropriate motion.

2A. Records of Administrative Proceedings, filed by the administrative agency, shall comply in full with Supreme Judicial Court Rule 1:24, if practicable given size and applicable filing deadlines. Otherwise, the agency should:

(a) Make reasonable efforts to segregate, redact and file publicly all portions of the record that can practically be redacted within the filing deadline, including in all cases a redacted copy of the decision under review; and

(b) separately file all other portions in one or more volumes, each having a first page that bears the legend: **"FILED UNDER PROVISIONAL MOTION TO IMPOUND,"** together with such a motion, which need not be served pursuant to Superior Court Rule 9A. Documents bearing that legend shall NOT be impounded without a hearing in compliance with Trial Court Rule VIII, but shall be segregated from the rest of the file in the same manner already employed by clerks' offices for third-party production of medical records, phone records and the like. The clerk shall note the existence of the segregated volume(s) on the docket sheet. The provisional motion to impound will be forwarded to the session judge for Rule VIII notice, hearing and findings ONLY if a non-party seeks to review the documents.

Notwithstanding the above, an agency need not redact from an administrative record any material that is in a public record.

3. The following motions raising preliminary matters must be served in accordance with Superior Court Rule 9A not later than twenty (20) days after service of the record by the administrative agency.

(a) Motions authorized by Mass. R. Civ. P. 12(b) or 12(e).

(b) Motion for leave to present testimony of alleged irregularities in procedure before the agency, not shown in the record (G. L. c. 30A, § 14(5)).

(c) Motion for leave to present additional evidence (G. L. c. 30A, § 14(6)).

Any party failing to serve such a motion within the prescribed time limit, or within any court-ordered extension, shall be deemed to have waived any such motion (unless relating to jurisdiction) and the case shall proceed solely on the basis of the record. Any such motion shall be promptly resolved in accordance with Superior Court Rule 9A. If the motion specified in (c) is allowed, all further proceedings shall be stayed until the administrative agency has complied with the provisions of G. L. c. 30A, § 14(6).

4. A claim for judicial review shall be resolved through a motion for judgment on the pleadings, Mass. R. Civ. P. 12(c), in accordance with Superior Court Rule 9A except as otherwise provided by this Standing Order, unless the Court's decision on any motion specified in part 3 above has made such a resolution inappropriate. A plaintiff's Rule 12(c) motion and supporting memorandum shall be served within thirty (30) days of the service of the record or of the Court's decision on any motion specified in part 3 above, whichever is later. A defendant's response shall be deemed to include a cross-motion for judgment on the pleadings pursuant to Mass. R. Civ. P. 12(c) (which should be noted in the caption of the response) and shall be served within thirty (30) days after service of the plaintiffs motion and memorandum. The plaintiff shall then promptly file the motion materials in accordance with Superior Court Rule 9A. The Court may grant an extension of time to file for good cause shown. Memoranda shall include specific page citations to matters in the record.

5. The Clerk or her/his designee will schedule a hearing date after receiving the motion materials. No pre-trial conference will be held, and no pre-trial memorandum filed, unless specifically ordered by the Court. No testimony or other evidence shall be presented at the hearing, and the review shall be confined to the record. A party may waive oral argument and submit on the brief by filing a written notice. Such waiver by a party shall not affect the right of any other party to appear and present oral argument.

Adopted effective April 1, 1996. Amended effective January 4, 1999; November 1, 2000; March 18, 2002. Amended December 5, 2014, effective February 1, 2015; December 2, 2016, effective January 1, 2017.

Standing Order 1–06. Continuances of Trial [Repealed]

Repealed and replaced by Rule 33, effective January 1, 2016.

Standing Order 1–07. Consolidation of Superior Court Cases [Repealed]

Repealed and replaced by Rule 31, effective January 1, 2016.

Standing Order 1–09. Written Discovery [Repealed]

Repealed and replaced by Rule 30A, effective January 1, 2016.

Standing Order 1–15. Participation in Juror Voir Dire by Attorneys and Self–Represented Parties [Rescinded]

Adopted December 5, 2014, effective February 2, 2015. Superseded by Superior Court Rule 6, effective September 1, 2017.

Standing Order 2–15. Exceptions to Notice Requirement of Trial Court Rule VIII, Uniform Rules on Impoundment Procedure (URIP) [Rescinded]

Adopted effective October 1, 2015. Superseded by Superior Court Rule 18, effective September 1, 2017.

Joint Standing Order 1–16. Authority of the Judge with Respect to Communication with Specialty Court Teams

This Standing Order is promulgated by the Chief Justice of the Trial Court pursuant to G. L, c. 211B, Section 9 and shall constitute authorization by law as referenced in Rule 2.9 (A)(2) of the Code of Judicial Conduct (effective January 1, 2016).

For purposes of this Order:

Specialty Court means a specifically designated court session that focuses on individuals with underlying medical, mental health, substance abuse, or other issues that contribute to the reasons such individuals are before the courts. Specialty court shall also mean Veterans Treatment Court and Homelessness Court. Specialty court sessions integrate treatment and services with judicial case oversight and intensive court supervision. Examples Include drug courts, mental health courts, veterans' courts, and tenancy preservation programs.

A Staffing shall refer to a regularly scheduled, informal conference not occurring in open court, the purpose of which is to permit the presiding judge and others, including counsel, to discuss a participant's progress in the specialty court, treatment recommendations, or responses to participant compliance issues.

IT IS THEREFORE ORDERED:

A judge presiding over a specialty court shall have the authority to initiate, permit or otherwise consider ex parte communications about defendants, juveniles or probationers with members of the specialty court team at a staffing or by written documents provided to all members of the specialty court team, The purpose of this authority is to allow judges in their role in presiding over specialty court sessions, and only in that capacity, to assume a more interactive role with parties, treatment providers, probation officers, social workers and others, than Rule 2.9 of the Code of Judicial Conduct would otherwise permit.

Adopted effective January 7, 2016.

Joint Standing Order 2–16. Uniform Interdepartmental Procedures for Probation Violation Proceedings

This Standing Order is promulgated by the Chief Justice of the Trial Court pursuant to G. L, c. 211B, Section 9 and stands effective October 3, 2016.

1. Application

This Order shall apply to the Superior Court, District Court, Boston Municipal Court and Juvenile Court Departments.

2. Purpose

This Order sets forth requirements regarding communication among the above-named departments of the Trial Court when an individual who is the subject of a probation order in one of these departments is charged with a new offense in another of these departments. Its purpose is to ensure that this required interdepartmental communication relating to the commencement of probation violation proceedings as a result of alleged new criminal behavior by a probationer, and the potential custody and transport of that probationer between different court departments, occur in a timely, informed and efficient manner. This Order does not apply to an individual who is the subject of a probation order issued prior to a trial or the formal submission and acceptance of a plea of guilty or an admission to sufficient facts, as provided in G.L. c. 276, § 87 ("pretrial probation").

3. Definition of Terms

As used in this Order, the terms below shall have the following meanings:

"Criminal:" includes delinquency or youthful offender.

"Criminal Court:" a court division of the Boston Municipal, District, or Juvenile Court or the Superior Court.

The terms used in this Order and the form promulgated by the Chief Justice of the Trial Court pursuant to Section 9 have been defined to include terminology associated with juvenile cases and proceedings and the Juvenile Court. They have been defined in this manner for the purposes of convenience and ease of reading and are applicable to this Order and form only. The terms as appearing in this Order and form do not change the meaning of the terminology used in adult and juvenile proceedings as defined and set forth by case law and statutes. Other than for the purposes of this Order and form, adult and juvenile terms are not interchangeable.

4. Intra-Departmental Communications

This Order does not apply to intra-departmental communications, transport of probationers, or use of the warrant management system, which may be the subject of rules or standing orders issued by and applicable within individual court departments.

5. Information to be Sent from the Criminal Court; Custody of Probationer

When an individual appears on a new criminal charge before a criminal court, and that individual is the subject of a probation order issued by a court in a different department of the Trial Court, the probation department of the criminal court shall transmit to the probation department of the court having responsibility for the supervision of the probationer (the "probation court") information and requests for information, including information regarding the possible service of a notice of violation on, and transport of, the probationer. This transmission shall be made by means of the form referred to in Section 9, below.

The transmission from the criminal court shall be sent electronically and promptly, to the probation officer in the probation court listed as the probation officer on duty in the probation court or, if there is no probation officer on duty, to the Chief Probation Officer of the probation court. The transmission shall be sent while the probationer is at the criminal court. When necessary, the criminal court may order the probationer held in custody until the procedures required by this Order are completed.

6. Information to be Returned by the Probation Court; Time Limit

The probation department of the probation court shall respond electronically, to the probation officer who transmitted the request for information from the criminal court. The response shall include information regarding service of a notice of violation on, and transport of, the probationer. This response shall be transmitted within two hours or within such time limit as extended, as provided in Section 7, such time limit to be measured from the time indicated on the transmission, and shall be set forth on the form referred to in Section 9, below.

If the probation department is requesting that the probationer be transported, the probation department shall request the issuance of an arrest warrant for a violation of probation ("warrant") from a judge in the probation court. If the judge issues such warrant, the clerk's office shall enter it promptly into the Warrant Management System and the probation department shall provide the criminal court with a notice of violation that cites the violation(s).

If the probation department is not requesting that the probationer be transported and is requesting that the probationer be served with a notice of violation, the probation department shall provide the probation department of the criminal court with a notice of violation that cites the violation(s) and indicates the date and time of the probationer's required appearance in the probation court.

7. Action by the Criminal Court

The criminal court shall await receipt of the information from the probation court for a period of two hours measured from the time of the transmission of the request for that information. This two-hour time limit may be extended by the criminal court.

Upon the timely receipt of the required information from the probation court and, if the probation court has issued a warrant, the criminal court shall serve on the probationer, in hand, a notice of violation on behalf of the probation court and shall either order transport of the probationer on such warrant or defer transport on the warrant until the termination of any custody ordered by the criminal court judge in the new criminal case. In the event that no warrant has been issued by the probation court, and the probation department has provided a notice of violation to the probation department of the criminal court, the criminal court shall serve such notice on the probationer, in hand, on behalf of the probation court.

If the probation department of the probation court does not provide the required information or a notice of violation to the probation department of the criminal court in the manner set forth in Section 6, the criminal court need not take any further action regarding the probation matter. In such instances, the probation department of the criminal court shall make an appropriate entry into its records.

8. Action by the Probation Court

Upon delivery of the probationer into the custody of the probation court on the warrant, and not withstanding any provision of this Order, the form promulgated pursuant to section 9, or the reason for the warrant as it may appear in the Warrant Management System, the probation court shall proceed on the violation of probation matter in accordance with applicable law and respective departmental rule or standing order.

9. Form to be Promulgated by the Chief Justice of the Trial Court

The transmittal of information between courts as required by this Order shall proceed by means of a form promulgated by the Chief Justice of the Trial Court. This form shall include such specific information requirements, data elements and attachments as the Chief Justice may deem appropriate, provided that nothing in this Order shall be construed to prohibit the use of telephone communication to supplement the use of such form and to achieve its purpose.

10. Probation Department Procedures and Record Keeping

Implementation of this Order by the Massachusetts Probation Service, including record keeping requirements, shall be as set forth in such instructions and regulations consistent with the provisions of this Order as may be deemed appropriate by the Commissioner of Probation.

Adopted August 18, 2016, effective October 3, 2016.

Standing Order 1–17. Waiver of Detailed Written Findings of Fact Under Superior Court Rule 20(2)(h) [Rescinded]

Adopted December 2, 2016, effective January 1, 2017. Superseded by amendment to Superior Court Rule 20 and rescinded, effective March 1, 2018.

Standing Order 2–17. Limited Assistance Representation [Rescinded]

Adopted April 6, 2017, effective June 1, 2017. Rescinded December 27, 2018, effective February 1, 2019. See, now, Uniform Trial Court Rule XVI. Limited Assistance Representation.

Standing Order 1–20. Videoconferencing of Court Events

Applicable to All Counties

1. This standing order is promulgated under the Trial Court Revised Policy for Videoconferencing, Revised November 2019 (Policy). The Policy recognizes the benefits of regular use of videoconferencing across the Commonwealth to reduce costs, to address safety concerns and delays associated with transportation of prisoners and detainees, and to provide cost savings and access to justice in cases where experts and witnesses are located outside a county or the Commonwealth.

Under the Policy, any department of the Trial Court may, by standing order, implement videoconferencing of court events identified by the departmental Chief Justice. This standing order identifies court events for which videoconferencing is presumptively used in all counties of the Superior Court, as well as other events for which videoconferencing is permitted.

2. The following court events shall presumptively be conducted by videoconferencing:

a. bail review hearings;

b. non-testimonial hearings for review of dangerousness determinations made under G. L. c. 276, § 58A;

c. non-evidentiary hearings in civil matters involving incarcerated persons;

3. Videoconferencing shall be permitted for medical malpractice tribunals conducted under G. L. c. 231, § 60B, and for any other event not specified in paragraph 2 above, upon court order or by agreement of the parties, provided that videoconferencing shall not be permitted in any proceeding in which constitutional, statutory, or other legal authority grants a right to physical presence at the event and that right has not been waived. Factors relevant to a court's determination whether to order that a proceeding be conducted by videoconferencing include, but are not limited to:

a. the nature of the proceeding, including whether it is civil or criminal;

b. any agreement of the parties or waiver of any right to physical appearance;

c. any efforts to procure the physical presence of a party, witness, or other participant and the cost of physical appearance in relation to the importance of presence in civil cases;

d. any security or health risks of physical presence, in relation to any corresponding risks at the remote site;

e. any other factors affecting convenience to and safety of the parties and the public.

4. To promote the orderly use and proper operation of videoconferencing equipment, the Clerk in each county shall designate a primary videoconferencing coordinator and a backup coordinator, who will be trained by the Judicial Information Services Department.

5. The videoconferencing coordinator should consult the Policy in conjunction with this standing order, because the Policy provides guidance on the proper operation of videoconferencing equipment, including steps that the court may take in the event of an equipment malfunction, as well as procedures relevant to consultations between criminal defendants and their counsel.

Adopted Jan. 6, 2020, eff. Feb. 1, 2020.

RULES OF THE COMMISSION ON JUDICIAL CONDUCT

Table of Rules

Scope and Title

These rules govern the procedures of the Commission on Judicial Conduct in the exercise of its jurisdiction pursuant to Chapter 211C of the General Laws as appearing in St.1987, c. 656, and apply to proceedings which are initiated on or after April 1, 1988. These rules shall be known and may be cited as the Rules of the Commission of Judicial Conduct (R.C.J.C.). (Any proceedings initiated prior to April 1, 1988, shall be governed by the rules which were in effect under Chapter 211C before April 1, 1988.)

Rule 1. Definitions

A. "Anonymous Complaint" means a complaint, written or oral, received by the Commission, in which the identity of the complainant is not revealed.

B. "Chairman" and "Vice Chairman" refer to members of the Commission elected as such by vote of the Commission. Whenever used in these rules, the word "Chairman" shall include, in the absence of the Chairman, the Vice Chairman or other member acting as Chairman.

C. "Commission" means the Commission on Judicial Conduct.

D. "Complainant" means a person or entity who has communicated to the Commission a complaint against a judge. The Commission may also, in its discretion, treat as a complainant, for purposes of notice and any other rights afforded to a complainant under these rules, a person or entity who has reported judicial conduct to a third party, although not directly to the Commission, provided that such person or entity is or was directly affected by the conduct.

E. "Complaint" means any oral or written statement which alleges judicial misconduct or physical or mental disability of a judge.

F. "Conditions on the Judge's Conduct," for purposes of G.L. c. 211C, section 8(1)(c), shall include but not be limited to:

(1) education;

(2) training;

(3) mentoring;

(4) foreclosing eligibility for recall;

(5) an agreed-upon press release to be issued, with no other public comment on the matter by either party;

(6) requiring that a decision in a court case be issued by a certain date;

(7) periodic status reports;

(8) meeting with Commission members and/or staff;

(9) writing an apology to a person or to the public;

(10) requiring the judge to caution the judge's family members regarding misuse of their relationship to the judge;

(11) agreeing never to mediate, hear or rule on any matters involving the attorneys who investigated and prosecuted the matter, or their firms;

(12) insuring that official audio equipment is recording at all times during court proceedings;

(13) holding conferences on the record;

(14) otherwise requiring a judge to comply with the law, the Code of Judicial Conduct and other rules, regulations, orders and procedures.

(15) If the Commission finds that a condition not specified herein would be appropriate, the Commission may file under seal a request with the Supreme Judicial Court to rule within fourteen days as to whether that condition is permissible in this category, without disclosing the identity of the judge.

    (a) If the Court does not rule within fourteen days, the Commission may assume that the condition is permissible in this category.

G. "Executive Director" means the Executive Director of the Commission or a member of the Commission's staff acting under the Executive Director's supervision.

H. "Judge" means a judge or justice of any court of this Commonwealth.

I. "Notoriety" means broad public knowledge.

J. "Reasonable Information" means any information, including reports in the news media, which comes to the attention of the Commission and which contains credible allegations about a judge that, if true, would constitute misconduct or disability within the jurisdiction of the Commission under Chapter 211C.

K. "Shall is mandatory; "may" is permissive.

L. "Special Counsel" means an attorney, appointed by the Supreme Judicial Court at the request of the Commission, to conduct investigations, to make recommendations to the Commission, and/or to present evidence at a hearing, with respect to a complaint or charges against a judge, or to take any other action related thereto which the Commission may direct.

M. "Statement of Allegations" means a clear statement of the allegations against a judge and the alleged facts forming their basis.

N. "Sworn Complaint" means a detailed written complaint which the complainant signs under oath and files, at the request of the Commission.

Amended September 14, 1999, effective October 1, 1999; May 8, 2007, effective July 1, 2007; January 29, 2015, effective March 1, 2015.

Rule 2.   Composition of Commission

A. The composition of the Commission and terms of its members are as provided in Chapter 211C.

B. A member of the Commission shall not participate in any proceeding in which the impartiality of that member might reasonably be questioned. Disqualification pursuant to this section shall be by the member involved or by affirmative vote of at least five (5) members of the Commission.

(1) Upon the call of the Chairman, an alternate member shall serve in place of a member of the Commission who has been disqualified from participating in a Commission proceeding or is otherwise unable to serve. Whenever an alternate member is called to serve in the place of a member of the Commission, the judge in question and the complainant shall be so notified.

C. If a Commission member ceases to be qualified for the appointment to represent the category for which he was appointed, resigns, or becomes permanently unable to serve for any reason, a vacancy shall occur. An appointment to fill a vacancy for the duration of the unexpired term shall be made by the appropriate appointing authority forthwith.

Rule 3.   Organization of Commission

A. A Chairman and Vice Chairman shall be elected annually by the members of the Commission.

B. Meetings of the Commission shall be held upon the call of the Chairman or the written request of at least three members of the Commission. Meetings shall not be held on less than three days notice; but this requirement may be waived by consent of all the members. The Chairman shall preside at meetings of the Commission, and the Vice Chairman shall act in the absence or disqualification of the Chairman. In the absence or disqualification of both the Chairman and the Vice Chairman, the members shall select one among them as acting Chairman.

C. A quorum of the Commission shall consist of five members, including at least one judge, one member of the bar who is not a judge, and one lay person who is not a member of the bar. An affirmative vote of at least five members of the

Commission is required to dismiss, informally adjust, or otherwise dispose of a proceeding; to issue formal charges against a judge; or to make recommendations to the Supreme Judicial Court regarding disciplinary action. A vote may be taken by telephone when a decision is required sooner than a meeting could be held, unless any member objects.

Rule 4.   Jurisdiction of the Commission

A. The Commission shall have the authority to receive information, conduct investigations and hearings, and make recommendations to the Supreme Judicial Court concerning allegations of judicial misconduct or disability.

B. The Commission's jurisdiction shall include the conduct of all active judges prior to, as well as during, their service in judicial office and shall also include the conduct of a retired judge who has been recalled.

Rule 5.   Confidentiality

A. All proceedings prior to a determination of sufficient cause and the filing of formal charges shall be confidential.

B. Records, files, and reports of the Commission shall be confidential, and no disclosure shall be made, except as follows:

(1) Upon waiver in writing by the judge at any stage of the proceedings;

(2) Upon inquiry by an appointing authority or by a state or federal agency conducting investigations on behalf of such authority in connection with the selection or appointment of judges; or upon inquiry in connection with the assignment or recall of a retired judge to judicial duties, by or on behalf of the assigning authority, in which case the Commission may:

(a) divulge whatever information is a matter of public record; and

(b) after obtaining the judge's signed waiver, divulge other relevant information; or

(c) divulge other relevant information after giving written notice to the judge affected of its intention to do so and allowing the judge seven (7) days to respond.

(3) In cases in which the subject matter has become public, the Commission may issue such statements as it deems appropriate in order to confirm the pendency of the investigation, to clarify the procedural aspects of the proceedings, to explain the right of the judge to a fair hearing, or to state that the judge denies the allegations;

(4) Upon filing of formal charges, in which case only the formal charges, the answer thereto, the evidentiary hearings thereon, and the final recommendation by the Commission as to disposition shall become public, except as provided in paragraph D below.

C. Where the circumstances necessitating the initiation of an inquiry include notoriety, or where the conduct in question is a matter of public record, information concerning the lack of cause to proceed may be released by the Commission.

D. Proceedings may remain confidential, even after a finding of sufficient cause, if the judge, the Commission, and the complainant, if any, all concur.

E. If, in the course of its proceedings, the Commission becomes aware of credible evidence that any person has committed a crime, the Commission may report such evidence to the appropriate law enforcement agency.

Rule 6. Commission Proceedings: Initial Stages; General Provisions

A. Initiation of Proceeding. A Commission proceeding relating to the conduct of a judge is initiated when the Commission receives a written or oral complaint, or when the Commission by motion creates its own complaint, on the basis of reasonable information.

B. Screening. The Executive Director shall cause each complaint to be screened promptly upon its receipt. The screening may include communication with the complainant, if any, to clarify the contents of the complaint, but shall not include any investigation of the allegations set forth in the complaint.

C. Docketing and Notification.

(1) If the Executive Director determines after screening that the complaint does not set forth facts concerning a judge's conduct which, if true, would constitute misconduct or disability within the Commission's jurisdiction, the Executive Director shall notify the complainant that the complaint will not be docketed or investigated by the Commission.

(2) If the Executive Director determines after screening a complaint that it alleges specific facts which, if true, would constitute misconduct or disability within the Commission's jurisdiction, the Executive Director shall docket the complaint.

(3) Except as provided in Rules 6(D), 6(E), 6(F) and 6(G), the Executive Director shall notify the judge of the complaint promptly after it is docketed. Notification shall be by certified mail or registered mail, addressed to the judge's last known place of residence, unless the judge has requested a different mailing address or the use of regular mail. Except where notice of the complaint is delayed or withheld pursuant to Rule 6(G), the Executive Director shall not conduct any inquiry into or investigation of the complaint until notice has been sent to the judge.

D. Frivolous or Unfounded Complaints. If, on the basis of screening, the Executive Director is of the opinion that a docketed complaint is frivolous or unfounded, the Executive Director shall promptly recommend its dismissal to the Commission before notifying the judge of the complaint. If a majority of the Commission votes to dismiss the complaint, the Executive Director shall promptly notify the complainant, if any, of the dismissal and the judge of both the complaint and its dismissal. If a majority of the Commission does not vote to dismiss the complaint, except as provided in Rule 6(G), the Executive Director shall promptly notify the judge of the complaint in accordance with Rule 6(C)(3).

E. Stale Complaints. When a complaint is docketed in which the allegations arise out of acts or omissions all occurring more than one year prior to the date the complaint was filed, the Executive Director shall, before notifying the judge of the complaint and before undertaking any inquiry or investigation of its allegations, make a recommendation to the Commission as to whether there exists good cause to investigate the complaint. If a majority of the Commission determines that there is not good cause to investigate the complaint, the complaint shall be dismissed without investigation, and the complainant, if any, as well as the judge, shall be so notified. If a majority of the Commission determines that there is good cause to investigate the complaint, except as provided in Rule 6(G), the Executive Director shall notify the judge of the complaint pursuant to Rule 6(C)(3). When a complaint alleges a pattern of recurring misconduct the last episode of which is alleged to have occurred less than one year prior to the filing of the complaint, a determination by the Commission of "good cause" pursuant to this Rule is not necessary.

F. Anonymous Complaints. Following the docketing of an anonymous complaint pursuant to Rule 6(C)(2), the Executive Director shall not conduct any inquiry or investigation of it unless the Commission, upon the recommendation of the Executive Director, determines by majority vote that the allegations of the anonymous complaint would, if true, constitute misconduct or disability within the jurisdiction of the Commission, and the seriousness or the notoriety of the misconduct alleged outweighs the potential prejudicial effect of an investigation into the merits of the complaint. If the Commission does not make such a determination, the complaint shall be dismissed, and the Executive Director shall promptly notify the judge of both the complaint and its dismissal. If the Commission does make such a determination, except as provided in Rule 6(G), the Executive Director shall promptly notify the judge of the anonymous complaint in accordance with Rule 6(C)(3).

G. Withholding Notification. If the Executive Director is of the opinion that, because of the nature of the complaint or the identity of the complainant, notification to the judge would create a substantial risk that evidence material to its investigation might be lost or destroyed, or that there is a substantial danger of reprisal or retaliation by the judge against the complainant or any other person mentioned in the complaint, the Executive Director shall recommend to the Commission that notice of the complaint to the judge be delayed or that notice of certain information in the complaint be delayed. No inquiry or investigation into the complaint beyond the screening process shall take place until the Commission has voted on the Executive Director's recommendation.

(1) If a majority of the Commission does not vote to approve any delay in notifying the judge of the complaint in whole or in part, the Executive Director shall promptly notify the judge of the complaint in accordance with Rule 6(C)(2).

(2) If a majority of the Commission determines that notice to the judge of the complaint in its entirety would create a substantial risk of lost or destroyed evidence or of reprisal, the Commission shall vote to approve the delay in notifying the judge of the complaint in whole or in part. If the Commission approves a delay in providing notice to the judge of any portion of the complaint, the Executive Director shall proceed with an investigation of the complaint pursuant to Rule 6H. If the Commission approves a delay in providing notice to the judge of certain information in the complaint such as the identity of the complainant, the Executive Director shall promptly notify the judge in accordance with Rule 6(C)(3) of all portions of the complaint for which no delay was approved before proceeding with any investigation.

(3) Notice of a complaint may be delayed pursuant to this paragraph only until the Commission obtains the necessary evidence or the risk of reprisal ends.

(4) The Commission shall take reasonable steps to insure that as much notice as possible of the complaint's allegations is provided to the judge at the earliest time feasible in accordance with this Rule.

H. Investigation. Unless a complaint is dismissed pursuant to Rule 6(D), 6(E) or 6(F), and except as provided in Rule 6G, after notice is given to the judge pursuant to Rule 6(C)(3), the Executive Director shall initiate a discreet and confidential investigation and evaluation of the complaint.

I. Request for Special Counsel. If in the course of an investigation the Executive Director concludes that Special Counsel is required, the Executive Director shall recommend that the Commission request the appointment of a Special Counsel by the Supreme Judicial Court. The Commission may also take such action upon its own motion.

J. Sworn Complaint or Statement of Allegations. Within ninety (90) days after the initiation of proceedings, the Executive Director shall recommend to the Commission whether there is adequate reason to proceed to the preparation of a Sworn Complaint or Statement of Allegations.

(1) The Commission shall so decide by majority vote.

(2) If the Executive Director recommends that further investigation is necessary before making this determination, the Commission may vote to continue the investigation on a month-to-month basis.

(3) If the Commission finds that there is sufficient cause to proceed, the complainant, if any, shall be asked to file a detailed, signed, Sworn Complaint against the judge. The Sworn Complaint shall state the facts constituting the alleged misconduct. Immediately upon receipt of the Sworn Complaint, the Executive Director shall make written acknowledgment thereof to the complainant.

(4) When a Sworn Complaint is not obtained, a Statement of Allegations against the judge and the alleged facts forming their basis shall be prepared by the Executive Director. Where more than one act of misconduct is alleged, each act should be clearly set forth in the Sworn Complaint, or in the Statement of Allegations, as the case may be.

(5) In any case where the judge has not yet been notified of the entire complaint pursuant to Rule 6(G), if the Commission determines by majority vote that there remains an ongoing danger of reprisal, the Sworn Complaint or the Statement of Allegations may be drafted so as to conceal the complainant's identity.

K. Same; Service. The judge shall immediately be served with a copy of the Sworn Complaint or Statement of Allegations.

L. Same; Answer. Within twenty-one (21) days after the service of the Sworn Complaint or the Statement of Allegations, the judge may file a written answer with the Executive Director and may request a personal appearance before the Commission, in lieu of or in addition to a written response. If the judge elects to appear personally, his or her statement shall be recorded.

M. Same; Dismissal. After the judge's answer and personal appearance, if any, the Commission may terminate the proceeding and dismiss the complaint and, in that event, shall give notice to the judge and the complainant that it has found insufficient cause to proceed.

N. Same; Amendment. Amendment of the allegations regarding the misconduct of a judge, whether presented to the Commission in a Sworn Complaint or in a Statement of Allegations, shall be permitted prior to a finding of sufficient cause, provided that notice thereof and an opportunity further to respond within twenty-one (21) days is given to the judge.

O. Right to Counsel. The judge shall be entitled to counsel of the judge's own choice.

P. Right to Compel Attendance of Witnesses and Inspection of Records. At any stage of the proceeding, the Commission or its designee may administer oaths or affirmations and shall be entitled to compel the attendance and testimony of witnesses, including the judge himself or herself, and the production of papers, books, accounts, documents, electronic recordings, other tangible things, or any other relevant evidence or testimony.

(1) Upon receiving the Sworn Complaint or Statement of Allegations, the judge shall become entitled to compel by subpoena the attendance and testimony of witnesses through depositions, and to provide for the inspection of documents, books, accounts, written or electronically-recorded statements, and other records.

(2) Witnesses may be interviewed, whether or not under oath and whether or not their statements are memorialized, without the presence of other participants. In other circumstances, statements may be taken as depositions, in accordance with Rule 9.

Q. Privilege. A complaint submitted to the Commission or its staff, or testimony with respect thereto, shall be absolutely privileged. No civil action predicated on the complaint shall be instituted against a complainant or a witness, or against counsel to either of them.

R. Recommendation Concerning Assignment. At any time the Commission may recommend to the Supreme Judicial Court, or to the Chief Justice of the Trial Court and the appropriate Chief Justice, the non-assignment or special assignment of a judge, pending the final disposition of a proceeding. The Commission shall state the reasons for its recommendation. A copy of any such recommendation shall be sent by the Commission to the judge.

S. Consultation. In the course of a proceeding, the Commission may consult with the Chief Justice of the Trial Court and the appropriate Chief Justice about administrative matters.

T. Record of Commission Proceedings. The Commission shall keep a record of all proceedings concerning a judge. The Commission's findings, conclusions and recommendations shall be entered in the record.

U. Extensions of Time. The Chairman of the Commission may for good cause extend the time for the filing of an answer, discovery, commencement of a hearing, or transmittal of the Hearing Officer's report, and any other time limit set herein.

V. Enforcement of an agreement for Informal Adjustment shall be by the Commission, or, upon application by the Commission to the Supreme Judicial Court, by the Court.

Amended September 14, 1999, effective October 1, 1999; May 8, 2007, effective July 1, 2007; January 29, 2015, effective March 1, 2015.

Rule 7. Sufficient Cause for Formal Charges

A. Following the expiration of the twenty-one (21) days allowed for the judge's response, for any proceeding not dismissed, the Commission shall thereafter hold a formal meeting which shall be conducted in private, at which the rules of evidence need not be observed. The judge shall have the right to make a personal appearance with his attorney, but not to be present during the Commission deliberations.

B. At this meeting the Commission shall vote to dispose of the case in one of the following ways:

(1) If it finds that there has been no misconduct, the Executive Director shall be instructed to send the judge and the complainant notice of dismissal.

(2) If it finds that there has been misconduct for which a private reprimand constitutes adequate discipline, and if the judge consents, it shall issue the reprimand. The complainant shall be notified that the matter has been so resolved.

(3) If it finds that there has been conduct that is or might be cause for discipline but for which an informal adjustment is appropriate, it may, with the agreement of the judge, so inform or admonish the judge, direct professional counseling or assistance for the judge, or impose conditions on the judge's future conduct. The complainant shall be notified that the matter has been so resolved. When either conditions or treatment is prescribed, the Commission shall provide for supervision, enforcement thereof, or both.

(4) If it finds by a preponderance of the credible evidence that there is sufficient cause to believe that there has been misconduct of a nature requiring a formal disciplinary proceeding, the Commission shall issue formal charges against the judge. A copy of the formal charges shall be served promptly upon the judge, and the judge shall have ten (10) days to respond.

(5) If it finds that there has been conduct that is or might be cause for discipline and for which direct submission to the Supreme Judicial Court is appropriate, it may, with the agreement of the judge, make a direct submission in accordance with Rule 13.

Amended May 8, 2007, effective July 1, 2007.

Rule 8. Scheduling of Formal Hearing

A. Upon the filing of the judge's written response to the formal charges or the expiration of the time for its filing, a copy of the formal charges and of the judge's written response shall be filed with the Supreme Judicial Court, which shall promptly appoint a Hearing Officer.

B. Immediately upon the appointment of a Hearing Officer by the Supreme Judicial Court, the Commission shall schedule a hearing to take place in not less than thirty (30) nor more than sixty (60) days. The Commission shall immediately notify the judge and all counsel of the time and place for the hearing.

Rule 9. Discovery During the Formal Proceeding Stage

A. Attached to the notice required by Rule 7B(4) shall be further notice that the Commission shall, within a reasonable time, make available for inspection upon the written request of the judge all books, papers, records, documents, electronic recordings, and other tangible things within the custody and control of the Commission which are relevant to the issues of the disciplinary proceeding, and any written or electronically recorded statements within the custody and control of the Commission which are relevant to the issues of the disciplinary proceeding. The failure of the Commission to furnish timely any such materials provided for herein shall not affect the validity of any proceedings before the Commission, provided that such failure is not substantially prejudicial to the judge.

B. Within thirty (30) days after service of the formal charges, the Commission or the judge

(1) May upon written request to the appropriate party prior to the hearing:

(a) Have made available to him for inspection and copying within a reasonable period of time all books, papers, records, documents, electronic recordings, or other tangible things which that party intends to present at a hearing.

(b) Obtain the names and addresses of witnesses to the extent known to a party in the proceeding, including an identification of those intended to be called to testify at the hearing.

(c) Have made available to him for inspection and copying within a reasonable period of time any written or electronically recorded statements made by witnesses who will be called to give testimony at the hearing.

(2) May, upon written application to the Commission, upon such terms and conditions as the Commission may impose:

(a) Depose within or without the Commonwealth persons having relevant testimony. The complete record of the testimony so taken shall be made and preserved by stenographic record or electronic recording.

(i) The written application to the Commission shall state the name and post office address of the witness, the subject matter concerning which the witness is expected to testify, the time and place of taking the deposition, and the reason why such deposition should be taken.

(ii) Unless notice is waived, no deposition shall be taken except after at least seven (7) days notice to the other parties.

(iii) Unless otherwise directed by the Commission, the deponent may be examined regarding any matter not privileged which is relevant to the subject matter of the proceedings. Parties shall have the right of cross-examination, and objection. In making objections to questions or evidence, the grounds relied upon shall be stated briefly, but no transcript filed by the notarial officer shall include argument or debate. Objections to questions or evidence shall be noted by the notarial officer upon the deposition, but he shall not have the power to decide on the competency, materiality, or relevancy of evidence. Objections to the competency, relevancy, or materiality of the testimony are not waived by failure to make them before or during the taking of the deposition.

(b) Subpoena relevant witnesses and documents.

(c) Seek any limitation or protection for any discovery permitted by this rule.

C. Nothing in these rules shall be construed to require the discovery of any report made to the Commission by special counsel or other person conducting an investigation for the Commission. Furthermore, in granting discovery the Commission shall protect against disclosure of the mental impressions, conclusions, opinions, or legal theories of an attorney or other representative of a witness or party in these proceedings.

D. Other issues relative to discovery which are not covered in these rules shall be addressed or resolved in accordance with the comparable provisions of the Massachusetts Rules of Civil Procedure.

Rule 10. Formal Hearing

A. The formal hearing shall be conducted before the Hearing Officer appointed by the Supreme Judicial Court.

B. The hearing shall be open to the public. The rules of evidence applicable to civil proceedings in Massachusetts shall apply, and all testimony shall be under oath. Commission attorneys, or special counsel retained for the purpose, shall present the case. The judge whose conduct is in question shall be permitted to adduce evidence and produce and cross-examine witnesses. The Commission shall have the burden of proving the charges by clear and convincing evidence. Every hearing shall be transcribed.

C. The formal charges may be amended after commencement of the public hearing only if the amendment is technical in nature and if the judge and his counsel are given adequate time to prepare a response.

Rule 11. Post–Hearing Procedure

A. Within thirty (30) days after the conclusion of the hearing, the Hearing Officer shall submit to the Commission and to the judge a report which shall contain proposed findings and recommendations, the transcripts of testimony, and all exhibits.

B. Upon receipt of the report of the Hearing Officer, the Commission shall send a copy of the report to the complainant forthwith.

C. Within twenty (20) days after receipt of such report, counsel for the judge and for the Commission shall each be allowed to submit to the Commission written objections to the proposed findings and recommendations. Any such objections shall become part of the record.

D. Within the same twenty (20) day period the judge and the complainant, if any, may file a written request to be heard before the Commission regarding its recommendation for discipline.

E. If either participant does so request, notice shall be given to both as to the scheduled time and place for such hearing, at least seven (7) days in advance. Such hearing shall

be public, but Commission deliberations regarding such recommendation shall be conducted in executive session.

F. Unless there is good cause for delay, the Commission shall reach a decision on the basis of the full record within ninety (90) days after the hearing concerning recommendation for discipline, if there is such a hearing, or otherwise within ninety (90) days after receipt of the Hearing Officer's report. Its conclusions may differ from those proposed by the Hearing Officer. Its decision shall state specific reasons for all conclusions and recommendations.

Rule 12. Cases Involving Allegations of Mental or Physical Disability

In considering allegations of mental or physical disability, the Commission shall, insofar as applicable and except as provided below pursuant to Chapter 211C, section 10, follow procedures established by these rules.

A. If, in a matter relating to mental or physical disability, the Commission finds facts supporting sufficient cause to believe that a judge has a mental or physical disability that may be affecting the judge's ability to perform judicial duties and the judge is not represented by counsel, the Commission shall request that the Supreme Judicial Court appoint an attorney to represent the judge. Where the Commission has not made a request for counsel, at any stage of proceedings on a complaint alleging judicial disability, a judge may request that the Commission seek appointment of counsel to represent the judge and the Commission shall then request that the Court appoint an attorney to represent the judge. Any attorney appointed to represent the judge shall be compensated by the Commission according to the guidelines and rates set forth for special masters by Superior Court Rule 49.

B. If a sworn complaint or statement of allegations involves the current or past mental or physical health of a judge, a denial of the alleged disability or condition shall constitute a waiver of medical privilege and the judge shall be required to produce any and all medical records relevant to the question of whether the judge has a mental or physical disability that may be affecting the judge's ability to perform judicial duties.

C. In the event of a waiver of medical privilege, the judge shall be deemed to have consented to an examination by a qualified medical practitioner designated by the Commission. The report of the medical practitioner shall be furnished to the Commission and the judge. The judge's attorney and/or his or her representative may be present for any such examination.

Amended August 29, 2019, effective October 1, 2019.

Rule 13. Direct Submission to the Supreme Judicial Court

At any stage of a proceeding the Commission may, with the agreement of the judge, elect one of the following methods for direct submission to the Supreme Judicial Court.

A. Final Submission Upon Agreed Facts.

(1) The Commission and the judge will prepare and sign an Agreement for Final Submission to the Supreme Judicial Court Upon Agreed Facts. The Agreement will contain:

(a) A waiver by the judge of the right to a formal hearing.

(b) A stipulation by the judge to facts sufficient, in the judgment of the Commission, to establish judicial misconduct.

(c) A statement of the section(s) of the Code of Judicial Conduct which the Commission alleges, and the judge agrees, the judge has violated.

(d) Statements by the Commission and by the judge of their joint or disparate recommendations for discipline by the Supreme Judicial Court.

(e) Agreement by the Commission and the judge that the Supreme Judicial Court may accept or reject the recommendations of the Commission or the judge or may impose whatever discipline it deems appropriate.

(f) Acknowledgment by the Commission and the judge that the decision of the Supreme Judicial Court will constitute the final disposition of the case.

(g) A waiver by the judge of any confidentiality rights that would preclude submission of the matter to, or disclosure of the matter by, the Supreme Judicial Court, including the items to be submitted as specified herein, and the Supreme Judicial Court's disposition of the case.

(2) The Commission will submit to the Supreme Judicial Court under seal:

(a) The Agreement for Final Submission Upon Agreed Facts.

(b) A copy of the complaint, statement of allegations and formal charges, if any, and all responses.

(c) Any other information agreed to by the parties.

(3) The Supreme Judicial Court may accept or reject the recommendation of either the Commission or the judge or may impose whatever discipline it deems appropriate.

B. Conditional Submission Upon Acknowledged Evidence

(1) The Commission and the judge will prepare and sign an Agreement for Conditional Submission to the Supreme Judicial Court Upon Acknowledged Evidence. The Agreement will contain:

(a) A waiver by the judge of the right to a formal hearing.

(b) A Statement of Evidence which in the Commission's view provides a basis for a finding of misconduct. The Statement of Evidence will identify the section(s) of the Code of Judicial Conduct which the Commission alleges the judge to have violated.

(c) An acknowledgment by the judge that the evidence set forth in the Statement of Evidence, if presented to and accepted by a Hearing Officer at a formal hearing as clear and convincing, would support a finding of such misconduct.

(d) A recommendation to the Supreme Judicial Court, agreed to by both the Commission and the judge, regarding appropriate discipline.

(e) Agreement by the Commission and the judge that (i) if the Supreme Judicial Court accepts their agreed recommendation for discipline, the decision of the Supreme Judicial Court will constitute the final disposition of the case; and (ii) if the Supreme Judicial Court does not accept their agreed recommendation, the Commission will proceed to consider and dispose of the complaint in accordance with these Rules, which disposition may include issuance of formal charges.

(f) A waiver by the judge of any confidentiality rights that would preclude submission of the matter to the Supreme Judicial Court, including the items to be submitted as specified herein.

(g) Agreement by the Commission and the judge that the submission will be made on condition that it be impounded by the Supreme Judicial Court.

(2) The Commission will submit to the Supreme Judicial Court:

(a) The Agreement for Conditional Submission Upon Acknowledged Evidence.

(b) A copy of the complaint, statement of allegations and formal charges, if any, and all responses.

(c) Any other information agreed to by the parties.

(3) The Supreme Judicial Court may accept or reject the recommended discipline agreed to by the Commission and the judge but may not at this stage impose other discipline.

C. The Supreme Judicial Court may request additional information from the parties or schedule oral argument before acting on a final or conditional submission.

D. If the Commission and the judge fail to agree upon an Agreement for Final or Conditional Submission to the Supreme Judicial Court under either 13.A. or 13.B. above, the Commission will proceed to consider and dispose of the complaint in accordance with these Rules, which disposition may include issuance of formal charges.

Approved May 8, 2007, effective July 1, 2007.

APPENDIX—M.G.L.A. CHAPTER 211C. COMMISSION ON JUDICIAL CONDUCT

Table of Sections

Section 1. Establishment; Membership; Expenses; Term; Chairman

There shall be a commission on judicial conduct consisting of nine members. Three judges shall be appointed by the justices of the supreme judicial court, none of whom shall be justices of said court and no two of whom shall be from the same department of the trial court. Three members of the bar shall be appointed by the chief justice of the trial court, none of whom shall be judges. Three members shall be appointed by the governor, none of whom shall be members of the bar. The members of the commission shall serve without compensation, but shall be reimbursed for all expenses reasonably incurred by them in the performance of their duties. Members of the commission shall serve for six year terms. Commission membership shall terminate if a member ceases to be qualified for the appointment. A vacancy shall be filled by the appointing authority for the remainder of the term. Upon the expiration of the term of office of a member, his successor shall be appointed in the manner aforesaid. No person shall succeed himself as a member of the commission except when his membership is due to an appointment to fill a vacancy for the remainder of an unexpired term. One or more alternate members, as necessary, shall be selected in the manner prescribed for initial appointments in each representative class, and shall serve at the call of the chairman to take the place of those who are disqualified from participating in a commission proceeding pursuant to commission rules.

Added by St.1978, c. 478, § 114. Amended by St.1987, c. 656, § 1; St.2011, c. 93, § 62, eff. July 1, 2012.

Section 2. Investigations, Hearings and Recommendations

(1) All judges of the trial court, the appeals court and the supreme judicial court shall be subject to discipline pursuant to this chapter. The commission on judicial conduct shall have the authority to receive information, investigate, conduct hearings, and make recommendations to the supreme judicial court concerning allegations of judicial misconduct and allegations of mental or physical disability affecting a judge's performance.

(2) The commission shall have jurisdiction over investigations and recommendations regarding discipline arising from the conduct of all judges, including any retired judge who is assigned to perform the duties of a judge for a temporary period. This jurisdiction shall include all conduct that occurred prior to a judge's assuming judicial office, and conduct of a lawyer who is no longer a judge that occurred while he held judicial office; provided, however, that in evaluating such conduct, the commission shall give substantial weight to relevant decisions of the supreme judicial court and the board of bar overseers regarding bar discipline. The foregoing shall not be construed to derogate the inherent authority of the supreme judicial court to supervise and discipline judges, the authority of the governor with the consent of the council to remove a judge upon the address of both houses of the legislature or to retire a judge involuntarily because of advanced age or mental or physical disability, the authority of the legislature to remove a judge through impeachment, or the supervisory authority of the chief justices of the appeals and supreme judicial courts or of the chief and department administrative justices of the trial court.

(3) Except where the commission determines otherwise for good cause, the commission shall not deal with complaints arising out of acts or omissions occurring more than one year prior to the date commission proceedings are initiated pursuant to section five; provided, however, that, when the last episode of an alleged pattern of recurring judicial conduct arises within the one year period, the commission may consider all prior acts or omissions related to such alleged pattern of conduct.

(4) In the absence of fraud, corrupt motive, bad faith, or clear indication that the judge's conduct violates the code of judicial conduct, the commission shall not take action against a judge for making findings of fact, reaching a legal conclusion, or applying the law as he understands it. Commission proceedings shall not be a substitute for an appeal.

(5) Grounds for discipline shall include:

(a) conviction of a felony;

(b) willful misconduct in office;

(c) willful misconduct which, although not related to judicial duties, brings the judicial office into disrepute;

(d) conduct prejudicial to the administration of justice or conduct unbecoming a judicial officer, whether conduct in office or outside of judicial duties, that brings the judicial office into disrepute; or

(e) any conduct that constitutes a violation of the codes of judicial conduct or professional responsibility.

Added by St.1978, c. 478, § 114. Amended by St.1987, c. 656, § 1.

Section 3. Report; Appropriations; Offices; Rules; Immunity; Executive Director; Proceedings

(1) The commission shall report only to the supreme judicial court. The commission shall be allowed for its purposes annually such amount as shall be appropriated for it by the general court. The commission shall be provided with adequate offices. The commission may adopt rules of procedure, without compliance with the provisions of chapter thirty A, but subject to the approval of the supreme judicial court, and may develop appropriate forms for its proceedings. Such rules shall establish reasonable time limits for all stages of commission proceedings and standards for extending time limits applicable to commission proceedings.

(2) Members of the commission, hearing officers, commission counsel, and staff shall be absolutely immune from suit for all conduct in the course of their official duties. A complaint submitted to the commission or its staff and communications related to the complaint shall be absolutely privileged, and no civil action predicated on the complaint or on such a communication may be instituted against any complainant or witness or his counsel; provided however, such immunity from suit shall apply only to communications to the commission or its staff and shall not apply to public disclosure of information contained in or relating to the complaint.

(3) The commission shall appoint an executive director who shall serve at the pleasure of the commission. The executive director shall be a member of the Massachusetts bar, shall serve full time, and shall not engage in the practice of law. The executive director shall receive an annual salary, subject to appropriation, which is fixed by the commission consistent with classification and compensation policies of the supreme judicial court, and such expenses as are approved by the commission and incurred in the discharge of the executive director's duties.

(4) The executive director shall have duties and responsibilities as prescribed by the commission, including the authority to:

(a) receive information, allegations, and complaints;

(b) make preliminary evaluations;

(c) screen complaints;

(d) conduct investigations;

(e) recommend dispositions;

(f) maintain the commission's records;

(g) maintain statistics concerning the operation of the commission and make them available to the commission and to the supreme judicial court;

(h) prepare the commission's budget for approval by the commission and administer its funds;

(i) employ and supervise other members of the commission's staff;

(j) prepare the annual report of the commission's activities required pursuant to section four; and

(k) employ, with the approval of the commission and subject to appropriation, special counsel, private investigators, or other experts, and clerical assistants, as necessary to investigate and process matters before the commission and before the supreme judicial court. Neither the attorney general's staff nor law enforcement officers shall be employed for this purpose.

(5) The supreme judicial court may delegate the power to enforce process in commission proceedings to another appropriate court. A witness at any stage of commission proceedings may rely on any privilege applicable to civil proceedings.

Added by St.1978, c. 478, § 114. Amended by St.1983, c. 622; St.1987, c. 656, § 1.

Section 4. Annual Report

The commission shall submit annually to the general court and the supreme judicial court a report of its activities together with recommendations. This report shall be a matter of public record and shall be printed as a public document.

Added by St.1978, c. 478, § 114.

Section 5. Initiation of Proceedings; Inquiry, Investigation and Evaluation; Detailed Complaint or Statement of Allegations; Formal Charges

(1) Commission proceedings relating to the conduct of a judge may be initiated by an oral or written complaint stating facts that if true, would be grounds for discipline, or by the commission's own motion when the commission receives reasonable information, including reports in the news media, as to conduct that appears to constitute grounds for discipline. Upon receipt of such complaint or adoption of such motion, the commission shall promptly notify the judge, except as provided in subdivision (2), and shall conduct a prompt, discreet and confidential inquiry, investigation and evaluation.

(2) The commission shall notify the judge of the proceedings and their subject matter before commencing any inquiry, investigation or evaluation in all cases except as follows:

(a) where, because of the nature of the complaint, delay is necessary in order to preserve evidence, notice may be delayed until such evidence is obtained, until the matter is dismissed, or until the sworn complaint or statement of allegations is served pursuant to subdivision (6), whichever occurs first;

(b) where the identity of the complainant could be readily determined by the judge from the nature of the complaint and there is a danger of reprisal against the complainant, notice may be delayed until the danger of reprisal ends, until the matter is dismissed, or until the sworn complaint or statement of allegations is served pursuant to subdivision (6), whichever occurs first; provided, however, that in any such case where there is an ongoing danger of reprisal, the notice and the statement of allegations may be drafted so as to conceal the complainant's identity.

(3) The commission shall discourage and shall promptly dismiss complaints which are frivolous, unfounded or outside commission jurisdiction. The commission shall notify the judge and the complainant, if any, of such dismissal in accordance with the provisions of subdivisions (1), (2) and (10).

(4) At any stage of the proceeding, the commission shall be entitled within the time limits established by commission rule to compel by subpoena the attendance and testimony of witnesses, including the judge, and to provide for the inspection of documents, books, accounts, and other records.

(5) After a thorough inquiry, investigation and evaluation, the executive director shall recommend to the commission, and the commission shall determine, by majority vote, whether there is adequate reason to proceed to the preparation of a detailed complaint or statement of allegations. If so, the commission shall request that the complainant file a detailed sworn complaint against the judge. When a sworn complaint is not obtained, the executive director shall prepare a clear statement of the allegations against the judge and the alleged facts forming their basis. Said complaint or statement of allegations shall clearly set forth each act of misconduct where more than one act of misconduct is alleged, and shall state clearly the provision of statute, code of judicial conduct or code of professional responsibility alleged to have been violated by each alleged act of misconduct.

(6) The judge shall be served promptly with a copy of the sworn complaint or statement of allegations.

(7) The judge shall have twenty-one days after receipt of the sworn complaint or statement of allegations to respond in writing to the charges and, if he wishes, to file a written request for a personal appearance before the commission.

(8) The judge shall be entitled to counsel of his own choice. After the judge is served with the sworn complaint or statement of allegations, he shall be entitled before the issuance of formal charges and within the time limits established by commission rule to compel by subpoena the attendance and testimony of witnesses through depositions, and to provide for the inspection of documents, books, accounts, written or electronically recorded statements, and other records. The judge may file written material for commission consideration before the issuance of formal charges.

(9) If the judge requests a personal appearance before the commission, he may be accompanied by counsel, his statement and that of his counsel shall be recorded, and the commission shall not issue formal charges until after such personal appearance.

(10) If at any time prior to the issuance of formal charges the commission determines that it does not have sufficient cause to proceed, the commission shall terminate the proceedings by closing the investigation or dismissing the complaint or the statement of allegations. In that event, the commission shall give notice to the complainant, if any, and to the judge that it has found insufficient cause to proceed. The file in any matter so terminated shall be closed.

(11) The commission may not refer subsequently to a file closed before the issuance of formal charges except in the following circumstances:

(a) in a subsequent proceeding that raises similar allegations against the judge and indicates a pattern of recurring judicial misconduct;

(b) in a subsequent proceeding alleging conduct in violation of conditions imposed as part of an informal adjustment pursuant to subdivision (1) of section eight;

(c) in connection with a decision as to the recommended sanction to be imposed in a subsequent proceeding.

(12) The commission may, upon notice to the judge, amend the allegations prior to a finding of sufficient cause to issue formal charges. The judge may amend his written response or submit additional written material for commission consideration before such finding.

(13) After the judge's personal appearance pursuant to subdivision (9), if any, and after the expiration of any time limit upon written submissions by the judge pursuant to subdivisions (8) and (12), the commission shall determine whether there is sufficient cause to issue formal charges. A finding of sufficient cause to issue formal charges shall require the concurrence of the majority of all commission members that there is a preponderance of credible evidence that the judge's conduct constitutes grounds for discipline.

(14) When sufficient cause is found, the commission shall issue formal charges stating those allegations as to which sufficient cause is found. A copy of the formal statement of charges shall be served promptly upon the judge and the judge shall have ten days to respond. Immediately thereafter, a copy of such formal statement of charges and of the judge's written response shall be filed with the supreme judicial court, which shall promptly appoint a hearing officer. Confidentiality shall cease upon this filing, as provided in section six, and after this filing the proceedings shall be governed by the provisions of section seven.

Added by St.1987, c. 656, § 2.

Section 6.   Confidentiality

(1) Except as provided in this section, all proceedings of the commission shall be confidential until there has been a determination of sufficient cause and formal charges have been filed with the supreme judicial court. The commission shall ensure that a procedure applicable to commission members, counsel and staff is established for enforcing confidentiality.

(2) Notwithstanding the provisions of subdivision (1), the judge may waive his right to confidentiality prior to a finding of sufficient cause. In addition, in any case in which the subject matter becomes public, through independent sources or through a waiver of confidentiality by the judge, the commission may issue such statements as it deems appropriate in order to confirm the pendency of the investigation, to clarify the procedural aspects of the disciplinary proceedings, to explain the right of the judge to a fair hearing without prejudgment, or to state that the judge denies the allegations.

(3) If the inquiry was initiated as a result of notoriety or because of conduct that is a matter of public record, and is subsequently terminated because there is insufficient cause to proceed, information concerning the insufficiency of cause to proceed may be released by the commission.

(4) Notwithstanding any other provision of this chapter to the contrary, proceedings pursuant to this chapter may remain confidential, even after a finding of sufficient cause, if the judge, the commission, and the complainant, if any, all concur.

(5) If any federal agency, the judicial nominating council, or any like agency for screening candidates for judicial appointment which succeeds the judicial nominating council, seeks information or written materials from the commission concerning a judge, in connection with his selection or appointment as a judge, information may be divulged in accordance with procedures prescribed by commission rule, including reasonable notice to the judge affected, unless the judge signs a waiver of the right to such notice. If, in connection with the assignment of a retired judge to judicial duties, the chief justice of the supreme judicial court or the appeals court or the chief justice of the trial court seeks information or written materials from the commission about the judge, information may be divulged in accordance with procedures prescribed by commission rule, including reasonable notice to the judge affected, unless the judge signs a waiver of the right to such notice.

Added by St.1987, c. 656, § 2. Amended by St.2011, c. 93, § 63, eff. July 1, 2012.

Section 7. Hearing; Recommendation for Discipline; Attorneys' Fees

(1) The commission shall schedule a hearing without undue delay after the appointment of the hearing officer by the supreme judicial court. The commission shall schedule the time and place of the hearing, and shall notify the judge and all counsel of the hearing. The judge shall be afforded ample opportunity to prepare for the hearing and may amend his written response to the charges.

(2) The judge and the commission shall each be entitled to discovery to the extent available in civil proceedings, within the time limits provided by commission rules. The judge and the commission shall each be entitled to compel by subpoena the attendance and testimony of witnesses, including the judge, and to provide for the inspection of documents, books, accounts, and other records.

(3) The formal hearing shall be public and shall be conducted before the hearing officer appointed by the supreme judicial court. At the hearing, all testimony shall be under oath, the rules of evidence applicable to civil proceedings shall apply, and the judge shall be accorded due process of law.

(4) An attorney or attorneys of the commission staff, or special counsel retained for the purpose, shall present the matter to the hearing officer. The commission shall have the burden of proving the charges by clear and convincing evidence. The judge and the commission shall be permitted to present evidence and cross-examine witnesses, subject to the rules of evidence applicable to civil proceedings.

(5) The raising of mental or physical condition as a defense constitutes a waiver of medical privilege.

(6) By leave of the commission or with the consent of the judge, the statement of charges may be amended after commencement of the hearing only if the amendment is technical in nature and the judge and his counsel are given adequate time to prepare a response.

(7) Every hearing shall be transcribed.

(8) The hearing officer shall submit to the commission and to the judge a report containing proposed findings and recommendations, the transcripts of testimony and all exhibits. Counsel for the judge and commission shall have twenty days after receipt of such report to submit written objections to the findings and recommendations, and said objections shall become part of the record.

(9) Before the commission reaches its decision, the judge and the complainant, if any, shall have the right to be heard before the commission regarding its recommendation for discipline, and their statements shall be transcribed. Such hearing shall be public, but commission deliberations regarding such recommendation shall be conducted in executive session. The commission shall reach a decision on the basis of the full record within ninety days after such hearing, unless there is good cause for delay. Its conclusions may differ from those proposed by the hearing officer. Its decision shall state specific reasons for all conclusions and recommendations.

(10) A recommendation for discipline shall be reported to the supreme judicial court only if a majority of all members of the commission concur that discipline should be recommended. Any dissent as to the need for or the form of discipline shall be transmitted with the majority decision. A copy of said recommendation and dissent shall be given to the judge and shall become part of the public record. The entire record, including transcripts, exhibits and the hearing officer's report, shall be transmitted to the supreme judicial court.

(11) If a majority of the members of the commission concur that discipline should not be recommended, the matter shall be dismissed, and the judge and complainant, if any, shall be notified of such dismissal.

(12) The provisions of subdivisions (10) and (11) shall not be construed to prohibit the commission from disposing of the matter by informal adjustment pursuant to section eight as a result of commission deliberations regarding a recommendation for discipline.

(13) The expense of witnesses shall be borne by the party that calls them unless:

(a) physical or mental disability of the judge is in issue, in which case the commission shall reimburse the judge for the reasonable expenses of the witnesses whose testimony related to the disability; or

(b) the supreme judicial court determines that the imposition of costs and expert witness fees will work a financial hardship or injustice upon him and orders that those fees be reimbursed.

(14) All witnesses shall receive fees and expenses in the same manner as witnesses in civil actions before the courts. A transcript of all proceedings shall be provided to the judge without cost. Except as provided in subdivision (13), costs of all proceedings shall be at public expense.

(15) With the approval of the supreme judicial court, a judge shall be entitled to the payment of reasonable attorneys' fees by the commonwealth in any case where the matter is dismissed by the commission at any stage after the filing of a sworn complaint or statement of charges, where the supreme judicial court determines despite a commission recommendation for discipline that no sanction is justified, or where the supreme judicial court determines that justice will be served by the payment of such fees.

Added by St.1987, c. 656, § 2.

Section 8. Informal Adjustment; Sanctions

(1) With the agreement of the judge, the commission may by informal adjustment dispose of a complaint at any stage of the proceedings by:

(a) informing or admonishing the judge that his conduct is or may be cause for discipline;

(b) directing professional counseling and assistance for the judge;

(c) imposing conditions on the judge's conduct; or

(d) persuading a judge to retire voluntarily.

(2) The commission may dismiss a sworn complaint, a statement of allegations or a formal statement of charges as unjustified or unfounded at any stage during the proceedings.

(3) The commission may issue a private reprimand with the consent of the judge.

(4) The commission may recommend to the supreme judicial court one or more of the following sanctions:

(a) removal;

(b) retirement;

(c) imposition of discipline as an attorney;

(d) imposition of limitations or conditions on the performance of judicial duties;

(e) public or private reprimand or censure;

(f) imposition of a fine;

(g) assessment of costs and expenses;

(h) imposition of any other sanction which is reasonable and lawful.

Added by St.1987, c. 656, § 2.

Section 9. Charges Against Supreme Judicial Court Member

The chief justice and the six most senior justices of the appeals court other than the chief justice shall serve in the place of the supreme judicial court when charges are brought against a member of the supreme judicial court.

Added by St.1987, c. 656, § 2.

Section 10. Physical or Mental Disabilities

(1) The commission shall have authority to receive information, investigate, conduct hearings, and make recommendations to the court relating to mental or physical disability affecting a judge's performance.

(2) In carrying out its responsibilities regarding physical or mental disabilities, the commission shall follow the same procedures that it employs with respect to discipline for misconduct.

(3) If the judge in a matter relating to physical or mental disability is not represented by counsel, the commission shall appoint an attorney to represent him at public expense.

(4) If a complaint involves the physical or mental condition of the judge, a denial of the alleged condition shall constitute a waiver of medical privilege and the judge shall be required to produce his medical records.

(5) If medical privilege is waived, the judge shall be deemed to have consented to a physical or mental examination by a qualified medical practitioner designated by the commission. The report of the medical practitioner shall be furnished to the commission and the judge.

Added by St.1987, c. 656, § 2.

Section 11. Advisory Committee

The supreme judicial court may establish an advisory committee on the code of judicial conduct, which may render advisory opinions to judges at their request or on its own motion.

Added by St.1987, c. 656, § 2.

RULES OF THE BOARD OF BAR OVERSEERS

Table of Sections

CHAPTER 1.   GENERAL PROVISIONS

Section 1.1.   Title

These rules shall be known and may be cited as the "Rules of the Board of Bar Overseers", and are hereby promulgated pursuant to Supreme Judicial Court Rule 4:01, Section 5(3)(h).

Adopted effective April 9, 2009.

Section 1.2.   Definitions

Subject to additional definitions contained in subsequent provisions of these Rules, the following words and phrases shall have, unless the context clearly indicates otherwise, the meanings given to them in this section.

ADMINISTRATOR: The Administrator as established by Section 5.5 of these Board Rules.

BAR COUNSEL: Bar Counsel or Bar Counsel's designee.

BOARD: The Board of Bar Overseers as appointed from time to time by the Supreme Judicial Court.

BOARD CHAIR: The Chair of the Board of Bar Overseers.

BOARD RULES: The provisions of the Rules of the Board of Bar Overseers of the Commonwealth of Massachusetts. Also referred to as "these Rules."

CHARGING MEMORANDUM: A confidential memorandum prepared by Bar Counsel solely for the consideration of a Reviewing Board Member when discipline is recommended which describes the investigation undertaken, the disciplinary charges to be brought, the facts uncovered by the investigation which support the charges, the Respondent's disciplinary history, if any, and Bar Counsel's reasons for recommending that discipline be imposed.

COMPLAINANT: Any person who has filed a complaint.

COMPLAINT: A statement of alleged misconduct or request for investigation filed with the Board or Bar Counsel pursuant to Sections 2.1 through 2.4 of these Rules.

COURT: Supreme Judicial Court of the Commonwealth of Massachusetts.

DISCIPLINARY RULES: S.J.C. Rules 3:07 and Chapter 4.

EXPEDITED HEARING: A proceeding under section 8(4) of S.J.C. Rule 4:01 following a lawyer's rejection of an admonition.

FORMAL CHARGES: Charges filed pursuant to Chapter 3 of these Rules in which Bar Counsel seeks public discipline.

FORMAL PROCEEDING: A proceeding subject to Chapter 3 of these Board Rules in which Bar Counsel seeks public discipline.

HEARING COMMITTEE: A hearing committee appointed by the Board under section 5(3)(c) of S.J.C. Rule 4:01. Unless otherwise provided herein, the words "hearing committee" used throughout this rule shall also mean a hearing panel of the Board or a special hearing officer.

INFORMATION: Proceedings filed by the Board in the Supreme Judicial Court in any case where disbarment or suspension of a lawyer is sought or recommended or when a lawyer or Bar Counsel has appealed from a Board decision to administer a public reprimand or to dismiss a case or to administer an admonition after formal proceedings.

INVESTIGATION: Inquiry into facts under the direction of Bar Counsel or the Board with respect to alleged misconduct or to reinstatement.

NOTARIAL OFFICER: An officer authorized under Section 4.12 of these Rules to take depositions for use before a hearing committee, hearing panel, or special hearing officer.

PARTIES: The parties to a proceeding under these Rules are Bar Counsel and the Respondent.

PETITION FOR DISCIPLINE: A formal pleading filed by Bar Counsel with the Board pursuant to section 8(3) of the Supreme Judicial Court Rule 4:01 requesting disciplinary action by the Board for alleged violations of the Rules of Professional Conduct or Supreme Judicial Court Rule 4:01.

PROOF OF SERVICE: A certificate of service complying with Sections 3.11 and 3.12 of these Board Rules.

RESPONDENT: A lawyer admitted to or engaging in the practice of law in this Commonwealth or any lawyer specially admitted by a Court of this Commonwealth for a particular proceeding, who in either case is alleged to have been guilty of misconduct in a complaint.

REVIEWING BOARD MEMBER: A member of the Board who has been designated by the Board Chair to review recommendations submitted by Bar Counsel.

SPECIAL HEARING OFFICER: A lawyer appointed by the Board to hear charges of misconduct when, in view of the anticipated length of the hearing or for other reasons, the Board determines that a speedy and just disposition would be better accomplished by such appointment than by referring the matter to a hearing committee or panel of the Board.

Adopted effective April 9, 2009.

CHAPTER 2.   INVESTIGATIONS AND INFORMAL PROCEEDINGS

SUBCHAPTER A.   PRELIMINARY PROVISIONS

Section 2.1.   Initiation of Investigations

(a) **At Direction of Board**. Upon the order of the Board, Bar Counsel shall undertake and complete an investigation of the conduct of any lawyer as may be specified in the order.

(b) By Bar Counsel.

(1) Bar Counsel shall undertake and complete an investigation of all matters involving alleged violations of the Rules of Professional Conduct filed in accordance with Section 2.2 of these Rules, provided that Bar Counsel need not pursue any matter that Bar Counsel in his or her discretion determines to be frivolous or to fall outside the Board's jurisdiction or to involve allegations that do not warrant further action. Bar Counsel need not investigate any complaint arising out of acts or omissions occurring more than six years prior to the date of the complaint.

(2) Bar Counsel may undertake an investigation of any conduct by a lawyer which may violate the Rules of Professional Conduct.

Adopted effective April 9, 2009.

Section 2.2.   Contents of Complaint

Each complaint relating to alleged misconduct of a lawyer shall be in writing and signed by the complainant and shall contain a brief statement of the facts upon which the complaint is based. Verifications of the complaint shall not be required. If necessary, Bar Counsel will assist the complainant in reducing the complaint to writing.

Adopted effective April 9, 2009.

Section 2.3.   [Reserved]

Reserved effective April 9, 2009.

Section 2.4.   Complaints Against Bar Counsel and the Board

Complaints against the bar counsel, assistant bar counsel or any member of the Board involving alleged violations of the Rules of Professional Conduct shall be submitted directly to the Board for disposition pursuant to Section 5.6(c)(2) of these Rules.

Adopted effective April 9, 2009.

Section 2.5.   [Reserved]

Reserved effective April 9, 2009.

Section 2.6.   Notification to Respondent

Before making a recommendation of admonition or prosecution of formal charges as provided in Sections 2.7(3)(A) or 2.7(3)(C) of these Rules, Bar Counsel shall forward to the Respondent a request for a statement of the Respondent's position, notifying the Respondent of:

(1) the nature of the complaint, and, if the investigation has been initiated by the filing of a written complaint and unless Bar Counsel determines otherwise for good cause, the name and address of the complainant;

(2) the Respondent's right and obligation to state his or her position with respect to the allegations against him or her within 20 days from the date of such notice unless a shorter time is fixed by Bar Counsel in such notice, and

(3) the fact that a copy of the Respondent's reply to the complaint may be forwarded to the complainant.

Failure of the Respondent to cooperate with Bar Counsel's request and any subsequent investigation may result in disciplinary action or administrative suspension under Supreme Judicial Court Rule 4:01, section 3.

Adopted effective April 9, 2009.

Section 2.7. Bar Counsel's Recommendation

Following completion of any investigation of the complaint that he or she deems appropriate and after consideration of any statement of position filed by the Respondent, Bar Counsel may take any one of the following actions:

(1) Close the complaint or make a determination that a complaint need not be pursued, subject to the notification requirements of Section 2.10.

(2) Close a matter after adjustment, informal conference, or reference to and completion of diversion to an alternative educational, remedial, or rehabilitative program.

(3) Recommend to the Board:

(A) that an admonition be administered in those cases in which a violation of the Rules of Professional Conduct is found which is determined to be of insufficient gravity to warrant the prosecution of formal charges; or

(B) that public discipline be imposed by agreement; or

(C) that formal charges be instituted.

Adopted effective April 9, 2009.

Section 2.8. Review of Bar Counsel's Recommendation

(a) Recommendation Other Than That Formal Charges Be Prosecuted.

(1) Bar Counsel shall submit to a Reviewing Board Member, along with the file, Bar Counsel's recommendation that an admonition be administered, or any request from a complainant for review of Bar Counsel's determination not to pursue or to close a complaint pursuant to Section 2.7(1) and 2.10(1) of these Rules. When Bar Counsel's recommendation is to administer an admonition, Bar Counsel shall prepare and provide to the Reviewing Board Member a charging memorandum.

(2) The Reviewing Board Member may adopt, reject, or modify Bar Counsel's recommendation. If the Reviewing Board Member modifies or rejects the recommendation of Bar Counsel, he or she shall set forth this determination and the reasons therefor on the recommendation form. The Reviewing Board Member may confer with Bar Counsel in making his or her determination.

(b) Recommendation That Formal Charges Be Prosecuted (No Agreement).

(1) *Bar Counsel's Recommendation.* When the prosecution of formal charges is recommended pursuant to Section 2.7(3)(C) of these rules or when, before the appointment of a hearing committee, hearing panel, or special hearing officer, Bar Counsel seeks to amend a previously approved petition for discipline by adding or deleting charges, Bar Counsel shall

prepare a petition for discipline or an amended petition for discipline and a charging memorandum or revised charging memorandum and submit these documents for approval pursuant to Section 2.8(b)(2) of these rules. After such appointment, any request by Bar Counsel to amend a previously approved petition, by deleting any charge or paragraph, shall be presented by motion and decided in accordance with Sections 3.16(2) and 3.18 of these rules. Any request by Bar Counsel to bring additional charges against a respondent named in an approved and pending petition for discipline shall be presented for approval as set forth in the first sentence of this subsection, whether or not a hearing committee, hearing panel, or special hearing officer has been appointed to hear the previously approved petition.

(2) *Transmission of File.* Bar Counsel shall forward to the Reviewing Board Member the documents set forth in subsection (b)(1) and the file.

(3) *Standard of Review.* In reviewing a recommendation to prosecute formal charges or to add or delete previously approved charges, the Reviewing Board Member shall make a determination

(A) whether the charging memorandum or revised charging memorandum supports the charges in the petition for discipline or the amended petition for discipline, and, if applicable, whether the revised charging memorandum adequately justifies the deletion of previously approved charges, and

(B) whether, if the charges in the petition for discipline or amended petition for discipline were to be proved by a preponderance of the evidence, the case would warrant public discipline.

(4) *Action by Reviewing Board Member.* The Reviewing Board Member may approve, modify, or reject Bar Counsel's recommendations under section (b)(1). If the Reviewing Board Member modifies or rejects Bar Counsel's recommendation, he or she shall set forth this determination and the reasons therefor on the recommendation forms. The Reviewing Board Member may confer with Bar Counsel in making his or her determination.

(5) *Use of Charging Memorandum.* The Charging Memorandum shall be considered only by the Reviewing Board Member and by the Board Chair on appeal pursuant to section 2.9 of these rules and shall not be provided to the hearing committee, hearing panel, or special hearing officer, or to the Board.

(c) Recommendation that Public Discipline be Imposed by Agreement. When the parties recommend under Section 2.7(3)(B) of these Rules that public discipline be imposed by agreement, Bar Counsel shall prepare a petition for discipline and the matter shall be referred directly to the Board under the procedures set forth in Section 3.19(d) and (e).

Adopted effective April 9, 2009. Amended June 21, 2017, effective September 1, 2017.

Section 2.9. Appeal by Bar Counsel From Modification or Rejection of Recommendation

(a) General Rule. Bar Counsel may appeal to the Board Chair from a modification or rejection of his or her recommendation by the Reviewing Board Member.

The appeal shall state briefly the grounds relied upon by Bar Counsel for the appeal and shall be filed with the Board within 14 days after the decision by the Reviewing Board Member was noted, which time limit is jurisdictional.

(b) Action by Chair. The Board Chair shall consider the appeal and may in his or her discretion adopt, modify, or reject any action recommended by Bar Counsel or by the Reviewing Board Member.

(c) Review by Board. When Bar Counsel's recommendation is that formal charges be prosecuted, Bar Counsel may appeal the decision of the Board Chair to the full Board. The appeal shall state briefly the grounds relied upon by Bar Counsel for the appeal and shall be filed with the Board within 14 days after the decision of the Board Chair is filed, which time limit is jurisdictional. The Board Chair's determination as to Bar Counsel's recommendation of an admonition shall be final and not subject to objection under Section 2.9(e).

(d) Appeals Administrative. Appeals under this section shall be administrative and not adversary in nature. Copies of the appeal shall be available only to the Board, and the Respondent shall not be deemed a party to the appeal or have any right to be heard with respect thereto.

(e) Filing of Information. If Bar Counsel objects to having the matter concluded by dismissal, the Board shall file an Information pursuant to section 3.58 of these rules.

Adopted effective April 9, 2009.

Section 2.10.   Notification of Disposition of Complaint

(1) When Bar Counsel determines not to investigate a complaint or to close a complaint, Bar Counsel shall notify the complainant that the complaint is not being pursued, or, if a file has been opened, the complainant and the Respondent that the complaint has been closed.

(A) Bar Counsel's notice to the complainant shall include (i) the reasons for not investigating a complaint or for closing the file and (ii) a letter from the Board advising the complainant that he or she has a right to request review of Bar Counsel's decision by a member of the Board and that such request must be made in writing no later than 14 days after the date of notification by Bar Counsel. Bar Counsel's notice may include, if appropriate, information concerning other forums for consideration of the complaint.

(B) If the complainant requests review of Bar Counsel's decision under this section, Bar Counsel shall transmit the file to the Board for review pursuant to Section 2.8 of these Rules.

(2) When the matter has been disposed of after adjustment, informal conference, or diversion to an alternative educational, remedial, or rehabilitative program, Bar Counsel shall so notify the complainant and the Respondent.

(3) In any event, Bar Counsel may notify the complainant, if appropriate, that the complainant may present his or her complaint to another jurisdiction, to a fee disputes committee or to any other duly constituted forum for the consideration of the complaint.

(4) If an admonition is administered, the complainant shall be notified after the admonition becomes final. If a public reprimand by agreement is imposed, an Information is filed by agreement of the parties with approval of the Board, or formal proceedings are commenced, the complainant shall be notified at the time that occurs.

Adopted effective April 9, 2009.

SUBCHAPTER B.   FINAL DISPOSITION WITHOUT FORMAL PROCEEDINGS

Section 2.11.   Admonition

When the matter is being disposed of by an admonition, Bar Counsel shall make service of the admonition on the Respondent, together with a summary of the basis for the admonition and written notice of the Respondent's right to demand in writing within 14 days of the date of service that the admonition be vacated and a hearing provided, as set forth in Section 2.12. The notice served with the admonition shall advise the Respondent that failure to demand within 14 days that the admonition be vacated and to submit a written statement of objections as provided in Section 2.12 constitutes consent to the admonition and that failure to set forth matters in mitigation constitutes waiver of the right to introduce evidence of mitigation at the hearing. A record shall be made of the fact of and basis for the admonition, which record shall be retained as provided in Section 5.10 of these Rules.

Adopted effective April 9, 2009.

Section 2.12.   Demand by Respondent for Hearing on Admonition

(1) *General Provisions:* A Respondent shall be entitled to demand that an admonition be vacated and a hearing provided.

The demand shall be in writing and shall be filed with the Board, and a copy served on Bar Counsel, within 14 days after the date of service of the admonition, which time limit is jurisdictional. The Respondent must submit with the demand a statement of objections to the factual allegations and disciplinary rule violations set forth in the summary served with the admonition pursuant to Section 2.11. The statement of objections must specify the reasons in detail for rejecting the admonition and include any matters in mitigation. Failure of the Respondent to demand within 14 days that the admonition be vacated and to provide a statement of objections constitutes consent to the admonition and failure to set forth matters in mitigation constitutes waiver of the right to introduce evidence of mitigation at hearing.

(2) *Additional Procedural Requirements:*

(a) All proceedings and the record shall be confidential pursuant to Section 3.22(b).

(b) No investigatory subpoenas shall be issued after expedited disciplinary proceedings are commenced.

(c) The matter shall be assigned to a special hearing officer and shall be set for hearing within 30 days of the filing of proceedings except for good cause shown.

(d) In addition to the notice of hearing requirements of Section 3.21, the notice of hearing for expedited hearings shall also set a date for the exchange between or among the parties of witness lists and exhibits that the party intends to use in his or her case-in-chief or for matters in aggravation or mitigation; a date for their exchange of objections to proposed witnesses and identified exhibits and supplemental designation of exhibits and witnesses; and a date for filing with the Board of final witness and exhibit lists and objections thereto, agreed exhibits, and any stipulations of the parties.

(e) Except for good cause shown, a prehearing conference shall not be held prior to an expedited disciplinary hearing.

(f) The burden of proof in such hearing shall be as set forth in Section 3.28.

(g) Except for good cause shown, no briefs or requests for findings and rulings shall be filed following an expedited disciplinary hearing.

Adopted effective April 9, 2009.

SUBCHAPTER C. DEFERMENTS

Section 2.13. Deferment of Matters Involving Related Pending Civil or Criminal Litigation

A motion for deferment of action under Supreme Judicial Court Rule 4:01, Section 11, may be made by the Respondent or Bar Counsel. Such motion shall be filed in the office of the Board and served on the opposing party. The other party may file and serve a written response thereto within seven days thereafter.

After the response to a motion for deferment has been filed, or after the time for filing a response has elapsed, the matter shall be decided in accordance with Section 3.18 of these rules.

Adopted effective April 9, 2009. Amended June 21, 2017, effective September 1, 2017.

CHAPTER 3. DISCIPLINARY PROCEEDINGS

SUBCHAPTER A. PRELIMINARY PROVISIONS

Section 3.1. Construction of Chapter

This chapter is promulgated for the purpose of assisting Bar Counsel, the Respondent and the Board to develop the facts relating to, and to reach a just and proper determination of complaints. The Board will not hold any action of a hearing committee, hearing panel, or special hearing officer invalid by reason of any nonprejudicial irregularity, or for any error not resulting in a miscarriage of justice.

Adopted effective April 9, 2009.

Section 3.2. Procedure to Apply

Except where inconsistent with these Rules, proceedings before hearing committees, hearing panels, special hearing officers and the Board shall conform generally to the practice in adjudicatory proceedings under Chapter 30A of the General Laws (State Administrative Procedure).

Adopted effective April 9, 2009.

Section 3.3. Filing; Timely Filing Required

Pleadings or other papers in formal proceedings shall be filed at the office of the Board and copies sent or delivered by the filing party to each member of the hearing committee or panel or special hearing officer unless otherwise directed. If the filing of a pleading or paper is subject to a time limit, it must be received at the office of the Board within the time limit. Except as otherwise provided by these Rules, on motion filed within the time limits established by this section, the Board Chair may shorten or extend the time for filing for good cause shown. The date of receipt by the office of the Board, and not the date of deposit in the mails, is determinative.

Adopted effective April 9, 2009.

Section 3.4. Representation of Respondent

(a) **Appearance Pro Se.** When a Respondent appears in his or her own behalf in a disciplinary proceeding, the Respondent shall file with the Board, with proof of service upon Bar Counsel, an address, including a street address, at which any notice or other written communication may be sent and a telephone number where the Respondent can be reached.

(b) **Representation of Respondent by Counsel.** When a Respondent is represented by counsel in a disciplinary proceeding, counsel shall file with the Board, with proof of service upon Bar Counsel, a written notice of such appearance, which shall state his or her name, address and telephone number, the name and address of the Respondent on whose behalf he or she appears, and the caption and file number of the subject proceeding. Thereafter, any notice or other written communication required to be served on or furnished to a Respondent may be sent to the counsel of record for such Respondent at the stated address of the counsel in lieu of transmission to the Respondent.

(c) **Service.** Any notice or pleading required to be served on the Respondent personally under these Rules may be served in hand or by addressing it by certified, registered, or first class mail to the address furnished by the Respondent during the proceeding. If the Respondent has not furnished an address during the proceeding, service may be made by addressing it by certified, registered, or first class mail to the address furnished in the last registration statement filed by the Respondent in accordance with Supreme Judicial Court Rule 4:02. Service by mail is complete upon mailing.

(d) Assistance in Obtaining Counsel for a Respondent. If a Respondent in a disciplinary proceeding desires counsel and cannot afford to retain counsel, then, upon application, the Board will seek to assist the Respondent to obtain counsel either at a reduced or no cost. Nothing in this subsection (d) accords any substantive right to the Respondent with respect to the appointment or payment of counsel.

(e) Policies Relating to Conflicts of Interest.

(1) No member of the Board, or partner or associate of a Board member, shall appear as counsel for a Respondent in a disciplinary proceeding, provided that no partner or associate of a Board member shall be required to withdraw from a disciplinary proceeding pending at the time the Board member commences his or her term.

(2) No member of any hearing committee or hearing panel, and no special hearing officer shall appear as counsel for a Respondent in a disciplinary proceeding.

(3) No partner or associate of a hearing committee member shall appear as counsel for a Respondent in a disciplinary proceeding before the hearing committee on which the said hearing committee member serves. No partner or associate of a special hearing officer shall appear as counsel for a Respondent in a disciplinary proceeding before the special hearing officer.

(4) No member of the Board or of any hearing committee shall appear voluntarily or make a submission as a character witness in a disciplinary or reinstatement proceeding.

Adopted effective April 9, 2009.

Section 3.5. Format of Pleadings and Documents

(a) Format. Pleadings or other documents filed in disciplinary proceedings shall be typed on letter size paper, 8½ inches wide by 11 inches long.

(b) Binding. Pleadings and other documents, other than correspondence, shall be bound by staples only.

(c) Incorporation by Reference. Any document on file with the Board in a disciplinary proceeding may be incorporated by reference into a subsequently filed pleading or other document.

(d) Identification. Pleadings or other documents filed in a disciplinary proceeding shall set forth:

(1) The caption and docket number of the proceeding.

(2) A brief descriptive title of the pleading or document.

(e) Copies. All pleadings or other documents filed in a disciplinary proceeding (other than correspondence) shall be filed with the Board. In any matter pending before a hearing committee, a hearing panel, or a special hearing officer, a conformed copy of each such paper, including all exhibits, if any, shall be furnished to the special hearing officer and to each member of the hearing committee or hearing panel. Whenever necessary or convenient, the Board, the hearing committee, the hearing panel, or the special hearing officer may order that a greater or lesser number of copies be filed.

Adopted effective April 9, 2009.

Section 3.6. Execution

(a) Signature. Except as may be otherwise ordered or requested by the Board the original of each pleading or other document shall be signed in ink by the party or the party's counsel, and shall show the office address and telephone number of such party or counsel. All other copies filed shall be fully conformed thereto.

(b) Effect. The signature of the person subscribing any document filed in a disciplinary proceeding constitutes a certificate that the signer has read the document being subscribed and filed, and knows the contents thereof; that if executed in any representative capacity, the document has been subscribed and executed in the capacity specified upon the document with full power and authority to do so; that the contents are true as stated, except as to matters and things, if any, stated on information and belief, and that as to those matters and things, the signer believes them to be true.

(c) Verification. No written statement in any proceeding required to be verified by affidavit shall be required to be verified by oath or affirmation if it contains or is verified by a written declaration that it is made under the penalties of perjury.

Adopted effective April 9, 2009.

Section 3.7. Continuances

(a) Avoidance of Delay. All disciplinary proceedings under these Rules shall be as expeditious as possible, and all time limits shall be mandatory and not discretionary.

(b) Continuances. A motion for an extension of time or for a continuance in a disciplinary proceeding may be granted for good cause shown, and it shall be decided in accordance with the provisions of Section 3.18(a) of these rules concerning matters not reserved for decision by the Board.

(c) Absence of Hearing Committee or Hearing Panel Member. The absence of a committee or panel member from any hearing shall not be cause for continuing the hearing as long as a quorum of the hearing committee or panel is present. Such member may participate fully in all deliberations of the committee so long as the transcript of the hearing at which he or she was absent is available to him or her.

Adopted effective April 9, 2009. Amended June 21, 2017, effective September 1, 2017.

Section 3.8. Service of Documents by the Board

Orders, notices and documents other than subpoenas originating with the Board shall be served by the Board by delivery in person or by mailing a copy thereof to the person to be served or the person's counsel.

Adopted effective April 9, 2009.

Section 3.9. Service of Documents by a Party

All pleadings, briefs and other documents filed in disciplinary proceedings, when filed or tendered to the Board for filing, shall be served upon all parties to the proceeding. Such service shall be made by delivery in person or by mail.

Adopted effective April 9, 2009.

Section 3.10. Date of Service of Documents

The date of service shall be the day when the document served is deposited in the United States mail, or is delivered in person, as the case may be.

Adopted effective April 9, 2009.

Section 3.11. Proof of Service of Documents

There shall accompany and be attached to the original of each pleading or other document filed with the Board, when service is required to be made by the parties, a certificate of service substantially in the form prescribed by Section 3.12 of these Rules. All other copies filed shall be fully conformed thereto.

Adopted effective April 9, 2009.

Section 3.12. Form of Certificate of Service

I hereby certify that I have this day served by (indicate method of service) the foregoing document upon all parties of record in this proceeding. Dated this ___ day of _____, ___.

_____

(Signature)

Counsel for _____

Adopted effective April 9, 2009.

SUBCHAPTER B. PRE–HEARING PROCEEDINGS

Section 3.13. Institution of Disciplinary Proceedings

(a) Bar Counsel shall institute formal disciplinary proceedings by filing with the Board a petition under Section 3.14 of these Rules in either of the following cases:

(1) Pursuant to a referral from the Supreme Judicial Court under Bar Disciplinary Rule 4:01, sections 12(4) and (5), following the conviction of the Respondent for a crime.

(2) Pursuant to a determination to institute formal proceedings made under Chapter 2 of these Rules.

(b) When the Respondent vacates an admonition and demands a hearing, Bar Counsel shall institute expedited disciplinary proceedings under section 8(4) of S.J.C. Rule 4:01 and Section 2.12 of these Rules.

Adopted effective April 9, 2009.

Section 3.14. Petition for Discipline

(a) **Caption.** A petition for discipline shall be captioned as follows:

_____

BAR COUNSEL,

   Petitioner

vs.   File No.

James Roe,

   Respondent

_____

(b) **Contents.** The petition shall set forth specific charges of alleged misconduct.

Adopted effective April 9, 2009.

Section 3.15. Service of Petition On Respondent and Answer

(a) A copy of the petition shall be served together with a notice from the Board which shall

(1) Set twenty days after such service upon the Respondent as the time for answering.

(2) Advise the Respondent that failure to file a timely answer to the petition shall be deemed an admission of the charges and that averments in the petition are admitted when not denied in the answer.

(3) Advise the Respondent that failure without good cause to file a timely answer shall be deemed an act of professional misconduct in violation of Supreme Judicial Court Rule 4:01, Section 3(1)(c), and shall be grounds for administrative suspension pursuant to Supreme Judicial Court Rule 4:01, Section 3(2).

(b) Service of the petition shall be made by Bar Counsel.

(c) The Respondent shall file an answer with the Board and serve a copy on Bar Counsel.

(d) **Contents of Answer.** The answer shall be in writing, and shall state fully and completely the nature of the defense. The answer shall admit or deny specifically, and in reasonable detail, each material allegation of the petition and state clearly and concisely the facts and matters of law relied upon. Averments in the petition are admitted when not denied in the answer in accordance with this section.

(e) **Failure to Answer In Accordance With the Rules.** The allegations in the petition for discipline shall be deemed admitted if the Respondent fails to file a timely answer.

(f) **Request to Be Heard in Mitigation.** The Respondent shall include in the answer any facts in mitigation and may request that a hearing be held on the issue of mitigation. Failure to include facts in mitigation constitutes a waiver of the right to present evidence of those facts.

(g) **Procedure upon Failure to Answer.** If no answer is filed within the time limit established by this section, the Board shall promptly notify the Respondent that the allegations of the petition have been deemed admitted and that the opportunity to present evidence in mitigation has been waived. Unless Bar Counsel requests a hearing on matters in aggravation, the Board shall consider the matter of disposition on the basis of the admitted charges. The Board may order the parties to submit briefs.

(h) **Motion for Relief from Default.** Within twenty days of the date of the notice required by subsection (g) of this section, the Respondent may file and serve a motion for relief from default. For good cause shown, the Board Chair may order that the default be removed and that the Respondent be permitted to file an answer on or before a date determined by the Board Chair.

Adopted effective April 9, 2009.

Section 3.16. Amendment of Pleadings or Other Filings

(1) Before the appointment of a hearing committee, hearing panel, or special hearing officer, a request by Bar Counsel to amend a petition for discipline by adding or deleting charges shall be decided in accordance with Section 2.8(b)(1) and (2) of these rules.

(2) After the appointment of a hearing committee, hearing panel or special hearing officer, a motion by Bar Counsel to amend a petition for discipline by deleting charges or, with respect to a motion to amend filed at any time by the respondent motions to amend the pleadings or other filings shall be decided in accordance with the provisions of Section 3.18 of these rules concerning motions not reserved for action by the Board. A request by Bar Counsel to bring additional charges against a respondent shall be presented to a reviewing board member in accordance with Section 2.8(b) of these rules. A motion to amend a petition to consolidate for hearing any such newly-approved charges with the charges in a previously approved petition shall be presented to and decided by the hearing committee, hearing panel, or special hearing officer.

(3) If a motion by Bar Counsel to dismiss a charge is allowed pursuant to Subsection (2) of this rule, a respondent may by motion request a determination by a reviewing board member on whether the amended petition satisfies the standard of review under Subsection 2.8(b)(3)(B) of these rules for prosecution of formal charges warranting public discipline and, if not, whether the matter should proceed pursuant to the provisions of Supreme Judicial Court Rule 4:01, § 8(4), governing expedited hearings concerning the imposition of an admonition.

Adopted April 9, 2009. Amended June 21, 2017, effective September 1, 2017.

Section 3.17. Discovery

(a) **Scope.** Within 20 days following the filing of an answer, Bar Counsel and the Respondent shall exchange the names and addresses of all persons having knowledge of facts relevant to the proceedings. Bar Counsel and the Respondent shall, within 10 days, comply with reasonable requests made within 30 days following the filing of an answer for (1) non-privileged information and evidence relevant to the charges or the Respondent, and (2) other material upon good cause shown to the chair of the hearing committee, hearing panel or special hearing officer. Applications for depositions may be made pursuant to Sections 4.9 or 4.10.

(b) **Resolution of Disputes.** Any dispute arising under this rule shall be resolved by motion decided in accordance with Section 3.18 of these rules.

Adopted effective April 9, 2009. Amended June 21, 2017, effective September 1, 2017.

Section 3.18. Motions

(a) **General Provisions.**

(1) Until the appointment of a hearing committee, hearing panel, or special hearing officer, all motions shall be decided by the Board chair or a Board member designated by the Board chair. Thereafter, and excepting motions for issue preclusion, all motions not reserved for action by the Board, as described below, shall be decided by the special hearing officer or the chair of the hearing committee or hearing panel. Motions for issue preclusion are reserved for action by the Board chair or, when so designated by the Board chair, by another Board member, the special hearing officer, the chair of the hearing committee, or the chair of the hearing panel.

(2) Motions reserved for action by the Board shall be decided as set forth in Subsection (b), below.

(3) All motions shall be filed at least ten days before the hearing, except by leave granted by the Board chair, the special hearing officer or the chair of the hearing committee or the hearing panel.

(4) A party wishing to respond to a motion must file a response within seven days after service of the motion. The time for filing a response shall not be shortened or extended except for good cause shown.

(5) No motion or response grounded on facts shall be considered unless the facts are verified by affidavit, are established by the pleadings or the record, or are agreed to by the parties in writing.

(6) All motions shall be determined on the papers, without hearing or oral argument, except as may be permitted in the discretion of the person authorized by this rule to decide the motion.

(7) Except as to the allowance of a respondent's motion to dismiss under Subsection (c), matters falling within Sections 3.16(3) and 3.22 of these rules, and rulings that the moving party alleges exceed the jurisdiction or authority of the chair of the hearing committee or panel, special hearing officer, or Board chair (or designee), rulings on motions shall control the subsequent course of the proceeding and shall not be appealed or reviewed prior to the issuance of the hearing report

(b) **Motions Reserved For Action By The Board.**

The following motions are reserved for action by the Board chair or a Board member designated by the Board chair: a motion by a respondent to dismiss the petition for discipline or any charge or set of charges contained in the petition: a motion for leave to take a discovery deposition after the commencement of formal disciplinary proceedings under B.B.O. Rules, Section 4.9; a motion for a protective order under Supreme Judicial Court Rule 4:01, Section 20 and B.B.O. Rules, Section 3.22; a motion to stay or defer proceedings, including motions under Supreme Judicial Court Rule

4:01, Section 11 and B.B.O. Rules, Section 2.13: and a motion pursuant to B.B.O. Rules, Section 3.16(3).

(c) Motions to Dismiss.

(1) The respondent's filing of a motion to dismiss shall not by itself stay a scheduled hearing.

(2) Bar Counsel may appeal from a dismissal of a petition or charge by filing a brief on appeal within seven days after service of the decision. The respondent may file a response within seven days after service of such appeal. The appeal shall be decided by the Board at its next meeting after the response period has expired. Dismissal of a charge does not stay proceedings on other charges in the petition for discipline.

(3) A motion by Bar Counsel to dismiss or discontinue an entire petition for discipline, or any charge or set of charges contained therein, shall be determined in accordance with Sections 2.8(b)(1) and 3.16 of these rules. The dismissal or discontinuance, at the request of Bar Counsel, of a petition, or any charge or set of charges contained therein, shall act as a dismissal with prejudice.

Adopted effective April 9, 2009. Amended June 21, 2017, effective September 1, 2017.

Section 3.19. Assignment for Hearing

(a) Hearing shall be held before a hearing committee, a hearing panel, a special hearing officer, or the full Board, at the discretion of the Board Chair. Unless otherwise stated the words "hearing committee" as appearing in Sections 3.20 through 3.49 of the Rules shall also mean a special hearing officer, a hearing panel or the full Board, where appropriate.

(b) If there are any contested issues raised by the answer, or if the Respondent requests the opportunity to be heard in mitigation, the matter shall be assigned for hearing to an appropriate hearing committee, hearing panel, special hearing officer, or to the full Board.

(c) In the event the Respondent files an answer admitting the charges, and does not therein request the opportunity to be heard in mitigation, but does not reach agreement with Bar Counsel on disposition, then the matter shall be assigned to a hearing committee, a panel of the Board or the full Board for hearing on disposition at which the parties shall be given the opportunity to present recommendations and argument on disposition, and evidence of prior disciplinary action or the lack thereof.

(d) In the event the Respondent files an answer admitting the charges, does not therein request the opportunity to be heard in mitigation, and reaches agreement with Bar Counsel on a joint recommendation that the matter be concluded by a public reprimand or a suspension, then the matter shall be referred directly to the Board. If the Board agrees that a joint recommendation for a public reprimand is appropriate under the circumstances, the Board shall order a public reprimand without further proceedings. If the Board agrees that a

joint recommendation for suspension is appropriate under the circumstances, it shall file an Information against the Respondent in accordance with Section 3.58 of these Rules. A tie vote by the Board on a joint recommendation shall constitute a rejection of the recommendation.

(e) If the Board rejects the parties' joint recommendation filed under Section 3.19(d) of these Rules, it shall issue a preliminary decision explaining the reasons for such rejection, and the parties shall have fourteen days from the date of service of the vote on the parties to file further briefs in support of the recommended disposition. If the Board thereafter upholds its preliminary decision to reject the joint recommendation of the parties, the Board shall state the reasons for its vote and the matter shall proceed pursuant to the provisions of Disciplinary Rule 4:01, Section 8(6), and Sections 3.55–3.58 of these Rules unless the parties have reserved the right to a hearing on the charges or on discipline. If the parties have reserved the right to a hearing, they may, unless they have otherwise agreed, then amend their pleadings without prejudice, and the matter shall be assigned for hearing to an appropriate hearing committee, special hearing officer, a hearing panel of the Board, or to the full Board.

(f) Composition of Committee. If the matter is assigned to a hearing committee or hearing panel, the Board Chair or his or her designee shall designate the one of the members of the hearing committee or hearing panel to serve as chair.

Adopted effective April 9, 2009.

Section 3.20. Place of Hearing

Unless the Board Chair or the Chair's designee specifies a different venue, a hearing on a petition for discipline shall take place at the offices of the Board. The Board chair or the chair's designee shall consider the convenience of the complainant, witnesses, the Respondent and hearing committee in selecting a hearing location.

Adopted effective April 9, 2009.

Section 3.21. Notice of Hearing

The Board Chair or the Chair's designee shall give notice to the parties of the date and place set for hearing.

The notice of hearing shall be served at least fifteen days in advance thereof and shall advise the Respondent that the Respondent is entitled to be represented by counsel, to cross-examine witnesses, and to present evidence in his or her own behalf. The notice shall further advise the Respondent that failure to appear at a hearing shall be deemed an act of professional misconduct in violation of Supreme Judicial Court Rule 4:01, Section 3(1)(c), and shall be grounds for administrative suspension pursuant to Supreme Judicial Court Rule 4:01, Section 3(2).

Adopted effective April 9, 2009.

SUBCHAPTER C. HEARINGS

Section 3.22. Public Access to Proceedings; Protective Orders

(a) Except as otherwise provided in this section and in Supreme Judicial Court Rule 4:01, Section 20, the Board and Bar Counsel shall keep confidential all information involving allegations of misconduct by a lawyer.

(b) Expedited disciplinary hearings pursuant to Supreme Judicial Court Rule 4:01, section 8(4) and Section 2.12 of these Rules shall be confidential. If, after hearing, the special hearing officer recommends that the matter be remanded for formal proceedings, the matter becomes public when a petition for discipline is served as set forth in subsection (c) of this rule.

(c) Upon the service of a petition for discipline, the Board's proceedings are open to the public, except for:

(1) deliberations of the hearing committee, the hearing panel, the special hearing officer or the Board, and documents reflective of those deliberations, including without limitation charging memoranda, draft reports, and minutes of Board meetings;

(2) information with respect to which the Board has issued a protective order under paragraph (d) hereof;

(3) information with respect to which the Supreme Judicial Court has issued a protective order on appeal from a Board decision denying such order; or

(4) further proceedings following the recommendation by a hearing committee, a hearing panel, a special hearing officer or an appeal panel, or following an order of the Board or the Supreme Judicial Court, that an admonition be imposed or that a petition for discipline be dismissed. In such event, the record shall be sealed and the proceedings shall be closed until and unless the Board or the Supreme Judicial Court orders otherwise.

(d) In order to protect the interests of a complainant, witness, third party, or Respondent-attorney, the Board may, upon motion of Bar Counsel or any affected person and for good cause shown, issue a protective order prohibiting the disclosure of specific information otherwise privileged or confidential and direct that the proceedings be conducted so as to implement the order, including requiring that the hearing be conducted in such a way as to preserve the confidentiality of the information that is the subject of the application. A motion for a protective order shall be decided in accordance with Section 3.18 of these rules. If bar discipline or other professional discipline has been imposed on the Respondent on a prior occasion, in this Commonwealth or elsewhere, the fact that the discipline imposed is or has been confidential shall not constitute good cause for the issuance of a protective order. Bar Counsel or any affected person may appeal from an order granting or denying a motion for a protective order by filing a notice of appeal with the Clerk of the Supreme Judicial Court for Suffolk County within seven days after the date of the notice of the Board's action, which time limit shall be jurisdictional. The pendency of such an appeal shall not be grounds to stay proceedings before a hearing committee, a hearing panel, a special hearing officer, or any panel of the Board.

Adopted effective April 9, 2009. Amended June 21, 2017, effective September 1, 2017.

Section 3.23. Mandatory Prehearing Conferences

(a) General Provisions.

(1) In all cases, except for matters arising from a conviction of a crime and expedited hearings pursuant to Section 2.12, a prehearing conference shall be held. A prehearing conference shall be held in conviction cases if a party requests such a conference within 30 days after the answer is filed. Except for good cause shown, a prehearing conference shall not be held prior to an expedited disciplinary hearing pursuant to Section 2.12 of these Rules.

(2) The conference shall be conducted by the chair of the hearing committee or hearing panel or the special hearing officer. Additional conferences may be held as necessary.

(3) The Respondent, the Respondent's attorney if the Respondent is represented by counsel, and Bar Counsel shall attend the prehearing conference.

(4) The parties and counsel shall be fully prepared for a useful discussion and resolution, to the extent possible, of all procedural and substantive issues in the proceeding and shall be fully authorized to make commitments regarding those matters.

(5) Except as to orders that the moving party alleges exceed the jurisdiction or authority of the chair of the hearing committee or panel, special hearing officer, or Board Chair, orders entered at a prehearing conference shall control the subsequent course of the proceeding and shall not be appealed or reviewed prior to the issuance of the hearing report.

(6) Prehearing deadlines set at a prehearing conference shall not be extended except for good cause shown.

(b) Purpose of Prehearing Conference and Action at Conference. At the mandatory prehearing conference, the following matters may be considered and orders thereon entered:

(1) Settling any discovery disputes within the jurisdiction of the hearing committee, hearing panel or special hearing officer.

(2) Identifying contested issues.

(3) Obtaining admissions or stipulations as to facts not in dispute, the authenticity of documents, and other matters that might properly shorten the hearing.

(4) Limiting the number of witnesses.

(5) Setting deadlines for the completion of any approved depositions ordered by or under the supervision of the chair of the hearing committee or panel or special hearing officer and for filing motions in limine and other prehearing motions.

(6) Establishing a date for the exchange between or among the parties of witness and exhibit lists and exhibits intended for use in the party's case-in-chief or for matters in aggrava-

tion and mitigation; a date for the parties' exchange of objections to proposed witnesses and exhibits and supplemental designation of witnesses and exhibits; and a date for filing final witness and exhibit lists and objections thereto, agreed exhibits, and any stipulations of the parties.

(a) When a party proposes to introduce testimony from an expert witness, the party shall be required to disclose the qualifications of the expert and the subject matter on which the expert is expected to testify and to state the substance of facts and opinions to which the expert is expected to testify and a summary of the grounds for each opinion.

(b) When the Respondent has placed his or her physical or mental status in issue, the Respondent shall identify and disclose to Bar Counsel in writing the dates and nature of every condition that the Respondent claims may have affected his or her professional conduct or is otherwise in issue and for which he or she has received consultation, evaluation, treatment, counseling or other services. For each such condition, the Respondent shall provide to Bar Counsel (1) the name and address of every hospital, doctor, therapist, counselor and other provider from whom the Respondent received any services, (2) all hospital, medical, psychiatric, psychological, counseling and other records and reports in the Respondent's possession and control, (3) an executed release, in a form acceptable to the provider, authorizing Bar Counsel or Bar Counsel's representatives to communicate with and received all available records and information from each provider.

(c) The objections to a witness or exhibit must be specified, and, if an objection is made to the authenticity of a proposed exhibit, must be further supported by a specified good faith basis questioning the authenticity of the document. Objections not made timely and in accordance with these requirements and the prehearing orders are waived. A party shall be precluded from calling any witness and introducing in evidence any document not disclosed by that party in accordance with these requirements and the prehearing orders, except upon a showing that the witness or exhibit was not earlier known to or ascertainable by the party or for other good cause shown.

(7) Confirming or rescheduling the hearing date.

(8) Such other matters as may properly be dealt with to assist in the prompt and orderly conduct and disposition of the proceeding.

Amended effective April 9, 2009.

Section 3.24.   [Reserved]

Reserved effective April 9, 2009.

Section 3.25.   Authority of Hearing Committee, Hearing Panel, or Special Hearing Officer at Prehearing Conferences

The person presiding at any prehearing conference may make rulings as to procedural matters which the committee would be authorized to rule upon during the course of the proceeding and which it appears may appropriately and usefully be disposed of at an early stage. In addition, where it appears that the proceeding would be substantially expedited

by distribution of proposed exhibits reasonably in advance of the hearing session, the person presiding may, with due regard for the convenience of the Respondent and Bar Counsel, direct such advance distribution by a prescribed date.

Adopted effective April 9, 2009.

Section 3.26.   Rulings of Hearing Committee, Hearing Panel, or Special Hearing Officer At Prehearing Conferences

The rulings made at such conference shall control the subsequent course of the hearing, unless modified by the Board chair for good cause shown.

Adopted effective April 9, 2009.

Section 3.27.   Appearances

The hearing committee, hearing panel, or special hearing officer shall cause to be entered upon the record all appearances, with a notation in whose behalf each appearance is made.

Adopted effective April 9, 2009.

Section 3.28.   Burden of Proof

In all disciplinary proceedings Bar Counsel shall have the burden of proof by a preponderance of the evidence, shall initiate the presentation of evidence, and may present rebuttal evidence. The Respondent shall have the burden of proof by a preponderance of the evidence on affirmative defenses and matters in mitigation.

Adopted effective April 9, 2009.

Section 3.29.   Presentation by the Parties

(a) **General Rule.** Respondent and Bar Counsel shall have the right to present evidence, cross-examine, object, argue, and make appropriate motions. The hearing and other proceedings shall proceed with all reasonable diligence and with the least practicable delay.

(b) **Objections.** When objections to the admission or exclusion of evidence or other procedural objections are made, the grounds relied upon shall be stated briefly, if so requested by the hearing committee, hearing panel, or special hearing officer, and may be stated briefly if no such request is made. Formal exceptions are unnecessary.

Adopted effective April 9, 2009.

Section 3.30.   Limiting Number of Witnesses

The hearing committee, hearing panel, or special hearing officer may limit appropriately the number of witnesses who may be heard upon any issue to eliminate unduly repetitious or cumulative evidence without prejudice to the substantive rights of any party.

Adopted effective April 9, 2009.

Section 3.31.   Additional Evidence

At the hearing, the hearing committee, hearing panel, or special hearing officer may, if deemed advisable, and subject to appropriate order to protect the substantive rights of any party, authorize any party to file specific documentary evidence as a part of the record within a fixed time, expiring not less than ten days before the date fixed for filing and serving briefs.

Adopted effective April 9, 2009.

Section 3.32. Motions

Any motion made during the hearing shall be filed with the Board, with a copy provided to each member of the hearing committee or hearing panel, or to the special hearing officer, and shall be served upon the opposing party, who shall have such time to respond as the hearing committee, hearing panel, or special hearing officer allows. All such motions shall be decided in accordance with Section 3.18 of these rules.

Adopted effective April 9, 2009. Amended June 21, 2017, effective September 1, 2017.

Section 3.33. Transcript

(a) **General Rule.** Except as may be ordered by the hearing committee, hearing panel, or special hearing officer for good cause shown, hearings shall be reported by a reporter designated by the office of the Board or by the chair of the committee hearing the case. A transcript of the proceedings shall be a part of the record. Such transcript shall include a verbatim report of the hearings including oral argument, if any, and nothing shall be omitted therefrom, except as may be directed on the record by the hearing committee, hearing panel, or special hearing officer. After the closing of the record, there shall not be received in evidence or considered as part of the record any document submitted after the close of testimony except as provided in Section 3.31 of these Rules.

(b) **Waiver of Transcript.** By agreement of Bar Counsel, the Respondent or the Respondent's counsel and the hearing committee, hearing panel, or special hearing officer, a transcript of the proceedings may be waived and in that event the stenographic notes or other recording shall be a part of the record.

(c) **Order by Board for Transcript.** Notwithstanding a waiver pursuant to paragraph (b) of this section, the Board may in its discretion direct that a transcript be prepared.

Adopted effective April 9, 2009.

Section 3.34. Transcript Corrections

Corrections in the official transcript may be made only to make it conform to the evidence presented at the hearing. No corrections or physical changes shall be made in or upon the official transcript of the hearing, except as provided in this section. Transcript corrections agreed to by all parties shall be made on the transcript by the special hearing officer or the hearing committee or panel chair, if and when approved by the hearing committee, hearing panel, or special hearing officer, at any time during the hearing or after the close of the hearing, as may be permitted by the hearing committee, hearing panel, or special hearing officer, but not less than ten days in advance of the time fixed for filing briefs. The hearing committee, hearing panel, or special hearing officer may call for the submission of proposed corrections and may make

disposition thereof at appropriate times during the course of a proceeding.

Adopted effective April 9, 2009.

Section 3.35. Copies of Transcripts

The Board will obtain an original of the transcript. A Respondent desiring a copy of such transcript may obtain such copy at his or her own expense from the official reporter. Any witness may obtain from the official reporter at his or her own expense a copy of the transcript of his or her own testimony.

Adopted effective April 9, 2009.

Section 3.36. Oral Examination

Witnesses shall be examined orally under oath or affirmation unless the testimony is taken by deposition as provided in Section 4.10 of these Rules or the facts are stipulated in the manner provided in Section 3.23 of these Rules or in Section 3.38 of these Rules.

Adopted effective April 9, 2009.

Section 3.37. [Reserved]

Reserved effective April 9, 2009.

Section 3.38. Presentation and Effect of Stipulations

Independently of the orders or rulings issued as provided by Section 3.23 of these Rules, the parties may stipulate as to any relevant matters of fact or the authenticity of any relevant documents. Such stipulations may be received in evidence at a hearing, and when so received shall be binding on the parties with respect to the matters therein stipulated.

Adopted effective April 9, 2009.

Section 3.39. Admissibility of Evidence

In any proceeding the admissibility of evidence shall be governed by the Rules of Evidence observed in adjudicatory proceedings under Chapter 30A of the General Laws (State Administrative Procedure).

Adopted effective April 9, 2009.

Section 3.40. Reception and Ruling on Evidence

The hearing committee, hearing panel, or special hearing officer shall rule on the admissibility of all evidence. The number of witnesses to be heard on any issue may be limited appropriately as provided in Section 3.30 of these Rules.

Adopted effective April 9, 2009.

Section 3.41. Copies of Exhibits to Parties, Special Hearing Officers, and Hearing Committee or Panel Members

Except as otherwise provided in these Rules, when exhibits of a documentary character are offered in evidence, copies shall be furnished to the parties present at the hearing, and copies of each exhibit of documentary character shall be furnished for the use of the special hearing officer and for each member of the hearing committee or hearing panel, unless the parties and the hearing committee, hearing panel, or special hearing officer waive the receipt of such copies.

Adopted effective April 9, 2009.

Section 3.42. Closing Argument

If the hearing committee, hearing panel, or special hearing officer decides to entertain closing argument, it shall do so directly following the taking of testimony in each proceeding except for good cause shown.

Adopted effective April 9, 2009.

Section 3.43. Time for Filing of Briefs

After a formal disciplinary proceeding, any party may file a brief and requests for findings and rulings with the hearing committee, hearing panel, or special hearing officer within 30 days of the receipt of the final transcript of the hearing or such other shorter period of time as may be fixed by the chair or the special hearing officer. No extensions shall be granted for the filing of proposed findings and rulings or briefs except for good cause shown.

Adopted effective April 9, 2009.

Section 3.44. Content and Form of Briefs

(a) **General Rule.** Briefs should normally contain:

(1) A concise statement of the case.

(2) A discussion or statement of the evidence relied upon by the party filing, with specific reference to the pages of the record or exhibits where such evidence appears.

(3) Proposed findings and conclusions together with the reasons and authorities therefor, separately stated.

(b) **Exhibits.** Exhibits shall not be reproduced in the brief, but may, if desired, be reproduced in an appendix to the brief.

Adopted effective April 9, 2009.

Section 3.45. Filing and Service of Briefs

Briefs not filed and served on or before the date fixed therefor shall not be accepted for filing except by special permission of the hearing committee, hearing panel, or special hearing officer. Except where filing of a different number is permitted or directed by the hearing committee, hearing panel, or special hearing officer, a copy of each brief shall be furnished for the use of each member of the committee or panel.

Adopted effective April 9, 2009.

Section 3.46. Filing of Report

The hearing committee, hearing panel, or special hearing officer shall report promptly to the Board its findings, conclusions and recommendations, together with a record of the proceedings before it.

Adopted effective April 9, 2009.

Section 3.47. Contents of Report

The report of the hearing committee, hearing panel, or special hearing officer shall be accompanied by Form BBO–11 and shall set forth:

(1) A concise statement of the case, including a citation of each rule of the Disciplinary Rules found to have been violated by the Respondent;

(2) Its rulings on admission of evidence and other procedural matters, which may be set forth by reference to the pages of the transcript wherein such rulings are recorded;

(3) Findings of fact;

(4) Conclusions of law; and

(5) Recommended disposition of the petition.

Adopted effective April 9, 2009.

Section 3.48. Report a Part of the Record

All reports shall become a part of the record.

Adopted effective April 9, 2009.

Section 3.49. Service of Report

All reports shall be filed with the Board, which shall serve copies thereof upon Respondent and Bar Counsel.

Adopted effective April 9, 2009.

SUBCHAPTER D. REVIEW BY BOARD

Section 3.50. Procedure on Appeal

(a) **Procedure to Object to Report of Hearing Committee, Hearing Panel, or Special Hearing Officer.** Any party objecting to the findings or recommendations of a hearing committee, hearing panel, or special hearing officer shall, within 20 days after the service of a copy of the report or within such other longer or shorter time as may reasonably be fixed by a Board member, file a brief on appeal. A brief opposing the appeal, and raising any cross-appeal, may be filed in response to a brief on appeal within 20 days after the filing of a brief on appeal or within such other longer or shorter time as may reasonably be fixed by a Board member. If a cross-appeal is claimed in a brief opposing the appeal, the party filing the original appeal may file a brief in response to the cross-appeal within 20 days after the filing of the cross-appeal or within such other longer or shorter time as may reasonably be fixed by a Board member. No further response will be entertained unless allowed or requested by the Board or a Board member.

(b) **Oral Argument.** Appeals from expedited hearings shall be decided upon the papers. For formal proceedings, oral argument shall be deemed waived unless expressly requested in a brief on appeal or brief opposing appeal. Oral argument shall be permitted at the discretion of the Board. The Board or the Appeal Panel may restrict the issues which may be argued orally.

(c) Waiver of Objections. A party will be conclusively deemed to have waived all objections to the findings, conclusions and recommendations of the hearing committee, hearing panel, or special hearing officer and to have stipulated to the waiver of oral argument and submission of briefs unless the party files an appeal as provided in subsection (a) of this section.

(d) Assignment of Appeals. If there is an appeal from the findings and recommendations of a hearing committee, hearing panel, or special hearing officer, the Board shall either hear the matter itself or assign it to an appeal panel of three members of the Board to be designated by the Board or the Chair of the Board.

(e) Procedure Before an Appeal Panel of the Board. If a matter is heard before an appeal panel of the Board, such panel may determine the matter upon the record and the briefs before it or after any oral argument or may remand the case to the hearing committee, hearing panel, or special hearing officer for the taking of further evidence. The appeal panel shall promptly report its findings of fact, conclusions of law and recommendations to the Board. Such report shall be served upon the Bar Counsel and the Respondent, either of whom may, within seven days thereafter, file with the Board objections to such report. Opposition to such objections may be filed with the Board within seven days after the service of said objections on the opposing party.

(f) Review of the Appeal Panel Report by the Board. Following the filing of a panel report and the expiration of the time allowed for the filing of objections thereto, the Board shall review the matter on the entire record including previously filed briefs and objections. Members of the appeal panel shall not be disqualified from participation in the deliberations and voting of the Board. The Board may remand the matter to the hearing committee, the hearing panel, or the special hearing officer for the taking of further evidence.

(g) Procedure on Appeal When the Matter Has Been Heard by a Hearing Panel of the Board. If an appeal has been filed from the findings and recommendations of a hearing panel of the Board, the Board may determine such appeal on the record and briefs before it or after any oral argument that it in its own discretion deems necessary. The Board may remand the matter to the hearing panel for the taking of further evidence.

Adopted effective April 9, 2009. Amended effective September 1, 2011.

Section 3.51. Content and Form of Briefs On Appeal

(a) Briefs on Appeal.

(1) The briefs on appeal shall contain:

(i) A short statement of the case.

(ii) A summary of the basic position of the party filing.

(iii) The grounds upon which the appeal rests.

(iv) The argument in support of the appeal with appropriate references to the record and legal authorities.

(2) There may also be included specific findings and conclusions proposed in lieu of those from which the appeal is being taken and any proposed additional findings and conclusions.

(3) Appeal from a recommended disposition shall specify the portions thereof from which the appeal is being taken, and may set forth a disposition suggested in lieu of that recommended by the hearing committee, hearing panel, or special hearing officer.

(b) Briefs Opposing Appeals. Briefs opposing appeals shall generally follow the same style prescribed for briefs on appeal, but may omit a statement of the case so far as it is correctly stated in the brief on appeal.

(c) Format and Number of Briefs. One original of each brief shall be filed with the Board and a copy served on the opposing party. Briefs shall be stapled, not bound.

Adopted effective April 9, 2009.

Section 3.52. Review by Board When There Has Been No Appeal

When the time for filing an appeal under Section 3.50 has expired and neither the Bar Counsel nor the Respondent has filed an appeal with the Board, the Board shall review the case. In the event the Board makes a preliminary determination that the decision of the hearing committee, hearing panel, or special hearing officer should not be affirmed, it shall give the parties appropriate notice thereof and an opportunity to file briefs, and the Board may then proceed to take such action as it could have taken had an appeal been filed.

Adopted effective April 9, 2009.

Section 3.53. Action by Board

The Board shall review and may adopt the findings of fact made by the hearing committee, hearing panel, or special hearing officer or revise any findings which it determines to be erroneous, paying due respect to the role of the hearing committee, hearing panel, or special hearing officer as the sole judge of the credibility of the testimony presented at the hearing. The Board may adopt or modify the recommendation of the hearing committee, hearing or appeal panel, or special hearing officer. Whenever the Board modifies the findings or recommendations, it shall state the reasons therefor in its vote or in a memorandum.

Adopted effective April 9, 2009.

Section 3.54. [Repealed]

Repealed effective September 1, 2011.

Section 3.55. Dismissal of Proceeding

In the event that the Board determines that a proceeding should be dismissed, it shall so notify the parties and Bar Counsel shall notify the complainant.

Adopted effective April 9, 2009.

Section 3.56. Admonition and Public Reprimand

(a) Notice to Respondent. In the event that the Board determines that the proceedings should be concluded by admonition or public reprimand, it shall serve a copy of the vote and memorandum (if any) on the parties. The vote and memorandum shall constitute the admonition or public reprimand. In the event that the court orders an admonition or a public reprimand, the order of the court shall constitute the admonition or public reprimand.

(b) Permanent Record. A permanent record shall be made of the fact of and basis for the admonition or public reprimand. The fact of the receipt of an admonition or public reprimand shall not affect the good standing of the Respondent as a lawyer.

(c) Confidentiality of Admonition. The Board and the bar counsel shall keep the fact of the receipt of an admonition confidential; provided, however, that in response to specific inquiry as to the outcome of a public hearing which has been concluded by admonition, the Board or Bar Counsel may disclose that an admonition was imposed. The admonition shall be subject to limited disclosure under Supreme Judicial Court Rule 4:01, Section 20(2).

Adopted effective April 9, 2009.

Section 3.57. Demand for Filing of Information

(a) In the event the Respondent or Bar Counsel is unwilling to accede to the determination of the Board that formal proceedings should be concluded by dismissal, admonition, or public reprimand, the party aggrieved may demand that the Board file an Information. The demand shall be in writing and shall be filed with the Board within 20 days after the date of service of the Board's vote and memorandum, which time limit is jurisdictional.

(b) The decision of the Board following an appeal by either party from the determination of a special hearing officer after an expedited disciplinary hearing shall be final and there shall be no right by either Bar Counsel or the Respondent to demand that an Information be filed.

Adopted effective April 9, 2009.

Section 3.58. Filing an Information

In the event that the Board shall determine that the matter should be concluded by suspension or disbarment, or in the event the Respondent or Bar Counsel files a written demand for the filing of an Information as authorized by Section 3.57 of these Rules, the Board shall file with the Clerk of the Supreme Judicial Court for Suffolk County an Information, together with the entire record of its proceedings.

Adopted effective April 9, 2009.

SUBCHAPTER E. REOPENING OF RECORD

Section 3.59. Reopening on Application of Party

(a) Petition to Reopen. At any time after the conclusion of a hearing in a proceeding, and before a report has been issued, any party may file with the hearing committee, hearing panel, or special hearing officer a petition to reopen the proceeding for the purpose of taking additional evidence. If a petition to reopen is filed after the issuance of a report by the hearing committee, hearing panel, or special hearing officer, it shall be filed with the Board. Such petition shall set forth clearly the material changes of fact or of law alleged to have occurred since the conclusion of the hearing or other good cause justifying reopening the hearing.

(b) Responses. Within ten days following the service of such petition, any other party may file an answer thereto, and in default thereof shall be deemed to have waived any objection to the granting of such petition.

(c) Action on Petition. As soon as practicable after the filing of responses to such petitions or default thereof, as the case may be, the hearing committee, hearing panel, the special hearing officer, or the Board shall grant or deny such petition. There shall be no hearing on such petition unless the hearing committee, hearing panel, the special hearing officer, or the Board shall so direct.

Adopted effective April 9, 2009.

Section 3.60. Reopening by Hearing Committee or Panel

At any time prior to the filing of its report a hearing committee, hearing panel, or special hearing officer may reopen the proceeding sua sponte to receive further evidence if there is reason to believe that facts or law require, or that the public interest requires, the reopening of such proceeding.

Adopted effective April 9, 2009.

Section 3.61. Reopening by Board Action

At any time prior to the issuance by the Board of its decision in a proceeding, the Board may, without motion, reopen the proceeding and remand to a hearing committee, hearing panel, or special hearing officer to receive further evidence if the Board has reason to believe that conditions of fact or law have so changed as to require, or that the public interest requires, the reopening of such proceeding.

Adopted effective April 9, 2009.

SUBCHAPTER F. REINSTATEMENT

Section 3.62. Procedure on Petitions for Reinstatement Generally

The Board will assign a reinstatement petition for hearing upon receipt of (a) a copy of the petition from the Clerk of the Supreme Judicial Court for Suffolk County; (b) four fully completed copies of Part I of the reinstatement questionnaire set out in section 3.63; (c) a certificate of service showing that one copy of the petition and the originals of both Part I and

Part II of the reinstatement questionnaire have been served upon Bar Counsel; and (d) the costs deposit required under section 3.64.

Adopted effective April 9, 2009.

Section 3.63. Reinstatement Questionnaire

The petitioner shall set forth, fully and accurately under the penalties of perjury, the information requested in Parts I and II of the reinstatement questionnaire set out as an appendix to these rules. Part I of the questionnaire shall become a part of the record in the reinstatement proceedings. Information contained in Part II, filed with Bar Counsel, shall be admitted in evidence at either party's request during the reinstatement proceedings subject to redaction or protective order where warranted.

Adopted effective April 9, 2009.

Section 3.64. Costs Deposit

The reinstatement questionnaire shall be accompanied by a deposit of $500 for costs. No hearing shall be scheduled until the costs deposit is paid in full.

Adopted effective April 9, 2009.

Section 3.65. Hearing Procedures

The provisions of these Rules applicable to formal proceedings shall, so far as relevant, govern the procedures before hearing committees, hearing panels, special hearing officers, and the Board upon petitions for reinstatement, except that the petitioner shall have the burden of demonstrating that he or she has the moral qualifications, competency and learning in the law required for admission to practice law in the Commonwealth, and that his or her resumption of the practice of law shall not be detrimental to the integrity and standing of the bar, the administration of justice, or to the public interest.

Adopted effective April 9, 2009.

Section 3.66. Expenses of Reinstatement Proceedings

The Board may recommend that the Court direct that the petitioner pay all necessary expenses incurred in connection with a petition for reinstatement, including the cost of notices published pursuant to Section 3.67 of these Rules. The expenses a petitioner is required to pay pursuant to this section shall be reduced by the costs deposit payment required by Section 3.64 above.

Adopted effective April 9, 2009.

Section 3.67. Public Notice of Reinstatement Proceedings

Hearings on petitions for reinstatement shall be open to the public. At least two weeks prior to a scheduled hearing, the Board shall cause notices of the filing of the petition and of the time, date, and place of the hearing to be published in a newspaper designated by the Court as an authorized source for the publication of all rules of court and other notices and in newspapers of general circulation serving the community in which the petitioner resides and the community in which the office listed on the petitioner's last registration statement was located.

Adopted effective April 9, 2009.

CHAPTER 4. MISCELLANEOUS MATTERS

SUBCHAPTER A. RESIGNATIONS

Section 4.1. Resignation by Lawyers Under Disciplinary Investigation

A lawyer who wishes to resign in accordance with Supreme Judicial Court Rule 4:01, Section 15, shall file a request for resignation and an affidavit with the Board. The Board shall serve the request and affidavit on Bar Counsel, who shall within seven days, or such further time as may be allowed by a Board member, file with the Board a statement containing Bar Counsel's recommendation and the reasons therefor, such statement to be served upon the Respondent.

The Board may order any hearing or investigation it deems appropriate. Upon reaching its determination, the Board shall file its recommendation and the entire record of any hearing held with the Court.

Adopted effective April 9, 2009.

SUBCHAPTER B. EXPUNCTION

Section 4.2. Expunction of Records

(a) Expunction Upon the Expiration of Six Years. The records of a matter that Bar Counsel in his or her discretion has determined does not warrant investigation pursuant to Section 2.1(b)(1), and of a complaint against a lawyer that has been closed and not subsequently reopened shall be destroyed and expunged following the expiration of six years from the date the complaint was closed unless a complaint has been filed in the intervening six-year period. In the event a complaint is so filed or reopened, the records shall not be destroyed and expunged until the expiration of six years from the date on which all complaints have been closed and not reopened.

(b) Reserved.

(c) Expunction for Bank Error. In the event a complaint has been docketed solely on account of a report made by a financial institution that it has dishonored an instrument presented against a lawyer's trust account and it is established that the instrument was dishonored solely due to error on the part of the financial institution, the lawyer shall be entitled, upon request made after the closing of the complaint, to have the records of the complaint destroyed and expunged.

(d) Procedure. Whenever, pursuant to the preceding subparagraphs (a) and (c), records are to be destroyed and expunged, Bar Counsel shall destroy all records within Bar Counsel's custody and control that indicate that the complaint was filed against the lawyer, and shall destroy all records and files pertaining thereto. Bar Counsel may separately maintain any investigative records that may pertain to matters other than the specific complaint or complaint against the lawyer, but such records shall not bear any indication of the specific complaint or complaint expunged.

(e) Nonapplicability. This section does not apply to the records of a complaint which gave rise to an admonition even if such complaint has been dismissed pursuant to Section 4.3(a) of these Rules.

Adopted effective April 9, 2009.

SUBCHAPTER C.   VACATING AN ADMONITION

Section 4.3.   Vacating an Admonition and Dismissal of the Underlying Complaint

(a) Vacating and Dismissal Upon the Expiration of Eight Years. Upon the expiration of eight years from the receipt of an admonition by a lawyer, if Bar Counsel determines that there has been no intervening disciplinary action taken with reference to the lawyer and there is no complaint then pending against him or her, Bar Counsel shall vacate the admonition and dismiss the complaint which gave rise to it.

Adopted effective April 9, 2009.

SUBCHAPTER D.   SUBPOENAS

Section 4.4.   Investigatory Subpoenas

(a) At any stage of the investigation, Bar Counsel may request that the Board issue a subpoena requiring the attendance and testimony of a witness, including the Respondent, and the production of any evidence, including books, records, correspondence or documents, relating to any matter in question in the investigation.

(b) The request shall be made in writing to a member of the Board, who may forthwith issue the subpoena.

(c) The subpoena shall require a witness to appear before Bar Counsel at a specified date and time and shall specify any evidence to be produced. Bar Counsel may take the testimony electronically or otherwise. Respondent shall not be entitled to be present, but Bar Counsel shall provide Respondent with a copy of any recorded testimony prior to any hearing on a petition for discipline.

(d) If a subpoena is issued subsequent to the filing of a petition for discipline and if the testimony is to be recorded electronically or otherwise, the Respondent shall be entitled to be present and participate in the examination of any such witness whose testimony is to be recorded and in the examination of any documents produced by such subpoena. No investigatory subpoenas shall be issued after expedited disciplinary proceedings are commenced pursuant to Section 2.12 of these Rules.

Adopted effective April 9, 2009.

Section 4.5.   Hearing Subpoenas

(a) Bar Counsel and the Respondent may request that the hearing committee, hearing panel, special hearing officer, or the Board issue a subpoena requiring the attendance and testimony of a witness, including the Respondent, and the production of any evidence, including books, records, correspondence or documents, relating to any matter in question in the proceeding.

(b) The request shall be made in writing to a member of the hearing committee or panel, or to the special hearing officer, or to a member of the Board who may forthwith issue the subpoena.

(c) The subpoena shall require a witness to appear before the Board, a hearing panel, the hearing committee, or the special hearing officer, or at a deposition conducted pursuant to Sections 4.9 to 4.15 of these Rules, at a specified date and time. The subpoena shall also specify the evidence, if any, to be produced and the date for production, which may be prior to the hearing. The parties shall each be entitled to inspect or copy any materials produced pursuant to such subpoena.

(d) The Board, the hearing committee, hearing panel, or special hearing officer may, on its own motion, subpoena any witness to appear and give testimony or produce evidence at any hearing.

Adopted effective April 9, 2009.

Section 4.5A.   Reciprocal Subpoenas

(a) Whenever a subpoena has been duly approved under the law of another jurisdiction for use in lawyer discipline or disability proceedings, Bar Counsel may request that the Board issue a subpoena requiring the attendance and testimony of the witness in this Commonwealth and the production of any evidence, including books, records, correspondence or documents, relating to the matter in question.

(b) The request shall be made in writing to a member of the Board, who may forthwith issue the subpoena.

(c) The subpoena shall require a witness to appear before Bar Counsel at a specified date and time and shall specify any evidence to be produced. Bar Counsel may take the testimony electronically or otherwise.

Adopted effective April 9, 2009.

Section 4.5B. Taking Out-of-State Depositions Pursuant to Subpoena

(a) Implementing the provisions of Subchapter E regarding the taking of depositions pursuant to Sections 4.9 and 4.10 out of state, Bar Counsel and/or the respondent may request that the hearing committee, hearing panel, special hearing officer, or the Chair approve the taking of out-of-state depositions pursuant to subpoena requiring the attendance of a witness and/or the production of any evidence, including books, records, correspondence, or documents, relating to any matter in question in the proceeding.

(b) Upon such approval having been given, the Board shall issue a request, addressed to the disciplinary board or entity in the jurisdiction in which the deposition is to be taken, that the latter issue a subpoena requiring the attendance and testimony of the witness in the out-of-state jurisdiction and the production of any evidence, including books, records, correspondence, or documents, relating to the matter in question. The request shall state that the Board has approved the taking of such deposition and shall specify the date, time, and place for the taking of the deposition.

(c) In the event that the disciplinary board in the out-of-state jurisdiction in which the deposition is to be taken either cannot issue, or declines to issue, a subpoena for the taking of such deposition, Bar Counsel and/or the respondent may apply to the Supreme Judicial Court for Suffolk County, citing such approval; for leave to take such deposition pursuant to the provisions of G.L. c. 223A, § 10 (Letters Rogatory). For purposes of such application, a disciplinary matter before the Board shall be considered "an action pending in this Commonwealth" within the meaning of G.L. c. 223A, § 10.

(d) Depositions in an out-of-state jurisdiction shall be taken before an officer, not being counsel for any of the parties, authorized to administer oaths by the laws of the United States or of the place where the examination is held.

Adopted effective September 1, 2011.

Section 4.6. Service

Each subpoena issued in accordance with this subchapter shall be served in the manner provided for service of summonses in the Courts of the Commonwealth. Alternatively, service may be made upon any lawyer in hand or by certified, registered, or first class mail addressed to the lawyer at either the residence or office address furnished in the last registration statement filed by the lawyer in accordance with S. J. C. Rule 4:02. A copy of each investigative subpoena served on a person other than the Respondent shall be mailed to the Respondent. No witness fee or travel allowance shall be paid or tendered to any Respondent subpoenaed hereunder.

Adopted effective April 9, 2009.

Section 4.7. Confidentiality of Investigatory Subpoenas

(a) Each investigatory subpoena shall clearly indicate on its face that it is issued in connection with a confidential investigation under Bar Disciplinary Rules of Chapter Four of the Supreme Judicial Court, and the Board and the Office of Bar Counsel will conduct themselves so as to maintain the absolute confidentiality of the investigation.

(b) Each subpoena shall state on its face that a person subpoenaed may consult with counsel.

(c) Whenever records of a lawyer's clients' trust fund account are subpoenaed, all steps necessary to maintain the confidentiality to which clients are entitled shall be taken by Bar Counsel and the Board, hearing committee, hearing panel, or special hearing officer.

Adopted effective April 9, 2009.

Section 4.8. Motions to Quash

A motion to quash any subpoena issued hereunder may be filed with the Board. The motion shall state the grounds on which it is based, and any fact alleged shall be supported by affidavit filed with the motion. The motion and affidavit shall be served upon the Respondent or Bar Counsel or both as the case may be, who shall within seven days after receipt thereof file any opposition thereto with the Board. The motion shall be promptly decided by the Chair of the Board, the Chair of the hearing committee or the hearing panel, or the special hearing officer, either upon the documents or after any hearing held.

Amended effective April 9, 2009.

SUBCHAPTER E. DEPOSITIONS

Section 4.9. Availability of Depositions

(a) **Discovery Depositions.** After the institution of formal disciplinary proceedings pursuant to Supreme Judicial Court Rule 4:01, Section 8(3), and the filing of an answer by the Respondent, a party may obtain discovery by deposition upon oral examination, subject to the following terms and conditions:

(1) Any party may file a written notice and motion with the Board pursuant to Section 4.11 (a) of these rules, requesting the deposition upon oral examination, or by telephone or audio-visual means, of any person and that any evidence, including books, records, correspondence or documents, relat-

ing to the matter be produced at the same time. Any other party may file and serve a response to the motion within seven days after service of the motion. All such notices and motions shall be decided in accordance with Section 3.18 of these rules.

(2) A motion to take a discovery deposition shall be allowed only upon a showing of a substantial need for the deposition in the preparation of the applicant's case, taking into consideration:

(A) The nature and complexity of the case and the need to assure an expeditious, economical and fair proceeding.

(B) Whether the information sought or its substantial equivalent has been provided or was available by other means, taking into consideration the formal or informal discovery that has already occurred.

(C) The prevention of embarrassment, oppression, or undue burden, including economic burden, that the deposition may cause the deponent.

The order permitting the deposition may specify or restrict the subject matter upon which the deponent may be examined.

(b) Discovery depositions shall be conducted as set forth in Sections 4.11 through 4.15, subject to such terms and conditions as the Board Chair or the Chair's designee may order, including supervision, length, location, and timing of the deposition. Depositions must be completed within 21 days prior to the commencement of hearing, unless otherwise ordered for good cause shown.

Adopted effective April 9, 2009. Amended June 21, 2017, effective September 1, 2017.

Section 4.10. Testimonial Depositions of Unavailable Witnesses

(a) Depositions Prior to the Commencement of Formal Proceedings. If at any stage of the investigation by Bar Counsel prior to the filing of a petition for discipline it appears that a prospective witness may no longer be subject to service of a subpoena or may become unable to attend or testify at a hearing because of age, illness or other infirmity, Bar Counsel or the Respondent may request that the Board order a deposition to preserve the testimony of the witness. The request shall be made in writing to the Board Chair or the Chair's designee pursuant to Section 4.11(a). If the Chair or the Chair's designee deems it to be in the interest of justice that the testimony of the prospective witness be taken and preserved, he or she shall order that the testimony of the witness be taken by deposition and that any evidence, including books, records, correspondence or documents, relating to any matter in question in the investigation be produced at the same time.

(b) Depositions After Commencement of Formal Proceedings. After the institution of formal disciplinary proceedings pursuant to Rule 4:01, section 8(3), and the filing of an answer by the Respondent, applications for the taking of testimony by deposition of those witnesses not subject to service of a subpoena or unable to attend a hearing due to age, illness or other infirmity shall be approved by the Board Chair or the Chair's designee or by the hearing committee, hearing panel, or special hearing officer to which the matter has been referred. Depositions must be completed within 21 days prior to the commencement of the hearing, unless otherwise ordered for good cause shown.

(c) Notice and Application. A written notice and application to take a testimonial deposition pursuant to subsections (a) and (b) when the matter has not been referred to a special hearing officer, hearing committee, or hearing panel shall be submitted by the party proposing to take such deposition to the other parties and to the Board Chair. Otherwise, written notice and application shall be submitted to the other parties and to the special hearing officer, hearing committee or hearing panel.

(d) Testimonial Depositions under this section shall be conducted as set forth in Sections 4.11 through 4.15.

Adopted effective April 9, 2009.

Section 4.11. Application for and Authorization of Taking Deposition

(a) In any application to take a deposition filed pursuant to Sections 4.9 or 4.10 and in addition to any other requirements specified by these Rules, the party desiring to take the deposition shall state the name and post office address of the witness, the subject matter concerning which the witness is expected to testify, the time and place of taking the deposition, the name and post office address of the notarial officer before whom it is desired that the deposition be taken, and the reason that such deposition should be taken. Any other party may file and serve a response to an application within seven days after service of the application.

(b) If an application for the taking of a deposition is allowed, the Board Chair or the Chair's designee, or the special hearing officer, hearing committee, or hearing panel to which application was made under Section 4.10(c), within a reasonable time in advance of the time fixed for taking testimony, will issue and serve upon the parties an authorization form naming the witness whose deposition is to be taken, and the time, place and notarial officer before whom the witness is to testify, but such time, place and notarial officer so specified may or may not be the same as those named in the notice and application. If required, the Board Chair or the Chair's designee shall issue a subpoena to compel the witness's attendance at the deposition.

(c) Upon motion, the Board Chair or the Chair's designee may enter protective orders regarding further terms and conditions under which depositions may be taken, including without limitation, the number, length, time and place, the scope or subject matter and the allocation of expenses. The Board Chair or the Chair's designee may also order that depositions cease. After the petition for discipline and answer have been referred to a special hearing officer, hearing committee or hearing panel, the special hearing officer or chair of the committee or panel may enter the same orders and take the same actions pursuant to this paragraph as the Board Chair.

Adopted effective April 9, 2009.

Section 4.12. Officer Before Whom Deposition Is Taken

(a) Within the United States. A deposition may be taken before the Board Chair or the Chair's designee, a single member of the hearing committee or hearing panel, or before the special hearing officer, or before a person authorized under either Section 2(a) or Section 2(b) of Rule 1:02(A) of the Supreme Judicial Court insofar as these sections deal with depositions to be taken within the United States or before any other person authorized to administer oaths not being counsel for any of the parties, or interested in the proceeding or investigation, according to such designation as may be made in the authorization form.

(b) In Foreign Countries. Where such deposition is taken in a foreign country, it may be taken before a secretary of an embassy or legation, consul general, consul, vice-consul or consular agent of the United States or before such persons as authorized by Section 2(b) of Rule 1:02(A) of the Supreme Judicial Court insofar as this section deals with depositions to be taken in foreign countries, or before such person or officer as may be designated in the authorization form or agreed upon by the parties by stipulation in writing filed with and approved by the hearing committee, hearing panel, or special hearing officer.

Adopted effective April 9, 2009.

Section 4.13.   Oath and Reduction to Writing

(a) General Rule. Every person whose testimony is taken by deposition shall be sworn, or shall affirm concerning the matter about which he or she shall testify, before any questions are put or testimony given. The testimony shall be reduced to writing by the notarial officer, or under the notarial officer's direction. When the testimony is fully transcribed the deposition shall be submitted to the witness for inspection and signing and shall be read to or by the witness and shall be signed by the witness, unless the inspection, reading and signing are waived by the witness and by all parties who attended the taking of the deposition, or the witness is ill or cannot be found or refuses to sign. Any changes in form or substance which the witness desires to make shall be entered upon the deposition by the notarial officer with a statement of the reasons given by the witness for making the changes. If the deposition is not signed by the witness, the notarial officer shall certify it in the usual form and state on the record the fact of the waiver or of the illness or absence of the witness or the refusal to sign together with the reason, if any, given therefor; and the deposition may then be used as fully as though signed, unless the hearing committee, hearing panel, or special hearing officer or the Board holds that the reasons given for the refusal to sign require rejection of the deposition in whole or in part.

(b) Transmission.

(1) For depositions taken pursuant to Section 4.10(b) and unless otherwise directed in the authorization form, after the deposition has been certified, it shall, together with the number of copies specified in the authorization, the copies being made by such notarial officer or under the notarial officer's direction, be forwarded by such notarial officer in a sealed envelope addressed to the office of the Board at Boston, Massachusetts, with sufficient stamps for postage affixed. Upon receipt thereof, the Board shall file the original in the proceeding and shall forward a copy to each party, the special hearing officer, and to each member of the hearing committee or panel.

(2) For all other depositions, the party taking the deposition shall give prompt notice of its receipt to all other parties.

Upon payment of the reasonable charges therefor, the notarial officer shall furnish a copy of the deposition to any party or the deponent.

Adopted effective April 9, 2009.

Section 4.14.   Scope and Conduct of Examination

The witness may be examined regarding any matter not privileged that is relevant to the subject matter of the proceedings and is within the areas of inquiry specified by the order permitting the deposition. Parties shall have the right of cross-examination and objection. In making objections to questions or evidence, the grounds relied upon shall be stated briefly, but no transcript filed by the notarial officer shall include argument or debate.

(a) If a deposition is not being taken in the presence of the special hearing officer, member of the hearing committee or member of the Board, objections to questions or evidence shall be noted by the notarial officer upon the deposition, but the notarial officer shall not have the power to decide on the competency, materiality or relevancy of the evidence. In such case, objections to the competency of a witness or to the competency, relevancy or materiality of the testimony are not waived by failure to make them before or during the taking of the deposition.

(b) If a deposition is being taken in the presence of the special hearing officer, member of the hearing committee or member of the Board, the individual so presiding shall rule on all objections. It is not grounds for objection at a discovery deposition that the information sought will be inadmissible at hearing if the information sought appears reasonably calculated to lead to the discovery of admissible evidence and is within the scope of the order permitting the deposition. The fact that an objection is overruled will not preclude a party from raising the same objection at hearing and the fact that an objection is allowed will not preclude a party from examining the witness on the same subject matter at hearing.

Adopted effective April 9, 2009.

Section 4.15.   Status of Deposition as Part of Record

No part of a deposition taken pursuant to Section 4.9 of this rule shall constitute a part of the record in the proceeding, unless offered in evidence before the hearing committee, hearing panel, or special hearing officer. At the hearing, any part or all of a deposition, so far as admissible under the Rules of evidence applied as though the witness were then present and testifying, may be admitted in evidence.

Adopted effective April 9, 2009.

Section 4.16.   [Reserved]

Reserved effective April 9, 2009.

SUBCHAPTER F.   NOTIFICATION OF DISBARMENT, RESIGNATION, SUSPENSION, TEMPORARY SUSPENSION, OR DISABILITY INACTIVE STATUS

Section 4.17.   Form of Notification

(a) A lawyer who has been disbarred, suspended, temporarily suspended, or placed on disability inactive status, or a lawyer who has resigned pursuant to the provisions of section 15 of Supreme Judicial Court Rule 4:01, shall

Complete and send to each court or agency in which the lawyer appears for any party a copy of the form Notification to Court or Agency prepared by the Board.

Complete and send to all clients being represented in pending matters and to all wards, heirs, and beneficiaries for whom the lawyer serves as guardian, executor, administrator, trustee, attorney-in-fact, or other fiduciary a copy of the form Notification to Clients, Wards, Heirs, and Beneficiaries prepared by the Board.

Complete and send to the lawyer or lawyers for each party in each pending litigation matter or administrative proceeding a copy of the form Notification to Counsel in Litigation Matters prepared by the Board.

(b) A notice substantially in the language of the form prepared by the Board may be used in lieu of a copy of the form.

Adopted effective April 9, 2009.

Section 4.18.   [Reserved]

Reserved effective April 9, 2009.

Section 4.19.   [Reserved]

Reserved effective April 9, 2009.

Section 4.20.   Affidavit of Compliance

The affidavit of compliance required by S.J.C. Rule 4:01, Section 17(5), shall be submitted on the form Affidavit of Compliance prepared by the Board or in substantially the language that form.

Adopted effective April 9, 2009.

SUBCHAPTER G.   RECUSAL

Section 4.21.   General Rule

(a) A Board member, hearing committee member, or special hearing officer shall disqualify himself or herself in any matter in which his or her impartiality might reasonably be questioned.

(b) "Impartiality" denotes absence of bias or prejudice in favor of, or against, any party, as well as maintaining an open mind in considering issues involved in the matter.

(c) A Board member, hearing committee member, or special hearing officer is disqualified where he or she has personal knowledge of disputed evidentiary facts involved in the matter or has previously expressed a view concerning its outcome or has a financial interest in the outcome.

Adopted effective September 1, 2011.

Section 4.22.   Recusal

The Chair shall not be disqualified from subsequent consideration or decision of a matter solely on the ground that he or she ruled on a motion or an appeal in his or her capacity as Chair.

Adopted effective September 1, 2011.

Section 4.23.   Recusal of a Board Member

(a) A Board member who has participated as a reviewing Board member in the decision to institute formal proceedings pursuant to Section 2.8 of these Rules, or as a member of a hearing committee or hearing panel or as a special hearing officer in an evidentiary hearing resulting in findings of fact and recommendations, shall be disqualified from participation in subsequent deliberations and voting of the Board in such matter.

(b) A Board member who has been a member of an Appeal Panel shall not be disqualified from participation in subsequent deliberations and voting of the Board.

Adopted effective September 1, 2011.

CHAPTER 5.   ORGANIZATION AND ADMINISTRATION

SUBCHAPTER A.   THE BOARD OF BAR OVERSEERS

Section 5.1.   Meetings of the Board

(a) Call and Notice. Meetings shall be held upon the call in writing of the Chair or of any two members of the Board at any place in the City of Boston designated for such purpose by resolution of the Board or in the absence of such resolution as designated by the Chair. Notice of special meetings shall be given in person or by telephone or telegraph to each member of the Board (at the address furnished to the office of the Board for that purpose) at least 24 hours prior to the time fixed for the special meeting. Notice of a special meeting may be waived in writing and shall be waived by attendance at the meeting.

(b) Organization. The Chair shall preside at meetings of the Board. In his or her absence, disqualification, or recusal, one of the following persons in the order stated shall preside or rule, as the case may be:

(1) The Vice–Chair.

(2) An Acting Chair selected by the Board for such purpose.

Adopted effective April 9, 2009.

Section 5.2. Conference Telephone Meetings

One or more members of the Board may participate in a meeting of the Board by means of conference telephone or similar communications equipment by means of which all persons participating in the meeting can hear each other. Participation in a meeting pursuant to this section shall constitute presence in person at such meeting.

Adopted effective April 9, 2009.

SUBCHAPTER B. ADMINISTRATION

Section 5.5. The Administrator

The Board shall appoint an Administrator who shall perform the duties assigned by the Board and imposed by these Rules.

Adopted effective April 9, 2009.

Section 5.6. Communications and Filings Generally

(a) **General Rule.** All communications to the Board and pleadings should be addressed to the Board at its office. Except as authorized by Sections 2.8(a)(2) and 2.8(b)(4) of these Rules, parties shall not communicate regarding a disciplinary matter with members of the Board, hearing committee members, or special hearing officers on an *ex parte* basis. All communications should clearly designate the file number, or similar identifying symbols, if any, employed by the Board or Bar Counsel, and should set forth a short title, the address of the person communicating, the party represented, and how responses should be sent if not by first class mail.

(b) **Pleadings.** All pleadings and other documents filed pursuant to any provisions of Chapter 3 of these Rules shall comply with the applicable provisions of such section.

(c) **Transmission of Complaints.**

(1) Except as otherwise provided in this subsection, all complaints received by the Board against lawyers shall be transmitted forthwith to the Bar Counsel.

(2) Complaints received against Bar Counsel, Assistant Bar Counsel or any member of the Board or its staff involving

Section 5.3. Agenda

An agenda for each meeting of the Board shall be prepared by the Chair, or in his or her absence by the Vice–Chair or Acting Chair.

Adopted effective April 9, 2009.

Section 5.4. Members Not to Be Voluntary Character Witnesses

No member of the Board shall appear voluntarily as a character witness in a disciplinary proceeding.

Adopted effective April 9, 2009.

alleged violations of the Disciplinary Rules shall be transmitted directly to the Board.

Adopted effective April 9, 2009.

Section 5.7. Dockets

(a) **Numbering.** Complaints submitted to the Board pursuant to Section 5.6(c)(2) of these Rules shall be assigned a docket number consisting of the letters "BBO" and the last two digits of the calendar year in which the matter is docketed, which shall be preceded by the serial number of the matter in such calendar year, e.g.: 1 BBO 97 et seq.

(b) **Petitions for Reinstatement.** Petitions for reinstatement shall be docketed to the number assigned by the Supreme Judicial Court

Adopted effective April 9, 2009.

Section 5.8. Records

The Administrator shall maintain permanent records of all matters processed by the Board and the disposition thereof. This paragraph shall not be construed to require the permanent retention of correspondence, transcripts, briefs and other similar documents which underlie the final disposition of a matter by the Board, but shall include the findings of any hearing committee, hearing panel, or special hearing officer and the action and any related opinion or opinions of the Board with respect thereto, and any other information which these Rules expressly require to be made a matter of record.

Adopted effective April 9, 2009.

SUBCHAPTER C. BAR COUNSEL

Section 5.9. Practice of Law by Bar Counsel Prohibited

Bar Counsel, Assistant Bar Counsel, and Board staff shall not engage in private practice, except that the Board may agree to a reasonable period of transition after appointment.

Adopted effective April 9, 2009.

Section 5.10. Retention of Records by Bar Counsel

Subject to the provisions of Supreme Judicial Court Rule 4:01, Section 7(5), and Section 4.2 of these Rules relating to the expunction of certain closed and dismissed matters, Bar Counsel shall maintain permanent records of all matters presented to the Office of the Bar Counsel and the disposition thereof, provided that Bar Counsel need not permanently retain correspondence, memoranda, transcripts and other simi- lar documents which underlie the final disposition of a matter by dismissal or closing.

Adopted effective April 9, 2009.

SUBCHAPTER D.   HEARING COMMITTEES

Section 5.11.   Service On Other Hearing Committees

Members of any one hearing committee may serve on any other hearing committee in specific cases as need arises as determined by the Board Chair or the Chair's designee.

Adopted effective April 9, 2009.

Section 5.12.   Duties of Chair

The Chair of a hearing committee shall be the presiding officer at all hearings held by the committee and, unless otherwise directed by the committee with respect to particular questions or issues, shall make all rulings on admissibility of evidence and other procedural matters arising in connection with formal proceedings.

Adopted effective April 9, 2009.

Section 5.13.   Meetings of Hearing Committees

Except as otherwise provided by these Rules, meetings and proceedings of a hearing committee shall be governed insofar as applicable by the provisions of these Rules governing meetings and proceedings of the Board.

Adopted effective April 9, 2009.

APPENDIX 1.   APPLICATION FOR REINSTATEMENT

APPENDIX.   Application for Reinstatement

COMMONWEALTH OF MASSACHUSETTS
BOARD OF BAR OVERSEERS
OF THE SUPREME JUDICIAL COURT

```
                    )
                    ) In Re
                    ) APPLICATION FOR
                    ) REINSTATEMENT
                    ) AS AN ATTORNEY AT LAW
                    )
                    ) SJC No.:
```

REINSTATEMENT QUESTIONNAIRE Part I

Filing and Service Instructions

In accordance with the provisions of Sections 3.62 and 3.63 of the Rules of the Board of Bar Overseers, the petitioner shall complete the Reinstatement Questionnaire, setting forth fully and accurately the information requested under the pains and penalties of perjury. Part I of this Questionnaire, as filed with the Board, shall become part of the record in the reinstatement proceeding.

1. **File with the Court.** The petitioner must file the Petition for Reinstatement with the Clerk of the Supreme Judicial court for Suffolk County. The Reinstatement Questionnaire should not be part of this filing.

2. **File with the Board.** When the Petition for Reinstatement is filed with the Court, the petitioner must also file one copy with the Board of Bar Overseers, along with four copies of Part I only of the Reinstatement Questionnaire and a check in the amount of $500.

3. **Serve Upon Bar Counsel.** When the Petition for Reinstatement is filed with the Board and the Court, the petitioner must also serve one copy on Bar Counsel, along with the originals of Part I and Part II of the Reinstatement Questionnaire.

4. **Supplementation of Responses.** The petitioner is under a duty seasonably to supplement or amend any prior response that the petitioner knows or has come to know (a) was incorrect when made or (b) was correct when made but is no longer true or complete.

1. **Personal Information**

    A.   Full Name:

    B.   Current Mailing Address:

    C.   Telephone Number(s):

    D.   E-mail address:

2. **Professional Status**

    A.   List each jurisdiction, court, and tribunal to which you have been admitted to practice with the dates of each admission. State your current status in each jurisdiction listed and state whether or not the jurisdiction was advised of the disciplinary action or transfer to disability inactive status ordered by the Supreme Judicial Court for the Commonwealth of Massachusetts.

    B.   Describe the misconduct that led to your suspension, disbarment, or resignation from the practice of law. If you were transferred to disability inactive status, describe the physical or mental disability which led to your transfer to disability inactive status. Attach to this Questionnaire a copy of the order of disbarment, suspension, acceptance of resignation, or transfer to disability inactive status entered by the Supreme Judicial Court together with the opinion of the Court or the summary published by the Board of Bar Overseers.

    C.   Attach to this Questionnaire a copy of all orders of reprimand, suspension, disbarment, acceptance of resignation, or transfer to disability inactive status entered by any other jurisdiction or tribunal together with the published opinion or summary.

    D.   If the sanction was imposed following the conviction of a crime, attach a copy of the judgment of conviction. Provide the name and address of your probation or parole officer, if any. If you have been discharged from probation or parole, attach the order or certificate of release.

3. Conduct since sanction imposed

Unless otherwise specified, this section pertains to conduct during the period of disbarment, suspension, resignation or disability in active status

A. Describe in detail your occupation or employment and provide the name and address of each employer, together with the name of each of your immediate supervisor(s), a description of each employment, the dates of each, and the reason(s) for leaving;

(1) If self-employed, provide the name and address of each business or occupation, together with a description of each such business or occupation and the dates of each.

B. List and describe all charitable endeavors, community work, and other activities in which you have engaged which you consider relevant to your current moral character and fitness to practice law.

C. State whether any charges, formal or informal, of fraud, malpractice, or errors or omissions were made or claimed against you. For each such charge or claim, state the date it was made, the name and current address of the claimant(s), the substance of the claims or charge, the forum where the charges are being or were considered, if any, and its current status.

D. List all claims paid by the Clients' Security Board as restitution on your account. As to each claim, list the name of the claimant, the CSB docket number, the amount of the award, the date of the award, and the date of your reimbursement to the Clients' Security Board. This information may be obtained by calling the Clients' Security Board at (617) 728–8700.

E. Describe all financial or other actions taken by you or on your behalf to make restitution or provide other appropriate compensation or payment to persons injured by your professional misconduct. If you have not made restitution, compensation, or payment, please set forth your reasons for not doing so.

F. Give the date(s) you took the MPRE and attach a certification that you obtained a passing score to this Questionnaire.

G. List all courses taken by you to acquire or maintain learning in the law and knowledge of your ethical obligations. As to each, list the name of the course, the school or program sponsoring the course, the date or dates of attendance, and, if applicable, the grade you received in the course. Please attach to the Questionnaire certificates of attendance.

H. List by name and author, if applicable, all periodicals, newspapers, and books to which you have regularly subscribed or which you have read which you believe have assisted you in acquiring or maintaining learning in the law and knowledge of your ethical obligations.

I. List every civil or administrative action commenced or pending in any jurisdiction in which you were a party or in which you had or claimed an interest, and for each such action list the date on which it was commenced, the case caption, the court, and docket number. Provide a summary of the allegations made in each such action, its final disposition if any, and its current status. If judgment entered against you, state the amount of the judgment and whether or not you have paid the judgment.

J. Criminal, administrative, or investigative proceedings.

(1) List every matter involving you arrest or prosecution in any jurisdiction for any crime, whether felony or misdemeanor. Identify each charge brought, the disposition of the charge, if any, and its current status.

(2) State whether or not you have been a target of a Federal or State investigation into alleged criminal conduct and state whether or not you gave testimony or information to any such authority under a grant of immunity. If so, please identify the authority conducting each investigation; the name, title, and address of the prosecutor conducting each investigation; and the date and the matter in which you testified.

K. State whether you have made any application for reinstatement or original admission as an attorney at law in any jurisdiction, or any application for other license requiring proof of good character for its procurement. For each such application, please state the date of the application, the name and address of the authority to whom it was addressed, whether or not any hearing was held in connection with you application, and the disposition thereof.

L. List all procedures or inquiries held concerning your standing as a member of any profession or organization, or holder of any license or office, which involved your censure, removal, suspension, revocation of license, or discipline; and as to each such procedure or inquiry, state the dates, facts, and the disposition thereof, and the name and address of the authority in possession of the record thereof.

4. Practice after Reinstatement

A. Describe your plans for practicing law if you are reinstated. Include the nature of the intended practice; the type and volume of cases you intend or expect to handle; the field or fields in which you intend to concentrate, if any; whether you intend to be a sole practitioner or to be associated with others; the intended location of your practice; your intended procedures for docket control and office management; and your intended procedures for maintaining client and other trust funds.

B. Identify by name and address all persons with whom you plan to associate as well as those on whom you intend to rely as mentors, supervisors, monitors, or accountants if you are reinstated. Explain how you expect each person so identified to function or assist you in connection with your practice of law.

C. Describe the efforts you have undertaken to be covered by professional liability insurance if you are reinstated and state the results of those efforts.

5. References

A. List names, address, and telephone numbers of three references, at least two of whom are members in good standing of the Massachusetts Bar, who would recommend your reinstatement to the Bar of this Commonwealth and who would attest to your character and conduct since disbarment or suspension.

1. _____
2. _____
3. _____

6. Personal Statement

Provide a concise statement of facts to justify your reinstatement to the Bar of this Commonwealth.

I, _____, being duly sworn, state as follows:

That all of the information contained in the foregoing Reinstatement Questionnaire is true and correct to the best of my knowledge and that I am aware of my obligation to supplement responses as set forth in the filing and service instructions for the Questionnaire Part I;

That I have fully abided by the terms of the order of discipline or disability inactive status; I have not practiced law, identified myself as "Esq." or "Esquire," or otherwise held myself out as an attorney during the term of my disbarment, resignation, suspension, or disability inactive status; I have not listed myself as a lawyer on any sign, letterhead or stationery, or in any directory, or in any electronic or computer-accessed media; I have not engaged in paralegal work during the term of my disbarment, resignation, suspension, or disability inactive status; and I have not been employed by a lawyer in any capacity during said term, except as authorized by the Supreme Judicial Court on [date] or as described above.

_____(signature)

Sworn to and subscribed before me this __ day of _____, 20 __.

_____Notary Public

(SEAL) My Commission Expires: _____

COMMONWEALTH OF MASSACHUSETTS
BOARD OF BAR OVERSEERS
OF THE SUPREME JUDICIAL COURT
_____

)
)   In Re
)   APPLICATION FOR
)   REINSTATEMENT
)   AS AN ATTORNEY AT LAW
)
)   SJC No.

_____

REINSTATEMENT QUESTIONNAIRE Part II

Filing and Service Instructions

In accordance with the provisions of Sections 3.62 and 3.63 of the Rules of the Board of Bar Overseers, the petitioner shall complete the Reinstatement Questionnaire, setting forth fully and accurately the information requested under the pains and penalties of perjury. Part I of this Questionnaire, as filed with the Board, shall become part of the record in the reinstatement proceeding.

1. **File with the Court.** The petitioner must file the Petition for Reinstatement with the Clerk of the Supreme Judicial court for Suffolk County. The Reinstatement Questionnaire should not be part of this filing.

2. **File with the Board.** When the Petition for Reinstatement is filed with the Court, the petitioner must also file one copy with the Board of Bar Overseers, along with four copies of Part I only of the Reinstatement Questionnaire and a check in the amount of $500.

3. **Serve Upon Bar Counsel.** When the Petition for Reinstatement is filed with the Board and the Court, the petitioner must also serve one copy on Bar Counsel, along with the originals of Part I and Part II of the Reinstatement Questionnaire.

4. **Supplementation of Responses.** The petitioner is under a duty seasonably to supplement or amend any prior response that the petitioner knows or has come to know (a) was incorrect when made or (b) was correct when made but is no longer true or complete.

1. Personal Information

A. Full Name:

B. Current Mailing Address and Street Address:

C. Social Security Number:

D. Date of Birth:

E. Marital Status:

F. For each of your dependents, state the full name, address, date of birth, and relationship:

G. List all residences maintained by you during the period of discipline or disability inactive status, with the names and addresses of landlords, if any.

2. Financial Information

A. List your gross monthly salary, commissions, or earnings from each employment, occupation, or business that you have engaged in during the period of your disbarment, suspension, resignation, or disability inactive status.

B. List your monthly income from all sources other than employment, occupation, or business, including gifts and loans, and the sources from which all such earnings and income were derived, during the period of your disbarment, suspension, resignation, or disability inactive status, or during the eight (8) years preceding the filing of the petition for reinstatement, whichever is less.

C. List all monthly expenses during the period of your disbarment, suspension, resignation, or disability inactive status, or during the eight (8) years preceding the filing of the petition for reinstatement, whichever is less.

D. Are you subject to an order or agreement to pay child and/or spousal support? If yes, attach a copy of the support order or agreement and proof that such payments are current.

E. Since the date of your disbarment, suspension, resignation, or transfer to disability inactive status, have you commenced proceedings in any capacity in bankruptcy or given an assignment for the benefit of creditors? If so, please give the case name(s), docket number(s), the name and address of assignee, and identify the court(s) where the proceedings related to such action were commenced, and describe the status of each.

F. Tax returns

(1) State whether or not you have filed all State and Federal income tax returns for the previous eight (8) years.

(2) Attach to Part II (not Part I) of this Questionnaire copies of all Federal income tax returns filed by you or on your behalf in any capacity for eight (8) years preceding the filing of the petition for reinstatement or for all tax years including and since the date of your suspension, disbarment, resignation, or transfer to disability inactive status, whichever is less.

(3) State whether or not you will provide the Board or Bar Counsel upon demand the authorization required by governmental taxing authorities to release the original returns.

G. Assets

(1) List all real estate which you owned or record or in which you have or had a beneficial interest at any time from the date of the order of disbarment, resignation, suspension, or transfer to disability inactive status to the present. For each such property, list its location, and current fair market value, or, if disposed of, the fair market value as of the date of the order of discipline or transfer to disability inactive status, the date of its disposition, and the consideration paid.

(2) List all other assets of a value of or exceeding $1,000 to which you have or held title or in which you have had a beneficial interest at any time during the period of disbarment, resignation, suspension, or disability inactive status. For each, identify the nature of the asset, its location, and its current value, or, if disposed of, the value of the asset as of the date of the order imposing discipline or transferring you to disability inactive status, the date of disposition of the asset, and the amount received for it.

H. Financial obligations

(1) List all your financial obligations not previously listed, above, as of the date of the filing of the petition for reinstatement. For each such obligation, list the name and address of the creditor or oblige, the amount of the obligation, the date the obligation was incurred, whether the obligation is fixed or disputed, and whether any agreement or judgment exists regarding the obligation. Please attach a copy of any such agreement or judgment. If no writing exists regarding the agreement for payment, please provide the name and address of the individual with whom the agreement was made and set forth the terms of the agreement and the date on which it was made. If the creditor is either the Massachusetts Department of Revenue (DOR) or the Internal Revenue Service (IRS), please provide a release on a form approved by the IRS and the DOR which will permit the Office of Bar Counsel and the Board of Bar Overseers to obtain information regarding your tax or support obligations.

(2)(a) List the names of all financial institutions in which you are or were signatory to accounts, safe deposit boxes, deposits or loans during the period of discipline or disability inactive status.

(b) Please state the number of each account, box, deposit, or loan; the date each account, box, deposit, or loan was opened, approved, or made; and the date each account, box, or loan was closed, discharged, or paid.

3. **Professional Status Information**

List the names and addresses of all persons who complained or testified against you in the proceeding which resulted in your resignation, disbarment, or suspension in this Commonwealth and in any other jurisdiction or court.

4. **Emotional Disorder/Addiction/Substance Abuse Information**

If you have been incapacitated from employment or from carrying out employment due to any physical or emotional impairment, alcoholism, use of prescription or non-prescription drugs, or other reason since the effective date of the discipline; or if you are seeking reinstatement from an order transferring you to disability inactive status; or if you raised in mitigation during any proceeding regarding your license to practice law or any other profession a claim that your physical or mental condition caused or contributed to the alleged misconduct. Describe the nature of the impairment or disability, its effect on your ability to obtain or maintain employment, and the treatment sought to address the impairment or disability. Provide the name and address of each institution and provider who has provided or who is providing treatment or consultation to you, the dates of treatment, and your current diagnosis or prognosis.

Additional Statement:

Provide a statement as to any other matter not previously described in the Questionnaire which should, in the interest of full disclosure, be brought to the attention of the Board of Bar Overseers in considering your petition for reinstatement.

I, _____, being duly sworn, state as follows:

That all of the information contained in the foregoing Reinstatement Questionnaire is true and correct to the best of my knowledgeand that I am aware of my obligation to supplement responses as set forth in the filing and service instructions for the Questionnaire Part II;

That I authorize all providers who have examined or treated me and all institutions in which I have been examined or treated for any physical or mental disorder or addiction since the date of the order imposing discipline or transferring me to disability inactive status to provide to agents and employees of the Office of Bar Counsel and the Board of Bar Overseers all hospital and medical records, reports, treatment notes, and information regarding care, consultation, evaluation, diagnosis and prognosis, and I will cooperate with the Office of Bar Counsel and the Board of Bar Overseers in providing such further information and authorizations as required to release information to the Office of Bar Counsel and the Board of Bar Overseers;

That I further authorize all financial institutions listed in response to question 2(H)(2) to provide to agents or employees of the Office of Bar Counsel and the Board of Bar Overseers copies of statements of account, canceled checks, box records, and loan records, and I will cooperate with the Office of Bar Counsel and the Board of Bar Overseers in providing such further information and authorizations as required to release information to the Office of Bar Counsel and the Board of Bar Overseers.

_____
(signature)

Sworn to and subscribed before me this ___ day of _____, 20 ___.

_____Notary Public

(SEAL) My commission expires: _____

Adopted effective April 9, 2009.

CLIENTS' SECURITY BOARD RULES

Rule 1. General Statement

The Clients' Security Board adopted these rules pursuant to Rule 4:06, Section 1(A), of the Rules of the Supreme Judicial Court (S.J.C.). They provide for the administration of the Clients' Security Fund, the procedures for the presentation, consideration, and payment of claims, and the exercise of the Board's powers and duties under the Rules of the Supreme Judicial Court (S.J.C.).

Repealed, readopted and amended June 26, 2019, effective September 1, 2019.

Rule 2. Definitions

For the purpose of these rules, the following definitions shall apply:

(A) The "Board" shall mean the Clients' Security Board established pursuant to S.J.C. Rule 4:04, Section 1.

(B) The "Fund" shall mean the Clients' Security Fund held by the Board pursuant to S.J.C. Rule 4:04, Section 1.

(C) An "attorney," "lawyer," or "respondent" shall mean a person who is or was a member of the bar of the Commonwealth. For the purpose of these rules, the attorney must have died, been disbarred or suspended from the practice of law, resigned from the bar of the Commonwealth (S.J.C. Rules 4:01, Section 15; 4:05, Section 1), or continued to act as if the attorney were a member of the bar in good standing while under suspension, disbarment, or resignation.

(D) "Client" shall mean a person who suffered a reimbursable loss resulting from an attorney acting either as an attorney or fiduciary as provided in S.J.C. Rule 4:04, Section 1.

(E) "Dishonest Conduct" shall mean wrongful acts committed by an attorney such as theft, embezzlement of money, or the wrongful taking or conversion of money, property, or other things of value, regardless of where the conduct occurred, including but not limited to:

(1) Failing to refund unearned fees received in advance as required by Rule 1.16(d) of the Massachusetts Rules of Professional Conduct;

(2) Borrowing of money from a client without intention to repay it, or with disregard of the attorney's ability or reasonably anticipated ability to repay it; and

(3) Settling a case without authorization and misappropriating the settlement proceeds. When an attorney has mis-appropriated settlement proceeds in a contingent fee case, the Board may review the facts and, in its discretion, conclude that the attorney settled the case for less than full value and reimburse the claimant for any legal fees that the attorney received.

(F) A "Reimbursable Loss" shall mean the loss of a client's money or other property caused by the dishonest conduct of an attorney that arose out of an attorney-client or a fiduciary relationship.

(G) A reimbursable loss shall not include:

(1) Any loss to the extent the client has recovered or may recover from a collateral source such as, but not limited to, a bond, a surety agreement, or insurance contract;

(2) Any loss arising solely out of an investment, lending, personal, or business relationship; or

(3) Any consequential or incidental damages, such as lost interest, or lawyer's fees or other costs incurred in seeking recovery of a loss.

In cases of hardship, the Board may, in its discretion, recognize as a reimbursable loss a claim that would otherwise be excluded hereunder.

Repealed, readopted and amended June 26, 2019, effective September 1, 2019.

Rule 3. Organization

A. Meetings.

(1) The Board shall meet at least quarterly. The Board shall elect a treasurer and a secretary who shall serve until the Board elects a different member to assume the responsibilities of either office.

(2) The Board may hold other meetings upon the call of the Chair or a majority of the members, with reasonable notice to the members.

(3) A majority of Board members shall constitute a quorum. A majority of the members present at a duly constituted meeting may exercise any powers held by the Board.

B. Duties of Officers.

(1) The Chair shall preside at all meetings of the Board and shall coordinate and supervise the administrative activities of the Board and of the Fund. The Chair may delegate the administrative activities to the Executive Director of the

Board of Bar Overseers pursuant to S.J.C. Rule 4:06, Section 1(G). The Vice–Chair shall preside at meetings in the absence of the Chair and shall have such additional duties as the Chair or the Board shall designate.

(2) The treasurer shall have custody of the money and other assets of the Fund, receive all payments to the Fund, make disbursements from the Fund authorized by the Board, invest the monies of the Fund in the manner authorized by the Board, cause an annual audit to be made of the Fund, maintain appropriate financial records, and file such tax or information returns as may be required. The Board shall obtain and file with the secretary a surety company bond in the amount of at least $500,000, and covering all members of the Board. The Board may delegate some or all of its duties under this paragraph (2) to the general counsel and staff.

(3) In conjunction with the general counsel the secretary shall prepare and maintain minutes of each meeting of the Board. The secretary shall have such other duties as the Chair or the Board shall designate.

C. Staff of the Board.

(1) The Board may employ and cause to be compensated an executive director, general counsel, additional counsel, an administrative assistant, and any other employees as are necessary for the performance of the Board's work. At the Board's discretion, one person may serve as both the Board's executive director and general counsel. The Board's executive director or the general counsel if the Board does not have an executive director, shall be responsible for overseeing and managing the Board's staff.

Amended October 1, 1998, effective November 2, 1998. Repealed, readopted and amended June 26, 2019, effective September 1, 2019.

Rule 4. Investment of the Fund

Money paid into the Fund may, upon authorization by the Board, be invested in any of the following:

(A) Bonds, notes, or other securities of or guaranteed by the United States or any Federal agency;

(B) Bonds, notes, or other securities of or guaranteed by the Commonwealth of Massachusetts;

(C) Interest-bearing accounts or certificates of any federally insured bank, trust company, savings bank, or savings and loan association; or

(D) Any fund insured by the Federal Deposit Insurance Corporation.

In addition, not less than twenty-five percent (25%) of the Fund shall be held in a money market fund or in investments maturing within three months.

Repealed, readopted and amended June 26, 2019, effective September 1, 2019.

Rule 5. Filing a Claim

A. Claim Form.

(1) A claimant shall apply to the Board in writing, on a form supplied by the Board, containing the following information:

(a) The claimant's name, home and business addresses, and occupation;

(b) The name and address (including the address at the time the claim arose) of the attorney involved;

(c) A summary of the attorney's actions;

(d) The date and circumstances under which the claimant discovered the loss;

(e) The efforts made to obtain reimbursement from the attorney or any third party;

(f) The total amount of the claimant's loss, including how the claimant calculated the amount of the loss;

(g) The name and address of any attorney or other person assisting or representing the claimant in connection with the claim;

(h) The claimant's signature or other verification; and

(i) How claimant learned of the Fund.

(2) The claimant shall include with the claim form all supporting documentation of the events giving rise to the claim.

(3) A claimant shall provide a financial statement and when requested by the Board tax returns.

B. The Board may, in its discretion, require the exhaustion of all reasonable remedies before processing a claim or reimbursing a loss. Such remedies may include, but are not limited to, pursuing recovery under a bond, from a surety, from a professional liability insurance carrier, by filing a civil action, or by reporting the loss to appropriate criminal authorities. A claimant's failure to cooperate in the disciplinary proceedings against the lawyer shall not bar the granting of relief from the Fund.

C. The claim form and supporting documentation shall be sent by mail or hand-delivery to Clients' Security Board, 99 High Street, 2nd Floor, Boston, MA 02110–2320. The claim form and supporting documentation may also be e-mailed to: info@masscsb.org.

Amended October 1, 1998, effective November 2, 1998. Repealed, readopted and amended June 26, 2019, effective September 1, 2019.

Rule 6. Processing a Claim

A. The general counsel shall cause reasonable investigation to be made of all claims filed with the Board.

B. Any member of the Board who has or has had a lawyer-client or financial relationship with a claimant or respondent, or is related by blood or marriage to either the claimant or respondent, shall not participate in the investigation or adjudication of any claim involving that claimant or that respondent.

C. As soon as practicable after receiving a claim, the Board shall send a copy of the claim by any reasonable method to the last known address of the attorney who is the subject of the claim. The attorney shall have twenty days from the date of mailing to file an answer with the Board.

D. If the claim does not meet the requirements of S.J.C. Rule 4:05, Section 1 but bar disciplinary proceedings are pending, general counsel shall notify the claimant of the requirements of Rule 4:05, Section 1. General counsel shall maintain the claim in an inactive status and periodically determine from the Board of Bar Overseers the status of the disciplinary proceedings. The Board shall use any information from the Board of Bar Overseers solely to investigate and resolve claims. The Board shall maintain any such information as confidential.

E. In determining whether it would be more appropriate for the Fund or the fund of another jurisdiction to pay a claim, the Board should consider the following factors:

(1) the fund(s) into which the attorney was required to pay an annual assessment or into which an appropriation was made on behalf of the attorney by the bar association or otherwise;

(2) the domicile of the attorney;

(3) the domicile of the client;

(4) the residence(s) of the attorney;

(5) the number of years the attorney has been licensed in each jurisdiction;

(6) the location of the attorney's principal office and other offices;

(7) where the attorney-client relationship arose;

(8) where the attorney performed the legal services;

(9) whether at the time the attorney performed the legal services, the attorney was engaged in the unauthorized practice of law as defined by the jurisdiction in which the attorney performed the legal services;

(10) any negligence or conduct of the claimant that may have contributed to the loss; and

(11) any other significant contacts with Massachusetts or another jurisdiction.

Repealed, readopted and amended June 26, 2019, effective September 1, 2019.

Rule 7. Consideration and Payment of Claims

A. Upon determination by general counsel that a claim is ready for adjudication, the Board shall decide the matter upon the record before it or after such hearing as the Board in its discretion deems necessary. In the event the Board determines that a hearing is not necessary, it shall cause the parties to be notified that the Board will consider the claim without hearing.

B. As an alternative to the Board hearing a matter, the Chair may designate one or more members of the Board as hearing members, who shall consider the Board's file, decide to hear the claim, make further investigation as they may deem appropriate, and make recommendations to the Board for disposition of the claim.

C. The Board may hold hearings at the Board's offices or other places mutually convenient to the Board members and the claimant. The Board may make a recording or transcript of each hearing solely for its administrative purposes.

D. The Board shall send notice of hearing by any reasonable method to the claimant, claimant's counsel, the respondent at the respondent's last known address, and the respondent's counsel.

E. The Board, in acting on each claim, shall take into account the standards and factors set forth in S.J.C. Rule 4:05, Section 3.

F. As soon as practicable, the Board shall send notice of its determination by any reasonable method to the claimant, claimant's counsel, respondent, and respondent's counsel.

G. The Board shall make payment of an allowed claim as soon as practicable following its adjudication and may make payment by any reasonable method giving consideration to a claimant's circumstances and the Board's need for documentation of the claimant's receipt of payment. Before the Board makes payment, it shall obtain a subrogation agreement from the claimant.

H. Upon the request of a claimant, respondent, or member of the Board, the Board in its discretion may reconsider its adjudication of a claim. Unless the time is extended by the Board, a claimant or respondent shall file a request with the Board within thirty days after the date of the Board's adjudication. The request shall state in writing and with particularity the facts on which reconsideration is sought. Except as provided herein, an adjudication of the Board is final and the Board shall give no further consideration to the original claim form or subsequent claim forms based upon substantially the same allegations.

I. Any payment of claims shall be a matter of grace, not right, and no client, beneficiary, employer, organization, or other person shall have any right or interest in the Fund. No decision to allow or deny reimbursement shall be subject to judicial review in a court of either appellate or original jurisdiction.

Amended September 29, 1993, effective November 1, 1993; amended effective August 1, 1994; amended December 11, 2003, effective January 1, 2004. Repealed, readopted and amended June 26, 2019, effective September 1, 2019.

Rule 8. Confidentiality

The Board shall keep confidential all claim forms, proceedings, investigations, claimants' and respondents' financial information, and reports involving specific claims received and payments made from the Fund. The Board and its staff shall maintain the confidentiality of the claimants, investigations, and proceedings. This provision shall not be construed to:

(A) to deny relevant information to the Board of Bar Overseers, to a court or investigative agency of proper jurisdiction, to an authorized agency investigating the qualifications of a judicial candidate, or claim form for governmental employment;

(B) to prohibit the release of statistical or summary information that does not disclose the identity of the parties; or

(C) to prohibit the release of publicity after the Board has made an award in a manner that is consistent with the provisions of this section.

Adopted June 26, 2019, effective September 1, 2019.

Rule 9. Subrogation for Reimbursement Made

As a condition of reimbursement, a claimant must execute a subrogation agreement on a form prepared by the Board. The Board shall be subrogated to the rights of a claimant to the extent of the amount of reimbursement made by the Board, and, where practicable, will seek recovery for the Fund. The Board may bring an action either in the name of the claimant or in the name of the Board, and, as a condition of reimbursement, the claimant shall agree to cooperate with the Board in the prosecution of such action.

Former Rule 8 amended October 1, 1998, effective November 2, 1998. Repealed, readopted, renumbered and amended June 26, 2019, effective September 1, 2019.

Rule 10. Attorney's Fees

Any attorney representing a claimant before the Board shall do so as a public service and shall not receive any portion of the award or any fee from the claimant for services related to the Board's proceedings.

Former Rule 9 repealed, readopted, renumbered and amended June 26, 2019, effective September 1, 2019.

Rule 11. Insurance of Approved Claims

The Board may insure the payment of claims approved by the Board with such insurance carrier or carriers as it may from time to time elect and may, in such event, authorize the treasurer to pay out of the Fund such premiums as it shall approve.

Former Rule 10 repealed, readopted and renumbered June 26, 2019, effective September 1, 2019.

Rule 12. Publicity

A. The Board shall have the discretion to publicize its activities, decisions, and awards so long as any publicity adheres to the confidentiality requirements set forth in Rule 8.

B. After awards are made the Board may publicize its awards by disclosing the name of, and other information pertaining to, an attorney who has caused a reimbursable loss. The Board may withhold such information in those cases where it finds the existence of mitigating circumstances.

Former Rule 11 repealed, readopted, renumbered and amended June 26, 2019, effective September 1, 2019.

Rule 13. General Provisions

A. The Board may waive technical adherence to these rules to achieve the objectives of S.J.C. Rules 4:04 to 4:08, inclusive.

B. The Board may amend these rules at any time by a majority vote, subject to the approval of the Supreme Judicial Court.

Former Rule 12 repealed, readopted, renumbered and amended June 26, 2019, effective September 1, 2019.

RULES OF PRACTICE AND PROCEDURE OF THE APPELLATE TAX BOARD

Promulgated Pursuant to G.L. c. 58A, § 8

Table of Sections

SECTION I. 831 CMR 1.00 APPELLATE TAX BOARD RULES OF PRACTICE AND PROCEDURE

Section 1.01. Appearance and Practice Before the Board

Persons may appear and act for themselves, or for partnerships of which they are members, or for corporations of which they are officers, or for boards of which they are members, in any proceeding before the Board.

Attorneys at law admitted to practice before the courts of the Commonwealth may practice before the Board. Attorneys shall conduct themselves in a manner conforming to the disciplinary rules of the Supreme Judicial Court of Massachusetts.

Notice of any change of attorney or representative shall be given promptly to the clerk and to the adverse party.

The Board may for cause deny or suspend the right of any person to practice before it.

Section 1.02. Form, Style and Size of Papers

All papers filed with the Board, except exhibits and forms supplied by the Board, shall be either printed or typewritten on one side only of plain white paper measuring eight and one-half by eleven inches with adequate margins and shall be clearly legible, and shall be signed by the party or his or her attorney.

Section 1.03. Petition Under Formal Procedure

The petition shall contain all facts and dates necessary for the determination of the Board's jurisdiction and shall contain in substance the following:

(1) A caption in the following form:

The Commonwealth of Massachusetts
Appellate Tax Board

Docket No. _____

_____
Appellant

_____
Appellee

PETITION UNDER FORMAL PROCEDURE

(2) A clear and concise statement of the nature of the tax or other matter in controversy and of the facts on which the appellant relies, giving all dates on which required filings were made and the date of notice of the decision or determination from which the appeal is taken. If the appeal is from the refusal to abate a tax, describe the property or commodity taxed and state the valuation made by the taxing authority, the rate and amount of the tax, the year for which it was assessed, the date of any tax bill for local property, the amount and date of any payment made, and the date and manner of application for abatement to the taxing authority.

(3) A clear and concise statement of the appellant's objections to the decision or determination appealed from, and of the contentions of law, if any, which the appellant desires to raise.

(4) A prayer setting forth the relief sought.

(5) The name, address, and telephone number of the appellant and his attorney.

Appeals involving real estate or tangible personal property taxes for two or more years shall not be included in one petition.

Where two or more parcels of real estate are included in one decision of a board of assessors, the Board in its discretion may require that each parcel be the subject of a separate petition.

The Commissioner of Revenue or the board of assessors of a city or town, as the case may be, shall be designated as appellee by his or its official title, without naming the individual or individuals holding the office, and if, while the appeal is pending, a change occurs in the individual or individuals holding the office, the appeal shall not abate, and no substitution of parties shall be necessary.

Section 1.04. Filing of Petition Under Formal Procedure and Service Thereof

(1) The petition shall be filed with the clerk and shall be signed by the appellant or his attorney. The appellant shall forthwith serve a copy thereof, stamped with the Board's docket number, upon the appellee in hand, or by first class

mail, postage prepaid, addressed to the usual place of business of the appellee.

(2) The appellant shall, not later than ten days after filing the petition, file with the clerk a signed acknowledgment of service or a certificate that a copy of the petition has been served upon upon the appellee in hand or mailed by first class mail, postage prepaid, to the usual place of business of the appellee, giving the address to which the copy has been mailed and the date of mailing.

(3) Failure to conform to the requirements of this rule or of 831 CMR 1.03 shall be ground, in the discretion of the Board, for dismissal of the appeal.

Amended effective May 4, 2007.

Section 1.05. Petition for Late Entry

A petition for late entry of an appeal as provided in M.G.L. c. 59, § 65C, shall contain a statement of the circumstances which constitute the accident or mistake upon which the petition for late entry is based. Upon the filing of such petition the clerk shall mail a notice thereof to the appropriate assessors by registered or certified mail within five days from the date of said filing, together with a copy of said petition. Said notice shall set a date for hearing of said petition not later than twenty days from the date of filing thereof, notice of which shall be given to the appellant.

Section 1.06. Small Claims Procedure

(1) In petitions seeking an abatement of tax from the Commissioner of Revenue related to any tax or excise specified in M.G.L. c. 62C, § 2, unless the appellant affirmatively requests that the case be heard under the formal procedure under M.G.L. c. 58A, § 7, the small claims procedure under M.G.L. c. 58A, § 7B shall govern in any case in which the amount of tax placed in dispute by the petition does not exceed:

(a) $25,000 for any taxable year, in the case of a tax imposed by taxable year;

(b) $25,000 for any calendar year, in the case of a tax imposed by calendar year;

(c) $25,000 for any calendar year, in the case of a tax imposed by M.G.L. chapters 64A through 64J, and M.G.L. c. 138, § 21;

(d) $25,000 in the case of a tax imposed by M.G.L. c. 65c; or

(e) $25,000 for any taxable event or transaction in the case of any other tax.

(f) For purposes of M.G.L. c. 58A, § 7B, the amount of any tax or excise placed in dispute does not include any interest, penalty, or addition to tax imposed by M.G.L. c. 62C or any statute referred to in M.G.L. c. 62C, § 2. If, however, only the imposition or the amount of interest and/or penalties is in dispute, the interest and penalties shall not exceed $25,000 for any period or transaction as specified in 831 CMR 1.06(1)(a) through (e).

If the amount in dispute exceeds these limitations, but not substantially, and the appellant is willing to limit his or her potential abatement to the applicable qualifying amount, the small claims procedure may be elected in accordance with M.G.L. c. 58A, § 7B(f). Amounts in dispute exceeding the qualifying limits by 10% or less shall be presumed not to be substantial for these purposes. Amounts exceeding the qualifying limits by more than 10% shall be presumed to be substantial for these purposes.

At any time at least 30 days prior to the commencement of the hearing, a party who has previously filed, after January 1, 1999, a petition under the formal procedure pursuant to M.G.L. c. 58A, § 7, but who qualifies and now wishes to elect the small claims procedure, may request by motion that the proceedings be transferred to the small claims procedure.

(2) The appellant shall file a petition containing a statement of the facts, the amount claimed in abatement and the reason or reasons the party disagrees with the Commissioner of Revenue's refusal to abate. The petition shall also include at least the following information:

(a) the type of tax at issue and the tax periods or transaction dates involved;

(b) the date the return at issue (if any) was filed;

(c) the date of any assessment by the Commissioner of Revenue;

(d) the date(s) on which the tax was paid;

(e) the date the taxpayer filed the application for abatement;

(f) the date of the Commissioner of Revenue's denial of the application for abatement;

(g) an address and telephone number where the appellant may be contacted and where service of notices and other papers concerning the appeal may be made;

(h) such other information as the Board may require; and

(i) the signature of the taxpayer or its authorized representative.

(3) An appellant filing a petition governed by the small claims procedure shall, at the time of filing the small claims petition or as soon thereafter as the Board may order, pay to the clerk the appropriate entry fee provided in M.G.L. c. 58A, § 7 and shall file a written waiver of the right to appeal to any court in accordance with M.G.L. c. 58A, § 7B. Petition and waiver of appeal forms will be supplied by the clerk upon request.

(4) An appellant shall file with the clerk an original and two copies of the small claims petition and the waiver. Within five business days after receipt of the petition, the clerk shall notify the parties to confirm scheduling of the case and shall serve one copy of the small claims petition on the Commissioner and return one copy to the appellant.

(5) At any time before the commencement of the hearing, the Board on its own motion or at the request of the Commissioner of Revenue, in accordance with M.G.L. c. 58A, § 7B(e), order the small claims designation removed and the proceedings transferred to the formal procedure. In appeals where the Commissioner establishes that there is a recurring issue of law and the aggregate tax at issue, taking into account other similarly situated taxpayers, is over $250,000, or the Board determines that the issue to be addressed is not suitable for small-claims resolution, the appeal will be transferred to the formal procedure.

(6) Within 25 days of the service of the small claims petition or at such other time as the Board may order, the Commissioner shall file with the Board and serve upon the appellant an Answer, similar to that required under the formal procedure provided in M.L. c. c. 58A, § 7, to the allegations contained in the small claims petition. The failure of the Commissioner to specifically admit or deny an allegation concerning which he does not have sufficient information at the time of filing of the Answer shall not constitute a deemed admission of the allegation.

(7) Procedural and non-dispositive motions in small claims cases may be filed only with leave of the Board and, where such leave is granted, shall be filed and heard in the regular motion session in accordance with the provisions of 831 CMR 1.16. Leave is not required to file a motion to remove the small claims designation and transfer the appeal to the formal procedure or to file a motion to transfer an appeal from the formal to the small claims docket.

(8) Dispositive motions in small claims cases shall be filed in writing and served upon the opposing party not later than seven days prior to the hearing of the case. Dispositive motions shall be heard at the hearing of the small claims case and not separately at the regular or a special motion session.

(9) All forms of pre-trial discovery will not be permitted in small claims cases except upon prior motion and a showing that the information sought is essential to the moving party's case, the information is not available from other sources, and the method of seeking the information is the least expensive and intrusive available.

(10) Hearings of small claims cases will be conducted as informally as possible consistent with orderly procedure and any evidence deemed by the Board to have probative value shall be admissible. Hearings of small claims cases shall not be stenographically recorded, except that the Board may have stenographic notes of hearings taken for its own information only which will not be open to the inspection or available for the use of the parties. A hearing on a motion to remove the small claims designation of any appeal may be stenographically recorded at the request of any party following the procedures in 831 CMR 1.28.

(11) Neither briefs nor oral arguments will be required in small claims cases, but the Board on its own motion or upon motion of either party may permit the filing of briefs.

(12) The small claims procedure is available in all appeals in which the petition initiating the appeal is filed with the Board on or after January 1, 1999.

(13) Each small claims case will be automatically advanced for speedy hearing by the Board.

(14) In appeals pending under the small claims procedure, the appellant may be represented by a person of appellant's choosing upon written authorization of the appellant and leave of the Board. The other non-conflicting provisions of 831 CMR 1.01 shall remain in effect under the small claims procedure.

(15) The provisions of 831 CMR 1.24 regarding subpoenas and the summonsing of witnesses shall be applicable under the small claims procedure.

(16) No requests for findings of fact and rulings of law shall be allowed under the small claims procedure.

(17) The Board will issue a brief written summary of the reasons for its decision in each case decided under the small claims procedure. The Board shall not issue findings of fact and reports in cases decided under the small claims procedure.

(18) Decisions issued under the small claims procedure shall not be reviewed by any court and shall not be used as precedent in any other case.

Section 1.07. Informal Procedure: Statement and Waiver of Appeal

(1) A party may elect to file an appeal under the informal procedure in accordance with M.G.L. c. 58A, § 7A. A party electing the informal procedure shall file a written statement of the facts in the case and of the amount claimed in abatement, as well as the following:

(a) dates necessary to establish jurisdiction

(b) the assessed value of the real or personal property

(c) the tax rate

(d) the tax assessed

(e) an address and telephone number where service of notices and other papers concerning the appeal may be made

(f) such further information as the clerk may require

(2) A party electing the informal procedure shall, at the time of filing the statement under the informal procedure, file a written waiver of the right of appeal in accordance with M.G.L. c. 58A, § 7A. Forms on which statements may be made and the waiver of appeal forms will be supplied by the clerk.

(3) No statement shall relate to an assessment on more than one parcel of real estate, unless the Board specifically permits it. If the assessed value of the property does not exceed twenty thousand dollars, the statement will be made out for the appellant, on request, by the clerk or an assistant clerk.

Section 1.08. Filing of Statement Under the Informal Procedure and Service Thereof

The appellant shall file with the clerk an original and two copies of the statement under informal procedure together with the waiver. The clerk shall promptly serve one copy of the statement upon the appellee and return one copy to the appellant.

Section 1.09. Transfer Procedure

If the assessed value of the property exceeds twenty thousand dollars, the appellee, within thirty days of the date of service of such statement, may elect to have the appeal heard under the formal procedure by so notifying the clerk in writing and by paying to the clerk the transfer fee provided by statute. The clerk shall thereupon transfer the appeal to the formal procedure, and shall give notice of the transfer promptly to both parties. If so transferred, the statement shall be considered to be a petition and service thereof to be service of the petition, and the waiver of the right of appeal shall be void; otherwise the informal procedure shall be deemed to have

been accepted and all right of appeal waived by the appellee, except as provided under the informal procedure.

Section 1.10. Fees

The appellant shall at the time of filing the petition or statement pay to the clerk an entry fee in accordance with the following schedule:

Appeals from Board of Assessors; all property with assessed value $20,000 or less	$10.00
Appeals from Board of Assessors; all property with assessed value over $20,000 or not in excess of $100,000	$50.00
Appeals from Board of Assessors; all property with assessed value over $100,000 and not in excess of $999,000	$100.00
Appeals from Board of Assessors; all property with assessed value over $1,000,000	$0.10 per $1,000 of assessed value. Maximum fee: $5,000
Appeals from Commissioner of Revenue except Small Claims appeals	$0.10 per $100 of tax abatement requested Minimum fee: $65.00 Maximum fee: $5,000
Appeals from Commissioner of Revenue; Small Claims appeals	$50.00
Transfer by municipality from Informal to Formal Procedure	$65.00

Amended effective November 8, 2001; August 30, 2002.

Section 1.11. Dockets

The clerk shall assign to each appeal a docket number and shall notify the parties thereof. The docket number assigned to each appeal entered under the informal procedure shall be preceded by the letter X and a separate numerical order shall be maintained for each procedure.

Section 1.12. Answers, Responsive Pleadings and Service Thereof

(1) The appellee shall file an answer with the clerk within thirty days of the service of the petition or statement or within such further time as the Board may allow. If a party files an amended petition pursuant to 831 CMR 1.14, the appellee shall file an answer or amended answer within thirty days of service of the amended petition or such other time as the Board may allow.

(2) In lieu of filing an answer, the appellee may file a motion to dismiss the appeal or other motions identified in 831 CMR 1.16(6). If the motion to dismiss or other motion identified in 831 CMR 1.16(6) is denied, the appellee shall file the answer within ten days of the denial of the motion or within such further time as the Board may allow.

(3) Pursuant to M.G.L. c. 58A, § 7, in an appeal under M.G.L. c. 59, §§ 64 or 65, no answer need be filed where the appellee contests no allegation of the appellant other than overvaluation or improper classification of the property at issue.

(4) The appellee shall serve a copy of the answer upon the appellant or his or her attorney or agent of record, by first class mail, postage prepaid. The answer shall contain in substance the following:

(a) A specific admission or denial of each allegation of fact contained in the petition.

(b) A clear and concise statement of any other facts or rulings of law upon which the appellee relies.

(c) An address and phone number where service of notices and other papers concerning the appeal may be made.

Amended effective May 4, 2007.

Section 1.13. Alternative Delivery Services and Substantiating Marks

(1) Generally, a document is considered filed when it is received by the Board. However, if a document is delivered by the United States mail after the due date in a postage prepaid, properly addressed envelope, then the date of the United States postmark is deemed to be the date of delivery if the date of the postmark is on or before the due date (the "postmark rule"). Pursuant to the authority granted by G.L. c. 58A, § 7, G.L. c. 59, § 64, and G.L. c. 62C, § 39, the Board hereby designates the following alternative delivery services and substantiating marks which the Board will recognize in applying the postmark rule:

(a) Registered mail: The date of registration is treated as the postmark date for purposes of the postmark rule.

(b) Certified mail: The date of the postmark on the sender's receipt is treated as the postmark date for purposes of the postmark rule.

(c) Certificate of mailing: The date produced or affixed by the United States Post Office on a Certificate of Mailing is treated as the postmark date for purposes of this postmark rule.

(d) With respect to the following alternative delivery services, only a substantiating mark produced or affixed by the delivery service, and not by the party relying on the mark, will be treated as the postmark for purposes of the postmark rule:

A. Airborne Express (Airborne), including Overnight Air Express Service, Next Afternoon Service, and Second Day Service;

B. DHL Worldwide Express (DHL), including DHL "Same Day" service and DHL USA Overnight;

C. Federal Express (FedEx), including FedEx Priority Overnight, FedEx Standard Overnight, and FedEx 2Day; and

D. United Parcel Service (UPS), including UPS Next Day Air, UPS Next Day Air Saver, UPS 2nd Day Air A.M., and UPS 2nd Day Air;

E. The Board may determine, on a case-by-case basis, whether any other private delivery service may qualify as an alternative delivery service for purposes of applying the postmark rule. The Board will consider the criteria enumerated in Rev. Proc. 97–19 of the Internal Revenue Service in making this determination. See 1997–1 C.B. 644.

In the event that a postmark or other authorized substantiating mark is illegible, the Board may make such inferences concerning the date of mailing or delivery to an alternative delivery service as are consistent with the purposes of the foregoing statutes and this rule.

Adopted effective May 4, 2007.

Section 1.14. Amended and Supplemental Pleadings

Parties may amend their pleadings, at any time before the decision of the Board, by consent of the adverse party or by leave of the Board.

A further and better statement of the nature of the claim or defense, or of any matter stated in any pleading, may be ordered by the Board in its discretion.

Section 1.15. Substitution of Parties

(1) In the event of the death of the appellant, or for other cause, the Board may order the substitution of the proper parties.

In case of the death of the appellant the executor/trix or administrator/trix may appear to prosecute the petition or appeal.

(2) All motions for substitution of a party shall be filed with the Board and served upon all parties to the appeal in accordance with the provisions of 831 CMR 1.16 and M.G.L. c. 58A, § 9. The Board may order further service in its discretion.

Section 1.16. Motions

(1) Motions must be in writing and a copy served upon the adverse party or his or her attorney. However, motions also may be made orally but must be reduced to writing within such time as the Board shall order.

(2) Motions will be heard on Mondays at 10:00 A.M. If a holiday falls on a Monday, motions will be heard on Tuesday.

(3) The moving party shall file a written motion, and notice of the hearing thereof, with the Board and shall serve a copy on the adverse party or his or her attorney not less than seven days before the date specified for the hearing, unless a different period is fixed by the Board. A Notice of Motion and Certificate of Service must accompany the motion when filed with the Board. When a motion is supported by affidavit, the moving party shall serve the affidavit with the motion and opposing affidavits may be filed and served not later than one day before the hearing, unless the Board permits them to be filed and served at some other time.

(4) Motions may be heard by telephone on Mondays at 11:00 A.M., or on Tuesday where a holiday falls on a Monday, upon request of a party with approval of the Board. The notice and service requirements are the same as provided above. The clerk shall initiate all such telephonic motions unless other arrangements have been made and approved by the Board.

(5) If a party fails to appear at the time set for hearing, the Board may proceed ex parte.

(6) Objections to the form of pleadings shall be made by motion to require the pleadings to be amended, specifically pointing out the matter objected to. If granted, the pleading shall be amended within such time as the Board may order, and if not so amended, the Board will make such order, or dispose of the case in such manner as justice shall require.

(7) Objections to the sufficiency of pleadings or to the jurisdiction of the Board shall be made by motion to dismiss, or to strike, or to take the petition as confessed, or by other appropriate motion stating specifically the ground of objection.

Section 1.17.   [Repealed]

Section 1.18.   Answer and Hearing of Appeals Under M.G.L. c. 58, § 14

When a board of assessors appeals to the Board from a determination of the Commissioner, under M.G.L. c. 58, § 14, the answer of the Commissioner shall be filed within five days of the filing of the petition and the board may give a hearing to the assessors not later than July fifteenth following such determination, as provided by M.G.L. c. 58, § 14.

Section 1.19.   Hearing List

(1) The clerk shall place appeals on the hearing list in their numerical order, unless the Board otherwise directs.

(2) The clerk shall send notices of hearing dates to the parties or to their attorneys.

(3) The chairman will provide for the speedy hearing of all appeals to be heard under the informal procedure.

(4) Appeals may, in the discretion of the Board, be assigned for hearing outside the city of Boston, or be placed on a reserve list for good cause shown, as, for example, to await the decision in some other case.

(5) In the discretion of the Board, petitions for abatement of taxes assessed upon real estate situated in the same general locality of the same town may be heard together, irrespective of the identity of the appellants.

(6) Continuances and postponements may be ordered by the Board on its own motion, or may be granted by it in its discretion on motion of either party.

(7) If any party fails to appear at the time set for hearing, the Board may proceed ex parte.

Section 1.20.   Decisions by a Single Member

(1) A single member of the Board may decide the following types of cases:

(a) Any appeal from a decision of a board of assessors in which the assessed value of the property involved does not exceed $500,000 may be decided by the member hearing the appeal.

(b) Any appeal from a decision of a board of assessors in which the value of the property involved exceeds $500,000 but does not exceed $750,000 may be decided by the member hearing the appeal if both the appellant and the appellee give written consent to a decision by a single member.

(c) Any appeal filed under the informal procedure pursuant to § 7A in which the assessed value is less than $1,000,000.

(d) Any appeal filed under the small-claims procedure pursuant to § 7B may be decided by the member hearing the appeal.

(2) In any such appeal, upon request and upon the filing of such written consent, when required, the appeal shall be advanced for speedy hearing.

(3) In the discretion of the member hearing the appeal, the appeal may be submitted to the full Board for decision.

Amended effective May 4, 2007.

Section 1.21.   Dismissal of Settled and Old Appeals

(1) When notice of the settlement of a pending appeal is received by the clerk from either party, unless a withdrawal of the petition or agreement for decision is filed forthwith, the clerk shall inform both parties or their attorneys by mail that the appeal should be disposed of by filing a withdrawal of the petition or agreement for decision according to the terms of the settlement. Unless within thirty days thereafter such a withdrawal of the petition or agreement for decision is filed with the clerk, or unless notice is received from the other party that the appeal has not been settled, the appeal shall be marked inactive by the clerk, who shall inform both parties by mail of such marking.

(2) Any appeal which has remained on the docket for three years preceding, without action shown upon the docket, other than placing on the hearing list or the filing or withdrawal of an appearance, or the filing of interrogatories, shall, unless the appeal has been placed on a reserve list, be marked inactive, and the clerk shall inform both parties by mail of such marking.

Upon motion of either party the Board may restore to the active list any appeal marked inactive.

If within one year after an appeal has been marked inactive it has not been heard or disposed of, it shall, unless the Board shall otherwise order, be dismissed, and entry of such dismissal shall be made on the docket by the clerk without further notice or order.

Section 1.22.   Scope of Hearing

(1) The Board will not consider, unless equity and good conscience so require, any issue of fact or contention of law not specifically set out in the petition or raised in the answer, except as otherwise provided by M.G.L. c. 58A, § 12C.

Issues sufficient in themselves to determine the decision of the Board or to narrow the scope of the hearing may be separately heard and disposed of in the discretion of the Board.

(2) The originals or, upon leave of the Board, photostatic copies of the following documents should be introduced in evidence:

(a) The tax return or list, if any, filed by the taxpayer, with the date of filing.

(b) The notice of intention to assess by the Commissioner, if any, with the date of notice.

(c) The original assessment, or other determination in issue, with the date of notice.

(d) The tax bill or notice of tax, with date of payment, if paid, and the amount of interest paid.

(e) The application for abatement, or other petition filed with the Commissioner, or with the board of assessors, with the date of filing.

(f) The notice from the Commissioner or from the board of assessors of the decision or determination on the application or other petition, with the date when the notice was given, or the fact that no decision was made.

(g) On appeals for exemption under M.G.L. c. 59, § 5, clause third, all forms required under clause third with the date of filing.

Section 1.23. Agreed Statement of Facts

The parties may, by stipulation in writing filed with the Board, agree upon any facts involved in the appeal.

Section 1.24. Subpoenas

(1) Either party may summon witnesses or may require the production of papers in the same manner in which witnesses may be summoned and papers may be required to be produced for the purpose of trial in the courts.

(2) Any member of the Board may summon and examine witnesses and require, by subpoena signed by the member, the production of all returns, books, papers, documents, correspondence and other evidence pertinent to the matter under inquiry, at any designated place of hearing.

Section 1.25. Interrogatories to A Party

Either party, except in appeals under the informal procedure, may interrogate the adverse party for the discovery of facts and documents admissible in evidence at the hearing. Interrogatories and answers shall be filed with the clerk and orders with respect thereto may be made by the Board in the manner provided by and according to the requirements and limitations of M.G.L. c. 231, §§ 61 to 67, inclusive.

Section 1.26. Depositions

(1) When either party proposes to take a deposition, such party shall file a motion with the Board requesting permission to do so. The motion shall set forth the following:

(a) The name, residence and post office address of each witness whose deposition is proposed to be taken.

(b) The matters concerning which the witness is to testify, together with a statement of the reasons why it is desired to take the deposition.

(c) The time and place of taking the proposed deposition.

(2) The motion shall be served and marked in accordance with 831 CMR 1.16 of the Board.

(3) Approval to take a deposition, either within or without the Commonwealth, may be granted in the sole discretion of the Board.

(4) If permission to take a deposition is granted, the procedures set forth in Rule 30 of the Massachusetts Rules of Civil Procedure will be followed by the parties.

Section 1.27. Documentary Evidence and Other Public Records

(1) Evidence as to the contents of books, documents, records and other papers may, in the discretion of the Board, be given by oral testimony.

(2) When books, documents, records and other papers have been received in evidence, a clear and legible copy thereof or of so much thereof as may be material or relevant, may, in the discretion of the Board, be substituted therefore.

(3) The originals of books, documents, records, models, diagrams and other exhibits introduced in evidence before the Board may be withdrawn from the custody of the Board in such manner and upon such terms as the Board in its discretion may prescribe.

(4) All "public records" as defined in G.L. c. 4, § 7, cl. 26, and all documents and other materials referred to in G.L. c. 58A, § 13, shall be available for public inspection at reasonable times and shall not be subject to protective orders.

(5) The Board may take judicial notice of matters of law and fact to the same extent that such matters may be the subject of judicial notice in Massachusetts courts. Such matters include federal and state statutes and cases and regulations of the Internal Revenue Service and Commissioner of Revenue. However, proof of municipal law, including bylaws, ordinances, regulations, and adoption of state local option statutes must be made by testimony of a municipal official or by certified copy of the municipal law or action in question.

Amended effective May 4, 2007.

Section 1.28. Stenographic Report of Evidence

(1) At the request of any party, made before any evidence is offered, the Board will order that all proceedings in a pending appeal be officially reported by a stenographer. Notice of such request shall be given to the clerk at least one day before the appeal is reached for hearing, but the Board in its discretion may permit later notice. The cost of reporting a proceeding officially shall include in every case the cost of one transcript for the Board, and additional transcripts may be obtained by any party from the stenographer upon the terms and conditions fixed by the contract of the Board with the stenographer. The party or parties requesting such report shall deposit with the clerk an amount equal to the cost thereof, as estimated by the clerk, at the time of making such request, and shall from time to time thereafter, on demand therefor, deposit with him such further amounts as in his judgment may be necessary to meet such cost. As soon after the hearing as the clerk shall ascertain the actual cost of such report, he shall refund to the depositor any excess deposit over the actual cost thereof, and he shall require the deposit of any

deficit from the party or parties requesting the report. No proceeding shall be reported officially unless the amounts required have been deposited as herein provided. Unless so reported no portion of the evidence will be included in the record in an appeal to the Appeals Court or the Supreme Judicial Court.

(2) Where any proceeding has been ordered officially reported and the cost of reporting thereof shall not be deposited by either party at any time with the clerk as required by the Board, the order for an official report shall become ineffective and no part of said proceeding shall be regarded as officially reported, but the stenographer shall furnish to the Board, without cost to the Commonwealth, a transcribed copy of so much of the proceeding as has already been taken.

(3) Stenographic notes of hearings taken and transcripts thereof prepared in proceedings which are not officially reported at the request of a party shall be for the information of the Board only, and will not be open to the inspection or available for the use of the parties.

Section 1.29. Requests for Findings and Rulings

Requests for findings of fact and rulings of law, if any are made, shall be filed under separate headings, and a copy given to the adverse party either before or at the time of the hearing, or after the hearing within a time to be fixed by the Board.

Section 1.30. Briefs

Briefs may be filed either before or at the time of the hearing, or after the hearing within a time to be fixed by the Board. Three copies of each brief shall be furnished to the Board and one copy shall be served on the adverse party.

Section 1.31. Submission Without Oral Argument

An appeal in which no issue of fact is raised, or in which the parties file an agreed statement of facts or in which evidence of contested facts has been introduced otherwise than by oral hearing before the Board, may be submitted to the Board for decision by either or both parties, on briefs without oral argument, but the Board may, in its discretion, require appearance for argument.

Section 1.32. Request for Report

After the promulgation of a decision under the formal procedure without findings of fact, the Board will make such findings and report thereon when a request therefor is filed by either party with the clerk within ten days of the date of the decision as prescribed by M.G.L. c. 58A, § 13. The requesting party shall send a copy of the request to the adverse party.

Section 1.33. Computation for Final Determination

When the Board determines the facts in any appeal and withholds final decision of the amount entered, the parties shall, if they are in agreement as to that amount, file with the clerk a computation showing the amount to be entered. If the parties do not agree as to the amount, either of them may file with the clerk a computation thereof. The matter shall be placed upon the motion list for hearing in due course and the Board shall determine the correct amount and enter final decision. 831 CMR 1.33 is not to be regarded as affording an opportunity for rehearing or reconsideration.

Section 1.34. Costs

Costs may be taxed against a party to the appeal as provided in M.G.L. c. 58A, §§ 12 and 12A and M.G.L. c. 59, § 64, in the discretion of the Board.

Section 1.35. Claim of Appeal

A claim of appeal shall be filed with the clerk of the Board in accordance with the *Massachusetts Rules of Appellate Procedure*, which rules shall govern such appeal. For the purposes of Rule 4 of the *Massachusetts Rules of Appellate Procedure*, the date the Board's decision is promulgated shall be the date of the entry of judgment unless a timely request for findings of fact and report is made, in which case, the date of promulgation of the Board's findings of fact and report shall be the date of the entry of judgment.

The record will be prepared in accordance with the relevant provisions of Rules 8 and 9 of the Massachusetts Rules of the Appellate Procedure.

Section 1.36. [Repealed]

Section 1.37. Practice and Procedure

(1) Except as herein otherwise provided, the practice and procedure before the Board shall conform to that heretofore prevailing in equity causes in the courts of the Commonwealth prior to the adoption of the Massachusetts Rules of Civil Procedure; but the Board reserves the right to make hearings and proceedings as informal as possible, to the end that substance and not form shall govern, and that a final determination of all matters before it may be promptly reached.

(2) In proceedings under the informal procedure, all formal rules of pleadings, practice and evidence will be eliminated to the extent that the Board member or members holding the hearing may consider practicable.

Section 1.38. [Repealed]

SECTION II. FORMS

Introductory Statement

These are only suggested forms and are subject to amendments as circumstances may render necessary or expedient.

Form 1. Petition Under Formal Procedure—City and Town Assessors Appeals

THE COMMONWEALTH OF MASSACHUSETTS
APPELLATE TAX BOARD

PETITION UNDER FORMAL PROCEDURE
APPEAL FROM ASSESSORS' DENIAL OF ABATEMENT APPLICATION

Docket No. **F-**_____

_____
Appellant (Print full name of each appellant)

vs.

BOARD OF ASSESSORS OF THE CITY(TOWN) OF _____
Appellee

1. This is an appeal from the refusal of the appellee to abate a tax assessed (or grant an exemption under Clause _____) for the fiscal year _____ on property owned or occupied by the appellant on January 1, _____.

2. The address or location of the property is _____.

3. Property type: ☐ *single-family residence;* ☐ *condominium;* ☐ *multi-family;* ☐ *apartment building;* ☐ *hotel;* ☐ *office building;* ☐ *retail building;* ☐ *industrial building;* ☐ *other real estate (describe)*_____ ☐ *personal property (describe):* _____

4. The appellee valued the property at $_____ and assessed a tax thereon at the rate of $_____ per $1000 in the total amount of $_____.

5. Dates on which taxes were paid:_____; Amount of interest, if any:_____

6. Date the appellant applied for an abatement in writing to the appellee:_____

7. Date the appellee denied the abatement:_____; if a partial abatement was granted, date and amount of assessment after the partial abatement: (date):_____; amount_____ ___(attach copy of abatement certificate)

8. The appellant is aggrieved by the decision of the appellee and contends that the property was overvalued and/or the following claim(s): _____ _____

9. The appellant requests that a hearing be held upon this petition and that the Board grant an abatement.

10. Mailing address of appellant:_____

11. Service of papers in connection with this appeal may be made on appellant or his/her attorney at:

(Print Name)_____ (Print Address)_____

(Attorney's BBO Number)_____ (Tel. No.)(_____) _____

_____
Signature

APPELLANT MUST FILE AN ORIGINAL AND TWO COPIES OF THIS FORM

Form 2.   Statement Under Informal Procedure—City and Town Assessors Appeals

THE COMMONWEALTH OF MASSACHUSETTS
APPELLATE TAX BOARD

STATEMENT UNDER INFORMAL PROCEDURE

APPEAL FROM ASSESSORS' DENIAL OF ABATEMENT APPLICATION

Docket No. **X-**_____

_____
Appellant (Print full name of each appellant)

vs.

BOARD OF ASSESSORS OF THE CITY(TOWN) OF _____
Appellee

1. This is an appeal from the refusal of the appellee to abate a tax assessed (or grant an exemption under Clause ___ ___) for the fiscal year _____ on property owned or occupied by the appellant on January 1, _____.

2. The address or location of the property is _____.

3. Property type: ☐ *single-family residence;* ☐ *condominium;* ☐ *multi-family* ☐ *apartment building;* ☐ *hotel;* ☐ *office;* ☐ *retail;* ☐ *industrial;* ☐ *other real estate (describe)*_____ ☐ *personal property (describe)*: _____

4. The appellee valued the property at $_____ and assessed a tax thereon at the rate of $_____ per $1000 in the total amount of $_____.

5. Dates on which taxes were paid:_____; Amount of interest, if any:_____

6. Date the appellant applied for an abatement in writing to the appellee:_____

7. Date the appellee denied the abatement:_____; if a partial abatement was granted, date of partial abatement and amount of assessment after the partial abatement: (date):_____; (amount):_____(attach copy of abatement certificate)

8. The appellant is aggrieved by the decision of the appellee and contends that the property was overvalued and/or the following claim(s):_____; and requests that a hearing be held and that the Board grant an abatement.

9. Mailing address of appellant:_____

10. Service of papers in connection with this appeal may be made on appellant or his/her attorney at:

(Print Name)_____ (Print Address)_____

(Attorney's BBO Number)_____ (Tel. No.)(_____) _____

_____
Signature

APPELLANT MUST FILE AN ORIGINAL AND TWO COPIES OF THIS FORM

WAIVER OF APPEAL AND ELECTION OF INFORMAL PROCEDURE

The appellant hereby waives any right of appeal to the Appeals Court or Supreme Judicial Court from any decision of the Appellate Tax Board, except upon questions of law raised by the pleadings, or by an agreed statement of facts, or shown by the report of the Board, and elects the informal procedure for the determination of the petition for abatement in the above-named appeal. By electing the informal procedure, the appellant waives any right to a report of the Board or other statement of reasons for the Board's decision pursuant to G.L. c. 58A, §13. The Appellant's waiver of the right of appeal and the right to a report or other statement of reasons for the Board's decision shall be void if the appeal is transferred by the appellee to the formal procedure pursuant to G.L. c. 58A, §7A.

Signature (MUST BE SIGNED) _____

APPELLANT MUST FILE AN ORIGINAL AND TWO COPIES OF THIS FORM

Form 3. Petition for Late Entry of an Appeal

COMMONWEALTH OF MASSACHUSETTS
APPELLATE TAX BOARD

Docket No. P.L.E. _____

_____, Petitioner.

BOARD OF ASSESSORS OF THE CITY (TOWN) OF _____, Respondent.

PETITION FOR LATE ENTRY OF AN APPEAL

1. This is a petition for leave to enter late under G.L. c. 59, s. 65C, an appeal under G. L. c. 59, s. 65.

2. On January 1, 20__, the petitioner was the owner (or a tenant under obligation to pay more than one-half the taxes thereon) of a parcel of real estate situated at

_____ and consisting of (Describe briefly)
    (street and number, if any)

3. The respondent valued the property at $_____ and assessed to _____
                                                             (Name of person assessed)
a tax thereon, at the rate of $_____ per $1,000, in the amount of $_____.

4. On _____, 20__, the petitioner applied in writing to the respondent on a form approved by the Commissioner of Revenue for an abatement of the tax, including in the application a sufficient description of the particular real estate as to which an abatement was requested. The respondent has failed to act on the application prior to the expiration of three months from the date of filing and failed to notify the petitioner of such inaction in writing within ten days.

5. The tax was paid on _____, 20__, with $_____ interest. (If the tax has not been paid, or if partial payment has been made, state that fact giving the amount and date of any partial payment.)

6. The petitioner had a right to appeal under G.L. c. 59, s. 65, as amended, but due to accident or mistake failed to do so within the time therein prescribed for the reason that _____
_____.

7. The petitioner, therefore, requests a hearing on this petition and prays that the petitioner be granted leave to file an appeal.

8. Service of papers in connection with this petition may be made on the appellant or his/her attorney at
_____, addressed to _____
_____(Tel. No. _____)

_____
                   Signature

(Note: This petition must be filed within Two Months after the appeal should have been entered.)

Form 4. Certificate of Service (Formal or Informal Procedure)
THE COMMONWEALTH OF MASSACHUSETTS
APPELLATE TAX BOARD

Docket No.:_____

_____
Appellant

vs.

Board of Assessors of the City (Town) of_____._____
Appellee

<u>CERTIFICATE OF SERVICE</u>

I, _____, appellant or attorney for appellant,

hereby certify that on _____ a copy of the petition in connection

with the above-described appeal was mailed by first class mail, postage prepaid, (or)

delivered in hand, to the usual place of business of the appellee, addressed to it at City

(Town) Hall, _____, Massachusetts.

Attached hereto is the Post Office Receipt and the Return Receipt.

_____
(Signature)

<u>Attach Receipts Here</u>.

Form 5. Withdrawal of Petition (Formal or Informal Procedure)

THE COMMONWEALTH OF MASSACHUSETTS
APPELLATE TAX BOARD

Docket No.:_____

_____
Appellant

vs.

Board of Assessors of the City (Town) of_____
Appellee

Location of Property_____

WITHDRAWAL

The above appeal is hereby withdrawn.

_____
Appellant

By_____
Attorney

_____
Address

(Tel. No._____)

W
I
T
H
D
R
A
W
A
L

Form 6.   Petition Under Formal Procedure—Department of Revenue Appeals

THE COMMONWEALTH OF MASSACHUSETTS
APPELLATE TAX BOARD

PETITION UNDER FORMAL PROCEDURE

APPEAL FROM COMMISSIONER OF REVENUE'S DENIAL OF ABATEMENT APPLICATION

Docket No. **C-**_____

_____
Appellant (full name of Appellant(s))
v.

COMMISSIONER OF REVENUE
Appellee

1.   This is an appeal from the refusal of the Appellee to: ☐ abate a tax, ☐ classify a business: ☐ other (describe) _____.

2.   Type of tax involved: ☐ *income;* ☐ *sales/use;* ☐ *corporate excise;* ☐ *other (describe)* _____
___.

3.   List the period(s) for which the tax was assessed:
_____.

4.   Provide the following information regarding the disputed assessment: date of assessment
_____, amount of the assessment: (tax) $_____, (interest) $_____,
(penalties) $_____,

5.   Date tax return(s) was (were) filed? _____.

6.   Date tax was paid: _____.

7.   Date the Appellant applied in writing to the Appellee for an abatement of the tax:_____
___.

8.   Date Appellee denied the abatement application or granted a partial abatement (include amount of partial abatement, if applicable):_____.

9.   The Appellant is aggrieved by the decision of the Appellee and objects thereto on the grounds that (give a concise statement of reasons and supporting facts; attach additional sheet if necessary.):

_____
_____

10.   The Appellant requests that a hearing be held on this petition and that and that such portion of the tax as may be determined to be excessive be abated, and for such further relief as may be proper.

11.   [Optional] If the amount at issue for each tax year does not exceed $25,000 or if only penalties are at issue, the appellant may request, by checking the box at the end of this paragraph, that the Appellate Tax Board conduct a mediation session to facilitate resolution of this appeal prior to a hearing. Election of mediation has no effect on the Appellant's right to a hearing if mediation should prove unsuccessful. ☐

12.   Service of papers in connection with this appeal may be made on Appellant or his/her attorney at:

(Name) _____ (Tel. No.)_____

(Address)_____

(Email)_____

_____
Signature

APPELLANT MUST FILE AN ORIGINAL AND TWO COPIES OF THIS FORM

Form 7.   Petition Under Small Claims Procedure—Department of Revenue Appeals

THE COMMONWEALTH OF MASSACHUSETTS
APPELLATE TAX BOARD

PETITION UNDER SMALL CLAIMS PROCEDURE

Docket No. S_____

_____
Appellant (full name of Appellant(s))

v.

COMMISSIONER OF REVENUE
Appellee

1. This is an appeal from the refusal of the Appellee to abate (state type of tax) _____ with respect to (list applicable tax period(s) or transaction date(s)) _____.

2. Provide the following information regarding the disputed assessment: date of the assessment _____; amount of the assessment (tax) $_____, (interest) $_____, (penalties) $_____.

3. Was a tax return filed? _____. If yes, on what date? _____.

4. The tax was paid on (date) _____; if applicable, amount of tax that remains unpaid _____.

5. On (date)_____, the Appellant applied in writing to the Appellee for an abatement of the tax.

6. On (date)_____, the Appellee denied the application for abatement or granted a partial abatement of

   $_____

7. The Appellant is aggrieved by the decision of the Appellee and objects thereto on the grounds that (give a concise statement of reasons and supporting facts; attach additional sheet if necessary):

   _____

   _____

8. The Appellant requests that a hearing be held on this petition and that such portion of the tax as may be determined to be excessive be abated, and for such further relief as may be proper.

9. [Optional] By checking the box at the end of this paragraph, the Appellant requests that prior to a hearing, the Appellate Tax Board conduct a mediation session to facilitate resolution of this appeal. Election of mediation has no effect on the Appellant's right to a hearing.

10. Service of papers in connection with this appeal may be made on the Appellant or his/her attorney at:

(Name)_____   (Tel. No.)_____

(Address)_____

(Email)_____

_____
Signature   (MUST BE SIGNED)

_____

WAIVER OF RIGHT TO APPEAL

The Appellant hereby waives the right to appeal to any court from any decision of the Appellate Tax Board issued under the small claims procedure. General Laws c. 58A, § 7B provides that this waiver shall be void if the appeal is transferred to the formal procedure.

_____
Signature   (MUST BE SIGNED)

Form 8.   Certificate of Service (Formal Procedure—Department of Revenue Appeals)

THE COMMONWEALTH OF MASSACHUSETTS
APPELLATE TAX BOARD

Docket No.:_____

_____
Appellant

vs.

COMMISSIONER OF REVENUE
Appellee

<u>CERTIFICATE OF SERVICE</u>

I, _____, appellant or attorney for appellant,

hereby certify that on _____ a copy of the petition in connection

with the above-described appeal was mailed by first class mail, postage prepaid, (or)

delivered in hand, to the usual place of business of the appellee, addressed to it at the

Department of Revenue in Boston, Massachusetts.

Attached hereto is the Post Office Receipt and the Return Receipt.

_____
(Signature)

<u>Attach Receipts Here</u>.

Form 9.   Withdrawal of Petition (Formal or Small Claims Procedure—Department of Revenue Appeals)

THE COMMONWEALTH OF MASSACHUSETTS
APPELLATE TAX BOARD

Docket No.:_____

_____
Appellant

vs.

COMMISSIONER OF REVENUE
Appellee

<u>WITHDRAWAL</u>

The above appeal is hereby withdrawn.

_____
Appellant

By_____
Attorney

_____
Address

(Tel. No._____)

W
I
T
H
D
R
A
W
A
L

Form 10.   Agreement as to the Fair Cash Value and Decision

THE COMMONWEALTH OF MASSACHUSETTS
Appellate Tax Board
100 Cambridge Street
Suite 200
Boston, Massachusetts 02114

(617) 727-3100
(617) 727-6234 FAX

Docket No. _____

_____

APPELLANT

BOARD OF ASSESSORS OF THECITY (TOWN) OF

_____

APPELLEE

<u>AGREEMENT AS TO FAIR CASH VALUE AND DECISION</u>

It is hereby agreed by and between the parties to the above entitled appeal

that the fair cash value of the property located at _____,

on January 1, 2____, was $_____, that it was overvalued to the

extent of $_____, and that the Appellate Tax Board may grant an

abatement of the tax in the amount of $_____.

Date :_____   _____

                                                Appellant (or Attorney for appellant)

                                          _____

                                                Appellee (or Attorney for appellee)

MASSACHUSETTS GUIDE TO EVIDENCE
2019 Edition

Publisher's Note

Thomson Reuters has been given permission to reprint the Massachusetts Guide to Evidence from the Massachusetts Supreme Judicial Court.

Table of Sections

ARTICLE I.   GENERAL PROVISIONS

Section 101.   Title

This volume may be referenced as the *Massachusetts Guide to Evidence*.

NOTE

The volume may be cited as Mass. G. Evid. § xxx (2019).

Section 102.   Purpose and Construction

The sections contained in this Guide summarize the law of evidence applied in proceedings in the courts of the Commonwealth of Massachusetts as set forth in the Massachusetts General Laws, common law, and rules of court, and as required by the Constitutions of the United States and Massachusetts.

The provisions contained in this Guide may be cited by lawyers, parties, and judges, but are not to be construed as adopted rules of evidence or as changing the existing law of evidence.

NOTE

The Advisory Committee has made every effort to provide the most accurate and clear statement of the law of evidence in Massachusetts as it exists at the time of the publication of this Guide. Importantly, these provisions are not to be interpreted as a set of formal or adopted rules of evidence, and they do not change Massachusetts law. Because Massachusetts has not adopted rules of evidence, the development of Massachusetts evidence law continues to be based on the common law and legislative processes. This Guide is intended to collect the law of evidence from those common law and legislative sources, and to make it readily accessible to judges, lawyers, and parties in Massachusetts courts so that judicial and administrative proceedings may be conducted fairly, efficiently, and without unjustifiable expense and delay.

The Guide tracks the general organization and structure of the Federal Rules of Evidence, but numerous sections have been changed or added to reflect the differences between Federal and Massachusetts law. Where the Advisory Committee determined that Federal law and Massachusetts law are consistent or very similar, the Guide uses the language of the Federal rule and identifies any minor differences in the Note accompanying that section. Sections of the Guide that are derived from Massachusetts statutes track the language of the statute as closely as possible, and the accompanying Note identifies the statute that provides the basis for the section. In all cases, the Note to each section identifies the authority on which the section is based, as well as other relevant authorities that may be helpful in interpreting or applying the section.

Discretion.   Whether evidence should be admitted or excluded often reduces to the exercise of discretion, especially when the parties disagree about whether the evidence is relevant (see Section 401, Test for Relevant Evidence), or whether the probative value of the evidence is substantially outweighed by the danger of unfair prejudice, confusion of the issues, misleading the jury, being unnecessarily time consuming, or needless presentation of cumulative evidence (see Section 403, Excluding Relevant Evidence for Prejudice, Confusion, Waste of Time, or Other Reasons). At one time, a discretionary decision was considered to be one that involved a choice made by the judge that was subject to review and reversal in only the most rare and unusual circumstances when it was shown that "no conscientious judge acting intelligently could honestly have taken the view expressed by him." See Commonwealth v. Bys, 370 Mass. 350, 361 (1976), quoting Davis v. Boston Elevated Ry. Co., 235 Mass. 482, 502 (1920). In recent years, appellate courts have established a variety of guidelines for the exercise of discretion by trial judges. See, e.g., Commonwealth v. Aviles, 461 Mass. 60, 73 (2011) (first complaint doctrine set forth in Section 413 is guideline to regulate exercise of judicial discretion); Commonwealth v. Heang, 458 Mass. 827, 850 (2011) (guideline for how expert witnesses may express degree of certitude in support of their opinions); Commonwealth v. Britto, 433 Mass. 596, 613–614 (2001) (guidelines for questioning of witnesses by jurors); Commonwealth v. Festa, 369 Mass. 419, 429–430 (1976) (guidelines for the use of interpreters); Commonwealth v. Bourgeois, 68 Mass. App. Ct. 433, 437 n.10 (2007) (discussing Lampron–Dwyer protocol established to regulate access to records in hands of third party).

In keeping with this trend in the law toward guided discretion, see, in particular, Lonergan–Gillen v. Gillen, 57 Mass. App. Ct. 746, 748–749 (2003), the Supreme Judicial Court has recalibrated the standard of review for discretionary decisions:

"An appellate court's review of a trial judge's decision for abuse of discretion must give great deference to the judge's exercise of discretion; it is plainly not an abuse of discretion simply because a reviewing court would have reached a different result. But the 'no conscientious judge' standard is so deferential that, if actually applied, an abuse of discretion would be as rare as flying pigs. When an appellate court concludes that a judge abused his or her discretion, the court is not, in fact, finding that the judge was not conscientious or, for that matter, not intelligent or honest. Borrowing from other courts, we think it more accurate to say that a judge's discretionary decision constitutes an abuse of discretion where we conclude the judge made 'a clear error of judgment in weighing' the factors relevant to the decision, such that the decision falls outside the range of reasonable alternatives."

L.L. v. Commonwealth, 470 Mass. 169, 185 n.27 (2014). The following is a list of situations where the new abuse of discretion standard has been applied.

Generally.

- *Admissibility of Excited Utterances.* Commonwealth v. Rodriguez, 90 Mass. App. Ct. 315, 318–319 (2016).

- *Admissibility of Expert Testimony.* Commonwealth v. Snyder, 475 Mass. 445, 452 (2016); Commonwealth v. Coates, 89 Mass. App. Ct. 728, 733 (2016).

- *Admissibility of Prior Bad Acts for Nonpropensity Purpose.* Commonwealth v. Veiovis, 477 Mass. 472, 482 (2017); Commonwealth v. Robertson, 88 Mass. App. Ct. 52, 54 (2015).

- *Admissibility of Statements Not Admitted for Their Truth.* Commonwealth v. Barbosa, 477 Mass. 658, 672 (2017).

- *Motion to Reopen Evidence to Allow Additional Testimony.* Clark v. Leisure Woods Estates, Inc., 89 Mass. App. Ct. 87, 95–96 (2016).

- *Remedy for Violation of Sequestration Order.* Commonwealth v. Neves, 474 Mass. 355, 368 (2016).

- *Sanctions for Attorney Misconduct.* Wong v. Luu, 472 Mass. 208, 220 (2015).

- *Weighing Probative Value of Evidence Versus Risk of Unfair Prejudice.* Commonwealth v. Facella, 478 Mass. 393, 407 (2017); Commonwealth v. Dew, 478 Mass. 304, 315 (2017); Commonwealth v. Hammond, 477 Mass. 499, 505 (2017).

Criminal Cases.

- *Admissibility of Eyewitness Identification Not Arising from Police Procedure.* Commonwealth v. Johnson, 473 Mass. 594, 602 (2016).

- *Direct Appeal from Conviction of First–Degree Murder Under G. L. c. 278, § 33E.* Commonwealth v. Chatman, 473 Mass. 840, 846 (2016).

- *Dismissal of Criminal Complaint Without Prejudice.* Commonwealth v. Butler, 87 Mass. App. Ct. 183, 186–187 (2015).

- *Lay Witness Identification of Firearm.* Commonwealth v. Thomas, 476 Mass. 451, 465 (2017). Cross-Reference: Note "Inanimate Objects" to Section 1112(a), Eyewitness Identification Generally.

- *Motion to Discharge Counsel.* Commonwealth v. Castano, 478 Mass. 75, 88 (2017).

- *Motion for Mistrial.* Commonwealth v. Bryan, 476 Mass. 351, 352–353 (2017).

- *Motion for New Trial.* Commonwealth v. Duart, 477 Mass. 630, 634 (2017); Commonwealth v. Ellis, 475 Mass. 459, 476 (2016); Commonwealth v. DiBenedetto, 475 Mass. 429, 442 (2016).

- *Motion to Reduce Verdict from Second–Degree Murder to Manslaughter.* Commonwealth v. Grassie, 476 Mass. 202, 214 (2017).

- *Motion for Resentencing.* Commonwealth v. Perez, 477 Mass. 677, 682 (2017).

Civil Cases.

- *Application of Judicial Estoppel.* Murphy v. Wachovia Bank of Del., 88 Mass. App. Ct. 9, 16–17 (2015).

- *Award of Attorney's Fees.* Schechter v. Schechter, 88 Mass. App. Ct. 239, 260 (2015).

- *Characterization of Income for Calculation of Child Support.* Hoegen v. Hoegen, 89 Mass. App. Ct. 6, 9–10 (2016).

- *Child Custody and Child Support Orders.* Rosenwasser v. Rosenwasser, 89 Mass. App. Ct. 577, 580 (2016); Ventrice v. Ventrice, 87 Mass. App. Ct. 190, 196 (2015); Murray v. Super, 87 Mass. App. Ct. 146, 148 (2015).

- *Civil Action in Nature of Certiorari.* Frawley v. Police Comm'r of Cambridge, 473 Mass. 716, 729 (2016).

- *Motion to Alter or Amend Judgment as to Damages.* Quarterman v. City of Springfield, 91 Mass. App. Ct. 254, 260 (2017).

Miscellaneous.

- *Grant of Parole to Juvenile Homicide Offender.* Diatchenko v. District Attorney for the Suffolk Dist., 471 Mass. 12, 31 (2015).

- *Prisoner's Petition for Name Change.* Jaynes, petitioner, 88 Mass. App. Ct. 745, 747 (2015).

- *Section 403 Balancing Test.* Commonwealth v. Gomes, 475 Mass. 775, 785 (2016).

Section 103. Rulings on Evidence, Objections, and Offers of Proof

(a) Preserving a Claim of Error. A party may claim error in a ruling to admit or exclude evidence only if the error injuriously affects a substantial right of the party and,

    (1) if the ruling admits evidence, a party, on the record,

        (A) timely objects or moves to strike and

(B) states the specific ground, unless it was apparent from the context, or,

(2) if the ruling excludes evidence, a party informs the court of its substance by an offer of proof, unless the substance was apparent from the context.

(b) Preliminary Evidentiary Motions: Effect on Appellate Rights. Where a party fails to object to the admission of evidence at trial, the party's appellate rights with respect to the admission of that evidence are preserved only if the party raised the same specific objection to the very same evidence in a motion in limine, and the motion was heard and denied.

(c) Court's Statement About the Ruling; Directing an Offer of Proof. The court may make any statement about the character or form of the evidence, the objection made, and the ruling. The court may direct that an offer of proof be made in question-and-answer form.

(d) Preventing the Jury or Witnesses from Hearing Inadmissible Evidence. To the extent practicable, the court must conduct a jury trial so that inadmissible evidence is not suggested to the jury or witnesses by any means.

(e) Substantial Risk of a Miscarriage of Justice. In criminal and sexually dangerous person cases, a court is required to consider an unpreserved error to determine whether there has been a substantial risk of a miscarriage of justice.

(f) Motions in Limine. Where the issue can reasonably be anticipated, a motion in limine should be filed prior to trial.

(g) Exclusion as Sanction. Although the court should impose the least severe sanction necessary to remedy the prejudice to the innocent party, nothing in this section precludes a court from excluding evidence as a sanction for a violation of a discovery rule, order, or other obligation imposed on a party in a civil or criminal case.

NOTE

Subsection (a). This subsection is derived from G. L. c. 231, § 119, which states as follows:

"No error in either the admission or the exclusion of evidence and no error or defect in any ruling or order or anything done or omitted by the trial court or by any of the parties is ground for modifying or otherwise disturbing a judgment or order unless the appeals court or the supreme judicial court deems that the error complained of has injuriously affected the substantial rights of the parties. If either court finds that the error complained of affects only one or some of the issues or parties involved it may affirm the judgment as to those issues or parties unaffected and may modify or reverse the judgment as to those affected."

See also G. L. c. 231, § 132 (stating that no new trial in a civil proceeding may be granted based upon the improper admission or exclusion of evidence unless the error injuriously affected the proponent's substantial rights). To determine whether a substantial right was injuriously affected by the exclusion of evidence

"the appropriate test is whether the proponent of erroneously excluded, relevant evidence has made a plausible showing that the trier of fact might have reached a different result if the evidence had been before it. Thus the erroneous exclusion of relevant evidence is reversible error unless, on the record, the appellate court can say with substantial confidence that the error would not have made a material difference."

DeJesus v. Yogel, 404 Mass. 44, 48–49 (1989).

Judicial Duty to Give Curative Instruction. In a criminal case, if defense counsel is unable to present certain evidence promised in an opening statement because the court changes an earlier ruling, the danger of prejudice is so great that the judge must give the jury an explanation why the defendant could not keep the promise made in the opening statement. Commonwealth v. Chambers, 465 Mass. 520, 534–535 (2013) (alternatively, the judge may decline to give the curative instruction and instead allow the defendant to present the evidence).

Subsection (a)(1). This subsection is derived from Commonwealth v. Marshall, 434 Mass. 358, 365 (2001), and Commonwealth v. Pickles, 364 Mass. 395, 399 (1973). "[O]bjections to evidence, or to any challenged order or ruling of the trial judge, are not preserved for appeal unless made in a precise and timely fashion, as soon as the claimed error is apparent." Commonwealth v. Perryman, 55 Mass. App. Ct. 187, 192 (2002). But see Commonwealth v. DePina, 476 Mass. 614, 624 n.9 (2017) (In a joint trial, one defendant's objection, which put the judge on notice of the basis of the objection, "served the purpose of the requirement of a contemporaneous objection[,]" thus preserving the appellate rights of both defendants.). "The purpose of requiring an objection is to afford the trial judge an opportunity to act promptly to remove from the jury's consideration evidence which has no place in the trial." Abraham v. Woburn, 383 Mass. 724, 726 n.1 (1981). If a timely objection is not made, the evidence is properly admitted, and the fact finder is entitled to give it such probative effect as it deems appropriate. See Commonwealth v. Proia, 92 Mass. App. Ct. 824, 827–828 (2018). But any objected-to statement at trial "is only worth what it is worth." Commonwealth v. Drapaniotis, 89 Mass. App. Ct. 267, 274–276 (2016).

In both jury trials and jury-waived trials, counsel have the obligation to make timely objections. See Commonwealth v. Freeman, 352 Mass. 556, 563–564 (1967) (jury trials); Commonwealth v. Mazzone, 55 Mass. App. Ct. 345, 348 (2002) (jury–waived trials). Counsel have the same duty to make objections to improper questions by a judge as they do when the questions are asked by opposing counsel. Commonwealth v. Watkins, 63 Mass. App. Ct. 69, 72–73 (2005). Generally, counsel should make an objection to a question before the answer is given. See Commonwealth v. Baptiste, 372 Mass. 700, 706 (1977). Self-represented litigants are bound by the same rules of procedure as litigants with counsel. Mains v. Commonwealth, 433 Mass. 30, 35–36 (2000).

"When objecting, counsel should state the specific ground of the objection unless it is apparent from the context." Commonwealth v. Marshall, 434 Mass. at 365, quoting P.J. Liacos, Massachusetts Evidence § 3.8.3, at 85 (7th ed. 1999). See Mass. R. Civ. P. 46; Mass. R. Crim. P. 22. The court may ask the party objecting to the admission or exclusion of evidence to state the precise ground for the objection. See Rule 8 of the Rules of the Superior Court. Further argument or discussion of the grounds is not allowed unless the court requests it. Id. The need for an exception has been abolished by Mass. R. Civ. P. 46 and Mass. R. Crim. P. 22.

A motion to strike is used to eliminate an answer that is objectionable either on substantive grounds or on the ground that it is nonresponsive. Commonwealth v. Pickles, 364 Mass. at 399. When testimony is subject to an objection that is sustained, but not followed by a motion to strike, the issue is not preserved. When an answer is nonresponsive and objectionable, a subsequent objection or a motion to strike is necessary to preserve the issue. Commonwealth v. Womack, 457 Mass. 268, 272–273 (2010); Commonwealth v. Rosado, 59 Mass. App. Ct. 913, 914 (2003).

As to the court's instructions to the jury, an objection is necessary to preserve an issue regarding the giving or failure to give an instruction. See Mass. R. Civ. P. 51(b); Mass. R. Crim. P. 24(b). See also Harlow v. Chin, 405 Mass. 697, 703 n.5 (1989); Commonwealth v. Barbosa, 399 Mass. 841, 844 (1987). Counsel should renew any prior objection with specificity following the charge. Fein v. Kahan, 36 Mass. App. Ct. 967, 968 n.4 (1994).

Subsection (a)(2). This subsection is derived from Commonwealth v. Chase, 26 Mass. App. Ct. 578, 581 (1988), and Mass. R. Civ. P. 43(c). "[A]n offer of proof is required to preserve the right to appellate review of the denial of an offer to introduce evidence through the direct examination of a witness." Commonwealth v. Chase, 26 Mass. App. Ct. at 581.

The offer of proof should state or summarize the testimony or evidence and show that the proponent would be prejudiced by the exclusion of the offered evidence. Holmgren v. LaLiberte, 4 Mass. App. Ct. 820, 821 (1976). The court may consider only so much of the offer of proof that is responsive to the excluded question or evidence and apparently within the witness's knowledge. Coral Gables, Inc. v. Beerman, 296 Mass. 267, 268–269 (1936). An offer of proof that fails to satisfy the statutory or common-law requirements for the admissibility of the evidence will lead to the exclusion of the evidence. See Rockport Granite Co. v. Plum Island Beach Co., 248 Mass. 290, 295 (1924).

An offer of proof is not necessary where the context is clear, see Commonwealth v. Donovan, 17 Mass. App. Ct. 83, 88 (1983), or where there is no doubt what the testimony will be, see Commonwealth v. Caldron, 383 Mass. 86, 89 n.2 (1981); Commonwealth v. Smith, 163 Mass. 411, 429 (1895).

If the evidence is excluded on cross-examination, an offer of proof generally need not be made, Stevens v. William S. Howe Co., 275 Mass. 398, 402 (1931), although there is a "relatively rare group of cases where, if the purpose or significance of the question is obscure and the prejudice to the cross-examiner is not clear ... the record must disclose the cross-examiner's reason for seeking an answer to an excluded question." Breault v. Ford Motor Co., 364 Mass. 352, 358 (1973).

Subsection (b). This subsection is derived from Commonwealth v. Grady, 474 Mass. 715 (2016), in which the Supreme Judicial Court held that,

"[g]oing forward, we dispense with any distinction, at the motion in limine stage, between objections based on constitutional grounds and objections based on other grounds. We will no longer require a defendant to object to the admission of evidence at trial where he or she has already sought to preclude the very same evidence at the motion in limine stage, and the motion was heard and denied."

Id. at 719. See also Commonwealth v. Almele, 474 Mass. 1017 (2016) (decided the same day as Grady). However, to be safe, the Supreme Judicial Court has recommended that the "better practice" is for a party "to object at trial even if he or she has already raised an objection prior to trial." Commonwealth v. Almele, 474 Mass. at 1018. See Commonwealth v. Santana, 477 Mass. 610, 620 n.7 (2017) (motion in limine objecting to "tooth mark" evidence based on lack of expert testimony to explain significance does not preserve hearsay objection to investigator's statement that he was told someone may have bitten the duct tape). The court also indicated that judges should no longer engage in the practice of "preserving" or "saving" a party's rights when ruling on a motion in limine because this practice may lull the party into not "voicing a necessary objection at trial." Commonwealth v. Almele, 474 Mass. at 1019; Commonwealth v. Grady, 474 Mass. at 721.

Subsection (c). The first sentence is derived from Mass. R. Civ. P. 43(c). As to the second sentence, if the court sustains an objection to a question, the court may permit the witness to answer the question in order to satisfy the need for an offer of proof.

Subsection (d). This subsection is derived generally from Mass. R. Civ. P. 43(c), Mass. R. Civ. P. 51(b), and Mass. R. Crim. P. 24(b). See Commonwealth v. Scullin, 44 Mass. App. Ct. 9, 14 (1997) ("[I]t is essential that [the court] take steps to ensure that the jury is not exposed to the questionable evidence before the issue of admissibility is finally decided. Failing to follow this course places the opponent of the evidence in a difficult situation, and may create an unfair advantage for the proponent of the testimony, especially in the event the evidence ultimately is excluded."). See also Ruszcyk v. Secretary of Pub. Safety, 401 Mass. 418, 422 (1988). Cross–Reference: Section 611(a), Mode and Order of Examining Witnesses and Presenting Evidence: Control by the Court.

The court has the discretion to employ any one of several methods to determine preliminary questions while insulating the jury from inadmissible evidence. These methods range from pretrial motions to suppress or motions in limine, to conducting proceedings during trial at sidebar, in chambers, or while the jury is absent from the courtroom. The court also has discretion whether to rule on the admissibility of evidence in advance of the trial by a motion in limine or to wait until the issue arises at trial. See Commonwealth v. Olsen, 452 Mass. 284, 292–293 (2008) (trial judge properly declined to rule in advance on motion in limine to permit defendant to call twenty-two witnesses to testify to the fact that the prosecution's chief witness had a poor reputation in the community for truth-telling, leaving the issue to be decided as it arose with particular witnesses).

Subsection (e). This subsection is derived from R.B., petitioner, 479 Mass. 712, 717 (2018); Commonwealth v. Alphas, 430 Mass. 8, 13 (1999); Commonwealth v. Freeman, 352 Mass. 556, 561–564 (1967); and Commonwealth v. Watkins, 63 Mass. App. Ct. 69, 72–73 (2005). See also G. L. c. 278, § 33E.

As stated above, a timely objection at trial is required to preserve an issue for appellate review. If an objection was not made, the appellate court can consider an issue but does so under a limited standard of review. For cases other than capital cases on direct appeal, the appellate court will apply the so-called Freeman standard to unpreserved trial errors and analyze whether the error created a substantial risk of a miscarriage of justice. Commonwealth v. Alphas, 430 Mass. at 13. The proper standard of review for a noncapital offense is as follows:

"An error creates a substantial risk of a miscarriage of justice unless we are persuaded that it did not 'materially influence[]' the guilty verdict. In making that determination, we consider the strength of the Commonwealth's case against the defendant (without consideration of any evidence erroneously admitted), the nature of the error, whether the error is 'sufficiently significant in the context of the trial to make plausible an inference that the jury's result might have been otherwise but for the error,' and whether it can be inferred 'from the record that counsel's failure to object was not simply a reasonable tactical decision.'" (Citations and footnotes omitted.)

Id. However, the application of the more stringent standard of review based on counsel's failure to object does not, standing alone, create a substantial risk of a miscarriage of justice. Commonwealth v. Vargas, 475 Mass. 338, 358 n.28 (2016). Under G. L. c. 278, § 33E, in any case in which the defendant was found guilty of murder in the first degree, see Commonwealth v. Francis, 450 Mass. 132, 137 n.5 (2007), the Supreme Judicial Court has a special duty and plenary authority to review the whole case, on the law and the evidence, and may order a new trial or reduce the verdict even in the absence of an objection. See Commonwealth v. Wright, 411 Mass. 678, 682 n.1 (1992). A trial judge may reduce a jury verdict to any lesser included offense "to ensure that the result in every criminal case is consonant with justice." Commonwealth v. Chhim, 447 Mass. 370, 381 (2006); G. L. c. 278, § 11; Mass. R. Crim. P. 25(b)(2). This power, which is designed to rectify a disproportionate verdict, or ameliorate injustice caused by the Commonwealth, defense counsel, the jury, the judge's own error, or the interaction of several causes, should be used sparingly. Commonwealth v. Keough, 385 Mass. 314, 316–321 (1982). A judge considering a motion to reduce a verdict may rely on essentially the same considerations as does the Supreme Judicial Court when deciding whether to reduce a verdict to a lesser degree of guilt pursuant to G. L. c. 278, § 33E. Commonwealth v. Pagan, 471 Mass. 537, 543 (2015).

Subsection (f). This subsection is derived from Commonwealth v. Spencer, 465 Mass. 32, 42 (2013).

Purpose. Massachusetts practice encourages the use of motions in limine. Motions in limine are useful to clarify or simplify the issues that need to be addressed prior to trial and to prevent irrelevant, inadmissible, or prejudicial matters from being considered by the trier of fact. See Commonwealth v. Lopez, 383 Mass. 497, 500 n.2 (1981). Such motions should be "narrowly limited to focus on a discrete issue or item of anticipated evidence," and "must not be used to choke off a valid defense in a criminal action, or to 'knock out' the entirety of the evidence supporting a defense before it can be heard by the jury." Commonwealth v. O'Malley, 14 Mass. App. Ct. 314, 324–325 (1982). See also Commonwealth v. Hood, 389 Mass. 581, 594 (1983); J.D.H. v. P.A.H., 71 Mass. App. Ct. 285, 290 (2008) (court may rely on evidence excluded in motion in limine where moving party later introduces the evidence where it is favorable to nonmoving party). A judge has discretion to reconsider an earlier or previous ruling on a motion in limine. Commonwealth v. Dabney, 478 Mass. 839, 852 (2018).

Timing. While a motion in limine may be filed during trial in advance of the evidence being offered, Commonwealth v. Spencer, 465 Mass. 32, 42 (2013), there is a preference for filing and ruling on such motions in advance of trial since it may affect counsels' conduct of the trial. See Commonwealth v. Woodbine, 461 Mass. 720, 735 n.21 (2012); Commonwealth v. Diaz, 383 Mass. 73, 81 (1981). In some cases, such as where there are challenges to the reliability of expert witness testimony, a pretrial motion in limine is required to preserve the opposing party's rights. Commonwealth v. Sparks, 433 Mass. 654, 659 (2001). A judge retains the discretion to reserve on a ruling until the evidence is presented at trial.

Illustrations. Cases involving common examples of motions in limine include the following: McLaughlin v. City of Lowell, 84 Mass. App. Ct. 45, 70 (2013) (application of collateral estoppel or issue preclusion); Scott v. Garfield, 454 Mass. 790, 802 (2009) (issues relating to collateral source rule and amount of medical bills); N.E. Physical Therapy Plus, Inc. v. Liberty Mut. Ins. Co., 466 Mass. 358, 360 (2013) (admissibility of data compilations pursuant to G. L. c. 233, § 79B); Vassallo v. Baxter Healthcare Corp., 428 Mass. 1, 9 (1998) (Daubert-type motions relating to admissibility of expert testimony); Croall v. Massachusetts Bay Transp. Auth., 26 Mass. App. Ct. 957, 959 (1988) (similar occurrences); and McDaniel v. Pickens, 45 Mass. App. Ct. 63, 67 (1998) (evidence of insurance offered to show bias).

A motion in limine may be used to obtain a ruling in advance of trial on whether a statement is subject to the rule against hearsay or whether the probative value of otherwise relevant evidence is substantially outweighed by its prejudicial effect. Commonwealth v. Spencer, 465 Mass. 32, 42 (2013). A motion in limine is also a useful method for obtaining a ruling on the admissibility of evidence of prior bad acts, see Commonwealth v. Leonard, 428 Mass. 782 (1999), as well as on evidence of prior criminal convictions and the application of the rape-shield law. See Commonwealth v. Harris, 443 Mass. 714 (2005). A motion in limine is commonly used to obtain a ruling in advance of trial on the admissibility of evidence under the first complaint doctrine. See, e.g., Commonwealth v. Aviles, 461 Mass. 60, 63–66 (2011).

Subsection (g). The trial court's ruling on the exclusion of evidence as a sanction is reviewable for an abuse of discretion. Commonwealth v. Sanford, 460 Mass. 441, 445 (2010). Sanctions are to be appropriately tailored to cure prejudice relating to a party's noncompliance with its discovery obligations and to ensure a fair trial. Commonwealth v. Carney, 458 Mass. 418, 427–428 (2010). Factors to be considered include the prevention of surprise, the effectiveness of sanctions short of exclusion of evidence, the presence or absence of bad faith, the prejudice to the nonoffending party, and the materiality of the evidence. Commonwealth v. Reynolds, 429 Mass. 388, 398 (1999). But see Commonwealth v. Giontzis, 47 Mass. App. Ct. 450, 462–463 (1999) (not prejudicial error to allow Commonwealth's undisclosed rebuttal witness to testify even though there was evidence of surprise and bad faith).

Generally, the judge should impose the least severe sanction necessary to remedy the prejudice to the innocent party. Keene v. Brig-

ham & Women's Hosp., Inc., 439 Mass. 223, 235 (2003). See Wiedmann v. Bradford Group, Inc., 444 Mass. 698, 704–705 (2005) (oral testimony may be excluded as sanction for destruction of supporting documents). Exclusion of evidence as a sanction need not be based on an intentional act, but there must be some fault attributable to the sanctioned party. Kippenhan v. Chaulk Servs., Inc., 428 Mass. 124, 127 (1998).

While a trial judge may exclude expert testimony for failure to comply with discovery, the judge must consider other options, including a sua sponte continuance of the trial or an order for a deposition of the late-identified expert. Morgan v. Jozus, 67 Mass. App. Ct. 17, 24 (2006). A pretrial motion to compel is not a prerequisite for relief for the innocent party. Mohamed v. Fast Forward, Inc., 41 Mass. App. Ct. 643, 648 (1996).

Cross–Reference: Section 1102, Spoliation or Destruction of Evidence; Mass. R. Crim. P. 14(c); Mass. R. Civ. P. 37.

Section 104. Preliminary Questions

(a) In General. The court must decide any preliminary question about whether a witness is qualified or competent, a privilege exists, or evidence is admissible. In so deciding, the court is not bound by the law of evidence, except that on privilege.

(b) Relevance That Depends on a Fact. When the relevance of evidence depends on whether a fact exists, proof must be introduced sufficient to support a finding that the fact does exist. The court may admit the proposed evidence, de bene, on the condition that the proof be introduced later. Evidence so admitted is subject to a motion to strike if that proof is not forthcoming.

(c) Conducting a Hearing So That the Jury Cannot Hear It. The court must conduct any hearing on a preliminary question so that the jury cannot hear it if

    (1) the hearing involves the admissibility of a confession or

    (2) justice so requires.

(d) Cross–Examining a Defendant in a Criminal Case. By testifying on a preliminary question, a defendant in a criminal case does not become subject to cross-examination on other issues in the case, except issues that affect the witness's credibility.

(e) Evidence Relevant to Weight and Credibility. The law stated in this section does not limit a party's right to introduce before the jury evidence that is relevant to the weight or credibility of other evidence.

NOTE

Subsection (a). This subsection is derived from Nally v. Volkswagen of Am., Inc., 405 Mass. 191, 197–198 (1989), and Commonwealth v. Figueroa, 56 Mass. App. Ct. 641, 646 (2002). See also Gorton v. Hadsell, 63 Mass. 508, 511 (1852) (explaining that Massachusetts follows the orthodox principle under which "it is the province of the judge . . . to decide all questions on the admissibility of evidence. It is also his province to decide any preliminary questions of fact, however intricate, the solution of which may be necessary to enable him to determine the other question of admissibility."). The court may consider, in appropriate circumstances, representations of counsel and summary testimony. When the credibility of witnesses is in dispute on a preliminary question of fact, the court's determination is final. See Commonwealth v. Lyons, 426 Mass. 466, 470 (1998); Davis v. Boston Elevated Ry. Co., 235 Mass. 482, 502 (1920). The general rule in all cases, except as to waiver of Miranda rights and the voluntariness of defendants' statements in criminal cases, is that the judge's findings of preliminary facts on which the admissibility of evidence depends need only be by a fair preponderance of the evidence. See Care & Protection of Laura, 414 Mass. 788, 792 (1993); Commonwealth v. Polian, 288 Mass. 494, 498–499 (1934). As to the waiver of Miranda rights and the issue of voluntariness, the standard under Massachusetts law is proof beyond a reasonable doubt. Commonwealth v. Day, 387 Mass. 915, 920 (1983).

When the preliminary question involves the applicability of a privilege and the substance of the proposed testimony or evidence is not known to the court, it may be necessary to require that the party or witness asserting the privilege make a disclosure in camera of enough of the evidence to enable the court to make a preliminary determination. See Commonwealth v. Collett, 387 Mass. 424, 436 (1982) (in camera review may be appropriate in determining applicability of client-social worker privilege); Notes to Section 511(b), Privilege Against Self–Incrimination: Privilege of a Witness (discussing Commonwealth v. Martin, 423 Mass. 496 [1996]). See also Carr v. Howard, 426 Mass. 514, 531 (1998) (medical peer review privilege). An in camera hearing should not be used unless the court is not able to determine the existence of the privilege from the record. Commonwealth v. Martin, 423 Mass. at 504–505. See, e.g., Bays v. Theran, 418 Mass. 685, 693 (1994); Bougas v. Chief of Police of Lexington, 371 Mass. 59, 65–66 (1976). Whether a privilege exists on behalf of a minor or incapacitated person is a preliminarily determination made by the court. If a privilege exists, the court appoints a guardian ad litem or guardian to waive or assert the privilege. G. L. c. 233, § 20B. See Adoption of Diane, 400 Mass. 196, 200–202 (1987).

Preliminary questions involving the voluntariness of a defendant's statement, whether there was a valid waiver of the rights required by Miranda v. Arizona, 384 U.S. 436 (1966), or whether an identification was unnecessarily suggestive, should be raised in advance of trial by a motion to suppress. See Mass. R. Crim. P. 13(c)(1), (2). When voluntariness is a live issue and is challenged by a pretrial motion to suppress or an objection at trial, the court shall conduct an evidentiary hearing. See Commonwealth v. Adams, 389 Mass. 265, 269–270 (1983); Commonwealth v. Miller, 68 Mass. App. Ct. 835, 842 (2007); Commonwealth v. Gonzalez, 59 Mass. App. Ct. 622, 624 (2003); Commonwealth v. Florek, 48 Mass. App. Ct. 414, 419 (2000). However, if a pretrial motion to suppress was heard and determined in advance of trial, and the evidence at trial is not materially different, the trial judge has no duty to rehear the motion based on an objection made at trial. See Commonwealth v. Parker, 412 Mass. 353, 356 (1992).

In some criminal cases, there are certain preliminary facts which, after being found by the judge, must also be submitted to the jury. In those situations, the judge must instruct the jury to disregard the evidence if they do not believe that those preliminary facts exist. See, e.g., Commonwealth v. Tavares, 385 Mass. 140, 152 (humane practice rule), cert. denied, 457 U.S. 1137 (1982); Commonwealth v. Key, 381 Mass. 19, 22 (1980) (dying declaration); Commonwealth v. Boyer, 52 Mass. App. Ct. 590, 598 (2001) (statements by joint venturers). See also G. L. c. 233, § 78 (business records). Cross–Reference: Section 1101(c)(3), Applicability of Evidentiary Sections: Where Inapplicable: Certain Other Proceedings.

For a comprehensive discussion of the difference between preliminary questions of fact upon which admissibility is determined by the judge under Mass. G. Evid. § 104(a) and the judge's determinations of conditional relevance under Mass. G. Evid. § 104(b), see Commonwealth v. Bright, 463 Mass. 421, 427–429 (2012).

Subsection (b). This subsection is derived from Commonwealth v. Perry, 432 Mass. 214, 234 (2000); Commonwealth v. Leonard, 428 Mass. 782, 785–786 (1999); Fauci v. Mulready, 337 Mass. 532, 540 (1958); and Harris–Lewis v. Mudge, 60 Mass. App. Ct. 480, 485 n.4 (2004). "Relevancy conditioned on fact" means that the judge is satisfied that a reasonable jury could find that the event took place or the condition of fact was fulfilled. Commonwealth v. Leonard, 428 Mass. at 785–786. See, e.g., Commonwealth v. Gambora, 457 Mass.

715, 730 (2010) (expert shoe-print evidence was relevant because reasonable jury could have found that police seizure of sneaker "from a closet in a bedroom at the defendant's mother's home—a room where the police also found personal papers bearing the defendant's name and photographs of him"—warranted an inference that the sneaker belonged to him, and therefore made it relevant). Contrast Section 104(a) (judge finds facts by preponderance of evidence).

In the event that the foundation evidence is not subsequently produced, the court has no duty to strike the evidence, admitted de bene, on its own motion. Commonwealth v. Sheppard, 313 Mass. 590, 595–596 (1943); Harris–Lewis v. Mudge, 60 Mass. App. Ct. at 485 n.4. If the objecting party fails to move to strike the evidence, the court's failure to strike it is not error. Muldoon v. West End Chevrolet, Inc., 338 Mass. 91, 98 (1958). See Commonwealth v. Navarro, 39 Mass. App. Ct. 161, 166 (1995). See also Section 611(a), Mode and Order of Examining Witnesses and Presenting Evidence: Control by the Court.

Subsection (c). This subsection is derived from Fed. R. Evid. 104(c) and Proposed Mass. R. Evid. 104(c) and is consistent with Massachusetts law. See Ruszcyk v. Secretary of Pub. Safety, 401 Mass. 418, 422–423 (1988).

Subsection (d). This subsection is derived from Fed. R. Evid. 104(d) and Proposed Mass. R. Evid. 104(d) and is consistent with Massachusetts law. See Commonwealth v. Judge, 420 Mass. 433, 444–446 (1995). It is well established that a defendant's testimony in support of a motion to suppress evidence may not be admitted against him or her at trial on the issue of guilt. See Simmons v. United States, 390 U.S. 377, 394 (1968). Such testimony may, however, be used for purposes of impeachment at trial if the defendant elects to testify. See Commonwealth v. Judge, 420 Mass. at 446 n.9 (the fact that defendant's testimony at suppression hearing may later be used at trial does not mean the scope of cross-examination of defendant at preliminary hearing should be limited). See also United States v. Smith, 940 F.2d 710, 713 (1st Cir. 1991) (defendant's testimony at a pretrial hearing can be used against him for impeachment purposes at trial); Care & Protection of M.C., 479 Mass. 246, 262 & n.9 (2018) (testimony at care and protection proceeding ordinarily not admissible at future criminal proceeding and can only be used for impeachment purposes if prior testimony "differ[s] significantly").

Subsection (e). This subsection is based on the long-standing principle that, in cases tried to a jury, questions of admissibility are for the court, while the credibility of witnesses and the weight of the evidence are questions for the jury. See Vassallo v. Baxter Healthcare Corp., 428 Mass. 1, 13 (1998); Commonwealth v. Festa, 369 Mass. 419, 424–425 (1976); Commonwealth v. Williams, 105 Mass. 62, 67 (1870).

Section 105. Limiting Evidence That Is Not Admissible Against Other Parties or for Other Purposes

If the court admits evidence that is admissible against a party or for a purpose—but not against another party or for another purpose—the court, on timely request, must restrict the evidence to its proper scope and instruct the jury accordingly.

NOTE

This section is derived from Commonwealth v. Carrion, 407 Mass. 263, 275 (1990) ("Evidence admissible for one purpose, if offered in good faith, is not inadmissible by the fact that it could not be used for another purpose."). If there is no request for a limiting instruction, the evidence is before the trier of fact for all purposes. See, e.g., Commonwealth v. Roberts, 433 Mass. 45, 48 (2000); Commonwealth v. Hollyer, 8 Mass. App. Ct. 428, 431 (1979).

A party must ask for an instruction limiting the scope of the evidence, if one is desired, at the time the evidence is admitted.

Commonwealth v. Roberts, 433 Mass. at 48. "[T]here is no requirement that the judge give limiting instructions sua sponte." Commonwealth v. Sullivan, 436 Mass. 799, 809 (2002). "A judge may refuse to limit the scope of the evidence where the objecting party fails to request limiting instructions when the evidence is introduced." Commonwealth v. Roberts, 433 Mass. at 48. "After the close of the evidence it is too late to present as of right a request for a ruling that the evidence be stricken." Id.

The trial judge has discretion in determining how to formulate limiting instructions. A trial judge may point the jury to issues of fact and conflicts of testimony, including which factors to consider when evaluating such testimony. This is permissible as long as "the judge clearly places the function of ultimate appraisal of the testimony upon the jury." Barrette v. Hight, 353 Mass. 268, 271 (1967).

Instructions Required. Once the judge has determined that the evidence is admissible under Section 403, Excluding Relevant Evidence for Prejudice, Confusion, Waste of Time, or Other Reasons, or Section 404(b), Character Evidence; Crimes or Other Acts: Crimes, Wrongs, or Other Acts, a limiting instruction is required where, even though the evidence is admissible for one purpose, there is a risk that the evidence will be improperly used for an inadmissible purpose. See Commonwealth v. McGee, 467 Mass. 141, 158 (2014) (a firearm that could not have been used to shoot victim, but that was offered to establish that defendant was familiar with firearms, was admissible only if accompanied by limiting instruction that it could not be taken as propensity evidence). Where evidence is admitted for a limited purpose, the judge should instruct the jury in accordance with the specific purpose for which the evidence was admitted. Commonwealth v. Howard, 479 Mass. 52, 67–68 (2018).

Timing of Limiting Instructions. Although contemporaneous limiting instructions are preferred, a judge has discretion as to the timing of a limiting instruction. Commonwealth v. Facella, 478 Mass. 393, 402–403 (2017) (no error where judge gave limiting instruction immediately following witness's direct examination, rather than during the testimony, as requested).

Section 106. Doctrine of Completeness

(a) Remainder of Writings or Recorded Statements. If a party introduces all or part of a writing or recorded statement, the court may permit an adverse party to introduce any other part of the writing or statement that is (1) on the same subject, (2) part of the same writing or conversation, and (3) necessary to an understanding of the admitted writing or statement.

(b) Curative Admissibility. When the erroneous admission of evidence causes a party to suffer significant prejudice, the court may permit incompetent evidence to be introduced to cure or minimize the prejudice.

NOTE

Subsection (a). This subsection is derived from Commonwealth v. Aviles, 461 Mass. 60, 74 (2011). See Mass. R. Civ. P. 32(a)(4). "When a party introduces a portion of a statement or writing in evidence the doctrine of verbal completeness allows admission of other relevant portions of the same statement or writing which serve to 'clarify the context' of the admitted portion." Commonwealth v. Carmona, 428 Mass. 268, 272 (1998), quoting Commonwealth v. Robles, 423 Mass. 62, 69 (1996). "The purpose of the doctrine is to prevent one party from presenting a fragmented and misleading version of events by requiring the admission of other relevant portions of the same statement or writing which serve to clarify the context of the admitted portion" (citations and quotations omitted). Commonwealth v. Eugene, 438 Mass. 343, 351 (2003). "The portion of the statement sought to be introduced must qualify or explain the segment previously introduced" (citations and quotations omitted). Commonwealth v. Richardson, 59 Mass. App. Ct. 94, 99 (2003). See, e.g., Commonwealth v. Aviles, 461 Mass. at 74 (where defendant offered portion of victim's testimony describing touching of her buttocks, Commonwealth was properly permitted to offer testimony about touching of vaginal area, as both answers pertained to issue of where defendant had touched victim and were made during the same line of questioning).

The decision as to when the remainder of the writing or statement is admitted is left to the discretion of the judge, but the "better practice is to require an objection and contemporaneous introduction of the complete statements when the original statement is offered." McAllister v. Boston Hous. Auth., 429 Mass. 300, 303 (1999). See Section 611(a), Mode and Order of Examining Witnesses and Presenting Evidence: Control by the Court. Compare Commonwealth v. Thompson, 431 Mass. 108, 115, cert. denied, 531 U.S. 864 (2000) (doctrine is not applicable to defendant's effort to admit alibi portion of his or her statement that has nothing to do with statement offered by Commonwealth), with Commonwealth v. Crayton, 470 Mass. 228, 230 (2014) (in prosecution for possession of child pornography, it was error to admit defendant's statement to police that he had been using a particular computer at library while excluding his contemporaneous denial that he had viewed child pornography on that computer).

Subsection (b). This subsection is derived from Commonwealth v. Ruffen, 399 Mass. 811, 813–814 (1987) ("The curative admissibility doctrine allows a party harmed by incompetent evidence to rebut that evidence only if the original evidence created significant prejudice."). See also Commonwealth v. Reed, 444 Mass. 803, 810–811 (2005) (court required to admit evidence); Burke v. Memorial Hosp., 29 Mass. App. Ct. 948, 950 (1990), citing Commonwealth v. Wakelin, 230 Mass. 567, 576 (1918).

ARTICLE II. JUDICIAL NOTICE

Section 201. Judicial Notice of Adjudicative Facts

(a) Scope. This section governs judicial notice of an adjudicative fact only, not a legislative fact.

(b) Kinds of Facts That May Be Judicially Noticed. The court may judicially notice a fact that is not subject to reasonable dispute because it

    (1) is generally known within the trial court's territorial jurisdiction or

    (2) can be accurately and readily determined from sources whose accuracy cannot reasonably be questioned.

(c) When Taken. A court may take judicial notice at any stage of the proceeding, whether requested or not, except a court shall not take judicial notice in a criminal trial of any element of an alleged offense.

(d) Opportunity to Be Heard. On timely request, a party is entitled to be heard on the propriety of taking judicial notice and the nature of the fact to be noticed. If the court takes judicial notice before notifying a party, the party, on request, is still entitled to be heard.

(e) Instructing the Jury. In a civil case, the court must instruct the jury to accept the noticed fact as conclusive. In a criminal case, the court must instruct the jury that it may or may not accept the noticed fact as conclusive.

NOTE

Subsection (a). There is a settled distinction between "adjudicative facts" and "legislative facts." See Cast Iron Soil Pipe Inst. v. Board of State Examiners of Plumbers & Gas Fitters, 8 Mass. App. Ct. 575, 586 (1979), and cases cited. Adjudicative facts are "the kind of facts that go to a jury in a jury case." Reid v. Acting Comm'r of the Dep't of Community Affairs, 362 Mass. 136, 142 (1972), quoting Davis, Administrative Law Treatise § 7.02. Legislative facts are those facts, including statistics, policy views, and other information, that constitute the reasons for legislation or administrative regulations. See Massachusetts Fed'n of Teachers, AFT, AFL–CIO v. Board of Educ., 436 Mass. 763, 772 (2002). Accord United States v. Bello, 194 F.3d 18, 23 (1st Cir. 1999). Judges "should use great caution before conducting independent research into factual matters, particularly on the internet." Commonwealth v. Hilaire, 92 Mass. App. Ct. 784, 789 & n.7 (2018) (demographic data used to identify defendant as perpetrator of home invasion was adjudicatory fact not appropriate for judicial notice), citing ABA Comm. on Ethics and Prof'l Responsibility, Independent Factual Research by Judges Via the Internet, Formal Op. 478 (2017).

The Supreme Judicial Court is "not inclined towards a narrow and illiberal application of the doctrine of judicial notice." Finlay v. Eastern Racing Ass'n, Inc., 308 Mass. 20, 27 (1941).

For an extensive list of matters on which a court may take judicial notice, see W.G. Young, J.R. Pollets, & C. Poreda, Annotated Guide to Massachusetts Evidence § 201 (2017–2018 ed.).

Subsection (b)(1). This subsection is derived from Nantucket v. Beinecke, 379 Mass. 345, 352 (1979). See also Commonwealth v. Kingsbury, 378 Mass. 751, 754 (1979). Accord Dimino v. Secretary of Commonwealth, 427 Mass. 704, 707 (1998) ("Factual matters which are 'indisputably true' are subject to judicial notice" [citations omitted].).

Subsection (b)(2). This subsection is derived from Commonwealth v. Green, 408 Mass. 48, 50 n.2 (1990). See also Commonwealth v. Kingsbury, 378 Mass. 751, 754 (1979). Accord Commonwealth v. Greco, 76 Mass. App. Ct. 296, 301 & n.11 (2010) ("judge did not err in taking judicial notice of the single and indisputable fact that, based upon the PDR [Physician's Desk Reference], Seroquel is the brand name for the generic drug quetiapine," while "not suggest[ing] that the PDR may be judicially noticed for other purposes"); Federal Nat'l Mtge. Ass'n v. Therrian, 42 Mass. App. Ct. 523, 525 (1997) ("facts which are ... verifiably true [e.g., Lynn is in Essex County] are susceptible of judicial notice"). "Judicial notice is not to be extended to personal observations of the judge or juror." Nantucket v. Beinecke, 379 Mass. 345, 352 (1979), citing Duarte, petitioner, 331 Mass. 747, 749–750 (1954). See also Commonwealth v. Kirk, 39 Mass. App. Ct. 225, 229 (1995) ("judicial notice ... cannot be taken of material factual issues that can only be decided by the fact finder on competent evidence"). Cf. Commonwealth v. Hilaire , 92 Mass. App. Ct. 784, 789 (2018) (inappropriate for a motion judge to take judicial notice of demographic data in order to "connect a defendant to the description of suspects or to a crime").

In Yankee Atomic Elec. Co. v. Secretary of the Commonwealth, 402 Mass. 750, 759 n.7 (1988), the court explained the difference between "judicial notice" of facts and "official notice" of facts. The latter includes matters that are "indisputably true," as well as other factual matters that an agency may take notice of due to its special familiarity with the subject matter. See G. L. c. 30A, § 6.

Court Records and Prior Proceedings. "[A] judge may take judicial notice of the court's records in a related action." Jarosz v. Palmer, 436 Mass. 526, 530 (2002). See also Adoption of Zak, 90 Mass. App. Ct. 840, 844 n.7 (2017); Home Depot v. Kardas, 81 Mass. App. Ct. 27, 28 (2011). In contrast, "[a] judge may not take judicial notice of facts or evidence brought out at a prior hearing that are not also admitted in evidence at the current hearing." Commonwealth v. O'Brien, 423 Mass. 841, 848–849 (1996); Furtado v. Furtado, 380 Mass. 137, 140 n.1 (1980); Ferriter v. Borthwick, 346 Mass. 391, 393 (1963).

See also Care & Protection of Zita, 455 Mass. 272, 283 (2009) ("We recognize the challenges that confront a judge who has presided over a case that is closely related to a new proceeding; it may be impossible to erase a judge's memory of the prior case. But each party is entitled to an impartial magistrate and a decision based on the evidence presented in her case.").

Cross–Reference: Section 1115(f)(3), Evidentiary Issues in Care and Protection, Child Custody, and Termination of Parental Rights Cases: Other Evidence: Judicial Findings from Prior Proceedings.

Subsection (c). This subsection, which is derived from Fed. R. Evid. 201(d) and Proposed Mass. R. Evid. 201(f), reflects the Massachusetts practice that judicial notice may be taken at any time by a trial or appellate court. Maguire v. Director of Office of Medicaid, 82 Mass. App. Ct. 549, 551 n.5 (2012); Commonwealth v. Grinkley, 44 Mass. App. Ct. 62, 69 n.9 (1997). While there is no express authority for the proposition that judicial notice is discretionary in connection with adjudicative facts, see Commonwealth v. Finegan, 45 Mass. App. Ct. 921, 922 (1998), the principle follows logically from the settled proposition that when there are no disputed facts, a legal dispute is ripe for a decision by the court. See Jackson v. Longcope, 394 Mass. 577, 580 n.2 (1985) (judicial notice may be taken by the court in connection with a motion to dismiss under Mass. R. Civ. P. 12[b][6]); Commonwealth v. Kingsbury, 378 Mass. 751, 754–755 (1979) ("The right of a court to take judicial notice of subjects of common knowledge is substantially the same as the right of jurors to rely on their common knowledge."). See also Commonwealth v. Marzynski, 149 Mass. 68, 72 (1889) (court took judicial notice that cigars were not drugs or medicine and properly excluded expert opinions stating the contrary). Courts may take judicial notice of their own records. See, e.g., Jarosz v. Palmer, 436 Mass. 526, 530 (2002). But see Commonwealth v. Berry, 463 Mass. 800, 804 n.6 (2012) (appellate court will not take judicial notice of contents of police report included in trial court file where report was not introduced into evidence or considered by motion judge and was not made part of record on appeal).

Criminal Cases. The defendant's constitutional right to trial by jury means that the "trier of fact, judge or jury, cannot be compelled to find against the defendant as to any element of the crime." Commonwealth v. Pauley, 368 Mass. 286, 291 (1975). Although the court may take judicial notice of an adjudicative fact in a criminal case, see Commonwealth v. Green, 408 Mass. 48, 50 & n.2 (1990), "[t]he proper practice in a criminal trial is to submit all factual issues to the jury, including matters of which the judge may take judicial notice." Commonwealth v. Kingsbury, 378 Mass. 751, 755 (1979), citing Fed. R. Evid. 201(g) (currently codified at Fed. R. Evid. 201[f]).

Subsection (d). This subsection is derived from the principle, grounded in due process considerations, that a party has a right to notice of matters that the court will adjudicate. See Department of Revenue v. C.M.J., 432 Mass. 69, 76 n.15 (2000), and cases cited. Even in situations where information is appropriate for judicial notice under Section 201(b)(2), it should not be taken without notice to the parties and an opportunity to be heard. Commonwealth v. Hilaire, 92 Mass. App. Ct. 784, 789 (2018) (motion judge improperly took judicial notice of adjudicatory fact after evidentiary hearing concluded and without notice to [or input from] the parties).

Subsection (e). The first sentence of this subsection, which is taken verbatim from Fed. R. Evid. 201(f), reflects Massachusetts practice. It is consistent with and follows from the principle set forth in Section 201(c). The second sentence is derived from Commonwealth v. Kingsbury, 378 Mass. 751, 754–755 (1979), and Commonwealth v. Finegan, 45 Mass. App. Ct. 921, 923 (1998), where the courts noted that any fact that is the subject of judicial notice in a criminal case must be given to the jury for its determination. See generally United States v. Bello, 194 F.3d 18, 22–26 (1st Cir. 1999) (explaining relationship between Fed. R. Evid. 201[b] and Fed. R. Evid. 201[g], currently codified at Fed. R. Evid. 201[f]).

Section 202. Judicial Notice of Law

(a) Mandatory. A court shall take judicial notice of

(1) the General Laws of the Commonwealth, public acts of the Massachusetts Legislature, the common law of Massachusetts, rules of court, the contents of the Code of Massachusetts Regulations, and Federal statutes, and

(2) the contents of Federal regulations and the laws of foreign jurisdictions that are brought to the court's attention.

(b) Permissive. A court may take judicial notice of the contents of Federal regulations and the laws of foreign jurisdictions not brought to its attention, legislative history, municipal charters, and charter amendments.

(c) Not Permitted. A court is not permitted to take judicial notice of municipal ordinances, town bylaws, special acts of the Legislature, or regulations not published in the Code of Massachusetts Regulations.

NOTE

Subsections (a)(1) and (2). These subsections are derived from 44 U.S.C. § 1507 (contents of the Federal Register shall be judicially noticed); G. L. c. 30A, § 6 (regulations published in the Code of Massachusetts Regulations shall be judicially noticed); and G. L. c. 233, § 70 ("The courts shall take judicial notice of the law of the United States or of any state, territory or dependency thereof or of a foreign country whenever the same shall be material."). See also Cohen v. Assessors of Boston, 344 Mass. 268, 269 (1962); Ralston v. Commissioner of Agric., 334 Mass. 51, 53–54 (1956); Mastrullo v. Ryan, 328 Mass. 621, 622 (1952); Brodsky v. Fine, 263 Mass. 51, 54 (1928).

The party which seeks to have the court notice or apply any foreign law has the burden of bringing it to the court's attention. See Mass. R. Crim. P. 39(b) ("The court shall upon request take judicial notice of the law of the United States or of any state, territory, or dependency thereof or of a foreign country whenever it shall be material."); Mass. R. Civ. P. 44.1 ("A party who intends to raise an issue concerning the law of the United States or of any state, territory or dependency thereof or of a foreign country shall give notice in his pleadings or other reasonable written notice. The court, in determining such law, may consider any relevant material or source, including testimony, whether or not submitted by a party or admissible under Rule 43. The court's determination shall be treated as a ruling on a question of law.").

Subsection (b). This subsection is derived from G. L. c. 43B, § 12; Commonwealth v. Lys, 481 Mass. 1, 10 (2018) (notice of "temporary protected status" designation for foreign nationals issued by Secretary of Homeland Security and published in Federal Register); Blue Hills Cemetery, Inc. v. Board of Registration in Embalming & Funeral Directing, 379 Mass. 368, 375 n.10 (1979), citing Pereira v. New England LNG Co., 364 Mass. 109, 122 (1973) (notice of legislative history is permissive); and New England Trust Co. v. Wood, 326 Mass. 239, 243 (1950) (notice of charters and charter amendments of cities and towns).

Subsection (c). Courts "will not take judicial cognizance of municipal ordinances, or of special acts of the Legislature" (citations omitted). Brodsky v. Fine, 263 Mass. 51, 54 (1928). Furthermore, "[t]he general rule in Massachusetts is that courts do not take judicial notice of regulations [not included in the Code of Massachusetts Regulations]; they must be put in evidence" (citations and quotations omitted). Peters v. Haymarket Leasing, Inc., 64 Mass. App. Ct. 767, 775 n.11 (2005). Printed copies of legislative acts and resolves and attested copies of municipal ordinances, bylaws, rules, and regulations are admissible. G. L. c. 233, § 75. The contents of a municipal bylaw or ordinance may also be proved by the oral testimony of police officers. Commonwealth v. Bones, 93 Mass. App. Ct. 681, 685–686 (2018).

ARTICLE III. INFERENCES, PRIMA FACIE EVIDENCE, AND PRESUMPTIONS

Section 301. Civil Cases

(a) Scope. This section applies to all civil actions and proceedings, except as otherwise specifically provided by a statute, the common law, a rule, or a regulation.

(b) Inferences. An inference is a step in reasoning that the fact finder may make from evidence that has been accepted as believable. A fact may be inferred even though the relationship between the basic fact and the inferred fact is not necessary or inescapable, so long as it is reasonable and possible.

(c) Prima Facie Evidence. Where a statute or regulation provides that a fact or group of facts is prima facie evidence of another fact at issue, the party against whom the prima facie evidence is directed has the burden of production to rebut or meet such prima facie evidence. If that party fails to come forward with evidence to rebut or meet the prima facie evidence, the fact at issue is to be taken by the fact finder as established. Where evidence is introduced sufficient to warrant a finding contrary to the fact at issue, the fact finder is permitted to consider the prima facie evidence as bearing on the fact at issue, but it must be weighed with all other evidence to determine whether a particular fact has been proved. Prima facie evidence does not shift the burden of persuasion, which remains throughout the trial on the party on whom it was originally cast.

(d) Presumptions. A presumption imposes on the party against whom it is directed the burden of production to rebut or meet that presumption. The extent of that burden may be defined by statute, regulation, or the common law. If that party fails to come forward with evidence to rebut or meet that presumption, the fact is to be taken by the fact finder as established. If that party comes forward with evidence to rebut or meet the presumption, the presumption shall have no further force or effect. A presumption does not shift the burden of persuasion, which remains throughout the trial on the party on whom it was originally cast.

NOTE

Subsection (b). This subsection is derived from Commonwealth v. Dinkins, 440 Mass. 715, 720–721 & n.8 (2004), and DeJoinville v. Commonwealth, 381 Mass. 246, 253 n.13 (1980). "In this formulation, 'possible' is not a lesser alternative to 'reasonable.' Rather, the two words function in a synergistic manner: each raises the standard imposed by the other." Commonwealth v. Dinkins, 440 Mass. at 721. "[W]e have permitted, in carefully defined circumstances, a jury to make an inference based on an inference to come to a conclusion of guilt or innocence. But we require that each inference must be a reasonable and logical conclusion from the prior inference; we have made clear that a jury may not use conjecture or guesswork to choose between alternative inferences." Commonwealth v. Dostie, 425 Mass. 372, 376 (1997). See, e.g., Commonwealth v. White, 452 Mass. 133, 136 (2008) (concluding that there was sufficient evidence connecting the defendant to a gun found at the crime scene, the court observed that "[w]e do not require that every inference be premised on an independently proven fact"). For a lengthy list of inferences, see W.G. Young, J.R. Pollets, & C. Poreda, Annotated Guide to Massachusetts Evidence § 301 (2017–2018 ed.). See also Model Jury Instructions for Use in the District Court § 3.03 (Mass. Cont. Legal Educ. 2003).

Subsection (c). This subsection is derived from Burns v. Commonwealth, 430 Mass. 444, 450–451 (1999); Ford Motor Co. v. Barrett, 403 Mass. 240, 242–243 (1988); and Cook v. Farm Serv. Stores, Inc., 301 Mass. 564, 566 (1938). For a list of statutes that involve prima facie evidence, see W.G. Young, J.R. Pollets, & C. Poreda, Annotated Guide to Massachusetts Evidence § 301 (2017–2018 ed.). See also Model Jury Instructions for Use in the District Court § 3.03 (Mass. Cont. Legal Educ. 2003).

Subsection (d). This subsection is based on the predominant approach in Massachusetts whereby a presumption shifts the burden of production and disappears when the opposing party meets its burden by offering evidence to rebut the presumption. However, the disappearance of the presumption does not prevent the fact finder from drawing an inference from one or more basic facts that is consistent with the original presumption. See Standerwick v. Zoning Bd. of Appeals of Andover, 447 Mass. 20, 34–35 (2006), quoting Epstein v. Boston Hous. Auth., 317 Mass. 297, 302 (1944) (in the context of the statutory provision that an abutter is presumed to have standing in cases arising under G. L. c. 40A, the court observed that "[a] presumption does not shift the burden of proof; it is a rule of evidence that aids the party bearing the burden of proof in sustaining that burden by 'throw[ing] upon his adversary the burden of going forward with evidence.'"); Jacobs v. Town Clerk of Arlington, 402 Mass. 824, 826–827 (1988) (rebuttable presumption of death). The quantum of evidence required to rebut the presumption may vary. See Yazbek v. Board of Appeal on Motor Vehicle Liab. Policies & Bonds, 41 Mass. App. Ct. 915, 916 (1996).

In civil cases, presumptions ordinarily require a party against whom the presumption is directed to come forward with some evidence to rebut the presumption; they ordinarily impose a burden of production, not persuasion, on that party. What has been termed an irrebuttable or conclusive presumption is not a rule of evidence, but rather a rule of substantive law designed to address a social policy, and cannot be rebutted by evidence. W.G. Young, J.R. Pollets, & C. Poreda, Annotated Guide to Massachusetts Evidence § 301 (2017–2018 ed.), citing Commonwealth v. Clerk–Magistrate of the W. Roxbury Div. of the Dist. Ct. Dep't, 439 Mass. 352, 354–356 (2003), and Commonwealth v. Dunne, 394 Mass. 10, 18 (1985). See G. L. c. 152, § 32(e); Carey's Case, 66 Mass. App. Ct. 749, 755–758 (2006).

A presumption may give rise to a constitutional question even in civil cases. See, e.g., Care & Protection of Erin, 443 Mass. 567, 571 (2005) ("[I]n cases that involve severing parental rights, the presumption that a child, who had been in the care of the department for more than one year, would have her best interests served by granting a petition for adoption or dispensing with the need for parental consent to adoption, violates the parents' due process rights because it shifts the burden to the parent affirmatively to prove fitness and to prove that the best interests of the child would be served by maintaining parental rights."). For presumptions governing child custody cases, see G. L. c. 208, §§ 31 and 31A; G. L. c. 209, § 38; G. L. c. 209A; and G. L. c. 209C, §§ 6 and 10(b). See also Custody of Kali, 439 Mass. 834, 844 (2003) ("The required considerations of G. L. c. 209C, § 10[a] . . . do [not] create a presumption that the caretaker with whom the child is primarily residing will be awarded permanent custody."); Della Corte v. Ramirez, 81 Mass. App. Ct. 906, 907 (2012) (presumption of parentage applies to child of same-sex couple who were married at time of child's birth). For a further list of presumptions, see W.G. Young, J.R. Pollets, & C. Poreda, Annotated Guide to Massachusetts Evidence § 301 (2017–2018 ed.). See also Model Jury Instructions for Use in the District Court § 3.07 (Mass. Cont. Legal Educ. 2003).

Section 302.   Criminal Cases

(a) Scope. This section governs the operation of inferences, prima facie evidence, and presumptions in criminal cases.

(b) Inferences. The jury generally may draw inferences in a criminal case in the same manner as in a civil case.

(c) Prima Facie Evidence. Prima facie evidence means that proof of the first fact permits, but does not require, the fact finder, in the absence of competing evidence, to find that the second fact is true beyond a reasonable doubt. Where there is contrary evidence, the first fact continues to constitute some evidence of the fact to be proved, remaining throughout the trial probative on issues to which it is relevant.

(d) Presumptions. The term "presumption" should not be used in connection with the Commonwealth's burden of proof.

(1) The defendant cannot be required to satisfy the burden of disproving a fact that is essential to a finding or verdict of guilty.

(2) The defendant may be required to satisfy a burden of production.

NOTE

Subsection (a). Constitutional principles restrict the manner in which concepts such as inferences, prima facie evidence, and presumptions are permitted to operate in criminal cases. "[T]he Due Process Clause protects the accused against conviction except upon proof beyond a reasonable doubt of every fact necessary to constitute the crime with which he is charged." In re Winship, 397 U.S. 358, 364 (1970). "[I]t is constitutionally impermissible to shift to a defendant the burden of disproving an element of a crime charged." Commonwealth v. Moreira, 385 Mass. 792, 794 (1982). Likewise, "[d]ue process requires that the State disprove beyond a reasonable doubt those 'defenses' that negate essential elements of the crime charged." Commonwealth v. Robinson, 382 Mass. 189, 203 (1981). Therefore, a conclusive or mandatory presumption or inference in any form which has the effect of relieving the jury of the duty of finding a fact essential to proof of the defendant's guilt on a criminal charge beyond a reasonable doubt based on evidence offered at trial, or which imposes on a defendant a burden of persuasion as to such a fact, conflicts with the presumption of innocence and violates due process. See Sandstrom v. Montana, 442 U.S. 510, 523–524 (1979); Patterson v. New York, 432 U.S. 197, 210 (1977); Commonwealth v. Stokes, 374 Mass. 583, 589–590 (1978). Further, "[a] permissive inference cannot have the effect of reducing the Commonwealth's burden to prove a crime beyond a reasonable doubt." Commonwealth v. Littles, 477 Mass. 382, 388 (2017).

Subsection (b). This subsection is derived from DeJoinville v. Commonwealth, 381 Mass. 246, 253 (1980), and Gagne v. Commonwealth, 375 Mass. 417, 422–423 (1978). While a jury generally may draw inferences in a criminal case in the same manner as in a civil case, drawing an inference in a criminal case is not a substitute for the separate determination of whether the defendant's guilt has been established beyond a reasonable doubt. See Commonwealth v. Waite, 422 Mass. 792, 805–806 (1996); Commonwealth v. Little, 384 Mass. 262, 267 (1981).

Cross–Reference: Section 301(b), Civil Cases: Inferences.

Subsection (c). This subsection is derived from Commonwealth v. Maloney, 447 Mass. 577, 581 (2006). See also Commonwealth v. Chappee, 397 Mass. 508, 520 (1986); Commonwealth v. Pauley, 368 Mass. 286, 291–292 (1975).

There are numerous statutes that designate certain evidence as having prima facie effect. See, e.g., G. L. c. 22C, § 39 (certificate of chemical analysis of narcotics); G. L. c. 46, § 19 (birth, marriage, or death certificate); G. L. c. 90, § 24(4) (court record of a prior conviction if accompanied by other documentation); G. L. c. 185C, § 21 (report of inspector in housing court); G. L. c. 233, § 79F (certificate of public way); G. L. c. 269, § 11C (firearm with obliterated serial number).

"Such provisions serve to identify evidence that the Commonwealth may introduce to meet its burden and which, while just as probative as other evidence, is less burdensome to produce. They do not, however, alter the Commonwealth's substantive burden of proof, render admissible any evidence that previously was inadmissible, or render sufficient any evidence that necessarily was insufficient beforehand." (Citation omitted.)

Commonwealth v. Maloney, 447 Mass. at 581–582. Such statutes may be unconstitutional unless there is a "strong, logical connection" between the basic fact and the inferred fact. Commonwealth v. Littles, 477 Mass. 382, 385–386 (2017) (failure to make good on dishonored check within two days cannot be prima facie evidence of intent to defraud).

Subsection (d). This subsection is derived from Commonwealth v. Moreira, 385 Mass. 792, 797 (1982), where the Supreme Judicial Court stated that "[t]he word 'presumption' must be given an explanation consistent with the meaning of inference. The safer course, perhaps, is to avoid the use of the word 'presumption,' in any context which includes the burden of proof in criminal cases." See also Commonwealth v. McInerney, 373 Mass. 136, 149 (1977) (explaining the problems that arise when the terms "presumption" and "inference" are used interchangeably). Additionally, in instructing a jury, the judge should explain that inferences operate only permissively, and that the jury are not required to accept any fact based on prima facie evidence. See Commonwealth v. Niziolek, 380 Mass. 513, 521–522 (1980); Commonwealth v. Pauley, 368 Mass. 286, 291–292 (1975). See also Commonwealth v. Corriveau, 396 Mass. 319, 340 (1985).

Subsection (d)(1). This subsection is derived from Commonwealth v. Moreira, 385 Mass. 792, 794–797 (1982), and Commonwealth v. McDuffee, 379 Mass. 353, 363–364 (1979). See also In re Winship, 397 U.S. 358, 364 (1970) ("[T]he Due Process Clause protects the accused against conviction except upon proof beyond a reasonable doubt of every fact necessary to constitute the crime with which he is charged.").

Subsection (d)(2). This subsection is derived from Commonwealth v. Cabral, 443 Mass. 171, 179 (2005), and cases cited. See id. ("[W]here a defendant asserts an affirmative defense, he takes on a burden of production, because the Commonwealth has no burden of disproving an affirmative defense unless and until there is evidence supporting such defense" [citation and quotation omitted].). This principle is illustrated by Commonwealth v. Vives, 447 Mass. 537, 541 (2006), where the court explained that

"[t]he Commonwealth's burden to disprove the affirmative defense of honest and reasonable claim arises once the defendant has met his own burden of production. Thus, if any view of the evidence would support a factual finding that the defendant was acting as creditor to the victim's debtor, the defendant has met his burden of production and it is incumbent on the Commonwealth to disprove the defense." (Citation and quotation omitted.)

The evidence supporting an affirmative defense "may be contained in the Commonwealth's case, the defendant's case, or the two in combination." Commonwealth v. Galvin, 56 Mass. App. Ct. 698, 699 (2002), citing Commonwealth v. Rodriguez, 370 Mass. 684, 688 n.5 (1976). In determining whether sufficient evidence supports an affirmative defense, the evidence must be viewed in the light most favorable to the defendant. Id.

In Commonwealth v. Vives, 447 Mass. at 541 n.3, the court also made it clear that a defendant may be required to carry the burden of production as to an affirmative defense that relates directly to an element of the crime. Commonwealth v. Dorvil, 472 Mass. 1, 13 (2015) (where there is some evidence that a parent used reasonable force in disciplining a minor child, the Commonwealth bears the burden of disproving at least one prong of the parental privilege), citing Commonwealth v. Glacken, 451 Mass. 163, 167 (2008). See, e.g., Commonwealth v. Rodriguez, 370 Mass. at 687–688 (in prosecution for assault and battery, Commonwealth has no duty to affirmatively disprove that the defendant acted in self-defense until there is some evidence in the case to warrant such a finding).

Firearm: Defense of License. In a prosecution of a firearm charge, the defendant must give the Commonwealth notice that he or she intends to raise the defense of license and produce "some evidence" of a license, at which time the burden shifts to the Commonwealth to prove the absence of a license beyond a reasonable doubt. Commonwealth v. Gouse, 461 Mass. 787, 806 (2012). However, when the charge results from alleged illegal possession of a firearm by a coventurer, the defendant must give notice of the defense but is not required to produce any evidence of the existence of the codefendant's firearm license, as he or she has no better access to that information than the Commonwealth. Commonwealth v. Humphries, 465 Mass. 762, 771 (2013).

Lack of Criminal Responsibility. The presumption of sanity is not truly a presumption but rather is an inference that a defendant is "probably criminally responsible." Commonwealth v. Lawson, 475 Mass. 806, 807 (2016). Where a defendant relies on a defense of lack of criminal responsibility and there is some supporting evidence, the inference of sanity alone "cannot support a finding that a defendant is criminally responsible beyond a reasonable doubt." Id. However, expert testimony is not needed in every case, and the Commonwealth may rely on the "circumstances of the offense," including the defendant's words and deeds around the offense, to prove a defendant's criminal responsibility. Id.

ARTICLE IV.　RELEVANCY AND ITS LIMITS

Section 401.　Test for Relevant Evidence

Evidence is relevant if

(a) it has any tendency to make a fact more or less probable than it would be without the evidence and

(b) the fact is of consequence in determining the action.

NOTE

This section is derived from Commonwealth v. Schuchardt, 408 Mass. 347, 350 (1990), and is nearly identical to Fed. R. Evid. 401. See also Commonwealth v. Kennedy, 389 Mass. 308, 310 (1983) (citing with approval Proposed Mass. R. Evid. 401). Massachusetts law accords relevance a liberal definition. See Commonwealth v. Fayer-

weather, 406 Mass. 78, 83 (1989) ("rational tendency to prove an issue in the case"); Commonwealth v. Vitello, 376 Mass. 426, 440 (1978) ("renders the desired inference more probable than it would be without the evidence"). Compare Commonwealth v. Scesny, 472 Mass. 185, 198–199 (2015) (testimony that witness was "pretty certain" defendant had been a patron at a bar was relevant and properly admitted), with Commonwealth v. Caruso, 476 Mass. 275, 291 (2017) ("without evidence that the defendant had accessed [the information depicted in the admitted screenshots of the defendant's computer, the screenshots] had no tendency to affect the probability of any material fact"). The concept of relevancy has two components: (1) the evidence must have some tendency (probative value) to prove or disprove a particular fact, and (2) that particular fact must be material to an issue (of consequence) in the case. Harris–Lewis v. Mudge, 60 Mass. App. Ct. 480, 485 (2004).

To be admissible, it is not necessary that the evidence be conclusive of the issue. Commonwealth v. Ashley, 427 Mass. 620, 624–625 (1998). It is sufficient if the evidence constitutes a link in the chain of proof. Commonwealth v. Arroyo, 442 Mass. 135, 144 (2004). "Evidence must go in by piecemeal, and evidence having a tendency to prove a proposition is not inadmissible simply because it does not wholly prove the proposition. It is enough if in connection with other evidence it helps a little." Commonwealth v. Tucker, 189 Mass. 457, 467 (1905).

> "The general pattern of our cases on the alleged remoteness in time or space of particular evidence indicates two general principles. If the evidence has some probative value, decisions to admit the evidence and to leave its weight to the jury have been sustained. The exclusion on the ground of remoteness of relevant evidence has generally not been sustained. The cases have recognized a range of discretion in the judge." (Citations and footnote omitted.)

DeJesus v. Yogel, 404 Mass. 44, 47 (1989). To be relevant, evidence must not be too remote in time from the date of the crime. See, e.g., Commonwealth v. Corliss, 470 Mass. 443, 450–451 (2015) (judge was warranted in reasoning that sixteen-month interval between shooting and time witness saw defendant loading bullets into a firearm was not too remote because a person would retain knowledge of how to use a firearm). See also Crowe v. Ward, 363 Mass. 85, 88–89 (1973) (admissibility of weather reports as proof of conditions at some distance away from the reported observations).

Reliance is placed upon the trial judge's discretion to exclude evidence whose probative value is "substantially outweighed" by risk of unfair prejudice, confusion, or waste of time. Commonwealth v. Bonds, 445 Mass. 821, 831 (2006). Although omitted in a number of cases, a proper explanation of this balancing test includes the term "substantially." See Note to Section 403, Excluding Relevant Evidence for Prejudice, Confusion, Waste of Time, or Other Reasons.

Section 402. General Admissibility of Relevant Evidence

Relevant evidence is admissible unless any of the following provides otherwise:

(a) the United States Constitution,

(b) the Massachusetts Constitution,

(c) a statute, or

(d) other provisions of the Massachusetts common law of evidence.

Irrelevant evidence is not admissible.

NOTE

This section is derived from Commonwealth v. DelValle, 443 Mass. 782, 793 (2005), and Commonwealth v. Owen, 57 Mass. App. Ct. 538, 547 (2003). Unless relevant, evidence will not be admitted because it does not make a fact in dispute more or less probable than it would be without the evidence. See Commonwealth v. Seabrooks, 425 Mass. 507, 512 n.7 (1997). But the converse is not true, which is to say that not all relevant evidence will be admitted. See Commonwealth v. Vitello, 376 Mass. 426, 440 (1978) ("all relevant evidence is admissible unless barred by an exclusionary rule"); Poirier v. Plymouth, 374 Mass. 206, 210 (1978) (same).

Relevant evidence may be excluded for any number of reasons. See, e.g., G. L. c. 233, § 20 (evidence of a private conversation between spouses is inadmissible); Commonwealth v. Kater, 432 Mass. 404, 416–417 (2000) (hypnotically aided testimony is not admissible); Commonwealth v. Harris, 371 Mass. 462, 467–468 (1976) (constitutional mandate forbids admission of a coerced confession regardless of its

relevance); Commonwealth v. Kartell, 58 Mass. App. Ct. 428, 432 (2003) (relevant evidence excluded on grounds it was too remote). "Alleged defects in the chain of custody usually go to the weight of the evidence and not its admissibility." Commonwealth v. Viriyahiranpaiboon, 412 Mass. 224, 230 (1992); Section 403, Excluding Relevant Evidence for Prejudice, Confusion, Waste of Time, or Other Reasons (relevant evidence may be excluded if its probative value is substantially outweighed by the risk of unfair prejudice, confusion, etc.). There may be circumstances where portions of documentary evidence should be excluded or redacted to protect personal privacy. See Matter of the Enforcement of a Subpoena, 436 Mass. 784, 794 (2002).

For an illustration of the rule barring the admission of irrelevant evidence, see Commonwealth v. Hampton, 91 Mass. App. Ct. 852, 854–855 (2017) (use of adult pornography "wholly irrelevant" to prove charges of sexual assault on child).

Cross–Reference: Note "Address of Witness" to Section 501, Privileges Recognized Only as Provided.

Section 403. Excluding Relevant Evidence for Prejudice, Confusion, Waste of Time, or Other Reasons

The court may exclude relevant evidence if its probative value is substantially outweighed by a danger of one or more of the following: unfair prejudice, confusing the issues, misleading the jury, undue delay, wasting time, or needlessly presenting cumulative evidence.

NOTE

This section is derived from Ruszcyk v. Secretary of Pub. Safety, 401 Mass. 418, 423 (1988) (adopting the principles expressed in Proposed Mass. R. Evid. 403). See Commonwealth v. Bonds, 445 Mass. 821, 831 (2006); Gath v. M/A-Com, Inc., 440 Mass. 482, 490–491 (2003); Commonwealth v. Beausoleil, 397 Mass. 206, 217 (1986); Commonwealth v. Cruz, 53 Mass. App. Ct. 393, 407–408 (2001).

This section states the general rule that all relevant evidence may be excluded when its probative value is "substantially outweighed," not simply outweighed, by the danger of unfair prejudice, confusion of the issues, misleading the jury, being unnecessarily time consuming, or needless presentation of cumulative evidence. See Commonwealth v. Crayton, 470 Mass. 228, 249 & n.27 (2014) (acknowledging this as general rule and explaining that more exacting standard is applicable when relevant evidence consists of prior bad act evidence under Section 404[b]). See also Commonwealth v. Kindell, 84 Mass. App. Ct. 183, 187–188 (2013) (measure of prejudice is not simply whether evidence is adverse to party opposed to it, but instead whether it is unfairly prejudicial). While a majority of the cases stand for the proposition that relevant evidence may be excluded if its probative value is "substantially" outweighed by its prejudicial effect—see, e.g., Commonwealth v. Bonds, 445 Mass. at 831; Commonwealth v. Stroyny, 435 Mass. 635, 641 (2002); Commonwealth v. Otsuki, 411 Mass. 218, 236 (1991)—others state that the probative value must be merely outweighed by the prejudicial effect. See, e.g., Commonwealth v. Rosario, 444 Mass. 550, 557 (2005); Commonwealth v. Reynolds, 429 Mass. 388, 395 (1999). These latter cases, however, rely on cases which include the term "substantial" when explaining the balancing test. See, e.g., Commonwealth v. Chalifoux, 362 Mass. 811, 816 (1973) (relied on by cases which Commonwealth v. Rosario, 444 Mass. at 556–557, relied on); Commonwealth v. Otsuki, 411 Mass. at 236 (relied on by Commonwealth v. Reynolds, 429 Mass. at 395).

Unfair Prejudice. "[T]rial judges must take care to avoid exposing the jury unnecessarily to inflammatory material that might inflame the jurors' emotions and possibly deprive the defendant of an impartial jury." Commonwealth v. Berry, 420 Mass. 95, 109 (1995). See, e.g., Commonwealth v. Bishop, 461 Mass. 586, 596–597 (2012) ("before a judge admits evidence that a defendant used [a racial slur] to describe a man of color, the judge must be convinced that the probative weight of such evidence justifies this risk"). Unfair prejudice also results when the trier of fact uses properly admitted evidence for an impermissible purpose, for example by relying on the truth of an out-of-court statement that was admitted for a nonhearsay purpose or, when evidence of a person's prior bad act is admitted under Section 404(b), by considering that evidence as indicating that person's propensity to commit such acts. See, e.g., Commonwealth v. Rosario, 430 Mass. 505, 509–510 (1999); Commonwealth v. Fidalgo, 74 Mass. App. Ct. 130, 133 (2009).

In balancing probative value against risk of prejudice, the fact that the evidence goes to a central issue in the case weighs in favor of admission. See Commonwealth v. Martinez, 476 Mass. 186, 194–195 (2017) (audio-video recording of news broadcast not unfairly prejudicial where judge explained that it was not admitted for its truth, required extensive redactions, and provided limiting instructions as to its use); Gath v. M/A–Com, Inc., 440 Mass. 482, 490–491 (2003). Unfair prejudice does not mean that the evidence sought to be excluded is particularly probative evidence harmful to the opponent of the evidence. An illustrative weighing of probative value against unfair prejudice arises regarding the admissibility of photographs of the victim (especially autopsy) or the crime scene. See generally Commonwealth v. Bell, 473 Mass. 131, 142–145 (2015); Commonwealth v. Zhan Tang Huang, 87 Mass. App. Ct. 65, 77–78 (2015); Commonwealth v. Prashaw, 57 Mass. App. Ct. 19, 24–25 (2003). Evidence of a defendant's prior bad act may be unfairly prejudicial and therefore inadmissible to prove the crime charged, but it may be admissible for other purposes (e.g., common plan, pattern of conduct, identity, absence of accident, motive). See Commonwealth v. Holloway, 44 Mass. App. Ct. 469, 475 (1998). See also Commonwealth v. Fidalgo, 74 Mass. App. Ct. 130, 133–134 (2009) (evidence that the defendant had been a passenger in three prior automobile accidents over the past nine years in which she had claimed injuries and sought damages was not relevant in a prosecution of the defendant for filing a false motor vehicle insurance claim because it showed nothing about the character of the prior claims and yet had the potential for prejudice since the case was essentially a credibility contest). The effectiveness of limiting instructions in minimizing the risk of unfair prejudice should be considered in the balance. Commonwealth v. Dunn, 407 Mass. 798, 807 (1990). See also Section 404(b), Character Evidence; Crimes or Other Acts: Crimes, Wrongs, or Other Acts.

Confusion of Issues and Misleading the Jury. The trial judge has discretion to exclude relevant evidence if it has potential for confusing and misleading the fact finder. Commonwealth v. Rosa, 422 Mass. 18, 25 (1996); Commonwealth v. Beausoleil, 397 Mass. 206, 217 (1986); Lally v. Volkswagen Aktiengesellschaft, 45 Mass. App. Ct. 317, 332 (1998) (admissibility of a test, experiment, or reenactment requires consideration of "whether the evidence is relevant, the extent to which the test conditions are similar to the circumstances surrounding the accident, and whether the [experiment, demonstration, or reenactment] will confuse or mislead the jury" [quotation and citation omitted]). See Commonwealth v. Dabney, 478 Mass. 839, 859–860 (2018) (exclusion of impeachment evidence consisting of advertising invoices is not an abuse of discretion where the admission of such evidence was likely to confuse the jury in the absence of company testimony explaining record-keeping practices).

Unnecessarily Time Consuming. The trial judge has discretion to exclude evidence if it is unduly time consuming. Commonwealth v. Cruz, 53 Mass. App. Ct. 393, 407–408 (2001).

Cumulative Evidence. The trial judge has discretion to exclude evidence if it is merely cumulative. Commonwealth v. Bonds, 445 Mass. 821, 831 (2006). See Fitchburg Gas & Elec. Light Co. v. Department of Telecomm. & Energy, 440 Mass. 625, 641 (2004) (no error in excluding testimony that would be "merely cumulative of the uncontroverted evidence"); Commonwealth v. Taghizadeh, 28 Mass. App. Ct. 52, 60–61 (1989) (evidence that is relevant to an essential element of a crime, claim, or defense is not cumulative and subject to

exclusion simply because an opposing party offers to stipulate to the fact at issue). See also Old Chief v. United States, 519 U.S. 172 (1997).

Courtroom Experiments and Demonstrations. In order to admit evidence of an in-court or out-of-court demonstration or experiment, the proponent must establish to the satisfaction of the judge that "the conditions or circumstances were in general the same in the illustrative case and the case in hand." Commonwealth v. Makarewicz, 333 Mass. 575, 592 (1956). See, e.g., Commonwealth v. Corliss, 470 Mass. 443, 454–456 (2015) (judge did not abuse his discretion by excluding video of perpetrator committing the offense with a superimposed height chart created by defense expert on grounds that under the circumstances it was misleading; judge did admit height chart as a separate exhibit, along with expert witness testimony about limitations of the surveillance video); Commonwealth v. McGee, 469 Mass. 1, 7 (2014) (judge did not abuse his discretion in permitting child witness, then six years old, to use a couch to demonstrate how victim was positioned as defendant killed her); Commonwealth v. Perryman, 55 Mass. App. Ct. 187, 192–193 (2002) (judge did not abuse her discretion in permitting jurors during trial to look through telescope used by police officer to spot defendant in alleged drug transaction).

Evidence of Similar Occurrences. Evidence of similar occurrences may be admitted if there is substantial identity between the occurrences and there is minimal danger of unfairness, jury confusion, or wasted time. See Denton v. Park Hotel, Inc., 343 Mass. 524, 527 (1962); Robitaille v. Netoco Community Theatre of N. Attleboro, Inc., 305 Mass. 265, 267–268 (1940). The test of substantial identity is "fact and case specific, ... one of relevance." Dubuque v. Cumberland Farms, Inc., 93 Mass. App. Ct. 332, 345 (2018) (internal report describing 485 car strikes at Cumberland Farms locations properly admitted because it was substantially similar, "relevant to the jury's consideration of whether the risk was foreseeable and whether Cumberland Farms was aware of that risk"). The nonoccurrence of an event may be admissible to rebut an allegation that a dangerous condition existed at a particular time. Haskell v. Boat Clinton–Serafina, Inc., 412 F.2d 896, 896–897 (1st Cir. 1969).

The requirement of substantial identity is not met when the other occurrence or occurrences "may have been the consequence of idiosyncratic circumstances" and therefore irrelevant to the case being tried. Read v. Mt. Tom Ski Area, Inc., 37 Mass. App. Ct. 901, 902 (1994); Robitaille v. Netoco Community Theatre of N. Attleboro, Inc., 305 Mass. at 266–267 (substantial identity in the circumstances is only the first element; "[u]nless a comparison of the circumstances and causes of the two injuries is made, the injury to another is without significance"). Evidence of similar occurrences may be admissible to show the following:

Causation. Carter v. Yardley & Co., 319 Mass. 92, 94 (1946) (other instances of skin irritation caused by defendant's perfume properly admitted to show causation); Shea v. Glendale Elastic Fabrics Co., 162 Mass. 463, 464–465 (1894) (evidence that other people who worked in the defendant's mill, under similar conditions, became ill from lead poisoning was admissible to prove cause of the illness). But see Reil v. Lowell Gas Co., 353 Mass. 120, 135–136 (1967) (after an explosion at a gas plant, evidence of multiple fires at that plant and another plant owned by the defendant were inadmissible because those incidents "would have been little help in determining the cause of the explosion on [the date in question]").

Notice. Santos v. Chrysler Corp., 430 Mass. 198, 202–205 (1999) (judge did not abuse her discretion in admitting the testimony of six Chrysler minivan owners regarding other braking incidents involving their minivans, as well as National Highway Transportation Safety Administration [NHTSA] vehicle owners' questionnaires submitted by the six owners to establish notice of defect); Elwell v. Del Torchio, 349 Mass. 766, 766 (1965) (Where the plaintiff was injured by a stairway railing giving way, "[t]here was no error in admitting the evidence of a similar accident occurring about a year before and disclosed to one of the defendants. Such testimony was relevant to show knowledge of the defect."). But see Crivello v. All–Pak Mach. Sys., 446 Mass. 729, 737–738 (2006) (evidence of prior accidents involving a bagging machine were properly excluded because the evidence did not establish that the defendants were aware of any accidents).

Rebuttal of Claim of Impossibility. Griffin v. General Motors Corp., 380 Mass. 362, 365–366 (1980) (results of an experiment on the air filtration system of the same model car that was at issue in the case were admissible to rebut the defendant's theory that it was impossible for fumes from the engine compartment to enter the passenger compartment).

Absence of Complaint. Carrel v. National Cord & Braid Corp., 447 Mass. 431, 447–448 (2006) (absence of oral or written complaints concerning a bungee cord admissible to rebut questions regarding failure to conduct product testing); Silver v. New York Cent. R.R. Co., 329 Mass. 14, 19–21 (1952) (evidence that eleven other passengers in the plaintiff's train car did not complain about the temperature to a porter would be admissible if the other passengers were in a substantially similar situation, if the porter's duties included receiving such complaints and he was present to receive complaints on that day, and if it was unlikely that the other passengers complained to another employee); Schuler v. Union News Co., 295 Mass. 350, 352 (1936) (absence of complaints of illness after people ate at defendant's restaurant was admissible to rebut claim that the defendant's turkey sandwich caused the plaintiff's sickness).

Absence of Dangerous Condition. Haskell v. Boat Clinton–Serafina, Inc., 412 F.2d 896, 896–897 (1st Cir. 1969) (evidence that no similar accidents had occurred was admissible to rebut a claim that the plaintiff slipped on a thick patch of slime on the deck of the ship). But see Marvin v. City of New Bedford, 158 Mass. 464, 467 (1893) (evidence that no accidents had occurred on a highway was inadmissible to prove that a defect in the road did not exist).

Foreseeability. Whitaker v. Saraceno, 418 Mass. 196, 199 (1994) (previous occurrences of similar criminal acts on defendant's premises may be considered in determining whether the event in question was foreseeable).

Exclusion as a Sanction. See Section 103(g), Rulings on Evidence, Objections, and Offers of Proof: Exclusion as Sanction; Section 1102, Spoliation or Destruction of Evidence.

Constitutional Considerations. In a criminal case, the defendant has a constitutional right to present a complete defense; however, this right does not deprive the trial judge of discretion to exclude evidence that is repetitive, only marginally relevant, or that creates an undue risk of unfair prejudice or confusion of the issues. See Commonwealth v. Kartell, 58 Mass. App. Ct. 428, 433 n.2 (2003). See also Commonwealth v. Carroll, 439 Mass. 547, 552 (2003); Commonwealth v. Edgerly, 372 Mass. 337, 343 (1977); Commonwealth v. Strickland, 87 Mass. App. Ct. 46, 54–55 (2015).

Weapons Evidence. Evidence that the defendant possessed a weapon that could have been used to commit the crime is admissible to show that the defendant had the means to commit the crime. See, e.g., Commonwealth v. Barbosa, 463 Mass. 116, 122 (2012); Commonwealth v. Ashman, 430 Mass. 736, 744 (2000); Commonwealth v. Toro, 395 Mass. 354, 356 (1985). See also Commonwealth v. Vazquez, 478 Mass. 443, 449 (2017) (no abuse of discretion to admit evidence of prior possession of firearm absent definitive forensic evidence that it could not have been used in commission of the crime). The evidence need not establish that the defendant possessed the weapon at the time the crime was committed. See Commonwealth v. Corliss, 470 Mass. 443, 450–451 (2015) (sixteen months before murder); Commonwealth v. McLaughlin, 352 Mass. 218, 229–230 (1967) (approximately one year after murder). See also Commonwealth v. Holley, 478 Mass. 508, 532–534 (2017) (evidence of prior gun theft was relevant to show that defendant had means of committing the crime; risk that jury would use evidence to conclude that defendant "had a propensity to commit this particular crime was low" where type of crime charged in underlying matter was different); Commonwealth v. Brown, 477 Mass. 805,

820 (2017) (photographs taken a few weeks prior to the crime showing defendant brandishing firearm used in commission of the crime admissible). By contrast, evidence of a type of weapon unconnected to the crime is generally inadmissible. See Commonwealth v. Veiovis, 477 Mass. 472, 486 (2017) (error to admit evidence of spiked baseball bat because there was "no evidence" that the bat could have been used to commit the crime); Commonwealth v. Valentin, 474 Mass. 301, 305–308 (2016) (evidence of defendant's "ownership of weapons other than the weapon used in the shootings" had little or no relevance and portrayed the defendant "as someone who was likely to commit murder, the crime with which he was charged"). Evidence of a firearm not connected to the crime may be admissible for the limited purpose of demonstrating that the defendant had access to, and knowledge of, firearms. Commonwealth v. Holley, 478 Mass. at 533. However, the evidence should be excluded if its probative value is outweighed by the danger of unfair prejudice to the defendant. See Commonwealth v. McGee, 467 Mass. 141, 157–158 (2014); Commonwealth v. Barbosa, 463 Mass. 116, 122–123 (2012).

Limiting Instruction. A limiting instruction to the jury as to the proper use of evidence that the defendant possessed a weapon that could have been used in the commission of the crime is not required. Commonwealth v. Holley, 478 Mass. at 533 n.25. In contrast, where a weapon could not have been used in the commission of the crime, a limiting instruction to the jury as to the proper use of the evidence is "often" required. Id.

Section 404. Character Evidence; Crimes or Other Acts

(a) Character Evidence.

(1) Prohibited Uses. Evidence of a person's character or a character trait is not admissible to prove that on a particular occasion the person acted in accordance with the character or trait.

(2) Exceptions for a Defendant or Victim in a Criminal Case. The following exceptions apply in a criminal case:

(A) a defendant may offer evidence, in reputation form only, of the defendant's pertinent trait, and if the evidence is admitted, the prosecutor may offer evidence to rebut it;

(B) where the identity of the first aggressor or the first to use deadly force is in dispute, a defendant may offer evidence of specific incidents of violence allegedly initiated by the victim, or by a third party acting in concert with or to assist the victim, whether known or unknown to the defendant, and the prosecution may rebut the same with specific incidents of violence by the defendant; and

(C) a defendant may offer evidence known to the defendant prior to the incident in question of the victim's reputation for violence, of specific instances of the victim's violent conduct, or of statements made by the victim that caused reasonable apprehension of violence on the part of the defendant.

(3) Exceptions for a Witness. Evidence of a witness's character for truthfulness or untruthfulness may be admitted under Sections 607, 608, and 609.

(b) Crimes, Wrongs, or Other Acts.

(1) Prohibited Uses. Evidence of a crime, wrong, or other act is not admissible to prove a person's character in order to show that on a particular occasion the person acted in accordance with the character.

(2) Permitted Uses. This evidence may be admissible for another purpose, such as proving motive, opportunity, intent, preparation, plan, knowledge, identity, absence of mistake, or lack of accident. However, evidence of other bad acts is inadmissible where its probative value is outweighed by the risk of unfair prejudice to the defendant, even if not substantially outweighed by that risk. Evidence of such an act is not admissible in a criminal case against a defendant who was prosecuted for that act and acquitted.

NOTE

Subsection (a). This subsection is derived from Commonwealth v. Helfant, 398 Mass. 214, 224 (1986), and Commonwealth v. Bonds, 445 Mass. 821, 829 (2006). Massachusetts follows the universally recognized rule against "propensity" evidence, i.e., evidence of a person's character through reputation or specific acts (see Section 404[b]) offered to suggest that the person acted in conformity with that character or trait on the occasion in question is inadmissible. See Maillet v. ATF–Davidson Co., 407 Mass. 185, 187–188 (1990); Commonwealth v. Doherty, 23 Mass. App. Ct. 633, 636–637 (1987). See also Commonwealth v. Reddy, 85 Mass. App. Ct. 104, 108 (2014) (admission of unredacted Chapter 209A order that stated "THERE IS A SUBSTANTIAL LIKELIHOOD OF IMMEDIATE DANGER OF ABUSE" was error in prosecution for violation of order, as it constituted improper predictive or propensity evidence). In Figueiredo v. Hamill, 385 Mass. 1003, 1003–1005 (1982), for example, the Supreme Judicial Court explained the difference between evidence of habit (a regular way of doing things) and evidence of character (a general description of one's disposition), and held that evidence offered by the defendant that the decedent acted in a "habitually reckless manner" was inadmissible evidence of the decedent's character. There is a distinction between criminal profile evidence (evidence of whether the defendant shares characteristics common to individuals who commit a particular crime) and character evidence (traits personal to the defendant). Commonwealth v. Coates, 89 Mass. App. Ct. 728, 735 (2016) (holding that criminal profile evidence offered to show that defendant did not have pedophilic tendencies was irrelevant and inadmissible). The prosecution may not offer in its case-in-chief evidence that the defendant is a violent or dishonest person in order to demonstrate that the defendant has a propensity to commit the crime charged. Commonwealth v. Mullane, 445 Mass. 702, 708–709 (2006). See also Commonwealth v. Roe, 90 Mass. App. Ct. 801, 807–808 (2016) (even where normally inadmissible evidence of character may be admitted for permissible purpose, failure to guide jury on their use of this evidence through proper instruction is prejudicial error). But see Commonwealth v. Adjutant, 443 Mass. 649, 664 (2005), discussed in the notes to Section 404(a)(2)(B). As Justice Cardozo stated, "the law has set its face against the endeavor to fasten guilt upon him by proof of character or experience predisposing to an act of crime." People v. Zackowitz, 254 N.Y. 192, 197, 172 N.E. 466, 468 (1930).

While Section 404(a) applies in both civil and criminal cases, the exceptions in (2) apply only in criminal cases, while the exception in (3) applies in both civil and criminal cases.

Subsection (a)(2)(A). This subsection is derived from Commonwealth v. Nagle, 157 Mass. 554, 554–555 (1893), and Commonwealth v. Brown, 411 Mass. 115, 117–118 (1991). According to long-standing practice, the defendant may introduce evidence of his or her own good character—in reputation form only—to show that he or she is not the type of person to commit the crime charged. See Commonwealth v. Belton, 352 Mass. 263, 267–269 (1967). The defendant is limited to introducing reputation evidence of traits that are involved in the charged crime. Commonwealth v. Beal, 314 Mass. 210, 229–230 (1943).

The prosecution has the right to cross-examine for impeachment purposes the defendant's character witnesses on matters that are inconsistent with the character trait to which the witness has testified, including specific instances of bad conduct or criminal activity. See Commonwealth v. Oliveira, 74 Mass. App. Ct. 49, 53 (2009) (When, in a prosecution for assault and battery, the defendant testified to his character for peacefulness, the trial judge did not abuse her discretion by ruling that the Commonwealth was entitled to cross-examine the defendant based on his prior convictions for the same offenses involving the same victim to rebut his credibility as to his character, even though the Commonwealth's motion in limine to use these prior convictions for impeachment purposes had been denied prior to trial.). See also Section 405(a), Methods of Proving Character: By Reputation. The prosecution may also present rebuttal evidence of the defendant's bad character in reputation form. Commonwealth v. Maddocks, 207 Mass. 152, 157 (1910).

Subsection (a)(2)(B). This subsection is derived from Commonwealth v. Adjutant, 443 Mass. 649, 664 (2005); Commonwealth v. Pring–Wilson, 448 Mass. 718, 737 (2007); and Commonwealth v. Chambers, 465 Mass. 520, 529–530 (2013). Where a claim of self-defense is asserted and the identity of the first aggressor is in dispute, trial courts have discretion to admit a defendant's evidence of specific incidents of violence allegedly initiated by the victim even if unknown to the defendant. Commonwealth v. Adjutant, 443 Mass. at 664. The Adjutant rule does not permit evidence of the victim's participation in athletic activities such as boxing or martial arts on the issue of whether the victim was the first aggressor, although such activities may, if known to the defendant, be relevant to a claim of self-defense based on the defendant's reasonable fear of the victim. Commonwealth v. Amaral, 78 Mass. App. Ct. 557, 559 (2011). If known to the defendant, the specific act evidence goes to the defendant's state of mind, Commonwealth v. Simpson, 434 Mass. 570, 577 (2001); if the defendant was not aware of the violent acts of the victim, the evidence goes merely to the propensity of the victim to attack. Commonwealth v. Adjutant, 443 Mass. at 661–662. See generally id. at 665 (courts "favor the admission of concrete and relevant evidence of specific acts over more general evidence of the victim's reputation for violence"). The rule announced in Commonwealth v. Adjutant is a "new common-law rule of evidence" to be applied prospectively only. Id. at 667. See also Commonwealth v. Clemente, 452 Mass. 295, 304–305 (2008) (declining to apply the Adjutant rule retrospectively). Judicial discretion to admit evidence of specific acts of violence on the question of who was the first aggressor extends to third parties acting in concert with or to assist the victim. Commonwealth v. Lopes, 89 Mass. App. Ct. 560, 564 (2016). Where the identity of either the initial aggressor or the first person to use or threaten deadly force is not in dispute, evidence of the victim's history of violence is not admissible. See Commonwealth v. Vargas, 475 Mass. 338, 346–348 (2016) (victim's history of violence inadmissible where both defendant and prosecution witnesses were "consistent in their portrayal of the victim as the initial aggressor").

If the defendant introduces evidence of specific instances of the victim's violent conduct to help establish the identity of the first aggressor, the prosecution may rebut by introducing evidence of the victim's propensity for peacefulness. Commonwealth v. Adjutant, 443 Mass. at 666 n.19. See Commonwealth v. Lapointe, 402 Mass. 321, 325 (1988). The Commonwealth is also permitted to rebut such evidence by introducing specific instances of the defendant's prior violent acts. Commonwealth v. Morales, 464 Mass. 302, 310–311 (2013). In such cases, as in traditional Adjutant-type cases, the judge must exercise discretion and determine whether the probative value of the proposed testimony about who was the first to use deadly force is substantially outweighed by its prejudicial effect. Commonwealth v. Chambers, 465 Mass. 520, 531 (2013).

Cross–Reference: Section 412, Sexual Behavior or Sexual Reputation (Rape–Shield Law).

Subsection (a)(2)(C). This subsection is derived from Commonwealth v. Sok, 439 Mass. 428, 434–435 (2003), and Commonwealth v. Fontes, 396 Mass. 733, 735–736 (1986). The evidence may be offered to prove the defendant's state of mind and the reasonableness of his or her actions in claiming to have acted in self-defense so long as the defendant knew about it prior to the incident in question. See Commonwealth v. Edmonds, 365 Mass. 496, 502 (1974).

Subsection (a)(3). This subsection is derived from Commonwealth v. Daley, 439 Mass. 558, 563 (2003). See Notes to Sections 607, Who May Impeach a Witness; 608, A Witness's Character for Truthfulness or Untruthfulness; and 609, Impeachment by Evidence of Conviction of Crime.

Subsection (b)(1). This subsection is derived from Commonwealth v. Clifford, 374 Mass. 293, 298 (1978), and Maillet v. ATF–Davidson Co., 407 Mass. 185, 188 (1990). Evidence of a prior bad act may not be admitted to show the defendant has a bad character or a propensity to commit the crime charged. See Commonwealth v. Valentin, 474 Mass. 301, 307–308 (2016) (admission of evidence concerning defendant's ownership of weapons other than weapon used to commit crime was improper because it "portrayed him as someone who was likely to commit murder, the crime which was charged"). "This rule stems from the belief that such evidence forces the defendant to answer accusations not set forth in the indictment, confuses his defense, diverts the attention of the jury, and may create undue prejudice against him." Commonwealth v. Clifford, 374 Mass. at 298. Even evidence of lawful conduct can be excluded as a prior "bad act." See Commonwealth v. Valentin, 474 Mass. at 307–308 (lawful ownership of weapons and ammunition). This rule applies to both civil and criminal cases. Maillet v. ATF–Davidson Co., 407 Mass. at 188 (evidence that plaintiff once before had a beer at work at an unspecified time and date prior to workplace accident).

Subsection (b)(2). This subsection is derived from Commonwealth v. Crayton, 470 Mass. 228 (2014); Commonwealth v. Helfant, 398 Mass. 214, 224–225 (1986); and G. L. c. 233, § 23F. "[W]hile evidence of other ... wrongful behavior may not be admitted to prove the character or propensity of the accused as enhancing the probability that he committed the offence[,] ... it is admissible for other relevant probative purposes." Commonwealth v. Tobin, 392 Mass. 604, 613 (1984), quoting Commonwealth v. Chalifoux, 362 Mass. 811, 815–816 (1973). See Commonwealth v. Rutherford, 476 Mass. 639, 649 (2017) (uncharged conduct involving possession of weapons permissible to show defendant's state of mind; prejudicial impact limited by prompt and thorough limiting instruction); Commonwealth v. McGee, 467 Mass. 141, 156 (2014) (firearm that could not have been used to shoot victim, but that was offered to establish that defendant was familiar with firearms, was admissible only if accompanied by limiting instruction that it could not be taken as propensity evidence).

Thus, the prosecution may not offer proof of the defendant's other bank robberies to paint the defendant as a "bank robber" or criminal type; but if the modus operandi of a prior bank robbery functions as an identifying feature because it is so distinctive as to be like a signature, it may be admitted to connect the defendant to the bank robbery which shares the same modus operandi. See Commonwealth v. Jackson, 428 Mass. 455, 459–460 (1998). See also Huddleston v. United States, 485 U.S. 681, 685 (1988) (noting that Fed. R. Evid. 404(b) "applies in both civil and criminal cases"); Dahms v. Cognex Corp., 455 Mass. 190, 201 (2009) (trial judge did not err when, after careful consideration, he admitted evidence of female employee's clothing, speech, and conduct, which was admissible in context of sexually hostile work environment to show she was not substantially offended by employer, not barred as irrelevant character and propensity evidence).

It is not a foundational requirement for the admissibility of other bad act evidence under Section 404(b) that the Commonwealth show either that the evidence is necessary or that there is no alternative way to prove its case. Commonwealth v. Copney, 468 Mass. 405, 411–413 (2014).

Evidence of prior crimes or other bad acts is not admissible unless, as a matter of conditional relevance—see Section 104(b), Preliminary Questions: Relevance That Depends on a Fact—the judge is satisfied that a reasonable jury could find that the event took place. Commonwealth v. Leonard, 428 Mass. 782, 785–786 (1999).

The evidence must be probative of a subsidiary fact at issue and not be too remote in time. Commonwealth v. Butler, 445 Mass. 568, 574 (2005); Commonwealth v. Trapp, 396 Mass. 202, 206–207 (1985). The same standards govern the admission of subsequent bad acts. Commonwealth v. Centeno, 87 Mass. App. Ct. 564, 566–567 (2015). See also Commonwealth v. Crayton, 470 Mass. 228, 248–252 (2014) (in prosecution for possession of child pornography on library computer, abuse of discretion to admit handdrawn, pornographic sketches of children found in defendant's jail cell ten months after charged event, where primary factual issue was identity of person who used the library computer to view child pornography).

Prior bad acts against someone other than the victim may be admissible if connected in time, place, or other relevant circumstances. Commonwealth v. Robertson, 88 Mass. App. Ct. 52, 55 (2015).

Due to the "inherent prejudice" associated with evidence of other bad acts, even when such evidence is relevant for a proper purpose other than propensity, the evidence should be excluded whenever "the risk of unfair prejudice outweighs its probative value." Commonwealth v. Crayton, 470 Mass. at 249 & n.27. See Commonwealth v. Woollam, 478 Mass. 493, 500–501 (2017) (where offered to establish motive in prosecution for first-degree murder, "testimony regarding the changes in the defendant once he began using drugs" was "more prejudicial than probative" where it included statement that defendant had become "a little more violent"). This is a more exacting standard than the standard set forth in Section 403, Excluding Relevant Evidence for Prejudice, Confusion, Waste of Time, or Other Reasons. When an objection to a prior bad act is raised, the judge's weighing of the probative value and prejudicial effect of the challenged evidence should be placed on the record for the benefit of the parties and the appellate court. Commonwealth v. Proia, 92 Mass. App. Ct. 824, 828 n.7 (2018).

As the Appeals Court has observed, "all cases where prior bad acts are offered invite consideration of the potency of this type of evidence, the risk that it may be misused, and the importance, in jury trials, of delivering careful limiting instructions." Commonwealth v. Gollman, 51 Mass. App. Ct. 839, 845 (2001), rev'd on other grounds, 436 Mass. 111, 113–115 (2002) (extensive discussion). See Commonwealth v. Roe, 90 Mass. App. Ct. 801, 807 (2016) (conviction reversed where witness testified to prior bad act ruled inadmissible in earlier motion in limine and judge failed to give full and prompt curative instruction). See generally Peter W. Agnes, Jr., Guided Discretion in Massachusetts Evidence Law: Standards for the Admissibility of Prior Bad Acts Against the Defendant, 13 Suffolk J. Trial & App. Advoc. 1 (2008).

Even if the evidence of another bad act is found to be more probative than unfairly prejudicial, it may be barred by the collateral estoppel principles of Article 12 of the Massachusetts Declaration of Rights if the defendant was prosecuted for the prior act and acquitted. See Commonwealth v. Dorazio, 472 Mass. 535, 547–548 (2015).

The corroboration requirement of G. L. c. 277, § 63, is not satisfied without independent corroborating evidence of the "specific criminal act at issue" and cannot be satisfied with only evidence of uncharged sexual misconduct. Commonwealth v. White, 475 Mass. 724, 736–738 (2016).

Cross–Reference: Section 105, Limited Admissibility; Section 403, Grounds for Excluding Relevant Evidence; Section 405, Methods of Proving Character; Section 406, Routine Practice of Business; Individual Habit; Section 611(b)(2), Manner and Order of Interrogation and Presentation: Scope of Cross–Examination: Bias and Prejudice.

Illustrations.

- *Criminal Activity.* Commonwealth v. Brown, 477 Mass. 805, 819–820 (2017) (evidence of uncharged armed robbery occurring earlier in day introduced to prove coventurer's intent to participate in subsequent armed robbery later that evening); Commonwealth v. Mazariego, 474 Mass. 42, 56 (2016) (history of bringing prostitutes to location relevant to show intent, similarity in location of past encounters, absence of mistake, and level of involvement in planning crime); Commonwealth v. Robidoux, 450 Mass. 144, 158 (2007) (evidence of prior starvation of child properly admitted to present full picture of events surrounding incident at issue); Commonwealth v. Walker, 442 Mass. 185, 201–203 (2004) (evidence tending to show that defendant previously engaged in similar, uncharged, criminal behavior admissible to show plan, common scheme, or course of conduct); Commonwealth v. Source One Assocs., Inc., 436 Mass. 118, 128–129 (2002) (trial judge properly allowed evidence of telephone calls similar to ones at issue at trial for purposes of showing that defendants were familiar with using ruses and false pretenses to obtain personal financial information); Commonwealth v. Leonard, 428 Mass. 782, 785, 787–788 (1999) (evidence of uncharged prior arson in murder prosecution properly admitted to show identity/modus operandi); Commonwealth v. Cordle, 404 Mass. 733, 736, 743–744 (1989) (evidence of prior break-in for which defendant was arrested and charged but never prosecuted properly admitted to show entire relationship between victim and defendant, state of mind, identification, knowledge, and motive).

- *Defense of Entrapment.* For cases involving the defense of entrapment, compare Commonwealth v. Buswell, 468 Mass. 92, 104–105 (2014) (admissibility of prior bad acts when defense is entrapment), with Commonwealth v. Denton, 477 Mass. 248, 252 (2017) (risk of prejudice may require exclusion if prior bad acts are too remote in time).

- *Domestic Violence.* Commonwealth v. Almeida, 479 Mass. 562, 567–569 (2018) (evidence of defendant's previous threat to stab his girlfriend to death admissible to show the parties' violent relationship); Commonwealth v. Oberle, 476 Mass. 539, 550–552 (2017) (allowing previous domestic violence incident by defendant against victim to be admitted in prosecution for subsequent domestic violence to show nature of relationship between the two, and to show intent, motive, and absence of mistake or accident); Commonwealth v. Miller, 475 Mass. 212, 229–230 (2016) (evidence of domestic violence committed by defendant against his girlfriend, which led to confrontation between defendant and murder victim, properly admitted to show "contentious nature" of relationship between defendant and victim, which provided motive for killing).

- *Drug Use.* Commonwealth v. O'Laughlin, 446 Mass. 188, 208–209 (2006) (evidence that defendant smoked crack cocaine and sought to obtain additional cocaine the night of the incident relevant to prove motive to rob to get more drugs); Commonwealth v. Mendes, 441 Mass. 459, 466 (2004) (defendant's history of spending his wife's money on drugs and prostitutes and prior arguments over financial issues properly admitted to prove financial motive for wife's murder).

- *Gang Affiliation.* Commonwealth v. Lopes, 478 Mass. 593, 604–605 (2018) (evidence of gang affiliation admissible to show motive and intent); Commonwealth v. Akara, 465 Mass. 245, 267–268 (2013) (use of gang affiliation to establish joint venture between codefendants).

- *Grooming Evidence.* Commonwealth v. McDonagh, 480 Mass. 131, 135 n.6 (2018) (evidence of grooming, e.g., exposing a child to child pornography to reduce the child's inhibitions for sexual activity with defendant, may be admissible if relevant for nonpropensity purposes).

- *Incarceration.* Commonwealth v. Rakes, 478 Mass. 22, 42–44 (2017) (evidence of defendant's prior incarceration, including certificate of parole, VAX transportation sheet, and booking sheet page with attached photographs, along with his statement that he "wasn't about to do any more time," admissible to prove defendant's identity and motive to kill victim).

- *Police Investigations.* Commonwealth v. Mullane, 445 Mass. 702, 708–710 (2006) (evidence of prior investigation into prostitution at

commercial property properly admitted to prove property owner's knowledge of illicit sexual activity occurring at property).

- *Possession of a Gun.* Commonwealth v. Howard, 479 Mass. 52, 66–67 (2018) (testimony that defendant had gun in vehicle before victim was hired admissible to rebut defendant's claim that he had brought gun to work due to fear of victim).

- *Prior Sexual Offenses.* Commonwealth v. Childs, 94 Mass. App. Ct. 67, 71–75, 78–79 (2018) (evidence of uncharged conduct was properly admitted to show that the relationship between the defendant and the victim "was one of continuous sexual abuse" and to rebut any claim of accident or mistake where the judge excluded the "two most damaging incidents of uncharged conduct," the uncharged conduct did not overwhelm the evidence of charged conduct, and the judge "forcefully limited" the jury's use of the uncharged conduct through limiting instructions "before the victim's testimony about the uncharged conduct, again after that testimony, and yet a third time in the final charge").

- *Racial Animus.* Commonwealth v. Cruzado, 480 Mass. 275, 278–279 (2018) (defendant's use of highly charged racial slur in reference to murder victim properly admitted to show animus toward African–Americans and therefore motive for killing).

- *Statements.* Commonwealth v. Sullivan, 436 Mass. 799, 809 (2002) (evidence that defendant stated that he liked to rob jewelry stores properly admitted to prove intent to commit robbery in felony-murder prosecution); Commonwealth v. Bradshaw, 86 Mass. App. Ct. 74, 76 (2014) (in prosecution for rape of child, defendant's statement that he was attracted to young boys was admissible for limited purpose of revealing his motive or intent).

- *Violent Interests or Conduct.* Commonwealth v. Veiovis, 477 Mass. 472, 482–486 (2017) (where evidence showed that unidentified perpetrator "enjoyed cutting the victims up," amputation drawings from defendant's home admissible to show identity, state of mind, and motive; drawings were not modus operandi evidence); Commonwealth v. Forte, 469 Mass. 469, 480 (2014) (instances of aggressive conduct in hours preceding murder to illustrate angry state of mind).

Section 405. Methods of Proving Character

(a) By Reputation. Except as provided in (b) and (c), when evidence of a person's character or a character trait is admissible, it may be proved by testimony about the person's reputation only. On cross-examination of the character witness, the court may allow impeachment by an inquiry into relevant specific instances of the person's conduct.

(b) By Specific Instances of Conduct. When a person's character or a character trait is an essential element of a charge, claim, or defense, the character or trait may also be proved by relevant specific instances of the person's conduct.

(c) By Violent Character of the Victim. See Section 404(a)(2), Character Evidence; Crimes or Other Acts: Character Evidence: Exceptions for a Defendant or Victim in a Criminal Case.

NOTE

Subsection (a). This subsection is derived from Commonwealth v. Roberts, 378 Mass. 116, 129 (1979), and Commonwealth v. Piedra, 20 Mass. App. Ct. 155, 160 (1985). Character may only be introduced through evidence of general reputation, except as provided by G. L. c. 233, § 21 (evidence of person's prior conviction is admissible to impeach his or her credibility), and Section 609, Impeachment by Evidence of Conviction of Crime. See Commonwealth v. Binkiewicz, 342 Mass. 740, 755 (1961). Unlike Federal law, general reputation cannot be proven by evidence of personal opinions or isolated acts. Commonwealth v. Walker, 442 Mass. 185, 198–199 (2004); Commonwealth v. Benjamin, 430 Mass. 673, 678 n.6 (2000). Reputation evidence must be based on one's reputation in the community or at that person's place of work or business. Commonwealth v. Walker, 442 Mass. at 198. See G. L. c. 233, § 21A (work or business); Commonwealth v. Dockham, 405 Mass. 618, 631 (1989) (community). A witness's testimony must be based on the witness's knowledge of the person's reputation in the community, not of the opinions of a limited number of people. Commonwealth v. Gomes, 11 Mass. App. Ct. 933, 933–934 (1981); Commonwealth v. LaPierre, 10 Mass. App. Ct. 871, 871 (1980). Contrast Commonwealth v. Walker, 442 Mass. at 197–199 (declining to adopt Proposed Mass. R. Evid. 405[a], which would permit character witnesses to testify not only about the defendant's reputation in the community, but also about their own opinion of the defendant's character).

A witness who testifies to a person's reputation is then subject to cross-examination for impeachment purposes "as to his awareness of rumors or reports of prior acts of misconduct by the [person], including prior arrests or convictions, that are inconsistent or conflict with the character trait to which the witness has testified." Commonwealth v. Montanino, 27 Mass. App. Ct. 130, 136 (1989). The prosecution may also present rebuttal evidence of a defendant's bad reputation. Commonwealth v. Maddocks, 207 Mass. 152, 157 (1910).

Subsection (b). This subsection is derived from Care & Protection of Martha, 407 Mass. 319, 325 n.6 (1990). "[P]ast parental conduct [is] relevant to the issue of current parental fitness where that conduct [is] not too remote, especially where the evidence support[s] the continuing vitality of such conduct." Adoption of Larry, 434 Mass. 456, 469 (2001). For example, a person's prior criminal history as maintained by the Commissioner of Probation (a Criminal Activity Record Information report) is admissible where character is directly at issue, as in child custody and adoption cases. See Custody of Vaughn, 422 Mass. 590 (1996) (domestic violence); Care & Protection of Frank, 409 Mass. 492 (1991) (substance abuse); Custody of Two Minors, 396 Mass. 610, 621 (1986) ("prior patterns of parental neglect or misconduct"). Specific act evidence may be admitted in those cases where character is directly at issue, such as negligent entrustment actions, see Leone v. Doran, 363 Mass. 1, 13–14, modified on other grounds, 363 Mass. 886 (1973); negligent hiring actions, see Foster v. Loft, Inc., 26 Mass. App. Ct. 289, 290–291 (1988); and when a defendant raises the defense of entrapment, see Commonwealth v. Buswell, 468 Mass. 92, 104–105 (2014).

Subsection (c). See Notes to Section 404(a)(2), Character Evidence; Crimes or Other Acts: Character Evidence: Exceptions for a Defendant or Victim in a Criminal Case.

Section 406.   Routine Practice of a Business; Habit of an Individual

(a) Routine Practice of a Business. Evidence of the routine practice of a business organization or of one acting in a business capacity, if established through sufficient proof, may be admitted to prove that on a particular occasion the organization or individual acted in accordance with the routine practice.

(b) Individual Habit. Evidence of an individual's personal habit is not admissible to prove action in conformity with the habit on a particular occasion.

NOTE

This section is derived from Palinkas v. Bennett, 416 Mass. 273, 276–277 (1993). "A habit is a regular response to a repeated situation with a specific type of conduct." Id. at 277. A trial judge has discretion in distinguishing between a routine practice of a business and a personal habit. Id.

Subsection (a). Evidence of a routine practice or custom of a business is admissible to prove that the business acted in conformity therewith. See, e.g., Commonwealth v. Torrealba, 316 Mass. 24, 30

(1944) (custom of selling goods with receipt); Santarpio v. New York Life Ins. Co., 301 Mass. 207, 210 (1938) (custom of submitting insurance applications); Prudential Trust Co. v. Hayes, 247 Mass. 311, 314–315 (1924) (custom of sending letters).

"Massachusetts draws a distinction between evidence of personal habit and evidence of business habit or custom. Evidence of a person's habits is inadmissible to prove whether an act was performed in accordance with the habit ... [F]or the purpose of proving that one has or has not done a particular act, it is not competent to show that he has or has not been in the habit of doing other similar acts. Despite this rule, evidence of business habits or customs is admissible to prove that an act was performed in accordance with the habit ... The fact that a habit is done by only one individual does not bar it from being a business habit." (Quotation and citations omitted.)

Palinkas v. Bennett, 416 Mass. 273, 276 (1993). See Ladd v. Scudder Kemper Invs., Inc., 433 Mass. 240, 243 (2001) (business includes sole proprietorship); Mumford v. Coghlin, 249 Mass. 184, 188 (1924) (notary's procedure of protesting notes); Mayberry v. Holbrook, 182 Mass. 463, 465 (1903) (physician's records of rendering services). A person is competent to testify about a routine business practice if the person is familiar with the practice. O'Connor v. SmithKline Bio–Science Labs., Inc., 36 Mass. App. Ct. 360, 365 (1994). Cf. Section 601, Competency.

Subsection (b). Unlike Federal practice, evidence of an individual's personal habit is not admissible to prove action in conformity therewith. See Davidson v. Massachusetts Cas. Ins. Co., 325 Mass. 115, 122 (1949). See also Commonwealth v. Wilson, 443 Mass. 122, 138 (2004) (owner's personal, not business, habit of locking door would be inadmissible); Figueiredo v. Hamill, 385 Mass. 1003, 1004–1005 (1982) (evidence that pedestrian accident victim habitually acted in reckless manner properly excluded).

Habit Versus Character. The distinction between habit and character is often difficult to make: habit "is the person's regular practice of meeting a particular kind of situation with a specific type of conduct," whereas character "is a generalized description of one's disposition, or of one's disposition in respect to a general trait, such as honesty, temperance, or peacefulness." Figueiredo v. Hamill, 385 Mass. at 1004, quoting Advisory Committee Notes, Fed. R. Evid. 406.

Section 407.   Subsequent Remedial Measures

(a) Prohibited Uses. When measures are taken that would have made an earlier injury or harm less likely to occur, evidence of the subsequent measures is not admissible to prove negligence or culpable conduct in connection with the event.

(b) Exceptions. The court may admit this evidence for another purpose, such as impeachment or, if disputed, proving ownership, control, or the feasibility of precautionary measures.

NOTE

This section is derived from doCanto v. Ametek, Inc., 367 Mass. 776, 780 (1975), and Simmons v. Monarch Mach. Tool Co., 413 Mass. 205, 214 (1992), abrogated on other grounds by Vassallo v. Baxter Healthcare Corp., 428 Mass. 1, 20–23 (1998).

Subsection (a). Evidence of the following subsequent remedial measures has been excluded: sanding stairs or the street, Barnett v. Lynn, 433 Mass. 662, 666 n.5 (2001); National Laundry Co. v. Newton, 300 Mass. 126, 127 (1938); installation of a flashing light signal at a railroad crossing, Ladd v. New York, N.H. & H.R. Co., 335 Mass. 117, 120 (1956); repositioning a barrier across a sidewalk, Manchester v. City of Attleboro, 288 Mass. 492, 493 (1934); and precautions taken to avoid another collapse of a trench, Shinners v. Proprietors of Locks &

Canals on Merrimack River, 154 Mass. 168, 169–171 (1891). The rule has been extended to exclude the results of a defendant's investigation into the causes of an accident. See Martel v. Massachusetts Bay Transp. Auth., 403 Mass. 1, 5 (1988).

Subsection (b). Evidence of a subsequent remedial measure is admissible to prove issues other than negligence. See Santos v. Chrysler Corp., 430 Mass. 198, 207–208 (1999) (manufacturer on notice of product defect); Schaeffer v. General Motors Corp., 372 Mass. 171, 175–176 (1977) (feasibility of giving adequate warnings); doCanto v. Ametek, Inc., 367 Mass. 776, 780–781 (1975) (feasibility of safety improvements); Reardon v. Country Club at Coonamessett, Inc., 353 Mass. 702, 704–705 (1968) (knowledge of the danger at time of accident); Finn v. Peters, 340 Mass. 622, 625 (1960) (ownership or control over the premises). Evidence of a preaccident remedial measure is also admissible for the same purposes. See doCanto v. Ametek, Inc., 367 Mass. at 780; Torre v. Harris–Seybold Co., 9 Mass. App. Ct. 660, 676 (1980).

When a party offers evidence of remedial measures to prove an issue other than negligence, the judge should determine whether it is relevant, see Section 402, General Admissibility of Relevant Evidence, and, if so, whether the probative value of the evidence is substantially outweighed by the danger of unfair prejudice, see Section 403, Excluding Relevant Evidence for Prejudice, Confusion, Waste of Time, or Other Reason. If the judge admits the evidence, the judge should, upon request, instruct the jury that the evidence cannot be considered as an admission of negligence or fault. See Section 105, Limiting Evidence That Is Not Admissible Against Other Parties or for Other Purpose; Section 403, Excluding Relevant Evidence for Prejudice, Confusion, Waste of Time, or Other Reason.

Section 408. Compromise Offers and Negotiations in Civil Cases

(a) Prohibited Uses. Evidence of the following is not admissible—on behalf of any party—either to prove or disprove the validity or amount of a disputed claim:

(1) furnishing, promising, or offering—or accepting, promising to accept, or offering to accept—a valuable consideration in compromising or attempting to compromise the claim or any other claim, and

(2) conduct or a statement made during compromise negotiations about the claim.

(b) Exceptions. The court may admit this evidence for another purpose, such as proving a witness's bias or prejudice or other state of mind, negating a contention of undue delay, or proving an effort to obstruct a criminal investigation or prosecution.

NOTE

This section is derived from Proposed Mass. R. Evid. 408, which was adopted in principle in Morea v. Cosco, Inc., 422 Mass. 601, 603–604 (1996). But see Zucco v. Kane, 439 Mass. 503, 510 (2003) ("even if we were to adopt the segment of [Proposed Mass. R. Evid. 408] pertaining to statements made during negotiations …"). "This rule is founded in policy, that there may be no discouragement to amicable adjustment of disputes, by a fear, that if not completed, the party amicably disposed may be injured" (quotation and citation omitted). Strauss v. Skurnik, 227 Mass. 173, 175 (1917).

Evidence that a defendant compromised or offered to compromise a claim arising from the same transaction with a third person not a party to the action is not admissible to prove the defendant's liability to the plaintiff. Murray v. Foster, 343 Mass. 655, 659–660 (1962); Ricciutti v. Sylvania Elec. Prods., Inc., 343 Mass. 347, 349 (1961). A closing agreement between the Internal Revenue Service and the plaintiff constitutes a settlement of a claim and is inadmissible on the

question of liability. National Grid Holdings, Inc. v. Commissioner of Revenue, 89 Mass. App. Ct. 506, 520 (2016). In mitigation of damages, however, a defendant is entitled to the admission of evidence of a settlement amount between the plaintiff and a joint tortfeasor on account of the same injury, but such evidence is for the judge only and not the jury to consider. See Morea v. Cosco, Inc., 422 Mass. at 602–603.

Evidence of a compromise or offer to compromise may be admitted (with limiting instructions) for a purpose other than to prove liability or the invalidity of the claim, such as to impeach the credibility of a witness. See Zucco v. Kane, 439 Mass. at 509–510; Cottam v. CVS Pharmacy, 436 Mass. 316, 327–328 (2002). For example, in an employment discrimination case, statements contained in settlement correspondence were properly admitted as probative of the employer's state of mind. Dahms v. Cognex Corp., 455 Mass. 190, 199 (2009).

There can be no offer to compromise a claim unless there is indication that there is a potential lawsuit. See Hurwitz v. Bocian, 41 Mass. App. Ct. 365, 372–373 (1996). Whether a particular conversation constitutes a settlement offer or admission may require the resolution of conflicting testimony and is a preliminary question for the trial judge. Marchand v. Murray, 27 Mass. App. Ct. 611, 615 (1989). See Section 104(a), Preliminary Questions: In General. A unilateral statement that a party will "take care of" a loss will be treated as an admission of liability, not an offer to compromise. See, e.g., Cassidy v. Hollingsworth, 324 Mass. 424, 425–426 (1949) (defendant's statement made after accident that "I guess I owe you a fender" held to be admission of liability); Bernasconi v. Bassi, 261 Mass. 26, 28 (1927) (defendant's statement "I fix it up, everything," held to be admission of liability); Dennison v. Swerdlove, 250 Mass. 507, 508–509 (1925) (defendant's statement immediately after automobile accident that he would "adjust the damage to your car" was an admission of fault). An expression of sympathy does not qualify as either an offer to compromise or an admission of liability. See Section 409, Expressions of Sympathy in Civil Cases; Offers to Pay Medical and Similar Expenses.

Admissions made on the face of settlement documents are admissible. Zucco v. Kane, 439 Mass. at 510–511. Where, however, the parties "understood at [the time of the negotiations] that what was said at that time was said without prejudice to either party," admissions of fact will not be admissible at trial (quotation omitted). Garber v. Levine, 250 Mass. 485, 490 (1925). However, evidence of conduct or statements made during such negotiations on collateral matters are admissible for their truth. See Wagman v. Ziskind, 234 Mass. 509, 510–511 (1920); Harrington v. Lincoln, 70 Mass. 563, 567 (1855); Dickinson v. Dickinson, 50 Mass. 471, 474–475 (1845). Cf. G. L. c. 233, § 23D (admissibility of benevolent statements, writings, or gestures relating to accident victims); Section 514, Mediation Privilege (under G. L. c. 233, § 23C, any communications made in course of mediation proceedings and in presence of mediator are not admissible, except where mediating labor disputes).

Cross–Reference: Section 403, Excluding Relevant Evidence for Prejudice, Confusion, Waste of Time, or Other Reasons.

Section 409. Expressions of Sympathy in Civil Cases; Offers to Pay Medical and Similar Expenses

(a) Expressions of Sympathy in Civil Cases. Statements, writings, or benevolent gestures expressing sympathy or a general sense of benevolence relating to the pain, suffering, or death of a person involved in an accident and made to such person or to the family of such person shall be inadmissible as evidence of an admission of liability in a civil action.

(b) Payment of Medical and Similar Expenses. Evidence of furnishing, promising to pay, or offering to pay medical, hospital, or similar expenses resulting from an injury is not admissible to prove liability for the injury.

(c) Medical Malpractice Claims. Any expression of benevolence, regret, apology, sympathy, commiseration, condolence, compassion, mistake, error, or a general sense of concern made by a health care provider, a facility, or an employee or agent of a health care provider or facility to the patient, a relative of the patient, or a representative of the patient, and that relates to an unanticipated outcome, shall be inadmissible as evidence in a medical malpractice action, unless the maker of the statement, or a defense expert witness, when questioned under oath during the litigation about facts and opinions regarding any mistakes or errors that occurred, makes a contradictory or inconsistent statement as to material facts or opinions, in which case the statements and opinions made about the mistake or error shall be admissible for all purposes.

NOTE

Subsection (a). This subsection is taken verbatim from G. L. c. 233, § 23D. See Gallo v. Veliskakis, 357 Mass. 602, 606 (1970); Casper v. Lavoie, 1 Mass. App. Ct. 809, 810 (1973). See also Denton v. Park Hotel, Inc., 343 Mass. 524, 528 (1962) (expressions of sympathy have "no probative value as an admission of responsibility or liability," and "[c]ommon decency should not be penalized by treating such statements as admissions").

Subsection (b). This subsection is derived from Gallo v. Veliskakis, 357 Mass. 602, 606 (1970), and Wilson v. Daniels, 250 Mass. 359, 364 (1924). This subsection is based on the public policy of encouraging a person to act "as a decent citizen with proper humane sensibilities" without having to admit liability (citations omitted). Lyons v. Levine, 352 Mass. 769, 769 (1967). Statements that accompany offers of payment are not excluded under this section if otherwise admissible. See Gallo v. Veliskakis, 357 Mass. at 606 (defendant's statements of sympathy and that he would take care of the medical bills were inadmissible because they "had no probative value as an admission of responsibility or liability" [citations omitted]). Cf. G. L. c. 231, § 140B (evidence of advanced payments to injured person by insurer is not admissible to prove liability).

Subsection (c). This subsection is taken nearly verbatim from G. L. c. 233, § 79L (effective November 4, 2012).

Section 410.   Pleas, Offers of Pleas, and Related Statements

(a) Prohibited Uses. In a civil or criminal case, evidence of the following is not admissible against the defendant who made the plea or participated in the plea discussions:

(1) a guilty plea that was later withdrawn or rejected,

(2) a nolo contendere plea,

(3) an admission to sufficient facts, or

(4) a statement made in connection with, and relevant to, any of the foregoing withdrawn or rejected pleas or admissions.

(b) Exception. The court may admit a statement described in Subsection (a)(4) in a criminal proceeding for perjury if the defendant made the statement under oath, on the record, and with counsel present.

NOTE

This section is taken from Mass. R. Crim. P. 12(f). Rule 12(f) bars the use in evidence in any criminal or civil proceeding of a withdrawn guilty plea, a withdrawn plea of nolo contendere, a withdrawn admission of sufficient facts, or a withdrawn offer of the same. See Mass.

R. Crim. P. 12(f). But see Aetna Cas. & Sur. Co. v. Niziolek, 395 Mass. 737, 747–750 (1985) (guilty plea, not withdrawn, is an admission of material facts alleged in complaint or indictment and is admissible as evidence of an admission in subsequent civil case without having preclusive effect); Hopkins v. Medeiros, 48 Mass. App. Ct. 600, 613 (2000) ("An admission to sufficient facts may be introduced against the defendant in a subsequently litigated civil suit arising out of the same incident on the theory that the proceeding was the functional equivalent of a guilty plea, with the same degree of finality" [quotations and citation omitted].); Section 801(d)(2)(A), Definitions: Statements That Are Not Hearsay: An Opposing Party's Statement. Except in a prosecution for perjury, the bar applies to any statement made in the course of the plea negotiations as long as it is relevant to the negotiations. See Mass. R. Crim. P. 12(f).

Unlike Fed. R. Evid. 410, the statements in question need not have been made to an attorney for the prosecuting authority to qualify for exclusion. See Commonwealth v. Wilson, 430 Mass. 440, 442–443 (1999). Rule 12(f) excludes only statements made during "plea negotiations," not the apparently broader "plea discussions" referred to in Fed. R. Evid. 410. Id. at 443 (while statements to a detective could be excluded under Mass. R. Crim. P. 12[f], the statements were nonetheless admissible because they were not made during plea negotiations). On the issue of what constitutes plea negotiations, see Commonwealth v. Smiley, 431 Mass. 477, 482 n.3 (2000) (holding there were no plea negotiations where prosecutor made no promises, commitments, or offers and defendant did not give his statement only in consideration of a benefit offered by prosecutor), and Commonwealth v. Luce, 34 Mass. App. Ct. 105, 111–112 (1993) (meetings between defendant, counsel, and government officers did not constitute plea bargaining).

A refusal to plead guilty is not admissible when offered by the defendant to prove consciousness of innocence. See Commonwealth v. DoVale, 57 Mass. App. Ct. 657, 662–663 (2003).

Section 411.   Insurance

Evidence that a person or entity was or was not insured against liability is not admissible to prove whether the person or entity acted negligently or otherwise wrongfully. But the court may admit evidence of insurance for another purpose, such as proving a witness's bias or prejudice or proving agency, ownership, or control.

NOTE

The first sentence of this section is derived from Goldstein v. Gontarz, 364 Mass. 800, 807–814 (1974) (extensive discussion of principles and authorities), and Leavitt v. Glick Realty Corp., 362 Mass. 370, 372 (1972). The exclusion covers (1) evidence offered by the plaintiff that the defendant is insured, (2) evidence offered by the defendant that the plaintiff has received third-party compensation for an injury, (3) evidence offered by the defendant that he or she is not protected by insurance, and (4) evidence offered by the plaintiff that he or she has no resort to insurance or other coverage for the loss. Goldstein v. Gontarz, 364 Mass. at 808–810.

The second sentence of this section is derived from Fed. R. Evid. 411 and Proposed Mass. R. Evid. 411 and is consistent with Massachusetts law. Evidence of insurance coverage may be admissible where the issue of control over the covered premises is disputed because the jury could properly infer "that the defendants would not have deemed it prudent to secure indemnity insurance on [an area] not within their control, or for the careless management or defective condition of which they could not be held responsible." Perkins v. Rice, 187 Mass. 28, 30 (1904). A blanket insurance policy covering more than one location is not, however, admissible to show control. See Camerlin v. Marshall, 411 Mass. 394, 398 (1991).

Evidence of insurance coverage or lack thereof may be admissible to establish the bias of a witness. Goldstein v. Gontarz, 364 Mass. 800, 812 (1974). See Corsetti v. Stone Co., 396 Mass. 1, 16–21 (1985);

McDaniel v. Pickens, 45 Mass. App. Ct. 63, 66–67 (1998); Commonwealth v. Danis, 38 Mass. App. Ct. 968, 968 (1995). See also Masters v. Khuri, 62 Mass. App. Ct. 467, 471–472 (2004); Harris–Lewis v. Mudge, 60 Mass. App. Ct. 480, 487–488 (2004).

Inadmissibility Due to Prejudicial Effect. Evidence of an insurance policy may still be excluded where its prejudicial effect substantially outweighs its probative value after contemplating the effectiveness of a limiting instruction. See Goldstein v. Gontarz, 364 Mass. 800, 812–813 (1974). See also Shore v. Shore, 385 Mass. 529, 530–532 (1982) (appropriate instructions could have cured possible prejudice from excluded evidence of insurance policy). But see McDaniel v. Pickens, 45 Mass. App. Ct. 63, 70 (1998) (raising but not reaching the issue of "whether jurors have attained to such a level of sophistication that they can take insurance and related things in stride when properly instructed" [citations omitted]).

Collateral Source Rule. Evidence of collateral source payments is generally not admissible to reduce the amount of damages recoverable, but may be admissible if probative of a relevant issue, such as impeaching the plaintiff's credibility or showing motive. See Corsetti v. Stone Co., 396 Mass. 1, 16–21 (1985); Savers Prop. & Cas. Ins. Co. v. Admiral Ins. Agency, Inc., 61 Mass. App. Ct. 158, 165–166 (2004), and cases cited; Rolanti v. Boston Edison Corp., 33 Mass. App. Ct. 516, 524–525 (1992).

The full amount of a medical or hospital bill is admissible as evidence of the reasonable value of the services rendered to the injured person, even where the amount actually paid by a private or public insurer is less than that amount. The actual amount paid by insurance is not admissible, but the defendant may offer evidence to establish the range of payments accepted by that provider for that particular service. Law v. Griffith, 457 Mass. 349, 353–354 (2010). See G. L. c. 233, § 79G. The court may instruct the jury that any amounts paid by insurance are subject to recoupment by the payor. Scott v. Garfield, 454 Mass. 790, 801 (2009). The amounts actually paid to the health providers by the health insurer must be redacted on medical bills admitted into evidence. Id.

Unless it is relevant for some other purpose, evidence of a settlement with another defendant is not admissible to reduce the amount of damages, but the court should make the appropriate deduction after the verdict. Morea v. Cosco, Inc., 422 Mass. 601, 603 (1996). In most cases, the verdict in a motor vehicle liability case will be reduced by the amount of any personal injury protection benefits received by the plaintiff. G. L. c. 90, § 34M. In a medical malpractice case, the defendant may, at a postverdict hearing, offer evidence to the court as to the amount of medical bills that have been covered by insurance. The amount of any such bills, less the amount of any premiums paid by the plaintiff for one year prior to the accrual of the cause of action, shall be deducted from the itemized verdict. This procedure does not apply to any payor who has subrogation rights based on any Federal law. G. L. c. 231, § 60G.

Section 412. Sexual Behavior or Sexual Reputation (Rape–Shield Law)

(a) Prohibited Uses. Except as otherwise provided, the following evidence is not admissible in a civil or criminal proceeding involving alleged sexual misconduct:

(1) evidence offered to prove that a victim engaged in other sexual behavior or

(2) evidence offered to prove a victim's sexual reputation.

(b) Exceptions. The court may admit the following evidence in a criminal case:

(1) evidence of specific instances of a victim's sexual behavior with respect to the person accused of the sexual misconduct;

(2) evidence of specific instances of a victim's recent sexual behavior if offered to prove that someone other than the defendant was the source of any physical feature, characteristic, or condition of the victim; and

(3) evidence whose exclusion would violate the defendant's constitutional rights.

(c) Procedure to Determine Admissibility.

(1) Motion. If a party intends to offer evidence under Subsection (b), the party must file a motion and an offer of proof.

(2) Hearing. Before admitting evidence under this section, the court must conduct a hearing, in open court, unless the judge makes appropriate findings to support courtroom closure. The judge must find that the weight and relevance (probative value) of the evidence is sufficient to outweigh its prejudicial effect to the victim. The court must make and file a written finding, but its finding must not be made available to the jury.

(d) Definition of "Victim." In this section, "victim" includes an alleged victim.

NOTE

Subsection (a). This subsection is derived from G. L. c. 233, § 21B, and Commonwealth v. Domaingue, 397 Mass. 693, 696–700 (1986). Evidence of a victim's sexual conduct cannot be introduced at a trial for any of the crimes on this nonexhaustive list: G. L. c. 265, §§ 13B, 13F, 13H, 22, 22A, 23, 24, and 24B, and G. L. c. 272, § 29A. Evidence in the form of reputation or opinion is not admissible to prove the complainant's reputation for unchastity. See Commonwealth v. Joyce, 382 Mass. 222, 227–228 (1981) (the rape-shield statute "reverses the common law rule under which evidence of the complainant's general reputation for unchastity was admissible" [citation omitted]). Note that the cases use the terms "victim" and "complainant" interchangeably.

"The rape-shield statute is principally designed to prevent defense counsel from eliciting evidence of the victim's promiscuity as part of a general credibility attack." Commonwealth v. Fitzgerald, 412 Mass. 516, 523 (1992). "The policy rationale for this law is that evidence of the victim's prior sexual conduct might divert attention from the alleged criminal acts of the defendant, inappropriately putting the victim on trial" (citations omitted). Commonwealth v. Houston, 430 Mass. 616, 621 (2000). In Commonwealth v. Parent, 465 Mass. 395, 404–405 (2013), the Supreme Judicial Court held that the trial judge did not abuse her discretion in ruling that a witness who overheard the victim speaking on a cell phone could testify that the victim invited a boy to visit her on the evening of the alleged sexual assault but would not be permitted to testify that the victim was overheard promising to engage in oral sex.

Subsection (b)(1). This subsection is taken from G. L. c. 233, § 21B. The complainant's prior sexual activity with the defendant may be relevant to the issue of consent, particularly to show the complainant's emotion to that particular defendant. Commonwealth v. Grieco, 386 Mass. 484, 488 (1982). Cf. Commonwealth v. Fionda, 33 Mass. App. Ct. 316, 321–322 (1992) (provocative conversation and kissing on prior occasion not probative of consent to intercourse on later occasion).

Subsection (b)(2). This subsection is taken from G. L. c. 233, § 21B. Prior acts with another person may be relevant to establishing an alternative cause for the complainant's physical condition. See, e.g., Commonwealth v. Fitzgerald, 402 Mass. 517, 521–522 (1988), S.C., 412 Mass. 516, 521–525 (1992) (presence of sperm where defendant underwent a vasectomy); Commonwealth v. Cardoza, 29 Mass. App. Ct. 645, 648–649 (1990) (presence of foreign pubic hair not belonging to defendant should have been admitted).

Subsection (b)(3). This subsection is derived from Commonwealth v. Joyce, 382 Mass. 222, 227–229 (1981). While a defendant has a constitutional right to present a full defense, that right is not unfettered. See Commonwealth v. Thevenin, 33 Mass. App. Ct. 588, 592–593 (1992). To overcome the restrictions contained in the rape-shield statute, the defense must be "based on more than a vague hope or speculation," and a defendant cannot conduct "an unbounded or freewheeling cross-examination" that invites the jury to conjecture. Id.

"Where evidence of bias is available by other means, no evidence of the complainant's prior sexual history should be admitted." Commonwealth v. Gagnon, 45 Mass. App. Ct. 584, 589 (1998). See also Commonwealth v. Pyne, 35 Mass. App. Ct. 36, 38 (1993), citing Commonwealth v. Elder, 389 Mass. 743, 751 nn.11–12 (1983). Cf. Commonwealth v. Stockhammer, 409 Mass. 867, 875 (1991) (specific act evidence may be used to demonstrate the complainant's bias or motive to fabricate). Evidence may be used to show that the complainant made prior false allegations of rape or abuse. See Commonwealth v. Bohannon, 376 Mass. 90, 94–95 (1978) (evidence admissible where witness was the complainant at trial, consent was central issue, complainant's testimony was inconsistent and confused, and there was independent basis for concluding that prior allegations were false). Cf. Commonwealth v. Talbot, 444 Mass. 586, 590–591 (2005); Commonwealth v. Blair, 21 Mass. App. Ct. 625, 626–629 (1986). A defendant may introduce evidence that a complainant has been subjected to past sexual abuse to explain the complainant's inappropriate knowledge of sexual matters. See Commonwealth v. Ruffen, 399 Mass. 811, 814–817 (1987). See also Commonwealth v. Beaudry, 445 Mass. 577, 580–586 (2005). A trial judge has discretion to admit evidence of a complainant's prior conviction for a sexual offense, but must take into consideration the objectives of the rape-shield statute. See Commonwealth v. Harris, 443 Mass. 714, 723–728 (2005) (harmonizing G. L. c. 233, §§ 21 and 21B). "The judge must determine whether the weight and relevance of the proffered evidence of bias or motive to lie is sufficient to outweigh its prejudicial effect to the victim" (internal citation omitted). Commonwealth v. Noj, 76 Mass. App. Ct. 194, 198–199 (2010). See also Commonwealth v. Thomas, 89 Mass. App. Ct. 422, 425–427 (2016) (no error in excluding rape victim's prior convictions for "prostitution-related offenses" where "nothing about the facts" gave victim motive to lie, and case did not involve consent defense).

Conversely, "[i]n the exercise of this discretion a trial judge should consider the important policies underlying the rape-shield statute. He should exclude evidence of specific instances of a complainant's sexual conduct in so far [sic] as that is possible without unduly infringing upon the defendant's right to show bias." Commonwealth v. Joyce, 382 Mass. 222, 231 (1981).

Subsection (c). This subsection is derived from G. L. c. 233, § 21B; Commonwealth v. Jones, 472 Mass. 707, 720–731 (2015); and Commonwealth v. Harris, 443 Mass. 714, 721 (2005). See Commonwealth v. Cortez, 438 Mass. 123, 129–130 (2002); Commonwealth v. Joyce, 382 Mass. 222, 232–233 (1981) (Braucher, J., concurring).

In Commonwealth v. Jones, 472 Mass. 707 (2015), the Supreme Judicial Court held that the Sixth Amendment right to a public trial applies to a rape-shield hearing. Despite the language of G. L. c. 233, § 21B, before closing the courtroom, the court must make case-specific findings in accordance with the four-part test articulated in Waller v. Georgia, 467 U.S. 39, 48 (1984):

"[1] the party seeking to close the hearing must advance an overriding interest that is likely to be prejudiced; [2] the closure must be no broader than necessary to protect that interest; [3] the trial court must consider reasonable alternatives to closing the proceeding; and [4] it must make findings adequate to support the closure."

Cross–Reference: Section 403, Excluding Relevant Evidence for Prejudice, Confusion, Waste of Time, or Other Reason; Note "Validity of Claim of Privilege" to Section 511(b), Privilege Against Self–Incrimination: Privilege of a Witness.

Section 413. First Complaint of Sexual Assault

(a) **Admissibility of First Complaint.** Testimony by the recipient of a complainant's first complaint of an alleged sexual assault regarding the fact of the first complaint and the circumstances surrounding the making of that first complaint, including details of the complaint, is admissible for the limited purpose of assisting the jury in determining whether to credit the complainant's testimony about the alleged sexual assault, not to prove the truth of the allegations.

(b) **Admissibility of Additional Reports of a Sexual Assault Under an Alternative Evidentiary Basis.** When otherwise admissible testimony or evidence other than the first complaint includes or implies that a report of a sexual assault was made, it may be admitted only if the trial judge determines that (1) it serves an evidentiary purpose other than to corroborate the testimony of the alleged victim and (2) its probative value outweighs its prejudicial effect.

NOTE

Subsection (a). This subsection is taken nearly verbatim from Commonwealth v. King, 445 Mass. 217, 218–219 (2005), cert. denied, 546 U.S. 1216 (2006). In Commonwealth v. King, the Supreme Judicial Court replaced the doctrine of "fresh complaint" with that of "first complaint." Id. at 241–248. See also Commonwealth v. Aviles, 461 Mass. 60, 71 (2011) (reaffirming the first complaint doctrine and explaining that it is not an "evidentiary rule" but rather a "body of governing principles to guide a trial judge on the admissibility of first complaint evidence").

"The doctrine seeks to balance the interest of two competing concerns: that a complainant (who . . . may be still a child) has her credibility fairly judged on the specific facts of the case rather than unfairly by misguided stereotypical thinking; and that the defendant receive a trial that is free from irrelevant and potentially prejudicial testimony."

Commonwealth v. Arana, 453 Mass. 214, 228 (2009).

"Under the new doctrine . . . the recipient of a complainant's first complaint of an alleged sexual assault may testify about the fact of the first complaint and the circumstances surrounding the making of that first complaint. The witness may also testify about the details of the complaint. The complainant may likewise testify to the details of the first complaint (i.e., what she told the first complaint witness), as well as why the complaint was made at that particular time. Testimony from additional complaint witnesses is not admissible."

Commonwealth v. King, 445 Mass. at 218–219.

The first complaint rule not only applies to statements of the complaining witness, as a "neutral" rule of evidence, it is applicable whenever the credibility of an allegation of sexual assault is at issue. Therefore, the first complaint doctrine is available to the defendant in a sexual assault prosecution who claims to have been sexually assaulted by the complainant, because "such a defendant faces the same credibility obstacle in proving his or her defense as the Commonwealth faces in proving the indictment." Commonwealth v. Mayotte, 475 Mass. 254, 260 (2016).

Role of the Trial Judge. The following sections of this Note amplify the doctrinal framework set forth in the guideline. Regarding this "body of governing principles," the Supreme Judicial Court has explained that the trial judge "is in the best position to determine the scope of admissible evidence, keeping in mind the underlying goals of the first complaint doctrine, our established first complaint jurisprudence, and our guidelines for admitting or excluding relevant evidence." Commonwealth v. Aviles, 461 Mass. 60, 73 (2011). The exercise of discretion as to whether evidence is admissible under the first complaint doctrine is fact specific and requires the trial judge to conduct a careful and thorough analysis based on the principles set forth in this Note. "Once a judge has carefully and thoroughly analyzed these considerations, and has decided that proposed first complaint evidence is admissible, an appellate court shall review that determination under an abuse of discretion standard." Id.

Applicability of First Complaint Doctrine. The first complaint doctrine is not applicable to cases in which neither the fact of a sexual assault nor the consent of the complainant is at issue. Commonwealth v. King, 445 Mass. 217, 247 (2005).

"First complaint testimony, including the details and circumstances of the complaint, will be considered presumptively relevant to a complainant's credibility in most sexual assault cases where the fact of the assault or the issue of consent is contested. However, where neither the occurrence of a sexual assault nor the complainant's consent is at issue [i.e., identity of the perpetrator], the evidence will serve no corroborative purpose and will not be admissible under the first complaint doctrine."

Id.

Identifying the First Complaint. That the complainant's first report of a sexual assault is abbreviated in nature does not change its status as the first complaint. See Commonwealth v. Stuckich, 450 Mass. 449, 455–456 (2008). A victim's report of a sexual assault may qualify as a first complaint even if it does not include the identity of the perpetrator. Commonwealth v. Asenjo, 477 Mass. 599, 603 (2017). A first complaint witness is not disqualified from testifying where the alleged victim previously disclosed only physical abuse to that witness. Commonwealth v. Rivera, 83 Mass. App. Ct. 581, 584 (2013). While ordinarily there will be only one first complaint witness, two first complaint witnesses may testify in circumstances "where each witness testifies to disclosures years apart concerning different periods of time and escalating levels of abuse, which constitute different and more serious criminal acts committed over a lengthy period." Commonwealth v. Kebreau, 454 Mass. 287, 288–289 (2009). See Commonwealth v. Aviles, 461 Mass. 60, 71 n.9 (2011) (distinguishing Kebreau and limiting first complaint to initial disclosure of "touching" where subsequent disclosure of rape could have been disclosed by complainant as part of her first complaint); Commonwealth v. Lewis, 91 Mass. App. Ct. 651, 659–661 (2017) (two first complaints admissible where each complaint concerned a separately charged rape, and each piece of evidence was carefully limited to the facts of one rape). The fact that the complainant tells someone that he or she is upset, unhappy, or scared is not a first complaint. See Commonwealth v. Murungu, 450 Mass. 441, 446 (2008). "Law enforcement officials, as well as investigatory, medical, or social work professionals, may testify to the complaint only where they are in fact the first to have heard of the assault, and not where they have been told of the alleged crime after previous complaints or after an official report." Commonwealth v. King, 445 Mass. at 243.

The first complaint evidence could be in the form of a recorded 911 emergency telephone call, a letter, or a G. L. c. 209A abuse prevention complaint affidavit; a live witness is not required. Commonwealth v. Stuckich, 450 Mass. at 455–456; Commonwealth v. Lewis, 91 Mass. App. Ct. at 661–662.

Limiting Instruction Required. Whenever first complaint evidence is admitted, whether through the complainant or the first complaint witness, the court must give the jury a limiting instruction. Commonwealth v. King, 445 Mass. 217, 219, 247–248 (2005). The instruction must be given contemporaneously with the first complaint testimony and again during the final instruction. Id. at 248.

Determination of Who Is the First Complaint Witness. The determination of who is the first complaint witness is a preliminary question of fact for the trial judge. Commonwealth v. Stuckich, 450 Mass. 449, 455–456 (2008). See Section 104(a), Preliminary Questions: In General.

Scope of the Doctrine. The first complaint doctrine applies only if the complainant is available for cross-examination about the first complaint. Commonwealth v. King, 445 Mass. 217, 247 n.27 (2005). "The timing by the complainant in making a complaint will not disqualify the evidence, but is a factor the jury may consider in deciding whether the first complaint testimony supports the complainant's credibility or reliability." Id. at 219. The first complaint doctrine applies even to cases in which there is a percipient witness (in addition to the victim) to the sexual assault. See Commonwealth v. Hartnett, 72 Mass. App. Ct. 467, 470 (2008). An alleged victim's inability to recall the details of the first complaint goes to the weight and not the admissibility of the testimony by the first complaint witness. See Commonwealth v. Wallace, 76 Mass. App. Ct. 411, 415 (2010).

The first complaint witness may "testify to the details of the complaint itself. By details, we mean that the witness 'may testify to the complainant's statements of the facts of the assault.'" Commonwealth v. King, 445 Mass. at 244, quoting Commonwealth v. Quincy Q., 434 Mass. 859, 874 (2001). The witness

"may testify to the circumstances surrounding the initial complaint, [including] his or her observations of the complainant during the complaint; the events or conversations that culminated in the complaint; the timing of the complaint; and other relevant conditions that might help a jury assess the veracity of the complainant's allegations or assess the specific defense theories as to why the complainant is making a false allegation" (citation omitted).

Id. at 246.

Complete congruence between the testimony of the complainant and the testimony of the first complaint witness is not required; the first complaint witness cannot fill in missing elements in the Commonwealth's case. Under Section 403, the trial judge has discretion to exclude details absent from the complainant's testimony. Commonwealth v. Rivera, 83 Mass. App. Ct. 581, 586 nn.5–6 (2013).

The alleged victim is permitted to testify to what he or she told the first complaint witness and why the complaint was made (1) when the first complaint witness or a court-approved substitute first complaint witness testifies at trial to those details, (2) when the first complaint witness is deceased, or (3) when the judge decides there is a compelling reason for the absence of the first complaint witness that is not the Commonwealth's fault. Commonwealth v. King, 445 Mass. at 245 & n.24.

A statement that qualifies as a spontaneous utterance by the victim reporting the assault also constitutes first complaint evidence such that an additional first complaint witness should not be permitted to testify, even if what that witness has to offer is more detailed or complete. Commonwealth v. McGee, 75 Mass. App. Ct. 499, 502–503 (2009); Commonwealth v. Davis, 54 Mass. App. Ct. 756, 765 (2002).

Substitution of a Witness. Where feasible, the first person told of the alleged sexual assault should be the initial or first complaint witness to testify. Commonwealth v. King, 445 Mass. 217, 243–244 (2005). In Commonwealth v. Murungu, 450 Mass. 441, 445–448 (2008), the Supreme Judicial Court identified two exceptions to the first complaint doctrine. A person other than the first recipient of information from the complainant is allowed to testify as the first complaint witness (1) if the victim's disclosure to the "first person does not constitute a complaint," or (2) if the victim complains first to an individual who "has an obvious bias or motive to . . . distort the victim's remarks." Id. at 446. The court explained that in Commonwealth v. King, it had not "set forth an exhaustive list of appropriate substitutions." Id. at 445. "Other exceptions are permissible based on the purpose and limitations of the first complaint doctrine." Id. See also Commonwealth v. Hanino, 82 Mass. App. Ct. 489, 491 (2012) (feigning).

Even when the complainant has disclosed information about the sexual assault to a person with no obvious bias against the complainant, the trial judge has discretion to allow the Commonwealth to substitute another witness as the first complaint witness in circumstances "where [that person] is unavailable, incompetent, or too young to testify meaningfully ..." Commonwealth v. King, 445 Mass. at 243–244. See, e.g., Commonwealth v. Roby, 462 Mass. 398, 407–408 (2012) (where two child victims initially first told each other about defendant's inappropriate touching, it was proper to allow first adult [and first noncomplainant] told about the sexual assaults to testify as first complaint witness); Commonwealth v. Thibeault, 77 Mass. App. Ct. 419, 421–423 (2010) (child's mother could be substituted as witness for child's father where father was first person to whom child complained but he appeared to have fled the Commonwealth and could not be located at time of trial).

Impeachment of First Complaint Witness. The court has discretion to permit the Commonwealth to impeach the first complaint witness by means of prior inconsistent statements in circumstances in which the court determines that the witness is feigning a lack of memory as to significant details of the first complaint. See Commonwealth v. Hanino, 82 Mass. App. Ct. 489, 497–498 (2012) (testimony of two police officers regarding statements made to them by first complaint witness and inconsistent with witness's in-court testimony was admissible for limited purpose of impeaching witness's in-court testimony and thus was not impermissible, multiple complaint hearsay).

Subsection (b). This subsection is derived from Commonwealth v. Dargon, 457 Mass. 387, 399–400 (2010); Commonwealth v. Arana, 453 Mass. 214, 224–229 (2009); and Commonwealth v. Stuckich, 450 Mass. 449, 457 (2008).

"Evidence of a subsequent complaint is not admissible simply because a separate evidentiary rule applies (e.g., the statement is not hearsay, or it falls within an exception to the hearsay rule). If independently admissible evidence ... serves no purpose other than to repeat the fact of a complaint and therefore corroborate the complainant's accusations, it is inadmissible. However, if that evidence does serve a purpose separate and apart from the first complaint doctrine, the judge may admit it after careful balancing of the testimony's probative and prejudicial value." (Quotations and citations omitted.)

Commonwealth v. Dargon, 457 Mass. at 399–400. See also Commonwealth v. Santos, 465 Mass. 689, 700–701 (2013) (mother's description of son's appearance and demeanor after alleged sexual assault admissible to show victim's state of mind at the time); Commonwealth v. Parent, 465 Mass. 395, 403–404 (2013) (claim of fabrication alone is insufficient to open the door to the admission of multiple complaints); Commonwealth v. Aviles, 461 Mass. 60, 67 (2011) (testimony of both complainant and first complaint witness pertaining to subsequent disclosure, though not admissible under first complaint doctrine, was properly admitted to rebut the defendant's suggestion that complainant's accusations were fabricated); Commonwealth v. McCoy, 456 Mass. 838, 851 (2010) (admission of mother's testimony that she and victim had conversation about assault, even without details of conversation, was error when testimony did not serve "any additional purpose"); Commonwealth v. Starkweather, 79 Mass. App. Ct. 791, 799–803 (2011) (applying Dargon and Arana analysis to several aspects of police involvement and investigation); Commonwealth v. Monteiro, 75 Mass. App. Ct. 489, 495 (2009) (admission of testimony indicating that complainant had made reports of sexual abuse to his mother, the Department of Social Services, and the district attorney's office, without any more details, in circumstances where the father was the first complaint witness, was error). Contrast Commonwealth v. Santos, 465 Mass. at 701 (in a prosecution for rape, the judge did not abuse her discretion in allowing the Commonwealth to introduce testimony from the victim's mother, a non-first complaint witness, about the victim's appearance and demeanor to rebut the defense's theory that the incident was fabricated where the "testimony did not repeat any details of the event, was relevant, and not merely cumulative of the [first complaint witness's] testimony"); Commonwealth v. Lawton, 82 Mass. App. Ct. 528, 536–538 (2012) (victim's statements to SAIN [Sexual Abuse Intervention Network] interviewer not offered as

additional complaint testimony, but were independently relevant to contradict impeachment of victim and to rebut defendant's theory of suggestibility).

The question whether testimony concerning multiple complaints is permissible "is fact-specific and requires, in the first analysis, a careful evaluation of the circumstances by the trial judge." Commonwealth v. Kebreau, 454 Mass. 287, 296 (2009). In Commonwealth v. Ramsey, 76 Mass. App. Ct. 844, 849 (2010), the Appeals Court explained that medical records that included statements by the alleged victim pointing to the defendant as the perpetrator of the sexual assault and statements of hospital personnel repeating the allegations, conclusory statements of rape, and a diagnosis of incest, which the judge found admissible under the hospital records exception to the hearsay rule, should not have been admitted at trial because the judge had not determined that the evidence served a purpose other than to corroborate the victim and had not carefully balanced its probative value and prejudicial effect.

"In [Commonwealth v.] Arana, [453 Mass. 214, 227 (2009)], further evidence of complaint was admissible in order to rebut the defendant's allegation that the complainant fabricated the accusations to provide a basis for a civil lawsuit. In Commonwealth v. Kebreau, 454 Mass. 287, 299 (2009), such evidence was admissible because the defense exploited discrepancies in the testimony of one of the victims and had 'opened the door on cross-examination'; thus 'the Commonwealth was entitled to attempt to rehabilitate the witness.'"

Commonwealth v. Ramsey, 76 Mass. App. Ct. at 850 n.12. See also Commonwealth v. Saunders, 75 Mass. App. Ct. 505, 509 (2009) (defense counsel cross-examined victim about reports she allegedly made that someone other than defendant got her pregnant; this opened the door to permit the Commonwealth to offer evidence of statements made by the victim about the defendant's conduct to persons other than the first complaint witness).

SAIN Evidence. A SANE (sexual abuse nurse examiner) is permitted to testify about the SAIN (Sexual Abuse Intervention Network) evidence kit used in the examination of a person alleged to be the victim of a sexual assault and the sexual assault examination process, provided it is either to provide background for the nurse's testimony about the examination of the alleged victim or to lay a foundation for the admission of physical evidence. See Commonwealth v. Dargon, 457 Mass. 387, 398 n.13 (2010). On the other hand, in Commonwealth v. Monteiro, 75 Mass. App. Ct. 489, 493–494 (2009), the Appeals Court found that the inclusion of testimony from a police detective who watched a tape of the SAIN interview and who described the interview process and indicated that as a result he continued with his investigation was error because it suggested that the SAIN interviews take place when persons are thought to be victims of sexual assault and implied that the detective found the complainant credible. In addition, the printed forms that are filled out by the SAIN interviewer (Forms 2 and 3) based on questions put to the alleged victim are not admissible, because the printing suggests that a sexual assault took place. See Commonwealth v. Dargon, 457 Mass. at 398 n.13.

Section 414. Industry and Safety Standards

Safety rules, governmental regulations or ordinances, and industry standards may be offered by either party in civil cases as evidence of the appropriate care under the circumstances.

NOTE

This section is derived from Torre v. Harris–Seybold Co., 9 Mass. App. Ct. 660, 671 (1980). Like the safety rules themselves, evidence of an employee's violation of his or her employer's safety rules is admissible as evidence of negligence. Lev v. Beverly Enters. Mass., Inc., 457 Mass. 234, 245 (2010). A company's or industry's "custom and practice," even when not embodied in a written policy, is also admissible. Commonwealth v. Angelo Todesca Corp., 446 Mass. 128, 137–138 (2006). A violation of such rules or regulations, while some evidence of negligence, is not conclusive. St. Germaine v. Prendergast, 411 Mass. 615, 620 (1992). The rule or regulation cannot, however, create a duty where none exists and is admissible only if the harm is of the kind intended to be prevented. Lev v. Beverly Enters. Mass., Inc., 457 Mass. at 246–247.

Cross–Reference: Section 803(17), Hearsay Exceptions; Availability of Declarant Immaterial: Statements of Facts of General Interest; Section 803(18), Hearsay Exceptions; Availability of Declarant Immaterial: Learned Treatises.

ARTICLE V. PRIVILEGES AND DISQUALIFICATIONS

Introductory Note

(a) General Duty to Give Evidence. A privilege is an exception to the general duty of a witness to offer evidence. Commonwealth v. Corsetti, 387 Mass. 1, 5 (1982).

(b) Interpretation of Privileges. "Testimonial privileges are exceptions to the general duty imposed on all people to testify, and therefore must be strictly construed" (quotations and citations omitted). Commonwealth v. Oliveira, 438 Mass. 325, 330 (2002). See also Matter of a Grand Jury Subpoena, 430 Mass. 590, 593–594, 597–599 (2000); Commonwealth v. Corsetti, 387 Mass. 1, 5 (1982). In criminal cases, even statutory privileges may be pierced when necessary to preserve a defendant's constitutional rights. See Commonwealth v. Dwyer, 448 Mass. 122, 144 (2006).

(c) Most Privileges Are Not Self–Executing. Most privileges require "some action by the patient or client . . . to 'exercise' the privilege." Commonwealth v. Oliveira, 438 Mass. 325, 331 (2002) (psychotherapist–patient privilege). See Commonwealth v. Pelosi, 441 Mass. 257, 261 (2004) (social worker-client privilege); District Attorney for the Plymouth Dist. v. Board of Selectmen of Middleborough, 395 Mass. 629, 633–634 (1985) (attorney–client privilege); Commonwealth v. Brennan, 386 Mass. 772, 780 (1982) (privilege against self-incrimination). The Legislature can create a privilege that is automatic and that does not require any action on the part of the holder of the privilege. See Commonwealth v. Oliveira, 438 Mass. at 331 n.7 ("the sexual assault counsellor-victim privilege created by G. L. c. 233, § 20J . . . does not suggest that the victim need do anything to 'exercise' the privilege contained therein, or to 'refuse' to disclose the communications, or to 'prevent' the counsellor from disclosing the communications."). See also Borman v. Borman, 378 Mass. 775, 787 (1979) (Code of Professional Responsibility applicable to lawyers is self-executing). In the case of a privilege that is not self-executing, it may be appropriate for the proponent of the privilege to temporarily assert the privilege pending notice to the party which holds the privilege. See Commonwealth v. Oliveira, 438 Mass. at 332 n.8.

(d) Confidentiality Versus Privilege. There is a distinction between a duty of confidentiality and an evidentiary privilege. See Commonwealth v. Vega, 449 Mass. 227, 229 n.7 (2007, citing Commonwealth v. Brandwein, 435 Mass. 623, 628 n.7 (2002). A duty of confidentiality obligates one, such as a professional, to keep certain information, often about a client or patient, confidential. It also may impose an obligation on a State agency. See G. L. c. 66A, §§ 1, 2. See also G. L. c. 233, § 20M (confidential communication between human trafficking victim and victim's caseworker).

"A provider's obligation to keep matters confidential may stem from a statute imposing such an obligation (oftentimes with a host of exceptions to that obligation), or may arise as a matter of professional ethics." Commonwealth v. Oliveira, 438 Mass. 325, 335 (2002). When a duty of confidentiality is set forth in a statute, there may or may not be an accompanying evidentiary privilege. See Commonwealth v. Vega, 449 Mass. at 233–234 (holding that G. L. c. 112, § 172, imposes a duty of confidentiality and creates an evidentiary privilege). Sometimes, the duty of confidentiality and the corresponding evidentiary privilege are set forth in separate statutes. See, e.g., G. L. c. 112, §§ 135A and 135B (social workers), and G. L. c. 112, § 129A, and G. L. c. 233, § 20B (psychologists and psychotherapists). In other cases, the duty of confidentiality and a privilege exist in the same statute. See Commonwealth v. Vega, 449 Mass. at 232, citing G. L. c. 233, § 20J (sexual assault counselors) and G. L. c. 233, § 20K (domestic violence counselors).

In some circumstances, when a provider breaches a duty of confidentiality, the absence of an accompanying evidentiary privilege may permit a party in litigation to gain access to the information or to offer it in evidence. See Commonwealth v. Brandwein, 435 Mass. at 628–629 (access to information improperly disclosed by a nurse in violation of her professional duty of confidentiality was not otherwise covered by an evidentiary privilege); Commonwealth v. Senior, 433 Mass. 453, 457 n.5 (2001) (noting the distinction between the confidentiality of medical and hospital records under G. L. c. 111, § 70, and the absence of a physician-patient privilege).

(e) Impounding Versus Sealing. In Pixley v. Commonwealth, 453 Mass. 827 (2009), the Supreme Judicial Court addressed the difference between impounding and sealing:

"The terms 'impounded' and 'sealed' are closely related and often used interchangeably, but are meaningfully different. Under the Uniform Rules o[n] Impoundment Procedure 1708 (LexisNexis 2008), which governs impoundment in civil proceedings and guides practice in criminal matters as well, 'impoundment' means 'the act of keeping some or all of the papers, documents, or exhibits, or portions thereof, in a case separate and unavailable for public inspection.' Rule 1 of the Uniform Rules o[n] Impoundment Procedure. Consequently, an order of impoundment prevents the public, but not the parties, from gaining access to impounded material, unless otherwise ordered by the court. A document is normally ordered 'sealed' when it is intended that only the court have access to the document, unless the court specifically orders limited disclosure. Therefore, we directed in Commonwealth v. Martin, [423 Mass. 496, 505 (1996),] that the record of the in camera hearing 'should be kept, under seal.' Similarly, we ordered that privileged psychological or counseling records of an alleged victim of a sexual assault be 'retained in court under seal,' but permitted defense counsel to have access pursuant to a strict protective order. Commonwealth v. Dwyer, 448 Mass. 122, 146 (2006)."

Pixley v. Commonwealth, 453 Mass. at 836 n.12. Martin hearings are discussed in the Note to Section 511(b), Privilege Against Self–Incrimination: Privilege of a Witness. The Lampron–Dwyer protocol is summarized in Section 1108, Access to Third–Party Records Prior to Trial in Criminal Cases (Lampron–Dwyer Protocol).

(f) Examples of Relationships in Which There May Be a Duty to Treat Information as Confidential Even Though There Is No Testimonial Privilege. Examples include the following:

(1) Patient Medical Information. There is no doctor-patient privilege recognized under Massachusetts law. Bratt v. International Business Machs. Corp., 392 Mass. 508, 522–523 n.22 (1984). See also Commonwealth v. Senior, 433 Mass. 453, 456–457 (2001); Tower v. Hirschhorn, 397 Mass. 581, 588 (1986). However, physicians have a duty not to make out-of-court disclosures of medical information about the patient without the patient's consent, Alberts v. Devine, 395 Mass. 59, 67–68, cert. denied sub nom. Carroll v. Alberts, 474 U.S. 1013 (1985), unless disclosure is necessary to meet a serious danger to the patient or others. Id. A breach of doctor-patient confidentiality does not require exclusion of the evidence, Commonwealth v. Senior, 433 Mass. at 457 n.5, citing Schwartz v. Goldstein, 400 Mass. 152, 153 (1987), but may subject the offending doctor to an action for damages. Alberts v. Devine, 395 Mass. at 65–69.

(2) Student Records. "There is no privilege which would prevent the introduction of relevant school records in evidence at a trial." Commonwealth v. Beauchemin, 410 Mass. 181, 185 (1991). However, the Legislature has recognized that privacy interests are at stake. School records pertaining to specific individuals are not subject to disclosure under our public records law if disclosure "may constitute an unwarranted invasion of personal privacy." G. L. c. 4, § 7, Twenty-sixth (c). See also G. L. c. 66, § 10. Access to student records is also restricted under regulations promulgated by the State board of education pursuant to G. L. c. 71, § 34D. See Commonwealth v. Buccella, 434 Mass. 473, 477 (2001) (third persons may access "student records" only with written consent from student or student's parents unless an exception promulgated by regulation applies).

(3) Special Needs Student Records. Records of the clinical history and evaluations of students with special needs created or maintained in accordance with G. L. c. 71B "shall be confidential." G. L. c. 71B, § 3.

(4) News Sources and Nonpublished Information. Before ordering a reporter to divulge a source and the information gathered, a judge must "consider the effect of compelled disclosure on values underlying the First Amendment and art. 16." Petition for Promulgation of Rules Regarding the Protection of Confidential News Sources & Other Unpublished Info., 395 Mass. 164, 171 (1985). Accordingly, a judge must balance the public interest in the use of every person's evidence against the public interest in protecting the free flow of information. Matter of a John Doe Grand Jury Investigation, 410 Mass. 596, 599 (1991). See also Ayash v. Dana–Farber Cancer Inst., 443 Mass. 367, 403 n.33 (2005).

(5) Certain Documents, Records, and Reports. A non-exhaustive list of confidentiality statutes includes the following:

    G. L. c. 4, § 6, Twenty-sixth (documents and records);

    G. L. c. 6, § 167 et seq. (Criminal Offender Record Information [C.O.R.I.]);

    G. L. c. 41, § 97D (reports of rape and sexual assault);

    G. L. c. 66A, §§ 1, 2 (personal data held by Commonwealth agencies);

    G. L. c. 111, §§ 70, 70E (hospital records);

    G. L. c. 111, § 70F (HIV test results);

    G. L. c. 111, § 70G (genetic testing);

    G. L. c. 111B, § 11 (alcohol treatment);

    G. L. c. 111E, § 18 (drug treatment);

    G. L. c. 112, § 129A (psychologist-patient communications);

    G. L. c. 119, § 51E (Department of Children and Families records);

    G. L. c. 119, §§ 60–60A (juvenile records);

    G. L. c. 123, §§ 36–36A (Department of Mental Health records);

    G. L. c. 123B, § 17 (Department of Developmental Services records);

    G. L. c. 127, § 29 (Department of Correction records);

    G. L. c. 127, § 130 (parole board); and

    G. L. c. 148, § 32 (fire insurance).

There are also numerous regulations (Code Mass. Regs.) which contain confidentiality requirements.

(6) Applicability of Federal Law. The Constitution of the United States or an act of Congress may govern the applicability of a privilege in Massachusetts State courts. See, e.g., 23 U.S.C. § 409 (protecting from disclosure in discovery or at trial and in Federal or State court proceedings information "compiled or collected" in connection with certain Federal highway safety programs); Pierce County v. Guillen, 537 U.S. 129, 146–148 (2003) (23 U.S.C. § 409 is a valid exercise of congressional power under the commerce clause and is binding on the States). Accord Boyd v. National R.R. Passenger Corp., 62 Mass. App. Ct. 783, 795–797 (2005). Access to records also may be restricted by Federal law. See, e.g., Commonwealth v. Nathaniel N., 54 Mass. App. Ct. 200, 206 (2002); Health Insurance Portability and Accountability Act (of 1996) (HIPAA), Pub. L. No. 104–191 (codified as amended at 42 U.S.C. § 1320d et seq.).

(g) Production of Presumptively Privileged Records from Nonparties Prior to Trial in Criminal Cases. Whenever a party in a criminal case seeks production of any records (privileged or nonprivileged) from nonparties prior to trial, Mass. R. Crim. P. 17(a)(2) must be satisfied. Commonwealth v. Lampron, 441 Mass. 265, 268 (2004). See also Commonwealth v. Odgren, 455 Mass. 171, 187 (2009). When Mass. R. Crim. P. 17(a)(2) has been satisfied and a nonparty has produced records to the court, the protocol set forth in Commonwealth v. Dwyer, 448 Mass. 122, 139–147 (2006), governs review or disclosure of presumptively privileged records by defense counsel. To reference the forms promulgated by the Supreme Judicial Court, see http://perma.cc/45WM–J4NE.

Cross–Reference: Section 1108, Access to Third–Party Records Prior to Trial in Criminal Cases (Lampron–Dwyer Protocol).

(h) Nonevidentiary Privileges. There are certain so-called privileges which concern nonevidentiary areas. Basically, they are defenses to suit and include the following:

(1) Immunity from Liability (Litigation Privilege). Written or oral communications made by a party, witness, or attorney prior to, in the institution of, or during and as a part of a judicial proceeding involving said party, witness, or attorney are absolutely privileged even if uttered maliciously or in bad faith. See Correllas v. Viveiros, 410 Mass. 314, 319–321 (1991); Sriberg v. Raymond, 370 Mass. 105, 108 (1976); Mezullo v. Maletz, 331 Mass. 233, 236 (1954). The absolute privilege applies to statements made in a letter by an employee to a former employer explaining that the reason for his or her resignation was sexual harassment and indicating an intention to pursue the matter with the Equal Employment Opportunity Commission (EEOC) and the Massachusetts Commission Against Discrimination (MCAD). Further, the absolute privilege extends to similar statements made in a subsequent filing with the EEOC. Visnick v. Caulfield, 73 Mass. App. Ct. 809, 812–813 (2009). The privilege protects speech and does not extend to conduct in furtherance of litigation, such as filing a lawsuit. Gillette Co. v. Provost, 91 Mass. App. Ct. 133, 140–143 (2017). The absolute privilege is based on the view that "it is more important that witnesses be free from the fear of civil liability for what they say than that a person who has been defamed by their testimony have a remedy." Aborn v. Lipson, 357 Mass. 71, 72 (1970). Accord Hoar v. Wood, 44 Mass. 193, 196–198 (1841) (same point with reference to statements by an attorney at trial). Contrast Kobrin v. Gastfriend, 443 Mass. 327, 342 n.17 (2005) (Anti–SLAPP statute, G. L. c. 231, § 59H, supersedes the common-law immunity against allegedly defamatory statements made by an expert witness called by the board of registration in medicine to testify against a medical doctor in a disciplinary proceeding).

A privilege attaches "[w]here a communication to a prospective defendant relates to a proceeding which is contemplated in good faith and which is under serious consideration." Sriberg v. Raymond, 370 Mass. at 109.

"[A]n attorney's statements are privileged where such statements are made by an attorney engaged in his function as an attorney whether in the institution or conduct of litigation or in conferences and other communications preliminary to litigation. The litigation privilege recognized in our cases, however, would not appear to encompass the defendant attorneys' conduct in counselling and assisting their clients in business matters generally." (Citations, quotation, and footnote omitted.)

Kurker v. Hill, 44 Mass. App. Ct. 184, 192 (1998). See Harmon Law Offices, P.C. v. Attorney Gen., 83 Mass. App. Ct. 830, 838 (2013) (privilege not applicable because law firm failed to establish that documents sought by attorney general related to judicial proceedings contemplated or instituted by law firm).

(2) Legislative Deliberation Privilege. Conduct or speech by a member of the Legislature in the course of exercising the member's duties as a legislator is absolutely privileged and cannot be the basis of any criminal or civil prosecution. See Article 21 of the Massachusetts Declaration of Rights ("[t]he freedom of deliberation, speech and debate, in either house of the legislature, is so essential to the rights of the people, that it cannot be the foundation of any accusation or prosecution, action or complaint, in any other court or place whatsoever"). This provision also establishes a privilege applicable to "the giving of a vote, to the making of a written report, and to every other act resulting from the nature, and in the execution, of the office." Coffin v. Coffin, 4 Mass. 1, 27 (1808).

(3) Fair Report Privilege. The fair report privilege is a common-law rule that protects from liability the republisher of a newsworthy account of one person's defamation of another so long as it is fair and accurate. See Howell v. Enterprise Publ. Co., LLC, 455 Mass. 641, 650–651 (2010), and cases cited.

"The privilege recognizes that (1) the public has a right to know of official government actions that affect the public interest, (2) the only practical way many citizens can learn of these actions is through a report by the news media, and (3) the only way news outlets would be willing to make such a report is if they are free from liability, provided that their report was fair and accurate."

ELM Med. Lab, Inc. v. RKO Gen., Inc., 403 Mass. 779, 782 (1989).

"The privilege is not absolute" and "may be 'be vitiated by misconduct on the newspapers' part, but that misconduct must amount to more than negligent, or even knowing, republication of an inaccurate official statement. To defeat the privilege, a plaintiff must either show that the publisher does not give a fair and accurate report of the official statement [or action], or malice.'" Howell v. Enterprise Publ. Co., LLC, 455 Mass. at 651 n.8, quoting Yohe v. Nugent, 321 F.3d 35, 44 (1st Cir. 2003). Newspapers are on "solid ground" when they report on "formal (as opposed to informal) governmental (as opposed to private) proceedings and actions." Howell v. Enterprise Publ. Co., LLC, 455 Mass. at 655–656. In such cases, "the privilege extends to reports of official actions based on information provided by nonofficial third-party sources." Id. at 658.

"If, however, the source is an unofficial or anonymous one, a report based on that source runs a risk that the underlying official action will not be accurately and fairly described by the source, and therefore will not be protected by the privilege, or that the information provided will go beyond the bounds of the official action and into unprivileged territory" (footnote omitted).

Id. at 659. "Whether a report was fair and accurate is a matter of law to be determined by a judge unless there is a basis for divergent views" (citation omitted). Id. at 661.

(4) Communications with Board of Bar Overseers and Bar Counsel. In Bar Counsel v. Farber, 464 Mass. 784, 787 (2013), the Supreme Judicial Court interpreted S.J.C. Rule 4:01, § 9, to provide a complainant with "absolute immunity from any civil liability with respect to his complaint and its allegations and ... with respect to testimony that the complainant may provide in the course of a proceeding before a hearing committee of the board." Id. at 787. The court further explained that the rule does not extend this immunity to statements made or testimony provided by the complainant "to a person or entity outside a bar discipline proceeding." Id. This is true even when the communication to someone outside a bar disciplinary proceeding is identical to the protected communication. Id. at 793.

(5) Legitimate Business Interest. There is a conditional privilege to publish defamatory matter if the publication is reasonably necessary to the protection or furtherance of a legitimate business interest. Bratt v. International Business Machs. Corp., 392 Mass. 508, 512–513 (1984). The business interest privilege applies to protect communications between two parties with a common interest in the subject matter of the communication. Downey v. Chutehall Constr. Co., 86 Mass. App. Ct. 660, 666 (2014).

Section 501. Privileges Recognized Only as Provided

Except as otherwise provided by constitution, statute, rules promulgated by the Supreme Judicial Court, or the common law, no person has a privilege to

(a) refuse to be a witness,

(b) refuse to disclose any matter,

(c) refuse to produce any object or writing, or

(d) prevent another from being a witness or disclosing any matter or producing any object or writing.

NOTE

This section, which is taken nearly verbatim from Proposed Mass. R. Evid. 501, reflects Massachusetts practice. Subsections (a), (b), and (c) follow the "longstanding principle that the public ... has a right to every man's evidence" (quotations omitted). Matter of Roche, 381 Mass. 624, 633 (1980). See also G. L. c. 233, § 20 ("[a]ny person of sufficient understanding, although a party, may testify in any proceeding, civil or criminal, in court or before a person who has authority to receive evidence").

"A witness may not decline to respond to a proper question on the ground that his answer might embarrass him (or another) ... Nor can fear of harm to the witness generally be offered as an excuse for declining testimony. Relief of witnesses on this ground would encourage intimidation of those in possession of information and proclaim a sorry confession of weakness of the rule of law" (citation omitted).

Commonwealth v. Johnson, 365 Mass. 534, 543–544 (1974). Subsection (d) is derived from Commonwealth v. Edwards, 444 Mass. 526, 536 (2005) ("forfeiture by wrongdoing" doctrine adopted).

The Supreme Judicial Court has the power to create privileges under the common law. Babets v. Secretary of Human Servs., 403 Mass. 230, 234 (1988). However, the creation of a new privilege or the expansion of an existing privilege is usually left to the Legislature, which is better equipped to weigh competing social policies or interests. Matter of a Grand Jury Subpoena, 430 Mass. 590, 597–598 (2000).

Address of Witness. A party seeking to elicit information about the home or employment address of a witness must demonstrate that the information is relevant in accordance with Section 402, General Admissibility of Relevant Evidence. However, "the very starting point in exposing falsehood and bringing out the truth through cross-examination must necessarily be to ask the witness who he is and where he lives" (quotations and citation omitted). Smith v. Illinois, 390 U.S. 129, 131 (1968). Nonetheless, such evidence may be excluded if the trial judge makes a preliminary finding that any relevance is outweighed by the risks to the safety of the witness. See Commonwealth v. McGrath, 364 Mass. 243, 250–252 (1973). In a criminal case, the trial judge must weigh the safety concerns of the witness against the defendant's right to confrontation. See McGrath v. Vinzant, 528 F.2d 681, 685 (1st Cir. 1976). A witness's general concerns for privacy or personal safety, without more, are not sufficient to overcome the defendant's right to confrontation under Article 12 of the Massachusetts Declaration of Rights and the Sixth Amendment. See Commonwealth v. Johnson, 365 Mass. 534, 544–547 (1974). See also Commonwealth v. Francis, 432 Mass. 353, 357 (2000) (In a murder case, Supreme Judicial Court relied on McGrath and upheld trial judge's ruling that "defense counsel could ask Rodriguez whether he was engaged in an occupation other than selling drugs, but not his specific employment or his employment address, and whether he now lived in western Massachusetts or in Connecticut, but not his city of residence or residential address. He also prohibited defense counsel from investigating these matters."); Commonwealth v. Righini, 64 Mass. App. Ct. 19, 25–26 n.5 (2005) (relying on reasoning of McGrath to explain why criminal defendants are ordinarily not entitled to obtain dates of birth of police witnesses). The existence of valid safety concerns on the part of a witness may be inherent in the nature of the criminal charges. Commonwealth v. Francis, 432 Mass. at 358 n.3.

Section 502. Attorney–Client Privilege

(a) Definitions. As used in this section, the following words shall have the following meanings:

(1) A "client" is a person, public officer, or corporation, association, or other entity, either public or private, who is rendered professional legal services by an attorney, or who consults an attorney with a view to obtaining professional legal services.

(2) A "representative of the client" may include the client's agent or employee.

(3) An "attorney" is a person who is authorized to practice law.

(4) A "representative of the attorney" is one used by the attorney to assist the attorney in providing professional legal services.

(5) A communication is "confidential" if it is not intended to be disclosed to third persons other than those to whom disclosure is made to obtain or provide professional legal services to the client, and those reasonably necessary for the transmission of the communication.

(b) General Rule of Privilege. A client has a privilege to refuse to disclose and to prevent others from disclosing confidential communications made for the purpose of obtaining or providing professional legal services to the client as follows:

(1) between the client or the client's representative and the client's attorney or the attorney's representative,

(2) between the client's attorney and the attorney's representative,

(3) between those involved in a joint defense,

(4) between representatives of the client or between the client and a representative of the client, or

(5) among attorneys and their representatives representing the same client.

(c) Who May Claim the Privilege. The privilege may be claimed by the client, the client's guardian or conservator, the personal representative of a deceased client, or the successor, trustee, or similar representative of a corporation, association, or other organization whether or not in existence at the time the privilege is claimed. The attorney or the attorney's representative at the time of the communication is presumed to have authority to claim the privilege but only on behalf of the client.

(d) Exceptions. The attorney-client privilege does not apply to the following:

(1) Furtherance of Crime or Fraud. If the services of the attorney were sought or obtained to commit or to plan to commit what the client knew or reasonably should have known was a crime or fraud;

(2) Claimants Through Same Deceased Client. As to a communication relevant to an issue between parties who claim through the same deceased client, regardless of whether the claims are by testate or intestate succession or by inter vivos transaction;

(3) Breach of Duty or Obligation. As to a communication relevant to an issue of breach of duty between an attorney and client;

(4) Document Attested by an Attorney. As to a communication relevant to an issue concerning an attested document to which the attorney is an attesting witness;

(5) Joint Clients. As to a communication relevant to a matter of common interest between or among two or more clients if the communication was made by any one of them to an attorney retained or consulted in common, when offered in an action between or among any of the clients; or

(6) Public Officer or Agency. [Privilege not recognized]

NOTE

Introduction. The Supreme Judicial Court has defined the attorney-client privilege as follows:

"The classic formulation of the attorney-client privilege . . . is found in 8 J. Wigmore, Evidence § 2292 (McNaughton rev. ed. 1961): (1) Where legal advice of any kind is sought (2) from a professional legal adviser in his capacity as such, (3) the communications relating to that purpose, (4) made in confidence (5) by the client, (6) are at his instance permanently protected (7) from disclosure by himself or by the legal adviser, (8) except the protection be waived. The purpose of the privilege is to enable clients to make full disclosure to legal counsel of all relevant facts . . . so that counsel may render fully informed legal advice with the goal of promot[ing] broader public interests in the observance of law and administration of justice." (Quotations and citations omitted.)

Commissioner of Revenue v. Comcast Corp., 453 Mass. 293, 303 (2009).

"The existence of the privilege and the applicability of any exception to the privilege is a question of fact for the judge. The burden of proving that the attorney-client privilege applies to a communication rests on the party asserting the privilege. This burden extends not only to a showing of the existence of the attorney-client relationship but to all other elements involved in the determination of the existence of the privilege, including (1) the communications were received from a client during the course of the client's search for legal advice from the attorney in his or her capacity as such; (2) the

communications were made in confidence; and (3) the privilege as to these communications has not been waived." (Citations omitted.)

Matter of the Reorganization of Elec. Mut. Liab. Ins. Co. (Bermuda), 425 Mass. 419, 421 (1997). This privilege is not self-executing. See District Attorney for the Plymouth Dist. v. Board of Selectmen of Middleborough, 395 Mass. 629, 633–634 (1985).

Subsection (a)(1). This subsection, which is taken nearly verbatim from Proposed Mass. R. Evid. 502(a)(1), reflects Massachusetts practice. The term "client" includes more than simply natural persons. See Mass. R. Prof. C. 1.13 (2015). See also Matter of a Grand Jury Investigation, 437 Mass. 340, 351–352 (2002); Bays v. Theran, 418 Mass. 685, 690 (1994).

An attorney-client relationship may be expressly created or implied as a matter of law. Cesso v. Todd, 92 Mass. App. Ct. 131, 135 (2017). An attorney-client relationship may be implied "when (1) a person seeks advice or assistance from an attorney, (2) the advice or assistance sought pertains to matters within the attorney's professional competence, and (3) the attorney expressly or impliedly agrees to give or actually gives the desired advice or assistance." DeVaux v. American Home Assur. Co., 387 Mass. 814, 817–818 (1983), quoting Kurtenback v. TeKippe, 260 N.W.2d 53 (Iowa 1977). See Cesso v. Todd, 92 Mass. App. Ct. at 135. The attorney-client privilege survives the death of the client. Matter of a John Doe Grand Jury Investigation, 408 Mass. 480, 483 (1990).

Subsection (a)(2). This subsection is derived from Ellingsgard v. Silver, 352 Mass. 34, 40 (1967) ("The attorney-client privilege may extend to communications from the client's agent or employee to the attorney."). The Supreme Judicial Court has yet to determine the scope of the privilege when the client is an organization such as a corporation. See Judge Rotenberg Educ. Ctr., Inc. v. Commissioner of the Dep't of Mental Retardation, 424 Mass. 430, 457 n.26 (1997) (attorney-client privilege not automatically extended to all employees of corporation who communicate with corporation's attorney). Cf. Messing, Rudavsky & Weliky, P.C. v. President & Fellows of Harvard College, 436 Mass. 347, 357 (2002) (a lawyer is barred from ex parte contact with employees of a corporation, under the rule of professional responsibility prohibiting a lawyer from communicating with a represented party in the absence of that party's counsel, only as to employees who exercise managerial responsibility with regard to the subject of pending litigation, those alleged to have committed wrongful actions at issue in the litigation, and employees with authority to make decisions about the course of litigation or having management authority sufficient to speak for and bind the corporation).

Subsection (a)(3). This subsection is derived from Barnes v. Harris, 61 Mass. 576, 576–577 (1851).

Subsection (a)(4). This subsection, which is taken nearly verbatim from Proposed Mass. R. Evid. 502(a)(4), reflects Massachusetts practice. In Foster v. Hall, 29 Mass. 89 (1831), the court explained that the attorney-client privilege applied to communications to members of the legal profession, and also to those who "facilitate the communication between attorney and client, as interpreters, agents, and attorneys' clerks" (citations omitted). Id. at 94.

Subsection (a)(5). This subsection is derived from Commissioner of Revenue v. Comcast Corp., 453 Mass. 293 (2009), and DaRosa v. City of New Bedford, 471 Mass. 446 (2015). In general, "information contained within a communication need not itself be confidential for the communication to be deemed privileged; rather the communication must be made in confidence—that is, with the expectation that the communication will not be divulged." Commissioner of Revenue v. Comcast Corp., 453 Mass. at 305. Thus, "[c]ommunications between an attorney and his client are not privileged, though made privately, if it is understood that the information communicated is to be conveyed to others." Peters v. Wallach, 366 Mass. 622, 627 (1975).

The Supreme Judicial Court, however, has recognized a derivative attorney-client privilege that "can shield communications of a third party employed to facilitate communication between the attorney and client and thereby assist the attorney in rendering legal advice to the client." Commissioner of Revenue v. Comcast Corp., 453 Mass. at 306, citing United States v. Kovel, 296 F.2d 918, 921–922 (2d Cir. 1961). See also Hanover Ins. Co. v. Rapo & Jepsen Ins. Servs., Inc., 449 Mass. 609, 616 (2007). "The purpose of the derivative attorney-client privilege is to maintain the [attorney-client] privilege for communications between the attorney and the client in circumstances where a third party's presence would otherwise constitute a waiver of the privilege." DaRosa v. City of New Bedford, 471 Mass. at 463–464.

But the derivative attorney-client privilege is "sharply limited in scope." DaRosa v. City of New Bedford, 471 Mass. at 463. "It attaches only when the third party's role is to clarify or facilitate communications between attorney and client, as where the third party functions as a translator between the client and the attorney, and is therefore nearly indispensable or serves some specialized purpose in facilitating the attorney-client communications" (quotations, citations, and brackets omitted). Id. "The privilege does not apply simply because 'an attorney's ability to represent a client is improved, even substantially, by the assistance' of an expert." Id., quoting Commissioner of Revenue v. Comcast Corp., 453 Mass. at 307.

> "In short, the derivative attorney-client privilege protects otherwise privileged communications between an attorney and client despite the presence of a third party where, without the assistance of the third party, what the client says would be 'Greek' to the attorney, either because the client is actually speaking in Greek or because the information provided by the client is so technical in nature that it might as well be spoken in Greek if there were not an expert to interpret it for the attorney."

DaRosa v. City of New Bedford, 471 Mass. at 463 (concluding that communications at issue failed to meet this test because, even if third party's analysis were "critical" to attorney's ability to effectively represent his client, third party was "translating" public record technical data, "*not* confidential communications from the client"). See also Commissioner of Revenue v. Comcast Corp., 453 Mass. at 309 (concluding that derivative attorney-client privilege did not apply because attorney's "purpose in consulting [third party] was to obtain advice about Massachusetts tax law, not to assist [attorney] with comprehending his client's information.").

Subsection (b). Subsections (b)(1), (2), (4), and (5) are derived from Proposed Mass. R. Evid. 502(b), which was cited with approval in Purcell v. District Attorney for the Suffolk Dist., 424 Mass. 109, 115 (1997) ("The attorney-client privilege applies only when the client's communication was for the purpose of facilitating the rendition of legal services."). See McCarthy v. Slade Assocs., Inc., 463 Mass. 181, 191 n.21 (2012) (privilege applies to confidential communications by attorney as well as client). Subsection (b)(3) is derived from Hanover Ins. Co. v. Rapo & Jepsen Ins. Servs., Inc., 449 Mass. 609, 614–617 (2007), where the Supreme Judicial Court recognized the "common interest doctrine" and adopted the principle of the Restatement (Third) of the Law Governing Lawyers § 76(1) (2000), which states as follows:

> "If two or more clients with a common interest in a litigated or nonlitigated matter are represented by separate lawyers and they agree to exchange information concerning the matter, a communication of any such client that otherwise qualifies as privileged . . . that relates to the matter is privileged as against third persons. Any such client may invoke the privilege, unless it has been waived by the client who made the communication."

This principle expresses the component of the doctrine known as "joint defense agreements," "joint defense privilege," or "joint prosecution privilege." See also Proposed Mass. R. Evid. 502(b)(3). In Hanover Ins. Co. v. Rapo & Jepsen Ins. Servs., Inc., 449 Mass. at 618, the Supreme Judicial Court explained that the common-interest doctrine depends on communications that are protected by the attorney-client privilege and is simply an exception to the waiver of the privilege. Thus, there is no requirement of a writing. Id. at 618. The court also explained that the legal interests of the parties do not have to be

identical in order for the common-interest doctrine to apply. Parties will be deemed to have a common interest when they "share a sufficiently similar interest and attempt to promote that interest by sharing a privileged communication" (quotation and citation omitted). Id. at 619. Finally, the Supreme Judicial Court also noted that Section 76(2) of the Restatement is consistent with Massachusetts law. Id. at 614 n.4. Section 76(2) states that "[u]nless the clients have agreed otherwise, a communication described in Subsection (1) is not privileged as between clients described in Subsection (1) in a subsequent adverse proceeding between them." Id., quoting Restatement (Third) of the Law Governing Lawyers § 76(2) (2000).

Subsection (c). This subsection, which is taken nearly verbatim from Proposed Mass. R. Evid. 502(c), reflects Massachusetts practice. See District Attorney for the Norfolk Dist. v. Magraw, 417 Mass. 169, 172–173 (1994). In the case of litigation between a corporation and its shareholders, the corporation may assert the privilege against a shareholder whose interests are opposed to the corporation's interests, because the privilege belongs to the corporation and not to the individual shareholders. See Chambers v. Gold Medal Bakery, Inc., 464 Mass. 383, 392 (2013); Clair v. Clair, 464 Mass. 205, 218 (2013). A law firm may claim the attorney-client privilege for communications between law firm attorneys and the firm's in-house counsel against a client who threatens a malpractice claim against the firm if (1) the law firm has designated an attorney or attorneys within the firm to represent the firm as in-house counsel; (2) the in-house counsel has not performed any work on the client matter at issue or a substantially related matter; (3) the time spent by the attorneys in these communications with in-house counsel is not billed to a client; and (4) the communications are made in confidence and kept confidential. RFF Family Partnership LLP v. Burns & Levinson LLP, 465 Mass. 702, 703 (2013).

Subsection (d)(1). This subsection is taken nearly verbatim from Proposed Mass. R. Evid. 502(d)(1), which the Supreme Judicial Court described as an adequate definition of the crime-fraud exception to the attorney-client privilege. Purcell v. District Attorney for the Suffolk Dist., 424 Mass. 109, 112 (1997). See also Mass. R. Prof. C. 1.6(b)(3) (2015). "Th[e] exception applies only if the client or prospective client seeks advice or assistance in furtherance of criminal conduct." Purcell v. District Attorney for the Suffolk Dist., 424 Mass. at 115. See Matter of a Grand Jury Investigation, 453 Mass. 453, 459 (2009) ("a client's communications to his lawyer threatening harm are privileged unless the crime-fraud exception applies").

Subsection (d)(2). This subsection, which is taken nearly verbatim from Proposed Mass. R. Evid. 502(d)(2), reflects Massachusetts practice. See Phillips v. Chase, 201 Mass. 444, 449 (1909).

Subsection (d)(3). This subsection, which is taken nearly verbatim from Proposed Mass. R. Evid. 502(d)(3), reflects Massachusetts practice. See Mass. R. Prof. C. 1.6(b) (2015); GTE Prods. Corp. v. Stewart, 421 Mass. 22, 32 (1995) (there are limits to the extent to which in-house counsel may disclose client confidences in pursuing a claim of wrongful discharge); Commonwealth v. Brito, 390 Mass. 112, 119 (1983) ("[T]rial counsel's obligation may continue to preserve confidences whose disclosure is not relevant to the defense of the charge of his ineffectiveness as counsel.").

Subsection (d)(4). This subsection, which is taken nearly verbatim from Proposed Mass. R. Evid. 502(d)(4), reflects Massachusetts practice. See Foster v. Hall, 29 Mass. 89, 98–99 (1831).

Subsection (d)(5). This subsection, which is taken nearly verbatim from Proposed Mass. R. Evid. 502(d)(5), reflects Massachusetts practice. See Beacon Oil Co. v. Perelis, 263 Mass. 288, 293 (1928); Thompson v. Cashman, 181 Mass. 36, 37 (1902).

Subsection (d)(6). In Suffolk Constr. Co. v. Division of Capital Asset Mgt., 449 Mass. 444, 450 (2007), the Supreme Judicial Court held that "confidential communications between public officers and employees and governmental entities and their legal counsel undertaken for the purpose of obtaining legal advice or assistance are protected under the normal rules of the attorney-client privilege." Thus, the Supreme Judicial Court rejected the proposed limitation on the attorney-client privilege for public employees and governmental entities found in Proposed Mass. R. Evid. 502(d)(6). Id. at 452 n.12. Additionally, the Supreme Judicial Court held that its decision in General Elec. Co. v. Department of Envtl. Protection, 429 Mass. 798, 801–806 (1999), which states that under the Massachusetts public records statute, G. L. c. 66, § 10, documents held by a State agency are not protected from disclosure under the attorney work-product doctrine, but rather enjoy the more limited protection of the so-called "deliberative process" exemption found in G. L. c. 4, § 7, Twenty-sixth (d), did not limit the applicability of the attorney-client privilege as to written communications between government officials and entities and their counsel.

> "With the attorney-client privilege, the principal focus is on encouraging the client to communicate freely with the attorney; with work-product, it is on encouraging careful and thorough preparation by the attorney. As a result, there are differences in the scope of the protection. For example, the privilege extends only to client communications, while work product encompasses much that has its source outside client communications. At the same time, the privilege extends to client-attorney communications whenever any sort of legal services are being provided, but the work-product protection is limited to preparations for litigation."

Suffolk Constr. Co. v. Division of Capital Asset Mgt., 449 Mass. at 456, quoting E.S. Epstein, The Attorney–Client Privilege and the Work–Product Doctrine 477 (4th ed. 2001).

Work–Product Doctrine. The work-product doctrine is not an evidentiary privilege, but rather a discovery rule which

> "protects a client's nonlawyer representatives, protecting from discovery documents prepared by a party's representative 'in anticipation of litigation.' The protection is qualified, and can be overcome if the party seeking discovery demonstrates 'substantial need of the materials' and that it is 'unable without undue hardship to obtain the substantial equivalent of the materials by other means.' There is a further limitation: the court is to 'protect against disclosure of the mental impressions, conclusions, opinions, or legal theories of an attorney or other representative of a party concerning the litigation.' This so-called 'opinion' work product is afforded greater protection than 'fact' work product."

Commissioner of Revenue v. Comcast Corp., 453 Mass. 293, 314 (2009), quoting Mass. R. Civ. P. 26(b)(3).

> "The work product doctrine, drawn from the well-known case of Hickman v. Taylor, 329 U.S. 495 (1947), is intended to enhance the vitality of an adversary system of litigation by insulating counsel's work from intrusions, inferences, or borrowings by other parties as he prepares for the contest. Originally developed in connection with civil litigation, the doctrine has been extended to criminal cases. United States v. Nobles, 422 U.S. 225, 238 (1974)." (Citations omitted.)

Ward v. Peabody, 380 Mass. 805, 817 (1980). It is codified in Massachusetts and applicable in both civil and criminal cases. See Mass. R. Civ. P. 26(b)(3); Mass. R. Crim. P. 14(a)(5). The protections afforded by the work-product doctrine can be waived by the attorney. Adoption of Sherry, 435 Mass. 331, 336 (2001). See also Matter of the Reorganization of Elec. Mut. Liab. Ins. Co. (Bermuda), 425 Mass. 419, 423 (1997) (no waiver when disclosure of work-product is due to inadvertence and adequate steps were taken to maintain the confidentiality of the information).

Scope of the Work–Product Doctrine in the Public Records Context. In DaRosa v. City of New Bedford, 471 Mass. 446 (2015), the Supreme Judicial Court addressed the work-product doctrine as it applies to public records:

> "[O]pinion work product that was prepared in anticipation of litigation or for trial by or for a party or party representative is

protected from discovery to the extent provided under Mass. R. Civ. P. 26(b)(3), even where the opinion work product has been made or received by a State or local government employee. So is fact work product that is prepared in anticipation of litigation or for trial where it is not a reasonably completed study or report, or, if it is reasonably completed, is interwoven with opinions or analysis leading to opinions. Other fact work product that has been made or received by a State or local government employee must be disclosed in discovery, even if it would be protected from discovery under rule 26(b)(3) were it not a public record."

DaRosa v. City of New Bedford, 471 Mass. at 462. If any work product is not a "public record" because it falls within the exemption found in G. L. c. 4, § 7, Twenty-sixth (d) (or any another exemption), the work product may not be ordered to be produced in discovery unless the third-party defendants have made the required showing of need to justify disclosure of this work product under Mass. R. Civ. P. 26(b)(3). Id. at 464.

Burden of Proof. Initially, the burden is on the party asserting the work-product doctrine to demonstrate that the document was prepared in anticipation of litigation. If that burden is met, the burden shifts to the party seeking access to the document to prove that it cannot obtain the substantial equivalent of the document without undue hardship. If the material is opinion work product, the party seeking access to it must make, at a minimum, a "far stronger showing of necessity and unavailability by other means." Upjohn Co. v. United States, 449 U.S. 383, 402 (1981). See Commissioner of Revenue v. Comcast Corp., 453 Mass. 293, 315 (2009).

In Comcast Corp., the Supreme Judicial Court further explained that the phrase "in anticipation of litigation" has been defined by courts in two different ways: (1) whether the documents "are prepared 'primarily or exclusively to assist in litigation'—a formulation that would potentially exclude documents containing analysis of expected litigation, if their primary, ultimate, or exclusive purpose is to assist in making the business decision," and (2) whether the documents "were prepared 'because of' existing or expected litigation—a formulation that would include such documents, despite the fact that their purpose is not to 'assist in' litigation" (citation omitted). Id. at 316. In Comcast Corp., the Supreme Judicial Court adopted the second of these two formulations as the law in Massachusetts:

> "The 'because of' test 'appropriately focuses on both what should be eligible for the [r]ule's protection and what should not.' Thus, a document is within the scope of the rule if, 'in light of the nature of the document and the factual situation in the particular case, the document can be fairly said to have been prepared *because of* the prospect of litigation'" (citations omitted).

Id. at 316–317 ("a litigation analysis prepared so that a party can make an informed business decision is afforded the protections of the work-product doctrine"; additionally, memos prepared for counsel by the accountant that were not protected by the attorney-client privilege also fall within the scope of the opinion work-product doctrine).

Opinion work product relating to a different case is nonetheless entitled to work-product protection, although it may require a lesser showing to overcome the work-product rule. McCarthy v. Slade Assocs., Inc., 463 Mass. 181, 198 n.37 (2012).

Waiver. For issues relating to waiver, see Section 523, Waiver of Privilege.

Section 503. Psychotherapist–Patient Privilege

(a) Definitions. As used in this section, the following words shall have the following meanings:

(1) A "patient" is a person who, during the course of diagnosis or treatment, communicates with a psychotherapist.

(2) A "psychotherapist" is (A) a person licensed to practice medicine who devotes a substantial portion of his or her time to the practice of psychiatry; (B) a person who is licensed as a psychologist by the board of registration of psychologists or a graduate of, or student enrolled in, a doctoral degree program in psychology at a recognized educational institution, who is working under the supervision of a licensed psychologist; or (C) a person who is a registered nurse licensed by the board of registration in nursing whose certificate of registration has been endorsed authorizing the practice of professional nursing in an expanded role as a psychiatric nurse mental health clinical specialist.

(3) "Communications" includes conversations, correspondence, actions, and occurrences relating to diagnosis or treatment before, during, or after institutionalization, regardless of the patient's awareness of such conversations, correspondence, actions, and occurrences, and any records, memoranda, or notes of the foregoing.

(b) Privilege. Except as hereinafter provided, in any court proceeding and in any proceeding preliminary thereto, and in legislative and administrative proceedings, a patient shall have the privilege of refusing to disclose, and of preventing a witness from disclosing, any communication, wherever made, between said patient and a psychotherapist relative to the diagnosis or treatment of the patient's mental or emotional condition. This privilege shall also apply to patients engaged with a psychotherapist in marital therapy, family therapy, or consultation in contemplation of such therapy. If a patient is incompetent to exercise or waive such privilege, a guardian shall be appointed to act in his or her behalf under this section. A previously appointed guardian shall be authorized to so act.

(c) Effect of Exercise of Privilege. Upon the exercise of the privilege granted by this section, the judge or presiding officer shall instruct the jury that no adverse inference may be drawn therefrom.

(d) Exceptions. The privilege granted hereunder shall not apply to any of the following communications:

(1) **Disclosure to Establish Need for Hospitalization or Imminently Dangerous Activity.** A disclosure made by a psychotherapist who, in the course of diagnosis or treatment of the patient, determines that the patient is in need of treatment in a hospital for mental or emotional illness or that there is a threat of imminently dangerous activity by the patient against himself or herself or another person, and on the basis of such determination discloses such communication either for the purpose of placing or retaining the patient in such hospital, provided, however, that the provisions of this section shall continue in effect after the patient is in said hospital, or placing the patient under arrest or under the supervision of law enforcement authorities;

(2) **Court–Ordered Psychiatric Exam.** A disclosure made to a psychotherapist in the course of a psychiatric examination ordered by the court, provided that such disclosure was made after the patient was informed that the communication would not be privileged, and provided further that such communications shall be admissible only on issues involving the patient's mental or emotional condition but not as a confession or admission of guilt;

(3) **Patient Raises the Issue of Own Mental or Emotional Condition as an Element of Claim or Defense.** A disclosure in any proceeding, except one involving child custody, adoption, or adoption consent, in which the patient introduces the patient's mental or emotional condition as an element of a claim or defense, and the judge or presiding officer finds that it is more important to the interests of justice that the communication be disclosed than that the relationship between patient and psychotherapist be protected;

(4) **Party Through Deceased Patient Raises Issue of Decedent's Mental or Emotional Condition as Element of Claim or Defense.** A disclosure in any proceeding after the death of a patient in which the patient's mental or emotional condition is introduced by any party claiming or defending through, or as a beneficiary of, the patient as an element of the claim or defense, and the judge or presiding officer finds that it is more important to the interests of justice that the communication be disclosed than that the relationship between patient and psychotherapist be protected;

(5) **Child Custody and Adoption Cases.** A disclosure in any case involving child custody, adoption, or the dispensing with the need for consent to adoption in which, upon a hearing in chambers, the judge, in the exercise of his or her discretion, determines that the psychotherapist has evidence bearing significantly on the patient's ability to provide suitable care or custody, and that it is more important to the welfare of the child that the communication be disclosed than that the relationship between patient and psychotherapist be protected; provided, however, that in such cases of adoption or the dispensing with the need for consent to adoption, a judge shall first determine that the patient has been informed that such communication would not be privileged;

(6) **Claim Against Psychotherapist.** A disclosure in any proceeding brought by the patient against the psychotherapist, and in any malpractice, criminal, or license revocation proceeding, in which disclosure is necessary or relevant to the claim or defense of the psychotherapist; or

(7) **Child Abuse or Neglect.** A report to the Department of Children and Families of reasonable cause to believe that a child under the age of eighteen has suffered serious physical or emotional injury resulting from sexual abuse, pursuant to G. L. c. 119, § 51A.

(8) **Exception.** In criminal actions, such confidential communications may be subject to discovery and may be admissible as evidence, subject to applicable law.

NOTE

Subsection (a). This subsection is taken nearly verbatim from G. L. c. 233, § 20B.

Subsection (b). This subsection is taken nearly verbatim from G. L. c. 233, § 20B. The psychotherapist-patient privilege recognizes the critical role of confidentiality in this medical specialty. Usen v. Usen, 359 Mass. 453, 457 (1971). This privilege is not self-executing. Commonwealth v. Oliveira, 438 Mass. 325, 331 (2002). See also Commonwealth v. Pickering, 479 Mass. 589, 596–597 (2018). The Supreme Judicial Court has left open whether privilege applies in group therapy settings.

Scope of the Privilege. "The privilege gives the patient the right to refuse to disclose and to prevent another witness from disclosing any communication between patient and psychotherapist concerning diagnosis or treatment of the patient's mental condition." Commonwealth v. Clancy, 402 Mass. 664, 667 (1988). The privilege is case-specific, and a waiver in one proceeding is not a waiver in a subsequent proceeding. Care & Protection of M.C., 479 Mass. 246, 263 (2018). The privilege does not protect the facts of the hospitalization or treatment, the dates, or the purpose of the hospitalization or treatment, if such purpose does not implicate communications between the witnesses and the psychotherapist. Commonwealth v. Clancy, 402 Mass. at 667. See Commonwealth v. Kobrin, 395 Mass. 284, 294 (1985) (holding, in context of grand jury investigation into Medicaid fraud, that patient diagnosis is not privileged but portions of records that "reflect patients' thoughts, feelings, and impressions, or contain the substance of the psychotherapeutic dialogue are protected").

The privilege is evidentiary and applies only "in any court proceeding and in any proceeding preliminary thereto and in legislative and administrative proceedings." G. L. c. 233, § 20B. See Commonwealth v. Brandwein, 435 Mass. 623, 628–630 (2002) (psychotherapist not prohibited by G. L. c. 233, § 20B, from informing police of statements made to her in her office by a client who confessed to a robbery and turned over a firearm).

Presence of Third Party. A conversation with a psychotherapist may still be privileged under G. L. c. 233, § 20B, notwithstanding the presence of a required police guard. See Commonwealth v. Waweru, 480 Mass. 173, 185 (2018).

Subsection (c). This subsection is taken verbatim from G. L. c. 233, § 20B.

Subsection (d)(1). This subsection is taken nearly verbatim from G. L. c. 233, § 20B(a). See Walden Behavioral Care v. K.I., 471 Mass. 150, 154 (2015).

Subsection (d)(2). This subsection is taken nearly verbatim from G. L. c. 233, § 20B(b). See Commonwealth v. Lamb, 365 Mass. 265, 270 (1974) (patient's communications to a psychotherapist in a court-ordered evaluation may not be disclosed against the patient's wishes absent a warning that the communications would not be privileged). See also Commonwealth v. Harris, 468 Mass. 429, 452 (2014) (Lamb warnings given at the beginning of court-ordered competency evaluations should contain a warning that the results of the competency evaluation may be used against the defendant where the defendant offers evidence at trial in support of a defense of lack of criminal responsibility.).

In the absence of a court order, a Lamb-type warning is not required where the examiner is a diagnosing or treating psychotherapist of a patient involuntarily committed to a mental health facility pursuant to G. L. c. 123, § 12(b). Walden Behavioral Care v. K.I., 471 Mass. 150, 154 (2015). Contrast Department of Youth Servs. v. A Juvenile, 398 Mass. 516, 524–526 (1986).

Subsection (d)(3). This subsection is taken nearly verbatim from G. L. c. 233, § 20B(c). In Commonwealth v. Dung Van Tran, 463 Mass. 8, 20–21 (2012), the Supreme Judicial Court found that the defendant did not put his mental or emotional condition in issue where "the defense was not that the defendant was incapable of forming the intent necessary to support conviction but, rather, that he lacked the requisite intent to harm another." Id. at 20. The court held that the "Commonwealth may not introduce against a defendant statements protected by the psychotherapist-patient privilege on the ground that the defendant himself placed his mental or emotional condition in issue, unless the defendant has at some point in the proceedings asserted a defense based on his mental or emotional condition, defect, or impairment." Id. at 21. See Care & Protection of M.C., 479 Mass. 246, 263 (2018) (introduction of psychiatric evidence at care and protection proceeding does not waive privilege, and such evidence is not admissible at criminal trial unless privilege holder puts mental health at issue).

Subsection (d)(4). This subsection is taken nearly verbatim from G. L. c. 233, § 20B(d).

Subsection (d)(5). This subsection is taken nearly verbatim from G. L. c. 233, § 20B(e). Upon a party's assertion of the psychotherapist-patient privilege, the judge, and not a guardian ad litem, must inspect the psychotherapist's records in camera to determine whether the records are subject to the privilege. See P.W. v. M.S., 67 Mass. App. Ct. 779, 785–786 (2006). A judge may appoint a discovery master or additional guardian ad litem to assist in the process of reviewing records, but the judge must make the determination whether the privilege applies to the records. See id. at 786 & n.10.

Subsection (d)(6). This subsection is taken nearly verbatim from G. L. c. 233, § 20B(f).

Subsection (d)(7). This subsection is derived from G. L. c. 119, § 51A.

Subsection (d)(8). This subsection is derived from Commonwealth v. Dwyer, 448 Mass. 122, 145–146 (2006) (establishing protocol in criminal cases governing access to and use of material covered by statutory privilege). See Introductory Note to Article V, Privileges and Disqualifications.

Section 504. Spousal Privilege and Disqualification; Parent–Child Disqualification

(a) Spousal Privilege.

(1) General Rule. A spouse shall not be compelled to testify in the trial of an indictment, complaint, or other criminal proceeding brought against the other spouse.

(2) Who May Claim the Privilege. Only the witness-spouse may claim the privilege.

(3) Exceptions. This privilege shall not apply in civil proceedings, or in any prosecution for nonsupport, desertion, neglect of parental duty, or child abuse, including incest.

(b) Spousal Disqualification.

(1) General Rule. In any proceeding, civil or criminal, a witness shall not testify as to private conversations with a spouse occurring during their marriage.

(2) Exceptions. This disqualification shall not apply to

(A) a proceeding arising out of or involving a contract between spouses;

(B) a proceeding to establish paternity or to modify or enforce a support order;

(C) a prosecution for nonsupport, desertion, or neglect of parental duty;

(D) child abuse proceedings, including incest;

(E) any criminal proceeding in which a spouse has been charged with a crime against the other spouse;

(F) a violation of a vacate, restraining, or no-contact order or judgment issued by a Massachusetts court or a similar protection order from another jurisdiction;

(G) a declaration of a deceased spouse if the court finds that it was made in good faith and upon the personal knowledge of the declarant; or

(H) a criminal proceeding in which the private conversation reveals a bias or motive on the part of a spouse testifying against his or her spouse.

(c) Parent–Child Disqualification.

(1) Definitions. As used in this subsection, the following words shall have the following meanings:

(A) Minor Child. A "minor child" is any person under eighteen years of age.

(B) Parent. A "parent" is the biological or adoptive parent, stepparent, legal guardian, or other person who has the right to act in loco parentis for the minor child referred to in Subsection (c)(1)(A).

(2) Disqualification. A parent shall not testify against the parent's minor child and a minor child shall not testify against the child's parent in a proceeding before an inquest, grand jury, trial of an indictment or complaint, or any other criminal, delinquency, or youthful offender proceeding in which the victim in the proceeding is not a family member and does not reside in the family household. In a case in which the victim is a family member and resides in the family household, the parent shall not testify as to any communication with the minor child that was for the purpose of seeking advice regarding the child's legal rights.

NOTE

Subsection (a)(1). This subsection is taken nearly verbatim from G. L. c. 233, § 20, Second.

The existence of the privilege depends on whether the spouse who asserts it is then married. The privilege applies even if the spouse was not married at the time of the events that are the subject of the criminal trial, and even if the spouse who asserts the privilege had testified in an earlier proceeding or trial. See Commonwealth v. DiPietro, 373 Mass. 369, 382 (1977). There is no common-law privilege, similar to the spousal privilege, applicable to unmarried cohabitants. Commonwealth v. Diaz, 422 Mass. 269, 274 (1996).

The privilege not to testify against a spouse applies regardless of whether the proposed testimony would be favorable or unfavorable to the other spouse. Commonwealth v. Maillet, 400 Mass. 572, 578 (1987). The privilege is broad and it applies even though a spouse is called to give testimony concerning "persons other than the spouse." Matter of a Grand Jury Subpoena, 447 Mass. 88, 97 (2006).

The privilege applies to testimony at trial and not to testimony before a grand jury. See Matter of a Grand Jury Subpoena, 447 Mass. at 99. (court finds it unnecessary to "decide whether, or to what extent, the spousal privilege may be invoked in pretrial [or posttrial] proceedings"). But see Commonwealth v. Szerlong, 457 Mass. 858, 864 (2010) (spousal privilege applied at pretrial hearing on motion in limine). The court should conduct a voir dire, outside the presence of the jury, and may inquire of the witness whether he or she will assert the privilege or otherwise refuse to testify. Id. at 864 n.10, citing Commonwealth v. Fisher, 433 Mass. 340, 350 (2001). However, a "spouse cannot be forced to testify regarding [his or] her reasons for doing so." Id. The privilege does not apply to posttrial evidentiary hearings where the spouse is not a defendant. Commonwealth v. Cotto, 471 Mass. 97, 118–119 (2015).

Subsection (a)(2). This subsection is derived from Commonwealth v. Spencer, 212 Mass. 438, 451 (1912). See also Commonwealth v. Stokes, 374 Mass. 583, 595 (1978).

A spouse may testify against the other spouse if he or she is willing to do so. Commonwealth v. Saltzman, 258 Mass. 109, 110 (1927). The defendant-spouse has no standing to object to his or her spouse's testimony. Commonwealth v. Stokes, 374 Mass. at 595. When a spouse decides to waive the privilege and testify against his or her spouse in a criminal proceeding, the judge should be satisfied, outside the presence of the jury, that the waiver is knowing and voluntary. Id. at 595 n.9.

Subsection (a)(3). This subsection is derived from G. L. c. 233, § 20, Second, and G. L. c. 273, § 7. See Three Juveniles v. Commonwealth, 390 Mass. 357, 361 (1983) (privilege inapplicable in civil proceedings), cert. denied, 465 U.S. 1068 (1984).

Subsection (b)(1). This subsection is derived from G. L. c. 233, § 20, First.

The disqualification, unlike the privilege, bars either spouse from testifying to private conversations with the other, even where both spouses wish the communication to be revealed. Gallagher v. Goldstein, 402 Mass. 457, 459 (1988). "The contents of private conversations are absolutely excluded, but the statute does not bar evidence as to the fact that a conversation took place" (citations omitted). Id. The disqualification survives the death of a spouse, see Dexter v. Booth, 84 Mass. 559, 561 (1861), except in civil cases subject to G. L. c. 233, § 65 ("In any action or other civil judicial proceeding, a declaration of a deceased person shall not be inadmissible in evidence as hearsay or as private conversation between husband and wife, as the case may be, if the court finds that it was made in good faith and upon the personal knowledge of the declarant."). See Section 504(b)(2)(G), Spousal Privilege and Disqualification; Parent–Child Disqualification: Spousal Disqualification: Exceptions.

Whether a conversation was "private" is a question of preliminary fact for the trial judge. Commonwealth v. Stokes, 374 Mass. 583, 595 (1978). Where children are present, "[i]t is for the trial judge to determine whether the conversation was overheard by the children and whether the children were 'of sufficient intelligence at the time to pay attention, and to understand what was being said.'" Id., quoting Freeman v. Freeman, 238 Mass. 150, 161 (1921). In the absence of an objection, evidence of private conversations is admissible and may be given its full probative value. Id. at 595 n.8. However, if there is an objection, the conversation is excluded even if neither spouse objects to the conversation being admitted. Gallagher v. Goldstein, 402 Mass. at 461; Commonwealth v. Salyer, 84 Mass. App. Ct. 346, 354 (2013). The conversation remains private, and thus inadmissible, even if one of the spouses discloses the conversation to a third party. Commonwealth v. Garcia, 476 Mass. 822, 827 (2017).

The disqualification applies only to conversations, not to other types of communications. For example, written communications are not included. Commonwealth v. Szczuka, 391 Mass. 666, 678 n.14 (1984). A spouse is not barred from testifying that a conversation took place, and, as a result, that he or she did something. See Sampson v. Sampson, 223 Mass. 451, 458–459 (1916). The disqualification does not bar a third person who overheard the "private conversation" from testifying to its contents. Commonwealth v. O'Brien, 377 Mass. 772, 774–775 (1979). See also Martin v. Martin, 267 Mass. 157, 159 (1929).

"[W]ords constituting or accompanying abuse, threats, or assaults of which the other spouse is the victim" are not regarded as private conversation for the purpose of the disqualification. Commonwealth v. Gillis, 358 Mass. 215, 218 (1970). See also Commonwealth v. Foxworth, 473 Mass. 149, 159–160 (2015). Complaints and exclamations of pain and suffering are also not private conversations for the purpose of the disqualification. Commonwealth v. Jardine, 143 Mass. 567, 567–568 (1887).

The disqualification depends upon the existence of the marriage at the time of the communication; it does not prohibit testimony by a spouse as to communications made prior to the marriage. Commonwealth v. Azar, 32 Mass. App. Ct. 290, 304 (1992), remanded for new trial on other grounds, 435 Mass. 675 (2002). See also Commonwealth v. Barronian, 235 Mass. 364, 366 (1920).

The Supreme Judicial Court has left open whether the disqualification would bar testimony of a spouse when husband and wife are jointly engaged in criminal activity. Commonwealth v. Walker, 438 Mass. 246, 254 n.4 (2002).

The defendant's constitutional right to confront witnesses may trump the statutory disqualification. "To determine whether the [marital] disqualification should yield to the invoked constitutional rights [in a criminal case the court] look[s] to whether the evidence at issue if admitted might have had a significant impact on the result of the trial" (quotations and citations omitted). Commonwealth v. Perl, 50 Mass. App. Ct. 445, 453 (2000) (upholding exclusion of private conversations which would have been cumulative of other evidence).

"Where [G. L. c. 233, § 20] confers a testimonial privilege, the language of the statute is to be strictly construed." Matter of a Grand Jury Subpoena, 447 Mass. 88, 90 (2006).

Subsection (b)(2)(A). This subsection is derived from G. L. c. 233, § 20, First.

Subsection (b)(2)(B). This subsection is derived from G. L. c. 233, § 20, First. Spousal disqualification does not apply in any Chapter 209C action. See G. L. c. 209C, § 16(c). It also does not apply to any action to establish paternity, support, or both under the Massachusetts Uniform Interstate Family Support Act (Chapter 209D), or to enforce a child support or alimony order. See G. L. c. 209D, § 3–316(h).

Subsection (b)(2)(C). This subsection is derived from G. L. c. 233, § 20, First.

Subsection (b)(2)(D). This subsection is derived from G. L. c. 233, § 20, First. See Commonwealth v. Burnham, 451 Mass. 517, 521–522 (2008) (the statutory exception to the applicability of the marital disqualification in child abuse cases applies to both civil and criminal proceedings).

Subsection (b)(2)(E). This subsection is derived from G. L. c. 233, § 20, First.

Subsection (b)(2)(F). This subsection is derived from G. L. c. 233, § 20, First.

Subsection (b)(2)(G). This subsection is taken nearly verbatim from G. L. c. 233, § 65.

Subsection (b)(2)(H). This subsection is derived from Commonwealth v. Sugrue, 34 Mass. App. Ct. 172, 175–178 (1993), where the Appeals Court explained that the criminal defendant's constitutional right to confrontation and to a fair trial outweighed the public policy behind the spousal disqualification.

Subsection (c)(1)(A). This subsection is derived from G. L. c. 4, § 7, Forty-eighth.

Subsection (c)(1)(B). This subsection is derived from G. L. c. 233, § 20, Fourth.

Subsection (c)(2). This subsection is derived from G. L. c. 233, § 20, Fourth. The statutory disqualification does not prohibit the child from testifying in a civil case, including but not limited to a divorce or custody case.

The Supreme Judicial Court has declined to recognize a testimonial privilege that parents could exercise to avoid being compelled to testify in criminal proceedings about confidential communications with their children. See Matter of a Grand Jury Subpoena, 430 Mass. 590, 590–591 (2000) ("the Legislature, in the first instance, is the more appropriate body to weigh the relative social policies and address whether and how such a privilege should be created").

Section 505. Domestic Violence Victims' Counselor Privilege

(a) Definitions. The definitions that follow apply to this section unless the context clearly requires otherwise.

(1) Abuse. "Abuse" means causing or attempting to cause physical harm; placing another in fear of imminent physical harm; or causing another to engage in sexual relations against his or her will by force, threat of force, or coercion.

(2) Confidential Communication. A "confidential communication" is information transmitted in confidence by and between a victim and a domestic violence victims' counselor by a means which does not disclose the information to a person other than a person present for the benefit of the victim, or to those to whom disclosure of such information is reasonably necessary to the counseling and assisting of such victim. The term "information" includes, but is not limited to, reports, records, working papers, or memoranda.

(3) Domestic Violence Victims' Counselor. A "domestic violence victims' counselor" is a person who is employed or volunteers in a domestic violence victim's program; who has undergone a minimum of twenty-five hours of training; who reports to and is under the direct control and supervision of a direct service supervisor of a domestic violence victims' program; and whose primary purpose is the rendering of advice, counseling, or assistance to victims of abuse.

(4) Domestic Violence Victims' Program. A "domestic violence victims' program" is any refuge, shelter, office, safe home, institution or center established for the purpose of offering assistance to victims of abuse through crisis intervention, medical, legal, or support counseling.

(5) Victim. A "victim" is a person who has suffered abuse and who consults a domestic violence victims' counselor for the purpose of securing advice, counseling, or assistance concerning a mental, physical, or emotional condition caused by such abuse.

(b) Privilege. A domestic violence victims' counselor shall not disclose confidential communications between the counselor and the victim of domestic violence without the prior written consent of the victim. Such confidential communication shall not be subject to discovery in any civil, legislative, or administrative proceeding without the prior written consent of the victim to whom such confidential communication relates, except as provided in Subsection (c).

(c) Exception. In criminal actions, such confidential communications may be subject to discovery and may be admissible as evidence, subject to applicable law.

NOTE

This section is derived from G. L. c. 233, § 20K; Commonwealth v. Dwyer, 448 Mass. 122, 143 n.25 (2006) (characterizing records prepared by domestic violence victims' counselor as privileged); and Commonwealth v. Tripolone, 425 Mass. 487, 489 (1997) (same). The specific provision in G. L. c. 233, § 20K, for in camera judicial review prior to an order allowing any discovery of material covered by the domestic violence victims' counselor privilege is different from the procedure recently established by the Supreme Judicial Court in Commonwealth v. Dwyer, 448 Mass. at 145–146. See Introductory Note to Article V, Privileges and Disqualifications.

Section 506. Sexual Assault Counselor– Victim Privilege

(a) Definitions. The definitions that follow apply to this section unless the context clearly requires otherwise.

(1) Rape Crisis Center. A "rape crisis center" is any office, institution, or center offering assistance to victims of sexual assault and the families of such victims through crisis intervention, medical, and legal counseling.

(2) Sexual Assault Counselor. A "sexual assault counselor" is a person who (A) is employed by or is a volunteer in a rape crisis center; (B) has undergone thirty-five hours of training; (C) reports to and is under the direct control and supervision of a licensed social worker, nurse, psychiatrist, psychologist, or psychotherapist; and (D) has the primary purpose of rendering advice, counseling, or assistance to victims of sexual assault.

(3) **Victim.** A "victim" is a person who has suffered a sexual assault and who consults a sexual assault counselor for the purpose of securing advice, counseling, or assistance concerning a mental, physical, or emotional condition caused by such sexual assault.

(4) **Confidential Communication.** A "confidential communication" is information transmitted in confidence by and between a victim of sexual assault and a sexual assault counselor by a means which does not disclose the information to a person other than a person present for the benefit of the victim, or to those to whom disclosure of such information is reasonably necessary to the counseling and assisting of such victim. The term includes all information received by the sexual assault counselor which arises out of and in the course of such counseling and assisting, including, but not limited to, reports, records, working papers, or memoranda.

(b) **Privilege.** A confidential communication as defined in Subsection (a)(4) shall not be disclosed by a sexual assault counselor, is not subject to discovery, and is inadmissible in any criminal or civil proceeding without the prior written consent of the victim to whom the report, record, working paper, or memorandum relates. Nothing in this section shall be construed to limit the defendant's right of cross-examination of such counselor in a civil or criminal proceeding if such counselor testifies with such written consent.

(c) **Exception.** In criminal actions, such confidential communications may be subject to discovery and may be admissible as evidence, subject to applicable law.

NOTE

Subsection (a). This subsection is taken nearly verbatim from G. L. c. 233, § 20J.

Subsection (b). This subsection is taken nearly verbatim from G. L. c. 233, § 20J. See Commonwealth v. Dwyer, 448 Mass. 122, 143 n.25 (2006) (characterizing records prepared by sexual assault victims' counselor as privileged).

This privilege protects only confidential communications between the victim and the counselor and does not extend to the date, time, or fact of the communication. Commonwealth v. Neumyer, 432 Mass. 23, 29 (2000). The victim's testimony to the content of a privileged communication under this section does not constitute a waiver of the privilege unless the testimony is given with knowledge of the privilege and an intent to waive it. Id. at 35–36. See Section 523(b), Waiver of Privilege: Conduct Constituting Waiver.

Subsection (c). This subsection is derived from Commonwealth v. Dwyer, 448 Mass. 122, 145–146 (2006) (establishing protocol in criminal cases governing access to and use of material covered by privilege). See Introductory Note to Article V, Privileges and Disqualifications.

Section 507. Social Worker–Client Privilege

(a) **Definitions.** As used in this section, the following words shall have the following meanings:

(1) **Client.** A "client" is a person with whom a social worker has established a social worker-client relationship.

(2) **Communications.** "Communications" includes conversations, correspondence, actions, and occurrences regardless of the client's awareness of such conversations, correspondence, actions, and occurrences and any records, memoranda, or notes of the foregoing.

(3) **[Reserved]**

(4) **Social Worker.** As used in this section, a "social worker" is a social worker licensed pursuant to the provisions of G. L. c. 112, § 132, or a social worker employed in a State, county, or municipal governmental agency.

(b) **Privilege.** A client shall have the privilege of refusing to disclose and of preventing a witness from disclosing any communication, wherever made, between said client and a social worker relative to the diagnosis or treatment of the client's mental or emotional condition. If a client is incompetent to exercise or waive such privilege, a guardian shall be appointed to act in the client's behalf under this section. A previously appointed guardian shall be authorized to so act.

(c) **Exceptions.** The privilege in Subsection (b) shall not apply to any of the following communications:

(1) if a social worker, in the course of making a diagnosis or treating the client, determines that the client is in need of treatment in a hospital for mental or emotional illness or that there is a threat of imminently dangerous activity by the client against the client or another person, and on the basis of such determination discloses such communication either for the purpose of placing or retaining the client in such hospital; provided, however, that the provisions of this section shall continue in effect after the client is in said hospital, or placing the client under arrest or under the supervision of law enforcement authorities;

(2) if a judge finds that the client, after having been informed that the communications would not be privileged, has made communications to a social worker in the course of a psychiatric examination ordered by the court; provided, however, that such communications shall be admissible only on issues involving the client's mental or emotional condition and not as a confession or admission of guilt;

(3) in any proceeding, except one involving child custody, adoption, or adoption consent, in which the client introduces his or her mental or emotional condition as an element of a claim or defense, and the judge or presiding officer finds that it is more important to the interests of justice that the communication be disclosed than that the relationship between client and social worker be protected;

(4) in any proceeding after the death of a client in which the client's mental or emotional condition is introduced by any party claiming or defending through or as a beneficiary of the client as an element of the claim or defense, and the judge or presiding officer finds that it is more important to the interests of justice that the communication be disclosed than that the relationship between client and social worker be protected;

(5) in the initiation of proceedings under G. L. c. 119, §§ 23(a)(3) and 24, or G. L. c. 210, § 3, or to give testimony in connection therewith;

(6) in any proceeding whereby the social worker has acquired the information while conducting an investigation pursuant to G. L. c. 119, § 51B;

(7) in any other case involving child custody, adoption, or the dispensing with the need for consent to adoption in which, upon a hearing in chambers, the judge, in the exercise of his or her discretion, determines that the social worker has evidence bearing significantly on the client's ability to provide suitable care or custody, and that it is more important to the welfare of the child that the communication be disclosed than that the relationship between client and social worker be protected; provided, however, that in such case of adoption or the dispensing with the need for consent to adoption, a judge shall determine that the client has been informed that such communication would not be privileged;

(8) in any proceeding brought by the client against the social worker and in any malpractice, criminal, or license revocation proceeding in which disclosure is necessary or relevant to the claim or defense of the social worker; or

(9) in criminal actions, such privileged communications may be subject to discovery and may be admissible as evidence, subject to applicable law.

NOTE

Subsections (a)(1)–(2). These subsections are taken nearly verbatim from G. L. c. 112, § 135.

Subsection (a)(4). This subsection is taken nearly verbatim from G. L. c. 112, §§ 135A and 135B. See Bernard v. Commonwealth, 424 Mass. 32, 35 (1996) (State police trooper employed as a peer counselor qualified as a social worker for purposes of this section).

Subsection (b). This subsection is taken nearly verbatim from G. L. c. 112, § 135B. See Commonwealth v. Pelosi, 441 Mass. 257, 261 n.6 (2004) (characterizing records prepared by clients' social worker as privileged; privilege is not self-executing).

Subsections (c)(1)–(8). These subsections are taken nearly verbatim from G. L. c. 112, § 135B.

The social worker-client privilege is set forth in G. L. c. 112, § 135B. General Laws c. 112, § 135A, addresses the general duty of confidentiality of certain social workers. See Commonwealth v. Pelosi, 441 Mass. 257, 261 n.6 (2004). The privilege is not self-executing. See Commonwealth v. Oliveira, 438 Mass. 325, 331 (2002).

Subsection (c)(9). This subsection is derived from Commonwealth v. Dwyer, 448 Mass. 122, 145–146 (2006) (establishing protocol in criminal cases governing access to and use of material covered by statutory privilege). See Introductory Note to Article V, Privileges and Disqualifications.

Section 508. Allied Mental Health or Human Services Professional Privilege

(a) Definitions. As used in this section, an "allied mental health and human services professional" is a licensed marriage and family therapist, a licensed rehabilitation counselor, a licensed mental health counselor, or a licensed educational psychologist.

(b) Privilege. Any communication between an allied mental health or human services professional and a client shall be deemed to be confidential and privileged.

(c) Waiver. This privilege shall be subject to waiver only in the following circumstances:

(1) where the allied mental health and human services professional is a party defendant to a civil, criminal, or

disciplinary action arising from such practice in which case the waiver shall be limited to that action;

(2) where the client is a defendant in a criminal proceeding and the use of the privilege would violate the defendant's right to compulsory process and right to present testimony and witnesses in his or her behalf;

(3) when the communication reveals the contemplation or commission of a crime or a harmful act; and

(4) where a client agrees to the waiver, or in circumstances where more than one person in a family is receiving therapy, where each such family member agrees to the waiver.

(d) Mental Health Counselor Exception. With respect to a mental health counselor, the privilege does not apply to the following communications:

(1) if a mental health counselor, in the course of diagnosis or treatment of the client, determines that the client is in need of treatment in a hospital for mental or emotional illness or that there is a threat of imminently dangerous activity by the patient against himself or herself or another person and, on the basis of the determination, discloses the communication either for the purpose of placing or retaining the client in the hospital, although this section shall continue in effect after the patient is in the hospital or placed under arrest or under the supervision of law enforcement authorities;

(2) if a judge finds that the client, after having been informed that a communication would not be privileged, has made a communication to a mental health counselor in the course of a psychiatric examination ordered by the court, although the communication shall be admissible only on issues involving the patient's mental or emotional condition and not as a confession or admission of guilt;

(3) in a proceeding, except one involving child custody, in which the client introduces his or her mental or emotional condition as an element of his or her claim or defense, and the judge or presiding officer finds that it is more important to the interests of justice that the communication be disclosed than that the relationship between client and mental health counselor be protected;

(4) in a proceeding after the death of a client in which the client's mental or emotional condition is introduced by any party claiming or defending through or as beneficiary of the patient as an element of the claim or the defense and the judge or presiding officer finds that it is more important to the interests of justice that the communication be disclosed than that the relationship between client and mental health counselor be protected;

(5) in the initiation of proceedings under G. L. c. 119, § 23(a)(3) or § 24, or G. L. c. 210, § 3, to give testimony in connection therewith;

(6) in a proceeding whereby the mental health counselor has acquired the information while conducting an investigation pursuant to G. L. c. 119, § 51B;

(7) in a case involving child custody, adoption, or the dispensing with the need for consent to adoption where, upon a hearing in chambers, the court exercises its discretion to determine that the mental health counselor has

evidence bearing significantly on the client's ability to provide suitable care or custody, and it is more important to the welfare of the child that the communication be disclosed than that the relationship between client and mental health counselor be protected, although in the case of adoption or the dispensing with the need for consent to adoption, the court shall determine that the client has been informed that the communication should not be privileged; or

(8) in a proceeding brought by the client against the mental health counselor and in any malpractice, criminal, or license revocation proceeding in which disclosure is necessary or relevant to the claim or defense of the mental health counselor.

(e) Exception. In criminal actions, such privileged communications may be subject to discovery and may be admissible as evidence, subject to applicable law.

NOTE

Subsection (a). This subsection is taken nearly verbatim from G. L. c. 112, § 163. General Laws c. 112, § 165, outlines license eligibility. A licensed educational psychologist must also be certified as a school psychologist by the Massachusetts Department of Education. G. L. c. 112, § 163.

Subsections (b) and (c). These subsections are taken nearly verbatim from G. L. c. 112, § 172. See Commonwealth v. Vega, 449 Mass. 227, 231 (2007) (the statute creates an evidentiary privilege as well as a confidentiality rule).

These subsections do not prohibit a third-party reimburser from inspecting and copying any records relating to diagnosis, treatment, or other services provided to any person for which coverage, benefit, or reimbursement is claimed, so long as access occurs in the ordinary course of business and the policy or certificate under which the claim is made provides that such access is permitted. G. L. c. 112, § 172. Further, this section does not apply to access to such records pursuant to any peer review or utilization review procedures applied and implemented in good faith. G. L. c. 112, § 172.

Subsection (d). This subsection is taken nearly verbatim from G. L. c. 112, § 172A. General Laws c. 112, § 172A, deals with the evidentiary privilege held by clients of mental health providers in court proceedings, while G. L. c. 112, § 172, deals with the confidentiality requirement adhered to by mental health providers. The confidentiality requirement need not be invoked by the client to be in effect, but it can be waived under certain circumstances covered in G. L. c. 112, § 172.

General Laws c. 119, § 23(a)(3), deals with children who are without proper care due to the death or incapacity, unfitness, or unavailability of a parent or guardian. General Laws c. 119, § 24, involves petitions and testimony regarding abuse or neglect of children. General Laws c. 210, § 3, involves petitions for adoption. General Laws c. 119, § 51B, involves investigations regarding the abuse or neglect of children.

In the absence of a court order, a warning in accordance with Commonwealth v. Lamb, 365 Mass. 265, 270 (1974), is not required where the examiner is a diagnosing or treating psychotherapist of a patient involuntarily committed to a mental health facility pursuant to G. L. c. 123, § 12(b). Walden Behavioral Care v. K.I., 471 Mass. 150, 154 (2015). Contrast Department of Youth Servs. v. A Juvenile, 398 Mass. 516, 524–526 (1986) (Lamb warning required when department ordered psychiatrist to interview juvenile in its custody).

Cross–Reference: Section 503(d)(2), Psychotherapist–Patient Privilege: Exceptions: Court–Ordered Psychiatric Exam.

Subsection (e). This subsection is derived from Commonwealth v. Dwyer, 448 Mass. 122, 145–146 (2006) (establishing protocol in criminal cases governing access to and use of material covered by statutory

privilege). See Introductory Note to Article V, Privileges and Disqualifications.

Section 509. Identity of Informer, Surveillance Location, and Protected Witness Privileges

(a) Identity of Informer. The identity of persons supplying the government with information concerning the commission of a crime may be privileged in both civil and criminal cases. The existence and validity of the privilege is determined in two stages:

(1) **Stage One.** The judge must first determine whether the Commonwealth has properly asserted the privilege by showing that disclosure would endanger the informant or otherwise impede law enforcement efforts. If such a finding is made, the judge must determine whether the defendant has offered some evidence that the privilege should be set aside on grounds that it interferes with the defense.

(2) **Stage Two.** If the judge finds that the privilege has been properly asserted and that, if recognized, it would interfere with the defense, the judge must undertake a balancing test in order to determine whether disclosure of the informant's identity and information is sufficiently relevant and helpful to the defense. The judge must consider the crime charged, the possible defenses, the possible significance of the privileged testimony, and other relevant factors in balancing the public interest in the free flow of information and the individual's interest in preparing a defense. There is no privilege under this subsection when the identity of the informer has been disclosed by the government or by the informer, or the court determines that it is otherwise known.

(b) Surveillance Location. The exact location, such as the location of a police observation post, used for surveillance is privileged, except there is no privilege under this subsection when a defendant shows that revealing the exact surveillance location would provide evidence needed to fairly present the defendant's case to the jury.

(c) Protected Witness. The identity and location of a protected witness and any other matter concerning a protected witness or the Commonwealth's witness protection program is privileged in both civil and criminal cases, except there is no privilege as to the identity and location of the protected witness under this subsection when

(1) the prosecuting officer agrees to a disclosure after balancing the danger posed to the protected witness, the detriment it may cause to the program, and the benefit it may afford to the public or the person seeking discovery, or

(2) disclosure is at the request of a local, State, or Federal law enforcement officer or is in compliance with a court order in circumstances in which the protected witness is under criminal investigation for, arrested for, or charged with a felony.

(d) Who May Claim. These privileges may be claimed by the government.

NOTE

Subsection (a). This subsection is derived from Commonwealth v. Bonnett, 472 Mass. 827, 846–851 (2015), and Roviaro v. United States, 353 U.S. 53, 59–62 (1957); the last sentence is derived from Commonwealth v. Congdon, 265 Mass. 166, 175 (1928), and Pihl v. Morris, 319 Mass. 577, 579 (1946). See also Commonwealth v. Dias, 451 Mass. 463, 469 (2008) ("part of the balance [between the defendant's right to present a defense and the public interest in protecting the free flow of information] involves weighing the potential danger to the informant").

The showing that must be made by the defendant in Stage One in order to trigger the balancing test as part of Stage Two is "relatively undemanding" because "the details concerning privileged information sought by the defendant ordinarily are not in his or her possession." Commonwealth v. Bonnett, 472 Mass. at 847. In determining whether disclosure would be relevant and helpful to the defense, judges must consider whether "knowledge of the informant's identity can offer substantial aid to the defense even if the informant himself cannot provide testimony sufficiently relevant and reliable to be admitted at trial." Id. at 849.

"[T]he government is not required to disclose the identity of an informant who is a mere tipster and not an active participant in the offense charged." Commonwealth v. Brzezinski, 405 Mass. 401, 408 (1989), quoting United States v. Alonzo, 571 F.2d 1384, 1387 (5th Cir. 1978), cert. denied, 439 U.S. 847 (1978). Accord McCray v. Illinois, 386 U.S. 300, 308–309 (1967). See also Commonwealth v. Martin, 362 Mass. 243, 245 (1972) (trial judge "reasonably refused to permit inquiry about an informant who seems merely to have told the police where the defendants were living together"); Commonwealth v. McKay, 23 Mass. App. Ct. 966, 967 (1987) (trial judge was not required to order disclosure of the identity of two inmates who informed on the defendant, although their statements were disclosed and they were not called as witnesses at trial by the Commonwealth). When the informant "is an active participant in the alleged crime or the only nongovernment witness, disclosure [of the identity of the informant] usually has been ordered." Commonwealth v. Lugo, 406 Mass. 565, 572 (1990).

The privilege may expire. The public records statute, G. L. c. 66, § 10, provides an independent right of access to records and documents that were covered by the privilege if the reason for the privilege no longer exists. See, e.g., District Attorney for the Norfolk Dist. v. Flatley, 419 Mass. 507, 511–512 (1995) (discussing Bougas v. Chief of Police of Lexington, 371 Mass. 59, 66 [1976], and WBZ–TV4 v. District Attorney for the Suffolk Dist., 408 Mass. 595, 602–604 [1990]).

Dual Sovereignty. In general, a defendant who seeks exculpatory information about a Federal informant must follow the prescribed Federal procedure for requesting informant information. Commonwealth v. Ayala, 481 Mass. 46, 56–57 (2018). When the defendant seeks an order to have the Commonwealth obtain informant information from the Federal government, the judge should consider "(i) the potential unfairness to the defendant; (ii) the defendant's lack of access to evidence; (iii) the burden on the prosecutor of obtaining the evidence; and (iv) the degree of cooperation between State and Federal authorities, both in general and in the particular case." Commonwealth v. Donahue, 396 Mass. 590, 599 (1986). The judge may not simply rely on the independent sovereignty of the United States as justification for failing to order disclosure of the informant's identity if disclosure is otherwise appropriate under this subsection. Commonwealth v. Bonnett, 472 Mass. 827, 845 (2015). The remedy for the Commonwealth's failure to comply with an order of disclosure in such a case is dismissal of the criminal charge. Id.

Challenges to the Sufficiency of an Affidavit. When a defendant challenges the sufficiency of an affidavit in support of a search warrant, the court's review "begins and ends with the 'four corners of the affidavit.'" Commonwealth v. O'Day, 440 Mass. 296, 297 (2003), quoting Commonwealth v. Villella, 39 Mass. App. Ct. 426, 428 (1995). The defendant has the burden of establishing by a preponderance of the evidence that the affidavit contains false statements. See Commonwealth v. Nine Hundred & Ninety-two Dollars, 383 Mass. 764, 767, 769 (1981). Intentionally or recklessly omitted material may satisfy the defendant's burden. See Commonwealth v. Long, 454 Mass. 542, 552 (2009). A negligent misrepresentation by the affiant is not a basis

for relief. See Commonwealth v. Amral, 407 Mass. 511, 520 (1990); Commonwealth v. Nine Hundred & Ninety-two Dollars, 383 Mass. at 771–772. If the affidavit contains false statements, the court must simply assess whether it establishes probable cause without reliance on the false statements. See Commonwealth v. Amral, 407 Mass. at 519. Cf. Commonwealth v. Nine Hundred & Ninety-two Dollars, 383 Mass. at 768 (leaving open whether suppression of evidence should be ordered under Article 14 of the Massachusetts Declaration of Rights when there has been a deliberately false, though nonmaterial, misstatement by the affiant).

Amral Hearing. In keeping with the "four corners rule," the court should not take any action simply based on an allegation that the affidavit contains false information. Only if the defendant makes an initial showing that "cast[s] a reasonable doubt on the veracity of material representations made by the affiant concerning a confidential informant" is the court required to act (citations omitted). Commonwealth v. Youngworth, 55 Mass. App. Ct. 30, 38 (2002), cert. denied, 538 U.S. 1064 (2003). The first step is to conduct an in camera hearing. See Commonwealth v. Ramirez, 416 Mass. 41, 53–54 (1993). The informant may be ordered to appear and submit to questions by the court at this "Amral hearing"; however, the identity of the informant is not revealed. The court has discretion to permit the prosecutor to attend this hearing. Neither the defendant nor defense counsel is permitted to attend. See Commonwealth v. Amral, 407 Mass. at 525. If the court is satisfied that the informant exists and that the defendant's allegations of false statements are not substantiated, there is no further inquiry. On the other hand, if the defendant makes "a substantial preliminary showing that a false statement knowingly and intentionally, or with reckless disregard for the truth, was included by the affiant in the warrant affidavit," the court must take the next step (citation omitted). Commonwealth v. Youngworth, 55 Mass. App. Ct. at 37–38. In this situation, the defendant is entitled to an evidentiary hearing and to the disclosure of the identity of the informant. The burden of proof at this hearing rests with the defendant to establish that the affiant presented the magistrate with false information purposely or with reckless disregard for its truth. If it is shown that an affidavit in support of a warrant contains false information that was material to the determination of probable cause, suppression of the evidence is required. See Franks v. Delaware, 438 U.S. 154, 155–156 (1978); Commonwealth v. Amral, 407 Mass. at 519–520.

Entrapment Defense. Where a defendant seeks disclosure of otherwise privileged information to support an entrapment defense, the question is whether the defense has been "appropriately raised . . . by the introduction of some evidence of inducement by a government agent or one acting at his direction." Commonwealth v. Madigan, 449 Mass. 702, 707 (2007), quoting Commonwealth v. Miller, 361 Mass. 644, 651–652 (1972). "The types of conduct that possess the indicia of inducement include 'aggressive persuasion, coercive encouragement, lengthy negotiations, pleading or arguing with the defendant, repeated or persistent solicitation, persuasion, importuning, and playing on sympathy or other emotion.'" Id. at 708, quoting Commonwealth v. Tracy, 416 Mass. 528, 536 (1993). See Commonwealth v. Elias, 463 Mass. 1015, 1016 (2012) (where defendant's affidavit states facts sufficient to raise an entrapment defense if informant were an individual named in the affidavit, trial court may require the Commonwealth to affirm whether informant is that individual); Commonwealth v. Mello, 453 Mass. 760, 765 (2009) (reversing trial judge's order that Commonwealth must disclose the identity of an unnamed informant because the defendant's proffer showed no more than a solicitation; duty to disclose identity of an undercover police officer or unnamed informant does not carry over to a second unnamed informant unless the second informant participated in the first informant's inducement).

In Camera Hearing. Unless the relevancy and materiality of the information sought is readily apparent, the party seeking access to the information has the burden to provide the trial judge with the basis for ordering the disclosure. Commonwealth v. Swenson, 368 Mass. 268, 276 (1975). When it is not clear from the record whether disclosure of the informant's identity is required, the court has discretion to hold an in camera hearing to assist in making that determination. Commonwealth v. Dias, 451 Mass. 463, 472 n.15 (2008) ("The nature of the in camera hearing is left to the judge."). In exceptional circumstances, a motion for the disclosure of the identity of an informant may be based on an ex parte affidavit in order to safeguard the defendant's privilege against self-incrimination. However, in such a case, before any order of disclosure is made, the Commonwealth must be given a summary or redacted version of the defendant's affidavit and an opportunity to oppose the defendant's motion. Commonwealth v. Shaughessy, 455 Mass. 346, 357–358 (2009).

Subsection (b). This subsection is derived from Commonwealth v. Lugo, 406 Mass. 565, 570–574 (1990), and Commonwealth v. Rios, 412 Mass. 208, 210–213 (1992). It would be a violation of the defendant's right to confrontation to preserve the confidentiality of a surveillance site by permitting the trier of fact to hear testimony from a witness outside of a defendant's presence. Commonwealth v. Rios, 412 Mass. at 212–213.

Subsection (c). This subsection is derived from St. 2006, c. 48, § 1, inserting G. L. c. 263A, entitled "Witness Protection in Criminal Matters." As for the right of the defense to have access to a Commonwealth witness, see Commonwealth v. Balliro, 349 Mass. 505, 515–518 (1965).

Subsection (d). This subsection is derived from Commonwealth v. Johnson, 365 Mass. 534, 544 (1974).

Section 510. Religious Privilege

(a) Definitions. As used in this section, the following words shall have the following meanings:

(1) A "clergyman" includes a priest, a rabbi, an ordained or licensed minister of any church, or an accredited Christian Science practitioner.

(2) A "communication" is not limited to conversations, and includes other acts by which ideas may be transmitted from one person to another.

(3) "In his professional character" means in the course of discipline enjoined by the rules or practice of the religious body to which the clergyman belongs.

(b) Privilege. A clergyman shall not disclose a confession made to him in his professional character without the consent of the person making the confession. Nor shall a clergyman testify as to any communication made to him by any person seeking religious or spiritual advice or comfort, or as to his advice given thereon in the course of his professional duties or in his professional character, without the consent of such person.

(c) Child Abuse. Any clergyman shall report all cases of child abuse, but need not report information solely gained in a confession or similarly confidential communication in other religious faiths. Nothing shall modify or limit the duty of a clergyman to report a reasonable cause that a child is being injured when the clergyman is acting in some other capacity that would otherwise make him a reporter.

NOTE

Subsection (a)(1). This subsection is taken nearly verbatim from G. L. c. 233, § 20A. In Commonwealth v. Kebreau, 454 Mass. 287, 301 (2009), the Supreme Judicial Court noted that the privilege is strictly construed and applies only to communications where a penitent "seek[s] religious or spiritual advice or comfort." In Commonwealth v. Marrero, 436 Mass. 488, 495 (2002), the Supreme Judicial Court declined to include the manager of a "Christian rehabilitation center"

for drug addicts and alcoholics, who was not an ordained or licensed minister, within the definition of "clergyman." The court also noted it was not an appropriate case to consider adopting the more expansive definition of "clergyman" found in Proposed Mass. R. Evid. 505(a)(1). Id.

Subsection (a)(2). This subsection is taken nearly verbatim from Commonwealth v. Zezima, 365 Mass. 238, 241 (1974), rev'd on other grounds, 387 Mass. 748 (1982).

Subsection (a)(3). This subsection is taken nearly verbatim from G. L. c. 233, § 20A. See Commonwealth v. Vital, 83 Mass. App. Ct. 669, 673–674 (2013) (a communication by the defendant to his pastor with a request that it be passed on to a person who was the alleged victim of a sexual assault by the defendant was not covered by the privilege because the defendant's purpose was not to receive "religious or spiritual advice or comfort," but instead to circumvent the terms of a restraining order).

Subsection (b). This subsection is taken nearly verbatim from G. L. c. 233, § 20A. It is a preliminary question of fact for the trial judge whether a communication to a clergyman is within the scope of the privilege. Commonwealth v. Zezima, 365 Mass. 238, 242 n.4 (1974), rev'd on other grounds, 387 Mass. 748 (1982). See Commonwealth v. Nutter, 87 Mass. App. Ct. 260, 264–265 (2015) (communication made after pastoral relationship had ended was not privileged).

Subsection (c). This subsection is taken nearly verbatim from G. L. c. 119, § 51A.

Section 511. Privilege Against Self–Incrimination

(a) Privilege of Defendant in Criminal Proceeding.

(1) Custodial Interrogation. A person has a right to refuse to answer any questions during a custodial interrogation.

(2) Refusal Evidence.

(A) No Court Order or Warrant. In the absence of a court order or warrant, evidence of a person's refusal to provide real or physical evidence, or to cooperate in an investigation ordered by State officials, is not admissible in any criminal proceeding, except to challenge evidence of cooperation elicited by the defendant.

(B) Court Order or Warrant. When State officials have obtained a court order or warrant for physical or real evidence, a person's refusal to provide the real or physical evidence is admissible in any criminal proceeding.

(3) Compelled Examination. A defendant has a right to refuse to answer any questions during a court-ordered examination for criminal responsibility.

(4) At a Hearing or Trial. A defendant has a right to refuse to testify at any criminal proceeding.

(b) Privilege of a Witness. Every witness has a right, in any proceeding, civil or criminal, to refuse to answer a question unless it is perfectly clear, from a careful consideration of all the circumstances, that the testimony cannot possibly have a tendency to incriminate the witness.

(c) Exceptions.

(1) Waiver by Defendant's Testimony. When a defendant voluntarily testifies in a criminal case, the defendant waives his or her privilege against self-incrimination to the extent that the defendant may be cross-examined on all relevant and material facts regarding that case.

(2) Waiver by Witness's Testimony. When a witness voluntarily testifies regarding an incriminating fact, the witness may thereby waive the privilege against self-incrimination as to subsequent questions seeking related facts in the same proceeding.

(3) Limitation. A waiver by testimony under Subsection (c)(1) or (c)(2) is limited to the proceeding in which it is given and does not extend to subsequent proceedings.

(4) Required Records. A witness may be required to produce required records because the witness is deemed to have waived his or her privilege against self-incrimination in such records. Required records, as used in this subsection, are those records required by law to be kept in order that there may be suitable information of transactions which are the appropriate subjects of governmental regulation and the enforcement of restrictions validly established.

(5) Immunity. In any investigation or proceeding, a witness shall not be excused from testifying or from producing books, papers, or other evidence on the ground that the testimony or evidence required may tend to incriminate the witness or subject him or her to a penalty or forfeiture if the witness has been granted immunity with respect to the transactions, matters, or things concerning which the witness is compelled, after having claimed his or her privilege against self-incrimination, to testify or produce evidence by a justice of the Supreme Judicial Court, Appeals Court, or Superior Court.

(6) Foregone Conclusion. Where a defendant is ordered by the court to produce information, the act of production does not involve testimonial communication and therefore does not violate the defendant's privilege against self-incrimination if the facts communicated already are known to the government and add little or nothing to the sum total of the government's information.

(d) Use of Suppressed Statements. The voluntary statement of a defendant that has been suppressed because of a Miranda violation may nevertheless, in limited circumstances, be used for impeachment purposes.

NOTE

Subsection (a). The Fifth Amendment to the Constitution of the United States provides that "[n]o person . . . shall be compelled in any criminal case to be a witness against himself." Similarly, Article 12 of the Declaration of Rights of the Massachusetts Constitution provides that "[n]o subject shall . . . be compelled to accuse, or furnish evidence against himself." These provisions protect a person from the compelled production of testimonial communications. See Blaisdell v. Commonwealth, 372 Mass. 753, 758–759 (1977). See also Commonwealth v. Brennan, 386 Mass. 772, 776 (1982). When the privilege is applicable, it may be overcome only by an adequate grant of immunity or a valid waiver. Blaisdell v. Commonwealth, 372 Mass. at 761. Under both Article 12 and the Fifth Amendment, the privilege does not apply to a corporation. Hale v. Henkel, 201 U.S. 43, 74–75 (1906); Matter of a John Doe Grand Jury Investigation, 418 Mass. 549, 552 (1994). Whether the privilege exists, its scope, and whether it has been waived are preliminary questions for the court to decide under Section 104(a), Preliminary Questions: In General.

Subsection (a)(1). This subsection is derived from the Fifth Amendment to the United States Constitution and Miranda v. Arizona, 384 U.S. 436, 444 (1966). The Miranda doctrine, including its accompanying exclusionary rule, has been developed and explained in numerous decisions of the United States Supreme Court and the appellate courts of Massachusetts. See E.B. Cypher, Criminal Practice and

Procedure § 7.13 et seq. (4th ed. 2014). "[E]vidence of a criminal defendant's postarrest, post-Miranda silence cannot be used for the substantive purpose of permitting an inference of guilt." Commonwealth v. Mahdi, 388 Mass. 679, 694 (1983). See Doyle v. Ohio, 426 U.S. 610, 619 (1976). The limited exceptions where evidence of a defendant's postarrest, post-Miranda silence may be admissible include to

> "explain[] why a police interview of the defendant abruptly ended [when] the jury would be confused without the explanation; rebut[] the defendant's suggestion at trial that some impropriety on the part of the police prevented him from completing his statement to them; and rebut[] a claim by the defendant that he had given the police at the time of his arrest the same exculpatory explanation as he was presenting to the jury at trial" (citations omitted).

Commonwealth v. Letkowski, 469 Mass. 603, 611–612 (2014).

Preference for Recording Certain Custodial Interrogations. Where the prosecution presents evidence of an unrecorded confession or statement made during a custodial interrogation, a criminal defendant is entitled, upon request, to a jury instruction advising that the State's highest court has expressed a preference that a custodial interrogation in a place of detention be recorded "whenever practicable." Commonwealth v. DiGiambattista, 442 Mass. 423, 447 (2004). In such a case, the jury should be instructed to weigh the evidence of the defendant's statement "with great caution and care" and be advised that "the absence of a recording permits (but does not compel) them to conclude that the Commonwealth has failed to prove voluntariness beyond a reasonable doubt." Id. at 447–448. The defendant has the right to refuse to have the interrogation recorded. Commonwealth v. Tavares, 81 Mass. App. Ct. 71, 73 (2011). The Commonwealth also has the right to introduce evidence that the defendant refused to have the interrogation recorded, even in circumstances where the defendant does not challenge the voluntariness of the statement or make an issue of the lack of a recording. Commonwealth v. DaSilva, 471 Mass. 71, 80 (2015). The defendant is entitled to a DiGiambattista instruction even where he or she requests a recording not be created or requests it be interrupted or ceased. Commonwealth v. Santana, 477 Mass. 610, 623–624 (2017). The DiGiambattista instruction may include reference to the defendant's decision not to have a custodial statement recorded. See Commonwealth v. Rousseau, 465 Mass. 372, 391–393 (2013). The Supreme Judicial Court has, however, stated that "the better practice is not to instruct juries that defendants have a 'right' to refuse recording." Commonwealth v. Alleyne, 474 Mass. 771, 785 (2016). The DiGiambattista rule does not apply when the police station interview of the defendant is noncustodial. See, e.g., Commonwealth v. Issa, 466 Mass. 1, 19–21 (2013).

Regarding situations where an interpreter is used to translate a defendant's custodial statements, in Commonwealth v. AdonSoto, 475 Mass. 497, 507 (2016), the Supreme Judicial Court stated, citing DiGiambattista, as follows: "We now announce a new protocol . . . Going forward, and where practicable, we expect that all interviews and interrogations using interpreter services will be recorded."

Cross–Reference: Section 604, Interpreters.

Subsection (a)(2). This subsection is derived from Commonwealth v. Delaney, 442 Mass. 604, 609–611 (2004), and from Commonwealth v. Jones, 477 Mass. 307, 326–328 (2017). The privilege against self-incrimination, under both Federal and State law, protects only against the production of communications or testimony compelled by the government. See Bellin v. Kelley, 48 Mass. App. Ct. 573, 581 n.13 (2000), and cases cited. It does not prevent the government from forcing a person to produce real or physical evidence, such as fingerprints, photographs, lineups, blood samples, handwriting, and voice exemplars. Commonwealth v. Brennan, 386 Mass. 772, 776–777, 783 (1982) (standard field sobriety tests do not implicate the privilege). The privilege against self-incrimination does not forbid the compelled production of certain statements that are necessarily incidental to the production of real or physical evidence. See Commonwealth v. Burgess, 426 Mass. 206, 220 (1997). On the other hand, testimonial evidence which reveals a person's knowledge or thoughts concerning some fact is protected. Commonwealth v. Brennan, 386 Mass. at 778. In some respects, Article 12 provides greater protections than the Fifth Amendment. See Attorney Gen. v. Colleton, 387 Mass. 790, 796 (1982); Commonwealth v. Hughes, 380 Mass. 583, 595 (1980). Compare Braswell v. United States, 487 U.S. 99, 109, 117–118 (1988) (Fifth Amendment privilege not applicable to order requiring custodian of corporate records to produce them even though the records would tend to incriminate the custodian because he is only acting as a representative of the corporation when he responds to the order), with Commonwealth v. Doe, 405 Mass. 676, 678–680 (1989) (describing result in Braswell v. United States as a "fiction" and holding that the privilege under Article 12 is fully applicable to protect custodian of corporate records from duty to produce them in circumstances in which act of production would incriminate the custodian as well as the corporation). However, evidence that a defendant failed to take a breathalyzer test properly after consenting is admissible. See Commonwealth v. AdonSoto, 475 Mass. 497, 501 (2016) (no error to admit evidence of defendant's failure to perform breathalyzer test properly after giving consent where such evidence did not constitute evidence of refusal, and where the defendant's consent was all that was required for admissibility).

Refusal Evidence. In Opinion of the Justices, 412 Mass. 1201, 1208 (1992), the Supreme Judicial Court opined that legislation permitting the Commonwealth to offer evidence of a person's refusal to take a breathalyzer test would violate the privilege against self-incrimination under Article 12 because such evidence reveals the person's thought processes, i.e., it indicates the person has doubts or concerns about the outcome of the test, and thus constitutes testimonial evidence, the admission of which into evidence would violate the privilege under Article 12 of the Massachusetts Declaration of Rights. Federal law and the law of most other States is to the contrary. See South Dakota v. Neville, 459 U.S. 553, 560–561 (1983). See also Commonwealth v. Conkey, 430 Mass. 139, 142 (1999) ("evidence admitted to show consciousness of guilt is always testimonial because it tends to demonstrate that the defendant knew he was guilty"). If evidence of the defendant's refusal to take a breathalyzer, or other alcohol-related test, is erroneously introduced at trial, the defendant has the right to a jury instruction pursuant to Commonwealth v. Downs, 53 Mass. App. Ct. 195, 198 (2001), that jurors are not to consider the lack of any alcohol-test evidence during deliberations. Id. It is the defendant's decision whether a Downs instruction is given; the instruction cannot be given over the defendant's objection, and the judge should not give the instruction sua sponte. See Commonwealth v. Wolfe, 478 Mass. 142, 149–150 (2017). The reasoning employed by the Supreme Judicial Court in Opinion of the Justices, 412 Mass. at 1208–1211, has been extended to other circumstances in which a person refuses to take a test, or to supply the police with real or physical evidence in the absence of a court order or warrant. See, e.g., Commonwealth v. Conkey, 430 Mass. at 141–143 (evidence of a defendant's failure to appear at a police station for fingerprinting); Commonwealth v. Hinckley, 422 Mass. 261, 264–265 (1996) (evidence of a defendant's refusal to turn over sneakers for comparison with prints at a crime scene is not admissible); Commonwealth v. McGrail, 419 Mass. 774, 779–780 (1995) (evidence of refusal to submit to field sobriety tests is not admissible); Commonwealth v. Zevitas, 418 Mass. 677, 683 (1994) (evidence of refusal to submit to a blood alcohol test under G. L. c. 90, § 24, is not admissible); Commonwealth v. Lydon, 413 Mass. 309, 313–315 (1992) (evidence of a defendant's refusal to let his hands be swabbed for the presence of gunpowder residue is not admissible). See also Commonwealth v. Buckley, 410 Mass. 209, 214–216 (1991) (a suspect may be compelled to provide a handwriting exemplar); Commonwealth v. Burke, 339 Mass. 521, 534–535 (1959) (defendant may be required to go to the courtroom floor and strike a pose for identification purposes). Contrast Commonwealth v. Delaney, 442 Mass. 604, 607–612 & n.8 (2004) (explaining that although a warrant involves an element of compulsion, it leaves the individual with no choice other

than to comply unlike the compulsion that accompanies a police request for information or evidence during the investigative stage; therefore, the Commonwealth may offer evidence of a defendant's resistance to a warrant or court order without violating Article 12); Commonwealth v. Brown, 83 Mass. App. Ct. 772, 778–779 (2013) (statements by defendant while performing field sobriety tests expressing difficulty with or inability to do the test are admissible).

However, evidence of refusal may be admissible where the defendant "opens the door" by introducing evidence of cooperation. Commonwealth v. Jones, 477 Mass. 307, 326–328 (2017); Commonwealth v. Beaulieu, 79 Mass. App. Ct. 100, 104 (2001) (where defense counsel elicited testimony that defendant was not subjected to field sobriety test, Commonwealth was entitled to elicit testimony that defendant refused); Commonwealth v. Johnson, 46 Mass. App. Ct. 398, 405–406 (1999) (where defendant testified that he "did not disguise his voice" during identification procedure, Commonwealth was entitled to elicit testimony that defendant twice failed to show up for voice identification).

Cross–Reference: Section 525(b)(1), Comment upon or Inference from Claim of Privilege: Criminal Case; Section 613(a)(2), Prior Statements of Witnesses, Limited Admissibility: Prior Inconsistent Statement: Examining Other Witness; Section 613(a)(3), Prior Statements of Witnesses, Limited Admissibility: Prior Inconsistent Statement: Disclosure of Extrinsic Evidence.

Subsection (a)(3). This subsection is derived from the Fifth Amendment to the United States Constitution; Article 12 of the Massachusetts Declaration of Rights; G. L. c. 233, § 23B; and Blaisdell v. Commonwealth, 372 Mass. 753 (1977). At any stage of the proceeding, the trial judge may order a defendant to submit to an examination by one or more qualified physicians or psychologists under G. L. c. 123, § 15(a), on the issue of competency or criminal responsibility.

Competency Examinations. A competency examination does not generally implicate a person's privilege against self-incrimination because it is concerned with whether the defendant is able to confer intelligently with counsel and to competently participate in the trial of his or her case, and not whether he or she is guilty or innocent. See Seng v. Commonwealth, 445 Mass. 536, 545 (2005). If the competency examination ordered by the court under G. L. c. 123, § 15(a), results in an opinion by the qualified physician or psychologist that the defendant is not competent, the court may order an additional examination by an expert selected by the Commonwealth. G. L. c. 123, § 15(a). "In the circumstances of a competency examination, G. L. c. 233, § 23B, together with the judge-imposed strictures of [Mass. R. Crim. P.] 14(b)(2)(B), protects the defendant's privilege against self-incrimination." Seng v. Commonwealth, 445 Mass. at 548.

Use of Statements Made During Competency Examinations in Connection with Criminal Responsibility. Generally, a patient's communications to a psychotherapist in a court-ordered evaluation under G. L. c. 123, § 15, may not be disclosed against the patient's wishes absent a warning that the communications would not be privileged. See Commonwealth v. Lamb, 365 Mass. 265, 270 (1974).

Criminal Responsibility Examinations. A defendant must give written notice to the Commonwealth if he or she intends at trial to raise his or her mental condition at the time of the alleged crime, or if he or she intends to introduce expert testimony on his or her mental condition at any stage of the proceeding. Mass. R. Crim. P. 14(b)(2)(A). Where a defendant's expert witness will rely on statements of the defendant as to his or her mental condition, the court, on its own motion or on motion of the Commonwealth, may order the defendant to submit to an examination by a court-appointed examiner in accordance with the terms and conditions set forth in Rule 14(b)(2)(B). This procedure adequately safeguards a defendant's privilege against self-incrimination. See Mass. R. Crim. P. 14(b)(2)(B); Blaisdell v. Commonwealth, 372 Mass. 753, 766–769 (1977). The results of a competency evaluation may be used against the defendant where the defendant offers evidence at trial in support of a defense of lack of criminal responsibility, thereby waiving the privilege; Lamb warnings given at the beginning of court-ordered competency evaluations should contain a warning to that effect. Commonwealth v. Harris, 468 Mass. 429, 452 (2014).

Rule 14(b)(2)(C) establishes a "reciprocal discovery process" to ensure that both the defendant's expert and the court-appointed examiner have "equal access to the information they collectively deem necessary to conduct an effective forensic examination and produce a competent report." Reporters' Notes to Mass. R. Crim. P. 14(b)(2)(C). See Commonwealth v. Hanright, 465 Mass. 639, 644 (2013) ("It is only fair that the Commonwealth have the opportunity to rebut the defendant's mental health evidence using the same resources that should be made available to defendant's medical expert."). Under the rule, within fourteen days of the court's designation of the court-appointed examiner, the defendant must make available to the examiner (1) all mental health records concerning the defendant in defense counsel's possession; (2) all medical records concerning the defendant in defense counsel's possession; and (3) all raw data from any tests or assessments administered or requested by the defendant's expert. Mass. R. Crim. P. 14(b)(2)(C)(i). This duty of production extends beyond the initial fourteen-day period. Mass. R. Crim. P. 14(b)(2)(C)(ii). The examiner also may request additional records under seal from "any person or entity" by following the procedure set forth in Rule 14(b)(2)(C)(iii); this same provision provides that if the court allows any part of an examiner's request, the defendant may make copies of the same records. At the conclusion of the court-ordered examination, the examiner must make available to the defendant all raw data from any tests or assessments administered to the defendant during the examination. Mass. R. Crim. P. 14(b)(2)(C)(iv). "By ensuring that the experts are working from a common, comprehensive set of records and objective, test-generated data, the rule advances the reliability and fairness of the examinations and the ensuing reports, and it promotes efficiency in the examination process." Reporters' Notes to Mass. R. Crim. P. 14(b)(2)(C).

Although Rule 14(b)(2)(C)(i) requires that the defendant produce only those mental health and medical records possessed by defense counsel, the rule "intends as wide a reach as is reasonably possible, covering every such record that the defense collected in the course of considering whether to assert this defense." Reporters' Notes to Mass. R. Crim. P. 14(b)(2)(C). Any concern that the defense "overlooked" or "chose not to collect" certain records is counterbalanced by the ability of the court-appointed examiner to request additional records. Id.

Subsection (a)(4). This subsection is derived from the Fifth Amendment to the United States Constitution; Article 12 of the Massachusetts Declaration of Rights; and G. L. c. 233, § 20, Third. Generally, in determining the existence of the privilege, the judge is not permitted to pierce the privilege. See Section 104(a), Preliminary Questions: In General. This privilege is not self-executing. See Commonwealth v. Brennan, 386 Mass. 772, 780 (1982).

Subsection (b). This subsection is derived from the Fifth Amendment to the United States Constitution; Article 12 of the Massachusetts Declaration of Rights; Wansong v. Wansong, 395 Mass. 154, 157–158 (1985) (civil proceeding); and Commonwealth v. Baker, 348 Mass. 60, 62–63 (1964) (criminal proceeding). See also Lefkowitz v. Turley, 414 U.S. 70, 77 (1973) ("The [Fifth] Amendment not only protects the individual against being involuntarily called as a witness against himself in a criminal prosecution but also privileges him not to answer official questions put to him in any other proceeding, civil or criminal, formal or informal, where the answers might incriminate him in future criminal proceedings."). The test used to determine whether an answer might incriminate the witness is the same under both Federal and State law. See Malloy v. Hogan, 378 U.S. 1, 11 (1964). See also Commonwealth v. Lucien, 440 Mass. 658, 665 (2004); Commonwealth v. Funches, 379 Mass. 283, 289 (1979). Also, under both Federal and State law, a public employee cannot be discharged or disciplined solely because the employee asserts his or her privilege against self-incrimination in response to questions by the public employer. Furtado v. Plymouth, 451 Mass. 529, 530 n.2 (2008). In Furtado, the Supreme Judicial Court interpreted the "criminal investigations" exception to G. L. c. 149, § 19B, which forbids the use of lie detector tests in the employment context except in very limited circumstances, as permitting a police chief to require a police officer under departmental investigation to submit to a lie detector test as a condition of his continued employment on grounds that there was an investigation of possible criminal activity, even though the police officer had been granted transactional immunity and could not be prosecuted criminally for that conduct. Id. at 532–538. Unlike other testimonial privileges, the privilege against self-incrimination should be liberally construed in favor of the person claiming it. Commonwealth v. Koonce, 418 Mass. 367, 378 (1994). This privilege is not self-executing. See Commonwealth v. Brennan, 386 Mass. 772, 780 (1982).

Validity of Claim of Privilege. Whenever a witness or the attorney for a witness asserts the privilege against self-incrimination, the judge "has a duty to satisfy himself that invocation of the privilege is proper in the circumstances." Commonwealth v. Martin, 423 Mass. 496, 503 (1996). The mere assertion of the privilege is not sufficient. The witness or counsel must show "a real risk" that answers to the questions will tend to indicate "involvement in illegal activity," as opposed to "a mere imaginary, remote or speculative possibility of prosecution." Id. at 502. The witness is only required to "open the door a crack." Id. at 504–505, quoting In re Brogna, 589 F.2d 24, 28 n.5 (1st Cir. 1978). "A witness also is not entitled to make a blanket assertion of the privilege. The privilege must be asserted with respect to particular questions, and the possible incriminatory potential of each proposed question, or area which the prosecution might wish to explore, must be considered." Commonwealth v. Martin, 423 Mass. at 502. If, however, it is apparent that most, if not all, of the questions will expose the witness to self-incrimination, and there is no objection, it is not necessary for the witness to assert the privilege as to each and every question. Commonwealth v. Sueiras, 72 Mass. App. Ct. 439, 445–446 (2008).

Martin Hearing. In general, the judge's verification of the validity of the privilege should be based on information provided in open court. Commonwealth v. Alicea, 464 Mass. 837, 843 (2013). "Only in those rare circumstances where the information is inadequate to allow the judge to make an informed determination should the judge conduct an in camera Martin hearing." Commonwealth v. Jones, 472 Mass. 707, 728 (2015), quoting Pixley v. Commonwealth, 453 Mass. 827, 833 (2009). Neither the defendant nor counsel has a right to be present during a Martin hearing. Commonwealth v. Clemente, 452 Mass. 295, 318 (2008). If the judge rules that there is a valid basis for the witness to assert the privilege, the defendant has no right to call that witness. Pixley v. Commonwealth, 453 Mass. at 834. At the conclusion of a Martin hearing, the trial judge should seal the transcript or tape of the hearing, which may be reopened "only by an appellate court on appellate review." Id. at 836–837.

Grand Jury Witness. The prosecutor must advise a witness that he or she is a target of the investigation or there is a "substantial likelihood" that the witness will be indicted, and the witness must be advised before testifying that "(1) he or she may refuse to answer any question if a truthful answer would tend to incriminate the witness, and (2) anything that he or she does say may be used against the witness in a subsequent legal proceeding." Commonwealth v. Woods, 466 Mass. 707, 720 (2014). See G. L. c. 277, § 14A (witness with counsel has the right to counsel's presence before the grand jury). See also Supreme Judicial Court Committee on Grand Jury Proceedings: Final Report (June 2018), at http://perma.cc/3CN6-8BZ6.

Noncriminal Proceedings. "A person may not seek to obtain a benefit or to turn the legal process to his advantage while claiming the privilege as a way of escaping from obligations and conditions that are normally incident to the claim he makes." Mello v. Hingham Mut. Fire Ins. Co., 421 Mass. 333, 338 (1995) (party seeking to recover insurance benefits as a result of a fire loss properly had summary judgment entered against him for refusing to submit to an examination required by his policy on grounds that his answers to questions would tend to incriminate him). See also Department of Revenue v. B.P., 412 Mass. 1015, 1016 (1992) (in paternity case, court may draw adverse inference against party who asserts privilege and refuses to submit to blood and genetic marker testing); Wansong v. Wansong, 395 Mass. 154, 157–158 (1985) (dismissal of complaint for divorce without prejudice as discovery sanction); Adoption of Cecily, 83 Mass. App. Ct. 719, 727 (2013) (in termination of parental rights case, court may draw adverse inference against parent who invokes privilege, even though criminal charges are pending). In addition, the court has discretion to reject claims by parties that they are entitled to continuances of administrative proceedings or civil trials until after a criminal trial because they will not testify for fear of self-incrimination. See Oznemoc, Inc. v. Alcoholic Beverages Control Comm'n, 412 Mass. 100, 105 (1992); Kaye v. Newhall, 356 Mass. 300, 305–306 (1969). Whenever a court faces a decision about the consequence of a party's assertion of the privilege in a civil case, "the judge's task is to balance any prejudice to the other civil litigants which might result ... against the potential harm to the party claiming the privilege if he is compelled to choose between defending the civil action and protecting himself from criminal prosecution" (citations and quotations omitted). Wansong v. Wansong, 395 Mass. at 157.

The existence of the privilege against self-incrimination does not shield a witness, other than a defendant in a criminal case, from being called before the jury to give testimony. See Kaye v. Newhall, 356 Mass. at 305. The trial judge has discretion to deny a defense request for process to bring an out-of-State witness back for trial based on evidence that there is a factual basis for the witness to assert his or her privilege against self-incrimination and a representation by the witness's attorney that the witness will invoke his or her privilege if called to testify. Commonwealth v. Sanders, 451 Mass. 290, 294–295 (2008). The assertion of the privilege by a party or a witness in a civil case may be the subject of comment by counsel, and the jury may be permitted to draw an adverse inference against a party as a result. See Section 525(a), Comment upon or Inference from Claim of Privilege: Civil Case.

Subsection (c)(1). This subsection is derived from Jones v. Commonwealth, 327 Mass. 491, 493 (1951). In such a case, the cross-examination is not limited to the scope of direct examination and may include inquiry about any matters that may be made the subject of impeachment. See, e.g., G. L. c. 233, § 21; Commonwealth v. Seymour, 39 Mass. App. Ct. 672, 675 (1996).

Subsection (c)(2). This subsection is derived from Taylor v. Commonwealth, 369 Mass. 183, 189–191 (1975). Though a witness may waive the privilege against self-incrimination as to subsequent questions by voluntarily testifying regarding an "incriminating fact," if a question put to the witness poses "a real danger of legal detriment," i.e., the answer might provide another link in the chain of evidence leading to a conviction, the witness may still have a basis for asserting the privilege against self-incrimination. See Commonwealth v. Funches, 379 Mass. 283, 290–291 & nn.8–10 (1979). In Commonwealth v. King, 436 Mass. 252, 258 n.6 (2002), the Supreme Judicial Court explained the scope of this doctrine by stating that "[t]he waiver, once made, waives the privilege only with respect to the same proceeding; the witness may once again invoke the privilege in any subsequent proceeding." See Commonwealth v. Martin, 423 Mass. 496, 500–501 (1996) (waiver of privilege before grand jury does not waive privilege at trial); Commonwealth v. Borans, 388 Mass. 453, 457–458 (1983) (same). See also Care & Protection of M.C., 479 Mass. 246, 261 (2018) (waiver of privilege at trial on termination of parental rights does not waive privilege in subsequent criminal trial). A voir dire hearing, held on the day of trial, is the same proceeding as the trial for purposes of the doctrine of waiver by testimony. Luna v. Superior Court, 407 Mass. 747, 750–751, cert. denied, 498 U.S. 939 (1990) (privilege could not be claimed at trial where witness had submitted incriminating affidavit in connection with pretrial motion and testified at pretrial hearing); Commonwealth v. Penta, 32 Mass. App. Ct. 36, 45–46 (1992)

(witness who testified at motion to suppress, recanted that testimony in an affidavit, and testified at hearing on motion to reconsider could not invoke the privilege at trial). See also Commonwealth v. Judge, 420 Mass. 433, 445 n.8 (1995) (hearing on motion to suppress is same proceeding as trial for purposes of waiver by testimony).

The trial judge may be required to caution a witness exhibiting "ignorance, confusion, or panic ... or other peculiar circumstances" in order for a voluntary waiver to be established. Taylor v. Commonwealth, 369 Mass. at 192. The proper exercise of this judicial discretion "involves making a circumstantially fair and reasonable choice within a range of permitted options." Lonergan–Gillen v. Gillen, 57 Mass. App. Ct. 746, 748–749 (2003). Ultimately, whether a voluntary waiver has occurred is a question of fact for the trial judge. See Commonwealth v. King, 436 Mass. at 258–259.

Subsection (c)(3). This subsection is derived from Taylor v. Commonwealth, 369 Mass. 183, 190–191 (1975). See also Commonwealth v. Martin, 423 Mass. 496, 500 (1996) (grand jury proceedings and the defendant's subsequent indictment are separate proceedings); Commonwealth v. Johnson, 175 Mass. 152, 153 (1900); Commonwealth v. Mandile, 17 Mass. App. Ct. 657, 662 (1984).

Subsection (c)(4). This subsection is derived from Stornanti v. Commonwealth, 389 Mass. 518, 521–522 (1983) ("The required records exception applies when three requirements are met: First, the purposes of the State's inquiry must be essentially regulatory; second, information is to be obtained by requiring the preservation of records of a kind which the regulated party has customarily kept; and third, the records themselves must have assumed 'public aspects' which render them at least analogous to public documents" [quotations and citation omitted].). See also Matter of Kenney, 399 Mass. 431, 438–441 (1987) (court notes that if the records in question are required to be kept by lawyers there is nothing incriminating about the fact that they exist and are in the possession of the lawyer required to produce them).

Subsection (c)(5). This subsection is derived from Article 12 of the Massachusetts Declaration of Rights; G. L. c. 233, § 20C; and Attorney Gen. v. Colleton, 387 Mass. 790, 796–801 (1982), quoting and citing Emery's Case, 107 Mass. 172, 185 (1871) (Article 12 requires transactional and not merely use or derivative use immunity to overcome the privilege against self-incrimination). See also G. L. c. 233, §§ 20D–20I (statutes governing the granting of immunity); Commonwealth v. Austin A., 450 Mass. 665, 669–670 (2008) (grant of immunity in Superior Court applicable to testimony in Juvenile Court). The Federal Constitution only requires use immunity to overcome the privilege against self-incrimination. See Kastigar v. United States, 406 U.S. 441 (1972). A conviction cannot be based solely on immunized testimony. There must be some corroborating evidence of at least one element of proof essential to convict the defendant. Commonwealth v. Resende, 476 Mass. 141, 152 (2017). See also G. L. c. 233, § 20I.

Subsection (c)(6). This subsection is taken nearly verbatim from Commonwealth v. Gelfgatt, 468 Mass. 512, 522–523 (2014), quoting Fisher v. United States, 425 U.S. 391, 410–411 (1976) ("for the exception to apply, the government must establish its knowledge of [1] the existence of the evidence demanded; [2] the possession or control of that evidence by the defendant; and [3] the authenticity of the evidence").

Subsection (d). This subsection is derived from Commonwealth v. Harris, 364 Mass. 236, 241–242 (1973), which permits statements obtained without a valid waiver of Miranda rights to be used for impeachment of a defendant who testifies at trial if the statements are voluntary and trustworthy. See Commonwealth v. Mahnke, 368 Mass. 662, 694–696 (1975) (statement obtained in violation of defendant's right to counsel admissible for impeachment). See also Commonwealth v. Mulgrave, 472 Mass. 170, 181 (2015) (general subject matter of defendant's responses during questioning admissible to impeach defendant's position that he was noncommunicative during booking process and thus unable to comprehend his Miranda rights); Commonwealth v. Rivera, 425 Mass. 633, 637–638 (1997) (defendant's prior inconsistent statements made at suppression hearing admissible to impeach his testimony at trial). A coerced or involuntary statement may not be used for any purpose, including impeachment. Commonwealth v. Harris, 364 Mass. at 241. See Commonwealth v. Durand, 457 Mass. 574, 590–591 (2010) (defendant's statements previously suppressed as involuntary not admissible on prosecution's redirect of police officer, even where cross-examination arguably opened the door). Evidence obtained in violation of a defendant's substantive constitutional rights, as opposed to violations of "prophylactic" Miranda rules, is not admissible for any purpose. Commonwealth v. Fini, 403 Mass. 567, 571 (1988) (statement obtained by warrantless electronic eavesdropping in private home in violation of Article 14 of the Massachusetts Declaration of Rights inadmissible for any purpose). Cf. Commonwealth v. Domaingue, 397 Mass. 693, 702 (1986) (transcript of warrantless recording of defendant's conversation made in restaurant could be used to refresh defendant's recollection without disclosing substance of defendant's statement).

Supplement to the 2019 Guide to Evidence

Subsection (a)(1). *Privilege Against Self-Incrimination: Privilege of Defendant in Criminal Proceeding, Custodial Interrogation.* Commonwealth v. Lajoie, 95 Mass. App. Ct. 10, 14–15 (2019). The court found Miranda warning formulation that "you have the right to an attorney" and that if you cannot afford an attorney, one will be appointed "prior to questioning" adequately conveyed the "equivalent" of a Miranda warning, emphasizing that "courts should focus on the totality of the warnings conveyed, rather than their precise form." Id. at 14-15.

Subsection (c)(6). *Privilege Against Self-Incrimination: Exceptions, Foregone Conclusion.* Commonwealth v. Jones, 481 Mass. 540, 542–543 (2019). "When the Commonwealth seeks an order pursuant to our decision in Gelfgatt . . . compelling a defendant to decrypt an electronic device by entering a password, art. 12 requires the Commonwealth to prove that the defendant knows the password beyond a reasonable doubt for the foregone conclusion exception to apply." Id. at 542-543.

"[A] judge acting on a renewed Gelfgatt motion may consider additional information without first finding that it was not known or not reasonably available to the Commonwealth at the time the earlier Gelfgatt motion was filed." Id. at 543.

Section 512. Jury Deliberations

See Section 606(b), Juror's Competency as a Witness: During an Inquiry into the Validity of a Verdict or Indictment.

Section 513. Medical Peer Review Privilege

(a) Definitions.

(1) As used in this section, "medical peer review committee" is a committee of a State or local professional society of health care providers, including doctors of chiropractic, or of a medical staff of a public hospital or licensed hospital or nursing home or health maintenance organization organized under G. L. c. 176G, provided the medical staff operates pursuant to written bylaws that have been approved by the governing board of the hospital or nursing home or health maintenance organization or a committee of physicians established pursuant to Section 12 of G. L. c. 111C for the purposes set forth in G. L. c. 111, § 203(f), which committee has as its function the evaluation or improvement of the quality of health care rendered by providers of health care services, the determination whether health care services were performed in compliance with the applicable standards of care, the determination whether the cost of health care services were performed in compliance with the applicable standards of care, determination whether the cost of the health care services rendered was considered reasonable by the providers of health services in the area, the determination of whether a health care provider's actions call into question such health care provider's fitness to provide health care services, or the evaluation and assistance of health care providers impaired or allegedly impaired by reason of alcohol, drugs, physical disability, mental instability, or otherwise; provided, however, that for purposes of Sections 203 and 204 of G. L. c. 111, a nonprofit corporation, the sole voting member of which is a professional society having as members persons who are licensed to practice medicine, shall be considered a medical peer review committee; provided, further, that its primary purpose is the evaluation and assistance of health care providers impaired or allegedly impaired by reason of alcohol, drugs, physical disability, mental instability, or otherwise.

(2) "Medical peer review committee" also includes a committee of a pharmacy society or association that is authorized to evaluate the quality of pharmacy services or the competence of pharmacists and suggest improvements in pharmacy systems to enhance patient care, or a pharmacy peer review committee established by a person or entity that owns a licensed pharmacy or employs pharmacists that is authorized to evaluate the quality of pharmacy services or the competence of pharmacists and suggest improvements in pharmacy systems to enhance patient care.

(b) Privilege.

(1) Proceedings, Reports, and Records of Medical Peer Review Committee. The proceedings, reports, and records of a medical peer review committee shall be confidential and shall be exempt from the disclosure of public records under Section 10 of G. L. c. 66, shall not be subject to subpoena or discovery prior to the initiation of a formal administrative proceeding pursuant to G. L. c. 30A, and shall not be subject to subpoena or discovery, or introduced into evidence, in any judicial or administrative proceeding, except proceedings held by the boards of registration in medicine, social work, or psychology or by the Department of Public Health pursuant to G. L. c. 111C, and no person who was in attendance at a meeting of a medical peer review committee shall be permitted or required to testify in any such judicial or administrative proceeding, except proceedings held by the boards of registration in medicine, social work, or psychology or by the Department of Public Health pursuant to G. L. c. 111C, as to the proceedings of such committee or as to any findings, recommendations, evaluations, opinions, deliberations, or other actions of such committee or any members thereof.

(2) Work Product of Medical Peer Review Committee. Information and records which are necessary to comply with risk management and quality assurance programs established by the board of registration in medicine and which are necessary to the work product of medical peer review committees designated by the patient care assessment coordinator are subject to the protections afforded to materials subject to Subsection (b)(1), except that such information and records may be inspected, maintained, and utilized by the board of registration in medicine, including but not limited to its data repository and disciplinary unit. Such information and records inspected, maintained, or utilized by the board of registration in medicine shall remain confidential, and not subject to subpoena, discovery, or introduction into evidence, consistent with Subsection (b)(1), except that such records may not remain confidential if disclosed in an adjudicatory proceeding of the board of registration in medicine.

(c) Exceptions. There is no restriction on access to or use of the following, as indicated:

(1) Documents, incident reports, or records otherwise available from original sources shall not be immune from subpoena, discovery, or use in any such judicial or administrative proceeding merely because they were presented to such committee in connection with its proceedings.

(2) The proceedings, reports, findings, and records of a medical peer review committee shall not be immune from subpoena, discovery, or use as evidence in any proceeding against a member of such committee who did not act in good faith and in a reasonable belief that based on all of the facts the action or inaction on his or her part was warranted. However, the identity of any person furnishing information or opinions to the committee shall not be disclosed without the permission of such person.

(3) An investigation or administrative proceeding conducted by the boards of registration in medicine, social work, or psychology or by the Department of Public Health pursuant to G. L. c. 111C.

(d) Testimony Before Medical Peer Review Committee. A person who testifies before a medical peer review committee or who is a member of such committee shall not be prevented from testifying as to matters known to such person independent of the committee's proceedings, provided that, except in a proceeding against a witness in Subsection (c)(2), neither the witness nor members of the committee may be questioned regarding the witness's testimony before such committee, and further provided that committee members may not be questioned in any proceeding about the identity of any person furnishing information or opinions to the committee, opinions formed by them as a result of such committee proceedings, or about the deliberations of such committee.

(e) Non–Peer Review Records and Testimony. Records of treatment maintained pursuant to G. L. c. 111, § 70, or incident reports or records or information which are not necessary to comply with risk management and quality assurance programs established by the board of registration in medicine shall not be deemed to be proceedings, reports, or records of a medical peer review committee; nor shall any person be prevented from testifying as to matters known by such person independent of risk management and quality assurance programs established by the board of registration in medicine.

NOTE

Introduction. The medical peer review privilege, unlike so many other privileges, is not based on the importance of maintaining the confidentiality between a professional and a client, but rather was established to promote rigorous and candid evaluation of professional performance by a provider's peers. See Beth Israel Hosp. Ass'n v. Board of Registration in Med., 401 Mass. 172, 182–183 (1987). This is accomplished by requiring hospitals and medical staffs to establish procedures for medical peer review proceedings, see G. L. c. 111, § 203(a), and by legal safeguards against the disclosure of the identity

of physicians who participate in peer review and immunity to prevent such physicians from civil liability. See Ayash v. DanaFarber Cancer Inst., 443 Mass. 367, 396, cert. denied, 546 U.S. 927 (2005).

Subsection (a)(1). This subsection is taken nearly verbatim from G. L. c. 111, § 1.

Subsection (a)(2). This subsection is taken nearly verbatim from G. L. c. 111, § 1. A licensed pharmacy is permitted to establish a pharmacy peer review committee:

"A licensed pharmacy may establish a pharmacy peer review committee to evaluate the quality of pharmacy services or the competence of pharmacists and suggest improvements in pharmacy systems to enhance patient care. The committee may review documentation of quality-related activities in a pharmacy, assess system failures and personnel deficiencies, determine facts, and make recommendations or issue decisions in a written report that can be used for contiguous quality improvement purposes. A pharmacy peer review committee shall include the members, employees, and agents of the committee, including assistants, investigators, attorneys, and any other agents that serve the committee in any capacity."

G. L. c. 111, § 203(g).

Subsection (b). Both Subsection (b)(1), which is taken nearly verbatim from G. L. c. 111, § 204(a), and Subsection (b)(2), which is taken nearly verbatim from G. L. c. 111, § 205(b), "shield information from the general public and other third parties to the same extent, [but] only information protected by § 204(a) [Subsection (b)(1)] is shielded from the board [of registration in medicine] prior to the commencement of a G. L. c. 30A proceeding." Board of Registration in Med. v. Hallmark Health Corp., 454 Mass. 498, 508 (2009). "Determining whether the medical peer review privilege applies turns on the way in which a document was created and the purpose for which it was used, not on its content. Examining that content in camera will therefore do little to aid a judge . . ." Carr v. Howard, 426 Mass. 514, 531 (1998). However, the peer review privilege does not prevent discovery into the process by which a given record or report was created in order to determine whether the information sought falls within the privilege. Id.

Subsection (b)(1). This subsection applies to "proceedings, reports and records of a medical peer review committee." G. L. c. 111, § 204(a). Material qualifies for protection under this subsection if it was created "by, for, or otherwise as a result of a 'medical peer review committee.'" Board of Registration in Med. v. Hallmark Health Corp., 454 Mass. 498, 509 (2009), quoting Miller v. Milton Hosp. & Med. Ctr., Inc., 54 Mass. App. Ct. 495, 499 (2002). See Carr v. Howard, 426 Mass. 514, 522 n.7 (1998) (asserting privilege of G. L. c. 111, § 204[a], [Subsection (b)(1)] requires evidence that materials sought "were not merely 'presented to [a] committee in connection with its proceedings,' . . . but were, instead, *themselves*, 'proceedings, reports and records' of a peer review committee under § 204(a)").

Subsection (b)(2). This subsection applies to materials that, while not necessarily "proceedings, reports and records" of a peer review committee, are nonetheless "necessary to comply with risk management and quality assurance programs established by the board and which are necessary to the work product of medical peer review committees." G. L. c. 111, § 205(b). Such materials include "incident reports required to be furnished to the [board] or any information collected or compiled by a physician credentialing verification service operated by a society or organization of medical professionals for the purpose of providing credentialing information to health care entities." Id. The protections afforded to materials covered by Subsection (b)(2) differ from those afforded by Subsection (b)(1) in that documents protected by Subsection (b)(2) "may be inspected, maintained and utilized by the board of registration in medicine, including but not limited to its data repository and disciplinary unit," and this subsection does not require that such access be conditioned on the commencement of a formal adjudicatory proceeding. G. L. c. 111, § 205(b).

Subsection (c). This subsection is taken nearly verbatim from G. L. c. 111, § 204(b), and Pardo v. General Hosp. Corp., 446 Mass. 1, 11–12 (2006), where the Supreme Judicial Court observed that

> "the privilege can only be invaded on some threshold showing that a member of a medical peer review committee did not act in good faith in connection with his activities as a member of the committee, for example did not provide the medical peer review committee with a full and honest disclosure of all of the relevant circumstances, but sought to mislead the committee in some manner."

In Pardo, the court held that the privilege was not overcome by the allegation that a member of the committee initiated an action for a discriminatory reason. Id. See also Vranos v. Franklin Med. Ctr., 448 Mass. 425, 447 (2007).

Subsection (d). This subsection is taken nearly verbatim from G. L. c. 111, § 204(c).

Subsection (e). This subsection is taken nearly verbatim from G. L. c. 111, § 205.

Section 514. Mediation Privilege

(a) Definition. For the purposes of this section, a "mediator" shall mean a person not a party to a dispute who enters into a written agreement with the parties to assist them in resolving their disputes and has completed at least thirty hours of training in mediation, and who either (1) has four years of professional experience as a mediator, (2) is accountable to a dispute resolution organization which has been in existence for at least three years, or (3) has been appointed to mediate by a judicial or governmental body.

(b) Privilege Applicable to Mediator Work Product. All memoranda and other work product prepared by a mediator and a mediator's case files shall be confidential and not subject to disclosure in any judicial or administrative proceeding involving any of the parties to any mediation to which such materials apply.

(c) Privilege Applicable to Parties' Communications. Any communication made in the course of and relating to the subject matter of any mediation and which is made in the presence of such mediator by any participant, mediator, or other person shall be a confidential communication and not subject to disclosure in any judicial or administrative proceeding.

(d) Privilege Applicable in Labor Disputes. Any person acting as a mediator in a labor dispute who receives information as a mediator relating to the labor dispute shall not be required to reveal such information received by him or her in the course of mediation in any administrative, civil, or arbitration proceeding. This provision does not apply to criminal proceedings.

NOTE

Subsections (a), (b), and (c). These subsections are derived from G. L. c. 233, § 23C. Although there are no express exceptions to the privilege set forth in Subsections (a), (b), and (c), the Supreme Judicial Court has recognized that the mediation privilege is subject to the doctrine of "at issue" waiver. See Bobick v. United States Fid. & Guar. Co., 439 Mass. 652, 658 n.11 (2003), citing Darius v. City of Boston, 433 Mass. 274, 277–278 (2001), and cases cited. See also Section 523(b)(2), Waiver of Privilege: Conduct Constituting Waiver.

Subsection (d). This subsection is derived from G. L. c. 150, § 10A.

Section 515. Investigatory Privilege

Unless otherwise required by law, information given to governmental authorities in order to secure the enforcement of law is subject to disclosure only within the discretion of the governmental authority.

NOTE

This section is derived from Worthington v. Scribner, 109 Mass. 487, 488–489 (1872), and Attorney Gen. v. Tufts, 239 Mass. 458, 490–491 (1921). See also District Attorney for the Norfolk Dist. v. Flatley, 419 Mass. 507, 510–511 (1995).

Although this privilege is described as "absolute," it is qualified by the duty of the prosecutor to provide discovery to a person charged with a crime. See Mass. R. Crim. P. 14. Moreover, as to certain kinds of information, the privilege is also qualified by the Massachusetts public records law. See G. L. c. 66, § 10. General Laws c. 4, § 7, Twenty-sixth (f), provides that investigatory materials, including information covered by this privilege, are regarded as a public record and thus subject to disclosure even though the material is compiled out of the public view by law enforcement or other investigatory officials, provided that the disclosure of the investigatory materials would not "so prejudice the possibility of effective law enforcement that such disclosure would not be in the public interest." Rafuse v. Stryker, 61 Mass. App. Ct. 595, 597 (2004), quoting Bougas v. Chief of Police of Lexington, 371 Mass. 59, 62 (1976). See Worcester Telegram & Gazette Corp. v. Chief of Police of Worcester, 436 Mass. 378, 383 (2002) (describing the process for determining whether material is exempt from disclosure as a public record).

Cross–Reference: Section 509, Identity of Informer, Surveillance Location, and Protected Witness Privileges.

Section 516. Political Voter Disqualification

A voter who casts a ballot may not be asked and may not disclose his or her vote in any proceeding unless the court finds fraud or intentional wrongdoing.

NOTE

This section is derived from McCavitt v. Registrars of Voters, 385 Mass. 833, 848–849 (1982), in which the court held "that the right to a secret ballot is not an individual right which may be waived by a good faith voter." Id. at 849.

Cross–Reference: Section 511, Privilege Against Self–Incrimination.

Section 517. Trade Secrets

[Privilege not recognized]

NOTE

In Gossman v. Rosenberg, 237 Mass. 122, 124 (1921), the Supreme Judicial Court held that a witness could not claim a privilege as to trade secrets. Cf. Proposed Mass. R. Evid. 507. However, public access to information about trade secrets in a public agency's possession may be limited. See G. L. c. 4, § 7, Twenty-sixth (g) (excluding from the definition of "public records" any "trade secrets or commercial or financial information voluntarily provided to an agency for use in developing governmental policy and upon a promise of confidentiality"). The confidentiality of trade secrets also may be maintained by means of a protective order whereby a court may protect from disclosure during discovery "a trade secret or other confidential research, development, or commercial information." Mass. R. Civ. P. 26(c)(7). See also Mass. R. Crim. P. 14(a)(5). The court may issue such a protective order on motion by a party or by the person from whom discovery is sought and if good cause is shown. Mass. R. Civ. P. 26(c)(7).

Section 518. Executive or Governmental Privilege

[Privilege not recognized]

NOTE

Unlike the Federal system, neither the Massachusetts courts nor the Legislature has established a "deliberative process privilege" that prevents a party from obtaining documents from a public officer or agency that record the deliberative process leading up to a decision by the officer or agency. See District Attorney for the Norfolk Dist. v. Flatley, 419 Mass. 507, 509–510 (1995). Likewise, there is no "executive privilege" under the Massachusetts Constitution similar to the privilege which exists under the Federal Constitution. Compare Babets v. Secretary of Human Servs., 403 Mass. 230, 231 (1988) (doctrine of separation of powers does not require recognition of "executive privilege"), with United States v. Nixon, 418 U.S. 683, 711 (1974) (recognizing that separation of powers under Federal Constitution implies a qualified privilege for presidential communications in performance of president's responsibilities).

Access to inter-agency or intra-agency reports, papers, and letters relating to the development of policy is governed by G. L. c. 66, § 10, the public records statute. This law creates a presumption that all records are public, G. L. c. 66, § 10(c), and places on the custodian of the record the burden of establishing that a record is exempt from disclosure because it falls within one of a series of specifically enumerated exemptions set forth in G. L. c. 4, § 7, Twenty-sixth. Id. Under G. L. c. 4, § 7, Twenty-sixth (d), the following material is exempt from public disclosure: "inter-agency or intra-agency memoranda or letters relating to policy positions being developed by the agency; but this subclause shall not apply to reasonably completed factual studies or reports on which the development of such policy positions has been or may be based." Id. "The Legislature has ... chosen to insulate the deliberative process from scrutiny only until it is completed, at which time the documents thereby generated become publicly available." Babets v. Secretary of Human Servs., 403 Mass. at 237 n.8.

Section 519. State and Federal Tax Returns

(a) **State Tax Returns.**

(1) **Disclosure by Commissioner of Revenue.** The disclosure by the commissioner, or by any deputy, assistant, clerk or assessor, or other employee of the Commonwealth or of any city or town therein, to any person but the taxpayer or the taxpayer's representative, of any information contained in or set forth by any return or document filed with the commissioner is prohibited.

(2) **Production by Taxpayer.** Massachusetts State tax returns are privileged, and a taxpayer cannot be compelled to produce them in discovery.

(3) **Exceptions.** Subsection (a)(1) does not apply in proceedings to determine or collect the tax, or to certain criminal prosecutions.

(b) **Federal Tax Returns.**

(1) **General Rule.** Federal tax returns are subject to a qualified privilege. The taxpayer is entitled to a presumption that the returns are privileged and are not subject to discovery.

(2) **Exceptions.** A taxpayer who is a party to litigation can be compelled to produce Federal tax returns upon a showing of substantial need by the party seeking to compel production.

NOTE

Subsection (a). This subsection is taken nearly verbatim from G. L. c. 62C, § 21(a). General Laws c. 62C, § 21(b), sets forth twenty-three exceptions, most of which pertain to limited disclosures of tax information to other government agencies or officials.

The commissioner also has authority to disclose tax information to the Secretary of the Treasury of the United States and certain tax officials in other jurisdictions. See G. L. c. 62C, § 22.

A violation of G. L. c. 62C, § 21, may be punishable as a misdemeanor. G. L. c. 62C, § 21(c).

The privilege applicable to State tax returns in the hands of the taxpayer is set forth in Finance Comm'n of Boston v. Commissioner of Revenue, 383 Mass. 63, 67–72 (1981). See also Leave v. Boston Elevated Ry. Co., 306 Mass. 391, 402–403 (1940). Nothing in this subsection prohibits the courts from requiring a party, in appropriate circumstances, to disclose tax documents to another party during the litigation process. See, e.g., Rule 410 of the Supplemental Rules of the Probate and Family Court (requiring certain parties to disclose "federal and state income tax returns and schedules for the past three [3] years and any non-public, limited partnership and privately held corporate returns for any entity in which either party has an interest together with all supporting documentation for tax returns, including but not limited to W–2's, 1099's, 1098's, K–1, Schedule C and Schedule E").

Subsection (b). This subsection is derived from Finance Comm'n of Boston v. McGrath, 343 Mass. 754, 766–768 (1962).

The conditional privilege against disclosure of the contents of Federal tax returns does not forbid disclosure of the defendant's failure to file such a return. A.C. Vaccaro, Inc. v. Vaccaro, 80 Mass. App. Ct. 635, 639–640 (2011).

Section 520. Tax Return Preparer

(a) **Definition.** For the purposes of this section, a person is engaged in the business of preparing tax returns if the person advertises, or gives publicity to the effect that the person prepares or assists others in the preparation of tax returns, or if he or she prepares or assists others in the preparation of tax returns for compensation.

(b) **Privilege.** No person engaged in the business of preparing tax returns shall disclose any information obtained in the conduct of such business, unless such disclosure is consented to in writing by the taxpayer in a separate document, or is expressly authorized by State or Federal law, or is necessary to the preparation of the return, or is made pursuant to court order.

NOTE

This section is taken nearly verbatim from G. L. c. 62C, § 74. A violation of this statute may be punishable as a misdemeanor.

Section 521. Sign Language Interpreter–Client Privilege

(a) **Definitions.** For the purpose of this section, the following words shall have the following meanings:

(1) **Client.** A "client" is a person rendered interpreting services by a qualified interpreter.

(2) **Qualified Interpreter.** A "qualified interpreter" is a person skilled in sign language or oral interpretation and transliteration, has the ability to communicate accurately with a deaf or hearing-impaired person, and is able to

translate information to and from such hearing-impaired person.

(3) Confidential Communication. A communication is confidential if a client has a reasonable expectation or intent that it not be disclosed to persons other than those to whom such disclosure is made.

(b) Privilege. A client has a privilege to prevent a qualified interpreter from disclosing a confidential communication between one or more persons where the communication was facilitated by the interpreter.

NOTE

Subsection (a). This subsection is derived nearly verbatim from G. L. c. 221, § 92A. The statute's definition of a "qualified interpreter" states that "[a]n interpreter shall be deemed qualified or intermediary as determined by the Office of Deafness, based upon the recommendations of the Massachusetts Registry of the Deaf, the Massachusetts State Association of the Deaf and other appropriate agencies." G. L. c. 221, § 92A.

Subsection (b). This subsection is derived nearly verbatim from G. L. c. 221, § 92A. The portion of G. L. c. 221, § 92A, that establishes the privilege references "a certified sign language interpreter," but the statute does not specifically define that term. Accordingly, to be consistent with the terms actually defined in G. L. c. 221, § 92A, this subsection uses the term "qualified interpreter." There is no case law in Massachusetts which defines the scope of this privilege.

Appointment of Interpreter. The interpreter must be appointed by the court as part of a court proceeding. See G. L. c. 221, § 92A ("In any proceeding in any court in which a deaf or hearing-impaired person is a party or a witness ... such court ... shall appoint a qualified interpreter to interpret the proceedings"). See also Mass. R. Crim. P. 41 ("The judge may appoint an interpreter or expert if justice so requires and may determine the reasonable compensation for such services and direct payment therefor."); Mass. R. Civ. P. 43(f) ("The court may appoint an interpreter of its own selection and may fix his reasonable compensation. The compensation shall be paid out of funds provided by law or by one or more of the parties as the court may direct, and may be taxed ultimately as costs, in the discretion of the court.").

Cross–Reference: Section 604, Interpreters; "Standards and Procedures of the Office of Court Interpreter Services," 1143 Mass. Reg. 15 (Nov. 13, 2009), at http://perma.cc/RPE2–85CA.

Section 522.   Interpreter–Client Privilege

(a) Definitions. For the purpose of this section, the following words shall have the following meanings:

(1) Interpreter. An "interpreter" is a person who is readily able to interpret written and spoken language simultaneously and consecutively from English to the language of the non-English speaker or from said language to English.

(2) Non–English Speaker. A "non-English speaker" is a person who cannot speak or understand, or has difficulty in speaking or understanding, the English language, because he or she uses only or primarily a spoken language other than English.

(b) Privilege. Disclosures made out of court by communications of a non-English speaker through an interpreter to another person shall be a privileged communication, and the interpreter shall not disclose such communication without permission of the non-English speaker.

(c) Scope. The privilege applies when the non-English speaker had a reasonable expectation or intent that the communication would not be disclosed.

NOTE

Subsection (a). This subsection is derived nearly verbatim from G. L. c. 221C, § 1.

Subsection (b). This subsection is derived nearly verbatim from G. L. c. 221C, § 4(c). See Section 4.06 of the "Standards and Procedures of the Office of Court Interpreter Services," 1143 Mass. Reg. 15 (Nov. 13, 2009), which is available at http://perma.cc/RPE2–85CA ("Court interpreters shall protect the confidentiality of all privileged and other confidential information.").

Subsection (c). This subsection is derived nearly verbatim from G. L. c. 221C, § 4(c). There is no case law in Massachusetts that defines the scope of this privilege.

Right to Assistance of an Interpreter. General Laws c. 221C, § 2, states as follows:

"A non-English speaker, throughout a legal proceeding, shall have a right to the assistance of a qualified interpreter who shall be appointed by the judge, unless the judge finds that no qualified interpreter of the non-English speaker's language is reasonably available, in which event the non-English speaker shall have the right to a certified interpreter, who shall be appointed by the judge."

See Mass. R. Crim. P. 41 ("The judge may appoint an interpreter or expert if justice so requires and may determine the reasonable compensation for such services and direct payment therefor."); Mass. R. Civ. P. 43(f) ("The court may appoint an interpreter of its own selection and may fix his reasonable compensation. The compensation shall be paid out of funds provided by law or by one or more of the parties as the court may direct, and may be taxed ultimately as costs, in the discretion of the court."). See also G. L. c. 221C, § 3 (waiver of right to interpreter).

Procedural Issues. The statute requires the interpreter to swear or affirm to "make true and impartial interpretation using [the interpreter's] best skill and judgment in accordance with the standards prescribed by law and the ethics of the interpreter profession." G. L. c. 221C, § 4(a). The statute also states that "[i]n any proceeding, the judge may order all of the testimony of a non-English speaker and its interpretation to be electronically recorded for use in audio or visual verification of the official transcript of the proceedings." G. L. c. 221C, § 4(b).

Cross–Reference: Section 604, Interpreters; "Standards and Procedures of the Office of Court Interpreter Services," 1143 Mass. Reg. 15 (Nov. 13, 2009), at http://perma.cc/RPE2–85CA.

Section 523.   Waiver of Privilege

(a) Who Can Waive. A privilege holder or his or her legally appointed guardian, administrator, executor, or heirs can waive the privilege.

(b) Conduct Constituting Waiver. Except as provided in Section 524, Privileged Matter Disclosed Erroneously or Without Opportunity to Claim Privilege, a privilege is waived if the person upon whom this Article confers a privilege against disclosure

(1) voluntarily discloses or consents to disclosure of any significant part of the privileged matter or

(2) introduces privileged communications as an element of a claim or defense.

(c) Conduct Not Constituting Waiver. A person upon whom this Article confers a privilege against disclosure does not waive the privilege if

(1) the person merely testifies as to events which were a topic of a privileged communication, or

(2) there is an unintentional disclosure of a privileged communication and reasonable precautions were taken to prevent the disclosure.

NOTE

Subsection (a). This subsection is derived from Phillips v. Chase, 201 Mass. 444, 449 (1909), and District Attorney for the Norfolk Dist. v. Magraw, 417 Mass. 169, 173–174 (1994). See also G. L. c. 233, § 20B; Adoption of Diane, 400 Mass. 196, 201, 202 n.4 (1987). Waiver by one or more, but not all, jointly represented clients does not waive the attorney-client privilege as to the nonwaiving party, even as to documents or other information already disclosed by a waiving party. ZVI Constr. Co., LLC v. Levy, 90 Mass. App. Ct. 412, 424–425 (2016).

Subsection (b)(1). This subsection is derived from Matter of the Reorganization of Elec. Mut. Liab. Ins. Co. (Bermuda), 425 Mass. 419, 423 n.4 (1997), where the Supreme Judicial Court noted that Proposed Mass. R. Evid. 510 was consistent with the views of the court.

Subsection (b)(2). This subsection is derived from the concept of an "at issue" waiver which the Supreme Judicial Court recognized in Darius v. City of Boston, 433 Mass. 274, 284 (2001). An "at issue" waiver is not a blanket waiver of the privilege, but rather "a limited waiver of the privilege with respect to what has been put 'at issue.'" Id. at 283. See, e.g., Global Investors Agent Corp. v. National Fire Ins. Co. of Hartford, 76 Mass. App. Ct. 812, 818–820 (2010) (determining that a limited at-issue waiver of the plaintiff's attorney-client privilege occurred because its claim for consequential damages was based in part on the advice it received from its attorney in the underlying action). See also Commonwealth v. Brito, 390 Mass. 112, 119 (1983) ("Once such a charge [of ineffectiveness of counsel] is made, the attorney-client privilege may be treated as waived at least in part, but trial counsel's obligation may continue to preserve confidences whose disclosure is not relevant to the defense of the charge of his ineffectiveness as counsel."). Doe v. American Guar. & Liab. Co., 91 Mass. App. Ct. 99, 103 (2017) (privilege waived if client's statement is relevant to action client brought against counsel). In addition, the party seeking to invoke the doctrine of an "at issue" waiver must establish that the privileged information is not available from any other source. Darius v. City of Boston, 433 Mass. at 284.

Subsection (c)(1). This subsection is derived from Commonwealth v. Goldman, 395 Mass. 495, 499–500, cert. denied, 474 U.S. 906 (1985). Though a witness does not waive the privilege merely by testifying as to events which were a topic of a privileged communication, a waiver occurs when the witness testifies as to the specific content of an identified privileged communication. Id. In Commonwealth v. Goldman, the Supreme Judicial Court specifically left open the question whether in a criminal case the rule embodied in this subsection would have to yield to the defendant's constitutional right of confrontation. Id. at 502 n.8. See also Commonwealth v. Pickering, 479 Mass. 589, 597 n.9 (2018) (prior statement to police on same subject matter does not automatically waive privilege); Commonwealth v. Neumyer, 432 Mass. 23, 29 (2000) (waiver of sexual assault counselor privilege); Commonwealth v. Clancy, 402 Mass. 664, 668–669 (1988) (waiver of patient-psychotherapist privilege).

Subsection (c)(2). This subsection is derived from Matter of the Reorganization of Elec. Mut. Liab. Ins. Co. (Bermuda), 425 Mass. 419, 422–423 (1997). See also Adoption of Sherry, 435 Mass. 331, 336 (2001).

Rule 502 of the Federal Rules of Evidence, Waivers in Federal Proceedings. On September 19, 2008, Rule 502 of the Federal Rules of Evidence was enacted. See Pub. L. No. 110–322, 110th Cong., 2d Sess. The rule is applicable "in all proceedings commenced after the date of enactment . . . and, insofar as is just and practicable, in all proceedings pending" on that date. The rule was developed in response to concerns about the rising cost of discovery, especially electronic discovery, in Federal proceedings in which among the thousands or hundreds of thousands of documents that are produced by a party in response to a discovery request, the producing party may inadvertently include one or a handful of documents that are covered by the attorney-client privilege or the work-product protection. Prior to the adoption of this rule, there was no uniform national standard governing the determination of when such a mistake would lead to a ruling that the privilege or protection had been waived. As a result, a party was forced to examine each and every document produced in discovery in order to avoid the risk of an inadvertent waiver.

Rule 502 of the Federal Rules of Evidence does not alter the law that governs whether a document is subject to the attorney-client privilege or the work-product protection in the first instance. Under Fed. R. Evid. 501, unless State law, the Federal Constitution, or a Federal statute controls, the existence of a privilege in Federal proceedings "shall be governed by the principles of the common law." However, Fed. R. Evid. 502 does establish a single national standard that protects parties against a determination by a Federal court, a Federal agency, a State court, or a State agency that an inadvertent disclosure of privileged or protected material constitutes a wholesale waiver of the privilege or protection as to other material that has not been disclosed.

Rule 502(a) of the Federal Rules of Evidence addresses when a waiver of either the attorney-client privilege or the work-product protection extends to undisclosed material. It provides that a waiver of the privilege or protection does not extend to undisclosed material unless (1) the waiver is intentional, (2) the disclosed and undisclosed material concern the same subject matter, and (3) both the disclosed and undisclosed material should in fairness be considered together. Rule 502(b) of the Federal Rules of Evidence addresses inadvertent disclosures. It is similar to Section 523(c)(2), Waiver of Privilege: Conduct Not Constituting Waiver, except that the Federal rule requires that to avoid a waiver the holder of the privilege must promptly take reasonable steps to rectify the erroneous disclosure. Fed. R. Evid. 502(b)(3). Rule 502(c) of the Federal Rules of Evidence provides that disclosures made in State court proceedings will not operate as a waiver in Federal proceedings so long as the disclosure is not regarded as a waiver under either Fed. R. Evid. 502(a) or 502(b), or the law of the State where the disclosure occurred. Rule 502(d) of the Federal Rules of Evidence provides that a Federal court order that the privilege or the protection is not waived by a disclosure is binding on both Federal and State courts. Rule 502(e) of the Federal Rules of Evidence provides that an agreement on the effect of the disclosure between the parties in a Federal proceeding is binding only on the parties to the agreement, unless it is incorporated into a court order. Rule 502(f) of the Federal Rules of Evidence expressly makes the rule applicable to State and Federal proceedings, "even if State law provides the rule of decision." Rule 502(g) of the Federal Rules of Evidence contains definitions of the terms "attorney-client privilege" and "work-product protection."

Section 524. Privileged Matter Disclosed Erroneously or Without Opportunity to Claim Privilege

A claim of privilege is not defeated by a disclosure erroneously made without an opportunity to claim the privilege.

NOTE

This section is derived from Commonwealth v. Neumyer, 432 Mass. 23, 35–36 (2000) (no waiver where record holder unaware of probable cause hearing and victim "was hardly in a position to be aware of her rights"). See also Commonwealth v. Dwyer, 448 Mass. 122, 145–146 (2006).

Section 525. Comment upon or Inference from Claim of Privilege

(a) Civil Case. Comment may be made and an adverse inference may be drawn against a party when that party, or in certain circumstances a witness, invokes a privilege.

(b) Criminal Case.

(1) No comment may be made and no adverse inference may be drawn against a defendant who invokes the privilege against self-incrimination or against a defendant for calling a witness who invokes a privilege that belongs to the witness and not to the defendant.

(2) In a case tried to a jury, the assertion of a privilege should be made outside the presence of the jury whenever reasonably possible.

NOTE

Subsection (a). This subsection is derived from the long-standing rule in Massachusetts that an adverse inference may be drawn against a party who invokes a testimonial privilege in a civil case. Phillips v. Chase, 201 Mass. 444, 450 (1909) (attorney-client privilege). This principle applies equally to cases involving custody or parental access to a child. See Custody of Two Minors, 396 Mass. 610, 616–617 (1986); Care & Protection of Quinn, 54 Mass. App. Ct. 117, 121 (2002); Adoption of Nadia, 42 Mass. App. Ct. 304, 307–308 (1997). Drawing the adverse inference in a civil case does not infringe on the party's privilege against self-incrimination under either Article 12 of the Declaration of Rights of the Massachusetts Constitution or the Fifth Amendment to the Constitution of the United States. Kaye v. Newhall, 356 Mass. 300, 305–306 (1969) (attorney-client privilege). It makes no difference that criminal matters are pending at the time. Frizado v. Frizado, 420 Mass. 592, 596 (1995) (privilege against self-incrimination).

In Labor Relations Comm'n v. Fall River Educators' Ass'n, 382 Mass. 465, 471–472 (1981), the Supreme Judicial Court expanded the rule to allow an adverse inference to be drawn against an organizational party as a result of a claim of the privilege against self-incrimination by its officers who had specific knowledge of actions taken on behalf of the organization in connection with the underlying claim. In Lentz v. Metropolitan Prop. & Cas. Ins. Co., 437 Mass. 23, 26–32 (2002), the Supreme Judicial Court expanded the principle even further to include circumstances in which the court finds, as a preliminary question of fact, that the witness who invokes the privilege against self-incrimination is acting on behalf of or to further the interests of one of the parties. The Supreme Judicial Court also noted that the potential for prejudice can be reduced by limiting the number of questions that may be put to the witness who invokes the privilege, and by a limiting instruction. Id. at 30–31.

Counsel has the right to comment on an opposing party's failure to testify in a civil case. See Kaye v. Newhall, 356 Mass. at 305; Silveira v. Kegerreis, 12 Mass. App. Ct. 906, 906–907 (1981).

When a nonparty witness is closely aligned with a party in a civil case, and the nonparty witness invokes the privilege against self-incrimination, the jury should be instructed that the witness may invoke the privilege for reasons unrelated to the case on trial, and that they are permitted, but not required, to draw an inference adverse to the party from the witness's invocation of the privilege against self-incrimination. The jury is permitted to draw an inference adverse to a party from the witness's invocation of the privilege against self-incrimination. Lentz v. Metropolitan Prop. & Cas. Ins. Co., 437 Mass. at 26–32.

Subsection (b)(1). This subsection is derived from Article 12 of the Declaration of Rights of the Massachusetts Constitution and the Fifth Amendment to the Constitution of the United States, as well as from G. L. c. 233, § 20, Third, and G. L. c. 278, § 23. See Commonwealth v. Goulet, 374 Mass. 404, 412 (1978). See also Commonwealth v. Szerlong, 457 Mass. 858, 869–870 n.13 (2010). In Commonwealth v. Vallejo, 455 Mass. 72, 78–81 (2009), the Supreme Judicial Court adopted the reasoning of Commonwealth v. Russo, 49 Mass. App. Ct. 579 (2000), and held that a defendant's privilege against self-incrimination may be violated by comments made by a codefendant's counsel on the defendant's pretrial silence or the defendant's decision not to testify. For a discussion of the numerous cases dealing with the issue of whether a remark by a judge, a prosecutor, or a co-counsel constitutes improper comment on the defendant's silence, see M.S. Brodin & M. Avery, Massachusetts Evidence § 5.14.8 (2018 ed.). A defendant may have the right to simply exhibit a person before the jury without questioning the person. See Commonwealth v. Rosario, 444 Mass. 550, 557–559 (2005). When there is a timely request made by the defense, the trial judge must instruct the jury that no adverse inference may be drawn from the fact that the defendant did not testify. See Carter v. Kentucky, 450 U.S. 288, 305 (1981); Commonwealth v. Sneed, 376 Mass. 867, 871–872 (1978). See also Commonwealth v. Rivera, 441 Mass. 358, 371 n.9 (2004) ("We remain of the view that judges should not give the instruction when asked not to do so. We are merely saying that it is not per se reversible error to do so.").

Subsection (b)(2). This subsection is derived from Commonwealth v. Martin, 372 Mass. 412, 413, 421 n.17 (1977) (privilege against self-incrimination), and Commonwealth v. Labbe, 6 Mass. App. Ct. 73, 79–80 (1978) (spousal privilege). "Where there is some advance warning that a witness might refuse to testify, the trial judge should conduct a voir dire of the witness, outside the presence of the jury, to ascertain whether the witness will assert some privilege or otherwise refuse to answer questions." Commonwealth v. Fisher, 433 Mass. 340, 350 (2001). If the witness asserts the privilege or refuses to testify before the jury when it was not anticipated, the judge should give a forceful cautionary instruction to the jury. Commonwealth v. Hesketh, 386 Mass. 153, 157–159 (1982).

Section 526. Unemployment Hearing Privilege

(a) Statutory Bar on the Use of Information from Unemployment Hearing. Subject to the exceptions listed in Subsection (b), information secured during an unemployment hearing is absolutely privileged, is not public record, and is not admissible in any action or proceeding.

(b) Exceptions. Such information may be admissible only in the following actions or proceedings:

(1) criminal or civil cases brought pursuant to G. L. c. 151A where the department or Commonwealth is a necessary party,

(2) civil cases relating to the enforcement of child support obligations,

(3) criminal prosecutions for homicide, and

(4) criminal prosecutions for violation of Federal law.

NOTE

This section is derived from G. L. c. 151A, § 46, and Tuper v. North Adams Ambulance Serv., Inc., 428 Mass. 132, 137 (2008) ("Information secured pursuant to [G. L. c. 151A] is confidential, is for the exclusive use and information of the department in the discharge of its duties, is not a public record, and may not be used in any action or proceeding."). A violation of this statute may be punishable as a misdemeanor.

Section 527.   Judicial Deliberation Privilege

A judge has an absolute privilege to refuse to disclose the mental impressions and thought processes relied on in reaching a decision, whether harbored internally or memorialized in nonpublic material.

NOTE

This section is derived from Matter of the Enforcement of a Subpoena, 463 Mass. 162 (2012). In that case, the Supreme Judicial Court quashed so much of a subpoena issued by the Commission on Judicial Conduct to a judge as related to the judge's internal thought processes and deliberative communications. Id. at 178. The court recognized an absolute judicial deliberation privilege that protects the judge's "mental impressions and thought processes in reaching a judicial decision, whether harbored internally or memorialized in other nonpublic material." Id. at 174. The court additionally ruled that "the privilege also protects confidential communications among judges and between judges and court staff made in the course of and related to their deliberative processes in particular cases." Id. This absolute but narrowly tailored privilege "does not cover a judge's memory of nondeliberative events in connection with cases in which the judge participated. Nor does the privilege apply to inquiries into whether a judge was subjected to improper 'extraneous influences' or ex parte communications during the deliberative process." Id. at 174–175.

The privilege also does not apply "when a judge is a witness to or was personally involved in a circumstance that later becomes the focus of a legal proceeding." Id. at 175.

Section 528.   Union Member—Union Privilege

[Privilege not recognized]

NOTE

In Chadwick v. Duxbury Pub. Sch., 475 Mass. 645 (2016), the Supreme Judicial Court declined to read a privilege for communications between a union member and his or her union into the provisions of G. L. c. 150E. In that case, the plaintiff filed a civil suit against the defendant seeking monetary damages after she was dismissed from her teaching position. The court found that Chapter 150E was designed to "protect the right of public employees to organize and to protect unions and their members from intrusion or control by the employer in the collective bargaining context," and that the Legislature did not intend "to protect the confidentiality of union member-union communications in a private lawsuit brought by the union member against the employer." Chadwick v. Duxbury Pub. Sch., 475 Mass. at 650–651. The court also declined to create the privilege judicially, saying that the Legislature is better equipped to create such a privilege. Id. at 655.

ARTICLE VI.   WITNESSES

Section 601.   Competency

(a) Generally. Every person is competent to be a witness unless a statute or the Massachusetts common law of evidence provides otherwise.

(b) Rulings. A person is competent to be a witness if he or she has

    (1) the general ability or capacity to observe, remember, and give expression to that which he or she has seen, heard, or experienced, and

    (2) an understanding sufficient to comprehend the difference between truth and falsehood, the wickedness of the latter, and the obligation and duty to tell the truth, and, in a general way, belief that failure to perform the obligation will result in punishment.

(c) Preliminary Questions. While the competency of a witness is a preliminary question of fact for the judge, questions of witness credibility are to be resolved by the trier of fact.

NOTE

Subsection (a). This subsection is derived from G. L. c. 233, § 20. See Commonwealth v. Monzon, 51 Mass. App. Ct. 245, 248–249 (2001). A person otherwise competent to be a witness may still be disqualified from testifying. See, e.g., G. L. c. 233, § 20 (with certain exceptions, "neither husband nor wife shall testify as to private conversations with the other"; "neither husband nor wife shall be compelled to testify in the trial of an indictment, complaint or other criminal proceeding against the other"; "defendant in the trial of an indictment, complaint or other criminal proceeding shall, at his own request . . . be allowed to testify"; and "an unemancipated, minor child, living with a parent, shall not testify before a grand jury, trial of an indictment, complaint or other criminal proceeding, against said parent"). See also Section 504, Spousal Privilege and Disqualification; Parent–Child Disqualification; Section 511, Privilege Against Self–Incrimination. Cf. Mass. R. Civ. P. 43(a) (witness testimony, and assessment of the competency of

a witness, must be done orally in open court); Hayden v. Hayden, 15 Mass. App. Ct. 915, 916 (1983) ("The probate judge acted well within his sound discretion in declining to have a conference in camera with the son of the parties, then twelve years old . . .").

Subsection (b). This subsection is taken nearly verbatim from Commonwealth v. Allen, 40 Mass. App. Ct. 458, 461 (1996). This test applies to all potential witnesses. Commonwealth v. Brusgulis, 398 Mass. 325, 329 (1986). Neither the inability of a witness to remember specific details of events nor inconsistencies in the testimony render the witness incompetent to testify, so long as the witness demonstrates "the general ability to observe, remember and recount." Commonwealth v. Trowbridge, 419 Mass. 750, 755 (1995); Commonwealth v. Thibeault, 77 Mass. App. Ct. 419, 424–428 (2010) (six year old permitted to testify about incidents that occurred when she was five despite inconsistencies in her ability to observe, remember, and recount facts and her initial difficulty with concept of a promise in connection with duty to tell the truth). See Commonwealth v. Gamache, 35 Mass. App. Ct. 805, 806–809 (1994) (five year old permitted to testify about incidents that allegedly took place when the child was twenty-one and thirty-three months old despite inconsistencies and her inability to recall every detail in her testimony). "The tendency, moreover, except in quite clear cases of incompetency, is to let the witness testify and have the triers make any proper discount for the quality of her understanding" (quotations omitted). Commonwealth v. Whitehead, 379 Mass. 640, 656 (1980). See, e.g., Commonwealth v. Brusgulis, 398 Mass. at 329 (child); Commonwealth v. Sires, 370 Mass. 541, 546 (1976) (alcoholic); Commonwealth v. Aitahmedlamara, 63 Mass. App. Ct. 76, 78 (2005) (developmentally disabled); Commonwealth v. Hiotes, 58 Mass. App. Ct. 255, 256 (2003) (mental illness).

Subsection (c). The initial segment of this subsection is derived from Demoulas v. Demoulas, 428 Mass. 555, 562–563 (1998); the remainder of the subsection is derived from Commonwealth v. Jackson, 428 Mass. 455, 466 (1998). The question of the competency of a potential witness is within the discretion of the trial judge, who has "wide discretion . . . to tailor the competency inquiry to the particular circumstances and intellect of the witness." Commonwealth v. Brusgulis, 398 Mass. 325, 329–330 (1986). When competency is challenged, a judge usually conducts a voir dire examination of the potential witness, but may require a physician or other expert to examine the potential witness's mental condition where appropriate. Demoulas v. Demoulas, 428 Mass. at 563. See G. L. c. 123, § 19; G. L. c. 233, § 23E. Cf. Mass. R. Civ. P. 43(a) (witness testimony, and assessment of the competency of a witness, must be done orally in open court). "Although competency must of course be determined before a witness testifies, the judge may reconsider his decision, either sua sponte or on motion, if he entertains doubts about the correctness of the earlier ruling." Commonwealth v. Brusgulis, 398 Mass. at 331.

Competency of Criminal Defendant. A defendant in a criminal case is competent so long as the defendant has a "sufficient present ability to consult with his [or her] lawyer with a reasonable degree of rational understanding and . . . a rational as well as factual understanding of the proceedings." Commonwealth v. Hung Tan Vo, 427 Mass. 464, 468–469 (1998), quoting Commonwealth v. Vailes, 360 Mass. 522, 524 (1971), quoting Dusky v. United States, 362 U.S. 402, 402 (1960). The trial judge has a duty to act sua sponte whenever there is "a substantial question of possible doubt" as to the defendant's competency to stand trial. See Commonwealth v. Hill, 375 Mass. 50, 62 (1978).

It is not necessary to suspend all pretrial proceedings because a defendant is not competent. See Abbott A. v. Commonwealth, 458 Mass. 24, 33 (2010) (concluding it is not a per se violation of due process for the Commonwealth to proceed against incompetent person at bail hearing or dangerousness hearing). Contra Commonwealth v. Torres, 441 Mass. 499, 505–507 (2004) (stating due process may be violated if defense counsel is unable to communicate at all with client during bail hearing or hearing on rendition).

Section 602.   Need for Personal Knowledge

A witness may testify to a matter only if evidence is introduced sufficient to support a finding that the witness has personal knowledge of the matter. Evidence to prove personal knowledge may consist of the witness's own testimony. This section does not apply to a witness's expert opinion testimony under Section 703.

NOTE

This section is taken from Fed. R. Evid. 602 and Proposed Mass. R. Evid. 602 and is consistent with Massachusetts law. See Commonwealth v. Cintron, 435 Mass. 509, 521 (2001); Malchanoff v. Truehart, 354 Mass. 118, 121–122 (1968); Commonwealth v. Wolcott, 28 Mass. App. Ct. 200, 207 (1990).

The personal-knowledge requirement also applies to hearsay declarants. See, e.g., Commonwealth v. Drapaniotis, 89 Mass. App. Ct. 267, 274–276 (2016) (reversing conviction of firearm offense, based on insufficiency of evidence, where sole evidence on element of gun's operability was gun owner's testimony of hearsay statement by salesman, admitted without objection but not supported by any indication of salesman's personal knowledge).

Cross–Reference: Section 104(b), Preliminary Questions: Relevance That Depends on a Fact; Section 601, Competency; Section 703, Bases of Opinion Testimony by Experts. Cf. Section 402, General Admissibility of Relevant Evidence; Section 403, Excluding Relevant Evidence for Prejudice, Confusion, Waste of Time, or Other Reasons; Section 701, Opinion Testimony by Lay Witnesses.

Section 603.   Oath or Affirmation to Testify Truthfully

Before testifying, a witness must give an oath or affirmation to testify truthfully. It must be in a form designed to impress that duty on the witness's conscience.

NOTE

This section is taken from Fed. R. Evid. 603 and Proposed Mass. R. Evid. 603 and is consistent with Massachusetts law. See G. L. c. 233, §§ 15–19. See also Mass. R. Civ. P. 43(d) ("Whenever under these rules an oath is required to be taken, a solemn affirmation under the penalties of perjury may be accepted in lieu thereof."). "Although taking [the traditional] oath is the customary method for signifying one's recognition that consequences attend purposeful falsehood, it is not the only method for doing so. The law requires some affirmative representation that the witness recognizes his or her obligation to tell the truth. See G. L. c. 233, §§ 17–19." Adoption of Fran, 54 Mass. App. Ct. 455, 467 (2002). A judge is not permitted to waive an oath or affirmation. Commonwealth v. Stewart, 454 Mass. 527, 531 (2009).

"A child witness does not have to understand fully the obligation of an oath, but must show a general awareness of the duty to be truthful and the difference between a lie and the truth." Commonwealth v. Ike I., 53 Mass. App. Ct. 907, 909 (2002). "With children, recognition of that obligation [to tell the truth] sometimes is more effectively obtained through careful questioning of the child than through recitation of what to the child may be a meaningless oath or affirmation." Adoption of Fran, 54 Mass. App. Ct. at 467 n.17. A judge's exchanges with a child and his or her discretionary conclusion that the child understands the difference between the truth and lying and the importance of testifying truthfully "effectively serve[s] the underlying purpose of the oath, and no more [can] be reasonably required of an infant deemed competent to testify, but manifestly lacking in theological understanding." Commonwealth v. McCaffrey, 36 Mass. App. Ct. 583, 590 (1994).

Section 604.   Interpreters

An interpreter must be qualified and must give an oath or affirmation to make a true translation.

NOTE

This section is derived from Fed. R. Evid. 604 and Proposed Mass. R. Evid. 604 and is consistent with Massachusetts law. See Commonwealth v. Festa, 369 Mass. 419, 429–430 (1976) (establishing guidelines for when witnesses testify through an interpreter). See G. L. c. 221C, § 2 (a non-English speaker has the right to an interpreter throughout the proceedings, whether criminal or civil); Mass. R. Civ. P. 43(f); Mass. R. Crim. P. 41. The trial judge has discretion to appoint an interpreter. Commonwealth v. Esteves, 46 Mass. App. Ct. 339, 345, reversed and remanded on other grounds, 429 Mass. 636 (1999). "[W]hen a witness testifies in a foreign language, the English translation is the only evidence, not the testimony in the original language." Id. All spoken-language court interpreters and court interpreters who provide services to the Trial Court for deaf and hard-of-hearing persons are governed by the "Standards and Procedures of the Office of Court Interpreter Services," 1143 Mass. Reg. 15 (Nov. 13, 2009), which include a Code of Professional Conduct that includes the subjects of conflict of interest, confidentiality, and interpreting protocols. See http://perma.cc/RPE2–85CA. Where a party seeks to admit a translation of a recorded statement made in a foreign language, the English-language transcript must be provided to opposing counsel sufficiently in advance to allow the parties to determine whether an agreement can be reached about its accuracy. If the parties are unable to agree on the accuracy of a single translation, each side may offer its own transcript through the testimony of a qualified translator. The foreign-language recording may not be admitted unless accompanied by an English translation. Commonwealth v. Portillo, 462 Mass. 324, 328–329 (2012). See also Commonwealth v. Lujan, 93 Mass. App. Ct. 95, 102–103 (2018) (although police not required to use certified or independent interpreters when questioning suspects, chosen interpreter must be competent).

Cross–Reference: Note "Preference for Recording Certain Custodial Interrogations" to Section 511(a)(1), Privilege Against Self–Incrimination: Privilege of Defendant in Criminal Proceeding: Custodial

Interrogation; Section 521, Sign Language Interpreter–Client Privilege; Section 522, Interpreter–Client Privilege; "Standards and Procedures of the Office of Court Interpreter Services," 1143 Mass. Reg. 15 (Nov. 13, 2009), available at http://perma.cc/RPE2–85CA.

Section 605. Competency of Judge as Witness

The presiding judge may not testify as a witness at the trial.

NOTE

This section states the first sentence of Fed. R. Evid. 605 and Proposed Mass. R. Evid. 605. While there are no Massachusetts statutes or cases on point, the proposition appears so clear as to be beyond question. See generally S.J.C. Rule 3:09, Canon 3(E) (judicial disqualification); Glenn v. Aiken, 409 Mass. 699, 703 (1991) ("calling a judge as a witness to opine on what ruling he might have made on a particular hypothesis" is disfavored). Cf. Guardianship of Pollard, 54 Mass. App. Ct. 318, 322–323 (2002) (judge who served as guardian ad litem prior to becoming judge not disqualified from testifying in guardianship proceeding before a different judge and from being cross-examined on her guardian ad litem report).

Section 606. Juror's Competency as a Witness

(a) At the Trial. A juror may not testify as a witness before the other jurors at the trial. If a juror is called to testify, the court must give a party an opportunity to object outside the jury's presence.

(b) During an Inquiry into the Validity of a Verdict or Indictment.

(1) Prohibited Testimony or Other Evidence. During an inquiry into the validity of a verdict or indictment, a juror may not testify about any statement made or incident that occurred during the jury's deliberations, the effect of anything on that juror's or another juror's vote, or any juror's mental processes concerning the verdict or indictment. The court may not receive a juror's affidavit or evidence of a juror's statement on these matters.

(2) Exceptions. A juror may testify about whether

(A) extraneous prejudicial information was improperly brought to the jury's attention or

(B) an outside influence was improperly brought to bear on any juror.

NOTE

Subsection (a). This subsection, which is taken verbatim from Fed. R. Evid. 606(a) and is nearly identical to Proposed Mass. R. Evid. 606(a), reflects Massachusetts practice.

Subsection (b). This subsection is taken from Proposed Mass. R. Evid. 606(b) and is derived from Commonwealth v. Tavares, 385 Mass. 140, 153–157, cert. denied, 457 U.S. 1137 (1982), and Commonwealth v. Fidler, 377 Mass. 192, 196–198 (1979). In Commonwealth v. Tavares, 385 Mass. at 155 n.25, the court stated that Proposed Mass. R. Evid. 606(b) "is the federal rule, and is in accord with the current Massachusetts rule admitting evidence of extraneous information and excluding evidence of mental processes" (quotation and citations omitted). See also Commonwealth v. Walker, 379 Mass. 297, 304 (1979); Woodward v. Leavitt, 107 Mass. 453, 466–467 (1871); Commonwealth v. Hanlon, 44 Mass. App. Ct. 810, 816 (1998).

The Doctrine of "Extraneous Matter." In Commonwealth v. Fidler, 377 Mass. at 200, the court held that "if specific facts not mentioned at trial concerning one of the parties or the matter in litigation were brought to the attention of the deliberating jury by a juror ... such misconduct may be proved by juror testimony." The

court cautioned, however, that "evidence concerning the subjective mental processes of jurors" is not admissible to impeach their verdict. Id. at 198. The challenge for courts is to make the distinction between "overt factors and matters resting in a juror's consciousness." Id. See Commonwealth v. Heang, 458 Mass. 827, 858 (2011) (pressure from other jurors during deliberation was not extraneous influence). In Commonwealth v. Guisti, 434 Mass. 245 (2001), the court offered further guidance by defining the concept of an "extraneous matter." "An extraneous matter is one that involves information not part of the evidence at trial and raises a serious question of possible prejudice" (citations and quotation omitted). Id. at 251. Some illustrations of this concept include "(1) unauthorized views of sites by jurors; (2) improper communications to the jurors by third persons; or (3) improper consideration of documents not in evidence" (citations omitted). Commonwealth v. Fidler, 377 Mass. at 197. See Fitzpatrick v. Allen, 410 Mass. 791 (1991) (home medical reference book brought into jury room); Markee v. Biasetti, 410 Mass. 785 (1991) (jurors took unauthorized view and made measurements at accident scene). See also Commonwealth v. Blanchard, 476 Mass. 1026, 1026–1027 (2017) (judge's binder containing information not in evidence at trial, inadvertently brought to jury room during deliberations, constitutes extraneous materials). But see Commonwealth v. Miller, 475 Mass. 212 (2016) (gun magazine not prejudicial).

Extraneous Matter Prior to Discharge. In Commonwealth v. Blanchard, 476 Mass. 1026 (2017), the Supreme Judicial Court ruled that, in a case in which exposure to extraneous matter is revealed before the jury is discharged, as opposed to after a verdict is announced and the jury excused,

> "the judge should ask the juror whether he or she read, saw, heard, or otherwise became aware of the extraneous materials during the jury's deliberations. The judge should then inquire into the effect of the exposure on the particular juror, with the focus of the question or questions being whether the juror can deliberate without being influenced by the materials. In asking about the effect of the extraneous materials on the individual juror, the judge should caution the juror not to speculate about the effect on any other juror or on the jury as a whole.

> [A] prefatory instruction by the judge to each juror about the need to avoid telling the judge anything about the substance of the jury's deliberations may be useful."

Id. at 1027–1028.

Contacting Jurors Post-Discharge. A lawyer's ability to contact jurors after the verdict is regulated by Mass. R. Prof. C. 3.5 (2015) and Commonwealth v. Moore, 474 Mass. 541 (2016). In Moore, the Supreme Judicial Court modified the prohibition against attorney-originated communications established by Commonwealth v. Fidler. Id. at 548. The court discussed the revisions to Mass. R. Prof. C. 3.5, effective July 1, 2015, noting that the prohibition against inquiring into the substance of jury deliberations remained intact. Attorneys may initiate contact with jurors, but only after giving opposing counsel five business days' notice. The notice must include "a description of the proposed manner of contact and the substance of any proposed inquiry to the jurors, and, where applicable, a copy of any letter or other form of written communication the attorney intends to send." Commonwealth v. Moore, 474 Mass. at 551–552. If a communication with a juror leads the lawyer to suspect that there was an extraneous influence on the jury, the lawyer may obtain an affidavit from the juror without prior court approval, but the affidavit "must focus on extraneous influences, and not the substance of the jury's deliberations or the individual or collective thought processes of the juror or the jury as a whole." Id.

Procedure for Determining Whether Jury Was Influenced by an "Extraneous Matter." A party alleging that a jury was exposed to a significant extraneous influence "bears the burden of demonstrating that the jury were in fact exposed to the extraneous matter. To meet this burden he may rely on juror testimony." Commonwealth v. Fidler, 377 Mass. 192, 201 (1979).

Further inquiry by the court is not required where "there has been no showing that specific facts not mentioned at trial concerning one of the parties or the matter in litigation were brought to the attention of the deliberating jury" (emphasis and quotations omitted). Commonwealth v. Drumgold, 423 Mass. 230, 261 (1996). See Commonwealth v. McQuade, 46 Mass. App. Ct. 827, 833 (1999). "The question whether the party seeking an inquiry has made such a showing is properly addressed to the discretion of the trial judge." Commonwealth v. Dixon, 395 Mass. 149, 152 (1985). There is always a danger that when questioned about the existence of an extraneous matter a juror will respond

> "with an answer that inappropriately reveals aspects of the deliberations. Giving cautionary instructions to each juror at the outset of the inquiry and, if necessary, again during the inquiry will reduce the likelihood of answers that stray into revelation of the jury's thought process. The jurors can be instructed to respond about any information that was not mentioned during the trial (appropriate), but not to describe how the jurors used that information or the effect of that information on the thinking of any one or more jurors (inappropriate). Once any juror has established that extraneous information was mentioned, by whom, and whether anyone said anything else about the extraneous information (not what they thought about it or did with it), the inquiry of that juror is complete. As soon as the judge determines that the defendant has satisfied his burden of establishing the existence of an extraneous influence, the questioning of all jurors should cease."

Commonwealth v. Kincaid, 444 Mass. 381, 391–392 (2005).

A defendant seeking a new trial bears the burden of showing that the jury was exposed to extraneous material, at which point the burden shifts to the Commonwealth to prove beyond a reasonable doubt that the defendant was not prejudiced by the exposure. Commonwealth v. Fidler, 377 Mass. at 201. See Commonwealth v. Miller, 475 Mass. 212, 221–222 (2016) (Where the extraneous matter was "not attached to any crucial issue" in the case, and there was substantial evidence of the defendant's guilt, the trial judge properly refused to grant a new trial even though a juror had brought a gun magazine to the jury room.). The same burden-shifting approach applies in a civil case, except that the party opposing the new trial need only show that there is "no reasonable likelihood of prejudice" from the extraneous material. Fitzpatrick v. Allen, 410 Mass. 791, 796 (1991); Markee v. Biasetti, 410 Mass. 785, 788–789 (1991).

Ethnic or Racial Bias. When the defendant files an affidavit from one or more jurors stating that another juror made a statement "that reasonably demonstrates racial or ethnic bias" and the jury's credibility is at issue, the judge must first determine whether the defendant has proved by a preponderance of the evidence that the juror made the biased statement. Commonwealth v. McCowen, 458 Mass. 461, 494 (2010). Second, if the answer to the first question is "yes," the judge must determine whether the defendant has proved by a preponderance of the evidence

> "that the juror who made the statements was actually biased because of the race or ethnicity of a defendant, victim, defense attorney, or witness. A juror is actually biased where her racial or ethnic prejudice, had it been revealed or detected at voir dire, would have required as a matter of law that the juror be excused from the panel for cause." (Citations omitted.)

Id. at 495. A juror's statement may establish such a strong inference of actual bias "that proof of the statement alone may suffice." Id. at 496. Nevertheless, a judge must typically consider the statement's content and the context in which it was made to decide if it shows the juror's actual racial or ethnic bias, or if it could be interpreted in a way that fails to establish bias. Id. A criminal defendant who has proven a juror's actual bias is entitled to a new trial without demonstrating that the jury's verdict was affected by the juror's bias. Id. Third,

even if the defendant fails to prove that the juror was actually biased, if the answer to the first question is "yes," the judge must determine "whether the statements so infected the deliberative process with racially or ethnically charged language or stereotypes that it prejudiced the defendant's right to have his guilt decided by an impartial jury on the evidence admitted at trial" (citations omitted). Id. at 496–497. Even though racial or ethnic bias is not an extraneous matter, see Commonwealth v. Laguer, 410 Mass. 89, 97 (1991), this third question is subject to the same analysis used to evaluate extraneous influences on the jury. If the defendant meets his or her burden of establishing that the statement was made, "the burden then shifts to the Commonwealth to show beyond a reasonable doubt that the defendant was not prejudiced by the jury's exposure to these statements." Commonwealth v. McCowen, 458 Mass. at 497. In making this determination, the judge must not receive any evidence concerning the effect of the statement on the thought processes of the jurors, but instead must focus on its "probable effect" on a "hypothetical average jury." Id.

Discharge of a Juror During Empanelment. Even prior to trial, a potential juror who may not be impartial due to the effect of an extraneous matter such as bias or prejudice may be excused by the court. See G. L. c. 234, § 28; G. L. c. 234A, § 39; Mass. R. Crim. P. 20(b)(2). If the jury has not been sworn, the judge has discretion to excuse a juror without a hearing or a showing of extreme hardship based on information that the juror may not be indifferent. See Commonwealth v. Gambora, 457 Mass. 715, 731–732 (2010) (juror dismissed based on report by court officer that she was observed in the hallway during a break speaking to persons who then joined a group which included members of the defendant's family); Commonwealth v. Duddie Ford Inc., 409 Mass. 387, 392 (1991). "It is generally within the judge's discretion . . . to determine when there exists a substantial risk that extraneous issues would influence the jury such that an individual voir dire of potential jurors is warranted." Commonwealth v. Holloway, 44 Mass. App. Ct. 469, 472 (1998).

Discharge of a Juror During Trial. In Commonwealth v. Jackson, 376 Mass. 790 (1978), the Supreme Judicial Court addressed the procedure for evaluating the effect of possibly prejudicial material on members of the jury and the proper judicial response:

> "When material disseminated during trial is reliably brought to the judge's attention, he should determine whether the material goes beyond the record and raises a serious question of possible prejudice. A number of factors may be involved in making that determination, including the likelihood that the material reached one or more jurors. If the judge finds that the material raises a serious question of possible prejudice, a voir dire examination of the jurors should be conducted. The initial questioning concerning whether any juror saw or heard the potentially prejudicial material may be carried on collectively, but if any juror indicates that he or she has seen or heard the material, there must be individual questioning of that juror, outside of the presence of any other juror, to determine the extent of the juror's exposure to the material and its effects on the juror's ability to render an impartial verdict."

Id. at 800–801. The trial judge must determine the nature of the extraneous matter before exercising discretion as to whether to discharge a juror. See id. (individualized questioning of juror appropriate given concerns of exposure to prejudicial media publicity during trial). See, e.g., Commonwealth v. Alicea, 464 Mass. 837, 848–849 (2013) (judge has "considerable discretion" to ensure that jurors remain impartial and indifferent; when jurors reported to court officer that one juror had made up his mind, judge was warranted in giving jury forceful instruction and appointing foreperson early to ensure compliance with instructions, rather than conducting voir dire); Commonwealth v. Stewart, 450 Mass. 25, 39 (2007) (trial judge acted properly in asking jury collectively whether anyone had seen anything while coming into or exiting courtroom based on court officer's report that door to lockup had been left open while defendant was inside cell); Commonwealth v. John, 442 Mass. 329, 339–340 (2004) (no error in declining to discharge juror who expressed personal fear due to nature of case); Commonwealth v. Maldonado, 429 Mass. 502, 506–507 (1999) (judge did not abuse her discretion in removing one juror who expressed fear for her personal safety as a result of evidence of defendant's association with a gang); Commonwealth v. Chambers, 93 Mass. App. Ct. 806, 813–815 (2018) (judge did not abuse his discretion in allowing a juror to remain empanelled following multiple colloquies between himself and the juror to allay the juror's concerns about jury duty impacting his studies and to correct the juror's personal opinions and assumptions regarding the applicable law and the function of the jury generally). See also Commonwealth v. Francis, 432 Mass. 353, 369–370 (2000). Cf. Commonwealth v. Fredette, 56 Mass. App. Ct. 253, 259 (2002) (judge erred in accepting a juror's note about a matter of extraneous influence without making inquiry of the juror).

Sleeping Jurors. A judge must intervene promptly whenever he or she observes or receives a reliable report that a juror is asleep. Commonwealth v. Villalobos, 478 Mass. 1007, 1008 (2017). By contrast, "[w]here a judge has only tentative information that a juror may be sleeping, it is sufficient to note the report and monitor the situation." Commonwealth v. Alleyne, 474 Mass. 771, 778 (2016). See Commonwealth v. Vaughn, 471 Mass. 398, 413 (2015) ("report of a sleeping juror was not sufficiently reliable to warrant further action"). If a judge makes a "preliminary conclusion that information about a juror's inattention is reliable, the judge must take further steps to determine the appropriate intervention." Commonwealth v. McGhee, 470 Mass. 638, 644 (2015). Although a judge has "substantial discretion in this area," "[t]ypically, the next step is to conduct a voir dire of the potentially inattentive juror, in an attempt to investigate whether that juror 'remains capable of fulfilling his or her obligation to render a verdict based on all of the evidence.'" Id., quoting Commonwealth v. Dancy, 75 Mass. App. Ct. 175, 181 (2009). The judge has discretion as to the nature of the intervention and is not required to conduct a voir dire in every complaint regarding jury attentiveness. Commonwealth v. Beneche, 458 Mass. 61, 78 (2010). Compare Commonwealth v. Ray, 467 Mass. 115, 134 (2014) (no error in declining to discharge juror observed sleeping at various points in the trial after judge conducted voir dire of juror and satisfied herself that juror could fairly participate in deliberations), with Commonwealth v. McGhee, 470 Mass. at 642–646 (failure of trial judge to conduct further inquiry concerning report of sleeping juror necessitated new trial).

Discharge of a Deliberating Juror. The problems associated with the effect of an extraneous matter on the jury also may arise before the jury returns a verdict. General Laws c. 234, § 26B, provides that if, at any time after a case has been submitted to the jury and before the jury have agreed on a verdict, a juror "dies, or becomes ill, or is unable to perform his duty for any other good cause shown to the court," the judge may discharge the juror, substitute an alternate selected by lot, and permit the jury to renew their deliberations. See Mass. R. Crim. P. 20(d)(3). "[G]ood cause includes only reasons personal to a juror, that is, reasons unrelated to the issues of the case, the juror's views on the case, or his relationship with his fellow jurors" (quotations omitted). Commonwealth v. Francis, 432 Mass. 353, 368 (2000). The judge must conduct a hearing before a juror is discharged. See Commonwealth v. Holley, 478 Mass. 508, 529–531 (2017) (judge did not err in dismissing juror who became ill during deliberations where "the judge telephoned the juror in the presence of counsel, questioned her, invited counsel to suggest further questions, and made specific findings of good cause"; no error in judge rejecting "defense counsel's request that he ask the juror about her ability to deliberate, as that question came close to touching upon the content of the deliberations"); Commonwealth v. McCowen, 458 Mass. 461, 488–489 (2010) (after jury reported it was deadlocked, judge was warranted in removing deliberating juror based on a finding that a "palpable conflict" existed due to the arrest of the father of the juror's son, who was being prosecuted by the same district attorney's office that was prosecuting the case on trial). Great care must be taken in such cases that a dissenting juror is not allowed to avoid the responsibility of jury service. See, e.g., Commonwealth v. Garcia, 84 Mass. App. Ct. 760,

770 (2014) (judge improperly dismissed deliberating juror without first determining a valid reason, personal to the juror and unrelated to juror's views about the case or relations with other jurors); Commonwealth v. Rodriguez, 63 Mass. App. Ct. 660, 675–676 (2005) (holding that discharge of deliberating juror was error).

Required Instruction After Discharge of Deliberating Juror. After dismissing a deliberating juror, the judge "must instruct the jury to disregard all prior deliberations and begin its deliberations again" (quotation omitted). Commonwealth v. Connor, 392 Mass. 838, 844 n.2 (1984). See Commonwealth v. Holley, 478 Mass. 508, 530–531 (2017) (holding it was sufficient to instruct jury to begin their deliberations "anew with a new jury of twelve people" and "not to simply pick up where [they] left off" where juror's illness was "clearly a personal problem"); Commonwealth v. Zimmerman, 441 Mass. 146, 151 (2004) ("A judge is not required in every case to adhere to the precise language we used in [Connor].").

Section 607. Who May Impeach a Witness

Any party, including the party that called the witness, may attack the witness's credibility. However, the party who calls a witness may not impeach that witness by evidence of bad character, including reputation for untruthfulness or prior convictions.

NOTE

This section is derived from G. L. c. 233, § 23, and Walter v. Bonito, 367 Mass. 117, 121–123 (1975). In Walter, the Supreme Judicial Court recognized that Labrie v. Midwood, 273 Mass. 578, 581–582 (1931), held that G. L. c. 233, § 22 (party's right to call and cross-examine adverse witness) does not override G. L. c. 233, § 23. See also Mass. R. Civ. P. 43(b). It is not a violation of this principle to permit a witness to testify about a prior criminal conviction in direct examination. Commonwealth v. Daley, 439 Mass. 558, 563 (2003). The reason for permitting a party to bring out the criminal record of his or her own witness is not impeachment, but rather "to avoid having the jury draw the inference that the party calling the witness had misled or deceived the jury as to the background of the witness." Commonwealth v. Blodgett, 377 Mass. 494, 502 (1979). See Commonwealth v. DePina, 476 Mass. 614, 631 (2017) (eliciting testimony on direct examination that witness was not honest with police due to fear of cooperating was not vouching, but was proper in anticipation of impeachment on cross-examination).

"[A] party cannot rely on this statutory right [G. L. c. 233, § 23] to call a witness whom he knows beforehand will offer no testimony relevant to an issue at trial solely for the purpose of impeaching that witness with prior inconsistent statements that would otherwise be inadmissible." Commonwealth v. McAfee, 430 Mass. 483, 489–490 (1999).

When impeaching one's own witness through a prior inconsistent statement, the proponent must bring the statement to the attention of the witness with sufficient circumstances to alert the witness to the particular occasion the prior statement was made and allow the witness an opportunity to explain the statement. See Section 613, Prior Statements of Witnesses, Limited Admissibility.

Subsequent to impeachment, questions concerning a witness's fear in testifying are not per se improper on redirect examination. Commonwealth v. Mitchell, 89 Mass. App. Ct. 13, 27–28 (2016), citing Commonwealth v. Auguste, 418 Mass. 643, 647 (1994).

This Guide includes specific sections dealing with impeachment by evidence of character (Sections 608 and 609), impeachment by prior inconsistent statements (Section 613), impeachment by reference to bias or prejudice (Section 611[b]), and evidence of religious beliefs (Section 610). Other methods of impeachment—e.g., improper motive, impairment of testimonial faculties, and contradiction—remain available and fall within the scope of Sections 102, Purpose and Construction; 410, Pleas, Offers of Pleas, and Related Statements; 403, Excluding Relevant Evidence for Prejudice, Confusion, Waste of Time, or Other Reasons; and 611, Mode and Order of Examining Witnesses and Presenting Evidence.

Section 608.   A Witness's Character for Truthfulness or Untruthfulness

(a) **Reputation Evidence.** A witness's credibility may be attacked or supported by testimony about the witness's reputation for having a character for truthfulness or untruthfulness. But evidence of truthful character is admissible only after the witness's character for truthfulness has been attacked.

(b) **Specific Instances of Conduct.** In general, specific instances of misconduct showing the witness to be untruthful are not admissible for the purpose of attacking or supporting the witness's credibility.

NOTE

Subsection (a). This subsection is derived from Commonwealth v. Dockham, 405 Mass. 618, 631 (1989), and Commonwealth v. Daley, 439 Mass. 558, 563 (2003). Cf. Commonwealth v. Daley, 439 Mass. at 562–563 (evidence of person's bad character generally inadmissible to prove action in conformity therewith); Section 404, Character Evidence; Crimes or Other Acts.

Unlike under Federal law, character for truthfulness cannot be proven by evidence of personal opinions or isolated acts. See Commonwealth v. Walker, 442 Mass. 185, 197–198 (2004) (declining to adopt original Proposed Mass. R. Evid. 405[a]); Commonwealth v. Benjamin, 430 Mass. 673, 678 n.6 (2000). Reputation evidence must be based on one's reputation in the community or at the person's place of work or business. Commonwealth v. Walker, 442 Mass. at 198. See G. L. c. 233, § 21A (work or business); Commonwealth v. Dockham, 405 Mass. at 631 (community). A witness's testimony must be based on the witness's knowledge of the person's reputation in the community, not of the opinions of a limited number of people. Commonwealth v. LaPierre, 10 Mass. App. Ct. 871, 871 (1980). See Commonwealth v. Phachansiri, 38 Mass. App. Ct. 100, 109 (1995); Commonwealth v. Gomes, 11 Mass. App. Ct. 933, 933–934 (1981).

The provision regarding testimony of the witness's reputation for having a character for truthfulness or untruthfulness is derived from Commonwealth v. Favorito, 9 Mass. App. Ct. 138, 140 (1980). "Evidence irrelevant to the issue at trial or to the witness's reputation for truth and veracity is inadmissible to impeach a witness." Commonwealth v. Cancel, 394 Mass. 567, 572 (1985).

The provision limiting the admissibility of evidence of truthful character to after the witness's character for truthfulness has been attacked is derived from Commonwealth v. Sheline, 391 Mass. 279, 288 (1984), and Commonwealth v. Grammo, 8 Mass. App. Ct. 447, 455 (1979). This limitation does not restrict the right of a defendant in a criminal case to offer evidence of his or her reputation for a character trait that would suggest he or she is not the type of person who would commit the crime charged. See Section 404(a)(2)(A), Character Evidence; Crimes or Other Acts: Character Evidence: Exceptions for a Defendant or Victim in a Criminal Case. Neither "the offering of testimony that contradicts the testimony of a witness" nor "the introduction of prior out-of-court statements of a witness constitute[s] an attack on the witness's character for truthfulness," because "[t]he purpose and only direct effect of the evidence are to show that the witness is not to be believed in [that] instance." Commonwealth v. Sheline, 391 Mass. at 288–289.

Subsection (b). This subsection is derived from Commonwealth v. LaVelle, 414 Mass. 146, 151 (1993), and Commonwealth v. Bregoli, 431 Mass. 265, 275 (2000). This applies whether or not the witness is a party, Commonwealth v. Binkiewicz, 342 Mass. 740, 755 (1961), and

whether the witness is impeached by cross-examination, Commonwealth v. Turner, 371 Mass. 803, 810 (1977), or by the introduction of extrinsic evidence, Commonwealth v. LaVelle, 414 Mass. at 151. On several occasions, the Supreme Judicial Court has declined to adopt Fed. R. Evid. 608(a) and Proposed Mass. R. Evid. 608(b), which permit inquiry into the details of prior instances of misconduct if probative of the witness's character for veracity. See Commonwealth v. Lopes, 478 Mass. 593, 606 (2018) (police officer's conduct from internal affairs investigation five years earlier was not admissible as specific instance of misconduct); Commonwealth v. Almonte, 465 Mass. 224, 241 (2013).

The Supreme Judicial Court has "chiseled" a narrow exception to the rule that the testimony of a witness may not be impeached with specific acts of prior misconduct, recognizing that in special circumstances (to date, only rape and sexual assault cases) the interest of justice would forbid its strict application. Commonwealth v. LaVelle, 414 Mass. at 151–152. In Commonwealth v. Bohannon, 376 Mass. 90, 94–96 (1978), the special circumstances warranting evidence of the prior accusations were that (1) the witness was the victim in the case on trial; (2) the victim/witness's consent was the central issue at trial; (3) the victim/witness was the only Commonwealth witness on the issue of consent; (4) the victim/witness's testimony was inconsistent and confused; and (5) there was a basis in independent third-party records for concluding that the victim/witness's prior accusation of the same type of crime had been made and was false. Not all of the Bohannon circumstances must be present for the exception to apply. Commonwealth v. Nichols, 37 Mass. App. Ct. 332, 337 (1994).

Section 609.   Impeachment by Evidence of Conviction of Crime

(a) **Generally.** A party may seek to impeach the credibility of a witness by means of the court record of the witness's conviction or a certified copy, but may not make reference to the sentence that was imposed, subject to Section 403 and the following requirements:

(1) **Misdemeanor.** A misdemeanor conviction cannot be used after five years from the date on which sentence was imposed, unless the witness has subsequently been convicted of a crime within five years of the time he or she testifies.

(2) **Felony Conviction Not Resulting in Committed State Prison Sentence.** A felony conviction where no sentence was imposed, a sentence was imposed and suspended, a fine was imposed, or a sentence to a jail or house of correction was imposed cannot be used after ten years from the date of conviction (where no sentence was imposed) or from the date of sentencing, unless the witness has subsequently been convicted of a crime within ten years of the time he or she testifies. For the purpose of this paragraph, a plea of guilty or a finding or verdict of guilty shall constitute a conviction within the meaning of this section.

(3) **Felony with State Prison Sentence Imposed.** A felony conviction where a sentence to a State prison was imposed cannot be used after ten years from the date of expiration of the minimum term of imprisonment, unless the witness has subsequently been convicted of a crime within ten years of the time he or she testifies.

(4) **Traffic Violation.** A traffic violation conviction where only a fine was imposed cannot be used unless the witness has been convicted of another crime or crimes within five years of the time he or she testifies.

(5) **Juvenile Adjudications of Delinquency or Youthful Offender.** Adjudications of delinquency or youthful offender may be used in subsequent delinquency or criminal

proceedings in the same manner and to the same extent as prior criminal convictions.

(b) Effect of Being a Fugitive. For the purpose of this section, any period during which the defendant was a fugitive from justice shall be excluded in determining time limitations under the provisions of this section.

NOTE

This section is derived from G. L. c. 233, § 21, except for Subsection (a)(5), which is derived from G. L. c. 119, § 60.

Definition of Conviction. For the purpose of impeachment, a conviction "means a judgment that conclusively establishes guilt after a finding, verdict, or plea of guilty." Forcier v. Hopkins, 329 Mass. 668, 670 (1953), and cases cited. Thus, a case that is continued without a finding, with or without an admission, is not a conviction and may not be used for impeachment under this section. See Wilson v. Honeywell, Inc., 409 Mass. 803, 808–809 (1991). See also Commonwealth v. Pon, 469 Mass. 296, 298 (2014); Commonwealth v. Norwell, 423 Mass. 725, 726 (1996); Commonwealth v. Jackson, 45 Mass. App. Ct. 666, 670 (1998).

Misdemeanors/Probation. A misdemeanor conviction for which a defendant was placed on probation cannot be used for impeachment, because straight probation does not constitute a "sentence" for purposes of the statute. Commonwealth v. Stewart, 422 Mass. 385, 387 (1996).

Probation Violation. The proper use of probation violations is as follows:

"Although convictions within the time frames established by G. L. c. 233, § 21 . . ., may be used to impeach a witness's character for truthfulness, probation violations may not be so used. Nevertheless, probation violations may be used 'to show bias on the part of the witness who might want to give false testimony to curry favor with the prosecution with respect to his case.' Commonwealth v. DiMuro, 28 Mass. App. Ct. 223, 228 (1990)." (Citation omitted.) Commonwealth v. Roberts, 423 Mass. 17, 20–21 (1996).

Suspended Sentence. A suspended sentence constitutes a sentence. Forcier v. Hopkins, 329 Mass. 668, 670–671 (1953).

Fine. A fine constitutes a sentence. Commonwealth v. Ortiz, 47 Mass. App. Ct. 777, 781 (1999).

Scope. "[C]onvictions relevant to credibility are not limited to crimes involving dishonesty or false statements." Commonwealth v. Smith, 450 Mass. 395, 407 (2008).

Discretion. The judge must exercise discretion before deciding whether to admit prior convictions for impeachment. Commonwealth v. Ruiz, 400 Mass. 214, 215 (1987). The factors that are relevant to the exercise of discretion include "whether the prior conviction is substantially similar to the crime charged, whether the prior conviction involves a crime implicating truthfulness, whether there were other prior convictions that the Commonwealth could have used to impeach the defendant, and whether the judge conducted the required balancing test." Commonwealth v. Little, 453 Mass. 766, 773 (2009). The balancing test is the one set forth in Section 403, Excluding Relevant Evidence for Prejudice, Confusion, Waste of Time, or Other Reason. See, e.g., Commonwealth v. Roucoulet, 22 Mass. App. Ct. 603, 608 (1986) (reversing conviction in drug case based on improper admission of prior criminal convictions for drug offenses). A judge is not required to exercise discretion in the absence of an objection or motion in limine. Commonwealth v. Bly, 444 Mass. 640, 653 (2005). The discretion to exclude prior convictions applies equally to the testimony of parties and other witnesses. Commonwealth v. Manning, 47 Mass. App. Ct. 923, 923 (1999). "The defendant may challenge the judge's ruling even if he never testifies." Commonwealth v. Little, 453 Mass. at 773. But see Section 103(b), Rulings on Evidence, Objections, and Offers of Proof: Preliminary Evidentiary Motions: Effect on Appellate Rights. "Generally, in order for the prejudicial effect to outweigh the probative value of prior conviction evidence, the 'prior conviction must be substantially similar to the charged offense'" (emphasis omitted). Commonwealth v. Leftwich, 430 Mass. 865, 869 (2000), quoting Commonwealth v. Drumgold, 423 Mass. 230, 250 (1996). However, "[a]lthough similarity of an offense weighs in favor of exclusion, there is no per se rule of exclusion of prior conviction of a similar crime for which the defendant is on trial." Commonwealth v. Bly, 444 Mass. at 654. A trial judge has discretion to permit impeachment of a sexual assault complaining witness by prior convictions of sexual offenses (which would otherwise be inadmissible under the rape-shield statute, G. L. c. 233, § 21B), but in exercising that discretion, the judge must consider the purposes of the rape-shield statute. Commonwealth v. Harris, 443 Mass. 714, 726–728 (2005). See Section 412, Sexual Behavior or Sexual Reputation (Rape–Shield Law).

Proof of Conviction. The conviction must be proven by production of a court record or a certified copy. Commonwealth v. Puleio, 394 Mass. 101, 104 (1985). But see Commonwealth v. Hamilton, 459 Mass. 422, 439 (2011) (proof of prior conviction for purpose other than to impeach truthfulness of witness does not require court record or certified copy). An attorney must have a reasonable evidentiary basis for any question concerning a prior criminal conviction. See Commonwealth v. Johnson, 441 Mass. 1, 5 n.4 (2004). It is presumed that the defendant was represented by counsel in the underlying conviction, and the Commonwealth does not have to prove representation unless the defendant makes a showing that the conviction was obtained without counsel or a waiver of counsel. Commonwealth v. Saunders, 435 Mass. 691, 695–696 (2002).

Evidence of Conviction. When a record of a witness's criminal conviction is introduced for impeachment purposes, the conviction must be left unexplained; but when "cross-examination goes beyond simply establishing that the witness is the person named in the record of conviction, the proponent of the witness may, in the judge's discretion, properly inquire on redirect examination about those collateral matters raised during the cross-examination." Commonwealth v. McGeoghean, 412 Mass. 839, 843 (1992). See Commonwealth v. Kalhauser, 52 Mass. App. Ct. 339, 343–345 (2001). Any reference to the length of the sentenced imposed should be excluded. Commonwealth v. Eugene, 438 Mass. 343, 352–353 (2003).

A witness may testify about his or her prior convictions for criminal conduct on direct examination in order to blunt the anticipated use of such evidence on cross-examination. Commonwealth v. Daley, 439 Mass. 558, 563 (2003). See Commonwealth v. Blodgett, 377 Mass. 494, 502 (1979). Despite an earlier in limine order excluding evidence of a prior conviction, a witness who testifies untruthfully opens the door to admission of previously excluded evidence to rebut the false testimony. Commonwealth v. Roderick, 429 Mass. 271, 273–275 (1999). Evidence of a stale prior conviction, although inadmissible under G. L. c. 233, § 21, may still be admissible for probative nonimpeachment purposes. Commonwealth v. Jacobs, 6 Mass. App. Ct. 867, 868 (1978). See Commonwealth v. Lavoie, 47 Mass. App. Ct. 1, 4 n.7 (1999).

Redaction. A prior conviction should either be introduced with a description of its nature or excluded entirely, as "[m]asking the nature of the prior offense . . . is more likely to affect the defendant unfairly than receipt in evidence of the unvarnished conviction." Commonwealth v. Ioannides, 41 Mass. App. Ct. 904, 905–906 (1996). However, the judge has discretion to redact the nature of the prior offense and restrict impeachment to the fact of a conviction of "a felony" if redaction is requested by the defendant. Commonwealth v. Kalhauser, 52 Mass. App. Ct. 339, 342 (2001). Any extraneous entries included in the record of criminal conviction should not be shown to the jury, and if, in the judge's opinion, masking the extraneous material risks inducing the jury to speculate about the missing portions of the record, the judge should refuse to mark the records as exhibits. Commonwealth v. Ford, 397 Mass. 298, 300 (1986).

Pardons, Sealing of Record, Expungement, Commutation of Sentence, Appeal Pending. A criminal record that has been sealed is not subject to mandatory discovery and is not available for impeachment. Wing v. Commissioner of Probation, 473 Mass. 368, 370–371 (2015). It appears that pardons and expunged records are likewise unavailable. See Commonwealth v. Childs, 23 Mass. App. Ct. 33, 35 (1986), aff'd, 400 Mass. 1006 (1987). Conversely, it appears that the commutation of a sentence may be used. Rittenberg v. Smith, 214 Mass. 343, 347 (1913) ("The commutation of the sentence did not do away with the conviction. Only a full pardon could do that."). It also appears that the pendency of an appeal does not prevent the use of a conviction for impeachment purposes. The fact that a defendant's prior conviction was vacated after the trial in which it was used to impeach him did not affect its status as a "final judgment" for purposes of G. L. c. 233, § 21. Commonwealth v. DiGiambattista, 59 Mass. App. Ct. 190, 199 (2003), judgment rev'd on other grounds, 442 Mass. 423 (2004). See Fed. R. Evid. 609(e); Proposed Mass. R. Evid. 609(f). The term conviction means "a judgment that conclusively establishes guilt after a finding, verdict, or plea of guilty … In a criminal case the sentence is the judgment." Forcier v. Hopkins, 329 Mass. 668, 670–671 (1953). "The sentence[,] until reversed in some way provided by the law, stands as the final judgment binding upon everybody." Commonwealth v. Dascalakis, 246 Mass. 12, 20 (1923).

Section 610.   Religious Beliefs or Opinions

Evidence of a witness's religious beliefs or opinions is not admissible to attack or support the witness's credibility.

NOTE

This section is derived from Commonwealth v. Dahl, 430 Mass. 813, 822–823 (2000) (citing with approval Proposed Mass. R. Evid. 610), and G. L. c. 233, § 19 ("evidence of [a person's] disbelief in the existence of God may not be received to affect his credibility as a witness"). Though not admissible as to credibility, evidence that relates to a person's religious beliefs is not per se inadmissible. See Commonwealth v. Kartell, 58 Mass. App. Ct. 428, 436–437 (2003) (evidence of defendant's religious beliefs admissible for relevant purpose of showing defendant was jealous of victim); Commonwealth v. Murphy, 48 Mass. App. Ct. 143, 145 (1999) (to establish that a child witness is competent to testify, "a question whether the child believes in God and a question whether the child recognizes the witness's oath as a promise to God are within tolerable limits to test whether the witness's oath meant anything to the child witness").

Section 611.   Mode and Order of Examining Witnesses and Presenting Evidence

(a) **Control by the Court.** The court should exercise reasonable control over the mode and order of examining witnesses and presenting evidence so as to

(1) make those procedures effective for determining the truth,

(2) avoid wasting time, and

(3) protect witnesses from harassment or undue embarrassment.

The court has discretion to admit evidence conditionally upon the representation that its relevancy will be established by evidence offered subsequently.

(b) **Scope of Cross–Examination.**

(1) **In General.** A witness is subject to reasonable cross-examination on any matter relevant to any issue in the case, including credibility and matters not elicited during direct examination. There must be a reasonable and good-faith basis for questions asked on cross-examination. The trial judge may restrict the scope of cross-examination in the exercise of judicial discretion.

(2) **Bias and Prejudice.** Reasonable cross-examination to show bias and prejudice is a matter of right which cannot be unreasonably restricted.

(c) **Leading Questions.** Leading questions should not be used on direct examination except as necessary to develop the witness's testimony. Ordinarily, the court should allow leading questions

(1) on cross-examination and

(2) when a party calls a hostile witness, an adverse party, or an officer or agent of an adverse corporate party, or an investigator appointed under G. L. c. 119, § 21A.

(d) **Rebuttal Evidence.** The trial judge generally has discretion to permit the introduction of rebuttal evidence in civil and criminal cases. In certain limited circumstances, a party may introduce rebuttal evidence as a matter of right. There is no right to present rebuttal evidence that only supports a party's affirmative case.

(e) **Scope of Subsequent Examination.** The scope of redirect and recross-examination is within the discretion of the trial judge.

(f) **Reopening.** The court has discretion to allow a party to reopen its case.

(g) **Stipulations.**

(1) **Form and Effect.** A stipulation is a voluntary agreement between opposing parties concerning some relevant fact, claim, or defense and may include agreements in both civil and criminal cases to simplify the issues for trial. A stipulation as to a matter of law is not binding on the court. A judge may require a stipulation be reduced to writing. A party is bound by its stipulation in the absence of consideration unless relief is granted by the court. In order to avoid a failure of justice, a court may at any time relieve a party from its stipulation.

(2) **Essential Element.** A stipulation as to a fact constituting an essential element of a crime or a fact material to the proof of the crime must be presented in some manner to the jury as part of the evidence of the case.

NOTE

Subsection (a). This subsection is derived from Commonwealth v. Rooney, 365 Mass. 484, 496 (1974); Goldman v. Ashkins, 266 Mass. 374, 380 (1929); Chandler v. FMC Corp., 35 Mass. App. Ct. 332, 338 (1993); and Albano v. Jordan Marsh Co., 2 Mass. App. Ct. 304, 311 (1974). See Commonwealth v. Edward, 75 Mass. App. Ct. 162, 171 n.12 (2009) (closing courtroom to the public during any portion of a trial implicates defendant's constitutional rights and must be preceded by a hearing and adequate findings of fact). The judge's discretion to impose reasonable limits on the length of the direct and cross-examination of witnesses does not permit the judge to impose arbitrary time limits that prevent a party from presenting its case. Chandler v. FMC Corp., 35 Mass. App. Ct. at 338. See also Commonwealth v. Conley, 34 Mass. App. Ct. 50, 59–60 & n.4 (1993) (improper for court to systematically screen a party's direct evidence at sidebar before witnesses are permitted to be called).

Evidence may be conditionally admitted (admitted de bene) upon the representation of counsel that additional evidence will be produced providing the foundation for the evidence offered. Harris–Lewis v. Mudge, 60 Mass. App. Ct. 480, 485 n.4 (2004). See Commonwealth v.

Perry, 432 Mass. 214, 234–235 (2000). In the event that the foundation evidence is not subsequently produced, the court has no duty to strike the evidence admitted de bene on its own motion. Commonwealth v. Sheppard, 313 Mass. 590, 595–596 (1943). If the objecting party fails to move to strike the evidence, the court's failure to strike it is not error. Muldoon v. West End Chevrolet, Inc., 338 Mass. 91, 98 (1958). See Commonwealth v. Navarro, 39 Mass. App. Ct. 161, 166 (1995). See Section 104(b), Preliminary Questions: Relevance That Depends on a Fact.

A self-represented litigant is bound by the same rules as those that guide attorneys. International Fid. Ins. Co. v. Wilson, 387 Mass. 841, 847 (1983). However, "[w]hether a party is represented by counsel at a trial or represents himself, the judge's role remains the same. The judge's function at any trial is to be 'the directing and controlling mind at the trial, and not a mere functionary to preserve order and lend ceremonial dignity to the proceedings'" (citations omitted). Commonwealth v. Sapoznik, 28 Mass. App. Ct. 236, 241–242 n.4 (1990), quoting Commonwealth v. Wilson, 381 Mass. 90, 118 (1980). See also Judicial Guidelines for Civil Hearings Involving Self–Represented Litigants, The Commonwealth of Massachusetts Administrative Office of the Trial Court (2006).

Subsection (b)(1).

In General. The first sentence of this subsection is derived from Beal v. Nichols, 68 Mass. 262, 264 (1854); Davis v. Hotels Statler Co., 327 Mass. 28, 29–30 (1951); and Commonwealth v. Taylor, 32 Mass. App. Ct. 570, 575 (1992). It reflects the Massachusetts practice of permitting cross-examination on matters beyond the subject matter of the direct examination. See Nuger v. Robinson, 32 Mass. App. Ct. 959, 959–960 (1992). Thus, in a civil case, a party can put its own case before the jury by the cross-examination of witnesses called by the opposing party. See Moody v. Rowell, 34 Mass. 490, 499 (1835).

Criminal Cases. The defendant has a right to confront and cross-examine the witnesses against him or her under both the Sixth Amendment to the United States Constitution and Article 12 of the Declaration of Rights. Commonwealth v. Garcia, 470 Mass. 24, 35 (2014). See Commonwealth v. Seeley, 467 Mass. 617, 623–625 (2014); Commonwealth v. Farley, 443 Mass. 740, 748 (2005); Commonwealth v. Vardinski, 438 Mass. 444, 449–451 (2003); Commonwealth v. Tanso, 411 Mass. 640, 650 (1992). See also Commonwealth v. Bergstrom, 402 Mass. 534, 541–551 (1988) (discussing defendant's right to "face-to-face" confrontation under Article 12).

Fairness to the Commonwealth. The Commonwealth has a common-law right to reasonable cross-examination of witnesses called by the defendant. See Commonwealth v. Gagnon, 408 Mass. 185, 192 (1990). See also Commonwealth v. Lawton, 82 Mass. App. Ct. 528, 537–538 (2012).

Reasonable and Good–Faith Basis for Cross–Examination. The second sentence of this subsection is derived from Commonwealth v. Johnston, 467 Mass. 674, 699 (2014); Commonwealth v. Jenkins, 458 Mass. 791, 795 (2011); and Commonwealth v. Christian, 430 Mass. 552, 561 (2000), overruled on other grounds by Commonwealth v. Paulding, 438 Mass. 1 (2002). For examples of cross-examination without an adequate basis, see Commonwealth v. Cruzado, 480 Mass. 275, 281 (2018) (improper to cross-examine on whether witness was known cocaine dealer when only evidence of drug dealing was an arrest for possession of heroin three years before crime); Commonwealth v. McCoy, 59 Mass. App. Ct. 284, 289 (2003) ("prosecutor should not have been allowed to impugn the defendant's character by insinuating his knowing intimacy with a drug criminal, particularly when that alleged criminality was never established"); and Commonwealth v. Brissett, 55 Mass. App. Ct. 862, 864–865 (2002) (lack of necessary foundation for cross-examination of defendant and defendant's alibi witness about why they had not come forward earlier).

There is no requirement that the cross-examiner be prepared to present admissible evidence to support a question. Commonwealth v. White, 367 Mass. 280, 284 (1975) (prosecutor was permitted to cross-examine witness about statements made to him by witness, even though he could not offer substantive evidence of statements without withdrawing from case and becoming a witness himself). However, the trial judge may require counsel to disclose the basis for a question to the judge and may curtail further questioning in the face of a witness's consistent denials. See Commonwealth v. Johnson, 441 Mass. 1, 4–5 (2004); Commonwealth v. Christian, 430 Mass. at 562. For other cases addressing the problem of cross-examination by innuendo, see Commonwealth v. Knowles, 92 Mass. App. Ct. 617, 620 (2018); Commonwealth v. Peck, 86 Mass. App. Ct. 34, 39–40 (2014); and Commonwealth v. Delrio, 22 Mass. App. Ct. 712, 721 (1986).

Impeachment by Prearrest Silence. "[I]mpeachment of a defendant with the fact of his pre-arrest silence should be approached with caution, and, whenever it is undertaken, it should be prefaced by a proper demonstration that it was 'natural' to expect the defendant to speak in the circumstances"; "the use of [pretrial silence] for impeachment purposes cannot be justified in the absence of unusual circumstances." Commonwealth v. Nickerson, 386 Mass. 54, 62 & n.6 (1982). See Commonwealth v. Gardner, 479 Mass. 764, 772 (2018) (despite the fact that self-defense was asserted four days after the arrest, the prosecutor's reference to the defendant's prearrest silence was improper); Commonwealth v. Martinez, 34 Mass. App. Ct. 131, 132–133 (1993).

Before a witness for the defense may be impeached for not coming forward and disclosing to the police or the prosecutor exculpatory information before the trial, prosecutors are required to lay a foundation by establishing (1) that the witness knew of the pending charges in sufficient detail to realize that the witness possessed exculpatory information, (2) that the witness had reason to make the information available, and (3) that the witness was familiar with the means of reporting it to the proper authorities. See Commonwealth v. Horne, 466 Mass. 440, 447–449 (2013); Commonwealth v. Washington, 459 Mass. 32, 42–43 (2011); Commonwealth v. Hart, 455 Mass. 230, 239–240 (2009).

Credibility of Other Witnesses. "[A] witness cannot be asked to assess the credibility of his testimony or that of other witnesses." Commonwealth v. Dickinson, 394 Mass. 702, 706 (1985). In cases tried to a jury and involving a "duel of credibility," repeated questions asking the defendant to comment of the truthfulness of another witness is prejudicial error. Commonwealth v. Triplett, 398 Mass. 561, 567 (1986). See Commonwealth v. Long, 17 Mass. App. Ct. 707, 708 (1984); Commonwealth v. Ward, 15 Mass. App. Ct. 400, 401 (1983).

Judicial Discretion to Limit Cross–Examination. The third sentence of this subsection is derived from the following cases: Commonwealth v. Mercado, 456 Mass. 198, 202–204 (2010); Commonwealth v. Clifford, 374 Mass. 293, 305 (1978); Commonwealth v. Smith, 329 Mass. 477, 479 (1952); and Guinan v. Famous Players–Lasky Corp., 267 Mass. 501, 523 (1929). See also Commonwealth v. Mahdi, 388 Mass. 679, 693 (1983) (questions that are designed to appeal "to racial, religious, or ethnic prejudices are especially incompatible with the concept of a fair trial because of the likelihood that such references will sweep jurors beyond a fair and calm consideration of the evidence" [quotation omitted]); Commonwealth v. Rooney, 365 Mass. 484, 496 (1974) (trial judge has "power to keep the examination of witnesses within the limits of common decency and fairness," and "duty to exercise that power promptly and firmly when it becomes necessary to do so"); Fialkow v. DeVoe Motors, Inc., 359 Mass. 569, 572 (1971) ("The trial judge, with the benefit of his presence in a vantage position when the alleged improper statement or argument is made, is in the best position to decide what corrective measures, if any, are required and when they should be taken.").

The trial judge also has the right to limit cross-examination when necessary to protect the safety of the witness. See Commonwealth v. Francis, 432 Mass. 353, 357–358 (2000). See also Note "Address of Witness" to Section 501, Privileges Recognized Only as Provided. When due to a witness's lack of cooperation or the assertion of the privilege against self-incrimination the defendant is prevented from cross-examining a witness, the judge may be required to strike the direct testimony of that witness. Commonwealth v. Santiago, 30 Mass. App. Ct. 207, 221 (1991).

For cases in which a judge failed to properly exercise discretion, see Commonwealth v. Reynolds, 429 Mass. 388, 391–392 (1999) (conviction reversed because scope of cross-examination of police officers too limited; "[i]t is well settled that a defendant has a right to expose inadequacies of police investigation"); Commonwealth v. Miles, 420 Mass. 67, 72–73 (1995) (judge erred in preventing defendant from cross-examining police officer about other suspects in circumstances where rape victim did not see perpetrator's face); and Commonwealth v. Murphy, 57 Mass. App. Ct. 586, 589 (2003) ("Trials are a search for truth, not socialized stonings. Consequently, witnesses must not be subjected to questions that go beyond the bounds of proper cross-examination merely to harass, annoy or humiliate.").

The defendant's right to confrontation is not denied when, on cross-examination, a witness refuses to answer questions relating exclusively to collateral matters. See Commonwealth v. Dwyer, 10 Mass. App. Ct. 707, 713 (1980). Compare Commonwealth v. Almeida, 452 Mass. 601, 607 (2008) (defendant was not denied his right to confront a key identification witness who was unable to recall numerous details; "[i]t was entirely reasonable for the witness to have no memory of some of the information sought by many of the questions"), and Commonwealth v. Amirault, 404 Mass. 221, 234–235 (1989) (lapse of memory by witness on cross-examination did not deny defendant right to confrontation), with Commonwealth v. Funches, 379 Mass. 283, 292 (1979) (trial judge was required to strike witness's direct testimony when witness asserted privilege against self-incrimination during cross-examination), and Commonwealth v. Johnson, 365 Mass. 534, 543–544 (1974) (defendant denied right to confrontation when judge, concerned for safety of witness, ordered witness to not answer questions on cross-examination).

Cross–Reference: Section 405(a), Methods of Proving Character: By Reputation; Section 1113(b)(3)(E), Opening Statement and Closing Argument; Applicable to Criminal and Civil Cases: Closing Argument: Improper Argument.

Subsection (b)(2). This subsection is derived from Commonwealth v. Martinez, 384 Mass. 377, 380–381 (1981); Commonwealth v. Michel, 367 Mass. 454, 459 (1975); and Commonwealth v. Russ, 232 Mass. 58, 79 (1919).

"[W]here . . . facts are relevant to a showing of bias or motive to lie, any general evidentiary rule of exclusion must give way to the constitutionally based right of effective cross-examination." Commonwealth v. Joyce, 382 Mass. 222, 231 (1981), citing Davis v. Alaska, 415 U.S. 308, 316–318 (1974), and Chambers v. Mississippi, 410 U.S. 284 (1973). "A judge may not restrict cross-examination of a material witness by foreclosing inquiry into a subject that could show bias or prejudice on the part of the witness." Commonwealth v. Aguiar, 400 Mass. 508, 513 (1987). See Commonwealth v. Kindell, 84 Mass. App. Ct. 183, 186–189 (2013). This right applies with special force whenever there is evidence that the testimony of a witness is given in exchange for some anticipated consideration or reward by the government, see Commonwealth v. Barnes, 399 Mass. 385, 392 (1987); Commonwealth v. O'Neil, 51 Mass. App. Ct. 170, 178–181 (2001), or when it concerns the subject of identification. See Commonwealth v. Vardinski, 438 Mass. 444, 450 (2003).

However, the trial judge has considerable discretion to limit such cross-examination when it becomes redundant or touches on matters of tangential materiality. See Commonwealth v. Parent, 465 Mass. 395, 405–406 (2013); Commonwealth v. Jordan, 439 Mass. 47, 55 (2003); Commonwealth v. Noj, 76 Mass. App. Ct. 194, 198–199 (2010). See also Commonwealth v. Durand, 475 Mass. 657, 662–663 (2016) (court found that judge's ruling prohibiting defendant's cross-examination of expert concerning e-mail message was not abuse of discretion where defendant argued e-mail message was basis of expert's termination from his position with chief medical examiner's office).

Subsection (c). This subsection is derived from G. L. c. 233, § 22; Carney v. Bereault, 348 Mass. 502, 510 (1965); and Mass. R. Civ. P. 43(b). "[T]he decision whether to allow leading questions should be left for the most part to the wisdom and discretion of the trial judge instead of being restricted by the mechanical operation of inflexible rules" (citations and quotation omitted). Commonwealth v. Flynn, 362 Mass. 455, 467 (1972). See Commonwealth v. Monahan, 349 Mass. 139, 162–163 (1965) (rulings on whether witness is hostile and whether cross-examination of the witness by his or her proponent are permitted are within discretion of trial judge). Some judges in Massachusetts require that when the subject of the cross-examination enters material not covered on direct, the attorney should no longer use leading questions.

Although as a general rule leading questions should not be used on direct examination, there are many instances where they are permitted in the discretion of the judge. See, e.g., DiMarzo v. S. & P. Realty Corp., 364 Mass. 510, 512 (1974) (refresh memory); Commonwealth v. Aronson, 330 Mass. 453, 460 (1953) (witness under stress); Gray v. Kelley, 190 Mass. 184, 187 (1906) (elderly witness); Commonwealth v. Lamontagne, 42 Mass. App. Ct. 213, 217–218 (1997) (child witness).

The use of leading questions on direct examination of an adverse party is authorized by statute. G. L. c. 233, § 22 ("A party who calls the adverse party as a witness shall be allowed to cross-examine him. In case the adverse party is a corporation, an officer or agent thereof, so called as a witness, shall be deemed such an adverse party for the purposes of this section."); Mass. R. Civ. P. 43(b) ("A party may call an adverse party or an officer, director, or managing agent of a public or private corporation or of a partnership or association which is an adverse party, and interrogate him by leading questions and contradict and impeach him in all respects as if he had been called by the adverse party."). When a party calls an adverse witness, that party may inquire by means of leading questions. See Mass. R. Civ. P. 43(b). Cf. G. L. c. 233, § 22. However, such examination is limited by G. L. c. 233, § 23, concerning impeachment of one's own witness. See Walter v. Bonito, 367 Mass. 117, 122 (1975). If a party is called as an adverse witness by opposing counsel, the trial judge may, in his or her discretion, permit leading questions on cross-examination. See Westland Hous. Corp. v. Scott, 312 Mass. 375, 383–384 (1942). See also G. L. c. 119, § 21A (the examination of an investigator "shall be conducted as though it were on cross-examination").

Subsection (d). This subsection is derived from Commonwealth v. Roberts, 433 Mass. 45, 51 (2000), and Commonwealth v. Guidry, 22 Mass. App. Ct. 907, 909 (1986). A party may not present rebuttal evidence that only "supports a party's affirmative case." Drake v. Goodman, 386 Mass. 88, 92 (1982). In other words, a party may not "present one theory of causation in his case-in-chief and, as a matter of right, present a different theory of causation in rebuttal." Id. at 93. This is especially true when a party is aware of the evidence prior to trial and could have presented it as part of the case-in-chief. Id.

Subsection (e). This subsection is derived from Commonwealth v. Maltais, 387 Mass. 79, 92 (1982) (redirect examination), and Commonwealth v. O'Brien, 419 Mass. 470, 476 (1995) (recross-examination). See Commonwealth v. Andrade, 468 Mass. 543, 549–550 (2014) (holding that on redirect examination of an immunized witness who had been impeached on cross-examination about lying to the police and to the grand jury, it was appropriate over objection to permit the prosecutor to ask the witness whether he "told the truth to the jury today about what [the defendant] told [him] about the murder of [the victim]" and explaining that, viewed in context, the prosecutor was not asking the witness to comment on his own credibility, but instead to rebut the implication of the cross-examination that the witness's testimony was false. Cf. Mass. R. Dom. Rel. P. 43(b).

Subsection (f). This subsection is derived from Kerr v. Palmieri, 325 Mass. 554, 557 (1950) ("As a general proposition, the granting of a motion to permit additional evidence to be introduced after the trial has been closed rests in the discretion of the trial judge."). See also Commonwealth v. Moore, 52 Mass. App. Ct. 120, 126–127 (2001) ("We also add that the decision whether to reopen a case is one that cannot be made in an arbitrary or capricious manner. It would be a wise practice in the future for trial judges to place on the record their reasons for exercising their discretion either for or against reopening the case.").

Criminal Cases. The constitutional rights of the defendant in a criminal case limit the discretion of the court to allow the Commonwealth to reopen. It is only within the court's discretion

"to permit reopening when mere inadvertence or some other compelling circumstance . . . justifies a reopening and no substantial prejudice will occur. If the court in the exercise of cautious discretion allows the prosecution to reopen its case before the defendant begins its defense, that reopening does not violate either the rules of criminal procedure or the defendant's right not to be put twice in jeopardy."

Commonwealth v. Cote, 15 Mass. App. Ct. 229, 241 (1983), quoting United States v. Hinderman, 625 F.2d 994, 996 (10th Cir. 1980). See Commonwealth v. Costa, 88 Mass. App. Ct. 750, 753–755 (2015) (trial judge properly permitted Commonwealth to reopen its case and present additional evidence regarding breathalyzer accuracy where defendant had deliberately concealed basis for his objection to results, thus depriving prosecution of opportunity to address factual basis for challenge in first instance). Compare Commonwealth v. Hurley, 455 Mass. 53, 68 (2009) (where police officer had gestured at and nodded to the defendant during his testimony, but had not formally identified the defendant on the record, trial judge did not err in permitting the Commonwealth to reopen its case to offer this minimal identification evidence), with Commonwealth v. Zavala, 52 Mass. App. Ct. 770, 779 (2001) (trial judge committed prejudicial error in allowing the Commonwealth to reopen its case to prove an essential element of the offense, previously neglected, where the burden of proving that element was clearly the Commonwealth's and the omission was identified by the defendant's motion). See also Commonwealth v. Hurley, 455 Mass. at 68, for a survey of cases.

Subsection (g)(1). This subsection is derived from Fanciullo v. B.G. & S. Theatre Corp., 297 Mass. 44, 51 (1937); Gurman v. Stowe–Woodward, 302 Mass. 442, 448 (1939); and Goddard v. Goucher, 89 Mass. App. Ct. 41, 45 (2016). See Mass. R. Civ. P. 36(b) (effect of admissions). See also Commonwealth v. Buswell, 468 Mass. 92, 104–105 (2014) (where rationale for stipulation changes, court has discretion to relieve a party of the stipulation); Loring v. Mercier, 318 Mass. 599, 601 (1945) (court "may vacate a stipulation made by the parties if it is deemed improvident or not conducive to justice").

In Mitchell v. Walton Lunch Co., 305 Mass. 76, 80 (1939), the court observed that "[n]othing is more common in practice or more useful in dispatching the business of the courts than for counsel to admit undisputed facts." Brocklesby v. City of Newton, 294 Mass. 41, 43 (1936).

A stipulation may affect the standard of review on appeal. See Commonwealth v. Phoenix, 409 Mass. 408, 420 (1991) (stipulation as to the admissibility of scientific evidence). A stipulation may bind a party in subsequent trials. Household Fuel Corp. v. Hamacher, 331 Mass. 653, 656–657 (1954).

Binding Admissions. A binding admission, sometimes referred to as a judicial admission, "is a proposition of fact in the form of acts or declarations during the course of judicial proceedings which conclusively determine an issue." Wood v. Roy Lapidus, Inc., 10 Mass. App. Ct. 761, 765 (1980). It is binding on the party making it. Quinn v. Mar–Lees Seafood, LLC, 69 Mass. App. Ct. 688, 697 (2007). A judicial admission "relieve[s] the other party of the necessity of presenting evidence on that issue" (quotation omitted). General Elec. Co. v. Board of Assessors of Lynn, 393 Mass. 591, 603 n.8 (1984). A judicial admission does not require an agreement between the parties, but may arise whenever "a party causes the judge to understand that certain facts are admitted or that certain issues are waived or abandoned." Dalton v. Post Publ. Co., 328 Mass. 595, 599 (1952). In a civil

case, a party or a party's authorized agent, such as a party's lawyer, is authorized to make statements of fact that may be deemed judicial admissions. Turners Falls Ltd. Partnership v. Board of Assessors of Montague, 54 Mass. App. Ct. 732, 737 (2002). A judicial admission may take the form of statements of fact made in pleadings, G. L. c. 231, § 87; a statement made in an opening, see Beaumont v. Segal, 362 Mass. 30, 32 (1972); or a response to a request for admissions under Mass. R. Civ. P. 36(b). See also Quinn v. Mar–Lees Seafood, LLC, 69 Mass. App. Ct. at 697 (party's testimony as to facts peculiarly within his knowledge is binding). However, the testimony of a party's expert witness is not a judicial admission. Turners Falls Ltd. Partnership v. Board of Assessors of Montague, 54 Mass. App. Ct. at 738.

A judge has discretion to relieve a party from the binding effect of a judicial admission that was the consequence of inadvertence and may permit a party to introduce corrective evidence. Id. at 737. See also Mass. R. Civ. P. 36. When a party delays seeking relief until trial has commenced, Rule 36(b) impliedly adopts a stricter standard of preventing "manifest injustice." Reynolds Aluminum Bldg. Prods. Co. v. Leonard, 395 Mass. 255, 260 n.9 (1985). An admission that is not amended or withdrawn cannot be "ignored by the court even if the party against whom it is directed offers more credible evidence" (citations omitted). Houston v. Houston, 64 Mass. App. Ct. 529, 533 (2005).

Nonbinding Admissions. A nonbinding admission, sometimes referred to as an evidentiary admission, is the "conduct of a party while not on the stand used as evidence against him at trial. The conduct may be in the form of an act, a statement, or a failure to act or make a statement." General Elec. Co. v. Board of Assessors of Lynn, 393 Mass. 591, 603 (1984). Evidentiary admissions, unlike judicial admissions, are not binding on a party, and a party may offer evidence that is inconsistent with an evidentiary admission. Id. "Unlike most prior inconsistent statements, an evidentiary admission is admissible for substantive purposes, not merely on the narrow issue of credibility." Id. Thus, the jury or fact finder can find that a fact is true on the basis on an evidentiary admission. Evidentiary admissions include answers to deposition questions, see Mass. R. Civ. P. 32(a)(2), and answers to interrogatories, see G. L. c. 231, § 89.

Cross–Reference: Section 801(d)(2)(C)–(D), Definitions: Statements That Are Not Hearsay: An Opposing Party's Statement.

Subsection (g)(2). This subsection is derived from Commonwealth v. Ortiz, 466 Mass. 475, 481–487 (2013).

Supplement to the 2019 Guide to Evidence

Subsection (a)(3). *Mode and Order of Examining Witnesses and Presenting Evidence: Control by the Court.* Commonwealth v. Chicas, 481 Mass. 316, 318–322 (2019). In general, "[t]here is no reason to believe that the fact that the witnesses may not have been legal residents of the United States was evidence of their ability to be truthful. In reality, a witness's status as an undocumented immigrant, for a variety of reasons, would make the witness less likely to cooperate with the government." Id. at 321–322.

Whether a party may ask questions about a witness's citizenship status on cross-examination to explore bias "depends on a showing that the witness was testifying in order to curry favor with the Commonwealth." Id. at 321.

"[A]fter the witnesses testified that they had not talked about their citizenship status with the Commonwealth, their status became irrelevant as to motive to lie." Id. at 321.

A judge may also limit cross-examination on the subject of citizenship status to prevent embarrassment and harassment of the witness. Id., citing Mass. G. Evid. § 611(a)(3) (2018).

Subsection (b)(2). *Mode and Order of Examining Witnesses and Presenting Evidence: Scope of Cross-Examination, Bias and Prejudice.* Commonwealth v. Chicas, 481 Mass. 316, 318–322 (2019). In general, "[t]here is no reason to believe that the fact that the witnesses may not have been legal residents of the United States was evidence of their ability to be truthful. In reality, a witness's status as an undocumented immigrant, for a variety of reasons, would make the witness less likely to cooperate with the government." Id. at 321–322.

Whether a party may ask questions about a witness's citizenship status on cross-examination to explore bias "depends on a showing that the witness was testifying in order to curry favor with the Commonwealth." Id. at 321.

"[A]fter the witnesses testified that they had not talked about their citizenship status with the Commonwealth, their status became irrelevant as to motive to lie." Id. at 321.

A judge may also limit cross-examination on the subject of citizenship status to prevent embarrassment and harassment of the witness. Id., citing Mass. G. Evid. § 611(a)(3) (2018).

Section 612.   Writing or Object Used to Refresh Memory

(a) While Testifying.

(1) General Rule. When a testifying witness's memory is exhausted as to a matter about which he or she once had knowledge, the witness's memory may be refreshed, in the presence of the jury, with any writing or other object that permits the witness to further testify from his or her own memory. The writing or object should not be read from or shown to the jury.

(2) Production and Use.

(A) When a testifying witness uses a writing or object to refresh his or her memory, an adverse party is entitled to the production of the writing or object after it is shown to the witness and before cross-examination, even if it contains information subject to work-product protection.

(B) A party entitled to the production of a writing or object under this section is entitled to examine the writing or so much of it as relates to the case on trial, may cross-examine about it, and may introduce it in evidence to show that it could not or did not aid the witness in any legitimate way.

(b) Before Testifying.

(1) Production. If, before testifying, a witness uses a writing or object to refresh his or her memory for the purpose of testifying, an adverse party has no absolute right to the production and inspection of the writing or object. The trial judge, however, in his or her discretion, may, at the request of the adverse party, order production of the writing or object at the trial, hearing, or deposition in which the witness is testifying if it is practicable and the interests of justice so require.

(2) Admissibility. Where the adverse party at trial calls for a writing or other object from his or her opponent that was used to refresh the witness's memory prior to trial, does so in front of the jury, and receives and examines it, the writing or other object may be offered in evidence by the producing party when necessary to prevent the impression of evasion or concealment, even though it would have been incompetent if it had not been called for and examined.

(3) Suppressed Statement. If, before testifying in a criminal case, a witness uses a suppressed statement to refresh his or her memory for the purpose of testifying, the judge must conduct a voir dire to establish that the witness

has a present recollection of the event to which he or she is testifying.

NOTE

Subsection (a)(1). This subsection is derived from Commonwealth v. O'Brien, 419 Mass. 470, 478–479 (1995) (citing with approval Proposed Mass. R. Evid. 612), and Bendett v. Bendett, 315 Mass. 59, 63 (1943). A witness may use a writing or other object to refresh a failing memory. Commonwealth v. O'Brien, 419 Mass. at 478. The witness's testimony, however, must be the product of present recollection. See Commonwealth v. Hoffer, 375 Mass. 369, 376 (1978). This subsection should not be confused with the doctrine of past recollection recorded.

Cross–Reference: Section 803(5), Hearsay Exceptions; Availability of Declarant Immaterial: Past Recollection Recorded.

Subsection (a)(2)(A). This subsection is derived from Commonwealth v. O'Brien, 419 Mass. 470, 478–480 (1995). "[W]hen materials protected by the work product doctrine are used by the examiner to refresh a witness's recollection on the stand, the protection afforded by the work product doctrine is waived and the opponent's attorney is entitled to inspect the writing." Id. at 478. Other Federal and State courts that have addressed this issue have concluded that using "protected material to refresh a witness's recollection on the stand constitutes waiver of that protection." Id. at 479.

Subsection (a)(2)(B). This subsection is taken nearly verbatim from Bendett v. Bendett, 315 Mass. 59, 62–63 (1943) (allowing adverse party to show that writing or object did not or could not have refreshed the memory of the witness).

Subsection (b)(1). This subsection is derived from Leonard v. Taylor, 315 Mass. 580, 583–584 (1944), citing Goldman v. United States, 316 U.S. 129, 132 (1942). This rule has been the subject of considerable criticism. See Commonwealth v. O'Brien, 419 Mass. 470, 479 n.5 (1995) ("Presently, the more controversial issue, and the one on which courts are still somewhat unclear, is whether an adverse party has a right under [Fed. R. Evid.] 612 to inspect protected and privileged documents used by the witness to refresh her recollection *prior* to testifying."); Commonwealth v. Marsh, 354 Mass. 713, 721–722 (1968) ("It is an artificial distinction to allow inspection of notes used on the stand to refresh recollection and to decline it where the witness inspects his notes just before being called to the stand.").

Subsection (b)(2). This subsection is derived from Leonard v. Taylor, 315 Mass. 580, 581–584 (1944). The purpose of this rule is to protect the opposing party from the impression of evasion and concealment from a "bold and dramatic demand" by the adverse party—not to make otherwise inadmissible evidence admissible—and should therefore be used sparingly. See id. at 582–583.

Cross–Reference: Section 106(b), Doctrine of Completeness: Curative Admissibility.

Subsection (b)(3). This subsection is derived from Commonwealth v. Woodbine, 461 Mass. 720, 731 (2012), where the court stated as follows:

"We do not decide today that it is impermissible for a witness to testify concerning an event after his memory has been refreshed by his review, before taking the stand, of material that is suppressed due to violations of a defendant's rights under the Fifth Amendment to the United States Constitution and art. 12 of the Massachusetts Declaration of Rights. However, before such a witness is permitted to testify, the judge must ensure that the Commonwealth has met its burden of establishing that the witness will testify not from a memory of the suppressed statement, which by definition is not to be placed in evidence, but from an independent memory of the separate event. This requires that the judge conduct a voir dire through which the basis for the witness's assertion that he or she has a present recollection of the separate event may be thoroughly examined."

Section 613. Prior Statements of Witnesses, Limited Admissibility

(a) Prior Inconsistent Statements.

(1) Examining Own Witness. A party who produces a witness may prove that the witness made prior statements inconsistent with his or her present testimony; but before proof of such inconsistent statements is given, the party must lay a foundation by asking the witness if the prior statements were in fact made and by giving the witness an opportunity to explain.

(2) Examining Other Witness. Extrinsic evidence of a prior inconsistent statement by a witness, other than a witness covered under Subsection (a)(1), is admissible whether or not the witness was afforded an opportunity to explain or deny the inconsistency.

(3) Disclosure of Extrinsic Evidence. In examining a witness, other than a witness covered under Subsection (a)(1), concerning a prior statement made by such witness, whether written or not, the statement need not be shown nor its contents disclosed to the witness at that time, but on request the same shall be shown or disclosed to opposing counsel.

(4) Collateral Matter. Extrinsic evidence to impeach a witness on a collateral matter is not admissible as of right, but only in the exercise of sound discretion by the trial judge.

(b) Prior Consistent Statements.

(1) Generally Inadmissible. A prior consistent statement by a witness is generally inadmissible.

(2) Exception. If the court makes a preliminary finding that there is a claim that the witness's in-court testimony is the result of recent contrivance or a bias, and the prior consistent statement was made before the witness had a motive to fabricate or the occurrence of the event indicating a bias, the evidence may be admitted for the limited purpose of rebutting the claim of recent contrivance or bias.

NOTE

Subsection (a)(1). This subsection is derived from G. L. c. 233, § 23, and Commonwealth v. Scott, 408 Mass. 811, 824 n.14 (1990). See Sherman v. Metropolitan Transit Auth., 345 Mass. 777, 778 (1963); Commonwealth v. Anselmo, 33 Mass. App. Ct. 602, 609 (1992). If the witness denies making the prior statement, he or she need not be given the opportunity to explain it. Commonwealth v. Scott, 408 Mass. at 824 n.14. See Commonwealth v. Festa, 369 Mass. 419, 425–426 (1976).

Cross–Reference: Section 607, Who May Impeach a Witness.

Subsections (a)(2) and (3). These subsections are derived from Hubley v. Lilley, 28 Mass. App. Ct. 468, 472, 473 n.7 (1990). See also Commonwealth v. Parent, 465 Mass. 395, 398–402 (2013). Opposing counsel has a right to examine the statement before conducting any further inquiry of the witness to prevent selective quotation of the prior statement by the questioner and to insure that the witness has an opportunity to explain or elaborate on the alleged inconsistencies. Hubley v. Lilley, 28 Mass. App. Ct. at 472, 473 n.7. This right arises after the examination of the witness under Subsection (a)(1) or (a)(2) and does not permit counsel to make a demand for a document before the jury during opposing counsel's cross-examination. See Section 103(d), Rulings on Evidence, Objections, and Offers of Proof: Preventing the Jury or Witnesses from Hearing Inadmissible Evidence. Such

conduct may warrant the court admitting extrinsic evidence of the prior inconsistent statement. See Section 612(b)(2), Writing or Object Used to Refresh Memory: Before Testifying: Admissibility.

A prior inconsistent statement offered to impeach one's own witness, Subsection (a)(1), or an opposing party's witness, Subsection (a)(2), is not admissible for its truth unless (1) there is no objection or (2) it falls within the exception set forth in Section 801(d)(1)(A), Definitions: Statements That Are Not Hearsay: A Declarant–Witness's Prior Statement, or another hearsay exception. See Commonwealth v. Jones, 439 Mass. 249, 261–262 (2003); Commonwealth v. Keevan, 400 Mass. 557, 562 (1987); Commonwealth v. Balukonis, 357 Mass. 721, 726 n.6 (1970).

Prior Statements That Qualify as Inconsistent. "It is not necessary that the prior statement contradict in plain terms the testimony of the witness." Commonwealth v. Simmonds, 386 Mass. 234, 242 (1982). "It is enough if the proffered testimony, taken as a whole, either by what it says or by what it omits to say, affords some indication that the fact was different from the testimony of the witness whom it is sought to contradict." Commonwealth v. Hesketh, 386 Mass. 153, 161 (1982). An omission in a prior statement may render that statement inconsistent "when it would have been natural to include the fact in the initial statement." Commonwealth v. Ortiz, 39 Mass. App. Ct. 70, 72 (1995). See also Langan v. Pignowski, 307 Mass. 149 (1940). It follows that a witness who denies making an earlier statement may be impeached with it, while a witness who is unable to remember the earlier statement, but does not deny making it, may have his or her recollection refreshed. See Section 612(a)(1), Writing or Object Used to Refresh Memory: While Testifying: General Rule. However, "a witness who has actually made a statement contradictory to trial testimony cannot escape impeachment simply by saying she does not remember making the statement." Commonwealth v. Parent, 465 Mass. 395, 401 (2013). Ordinarily, "[t]here is no inconsistency between a present failure of memory on the witness stand and a past existence of memory" (citation and quotation omitted). Commonwealth v. Martin, 417 Mass. 187, 197 (1994). However, if the trial judge makes a preliminary determination (see Section 104[a], Preliminary Questions: In General) that the witness's present failure of memory is fabricated, the witness's prior detailed statement is admissible for impeachment purposes. See Commonwealth v. Sineiro, 432 Mass. 735, 742–743 & n.7 (2000). Cf. Note "Feigning Lack of Memory" to Section 801(d)(1)(A), Definitions: Statements That Are Not Hearsay: A Declarant–Witness's Prior Statement (feigning lack of memory may result in the admission of a prior statement, not simply for impeachment purposes, but also for its truth). A witness who gives a detailed account of an incident at trial but who indicated at some earlier point in time only limited or no memory of the details of the incident may be impeached with that earlier failure of memory. Commonwealth v. Granito, 326 Mass. 494, 500 (1950).

Prior Silence or Inaction for Impeachment. Trial judges must proceed with caution when the Commonwealth seeks to impeach the defendant with his or her pretrial silence. See Doyle v. Ohio, 426 U.S. 610, 611, 617, 618 (1976) (use of defendant's postarrest silence violates Federal due process); Commonwealth v. Connolly, 454 Mass. 808, 828 (2009) (same). In Massachusetts, even use of the defendant's prearrest silence may violate Article 12 of the Declaration of Rights. See Harris v. New York, 401 U.S. 222, 226 (1971); Commonwealth v. Ly, 454 Mass. 223, 228 (2009); Commonwealth v. Harris, 364 Mass. 236, 240–241 (1973); Commonwealth v. Sazama, 339 Mass. 154, 157–158 (1959). See also Section 511(a)(2), Privilege Against Self–Incrimination: Privilege of Defendant in Criminal Proceeding: Refusal Evidence. Although a statement obtained in violation of a person's rights under the Fourth and Fourteenth Amendments to the Constitution of the United States may be used for impeachment purposes, see United States v. Havens, 446 U.S. 620, 627–628 (1980), Article 14 of the Declaration of Rights forbids the use of evidence in the case of electronic eavesdropping in or about a private home. Compare Commonwealth v. Fini, 403 Mass. 567, 573–574 (1988) (excluding statements), with Commonwealth v. Eason, 427 Mass. 595, 600–601 (1998) (admitting statements).

If a witness previously remained "silent in circumstances in which he naturally would have been expected to deny some asserted fact ... the jury may consider the failure to respond in assessing the veracity of the witness in testifying contrary to the fact that was adoptively admitted by his silence." Commonwealth v. Nickerson, 386 Mass. 54, 57 (1982). In circumstances where it "would not be natural for a witness to provide the police before trial with exculpatory information," this omission is admissible to impeach the witness at trial only after first establishing "[1] that the witness knew of the pending charges in sufficient detail to realize that he possessed exculpatory information, [2] that the witness had reason to make the information available, [and] [3] that he was familiar with the means of reporting it to the proper authorities ..." Commonwealth v. Hart, 455 Mass. 230, 238–239 (2009). See Id. at 239–240 (abolishing requirement that prosecutor needs to "elicit from the witness that she was not asked by the defendant or the defense attorney to refrain from disclosing her exculpatory information to law enforcement authorities"). Contrast Commonwealth v. Gardner, 479 Mass. 764, 772 (2018) (In a claim for self-defense, cross-examination of the defendant about his failure to contact the police between the victim's death and his arrest was improper because it would not have been natural for the defendant to contact the police). The Supreme Judicial Court has observed that

"[t]here are some circumstances, though, in which it would not be natural for a witness to provide the police before trial with exculpatory information, such as when the witness does not realize she possesses exculpatory information, when she thinks that her information will not affect the decision to prosecute, or when she does not know how to furnish such information to law enforcement."

Commonwealth v. Hart, 455 Mass. at 238. The principles applicable to impeachment of a witness by failure to provide exculpatory information apply to tangible evidence as well as oral testimony. Commonwealth v. Issa, 466 Mass. 1, 15–16 (2013).

Cross–Reference: Section 525(b), Comment upon or Inference from Claim of Privilege: Criminal Case; Section 104(d), Preliminary Questions: Cross–Examining a Defendant in a Criminal Case; Section 1113(b)(3)(E), Opening Statement and Closing Argument; Applicable to Criminal and Civil Cases: Closing Argument: Improper Argument.

Impeachment by Omission in a Statement. An omission from an earlier statement may qualify as a prior inconsistent statement. Commonwealth v. Perez, 460 Mass. 683, 699 (2011) (absence of journal entry regarding visit from defendant on night of murder qualified as prior inconsistent statement to trial testimony that defendant visited witness in person on night of murder), and cases cited.

Subsection (a)(4). This subsection is derived from Commonwealth v. Farley, 443 Mass. 740, 751 (2005), quoting Commonwealth v. Chase, 372 Mass. 736, 747 (1977), citing Commonwealth v. Doherty, 353 Mass. 197, 213–214 (1967), cert. denied, 390 U.S. 982 (1968). See also Commonwealth v. Zezima, 365 Mass. 238, 242 n.5 (1974), rev'd on other grounds, 387 Mass. 748 (1982); Leone v. Doran, 363 Mass. 1, 15–16 (1973), modified on other grounds, 363 Mass. 886 (1973); Commonwealth v. Connolly, 308 Mass. 481, 495 (1941). This principle is based on the practical need to keep a case from getting out of control. See Abramian v. President & Fellows of Harvard College, 432 Mass. 107, 120 (2000). The better practice is to exclude such evidence in a criminal case when it bears on a defendant's character. Commonwealth v. Ferguson, 425 Mass. 349, 355–356 n.6 (1997).

Although there is discretion involved in determining whether to admit or exclude evidence offered for impeachment, when the impeaching evidence is directly related to testimony on a central issue in the case, there is no discretion to exclude it. See Commonwealth v. McGowan, 400 Mass. 385, 390–391 (1987). See also Section 403, Excluding Relevant Evidence for Prejudice, Confusion, Waste of Time, or Other Reasons; Section 611(d), Mode and Order of Examining Witnesses and Presenting Evidence: Rebuttal Evidence. When the

extrinsic evidence relates exclusively to a collateral matter, the discretion of the trial judge has been described as "nearly unreversible." Commonwealth v. Roberts, 433 Mass. 45, 51 (2000), quoting Commonwealth v. Johnson, 41 Mass. App. Ct. 81, 89 (1996).

"Because bias, prejudice, and motive to lie are not considered collateral matters, they may be demonstrated by extrinsic proof as well as on cross-examination. There is no requirement that the opponent cross-examine on the matter as a foundation prior to offering extrinsic evidence." (Citations omitted.) Commonwealth v. Hall, 50 Mass. App. Ct. 208, 213 n.7 (2000), quoting P.J. Liacos, Massachusetts Evidence § 6.9, at 299–300 (7th ed. 1999).

Subsection (b). This subsection is derived from Commonwealth v. Novo, 449 Mass. 84, 93 (2007), and Commonwealth v. Kindell, 44 Mass. App. Ct. 200, 202 (1998). "The reason for the rule is that the testimony of a witness in court should not need—and ought not—to be 'pumped up' by evidence that the witness said the same thing on some prior occasion." Commonwealth v. Kindell, 44 Mass. App. Ct. at 202–203. "The trial judge has a range of discretion in determining whether a suggestion of recent contrivance exists in the circumstances." Commonwealth v. Zukoski, 370 Mass. 23, 27 (1976). The judge should make preliminary findings on the record that a party has claimed that a witness's in-court testimony is the result of recent contrivance or bias, and that the prior consistent statement was made before the witness had a motive to fabricate or before the occurrence of an event indicating bias. See Commonwealth v. Caruso, 476 Mass. 275, 284 & n.5 (2017). However, "the impeachment of a witness by prior inconsistent statements or omissions does not, standing alone, entitle the adverse party to introduce other prior statements made by the witness that are consistent with his trial testimony." Commonwealth v. Bruce, 61 Mass. App. Ct. 474, 482 (2004), citing Commonwealth v. Retkovitz, 222 Mass. 245, 249–250 (1915). See also Commonwealth v. Hatzigiannis, 88 Mass. App. Ct. 395, 399–400 (2015) (rehabilitation by prior consistent statement improper where theory of impeachment was mistaken perception or there was no suggestion of recent fabrication). Such statements "should be allowed only with caution, and where the probative value for the proper purpose is clear." Commonwealth v. Lareau, 37 Mass. App. Ct. 679, 683 (1994), quoting Commonwealth v. Darden, 5 Mass. App. Ct. 522, 528 (1977).

Although the admission of cumulative accounts of prior consistent statements may create a danger of improper bolstering, multiple prior consistent statements are admissible if each statement is relevant to rebut various claims of recent contrivance. Commonwealth v. Lessieur, 472 Mass. 317, 325–326 (2015). The judge may admit a prior consistent statement on direct examination, prior to any impeachment, if it is obvious that a claim of recent contrivance will be made (e.g., when a party makes a statement in his or her opening statement that he or she will attack the credibility of the witness on cross-examination on the basis of recent contrivance). See Commonwealth v. Barbosa, 457 Mass. 773, 797–798 (2010) (opponent's opening statement suggested recent contrivance).

A prior consistent statement that does not meet the requirements of this subsection nonetheless may be admissible on other grounds. See Commonwealth v. Tennison, 440 Mass. 553, 562–564 (2003) (verbal completeness). The prior consistent statement may be admissible not only if made before the motive to fabricate arose, but also if made at a time when the motive to fabricate no longer exists. Commonwealth v. Aviles, 461 Mass. 60, 69–70 (2011) (prior consistent statement made after victim moved back to grandmother's house admissible to rebut inference that victim had fabricated accusation of abuse to provide basis for moving out of defendant's home and back to grandmother's).

Cross–Reference: Section 413, First Complaint of Sexual Assault; Section 611(a), Mode and Order of Examining Witnesses and Presenting Evidence: Control by the Court; Note to Section 801(d)(1)(B), Definitions: Statements That Are Not Hearsay: A Declarant–Witness's Prior Statement; Section 801(d)(1)(C), Definitions: Statements

That Are Not Hearsay: A Declarant–Witness's Prior Statement; Section 1104, Witness Cooperation Agreements.

Section 614. Calling and Examination of Witnesses by Court or Jurors

(a) Calling. When necessary in the interest of justice, the court may call a witness on its own or at a party's request. Each party is entitled to cross-examine the witness.

(b) Examining by Court. The court may examine a witness to clarify an issue, to prevent perjury, or to develop trustworthy testimony, provided that the judge remains impartial.

(c) Objections. A party may object to the court's calling or examining a witness, but the objection should be made outside the presence of the jury.

(d) Examining by Jurors. The court, in its discretion, may allow questions posed by the jury, subject to the following procedures:

(1) The judge should instruct the jury that they will be given the opportunity to pose questions to witnesses.

(2) Jurors' questions need not be limited to important matters, but may also seek clarification of a witness's testimony.

(3) The judge should emphasize to jurors that, although they are not expected to understand the technical rules of evidence, their questions must comply with those rules, and so the judge may have to alter or to refuse a particular question.

(4) The judge should emphasize that, if a particular question is altered or refused, the juror who poses the question must not be offended or hold that against either party.

(5) The judge should tell the jurors that they should not give the answers to their own questions or questions by other jurors a disproportionate weight.

(6) These instructions should be given before the testimony begins and repeated during the final charge to the jury before they begin deliberations.

(7) All questions should be submitted in writing to the judge, with the juror's identification number included on each question.

(8) On submission of questions, counsel should have an opportunity, outside the hearing of the jury, to examine the questions with the judge, make any suggestions, or register objections.

(9) Counsel should be given an opportunity to reexamine a witness after juror interrogation with respect to the subject matter of the juror questions.

NOTE

Subsection (a). This subsection is derived from *Quincy Trust Co. v. Taylor*, 317 Mass. 195, 198 (1944). See also Henry T. Lummus, *The Trial Judge* 19–21 (Chicago, The Foundation Press 1937).

Subsection (b). This subsection is derived from *Commonwealth v. Lucien*, 440 Mass. 658, 664 (2004), and *Commonwealth v. Fitzgerald*, 380 Mass. 840, 846–847 (1980). See *Commonwealth v. Festa*, 369 Mass. 419, 422 (1976) ("There is no doubt that a judge can properly question a witness, albeit some of the answers may tend to reinforce the Commonwealth's case, so long as the examination is not partisan in

nature, biased, or a display of belief in the defendant's guilt."); *Commonwealth v. Fiore*, 364 Mass. 819, 826–827 (1974) ("The judge has a right, and it is perhaps sometimes a duty, to intervene on occasion in the examination of a witness … Here a discrepancy appeared between the proffered testimony and earlier testimony of the same witnesses. A likely possibility existed that each witness would perjure himself or admit to perjury in his prior statement. As this became evident to the judge, he indulged in no transgression when for the benefit of the witness and to aid in developing the most trustworthy evidence he took a hand in indicating to the witness the extent of the inconsistencies. In this case the questioning by the judge was not clearly biased or coercive." [Citations omitted.]). Accord *Adoption of Seth*, 29 Mass. App. Ct. 343, 351 (1990). See also *Commonwealth v. Hanscomb*, 367 Mass. 726, 732 (1975) (Hennessey, J., concurring) ("The judge need not be mute; he is more than a referee. Justice may require that he ask questions at times. However, the primary principle in jury trials is that he must use this power with restraint."). Compare *Commonwealth v. Watkins*, 63 Mass. App. Ct. 69, 74 (2005) (trial judge's questions were appropriate because they helped to clarify the testimony), with *Commonwealth v. Hassey*, 40 Mass. App. Ct. 806, 810–811 (1996) (judge's cross-examination of defense witnesses "too partisan" and lacked appropriate foundation).

Subsection (c). This subsection is derived from *Commonwealth v. Fitzgerald*, 380 Mass. 840, 846 (1980). Despite "the natural reluctance of trial counsel to object to questions or comments coming from a judge, sometimes trial counsel's duty to protect his client's rights requires him to object, preferably at the bench out of the jury's hearing." Id. Where a party fails to object at trial to questions by the judge, any error by the trial judge is reviewed for a substantial risk of a miscarriage of justice. *Commonwealth v. Gomes*, 54 Mass. App. Ct. 1, 5 (2002).

Subsection (d). This subsection is taken nearly verbatim from *Commonwealth v. Britto*, 433 Mass. 596, 613–614 (2001). See also *Commonwealth v. Urena*, 417 Mass. 692, 701–703 (1994). In addition to the procedures outlined in Subsection (d), the judge should instruct the jury "not to let themselves become aligned with any party, and that their questions should not be directed at helping or responding to any party"; the judge should also instruct the jurors "not to discuss the questions among themselves but, rather each juror must decide independently any questions he or she may have for a witness." *Commonwealth v. Britto*, 433 Mass. at 613–614. Upon counsels' review of the submitted questions, "[t]he judge should rule on any objections at [that] time, including any objection that the question touches on a matter that counsel purposefully avoided as a matter of litigation strategy, and that, if asked, will cause particular prejudice to the party." Id. at 614. Finally, the scope of the reexamination of the witness after juror interrogation "should ordinarily be limited to the subject matter raised by the juror question and the witness's answer. The purpose of reexamination is two fold. First, it cures the admission of any prejudicial questions or answers; and second, it prevents the jury from becoming adversary in its interrogation." (Citation omitted.) Id. at 614.

Section 615. Sequestration of Witnesses

At a party's request, the court may order witnesses excluded so that they cannot hear other witnesses' testimony. Or the court may do so on its own. But the court may not exclude any parties in a civil proceeding, nor the defendant in a criminal proceeding.

NOTE

This section is derived from *Zambarano v. Massachusetts Turnpike Auth.*, 350 Mass. 485, 487 (1966), and Mass. R. Crim. P. 21 ("Upon his own motion or the motion of either party, the judge may, prior to or during the examination of a witness, order any witness or witnesses other than the defendant to be excluded from the courtroom."). See *Commonwealth v. Therrien*, 359 Mass. 500, 508 (1971) (court may except from general sequestration order a witness deemed "essential to the management of the case").

"Sequestration of witnesses lies in the discretion of the trial judge." Zambarano v. Massachusetts Turnpike Auth., 350 Mass. at 487. See Commonwealth v. Herndon, 475 Mass. 324, 336 (2016) (trial judge properly found that defendant's sister's Facebook posts were sufficiently relevant to justify naming her as potential witness subject to sequestration order, and that adding her to witness list was not pretext to exclude her from courtroom); Commonwealth v. Perez, 405 Mass. 339, 343 (1989) (court has discretion to exempt police officer in charge of investigation from sequestration order). Upon a violation of a sequestration order, a trial judge has discretion in taking remedial action. See, e.g., Commonwealth v. Neves, 474 Mass. 355, 367–368 (2016) (no abuse of discretion in denying motion to strike testimony of

witness who had violated sequestration order where defense counsel stated he was "satisfied" with judge's "instructional remedy" to jury); Custody of a Minor (No. 2), 392 Mass. 719, 726 (1984) (trial judge may exclude testimony of person who violates sequestration order); Commonwealth v. Navarro, 2 Mass. App. Ct. 214, 223 (1974) ("but even in a case where a violation of sequestration order is wilful a trial judge might for good reason prefer to invoke contempt proceedings rather than declare a mistrial").

The second sentence of this section is derived from the Sixth and Fourteenth Amendments to the United States Constitution, and Article 12 of the Declaration of Rights of the Massachusetts Constitution. See also Commonwealth v. Nwachukwu, 65 Mass. App. Ct. 112, 117–120 (2005). Civil litigants also have a right to be present during the trial. See White v. White, 40 Mass. App. Ct. 132, 141–142 (1996).

ARTICLE VII. OPINION AND EXPERT EVIDENCE

Section 701. Opinion Testimony by Lay Witnesses

If a witness is not testifying as an expert, testimony in the form of an opinion is limited to one that is

(a) rationally based on the witness's perception;

(b) helpful to a clear understanding of the witness's testimony or in determining a fact in issue; and

(c) not based on scientific, technical, or other specialized knowledge within the scope of Section 702.

NOTE

This section, which is taken nearly verbatim from Fed. R. Evid. 701, reflects Massachusetts practice. See Noyes v. Noyes, 224 Mass. 125, 129 (1916); Commonwealth v. Sturtivant, 117 Mass. 122, 133, 137 (1875); Commonwealth v. Brusgulis, 41 Mass. App. Ct. 386, 390–391 (1996). "While an expert opinion is admissible only where it will help jurors interpret evidence that lies outside of common experience, a lay opinion is admissible only where it lies within the realm of common experience" (quotation omitted). Commonwealth v. Canty, 466 Mass. 535, 541–542 (2013). "The rule that witnesses in describing conduct should tell what they saw and heard does not foreclose the use of words of summary description." Kane v. Fields Corner Grille, Inc., 341 Mass. 640, 647 (1961) (judge had the discretion to permit witnesses to use the words "boisterous" and "in an arrogant manner" in describing the actions of a person they observed). Accord Commonwealth v. Bonomi, 335 Mass. 327, 339 (1957) (condition of nervousness or happiness); Commonwealth v. Fuller, 66 Mass. App. Ct. 84, 91 (2006). See also Commonwealth v. Bonds, 445 Mass. 821, 830 (2006); McGrath v. Fash, 244 Mass. 327, 329 (1923) (witness permitted to testify that "all of a sudden this truck came around the corner on two wheels, and zigzagging across the street and appeared to be out of the control of the driver"); Commonwealth v. Rodziewicz, 213 Mass. 68, 69 (1912) (it was error to permit a police investigator to identify points of origin of a fire based simply on observations about condition of the burned structure).

Ultimately, the admission of summary descriptions of observed facts is left to the discretion of the trial judge. Kane v. Fields Corner Grille, Inc., 341 Mass. at 647 ("Trials are not to be delayed and witnesses made inarticulate by too nice objections or rulings as to the use of such descriptive words."). See Commonwealth v. Barbosa, 477 Mass. 658, 673–674 (2017) (witness may testify about time discrepancy between video surveillance footage and GPS data to explain "investigative significance" of evidence. A witness may not express an opinion about the credibility of another witness. See Commonwealth v. Triplett, 398 Mass. 561, 567 (1986).

Illustrations. When, due to the complexity of expressing the observation, such evidence might otherwise not be available, witnesses

are permitted, out of necessity, to use "shorthand expressions" to describe observed facts such as the identity, size, distance, and speed of objects; the length of the passage of time; and the age, identity, and conduct of persons. See Commonwealth v. Tracy, 349 Mass. 87, 95–96 (1965); Noyes v. Noyes, 224 Mass. 125, 129–130 (1916); Ross v. John Hancock Mut. Life Ins. Co., 222 Mass. 560, 562 (1916).

Cellular Phone Positioning. A lay witness is not permitted to testify to the intra-cell site position of a phone user because the testimony requires specialized knowledge that relates to the scientific and technological features of cell sites. Commonwealth v. Gonzalez, 475 Mass. 396, 412 n.37 (2016).

Identity. In some circumstances, lay witnesses are permitted to identify a person in a photograph or on videotape. Compare Commonwealth v. Vitello, 376 Mass. 426, 459–460 & n.29 (1978) (allowing police officer to testify that a photograph selected by a witness depicted the defendant because his appearance had changed since the date of the offense), and Commonwealth v. Pleas, 49 Mass. App. Ct. 321, 323–329 (2000) (allowing police officer to testify that man depicted in a surveillance videotape who was holding the victim was the defendant "because [1] the image in the videotape and the prints made from it were of poor quality . . .; [2] [the officer] had long familiarity with the defendant that enabled him to identify an indistinct picture of the defendant; [3] there was some change in the appearance of the defendant at trial and as he generally presented in everyday life outdoors; and [4] the acquaintanceship of [the officer] with the defendant, as it was presented to the jury, was social rather than tied to [the officer's] duties as a police officer"), with Commonwealth v. Austin, 421 Mass. 357, 365–366 (1995) (excluding testimony of police officer identifying person in a surveillance videotape as the defendant because the jury was equally capable of making the determination), and Commonwealth v. Nassar, 351 Mass. 37, 41–42 (1966) (because a sketch and a photograph of the defendant were in evidence, the jury did not require any assistance from a witness who was asked whether they were a likeness of the defendant). See also Commonwealth v. Connolly, 91 Mass. App. Ct. 580, 591–593 (2017) (police officer's testimony that person in surveillance video that was inadvertently erased was the defendant was not helpful to jury without foundation providing "enough information to allow the jury to conduct an independent assessment of the accuracy and reliability of his identifications"; rejecting categorical approach to exclusion of such evidence).

Intent. This section does not permit a witness to express an opinion about what someone was intending or planning to do based on an observation of the person. See Commonwealth v. Jones, 319 Mass. 228, 230 (1946).

Mental Capacity. A lay opinion as to sanity or mental capacity is permitted only by an attesting witness to a will and only as to the testator's mental condition at the time of its execution. See Holbrook v. Seagrave, 228 Mass. 26, 29 (1917); Commonwealth v. Spencer, 212

Mass. 438, 447 (1912). "Although a lay witness may not testify about whether another person suffered from mental illness, such a witness is permitted to 'testify to facts observed.'" Commonwealth v. Sliech-Brodeur, 457 Mass. 300, 330 n.43 (2010), quoting Commonwealth v. Monico, 396 Mass. 793, 803 (1986).

Sobriety.

—*Alcohol.* A police officer or lay witness may provide an opinion, in summary form, about another person's sobriety, provided there exists a basis for that opinion. Commonwealth v. Orben, 53 Mass. App. Ct. 700, 704 (2002). Where a defendant is charged with operating a vehicle while under the influence of alcohol, a police officer who observed the defendant may offer an opinion as to the defendant's level of intoxication but may not offer an opinion as to whether the defendant's intoxication impaired his ability to operate a motor vehicle, because the latter comes too close to an opinion on the defendant's guilt. Commonwealth v. Canty, 466 Mass. 535, 545 (2013). As a lay witness, a police officer may testify to the administration and results of field sobriety tests that measure a person's balance, coordination, and acuity of mind in understanding and performing simple instructions, as a juror understands from common experience and knowledge that "intoxication leads to diminished balance, coordination, and mental acuity." Commonwealth v. Sands, 424 Mass. 184, 187 (1997) (contrasting the Horizontal Gaze Nystagmus Test, which requires expert testimony, from "ordinary" field sobriety tests such as a nine-step walk and turn and recitation of the alphabet); Id. at 186 ("Expert testimony on the scientific theory is needed if the subject of expert testimony is beyond the common knowledge or understanding of the lay juror.").

—*Marijuana.* Where a defendant is charged with operating a motor vehicle under the influence of marijuana, a police officer may testify as a lay witness as to his or her observations of the defendant's performance of the one-leg stand test and the nine-step walk-and-turn test. Commonwealth v. Gerhardt, 477 Mass. 775, 783 (2017). These observations are admissible to the extent that they are probative of "a defendant's balance, coordination, ability to retain and follow directions, and ability to perform tasks requiring divided attention," as well as "the presence or absence of other skills necessary for the safe operation of a motor vehicle." Id. However, a police officer may not testify that a defendant charged with operating under the influence of marijuana "passed" or "failed" a field sobriety test. Id. at 784. Lay witnesses and police officers also may not present testimony indicating that, in their opinion, a defendant was under the influence of marijuana. Id. A testifying witness "should" refer to field sobriety tests as "roadside assessments." Id. at 785.

Sounds.
In Commonwealth v. Sturtivant, 117 Mass. 122, 133 (1875), the Supreme Judicial Court stated that a witness "may state his opinion in regard to sounds, their character, from what they proceed, and the direction from which they seem to come."

Struggle.
An experienced police officer, or possibly even a lay witness, could opine on whether a scene was suggestive of a struggle. Commonwealth v. Burgess, 450 Mass. 422, 436 n.8 (2008).

Value.
Depending on the circumstances, opinion testimony about the value of real or personal property may be given by lay witnesses or expert witnesses. With regard to lay witnesses,

"[t]he rule which permits the owner of real or personal property to testify as to its value does not rest upon the fact that he holds the legal title. The mere holding of the title to property by one who knows nothing about it and perhaps has never even seen it does not rationally and logically give him any qualification to express an opinion as to its value. Ordinarily an owner of property is actually familiar with its characteristics, has some acquaintance with its uses actual and potential and has had experience in dealing with it. It is this familiarity, knowledge and experience, not the holding of the title, which qualify him to testify to its value."

Menici v. Orton Crane & Shovel Co., 285 Mass. 499, 503 (1934). Accord von Henneberg v. Generazio, 403 Mass. 519, 524 (1988) (same rule applied to landowner's opinion as to damages to his property caused by filling of drainage ditch by abutter); Turner v. Leonard, Inc., 17 Mass. App. Ct. 909, 910–911 (1983) (owner was not so familiar with his automobile to permit him to offer an opinion as to its value). A lay witness also may testify to the value of his or her own services. Berish v. Bornstein, 437 Mass. 252, 273 (2002).

Section 702. Testimony by Expert Witnesses

A witness who is qualified as an expert by knowledge, skill, experience, training, or education may testify in the form of an opinion or otherwise if

(a) the expert's scientific, technical, or other specialized knowledge will help the trier of fact to understand the evidence or to determine a fact in issue;

(b) the testimony is based on sufficient facts or data;

(c) the testimony is the product of reliable principles and methods; and

(d) the expert has reliably applied the principles and methods to the facts of the case.

NOTE

Introduction. This section, which is based upon Fed. R. Evid. 702 and Proposed Mass. R. Evid. 702, reflects Massachusetts law. There are two methods by which the judge may satisfy his or her duty as the gatekeeper to ensure that expert witness testimony is reliable: (1) the "Frye" test, i.e., general acceptance in the relevant scientific community, or (2) a Daubert–Lanigan analysis. Commonwealth v. Powell, 450 Mass. 229, 238 (2007). See Daubert v. Merrell Dow Pharms., Inc., 509 U.S. 579, 585–595 (1993), and Commonwealth v. Lanigan, 419 Mass. 15, 24–26 (1994).

It is important to distinguish between the words used to express the principle of Massachusetts law set forth in this section and the application of the principle in specific cases. As the following notes indicate, the framework used under the Federal rules and in Massachusetts is the same, and each approach is specifically described as flexible. The principal difference is that in Massachusetts, the trial judge satisfies his or her gatekeeper responsibilities under Subsections (b) and (c) once the proponent of the evidence establishes that it is generally accepted by the relevant scientific community. See Commonwealth v. Patterson, 445 Mass. 626, 640–641 (2005); Commonwealth v. Sands, 424 Mass. 184, 185–186 (1997). Compare Commonwealth v. Lanigan, 419 Mass. at 26 ("We accept the basic reasoning of the Daubert opinion because it is consistent with our test of demonstrated reliability. We suspect that general acceptance in the relevant scientific community will continue to be the significant, and often the only, issue."), and Canavan's Case, 432 Mass. 304, 314 n.5 (2000) ("Application of the Lanigan test requires flexibility. Differing types of methodology may require judges to apply differing evaluative criteria to determine whether scientific methodology is reliable. In the Lanigan case, we established various guideposts for determining admissibility including general acceptance, peer review, and testing."), with Daubert v. Merrell Dow Pharms., Inc., 509 U.S. at 594–595 ("The inquiry envisioned by [Fed. R. Evid.] 702 is, we emphasize, a flexible one. Its overarching subject is the scientific validity—and thus the evidentiary relevance and reliability—of the principles that underlie a proposed submission."), and Kumho Tire Co. v. Carmichael, 526 U.S. 137, 141 (1999) ("[T]he test of reliability is 'flexible,' and Daubert's list of specific factors neither necessarily nor exclusively applies to all experts or in every case."). See also Kumho Tire Co. v. Carmichael, 526 U.S. at 150 ("Daubert makes clear that the factors it mentions do *not* constitute a 'definitive checklist or test.' [Daubert v. Merrell Dow Pharms., Inc., 509 U.S.] at 593. And Daubert adds that the gatekeeping inquiry must be 'tied to the facts' of a particular 'case.' Id. at

591." [Quotation and citation omitted.]); Daubert v. Merrell Dow Pharms., Inc., 509 U.S. at 594 ("Widespread acceptance can be an important factor in ruling particular evidence admissible, and a known technique which has been able to attract only minimal support within the community[] may properly be viewed with skepticism" [quotation and citation omitted].).

Hearing. An evidentiary hearing is not always necessary to comply with Commonwealth v. Lanigan, 419 Mass. 15 (1994). See Palandjian v. Foster, 446 Mass. 100, 111 (2006); Vassallo v. Baxter Healthcare Corp., 428 Mass. 1, 1–13 (1998) (trial judge properly relied on affidavits and transcripts of testimony from other cases). However, as the Supreme Judicial Court noted, "we have not 'grandfathered' any particular theories or methods for all time, especially in areas where knowledge is evolving and new understandings may be expected as more studies and tests are conducted." Commonwealth v. Shanley, 455 Mass. 752, 763 n.15 (2010) (court acknowledged it was prudent for trial judge to conduct an evidentiary hearing in connection with expert testimony about dissociative amnesia because of "the evolving nature of scientific and clinical studies of the brain and memory"); Commonwealth v. Camblin, 471 Mass. 639, 648 (2015) (fact that the Legislature may prescribe rules of evidence and methods of proof employed in trials "does not mean that the reliability of every type of evidence the Legislature may deem admissible, particularly in a criminal case, is automatically insulated from challenge and review on reliability grounds"). To preserve an objection to expert testimony on grounds it is not reliable, a defendant must file a pretrial motion and request a hearing on the subject. See Commonwealth v. Sparks, 433 Mass. 654, 659 (2001). See also Commonwealth v. Cole, 473 Mass. 317, 328 (2015) (defendant who wished to challenge the scientific reliability of program used to calculate probability of DNA match should have filed a pretrial motion stating grounds and requesting Daubert–Lanigan hearing). A trial judge's decision on whether expert witness evidence meets the Lanigan standard of reliability is reviewed on appeal under an abuse of discretion standard. See General Elec. Co. v. Joiner, 522 U.S. 136, 141–143 (1997); Canavan's Case, 432 Mass. 304, 311–312 (2000).

Five Foundation Requirements. The proponent of expert witness testimony has the burden of establishing the five foundation requirements for the admission of such testimony under this section. See Commonwealth v. Barbosa, 457 Mass. 773, 783 (2010) (explaining the five foundation requirements). First, the proponent must establish that the expert witness testimony will assist the trier of fact. See Commonwealth v. Francis, 390 Mass. 89, 98 (1983); Commonwealth v. Rodziewicz, 213 Mass. 68, 69–70 (1912). Second, the proponent must demonstrate that the witness is qualified as an expert in the relevant area of inquiry. See Commonwealth v. Frangipane, 433 Mass. 527, 535–536 (2001); Commonwealth v. Boyd, 367 Mass. 169, 182 (1975). Third, the proponent must demonstrate that the facts or data in the record are sufficient to enable the witness to give an opinion that is not merely speculation. See Lightlab Imaging, Inc. v. Axsun Techs., Inc., 469 Mass. 181, 191 (2014). Fourth, the expert opinion must be based on a body of knowledge, a principle, or a method that is reliable. Commonwealth v. Lanigan, 419 Mass. 15, 26 (1994). Fifth, the proponent must demonstrate that the expert has applied the body of knowledge, the principle, or the method in a reliable manner to the particular facts of the case. See Commonwealth v. Patterson, 445 Mass. 626, 645–648 (2005); Commonwealth v. McNickles, 434 Mass. 839, 850 (2001).

Each of these five foundation requirements is a preliminary question of fact for the trial judge to determine under Section 104(a), Preliminary Questions: In General. The trial judge has "broad discretion" in making these determinations. Commonwealth v. Robinson, 449 Mass. 1, 5 (2007). In making these preliminary determinations, the trial judge may be required to resolve disputes as to the credibility of witnesses. Commonwealth v. Patterson, 445 Mass. at 647–648. Expert witness testimony should not be deemed unreliable simply because there is a disagreement of opinion or in terms of the level of confidence among the experts. See Commonwealth v. Torres, 442 Mass. 554, 581 (2004).

The judge has no authority to exclude the evidence because he or she disagrees with the expert's opinion or finds the testimony unpersuasive. See Commonwealth v. Roberio, 428 Mass. 278, 281 (1998) ("Once the expert's qualifications were established and assuming the expert's testimony met the standard of Commonwealth v. Lanigan, 419 Mass. 15 [1994], the issue of credibility was for a jury, not the judge."). When an expert's opinion is based on the analysis of complex facts, the failure of the expert to account for all the variables goes to its weight and not its admissibility. Salvas v. Wal–Mart Stores, Inc., 452 Mass. 337, 359–360 (2008). See id. at 351–360 (expert witness with doctorate in psychology and mathematics used statistical methods to evaluate large body of employee records to account for missing records and to opine that employer had wrongfully deprived employees of compensation).

First Foundation Requirement: Assistance to the Trier of Fact. "The role of an expert witness is to help jurors interpret evidence that lies outside of common experience." Commonwealth v. Tanner, 45 Mass. App. Ct. 576, 581 (1998). Thus, expert testimony may be excluded when it will not assist the jury. See Commonwealth v. Tolan, 453 Mass. 634, 648 (2009) (trial judge has discretion "to preclude expert testimony on commonly understood interrogation methods"); Commonwealth v. Bly, 448 Mass. 473, 496 (2007) (trial judge did not abuse his discretion in excluding expert witness testimony on the subject of cross-racial identification). Expert witness testimony also may be excluded because it is cumulative. See Anthony's Pier Four, Inc. v. HBC Assocs., 411 Mass. 451, 482 (1991). Expert witness testimony may be excluded because it does not fit the facts of the case. See Ready, petitioner, 63 Mass. App. Ct. 171, 179 (2005) (concluding that a diagnostic test known as the Abel Assessment of Sexual Interest [AASI] was of no value to the fact issues facing the jury). See generally Section 403, Excluding Relevant Evidence for Prejudice, Confusion, Waste of Time, or Other Reason. Finally, expert witness testimony may be excluded as not probative of a material fact in dispute and thus of no assistance to the jury when it amounts to a mere guess or conjecture. See Kennedy v. U–Haul Co., 360 Mass. 71, 73–74 (1971). See also Section 402, General Admissibility of Relevant Evidence. There are circumstances, however, in which an expert witness's opinion as to a possibility will have probative value. See Commonwealth v. Federico, 425 Mass. 844, 852 (1997). The trial judge has discretion to determine whether expert witness testimony will assist the trier of fact. See, e.g., Commonwealth v. Francis, 390 Mass. 89, 95–102 (1983) (expert witness testimony on the reliability of eyewitness identification evidence); Commonwealth v. Trainor, 374 Mass. 796, 801 (1978) ("A properly conducted public opinion survey, offered through an expert in conducting such surveys, is admissible in an obscenity case if it tends to show relevant standards in the Commonwealth.").

Second Foundation Requirement: Qualifications of the Expert. "The crucial issue in determining whether a witness is qualified to give an expert opinion is whether the witness has sufficient education, training, experience and familiarity with the subject matter of the testimony" (quotations and citation omitted). Commonwealth v. Richardson, 423 Mass. 180, 183 (1996). See Adoption of Hugo, 428 Mass. 219, 232–234 (1998) (license clinical social worker); Custody of Michel, 28 Mass. App. Ct. 260, 266 (1990) (investigator appointed under G. L. c. 119, § 24). Qualification of a witness as an expert in accordance with Section 104(a), Preliminary Questions: In General, does not always require an explicit ruling on the record by the judge. However, if a formal ruling is made, it should be made outside the hearing of the jury. Id. at 184.

"Whether an expert determined to be qualified in one subject is also qualified to testify in another, related subject will depend on the circumstances of each case, and, where an expert has been determined to be qualified, questions or criticisms as to whether the basis of the expert's opinion is reliable go to the weight, and not the admissibility, of the testimony."

Commonwealth v. Crouse, 447 Mass. 558, 569 (2006) (noting that there must always be a first time for every expert witness). However, the trial judge, acting as the gatekeeper, must enforce boundaries between areas of expertise within which the expert is qualified and areas that require different training, education, and experience and within which the expert is not qualified. See Commonwealth v. Frangipane, 433 Mass. 527, 535 (2001) (social worker qualified to testify as an expert witness that abused children may experience dissociative memory loss and recovered memory, but was not qualified to testify about how trauma victims store and retrieve or dissociate memories); Commonwealth v. Bouley, 93 Mass. App. Ct. 709, 714–715 (2018) (EMT qualified to opine that defendant had overdosed on opioids).

Third Foundation Requirement: Knowledge of Sufficient Facts or Data in the Record. The basis of expert opinion may include the factors set forth in Section 703, namely: (a) facts observed by the witness or otherwise in the witness's direct personal knowledge; (b) evidence already in the record or which the parties represent will be presented during the course of the proceedings, which facts may be assumed to be true in questions put to the witness; and (c) facts or data not in evidence if the facts or data are independently admissible in evidence and are a permissible basis for an expert to consider in formulating an opinion. See Section 703, Bases of Opinion Testimony by Experts; LaClair v. Silberline Mfg. Co., 379 Mass. 21, 32 (1979). See also Department of Youth Servs. v. A Juvenile, 398 Mass. 516, 531 (1986). This requirement means the expert witness

"must have sufficient familiarity with the particular facts to reach a meaningful expert opinion. The relevant distinction is between an opinion based upon speculation and one adequately grounded in facts. Although a trial judge has some discretion in making that distinction, it may be an abuse of discretion to disallow expert testimony which is based upon reasonably adequate familiarity with the facts." (Citations omitted.)

Fourth St. Pub, Inc. v. National Union Fire Ins. Co., 28 Mass. App. Ct. 157, 161 (1989). Contrast Commonwealth v. Talbot, 444 Mass. 586, 589 (2005) (no error in excluding defense expert who was proffered to testify about the effects of hypoglycemic shock in view of the absence of any evidence that the defendant experienced such a condition at the time of the offense); Commonwealth v. Laliberty, 373 Mass. 238, 241 (1977) (opinion concerning defense of lack of criminal responsibility not admissible absent evidence that defendant suffered from mental disease or defect at time of crime).

Fourth Foundation Requirement: Reliability of Principle or Method Used by the Expert. Both the United States Supreme Court, applying Fed. R. Evid. 702 in Daubert v. Merrell Dow Pharms., Inc., 509 U.S. 579 (1993), and the Supreme Judicial Court applying the common law in Commonwealth v. Lanigan, 419 Mass. 15 (1994), agree on the fundamental requirement that "[i]f the process or theory underlying [an] ... expert's opinion lacks reliability, that opinion should not reach the trier of fact." Commonwealth v. Lanigan, 419 Mass. at 26. Both the Supreme Court and the Supreme Judicial Court require the trial judge to act as a gatekeeper to ensure that the expert witness testimony that is considered by the jury meets minimum standards of reliability. The variation between the two approaches is that Massachusetts law makes general acceptance the default position and a Daubert analysis an alternative method of establishing reliability. Under Fed. R. Evid. 702, Federal courts must consider five nonexclusive factors in assessing reliability, one of which is the traditional test that looked at whether the principle or method was generally accepted in the relevant scientific community. See Frye v. United States, 293 F. 1013 (D.C. Cir. 1923). "[G]eneral acceptance in the relevant community of the theory and process on which an expert's testimony is based, on its own, continues to be sufficient to establish the requisite reliability for admission in Massachusetts courts regardless of other Daubert factors." Commonwealth v. Patterson, 445 Mass. 626, 640 (2005) (latent fingerprint identification theory). See Commonwealth v. Frangipane, 433 Mass. 527, 538 (2001) (Lanigan hearing not necessary where qualified expert testimony has been

accepted as reliable in the past in Massachusetts appellate cases). "Where general acceptance is not established by the party offering the expert testimony, a full Daubert analysis provides an alternate method of establishing reliability." Commonwealth v. Patterson, 445 Mass. at 641. These alternative, Daubert considerations include the ability to test the theory, existence of peer-reviewed publications supporting it, existence of standards for controlling or maintaining it, and known or potential error rates. See Daubert v. Merrell Dow Pharms., Inc., 509 U.S. at 593–594. "A Daubert–Lanigan inquiry does not end once it is determined that an expert's methodology is generally accepted. In Lightlab Imaging, Inc. v. Axsun Techs., Inc., 469 Mass. 181, 189–191 (2014), the plaintiff claimed the judge erred in excluding expert witness testimony about lost profits because the witness used the discounted cash flow (DCF) method that is generally regarded as a reliable methodology. However, the judge found a specific aspect of the expert witness's methodology to be speculative. In particular, the witness relied on a theory known as "first mover advantage," which posits that "firms that innovate often capture long-term benefits from doing so, thanks to various first mover advantages." It was within the judge's discretion to conclude that the use of "first mover advantage" in the witness's methodology rendered that methodology incapable of being validated and tested.

In determining reliability, "[a] judge may also look to his own common sense, as well as the depth and quality of the proffered expert's education, training, experience, and appearance in other courts to determine reliability" (quotation and citation omitted). Commonwealth v. Pasteur, 66 Mass. App. Ct. 812, 826 (2006). See also Commonwealth v. Powell, 450 Mass. 229, 239 (2007) (holding a court may consider an appellate decision from a different jurisdiction).

In making the reliability determination it is also important that

"[a] relevant scientific community must be defined broadly enough to include a sufficiently broad sample of scientists so that the possibility of disagreement exists, ... and ... trial judges [must] not ... define the relevant scientific community so narrowly that the expert's opinion will inevitably be considered generally accepted. In the context of technical forensic evidence, the community must be sufficiently broad to permit the potential for dissent."

Commonwealth v. Patterson, 445 Mass. at 643, quoting Canavan's Case, 432 Mass. 304, 314 n.6 (2000). See Canavan's Case, 432 Mass. at 313–316 (holding that the requirement of reliability under Lanigan extends to expert opinions based on personal observations and clinical experience, including medical expert testimony concerning diagnosis and causation). The testimony of a substitute medical examiner who did not perform or witness the autopsy is not, for that reason, unreliable. Commonwealth v. Williams, 475 Mass. 705, 720 (2016).

The requirements of Lanigan, as amplified in Canavan's Case, do not apply fully as to the standard of care in a medical negligence case. Palandjian v. Foster, 446 Mass. 100, 108–109 (2006) ("How physicians practice medicine is a fact, not an opinion derived from data or other scientific inquiry by employing a recognized methodology. However, when the proponent of expert testimony incorporates scientific fact into a statement concerning the standard of care, that science may be the subject of a Daubert-Lanigan inquiry." [Quotation and citation omitted.]).

The application of the Daubert–Lanigan factors in cases involving the "hard" sciences may not apply in the same way in cases involving the "soft" sciences. See Daubert v. Merrell Dow Pharms., Inc., 509 U.S. at 593–594; Commonwealth v. Lanigan, 419 Mass. at 25–26. See also Mark S. Brodin, Behavioral Science Evidence in the Age of Daubert: Reflections of a Skeptic, 73 U. Cin. L. Rev. 867 (2005). The Supreme Judicial Court has stated as follows:

"Observation informed by experience is but one scientific technique that is no less susceptible to Lanigan analysis than other types of scientific methodology. The gatekeeping function pursuant to Lanigan is the same regardless of the nature of the methodology used: to determine whether 'the process or theory underlying a scientific expert's opinion lacks reliability [such] that [the] opinion should not reach the trier of fact.' Commonwealth v. Lanigan, 419 Mass. 15, 26 (1994). Of course, even though personal observations are not excepted from Lanigan analysis, in many cases personal observation will be a reliable methodology to justify an expert's conclusion. If the proponent can show that the method of personal observation is either generally accepted by the relevant scientific community or otherwise reliable to support a scientific conclusion relevant to the case, such expert testimony is admissible."

Canavan's Case, 432 Mass. at 313–314. See, e.g., Commonwealth v. Shanley, 455 Mass. 752, 766 (2010) ("[T]he judge's finding that the lack of scientific testing did not make unreliable the theory that an individual may experience dissociative amnesia was supported in the record, not only by expert testimony but by a wide collection of clinical observations and a survey of academic literature.").

In several cases, the Supreme Judicial Court has relied on the discussion of forensic methods contained in a 2009 report by the National Research Council entitled Strengthening Forensic Science in the United States: A Path Forward 134–135 (2009) (NAS Report). See, e.g., Commonwealth v. Fernandez, 458 Mass. 137, 149 n.17 (2010) (citing NAS Report that the "near universal" laboratory test for drug identity is the "gas chromatography-mass spectrometry" test); Commonwealth v. Barbosa, 457 Mass. 773, 788 n.13 (2010) (citing NAS Report for proposition that nuclear DNA analysis is the standard against which many other forensic individualization techniques are judged). In Commonwealth v. Gambora, 457 Mass. 715, 724–727 (2010), the defendant challenged the scientific basis of the latent fingerprint identification methodology known as ACE–V, which was criticized in the NAS Report. The Supreme Judicial Court observed that "[t]he NAS Report does not conclude that fingerprint evidence is so unreliable that courts should no longer admit it. The Report does, however, stress the subjective nature of the judgments that must be made by the fingerprint examiner at every step of the ACE–V process . . ."

The Supreme Judicial Court has not addressed the standard to apply to evidence that meets the general acceptance test but is opposed on grounds that it is nonetheless unreliable. "Given that knowledge is constantly expanding, and that scientific principles are frequently modified in light of new discoveries or theories, it is inconsistent with the reliability requirement to permit any theories or methods to be 'grandfathered' as admissible evidence." M.S. Brodin & M. Avery, Massachusetts Evidence § 7.5.1, at 419 (8th ed. 2007). See Commonwealth v. Camblin, 471 Mass. 639, 650 (2015) (despite statutory authorization, where evidence offered from breathalyzer machine utilizing new methodology not previously shown to be reliable, Lanigan hearing was required).

Fifth Foundation Requirement: Reliability of the Application of the Principle or Method to the Specific Facts of the Case. See Commonwealth v. Colturi, 448 Mass. 809, 815–817 (2007) (results of otherwise valid breathalyzer test is admissible to establish blood alcohol level at the time of the offense without expert witness testimony on the theory of retrograde extrapolation so long as the test was administered within three hours of the offense); Commonwealth v. McNickles, 434 Mass. 839, 847–850 (2001) (disagreement among experts regarding the reliability of the application of a statistical method known as "likelihood ratios" to mixed samples of DNA evidence went to the weight, but not the admissibility, of the expert witness evidence). But see Lightlab Imaging, Inc. v. Axsun Techs., Inc., 469 Mass. 181, 192–194 (2014) (the judge did not abuse her discretion in excluding the expert witness's opinion because the expert's estimate of lost profits was based on speculation about the availability of future funding for the business); Smith v. Bell Atlantic, 63 Mass. App. Ct. 702, 718–719 (2005) (even though expert witness was qualified and employed a reliable diagnostic method, her lack of knowledge of the details of the patient's life called into question the reliability of her opinion and justified its exclusion in judge's discretion).

Duty to Consult with Expert. In cases where scientific evidence is central to the defense, counsel may have a duty to consult with an appropriate expert. See Commonwealth v. Field, 477 Mass. 553, 556–558 (2017) (error for counsel not to consult with mental health expert regarding defense of mental impairment, but error not likely to have affected verdict). Where science critical to a defense is evolving with new research findings, it may be manifestly unreasonable and present a substantial risk of a miscarriage of justice for counsel to fail to consult or present an expert who could offer evidence in support of the defense. See Commonwealth v. Epps, 474 Mass. 743 (2016) (ineffective assistance of counsel requiring new trial where counsel failed to consult or present expert on possibility of accidental fall as substantial defense in prosecution based upon shaken baby syndrome); Commonwealth v. Millien, 474 Mass. 417 (2016) (failure to consult or call expert on science of shaken baby syndrome). Cf. Commonwealth v. Ayala, 481 Mass. 46, 64 n.20 (2018) (no duty to consult expert in eyewitness identification at time of 2009 trial, when "retention of experts on eyewitness identification was not as prevalent as it is today").

Profile Evidence. Using a criminal profile to suggest that a defendant committed an act by comparing him or her to stereotypes is inadmissible as not relevant and inherently prejudicial. Commonwealth v. Day, 409 Mass. 719, 723 (1991) (testimony that defendant fit "child battering" profile inadmissible). Similarly, it is inadmissible for an expert to provide so-called negative profile evidence by testifying that the defendant does not match a particular profile. Commonwealth v. Horne, 476 Mass. 222, 227–228 (2017) (testimony that defendant did not fit description of drug addict and so possessed drugs for purposes of distribution is inadmissible). See also Commonwealth v. Coates, 89 Mass. App. Ct. 728, 735 (2016).

Cross-Reference: Section 404(a), Character Evidence; Crimes or Other Acts: Character Evidence.

Certitude of Expert Witness Opinion. In Commonwealth v. Heang, 458 Mass. 827 (2011), the Supreme Judicial Court explained that when an expert witness offers an opinion that is empirically based but subjective in nature, such as whether a cartridge or casing was fired from a particular firearm, it is not permissible for the witness to imply that the opinion has a statistical or mathematical basis. "Phrases that could give the jury an impression of greater certainty, such as 'practical impossibility' and 'absolute certainty' should be avoided. The phrase 'reasonable degree of scientific certainty' should also be avoided because it suggests that forensic ballistics is a science, where it is clearly as much an art as a science." (Citation and footnote omitted.) Id. at 849. In Heang, the Supreme Judicial Court provided the following examples of the degree of certitude that an expert witness may express when the opinion is empirically based but subjective in nature: for firearm or ballistics identification, a "reasonable degree of ballistics certainty," Id. at 848–849; for medical examiner and pathologist opinions, a "reasonable degree of medical certainty," id. at 849, citing Commonwealth v. Nardi, 452 Mass. 379, 383 (2008); Commonwealth v. DelValle, 443 Mass. 782, 788 (2005); for clinical diagnoses, a "reasonable degree of scientific certainty," Commonwealth v. Roberio, 428 Mass. 278, 280 (1998); and for psychological opinions, a "reasonable degree of psychological certainty," Commonwealth v. Wentworth, 53 Mass. App. Ct. 82, 86 (2001). It may also be error for a fingerprint expert to state with absolute certainty that a particular latent print matches a known fingerprint. Commonwealth v. Gambora, 457 Mass. 715, 727–728 (2010). In Heang, the court also noted that there are forensic disciplines that permit expert witness opinion to be expressed to a mathematical or statistical certainty. Commonwealth v. Heang, 458 Mass. at 849, citing Commonwealth v. Mattei, 455 Mass. 840, 850–853 (2010) (because it is possible to say to mathematical degrees of statistical certainty that one DNA profile matches another, test results and opinions regarding DNA profile must be accompanied by testimony explaining likelihood of that match occurring in general population).

Illustrations.

Abused Children. See Commonwealth v. Federico, 425 Mass. 844, 847–848 (1997).

Battered Woman Syndrome. The defendant has a statutory right under G. L. c. 233, § 23F, to present such evidence "where certain specified defenses are asserted." Commonwealth v. Asenjo, 477 Mass. 599, 607–609 (2017) ("Section 23F is more permissive than the common law bases for expert opinions outlined in Mass. G. Evid. § 703.").

Bloodstain Analysis. See Commonwealth v. Vasquez, 462 Mass. 827, 844–846 (2012); Commonwealth v. Powell, 450 Mass. 229, 237–241 (2007).

Breath Test Analysis. See Commonwealth v. Camblin, 478 Mass. 469, 480 (2017).

Capacity to Contract. See Sparrow v. Demonico, 461 Mass. 322, 327–330 (2012).

Cause and Origin of Fire. See Commonwealth v. Rosario, 477 Mass. 69, 80–81 (2017); Commonwealth v. Goodman, 54 Mass. App. Ct. 385, 389–393 (2002).

Computer Simulations. Evidence consisting of computer-generated models or simulations is treated like other scientific tests; admissibility is conditioned "on a sufficient showing that: (1) the computer is functioning properly; (2) the input and underlying equations are sufficiently complete and accurate (and disclosed to the opposing party, so that they may challenge them); and (3) the program is generally accepted by the appropriate community of scientists." Commercial Union Ins. Co. v. Boston Edison Co., 412 Mass. 545, 549–550 (1992).

Contribution of Alcohol to Personal Injury. See Baudanza v. Comcast of Mass. I, Inc., 454 Mass. 622, 631–633 (2009).

Coprophilia (Sexual Fetish). See Commonwealth v. Lawton, 82 Mass. App. Ct. 528, 538–539 (2012).

Development of Adolescent Brain. See Commonwealth v. Okoro, 471 Mass. 51, 66–67 (2015) (expert properly permitted to testify regarding development of adolescent brain and how it might affect a particular juvenile's capacity for impulse control and reasoned decision-making at time in question as it relates to juvenile's ability to form specific intent for murder but may not opine that no juvenile of that age could form specific intent).

Dissociative Memory Loss. See Commonwealth v. Polk, 462 Mass. 23, 32–36 (2012).

Dissociative Trance Disorder. See Commonwealth v. Montanez, 55 Mass. App. Ct. 132, 144–146 (2002).

Distributing Heroin. See Commonwealth v. Miranda, 441 Mass. 783, 792–795 (2004).

DNA. See Commonwealth v. Dixon, 458 Mass. 446, 453 (2010) ("[a] properly generated DNA profile is a string of code that exclusively identifies a person's hereditary composition with near infallibility"); Commonwealth v. Mattei, 455 Mass. 840, 847–852 (2010) (evidence that DNA test failed to exclude defendant "without accompanying evidence that properly interprets that result creates a greater risk of misleading the jury and unfairly prejudicing the defendant than admission of a 'match' without accompanying statistics"). There is a distinction between nonexclusion (the defendant is not excluded as a contributor of the sample) and inconclusive (insufficient sample material, contamination, or some other problem) DNA results. "Evidence that a defendant is not excluded could suggest to the jury that a link would be more firmly established if only more [sample] were available for testing. Such evidence should not [be] admitted without accompanying statistical explanation of the meaning of nonexclusion." Commonwealth v. Cameron, 473 Mass. 100, 106 (2015); Commonwealth v. Lally, 473 Mass. 693, 702–704 (2016). Inconclusive DNA results are not relevant absent a Bowden defense. Commonwealth v. Cameron, 473 Mass. at 107 n.8. See Section 1107, Inadequate Police Investigation Evidence.

Extrapolation. Extrapolation evidence to determine the weight of drugs is permissible, and any objections to its admissibility should be raised by way of pretrial motion. Commonwealth v. Crapps, 84 Mass. App. Ct. 442, 445–449 (2013).

False Confessions. See Commonwealth v. Hoose, 467 Mass. 395, 413–420 (2014).

Field Testing Drugs. See Commonwealth v. Fernandez, 458 Mass. 137, 151 (2010); Commonwealth v. Rodriguez, 92 Mass. App. Ct. 774, 779–780 (2018).

Fingerprints. See Commonwealth v. Patterson, 445 Mass. 626, 641–655 (2005). See also Commonwealth v. Joyner, 467 Mass. 176, 177 (2014) (testimony of fingerprint expert did not violate prohibition against expressing an opinion to a scientific certainty that there was a match). Where a fingerprint is the only identification evidence, the Commonwealth must prove beyond a reasonable doubt that the fingerprint was placed during the commission of the charged crime. Commonwealth v. French, 476 Mass. 1023, 1024–1025 (2017). Unlike DNA evidence, the statistical significance of an opinion about a match is not a foundational requirement, but may affect the weight of the evidence. Commonwealth v. Wadlington, 467 Mass. 192 (2014). Cf. Commonwealth v. Gambora, 457 Mass. 715, 724–725 (2010) (considering report by National Research Council, Strengthening Forensic Science in the United States: A Path Forward 102–104, 136–145 [2009]).

Firearm Identification (Forensic Ballistics). See Commonwealth v. Heang, 458 Mass. 827, 847–848 (2011) (adopting "guidelines" for the admissibility of expert firearm identification testimony that [1] require documentation of the basis of the expert's opinion before trial, which the Commonwealth must disclose to the defense in discovery; [2] require an explanation by the expert to the jury of the theories and methodologies underlying the field of forensic ballistics before offering any opinions; and [3] limit the degree of certitude that the qualified expert may express about whether a particular firearm fired a specific projectile or cartridge to a "reasonable degree of ballistic certainty").

Gang Membership. See Commonwealth v. Barbosa, 477 Mass. 658, 667–669 (2017).

Gunshot Residue. See Commonwealth v. Johnson, 463 Mass. 95, 107–108 (2012); Commonwealth v. Heang, 458 Mass. 827, 851 (2011).

Personality Testing. See Ready, petitioner, 63 Mass. App. Ct. 171, 172–179 (2005).

Posttraumatic Stress Disorder. See Commonwealth v. Anestal, 463 Mass. 655, 658 n.5 (2012); Commonwealth v. Crawford, 429 Mass. 60, 67 (1999).

Retrograde Extrapolation. See Commonwealth v. Senior, 433 Mass. 453, 458–462 (2001). But see Commonwealth v. Dacosta, 85 Mass. App. Ct. 386, 386–388 (2014) (breath test within fifty minutes of arrest permits inference of blood alcohol content above 0.08 percent without need for expert witness testimony).

Sexual Assault Evidence. See Commonwealth v. Scesny, 472 Mass. 185, 194–196 (2015) (testimony regarding what evidence criminologist would expect to have found if victim pulled up her underwear and pants following intercourse).

Sexually Dangerous Persons. See Commonwealth v. George, 477 Mass. 331, 341–342 (2017) (Static-99R risk assessment tool's raw score and risk percentage are admissible; Static-99R risk category labels are inadmissible, as they do not provide sincere, numeric estimates of recidivism risk); Commonwealth v. Ortiz, 93 Mass. App. Ct. 381, 389 (2018) (no abuse of discretion in excluding penile plethysmograph [PPG] examination results on issue of likelihood of sexual reoffense).

Shaken Baby Syndrome. See Commonwealth v. Epps, 474 Mass. 743 (2016); Commonwealth v. Millien, 474 Mass. 417 (2016).

Susceptibility to Suggestiveness. See Commonwealth v. Soares, 51 Mass. App. Ct. 273, 280–282 (2001).

Valuation of Business Interest. In divorce cases, the judge may accept one expert valuation over another or reject expert opinion altogether and arrive at a valuation on other evidence, but he or she may not reach a valuation that varies from the requirements of the equitable distribution statute. G. L. c. 208, § 34. See Adams v. Adams, 459 Mass. 361, 380–381 (2011); Bernier v. Bernier, 449 Mass. 774 (2007).

Valuation of Real Estate. There is no requirement that the person testifying as an expert have sales or practical experience in the locality about which they are testifying. See McLaughlin v. Board of Selectman of Amherst, 422 Mass. 359, 362–363 (1996). A real estate broker or appraiser with "sufficient experience and knowledge of values of other similar real estate in the particular locality" may testify. Lee Lime Corp. v. Massachusetts Turnpike Auth., 337 Mass. 433, 436 (1958). A witness who had "worked as an appraiser" and "was in the process of earning professional designations in the appraisal field" may testify as an expert in real estate. See Lavin v. Lavin, 24 Mass. App. Ct. 929, 931 (1987). An expert witness may use the depreciated reproduction cost method to form an opinion as to the value of real estate when the judge finds that there is a justification for the use of this disfavored approach. Correia v. New Bedford Redev. Auth., 375 Mass. 360, 362–367 (1978).

For examples of cases applying this section, see M.S. Brodin & M. Avery, Massachusetts Evidence §§ 7.4–7.6 (2018 ed.); 2 M.G. Perlin & D. Cooper, Proof of Cases in Massachusetts §§ 71:1–71:23 (2017–2018 ed.); and W.G. Young, J.R. Pollets, & C. Poreda, Annotated Guide to Massachusetts Evidence § 702 (2017–2018 ed.).

Jury Instructions. See Commonwealth v. Hinds, 450 Mass. 1, 12 n.7 (2007).

Cross–Reference: Section 703, Bases of Opinion Testimony by Experts.

Section 703.   Bases of Opinion Testimony by Experts

The facts or data in the particular case upon which an expert witness bases an opinion or inference may be those perceived by or made known to the witness at or before the hearing. These include (a) facts observed by the witness or otherwise in the witness's direct personal knowledge; (b) evidence already in the record or that will be presented during the course of the proceedings, which facts may be assumed to be true in questions put to the witness; and (c) facts or data not in evidence if the facts or data are independently admissible in evidence and are a permissible basis for an expert to consider in formulating an opinion.

NOTE

This section is derived from Department of Youth Servs. v. A Juvenile, 398 Mass. 516, 531 (1986); LaClair v. Silberline Mfg. Co., 379 Mass. 21, 32 (1979); and Commonwealth v. Russ, 232 Mass. 58, 73 (1919). See Commonwealth v. Piantedosi, 478 Mass. 536, 541–546 (2017). Massachusetts has not fully adopted Fed. R. Evid. 703, or Proposed Mass. R. Evid. 703, which would permit opinions based on inadmissible evidence if it is of a type reasonably relied upon by experts in the relevant field.

"When an expert provides the jury with an opinion regarding the facts of the case, that opinion must rest on a proper basis, else inadmissible evidence might enter in the guise of expert opinion. The expert must have knowledge of the particular facts from firsthand observation, or from a proper hypothetical question posed by counsel, or from unadmitted evidence that would nevertheless be admissible."

Commonwealth v. Waite, 422 Mass. 792, 803 (1996). See id. at 803–804 (psychologist called by the defense in a murder trial could opine on the defendant's mental impairment at the time of the offense based on the witness's interview with the defendant five weeks after the killings,

and the contents of police and medical records, but not on the basis of a psychiatrist's earlier "preliminary diagnosis" that was not shown to be reliable and independently admissible). Accord Vassallo v. Baxter Healthcare Corp., 428 Mass. 1, 15–16 (1998) ("The judge properly prevented the defendants' experts [as well as the plaintiffs' experts] from testifying on direct examination to the out-of-court opinions of other scientists in the absence of some specific exception to the hearsay rule [none was shown]."). But see Commonwealth v. Asenjo, 477 Mass. 599, 607–609 (2017) (error to exclude expert testimony regarding battered woman syndrome where G. L. c. 233, § 23F, provides independent statutory basis for admission of evidence, as statute is more permissive than common law embodied in Section 703 and permits expert testimony based solely on defendant's assertion of certain specified defenses).

Regarding Section 703(b), unless the evidence is capable of only one interpretation, the question to the expert witness must refer to specific portions of the record. See Connor v. O'Donnell, 230 Mass. 39, 42 (1918).

Regarding Section 703(c), in determining whether facts or data are independently admissible, it is not whether the forms in which such facts or data exist satisfy evidentiary requirements. Rather, the court will determine whether the underlying facts or data would potentially be admissible through appropriate witnesses. Such witnesses need not be immediately available in court to testify. See Commonwealth v. Markvart, 437 Mass. 331, 337–338 (2002), citing Department of Youth Servs. v. A Juvenile, 398 Mass. at 531. But see Custody of Michel, 28 Mass. App. Ct. 260, 267 (1990) (applying G. L. c. 119, § 24).

On direct examination, the expert witness may testify to the basis of his or her opinion regarding (1) facts within the witness's personal knowledge; (2) facts in evidence; or (3) with approval of the court, facts that a party will put in evidence. However, "it is settled that an expert witness may not, under the guise of stating the reasons for his opinion, testify to matters of hearsay in the course of his direct examination unless such matters are admissible under some statutory or other recognized exception to the hearsay rule." Commonwealth v. Nardi, 452 Mass. 379, 392 (2008), quoting Grant v. Lewis/Boyle, Inc., 408 Mass. 269, 273 (1990), quoting Kelly Realty Co. v. Commonwealth, 3 Mass. App. Ct. 54, 55–56 (1975). The limitation on the direct-examination testimony of expert witnesses operates in both civil and criminal cases and applies to both sides. Commonwealth v. Chappell, 473 Mass. 191, 204 (2015) (this evidentiary rule does not violate defendant's right to present a full defense). On cross-examination, the defendant may choose to elicit the underlying facts or data, thereby waiving his or her rights under the confrontation clause. Commonwealth v. Barbosa, 457 Mass. 773, 785 (2010).

Cross–Reference: Section 705, Disclosure of Facts or Data Underlying Expert Opinion.

Limitation on Cross–Examination. On cross-examination of an expert, a judge may exclude evidence as unfairly prejudicial, see Section 403, even if the expert is aware of those facts, if the facts were not relied upon as part of the expert's opinion, do not clarify or discredit the opinion, and serve only to focus the jury on those facts. Commonwealth v. Anestal, 463 Mass. 655, 667–668 (2012) (prior bad acts excluded).

Risk of Inaccurate Forensic Analysis. In Commonwealth v. Barbosa, 457 Mass. 773 (2010), the Supreme Judicial Court addressed the risk of inaccurate forensic analysis as follows:

"Our common-law rules of evidence protect a defendant in various ways from the risk of inaccurate forensic analysis. Where there is reason to believe that evidence has been mislabeled or mishandled or that data have been fabricated or manipulated, a defendant may challenge the admissibility of an expert opinion relying on such evidence or data in a Daubert–Lanigan hearing, because an opinion must rest on evidence or data that provide 'a permissible basis' for an expert to formulate an opinion. A defendant may also challenge the admissibility of an opinion where an expert relies solely on the conclusions of the testing analyst, without knowledge of the procedures employed by the testing analyst or the underlying data and evidence that are generally contained in worksheets, because a conclusory opinion alone may not be a permissible basis on which an expert may rest an opinion. Where an expert opinion survives a Daubert–Lanigan challenge or where ... the defendant does not challenge the admissibility of the expert's opinion, the defendant may still ... cross-examine the testifying expert as to the risk of evidence being mishandled or mislabeled or of data being fabricated or manipulated, and as to whether the expert's opinion is vulnerable to these risks." (Citations omitted.)

Id. at 790–791.

Substituted Experts.

Meaningful Opportunity to Cross–Examine. The Massachusetts common law of evidence is more protective of confrontation rights than the Sixth Amendment to the United States Constitution in that it requires that the defendant have "a meaningful opportunity to cross-examine the expert about her opinion and the reliability of the facts or data that underlie her opinion." Commonwealth v. Tassone, 468 Mass. 391, 399–402 (2014). In Tassone, the Supreme Judicial Court explained that, where an expert opines on the cause of death in a homicide case, "a defendant will generally have a meaningful opportunity to cross-examine the expert witness regarding possible flaws in the opinion based on the underlying autopsy report and notes, and photographs taken during the autopsy," regardless of whether the witness performed the autopsy or is a substitute expert. Id. at 400. However, "where a DNA expert offers an opinion regarding a DNA match, a meaningful opportunity for cross-examination means that a defendant must have the opportunity substantively to explore the 'risk of evidence being mishandled or mislabeled, or of data being fabricated or manipulated, and ... whether the expert's opinion is vulnerable to these risks.'" Id. at 400, quoting Commonwealth v. Barbosa, 457 Mass. 773, 790 (2010). Thus, in Tassone, the court held that, where the substitute DNA analyst was not affiliated with the laboratory where the DNA testing was conducted and there was no showing that she had any personal knowledge of that lab's evidence-handling protocols, the defendant was denied the opportunity to explore through cross-examination whether the testing was flawed. The court distinguished Commonwealth v. Greineder, 464 Mass. 580 (2013), where the substitute DNA expert was the forensic laboratory director of the facility where the DNA testing was conducted and was personally aware of the DNA testing process employed by the laboratory. Compare Commonwealth v. Sanchez, 476 Mass. 725, 734 (2017) (fire inspector who was present for electrician's inspection of arson site could testify and be meaningfully cross-examined about his own observations), with Commonwealth v. Jones, 472 Mass. 707, 715–716 (2015) (where DNA expert's knowledge of how DNA samples had been collected was derived from form completed by person who had collected the specimens from victim's body, no meaningful opportunity to cross-examine witness).

DNA Analyst. Where the prosecution offers an opinion about a DNA profile match without calling the DNA analyst who conducted the testing of the crime scene DNA, the prosecution must, at a minimum, call an expert affiliated with the laboratory where the testing took place. Commonwealth v. Tassone, 468 Mass. 391, 402 (2014). Where the testifying expert has personal knowledge of the testing laboratory's procedures, the witness may give an opinion about a DNA match, even though the basis is in whole or in part evidence collected or created by an absent DNA analyst. See Commonwealth v. Greineder, 464 Mass. 580, 583–584 (2013). However, an expert who has no knowledge of how the sample was collected cannot testify to the location from which the sample was collected. Commonwealth v. Jones, 472 Mass. 707, 716–717 n.3 (2015) (no meaningful opportunity to cross-examine testifying DNA expert about how specimen was collected).

Medical Examiner. A substitute medical examiner may not testify to the observations, findings, or opinions made by an absent medical examiner. In accordance with Section 705, a medical examiner may testify to his or her opinion even though the basis is in whole or in part evidence collected or created by the absent medical examiner. See Commonwealth v. Seino, 479 Mass. 463, 466–468 (2018) (substitute medical examiner may offer opinion as to cause of death based upon review of independently admissible documents contained in original medical examiner's file); Commonwealth v. Nardi, 452 Mass. 379, 388 (2008). See Commonwealth v. Tassone, 468 Mass. 391, 402 (2014) (autopsy report, notes, and photo-graphs provide defendant with "meaningful basis" to cross-examine substitute witness about possible flaws in his or her opinion). The Commonwealth is not required to show that the medical examiner who performed an autopsy is unavailable for a substitute medical examiner to testify. Commonwealth v. Reavis, 465 Mass. 875, 881–882 (2013). See also Commonwealth v. Williams, 475 Mass. 705, 719 (2016).

Cross–Reference: Section 702, Testimony by Expert Witnesses; Section 705, Disclosure of Facts or Data Underlying Expert Opinion; Introductory Note to Article VIII, Hearsay.

Section 704.   Opinion on Ultimate Issue

An opinion is not objectionable just because it embraces an ultimate issue.

NOTE

This section is derived from Proposed Mass. R. Evid. 704; Commonwealth v. Woods, 419 Mass. 366, 374–375 (1995); and Simon v. Solomon, 385 Mass. 91, 105 (1982). The critical question is not whether the opinion touches on the ultimate issue, but whether it satisfies Sections 403, Excluding Relevant Evidence for Prejudice, Confusion, Waste of Time, or Other Reasons; 701, Opinion Testimony by Lay Witnesses; 702, Testimony by Expert Witnesses; and any other applicable sections. See Commonwealth v. Goddard, 476 Mass. 443, 446–447 (2017); Commonwealth v. Canty, 466 Mass. 535, 543 (2013); Martel v. Massachusetts Bay Transp. Auth., 403 Mass. 1, 3–4 (1988); Commonwealth v. LaCorte, 373 Mass. 700, 705 (1977); Commonwealth v. Almeida, 34 Mass. App. Ct. 901, 902–903 (1993); Commonwealth v. Lopes, 25 Mass. App. Ct. 988, 990 (1988), citing Commonwealth v. Sendele, 18 Mass. App. Ct. 755, 760 (1984). Accord M.S. Brodin & M. Avery, Massachusetts Evidence § 7.3.2 (2018 ed.).

At least four different, but related, reasons are given for the exclusion of opinion evidence on an ultimate issue. First, such opinions offer no assistance to the fact finders "because the jury are capable of making that assessment without an expert's aid." Commonwealth v. Colin C., 419 Mass. 54, 60 (1994). See Commonwealth v. Andujar, 57 Mass. App. Ct. 529, 531 (2003). Second, "[o]n such questions, the influence of an expert's opinion may threaten the independence of the jury's decision." Simon v. Solomon, 385 Mass. 91, 105 (1982). Third, such questions call for opinions on matters of law or mixed questions of law and fact, and the jury must be allowed to draw their own conclusions from the evidence. See Commonwealth v. Hesketh, 386 Mass. 153, 161–162 (1982). Fourth, expert opinion in the form of conclusions about the credibility of a witness or a party are beyond the scope of the witness's expertise and in the realm of speculation and conjecture. See Commonwealth v. Gardner, 350 Mass. 664, 666 (1966).

Improper Vouching. Expert witness testimony which simply amounts to an opinion on the credibility of a witness is inadmissible as improper vouching; credibility is an issue reserved for the jury that does not re-quire the assistance of an expert. This issue commonly arises in sexual abuse cases, in which an expert witness may testify to general characteristics to assist the jury's understanding, but may not compare the alleged victim to those characteristics. Commonwealth v. Richardson, 423 Mass. 180, 185–186 (1996), quoting Commonwealth v. Trowbridge, 419 Mass. 750, 759 (1995) ("[a]lthough expert testimony on the general behavioral characteristics of sexually abused children is permissible, an expert may not refer or compare the child to those general characteristics"). See Commonwealth v. Jewett, 442 Mass.

356, 368 (2004) ("in the absence of special circumstances, an expert may not be asked whether a rape or sexual assault has occurred"). Testimony about profiling is generally inadmissible. Commonwealth v. Coates, 89 Mass. App. Ct. 728, 733–737 (2016) (trial judge properly excluded criminal-profile testimony that defendant did not fit profile of pedophile); Commonwealth v. Aspen, 85 Mass. App. Ct. 278, 282–284 (2014), citing Commonwealth v. Federico, 425 Mass. 844, 849 (1997) (conviction reversed where expert gave profile testimony relating to intrafamilial sexual abuse that closely resembled complainant's family makeup and dynamic).

Testimony by an expert who has also treated the victim must be carefully scrutinized to avoid the implication that the expert's contact with the victim gives the expert special knowledge about credibility. See Commonwealth v. Quinn, 469 Mass. 641, 646 (2014) (risk of improper vouching was "especially acute" because expert witness had treated victim for months); Commonwealth v. Trowbridge, 419 at 759–760. The rule against vouching does not prohibit an expert from explaining physical findings or characteristics and their significance, See, e.g., Commonwealth v. Alvarez, 480 Mass. 299, 314 (2018) (general statements by treating physician that it is "very uncommon" to find physical genital injury in sexual abuse victim and that "absence of physical trauma is not inconsistent with abuse" do not constitute implicit vouching). Cf. Commonwealth v. Burgess, 450 Mass. 422, 436 (2008) ("the prosecutor [improperly] asked [the Commonwealth's expert] to comment on the credibility of the Commonwealth's theory of the case by asking whether its theory was 'consistent' with [the expert's] observations").

Illustrations. For examples of cases applying this section, see M.S. Brodin & M. Avery, Massachusetts Evidence § 7.3 (2018 ed.), and 2 M.G. Perlin & D. Cooper, Proof of Cases in Massachusetts § 71.4 (2017–2018 ed.).

Operating Under the Influence Cases. In Commonwealth v. Canty, 466 Mass. 535, 541 (2013), the court explained that the limitation on testimony that amounts to an opinion as to guilt or innocence applies to the lay witness as well as to the expert witness. Cross-Reference: Section 701, Opinion Testimony by Lay Witnesses.

Opinions About the Law Versus the Facts. Legal questions, as to which testimony is not permitted, should be distinguished from factual conclusions, as to which testimony is proper. The line between a "conclusion of law" and an "ultimate factual issue" is sometimes blurred. Commonwealth v. Little, 453 Mass. 766, 769 (2009) ("Narcotics investigators may testify as experts to describe how drug transactions occur on the street . . . [such as] testimony on the use of lookouts in drug transactions, and the significance of the purity of seized drugs. We have also repeatedly held that there is no error in allowing a police detective to testify that in his opinion the amount of drugs possessed by the defendant was not consistent with personal use but was consistent with an intent to distribute." [Citations and quotations omitted.]). See Commonwealth v. Roderiques, 78 Mass. App. Ct. 515, 522 (2010) (pediatrician allowed to testify that baby's injuries were not accidental); Puopolo v. Honda Motor Co., 41 Mass. App. Ct. 96, 99 (1996) (expert should have been permitted to testify that vehicle was unreasonably dangerous even though special question given to jury was framed in nearly identical language). Cf. Commonwealth v. Brady, 370 Mass. 630, 635 (1976) (insurance agent may not testify to applicability of insurance coverage); Perry v. Medeiros, 369 Mass. 836, 842 (1976) (building inspector cannot give opinion interpreting building code); Commonwealth v. Coleman, 366 Mass. 705, 711 (1975) (medical examiner not permitted to testify that death was "homicide"); DeCanio v. School Comm. of Boston, 358 Mass. 116, 125–126 (1970) (expert could not testify that "suspension and dismissal of probationary teachers without a hearing 'would have no legitimate educational purpose'"); Commonwealth v. Gardner, 350 Mass. 664, 666–667 (1966) (doctor in rape prosecution cannot testify to "forcible entry"); S.D. Shaw & Sons v. Joseph Rugo, Inc., 343 Mass. 635, 639 (1962) (witness may not give opinion as to whether certain work was included in contract specification); Commonwealth v. Ross, 339 Mass. 428, 435 (1959) (guilt); Foley

v. Hotel Touraine Co., 326 Mass. 742, 745 (1951) (treasurer of corporation could not testify on question whether assistant manager had "ostensible authority" on day of accident); Silva v. Norfolk & Dedham Mut. Fire Ins. Co., 91 Mass. App. Ct. 413, 420 (2017) (testimony in action brought under G. L. c. 176D that insurer's action was "unfair and deceptive" properly excluded). But see Ford v. Boston Hous. Auth., 55 Mass. App. Ct. 623, 626 (2002) (expert testimony explaining requirements of complicated code was not per se inadmissible; judge had discretion to admit expert opinion of building inspector that "if the door was locked at the time of the accident . . . that would have been noncompliance with the State building code").

Section 705. Disclosure of Facts or Data Underlying Expert Opinion

Unless the court orders otherwise, an expert may state an opinion—and give the reasons for it—without first testifying to the underlying facts or data. But the expert may be required to disclose those facts or data on cross-examination.

NOTE

This section is taken from Proposed Mass. R. Evid. 705, which the Supreme Judicial Court adopted in Department of Youth Servs. v. A Juvenile, 398 Mass. 516, 532 (1986).

"The rule is aimed principally at the abuse of the hypothetical question. It does not eliminate the availability of the hypothetical question, but only the requirement of its use . . . The thrust of the rule is to leave inquiry regarding the basis of expert testimony to cross-examination, which is considered an adequate safeguard."

Id., quoting Advisory Committee's Note on Proposed Mass. R. Evid. 705. Under Massachusetts law, for purposes of direct examination, there is a "distinction between an expert's opinion on the one hand and the hearsay information that formed the basis of the opinion on the other, holding the former admissible and the latter inadmissible." Commonwealth v. Greineder, 464 Mass. 580, 584 (2013). However, on cross-examination, the opposing party may choose to elicit the hearsay basis for an opinion offered on direct examination. See Commonwealth v. Nardi, 452 Mass. 379, 387–395 (2008). In Commonwealth v. Barbosa, 457 Mass. 773, 785–787 (2010), the Supreme Judicial Court stated the direct examination of an expert on facts not in evidence

"is limited to the expert's opinion and matters of which the expert had personal knowledge, such as her training and experience, and the protocols generally accepted in her field of expertise. Only the defendant can open the door on cross-examination to testimony regarding the basis for the expert's opinion, which may invite the expert witness to testify to facts or data that may be admissible in evidence but have not yet been admitted in evidence."

Accord Commonwealth v. Leng, 463 Mass. 779, 783–785 (2012); Commonwealth v. Nardi, 452 Mass. 379, 387–395 (2008).

Cross–Reference: Introductory Note to Article VIII, Hearsay.

Limitation on Cross–Examination. Under certain circumstances, the requirement that the expert disclose underlying facts or data on cross-examination may be limited by Section 403 considerations. See Commonwealth v. Anestal, 463 Mass. 655, 668–669 (2012). In Anestal, the court held that

"[o]nce the Commonwealth sought to inquire over objection about this prior bad act evidence, it was incumbent on the judge in the sound exercise of his discretion to ascertain whether the evidence was probative and, if so, whether that probative value was substantially outweighed by the danger of unfair prejudice to the defendant."

Id. at 669. This inquiry should take place at sidebar, or the judge should conduct a voir dire. Id. at 669 n.20.

Section 706. Court–Appointed Experts

(a) Appointment. If legally permissible, the court, on its own or at the request of a party, may appoint an expert. Unless mandated by law to accept the assignment, the expert shall have the right to refuse such appointment. The court, after providing an opportunity to the parties to participate, shall inform the expert of his or her duties. The expert may be required to testify.

(b) Compensation. Expert witnesses so appointed are entitled to reasonable compensation, as set by the court, unless controlled by statute or rule. Except as otherwise provided by law, the compensation shall be paid by the parties in such proportion and at such time as the court directs, and thereafter charged in like manner as other costs.

(c) Disclosure of Appointment. The fact that the court appointed the expert witness shall not be disclosed to the jury.

(d) Parties' Choice of Their Own Experts. This section does not limit a party in calling its own experts.

NOTE

This section is derived from Commonwealth v. O'Brien, 423 Mass. 841, 855 n.24 (1996); Fed. R. Evid. 706; and Proposed Mass. R. Evid. 706, and reflects the Massachusetts practice of making widespread use of court-appointed experts. See, e.g., G. L. c. 119, §§ 21, 24 (court-appointed expert to assist in determination of cases involving children in need of services); G. L. c. 123, § 15(a)–(c) (court-appointed expert to assess criminal defendant's competency to stand trial or criminal responsibility); G. L. c. 123, § 15(e) (court-appointed expert to render opinion to assist court in sentencing defendant); G. L. c. 190B, § 5–303(e) (court-appointed expert to assess mental health of a person who may be in need of guardianship); G. L. c. 215, § 56A (guardian ad litem to investigate facts for the Probate and Family Court relating to care, custody, and maintenance of children); Brodie v. Jordan, 447 Mass. 866, 867 (2006) (expert witness appointed by court to render opinion on the value of corporation's net assets); Commonwealth v. Berry, 420 Mass. 95, 103 (1995) (judge warranted in relying upon opinion of court-appointed expert); Commonwealth v. Aponte, 391 Mass. 494, 497–498 (1984) (court-appointed expert in statistical analysis in social sciences to assist in resolution of challenge to method of grand jury selection in Essex County); Gilmore v. Gilmore, 369 Mass. 598, 604–605 (1976) (use of court-appointed guardian ad litem for investigation in child custody cases); Munshani v. Signal Lake Venture Fund II, LP, 60 Mass. App. Ct. 714, 717 (2004) (court-appointed expert to assess authenticity of an electronic communication).

Failure to seek funds to consult or retain an expert where there is new scientific research and the science is evolving, which could provide a substantial ground of defense, may constitute ineffective assistance of counsel. Commonwealth v. Millien, 474 Mass. 417 (2016) (failure to consult or call expert on shaken baby syndrome).

ARTICLE VIII.   HEARSAY

Introductory Note

(a) Confrontation Clause and Hearsay in Criminal Cases. In considering the following sections, it is necessary to recognize the distinction between hearsay rules and the requirements of the confrontation clause of the Sixth Amendment to the Constitution of the United States and Article 12 of the Declaration of Rights. Even if an out-of-court statement would be admissible for its truth under the hearsay rule, it must still satisfy the requirements of the confrontation clause and Article 12. Other than situations dealing with the defendant's right to physically confront child witnesses, see Subsection (c) below, Article 12 provides no greater protections with respect to the admissibility of hearsay than does the confrontation clause. Commonwealth v. DeOliveira, 447 Mass. 56, 57 n.1 (2006), citing Commonwealth v. Whelton, 428 Mass. 24, 28 (1998), and Commonwealth v. Childs, 413 Mass. 252, 260 (1992).

In Crawford v. Washington, 541 U.S. 36, 54 (2004), the United States Supreme Court explained that the Sixth Amendment expressed the common-law right of the defendant in a criminal case to confrontation, and that it was subject only to those exceptions that existed at the time of the amendment's framing in 1791. As a result, the Supreme Court held that "testimonial statements" of a witness for the government in a criminal case who is not present at trial and subject to cross-examination are not admissible unless the witness is unavailable and the defendant had a prior opportunity to cross-examine the witness. Id. at 53–54. Accord Commonwealth v. Gonsalves, 445 Mass. 1, 14 (2005), cert. denied, 548 U.S. 926 (2006) ("constitutional provision of the confrontation clause trumps [our own] rules of evidence"). In Commonwealth v. Lao, 450 Mass. 215, 223 (2007), the Supreme Judicial Court held that "the protection provided by art. 12 is coextensive with the guarantees of the Sixth Amendment to the United States Constitution."

The Supreme Judicial Court has expressed the following analytical approach to determine whether out-of-court statements constitute admissible evidence:

"When the Commonwealth offers an out-of-court statement in a criminal case, the evidentiary and potential confrontation clause issues can prove challenging. The following conceptual approach may be helpful: First, is the out-of-court statement being offered to establish the truth of the words contained in the statement? In other words, is the out-of-court statement hearsay? If the out-of-court statement is offered for any purpose other than its truth, then it is not hearsay and the confrontation clause is not implicated. Second, if the evidence is hearsay, does the statement fall within an exception to the rule against hearsay? Third, if the hearsay falls within an exception, is the hearsay 'testimonial'? Fourth, if the hearsay is testimonial, has the out-of-court declarant been previously subject to cross-examination and is the out-of-court declarant 'unavailable' as a matter of law, such that the testimonial hearsay does not offend the confrontation clause?"

Commonwealth v. Caruso, 476 Mass. 275, 295 n.15 (2017).

(1) Testimonial Versus Nontestimonial; the Primary Purpose Test. The United States Supreme Court and the Supreme Judicial Court use the primary purpose test to determine whether a statement is testimonial or nontestimonial. See Michigan v. Bryant, 562 U.S. 344 (2011); Davis v. Washington, 547 U.S. 813 (2006); Commonwealth v. Celester, 473 Mass. 553, 562–563 (2016); Commonwealth v. Beatrice, 460 Mass. 255 (2011); Commonwealth v. Smith, 460 Mass. 385 (2011); Commonwealth v. Wilson, 94 Mass. App.

Ct. 416, 425–428 (2018); Commonwealth v. Rodriguez, 90 Mass. App. Ct. 315, 321 (2016). The primary purpose test's key analysis is whether the statement is procured with the primary purpose of creating an out-of-court substitute for trial testimony. Commonwealth v. Beatrice, 460 Mass. at 260–262 (holding that statements are testimonial when "the primary purpose . . . is to establish or prove past events potentially relevant to later criminal prosecution"). The primary purpose test is objective, and "the relevant inquiry into the parties' statements and actions is not the subjective or actual purpose of the particular parties, but the purpose that reasonable participants would have had, as ascertained from the parties' statements and actions and the circumstances in which the encounter occurred." Michigan v. Bryant, 562 U.S. at 360. See Commonwealth v. Cole, 473 Mass. 317, 329–330 (2015) (computer software used to calculate the statistical probability of a DNA match was not testimonial, as program's creator would not anticipate that the probability statistics would be used to prosecute this particular defendant). See also Commonwealth v. Smith, 460 Mass. at 394 ("[T]he 'primary purpose' inquiry [is] objective. The parties' subjective motives or intentions are largely irrelevant."). The United States Supreme Court has noted that under the primary purpose test, "[s]tatements by very young children will rarely, if ever, implicate the Confrontation Clause." Ohio v. Clark, 135 S. Ct. 2173, 2182 (2015). The following factors are relevant to an analysis under the primary purpose test.

(A) *Whether an Emergency Exists.* In Davis v. Washington, 547 U.S. 813, 822 (2006), the United States Supreme Court held as follows:

"Statements are nontestimonial when made in the course of police interrogation under circumstances objectively indicating that the primary purpose of the interrogation is to enable police assistance to meet an ongoing emergency. They are testimonial when the circumstances objectively indicate that there is no such ongoing emergency, and that the primary purpose of the interrogation is to establish or prove past events potentially relevant to later criminal prosecution."

In Michigan v. Bryant, 562 U.S. 344, 363–366 (2011), the Supreme Court held that "whether an emergency exists and is ongoing is a highly context-dependent inquiry" and explained that "'a conversation which begins as an interrogation to determine the need for emergency assistance' can 'evolve into testimonial statements,'" and "[a] conversation that begins with a prosecutorial purpose may nevertheless devolve into nontestimonial statements if an unexpected emergency arises."

In Commonwealth v. Beatrice, 460 Mass. 255, 259–260 (2011), and Commonwealth v. Smith, 460 Mass. 385, 392–393 (2011), both decided after Michigan v. Bryant, the Supreme Judicial Court identified a nonexhaustive list of factors relevant to determining whether an ongoing emergency exists at the time a declarant makes statements to a law enforcement agent:

- whether an armed assailant poses a substantial threat to the public at large, the victim, or the responding officers;

- the type of weapon that has been employed;

- the severity of the victim's injuries;

- the formality of the interrogation;

- the involved parties' statements and actions; and

- whether the victim's safety is at substantial imminent risk.

See Commonwealth v. Beatrice, 460 Mass. at 260–262; Commonwealth v. Smith, 460 Mass. at 393–394. See also Commonwealth v. Middlemiss, 465 Mass. 627, 635–636 (2013) (applying Beatrice factors to statements shooting victim made to 911 operator).

In Michigan v. Bryant, 562 U.S. 344, 366 (2011), the Supreme Court additionally explained that "whether an ongoing emergency exists is simply one factor—[although] an important factor—that informs the ultimate inquiry regarding the 'primary purpose' of an interrogation." "[T]here may be other circumstances, aside from ongoing emergencies, when a statement is not procured with a primary purpose of creating an out-of-court substitute for trial testimony." Id. at 358.

(B) *The Formality of the Statements and the Actions of the Parties Involved.* The formality of an interrogation is an important factor for determining whether a statement was procured with a primary purpose of creating an out-of-court substitute for trial testimony. Michigan v. Bryant, 562 U.S. at 367. In Michigan v. Bryant, 562 U.S. 344 (2011), the United States Supreme Court held that questioning that occurred in an exposed, public area, prior to the arrival of emergency medical services (when the declarant had been shot in the abdomen and the armed assailant was still at large), and in a disorganized fashion, was informal and "distinguishable from [a] formal station-house interrogation." Id. at 366.

The statements of a declarant and the actions of both the declarant and interrogators also provide objective evidence of the interrogation's primary purpose. Id. at 367. The Supreme Court explained that looking to the content of both the questions and the answers is an important factor in the primary purpose test because both interrogators and declarants may have mixed motives. Id. Police officers' dual responsibilities as both first responders and criminal investigators may lead them to act with different motives simultaneously or in quick succession. Id. Likewise, during an ongoing emergency, victims may make statements they think will help end the threat to their safety but may not envision these statements being used for prosecution. Id. Alternatively, a severely injured victim may lack the ability to have any purpose at all in answering questions. Id. The inquiry is still objective, however, and it focuses on the understanding and purpose of a reasonable victim in the actual victim's circumstances, which prominently include the victim's physical state. Id.

(C) *Whether the Statements Were Made to Non-Law Enforcement Personnel.* In Ohio v. Clark, 135 S. Ct. 2173 (2015), the United States Supreme Court concluded that statements made to non-law enforcement personnel "are much less likely to be testimonial than statements to law enforcement officers." Id. at 2181. The Supreme Judicial Court, by comparison, has stated that although "out-of-court statements made in response to questions from people who are not law enforcement agents" are not "per se testimonial," they are "testimonial in fact" if "a reasonable person in the declarant's position would anticipate the statement's being used against the accused in investigating and prosecuting a crime." Commonwealth v. Gonsalves, 445 Mass. 1, 11–13 (2005), cert. denied, 548 U.S. 926 (2006). See Commonwealth v. Celester, 473 Mass. 553, 563 (2016) (shooting victim's response to bystander's question, "Who shot you?" was not testimonial in fact because of gravity of victim's injuries and immediate threat they posed to him).

"[W]here statements contained in hospital medical records demonstrate, on their face, that they were included for the purpose of medical treatment, that evident purpose renders the statements both nontestimonial as to the author of the record, and as falling within the scope of [G. L. c. 233,] § 79." Commonwealth v. Irene, 462 Mass. 600, 618 (2012).

(2) Records Admitted Without Live Testimony. Many cases since Crawford v. Washington, 541 U.S. 36 (2004), have challenged the admissibility of certificates attested to by nontestifying experts. In Melendez–Diaz v. Massachusetts, 557 U.S. 305 (2009), the United States Supreme Court held that the reasoning of Crawford applied to certain certificates of analysis that had been frequently introduced in criminal trials to establish that a substance was a "controlled substance" under G. L. c. 94C. The Supreme Court held that a drug certificate in the form of an affidavit by the analyst was a testimonial statement because it was prepared with the knowledge that it would be used at trial, and thus its admission in evidence over the defendant's objection violated the confrontation clause of the Sixth Amendment because the technician or scientist who made the findings set forth in the certificate was not made available for questioning by the defense. As a result, the United States Supreme Court reversed the decision of the Appeals Court in Commonwealth v. Melendez–Diaz, 69 Mass. App. Ct. 1114 (2007) (unpublished), and effectively overruled the decision of the Supreme Judicial Court in Commonwealth v. Verde, 444 Mass. 279, 283–285 (2005). Analytical certificates made under oath by chemists or ballisticians that a substance is a drug, is of a specific weight, or both, or that a thing is a working firearm, "are functionally identical to live, in-court testimony, doing 'precisely what a witness does on direct examination'" (emphasis deleted). Melendez–Diaz v. Massachusetts, 557 U.S. at 310–311, quoting Davis v. Washington, 547 U.S. 813, 830 (2006). See also Commonwealth v. Brown, 75 Mass. App. Ct. 361, 363 (2009) (applying Melendez–Diaz holding to ballistics certificate).

In Melendez–Diaz v. Massachusetts, 557 U.S. 305, 306–309 (2009), the Supreme Court explicitly rejected the idea that an analyst's testimony was the only way to prove the chemical composition of a substance. In Commonwealth v. MacDonald, 459 Mass. 148 (2011), the Supreme Judicial Court stated as follows:

"Melendez–Diaz stands for the proposition that if a certificate of drug analysis is used, it must be accompanied by the testimony of an analyst so that the defendant's right to confrontation is preserved. However, nowhere does the decision state that where . . . a prosecutor

uses the opinion testimony of an expert to establish the composition of a drug, that testimony requires corroboration . . . A prosecutor's decision to proceed without a certificate of drug analysis does not violate the holding in Melendez–Diaz."

Id. at 155–156.

In Commonwealth v. Zeininger, 459 Mass. 775 (2011), the Supreme Judicial Court held that statements contained in an annual certification and accompanying diagnostic records, attesting to the proper functioning of a breath-testing machine used to test the defendant's blood alcohol content, were not testimonial, and that the defendant's confrontation rights were not violated by the admission of the certification and records without the live testimony of the technician who had performed the certification test on the machine. Id. at 788–789. The critical distinction that "ma[de] all the difference" was that the certificate of analysis in Melendez–Diaz resembled "the type of 'ex parte in-court testimony or its functional equivalent' at the nucleus of the confrontation clause" because it was particularized and performed in aid of a prosecution seeking to prove the commission of a past act, while the Office of Alcohol Testing certification records were generalized and performed prospectively in primary aid of the administration of a regulatory program. Id., quoting Crawford v. Washington, 541 U.S. 36, 51–52 (2004).

In Bullcoming v. New Mexico, 564 U.S. 647 (2011), the United States Supreme Court decided five to four that a blood alcohol analysis report, which certified that the defendant's blood alcohol concentration was well above the threshold for aggravated driving while intoxicated under New Mexico law, and which was introduced at trial through the testimony of an analyst who had not performed the certification, was testimonial within the meaning of the confrontation clause. The Supreme Court found that the laboratory report in Bullcoming resembled those in Melendez–Diaz "[i]n all material respects." Id. at 664.

In Commonwealth v. Parenteau, 460 Mass. 1 (2011), the Commonwealth introduced in evidence a certificate from the Registry of Motor Vehicles attesting that a notice of license suspension or revocation was mailed to the defendant; the Commonwealth did not present any testimony from a witness on behalf of the registry. The Supreme Judicial Court held that the certificate was testimonial in nature and that its admission without testimony from the preparers violated the confrontation clause. Id. at 8–9. The court explained that one "must examine carefully the purpose for which [a document is] created" when "determining the admissibility of a particular business record." Id. at 10. In Parenteau, the business record was created two months after the criminal complaint was issued and therefore was "plainly" created to establish an element of the statutory offense at trial. Id. at 8. Importantly, the court noted that "[i]f such a record had been created at the time the notice was mailed and preserved by the registry as part of the administration of its regular business affairs, then it would have been admissible at trial." Id. at 10. See also Commonwealth v. Ellis, 79 Mass. App. Ct. 330 (2011).

The admission of a properly completed and returned G. L. c. 209A return of service absent the testimony of the officer who completed it does not violate a defendant's confrontation clause rights. Commonwealth v. Shangkuan, 78 Mass. App. Ct. 827, 833–834, 837 (2011) ("[T]he primary purpose for which the return of service in this case was created is to serve the routine administrative functions of the court system, ensuring that the defendant received the fair notice to which he is statutorily and constitutionally entitled . . . , establishing a time and manner of notice for purposes of determining when the order expires or is subject to renewal, and assuring the plaintiff that the target of the order knows of its existence. The return of service here was not created for the purpose of establishing or proving some fact at a potential future criminal trial."). See also Commonwealth v. Bigley, 85 Mass. App. Ct. 507, 515–516 (2014) (defendant's Registry of Motor Vehicles record may be admitted without testimony as it is an automatically generated list regularly maintained by registry in the administration of its regular business affairs); Commonwealth v. Fox, 81 Mass. App. Ct. 244, 246 (2012) (sexual offender registry records are admissible as business records without violation of confrontation clause because they are not created to prove fact at trial). In Commonwealth v. Carr, 464 Mass. 855, 876 (2013), the Supreme Judicial Court held that a statement by the medical examiner in the death certificate that the victim's death was the result of a "gunshot wound of the head with fracture of the skull and perforation of the brain" was testimonial based on the obvious purpose for which it will be used in the case of a homicide and the statutory duties of the medical examiner. Id. at 876.

(3) Expert Testimony. In the years since Melendez–Diaz v. Massachusetts, 557 U.S. 305 (2009), was decided, the United States Supreme Court and the Supreme Judicial Court have considered to what extent that case alters procedures governing the admissibility of expert testimony. That debate is ongoing.

In Commonwealth v. Barbosa, 457 Mass. 773, 785–787 (2010), the Supreme Judicial Court held that Melendez–Diaz does not "purport to alter the rules governing expert testimony" and does not, therefore, forbid one expert from testifying and offering an opinion on the basis of an examination of tests performed and data collected by others, so long as the witness does not testify to the details of the hearsay on direct examination. See also Commonwealth v. Phim, 462 Mass. 470, 479 (2012), and Commonwealth v. Greineder, 458 Mass. 207, 235–239 (2010), vacated and remanded in light of Williams v. Illinois, 567 U.S. 50 (2012).

In Bullcoming v. New Mexico, 564 U.S. 647 (2011), the United States Supreme Court held five to four that admission in evidence of a blood alcohol analysis report, which certified that the defendant's blood alcohol concentration was well above the threshold for aggravated driving while intoxicated under New Mexico law, and which was introduced at trial through the testimony of an analyst who had not performed the certification, violated the confrontation clause. The Supreme Court found that the laboratory report in Bullcoming resembled those in Melendez–Diaz "[i]n all material respects." Id. at 664.

In Commonwealth v. Munoz, 461 Mass. 126, 132 (2011), vacated and remanded in light of Williams v. Illinois, 567 U.S. 50 (2012), the Supreme Judicial Court opined that Bullcoming did not call Barbosa into question. In Munoz, the court affirmed the distinction between a substitute analyst's permissible testimony as to independent opinions based on data generated by a nontestifying analyst and a substitute analyst's impermissible testimony as to the testing analyst's reports and conclusions.

Several days after the decision in Munoz, the United States Supreme Court held five to four that the testimony of a forensic specialist identifying a match between the defendant's blood sample and a DNA sample taken from the victim's vaginal swab was admissible even where the specialist did not work for the outside lab that had produced the DNA sample. Williams v. Illinois, 567 U.S. at 56. Writing for four Justices, Justice Alito found that the specialist's testimony regarding the DNA match was not admitted for its truth, but for the limited purpose of explaining the basis for her own independent expert opinion. Id. at 72. In the opinion of the same four Justices, the underlying DNA report was nontestimonial since it was prepared to catch an unknown rapist who was still at large, not for the primary purpose of accusing a targeted individual. Id. at 84. In a concurrence, Justice Thomas found no confrontation clause violation because the underlying DNA report lacked "the requisite 'formality and solemnity' to be considered 'testimonial' for purposes of the confrontation clause." Id. at 103 (Thomas, J., concurring). In dissent, Justice Kagan, joined by three other Justices, found the DNA report to be precisely the sort of testimonial evidence barred by the decisions in Melendez–Diaz and Bullcoming. Id. at 133–135, 140–141 (Kagan, J., dissenting).

In Commonwealth v. Greineder, 464 Mass. 580, 592–602 (2013), on remand from the United States Supreme Court, the Supreme Judicial Court affirmed its earlier ruling. In that case, the testifying DNA analyst was not the analyst who had performed the tests and written the report on which her opinion testimony was based, although she was the forensic laboratory director of the same company. The court reasoned that Massachusetts evidence law, which permits opinion testimony that is based on data that is hearsay, but prohibits the admission of such a hearsay basis on direct examination of the expert, provides the defendant with more protection than the confrontation clause as interpreted by the United States Supreme Court in Williams v. Illinois, 567 U.S. 50 (2012), especially where, as here, the expert was able to be meaningfully cross-examined on the reliability of the testing procedures that produced the data underlying her opinion.

Two years later, in Commonwealth v. Jones, 472 Mass. 707, 713–715 (2015), the Supreme Judicial Court reversed a conviction based on testimony of a DNA expert as to the location on the victim's body from which the DNA samples had been collected, where the DNA expert's knowledge of how the DNA samples had been gathered was derived from a form completed by the nurse who had collected the specimens from the victim's body. The court concluded that this violated two principles of Greineder: one, the expert may not testify to hearsay on direct examination, and two, the expert must have the capacity to be meaningfully cross-examined about the reliability of the underlying data.

(b) Confrontation Clause Inapplicable. Under certain conditions, the confrontation clause of the Federal and State Constitutions does not bar the admission of testimonial statements, introduced for purposes other than establishing the truth of the matter asserted, in criminal cases even though the declarant is not available for cross-examination. Commonwealth v. Hurley, 455 Mass. 53, 65 n.12 (2009). See Commonwealth v. Pelletier, 71 Mass. App. Ct. 67, 69–72 (2008) (wife's statement was properly admitted for a limited purpose other than its truth even though she did not testify at the defendant's trial).

(c) Child Witness: Massachusetts Law Versus Federal Law. Based on differences in the language of the Sixth Amendment (defendant's right to be "confronted with the witnesses against him") and Article 12 of the Declaration of Rights (defendant's right to "meet the witnesses against him face to face"), the State Constitution has been interpreted by the Supreme Judicial Court to provide a criminal defendant more protection than the Sixth Amendment in certain respects. Compare Maryland v. Craig, 497 U.S. 836, 844–850 (1990) (confrontation clause does not guarantee criminal defendants an absolute right to a face-to-face meeting with the witnesses against them at trial; upholding constitutionality of a procedure whereby a young child alleged to have been the victim of a sexual assault testified at trial outside the courtroom but was visible to defendant and jury on a monitor), with Commonwealth v. Amirault, 424 Mass. 618, 631–632 (1997) (Article 12 requires that the jury be allowed to assess the encounter between the witness and the defendant with the witness testifying in the face of the defendant; in certain circumstances, however, the encounter between the defendant and the child witness may take place outside the courtroom and be presented at trial by videotape. See also Commonwealth v. Bergstrom, 402 Mass. 534, 541–542 (1988).

See also G. L. c. 278, § 16D (courts may order the use of a "suitable alternative procedure" to take the testimony of a child witness, including recording on videotape or simultaneous electronic transmission, upon a finding that testifying in open court or before the defendant will likely traumatize the child witness).

(d) Waiver of Right to Confrontation. The right to confrontation may be waived. See Commonwealth v. Szerlong, 457 Mass. 858, 860–861 (2010) (doctrine of forfeiture by wrongdoing extinguishes right to confrontation); Commonwealth v. Chubbuck, 384 Mass. 746, 751 (1981) (defendant waived right to be present at trial based on persistent disruptive behavior in the courtroom); Commonwealth v. Flemmi, 360 Mass. 693, 694 (1971) (if defendant is voluntarily absent after trial begins, "the court may proceed without the defendant"). See also Mass. R. Crim. P. 18(a)(1) ("If a defendant is present at the beginning of a trial and thereafter absents himself without cause or without leave of court, the trial may proceed to a conclusion in all respects except the imposition of sentence as though the defendant were still present."). A defendant must be competent to plead guilty in order to waive his or her presence at trial. Commonwealth v. L'Abbe, 421 Mass. 262, 268–269 (1995).

Section 801. Definitions

The following definitions apply under this Article:

(a) Statement. "Statement" means a person's oral assertion, written assertion, or nonverbal conduct, if the person intended it as an assertion.

(b) Declarant. "Declarant" means the person who made the statement.

(c) Hearsay. "Hearsay" means a statement that

(1) the declarant does not make while testifying at the current trial or hearing, and

(2) a party offers in evidence to prove the truth of the matter asserted in the statement.

(d) Statements That Are Not Hearsay. A statement that meets the following conditions is not hearsay:

(1) A Declarant–Witness's Prior Statement. The declarant testifies and is subject to cross-examination about a prior statement, and the statement

(A) (i) is inconsistent with the declarant's testimony; (ii) was made under oath before a grand jury, or at an earlier trial, a probable cause hearing, or a deposition, or in an affidavit made under the penalty of perjury in a G. L. c. 209A proceeding; (iii) was not coerced; and (iv) is more than a mere confirmation or denial of an allegation by the interrogator;

(B) [for a discussion of prior consistent statements, which are not admissible substantively under Massachusetts law, see Section 613(b), Prior Statements of Witnesses, Limited Admissibility: Prior Consistent Statements]; or

(C) identifies a person as someone the declarant perceived earlier.

(2) An Opposing Party's Statement. The statement is offered against an opposing party and

(A) was made by the party;

(B) is one the party manifested that it adopted or believed to be true;

(C) was made by a person whom the party authorized to make a statement on the subject, or who was authorized to make true statements on the party's behalf concerning the subject matter;

(D) was made by the party's agent or employee on a matter within the scope of that relationship and while it existed; or

(E) was made by the party's coconspirator or joint venturer during the cooperative effort and in furtherance of its goal, if the existence of the conspiracy or joint venture is shown by evidence independent of the statement.

NOTE

Subsection (a). This subsection is taken from Commonwealth v. Baker, 20 Mass. App. Ct. 926, 928 n.3 (1985), quoting with approval the definition of a "statement" contained in Fed. R. Evid. 801(a) and Proposed Mass. R. Evid. 801(a).

To be hearsay, the statement, whether verbal or nonverbal, must be intended as an assertion. See Bacon v. Charlton, 61 Mass. 581, 586 (1851) (distinguishing between groans and exclamations of pain, which are not hearsay, and anything in the nature of narration or statement). Cf. Commonwealth v. DeJesus, 87 Mass. App. Ct. 198, 201–202 (2015) (checkmarks on photocopies of currency made to indicate a match with bills in defendant's pocket are hearsay when offered to prove the match).

"[C]onduct can serve as a substitute for words, and to the extent it communicates a message, hearsay considerations apply." Commonwealth v. Gonzalez, 443 Mass. 799, 803 (2005). "[O]ut-of-court conduct, which by intent or inference expresses an assertion, has been regarded as a statement and therefore hearsay if offered to prove the truth of the matter asserted. See Bartlett v. Emerson, [73 Mass. 174, 175–176] (1856) (act of pointing out boundary marker inadmissible hearsay)." Opinion of the Justices, 412 Mass. 1201, 1209 (1992) (legislation that would permit the Commonwealth to admit evidence of a person's refusal to take a breathalyzer test violates the privilege against self-incrimination because it reveals the person's thought process and is thus tantamount to an assertion).

Computer Records. For hearsay purposes, whether a computer record contains a statement depends on if the record is "computer-generated," "computer-stored," or a hybrid of both. Commonwealth v. Thissell, 457 Mass. 191, 197 n.13 (2010). Computer-generated records are created solely by the electrical or mechanical operation of a computer. Id. See Commonwealth v. Royal, 89 Mass. App. Ct. 168, 171–172 (2016) (examples include "automated teller machine receipts, log-in records from Internet service providers, and telephone records"). "Because computer-generated records, by definition, do not contain a statement from a person, they do not necessarily implicate hearsay concerns." Commonwealth v. Thissell, 457 Mass. at 197 n.13 (reliability of generative process that created record addressed by rules of authentication). See, e.g., Commonwealth v. Woollam, 478 Mass. 493, 498 (2017) (cellular telephone call logs); Commonwealth v. Perez, 89 Mass. App. Ct. 51, 56 (2016) (automatically generated bank withdrawal records). Conversely, computer-stored records are electronic records generated by humans that are maintained on a computer system. Commonwealth v. Thissell, 457 Mass. at 197 n.13. See Commonwealth v. Royal, 89 Mass. App. Ct. at 171–172 (examples include "electronic mail messages, online posts, and word processing files"). Computer-stored records generally implicate the hearsay rule because these records contain human statements and assertions that have been reduced to electronic form and are merely stored on a computer system. Commonwealth v. Thissell, 457 Mass. at 197 n.13. See, e.g., Commonwealth v. Royal, 89 Mass. App. Ct. at 171–172 (Registry of Motor Vehicle records requiring human action to create and retrieve the records). Hybrid records are comprised of both computer-stored records (containing human statements) and computer-generated data. Commonwealth v. Thissell, 457 Mass. at 197 n.13 (hybrid records may implicate both hearsay and authentication issues).

Subsection (b). This subsection is identical to Fed. R. Evid. 801(b). While no Massachusetts case has defined "declarant," the term has been commonly used in Massachusetts case law to mean a person who makes a statement. See, e.g., Commonwealth v. DeOliveira, 447 Mass. 56, 57–58 (2006); Commonwealth v. Zagranski, 408 Mass. 278, 285 (1990). See also Webster's Third New International Dictionary 586 (2002), which defines "declarant" as a person "who makes a declaration" and "declaration" as "a statement made or testimony given by a witness."

Subsection (c). This subsection is derived from Commonwealth v. Cohen, 412 Mass. 375, 393 (1992), quoting McCormick, Evidence § 246, at 729 (3d ed. 1984), and Fed. R. Evid. 801(c). See Commonwealth v. Cordle, 404 Mass. 733, 743 (1989); Commonwealth v. Randall, 50 Mass. App. Ct. 26, 27 (2000). See also Commonwealth v. Silanskas, 433 Mass. 678, 693 (2001) ("Hearsay is an out-of-court statement offered to prove the truth of the matter asserted."); G.E.B. v. S.R.W., 422 Mass. 158, 168 (1996), quoting Commonwealth v. Keizer, 377 Mass. 264, 269 n.4 (1979) ("Hearsay is an 'extrajudicial statement offered to prove the truth of the matter asserted.'"); Commonwealth v. DelValle, 351 Mass. 489, 491 (1966) ("The broad rule on hearsay evidence interdicts the admission of a statement made out of court which is offered to prove the truth of what it asserted."). If a witness at trial affirms the truth of a statement made out of court, the witness adopts it and it is not hearsay. Commonwealth v. Sanders, 451 Mass. 290, 302 n.8 (2008). Whether the witness has adopted his or her out-

of-court statement is a question of fact for the jury and not a preliminary question for the judge. Id. at 302. See Commonwealth v. Bradshaw, 94 Mass. App. Ct. 477, 481 (2018) (live-witness testimony based on direct experience not hearsay).

"The theory which underlies exclusion is that with the declarant absent the trier of fact is forced to rely upon the declarant's memory, truthfulness, perception, and use of language not subject to cross-examination." Commonwealth v. DelValle, 351 Mass. at 491.

Evidence Admitted for Nonhearsay Purpose. "The hearsay rule forbids only the testimonial use of reported statements." Commonwealth v. Miller, 361 Mass. 644, 659 (1972). Accord Commonwealth v. Fiore, 364 Mass. 819, 824 (1974), quoting Wigmore, Evidence § 1766 (3d ed. 1940) (out-of-court utterances are hearsay only when offered "for a special purpose, namely, as assertions to evidence the truth of the matter asserted"). Thus, when out-of-court statements are offered for a reason other than to prove the truth of the matter asserted or when they have independent legal significance, they are not hearsay. There are many nonhearsay purposes for which out-of-court statements may be offered, such as the following:

- *Proof of "Verbal Acts" or "Operative" Words.* See Commonwealth v. Alvarez, 480 Mass. 1017, 1019 (2018) (statement in a text message asking to buy drugs is composed of the words of a crime and does not constitute hearsay); Commonwealth v. McLaughlin, 431 Mass. 241, 246 (2000) ("[e]vidence of the terms of that oral agreement was not offered for the truth of the matters asserted, but as proof of an 'operative' statement, i.e., existence of a conspiracy"); Charette v. Burke, 300 Mass. 278, 280–281 (1938) (father's remark to a child before leaving the child to go into the house ["Wait where you are while I go inside to get you a cookie"] was a "verbal act" and not hearsay); Commonwealth v. Perez, 89 Mass. App. Ct. 51, 55–56 (2016) (withdrawal and deposit slips used by defendant accused of theft from customer bank accounts were legally operative verbal acts and not hearsay); Shimer v. Foley, Hoag & Eliot, LLP, 59 Mass. App. Ct. 302, 310 (2003) (evidence of the terms of a contract used to establish lost profits is not hearsay because it is not an assertion).

- *To Show Notice or Other Effect on Hearer.* See Commonwealth v. Santana, 477 Mass. 610, 621–622 (2017) (interrogating police officer's statement that he had information that defendant had been inside apartment where murder was committed admissible to "contextualize" defendant's "arguably exculpatory" statement that he had been just outside apartment, thus avoiding improper suggestion that defendant had gratuitously placed himself at murder scene); Commonwealth v. Spinucci, 472 Mass. 872, 882–883 (2015) (statements made within defendant's earshot, indicating codefendant's possession of a knife, were not hearsay when offered to show defendant's knowledge that codefendant had a knife); Pardo v. General Hosp. Corp., 446 Mass. 1, 18–19 (2006) (memorandum admissible to show notice); A.W. Chesterton Co. v. Massachusetts Insurers Insolvency Fund, 445 Mass. 502, 515–516 (2005) (knowledge of insurance reserves not listed in response to question on insurance application regarding potential losses); Commonwealth v. Bregoli, 431 Mass. 265, 273 (2000) (other declarants' knowledge of facts relating to crime to rebut Commonwealth's claim that only killer would be aware of facts); Vassallo v. Baxter Healthcare Corp., 428 Mass. 1, 17 (1998) (other complaints about product admissible as evidence that manufacturer was on notice of defect); Mailhiot v. Liberty Bank & Trust Co., 24 Mass. App. Ct. 525, 529 n.5 (1987) (instructions given to the plaintiff by bank examiners about how to handle a problem were not assertions and thus not hearsay). Cf. Commonwealth v. Daley, 55 Mass. App. Ct. 88, 94 n.9 (2002) (a passerby's remark ["Hey, are you all right?"], if offered as an assertion that the victim was in distress, would be hearsay, but if offered to explain why the defendant fled, and thus not as an assertion, would not be hearsay), S.C., 439 Mass. 558 (2003).

- *To Show "the State of Police Knowledge."* Out-of-court statements to a police investigator may sometimes be admitted for the nonhearsay purpose of showing "the state of police knowledge," because "an arresting or investigating officer should not be put in the false position of seeming just to have happened upon the scene; he should be allowed some explanation of his presence and conduct." Commonwealth v. Cohen, 412 Mass. 375, 393 (1992). See Commonwealth v. Miller, 361 Mass. 644, 659 (1972) (out-of-court statements are admissible when offered to explain why police approached defendant to avoid misimpression that police acted arbitrarily in singling out defendant for investigation). However, "[t]estimony of this kind carries a high probability of misuse, because a witness may relate historical aspects of the case, replete with hearsay statements in the form of complaints and reports[,] even when not necessary to show state of police knowledge" (quotation omitted). Commonwealth v. Rosario, 430 Mass. 505, 510 (1999). Such evidence, therefore, (1) is permitted only through the testimony of a police officer, who must testify only on the basis of his or her own knowledge; (2) is limited to the facts required to establish the officer's state of knowledge; (3) is allowed only when the police action or state of police knowledge is relevant to an issue in the case. Commonwealth v. Sullivan, 478 Mass. 369, 376 (2017).

Cross–Reference: Section 105, Limiting Evidence That Is Not Admissible Against Other Parties or for Other Purposes.

- As Circumstantial Evidence of Declarant's State of Mind. Where the declarant asserts his or her own state of mind (usually by words describing the state of mind), the statement is hearsay and is admissible only if it falls within the hearsay exception. See Section 803(3)(B), Hearsay Exceptions; Availability of Declarant Immaterial: Then–Existing Mental, Emotional, or Physical Condition, and the accompanying note. However, when the statement conveys the speaker's state of mind only circumstantially (usually because the words themselves do not describe the state of mind directly), it is not hearsay. See, e.g., Commonwealth v. Cruzado, 480 Mass. 275, 280 (2018) (testimony that victim had concluded that defendant had stolen his cell phone properly admitted to show ill will between defendant and victim); Commonwealth v. Romero, 464 Mass. 648, 652 n.5 (2013) (defendant's statement that passenger in his vehicle had shown him a gun was admissible to show defendant's knowledge that gun was in car, as well as being admission of a party-opponent); Commonwealth v. Montanez, 439 Mass. 441, 447–448 (2003) (evidence of victim's statement to her friend was properly admitted to establish victim's state of mind [concern for her family's shame and diminished economic circumstances if abuser were removed from her home], which helped explain her delay in reporting an episode of sexual abuse and thus was not hearsay). Contrast Section 803(3)(B)(ii), Hearsay Exceptions; Availability of Declarant Immaterial: Then–Existing Mental, Emotional, or Physical Condition.

- As Circumstantial Evidence of the Nature of a Place or a Thing. Sometimes out-of-court statements that do not directly describe the nature or character of a place or an object can nevertheless be probative of that nature or character. In such cases, the statements are treated as nonhearsay. See, e.g., Commonwealth v. Massod, 350 Mass. 745, 748 (1996) (statements over telephone not hearsay when used to show that telephone was apparatus used for registering bets on horse races); Commonwealth v. DePina, 75 Mass. App. Ct. 842, 850 (2009) (conversation of police officer on defendant's cellular telephone was admissible as evidence of nature of the cellular telephone as instrument used in cocaine distribution); Commonwealth v. Washington, 39 Mass. App. Ct. 195, 199–201 (1995) (conversations of police officer with callers to defendant's beeper not hearsay when used to show that beeper was used for drug transactions). See also Commonwealth v. Purdy, 459 Mass. 442, 452 (2011) (words soliciting sexual act have independent legal significance and are not hearsay); Commonwealth v. Mullane, 445 Mass. 702, 711 (2006) (portion of conversation regarding negotiation for "extras" between police detective and "massage therapist" were not hearsay).

Prior Statements Used to Impeach or Rehabilitate. Ordinarily, the out-of-court statements of a testifying witness are hearsay if they are offered to prove the truth of the statement. Prior inconsistent statements are usually admissible only for the limited purpose of impeaching the credibility of the witness. But see Subsection (d)(1)(A) and the accompanying note. A witness's prior consistent statements are not admissible substantively under Massachusetts law, but they may be admissible for certain other purposes. See for example Section 413, First Complaint of Sexual Assault, and Section 613(b), Prior Statements of Witnesses, Limited Admissibility: Prior Consistent Statements.

Cross–Reference: Section 105, Limiting Evidence That Is Not Admissible Against Other Parties or for Other Purposes.

Nonverbal Conduct Excluded as Hearsay. See Commonwealth v. Todd, 394 Mass. 791, 797 (1985) (explaining that the destruction of her marriage license could be considered "an extrajudicial, nonverbal assertion of the victim's intent which, if introduced for the truth of the matter asserted, would be, on its face, objectionable as hearsay"); Bartlett v. Emerson, 73 Mass. 174, 175–176 (1856) (testimony about another person's act of pointing out a boundary marker was an assertion of a fact and thus inadmissible as hearsay); Commonwealth v. Ramirez, 55 Mass. App. Ct. 224, 227 (2002) (a business card offered to establish a connection between the defendant and a New York address on the card was hearsay because it was used as an assertion of a fact); Commonwealth v. Kirk, 39 Mass. App. Ct. 225, 229–230 (1995) (conduct of a police officer who served a restraining order on the defendant offered to establish the identity of that person as the perpetrator was hearsay because its probative value depended on the truth of an assertion made in the papers by the victim that the defendant was the same person named in the complaint).

When an out-of-court statement is offered for a nonhearsay purpose, after considering the effectiveness of a Section 105 limiting instruction it is necessary to weigh the risk of unfair prejudice that would likely result if the jury misused the statement. See Section 403, Excluding Relevant Evidence for Prejudice, Confusion, Waste of Time, or Other Reason. In criminal cases, that risk can have confrontation clause implications.

Cross–Reference: Section 105, Limiting Evidence That Is Not Admissible Against Other Parties or for Other Purposes; Section 803(3)(B)(ii), Hearsay Exceptions; Availability of Declarant Immaterial: Then–Existing Mental, Emotional, or Physical Condition.

Subsection (d). This subsection addresses out-of-court statements that are admissible for their truth. Section 613, Prior Statements of Witnesses, Limited Admissibility, addresses prior statements for the limited purposes only of impeachment and rehabilitation.

Subsection (d)(1)(A). Massachusetts generally adheres to the orthodox rule that prior inconsistent statements are admissible only for the limited purpose of impeaching the credibility of a witness's testimony at trial and are inadmissible hearsay when offered to establish the truth of the matters asserted. See Section 613(a)(1), Prior Statements of Witnesses, Limited Admissibility: Prior Inconsistent Statements: Examining Own Witness, and Section 613(a)(2), Prior Statements of Witnesses, Limited Admissibility: Prior Inconsistent Statements: Examining Other Witness. However, in Commonwealth v. Daye, 393 Mass. 55, 66 (1984), the Supreme Judicial Court adopted the principles of Proposed Mass. R. Evid. 801(d)(1)(A) allowing prior inconsistent statements made before a grand jury to be admitted substantively. The Daye rule has been extended to cover prior inconsistent statements made in other proceedings as well. See Commonwealth v. Sineiro, 432 Mass. 735 (2000) (probable cause hearings); Commonwealth v. Newman, 69 Mass. App. Ct. 495 (2007) (testimony given at an accomplice's trial). Commonwealth v. Ragland, 72 Mass. App. Ct. 815, 823 n.9 (2008), made it clear in dicta that the same principles would apply to admission of prior inconsistent deposition evidence given under oath. See also Commonwealth v. Belmer, 78 Mass. App. Ct. 62, 64 (2010) (prior inconsistent statement may be admissible for its full probative value where the witness has signed a written affidavit under penalties of perjury in support of an application for a restraining order pursuant to G. L. c. 209A and that witness is subject to cross-examination).

Two general requirements for the substantive use of such statements are (1) that there is an opportunity to cross-examine the declarant and (2) that the prior testimony was in the declarant's own words and was not coerced. In addition, if the prior inconsistent statement is relied on to establish an essential element of a crime, the Commonwealth must offer at least some additional evidence on that element in order to support a conclusion of guilt beyond a reasonable doubt. Commonwealth v. Daye, 393 Mass. at 73–75. However, the additional evidence need not be sufficient in itself to establish the element. Commonwealth v. Noble, 417 Mass. 341, 345 & n.3 (1994). The corroboration requirement thus concerns the sufficiency of the evidence, not its admissibility. Commonwealth v. McGhee, 472 Mass. 405, 422–423 (2015); Commonwealth v. Clements, 436 Mass. 190, 193 (2002). The prior testimony should be introduced by having it read directly into the record, either by a single reader or by two persons reading responsively, making clear which portions are questions and which are answers. Commonwealth v. Andrade, 481 Mass. 139, 144 (2018).

Feigning Lack of Memory. Prior statements included in Section 801(d)(1)(A) may be admitted substantively against a witness as inconsistent with a claimed lack of memory if that witness is available for cross-examination and subject to the requirements of this subsection, Section 801(d)(1)(A), provided the trial judge follows the requirements set forth in Commonwealth v. Daye, 393 Mass. 55, 73–74 (1984), and Commonwealth v. Sineiro, 432 Mass. 735, 745 & n.12 (2000). Before admitting such testimony, the judge must make preliminary findings of fact that (1) the witness is in fact feigning lack of memory, (2) the testimony was not coerced, and (3) the testimony was in the witness's own words and is more than a mere confirmation or denial of an allegation by the interrogator. Commonwealth v. DePina, 476 Mass. 614, 620–621 (2017). See Commonwealth v. Evans, 439 Mass. 184, 190 (2003); Commonwealth v. Silvester, 89 Mass. App. Ct. 350, 355–356 (2016). At a party's request, the judge may conduct a voir dire to make these findings. Commonwealth v. Sineiro, 432 Mass. at 739. A trial judge's findings are "entitled to substantial deference and are 'conclusive as long as . . . supported by the evidence.'" Commonwealth v. DePina, 476 Mass. at 621, quoting Commonwealth v. Maldonado, 466 Mass. 742, 756, cert. denied, 134 S. Ct. 2312 (2014), quoting Commonwealth v. Sineiro, 432 Mass. at 742 n.6. "[W]here grand jury testimony relates to an essential element of the offense, the Commonwealth must offer corroborative evidence, in addition to that testimony, in order to sustain a conviction." Id. at 621 n.5 (corroboration requirement "goes to the sufficiency of the evidence rather than to its admissibility"). A judge's finding of witness feigning is often based on a careful examination of the witness's demeanor and testimony in light of the judge's experience. See Commonwealth v. Sineiro, 432 Mass. at 740; Commonwealth v. Newman, 69 Mass. App. Ct. 495, 497 (2007). See, e.g., Commonwealth v. Figueroa, 451 Mass. 566, 573–574, 576–577 (2008) (judge concluded that witness was feigning when he was able to recall many specific events of the evening in question but was unable to recall the portion of his grand jury testimony in which he said the defendant admitted to shooting someone, and a transcript failed to refresh his memory); Commonwealth v. Tiexeira, 29 Mass. App. Ct. 200, 204 (1990) (judge observed how the witness's detailed account of the evening was conspicuously vague regarding the defendant's encounter with the victim). Regardless of the judge's conclusion at voir dire, the jury shall not be told of the judge's preliminary determination that the witness is feigning. Commonwealth v. Sineiro, 432 Mass. at 742 n.6.

"Where a witness testifies at trial and is cross-examined, any limitation on the effectiveness or substance of that cross-examination stemming from feigned memory loss generally does not implicate the confrontation clause." Commonwealth v. DePina, 476 Mass. at 622. See also Commonwealth v. Stewart, 454 Mass. 527, 533 (2009) (genuine

total loss of memory preventing cross-examination may preclude admission of grand jury testimony).

Cross–Reference: Introductory Note (a) to Article VIII, Hearsay.

Subsection (d)(1)(B). In Commonwealth v. Cruz, 53 Mass. App. Ct. 393, 401 & n.10 (2001), the Appeals Court noted that the Supreme Judicial Court has not adopted Proposed Mass. R. Evid. 801(d)(1)(B) as to the admission of prior consistent statements as substantive evidence, rather than merely for the purpose of rehabilitating the credibility of a witness-declarant who has been impeached on the ground that his or her trial testimony is of recent contrivance. See also Commonwealth v. Thomas, 429 Mass. 146, 161–162 (1999) (prior consistent statement admissible to rebut suggestion of recent contrivance); Commonwealth v. Kater, 409 Mass. 433, 448 (1991) ("prior consistent statements of a witness may be admitted where the opponent has raised a claim or inference of recent contrivance, undue influence, or bias"); Commonwealth v. Zukoski, 370 Mass. 23, 26–27 (1976) ("[A] witness's prior consistent statement is admissible where a claim is made that the witness's in-court statement is of recent contrivance or is the product of particular inducements or bias . . . Unless admissible on some other ground to prove the truth of the facts asserted, such a prior consistent statement is admissible only to show that the witness's in-court testimony is not the product of the asserted inducement or bias or is not recently contrived as claimed").

Cross–Reference: Section 413, First Complaint of Sexual Assault.

Subsection (d)(1)(C). This subsection is derived from Commonwealth v. Cong Duc Le, 444 Mass. 431, 432, 436–437 (2005), where the Supreme Judicial Court "adopt[ed] the modern interpretation of the rule" expressed in Proposed Mass. R. Evid. 801(d)(1)(C), which, like its Federal counterpart, states that "[a] statement is not hearsay . . . if '[t]he declarant testifies at the trial or hearing and is subject to cross-examination concerning the statement, and the statement is . . . one of identification of a person [made] after perceiving [the person].'" It is not necessary that the declarant make an in-court identification. See Commonwealth v. Machorro, 72 Mass. App. Ct. 377, 379–380 (2008) (police officer allowed to testify to extrajudicial identification of the assailant by two victims who were present at trial and subject to cross-examination even though one victim could not identify the assailant [although she recalled being present at his arrest and was certain that the person arrested was the assailant] and the other victim was not asked to make an identification at trial). The third party's testimony about the identification may not be admitted until after the Commonwealth has questioned the eyewitness about the identification. Commonwealth v. Herndon, 475 Mass. 324, 335 (2016). This subsection applies to an out-of-court identification based on a witness's familiarity with the person identified and is not limited to a photographic array, showup, or other identification procedure. Commonwealth v. Adams, 458 Mass. 766, 770–776 (2011). Multiple versions of an extrajudicial identification may be admissible for substantive purposes. Id. at 773.

Under this subsection, whether and to what extent third-party testimony about a witness's out-of-court identification may be admitted in evidence no longer turns on whether the identifying witness acknowledges or denies the extrajudicial identification at trial. See Commonwealth v. Cong Duc Le, 444 Mass. at 439–440. The third-party testimony will be admitted for substantive purposes as long as the cross-examination requirement is satisfied. Id. As the court explained, it is for the jury to "determine whose version to believe— the witness who claims not to remember or disavows the prior identification (including that witness's version of what transpired during the identification procedure), or the observer who testifies that the witness made a particular prior identification." Id. at 440. Prior identification evidence, even if disputed, may be considered in light of all the other evidence relevant to the perpetrator's identity. Id. See also Commonwealth v. Silvester, 89 Mass. App. Ct. 350, 357 (2016) (admission of videotape of witness selecting photograph of defendant from photo array did not violate defendant's confrontation rights where witness was available for cross-examination).

Cross-Reference: Section 1112(d), Eyewitness Identification: Testimony of Third-Party Observer.

Facts Accompanying an Identification. Identification evidence has no meaning absent context, and the extent of the statement needed to provide context varies from case to case. Commonwealth v. Adams, 458 Mass. 766, 772 (2011). Thus, the contents of a witness's statement are admissible under this rule only so far as they are relevant to the issue of identification. Id. This issue should be the subject of a motion in limine. Id. See also Commonwealth v. Walker, 460 Mass. 590, 608–609 (2011).

Cross–Reference: Section 1112, Eyewitness Identification.

Subsection (d)(2). This subsection defines admissions by a party-opponent as not hearsay, consistent with recent Supreme Judicial Court decisions, the Federal Rules of Evidence, and the Proposed Massachusetts Rules of Evidence. See Commonwealth v. Mendes, 441 Mass. 459, 467 (2004); Commonwealth v. Allison, 434 Mass. 670, 676 n.5 (2001); Commonwealth v. DiMonte, 427 Mass. 233, 243 (1998), citing Proposed Mass. R. Evid. 801(d)(2); Fed. R. Evid. 801(d)(2); Proposed Mass. R. Evid. 801(d)(2). In some cases, the court has ruled that out-of-court statements by a party-opponent are admissible as an exception to the hearsay rule. See Commonwealth v. DeBrosky, 363 Mass. 718, 724 (1973); Commonwealth v. McKay, 67 Mass. App. Ct. 396, 403 n.13 (2006).

Subsection (d)(2)(A). This subsection is derived from Commonwealth v. Marshall, 434 Mass. 358, 365–366 (2001), quoting P.J. Liacos, Massachusetts Evidence § 8.8.1 (7th ed. 1999). See also Commonwealth v. McCowen, 458 Mass. 461, 485–486 (2010) (defendant's out-of-court statement offered for its truth is hearsay and not admissible when not offered by the Commonwealth); Care & Protection of Sophie, 449 Mass. 100, 110 n.14 (2007) (no requirement that the statement of a party-opponent be contradictory or against the party-opponent's interest); Commonwealth v. Bonomi, 335 Mass. 327, 347 (1957) ("An admission in a criminal case is a statement by the accused, direct or implied, of facts pertinent to the issue, which although insufficient in itself to warrant a conviction tends in connection with proof of other facts to establish his guilt"); Hopkins v. Medeiros, 48 Mass. App. Ct. 600, 613 (2000) ("The evidence of [the defendant's] admission to sufficient facts was admissible as an admission of a party opponent."); Section 410, Pleas, Offers of Pleas, and Related Statements.

A defendant's unequivocal denial that he or she has committed a charged crime is not admissible in evidence. Commonwealth v. Nawn, 394 Mass. 1, 4 (1985). Both the denial and the accusation it denies are inadmissible as hearsay. Commonwealth v. Spencer, 465 Mass. 32, 46 (2013). The rule barring evidence of a defendant's denial applies only to denials of accusations of criminal activity and not to other denials. See Commonwealth v. Cruzado, 480 Mass. 275, 277–278 (2018) (investigators' questions about whether defendant recognized a photograph of murder victim and defendant's denials properly admitted because questions did not accuse defendant of criminal activity). This rule does not prohibit evidence of a defendant's false factual statements or omissions to show consciousness of guilt. See Commonwealth v. Lavalley, 410 Mass. 641, 649–650 (1991) (impeachment of defendant's trial testimony by showing difference from his pretrial statement to police was evidence of consciousness of guilt and did not amount to impermissible comment on his denial or failure to deny the offense). See also Commonwealth v. Lewis, 465 Mass. 119, 127 (2013) (defendant's ambiguous statement that could be construed as consciousness of guilt ["I'll beat this"] is admissible and subject to parties' arguments about proper interpretation).

While a discussion of the constitutional and common-law principles governing the admissibility of confessions is beyond the scope of this Guide, the law is that a statement, admission, or confession by a person is not admissible in a criminal proceeding if it was not made voluntarily. See, e.g., Commonwealth v. Cryer, 426 Mass. 562, 571 (1998); Commonwealth v. Tavares, 385 Mass. 140, 146 (1982); Commonwealth v. Mahnke, 368 Mass. 662, 679–691 (1975).

Discovery Material. Under this subsection, deposition answers by an opposing party, Mass. R. Civ. P. 32(a)(2), interrogatory answers by an opposing party, G. L. c. 231, § 89, and responses to requests for admission of facts, Mass. R. Civ. P. 36(b), are not subject to a hearsay objection and thus may be used by the opponent for any permissible purpose. See Federico v. Ford Motor Co., 67 Mass. App. Ct. 454, 460–461 (2006); Beaupre v. Cliff Smith & Assocs., 50 Mass. App. Ct. 480, 484 n.8 (2000).

Criminal Cases. The principle that the admission of a party-opponent, without more, is admissible is superseded by the requirements of the confrontation clause:

"[W]here a nontestifying codefendant's statement expressly implicates the defendant, leaving no doubt that it would prove to be powerfully incriminating, the confrontation clause of the Sixth Amendment to the United States Constitution has been offended, notwithstanding any limiting instruction by the judge that the jury may consider the statement only against the codefendant."

Commonwealth v. Vallejo, 455 Mass. 72, 83 (2009) (discussing Bruton v. United States, 391 U.S. 123 [1968]). See also Commonwealth v. Resende, 476 Mass. 141, 150 (2017) ("Where a nontestifying codefendant's statement does not inculpate a defendant directly, but does inculpate the defendant when combined with other evidence, a limiting instruction [that the statement may not be used as evidence against the defendant] may be sufficient to cure the prejudice."); Commonwealth v. Vasquez, 462 Mass. 827, 842–844 (2012) (statement made by nontestifying defendant to police admissible where statement did not expressly or "obviously" refer directly to defendant).

Subsection (d)(2)(B). This subsection is taken verbatim from Fed. R. Evid. 801(d)(2)(B) and is consistent with Massachusetts law. See also Proposed Mass. R. Evid. 801(d)(2)(B). "Where a party is confronted with an accusatory statement which, under the circumstances, a reasonable person would challenge, and the party remains silent or responds equivocally, the accusation and the reply may be admissible on the theory that the party's response amounts to an admission of the truth of the accusation." Commonwealth v. MacKenzie, 413 Mass. 498, 506 (1992). Accord Commonwealth v. Braley, 449 Mass. 316, 320–321 (2007); Zucco v. Kane, 439 Mass. 503, 507–508 (2003); Commonwealth v. Silanskas, 433 Mass. 678, 694 (2001). This is commonly referred to as an "adoptive admission."

Admission by Silence. For an admission by silence to be admissible it must be apparent that the party has heard and understood the statement, had an opportunity to respond, and the context was one in which the party would have been expected to respond. Commonwealth v. Olszewski, 416 Mass. 707, 719 (1993), cert. denied, 513 U.S. 835 (1994). See Commonwealth v. DePina, 476 Mass. 614, 624 (2017); Leone v. Doran, 363 Mass. 1, 16, modified on other grounds, 363 Mass. 886 (1973). "Because silence may mean something other than agreement or acknowledgment of guilt (it may mean inattention or perplexity, for instance), evidence of adoptive admissions by silence must be received and applied with caution." Commonwealth v. Babbitt, 430 Mass. 700, 705 (2000). See generally Commonwealth v. Nickerson, 386 Mass. 54, 61 n.6 (1982) (cautioning against use of a defendant's prearrest silence to show consciousness of guilt and indicating such evidence is admissible only in "unusual circumstances"). Accordingly, adoption by silence can be imputed to a defendant only for statements that "clearly would have produced a reply or denial on the part of an innocent person." Commonwealth v. Brown, 394 Mass. 510, 515 (1985).

"No admission by silence may be inferred, however, if the statement is made after the accused has been placed under arrest[, see Commonwealth v. Kenney, 53 Mass. 235, 238 (1847); Commonwealth v. Morrison, 1 Mass. App. Ct. 632, 634 (1973); Commonwealth v. Cohen, 6 Mass. App. Ct. 653, 657 (1978)], after the police have read him his Miranda rights[, see Commonwealth v. Rembiszewski, 363 Mass. 311, 316 (1973)], or after he has been so significantly deprived of his freedom that he is, in effect, in police custody[, see Commonwealth v. Corridori, 11 Mass. App. Ct. 469, 480 (1981)]."

Commonwealth v. Stevenson, 46 Mass. App. Ct. 506, 510 (1999), quoting Commonwealth v. Ferrara, 31 Mass. App. Ct. 648, 652 (1991).

Admission by Conduct. "An admission may be implied from conduct as well as from words." Commonwealth v. Bonomi, 335 Mass. 327, 348 (1957). For instance,

"[a]ctions and statements that indicate consciousness of guilt on the part of the defendant are admissible and together with other evidence, may be sufficient to prove guilt ... [T]his theory usually has been applied to cases where a defendant runs away ... or makes intentionally false and misleading statements to police ... or makes threats against key witnesses for the prosecution ..."

Commonwealth v. Montecalvo, 367 Mass. 46, 52 (1975). See also Olofson v. Kilgallon, 362 Mass. 803, 806 (1973), citing Hall v. Shain, 291 Mass. 506, 512–513 (1935). For a thorough discussion of the evidentiary and constitutional issues surrounding the use of a defendant's prearrest silence or conduct to establish consciousness of guilt, see Commonwealth v. Irwin, 72 Mass. App. Ct. 643, 648–656 (2008). "[A] judge should instruct the jury [1] that they are not to convict a defendant on the basis of evidence of [conduct] alone, and [2] that they may, but need not, consider such evidence as one of the factors tending to prove the guilt of the defendant" (citation omitted). Commonwealth v. Toney, 385 Mass. 575, 585 (1982).

Subsection (d)(2)(C). This subsection is derived from Sacks v. Martin Equip. Co., 333 Mass. 274, 279–280 (1955).

This subsection covers the admissibility of statements by an agent who has been authorized by the principal to speak on his behalf. See Simonoko v. Stop & Shop, Inc., 376 Mass. 929, 929 (1978) (concluding there was no showing of the manager's authority to speak for the defendant). Contrast Subsection (d)(2)(D), which deals with statements of agents.

Subsection (d)(2)(D). This subsection is derived from Ruszcyk v. Secretary of Pub. Safety, 401 Mass. 418, 420–423 (1988), in which the Supreme Judicial Court adopted Proposed Mass. R. Evid. 801(d)(2)(D). Under some circumstances, inconsistent statements by a prosecutor at successive trials may be admissible as admissions of a party-opponent. See Commonwealth v. Keo, 467 Mass. 25, 33 n.21 (2014).

To determine whether a statement qualifies as a vicarious admission, the judge first must decide as a preliminary question of fact whether the declarant was authorized to act on the matters about which he or she spoke. See Herson v. New Boston Garden Corp., 40 Mass. App. Ct. 779, 791 (1996). If the judge finds that the declarant was so authorized, the judge must then decide whether the probative value of the statement was substantially outweighed by its potential for unfair prejudice. Id. In so doing,

"the judge should consider the credibility of the witness; the proponent's need for the evidence, e.g., whether the declarant is available to testify; and the reliability of the evidence offered, including consideration of whether the statement was made on firsthand knowledge and of any other circumstances bearing on the credibility of the declarant. Ruszcyk v. Secretary of Pub. Safety, [401 Mass.] at 422–423" (footnote and quotation omitted).

Thorell v. ADAP, Inc., 58 Mass. App. Ct. 334, 339–340 (2003). The out-of-court statements of the agent are hearsay and thus inadmissible for the purpose of proving the existence of the agency; however, the agency may be shown through the agent's testimony at trial. Campbell v. Olender, 27 Mass. App. Ct. 1197, 1198 (1989).

Subsection (d)(2)(E). This subsection is derived from Commonwealth v. Bongarzone, 390 Mass. 326, 340 (1983), which relied on Proposed Mass. R. Evid. 801(d)(2)(E) and the identical Fed. R. Evid. 801(d)(2)(E). See also Commonwealth v. Rakes, 478 Mass. 22, 38–43 (2017); Commonwealth v. Carriere, 470 Mass. 1, 10 (2014). This exception is based on the belief that the shared acts and interests of

coventurers engaging in a criminal enterprise tend to some degree to assure that statements made between them will be at least minimally reliable. Commonwealth v. Bongarzone, 390 Mass. at 340.

"[A] statement made by a coconspirator or joint venturer may be admitted for its truth against the other coconspirators or joint venturers." Commonwealth v. Mattier, 474 Mass. 261, 276–277 (2016). Before admitting such evidence, a judge "must find, by a preponderance of the evidence, the existence of a joint venture independent of the statement being offered." Commonwealth v. Holley, 478 Mass. 508, 534–535 (2017). "This determination permits the statement to be placed in front of the jury, but does not suffice for the jury to consider it as bearing on the defendant's guilt." Commonwealth v. Rakes, 478 Mass. 22, 37 (2017). Instead, before they consider the statement for such purpose, "the jury must make their own independent determination, again based on a preponderance of the evidence other than the statement itself, that a joint venture existed and that the statement was made in furtherance thereof" (quotation omitted). Commonwealth v. Holley, 478 Mass. at 534. "Alternatively, the statement may be admitted provisionally, subject to a motion to strike should the evidence presented ... fail to establish the existence of a joint venture." Commonwealth v. Rakes, 478 Mass. at 37 n.11. A statement otherwise inadmissible under the joint venture exception may be admissible for nonhearsay purposes. Commonwealth v. Brown, 474 Mass. 576, 587–588 (2016) (statement may serve as "foundation for later showing, through other admissible evidence," that defendant's statements were false).

Statements probative of a declarant's intent to enter into a joint venture are admissible under the joint venture exception even if the joint venture has not yet begun. Commonwealth v. Rakes, 478 Mass. at 39. Statements made after completion of a crime may be admissible if made in an effort to conceal a crime, even if made years after the crime. Commonwealth v. Winquist, 474 Mass. 517, 522–524 (2016). This exception extends to situations where "the joint venturers are acting to conceal the crime that formed the basis of the criminal enterprise," Commonwealth v. Ali, 43 Mass. App. Ct. 549, 561 (1997), quoting Commonwealth v. Angiulo, 415 Mass. 502, 519 (1993), but it "does not apply after the criminal enterprise has ended, as where a joint venturer has been apprehended and imprisoned." Commonwealth v. Colon-Cruz, 408 Mass. 533, 543 (1990). Cf. Commonwealth v. Rakes, 478 Mass. at 41–42 (statement made by incarcerated coventurer approximately fifteen years after commission of the crime deemed admissible because it demonstrated that joint venturers "remained actively engaged in an effort to conceal their . . . crimes"). Thus, a confession or admission of a coconspirator or joint venturer made after the termination of the conspiracy or joint venture is not admissible as a vicarious statement of another member of the conspiracy or joint venture. Commonwealth v. Bongarzone, 390 Mass. 326, 340 n.11 (1983), citing Commonwealth v. White, 370 Mass. 703, 708–712 (1976). Cf. Commonwealth v. Leach, 73 Mass. App. Ct. 758, 766 (2009) (although statements made by codefendants occurred after they were in custody, statements were made shortly after crime and for purpose of concealing crime and thus became admissible against each defendant).

Use of Depositions at Trial. In addition to substantive evidentiary issues, which are resolved in the same manner as if the deponent were testifying in court, the use of depositions at trial sometimes raises hearsay issues. The deposition of an adverse party or an authorized agent of a party is not hearsay under Section 801(d)(2). See Mass. R. Civ. P. 32(a)(2). Rule 30A(m) of the Massachusetts Rules of Civil Procedure creates a hearsay exception for certain audiovisual depositions of treating physicians and expert witnesses taken by the party offering the witness. Objections to the deposition testimony taken under this rule are waived if not brought to the court's attention twenty-one days before trial. Rothkopf v. Williams, 55 Mass. App. Ct. 294, 298–299 (2002). The audiovisual recording of a deposition offered at trial becomes part of the record, but should not be admitted as an exhibit. McSweeney v. Build Safe Corp., 417 Mass. 610, 612 (1994). See Mass. R. Civ. P. 30A(k)(4).

Any party may introduce the deposition testimony of a witness who is unavailable at trial. Mass. R. Civ. P. 32(a)(4). In addition to the grounds for unavailability enumerated in Rule 32(a)(4), a witness who holds a valid Fifth Amendment privilege is deemed unavailable. Hasouris v. Sorour, 92 Mass. App. Ct. 607, 614–615 (2018). The proponent of the use of the deposition must demonstrate the witness's unavailability (unavailability cannot be presumed; the trial judge must make a particularized inquiry). The party against whom the deposition testimony is offered must have had the opportunity to cross-examine the witness prior to trial. Frizzell v. Wes Pine Millwork, Inc., 4 Mass. App. Ct. 710, 712 (1976). A deposition from an unrelated action is not admissible against a party who was not present or represented at the earlier deposition. Martin v. Roy, 54 Mass. App. Ct. 642, 647 (2002); Kirby v. Morales, 50 Mass. App. Ct. 786, 790 (2001). "If only part of a deposition is offered in evidence by a party, an adverse party may require him to introduce any other part which ought in fairness to be considered with the part introduced, and any party may introduce any other parts." Mass. R. Civ. P. 32(a)(4). Cf. Section 106, Doctrine of Completeness.

Cross-Reference: Section 804(b)(1), Hearsay Exceptions; Declarant Unavailable: The Exceptions: Prior Recorded Testimony.

Section 802.　The Rule Against Hearsay

Hearsay is not admissible unless any of the following provides otherwise:

(a) case law,

(b) a statute, or

(c) a rule prescribed by the Supreme Judicial Court.

NOTE

This section is derived from Commonwealth v. Markvart, 437 Mass. 331, 335 (2002) ("hearsay not otherwise admissible under the rules of evidence is inadmissible at the trial … unless specifically made admissible by statute"). There is no "innominate" or catchall exception to the hearsay rule in Massachusetts whereby hearsay may be admitted on an ad hoc basis provided that there are circumstantial guarantees of trustworthiness. See Commonwealth v. Pope, 397 Mass. 275, 281–282 (1986); Commonwealth v. Meech, 380 Mass. 490, 497 (1980); Commonwealth v. White, 370 Mass. 703, 713 (1976). Contrast Fed. R. Evid. 807.

In addition to exceptions established by case law, several Massachusetts statutes and rules provide exceptions to the rule against hearsay, including, but not limited to the following:

G. L. c. 79, § 35 (assessed valuation of real estate);

G. L. c. 111, § 195 (certain lead inspection reports);

G. L. c. 119, § 24 (court investigation reports);

G. L. c. 119, §§ 51A, 51B (Department of Children and Families reports);

G. L. c. 123A, §§ 6A, 9 (sexually dangerous person statute);

G. L. c. 152, §§ 20A, 20B (medical reports);

G. L. c. 175, § 4(7) (report of Commissioner of Insurance);

G. L. c. 185C, § 21 (housing inspection report);

G. L. c. 233, § 65 (declaration of deceased person);

G. L. c. 233, § 65A (answers to interrogatories of deceased party);

G. L. c. 233, § 66 (declarations of testator);

G. L. c. 233, § 69 (records of other courts);

G. L. c. 233, § 70 (judicial notice of law);

G. L. c. 233, § 79B (publicly issued compilations of fact);

G. L. c. 233, § 79C (treatises in malpractice actions);

G. L. c. 233, § 79F (certificate of public way);

G. L. c. 233, § 79G (medical and hospital bills);

G. L. c. 233, § 79H (medical reports of deceased physicians);

G. L. c. 239, § 8A, ¶ 3 (board of health inspection report if certified by inspector who conducted the inspection);

Mass. R. Civ. P. 32(a)(3) (depositions); and

Mass. R. Crim. P. 35(g) (depositions).

If no objection to the hearsay statement is made and it has been admitted, it "may be weighed with the other evidence, and given any evidentiary value which it may possess." Mahoney v. Harley Private Hosp., Inc., 279 Mass. 96, 100 (1932). In a criminal case, the admission of such a statement will be reviewed to determine whether its admission created a substantial risk of a miscarriage of justice. See Commonwealth v. Keevan, 400 Mass. 557, 562 (1987).

Section 803.　Hearsay Exceptions;　Availability of Declarant Immaterial

The following are not excluded by the hearsay rule, even though the declarant is available as a witness:

(1) Present Sense Impression. [Exception not recognized]

(2) Excited Utterance (Spontaneous Utterance). A spontaneous utterance if (A) there is an occurrence or event sufficiently startling to render inoperative the normal reflective thought processes of the observer, and (B) the declarant's statement was a spontaneous reaction to the occurrence or event and not the result of reflective thought.

(3) Then–Existing Mental, Emotional, or Physical Condition.

(A) Expressions of present physical condition such as pain and physical health.

(B)(i) Statements of a person as to his or her present friendliness, hostility, intent, knowledge, or other mental condition are admissible to prove such mental condition.

(ii) Statements, not too remote in time, which indicate an intention to engage in particular conduct, are admissible to prove that the conduct was, in fact, put in effect. Statements of memory or belief to prove the fact remembered or believed do not fall within this exception.

(iii) Declarations of a testator cannot be received to prove the execution of a will, but may be shown to show the state of mind or feelings of the testator.

(4) Statements for Purposes of Medical Diagnosis or Treatment. Statements made for the purpose of medical diagnosis or treatment describing medical history, pain, symptoms, condition, or cause, but not as to the identity of the person responsible or legal significance of such symptoms or injury.

(5) Past Recollection Recorded.

(A) A previously recorded statement may be admissible if (i) the witness has insufficient memory to testify fully and accurately, (ii) the witness had firsthand knowledge of the facts recorded, (iii) the witness can testify that the recorded statement was truthful when made, and (iv) the witness made or adopted the recorded statement when the events were fresh in the witness's memory.

(B) The recorded statement itself may be admitted in evidence, although the original of the statement must be produced if procurable.

(6) Business and Hospital Records.

(A) Entry, Writing, or Record Made in Regular Course of Business. A business record shall not be inadmissible because it is hearsay or self-serving if the court finds that (i) the entry, writing, or record was made in good faith; (ii) it was made in the regular course of business; (iii) it was made before the beginning of the civil or criminal proceeding in which it is offered; and (iv) it was the regular course of such business to make such memorandum or record at the time of such act, transaction, occurrence, or event, or within a reasonable time thereafter.

(B) Hospital Records. Records kept by hospitals pursuant to G. L. c. 111, § 70, shall be admissible as evidence so far as such records relate to the treatment and medical history of such cases, but nothing contained therein shall be admissible as evidence which has reference to the question of liability. Records required to be kept by hospitals under the law of any other United States jurisdiction may be admissible.

(C) Medical and Hospital Services.

(i) Definitions.

(a) Itemized Bills, Records, and Reports. As used in this section, "itemized bills, records, and reports" means itemized hospital or medical bills; physician or dentist reports; hospital medical records relating to medical, dental, hospital services, prescriptions, or orthopedic appliances rendered to or prescribed for a person injured; or any report of any examination of said injured person including, but not limited to, hospital medical records.

(b) Physician or Dentist. As used in this section, "physician or dentist" means a physician, dentist, or any person who is licensed to practice as such under the laws of the jurisdiction within which such services were rendered, as well as chiropodists, chiropractors, optometrists, osteopaths, physical therapists, podiatrists, psychologists, and other medical personnel licensed to practice under the laws of the jurisdiction within which such services were rendered.

(c) Hospital. As used in this section, "hospital" means any hospital required to keep records under G. L. c. 111, § 70, or which is in any way licensed or regulated by the laws of any other State, or by the laws and regulations of the United States of America, including hospitals of the Veterans Administration or similar type institutions, whether incorporated or not.

(d) Health Maintenance Organization. As used in this section, "health maintenance organization" shall have the same meaning as defined in G. L. c. 176G, § 1.

(ii) Admissibility of Itemized Bills, Records, and Reports. In any civil or criminal proceeding, itemized bills, records, and reports of an examination of or for services rendered to an injured person are admissible as evidence of the fair and reasonable charge for such services, the necessity of such services or treatments, the diagnosis, prognosis, opinion as to the proximate cause of the condition so diagnosed, or the opinion as to disability or incapacity, if any, proximately resulting from the condition so diagnosed, provided that

(a) the party offering the evidence gives the opposing party written notice of the intention to offer the evidence, along with a copy of the evidence, by mailing it by certified mail, return receipt requested, not less than ten days before the introduction of the evidence;

(b) the party offering the evidence files an affidavit of such notice and the return receipt is filed with the clerk of the court after said receipt has been returned; and

(c) the itemized bill, record, or report is subscribed and sworn to under the penalties of perjury by the physician, dentist, authorized agent of a hospital or health maintenance organization rendering such services, or by the pharmacist or retailer of orthopedic appliances.

(iii) Calling the Physician or Dentist as a Witness. Nothing contained in this subsection limits the right of a party to call the physician or dentist, or any other person, as a witness to testify about the contents of the itemized bill, record, or report in question.

(7) Absence of Entry in Records Kept in Accordance with Provisions of Section 803(6). The absence of an entry in records of regularly conducted activity, or testimony of a witness that he or she has examined records and not found a particular entry or entries, is admissible for purposes of proving the nonoccurrence of the event.

(8) Official/Public Records and Reports.

(A) Record of Primary Fact. A record of a primary fact, made by a public officer in the performance of an official duty, is competent evidence as to the existence of that fact.

(B) Prima Facie Evidence. Certain statutes provide that the admission of facts contained in certain public records constitute prima facie evidence of the existence of those facts.

(C) Record of Investigations. Record of investigations and inquiries conducted, either voluntarily or pursuant to requirement of law, by public officers concerning causes and effects involving the exercise of judgment and discretion, expressions of opinion, and making conclusions are not admissible in evidence as public records, unless specifically authorized by statute.

(9) Public Records of Vital Statistics. A town clerk's record of birth, marriage, or death is prima facie evidence of the facts recorded, but nothing contained in the record of a death that refers to the question of liability for causing the death is admissible in evidence.

(10) Absence of a Public Record. Testimony—or a certification under Section 902—that a diligent search failed to disclose a public record or statement is admissible in evidence if the testimony or certification is offered to prove that

(A) the record or statement does not exist, or

(B) a matter did not occur or exist, if a public office regularly kept a record or statement for a matter of that kind.

(11) Records of Religious Organizations. [Exception not recognized]

(12) Marriage, Baptismal, and Similar Certificates. [Exception not recognized]

(13) Family Records. A statement of fact about personal or family history contained in a family record, such as a Bible, genealogy, chart, engraving on a ring, inscription on a portrait, or engraving on an urn or burial marker or a similar item is admissible in evidence.

(14) Records or Documents Affecting an Interest in Property. A registry copy of a document purporting to prove or establish an interest in land is admissible as proof of the content of the original recorded document and its execution and delivery by each person who signed it. However, the grantee or entity claiming present ownership interest of the property must account for the absence of the original document before offering the registry copy.

(15) Statements in Documents Affecting an Interest in Property. Statements of a person's married or unmarried status, kinship or lack of kinship, or of the date of the person's birth or death which relate or purport to relate to the title to land and are sworn to before any officer authorized by law to administer oaths may be filed for record and shall be recorded in the registry of deeds for the county where the land or any part thereof lies. Any such statement, if so recorded, or a certified copy of the record thereof, insofar as the facts stated therein bear on the title to land, shall be admissible in evidence in support of such title in any court in the Commonwealth in proceedings relating to such title.

(16) Statements in Ancient Documents. A statement in a document that is at least thirty years old and whose authenticity is established is admissible in evidence.

(17) Statements of Facts of General Interest. Statements of facts of general interest to persons engaged in an occupation contained in a list, register, periodical, book, or other compilation, issued to the public, shall, in the discretion of the court, if the court finds that the compilation is published for the use of persons engaged in that occupation and commonly is used and relied upon by them, be admissible in civil cases as evidence of the truth of any fact so stated.

(18) Learned Treatises.

(A) Use in Medical Malpractice Actions. Statements of facts or opinions on a subject of science or art contained in a published treatise, periodical, book, or pamphlet shall, insofar as the court shall find that the said statements are relevant and that the writer of such statements is recognized in his or her profession or calling as an expert on the subject, be admissible in actions of contract or tort for malpractice, error, or mistake against physicians, surgeons, dentists, optometrists, hospitals, and sanitaria, as evidence tending to prove said facts or as opinion evidence; provided, however, that the party intending to offer as evidence any such statements shall, not less than thirty days before the trial of the action, give the adverse party or that party's attorney notice of such intention, stating the name of the writer of the statements; the title of the treatise, periodical, book, or pamphlet in which they are contained; the date of publication of the same; the name of the publisher of the same; and wherever possible or practicable the page or pages of the same on which the said statements appear.

(B) Use in Cross–Examination of Experts. To the extent called to the attention of an expert witness upon cross-examination, statements contained in published treatises, periodicals, or pamphlets on a subject of history, medicine, or other science or art, established as a reliable authority by the testimony or admission of the witness or by other expert testimony or by judicial notice. If admitted, the statements may be read into evidence, but may not be received as exhibits.

(19) Reputation Concerning Personal or Family History. A reputation within a family as to matters of pedigree, such as birth, marriage, and relationships between and among family members, may be testified to by any member of the family.

(20) Reputation Concerning Boundaries or General History. Evidence of a general or common reputation concerning the existence or nonexistence of a boundary or other matter of public or general interest concerning land or real property is admissible.

(21) Reputation Concerning Character. A witness with knowledge may testify to a person's reputation as to a trait of character, as provided in Sections 404, 405, and 608.

(22) Judgment of a Previous Conviction. Evidence of a final judgment of conviction is admissible if

(A) the judgment was entered after a trial or guilty plea, but not a nolo contendere plea;

(B) the conviction was for a crime punishable by death or by confinement for more than a year;

(C) the evidence is admitted to prove any fact essential to the judgment; and

(D) when offered by the prosecutor in a criminal case for a purpose other than impeachment, the judgment was against the defendant.

The pendency of an appeal may be shown but does not affect admissibility.

(23) Judgment as to Personal, Family, or General History, or Boundaries. [Exception not recognized]

(24) Out-of-Court Statement of Child Describing Sexual Contact in Proceeding to Place Child in Foster Care.

(A) Admissibility in General. Any out-of-court statements of a child under the age of ten describing any act of sexual contact performed on or with the child, or the circumstances under which it occurred, or identifying the perpetrator offered in an action brought under G. L. c. 119, §§ 23(C) and 24, shall be admissible; provided, however that

(i) the person to whom the statement was made, or who heard the child make the statement, testifies;

(ii) the judge finds that the statement is offered as evidence of a material fact and is more probative on the point for which it is offered than any other evidence which the proponent can procure through reasonable effort;

(iii) the judge finds pursuant to Subsection (24)(B) that such statement is reliable; and

(iv) the judge's reasons for relying on the statement appear in the judge's findings pursuant to Subsection (24)(C).

(B) Reliability of Statement. A judge must assess the reliability of the out-of-court statement by considering the following factors:

(i) the timing of the statement, the circumstances in which it was made, the language used by the child, and the child's apparent sincerity or motive in making the statement;

(ii) the consistency over time of a child's statement concerning abuse, expert testimony about a child's ability to remember and to relate his or her experiences, or other relevant personality traits;

(iii) the child's capacity to remember and to relate, and the child's ability to perceive the necessity of telling the truth; and

(iv) whether other admissible evidence corroborates the existence of child abuse.

(C) Findings on the Record. The judge's reasons for relying on the statement must appear clearly in the specific and detailed findings the judge is required to make in a care and protection case.

(D) Admissibility by Common Law or Statute. An out-of-court statement admissible by common law or by statute shall remain admissible notwithstanding the provisions of this section.

NOTE

Confrontation Clause. In a criminal case, an out-of-court statement offered against the defendant for its truth must first satisfy a hearsay exception and then satisfy the confrontation clause. Commonwealth v. Wilson, 94 Mass. App. Ct. 416, 421 (2018). For a discussion of the relationship between the confrontation clause and the hearsay exceptions stated in Section 803, refer to the Introductory Note to Article VIII, Hearsay.

Subsection (1). To date, the present sense impression exception has not been adopted in Massachusetts. See Commonwealth v. Mandeville, 386 Mass. 393, 398 n.3 (1982).

Subsection (2). This subsection is taken nearly verbatim from Commonwealth v. Santiago, 437 Mass. 620, 623 (2002). See also Commonwealth v. McLaughlin, 364 Mass. 211, 221–222 (1973); Commonwealth v. Wilson, 94 Mass. App. Ct. 416, 424 n.9 (2018) (describing history of excited utterance or spontaneous exclamation exception). In determining whether a statement qualifies under this exception, the trial judge should consider whether the statement was made "under the stress of an exciting event and before the declarant has had time to contrive or fabricate the remark" (citations omitted). Commonwealth v. Baldwin, 476 Mass. 1041, 1042 (2017). The judge should consider such factors as whether the statement was made in the same location as the precipitating event, the temporal proximity to the event, and the age, spontaneity, and degree of excitement of the declarant. Id. "The statement itself may be taken as proof of the exciting event." Commonwealth v. Nunes, 430 Mass. 1, 4 (1999). See Commonwealth v. King, 436 Mass. 252, 255 (2002). The proponent of the evidence is not required to show that the spontaneous utterance qualifies, characterizes, or explains the underlying event as long as the court is satisfied that the statement was the product of a startling event and not the result of conscious reflection. See Commonwealth v. Santiago, 437 Mass. at 624–627.

"[T]he nexus between the statement and the event that produced it is but one of many factors to consider in determining whether the declarant was, in fact, under the sway of the exciting event when she made the statement . . . It illuminates the second aspect of the test; it is not an independent requirement, in the same respect that the lapse of time between the startling event and the declarant's statement is not an independent requirement."

Commonwealth v. Santiago, 437 Mass. at 625–626. See Commonwealth v. Gomes, 475 Mass. 775, 788 (2016) ("[t]he circumstances of being the target of a drive-by shooting and actually being shot were certainly enough to permit a reasonable finding" that declarant was "sufficiently startled to render inoperative his normal reflective thought processes").

"[T]here can be no definite and fixed limit of time [between the incident and the statement]. Each case must depend upon its own circumstances." Commonwealth v. McLaughlin, 364 Mass. at 223, quoting Rocco v. Boston-Leader, Inc., 340 Mass. 195, 196–197 (1960). See Commonwealth v. Crawford, 417 Mass. 358, 362 (1994) (statements need not be strictly contemporaneous with the exciting cause; a child's statement five hours later correctly admitted). See also Commonwealth v. Grant, 418 Mass. 76, 81 (1994) (same). "But the length of time between the incident and statement is important; the further the statement from the event, the more difficult it becomes to determine whether the statement is the result of reflection, influenced by other factors." Commonwealth v. DiMonte, 427 Mass. 233, 239 (1998). See Commonwealth v. Barbosa, 477 Mass. 658, 672–673 (2017) (witness's emotional demeanor and physical illness sufficient to demonstrate that statements were spontaneous reaction to murder).

A writing may qualify as a spontaneous utterance. See Commonwealth v. DiMonte, 427 Mass. at 238–240. See also Commonwealth v. Mulgrave, 472 Mass. 170, 176 (2015) (text message). However, "[b]ecause a writing is more suspect as a spontaneous exclamation than is an oral statement, the circumstances of the writing would have to include indicia of reliability even more persuasive than those required for an oral statement before [the court] could conclude that the writing qualified as a spontaneous exclamation." Commonwealth v. DiMonte, 427 Mass. at 239. The "heightened indicia of reliability" requirement does not impose an additional test for written statements but is meant "only to ensure that a writing, which generally is a product of reflection, meets the spontaneity requirement." Commonwealth v. Mulgrave, 472 Mass. at 177. Other than increased scrutiny on the spontaneity element, "the analysis is the same as for an oral statement." Id.

A bystander's spontaneous utterance may be admissible. See Commonwealth v. Harbin, 435 Mass. 654, 657–658 (2002). "Although witnesses may not testify unless evidence is introduced sufficient to support a finding that they have personal knowledge of the matter about which they are testifying, there is no requirement that the declarant have been a participant in the exciting event" (citation omitted). Id. at 657. But see Commonwealth v. Alcantara, 471 Mass. 550, 558–559 (2015) (recording of 911 call containing information outside of caller's personal knowledge was admissible as excited utterance where information was acquired by caller from person who had personal knowledge and whose statement to caller also was excited utterance).

A statement made in response to a question may qualify as a spontaneous utterance. See Commonwealth v. Simon, 456 Mass. 280, 296 (2010); Commonwealth v. Wilson, 94 Mass. App. Ct. 416, 423–424 (2018) (declarant's responses to questions during 911 call and initial response to police questioning at the scene concerning defendant's whereabouts admissible as excited utterances); Commonwealth v. Guaman, 90 Mass. App. Ct. 36, 42–43 (2016) (nine-year-old's call to 911 to report her uncle was driving drunk with his young son in the car, made because of caller's concern that her cousin was in danger, was admissible as excited utterance even though some statements were made in response to dispatcher's questions). But see Commonwealth v. McCoy, 456 Mass. 838, 849 (2010) (statements made by victim of sexual assault during interview by sexual assault nurse examiner at hospital lacked requisite degree of spontaneity to qualify as excited utterances).

Confrontation in Criminal Cases. "When the Commonwealth in a criminal case seeks to admit the excited utterance of a declarant who is not a witness at trial or has completed his testimony at trial, the judge should conduct a careful voir dire, evidentiary if needed, before admitting the excited utterance in evidence." Commonwealth v. Hurley, 455 Mass. 53, 68 n.14 (2009) (statement, if testimonial, would be barred by the confrontation clause).

Subsection (3)(A). This subsection is derived from Murray v. Foster, 343 Mass. 655, 658 (1962). See Weeks v. Boston Elevated Ry. Co., 190 Mass. 563, 564–565 (1906) (witness permitted to testify that decedent remarked that the "carriage never rode so hard before"; "[t]his may well be regarded as an expression and indication of then present pain or weakness"); Simmons v. Yurchak, 28 Mass. App. Ct. 371, 373–375, 375 n.6 (1990) (upholding trial court's refusal to apply Proposed Mass. R. Evid. 803[3] while noting that "[i]t is not self-evident that Proposed Mass. R. Evid. 803[3] propounds a more expansive hearsay exception than the common law 'expression of pain'").

Subsection (3)(B). The principle contained in the following three subsections is also known as the "state-of-mind exception." This exception applies only to statements that assert the declarant's own state of mind directly (usually by words describing the state of mind). See, e.g., Commonwealth v. Woollam, 478 Mass. 493, 499 (2017) (text messages were admissible under state of mind exception to hearsay rule because they "were offered to show proof of motive for the killing"); Pardo v. General Hosp. Corp., 446 Mass. 1, 18–19 (2006) (memorandum and letter admissible to show nondiscriminatory state of mind at time employment actions were taken); Commonwealth v. White, 32 Mass. App. Ct. 949, 949 (1992) (in prosecution for sexual abuse of a child, mother's out-of-court statement that, even if defendant didn't do it, "I still hope that all sorts of nasty things happen to him" was admissible under state-of-mind exception as an expression of her hostility toward defendant to prove her bias as prosecution witness). But see Commonwealth v. Whitman, 453 Mass. 331, 341–342 (2009) (defendant's statement that he heard voices inadmissible, as it pertained to the past, not the present). For statements that convey the declarant's state of mind circumstantially or that are probative of another's state of mind, see the Note "Evidence Admitted for Non-hearsay Purpose" to Section 801(c), Definitions: Hearsay.

Evidence of a person's state of mind, whether hearsay (and offered under this exception) or nonhearsay, is admissible only if the state of mind is relevant and if the probative value of the proffered evidence is not substantially outweighed by the risk of unfair prejudice to the opponent. See Section 403, Excluding Relevant Evidence for Prejudice, Confusion, Waste of Time, or Other Reason. Statements offered to show state of mind often include assertions of facts that led to that state of mind (e.g., the victim's out-of-court statements describing the defendant's threats or assaults offered as evidence of the victim's determination to end the relationship with the defendant). The out-of-court statement of those facts would ordinarily be inadmissible hearsay, and the trier of fact's reliance on the truth of those facts would therefore be unfairly prejudicial to the opponent. This danger is especially acute in criminal cases, where confrontation clause rights are also at stake when hearsay is admitted against a defendant. See Introductory Note to Article VIII, Hearsay. Before such evidence is admitted, the trial court must conduct a careful review of the probative value of the evidence and the risk of unfair prejudice under Section 403. See Commonwealth v. Magraw, 426 Mass. 589 (1998) (new trial granted because of erroneous admission of murder victim's statements to show her fear of defendant). In addition to carrying this enhanced risk of unfair prejudice, evidence of the victim's state of mind often has limited probative value. A murder victim's statements of fear of the defendant alone are not relevant to prove motive. Commonwealth v. Qualls, 425 Mass. 163, 169 (1997). When a victim's state of mind is offered to prove a defendant's motive, it is usually not relevant unless the state of mind was known to the defendant, and the defendant was likely to respond to it. Id. at 167. See Commonwealth v. Watkins, 473 Mass. 222, 238 (2015). See also Commonwealth v.

Castano, 478 Mass. 75, 85–86 (2017) (victim's intent to end relationship with defendant). However,

"[a] murder victim's state of mind becomes a material issue if the defendant opens the door by claiming that the death was a suicide or a result of self-defense, that the victim would voluntarily meet with or go someplace with the defendant, or that the defendant was on friendly terms with the victim."

Commonwealth v. Magraw, 426 Mass. at 594.

"Where evidence of the victim's state of mind is admitted, it may only be used to prove that state of mind, and not to prove the truth of what was stated or that a defendant harbored certain thoughts or acted in a certain way. Therefore, on the defendant's request, the jury must be given an instruction on the limited use of state of mind evidence."

Id. at 594–595, citing Commonwealth v. Costa, 354 Mass. 757 (1968).

Subsection (3)(B)(i). This subsection is taken nearly verbatim from Commonwealth v. Caldron, 383 Mass. 86, 91 (1981). See Commonwealth v. Mendes, 441 Mass. 459, 466 (2004); Commonwealth v. Ferreira, 381 Mass. 306, 310–311 (1980); Commonwealth v. Wampler, 369 Mass. 121, 123 (1975).

Subsection (3)(B)(ii). The first sentence of this subsection is taken verbatim from Commonwealth v. Ferreira, 381 Mass. 306, 310 (1980). Accord Commonwealth v. Trefethen, 157 Mass. 180, 183–184 (1892) (murder conviction reversed because trial judge improperly excluded evidence that victim, who was unmarried and pregnant at time of her death, told fortune teller the day before her drowning that she was going to drown herself). See Commonwealth v. Ortiz, 463 Mass. 402, 409–410 (2012) (murder victim told family she was going to go meet defendant after dinner); Commonwealth v. Fernandes, 427 Mass. 90, 95 (1998) ("A declarant's threat to 'get' or kill someone is admissible to show that the declarant had a particular state of mind and that he carried out his intent."); Commonwealth v. Vermette, 43 Mass. App. Ct. 789, 801–802 (1997) (proper to admit statement of intention to lie and confess to shooting for purpose of showing that declarant carried out that intent). In a prosecution for murder, a victim's statement of intent to meet with the defendant, made immediately before the murder, is sometimes admissible. See Commonwealth v. Britt, 465 Mass. 87, 90 (2013) (admission of victim's statement that he was going to meet defendant to get his money not error, as statement did not necessarily mean that defendant had previously agreed to a meeting, and it was cumulative of other evidence of a preplanned meeting). See also Commonwealth v. Ortiz, 463 Mass. at 409–410 (murder victim's statement to daughter that she was going to pick up defendant at a restaurant admissible, because statement expressed only victim's "present intent to act," not defendant's, and there was other evidence that defendant was with victim at time of murder). In each of the above cases, there was independent evidence of the defendant's presence at the place in question.

The second sentence of this subsection is derived from Commonwealth v. Lowe, 391 Mass. 97, 104–105, cert. denied, 469 U.S. 840 (1984). See Commonwealth v. Pope, 397 Mass. 275, 281 (1986) ("exception applies only to the declarant's present intent to act, not to past conduct"). See also Commonwealth v. Seabrooks, 425 Mass. 507, 512 (1997) ("[a]llowing hearsay statements generally under the state-of-mind exception would entirely eviscerate the hearsay rule and its important purpose of securing the correctness and completeness of testimony through cross-examination"). Accord Shepard v. United States, 290 U.S. 96, 105–106 (1933).

Subsection (3)(B)(iii). This subsection is taken nearly verbatim from Mahan v. Perkins, 274 Mass. 176, 179–180 (1931). See id. at 180 ("[Testator's] declarations showing her intention, plan or purpose should not be received to support the proponent's contention that the will was signed by her and attested by [the witness].")

Subsection (4). This subsection is derived from Commonwealth v. Comtois, 399 Mass. 668, 675 (1987), and Commonwealth v. Howard,

355 Mass. 526, 528–529 (1969). See Commonwealth v. Arana, 453 Mass. 214, 231 (2009); Commonwealth v. DeOliveira, 447 Mass. 56, 62 (2006). If made for the purpose of receiving medical advice, the statements are admissible under this subsection even if made after the commencement of the action. Barber v. Merriam, 93 Mass. 322, 326 (1865).

While the appellate cases cited in this note related to physicians, nothing in the reasoning of those cases exclude other health care professionals. See Bouchie v. Murray, 376 Mass. 524, 527–528 (1978).

Cross–Reference: Section 803(6)(C), Hearsay Exceptions; Availability of Declarant Immaterial: Business and Hospital Records: Medical and Hospital Services.

Subsection (5)(A). This subsection is derived from Commonwealth v. Nolan, 427 Mass. 541, 543 (1998), and Commonwealth v. Bookman, 386 Mass. 657, 663–664 (1982). A witness does not have to have a complete lack of memory; all that is required is that the witness cannot testify fully. Commonwealth v. Nolan, 427 Mass. at 544.

"As to the fourth element of the foundation, where the recording was made by another, it must be shown that the witness adopted the writing 'when the events were fresh in [the witness's] mind'" (emphasis omitted). Commonwealth v. Evans, 439 Mass. 184, 189–190 (2003), quoting Commonwealth v. Bookman, 386 Mass. at 664. See Commonwealth v. Fryar, 414 Mass. 732, 746 (1993), cert. denied, 522 U.S. 1033 (1997). The requirement that the recording be made when the events were fresh in the witness's memory has been interpreted broadly. See Catania v. Emerson Cleaners, Inc., 362 Mass. 388, 389–390 (1972) (holding that statement given approximately eight months after accident admissible as a past recollection recorded). But see Kirby v. Morales, 50 Mass. App. Ct. 786, 791–792 (2001) (one year insufficient).

Subsection (5)(B). This subsection is derived from Fisher v. Swartz, 333 Mass. 265, 267–271 (1955). In Fisher, the court cautioned that it was not

"laying down a hard and fast rule that in every 'past recollection recorded' situation the writing used by the witness must always be admitted in evidence, and that it is error to exclude it ... It is conceivable that there might be situations where the probative value of the writing as evidence might be outweighed by the risk that its admission might create substantial danger of undue prejudice or of misleading the jury. In such a case the trial judge in the exercise of sound discretion might be justified in excluding the writing."

Id. at 270. See Commonwealth v. Bookman, 386 Mass. 657, 664 (1982) (error to admit grand jury testimony of the witness as past recollection recorded). The witness may read from the writing during the witness's testimony, or the writing may be admitted.

The past recollection recorded exception should not be confused with the doctrine of refreshing memory. See Section 612, Writing or Object Used to Refresh Memory. For a discussion of the distinction between the two, see Fisher v. Swartz, 333 Mass. at 267.

Subsection (6)(A). This subsection is taken nearly verbatim from G. L. c. 233, § 78. See Beal Bank, SSB v. Eurich, 444 Mass. 813, 815 (2005); Commonwealth v. Trapp, 396 Mass. 202, 208 (1985). See, e.g., Commonwealth v. Fulgiam, 477 Mass. 20, 39–43 (2017) ("ten-print" fingerprint cards); Adoption of Paula, 420 Mass. 716 (1995) (in care and protection proceeding, police report containing officer's firsthand account of conditions in the marital home during execution of search warrant was admissible as business record); Johnson v. MBTA, 418 Mass. 783, 786 (1994) (results of laboratory test); Commonwealth v. Sellon, 380 Mass. 220, 230 & n.15 (1980) (In admitting police journal entry fixing the time a telephone call was received, the Supreme Judicial Court noted that "[t]he operations of the instrumentalities of government constitute 'business' within the meaning of the statute" [citation omitted].); Commonwealth v. Walker, 379 Mass. 297, 302 (1979) (police record of stolen car report); Commonwealth v. Albino, 81 Mass. App. Ct. 736, 737–738 (2012) (notification letters from Sex Offender Registry Board to police department). In a criminal pro-

ceeding where the judge admits a business record under this exception, the questions of fact serving as a basis for its admissibility must be submitted to the jury. G. L. c. 233, § 78. See Commonwealth v. Reyes, 19 Mass. App. Ct. 1017, 1019 (1985). Cf. G. L. c. 233, § 79J (certification, inspection, and copies of business records).

The trial judge may, as a condition to admissibility of business records, require the party offering the business record into evidence to call a witness who has personal knowledge of the facts stated in the record. G. L. c. 233, § 78. See Burns v. Combined Ins. Co. of Am., 6 Mass. App. Ct. 86, 92 (1978). The foundation for the admission of a business record need not be established through the testimony of a designated keeper of records, provided that the testifying witness has an adequate understanding of the business's record-keeping system. Commonwealth v. Driscoll, 91 Mass. App. Ct. 474, 480 (2017). A trial judge must first determine if the writing itself qualifies as a business record, and then determine "whether all or only some of the material and information contained in the document qualifies as being within the scope of the statutory exception." Wingate v. Emery Air Freight Corp., 385 Mass. 402, 408 (1982) (Liacos, J., concurring). A business record is admissible even when its preparer has relied on the statements of others because the personal knowledge of the entrant or maker affects only the weight of the record, not its admissibility. Id. at 406. However, "unless statements on which the preparer relies fall within some other exception to the hearsay rule, the proponent must show that all persons in the chain of communication, from the observer to the preparer, reported the information as a matter of business duty or business routine." Id. See NationsBanc Mtge. Corp. v. Eisenhauer, 49 Mass. App. Ct. 727, 733–735 (2000) (where records made by one business were transferred to another, latter business unable to admit the records under business record exception because records were made by former business). But see Commonwealth v. Albino, 81 Mass. App. Ct. 736, 738 (2012) (business record of one business may be admissible as business record of second business where record is integrated into records of second business and relied on by that business), citing Beal Bank SSB v. Eurich, 444 Mass. 813, 815 (2005).

"[T]he business records hearsay exception in [G. L. c. 233,] § 78 may not be used to expand the scope of the hearsay exception for hospital medical records." Commonwealth v. Irene, 462 Mass. 600, 616 (2012). "The admissibility of statements in medical records is limited by the provisions in G. L. c. 233 relating to hospital records, including §§ 79 and 79G." Id.

Opinions contained in business records are not admissible unless they fall within some other exception to the hearsay rule. See Julian v. Randazzo, 380 Mass. 391, 392–393 (1980); Burke v. Memorial Hosp., 29 Mass. App. Ct. 948, 949–950 (1990). Cf. Section 803(6)(C), Hearsay Exceptions; Availability of Declarant Immaterial: Business and Hospital Records: Medical and Hospital Services (provides, under certain circumstances, for the admission of opinion contained in medical, dental, and other identified records and reports). Even if a document satisfies the business record exception, the trial judge retains the discretion to consider the reliability of the evidence offered. N.E. Physical Therapy Plus, Inc. v. Liberty Mut. Ins. Co., 466 Mass. 358, 367 n.10 (2013). Cross–Reference: Section 803(17), Hearsay Exceptions; Availability of Declarant Immaterial: Statements of Facts of General Interest.

Police Reports. Police reports are generally admissible as business records under this subsection. Commonwealth v. Walker, 379 Mass. 297, 302 (1979); Carey v. New Yorker of Worcester, Inc., 355 Mass. 450, 453 (1969). Thus, the reporting officers' firsthand observations as recorded in their reports are admissible. Adoption of Paula, 420 Mass. 716, 727 (1995) (responding officers' description of open beer cans, drinking by underage guests, inadequate sleeping arrangements for the children, broken window, and weapons openly displayed). Such reports are admissible as an exception to the hearsay rule even when the preparer has relied on statements made by others in the regular course of the preparer's record-keeping duties (such as fellow police officers) because, under G. L. c. 233, § 78, "'personal knowledge by the entrant or maker' is a matter affecting the weight (rather than the admissibility) of the record." Wingate v. Emery Air Freight Corp., 385 Mass. 402, 406 (1982), quoting G. L. c. 233, § 78. However, "second-level" hearsay, such as statements of bystanders or witnesses, should be redacted, as these statements are not made admissible by G. L. c. 233, § 78. See Commonwealth v. Happnie, 3 Mass. App. Ct. 193, 199 (1975), overruled in part on other grounds by Commonwealth v. Szerlong, 457 Mass. 858, 869 (2010); Kelly v. O'Neil, 1 Mass. App. Ct. 313, 316–317 (1973). Cf. Commonwealth v. Walker, 379 Mass. at 302 (statements made by unidentified caller to police cadet who authored report not offered for their truth). Further, the admittance of police reports as business records applies only to factual observations and does not permit the admission of opinions contained in the report. Julian v. Randazzo, 380 Mass. 391, 393 (1980). Police reports may be considered as evidence at a probation revocation hearing even when the reporting officer does not testify and even when they contain second-level hearsay, so long as they are deemed sufficiently reliable. See Commonwealth v. Durling, 407 Mass. 108, 120–122 (1990) (personal observations of nontestifying officer); Commonwealth v. Foster, 77 Mass. App. Ct. 444, 450 (2010) (witness statement contained in police report). Police reports relating to prior sexual offenses are admissible in Sexually Dangerous Person proceedings pursuant to G. L. c. 123A, § 14(c), even when they contain hearsay statements. Commonwealth v. Given, 441 Mass. 741, 745–746 (2004).

Criminal Cases. A record or report that qualifies as an exception to the hearsay rule under this subsection may nevertheless be inadmissible if it contains testimonial statements in violation of the confrontation clause. See Melendez–Diaz v. Massachusetts, 557 U.S. 305, 310–311 (2009). Additionally, Massachusetts statutory law provides that in criminal cases tried to a jury, "all questions of fact which must be determined by the court as the basis for the admissibility of the evidence involved shall be submitted to the jury." G. L. c. 233, § 78. As a result, in criminal cases involving business records, unless the defendant agrees otherwise, the judge not only must make the four preliminary determinations of fact set forth in Subsection (6)(A), but must instruct the jury that they too must find these facts by a preponderance of the evidence before they consider the contents of the business record. See Commonwealth v. Oppenheim, 86 Mass. App. Ct. 359, 367 (2014).

Subsection (6)(B). This subsection is derived from G. L. c. 233, § 79. See Commonwealth v. Sheldon, 423 Mass. 373, 376 (1996). A hospital record is admissible at trial if the trial judge finds that (1) it is the type of record contemplated by G. L. c. 233, § 79; (2) the information is germane to the patient's treatment or medical history; and (3) the information is recorded from the personal knowledge of the entrant or from a compilation of the personal knowledge of those under a medical obligation to transmit such information. Bouchie v. Murray, 376 Mass. 524, 531 (1978). See Commonwealth v. Ackerman, 476 Mass. 1033, 1034 (2017) (even where medical record does not expressly state that blood alcohol test was performed as part of medical treatment, circumstances surrounding test may permit that inference). Compare Commonwealth v. Sheldon, 423 Mass. at 375–377 (blood alcohol tests conducted solely to prove the defendant's sobriety, in circumstances in which there was no hospital protocol for conducting such a test, do not qualify for admission under G. L. c. 233, § 79), with Commonwealth v. Dyer, 77 Mass. App. Ct. 850, 855–856 (2010) (blood alcohol test results ordered by physician exclusively for the medical evaluation and treatment of the defendant qualify for admission under G. L. c. 233, § 79). The party offering the record into evidence has the burden of proving the statutory requirements, Commonwealth v. Dunne, 394 Mass. 10, 16 (1985), and need not give advance notice of the intent to offer the record in evidence, Commonwealth v. McCready, 50 Mass. App. Ct. 521, 524–525 (2000). Cf. G. L. c. 233, § 79G (ten days' advance notice required). The trial judge has discretion to exclude portions of an otherwise admissible medical record in accordance with Sections 402, General Admissibility of Relevant Evidence; 403, Excluding Relevant Evidence for Prejudice, Confusion, Waste of Time, or Other Reasons; and 611(a), Mode and

Order of Examining Witnesses and Presenting Evidence: Control by the Court. See Commonwealth v. Francis, 450 Mass. 132, 138–139 (2007). See also Commonwealth v. Hamel, 91 Mass. App. Ct. 349, 352 (2017) (in prosecution for sexual assault of child, error to admit medical records with diagnosis of "irritant dermatitis" of penis in absence of expert testimony that condition was caused by rubbing described by alleged victim).

"[V]oluntary statements of third persons appearing in the record are not admissible unless they are offered for reasons other than to prove the truth of the matter contained therein or, if offered for their truth, come within another exception to the hearsay rule ..." Bouchie v. Murray, 376 Mass. at 531. The Supreme Judicial Court has noted that G. L. c. 233, § 79,

"may be read to permit the admission of a medical history taken from a person with reason to know of the patient's medical history by virtue of his or her relationship to the patient. Such a history may contain personal knowledge gained from observation or knowledge gained from an intimate relationship. We think that [G. L. c. 233, § 79] should be read to include such statements if made for purposes of medical diagnosis or treatment and if the declarant's relationship to the patient and the circumstances in which the statements are made guarantees their trustworthiness."

Id. at 531. In Commonwealth v. Dube, 413 Mass. 570, 573 (1992), the court noted that Section 79 has been interpreted liberally to allow "the admission of a record that relates directly and primarily to the treatment and medical history of the patient," even if facts pertaining to liability but only incidental to medical treatment have also been admitted. See Commonwealth v. DiMonte, 427 Mass. 233, 242 (1998).

"[General Laws c. 233, § 79,] relies on a 'pragmatic test of reliability' that permits the introduction of records containing even second level hearsay provided the information in the record is of a nature that is relied on by medical professionals in administering health care... While creating an exception to the hearsay rule, the statute does not permit the admission of hospital records that are facially unreliable."

Commonwealth v. Johnson, 59 Mass. App. Ct. 164, 167 (2003), citing Doyle v. Dong, 412 Mass. 682, 687 (1992). See generally Petitions of the Dep't of Social Servs. to Dispense with Consent to Adoption, 399 Mass. 279, 287–288 (1987) (privileged material should be redacted).

Illustrations. Notations on Form 2 in the "Sexual Assault Evidence Collection Kit" made by the SANE (sexual assault nurse examiner) based on statements by the complainant about how he or she received his or her injuries are admissible because they assist the SANE in conducting the examination, even though the information is also collected to assist investigators. Commonwealth v. Dargon, 457 Mass. 387, 396 (2010). However, the printed form should not be admitted because it suggests a sexual assault occurred. Id. Notations on hospital intake forms stating that a patient was "assaulted" should be redacted. Commonwealth v. DiMonte, 427 Mass. at 241–242. In DiMonte, several references to the facts of the alleged assault, including "Pt. struck in the face [with] fist" and "reports having a plastic container thrown [at] her which struck her [right] forehead," were admissible. Id. at 241. Statements consisting of self-diagnosis should be redacted. Commonwealth v. Hartman, 404 Mass. 306, 316–317 (1989). In Commonwealth v. Concepcion, 362 Mass. 653, 654–655 (1972), hospital records where (a) under the heading "Nature of Illness" appeared the words "? Assaulted– ? Raped," (b) under the heading "History and Physical Exam" appeared the words "History of recent rape," and (c) under the heading "Diagnosis" appeared the notation "? Rape," the doctor's opinions were related to the treatment and medical history. Blood tests bearing on the patient's degree of intoxication are admissible; entries made by observing nurses are also admissible. Commonwealth v. McCready, 50 Mass. App. Ct. 521, 524 (2000). In Commonwealth v. Baldwin, 24 Mass. App. Ct. 200, 202 (1987), a "[d]iagnosis" of "sexual molestation," a term "synonymous to laymen with indecent assault and battery," should have been redacted.

Cf. Commonwealth v. Patton, 458 Mass. 119 (2010) (SAIN [Sexual Abuse Intervention Network] report may be admissible in probation violation hearings).

Subsection (6)(C). This subsection is derived from G. L. c. 233, § 79G. The text in this subsection places the statutory language in more straightforward language and also incorporates the case law. The practitioner, however, is cautioned to check the precise statutory language.

This statute applies to criminal cases as well as to civil cases, and its scope is much broader than that of G. L. c. 233, § 79. Commonwealth v. Schutte, 52 Mass. App. Ct. 796, 798–800 (2001). See generally Grant v. Lewis/Boyle, Inc., 408 Mass. 269, 274 (1990) (declining to adopt Proposed Mass. R. Evid. 803[6] for the purpose of admitting physician's reports given the "carefully crafted provisions of § 79G").

Scope. This subsection establishes a broad exception to the hearsay rule which overlaps to some degree with the hospital records exception provided in Section 803(6)(B), Hearsay Exceptions; Availability of Declarant Immaterial: Business and Hospital Records: Hospital Records. See McHoul, petitioner, 445 Mass. 143, 151 (2005); Ortiz v. Stein, 31 Mass. App. Ct. 643, 645 (1991). But see Brusard v. O'Toole, 45 Mass. App. Ct. 288, 295 (1998) (G. L. c. 233, § 79G, would not allow the admission in evidence of hospital policies and procedures). In some respects, however, this subsection is broader than the exception for hospital records found in Section 803(6)(B) because

> "reports admissible under § 79G may include the 'opinion of such physician . . . as to proximate cause of the condition so diagnosed, . . .' and 'the opinion of such physician . . . as to disability or incapacity, if any, proximately resulting from the condition so diagnosed . . .' These are not matters usually found in a medical record but do pertain to issues commonly involved in personal injury claims and litigation. Thus, the concerns that require redaction of information not germane to the patient's treatment in medical records under § 79, see, e.g., Bouchie v. Murray, 376 Mass. 524, 531 (1978), are overridden by express language in § 79G."

Commonwealth v. Schutte, 52 Mass. App. Ct. at 799–800. Also, since the term "report" is not defined in G. L. c. 233, § 79G, a properly attested letter from a person's treating physician explaining the patient's medical condition and its effects based on the physician's personal observations can be qualified as a report. Id. Ambulance records are admissible under Section 79G, as the certification requirements for EMTs are similar in nature to the licensure requirements for other medical personnel contained in the statute whose reports are admissible. Commonwealth v. Palacios, 90 Mass. App. Ct. 722, 726 (2016).

The full amount of a medical or hospital bill is admissible as evidence of the reasonable value of the services rendered to the injured person, even where the amount actually paid by a private or public insurer is less than that amount. Law v. Griffith, 457 Mass. 349, 353–354 (2010), citing G. L. c. 233, § 79G.

Cross–Reference: G. L. c. 233, § 79H (medical records of deceased physicians); Section 411, Insurance; Section 902(k), Evidence That is Self–Authenticating: Certified Copies of Hospital and Other Records of Treatment and Medical History.

Requirements for Admissibility. Reports offered under G. L. c. 233, § 79G, as opposed to G. L. c. 233, § 78, are admissible even if prepared in anticipation of litigation. See O'Malley v. Soske, 76 Mass. App. Ct. 495, 498–499 (2010); Commonwealth v. Schutte, 52 Mass. App. Ct. 796, 799 n.3 (2001). Medical reports which deal with an injured person's "diagnosis, prognosis, opinion as to the proximate cause of the condition so diagnosed, or the opinion as to disability or incapacity," see Section 803(6)(C)(ii), must be by a physician, as that term is defined in the subsection, who treated or examined the injured person. See Ortiz v. Stein, 31 Mass. App. Ct. at 645–646. See also Gompers v. Finnell, 35 Mass. App. Ct. 91, 93 (1993) ("Nothing in § 79G authorizes one not a physician or dentist to offer an expert opinion that a patient's physical symptoms resulted from a particular

accident or incident."). If a record contains such an opinion, however, it may satisfy the plaintiff's burden of proof on the issue of causation in a medical negligence case. See Bailey v. Cataldo Ambulance Serv., Inc., 64 Mass. App. Ct. 228, 234–236 (2005) (explaining that there is no requirement that an expert opinion on causation contain the phrase "to a reasonable degree of medical certainty").

General Laws c. 233, § 79G, requires that a party who seeks to offer the report of a physician or dentist at trial must serve opposing counsel at least ten days in advance of trial with notice and a copy of the report by the physician or dentist. See Adoption of Seth, 29 Mass. App. Ct. 343, 351–352 (1990). However, the attestation by the physician or dentist does not have to be included with the notice so long as it is present when the evidence is offered at trial. See Grant v. Lewis/Boyle, Inc., 408 Mass. 269, 274 (1990); Knight v. Maersk Container Serv. Co., 49 Mass. App. Ct. 254, 256 (2000).

Cross–Reference: G. L. c. 233, § 79H; Section 902(k), Evidence That is Self–Authenticating: Certified Copies of Hospital and Other Records of Treatment and Medical History.

Subsection (7). This subsection is derived from McNamara v. Honeyman, 406 Mass. 43, 54 n.10 (1989), and Commonwealth v. Scanlan, 9 Mass. App. Ct. 173, 182 (1980). See Johnson v. Wilmington Sales, Inc., 5 Mass. App. Ct. 858, 858 (1977). Where testimony is offered, proof of the fact that an entry does not exist does not require the production of the records themselves or the laying of a foundation for the introduction of secondary evidence. Commonwealth v. Scanlan, 9 Mass. App. Ct. at 182. See Commonwealth v. Torrealba, 316 Mass. 24, 30 (1944); Johnson v. Wilmington Sales, Inc., 5 Mass. App. Ct. at 858.

Subsection (8). This subsection is derived from Commonwealth v. Slavski, 245 Mass. 405, 415 (1923). See Custody of Two Minors, 19 Mass. App. Ct. 552, 559 (1985) (noting that it is "sound practice" for judge to give notice to parties if judge intends to use court investigator or guardian ad litem report where neither party offered report into evidence). Cf. G. L. c. 233, § 76 (admissibility of authenticated government records); Mass. R. Civ. P. 44 (proof of official records); Mass. R. Crim. P. 40 (same). The admission of a record of a primary fact created for routine government administrative functions does not violate the confrontation clause. Commonwealth v. Shangkuan, 78 Mass. App. Ct. 827, 833–834 (2011) (officer's return of service, required by court rule to be completed and filed in court, is nontestimonial because it was not "created solely for use in a pending criminal prosecution," even though it might later be used for proving notice to a defendant).

Under the common law, a report or record does not become an official record for the purpose of this exception merely because it is filed with a governmental agency. See Commonwealth v. Williams, 63 Mass. App. Ct. 615, 619 (2005); Kelly v. O'Neil, 1 Mass. App. Ct. 313, 319 (1973). A hearsay statement recorded in an official record, if made by someone other than the public officer making the record, is not admissible under this exception, although it may be admissible if it falls within another hearsay exception. See Sklar v. Beth Israel Deaconess Med. Ctr., 59 Mass. App. Ct. 550, 556 n.8 (2003). Evaluative reports, opinions, and conclusions contained in a public report are not admissible at common law. Commonwealth v. Nardi, 452 Mass. 379, 387–395 (2008) (ruling that the findings of a medical examiner concerning the nature and extent of the victim's injuries and his or her ultimate opinion as to the cause of death were not statements of fact excluded by the hearsay rule, but instead were evaluative statements that fell outside the public record exception); Mattoon v. City of Pittsfield, 56 Mass. App. Ct. 124, 135 (2002). See Middlesex Supply, Inc. v. Martin & Sons, Inc., 354 Mass. 373, 374–375 (1968); Herson v. New Boston Garden Corp., 40 Mass. App. Ct. 779, 792–793 (1996).

The following statutes provide for the admission of facts contained in public records as prima facie evidence (examples of the records covered are in parentheses): G. L. c. 46, § 19 (birth, marriage, and death records); G. L. c. 79, § 35 (assessed valuation of real property);

G. L. c. 90, § 30 (records of the Registry of Motor Vehicles); G. L. c. 123A, § 14(c) (public records at trial on whether person is sexually dangerous); and G. L. c. 185C, § 21 (report of housing inspector). But see Commonwealth v. Almonte, 465 Mass. 224, 242 (2013) (the preferred practice is to redact means and manner of death before admitting death certificate into evidence). Conclusions contained in public records may be made admissible by statute. Shamlian v. Equitable Acc. Co., 226 Mass. 67, 69–70 (1917).

Mortality Tables. In Harlow v. Chin, 405 Mass. 697, 714 (1989), the Supreme Judicial Court addressed the admissibility of mortality tables:

"Mortality tables, though not conclusive proof of life expectancy, help furnish a basis for the jury's estimation. The tables themselves are admissible regardless of the poor health or extra-hazardous occupation of the person whose life expectancy is being estimated. When the opposing side believes that the person in question, because of poor health, has a lower life expectancy than that reflected in the mortality tables, the usual remedy is to offer evidence to that effect and argue the point to the jury." (Citations omitted.)

Criminal Cases. A record or report that qualifies as an exception to the hearsay rule under this subsection may nevertheless be inadmissible if it contains testimonial statements in violation of the confrontation clause. See Melendez–Diaz v. Massachusetts, 557 U.S. 305, 310–311 (2009). See also Introductory Note to Article VIII, Hearsay.

Subsection (9). This subsection is taken nearly verbatim from G. L. c. 46, § 19. See Commonwealth v. Lykus, 406 Mass. 135, 144 (1989), cert. denied, 519 U.S. 1126 (1997). See also Miles v. Edward Tabor M.D., Inc., 387 Mass. 783, 786 (1982). Records from foreign countries are not admissible under G. L. c. 46, § 19, or G. L. c. 207, § 45. Vergnani v. Guidetti, 308 Mass. 450, 457 (1941). Cf. G. L. c. 46, § 19C ("The commissioner of public health shall use the seal of the department of public health for the purpose of authenticating copies of birth, marriage and death records in his department, and copies of such records when certified by him and authenticated by said seal, shall be evidence like the originals."). General Laws c. 46, § 19, makes the town clerk certificate admissible in evidence, but not with respect to liability. See Wadsworth v. Boston Gas Co., 352 Mass. 86, 93 (1967). See also G. L. c. 207, § 45 ("The record of a marriage made and kept as provided by law by the person by whom the marriage was solemnized, or by the clerk or registrar, or a copy thereof duly certified, shall be prima facie evidence of such marriage.").

Subsection (10). This subsection, which is taken from Proposed Mass. R. Evid. 803(10), reflects Massachusetts practice. See Mass. R. Civ. P. 44(b); Mass. R. Crim. P. 40(b); Blair's Foodland, Inc. v. Shuman's Foodland, Inc., 311 Mass. 172, 175–176 (1942).

Subsection (11). No cases or statutes were located on this issue. Cf. Section 803(6)(A), Hearsay Exceptions; Availability of Declarant Immaterial: Business and Hospital Records: Entry, Writing, or Record Made in Regular Course of Business.

Cross–Reference: Section 804(b)(7), Hearsay Exceptions; Declarant Unavailable: The Exceptions: Religious Records.

Subsection (12). No cases or statutes were located on this issue. Cf. Section 804(b)(7), Hearsay Exceptions; Declarant Unavailable: The Exceptions: Religious Records; Kennedy v. Doyle, 92 Mass. 161, 168 (1865) (baptismal record admissible where maker is deceased).

Subsection (13). This subsection, which is taken from Proposed Mass. R. Evid. 803(13), reflects Massachusetts practice. See North Brookfield v. Warren, 82 Mass. 171, 174–175 (1860). Cf. Section 803(9), Hearsay Exceptions; Availability of Declarant Immaterial: Public Records of Vital Statistics; Section 804(b)(5)(A), Hearsay Exceptions; Declarant Unavailable: The Exceptions: Statutory Exceptions in Civil Cases: Declarations of Decedent.

Subsection (14). This subsection is derived from Scanlan v. Wright, 30 Mass. 523, 527 (1833), and Commonwealth v. Emery, 68 Mass. 80, 81–82 (1854).

Subsection (15). This subsection is taken nearly verbatim from G. L. c. 183, § 5A.

Subsection (16). This subsection is derived from Cunningham v. Davis, 175 Mass. 213, 219 (1900) ("It is a general rule that deeds appearing to be more than 30 years old, which come from the proper custody, and are otherwise free from just grounds of suspicion, are admissible without any proof of execution."). See Whitman v. Shaw, 166 Mass. 451, 460–461 (1896) (ancient plan and field notes); Drury v. Midland R.R. Co., 127 Mass. 571, 581 (1879) (old plans admitted for purposes of establishing location of a creek). Cf. Section 901(b)(8), Authenticating or Identifying Evidence: Examples: Evidence About Ancient Documents.

Cross–Reference: Section 403, Excluding Relevant Evidence for Prejudice, Confusion, Waste of Time, or Other Reason; Section 805, Hearsay within Hearsay.

Subsection (17). This subsection is taken verbatim from G. L. c. 233, § 79B. The word "'compilation,' as used in the statute, connotes simple objective facts, and not conclusions or opinions." Mazzaro v. Paull, 372 Mass. 645, 652 (1977). The trial judge must make "preliminary findings that the proposed exhibit is (1) issued to the public, (2) published for persons engaged in the applicable occupation, and (3) commonly used and relied on by such persons." Id. See Fall River Sav. Bank v. Callahan, 18 Mass. App. Ct. 76, 83–84 (1984); Torre v. Harris–Seybold Co., 9 Mass. App. Ct. 660, 672–673 (1980). The judge has the discretion to consider the reliability of the information as a factor in determining the admissibility of the compilation, even where the statutory requirements are satisfied. See N.E. Physical Therapy Plus, Inc. v. Liberty Mut. Ins. Co., 466 Mass. 358, 366–367 (2013) (judge did not abuse his discretion in excluding statistical summaries derived from compilation of raw data voluntarily submitted by participating insurance companies where accuracy and reliability of raw data had not been established).

See generally G. L. c. 106, § 2–724 ("Whenever the prevailing price or value of any goods regularly bought and sold in any established commodity market is in issue, reports in official publications or trade journals or in newspapers or periodicals of general circulation published as the reports of such market shall be admissible in evidence. The circumstances of the preparation of such a report may be shown to affect its weight but not its admissibility.").

Subsection (18)(A). This subsection is taken nearly verbatim from G. L. c. 233, § 79C. See Commonwealth v. Johnson, 59 Mass. App. Ct. 164, 170 (2003) ("pill book" purchased from pharmacy purporting to describe effects of prescription drugs not admissible as learned treatise); Simmons v. Yurchak, 28 Mass. App. Ct. 371, 375–377 (1990) (instructional videotape not admissible as learned treatise). Statements from a treatise satisfying the requirements of G. L. c. 233, § 79C, may also be used in medical malpractice tribunals. See G. L. c. 231, § 60B.

"When determining the admissibility of a published treatise under G. L. c. 233, § 79C, we interpret the 'writer of such statements' to mean the treatise author, not the author of each individual item incorporated into the treatise text." Brusard v. O'Toole, 429 Mass. 597, 606 (1999). "[T]he 'writer' of a statement contained in an authored treatise is the author of the treatise, and the 'writer' of a statement contained in a periodical or similarly edited publication is the author of the specific article in which the statement is contained." Id. The biographical data about the author in the front of the treatise may not be used to establish the expertise of the author, see Redding-ton v. Clayman, 334 Mass. 244, 247 (1956), but an opponent witness who admits that the author of the treatise is a recognized expert in the field is sufficient, see Thomas v. Ellis, 329 Mass. 93, 98, 100 (1952). "The statutory notice of the intent to introduce a treatise required by G. L. c. 233, § 79C, requires that 'the date of publication' of the treatise be specified. The edition of a treatise, if applicable, should be specified, and parties should be permitted to introduce statements from only that edition." Brusard v. O'Toole, 429 Mass. at 606 n.13.

Subsection (18)(B). This subsection is derived from Commonwealth v. Sneed, 413 Mass. 387, 396 (1992), in which the Supreme Judicial Court adopted Proposed Mass. R. Evid. 803(18). Treatises are not available to bolster direct examination. Brusard v. O'Toole, 429 Mass. 597, 601 n.5 (1999). But see Commonwealth v. Sneed, 413 Mass. at 396 n.8 ("We can imagine a situation in which, in fairness, portions of a learned treatise not called to the attention of a witness during cross-examination should be admitted on request of the expert's proponent in order to explain, limit, or contradict a statement ruled admissible under [Section] 803[(18)]."). This subsection "contemplates that an authored treatise, and not the statements contained therein, must be established as a reliable authority." Brusard v. O'Toole, 429 Mass. at 602–603. The contents of the specific article, Web page, or other material must be shown to have been authored or prepared by a person established to be a "reliable authority" pursuant to one of the means spelled out in Section 803(18)(B). Kace v. Liang, 472 Mass. 630, 644 (2015).

"[The] opponent of the expert witness [must] bring to the witness's attention a specific statement in a treatise that has been established, to the judge's satisfaction, as a reliable authority. The witness should be given a fair opportunity to assess the statement in context and to comment on it, either during cross-examination or on redirect examination. The judge, of course, will have to determine the relevance and materiality of the statement and should consider carefully any claimed unfairness or confusion that admission of the statement may create."

Commonwealth v. Sneed, 413 Mass. at 396. This is a preliminary question of fact for the judge. See Section 104(a), Preliminary Questions: In General.

Subsection (19). This subsection is derived from Butrick v. Tilton, 155 Mass. 461, 466 (1892). See Cadorette v. United States, 988 F.2d 215, 220–222 (1st Cir. 1993). But see Haddock v. Boston & Maine R.R., 85 Mass. 298, 301 (1862).

Subsection (20). This subsection is derived from Enfield v. Woods, 212 Mass. 547, 551–552 (1912) (admitting reputation evidence regarding existence or nonexistence of public ownership of land). See G. L. c. 139, § 9 ("For the purpose of proving the existence of the nuisance the general reputation of the place shall be admissible as evidence."); Commonwealth v. United Food Corp., 374 Mass. 765, 767 n.2 (1978) (G. L. c. 139, § 9, is a statutory exception to hearsay rule).

Subsection (21). This exception deals only with the hearsay aspect of evidence of reputation. For additional restrictions on the use of such evidence, see Sections 404, Character Evidence; Crimes or Other Act; 405, Methods of Proving Character; and 608, A Witness's Character for Truthfulness or Untruthfulness.

Subsection (22). This subsection is derived from Flood v. Southland Corp., 416 Mass. 62, 70 (1993), in which the Supreme Judicial Court adopted Proposed Mass. R. Evid. 803(22). See Commonwealth v. Powell, 40 Mass. App. Ct. 430, 435–436 (1996) (error where trial court instructed jury it could consider prior guilty plea of alleged joint venturer to charge of armed robbery as circumstantial evidence of presence of gun in subsequent trial of other joint venturer on same charge). "[A] plea of guilty is admissible in evidence as an admission in subsequent civil litigation, but is not conclusive." Aetna Cas. & Sur. Co. v. Niziolek, 395 Mass. 737, 747 (1985). Cf. Section 609, Impeachment by Evidence of Conviction of Crime; Section 410, Pleas, Offers of Pleas, and Related Statements; Mass. R. Crim. P. 12(f).

Subsection (23). No cases or statutes were located on this issue.

Subsection (24)(A). Subsections (24)(A) through (A)(ii) are taken nearly verbatim from G. L. c. 233, § 83(a). Subsections (24)(A)(iii) and (iv) are derived from Care & Protection of Rebecca, 419 Mass. 67, 78, 80 (1994). There is no requirement that the child be unavailable.

Id. at 76–77. When a care and protection proceeding is joined with a petition to dispense with consent to adoption, admissibility of a child's out-of-court statements should comply with the stricter requirements of G. L. c. 233, § 82, not § 83. Adoption of Tina, 45 Mass. App. Ct. 727, 733 (1998).

Subsection (24)(B). This subsection is taken nearly verbatim from Care & Protection of Rebecca, 419 Mass. 67, 79–80 (1994). The judge may question the child through a voir dire. Id. The reliability of statements contained in an investigator's report can be assessed by cross-examining the investigator. Care & Protection of Leo, 38 Mass. App. Ct. 237, 241–242 (1995).

Subsection (24)(C). This subsection is taken nearly verbatim from Care & Protection of Rebecca, 419 Mass. 67, 80 (1994).

Subsection (24)(D). This subsection is taken verbatim from G. L. c. 233, § 83(b).

Section 804. Hearsay Exceptions; Declarant Unavailable

(a) Criteria for Being Unavailable. A declarant is considered to be unavailable as a witness if the declarant

    (1) is exempted from testifying about the subject matter of the declarant's statement because the court rules that a privilege applies;

    (2) refuses to testify [this criterion not recognized];

    (3) testifies to not remembering the subject matter [this criterion not recognized];

    (4) cannot be present or testify at the trial or hearing because of death or a then-existing infirmity, physical illness, or mental illness; or

    (5) is absent from the trial or hearing and the statement's proponent has not been able to procure the declarant's attendance by process or other reasonable means.

But this Subdivision (a) does not apply if the statement's proponent procured or wrongfully caused the declarant's unavailability as a witness in order to prevent the declarant from attending or testifying.

(b) The Exceptions. The following are not excluded by the rule against hearsay if the declarant is unavailable as a witness:

    (1) Prior Recorded Testimony. Testimony that

    (A) was given as a witness at a trial, hearing, or lawful deposition, whether given during the current proceeding or a different one, and

    (B) is now offered against a party who had—or, in a civil case, whose predecessor in interest had—an opportunity and similar motive to develop it by direct, cross-, or redirect examination.

    (2) Statement Made Under the Belief of Imminent Death. In a prosecution for homicide, a statement that a declarant, who believed that the declarant's death was imminent and who died shortly after making the statement, made about the cause or circumstances of the declarant's own impending death or that of a co-victim.

    (3) Statement Against Interest. A statement that a reasonable person in the declarant's position would have made only if the person believed it to be true because, when made, it was so contrary to the declarant's proprietary or pecuniary interest or had so great a tendency to invalidate the declarant's claim against someone else, or to expose the declarant to civil or criminal liability. In a criminal case, the exception does not apply to a statement that tends to expose the declarant to criminal liability and is offered to exculpate the defendant, or is offered by the Commonwealth to inculpate the defendant, unless corroborating circumstances clearly indicate the trustworthiness of the statement.

(4) Statement of Personal History.

(A) A statement concerning the declarant's own birth, adoption, legitimacy, ancestry, marriage, divorce, or relationship by blood, even though the declarant had no way of acquiring personal knowledge of the matter stated.

(B) A statement regarding those matters concerning another person to whom the declarant is related [exception not recognized].

(5) Statutory Exceptions in Civil Cases.

(A) Declarations of Decedent. In any action or other civil judicial proceeding, a declaration of a deceased person shall not be inadmissible in evidence as hearsay or as private conversation between husband and wife, as the case may be, if the court finds that it was made in good faith and upon the personal knowledge of the declarant.

(B) Deceased Party's Answers to Interrogatories. If a party to an action who has filed answers to interrogatories under any applicable statute or any rule of the Massachusetts Rules of Civil Procedure dies, so much of such answers as the court finds have been made upon the personal knowledge of the deceased shall not be inadmissible as hearsay or self-serving if offered in evidence in said action by a representative of the deceased party.

(C) Declarations of Decedent in Actions Against an Estate. If a cause of action brought against an executor or administrator is supported by oral testimony of a promise or statement made by the testator or intestate of the defendant, evidence of statements, written or oral, made by the decedent, memoranda and entries written by the decedent, and evidence of the decedent's acts and habits of dealing, tending to disprove or to show the improbability of the making of such promise or statement, shall be admissible.

(D) Reports of Deceased Physicians in Tort Actions. In an action of tort for personal injuries or death, or for consequential damages arising from such personal injuries, the medical report of a deceased physician who attended or examined the plaintiff, including expressions of medical opinion, shall, at the discretion of the trial judge, be admissible in evidence, but nothing therein contained which has reference to the question of liability shall be so admissible. Any opposing party shall have the right to introduce evidence tending to limit, modify, contradict, or rebut such medical report. The word "physician" as used in this section shall not include any person who was not licensed to practice medicine under the laws of the jurisdiction within which such medical attention was given or such examination was made.

(E) Medical Reports of Disabled or Deceased Physicians as Evidence in Workers' Compensation Proceedings. In proceedings before the industrial accident board, the medical report of an incapacitated, disabled, or deceased physician who attended or examined the employee, including expressions of medical opinion, shall, at the discretion of the member, be admissible as evidence if the member finds that such medical report was made as the result of such physician's attendance or examination of the employee.

(6) Statement Offered Against a Party That Wrongfully Caused the Declarant's Unavailability. A statement offered against a party if the court finds (A) that the witness is unavailable; (B) that the party was involved in, or responsible for, procuring the unavailability of the witness; and (C) that the party acted with the intent to procure the witness's unavailability.

(7) Religious Records. Statements of fact made by a deceased person authorized by the rules or practices of a religious organization to perform a religious act, contained in a certificate that the maker performed such act, and purporting to be issued at the time of the act or within a reasonable time thereafter.

(8) Admissibility in Criminal Proceedings of a Child's Out-of-Court Statement Describing Sexual Contact. General Laws c. 233, § 81, was adopted prior to the United States Supreme Court's decisions in Crawford v. Washington, 541 U.S. 36 (2004), and Davis v. Washington, 547 U.S. 813 (2006), as well as the Supreme Judicial Court's decisions in Commonwealth v. Gonsalves, 445 Mass. 1 (2005), cert. denied, 548 U.S. 926 (2006), and Commonwealth v. Amirault, 424 Mass. 618 (1997). These decisions call into question the constitutionality of this subsection.

(A) Admissibility in General. An out-of-court statement of a child under the age of ten describing an act of sexual contact performed on or with the child, the circumstances under which it occurred, or which identifies the perpetrator shall be admissible as substantive evidence in any criminal proceeding; provided, however, that

(i) the statement is offered as evidence of a material fact and is more probative on the point for which it is offered than any other evidence which the proponent can procure through reasonable efforts,

(ii) the person to whom the statement was made or who heard the child make the statement testifies,

(iii) the judge finds pursuant to Subsection (b)(8)(B) that the child is unavailable as a witness,

(iv) the judge finds pursuant to Subsection (b)(8)(C) that the statement is reliable, and

(v) the statement is corroborated pursuant to Subsection (b)(8)(D).

(B) Unavailability of Child. The proponent of such statement shall demonstrate a diligent and good-faith effort to produce the child and shall bear the burden of showing unavailability. A finding of unavailability shall be supported by specific findings on the record, describing facts with particularity, demonstrating that

(i) the child is unable to be present or to testify because of death or physical or mental illness or infirmity;

1249

(ii) by a ruling of the court, the child is exempt on the ground of privilege from testifying concerning the subject matter of such statement;

(iii) the child testifies to a lack of memory of the subject matter of such statement;

(iv) the child is absent from the hearing and the proponent of such statement has been unable to procure the attendance of the child by process or by other reasonable means;

(v) the court finds, based upon expert testimony from a treating psychiatrist, psychologist, or clinician, that testifying would be likely to cause severe psychological or emotional trauma to the child; or

(vi) the child is not competent to testify.

(C) Reliability of Statement. If a finding of unavailability is made, the out-of-court statement shall be admitted if the judge further finds,

(i) after holding a separate hearing, that such statement was made under oath, that it was accurately recorded and preserved, and that there was sufficient opportunity to cross-examine, or

(ii) after holding a separate hearing and, where practicable and where not inconsistent with the best interests of the child, meeting with the child, that such statement was made under circumstances inherently demonstrating a special guarantee of reliability.

For the purposes of finding circumstances demonstrating reliability pursuant to this subsection, a judge may consider whether the relator documented the child witness's statement and shall consider the following factors:

(a) the clarity of the statement, meaning the child's capacity to observe, remember, and give expression to that which such child has seen, heard, or experienced; provided, however, that a finding under this clause shall be supported by expert testimony from a treating psychiatrist, psychologist, or clinician;

(b) the time, content, and circumstances of the statement; and

(c) the child's sincerity and ability to appreciate the consequences of such statement.

(D) Corroborating Evidence. The out-of-court statement must be corroborated by other independently admitted evidence.

(E) Admissibility by Common Law or Statute. An out-of-court statement admissible by common law or by statute shall remain admissible notwithstanding the provisions of this section.

(9) Out–of–Court Statement of Child Describing Sexual Contact in Civil Proceeding, Including Termination of Parental Rights.

(A) Admissibility in General. The out-of-court statements of a child under the age of ten describing any act of sexual contact performed on or with the child, the circumstances under which it occurred, or which identifies the perpetrator shall be admissible as substantive evidence in any civil proceeding, except proceedings brought under G. L. c. 119, §§ 23(C) and 24; provided, however, that

(i) such statement is offered as evidence of a material fact and is more probative on the point for which it is offered than any other evidence which the proponent can procure through reasonable efforts,

(ii) the person to whom such statement was made or who heard the child make such statement testifies,

(iii) the judge finds pursuant to Subsection (b)(9)(B) that the child is unavailable as a witness,

(iv) the judge finds pursuant to Subsection (b)(9)(C) that such statement is reliable, and

(v) such statement is corroborated pursuant to Subsection (b)(9)(D).

(B) Unavailability of Child. The proponent of such statement shall demonstrate a diligent and good-faith effort to produce the child and shall bear the burden of showing unavailability. A finding of unavailability shall be supported by specific findings on the record, describing facts with particularity, demonstrating that

(i) the child is unable to be present or to testify because of death or existing physical or mental illness or infirmity;

(ii) by a ruling of the court, the child is exempt on the ground of privilege from testifying concerning the subject matter of such statement;

(iii) the child testifies to a lack of memory of the subject matter of such statement;

(iv) the child is absent from the hearing and the proponent of such statement has been unable to procure the attendance of the child by process or by other reasonable means;

(v) the court finds, based upon expert testimony from a treating psychiatrist, psychologist, or clinician, that testifying would be likely to cause severe psychological or emotional trauma to the child; or

(vi) the child is not competent to testify.

(C) Reliability of Statement. If a finding of unavailability is made, the out-of-court statement shall be admitted if the judge further finds,

(i) after holding a separate hearing, that such statement was made under oath, that it was accurately recorded and preserved, and that there was sufficient opportunity to cross-examine, or

(ii) after holding a separate hearing and, where practicable and where not inconsistent with the best interests of the child, meeting with the child, that such statement was made under circumstances inherently demonstrating a special guarantee of reliability.

For the purposes of finding circumstances demonstrating reliability pursuant to this subsection, a judge may consider whether the relator documented the child witness's statement and shall consider the following factors:

(a) the clarity of the statement, meaning the child's capacity to observe, remember, and give expression to that which such child has seen, heard, or experienced; provided, however, that a finding under this clause shall be supported by expert testimony from a treating psychiatrist, psychologist, or clinician;

(b) the time, content, and circumstances of the statement;

(c) the existence of corroborative evidence of the substance of the statement regarding the abuse, including either the act, the circumstances, or the identity of the perpetrator; and

(d) the child's sincerity and ability to appreciate the consequences of the statement.

(D) Corroborating Evidence. The out-of-court statement must be corroborated by other independently admitted evidence.

(E) Admissibility by Common Law or Statute. An out-of-court statement admissible by common law or by statute shall remain admissible notwithstanding the provisions of this section.

NOTE

Confrontation Clause. In a criminal case, a hearsay statement offered against the defendant must satisfy both the confrontation clause and one of the hearsay exceptions. For a discussion of the relationship between the confrontation clause and the hearsay exceptions stated in Section 804, refer to the Introductory Note to Article VIII, Hearsay.

Introduction. Section 804 defines hearsay exceptions that are conditioned upon a showing that the declarant is unavailable. Section 804(a) defines the requirement of unavailability that applies to all the hearsay exceptions in Section 804(b). The second paragraph of Section 804(a) is consistent with the doctrine of forfeiture by wrongdoing adopted by the Supreme Judicial Court in Commonwealth v. Edwards, 444 Mass. 526, 540 (2005).

The exceptions that apply when the declarant of the out-of-court statement is unavailable address only the evidentiary rule against hearsay, except in the context of forfeiture by wrongdoing. See Section 804(b)(6), Hearsay Exceptions; Declarant Unavailable: The Exceptions: Statement Offered Against a Party That Wrongfully Caused the Declarant's Unavailability. In criminal cases, the admissibility at trial of an out-of-court statement against the defendant also requires consideration of the constitutional right to confrontation under the Sixth Amendment to the United States Constitution and Article 12 of the Massachusetts Declaration of Rights. For a discussion of the relationship between the confrontation clause and the hearsay exceptions stated in Section 804, refer to the Introductory Note to Article VIII, Hearsay.

A defendant invoking the Fifth Amendment privilege against self-incrimination only makes himself or herself unavailable to another party, but the defendant is not unavailable as to himself or herself. See Commonwealth v. Labelle, 67 Mass. App. Ct. 698, 701 (2006). It should not be presumed that an absent witness may invoke his or her privilege against self-incrimination. See Commonwealth v. Lopera, 42 Mass. App. Ct. 133, 137 n.3 (1997). But where the declarant is a codefendant and joint venturer in the crimes charged against the defendant, and the declarant's out-of-court statements directly implicate the declarant in the criminal enterprise, the unavailability requirement is satisfied because the defendant undoubtedly would invoke the Fifth Amendment privilege. See Commonwealth v. Charles, 428 Mass. 672, 677–679 (1999).

Cross-Reference: Note "Use of Depositions at Trial" to Section 801, Definitions.

Subsection (a)(1). This subsection is derived from Commonwealth v. Canon, 373 Mass. 494, 499–500 (1977), cert. denied, 435 U.S. 933 (1978) (valid invocation of privilege against self-incrimination rendered witness unavailable). Unavailability is not defined simply in terms of lack of physical presence, but stems from the inability of opposing counsel to cross-examine the witness. Commonwealth v. DiPietro, 373 Mass. 369, 392– 394 (1977). Accord Commonwealth v. Negron, 441 Mass. 685, 688–691 (2004) (valid claim of spousal privilege by defendant's wife rendered her unavailable). However, a claim of privilege will not be presumed simply because a witness might have a basis for asserting it if the witness had appeared and been called to testify. See Commonwealth v. Charros, 443 Mass. 752, 767–768 (2005).

Subsection (a)(2). The Supreme Judicial Court has not yet adopted Proposed Mass. R. Evid. 804(a)(2), which, like the Federal rule, provides that a witness who persists in refusing to testify concerning the subject matter of his or her statement may be deemed to be unavailable. See Commonwealth v. Rosado, 480 Mass. 540, 549 (2018) (explaining that absent the assertion of a privilege against self-incrimination, a witness's refusal to testify does not render the witness unavailable for purposes of the hearsay exception for prior recorded testimony).

Subsection (a)(3). Massachusetts law does not recognize lack of memory of the subject matter of the testimony as a basis for finding that the witness is unavailable. Commonwealth v. Bray, 19 Mass. App. Ct. 751, 758 (1985). Cf. A.T. Stearns Lumber Co. v. Howlett, 239 Mass. 59, 61 (1921) (declining to extend doctrine of past recollection recorded to permit introduction of prior recorded testimony that witness had no present memory of but recalled was the truth).

Subsection (a)(4). This subsection is derived from Commonwealth v. Bohannon, 385 Mass. 733, 742 (1982) ("death or other legally sufficient reason"), and cases cited. See Commonwealth v. Mustone, 353 Mass. 490, 491–492 (1968) (death of witness). In Ibanez v. Winston, 222 Mass. 129, 130 (1915), the Supreme Judicial Court observed that although the death or insanity of a witness would supply the basis for a finding of unavailability, the mere fact that a witness had returned to Spain, without more, did not demonstrate that he was unavailable. However, in Commonwealth v. Hunt, 38 Mass. App. Ct. 291, 295 (1995), the Appeals Court noted that

"[w]hen a witness is outside of the borders of the United States and declines to honor a request to appear as a witness, the unavailability of that witness has been conceded because a State of the United States has no authority to compel a resident of a foreign country to attend a trial here."

In Commonwealth v. Housewright, 470 Mass. 665, 671–674 (2015), the Supreme Judicial Court provided a framework to analyze whether a witness is "unavailable because of illness or infirmity" in criminal cases where the Commonwealth is the proponent of the evidence. The Commonwealth must show that there is "an unacceptable risk that the witness's health would be significantly jeopardized if the witness were required to testify in court" by providing "reliable, up-to-date information sufficient to permit the judge to make an independent finding." Id. at 671. In assessing the probability that the witness's appearance will cause an adverse health consequence, the court should consider "the severity of the adverse health consequence, such as whether it would be life-threatening, the importance of the testimony in the context of the case, and the extent to which the live trial testimony would likely differ from the prior recorded testimony," id. at 672, and whether a continuance of the trial or a deposition of the witness is appropriate, considering both the witness's health and interest of justice. Id. at 672–673. The Commonwealth must make a good-faith effort to produce the witness at trial and must promptly inform the court and the defendant of the claimed unavailability. See Commonwealth v. Dorisca, 88 Mass. App. Ct. 776, 779–783 (2015) (trial judge erred in basing determination of witness's unavailability on prosecutor's statement that witness had recently gone into labor, without making inquiry into Housewright factors).

Subsection (a)(5). This subsection is derived from Commonwealth v. Charles, 428 Mass. 672, 678 (1999) ("We accept as a basis of unavailability the principles expressed in Rule 804[a][5] of the Federal Rules of Evidence [1985]"). A judge must be satisfied that the proponent engaged in a "good faith effort" to find and produce a witness at trial before allowing prior recorded testimony in evidence. Commonwealth v. Sena, 441 Mass. 822, 832 (2004). Such a determination "depends upon what is a reasonable effort in light of the peculiar facts of the case." Id.; Commonwealth v. Rosado, 480 Mass. 540, 549 (2018) (Commonwealth failed to show that person "served with out-of-State process and ordered to come to Massachusetts" was unavailable where person "informed the prosecutor that she did not want to return" but nothing indicated that "the Commonwealth was unable to compel her appearance"). See Commonwealth v. Roberio, 440 Mass. 245, 248 (2003) (where prosecutor established unavailability before trial of witness who is then located out of State during trial, court is not required to suspend trial to obtain presence of witness); Commonwealth v. Charles, 428 Mass. at 678 (evidence that declarant is a fugitive satisfies unavailability requirement); Commonwealth v. Pittman, 60 Mass. App. Ct. 161, 169–170 (2003) (witness who ignored defense counsel's subpoena and instead attended an out-of-State funeral was unavailable). Contrast Ruml v. Ruml, 50 Mass. App. Ct. 500, 508–509 (2000) (self-imposed exile from Massachusetts does not satisfy unavailability requirement); Commonwealth v. Hunt, 38 Mass. App. Ct. 291, 295–296 (1995) (fact that prospective witness is a foreign national outside United States does not excuse proponent of statement from making diligent effort to locate and secure attendance of witness). "When former testimony is sought to be offered against the accused, the degree of 'good faith' and due diligence is greater than that required in other situations." Commonwealth v. Bohannon, 385 Mass. 733, 745 (1982).

Subsection (b)(1). This subsection is derived from Commonwealth v. Meech, 380 Mass. 490, 494 (1980), and Commonwealth v. DiPietro, 373 Mass. 369, 380–385 (1977). Rule 32(a)(3) of the Massachusetts Rules of Civil Procedure permits the use of deposition testimony in several enumerated situations where the witness is unavailable. Rule 32(a)(4) allows the trial judge to permit the use of deposition testimony in "exceptional circumstances." An audiovisual deposition may be used in the same manner as a stenographic deposition. Mass. R. Civ. P. 30A(i). See Hasouris v. Sorour, 92 Mass. App. Ct. 607, 614–615 (2018) (use of deposition in civil trial where party is unable to provide attendance of witness by subpoena pursuant to Mass. R. Civ. P. 32[a][3][D]). See also Mass. R. Crim. P. 35 (use of depositions in proceedings).

"The prior recorded testimony exception to the hearsay rule applies 'where the prior testimony was given by a person, now unavailable, in a proceeding addressed to substantially the same issues as in the current proceeding, with reasonable opportunity and similar motivation on the prior occasion for cross-examination of the declarant by the party against whom the testimony is now being offered.'"

Commonwealth v. Fisher, 433 Mass. 340, 355 (2001), quoting Commonwealth v. Trigones, 397 Mass. 633, 638 (1986). The party against whom the testimony is being offered need not actually cross-examine the declarant; only an adequate opportunity to cross-examine the declarant is required. Commonwealth v. Canon, 373 Mass. 494, 499–501 (1977), cert. denied, 435 U.S. 933 (1978). See Commonwealth v. Hurley, 455 Mass. 53, 62–63 (2009) ("A defendant is not entitled under the confrontation clause to a cross-examination that is 'effective in whatever way, and to whatever extent the defense might wish.' Rather, what is essential is that the 'trier of fact [have] a satisfactory basis for evaluating the truth of the prior statement.'" [Citations omitted.]).

In a civil trial, a valid invocation of the privilege against self-incrimination makes a witness unavailable for purposes of admitting deposition testimony under this exception. Hasouris v. Sorour, 92

Mass. App. Ct. at 611–612. A judge must make a particularized inquiry as to whether particular questions or areas of examination or cross-examination would tend to incriminate the party. Id. at 614.

The Supreme Judicial Court has applied this hearsay exception when the prior recorded testimony was given at a probable cause hearing, see Commonwealth v. Mustone, 353 Mass. 490, 492–494 (1968), and at a pretrial dangerousness hearing under G. L. c. 276, § 58A. See Commonwealth v. Hurley, 455 Mass. at 63 & n.9 (noting that there is "no general rule that a witness's prior testimony at a pretrial detention hearing is always admissible at trial if that witness becomes unavailable."). See also id. at 66–67 (when an excited utterance is admitted at a pretrial hearing as an exception to the hearsay rule in circumstances in which the defendant is not given an opportunity to cross-examine the declarant about the facts described in the excited utterance, the admission of the evidence violates the confrontation clause). Cf. Commonwealth v. Arrington, 455 Mass. 437, 442–445 (2009) (upholding order that excluded from trial the alleged victim's testimony at a pretrial dangerousness hearing under G. L. c. 276, § 58, on grounds that due to her medical condition [late stage cancer], defense counsel was deprived of reasonable opportunity for cross-examination).

In Commonwealth v. Clemente, 452 Mass. 295, 313–315 (2008), the Supreme Judicial Court held that this hearsay exception is not generally applicable to prior recorded testimony before the grand jury because the testimony of such witnesses is usually far more limited than at trial and is often presented without an effort to corroborate or discredit it. "If, however, the party seeking the admission of the grand jury testimony can establish that the Commonwealth had an opportunity and similar motive to develop fully a (now unavailable) witness's testimony at the grand jury, that earlier testimony would be admissible." Id. at 315.

The declarant's prior testimony must be able to be "substantially reproduced in all material particulars." Commonwealth v. Martinez, 384 Mass. 377, 381 (1981). See G. L. c. 233, § 80 (official transcripts); Commonwealth v. DiPietro, 373 Mass. 369, 392–394 (1977) (unofficial transcripts); Commonwealth v. Vaden, 373 Mass. 397, 400 (1977) (tape recordings, whether official or unofficial); Commonwealth v. Janovich, 55 Mass. App. Ct. 42, 45 (2002) (witness present at prior proceeding).

Subsection (b)(2). This subsection is derived from Commonwealth v. Polian, 288 Mass. 494, 497 (1934), and Commonwealth v. Vona, 250 Mass. 509, 511 (1925). See Commonwealth v. Gonzalez, 469 Mass. 410, 419–420 (2014). This common-law exception is not subject to the defendant's right to confrontation. See Commonwealth v. Nesbitt, 452 Mass. 236, 251 (2008) ("Thus, in the unique instance of dying declarations, we ask *only* whether the statement is admissible as a common-law dying declaration, and not whether the statement is testimonial."). The "dying declaration" allows testimony as to the victim's statements concerning the circumstances of the killing and the identity of the perpetrator. Commonwealth v. Polian, 288 Mass. at 500. It may be in the form of oral testimony, gestures, or a writing made by the victim. See Commonwealth v. Casey, 65 Mass. 417, 422 (1853) (victim who was mortally wounded and unable to speak, but conscious, confirmed identity of perpetrator by squeezing the hand of her treating physician who asked her if it was "Mr. Casey, who worked for her husband"). The Supreme Judicial Court has left open the question whether a defendant's right to confrontation is applicable to the current, expanded concept of the dying declaration exception. See Commonwealth v. Nesbitt, 452 Mass. at 252 n.17, citing G. L. c. 233, § 64 (addressing admissibility of dying declarations of a female whose death results from an unlawful abortion in violation of G. L. c. 272, § 19), and Commonwealth v. Key, 381 Mass. 19, 26 (1980) (expanding the common-law exception by admitting a dying declaration to prove the homicides of other common victims).

The declarant's belief of impending death may be inferred from the surrounding circumstances, including the character of the injury sustained. See Commonwealth v. Moses, 436 Mass. 598, 602 (2002) ("Jenkins had been shot four times shortly before making the statement. Two bullets had pierced his chest, one of which had lodged in his spine. When police and emergency personnel arrived, he was 'very frightened,' grimacing in pain, bleeding, and asking for oxygen. He asked a treating emergency medical technician if he were going to die. She told him that 'it didn't look too good' for him. In the circumstances, it was not error for the judge to find that Jenkins believed at the time he made the statements that death was imminent."); Commonwealth v. Niemic, 427 Mass. 718, 724 (1998) ("The evidence showed that, when the officer found the victim, he had been stabbed in the heart and was bleeding profusely. There was also testimony that, at the hospital, he was 'breathing heavily' and 'appeared to be having a hard time' and that the officer questioning him 'had to work to get his attention to focus.' It was permissible to infer from this that the victim was aware that he was dying.").

Before admitting the dying declaration, the trial judge must first determine by a preponderance of the evidence that the requisite elements of a dying declaration are satisfied. Commonwealth v. Green, 420 Mass. 771, 781–782 (1995). If the statement is admitted, the judge must then instruct the jury that they must also find by a preponderance of the evidence that the same elements are satisfied before they may consider the substance of the statement. Id.

The broader statutory exception for declarations of a deceased person set forth in G. L. c. 233, § 65, applies only in civil cases. Commonwealth v. Dunker, 363 Mass. 792, 794 n.1 (1973).

Subsection (b)(3). This subsection is derived from Commonwealth v. Carr, 373 Mass. 617, 622–624 (1977), and Commonwealth v. Charles, 428 Mass. 672, 679 (1999). See also Williamson v. United States, 512 U.S. 594 (1994). This subsection is applicable only to "statements made by witnesses, not parties to the litigation or their privies or representatives." Commonwealth v. McLaughlin, 433 Mass. 558, 565 (2001), quoting P.J. Liacos, Massachusetts Evidence § 8.10 (7th ed. 1999). This exception against penal interest is applicable in civil and criminal cases. See Zinck v. Gateway Country Store, Inc., 72 Mass. App. Ct. 571, 575 (2008). The admission by a party-opponent need not be a statement against the declarant's penal or proprietary interest. See Section 801(d)(2), Definitions: Statements That Are Not Hearsay: An Opposing Party's Statement.

A declarant's narrative may include self-inculpatory and self-exculpatory elements.

"[A]pplication of the evidentiary rule concerning declarations against penal interest to a full narrative requires breaking out which parts, if any, of the declaration are actually against the speaker's penal interest. Further, application of the hearsay exception requires determination whether the declaration has an evidentiary connection and linkage to the matters at hand in the trial."

Commonwealth v. Marrero, 60 Mass. App. Ct. 225, 229 (2003). When the self-inculpatory aspect of the narrative is very limited, the trial judge has discretion either to exclude it entirely or "to allow it in with some limited 'necessary surrounding context' to prevent its significance from being distorted" by opposing counsel. Commonwealth v. Dejarnette, 75 Mass. App. Ct. 88, 99 (2009).

The judge's role in determining the admissibility of a statement against interest is to determine "whether, in light of the other evidence already adduced or to be adduced, there is some reasonable likelihood that the statement could be true." Commonwealth v. Drew, 397 Mass. 65, 76 (1986). This means that in accordance with Section 104(b), Preliminary Questions: Relevance That Depends on a Fact, the question whether to believe the declarant's statement is ultimately for the jury. Id.

A statement may qualify for admission as a declaration against penal interest even though it supplies circumstantial, and not direct, evidence of the declarant's guilt. See Commonwealth v. Charles, 428 Mass. 672, 679 (1999). In Commonwealth v. Charles, the Supreme Judicial Court also indicated that even though the exception does not explicitly require corroboration when the statement is introduced against the defendant, it would follow the majority rule and require it

in such cases. Id. at 679 n.2. See, e.g., Commonwealth v. Pope, 397 Mass. 275, 280 (1986) (reversing defendant's conviction based on erroneous admission of extrajudicial statement of a deceased witness; "[w]e do not believe that concern for penal consequence would inspire a suicide victim to truthfulness").

In criminal cases, "[i]n applying the corroboration requirement, judges are obliged to ... consider as relevant factors the degree of disinterestedness of the witnesses giving corroborating testimony as well as the plausibility of that testimony in the light of the rest of the proof." Commonwealth v. Carr, 373 Mass. at 624. The Supreme Judicial Court has explained that

"behind the corroboration requirement of [Fed. R. Evid.] 804(b)(3) lurks a suspicion that a reasonable man might sometimes admit to a crime he did not commit. A classic example is an inmate, serving time for multiple offenses, who has nothing to lose by a further conviction, but who can help out a friend by admitting to the friend's crime."

Commonwealth v. Drew, 397 Mass. at 74 n.8. The Supreme Judicial Court has stated that

"[o]ther factors the judge may consider are: the timing of the declaration and the relationship between the declarant and the witness, the reliability and character of the declarant, whether the statement was made spontaneously, whether other people heard the out-of-court statement, whether there is any apparent motive for the declarant to misrepresent the matter, and whether and in what circumstances the statement was repeated" (citation omitted).

Id. at 76. However,

"[i]n determining whether the declarant's statement has been sufficiently corroborated to merit its admission in evidence, the judge should not be stringent. A requirement that the defendant corroborate the declarant's entire statement, for example, may run afoul of the defendant's due process rights ... If the issue of sufficiency of the defendant's corroboration is close, the judge should favor admitting the statement. In most such instances, the good sense of the jury will correct any prejudicial impact." (Citation omitted.)

Id. at 75 n.10. See Commonwealth v. Nutbrown, 81 Mass. App. Ct. 773, 779–780 (2012) (in deciding whether statement is "trustworthy," trial judge must look only to credibility of declarant, leaving it to jury to determine credibility of witness who testifies to declaration). There is no requirement that when the statement is offered by the defendant, the exculpatory portion must also inculpate the declarant. See Commonwealth v. Keizer, 377 Mass. 264, 270 (1979).

Subsection (b)(4)(A). This subsection is derived from Haddock v. Boston & Maine R.R., 85 Mass. 298, 300–301 (1862), and Butrick v. Tilton, 155 Mass. 461, 466 (1892). In Haddock v. Boston & Maine R.R., 85 Mass. at 298–299, the court allowed a witness to testify that she came into ownership of the property through her mother and grandmother even though the only basis for her knowledge was what the person she alleged to be her mother said to her. In Butrick v. Tilton, 155 Mass. at 466, also a dispute over title to real property, the court permitted the alleged owner's granddaughter to testify as to how her grandfather came into ownership of the real estate, and that a cousin who owned the property before her grandfather died without children, based exclusively on what other family members told her and without any personal knowledge. See also Section 803(13), Hearsay Exceptions; Availability of Declarant Immaterial: Family Records; Section 803(19), Hearsay Exceptions; Availability of Declarant Immaterial: Reputation Concerning Personal or Family History.

Subsection (b)(4)(B). Massachusetts has not yet had occasion to consider Fed. R. Evid. 804(b)(4)(B), which extends the principle of Section 804(b)(4)(A) to others to whom the declarant is related by "blood, adoption or marriage," or to whom the declarant is so "intimately associated with ... as to be likely to have accurate information concerning the matter declared."

Subsection (b)(5)(A). This subsection is taken verbatim from G. L. c. 233, § 65. This hearsay exception applies in "all civil cases." Harrison v. Loyal Protective Life Ins. Co., 379 Mass. 212, 219 (1979). It does not apply in criminal proceedings. Commonwealth v. Cyr, 425 Mass. 89, 94 n.9 (1997). Nor is it available to a party attempting to perpetuate the testimony of a person who is expected to die shortly. Anselmo v. Reback, 400 Mass. 865, 868–869 (1987). See G. L. c. 233, §§ 46, 47; Mass. R. Civ. P. 27(a) (requirements to perpetuate testimony). The proponent of the evidence has the burden of establishing the foundational requirements of good faith and personal knowledge for the admissibility of the evidence. Kelley v. Jordan Marsh Co., 278 Mass. 101, 106 (1932). Whether the proponent has met this burden, including proof that the statement was actually made, is a preliminary question of fact for the trial judge under Section 104(a), Preliminary Questions: In General. See Slotofski v. Boston Elevated Ry. Co., 215 Mass. 318, 321 (1913).

The only ground of unavailability is the death of the declarant. G. L. c. 233, § 65. In the absence of a finding of good faith, the statement is not admissible. See Barbosa v. Hopper Feeds, Inc., 404 Mass. 610, 620 (1989) (excluding declaration because it was made after the injury suffered by the plaintiff and at the time when the now-deceased person had an incentive to fabricate). "In general [the declarations] must be derived from the exercise of the declarant's own senses as distinguished from opinions based upon data observed by him or furnished by others." Little v. Massachusetts N.E. St. Ry. Co., 223 Mass. 501, 504 (1916). "The declarations of the deceased may be in writing and need not be reproduced in the exact words used by the declarant" (citations omitted). Bellamy v. Bellamy, 342 Mass. 534, 536 (1961). See id. (oral statements also admissible).

Subsection (b)(5)(B). This subsection is taken verbatim from G. L. c. 233, § 65A. See Thornton v. First Nat'l Stores, Inc., 340 Mass. 222, 225 (1960). See also Mass. R. Civ. P. 33 (interrogatories to parties).

Subsection (b)(5)(C). This subsection is taken nearly verbatim from G. L. c. 233, § 66. In Rothwell v. First Nat'l Bank, 286 Mass. 417, 421 (1934), the Supreme Judicial Court explained the difference between Section 65 and Section 66 of G. L. c. 233. "[Section 66] is narrower than the other, in that it relates to the declarations or conduct of one person in one sort of case. But it requires no preliminary finding of good faith or other conditions. These two statutes operate concurrently and independently." Id. See Greene v. Boston Safe Deposit & Trust Co., 255 Mass. 519, 524 (1926).

Subsection (b)(5)(D). This subsection is taken verbatim from G. L. c. 233, § 79H.

Subsection (b)(5)(E). This subsection is taken verbatim from G. L. c. 152, § 20B. The statutory exception, however, might not overcome the further objection that it contains hearsay-within-hearsay in the form of statements to the employee's physician about how an injury occurred. See Fiander's Case, 293 Mass. 157, 164 (1936).

Subsection (b)(6). This subsection is derived from Commonwealth v. Edwards, 444 Mass. 526, 540 (2005). See Giles v. California, 554 U.S. 353, 373 (2008) (holding that the Sixth Amendment right to confrontation is not forfeited by wrongdoing unless the defendant acted with the intent to render the witness unavailable); Crawford v. Washington, 541 U.S. 36, 62 (2004) ("[T]he rule of forfeiture by wrongdoing [which we accept] extinguishes confrontation claims on essentially equitable grounds."). The Massachusetts common-law doctrine expressed in this subsection is fully consistent with the Federal doctrine set forth in Fed. R. Evid. 804(b)(6):

"By requiring that the defendant actively assist the witness in becoming unavailable with the intent to make her unavailable, our doctrine of forfeiture by wrongdoing is at least as demanding as Fed. R. Evid. 804(b)(6), which permits a finding of forfeiture where the defendant 'acquiesced' in conduct that was intended to, and did, make the witness unavailable to testify."

Commonwealth v. Szerlong, 457 Mass. 858, 862–863 (2010). See Commonwealth v. Rosado, 480 Mass. 540, 544–545 (2018) (whether the Commonwealth has met its burden to invoke the doctrine of forfeiture by wrongdoing "is a preliminary question of fact on the admissibility of evidence that is decided by a judge"). Even where the right of confrontation is forfeited by wrongdoing, due process requires that the statement be reliable. Commonwealth v. Rosado, 480 Mass. at 544 n.3 (citing Szerlong).

"A defendant's involvement in procuring a witness's unavailability need not consist of a criminal act, and may include a defendant's collusion with a witness to ensure that the witness will not be heard at trial." Commonwealth v. Edwards, 444 Mass. at 540. In Edwards, the Supreme Judicial Court elaborated on the scope of this exception.

"A finding that a defendant somehow influenced a witness's decision not to testify is not required to trigger the application of the forfeiture by wrongdoing doctrine where there is collusion in implementing that decision or planning for its implementation. Certainly, a defendant must have contributed to the witness's unavailability in some significant manner. However, the causal link necessary between a defendant's actions and a witness's unavailability may be established where (1) a defendant puts forward to a witness the idea to avoid testifying, either by threats, coercion, persuasion, or pressure; (2) a defendant physically prevents a witness from testifying; or (3) a defendant actively facilitates the carrying out of the witness's independent intent not to testify. Therefore, in collusion cases (the third category above) a defendant's joint effort with a witness to secure the latter's unavailability, regardless of whether the witness already decided 'on his own' not to testify, may be sufficient to support a finding of forfeiture by wrongdoing." (Footnote omitted.)

Id. at 540–541. "[W]here the defendant has had a meaningful impact on the witness's unavailability, the defendant may have forfeited confrontation and hearsay objections to the witness's out-of-court statements, even where the witness modified the initial strategy to procure the witness's silence." Id. at 541. See also Commonwealth v. Szerlong, 457 Mass. at 865–866 (evidence that defendant married alleged victim of his assault with the intent to enable her to exercise her spousal privilege at trial supported application of the doctrine of forfeiture by wrongdoing and thus the use of his wife's hearsay statements made before the marriage, even though it may not have been defendant's sole or primary purpose).

The proponent of the statement must prove that the opposing party procured the witness's unavailability by a preponderance of the evidence. Commonwealth v. Edwards, 444 Mass. at 542. "[P]rior to a determination of forfeiture, the parties should be given an opportunity to present evidence, including live testimony [and the unavailable witness's out-of-court statements], at an evidentiary hearing outside the jury's presence." Id. at 545. The trial judge should make the findings required by Commonwealth v. Edwards either orally on the record or in writing. Commonwealth v. Szerlong, 457 Mass. at 864 n.9. See also Commonwealth v. Rosado, 480 Mass. 540, 546 (2018) (doctrine of forfeiture inapplicable in circumstances in which defendant's misconduct was directed against testimony by witness at another trial against another person).

Subsection (b)(7). This subsection is derived from Kennedy v. Doyle, 92 Mass. 161, 168 (1865) (where the court admitted a baptismal record showing child's date of birth as evidence of the person's age when a contract had been made, in circumstances in which the entry was in the hand of the parish priest who had been the custodian of the book; Supreme Judicial Court observed that "[a]n entry made in the performance of a religious duty is certainly of no less value than one made by a clerk, messenger or notary, an attorney or solicitor or a physician, in the course of his secular occupation."). Contrast Derinza's Case, 229 Mass. 435, 443 (1918) (copies of what purported to be a marriage certificate from a town in Italy not admitted in evidence; Supreme Judicial Court observed that there was no "evidence respecting their character, the circumstances under which the records were kept, or the source from which the certificates came. No one testified that they were copies of an official original. There was no authentication of them as genuine by a consular officer of the United States. There was absolutely nothing beyond the bare production of the copies of the certificates. In the absence of a statute making such certificates admissible by themselves, or something to show that they were entitled to a degree of credence, they were not competent."). See Section 803(6), Hearsay Exceptions; Availability of Declarant Immaterial: Business and Hospital Records.

Subsection (b)(8)(A). Subsections (b)(8)(A) through (b)(8)(A)(iv) are taken nearly verbatim from G. L. c. 233, § 81(a), and Subsection (b)(8)(A)(v) is derived from Commonwealth v. Colin C., 419 Mass. 54, 64–66 (1994). See generally Opinion of the Justices, 406 Mass. 1201 (1989) (concluding that bill on related topic would, if enacted, offend the Massachusetts Constitution). The prosecution must give prior notice to the criminal defendant that it will seek to admit hearsay statements under this statute. Commonwealth v. Colin C., 419 Mass. at 64. It must also show a compelling and necessary need to use this procedure by more than a preponderance of evidence. Id. at 64–65.

Subsection (b)(8)(B). This subsection is taken nearly verbatim from G. L. c. 233, § 81(b). See Section 804(a), Hearsay Exceptions; Declarant Unavailable: Criteria for Being Unavailable. A judge's reasons for finding a child incompetent to testify should not be the same reasons for doubting the reliability of the child's out-of-court statements. Commonwealth v. Colin C., 419 Mass. 54, 65 (1994).

Subsection (b)(8)(C). This subsection is taken nearly verbatim from G. L. c. 233, § 81(c). The separate hearing regarding the reliability of the out-of-court statement must be on the record, and the judge's determination of reliability must be supported by specific findings on the record. Commonwealth v. Colin C., 419 Mass. 54, 65 (1994). See Commonwealth v. Joubert, 38 Mass. App. Ct. 943, 945 (1995). The statement must be substantially reliable to be admissible. Commonwealth v. Joubert, 38 Mass. App. Ct. at 945. See Commonwealth v. Almeida, 433 Mass. 717, 719–720 (2001) (statements of sleeping child were not admissible because they lacked indicia of reliability). The defendant and his or her counsel should be given the opportunity to attend the hearing if it would not cause the child witness severe emotional trauma. Commonwealth v. Colin C., 419 Mass. at 65.

Subsection (b)(8)(D). This subsection is derived from Commonwealth v. Colin C., 419 Mass. 54, 66 (1994).

Subsection (b)(8)(E). This subsection is taken nearly verbatim from G. L. c. 233, § 81(d).

Subsection (b)(9)(A). Subsections (b)(9)(A)(i) through (iv) are taken nearly verbatim from G. L. c. 233, § 82, and Subsection (b)(9)(A)(v) is derived from Adoption of Quentin, 424 Mass. 882, 893 (1997). See Commonwealth v. Colin C., 419 Mass. 54, 64–66 (1994) (establishing additional procedural requirements for admitting hearsay statements of child under G. L. c. 233, § 81). The Department of Children and Families must give prior notice to the parents that it will seek to admit hearsay statements under this statute. Adoption of Quentin, 424 Mass. at 893. It must also show a compelling and necessary need to use this procedure by more than a preponderance of evidence. Id. See also Adoption of Arnold, 50 Mass. App. Ct. 743, 752 (2001); Adoption of Tina, 45 Mass. App. Ct. 727, 733–734 (1998) (recognizing additional procedural requirements). When a care and protection proceeding is joined with a petition to dispense with consent to adoption, admissibility of a child's hearsay statements should comply with the stricter requirements of G. L. c. 233, § 82, not § 83. Adoption of Tina, 45 Mass. App. Ct. at 733 n.10. The phrase "child under the age of ten" refers to the age of the child at the time the statement was made, not the child's age at the time of the proceeding. Adoption of Daisy, 460 Mass. 72, 78 (2011).

Subsection (b)(9)(B). This subsection is taken nearly verbatim from G. L. c. 233, § 82(b). See Adoption of Sean, 36 Mass. App. Ct.

261, 266 (1994). See also Section 804(a), Hearsay Exceptions; Declarant Unavailable: Criteria for Being Unavailable.

Subsection (b)(9)(C). This subsection is taken nearly verbatim from G. L. c. 233, § 82(c). Note that it appears that the Legislature inadvertently omitted from G. L. c. 233, § 82, the following: "finds: (1) after holding a separate hearing, that such ..." We have inserted that language in the subsection above. See Adoption of Quentin, 424 Mass. 882, 890 n.5 (1997) (noting omission). A judge must make sufficient findings of reliability to admit the statements. See Adoption of Tina, 45 Mass. App. Ct. 727, 733 (1998); Edward E. v. Department of Social Servs., 42 Mass. App. Ct. 478, 484–486 (1997). The separate hearing regarding the reliability of the out-of-court statement must be on the record, and the judge's determination of reliability must be supported by specific findings on the record. Adoption of Quentin, 424 Mass. at 893. See Commonwealth v. Colin C., 419 Mass. 54, 65 (1994). See also Adoption of Olivette, 79 Mass. App. Ct. 141, 149–150 (2011).

Subsection (b)(9)(D). This subsection is derived from Adoption of Quentin, 424 Mass. 882, 893 (1997). See Commonwealth v. Colin C., 419 Mass. 54, 66 (1994). See also Adoption of Arnold, 50 Mass. App. Ct. 743, 753 (2001) (examples of corroborating evidence).

Subsection (b)(9)(E). This subsection is taken verbatim from G. L. c. 233, § 82(d).

Supplement to the 2019 Guide to Evidence

Subsection (a)(3). *Hearsay Exceptions; Declarant Unavailable: Criteria for Being Unavailable.* Hedberg v. Wakamatsu, 482 Mass. 613, 616-618 (2019). The Court held that a declarant in a civil case who testifies to a lack of memory will be deemed unavailable, thus permitting the admission of out-of-court statements falling within one of the exceptions in Section 804(b). The declarant's lack of memory is a preliminary question of fact for the trial judge.

Section 805. Hearsay Within Hearsay

Hearsay within hearsay is not excluded by the rule against hearsay if each part of the combined statements conforms with an exception to the rule in accordance with the common law, a statute, or a rule of court.

NOTE

This section is derived from Commonwealth v. Gil, 393 Mass. 204, 218 (1984), and Bouchie v. Murray, 376 Mass. 524, 528–530 (1978). See Commonwealth v. McDonough, 400 Mass. 639, 643 n.8 (1987). This type of layered hearsay is commonly referred to as "multiple hearsay," see Commonwealth v. Gil, 393 Mass. at 218; "totem pole hearsay," see Commonwealth v. Santiago, 437 Mass. 620, 627 n.4 (2002); or "hearsay within hearsay," see Fed. R. Evid. 805. The decisions in Bouchie v. Murray, 376 Mass. at 528–530, and Custody of Tracy, 31 Mass. App. Ct. 481, 484–486 (1991), illustrate the principle that under the terms of certain exceptions to the hearsay rule, the statements of multiple out-of-court declarants appearing in a single report or writing may be admissible, provided that each such statement falls within the applicable hearsay exception. See also Commonwealth v. DePina, 476 Mass. 614, 623 (2017); Commonwealth v. Alcantara, 471 Mass. 550, 558–559 (2015).

Use of "totem pole hearsay" or "multiple hearsay" must conform to the principles of due process. The party against whom such evidence is to be used must have a meaningful opportunity to rebut the adverse evidence. Brantley v. Hampden Div. of the Probate & Family Ct. Dep't, 457 Mass. 172, 185–186 (2010) (documents "comprised of abbreviated oral summaries of voluminous records made by persons who may have no firsthand experience with the case" were unreliable and judge's consideration of such documents could run afoul of litigants' due process rights).

Section 806. Attacking and Supporting Credibility of Hearsay Declarant

When a hearsay statement has been admitted in evidence, the declarant's credibility may be attacked, and then supported, by any evidence that would be admissible for those purposes if the declarant had testified as a witness. The court may admit evidence of the declarant's inconsistent statement or conduct, regardless of when it occurred or whether the declarant had an opportunity to explain or deny it. If the party against whom the statement was admitted calls the declarant as a witness, the party may examine the declarant on the statement as if on cross-examination.

NOTE

This section is taken from Commonwealth v. Mahar, 430 Mass. 643, 649 (2000), in which the Supreme Judicial Court "accept[ed] the principles of proposed [Mass. R. Evid.] 806." See Commonwealth v. Gray, 463 Mass. 731, 748 & n.17 (2012) (quoting with approval Mass. G. Evid.§ 806 and ruling that grand jury testimony of unavailable witness Jamison, who identified photograph of person other than defendant as perpetrator, was erroneously precluded to impeach witness's testimony at trial that Jamison had identified defendant). See also Commonwealth v. Pina, 430 Mass. 66, 76 (1999) ("We now adopt the rule in the circumstances of this case."); Commonwealth v. Sellon, 380 Mass. 220, 224 n.6 (1980).

Section 807. Residual Exception

[Exception not recognized]

NOTE

Unlike the Federal Rules of Evidence, Massachusetts does not recognize a "residual" exception to the hearsay rule. The Supreme Judicial Court, however, has recognized "a narrow, constitutionally based exception to the hearsay rule, which applies where otherwise inadmissible hearsay is critical to the defense and bears persuasive guarantees of trustworthiness." Commonwealth v. Drayton, 473 Mass. 23, 25 (2015) (Drayton I). See also Commonwealth v. Drayton, 479 Mass. 479 (2018) (Drayton II). The court noted that it had previously recognized a criminal defendant's right to admit "otherwise inadmissible hearsay evidence to support the assertion that a third party is the true culprit, provided certain conditions are met," and that it identified "no persuasive reasons for confining [its] recognition of a constitutionally based hearsay exception to the context of third-party culprit evidence." Drayton I, 473 Mass. at 36. Nevertheless, the court emphasized that this narrow hearsay exception should be used only on the rare occasion when "otherwise inadmissible evidence is both truly critical to the defense's case and bears persuasive guarantees of trustworthiness." Id. at 40. See generally id. at 33–38 (discussing Chambers v. Mississippi, 410 U.S. 284 [1973]). See also Commonwealth v. Dame, 473 Mass. 524, 533 n.17 (2016) (defendant's sister's exculpatory hearsay statements to police were neither "critical to the defense" nor bearing "persuasive guarantees of trustworthiness").

Cross–Reference: Note to Section 1105, Third-Party Culprit Evidence.

ARTICLE IX. AUTHENTICATION AND IDENTIFICATION

Section 901. Authenticating or Identifying Evidence

(a) In General. To satisfy the requirement of authenticating or identifying an item of evidence, the proponent must produce evidence sufficient to support a finding that the item is what the proponent claims it is.

(b) Examples. The following are examples only—not a complete list—of evidence that satisfies the requirement:

(1) Testimony of a Witness with Knowledge. Testimony that an item is what it is claimed to be.

(2) Nonexpert Opinion About Handwriting. A nonexpert's opinion that handwriting is genuine, based on a familiarity with it that was not acquired for the current litigation.

(3) Comparison by an Expert Witness or the Trier of Fact. A comparison with an authenticated specimen by an expert witness or the trier of fact.

(4) Distinctive Characteristics and the Like. The appearance, contents, substance, internal patterns, or other distinctive characteristics of the item, taken together with all the circumstances.

(5) Opinion About a Voice. An opinion identifying a person's voice—whether heard firsthand or through mechanical or electronic transmission or recording—based on hearing the voice at any time under circumstances that connect it with the alleged speaker.

(6) Evidence About a Telephone Conversation. For a telephone conversation, evidence that a call was made to the number assigned at the time to

(A) a particular person, if circumstances, including self-identification, show that the person answering was the one called, or

(B) a particular business, if the call was made to a business and the call related to business reasonably transacted over the telephone.

(7) Evidence About Public Records.

(A) Originals. Evidence that a document was recorded or filed in a public office as authorized by law, or that a purported public record or statement is from the office where items of this kind are kept.

(B) Copies. A copy of any of the items described in Subsection (7)(A), if authenticated by the attestation of the officer who has charge of the item, is admissible on the same terms as the original.

(8) Evidence About Ancient Documents. For a document, evidence that it

(A) is in a condition that creates no suspicion about its authenticity;

(B) was in a place where, if authentic, it would likely be; and

(C) is at least thirty years old when offered.

(9) Evidence About a Process or System. Evidence describing a process or system and showing that it produces an accurate result.

(10) Methods Provided by a Statute or Rule. Any method of authentication or identification allowed by a rule of the Supreme Judicial Court, by statute, or by the Massachusetts Constitution.

(11) Electronic or Digital Communication. Electronic or digital communication, by confirming circumstances that would allow a reasonable fact finder to conclude that this evidence is what its proponent claims it to be. Neither expert testimony nor exclusive access is necessary to authenticate the source.

NOTE

Subsection (a). This subsection is derived from Commonwealth v. LaCorte, 373 Mass. 700, 704 (1977), where the court acknowledged that a police witness at the trial properly authenticated a fingerprint card by his testimony that it was the same card he used to record the defendant's prints at the time of the defendant's arrest. "[P]roof of authenticity usually takes the form of testimony of a qualified witness either (1) that the thing is what its proponent represents it to be, or (2) that circumstances exist which imply that the thing is what its proponent represents it to be." Commonwealth v. LaCorte, 373 Mass. at 704, quoting W.B. Leach & P.J. Liacos, Massachusetts Evidence 265 (4th ed. 1967). Authentication is a preliminary question of fact under Section 104(b), Preliminary Questions: Relevance That Depends on a Fact. This requires the judge to determine whether sufficient evidence exists for a reasonable jury (or fact finder in a jury-waived case) to find by a preponderance of the evidence that the matter in question is what its proponent claims. Commonwealth v. Oppenheim, 86 Mass. App. Ct. 359, 366–367 (2014). See Commonwealth v. Duddie Ford Inc., 28 Mass. App. Ct. 426, 435 n.10 (1990), aff'd in part, rev'd in part, 409 Mass. 387 (1991), quoting Proposed Mass. R. Evid. 901(a). This principle is applicable to photographs as well as other forms of documentary evidence. Commonwealth v. Figueroa, 56 Mass. App. Ct. 641, 646 (2002) ("Photographs usually are authenticated directly through competent testimony that the scene they show is a fair and accurate representation of something the witness actually saw. But authenticity also can be established circumstantially by evidence sufficient to support a finding that the matter in question is what its proponent claims. Proposed Mass. R. Evid. 901[a]." [Quotation and citations omitted.]). See also Commonwealth v. Heang, 458 Mass. 827, 855–856 (2011) (store surveillance video properly authenticated by testimony of customer who had been there several hours before shootings, as well as by detective's description of process by which videotape was copied from store's system).

An item of evidence must be authenticated even if the item is presented only through testimony and is not itself admitted. See Commonwealth v. Connolly, 91 Mass. App. Ct. 580, 587–588 (2017) (foundational requirements for video surveillance tape). Cross-Reference: Note "Identity" to Section 701, Opinion Testimony by Lay Witnesses.

Subsection (b)(1). This subsection is derived from Commonwealth v. LaCorte, 373 Mass. 700, 704 (1977), quoting W.B. Leach & P.J. Liacos, Massachusetts Evidence 265 (4th ed. 1967). See also Commonwealth v. Driscoll, 91 Mass. App. Ct. 474, 478–479 (2017) (testimony of insurance adjuster indicating that copied document was coverage selections page of defendant's insurance policy satisfied attestation requirement set forth in G. L. c. 233, § 79A); Commonwealth v. Wheeler, 42 Mass. App. Ct. 933, 935 (1997).

Subsection (b)(2). This subsection is derived from Commonwealth v. Ryan, 355 Mass. 768, 770–771 (1969). See also Commonwealth v. O'Connell, 438 Mass. 658, 667 (2003). Before the lay opinion evidence is admitted, the trial judge must determine that the witness has sufficient familiarity with the genuine handwriting of the person in question to express an opinion that the specimen was written by that person. Nunes v. Perry, 113 Mass. 274, 276 (1873). See Section 104(b), Preliminary Questions: Relevance That Depends on a Fact. However, when the evidence includes both authentic samples of the person's handwriting and samples of questionable origin, and where the witness has no prior familiarity, there is no necessity for lay opinion testimony and it should not be admitted. See Noyes v. Noyes, 224 Mass. 125, 130 (1916) ("The opinion of the jury under such circumstances is quite as good as that of the witness of ordinary experience who has no particular acquaintance with the genuine handwriting. There is, under such circumstances, no occasion for the opinion of the outsider of only ordinary intelligence.").

Subsection (b)(3). This subsection is derived from Commonwealth v. O'Connell, 438 Mass. 658, 662–663 (2003). Whether a specimen of handwriting is genuine, i.e., the handwriting of a named person, is a preliminary question of fact for the trial judge. See Davis v. Meenan, 270 Mass. 313, 314–315 (1930). See also Section 104(a), Preliminary Questions: In General. In a criminal case, if this issue is disputed, the trial judge also should submit the question to the jury. See Commonwealth v. Tucker, 189 Mass. 457, 473–474 (1905).

If a genuine specimen of handwriting is in evidence, the jury is capable of comparing a specimen of handwriting to it to determine whether the specimen is genuine. Commonwealth v. O'Laughlin, 446 Mass. 188, 209 (2006). In the discretion of the court, the testimony of an expert witness may be admissible. Moody v. Rowell, 34 Mass. 490, 496–497 (1835).

Subsection (b)(4). This subsection is derived from Irving v. Goodimate Co., 320 Mass. 454, 459–460 (1946) (contents of letter used to authenticate signature). For example, hospital records showing the name of a patient that was the same alias used by the defendant in the past, with the same date of birth and the same mother's name, where the patient was treated for a leg injury similar to that which the victim's friend described inflicting on the attacker, provided sufficient foundation to allow the jury to conclude that the defendant was the individual whose hospital records were admitted into evidence. Commonwealth v. Cole, 473 Mass. 317, 321–323 (2015). See also Connecticut v. Bradish, 14 Mass. 296, 300 (1817) (reply letter doctrine); Commonwealth v. Biesiot, 91 Mass. App. Ct. 820, 824–826 (2017) (graffiti tags); Commonwealth v. Figueroa, 56 Mass. App. Ct. 641, 645–647 (2002) (contents of photographs and authenticating circumstances).

Subsection (b)(5). This subsection is taken from Commonwealth v. Williams, 8 Mass. App. Ct. 283, 291 (1979), quoting Fed. R. Evid. 901(b)(5). See also Commonwealth v. Lykus, 367 Mass. 191, 201 n.4 (1975); Lord Elec. Co. v. Morrill, 178 Mass. 304, 306 (1901). On the other hand, "[a] caller's mere self-identification, without more, is insufficient authentication to admit the substance of a telephone conversation." Commonwealth v. Howard, 42 Mass. App. Ct. 322, 324 (1997). Cf. Commonwealth v. Hartford, 346 Mass. 482, 488 (1963) (identification of caller by witness is permitted when caller identifies himself and there is other circumstantial evidence pointing to his or her identity). Apart from whether a witness is sufficiently familiar with a voice to identify the speaker, an in-court voice identification may be excluded on grounds that it was the product of an unnecessarily suggestive identification procedure. See Commonwealth v. Saunders, 50 Mass. App. Ct. 865, 874 (2001).

Subsection (b)(6). This subsection is derived from Massachusetts Northeastern St. Ry. Co. v. Plum Island Beach Co., 255 Mass. 104, 114–115 (1926). See Commonwealth v. Anderson, 404 Mass. 767, 769–770 (1989); Bond Pharmacy, Inc. v. Cambridge, 338 Mass. 488, 490–491 (1959); Commonwealth v. Loach, 46 Mass. App. Ct. 313, 316 (1999).

Subsection (b)(7)(A). This subsection is derived from Kaufmann v. Kaitz, 325 Mass. 149, 151 (1949). See Bowes v. Inspector of Bldgs. of Brockton, 347 Mass. 295, 296 (1964) (authentication of city ordinance by city clerk). See also G. L. c. 233, § 73 (foreign oaths and affidavits, if taken or administered by a duly authorized notary public "within the jurisdiction for which he is commissioned, and certified under his official seal, shall be as effectual in this commonwealth as if administered or taken and certified by a justice of the peace therein"); G. L. c. 233, § 74 ("Acts of incorporation shall be held to be public acts and as such may be declared on and given in evidence."). Cf. G. L. c. 233, § 75 ("[P]rinted copies of any city ordinances ... shall be admitted without certification or attestation, but, if their genuineness is questioned, the court shall require such certification or attestation thereof as it deems necessary.").

There are a number of statutory provisions dealing with authentication. See, e.g., G. L. c. 233, § 69 (admissibility of records and court proceedings of a court of another State or of the United States if authenticated "by the attestation of the clerk or other officer who has charge of the records of such court under its seal."); G. L. c. 233, § 73 (foreign oaths and affidavits); G. L. c. 233, § 74 (acts of incorporation); G. L. c. 233, § 75 (municipal ordinances); G. L. c. 233, § 76 (documents filed with governmental departments); G. L. c. 233, § 76A (documents filed with Securities and Exchange Commission); G. L. c. 233, § 76B (documents filed with Interstate Commerce Commission); G. L. c. 233, § 77 (copies of records, books, and accounts of banks and trust companies).

Subsection (b)(7)(B). This subsection is derived from G. L. c. 233, § 76; G. L. c. 90, § 30; Mass. R. Civ. P. 44(a)(1); Mass. R. Crim. P. 40(a)(1); and Commonwealth v. Deramo, 436 Mass. 40, 47–48 (2002).

"[A]n attested copy of a document is one which has been examined and compared with the original, with a certificate or memorandum of its correctness signed by the persons who have examined it. Thus, to qualify as an attested copy there must be a written and signed certification that it is a correct copy. The attestation of an official having custody of an official record is the assurance given by the certifier that the copy submitted is accurate and genuine as compared to the original." (Citations and quotations omitted.)

Id. In Commonwealth v. Deramo, the Supreme Judicial Court held that "[m]erely making a copy of the original attestation along with a copy of the underlying record does not serve the purpose of the attestation requirement." Id. at 48. See id. (concluding that a copy of the defendant's driver history from the Registry of Motor Vehicles was improperly admitted into evidence because it was not supported by an original attestation, but only by a copy of the attestation). Unless a statute or regulation provides otherwise, an attestation does not have to take the form of an original signature; it need only be an original mark, such as a stamp or facsimile. See Commonwealth v. Martinez–Guzman, 76 Mass. App. Ct. 167, 170 (2010) (holding that documents bearing the original stamped signature of the Registrar of Motor Vehicles were properly authenticated).

Any error in admitting a copy of a public record may be cured by comparing it to a properly authenticated record. Commonwealth v. Deramo, 436 Mass. at 49. See also G. L. c. 233, § 68 (proof of the genuineness of a signature to an attested instrument may be by the same methods used for proof of any signature).

Proof of Specific Types of Records. Records and court proceedings of a court of the United States or another State are admissible when relevant if authenticated "by the attestation of the clerk or other officer who has charge of the records of such court under its seal." G. L. c. 233, § 69. Printed copies of State statutes, acts, or resolves "which are published under its authority," and copies of city ordinances, town bylaws, and the rules and regulations of a board of alderman, "if attested by the clerk of such city or town, shall be admitted as sufficient evidence thereof in all courts of law and on all occasions." G. L. c. 233, § 75. Printed copies of rules and regulations of a State department, commission, board, or officer of the Commonwealth or any city or town authorized to adopt them, printed copies of city ordinances or town bylaws, or copies of the United States Code Annotated, the United States Code Service, and all Federal regulations, "shall be admitted without certification or attestation, but, if their genuineness is questioned, the court shall require such certification or attestation as it deems necessary." G. L. c. 233, § 75. Copies of books, papers, documents, and records in any department of State or local government, when attested by the officer in charge of the items, "shall be competent evidence in all cases equally with the originals . . ." G. L. c. 233, § 76 (in most cases the genuineness of that officer's signature shall be attested by the Secretary of the Commonwealth or the clerk of a city or town, as the case may be). See also G.

L. c. 233, § 76A (authentication of documents filed with the Securities and Exchange Commission); G. L. c. 233, § 76B (authentication of documents filed with the Interstate Commerce Commission). Copies of records of banks doing business in the Commonwealth are admissible in evidence on the same terms as originals if accompanied by an affidavit, taken before and under the seal of a clerk of a court of record or notary, "stating that the affiant is the officer having charge of the original records, books and accounts, and that the copy is correct and is full" insofar as it relates to the subject matter in question. G. L. c. 233, § 77. See also G. L. c. 233, § 77A (bank statement showing payment of a check or other item, if accompanied by a legible copy of the check or other item, "is competent evidence in all cases" and prima facie proof of payment of the amount of the check or other item).

Subsection (b)(8). This subsection is derived from Whitman v. Shaw, 166 Mass. 451, 456–461 (1896). See also Green v. Chelsea, 41 Mass. 71, 76–77 (1836). Compare Fed. R. Evid. 901(b)(8) and Proposed Mass. R. Evid. 901(b)(8), which shorten the period from thirty to twenty years.

Subsection (b)(9). This subsection is derived from Commonwealth v. Whynaught, 377 Mass. 14, 19 (1979) (radar), and De Forge v. New York, New Haven & Hartford R.R. Co., 178 Mass. 59, 62–63 (1901) (X-ray).

Subsection (b)(10). This subsection simply establishes that this section is not exclusive. For example, the authenticity of a writing which a party intends to offer at trial may be established prior to trial by a demand for an admission as to genuineness under G. L. c. 231, § 69. See Waldor Realty Corp. v. Planning Bd. of Westborough, 354 Mass. 639, 640 (1968). See also Mass. R. Crim. P. 11(a)(2)(A) ("Agreements reduced to writing in the conference report shall be binding on the parties and shall control the subsequent course of the proceeding."); Mass. R. Civ. P. 44(c) (authentication of official records or the lack thereof from the Commonwealth or a foreign jurisdiction may be accomplished "by any other method authorized by law"). Also, certain statutes provide that records may be authenticated as part of a hearsay exception by means of an affidavit. See, e.g., G. L. c. 233, §§ 79, 79G, 79J.

Subsection (b)(11). This subsection is derived from Commonwealth v. Purdy, 459 Mass. 442, 450 (2011), where the court held that the same basic principles of authentication apply to e-mails and other forms of electronic communication as apply to, for example, telephone calls and handwritten letters. Evidence that a person's name is written as the author of an e-mail or that the electronic communication originates from an e-mail or social-networking website that bears the person's name is not, standing alone, sufficient to authenticate the communication as having been authored, posted, or sent by the person. There must be some "confirming circumstances" sufficient for a reasonable jury to find by a preponderance of the evidence that the person authored, posted, or sent the communication. Id. at 450. In Purdy, the confirming circumstances were that the e-mails were found on the hard drive of the computer that the defendant acknowledged owning and to which he supplied all necessary passwords, and at least two e-mails contained either an attached photograph of the defendant or a self-characterization. Id. at 450–451. "The defendant's uncorroborated testimony that others used his computer regularly . . . was relevant to the weight, not the admissibility, of the[] messages." Id. at 451. The court stated that neither expert testimony nor exclusive access is necessary to authenticate the authorship of an e-mail. Id. at 451 n.7. See also Commonwealth v. Alden, 93 Mass. App. Ct. 438, 441 (2018) (In addition to the content of the text message, the witness's prior relationship with the defendant and her use of the telephone number to communicate with the defendant over a significant period of time provided the necessary link providing the confirming circumstances.); Commonwealth v. Gilman, 89 Mass. App. Ct. 752, 758–759 (2016) (Facebook chat messages authenticated by location on laptops solely used by defendant, defendant's name and picture associated with account sending and receiving messages, initiation of chat sessions via text message, and references to personal details within messages); Commonwealth v. Oppenheim, 86 Mass. App. Ct. 359, 366–367 (2014); Commonwealth v. Foster F., 86 Mass. App. Ct. 734, 737 (2014) (messages on social-networking website provided adequate confirming circumstances for reasonable jury to find defendant authored messages, as required for messages to be admissible, where defendant appeared at park to play dating game with victim and victim's friends exactly as person sending messages from the social-networking account had proposed); Commonwealth v. Amaral, 78 Mass. App. Ct. 671, 674–675 (2011) (e-mails authenticated by actions of defendant who, for example, appeared at time and place indicated in an e-mail and answered telephone number provided in another e-mail).one number provided in another e-mail).

Section 902.   Evidence That Is Self–Authenticating

Extrinsic evidence of authenticity, as a condition precedent to admissibility, is not required with respect to the following:

(a) Court Records Under Seal. The records and judicial proceedings of a court of another State or of the United States, if authenticated by the attestation of the clerk or other officer who has charge of the records of such court under its seal.

(b) Domestic Official Records Not Under Seal. An official record kept within the Commonwealth, or an entry therein, when admissible for any purpose, may be evidenced by an official publication thereof or by a copy attested by the officer having legal custody of the record, or by that officer's deputy. If the record is kept in any other State, district, Commonwealth, territory, or insular possession of the United States, or within the Panama Canal Zone, the Trust Territory of the Pacific Islands, or the Ryukyu Islands, any such copy shall be accompanied by a certificate that such custodial officer has custody of the record.   This certificate may be made by a judge of a court of record of the district or political subdivision in which the record is kept, authenticated by the seal of the court, or may be made by any public officer having a seal of office and having official duties in the district or political subdivision in which the record is kept, authenticated by the seal of the office.

(c) Foreign Official Records. A foreign official record, or an entry therein, when admissible for any purpose, attested by a person authorized to make the attestation and accompanied by a final certification as to the genuineness of the signature and official position (1) of the attesting person or (2) of any foreign official whose certificate of genuineness of signature and official position relates to the attestation or is in a chain of certificates of genuineness of signature and official position relating to the attestation. A final certification may be made by a secretary of embassy or legation, consul general, consul, vice consul, or consular agent of the United States, or a diplomatic or consular official of the foreign country assigned or accredited to the United States. If reasonable opportunity has been given to all parties to investigate the authenticity and accuracy of the documents, the court may, for good cause shown, (1) admit an attested copy without final certification or (2) permit the foreign official record to be evidenced by an attested summary with or without a final certification.

(d) Certified Copies of Public Records. Copies of public records, of records described in Sections 5, 7, and 16 of G. L. c. 66, and of records of banks, trust companies, insurance companies, and hospitals, whether or not such records or copies are made by the photographic or microphotographic process if there is annexed to such copies an affidavit, taken before a clerk of a court of record or notary public, under the seal of such court or notary, stating that the affiant is the officer having charge of the original records, books, and accounts, and that the copy is correct and is full so far as it relates to the subject matter therein mentioned.

(e) Official Publications.

(1) Printed copies of all statutes, acts, and resolves of the Commonwealth, public or private, which are published under its authority, and copies of the ordinances of a city, the bylaws of a town, or the rules and regulations of a board of aldermen, if attested by the clerk of such city or town.

(2) Printed copies of rules and regulations purporting to be issued by authority of any department, commission, board, or officer of the Commonwealth or of any city or town having authority to adopt them, or printed copies of any city ordinances or town bylaws or printed copies of the United States Code Annotated or the United States Code Service and all Federal regulations, without certification or attestation; provided, however, that if their genuineness is questioned, the court shall require such certification or attestation thereof as it deems necessary.

(3) Copies of books, papers, documents, and records in any department of the Commonwealth or of any city or town, authenticated by the attestation of the officer who has charge of the same; provided that the genuineness of the signature of such officer shall be attested by the Secretary of the Commonwealth under its seal or by the clerk of such city or town except in the case of books, papers, documents, and records of the Department of Telecommunications and Energy in matters relating to common carriers, and of the Registry of Motor Vehicles.

(4) The Massachusetts Register.

(f) Certain Newspapers. Certified copies of any newspaper, or part thereof, made by the photographic or microphotographic process deposited in any public library or a library of any college or university located in the Commonwealth.

(g) Trade Inscriptions. A trademark or trade name affixed on a product indicating origin.

(h) Acknowledged Documents. All oaths and affidavits administered or taken by a notary public, duly commissioned and qualified by authority of any other State or government, within the jurisdiction for which the notary is commissioned, and certified under an official seal; such documents shall be as effectual in this Commonwealth as if administered or taken and certified by a justice of the peace therein.

(i) Commercial Paper and Related Documents. Commercial paper, a signature on it, and related documents, to the extent allowed by general commercial law.

(j) Presumptions Created by Law. A signature, document, or anything else that a law of the United States or this Commonwealth declares to be presumptively or prima facie genuine or authentic.

(k) Certified Copies of Hospital and Other Records of Treatment and Medical History. Records or copies of records kept by any hospital, dispensary or clinic, or sanitarium, if certified by affidavit by the person in custody thereof to be true and complete.

(*l*) Copies of Hospital and Other Records of Itemized Bills and Reports. Itemized bills and reports, including hospital medical records and examination reports, relating to medical, dental, hospital services, prescriptions, or orthopedic appliances rendered to a person injured, if (1) it is subscribed and sworn to under the penalties of perjury by the physician, dentist, authorized agent of a hospital or health maintenance organization, pharmacist, or retailer of orthopedic appliances rendering such services; (2) the party offering the evidence gives the opposing party written notice of the intention to offer the evidence, along with a copy of the evidence, by mailing it by certified mail, return receipt requested, not less than ten days before the introduction of the evidence; and (3) the party offering the evidence files an affidavit of such notice and the return receipt is filed with the clerk of the court after said receipt has been returned.

(m) Copies of Bills for Genetic Marker Tests and for Prenatal and Postnatal Care. Copies of bills for genetic marker tests and for prenatal and postnatal health care of the mother and child, furnished to the adverse party at least ten days before trial, shall be admissible in evidence to prove the amount of the charges billed and that the charges were reasonable, necessary, and customary.

(n) Results of Genetic Marker Tests. In an action to establish the paternity of a child born out of wedlock, the report of the results of genetic marker tests, including a statistical probability of the putative father's paternity based upon such tests, unless a party objects in writing to the test results upon notice of the hearing date or within thirty days prior to the hearing, whichever is shorter.

NOTE

Subsection (a). This subsection is derived from G. L. c. 233, § 69. See also Mass. R. Crim. P. 39(a).

Subsection (b). This subsection is derived from Mass. R. Civ. P. 44(a)(1) and Mass. R. Crim. P. 40(a)(1).

Subsection (c). This subsection is derived from Mass. R. Civ. P. 44(a)(2) and Mass. R. Crim. P. 40(a)(2).

Subsection (d). This subsection is derived from G. L. c. 233, §§ 77 and 79A.

Subsection (e)(1). This subsection is derived from G. L. c. 233, § 75.

Subsection (e)(2). This subsection is derived from G. L. c. 233, § 75.

Subsection (e)(3). This subsection is derived from G. L. c. 233, § 76.

Subsection (e)(4). This subsection is derived from G. L. c. 30A, § 6 ("The publication in the Massachusetts Register of a document creates a rebuttable presumption [1] that it was duly issued, prescribed, or promulgated; [2] that all the requirements of this chapter and regulations prescribed under it relative to the document have been complied with; and [3] that the text of the regulations as published in the Massachusetts Register is a true copy of the attested regulation as filed by the agency.").

Subsection (f). This subsection is derived from G. L. c. 233, § 79D ("Copies of any newspaper, or part thereof made by photographic or microphotographic process deposited in any public library or a library of any college or university located in the commonwealth, shall, when duly certified by the person in charge thereof, be admitted in evidence

equally with the originals."). See also Section 901(b)(1), Authenticating or Identifying Evidence: Examples: Testimony of a Witness with Knowledge.

Subsection (g). This subsection is derived from Smith v. Ariens Co., 375 Mass. 620, 621–623 (1978), and Doyle v. Continental Baking Co., 262 Mass. 516, 519 (1928). In Smith v. Ariens Co., 375 Mass. at 623, the presence of the defendant's name on the decal on a snowmobile was sufficient to identify the defendant as the manufacturer of the snowmobile. In Doyle v. Continental Baking Co., 262 Mass. at 519, the label on which the defendant's name appeared was sufficient to identify the defendant as the manufacturer of the defective bread. See also G. L. c. 156B, § 11(a) (a corporation is not permitted to use the corporate name or trademark of another corporation registered or doing business in this Commonwealth without their consent).

"Several rationales underlie the acceptance of this rule. First, since trademarks and trade names are protected under statutes, the probability that a particular name will be used by another corporation is very low. Second, since the probability is very high that the corporation whose name appears on a product is the corporation which manufactured the product, judicial efficiency will be served by allowing the identity of the name on a product and the defendant's name to satisfy the plaintiff's burden of identifying the defendant as the manufacturer. Finally, the presence of trademarks or trade names on products is accepted and relied on in daily life as sufficient proof of the manufacturer of the product. This common acceptance, which has been reinforced by manufacturers' advertising, indicates that the identity of a corporation's name and the name on a product should be sufficient to identify that corporation as the manufacturer." (Citations omitted.)

Smith v. Ariens Co., 375 Mass. at 622.

Subsection (h). This subsection is derived from G. L. c. 233, § 73. See also Mass. R. Civ. P. 43(d).

Subsection (i). This subsection is derived from various statutes and commercial law. See, e.g., G. L. c. 106, § 1–202 (document authorized or required by a contract to be issued by a third party is prima facie evidence of its own authenticity); G. L. c. 233, § 76A (records of the Securities and Exchange Commission must be attested by an officer or person who has charge of the same and under a certificate of a member); G. L. c. 233, § 76B (printed copies of rate schedules filed with the Interstate Commerce Commission are admissible without certification); G. L. c. 233, § 77 (copies from the records, books, and accounts of banks and trust companies doing business in the Commonwealth must have an affidavit taken before a notary stating that the officer has charge of the original records); G. L. c. 233, § 78 (business records shall be admissible if the court finds the record was made in good faith, in the regular course of business, before the beginning of legal proceedings, and the person who made the entry has personal knowledge of the facts stated in the record).

Subsection (j). This subsection is derived from statutes which deal with authentication not covered in other areas of Article IX, Authentication and Identification. See, e.g., G L. c. 9, § 11 (Great Seal); G. L. c. 111, § 195 (certified copy of reports of State laboratory for lead and lead poisoning); G. L. c. 209C, § 17 (in an action to establish paternity of a child born out of wedlock, the report of the results of genetic marker tests shall be admissible without proof of authenticity); G. L. c. 233, § 79B (published statements of fact of general interest to persons engaged in an occupation shall be admissible in the court's discretion in civil cases); G. L. c. 233, § 79C (published facts or opinions on a subject of science or art shall be admissible in actions of contract or malpractice, conditioned on the court finding that said statements are relevant and that the writer is recognized in his or her profession as an expert on the subject); G. L. c. 233, § 80 (stenographic transcripts).

Subsection (k). This subsection is derived from G. L. c. 233, § 79. "[Section 79] was enacted primarily to relieve the physicians and nurses of public hospitals from the hardship and inconvenience of attending court as witnesses to facts which ordinarily would be found recorded in the hospital books" (citation omitted). Bouchie v. Murray, 376 Mass. 524, 527 (1978).

Cross–Reference: Section 803(6)(B), Hearsay Exceptions; Availability of Declarant Immaterial: Business and Hospital Records: Hospital Records.

Subsection (*l*). This subsection is derived from G. L. c. 233, § 79G. Under Section 79G, in addition to those already noted are "chiropodists, chiropractors, optometrists, osteopaths, physical therapists, podiatrists, psychologists and other medical personnel licensed to practice under the laws of the jurisdiction within which such services were rendered." This subsection applies to both civil and criminal cases. See Commonwealth v. Schutte, 52 Mass. App. Ct. 796, 797–800 (2001).

Cross–Reference: Section 803(6)(C), Hearsay Exceptions; Availability of Declarant Immaterial: Business and Hospital Records: Medical and Hospital Services.

Subsection (m). This subsection is taken verbatim from G. L. c. 209C, § 16(f).

Subsection (n). This subsection is derived from G. L. c. 209C, § 17. Such reports shall not be admissible absent sufficient evidence of intercourse between the mother and the putative father during the period of probable conception and shall not be considered as evidence of the occurrence of intercourse between the mother and the putative father. Id. There is nothing in the statute that requires the test to be court ordered in order to be admissible. Department of Revenue v. Sorrentino, 408 Mass. 340, 344 (1990).

Section 903. Subscribing Witness's Testimony

A subscribing witness's testimony is necessary to authenticate a writing only if required by the law of the jurisdiction that governs its validity.

NOTE

This section is derived from G. L. c. 233, § 68, and Mass. R. Civ. P. 8(b) ("The signature to an instrument set forth in any pleading shall be taken as admitted unless a party specifically denies its genuineness.").

Authentication of wills in uncontested proceedings is governed by the Massachusetts Uniform Probate Code, G. L. c. 190B. Authentication of a will in a contested proceeding requires a greater level of support. See Goodwin v. Riordan, 333 Mass. 317, 318–319 (1955); Werber v. Werber, 62 Mass. App. Ct. 927, 927–928 (2004).

ARTICLE X.   CONTENTS OF WRITINGS AND RECORDS

Section 1001. Definitions That Apply to This Article

The following definitions apply under this Article:

(a) Writings and Records. "Writings" and "records" are documents that consist of letters, words, numbers, or their equivalent. Photographs, composite pictures, tape recordings, videotapes, and digital images are not writings or records.

(b) Original. An "original" of a writing or record means the writing or record itself or any copy intended to have the same effect by the person who executed or issued it.

(c) Duplicate. A "duplicate" is a copy of a writing or record that is not intended to be an original, the copies being no more than secondary evidence of the original.

NOTE

Subsection (a). This subsection is derived from Commonwealth v. Duhamel, 391 Mass. 841, 844 (1984) (tape recording); Commonwealth v. Weichell, 390 Mass. 62, 77 (1983), cert. denied, 465 U.S. 1032 (1984) (photographs); Commonwealth v. Balukonis, 357 Mass. 721, 725 (1970) (composite pictures); Smith v. Palmer, 60 Mass. 513, 520–521 (1850) (best evidence); and Commonwealth v. Leneski, 66 Mass. App. Ct. 291, 294 (2006) (videotapes or digital images).

This section is not as extensive as Fed. R. Evid. 1001 and Proposed Mass. R. Evid. 1001(1), both of which cover recordings and photographs. "The best evidence rule is applicable to only those situations where the contents of a writing are sought to be proved" (citation omitted). Commonwealth v. Balukonis, 357 Mass. at 725. "[T]his rule is usually regarded ... as not applicable to any objects but writings ... So far, then, as concerns objects not writings, a photographic representation could be used without accounting for the original." Id. at 725, quoting Wigmore, Evidence § 796 (3d ed. 1940). See also Commonwealth v. McKay, 67 Mass. App. Ct. 396, 402–403 (2006).

Subsection (b). This subsection is derived from Quinn v. Standard Oil Co., 249 Mass. 194, 201 (1924), and Peaks v. Cobb, 192 Mass. 196, 196–197 (1906).

Subsection (c). This subsection is derived from Augur Steel Axle & Gearing Co. v. Whittier, 117 Mass. 451, 455 (1875) (as to letter-press copy of an original letter in possession of adverse party, "[t]here was sufficient foundation for the admission of secondary evidence of the contents of the letter"). See also Meehan v. North Adams Sav. Bank, 302 Mass. 357, 363–364 (1939) (admissibility of copy of a letter upheld, not to prove its contents, but to prove the opponent had received the original letter).

Section 1002. Requirement of Original (Best Evidence Rule)

An original writing or record is required in order to prove its content unless these sections, a statute, or the common law provides otherwise.

NOTE

This section is derived from Commonwealth v. Ocasio, 434 Mass. 1, 6 (2001), where the court explained as follows:

> "The best evidence rule provides that, where the contents of a document are to be proved, the party must either produce the original or show a sufficient excuse for its nonproduction. The rule is a doctrine of evidentiary preference principally aimed, not at securing a writing at all hazards and in every instance, but at securing the best obtainable evidence of its contents. Thus, where the original has been lost, destroyed, or is otherwise unavailable, its production may be excused and other evidence of its contents will be admissible, provided that certain findings are made." (Quotation and citations omitted; emphasis omitted.)

See also Commonwealth v. Stevens, 155 Mass. 291, 292 (1892); Commonwealth v. Silva, 61 Mass. App. Ct. 28, 35–37 (2004) (written inventory search policy of police department is the best evidence of that policy and such documents should be offered in evidence to prove it exists).

The best evidence rule does not apply where the writing is so simple that the possibility of error is negligible. See Commonwealth v. Blood, 77 Mass. 74, 77 (1858).

"The best evidence rule [applies] to only those situations where the contents of a writing are sought to be proved." Commonwealth v. Balukonis, 357 Mass. 721, 725 (1970). See Commonwealth v. DeJesus, 87 Mass. App. Ct. 198, 201 (2015) (original currency not required where only question was whether photocopy of bills used in undercover operation matched bills found in defendant's pocket after drug transaction). The rule does not apply to photographs, Commonwealth v. Weichell, 390 Mass. 62, 77 (1983), cert. denied, 465 U.S. 1032 (1984); composite pictures, Commonwealth v. Balukonis, 357 Mass. at 725; tape recordings, Commonwealth v. Duhamel, 391 Mass. 841, 844 (1984); or videotapes or digital images, Commonwealth v. Leneski, 66 Mass. App. Ct. 291, 294 (2006). The introduction of such evidence is subject to other requirements, i.e., relevancy and authentication. Id.

The admission of photographs, composite drawings, tape recordings, or digital images is within the discretion of the trial judge, provided that the evidence is accurate, similar enough to circumstances at the time in dispute to be relevant and helpful to the jury in its deliberations, and its probative value outweighs any prejudice to the other party. See Renzi v. Paredes, 452 Mass. 38, 52 (2008); Commonwealth v. Duhamel, 391 Mass. at 844–845; Commonwealth v. Balukonis, 357 Mass. at 725–726; Commonwealth v. Leneski, 66 Mass. App. Ct. at 294; Henderson v. D'Annolfo, 15 Mass. App. Ct. 413, 428–429 (1983). A witness may testify that a photograph or digital image is substantially similar to the original as long as the witness is familiar with the details pictured even though the witness is not the photographer. Renzi v. Paredes, 452 Mass. at 52. "Concerns regarding the completeness or production of the image go to its weight and not its admissibility." Id.

"The best evidence rule does not forbid the use of 'copies' of electronic records (including e-mails and text messages and other computer data files), because there is no 'original' in the traditional sense" (citations omitted). Commonwealth v. Salyer, 84 Mass. App. Ct. 346, 356 n.10 (2013). Cf. G. L. c. 233, § 79K. "However, oral testimony designed to prove the contents of an electronic record is barred for the same reasons as those underlying the best evidence rule." Commonwealth v. Salyer, 84 Mass. App. Ct. at 356 n.10.

Section 1003. Admissibility of Duplicates

Where the original has been lost, destroyed, or otherwise made unavailable, its production may be excused and other evidence of its contents will be admissible, provided that certain findings are made as outlined in Section 1004.

NOTE

This section is taken nearly verbatim from Commonwealth v. Ocasio, 434 Mass. 1, 6 (2001).

"As a threshold matter, the proponent must offer evidence sufficient to warrant a finding that the original once existed. If the evidence warrants such a finding, the judge must assume its existence, and then determine if the original had become unavailable, otherwise than through the serious fault of the proponent and that reasonable search had been made for it." (Citation, quotation, and ellipsis omitted.)

Id. at 6–7.

A number of statutes make duplicates admissible on the same terms as originals. See, e.g., G. L. c. 233, § 76 (attested-to records of governmental departments); G. L. c. 233, § 76A (properly authenticated copies of documents filed with the Securities and Exchange Commission); G. L. c. 233, § 77 (copies of books, etc., of trust companies and banks); G. L. c. 233, § 79A (duly certified copies of public, bank, insurance, and hospital records); G. L. c. 233, § 79D (duly certified copies of newspapers made by photographic process and deposited in certain public and college libraries); G. L. c. 233, § 79E (reproductions made in the regular course of business); G. L. c. 233, § 79K (duplicate of a computer data file or program file unless issue as to authenticity or unfair to admit). See also G. L. c. 233, § 78 (court "may" order originals).

Section 1004. Admissibility of Other Evidence of Content

An original is not required, and other evidence of the content of the writing or record is admissible, if

(a) all the originals are lost or destroyed, and not by the proponent acting in bad faith;

(b) an original cannot be obtained by any available judicial process;

(c) the party against whom the original would be offered had control of the original; was at that time put on notice, by pleadings or otherwise, that the original would be a subject of proof at the trial or hearing; and fails to produce it at the trial or hearing; or

(d) the writing or record is not closely related to a controlling issue.

NOTE

This section is taken from Fed. R. Evid. 1004 and Proposed Mass. R. Evid. 1004, both of which reflect Massachusetts practice.

Subsection (a). This subsection is derived from Commonwealth v. Ocasio, 434 Mass. 1, 7 (2001), quoting Proposed Mass. R. Evid. 1004(a). See also Old Colony Trust Co. v. Shaw, 348 Mass. 212, 219 (1964); Fauci v. Mulready, 337 Mass. 532, 540–542 (1958); Joannes v. Bennett, 87 Mass. 169, 172–173 (1862); Capitol Bank & Trust Co. v. Richman, 19 Mass. App. Ct. 515, 520–521 (1985).

"[I]n order to permit proof by secondary evidence of the contents of [a lost original], the trial judge must make preliminary findings that the original had become unavailable, otherwise than through the serious fault of the proponent . . . and that reasonable search had been made for it." Fauci v. Mulready, 337 Mass. at 540.

Subsection (b). This subsection is derived from Topping v. Bickford, 86 Mass. 120, 122 (1862), and Commonwealth v. Smith, 151 Mass. 491, 495 (1890).

Subsection (c). This subsection is derived from Fisher v. Swartz, 333 Mass. 265, 271 (1955) (defendant had an original in court and refused to produce it on plaintiff's request so secondary evidence was admitted), and Commonwealth v. Slocomb, 260 Mass. 288, 291 (1927) (when pleadings disclose proof of a document that will be necessary at trial, no further notice is necessary, and if the party fails to produce the document, secondary evidence is admissible). Cf. Cregg v. Puritan Trust Co., 237 Mass. 146, 149–150 (1921) ("The failure of the defendant to produce its books and accounts when summoned by a subpoena *duces tecum* conferred authority on the court to compel that production by proper process, and authorized the plaintiff to introduce parol evidence of the contents of such books and records. A like result follows upon the failure of a party at the trial to produce on reasonable demand writings which are material to the issue. The failure to produce documents on demand at a trial or on the subpoena *duces tecum*, is not in itself evidence of the alleged contents of such documents." [Citations omitted.]).

Subsection (d). This subsection is derived from Smith v. Abington Sav. Bank, 171 Mass. 178, 184 (1898). See also Commonwealth v. Borasky, 214 Mass. 313, 317 (1913) (defendant's objection to testimony of physician, who performed autopsy, on the ground that the record was the best evidence, was properly overruled as "[t]he testimony of the witness who was present and observed the condition revealed by the autopsy was admissible"); Beauregard v. Benjamin F. Smith Co., 213 Mass. 259, 264 (1913) (sheriff was permitted to testify as to where he served the defendant without producing the official return of service); Eagle Bank at New Haven v. Chapin, 20 Mass. 180, 182–183 (1825) (parol evidence of a notice to an endorser admissible without calling on the party to produce the written notice received by him).

Section 1005.   Official Records

(a) Authentication.

(1) **Domestic.** An official record kept within the Commonwealth, or an entry therein, when admissible for any purpose, may be evidenced by an official publication thereof or by a copy attested by the officer having legal custody of the record, or by that officer's deputy. If the record is kept in any other State, district, Commonwealth, territory, or insular possession of the United States, or within the Panama Canal Zone, the Trust Territory of the Pacific Islands, or the Ryukyu Islands, any such copy shall be accompanied by a certificate that such custodial officer has the custody. This certificate may be made by a judge of a court of record of the district or political subdivision in which the record is kept, authenticated by the seal of the court, or may be made by any public officer having a seal of office and having official duties in the district or political subdivision in which the record is kept, authenticated by the seal of the office.

(2) **Foreign.** A foreign official record, or an entry therein, when admissible for any purpose, may be evidenced by an official publication thereof, or a copy thereof, attested by a person authorized to make the attestation and accompanied by a final certification as to the genuineness of the signature and official position (A) of the attesting person or (B) of any foreign official whose certificate of genuineness of signature and official position relates to the attestation or is in a chain of certificates of genuineness of signature and official position relating to the attestation. A final certification may be made by a secretary of embassy or legation, consul general, consul, vice consul, or consular agent of the United States, or a diplomatic or consular official of the foreign country assigned or accredited to the United States. If reasonable opportunity has been given to all parties to investigate the authenticity and accuracy of the documents, the court may, for good cause shown, (A) admit an attested copy without final certification or (B) permit the foreign official record to be evidenced by an attested summary with or without a final certification.

(b) Lack of Record.

A written statement that after diligent search no record or entry of a specified tenor is found to exist in the records designated by the statement, authenticated as provided in Subsection (a)(1) of this section in the case of a domestic record or complying with the requirements of Subsection (a)(2) of this section for a summary in the case of a foreign record, is admissible as evidence that the records contain no such record or entry.

(c) Other Proof.

This section does not prevent the proof, by any other method authorized by law, of the existence of, or the lack of, an official record, or of entry, or lack of entry therein.

NOTE

This section is taken nearly verbatim from Mass. R. Civ. P. 44 and Mass. R. Crim. P. 40.

Section 1006.   Summaries to Prove Content

The proponent may use a summary, chart, or the like to prove the content of voluminous writings or records that cannot be conveniently examined in court. The proponent must make the originals or duplicates available for examination or copying, or both, by other parties at a reasonable time and place. The court may order the proponent to produce the underlying documents or records in court.

NOTE

This section, which is taken nearly verbatim from Fed. R. Evid. 1006, reflects Massachusetts practice. See Fed. R. Evid. 1006.

"[I]n a trial embracing so many details and occupying so great a length of time... during which a great mass of books and documents were put in evidence, concise statements of their content verified by persons who had prepared them from the originals were the only means for presenting to the jury an intelligible view of the issues involved" (quotation and citations omitted). Commonwealth v. Greenberg, 339 Mass. 557, 582 (1959). See also the cases cited in Section 611(a), Mode and Order of Examining Witnesses and Presenting Evidence: Control by the Court.

"[C]are must be taken to insure that summaries accurately reflect the contents of the underlying documents and do not function as pedagogical devices that unfairly emphasize part of the proponent's proof" (quotations and citations omitted). Welch v. Keene Corp., 31 Mass. App. Ct. 157, 165–166 (1991). The witness presenting the summary is not permitted to state deductions or inferences, but may testify as to the results of his or her computations. Commonwealth v. Greenberg, 339 Mass. at 582. The court may order that the original be produced. Cf. Cornell–Andrews Smelting Co. v. Boston & P.R. Corp., 215 Mass. 381, 390–391 (1913).

For a thoughtful discussion of Section 1006, its relation to Fed. R. Evid. 1006, and its application to summaries of evidence, see Commonwealth v. Wood, 90 Mass. App. Ct. 271 (2016), which is instructive. There, the Commonwealth, as part of its case against a defendant on trial for assault with a deadly weapon, showed the jury a PowerPoint presentation that was a "compilation of various pages chosen from previously-admitted exhibits." Id. at 276. The presentation included cellular phone records; condensed versions of text messages between the defendant, the victim, and a third party; call logs; and maps showing the victim's movement based on data from his GPS tracking bracelet. Id. The Appeals Court held that because the presentation selectively presented excerpts of other exhibits in evidence in such a way that it served to both bolster the Commonwealth's case and rebut the defendant's defense, it was "not merely a neutral summary. It was 'more akin to argument than evidence since [it] organizes the jury's examination of testimony and documents already admitted in evidence.'" Id. at 277, quoting United States v. Bray, 139 F.3d 1104, 1111 (6th Cir. 1998). However, the court found that although the presentation was erroneously admitted, its admission did not prejudice the defendant because "all of the material in [the presentation] was previously admitted in evidence and ... added little to the Commonwealth's case and detracted little from the defendant's theory at trial." Id. at 282.

Section 1007.   Testimony or Statement of Party to Prove Content

The proponent may prove the content of a written statement of the party against whom the evidence is offered without producing or accounting for the original.

NOTE

This section is taken from Smith v. Palmer, 60 Mass. 513, 521 (1850). See also Cooley v. Collins, 186 Mass. 507, 509–510 (1904); Clarke v. Warwick Cycle Mfg. Co., 174 Mass. 434, 435 (1899).

Section 1008.   Functions of Judge and Fact Finder

Before secondary evidence of the contents of a writing or record may be admitted, the proponent must offer evidence sufficient to warrant a finding that an original once existed. If the evidence warrants such a finding, the judge must assume its existence and then determine if the original is unavailable, not through the serious fault of the proponent, and if reasonable search has been made for it. If the judge makes these findings in favor of the proponent, the judge must allow secondary evidence to establish the contents of the original writing or record. Once the secondary evidence is admitted, it is for the trier of fact to determine the weight, if any, to give the secondary evidence.

NOTE

This section is derived from Fauci v. Mulready, 337 Mass. 532, 540–542 (1958), and Dana v. Kemble, 36 Mass. 112, 114 (1837). See also Commonwealth v. Ocasio, 434 Mass. 1, 6–7 (2001); Old Colony Trust Co. v. Shaw, 348 Mass. 212, 219 (1964); Capitol Bank & Trust Co. v. Richman, 19 Mass. App. Ct. 515, 520–522 (1985); Buker v. Melanson, 8 Mass. App. Ct. 325, 330–331 (1979). If secondary evidence is admitted, it is then up to the trier of fact to decide, when it is an issue, whether the document ever existed. Fauci v. Mulready, 337 Mass. at 542.

"[T]here are no degrees in secondary evidence, so that a party authorized to resort to it is compelled to produce one class of such evidence rather than another." Commonwealth v. Smith, 151 Mass. 491, 495 (1890).

ARTICLE XI. MISCELLANEOUS SECTIONS

Section 1101. Applicability of Evidentiary Sections

(a) Proceedings to Which Applicable. Except as provided in Subsection (c), these sections apply to all actions and proceedings in the courts of the Commonwealth.

(b) Privileges. The provisions of Article V apply at all stages of all actions, cases, and proceedings.

(c) Where Inapplicable. These sections (other than those concerning privileges) do not apply in the following situations:

(1) Preliminary Determinations of Fact. The determination of questions of fact preliminary to the admissibility of evidence when the determination is to be made by the judge under Section 104(a).

(2) Grand Jury Proceedings. Proceedings before grand juries.

(3) Certain Other Proceedings. Most administrative proceedings; bail proceedings; bar discipline proceedings; civil motor vehicle infraction hearings; issuance of process (warrant, complaint, capias, summons); precomplaint, show cause hearings; civil commitment proceedings for alcohol and substance abuse; pretrial dangerousness hearings; prison disciplinary hearings; probation violation hearings; restitution hearings; sentencing; sexual offender registry board hearings; small claims sessions; and summary contempt proceedings.

(d) Motions to Suppress. The law of evidence does not apply with full force at motion to suppress hearings. As to the determination of probable cause or the justification of government action, out-of-court statements are admissible.

NOTE

Subsection (a). This subsection summarizes the current practice in Massachusetts courts. "The rules of evidence stand guard to ensure that only relevant, reliable, noninflammatory considerations may shape fact finding. Without these rules, there would be nothing to prevent trials from being resolved on whim, personal affections, or prejudice." Adoption of Sherry, 435 Mass. 331, 338 (2001). In addition to trials, therefore, the law of evidence applies at hearings on motions. See Thorell v. ADAP, Inc., 58 Mass. App. Ct. 334, 340–341 (2003).

Subsection (b). Privileges are covered in Article V, Privileges and Disqualifications.

Subsection (c)(1). See Note to Section 104(a), Preliminary Questions: In General.

Subsection (c)(2). This subsection is derived from Commonwealth v. Gibson, 368 Mass. 518, 522–525 (1975), and Mass. R. Crim. P. 4(c). See Reporters' Notes to Mass. R. Crim. P. 4(c) ("evidence which is not legally competent at trial is sufficient upon which to base an indictment").

Subsection (c)(3). Evidence bearing directly on probable cause, such as what a witness, a police officer, or a probation officer tells a court in connection with a request for an arrest warrant, a probation violation warrant, a warrant of apprehension, a search warrant, a capias, or a summons, or in support of a criminal complaint or as justification for a search and seizure, is not objectionable on grounds of hearsay in a judicial proceeding to determine probable cause. Commonwealth v. Fletcher, 435 Mass. 558, 567 (2002); Commonwealth v. Weiss, 370 Mass. 416, 418 (1976); Commonwealth v. Rosenthal, 52 Mass. App. Ct. 707, 709 n.3 (2001). While the traditional rules of evidence may not apply in these situations, the evidence must still be reliable and trustworthy. See Abbott A. v. Commonwealth, 458 Mass. 24, 34–35 (2010); Brantley v. Hampden Div. of the Probate & Family Ct. Dep't, 457 Mass. 172, 184–185 (2010); Commonwealth v. Wilcox, 446 Mass. 61, 71 (2006).

This subsection identifies the various miscellaneous proceedings to which the rules of evidence are not applicable, including the following:

209A Hearings. See Silvia v. Duarte, 421 Mass. 1007, 1008 (1995); Frizado v. Frizado, 420 Mass. 592, 597–598 (1995).

Administrative Proceedings. See G. L. c. 30A, § 11(2); 452 Code Mass. Regs. § 1.11(5); Costa v. Fall River Hous. Auth., 453 Mass. 614, 627 (2009); Rate Setting Comm'n v. Baystate Med. Ctr., 422 Mass. 744, 752–755 (1996); Goodridge v. Director of Div. of Employment Sec., 375 Mass. 434, 436 n.1 (1978). See also Care & Protection of Rebecca, 419 Mass. 67, 83 (1994) (a witness at such a proceeding is not permitted to express an opinion about the credibility of another witness).

Bail Proceedings. See Paquette v. Commonwealth, 440 Mass. 121, 133 (2003) (bail revocation proceedings); Querubin v. Commonwealth, 440 Mass. 108, 118 (2003) (G. L. c. 276, § 57, proceedings); Snow v. Commonwealth, 404 Mass. 1007, 1007 (1989).

Bar Discipline Proceedings. See Matter of Abbott, 437 Mass. 384, 393 (2002).

Civil Commitment Hearings for Alcohol and Substance Use Disorders. See G. L. c. 123, § 35; Matter of G.P., 473 Mass. 112, 128–129 (2015). See also Section 1118, Civil Commitment Hearings for Alcohol and Substance Use Disorders.

Civil Motor Vehicle Infraction Hearings. See G. L. c. 90, § 20 (traffic citation). Under the Uniform Rules on Civil Motor Vehicle Infractions, the formal rules of evidence do not apply. See Commonwealth v. Curtin, 386 Mass. 587, 588 n.3 (1982). The same holds true for cases involving parking tickets under G. L. c. 90, § 20C. See Lemaine v. City of Boston, 27 Mass. App. Ct. 1173, 1175 (1989).

Issuance of Process (Warrant, Capias, Summons). See Commonwealth v. Weiss, 370 Mass. 416, 418 (1976); Commonwealth v. Young, 349 Mass. 175, 179 (1965); Commonwealth v. Lehan, 347 Mass. 197, 206 (1964); Commonwealth v. Rosenthal, 52 Mass. App. Ct. 707, 709 n.3 (2001).

Precomplaint Hearings. See G. L. c. 218, § 35A. The formal rules of evidence do not apply at a hearing conducted pursuant to G. L. c. 218, § 35A. Commonwealth v. Clerk–Magistrate of the W. Roxbury Div. of the Dist. Ct. Dep't, 439 Mass. 352, 357–358 (2003); Commonwealth v. DiBennadetto, 436 Mass. 310, 314–315 (2002) (no right to cross-examine witness).

Pretrial Dangerousness Hearings. See G. L. c. 276, § 58A(4); Abbott A. v. Commonwealth, 458 Mass. 24, 30–33 (2010); Mendonza v. Commonwealth, 423 Mass. 771, 785–786 (1996). By statute, a judge must consider hearsay contained either in a police report or a statement of a victim or witness at a dangerousness hearing. G. L. c. 276, § 58A(4). Before being able to summons the victim or the victim's family to the hearing, a defendant must make a motion to the court prior to the issuance of the summons. The defendant must demonstrate a good-faith basis that there is a reasonable belief that the testimony of the witness will support a conclusion for conditions of release. G. L. c. 276, § 58A(4).

Prison Disciplinary Hearings. See Murphy v. Superintendent, Mass. Correctional Inst., 396 Mass. 830, 834 (1986).

Probation Violation Hearings. See Commonwealth v. Bukin, 467 Mass. 516, 522 (2014) (hearsay admissible in probation violation hearings as long as it is determined to be substantially reliable); Commonwealth v. Durling, 407 Mass. 108, 117–118 (1990) (hearsay evidence must still bear substantial indicia of reliability and trustworthiness). See also Rule 7 of the District Court Rules for Probation Violation Proceedings.

Restitution Hearings. See Section 1114, Restitution.

Sentencing. See Commonwealth v. Goodwin, 414 Mass. 88, 92 (1993) (a judge may consider many factors, including hearsay). See also G. L. c. 276, § 85; Mass. R. Crim. P. 28(d); Commonwealth v. Stuckich, 450 Mass. 449, 461–462 (2008) (evidence of uncharged conduct is admissible and relevant to the character of the offender, but may not be used to increase the punishment).

Sexual Offender Registry Board Hearings. See G. L. c. 6, § 178L(2); 803 Code Mass. Regs. § 1.19(1).

Small Claims. See generally G. L. c. 218, §§ 21, 22.

Summary Contempt Proceedings. See Mass. R. Crim. P. 43.

Subsection (d). This subsection is derived from United States v. Matlock, 415 U.S. 164, 172–175 (1974), and Commonwealth v. Young, 349 Mass. 175, 179 (1965). While out-of-court statements are admissible as to the determination of probable cause or the justification of government action, other evidence that would be incompetent under the rules of evidence is not admissible at suppression hearings or other proceedings in which probable cause is challenged. If a defendant testifies at a motion to suppress hearing and subsequently testifies at trial, his or her testimony from the motion to suppress hearing may be used to impeach his or her credibility at the later trial. Commonwealth v. Rivera, 425 Mass. 633, 637–638 (1997).

Cross–Reference: Section 1112, Eyewitness Identification.

Section 1102.   Spoliation or Destruction of Evidence

A judge has the discretion to impose sanctions for the spoliation or destruction of evidence, whether negligent or intentional, in the underlying action in which the evidence would have been offered.

NOTE

This section is derived from Keene v. Brigham & Women's Hosp., Inc., 439 Mass. 223, 235–236 (2003), and Commonwealth v. Henderson, 411 Mass. 309, 311–312 (1991). See also Mass. R. Civ. P. 37(b); Kippenhan v. Chaulk Servs., Inc., 428 Mass. 124, 126–129 (1998); Nally v. Volkswagen of Am., Inc., 405 Mass. 191, 197 (1989). The mere fact that evidence is missing and was in the possession of a party, without more, is insufficient to establish spoliation. Sullivan v. Connolly, 91 Mass. App. Ct. 56, 58–59 (2017). There is no tort cause of action for spoliation or destruction of evidence. See Fletcher v. Dorchester Mut. Ins. Co., 437 Mass. 544, 547 (2002).

"Sanctions may be appropriate for the spoliation of evidence that occurs even before an action has been commenced, if a litigant or its expert knows or reasonably should know that the evidence might be relevant to a possible action. The threat of a lawsuit must be sufficiently apparent, however, that a reasonable person in the spoliator's position would realize, at the time of spoliation, the possible importance of the evidence to the resolution of the potential dispute." (Citations omitted.)

Kippenhan v. Chaulk Servs., Inc., 428 Mass. at 127. "While a duty to preserve evidence does not arise automatically from a nonparty's mere knowledge, there are ways that that duty may be imposed on a nonparty." Fletcher v. Dorchester Mut. Ins. Co., 437 Mass. at 548. For example, a witness served with a subpoena duces tecum must preserve evidence in his or her control when the subpoena is received, or a third-party witness may enter into an agreement to preserve evidence. Id. at 549.

Civil Cases. "[S]anctions for spoliation are carefully tailored to remedy the precise unfairness occasioned by that spoliation. A party's claim of prejudice stemming from spoliation is addressed within the context of the action that was allegedly affected by that spoliation." Fletcher v. Dorchester Mut. Ins. Co., 437 Mass. 544, 551 (2002). "As a general rule, a judge should impose the least severe sanction necessary to remedy the prejudice to the nonspoliating party." Keene v. Brigham & Women's Hosp., Inc., 439 Mass. 223, 235 (2003).

"[I]n a civil case, where an expert has removed an item of physical evidence and the item has disappeared, or the expert has caused a change in the substance or appearance of such an item in such circumstances that the expert knows or reasonably should know that that item in its original form may be material to litigation, the judge, at the request of a potentially prejudiced litigant, should preclude the expert from testifying as to his or her observations of such items before he or she altered them and as to any opinion based thereon. The rule should be applied without regard for whether the expert's conduct occurred before or after the expert was retained by a party to the litigation."

Nally v. Volkswagen of Am., Inc., 405 Mass. 191, 197–198 (1989). See also Bolton v. MBTA, 32 Mass. App. Ct. 654, 655–657 (1992) (extending rule to cover spoliation of evidence by a party after expert inspection).

"The spectrum of remedies [also] includes allowing the party who has been aggrieved by the spoliation to present evidence about the preaccident condition of the lost evidence and the circumstances surrounding the spoliation, as well as instructing the jury on the inferences that may be drawn from spoliation" (citations omitted). Gath v. M/A–Com, Inc., 440 Mass. 482, 488 (2003). A judge may preclude testimony that is dispositive of the ultimate merits of the case. Fletcher v. Dorchester Mut. Ins. Co., 437 Mass. at 550. Once the moving party produces evidence sufficient to establish that another party lost or destroyed evidence that the litigant or its expert knew or reasonably should have known might be relevant to a pending or potential case, the burden shifts to the nonmoving party to prove that it was not at fault. Scott v. Garfield, 454 Mass. 790, 799 (2009). See also Nally v. Volkswagen of Am., Inc., 405 Mass. at 195, 199 (defendant entitled to summary judgment if excluded testimony prevents plaintiff from making prima facie case).

For the extreme sanction of dismissal or entering a default judgment, ordinarily a finding of willfulness or bad faith is necessary. Keene v. Brigham & Women's Hosp., Inc., 439 Mass. at 235–236.

Criminal Cases. In Commonwealth v. DiBenedetto, 427 Mass. 414, 419 (1998), the court addressed the appropriate remedial action in criminal cases:

> "[W]hen potentially exculpatory evidence is lost or destroyed, a balancing test is employed to determine the appropriateness and extent of remedial action. The courts must weigh the culpability of the Commonwealth, the materiality of the evidence and the potential prejudice to the defendant. To establish prejudice, the defendant must show a reasonable possibility, based on concrete evidence rather than a fertile imagination, that access to the [material] would have produced evidence favorable to [the defendant's] cause." (Quotations and citation omitted.)

See also Mass. R. Crim. P. 14(c); Commonwealth v. Olszewski, 416 Mass. 707, 714 (1993), cert. denied, 513 U.S. 835 (1994); Commonwealth v. Willie, 400 Mass. 427, 432–433 (1987); Commonwealth v. Heath, 89 Mass. App. Ct. 328, 335–337 (2016) (conviction reversed for improper calibration of factors of culpability and potential prejudice relating to destroyed evidence, and for insufficiency of remedial action). Remedial action in the form of sanctions or a "missing evidence" instruction is not appropriate unless the defendant meets "his initial burden of showing a reasonable possibility that the lost evidence was exculpatory." Commonwealth v. Kee, 449 Mass. 550, 554 (2007). If remedial action is required, the judge has the discretion to fashion a remedy that will protect the defendant's rights. See, e.g., Commonwealth v. Kee, 449 Mass. at 557–558 (missing evidence instruction); Commonwealth v. Harwood, 432 Mass. 290, 303 (2000) (suppression of evidence). Cf. Commonwealth v. Sasville, 35 Mass. App. Ct. 15, 28 (1993) (dismissal appropriate only where the harm is irremediable). With reference to the Commonwealth's duty to preserve evidence, see Commonwealth v. Williams, 475 Mass. 705, 722–723 (2016).

Section 1103. Sexually Dangerous Person Proceedings

(a) In General. A person who has been convicted of a sex offense may be confined indefinitely for treatment after the termination of the person's criminal sentence if the person is found to be a sexually dangerous person (SDP) in accordance with statutory procedures and based on the testimony of a qualified examiner.

(b) Proceedings. In proceedings for the commitment or discharge of a person alleged to be a sexually dangerous person, hearsay evidence is not admissible, except as provided in Subsections (b)(1) and (b)(2) of this section.

(1) Hearsay That Is Admissible. Hearsay consisting of reports or records relating to a person's criminal conviction, adjudication of juvenile delinquency or as a youthful offender, the person's psychiatric and psychological records, and a variety of records created or maintained by the courts and other government agencies, as more particularly defined by statute, is admissible in SDP proceedings.

(2) Hearsay That May Be Admissible. In addition to hearsay admissible under Subsection (b)(1), other hearsay may be admissible if it concerns uncharged conduct of the person and is closely related in time and circumstance to a sexual offense for which the person was convicted or adjudicated a juvenile delinquent or youthful offender.

NOTE

Subsection (a). This subsection is derived from Johnstone, petitioner, 453 Mass. 544, 547 (2009) (discussing G. L. c. 123A, §§ 12–14),

and Green, petitioner, 475 Mass. 624 (2016). Expert witness testimony by a credible qualified examiner is required for a judge or a jury to make the determination that a person is sexually dangerous, and the jury must be instructed to that effect. Green, petitioner, 475 Mass. at 625–626.

The current Massachusetts law, G. L. c. 123A, was adopted in 1999, St. 1999, c. 74, §§ 3–8, and is the successor to an earlier statutory scheme for the civil commitment of sexually dangerous persons (St. 1958, c. 646) that was repealed by St. 1990, c. 150, § 304. As a result, the population of the Massachusetts Treatment Center includes persons who are confined under commitment orders made prior to 1990 and subsequent to 1999. Each population has a right to file a petition in the Superior Court each year that requires a redetermination of whether they remain sexually dangerous. See G. L. c. 123A, § 9. The law provides for trial by jury and affords the individual the right to counsel, the right to present evidence, and the right to cross-examine adverse witnesses. Unless the Commonwealth proves that the person remains sexually dangerous beyond a reasonable doubt, the person must be released. See Commonwealth v. Nieves, 446 Mass. 583, 587, 593–594 (2006) (explaining the statutory procedures governing commitment and discharge under G. L. c. 123A). See also Commonwealth v. Curran, 478 Mass. 630, 636 (2018) (right of incompetent defendant to raise defenses in these proceedings includes right to provide expert testimony regarding lack of criminal responsibility). The criteria for commitment are set forth in the definition of a "sexually dangerous person" found in G. L. c. 123A, § 1. See Commonwealth v. Boucher, 438 Mass. 274, 275–281 (2002).

Subsection (b). "It is settled that hearsay not otherwise admissible under the rules of evidence is inadmissible at the trial of a sexually dangerous person petition unless specifically made admissible by statute" (citations omitted). Commonwealth v. Markvart, 437 Mass. 331, 335 (2002). Thus, the catch-all provision found in G. L. c. 123A, § 14(c) ("Any other evidence" tending to show that the person is sexually dangerous), is not interpreted to make any and all hearsay evidence admissible in SDP proceedings. McHoul, petitioner, 445 Mass. 143, 147 n.2 (2005). See also id. at 151 n.6 ("For example, there is no hearsay exception that would allow a party to introduce his own prior statements in the various reports and records; if offered by the petitioner, his own statements would not be the admission of a party opponent."). Live-witness testimony based on direct experience, the substance of which may also be memorialized in a report, is not hearsay and is not affected by G. L. c. 123A, § 14(c). Commonwealth v. Bradshaw, 94 Mass. App. Ct. 477, 481 (2018). It is equally settled that documents made admissible by statute in SDP proceedings such as police reports, psychological assessments, notes about treatment, and the like, are not subject to redaction simply because they contain hearsay statements. See McHoul, petitioner, 445 Mass. at 147–148, 151 n.6.

> "When the Legislature identified the specific records and reports that were to be admissible in sexually dangerous person proceedings, it did so with full knowledge that they routinely contain information derived from hearsay sources. Having made such records and reports 'admissible,' the Legislature did not intend that the documents be reduced to isolated shreds of partial information that would result from the application of hearsay rules to each individual entry in the documents."

Id. at 150. See also Commonwealth v. Reese, 438 Mass. 519, 527 (2003) (G. L. c. 123A, § 14[c], does not supersede the requirements of the learned treatise exception to the hearsay rule).

Miscellaneous Evidentiary Rulings. The Supreme Judicial Court and Appeals Court have addressed several other evidentiary questions that relate to these specialized proceedings. See Johnstone, petitioner, 453 Mass. 544, 550 (2009) (although the annual report of the Community Access Board as to a civilly committed person's sexual dangerousness is admissible in discharge proceedings under G. L. c. 123A, § 9, the Commonwealth cannot proceed to trial unless at least one of the two qualified examiners opines that the petitioner is a sexually dangerous person); Commonwealth v. Connors, 447 Mass. 313, 317–319 (2006) (although the allegedly sexually dangerous person has a right to refuse to speak to the qualified examiners, he or she may not offer his or her own expert testimony, based on his or her statements made to his or her own experts, while refusing to answer the questions of the qualified examiners); Commonwealth v. Nieves, 446 Mass. 583, 587, 593–594 (2006) (civil commitment of an incompetent person under G. L. c. 123A is not unconstitutional even though no effective treatment is available); Commonwealth v. Callahan, 440 Mass. 436, 439–442 (2004) (G. L. c. 123A, § 13[b], which requires that certain material about a person alleged to be a sexually dangerous person be given to the qualified examiners, does not supersede the patient-psychotherapist privilege); Wyatt, petitioner, 428 Mass. 347, 355–359 (1998) (questions concerning the relevancy and probative value of evidence offered in proceedings under G. L. c. 123A are within the discretion of the trial judge in accordance with Sections 401–403 of this Guide); Commonwealth v. Bradshaw, 94 Mass. App. Ct. 477, 482 n.8 (2018) (in SDP proceedings, evidence of uncharged sexual misconduct against other children was "inherently relevant and probative on the question of the likelihood of reoffending in the future"); Commonwealth v. Dinardo, 92 Mass. App. Ct. 715, 722 (2018) (report of Commonwealth's expert psychologist retained prior to filing of petition to commit defendant as a sexually dangerous person, and who was not a designated qualified examiner or defendant's treating psychiatric specialist, admissible at trial pursuant to G. L. c. 123A, § 14[c]); Gammell, petitioner, 86 Mass. App. Ct. 8, 9 (2014) (qualified examiner was permitted to testify at trial as to his opinion regarding the credibility of statements made by petitioner during evaluation of sexual dangerousness); Kenney, petitioner, 66 Mass. App. Ct. 709, 714–715 (2006) (admissibility of juvenile court records in SDP cases); Commonwealth v. Bradway, 62 Mass. App. Ct. 280, 287 (2004) (if reports of qualified examiners are admitted pursuant to G. L. c. 123A, § 14[c], the author of report must be made available for cross-examination).

Hearsay Evidence Excluded. Police reports and out-of-court statements of witnesses from cases in which the charges have been dismissed or nolle prossed or in which the defendant was found not guilty are not statements of "prior sexual offenses," as set forth in G. L. c. 123A, § 14(c), and thus are inadmissible as hearsay. See Commonwealth v. Markvart, 437 Mass. 331, 335–336 (2002). However, this does not mean that the testimony of witnesses with personal knowledge of the facts in cases that were dismissed or nolle prossed cases would be inadmissible in SDP cases. See id. at 337. Similarly, "Markvart does not limit a witness's ability to testify about uncharged sexual misconduct during a trial on a sexually dangerous person petition." Commonwealth v. Bradshaw, 94 Mass. App. Ct. 477, 481–482 (2018).

Subsection (b)(1). This subsection is derived from G. L. c. 123A, §§ 6A, 9, and 14(c). In proceedings for the initial commitment of a person under Section 12 (including the preliminary, probable cause hearing) and the discharge of committed persons under Section 9, the Legislature has removed many of the barriers against the admissibility of hearsay evidence. See G. L. c. 123A, §§ 6A, 9, 14(c). The case law has harmonized these sections so that the general rule is that hearsay admissible in a proceeding under G. L. c. 123A, § 12, is also admissible in a proceeding under Section 9. These statutory provisions permit psychiatrists or psychologists who are qualified examiners, see G. L. c. 123A, § 1, to testify as experts without an independent determination by the court that they are qualified and that their testimony meets standards of reliability under Section 702, Testimony by Expert Witnesses. See Commonwealth v. Bradway, 62 Mass. App. Ct. 280, 285–289 (2004) (admission of testimony and reports of qualified examiners as to a person's sexual dangerousness does not require the court to assess reliability under the standards established in Daubert v. Merrell Dow Pharms., Inc., 509 U.S. 579 [1993], and Commonwealth v. Lanigan, 419 Mass. 15 [1994]). Cf. Ready, petitioner, 63 Mass. App. Ct. 171, 172–179 (2005) (in a Section 9 proceeding, the trial judge was correct in excluding the results of the Abel

Assessment for Sexual Interest test administered by an independent expert witness for the petitioner on grounds that it was not generally accepted by the relevant scientific community and thus not reliable under the Daubert-Lanigan standard).

Hearsay Evidence Expressly Made Admissible by Statute. Under G. L. c. 123A, § 6A, reports by the community access board of evaluations of residents of the Massachusetts Treatment Center are admissible in proceedings for discharge under G. L. c. 123A, § 9. Under G. L. c. 123A, §§ 9 and 14(c), reports prepared by qualified examiners are admissible. The phrase "psychiatric and psychological records" in G. L. c. 123A, § 9, includes the reports prepared by psychiatrists and psychologists who have been retained as expert witnesses by the petitioner in connection with a Section 9 petition for examination and discharge. Santos, petitioner, 461 Mass. 565, 573 (2012). The cognate phrase in G. L. c. 123A, § 14(c), will be interpreted in the same manner. Id. at 573 n.10. There also is a broad exemption from the hearsay rule found in G. L. c. 123A, § 14(c), which states that the following records are admissible in proceedings under G. L. c. 123A, § 12, for the initial commitment of an offender as a sexually dangerous person:

> "Juvenile and adult court probation records, psychiatric and psychological records and reports of the person named in the petition, including the report of any qualified examiner, as defined in section 1, and filed under this chapter, police reports relating to such person's prior sexual offenses, incident reports arising out of such person's incarceration or custody, oral or written statements prepared for and to be offered at the trial by the victims of the person who is the subject of the petition and any other evidence tending to show that such person is or is not a sexually dangerous person shall be admissible at the trial if such written information has been provided to opposing counsel reasonably in advance of trial."

See also Commonwealth v. Morales, 60 Mass. App. Ct. 728, 730 (2004) ("[Department of Social Services] reports and grand jury minutes containing information about victims of sexual offenses committed against them by a defendant convicted of those offenses are directly admissible in evidence at trials on petitions brought under G. L. c. 123A, § 14[a]"). Under G. L. c. 123A, § 9, either side may introduce in evidence the report of a qualified examiner, the petitioner's "juvenile and adult court and probation records," the petitioner's "psychiatric and psychological records," and the Department of Correction's updated annual progress report pertaining to the petitioner. Constitutional challenges to the Legislature's relaxation of the rule against the admissibility of hearsay in SDP cases were considered and rejected by the Supreme Judicial Court in Commonwealth v. Given, 441 Mass. 741, 746–748 (2004).

When Hearsay Evidence Is the Basis of Expert Testimony. In Commonwealth v. Markvart, 437 Mass. 331, 336–339 (2002), the Supreme Judicial Court applied Department of Youth Servs. v. A Juvenile, 398 Mass. 516, 531 (1986), see Section 703(c), Bases of Opinion Testimony by Experts, and harmonized the demands of the more general law of evidence and the special statutory exemptions from the hearsay rule found in G. L. c. 123A, §§ 9 and 14(c). The Supreme Judicial Court held that in an SDP proceeding, a qualified examiner could base an expert opinion on police reports and witness statements pertaining to the sex offender even though the information is not in evidence, as long as the information could be admitted if the witnesses were called to testify. Commonwealth v. Markvart, 437 Mass. at 337–338. Because the statutes, G. L. c. 123A, §§ 9 and 14(c), make the reports of these qualified examiners admissible, any independently admissible hearsay contained in such reports that is not admitted during the trial must be redacted from the reports before it is presented to the jury. Id. at 339. The reason why redaction is required in such cases is not because the qualified examiner's report contains hearsay within hearsay, but rather because the report is the equivalent of an expert witness's direct testimony which cannot be used as a vehicle for putting before the jury facts not in evidence. See McHoul, petitioner, 445 Mass. 143, 148 n.4 (2005).

Subsection (b)(2). This subsection is derived from *Commonwealth v. Given*, 441 Mass. 741, 745 (2004). The Supreme Judicial Court explained that in proceedings under G. L. c. 123A, § 9 or § 12, G. L. c. 123A, § 14(c), makes admissible evidence of uncharged conduct when it is closely related in time and circumstance to the underlying sexual offense. Id. Cf. id. at 746 n.6 ("We do not consider or decide whether statements in a police report that include information concerning uncharged misconduct completely unrelated in time and circumstance to the underlying sexual offense must be redacted.").

Standard of Review. "Given the fundamental liberty interest at stake in sexual dangerousness proceedings, we consider it appropriate to review arguments that are raised for the first time on appeal. When evaluating such unpreserved arguments, we apply the same standard governing criminal cases: review for a substantial miscarriage of justice." *R.B., petitioner*, 479 Mass. 712, 717 (2018).

Cross-Reference: Section 103(e), Rulings on Evidence, Objections, and Offers of Proof: Substantial Risk of a Miscarriage of Justice.

Section 1104. Witness Cooperation Agreements

In a criminal case in which there is a written agreement between the Commonwealth and a witness in which the Commonwealth makes a promise to the witness in relation to the charges or the sentence in exchange for the testimony of the witness at trial, the use and admission of the agreement by the Commonwealth at trial is within the discretion of the trial judge subject to the following guidelines:

(a) On direct examination, the prosecution may properly bring out the fact that the witness has entered into a plea agreement and that the witness generally understands his or her obligations under it.

(b) The agreement itself is admissible. The timing of the admission of the agreement is within the judge's discretion. The judge may defer admission of the agreement until redirect examination, after the defendant has undertaken to impeach the witness's credibility by showing that the witness had struck a deal with the prosecution in order to obtain favorable treatment.

(c) References to a witness's obligation to tell the truth, any certification or acknowledgment by his or her attorney, and any provision that suggests that the Commonwealth has special knowledge as to the veracity of the witness's testimony should be redacted from the agreement, on request.

(d) Ordinarily, questions by the prosecutor about the duty of the witness to tell the truth and the reading of the agreement are not permitted until redirect examination and after the witness has been cross-examined on the matter.

(e) Care must be taken by the Commonwealth not to suggest, by questions or argument, that it has knowledge of the credibility of the witness independent of the evidence.

(f) The trial judge must instruct the jury by focusing their attention on the particular care they should give in evaluating testimony given pursuant to a plea agreement that is contingent on the witness's telling the truth.

NOTE

Subsections (a) and (b). These subsections are taken nearly verbatim from *Commonwealth v. Ciampa*, 406 Mass. 257, 264 (1989). See also *Commonwealth v. Rivera*, 430 Mass. 91, 96 (1999).

Subsection (c). This subsection is derived from *Commonwealth v. Conkey*, 430 Mass. 139, 147 (1999), and *Commonwealth v. Ciampa*, 406 Mass. 257, 261–262 (1989).

Subsections (d) and (e). These subsections are derived from *Commonwealth v. Rivera*, 430 Mass. 91, 96–97 (1999), and *Commonwealth v. Ciampa*, 406 Mass. 257, 264–265 (1989). See also *Commonwealth v. Webb*, 468 Mass. 26, 32–34 (2014) (no error in permitting prosecutor to inquire on direct examination into witness's agreement to provide truthful testimony after defense counsel had attacked witness's credibility during opening statement).

Subsection (f). This subsection is derived from *Commonwealth v. Ciampa*, 406 Mass. 257, 266 (1989), and *Commonwealth v. Asmeron*, 70 Mass. App. Ct. 667, 675 (2007). See *Commonwealth v. Meuse*, 423 Mass. 831, 832 (1996) (reversible error where prosecutor vouched for witness testifying pursuant to plea agreement and judge failed to give *Ciampa*-type instruction); *Commonwealth v. Daye*, 411 Mass. 719, 739–740 (1992) (no special instruction necessary as it did not appear that evidence presented realistic possibility that jury would believe witness's testimony based on her agreement to tell truth); *Commonwealth v. Colon*, 408 Mass. 419, 445 (1990) (no special instructions necessary where plea agreement does not condition immunization on truthfulness).

General Application. The above guidelines also apply to nonbinding pretrial "agreements." See *Commonwealth v. Davis*, 52 Mass. App. Ct. 75, 78–79 & n.7 (2001) (holding that *Ciampa's* prophylactic measures are applicable in circumstances in which Commonwealth witness testified that, after he was charged with distribution of marijuana, he agreed to help police arrest others involved in illegal sale of drugs in exchange for nonspecific "consideration" from prosecution). A defendant has the right to bring to the attention of the jury any "quid pro quo" agreement between the prosecution and a testifying witness, whether formal or informal, written or unwritten. See id. at 78 n.7; *Commonwealth v. O'Neil*, 51 Mass. App. Ct. 170, 179 (2001).

In *Commonwealth v. Prater*, 431 Mass. 86, 98 (2000), the Supreme Judicial Court indicated that the "better practice" is for the trial judge to include in the cautionary instruction a warning that the jury should not consider an accomplice's guilty plea as evidence against the defendant.

An agreement that obligates a witness to testify to some particular version of the facts in exchange for a charge or sentence concession would be grounds for a motion to preclude the testimony or to strike it. See *Commonwealth v. Ciampa*, 406 Mass. 257, 261 n.5 (1989) ("Testimony pursuant to a plea agreement made contingent on obtaining ... a conviction, as a result of the witness's testimony, would presumably present too great an inducement to lie, [and] would not meet the test of fundamental fairness."). See also *Commonwealth v. Colon–Cruz*, 408 Mass. 533, 553 (1990) ("[W]e do not condone the use of agreements which do not require a witness to tell the truth. Such agreements are antithetical to the fair administration of justice ... [F]uture plea agreements [should] be drafted so as to make the obligation to testify truthfully clear to the witness[.]").

Cross–Reference: Section 611(b)(2), Mode and Order of Examining Witnesses and Presenting Evidence: Scope of Cross–Examination: Bias and Prejudice.

Section 1105. Third–Party Culprit Evidence

Evidence that a third party committed the crimes charged against the defendant, or had the motive, intent, and opportunity to commit the crimes, is admissible provided that the evidence has substantial probative value. In making this determination, the court must make a preliminary finding (a) that the evidence is relevant, (b) that the evidence will not tend to prejudice or confuse the jury, and (c) that there are other substantial connecting links between the crime charged and a third party or between the crime charged and another crime that could not have been committed by the defendant.

NOTE

This section is derived from Commonwealth v. Silva–Santiago, 453 Mass. 782, 800–801 (2009); Commonwealth v. Jewett, 392 Mass. 558, 562 (1984); Commonwealth v. Murphy, 282 Mass. 593, 597–598 (1933); and Commonwealth v. Abbott, 130 Mass. 472, 475 (1881). See Commonwealth v. Buckman, 461 Mass. 24, 29–30 (2011) (trial judge had discretion to rule in advance of trial that defendant had not made adequate showing that three potential culprits were connected to the crime, and that defendant should provide advance warning to court before offering evidence or argument at trial of third-party culprit). The admission of evidence under this section does not require the trial judge to give a specific instruction on third-party culprit evidence so long as the jury instructions adequately convey the Commonwealth's burden to prove beyond a reasonable doubt that the defendant committed the crime charged. Commonwealth v. Hoose, 467 Mass. 395, 412–413 (2014).

In Commonwealth v. Rosa, 422 Mass. 18, 22 (1996), the Supreme Judicial Court observed that

"[i]f the defense offers its own theory of the case (beyond merely putting the government to its proof), its evidence must have a rational tendency to prove the issue the defense raises, and the evidence cannot be too remote or speculative. Evidence that another person committed the crime charged also poses a real threat of prejudice, especially the risk of confusing jurors by diverting their attention to wholly collateral matters involving persons not on trial."

For example, in Commonwealth v. Rosa, the Supreme Judicial Court upheld the trial judge's exclusion of so-called third-party culprit evidence consisting of the fact that there was another person awaiting trial with a record for crimes of violence and who was held in the same jail as the defendant. Id. at 24–25. Even though this other person had been mistaken for the defendant by his lawyer and had lived in the same neighborhood as the defendant at the time of the murder, the court upheld the trial judge's decision to exclude the evidence. The court concluded that "[w]ithout more, these are fairly common similarities that do not require the admission of evidence of similar crimes." Id. at 23. The court contrasted Commonwealth v. Keizer, 377 Mass. 264, 267 (1979), where it held that the trial judge should have admitted evidence "because there were substantial connecting links between the robbery charged and another robbery in which the defendant could not have participated." Commonwealth v. Rosa, 422 Mass. at 23. The court noted that in Keizer,

"[n]ot only did the two crimes share an identical modus operandi with several distinctive features, but the two robberies also had one common perpetrator (each robbery was by a team of three perpetrators). We also found distinctive a specific link between the identification testimony against the defendant and the identity of the perpetrators of the similar crime (only one witness could identify defendant, and same witness also identified common perpetrator of two crimes)."

Id. at 23, citing Commonwealth v. Keizer, 377 Mass. at 268 n.2.

The mere fact that a third party had the motive, intent, and opportunity to commit the crime, however, does not make evidence about that person and his or her possible culpability admissible. Commonwealth v. O'Brien, 432 Mass. 578, 588–589 (2000) (explaining that evidence that the victim had expressed fear of the third party in circumstances in which there were no substantial links between the third party and the crime was not admissible because it amounted to nothing more than the witness's opinion that the third party committed the crime). Accord Commonwealth v. Buckman, 461 Mass. 24, 29–30 (2011); Commonwealth v. Rice, 441 Mass. 291, 305–306 (2004); Commonwealth v. DiBenedetto, 427 Mass. 414, 420–421 (1998). See also Commonwealth v. Wood, 469 Mass. 266, 278 (2014) (affirming exclusion of statements offered in furtherance of a Bowden defense

where there was no evidence suggesting that the third party was in any way involved in the victim's death); Commonwealth v. Smith, 461 Mass. 438, 446–448 (2012) (affirming exclusion of statements suggesting murder victim feared unknown persons because statements failed to establish connection between the unknown persons and the murder).

Where the Commonwealth seeks to obtain a DNA buccal swab from a third party in order to foreclose a possible third-party culprit defense, it bears the burden of establishing probable cause that a crime has been committed and that the sample probably will provide evidence relevant to the question of the defendant's guilt. Commonwealth v. Kostka, 471 Mass. 656, 659 (2015) (DNA buccal swab of defendant's twin brother).

Constitutional Considerations. "The defendant has a constitutional right to present evidence that another may have committed the crime." Commonwealth v. Keohane, 444 Mass. 563, 570 (2005). State evidence rules which effectively bar the introduction of third-party culprit evidence deprive a defendant of his or her right to present a meaningful defense and violate the due process clause of the Fourteenth Amendment. See Holmes v. South Carolina, 547 U.S. 319 (2006); Chambers v. Mississippi, 410 U.S. 284 (1973). Hearsay evidence is admissible as third-party culprit evidence even though it does not fall within a hearsay exception, but "only if, in the judge's discretion, the evidence is otherwise relevant, will not tend to prejudice or confuse the jury, and there are other substantial connecting links to the crime." Commonwealth v. Silva–Santiago, 453 Mass. 782, 801 (2009), and cases cited; Commonwealth v. Alcantara, 471 Mass. 550, 559–561 (2015). See Commonwealth v. Drew, 397 Mass. 65, 72 (1986) (noting that in "rare circumstances," the defendant's constitutional right to present a defense may require the admission of third-party culprit evidence). However, "[a] defendant has no 'constitutional right to the admission of unreliable hearsay.'" Commonwealth v. Burnham, 451 Mass. 517, 526 (2008), quoting Commonwealth v. Evans, 438 Mass. 142, 156 (2002), cert. denied, 538 U.S. 966 (2003). Accord Commonwealth v. Morgan, 449 Mass. 343, 358 (2007) (explaining that an absent witness's statement that a third party told her that he had shot the victim was not admissible as a statement against penal interest or as third-party culprit evidence in circumstances in which the third party denied making the statement when interviewed by the police and where there was no corroboration). Hearsay evidence which does not qualify as third-party culprit evidence may nonetheless be admissible for a different but related purpose of establishing the inadequacy of the police investigation. See Commonwealth v. Silva–Santiago, 453 Mass. at 802 (explaining that based on the reasoning in Commonwealth v. Bowden, 379 Mass. 472, 486 (1980), "information regarding a third-party culprit, whose existence was known to the police but whose potential involvement was never investigated, may be admissible under a Bowden defense even though it may not otherwise be admissible under a third-party culprit defense"). Before such evidence is admitted, the judge should conduct a voir dire to determine whether the third-party culprit evidence was provided to the police and whether its admission would be more prejudicial than probative. Id. at 802–803.

Cross–Reference: Section 1107, Inadequate Police Investigation Evidence.

Section 1106. Abuse Prevention and Harassment Prevention Proceedings

In all civil proceedings under G. L. c. 209A (abuse prevention) and G. L. c. 258E (harassment prevention), the rules of evidence should be applied flexibly by taking into consideration the personal and emotional nature of the issues involved, whether one or both of the parties is self-represented, and the need for fairness to all parties.

NOTE

Introduction. This section is derived from G. L. c. 209A; Frizado v. Frizado, 420 Mass. 592, 597–598 (1995); S.T. v. E.M., 80 Mass. App. Ct. 423, 429–430 (2011); and O'Brien v. Borowski, 461 Mass. 415 (2012). Civil proceedings under G. L. c. 209A are commenced by filing a civil complaint. G. L. c. 209A, § 3A. Violations of orders issued under G. L. c. 209A are punishable as crimes. G. L. c. 209A, §§ 3B, 7. The remedies that may be ordered by the court are set forth in G. L. c. 209A, §§ 3 and 3B. Initially, a temporary order may be issued, ex parte, if the plaintiff demonstrates abuse. Abuse is defined as "the occurrence of one or more of the following acts between family or household members: (a) attempting to cause or causing physical harm; (b) placing another in fear of imminent serious physical harm; [or] (c) causing another to engage involuntarily in sexual relations by force, threat or duress." G. L. c. 209A, § 1. When courts are closed, emergency relief is available to any person who "demonstrates a substantial likelihood of immediate danger of abuse." G. L. c. 209A, § 5. Whenever a court issues a temporary order, the defendant has a right to be heard no later than ten business days after such order. This hearing constitutes a civil, jury-waived trial. At the temporary hearing and at any subsequent trial or hearing, the Supreme Judicial Court has observed that "the rules of evidence need not be followed, provided that there is fairness in what evidence is admitted and relied on." Frizado v. Frizado, 420 Mass. at 597–598. For additional information, see Guidelines for Judicial Practice, Abuse Prevention Proceedings, at http://perma.cc/LN2Q-8672.

Evidentiary Principles Applicable in G. L. c. 209A Proceedings. In determining whether and how to apply the law of evidence, the Supreme Judicial Court in Frizado v. Frizado, 420 Mass. 592 (1995), offered the following guidelines.

> "[First, t]he burden is on the complainant to establish facts justifying the issuance and continuance of an abuse prevention order. The court must on request grant a defendant an opportunity to be heard on the question of continuing the temporary order and of granting other relief. That opportunity, however, places no burden on a defendant to testify or to present evidence. The defendant need only appear at the hearing." (Quotation omitted.)

Frizado v. Frizado, 420 Mass. at 596, quoting G. L. c. 209A, § 4.

Second, the plaintiff's burden of proof is preponderance of the evidence. Frizado v. Frizado, 420 Mass. at 597. See M.G v. G.A., 94 Mass. App. Ct. 139, 148 (2018) (Judges may not "dismiss a complaint at the close of the plaintiff's case simply because they do not believe some or all of the plaintiff's testimony. Instead, the resolution of questions of credibility, ambiguity, and contradiction must await the close of the evidence.").

Third, an adverse inference can be drawn by the court from the defendant's failure to testify in a G. L. c. 209A proceeding. The fact that the defendant may refuse to testify on the ground of self-incrimination does not bar the taking of an adverse inference. However, the adverse inference alone is not sufficient to justify the issuance of an abuse prevention order. Frizado v. Frizado, 420 Mass. at 596. See also Smith v. Joyce, 421 Mass. 520, 523 n.1 (1995) (a judge may not issue a restraining order "simply because it seems to be a good idea or because it will not cause the defendant any real inconvenience"). The plaintiff is still permitted to call the defendant as a witness even though the defendant is able to assert the privilege against self-incrimination. S.T. v. E.M., 80 Mass. App. Ct. 423, 429 (2011).

Fourth, "[b]ecause a G. L. c. 209A proceeding is a civil, and not a criminal, proceeding, the constitutional right to confront witnesses and to cross-examine them set forth in art. 12 of the Declaration of Rights has no application." Frizado v. Frizado, 420 Mass. at 596 n.3.

Fifth, "[t]he right of the defendant to be heard includes his right to testify and to present evidence." Frizado v. Frizado, 420 Mass. at 597. It is not sufficient to hear from the defendant's attorney and to deny the defendant the opportunity to present evidence. C.O. v. M.M., 442 Mass. 648, 657 (2004). The plaintiff has a corresponding right to present evidence prior to the judge vacating any part of an abuse prevention order. Singh v. Capuano, 468 Mass. 328, 331 (2014); S.T. v. E.M., 80 Mass. App. Ct. at 429–430.

Sixth, with respect to cross-examination, "[t]he judge's discretion in restricting cross-examination may not be unlimited in particular situations." Frizado v. Frizado, 420 Mass. at 598 n.5. The Supreme Judicial Court cautioned against "the use of cross examination for harassment or discovery purposes. However, each side must be given a meaningful opportunity to challenge the other's evidence." Id. See C.O. v. M.M., 442 Mass. at 656–658 (defendant's due process rights were violated when the court refused to permit him to cross-examine witnesses or to present evidence).

Termination of an Order. A defendant who seeks to terminate a permanent G. L. c. 209A order must prove by clear and convincing evidence that there has been a significant change in circumstances such that the protected party no longer has a reasonable fear of imminent serious physical harm from the defendant, and that continuation of the order would therefore not be equitable. The mere passage of time, during which the defendant has complied with the order, is not alone sufficient to justify termination. MacDonald v. Caruso, 467 Mass. 382, 388–389 (2014).

Harassment Prevention Proceedings (G. L. c. 258E). There are many parallels between proceedings brought under G. L. c. 209A and those brought under G. L. c. 258E. See F.A.P. v. J.E.S., 87 Mass. App. Ct. 595, 602 (2015). The considerations set forth above regarding the conduct of a G. L. c. 209A proceeding also apply to proceedings conducted pursuant to G. L. c. 258E. See O'Brien v. Borowski, 461 Mass. 415 (2012).

In order to obtain a harassment prevention order pursuant to G. L. c. 258E, a plaintiff must demonstrate that the act or acts of the defendant fit within the statutory definition of harassment set forth in G. L. c. 258E, § 1. Harassment is defined in various ways under the statute. Harassment is first defined as "3 or more acts of willful and malicious conduct aimed at a specific person committed with the intent to cause fear, intimidation, abuse or damage to property and that does in fact cause fear, intimidation, abuse or damage to property." G. L. c. 258E, § 1. Additionally, "an act that . . . by force, threat or duress causes another to involuntarily engage in sexual relations" constitutes harassment under the statute. Id. Finally, harassment includes a violation of the stalking statute, the criminal harassment statute, or any of the ten sex-crime statutes listed in G. L. c. 258E, § 1. Id. See A.S.R. v. A.K.A., 92 Mass. App. Ct. 270, 274–275 (2017) (discussing various definitions of harassment under G. L. c. 258E); F.A.P. v. J.E.S., 87 Mass. App. Ct. at 598–599 (same).

An adverse inference may be drawn against a defendant, including a juvenile, who fails to testify at a 258E hearing. See A.P. v. M.T., 92 Mass. App. Ct. 156, 166 (2017).

Section 1107. Inadequate Police Investigation Evidence

(a) Admissibility. Evidence that certain tests were not conducted, that certain police procedures were not followed, or that certain information known to the police about another suspect was not investigated, in circumstances in which it was reasonable to expect that the police should have conducted such tests, followed such procedures, or investigated such information, is admissible.

(b) Jury Instruction. If evidence under Subsection (a) is admitted, it is within the judge's discretion whether to give a specific instruction to the jury. In the absence of an instruction, counsel may argue the issue, provided the argument is based on the evidence in the record and any permissible inferences taken from that evidence.

NOTE

Subsection (a). This subsection is derived from Commonwealth v. Bowden, 379 Mass. 472, 486 (1980), and cases cited. See Commonwealth v. Silva–Santiago, 453 Mass. 782, 801 (2009) ("[T]he inference that may be drawn from an inadequate police investigation is that the evidence at trial may be inadequate or unreliable because the police failed to conduct the scientific tests or to pursue leads that a reasonable police investigation would have conducted or investigated, and these tests or investigation reasonably may have led to significant evidence of the defendant's guilt or innocence."); Commonwealth v. Phinney, 446 Mass. 155, 165 (2006) ("Defendants have the right to base their defense on the failure of police adequately to investigate a murder in order to raise the issue of reasonable doubt as to the defendant's guilt . . .."). Compare Commonwealth v. Mattei, 455 Mass. 840, 857–860 (2010) (In a prosecution for attempted rape in which the defendant, a convict on work release, sought to demonstrate misidentification based on an inadequate police investigation because the police did not investigate three other Housing Authority employees who were on duty at the time who had criminal histories, it was error to refuse to permit the defense to question the police about their knowledge of the criminal histories of these employees.) with Commonwealth v. Alcantara, 471 Mass. 550, 561–563 (2015) (judge did not abuse her discretion in excluding proposed Bowden evidence as not probative of police thoroughness and likely to confuse jury). The judge must conduct a voir dire hearing to determine whether the third-party culprit information had been furnished to the police, and whether the probative value of the Bowden evidence is not substantially outweighed by the risk of unfair prejudice to the Commonwealth from diverting the jury's attention to collateral matters. Commonwealth v. Moore, 480 Mass. 799, 809 n.9 (2018).

The Bowden defense "is a two-edged sword for the defendant, because it opens the door for the Commonwealth to offer evidence explaining why the police did not follow the line of investigation suggested by the defense" (citations omitted). Commonwealth v. Silva-Santiago, 453 Mass. at 803 n.25. "[T]he more wide-ranging the defendant's attack on the police investigation, the broader the Commonwealth's response may be." Commonwealth v. Avila, 454 Mass. 744, 754–755 (2009) ("Here, the Bowden claim was an expansive one, calling into question police competence and judgment about both the leads that were not pursued and those that were. In response, the Commonwealth was entitled to elicit testimony about why the investigators chose the particular investigative path they did . . . ."). See Commonwealth v. Wiggins, 477 Mass. 732, 743–744 (2017) (testimony that evidence collected during defendants' booking was removed from police custody by someone who was not a member of law enforcement properly admitted where defendants "attempted to raise a Bowden defense" and challenged the competence of investigators at trial).

Under a Bowden defense, information regarding a third-party culprit whose existence was known to the police but whose potential involvement was never investigated may be admissible to prove that the police knew of the possible suspect and failed to take reasonable steps to investigate the suspect. This information is not hearsay because it is not offered to show the truth of the matter asserted, but simply to show that the information was provided to the police. Therefore, it need not meet the standard set to admit hearsay evidence regarding a third-party culprit, including the substantial connecting links. See Commonwealth v. Reynolds, 429 Mass. 388, 391–392 (1999) (police detective could testify to what confidential informants had told him about suspect's motive and opportunity to kill the victim, despite the confidential informants' potential lack of first-hand knowledge). There is a lessened risk of prejudice to the Commonwealth from the admission of evidence of a Bowden defense because the police are able to explain what they did to determine that the suspect was not guilty of the crime. See Id. at 391 n.1. In contrast to the third-party culprit defense, where evidence may be admitted regardless of whether the police knew of the suspect, third-party culprit information is admissible under a Bowden defense only if the police had learned of it during the investigation and failed to

reasonably act on the information. Commonwealth v. Silva-Santiago, 453 Mass. at 802–803.

Cross–Reference: Section 1105, Third–Party Culprit Evidence.

Subsection (b). This subsection is derived from Commonwealth v. Bowden, 379 Mass. 472, 486 (1980). The admission of Bowden evidence does not require the trial judge to give a special instruction to the jury. Instead, the judge is simply required not to take the issue of the adequacy of the police investigation away from the jury. See Commonwealth v. Williams, 439 Mass. 678, 687 (2003). The Appeals Court, while recognizing such discretion, has suggested that "it might be[ ] preferable for the judge to inform the jurors that the evidence of police omissions could create a reasonable doubt." Commonwealth v. Reid, 29 Mass. App. Ct. 537, 540–541 (1990).

Defense counsel has a right to argue to the jury that they should draw an adverse inference against the Commonwealth from the failure of the police to preserve and introduce material evidence or to perform probative tests. See Arizona v. Youngblood, 488 U.S. 51 (1988) (while police have no constitutional duty to perform any particular test, defense may argue to jury that a particular test may have been exculpatory). While a judge is not required to instruct the jury that they may draw such an inference, the defendant is entitled to make such an argument, and in such a case it is error to caution the jury against drawing any inferences from the absence of evidence. Commonwealth v. Person, 400 Mass. 136, 140 (1987); Commonwealth v. Gilmore, 399 Mass. 741, 745 (1987); Commonwealth v. Bowden, 379 Mass. 472, 485–486 (1980); Commonwealth v. Rodriguez, 378 Mass. 296, 308 (1979); Commonwealth v. Jackson, 23 Mass. App. Ct. 975, 975–976 (1987); Commonwealth v. Flanagan, 20 Mass. App. Ct. 472, 475–477 (1985). The standard instruction that a jury should decide the case based solely on the evidence, given as part of the final instructions and not in response to an argument by defense counsel or a jury question, does not impermissibly limit the jury's consideration of a Bowden defense. Commonwealth v. Alvarez, 480 Mass. 299, 317–318 (2018).

Section 1108. Access to Third–Party Records Prior to Trial in Criminal Cases (Lampron–Dwyer Protocol)

(a) Filing and Service of the Motion.

(1) Whenever in a criminal case a party seeks to summons books, papers, documents, or other objects (records) from any nonparty individual or entity prior to trial, the party shall file a motion pursuant to Mass. R. Crim. P. 17(a)(2), stating the name and address of the custodian of the records (record holder) and the name, if any, of the person who is the subject of the records (third-party subject), for example, a complainant, and describing, as precisely as possible, the records sought. The motion shall be accompanied by an affidavit as required by Mass. R. Crim. P. 13(a)(2) and Commonwealth v. Lampron, 441 Mass. 265 (2004) (Lampron).

(2) The moving party shall serve the motion and affidavit on all parties.

(3) The Commonwealth shall forward copies of the motion and affidavit to the record holder and (where applicable) to the third-party subject, and notify them of the date and place of the hearing on the motion. The Commonwealth shall also inform the record holder and third-party subject that (i) the Lampron hearing shall proceed even if either of them is absent; (ii) the hearing shall be the third-party subject's only opportunity to address the court; (iii) any statutory privilege applicable to the records sought shall

remain in effect unless and until the third-party subject affirmatively waives any such privilege, and that failure to attend the hearing shall not constitute a waiver of any such privilege; and (iv) if the third-party subject is the victim in the case, he or she has the opportunity to confer with the prosecutor prior to the hearing.

(b) The Lampron Hearing and Findings.

(1) A party moving to summons documents pursuant to Mass. R. Crim. P. 17(a)(2) prior to trial must establish good cause by showing (i) that the documents are evidentiary and relevant; (ii) that they are not otherwise procurable reasonably in advance of trial by exercise of due diligence; (iii) that the party cannot properly prepare for trial without such production and inspection in advance of trial, and that the failure to obtain such inspection may tend unreasonably to delay the trial; and (iv) that the application is made in good faith and is not intended as a general fishing expedition.

(2) At the Lampron hearing, the judge shall hear from all parties, the record holder, and the third-party subject, if present. The record holder and third-party subject shall be heard on whether the records sought are relevant or statutorily privileged.

(3) Following the Lampron hearing, and in the absence of having reviewed the records, the judge shall make oral or written findings with respect to the records sought from each record holder indicating (i) that the party seeking the records has or has not satisfied the requirements of Mass. R. Crim. P. 17(a)(2), and (ii) that the records sought are or are not presumptively privileged. A judge's determination that any records sought are presumptively privileged shall not be appealable as an interlocutory matter and shall carry no weight in any subsequent challenge that a record is in fact not privileged.

(c) Summons and Notice to Record Holder.

(1) If all Mass. R. Crim. P. 17(a)(2) requirements have been met and there has been a finding that the records sought are not presumptively privileged or the third-party subject has waived all applicable statutory privileges, the judge shall order a summons to issue directing the record holder to produce all responsive records to the applicable clerk of the court on the return date stated in the summons. The clerk shall maintain the records in a location separate from the court file, and the records shall be made available for inspection by counsel, as provided in Subsection (d)(1) below. The records shall not be made available for public inspection unless and until any record is filed in connection with a proceeding in the case or introduced in evidence at the trial.

(2) Where a judge has determined that some or all of the requested records are presumptively privileged, the summons shall so inform the record holder and shall order the record holder to produce such records to the clerk of the court in a sealed envelope or box marked "PRIVILEGED," with the name of the record holder, the case name and docket number, and the return date specified on the summons. The clerk shall maintain the records in a location separate from the court file, clearly designated "presumptively privileged records," and the records shall not be available for inspection except by counsel as provided in

Subsection (d)(2). The records shall not be made available for public inspection unless and until any record is introduced in evidence at trial.

(d) Inspection of Records.

(1) **Nonpresumptively Privileged Records.** The clerk of court shall permit counsel who obtained the summons to inspect and copy all records that are not presumptively privileged. When the defendant is the moving party, the Commonwealth's ability to inspect or copy the records is within a judge's discretion.

(2) **Presumptively Privileged Records.**

(A) The clerk of court shall permit only defense counsel who obtained the summons to inspect the records, and only on counsel's signing and filing a protective order in a form approved by the court. The protective order shall provide that any violation of its terms and conditions shall be reported to the Board of Bar Overseers by anyone aware of such violation.

(B) [The Supreme Judicial Court has not reached the issue of whether the procedures governing defense counsel's review of presumptively privileged records also apply to the Commonwealth.]

(e) Challenge to Privilege Designation.

(1) If, on inspection of the records, defense counsel believes that any record or portion thereof is in fact not privileged, then in lieu of or in addition to a motion to disclose or introduce at trial (see Subsections (f) and (g) below), counsel may file a motion to release specified records or portions thereof from the terms of the protective order.

(2) Defense counsel shall provide notice of the motion to all parties. Prior to the hearing, counsel for the Commonwealth shall be permitted to review such records in order to respond to the motion, subject to signing and filing a protective order as provided in Subsection (d)(2) above.

(3) If a judge determines that any record or portion thereof is not privileged, the record shall be released from the terms of the protective order and may be inspected and copied as provided in Subsection (d)(1) above.

(f) Disclosure of Presumptively Privileged Records.

(1) If defense counsel who obtained the summons believes that the copying or disclosure of some or all of any presumptively privileged record to other persons (for example, the defendant, an investigator, an expert) is necessary to prepare the case for trial, counsel shall file a motion to modify the protective order to permit copying or disclosure of particular records to specifically named individuals. The motion shall be accompanied by an affidavit explaining with specificity the reason why copying or disclosure is necessary; the motion and the affidavit shall not disclose the content of any presumptively privileged record. Counsel shall provide notice of the motion to all parties.

(2) Following a hearing, and in camera inspection of the records by the judge where necessary, a judge may allow the motion only on making oral or written findings that the copying or disclosure is necessary for the defendant to prepare adequately for trial. The judge shall consider alternatives to full disclosure, including agreed to stipula-

tions or disclosure of redacted portions of the records. Before disclosure is made to any person specifically authorized by the judge, that person shall sign a copy of the court order authorizing disclosure. This court order shall clearly state that a violation of its terms shall be punishable as criminal contempt.

(3) All copies of any documents covered by a protective order shall be returned to the court on resolution of the case, i.e., on a change of plea or at the conclusion of any direct appeal following a trial or dismissal of the case.

(g) Use of Presumptively Privileged Records at Trial.

(1) A defendant seeking to introduce at trial some or all of any presumptively privileged record shall file a motion in limine at or before any final pretrial conference.

(2) Counsel for the Commonwealth shall be permitted to review enough of the presumptively privileged records to be able to respond adequately to the motion in limine, subject to signing and filing a protective order as provided in Subsection (d)(2) above.

(3) The judge may allow the motion only on making oral or written findings that introduction at trial of a presumptively privileged record is necessary for the moving defendant to obtain a fair trial. Before permitting the introduction in evidence of such records, the judge shall consider alternatives to introduction, including an agreed to stipulation or introduction of redacted portions of the records.

(h) Preservation of Records for Appeal. Records produced in response to a Mass. R. Crim. P. 17(a)(2) summons shall be retained by the clerk of court until the conclusion of any direct appeal following a trial or dismissal of a case.

NOTE

Introduction. In criminal cases, pretrial discovery is limited to information and objects in the possession or control of the parties and is governed principally by Mass. R. Crim. P. 14. When a party seeks access in advance of trial to books, papers, documents, or objects (records, privileged or nonprivileged) that are in the hands of a third party, such requests are governed by Mass. R. Crim. P. 17(a)(2). Commonwealth v. Odgren, 455 Mass. 171, 186–187 (2009) (both prosecutor and defense counsel must follow the procedures contained in Mass. R. Crim. P. 17 and obtain prior judicial approval to obtain access before trial to any records in the hands of a third party, whether privileged or not). See Commonwealth v. Lampron, 441 Mass. 265, 268 (2004). See also Commonwealth v. Hart, 455 Mass. 230, 243 (2009) (Mass. R. Crim. P. 17[a][2] is the exclusive method to obtain records from a third party prior to trial); Commonwealth v. Hunt, 86 Mass. App. Ct. 494, 495 (2014) (affidavit accompanying motion for records must meet the specificity requirements of Mass. R. Crim. P. 17[a][2]). When Mass. R. Crim. P. 17(a)(2) has been satisfied and a nonparty has produced records to the court, the protocol set forth in Commonwealth v. Dwyer, 448 Mass. 122, 139–147 (2006), governs review or disclosure of presumptively privileged records by defense counsel. To reference the forms promulgated by the Supreme Judicial Court, see http://perma.cc/45WM–J4NE.

At trial, a defendant seeking records must proceed under Mass. R. Crim. P. 17(a)(2). The Commonwealth may proceed under either Mass. R. Crim. P. 17(a)(2) or G. L. c. 277, § 68. See Commonwealth v. Hart, 455 Mass. at 243 (a subpoena issued under G. L. c. 277, § 68, may only request a third party to produce records to a court on the day of the trial). Records held in the victim's compensation file maintained by the attorney general, a third party, are accessible under Mass. R. Crim. P. 17(a)(2). Commonwealth v. Torres, 479 Mass. 641, 650–651 (2018).

Subsection (a). This subsection is derived from Commonwealth v. Lampron, 441 Mass. 265, 268 (2004). See also Commonwealth v. Odgren, 455 Mass. 171, 187 (2009) (Lampron procedures apply to both prosecution and defense).

Subsection (b). This subsection is derived generally from Commonwealth v. Lampron, 441 Mass. 265, 268 (2004), and Commonwealth v. Dwyer, 448 Mass. 122, 148 (2006). "The Commonwealth's inability to locate either the record holder or the third-party subject shall not delay the Lampron hearing." Id. at 148 n.2.

In Commonwealth v. Lampron, 441 Mass. 265 (2004), the Supreme Judicial Court followed Federal law as enunciated in United States v. Nixon, 418 U.S. 683, 699–700 (1974), and held that a party moving to summons documents pursuant to Mass. R. Crim. P. 17(a)(2) prior to trial must establish good cause by showing the following:

"(1) that the documents are evidentiary and relevant; (2) that they are not otherwise procurable reasonably in advance of trial by exercise of due diligence; (3) that the party cannot properly prepare for trial without such production and inspection in advance of trial and that the failure to obtain such inspection may tend unreasonably to delay the trial; and (4) that the application is made in good faith and is not intended as a general 'fishing expedition.'"

Commonwealth v. Lampron, 441 Mass. at 269. Accord Commonwealth v. Mitchell, 444 Mass. 786, 792 (2005) (summarizing these requirements as "relevance, admissibility, necessity, and specificity"). See Commonwealth v. Jones, 478 Mass. 65, 68–72 (2017) (in sexual abuse prosecution, trial judge did not abuse discretion in refusing to issue summonses for privileged records where defendant's showing of relevance was "too speculative"); Commonwealth v. Olivier, 89 Mass. App. Ct. 836, 844–846 (2016) (trial judge correctly denied motion for release of privileged records where defendant failed to present evidence of connection between diagnosis in records and victim's actions); Commonwealth v. Rivera, 83 Mass. App. Ct. 581, 588–589 (2013) (judge properly denied defendant's pretrial motion seeking access to complainant's preabuse mental health records based only on belief that they might yield evidence concerning her credibility).

"Presumptively privileged records are those prepared in circumstances suggesting that some or all of the records sought are likely protected by a statutory privilege, for example, a record prepared by one who holds himself or herself out as a psychotherapist, see G. L. c. 233, § 20B; a social worker, see G. L. c. 112, § 135B; a sexual assault counsellor, see G. L. c. 233, § 20J; or a domestic violence victims' counsellor, see G. L. c. 233, § 20K."

Commonwealth v. Dwyer, 448 Mass. at 148. Because the judge will not have viewed any of the records sought by the defendant, "the judge shall make such determination based on the identity of the record holder or record preparer (if known) and any additional information adduced at the Lampron hearing. The defendant shall have the burden of showing that records are not presumptively privileged." Id. at 148 n.3.

Subsection (c). This subsection is derived generally from Commonwealth v. Lampron, 441 Mass. 265 (2004), and Commonwealth v. Dwyer, 448 Mass. 122 (2006).

"Some records, although not presumptively privileged, may contain information of a personal or confidential nature, such as medical or school records. See, e.g., G. L. c. 71B, § 3 (special education records); G. L. c. 111, §§ 70, 70E (hospital records). The judge may, in his or her discretion, order such records produced subject to an appropriate protective order." Commonwealth v. Dwyer, 448 Mass. at 149 n.5.

Subsection (d). This subsection is derived generally from Commonwealth v. Dwyer, 448 Mass. 122, 149 (2006). A judge may order that even nonpresumptively privileged records be subject to an appropriate protective order. Id. at 149 n.5 (Appendix).

"The Commonwealth may inspect or copy any records if prior consent is given by the record holder and third-party subject (where applicable)." Id. at 149 n.7. With respect to nonpresumptively privileged records, Subsection (d)(1), a party may have production obligations pursuant to Mass. R. Crim. P. 14 or other pretrial agreements. See Commonwealth v. Mitchell, 444 Mass. 786, 800 (2005).

Subsection (e). This subsection is taken nearly verbatim from Commonwealth v. Dwyer, 448 Mass. 122, 149–150 (2006).

Subsection (f). This subsection is taken nearly verbatim from Commonwealth v. Dwyer, 448 Mass. 122, 150 (2006).

Subsection (g). This subsection is taken nearly verbatim from Commonwealth v. Dwyer, 448 Mass. 122, 150 (2006).

Subsection (h). This subsection is taken nearly verbatim from Commonwealth v. Dwyer, 448 Mass. 122, 150 (2006).

Section 1109.   View

(a) Availability.

(1) Upon motion in civil and criminal cases, the court has discretion to allow the jury, accompanied by the judge, or, in a matter tried without a jury, the judge to take a view of the premises or place in question or any property matter or thing relative to the case.

(2) In a limited class of civil cases, a party has the right, upon request, to a view.

(b) Conduct. Counsel may point out the essential features of the place or thing that is the subject of the view, but no comment or discussion is permitted. No witnesses are heard. Jurors are not permitted to ask questions. The presence of the defendant in a criminal case is left to the judge's discretion.

(c) Status. Observations made by the jury or by the judge on a view may be used by the finder of fact in making a decision.

(d) Costs. In a civil case, the expenses of taking a view shall be paid by the party who makes the motion or in accordance with an agreement between or among some or all of the parties, and may be taxed as costs if the party or parties who advanced them prevails. In a criminal case, the expenses of taking a view shall be paid by the Commonwealth.

NOTE

Subsection (a)(1). This subsection is derived from Commonwealth v. Gedzium, 259 Mass. 453, 462 (1927); Madden v. Boston Elevated Ry. Co., 284 Mass. 490, 493–494 (1933); Commonwealth v. Gomes, 459 Mass. 194, 201–202 (2011); and G. L. c. 234, § 35. In the administrative context, the judge or fact finder also may have the right to conduct a view. See, e.g., G L. c. 152, § 2 (Authority of the Division of Industrial Accidents to "make all necessary inspections and investigations relating to causes of injuries for which compensation may be claimed . . .").

The court has the discretion to take a view any time after the jury is sworn. See Yore v. City of Newton, 194 Mass. 250, 253 (1907) (court permitted jury to take a view after deliberations had begun).

The court may exercise its discretion to deny a motion for a view when visiting a particular location would not fairly represent the way it appeared or the conditions that existed at the time of the events that are the subject of the trial. See Commonwealth v. Cataldo, 423 Mass. 318, 327 n.8 (1996). However, even though the appearance of premises or a thing has changed, if the premises or thing in its altered condition would be helpful to the jury in understanding the evidence the court has discretion to permit a view. See Commonwealth v. Welansky, 316 Mass. 383, 401–402 (1944) (there was no error in

permitting the jury to take a view of a nightclub after a fire had severely damaged it and caused the death of numerous persons who were trapped inside). The court may deny a motion for a view because it will not contribute to the jury's understanding of the evidence at trial. See Commonwealth v. Cambell, 378 Mass. 680, 704–705, cert. denied, 488 U.S. 847 (1979).

Subsection (a)(2). This subsection is derived from G. L. c. 80, § 9 (betterment assessments); G. L. c. 79, § 22 (eminent domain); and G. L. c. 253, § 7 (mill flowage).

Subsection (b). This subsection is derived from Commonwealth v. Dascalakis, 246 Mass. 12, 29–30 (1923). "Generally, an impropriety occurring on a view may be cured by cautionary instructions." Commonwealth v. Cresta, 3 Mass. App. Ct. 560, 562 (1975), citing Commonwealth v. Madeiros, 255 Mass. 304, 313 (1926).

The defendant has no right to be present at a view; the judge has discretion to impose reasonable restrictions on the defendant's presence and conduct. Commonwealth v. Corliss, 470 Mass. 443, 448 (2015). "A defendant is not entitled of right to confer with his counsel during a view." Commonwealth v. Gagliardi, 29 Mass. App. Ct. 225, 237 (1990).

Subsection (c). This subsection is derived from Commonwealth v. Curry, 368 Mass. 195 (1975), where the Supreme Judicial Court stated that

"[t]he chief purpose (of a view) is to enable the jury to understand better the testimony which has or may be introduced. The function of the jury . . . is simply to observe. Although what is seen on the view may be used by the jury in reaching their verdict, in a strict and narrow sense a view may be thought not to be evidence." (Citations omitted.)

Id. at 197–198. See also Berlandi v. Commonwealth, 314 Mass. 424, 451 (1943) ("A view is not technically evidence and subject to all the principles applicable to evidence . . . [but] it inevitably has the effect of evidence" [citations and quotation omitted].); Commonwealth v. Perryman, 55 Mass. App. Ct. 187, 193–194 n.1 (2002) (a view is analogous to a courtroom demonstration or the use of a chalk; observations made on a view can be used "to illustrate testimony and assist the jury in weighing the evidence they hear" so long as the conditions are similar to the circumstances of the matter to be proved).

Subsection (d). This subsection is derived from G. L. c. 234, § 35.

Section 1110.   Consciousness of Guilt or Liability

(a) Criminal Cases. In a criminal case, the Commonwealth may offer evidence of a defendant's conduct that occurred subsequent to the commission of the crime if

(1) the evidence reflects a state of consciousness of guilt;

(2) the evidence supports the inference that the defendant committed the act charged;

(3) the evidence is, with other evidence, together with reasonable inferences, sufficient to prove guilt; and

(4) the inflammatory nature of the conduct does not substantially outweigh its probative value.

Evidence of consciousness of guilt alone is not sufficient to support a verdict or finding of guilt. The judge should instruct the jury accordingly.

(b) Civil Cases. Subject to Sections 407–411, in a civil case, a party may offer evidence of another party's conduct that occurred subsequent to the commission of the alleged act or acts that give rise to the cause of action if the evidence

(1) reflects a state of consciousness of liability of that party;

(2) supports the inference that the party against whom the evidence is offered is liable; and

(3) is, with other evidence, together with reasonable inferences, sufficient to prove liability.

Evidence of consciousness of liability alone cannot sustain the burden to establish liability. The judge should instruct the jury accordingly.

(c) Rebuttal. The party against whom the evidence is offered has the right to offer evidence explaining the reason or reasons for the conduct to negate any adverse inference.

NOTE

Subsection (a). This subsection is derived from Commonwealth v. Vick, 454 Mass. 418, 423 (2009), and Commonwealth v. Toney, 385 Mass. 575, 584–585 & n.4 (1982). Where self-defense is an issue and the defendant objects to an instruction on consciousness of guilt, the trial judge should first consider whether to instruct on flight as evidence of consciousness of guilt. If the instruction is given, the judge should focus first on possible innocent reasons for flight, and that the conduct does not necessarily reflect feelings of guilt, but may be consistent with self-defense. Commonwealth v. Morris, 465 Mass. 733, 738–739 (2013). The Commonwealth may properly argue consciousness of guilt even if a jury instruction is not requested or not given. Commonwealth v. Franklin, 465 Mass. 895, 915 (2013). Compare Section 1111, Missing Witness.

Illustrations. The following conduct may be offered as evidence of consciousness of guilt:

- flight itself, regardless of whether the police were actively searching for the defendant, Commonwealth v. Figueroa, 451 Mass. 566, 579 (2008);

- flight after discovery by the party that he or she was about to be arrested or charged with an offense, Commonwealth v. Jackson, 391 Mass. 749, 758 (1984);

- attempted escape while awaiting trial, Commonwealth v. Fritz, 472 Mass. 341, 350 (2015);

- flight from a defendant's "usual environs," Commonwealth v. Siny Van Tran, 460 Mass. 535, 553 (2011);

- an intentionally false statement made to police or another person before or after arrest, Commonwealth v. Martinez, 476 Mass. 186, 197 (2017);

- use of a false name to conceal his or her identity, Commonwealth v. Vick, 454 Mass. 418, 424 (2009); Commonwealth v. Carrion, 407 Mass. 263, 276 (1990);

- intentional attempts to intimidate, coerce, threaten, or bribe a witness, Commonwealth v. Vick, 454 Mass. at 423; Commonwealth v. Toney, 385 Mass. 575, 584 n.4 (1982);

- alteration of a defendant's appearance after a crime to conceal physical characteristics, Commonwealth v. Carrion, 407 Mass. at 277; or

- an intentional attempt to conceal, destroy, or falsify evidence, Commonwealth v. Stuckich, 450 Mass. 449, 453 (2008).

The following conduct should not be admitted as evidence of consciousness of guilt:

- flight, where the issue is misidentification and there is no dispute that the person who fled the scene committed the offense, Commonwealth v. Bastaldo, 472 Mass. 16, 33–36 (2015); cf. Commonwealth v. Lopez, 87 Mass. App. Ct. 642, 647 (2015) (flight may be admitted as evidence of consciousness of guilt even when identification is an issue so long as it is not certain person fleeing committed the crime);

- evidence that the defendant lied during trial testimony, Commonwealth v. Edgerly, 390 Mass. 103, 110 (1983) (disfavoring such evidence; "[c]omment to a jury on the consequences of a criminal defendant's lying in the course of his testimony must be made with care, and customarily should be avoided because it places undue emphasis on only one aspect of the evidence");

- a defendant's failure to appear at trial, except where the Commonwealth can show the defendant had knowledge of the scheduled date, Commonwealth v. Hightower, 400 Mass. 267, 269 (1987); Commonwealth v. Addy, 79 Mass. App. Ct. 835, 841 (2011); see also Commonwealth v. Zammuto, 89 Mass. App. Ct. 80, 82–83 (2016); cf. Commonwealth v. Muckle, 59 Mass. App. Ct. 631, 639–640 (2003) (where defendant is defaulted midtrial, judge should conduct voir dire to determine if Commonwealth can show requisite foundation); or

- the denial or failure to deny guilt during a police interrogation, Commonwealth v. Diaz, 453 Mass. 266, 273–274 (2009); Commonwealth v. Haas, 373 Mass. 545, 558–562 (1977).

In a charge of murder, consciousness of guilt "is rarely relevant to the issue of premeditation," Commonwealth v. Dagenais, 437 Mass. 832, 843–844 (2002), and it should not be used as proof that a homicide was murder rather than manslaughter. See Commonwealth v. Clemente, 452 Mass. 295, 334 (2008); Commonwealth v. Lowe, 391 Mass. 97, 108 n.6 (1984); Commonwealth v. Niland, 45 Mass. App. Ct. 526, 529 (1998). However, in a homicide case, consciousness-of-guilt evidence may be "relevant to an assessment of the defendant's mental state and whether he was criminally responsible." Commonwealth v. Chappell, 473 Mass. 191, 207 (2015).

Jury Instruction on Evidence of Consciousness of Guilt. If evidence of consciousness of guilt is admitted, the court should instruct the jury (1) that they are not to convict the defendant on the basis of the offered evidence alone, and (2) that they may, but need not, consider such evidence as one of the factors tending to prove the guilt of the defendant. Upon request, the jury must be further instructed (1) that the conduct does not necessarily reflect feelings of guilt, since there are numerous reasons why an innocent person might engage in the conduct alleged, and (2) that even if the conduct demonstrates feelings of guilt, it does not necessarily mean that the defendant is guilty in fact, because guilty feelings are sometimes present in innocent people. See Commonwealth v. Toney, 385 Mass. 575, 584–585 (1982); Commonwealth v. Estrada, 25 Mass. App. Ct. 907, 908 (1987). See also Commonwealth v. Vick, 454 Mass. 418, 424 (2009).

Evidence of Consciousness of Innocence. "Consciousness of innocence is a subject properly left to the give and take of argument, without jury instructions." Commonwealth v. Lam, 420 Mass. 615, 619–620 (1995). In some instances, however, such evidence is not admissible. See Commonwealth v. Cassidy, 470 Mass. 201, 218–219 (2014) (judge properly excluded evidence of a telephone call and note to explain reason for fleeing); Commonwealth v. Martinez, 437 Mass. 84, 88 (2002) (offer to submit to polygraph inadmissible).

Cross-Reference: Section 410, Pleas, Offers of Pleas, and Related Statements; Section 1102, Spoliation or Destruction of Evidence.

Subsection (b). This subsection is derived from Sheehan v. Goriansky, 317 Mass. 10, 16–17 (1944), and City of Boston v. Santosuosso, 307 Mass. 302, 349 (1940). Evidence of consciousness of liability alone cannot sustain the burden to establish liability. Olofson v. Kilgallon, 362 Mass. 803, 806 (1973); Miles v. Caples, 362 Mass. 107, 114 (1972).

Illustrations. The following conduct may be offered as evidence of consciousness of liability:

- providing false or inconsistent statements, McNamara v. Honeyman, 406 Mass. 43, 54 n.10 (1989);

- leaving the scene of an accident without identifying himself or herself, Olofson v. Kilgallon, 362 Mass. 803, 806 (1973);

- providing a false name or statement to police, Parsons v. Ryan, 340 Mass. 245, 248 (1960);

- providing intentionally false testimony, Sheehan v. Goriansky, 317 Mass. 10, 16–17 (1944);

- transferring property immediately prior to the beginning of litigation, Credit Serv. Corp. v. Barker, 308 Mass. 476, 481 (1941);

- suborning a witness to provide false testimony, bribing a juror, or suppressing evidence, Bennett v. Susser, 191 Mass. 329, 331 (1906); or

- destroying potential evidence, Gath v. M/A–Com, Inc., 440 Mass. 482, 489–491 (2003).

Cross–Reference: Section 407, Subsequent Remedial Measures; Section 408, Compromise Offers and Negotiations in Civil Case; Section 409, Expressions of Sympathy in Civil Cases; Offers to Pay Medical and Similar Expenses; Section 410, Pleas, Offers of Pleas, and Related Statements; Section 411, Insurance; Section 1102, Spoliation or Destruction of Evidence.

Jury Instruction on Evidence of Consciousness of Liability. Upon request, the judge should instruct the jury that they may, but are not required to, draw an inference; that any such inference must be reasonable in light of all the circumstances; that the weight of the evidence is for the jury to decide; that there may be innocent explanations for the conduct; and that the conduct does not necessarily reflect feelings of liability or responsibility. See Commonwealth v. Toney, 385 Mass. 575, 584–585 (1982) (it was for jury to decide which explanation for defendant's departure from scene was most credible). See also Sheehan v. Goriansky, 317 Mass. 10, 16–17 (1944) (whether evidence of defendant's conduct indicated consciousness of liability was for jury to decide); Hall v. Shain, 291 Mass. 506, 512 (1935) (jury to decide whether driver's failure to contact police after accident was because of consciousness of liability).

Subsection (c). This subsection is derived from Commonwealth v. Chase, 26 Mass. App. Ct. 578, 580–581 (1988), and Commonwealth v. Kerrigan, 345 Mass. 508, 513 (1963).

Section 1111. Missing Witness

(a) Argument by Counsel. Counsel is not permitted to make a missing-witness argument without first obtaining judicial approval; if approval is granted, the court must give a missing witness instruction.

(b) Jury Instruction. The court may instruct the jury that an adverse inference may be drawn from a party's failure to call a witness when

(1) the witness is shown to be available;

(2) the witness is friendly, or at least not hostile, to the party;

(3) the witness is expected to give noncumulative testimony of distinct importance to the case; and

(4) there is no logical or tactical explanation for the failure to call the witness.

NOTE

Subsection (a). This subsection is derived from Commonwealth v. Pena, 455 Mass. 1, 16–17 (2009); Commonwealth v. Saletino, 449 Mass. 657, 670 (2007); and Commonwealth v. Ortiz, 61 Mass. App. Ct. 468, 471 (2004). See Hoffman v. Houghton Chem. Corp., 434 Mass. 624, 640 (2001) (same principles apply in civil cases). The missing witness argument and the missing witness instruction are interrelated. The preferred practice is for counsel and the court to discuss the matter of a missing witness argument before the closing arguments. See Commonwealth v. Williams, 450 Mass. 894, 907 (2008). If the trial judge

decides not to give the instruction, counsel is not permitted to make the argument. Commonwealth v. Saletino, 449 Mass. at 670–672.

In Commonwealth v. Saletino, 449 Mass. 657 (2007), the Supreme Judicial Court explained the critical distinction between argument by counsel that the evidence is insufficient, and the missing witness argument:

"A defendant has wide latitude in every case to argue that the Commonwealth has failed to present sufficient evidence and, in this sense, that there is an 'absence' of proof or that evidence is 'missing.' That is distinctly different from a missing witness argument, however. In the former, the defendant argues that the evidence that has been produced is inadequate; the defendant may even legitimately point out that a specific witness or specific evidence has not been produced; but the defendant does not argue or ask the jury to draw any conclusions as to the substance of the evidence that has not been produced. In the latter, the defendant points an accusatory finger at the Commonwealth for not producing the missing witness and urges the jury to conclude affirmatively that the missing evidence would have been unfavorable to the Commonwealth. That is the essence of the adverse inference."

Id. at 672. Accord Commonwealth v. Pena, 455 Mass. at 17; Sullivan v. Connolly, 91 Mass. App. Ct. 56, 57–58 (2017).

Subsection (b). This subsection is derived from Commonwealth v. Saletino, 449 Mass. 657, 668 (2007), and Commonwealth v. Anderson, 411 Mass. 279, 280 n.1 (1991). See also Commonwealth v. Franklin, 366 Mass. 284, 292–295 (1974). The instruction permits the jury, "if they think reasonable in the circumstances, [to] infer that the person, had he been called, would have given testimony unfavorable to the party." Id.

Whether to allow argument and give a missing witness instruction is within the discretion of the trial judge, even when the foundation requirements are met. Commonwealth v. Thomas, 429 Mass. 146, 151 (1999). It is a highly fact-specific decision, and it cannot be insisted on as a matter of right. Id. "Because the inference, when it is made, can have a seriously adverse effect on the noncalling party—suggesting, as it does, that the party has willfully attempted to withhold or conceal significant evidence—it should be invited only in clear cases, and with caution." Commonwealth v. Williams, 450 Mass. 894, 900–901 (2008), quoting Commonwealth v. Schatvet, 23 Mass. App. Ct. 130, 134 (1986). If the instruction is given, the court must take care not to negate its effect by instructing the jury not to consider anything beyond the evidence actually introduced at trial. See Commonwealth v. Remedor, 52 Mass. App. Ct. 694, 701 (2001).

Foundation for the Instruction. In Commonwealth v. Broomhead, 67 Mass. App. Ct. 547 (2006), the court stated as follows:

"In order to determine whether there has been a sufficient foundation for a missing witness instruction, we look at (1) whether the case against the defendant is [so strong that,] faced with the evidence, the defendant would be likely to call the missing witness if innocent; (2) whether the evidence to be given by the missing witness is important, central to the case, or just collateral or cumulative; (3) whether the party who fails to call the witness has superior knowledge of the whereabouts of the witness; and (4) whether the party has a 'plausible reason' for not producing the witness."

Id. at 552, quoting Commonwealth v. Alves, 50 Mass. App. Ct. 796, 802 (2001). Even where the foundational requirements are met, the judge has discretion to decline to give the instruction and refuse to permit the argument if the judge finds that an adverse inference is not warranted. Commonwealth v. Pena, 455 Mass. 1, 17 n.15 (2009).

Is the "Missing Witness" Available? Availability is "the likelihood that the party against whom the inference is to be drawn would be able to procure the missing witness'[s] physical presence in court." Commonwealth v. Happnie, 3 Mass. App. Ct. 193, 197 (1975). Availability does not necessarily require proof of "actual physical whereabouts," but the court will look at whether the party made reasonable efforts to produce the witness under the circumstances. Commonwealth v. Luna, 46 Mass. App. Ct. 90, 95–96 nn.3 & 6 (1998). Compare Commonwealth v. Smith, 49 Mass. App. Ct. 827, 830–831 (2000) (basis to conclude that witnesses lived in area and no showing of impediment to obtaining their testimony), with Commonwealth v. Ortiz, 67 Mass. App. Ct. 349, 350 (2006) (defendant not entitled to missing witness instruction where he failed to show that prosecutor had knowledge of witness's whereabouts).

A missing witness instruction is not warranted where a witness is equally available to both sides. Commonwealth v. Cobb, 397 Mass. 105, 108 (1986). For example, in Commonwealth v. Hoilett, 430 Mass. 369, 376 (1999), the court ruled the instruction was not warranted because both sides had the same contact information for a witness who was not aligned with either side. The instruction may properly be given where the missing witness is more friendly to one side than the other, even if the witness was available to the party requesting the instruction. See Commonwealth v. Thomas, 429 Mass. 146, 151–152 (1999). See also Hoffman v. Houghton Chem. Corp., 434 Mass. 624, 641 (2001) (defendant corporation's vice president not absent where plaintiff could have subpoenaed him to testify).

Is the "Missing Witness" Friendly, or At Least Not Hostile, to the Party? "The jury should ordinarily be instructed not to draw inferences from the neglect of a defendant to call witnesses, unless it appears to be within his power to call others than himself, and unless the evidence against him is so strong that, if innocent, he would be expected to call them." Commonwealth v. Finnerty, 148 Mass. 162, 167 (1889). See Commonwealth v. Rollins, 441 Mass. 114, 118–119 (2004); Commonwealth v. Thomas, 429 Mass. 146, 152 (1999). See also Grady v. Collins Transp. Co., 341 Mass. 502, 509 (1960) ("The plaintiff's testimony was uncorroborated and was opposed by that of three witnesses, which, if accepted, showed his admitted fault to be the cause of the accident. The names of the plaintiff's companions had been given to his counsel. There was very substantial likelihood that, notwithstanding the nine year interval, one or more of them lived in Worcester or near by [sic].").

Would the "Missing Witness" Give Noncumulative Testimony of Importance? A missing witness instruction is warranted where the witness would be expected to give testimony "of distinct importance to the case." Commonwealth v. Schatvet, 23 Mass. App. Ct. 130, 134 (1986). In determining the potential importance of the missing witness's testimony, the court may consider whether the case against the party is so strong that the party would be likely to call the missing witness to rebut it. Commonwealth v. Broomhead, 67 Mass. App. Ct. 547, 552 (2006). See Commonwealth v. Rollins, 441 Mass. at 119 (proper to give missing witness instruction where defendant failed to call "good friend" who was with him at time of his arrest for OUI); Commonwealth v. Caldwell, 36 Mass. App. Ct. 570, 581–582 (1994) (defendant failed to call as alibi witness a cousin who supposedly let him into apartment at time of charged attack). Compare Commonwealth v. Graves, 35 Mass. App. Ct. 76, 81 (1993) (failure to call alibi witness who was "central" to defense), with Commonwealth v. Thomas, 439 Mass. 362, 370 (2003) (absent witness's testimony would have been "merely corroborative").

Is There an Explanation for Failure to Call a "Missing Witness"? 'If the circumstances, considered by ordinary logic and experience, suggest a plausible reason for nonproduction of the witness, the jury should not be advised of the inference." Commonwealth v. Anderson, 411 Mass. 279, 282–283 (1991). Thus, it is not error to refuse the instruction where it appears the witness may have been withheld because of his or her prior criminal record. Commonwealth v. Saletino, 449 Mass. 657, 668–669 (2007). See Commonwealth v. Figueroa, 413 Mass. 193, 197 (1992) (witnesses of limited mental capacity); Commonwealth v. Ortiz, 61 Mass. App. Ct. 468, 472–473 (2004) (defense counsel believed, albeit mistakenly, that witness had been subpoenaed and had failed to appear such that further efforts to compel his presence would be futile); Commonwealth v. Gagliardi, 29

Mass. App. Ct. 225, 244 (1990) (witness was reluctant to testify because of fear of intimidation by persons related to defendant). Contrast Brownlie v. Kanzaki Specialty Papers, Inc., 44 Mass. App. Ct. 408, 420 (1998) (affidavit of company official stating only that "compelling business reasons" mandated his return to Japan did not provide judge with plausible explanation for his absence).

Criminal Cases. The judge must inform the jury in a criminal case that they may not draw an adverse inference from the defendant's failure to call a witness unless and until they find beyond a reasonable doubt that if the witness had been called he or she would have given testimony unfavorable to the defendant. Commonwealth v. Niziolek, 380 Mass. 513, 522 (1980). The inference may also be applied to a situation where evidence is "missing." See Commonwealth v. Kee, 449 Mass. 550, 558 (2007).

Cross–Reference: Section 1102, Spoliation or Destruction of Evidence.

Section 1112. Eyewitness Identification

(a) **Eyewitness Identification Generally.** The admissibility of eyewitness identification evidence is governed both by Article 12 of the Massachusetts Declaration of Rights and common-law principles of fairness.

(b) **Out–of–Court Identification.**

(1) **Photographic Array.**

(A) **Suppression of Identification.** Identification based on a pretrial photographic procedure is not subject to suppression unless the procedures employed in showing the photographic array were unnecessarily suggestive and conducive to mistaken identification. In making this ruling, the trial judge should consider

(i) whether the police properly informed the party making the identification that (1) the wrongdoer may or may not be in the depicted photographs, (2) it is just as important to clear a person from suspicion as to identify a person as the wrongdoer, (3) the depicted individuals may not appear exactly as they did on the date of the incident because features such as weight and head and facial hair may change, and (4) the investigation will continue regardless of whether an identification is made;

(ii) whether the party making the identification was asked to state how certain he or she is of any identification;

(iii) whether the array was composed of persons who possess reasonably similar features and characteristics; and

(iv) whether the array contained at least five fillers for every photograph of the suspect.

(B) **Suggestive Police Procedures.** If the trial judge finds that the police procedures employed in the showing of the photographic array were so unnecessarily suggestive and conducive to mistaken identity as to deny the defendant due process of law, the Commonwealth may offer evidence of the identification only if it establishes by clear and convincing evidence that the proffered identification has a source independent of the suggestive photographic array.

(C) **Admissibility of Photographs.** Police photographs used in an out-of-court identification may be admitted if (i) the prosecution demonstrates some need for their introduction, (ii) the photographs are offered in a form that does not imply a prior criminal record, and (iii) the manner of their introduction does not call attention to their source.

(2) Lineup. The considerations present with photographic arrays also apply to identifications resulting from lineups.

(3) Showup. Showup identifications are generally disfavored. However, for good cause shown, the trial judge may admit evidence of such an identification if the showup was not unnecessarily or impermissibly suggestive. This determination involves an inquiry of whether the Commonwealth has shown that police had good cause to use a one-on-one identification procedure and whether police avoided any special elements of unfairness.

(4) Suggestive Identification Not Resulting from Police Procedures. An identification will be suppressed even in the absence of constitutional concerns or police action if admitting the identification would violate common-law principles of fairness.

(c) In–Court Identification.

(1) Where There Has Been an Out–of–Court Identification.

    (A) Generally, an in-court identification of the defendant by an eyewitness who was present during commission of the crime is admissible if the eyewitness (i) participated before trial in an identification procedure and (ii) has made an unequivocal, positive identification of the defendant.

    (B) If the out-of-court identification is determined to have been the result of unnecessarily suggestive police procedures, an in-court identification is not admissible unless the Commonwealth establishes, by clear and convincing evidence, that it has a source independent of and unrelated to the unnecessarily suggestive out-of-court identification.

    (C) If the suggestiveness did not arise from police conduct, and the out-of-court identification was suppressed under common-law principles of fairness, a subsequent in-court identification cannot be admitted.

(2) Where There Has Been No Out–of–Court Identification.

    (A) If an eyewitness who was present during the commission of a crime did not participate before trial in an identification procedure or has made something less than an unequivocal, positive identification, an in-court identification is not admissible unless there is good reason for its admission.

    (B) In cases subject to Subsection (c)(2)(A), the Commonwealth must move in limine to admit the in-court identification. The Commonwealth has the burden of production on whether there is good reason for admitting the in-court identification. The defendant has the burden of persuasion to establish that an in-court identification would be unnecessarily suggestive and that there is not good reason for it.

(d) Testimony of Third-Party Observer. If the eyewitness testifies at trial and is subject to cross-examination, a third party who observed the eyewitness's out-of-court identification may testify about that identification (1) where the eyewitness cannot identify a defendant at trial but acknowledges having made an out-of-court identification of the defendant, or (2) where the eyewitness denies or fails to remember having made an identification. The third party's testimony about the identification may not be admitted until after the Commonwealth has questioned the eyewitness about the identification. The third party's testimony about the out-of-court identification is admissible as substantive evidence.

(e) Expert Testimony. Expert testimony on the issue of eyewitness identification is admissible at the discretion of the trial judge.

(f) Jury Instruction.

(1) Positive Eyewitness Identification. Where the jury heard eyewitness evidence that positively identified the defendant and the identification of the defendant as the person who committed or participated in the alleged crime is contested, the judge should give the Model Eyewitness Identification Instruction.

(2) Partial Eyewitness Identification. Upon request, where an eyewitness partially identified the defendant, the judge should give some variation of the Model Eyewitness Identification Instruction that includes information about the risk of an honest but mistaken observation.

(3) Cross-Racial Identification. The judge should omit the cross-racial component of the Model Eyewitness Identification Instruction only if all parties agree that there was no cross-racial identification. Where the instruction is given, the judge has discretion to add references to ethnicity.

(4) Failure to Identify or Inconsistent Identification. The judge should instruct the jury to consider whether a witness ever failed to identify the defendant or made an identification that was inconsistent with the identification that the witness made at the trial.

(5) Preliminary/Contemporaneous Instruction. Upon request, before opening statements or immediately before or after the testimony of an identifying witness, the judge must give the Preliminary/Contemporaneous Instruction.

NOTE

Subsection (a). This subsection is derived from Commonwealth v. Crayton, 470 Mass. 228 (2014). See also Commonwealth v. Walker, 460 Mass. 590 (2011); Commonwealth v. Jones, 423 Mass. 99 (1996).

In both Crayton and Walker, the Supreme Judicial Court explained that Massachusetts law follows a per se rule of exclusion for unnecessarily suggestive identifications and, as a result, is more favorable to the defendant than Federal law, which permits the admission of such identifications so long as the judge finds that they are reliable under the totality of the circumstances. In Crayton, the court added that, in Massachusetts, an identification made under "'especially suggestive circumstances' even where the circumstances did not result from improper police activity is also in contrast with the United States Supreme Court jurisprudence" (quotation and citations omitted). Commonwealth v. Crayton, 470 Mass. at 235. Because Massachusetts constitutional and common law is more favorable to the defendant, there is no need to separately consider Federal law on questions relating to the admission of eyewitness identification.

In Walker, the court added that

"[b]ecause eyewitness identification is the greatest source of wrongful convictions but also an invaluable law enforcement tool in obtaining accurate convictions, and because the research regarding eyewitness identification procedures is complex and evolving, we shall convene a study committee to consider how we can best deter unnecessarily suggestive procedures and whether existing model jury instructions provide adequate guidance to juries in evaluating eyewitness testimony."

Commonwealth v. Walker, 460 Mass. at 604 n.16. The study committee filed its report on July 25, 2013. See Supreme Judicial Court Study Group on Eyewitness Evidence, Report and Recommendations to the Justices (July 25, 2013), at http://perma.cc/52L8–C6SQ. See also Identifying the Culprit: Assessing Eyewitness Identification (2014) (report of the National Research Council of the National Academies of Science; prepublication copy available at http://perma.cc/6SRE–8UHR).

Inanimate Objects. Under some circumstances, due process principles may apply to the identification of an inanimate object:

"Due process may be denied by admitting in evidence an identification of an inanimate object where, first, the police knew or reasonably should have known that identification of the object effectively identifies the defendant as the perpetrator of the crime and where, second, the police needlessly and strongly suggested to the witness that the object is the object at issue."

Commonwealth v. Thomas, 476 Mass. 451, 466–467 (2017). The Supreme Judicial Court has urged police departments to devise a protocol for identification of inanimate objects and suggested elements of such a protocol for police departments to consider. Id. at 467–468. See also Commonwealth v. Bresilla, 470 Mass. 422, 429 (2015).

Subsection (b)(1)(A)(i). This subsection is derived from Commonwealth v. Walker, 460 Mass. 590, 600 (2011), making mandatory the protocol adopted in Commonwealth v. Silva–Santiago, 453 Mass. 782, 797–798 (2009). While the Supreme Judicial Court has not yet required a double-blind procedure where the identification procedure is conducted by a law enforcement officer who does not know the identity of the suspect, it has recognized that such a process is the better practice to eliminate the risk of conscious or unconscious suggestion. Id. at 797.

Subsection (b)(1)(A)(ii). This subsection is derived from Commonwealth v. Silva–Santiago, 453 Mass. 782, 797–798 (2009).

Subsection (b)(1)(A)(iii). This subsection is derived from Commonwealth v. Silva–Santiago, 453 Mass. 782, 795 (2009). See, e.g., Commonwealth v. Arzola, 470 Mass. 809, 813 (2015) (after victim had given description of assailant that included a gray shirt, identification was not unnecessarily suggestive where victim explicitly stated that his identification was based on defendant's facial features, hair, complexion, and eyes, even though defendant was the only subject wearing gray shirt).

Subsection (b)(1)(A)(iv). This subsection is derived from Commonwealth v. Walker, 460 Mass. 590, 602–603 (2011). Unless there are exigent circumstances, the police should not show a witness a photographic array that contains fewer than five fillers for every suspect photograph. Id. at 603–604.

Subsection (b)(1)(B). This subsection is derived from Commonwealth v. Johnson, 473 Mass. 594 (2016), and Commonwealth v. Warren, 403 Mass. 137, 139 (1988). Cf. Commonwealth v. Forte, 469 Mass. 469, 477 (2014).

In Johnson, the Supreme Judicial Court indicated that it will, in an appropriate case, determine whether the reasoning in Commonwealth v. Crayton, 470 Mass. 228 (2014), and Commonwealth v. Collins, 470 Mass. 255 (2014), dictates elimination or revision of the independent-source doctrine. Commonwealth v. Johnson, 473 Mass. at 602–603.

Subsection (b)(1)(C). This subsection is derived from Commonwealth v. Cruz, 445 Mass. 589, 592 (2005).

Subsection (b)(3). This subsection is derived from Commonwealth v. Martin, 447 Mass. 274, 279 (2006). See also Commonwealth v. Crayton, 470 Mass. 228, 235 (2014); Commonwealth v. Amaral, 81 Mass. App. Ct. 143, 148–149 (2012). Good cause may be based on (1) the nature of the crime and concerns for public safety, (2) the need for efficient investigation in the aftermath of a crime, and (3) the usefulness of prompt confirmation of the accuracy of information. Commonwealth v. Rivera, 91 Mass. App. Ct. 796, 801 (2017). Good cause is required for this analysis, not "good faith." Commonwealth v. Carlson, 92 Mass. App. Ct. 710, 713 n.3 (2018). The availability of an alternative identification procedure does not necessarily make an identification unduly suggestive. Commonwealth v. Martinez, 67 Mass. App. Ct. 788, 793 (2006). A delay in time between the crime and the showup is one factor in determining whether the identification is inherently or unnecessarily suggestive, but such a delay does not make it per se inadmissible. Commonwealth v. Levasseur, 32 Mass. App. Ct. 629, 636 (1990). E.g., Commonwealth v. Pearson, 87 Mass. App. Ct. 720, 724–725 (2015) (showup procedure following victim's spontaneous encounter with perpetrator fifty-three days after assault not unnecessarily suggestive). The defendant may argue to the jury that as an alternative to a one-on-one showup, it would have been fairer to ask the witness to pick the defendant out of a group of similar individuals. Commonwealth v. Gonzalez, 28 Mass. App. Ct. 906, 908 (1989).

Subsection (b)(4). This subsection is derived from Commonwealth v. Jones, 423 Mass. 99, 108–109 (1996) (in-court identification suppressed even in the absence of constitutional concerns or police action where admitting the identification would violate common-law principles of fairness). See Commonwealth v. McCray, 93 Mass. App. Ct. 835, 841 (2018) (identification of defendant by witness who drove by and observed police officer in process of arresting defendant was not the result of "police procedure" and would be analyzed under common-law principles of fairness). See also Commonwealth v. McEvoy, 93 Mass. App. Ct. 308, 321 (2018) (after rejecting defendant's argument that out-of-court identification based on a photo array was unnecessarily suggestive, court considered and rejected argument that the probative value of the identification was so minimal as to be substantially outweighed by the danger of unfair prejudice).

Subsection (c). This subsection is derived from Commonwealth v. Crayton, 470 Mass. 228, 233–245 (2014), and Commonwealth v. Collins, 470 Mass. 255, 259–267 (2014), which apply prospectively to trials that commence after December 17, 2014. In both Crayton and Collins, the Supreme Judicial Court explained that the new rule was not mandated by the State constitution, but rather was a rule of the common law.

In Crayton, the court noted that the usual "good reasons" for conducting an out-of-court showup—"concerns for public safety," "efficient police investigation[s]," and the value of rapid confirmation of investigatory details—"will never justify an in-court showup." Commonwealth v. Crayton, 470 Mass. at 242. In Crayton, the court recognized two circumstances that may qualify as "good reasons" for not conducting an out-of-court identification procedure: the first is "where the eyewitness was familiar with the defendant before the commission of the crime, such as where a victim testifies to a crime of domestic violence," and the second is "where the witness is an arresting officer who was also an eyewitness to the commission of the crime, and the identification merely confirms that the defendant is merely the person who was arrested for the charged crime." Id. In Collins, the court added that

"'good reason' will not often exist where a witness has earlier failed to make a positive identification. In these circumstances, for an in-court showup to be admissible, it would need to be justified by some other 'good reason' for permitting a suggestive identification procedure, which usually would require a showing that the in-court identification is more reliable than the witness's earlier failure to make a positive identification and that it poses little risk of misidentification despite its suggestiveness."

Commonwealth v. Collins, 470 Mass. at 265.

The court specifically left open whether this new rule should apply to in-court identifications of the defendant by eyewitnesses who were not present during the commission of the crime but who may have observed the defendant before or after the crime. Commonwealth v. Crayton, 470 Mass. at 242 n.17; Commonwealth v. Collins, 470 Mass. at 265 n.15.

Subsection (c)(1)(A). The requirement that the out-of-court identification must have been "unequivocal" stems from Commonwealth v. Collins, 470 Mass. 255, 266 (2014), where the Supreme Judicial Court stated that

"[i]n the future, where an eyewitness to a crime has not made an unequivocal positive identification of the defendant before trial but the prosecutor nonetheless intends to ask the eyewitness to make an in-court identification of the defendant, we impose the same burden on the prosecutor as we did in [Commonwealth v.] Crayton[, 470 Mass. 228, 242 (2014),] to move in limine to admit the in-court identification, preferably before trial."

An unequivocal positive identification exists where the witness "identifies the defendant as the perpetrator, such that the statement of identification is clear and free from doubt." Commonwealth v. Dew, 478 Mass. 304, 315 (2017). The prior-identification requirement may be satisfied where the witness observed the defendant commit the crime and identified the defendant to police at the scene of the crime. Commonwealth v. Stewart, 94 Mass. App. Ct. 485, 488 (2018).

Subsection (c)(1)(B). This subsection is derived from Commonwealth v. Johnson, 420 Mass. 458, 463 (1995), as further elaborated by Commonwealth v. Johnson, 473 Mass. 594 (2016). The prosecution may introduce only an identification that is not the product of the suggestive identification. If the out-of-court identification was the result of unnecessarily suggestive police procedures, such an identification must have an independent source, as demonstrated by clear and convincing evidence. In the 2016 Johnson case, the Supreme Judicial Court indicated that it will, in an appropriate case, determine whether the reasoning in Commonwealth v. Crayton, 470 Mass. 228 (2014), and Commonwealth v. Collins, 470 Mass. 255 (2014), dictates elimination or revision of this independent-source doctrine. Commonwealth v. Johnson, 473 Mass. at 602–603. An in-court identification will be suppressed where either the physical presence of the witness in court or the witness's basis of knowledge for the identification was procured in violation of the Fourth Amendment to the United States Constitution. Commonwealth v. Greenwood, 78 Mass. App. Ct. 611, 621 (2011).

Subsection (c)(1)(C). This subsection is derived from Commonwealth v. Johnson, 473 Mass. 594 (2016). If an out-of-court identification was declared inadmissible under common-law principles of fairness, a subsequent in-court identification by the same person cannot be admitted. The independent-source doctrine does not apply. Id. at 603.

Subsection (d). This subsection is derived from Commonwealth v. Cong Duc Le, 444 Mass. 431, 441–442 (2005). Identification testimony must be accompanied by an accusation relevant to the issue before the court or some form of exclusionary statement.

"[A]n eyewitness's out-of-court statement identifying a defendant as the person shooting at the eyewitness's friend is part of the context of the identification, but a statement regarding the number of shots fired, the color of the firearm, and the defendant's behavior after the shooting goes beyond the context of the identification of the shooter" (citation omitted).

Commonwealth v. Walker, 460 Mass. 590, 608 (2011). The Commonwealth is required to question the alleged eyewitness about the prior identification before it seeks to introduce substantive evidence of that identification through a third party. This procedure is necessary to provide the defendant with adequate notice about the identification and to permit the defendant to cross-examine the alleged eyewitness. Commonwealth v. Herndon, 475 Mass. 324, 334 (2016). The opportunity to recall the declarant witness after the statement has been introduced through a third party does not satisfy the requirement of meaningful cross-examination, as it is too limited and inappropriately places a "strategic burden on the non-offering party." Id., quoting Smith v. State, 669 A.2d 1, 8 (Del. 1995). The third-party testimony of the declarant is admissible for probative purposes even if that third party was not a percipient observer of the entire identification process, including observing the declarant in the act of identifying the particular person. Commonwealth v. Raedy, 68 Mass. App. Ct. 440, 448–449 (2007). The testimony of the third-party witness who observed the out-of-court identification is governed by Section 801(d)(1)(C), Definitions: Statements Which Are Not Hearsay: Prior Statement by Witness.

Subsection (e). This subsection is derived from Commonwealth v. Bly, 448 Mass. 473, 495 (2007). The judge must conclude the subject of the expert opinion is one on which the jurors need assistance, and that they will not be confused or misled by the testimony. The tests and circumstances on which the opinion rests must provide a basis for determining it is reliable. The testimony must be sufficiently tied to the facts of the case so that it will aid the jury. Commonwealth v. Santoli, 424 Mass. 837, 844 (1997).

Subsection (f). This subsection is derived from the Model Jury Instructions on Eyewitness Identification set forth at 473 Mass. 1051 (2015). The instructions include the Model Eyewitness Identification Instruction and the Preliminary/Contemporaneous Instruction. The Model Eyewitness Identification Instruction should be given "unless a judge determines that different language would more accurately or clearly provide comparable guidance to a jury or better promote the fairness of the trial." Model Jury Instructions on Eyewitness Identification, 473 Mass. at 1051. For the entire statement of the justices, see https://perma.cc/KH5B–J9YQ.

Section 1113. Opening Statement and Closing Argument; Applicable to Criminal and Civil Cases

(a) Opening Statement.

(1) Purpose. The proper function of an opening statement is to outline in a general way the nature of the case that a party expects to be able to prove or support by admissible evidence. The expectation must be reasonable and grounded in good faith. Except for a prosecutor in a criminal case, a party may discuss evidence expected to be offered by an opponent. Argument for or against either party is not permitted.

(2) Directed Verdict, Finding of Not Guilty, or Mistrial. If the evidence outlined in an opening statement is insufficient as a matter of law to sustain that party's burden of proof, or to establish a cause of action, the court has discretion to direct a verdict against that party.

(b) Closing Argument.

(1) Critical Stage. Closing argument is not evidence but is a critical stage of a trial that requires advance preparation and knowledge of the principles expressed in this section.

(2) Permissible Argument. Closing argument must be based on the evidence and the fair inferences from the evidence. It may contain enthusiastic rhetoric, strong advocacy, and excusable hyperbole. It is permissible to argue from the evidence that a witness, document, or other evidence is or is not credible, as well as to suggest the conclusions, if any, that should be drawn from the evidence. A party may urge jurors to rely on common sense and life experience as long as the subject matter at issue does not require expert knowledge. In civil actions in the Superior

Court, parties, through their counsel, may suggest a specific monetary amount for damages at trial.

(3) Improper Argument. The following are not permissible in a closing argument:

(A) to misstate the evidence, to refer to facts not in evidence (including excluded matters), to use evidence for a purpose other than the limited purpose for which it was admitted, or to suggest inferences not fairly based on the evidence;

(B) to state a personal opinion about the credibility of a witness, the evidence, or the ultimate issue of guilt or liability;

(C) to appeal to the jurors' emotions, passions, prejudices, or sympathies;

(D) to ask the jurors to put themselves in the position of any person involved in the case;

(E) to misstate principles of law, to make any statement that shifts the burden of proof, or to ask the finder of fact to infer guilt based on the defendant's exercise of a constitutional right; and

(F) to ask the jury to disregard the court's instructions.

(c) Objections. An objection to a statement in an opening or closing, to be timely, must be made no later than the conclusion of the opponent's opening or closing. If counsel is dissatisfied with a judge's curative or supplemental instruction, an additional objection must be made.

(d) Duty of the Court. A trial judge has a duty to take appropriate action to prevent and remedy error in opening statements and closing arguments.

NOTE

Subsection (a). An opening statement is generally limited to fifteen minutes. See Mass. R. Crim. P. 24(a)(2); Rule 7 of the Rules of the Superior Court. The defendant may present an opening statement immediately after the plaintiff's opening or may choose to defer his or her opening until after the close of the plaintiff's case. See Commonwealth v. Dupree, 16 Mass. App. Ct. 600, 603 (1983) (discussing tactical considerations that may affect decision whether to defer opening until after conclusion of Commonwealth's case).

Subsection (a)(1). This subsection is derived from Commonwealth v. Croken, 432 Mass. 266, 268 (2000); Commonwealth v. Fazio, 375 Mass. 451, 454 (1978); and Posell v. Herscovitz, 237 Mass. 513, 514 (1921). There is no place for inflammatory rhetoric in an opening statement. See Commonwealth v. Siny Van Tran, 460 Mass. 535, 554 (2011); Commonwealth v. Silva, 455 Mass. 503, 514 (2009) ("The prosecutor's opening remark, describing the killing as cold blooded, was improper argument for an opening."). But see Commonwealth v. Johnson, 429 Mass. 745, 748 (1999). Simply because a statement made in a reasonable, good-faith belief that the evidence would materialize at trial turns out not to be true does not mean the statement constitutes error. See Commonwealth v. Fazio, 375 Mass. at 457. Accord Commonwealth v. Qualls, 440 Mass. 576, 586 (2003) (holding that absent a showing of bad faith or prejudice, the fact that certain evidence cited in an opening statement fails to materialize is not a ground for reversal). Neither unreasonableness or bad faith is to be presumed. Commonwealth v. Errington, 390 Mass. 875, 883 (1984). Just because statements of a coconspirator the prosecutor believes to be admissible against the defendant are ruled inadmissible when offered at trial does not establish that the prosecutor acted in bad faith in referring to the statements in his or her opening statement. See Commonwealth v. Morgan, 449 Mass. 343, 361 (2007).

"[A] judge, acting within his discretion, may limit the scope of the prosecutor's and defense counsel's opening statements to evidence counsel expects to introduce." Commonwealth v. Truong, 34 Mass. App. Ct. 668, 671 (1993). See also Commonwealth v. Medeiros, 15 Mass. App. Ct. 913, 913–914 (1983) (no abuse of discretion in refusing to permit an opening statement when defense counsel "announced no more than a hope to puncture the Commonwealth's case somehow through cross-examination"; but, "[i]f defense counsel reasonably expects on cross-examination to elicit specific evidence, . . . a defense opening stating such [evidence] would be proper"); Commonwealth v. Dupree, 16 Mass. App. Ct. 600, 602–603 (1983) ("To deny the defendant the right to open at the commencement of the trial without inquiry into the [content] of the proposed statement was error. To attempt to evaluate the extent of the prejudice which ensued would be an exercise in speculation, and, therefore, we reverse."). There may be special circumstances where a statement may be so "irretrievably and fatally prejudicial to the defendant" that a prosecutor should have "no doubt" as to its admissibility before including it in the opening. See Commonwealth v. Fazio, 375 Mass. at 455, discussing Commonwealth v. Bearse, 358 Mass. 481, 487 (1987). If there is a question asked as to the existence or admissibility of evidence, the matter may be brought to the judge by way of a motion in limine. See Commonwealth v. Spencer, 465 Mass. 32, 42 (2013). Cross–Reference: Section 103(f), Rulings on Evidence, Objections, and Offers of Proof: Motions in Limine.

Disciplinary Authority. See Mass. R. Prof. C. 3.4(e), 8.4(d) (2015); Admonition No. 00–51, 16 Mass. Att'y Discipline Rep. 528 (2000), at http://perma.cc/NB7Y-7BES (in opening statement, prosecutor described evidence that he was not in a position to produce).

Subsection (a)(2). This subsection is derived from Douglas v. Whittaker, 324 Mass. 398, 399 (1949), and Commonwealth v. Lowder, 432 Mass. 92, 102 (2000). The power to direct a verdict should be exercised with "great caution" because the outline of the evidence in the opening may not always fully describe the evidence at trial. See Hubert v. Melrose–Wakefield Hosp. Ass'n, 40 Mass. App. Ct. 172, 176 (1996), quoting from Upham v. Chateau de Ville Dinner Theatre, Inc., 380 Mass. 350, 351 n.2 (1980). Thus, in close cases, the motion should be denied. Douglas v. Whittaker, 324 Mass. at 400. However, where the facts stated do not constitute a cause of action, a verdict is properly directed because "the court and jury's time, the public purse, and the defendant's time and purse ought not to be wasted." Sereni v. Star Sportswear Mfg. Corp., 24 Mass. App. Ct. 428, 431 (1987). In a criminal case, the judge should not allow a motion for a required finding of not guilty after the opening unless the prosecutor is made aware of the problem and given an opportunity to correct it, and it is clear that the defendant cannot be lawfully convicted. Commonwealth v. Lowder, 432 Mass. at 100–101. See Island Transp. Co. v. Cavanaugh, 54 Mass. App. Ct. 650, 654 (2002) (preference for civil cases to be decided upon "sworn evidence rather than an anticipatory statement of counsel" unless opening statement fails to describe the elements of a cause of action).

Cross–Reference: Section 611(f), Mode and Order of Examining Witnesses and Presenting Evidence: Reopening.

Subsection (b). A party is generally allowed thirty minutes for closing argument in a civil case. Mass. R. Civ. P. 51(a). "The defendant shall present his closing argument first." Mass. R. Crim. P. 24(a)(1). "A trial judge has broad discretion in limiting the time for closing argument." Commonwealth v. Mahar, 6 Mass. App. Ct. 875, 875–876 (1978). See also Commonwealth v. Rocheteau, 74 Mass. App. Ct. 17, 22 (2009). "[J]udges who intend to enforce a time limit [on closing argument should] make clear to counsel before closing argument the limit to be imposed and the possibility that the judge will warn them of the time remaining." Commonwealth v. Brown, 462 Mass. 620, 633 n.11 (2012).

The defendant in a criminal case has a right under the Sixth Amendment to the United States Constitution to make a closing argument at trial. Commonwealth v. Marvin, 417 Mass. 291, 292

(1994). This right applies in cases in which the defendant represents himself or herself as well. Herring v. New York, 422 U.S. 853, 864 n.18 (1975). See also Commonwealth v. Martelli, 38 Mass. App. Ct. 669, 669–672 (1995) (failure to allow defense to present closing argument is structural error and requires reversal even absent objection).

Subsection (b)(1). This subsection is derived from Herring v. New York, 422 U.S. 853, 862 (1975), and Commonwealth v. Farley, 432 Mass. 153, 157 (2000).

Subsection (b)(2). The first sentence of this subsection is taken nearly verbatim from Commonwealth v. Pettie, 363 Mass. 836, 840 (1973), and Mason v. General Motors Corp., 397 Mass. 183, 192 (1986). See also Commonwealth v. Haas, 398 Mass. 806, 812 (1986); Teller v. Schepens, 25 Mass. App. Ct. 346, 352–353 (1988). The second sentence is derived from Commonwealth v. Costa, 414 Mass. 618, 629 (1993). See also Commonwealth v. Brown, 46 Mass. App. Ct. 279, 283 (1999) (prosecutor's comment fell into category of enthusiastic rhetoric, strong advocacy, and excusable hyperbole). The third sentence is derived from Commonwealth v. Kee, 449 Mass. 550, 560 (2007). See also Commonwealth v. Grimshaw, 412 Mass. 505, 510 (1992); Commonwealth v. Ferreira, 381 Mass. 306, 316 (1980) ("Counsel may also attempt to assist the jury in their task of analyzing, evaluating, and applying evidence. Such assistance includes suggestions by counsel as to what conclusion the jury should draw from the evidence."); Commonwealth v. Haas, 373 Mass. 545, 557 n.11 (1977) ("Counsel may 'fit all the pieces of evidence together so that they form a comprehensive and comprehensible picture for the jury.'"). The fourth sentence is derived from Commonwealth v. Oliveira, 431 Mass. 609, 613 (2000). Counsel may argue that a witness is mistaken or lying when the argument is expressed as a conclusion to be drawn from the evidence and not as a personal opinion. See Commonwealth v. Murchison, 418 Mass. 58, 60 (1994) (defense counsel was entitled to argue from the evidence that police officers had lied). The last sentence of this subsection is derived from G. L. c. 231, § 13B. The Supreme Judicial Court has noted its concern with unfair tactics where, "[a]lthough the prosecutor's comment d[oes] not violate the letter of the judge's order, it undoubtedly undermine[s] the spirit of the ruling." Commonwealth v. Durand, 475 Mass. 657, 672 (2016). In Durand, the court, while concluding there was no prejudicial error, noted that the prosecutor's comment "unfairly suggested that the defendant withheld . . . information, and that this act reflected consciousness of guilt." Id.

References to the View. Counsel may ask the jury in a closing to consider things they saw on a view. Commonwealth v. Fitzgerald, 376 Mass. 402, 420 (1978). Cross-Reference: Section 1109, View.

Common Sense; Common Experience. Counsel may ask the jury to use their common sense and to apply their common experience to the evidence. See Commonwealth v. Jefferson, 461 Mass. 821, 836 (2012); Commonwealth v. Santiago, 425 Mass. 491, 498 (1997), cert. denied, 525 U.S. 1003 (1998). Cf. Commonwealth v. Salazar, 481 Mass. 105, 116–117 (2018) (prosecutor's suggestion that jurors should consult "moral compass" was troublesome and approached improper appeal to emotions). Contrast Commonwealth v. Hrabak, 57 Mass. App. Ct. 648, 654 (2003) (improper for prosecutor to urge jurors to infer from their own knowledge and experience that six-year-old child's rectum could accommodate a penis without showing any injury, as this is beyond knowledge of ordinary layperson).

Stipulation or Transcript. Counsel may read from or quote any transcript or stipulation that has been admitted in evidence "so long as [counsel] furnishes opposing counsel with a copy of the transcript [or stipulation] from which he or she expects to read." Commonwealth v. Delacruz, 443 Mass. 692, 694–696 (2005).

Special Role of the Prosecutor. The prosecutor performs a special function in representing the Commonwealth. The interest of the prosecutor is "not that [he] shall win a case, but that justice shall be done . . . It is as much his duty to refrain from improper methods calculated to produce a wrongful conviction as it is to use every legitimate means to bring about a just one." Commonwealth v. Keo, 467 Mass. 25, 35–36 (2014), quoting Berger v. United States, 295 U.S.

78, 88 (1935). See also Commonwealth v. Shelley, 374 Mass. 466, 472 (1978) ("The prosecuting attorney is the representative not of an ordinary party to a controversy, but of a sovereignty whose obligation to govern impartially is as compelling as its obligation to govern at all; and whose interest, therefore, in a criminal prosecution is not that it shall win a case, but that justice shall be done.").

"We have never criticized a prosecutor for arguing forcefully for a conviction based on the evidence and on inferences that may reasonably be drawn from the evidence. On the other hand, a prosecutor should not refer to the defendant's failure to testify, misstate the evidence or refer to facts not in evidence, interject personal belief in the defendant's guilt, play on racial, ethnic, or religious prejudice or on the jury's sympathy or emotions, or comment on the consequences of a verdict . . . [P]rosecutors are held to a stricter standard of conduct than are errant defense counsel and their clients . . ." (Citations and footnotes omitted.)

Commonwealth v. Kozec, 399 Mass. 514, 516–519 (1987). See also Commonwealth v. Mahdi, 388 Mass. 679, 693 (1983).

Within reason, prosecutors may comment on the tactics and strategy of the defense. Compare Commonwealth v. Felder, 455 Mass. 359, 369 (2009), citing Commonwealth v. Jackson, 428 Mass. 455, 463 (1998) ("When read in context, there was no error in the prosecutor's limited references to the attempts by defense counsel to create 'smoke screen[s].'"); Commonwealth v. Espada, 450 Mass. 687, 699 (2008) (not improper for prosecutor to refer to defendant's "story as 'ridiculous'"); Commonwealth v. Raposa, 440 Mass. 684, 697 (2004) ("[T]he prosecutor stated, 'I mean, thank goodness you folks have notes, if I was sitting there listening to [defense counsel] tell you what the evidence was. Thank goodness you have the notes, because it's not what [defense counsel] tells you the evidence is.' The prosecutor went on to characterize defense counsel as an attorney able to 'spin gold from straw.' Our cases have upheld the use of language of this nature."); and Commonwealth v. MacDonald (No. 1), 368 Mass. 395, 401 (1975) ("Comment by the prosecutor on the tactics of the defense, based on the evidence and what the jury could observe in the court room, is permissible"), with Commonwealth v. Gentile, 437 Mass. 569, 580–581 (2002) ("Characterizing the defense tactic as 'despicable' goes beyond labeling it as unworthy of belief or lacking in merit and smacks more of an ad hominem attack."); Commonwealth v. Fernandes, 436 Mass. 671, 674 (2002) (improper to characterize defense counsel as "obscuring the truth or intentionally misleading the jury"); and Commonwealth v. McCravy, 430 Mass. 758, 764 (2000) (prosecutor may address a particular point in defense counsel's closing argument as a sham, but he or she may not characterize the entire defense as such). See also Commonwealth v. Silanskas, 433 Mass. 678, 702–703 (2001) (improper to comment on length of defense closing).

A prosecutor must be careful in making comments about defense counsel. See Commonwealth v. Lewis, 465 Mass. 119, 132 (2013) (Prosecutor's closing argument improperly disparaged defense counsel.); Commonwealth v. Scott, 463 Mass. 561, 574 (2012) ("[S]ome of the prosecutor's personal comments about defense counsel went beyond the bounds of proper argument."); Commonwealth v. Hawley, 380 Mass. 70, 84–85 (1980) (concluding that "impropriety lay in the prosecutor's suggestion that defense counsel was an active participant, if not the leader or mastermind, in the commission of the crimes of perjury"); Commonwealth v. Burts, 68 Mass. App. Ct. 684, 687–688 (2007) ("Criticisms of the defendant's attorney, including the prosecutor's urging of the jurors to be angry with the attorney, were improper and, among other things, impugned two basic constitutional rights, that of counsel, as well as the right of a defendant to make his defense."); Commonwealth v. Awad, 47 Mass. App. Ct. 139, 142 (1999) ("Disparaging remarks about the qualifications or motivations of defense counsel, or lawyers in general, are disfavored.").

Similarly, a prosecutor may not engage in "prejudicial name-calling." Commonwealth v. Rivera, 52 Mass. App. Ct. 321, 328 (2001) ("We have cautioned counsel for the Commonwealth to avoid prejudicial name-calling."). See also Commonwealth v. Rutherford, 476 Mass. 639,

644 (2017) (arguing that an expert "needs to become a human being" is inappropriate); Commonwealth v. Cosme, 410 Mass. 746, 754 (1991) (prosecutor's comments regarding two defense witnesses were "tasteless and improper"); Commonwealth v. Saunders, 75 Mass. App. Ct. 505, 511 (2009) ("A prosecutor should not use extreme epithets to characterize the defendant.").

"A prosecutor's role at a trial does not change where the defendant represents himself." Commonwealth v. Sapoznik, 28 Mass. App. Ct. 236, 240 n.3 (1990).

The disciplinary authority governing the special responsibilities of a prosecutor is Mass. R. Prof. C. 3.8(h) (1999).

Retaliatory Reply. Fighting fire with fire does not mean that a party has a right to exceed the proper bounds of closing argument because defense counsel did so. It means only that "a prosecutor may properly comment to correct 'an erroneous impression created by opposing counsel.'" Commonwealth v. Kozec, 399 Mass. 514, 519 n.9 (1987), quoting Commonwealth v. Bradshaw, 385 Mass. 244, 277 (1982). Compare Commonwealth v. Rivera, 425 Mass. 633, 647 (1997) ("The prosecutor was entitled to respond to defense counsel's improper suggestions regarding the use of prior convictions, and his reminder to the jury of the limited use of the defendant's prior convictions, although not artful, is not a ground for reversal."), and Commonwealth v. Prendergast, 385 Mass. 625, 633–634 (1982) (The defense counsel cited the defendant's hospital records as evidence that the defendant was mentally ill and dangerous and, therefore, not criminally responsible. The prosecutor's statement that the hospital records did not prevent the jury from finding the defendant criminally responsible was within his "right of retaliatory reply."), with Commonwealth v. McCoy, 59 Mass. App. Ct. 284, 296 (2003) (prosecutor "exceeded the bounds of fair, corrective response" when he "impermissibly appealed to the jury's emotional concern for crime-free streets by inferentially urging their trust in the police witnesses who had long protected those streets").

Subsection (b)(3)(A). This subsection is derived from Commonwealth v. Beaudry, 445 Mass. 577, 580 (2005); Commonwealth v. Pearce, 427 Mass. 642, 646 (1998); and Hart v. Morris & Co., 259 Mass. 211, 214–215 (1927). The right to argue inferences from the evidence does not include the right to "lead the jury to an improper inference not from the evidence but from the apparent personal knowledge of the attorney." Commonwealth v. Nordstrom, 364 Mass. 310, 315 (1973). See also Commonwealth v. Jones, 471 Mass. 138, 147–149 (2015) (improper for prosecutor to argue that defendant might have assaulted another victim if child had not moved away).

For the rule that a party may not misstate the evidence, see Commonwealth v. Sanders, 451 Mass. 290, 298–300 (2008) (multiple misstatements of evidence); Commonwealth v. Coren, 437 Mass. 723, 731 (2002) ("We conclude that the prosecutor exceeded the scope of proper argument by misstating important aspects of the testimony beyond inferences that might reasonably have been drawn from the evidence, and thereby committed error."); Commonwealth v. Sheehan, 435 Mass. 183, 191 (2001) (prosecutor had "no support in the evidence for labelling the defendant a 'predator,' and the remark [therefore] was unwarranted"); Commonwealth v. Daley, 66 Mass. App. Ct. 254, 257 (2006) (prosecutor misstated the evidence when he told the jury that trooper "detected a 'strong' odor of alcohol"); Commonwealth v. Vazquez, 65 Mass. App. Ct. 305, 312 (2005) (prosecutor misstated evidence when describing length of a kiss); and Commonwealth v. Gonzalez, 59 Mass. App. Ct. 622, 629 (2003) (no "basis in the evidence" for prosecutor's "suggestion of a possibility that the defendant might have possessed a weapon at the time of his arrest").

For the rule that a party may not refer to facts not in evidence, see Commonwealth v. Alvarez, 480 Mass. 299, 310 (2018) (reversible error for prosecutor to cite facts not in evidence that directly corroborated testimony of child rape victim; error not cured by general instruction to decide case based solely on admitted evidence); Commonwealth v. Dirgo, 474 Mass. 1012, 1013–1014 (2016) (A party cannot suggest that evidence would have been available but for a prohibition of law, in this case, the first complaint doctrine. It was error for the prosecutor to argue she could have provided a "parade" of witnesses to corroborate the complainant's testimony but for the first complaint doctrine.); Commonwealth v. Harris, 443 Mass. 714, 732 (2005) ("Counsel may not, in closing, 'exploit[] the absence of evidence that had been excluded at his request.' Such exploitation of absent, excluded evidence is 'fundamentally unfair' and 'reprehensible.'" [Citations omitted.]); Commonwealth v. Daley, 439 Mass. 558, 565 & n.3 (2003) (error for prosecutor to argue that "the defendant's 'character' as a dealer in crack cocaine and as a 'thief' should be used by the jury in assessing his credibility"); Commonwealth v. Grimshaw, 412 Mass. 505, 508 (1992) ("A prosecutor is barred from referring in closing argument to matter that has been excluded from evidence, and a prosecutor should also refrain from inviting an inference from the jury about the same excluded subject matter" [citation omitted].); Commonwealth v. Demetrius D., 94 Mass. App. Ct. 12, 20 (2018) (counsel who opposes a motion in limine to introduce evidence may not later exploit the absence of that evidence if the motion is denied); and Commonwealth v. Chambers, 93 Mass. App. Ct. 806, 821 (2018) (not error for prosecutor to state that the victims and witness gave statements identifying the defendant because the argument "was properly based on the reasonable inferences from the evidence").

For the rule that a party may not use evidence for a purpose other than the limited purpose for which it was admitted, see Commonwealth v. Cheremond, 461 Mass. 397, 413–414 (2012); Commonwealth v. Daley, 439 Mass. 558, 565–566 & n.3 (2003); Commonwealth v. Bregoli, 431 Mass. 265, 277–278 (2000); Commonwealth v. McIntyre, 430 Mass. 529, 543 (1999); Commonwealth v. Rosa, 412 Mass. 147, 156 (1992) ("A prosecutor may not present to the jury evidence admitted for a limited purpose as if it were substantive evidence."); and Commonwealth v. Burns, 49 Mass. App. Ct. 677, 683 (2000) (where prosecutor impeached witness with grand jury testimony, subsequent "substantive use" of same testimony in closing argument was improper). See also Commonwealth v. Howard, 469 Mass. 721, 738 (2014) (even when evidence of prior bad acts has been properly admitted, it is improper to cite that evidence in support of propensity-based argument in closing).

It is improper to argue that a witness should be believed because the witness appeared in court to testify. See Commonwealth v. Polk, 462 Mass. 23, 39 (2012). While a prosecutor may argue that a testifying defendant has an interest in the outcome of a case and this may affect his or her credibility, it is improper to argue that the testimony of the criminal defendant is inherently incredible simply because he or she is on trial. Commonwealth v. Niemic, 472 Mass. 665, 674–675 (2015). A prosecutor must proceed with great caution before suggesting that a child who is alleged to be the victim of a sexual assault could only have acquired knowledge of sexual acts from the experience of victimization. See Commonwealth v. Beaudry, 445 Mass. 577, 580, 581–582 (2005) (declining to assume that twelve-year-old child is unfamiliar with sexual acts and terminology, while noting that an argument that a child had age-inappropriate knowledge could be made if supported by expert witness testimony); Commonwealth v. Helberg, 73 Mass. App. Ct. 175, 179 (2008), quoting Commonwealth v. Fuller, 22 Mass. App. Ct. 152, 158 (1986) ("[A] prosecutor may not suggest that a child sexual abuse victim 'wouldn't have that kind of idea in her head unless something like that happened to her.'").

Disciplinary Authority. See Mass. R. Prof. C. 3.4(e) (2015), 3.8(i) (1999), 8.4(d) (2015); Private Reprimand No. 91–21, 7 Mass. Att'y Discipline Rep. 356 (1991) (among other issues, lawyer in administrative proceeding alluded in closing to matters ruled inadmissible); Admonition No. 05–04, 21 Mass. Att'y Discipline Rep. 671 (2005), at http://perma.cc/Y8R2-ZWEJ (among other issues, prosecutor referred in closing arguments to police reports excluded from evidence as hearsay); and Admonition No. 01–20, 17 Mass. Att'y Discipline Rep. 694 (2001), at http://perma.cc/R5FD-E5JX (prosecutor referred in closing argument to defendant's prior convictions, despite instructions from judge not to do so).

Use of Props. Counsel may not display objects not in evidence and should discuss any "plan to employ dramatic props with the judge during the pre-argument conference." Commonwealth v. Hoppin, 387 Mass. 25, 30–32 (1982).

Use of Chalks. A judge has "considerable, but not unrestrained, discretion as to the degree to which chalks can be used" to illustrate the evidence for the jury and to make use of such aids in closing argument (citation omitted). Commonwealth v. Walker, 10 Mass. App. Ct. 255, 264 (1980). See also Goldstein v. Gontarz, 364 Mass. 800, 814 (1974) ("Permission to use a blackboard as a graphic aid is discretionary with the trial judge.").

Collateral Sources. In general, information of "outside source" compensation is legally irrelevant and should not be referred to in the closing argument. See Goldstein v. Gontarz, 364 Mass. 800, 808–809 (1974). See also Commonwealth v. Murray, 22 Mass. App. Ct. 984, 985 (1986) (improper to suggest that victim of theft had recovered his loss because recovery would not diminish the crime).

Missing Witnesses. If the trial judge declines to give a missing witness instruction, counsel is not permitted to argue that an adverse inference should be drawn against the other side for not calling the witness. Commonwealth v. Saletino, 449 Mass. 657, 670–672 (2007). However, a party is permitted to argue consciousness of guilt or liability even without a jury instruction. Commonwealth v. Franklin, 465 Mass. 895, 915 (2013). See also Commonwealth v. Saletino, 449 Mass. at 671–672 (explaining that defense counsel is always permitted to argue that Commonwealth has not produced sufficient evidence to warrant conviction beyond a reasonable doubt).

Subsection (b)(3)(B). This subsection is derived from Commonwealth v. Kee, 449 Mass. 550, 560 (2007); See Commonwealth v. Lopes, 478 Mass. 593, 607 (2018) (prosecutor's characterizations of the defense argument as an "insult," "farce," and "distraction" were overly aggressive but did not require reversal, particularly in light of the judge's curative instruction); Warren v. Edgeco, Inc., 8 Mass. App. Ct. 171, 177 (1979). "The jury are presumed to recognize that the prosecutor is an advocate, not a witness." Commonwealth v. Mitchell, 428 Mass. 852, 856–857 (1999) (prosecutor's "use of phrases 'I think,' 'I suggest,' to preface some remarks did not, viewed in their proper context, imply that the prosecutor had personal knowledge or was stating a personal belief"). "Where credibility is at issue, it is certainly proper for counsel to argue from the evidence why a witness should be believed." Commonwealth v. Thomas, 401 Mass. 109, 116 (1987). A prosecutor may make a fair response to an attack on the credibility of a government witness. Commonwealth v. Chavis, 415 Mass. 703, 713 (1993). See also Commonwealth v. Brewer, 472 Mass. 307, 315 (2015) (prosecutor's statement that jury had "no reason to doubt" witness was a proper response to defense's assertion that witness was not credible). An argument that a witness had a motive to lie must be based on the evidence. Commonwealth v. Murchison, 418 Mass. 58, 61 (1994). Counsel should avoid phrases such as "I think," "I feel," and "I believe" because they express a personal opinion concerning the credibility of witnesses. See Commonwealth v. Finstein, 426 Mass. 200, 205 n.1 (1997). In contrast, repeated use of the pronoun "we" is troubling. See Commonwealth v. Burts, 68 Mass. App. Ct. 684, 688–689 (2007) ("We are troubled by the prosecutor's repeated use of the pronoun 'we,' which, when considered in light of the substance of some of those statements and phrases, conveyed, at least inferentially, the prosecutor's belief or opinion about either certain evidence or the credibility of certain witnesses.").

Disciplinary Authority. See Mass. R. Prof. C. 3.4(e) (2015), 3.8(i) (1999), 8.4(d) (2015); Matter of the Discipline of an Attorney, 2 Mass. Att'y Discipline Rep. 110, 112 (1980) (among other problems with closing argument, prosecutor said—as to defendant's testimony to the contrary—"believe me," no one in Chelsea is selling heroin at half price, and that "I would guess" the defendant supplemented his income by selling drugs); and Private Reprimand No. 91–21, 7 Mass. Att'y Discipline Rep. 356 (1991) (among other issues, lawyer in closing

argument in administrative proceeding presented his personal opinion on merits of case).

Improper Vouching. "Improper vouching occurs if 'an attorney expresses a personal belief in the credibility of a witness, or indicates that he or she has knowledge independent of the evidence before the jury.'" Commonwealth v. Ortega, 441 Mass. 170, 181 (2004), quoting Commonwealth v. Wilson, 427 Mass. 336, 352 (1998). Thus, argument based on an attorney's "own subjective assessment of the evidence is improper." Commonwealth v. Santiago, 425 Mass. 491, 498 (1997). See also Commonwealth v. Earltop, 372 Mass. 199, 203 (1977) (error for prosecutor to argue that he was "firmly convinced in [his] mind" of defendant's guilt). Cf. Commonwealth v. Kozec, 399 Mass. 514, 521 (1987) ("It is not improper to make a factually based argument that, due to the demeanor, disclosed circumstances, and appearance of a witness, a particular witness should be believed or disbelieved.").

Plea Agreements. Where a plea agreement requires a witness to give truthful testimony, the prosecutor must avoid any argument that the government has special knowledge or a method to determine the witness's veracity. See Commonwealth v. Marrero, 436 Mass. 488, 501 (2002) ("[A]lthough the prosecutor was free to encourage the jury to read the [plea and immunity] agreement (especially in light of the defendants' closing arguments to the jury that [the witness] was a 'pretty street smart' witness and one who 'got her deal' under which she 'ha[d] to testify a certain way'), he should not have stated that [the witness] 'tells the truth, at least that's as far as [he] could follow it'" [footnote omitted].); Commonwealth v. Ciampa, 406 Mass. 257, 265 (1989) ("A prosecutor in closing argument may restate the government's agreement with the witness and may argue reasonable inferences from the plea agreement's requirement of truthful testimony. If, however, a prosecutor goes beyond the terms and circumstances of the plea agreement and suggests that the government has special knowledge by which it can verify the witness's testimony, reversible error may occur." [Citations omitted.]).

Disciplinary Authority. See Mass. R. Prof. C. 3.4(e) (2015), 3.8(h), (i) (1999), 8.4(d) (2015); Matter of Nelson, 25 Mass. Att'y Discipline Rep. 413 (2009), at http://perma.cc/86SC–PSRJ (among other issues with closing argument, prosecutor improperly vouched for witnesses, claiming, as to one, to have verified witness's account by following his route to crime scene and, as to other, to have "looked at" witness and seen how he had turned his life around); and Matter of the Discipline of an Attorney, 2 Mass. Att'y Discipline Rep. 110 (1980) (among other problems with closing argument, prosecutor appeared to vouch for credibility of police witnesses).

Subsection (b)(3)(C). This subsection is derived from Commonwealth v. Kozec, 399 Mass. 514, 517 (1987); Commonwealth v. Smith, 387 Mass. 900, 909–910 (1983); Commonwealth v. Shelley, 374 Mass. 466, 470 (1978); London v. Bay State Ry. Co., 231 Mass. 480, 485–486 (1919); and Commonwealth v. Vazquez, 65 Mass. App. Ct. 305, 312 (2005).

It is permissible to argue relevant inferences from the evidence, even where the subject matter is potentially gruesome or inflammatory, but care must be given not to urge the jury to go beyond the proper use of such evidence and to make a decision based on improper considerations. See Commonwealth v. Raymond, 424 Mass. 382, 389–390 (1997) ("the gruesomeness of the crimes and the suffering of the victims were relevant to the issue whether the defendant's actions constituted extreme atrocity or cruelty"). See also Commonwealth v. Rutherford, 476 Mass. 639, 644 (2017) (improper to argue that defendant thought victim's life was worth $500 because defendant sold one of victim's television sets, among many stolen items, for $500); Commonwealth v. Cadet, 473 Mass. 173, 181 (2015) (while court emphasized that "the better practice is for the prosecutor, defense counsel, the judge, and all of the witnesses to refrain from describing the person killed as the 'victim,'" jury was likely not swayed by the use of the term). Contrast Commonwealth v. Niemic, 472 Mass. 665, 675 (2015) (emotional impact of victim's death on witnesses who saw it was not a proper matter for consideration by jury and it was improper to comment on it); Commonwealth v. Lodge, 431 Mass. 461, 470–471 (2000) (improper to argue that victim was "entitled to the right to live and [the defendant] took it"); Commonwealth v. Hamilton, 426 Mass. 67, 75 (1997) (comment that "there is no greater wrong that can be done to an individual than to deprive him of his very existence" improperly appealed to jurors' sympathies); Commonwealth v. Ward, 28 Mass. App. Ct. 292, 295 (1990) (repeated references to extent of urban crime and duty to aid law-abiding citizens was an improper appeal to emotions and fear of jury). It is improper to comment on the defendant's lack of remorse. Commonwealth v. Borodine, 371 Mass. 1, 9 (1976). "The nature of an appeal to sympathy is not so much a misstatement of evidence as an obfuscation of 'the clarity with which the jury would look at the evidence and encourage the jury to find guilt even if the evidence does not reach the level of proof beyond a reasonable doubt.'" Commonwealth v. Guy, 454 Mass. 440, 445 (2009), quoting Commonwealth v. Santiago, 425 Mass. 491, 501 (1997), cert. denied, 525 U.S. 1003 (1998). "Comments that appeal to emotions are ones that have the effect of engendering the jury's anger toward the defendant or his counsel so as to evoke an emotional rather than an intellectual response." Commonwealth v. Seng, 436 Mass. 537, 556 (2002). Words such as "brutally" and "viciously" may be used when they are apt descriptions of the evidence. Commonwealth v. Mejia, 463 Mass. 243, 254 (2012). See also Commonwealth v. Rock, 429 Mass. 609, 615 (1999) ("While the prosecutor may, in opening statement or summation, 'tell the jury something of the person whose life ha[s] been lost in order to humanize the proceedings,' the testimony of a relative may not be elicited for the sole purpose of creating sympathy" [citation omitted].).

Disciplinary Authority. See Mass. R. Prof. C. 8.4(d) (2015); Matter of Nelson, 25 Mass. Att'y Discipline Rep. 413 (2009), at http://perma.cc/86SC–PSRJ (among other problems with closing argument, prosecutor improperly implied to jury that they should avenge victim); and Admonition No. 01–03, 17 Mass. Att'y Discipline Rep. 659 (2001), at http://perma.cc/R5FD–E5JX (prosecutor made improper appeal to jury in closing argument for sympathy for victim).

Illustrations.

- Attacking Credibility. See Commonwealth v. Fernandes, 478 Mass. 725, 743 (2018) (prosecutor's use of rhetorical questions regarding motive to testify and credibility of witnesses in closing argument was not improper vouching); Commonwealth v. Bishop, 461 Mass. 586, 598 (2012) (expert's billing rate is admissible as evidence of bias, and the jury may be reminded that an expert was retained by the defendant; "[b]ut it is improper for a prosecutor to suggest that an expert witness's testimony was 'bought' by a defendant or to characterize the witness as a 'hired gun' where, as here, there was no evidence that he was paid more than his customary fee"); Commonwealth v. Kee, 449 Mass. 550, 560 (2007) (prosecutor's comments in closing argument about experience of police witnesses proper to show why those witnesses should be believed and did not amount to improper vouching); Commonwealth v. Obershaw, 435 Mass. 794, 807 (2002) (permissible to call defendant a liar where there "was substantial evidence that defendant had changed his story between his statements to the police and his testimony at trial and that his account at trial strained credulity); Commonwealth v. Olszewski, 401 Mass. 749, 760 (1988), cert. denied, 513 U.S. 835 (1994) (prosecutor is not permitted to use "police on trial" maxim); Commonwealth v. Clary, 388 Mass. 583, 592 (1983) ("prosecutor's insinuations regarding the defendant's sexual preference clearly were likely to instigate prejudice against her").

- Resort to Stereotypes. Both prosecutors and defense counsel should refrain from what is termed "broad brushing" or arguments based on racial, ethnic, or gender stereotypes. See Commonwealth v. Murchison, 35 Mass. App. Ct. 269, 275 (1993), and cases cited. See also Commonwealth v. Rosario, 430 Mass. 505, 515–516 (1999) (describing defendant as a "monster"); Commonwealth v. Saunders, 75 Mass. App. Ct. 505, 511–512 (2009) (describing defendant as "[s]wooping down like a vulture").

- No Motive to Lie. There is no per se rule against a prosecutor's comment that a witness has no motive to lie when it is based on the evidence and is understood as a retaliatory reply to a defense attack on the credibility of the witness. See Commonwealth v. Smith, 450 Mass. 395, 408 (2008); Commonwealth v. Helberg, 73 Mass. App. Ct. 175, 179 (2008). If defense counsel challenges the credibility of the alleged victim in his or her closing argument, the prosecutor may invite the jury to consider whether the witness has a motive to lie and may identify the evidence that demonstrates the accuracy and reliability of the witness's testimony. See Commonwealth v. Polk, 462 Mass. 23, 39–40 (2012). Compare Commonwealth v. Ramos, 73 Mass. App. Ct. 824, 826 (2009) ("prosecutor may not . . . suggest to the jury that a victim's testimony is entitled to greater credibility merely by virtue of her willingness to come into court to testify"), with Commonwealth v. Pina, 430 Mass. 266, 269 (1999) (where there is evidence of a witness's fear of testifying, "a prosecutor may argue that it took 'courage' or 'character' for a witness to testify").

- Reference to Damages. In a civil case, "[a]n argument concerning money damages indulging in significant references to numerical amounts that have no basis in the record is improper. Repeated, substantive discussions of hypothetical damages in other circumstances, and especially references to verdicts in other cases, are not proper." Harlow v. Chin, 405 Mass. 697, 704 (1989).

- Justice to the Victim. In Commonwealth v. Niemic, 472 Mass. 665 (2015), the Supreme Judicial Court addressed appealing to the jury for justice for the victim:

> "It is improper for a prosecutor to characterize a criminal trial as a dispute between a deceased victim on the one hand, and the defendant on the other, and to exhort the jury to dispense justice *evenly* between them. The deceased is not a party to th[e] case. A criminal trial places the interests of the Commonwealth and the defendant against one another. An argument that asks the jury to give justice to the victim is an improper appeal to sympathy for the victim."

Id. at 676, citing Commonwealth v. Drumgold, 423 Mass. 230, 253 (1996).

Subsection (b)(3)(D). This subsection is derived from Commonwealth v. Finstein, 426 Mass. 200, 205 n.1 (1997), where the court cautioned against so-called "Golden Rule" arguments in which jurors are asked to place themselves or a relative in the shoes of a party, witness, or victim, and against defense counsel asking jurors to put themselves or a relative in the shoes of the defendant. See also Commonwealth v. Bizanowicz, 459 Mass. 400, 420 (2011); Commonwealth v. Valentin, 420 Mass. 263, 274 (1995) ("The prosecutor's suggestion, in effect that the jurors put themselves in the shoes of the two witnesses, was poorly phrased, and the argument should not have been made.").

Subsection (b)(3)(E). This subsection is derived from Commonwealth v. Amirault, 404 Mass. 221, 240 (1989). See Doyle v. Ohio, 426 U.S. 610, 618–619 (1976) (defendant's post-Miranda silence cannot be used against him), and Griffin v. California, 380 U.S. 609, 615 (1965) (defendant's decision not to testify at trial cannot be used against him).

Misstatements of Law. For the rule that a party may not make misstatements of law, see Commonwealth v. Scesny, 472 Mass. 185, 202 (2015) (error for prosecutor to repeatedly characterize admitted defense evidence related to third-party defense as "irrelevant and immaterial 'information,' unworthy of even being called 'evidence'"); Commonwealth v. Bins, 465 Mass. 348, 367 (2013); Commonwealth v. Morales, 461 Mass. 765, 783 (2012) ("We agree with the defendant that the prosecutor erroneously misstated the law of deliberately premeditated murder during his closing argument by improperly suggesting that on that theory of murder only an intent to kill was required to be proved."); Commonwealth v. Weaver, 400 Mass. 612, 615–616 (1987) (error for prosecutor to argue that his duty was to present all the evidence and to assist jury to discover the truth, whereas function of defense counsel was to create doubts in minds of the jury); Commonwealth v. Killelea, 370 Mass. 638, 646 (1976) (misstatement of meaning of not guilty by reason of insanity); and Commonwealth v. Pagano, 47 Mass. App. Ct. 55, 62 (1999) (misstatement of presumption of innocence). In particular, a party should not attempt to define "reasonable doubt." Commonwealth v. Snow, 30 Mass. App. Ct. 443, 447 (1991).

Although a party may not misstate principles of law, the party must be allowed to "argue the law as applied to the evidence." Bloom v. Town Taxi, Inc., 336 Mass. 78, 80 (1957) (new trial required where judge refused to allow the plaintiffs to "argue the law as applied to the evidence"; refusal "impaired the right of the plaintiffs to have their cases fully presented to the jury").

Shifting the Burden of Proof. Counsel may not make any statement that shifts the burden of proof. Commonwealth v. Johnson, 463 Mass. 95, 112 (2012), quoting Commonwealth v. Amirault, 404 Mass. 221, 240 (1989) ("As a general rule, a 'prosecutor ... cannot make statements that shift the burden of proof from the Commonwealth to the defendant.'"). See Commonwealth v. Fernandes, 478 Mass. 725, 741–742 (2018) (no burden shifting where prosecutor argued in response to defense counsel's closing argument that the evidence presented was not a series of coincidences and prosecutor used rhetorical questions to suggest that the defendant's defense was implausible); Commonwealth v. Silva, 471 Mass. 610, 622–623 (2015) (permissible for prosecutor to state that "there is not a scintilla of evidence to support [the proposition that the defendant was merely present,]" because statement was "directed at the defendant's defense and not at the defendant's failure to testify"); Commonwealth v. Trinh, 458 Mass. 776, 787 (2011) (prosecutor engaged in burden shifting when he suggested that defendant had "an affirmative duty to bring forth evidence of his innocence, thereby lessening the Commonwealth's burden to prove every element of a crime"); Commonwealth v. Miranda, 458 Mass. 100, 117 (2010) ("To the extent that the [prosecutor's] remarks may have implied the unstated observation that ... the defendant left the balance of the Commonwealth's evidence from these witnesses uncontested, this indirect implication does not approach the sort of burden shifting that results from direct comment on a defendant's failure to contradict testimony"); Commonwealth v. Stewart, 454 Mass. 527, 539–540 (2009) (no burden shifting where prosecutor stated "[t]here may be no trace evidence that places [the defendant] there ... but there is nothing that excludes him from being there; that proves he wasn't there"); Commonwealth v. Montez, 450 Mass. 736, 747 (2008) ("The prosecutor's statement that defense counsel never addressed the evidence about ... incidents was not a comment on the defendant's failure to present evidence, and it did not impermissibly shift the burden of proof to the defendant"); Commonwealth v. Silanskas, 433 Mass. 678, 700 (2001) ("[T]he Commonwealth may not comment on the defendant's failure to produce evidence."); Commonwealth v. Feroli, 407 Mass. 405, 408–409 (1990) ("A prosecutor is entitled to emphasize the strong points of the Commonwealth's case and the weaknesses of the defendant's case, even though he may, in so doing, prompt some collateral or passing reflection on the fact that the defendant declined to testify."); Commonwealth v. Ayoub, 77 Mass. App. Ct. 563, 567 (2010) ("We do not conclude, as the defendant proposes, that these statements amounted to improper personal comment on the defendant's credibility and suggested that the defendant had failed to prove his innocence. Rather, they constitute commentary on the weakness of the defendant's case.").

Denigration of Constitutional Rights. A prosecutor may not ask the finder of fact to infer guilt based on the defendant's exercise of a constitutional right. See Commonwealth v. Cook, 419 Mass. 192, 203 (1994) (improper for prosecutor to argue that "jury should 'not be intimidated by the phrase "beyond a reasonable doubt"'"); Commonwealth v. Thomas, 401 Mass. 109, 113 (1987), quoting Commonwealth v. Smith, 387 Mass. 900, 903 (1983) ("We reiterate that '[l]awyers shall not and must not misstate principles of law nor may their summations infringe or denigrate constitutional rights.'"); Commonwealth v. Person, 400 Mass. 136, 141 (1987) (prosecutor may not ask jury to draw inference of guilt from defendant's exercise of right to advice of

counsel); Commonwealth v. Hanino, 82 Mass. App. Ct. 489, 498 (2012), quoting Commonwealth v. Haraldstad, 16 Mass. App. Ct. 565, 574 (1983) ("Although it would have been preferable had the prosecutor avoided the word 'rehearsed,' there is a qualitative difference between implying that it is improper for counsel to prepare a witness and 'casting doubt on testimony by calling attention to extraordinary parallels between what a group of witnesses who could talk to each other have said on the stand'" [citation omitted].); Commonwealth v. Hughes, 82 Mass. App. Ct. 21, 29–31 (2012) ("plain error" for prosecutor to suggest in "closing argument that the jury could conclude that the Commonwealth's case was strong, because the defendant chose to put on witnesses even though he had no obligation to do so"); Commonwealth v. Dodgson, 80 Mass. App. Ct. 307, 314 (2011) ("A prosecutor should generally avoid using the term 'rehearse' because it may impinge on the defendant's right to prepare for trial."); Commonwealth v. Youngworth, 55 Mass. App. Ct. 30, 39–40 (2002) (prosecutor's statements were "not reasonably construable as 'inferentially attack[ing] the defendant for asserting his right to trial' or 'calling on the jury to punish him for exercising that right'").

Uncontradicted or Uncontested Evidence. The Supreme Judicial Court has stated that

> "[r]eferences to material facts as uncontradicted or uncontested invariably approach the border of the forbidden territory of speculation regarding the absence of testimony by the defendant. 'A claim that certain evidence is uncontested should be made with caution and only after careful reflection concerning the specific circumstances in which the defendant could have produced contradictory evidence.'"

Commonwealth v. Buzzell, 53 Mass. App. Ct. 362, 366–367 (2001), quoting Commonwealth v. Hawley, 380 Mass. 70, 83–84 (1980). See also Commonwealth v. Wilson, 443 Mass. 122, 132 (2004); Commonwealth v. Borodine, 371 Mass. 1, 10 (1976), cert. denied, 429 U.S. 1049 (1977) (prosecutor's references to facts as "uncontested" were improper because the defendant was the only person who could contradict them).

Commenting on Criminal Defendant's Silence or Testimony. Except in rare circumstances, the prosecutor may not comment on the defendant's invocation of his or her right to silence. Thus, a prosecutor may not make any statement that is "reasonably susceptible" of being interpreted as a comment on a defendant's decision not to testify. Commonwealth v. Pena, 455 Mass. 1, 19 (2009); Commonwealth v. Botelho, 87 Mass. App. Ct. 846, 853 (2015). Compare Commonwealth v. Beneche, 458 Mass. 61, 75–76 (2010) (prosecutor should not have mentioned defendant's statement, "I don't want to talk about it," because "a defendant's statements about his desire not to speak with police may suggest to the jury that the defendant is guilty simply because he chose to exercise his constitutional right to silence"), and Commonwealth v. Brum, 438 Mass. 103, 121 (2003) ("It does not appear that there was any need to resort to the defendant's invocation of his right to remain silent as a method of explaining any abrupt end to either interview, or any other permissible basis for admitting evidence of the defendant's refusal to answer further questions."), with Commonwealth v. Torres, 442 Mass. 554, 578 (2004) ("[W]e have recognized that, in some rare circumstances, a defendant's invocation of his right to remain silent may be presented to the jury in order to avoid juror confusion about why an interview ended abruptly"), and cases cited; Commonwealth v. Caputo, 439 Mass. 153, 166 (2003) ("prosecutor's reference in his closing statement to the defendant's invocation of his right to remain silent was permissible" because "defense counsel elicited [invocation], and because in his closing argument the prosecutor referred to the statement solely to challenge the defendant's claim of coercion"); and Commonwealth v. Martinez, 431 Mass. 168, 183 (2000) (although errors and prosecutorial misconduct occurred, considered individually and collectively, errors did not create substantial likelihood of miscarriage of justice).

A prosecutor's comments on "omissions" in the defendant's statement to the police following the defendant's receipt of Miranda warnings are not improper comments on the defendant's silence. See Commonwealth v. Lodge, 89 Mass. App. Ct. 415, 419 (2016).

In Commonwealth v. McCray, 40 Mass. App. Ct. 936, 937 (1996), the Appeals Court found that the Commonwealth properly conceded that the "prosecutor erred when he argued that the defendant had 'the benefit of [the complainant's] testimony over the course of the two days' and 'was able to conform her story with that.'" The Supreme Judicial Court has since explained that such comments are not necessarily improper. See Commonwealth v. Gaudette, 441 Mass. 762, 767 (2004) ("[A] prosecutor may, if there is a basis in the evidence introduced at trial, attack the credibility of a defendant on the ground that his testimony has been shaped or changed in response to listening to the testimony of other witnesses."). See also Commonwealth v. Mendez, 476 Mass. 512, 521–522 (2017) (prosecutor permissibly argued that defendant conformed his trial testimony to Commonwealth's evidence at trial when his initial statement to police officers on night of incident was different from his testimony at trial). The propriety of such a comment may depend on whether the defendant made a pretrial statement to police. See Commonwealth v. Person, 400 Mass. 136, 138–143 (1987) (prosecutor impermissibly commented on defendant's right to remain silent when he stated that the defendant, who had not made a statement prior to trial, sat through prosecutor's presentation at trial and fabricated a story that countered prosecution's theory of case).

Prearrest Silence. "[I]mpeachment of a defendant with the fact of his pre-arrest silence should be approached with caution, and, whenever it is undertaken, it should be prefaced by a proper demonstration that it was 'natural' to expect the defendant to speak in the circumstances"; "the use of [pretrial silence] for impeachment purposes cannot be justified in the absence of unusual circumstances." Commonwealth v. Nickerson, 386 Mass. 54, 62 & n.6 (1982). Compare Commonwealth v. Womack, 457 Mass. 268, 277–278 (2010) ("The defendant's silence in response to [the lieutenant's] query into his reason for standing outside the store for two seconds without entering was not an exercise of his right to remain silent, but a failure to respond to a particular question. As such it was admissible in evidence, and subject to comment" [citation omitted].), and Commonwealth v. Thompson, 431 Mass. 108, 118 (2000) ("[T]he prosecutor here did not comment on the defendant's failure to proclaim his innocence, but rather on his failure to ask appropriate questions that an innocent party would ordinarily ask. The defendant did not invoke at any time his right to stop the questioning and be silent. Instead, the defendant agreed to give a far-ranging statement over several hours. It was therefore proper for the prosecutor to comment on the fact that the defendant did not ask appropriate questions."), with Commonwealth v. Gardner, 479 Mass. 764, 772 (2018) (despite the fact that self-defense was asserted four days after the arrest, the prosecutor's reference to the defendant's prearrest silence was improper), and Commonwealth v. Haas, 373 Mass. 545, 558–559 (1977) (prosecutor's comments, asking jury to infer guilt from fact that defendant had not spontaneously volunteered his innocence during interrogation by police, were improper).

Statements Concerning the Role of the Jury. A prosecutor may not make any comment that could be interpreted to suggest that jurors have a duty to convict. Commonwealth v. Miller, 457 Mass. 69, 79–80 (2010); Commonwealth v. Francis, 450 Mass. 132, 140 (2007). Neither party may suggest that jurors may need to explain the verdict. Commonwealth v. Quinn, 61 Mass. App. Ct. 332, 334–335 (2004). "It [is] also inappropriate for the prosecutor to tell the jurors that they [are] the 'conscience of the community.' They bear no such burden; their role in a trial is limited to finding the facts on the basis of the evidence dispassionately and impartially." Commonwealth v. Mathews, 31 Mass. App. Ct. 564, 573 (1991), cert. denied sub nom. Mathews v. Rakiey, 504 U.S. 922 (1992). See also Commonwealth v. Scesny, 472 Mass. 185, 200 (2015) ("prosecutor's characterization of his role as representing the 'citizens' ran the risk of suggesting that the prosecutor was representing the jurors-as-citizens against the defendant, and in that way misrepresenting or at least confusing the jurors'

actual role as neutral fact finders"). A party should not discuss the consequences of a verdict with jury. See Commonwealth v. Duguay, 430 Mass. 397, 404 (1999) ("clearly error for the prosecutor to address the issue of punishment" with the jury); Commonwealth v. Ruddock, 428 Mass. 288, 292–293 (1998) ("Of course, a prosecutor should not argue to the jury that, if found not guilty by reason of insanity, a defendant will be released."). Finally, while jurors may be encouraged to examine the physical evidence, it is improper to suggest that they should conduct outside experiments or investigation. See Commonwealth v. Beauchamp, 424 Mass. 682, 691 (1997) ("the prosecutor should not encourage the jury to conduct experiments or to obtain outside information of any sort").

Disciplinary Authority. See Mass. R. Prof. C. 8.4(d) (2015) and Admonition No. 05–04, 21 Mass. Att'y Discipline Rep. 671 (2005), at http://perma.cc/Y8R2-ZWEJ (among other issues, prosecutor, without court authorization, improperly commented during closing on defendant's failure to call a witness).

Prosecutor's Comment on Defendant's Courtroom Appearance or Conduct. The appearance and demeanor of a person in a courtroom is evidence even if the person does not take the stand. See Commonwealth v. Roderick, 411 Mass. 817, 819 (1992) (mentally retarded victim who did not testify); Commonwealth v. Smith, 387 Mass. 900, 907 (1983) (defendant who did not testify); Commonwealth v. Houghton, 39 Mass. App. Ct. 94, 100 (1995) (victim who did testify). In a criminal case, "a prosecutorial argument that the jury should draw inferences against a defendant who did nothing but behave properly in the courtroom is improper." Commonwealth v. Young, 399 Mass. 527, 531 (1987) (reversal based on this improper comment by prosecutor: "Did you notice how he just sits there stone-faced, cool, never blinks an eye, doesn't get upset about anything? He's very in control. He doesn't show his emotions when he doesn't want to, does he?"); Commonwealth v. Kozec, 399 Mass. 514, 523 (1987) (unfair and improper for prosecutor to comment that "the defendant looked sorry when the victim testified because she knew the truth about what happened between them would come out"). See also Commonwealth v. Valliere, 366 Mass. 479, 494–495 (1974) (improper for prosecutor to suggest that defendant demonstrates consciousness of guilt by reading transcripts or suggesting questions to counsel). Contrast Commonwealth v. Cohen, 412 Mass. 375, 385–386 (1992); Commonwealth v. Pina, 406 Mass. 540, 548 (1998) (where evidence showed that defendant changed his hairstyle and shaved his mustache soon after crime, proper for prosecutor to pose argument during closing about why a person would do that); Commonwealth v. Smith, 387 Mass. 900, 907 (1983) (prosecutor's comments about defendant's demeanor during trial, including that he was "smirking," "laughing," and "squirming," were permissible where jury was entitled to observe demeanor of defendant and prosecutor did not suggest he had knowledge that jury did not share); Commonwealth v. Rogers, 43 Mass. App. Ct. 782, 787 (1997) (proper to refer to defendant's size in comparison to size of victim).

Use of Rhetorical Questions. Rhetorical questions are not per se impermissible. See Commonwealth v. Grant, 418 Mass. 76, 83 (1994), quoting Commonwealth v. Smallwood, 379 Mass. 878, 892 (1980) (It is "well settled that a prosecutor may ask the jury rhetorical questions that touch on the defendant's constitutional right to not incriminate himself without violating that right provided the questions are not 'of such a nature that a jury would naturally and necessarily construe them to be directed to the failure of the defendant to testify.'"); Commonwealth v. Habarek, 402 Mass. 105, 111 (1988) (no error in prosecutor asking rhetorically and in reference to motive, "Why? Why does a person do that?"); Commonwealth v. Lawton, 82 Mass. App. Ct. 528, 541–542 (2012); Commonwealth v. Flint, 81 Mass. App. Ct. 794, 807 (2012) ("In the face of ... direct assertions of evidence of improper motives underlying the victim's accusations, it was fair for the prosecutor to reply by asking the jury rhetorically, 'Why would a person make up something like this? What is the motive to fabricate? Are they being honest? Are they responsive to questions? Are they being direct? Do they appear to be forthcoming? Do they appear to be genuine? Do they sound as if they are giving contrived answers?"). See also Commonwealth v. Nelson, 468 Mass. 1, 12–13 (2014) (rhetorical question did not shift burden of proof to defendant).

Subsection (b)(3)(F). This subsection is derived from Fyffe v. Massachusetts Bay Transp. Auth., 86 Mass. App. Ct. 457, 478 (2014). "Jury nullification is inconsistent with a jury's duty to return a guilty verdict of the highest crime proved beyond a reasonable doubt." Commonwealth v. Kirwan, 448 Mass. 304, 319 (2007). See Commonwealth v. Fernette, 398 Mass. 658, 670–671 n.23 (1986) ("We recognize that jurors may return verdicts which do not comport with the judge's instructions. We do not accept the premise that jurors have a right to nullify the law on which they are instructed by the judge, or that the judge must inform them of their power."). Counsel should avoid any reference to the appellate process. Commonwealth v. Finstein, 426 Mass. 200, 205 n.1 (1997).

Subsection (c). This subsection is derived from Commonwealth v. Johnson, 374 Mass. 453, 458 (1978) (objection to closing argument not made until close of judge's final instructions is ordinarily not timely to preserve issue for appellate review), and Commonwealth v. Beaudry, 445 Mass. 577, 587 (2005) (timely objection to an improper closing argument followed by "focused, particularized [curative] instructions" is not sufficient to preserve for appeal the issue of adequacy of the instructions to cure the improper argument where defense counsel acquiesced in the curative instruction). See Harlow v. Chin, 405 Mass. 697, 706 (1989) (if judge fails to cure alleged error, counsel must bring judge's attention to alleged errors and omissions at end of charge).

Subsection (d). This subsection is derived from Commonwealth v. Witschi, 301 Mass. 459, 462 (1938); O'Neill v. Ross, 250 Mass. 92, 96–97 (1924); Posell v. Herscovitz, 237 Mass. 513, 514–515 (1921); and Commonwealth v. Truong, 34 Mass. App. Ct. 668, 671 (1993). The judge is "the directing and controlling mind at the trial, and not a mere functionary to preserve order and lend ceremonial dignity to the proceedings." Whitney v. Wellesley & Boston St. Ry. Co., 197 Mass. 495, 502 (1908). See also Beit v. Probate & Family Ct. Dep't, 385 Mass. 854, 859 (1982); Sussman v. Commonwealth, 374 Mass. 692, 697 (1978). In discussing the duty of the judge in the circumstances of Commonwealth v. Cabot, the Supreme Judicial Court stated as follows:

"It was the duty of the judge to emphasize the fact that the argument [by the prosecutor] had been grossly improper, to point out in plain, unmistakable language the particulars in which it was unwarranted and to instruct the jury to cast aside in their deliberations the improper considerations that had been presented to them, using such clear and cogent language as would correct the obviously harmful effect of the argument."

Commonwealth v. Cabot, 241 Mass. 131, 150–151 (1922). See also Commonwealth v. Pearce, 427 Mass. 642, 646 (1998) (trial judges have authority to interrupt "any argument" not "based solely on the evidence and all inferences therefrom"); Rolanti v. Boston Edison Corp., 33 Mass. App. Ct. 516, 529 (1992) ("It is well established under our practice that a trial judge must take 'rigorous and emphatic action' to counteract prejudicial statements made in front of the jury."). A judge has "considerable latitude" in the "choice of methods" to correct improper argument. Commonwealth v. Watson, 377 Mass. 814, 823 (1979), quoting Commonwealth v. Clark, 3 Mass. App. Ct. 481, 488 (1975). See Commonwealth v. Montecalvo, 367 Mass. 46, 56 (1975) (judge may guard against improper arguments by stopping counsel, instructing jury to disregard such an argument, or by combining both methods).

Responses to Improper Argument. For examples of proper responses to improper argument, see Rivera v. Club Caravan, Inc., 77 Mass. App. Ct. 17, 21 (2010) (trial judge was appropriately specific and forceful in instructing jury to disregard reference in opening statement to blood alcohol level that would not be admitted in evidence); Salter v. Leventhal, 337 Mass. 679, 698 (1958); and Hart v. Morris & Co., 259 Mass. 211, 215 (1927). A judge may not limit closing

arguments to the line of thought that the judge believes will prevail or is most consistent with the evidence. O'Driscoll v. Lynn & Boston R.R., 180 Mass. 187, 190 (1902). See also Gath v. M/A–Com, Inc., 440 Mass. 482, 495 (2003) (judge's instruction sufficient to correct improper argument on damages); Commonwealth v. Cutty, 47 Mass. App. Ct. 671, 675–676 (1999) (judge must not prevent party from making relevant arguments that are based on evidence and fair inferences from evidence).

"[A] judge need take no vow of silence. He is there to see that justice is done, or at least to see that the jury have a fair chance to do justice ... The judge ought not to let the jury be diverted from the real issue. The skill of counsel must not be allowed to mislead the jury by raising false issues or by appeals to emotion and prejudice ... It is not always easy for a judge to see his duty clearly. But a first-rate trial judge will find and tread the narrow path that lies between meddlesomeness on the one hand and ineffectiveness and impotence on the other."

Commonwealth v. Brown, 462 Mass. 620, 632 (2012), quoting Commonwealth v. Haley, 363 Mass. 513, 519 (1973).

Preventative Measures. There are several practical steps that judges may take to minimize the risk of error in closing arguments. One practice is to conduct a pre-closing argument conference to address the boundary lines of proper argument and any questions counsel may have. Commonwealth v. Finstein, 426 Mass. 200, 205 n.1 (1997). A judge also may wish to give a cautionary instruction to the jury before closing argument. See Commonwealth v. Olmande, 84 Mass. App. Ct. 231, 239–243 (2013) (Agnes, J., concurring).

Section 1114. Restitution

(a) Nature and Extent of Remedy. Restitution is a judicially determined penalty in the form of money or services imposed against the defendant in a criminal case or a juvenile in a delinquency case for the benefit of the victim of a crime. A judge may order restitution as a condition of probation provided that the judge finds, or the parties, in consultation with the probation department, agree, that (1) the victim has suffered economic loss that is causally related to the defendant's criminal conduct, (2) the award does not exceed the victim's economic loss, and (3) the defendant has the ability to pay the money or perform the services.

(b) Procedural Requirements. The defendant has the right to counsel and the right to be heard at a restitution hearing. Cross-examination of the victim is limited to the issue of restitution and does not extend to matters concerning guilt or innocence. Hearsay is admissible, but an award of restitution cannot rest entirely on unsubstantiated and unreliable hearsay. The Commonwealth has the burden of proving both a causal connection between the crime and the victim's economic loss and the amount of the loss by a preponderance of the evidence.

(c) Judicial Determination. The amount of restitution ordered by the court must be based on evidence presented to the court or on a stipulation by the parties. The judge must determine (1) the amount of actual economic loss proved, (2) the appropriate length of the probation period, and (3) the defendant's maximum monthly ability to pay. The defendant bears the burden of proving an inability to pay.

NOTE

Subsection (a). This subsection is derived from Commonwealth v. Henry, 475 Mass. 117 (2016); Commonwealth v. Denehy, 466 Mass. 723 (2014); Commonwealth v. McIntyre, 436 Mass. 829 (2002); Commonwealth v. Malick, 86 Mass. App. Ct. 174 (2014); and Commonwealth v. Avram A., 83 Mass. App. Ct. 208 (2013). See also G. L. c. 258B, § 1 (defining restitution as "money or services which a court orders a defendant to pay or render to a victim as part of the disposition"). Restitution is an "entirely judicially determined penalty" that is separate and distinct from "punishments such as imprisonment and fines that are accompanied by statutory prescriptions." Commonwealth v. Denehy, 466 Mass. at 737. There is no right to trial by jury in connection with an order for restitution. Commonwealth v. Nawn, 394 Mass. 1, 8–9 (1985).

In Commonwealth v. McIntyre, the court explained that to establish a nexus between the defendant's criminal conduct and the victim's loss, the Commonwealth must prove that the "loss . . . is causally connected to the offense and bears a significant relationship to the offense . . . [W]e look to the underlying facts of the charged offense, not the name of the crime [of which the defendant was convicted or] to which the defendant entered a plea." Commonwealth v. McIntyre, 436 Mass. at 835. The court's power to award restitution in criminal cases is "unquestionable" and derives from a judge's power to order conditions of probation under G. L. c. 276, §§ 87 and 87A, and G. L. c. 279, § 1. Commonwealth v. Denehy, 466 Mass. at 737. In Denehy, the Supreme Judicial Court rejected the argument that the constitutional principle that requires that certain factual determinations relating to sentencing must be found by a jury beyond a reasonable doubt does not apply to an award of restitution. Id. at 737–738. Restitution may not be ordered to reward anyone or to create an incentive for the dismissal of criminal charges. Commonwealth v. Rotonda, 434 Mass. 211, 221 (2001). Cf. G. L. c. 276, § 55 (accord and satisfaction). Restitution may be ordered as a condition of probation in the case of a conviction or a continuance without a finding. Commonwealth v. Rotonda, 434 Mass. at 221–222. An order of restitution is distinct from an order that the defendant pay the costs of the prosecution. See G. L. c. 280, § 6 (all such payments go to the Commonwealth not the victim). It is not necessary that the victim of a crime file a claim with an insurer to be eligible for restitution. Commonwealth v. Williams, 57 Mass. App. Ct. 917 (2003) (rescript).

The nexus between the defendant's criminal conduct and the economic loss suffered by the victim does not require proof of every element of each crime with which the defendant is charged. Instead, the Commonwealth must establish "a significant causal relationship" between the facts admitted by the defendant or that form the basis of the crimes of which he or she is convicted and the economic losses suffered by the victim. See Commonwealth v. Denehy, 466 Mass. at 723 (There was a sufficient nexus between the defendant's conviction for assault by means of a dangerous weapon and disorderly conduct and damage to the eyeglasses of the police officer attacked by the defendant even though the defendant was found not guilty of the charge of assault and battery on a police officer.); Commonwealth v. McIntyre, 436 Mass. at 835 (There was a sufficient causal relationship between damage to the victim's automobile and the defendant's conviction for stabbing the victim because, after the stabbing, the defendant returned to the scene and set his dog on the victim; eventually, as the victim retreated to his car to avoid the ongoing assault, the defendant kicked the victim's car door and fender.); Commonwealth v. Palmer P., 61 Mass. App. Ct. 230, 232 (2004) (Although the juvenile was found not delinquent of larceny, the facts related to the delinquency finding on the charge of breaking and entering during the daytime with intent to commit a felony was sufficient to support an order for restitution to the victim in the amount of $1,000 for the loss of his personal property.). But see Commonwealth v. Casanova, 65 Mass. App. Ct. 750, 750 (2006) (The evidence was not sufficient to establish a causal relationship between the victim's injuries as a result of being struck in the face and stomach by the defendant and the victim's decision one month later to withdraw from college, which caused him to incur a loss of $8,046 in tuition he had paid, although the court indicated that medical expenses, court-related travel expenses, property loss and damage, lost pay, and lost vacation days required to be used to attend court might be compensable as restitution.).

The Commonwealth must prove that the defendant's criminal conduct is the cause in fact of the victim's economic loss, and that such loss was a reasonably foreseeable consequence of the defendant's conduct. Negligent acts of the victim or a third party that occur after the defendant's criminal conduct do not necessarily break the causal connection between the defendant's criminal conduct and the victim's economic loss underlying an order of restitution. Commonwealth v. Buckley, 90 Mass. App. Ct. 177, 184 (2016) (due to miscommunication, victim was not notified for several months that police had recovered his vehicle and in interim had purchased replacement vehicle; negligence by third party did not break causal connection).

In Commonwealth v. Avram A., 83 Mass. App. Ct. 208 (2013), an order to pay restitution in the amount of $1,063.78 against a twelve-year-old juvenile who had admitted to sufficient facts for a delinquency finding was upheld, along with an order extending the juvenile's probation as a sanction for nonpayment of the restitution. The public policy of the Commonwealth favors the award of restitution to victims of crime "to the greatest extent possible." G. L. c. 258B, § 3. "There is no question that restitution is an appropriate consideration in a criminal sentencing." Commonwealth v. Nawn, 394 Mass. 1, 6 (1985), citing Novelty Bias Binding Co. v. Shevrin, 342 Mass. 714, 717 (1961). See also G. L. c. 276, § 92A (providing that upon conviction of any one of enumerated offenses, defendant is required to pay restitution "for any financial loss sustained by the victim of his crime, his dependents or an insurer").

Subsection (b). This subsection is derived from Commonwealth v. Denehy, 466 Mass. 723 (2014); Commonwealth v. Nawn, 394 Mass. 1, 6–8 (1985); and Commonwealth v. Casanova, 65 Mass. App. Ct. 750, 755–756 (2006). See Commonwealth v. Avram A., 83 Mass. App. Ct. 208 (2013) (in case involving two incidents of tagging, upholding restitution order based in part on estimates of cost of repairs made by examining photographs of damage); Commonwealth v. Williams, 57 Mass. App. Ct. 917 (2003) (rescript) (repair cost estimates by various vendors for damage to glass in building and vehicle rather than actual costs for repairs was sufficient to support award of restitution). The victim has the right to assistance from the prosecutor in documenting and obtaining restitution. See G. L. c. 258B, § 3(e). The prosecutor may offer testimony from the victim and expert witness testimony.

There is no right to a trial by jury in connection with an order for restitution. Commonwealth v. Nawn, 394 Mass. at 8–9.

Strict evidentiary rules are not imposed at a restitution hearing. Commonwealth v. Molina, 476 Mass. 388, 407 (2017). The defendant has a presumptive right to call witnesses, but the trial judge has the discretionary authority not to require a victim to testify, and to preclude the defendant from calling the victim as a witness, if the judge determines that the interest of insulating the victim from further trauma overcomes the defendant's presumptive right to call the victim.

"In particular, in determining whether the countervailing interests overcome the presumption after considering the totality of the circumstances, the judge conducting a restitution hearing should consider whether, based on an individualized assessment of the proposed witness, there is an unacceptable risk that the witness's physical, psychological, or emotional health would be significantly jeopardized if the witness were required to testify in court at the probation hearing."

Id. at 407–408.

Subsection (c). This subsection is derived from Commonwealth v. Henry, 475 Mass. 117 (2016). The Commonwealth bears the burden of proving that the victim's actual economic loss is causally connected to defendant's crime by a preponderance of the evidence. Id. at 121. The length of probation supervision imposed at the time of the sentence should not be based on the financial ability of the defendant but on the amount that will serve the dual goals of rehabilitation and protection of the public. Id. at 125. If the only basis for imposing probation is to collect restitution, the period of probation may be only for a brief period of time, thirty or sixty days. Id. at 125 n.8. Factors to be considered in determining the defendant's ability to pay are the financial resources of the defendant, including income and net assets, and defendant's financial obligations such as food, shelter, and clothing for the defendant and any dependents. Id. at 126. A payment order made as a condition of probation may not "cause a defendant a substantial financial hardship." Id. at 127. Restitution as a condition of probation is established at the monthly amount the defendant is able to pay multiplied by the number of months of probation, but no more than the actual economic loss. Id. at 125. Where the victim is a retailer, economic loss is based on the wholesale, not retail, price, unless the Commonwealth proves the items "would have been sold were they not stolen." Id. at 129.

Probation can be revoked or extended only upon a finding that the failure to pay the restitution amount was willful and that there was an ability to pay. Id. at 121. There can be no finding of a willful failure to pay where payment would cause substantial financial hardship to the defendant or his or her dependents. Commonwealth v. Bruno-O'Leary, 94 Mass. App. Ct. 44, 48 (2018). The probationer bears the burden of proof with respect to his or her inability to pay as a defense in probation violation proceedings. Id. at 49.

Refund if Conviction Is Invalidated. Where a conviction has been invalidated and it is determined that the case will not or cannot be retried, due process requires a refund of restitution payments (as well as certain other payments) made by the defendant. Commonwealth v. Martinez, 480 Mass. 777, 785 (2018), citing Nelson v. Colorado, 137 S. Ct. 1249 (2017). Because the only restitution ordered in Martinez was paid to a police department and refunded to the defendant, the Supreme Judicial Court expressly postponed deciding whether Nelson requires the Commonwealth to refund restitution paid by the defendant to a private victim.

Section 1115.　Evidentiary Issues in Care and Protection, Child Custody, and Termination of Parental Rights Cases

(a) General Rule. Evidence in child custody and child protective cases, both parental unfitness and termination of parental rights (TPR) proceedings, is admissible according to the rules of the common law and the Massachusetts General Laws.

(b) Official/Public Records and Reports.

(1) Probation Records, Including Criminal Activity Record Information (CARI). Adult probation records, including CARI, are official records that are admissible as evidence of a parent's character. Juvenile delinquency probation records are inadmissible in care and protection cases by operation of statute.

(2) Department of Children and Families (DCF) Records and Reports.

(A) G. L. c. 119, § 51A, Reports. Section 51A reports are admissible for the limited purpose of setting the stage.

(B) G. L. c. 119, § 51B, Investigation Reports. Primary facts contained in Section 51B investigations are admissible. Statements of opinion, conclusions, and judgment contained in these reports are not admissible.

(C) DCF Action Plans, Affidavits, Foster Care Review Reports, Case Review Reports, Family Assessments, and Dictation Notes. Primary facts contained in these DCF records are admissible as official records. Assessments prepared by private entities under contract with the DCF also are admissible as official records.

Statements of opinion, conclusions, and judgment contained in these reports are not admissible.

(3) Drug and Alcohol Treatment Records. Drug and alcohol treatment records are confidential under State and Federal law. Such records may, however, be released to the parties by judicial order after application showing good cause therefor, including the need to avert a substantial risk of death or serious bodily harm, which specifically includes incidents of suspected child abuse and neglect.

(4) School Records. School records generally are admissible as official records, with the exception of records of clinical history and evaluations of students with special needs.

(5) Police Reports. Police reports regarding police responses are admissible as business records insofar as the report is a record of the police officers' firsthand observations. Opinions and evaluations are not admissible. Hearsay statements within the report generally are not admissible unless the statement satisfies another hearsay exception.

(c) Written Court Reports.

(1) Court Investigation Reports. Written reports of court-appointed investigators are admissible.

(2) Guardian Ad Litem (GAL) Reports. Written guardian ad litem reports may properly be admitted into evidence and are entitled to such weight as the court sees fit to give them.

(3) Court–Appointed Special Advocate (CASA) Reports. Written CASA reports may properly be admitted into evidence and are entitled to such weight as the court sees fit to give them.

(4) Court–Ordered Psychiatric, Psychological, and Court Clinic Evaluation Reports. Written psychiatric, psychological, and Court Clinic evaluation reports generally are not admissible in evidence.

(d) Children's Out–of–Court Statements.

(1) Statements Not Related to Sexual Abuse. Out–of–court statements made by children that are not related to sexual abuse are admissible if they fall within an established exception to the hearsay rule or are offered for a nonhearsay purpose.

(2) Statements Related to Sexual Abuse.

(A) Cases Involving TPR. An out-of-court statement of a child under the age of ten describing any act of sexual contact performed on or with the child, the circumstances under which it occurred, or the identity of the perpetrator offered in a TPR trial is admissible, provided that the statement is offered as evidence of a material fact and is more probative on the point for which it is offered than any other evidence that the proponent can procure through reasonable efforts, that the person to whom the statement was made or who heard the child make the statement testifies, that the court finds that the child is "unavailable" as a witness, and that the court finds the statement to be reliable.

(B) Custody Proceedings Not Involving TPR. In care and protection cases and other child custody proceedings that do not involve termination of parental rights, a child's hearsay statement that describes any act of sexual contact performed on or with the child or the circumstances under which it occurred, or that identifies the perpetrator, is admissible, provided that the person to whom the statement was made or who heard the statement testifies, that the judge finds that the statement is offered as evidence of a material fact and is more probative on the point for which it is offered than any other evidence that the proponent can procure through reasonable effort, and that the judge finds the statement to be reliable.

(e) Testimony.

(1) Children. Children may testify in care and protection and TPR proceedings if the court determines, after consultation with the child's attorney, that the child is competent and willing to do so. Children may testify in child custody proceedings in Probate and Family Court at the discretion of the judge.

(2) Foster/Preadoptive Parents. Foster parents and preadoptive parents have the right to attend care and protection trials and to be heard, subject to the usual evidentiary rules, but are not parties to care and protection or TPR proceedings.

(3) Parents Called by Adverse Party. A parent may be called as a witness by an opposing party. An adverse party who calls the parent as a witness may question the parent witness according to the rules of cross-examination.

(4) Social Workers. A licensed social worker or social worker employed by a government agency may be called as a witness by any party. An adverse party who calls the social worker may question the social worker according to the rules of cross-examination. Regarding communications between a social worker and a client that are privileged under State law, the social worker may testify to any such communication that bears significantly on the client's ability to provide suitable care or custody if the court first determines (1) that the social worker has such evidence, (2) that it is more important to the welfare of the child that the communication be disclosed than that the social worker-client relationship be preserved, and, if a TPR case, (3) that the patient has been informed that any such disclosure would not be privileged.

(5) Psychotherapists. Psychotherapists may be called as witnesses in care and protection and TPR proceedings regarding disclosures by a patient that bear significantly on the patient's ability to provide suitable care and custody if the patient attempts to exercise the privilege at trial and the court then determines (1) that the psychotherapist has such evidence, (2) that it is more important to the welfare of the child that the information be disclosed than that the psychotherapist-patient relationship be preserved, and, if a TPR case, (3) that the patient has been informed that any such disclosure would not be privileged.

(6) Court–Appointed Investigators and G. L. c. 119, § 51B, Investigators. Court–appointed investigators appointed pursuant to G. L. c. 119, § 24, and investigators assigned to investigate G. L. c. 119, § 51A, reports pursuant to G. L. c. 119, § 51B, may be called as witnesses by any party for examination regarding the information contained in any such investigation report.

(7) Experts. Opinion testimony by persons qualified by the court as experts is admissible if it is based on scientific, technical, or specialized knowledge that will assist the trier of fact to understand the evidence or to determine a fact at issue.

(f) Other Evidence.

(1) Adoption Plans. Adoption plans prepared by the DCF are admissible.

(2) Bonding and Attachment Studies. Written reports of bonding and attachment studies are inadmissible. Evidence relevant to any such bonding and attachment study may be the subject of testimony from the evaluator.

(3) Judicial Findings from Prior Proceedings. Judicial findings from prior proceedings may be admissible if the findings are relevant, timely, and material.

(g) Adverse Inference from a Party's Failure to Appear. The court may draw an adverse inference against a party who has received notice and fails to appear, without good cause, at trial, as long as a case adverse to the nontestifying party has been presented.

NOTE

Subsection (a). This subsection is derived from G. L. c. 119, § 21A. Cross–Reference: Section 103, Rulings on Evidence, Objections, and Offers of Proof.

Subsection (b). This subsection is derived from Commonwealth v. Slavski, 245 Mass. 405, 415 (1923).

Subsection (b)(1). This subsection is derived from Adoption of Irwin, 28 Mass. App. Ct. 41, 43 (1989), and G. L. c. 276, § 100. Probation records, including CARI, are records of the court system and are by statute available for use by the courts of the Commonwealth. Adoption of Irwin, 28 Mass. App. Ct. at 43. It is unnecessary to qualify probation records as business records because they are admissible as official records. Id. While not necessarily conclusive, a parent's criminal record, as well as observations of his or her criminal conduct, are relevant as to the issue of parental fitness. Care & Protection of Frank, 409 Mass. 492, 495 (1991). "An adjudication of any child as a delinquent child ... or any disposition thereunder ... shall not be received in evidence or used against such child for any purpose in any proceedings in any court except in subsequent delinquency or criminal proceedings against the same person." G. L. c. 119, § 60.

Cross–Reference: Note to Section 405(b), Methods of Proving Character: By Specific Instances of Conduct.

Subsection (b)(2)(A). A "Section 51A report" is a report filed with the DCF that "details suspected child abuse or neglect." G. L. c. 119, § 21. Such reports are admissible to "set the stage," i.e., to explain the reasons for the filing of the petition. Care & Protection of Inga, 36 Mass. App. Ct. 660, 663–664 (1994), quoting Custody of Michel, 28 Mass. App. Ct. 260, 267 (1990). But see Adoption of Lorna, 46 Mass. App. Ct. 134, 141–142 (1999) (Lorna's injuries, which were the subject of an unsupported 1992 Section 51A report, taken in context with documented neglect in 1994 and abuse in 1995, establish a pattern of neglect and abuse probative of her mother's current unfitness.). Competent evidence regarding an incident that was the subject of an unsubstantiated Section 51A report may be admitted at trial against a parent as long as the evidence is "sufficient to convey to a high degree of probability that the proposition is true." Adoption of Rhona I, 57 Mass. App. Ct. 479, 484 (2003), quoting Adoption of Iris, 43 Mass. App. Ct. 95, 105 (1997).

Subsection (b)(2)(B). This subsection is derived from Custody of Michel, 28 Mass. App. Ct. 260, 267 (1990), and Adoption of George, 27 Mass. App. Ct. 265, 272 (1994). Section 51B reports are required government documents and "may be considered for statements of fact, e.g., that there was screaming or beating or no food." Custody of Michel, 28 Mass. App. Ct. at 267. Hearsay statements contained in these reports may only be admitted for the truth asserted therein if they are statements of primary fact, or if they satisfy some other established exception to the hearsay rule. Adoption of George, 27 Mass. App. Ct. at 272. "'Primary fact' is not a self-defining phrase, but at least connotes facts which can be recorded without recourse to discretion and judgment, e.g., the fire alarm sounded at 10:30 p.m.; it was raining lightly at the time of the accident; the child was placed with Mr. and Mrs. Doe . . ." Id. at 274. The exclusion of expressions of opinion, evaluation, or judgment from official records is a "practical working rule" that has exceptions. Id. at 272. "More leeway" relative to admissibility may be given to material that "smacks of opinion" if the source of the opinion is available for cross-examination. Id. at 274. Adoption of George does not address whether statements of identified, nonmandated reporters contained in 51B reports are admissible subject to redaction.

Subsection (b)(2)(C). This subsection is derived from Adoption of George, 27 Mass. App. Ct. 265 (1994); Care & Protection of Zita, 455 Mass. 272, 275 n.6, 279–280 (2009) (petitions in care and protection cases are not evidence, compared to DCF affidavits, which are official records; it is best practice to submit a sworn affidavit of a social worker in support of a request for emergency removal of a child, together with a petition); and Care & Protection of Bruce, 44 Mass. App. Ct. 758, 766 (1998) (DCF affidavits are reports of agents of the DCF and are admissible as official records if the author is available for cross-examination). Statements of primary fact contained in these DCF documents, including affidavits supporting care and protection petitions, are admissible under the official records exception to the hearsay rule, see Section 803(8), after redaction of expressions of opinion, evaluation, or judgment. Adoption of George, 27 Mass. App. Ct. at 271, 274–275. Service plans also are admissible under a statutory exception to the hearsay rule contained in G. L. c. 119, § 29. See the note for Subsection (b)(2)(B) above regarding the meaning of "primary fact," as well as regarding the extra "leeway" given to the admissibility of expressions of opinion, evaluation, or judgment included in these records. A private entity's assessment or case review performed under a contract with the DCF is admissible in the same manner as an official record prepared by the DCF because the private entity was required to conduct the assessment as an agent of the DCF. Adoption of Vidal, 56 Mass. App. Ct. 916, 916 (2002). Documents of the DCF formerly called "Service Plans" are now referred to as "Action Plans."

Because DCF social workers no longer perform G. L. c. 119, § 21A, investigations, former Subsection (b)(2)(D) and its note have been removed from Section 1115 of the Guide.

Subsection (b)(3). This subsection is derived from G. L. c. 111B, § 11 (alcoholism treatment records); G. L. c. 111E, § 18 (drug rehabilitation treatment records); and 42 U.S.C. § 290dd–2 (substance abuse treatment records). Federal regulations require that, before issuing an order for release of these records to one or more parties, the court must determine that "disclosure [of the information] is necessary to protect against an existing threat to life or of serious bodily injury, including circumstances which constitute suspected child abuse and neglect and verbal threats against third parties [(among other things)]." 42 C.F.R. § 2.63(a)(1)–(3). Orders of appointment issued to court-appointed investigators do not satisfy the requirements of State and Federal law and therefore do not permit the court investigator to obtain drug and alcohol treatment records where the specific factual determination necessary for release of these records has not been made by the appointing judge.

Cross–Reference: Introductory Note (f)(5) to Article V, Privileges and Disqualifications.

Subsection (b)(4). This subsection is derived from Introductory Note (f)(2) and (f)(3) to Article V, Privileges and Disqualifications. There is no privilege preventing the introduction of relevant school records in evidence at trial, and most school records are admissible as official records. See Introductory Note (f)(2) to Article V, Privileges and Disqualifications (student records). Records of the clinical history and evaluations of students with special needs, created or maintained in accordance with G. L. c. 71B, are confidential but not privileged. G. L. c. 71B, § 3. See Introductory Note (f)(3) (special needs student records) and Introductory Note (d) (confidentiality versus privilege) to Article V, Privileges and Disqualifications.

Subsection (b)(5). This subsection is derived from G. L. c. 233, § 78. See Adoption of Paula, 420 Mass. 716, 727 (1995); Julian v. Randazzo, 380 Mass. 391 (1980). Besides the ordinary business records hearsay exception, there is an additional business records exception permitting second-level hearsay where the proponent of a hearsay statement shows "that all persons in the chain of communication, from the observer to the preparer, reported the information as a matter of business duty or business routine." Irwin v. Town of Ware, 392 Mass. 745, 749 (1984), quoting Wingate v. Emery Air Freight Corp., 385 Mass. 402, 406 (1982).

Cross–Reference: Section 803(6)(A), Hearsay Exceptions; Availability of Declarant Immaterial: Business and Hospital Records: Entry, Writing, or Record Made in Regular Course of Business.

Subsection (c). This subsection is derived from G. L. c. 119, §§ 21A and 24.

Subsection (c)(1). By the express terms of G. L. c. 119, § 24, investigators' reports are admissible and become part of the record in care and protection cases. Care & Protection of Zita, 455 Mass. 272, 281 (2009), citing Custody of Michel, 28 Mass. App. Ct. 260, 265 (1990). As set forth in G. L. c. 119, § 21A, "[t]he person reporting may be called as a witness by any party for examination as to the statements made in the report." Hearsay statements, including multilevel hearsay, contained within the reports, including opinions, clinical observations, and recommendations, are admissible probatively as long as the declarant is identifiable and the parties have a fair opportunity to rebut the statements of both the investigator and his or her sources through cross-examination or other means. Care & Protection of Zita, 455 Mass. at 281; Gilmore v. Gilmore, 369 Mass. 598, 604–605 (1976); Adoption of Astrid, 45 Mass. App. Ct. 538, 546 (1998). This principle applies to hearsay statements of children against their parents that are contained in investigators' reports. Care & Protection of Inga, 36 Mass. App. Ct. 660, 664 (1994). "When a judge appoints an investigator under G. L. c. 119, § 24, it signifies the judge's expectation that the [investigator] has the training and specialized knowledge which will enable the [investigator] to make and report acute observations about the interactions of family members, and their respective mental conditions." Custody of Michel, 28 Mass. App. Ct. at 266. Opinions of the court investigator as to the credibility of another witness (including the credibility of any source) are not admissible. Commonwealth v. Triplett, 398 Mass. 561, 567 (1986) ("[I]t is a fundamental principle that 'a witness cannot be asked to assess the credibility of his testimony or that of other witnesses'" [citation omitted].).-

Subsection (c)(2). Guardian ad litem (GAL) reports are analogous to court investigator reports in that hearsay, including multilevel hearsay, generally is admissible. See the Note to Subsection (c)(1) above and Adoption of Sean, 36 Mass. App. Ct. 261, 263 (1994). Guardian ad litem reports containing hearsay in-formation are admissible, including multilevel hearsay and clinical evaluations, if the guardian ad litem is available to testify at trial and the source of the material is sufficiently identified so that the affected party has an opportunity to rebut any adverse or erroneous material contained therein. Adoption of Sean, 36 Mass. App. Ct. at 264. Adoption of Sean leaves open the question whether expert opinions contained in GAL reports are admissible. Id. It is "sound practice" for the judge to give notice to the parties if the judge intends to use the report. See Duro v. Duro, 392 Mass. 574, 575 (1984) (like guardian ad litem reports, reports of probation officers in the Probate and Family Court made pursuant to G. L. c. 276, § 85B, must be in writing and subject to cross-examination).

Subsection (c)(3). A CASA is analogous to a guardian ad litem. Adoption of Georgia, 433 Mass. 62, 68 (2000). See the Note to Subsection (c)(2) above. For a CASA report to be admitted into evidence, including reports containing multilevel hearsay, the CASA must be available to testify at trial, and the sources of the information contained in the report must be sufficiently identified so that the affected party has an opportunity to rebut. Id. at 68–69. A CASA is not automatically qualified to file a report containing the CASA's expert opinions or to testify as an expert simply by being a CASA. Rather, when an objection is made regarding a CASA's qualifications to render an expert opinion, the court must determine whether the CASA is qualified to do so. Id. at 68 n.6. Expressions of opinion of mental health professionals (including the CASA if so qualified) in a CASA report are not admissible, but factual observations and information contained in clinical evaluations may be admissible and entitled to whatever weight the judge may give them. Adoption of Sean, 36 Mass. App. Ct. 261, 264 (1994).

Subsection (c)(4). Written court-ordered psychiatric evaluation reports are inadmissible. Adoption of Seth, 29 Mass. App. Ct. 343, 351–352 (1990). Although those who conduct psychological evaluations, including psychological evaluations that are court ordered, may testify in child custody, care and protection, and TPR proceedings (see Subsections [e][4], [5], and [6] below), there is no exception to the hearsay rule pertaining to written reports of such evaluations.

Cross–Reference: Section 503(d)(2), Psychotherapist–Patient Privilege: Exceptions: Court–Ordered Psychiatric Exam; Section 503(d)(5), Psychotherapist–Patient Privilege: Exceptions: Child Custody and Adoption Cases.

Subsection (d)(1). This subsection is derived from Custody of Michel, 28 Mass. App. Ct. 260, 267 (1990), and Custody of Jennifer, 25 Mass. App. Ct. 241, 243 (1988). Children's out-of-court statements are not admissible for the truth of the matter asserted, but expressed preferences regarding where they want to live are admissible insofar as the statements reflect the mental state of the children at the time. A child's state of mind is often a material issue in child custody cases. Id. A child's out-of-court hearsay statement made to an expert witness may also be admissible, not for the truth of the matter asserted, but rather to indicate the basis of an expert opinion given by the witness. Id. Similarly, a child's statement may be admissible when used for diagnostic or treatment purposes. Id. at 268. See Mass. G. Evid. § 705.

A child's extrajudicial statement concerning a parent is not admissible as an admission by a party-opponent against that parent. Care & Protection of Sophie, 449 Mass. 100, 110 (2007); Mass. G. Evid. § 801(d)(2).

With respect to a child's privileged communications to a social worker or psychotherapist, exceptions exist that permit such statements to be admitted in certain circumstances. See Mass. G. Evid. §§ 503(d), 507(c). Children's out-of-court statements to court-appointed investigators are admissible where there is "an opportunity to refute the investigator and the investigator's sources through cross-examination and other means." Custody of Michel, 28 Mass. App. Ct. at 266. The child's parent must be allowed the opportunity to effectively rebut such hearsay when the child does not testify and the trial judge has no other means by which to assess the credibility and accuracy of the child's statements. Id.

Subsection (d)(2). This subsection is derived from G. L. c. 233, §§ 82 and 83. Cross–Reference: Section 503(d)(5), Psychotherapist–Patient Privilege: Exceptions: Child Custody and Adoption Cases; Section 803(24), Hearsay Exceptions; Availability of Declarant Immaterial: Out–of–Court Statement of Child Describing Sexual Contact in Proceeding to Place Child in Foster Care.

Subsection (d)(2)(A). This subsection is derived from G. L. c. 233, § 82. "Child under the age of ten" refers to the age of the child at the time the out-of-court statements were made, not the age of the child at the time of trial. Adoption of Daisy, 460 Mass. 72, 78–79 (2011). The

following procedures must be utilized in Section 82 proceedings: (1) the DCF must give prior notice to the parent of their intention to introduce a child's out-of-court statements regarding alleged sexual abuse; (2) the DCF must show by more than a mere preponderance of the evidence that a compelling need exists for use of such a procedure; (3) any separate hearing regarding the reliability of the child's out-of-court statements must be on the record; (4) specific findings must be issued that present the basis upon which the reliability of the statements was determined; and (5) independently admitted evidence must be presented that corroborates the out-of-court statements. See Mass. G. Evid.§ 804(b)(9); Adoption of Quentin, 424 Mass. 882, 892 (1997); Adoption of Olivette, 79 Mass. App. Ct. 141, 147 (2011), quoting Adoption of Arnold, 50 Mass. App. Ct. 743, 752 (2001).

Cross–Reference: Section 804(b)(9), Hearsay Exceptions; Declarant Unavailable: The Exceptions: Out-of-Court Statement of Child Describing Sexual Contact in Civil Proceeding, Including Termination of Parental Rights.

Subsection (d)(2)(B). This subsection is derived from G. L. c. 233, § 83. See Section 803(24), Hearsay Exceptions; Availability of Declarant Immaterial: Out–of–Court Statement of Child Describing Sexual Contact in Proceeding to Place Child in Foster Care. Where a care and protection case is joined with a TPR proceeding, the hearing should comply with the stricter requirements of G. L. c. 233, § 82. Adoption of Tina, 45 Mass. App. Ct. 727, 733 (1998).

Subsection (e)(1). This subsection is derived from G. L. c. 119, § 21A, and G. L. c. 233, § 20. Every person is competent to be a witness, unless excepted by statute or common law. This includes children of all ages who (1) have the ability to observe, remember, and give expression to that which they have seen, heard, or experienced and (2) have an understanding sufficient to comprehend the difference between truth and falsehood, their duty to tell the truth, that lying is wrong, and that failure to tell the truth will result in punishment. Mass. G. Evid. § 601(b). In care and protection and termination of parental rights proceedings, "[evidence] may include the testimony of the child if the court determines that the child is competent and willing, after consultation with counsel, if any, to testify." G. L. c. 119, § 21A (emphasis supplied). See Abbot v. Virusso, 68 Mass. App. Ct. 326, 337–338 (2007) (upholding judicial discretion regarding competency of child witnesses and discussing issues concerning in-camera interviews with children). Judges must be sensitive to a child's limited stamina and have considerable latitude to devise procedures and modify the usual rules of trial to accommodate child and other witnesses with special needs. See Commonwealth v. Brusgulis, 398 Mass. 325, 332 (1986).

Cross Reference: Section 601, Competency.

Subsection (e)(2). This subsection is derived from G. L. c. 119, § 29D. Foster and preadoptive parents have a statutory right to testify at trial. Such testimony must be taken as any other witness's, under oath and subject to cross-examination. Adoption of Sherry, 435 Mass. 331, 337 (2001).

Subsection (e)(3). This subsection is derived from G. L. c. 233, § 22. Absent a valid assertion of a Fifth Amendment privilege, a parent may be required to testify in care and protection and TPR proceedings. Adoption of Salvatore, 57 Mass. App. Ct. 929, 930 (2003). The burden is on the party asserting the Fifth Amendment privilege to establish its existence. Commonwealth v. Brennan, 386 Mass. 772, 780 (1982). Negative inferences may be drawn against a party who asserts the privilege. See Care & Protection of Sharlene, 445 Mass. 756, 767 (2006). See also Mass. G. Evid.§ 511. Whether to draw the adverse inference is a matter within the discretion of the judge, who should take into consideration all of the circumstances. See Adoption of Talik, 92 Mass. App. Ct. 367, 372 (2017).

Subsection (e)(4). This subsection is derived from G. L. c. 112, §§ 135, 135A, and 135B.

General Laws c. 112, § 135A, requires that from the initial phase of the professional relationship, a licensed social worker or social worker employed by a government agency shall inform the client about the confidential nature of their communications and not disclose any information acquired or revealed from the client except, inter alia, in the initiation of, or to give testimony in connection with, a proceeding under G. L. c. 119, § 24, to commit a child facing abuse or neglect to the custody of the department or agency, or to transfer custody by way of an emergency order, or to dispense with the need for consent to adoption of the child in the care or custody of the department or agency. G. L. c. 112, § 135A(e).

In any court proceeding or preliminary proceeding thereto, G. L. c. 112, § 135B, creates a privilege enabling a client to refuse to disclose, or prevent a witness from disclosing, any communication between the client and the social worker relative to the diagnosis or treatment of the client's mental or emotional condition. The exception to the privilege in this subsection is taken nearly verbatim from G. L. c. 112, § 135B(e), (f), and (g).

Cross–Reference: Section 104, Preliminary Questions; Section 507, Social Worker–Client Privilege.

Subsection (e)(5). This subsection is derived from G. L. c. 233, § 20B. See Section 503(a) for definitions of "psychotherapist," "patient," and "communications," and Section 503(b) and (d) for descriptions of, and exceptions to, the privilege. See also Commonwealth v. Lamb, 365 Mass. 265, 270 (1974). Because the privilege is not self-executing, the patient must attempt to assert it during the trial. Adoption of Carla, 416 Mass. 510, 515 (1993).

Cross–Reference: Introductory Note to Article V, Privileges and Disqualifications; Section 503, Psychotherapist–Patient Privilege.

Subsection (e)(6). This subsection is derived from G. L. c. 119, § 21A.

Subsection (e)(7). This subsection is modeled after Sections 702, 703, and 705. Massachusetts law, unlike Federal law, allows expert opinion on the ultimate issue. Mass. G. Evid. § 704. Expert testimony that simply "vouches" for the credibility of other witnesses, opines as to whether a child told the truth, makes legal conclusions, or renders an opinion within the common understanding of the trier of fact is inadmissible. See Mass. G. Evid. § 704. See also Care & Protection of Rebecca, 419 Mass. 67, 83 (1994); Adoption of Olivette, 79 Mass. App. Ct. 141, 152 (2011).

Cross–Reference: Section 702, Testimony by Expert Witnesses.

Subsection (f)(1). This subsection is derived from G. L. c. 210, § 3(c). Section 3(c) requires the court to consider the adoption plan by the DCF, which plan need not be in writing but may be presented to the court through testimony. Adoption of Stuart, 39 Mass. App. Ct. 380, 393–394 (1995). It is not necessary that the plan be fully developed or that the plan identify prospective adoptive parents, but it must have sufficient content and substance to permit the court to meaningfully evaluate and consider the suitability of the DCF adoption plan. Adoption of Lars, 46 Mass. App. Ct. 30, 31 (1998).

Subsection (f)(2). Bonding and attachment evaluators may testify in the same manner as any other witness. Expert opinions held by such evaluators are admissible subject to Sections 702, Testimony by Expert Witnesses, and 703, Bases of Opinion Testimony by Experts.

Cross–Reference: Section 201, Judicial Notice of Adjudicative Facts; Section 803(22), Hearsay Exceptions; Availability of Declarant Immaterial: Judgment of a Previous Conviction.

Subsection (f)(3). Findings of fact in a prior care and protection or termination of parental rights proceeding that are not "out of date, or the product of a proceeding where the parent may not have a compelling incentive to litigate," may be admitted in a subsequent proceeding to the extent that they are both relevant and material. Adoption of Paula, 420 Mass. 716, 721 (1995); Adoption of Darla, 56 Mass. App. Ct. 519, 520–521 (2002). The parties and the judge are not bound by the prior findings, which carry no special evidentiary weight, and evidence may be offered by any party as to any of the issues covered by the prior findings, either to support or contradict them.

Adoption of Paula, 420 Mass. at 722. Where a prior proceeding is on appeal, the better practice is for the judge to decline to admit the prior findings in the subsequent proceeding. Adoption of Simone, 427 Mass. 34, 43 (1998), citing Adoption of Paula, 420 Mass. at 722. See also Care & Protection of Zita, 455 Mass. 272, 283 (2009) (judge may not judicially notice facts or evidence brought out in a prior hearing or trial).

Subsection (g). This subsection is derived from Adoption of Talik, 92 Mass. App. Ct. 367, 370–373 (2017). Whether to draw the adverse inference is a matter within the discretion of the judge, who should take into consideration all of the circumstances. Id. at 372. No adverse inference may be drawn "unless a case against the interests of the affected party is presented, so that failure of the party to testify would be a fair subject of comment." Id., citing Custody of Two Minors, 396 Mass. 610, 616 (1986).

Section 1116. Peremptory Challenges of Potential Jurors

(a) General Principles. This section applies to the use of peremptory challenges in civil, criminal, and juvenile cases. Peremptory challenges of potential jurors, which generally do not have to be supported by a reason, may not be based on a belief that the juror is biased because of the juror's membership in a discrete community group, including groups based on gender, race, creed, religious belief, or national origin. Peremptory challenges may be based on a belief that a juror is biased as a result of factors such as age, employment, place of residence, educational level, income, demeanor, or conduct, or factors other than membership in a discrete community group.

(b) Objecting to a Peremptory Challenge. An objection to a peremptory challenge may be made by a party or the matter may be raised by the judge in the absence of an objection. Whether an objection to the exercise of a peremptory challenge should be overruled or sustained requires a three-stage analysis. The judge must make specific findings on the record at each stage.

(1) Stage One: Prima Facie Case of Unlawful Discrimination. There is a rebuttable presumption that a peremptory challenge is lawful. The party opposed to the peremptory challenge has the initial burden to present some evidence that the challenge is based on the juror's membership in a discrete community group and is not based on a personal characteristic of the juror. A single peremptory challenge may be sufficient to establish a prima facie case of unlawful discrimination. The judge must make an explicit finding on the record whether the presumption of regularity has been overcome.

(2) Stage Two: Burden Shifts to Party Exercising Challenge. Once the moving party has overcome the presumption of regularity, the burden shifts to the party which exercised the peremptory challenge to supply a group-neutral, bona fide reason for the peremptory challenge. The reason must be clear, reasonably specific, related to the case before the court, and personal to the juror. Good faith alone is insufficient. The judge must allow all parties to be heard and may take evidence.

(3) Stage Three: Evaluation of Group-Neutral Explanation. The judge must determine whether the explanation given by the party exercising the peremptory challenge is bona fide or a pretext. The judge must make two specific findings on the record regarding the explanation:

(A) whether the reason given for the peremptory challenge is based on a factor other than the juror's membership in a discrete community group, and

(B) whether the reason given for the peremptory challenge is genuine.

(c) Overruling the Objection. The judge must overrule the objection and allow the exercise of the peremptory challenge if the party opposed to the peremptory challenge has not established a prima facie case to overcome the presumption of regularity, or if the judge determines that

(1) the peremptory challenge was based on a specific reason other than the juror's membership in a discrete community group, and

(2) the reason given for the peremptory challenge was credible, genuine, and not a pretext.

(d) Sustaining the Objection. The judge must sustain the objection to the peremptory challenge if the judge determines that

(1) the peremptory challenge was not based on a specific reason other than the juror's membership in a protected class, or

(2) the reason given for the peremptory challenge was not credible or genuine, and was a pretext.

NOTE

Subsection (a). This subsection is derived from Commonwealth v. Soares, 377 Mass. 461, cert. denied, 444 U.S. 881 (1979). "Defendants have a right under the United States Constitution and the Massachusetts Declaration of Rights to be tried by an impartial jury." Commonwealth v. Obi, 475 Mass. 541, 550 (2016). All parties, including the Commonwealth, are entitled to a jury that has not been unfairly skewed. See Commonwealth v. Prunty, 462 Mass. 295, 308 (2012) (ensuring nondiscriminatory use of peremptory challenges is intended to benefit both sides in a criminal trial); Commonwealth v. Fruchtman, 418 Mass. 8, 13 (1994) ("[t]he Commonwealth is equally entitled to a fairly selected and representative jury ..."); Anderson-Mole v. University of Mass., 49 Mass. App. Ct. 723, 724 (2000) ("[c]ivil litigants, as well as parties in criminal cases, are entitled to a jury that has not been unfairly skewed"). Potential jurors are also entitled to the opportunity to serve on a jury without fear of being discriminated against. Commonwealth v. Prunty, 462 Mass. at 308. "An erroneous denial of a peremptory challenge is a structural error, requiring reversal without a showing of prejudice." Commonwealth v. Oberle, 476 Mass. 539, 545 (2017); Gates v. Flood, 57 Mass. App. Ct. 739, 742–743 (2003).

Protected Groups. The terms "discrete community group" and "protected group" reflect the language contained in Article 1 of the Declaration of Rights of the Constitution of the Commonwealth, as amended by Article 106 of the Amendments to the Massachusetts Constitution (Equal Rights Amendment), and include sex, race, color, creed, and national origin. Commonwealth v. Soares, 377 Mass. at 488 n.33. Contrast Commonwealth v. Lopes, 478 Mass. 593, 597–598 (2018); Commonwealth v. Oberle, 476 Mass. 539, 545 (2017) (age is not a discrete protected group for purposes of Batson–Soares peremptory challenges); Commonwealth v. Acen, 396 Mass. 472, 477–478 (1986) (non-English speakers and noncitizens are not protected groups); Commonwealth v. Matthews, 406 Mass. 380, 389 (1990) (suburban parents and caretakers of adolescent children are not protected groups); and Commonwealth v. Evans, 438 Mass. 142, 149–150 (2002), cert. denied, 538 U.S. 966 (2003) (college students are not a protected group). The Supreme Judicial Court "has not considered the question whether the exercise of a peremptory challenge to remove a juror because of his or her sexual orientation or because the juror was

transgendered would violate the guarantees of art. 12 or the equal protection clause." Commonwealth v. Smith, 450 Mass. 395, 405 (2008).

The party opposing the exercise of a peremptory challenge must demonstrate that the challenged juror is a member of a protected group. Commonwealth v. Suarez, 59 Mass. App. Ct. 111, 114 (2003). See Commonwealth v. Obi, 475 Mass. 541, 550–551 (2016) (judge's observation that juror wore headscarf traditionally worn by Muslim women and similar to that worn by Muslim victim was sufficient to establish juror's membership in discrete group). If there is a reasonable question about whether a prospective juror belongs to a protected class, the trial judge must assume membership in the class for purposes of the first step in the Batson–Soares analysis. Commonwealth v. Robertson, 480 Mass. 383, 395 (2018). Cf. Commonwealth v. Ortega, 480 Mass. 603, 607 n.8 (2018) (persons belonging to various "minority ethnic or racial groups" may not be "lumped together" when assessing whether a preemptory challenge is improper).

Subsection (b). This subsection is derived from Commonwealth v. Soares, 377 Mass. 461, 488, cert. denied, 444 U.S. 881 (1979). See Commonwealth v. Robertson, 480 Mass. 383, 395 (2018).

Either a party or the judge, sua sponte, may initially raise the issue of a potentially improper peremptory challenge. Commonwealth v. Maldonado, 439 Mass. 460, 463 (2003). See Commonwealth v. LeClair, 429 Mass. 313, 322 (1999) ("immaterial" whether issue is initially raised by judge or opposing party).

It is imperative that the judge make explicit findings on the record at each stage of the analysis. Commonwealth v. Maldonado, 439 Mass. at 465 (judge must make specific findings as to whether explanation for peremptory challenge is both adequate and genuine); Commonwealth v. Burnett, 418 Mass. 769, 771 (1994) (trial judge should make finding as to whether requisite prima facie showing of impropriety has been made).

Timing of the Objection. To preserve the issue of an improper peremptory challenge on appeal, the objection to the peremptory challenge must be made as soon as it becomes evident that a pattern of unlawful challenges exists and prior to empanelment. Commonwealth v. Smith, 450 Mass. 395, 406 (2008) (trial judge's obligation to assess propriety of peremptory challenge is not triggered where counsel fails to object or assert that pattern of improper exclusion has been established); Commonwealth v. Colon-Cruz, 408 Mass. 533, 550 (1990) (a record in which a party has not had an opportunity to explain the use of peremptory challenges is inadequate to raise a challenge to an allegedly impermissible peremptory challenge); Commonwealth v. Sosnowski, 43 Mass. App. Ct. 367, 372–373 (1997) (propriety of peremptory challenge could not be reviewed on appeal because defendant failed to object at trial).

Subsection (b)(1). The court begins with the presumption that the exercise of a peremptory challenge is proper. See Commonwealth v. Maldonado, 439 Mass. 460, 463 (2003); Commonwealth v. Curtiss, 424 Mass. 78, 80 (1997). To rebut that presumption, the party opposing the peremptory challenge must establish a prima facie case of discrimination by showing (1) a pattern of excluding members of a discrete group, or in some circumstances a single member of a discrete group, and (2) individuals are being excluded solely on the basis of their membership in that group. See Commonwealth v. Garrey, 436 Mass. 422, 428 (2002). The second prong of the prima facie case has been described as whether it was "likely" that peremptory challenges were used to exclude members of a protected class. See id. This burden has since been described as not "a terribly weighty one." Commonwealth v. Maldonado, 439 Mass. at 464 n.4. See Commonwealth v. Obi, 475 Mass. 541, 550–551 (2016) (prima facie case met where challenged juror was Muslim, defendant was Muslim, and no other prospective jurors appeared to be Muslim); Commonwealth v. Rodriguez, 457 Mass. 461, 472 (2010) (removal of sole Hispanic juror adequate to rebut presumption). But see Commonwealth v. Roche, 44 Mass. App. Ct. 372, 377–378 & n.3 (1998) (peremptory challenge of member of protected class does not, by itself, constitute prima facie showing of impropriety). However, the United States Supreme Court stated that the party opposing the peremptory challenge must offer "evidence sufficient to permit the trial judge to draw an inference that discrimination has occurred." Johnson v. California, 545 U.S. 162, 170 (2005) ("California's 'more likely than not' standard is at odds with the prima facie inquiry mandated by [Batson v. Kentucky, 476 U.S. 79 (1986)]").

Generally, a judge must make a finding that the prima facie case has been made before requiring the party who made the allegedly improper challenge to provide reasons for the peremptory challenge. Commonwealth v. Green, 420 Mass. 771, 776–777 (1995). See Commonwealth v. Calderon, 431 Mass. 21, 25–26 (2000) (requiring party exercising peremptory challenge to provide explanation may demonstrate implicit finding that prima facie case has been made). However, in the early stages of jury selection, the trial judge also has broad discretion to require an explanation without making the determination that a pattern of improper exclusion exists. See Commonwealth v. Scott, 463 Mass. 561, 571 (2012), quoting Commonwealth v. Van Winkle, 443 Mass. 230, 236 (2005) ("[w]here a venire contains 'a paucity of African-Americans' a judge has broad discretion to require an explanation without first making the determination that a pattern of improper exclusion exists"), quoting Commonwealth v. Garrey, 436 Mass. 422, 429 (2002).

To determine whether the party challenging a peremptory strike or strikes has established the prima facie showing, "a trial judge is to consider all of the relevant facts and circumstances." Commonwealth v. Jones, 477 Mass. 307, 322 (2017). See, e.g., Commonwealth v. Issa, 466 Mass. 1, 10 (2013) (judge did not abuse his discretion in considering other relevant circumstances, including prosecutor's statement that challenged juror looked familiar). "The inquiry ordinarily begins with the number and percentage of group members who have been excluded," which can, in certain circumstances, establish the prima facie showing. Commonwealth v. Jones, 477 Mass. at 322, citing Commonwealth v. Issa, 466 Mass. at 9. See Commonwealth v. Obi, 475 Mass. 541, 551 (2016). Other factors that may be considered in making the determination include

"the possibility of an objective group-neutral explanation for the strike or strikes; any similarities between excluded jurors and those, not members of the allegedly targeted group, who have been struck; differences among the various members of the allegedly targeted group who were struck; whether those excluded are members of the same protected group as the defendant or the victim; and the composition of the jurors already seated."

Commonwealth v. Jones, 477 Mass. at 322 & n.25 (recognizing that a judge's consideration of an objective group-neutral explanation for the strike in this stage overlaps with the analysis at the second and third stages). "This list of factors is neither mandatory nor exhaustive; a trial judge and a reviewing court must consider 'all relevant circumstances' for each challenged strike." Id. at 322 n.24, citing Batson v. Kentucky, 476 U.S. 79, 96 (1986).

Single Challenge May Be Sufficient. "A single peremptory challenge may be sufficient to make a prima facie showing that rebuts the presumption of proper use." Commonwealth v. Ortega, 480 Mass. 603, 606 (2018). See Commonwealth v. Issa, 466 Mass. 1, 9 (2013); Commonwealth v. Prunty, 462 Mass. 295, 306 n.15 (2012) (trial judge properly requested explanation for defendant's peremptory challenge of only African-American in venire). See also Commonwealth v. Maldonado, 439 Mass. 460, 463 n.3 (2003) ("the ultimate issue is not whether there is a 'pattern' of excluding a discrete group, but whether the challenge made to any member of the panel is impermissibly based on the juror's membership in one of the discrete groups protected under [Commonwealth v. Soares]").

Rebutting the Presumption of Propriety. It is within the trial judge's discretion to determine whether the party opposing the exercise of a peremptory challenge has rebutted the presumption of propriety. Commonwealth v. Issa, 466 Mass. at 10; Commonwealth v. Prunty, 462 Mass. at 304. See, e.g., Commonwealth v. Scott, 463 Mass. 561, 571 (2012) (judge did not abuse discretion in finding no pattern of discriminatory challenges); Commonwealth v. Aspen, 53 Mass. App. Ct. 259, 262 (2001) (appellate courts will not substitute their judgment for trial judge's concerning whether presumption has been rebutted if there is support for it on the record, because trial judge is in best position to decide if peremptory challenge appears improper).

Subsection (b)(2). If the trial judge finds that the prima facie case has been met, the burden shifts to the party who sought to exercise the challenge to provide, if possible, a justification for that challenge that is "group neutral" or unrelated to the prospective juror's group affiliation. Commonwealth v. Scott, 463 Mass. 561, 570 (2012); Commonwealth v. Prunty, 462 Mass. 295, 306 (2012). While general assertions are not enough, the level of specificity does not have to rise to the level of specificity required to remove a juror for cause. Commonwealth v. Cavotta, 48 Mass. App. Ct. 636, 638 (2000) (attitude, bearing, and demeanor of juror during voir dire may constitute sufficient basis for peremptory removal). See also Commonwealth v. Soares, 377 Mass. 461, 491, cert. denied, 444 U.S. 881 (1979); Commonwealth v. Mathews, 31 Mass. App. Ct. 564, 568 (1991), cert. denied sub nom. Mathews v. Rakiey, 504 U.S. 922 (1992). The trial judge must not provide the group-neutral reason for the preemptory challenge. See Commonwealth v. Fryar, 414 Mass. 732, 740–741 (1993) (although trial judge properly found prima facie case had been made, reversible error for judge to supply group-neutral reason instead of waiting to hear from party exercising challenge). After the party seeking to exercise the peremptory challenge asserts their group-neutral reason, the opposing party should be allowed to rebut the proffered explanation as mere pretext. See Commonwealth v. Maldonado, 439 Mass. 460, 464 n.6. (2003).

Subsection (b)(3). The third stage requires the judge to determine whether the reason provided was a bona fide reason for exercising the challenge or a mere pretext to avoid admitting facts of group discrimination. Commonwealth v. Soares, 377 Mass. 461, 491, cert. denied, 444 U.S. 881 (1979). In determining whether an explanation is bona fide or pretextual, the trial judge must make findings concerning two points: (1) whether the explanation is "adequate" and (2) whether the explanation is "genuine." Commonwealth v. Maldonado, 439 Mass. 460, 464 (2003). While the soundness of the proffered explanation may be a strong indicator of its genuineness, the two prongs of the analysis are not identical. Id. at 466.

The judge must make specific findings or provide an explanation which is ascertainable to an appellate court concerning whether the party asserting the challenge provided both an adequate and genuine explanation for the peremptory challenge. See Commonwealth v. Benoit, 452 Mass. 212, 220 (2008) (trial judge's specific findings aid appellate courts in ascertaining whether judge "considered both the adequacy and the genuineness of the proffered explanation, and did not conflate the two into a simple consideration of whether the explanation was 'reasonable' or 'group neutral'") (quotation omitted). See also Commonwealth v. Rodriguez, 457 Mass. 461, 470–471 (2010); Commonwealth v. Lacoy, 90 Mass. App. Ct. 427, 432 (2016). An appellate court is "not in a position to give deference to the judge's findings" when the record does not reflect the trial judge's independent evaluation and determination of the adequacy and credibility of the challenging party's proffered reason for the peremptory challenge. Commonwealth v. Benoit, 452 Mass. at 223.

Subsection (b)(3)(A). Adequacy refers to the soundness of the proffered explanation. Commonwealth v. Maldonado, 439 Mass. 460, 464–465 (2003). An explanation is adequate if it is clear and reasonably specific, personal to the juror and not based on the juror's group affiliation, and related to the particular case being tried. Id. Subjective challenges, such as a challenge to a juror's looks or gestures, or a party's "gut feeling," should rarely be accepted as adequate because such explanations can easily be used as pretexts for discrimination. Commonwealth v. Benoit, 452 Mass. 212, 219 (2008) (the inquiry must determine whether explanation is belatedly contrived to avoid admitting facts of group discrimination). See, e.g., Commonwealth v. Obi, 475 Mass. 541, 550–551 (2016) (defense counsel's "gut feeling" that juror would not be sympathetic to defendant was insufficient); Commonwealth v. Calderon, 431 Mass. 21, 27 n.4 (2000) (juror who smiled at defense counsel did not justify challenge). Similarly, mere affirmations of good faith are not sufficient. See Commonwealth v. Carleton, 36 Mass. App. Ct. 137, 144 (1994). A trial judge's determination that the explanation offered by the party exercising the peremptory challenge is adequate is within the sound discretion of the judge and will not be disturbed so long as there is support for the ruling in the record. Commonwealth v. Scott, 463 Mass. 561, 570 (2012). See Commonwealth v. Prunty, 462 Mass. 295, 309–310 (2012) (trial judge entitled to disbelieve defendant's facially race-neutral reason for exercising peremptory challenge); Commonwealth v. LeClair, 429 Mass. 313, 323 (1999).

Subsection (b)(3)(B). "An explanation is genuine if it is in fact the reason for the exercise of the challenge." Commonwealth v. Maldonado, 439 Mass. 460, 465 (2003). The mere denial of an improper motive is inadequate to establish the genuineness of the explanation. Id. A reasonable justification in the abstract must be rejected if the judge does not believe that it reflects the challenging party's actual thinking. Id. See Commonwealth v. Oberle, 476 Mass. 539, 546–547 (2017) (in domestic violence case in which defendant was charged with assaulting his female partner, trial judge did not abuse his discretion in finding a lack of genuineness of defendant's proffered reasons for peremptory challenge of woman juror after all three of defendant's previous peremptory challenges had been of women); Commonwealth v. Prunty, 462 Mass. 295, 309 (2012) (trial judge warranted in finding that defendant's challenge, allegedly based on juror's occupation, was not genuine); Commonwealth v. LeClair, 429 Mass. 313, 323 (1999) (affirming judge's disallowance of peremptory challenge after he determined that it was disingenuous).

If the trial judge determines that the peremptory challenge was improper, "the judge has the authority to fashion relief without declaring a mistrial." Commonwealth v. Reid, 384 Mass. 247, 254–255 (1981) (defendant's improper use of peremptory challenges of prospective male jurors authorized trial judge to strike all jurors and begin with a new venire).

Subsection (c). An objection to a peremptory challenge must be overruled if the prima facie case has not been made. See, e.g., Commonwealth v. Issa, 466 Mass. 1, 10 (2013) ("judge did not abuse his discretion in finding that the defendant had failed to rebut the presumption"); Commonwealth v. Scott, 463 Mass. 561, 571 (2012) (finding of no pattern of discriminatory challenges within judge's discretion).

Subsection (c)(1). An objection to a peremptory challenge must be overruled if the challenge was based on a factor other than the juror's membership in a discrete community group. See, e.g., Commonwealth v. Nom, 426 Mass. 152, 155 (1997) (explanation that prospective juror's prior domestic arrest was reason for challenge was based on factor other than juror's race); Commonwealth v. Barnoski, 418 Mass. 523, 533–534 (1994) (judge overruled objection to peremptory challenge and accepted prosecutor's specific examples of juror's demeanor as being reason for challenge, which were unrelated to juror's ethnicity).

Subsection (c)(2). An objection to a peremptory challenge must be overruled if the explanation for the challenge is credible, genuine, and not pretext. See, e.g., Commonwealth v. Rodriguez, 457 Mass. 461, 470–471 (2010) (explanation that challenge to prospective juror was based on juror's inability to follow instructions and experience in court was sufficient and credible).

Subsection (d)(1). An objection to a peremptory challenge must be sustained if the explanation for the challenge is not adequate. See, e.g., Commonwealth v. Obi, 475 Mass. 541, 552 (2016) (explanation that defense counsel had gut feeling that juror would not be sympathetic to defendant was not adequate); Commonwealth v. Rodriguez, 431 Mass. 804, 808–809 (2000) (after pattern of excluding female jurors was

established, defendant's attempt to challenge another female juror was invalid because not liking her looks was insufficient gender-neutral reason for peremptory challenge); Commonwealth v. Calderon, 431 Mass. 21, 26–28 (2000) (challenge based primarily on juror's husband's occupation inadequate).

Subsection (d)(2). An objection to a peremptory challenge must be sustained if the explanation for the challenge is not genuine and constitutes mere pretext. See, e.g., Commonwealth v. Prunty, 462 Mass. 295, 310 (2012) (explanation that peremptory challenge was used to remove juror based on her occupation was not genuine); Commonwealth v. Carvalho, 88 Mass. App. Ct. 840, 844 (2016) (explanation for challenge that "looking at the juror's experience, I don't feel that she would be a person that would be fair and equitable to my client" was not bona fide); Commonwealth v. Povez, 84 Mass. App. Ct. 660, 665 (2013) (explanation that juror was challenged because his father worked as a janitor in Federal court was adequate but not genuine).

Section 1117. Civil Commitment Hearings for Mental Illness

(a) Mental Health Commitment Hearings. In order to commit or retain a person in a mental health facility or in Bridgewater State Hospital, the petitioner must prove beyond a reasonable doubt that

(1) the respondent is mentally ill;

(2) by reason of that illness, the failure to commit or retain the respondent in a facility would create a likelihood of serious harm to the respondent or another; and

(3) if the respondent is already committed to a mental health facility or to Bridgewater State Hospital, discharge of the patient from said facility is imminent.

(b) Law of Evidence. The law of evidence applies in commitment hearings for persons with mental illness.

(c) Expert Opinion Testimony. Expert opinion testimony, whether by a treating psychiatrist or any other witness, is admissible if

(1) the expert witness testimony will assist the trier of fact;

(2) the witness is qualified as an expert in the relevant area of inquiry;

(3) the facts or data in the record are sufficient to enable the witness to give an opinion that is not merely speculation;

(4) the expert opinion is based on a body of knowledge, a principle, or a method that is reliable; and

(5) the expert has applied the body of knowledge, the principle, or the method in a reliable manner to the particular facts of the case.

(d) Basis for Expert Opinion. The facts or data upon which an expert witness may base an opinion or inference include

(1) facts observed by the witness or otherwise in the witness's direct personal knowledge;

(2) evidence already in the record or that will be presented during the course of the proceedings, which facts may be assumed to be true in questions put to the witness; and

(3) facts or data not in evidence if the facts or data are independently admissible in evidence and are a permissible basis for an expert to consider in formulating an opinion.

(e) Psychotherapist–Patient and Social Worker–Client Privileges. A patient shall have the privilege of refusing to disclose, and of preventing a witness from disclosing, any communication, wherever made, between that patient and a psychotherapist or between that patient and a social worker relative to the diagnosis or treatment of the patient's mental or emotional condition.

(1) The privilege does not apply to a disclosure made by a psychotherapist or social worker who, in the course of diagnosis or treatment of the patient, determines that the patient is in need of treatment in a hospital for mental or emotional illness or that there is a threat of imminently dangerous activity by the patient against himself or herself or another person, and who, on the basis of that determination, discloses such communication for the purpose of either placing or retaining the patient in such hospital, provided, however, that the provisions of this section shall continue in effect after the patient is in that hospital, or after placing the patient under arrest or under the supervision of law enforcement authorities.

(2) Whenever a psychiatrist, psychologist, or social worker interviews a patient on behalf of the Commonwealth with the purpose of preparing for a hearing, whether or not the interview was ordered by the court, the patient must be warned before the interview begins that everything said during the interview is not subject to privilege and may be presented against him or her in the hearing.

(A) The privilege must be knowingly and willfully waived for the contents of the conversation to be admissible at the hearing.

(B) No statement shall be admitted if such statement constitutes a confession or admission of guilt to the crime charged.

(f) Hospital Records. Records kept by hospitals pursuant to G. L. c. 111, § 70, and by mental health facilities pursuant to G. L. c. 123, § 36, shall be admissible as evidence if such records relate to the treatment and medical history of such cases. Records required to be kept by hospitals under the law of any other United States jurisdiction may be admissible.

(g) Medical Bills, Records, and Reports. Records and reports of an examination and itemized bills for services rendered are admissible as

(1) evidence of the necessity of such services or treatments;

(2) the diagnosis, prognosis, or opinion as to the proximate cause of the condition so diagnosed; or

(3) the opinion as to disability or incapacity, if any, proximately resulting from the condition so diagnosed.

NOTE

Subsection (a). This subsection is derived from G. L. c. 123, §§ 7, 8; Commonwealth v. Nassar, 380 Mass. 908, 912–914 (1980); and Superintendent of Worcester State Hosp. v. Hagberg, 374 Mass. 271, 276 (1978).

Subsection (a)(2). "Likelihood of serious harm" is defined in G. L. c. 123, § 1, as

"(1) a substantial risk of physical harm to the person himself as manifested by evidence of, threats of, or attempts at, suicide or serious bodily harm; (2) a substantial risk of physical harm to other persons as manifested by evidence of homicidal or other violent behavior or evidence that others are placed in reasonable fear of violent behavior and serious physical harm to them; or (3) a very substantial risk of physical impairment or injury to the person himself as manifested by evidence that such person's judgment is so affected that he is unable to protect himself in the community and that reasonable provision for his protection is not available in the community."

G. L. c. 123, § 1. The type of "serious harm" proven at the hearing must be the same as the type alleged in the petition. Matter of S.S., 2016 Mass. App. Div. 101, 103, citing Blixt v. Blixt, 437 Mass. 649, 665–666 (2002).

Subsection (a)(3). This subsection is derived from Acting Supt. of Bournewood Hosp. v. Baker, 431 Mass. 101, 105 (2000).

Subsection (b). This subsection is derived from the District Court's Standards of Judicial Practice: Civil Commitment and Authorization of Medical Treatment for Mental Illness, Standard 5:01 (2011) ("[G. L. c.] 123 proceedings are formal judicial determinations in which a substantial deprivation of liberty is at stake and there are no statutory provisions or case decisions suspending the rules of evidence").

Cross-Reference: Section 803(6)(C), Hearsay Exceptions; Availability of Declarant Immaterial: Business and Hospital Records: Medical and Hospital Services.

Subsection (c). This subsection is derived from Commonwealth v. Lanigan, 419 Mass. 15, 26 (1994), adopting the rule from Daubert v. Merrell Dow Pharms., Inc., 509 U.S. 579 (1993).

Cross-Reference: Section 702, Testimony by Expert Witnesses (including Note "Five Foundation Requirements").

Subsection (d). This subsection is derived from Department of Youth Servs. v. A Juvenile, 398 Mass. 516, 531–532 (1986), and Section 703, Bases of Opinion Testimony by Experts. Because expert testimony plays a crucial role in almost all proceedings under G. L. c. 123, §§ 7, 8, and 35, the most important evidentiary questions in such proceedings often arise from the basis of the expert's opinion. A testifying expert will usually review the patient's medical records, raising the same issues of reliable hearsay and privilege that would constrain the admission of those records into evidence. Adoption of Seth, 29 Mass. App. Ct. 343, 352 (1990); Section 1118(a), Civil Commitment Hearings for Alcohol and Substance Use Disorders: Civil Commitment Proceedings Pursuant to G. L. c. 123, § 35, for Individuals with Alcohol and Substance Use Disorders (commitment proceedings pursuant to G. L. c. 123, § 35, "shall include expert testimony"). Experts may also want to interview caregivers, family members, and other clinicians about the patient's history and behaviors. The contents of such conversations are not a permissible basis for an expert's opinion in hearings pursuant to G. L. c. 123, §§ 7 and 8 (unless they are subject to an exception to the rule against hearsay or are otherwise independently admissible) but may form the basis for an expert opinion in a hearing under G. L. c. 123, § 35, as long as the contents of the conversations are substantially reliable. Matter of G.P., 473 Mass. 112, 120–122 (2015); Department of Youth Servs. v. A Juvenile, 398 Mass. at 527, 531; Matter of J.W., 2016 Mass. App. Div. 74, 77–78. "If a party believes that an expert is basing an opinion on inadmissible facts or data, the party may request a voir dire to determine the basis of the expert opinion." Department of Youth Servs. v. A Juvenile, 398 Mass. at 532. If a party requests a voir dire on the expert's basis for opinion, the facts and data used to form that opinion should be evaluated as though they were themselves being admitted into evidence. Id. at 531; Adoption of Seth, 29 Mass. App. Ct. 343, 352 (1990).

Bases for Expert Opinion in Mental Health Hearings. The following is a list of common bases for expert opinion testimony in mental health hearings that are permissible as a foundation for expert opinion:

– Objective observations, whether made by the expert themselves or by nurses, doctors, or other treatment professionals recording them in hospital records. Adoption of Abigail, 23 Mass. App. Ct. 191, 199 (1986); G. L. c. 233, § 79. See also P.W. v. M.S., 67 Mass. App. Ct. 779, 787 (2002) (privilege does not preclude admission of conclusions based on objective indicia rather than on patient's statements).

– Medical history, including prior hospitalizations and diagnoses, if such diagnoses do not imply or contain privileged communications between a psychotherapist and patient, and such history is recorded in the medical records from a source with firsthand knowledge, meriting a presumption of reliability. Bouchie v. Murray, 376 Mass. 524, 531 (1978); Adoption of Saul, 60 Mass. App. Ct. 546, 552 (2004). See also Commonwealth v. Kobrin, 395 Mass. 284, 294 (1985); Section 803(6)(B), Hearsay Exceptions; Availability of Declarant Immaterial: Business and Hospital Records, and the accompanying note; Section 803(6)(C), Hearsay Exceptions; Availability of Declarant Immaterial: Business and Hospital Records: Medical and Hospital Services, and the accompanying note.

– Conversations with the respondent, subject to prior notice and waiver of the psychotherapist-patient privilege. Commonwealth v. Barboza, 387 Mass. 105, 108 (1982); Commonwealth v. Lamb, 365 Mass. 265, 270 (1974); Matter of Laura L., 54 Mass. App. Ct. 853, 857 (2002).

– Facts or data that may be hearsay but are otherwise independently admissible such as conversations about direct observations made by other clinicians, if not privileged, or by family members. See Commonwealth v. Markvart, 437 Mass. 331, 336–337 & n.4 (2002) (holding expert opinion may be based on hearsay if facts or data contained therein would be admissible if presented in another form).

The following is a list of common bases for expert opinion testimony in mental health hearings that are impermissible as a foundation for expert opinion:

– Hospital records or medical reports that contain or reference the contents of privileged communications. Adoption of Seth, 29 Mass. App. Ct. 343, 352 (1990).

– Diagnoses or other information that necessarily imply the contents of privileged communications. Adoption of Saul, 60 Mass. App. Ct. 546, 552 n.8 (2004); Adoption of Seth, 29 Mass. App. Ct. at 352.

– Conversations with the respondent not subject to prior warnings and a waiver of privilege. Department of Youth Servs. v. A Juvenile, 398 Mass. 516, 531–532 (1986); Commonwealth v. Lamb, 365 Mass. 265, 270 (1974).

– Other evidence that would be inadmissible if offered in the proceeding, including hearsay not noted above as permissible. Department of Youth Servs. v. A Juvenile, 398 Mass. 516, 531 (1986). See also Section 801, Definitions; Section 802, The Rule Against Hearsay.

Cross-Reference: Section 703, Bases of Opinion Testimony by Experts.

Subsection (e). This subsection is taken nearly verbatim from G. L. c. 233, § 20B, and G. L. c. 112, § 135B. Objective observations by a psychotherapist are admissible if not accompanied by any communication. Matter of Laura L., 54 Mass. App. Ct. 853, 861 (2002), citing Sheridan, petitioner, 412 Mass. 599, 605 (1992), and Adoption of Abigail, 23 Mass. App. Ct. 191, 198–199 (1986).

Cross-Reference: Section 503, Psychotherapist-Patient Privilege; Section 507, Social Worker–Client Privilege.

Subsection (e)(1). This subsection is taken nearly verbatim from G. L. c. 233, § 20B(a). The rule does not apply where the patient is already in the custody of the State or in an ordinary judicial proceeding. Commonwealth v. Lamb, 365 Mass. 265, 268 (1974). "The legislature's intention was to dispense with the privilege only when there is an imminent threat that a person who should be in custody

will instead be at large." Id. A treating psychiatrist may disclose the contents of privileged communications under this exception even if the conversation occurred during the course of an involuntary commitment under a section of G. L. c. 123. Walden Behavioral Care v. K.I., 471 Mass. 150, 157 (2015). The exception for G. L. c. 233, § 20B(a), is met as long as there is "an imminent threat that a person who should be in custody will instead be at large," the examination was conducted "to determine the care and treatment" needed by the patient, and the examination was not specifically ordered by a court or sought by the Commonwealth "for the purpose of supporting a petition seeking [the respondent's] involuntary commitment." Id. at 159.

Cross-Reference: Section 503(d)(1), Psychotherapist-Patient Privilege: Exceptions: Disclosure to Establish Need for Hospitalization or Imminently Dangerous Activity; Section 507(c)(1), Social Worker–Client Privilege: Exceptions.

Subsection (e)(2). This subsection is derived from Commonwealth v. Lamb, 365 Mass. 265, 270 (1974), and Department of Youth Servs. v. A Juvenile, 398 Mass. 516, 526 (1986). This exception only applies when an examination is conducted by or for the Commonwealth or under a court order and is conducted pursuant to, or in anticipation of, a future proceeding. Walden Behavioral Care v. K.I., 471 Mass. 150, 159–160 (2015); Commonwealth v. Seabrooks, 433 Mass. 439, 450–451 (2001).

Regarding communications that occur during any court-ordered examination, the privilege applies unless the Lamb warning was given and the privilege waived, even if the communications are proffered as evidence of imminent harm. Matter of Laura L., 54 Mass. App. Ct. 853, 858–859 (2002).

Any examination for the involuntary administration of medication pursuant to the provisions of G. L. c. 123, § 8B, requires the provision of the Lamb warning. See G. L. c. 123, § 8B(h) (The psychotherapist-patient privilege, established by G. L. c. 233, § 20B, "shall not prohibit the filing of reports or affidavits, or the giving of testimony, pursuant to this section, for the purpose of obtaining treatment of a patient, provided that such patient has been informed prior to making such communications that they may be used for such purpose and has waived the privilege."); Matter of T.M., 2017 Mass. App. Div. 99, 102 (hospital's motion to amend treatment plan was still a proceeding under G. L. c. 123, § 8B, in which the psychotherapist-patient privilege applies); In re Commitment of M.B., 2013 Mass. App. Div. 8, 11 ("unambiguously clear" that psychotherapist-patient privilege applies to proceedings under G. L. c. 123, § 8B).

Appointment of Guardian. If a patient cannot knowingly and voluntarily waive the statutory privilege, then a guardian should be appointed to act on the patient's behalf. G. L. c. 233, § 20B. A person may not be competent to waive the privilege if that person does not have "sufficient present ability to consult with his attorney with a reasonable degree of rational understanding" and does not have "a rational as well as factual understanding of the proceedings." Commonwealth v. Vailes, 360 Mass. 522, 524 (1971), quoting Dusky v. United States, 362 U.S. 402, 402 (1960). Where there is some doubt, the court should make an inquiry as to whether an individual is capable of making a knowing and voluntary waiver of the privilege. Commonwealth v. DelVerde, 401 Mass. 447, 451 n.8 (1988); Matter of Laura L., 54 Mass. App. Ct. 853, 857 (2002); Adoption of Kirk, 35 Mass. App. Ct. 533, 539 (1993).

Cross-Reference: Section 503(d)(2), Psychotherapist-Patient Privilege: Exceptions: Court-Ordered Psychiatric Exam.

Subsection (f). This subsection is derived from G. L. c. 233, § 79, and Bouchie v. Murray, 376 Mass. 524, 527–529 (1978). In the case of hospital admissions for psychiatric reasons, the fact and dates of such admissions are admissible as part of the medical record, and the reasons for such admissions are admissible if such reasons do not implicate any communications between a psychotherapist and patient. Commonwealth v. Clancy, 402 Mass. 664, 667 (1988). Privileged communications between a patient and psychotherapist or patient and social worker are not admissible under the hospital records exception. Usen v. Usen, 359 Mass. 453, 457 (1971). Records containing privileged information must be thoroughly redacted before they can be submitted into evidence. Commonwealth v. Clancy, 402 Mass. at 669. Records clearly within the privilege are not ordinarily open for examination by counsel because "the purpose of [G. L. c. 233, § 20B,] is to protect justifiable expectations of confidentiality." Id. at 667, citing Usen v. Usen, 359 Mass. at 457; Petitions of the Dep't of Social Servs. to Dispense with Consent to Adoption, 399 Mass. 279, 286 (1987). If a hospital record contains notations relating to psychiatric treatment by doctors and nurses who are not psychotherapists, it may be reviewed by counsel and admitted into evidence, as long as it is redacted to exclude communications or notes of communications between the patient and a psychotherapist. Petitions of the Dep't of Social Servs. to Dispense with Consent to Adoption, 399 Mass. at 288. Objective observations by a psychotherapist, social worker, nurse, or other party, recorded in the medical records, are admissible as long as they do not imply the contents of any privileged communication. Adoption of Abigail, 23 Mass. App. Ct. 191, 198–199 (1986).

Cross-Reference: Section 803(6)(B), Hearsay Exceptions; Availability of Declarant Immaterial: Business and Hospital Records: Hospital Records.

Subsection (g). This subsection is derived from G. L. c. 233, § 79G, and Section 803(6)(C), Hearsay Exceptions; Availability of Declarant Immaterial: Business and Hospital Records: Medical and Hospital Services.

Reports from a psychologist or psychiatrist are admissible by statute under G. L. c. 233, § 79G, but similar to the hospital records exception (see Subsection[f], above), a report by a treating psychotherapist may not contain or imply the contents of any privileged communication. G. L. c. 233, § 79G; Adoption of Seth, 29 Mass. App. Ct. 343, 353 (1990). These reports are admissible even if prepared in anticipation of litigation. O'Malley v. Soske, 76 Mass. App. Ct. 495, 498 (2010). The limit contained in G. L. c. 233, § 79, that information contained in medical records must be germane to the patient's treatment to be admissible, is expressly overridden in G. L. c. 233, § 79G, which permits the doctor's opinion on proximate cause, diagnosis, and prognosis, as well as treating information. Commonwealth v. Schutte, 52 Mass. App. Ct. 796, 799–800 (2001). Psychiatric diagnoses contained in medical reports are therefore admissible, but only as long as such diagnoses do not disclose the contents of any privileged communication. See Adoption of Saul, 60 Mass. App. Ct. 546, 552–553 n.8 (2004) (finding that diagnostic terms "schizophrenia" and "schizoaffective disorder" were not themselves privileged where such terms do not reveal the contents of privileged communications, while diagnoses of kleptomania, pathological gambling, or pedophilia, among others, may inherently convey some contents of privileged communication).

Cross-Reference: Section 803(6)(C), Hearsay Exceptions; Availability of Declarant Immaterial: Business and Hospital Records: Medical and Hospital Services.

Section 1118. Civil Commitment Hearings for Alcohol and Substance Use Disorders

(a) Civil Commitment Proceedings Pursuant to G. L. c. 123, §35, for Individuals with Alcohol and Substance Use Disorders. In order to involuntarily commit a person with an alcohol or substance use disorder, the court must find by clear and convincing evidence, based on a hearing which shall include expert testimony and may include other evidence, that

(1) the respondent is an individual with an alcohol or substance use disorder, and

(2) there is a likelihood of serious harm to the respondent, the petitioner, or any other person as a result of the respondent's alcohol or substance use disorder.

The respondent shall have the right to cross-examine witnesses, present independent expert evidence, call witnesses, and submit documents or other evidence.

(b) Hearsay in G. L. c. 123, § 35, Proceedings. The rules of evidence do not apply in proceedings to commit individuals with alcohol and substance use disorders, except that privileges and statutory disqualifications do apply.

(1) Hearsay evidence is admissible but may only be relied upon if the judge finds it to be substantially reliable.

(2) Hearsay may be found to be substantially reliable by weighing some or all of the following factors. These factors are nonexclusive, and there is no requirement that hearsay satisfy each of the criteria to be considered substantially reliable.

(A) The level of factual detail, rather than generalized and conclusory assertions.

(B) Whether the statement is based on personal knowledge and direct observation.

(C) Whether the statement is corroborated by other evidence.

(D) Whether the statement was provided under circumstances that support the veracity of the source.

(E) Whether the statement was provided by a disinterested witness.

(c) Refusal to Testify in G. L. c. 123, § 35, Proceedings. No adverse inference may be drawn from a respondent's refusal to testify or to speak with the examining clinician. The respondent's refusal to testify or speak with the examining clinician does not prohibit the clinician from offering an opinion despite such refusal and reporting such refusal to the court.

NOTE

Subsection (a). This subsection is derived from G. L. c. 123, § 35; Rule 6(a) of the Uniform Trial Court Rules for Civil Commitment Proceedings for Alcohol and Substance Use Disorders (2016); and Matter of G.P., 473 Mass. 112, 118–120 (2015).

Significant Statutory Amendment. An amendment to G. L. c. 123, § 35, effective on April 24, 2016, eliminated a requirement for "competent medical testimony" and replaced it with a requirement for "expert testimony." Although the decision in Matter of G.P., 473 Mass. at 118–120, discussed the former "competent medical testimony" language, the decision remains relevant regarding the "clear and convincing" standard.

Definitions. A person has a "substance use disorder" for the purpose of the statute if that person chronically or habitually consumes or ingests a substance to the extent that (1) such use substantially injures their health or substantially interferes with their social or economic functioning, or (2) that person has lost the power of self-control over the use of such controlled substances. G. L. c. 123, § 35.

Cross-Reference: Note to Section 1117(a)(2), Civil Commitment Hearings for Mental Illness: Mental Health Commitment Hearings (quoting definition of "likelihood of serious harm" from G. L. c. 123, § 1).

Subsection (b). This subsection is taken nearly verbatim from Rule 7(a) of the Uniform Trial Court Rules for Civil Commitment Proceedings for Alcoholic and Substance Abuse (2015), as approved of in Matter of G.P., 473 Mass. 112, 122 (2015) ("The flexible nature of due process permits accommodation of these circumstances by not requiring strict adherence to the rules so long as there is fairness in the proceeding."). Because expert testimony is required by statute in

G. L. c. 123, § 35, proceedings, it is essential that rules regarding the waiver of privilege be strictly adhered to when the court-appointed clinician interviews the respondent. See Commonwealth v. Lamb, 365 Mass. 265, 270 (1974); Section 1117(d)(3), Civil Commitment Hearings for Mental Illness: Basis for Expert Opinion (facts or data not in evidence).

Subsection (b)(1). This subsection is taken nearly verbatim from Rule 7(a) the Uniform Trial Court Rules for Civil Commitment Proceedings for Alcoholic and Substance Abuse (2015), as approved of in Matter of G.P., 473 Mass. 112, 122 (2015).

Subsection (b)(2). This subsection is derived from factors for weighing the reliability of hearsay in probation revocation hearings. Matter of G.P., 473 Mass. 112, 121–122 (2015); Commonwealth v. Patton, 458 Mass. 119, 132–133 (2010), citing Commonwealth v. Durling, 407 Mass. 108, 114–118 (1990), and Commonwealth v. Delaney, 36 Mass. App. Ct. 930, 932 (1994). In Matter of G.P., 473 Mass. 112 (2015), the Supreme Judicial Court discussed the requirement that hearsay be "substantially reliable" by relating it to the admissibility of such hearsay in probation revocation proceedings. Matter of G.P., 473 Mass. at 121–122, citing Commonwealth v. Patton, 458 Mass. at 132–133, and Commonwealth v. Durling, 407 Mass. at 114–118. The same factors apply for weighing whether to rely on hearsay evidence in support of commitment under G. L. c. 123, § 35. Matter of G.P., 473 Mass. at 122; Matter of J.W., 2016 Mass. App. Div. 74, 77. In Section 35 hearings the core goal, consistent with due process, is for the evidence to "provid[e] an accurate and reliable determination" of the underlying question of fact. Matter of G.P., 473 Mass. at 121–122; Commonwealth v. Durling, 407 Mass. at 116. Hearsay is presumptively reliable if it is admissible under standard evidentiary rules. Commonwealth v. Patton, 458 Mass. at 132; Commonwealth v. Durling, 407 Mass. at 118.

Cross-Reference: Section 801, Definitions; Section 803, Hearsay Exceptions; Availability of Declarant Immaterial; Section 804, Hearsay Exceptions; Declarant Unavailable.

Subsection (c). This subsection is derived from Rule 7(b) of the Uniform Trial Court Rules for Civil Commitment Proceedings for Alcohol and Substance Use Disorders (2016) and G. L. c. 123, § 35.

SUPPLEMENT TO THE MASSACHUSETTS 2019 GUIDE TO EVIDENCE

Applicable Section(s)	Case Name & Citation	Brief Description
§ 511(a)(1). Privilege Against Self-Incrimination: Privilege of Defendant in Criminal Proceeding, Custodial Interrogation.	**Commonwealth v. Lajoie**, 95 Mass. App. Ct. 10, 14-15 (2019).	The court found Miranda warning formulation that "you have the right to an attorney" and that if you cannot afford an attorney, one will be appointed "prior to questioning" adequately conveyed the "equivalent" of a Miranda warning, emphasizing that "courts should focus on the totality of the warnings conveyed, rather than their precise form." Id. at 14-15.
§ 511(c)(6). Privilege Against Self-Incrimination: Exceptions, Foregone Conclusion.	**Commonwealth v. Jones**, 481 Mass. 540, 542-543 (2019)	"When the Commonwealth seeks an order pursuant to our decision in Gelfgatt . . . compelling a defendant to decrypt an electronic device by entering a password, art. 12 requires the Commonwealth to prove that the defendant knows the password beyond a reasonable doubt for the foregone conclusion exception to apply." Id. at 542-543.

"[A] judge acting on a renewed Gelfgatt motion may consider additional information without first finding that it was not known or not reasonably available to the Commonwealth at the time the earlier Gelfgatt motion was filed." Id. at 543. |
| § 611(a)(3). Mode and Order of Examining Witnesses and Presenting Evidence; Control by the Court. | **Commonwealth v. Chicas**, 481 Mass. 316, 318-322 (2019) | In general, "[t]here is no reason to believe that the fact that the witnesses may not have been legal residents of the United States was evidence of their ability to be truthful. In reality, a witness's status as an undocumented immigrant, for a variety of reasons, would make the witness less likely to cooperate with the government." Id. at 321–322. |
| § 611(b)(2). Mode and Order of Examining Witnesses and Presenting | | Whether a party may ask questions about a witness's citizenship status on cross- |

Applicable Section(s)	Case Name & Citation	Brief Description
Evidence; Scope of Cross-Examination, Bias and Prejudice.		examination to explore bias "depends on a showing that the witness was testifying in order to curry favor with the Commonwealth." Id. at 321.
		"[A]fter the witnesses testified that they had not talked about their citizenship status with the Commonwealth, their status became irrelevant as to motive to lie." Id. at 321.
		A judge may also limit cross-examination on the subject of citizenship status to prevent embarrassment and harassment of the witness. Id., citing Mass. G. Evid. § 611(a)(3) (2018).
§ 804(a)(3). Hearsay Exceptions; Declarant Unavailable; Prior Recorded Testimony; Criteria for Being Unavailable.	**Hedberg v. Wakamatsu**, 482 Mass. 613, 616-618 (2019)	The Court held that a declarant in a civil case who testifies to a lack of memory will be deemed unavailable, thus permitting the admission of out-of-court statements falling within one of the exceptions in Section 804(b). The declarant's lack of memory is a preliminary question of fact for the trial judge.

Adopted July 30, 2019.

CONSOLIDATED INDEX FOR STATE RULES

Rules, Standing Orders and Forms Included	Citation Style

CIVIL, CRIMINAL, AND APPELLATE RULES

Rules of Civil Procedure	Rule ___
Rules of Criminal Procedure	Rule ___ (Crim.Proc.)
Rules of Appellate Procedure	Rule ___ (App.Proc.)
Interim Supplemental Rules of Appellate Procedure in Care and Protection Cases	Rule ___ (I.S.R.App. Proc.)

SUPREME JUDICIAL COURT

Rules of Supreme Judicial Court	Rule ___ (S.J.Ct.)
Standing Orders of Supreme Judicial Court	Standing Order (S.J.Ct.)
Interim Electronic Filing Rules for Pilot Courts	Rule ___ (E Filing)

APPEALS COURT

Appeals Court Rules for the Regulation of Appellate Practice	Rule ___ (App.Ct.)
Standing Orders of Appeals Court	Standing Order (App.Ct.)

TRIAL COURT

Uniform Summary Process Rules	Rule ___ (Sum.Proc.)
Uniform Magistrate Rules	Rule ___ (Mag.)
Uniform Small Claims Rules	Rule ___ (Small Claims)
Small Claims Standards	Foll. Small Claims Rules
Uniform Rule Requiring Disclosure of Pending and Concluded Care or Custody Matters	Trial Court Rule IV
Procedure Regulating the Issuance of Standing Orders	Trial Court Rule V
Uniform Rules for Permancy Hearings	Trial Court Rule VI
Uniform Rule on Civil Motor Vehicle Infractions	Trial Court Rule VII
Appendix of Forms	Appendix (Trial Ct.Rule VII)
Uniform Rules on Impoundment Procedure	Trial Court Rule VIII
Uniform Rules on Subpoenas to Court Officials	Trial Court Rule IX
Uniform Rule Requiring Disclosure of Present or Past Receipt of Public Assistance Benefits by Minor Children	Trial Court Rule X
Uniform Rule for Probable Cause Determination for Persons Arrested Without a Warrant	Trial Court Rule XI
Requests for Interdepartmental Judicial Assignments	Trial Court Rule XII
Standing Orders of the Trial Court	Standing Order ___ (T.Ct.)
Uniform Schedule of Fees For the Trial Court	Trial Court Fee Schedule
United Trial Court Rules for Civil Commitment Proceedings for Alcohol and Substance Abuse	Rule ___ (Substance Abuse)

DISTRICT COURTS AND BOSTON MUNICIPAL COURT

District/Municipal Courts	
Appendix of Forms	Appendix (Dist./Mun.Cts.) Form ___
Appendix, Boston Municipal Court Forms	Appendix (Bos.Mun.Ct.) Form ___
District/Municipal Courts Supplemental Rules of Civil Procedure	Rule ___ (Dist./Mun.Cts. Supp.)
District/Municipal Courts Rules for Appellate Division Appeal	Rule ___ (Dist./Mun.Cts.App.)
Special Rules of the District Courts	Rule ___ (Dist.Cts.Spec.)
Special Rules of the Boston Municipal Court	Rule ___ (Mun.Ct.Spec.)
District/Municipal Courts Rules of Criminal Procedure	Rule ___ (Dist./Mun.Cts.R.Crim.P.)
Rules of the Municipal Court of the City of Boston Sitting for Criminal Business	Rule ___ (Bos.Mun.Ct. Crim.)
District Court Department Supplemental Rules of Criminal Procedure	Rule ___ (Dist.Ct.Supp. R.Crim.Proc.)

CONSOLIDATED INDEX FOR STATE RULES

CONSOLIDATED INDEX FOR STATE RULES

CONSOLIDATED INDEX FOR STATE RULES

CONSOLIDATED INDEX FOR STATE RULES

CONSOLIDATED INDEX FOR STATE RULES

DOMESTIC RELATIONS PROCEDURE—Cont'd
Time—Cont'd
Filing financial statements, **Rule 401 (Prob.Cts.Supp.)**
Motions, **Rule 6 (Dom.Rel.)**
Transmittal of papers, **Rule 77 (Dom.Rel.)**
Uncontested divorce and annulment matters, corroborating witnesses, necessity, **Uniform Practices II (Prob. Cts.)**
Uniform magistrate rules, **Rule 1 et seq. (Mag.)**
Visitations. Children and Minors, this index
Voluntary dismissal, **Rule 41 (Dom.Rel.)**
Waiver,
Attorneys, contempt proceedings, **Rule 402 (Prob.Cts. Supp.)**
Counsel, contempt proceedings, **Rule 402 (Prob.Cts. Supp.)**
Defenses, **Rule 12 (Dom.Rel.)**
Living apart, **Rule 2 (Mag.)**
Witnesses, corroborating witnesses, necessity, uncontested divorce and annulment matters, **Uniform Practices II (Prob.Cts.)**

DOMESTIC VIOLENCE
See, also, Domestic Relations Procedure, generally, this index
Children and minors, special procedures, **Standing Order 1–10 (Prob.Ct.)**
Privileges and immunities, victims, counselors, **§ 505 (G.Evid.)**

DOMICILE AND RESIDENCE
Parties residence, pleadings, form of pleadings, **Rule 10**

DRAFT REPORTS
Model, form, **Appendix (Dist./Mun.Cts.), Form 33**

DRAFTS
Production of documents and things, **Rule 34**

DRAWINGS
Production of documents and things, **Rule 34**

DRUG ADDICTION
Alcoholics and Chemically Dependent Persons, generally, this index

DRUGS AND MEDICINE
Rogers orders, uncontested, review, **Standing Order 4–11 (Prob.Ct.)**

DUPLICATES
Evidence, **§ 1003 (G.Evid.)**

E FILING
Definitions, electronic filing, **Rule 1:25 (S.J.Ct.)**

E MAIL
Attorneys, address, registration, **Rule 4:02 (S.J.Ct.)**
Judgments and decrees, orders of court, notice, **Rule 77**

E SERVICE
Definitions, electronic filing, **Rule 1:25 (S.J.Ct.)**

EARLY CASE SETTLEMENT PROCESS
Probate and family courts, family-centered case resolution and management, **Standing Order 2–17 (Prob.Ct.)**

EDUCATION
Attorneys, qualifications, **Rule 3:01 (S.J.Ct.)**

EDUCATION—Cont'd
Bail magistrates, **Rule 6 (Bail)**
Divorce, this index

ELECTIONS
Contested elections, applicability of rules, **Rule 81**
Voters, privileges and immunities, **§ 516 (G.Evid.)**

ELECTRONIC ACCESS
Courts, **Rule 1:19 (S.J.Ct.)**
Records and recordation, **Trial Court Rule XIV**

ELECTRONIC APPLICATION FOR CRIMINAL COMPLAINT
Generally, **Standing Order 2–19 (T.Ct.)**

ELECTRONIC COMMUNICATIONS
Evidence, authentication, identification, **§ 901 (G.Evid.)**
Judgments and decrees, orders of court, notice, **Rule 77**

ELECTRONIC FILING
Generally, **Rule 1:25 (S.J.Ct.)**
Appeals court, **Standing Orders (App.Ct.)**
Housing courts, **Standing Order 1–20 (H.Ct.)**
Land court, **Standing Order 2–18 (Land Ct.)**
Probate and family courts, **Standing Order 1–16 (Prob. Ct.)**

ELECTRONIC RECORDING DEVICES
Sound Recording Devices, generally, this index

ELECTRONIC SERVICE
Definitions, electronic filing, **Rule 1:25 (S.J.Ct.)**

ELECTRONIC SIGNATURES
Definitions, electronic filing, **Rule 1:25 (S.J.Ct.)**
Electronic filing, **Rule 1:25 (S.J.Ct.)**
Orders of court, judgments and decrees, **Rule 1:25 (S.J.Ct.)**

ELECTRONICALLY CONVERTED PDFS
Definitions, electronic filing, **Rule 1:25 (S.J.Ct.)**

ELECTRONICALLY STORED INFORMATION
Discovery, **Rule 26**
Failure to provide, **Rule 37**
Production, **Rule 34**
Subpoenas, **Rule 45**

EMAIL
Attorneys, address, registration, **Rule 4:02 (S.J.Ct.)**
Judgments and decrees, orders of court, notice, **Rule 77**

EMBEZZLEMENT
Attorneys, clients security board, **Rule 1 et seq. (Client S.B.R.)**

EMERGENCY RULES
Civil support paternity actions, **Rule 209 (Dist.Cts.Spec.); Rule 306 (Mun.Ct.Spec.)**

EMPLOYMENT SECURITY
Hearings, privileges and immunities, **§ 526 (G.Evid.)**

ENLARGEMENT OR EXTENSION OF TIME
Generally, **Rule 6**

ENTRY OF JUDGMENT
Judgments and Decrees, this index

I-41

CONSOLIDATED INDEX FOR STATE RULES

CONSOLIDATED INDEX FOR STATE RULES

CONSOLIDATED INDEX FOR STATE RULES

CONSOLIDATED INDEX FOR STATE RULES

CONSOLIDATED INDEX FOR STATE RULES

CONSOLIDATED INDEX FOR STATE RULES

CONSOLIDATED INDEX FOR STATE RULES

CONSOLIDATED INDEX FOR STATE RULES

CONSOLIDATED INDEX FOR STATE RULES

CONSOLIDATED INDEX FOR STATE RULES

CONSOLIDATED INDEX FOR STATE RULES